INDEX OF ECONOMIC ARTICLES
In Journals and Collective Volumes

Index of Economic Articles

IN JOURNALS AND COLLECTIVE VOLUMES

Volume XXVIII · 1986

Part One—Subject Index

Prepared under the auspices of

THE JOURNAL OF ECONOMIC LITERATURE

of the

AMERICAN ECONOMIC ASSOCIATION

NASHVILLE, TENNESSEE
AMERICAN ECONOMIC ASSOCIATION
1989

Executive Office
1313 21st Avenue South, Nashville, Tennessee 37212

Library of Congress Catalog Card Number: 61–8020
International Standard Book Number: 0–917290–17–8
International Standard Serial Number: 0536–647X
Printed in the United States of America

TABLE OF CONTENTS

Part One
Introduction vii

Introductory Discussion vii
List of Journals Indexed x
List of Collective Volumes Indexed xvi
Four-Digit Classification System xxxv

Subject Index of Articles in Journals and Collective Volumes 1

000 General Economics; Theory; History; Systems 3
100 Economic Growth; Development; Planning; Fluctuations 154
200 Quantitative Economic Methods and Data 228
300 Domestic Monetary and Fiscal Theory and Institutions 276
400 International Economics 391
500 Administration; Business Finance; Marketing; Accounting 489
600 Industrial Organization; Technological Change; Industry Studies 524
700 Agriculture; Natural Resources 644
800 Manpower; Labor; Population 715
900 Welfare Programs; Consumer Economics; Urban and Regional Economics 825

Topical Guide to Classification Schedule li

Part Two
Index of Authors of Articles in Journals and Collective Volumes 905

INTRODUCTORY DISCUSSION

This volume of the *Index* lists, both by subject category and by author, articles in major economic journals and in collective volumes published during the year 1986. The articles listed include all articles published in English or with English summaries in the journals and books identified in the following sections. Part one includes the Subject Index of Articles in Journals and Collective Volumes, and Part Two consists of an alphabetical Author Index of all the articles indexed in Part One.

Relationship to JEL

This *Index* is prepared largely as an adjunct to the bibliographic activities of the *Journal of Economic Literature (JEL).* Economies of joint production are pursued throughout the production process. Journals included are those indexed in the *JEL* quarterly; collective volumes are selected from the annotated 1986 books; the classification system is a more detailed version of the *JEL* system.

Journals Included

The 303 journals listed represent, in general, those journals that we believe will be most helpful to research workers and teachers of economics. These journals are listed below on page x.

Generally, articles, notes, communications, comments, replies, rejoinders, as well as papers and formal discussions in proceedings and review articles have been indexed. There are some exceptions; only articles in English or with English summaries are included—this practice results in a slightly reduced coverage compared with the *JEL* quarterly. Articles lacking author identification are omitted, as are articles without economic content. Identical articles appearing in two different journals in 1986 are listed from both sources. The journal issues included usually fall within a single volume. When a volume of a journal overlaps two calendar years, for example, Fall 1985 to Summer 1986, we include the issues from the two volumes relating to 1986 as best we can determine.

Collective Volumes

The collective volumes consist of the following:

1. *Festschriften*
2. Conference publications with individual papers
3. Collected essays, original, by one or more authors
4. Collected essays, reprinted, by one or more authors
5. Proceedings volumes
6. Books of readings

All original articles in English are indexed with the exception of unsigned articles or articles without economic content. Reprinted articles are included on the basis that a researcher would be interested in knowing about another source of the article. The original publication dates are shown in italics on the citations of reprinted articles. Excerpts are not included. The same article appearing for the first time in different collective volumes in the same year is cited from both publications.

In the article citation, reference to the book in which the article appears is by author or editor of the volume. If the same person or persons wrote or edited more than one book included in the 1986 *Index,* it is indicated by a I or II appearing in both the source given in the article citation and the bibliographic reference in the book listing. If the same person wrote one book and edited another in 1986, the specification of "ed" in the reference indicates which book is being cited.

The collective volumes are listed alphabetically by author or editor beginning on page xvi and include a full bibliographic reference. If there is more than one edition, the publisher cited is the one on the copy the *JEL* received, usually the American publisher.

Arrangement

The *Index* consists of two parts:

1. A Subject Index in which the articles are arranged by subject.
2. An Author Index.

Part One—Subject Index

In Part One, all articles are listed alphabetically by first author under each 4-digit subject category. Joint authors are listed up to three; beyond that, only the first author is listed, followed by *et al.*

There is one exception to the alphabetical author arrangement. In the 0322 category, a subdivision of **History of Thought** entitled **Individuals,** the arrangement is first alphabetical by the individual discussed in the article and then alphabetical by the article's author.

Articles with empirical content or discussing a particular geographic area carry a geographic descriptor (see discussion below).

Classification System

The classification system is an expansion of the 3-digit classification system used in the *Journal of Economic Literature* to a 4-digit system with slightly over 300 subcategories. The classification system, itself, is shown beginning on page xxxv (Part One). In most cases the classification heading is self-explanatory; however, in some cases notes have been added to clarify the coverage or indicate alternative subject classifications. The basic approach in classification is from the point of view of the researcher rather than the teacher; course content does not necessarily coincide with subfields of our classification system. In all cases where there are two or more 4-digit classifications under a 3-digit category, there is a zero classification; in most instances this is labeled "General." The zero or general category has been used both as an inclusive and a residual category. For example, an article discussing *all* aspects of international trade theory appears in the general category. There are also some articles that do not fall in any of the individual subcategories, and these, too, are classified in the general or zero category.

The criterion used in the classifying process is whether persons interested in this topic would wish to have the article drawn to their attention. With the advent of the online ECONOMIC LITERATURE INDEX on DIALOG, the interpretation of "interest" has broadened slightly to include cross-classifications that indicate the subject matter, particularly in such categories as industry studies or occupational designations. Over half of the articles are classified in more than one subcategory. From time to time, we find it desirable to add subject classifications as particular topics become prominent or to change subject headings to make them more descriptive of the contents of the category.

Geographic Descriptors

Geographic descriptors appear in brackets at the end of any article entry in the Subject Index where the article cites data from or refers to a particular country or area. Research workers interested in these countries thus are made aware of the empirical content in the article. The descriptors used are countries or broader areas, such as Southeast Asia (S. E. Asia); articles referring to cities or regions within a country are classified under the country. In general, the country name is written out in full with some adaptations and abbreviations, *e.g.*, U.S. is used for United States, U.K. for United Kingdom, and U.S.S.R. for Union of Soviet Socialist Republics. Abbreviations include: W. for West, E. for East, S. for South, N. for North. A shortened name such as W. Germany is used rather than the correct, but longer, Federal Republic of Germany. When broader regions are used as descriptors, the article may or may not refer to the full unit. For example, OECD has been used at times when most, but not all, of the OECD member countries are referred to.

Index volumes prior to 1979 sometimes did not include geographic descriptors on articles listed under subject categories 1210, 1211, 1220, 1221, 1230, 1240, and 1241, involving general or comparative economic country studies. In the 1979 *Index* and later volumes, these articles carry geographic descriptors in order to facilitate online identification in the Economic Literature Index on DIALOG. Because the descriptor fields are limited to five, very general descriptors, such as LDCs (developing countries) and MDCs (developed countries), are often used on articles.

The fact that an article carries a geographic descriptor does not necessarily preclude its being primarily theoretical in nature. Any theoretical article drawing on empirical data to demonstrate its findings will carry a geographic descriptor.

Topical Guide to the Classification System

At the end of Part One there is an alphabetical listing of standard economic terms and concepts. References are to the appropriate 4-digit classification numbers, not to page numbers.

Part Two—Author Index

Part two consists of an alphabetical Author Index in which citations appear under each author (up to three) of an article. Wherever possible the full first name and middle initial or middle name(s) are used. Wherever it could be definitely ascertained, articles by the same person are grouped together with only one listing of the name. Authors' first names and initials are listed differently in various journals and books; for example, an individual may be identified as John L. Smith, J. L. Smith, or John Smith. Thus, despite our best efforts, we were left in doubt in several instances. Joint authors are listed up to three; beyond that, only the first author is listed, followed by *et al.* Under each author, articles are listed alphabetically. Names carrying prefixes are alphabetized according to the first *capitalized* letter, with occasional exceptions following national practices. Thus, van Arkadie would appear under A and D'Alabro under D.

LIST OF JOURNALS INDEXED 1986

Accounting Review, Vol. 61.

Acta Oeconomica, Vol. 36; Vol. 37.

L'Actualité Economique, Vol. 62.

African Economic History, Issue no. 15.

Agricultural Economics Research, Vol. 38.

American Economic Review, Vol. 76.

American Economist, Vol. 30.

American Historical Review, Vol. 91.

American Journal of Agricultural Economics, Vol. 68.
Title changed from **Journal of Farm Economics** in 1968.

American Journal of Economics and Sociology, Vol. 45.

American Political Science Review, Vol. 80.

American Real Estate and Urban Economics Association Journal, Vol. 14.

Annales d'Economie et de Statistique, Issues nos. 1–4, 1985.
Title changed from **Annales de l'INSEE in 1986.**

Annals of Public and Co-operative Economy, Vol. 57.

Annals of Regional Science, Vol. 20.

Antitrust Bulletin, Vol. 31.

Applied Economics, Vol. 18.

Atlantic Economic Journal, Vol. 14.

Aussenwirtschaft, Vol. 41.

Australian Bulletin of Labour, Vol. 12, Issue nos. 2–4; Vol. 13, Issue no. 1.

Australian Economic History Review, Vol. 26.
Title changed from **Business Archives and History** in 1967; entitled **Bulletin of the Business Archives Council of Australia** prior to 1962.

Australian Economic Papers, Vol. 25.

Australian Economic Review, Issue nos. 73–76.

Australian Journal of Agricultural Economics, Vol. 30.

Australian Tax Forum, Vol. 3.

Banca Nazionale del Lavoro—Quarterly Review, Issue nos. 156–159.

Bangladesh Development Studies, Vol. 14, Issue nos. 1–2.

British Journal of Industrial Relations, Vol. 24.

British Review of Economic Issues, Vol. 8

Brookings Papers on Economic Activity, Issue nos. 1–2, 1986.

Bulletin for International Fiscal Documentation, Vol. 40.

Bulletin of Economic Research, Vol. 38.
Title changed from **Yorkshire Bulletin of Economic and Social Research** in 1971.

Bulletin of Indonesian Economic Studies, Vol. 22.

Business Economics, Vol. 21.

Business History Review, Vol. 60.
Title changed from **Bulletin of the Business Historical Society** in 1954.

Cahiers Économiques de Bruxelles, Issue nos. 109–112.

Cambridge Journal of Economics, Vol. 10.

Canadian Journal of Agricultural Economics, Vol. 33, Annual Meeting and Workshop Proceedings; Vol. 34, Issue nos. 1–3, Workshop Proceedings.

Canadian Journal of Development Studies, Vol. 7, Issue no. 1.

Canadian Journal of Economics, Vol. 19.

Canadian Public Policy, Vol. 12; Supplement.

Carnegie–Rochester Conference Series on Public Policy, Vols. 24–25.
Vols. 1–17 were listed as supplements to the **Journal of Monetary Economics.**

Cato Journal, Vol. 5, Issue no. 3; Vol. 6, Issue nos. 1–2.

Cepal Review, Issue nos. 28–30.

Challenge, Vol. 28, Issue no. 6; Vol. 28, Issue nos. 1–5.

Chinese Economic Studies, Vol. 19, Issue nos. 2–4; Vol. 20, Issue no. 1.

Colección Estudios CIEPLAN, Issue nos, 19–20.

Comparative Economic Studies, Vol. 28.
Title changed from **ACES Bulletin** in 1985.

Conflict Management and Peace Science, Vol. 9, Issue no. 2.
Title changed from **Journal of Peace Science** in 1979–80.

Contemporary Policy Issues, Vol. 4, Issue nos. 1–4.

Cuadernos de Economia, Vol. 23.

Czechoslovak Economic Digest, Issue nos. 1–8, 1986.

Demography, Vol. 23.

Desarrollo Económico, Vol. 25, Issue no. 100; Vol. 26, Issue nos. 101–103.

Developing Economies, Vol. 24.

Eastern Economic Journal, Vol. 12.

Eastern European Economics, Vol. 24, Issue nos. 3–4; Vol. 25, Issue nos. 1–2.

Econometric Reviews, Vol. 5.

Econometrica, Vol. 54.

Economia (Portuguese Catholic University), Vol. 10.

Economia Internazionale, Vol. 39.

Economia e Lavoro, Vol. 20.

Economía et Política, Vol. 3.

Economic Analysis and Workers' Management, Vol. 20.

Economic Computation and Economic Cybernetics Studies and Research, Vol. 21.
Title changed from **Studii şi Cercetări Economicè** in 1974. Changed from issue numbers to volume numbers in 1978.

Economic Development and Cultural Change, Vol. 34, Issue nos. 2–4; Vol. 35, Issue no. 1.

Economic Forum, Vol. 16, Issue no. 1.
Title changed from **Intermountain Economic Review** in 1979.

Economic Geography, Vol. 62.

Economic History Review, Vol. 39.

Economic Inquiry, Vol. 24.
Title changed from **Western Economic Journal** in 1974.

Economic Journal, Vol. 96; Supplement.

Economic Modelling, Vol. 3.

Economic Notes, Issue nos. 1–3, 1986.

Economic Record, Vol. 62; Supplement.

Economic and Social Review, Vol. 17, Issue nos. 2–4; Vol. 18, Issue no. 1.

Economic Studies Quarterly, Vol. 37.

Economica, Vol. 53; Supplement.
Title changed from **Economica, N.S.** in 1974.

Económica, Vol. 32.

Economics of Education Review, Vol. 5.

Economics and Philosophy, Vol. 2.

Economics of Planning, Vol. 20.

Économie Appliquée, Vol. 39.

Économies et Sociétés, Vol. 20.

De Economist, Vol. 134.

Ekonomiska Samfundets Tidskrift, Vol. 39.

Empirica, Vol. 13.

Empirical Economics, Vol. 11.

Energy Economics, Vol. 8.

Energy Journal, Vol. 7.

Estudios Económico, Vol. 1.

European Economic Review, Vol. 30.

European Review of Agricultural Economics, Vol. 13.

Explorations in Economic History, Vol. 23.
Title changed from **Explorations in Entrepreneurial History** in 1969–70.

Federal Reserve Bank of Dallas Economic Review, January, March, May, July, September, November, 1986.

Federal Reserve Bank of Minneapolis Quarterly Review, Vol. 10.

Federal Reserve Bank of New York Quarterly Review, Vol. 11.

Federal Reserve Bank of Richmond Economic Review, Vol. 72.

Federal Reserve Bank of San Francisco Economic Review, Issue nos. 1–4, 1986.

Federal Reserve Bank of St. Louis Review, Vol. 68.

Federal Reserve Bulletin, Vol. 72.

Finance, Vol. 7.

Finance and Development, Vol. 23.

Financial Review, Vol. 21.

Fiscal Studies, Vol. 7.

Food Research Institute Studies, Vol. 20, Issue no. 1.

Foreign Affairs, Vol. 64, Issue nos. 2–5; Vol. 65, Issue no. 1.

Giornale degli Economisti e Annali di Economia, Vol. 45.

Greek Economic Review, Vol. 8.

Growth and Change, Vol. 17.

History of Political Economy, Vol. 18.

Hitotsubashi Journal of Economics, Vol. 27; Special Issue.

Hong Kong Economic Papers, Issue no. 17.

Housing Finance Review, Vol. 5.

Ifo-Studien, Vol. 32.

Indian Economic Journal, Vol. 33, Issue nos. 3–4; Vol. 34, Issue nos. 1–2.

Indian Economic Review, Vol. 21.

Indian Journal of Quantitative Economics, Vol. 2.

Industrial and Labor Relations Review, Vol. 39, Issue nos. 2–4; Vol. 40, Issue no. 1.

Industrial Relations, Vol. 25.

Industry and Development, Issue nos. 16–19.

Information Economics and Policy, Vol. 2.

Inquiry, Vol. 23.

International Economic Review, Vol. 27.

International Journal of Forecasting, Vol. 2, Issue nos. 2–4.

International Journal of Game Theory, Vol. 15, Issue no. 3.

International Journal of Industrial Organization, Vol. 4.

International Journal of Social Economics, Vol. 13.

International Journal of Transport Economics, Vol. 13.

International Labour Review, Vol. 125.

International Monetary Fund Staff Papers, Vol. 33.

International Organization, Vol. 40.

International Regional Science Review, Vol. 10.

International Review of Law and Economics, Vol. 6.

Investigaciones Economicas, Vol. 10.

Irish Journal of Agricultural Economics and Rural Sociology, Vol. 11.

Jahrbücher für Nationalökonomie und Statistik, Vol. 201.

Journal of Accounting and Economics, Vol. 8.

Journal of Accounting Research, Vol. 24; Supplement.

Journal of Agricultural Economics, Vol. 37.

Journal of the American Statistical Association, Vol. 81.

Journal of Applied Econometrics, Vol. 1.

Journal of Bank Research, Vol. 16, Issue no. 4; Vol. 17, Issue no. 1.

Journal of Banking and Finance, Vol. 10.

Journal of Behavioral Economics, Vol. 15.

Journal of Business, Vol. 59.

Journal of Business and Economic Statistics, Vol. 4.

Journal of Common Market Studies, Vol. 24, Issue nos. 3–4; Vol. 25, Issue nos. 1–2.

Journal of Comparative Economics, Vol. 10.

Journal of Consumer Affairs, Vol. 20.

Journal of Consumer Research, Vol. 12, Issue no. 4; Vol. 13, Issue nos. 1–3.

Journal of Cultural Economics, Vol. 10.

Journal of Developing Areas, Vol. 20, Issue nos. 2–4; Vol. 21, Issue no. 1.

Journal of Development Economics, Vols. 20–24.

Journal of Development Studies, Vol. 22, Issue nos. 2–4; Vol. 23, Issue no. 1.

Journal of Econometrics, Vols. 31–33.

Journal of Economic Behavior and Organization, Vol. 7.

Journal of Economic Development, Vol. 11.

Journal of Economic Dynamics and Control, Vol. 10.

Journal of Economic Education, Vol. 17.

Journal of Economic History, Vol. 46.

Journal of Economic Issues, Vol. 20.

Journal of Economic Literature, Vol. 24.

Journal of Economic and Social Measurement, Vol. 14.

Title changed from **Review of Public Data Use** in 1985.

Journal of Economic Studies, Vol. 13.

Journal of Economic Theory, Vols. 38–40.

Journal of Economics (Zeitschrift für Nationalökonomie), Vol. 46; Supplement.

Listed as **Zeitschrift für Nationalokonomie** prior to 1986.

Journal of Economics and Business, Vol. 38.

Title changed from **Economics and Business Bulletin** in 1972–73.

Journal of Energy and Development, Vol. 11, Issue no. 2; Vol. 12, Issue no. 1.

Journal of Environmental Economics and Management, Vol. 13.

Journal of European Economic History, Vol. 15.

Journal of Finance, Vol. 41.

Journal of Financial Economics, Vol. 15–17.

Journal of Financial and Quantitative Analysis, Vol. 21.

Journal of Financial Research, Vol. 9.

Journal of Futures Markets, Vol. 6.

Journal of Health Economics, Vol. 5.

Journal of Human Resources, Vol. 21.

Journal of Industrial Economics, Vol. 34, Issue nos. 3–4; Vol. 35, Issue nos. 1–2.

Journal of International Economics, Vols. 20–21.

Journal of Institutional and Theoretical Economics, Vol. 142.

Listed as **Zeitschrift für die gesamte Staatswissenchaft** prior to 1986.

Journal of International Money and Finance, Vol. 5; Supplement.

Journal of Labor Economics, Vol. 4.

Journal of Labor Research, Vol. 7.

Journal of Law and Economics, Vol. 29.

Journal of Law, Economics, and Organization, Vol. 2.

Journal of Macroeconomics, Vol. 8.

Journal of Mathematical Economics, Vol. 15.

Journal of Monetary Economics, Vols. 17–18.

Journal of Money, Credit and Banking, Vol. 18.

Journal of Policy Analysis and Management, Vol. 5, Issue nos. 2–4; Vol. 6, Issue no. 1.

Journal of Policy Modeling, Vol. 8.

Journal of Political Economy, Vol. 94.

Journal of Portfolio Management, Vol. 12, Issue nos. 2–4; Vol. 13, Issue no. 1.

Journal of Post Keynesian Economics, Vol. 8, Issue nos. 2–4; Vol. 9, Issue no. 1.

Journal of Public Economics, Vols. 29–31.

Journal of Quantitative Economics, Vol. 2.

Journal of Regional Science, Vol. 26.

Journal of Risk and Insurance, Vol. 53.

Journal of the Royal Statistical Society, Series A, Vol. 149.

Journal for Studies in Economics and Econometrics, Issue nos. 24–26.

Journal of Transport Economics and Policy, Vol. 20.

Journal of Urban Economics, Vols. 19–20.

Journal of World Trade Law, Vol. 20; Supplement.

Keio Economic Studies, Vol. 23.

Kobe University Economic Review, Issue no. 32.

Konjunkturpolitik, Vol. 32.

Kredit und Kapital, Vol. 19.

Kyklos, Vol. 39.

Labor History, Vol. 27.

Land Economics, Vol. 62.

Law and Contemporary Problems, Vol. 49.

Liiketaloudellinen Aikakauskirja, Vol. 35.

Lloyds Bank Review, Issue nos. 159–162.

Logistics and Transportation Review, Vol. 22.

Managerial and Decision Economics, Vol. 7.

Manchester School of Economics and Social Studies, Vol. 54.

Title changed from **The Manchester School** in 1939; entitled **The Manchester School of Economics, Commerce and Administration** prior to 1932.

Margin, Vol. 18, Issue nos. 2–4; Vol. 19, Issue no. 1.

Marine Resource Economics, Vol. 2, Issue nos. 3–4; Vol. 3.

Marketing Science, Vol. 5.

Matekon, Vol. 22, Issue nos. 3–4; Vol. 23, Issue nos. 1–2.
Title changed from **Mathematical Studies in Economics and Statistics in the USSR and Eastern Europe** in 1969.

Mathematical Social Sciences, Vols. 11–12.

Metroeconomica, Vol. 38.

METU—Studies in Development, Vol. 13.

Michigan Law Review, Vol. 84, Issue nos. 4–8; Vol. 85, Issue nos. 1–3.

Monthly Labor Review, Vol. 109.

National Institute Economic Review, Issue nos. 115–118.

National Tax Journal, Vol. 39.

National Westminster Bank Quarterly Review, February, May, August, November, 1986.

Nationaløkonomisk Tidsskrift, Vol. 124.

Natural Resources Journal, Vol. 26.

New England Economic Review, January/February, March/April, May/June, July/August, September/October, November/December, 1986.

New Zealand Economic Papers, Vol. 20.

OECD Economic Studies, Issue nos. 6–7, 1986.

Oxford Bulletin of Economics and Statistics, Vol. 48.
Title changed from **Bulletin Oxford University Institute of Economics and Statistics** in 1973; entitled **Bulletin of the Institute of Economics and Statistics** prior to 1972.

Oxford Economic Papers, Vol. 38; Supplement.

Oxford Review of Economic Policy, Vol. 2.

Pakistan Development Review, Vol. 25.

Pakistan Economic and Social Review, Vol. 24.

Pakistan Journal of Applied Economics, Vol. 5.

Pesquisa e Planejamento Econômico, Vol. 16.

Philippine Economic Journal, Vol. 25, Issue nos. 1–2.

Philippine Review of Economics and Business, Vol. 23.

Policy Sciences, Vol. 19.

Politica Economica, Vol. 2.

Population and Development Review, Vol. 12; Supplement.

Population Studies, Vol. 40.

Problems of Economics, Vol. 28, Issue nos. 9–12; Vol. 29, Issue nos. 1–8.

Public Budgeting and Finance, Vol. 6.

Public Choice, Vols. 48–51.

Public Finance, Vol. 41.

Public Finance Quarterly, Vol. 14, Issue nos. 1–3.

Quarterly Journal of Business and Economics, Vol. 25.
Title changed from **Nebraska Journal of Economics and Business** in 1983.

Quarterly Journal of Economics, Vol. 101.

Quarterly Review of Economics and Business, Vol. 26.

Rand Journal of Economics, Vol. 17, Issue nos. 1–3.
Title changed from **Bell Journal of Economics** in 1984.

Recherches Economiques de Louvain, Vol. 52.

Regional Science and Urban Economics, Vol. 16.

Regional Studies, Vol. 20.

Review of Black Political Economy, Vol. 14, Issue no. 4; Vol. 15, Issue nos. 1–2.

Review of Economic Conditions in Italy, Issue nos. 1–3, 1986.

Review of Economic Studies, Vol. 53.

Review of Economics and Statistics, Vol. 68.
Title changed from **The Review of Economic Statistics** in 1948.

Review of Income and Wealth, Vol. 32.

Review of Industrial Organization, Vol. 2, Issue no. 4; Vol. 3, Issue no. 1.

Review of Marketing and Agricultural Economics, Vol. 54.

Review of Radical Political Economics, Vol. 18.

Review of Regional Studies, Vol. 16.

Review of Social Economy, Vol. 44.

Revista Española de Economia, Vol. 3, Issue no. 1.

Revue d'Economie Politique, Vol. 96.

Revue Économique, Vol. 37.

Ricerche Economiche, Vol. 40.

Rivista Internazionale di Scienze Economiche e Commerciali, Vol. 33.

Scandinavian Economic History Review, Vol. 34.

Scandinavian Journal of Economics, Vol. 88.
Title changed from **Swedish Journal of Economics** in 1976; entitled **Ekonomisk Tidskrift** prior to 1965.

Schweizerische Zeitschrift für Volkswirtschaft und Statistik, Vol. 122.

Science and Society, Vol. 50.

Scottish Journal of Political Economy, Vol. 33.

Singapore Economic Review, Vol. 31.
Title changed from **Malayan Economic Review** in 1983.

Social Choice and Welfare, Vol. 3.

Social and Economic Studies, Vol. 35.

Social Science Quarterly, Vol. 67.

Social Security Bulletin, Vol. 49; Supplement.

South African Journal of Economics, Vol. 54.

Southern Economic Journal, Vol. 52, Issue nos. 3–4; Vol. 53, Issue nos. 1–2.

Southern Journal of Agricultural Economics, Vol. 18.

Soviet and Eastern European Foreign Trade, Vol. 22.

Soviet Economy, Vol. 2.

Statistica, Vol. 46, Issue no. 1.

Statistical Journal, Vol. 4, Issue nos. 1–2.

Studi Economici, Vol. 41.

Survey of Current Business, Vol. 66.

Tijdschrift Voor Economie en Management, Vol. 31.
Title changed from **Tijdschrift voor Economie** in 1975.

Urban Studies, Vol. 23.

Water Resources Research, Vol. 22.

Weltwirtschaftliches Archiv, Vol. 122.

Western Journal of Agricultural Economics, Vol. 11.

Wirtschaft und Recht, Vol. 38.

World Bank Economic Review, Vol. 1, Issue no. 1.

World Bank Research Observer, Vol. 1.

World Development, Vol. 14.

World Economy, Vol. 9.

Yale Journal on Regulation, Vol. 3, Issue no. 2; Vol. 4, Issue no. 1.

Yale Law Journal, Vol. 95, Issue nos. 3–8; Vol. 96, Issue nos. 1–2.

Zeitschrift für Betriebswirtschaft, Vol. 56.

Zeitschrift für die gesamte Staatswissenschaft.
See **Journal of Institutional and Theoretical Economics.**

Zeitschrift für Nationalökonomie.
See **Journal of Economics (Zeitschrift für Nationalökonomie).**

Zeitschrift für Wirtschafts- und Socialwissenschaften, Vol. 106.

LIST OF COLLECTIVE VOLUMES INDEXED 1986

Abegaz, Berhanu, ed. *The economic demography of mass poverty*. Studies in Third World Societies series, no. 29. Williamsburg, Va.: College of William and Mary, Department of Anthropology, 1986.

Adams, F. Gerard and Wachter, Susan M., eds. *Savings and capital formation: The policy options*. Lexington, Mass., and Toronto: Heath, Lexington Books, 1986.

Adams, Walter, ed. *The structure of American industry*. Seventh edition. New York: Macmillan; London: Collier Macmillan, [1950 . . .1982] 1986.

Adams, William James and Stoffaës, Christian, eds. *French industrial policy*. Washington, D.C.: Brookings Institution, 1986.

Adelman, Irma and Taylor, J. Edward, eds. *The design of alternative development strategies*. Rohtak, India: Jan Tinbergen Institute of Development Planning, 1986.

Aiginger, Karl, ed. *Weltwirtschaft und unternehmerische strategien*. Stuttgart: Fischer; Vienna: Österreichisches Institut für Wirtschaftsforschung, 1986.

Aiken, Linda H. and Mechanic, David, eds. *Applications of social science to clinical medicine and health policy*. New Brunswick, N.J.: Rutgers University Press, 1986.

Akerlof, George A. and Yellen, Janet L., eds. *Efficiency wage models of the labor market*. Cambridge; New York and Melbourne: Cambridge University Press, 1986.

Altmann, Franz-Lothar, ed. *Jahrbuch der wirtschaft Osteuropas (Yearbook of East-European economics)*. Vol. 11, no. 2. Munich and Vienna: Olzog, 1986.

Amann, Ronald and Cooper, Julian, eds. *Technical progress and Soviet economic development*. Oxford and New York: Blackwell, 1986.

Anderson, Kym and Hayami, Yujiro. *The political economy of agricultural protection: East Asia in international perspective*. With Aurelia George et al. Sydney; London and Boston: Allen and Unwin in association with the Australian National University, Australia–Japan Research Centre, 1986.

[Arrow, Kenneth J.] *Essays in honor of Kenneth J. Arrow*. Volume 1. *Social choice and public decision making*. Edited by Walter P. Heller, Ross M. Starr, and David A. Starrett. Cambridge; New York and Sydney: Cambridge University Press, 1986.

[Arrow, Kenneth J.] *Essays in honor of Kenneth J. Arrow*. Volume 2. *Equilibrium analysis*. Edited by Walter P. Heller, Ross M. Starr, and David A. Starrett. Cambridge; New York and Sydney: Cambridge University Press, 1986.

[Arrow, Kenneth J.] *Essays in honor of Kenneth J. Arrow*. Volume 3. *Uncertainty, information, and communication*. Edited by Walter P. Heller; Ross M. Starr and David A. Starrett. Cambridge; New York and Sydney: Cambridge University Press, 1986.

Artus, P. and Guvenen, O., eds. *International macroeconomic modelling for policy decisions*. In collaboration with F. Gagey. Advanced Studies in Theoretical and Applied Econometrics series, vol. 5. Dordrecht and Lancaster: Nijhoff; distributed in the U.S. and Canada by Kluwer Academic, Hingham, Mass., 1986.

Ashenfelter, Orley and Layard, Richard, eds. *Handbook of labor economics*. Volume 1. Handbooks in Economics series, no. 5. Amsterdam; Oxford and Tokyo: North-Holland; distributed in North America by Elsevier Science, New York, 1986.

Ashenfelter, Orley and Layard, Richard, eds. *Handbook of labor economics*. Volume 2. Handbooks in Economics series, no. 5. Amsterdam; Oxford and Tokyo: North-Holland; distributed in North America by Elsevier Science, New York, 1986.

Association of African Central Banks. *National financial policies and capital formation in Africa (Proceedings of a symposium), Cairo, Egypt*. Dakar, Senegal: African Centre for Monetary Studies, 1986.

Atack, Jeremy, ed. *Business and economic history, second series*. Volume 15. Champaign: University of Illinois, Bureau of Economic and Business Research 1986.

Axilrod, Stephen H., et al. *Debt, financial stability, and public policy: A symposium sponsored by the Federal Reserve Bank of Kansas City, Jackson Hole, Wyoming, August 27–29, 1986.* Kansas City: Federal Reserve Bank of Kansas City, 1986.

Axsäter, S.; Schneeweiss, Ch. and Silver, E., eds. *Multi-stage production planning and inventory control.* Lecture Notes in Economics and Mathematical Systems series, vol. 266. New York; Berlin and Tokyo: Springer, 1986.

Baark, Erik and Jamison, Andrew, eds. *Technological development in China, India and Japan: Cross-cultural perspectives.* New York: St. Martin's Press, 1986.

Baber, Colin and Williams, L. J., eds. *Modern South Wales: Essays in economic history.* Cardiff, U.K.: University of Wales Press; distributed by Humanities Press, Atlantic Highlands, N.J., 1986.

Backhaus, Klaus and Wilson, David T., eds. *Industrial marketing: A German–American perspective.* Berlin; New York and Tokyo: Springer, 1986.

Balassa, Bela and Giersch, Herbert, eds. *Economic incentives: Proceedings of a conference held by the International Economic Association at Kiel, West Germany.* New York: St. Martin's Press, 1986.

Bale, Malcolm D., ed. *Horticultural trade of the expanded European Community: Implications for Mediterranean countries.* World Bank Country Study series. Washington, D.C.: World Bank, 1986.

Bamberg, Günter and Spremann, Klaus, eds. *Capital market equilibria.* With contributions by G. Bamberg et al. New York; Berlin and Tokyo: Springer, 1986.

Baranzini, Mauro and Scazzieri, Roberto, eds. *Foundations of economics: Structures of inquiry and economic theory.* New York and Oxford: Blackwell, 1986.

Barfield, Claude E. and Schambra, William A., eds. *The politics of industrial policy.* Competing in a Changing World Economy Project series. Washington, D.C.: American Enterprise Institute for Public Policy Research, 1986.

Barney, Jay B. and Ouchi, William G., eds. *Organizational economics.* Jossey-Bass Management Series. Jossey-Bass Social and Behavioral Science Series. San Francisco and London: Jossey-Bass, 1986.

Başar, T., ed. *Dynamic games and applications in economics.* Lecture Notes in Economics and Mathematical Systems series, vol. 265. New York; Berlin and Tokyo: Springer, 1986.

Bassand, Michel, et al., eds. *Self-reliant development in Europe: Theory, problems, actions.* Aldershot, U.K., and Brookfield, Vt.: Gower, 1986.

Batey, P. W. and Madden, M., eds. *Integrated analysis of regional systems.* London Papers in Regional Science series, no. 15. London: Pion; distributed in the U.S. by Methuen, New York, 1986.

Baumol, William J. *Microtheory: Applications and origins.* Cambridge, Mass., and London: MIT Press, 1986.

Bean, Charles R.; Layard, P. Richard G. and Nickell, Stephen J., eds. *The rise in unemployment.* Paperback reprint. Oxford and New York: Blackwell, 1986.

Beckerman, Wilfred, ed. *Wage rigidity and unemployment.* Baltimore: Johns Hopkins University Press, 1986.

Belsley, David A. and Kuh, Edwin, eds. *Model reliability.* Cambridge, Mass., and London: MIT Press, 1986.

Ben-Porath, Yoram, ed. *The Israeli economy: Maturing through crises.* Cambridge, Mass., and London: Harvard University Press, 1986.

Bentkover, Judith D.; Covello, Vincent T. and Jeryl, Mumpower, eds. *Benefits assessment: The state of the art.* Technology, Risk and Society: An International Series in Risk Analysis. Dordrecht; Boston; Lancaster and Tokyo: Kluwer Academic, Reidel, 1986.

Berend, Iván T. and Borchardt, Knut, eds. *The impact of the Depression of the 1930s and its relevance for the contemporary world: Comparative studies prepared for the A/5 session of the 9th International Economic History Congress, 24–29 August, 1986, Bern, Switzerland.* Budapest: Karl Marx University of Economics, Academy Research Center of East-Central Europe; distributed by Kultura, Hungarian Foreign Trading Company, 1986.

BERG, ROBERT J. AND WHITAKER, JENNIFER SEYMOUR, eds. *Strategies for African development.* Berkeley, Calif., and London: University of California Press, 1986.

BERGMAN, EDWARD M., ed. *Local economies in transition: Policy realities and development potentials.* Duke Press Policy Studies series. Durham, N.C.: Duke University Press, 1986.

BERKOWITZ, MONROE AND HILL, M. ANNE, eds. *Disability and the labor market: Economic problems, policies, and programs.* Ithaca, N.Y.: Cornell University, New York State School of Industrial and Labor Relations, ILR Press, 1986.

BITTANTI, S., ed. *Time series and linear systems.* Lecture Notes in Control and Information Sciences series, vol. 86. Berlin; New York; London and Tokyo: Springer, 1986.

BJÖRKMAN, JAMES WARNER, ed. *The changing division of labor in South Asia: Women and men in India's society, economy, and politics.* Riverdale, Md.: Riverdale, 1986.

BLACK, R. D. COLLISON, ed. *Ideas in economics.* Totowa, N.J.: Barnes and Noble Books, 1986.

BLANCHARD, OLIVIER; DORNBUSCH, RUDIGER AND LAYARD, RICHARD, eds. *Restoring Europe's prosperity: Macroeconomic papers from the Centre for European Policy Studies.* Cambridge, Mass., and London: MIT Press, 1986.

BLAUG, MARK. *Economic history and the history of economics.* New York: New York University Press; distributed by Columbia University Press, 1986.

BLOCK, WALTER, ed. *Reaction: The new Combines Investigation Act.* Vancouver: Fraser Institute, 1986.

BLOCK, WALTER AND HEXHAM, IRVING, eds. *Religion, economics and social thought.* Vancouver: Fraser Institute, 1986.

BLUNDELL, RICHARD AND WALKER, IAN, eds. *Unemployment, search and labour supply.* Cambridge; New York and Sydney: Cambridge University Press, 1986.

BOADWAY, ROBIN W. AND MINTZ, JACK M., eds. *Policy forum on the business transfer tax.* Policy Forum series, no. 12. Kingston, Ontario: Queen's University, John Deutsch Institute for the Study of Economic Policy, 1986.

BOESEN, JANNIK, ET AL., eds. *Tanzania: Crisis and struggle for survival.* Uppsala: Scandinavian Institute of African Studies; distributed by Almqvist & Wiksell International, Stockholm, 1986.

BREIT, WILLIAM AND SPENCER, ROGER W., eds. *Lives of the laureates: Seven Nobel economists.* Cambridge: MIT Press, 1986.

BROMLEY, DANIEL W., ed. *Natural resource economics: Policy problems and contemporary analysis.* Recent Economic Thought Series. Dordrecht and Lancaster: Kluwer Nijhoff; distributed in the U.S. and Canada by Kluwer Academic, Hingham, Mass., 1986.

BROWNE, WILLIAM P. AND HADWIGER, DON F., eds. *World food policies toward agricultural interdependence.* Boulder, Colo.: Rienner, 1986.

BRUCE, ROBERT, ET AL., eds. *Handbook of Australian corporate finance.* Second edition. Honolulu: University of Hawaii Press, 1986.

BUCHANAN, JAMES M. *Liberty, market and state: Political economy in the 1980s.* New York: New York University Press, 1986.

BURTON, DANIEL F., ET AL., eds. *The jobs challenge: Pressures and possibilities.* Cambridge, Mass.: Harper & Row, Ballinger, 1986.

BURTON, JOHN, ET AL. *Keynes's* General Theory: *Fifty years on, its relevance and irrelevance to modern times.* Hobart Paperback series, no. 24. London: Institute of Economic Affairs; distributed in North America by Transatlantic Arts, Albuquerque, N.M., 1986.

BUTKIEWICZ, JAMES L.; KOFORD, KENNETH J. AND MILLER, JEFFREY B., eds. *Keynes' economic legacy: Contemporary economic theories.* New York; Eastbourne, U.K.; Toronto and Sydney: Praeger, 1986.

BUTLER, JAMES R. G. AND DOESSEL, DARREL P., eds. *Economics and health 1985: Proceedings of the Seventh Australian Conference of Health Economists.* Australian Studies in Health Service Administration series, no. 56. Kensington, New South Wales: University of New South Wales, School of Health Administration, 1986.

CAGAN, PHILLIP, ed. *Essays in contemporary economic problems, 1986: The impact of the Reagan program*. EDUARDO SOMENSATTO, Associate Editor. Washington, D.C.: American Enterprise Institute for Public Policy Research, 1986.

CAIRNCROSS, ALEC. *Economics and economic policy*. Oxford and New York: Blackwell, 1986.

CAMPBELL, COLIN D. AND DOUGAN, WILLIAM R., eds. *Alternative monetary regimes*. Baltimore and London: Johns Hopkins University Press, 1986.

CANTO, VICTOR A.; KADLEC, CHARLES W. AND LAFFER, ARTHUR B., eds. *The financial analyst's guide to fiscal policy*. New York; Eastbourne, U.K.; Toronto and Sydney: Greenwood Press, Praeger, 1986.

CAPIE, FORREST AND WOOD, GEOFFREY E., eds. *Financial crises and the world banking system*. New York: St. Martin's Press, 1986.

CAPPS, ORAL, JR. AND SENAUER, BENJAMIN, eds. *Food demand analysis: Implications for future consumption*. Blacksburg: Virginia Polytechnic Institute and State University, Department of Agricultural Economics, 1986.

CARTER, R. L.; CHIPLIN, B. AND LEWIS, M. K., eds. *Personal financial markets: An examination of the evolving markets for personal savings and financing in the United Kingdom and the United States*. Oxford: Allan; distributed by Humanities Press, Atlantic Highlands, N.J., 1986.

CASSON, MARK, ET AL. *Multinationals and world trade: Vertical integration and the division of labour in world industries*. In association with DAVID BARRY ET AL. London; Boston and Sydney: Allen & Unwin, 1986.

C. D. HOWE INSTITUTE. *Policy harmonization: The effects of a Canadian–American free trade area*. Toronto: Author; distributed by Prentice-Hall Canada, Scarborough, Ontario, 1986.

CHELIUS, JAMES, ed. *Current issues in workers' compensation: Papers presented at a conference sponsored by: The Institute of Management and Labor Relations and the Bureau of Economic Research, Rutgers, The State University of New Jersey; The New York State School of Industrial and Labor Relations, Cornell University; and The Economics Department, the University of Connecticut*. Kalamazoo, Mich.: W. E. Upjohn Institute for Employment Research, 1986.

CHEN, ANDREW H., ed. *Research in finance*. Volume 6. A Research Annual. Greenwich, Conn., and London: JAI Press, 1986.

CHENERY, HOLLIS; ROBINSON, SHERMAN AND SYRQUIN, MOSHE. *Industrialization and growth: A comparative study*. With contributions by GERSHON FEDER, ET AL. New York; Oxford; Toronto and Melbourne: Oxford University Press for the World Bank, 1986.

CHENG, HANG-SHENG, ed. *Financial policy and reform in Pacific Basin countries*. Lexington, Mass., and Toronto: Heath, Lexington Books, 1986.

CHICOINE, DAVID L. AND WALZER, NORMAN, eds. *Financing local infrastructure in nonmetropolitan areas*. New York: Greenwood Press, Praeger, 1986.

CLAUDON, MICHAEL P., ed. *World debt crisis: International lending on trial*. Cambridge, Mass.: Harper & Row, Ballinger, 1986.

CLAUSEN, A. W. *The development challenge of the eighties: A.W. Clausen at the World Bank. Major policy addresses, 1981–1986*. Washington, D.C.: World Bank, 1986.

COATS, A. W., ed. *Economists in international agencies: An exploratory study*. New York and London: Greenwood Press, Praeger, 1986.

COHN, ELCHANAN, ed. *Federal block grants to education*. Oxford; New York; Toronto and Sydney: Pergamon Press, 1986.

COLANDER, DAVID C., ed. *Incentive-based incomes policies: Advances in TIP and MAP*. Cambridge, Mass.: Harper & Row, Ballinger, 1986.

COLE, R. V. AND PARRY, T. G., eds. *Selected issues in Pacific island development: Papers from the Islands/Australia project*. Pacific Policy Papers series, no. 2. Canberra: Australian National University, National Centre for Development Studies, 1986.

[COLEMAN, D. C.] *Business life and public policy: Essays in honour of D.C. Coleman*. Edited by NEIL MCKENDRICK AND R. B. OUTHWAITE. Cambridge; New York and Melbourne: Cambridge University Press, 1986.

COLEMAN, JAMES S. *Individual interests and collective action: Selected essays*. Studies in Rationality and Social Change series. Cambridge; New York and Melbourne: Cambridge University Press in collaboration with Maison des Sciences de l'Homme, Paris, 1986.

COMISSO, ELLEN AND TYSON, LAURA D'ANDREA, eds. *Power, purpose, and collective choice: Economic strategy in socialist states.* Cornell Studies in Political Economy series. Ithaca and London: Cornell University Press, 1986.

COONTZ, STEPHANIE AND HENDERSON, PETA, eds. *Women's work, men's property: The origins of gender and class.* London: New Left Books, Verso; distributed in the U.S. and Canada by Schocken Books, New York, 1986.

COOPER, RICHARD N. *Economic policy in an interdependent world: Essays in world economics.* Cambridge, Mass., and London: MIT Press, 1986.

COX, ANDREW, ed. *State, finance and industry: A comparative analysis of post-war trends in six advanced industrial economies.* New York: St. Martin's Press, 1986.

COYNE, JOHN AND WRIGHT, MIKE, eds. *Divestment and strategic change.* Oxford: Allan; Totowa, N.J.: Barnes and Noble Books, 1986.

[CRUTCHFIELD, JAMES A.] *Natural resources economics and policy applications: Essays in honor of James A. Crutchfield.* Edited by EDWARD MILES, ROBERT PEALY, AND ROBERT STOKES. Foreword by BREWSTER C. DENNY. Public Policy Issues in Resource Management series. Seattle: Institute for Public Policy and Management, University of Washington Graduate School of Public Affairs, and Institute for Marine Studies; distributed by the University of Washington Press, Seattle and London, 1986.

CULYER, A. J. AND JÖNSSON, BENGT, eds. *Public and private health services: Complementarities and conflicts.* Oxford and New York: Blackwell, 1986.

CUMMINGS, R. G.; BROOKSHIRE, D. S. AND SCHULZE, W. D., eds. *Valuing environmental goods: An assessment of the contingent valuation method.* Totowa, N.J.: Littlefield, Adams; Rowman and Allanheld, 1986.

DABONI, L.; MONTESANO, A. AND LINES, M., eds. *Recent developments in the foundations of utility and risk theory.* Theory and Decision Library Series, vol 47. Dordrecht: Reidel; distributed in the U.S. and Canada by Kluwer Academic, Hingham, Mass., 1986.

DALE, RICHARD, ed. *Financial deregulation: The proceedings of a conference held by the David Hume Institute in May 1986.* Cambridge and Wolfeboro, N.H.: Woodhead-Faulkner, 1986.

DAMACHI, UKANDI G. AND SEIBEL, HANS DIETER, eds. *Management problems in Africa.* New York: St. Martin's Press, 1986.

DANSON, MIKE, ed. *Redundancy and recession: Restructuring the regions?* Norwich, U.K.: Geo Abstracts, Geo Books, 1986.

DANTWALA, M. L., ET AL. *Indian agricultural development since independence: A collection of essays.* New Delhi: Oxford and IBH, 1986.

DANZIGER, SHELDON H. AND WEINBERG, DANIEL H., eds. *Fighting poverty: What works and what doesn't.* Cambridge, Mass., and London: Harvard University Press, 1986.

DAY, RICHARD H. AND ELIASSON, GUNNAR, eds. *The dynamics of market economies.* Amsterdam and Oxford: North-Holland in cooperation with the Industrial Institute for Economic and Social Research, Stockholm; distributed in the U.S. and Canada by Elsevier Science, New York, 1986.

[DEAN, JOEL] *The economics of strategic planning: Essays in honor of Joel Dean. Partial proceedings of a conference sponsored by AT&T, Coopers and Lybrand, the Joel Dean Foundation, and the Graduate School of Business, Columbia University.* Edited by LACY GLENN THOMAS III. Lexington, Mass., and Toronto: Heath, Lexington Books, 1986.

DE ANTONI, F.; LAURO, N. AND RIZZI, A., eds. *Compstat: Proceedings in computational statistics, 7th symposium held at Rome 1986.* Heidelberg and Vienna: Physica, 1986.

DEMAC, DONNA A., ed. *Tracing new orbits: Cooperation and competition in global satellite development.* Columbia Studies in Business, Government, and Society series. New York: Columbia University Press, 1986.

DENNIS, BARBARA D., ed. *Proceedings of the Thirty-Eighth Annual Meeting: December 28–30, 1985, New York.* RRA Series. Madison, Wisc.: Industrial Relations Research Association, 1986.

DENOON, DAVID B. H., ed. *Constraints on strategy: The economics of Western security.* Washington, D.C.; London; Beijing and Toronto: Pergamon-Brassey's, 1986.

DICKE, DETLEV CHR., ed. *Foreign debts in the present and a new international economic order.* Progress and Undercurrents in Public International Law series, vol. 1. Fribourg, Switzerland: University Press; distributed by Westview Press, Boulder, Colo., 1986.

DIMAGGIO, PAUL J., ed. *Nonprofit enterprise in the Arts: Studies in mission and constraint.* Yale Studies on Nonprofit Organizations series. New York and Oxford: Oxford University Press, 1986.

DIXON, JOHN A. AND HUFSCHMIDT, MAYNARD M., eds. *Economic valuation techniques for the environment: A case study workbook.* Baltimore and London: Johns Hopkins University Press, 1986.

DONCKELS, RIK AND MEIJER, JANE N., eds. *Women in small business: Focus on Europe.* Assen, the Netherlands, and Wolfeboro, N.H.: Van Gorcum, 1986.

DORNBUSCH, RUDIGER. *Dollars, debts, and deficits.* Leuven, Belgium: Leuven University Press; Cambridge, Mass., and London: MIT Press, 1986.

[DORSEY, JASPER N. AND WIGGINS, BEN T.] *Telecommunications in the post-divestiture era: Essays in honor of Jasper N. Dorsey and Ben T. Wiggins.* Edited by ALBERT L. DANIELSEN AND DAVID R. KAMERSCHEN. Lexington, Mass., and Toronto: Heath, Lexington Books, 1986.

DOWDY, EDWIN, ed. *Marxist policies today: In socialist and capitalist countries.* St. Lucia, Queensland; London and New York: University of Queensland Press, 1986.

DUIGNAN, PETER AND JACKSON, ROBERT H., eds. *Politics and government in African states, 1960–1985.* London and Sydney: Croom Helm; Stanford, Calif.: Hoover Institution Press, 1986.

EASTER, WILLIAM K., ed. *Irrigation investment, technology, and management strategies for development.* Studies in Water Policy and Management, no. 9. Boulder, Colo., and London: Westview Press, 1986.

ECONOMIC COMMISSION FOR LATIN AMERICA AND THE CARIBBEAN (ECLAC). *Debt, adjustment, and renegotiation in Latin America: Orthodox and alternative approaches.* Boulder, Colo.: Rienner in cooperation with the United Nations, New York, 1986.

ECONOMIC COUNCIL OF CANADA. *Managing the legacy: Proceedings of a Colloquium on the Environment, December 1985.* Ottawa: Minister of Supply and Services Canada, Canadian Government Publishing Centre, 1986.

EDWARDS, JEREMY, ET AL., eds. *Recent developments in corporate finance.* Cambridge; New York and Melbourne: Cambridge University Press, 1986.

EDWARDS, RICHARD; GARONNA, PAOLO AND TÖDTLING, FRANZ, eds. *Unions in crisis and beyond: Perspectives from six countries.* Dover, Mass., and London: Auburn House, 1986.

EDWARDS, SEBASTIAN AND AHAMED, LIAQUAT, eds. *Economic adjustment and exchange rates in developing countries.* Chicago and London: University of Chicago Press, 1986.

EHRENBERG, RONALD G., ed. *Research in Labor economics.* Volume 8 (Part A). A Research Annual. Greenwich, Conn., and London: JAI Press, 1986.

EHRENBERG, RONALD G., ed. *Research in Labor economics.* Volume 8 (Part B). A Research Annual. Greenwich, Conn., and London: JAI Press, 1986.

ELBAUM, BERNARD AND LAZONICK, WILLIAM, eds. *The decline of the British economy.* Oxford; New York; Toronto and Singapore: Oxford University Press, 1986.

EL MALLAKH, RAGAEI, ed. *The Middle East, Pacific Basin, and the United States: Refining and petrochemicals. Proceedings of the Sixth International Area Conference.* Boulder, Colo.: The International Research Center for Energy and Economic Development, 1986.

ELSTER, JON, ed. *The multiple self.* Studies in Rationality and Social Change series. Cambridge; New York and Sydney: Cambridge University Press in collaboration with Maison des Sciences de l'Homme, Paris, 1986.

ELSTER, JON AND HYLLAND, AANUND, eds. *Foundations of social choice theory.* Studies in Rationality and Social Change series. Cambridge; New York and Sydney: Cambridge Univesity Press; Paris: Maison des Sciences de l'Homme, 1986.

ENGERMAN, STANLEY L. AND GALLMAN, ROBERT E., eds. *Long-term factors in American economic growth*. Studies in Income and Wealth series, vol. 51. Chicago and London: University of Chicago Press, 1986.

Eucken, Walter and Böhm, Franz, eds. *ORDO: Jahrbuch für die Ordnung von Wirtschaft und Gesellschaft*. Band 37. Stuttgart and New York: Fischer, 1986.

Faber, Malte, ed. *Studies in Austrian capital theory, investment and time*. Lecture Notes in Economics and Mathematical Systems series, vol. 277. New York; Berlin; London and Tokyo: Springer, 1986.

Fagen, Richard R.; Deere, Carmen Diana and Coraggio, José Luis, eds. *Transition and development: Problems of third world socialism*. MR/Censa Series on the Americas. New York: Monthly Review Press; Berkeley, Calif.: Center for the Study of the Americas, 1986.

Faulhaber, Gerald; Noam, Eli and Tasley, Roberta, eds. *Services in transition: The impact of information technology on the service sector*. Cambridge, Mass.: Harper & Row, Ballinger, 1986.

Federal Home Loan Bank of San Francisco. *Financial stability of the thrift industry: Proceedings of the Eleventh Annual Conference, December 12–13, 1985, San Francisco, California*. San Francisco: Author, 1986.

Federal Reserve Bank of Boston. *Economic consequences of tax simplification: Proceedings of a conference held at Melvin Village, New Hampshire, October 1985*. Federal Reserve Bank of Boston Conference Series, no.29. Boston: Author, 1986.

Feinberg, Richard E., et al. *Between two worlds: The World Bank's next decade*. New Brunswick, N.J., and Oxford: Transaction Books, 1986.

Findlay, Christopher and Garnaut, Ross, eds. *The political economy of manufacturing protection: Experiences of ASEAN and Australia*. Sydney; London and Boston: Allen & Unwin, 1986.

Fine, Ben, ed. *The value dimension: Marx versus Ricardo and Sraffa*. Economy and Society series. London and New York: Routledge and Kegan Paul, 1986.

[de Finetti, Bruno] *Bayesian inference and decision techniques: Essays in honor of Bruno de Finetti*. Edited by Prem K. Goel and Arnold Zellner. Studies in Bayesian Econometrics and Statistics series, vol. 6. Amsterdam and Oxford: North-Holland; distributed in the U.S. and Canada by Elsevier Science, New York, 1986.

Finn, Richard B., ed. *U.S.–Japan relations: Learning form competition. Annual Review, 1985*. Harvard University, Center for International Affairs, Program on U.S.–Japan Relations. New Brunswick, N.J., and Oxford: Transaction Books, 1986.

Finsinger, Jörg and Pauly, Mark V., eds. *The economics of insurance regulation: A cross-national study*. New York: St. Martin's Press, 1986.

Firth, Michael and Keane, Simon M., eds. *Issues in finance*. Oxford: Allan; distributed in the U.S. and Canada by Humanities Press, Atlantic Highlands, N.J., 1986.

Fischer, Stanley. *Indexing, inflation, and economic policy*. Cambridge, Mass., and London: MIT Press, 1986.

Fischer, Stanley, ed. *NBER Macroeconomics Annual 1986*. Cambridge, Mass., and London: MIT Press, 1986.

Fleming, Gretchen V. and Andersen, Ronald M., eds. *The municipal health services program: Can access be improved while controlling costs?* Research Series, no. 34. Chicago: Pluribus Press for the University of Chicago Center for Health Administration Studies, 1986.

Follain, James R., ed. *Tax reform and real estate*. Washington, D.C.: Urban Institute Press, 1986.

Fransman, Martin, ed. *Machinery and economic development*. New York: St. Martin's Press, 1986.

Franz, Alfred and Rainer, Norbert, eds. *Problems of compilation of input–output tables: Proceedings of an International Meeting organized by the Austrian Statistical Society, Baden near Vienna, Austria, 19–25 May, 1985*. Schriftenreihe der Österreichischen Statistischen Gesellschaft, band 2. Vienna: Orac, 1986.

Frederick, Kenneth D., ed. *Scarce water and institutional change*. With the assistance of Diana

C. Gibbons. Washington, D.C.: Resources for the Future; distributed by Johns Hopkins University Press, Baltimore, 1986.

Freeman, Christopher, ed. *Design, innovation and long cycles in economic development.* New York: St. Martin's Press, 1986.

Freeman, Richard B. and Holzer, Harry J., eds. *The black youth employment crisis.* National Bureau of Economic Research Project Report series. Chicago and London: University of Chicago Press, 1986.

Friedman, Benjamin M., ed. *Financing corporate capital formation.* National Bureau of Economic Research Project Report series. Chicago and London: University of Chicago Press, 1986.

Frisch, Helmut and Gahlen, Bernhard, eds. *Causes of contemporary stagnation: Proceedings of an international symposium held at the Institute for Advanced Studies, Vienna, Austria, October 10–12, 1984.* Studies in Contemporary Economics series. Berlin; New York and Tokyo: Springer, 1986.

Fuchs, Victor R. *The health economy.* Cambridge, Mass., and London: Harvard University Press, 1986.

Giersch, Herbert, ed. *The international debt problem: Lessons for the future.* Symposium series 1985. Tübingen, West Germany: Mohr, 1986.

Gilad, Benjamin and Kaish, Stanley, eds. *Handbook of behavioral economics.* Volume A. *Behavioral microeconomics.* Greenwich, Conn., and London: JAI Press, 1986.

Gilad, Benjamin and Kaish, Stanley, eds. *Handbook of behavioral economics.* Volume B. *Behavioral macroeconomics.* Greenwich, Conn., and London: JAI Press, 1986.

Gilroy, Curtis L., ed. *Army manpower economics.* Westview Special Studies in Military Affairs. Boulder, Colo., and London: Westview Press, 1986.

Glazier, Ira A. and De Rosa, Luigi, eds. *Migration across time and nations: Population mobility in historical contexts.* New York and London: Holmes & Meier, 1986.

Gold, Steven D., ed. *Reforming state tax systems.* Denver: National Conference of State Legislatures, 1986.

Goldberg, Walter H., ed. *Ailing steel: The transoceanic quarrel.* New York: St. Martin's Press, 1986.

Gomulka, Stanislaw. *Growth, innovation and reform in Eastern Europe.* Economics of Technological Change series. Madison: University of Wisconsin Press, 1986.

Gondolf, Edward W.; Marcus, Irwin M. and Dougherty, James P., eds. *The global economy: Divergent perspectives on economic change.* Boulder, Colo., and London: Westview Press, 1986.

Gordon, Robert J., ed. *The American business cycle: Continuity and change.* National Bureau of Economic Research Studies in Business Cycles series, vol. 25. Chicago and London: University of Chicago Press, 1986.

Goss, Barry A., ed. *Futures markets: Their establishment and performance.* New York: New York University Press; distributed by Columbia University Press, 1986.

Grassl, Wolfgang and Smith, Barry, eds. *Austrian economics: Historical and philisophical background.* New York: New York University Press, 1986.

Gray, Bradford H., ed. *For-profit enterprise in health care.* Washington, D.C.: National Academy Press, 1986.

Gray, H. Peter, ed. *Research in international business and finance.* Volume 5. *Uncle Sam as Host.* A Research Annual. Greenwich, Conn., and London: JAI Press, 1986.

Greenaway, David and Tharakan, P. K. M., eds. *Imperfect competition and international trade: The policy aspects of intra-industry trade.* Atlantic Highlands, N.J.: Humanities Press; Brighton, Sussex: Harvestor Press, Wheatsheaf Books, 1986.

Greenfield, Sidney M. and Strickon, Arnold, eds. *Entrepreneurship and social change.* Monographs in Economic Anthropology, no. 2. Lanham, N.Y., and London: University Press of America in cooperation with the Society for Economic Anthropology, 1986.

Grieson, Ronald E., ed. *Antitrust and regulation.* Lexington, Mass., and Toronto: Heath, Lexington Books, 1986.

GRILICHES, ZVI AND INTRILIGATOR, MICHAEL D., eds. *Handbook of Econometrics.* Volume 3. Handbooks in Economics series, book 2. Amsterdam; Oxford and Tokyo: North-Holland; distributed in the U.S. and Canada by Elsevier Science, New York, 1986.

HAFER, R. W., ed. *How open is the U.S. economy?* Lexington, Mass., and Toronto: Heath, Lexington Books, 1986. (I)

HAFER, R. W., ed. *The monetary versus fiscal policy debate: Lessons from two decades.* Totowa, N.J.: Littlefield, Adams; Rowman and Allanheld, 1986. (II)

HALL, GRAHAM, ed. *European industrial policy.* New York: St. Martin's Press, 1986.

HALL, PETER, ed. *Technology, innovation and economic policy.* New York: St. Martin's Press, 1986.

HAMILTON, GEOFFREY, ed. *Red multinationals or red herrings? The activities of enterprises from socialist countries in the West.* New York: St. Martin's Press, 1986.

HANSON, JAMES A. AND ROCHA, ROBERTO DE REZENDE. *High interest rates, spreads, and the costs of intermediation: Two studies.* Industry and Finance Series, vol. 18. Washington, D.C.: World Bank, 1986.

[HARCOURT, G. C.] *Controversies in political economy: Selected essays of G. C. Harcourt.* Edited by O. F. HAMOUDA. New York: New York University Press; distributed by Columbia University Press, 1986.

HARDOY, JORGE E. AND SATTERTHWAITE, DAVID, eds. *Small and intermediate urban centres: Their role in regional and national development in the third world.* Boulder, Colo.: Westview Press in association with the United Nations University, 1986.

HART, P. E., ed. *Unemployment and labour market policies.* National Institute of Economic and Social Research, Policy Studies Institute, and Royal Institute of International Affairs Joint Studies in Public Policy series, no. 12. Aldershot, U.K., and Brookfield, Vt.: Gower, 1986.

HARTLAND-THUNBERG, PENELOPE AND EBINGER, CHARLES K., eds. *Banks, petrodollars, and sovereign debtors: Blood from a stone?* Lexington, Mass., and Toronto: Heath, Lexington Books, 1986.

HARTLYN, JONATHAN AND MORLEY, SAMUEL A., eds. *Latin American political economy: Financial crisis and political change.* Boulder, Colo., and London: Westview Press, 1986.

HAUPT, GEORGES. *Aspects of international socialism, 1871–1914: Essays by Georges Haupt.* Translated by PETER FAWCETT. With a preface by ERIC HOBSBAWM. Studies in Modern Capitalism series. Cambridge; New York and Melbourne: Cambridge University Press; Paris: Éditions de la Maison des Sciences de l'Homme, 1986.

HAUSER, HEINZ, ed. *Promotion of direct investment in developing countries.* Swiss Institute for Research into International Economic Relations, Economic Structures, and Regional Science series, no. 11. Grüsch, West Germany: Rüegger, 1986. (I)

HAUSER, HEINZ, ed. *Protectionism and structural adjustment.* Swiss Institute for Research into International Economic Relations, Economic Structures, and Regional Science series, no. 12. Grüsch, West Germany: Rüegger, 1986. (II)

HAX, H.; KRAUS, W. AND TSUCHIYA, K., eds. *Structural change: The challenge to industrial societies.* Berlin; New York and Tokyo: Springer, 1986.

HAZELL, PETER; POMAREDA, CARLOS AND VALDÉS, ALBERTO, eds. *Crop insurance for agricultural development: Issues and experience.* With the assistance of JOAN STRAKER HAZELL. Baltimore and London: Johns Hopkins University Press for the International Food Policy Research Institute, 1986.

HELBURN, SUZANNE W. AND BRAMHALL, DAVID F., eds. *Marx, Schumpeter, Keynes: A centenary celebration of dissent.* Armonk, N.Y., and London: Sharpe, 1986.

HELLEINER, GERALD K, ed. *Africa and the International Monetary Fund: Papers presented at a symposium held in Nairobi, Kenya, May 13–15, 1985.* Washington, D.C.: International Monetary Fund, 1986.

HERBER, BERNARD P., ed. *Public finance and public debt: Proceedings of the 40th Congress of the International Institute of Public Finance, Innsbruck, 1984.* Detroit: Wayne State University Press, 1986.

Hertner, Peter and Jones, Geoffrey eds. *Multinationals: Theory and history.* Aldershot, U.K., and Brookfield, Vt.: Gower in association with the European Science Foundation, Strasbourg, 1986.

Hewlett, Sylvia Ann; Ilchman, Alice S. and Sweeney, John J., eds. *Family and work: Bridging the gap.* Cambridge, Mass.: Harper & Row, Ballinger, 1986.

Hills, Stephen M., ed. *The changing labor market: A longitudinal study of young men.* Lexington, Mass., and Toronto: Heath, Lexington Books, 1986.

Hirashima, S. and Muqtada, M., eds. *Hired labour and rural labour markets in Asia: Studies based on farm-level data.* New Delhi: International Labour Organisation, Asian Employment Programme, 1986.

[Hirshman, Albert O.] *Development, democracy, and the art of trespassing: Essays in honor of Albert O. Hirschman.* Edited by Alejandro Foxley, Michael S. McPherson, and Guillermo O'Donnell. Notre Dame, Ind.: University of Notre Dame Press for the Helen Kellogg Institute for International Studies, 1986.

Hogarth, Robin M. and Reder, Melvin W., eds. *Rational Choice: The Contrast between Economics and Psychology.* Chicago and London: University of Chicago Press, 1987.

Höhmann, Hans-Hermann; Nove, Alec and Vogel, Heinrich, eds. *Economics and politics in the USSR: Problems of interdependence.* Boulder, Colo., and London: Westview Press in cooperation with das Bundesinstitut für ostwissenschaftliche und internationale Studien/the Federal Institute for East European and International Studies, 1986.

Holton, Robert J. and Turner, Bryan S. *Talcott Parsons on economy and society.* New York and London: Routledge and Kegan Paul, 1986.

Holzer, H. Peter and Schoenfeld, Hanns-Martin W., eds. *Managerial accounting and analysis in multinational enterprises.* New York and Berlin: de Gruyter, 1986.

Humphreys, Thomas M. *Essays on inflation.* Fifth edition. Richmond: Federal Reserve Bank of Richmond, [1979 . . . 1983] 1986.

[Hutt, W. H.] *W. H. Hutt: An economist for the long run.* Edited by Morgan O. Reynolds. Chicago: Regnery Books, Gateway Editions for, and in association with, the Heritage Foundation, Washington, D.C., 1986.

Institute of Medicine and National Research Council, Committee on an Aging Society. *America's aging: Productive roles in an older society.* Washington, D.C.: National Academy Press, 1986.

International Monetary Fund, Research Department. *Staff studies for the* World Economic Outlook, *July 1986.* World Economic and Financial Surveys series. Washington, D.C.: Author, 1986.

Ioffe, Olimpiad S. and Janis, Mark W., eds. *Soviet law and economy.* University of Leyden, Documentation Office for East European Law, Law in Eastern Europe series, no. 32. Norwell, Mass.; Dordrecht and Lancaster: Kluwer Academic, Nijhoff, 1986.

Ippolito, Pauline M. and Scheffman, David T., eds. *Empirical approaches to consumer protection economics: Proceedings of a conference sponsored by the Bureau of Economics, Federal Trade Commission, April 26–27, 1984.* Washington, D.C.: Federal Trade Commission, 1986.

Islam, Rizwanul and Muqtada, M., eds. *Bangladesh: Selected issues in employment and development.* New Delhi: International Labour Organisation, Asian Employment Programme, 1986.

Isserman, Andrew M., ed. *Population change and the economy: Social science theories and models.* Dordrecht and Lancaster: Kluwer Academic, Kluwer-Nijhoff; distributed in the U.S. and Canada by Kluwer Academic, Hingham, Mass., 1986.

Jacobi, Otto, et al., eds. *Economic crisis, trade unions and the state.* London; Sydney and Dover, N.H.: Croom Helm, 1986. (I)

Jacobi, Otto, et al., eds. *Technological change, rationalisation and industrial relations.* New York: St. Martin's Press, 1986. (II)

Jain, Ajit and Matejko, Alexander, eds. *A critique of Marxist and non-Marxist thought.* New York; Eastbourne, U.K.; Toronto and Tokyo: Greenwood Press, Praeger, 1986.

JAO, Y. C. AND LEUNG, C. K., eds. *China's special economic zones: Polices, problems, and prospects.* Hong Kong; Oxford and New York: Oxford University Press, 1986.

JONES, RONALD W., ed. *International trade: Surveys of theory and policy. Selections from the* Handbook of International Economics. Amsterdam; Oxford and Tokyo: North-Holland; distributed in the U.S. and Canada by Elsevier Science, New York, 1986.

DE JONG, H. W. AND SHEPHERD, W. G., eds. *Mainstreams in Industrial Organization.* Book 1. *Theory and international aspects.* Studies in Industrial Organization series, vol. 6. Hingham, Mass.; Dordrecht and Lancaster: Kluwer Academic, 1986.

DE JONG, H. W. AND SHEPHERD, W. G., eds. *Mainstreams in industrial organization.* Book 2. *Policies: Antitrust, deregulation and industrial.* Studies in Industrial Organization series, vol. 6. Hingham, Mass.; Dordrecht and Lancaster: Kluwer Academic, 1986.

KAHAN, ARCADIUS. *Essays in Jewish social and economic history.* Edited by ROGER WEISS. With an introduction by JONATHAN FRANKEL. Chicago and London: University of Chicago Press, 1986.

KAHLER, MILES, ed. *The politics of international debt.* Cornell Studies in Political Economy series. Ithaca, N.Y., and London: Cornell University Press, 1986.

KALECKI, MICHAL. *Selected essays on economic planning.* Edited, translated, and introduced by JAN TOPOROWSKI. Cambridge; New York and Melbourne: Cambridge University Press, 1986.

KAPUR, BASANT K. *Studies in inflationary dynamics: Financial repression and financial liberalization in less developed countries.* Kent Ridge, Singapore: National University of Singapore, Singapore University Press, 1986.

KASER, M. C., ed. *The economic history of Eastern Europe, 1919–1975.* Volume 3. *Institutional change within a planned economy.* Oxford; New York; Toronto and Melbourne: Oxford University Press, Clarendon Press, 1986.

KASER, M. C. AND RADICE, E. A., eds. *The economic history of Eastern Europe, 1919–1975.* Volume 2. *Interwar policy, the war and reconstruction.* Oxford; New York; Toronto and Melbourne: Oxford University Press, Clarendon Press, 1986.

KAUFMAN, GEORGE G. AND KORMENDI, ROGER C., eds. *Deregulating financial services: Public policy in flux.* Mid America Institute for Public Policy Research Book series. Cambridge, Mass.: Harper & Row, Ballinger, 1986.

KEEBLE, DAVID AND WEVER, EGBERT, eds. *New firms and regional development in Europe.* London; Sydney and Dover, N.H.: Croom Helm, 1986.

KERN, ROSEMARY GIBSON AND WINDHAM, SUSAN R. *Medicaid and other experiments in state health policy.* With PAULA GRISWOLD. American Enterprise Institute Studies in Health Policy, no. 437. Washington, D.C.: American Enterprise Institute for Public Policy Research, 1986.

KHAN, KHUSHI M., ed. *Multinationals of the South: New actors in the international economy.* New York: St. Martin's Press, 1986.

KNOWLTON, WINTHROP AND ZECKHAUSER, RICHARD, eds. *American society: Public and private responsibilities.* Cambridge, Mass.: Harper & Row, Ballinger, 1986.

KOP, YAAKOV, ed. *Changing social policy: Israel, 1985–86.* Jerusalem: Center for Social Policy Studies in Israel, 1986.

KORNAI, JÁNOS. *Contradictions and dilemmas: Studies on the Socialist economy and society.* Translated by ILONA LUKÁCS, JULIANNA PARTI, BRIAN MCLEAN, AND GYÖRGY HAJDÚ. Cambridge, Mass., and London: MIT Press, 1986.

KRUGMAN, PAUL R., ed. *Strategic trade policy and the new international economics.* Cambridge, Mass., and London: MIT Press, 1986.

[LACHMANN, LUDWIG M.] *Subjectivism, intelligibility and economic understanding: Essays in honor of Ludwig M. Lachmann on his eightieth birthday.* Edited by ISRAEL M. KIRZNER. New York: New York University Press; distributed by Columbia University Press, 1986.

LAIRD, ROBBIN F. AND HOFFMANN, ERIK P., eds. *Soviet foreign policy in a changing world.* New York: Aldine, 1986.

LAL, DEEPAK AND WOLF, MARTIN, eds. *Stagflation, savings, and the state: Perspectives on the global economy.* World Bank Research Publication series. New York; Oxford; Toronto and Melbourne: Oxford University Press for the World Bank, 1986.

LANCASTER, CAROL AND WILLIAMSON, JOHN, eds. *African debt and financing.* Special Reports series, no. 5. Washington, D.C.: Institute for International Economics, 1986.

LANDAU, RALPH AND JORGENSON, DALE W., eds. *Technology and economic policy.* Cambridge, Mass.: Harper & Row, Ballinger, 1986.

LANDAU, RALPH AND ROSENBERG, NATHAN, eds. *The positive sum strategy: Harnessing technology for economic growth.* Washington, D.C.: National Academy Press, 1986.

LANE, DAVID, ed. *Labour and employment in the USSR.* New York: New York University Press, 1986.

LANGLOIS, RICHARD N., ed. *Economics as a process: Essays in the new institutional economics.* Cambridge; New York and Melbourne: Cambridge University Press, 1986.

LANGTON, JOHN AND MORRIS, R. J., eds. *Atlas of industrializing Britain, 1780–1914.* London and New York: Methuen, 1986.

[LASLETT, PETER] *The world we have gained: Histories of population and social structure. Essays presented to Peter Laslett on his seventieth birthday.* Edited by LLOYD BONFIELD, RICHARD M. SMITH, AND KEITH WRIGHTSON. Oxford and New York: Blackwell, 1986.

LAU, LAWRENCE J., ed. *Models of development: A comparative study of economic growth in South Korea and Taiwan.* San Francisco: Institute for Contemporary Studies Press, 1986.

LAWLER, EDWARD J., ed. *Advances in group processes.* Volume 3. A Research Annual. Greenwich, Conn., and London: JAI Press, 1986.

LAWRENCE, COLIN AND SHAY, ROBERT P., eds. *Technological innovation, regulation, and the monetary economy.* Cambridge, Mass.: Harper & Row, Ballinger, 1986.

LEE, DWIGHT R., ed. *Taxation and the deficit economy: Fiscal policy and capital formation in the United States.* Foreword by MICHAEL J. BOSKIN. Pacific Studies in Public Policy series. Inner Cities Research Programme Series, no. 4. Oxford; New York; Toronto and Melbourne: Oxford University Press, Clarendon Press, 1986.

LEONTIEF, WASSILY. *Input–output economics.* Second edition. New York and Oxford: Oxford University Press, [1966] 1986.

LEVER, WILLIAM AND MOORE, CHRIS, eds. *The cities in transition: Policies and agencies for the economic regeneration of Clydeside.* Inner Cities Research Programme Series, no. 4. Oxford; New York; Toronto and Melbourne: Oxford University Press, Clarendon Press, 1986.

LEWIS, JOHN P. AND KALLAB, VALERIANA, eds. *Development strategies reconsidered.* New Brunswick, N.J., and Oxford: Transaction Books, 1986.

LINDHOLM, RICHARD W., ed. *Examination of basic weaknesses of income as the major federal tax base.* New York and London: Greenwood Press, Praeger, 1986.

LIPSET, SEYMOUR MARTIN, ed. *Unions in transition: Entering the second century.* San Francisco: Institute for Contemporary Studies, ICS Press, 1986.

LIPSKY, DAVID B. AND LEWIN, DAVID, eds. *Advances in industrial and labor relations.* A Research Annual series, vol. 3. Greenwich, Conn., and London: JAI Press, 1986.

[LÖSCH, AUGUST] *Space–structure–economy: A tribute to August Lösch.* Edited by ROLF H. FUNCK AND ANTONI KUKLINSKI. Karlsruhe Papers in Economic Policy Research series, vol. 3. Karlsruhe, West Germany: von Loeper; distributed in the U.S. and Canada by Kober Press, San Fransciso, 1986.

MACFADYEN, ALAN J. AND MACFADYEN, HEATHER W., eds. *Economic psychology: Intersections in theory and application.* Amsterdam; Oxford and Tokyo: North-Holland; distributed in the U.S. and Canada by Elsevier Science, New York, 1986.

MACHARZINA, KLAUS AND STAEHLE, WOLFGANG H., eds. *European approaches to international management.* Berlin and New York: de Gruyter, 1986.

MACLEAN, DOUGLAS, ed. *Values at risk.* Maryland Studies in Public Philosophy series. Totowa, N.J.: Rowman and Allanheld, 1986.

MADDISON, ANGUS, ed. *Latin America, the Caribbean and the OECD: A dialogue on economic reality and policy options.* Development Centre Seminars series. Paris: Development Centre of the Organisation for Economic Co-operation and Development, 1986.

[MARSCHAK, JACOB] *Decision and organization: A volume in honor of Jacob Marschak.* Second edition. Edited by C. B. McGuire and Roy Radner. Minneapolis: University of Minnesota Press, [1972] 1986.

Mason, John [Sir]; Mathias, P. and Westcott, J. H., eds. *Predictability in science and society: A joint symposium of the Royal Society and the British Academy held on 20 and 21 March 1986.* London: The Royal Society and the British Academy, 1986.

Maunder, Allen and Renborg, Ulf, eds. *Agriculture in a turbulent world economy: Proceedings of the nineteenth international conference of agricultural economists, held at Málaga, Spain, 26 August–4 September 1985.* Aldershot, U.K., and Brookfield, Vt.: Gower, 1986.

May, Ernest R. and Fairbank, John K., eds. *America's China trade in historical perspective: The Chinese and American performance.* Harvard Studies in American–East Asian Relations series, no. 11. Cambridge, Mass.: Harvard University, Department of History, Committee on American–East Asian Relations in collaboration with Harvard University Council on East Asian Studies; distributed by Harvard University Press, Cambridge, Mass., and London, 1986.

McIntyre, John R. and Papp, Daniel S., eds. *The political economy of international technology transfer.* New York and London: Greenwood Press, Quorum Books, 1986.

Menken, Jane, ed. *World population and U.S. policy: The choices ahead.* American Assembly, Columbia University, series. New York and London: Norton; Markham, Ontario: Penguin Books Canada, 1986.

Mesa-Lago, Carmelo, ed. *Cuban studies.* Volume 16. Pittsburgh: University of Pittsburgh, Center for Latin American Studies, 1986.

Minnesota Tax Study Commission. *Final report of the Minnesota Tax Study Commission.* Volume 2. *Staff papers.* St. Paul: Butterworths, 1986.

Mirowski, Philip, ed. *The reconstruction of economic theory.* Recent Economic Thought Series. Norwell, Mass.; Dordrecht and Lancaster: Kluwer Academic, Kluwer-Nijhoff, 1986.

Mishan, Ezra J. *Economic myths and the mythology of economics.* Atlantic Highlands, N.J.: Humanities Press International, 1986.

Moores, Brian, ed. *Are they being served? Quality consciousness in service industries.* Oxford: Allan; distributed by Humanities Press, Atlantic Highlands, N.J., 1986.

Moorhouse, John C., ed. *Electric power: Deregulation and the public interest.* Foreword by Harold Demsetz. Pacific Studies in Public Policy series. San Francisco: Pacific Research Institute for Public Policy, 1986.

Moran, Theodore H., ed. *Investing in development: New roles for private capital?* New Brunswick, N.J., and Oxford: Transaction Books, 1986.

Morgan, Roger and Bray, Caroline, eds. *Partners and rivals in Western Europe: Britain, France and Germany.* European Centre for Political Studies, Policy Studies Institute series. Aldershot, U.K., and Brookfield, Vt.: Gower, 1986.

Morris, D. J., et al., eds. *Strategic behaviour and industrial competition.* Oxford; New York; Toronto and Melbourne: Oxford University Press, Clarendon Press, 1986.

Mueller, Dennis C. *The modern corporation: Profits, power, growth and performance.* Lincoln, Nebraska: University of Nebraska Press, 1986.

Musgrave, Richard A. *Public finance in a democratic society.* Volume 1. *Social goods, taxation and fiscal policy. Collected papers of Richard A. Musgrave.* New York: New York University Press; distributed by Columbia University Press, 1986.

Musgrave, Richard A. *Public finance in a democratic society.* Volume 2. *Fiscal doctrine, growth and institutions. Collected papers of Richard A. Musgrave.* New York: New York University Press; distributed by Columbia University Press, 1986.

Neary, J. Peter and van Wijnbergen, Sweder, eds. *Natural resources and the macroeconomy.* Cambridge, Mass.: MIT Press; Oxford: Blackwell, 1986.

Nemetz, Peter N., ed. *The Pacific Rim: Investment, development and trade.* Vancouver: University of British Columbia Press, 1986.

Nevitte, Neil and Kennedy, Charles H., eds. *Ethnic preference and public policy in developing states.* Boulder, Colo.: Rienner, 1986.

Nijkamp, Peter, ed. *Handbook of regional and urban economics.* Volume 1. *Regional economics.*

Handbooks in Economics series, no. 7. Amsterdam; New York; Oxford and Tokyo: North-Holland; distributed in the U.S. and Canada by Elsevier Science, New York, 1986. (I)

NIJKAMP, PETER, ed. *Technological change, employment and spatial dynamics: Proceedings of an international symposium on technological change and employment: Urban and regional dimensions, held at Zandvoort, the Netherlands, April 1–3, 1985.* Berlin; New York and Tokyo: Springer, 1986. (II)

NOLAN, PETER AND PAINE, SUZANNE, eds. *Rethinking socialist economics: A new agenda for Britain.* New York: St. Martin's Press, 1986.

NØRLUND, IRENE; CEDERROTH, SVEN AND GERDIN, INGELA, eds. *Rice societies: Asian problems and prospects.* Scandinavian Institute of Asian Studies, Studies on Asian Topics series, no. 10. London: Curzon Press; Riverdale, Md.: Riverdale, 1986.

NORMAN, G., ed. *Spatial pricing and differentiated markets.* London Papers in Regional Science series, no. 16. London: Pion; distributed in the U.S. by Methuen, New York, 1986.

NOVE, ALEC. *Socialism, economics and development.* London; Boston and Sydney: Allen & Unwin, 1986.

ONWUKA, RALPH I. AND ALUKO, OLAJIDE, eds. *The future of Africa and the new international economic order.* New York: St. Martin's Press, 1986.

PALMER, JOHN, ed. *The economics of patents and copyrights.* Research in Law and Economics series, vol. 8. Greenwich, Conn., and London: JAI Press, 1986.

PANCHAMUKHI, V. R., ET AL. *The third world and the world economic system.* Research and Information System for the Non-aligned and Other Developing Countries series. New Delhi: Radiant; distributed in North America by Humanities Press, Atlantic Highlands, N.J., 1986.

PANITCH, LEO. *Working-class politics in crisis: Essays on labour and the state.* London: New Left Books, Verso; distributed by Routledge, Chapman and Hall, New York, 1986.

PARKER, R. H.; HARCOURT, G. C. AND WHITTINGTON, G., eds. *Readings in the concept and measurement of income.* Second edition. Oxford: Allan; distributed by Humanities Press International, Atlantic Highlands, N.J., [1969] 1986.

PARKER, WILLIAM N., ed. *Economic history and the modern economist.* Oxford and New York: Blackwell, 1986.

PATEL, I. G. *Essays in economic policy and economic growth.* New York: St. Martin's Press, 1986.

[PATEL, SURENDRA] *World economy in transition: Essays presented to Surendra Patel on his sixtieth birthday.* Edited by KRISHNA AHOOJA-PATEL, ANNE GORDON DRABEK, AND MARC NERFIN. Oxford; New York; Toronto and Sydney: Pergamon Press, 1986.

PATRICK, HUGH, ed. *Japan's high technology industries: Lessons and limitations of industrial policy.* With the assistance of LARRY MEISSNER. Seattle and London: University of Washington Press; Tokyo: University of Tokyo Press, 1986.

PAU, L. F., ed. *Artificial intelligence in economics and management.* Amsterdam; Oxford and Tokyo: North-Holland; distributed in the U.S. and Canada by Elsevier Science, New York, 1986.

PEDEN, JOSEPH R. AND GLAHE, FRED R., eds. *The American family and the state.* Foreword by ROBERT NISBET. Pacific Studies in Public Policy series. San Francisco: Pacific Research Institute for Public Policy, 1986.

PELLEGRINI, LUCA AND REDDY, SRINIVAS K., eds. *Marketing Channels: Relationships and Performance.* Advances in Retailing Series. Lexington, Mass., and Toronto: Heath, Lexington Books, 1986.

PERRYMAN, M. RAY AND SCHMIDT, JAMES R., eds. *Regional econometric modeling.* International Series in Economic Modeling. Norwell; Mass.; Dordrecht and Lancaster: Kluwer Academic, Kluwer-Nijhoff, 1986.

PETERSON, GEORGE E. AND LEWIS, CAROL W., eds. *Reagan and the cities.* The Changing Domestic Priorities Series. Washington, D.C.: Urban Institute Press, 1986.

POHL, HANS AND RUDOLPH, BERND, eds. *German yearbook on business history, 1985.* Berlin; New York and Tokyo: Springer, 1986.

Pontecorvo, Giulio, ed. *The new order of the oceans: The advent of a managed environment.* New York and Gildford, U.K.: Columbia University Press, 1986.

Posner, Michael, ed. *Problems of international money, 1972–85: Papers presented at a seminar organized by the International Monetary Fund and the Overseas Development Institute in London in March 1985.* Washington, D.C.: International Monetary Fund; London: Overseas Development Institute, 1986.

Pozo, Susan, ed. *Essays on legal and illegal immigration: Papers presented in a seminar series conducted by the Department of Economics at Western Michigan University.* Kalamazoo, Mich.: W. E. Upjohn Institute for Employment Research, 1986.

Preeg, Ernest H. and Bendahmane, Diane B., eds. *New dimensions in foreign economic policy: Industrial—oil—banking.* Washington, D.C.: U.S. Department of State, Foreign Service Institute, Center for the Study of Foreign Affairs, 1986.

Pugel, Thomas A., ed. *Fragile interdependence: Economic issues in U.S.–Japanese trade and investment.* With Robert G. Hawkins. Lexington, Mass., and Toronto: Heath, Lexington Books, 1986.

Putnam, Bluford H. and Wilford, D. Sykes, eds. *The monetary approach to international adjustment.* Revised edition. New York and London: Greenwood Press, Praeger, [1978] 1986.

Putterman, Louis, ed. *The economic nature of the firm: A reader.* With the assistance of Randy Kroszner. Cambridge; New York and Melbourne: Cambridge University Press, 1986.

Raddock, David M., et al. *Assessing corporate political risk: A guide for international businessmen.* Totowa, N.J.: Littlefield, Adams; Rowman and Allanheld, 1986.

Ramanadham, V. V., ed. *Public enterprise: Studies in organisational structure.* London: Cass, 1986.

[Rapoport, Anatol] *Paradoxical effects of social behavior: Essays in honor of Anatol Rapoport.* Edited by Andreas Diekmann and Peter Mitter. Heidelberg and Vienna: Physica, 1986.

Ravenhill, John, ed. *Africa in economic crisis.* New York: Columbia University Press, 1986.

Redburn, F. Stevens; Buss, Terry F. and Ledebur, Larry C., eds. *Revitalizing the U.S. economy.* New York and London: Greenwood Press, Praeger, 1986.

Reserve Bank of New Zealand. *Financial policy reform.* Wellington, New Zealand: Author, 1986.

Reynolds, Lloyd G.; Masters, Stanley H. and Moser, Colletta H., eds. *Readings in labor economics and labor relations.* Fourth edition. Englewood Cliffs, N.J.: Prentice-Hall, [1974 . . .1982] 1986.

Richards, Alan, ed. *Food, states, and peasants: Analyses of the agrarian question in the Middle East.* Boulder, Colo., and London: Westview Press, 1986.

Rose, Richard and Shiratori, Rei, eds. *The welfare state: East and West.* Oxford; New York; Toronto and Melbourne: Oxford University Press, 1986.

Rose-Ackerman, Susan, ed. *The economics of nonprofit institutions: Studies in structure and policy.* Yale Studies on Nonprofit Organizations series. New York and Oxford: Oxford University Press, 1986.

Rosen, Harvey S., ed. *Studies in state and local public finance.* National Bureau of Economic Research Project Report series. Chicago and London: University of Chicago Press, 1986.

Rosenbloom, Richard S., ed. *Research on technological innovation, management and policy.* Volume 3. A Research Annual. Greenwich, Conn., and London: JAI Press, 1986.

Rosow, Jerome M., ed. *Teamwork: Joint labor–management programs in America.* New York; Oxford; Toronto and Sydney: Pergamon Press, 1986.

Roukis, George S. and Montana, Patrick J., eds. *Workforce management in the Arabian Peninsula: Forces affecting development.* Contributions in Economics and Economic History series, no. 67. New York and London: Greenwood Press, 1986.

Rushing, Francis W. and Brown, Carole Ganz, eds. *National policies for developing high technology industries: International comparisons.* Westview Special Studies in Science, Technology, and Public Policy series. Boulder, Colo., and London: Westview Press, 1986.

Saltzman, Sidney and Schuler, Richard E., eds. *The future of electrical energy: A regional perspective of an industry in transition.* New York and London: Greenwood Press, Praeger, 1986.

SAMUELSON, LARRY, ed. *Microeconomic theory.* Recent Economic Thought Series. Dordrecht, and Lancaster: Kluwer-Nijhoff; distributed in the U.S. and Canada by Kluwer Academic Publishers, Hingham, Mass., 1986.

SAMUELSON, PAUL A. *The collected scientific papers of Paul A. Samuelson.* Volume 5. Edited by KATE CROWLEY. Cambridge, Mass., and London: MIT Press, 1986.

SAUNDERS, ANTHONY AND WHITE, LAWRENCE J., eds. *Technology and the regulation of financial markets: Securities, futures, and banking.* Lexington Books/Salomon Brothers Center Series on Financial Institutions and Markets. Lexington, Mass., and Toronto: Heath, Lexington Books, 1986.

SAWHILL, JOHN C. AND COTTON, RICHARD, eds. *Energy conservation: Successes and failures.* Washington, D.C.: Brookings Institution, 1986.

SAXONHOUSE, GARY R. AND YAMAMURA, KOZO, eds. *Law and trade issues of the Japanese economy: American and Japanese perspectives.* Seattle and London: University of Washington Press; Tokyo: University of Tokyo Press, 1986.

SCHICK, ALLEN, ET AL. *Crisis in the budget process: Exercising political choice.* AEI Studies, no. 438. Washington, D.C.: American Enterprise Institute for Public Policy Research, 1986.

SCHOOLMAN, MORTON AND MAGID, ALVIN, eds. *Reindustrializing New York State: Strategies, implications, challenges.* Albany: State University of New York Press, 1986.

VON DER SCHULENBURG, J.-MATTHIAS GRAF, ed. *Essays in social security economics: Selected papers of a conference of the International Institute of Management, Wissenschaftszentrum, Berlin.* Microeconomics Studies series. New York; Berlin; London and Tokyo: Springer, 1986.

VON DER SCHULENBURG, J.-MATTHIAS GRAF AND SKOGH, GÖRAN, eds. *Law and economics and the economics of legal regulation.* International Studies in Economics and Econometrics series, vol. 13. Hingham, Mass.; Dordrecht and Lancaster: Kluwer Academic, 1986.

SCITOVSKY, TIBOR. *Human desire and economic satisfaction: Essays on the frontiers of economics.* New York: New York University Press, 1986.

SCOTT, ALLEN J. AND STORPER, MICHAEL, eds. *Production, work, and territory: The geographical anatomy of industrial capitalism.* Boston; London and Sydney: Allen & Unwin, 1986.

SEGURA, EDILBERTO L.; SHETTY, Y. T. AND NISHIMIZU, MIEKO, eds. *Fertilizer producer pricing in developing countries: Issues and approaches.* Industry and Finance Series, vol. 11. Washington, D.C.: World Bank, 1986.

[SELDON, ARTHUR] *The unfinished agenda: Essays on the political economy of government policy in honour of Arthur Seldon.* Edited by MARTIN J. ANDERSON. London: Institute of Economic Affairs; distributed in North America by Transatlantic Arts, Albuquerque, New Mexico, 1986.

SEMMLER, WILLI, ed. *Competition, instability, and nonlinear cycles: Proceedings of an internatonal conference, New School for Social Research, New York, USA, March 1985.* Lecture Notes in Economics and Mathematical Systems series, vol. 275. New York; Berlin; London and Tokyo: Springer, 1986.

SHADOW OPEN MARKET COMMITTEE. *Policy statement and position papers, March 16–17, 1986.* Rochester: University of Rochester, Graduate School of Management, Center for Research in Government Policy and Business, 1986. (I)

SHADOW OPEN MARKET COMMITTEE. *Policy statement and position papers, September 21–22, 1986.* Rochester: University of Rochester, Graduate School of Management, Center for Research in Government Policy and Business, 1986. (II)

SHAND, R. T., ed. *Off-farm employment in the development of rural Asia.* Volume 1. *Papers presented at a conference held in Chiang Mai, Thailand, 23 to 26 August 1983.* Canberra: Australian National University, National Centre for Development Studies, 1986.

SHAND, R. T., ed. *Off-farm employment in the development of rural Asia.* Volume 2. *Papers presented at a conference held in Chiang Mai, Thailand, 23 to 26 August 1983.* Canberra: Australian National University, National Centre for Development Studies, 1986.

SHARP, MARGARET, ed. *Europe and the new technologies: Six case studies in innovation and ad-*

justment. Cornell Studies in Political Economy series. Ithaca, N.Y.: Cornell University Press, 1986.

SHOME, PARTHASARATHI, ed. *Fiscal issues in South-east Asia: Comparative studies of selected economies*. Singapore; Oxford; New York and Toronto: Oxford University Press, 1986.

SHULMAN, MARSHALL D., ed. *East–West tensions in the third world*. The American Assembly, Columbia University, series. New York and London: Norton, 1986.

SIMON, JULIAN L. *Theory of population and economic growth*. Oxford and New York: Blackwell, 1986.

SINGH, INDERJIT; SQUIRE, LYN AND STRAUSS, JOHN, eds. *Agricultural household models: Extensions, applications, and policy*. Baltimore and London: Johns Hopkins University Press for the World Bank, 1986.

SJÖSTEDT, GUNNAR AND SUNDELIUS, BENGT, eds. *Free trade—managed trade? Perspectives on a realistic international trade order*. Westview Special Studies in International Economics and Business series. Boulder, Colo., and London: Westview Press in cooperation with the Swedish Institute of International Affairs, Stockholm, 1986.

SLATER, PAUL B. *Large scale data analytic studies in the social sciences*. Santa Barbara: University of California, Community and Organization Research Institute, 1986.

SLOAN, FRANK A.; BLUMSTEIN, JAMES F. AND PERRIN, JAMES M., eds. *Uncompensated hospital care: Rights and responsibilities*. Baltimore and London: Johns Hopkins University Press, 1986.

SMELSER, NEIL J. AND GERSTEIN, DEAN R., eds. *Behavioral and social science: Fifty years of discovery; In commemoration of the fiftieth anniversary of the "Ogburn Report," recent social trends in the United States*. Washington, D.C.: National Academy Press, 1986.

SMITH, KEITH, ed. *Soviet industrialisation and Soviet maturity*. Economy and Society series. London and New York: Routledge and Kegan Paul in associaton with Methuen, New York, 1986.

SMOLLAN, ROY, ed. *Black advancement in the South African economy*. New York: St. Martin's Press, 1986.

SNAPE, R. H., ed. *Issues in world trade policy: GATT at the Crossroads. Papers presented at a conference of the Centre of Policy Studies, Monash University, Australia*. New York: St. Martin's Press, 1986.

SNOW, MARCELLUS S. *Marketplace for telecommunications: Regulation and deregulation in industrialized democracies*. New York and London: Longman, 1986.

SOHN, IRA, ed. *Readings in input–output analysis: Theory and applications*. New York and Oxford: Oxford University Press, 1986.

SONNENSCHEIN, HUGO F., ed. *Models of economic dynamics: Proceedings of a workshop held at the IMA, University of Minnesota, Minneapolis, USA, October 24–28, 1983*. Lecture Notes in Economics and Mathematical Systems series, vol. 264. New York; Berlin and Tokyo: Springer, 1986.

SRINIVASAN, T. N. AND WHALLEY, JOHN, eds. *General equilibrium trade policy modeling*. Cambridge, Mass., and London: MIT Press, 1986.

STARK, ODED, ed. *Research in human capital and development*. Volume 4. *Migration, human capital and development*. A Research Annual. Greenwich, Conn. and London: JAI Press, 1986.

STAUFFER, ROBERT B. *The Philippines under Marcos: Failure of transnational developmentalism*. Sydney: University of Sydney, Transnational Corporations Research Project, 1986.

STEVENS, PAUL, ed. *International gas: Prospects and trends*. New York: St. Martin's Press, 1986.

STIGLER, GEORGE J. *The essence of Stigler*. Edited by KURT R. LEUBE AND THOMAS GALE MOORE. Foreword by W. GLENN CAMPBELL. Stanford, Calif.: Hoover Institution Press, 1986.

STIGLITZ, JOSEPH E. AND MATHEWSON, G. FRANK, eds. *New developments in the analysis of market structure: Proceedings of a conference held by the International Economic Association in Ottawa, Canada*. Cambridge, Mass.: MIT Press; London: Macmillan Press, 1986.

[STREETEN, PAUL] *Theory and reality in development. Essays in honour of Paul Streeten*. Edited by SANJAYA LALL AND FRANCES STEWART. New York: St. Martin's Press, 1986.

SUZUKI, YOSHIO AND YOMO, HIROSHI, eds. *Financial innovation and monetary policy: Asia and the West. Proceedings of the Second International Conference held by the Institute for Monetary and Economic Studies of the Bank of Japan.* Tokyo: University of Tokyo Press; distributed by Columbia University Press, 1986.

SWAMINATHAN, M. S. AND SINHA, S. K., eds. *Global aspects of food production.* Natural Resources and the Environment Series, vol. 20. London; Riverton, N.J., and Dehra Dun, India: Tycooly International, 1986.

SZENBERG, MICHAEL, ed. *Essays in economics: The John Commons Memorial Lectures.* Boulder, Colo., and London: Westview Press, 1986.

[TARSHIS, LORIE] *International monetary problems and supply-side economics: Essays in honour of Lorie Tarshis.* Edited by JON S. COHEN AND G. C. HARCOURT. New York: St. Martin's Press, 1986.

TAYLOR, RALPH B., ed. *Urban neighborhoods: Research and policy.* New York and London: Praeger, 1986.

TEICHOVA, ALICE; LÉVY-LEBOYER, MAURICE AND NUSSBAUM, HELGA, eds. *Multinational enterprise in historical perspective.* Cambridge; New York and Melbourne: Cambridge University Press; Paris: Editions de la Maison des Sciences de l'Homme, 1986.

DI TELLA, GUIDO AND PLATT, D. C. M., eds. *The political economy of Argentina, 1880–1946.* New York: St. Martin's Press; London: Macmillan Press, 1986.

THOMPSON, DENNIS L. AND RONEN, DOV, eds. *Ethnicity, politics, and development.* David M. Kennedy Center for International Studies monograph series, vol. 2. Boulder, Colo.: Rienner, 1986.

TOMA, EUGENIA FROEDGE AND TOMA, MARK, eds. *Central bankers, bureaucratic incentives, and monetary policy.* Financial and Monetary Policy Studies series, vol. 13. Hingham, Mass.; Dordrecht and Lancaster: Kluwer Academic, 1986.

TSOUKALIS, LOUKAS, ed. *Europe, America and the world economy.* New York and Oxford: Blackwell for the College of Europe, 1986.

TULLOCK, GORDON. *The economics of wealth and poverty.* New York: New York University Press; distributed by Columbia University Press, 1986.

TURNER, MICHAEL, ed. *Malthus and his time.* New York: St. Martin's Press, 1986.

UNITED NATIONS DEPARTMENT OF INTERNATIONAL ECONOMIC AND SOCIAL AFFAIRS. *Savings for development: Report of the Third International Symposium on the Mobilization of Personal Savings in Developing Countries, Yaoundé, Cameroon, 10–14 December 1984.* U.N. Publication Sales No. E.85.II.A.17. New York: United Nations, 1986.

UNITED NATIONS DEPARTMENT OF TECHNICAL CO-OPERATION FOR DEVELOPMENT. *Economic performance of public enterprises: Major issues and strategies for action.* New York: United Nations, 1986.

UNITED NATIONS DEPARTMENT OF TECHNICAL CO-OPERATION FOR DEVELOPMENT, DEVELOPMENT ADMINISTRATION DIVISION. *The role of the public sector in the mobilization of domestic financial resources in developing countries.* New York: United Nations, 1986.

USELDING, PAUL, ed. *Research in economic history.* Volume 10. A Research Annual. Greenwich, Conn., and London: JAI Press, 1986.

DE VRIES, MARGARET GARRITSEN. *The IMF in a changing world: 1945–85.* Washington, D.C.: International Monetary Fund, 1986.

WAGENER, H.-J. AND DRUKKER, J. W., eds. *The economic law of motion of modern society: A Marx–Keynes–Schumpeter centennial.* Cambridge; New York and Sydney: Cambridge University Press, 1986.

WALZER, NORMAN AND CHICOINE, DAVID L., eds. *Financing economic development in the 1980s: Issues and trends.* New York and London: Greenwood Press, Praeger, 1986.

WASOW, BERNARD AND HILL, RAYMOND D., eds. *The insurance industry in economic development.* New York and London: New York University Press, 1986.

WEISS, LEONARD W. AND KLASS, MICHAEL W., eds. *Regulatory reform: What actually happened.* Boston and Toronto: Little, Brown, 1986.

WHEELWRIGHT, TED, ed. *Consumers, transnational corporations and development.* Sydney: University of Sydney, Transnational Corporations Research Project, 1986.

WHITEHEAD, DAVID J., ed. *Economics education: A second handbook for economics teachers.* London; Melbourne; Portsmouth, N.H., and Kingston: Heinemann Educational Books, 1986.

WILLIAMSON, OLIVER E. *Economic Organization: Firms, markets and policy control.* New York: New York University Press, 1986.

WORLD BANK. *Recovery in the developing world: The London symposium on the World Bank's role.* Washington, D.C.: Author, 1986.

WRIGHT, GERALD C., JR.; RIESELBACH, LEROY N. AND DODD, LAWRENCE C., eds. *Congress and policy change.* New York: Agathon Press, 1986.

[YAMEY, BASIL] *Firms and markets: Essays in honour of Basil Yamey.* Edited by K. TUCKER AND C. BADEN FULLER. New York: St. Martin's Press, 1986.

YEUNG, Y. M. AND MCGEE, T. G., eds. *Community participation in delivering urban services in Asia.* Ottawa: International Development Research Centre, 1986.

YSANDER, BENGT-CHRISTER, ed. *Two models of an open economy.* Industriens Utrednigsinstitut series. Stockholm: Almqvist and Wiksell International, 1986.

ZAREMBKA, PAUL, ed. *Research in political economy.* Volume 9. A Research Annual. Greenwich, Conn., and London: JAI Press, 1986.

ZERBE, RICHARD O., JR., ed. *Research in law and economics.* Volume 9. A Research Annual. Greenwich, Conn., and London: JAI Press, 1986.

CLASSIFICATION SYSTEM

Editor's note: Notes on the *Classification System* further clarify the subject matter covered under specific categories or point out specific topics included. They also may contain cross references to other categories. In addition, the *Topical Guide* at the end of this volume provides an index to classification numbers appropriate for specific topics. Please note that "General" categories may include *both* detailed articles covering all subcategories and very general articles falling into no subcategory.

000 General Economics; Theory; History; Systems

010 General Economics 3

011 General Economics 3

0110 General 3

Includes general bibliographies. For bibliographies relating to subfield, see general category in subfield.

0112 Role of Economics; Role of Economists 4

0113 Relation of Economics to Other Disciplines 7

0114 Relation of Economics to Social Values 9

Articles where the values discussed refer to the "economic system" may appear in subcategories 0510 or 0520.

0115 Methods Used by Economists 11

For methodology, see also 0360.

012 Teaching of Economics 11

0120 Teaching of Economics 11

For teaching in specific subfields, see also general category in subfield.

020 General Economic Theory 14

0200 General Economic Theory 14

Articles referring to entire field of economic theory.

021 General Equilibrium and Disequilibrium Theory 17

0210 General Equilibrium and Disequilibrium Theory 17

For general equilibrium and disequilibrium in macroeconomic models, see 023 category. For computable general equilibrium models, see specific subject categories; for forecasting and policy simulations, see category 132; for discussions of solutions methods, see category 212 or 213.

022 Microeconomic Theory 20

0220 General 20

0222 Theory of the Household (consumer demand) 23

For empirical consumption function, see 921 category; for microfoundations of macroeconomic theory, see 0232. For consumer surplus, see also 0240.

0223 Theory of Production 27

Theory of the firm will generally appear here. For articles dealing with social objectives of the firm, see 5140. For theory of production functions for the economy as a whole, see 0234. For microtheory of investment, see also 5220. In general, empirical studies of production not used to illustrate theory will appear in industry studies, category 630.

0224 Theory of Factor Distribution and Distributive Shares 32

For macroeconomic factor (functional income) distribution, see 0235. For human capital theory, see 8510; for wage theory, see also 8210; for empirical wages, see 8242.

0225 Theory of Firm and Industry under Competitive Market Structures 33

0226 Theory of Firm and Industry under Imperfectly Competitive Market Structures 34

For studies of structure of industry, concentration ratios, see 6110; for policy toward monopoly, see 6120. For multimarket equilibrium, see 0210.

0227 Theory of Auction Markets 41

0228 Agent Theory 41

0229 Microeconomics of Intertemporal Choice 42

023 Macroeconomic Theory 43

0230 General 43

For business fluctuation theory, see also 1311; for stabilization theory and policies, see 1331; for inflation theory see 1342; for fiscal theory, see also 3212.

0232 Theory of Aggregate Demand: Consumption 49

For empirical studies of the consumption and saving functions, see 9211.

0233 Theory of Aggregate Demand: Investment 50

For microtheory of investment, see 0223 and 5220.

0234 Theory of Aggregate Supply 51

0235 Theory of Aggregate Distribution 55

For microeconomic factor distribution, see 0224; for empirical studies of income distribution, see 2213; for labor market theories, see also 8210.

0239 Macroeconomics of Intertemporal Choice 58

024 Welfare Theory 59

0240 General 59

For theory of public goods and the public goods sector, see also 3212. For the social welfare function, see also 0251; for equity and justice, see also 0251.

0242 Allocative Efficiency Including Theory of Cost/Benefit 62

Articles in this section are concerned with theory rather than empirical application of cost/benefit studies to specific subfields. For empirical applications see the subfield involved. See also, 0226 for welfare distortions owing to monopoly. See the 411 category for welfare aspects of trade theory and policy.

0243 Redistribution Analyses 65

0244 Externalities 66

See 7220 for pollution.

025 Social Choice 67

Includes theory and studies of collective decision.

0250 General 67

0251 Social Choice Theory 68

0252 Social Choice Studies: Voting, Committees, etc. 73

026 Economics of Uncertainty and Information; Game Theory and Bargaining Theory 76

0260 General 76

0261 Theory of Uncertainty and Information 77

0262 Game Theory and Bargaining Theory 82
For applications see specific subfields.
027 Economics of Centrally Planned Economies 86
0270 General 86
0271 Microeconomic Theory 87
0272 Macroeconomic Theory 88
030 History of Thought; Methodology 89
031 History of Economic Thought 89
0310 General 89
0311 Ancient, Medieval 89
0312 Preclassical 89
0313 Mercantilist 90
0314 Classical 90
0315 Austrian, Marshallian, Neoclassical 92
0316 General Equilibrium until 1945 93
0317 Socialist and Marxian until 1945 93
For current articles on figures such as Marx, see individuals, 0322; for articles on socialist systems in operation, see 0520.
0318 Historical and Institutional 95
032 History of Economic Thought (continued) 96
0321 Other Schools since 1800 96
0322 Individuals 96
Articles about individual figures in the history of thought are listed alphabetically by the person discussed.
0329 Other Special Topics 110
036 Economic Methodology 113
0360 Economic Methodology 113
040 Economic History 116
Studies covering solely the period prior to 1946, the end of World War II, are designated as historical. In general, the articles are cross-classified in the relevant subject categories.
041 Economic History: General 116
0410 General 116
0411 Development of the Discipline 117
0412 Comparative Intercountry or Intertemporal Economic History 117
042 Economic History: United States and Canada 118
0420 General 118
0421 History of Product Prices and Markets 120
0422 History of Factor Prices and Markets 121
0423 History of Public Economic Policy (all levels) 125
043 Economic History: Ancient and Medieval (until 1453) 127
Articles, irrespective of the geographic area involved, dealing with this time period are all listed in this group.
0430 General 127
0431 History of Product Prices and Markets 127
0432 History of Factor Prices and Markets 128
0433 History of Public Economic Policy (all levels) 128
044 Economic History: Europe 128
0440 General 128
0441 History of Product Prices and Markets 131
0442 History of Factor Prices and Markets 133
0443 History of Public Economic Policy (all levels) 135

045 Economic History: Asia 137
0450 General 137
0451 History of Product Prices and Markets 138
0452 History of Factor Prices and Markets 138
0453 History of Public Economic Policy (all levels) 138
046 Economic History: Africa 139
0460 General 139
0461 History of Product Prices and Markets 139
0462 History of Factor Prices and Markets 139
0463 History of Public Economic Policy (all levels) 139
047 Economic History: Latin America and Caribbean 139
0470 General 139
0471 History of Product Prices and Markets 139
0472 History of Factor Prices and Markets 139
0473 History of Public Economic Policy (all levels) 139
048 Economic History: Oceania 141
0480 General 141
0481 History of Product Prices and Markets 141
0482 History of Factor Prices and Markets 141
0483 History of Public Economic Policy (all levels) 141
050 Economic Systems 141
For studies of particular countries, as distinct from discussions of a system, see category 120.
0500 General 141
051 Capitalist Economic Systems: Market Economies 141
0510 Capitalist Economic Systems: Market Economies 141
Includes articles discussing or critiquing capitalist systems. Also includes articles on the cooperative as a system in predominantly market economies. Articles on mixed enterprise systems and nontheoretical articles on entrepreneurship also appear here (for theoretical articles on entrepreneurship and profits, see 0224).
052 Socialist and Communist Economic Systems 149
0520 Socialist and Communist Economic Systems 149
Articles discussing socialist or communist systems generally or in a specific country are included here. For theory, see the 027 category and for planning, see the 113 category. Studies of particular communist or socialist countries or of particular sectors in the countries will be found in either the country division (124 subcategories) or the appropriate subject category for the article. For example, an article dealing with agriculture in the Soviet Union would be classified in one of the 710 subcategories.
053 Comparative Economic Systems 154
0530 Comparative Economic Systems 154

100 Economic Growth; Development; Planning; Fluctuations
110 Economic Growth; Development; Planning Theory and Policy 154
For development theory see 1120; for empirical studies of an individual country, see category 120, or for primarily historical studies, 040.
111 Economic Growth Theory and Models 154
Does not include theory and analyses of productivity, which appear in 2260.
1110 Growth Theories 154

1112 One and Two Sector Growth Models and Related Topics 156
1113 Multisector Growth Models and Related Topics 156
1114 Monetary Growth Models 156
112 Economic Development Models and Theories 157
1120 Economic Development Models and Theories 157
To be distinguished from individual country studies, although there will be some overlap and cross classification; for agriculture and development, see also 7100; for theory of export-led development and for import substitution and development, see also 4114.
113 Economic Planning Theory and Policy 163
For regional planning theory see 9411; for regional planning models see 9413.
1130 General 163
1132 Economic Planning Theory 164
1136 Economic Planning Policy 165
114 Economics of War, Defense, and Disarmament 167
1140 Economics of War, Defense, and Disarmament 167
120 Country Studies 170
Country studies include complete country studies or broad studies involving several sectors of the economy, for centrally planned economies, see category 124. (The Index *has adopted the breakdown used by the World Bank.)*
121 Economic Studies of Developing Countries 170
1210 General 170
1211 Comparative Country Studies 171
1213 European Countries 172
1214 Asian Countries 172
1215 African Countries 174
1216 Latin American and Caribbean Countries 176
1217 Oceanic Countries 178
122 Economic Studies of Developed Countries 178
1220 General 178
1221 Comparative Country Studies 178
1223 European Countries 179
1224 Asian Countries 180
1225 African Countries
1227 Oceanic Countries 180
1228 North American Countries 180
123 Comparative Studies of Developing, Developed, and/or Centrally Planned Economies 181
1230 Comparative Studies of Developing, Developed, and/or Centrally Planned Economies 181
Includes comparisons of individual sectors.
124 Economic Studies of Centrally Planned Economies 182
1240 General
1241 Comparative Country Studies 182
1243 European Countries 182
For Yugoslavia, see 1213.
1244 Asian Countries 184
1246 Latin American and Caribbean Countries 184
130 Economic Fluctuations; Forecasting; Stabilization; Inflation 184
131 Economic Fluctuations 184
1310 General 184

1312 Economic Fluctuations: Theory 185
1313 Economic Fluctuations: Studies 188
132 Forecasting; Econometric Models 194
1320 General 194
1322 General Forecasts and Models 194
1323 Specific Forecasts and Models 199
For regional models see 9413.
1324 Forecasting and Econometric Models: Theory and Methodology 203
See also 2120.
133 General Outlook and Stabilization Theories and Policies 205
1330 General Outlook and General Economic Policy Discussions 205
1331 Stabilization Theories and Policies 210
1332 Wage and Price Controls 217
134 Inflation and Deflation 219
1340 General 219
Nontheoretical articles (in general).
1342 Inflation Theories; Studies Illustrating Inflation Theories 221

200 Quantitative Economic Methods and Data
210 Econometric, Statistical, and Mathematical Methods and Models 228
211 Econometric and Statistical Methods and Models 228
2110 General 228
The general category includes many small statistical problems that are not classified into independent categories but are important for the general theory of statistical inference.
2112 Inferential Problems in Simultaneous Equation Systems 229
2113 Distributed Lags and Serially Correlated Disturbance Terms; Inferential Problems in Single Equation Models 230
2114 Multivariate Analysis, Statistical Information Theory, and Other Special Inferential Problems; Queuing Theory; Markov Chains 234
2115 Bayesian Statistics and Bayesian Econometrics 235
2116 Time Series and Spectral Analysis 235
2117 Survey Methods; Sampling Methods 238
2118 Theory of Index Numbers and Aggregation 239
2119 Experimental Design; Social Experiments 239
See 215 category for experimental economic methods.
212 Construction, Analysis, and Use of Econometric Models 240
2120 Construction, Analysis, and Use of Econometric Models 240
For actual models, see category 132. Includes control theory applications to econometric models. Also includes the analysis and comparison of different modeling strategies.
213 Mathematical Methods and Models 247
2130 General 247
2132 Optimization Techniques 247
2133 Existence and Stability Conditions of Equilibrium 247
2134 Computational Techniques 248
2135 Construction, Analysis, and Use of Mathematical Programming Models 248
214 Computer Programs 249
2140 Computer Programs 249

215 Experimental Economic Methods 250
2150 Experimental Economic Methods 250
220 Economic and Social Statistical Data and Analysis 252
2200 General 252
For econometric and statistical methods see categories 211, 212, and 213.
221 National Income Accounting 253
2210 National Income Accounting Theory and Procedures 253
2212 National Income Accounts 254
2213 Income Distribution 258
For theory of income distribution see 0224 and 0235.
222 Input–Output 261
2220 Input–Output 261
For regional input–output studies see 9413; for theoretical general equilibrium models see 0210.
223 Financial Accounts 264
2230 Financial Accounts; Financial Statistics; Empirical Analyses of Capital Adequacy 264
224 National Wealth and Balance Sheets 265
2240 National Wealth and Balance Sheets 265
For consumer savings behavior, see 9211. For theories of bequests and intergenerational distribution of wealth, see 0243.
225 Social Indicators: Data and Analysis 267
2250 Social Indicators: Data and Analysis 267
226 Productivity and Growth: Theory and Data 268
2260 Productivity and Growth: Theory and Data 268
For productivity studies, see also 8250.
227 Prices 273
2270 Prices 273
228 Regional Statistics 276
2280 Regional Statistics 276
See also category 940.
229 Microdata and Database Analysis 276
2290 Microdata and Database Analysis 276

300 Domestic Monetary and Fiscal Theory and Institutions
310 Domestic Monetary and Financial Theory and Institutions 276
3100 General 276
311 Domestic Monetary and Financial Theory and Policy 278
3110 Domestic Monetary Theory and Policy 278
3112 Monetary Theory; Empirical Studies Illustrating Theory 280
Monetary theories of income determination are cross-referenced to 0230.
3116 Monetary Policy, Including All Central Banking Topics 295
For relationship to commercial banks, see also 3120; for relationship to credit policies, see also category 315; for general policy discussions, see 1330.
312 Commercial Banking 303
3120 Commercial Banking 303
Covers all aspects of commercial banks including regulation. For consumer credit see 3151; for mortgages see 3152.

313 Capital Markets 312
For business finance and investment, see 520 categories; for international finance, see 430 categories.
3130 General 312
3131 Capital Markets: Theory, Including Portfolio Selection, and Empirical Studies Illustrating Theory 313
For optimal bank portfolios, see also 3120; for valuation of the firm, see also 5220.
3132 Capital Markets: Empirical Studies, Including Regulation 321
Includes commodity markets. For foreign exchange markets see 4314.
314 Financial Intermediaries 334
3140 Financial Intermediaries 334
315 Credit to Business, Consumer, etc. (including mortgages) 338
3150 General 338
3151 Consumer Finance 338
3152 Mortgage Market 339
For effects on housing, see also 9320; for lending institutions see 3120 and 3140.
3153 Business Credit 340
320 Fiscal Theory and Policy; Public Finance 342
3200 General 342
321 Fiscal Theory and Policy 343
3210 General 343
For relationship to business cycles, see also category 131; for stabilization, see 1331; for general macro, see also 0230.
3212 Fiscal Theory; Empirical Studies Illustrating Fiscal Theory 344
3216 Fiscal Policy 354
Includes only central government fiscal policy; for state and local fiscal policy, see 324 category.
322 National Government Expenditures and Budgeting 357
3220 General 357
3221 National Government Expenditures 358
For welfare expenditure see 9110; for educational expenditure see 9120; for health expenditure see 9130.
3226 National Government Budgeting and Deficits 360
3228 National Government Debt Management 363
323 National Taxation, Revenue, and Subsidies 365
3230 National Taxation, Revenue, and Subsidies 365
For theory of taxation see also 3212; for negative income taxes see 9110; for social security taxes see 9150; for local taxes see 3242.
324 State and Local Government Finance 382
Includes theory of state and local public finance (see also 3212). For urban economics, see 930 category.
3240 General 382
3241 State and Local Government Expenditures and Budgeting 384
3242 State and Local Government Taxation, Subsidies, and Revenue 385
For national taxation see 3230.
3243 State and Local Government Borrowing 389
325 Intergovernmental Financial Relationships 390
3250 Intergovernmental Financial Relationships 390

400 International Economics
4000 General 391
Most articles pertaining to the New International Economic Order are classified here.
410 International Trade Theory 393
411 International Trade Theory 393
4110 General 393
For theory of international investment see 4410; for balance of payments theory see 4312.
4112 Theory of International Trade 393
4113 Theory of Protection 397
For theory of protection in relation to development see also 4114; for commercial policy see 4220.
4114 Theory of International Trade and Economic Development 399
For agriculture and development see also 7100; for multinationals and development see 4420; for international aid see 4430; for international investment see 4410.
420 Trade Relations; Commercial Policy; International Economic Integration 400
4200 General 400
421 Trade Relations 401
4210 Trade Relations 401
For trade policies designed to affect balance of payments, see 4312 and 4313.
422 Commercial Policy 416
4220 Commercial Policy 416
For theoretical aspects of commercial policy, see 4113.
423 Economic Integration 429
4230 General 429
4232 Theory of Economic Integration 429
4233 Economic Integration: Policy and Empirical Studies 430
430 International Finance 433
4300 General 433
431 Open Economy Macroeconomics; Exchange Rates 433
Includes short-term capital movements. For International Monetary Fund and other international monetary agencies and groups, see 4320; for lending aspects of the IMF, see 4430.
4310 General 433
4312 Open Economy Macroeconomic Theory: Balance of Payments and Adjustment Mechanisms 433
4313 Open Economy Macroeconomic Studies: Balance of Payments and Adjustment Mechanisms 440
4314 Exchange Rates and Markets: Theory and Studies 445
432 International Monetary Arrangements 458
4320 International Monetary Arrangements 458
433 Private International Lending 462
4330 Private International Lending 462
For aggregate debt service problem, see 4430.
440 International Investment and Foreign Aid 466
441 International Investment and Long-term Capital Movements 466
4410 General 466
4411 International Investment and Long-term Capital Movements: Theory 467

For theory of short-term capital movements and flows related to balance of payments adjustments, see 4312.
4412 International Investment and Long-term Capital Movements: Studies 468
For empirical studies of short-term capital movements and flows related to balance of payments adjustments, see also 4313.
442 International Business and Multinational Enterprises 471
4420 International Business and Multinational Enterprises 471
Includes multinational firm management and policies and also host country policies.
443 International Lending and Aid (public) 479
4430 International Lending and Aid (public) 479
Includes technical assistance and debt services.

500 Administration; Business Finance; Marketing; Accounting
5000 General 489
510 Administration 489
511 Organization and Decision Theory 489
5110 Organization and Decision Theory 489
For collective decision-making see 0250.
512 Managerial Economics 494
5120 Managerial Economics 494
513 Business and Public Administration 498
5130 General 498
For organization and decision theory see 5110; for managerial economics see 5120.
5131 Business Administration 499
5132 Public Administration 500
For administration of public enterprises, see 5131.
514 Goals and Objectives of Firms 500
5140 Goals and Objectives of Firms 500
See 0223 for theoretical discussions.
520 Business Finance and Investment 501
5200 Business Finance and Investment 501
521 Business Finance 502
5210 Business Finance 502
For multinational firm financing, see also 4420.
522 Business Investment 510
5220 Business Investment 510
For theory of investment by the firm see also 0223; for macro investment theory see also 0233; for capital markets and portfolio investment, see 313 categories.
530 Marketing and Advertising 514
531 Marketing and Advertising 514
5310 Marketing and Advertising 514
540 Accounting 519
541 Accounting 519
5410 Accounting 519

600 Industrial Organization; Technological Change; Industry Studies
6000 General
610 Industrial Organization and Public Policy 524

6100 General 524
611 Market Structure and Corporate Strategy 524
6110 Market Structure and Corporate Strategy 524
For microeconomic theory of monopoly, see also 0223, 0225, and 0226; for antitrust policy see 6120; for specific industry studies, see also the relevant industry study categories.
612 Public Policy Toward Monopoly and Competition 543
6120 Public Policy Toward Monopoly and Competition 543
For public utility regulation see 6130; for policy toward agriculture see 7130; for policy toward transportation see 6150; for policy toward commercial banks see 3120.
613 Regulation of Public Utilities 549
6130 Regulation of Public Utilities 549
For supply, demand, and technology studies for individual firms or industries in electric and gas utilities, see 6352.
614 Public Enterprises 552
6140 Public Enterprises 552
For public utilities operated as a public enterprise, see also 6131.
615 Economics of Transportation 556
6150 Economics of Transportation 556
For urban transportation, see also 9330; for subsidies, see also 3230 and 3242; for location theory, see 9411.
616 Industrial Policy 562
6160 Industrial Policy 562
619 Economics of Regulation 569
6190 Economics of Regulation 569
620 Economics of Technological Change 576
621 Technological Change; Innovation; Research and Development 576
6210 General 576
6211 Technological Change and Innovation 578
6212 Research and Development 589
For effects of taxes and subsidies, see also 3230.
630 Industry Studies 593
6300 General 593
Articles relating to all industrial sectors.
631 Industry Studies: Manufacturing 597
6310 General 597
6312 Metals (iron, steel, and other) 606
6313 Machinery (tools, electrical equipment, computers, communication equipment, and appliances) 609
6314 Transportation Equipment 611
6315 Chemicals, Drugs, Plastics, Ceramics, Glass, Cement, and Rubber 613
6316 Textiles, Leather, and Clothing 615
6317 Forest Products, Lumber, Paper, and Printing and Publishing 616
6318 Food Processing, Tobacco, and Beverages 617
6319 Other Industries 618
632 Industry Studies: Extractive Industries 618
6320 General 618
6322 Mining (metal, coal, and other nonmetallic minerals) 619
For coal see also 7230.

6323 Oil, Gas, and Other Fuels 619
See also 7230.
633 Industry Studies: Distributive Trades 623
6330 General 623
6332 Wholesale Trade 624
6333 Retail Trade 624
634 Industry Studies: Construction 625
6340 Construction 625
635 Industry Studies: Services and Related Industries 626
6350 General 626
6352 Electrical, Gas, Communication, and Information Services 627
For regulation of public utilities, see also 6130; for natural resource sources for the electrical and gas industries, see 7230; for conservation and pollution, see 7220.
6353 Personal Services 633
6354 Business and Legal Services 634
6355 Repair Services 634
6356 Insurance 634
6357 Real Estate 638
6358 Entertainment, Recreation, and Tourism 640
636 Nonprofit Industries: Theory and Studies 641
6360 Nonprofit Industries: Theory and Studies 641
For hospitals see 9130; for education see 9120; for entertainment see 6358.
640 Economic Capacity 643
641 Economic Capacity 643
6410 Economic Capacity 643

700 Agriculture; Natural Resources
710 Agriculture 644
7100 General 644
For agriculture and development see also 1120; for agricultural manpower see also 8131; for agricultural migrant labor see 8230.
711 Agricultural Supply and Demand Analysis 646
7110 Agricultural Supply and Demand Analysis 646
712 Agricultural Situation and Outlook 655
7120 Agricultural Situation and Outlook 655
713 Agricultural Policy, Domestic and International 657
7130 Agricultural Policy, Domestic and International 657
For farm subsidies see also 3230; for agricultural commodity agreements see also 4220.
714 Agricultural Finance 665
7140 Agricultural Finance 665
715 Agricultural Markets and Marketing; Cooperatives 667
7150 Agricultural Markets and Marketing; Cooperatives 667
For agricultural commodity agreements see also 7130 and 4220; for futures markets, see 3132.
7151 Corporate Agriculture 671
716 Farm Management 671
7160 Farm Management 671
717 Land Reform and Land Use 678
7170 General 678

		7171	Land Ownership and Tenure; Land Reform	678
		7172	Land Development; Land Use; Irrigation Policy *For urban and suburban land use, see category 930.*	679
	718		Rural Economics	683
		7180	Rural Economics	683
720			Natural Resources	688
		7200	General	688
	721		Natural Resources	688
		7210	General *For agricultural irrigation aspects, see 7172; for industrial use of natural resources, see appropriate category 630 subdivision; for water and gas utilities, see also 6130; for electricity, see also 6130 and 6352; for tax policies and natural resources, see also 3230 and 3242.*	688
		7211	Recreational Aspects of Natural Resources	697
	722		Conservation and Pollution	697
		7220	Conservation and Pollution *For theoretical aspects of externalities and public goods, see also 0240 and 0244; for tax policies and pollution, see also 3230 and 3242; for energy, see 7230.*	697
	723		Energy	705
		7230	Energy	705
730			Economic Geography	714
	731		Economic Geography	714
		7310	Economic Geography *For urban land see 9310; for regional problems see category 940.*	714
800			Manpower; Labor; Population	
		8000	General	715
810			Manpower Training and Development; Labor Force and Supply	715
		8100	General	
	811		Manpower Training and Development	715
		8110	Manpower Training and Development *Refers to government programs; for government sponsored programs for disadvantaged, see also 9110 and 9140; for educational investment in human capital, see also 8510; for executive training, see 5130.*	715
	812		Occupation	717
		8120	Occupation *Includes supply and demand studies by occupation. For employment studies, see 8243.*	717
	813		Labor Force *Includes labor force studies by industry.*	721
		8130	General	721
		8131	Agriculture	725
		8132	Manufacturing	725
		8133	Service	726
		8134	Professional	726
		8135	Government Employees	727
		8136	Construction	728
820			Labor Markets; Public Policy	728
		8200	General	728

821 Labor Economics 728
8210 Labor Economics: Theory and Empirical Studies Illustrating Theory 728
For empirical wage studies see 8242; for empirical studies of employment, vacancies, and unemployment see 8243. For distribution theory see also 0224 and 0235. For disguised unemployment in agriculture, see 8131 and also 8243.
822 Public Policy; Role of Government 740
8220 General 740
8221 Wages and Hours 741
8222 Workmen's Compensation and Vocational Rehabilitation 742
For other medical costs covered by employment, see 8242 and 9130.
8223 Factory Act and Safety Legislation 743
8224 Unemployment Insurance 744
For private pensions see 8242.
8225 Government Employment Policies (including employment services) 745
For unemployment studies see 8243.
8226 Employment in the Public Sector 746
See 8135 for statistical studies of government employees.
823 Labor Mobility; National and International Migration 747
8230 Labor Mobility; National and International Migration 747
For general migration see 8410.
824 Labor Market Studies, Wages, Employment 751
8240 General 751
8241 Geographic Labor Market Studies 753
Refers to labor market studies in specific geographical areas
8242 Wage, Hours, and Fringe Benefit Studies 754
8243 Employment Studies; Unemployment and Vacancies; Retirements and Quits 765
For labor force shifts see 8130; for labor market theory see 8210.
825 Productivity Studies: Labor, Capital, and Total Factor 781
8250 Productivity Studies: Labor, Capital, and Total Factor 781
826 Labor Markets: Demographic Characteristics 787
8260 Labor Markets: Demographic Characteristics 787
For economic effects of job discrimination involving minorities and women, see 9170.
830 Trade Unions; Collective Bargaining; Labor–Management Relations 791
8300 General 791
831 Trade Unions 792
8310 Trade Unions 792
832 Collective Bargaining 798
8320 General 798
8321 Collective Bargaining in the Private Sector 799
8322 Collective Bargaining in the Public Sector 801
833 Labor–Management Relations 802
8330 General 802
For labor–management problems covered by collective bargaining agreements, see category 832; for theory of the labor-managed firm, see 0223 or 0271.

8331 Labor–Management Relations in the Private Sector 804
8332 Labor–Management Relations in the Public Sector 807
Includes labor–management relations in socialist countries.
840 Demographic Economics 808
841 Demographic Economics 808
8410 Demographic Economics 808
For migration emphasizing labor market conditions, see 8230; for food supply, see also 7110; for nutrition, see also 9130.
850 Human Capital; Value of Human Life 821
851 Human Capital; Value of Human Life 821
8510 Human Capital; Value of Human Life 821
For educational expenditures, financing, structure, and demand, see 9120; for manpower training, see 8110; for government sponsored employment policy, see 8225.

900 Welfare Programs; Consumer Economics; Urban and Regional Economics
910 Welfare; Health; Education 825
9100 General 825
911 General Welfare Programs 825
9110 General Welfare Programs 825
For housing subsidies, see 9320.
912 Economics of Education 828
9120 Economics of Education 828
For investment in human capital, see 8510.
913 Economics of Health (including medical subsidy programs) 833
9130 Economics of Health (including medical subsidy programs) 833
For workmen's compensation, see 8222; for fringe benefits covering medical costs, see 8242; for general social security programs, see also 9150; for value of human life, see also 8510.
914 Economics of Poverty 844
9140 Economics of Poverty 844
For negative income tax see also 9110 and 3230; for rural poverty, see 7180.
915 Social Security 846
9150 Social Security 846
For all pensions see 8242; for medical subsidy programs, see 9130.
916 Economics of Law; Economics of Crime 849
9160 Economics of Law; Economics of Crime 849
For antitrust law, see 6120.
917 Economics of Minorities; Economics of Discrimination 854
9170 Economics of Minorities; Economics of Discrimination 854
For demographic characteristics in labor markets, see also 8260.
918 Economics of Aging 862
9180 Economics of Aging 862
920 Consumer Economics 863
921 Consumer Economics; Levels and Standards of Living 863
9210 General 863
For theory of the household see 0222; for theory of con-

sumption function and saving see also 0232; for consumers' cooperatives see 0510; for consumer finance see 3151.

9211 Living Standards, Composition of Overall Expenditures, and Empirical Consumption and Savings Studies 864

For consumer demand for or expenditures on specific commodities, see 9212; for distribution of wealth, see 2240.

9212 Expenditure Patterns and Consumption of Specific Items 870

For overall expenditure pattern see 9211.

9213 Consumer Protection 875

930 Urban Economics 877

9300 General 877

931 Urban Economics and Public Policy 877

9310 Urban Economics and Public Policy 877

932 Housing Economics 885

9320 Housing Economics (including nonurban housing) 885

For construction industry studies see 6340; for housing mortgages see 3152.

933 Urban Transportation Economics 889

9330 Urban Transportation Economics 889

For other transportation studies see 6150.

940 Regional Economics 890

941 Regional Economics 890

9410 General 890

For regional statistics see 2280.

9411 Theory of Regional Economics 891

9412 Regional Economic Studies 894

9413 Regional Economic Models and Forecasts 902

Subject Index of Articles in Current Periodicals and Collective Volumes

Abbreviated titles for journals are the same as those used in the *Journal of Economic Literature*. Full titles of journals may be found on pages x–xv.

Books have been identified by author or editor (noted *ed.*). In rare cases where two books by the same author appear, volumes are distinguished by I or II after the name. In some cases there appear two books by the same person, once as author, once as editor. These may be distinguished by *ed.* noted for the edited volume. Full titles and bibliographic references for books may be found on pages xvi–xxxiv.

Geographic descriptors when appropriate appear in brackets at the end of the article citation.

000 General Economics; Theory; History; Systems

010 General Economics

011 General Economics

0110 General

Beilock, Richard P.; Polopolus, Leo C. and Correal, Mario. Ranking of Agricultural Economics Department by Citations. *Amer. J. Agr. Econ.*, August 1986, *68*(3), pp. 595–604. **[G: U.S.]**

Benedict, Michael Les. Historians and the Continuing Controversy over Fair Use of Unpublished Manuscript Materials. *Amer. Hist. Rev.*, October 1986, *91*(4), pp. 859–81.

Blair, Dudley W.; Cottle, Rex L. and Wallace, Myles S. Faculty Ratings of Major Economics Departments by Citations: An Extension. *Amer. Econ. Rev.*, March 1986, *76*(1), pp. 264–67. **[G: U.S.]**

Buchanan, James M. The Related but Distinct 'Sciences' of Economics and of Political Economy. **In** *Buchanan, J. M.*, 1986, *1982*, pp. 28–39.

Davies, J. Kenneth. Mormonism and the Socio-Economic Order. *Int. J. Soc. Econ.*, 1986, *13*(3), pp. 64–79. **[G: U.S.]**

Desai, Meghnad. Men and Things. *Economica*, February 1986, *53*(209), pp. 1–10.

Dewald, William G.; Thursby, Jerry G. and Anderson, Richard G. Replication in Empirical Economics: The *Journal of Money, Credit and Banking Project*. *Amer. Econ. Rev.*, September 1986, *76*(4), pp. 587–603.

Diamond, Arthur M., Jr. What Is a Citation Worth? *J. Human Res.*, Spring 1986, *21*(2), pp. 200–215. **[G: U.S.]**

Dubiel, Ivo. Changes of Social Relevance in the Transplantation of Theories: The Examples of Economics and Agronomics. *CEPAL Rev.*, April 1986, (28), pp. 151–69.

Dyer, Alan W. Semiotics, Economic Development, and the Deconstruction of Economic Man. *J. Econ. Issues,* June 1986, *20*(2), pp. 541–49.

Epperson, J. E., et al. On a Name Change for the *Journal*. *Southern J. Agr. Econ.*, July 1986, *18*(1), pp. 161–68.

Feiner, Susan F. and Roberts, Bruce B. Marx and Keynes and Kalecki. *J. Econ. Issues*, December 1986, *20*(4), pp. 1135–36.

Fletcher, Daniel O. A Survey of Textbooks for Industrial Organization and Public Policy. *J. Econ. Educ.*, Spring 1986, *17*(2), pp. 141–51.

Geistfeld, Loren V. and Key, Rosemary. A Decade in Perspective 1975–84: Focus and Trends in the *Journal of Consumer Affairs*. *J. Cons. Aff.*, Summer 1986, *20*(1), pp. 65–76.

Gilley, Otis W. A Ranking of the Top U.S. Economics Departments by Research Productivity of Graduates: A Comment. *J. Econ. Educ.*, Fall 1986, *17*(4), pp. 307–09. **[G: U.S.]**

Golden, John, et al. Publication Performance of Fifty Top Economics Departments: A *Per Capita* Analysis. *Econ. Educ. Rev.*, 1986, *5*(1), pp. 83–86. **[G: U.S.]**

Hacken, Richard D. Scandinavian Social Economics since 1930: A Bibliographic Note. *Rev. Soc. Econ.*, October 1986, *44*(2), pp. 159–77. **[G: Scandinavia]**

Harcourt, Geoffrey C. Reflections on the Development of Economics as a Discipline. **In** *[Harcourt, G. C.]*, 1986, *1984*, pp. 9–45.

Heck, J. Louis and Bremser, Wayne G. Six Decades of *The Accounting Review:* A Summary of Author and Institutional Contributors. *Accounting Rev.*, October 1986, *61*(4), pp. 735–44.

Heck, J. Louis; Cooley, Philip L. and Hubbard, Carl M. Contributing Authors and Institutions to the *Journal of Finance:* 1946–1985. *J. Finance*, December 1986, *41*(5), pp. 1129–40.

Henderson, Margaret. Thesis Titles for Degrees in the United Kingdom 1984/85 and 1985/86. *Econ. J.*, March 1986, *96*(381), pp. 216–23. **[G: U.K.]**

Hogan, Timothy D. The Publishing Performance of U.S. Ph.D. Programs in Economics during the 1970s. *J. Human Res.*, Spring 1986, *21*(2), pp. 216–29. **[G: U.S.]**

Kindleberger, Charles P. My Working Philosophy. *Amer. Econ.*, Spring 1986, *30*(1), pp. 13–20.

Kindleberger, Charles P. Reversible and Irreversible Processes in Economics. *Challenge*, Sept./Oct. 1986, *29*(4), pp. 4–10. **[G: U.S.]**

011 General Economics

Koen, Vincent. La production française de connaissances économiques. Analyse bibliométrique. (The French Production of Economic Knowledge: A Bibliometric Analysis. With English summary.) *Revue Écon.*, January 1986, *37*(1), pp. 117–36. **[G: France]**

Laband, David N. A Ranking of the Top U.S. Economics Departments by Research Productivity of Graduates: Reply. *J. Econ. Educ.*, Fall 1986, *17*(4), pp. 311–14. **[G: U.S.]**

Laband, David N. A Ranking of the Top U.S. Economics Departments by Research Productivity of Graduates. *J. Econ. Educ.*, Winter 1986, *17*(1), pp. 70–76.

Laband, David N. Article Popularity. *Econ. Inquiry,* January 1986, *24*(1), pp. 173–80. **[G: U.S.]**

McDowell, John M. and Amacher, Ryan C. Economic Value of an In-House Editorship. *Public Choice,* 1986, *48*(2), pp. 101–12. **[G: U.S.]**

Modigliani, Franco. Bibliography of Franco Modigliani's Publications, 1944–1985. *Scand. J. Econ.*, 1986, *88*(2), pp. 335–53.

Nash, Michael. Business History at the Hagley Museum and Library. *Bus. Hist. Rev.*, Spring 1986, *60*(1), pp. 104–20. **[G: U.S.]**

Nato, Takatsugu. The Influence of Confucianism and Buddhism on Life-Innovators in the Japanese Socio-Economic Order. *Int. J. Soc. Econ.*, 1986, *13*(3), pp. 53–63. **[G: Japan]**

Parkin, Michael. Essays on and in the Chicago Tradition: A Review Essay. *J. Money, Credit, Banking,* February 1986, *18*(1), pp. 104–16.

Patinkin, Don. Essay on and in the Chicago Tradition: A Reply. *J. Money, Credit, Banking,* February 1986, *18*(1), pp. 116–21.

Pommerehne, Werner W. Die Reputation wirtschaftswissenschaftlicher Fachzeitschriften: Ergebnisse einer Befragung deutscher Ökonomen. (The Reputation of Economic Journals: Results of a Survey among German Economists. With English summary.) *Jahr. Nationalökon. Statist.*, May 1986, *201*(3), pp. 280–306. **[G: W. Germany]**

Reed, Dale. Holdings on United States Socialism and Communism at the Hoover Institution on War, Revolution and Peace. *Labor Hist.*, Fall 1986, *27*(4), pp. 506–28. **[G: U.S.]**

Reuter, Peter. The Social Costs of the Demand for Quantification. *J. Policy Anal. Manage.*, Summer 1986, *5*(4), pp. 807–12.

Rogers, Ruth R. The Kress Library of Business and Economics. *Bus. Hist. Rev.*, Summer 1986, *60*(2), pp. 281–88.

Samuelson, Paul A. Succumbing to Keynesianism. **In** *Samuelson, P. A.*, 1986, *1985*, pp. 283–90. **[G: U.S.]**

Slater, Paul B. A Citation-Based Taxonomy of Scientific Journals. **In** *Slater, P. B.*, 1986, pp. 125–53.

Stigler, George J. A Certain Galbraith in an Uncertain Age. **In** *Stigler, G. J.*, 1986, *1985*, pp. 352–59.

Stigler, George J. The Process and Progress of Economics. **In** *Stigler, G. J.*, 1986, *1983*, pp. 134–49.

Swanson, Dorothy. Annual Bibliography on American Labor History, 1985: Periodicals, Dissertations, and Research in Progress. *Labor Hist.*, Fall 1986, *27*(4), pp. 529–41. **[G: U.S.]**

Székely, Alberto. Transboundary Oil and Gas: Selected Bibliography. *Natural Res. J.*, Fall 1986, *26*(4), pp. 833–50.

Tollison, Robert D. and Goff, Brian L. Citation Practices in Economics and Physics. *J. Inst. Theoretical Econ.*, September 1986, *142*(3), pp. 581–87.

Uppal, J. S. Hinduism and Economic Development in South Asia. *Int. J. Soc. Econ.*, 1986, *13*(3), pp. 20–33. **[G: Asia]**

Venkateswarlu, Tadiboyina. Public Finance: Survey of Course Reading Materials in Academic Institutions. *Amer. Econ.*, Fall 1986, *30*(2), pp. 62–93.

Weiermair, Klaus. On the Economics of Institutional Change: An Institutional Change in Economics? *J. Econ. Issues,* June 1986, *20*(2), pp. 571–82. **[G: U.S.]**

Williams, C. Arthur, Jr. 1985 Annual Report of the Editor of the *Journal of Risk and Insurance. J. Risk Ins.*, March 1986, *53*(1), pp. 23–27. **[G: U.S.]**

Williamson, Oliver E. An Autobiographical Sketch. **In** *Williamson, O. E.*, 1986, pp. xi–xviii.

Wisman, Jon D. The Renaissance of Natural Law Cosmology: Free Markets and Fettered Minds. *Int. J. Soc. Econ.*, 1986, *13*(10), pp. 26–37.

0112 Role of Economics; Role of Economists

Baldwin, George B. Economics and Economists in the World Bank. **In** *Coats, A. W., ed.*, 1986, pp. 67–90.

Bannon, Bob. Fedwatching. *Bus. Econ.*, October 1986, *21*(4), pp. 43–47.

Baranzini, Mauro and Scazzieri, Roberto. Knowledge in Economics: A Framework. **In** *Baranzini, M. and Scazzieri, R., eds.*, 1986, pp. 1–87.

Baumol, William J. Microtheory: Applications and Origins: Introduction. **In** *Baumol, W. J.*, 1986, pp. viii–xxvii.

Benton, Raymond, Jr. Economics and Loss of Meaning. *Rev. Soc. Econ.*, December 1986, *44*(3), pp. 251–67.

Black, R. D. Collison. Dentists and Preachers. **In** *Black, R. D. C., ed.*, 1986, pp. 1–15.

Bliss, Christopher. Progress and Anti-progress in Economic Science. **In** *Baranzini, M. and Scazzieri, R., eds.*, 1986, pp. 363–76.

Bordo, Michael D. and Landau, Daniel. Advocacy and Neo Classical Economics. *Eastern Econ. J.*, Apr.-June 1986, *12*(2), pp. 94–102.

Boulding, Kenneth E. What Went Wrong with Economics? *Amer. Econ.*, Spring 1986, *30*(1), pp. 5–12.

Buchanan, James M. Better than Plowing. *Banca Naz. Lavoro Quart. Rev.*, December 1986, (159), pp. 359–75.

Buchanan, James M. Ideas, Institutions, and Political Economy: A Plea for Disestablishment.

Carnegie-Rochester Conf. Ser. Public Policy, Autumn 1986, *25*, pp. 245–57. **[G: U.S.]**

Buchanan, James M. and Tollison, Robert D. A Theory of Truth in Autobiography. *Kyklos*, 1986, *39*(4), pp. 507–17.

Bugra, Ayşe. Karl Polanyi and the Boundaries of Economics. *METU*, 1986, *13*(3–4), pp. 217–38.

Cairncross, Alec. Academics and Policy Makers. **In** *Cairncross, A.*, 1986, *1981*, pp. 21–36.

Cairncross, Alec. Economics in Theory and Practice. **In** *Cairncross, A.*, 1986, *1984*, pp. 1–20.

Clawson, Marion. Application of Economics to the Problems of Natural Resource Use, Development, and Policy. **In** *[Crutchfield, J. A.]*, 1986, pp. 25–41.

Coats, A. W. Economists in International Agencies: An Exploratory Study: Introduction. **In** *Coats, A. W., ed.*, 1986, pp. 1–35.

Coats, A. W. Economists in International Agencies: An Exploratory Study: Conclusions. **In** *Coats, A. W., ed.*, 1986, pp. 165–71.

Conyers, Diana. In Search of the Practical Academic: Lessons from the Study of Regional Administration. *Reg. Stud.*, October 1986, *20*(6), pp. 579–84.

Cooper, Kathleen M. NABE's Role: Fostering the Professional Growth of Business Economists. *Bus. Econ.*, April 1986, *21*(2), pp. 25–27. **[G: U.S.]**

Dahm, Helmut. The Role of Economics in Soviet Political Ideology. **In** *Höhmann, H.-H.; Nove, A. and Vogel, H., eds.*, 1986, pp. 17–40. **[G: U.S.S.R.]**

DeAngelo, David J. The Business Economist at Work: Pennsylvania Power and Light Co. *Bus. Econ.*, April 1986, *21*(2), pp. 57–59. **[G: U.S.]**

Dell, Sidney. Economics in the United Nations. **In** *Coats, A. W., ed.*, 1986, pp. 36–52.

Djojohadikusumo, Sumitro. Recollections of My Career. *Bull. Indonesian Econ. Stud.*, December 1986, *22*(3), pp. 27–39.

Eriksson, Tor. Kan den akademiska nationalekonomin ges förnyad livskraft? (Can Academic Economics Be Given Renewed Vitality? With English summary.) *Ekon. Samfundets Tidskr.*, 1986, *39*(3), pp. 163–68.

Ewing, Arthur F. Surendra Patel: The Man and the Economist. **In** *[Patel, S.]*, 1986, pp. xi–xix.

Fischer, Lewis. Sixty Years of Agricultural Economics at Macdonald College. *Can. J. Agr. Econ.*, Proceedings 1986, *34*, pp. 42–47. **[G: Canada]**

Fox, Karl A. Agricultural Economists as World Leaders in Applied Econometrics, 1917–33. *Amer. J. Agr. Econ.*, May 1986, *68*(2), pp. 381–86.

Foxley, Alejandro. After Authoritarianism: Political Alternatives. **In** *[Hirshman, A. O.]*, 1986, pp. 191–216. **[G: Chile]**

Frey, Bruno S. Economists Favour the Price System—Who Else Does? *Kyklos*, 1986, *39*(4), pp. 537–63.

Friedman, Milton. Economists and Economic Policy. *Econ. Inquiry*, January 1986, *24*(1), pp. 1–10.

Furtan, W. H. Educational Institutions and Scholarship in the Twenty-First Century. *Can. J. Agr. Econ.*, June 1986, *33*, pp. 111–17. **[G: Canada]**

Giersch, Herbert. Economics as a Public Good. *Banca Naz. Lavoro Quart. Rev.*, September 1986, (158), pp. 251–73.

Gilad, Benjamin. Go Industrial Young Man, and Then Go Behavioral. *Bus. Econ.*, April 1986, *21*(2), pp. 28–33. **[G: U.S.]**

Glejser, Herbert and Waelbroeck, Jean. A Few Words to the Readers. *Europ. Econ. Rev.*, February 1986, *30*(1), pp. 1–3. **[G: Europe]**

Hall, John B. Economic Thought and the Evolution of Institutions in Hungary. *J. Econ. Issues*, June 1986, *20*(2), pp. 593–600. **[G: Hungary]**

Harwell, R. Lynn and Rosson, C. Parr, III. Financial Crisis in Agriculture, a Southern Perspective: Discussion. *Southern J. Agr. Econ.*, July 1986, *18*(1), pp. 109–12. **[G: U.S.]**

Hicks, John R. Is Economics a Science? **In** *Baranzini, M. and Scazzieri, R., eds.*, 1986, pp. 91–101.

Highsmith, Robert J. Professional Developments and Opportunities. *J. Econ. Educ.*, Fall 1986, *17*(4), pp. 315–17. **[G: U.S.]**

Hoadley, Walter E. Tomorrow's Business Economist. *Bus. Econ.*, April 1986, *21*(2), pp. 5–10. **[G: U.S.]**

Hobsbawm, Eric. Aspects of International Socialism, 1871–1914: Essays by Georges Haupt: Preface. **In** *Haupt, G.*, 1986, pp. vii–xvii.

Hoskins, W. Lee. Professional Certification: An Idea in Search of a Problem. *Bus. Econ.*, April 1986, *21*(2), pp. 15–20. **[G: U.S.]**

Houck, James P.. Views on Agricultural Economics' Role in Economic Thought. *Amer. J. Agr. Econ.*, May 1986, *68*(2), pp. 375–80. **[G: U.S.]**

Johnson, D. Gale. Agricultural Economics, Contributions: Discussion [Views on Agricultural Economics' Role in Economic Thought]. *Amer. J. Agr. Econ.*, May 1986, *68*(2), pp. 395–96. **[G: U.S.]**

Johnson, Glenn L. Scope of Agricultural Economics. **In** *Maunder, A. and Renborg, U., eds.*, 1986, pp. 21–34.

Laden, Ben E. Business Economics—Preparing for the Future. *Bus. Econ.*, January 1986, *21*(1), pp. 13–16. **[G: U.S.]**

Leube, Kurt R. George J. Stigler: A Biographical Introduction. **In** *Stigler, G. J.*, 1986, pp. xiii–xix.

Love, Ross O. The Role of Extension in Dealing with Farm Families in Financial Crisis. *Southern J. Agr. Econ.*, July 1986, *18*(1), pp. 83–92. **[G: U.S.]**

Lukka, Kari. Taloustieteen metodologiset suuntaukset: liiketaloustieteen ja kansantaloustieteen vertailu. (Methodological Approaches in Economic Sciences: A Comparison between Business Economics and Economics. With English summary.) *Liiketaloudellinen Aikak.*, 1986, *35*(2), pp. 133–49.

Marris, Stephen. The Role of Economists in the OECD. **In** *Coats, A. W., ed.*, 1986, pp. 98–114. **[G: OECD]**

Maxwell, Simon. The Social Scientist in Farming Systems Research. *J. Agr. Econ.*, January 1986, *37*(1), pp. 25–35.

McCaleb, Thomas S. The Council of Economic Advisors after Forty Years. *Cato J.*, Fall 1986, *6*(2), pp. 687–93. **[G: U.S.]**

McMillan, Robert A. The Business Economist at Work: The BFGoodrich Company. *Bus. Econ.*, January 1986, *21*(1), pp. 58–60. **[G: U.S.]**

Meehan, Eugene J. A Critique of Economic Policymaking. **In** *Redburn, F. S.; Buss, T. F. and Ledebur, L. C., eds.*, 1986, pp. 200–227.

Meier, Alfred and Mettler, Daniel. Einfluss und Macht in der Wirtschaftspolitik. (Influence and Power in Economic Policy. With English summary.) *Schweiz. Z. Volkswirtsch. Statist.*, March 1986, *122*(1), pp. 37–59.

Mishan, Ezra J. The Mystique of Economic Expertise. **In** *Mishan, E. J.*, 1986, *1984*, pp. 78–107.

Mueller, Dennis C. An Autobiographical Essay. **In** *Mueller, D. C.*, 1986, pp. ix–xx.

Musgrave, Richard A. Alvin Hansen. **In** *Musgrave, R. A., Vol. 2*, 1986, *1976*, pp. 274–79.

Musgrave, Richard A. Public Finance in a Democratic Society: Introduction. **In** *Musgrave, R. A., Vol. 1*, 1986, pp. vii–xiii.

Nerlove, Marc. Agricultural Economics, Contributions: Discussion [Agricultural Economists as World Leaders in Applied Econometrics, 1917–33] [Future Challenges for Modeling in Agricultural Economics]. *Amer. J. Agr. Econ.*, May 1986, *68*(2), pp. 397–98.

Niskanen, William A. A Reflection on the Role of the Council of Economic Advisers. *Carnegie-Rochester Conf. Ser. Public Policy*, Autumn 1986, *25*, pp. 259–63. **[G: U.S.]**

Niskanen, William A. Economists and Politicians. *J. Policy Anal. Manage.*, Winter 1986, *5*(2), pp. 234–44.

Nordhaus, William D. The Council of Economic Advisers: Conscience or Advocate? *Carnegie-Rochester Conf. Ser. Public Policy*, Autumn 1986, *25*, pp. 265–77. **[G: U.S.]**

Nove, Alec. Soviet Economics and Soviet Economists: Some Random Observations. **In** *Nove, A.*, 1986, *1981*, pp. 104–27. **[G: U.S.S.R.]**

Nowzad, Bahram. The Perils of Prescription: Economics and the Macroeconomic Policy Adviser. *World Devel.*, Oct./Nov. 1986, *14*(10/11), pp. 1361–73.

Parker, William N. An Historical Introduction. **In** *Parker, W. N., ed.*, 1986, pp. 1–10.

Patel, I. G. Economic Theory and Economic Policy. **In** *Patel, I. G.*, 1986, pp. 101–16. **[G: India]**

Patterson, Gardner. The Role of Economists in the GATT Secretariat. **In** *Coats, A. W., ed.*, 1986, pp. 91–97.

Petit, Michel. The Status and the State of Agricultural Economics. **In** *Maunder, A. and Renborg, U., eds.*, 1986, pp. 793–803.

Pope, Rulon D. and Hallam, Arne. A Confusion of Agricultural Economists? A Professional Interest Survey and Essay. *Amer. J. Agr. Econ.*, August 1986, *68*(3), pp. 572–94. **[G: U.S.]**

Rostow, Walt W. My Life Philosophy. *Amer. Econ.*, Fall 1986, *30*(2), pp. 3–13.

Rothschild, Kurt W. Economic Theory: U.S.–European Linkages: A Journal Analysis. *Weltwirtsch. Arch.*, 1986, *122*(3), pp. 566–74. **[G: U.S.; EEC]**

Samuelson, Paul A. Economics in My Time. **In** *Samuelson, P. A.*, 1986, pp. 797–808.

Samuelson, Paul A. Has Economic Science Improved the System? **In** *Knowlton, W. and Zeckhauser, R., eds.*, 1986, pp. 299–315. **[G: U.S.]**

Samuelson, Paul A. Policy Advising in Economics. **In** *Samuelson, P. A.*, 1986, *1978*, pp. 980–81.

Schmitt, Günther. The Role of Institutions in Formulation of Agricultural Policy: Their Repercussions on the Challenges of an Agriculture in a Turbulent World Economy. **In** *Maunder, A. and Renborg, U., eds.*, 1986, pp. 390–403.

Schott, Francis H. Tomorrow's Business Economist—An Alternative View. *Bus. Econ.*, April 1986, *21*(2), pp. 11–14. **[G: U.S.]**

Schotter, Andrew. The Evolution of Rules. **In** *Langlois, R. N., ed.*, 1986, pp. 117–33.

Scitovsky, Tibor. Are Men Rational or Economists Wrong? **In** *Scitovsky, T.*, 1986, *1974*, pp. 70–82.

Scitovsky, Tibor. How to Bring Joy into Economics. **In** *Scitovsky, T.*, 1986, pp. 183–203.

Scitovsky, Tibor. Notes on the Producer Society. **In** *Scitovsky, T.*, 1986, *1972*, pp. 47–69.

Sen, Amartya K. Prediction and Economic Theory. **In** *Mason, J.; Mathias, P. and Westcott, J. H., eds.*, 1986, pp. 3–22.

Shillinglaw, Gordon. The Economics of Strategic Planning: Foreword. **In** *[Dean, J.]*, 1986, pp. xi–xiv.

Silber, Jacques G. Rationality, Self Interest and Coordination: On Some Current Controversies in Economics. *Econ. Notes*, 1986, (3), pp. 47–64.

Silk, Leonard. Communicating Economic Ideas and Controversies. *Amer. Econ. Rev.*, May 1986, *76*(2), pp. 141–44. **[G: U.S.]**

Solomon, Anthony. Economics, Ideology, and Public Policy. *Challenge*, July/Aug. 1986, *29*(3), pp. 11–17. **[G: U.S.]**

Sprinkel, Beryl W. The Value of Economic Analysis. *Bus. Econ.*, January 1986, *21*(1), pp. 17–21.

Stein, Herbert. The Washington Economics Industry. *Amer. Econ. Rev.*, May 1986, *76*(2), pp. 1–9. **[G: U.S.]**

Stigler, George J. A Sketch of the History of Truth in Teaching. **In** *Stigler, G. J.*, 1986, *1973*, pp. 368–72.

Stigler, George J. The Economist and the State. **In** *Stigler, G. J.*, 1986, *1965*, pp. 99–116.

Stigler, George J. The Process and Progress of Economics. **In** *Stigler, G. J.*, 1986, *1983*, pp. 134–49.

Sumner, Michael T. Are Economists Rational?

Appl. Econ., April 1986, *18*(4), pp. 453–56. **[G: U.K.]**

Tollison, Robert D. Economists as the Subject of Economic Inquiry. *Southern Econ. J.*, April 1986, *52*(4), pp. 909–22.

Van Dyke, Daniel T. How to Measure the Performance of a Business Economics Unit. *Bus. Econ.*, April 1986, *21*(2), pp. 21–24. **[G: U.S.]**

de Vries, Margaret Garritsen. The International Monetary Fund: Economists in Key Roles. **In** *Coats, A. W., ed.*, 1986, pp. 53–66.

de Vries, Margaret Garritsen. The IMF in a Changing World, 1945–85: The H. Johannes Witteveen Years, 1973–78. **In** *de Vries, M. G.*, 1986, *1978*, pp. 136–48.

de Vries, Margaret Garritsen. The IMF in a Changing World, 1945–85: The Decade of Pierre-Paul Schweitzer, 1963–73. **In** *de Vries, M. G.*, 1986, *1973*, pp. 85–93.

Walter, John D., Jr. The Business Economist at Work: Dow Corning Corporation. *Bus. Econ.*, July 1986, *21*(3), pp. 46–48. **[G: U.S.]**

0113 Relation of Economics to Other Disciplines

Altar, M. The Romanian School of Economic Cybernetics. *Econ. Computat. Cybern. Stud. Res.*, 1986, *21*(3), pp. 79–82. **[G: Romania]**

Alverson, Hoyt S. Culture and Economy: Games That "Play People." *J. Econ. Issues*, September 1986, *20*(3), pp. 661–79.

Buchanan, James M. Political Economy and Social Philosophy. **In** *Buchanan, J. M.*, 1986, *1985*, pp. 261–74.

Buchanan, James M. The Potential for Tyranny in Politics as Science. **In** *Buchanan, J. M.*, 1986, pp. 40–54.

Businaro, Ugo L. Applying the Biological Evolution Metaphor to Technological Innovation. **In** *Freeman, C., ed.*, 1986, pp. 104–20.

Chadwick-Jones, J. K. Social Exchange, Social Psychology and Economics. **In** *MacFadyen, A. J. and MacFadyen, H. W., eds.*, 1986, pp. 249–67.

Chisholm, Roderick M. Brentano on Preference, Desire and Intrinsic Value. **In** *Grassl, W. and Smith, B., eds.*, 1986, pp. 182–95.

Chrystal, K. Alec and Peel, David A. What Can Economics Learn from Political Science, and Vice Versa? *Amer. Econ. Rev.*, May 1986, *76*(2), pp. 62–65. **[G: U.K.]**

Cox, James C. and Isaac, R. Mark. Experimental Economics and Experimental Psychology: Ever the Twain Shall Meet? **In** *MacFadyen, A. J. and MacFadyen, H. W., eds.*, 1986, pp. 647–69.

Dooley, David and Catalano, Ralph. Do Economic Variables Generate Psychological Problems? Different Methods, Different Answers. **In** *MacFadyen, A. J. and MacFadyen, H. W., eds.*, 1986, pp. 503–46.

Elster, Jon. The Multiple Self: Introduction. **In** *Elster, J., ed.*, 1986, pp. 1–34.

Etzioni, Amitai. Founding a New Socioeconomics. *Challenge*, Nov./Dec. 1986, *29*(5), pp. 13–17.

Fabian, Reinhard and Simons, Peter M. The Second Austrian School of Value Theory. **In** *Grassl, W. and Smith, B., eds.*, 1986, pp. 37–101.

Filer, Randall K. People and Productivity: Effort Supply as Viewed by Economists and Psychologists. **In** *Gilad, B. and Kaish, S., eds., Vol. A*, 1986, pp. 261–87.

Fisher, Irving. The Economics of Accountancy. **In** *Parker, R. H.; Harcourt, G. C. and Whittington, G., eds.*, 1986, *1930*, pp. 66–81.

Fitzhenry, Roy. Parsons, Schutz and the Problem of *Verstehen*. **In** *Holton, R. J. and Turner, B. S.*, 1986, pp. 143–78.

Georgescu-Roegen, Nicholas. The Entropy Law and the Economic Process in Retrospect. *Eastern Econ. J.*, Jan.-Mar. 1986, *12*(1), pp. 3–25.

Gerstein, Dean R. Behavioral and Social Science: Fifty Years of Discovery: Introduction. **In** *Smelser, N. J. and Gerstein, D. R., eds.*, 1986, pp. 1–17.

Gilad, Benjamin and Kaish, Stanley. Behavioral Microeconomics: Introduction. **In** *Gilad, B. and Kaish, S., eds., Vol. A*, 1986, pp. xvii–xxiii.

Green, Sebastian. The Contribution of Anthropology to Economic Growth and Development. **In** *Gilad, B. and Kaish, S., eds., Vol. B*, 1986, pp. 201–13.

Grossbard-Shechtman, Amyra. Marriage and Productivity: An Interdisciplinary Analysis. **In** *Gilad, B. and Kaish, S., eds., Vol. A*, 1986, pp. 289–302.

Guran, M. The Romanian School of Economic Cybernetics and the Development of Informatics. *Econ. Computat. Cybern. Stud. Res.*, 1986, *21*(3), pp. 89–92. **[G: Romania]**

Heiner, Ronald A. Uncertainty, Signal-Detection Experiments, and Modeling Behavior. **In** *Langlois, R. N., ed.*, 1986, pp. 59–115.

Hirshleifer, Jack. Economics from a Biological Viewpoint. **In** *Barney, J. B. and Ouchi, W. G., eds.*, 1986, *1977*, pp. 319–71.

Hogarth, Robin M. and Reder, Melvin W. Perspectives from Economics and Psychology. **In** *Hogarth, R. M. and Reder, M. W., eds.*, 1986, pp. 1–23.

Hogarth, Robin M. and Reder, Melvin W. Perspectives from Economics and Psychology: Editor's Comments. *J. Bus.*, Part 2, October 1986, *59*(4), pp. S185–207.

Holton, Robert J. Talcott Parsons and the Theory of Economy and Society. **In** *Holton, R. J. and Turner, B. S.*, 1986, pp. 25–105.

Holton, Robert J. and Turner, Bryan S. Against Nostalgia: Talcott Parsons and a Sociology for the Modern World. **In** *Holton, R. J. and Turner, B. S.*, 1986, pp. 207–34.

Holton, Robert J. and Turner, Bryan S. Reading Parsons: Introductory Remarks. **In** *Holton, R. J. and Turner, B. S.*, 1986, pp. 1–24.

Isard, Walter. Reflections on the Relevance of Integrated Multiregion Models: Lessons from Physics. *Reg. Sci. Urban Econ.*, May 1986, *16*(2), pp. 165–80.

Kahneman, Daniel and Tversky, Amos. Choices,

Values, and Frames. **In** *Smelser, N. J. and Gerstein, D. R., eds.*, 1986, pp. 153–72.

Kent, Calvin A. A Christian Approach to Social Economics. *Int. J. Soc. Econ.*, 1986, *13*(3), pp. 80–92.

Kindleberger, Charles P. International Public Good without International Government. *Amer. Econ. Rev.*, March 1986, *76*(1), pp. 1–13.

Kornai, János. The Health of Nations: Reflections on the Analogy between the Medical Sciences and Economics. **In** *Kornai, J.*, 1986, *1983*, pp. 139–60.

Lee, Han Yu and Hayden, F. Gregory. DeGregori's *A Theory of Technology:* A Review Article. *J. Econ. Issues*, September 1986, *20*(3), pp. 799–804.

Lux, Kenneth and Lutz, Mark A. Economic Psychology: The Humanistic Perspective. **In** *MacFadyen, A. J. and MacFadyen, H. W., eds.*, 1986, pp. 383–424.

MacFadyen, Alan J. and MacFadyen, Heather Wood. Economic Psychology: Intersections in Theory and Application: Introduction. **In** *MacFadyen, A. J. and MacFadyen, H. W., eds.*, 1986, pp. 1–5.

MacFadyen, Alan J. and MacFadyen, Heather Wood. Other Concepts in Economic Psychology. **In** *MacFadyen, A. J. and MacFadyen, H. W., eds.*, 1986, pp. 441–95.

MacFadyen, Heather Wood. Motivational Constructs in Psychology. **In** *MacFadyen, A. J. and MacFadyen, H. W., eds.*, 1986, pp. 67–108.

MacFadyen, Heather Wood and MacFadyen, Alan J. Economic Psychology: Intersections in Theory and Application: Summary and Conclusions. **In** *MacFadyen, A. J. and MacFadyen, H. W., eds.*, 1986, pp. 673–78.

Maital, Sharone L.; Maital, Shlomo and Pollak, Nava. Economic Behavior and Social Learning. **In** *MacFadyen, A. J. and MacFadyen, H. W., eds.*, 1986, pp. 271–90.

Manara, Carlo Felice. L'economia e il metodo matematico. (Economics and Mathematical Method. With English summary.) *Econ. Polit.*, August 1986, *3*(2), pp. 179–86.

McKee, Arnold. The Passage from Theology to Economics. *Int. J. Soc. Econ.*, 1986, *13*(3), pp. 5–19. **[G: Canada]**

McLoughlin, Peter F. M. A Theory of Technology—Continuity and Change in Human Development: A Review Article. *J. Econ. Issues*, September 1986, *20*(3), pp. 785–98.

Meyer, Willi. Beyond Choice. **In** *[Lachmann, L. M.]*, 1986, pp. 221–35.

Middleton, Elliott. A Behavioral Model of "Animal Spirits." *Metroecon.*, February 1986, *38*(1), pp. 39–51.

Niskanen, William A. Economists and Politicians. *J. Policy Anal. Manage.*, Winter 1986, *5*(2), pp. 234–44.

Ohrenstein, Roman A. Value Analysis in Talmudic Literature in the Light of Modern Economics. *Int. J. Soc. Econ.*, 1986, *13*(3), pp. 34–52.

van Raaij, W. Fred. Causal Attributions in Economic Behavior. **In** *MacFadyen, A. J. and MacFadyen, H. W., eds.*, 1986, pp. 353–79.

van Raaij, W. Fred. Economic Phenomena from a Psychological Perspective: Economic Psychology. **In** *MacFadyen, A. J. and MacFadyen, H. W., eds.*, 1986, pp. 9–23.

Rubin, Paul H. Costs and Benefits of a Duty to Rescue. *Int. Rev. Law Econ.*, December 1986, *6*(2), pp. 273–76.

Samuelson, Paul A. Complete Genetic Models for Altruism, Kin Selection and Like-Gene Selection. **In** *Samuelson, P. A.*, 1986, *1983*, pp. 710–22.

Samuelson, Paul A. Maximizing and Biology. **In** *Samuelson, P. A.*, 1986, *1978*, pp. 697–709.

Schachter, Stanley, et al. Aggregate Variables in Psychology and Economics: Dependence and the Stock Market. **In** *Gilad, B. and Kaish, S., eds., Vol. B*, 1986, pp. 237–72. **[G: U.S.]**

Schmitt, Bernard. The Process of Formation of Economics in Relation to Other Sciences. **In** *Baranzini, M. and Scazzieri, R., eds.*, 1986, pp. 103–32.

Scitovsky, Tibor. How to Bring Joy into Economics. **In** *Scitovsky, T.*, 1986, pp. 183–203.

Shapira, Zur. On the Implications of Behavioral Decision Making Theory to Economics. **In** *MacFadyen, A. J. and MacFadyen, H. W., eds.*, 1986, pp. 621–44.

Simon, Herbert A. Rationality in Psychology and Economics. *J. Bus.*, Part 2, October 1986, *59*(4), pp. S209–24.

Simon, Herbert A. Rationality in Psychology and Economics. **In** *Hogarth, R. M. and Reder, M. W., eds.*, 1986, pp. 25–40.

Simon, Herbert A. The Failure of Armchair Economics. *Challenge*, Nov./Dec. 1986, *29*(5), pp. 18–25.

Sirgy, M. Joseph. A Quality-of-Life Derived from Maslow's Developmental Perspective: 'Quality' Is Related to Progressive Satisfaction of Hierarchy of Needs, Lower Order and Higher. *Amer. J. Econ. Soc.*, July 1986, *45*(3), pp. 329–42.

Stigler, George J. Economic Competition and Political Competition. **In** *Stigler, G. J.*, 1986, *1972*, pp. 117–33.

Taylor, Lester D. Opponent Processes and the Dynamics of Consumption. **In** *MacFadyen, A. J. and MacFadyen, H. W., eds.*, 1986, pp. 135–61.

Thaler, Richard H. The Psychology and Economics Conference Handbook: Comments. *J. Bus.*, Part 2, October 1986, *59*(4), pp. S279–84.

Thaler, Richard H. The Psychology and Economics Conference Handbook: Comments. **In** *Hogarth, R. M. and Reder, M. W., eds.*, 1986, pp. 95–100.

Tintner, Gerhard and Licari, Joseph A. The Stochastic View of Economics. **In** *Szenberg, M., ed.*, 1986, *1970*, pp. 23–32.

Turner, Bryan S. Parsons and His Critics: On the Ubiquity of Functionalism. **In** *Holton, R. J. and Turner, B. S.*, 1986, pp. 179–206.

Wisman, Jon D. The Renaissance of Natural Law Cosmology: Free Markets and Fettered Minds. *Int. J. Soc. Econ.*, 1986, *13*(10), pp. 26–37.

Wooster, Warren S. Immiscible Investigators: Oceanographers, Meteorologists, and Fishery Scientists. **In** *[Crutchfield, J. A.]*, 1986, pp. 374–86.

Wright, R. W. Economic Man vs. Existential Man. **In** *MacFadyen, A. J. and MacFadyen, H. W., eds.*, 1986, pp. 427–40.

Zaslavskaia, T. I. Economics through the Prism of Sociology. *Prob. Econ.*, September 1986, 29(5), pp. 21–40.

0114 Relation of Economics to Social Values

Abdul-Rauf, Muhammad. Islamic Social Thought: Comment. **In** *Block, W. and Hexham, I., eds.*, 1986, pp. 500–508.

Ahmad, Imad. Islamic Social Thought. **In** *Block, W. and Hexham, I., eds.*, 1986, pp. 465–91.

Ahmad, Imad. Islamic Social Thought: Reply. **In** *Block, W. and Hexham, I., eds.*, 1986, pp. 509–12.

Baum, Gregory. Recent Roman Catholic Social Teaching: A Shift to the Left. **In** *Block, W. and Hexham, I., eds.*, 1986, pp. 47–72. **[G: Canada]**

Benestad, J. Brian. Henry George and the Catholic Views of Morality and the Common Good, II: George's Proposals in the Context of Perennial Philosophy. *Amer. J. Econ. Soc.*, January 1986, *45*(1), pp. 115–23. **[G: George, Henry]**

Benne, Robert. Recent Roman Catholic Social Teaching: A Shift to the Left: Comment. **In** *Block, W. and Hexham, I., eds.*, 1986, pp. 72–81.

Bennett, John C. Religion, Economics and Social Thought: Overview. **In** *Block, W. and Hexham, I., eds.*, 1986, pp. 543–60.

Block, Walter. Judaism and the Market Mechanism: Comment. **In** *Block, W. and Hexham, I., eds.*, 1986, pp. 430–49.

Buchanan, James M. The Ethical Limits of Taxation. **In** *Buchanan, J. M.*, 1986, *1984*, pp. 165–77.

Buchanan, James M. The Moral Dimension of Debt Financing. **In** *Buchanan, J. M.*, 1986, *1985*, pp. 189–94.

Choudhury, Masudul Alam and Rahman, A. N. M. Azizur. Macroeconomic Relations in the Islamic Economic Order. *Int. J. Soc. Econ.*, 1986, *13*(6), pp. 60–78.

Feigenbaum, Susan. Judaism's Historical Response to Economic, Social and Political Systems: Comment. **In** *Block, W. and Hexham, I., eds.*, 1986, pp. 387–92.

Friedman, Marilyn A. Judaism and the Market Mechanism: Comment. **In** *Block, W. and Hexham, I., eds.*, 1986, pp. 421–30.

Gibbard, Allan. Risk and Value. **In** *MacLean, D., ed.*, 1986, pp. 94–112.

Goudzwaard, Bob. Christian Social Thought in the Dutch Neo-Calvinist Tradition. **In** *Block, W. and Hexham, I., eds.*, 1986, pp. 251–65. **[G: Netherlands]**

Goudzwaard, Bob. Christian Social Thought in the Dutch Neo-Calvinist Tradition: Reply. **In** *Block, W. and Hexham, I., eds.*, 1986, pp. 275–79. **[G: Netherlands]**

Goulet, Denis. Three Rationalities in Development Decision-making. *World Devel.*, Special Issue, Feb. 1986, *14*(2), pp. 301–17. **[G: Brazil]**

Grassl, Wolfgang. Markets and Morality: Austrian Perspectives on the Economic Approach to Human Behaviour. **In** *Grassl, W. and Smith, B., eds.*, 1986, pp. 139–81.

Grau, Joseph A. Corporate Management and Orthopraxis—Is Synergy Possible? *Int. J. Soc. Econ.*, 1986, *13*(1/2), pp. 7–19.

Hexham, Irving. Christian Social Thought in the Dutch Neo-Calvinist Tradition: Comment. **In** *Block, W. and Hexham, I., eds.*, 1986, pp. 265–75. **[G: Netherlands]**

Heyne, Paul. Clerical Laissez-Faire: A Study in Theological Economics. **In** *Block, W. and Hexham, I., eds.*, 1986, pp. 125–52.

Heyne, Paul. Clerical Laissez-Faire: A Study in Theological Economics: Reply. **In** *Block, W. and Hexham, I., eds.*, 1986, pp. 160–63.

Hickerson, Steven R. Instrumental Justice and Social Economics. *Rev. Soc. Econ.*, December 1986, *44*(3), pp. 268–80.

Hill, Lewis E. Pragmatism, Instrumental Value Theory and Social Economics: Comment. *Rev. Soc. Econ.*, October 1986, *44*(2), pp. 193–95. **[G: U.S.]**

Hill, Peter J. The World Council of Churches and Social and Economic Issues: Comment. **In** *Block, W. and Hexham, I., eds.*, 1986, pp. 355–59.

Hoy, Terry. Gustavo Gutierrez: Latin American Liberation Theology. *Int. J. Soc. Econ.*, 1986, *13*(9), pp. 3–16. **[G: Latin America]**

Kaltefleiter, Werner. Changes in Social Values: The Example of the Federal Republic of Germany. **In** *Hax, H.; Kraus, W. and Tsuchiya, K., eds.*, 1986, pp. 177–86. **[G: W. Germany]**

Kassis, Hanna E. Islamic Social Thought: Comment. **In** *Block, W. and Hexham, I., eds.*, 1986, pp. 492–500.

Kent, Calvin A. A Christian Approach to Social Economics. *Int. J. Soc. Econ.*, 1986, *13*(3), pp. 80–92.

Kolm, Serge-Christophe. The Buddhist Theory of 'No-Self.' **In** *Elster, J., ed.*, 1986, pp. 233–65.

Kucheman, Clark A. Classical Social Doctrine in the Roman Catholic Church: Comment. **In** *Block, W. and Hexham, I., eds.*, 1986, pp. 23–31.

Lutz, Mark A. Instrumental Value Theory and Social Economics: A Rejoinder. *Rev. Soc. Econ.*, October 1986, *44*(2), pp. 196–200. **[G: U.S.]**

Lutz, Mark A. and Lux, Kenneth. Neo-Humanistic Economics: A Comment [Is Neo-Humanistic Economics the New Paradigm for Social Economists?]. *Rev. Soc. Econ.*, October 1986, *44*(2), pp. 183–87.

MacLean, Douglas. Social Values and the Distribution of Risk. **In** *MacLean, D., ed.*, 1986, pp. 75–93.

Marty, Martin E. Clerical Laissez-Faire: A Study in Theological Economics: Comment. **In** *Block, W. and Hexham, I., eds.*, 1986, pp. 153–59.

McKee, Arnold. The Passage from Theology to Economics. *Int. J. Soc. Econ.*, 1986, *13*(3), pp. 5–19. **[G: Canada]**

McKendrick, Neil. 'Gentlemen and Players' Revisited: The Gentlemanly Ideal, the Business Ideal and the Professional Ideal in English Literary Culture. **In** *[Coleman, D. C.]*, 1986, pp. 98–136. **[G: U.K.]**

Mishan, Ezra J. Religion, Capitalism and Technology. **In** *Mishan, E. J.*, 1986, *1983*, pp. 194–224.

Mishan, Ezra J. The Road to Repression. **In** *Mishan, E. J.*, 1986, *1976*, pp. 131–68. **[G: MDCs]**

Mueller, Franz H. Catholic Social Doctrine between Scylla and Charybdis? Some Comments on Two Books. *Rev. Soc. Econ.*, April 1986, *44*(1), pp. 40–56.

Nitsch, Thomas O. Social Catholicism, Marxism and Liberation Theology: From Antithesis to Coexistence, Coalescence and Synthesis. *Int. J. Soc. Econ.*, 1986, *13*(9), pp. 52–74.

Novak, Michael. Religion, Economics and Social Thought: Overview. **In** *Block, W. and Hexham, I., eds.*, 1986, pp. 524–43.

O'Brien, John C. Ethical Norms in American Society: A Critique. *Int. J. Soc. Econ.*, 1986, *13*(10), pp. 50–63. **[G: U.S.]**

Ohrenstein, Roman A. Value Analysis in Talmudic Literature in the Light of Modern Economics. *Int. J. Soc. Econ.*, 1986, *13*(3), pp. 34–52.

Patel, I. G. Social Justice and Economic Development. **In** *Patel, I. G.*, 1986, pp. 128–37. **[G: India]**

Presser, Harriet B. Changing Values and Falling Birth Rates: Comment. *Population Devel. Rev.*, Supp. 1986, *12*, pp. 196–200. **[G: OECD]**

Preston, Ronald H. The Legacy of the Christian Socialist Movement in England. **In** *Block, W. and Hexham, I., eds.*, 1986, pp. 181–201. **[G: U.K.]**

Preston, Ronald H. The Legacy of the Christian Socialist Movement in England: Reply. **In** *Block, W. and Hexham, I., eds.*, 1986, pp. 208–12. **[G: U.K.]**

Preston, Samuel H. Changing Values and Falling Birth Rates. *Population Devel. Rev.*, Supp. 1986, *12*, pp. 176–95. **[G: OECD]**

Raines, J. Patrick and Jung, Clarence R. Knight on Religion and Ethics as Agents of Social Change: An Essay to Commemorate the Centennial of Frank H. Knight's Birth. *Amer. J. Econ. Soc.*, October 1986, *45*(4), pp. 429–39.

Rashid, Salim. Historical Notes on the Origins of Supply-Side Economics and Its Ethical Roots: Say's Law, Smith's Law, or Moral Law? *Quart. Rev. Econ. Bus.*, Winter 1986, *26*(4), pp. 22–34.

Rivkin, Ellis. Judaism's Historical Response to Economic, Social and Political Systems. **In** *Block, W. and Hexham, I., eds.*, 1986, pp. 375–87.

Rubin, Paul H. Costs and Benefits of a Duty to Rescue. *Int. Rev. Law Econ.*, December 1986, *6*(2), pp. 273–76.

Sadowsky, James A. Classical Social Doctrine in the Roman Catholic Church. **In** *Block, W. and Hexham, I., eds.*, 1986, pp. 3–23.

Scaperlanda, Anthony. Neo-Humanistic Economics and Social Economics, Revisited [Is Neo-Humanistic Economics the New Paradigm for Social Economists?]. *Rev. Soc. Econ.*, October 1986, *44*(2), pp. 188–92.

Schwartzman, Jack. Henry George and the Ethics of Economics. *Amer. J. Econ. Soc.*, January 1986, *45*(1), pp. 101–14.

Scitovsky, Tibor. The Place of Economic Welfare in Human Welfare. **In** *Scitovsky, T.*, 1986, *1973*, pp. 13–25.

Scott, Edward. The World Council of Churches and Social and Economic Issues. **In** *Block, W. and Hexham, I., eds.*, 1986, pp. 341–54.

Shapiro, Aharon. The Treatment of Poverty in the Talmud. *Int. J. Soc. Econ.*, 1986, *13*(6), pp. 54–59.

Shenfield, Arthur A. The Legacy of the Christian Socialist Movement in England: Comment. **In** *Block, W. and Hexham, I., eds.*, 1986, pp. 202–08. **[G: U.K.]**

Skok, Charles D. The Social Economics of *Gaudium et Spes (The Constitution on the Church in the Modern World)* of the Second Vatican Council. *Int. J. Soc. Econ.*, 1986, *13*(9), pp. 25–44.

Stigler, George J. The Goals of Economic Policy. **In** *Stigler, G. J.*, 1986, *1975*, pp. 89–98. **[G: U.S.]**

Tamari, Meir. Judaism and the Market Mechanism. **In** *Block, W. and Hexham, I., eds.*, 1986, pp. 393–421.

Tietzel, Manfred. Moral und Wirtschaftstheorie. (Morals and Economic Theory. With English summary.) *Z. Wirtschaft. Sozialwissen.*, 1986, *106*(2), pp. 113–37.

Tonsor, Stephen. Christian Political Economy: Malthus to Margaret Thatcher: Comment. **In** *Block, W. and Hexham, I., eds.*, 1986, pp. 118–23.

Waterman, A. M. C. Christian Political Economy: Malthus to Margaret Thatcher: Reply. **In** *Block, W. and Hexham, I., eds.*, 1986, pp. 123–24.

Waterman, A. M. C. Christian Political Economy: Malthus to Margaret Thatcher. **In** *Block, W. and Hexham, I., eds.*, 1986, pp. 99–117.

Weida, William J. and Gertcher, Franklin L. The Ethics and Economics of Foreign Sales of U.S.-Made Military Weapons. *Int. J. Soc. Econ.*, 1986, *13*(1/2), pp. 20–39. **[G: U.S.]**

Winter, J. M. Bernard Shaw, Bertold Brecht and the Businessman in Literature. **In** *[Coleman, D. C.]*, 1986, pp. 185–204. **[G: U.K.]**

Yunker, James A. In Defense of Utilitarianism: An Economist's Viewpoint. *Rev. Soc. Econ.*, April 1986, *44*(1), pp. 57–79.

0115 Methods Used by Economists

Breton, Yves. La place de la statistique et de l'arithmétique politique dans la méthodologie économique de Jean-Baptiste Say le temps des ruptures. (The Role of Statistics and Political Arithmetic in the Economic Methodology of Jean-Baptiste Say at the Time of the Ruptures. With English summary.) *Revue Écon.*, November 1986, *37*(6), pp. 1033–62.

Breton, Yves. Les économistes libéraux français et l'emploi des mathématiques en économie politique. 1800–1914. (The French Liberal Economists and the Use of Mathematics in Political Economy, 1800–1914. With English summary.) *Écon. Soc.*, March 1986, *20*(3), pp. 25–63. **[G: France]**

Demaria, Giovanni. Sul fondamento eurostico di alcuni strumenti analitici impiegati nelle logiche naturali dell'economia. (On the Heuristic Capacity of Some Analytical Tools Employed by the Natural Logic of Economics. With English summary.) *Rivista Int. Sci. Econ. Com.*, June-July 1986, *33*(6–7), pp. 529–44.

Grubel, Herbert G. and Boland, Lawrence A. On the Efficient Use of Mathematics in Economics: Some Theory, Facts and Results of an Opinion Survey. *Kyklos*, 1986, *39*(3), pp. 419–42.

Mirowski, Philip. Mathematical Formalism and Economic Explanation. **In** *Mirowski, P., ed.*, 1986, pp. 179–240.

Mishan, Ezra J. The Mystique of Economic Expertise. **In** *Mishan, E. J.*, 1986, *1984*, pp. 78–107.

012 Teaching of Economics

0120 Teaching of Economics

Aigner, Dennis J. and Thum, Frederick D. On Student Evaluation of Teaching Ability. *J. Econ. Educ.*, Fall 1986, *17*(4), pp. 243–65. **[G: U.S.]**

Anderson, Curt L. A Student-Participation Demonstration: The Short-run Production Process. *J. Econ. Educ.*, Winter 1986, *17*(1), pp. 57–60.

Anderton, Alain. Economics Education: Organising Economics Resources. **In** *Whitehead, D. J., ed.*, 1986, pp. 273–75.

Anderton, Alain. Economics Education: Using a Library. **In** *Whitehead, D. J., ed.*, 1986, pp. 279–83.

Anderton, Alain. Teaching Economics to the 13–16 Age Range: The Welfare State. **In** *Whitehead, D. J., ed.*, 1986, pp. 121–23.

Anderton, Alain. Teaching Economics to the 16–19 Age Range: The Theory of the Firm. **In** *Whitehead, D. J., ed.*, 1986, pp. 173–76.

Anderton, Alain. Teaching Economics to the 16–19 Age Range: Economic Efficiency. **In** *Whitehead, D. J., ed.*, 1986, pp. 176–78.

Appleyard, Dennis R. and Field, Alfred J., Jr. A Note on Teaching the Marshall–Lerner Condition. *J. Econ. Educ.*, Winter 1986, *17*(1), pp. 52–56.

Awh, Robert Y. Barriers to Better Economic Education: Analytical Errors That Persist in Economics Textbooks. *J. Econ. Educ.*, Summer 1986, *17*(3), pp. 195–200.

Boskin, Michael J. Some Thoughts on Teaching Principles of Macroeconomics. *J. Econ. Educ.*, Fall 1986, *17*(4), pp. 283–87. **[G: U.S.]**

Brietzke, Paul H. Another Law and Economics. **In** *Zerbe, R. O., Jr., ed.*, 1986, pp. 57–109.

Brimbel, Martin C. Teaching Economics to the 13–16 Age Range: Survey Work in Economics: Investigating Industry. **In** *Whitehead, D. J., ed.*, 1986, pp. 29–34.

Butler, David R. Teaching Economics to the 13–16 Age Range: Population. **In** *Whitehead, D. J., ed.*, 1986, pp. 92–95. **[G: U.K.]**

Butler, David R. Teaching Economics to the 13–16 Age Range: Money and Banking. **In** *Whitehead, D. J., ed.*, 1986, pp. 99–102.

Butler, David R. Teaching Economics to the 16–19 Age Range: Money and Banking. **In** *Whitehead, D. J., ed.*, 1986, pp. 206–08.

Carr, Nigel. Economics Education: An Evaluation of A-Level Textbooks. **In** *Whitehead, D. J., ed.*, 1986, pp. 244–50.

Chambers, Ian. Teaching Economics to the 13–16 Age Range: Cambridge O-Level Business Studies. **In** *Whitehead, D. J., ed.*, 1986, pp. 47–55. **[G: U.K.]**

Clark, J. H. The Financial Crisis of Farming: The Educators' Perspective. *Can. J. Agr. Econ.*, June 1986, *33*, pp. S16–25. **[G: Canada]**

Clarke, Paul. Teaching Economics to the 13–16 Age Range: Prices and Markets. **In** *Whitehead, D. J., ed.*, 1986, pp. 64–72.

Clarke, Paul. Teaching Economics to the 13–16 Age Range: Employment, Unemployment and Inflation. **In** *Whitehead, D. J., ed.*, 1986, pp. 102–09.

Cloninger, Dale O. and Hodgin, Robert. An Economic Analysis of Student-reported Grading Errors. *J. Econ. Educ.*, Winter 1986, *17*(1), pp. 25–33.

Collings, Lindsey. Economics Education: The Head of Department. **In** *Whitehead, D. J., ed.*, 1986, pp. 265–73.

Collings, Lindsey. Teaching Economics to the 16–19 Age Range: The Study Guide Approach. **In** *Whitehead, D. J., ed.*, 1986, pp. 128–30.

Cotterrell, Ann. Teaching Economics to the 16–19 Age Range: Economics in Further Education. **In** *Whitehead, D. J., ed.*, 1986, pp. 144–47.

Crowe, Douglas and Youga, Janet. Using Writing as a Tool for Learning Economics. *J. Econ. Educ.*, Summer 1986, *17*(3), pp. 218–22.

DeCanio, Stephen J. Student Evaluations of Teaching—A Multinomial Logit Approach. *J. Econ. Educ.*, Summer 1986, *17*(3), pp. 165–76. **[G: U.S.]**

Dunnill, Richard. Teaching Economics to the 13–16 Age Range: Economics in the Third Year: Two Approaches. **In** *Whitehead, D. J., ed.*, 1986, pp. 2–8.

Dunnill, Richard. Teaching Economics to the 13–16 Age Range: 'Starting Off!': Suggestions for

Beginning a Two-Year Course. In *Whitehead, D. J., ed.*, 1986, pp. 56–63.

Ellingham, Morag A. W. Teaching Economics to the 13–16 Age Range: Industry. In *Whitehead, D. J., ed.*, 1986, pp. 85–92.

Etner, F. L'enseignement économique dans les grandes écoles au XIXe siècle en France. (Economic Teaching in the French "grandes écoles" in the 19th Century. With English summary.) *Écon. Soc.*, October 1986, *20*(10), pp. 159–74.

Evans, Graham and Perrin, Norman. Teaching Economics to the 13–16 Age Range: Why Can't the English Teacher . . .? A Programme to Improve Written Communication in Economics. In *Whitehead, D. J., ed.*, 1986, *1981*, pp. 21–25.

Evans, Tony. Teaching Economics to the 13–16 Age Range: Producing a Local Economy Resources Pack. In *Whitehead, D. J., ed.*, 1986, pp. 34–38. **[G: U.K.]**

Fischer, Lewis. Sixty Years of Agricultural Economics at Macdonald College. *Can. J. Agr. Econ.*, Proceedings 1986, *34*, pp. 42–47. **[G: Canada]**

Fizel, John L. and Fiedler, John L. A Disaggregated Investigation of Learning Functions in Introductory Economics. *Econ. Educ. Rev.*, 1986, *5*(3), pp. 287–95.

Fizel, John L. and Johnson, Jerry D. The Effect of Macro/Micro Course Sequencing on Learning and Attitudes in Principles of Economics. *J. Econ. Educ.*, Spring 1986, *17*(2), pp. 87–98.

Furtan, W. H. Educational Institutions and Scholarship in the Twenty-First Century. *Can. J. Agr. Econ.*, June 1986, *33*, pp. 111–17. **[G: Canada]**

Gagey, Frédéric and Rey, Patrick. L'économie expérimentale comme outil pédagogique: Élaboration d'un jeu d'initiation à la microéconomie. (Experimental Economics Applied to Teaching: Elaboration of a Microeconomic Game. With English summary.) *Revue Écon.*, January 1986, *37*(1), pp. 5–30.

Goulet, Janet C. Survey of Intermediate Microeconomic Textbooks. *J. Econ. Educ.*, Summer 1986, *17*(3), pp. 229–33.

Grunin, Lori and Lindauer, David L. Economic Analysis in Plain English: A Course in Economic Journalism. *J. Econ. Educ.*, Summer 1986, *17*(3), pp. 223–28.

Hansen, W. Lee. Report of the Committee on Economic Education of the American Economic Association. *J. Econ. Educ.*, Spring 1986, *17*(2), pp. 157–58.

Hansen, W. Lee. What Knowledge Is Most Worth Knowing—For Economics Majors? *Amer. Econ. Rev.*, May 1986, *76*(2), pp. 149–52. **[G: U.S.]**

Hendry, David F. Using PC-GIVE in Econometrics Teaching. *Oxford Bull. Econ. Statist.*, February 1986, *48*(1), pp. 87–98.

Hertel, Thomas W. and McKinzie, Lance. Pseudo Data as a Teaching Tool: Application to the Translog, Multiproduct Profit Function. *Western J. Agr. Econ.*, July 1986, *11*(1), pp. 19–30.

Highsmith, Robert J. Professional Developments and Opportunities. *J. Econ. Educ.*, Fall 1986, *17*(4), pp. 315–17. **[G: U.S.]**

Hodkinson, Steve. Teaching Economics to the 13–16 Age Range: Economics Teaching and Consumer Education. In *Whitehead, D. J., ed.*, 1986, pp. 44–47.

Hodkinson, Steve. Teaching Economics to the 13–16 Age Range: On the Use of Photographs in Economics Teaching. In *Whitehead, D. J., ed.*, 1986, pp. 39–44.

Houser, Michael. Teaching Economics to the 16–19 Age Range: 'Actuality' in Economics Education: London-Based Experience Courses. In *Whitehead, D. J., ed.*, 1986, *1982*, pp. 157–64.

Jarvis, Ray. Teaching Economics to the 16–19 Age Range: The Use of Mini-charts. In *Whitehead, D. J., ed.*, 1986, pp. 148–53.

Jarvis, Ray. Teaching Economics to the 13–16 Age Range: An Economics Course for the Core Curriculum. In *Whitehead, D. J., ed.*, 1986, pp. 8–14.

Jones, Graham. Teaching Economics to the 16–19 Age Range: International Trade. In *Whitehead, D. J., ed.*, 1986, pp. 222–27.

Kähkönen, Juha and Leponiemi, Arvi. Uusia suuntauksia kauppakorkeakoulujen tutkimuksessa ja opetuksessa: Tuloksia maailman kauppakorkeakouluille tehdystä kyselystä. (New Trends in Research and Teaching in Business Schools. With English summary.) *Liiketaloudellinen Aikak.*, 1986, *35*(3), pp. 213–17.

Kennedy, Peter. The Bayesian Approach to Research in Economic Education. *J. Econ. Educ.*, Winter 1986, *17*(1), pp. 9–24.

King, Barrie. Teaching Economics to the 16–19 Age Range: Teaching on BTEC National: Sources of Finance. In *Whitehead, D. J., ed.*, 1986, pp. 209–11.

Kourilsky, Marilyn. School Reform: The Role of the Economic Educator. *J. Econ. Educ.*, Summer 1986, *17*(3), pp. 213–17.

Langrehr, Virginia B. and Langrehr, Frederick W. Course Requirements, Job Responsibilities, and Compensation for Financial Counselors: The Not-for-Profit Industry View. *J. Cons. Aff.*, Summer 1986, *20*(1), pp. 131–41. **[G: U.S.]**

Lawson, Luther D. and O'Donnell, Margaret G. Identifying Factors That Influence the Learning of Economics: A Sixth-Grade Case Study. *J. Econ. Educ.*, Summer 1986, *17*(3), pp. 177–85. **[G: U.S.]**

Leake, Andrew. Teaching Economics to the 16–19 Age Range: Social Economics. In *Whitehead, D. J., ed.*, 1986, pp. 194–97.

Leake, Andrew. Teaching Economics to the 16–19 Age Range: Teaching the Theory of Consumer Behaviour. In *Whitehead, D. J., ed.*, 1986, pp. 179–82.

Leech, Peter. Teaching Economics to the 13–16 Age Range: Division of Labour. In *Whitehead, D. J., ed.*, 1986, pp. 80–85.

Livesey, Frank. Economics Examinations at A-Level. **In** *Whitehead, D. J., ed.*, 1986, pp. 256–61.

Luker, Stuart. Teaching Economics to the 16–19 Age Range: Teaching the Economics of the Public Sector. **In** *Whitehead, D. J., ed.*, 1986, pp. 231–36.

Luker, Stuart. Teaching Economics to the 16–19 Age Range: Industrial Relations. **In** *Whitehead, D. J., ed.*, 1986, pp. 187–93.

MacDowell, Michael A. Increasing the Public's Understanding of Economics: What Can We Expect from the Schools? *Amer. Econ. Rev.*, May 1986, *76*(2), pp. 145–48. **[G: U.S.]**

MacDowell, Michael A. The School-Reform Debate: Response. *J. Econ. Educ.*, Summer 1986, *17*(3), pp. 210–12.

Marcousé, Ian. Economics Education: Projects for 14–16-Year-olds—A Positive Approach. **In** *Whitehead, D. J., ed.*, 1986, pp. 25–29.

Marder, Keith. Teaching Economics to the 16–19 Age Range: Government Policy. **In** *Whitehead, D. J., ed.*, 1986, pp. 227–31.

Mason, Jerry and Poduska, Bud. Financial Planner or Financial Counselor: The Differences Are Significant. *J. Cons. Aff.*, Summer 1986, *20*(1), pp. 142–47.

Miller, John A. and Weil, Gordon. Interactive Computer Lessons for Introductory Economics: Guided Inquiry—from Supply and Demand to Women in the Economy. *J. Econ. Educ.*, Winter 1986, *17*(1), pp. 61–68.

Miller, Merton H. The Academic Field of Finance: Some Observations on Its History and Prospects. *Tijdschrift Econ. Manage.*, 1986, *31*(4), pp. 395–408. **[G: U.S.]**

Minogue, Claire. Economics Education: 14–16 Textbooks—An Evaluation. **In** *Whitehead, D. J., ed.*, 1986, pp. 241–44.

Mixon, J. Wilson, Jr. On the Incidence of Excise Taxes on a Monopolist's Price: A Pedagogical Note. *J. Econ. Educ.*, Summer 1986, *17*(3), pp. 201–03.

Morris, Mike. Teaching Economics to the 16–19 Age Range: Supply, Demand and Price. **In** *Whitehead, D. J., ed.*, 1986, pp. 167–73.

Myers, Danny. Teaching Economics to the 16–19 Age Range: Making and Using Overhead Transparencies. **In** *Whitehead, D. J., ed.*, 1986, pp. 155–57.

Negus, Philip. Teaching Economics to the 16–19 Age Range: Pre-vocational Courses. **In** *Whitehead, D. J., ed.*, 1986, pp. 138–44.

Nieswiadomy, Michael. A Note on Comparing the Elasticities of Demand Curves. *J. Econ. Educ.*, Spring 1986, *17*(2), pp. 125–28.

Paisley, Robert. Teaching Economics to the 13–16 Age Range: International Trade and the Balance of Payments. **In** *Whitehead, D. J., ed.*, 1986, pp. 109–18. **[G: U.K.]**

Parker, William N. An Historical Introduction. **In** *Parker, W. N., ed.*, 1986, pp. 1–10.

Powell, Richard A. Teaching Economics to the 16–19 Age Range: Population and Demography. **In** *Whitehead, D. J., ed.*, 1986, pp. 182–86. **[G: U.K.]**

Rees, Albert. The Marketplace of Economic Ideas. *Amer. Econ. Rev.*, May 1986, *76*(2), pp. 138–40. **[G: U.S.]**

Regan, Trevor and Tree, Nigel. Teaching Economics to the 16–19 Age Range: Economics Tours Abroad. **In** *Whitehead, D. J., ed.*, 1986, *1983*, pp. 164–66.

Scheraga, Joel D. Instruction in Economics through Simulated Computer Programming. *J. Econ. Educ.*, Spring 1986, *17*(2), pp. 129–39.

Schout, Richard P. M. and Slangen, Louis H. G. The Individual Study System in Teaching General and Agricultural Economics: Methodology and Results. *Europ. Rev. Agr. Econ.*, 1986, *13*(1), pp. 107–22. **[G: Netherlands]**

Seldon, James R. A Note on the Teaching of Arc Elasticity. *J. Econ. Educ.*, Spring 1986, *17*(2), pp. 120–24.

Silk, Leonard. Communicating Economic Ideas and Controversies. *Amer. Econ. Rev.*, May 1986, *76*(2), pp. 141–44. **[G: U.S.]**

Spencer, Robert W. and Van Eynde, Donald F. Experiential Learning in Economics. *J. Econ. Educ.*, Fall 1986, *17*(4), pp. 289–94. **[G: U.S.]**

Thomas, Linda and Scriven, Malcolm. Economics Education: Internal Assessment. **In** *Whitehead, D. J., ed.*, 1986, pp. 251–56.

Thomas, Linda and Wall, Sara. Teaching Economics to the 13–16 Age Range: Teaching Mixed-Ability Groups. **In** *Whitehead, D. J., ed.*, 1986, pp. 14–18.

Thorne, Richard. Teaching Economics to the 13–16 Age Range: Public Finance. **In** *Whitehead, D. J., ed.*, 1986, pp. 119–21.

Tibbitt, Andrew. Teaching Economics to the 16–19 Age Range: Comparative Economics. **In** *Whitehead, D. J., ed.*, 1986, pp. 197–205.

Ţigănescu, E. Cybernetics Education and Economic Informatics. *Econ. Computat. Cybern. Stud. Res.*, 1986, *21*(3), pp. 93–97. **[G: Romania]**

Tighe, Michael. Teaching Economics to the 16–19 Age Range: National Income: An Introduction to Macroeconomics. **In** *Whitehead, D. J., ed.*, 1986, pp. 211–17.

Tinsley, Kevin. Teaching Economics to the 13–16 Age Range: Trade Unions. **In** *Whitehead, D. J., ed.*, 1986, pp. 95–99.

Titley, Brian. Teaching Economics to the 16–19 Age Range: The 'Wipe-clean' Wall Chart. **In** *Whitehead, D. J., ed.*, 1986, pp. 153–55.

Vaughan, Michael B. and Thomas, Wade L. Teaching the Theory of Monopolistic Competition: An Analytical Approach. *Atlantic Econ. J.*, July 1986, *14*(2), pp. 80.

Venkateswarlu, Tadiboyina. Labor Economics: Survey of Course Outlines in Universities in Canada and the United States of America. *Amer. Econ.*, Spring 1986, *30*(1), pp. 78–85. **[G: Canada; U.S.]**

Wall, Nancy. Teaching Economics to the 16–19 Age Range: Teaching Inflation, Unemployment and the Keynesian–Monetarist Debate. **In** *Whitehead, D. J., ed.*, 1986, pp. 218–21.

012 Teaching of Economics

Welford, Richard. Teaching Economics to the 16–19 Age Range: Computer-Assisted Learning in Economics Education. **In** *Whitehead, D. J., ed.*, 1986, pp. 130–34.

Wilkinson, Roy. Teaching Economics to the 16–19 Age Range: Data-Response Questions in Teaching A-Level Economics. **In** *Whitehead, D. J., ed.*, 1986, *1980*, pp. 135–38.

Willatt, Maurice. Teaching Economics to the 16–19 Age Range: Rethinking the Syllabus. **In** *Whitehead, D. J., ed.*, 1986, pp. 125–28.

Wilson, Robert. Economics Education: Some Ways of Enhancing the Use and Value of Audio-visual Aids. **In** *Whitehead, D. J., ed.*, 1986, pp. 238–41.

Wilson, Robert. Teaching Economics to the 13–16 Age Range: A Task-Oriented Approach to Teaching the Theory of the Firm. **In** *Whitehead, D. J., ed.*, 1986, pp. 73–80.

Wood, Keith. Economics Education: Teacher Groups for Curriculum Development. **In** *Whitehead, D. J., ed.*, 1986, pp. 262–64.

020 General Economic Theory

0200 General Economic Theory

Addleson, Mark. "Radical Subjectivism" and the Language of Austrian Economics. **In** *[Lachmann, L. M.]*, 1986, pp. 1–15.

Alchian, Armen A. Uncertainty, Evolution, and Economic Theory. **In** *Barney, J. B. and Ouchi, W. G., eds.*, 1986, *1950*, pp. 305–19.

Arrow, Kenneth J. Rationality of Self and Others in an Economic System. **In** *Hogarth, R. M. and Reder, M. W., eds.*, 1986, pp. 201–15.

Arrow, Kenneth J. Rationality of Self and Others in an Economic System. *J. Bus.*, Part 2, October 1986, *59*(4), pp. S385–99.

Bacharach, Michael O. L. The Problem of Agents' Beliefs in Economic Theory. **In** *Baranzini, M. and Scazzieri, R., eds.*, 1986, pp. 175–203.

Baranzini, Mauro and Scazzieri, Roberto. Knowledge in Economics: A Framework. **In** *Baranzini, M. and Scazzieri, R., eds.*, 1986, pp. 1–87.

Bartoli, Henri. Au-delà des confusions. Propositions hérétiques. (Beyond Confusion, Heretic Propositions. With English summary.) *Écon. Soc.*, April 1986, *20*(4), pp. 3–56.

Basile, Liliana. Causalità ed economia. (Causality and Economics. With English summary.) *Econ. Polít.*, August 1986, *3*(2), pp. 233–58.

Bausor, Randall. Time and Equilibrium. **In** *Mirowski, P., ed.*, 1986, pp. 93–135.

Bhagwati, Jagdish N. and Srinivasan, T. N. Religion as DUP Activity. *Public Choice*, 1986, *48*(1), pp. 49–54.

Bharadwaj, Krishna. Production and Exchange in Theories of Price Formation and Economic Transition. **In** *Baranzini, M. and Scazzieri, R., eds.*, 1986, pp. 339–60.

Bliss, Christopher. Progress and Anti-progress in Economic Science. **In** *Baranzini, M. and Scazzieri, R., eds.*, 1986, pp. 363–76.

Boulding, Kenneth E. What Went Wrong with Economics? *Amer. Econ.*, Spring 1986, *30*(1), pp. 5–12.

Chadwick-Jones, J. K. Social Exchange, Social Psychology and Economics. **In** *MacFadyen, A. J. and MacFadyen, H. W., eds.*, 1986, pp. 249–67.

Clower, Robert W. On the Behavioral and Rational Foundations of Economic Dynamics: Comment. **In** *Day, R. H. and Eliasson, G., eds.*, 1986, pp. 42–44.

Coats, A. W. Economic Methodology: Theory, Practice, and the Current State of Economics. *Kyklos*, 1986, *39*(1), pp. 109–15.

Cox, D. R. Statistics and Causal Inference: Comment. *J. Amer. Statist. Assoc.*, December 1986, *81*(396), pp. 963–64.

Dahmén, Erik. Företagarverksamheten i den ekonomiska teorien. (Entrepreneurial Activity in Economic Theory. With English summary.) *Ekon. Samfundets Tidskr.*, 1986, *39*(2), pp. 69–75.

Dahmén, Erik. Rights and Relations in Modern Economic Theory: Comment. **In** *Day, R. H. and Eliasson, G., eds.*, 1986, pp. 342–43.

Day, Richard H. Disequilibrium Economic Dynamics: A Post-Schumpeterian Contribution. **In** *Day, R. H. and Eliasson, G., eds.*, 1986, *1984*, pp. 51–70.

Day, Richard H. and Eliasson, Gunnar. Economic Behavior, Disequilibrium and Structural Change: From Micro Force to Macro Effect. **In** *Day, R. H. and Eliasson, G., eds.*, 1986, pp. 1–17.

Debreu, Gerard. Theoretical Models: Mathematical Forms and Economic Content. *Econometrica*, November 1986, *54*(6), pp. 1259–70.

Di Ruzza, Renato. Sraffa et la notion d'équilibre. (Sraffa and the Equilibrium Concept. With English summary.) *Écon. Appl.*, 1986, *39*(1), pp. 11–33.

Dnes, Antony W. Individualism in Contemporary Political Economy: A Review Article. *Scot. J. Polit. Econ.*, November 1986, *33*(4), pp. 391–95.

Dopfer, Kurt. Causality and Consciousness in Economics: Concepts of Change in Orthodox and Heterodox Economics. *J. Econ. Issues*, June 1986, *20*(2), pp. 509–23.

Ebeling, Richard M. Toward a Hermeneutical Economics: Expectations, Prices, and the Role of Interpretation in a Theory of the Market Process. **In** *[Lachmann, L. M.]*, 1986, pp. 39–55.

Eichner, Alfred S. Can Economics Become a Science? *Challenge*, Nov./Dec. 1986, *29*(5), pp. 4–12.

Eliasson, Gunnar. Rights and Relations in Modern Economic Theory: Comment. **In** *Day, R. H. and Eliasson, G., eds.*, 1986, pp. 346–50.

Ellerman, David P. Property Appropriation and Economic Theory. **In** *Mirowski, P., ed.*, 1986, pp. 41–92.

Eriksson, Tor. Kan den akademiska nationalekonomin ges förnyad livskraft? (Can Academic Economics Be Given Renewed Vitality? With

English summary.) *Ekon. Samfundets Tidskr.*, 1986, *39*(3), pp. 163–68.

Etzioni, Amitai. Founding a New Socioeconomics. *Challenge*, Nov./Dec. 1986, *29*(5), pp. 13–17.

Faber, Malte and Proops, John L. R. Time Irreversibilities in Economics: Some Lessons from the Natural Sciences. **In** *Faber, M., ed.*, 1986, pp. 294–316.

Feiwel, George R. Shafts from Arrow's Bow: Advance in and beyond Economic Theory. *Economia (Portugal)*, May 1986, *10*(2), pp. 229–75.

Frey, Bruno S. Economists Favour the Price System—Who Else Does? *Kyklos*, 1986, *39*(4), pp. 537–63.

Georgescu-Roegen, Nicholas. Man and Production. **In** *Baranzini, M. and Scazzieri, R., eds.*, 1986, pp. 247–80.

Georgescu-Roegen, Nicholas. The Entropy Law and the Economic Process in Retrospect. *Eastern Econ. J.*, Jan.-Mar. 1986, *12*(1), pp. 3–25.

Gilad, Benjamin and Kaish, Stanley. Behavioral Microeconomics: Introduction. **In** *Gilad, B. and Kaish, S., eds., Vol. A*, 1986, pp. xvii–xxiii.

Gowdy, John M. Neoclassical and Neo-Marxian Views of Scarcity: There Is a Free Lunch. *Rev. Radical Polit. Econ.*, Winter 1986, *18*(4), pp. 102–05.

Gram, Harvey. "Temporary General Equilibrium Theory": by Jean-Michael Grandmont: A Review Essay. *Eastern Econ. J.*, Jan.-Mar. 1986, *12*(1), pp. 81–86.

Helm, Dieter R. Price Formation and the Costs of Exchange. **In** *Baranzini, M. and Scazzieri, R., eds.*, 1986, pp. 205–20.

Hennings, Klaus H. The Exchange Paradigm and the Theory of Production and Distribution. **In** *Baranzini, M. and Scazzieri, R., eds.*, 1986, pp. 221–43.

Hicks, John R. Is Economics a Science? **In** *Baranzini, M. and Scazzieri, R., eds.*, 1986, pp. 91–101.

Hirschman, Alberto O. En contra de la parsimonia: tres formas fáciles para complicar alguans categorías del discurso económico. (Against Parsimony. With English summary.) *Colección Estud. CIEPLAN*, June 1986, (19), pp. 135–47.

Hoffman, Elizabeth; Marsden, James R. and Whinston, Andrew B. Using Different Economic Data Forms [Microeconomic Systems as an Experimental Science]. *J. Behav. Econ.*, Winter 1986, *15*, pp. 67–84.

Hogarth, Robin M. and Reder, Melvin W. Perspectives from Economics and Psychology: Editor's Comments. *J. Bus.*, Part 2, October 1986, *59*(4), pp. S185–207.

Hogarth, Robin M. and Reder, Melvin W. Perspectives from Economics and Psychology. **In** *Hogarth, R. M. and Reder, M. W., eds.*, 1986, pp. 1–23.

Hutchison, Terence W. Philosophical Issues that Divide Liberals: Omniscience or Omni-nescience about the Future? **In** *[Lachmann, L. M.]*, 1986, pp. 122–39.

Ickes, Barry W. Possibility Theorems, Incentives, and Progress in Economic Theory. **In** *Samuelson, L., ed.*, 1986, pp. 235–42.

Kunreuther, Howard. Comments [Rational Choice in Experimental Markets] [Fairness and the Assumptions of Economics]. *J. Bus.*, Part 2, October 1986, *59*(4), pp. S329–35.

Langlois, Richard N. Rationality, Institutions, and Explanation. **In** *Langlois, R. N., ed.*, 1986, pp. 225–55.

Langlois, Richard N. The New Institutional Economics: An Introductory Essay. **In** *Langlois, R. N., ed.*, 1986, pp. 1–25.

Levine, David P. Reconceptualizing Classical Economics. **In** *Mirowski, P., ed.*, 1986, pp. 13–40.

Littlechild, S. C. Three Types of Market Process. **In** *Langlois, R. N., ed.*, 1986, pp. 27–39.

Loasby, Brian J. Competition and Imperfect Knowledge: The Contribution of G. B. Richardson. *Scot. J. Polit. Econ.*, May 1986, *33*(2), pp. 145–58.

Lovell, Michael C. Tests of the Rational Expectations Hypothesis. *Amer. Econ. Rev.*, March 1986, *76*(1), pp. 110–24. **[G: U.S.]**

Lucas, Robert E., Jr. Adaptive Behavior and Economic Theory. **In** *Hogarth, R. M. and Reder, M. W., eds.*, 1986, pp. 217–42.

Lucas, Robert E., Jr. Adoptive Behavior and Economic Theory. *J. Bus.*, Part 2, October 1986, *59*(4), pp. S401–26.

Lux, Kenneth and Lutz, Mark A. Economic Psychology: The Humanistic Perspective. **In** *MacFadyen, A. J. and MacFadyen, H. W., eds.*, 1986, pp. 383–424.

MacFadyen, Alan J. Rational Economic Man: An Introduction Survey. **In** *MacFadyen, A. J. and MacFadyen, H. W., eds.*, 1986, pp. 25–66.

MacFadyen, Alan J. and MacFadyen, Heather Wood. Other Concepts in Economic Psychology. **In** *MacFadyen, A. J. and MacFadyen, H. W., eds.*, 1986, pp. 441–95.

MacFadyen, Heather Wood and MacFadyen, Alan J. Economic Psychology: Intersections in Theory and Application: Summary and Conclusions. **In** *MacFadyen, A. J. and MacFadyen, H. W., eds.*, 1986, pp. 673–78.

Matthaei, Julie A. "Neoclassical and Neo-Marxian Views of Scarcity: There Is a Free Lunch": A Response. *Rev. Radical Polit. Econ.*, Winter 1986, *18*(4), pp. 106–08.

Mirowski, Philip. Mathematical Formalism and Economic Explanation. **In** *Mirowski, P., ed.*, 1986, pp. 179–240.

Mirowski, Philip. Paradigms, Hard Cores, and Fuglemen in Modern Economic Theory. **In** *Mirowski, P., ed.*, 1986, pp. 1–11.

van Moeseke, Paul. Time and Cost Budgets. *Math. Soc. Sci.*, April 1986, *11*(2), pp. 129–38.

Montesano, Aldo. Variazioni sul tema generale dell'equilibrio economico. (Variations on the General Theme of Economic Equilibrium. With English summary.) *Econ. Polít.*, December 1986, *3*(3), pp. 335–38.

Musgrave, Richard A. Economics and the World Around It. **In** *Musgrave, R. A., Vol. 2,* 1986, *1980,* pp. 280–92.

Nicola, Pier Carlo. Economia matematica: centro della teoria economica o vuoto formalismo? (Mathematical Economics: Core of Economic Theory or Vacuous Formalism? With English summary.) *Econ. Polít.,* December 1986, *3*(3), pp. 379–95.

Nooteboom, Bart. Plausibility in Economics. *Econ. Philos.,* October 1986, *2*(2), pp. 197–224.

Olson, Mancur. On the Nature of Disequilibrium: Introduction. **In** *Day, R. H. and Eliasson, G., eds.,* 1986, pp. 475–81.

Pasinetti, Luigi L. Theory of Value—A Source of Alternative Paradigms in Economic Analysis. **In** *Baranzini, M. and Scazzieri, R., eds.,* 1986, pp. 409–31.

Plott, Charles R. Rational Choice in Experimental Markets. **In** *Hogarth, R. M. and Reder, M. W., eds.,* 1986, pp. 117–43.

Quadrio-Curzio, Alberto and Scazzieri, Roberto. The Exchange–Production Duality and the Dynamics of Economic Knowledge. **In** *Baranzini, M. and Scazzieri, R., eds.,* 1986, pp. 377–407.

van Raaij, W. Fred. Causal Attributions in Economic Behavior. **In** *MacFadyen, A. J. and MacFadyen, H. W., eds.,* 1986, pp. 353–79.

van Raaij, W. Fred. Economic Phenomena from a Psychological Perspective: Economic Psychology. **In** *MacFadyen, A. J. and MacFadyen, H. W., eds.,* 1986, pp. 9–23.

Saari, Donald G. Dynamical Systems and Mathematical Economics. **In** *Sonnenschein, H. F., ed.,* 1986, pp. 1–24.

Salanti, Andrea. Strumentalismo e fallibilismo in economia: una nota su alcune recenti interpretazioni. (Instrumentalism versus Fallibilism in Economics: A Note on Some Recent Interpretations. With English summary.) *Rivista Int. Sci. Econ. Com.,* June-July 1986, *33*(6–7), pp. 603–20.

Samuelson, Paul A. Foundations of Economic Analysis: Introduction to the Enlarged Edition. **In** *Samuelson, P. A.,* 1986, *1983,* pp. 846–57.

Schmitt, Bernard. The Process of Formation of Economics in Relation to Other Sciences. **In** *Baranzini, M. and Scazzieri, R., eds.,* 1986, pp. 103–32.

Schroeder, Edward A. and Lindbeck, Rudolph. A Problem with Marginal Analysis. *Atlantic Econ. J.,* March 1986, *14*(1), pp. 122. **[G: U.S.]**

Scitovsky, Tibor. Are Men Rational or Economists Wrong? **In** *Scitovsky, T.,* 1986, *1974,* pp. 70–82.

Sen, Amartya K. Prediction and Economic Theory. **In** *Mason, J.; Mathias, P. and Westcott, J. H., eds.,* 1986, pp. 3–22.

Shapira, Zur. On the Implications of Behavioral Decision Making Theory to Economics. **In** *MacFadyen, A. J. and MacFadyen, H. W., eds.,* 1986, pp. 621–44.

Sharefkin, Mark F. Disequilibrium Economic Dynamics: A Post-Schumpeterian Contribution: Comment. **In** *Day, R. H. and Eliasson, G., eds.,* 1986, pp. 71–74.

Sharefkin, Mark F. On the Behavioral and Rational Foundations of Economic Dynamics: Comment. **In** *Day, R. H. and Eliasson, G., eds.,* 1986, pp. 45–47.

Silber, Jacques G. Rationality, Self Interest and Coordination: On Some Current Controversies in Economics. *Econ. Notes,* 1986, (3), pp. 47–64.

Simon, Herbert A. On the Behavioral and Rational Foundations of Economic Dynamics: Reply. **In** *Day, R. H. and Eliasson, G., eds.,* 1986, pp. 48–49.

Simon, Herbert A. On the Behavioral and Rational Foundations of Economic Dynamics. **In** *Day, R. H. and Eliasson, G., eds.,* 1986, *1984,* pp. 21–41.

Simon, Herbert A. The Failure of Armchair Economics. *Challenge,* Nov./Dec. 1986, *29*(5), pp. 18–25.

Stigler, George J. The Process and Progress of Economics. **In** *Stigler, G. J.,* 1986, *1983,* pp. 134–49.

von Weizsäcker, Carl Christian. Rights and Relations in Modern Economic Theory. **In** *Day, R. H. and Eliasson, G., eds.,* 1986, *1984,* pp. 317–41.

Williamson, Oliver E. The Economics of Governance: Framework and Implications. **In** *Langlois, R. N., ed.,* 1986, pp. 171–202.

Williamson, Oliver E. Transaction-Cost Economics: The Governance of Contractual Relations. **In** *Barney, J. B. and Ouchi, W. G., eds.,* 1986, *1979,* pp. 98–129.

Winter, Sidney G. Comments [Rationality of Self and Others in an Economic System] [Adoptive Behavior and Economic Theory]. *J. Bus.,* Part 2, October 1986, *59*(4), pp. S427–34.

Winter, Sidney G. Comments [Rationality of Self and Others in an Economic System] [Adaptive Behavior and Economic Theory]. **In** *Hogarth, R. M. and Reder, M. W., eds.,* 1986, pp. 243–50.

Wold, Herman. Disequilibrium Economic Dynamics: A Post-Schumpeterian Contribution: Comment. **In** *Day, R. H. and Eliasson, G., eds.,* 1986, pp. 75–76.

Wright, R. W. Economic Man vs. Existential Man. **In** *MacFadyen, A. J. and MacFadyen, H. W., eds.,* 1986, pp. 427–40.

Ysander, Bengt-Christer. Rights and Relations in Modern Economic Theory: Comment. **In** *Day, R. H. and Eliasson, G., eds.,* 1986, pp. 344–45.

Zeckhauser, Richard. Behavioral versus Rational Economics: What You See Is What You Conquer: Comment. **In** *Hogarth, R. M. and Reder, M. W., eds.,* 1986, pp. 251–65.

Zeckhauser, Richard. Behavioral versus Rational Economics: What You See Is What You Conquer: Comments. *J. Bus.,* Part 2, October 1986, *59*(4), pp. S435–49.

021 General Equilibrium and Disequilibrium Theory

0210 General Equilibrium and Disequilibrium Theory

Abraham, H. Total Satiation and Competitive Equilibrium: A Comment. *S. Afr. J. Econ.*, June 1986, *54*(2), pp. 220–21.

Albrecht, James W.; Axell, Bo and Lang, Harald. General Equilibrium Wage and Price Distributions. *Quart. J. Econ.*, November 1986, *101*(4), pp. 687–706.

Allais, Maurice. The Concepts of Surplus and Loss and the Reformulation of the Theories of Stable General Economic Equilibrium and Maximum Efficiency. **In** *Baranzini, M. and Scazzieri, R., eds.*, 1986, pp. 135–74.

Allen, Beth. The Demand for (Differentiated) Information. *Rev. Econ. Stud.*, July 1986, *53*(3), pp. 311–23.

Anas, Alex and Cho, Joong Rae. Existence and Uniqueness of Price Equilibria: Theory and Application to Discrete Choice Models. *Reg. Sci. Urban Econ.*, May 1986, *16*(2), pp. 211–39.

Armstrong, Thomas E. and Richter, Marcel K. Existence of Nonatomic Core–Walras Allocations. *J. Econ. Theory*, February 1986, *38*(1), pp. 137–59.

Arrow, Kenneth J. Alternative Proof of the Substitution Theorem for Leontief Models in the General Case. **In** *Sohn, I., ed.*, 1986, *1951*, pp. 175–84.

Aumann, Robert J. and Drèze, Jacques H. Values of Markets with Satiation or Fixed Prices. *Econometrica*, November 1986, *54*(6), pp. 1271–1318.

Benassy, Jean-Pascal. On Competitive Market Mechanisms. *Econometrica*, January 1986, *54*(1), pp. 95–108.

Bergstrom, Theodore. Soldiers of Fortune? **In** *[Arrow, K. J.], Vol. 2*, 1986, pp. 57–80.

Bewley, Truman F. Dynamic Implications of the Form of the Budget Constraint. **In** *Sonnenschein, H. F., ed.*, 1986, pp. 117–23.

Bewley, Truman F. The Share Economy in General Equilibrium. *J. Compar. Econ.*, December 1986, *10*(4),pp. 457–59.

Blume, Lawrence and Jordan, James S. Introduction to Expectations Equilibrium. **In** *Sonnenschein, H. F., ed.*, 1986, pp. 206–12.

Boyd, John H. and Prescott, Edward C. Financial Intermediary-Coalitions. *J. Econ. Theory*, April 1986, *38*(2), pp. 211–32.

Brems, Hans. General Equilibrium after Schneider. *Weltwirtsch. Arch.*, 1986, *122*(2), pp. 213–22.

Brock, William A. A Revised Version of Samuelson's Correspondence Principle: Applications of Recent Results on the Asymptotic Stability of Optimal Control to the Problem of Comparing Long Run Equilibria. **In** *Sonnenschein, H. F., ed.*, 1986, pp. 86–116.

Brown, Donald J., et al. On a General Existence Theorem for Marginal Cost Pricing Equilibria. *J. Econ. Theory*, April 1986, *38*(2), pp. 371–79.

Campbell, D. E. Revealed Preference and Demand Correspondences. *J. Econ. Theory*, April 1986, *38*(2), pp. 364–70.

Chamley, Christophe. Optimal Taxation of Capital Income in General Equilibrium with Infinite Lives. *Econometrica*, May 1986, *54*(3), pp. 607–22.

Chichilnisky, Graciela. A General Equilibrium Theory of North–South Trade. **In** *[Arrow, K. J.], Vol. 2*, 1986, pp. 3–56.

Clower, Robert W. and Friedman, Daniel. Trade Specialists and Money in an Ongoing Exchange Economy. **In** *Day, R. H. and Eliasson, G., eds.*, 1986, pp. 115–29.

Coles, Jeffrey L. Equilibrium Turnpike Theory with Time-Separable Utility. *J. Econ. Dynam. Control*, September 1986, *10*(3), pp. 367–94.

Coricelli, Fabrizio and Siconolfi, Paolo. Equilibrio economico generale e macroeconomia: una critica della "nuova macroeconomia neoclassica." (General Economic Equilibrium and Macroeconomics: A Critique on the New Classical Macroeconomics. With English summary.) *Polit. Econ.*, April 1986, *2*(1), pp. 45–80.

Costrell, Robert M. Equilibrium and Optimality in a Mean-Variance Model. *Rand J. Econ.*, Spring 1986, *17*(1), pp. 122–32.

Coutinho, Paulo C. Non-optimality of Rational Expectations Equilibrium: The Complete Markets Case. *Rev. Econ. Stud.*, October 1986, *53*(5), pp. 883–84.

Dasgupta, Partha and Maskin, Eric. The Existence of Equilibrium in Discontinuous Economic Games, II: Applications. *Rev. Econ. Stud.*, January 1986, *53*(1), pp. 27–41.

Dasgupta, Partha and Maskin, Eric. The Existence of Equilibrium in Discontinuous Economic Games, I: Theory. *Rev. Econ. Stud.*, January 1986, *53*(1), pp. 1–26.

Day, Richard H. Disequilibrium Economic Dynamics: A Post-Schumpeterian Contribution: Reply. **In** *Day, R. H. and Eliasson, G., eds.*, 1986, pp. 77.

Day, Richard H. Trade Specialists and Money in an Ongoing Exchange Economy: Comment. **In** *Day, R. H. and Eliasson, G., eds.*, 1986, pp. 130–31.

Debreu, Gerard and Scarf, Herbert E. The Limit of the Core of an Economy. **In** *[Marschak, J.]*, 1986, *1972*, pp. 283–95.

Deneckere, Raymond J. and Pelikan, Steve. Competitive Chaos. *J. Econ. Theory*, October 1986, *40*(1), pp. 13–25.

DeSerpa, Allan C. Hotelling Models: A General Equilibrium Approach. *Southern Econ. J.*, April 1986, *52*(4), pp. 999–1009.

Donzelli, Franco. Temporary Equilibrium, Intertemporal Equilibrium and the "Complete Markets" Hypothesis. *Ricerche Econ.*, Apr.-Sept. 1986, *40*(2–3), pp. 214–48.

Dubey, Pradeep and Shubik, Martin. General Equilibrium and the Foundations of the Theory of Monopolistic Competition. *Rivista Int. Sci. Econ. Com.*, March 1986, *33*(3), pp. 207–19.

Duffie, Darrell. Competitive Equilibria in General Choice Spaces. *J. Math. Econ.*, 1986, *15*(1), pp. 1–23.

Duffie, Darrell. Stochastic Equilibria: Existence, Spanning Number, and the 'No Expected Financial Gain from Trade' Hypothesis. *Econometrica*, September 1986, *54*(5), pp. 1161–83.

Duffie, Darrell and Shafer, Wayne J. Equilibrium in Incomplete Markets: II; Generic Existence in Stochastic Economies. *J. Math. Econ.*, 1986, *15*(3), pp. 199–216.

Eckalbar, John C. Bilateral Trade in a Monetized Pure Exchange Economy. *Econ. Modelling*, April 1986, *3*(2), pp. 135–39.

Esteban, Joan M. A Characterization of the Core in Overlapping-Generations Economies [An Exact Consumption-Loan Model of Interest with or without the Social Contrivance of Money]. *J. Econ. Theory*, August 1986, *39*(2), pp. 439–56.

Estrup, Hector. Ligevægt og virkelighed. (Existence of Equilibrium in Economic Models and Their Real-World Interpretation. With English summary.) *Nationaløkon. Tidsskr.*, 1986, *124*(1), pp. 15–28.

Fehl, Ulrich. Spontaneous Order and the Subjectivity of Expectations: A Contribution to the Lachmann–O'Driscoll Problem. **In** *[Lachmann, L. M.]*, 1986, pp. 72–86.

Feiwel, George R. Shafts from Arrow's Bow: Advance in and beyond Economic Theory. *Economia (Portugal)*, May 1986, *10*(2), pp. 229–75.

Flaschel, Peter and Semmler, Willi. The Dynamic Equalization of Profit Rates for Input–Output Models with Fixed Capital. **In** *Semmler, W., ed.*, 1986, pp. 1–34.

Fradera, Isabel. Perfect Competition with Product Differentiation. *Int. Econ. Rev.*, October 1986, *27*(3), pp. 529–38.

Fujimoto, Takao. Non-linear Leontief Models in Abstract Spaces. *J. Math. Econ.*, 1986, *15*(2), pp. 151–56.

Funaki, Yukihiko and Kaneko, Mamoru. Economies with Labor Indivisibilities—Part I: Optimal Tax Schedules. *Econ. Stud. Quart.*, March 1986, *37*(1), pp. 11–29.

Funaki, Yukihiko and Kaneko, Mamoru. Economies with Labor Indivisibilities: Part II: Competitive Equilibria under Tax Schedules. *Econ. Stud. Quart.*, September 1986, *37*(3), pp. 199–222.

Gagey, Frédéric; Laroque, Guy and Lollivier, Stefan. Monetary and Fiscal Policies in a General Equilibrium Model. *J. Econ. Theory*, August 1986, *39*(2), pp. 329–57.

Gale, Douglas M. Bargaining and Competition Part II: Existence. *Econometrica*, July 1986, *54*(4), pp. 807–18.

Gale, Douglas M. Bargaining and Competition Part I: Characterization. *Econometrica*, July 1986, *54*(4), pp. 785–806.

Garrison, Roger W. From Lachmann to Lucas: On Institutions, Expectations, and Equilibrating Tendencies. **In** *[Lachmann, L. M.]*, 1986, pp. 87–101.

Geanakoplos, John D. and Polemarchakis, Herakles M. Existence, Regularity, and Constrained Suboptimality of Competitive Allocations When the Asset Market Is Incomplete. **In** *[Arrow, K. J.], Vol. 3*, 1986, pp. 65–95.

Geller, William. An Improved Bound for Approximate Equilibria [Approximate Equilibria with Bounds Independent of Preferences]. *Rev. Econ. Stud.*, April 1986, *53*(2), pp. 307–08.

Goodwin, Richard M. Swinging along the Autostrada. **In** *Semmler, W., ed.*, 1986, pp. 125–31.

Grandmont, Jean-Michel and Malgrange, Pierre. Nonlinear Economic Dynamics: Introduction. *J. Econ. Theory*, October 1986, *40*(1), pp. 3–12.

Greenberg, Joseph and Shitovitz, Benyamin. A Simple Proof of the Equivalence Theorem for Oligopolistic Mixed Markets. *J. Math. Econ.*, 1986, *15*(2), pp. 79–83.

Greenberg, Joseph and Weber, Shlomo. Strong Tiebout Equilibrium under Restricted Preferences Domain. *J. Econ. Theory*, February 1986, *38*(1), pp. 101–17.

Grossman, Sanford J. and Perry, Motty. Sequential Bargaining under Asymmetric Information. *J. Econ. Theory*, June 1986, *39*(1), pp. 120–54.

Guesnerie, Roger. Stationary Sunspot Equilibria in an *N* Commodity World. *J. Econ. Theory*, October 1986, *40*(1), pp. 103–27.

Hahn, Frank H. An Exercise in Non-Walrasian Analysis. **In** *[Arrow, K. J.], Vol. 2*, 1986, pp. 289–99.

Heller, Walter P. Coordination Failure under Complete Markets with Applications to Effective Demand. **In** *[Arrow, K. J.], Vol. 2*, 1986, pp. 155–75.

High, Jack. Equilibration and Disequilibration in the Market Process. **In** *[Lachmann, L. M.]*, 1986, pp. 111–21.

Hurwicz, Leonid. On the Stability of the Tatonnement Approach to Competitive Equilibrium. **In** *Sonnenschein, H. F., ed.*, 1986, pp. 45–48.

Ikeda, Takanobu. Does Quantity-Constrained Behavior Make the Conjecture Function Kinked? *Keio Econ. Stud.*, 1986, *23*(2), pp. 37–56.

Johansen, Leif. On the Theory of Dynamic Input–Output Models with Different Time Profiles of Capital Construction and Finite Lifetime of Capital Equipment. **In** *Sohn, I., ed.*, 1986, *1978*, pp. 295–313.

Jones, Larry E. Special Problems Arising in the Study of Economies with Infinitely Many Commodities. **In** *Sonnenschein, H. F., ed.*, 1986, pp. 184–205.

Jordan, James S. Instability in the Implementation of Walrasian Allocations. *J. Econ. Theory*, August 1986, *39*(2), pp. 301–28.

Kaneko, Mamoru and Yamamoto, Yoshitsugu. The Existence and Computation of Competitive Equilibria in Markets with an Indivisible Commodity. *J. Econ. Theory*, February 1986, *38*(1), pp. 118–36.

Keisler, H. Jerome. A Price Adjustment Model with Infinitesimal Traders. **In** *Sonnenschein, H. F., ed.*, 1986, pp. 69–85.

Kirman, Alan P. and Koch, K. J. Market Excess Demand in Exchange Economies with Identical Preferences and Collinear Endowments. *Rev. Econ. Stud.*, July 1986, *53*(3), pp. 457–63.

Kohn, Robert E. and Meisel, J. B. Total Satiation and Competitive Equilibrium: A Reply. *S. Afr. J. Econ.*, December 1986, *54*(4), pp. 440–41.

Koopmans, Tjalling C. Alternative Proof of the Substitution Theorem for Leontief Models in the Case of Three Industries. **In** *Sohn, I., ed.*, 1986, *1951*, pp. 185–91.

Kregel, J. A. Conceptions of Equilibrium: The Logic Choice and the Logic of Production. **In** *[Lachmann, L. M.]*, 1986, pp. 157–70.

Kuroki, Ryuzo. The Equalization of the Rate of Profit. **In** *Semmler, W., ed.*, 1986, pp. 35–50.

Lemche, S. Q. Remarks on Non-paternalism and the Second Theorem of Welfare Economics. *Can. J. Econ.*, May 1986, *19*(2), pp. 270–80.

Leontief, Wassily. Input–Output Analysis. **In** *Leontief, W.*, 1986, *1985*, pp. 19–40. **[G: U.S.]**

Leontief, Wassily. The Dynamic Inverse. **In** *Leontief, W.*, 1986, *1970*, pp. 294–320.

Mas-Colell, Andreu. Notes on Price and Quantity Tatonnement Dynamics. **In** *Sonnenschein, H. F., ed.*, 1986, pp. 49–68.

Mas-Colell, Andreu. The Price Equilibrium Existence Problem in Topological Vector Lattices. *Econometrica*, September 1986, *54*(5), pp. 1039–53.

Mestelman, Stuart. General Equilibrium Modelling of Industries with Production Externalities. *Can. J. Econ.*, August 1986, *19*(3), pp. 522–25.

Montesano, Aldo. Una riformulazione della teoria monetaria di Walras. (A Restatement of Walras' Theory of Money. With English summary.) *Rivista Int. Sci. Econ. Com.*, September 1986, *33*(9), pp. 901–38.

Nguyen, Trien T. and Whalley, John. Equilibrium under Price Controls with Endogenous Transactions Costs. *J. Econ. Theory*, August 1986, *39*(2), pp. 290–300.

Nicola, Pier Carlo. Equilibrio interpersonale temporaneo: un modello elementare senza banditore. (Temporary Interpersonal Equilibrium: An Elementary Model without Any Auctioneer. With English summary.) *Giorn. Econ.*, Mar.-Apr. 1986, *45*(3–4), pp. 113–47.

Novshek, William and Sonnenschein, Hugo. Quantity Adjustment in an Arrow–Debreu–McKenzie Type Model. **In** *Sonnenschein, H. F., ed.*, 1986, pp. 148–56.

Olsem, Jean-Pierre. Lat rationalité de l'équilibre concurrentiel général. (With English summary.) *Revue Écon. Polit.*, Nov.-Dec. 1986, *96*(6), pp. 625–41.

Palfrey, Thomas R. and Srivastava, Sanjay. Private Information in Large Economies. *J. Econ. Theory*, June 1986, *39*(1), pp. 34–58.

Perrings, Charles. Conservation of Mass and Instability in a Dynamic Economy-Environment System. *J. Environ. Econ. Manage.*, September 1986, *13*(3), pp. 199–211.

Postlewaite, Andrew and Schmeidler, David. Implementation in Differential Information Economies. *J. Econ. Theory*, June 1986, *39*(1), pp. 14–33.

Prescott, Edward C. Financial Structures as Communication Systems: Commentary. **In** *Lawrence, C. and Shay, R. P., eds.*, 1986, pp. 179–83.

ten Raa, Thijs. Applied Dynamic Input–Output with Distributed Activities. *Europ. Econ. Rev.*, August 1986, *30*(4), pp. 805–31. **[G: Poland]**

Raut, Lakishmi Kanta. Myopic Topologies on General Commodity Spaces. *J. Econ. Theory*, August 1986, *39*(2), pp. 358–67.

Read, Thomas T. Balanced Growth without Constant Returns to Scale. *J. Math. Econ.*, 1986, *15*(2), pp. 171–78.

Richard, Scott F. and Zame, William R. Proper Preferences and Quasi-concave Utility Functions. *J. Math. Econ.*, 1986, *15*(3), pp. 231–47.

Rogawski, J. and Shubik, Martin. A Strategic Market Game with Transactions Costs. *Math. Soc. Sci.*, April 1986, *11*(2), pp. 139–60.

Rosefielde, Steven. Competitive Market Socialism Revisited: Impediments to Efficient Price-Fixing. *Comp. Econ. Stud.*, Fall 1986, *28*(3), pp. 17–23.

Rossini, Gianpaolo. Alcune teorie della diffusione della moneta a confronto. (Money and Microeconomic Foundations: Some Comments. With English summary.) *Econ. Polít.*, August 1986, *3*(2), pp. 277–98.

Samuelson, Larry. Nonwalrasian Equilibria with Leading Behavior. *Oxford Econ. Pap.*, March 1986, *38*(1), pp. 31–58.

Samuelson, Paul A. Abstract of a Theorem Concerning Substitutability in Open Leontief Models. **In** *Sohn, I., ed.*, 1986, *1951*, pp. 192–95.

Samuelson, Paul A. Durable Capital Inputs: Conditions for Price Ratios to Be Invariant to Profit-Rate Changes. **In** *Samuelson, P. A.*, 1986, *1983*, pp. 375–94.

Sancho, Ferran. The Core of a Large Economy with Personal Risks. *Int. Econ. Rev.*, June 1986, *27*(2), pp. 407–14.

Sargent, Thomas J. Financial Structures as Communication Systems. **In** *Lawrence, C. and Shay, R. P., eds.*, 1986, pp. 184–88.

Scarf, Herbert E. Testing for Optimality in the Absence of Convexity. **In** *[Arrow, K. J.], Vol. 1*, 1986, pp. 117–34.

Shubik, Martin and Wooders, Myrna Holtz. Near-Markets and Market Games. *Econ. Stud. Quart.*, December 1986, *37*(4), pp. 289–99.

Singh, Nirvikar. Equilibrium Price Dispersion with Sequential Search. *J. Quant. Econ.*, July 1986, *2*(2), pp. 163–71.

Skott, Peter. On General Equilibrium Theory, Rationality and the Costs of Spurious Generality. *Brit. Rev. Econ. Issues*, Spring 1986, *8*(18), pp. 29–50.

021 General Equilibrium and Disequilibrium Theory

Sohn, Ira. Readings in Input–Output Analysis: Theory and Applications: Introduction. **In** *Sohn, I., ed.*, 1986, pp. 3–10.

Spear, Stephen E. and Srivastava, Sanjay. Markov Rational Expectations Equilibria in an Overlapping Generations Model. *J. Econ. Theory*, February 1986, *38*(1), pp. 35–62.

Starr, Ross M. Decentralized Trade in a Credit Economy. **In** *[Arrow, K. J.], Vol. 2*, 1986, pp. 105–20.

Stephan, Gunter. Competitive Finite Value Prices: A Complete Characterization. **In** *Faber, M., ed.*, 1986, *1985*, pp. 173–83.

Suda, Shinichi. Pareto Optimality and Monetary Competitive Equilibrium in the Overlapping Generations Model. *Keio Econ. Stud.*, 1986, *23*(1), pp. 79–96.

Takeda, Shigeo. Joint Production and a Discontinuous Switch of the Wage–Profit Frontier. *Econ. Stud. Quart.*, March 1986, *37*(1), pp. 54–66.

Tesfatsion, Leigh. Time Inconsistency of Benevolent Government Economies. *J. Public Econ.*, October 1986, *31*(1), pp. 25–52.

Thore, Sten. Spatial Disequilibrium. *J. Reg. Sci.*, November 1986, *26*(4), pp. 661–75.

Townsend, Robert M. Financial Structures as Communication Systems. **In** *Lawrence, C. and Shay, R. P., eds.*, 1986, pp. 163–78.

Williams, Steven R. Realization and Nash Implementation: Two Aspects of Mechanism Design. *Econometrica*, January 1986, *54*(1), pp. 139–51.

Woodford, Michael. Stationary Sunspot Equilibria in a Finance Constrained Economy. *J. Econ. Theory*, October 1986, *40*(1), pp. 128–37.

Yannelis, Nicholas C. and Zame, William R. Equilibria in Banach Lattices without Ordered Preferences. *J. Math. Econ.*, 1986, *15*(2), pp. 85–110.

Yoon, Chang-Ho. Rational Expectations Equilibrium in a Sequence of Asset Markets. *Int. Econ. Rev.*, October 1986, *27*(3), pp. 553–64.

Yu, Eden S. H. and Ingene, Charles A. Resource Allocation in a General Equilibrium Model of Production under Uncertainty: The Case of Variable Supply of Labor. *J. Econ. Theory*, December 1986, *40*(2), pp. 329–37.

022 Microeconomic Theory

0220 General

Abe, Kenzo; Okamoto, Hisayuki and Tawada, Makoto. A Note on the Production Possibility Frontier with Pure Public Intermediate Goods. *Can. J. Econ.*, May 1986, *19*(2), pp. 351–56.

Akerlof, George A. The Market for "Lemons": Quality Uncertainty and the Market Mechanism. **In** *Barney, J. B. and Ouchi, W. G., eds.*, 1986, *1970*, pp. 27–39. **[G: India]**

Allais, Maurice. Determination of Cardinal Utility According to an Intrinsic Invariant Model. **In** *Daboni, L.; Montesano, A. and Lines, M., eds.*, 1986, pp. 83–120.

Anderton, Alain. Teaching Economics to the 16–19 Age Range: Economic Efficiency. **In** *Whitehead, D. J., ed.*, 1986, pp. 176–78.

Arigoni, Anio O. Information Utility—Statistical and Semantical Features. **In** *Daboni, L.; Montesano, A. and Lines, M., eds.*, 1986, pp. 277–88.

Arnott, Richard J. and Stiglitz, Joseph E. Moral Hazard and Optimal Commodity Taxation. *J. Public Econ.*, February 1986, *29*(1), pp. 1–24.

Awh, Robert Y. Barriers to Better Economic Education: Analytical Errors That Persist in Economics Textbooks. *J. Econ. Educ.*, Summer 1986, *17*(3), pp. 195–200.

Barberá, Salvador and Pattanaik, Prasanta K. Falmagne and the Rationalizability of Stochastic Choices in Terms of Random Orderings. *Econometrica*, May 1986, *54*(3), pp. 707–15.

Basu, Kaushik. One Kind of Power. *Oxford Econ. Pap.*, July 1986, *38*(2), pp. 259–82.

Benson, Bruce L. and Faminow, Merle D. The Incentives to Organize and Demand Regulation: Two Ends against the Middle. *Econ. Inquiry*, July 1986, *24*(3), pp. 473–84.

Berg, Joyce E., et al. Controlling Preferences for Lotteries on Units of Experimental Exchange. *Quart. J. Econ.*, May 1986, *101*(2), pp. 281–306.

Berliant, Marcus C. A Utility Representation for a Preference Relation on a σ-Algebra. *Econometrica*, March 1986, *54*(2), pp. 359–62.

Bernard, Georges. The Present State of Utility Theory. **In** *Daboni, L.; Montesano, A. and Lines, M., eds.*, 1986, pp. 121–38.

Bernheim, B. Douglas and Ray, Debraj. On the Existence of Markov-Consistent Plans under Production Uncertainty. *Rev. Econ. Stud.*, October 1986, *53*(5), pp. 877–82.

Bös, Dieter. On Supporting the Maximization Postulate. *J. Behav. Econ.*, Winter 1986, *15*, pp. 35–39.

Bradley, Michael G. and Lehman, Dale E. Comparative Equilibrium versus Comparative Statics. *Can. J. Econ.*, August 1986, *19*(3), pp. 526–38.

Bray, Margaret M. and Savin, Nathan E. Rational Expectations Equilibria, Learning, and Model Specification. *Econometrica*, September 1986, *54*(5), pp. 1129–60.

Bruno, Sergio. Incertezza, complesità e crisi della "economia del controllo." (Uncertainty, Complexity and Crisis of the "Economics of Control." With English summary.) *Econ. Lavoro*, July-Sept. 1986, *20*(3), pp. 39–61.

Campbell, Donald T. Rationality and Utility from the Standpoint of Evolutionary Biology. *J. Bus.*, Part 2, October 1986, *59*(4), pp. S355–64.

Campbell, Donald T. Rationality and Utility from the Standpoint of Evolutionary Biology. **In** *Hogarth, R. M. and Reder, M. W., eds.*, 1986, pp. 171–80.

Coleman, James S. Psychological Structure and Social Structure in Economic Models. **In** *Hogarth, R. M. and Reder, M. W., eds.*, 1986, pp. 181–85.

Coleman, James S. Psychological Structure and Social Structure in Economic Models. *J. Bus.*, Part 2, October 1986, *59*(4), pp. S365–69.

Coutinho, Paulo C. Non-optimality of Rational Expectations Equilibrium: The Complete Markets Case. *Rev. Econ. Stud.*, October 1986, *53*(5), pp. 883–84.

Daboni, Luciano. Associative Means and Utility Theory. **In** *Daboni, L.; Montesano, A. and Lines, M., eds.*, 1986, pp. 149–51.

Daniel, Coldwell, III. The Process of Adjustment from One Long-run Equilibrium to Another: The Competitive Case. *Scot. J. Polit. Econ.*, August 1986, *33*(3), pp. 284–91.

Day, Richard H. On Endogenous Preferences and Adaptive Economizing. **In** *Day, R. H. and Eliasson, G., eds.*, 1986, pp. 153–70.

Day, Richard H. On Endogenous Preferences and Adaptive Economizing: Reply. **In** *Day, R. H. and Eliasson, G., eds.*, 1986, pp. 175.

Dekel, Eddie. An Axiomatic Characterization of Preferences under Uncertainty: Weakening the Independence Axiom. *J. Econ. Theory*, December 1986, *40*(2), pp. 304–18.

Dow, Gregory K. Stability Analysis for Profit-Responsive Selection Mechanisms. *Math. Soc. Sci.*, October 1986, *12*(2), pp. 169–83.

Dye, Ronald A. An Economic Analysis of Bankruptcy Statutes. *Econ. Inquiry*, July 1986, *24*(3), pp. 417–28.

Engelbrecht-Wiggans, Richard. Risk and Prices in Separable Utility Functions. *Managerial Dec. Econ.*, September 1986, *7*(3), pp. 215–17.

England, Richard W. Production, Distribution, and Environmental Quality: Mr. Sraffa Reinterpreted as an Ecologist. *Kyklos*, 1986, *39*(2), pp. 230–44.

Flaschel, Peter. Sraffa's Standard Commodity: No Fulfillment of Ricardo's Dream of an "Invariable Measure of Value." *J. Inst. Theoretical Econ.*, September 1986, *142*(3), pp. 588–602.

Flaschel, Peter. The Standard Commodity as a Tool of Economic Analysis: A Reply [Sraffa's Standard Commodity: No Fulfillment of Ricardo's Dream of an "Invariable Measure of Value"]. *J. Inst. Theoretical Econ.*, September 1986, *142*(3), pp. 623–25.

Friedman, Daniel. Two Microdynamic Models of Exchange. *J. Econ. Behav. Organ.*, June 1986, *7*(2), pp. 129–46.

Fujimoto, Takao. Non-linear Leontief Models in Abstract Spaces. *J. Math. Econ.*, 1986, *15*(2), pp. 151–56.

Furubotn, Eirik G. Efficiency and the Maximization Postulate: Another Interpretation. *J. Behav. Econ.*, Winter 1986, *15*, pp. 41–48.

Gibbard, Allan. A Characterization of Decision Matrices That Yield Instrumental Expected Utility. **In** *Daboni, L.; Montesano, A. and Lines, M., eds.*, 1986, pp. 139–48.

Goulet, Janet C. Survey of Intermediate Microeconomic Textbooks. *J. Econ. Educ.*, Summer 1986, *17*(3), pp. 229–33.

Hagen, Ole. Surviving Implications of Expected Utility Theory. **In** *Daboni, L.; Montesano, A. and Lines, M., eds.*, 1986, pp. 201–14.

Harsanyi, John C. Practical Certainty and the Acceptance of Empirical Statements. **In** *Daboni, L.; Montesano, A. and Lines, M., eds.*, 1986, pp. 27–41.

Hassin, Refael. Consumer Information in Markets with Random Product Quality: The Case of Queues and Balking. *Econometrica*, September 1986, *54*(5), pp. 1185–95.

Heiner, Ronald A. Uncertainty, Signal-Detection Experiments, and Modeling Behavior. **In** *Langlois, R. N., ed.*, 1986, pp. 59–115.

Hennings, Klaus H. The State of Microeconomics: An Historical Perspective. **In** *Samuelson, L., ed.*, 1986, pp. 265–71.

Hicks, John R. Rational Behavior—Observation or Assumption? **In** *[Lachmann, L. M.]*, 1986, pp. 102–10.

Hirshleifer, Jack. Economics from a Biological Viewpoint. **In** *Barney, J. B. and Ouchi, W. G., eds.*, 1986, *1977*, pp. 319–71.

Hossain, T. and Maxwell, P. Producers Surplus in a Dynamic Situation and the Welfare Gains from Price Stabilisation. *Australian Econ. Pap.*, June 1986, *25*(46), pp. 128–34.

Kahneman, Daniel; Knetsch, Jack L. and Thaler, Richard H. Fairness and the Assumptions of Economics. **In** *Hogarth, R. M. and Reder, M. W., eds.*, 1986, pp. 101–16.

Kahneman, Daniel; Knetsch, Jack L. and Thaler, Richard H. Fairness and the Assumptions of Economics. *J. Bus.*, Part 2, October 1986, *59*(4), pp. S285–300.

Kalai, Ehud. Strategic Behavior and Competition: An Overview. *J. Econ. Theory*, June 1986, *39*(1), pp. 1–13.

Kornai, János. The Soft Budget Constraint. *Kyklos*, 1986, *39*(1), pp. 3–30. **[G: Hungary; Yugoslavia; China; U.S.]**

Kunreuther, Howard. Comments [Fairness and the Assumptions of Economics] [Rational Choice in Experimental Markets]. **In** *Hogarth, R. M. and Reder, M. W., eds.*, 1986, pp. 145–51.

Kunreuther, Howard. Comments [Rational Choice in Experimental Markets] [Fairness and the Assumptions of Economics]. *J. Bus.*, Part 2, October 1986, *59*(4), pp. S329–35.

Kurz, Heinz D. and Salvadori, Neri. A Comment on Levine [Sraffa's *Production of Commodities by Means of Commodities*, Returns to Scale, Relevance, and Other Matters: A Note]. *J. Post Keynesian Econ.*, Fall 1986, *9*(1), pp. 163–65.

Laband, David N. Stoplight Sales and Sidewalk Solicitations: Some Simple Economics of Forced Consumption. *J. Econ. Behav. Organ.*, December 1986, *7*(4), pp. 403–14. **[G: U.S.]**

Lavoie, Donald C. The Market as a Procedure for Discovery and Conveyance of Inarticulate Knowledge. *Comp. Econ. Stud.*, Spring 1986, *28*(1), pp. 1–19.

Lee, Lung-Fei. The Specification of Multi-market Disequilibrium Econometric Models. *J. Econometrics*, August 1986, *32*(3), pp. 297–332.

Leibenstein, Harvey. On Relaxing the Maximization Postulate: Comments on and Responses to Contributors. *J. Behav. Econ.*, Winter 1986, *15*, pp. 57–63.

Leibenstein, Harvey. On Relaxing the Maximization Postulate. *J. Behav. Econ.*, Winter 1986, *15*, pp. 3–16.

Leonardi, Giorgio; Arcangeli, E. F. and Reggiani, A. Aggregate Revealed Preferences and Random Utility Theory. **In** *Daboni, L.; Montesano, A. and Lines, M., eds.*, 1986, pp. 231–48.

Levi, Isaac. The Paradoxes of Allais and Ellsberg. *Econ. Philos.*, April 1986, *2*(1), pp. 23–53.

Levine, A. L. Reply [Sraffa's *Production of Commodities by Means of Commodities*, Returns to Scale, Relevance, and Other Matters: A Note]. *J. Post Keynesian Econ.*, Fall 1986, *9*(1), pp. 166–68.

Lopes, Lola. What Naive Decision Makers Can Tell Us about Risk. **In** *Daboni, L.; Montesano, A. and Lines, M., eds.*, 1986, pp. 311–26.

Luce, R. Duncan. Comments [Fairness and the Assumptions of Economics] [Rational Choice in Experimental Markets]. **In** *Hogarth, R. M. and Reder, M. W., eds.*, 1986, pp. 153–59.

Luce, R. Duncan. Comments [Rational Choice in Experimental Markets] [Fairness and the Assumptions of Economics]. *J. Bus.*, Part 2, October 1986, *59*(4), pp. S337–45.

MacCrimmon, Kenneth R. and Wehrung, Donald A. Assessing Risk Propensity. **In** *Daboni, L.; Montesano, A. and Lines, M., eds.*, 1986, pp. 291–309.

MacMinn, Richard D. Search and the Market for Lemons. *Info. Econ. Policy*, June 1986, *2*(2), pp. 137–46.

Maital, Shlomo. Prometheus Rebound: On Welfare-Improving Constraints. *Eastern Econ. J.*, July-Sept. 1986, *12*(3), pp. 237–44.

Mak, King-Tim. On Separability: Functional Structure. *J. Econ. Theory*, December 1986, *40*(2), pp. 250–82.

Marschak, Thomas A. Independence versus Dominance in Personal Probability Axioms. **In** *[Arrow, K. J.], Vol. 3*, 1986, pp. 129–71.

Maskin, Eric. Optimal Bayesian Mechanisms. **In** *[Arrow, K. J.], Vol. 3*, 1986, pp. 229–38.

Milgrom, Paul and Roberts, John. Price and Advertising Signals of Product Quality. *J. Polit. Econ.*, August 1986, *94*(4), pp. 796–821.

Milgrom, Paul and Roberts, John. Relying on the Information of Interested Parties. *Rand J. Econ.*, Spring 1986, *17*(1), pp. 18–32.

Montesano, Aldo. A Measure of Risk Aversion in Terms of Preferences. **In** *Daboni, L.; Montesano, A. and Lines, M., eds.*, 1986, pp. 327–35.

Munera, Hector A. The Generalized Means Model (GMM) for Non-deterministic Decision Making: A Unified Treatment for the Two Contending Theories. **In** *Daboni, L.; Montesano, A. and Lines, M., eds.*, 1986, pp. 161–84.

Nordquist, Gerald L. State-Dependent Utility and Risk Aversion. **In** *Daboni, L.; Montesano, A. and Lines, M., eds.*, 1986, pp. 337–51.

Palfrey, Thomas R. and Srivastava, Sanjay. Private Information in Large Economies. *J. Econ. Theory*, June 1986, *39*(1), pp. 34–58.

Plott, Charles R. Rational Choice in Experimental Markets. *J. Bus.*, Part 2, October 1986, *59*(4), pp. S301–27.

Plott, Charles R. Rational Choice in Experimental Markets. **In** *Hogarth, R. M. and Reder, M. W., eds.*, 1986, pp. 117–43.

Plummer, Mark L. and Hartman, Richard C. Option Value: A General Approach. *Econ. Inquiry*, July 1986, *24*(3), pp. 455–71.

Polemarchakis, Herakles M., et al. Approximate Aggregation under Uncertainty. *J. Econ. Theory*, April 1986, *38*(2), pp. 189–210.

Pope, Robin. Consistency and Expected Utility Theory. **In** *Daboni, L.; Montesano, A. and Lines, M., eds.*, 1986, pp. 215–29.

Raut, Lakishmi Kanta. Myopic Topologies on General Commodity Spaces. *J. Econ. Theory*, August 1986, *39*(2), pp. 358–67.

Ricossa, Sergio. S'ha da fare questo matrimonio? (What about This Marriage? With English summary.) *Econ. Polít.*, April 1986, *3*(1), pp. 3–6.

Ronen, Joshua. On Relaxing the Maximization Postulate: A Note. *J. Behav. Econ.*, Winter 1986, *15*, pp. 49–53.

Rosen, Sherwin. Prizes and Incentives in Elimination Tournaments. *Amer. Econ. Rev.*, September 1986, *76*(4), pp. 701–15.

Rossi, Guido A. On Utility Functions in a Financial Context. **In** *Daboni, L.; Montesano, A. and Lines, M., eds.*, 1986, pp. 153–60.

Rozen, Marvin. On Relaxing the Maximization Postulate: A Comment. *J. Behav. Econ.*, Winter 1986, *15*, pp. 21–27.

Salvadori, Neri. Il capitale fisso come "specie" del "genere" produzione congiunta. (Fixed Capital as "Species" of "Genus" Joint Production. With English summary.) *Econ. Polít.*, April 1986, *3*(1), pp. 21–38.

Samuelson, Larry. An Affirmative View of Macroeconomic Theory. **In** *Samuelson, L., ed.*, 1986, pp. 1–29.

Samuelson, Larry. Nonwalrasian Equilibria with Leading Behavior. *Oxford Econ. Pap.*, March 1986, *38*(1), pp. 31–58.

Schefold, Bertram. The Standard Commodity as a Tool of Economic Analysis: A Comment [Sraffa's Standard Commodity: No Fulfillment of Ricardo's Dream of an "Invariable Measure of Value"]. *J. Inst. Theoretical Econ.*, September 1986, *142*(3), pp. 603–22.

Schotter, Andrew. On the Economic Virtues of Incompetency and Dishonesty. **In** *[Rapoport, A.]*, 1986, pp. 235–41.

Sen, Amartya K. Rationality and Uncertainty. **In** *Daboni, L.; Montesano, A. and Lines, M., eds.*, 1986, pp. 3–25.

Shen, T. Y. On Relaxing the Maximization Postulate: Putting X-Efficiency in Its Place at a Pinnacle. *J. Behav. Econ.*, Winter 1986, *15*, pp. 29–34.

Shweder, Richard A. Comments [Fairness and the Assumptions of Economics] [Rational Choice in Experimental Markets]. **In** *Hogarth,*

R. M. *and Reder, M. W., eds.*, 1986, pp. 161–70.

Shweder, Richard A. Comments [Rational Choice in Experimental Markets] [Fairness and the Assumptions of Economics]. *J. Bus.*, Part 2, October 1986, *59*(4), pp. S345–54.

Simon, Herbert A. Rationality in Psychology and Economics. *J. Bus.*, Part 2, October 1986, *59*(4), pp. S209–24.

Simon, Herbert A. Rationality in Psychology and Economics. **In** *Hogarth, R. M. and Reder, M. W., eds.*, 1986, pp. 25–40.

Simon, Herbert A. Theories of Bounded Rationality. **In** *[Marschak, J.]*, 1986, *1972*, pp. 153–76.

Skourtos, M. Market Processes in a Ricardian Framework: The Case of V. K. Dmitriev. *Metroecon.*, October 1986, *38*(3), pp. 229–55. **[G: U.K.]**

Stanley, T. D. Recursive Economic Knowledge: Hierarchy, Maximization and Behavioral Economics. *J. Behav. Econ.*, Winter 1986, *15*, pp. 85–99.

Stephan, Gunter. Competitive Finite Value Prices: A Complete Characterization. **In** *Faber, M., ed.*, 1986, *1985*, pp. 173–83.

Stern, Nicholas. A Note on Commodity Taxation: The Choice of Variable and the Slutsky, Hessian and Antonelli Matrices (SHAM). *Rev. Econ. Stud.*, April 1986, *53*(2), pp. 293–99.

Stoker, Thomas M. Simple Tests of Distributional Effects on Macroeconomic Equations. *J. Polit. Econ.*, August 1986, *94*(4), pp. 763–95.

Sugden, Robert. New Developments in the Theory of Choice under Uncertainty. *Bull. Econ. Res.*, January 1986, *38*(1), pp. 1–24.

Sugden, Robert. Regret, Recrimination and Rationality. **In** *Daboni, L.; Montesano, A. and Lines, M., eds.*, 1986, pp. 67–80.

Tomer, John F. On Relaxing the Maximization Postulate: A Comment. *J. Behav. Econ.*, Winter 1986, *15*, pp. 17.

Wakker, Peter. Concave Additively Decomposable Representing Functions and Risk Aversion. **In** *Daboni, L.; Montesano, A. and Lines, M., eds.*, 1986, pp. 249–62.

Wellisz, Stanislaw. On Relaxing the Maximization Postulate: A Comment. *J. Behav. Econ.*, Winter 1986, *15*, pp. 19–20.

Williams, Philip L. A Reconstruction of Marshall's Temporary Equilibrium Pricing Model. *Hist. Polit. Econ.*, Winter 1986, *18*(4), pp. 639–53.

Yaari, Menahem E. Univariate and Multivariate Comparisons of Risk Aversion: A New Approach. **In** *[Arrow, K. J.], Vol. 3*, 1986, pp. 173–87.

Ysander, Bengt-Christer. On Endogenous Preferences and Adaptive Economizing: Comment. **In** *Day, R. H. and Eliasson, G., eds.*, 1986, pp. 171–74.

Zaghini, Enrico. Natural Prices and Market Prices. An Interpretation of the Walrasian Theory of Accumulation. *Econ. Notes*, 1986, (1), pp. 10–59.

0222 Theory of the Household (consumer demand)

Abraham, H. Total Satiation and Competitive Equilibrium: A Comment. *S. Afr. J. Econ.*, June 1986, *54*(2), pp. 220–21.

Ainslie, George. Beyond Microeconomics. Conflict among Interests in a Multiple Self as a Determinant of Value. **In** *Elster, J., ed.*, 1986, pp. 133–75.

Alhadeff, David A. Microeconomics and the Experimental Analysis of Behavior. **In** *MacFadyen, A. J. and MacFadyen, H. W., eds.*, 1986, pp. 183–215.

Arai, Kazuhiro. Demand for and Supply of Price Information in Markets for Consumer Goods. *Hitotsubashi J. Econ.*, June 1986, *27*(1), pp. 35–47.

Back, Kerry. Concepts of Similarity for Utility Functions. *J. Math. Econ.*, 1986, *15*(2), pp. 129–42.

Basemann, R. L., et al. Correction [On Deviations between Neoclassical and GFT-Based True Cost-of-Living Indexes Derived from the Same Demand Function System]. *J. Econometrics*, July 1986, *32*(2), pp. 293.

Battalio, Raymond C.; Kagel, John H. and Phillips, Owen R. Optimal Prices and Animal Consumers in Congested Markets. *Econ. Inquiry*, April 1986, *24*(2), pp. 181–93.

Becker, Gary S. and Barro, Robert J. Altruism and the Economic Theory of Fertility. *Population Devel. Rev.*, Supp. 1986, *12*, pp. 69–76.

Behrman, Jere R.; Pollak, Robert A. and Taubman, Paul. Do Parents Favor Boys? *Int. Econ. Rev.*, February 1986, *27*(1), pp. 33–54. **[G: U.S.]**

Beltratti, Andrea. Preferenze temporali ed equilibri tenui nei modelli a generazioni sovrapposte. (Temporal Preferences and Tenuous Equilibria in Overlapping Generations Models. With English summary.) *Giorn. Econ.*, May-June 1986, *45*(5–6), pp. 317–23.

Bernheim, B. Douglas; Shleifer, Andrei and Summers, Lawrence H. The Strategic Bequest Motive. *J. Lab. Econ.*, Part 2, July 1986, *4*(3), pp. S151–82. **[G: U.S.]**

Blackorby, Charles and Donaldson, David. Can Risk–Benefit Analysis Provide Consistent Policy Evaluations of Projects Involving Loss of Life? *Econ. J.*, September 1986, *96*(383), pp. 758–73.

Boland, Lawrence A. Methodology and the Individual Decision Maker. **In** *[Lachmann, L. M.]*, 1986, pp. 30–38.

Bordley, Robert F. Satiation and Habit Persistence (or the Dieter's Dilemma). *J. Econ. Theory*, February 1986, *38*(1), pp. 178–84.

Boyer, Marcel. Corrigenda [Rational Demand and Expenditures Patterns under Habit Formation]. *J. Econ. Theory*, August 1986, *39*(2), pp. 464–66.

Bozzi, Rita Castellani and Tintori, Paolo Matrigali. Un modello di scelta del consumatore. (Consumer's Behaviour and Choice: A Model. With English summary.) *Ricerche Econ.*, Jan.-

Mar. 1986, *40*(1), pp. 82–95.

Bradley, Michael G. and Lehman, Dale E. Instrument-Dependent Randomness and Increases in Risk. *J. Econ. (Z. Nationalökon.)*, 1986, *46*(1), pp. 17–29.

Bridges, Douglas S. Numerical Representation of Interval Orders on a Topological Space. *J. Econ. Theory*, February 1986, *38*(1), pp. 160–66.

Camacho, Antonio. Individual Cardinal Utility, Interpersonal Comparisons, and Social Choice. **In** *Daboni, L.; Montesano, A. and Lines, M., eds.*, 1986, pp. 185–200.

Campbell, D. E. Revealed Preference and Demand Correspondences. *J. Econ. Theory*, April 1986, *38*(2), pp. 364–70.

Cejas, Horacio E. El efecto sustitución dentro de la ecuación de Slutsky y el nivel de utilidad. Enfoque finito. (The Slutsky Equation: Substitution Effect and Utility Level—A Finite Approach. With English summary.) *Económica (La Plata)*, Jan.-June 1986, *32*(1), pp. 3–19.

Chetty, V. K. and Jha, Shikha. Microeconomics of Rationing and Licensing. *J. Quant. Econ.*, July 1986, *2*(2), pp. 173–98.

Cotter, Kevin D. Similarity of Information and Behavior with a Pointwise Convergence Topology. *J. Math. Econ.*, 1986, *15*(1), pp. 25–38.

Dardanoni, Valentino. Consumption Decisions with Income Uncertainty and a Kinked Budget Constraint. *Metroecon.*, October 1986, *38*(3), pp. 317–22.

David, Paul A. Altruism and the Economic Theory of Fertility: Comment. *Population Devel. Rev.*, Supp. 1986, *12*, pp. 77–86.

Davidson, Donald. Judging Interpersonal Interests. **In** *Elster, J. and Hylland, A., eds.*, 1986, pp. 195–211.

Deaton, Angus S. Demand Analysis. **In** *Griliches, Z. and Intriligator, M. D., eds.*, 1986, pp. 1767–1839.

De Borger, Bruno. The Relation between Alternative Benefit Measures for Quantity Constrained Price Subsidies. *Europ. Econ. Rev.*, August 1986, *30*(4), pp. 893–907.

DeGroot, Morris H. Concepts of Information Based on Utility. **In** *Daboni, L.; Montesano, A. and Lines, M., eds.*, 1986, pp. 265–75.

Dutta, Bhaskar; Panda, Santosh C. and Pattanaik, Prasanta K. Exact Choice and Fuzzy Preferences. *Math. Soc. Sci.*, February 1986, *11*(1), pp. 53–68.

Earl, Peter E. A Behavioural Analysis of Demand Elasticities. *J. Econ. Stud.*, 1986, *13*(3), pp. 20–37.

Einhorn, Hillel J. and Hogarth, Robin M. Decision Making under Ambiguity. *J. Bus.*, Part 2, October 1986, *59*(4), pp. S225–50.

Einhorn, Hillel J. and Hogarth, Robin M. Decision Making under Ambiguity. **In** *Hogarth, R. M. and Reder, M. W., eds.*, 1986, pp. 41–66.

Epstein, Larry G. Intergenerational Preference Orderings. *Soc. Choice Welfare*, 1986, *3*(3), pp. 151–60.

Etzioni, Amitai. The Case for a Multiple-Utility Conception. *Econ. Philos.*, October 1986, *2*(2), pp. 159–83.

Fischer, Stanley. The Demand for Index Bonds. **In** *Fischer, S.*, 1986, *1975*, pp. 271–99.

Fishburn, Peter C. Alternatives to Expected Utility Theory for Risky Decisions. **In** *Samuelson, L., ed.*, 1986, pp. 31–52.

Fishburn, Peter C. and Rosenthal, Robert W. Noncooperative Games and Nontransitive Preferences. *Math. Soc. Sci.*, August 1986, *12*(1), pp. 1–7.

Frank, Robert H. The Nature of the Utility Function. **In** *MacFadyen, A. J. and MacFadyen, H. W., eds.*, 1986, pp. 113–32.

Fraser, R. W. Supply Responses, Risk Aversion and Covariances in Agriculture. *Australian J. Agr. Econ.*, August/December 1986, *30*(2–3), pp. 153–56.

Fuchs, Victor R. Time Preference and Health. **In** *Fuchs, V. R.*, 1986, *1982*, pp. 214–42. **[G: U.S.]**

Fuchs-Seliger, Susanne and Pfingsten, Andreas. Cost of Living Indices Based on Demand Functions. *J. Econ. (Z. Nationalökon.)*, 1986, *46*(1), pp. 49–64.

Fustier, Bernard. Contribution à la théorie de la demande floue. (With English summary.) *Revue Écon. Polit.*, Mar.-Apr. 1986, *96*(2), pp. 93–117.

Gaertner, Wulf. Zyklische Konsummuster. (Cyclical Consumption Patterns. With English summary.) *Jahr. Nationalökon. Statist.*, January 1986, *201*(1), pp. 54–65.

Gahvari, Firouz. A Note on Additivity and Diminishing Marginal Utility. *Oxford Econ. Pap.*, March 1986, *38*(1), pp. 185–86.

Gibbard, Allan. Interpersonal Comparisons: Preference, Good, and the Intrinsic Reward of a Life. **In** *Elster, J. and Hylland, A., eds.*, 1986, pp. 165–93.

Glycopantis, Dionysius. Some Demand Theory in Continuous Models. *Econ. Stud. Quart.*, March 1986, *37*(1), pp. 44–53.

Goering, Patricia A. Consumer Learning and Optimal Pricing Strategies for Products of Unknown Quality. **In** *Samuelson, L., ed.*, 1986, pp. 53–77.

Goering, Patricia A. Learning, Quality and Prices. *Info. Econ. Policy*, 1986, *2*(1), pp. 23–47.

Granovetter, Mark and Soong, Roland. Threshold Models of Interpersonal Effects in Consumer Demand. *J. Econ. Behav. Organ.*, March 1986, *7*(1), pp. 83–99.

Green, Richard C. and Srivastava, Sanjay. Expected Utility Maximization and Demand Behavior. *J. Econ. Theory*, April 1986, *38*(2), pp. 313–23.

Gronau, Reuben. Home Production—A Survey. **In** *Ashenfelter, O. and Layard, R., eds., Vol. 1*, 1986, pp. 273–304. **[G: U.S.]**

Grossbard-Shechtman, Amyra and Neuman, Shoshana. Economic Behavior, Marriage and Religiosity. *J. Behav. Econ.*, Spring/Summer 1986, *15*(1/2), pp. 71–85. **[G: Israel]**

Hagen, Ole. Some Paradoxes in Economics. **In**

[Rapoport, A.], 1986, pp. 13–25.

Harsanyi, John C. Individual Utilities and Utilitarian Ethics. **In** *[Rapoport, A.]*, 1986, pp. 1–12.

Hartzenberg, G. M. Errata [The Individual Welfare Function of Income]. *J. Stud. Econ. Econometrics*, November 1986, (26), pp. 1. **[G: Belgium; Netherlands]**

Hartzenberg, G. M. The Individual Welfare Function of Income. *J. Stud. Econ. Econometrics*, August 1986, (25), pp. 51–78. **[G: Netherlands; Belgium]**

Havlicek, Joseph, Jr. Food Demand Analysis: Implications for Future Consumption: Discussion. **In** *Capps, O., Jr. and Senauer, B., eds.*, 1986, pp. 87–90. **[G: U.S.]**

Holt, Charles A. Preference Reversals and the Independence Axiom. *Amer. Econ. Rev.*, June 1986, *76*(3), pp. 508–15.

Hu, Sheng Cheng. Uncertain Life Span, Risk Aversion, and the Demand for Pension Annuities. *Southern Econ. J.*, April 1986, *52*(4), pp. 933–47.

Huang, Kuo S. and Haidacher, Richard C. Projecting Aggregate Food Expenditures to the Year 2000. **In** *Capps, O., Jr. and Senauer, B., eds.*, 1986, pp. 67–85. **[G: U.S.]**

Jackson, Matthew O. Continuous Utility Functions in Consumer Theory: A Set of Duality Theorems. *J. Math. Econ.*, 1986, *15*(1), pp. 63–77.

Jackson, Matthew O. Integration of Demand and Continuous Utility Functions. *J. Econ. Theory*, April 1986, *38*(2), pp. 298–312.

Jha, Raghbendra. Optimal Labour Supply and the Accumulation of Human and Financial Capital with Capital Market Imperfections. *Indian Econ. Rev.*, Jan.-June 1986, *21*(1), pp. 21–39.

Johnson, Stan R., et al. Market Demand Functions. **In** *Capps, O., Jr. and Senauer, B., eds.*, 1986, pp. 1–33. **[G: Canada; U.S.]**

Jones, C. Vaughan. Rate Schedules and the Law of Demand. *Atlantic Econ. J.*, December 1986, *14*(4), pp. 96.

Kahneman, Daniel and Tversky, Amos. Choices, Values, and Frames. **In** *Smelser, N. J. and Gerstein, D. R., eds.*, 1986, pp. 153–72.

Karni, Edi and Schmeidler, David. Self-preservation as a Foundation of Rational Behavior under Risk. *J. Econ. Behav. Organ.*, March 1986, *7*(1), pp. 71–81.

Kelsey, D. Utility and the Individual: An Analysis of Internal Conflicts. *Soc. Choice Welfare*, July 1986, *3*(2), pp. 77–87.

Kim, Taesung and Richter, Marcel K. Nontransitive-Nontotal Consumer Theory. *J. Econ. Theory*, April 1986, *38*(2), pp. 324–63.

King, Mervyn A. Capital Market "Imperfections" and the Consumption Function. *Scand. J. Econ.*, 1986, *88*(1), pp. 59–80. **[G: U.K.]**

Kirman, Alan P. and Koch, K. J. Market Excess Demand in Exchange Economies with Identical Preferences and Collinear Endowments. *Rev. Econ. Stud.*, July 1986, *53*(3), pp. 457–63.

Kirzner, Israel M. Another Look at the Subjectivism of Costs. **In** *[Lachmann, L. M.]*, 1986, pp. 140–56.

Klein, Gary, et al. Simplified Assessment of Single and Multi-attribute Utility Functions. **In** *[de Finetti, B.]*, 1986, pp. 319–34.

Kohli, Ulrich. Direct Index Numbers and Demand Theory. *Australian Econ. Pap.*, June 1986, *25*(46), pp. 17–32.

Kohli, Ulrich. Robert Giffen and the Irish Potato: Note. *Amer. Econ. Rev.*, June 1986, *76*(3), pp. 539–42. **[G: Ireland]**

Kohn, Robert E. and Meisel, J. B. Total Satiation and Competitive Equilibrium: A Reply. *S. Afr. J. Econ.*, December 1986, *54*(4), pp. 440–41.

Kolm, Serge-Christophe. The Buddhist Theory of 'No-Self.' **In** *Elster, J., ed.*, 1986, pp. 233–65.

Koopmans, Tjalling C. Representation of Preference Orderings over Time. **In** *[Marschak, J.]*, 1986, *1972*, pp. 79–100.

Koopmans, Tjalling C. Representation of Preference Orderings with Independent Components of Consumption. **In** *[Marschak, J.]*, 1986, *1972*, pp. 57–78.

Lee, Ronald D. The Value and Allocation of Time in High-Income Countries: Implications for Fertility: Comment. *Population Devel. Rev.*, Supp. 1986, *12*, pp. 108–10.

Leigh, J. Paul. Accounting for Tastes: Correlates of Risk and Time Preferences. *J. Post Keynesian Econ.*, Fall 1986, *9*(1), pp. 17–31.

Liebhafsky, Herbert H. Peirce on the *Summum Bonum* and the Unlimited Community; Ayres on "The Criterion of Value." *J. Econ. Issues*, March 1986, *20*(1), pp. 5–20.

Loomes, Graham and Sugden, Robert. Disappointment and Dynamic Consistency in Choice under Uncertainty. *Rev. Econ. Stud.*, April 1986, *53*(2), pp. 271–82.

Lopez, Ramon E. Structural Models of the Farm Household That Allow for Interdependent Utility and Profit-Maximization Decisions. **In** *Singh, I.; Squire, L. and Strauss, J., eds.*, 1986, pp. 306–25. **[G: Canada]**

MacFadyen, Alan J. and MacFadyen, Heather Wood. Economic Psychology: Intersections in Theory and Application: Introduction. **In** *MacFadyen, A. J. and MacFadyen, H. W., eds.*, 1986, pp. 1–5.

MacFadyen, Heather Wood. Motivational Constructs in Psychology. **In** *MacFadyen, A. J. and MacFadyen, H. W., eds.*, 1986, pp. 67–108.

Maital, Sharone L.; Maital, Shlomo and Pollak, Nava. Economic Behavior and Social Learning. **In** *MacFadyen, A. J. and MacFadyen, H. W., eds.*, 1986, pp. 271–90.

Marshall, James D.; Knetsch, Jack L. and Sinden, J. A. Agents' Evaluations and the Disparity in Measures of Economic Loss. *J. Econ. Behav. Organ.*, June 1986, *7*(2), pp. 115–27.

Martin, Robert E. On Judging Quality by Price: Price Dependent Expectations, Not Price Dependent Preferences. *Southern Econ. J.*, January 1986, *52*(3), pp. 665–72.

Mason, Charles F. Cherries, Lemons, and the

FTC, Revisited [The Market for 'Lemons'] [Cherries, Lemons, and the FTC: Minimum Quality Standards in the Retail Used Automobile Industry]. *Econ. Inquiry,* April 1986, *24*(2), pp. 363–65. **[G: U.S.]**

McKenna, Christopher J. Theories of Individual Search Behaviour. *Bull. Econ. Res.,* September 1986, *38*(3), pp. 189–207.

Middleton, Elliott. Some Testable Implications of a Preference for Subjective Novelty. *Kyklos,* 1986, *39*(3), pp. 397–418.

Mongin, Philippe. Are "All-and-Some" Statements Falsifiable after All? The Example of Utility Theory. *Econ. Philos.,* October 1986, *2*(2), pp. 185–95.

Morgan, James N. Research on Choices with Alternatives, Related Choices, Related Choosers, and Use of Economic Insights. **In** *Gilad, B. and Kaish, S., eds., Vol. A,* 1986, pp. 127–43.

Musgrave, Richard A. Maximin, Uncertainty and the Leisure Trade-off. **In** *Musgrave, R. A., Vol. 2,* 1986, *1974,* pp. 246–53.

Orosel, Gerhard O. Tentative Notes on Prestige Seeking and Pareto-Efficiency. *J. Econ. (Z. Nationalökon.),* Supplementum 5, 1986, pp. 169–94.

Pashardes, Panos. Myopic and Forward Looking Behavior in a Dynamic Demand System. *Int. Econ. Rev.,* June 1986, *27*(2), pp. 387–97. **[G: U.K.]**

Peck, Richard M. and Srinagesh, Padmanabhan. Time Preference and Uncertain Lifetime. *Amer. Econ.,* Fall 1986, *30*(2), pp. 41–45.

Persson, Torsten. Capital Market "Imperfections" and the Consumption Function: Comment. *Scand. J. Econ.,* 1986, *88*(1), pp. 81–83. **[G: U.K.]**

Plummer, Mark L. Supply Uncertainty, Option Price, and Option Value: An Extension. *Land Econ.,* August 1986, *62*(3), pp. 313–18.

Poulson, Barry W. The Family and the State: A Theoretical Framework. **In** *Peden, J. R. and Glahe, F. R., eds.,* 1986, pp. 49–80.

Ravallion, Martin. On Expectations Formation When Future Welfare Is Contemplated. *Kyklos,* 1986, *39*(4), pp. 564–73.

Raymon, Neil. Price Ceilings, Product Quality and Consumer Welfare. *J. Econ. (Z. Nationalökon.),* 1986, *46*(4), pp. 369–95.

Reinganum, Jennifer F. and Wilde, Louis L. Equilibrium Verification and Reporting Policies in a Model of Tax Compliance. *Int. Econ. Rev.,* October 1986, *27*(3), pp. 739–60.

Richard, Scott F. and Zame, William R. Proper Preferences and Quasi-concave Utility Functions. *J. Math. Econ.,* 1986, *15*(3), pp. 231–47.

Roe, Terry and Graham-Tomasi, Theodore. Yield Risk in a Dynamic Model of the Agricultural Household. **In** *Singh, I.; Squire, L. and Strauss, J., eds.,* 1986, pp. 255–76. **[G: Dominican Republic]**

Roskamp, Karl W. Optimal Life Time Consumption Paths under Income and Property Taxes: Effects of Tax Structure Changes. *Public Finance,* 1986, *41*(1), pp. 1–7.

Samuelson, Paul A. St. Petersburg Paradoxes: Defanged, Dissected, and Historically Described. **In** *Samuelson, P. A.,* 1986, *1977,* pp. 133–64.

Samuelson, Paul A. and Sato, Ryuzo. Unattainability of Integrability and Definiteness Conditions in the General Case of Demand for Money and Goods. **In** *Samuelson, P. A.,* 1986, *1984,* pp. 177–93.

Sawhill, Isabel V. Economic Perspectives on the Family. **In** *Reynolds, L. G.; Masters, S. H. and Moser, C. H., eds.,* 1986, *1977,* pp. 30–40.

Schelling, Thomas C. The Mind as a Consuming Organ. **In** *Elster, J., ed.,* 1986, pp. 177–95.

Schultz, T. Paul. The Value and Allocation of Time in High-Income Countries: Implications for Fertility. *Population Devel. Rev.,* Supp. 1986, *12,* pp. 87–108. **[G: U.S.]**

Scitovsky, Tibor. Psychologizing by Economists. **In** *MacFadyen, A. J. and MacFadyen, H. W., eds.,* 1986, pp. 165–80.

Shackle, George L. S. The Origination of Choice. **In** *[Lachmann, L. M.],* 1986, pp. 281–87.

Singh, Inderjit; Squire, Lyn and Strauss, John. Agricultural Household Models: Methodological Issues. **In** *Singh, I.; Squire, L. and Strauss, J., eds.,* 1986, pp. 48–70.

Snow, Arthur and Warren, Ronald S., Jr. Price Level Uncertainty, Saving, and Labor Supply. *Econ. Inquiry,* January 1986, *24*(1), pp. 97–106.

Steedman, Ian and Krause, Ulrich. Goethe's *Faust,* Arrow's Possibility Theorem and the Individual Decision-taker. **In** *Elster, J., ed.,* 1986, pp. 197–231.

Strauss, John. The Theory and Comparative Statics of Agricultural Household Models: A General Approach. **In** *Singh, I.; Squire, L. and Strauss, J., eds.,* 1986, pp. 71–91.

Taylor, Lester D. Opponent Processes and the Dynamics of Consumption. **In** *MacFadyen, A. J. and MacFadyen, H. W., eds.,* 1986, pp. 135–61.

Thaler, Richard H. The Psychology and Economics Conference Handbook: Comments. *J. Bus.,* Part 2, October 1986, *59*(4), pp. S279–84.

Tonks, Ian. The Demand for Information and the Diffusion of a New Product. *Int. J. Ind. Organ.,* December 1986, *4*(4), pp. 397–408.

Torr, Christopher. Convergent and Divergent Expectations. **In** *[Lachmann, L. M.],* 1986, pp. 295–300.

Tversky, Amos and Kahneman, Daniel. Rational Choice and the Framing of Decisions. *J. Bus.,* Part 2, October 1986, *59*(4), pp. S251–78.

Tversky, Amos and Kahneman, Daniel. Rational Choice and the Framing of Decisions. **In** *Hogarth, R. M. and Reder, M. W., eds.,* 1986, pp. 67–94.

Weiss, Jeffrey H. Donations: Can They Reduce a Donor's Welfare? **In** *Rose-Ackerman, S., ed.,* 1986, pp. 45–54.

Weissenberger, Edgar. An Intertemporal System of Dynamic Consumer Demand Functions.

Europ. Econ. Rev., August 1986, *30*(4), pp. 859–91. **[G: U.K.]**

Weymark, John A. Bunching Properties of Optimal Nonlinear Income Taxes. *Soc. Choice Welfare*, 1986, *3*(3), pp. 213–32.

Wohlgenant, Michael K. Global Behavior of Demand Elasticities for Food: Implications for Demand Projections. **In** *Capps, O., Jr. and Senauer, B., eds.*, 1986, pp. 35–48.

Zamagni, Stefano. La teoria del consumatore nell'ultimo quarto di secolo: risultati, problemi, linee di tendenza. (Consumer Theory in the Last Quarter of a Century: Achievements, Problems, Perspectives. With English summary.) *Econ. Polít.*, December 1986, *3*(3), pp. 409–66.

Zaman, Asad. Microfoundations for the Basic Needs Approach to Development: The Lexicographic Utility Function. *Pakistan J. Appl. Econ.*, Summer 1986, *5*(1), pp. 1–11.

0223 Theory of Production

Aiginger, Karl. The Impact of Uncertainty on the Optimal Decision of Risk Neutral Firms. **In** *Daboni, L.; Montesano, A. and Lines, M., eds.*, 1986, pp. 355–73.

Akerlof, George A. Labor Contracts as Partial Gift Exchange. **In** *Akerlof, G. A. and Yellen, J. L., eds.*, 1986, *1982*, pp. 66–92.

Akerlof, George A. The Market for "Lemons": Quality Uncertainty and the Market Mechanism. **In** *Barney, J. B. and Ouchi, W. G., eds.*, 1986, *1970*, pp. 27–39. **[G: India]**

Albach, Horst. Allgemeine Betriebswirtschaftslehre Zum Gedenken an Erich Gutenberg. (With English summary.) *Z. Betriebswirtshaft*, July 1986, *56*(7), pp. 578–613.

Alchian, Armen A. and Demsetz, Harold. Production, Information Costs, and Economic Organization. **In** *Barney, J. B. and Ouchi, W. G., eds.*, 1986, *1972*, pp. 129–55.

Alchian, Armen A. and Demsetz, Harold. Production, Information Costs, and Economic Organization. **In** *Putterman, L., ed.*, 1986, *1972*, pp. 111–34.

Alvi, Eskander. The Production Process in a Competitive Economy: Comment. *Amer. Econ. Rev.*, December 1986, *76*(5), pp. 1200–1202.

Anderson, Ronald W. and Harris, Christopher J. A Model of Innovation with Application to New Financial Products. *Oxford Econ. Pap.*, Suppl. Nov. 1986, *38*, pp. 203–18.

Aoki, Masahiko. Horizontal vs. Vertical Information Structure of the Firm. *Amer. Econ. Rev.*, December 1986, *76*(5), pp. 971–83.

Appelbaum, Elie and Katz, Eliakim. Measures of Risk Aversion and Comparative Statics of Industry Equilibrium. *Amer. Econ. Rev.*, June 1986, *76*(3), pp. 524–29.

Arena, Richard and Torre, Dominique. Approche sraffaienne et théorie de la gravitation: une tentative de rapprochement. (Sraffian Approach and Gravitation Theory. With English summary.) *Écon. Appl.*, 1986, *39*(1), pp. 61–86.

Armour, Henry Ogden and Teece, David J. Organizational Structure and Economic Performance: A Test of the Multidivisional Hypothesis. **In** *Barney, J. B. and Ouchi, W. G., eds.*, 1986, *1978*, pp. 187–204.

Artus, Patrick and Migus, Bernard. Dynamique de l'investissement et de l'emploi avec cots d'ajustement sur le capital et le travail. (Investment and Employment Dynamics with Adjustment Costs on Capital and Labour. With English summary.) *Ann. Écon. Statist.*, Apr./June 1986, (2), pp. 75–99.

Artzner, Philippe; Simon, Carl P. and Sonnenschein, Hugo. Convergence of Myopic Firms to Long-run Equilibrium via the Method of Characteristics. **In** *Sonnenschein, H. F., ed.*, 1986, pp. 157–83.

Barney, Jay B. and Ouchi, William G. The Search for New Microeconomic and Organization Theory Paradigms. **In** *Barney, J. B. and Ouchi, W. G., eds.*, 1986, pp. 1–17.

Barzelay, Michael and Thomas, Lee R., III. Is Capitalism Necessary? A Critique of the Neoclassical Economics of Organization. *J. Econ. Behav. Organ.*, September 1986, *7*(3), pp. 225–33.

Baumol, William J. Optimal Depreciation Policy: Pricing the Products of Durable Assets. **In** *Baumol, W. J.*, 1986, pp. 111–29.

Baumol, William J. Scale Economies, Average Cost, and the Profitability of Marginal Cost Pricing. **In** *Baumol, W. J.*, 1986, *1976*, pp. 11–25.

Beladi, Hamid and Lyon, Kenneth S. The Effects of Risk Aversion When an Input Is Random: A Note. *Quart. J. Bus. Econ.*, Spring 1986, *25*(2), pp. 71–83.

Bell, Christopher Ross. Charles Ellet, Jr., and the Theory of Optimal Input Choice. *Hist. Polit. Econ.*, Fall 1986, *18*(3), pp. 485–95.

Betancourt, Roger R. A Generalization of Modern Production Theory. *Appl. Econ.*, August 1986, *18*(8), pp. 915–28.

Betancourt, Roger R. The Duration of Operations and the Estimation of Substitution Possibilities. *Europ. Econ. Rev.*, December 1986, *30*(6), pp. 1189–95.

Bidard, Christian. Baisse tendancielle du taux de profit et marchandise-étalon. (Falling Rate of Profit and the Standard Commodity. With English summary.) *Écon. Appl.*, 1986, *39*(1), pp. 139–54.

Bidard, Christian. Is von Neumann Square? *J. Econ. (Z. Nationalökon.)*, 1986, *46*(4), pp. 407–19.

Bidard, Christian. Production de marchandises, Corrigendum. (Production of Commodities, Corrigendum. With English summary.) *Écon. Appl.*, 1986, *39*(1), pp. 113–38.

Bivin, David G. Inventories and Interest Rates: A Critique of the Buffer Stock Model. *Amer. Econ. Rev.*, March 1986, *76*(1), pp. 168–76. **[G: U.S.]**

Blinder, Alan S. Can the Production Smoothing Model of Inventory Behavior Be Saved? *Quart.*

J. Econ., August 1986, *101*(3), pp. 431–53. **[G: U.S.]**

Boisvert, Richard N. A General Measure of Output-Variable Input Demand Elasticities: Comment. *Amer. J. Agr. Econ.*, August 1986, *68*(3), pp. 745–46.

Bol, Georg. On Technical Efficiency Measures: A Remark. *J. Econ. Theory*, April 1986, *38*(2), pp. 380–85.

Bonin, John P. Implicit-Contract Theory in Illyria: Comment [The Economics of a Labor-Managed Enterprise in the Short Run: An "Implict Contracts" Approach]. *J. Compar. Econ.*, March 1986, *10*(1), pp. 79–85.

Bonin, John P. and Fukuda, Wataru. The Multifactor Illyrian Firm Revisited. *J. Compar. Econ.*, June 1986, *10*(2), pp. 171–80.

Bowles, Samuel. The Production Process in a Competitive Economy: Walrasian, Neo-Hobbesian, and Marxian Models. **In** *Putterman, L., ed.*, 1986, *1985*, pp. 329–55.

Bowles, Samuel. The Production Process in a Competitive Economy: Reply. *Amer. Econ. Rev.*, December 1986, *76*(5), pp. 1203–04.

Brockhoff, Klaus. The Incentive Limits of Firms: A Comparative Institutional Assessment of Bureaucracy: Comment. **In** *Balassa, B. and Giersch, H., eds.*, 1986, pp. 231–34.

Brown, Donald J. Increasing Returns and the Share Economy. *J. Compar. Econ.*, December 1986, *10*(4), pp. 454–56.

Brown, Donald J., et al. On a General Existence Theorem for Marginal Cost Pricing Equilibria. *J. Econ. Theory*, April 1986, *38*(2), pp. 371–79.

Burkett, John P. Search, Selection, and Shortage in an Industry Composed of Labor-Managed Firms. *J. Compar. Econ.*, March 1986, *10*(1), pp. 26–40.

Chetty, V. K. and Jha, Shikha. Microeconomics of Rationing and Licensing. *J. Quant. Econ.*, July 1986, *2*(2), pp. 173–98.

Coase, Ronald H. The Nature of the Firm. **In** *Barney, J. B. and Ouchi, W. G., eds.*, 1986, *1937*, pp. 80–98.

Coase, Ronald H. The Nature of the Firm. **In** *Putterman, L., ed.*, 1986, *1937*, pp. 72–85.

Conte, Michael A. Entry of Worker Cooperatives in Capitalist Economies. *J. Compar. Econ.*, March 1986, *10*(1), pp. 41–47.

Day, Richard H. and Hanson, Kenneth A. Adaptive Economising, Technological Change and the Demand for Labour in Disequilibrium. **In** *Nijkamp, P., ed. (II)*, 1986, pp. 301–20.

Despotakis, Kostas A. Economic Performance of Flexible Functional Forms: Implications for Equilibrium Modeling. *Europ. Econ. Rev.*, December 1986, *30*(6), pp. 1107–43.

Dierker, Egbert. When Does Marginal Cost Pricing Lead to Pareto Efficiency? *J. Econ. (Z. Nationalökon.)*, Supplementum 5, 1986, pp. 41–66.

Dixon, Huw. Strategic Investment with Consistent Conjectures. *Oxford Econ. Pap.*, Suppl. Nov. 1986, *38*, pp. 111–28.

Dixon, Huw. Strategic Investment with Consistent Conjectures. **In** *Morris, D. J., et al., eds.*, 1986, pp. 111–28.

Dow, Gregory K. Control Rights, Competitive Markets, and the Labor Management Debate. *J. Compar. Econ.*, March 1986, *10*(1), pp. 48–61.

Ellerman, David P. Horizon Problems and Property Rights in Labor-Managed Firms. *J. Compar. Econ.*, March 1986, *10*(1), pp. 62–78.

Enos, J. L. Public Policy in an Economy with Different Types of Agents. **In** *Hall, P., ed.*, 1986, *1984*, pp. 172–200.

Estrin, Saul. Long-run Supply Responses under Self-Management: Reply. *J. Compar. Econ.*, September 1986, *10*(3), pp. 342–45.

Evans, David S. and Heckman, James J. A Test for Subadditivity of the Cost Function with an Application to the Bell System: Erratum. *Amer. Econ. Rev.*, September 1986, *76*(4), pp. 856–58.

Faber, Malte. Relationships between Modern Austrian and Sraffa's Capital Theory. **In** *Faber, M., ed.*, 1986, *1980*, pp. 44–59.

Färe, Rolf. Addition and Efficiency. *Quart. J. Econ.*, November 1986, *101*(4), pp. 861–65.

Färe, Rolf. On the Existence and Equivalence of Three Joint Production Functions. *Scand. J. Econ.*, 1986, *88*(4), pp. 669–74.

Färe, Rolf; Grosskopf, Shawna and Lovell, C. A. Knox. Scale Economies and Duality. *J. Econ. (Z. Nationalökon.)*, 1986, *46*(2), pp. 175–82.

Färe, Rolf and Logan, James. Regulation, Scale and Productivity: A Comment. *Int. Econ. Rev.*, October 1986, *27*(3), pp. 777–81.

Färe, Rolf and Primont, Daniel. On Differentiability of Cost Functions. *J. Econ. Theory*, April 1986, *38*(2), pp. 233–37.

Fershtman, Chaim and Muller, Eitan. Turnpike Properties of Capital Accumulation Games [Capital Accumulation Games of Infinite Duration]. *J. Econ. Theory*, February 1986, *38*(1), pp. 167–77.

Fishelson, Gideon. On the Behavior of a Noncompetitive Firm when the Supplies of Inputs Are Random. *J. Econ. Bus.*, December 1986, *38*(4), pp. 331–39.

Flacco, Paul R. and Kroetch, Brent G. Adjustment to Production Uncertainty and the Theory of the Firm. *Econ. Inquiry*, July 1986, *24*(3), pp. 485–95.

Fooladi, Iraj. The Effect of Proportional Profit Tax on the Level of Output, under Uncertainty. *Atlantic Econ. J.*, December 1986, *14*(4), pp. 90–94.

Franke, Reiner. Some Problems Concerning the Notion of Cost-Minimizing Systems in the Framework of Joint Production. *Manchester Sch. Econ. Soc. Stud.*, September 1986, *54*(3), pp. 298–307.

Frantz, Roger S. X-Efficiency in Behavioral Economics. **In** *Gilad, B. and Kaish, S., eds., Vol. A*, 1986, pp. 307–23.

Fraser, R. W. Uncertainty and Production Quotas. *Econ. Rec.*, September 1986, *62*(178), pp. 338–42.

French, George. Price Smoothing and Inventory Behavior. *J. Econ. Dynam. Control,* September 1986, *10*(3), pp. 353–66.

Fujimoto, Takao. Non-linear Leontief Models in Abstract Spaces. *J. Math. Econ.,* 1986, *15*(2), pp. 151–56.

Gangopadhyay, Shubhashis. Choice of Techniques, Employment and Poverty. *J. Quant. Econ.,* July 1986, *2*(2), pp. 199–212.

Giordano, James N. When Are Factor Inputs Gross Substitutes? *Eastern Econ. J.,* Jan.-Mar. 1986, *12*(1), pp. 53–59.

Goering, Patricia A. Consumer Learning and Optimal Pricing Strategies for Products of Unknown Quality. **In** *Samuelson, L., ed.,* 1986, pp. 53–77.

Goldstein, Jonathan P. Mark-Up Pricing over the Business Cycle: The Microfoundations of the Variable Mark-Up. *Southern Econ. J.,* July 1986, *53*(1), pp. 233–46.

Grabowski, Henry G. and Mueller, Dennis C. Life Cycle Effects on Corporate Returns on Retentions. **In** *Mueller, D. C.,* 1986, *1975,* pp. 138–52. **[G: U.S.]**

Griffiths, William E. A Bayesian Framework for Optimal Input Allocation with an Uncertain Stochastic Production Function. *Australian J. Agr. Econ.,* August/December 1986, *30*(2–3), pp. 128–52.

Gronchi, Sandro. On Investment Criteria Based on the Internal Rate of Return. *Oxford Econ. Pap.,* March 1986, *38*(1), pp. 174–80.

Grosskopf, Shawna. The Role of the Reference Technology in Measuring Productive Efficiency. *Econ. J.,* June 1986, *96*(382), pp. 499–513.

Groth, C. Different Indecomposability Concepts for a von Neumann Technology: A Note. *Metroecon.,* June 1986, *38*(2), pp. 157–66.

Haber, Lawrence J. Production Theory under Uncertain Inflation. *Atlantic Econ. J.,* September 1986, *14*(3), pp. 24–33.

Hackman, Steven T. A New, Geometric Proof of Shephard's Duality Theorem. *J. Econ. (Z. Nationalökon.),* 1986, *46*(3), pp. 299–304.

Hansson, Ingemar. Classical, Keynes' and Neoclassical Investment Theory—A Synthesis. *Oxford Econ. Pap.,* July 1986, *38*(2), pp. 305–16.

Hansson, Ingemar. Market Adjustment and Investment Determination under Rational Expectations. *Economica,* November 1986, *53*(212), pp. 505–14.

Harcourt, Geoffrey C. Investment-Decision Criteria, Capital-Intensity and the Choice of Techniques. **In** *[Harcourt, G. C.],* 1986, *1967,* pp. 113–44. **[G: U.K.; Europe]**

Haruna, Shoji. Long-run Supply Responses under Self-Management: Comment. *J. Compar. Econ.,* September 1986, *10*(3), pp. 338–41.

van den Heuvel, Paul. Nonjoint Production and the Cost Function: Some Refinements. *J. Econ. (Z. Nationalökon.),* 1986, *46*(3), pp. 283–97.

Hillman, Arye L. and Katz, Eliakim. Domestic Uncertainty and Foreign Dumping. *Can. J. Econ.,* August 1986, *19*(3), pp. 403–16.

Horvat, Branko. A Rejoinder [The Theory of the Worker-Managed Firm Revisited]. *Econ. Anal. Workers' Manage.,* 1986, *20*(4), pp. 417–18.

Horvat, Branko. Farewell to the Illyrian Firm. *Econ. Anal. Workers' Manage.,* 1986, *20*(1), pp. 23–29.

Horvat, Branko. The Illyrian Firm: An Alternative View: A Rejoinder. *Econ. Anal. Workers' Manage.,* 1986, *20*(4), pp. 411–16.

Horvat, Branko. The Theory of the Worker-Managed Firm Revisited. *J. Compar. Econ.,* March 1986, *10*(1), pp. 9–25.

Horvat, Branko. Workers' Management and the Market. **In** *Stiglitz, J. E. and Mathewson, G. F., eds.,* 1986, pp. 297–309. **[G: Yugoslavia]**

Inoue, Tadashi and Wegge, Leon L. On the Geometry of the Production Possibility Frontier. *Int. Econ. Rev.,* October 1986, *27*(3), pp. 727–37.

Jensen, Michael C. and Meckling, William H. Theory of the Firm: Managerial Behavior, Agency Costs, and Ownership Structure. **In** *Barney, J. B. and Ouchi, W. G., eds.,* 1986, *1976,* pp. 214–75.

Jorgenson, Dale W. Econometric Methods for Modeling Producer Behavior. **In** *Griliches,* Z. *and Intriligator, M. D., eds.,* 1986, pp. 1841–1915.

Just, Richard E. and Zilberman, David. Does the Law of Supply Hold under Uncertainty? *Econ. J.,* June 1986, *96*(382), pp. 514–24.

Kahn, Charles M. The Durable Goods Monopolist and Consistency with Increasing Costs. *Econometrica,* March 1986, *54*(2), pp. 275–94.

Katz, Eliakim. A Diagramatic Illustration of the Labour Cooperative, a Note. *Amer. Econ.,* Spring 1986, *30*(1), pp. 73–74.

Kokkelenberg, Edward C. and Bischoff, Charles W. Expectations and Factor Demand. *Rev. Econ. Statist.,* August 1986, *68*(3), pp. 423–31. **[G: U.S.]**

König, Heinz and Nerlove, Marc. Price Flexibility, Inventory Behavior, and Production Responses. **In** *[Arrow, K. J.], Vol. 2,* 1986, pp. 179–218. **[G: France; W. Germany]**

Kornai, János. "Hard" and "Soft" Budget Constraint. **In** *Kornai, J.,* 1986, *1980,* pp. 33–51.

Kroll, Mark and Johnson, Herb. A Note on Managerial Behavior and the Theory of the Firm. *J. Behav. Econ.,* Spring/Summer 1986, *15*(1/2), pp. 123–34.

Kuran, Timur. Price Adjustment Costs, Anticipated Inflation, and Output. *Quart. J. Econ.,* May 1986, *101*(2), pp. 407–18.

Kurz, Heinz D. Classical and Early Neoclassical Economists on Joint Production. *Metroecon.,* February 1986, *38*(1), pp. 1–37.

Laffont, Jean-Jacques and Tirole, Jean. Using Cost Observation to Regulate Firms. *J. Polit. Econ.,* Part 1, June 1986, *94*(3), pp. 614–41.

Landesmann, Michael A. Conceptions of Technology and the Production Process. **In** *Baran-*

zini, M. and Scazzieri, R., eds., 1986, pp. 281–310.

Lau, Lawrence J. and Ma, Barry K. Choice of Technique in a Putty-Clay Model of Production. *Eastern Econ. J.*, July-Sept. 1986, *12*(3), pp. 321–26.

Lazear, Edward P. Retail Pricing and Clearance Sales. *Amer. Econ. Rev.*, March 1986, *76*(1), pp. 14–32.

LeBlanc, Michael and Hrubovcak, James. Dynamic Input Demand: An Application to Agriculture. *Appl. Econ.*, July 1986, *18*(7), pp. 807–18. **[G: U.S.]**

Leibenstein, Harvey. The Prisoners' Dilemma in the Invisible Hand: An Analysis of Intrafirm Productivity. **In** *Putterman, L., ed.*, 1986, *1982*, pp. 170–78.

Lere, John C. Product Pricing Based on Accounting Costs [Theory of the Firm Facing Uncertain Demand]. *Accounting Rev.*, April 1986, *61*(2), pp. 318–24.

Levy, David T. and Haber, Lawrence J. An Advantage of the Multiproduct Firm: The Transferability of Firm-Specific Capital. *J. Econ. Behav. Organ.*, September 1986, *7*(3), pp. 291–302.

Loury, Glenn C. and Lewis, Tracy R. On the Profitability of Interruptible Supply. *Amer. Econ. Rev.*, September 1986, *76*(4), pp. 827–32.

Luenberger, David G. Control of Linear Dynamic Market Systems. *J. Econ. Dynam. Control*, September 1986, *10*(3), pp. 339–51.

Madžar, Ljubomir. The Illyrian Firm: An Alternative View. *Econ. Anal. Workers' Manage.*, 1986, *20*(4), pp. 401–10.

Maneschi, Andrea. A Comparative Evaluation of Sraffa's 'The Laws of Returns under Competitive Conditions' and Its Italian Precursor. *Cambridge J. Econ.*, March 1986, *10*(1), pp. 1–12.

Marion, Nancy Peregrim and Svensson, Lars E. O. Adjustment to Expected and Unexpected Oil Price Changes: Corrigendum. *Can. J. Econ.*, November 1986, *19*(4), pp. 816–17.

Marris, Robin and Mueller, Dennis C. The Corporation, Competition, and the Invisible Hand. **In** *Mueller, D. C.*, 1986, *1980*, pp. 261–97.

Martin, Robert E. Quality Choice under Labor-Management. *J. Compar. Econ.*, December 1986, *10*(4), pp. 400–413.

Masten, Scott E. Institutional Choice and the Organization of Production: The Make-or-Buy Decision. *J. Inst. Theoretical Econ.*, September 1986, *142*(3), pp. 493–509.

Mato Leal, Gonzalo and Ríos Rull, José V. Efectos de los créditos participativos públicos en la financiación de las empresas. (With English summary.) *Invest. Ecón.*, January 1986, *10*(1), pp. 173–84.

McCain, Roger A. Comments on Professor Horvat's Essay [The Economics of a Labor-managed Enterprise in the Short Run: An "Implicit Contracts" Approach]. *J. Compar. Econ.*, March 1986, *10*(1), pp. 86–87.

McClelland, John W.; Wetzstein, Michael E. and Musser, Wesley N. Returns to Scale and Size in Agricultural Economics. *Western J. Agr. Econ.*, December 1986, *11*(2), pp. 129–33.

McDonald, Robert and Siegel, Daniel. The Value of Waiting to Invest. *Quart. J. Econ.*, November 1986, *101*(4), pp. 707–27.

Meško, Ivan. Analysis of Business Process by Opportunity Costs. *Econ. Anal. Workers' Manage.*, 1986, *20*(3), pp. 307–10.

de Meza, David. Safety in Conformity but Profits in Deviance. *Can. J. Econ.*, May 1986, *19*(2), pp. 261–69.

Michel, Philippe. Dynamique de l'accumulation de capital en présence de contraintes de débouchés. (A Dynamic Analysis of Capital Accumulation with Expected Demand Constraints. With English summary.) *Ann. Écon. Statist.*, Apr./June 1986, (2), pp. 117–45.

Mills, David E. Flexibility and Firm Diversity with Demand Fluctuations. *Int. J. Ind. Organ.*, June 1986, *4*(2), pp. 203–15.

Miyazaki, Hajime. Labor–Management Bargaining: Contract Curves and Slutsky Equations. *J. Polit. Econ.*, December 1986, *94*(6), pp. 1225–45.

Modica, Salvatore. Investimento, incertezza e vincoli di liquidità. (Investment, Uncertainty, and Liquidity Constraints. With English summary.) *Giorn. Econ.*, Jan.-Feb. 1986, *45*(1–2), pp. 73–77.

Molesti, Romano. La teoria del costo di produzione in Pasquale Jannaccone. (Pasquale Jannaccone's Theory of the Cost of Production. With English summary.) *Rivista Int. Sci. Econ. Com.*, March 1986, *33*(3), pp. 261–80.

Mongin, Philippe. La controverse sur l'entreprise (1940–1950) et la formation de l'"irréalisme méthodologique." (The Controversy over the Enterprise (1940–1950) and the Building-Up of a "Lack of Methodological Realism." With English summary.) *Écon. Soc.*, March 1986, *20*(3), pp. 95–151.

Montias, J. Michael. On the Centralization and Decentralization of Economic Activities. **In** *Adelman, I. and Taylor, J. E., eds.*, 1986, pp. 171–89.

Montias, J. Michael. On the Labor-Managed Firm in a Competitive Environment. *J. Compar. Econ.*, March 1986, *10*(1), pp. 2–8.

Morrison, Catherine J. Structural Models of Dynamic Factor Demands with Nonstatic Expectations: An Empirical Assessment of Alternative Expectations Specifications. *Int. Econ. Rev.*, June 1986, *27*(2), pp. 365–86. **[G: U.S.]**

Mueller, Dennis C. A Life Cycle Theory of the Firm. **In** *Mueller, D. C.*, 1986, *1972*, pp. 119–37.

Mueller, Dennis C. A Theory of Conglomerate Mergers. **In** *Mueller, D. C.*, 1986, *1969*, pp. 155–70.

Mueller, Dennis C. The Modern Corporation: Profits, Power, Growth and Performance: Introduction. **In** *Mueller, D. C.*, 1986, pp. 1–11.

Mulligan, James G. Technical Change and Scale

Economies Given Stochastic Demand and Production. *Int. J. Ind. Organ.*, June 1986, *4*(2), pp. 189–201.

Naish, Howard F. Price Adjustment Costs and the Output–Inflation Trade-off. *Economica*, May 1986, *53*(210), pp. 219–30.

Nuti, Domenico Mario. Merger Conditions and the Measurement of Disequilibrium in Labour-Managed Economies. *Ann. Pub. Co-op. Econ.*, Jan.-March 1986, *57*(1), pp. 47–53.

Paroush, Jacob. Inflation, Search Costs and Price Dispersion. *J. Macroecon.*, Summer 1986, *8*(3), pp. 329–36.

Peck, S. C. Econometric Aspects of Firm Growth Behaviour. **In** *[Yamey, B.]*, 1986, pp. 133–58.

Pereira, Alfredo M. On the Computation of the Users' Cost of Capital in the Presence of Adjustments Costs. *Economia (Portugal)*, October 1986, *10*(3), pp. 447–52.

Pfouts, Ralph W. and Rosefielde, Steven. The Firm in Illyria: Market Syndicalism Reconsidered. *J. Compar. Econ.*, June 1986, *10*(2), pp. 160–70.

Phillips, Ronnie J. Marx, the Classical Firm, and Economic Planning. *J. Post Keynesian Econ.*, Winter 1985-86, *8*(2), pp. 266–76.

Pitelis, Christos N. and Sugden, Roger. The Separation of Ownership and Control in the Theory of the Firm: A Reappraisal. *Int. J. Ind. Organ.*, March 1986, *4*(1), pp. 69–86.

Plessner, Yakir and Shalit, Haim. Inflation, the Level of Investment, and Interest Rates. *Europ. Econ. Rev.*, December 1986, *30*(6), pp. 1169–87.

Prucha, Ingmar R. and Nadiri, M. Ishaq. A Comparison of Alternative Methods for the Estimation of Dynamic Factor Demand Models under Non-static Expectations. *J. Econometrics*, Oct./Nov. 1986, *33*(1/2), pp. 187–211.

Putterman, Louis G. The Economic Nature of the Firm: Overview. **In** *Putterman, L., ed.*, 1986, pp. 1–29.

Quadrio-Curzio, Alberto. Technological Scarcity: An Essay on Production and Structural Change. **In** *Baranzini, M. and Scazzieri, R., eds.*, 1986, pp. 311–38.

Radner, Roy. The Internal Economy of Large Firms. *Econ. J.*, Supplement 1986, *96*, pp. 1–22.

Ravid, S. A. and Sudit, E. F. Application of Production Standards in Complex Organizations under Uncertainty. *J. Econ. Bus.*, December 1986, *38*(4), pp. 307–16.

Rees, Ray. Indivisibilities, Pricing and Investment: The Case of the Second Best. *J. Econ. (Z. Nationalökon.)*, Supplementum 5, 1986, pp. 195–210.

Reynolds, Morgan O. Trade Unions in the Production Process Reconsidered. *J. Polit. Econ.*, April 1986, *94*(2), pp. 443–47.

Rosefielde, Steven. Behavioral Uncertainty and the Optimal Public Regulation of ELMF Systems: Comments on the State of Worker-Management Theory. *J. Compar. Econ.*, March 1986, *10*(1), pp. 88–90.

Rossana, Robert J. Wage and Hiring Dynamics with Storable Output. *J. Macroecon.*, Summer 1986, *8*(3), pp. 313–28.

Saloner, Garth. The Role of Obsolescence and Inventory Costs in Providing Commitment. *Int. J. Ind. Organ.*, September 1986, *4*(3), pp. 333–45.

Salvadori, Neri. Land and Choice of Techniques within the Sraffa Framework. *Australian Econ. Pap.*, June 1986, *25*(46), pp. 94–105.

Samuelson, Paul A. Paul Douglas's Measurement of Production Functions and Marginal Productivities. **In** *Samuelson, P. A.*, 1986, *1979*, pp. 203–19.

Sandelin, Bo. Some Unneoclassical Results in Neoclassical Investment Theory. *Australian Econ. Pap.*, June 1986, *25*(46), pp. 83–93.

Scarf, Herbert E. Neighborhood Systems for Production Sets with Indivisibilities. *Econometrica*, May 1986, *54*(3), pp. 507–32.

van Schijndel, Geert-Jan C. Th. Dynamic Behaviour of a Value Maximizing Firm under Personal Taxation. *Europ. Econ. Rev.*, October 1986, *30*(5), pp. 1043–62.

Scott, Allen J. Industrial Organization and Location: Division of Labor, the Firm, and Spatial Process. *Econ. Geogr.*, July 1986, *62*(3), pp. 215–31.

Sgro, Pasquale M. Factor Substitution and Discrimination in Labor Markets. *Southern Econ. J.*, April 1986, *52*(4), pp. 1103–14.

Shaffer, Sherrill. Small Firm Expansion and Demand Uncertainty. *Scot. J. Polit. Econ.*, May 1986, *33*(2), pp. 182–87.

Shapiro, Matthew D. The Dynamic Demand for Capital and Labor. *Quart. J. Econ.*, August 1986, *101*(3), pp. 513–42. **[G: U.S.]**

Sikdar, Soumyen. Technological Change and the Labour-Managed Firm. *J. Quant. Econ.*, January 1986, *2*(1), pp. 111–18.

Sinn, Hans-Werner. Risiko als Produktionsfaktor. (Risk as a Factor of Production. With English summary.) *Jahr. Nationalökon. Statist.*, November 1986, *201*(6), pp. 557–71.

Steindl, Alois, et al. On the Optimality of Cyclical Employment Policies: A Numerical Investigation. *J. Econ. Dynam. Control*, December 1986, *10*(4), pp. 457–66.

Stigler, George J. The Division of Labor Is Limited by the Extent of the Market. **In** *Stigler, G. J.*, 1986, *1951*, pp. 13–24.

Stigler, George J. The Economies of Scale. **In** *Stigler, G. J.*, 1986, *1958*, pp. 25–45. **[G: U.S.]**

Sueyoshi, Toshiyuki and Anselmo, Peter C. The Evans and Heckman Subadditivity Test: Comment. *Amer. Econ. Rev.*, September 1986, *76*(4), pp. 854–55.

Sun, Emily. A Simplified Exposition of the Profit-Maximization Model of the Firm. *Amer. Econ.*, Fall 1986, *30*(2), pp. 59–61.

Sutcliffe, C. and Bromwich, M. Investment Appraisal. **In** *Firth, M. and Keane, S. M., eds.*, 1986, pp. 44–58.

Takamasu, Akira. On the Production Possibility Frontier in a Sraffa–Leontief Economy. *Man-*

chester Sch. Econ. Soc. Stud.*, June 1986, *54*(2), pp. 202–07.

Takeda, Shigeo. Joint Production and a Discontinuous Switch of the Wage–Profit Frontier. *Econ. Stud. Quart.*, March 1986, *37*(1), pp. 54–66.

Thaler, Richard H. The Psychology and Economics Conference Handbook: Comments. **In** *Hogarth, R. M. and Reder, M. W., eds.*, 1986, pp. 95–100.

Tinbergen, Jan. Some Extensions and Refinements of Gottschalk's Estimation of Production Functions. **In** *Perryman, M. R. and Schmidt, J. R., eds.*, 1986, pp. 3–12. **[G: U.S.]**

Turnbull, Geoffrey Keith. Theory of the Firm under the Threat of Input Supply Interruption. *Southern Econ. J.*, January 1986, *52*(3), pp. 807–17.

Varela, Oscar and Olson, Richard E. A General Equilibrium Analysis of Financial Regulation. *J. Public Econ.*, August 1986, *30*(3), pp. 329–40.

Weissenberger, Edgar; Müller-Brockhausen, Gerd and Welsch, Heinz. A Factor Demand Model with Quasi-fixed Factors and Rational Expectations. *J. Econ. (Z. Nationalökon.)*, 1986, *46*(2), pp. 123–42. **[G: U.S.]**

Wernerfelt, Birger. Product Line Rivalry: Note. *Amer. Econ. Rev.*, September 1986, *76*(4), pp. 842–44.

White, Harry. Uncertainty and Factor Proportions [Factor Price Uncertainty with Variable Proportions]. *Can. J. Econ.*, November 1986, *19*(4), pp. 814–15.

Wilkins, Mira. Defining a Firm: History and Theory. **In** *Hertner, P. and Jones, G., eds.*, 1986, pp. 80–95.

Williamson, Oliver E. The Incentive Limits of Firms: A Comparative Institutional Assessment of Bureaucracy. **In** *Balassa, B. and Giersch, H., eds.*, 1986, pp. 204–30.

Williamson, Oliver E. The Multidivisional Structure. **In** *Barney, J. B. and Ouchi, W. G., eds.*, 1986, *1975*, pp. 163–87.

Williamson, Oliver E. Transaction-Cost Economics: The Governance of Contractual Relations. **In** *Barney, J. B. and Ouchi, W. G., eds.*, 1986, *1979*, pp. 98–129.

Winter, Sidney G. The Research Program of the Behavioral Theory of the Firm: Orthodox Critique and Evolutionary Perspective. **In** *Gilad, B. and Kaish, S., eds., Vol. A*, 1986, pp. 151–88.

Witt, Ulrich. Firms' Market Behavior under Imperfect Information and Economic Natural Selection. *J. Econ. Behav. Organ.*, September 1986, *7*(3), pp. 265–90.

Wodopia, Franz-Josef. Flow and Fund Approaches to Irreversible Investment Decisions. **In** *Faber, M., ed.*, 1986, pp. 195–207.

Wolinsky, Asher. The Nature of Competition and the Scope of Firms. *J. Ind. Econ.*, March 1986, *34*(3), pp. 247–59.

Wright, J. F. On Investment Criteria Based on the Internal Rate of Return: A Response. *Oxford Econ. Pap.*, March 1986, *38*(1), pp. 181–84.

Young, Richard A. A Note on "Economically Optimal Performance Evaluation and Control Systems": The Optimality of Two-Tailed Investigations. *J. Acc. Res.*, Spring 1986, *24*(1), pp. 231–40.

0224 Theory of Factor Distribution and Distributive Shares

Acheson, James M. Constraints on Entrepreneurship: Transaction Costs and Market Efficiency. **In** *Greenfield, S. M. and Strickon, A., eds.*, 1986, pp. 45–53.

Ball, Michael. On Marx's Theory of Agricultural Rent: A Reply. **In** *Fine, B., ed.*, 1986, *1980*, pp. 152–74.

Bidard, Christian. Production de marchandises, Corrigendum. (Production of Commodities, Corrigendum. With English summary.) *Écon. Appl.*, 1986, *39*(1), pp. 113–38.

Bidard, Christian. The Maximum Rate of Profits in Joint Production. *Metroecon.*, February 1986, *38*(1), pp. 53–66.

Blaug, Mark. Another Look at the Labour Reduction Problem in Marx. **In** *Blaug, M.*, 1986, *1982*, pp. 197–208.

Catephores, George. The Historical Transformation Problem—A Reply. **In** *Fine, B., ed.*, 1986, *1980*, pp. 180–84.

Collier, Irwin L., Jr. On Marxian Value, Exploitation, and the Transformation Problem: A Geometric Approach. *J. Compar. Econ.*, September 1986, *10*(3), pp. 325–37.

D'Agata, Antonio. Non-produced Means of Production in Sraffa's System: Basics, Non-basics and Quasi-basics. A Comment. *Cambridge J. Econ.*, December 1986, *10*(4), pp. 379–86.

Faber, Malte. Relationships between Modern Austrian and Sraffa's Capital Theory. **In** *Faber, M., ed.*, 1986, *1980*, pp. 44–59.

Fine, Ben. On the Historical Transformation Problem. **In** *Fine, B., ed.*, 1986, *1980*, pp. 185–87.

Fine, Ben. On Marx's Theory of Agricultural Rent. **In** *Fine, B., ed.*, 1986, *1979*, pp. 114–51.

Fine, Ben. On Marx's Theory of Agricultural Rent: A Rejoinder. **In** *Fine, B., ed.*, 1986, *1980*, pp. 175–79.

Flaschel, Peter and Semmler, Willi. The Dynamic Equalization of Profit Rates for Input–Output Models with Fixed Capital. **In** *Semmler, W., ed.*, 1986, pp. 1–34.

Gibson, Bill and McLeod, Darryl. Technical Change and the Theory of Rent: Reply [Non-produced Means of Production in Sraffa's System: Basics, Non-basics and Quasi-basics]. *Cambridge J. Econ.*, December 1986, *10*(4), pp. 387–91.

Harcourt, Geoffrey C. The Rate of Profits in Equilibrium Growth Models: A Review Article. **In** *[Harcourt, G. C.]*, 1986, *1973*, pp. 207–28.

von Hayek, Friedrich A. Maintaining Capital Intact: A Reply. **In** *Parker, R. H.; Harcourt, G. C. and Whittington, G., eds.*, 1986, *1941*, pp. 139–43.

Hicks, John R. Maintaining Capital Intact: A Further Suggestion. **In** *Parker, R. H.; Harcourt, G. C. and Whittington, G., eds.*, 1986, *1942*, pp. 144–50.

Horvat, Branko. The Theory of Rent. *Econ. Anal. Workers' Manage.*, 1986, *20*(2), pp. 109–18.

Klein, Benjamin; Crawford, Robert G. and Alchian, Armen A. Vertical Integration, Appropriable Rents, and the Competitive Contracting Process. **In** *Barney, J. B. and Ouchi, W. G., eds.*, 1986, *1978*, pp. 39–71. **[G: U.S.]**

Law, Peter J. The Effect of Regulation on Wages and Intermediate Product Prices under Bilateral Monopoly. *Bull. Econ. Res.*, September 1986, *38*(3), pp. 221–36.

Mott, Tracy. Marx, Keynes, and Schumpeter: A Synthesis with Special Emphasis on the Contributions of Michal Kalecki. **In** *Helburn, S. W. and Bramhall, D. F., eds.*, 1986, pp. 327–35.

Mueller, Dennis C. Information, Mobility and Profit. **In** *Mueller, D. C.*, 1986, *1976*, pp. 15–36.

Ochoa, Eduardo M. Is Reswitching Empirically Relevant? U.S. Wage-Profit–Rate Frontiers, 1947–1972. *Econ. Forum,* Winter 1986-1987, *16*(1), pp. 45–67. **[G: U.S.]**

Pigou, Arthur C. Maintaining Capital Intact. **In** *Parker, R. H.; Harcourt, G. C. and Whittington, G., eds.*, 1986, *1941*, pp. 135–38.

Samuelson, Paul A. Durable Capital Inputs: Conditions for Price Ratios to Be Invariant to Profit-Rate Changes. **In** *Samuelson, P. A.*, 1986, *1983*, pp. 375–94.

Samuelson, Paul A. Pseudo-maximization to the Rescue of Derived Factor Demand of a Competitive Industry. **In** *Samuelson, P. A.*, 1986, *1978*, pp. 101–32.

Sau, Ranjit. Ground Rent and Super Profit in the Sraffa System. *Indian Econ. Rev.*, Jan.-June 1986, *21*(1), pp. 51–60.

Steenge, Albert E. On the Wage–Profit Relation in a Sraffa System with Joint Production. *Revue Écon.*, September 1986, *37*(5), pp. 925–32.

Williamson, Oliver E. Managerial Discretion and Business Behaviour. **In** *Williamson, O. E.*, 1986, *1963*, pp. 6–31.

0225 Theory of Firm and Industry under Competitive Market Structures

Allen, Beth and Hellwig, Martin. Price-Setting Firms and the Oligopolistic Foundations of Perfect Competition. *Amer. Econ. Rev.*, May 1986, *76*(2), pp. 387–92.

Anderson, Richard K. and Enomoto, Carl E. Product Quality and Price Regulation: A General Equilibrium Analysis. *Economica*, February 1986, *53*(209), pp. 87–95.

Baumol, William J. Contestable Markets: An Uprising in the Theory of Industry Structure. **In** *Baumol, W. J.*, 1986, *1982*, pp. 40–54.

Blanchard, Olivier J. and Melino, Angelo. The Cyclical Behavior of Prices and Quantities: The Case of the Automobile Market. *J. Monet. Econ.*, May 1986, *17*(3), pp. 379–407.

Bond, Eric W. The Effect of Used Markets with Endogenous Replacement of Durable Goods. *Southern Econ. J.*, October 1986, *53*(2), pp. 422–31.

Brander, J. R. G. and Cook, B. A. The Market as a Commons: A Further Comment [The Market as an Open Access Commons: A Neglected Aspect of Excess Capacity]. *De Economist*, 1986, *134*(2), pp. 214–24.

Brown, Keith C. In Search of the Winner's Curse: Comment. *Econ. Inquiry*, July 1986, *24*(3), pp. 513–15.

Cox, James C. and Isaac, R. Mark. In Search of the Winner's Curse: Reply. *Econ. Inquiry*, July 1986, *24*(3), pp. 517–20.

Daniel, Coldwell, III. The Process of Adjustment from One Long-run Equilibrium to Another: The Competitive Case. *Scot. J. Polit. Econ.*, August 1986, *33*(3), pp. 284–91.

Fradera, Isabel. Perfect Competition with Product Differentiation. *Int. Econ. Rev.*, October 1986, *27*(3), pp. 529–38.

Gabszewicz, Jean Jaskold and Thisse, Jacques-François. On the Nature of Competition with Differentiated Products. *Econ. J.*, March 1986, *96*(381), pp. 160–72.

Greenhut, Melvin L. On Demand Curves and Spatial Pricing. **In** *Norman, G., ed.*, 1986, pp. 65–76.

Mashiyama, Koichi. The Relationship between Wholesale and Retail Prices and Speculation: The Case of a Middleman Economy. *Econ. Stud. Quart.*, March 1986, *37*(1), pp. 30–43.

Metcalfe, J. S. Technological Innovation and the Competitive Process. **In** *Hall, P., ed.*, 1986, *1984*, pp. 35–64.

Mills, David E. Flexibility and Firm Diversity with Demand Fluctuations. *Int. J. Ind. Organ.*, June 1986, *4*(2), pp. 203–15.

Pithyachariyakul, Pipat. Exchange Markets: A Welfare Comparison of Market Maker and Walrasian Systems. *Quart. J. Econ.*, February 1986, *101*(1), pp. 69–84.

Schweitzer, Arthur. Detrimental Competition. *J. Econ. Issues*, September 1986, *20*(3), pp. 681–707.

Shepherd, William G. On the Core Concepts of Industrial Economics. **In** *de Jong, H. W. and Shepherd, W. G., eds., Bk. 1*, 1986, pp. 23–67. **[G: U.S.]**

Silvestre, Joaquim. The Elements of Fixprice Microeconomics. **In** *Samuelson, L., ed.*, 1986, pp. 195–234.

Stigler, George J. Perfect Competition, Historically Contemplated. **In** *Stigler, G. J.*, 1986, *1983*, pp. 265–88.

Stiglitz, Joseph E. New Developments in the Analysis of Market Structure: Introduction. **In** *Stiglitz, J. E. and Mathewson, G. F., eds.*, 1986, pp. vii–xxiv.

022 Microeconomic Theory

0226 Theory of Firm and Industry under Imperfectly Competitive Market Structures

Abreu, Dilip. Extremal Equilibria of Oligopolistic Supergames. *J. Econ. Theory,* June 1986, *39*(1), pp. 191–225.

Abreu, Dilip; Pearce, David and Stacchetti, Ennio. Optimal Cartel Equilibria with Imperfect Monitoring. *J. Econ. Theory,* June 1986, *39*(1), pp. 251–69.

Admati, Anat R. and Pfleiderer, Paul. A Monopolistic Market for Information. *J. Econ. Theory,* August 1986, *39*(2), pp. 400–438.

Allen, Beth and Hellwig, Martin. Bertrand–Edgeworth Oligopoly in Large Markets. *Rev. Econ. Stud.,* April 1986, *53*(2), pp. 175–204.

Allen, Beth and Hellwig, Martin. Price-Setting Firms and the Oligopolistic Foundations of Perfect Competition. *Amer. Econ. Rev.,* May 1986, *76*(2), pp. 387–92.

Anderson, Ronald W. and Harris, Christopher J. A Model of Innovation with Application to New Financial Products. **In** *Morris, D. J., et al., eds.,* 1986, pp. 203–18.

Anderson, S. P. Equilibrium Existence in the Circle Model of Product Differentiation. **In** *Norman, G., ed.,* 1986, pp. 19–29.

Archibald, G. C.; Eaton, B. C. and Lipsey, Richard G. Address Models of Value Theory. **In** *Stiglitz, J. E. and Mathewson, G. F., eds.,* 1986, pp. 3–47.

Arvan, Lanny. Sunk Capacity Costs, Long-run Fixed Costs, and Entry Deterrence under Complete and Incomplete Information. *Rand J. Econ.,* Spring 1986, *17*(1), pp. 105–21.

d'Aspremont, Claude and Gabszewicz, Jean Jaskold. On the Stability of Collusion. **In** *Stiglitz, J. E. and Mathewson, G. F., eds.,* 1986, pp. 243–61.

Basile, Liliana and Salvadori, Neri. Kalecki's Pricing Theory: A Reply. *J. Post Keynesian Econ.,* Fall 1986, *9*(1), pp. 159–60.

Baumol, William J. Contestable Markets: An Uprising in the Theory of Industry Structure. **In** *Baumol, W. J.,* 1986, *1982,* pp. 40–54.

Baumol, William J. Minimum and Maximum Pricing Principles for Residual Regulation. **In** *Baumol, W. J.,* 1986, *1983,* pp. 151–64.

Baumol, William J. On the Proper Cost Tests for Natural Monopoly in a Multiproduct Industry. **In** *Baumol, W. J.,* 1986, *1977,* pp. 26–39.

Baumol, William J.; Panzar, J. C. and Willig, Robert D. On the Theory of Perfectly-Contestable Markets. **In** *Stiglitz, J. E. and Mathewson, G. F., eds.,* 1986, pp. 339–65.

Baumol, William J. and Willig, Robert D. Contestability: Developments since the Book. *Oxford Econ. Pap.,* Suppl. Nov. 1986, *38,* pp. 9–36. **[G: U.S.]**

Baumol, William J. and Willig, Robert D. Contestability: Developments since the Book. **In** *Morris, D. J., et al., eds.,* 1986, pp. 9–36.

Beckmann, Martin J. Competitive Mill and Uniform Pricing. **In** *Norman, G., ed.,* 1986, pp. 52–64.

Beckmann, Martin J. and Thisse, Jacques-François. The Location of Production Activities. **In** *Nijkamp, P., ed. (I),* 1986, pp. 21–95.

Belloc, Bernard. Quelques aspects normatifs du problème d'akerlof. Un exemple. (Some Normative Aspects of Akerlof's Problem. An Example. With English summary.) *Revue Écon.,* September 1986, *37*(5), pp. 783–803.

Bhattacharya, Sudipto; Chatterjee, Kalyan and Samuelson, Larry. Sequential Research and the Adoption of Innovations. **In** *Morris, D. J., et al., eds.,* 1986, pp. 219–43.

Blazenko, George. The Economics of Reinsurance. *J. Risk Ins.,* June 1986, *53*(2), pp. 258–77.

Bolle, Friedel. On the Oligopolistic Extraction of Non-renewable Common-Pool Resources. *Economica,* November 1986, *53*(212), pp. 519–27.

Bonanno, Giacomo. Advertising, Perceived Quality and Strategic Entry Deterrence and Accommodation. *Metroecon.,* October 1986, *38*(3), pp. 257–80.

Bonanno, Giacomo. Vertical Differentiation with Cournot Competition. *Econ. Notes,* 1986, (2), pp. 68–91.

Boyer, Marcel and Moreaux, Michel. Rationnement, anticipations rationnelles et équilibres de Stackelberg. (Rationing, Rational Expectations and Stackelberg Equilibria. With English summary.) *Ann. Écon. Statist.,* Jan./Mar. 1986, (1), pp. 55–73.

Braid, Ralph M. Stackelberg Price Leadership in Spatial Competition. *Int. J. Ind. Organ.,* December 1986, *4*(4), pp. 439–49.

Brennan, Timothy J. and Kimmel, Sheldon. Joint Production and Monopoly Extension through Tying. *Southern Econ. J.,* October 1986, *53*(2), pp. 490–501. **[G: U.S.]**

Bresnahan, Timothy F. and Salop, Steven C. Quantifying the Competitive Effects of Production Joint Ventures. *Int. J. Ind. Organ.,* June 1986, *4*(2), pp. 155–75. **[G: U.S.]**

Bucovetsky, Sam and Chilton, John. Concurrent Renting and Selling in a Durable-Goods Monopoly under Threat of Entry. *Rand J. Econ.,* Summer 1986, *17*(2), pp. 261–75.

Bulow, Jeremy I. An Economic Theory of Planned Obsolescence. *Quart. J. Econ.,* November 1986, *101*(4), pp. 729–49.

Cantarelli, Davide. Il monopsonio rivisitato. (Monopsony Revisited. With English summary.) *Rivista Int. Sci. Econ. Com.,* March 1986, *33*(3), pp. 221–46.

Caplin, Andrew S. and Nalebuff, Barry J. Multidimensional Product Differentiation and Price Competition. **In** *Morris, D. J., et al., eds.,* 1986, pp. 129–45.

Caplin, Andrew S. and Nalebuff, Barry J. Multidimensional Product Differentiation and Price Competition. *Oxford Econ. Pap.,* Suppl. Nov. 1986, *38,* pp. 129–45.

Capozza, D. R. and Van Order, Robert. Spatial Competition with Cross-Hauling. **In** *Norman, G., ed.,* 1986, pp. 77–84.

Champsaur, Paul and Rochet, Jean-Charles. Concurrence par les prix et variété des produits. (Price Competition and Product Variety.

With English summary.) *Ann. Écon. Statist.*, Jan./Mar. 1986, (1), pp. 153–73.

Chan, Yuk-Shee and Leland, Hayne E. Prices and Qualities: A Search Model. *Southern Econ. J.*, April 1986, *52*(4), pp. 1115–30.

Cherkes, Martin; Friedman, Joseph and Spivak, Avia. The Disinterest in Deregulation: Comment. *Amer. Econ. Rev.*, June 1986, *76*(3), pp. 559–63.

Coate, Malcolm B. An Analysis of Three Approaches to Market Definition. **In** *Zerbe, R. O., Jr., ed.*, 1986, pp. 29–43.

Colander, David C. On the Theory of Incentive Anti-inflation Plans. **In** *Colander, D. C., ed.*, 1986, pp. 129–38.

Cooper, Thomas E. Most-Favored-Customer Pricing and Tacit Collusion. *Rand J. Econ.*, Autumn 1986, *17*(3), pp. 377–88.

Cornes, Richard; Mason, Charles F. and Sandler, Todd. The Commons and the Optimal Number of Firms. *Quart. J. Econ.*, August 1986, *101*(3), pp. 641–46.

Cossutta, Dario and Grillo, Michele. Excess Capacity, Sunk Costs and Collusion: A Non-cooperative Bargaining Game: Some Considerations on the European Car Industry. *Int. J. Ind. Organ.*, September 1986, *4*(3), pp. 251–70. **[G: W. Europe]**

Cowling, Keith and Mueller, Dennis C. The Social Costs of Monopoly Power. **In** *Mueller, D. C.*, 1986, *1978*, pp. 223–47. **[G: U.S.; U.K.]**

Crampes, Claude. Les inconvénients d'un dépôt de brevet pour une entreprise innovatrice. (The Disadvantage of Patenting. With English summary.) *L'Actual. Econ.*, December 1986, *62*(4), pp. 521–34.

Cullis, John G. and Jones, Philip R. Rationing by Waiting Lists: An Implication. *Amer. Econ. Rev.*, March 1986, *76*(1), pp. 250–56. **[G: U.K.]**

Dana, Rose-Anne and Montrucchio, Luigi. Dynamic Complexity in Duopoly Games. *J. Econ. Theory*, October 1986, *40*(1), pp. 40–56.

Das, Satya P. and Niho, Yoshio. A Dynamic Analysis of Protection, Market Structure, and Welfare. *Int. Econ. Rev.*, June 1986, *27*(2), pp. 513–23.

Davidson, Carl and Deneckere, Raymond J. Long-run Competition in Capacity, Short-run Competition in Price, and the Cournot Model. *Rand J. Econ.*, Autumn 1986, *17*(3), pp. 404–15.

Delbono, Flavio. Proprietà dell'equilibrio di Nash in modelli di competizione tecnologica. (Properties of Nash Equilibrium in R&D Models. With English summary.) *Rivista Int. Sci. Econ. Com.*, December 1986, *33*(12), pp. 1167–83.

Demange, Gabrielle. Free Entry and Stability in a Cournot Model. *J. Econ. Theory*, December 1986, *40*(2), pp. 283–303.

Demange, Gabrielle and Ponssard, Jean-Pierre. Barrière de mobilité et concurrence dans un duopole. Essai de formalisation dans le cadre de la théorie des jeux. (Barriers to Mobility and Competition in a Duopoly: An Attempt to Formalize within the Context of Game Theory. With English summary.) *Ann. Écon. Statist.*, Jan./Mar. 1986, (1), pp. 35–53.

DeSerpa, Allan C. A Note on Second Degree Price Discrimination and Its Implications. *Rev. Ind. Organ.*, 1986, *2*(4), pp. 368–75.

DeSerpa, Allan C. Hotelling Models: A General Equilibrium Approach. *Southern Econ. J.*, April 1986, *52*(4), pp. 999–1009.

Dewey, Donald. Antitrust and Its Alternatives: A Compleat Guide to the Welfare Tradeoffs. **In** *Grieson, R. E., ed.*, 1986, pp. 1–27.

Dickson, Vaughan A. Efficiencies, Market Power and Horizontal Merger. *Rev. Ind. Organ.*, 1986, *3*(1), pp. 10–24.

Dickson, Vaughan A. Goals of Oligopolistic Firms: Comment. *Southern Econ. J.*, April 1986, *52*(4), pp. 1151–57. **[G: U.S.]**

Dixit, Avinash K. Comparative Statics for Oligopoly. *Int. Econ. Rev.*, February 1986, *27*(1), pp. 107–22.

Dixit, Avinash K. and Shapiro, Carl. Entry Dynamics with Mixed Strategies. **In** *[Dean, J.]*, 1986, pp. 63–79.

Dixon, Huw. Strategic Investment with Consistent Conjectures. *Oxford Econ. Pap.*, Suppl. Nov. 1986, *38*, pp. 111–28.

Dixon, Huw. Strategic Investment with Consistent Conjectures. **In** *Morris, D. J., et al., eds.*, 1986, pp. 111–28.

Dixon, Huw. The Cournot and Bertrand Outcomes as Equilibria in a Strategic Metagame. *Econ. J.*, Supplement 1986, *96*, pp. 59–70.

Dockner, Engelbert and Feichtinger, Gustav. Dynamic Advertising and Pricing in an Oligopoly: A Nash Equilibrium Approach. *J. Econ. Dynam. Control*, June 1986, *10*(1/2), pp. 37–39.

Dockner, Engelbert and Feichtinger, Gustav. Dynamic Advertising and Pricing in an Oligopoly: A Nash Equilibrium Approach. **In** *Başar, T., ed.*, 1986, pp. 238–51.

Donsimoni, Marie-Paule; Economides, Nicholas S. and Polemarchakis, Herakles M. Stable Cartels. *Int. Econ. Rev.*, June 1986, *27*(2), pp. 317–27.

Dowrick, Steve. von Stackelberg and Cournot Duopoly: Choosing Roles. *Rand J. Econ.*, Summer 1986, *17*(2), pp. 251–60.

Doyle, Chris. Intertemporal Price Discrimination, Uncertainty and Introductory Offers. *Econ. J.*, Supplement 1986, *96*, pp. 71–82.

Dubey, Pradeep and Shubik, Martin. General Equilibrium and the Foundations of the Theory of Monopolistic Competition. *Rivista Int. Sci. Econ. Com.*, March 1986, *33*(3), pp. 207–19.

Eaton, Jonathan and Grossman, Gene M. The Provision of Information as Marketing Strategy. *Oxford Econ. Pap.*, Suppl. Nov. 1986, *38*, pp. 166–83.

Economides, Nicholas S. Nash Equilibrium in Duopoly with Products Defined by Two Characteristics. *Rand J. Econ.*, Autumn 1986, *17*(3), pp. 431–39.

Ekelund, Robert B., Jr. and Saba, Richard P. Establishing Property Rights in Utility Franchises. **In** *Moorhouse, J. C., ed.*, 1986, pp. 425–45.

Encaoua, David; Geroski, Paul A. and Jacquemin, Alexis. Strategic Competition and the Persistence of Dominant Firms: A Survey. **In** *Stiglitz, J. E. and Mathewson, G. F., eds.*, 1986, pp. 55–86.

Encaoua, David; Jacquemin, Alexis and Moreaux, Michel. Global Market Power and Diversification. *Econ. J.*, June 1986, *96*(382), pp. 525–33.

Espitia, Manuel; Salas, Vicente and Vagüe, M. Jesús. Medidas de resultados empresariales: relevancia para los estudios sobre el poder de monopolio. (With English summary.) *Invest. Ecón.*, September 1986, *10*(3), pp. 427–48.

Farrell, Joseph. Moral Hazard as an Entry Barrier. *Rand J. Econ.*, Autumn 1986, *17*(3), pp. 440–49.

Farrell, Joseph and Saloner, Garth. Installed Base and Compatibility: Innovation, Product Preannouncements, and Predation. *Amer. Econ. Rev.*, December 1986, *76*(5), pp. 940–55.

Fehl, Ulrich. Wettbewerbliche Dimensionen des Oligopolmarktes. (Competitive Dimensions of the Oligopoly Market. With English summary.) **In** *Eucken, W. and Böhm, F., eds.*, 1986, pp. 141–53.

Felder, Joseph. Protectionism, Domestic Monopoly, and the Levels of Domestic Production and Consumption. *Quart. J. Bus. Econ.*, Autumn 1986, *25*(4), pp. 77–100. **[G: LDCs]**

Fershtman, Chaim and Muller, Eitan. Capital Investments and Price Agreements in Semicollusive Markets. *Rand J. Econ.*, Summer 1986, *17*(2), pp. 214–26.

Fishelson, Gideon. On the Behavior of a Noncompetitive Firm when the Supplies of Inputs Are Random. *J. Econ. Bus.*, December 1986, *38*(4), pp. 331–39.

Frantz, Roger S. X-Efficiency in Behavioral Economics. **In** *Gilad, B. and Kaish, S., eds., Vol. A*, 1986, pp. 307–23.

Fraysśe, Jean. Existence des équilibres de Cournot: un tour d'horizon. (Existence of a Cournot Equilibrium: A Survey. With English summary.) *Ann. Écon. Statist.*, Jan./Mar. 1986, (1), pp. 9–33.

French, George. Price Smoothing and Inventory Behavior. *J. Econ. Dynam. Control*, September 1986, *10*(3), pp. 353–66.

Fudenberg, Drew and Tirole, Jean. A "Signal-Jamming" Theory of Predation. *Rand J. Econ.*, Autumn 1986, *17*(3), pp. 366–76.

Fudenberg, Drew and Tirole, Jean. A Theory of Exit in Duopoly. *Econometrica*, July 1986, *54*(4), pp. 943–60.

Fujita, Masahisa and Thisse, Jacques-François. Spatial Competition with a Land Market: Hotelling and Von Thunen Unified. *Rev. Econ. Stud.*, October 1986, *53*(5), pp. 819–41.

Furth, Dave. Stability and Instability of Oligopoly. *J. Econ. Theory*, December 1986, *40*(2), pp. 197–228.

Gabszewicz, Jean Jaskold, et al. Segmenting the Market: The Monopolist's Optimal Product Mix. *J. Econ. Theory*, August 1986, *39*(2), pp. 273–89.

Gabszewicz, Jean Jaskold and Garella, Paolo. 'Subjective' Price Search and Price Competition. *Int. J. Ind. Organ.*, September 1986, *4*(3), pp. 305–16.

Gabszewicz, Jean Jaskold and Thisse, Jacques-François. On the Nature of Competition with Differentiated Products. *Econ. J.*, March 1986, *96*(381), pp. 160–72.

Gal-Or, Esther. Information Transmission—Cournot and Bertrand Equilibria. *Rev. Econ. Stud.*, January 1986, *53*(1), pp. 85–92.

Gee, J. M. A. and Jarvis, R. J. Costs and Social Welfare in the Theory of the Spatial Firm and Industry. **In** *Norman, G., ed.*, 1986, pp. 85–102.

Gerstner, Eitan. Peak Load Pricing in Competitive Markets. *Econ. Inquiry*, April 1986, *24*(2), pp. 349–61.

Ghemawat, Pankaj and Caves, Richard E. Capital Commitment and Profitability: An Empirical Investigation. **In** *Morris, D. J., et al., eds.*, 1986, pp. 94–110.

Gilbert, Richard J. Pre-emptive Competition. **In** *Stiglitz, J. E. and Mathewson, G. F., eds.*, 1986, pp. 90–123.

Gilbert, Richard J. and Vives, Xavier. Entry Deterrence and the Free Rider Problem. *Rev. Econ. Stud.*, January 1986, *53*(1), pp. 71–83.

Goering, Patricia A. Learning, Quality and Prices. *Info. Econ. Policy*, 1986, *2*(1), pp. 23–47.

Gottfries, Nils. Price Dynamics of Exporting and Import-Competing Firms. *Scand. J. Econ.*, 1986, *88*(2), pp. 417–36.

Gould, John P. Is the Rational Expectations Hypothesis Enough? **In** *Hogarth, R. M. and Reder, M. W., eds.*, 1986, pp. 187–93.

Gould, John P. Is the Rational Expectations Hypothesis Enough? *J. Bus.*, Part 2, October 1986, *59*(4), pp. S371–77.

Green, Jerry R. Vertical Integration and Assurance of Markets. **In** *Stiglitz, J. E. and Mathewson, G. F., eds.*, 1986, pp. 177–207.

Greenberg, Joseph and Shitovitz, Benyamin. A Simple Proof of the Equivalence Theorem for Oligopolistic Mixed Markets. *J. Math. Econ.*, 1986, *15*(2), pp. 79–83.

Greenhut, Melvin L. On Demand Curves and Spatial Pricing. **In** *Norman, G., ed.*, 1986, pp. 65–76.

Greenhut, Melvin L.; Mai, Chao-cheng and Norman, George. Impacts on Optimum Location of Different Pricing Strategies, Market Structures and Customer Distributions over Space. *Reg. Sci. Urban Econ.*, August 1986, *16*(3), pp. 329–51.

Grieson, Ronald E. and Singh, Nirvikar. Resale Price Maintenance: A Simple Analysis. **In** *Grieson, R. E., ed.*, 1986, pp. 127–33.

Grossman, Sanford J. and Hart, Oliver D. The Costs and Benefits of Ownership: A Theory of Vertical and Lateral Integration. *J. Polit. Econ.*, August 1986, *94*(4), pp. 691–719.

Gul, Faruk; Sonnenschein, Hugo and Wilson, Robert B. Foundations of Dynamic Monopoly and the Coase Conjecture. *J. Econ. Theory*, June 1986, *39*(1), pp. 155–90.

Hamilton, James L. and Lee, Soo Bock. The Paradox of Vertical Integration. *Southern Econ. J.*, July 1986, *53*(1), pp. 110–26.

Hansen, Robert G. A Model of Intra-brand Competition and Related Pricing Policies for Manufacturers. *Info. Econ. Policy*, June 1986, *2*(2), pp. 119–35.

Harrigan, Kathryn Rudie. Strategic Flexibility. **In** *[Dean, J.]*, 1986, pp. 81–111. **[G: U.S.]**

Harrington, Joseph E., Jr. Limit Pricing When the Potential Entrant Is Uncertain of Its Cost Function [Limit Pricing and Entry under Incomplete Information: An Equilibrium Analysis]. *Econometrica*, March 1986, *54*(2), pp. 429–37.

Hart, Oliver D. and Kreps, David M. Price Destabilizing Speculation. *J. Polit. Econ.*, October 1986, *94*(5), pp. 927–52.

Helmedag, Fritz. Long-run and Short-run Demand Response, Discount Rate, and Pricing. *Z. Wirtschaft. Sozialwissen.*, 1986, *106*(3), pp. 275–86.

Henderson, John S. and Henderson, Richard H. Perversity in Factor Demand Curves—Simulation and Theory. *Economica*, November 1986, *53*(212), pp. 515–18.

Hobbs, Benjamin F. Mill Pricing versus Spatial Price Discrimination under Bertrand and Cournot Spatial Competition. *J. Ind. Econ.*, December 1986, *35*(2), pp. 173–91.

Holt, Charles A. and Villamil, Anne P. A Laboratory Experiment with a Single-Person Cobweb. *Atlantic Econ. J.*, July 1986, *14*(2), pp. 51–54.

Hung, Chao-Shun. The Effects of Entry on Spatial Pricing and Their Implications in Industrial Economics. *Atlantic Econ. J.*, September 1986, *14*(3), pp. 18–23.

Hüpen, Rolf. Zur Theorie der Preisbildung beim Monopson. (On the Theory of Monopsony Pricing. With English summary.) *Jahr. Nationalökon. Statist.*, May 1986, *201*(3), pp. 257–63.

Ikeda, Takanobu. Does Quantity-Constrained Behavior Make the Conjecture Function Kinked? *Keio Econ. Stud.*, 1986, *23*(2), pp. 37–56.

Imai, Haruo. Bilateral Price-Setting in a Bilateral Monopoly Model. *Math. Soc. Sci.*, December 1986, *12*(3), pp. 279–301.

Jørgensen, Steffen. Optimal Dynamic Pricing in an Oligopolistic Market: A Survey. **In** *Başar, T., ed.*, 1986, pp. 179–237.

Judd, Kenneth L. and Petersen, Bruce C. Dynamic Limit Pricing and Internal Finance. *J. Econ. Theory*, August 1986, *39*(2), pp. 368–99.

Justman, Moshe. Intertemporal Dependence of Demand in an Imperfectly Competitive Market: A Differential Game Analysis. *Int. J. Ind. Organ.*, September 1986, *4*(3), pp. 271–86.

Kahn, Charles M. The Durable Goods Monopolist and Consistency with Increasing Costs. *Econometrica*, March 1986, *54*(2), pp. 275–94.

Kamien, Morton I. and Tauman, Yair. Fees versus Royalties and the Private Value of a Patent. *Quart. J. Econ.*, August 1986, *101*(3), pp. 471–91.

Kaminsky, Graciela Laura. Uncertainty, Expectations of Devaluation, and the Real Exchange Rate. *J. Devel. Econ.*, November 1986, *24*(1), pp. 29–57. **[G: Argentina]**

Katz, Michael L. and Shapiro, Carl. Product Compatibility Choice in a Market with Technological Progress. **In** *Morris, D. J., et al., eds.*, 1986, pp. 146–65.

Kirman, William I. and Masson, Robert T. Capacity Signals and Entry Deterrence. *Int. J. Ind. Organ.*, March 1986, *4*(1), pp. 25–42.

Klein, Benjamin; Crawford, Robert G. and Alchian, Armen A. Vertical Integration, Appropriable Rents, and the Competitive Contracting Process. **In** *Barney, J. B. and Ouchi, W. G., eds.*, 1986, *1978*, pp. 39–71. **[G: U.S.]**

Kolstad, Charles D. and Wolak, Frank A. Conjectural Variation and the Indeterminacy of Duopolistic Equilibria. *Can. J. Econ.*, November 1986, *19*(4), pp. 656–77. **[G: U.S.]**

Koutsoyiannis, A. Goals of Oligopolistic Firms: Reply. *Southern Econ. J.*, April 1986, *52*(4), pp. 1158–61. **[G: U.S.]**

Kubo, Yuji. Quality Uncertainty and Guarantee: A Case of Strategic Market Segmentation by a Monopolist. *Europ. Econ. Rev.*, October 1986, *30*(5), pp. 1063–79.

La Manna, Manfredi M. A. Workable Competition Deadweight Losses, and Demand Elasticities: Comment. *Manchester Sch. Econ. Soc. Stud.*, March 1986, *54*(1), pp. 99–103.

Lederer, Phillip J. and Hurter, Arthur P., Jr. Competition of Firms: Discriminatory Pricing and Location. *Econometrica*, May 1986, *54*(3), pp. 623–40.

Lee, Fred S. Reply: [Kalecki's Pricing Theory: Two Comments]. *J. Post Keynesian Econ.*, Fall 1986, *9*(1), pp. 161–62.

Lee, Fred S., et al. P. W. S. Andrews' Theory of Competitive Oligopoly: A New Interpretation. *Brit. Rev. Econ. Issues*, Autumn 1986, *8*(19), pp. 13–39.

Lewis, Tracy R.; Linsey, Robin and Ware, Roger. Long-term Bilateral Monopoly: The Case of an Exhaustible Resource. *Rand J. Econ.*, Spring 1986, *17*(1), pp. 89–104.

Löfgren, Karl Gustaf. The Spatial Monopsony: A Theoretical Analysis. *J. Reg. Sci.*, November 1986, *26*(4), pp. 707–30.

Loury, Glenn C. A Theory of 'Oil'igopoly: Cournot Equilibrium in Exhaustible Resource Markets with Fixed Supplies. *Int. Econ. Rev.*, June 1986, *27*(2), pp. 285–301.

Loury, Glenn C. and Lewis, Tracy R. On the Profitability of Interruptible Supply. *Amer. Econ. Rev.*, September 1986, *76*(4), pp. 827–32.

Lyons, Bruce R. The Welfare Loss Due to Strategic Investment in Excess Capacity. *Int. J. Ind. Organ.*, March 1986, *4*(1), pp. 109–19.

Magill, Michael J. P. and Nermuth, Manfred. On the Qualitative Properties of Futures Market Equilibrium. *J. Econ. (Z. Nationalökon.)*, 1986, *46*(3), pp. 233–52.

Mankiw, N. Gregory and Whinston, Michael D. Free Entry and Social Inefficiency. *Rand J. Econ.*, Spring 1986, *17*(1), pp. 48–58.

Mantakas, George. Duopolistic Conduct under Demand Uncertainty with Irreversible Capital Commitments. *Greek Econ. Rev.*, June 1986, *8*(1), pp. 21–40.

Markovits, Richard S. Monopolistic Competition and Second Best: Some New Conceptual Schemes. **In** *[Yamey, B.]*, 1986, pp. 181–98.

Martin, Robert E. Externality Regulation and the Monopoly Firm. *J. Public Econ.*, April 1986, *29*(3), pp. 347–62.

Martin, Robert E. Quality Choice under Labor-Management. *J. Compar. Econ.*, December 1986, *10*(4), pp. 400–413.

Mashiyama, Koichi. The Relationship between Wholesale and Retail Prices and Speculation: The Case of a Middleman Economy. *Econ. Stud. Quart.*, March 1986, *37*(1), pp. 30–43.

Maskin, Eric. The Existence of Equilibrium with Price-Setting Firms. *Amer. Econ. Rev.*, May 1986, *76*(2), pp. 382–86.

Mathewson, G. Frank and Winter, Ralph A. The Economics of Vertical Restraints in Distribution. **In** *Stiglitz, J. E. and Mathewson, G. F., eds.*, 1986, pp. 211–36.

McCormick, Robert E.; Shughart, William F., II and Tollison, Robert D. The Disinterest in Deregulation: Reply. *Amer. Econ. Rev.*, June 1986, *76*(3), pp. 564–65.

de Meza, David. Immiserising Invention: The Private and Social Returns to R&D under Oligopoly. *Int. J. Ind. Organ.*, December 1986, *4*(4), pp. 409–17.

Mirman, Leonard J.; Tauman, Yair and Zang, Israel. Ramsey Prices, Average Cost Prices and Price Sustainability. *Int. J. Ind. Organ.*, June 1986, *4*(2), pp. 123–40.

Mixon, J. Wilson, Jr. and Uri, Noel D. On the Optimal Pricing Policy of a Dominant Firm. *De Economist*, 1986, *134*(2), pp. 225–27.

Moore, Giora. Spatial Monopolistic Competition versus Spatial Monopoly: A Comment. *J. Econ. Theory*, February 1986, *38*(1), pp. 185.

Morris, Derek J., et al. Strategic Behaviour and Industrial Competition: An Introduction. **In** *Morris, D. J., et al., eds.*, 1986, pp. 1–8.

Morris, Derek J., et al. Strategic Behaviour and Industrial Competition: An Introduction. *Oxford Econ. Pap.*, Suppl. Nov. 1986, *38*, pp. 1–8.

Nakagome, Masaki. A Note on the Stability Property of Spatial Competition. *J. Reg. Sci.*, August 1986, *26*(3), pp. 605–11.

Neven, D. 'Address' Models of Differentiation. **In** *Norman, G., ed.*, 1986, pp. 5–18.

Nishimura, Kiyohiko G. Rational Expectations and Price Rigidity in a Monopolistically Competitive Market. *Rev. Econ. Stud.*, April 1986, *53*(2), pp. 283–92.

Norman, George. Market Strategy with Variable Entry Threats. **In** *Norman, G., ed.*, 1986, pp. 103–24.

Ofek, Hiam and Paroush, Jacob. Endogeneous Risk in Oligopolistic Competition and Quasi-Competitiveness in Cournot Markets. *Atlantic Econ. J.*, July 1986, *14*(2), pp. 1–8.

Okuguchi, Koji. Labor-Managed Bertrand and Cournot Oligopolies. *J. Econ. (Z. Nationalökon.)*, 1986, *46*(2), pp. 115–22.

Opp, Karl-Dieter. The Evolution of a Prisoner's Dilemma in the Market. **In** *[Rapoport, A.]*, 1986, pp. 149–67. **[G: W. Germany]**

Osborne, Martin J. and Pitchik, Carolyn. Price Competition in a Capacity-Constrained Duopoly. *J. Econ. Theory*, April 1986, *38*(2), pp. 238–60.

Osborne, Martin J. and Pitchik, Carolyn. The Nature of Equilibrium in a Location Model. *Int. Econ. Rev.*, February 1986, *27*(1), pp. 223–37.

de Palma, André; Labbé, M. and Thisse, Jacques-François. On the Existence of Price Equilibria under Mill and Uniform Delivered Price Policies. **In** *Norman, G., ed.*, 1986, pp. 30–42.

Paredes M., Ricardo. "Una revisión crítica a la literatura de colusión." (With English summary.) *Cuadernos Econ.*, August 1986, *23*(69), pp. 173–99.

Pasour, E. C., Jr. Monopoly Power, Taxation, and Entrepreneurship. **In** *Lee, D. R., ed.*, 1986, pp. 381–405.

Perloff, Jeffrey M. and Salop, Steven C. Firm-Specific Information, Product Differentiation, and Industry Equilibrium. **In** *Morris, D. J., et al., eds.*, 1986, pp. 184–202.

Perloff, Jeffrey M. and Salop, Steven C. Firm-Specific Information, Product Differentiation, and Industry Equilibrium. *Oxford Econ. Pap.*, Suppl. Nov. 1986, *38*, pp. 184–202.

Perrakis, Stylianos and Warskett, George. Uncertainty, Economies of Scale, and Barrier to Entry. *Oxford Econ. Pap.*, Suppl. Nov. 1986, *38*, pp. 58–74.

Perrakis, Stylianos and Warskett, George. Uncertainty, Economies of Scale, and Barrier to Entry. **In** *Morris, D. J., et al., eds.*, 1986, pp. 58–74.

Perry, Martin K. and Groff, Robert H. Trademark Licensing in a Monopolistically Competitive Industry. *Rand J. Econ.*, Summer 1986, *17*(2), pp. 189–200.

Perry, Motty and Wigderson, Avi. Search in a Known Pattern. *J. Polit. Econ.*, February 1986, *94*(1), pp. 225–30.

Pithyachariyakul, Pipat. Exchange Markets: A Welfare Comparison of Market Maker and Walrasian Systems. *Quart. J. Econ.*, February 1986, *101*(1), pp. 69–84.

van der Ploeg, Frederick. Inefficiency of Oligopolistic Resource Markets with ISO-Elastic Demand, Zero Extraction Costs and Stochastic Renewal. *J. Econ. Dynam. Control*, June 1986, *10*(1/2), pp. 309–14.

Polo, Michele. Recenti sviluppi nell'analisi della differenziazione del prodotto. (Recent Developments in the Analysis of Product Differentiation. With English summary.) *Giorn. Econ.*,

Mar.-Apr. 1986, *45*(3–4), pp. 171–200.

Porter, Robert H. A Note on Tacit Collusion under Demand Uncertainty. *Can. J. Econ.*, August 1986, *19*(3), pp. 556–58.

Quirmbach, Herman C. The Path of Price Changes in Vertical Integration. *J. Polit. Econ.*, October 1986, *94*(5), pp. 1110–19.

Quirmbach, Herman C. Vertical Integration: Scale Distortions, Partial Integration, and the Direction of Price Change. *Quart. J. Econ.*, February 1986, *101*(1), pp. 131–47.

Rampa, Lorenzo. Commercio e inflazione. Un'analisi dinamica dei prezzi in sistemi con intermediazione dei prodotti. (Commerce and Inflation. A Dynamic Analysis of Prices in Systems with Commercial Firms. With English summary.) *Ricerche Econ.*, Apr.-Sept. 1986, *40*(2–3), pp. 303–16.

Rao, T. V. S. Ramomahan. Welfare Economics of Organizational Decisions and Its Implications for Industrial Economics. *Indian Econ. J.*, Oct.-Dec. 1986, *34*(2), pp. 87–105.

Reagan, Patricia B. Resale Price Maintenance: A Re-examination of the Outlets Hypothesis. **In** *Zerbe, R. O., Jr., ed.*, 1986, pp. 1–12.

Reati, Angelo. The Deviation of Prices from Labour Values: An Extension to the Non-competitive Case. *Cambridge J. Econ.*, March 1986, *10*(1), pp. 35–42.

Reiber, William J. Trade Liberalization and Monopoly. *Indian Econ. J.*, Jan.-Mar. 1986, *33*(3), pp. 15–22.

Rey, Patrick and Tirole, Jean. The Logic of Vertical Restraints. *Amer. Econ. Rev.*, December 1986, *76*(5), pp. 921–39.

Rey, Patrick and Tirole, Jean. Vertical Restraints from a Principal–Agent Viewpoint. **In** *Pellegrini, L. and Reddy, S. K., eds.*, 1986, pp. 1–30.

Reynolds, Robert J. and Snapp, Bruce R. The Competitive Effects of Partial Equity Interests and Joint Ventures. *Int. J. Ind. Organ.*, June 1986, *4*(2), pp. 141–53.

Riordan, Michael H. A Note on Optimal Procurement Contracts. *Info. Econ. Policy*, September 1986, *2*(3), pp. 211–19.

Riordan, Michael H. Monopolistic Competition with Experience Goods. *Quart. J. Econ.*, May 1986, *101*(2), pp. 265–79.

Roberts, John. A Signaling Model of Predatory Pricing. **In** *Morris, D. J., et al., eds.*, 1986, pp. 75–93.

Roberts, John. A Signaling Model of Predatory Pricing. *Oxford Econ. Pap.*, Suppl. Nov. 1986, *38*, pp. 75–93.

Robson, Arthur J. The Existence of Nash Equilibria in Reaction Functions for Dynamic Models of Oligopoly. *Int. Econ. Rev.*, October 1986, *27*(3), pp. 539–44.

Rosenthal, Robert W. Dynamic Duopoly with Incomplete Customer Loyalties. *Int. Econ. Rev.*, June 1986, *27*(2), pp. 399–406.

Ross, David R. Learning to Dominate. *J. Ind. Econ.*, June 1986, *34*(4), pp. 337–53.

Ross, Thomas W. The Costs of Regulating Price Differences. *J. Bus.*, January 1986, *59*(1), pp. 143–56.

Rotemberg, Julio J. and Saloner, Garth. A Supergame-Theoretic Model of Price Wars during Booms. *Amer. Econ. Rev.*, June 1986, *76*(3), pp. 390–407. **[G: U.S.]**

Rothschild, R. The Stability of Cartels in Spatial Markets. **In** *Norman, G., ed.*, 1986, pp. 43–51.

Russell, Allen M.; Rickard, John A. and Howroyd, T. D. The Effects of Delays on the Stability and Rate of Convergence to Equilibrium of Oligopolies. *Econ. Rec.*, June 1986, *62*(177), pp. 194–98.

Rust, John. When Is It Optimal to Kill Off the Market for Used Durable Goods? *Econometrica*, January 1986, *54*(1), pp. 65–86.

Sakai, Yasuhiro. Cournot and Bertrand Equilibria under Imperfect Information. *J. Econ. (Z. Nationalökon.)*, 1986, *46*(3), pp. 213–32.

Salant, David J. Equilibrium in a Spatial Model of Imperfect Competition with Sequential Choice of Locations and Quantities. *Can. J. Econ.*, November 1986, *19*(4), pp. 685–715.

Saloner, Garth. The Role of Obsolescence and Inventory Costs in Providing Commitment. *Int. J. Ind. Organ.*, September 1986, *4*(3), pp. 333–45.

Salop, Steven C. Practices that (Credibly) Facilitate Oligopoly Co-ordination. **In** *Stiglitz, J. E. and Mathewson, G. F., eds.*, 1986, pp. 265–90.

Schwartz, Marius. The Nature and Scope of Contestability Theory. *Oxford Econ. Pap.*, Suppl. Nov. 1986, *38*, pp. 37–57.

Schwartz, Marius. The Nature and Scope of Contestability Theory. **In** *Morris, D. J., et al., eds.*, 1986, pp. 37–57.

Schwartz, Marius and Thompson, Earl A. Divisionalization and Entry Deterrence. *Quart. J. Econ.*, May 1986, *101*(2), pp. 307–21.

Schweitzer, Arthur. Detrimental Competition. *J. Econ. Issues*, September 1986, *20*(3), pp. 681–707.

Scitovsky, Tibor. Price Takers' Plenty: A Neglected Benefit of Monopoly Capitalism. **In** *Scitovsky, T.*, 1986, pp. 97–113.

Selten, Reinhard. Elementary Theory of Slack-Ridden Imperfect Competition. **In** *Stiglitz, J. E. and Mathewson, G. F., eds.*, 1986, pp. 126–44.

Sengupta, Jati K. Optimal Monopolistic Strategy under Demand Uncertainty. *J. Econ. (Z. Nationalökon.)*, 1986, *46*(2), pp. 101–13.

Shaffer, Sherrill. A Reverse Structural Test for the Degree of Monopoly Power. *Atlantic Econ. J.*, March 1986, *14*(1), pp. 124.

Shapiro, Carl. Exchange of Cost Information in Oligopoly. *Rev. Econ. Stud.*, July 1986, *53*(3), pp. 433–46.

Shepherd, William G. On the Core Concepts of Industrial Economics. **In** *de Jong, H. W. and Shepherd, W. G., eds., Bk. 1*, 1986, pp. 23–67. **[G: U.S.]**

Shupp, Franklin R. Limit Pricing in a Mature Market: A Dynamic Game Approach. *J. Econ.*

Dynam. Control, June 1986, *10*(1/2), pp. 67–71.

Silvestre, Joaquim. The Elements of Fixprice Microeconomics. **In** *Samuelson, L., ed.*, 1986, pp. 195–234.

Simpson, Paul and Waterson, Michael. Cartel Problems: The Incentive to Lie about Costs. *Bull. Econ. Res.*, September 1986, *38*(3), pp. 209–19.

Singh, Nirvikar. Equilibrium Price Dispersion with Sequential Search. *J. Quant. Econ.*, July 1986, *2*(2), pp. 163–71.

Siroën, Jean-Marc. Discrimination des prix différenciation des produits et échange international. (Price Discrimination, Product Differentiation and International Trade. With English summary.) *Revue Écon.*, May 1986, *37*(3), pp. 489–520.

Skinner, Andrew S. Edward Chamberlin: The Theory of Monopolistic Competition: A Re-orientation of the Theory of Value. *J. Econ. Stud.*, 1986, *13*(5), pp. 27–44.

Slade, Margaret E. Static Profitability as a Measure of Deviations from the Competitive Norm. *Managerial Dec. Econ.*, June 1986, *7*(2), pp. 113–18.

Sleuwaegen, Leo E. On the Nature and Significance of Collusive Price Leadership. *Int. J. Ind. Organ.*, June 1986, *4*(2), pp. 177–88.

Smith, W. James and Vaughan, Michael B. Economic Welfare, Price and Profit: The Deterrent Effect of Alternative Antitrust Regimes. *Econ. Inquiry*, October 1986, *24*(4), pp. 615–29.

Soldatos, Gerasimos T. On the Stability of Temporal Collusions. *Indian Econ. J.*, Oct.-Dec. 1986, *34*(2), pp. 65–70.

Solow, Robert M. Monopolistic Competition and the Multiplier. **In** *[Arrow, K. J.], Vol. 2*, 1986, pp. 301–15.

Spence, Michael. Cost Reduction, Competition and Industry Performance. **In** *Stiglitz, J. E. and Mathewson, G. F., eds.*, 1986, pp. 475–515.

Spulber, Daniel F. Second-Best Pricing and Cooperation. *Rand J. Econ.*, Summer 1986, *17*(2), pp. 239–50.

Stanford, William G. On Continuous Reaction Function Equilibria in Duopoly Supergames with Mean Payoffs. *J. Econ. Theory*, June 1986, *39*(1), pp. 233–50.

Stanford, William G. Subgame Perfect Reaction Function Equilibria in Discounted Duopoly Supergames Are Trivial. *J. Econ. Theory*, June 1986, *39*(1), pp. 226–32.

Steele, G. R. A Note on Labour Market Monopsony. *Indian Econ. J.*, Oct.-Dec. 1986, *34*(2), pp. 59–64.

Stigler, George J. A Theory of Oligopoly. **In** *Stigler, G. J.*, 1986, *1964*, pp. 153–78.

Stiglitz, Joseph E. New Developments in the Analysis of Market Structure: Introduction. **In** *Stiglitz, J. E. and Mathewson, G. F., eds.*, 1986, pp. vii–xxiv.

Stiglitz, Joseph E. Theory of Competition, Incentives and Risk. **In** *Stiglitz, J. E. and Mathewson, G. F., eds.*, 1986, pp. 399–446.

Suslow, Valerie Y. Commitment and Monopoly Pricing in Durable Goods Models. *Int. J. Ind. Organ.*, December 1986, *4*(4), pp. 451–60.

Sutton, John. Vertical Product Differentiation: Some Basic Themes. *Amer. Econ. Rev.*, May 1986, *76*(2), pp. 393–98.

Tilton, John E. and Mueller, Dennis C. Research and Development Costs as a Barrier to Entry. **In** *Mueller, D. C.*, 1986, *1969*, pp. 108–18.

Vaughan, Michael B. and Thomas, Wade L. Teaching the Theory of Monopolistic Competition: An Analytical Approach. *Atlantic Econ. J.*, July 1986, *14*(2), pp. 80.

Vislie, Jon. Joint Production and Market Structure: The Case of Oil and Natural Gas. *J. Econ. (Z. Nationalökon.)*, 1986, *46*(2), pp. 163–73.

Vives, Xavier. Commitment, Flexibility and Market Outcomes. *Int. J. Ind. Organ.*, June 1986, *4*(2), pp. 217–29.

Wan, Yieh-Hei. The Cournot Problem with Bounded Memory Strategies. **In** *Sonnenschein, H. F., ed.*, 1986, pp. 139–47.

Ware, Roger. A Model of Public Enterprise with Entry. *Can. J. Econ.*, November 1986, *19*(4), pp. 642–55.

Ware, Roger and Winter, Ralph A. Public Pricing under Imperfect Competition. *Int. J. Ind. Organ.*, March 1986, *4*(1), pp. 87–97.

Weiss, Nitzan and Lee, Phil. Sustainability of the Multiproduct Monopoly and Ramsey-Optimal Pricing. *J. Inst. Theoretical Econ.*, September 1986, *142*(3), pp. 473–92.

Werden, Gregory J. and Baumann, Michael G. A Simple Model of Imperfect Competition in Which Four Are Few but Three Are Not. *J. Ind. Econ.*, March 1986, *34*(3), pp. 331–35.

Wernerfelt, Birger. Product Line Rivalry: Note. *Amer. Econ. Rev.*, September 1986, *76*(4), pp. 842–44.

Westfield, Fred M. Vertical Industry Structure: An Analytical Scheme. **In** *Grieson, R. E., ed.*, 1986, pp. 253–66.

Williamson, Oliver E. The Economics of Antitrust: Transaction Cost Considerations. **In** *Williamson, O. E.*, 1986, pp. 197–249.

Williamson, Oliver E. The Vertical Integration of Production: Market Failure Considerations. **In** *Williamson, O. E.*, 1986, *1971*, pp. 85–100.

Williamson, Oliver E. Transaction-Cost Economics: The Governance of Contractual Relations. **In** *Williamson, O. E.*, 1986, *1979*, pp. 101–30.

Williamson, Oliver E. Vertical Integration and Related Variations on a Transaction-Cost Economics Theme. **In** *Stiglitz, J. E. and Mathewson, G. F., eds.*, 1986, pp. 149–74.

Williamson, Oliver E. What Is Transaction Cost Economics? **In** *Williamson, O. E.*, 1986, pp. 174–91.

Wolinsky, Asher. True Monopolistic Competition as a Result of Imperfect Information. *Quart. J. Econ.*, August 1986, *101*(3), pp. 493–511.

Zabel, Edward. Price Smoothing and Equilibrium in a Monopolistic Market. *Int. Econ. Rev.*, June 1986, *27*(2), pp. 349–63.

0227 Theory of Auction Markets

Bernheim, B. Douglas and Whinston, Michael D. Menu Auctions, Resource Allocation, and Economic Influence. *Quart. J. Econ.*, February 1986, *101*(1), pp. 1–31.

Brown, Keith C. In Search of the Winner's Curse: Comment. *Econ. Inquiry*, July 1986, *24*(3), pp. 513–15.

Chen, Yu-Min. An Extension to the Implementability of Reduced Form Auctions. *Econometrica*, September 1986, *54*(5), pp. 1249–51.

Cox, James C. and Isaac, R. Mark. In Search of the Winner's Curse: Reply. *Econ. Inquiry*, July 1986, *24*(3), pp. 517–20.

Davis, Douglas D. and Williams, Arlington W. The Effects of Rent Asymmetries in Posted Offer Markets. *J. Econ. Behav. Organ.*, September 1986, *7*(3), pp. 303–16.

Demange, Gabrielle; Gale, David and Sotomayor, Marilda. Multi-Item Auctions. *J. Polit. Econ.*, August 1986, *94*(4), pp. 863–72.

Güth, Werner and van Damme, Eric E. C. A Comparison of Pricing Rules for Auctions and Fair Division Games. *Soc. Choice Welfare*, 1986, *3*(3), pp. 177–98.

Hansen, Robert G. Sealed-Bid versus Open Auctions: The Evidence. *Econ. Inquiry*, January 1986, *24*(1), pp. 125–42. **[G: U.S.]**

Hoffman, Elizabeth and Marsden, James R. Testing Informational Assumptions in Common Value Bidding Models. *Scand. J. Econ.*, 1986, *88*(4), pp. 627–41. **[G: U.S.]**

Holt, Charles A.; Langan, Loren W. and Villamil, Anne P. Market Power in Oral Double Auctions. *Econ. Inquiry*, January 1986, *24*(1), pp. 107–23.

Kagel, John H. and Levin, Dan. The Winner's Curse and Public Information in Common Value Auctions. *Amer. Econ. Rev.*, December 1986, *76*(5), pp. 894–920. **[G: U.S.]**

Luton, Richard A. and McAfee, R. Preston. Sequential Procurement Auctions. *J. Public Econ.*, November 1986, *31*(2), pp. 181–95.

Lyon, Randolph M. Equilibrium Properties of Auctions and Alternative Procedures for Allocating Transferable Permits. *J. Environ. Econ. Manage.*, June 1986, *13*(2), pp. 129–52.

Naegelen, Florence. La malédiction du vainqueur dans les procédures d'appel d'offres. (The Winner's Curse in Auctions. With English summary.) *Revue Écon.*, July 1986, *37*(4), pp. 605–36.

Webb, L. Roy and de Jong, Piet. Competitive Bidding and the Price Mechanism. **In** *[Yamey, B.]*, 1986, pp. 109–29.

Wu, C. L. Government Land Sales in Hong Kong: Auctions and a Proposed Alternative. *Hong Kong Econ. Pap.*, 1986, (17), pp. 51–63. **[G: Hong Kong]**

0228 Agent Theory

Bernheim, B. Douglas and Whinston, Michael D. Common Agency. *Econometrica*, July 1986, *54*(4), pp. 923–42.

Bulmash, Samuel. An Agency Perspective of the Firm's Life-cycle. *Managerial Dec. Econ.*, June 1986, *7*(2), pp. 107–11.

Darrough, Masako N. and Stoughton, Neal M. Moral Hazard and Adverse Selection: The Question of Financial Structure. *J. Finance*, June 1986, *41*(2), pp. 501–13.

Demski, Joel S. and Sappington, David E. M. On the Timing of Information Release. *Info. Econ. Policy*, December 1986, *2*(4), pp. 307–16.

Dye, Ronald A. Optimal Monitoring Policies in Agencies. *Rand J. Econ.*, Autumn 1986, *17*(3), pp. 339–50.

Fama, Eugene F. and Jensen, Michael C. Separation of Ownership and Control. **In** *Barney, J. B. and Ouchi, W. G., eds.*, 1986, *1983*, pp. 276–98.

Foster, James E. and Wan, Henry Y., Jr. Involuntary Unemployment as a Principal–Agent Equilibrium. **In** *Akerlof, G. A. and Yellen, J. L., eds.*, 1986, *1984*, pp. 57–65.

Friedman, Debra. The Principal–Agent Problem in Labor–Management Negotiations. **In** *Lawler, E. J., ed.*, 1986, pp. 89–106.

Gaynor, Martin. Misperceptions, Moral Hazard and Incentives in Groups. *Managerial Dec. Econ.*, December 1986, *7*(4), pp. 279–82.

Green, Jerry R. and Laffont, Jean-Jacques. Incentive Theory with Data Compression. **In** *[Arrow, K. J.], Vol. 3*, 1986, pp. 239–53.

Green, Jerry R. and Laffont, Jean-Jacques. Partially Verifiable Information and Mechanism Design. *Rev. Econ. Stud.*, July 1986, *53*(3), pp. 447–56.

Holmstrom, Bengt and Ricart i Costa, Joan. Managerial Incentives and Capital Management. *Quart. J. Econ.*, November 1986, *101*(4), pp. 835–60.

Knoeber, Charles R. Golden Parachutes, Shark Repellents, and Hostile Tender Offers. *Amer. Econ. Rev.*, March 1986, *76*(1), pp. 155–67. **[G: U.S.]**

Lafuente Felez, Alberto and Salas Fumás, Vicente. Incentivos y participación pública en al promoción de empresas. (With English summary.) *Invest. Ecón.*, May 1986, *10*(2), pp. 379–403. **[G: Spain]**

Lal, Rajiv and Staelin, Richard. Salesforce Compensation Plans in Environments with Asymmetric Information. *Marketing Sci.*, Summer 1986, *5*(3), pp. 179–98.

Lambert, Richard A. Executive Effort and Selection of Risky Projects. *Rand J. Econ.*, Spring 1986, *17*(1), pp. 77–88.

Malcomson, James M. Rank–Order Contracts for a Principal with Many Agents. *Rev. Econ. Stud.*, October 1986, *53*(5), pp. 807–17.

Malcomson, James M. Work Incentives, Hierarchy, and Internal Labor Markets. **In** *Akerlof, G. A. and Yellen, J. L., eds.*, 1986, *1984*, pp. 157–78.

Malueg, David A. Efficient Outcomes in a Repeated Agency Model without Discounting. *J. Math. Econ.*, 1986, *15*(3), pp. 217–30.

McAfee, R. Preston and McMillan, John. Bidding

for Contracts: A Principal–Agent Analysis. *Rand J. Econ.*, Autumn 1986, *17*(3), pp. 326–38.

Odle, Curt J. and Gorman, Raymond F. Collusion among Many Agents. *J. Econ. Bus.*, February 1986, *38*(1), pp. 57–64.

Otsuka, Keijiro. Economics of Share Contract: A Survey in the Light of Theory of Agency–Principal Relationships. (In Japanese. With English summary.) *Econ. Stud. Quart.*, December 1986, *37*(4), pp. 351–72.

Radner, Roy. Repeated Moral Hazard with Low Discount Rates. **In** *[Arrow, K. J.], Vol. 3,* 1986, pp. 25–63.

Rey, Patrick and Tirole, Jean. Contraintes verticales: l'approche principal–agent. (Vertical Restraints: The Principal–Agent Approach. With English summary.) *Ann. Écon. Statist.*, Jan./Mar. 1986, (1), pp. 175–201.

Ricketts, Martin. The Geometry of Principal and Agent: Yet Another Use for the Edgeworth Box. *Scot. J. Polit. Econ.*, August 1986, *33*(3), pp. 228–48.

Shleifer, Andrei and Vishny, Robert W. Large Shareholders and Corporate Control. *J. Polit. Econ.*, Part 1, June 1986, *94*(3), pp. 461–88.

Steedman, Ian and Krause, Ulrich. Goethe's *Faust,* Arrow's Possibility Theorem and the Individual Decision-taker. **In** *Elster, J., ed.,* 1986, pp. 197–231.

Tirole, Jean. Hierarchies and Bureaucracies: On the Role of Collusion in Organizations. *J. Law, Econ., Organ.*, Fall 1986, *2*(2), pp. 181–214.

Tzur, Joseph. An Agency Model of Search for Alternatives. *J. Econ. Behav. Organ.*, September 1986, *7*(3), pp. 317–27.

Verrecchia, Robert E. Managerial Discretion in the Choice among Financial Reporting Alternatives. *J. Acc. Econ.*, October 1986, *8*(3), pp. 175–95.

0229 Microeconomics of Intertemporal Choice

Abel, Andrew B. Capital Accumulation and Uncertain Lifetimes with Adverse Selection. *Econometrica*, September 1986, *54*(5), pp. 1079–97.

Altonji, Joseph G. Intertemporal Substitution in Labor Supply: Evidence from Micro Data. *J. Polit. Econ.*, Part 2, June 1986, *94*(3), pp. S176–S215.

Beltratti, Andrea. Preferenze temporali ed equilibri tenui nei modelli a generazioni sovrapposte. (Temporal Preferences and Tenuous Equilibria in Overlapping Generations Models. With English summary.) *Giorn. Econ.*, May-June 1986, *45*(5–6), pp. 317–23.

Benveniste, Lawrence M. Pricing Optimal Distributions to Overlapping Generations: A Corollary to Efficiency Pricing [A Complete Characterization of Efficiency in a General Capital Accumulation Model]. *Rev. Econ. Stud.*, April 1986, *53*(2), pp. 301–06.

Benveniste, Lawrence M. and Cass, David. On the Existence of Optimal Stationary Equilibria with a Fixed Supply of Fiat Money: I. The Case of a Single Consumer. *J. Polit. Econ.*, April 1986, *94*(2), pp. 402–17.

Coles, Jeffrey L. Equilibrium Turnpike Theory with Time-Separable Utility. *J. Econ. Dynam. Control,* September 1986, *10*(3), pp. 367–94.

Dana, Rose-Anne and Montrucchio, Luigi. Dynamic Complexity in Duopoly Games. *J. Econ. Theory,* October 1986, *40*(1), pp. 40–56.

Davies, James B. Does Redistribution Reduce Inequality? *J. Lab. Econ.*, October 1986, *4*(4), pp. 538–59.

Donzelli, Franco. Temporary Equilibrium, Intertemporal Equilibrium and the "Complete Markets" Hypothesis. *Ricerche Econ.*, Apr.-Sept. 1986, *40*(2–3), pp. 214–48.

Epstein, Larry G. Implicitly Additive Utility and the Nature of Optimal Economic Growth. *J. Math. Econ.*, 1986, *15*(2), pp. 111–28.

Epstein, Larry G. Intergenerational Consumption Rules: An Axiomatization of Utilitarianism and Egalitarianism. *J. Econ. Theory,* April 1986, *38*(2), pp. 280–97.

Epstein, Larry G. Intergenerational Preference Orderings. *Soc. Choice Welfare,* 1986, *3*(3), pp. 151–60.

Esteban, Joan M. A Characterization of the Core in Overlapping-Generations Economies [An Exact Consumption-Loan Model of Interest with or without the Social Contrivance of Money]. *J. Econ. Theory,* August 1986, *39*(2), pp. 439–56.

Farmer, Roger E. A. Deficits and Cycles. *J. Econ. Theory,* October 1986, *40*(1), pp. 77–88.

Feltenstein, Andrew. An Intertemporal General Equilibrium Analysis of Financial Crowding Out: A Policy Model and an Application to Australia. *J. Public Econ.*, October 1986, *31*(1), pp. 79–104. **[G: Australia]**

Guesnerie, Roger. Stationary Sunspot Equilibria in an *N* Commodity World. *J. Econ. Theory,* October 1986, *40*(1), pp. 103–27.

Karni, Edi and Zilcha, Itzhak. Welfare and Comparative Statics Implications of Fair Social Security: A Steady-state Analysis. *J. Public Econ.*, August 1986, *30*(3), pp. 341–57.

Kemp, Murray C. and Kondo, Hitoshi. Overlapping Generations, Competitive Efficiency and Optimal Population. *J. Public Econ.*, July 1986, *30*(2), pp. 237–47.

Labadie, Pamela. Comparative Dynamics and Risk Premia in an Overlapping Generations Model. *Rev. Econ. Stud.*, January 1986, *53*(1), pp. 139–52.

Lahiri, Somdeb. Feasibility and Stability in Intertemporal Information Flows. *Econ. Planning,* 1986, *20*(2), pp. 104–30.

Leininger, Wolfgang. The Existence of Perfect Equilibria in a Model of Growth with Altruism between Generations. *Rev. Econ. Stud.*, July 1986, *53*(3), pp. 349–67.

Luenberger, David G. Control of Linear Dynamic Market Systems. *J. Econ. Dynam. Control,* September 1986, *10*(3), pp. 339–51.

Michel, Philippe. Dynamique de l'accumulation de capital en présence de contraintes de débouchés. (A Dynamic Analysis of Capital Accumulation with Expected Demand Constraints. With English summary.) *Ann. Écon. Statist.*, Apr./June 1986, (2), pp. 117–45.

Nerlove, Marc; Razin, Assaf and Sadka, Efraim. Tamaño de población socialmente óptimo. (With English summary.) *Cuadernos Econ.*, April 1986, *23*(68), pp. 3–23.

Nicola, Pier Carlo. Equilibrio interpersonale temporaneo: un modello elementare senza banditore. (Temporary Interpersonal Equilibrium: An Elementary Model without Any Auctioneer. With English summary.) *Giorn. Econ.*, Mar.-Apr. 1986, *45*(3–4), pp. 113–47.

Ravallion, Martin. On Expectations Formation When Future Welfare Is Contemplated. *Kyklos,* 1986, *39*(4), pp. 564–73.

Roskamp, Karl W. Optimal Life Time Consumption Paths under Income and Property Taxes: Effects of Tax Structure Changes. *Public Finance,* 1986, *41*(1), pp. 1–7.

Spear, Stephen E. and Srivastava, Sanjay. Markov Rational Expectations Equilibria in an Overlapping Generations Model. *J. Econ. Theory,* February 1986, *38*(1), pp. 35–62.

Sproule, Robert A. The Portfolio Effects of Increasing Asset-Return Uncertainty in a Two-Asset, Two-Period Model. *Rivista Int. Sci. Econ. Com.*, Oct.-Nov. 1986, *33*(10–11), pp. 1017–26.

Suda, Shinichi. Pareto Optimality and Monetary Competitive Equilibrium in the Overlapping Generations Model. *Keio Econ. Stud.*, 1986, *23*(1), pp. 79–96.

Veall, Michael R. Public Pensions as Optimal Social Contracts. *J. Public Econ.*, November 1986, *31*(2), pp. 237–51.

Yoshida, Masatoshi. Public Investment Criterion in an Overlapping Generations Economy. *Economica,* May 1986, *53*(210), pp. 247–63.

023 Macroeconomic Theory

0230 General

Allen, Larry and Price, Don. The Short-run Impact of Monetary and Fiscal Policy in a Two Sector Keynesian Model. *Amer. Econ.*, Spring 1986, *30*(1), pp. 40–50.

Allsbrook, Ogden O., Jr. Rational Expectations and Crowding-Out. *Kredit Kapital,* 1986, *19*(2), pp. 248–51.

Allsbrook, Ogden O., Jr. Real Velocity and Crowding-In. *S. Afr. J. Econ.*, June 1986, *54*(2), pp. 222–25.

Andersen, Leonall C. and Jordan, Jerry L. Monetary and Fiscal Actions: A Test of Their Relative Importance in Economic Stabilization. *Fed. Res. Bank St. Louis Rev.*, October 1986, *68*(8), pp. 29–44. **[G: U.S.]**

Arestis, Philip. Wages and Prices in the UK: The Post Keynesian View. *J. Post Keynesian Econ.*, Spring 1986, *8*(3), pp. 339–58. **[G: U.K.]**

Arestis, Philip; Driver, Ciaran and Rooney, J. The Real Segment of a UK Post Keynesian Model. *J. Post Keynesian Econ.*, Winter 1985-86, *8*(2), pp. 163–81. **[G: U.K.]**

Askari, Mostafa. A Non-nested Test of the New Classical Neutrality Proposition for Canada. *Appl. Econ.*, December 1986, *18*(12), pp. 1349–57. **[G: Canada]**

Assarsson, Bengt. Inflation and Relative-Price Variability—A Model for an Open Economy Applied to Sweden. *J. Macroecon.*, Fall 1986, *8*(4), pp. 455–69. **[G: Sweden]**

d'Autume, Antoine. Les anticipations rationnelles dans l'analyse macro-Économique. (Rational Expectations and Macroeconomic Analysis. With English summary.) *Revue Écon.*, March 1986, *37*(2), pp. 243–83. **[G: U.S.]**

d'Autume, Antoine and Michel, Philippe. Déséquilibre général et investissement. (General Disequilibrium and Investment. With English summary.) *Ann. Écon. Statist.*, Oct./Dec. 1986, (4), pp. 23–51.

Azariadis, Costas and Guesnerie, Roger. Sunspots and Cycles. *Rev. Econ. Stud.*, October 1986, *53*(5), pp. 725–37.

Barrère, Alain. Price System and Money-Wage System. *J. Post Keynesian Econ.*, Winter 1985-86, *8*(2), pp. 315–35.

Barsky, Robert B.; Mankiw, N. Gregory and Zeldes, Stephen P. Ricardian Consumers with Keynesian Propensities. *Amer. Econ. Rev.*, September 1986, *76*(4), pp. 676–91.

Batten, Dallas S. and Thornton, Daniel L. The Monetary–Fiscal Policy Debate and the Andersen–Jordan Equation. *Fed. Res. Bank St. Louis Rev.*, October 1986, *68*(8), pp. 9–17. **[G: U.S.]**

Baye, Michael R. and Cosimano, Thomas F. Erratic Monetary Policy and the Dispersion of Commodity Prices. *J. Macroecon.*, Spring 1986, *8*(2), pp. 201–12.

Beare, John B. Automatic Stabilizers? *J. Macroecon.*, Winter 1986, *8*(1), pp. 43–54.

Benavie, Arthur and Froyen, Richard I. A Balanced-Budget Constraint in Modern Stochastic Macromodels. *Southern Econ. J.*, July 1986, *53*(1), pp. 247–58.

Bivin, David G. Input and Output Inventories in a Disaggregated Macro-model. *J. Post Keynesian Econ.*, Spring 1986, *8*(3), pp. 478–96. **[G: U.S.]**

Blejer, Mario I. and Cheasty, Adrienne. Budgetary Policy and the Mobilization of Domestic Financial Resources. **In** *U.N., Dept. of Tech. Co-op. for Devel., Devel. Admin. Div.*, 1986, pp. 83–98.

Blinder, Alan S. Keynes after Lucas. *Eastern Econ. J.*, July-Sept. 1986, *12*(3), pp. 209–16.

Blinder, Alan S. Macroeconomic Implications of Profit Sharing: Comment. **In** *Fischer, S., ed.*, 1986, pp. 335–43. **[G: Japan]**

Blinder, Alan S. On the Share Economy . . . A Bottle Half Full. *Challenge,* Nov./Dec. 1986, *29*(5), pp. 51–52.

Blinder, Alan S. Ruminations on Karl Brunner's Reflections [Fiscal Policy in Macro Theory: A Survey and Evaluation]. **In** *Hafer, R. W., ed. (II),* 1986, pp. 117–26.

Borio, C. E. V. Do Contingent Rules Really Dominate Fixed Rules? *Econ. J.*, December 1986, *96*(384), pp. 1000–1010.

Boschen, John F. The Information Content of Indexed Bonds. *J. Money, Credit, Banking,* February 1986, *18*(1), pp. 76–87.

Bosworth, Barry P. What Would Keynes Have Thought of Rational Expectations? Comment. **In** *Butkiewicz, J. L.; Koford, K. J. and Miller, J. B., eds.,* 1986, pp. 52–55.

Branson, William H. Natural Resources and the Macroeconomy: A Theoretical Framework: Discussion: An International Macroeconomic Perspective. **In** *Neary, J. P. and van Wijnbergen, S., eds.,* 1986, pp. 50–52.

Breeden, Douglas T. Consumption, Production, Inflation and Interest Rates: A Synthesis. *J. Finan. Econ.,* May 1986, *16*(1), pp. 3–39.

Brems, Hans. Fünfzig Jahre General Theory. (General Theory at Fifty. With English summary.) *Jahr. Nationalökon. Statist.,* May 1986, *201*(3), pp. 213–21.

Brothwell, John F. *The General Theory* after Fifty Years: Why Are We Not All Keynesians Now? *J. Post Keynesian Econ.,* Summer 1986, *8*(4), pp. 531–47.

Brunner, Karl. Financial Markets and Macroeconomic Fluctuations: Comment. **In** *Butkiewicz, J. L.; Koford, K. J. and Miller, J. B., eds.,* 1986, pp. 88–94. **[G: U.S.]**

Brunner, Karl. Financial Markets and Macroeconomic Fluctuations: Rejoinder. **In** *Butkiewicz, J. L.; Koford, K. J. and Miller, J. B., eds.,* 1986, pp. 108–09. **[G: U.S.]**

Brunner, Karl. Fiscal Policy in Macro Theory: A Survey and Evaluation. **In** *Hafer, R. W., ed. (II),* 1986, pp. 33–116.

Brunner, Karl. Keynes's Intellectual Legacy. **In** *Burton, J., et al.,* 1986, pp. 59–67.

Brunner, Karl. What Would Keynes Have Thought of Rational Expectations? Comment. **In** *Butkiewicz, J. L.; Koford, K. J. and Miller, J. B., eds.,* 1986, pp. 59–61.

Budd, Alan P. On Keynesian Unemployment and the Unemployment of Keynes. **In** *Burton, J., et al.,* 1986, pp. 139–52.

Burmeister, Edwin and Wall, Kent D. The Arbitrage Pricing Theory and Macroeconomic Factor Measures. *Financial Rev.,* February 1986, *21*(1), pp. 1–20. **[G: U.S.]**

Burton, John. Fifty Years On: Background and Foreground. **In** *Burton, J., et al.,* 1986, pp. 3–24.

Canto, Victor A. and Miles, Marc A. On the Missing Equation—A Final Rejoinder. *J. Macroecon.,* Fall 1986, *8*(4), pp. 491–92.

Canto, Victor A. and Miles, Marc A. On the Missing Equation: A Reply. *J. Macroecon.,* Winter 1986, *8*(1), pp. 113–18.

Cantor, Richard. A Macroeconomic Model with Auction Markets and Nominal Contracts. *Amer. Econ. Rev.,* March 1986, *76*(1), pp. 204–11.

Carraro, Carlo. Indicatori sintetici della politica economica: teoria e applicazioni. (Synthetic Indicators of Macro Policy Goals: Theory and Applications. With English summary.) *Rivista Int. Sci. Econ. Com.,* June-July 1986, *33*(6–7), pp. 629–56. **[G: Italy]**

Caskey, John and Fazzari, Steven M. Macroeconomics and Credit Markets. *J. Econ. Issues,* June 1986, *20*(2), pp. 421–29.

Cecchetti, Stephen G. Testing Short-run Neutrality. *J. Monet. Econ.,* May 1986, *17*(3), pp. 409–23. **[G: U.S.]**

Chick, Victoria. The Evolution of the Banking System and the Theory of Saving, Investment and Interest. *Écon. Soc.,* Aug.-Sept. 1986, *20*(8–9), pp. 111–26.

Choudhury, Masudul Alam and Rahman, A. N. M. Azizur. Macroeconomic Relations in the Islamic Economic Order. *Int. J. Soc. Econ.,* 1986, *13*(6), pp. 60–78.

Chung, Pham. A Note on Policy Evaluation and Rational Expectations. *Public Finance,* 1986, *41*(1), pp. 139–46.

Colangelo, Giuseppe. Alcune riflessioni sulla questione dell'indeterminazione del livello dei prezzi nel caso di una politica del tasso d'interesse nei modelli con aspettative razionali. (Some Reflections on the Price Level Indeterminacy under an Interest Rate Policy Rule in Models with Rational Expectations. With English summary.) *Giorn. Econ.,* Jan.-Feb. 1986, *45*(1–2), pp. 79–89.

Cooper, Richard N. Macroeconomic Policy Adjustment in Interdependent Economies. **In** *Cooper, R. N.,* 1986, *1969*, pp. 155–78.

Coricelli, Fabrizio and Siconolfi, Paolo. Equilibrio economico generale e macroeconomia: una critica della "nuova macroeconomia neoclassica." (General Economic Equilibrium and Macroeconomics: A Critique on the New Classical Macroeconomics. With English summary.) *Polit. Econ.,* April 1986, *2*(1), pp. 45–80.

Corry, Bernard. Keynes's Economics: A Revolution in Economic Theory or in Economic Policy? **In** *Black, R. D. C., ed.,* 1986, pp. 211–37.

Costrell, Robert M. Interest, Profits, and Suboptimality in a Demand-Constrained Macro Model. *Econ. J.,* December 1986, *96*(384), pp. 919–41.

Cottrell, Allin F. The Endogeneity of Money and Money–Income Causality. *Scot. J. Polit. Econ.,* February 1986, *33*(1), pp. 2–27.

Coutinho, Paulo C. Non-optimality of Rational Expectations Equilibrium: The Complete Markets Case. *Rev. Econ. Stud.,* October 1986, *53*(5), pp. 883–84.

Cukierman, Alex and Meltzer, Allan H. A Theory of Ambiguity, Credibility, and Inflation under Discretion and Asymmetric Information. *Econometrica,* September 1986, *54*(5), pp. 1099–1128.

Dagum, Camilo. Analyzing Rational and Adaptive Expectations Hypotheses and Model Specifications. *Écon. Soc.,* November 1986, *20*(11), pp. 15–34.

Darby, Michael R. and Lothian, James R. Economic Events and Keynesian Ideas: The 1930s and the 1970s. **In** *Burton, J., et al.,* 1986, pp. 71–86.

Dasgupta, Partha. Natural Resources and the

Macroeconomy: A Theoretical Framework: Discussion: A Natural Resources Perspective. In *Neary, J. P. and van Wijnbergen, S., eds.*, 1986, pp. 53.

Davidson, Paul. Financial Markets and Macroeconomic Fluctuations: Comment. In *Butkiewicz, J. L.; Koford, K. J. and Miller, J. B., eds.*, 1986, pp. 94–102. **[G: U.S.]**

Davidson, Paul. What Would Keynes Have Thought of Rational Expectations? Comment. In *Butkiewicz, J. L.; Koford, K. J. and Miller, J. B., eds.*, 1986, pp. 58–59.

Davis, Steve J. Does Search Theory Provide a Micro Foundation for Keynesian Models and a Rationale for Policy Activism? A Review of Peter Diamond's Wicksell Lectures. *J. Monet. Econ.*, September 1986, *18*(2), pp. 209–16.

Day, Richard H. Unscrambling the Concept of Chaos through Thick and Thin: Reply [The Emergence of Chaos from Classical Economic Growth]. *Quart. J. Econ.*, May 1986, *101*(2), pp. 425–26.

Deane, Phyllis. Microeconomic Incentives and Macroeconomic Decline: Comment. In *Balassa, B. and Giersch, H., eds.*, 1986, pp. 54–58.

Deneckere, Raymond J. and Pelikan, Steve. Competitive Chaos. *J. Econ. Theory*, October 1986, *40*(1), pp. 13–25.

Deprez, Johan. Time in a Multi-industry, Fixed-Capital World. *J. Post Keynesian Econ.*, Winter 1985-86, *8*(2), pp. 249–65.

Dimand, Robert W. The Macroeconomics of the *Treatise on Money*. *Eastern Econ. J.*, Oct.-Dec. 1986, *12*(4), pp. 431–50.

Dos Santos Ferreira, Rodolphe. Is a Wider Choice Conducive to Stability? A Comment [Money, National Debt, and Economic Growth]. *J. Econ. Theory*, August 1986, *39*(2), pp. 457–63.

Dotsey, Michael and King, Robert G. Informational Implications of Interest Rate Rules. *Amer. Econ. Rev.*, March 1986, *76*(1), pp. 33–42.

Dow, Sheila C. Speculation and the Monetary Circuit with Particular Attention to the Eurocurrency Market. *Écon. Soc.*, Aug.-Sept. 1986, *20*(8–9), pp. 95–109.

Driskill, Robert A. and Sheffrin, Steven M. Is Price Flexibility Destabilizing? *Amer. Econ. Rev.*, September 1986, *76*(4), pp. 802–07.

Ellman, Michael. Images of a Socialist Economy: The End of the Statist Model. In *Nolan, P. and Paine, S., eds.*, 1986, pp. 359–73. **[G: U.K.]**

Evans, George W. Selection Criteria for Models with Non-uniqueness. *J. Monet. Econ.*, September 1986, *18*(2), pp. 147–57.

Felderer, Bernhard and Homburg, Stefan. Ein Fehlinterpretation des Keynesianischen Modells. (A Misinterpretation of the Keynesian Model. With English summary.) *Jahr. Nationalökon. Statist.*, September 1986, *201*(5), pp. 457–68.

Fethke, Gary and Policano, Andrew. Will Wage Setters Ever Stagger Decisions? [Wage Contingencies, the Pattern of Negotiation and Aggregate Implications of Alternative Contract Structures]. *Quart. J. Econ.*, November 1986, *101*(4), pp. 867–77.

Fineschi, Andrea. Classi sociali, agenti collettivi e analisi macroeconomica. (With English summary.) *Stud. Econ.*, 1986, *41*(28), pp. 23–62.

Flaschel, Peter and Picard, R. Problems Concerning the Dynamic Analysis of a Keynesian Model with Perfect Foresight. In *Semmler, W., ed.*, 1986, pp. 269–88.

Fourgeaud, Claude; Gouriéroux, Christian and Pradel, Jacqueline. Learning Procedures and Convergence to Rationality. *Econometrica*, July 1986, *54*(4), pp. 845–68.

Freeman, Scott. Inside Money, Monetary Contractions, and Welfare. *Can. J. Econ.*, February 1986, *19*(1), pp. 87–98.

Fremdling, Rainer. Microeconomic Incentives and Macroeconomic Decline: Comment. In *Balassa, B. and Giersch, H., eds.*, 1986, pp. 59–62.

Galeotti, Marcello and Gori, Franco. Global Analysis and Controls of an Irregular Economy Model. *J. Econ. Dynam. Control*, June 1986, *10*(1/2), pp. 205–12.

Garofalo, Giuseppe. Interdipendenza e processi causali nell'analisi monetaria. (With English summary.) *Stud. Econ.*, 1986, *41*(28), pp. 101–40.

Geanakoplos, John D. and Polemarchakis, Herakles M. Walrasian Indeterminacy and Keynesian Macroeconomics. *Rev. Econ. Stud.*, October 1986, *53*(5), pp. 755–79.

Gerdes, William D. Mr. Fisher and the Classics. *Amer. Econ.*, Spring 1986, *30*(1), pp. 66–72.

Gochoco, Maria S. Tests of the Money Neutrality and Rationality Hypotheses: The Case of Japan 1973–1985. *J. Money, Credit, Banking*, November 1986, *18*(4), pp. 458–66. **[G: Japan]**

Gordon, Robert J. Fiscal Policy in Macro Theory: A Survey and Evaluation: Comment. In *Hafer, R. W., ed. (II)*, 1986, pp. 127–36. **[G: U.S.]**

Gottardi, Piero. Decisioni di risparmio, scelte di portafoglio e politiche di finanziamento del disavanzo. (Saving Decisions, Portfolio Choices and Government Financial Policies. With English summary.) *Giorn. Econ.*, May-June 1986, *45*(5–6), pp. 263–93.

Gowdy, John M. Rational Expectations and Predictability. *J. Post Keynesian Econ.*, Winter 1985-86, *8*(2), pp. 192–200.

Grandmont, Jean-Michel. Stabilizing Competitive Business Cycles. *J. Econ. Theory*, October 1986, *40*(1), pp. 57–76.

Greenfield, Robert L. Walras's Law in Macroeconomic Disequilibrium. *Australian Econ. Pap.*, December 1986, *25*(47), pp. 257–60.

Guesnerie, Roger. Stationary Sunspot Equilibria in an *N* Commodity World. *J. Econ. Theory*, October 1986, *40*(1), pp. 103–27.

Hagen, Ole. Some Paradoxes in Economics. In *[Rapoport, A.]*, 1986, pp. 13–25.

Hahn, Frank H. "Of Marx and Keynes and Many Things." *Oxford Econ. Pap.*, July 1986, *38*(2), pp. 354–61.

Hamada, Fumimasa. A Macroeconomic Model with the Rate of Unemployment as a Risk Probability under the Government Budget Restraint. *Keio Econ. Stud.*, 1986, *23*(1), pp. 49–62.

Hamada, Koichi. The Impact of the General Theory in Japan. *Eastern Econ. J.*, Oct.-Dec. 1986, *12*(4), pp. 451–66. **[G: Japan]**

Heiner, Ronald A. Rational Expectations When Agents Imperfectly Use Information. *J. Post Keynesian Econ.*, Winter 1985-86, *8*(2), pp. 201–07.

Henin, Pierre-Yves. Équilibres avec rationnement d'une économie à planification centralisée et secteur parallèle: une analyse macroéconomique. (With English summary.) *Revue Écon. Polit.*, May-June 1986, *96*(3), pp. 217–38.

Hicks, John R. Towards a More "General Theory." *Econ. Polít.*, April 1986, *3*(1), pp. 7–19.

Hodgson, Geoff. The Limits to Keynes. **In** *Nolan, P. and Paine, S., eds.*, 1986, pp. 150–64.

Howitt, Peter. Conversations with Economists: A Review Essay. *J. Monet. Econ.*, July 1986, *18*(1), pp. 103–18.

Howitt, Peter. The Keynesian Recovery. *Can. J. Econ.*, November 1986, *19*(4), pp. 626–41.

Humphrey, Thomas M. Cumulative Process Models from Thornton to Wicksell. *Fed. Res. Bank Richmond Econ. Rev.*, May/June 1986, *72*(3), pp. 18–25.

Isaac, Alan G. Bursting Bubbles: Further Results. *J. Monet. Econ.*, May 1986, *17*(3), pp. 425–31.

Jacobsen, Hans Jørgen and Schultz, Christian. A Macro Model of Conjectural Equilibrium. *Scand. J. Econ.*, 1986, *88*(3), pp. 489–509.

Jaeger, Klaus. Stabilisierungspolitik in kurzfristigen Einkommens- und Beschäftigungsmodellen mit rationalen Erwartungen. (Stabilization Policy in Short-run Income and Employment Models with Rational Expectations. With English summary.) *Jahr. Nationalökon. Statist.*, July 1986, *201*(4), pp. 329–49.

Jarsulic, Marc. Growth Cycles in a Classical-Keynesian Model. **In** *Semmler, W., ed.*, 1986, pp. 252–68.

Jones, Ronald W. Natural Resources and the Macroeconomy: A Theoretical Framework: Discussion: A Trade Theoretic Perspective. **In** *Neary, J. P. and van Wijnbergen, S., eds.*, 1986, pp. 46–50.

Jordan, Jerry L. The Anderson–Jordan Approach after Nearly 20 Years. *Fed. Res. Bank St. Louis Rev.*, October 1986, *68*(8), pp. 5–8. **[G: U.S.]**

Jung, Woo S. Optimal Stabilization Policies under Rational Expectations. *Econ. Modelling*, April 1986, *3*(2), pp. 117–25.

Kapur, Basant K. Optimal Stabilization Policies for Less-developed Economies with Rational Expectations. **In** *Kapur, B. K.*, 1986, *1982*, pp. 69–91.

Kimbrough, Kent P. Inflation, Employment, and Welfare in the Presence of Transactions Costs. *J. Money, Credit, Banking*, May 1986, *18*(2), pp. 127–40.

King, Robert G. and Plosser, Charles I. Money as the Mechanism of Exchange. *J. Monet. Econ.*, January 1986, *17*(1), pp. 93–115.

Klausinger, Hansjörg. "Hayek Re-Analyzed": A Note [F. A. Hayek's "Prices and Production" Re-Analyzed]. *Jahr. Nationalökon. Statist.*, July 1986, *201*(4), pp. 422–28.

Klein, Philip A. Institutionalism and the New Classical Economics. *J. Econ. Issues*, June 1986, *20*(2), pp. 313–23.

Klein, Philip A. Reinventing the Square Wheel: A Behavioral Assessment of Inflation. **In** *Gilad, B. and Kaish, S., eds., Vol. B*, 1986, pp. 5–30.

Klotz, Ben P. and Meinster, David R. An Integration of CAPM with IS–LM Analysis into a Unified Theory of Aggregate Demand. *Southern Econ. J.*, January 1986, *52*(3), pp. 718–34.

van de Klundert, Theo C. Economic Resilience: A Two-Country Analysis. *De Economist*, 1986, *134*(1), pp. 25–41.

van de Klundert, Theo. C. and Peters, Peter J. Tax Incidence in a Model with Perfect Foresight of Agents and Rationing in Markets. *J. Public Econ.*, June 1986, *30*(1), pp. 37–59.

Koford, Kenneth J.; Butkiewicz, James L. and Miller, Jeffrey B. Keynes' Economic Legacy: Contemporary Economic Theories: Introduction. **In** *Butkiewicz, J. L.; Koford, K. J. and Miller, J. B., eds.*, 1986, pp. 1–24.

Kornai, János. The Reproduction of Shortage. **In** *Kornai, J.*, 1986, *1979*, pp. 6–32.

Kouri, Pentti J. K. Franco Modigliani's Contributions to Economics. *Scand. J. Econ.*, 1986, *88*(2), pp. 311–34.

Kregel, J. A. Shylock and Hamlet or Are There Bulls and Bears in the Circuit? *Écon. Soc.*, Aug.-Sept. 1986, *20*(8–9), pp. 11–22.

Kromphardt, Jürgen. The Contribution of Business Cycle Theories to the Explanation of the Actual Economic Slowdown. **In** *Frisch, H. and Gahlen, B., eds.*, 1986, pp. 70–85. **[G: W. Germany]**

de La Grandville, Olivier. Dynamics and Stability in IS–LM Models: A Re-examination. *J. Macroecon.*, Winter 1986, *8*(1), pp. 31–41.

de La Grandville, Olivier. Erratum [Dynamics and Stability in IS–LM Models]. *J. Macroecon.*, Fall 1986, *8*(4), pp. 402.

Laidler, David. The New-Classical Contributions to Macroeconomics. *Banca Naz. Lavoro Quart. Rev.*, March 1986, (156), pp. 27–55.

Leijonhufvud, Axel. What Would Keynes Have Thought of Rational Expectations? **In** *Butkiewicz, J. L.; Koford, K. J. and Miller, J. B., eds.*, 1986, pp. 25–52.

Leijonhufvud, Axel. What Would Keynes Have Thought of Rational Expectations? Reply. **In** *Butkiewicz, J. L.; Koford, K. J. and Miller, J. B., eds.*, 1986, pp. 61–63.

Leone, Alfredo M. Variabilidad de precios relativos en modelos de generaciones superpuestas. (Relative Prices Variability in Overlapping Generations Models. With English summary.) *Económica (La Plata)*, Jan.-June 1986, *32*(1), pp. 57–79.

Levine, David P. A Note on Wage Determination and Capital Accumulation. *J. Post Keynesian Econ.*, Spring 1986, *8*(3), pp. 463–77.

Levine, Paul. The Formulation of Robust Policies for Rival Rational Expectations Models of the Economy. *J. Econ. Dynam. Control*, June 1986, *10*(1/2), pp. 93–97.

Maes, Ivo. Did the Keynesian Revolution Retard the Development of Portfolio Theory? *Banca Naz. Lavoro Quart. Rev.*, December 1986, (159), pp. 407–21.

Maes, Ivo and Schokkaert, Erik. On Positivism and the Keynesian Revolution. *Tijdschrift Econ. Manage.*, 1986, *31*(1), pp. 81–91.

Mankiw, N. Gregory. Issues in Keynesian Macroeconomics: A Review Essay. *J. Monet. Econ.*, September 1986, *18*(2), pp. 217–23.

Mankiw, N. Gregory and Summers, Lawrence H. Money Demand and the Effects of Fiscal Policies. *J. Money, Credit, Banking*, November 1986, *18*(4), pp. 415–29.

Marini, Giancarlo. Employment Fluctuations and Demand Management. *Economica*, May 1986, *53*(210), pp. 209–18.

Matsukawa, Shigeru. The Equilibrium Distribution of Wage Settlements and Economic Stability. *Int. Econ. Rev.*, June 1986, *27*(2), pp. 415–37.

Matsuyama, Keisuke; Kojina, Mitsuhiro and Koken, Junichiro. Revisiting Phillips' Model by Applying the Root Locus Method. *Econ. Computat. Cybern. Stud. Res.*, 1986, *21*(3), pp. 43–68.

Mauleón, Iñaki. El déficit público y el mercado de trabajo en España: algunas conexiones e implicaciones. (With English summary.) *Invest. Ecón.*, September 1986, *10*(3), pp. 483–504. **[G: Spain]**

McCafferty, Stephen. Aggregate Demand and Interest Rates: A Macroeconomic Approach to the Term Structure. *Econ. Inquiry*, October 1986, *24*(4), pp. 521–33.

McCallum, Bennett T. Estimating the Long-run Relationship between Interest Rates and Inflation: A Reply. *J. Monet. Econ.*, July 1986, *18*(1), pp. 87–90.

McCallum, Bennett T. On "Real" and "Sticky-Price" Theories of the Business Cycle. *J. Money, Credit, Banking*, November 1986, *18*(4), pp. 397–414.

McDonald, John. An Econometric Test of Inflation Neutrality Using Observable Variables Only. *J. Macroecon.*, Spring 1986, *8*(2), pp. 193–99. **[G: U.S.]**

Mehrling, Perry G. A Classical Model of the Class Struggle: A Game-Theoretic Approach. *J. Polit. Econ.*, December 1986, *94*(6), pp. 1280–1303.

Meller, Patricio. Keynesianismo y monetarismo: discrepancias metodológicas. (With English summary.) *Desarrollo Econ.*, Oct.-Dec. 1986, *26*(103), pp. 389–422.

Minford, Patrick. Expectations and the Economy. **In** *Burton, J., et al.*, 1986, pp. 103–17.

Minford, Patrick. From Macro to Micro via Rational Expectations. **In** *[Seldon, A.]*, 1986, pp. 107–14.

Musgrave, Richard A. Alternative Budget Policies for Full Employment. **In** *Musgrave, R. A., Vol. 1*, 1986, *1945*, pp. 336–50.

Myatt, Anthony E. On the Non-existence of a Natural Rate of Unemployment and Kaleckian Micro Underpinnings to the Phillips Curve. *J. Post Keynesian Econ.*, Spring 1986, *8*(3), pp. 447–62.

Neary, J. Peter and van Wijnbergen, Sweder J. G. Natural Resources and the Macroeconomy: A Theoretical Framework. **In** *Neary, J. P. and van Wijnbergen, S., eds.*, 1986, pp. 13–45.

Obstfeld, Maurice and Rogoff, Kenneth. Ruling Out Divergent Speculative Bubbles. *J. Monet. Econ.*, May 1986, *17*(3), pp. 349–62.

Olson, Mancur. Microeconomic Incentives and Macroeconomic Decline. **In** *Balassa, B. and Giersch, H., eds.*, 1986, pp. 40–53.

Parguez, Alain. Au cœur du circuit ou quelques réponses aux énigmes du circuit. (Inside the Core or the First Principles of the General Theory of Circuit. With English summary.) *Écon. Soc.*, Aug.-Sept. 1986, *20*(8–9), pp. 23–39.

Parkin, Michael. The Output–Inflation Trade-off When Prices Are Costly to Change. *J. Polit. Econ.*, February 1986, *94*(1), pp. 200–224.

Pearlman, Joseph; Currie, David and Levine, Paul. Rational Expectations Models with Partial Information. *Econ. Modelling*, April 1986, *3*(2), pp. 90–105.

Pesaran, M. Hashem. Structural Keynesianism as an Alternative to Monetarism. **In** *Nolan, P. and Paine, S., eds.*, 1986, pp. 165–75. **[G: U.K.]**

Pissarides, Christopher A. What Would Keynes Have Thought of Rational Expectations? Comment. **In** *Butkiewicz, J. L.; Koford, K. J. and Miller, J. B., eds.*, 1986, pp. 55–57.

Pohjola, Matti. Applications of Dynamic Game Theory to Macroeconomics. **In** *Başar, T., ed.*, 1986, pp. 103–33.

Poterba, James M.; Rotemberg, Julio J. and Summers, Lawrence H. A Tax-Based Test for Nominal Rigidities. *Amer. Econ. Rev.*, September 1986, *76*(4), pp. 659–75. **[G: U.S.; U.K.]**

Potestio, Paola. Equilibrium and Employment in "The General Theory." *Giorn. Econ.*, July-Aug. 1986, *45*(7–8), pp. 363–88.

Presley, John R. J. M. Keynes and the Real Balance Effect. *Manchester Sch. Econ. Soc. Stud.*, March 1986, *54*(1), pp. 22–30.

Putnam, Bluford H. and Wilford, D. Sykes. Money, Income, and Causality in the United States and the United Kingdom. **In** *Putnam, B. H. and Wilford, D. S., eds.*, 1986, *1978*, pp. 59–65. **[G: U.S.; U.K.]**

Ramser, Hans J. Keynes-Literatur und die Relevanz makroökonomischer Lehrbuchmodelle. (Towards Keynesian Literature and the Relevance of Macroeconomic Textbook Models. With English summary.) *Jahr. Nationalökon. Statist.*, September 1986, *201*(5), pp. 441–56.

Rankin, N. Debt Policy under Fixed and Flexible

Prices. *Oxford Econ. Pap.*, November 1986, *38*(3), pp. 481–500.

Rao, B. Bhaskara. A Note on Employment, Labor Supply, and Real Wages in Market Disequilibrium. *J. Macroecon.*, Spring 1986, *8*(2), pp. 233–42. **[G: U.S.]**

Richards, Daniel J. The Macroeconomic Models and Expectations of Corporate Executives. *J. Post Keynesian Econ.*, Spring 1986, *8*(3), pp. 438–46. **[G: U.S.]**

Rousseas, Stephen. The Finance Motive, Keynes, and Post Keynesians. *Écon. Soc.*, Aug.-Sept. 1986, *20*(8–9), pp. 189–201.

Sakakibara, Kenichi. A Fisher–Brown Proposition for Speculative Bubbles. *J. Macroecon.*, Fall 1986, *8*(4), pp. 485–90.

Salant, Walter S. A Critical Look at Supply-Side Theory and a Brief Look at Some of Its International Aspects. **In** *[Tarshis, L.]*, 1986, pp. 108–24.

Salmon, Mark. The Principle of Effective Demand Revisited. *J. Econ. Dynam. Control*, June 1986, *10*(1/2), pp. 231–37.

Samuels, Warren J. What Aspects of Keynes's Economic Theories Merit Continued or Renewed Interest? One Interpretation. *J. Post Keynesian Econ.*, Fall 1986, *9*(1), pp. 3–16.

Samuelson, Larry. Nonwalrasian Equilibria with Leading Behavior. *Oxford Econ. Pap.*, March 1986, *38*(1), pp. 31–58.

Samuelson, Paul A. Evaluating Reaganomics. **In** *Samuelson, P. A.*, 1986, *1984*, pp. 901–08. **[G: U.S.]**

Samuelson, Paul A. Succumbing to Keynesianism. **In** *Samuelson, P. A.*, 1986, *1985*, pp. 283–90. **[G: U.S.]**

Samuelson, Paul A. What Would Keynes Have Thought of Rational Expectation? Comment. **In** *Samuelson, P. A.*, 1986, *1983*, pp. 291–300.

Sarantis, Nicholas C. A Note on Employment, Labor Supply, and Real Wages in Market Disequilibrium: A Reply. *J. Macroecon.*, Spring 1986, *8*(2), pp. 243–45. **[G: U.S.]**

Sardoni, Claudio. Marx and Keynes on Effective Demand and Unemployment. *Hist. Polit. Econ.*, Fall 1986, *18*(3), pp. 419–41.

Schlieper, Ulrich. Real Wages, Business Cycles and Unemployment. **In** *Frisch, H. and Gahlen, B., eds.*, 1986, pp. 145–58.

Semmler, Willi. On Nonlinear Theories of Economic Cycles and the Persistence of Business Cycles. *Math. Soc. Sci.*, August 1986, *12*(1), pp. 47–76.

Shaller, Douglas R. Still Missing [The Missing Equation: The Wedge Model Alternative]. *J. Macroecon.*, Fall 1986, *8*(4), pp. 493–95.

Shiller, Robert J. Financial Markets and Macroeconomic Fluctuations. **In** *Butkiewicz, J. L.; Koford, K. J. and Miller, J. B., eds.*, 1986, pp. 65–88. **[G: U.S.]**

Shiller, Robert J. Financial Markets and Macroeconomic Fluctuations: Reply. **In** *Butkiewicz, J. L.; Koford, K. J. and Miller, J. B., eds.*, 1986, pp. 105–08. **[G: U.S.]**

Sinclair, P. J. N. Interest, Employment and Money: An Editorial Note. *Oxford Econ. Pap.*, November 1986, *38*(3), pp. 363–66.

Singh, Harinder. When Are Expectations Rational? Some Vexing Questions and Behavioral Clues. *J. Behav. Econ.*, Spring/Summer 1986, *15*(1/2), pp. 191–209.

Smithin, John N. The Length of the Production Period and Effective Stabilization Policy. *J. Macroecon.*, Winter 1986, *8*(1), pp. 55–62.

Snippe, Jan. Varieties of Rational Expectations: Their Differences and Relations. *J. Post Keynesian Econ.*, Spring 1986, *8*(3), pp. 427–37.

Solow, Robert M. Another Possible Source of Wage Stickiness. **In** *Akerlof, G. A. and Yellen, J. L., eds.*, 1986, *1979*, pp. 41–44.

Solow, Robert M. Macroeconomic Theory and Government Action. **In** *Aiginger, K., ed.*, 1986, pp. 19–30.

Solow, Robert M. Monopolistic Competition and the Multiplier. **In** *[Arrow, K. J.], Vol. 2*, 1986, pp. 301–15.

Solow, Robert M. What Is a Nice Girl Like You Doing in a Place Like This? Macroeconomics after Fifty Years. *Eastern Econ. J.*, July-Sept. 1986, *12*(3), pp. 191–98.

Sørensen, Peter Birch. Errata: Countercyclical versus Passive Monetary Policy in a Medium-run Macro Model. *Scand. J. Econ.*, 1986, *88*(2), pp. 453.

Steindl, Frank G. General Equilibrium Models of Inflation and Interest Rates: Specification Considerations. *Kredit Kapital*, 1986, *19*(2), pp. 252–70.

Stiglitz, Joseph E. Financial Markets and Macroeconomic Fluctuations: Comment. **In** *Butkiewicz, J. L.; Koford, K. J. and Miller, J. B., eds.*, 1986, pp. 102–05. **[G: U.S.]**

Stoker, Thomas M. Simple Tests of Distributional Effects on Macroeconomic Equations. *J. Polit. Econ.*, August 1986, *94*(4), pp. 763–95.

Stournaras, Yannis A. The Fix-Price Method and the Welfare Implications of New Cambridge Macroeconomics. *Greek Econ. Rev.*, June 1986, *8*(1), pp. 41–59.

Strassl, Wolfgang. Keynes on Expectations and Uncertainty: Rational Expectations Equilibria with Asymmetric Information. *Bull. Econ. Res.*, May 1986, *38*(2), pp. 137–59.

Summers, Lawrence H. Estimating the Long-run Relationship between Interest Rates and Inflation: A Response. *J. Monet. Econ.*, July 1986, *18*(1), pp. 77–86.

Summers, Lawrence H. On the Share Economy: Prospects and Problems . . . *Challenge*, Nov./Dec. 1986, *29*(5), pp. 47–50.

Svensson, Lars E. O. Sticky Goods Prices, Flexible Asset Prices, Monopolistic Competition, and Monetary Policy. *Rev. Econ. Stud.*, July 1986, *53*(3), pp. 385–405.

Taylor, John B. An Appeal for Rationality in the Policy Activism Debate. **In** *Hafer, R. W., ed. (II)*, 1986, pp. 151–63.

Tobin, James. On the Welfare Macroeconomics of Government Financial Policy. *Scand. J. Econ.*, 1986, *88*(1), pp. 9–24.

Toufique, Kazi Ali. The IS LM Curves Re-revisited with the Aid of Geometry of International Trade—A Note. *Indian Econ. J.*, Jan.-

Mar. 1986, *33*(3), pp. 65–69.

Travaglini, Guido. Quattro modelli macroeconomici a confronto. Somiglianze e divergenze in merito alla struttura, alle implicazioni di politica economica e alla stabilita' asintotica. (With English summary.) *Econ. Int.*, February 1986, *39*(1), pp. 60–91.

Vandevelde, Franck. La thésaurisation dans le circuit de l'économie monétaire de production. (Hoarding in the Circuit of the Monetary Production Economy. With English summary.) *Écon. Soc.*, Aug.-Sept. 1986, *20*(8–9), pp. 41–66.

Velupillai, K. From the Fractals of Micro to the Chaos of Macro. *J. Econ. Dynam. Control*, June 1986, *10*(1/2), pp. 269–72.

Vicarelli, Fausto. Natural Laws and Economic Policy: Some Considerations on the Theoretical Foundations of the New Classical Macroeconomics. *J. Post Keynesian Econ.*, Winter 1985-86, *8*(2), pp. 298–314.

Vickers, Douglas. Time, Ignorance, Surprise, and Economic Decisions: A Comment on Williams and Findlay's "Risk and the Role of Failed Expectations in an Uncertain World." *J. Post Keynesian Econ.*, Fall 1986, *9*(1), pp. 48–57.

Weitzman, Martin L. Macroeconomic Implications of Profit Sharing. **In** *Fischer, S., ed.*, 1986, pp. 291–335. **[G: Japan]**

Weitzman, Martin L. The Simple Macroeconomics of Profit-Sharing. **In** *Beckerman, W., ed.*, 1986, pp. 171–99.

Wells, Paul. 'Mr Churchill' and the *General Theory*. **In** *[Tarshis, L.]*, 1986, pp. 8–27. **[G: U.K.]**

Williams, Edward E. and Findlay, M. Chapman, III. Risk and the Role of Failed Expectations in an Uncertain World. *J. Post Keynesian Econ.*, Fall 1986, *9*(1), pp. 32–47.

Woods, J. E. On the Matrix Multiplier. *Econ. Notes*, 1986, (1), pp. 167–78.

Yeager, Leland B. The Keynesian Heritage in Economics. **In** *Burton, J., et al.*, 1986, pp. 27–44.

0232 Theory of Aggregate Demand: Consumption

Adams, F. Gerard and Wachter, Susan M. Toward a National Consensus on Saving. **In** *Adams, F. G. and Wachter, S. M., eds.*, 1986, pp. 205–09.

Barth, James R.; Iden, George R. and Russek, Frank S. Government Debt, Government Spending, and Private Sector Behavior: Comment. *Amer. Econ. Rev.*, December 1986, *76*(5), pp. 1158–67. **[G: U.S.]**

Boskin, Michael J. Theoretical and Empirical Issues in the Measurement, Evaluation, and Interpretation of Postwar U.S. Saving. **In** *Adams, F. G. and Wachter, S. M., eds.*, 1986, pp. 11–43. **[G: U.S.]**

Chand, Sheetal K. and Otani, Ichiro. Aggregate Demand and the Coordination of Monetary and Fiscal Action. **In** *Shome, P., ed.*, 1986, pp. 173–97. **[G: Malaysia; Thailand; Philippines; S. Korea; Japan]**

Drobny, Andres and Speight, Alan. Consumption and Income: Some Simple Exercises with Panel Data. *Appl. Econ.*, July 1986, *18*(7), pp. 757–75. **[G: Austria]**

Fornero, Elsa. Teoria del ciclo vitale del risparmio e assicurazioni di rendita vitalizia: Un'applicazione al caso italiano. (Life Cycle Theory of Savings and Lifetime Annuity Insurance: An Application to the Italian Case. With English summary.) *Giorn. Econ.*, July-Aug. 1986, *45*(7–8), pp. 341–61. **[G: Italy]**

Friend, Irwin. The Policy Options for Stimulating National Saving. **In** *Adams, F. G. and Wachter, S. M., eds.*, 1986, pp. 45–63.

Hadjimatheou, George. Unemployment and Consumption: A Review of Theory and Evidence. *Brit. Rev. Econ. Issues*, Spring 1986, *8*(18), pp. 51–73. **[G: U.S.]**

Hall, Robert E. Liquidity Constraints, Fiscal Policy, and Consumption: Comments. *Brookings Pap. Econ. Act.*, 1986, (1), pp. 51–53. **[G: U.S.]**

Hall, Robert E. The Role of Consumption in Economic Fluctuations. **In** *Gordon, R. J., ed.*, 1986, pp. 237–55. **[G: U.S.]**

Hsu, Chen-Min. The Consumption Function and Intertemporal Spillover Effects. *J. Econ. Dynam. Control*, December 1986, *10*(4), pp. 443–55.

Hubbard, R. Glenn and Judd, Kenneth L. Liquidity Constraints, Fiscal Policy, and Consumption. *Brookings Pap. Econ. Act.*, 1986, (1), pp. 1–50. **[G: U.S.]**

James, Robert G. On Estimating the Variance of Permanent Income. *Atlantic Econ. J.*, December 1986, *14*(4), pp. 97.

Jha, Raghbendra. Optimal Labour Supply and the Accumulation of Human and Financial Capital with Capital Market Imperfections. *Indian Econ. Rev.*, Jan.-June 1986, *21*(1), pp. 21–39.

King, Mervyn A. Capital Market "Imperfections" and the Consumption Function. *Scand. J. Econ.*, 1986, *88*(1), pp. 59–80. **[G: U.K.]**

Kormendi, Roger C. and Meguire, Philip. Government Debt, Government Spending, and Private Sector Behavior: Reply. *Amer. Econ. Rev.*, December 1986, *76*(5), pp. 1180–87. **[G: U.S.]**

Miron, Jeffrey A. Seasonal Fluctuations and the Life Cycle–Permanent Income Model of Consumption. *J. Polit. Econ.*, December 1986, *94*(6), pp. 1258–79. **[G: U.S.]**

Modigliani, Franco. Life Cycle, Individual Thrift, and the Wealth of Nations. *Amer. Econ. Rev.*, June 1986, *76*(3), pp. 297–313. **[G: OECD]**

Modigliani, Franco and Sterling, Arlie. Government Debt, Government Spending and Private Sector Behavior: Comment. *Amer. Econ. Rev.*, December 1986, *76*(5), pp. 1168–79. **[G: U.S.]**

Montgomery, Edward. Where Did All the Saving Go? A Look at the Recent Decline in the Personal Saving Rate. *Econ. Inquiry*, October 1986, *24*(4), pp. 681–97. **[G: U.S.]**

Owens, Emiel W. Demographic Trends and Saving Propensities "A Revisit with Life Cycle

Theory." *Atlantic Econ. J.*, December 1986, *14*(4), pp. 106.

Patterson, K. D. The Stability of Some Annual Consumption Functions. *Oxford Econ. Pap.*, March 1986, *38*(1), pp. 1–30. **[G: U.K.]**

Pearce, I. F. and Thomas, S. H. Personal Savings and Transactions Balance Changes. *Manchester Sch. Econ. Soc. Stud.*, December 1986, *54*(4), pp. 380–90. **[G: U.K.]**

Persson, Torsten. Capital Market "Imperfections" and the Consumption Function: Comment. *Scand. J. Econ.*, 1986, *88*(1), pp. 81–83. **[G: U.K.]**

Pitelis, Christos N. The Pension Funds "Revolution" and the Managerialist Saving Function. *Scot. J. Polit. Econ.*, November 1986, *33*(4), pp. 383–90.

Pourgerami, Abbas; Perez, Felipe and Traore, Namatie. The Impact of Income Redistribution on Aggregate Consumption. *Atlantic Econ. J.*, December 1986, *14*(4), pp. 98.

Rao, B. Bhaskara. Alternative Aggregate Demand Functions in Macroeconomics. *Australian Econ. Pap.*, December 1986, *25*(47), pp. 261–64.

Samuelson, Paul A. Land and the Rate of Interest. **In** *Samuelson, P. A.*, 1986, *1979*, pp. 664–82.

Stanković, Fuada. The Relevance of the Phenomenon of "Conspicuous Consumption" for the General Theory of Consumption. *Econ. Anal. Workers' Manage.*, 1986, *20*(4), pp. 375–83.

Summers, Lawrence H. Liquidity Constraints, Fiscal Policy, and Consumption: Comments. *Brookings Pap. Econ. Act.*, 1986, (1), pp. 53–57. **[G: U.S.]**

von Ungern-Sternberg, Thomas. Inflation and the Consumption Function. *Weltwirtsch. Arch.*, 1986, *122*(4), pp. 741–44. **[G: U.K.]**

V'iugin, O. V. Modeling and Forecasting Household Savings to Take Account of Supply and Demand. *Matekon*, Fall 1986, *23*(1), pp. 64–81. **[G: Hungary; E. Germany; U.S.S.R.; Czechoslovakia]**

Walters, Alan. Consumption, Savings and the Multiplier. **In** *Burton, J., et al.*, 1986, pp. 89–100.

Weissenberger, Edgar. Consumption Innovations and Income Innovations: The Case of the United Kingdom and Germany. *Rev. Econ. Statist.*, February 1986, *68*(1), pp. 1–8. **[G: U.K.; W. Germany]**

0233 Theory of Aggregate Demand: Investment

Allsbrook, Ogden O., Jr. and Gilliam, Kenneth P. An Attenuated Exposition of the Ramsey–Keynes Rate of Saving. *Econ. Notes*, 1986, (3), pp. 70–84.

Asimakopulos, A. Finance, Investment and Saving: A Reply. *Cambridge J. Econ.*, March 1986, *10*(1), pp. 81–82.

Asimakopulos, A. Richardson on Asimakopulos on Finance: A Reply [Kalecki and Keynes on Finance, Investment and Saving]. *Cambridge J. Econ.*, June 1986, *10*(2), pp. 199–201.

Asimakopulos, Athanasios. Finance, Liquidity, Saving, and Investment. *J. Post Keynesian Econ.*, Fall 1986, *9*(1), pp. 79–90.

Bivin, David G. Inventories and Interest Rates: A Critique of the Buffer Stock Model. *Amer. Econ. Rev.*, March 1986, *76*(1), pp. 168–76. **[G: U.S.]**

Blanchard, Olivier J. Investment, Output, and the Cost of Capital: Comments. *Brookings Pap. Econ. Act.*, 1986, (1), pp. 153–58. **[G: U.S.]**

Blinder, Alan S. More on the Speed of Adjustment in Inventory Models. *J. Money, Credit, Banking*, August 1986, *18*(3), pp. 355–65.

Böge, Werner. Remarks on a Dynamic Game with Macroeconomic Investment. **In** *Faber, M., ed.*, 1986, pp. 259–66.

Böge, Werner; Faber, Malte and Güth, Werner. A Dynamic Game with Macroeconomic Investment Decisions under Alternative Market Structures. **In** *Faber, M., ed.*, 1986, *1982*, pp. 229–58.

Browne, F. X. Loan Market Price and Quantity Effects in a Production Smoothing Model of Inventory Investment. *Appl. Econ.*, June 1986, *18*(6), pp. 691–707. **[G: Ireland]**

Chowdhury, Abdur R.; Fackler, James S. and McMillin, W. Douglas. Monetary Policy, Fiscal Policy, and Investment Spending: An Empirical Analysis. *Southern Econ. J.*, January 1986, *52*(3), pp. 794–806. **[G: U.S.]**

Davidson, Paul. Finance, Funding, Saving, and Investment. *J. Post Keynesian Econ.*, Fall 1986, *9*(1), pp. 101–10.

Domar, Evsey D. and Musgrave, Richard A. Proportional Income Taxation and Risk-Taking. **In** *Musgrave, R. A., Vol. 1*, 1986, *1944*, pp. 108–31.

Falkinger, Josef. Investment under Uncertainty and the State of Confidence—A Note. *Empirica*, 1986, *13*(1), pp. 97–104.

Falkinger, Josef. Konjunkturelle Unsicherheit, längerfristiges Wachstumsklima und Investitionsverhalten. (Short-run Uncertainty, Long-run Growth-Climate, and Investment Behavior. With English summary.) *Jahr. Nationalök. Statist.*, September 1986, *201*(5), pp. 469–79.

Geweke, John. Fixed Investment in the American Business Cycle, 1919–83: Comment. **In** *Gordon, R. J., ed.*, 1986, pp. 336–40. **[G: U.S.]**

Gordon, Robert J. and Veitch, John M. Fixed Investment in the American Business Cycle, 1919–83: Reply. **In** *Gordon, R. J., ed.*, 1986, pp. 348–51. **[G: U.S.]**

Gordon, Robert J. and Veitch, John M. Fixed Investment in the American Business Cycle, 1919–83. **In** *Gordon, R. J., ed.*, 1986, pp. 267–335. **[G: U.S.]**

Gronchi, Sandro. A Note on Truncation. *Bull. Econ. Res.*, May 1986, *38*(2), pp. 161–67.

Gronchi, Sandro. On Investment Criteria Based on the Internal Rate of Return. *Oxford Econ. Pap.*, March 1986, *38*(1), pp. 174–80.

Hansson, Ingemar. Classical, Keynes' and Neoclassical Investment Theory—A Synthesis. *Oxford Econ. Pap.*, July 1986, *38*(2), pp. 305–16.

Harcourt, Geoffrey C. Investment-Decision Criteria, Capital-Intensity and the Choice of

Techniques. In *[Harcourt, G. C.]*, 1986, *1967*, pp. 113–44. **[G: U.K.; Europe]**

Kregel, J. A. A Note on Finance, Liquidity, Saving, and Investment. *J. Post Keynesian Econ.*, Fall 1986, *9*(1), pp. 91–100.

Lovell, Michael C. Investment, Output, and the Cost of Capital: Comments. *Brookings Pap. Econ. Act.*, 1986, (1), pp. 158–61. **[G: U.S.]**

Mauleón, Iñaki. La inversión en bienes de equipo: determinantes y estabilidad. (With English summary.) *Invest. Ecón.*, May 1986, *10*(2), pp. 251–78. **[G: Spain]**

Modica, Salvatore. Investimento, incertezza e vincoli di liquidità. (Investment, Uncertainty, and Liquidity Constraints. With English summary.) *Giorn. Econ.*, Jan.-Feb. 1986, *45*(1–2), pp. 73–77.

Mott, Tracy. Towards a Post-Keynesian Formulation of Liquidity Preference. *J. Post Keynesian Econ.*, Winter 1985-86, *8*(2), pp. 222–32.

Okuno, Nobuhiro. Public Investment and Unegalitarian Equilibrium. *Public Finance*, 1986, *41*(2), pp. 260–66.

Plessner, Yakir and Shalit, Haim. Inflation, the Level of Investment, and Interest Rates. *Europ. Econ. Rev.*, December 1986, *30*(6), pp. 1169–87.

Richardson, David R. Asimakopulos on Kalecki and Keynes on Finance, Investment and Saving. *Cambridge J. Econ.*, June 1986, *10*(2), pp. 191–98.

Shapiro, Matthew D. Investment, Output, and the Cost of Capital. *Brookings Pap. Econ. Act.*, 1986, (1), pp. 111–52. **[G: U.S.]**

Sims, Christopher A. Fixed Investment in the American Business Cycle, 1919–83: Comment. In *Gordon, R. J., ed.*, 1986, pp. 340–48. **[G: U.S.]**

Snippe, Jan. Finance, Saving and Investment in Keynes's Economics: A Reply. *Cambridge J. Econ.*, December 1986, *10*(4), pp. 373–77.

Terzi, Andrea. Finance, Investment and Saving: A Comment. *Cambridge J. Econ.*, March 1986, *10*(1), pp. 77–80.

von Thadden, Ernst-Ludwig. A Dynamic Macroeconomic Investment Game with Non-linear Saving Behaviour. In *Faber, M., ed.*, 1986, pp. 267–91.

Tilly, Richard H. Financing Industrial Enterprise in Great Britain and Germany in the Nineteenth Century: Testing Grounds for Marxist and Schumpeterian Theories? In *Wagener, H.-J. and Drukker, J. W., eds.*, 1986, pp. 123–55. **[G: U.K.; Germany]**

Ueda, Kazuo and Yoshikawa, Hiroshi. Financial Volatility and the *q* Theory of Investment. *Economica*, February 1986, *53*(209), pp. 11–27. **[G: Japan]**

Wodopia, Franz-Josef. Flow and Fund Approaches to Irreversible Investment Decisions. In *Faber, M., ed.*, 1986, pp. 195–207.

Wright, J. F. On Investment Criteria Based on the Internal Rate of Return: A Response. *Oxford Econ. Pap.*, March 1986, *38*(1), pp. 181–84.

Zabel, Edward. Price Smoothing, Inventory and Random Output. *Eastern Econ. J.*, July-Sept. 1986, *12*(3), pp. 313–20.

Zinn, Karl Georg. Does Uncertainy Imply a Bias in Favour of Unemployment and Stagnation? A Question to Bartmann, John and Others. *Jahr. Nationalökon. Statist.*, September 1986, *201*(5), pp. 531–34.

0234 Theory of Aggregate Supply

Ahmad, Syed. Sraffa Numeraire and Reswitching: A Note. *J. Macroecon.*, Summer 1986, *8*(3), pp. 381–85.

Aizenman, Joshua and Frenkel, Jacob A. Supply Shocks, Wage Indexation and Monetary Accommodation. *J. Money, Credit, Banking*, August 1986, *18*(3), pp. 304–22.

Altonji, Joseph G. Efficiency Wage Theories: A Partial Evaluation: Comment. In *Fischer, S., ed.*, 1986, pp. 276–85. **[G: U.S.]**

Andersen, Torben M. Fagforeninger, lønudvikling og arbejdsløshed. (Trade Unions and the Wage–Employment Nexus. With English summary.) *Nationaløkon. Tidsskr.*, 1986, *124*(3), pp. 241–58. **[G: Denmark]**

Arena, Richard and Torre, Dominique. Approche sraffaienne et théorie de la gravitation: une tentative de rapprochement. (Sraffian Approach and Gravitation Theory. With English summary.) *Écon. Appl.*, 1986, *39*(1), pp. 61–86.

Arnaudo, A. A., et al. Tipología del Desempleo en la Argentina 1950–84. (Typology of Argentine Unemployment 1950–84. With English summary.) *Económica (La Plata)*, July-December 1986, *32*(2), pp. 143–63. **[G: Argentina]**

Auernheimer, Leonardo. Variable Depreciation and Some of Its Implications. *Can. J. Econ.*, February 1986, *19*(1), pp. 99–113.

Azariadis, Costas. Theories of Wage Rigidity: Comment. In *Butkiewicz, J. L.; Koford, K. J. and Miller, J. B., eds.*, 1986, pp. 216–19.

Battinelli, Andrea. Variable Working Hours in a Simple Model of Macroeconomic Equilibrium with Rationing. *Econ. Lavoro*, Jan.-Mar. 1986, *20*(1), pp. 3–22.

Betancourt, Roger R. The Duration of Operations and the Estimation of Substitution Possibilities. *Europ. Econ. Rev.*, December 1986, *30*(6), pp. 1189–95.

Bidard, Christian. Production de marchandises, Corrigendum. (Production of Commodities, Corrigendum. With English summary.) *Écon. Appl.*, 1986, *39*(1), pp. 113–38.

Blanchard, Olivier J. Market Structure and Macroeconomic Fluctuations: Comments. *Brookings Pap. Econ. Act.*, 1986, (2), pp. 323–28.

Boddy, Raford and Alwan, Rami. Work Shifts and the Cyclical Behavior of Productivity and Real Wages. *J. Macroecon.*, Summer 1986, *8*(3), pp. 355–63.

Boggio, Luciano. Stability of Production Prices in a Model of General Interdependence. In *Semmler, W., ed.*, 1986, pp. 83–114.

Bosworth, Barry P. Financial Markets and Macroeconomic Fluctuations: Comment. In *Butkie-*

wicz, J. L.; Koford, K. J. and Miller, J. B., eds., 1986, pp. 133–35.

Boyer, Robert and Coriat, Benjamin. Technical Flexibility and Macro Stabilisation. *Ricerche Econ.*, Oct.-Dec. 1986, *40*(4), pp. 771–835. **[G: U.S.]**

Brunner, Karl. Theories of Wage Rigidity: Comment. **In** *Butkiewicz, J. L.; Koford, K. J. and Miller, J. B., eds.*, 1986, pp. 209–15.

Bureau, Dominique and Norotte, Michel. Réduire le chômage en modifiant le coût des facteurs de production: la réponse des modèles. (Reduction of Employment by Production Factor Cost Shifting: Answer from Macroeconomic Models. With English summary.) *Écon. Appl.*, 1986, *39*(4), pp. 739–55. **[G: France]**

Calmfors, Lars and Horn, Henrik. Employment Policies and Centralized Wage-Setting. *Economica*, August 1986, *53*(211), pp. 281–302.

Carlberg, Michael. Makroökonomik der Kapitalmangel-Arbeitslosigkeit. (Macroeconomics of Unemployment Due to Lack of Capital. With English summary.) *Kredit Kapital*, 1986, *19*(3), pp. 313–24.

Carlson, John A. Stocks, Shocks and Price-Output Decisions. *J. Macroecon.*, Summer 1986, *8*(3), pp. 257–77.

Catinat, Michel; Cette, Gilbert and Taddéi, Dominique. Réduction-réorganisation du temps de travail. (Reduction and Reorganisation of Working Time: A Macroeconomic Model of Disequilibrium. With English summary.) *Écon. Appl.*, 1986, *39*(4), pp. 757–92.

Chopra, Ajai and Montiel, Peter J. Output and Unanticipated Money with Imported Intermediate Goods and Foreign Exchange Rationing. *Int. Monet. Fund Staff Pap.*, December 1986, *33*(4), pp. 697–721. **[G: Philippines]**

Colander, David C. Financial Markets and Macroeconomic Fluctuations: Comment. **In** *Butkiewicz, J. L.; Koford, K. J. and Miller, J. B., eds.*, 1986, pp. 145–49.

Contini, B.; Galeotti, Marcello and Cugno, F. Inflation and the Irregular Economy: A Dynamic Analysis. *Metroecon.*, February 1986, *38*(1), pp. 67–84.

Cooper, Russell. Share Contracts and Macroeconomic Externalities. *J. Compar. Econ.*, December 1986, *10*(4), pp. 421–26.

Cross, Rod. Phelps, Hysteresis, and the Natural Rate of Unemployment. *Quart. J. Bus. Econ.*, Winter 1986, *25*(1), pp. 56–64.

D'Agata, Antonio. Non-produced Means of Production: Neo-Ricardians vs. Fundamentalists, a Comment. *Rev. Radical Polit. Econ.*, Winter 1986, *18*(4), pp. 93–99.

Davidson, Paul. Financial Markets and Macroeconomic Fluctuations: Comment. **In** *Butkiewicz, J. L.; Koford, K. J. and Miller, J. B., eds.*, 1986, pp. 135–43.

Davis, John and Minford, Patrick. Germany and the European Disease. *Rech. Écon. Louvain*, 1986, *52*(3–4), pp. 373–98. **[G: W. Germany]**

De Long, James Bradford and Summers, Lawrence H. Is Increased Price Flexibility Stabilizing? *Amer. Econ. Rev.*, December 1986, *76*(5), pp. 1031–44.

Delarue, Antoine. Circulation des marchandises et création de valeur: Une approche néoricardienne de la fonction distribution. (Commodity Flows andd Value Creation: A Neoricardian Approach to Trade. With English summary.) *Écon. Appl.*, 1986, *39*(1), pp. 87–111.

Diewert, W. Erwin and Morrison, Catherine J. Adjusting Output and Productivity Indexes for Changes in the Terms of Trade. *Econ. J.*, September 1986, *96*(383), pp. 659–79.

Duménil, Gérard and Lévy, D. Stability and Instability in a Dynamic Model of Capitalist Production. **In** *Semmler, W., ed.*, 1986, pp. 132–69.

Eichner, Alfred S. Post Keynesian View of Average Direct Cost: A Comment. *J. Post Keynesian Econ.*, Spring 1986, *8*(3), pp. 425–26.

Eisner, Robert. The Revolution Restored: Keynesian Unemployment, Inflation and Budget Deficits. *Eastern Econ. J.*, July-Sept. 1986, *12*(3), pp. 217–21.

Elliott, J. Walter and Sherony, Keith R. Employer Search Activities and Short-run Aggregate Labor Supply. *Southern Econ. J.*, January 1986, *52*(3), pp. 693–705. **[G: U.S.]**

Farmer, Karl. Gleichgewichtskonzept, Investitionsfunktion und Unterbeschäftigungsgleichgewicht. (Equilibrium Concepts, Investment Function and Unemployment Equilibrium. With English summary.) *Z. Wirtschaft. Sozialwissen.*, 1986, *106*(5), pp. 441–65.

Fehr, Ernest. A Theory of Involuntary Equilibrium Unemployment. *J. Inst. Theoretical Econ.*, June 1986, *142*(2), pp. 405–30.

Feltenstein, Andrew. Financial Crowding Out: Theory with an Application to Australia. *Int. Monet. Fund Staff Pap.*, March 1986, *33*(1), pp. 60–89. **[G: Australia]**

Fischer, Stanley. On Activist Monetary Policy with Rational Expectations. **In** *Fischer, S.*, 1986, *1980*, pp. 383–412. **[G: U.S.]**

Franke, Reiner. A Cross-over Gravitation Process in Prices and Inventories. **In** *Semmler, W., ed.*, 1986, pp. 51–82.

Fujimoto, Takao and Krause, Ulrich. Ergodic Price Setting with Technical Progress. **In** *Semmler, W., ed.*, 1986, pp. 115–24.

Gabszewicz, Jean Jaskold and Quinzii, M. The Dynamics of Capacity Adjustments in a Competitive Economy. *Europ. Econ. Rev.*, August 1986, *30*(4), pp. 729–48.

Gibson, Bill and Esfahani, Hadi S. Technical Change with Non-produced Means of Production. *Rev. Radical Polit. Econ.*, Winter 1986, *18*(4), pp. 100–101.

Gomulka, Stanislaw. Industrialisation and the Rate of Growth: Eastern Europe 1955–75. **In** *Gomulka, S.*, 1986, *1983*, pp. 92–102. **[G: E. Europe]**

Grant, James H. and Nichols, Len M. On the Existence of a Market for Second Hand Physical Capital: An Empirical Test of the Keynesian and Neoclassical Assumptions. *J. Macroecon.*,

Spring 1986, *8*(2), pp. 131–57. **[G: U.S.]**

Gylfason, Thorvaldur and Lindbeck, Assar. Endogenous Unions and Governments: A Game-Theoretic Approach. *Europ. Econ. Rev.*, February 1986, *30*(1), pp. 5–26.

Hall, Robert E. Market Structure and Macroeconomic Fluctuations. *Brookings Pap. Econ. Act.*, 1986, (2), pp. 285–322. **[G: U.S.]**

Hammad, Khalil. An Aggregate Production Function for Jordan. *METU*, 1986, *13*(3–4), pp. 287–98. **[G: Jordan]**

Heal, Geoffrey. Macrodynamics and Returns to Scale. *Econ. J.*, March 1986, *96*(381), pp. 191–98.

Helliwell, John F. Supply-Side Macro-economics. *Can. J. Econ.*, November 1986, *19*(4), pp. 597–625. **[G: Canada; U.S.; Selected OECD]**

Herce San Miguel, José Antonio. Presupuesto de Seguridad Social y oferta de factores en una economía de generaciones sucesivas. (With English summary.) *Invest. Ecón.*, January 1986, *10*(1), pp. 37–64.

Hercowitz, Zvi. The Real Interest Rate and Aggregate Supply. *J. Monet. Econ.*, September 1986, *18*(2), pp. 121–45. **[G: U.S.; Canada]**

Hoel, Michael. Employment and Allocation Effects of Reducing the Length of the Workday. *Economica*, February 1986, *53*(209), pp. 75–85.

Howitt, Peter. Wage Flexibility and Employment. *Eastern Econ. J.*, July-Sept. 1986, *12*(3), pp. 237–42.

Hubbard, R. Glenn. Market Structure and Macroeconomic Fluctuations: Comments. *Brookings Pap. Econ. Act.*, 1986, (2), pp. 328–36.

Humphrey, Thomas M. The Early History of the Phillips Curve. **In** *Humphreys, T. M.*, 1986, *1985*, pp. 91–98.

Inoue, Tadashi and Wegge, Leon L. On the Geometry of the Production Possibility Frontier. *Int. Econ. Rev.*, October 1986, *27*(3), pp. 727–37.

Jackman, Richard; Layard, Richard and Pissarides, Christopher A. Policies for Reducing the Natural Rate of Unemployment. **In** *Butkiewicz, J. L.; Koford, K. J. and Miller, J. B., eds.*, 1986, pp. 111–33.

Jorgenson, Dale W. and Yun, Kun-Young. The Efficiency of Capital Allocation. *Scand. J. Econ.*, 1986, *88*(1), pp. 85–107. **[G: U.S.]**

Kalmbach, Peter and Kurz, Heinz D. Economic Dynamics and Innovation: Ricardo, Marx and Schumpeter on Technological Change and Unemployment. **In** *Wagener, H.-J. and Drukker, J. W., eds.*, 1986, pp. 71–92.

Kantor, Laurence G. Inflation Uncertainty and Real Economic Activity: An Alternative Approach. *Rev. Econ. Statist.*, August 1986, *68*(3), pp. 493–500. **[G: U.S.]**

Katz, Lawrence F. Efficiency Wage Theories: A Partial Evaluation. **In** *Fischer, S., ed.*, 1986, pp. 235–76. **[G: U.S.]**

Knoester, Anthonie. Okun's Law Revisited. *Weltwirtsch. Arch.*, 1986, *122*(4), pp. 657–66. **[G: W. Germany; Netherlands; U.K.; U.S.]**

Kœig, Gilbert. Le concept keynesien de coût d'usage et les prévisons du producteur. (The Keynesian Concept of User Cost and the Producer's Short Term Expectations. With English summary.) *Revue Écon.*, July 1986, *37*(4), pp. 697–721.

Kohn, Robert E. The Rate of Interest in a Stationary Economy. *J. Macroecon.*, Summer 1986, *8*(3), pp. 373–80.

König, Heinz and Nerlove, Marc. Price Flexibility, Inventory Behavior, and Production Responses. **In** *[Arrow, K. J.], Vol. 2*, 1986, pp. 179–218. **[G: France; W. Germany]**

Kuran, Timur. Anticipated Inflation and Aggregate Employment: The Case of Costly Price Adjustment. *Econ. Inquiry*, April 1986, *24*(2), pp. 293–311.

Kurz, Heinz D. and Salvadori, Neri. A Comment on Levine [Sraffa's *Production of Commodities by Means of Commodities*, Returns to Scale, Relevance, and Other Matters: A Note]. *J. Post Keynesian Econ.*, Fall 1986, *9*(1), pp. 163–65.

Kurz, Mordecai. On Asymmetric Information, Unemployment, and Inflexible Wages. **In** *[Arrow, K. J.], Vol. 2*, 1986, pp. 219–49.

Laroque, Guy. Le chômage des années 1970 était-il classique? (The Unemployment of the 1970's: A Classical Unemployment Régime? With English summary.) *L'Actual. Econ.*, September 1986, *62*(3), pp. 349–64. **[G: France]**

Lavoie, Marc. Chômage classique et chômage keynésien: un prétexte aux politiques d'austérité. (Classical Unemployment and Keynesian Unemployment: A Pretext for Policies of Austerity. With English summary.) *Écon. Appl.*, 1986, *39*(2), pp. 203–38.

Layard, Richard. Financial Markets and Macroeconomic Fluctuations: Reply. **In** *Butkiewicz, J. L.; Koford, K. J. and Miller, J. B., eds.*, 1986, pp. 149–52.

Layard, Richard. Theories of Wage Rigidity: Comment. **In** *Butkiewicz, J. L.; Koford, K. J. and Miller, J. B., eds.*, 1986, pp. 215–16.

Lee, Fred S. Post Keynesian View of Average Direct Costs: A Critical Evaluation of the Theory and the Empirical Evidence. *J. Post Keynesian Econ.*, Spring 1986, *8*(3), pp. 400–424. **[G: U.S.]**

Levine, A. L. Reply [Sraffa's *Production of Commodities by Means of Commodities*, Returns to Scale, Relevance, and Other Matters: A Note]. *J. Post Keynesian Econ.*, Fall 1986, *9*(1), pp. 166–68.

Livshits, A. Criticism of Supply-Side Economics. *Prob. Econ.*, September 1986, *29*(5), pp. 76–94. **[G: U.S.]**

Lubian, Diego. Interessi nel tasso "naturale": una interpretazione della elevata e persistente disoccupazione attuale. (Hysteresis in the "Natural" Rate of Employment: An Interpretation of the High and Persistent Present Unemployment. With English summary.) *Giorn. Econ.*, Jan.-Feb. 1986, *45*(1–2), pp. 55–72. **[G: U.S.; U.K.; Japan; Italy; W. Germany]**

Malinvaud, Edmond. Jusqu'ou la rigueur salariale devrait-elle aller? Une exploration théorique de la question. (The Search for the Appropriate

Real Wage. With English summary.) *Revue Écon.*, March 1986, *37*(2), pp. 181–205.

Marris, Robin and Mueller, Dennis C. The Corporation, Competition, and the Invisible Hand. **In** *Mueller, D. C.*, 1986, *1980*, pp. 261–97.

Marsh, James Barney. Jacob Vanderlint and the Roots of Supply-Side Economics. *Eastern Econ. J.*, Jan.-Mar. 1986, *12*(1), pp. 63–72.

McCombie, John S. L. On Some Interpretations of the Relationship between Productivity and Output Growth. *Appl. Econ.*, November 1986, *18*(11), pp. 1215–25. **[G: OECD]**

McCombie, John S. L. Why Cutting Real Wages Will Not Necessarily Reduce Unemployment—Keynes and the "Postulates of the Classical Economics." *J. Post Keynesian Econ.*, Winter 1985-86, *8*(2), pp. 233–48.

Melese, Francois and Transue, William. Unscrambling Chaos through Thick and Thin [The Emergence of Chaos from Classical Economic Growth]. *Quart. J. Econ.*, May 1986, *101*(2), pp. 419–23.

Minford, Patrick. Rational Expectations and Monetary Policy. *Scot. J. Polit. Econ.*, November 1986, *33*(4), pp. 317–33.

Mirlesse, D. and Royer, D. Dynamique du chômage et attractions du plein-emploi. (Unemployment Dynamics and Full-Employment Attractions. With English summary.) *Écon. Appl.*, 1986, *39*(2), pp. 369–99.

Mitchell, Daniel J. B. Wages and Keynes: Lessons from the Past. *Eastern Econ. J.*, July-Sept. 1986, *12*(3), pp. 199–208. **[G: U.S.]**

Miyao, Takahiro. Marx's Transformation Problem and Sraffa's Standard Commodity. *Econ. Stud. Quart.*, September 1986, *37*(3), pp. 193–98.

Musgrave, Richard A. Maximin, Uncertainty and the Leisure Trade-off. **In** *Musgrave, R. A., Vol. 2*, 1986, *1974*, pp. 246–53.

Naish, Howard F. Price Adjustment Costs and the Output–Inflation Trade-off. *Economica*, May 1986, *53*(210), pp. 219–30.

Nakamura, Shinichiro. A Flexible Dynamic Model of Multiproduct Technology for the West German Economy. *J. Appl. Econometrics*, October 1986, *1*(4), pp. 333–44. **[G: W. Germany]**

Nguyen, Hong V. Money in the Aggregate Production Function: Reexamination and Further Evidence. *J. Money, Credit, Banking*, May 1986, *18*(2), pp. 141–51. **[G: U.S.]**

Nordhaus, William D. Can the Share Economy Cure Our Macroeconomic Woes? Probably Not. *J. Compar. Econ.*, December 1986, *10*(4), pp. 448–53.

Nordhaus, William D. Introduction to the Share Economy. *J. Compar. Econ.*, December 1986, *10*(4), pp. 416–20. **[G: U.S.]**

Peston, Maurice H. The Elementary Macroeconomic Consequences of Differing Public and Private Sector Wages. *Public Finance*, 1986, *41*(2), pp. 173–81.

Pissarides, Christopher A. Theories of Wage Rigidity: Comment. **In** *Butkiewicz, J. L.; Koford, K. J. and Miller, J. B., eds.*, 1986, pp. 206–09.

Rima, Ingrid H. The Pigou–Keynes Controversy about Involuntary Unemployment: A Half-Century Reinterpretation. *Eastern Econ. J.*, Oct.-Dec. 1986, *12*(4), pp. 467–77.

Rossana, Robert J. Wage and Hiring Dynamics with Storable Output. *J. Macroecon.*, Summer 1986, *8*(3), pp. 313–28.

Rouwendal, Jan. On the Production and Diffusion of Technological Change. **In** *Nijkamp, P., ed. (II)*, 1986, pp. 371–81.

Rouzaud, Catherine. Approches théoriques récentes du chômage imputable à l'absence d'ajustement du salaire. (Recent Wage Rigidity Explanations of Unemployment. With English summary.) *Écon. Appl.*, 1986, *39*(4), pp. 793–817.

Rübel, Gerhard. Arbeitszeit, Ersparnis und Leistungsbilanz—Eine intertemporale Untersuchung. (Working Hours, Savings and the Current Account—An Intertemporal Study. With English summary.) *Jahr. Nationalökon. Statist.*, March 1986, *201*(2), pp. 175–89.

Samanta, Subarna K. Price Surprises and Real Output: The Indian Evidence. *Indian Econ. J.*, Oct.-Dec. 1986, *34*(2), pp. 49–58. **[G: India]**

Samuelson, Paul A. Paul Douglas's Measurement of Production Functions and Marginal Productivities. **In** *Samuelson, P. A.*, 1986, *1979*, pp. 203–19.

Seidman, Laurence S. Financial Markets and Macroeconomic Fluctuations: Comment. **In** *Butkiewicz, J. L.; Koford, K. J. and Miller, J. B., eds.*, 1986, pp. 143–44.

Semmler, Willi. On a Microdynamics of a Nonlinear Macrocycle Model. **In** *Semmler, W., ed.*, 1986, pp. 170–99.

Simon, Julian L. and Steinmann, Gunter. The Effects of Population Size and Growth through Learning-by-Doing [The Economic Implications of Learning-by-Doing for Population Size and Growth]. **In** *Simon, J. L.*, 1986, *1984*, pp. 83–101.

Solimano, Andrés. Salarios Reales y Empleo Bajo Distintos Regímenes Macroeconómicos. Una Aplicación para Chile y Brasil. (With English summary.) *Cuadernos Econ.*, December 1986, *23*(70), pp. 343–71. **[G: Chile; Brazil]**

Solow, Robert M. Unemployment: Getting the Questions Right. *Economica*, Supplement 1986, *53*(210(S)), pp. S23–34.

Stephan, Gunter. A Neo-Austrian Approach to the Open-Endedness of the Future: An Overview. **In** *Faber, M., ed.*, 1986, pp. 132–43.

Stephan, Gunter. Roundaboutness, Nontightness and Malinvaud Prices in Multisector Models with Infinite Horizon. **In** *Faber, M., ed.*, 1986, pp. 154–72.

Stiglitz, Joseph E. Theories of Wage Rigidity. **In** *Butkiewicz, J. L.; Koford, K. J. and Miller, J. B., eds.*, 1986, pp. 153–206.

Stiglitz, Joseph E. Theories of Wage Rigidity: Reply. **In** *Butkiewicz, J. L.; Koford, K. J. and Miller, J. B., eds.*, 1986, pp. 219–21.

Stockman, Alan C. and Koh, Ai Tee. Open-Economy Implications of Two Models of Business

Fluctuations. *Can. J. Econ.*, February 1986, *19*(1), pp. 23–34.

Svensson, Lars-Gunnar. National Income and Marginal Taxes. *Scand. J. Econ.*, 1986, *88*(4), pp. 565–81.

Talamona, Mario. Bresciani Turroni, Keynes and the Problem of Unemployment in Italy. *Rev. Econ. Cond. Italy,* Sept.-Dec. 1986, (3), pp. 541–57. **[G: Italy]**

Tinbergen, Jan. Some Extensions and Refinements of Gottschalk's Estimation of Production Functions. **In** *Perryman, M. R. and Schmidt, J. R., eds.*, 1986, pp. 3–12. **[G: U.S.]**

Tobin, James. Inflation and Unemployment in the Share Economy. *J. Compar. Econ.*, December 1986, *10*(4), pp. 460–63.

Weiss, Laurence. Asymmetric Adjustment Costs and Sectoral Shifts. **In** *[Arrow, K. J.], Vol. 2*, 1986, pp. 251–64.

Weiss, Laurence. Efficiency Wage Theories: A Partial Evaluation: Comment. **In** *Fischer, S., ed.*, 1986, pp. 285–87. **[G: U.S.]**

Weitzman, Martin L. The Share Economy Symposium: A Reply. *J. Compar. Econ.*, December 1986, *10*(4), pp. 469–73.

Wilson, Thomas. Real Wages and Unemployment. *Banca Naz. Lavoro Quart. Rev.*, March 1986, (156), pp. 85–102. **[G: U.S.; U.K.]**

Winckler, Georg and Kunst, Robert. The Influence of Wage Rate Variations on the Level of Employment with and without an Exogenous Interest Rate. **In** *Frisch, H. and Gahlen, B., eds.*, 1986, pp. 186–200.

Wodopia, Franz-Josef. Time and Production: Period versus Continuous Analysis. **In** *Faber, M., ed.*, 1986, pp. 186–94.

Wörgötter, Andreas. Asymmetric Adjustment Costs and Price Stickiness. **In** *Frisch, H. and Gahlen, B., eds.*, 1986, pp. 201–16.

Wright, Randall. Job Search and Cyclical Unemployment. *J. Polit. Econ.*, February 1986, *94*(1), pp. 38–55.

Young, Jeffrey T. The Entrepreneur in Marx and Schumpeter: A Post-Keynesian Perspective. **In** *Helburn, S. W. and Bramhall, D. F., eds.*, 1986, pp. 183–95.

0235 Theory of Aggregate Distribution

Ahmad, Syed. A Pasinetti Theory of Relative Profit Share for the Anti-Pasinetti Case. *J. Post Keynesian Econ.*, Fall 1986, *9*(1), pp. 149–58.

Ahmad, Syed. Sraffa Numeraire and Reswitching: A Note. *J. Macroecon.*, Summer 1986, *8*(3), pp. 381–85.

Amadeo, Edward J. Crescimento, distribuição e utilização capacidade: um modelo neo-steindliano. (With English summary.) *Pesquisa Planejamento Econ.*, December 1986, *16*(3), pp. 689–711.

Bajt, Aleksander. Post-Keynesian Theory of the Labour-Managed Firm: Some Comments. *Econ. Anal. Workers' Manage.*, 1986, *20*(4), pp. 385–93.

Ball, Michael. On Marx's Theory of Agricultural Rent: A Reply. **In** *Fine, B., ed.*, 1986, *1980*, pp. 152–74.

Basile, Liliana and Salvadori, Neri. Kalecki's Pricing Theory: A Reply. *J. Post Keynesian Econ.*, Fall 1986, *9*(1), pp. 159–60.

Bauer, Otto. Otto Bauer's 'Accumulation of Capital' (1913). *Hist. Polit. Econ.*, Spring 1986, *18*(1), pp. 87–110.

Bernholz, Peter; Faber, Malte and Reiss, Winfried. A Neo-Austrian Two-Period Multisector Model of Capital. **In** *Faber, M., ed.*, 1986, *1978*, pp. 98–112.

Bidard, Christian. Baisse tendancielle du taux de profit et marchandise-étalon. (Falling Rate of Profit and the Standard Commodity. With English summary.) *Écon. Appl.*, 1986, *39*(1), pp. 139–54.

Bidard, Christian. The Maximum Rate of Profits in Joint Production. *Metroecon.*, February 1986, *38*(1), pp. 53–66.

Blaug, Mark. Another Look at the Labour Reduction Problem in Marx. **In** *Blaug, M.*, 1986, *1982*, pp. 197–208.

Böge, Werner. Remarks on a Dynamic Game with Macroeconomic Investment. **In** *Faber, M., ed.*, 1986, pp. 259–66.

Böge, Werner; Faber, Malte and Güth, Werner. A Dynamic Game with Macroeconomic Investment Decisions under Alternative Market Structures. **In** *Faber, M., ed.*, 1986, *1982*, pp. 229–58.

Bowles, Samuel; Gordon, David M. and Weisskopf, Thomas E. Power and Profits: The Social Structure of Accumulation and the Profitability of the Postwar U.S. Economy. *Rev. Radical Polit. Econ.*, Spring/Summer 1986, *18*(1/2), pp. 132–67. **[G: U.S.]**

Brush, Brian C. and Crane, Steven E. Wage Share, Market Power and Unionism: Rejoinder. *Manchester Sch. Econ. Soc. Stud.*, March 1986, *54*(1), pp. 190–12. **[G: U.S.]**

Carchedi, Guglielmo. The Logic of Prices as Values. **In** *Fine, B., ed.*, 1986, *1984*, pp. 215–39.

Carling, Alan. Forms of Value and the Logic of Capital. *Sci. Soc.*, Spring 1986, *50*(1), pp. 52–80.

Catephores, George. The Historical Transformation Problem—A Reply. **In** *Fine, B., ed.*, 1986, *1980*, pp. 180–84.

Chu, Yun-peng. Changes in Income Distribution over Time in a One-Sector Neoclassical Setting. *J. Devel. Econ.*, December 1986, *24*(2), pp. 359–70.

Cleaver, Harry. Karl Marx: Economist or Revolutionary? **In** *Helburn, S. W. and Bramhall, D. F., eds.*, 1986, pp. 121–46.

Collier, Irwin L., Jr. On Marxian Value, Exploitation, and the Transformation Problem: A Geometric Approach. *J. Compar. Econ.*, September 1986, *10*(3), pp. 325–37.

Cooper, Russell. Macroeconomic Implications of Profit Sharing: Comment. **In** *Fischer, S., ed.*, 1986, pp. 343–51. **[G: Japan]**

Coram, B. T. Marx, Roemer and the Theory of the Falling Rate of Profit. *Australian Econ. Pap.*, December 1986, *25*(47), pp. 265–71.

Cuyvers, Ludo. A Note on the Inequality Approach of the Labour Theory of Value. *Rech. Écon. Louvain*, 1986, *52*(1), pp. 85–94.

D'Agata, Antonio. Non-produced Means of Production in Sraffa's System: Basics, Non-basics and Quasi-basics. A Comment. *Cambridge J. Econ.*, December 1986, *10*(4), pp. 379–86.

D'Agata, Antonio. Non-produced Means of Production: Neo-Ricardians vs. Fundamentalists, a Comment. *Rev. Radical Polit. Econ.*, Winter 1986, *18*(4), pp. 93–99.

Diamond, Peter A. Intertemporal Aspects of Learning New Techniques: Implications for Efficiency and Distribution: Comment. *Scand. J. Econ.*, 1986, *88*(1), pp. 189–94.

Dolado, Juan J.; Malo de Molina, José Luis and Ortega, Eloísa. Respuesta en el deflactor del valor añadido en la industria ante variaciones en los costes laborales unitarios. (With English summary.) *Invest. Ecón.*, January 1986, *10*(1), pp. 163–72. **[G: Spain]**

Dostaler, Giles. Understanding the Significance of Piero Sraffa's Standard Commodity: A Note on the Marxian Notion of Surplus: "From Marx to Sraffa": Comments. *Hist. Polit. Econ.*, Fall 1986, *18*(3), pp. 463–69.

Faber, Malte. On the Development of Austrian Capital Theory. **In** *Faber, M., ed.*, 1986, pp. 12–43.

Faber, Malte. Relationships between Modern Austrian and Sraffa's Capital Theory. **In** *Faber, M., ed.*, 1986, *1980*, pp. 44–59.

Faber, Malte and Stephan, Gunter. Neo-Austrian Characterization of Proportional Prices with Positive Rate of Interest Relative to the Growth Rate. **In** *Faber, M., ed.*, 1986, pp. 144–53.

Faber, Malte, et al. On the Methodology of Strategic Interaction in Time. **In** *Faber, M., ed.*, 1986, pp. 210–28.

Faccarello, Gilbert. Understanding the Significance of Piero Sraffa's Standard Commodity: A Note on the Marxian Notion of Surplus: "Understanding Sraffa's Standard Commodity": A Comment. *Hist. Polit. Econ.*, Fall 1986, *18*(3), pp. 471–78.

Fine, Ben. Note: A Dissenting Note on the Transformation Problem. **In** *Fine, B., ed.*, 1986, *1983*, pp. 209–14.

Fine, Ben. On the Historical Transformation Problem. **In** *Fine, B., ed.*, 1986, *1980*, pp. 185–87.

Fine, Ben. On Marx's Theory of Agricultural Rent. **In** *Fine, B., ed.*, 1986, *1979*, pp. 114–51.

Fine, Ben. On Marx's Theory of Agricultural Rent: A Rejoinder. **In** *Fine, B., ed.*, 1986, *1980*, pp. 175–79.

Fine, Ben. The Value Dimension: Marx versus Ricardo and Sraffa: Introduction. **In** *Fine, B., ed.*, 1986, pp. 1–17.

Fineschi, Andrea. Classi sociali, agenti collettivi e analisi macroeconomica. (With English summary.) *Stud. Econ.*, 1986, *41*(28), pp. 23–62.

Fisunoglu, H. Mahir. Two Alternative Models for Explaining Capital Accumulation. *METU*, 1986, *13*(3–4), pp. 275–86.

Francesco, Drudi. Effetti redistributivi e di benessere di un'apertura a movimenti di capitale. (Effects of Capital Flows on Income Distribution and Welfare. A Review Article. With English summary.) *Giorn. Econ.*, July-Aug. 1986, *45*(7–8), pp. 433–62.

Ganssmann, Heiner. Transformations of Physical Conditions of Production: Steedman's Economic Metaphysics. **In** *Fine, B., ed.*, 1986, *1981*, pp. 94–113.

Gibson, Bill and Esfahani, Hadi S. Technical Change with Non-produced Means of Production. *Rev. Radical Polit. Econ.*, Winter 1986, *18*(4), pp. 100–101.

Gibson, Bill and McLeod, Darryl. Technical Change and the Theory of Rent: Reply [Non-produced Means of Production in Sraffa's System: Basics, Non-basics and Quasi-basics]. *Cambridge J. Econ.*, December 1986, *10*(4), pp. 387–91.

Glombowski, Jörg. Are There Macroeconomic Laws? The 'Law' of the Falling Rate of Profit Reconsidered: Comment. **In** *Wagener, H.-J. and Drukker, J. W., eds.*, 1986, pp. 64–70.

Glombowski, Jörg and Krüger, Michael. Some Extensions of a Classical Growth Cycle Model. **In** *Semmler, W., ed.*, 1986, pp. 212–51.

Goodwin, Richard M. Swinging along the Autostrada. **In** *Semmler, W., ed.*, 1986, pp. 125–31.

Goodwin, Richard M. Swinging along the Turnpike with von Neumann and Sraffa. *Cambridge J. Econ.*, September 1986, *10*(3), pp. 203–10.

Groenewegen, Peter. Professor Porta on the Significance of Understanding Sraffa's Standard Commodity and the Marxian Theory of Surplus: A Comment. *Hist. Polit. Econ.*, Fall 1986, *18*(3), pp. 455–62.

Harcourt, Geoffrey C. Some Cambridge Controversies in the Theory of Capital. **In** *[Harcourt, G. C.]*, 1986, *1969*, pp. 145–206.

Harris, Donald J. Are There Macroeconomic Laws? The 'Law' of the Falling Rate of Profit Reconsidered. **In** *Wagener, H.-J. and Drukker, J. W., eds.*, 1986, pp. 49–63.

von Hayek, Friedrich A. Maintaining Capital Intact: A Reply. **In** *Parker, R. H.; Harcourt, G. C. and Whittington, G., eds.*, 1986, *1941*, pp. 139–43.

Henley, Andrew. Wage Share, Market Power and Unionism: A Reply. *Manchester Sch. Econ. Soc. Stud.*, March 1986, *54*(1), pp. 104–08. **[G: U.S.]**

Hicks, John R. Maintaining Capital Intact: A Further Suggestion. **In** *Parker, R. H.; Harcourt, G. C. and Whittington, G., eds.*, 1986, *1942*, pp. 144–50.

Horvat, Branko. The Theory of Rent. *Econ. Anal. Workers' Manage.*, 1986, *20*(2), pp. 109–18.

Juillard, Michel. The Stability of the Reproduction Scheme: Theoretical Discussion and Empirical Evidence for the United States, 1948–1980. **In** *Semmler, W., ed.*, 1986, pp. 304–23. **[G: U.S.]**

Jungenfelt, Karl G. Intertemporal Aspects of Learning New Techniques: Implications for Efficiency and Distribution. *Scand. J. Econ.*, 1986, *88*(1), pp. 157–87.

Kuroki, Ryuzo. The Equalization of the Rate of Profit. **In** *Semmler, W., ed.*, 1986, pp. 35–50.

Laise, Domenico and Tucci, Michele. Una nota alla recensione di "Capitale, moneta e tempo." *Stud. Econ.*, 1986, *41*(29), pp. 187–98.

Lee, Fred S. Reply: [Kalecki's Pricing Theory: Two Comments]. *J. Post Keynesian Econ.*, Fall 1986, *9*(1), pp. 161–62.

Lianos, T. P. Marx on the Rate of Profit, the Rate of Profit of Enterprise and the Rate of Interest. *Acta Oecon.*, 1986, *37*(1–2), pp. 123–28.

Lindahl, Erik. The Concept of Income. **In** *Parker, R. H.; Harcourt, G. C. and Whittington, G., eds.*, 1986, *1933*, pp. 82–90.

Lindbeck, Assar. Pure Profits as Forced Saving: Comment. *Scand. J. Econ.*, 1986, *88*(1), pp. 131–35. **[G: France]**

Lipietz, Alain. Behind the Crisis: The Exhaustion of a Regime of Accumulation. A "Regulation School" Perspective on Some French Empirical Works. *Rev. Radical Polit. Econ.*, Spring/Summer 1986, *18*(1/2), pp. 13–32.

Lundberg, Erik. Pure Profits as Forced Saving: Comment. *Scand. J. Econ.*, 1986, *88*(1), pp. 137–40. **[G: France]**

Malinvaud, Edmond. Pure Profits as Forced Saving. *Scand. J. Econ.*, 1986, *88*(1), pp. 109–30. **[G: France]**

Malinvaud, Edmond. Reflecting on the Theory of Capital and Growth. *Oxford Econ. Pap.*, November 1986, *38*(3), pp. 367–85.

Miyao, Takahiro. Marx's Transformation Problem and Sraffa's Standard Commodity. *Econ. Stud. Quart.*, September 1986, *37*(3), pp. 193–98.

Moseley, Fred. Estimates of the Rate of Surplus-Value in the Postwar United States Economy. *Rev. Radical Polit. Econ.*, Spring/Summer 1986, *18*(1/2), pp. 169–89. **[G: U.S.]**

Nell, Edward J. Cyclical Growth: The Interdependent Dynamics of Industry and Agriculture. **In** *Semmler, W., ed.*, 1986, pp. 289–303.

Ochoa, Eduardo M. Is Reswitching Empirically Relevant? U.S. Wage-Profit–Rate Frontiers, 1947–1972. *Econ. Forum*, Winter 1986-1987, *16*(1), pp. 45–67. **[G: U.S.]**

Parys, Wilfried. Standard Commodities and the Transformation Problem. *Écon. Appl.*, 1986, *39*(1), pp. 181–90.

Pellengahr, Ingo. Austrians versus Austrians I: A Subjectivist View of Interest. **In** *Faber, M., ed.*, 1986, pp. 60–77.

Pellengahr, Ingo. Austrians versus Austrians II: Functionalist versus Essentialist Theories of Interest. **In** *Faber, M., ed.*, 1986, pp. 78–95.

Pigou, Arthur C. Maintaining Capital Intact. **In** *Parker, R. H.; Harcourt, G. C. and Whittington, G., eds.*, 1986, *1941*, pp. 135–38.

Porta, Pier Luigi. Understanding the Significance of Piero Sraffa's Standard Commodity: A Note on the Marxian Notion of Surplus. *Hist. Polit. Econ.*, Fall 1986, *18*(3), pp. 443–54.

Porta, Pier Luigi. Understanding the Significance of Piero Sraffa's Standard Commodity: A Rejoinder. *Hist. Polit. Econ.*, Fall 1986, *18*(3), pp. 479–84.

Reati, Angelo. La transformation des valeurs en prix non concurrentiels. (The Transformation of Labour Values into Non-competitive Prices. With English summary.) *Écon. Appl.*, 1986, *39*(1), pp. 155–79.

Reati, Angelo. The Deviation of Prices from Labour Values: An Extension to the Non-competitive Case. *Cambridge J. Econ.*, March 1986, *10*(1), pp. 35–42.

Reati, Angelo. The Rate of Profit and the Organic Composition of Capital in West German Industry from 1960 to 1981. *Rev. Radical Polit. Econ.*, Spring/Summer 1986, *18*(1/2), pp. 56–86. **[G: W. Germany]**

Reiss, Winfried and Faber, Malte. Own Rates of Interest in a General Multisector Model of Capital. **In** *Faber, M., ed.*, 1986, *1982*, pp. 113–31.

Rutherford, Robert P. Ricardo's Mantle. *Australian Econ. Pap.*, December 1986, *25*(47), pp. 206–21.

Salvadori, Neri. Replica [Capitale, moneta e tempo].(With English summary.) *Stud. Econ.*, 1986, *41*(29), pp. 199–201.

Samuelson, Paul A. Balanced-Growth Equilibrium in the General Multi-class Saving Model (Macroeconomic Distribution Theory/Neoclassical Imputation/NeoKeynesian Identities). **In** *Samuelson, P. A.*, 1986, *1977*, pp. 194–202.

Samuelson, Paul A. Land and the Rate of Interest. **In** *Samuelson, P. A.*, 1986, *1979*, pp. 664–82.

Samuelson, Paul A. The Role of Profits in a Mixed Economy: Changes in the Perceived Reality. **In** *Samuelson, P. A.*, 1986, *1978*, pp. 929–45.

Semmler, Willi. Competition, Instability, and Nonlinear Cycles: Introduction. **In** *Semmler, W., ed.*, 1986, pp. v–xii.

Shapiro, Matthew D. Capital and Saving in a Share Economy. *J. Compar. Econ.*, December 1986, *10*(4), pp. 444–47.

Solomons, David. Economic and Accounting Concepts of Income. **In** *Parker, R. H.; Harcourt, G. C. and Whittington, G., eds.*, 1986, *1961*, pp. 153–66.

Steenge, Albert E. On the Wage–Profit Relation in a Sraffa System with Joint Production. *Revue Écon.*, September 1986, *37*(5), pp. 925–32.

Stephan, Gunter. A Neo-Austrian Approach to the Open-Endedness of the Future: An Overview. **In** *Faber, M., ed.*, 1986, pp. 132–43.

Stephan, Gunter. Roundaboutness, Nontightness and Malinvaud Prices in Multisector Models with Infinite Horizon. **In** *Faber, M., ed.*, 1986, pp. 154–72.

Swanson, Paul A. The Labor Theory of Value and Fixed Capital. *Rev. Radical Polit. Econ.*, Fall 1986, *18*(3), pp. 44–64.

Tajnikar, Maks. Post-Keynesian Theory of the Labour-Managed Firm: A Rejoinder. *Econ. Anal. Workers' Manage.*, 1986, *20*(4), pp. 395–400.

Tajnikar, Maks. Reconstruction of the Theory of Distribution in the Labour-Managed Economy Following the Example of Post-Keynesian Economic Theory. *Econ. Anal. Workers' Manage.*, 1986, *20*(1), pp. 45–63.

023 Macroeconomic Theory

von Thadden, Ernst-Ludwig. A Dynamic Macroeconomic Investment Game with Non-linear Saving Behaviour. **In** *Faber, M., ed.*, 1986, pp. 267–91.

Vallageas, Bernard. Le problèmme de la nature du profit et de son agrégation dans le traité sur la monnaie et la théorie généale. (A Restatement of the Theory of Profit in Keynes's Treatise of Money and General Theory. With English summary.) *Écon. Soc.*, Aug.-Sept. 1986, *20*(8–9), pp. 171–88.

Zamkov, O. O. Mathematical Analysis of Extended Reproduction Schemata with a Changing Rate of Surplus Value. *Matekon,* Fall 1986, *23*(1), pp. 25–46.

Zinn, Karl Georg. Geldvermögen, Zinseinkommensquote und Inflation. (Financial Capital, Share of Interest Income and Inflation. With English summary.) *Jahr. Nationalökon. Statist.*, July 1986, *201*(4), pp. 350–69. **[G: W. Germany]**

0239 Macroeconomics of Intertemporal Choice

Ahmed, Shaghil. Temporary and Permanent Government Spending in an Open Economy: Some Evidence for the United Kingdom. *J. Monet. Econ.*, March 1986, *17*(2), pp. 197–224. **[G: U.K.]**

d'Autume, Antoine and Michel, Philippe. Déséquilibre général et investissement. (General Disequilibrium and Investment. With English summary.) *Ann. Écon. Statist.*, Oct./Dec. 1986, (4), pp. 23–51.

Balasko, Yves and Shell, Karl. Lump-sum Taxes and Transfers: Public Debt in the Overlapping-Generations Model. **In** *[Arrow, K. J.], Vol. 2,* 1986, pp. 121–53.

Benveniste, Lawrence M. and Cass, David. On the Existence of Optimal Stationary Equilibria with a Fixed Supply of Fiat Money: I. The Case of a Single Consumer. *J. Polit. Econ.*, April 1986, *94*(2), pp. 402–17.

Cuddington, John T. and Viñals, José M. Budget Deficits and the Current Account in the Presence of Classical Unemployment. *Econ. J.*, March 1986, *96*(381), pp. 101–19.

Cummings, Ronald G. and Pearse, Spencer R. The Intertemporal Problem: Comment. **In** *Bromley, D. W., ed.*, 1986, pp. 21–28.

Dehez, Pierre and Fitoussi, Jean-Paul. Indexation des salaires et fluctuations macroéconomiques. (With English summary.) *Revue Écon. Polit.*, May-June 1986, *96*(3), pp. 239–55.

Dehez, Pierre and Fitoussi, Jean-Paul. Wage Indexation and Macroeconomic Fluctuations. **In** *Beckerman, W., ed.*, 1986, pp. 201–17.

Dutton, John. Optimal Taxes on Foreign Investment in an Overlapping Generation Model. *Public Finance Quart.*, July 1986, *14*(3), pp. 289–311.

Elbers, C. and Weddepohl, H. N. Steady State Equilibria with Saving for Retirement in a Continuous Time Overlapping Generations Model. *J. Econ. (Z. Nationalökon.)*, 1986, *46*(3), pp. 253–82.

Faber, Malte, et al. On the Methodology of Strategic Interaction in Time. **In** *Faber, M., ed.*, 1986, pp. 210–28.

Farmer, Roger E. A. Deficits and Cycles. *J. Econ. Theory*, October 1986, *40*(1), pp. 77–88.

Gottardi, Piero. Decisioni di risparmio, scelte di portafoglio e politiche di finanziamento del disavanzo. (Saving Decisions, Portfolio Choices and Government Financial Policies. With English summary.) *Giorn. Econ.*, May-June 1986, *45*(5–6), pp. 263–93.

Gottardi, Piero. Risparmio e finanziamento del disavanzo pubblico in un'economia con generazioni sovrapposte. (Saving and Deficit-Financing in an Overlapping Generations Model. With English summary.) *Econ. Polít.*, December 1986, *3*(3), pp. 355–78.

Grandmont, Jean-Michel. Stabilizing Competitive Business Cycles. *J. Econ. Theory,* October 1986, *40*(1), pp. 57–76.

Grandmont, Jean-Michel and Laroque, Guy. Stability of Cycles and Expectations. *J. Econ. Theory*, October 1986, *40*(1), pp. 138–51.

Hahn, Frank H. and Solow, Robert M. Is Wage Flexibility a Good Thing? **In** *Beckerman, W., ed.*, 1986, pp. 1–19.

Heal, Geoffrey. The Intertemporal Problem. **In** *Bromley, D. W., ed.*, 1986, pp. 1–20.

Henin, Pierre-Yves and Zylberberg, André. Contrats indexés dans une économie monétaire. (Indexed Contracts in a Monetary Economy. With English summary.) *Ann. Écon. Statist.*, Apr./June 1986, (2), pp. 147–63.

Hsu, Chen-Min. The Consumption Function and Intertemporal Spillover Effects. *J. Econ. Dynam. Control*, December 1986, *10*(4), pp. 443–55.

Huffman, Gregory W. The Representative Agent, Overlapping Generations, and Asset Pricing. *Can. J. Econ.*, August 1986, *19*(3), pp. 511–21.

Lane, John and Leininger, Wolfgang. On Price Characterization and Pareto-Efficiency of Game Equilibrium Growth. *J. Econ. (Z. Nationalökon.),* 1986, *46*(4), pp. 347–67.

Leininger, Wolfgang. The Existence of Perfect Equilibria in a Model of Growth with Altruism between Generations. *Rev. Econ. Stud.*, July 1986, *53*(3), pp. 349–67.

Leone, Alfredo M. Variabilidad de precios relativos en modelos de generaciones superpuestas. (Relative Prices Variability in Overlapping Generations Models. With English summary.) *Económica (La Plata)*, Jan.-June 1986, *32*(1), pp. 57–79.

Modica, Salvatore. Temporary Equilibrium with Money, Unit-Elastic Price Expectations and Production Lags. *Econ. Notes*, 1986, (3), pp. 65–69.

Murphy, Robert G. Productivity Shocks, Nontraded Goods and Optimal Capital Accumulation. *Europ. Econ. Rev.*, October 1986, *30*(5), pp. 1081–95.

Musu, Ignazio. Analisi non walrasiana e modello *IS–LM:* una integrazione. (Non Walrasian

Analysis and the *IS–LM* Model: An Integration. With English summary.) *Ricerche Econ.*, Apr.-Sept. 1986, *40*(2–3), pp. 189–213.

Nishimura, Osamu and Nakao, Takeo. A Note on the Golden-Rule Condition in the Overlapping Generations Growth Model. *Manchester Sch. Econ. Soc. Stud.*, December 1986, *54*(4), pp. 420–24.

Phaneuf, Louis. Approche d'équilibre général stochastique du cycle économique: problèmes et réalisations. (The Stochastic General Equilibrium Approach to Business Cycles: Results and Problems. With English summary.) *L'Actual. Econ.*, March 1986, *62*(1), pp. 110–46.

Quirk, James P. The Intertemporal Problem: Comment. **In** *Bromley, D. W., ed.*, 1986, pp. 29–36.

Reichlin, Pietro. Equilibrium Cycles in an Overlapping Generations Economy with Production. *J. Econ. Theory*, October 1986, *40*(1), pp. 89–102.

Smith, Bruce. Limited Information, Money, and Competitive Equilibrium. *Can. J. Econ.*, November 1986, *19*(4), pp. 780–97.

Spear, Stephen E. and Srivastava, Sanjay. Markov Rational Expectations Equilibria in an Overlapping Generations Model. *J. Econ. Theory*, February 1986, *38*(1), pp. 35–62.

Suda, Shinichi. Pareto Optimality and Monetary Competitive Equilibrium in the Overlapping Generations Model. *Keio Econ. Stud.*, 1986, *23*(1), pp. 79–96.

Tanaka, Yasuhito. The Optimum Interest Rate under Uncertain Life Time. *Econ. Rev. (Keizai Kenkyu)*, January 1986, *37*(1), pp. 79–83.

van Wijnbergen, Sweder J. G. On Fiscal Deficits, the Real Exchange Rate and the World Rate of Interest. *Europ. Econ. Rev.*, October 1986, *30*(5), pp. 1013–23.

Woodford, Michael. Stationary Sunspot Equilibria in a Finance Constrained Economy. *J. Econ. Theory*, October 1986, *40*(1), pp. 128–37.

024 Welfare Theory

0240 General

Anderson, F. J. Valuing a Depletable Resource Endowment in an Open Economy. *Can. J. Econ.*, November 1986, *19*(4), pp. 730–44.

Balcer, Yves and Sadka, Efraim. Equivalence Scales, Horizontal Equity and Optimal Taxation under Utilitarianism. *J. Public Econ.*, February 1986, *29*(1), pp. 79–97.

Ball, Stephen W. Economic Equality: Rawls versus Utilitarianism. *Econ. Philos.*, October 1986, *2*(2), pp. 225–44.

Barry, Brian. Lady Chatterley's Lover and Doctor Fischer's Bomb Party: Liberalism, Pareto Optimality, and the Problem of Objectionable Preferences. **In** *Elster, J. and Hylland, A., eds.*, 1986, pp. 11–43.

Baumann, Michael G. and Kalt, Joseph P. Intertemporal Consumer Surplus in Lagged-Adjustment Demand Models: An Application to Natural Gas Pricing. *Energy Econ.*, January 1986, *8*(1), pp. 2–12. **[G: U.S.]**

Baumol, William J. The Public-Good Attribute as Independent Justification for Subsidy. **In** *Baumol, W. J.*, 1986, *1977*, pp. 101–10.

Baumol, William J. and Ordover, Janusz A. On the Optimality of Public-Goods Pricing with Exclusionary Devices. **In** *Baumol, W. J.*, 1986, *1977*, pp. 84–100.

Ben-Ner, Avner. Nonprofit Organizations: Why Do They Exist in Market Economies? **In** *Rose-Ackerman, S., ed.*, 1986, pp. 94–113.

Bergstrom, Theodore; Blume, Lawrence and Varian, Hal. On the Private Provision of Public Goods. *J. Public Econ.*, February 1986, *29*(1), pp. 25–49.

Besen, Stanley M. Private Copying, Reproduction Costs, and the Supply of Intellectual Property. *Info. Econ. Policy*, 1986, *2*(1), pp. 5–22.

Blackorby, Charles and Donaldson, David. Can Risk–Benefit Analysis Provide Consistent Policy Evaluations of Projects Involving Loss of Life? *Econ. J.*, September 1986, *96*(383), pp. 758–73.

Blair, Douglas H. and Pollak, Robert A. Rationality and Social Choice. **In** *Samuelson, L., ed.*, 1986, pp. 79–98.

Boyer, Marcel. Intertemporal Non-linear Pricing. *Can. J. Econ.*, August 1986, *19*(3), pp. 539–55.

Bronfenbrenner, Martin. Income Distribution and "Economic Justice." *J. Econ. Educ.*, Winter 1986, *17*(1), pp. 35–51. **[G: U.S.]**

Brümel, Wolfgang; Pethig, Rüdiger and von dem Hagen, Oskar. The Theory of Public Goods: A Survey of Recent Issues. *J. Inst. Theoretical Econ.*, June 1986, *142*(2), pp. 241–309.

Brunner, Johann K. A Two-Period Model on Optimal Taxation with Learning Incentives. *J. Econ. (Z. Nationalökon.)*, 1986, *46*(1), pp. 31–47.

Buchanan, James M. Our Times: Past, Present and Future. **In** *[Seldon, A.]*, 1986, pp. 31–38.

Buchanan, James M. The Ethical Limits of Taxation. **In** *Buchanan, J. M.*, 1986, *1984*, pp. 165–77.

Burrows, Paul. Nonconvexity Induced by External Costs on Production: Theoretical Curio or Policy Dilemma? *J. Environ. Econ. Manage.*, June 1986, *13*(2), pp. 101–28.

Carrica, J. L. Just Wages: The Law and Morality. *Int. J. Soc. Econ.*, 1986, *13*(9), pp. 17–24.

Coleman, James S. Beyond Pareto Optimality. **In** *Coleman, J. S.*, 1986, *1969*, pp. 33–62.

Coleman, James S. Individual Interests and Collective Action: Selected Essays: Introduction. **In** *Coleman, J. S.*, 1986, pp. 1–11.

Coleman, James S. Individual Interests and Collective Action. **In** *Coleman, J. S.*, 1986, *1966*, pp. 305–18.

Coleman, James S. The Possibility of a Social Welfare Function. **In** *Coleman, J. S.*, 1986, *1966*, pp. 63–84.

Coleman, Jules L. and Kraus, Jody. Rethinking the Theory of Legal Rights. *Yale Law J.*, June 1986, *95*(7), pp. 1335–71.

024 Welfare Theory

Coughlin, Peter J. Rights and the Private Pareto Principle. *Economica,* August 1986, *53*(211), pp. 303–20.

Cowling, Keith and Mueller, Dennis C. The Social Costs of Monopoly Power. **In** *Mueller, D. C.,* 1986, *1978,* pp. 223–47. **[G: U.S.; U.K.]**

Dasgupta, Partha. Positive Freedom, Markets and the Welfare State. *Oxford Rev. Econ. Policy,* Summer 1986, *2*(2), pp. 25–36.

Davidson, Donald. Judging Interpersonal Interests. **In** *Elster, J. and Hylland, A., eds.,* 1986, pp. 195–211.

De Borger, Bruno. The Relation between Alternative Benefit Measures for Quantity Constrained Price Subsidies. *Europ. Econ. Rev.,* August 1986, *30*(4), pp. 893–907.

Debroy, B. Decomposing Welfare Measures According to Groups of the Economy. *Margin,* July 1986, *18*(4), pp. 69–75. **[G: India]**

Delbono, Flavio. Giustizia distributiva e decisioni collettive: una nota su un recente saggio di Ackerman. (Distributive Justice and Collective Decisions: A Note on a Recent Book by Ackerman. With English summary.) *Econ. Polít.,* December 1986, *3*(3), pp. 397–408.

Dinopoulos, Elias and Wooton, Ian. A North–South Model of International Justice. *Can. J. Econ.,* November 1986, *19*(4), pp. 766–79.

Dye, Ronald A. and Antle, Rick. Cost-Minimizing Welfare Programs. *J. Public Econ.,* July 1986, *30*(2), pp. 259–65.

Edwards, Sebastian. Country Risk, Foreign Borrowing, and the Social Discount Rate in an Open Developing Economy. *J. Int. Money Finance,* Supp. March 1986, *5,* pp. S79–96. **[G: LDCs; Chile; Costa Rica]**

Feiwel, George R. Shafts from Arrow's Bow: Advance in and beyond Economic Theory. *Economia (Portugal),* May 1986, *10*(2), pp. 229–75.

Garner, C. Alan. Equity in Economic Relationships: Towards a Positive Theory. *J. Econ. Behav. Organ.,* September 1986, *7*(3), pp. 253–64.

Gibbard, Allan. Interpersonal Comparisons: Preference, Good, and the Intrinsic Reward of a Life. **In** *Elster, J. and Hylland, A., eds.,* 1986, pp. 165–93.

Gregory, Robin. Interpreting Measures of Economic Loss: Evidence from Contingent Valuation and Experimental Studies. *J. Environ. Econ. Manage.,* December 1986, *13*(4), pp. 325–37.

Güth, Werner and Hellwig, Martin. The Private Supply of a Public Good. *J. Econ. (Z. Nationalökon.),* Supplementum 5, 1986, pp. 121–59.

Guttman, Joel M. Matching Behavior and Collective Action: Some Experimental Evidence. *J. Econ. Behav. Organ.,* June 1986, *7*(2), pp. 171–98.

Harsanyi, John C. Utilitarian Morality in a World of Very Half-hearted Altruists. **In** *[Arrow, K. J.], Vol. 1,* 1986, pp. 57–73.

Hartzenberg, G. M. Errata [The Individual Welfare Function of Income]. *J. Stud. Econ. Econometrics,* November 1986, (26), pp. 1. **[G: Belgium; Netherlands]**

Hartzenberg, G. M. The Individual Welfare Function of Income. *J. Stud. Econ. Econometrics,* August 1986, (25), pp. 51–78. **[G: Netherlands; Belgium]**

Hatta, Tatsuo. Welfare Effects on Changing Commodity Tax Rates toward Uniformity. *J. Public Econ.,* February 1986, *29*(1), pp. 99–112.

Henderson, Dale W. Country Risk, Foreign Borrowing, and the Social Discount Rate in an Open Developing Economy: Comments. *J. Int. Money Finance,* Supp. March 1986, *5,* pp. 97–99. **[G: LDCs; Chile; Costa Rica]**

Hickerson, Steven R. Instrumental Justice and Social Economics. *Rev. Soc. Econ.,* December 1986, *44*(3), pp. 268–80.

James, Estelle. Contract Failure and Information Asymmetry: Comments. **In** *Rose-Ackerman, S., ed.,* 1986, pp. 154–58.

Johansson, Börje and Leonardi, Giorgio. Public Facility Location: A Multiregional and Multi-authority Decision Context. **In** *Nijkamp, P., ed. (I),* 1986, pp. 133–70.

Jorgenson, Dale W. Efficiency versus Equity in Economic Policy Analysis. **In** *Szenberg, M., ed.,* 1986, *1985,* pp. 105–21. **[G: U.S.]**

Karni, Edi and Zilcha, Itzhak. Welfare and Comparative Statics Implications of Fair Social Security: A Steady-state Analysis. *J. Public Econ.,* August 1986, *30*(3), pp. 341–57.

King, Mervyn A. A Pigovian Rule for the Optimum Provision of Public Goods. *J. Public Econ.,* August 1986, *30*(3), pp. 273–91.

Kolm, Serge-Christophe. L'allocation des ressources naturalles et le libéralisme. (The Allocation of Natural Resources and the Theory of Liberalism. With English summary.) *Revue Écon.,* March 1986, *37*(2), pp. 207–41.

Krashinsky, Michael. Transaction Costs and a Theory of the Nonprofit Organization. **In** *Rose-Ackerman, S., ed.,* 1986, pp. 114–32.

Lane, Robert E. Market Justice, Political Justice. *Amer. Polit. Sci. Rev.,* June 1986, *80*(2), pp. 383–402. **[G: U.S.]**

Lichtenberg, Erik and Zilberman, David. The Welfare Economics of Price Supports in U.S. Agriculture. *Amer. Econ. Rev.,* December 1986, *76*(5), pp. 1135–41. **[G: U.S.]**

Lindenberg, Siegwart. The Paradox of Privatization in Consumption. **In** *[Rapoport, A.],* 1986, pp. 297–310.

Littlechild, S. C. and Wiseman, Jack. The Political Economy of Restriction of Choice. *Public Choice,* 1986, *51*(2), pp. 161–72.

Maasoumi, Esfandiar. The Measurement and Decomposition of Multi-dimensional Inequality. *Econometrica,* July 1986, *54*(4), pp. 991–97.

Mack, Eric. The Ethics of Taxation: Rights versus Public Goods. **In** *Lee, D. R., ed.,* 1986, pp. 487–514.

Maital, Shlomo. Prometheus Rebound: On Welfare-Improving Constraints. *Eastern Econ. J.,* July-Sept. 1986, *12*(3), pp. 237–44.

Marshall, James D.; Knetsch, Jack L. and Sinden, J. A. Agents' Evaluations and the Disparity in Measures of Economic Loss. *J. Econ.*

Behav. Organ., June 1986, *7*(2), pp. 115–27.

McCormick, Ken. Towards a Definition of Waste in Economics: A Neoinstitutional Approach. *Rev. Soc. Econ.*, April 1986, *44*(1), pp. 80–92.

Mezzetti, Claudio. Libertà personale e principio paretiano sono compatibili? Un dilemma di teoria delle scelte sociali. (Is the Pareto Principles Compatible with Personal Liberty? A Dilemma in Social Choice Theory. With English summary.) *Econ. Polít.*, April 1986, *3*(1), pp. 61–91.

Mooney, Christopher P. Criteria for Justice. *Amer. J. Econ. Soc.*, April 1986, *45*(2), pp. 223–33.

Moreh, Jacob. Women, Men, and Society. *Kyklos*, 1986, *39*(2), pp. 209–29.

Morgan, Peter B.; McDonald, John and Woodfield, A. Affordability and Some Welfare Aspects of Indexation. *Econ. Rec.*, March 1986, *62*(176), pp. 37–48.

Moulin, Hervé. Characterizations of the Pivotal Mechanism. *J. Public Econ.*, October 1986, *31*(1), pp. 53–78.

Musgrave, Richard A. A Brief History of Fiscal Doctrine. **In** *Musgrave, R. A., Vol. 2*, 1986, *1985*, pp. 338–93.

Musgrave, Richard A. Provision for Social Goods. **In** *Musgrave, R. A., Vol. 1*, 1986, *1969*, pp. 41–58.

Musgrave, Richard A. Public Finance, Now and Then. **In** *Musgrave, R. A., Vol. 1*, 1986, *1983*, pp. 89–101.

Musgrave, Richard A. Samuelson on Public Goods. **In** *Musgrave, R. A., Vol. 2*, 1986, *1983*, pp. 319–34.

Musgrave, Richard A. The Voluntary Exchange Theory of Public Economy. **In** *Musgrave, R. A., Vol. 1*, 1986, *1939*, pp. 3–22.

Musgrave, Richard A. and Pazner, Elisha A. Liability Rules, Efficiency and Equity. **In** *Musgrave, R. A., Vol. 2*, 1986, *1980*, pp. 293–303.

Musgrave, Richard A. and Peacock, Alan. Classics in the Theory of Public Finance. **In** *Musgrave, R. A., Vol. 2*, 1986, *1958*, pp. 235–45.

Nas, Tevfik F.; Price, Albert C. and Weber, Charles T. A Policy-oriented Theory of Corruption. *Amer. Polit. Sci. Rev.*, March 1986, *80*(1), pp. 107–19.

Neill, Jon R. Bounds on the Willingness to Pay for Non-traded Goods: A Possibility Theorem [Observable Preferences for Public Goods]. *J. Public Econ.*, July 1986, *30*(2), pp. 267–72.

Nerlove, Marc; Razin, Assaf and Sadka, Efraim. Endogenous Population with Public Goods and Malthusian Fixed Resources: Efficiency or Market Failure. *Int. Econ. Rev.*, October 1986, *27*(3), pp. 601–09.

Nerlove, Marc; Razin, Assaf and Sadka, Efraim. Some Welfare Theoretic Implications of Endogenous Fertility. *Int. Econ. Rev.*, February 1986, *27*(1), pp. 3–31.

Nerlove, Marc; Razin, Assaf and Sadka, Efraim. Tamaño de población socialmente óptimo. (With English summary.) *Cuadernos Econ.*, April 1986, *23*(68), pp. 3–23.

Ng, Yew-Kwang. A Final Rejoinder [Beyond Pareto Optimality]. *J. Econ. (Z. Nationalöokon.)*, 1986, *46*(3), pp. 307–08.

Ng, Yew-Kwang. Beyond Pareto Optimality!! A Response. *J. Econ. (Z. Nationalöokon.)*, 1986, *46*(3), pp. 311–15.

Ng, Yew-Kwang. On the Welfare Economics of Population Control. *Population Devel. Rev.*, June 1986, *12*(2), pp. 247–66.

Ng, Yew-Kwang. Social Criteria for Evaluating Population Change: An Alternative to the Blackorby–Donaldson Criterion. *J. Public Econ.*, April 1986, *29*(3), pp. 375–81.

Oster, Sharon. Contract Failure and Information Asymmetry: Comments. **In** *Rose-Ackerman, S., ed.*, 1986, pp. 152–54.

Park, Wankyu. A Theoretical Analysis of the Efficient Provision of a Public Good. *J. Econ. Devel.*, July 1986, *11*(1), pp. 191–209.

Petersen, Niels Christian. A Public Choice Analysis of Parallel Public–Private Provision of Health Care. **In** *Culyer, A. J. and Jönsson, B., eds.*, 1986, pp. 67–85.

Plummer, Mark L. Supply Uncertainty, Option Price, and Option Value: An Extension. *Land Econ.*, August 1986, *62*(3), pp. 313–18.

Pöll, Günther. On the Graphical Analysis of the Ramsey-Problem. *Public Finance*, 1986, *41*(1), pp. 71–77.

Porta, Pier Luigi. Deontologia e apriorismo etico. (Deontology and Ethical Apriorism. With English summary.) *Rivista Int. Sci. Econ. Com.*, February 1986, *33*(2), pp. 165–84.

Raymon, Neil. Price Ceilings, Product Quality and Consumer Welfare. *J. Econ. (Z. Nationalöokon.)*, 1986, *46*(4), pp. 369–95.

Riley, J. M. Generalized Social Welfare Functionals: Welfarism, Morality and Liberty. *Soc. Choice Welfare*, December 1986, *3*(4), pp. 233–54.

Rob, Rafael. The Demand Revealing Mechanism. **In** *Samuelson, L., ed.*, 1986, pp. 121–38.

Roemer, John E. An Historical Materialist Alternative to Welfarism. **In** *Elster, J. and Hylland, A., eds.*, 1986, pp. 133–64.

Rose-Ackerman, Susan. Charitable Giving and "Excessive" Fundraising. **In** *Rose-Ackerman, S., ed.*, 1986, *1982*, pp. 333–46.

Samuels, Warren J. and Mercuro, Nicholas. Wealth Maximization and Judicial Decision-Making: The Issues Further Clarified [Posnerian Law and Economics on the Bench]. *Int. Rev. Law Econ.*, June 1986, *6*(1), pp. 133–37. **[G: U.S.]**

Samuelson, Paul A. Bergsonian Welfare Economics. **In** *Samuelson, P. A.*, 1986, *1981*, pp. 3–46.

Samuelson, Paul A. Reaffirming the Existence of "Reasonable" Bergson–Samuelson Social Welfare Functions. **In** *Samuelson, P. A.*, 1986, *1977*, pp. 47–54.

Samuelson, Paul A. When It Is Ethically Optimal to Allocate Money Income in Stipulated Fractional Shares. **In** *Samuelson, P. A.*, 1986, *1977*, pp. 55–75.

Schap, David. The Nonequivalence of Property Rules and Liability Rules. *Int. Rev. Law*

Econ., June 1986, *6*(1), pp. 125–32.

Scitovsky, Tibor. Equity. **In** *Scitovsky, T.*, 1986, *1964*, pp. 3–12.

Scitovsky, Tibor. Inequalities: Open and Hidden, Measured and Unmeasurable. **In** *Scitovsky, T.*, 1986, *1973*, pp. 26–34.

Scitovsky, Tibor. The Place of Economic Welfare in Human Welfare. **In** *Scitovsky, T.*, 1986, *1973*, pp. 13–25.

Seidl, Christian. A Final Note [Beyond Pareto Optimality]. *J. Econ. (Z. Nationalökon.)*, 1986, *46*(3), pp. 317.

Seidl, Christian. Beyond Pareto Optimality? A Comment. *J. Econ. (Z. Nationalöokon.)*, 1986, *46*(3), pp. 305–10.

Sen, Amartya K. Foundations of Social Choice Theory: An Epilogue. **In** *Elster, J. and Hylland, A., eds.*, 1986, pp. 213–48.

Slesnick, Daniel T. Welfare Distributional Change and the Measurement of Social Mobility. *Rev. Econ. Statist.*, November 1986, *68*(4), pp. 586–93. **[G: U.S.]**

Stell, Lance K. Close Encounters of the Lethal Kind: The Use of Deadly Force in Self-Defense. *Law Contemp. Probl.*, Winter 1986, *49*(1), pp. 113–24.

Stigler, George J. Free Riders and Collective Action: An Appendix to Theories of Economic Regulation. **In** *Stigler, G. J.*, 1986, *1974*, pp. 67–75. **[G: U.S.]**

Throsby, C. D. and Withers, Glenn A. Strategic Bias and Demand for Public Goods: Theory and an Application to the Arts. *J. Public Econ.*, December 1986, *31*(3), pp. 307–27. **[G: Australia]**

Trannoy, Alain. On Thon's Axiomatization of the Gini Index. *Math. Soc. Sci.*, April 1986, *11*(2), pp. 191–94.

Tullock, Gordon. Population Paradoxes. **In** *Tullock, G.*, 1986, pp. 183–92.

Tullock, Gordon. Wanted: New Public-Choice Theories. **In** *[Seldon, A.]*, 1986, pp. 15–27.

Weisbrod, Burton A. Toward a Theory of the Voluntary Nonprofit Sector in a Three-Sector Economy. **In** *Rose-Ackerman, S., ed.*, 1986, *1977*, pp. 21–44.

Weiss, Jeffrey H. Donations: Can They Reduce a Donor's Welfare? **In** *Rose-Ackerman, S., ed.*, 1986, pp. 45–54.

von Weizsäcker, Carl Christian. Free Entry into Telecommunications. **In** *Snow, M. S.*, 1986, pp. 20–41.

Wriglesworth, J. L. Two Simple Single-Profile Impossibilities. *Soc. Choice Welfare*, July 1986, *3*(2), pp. 89–97.

Zinam, Oleg. Impact of Ideology and Organizational Structures on Technology and Quality of Life. *Rivista Int. Sci. Econ. Com.*, January 1986, *33*(1), pp. 41–58. **[G: Global]**

0242 Allocative Efficiency Including Theory of Cost/Benefit

Allais, Maurice. The Concepts of Surplus and Loss and the Reformulation of the Theories of Stable General Economic Equilibrium and Maximum Efficiency. **In** *Baranzini, M. and Scazzieri, R., eds.*, 1986, pp. 135–74.

Anderson, Glen D. and Bishop, Richard C. The Valuation Problem. **In** *Bromley, D. W., ed.*, 1986, pp. 89–137.

Arnott, Richard J. and Stiglitz, Joseph E. Moral Hazard and Optimal Commodity Taxation. *J. Public Econ.*, February 1986, *29*(1), pp. 1–24.

Aumann, Robert J. and Drèze, Jacques H. Values of Markets with Satiation or Fixed Prices. *Econometrica*, November 1986, *54*(6), pp. 1271–1318.

Bandyopadhyay, Taradas. Rationality, Path Independence, and the Power Structure. *J. Econ. Theory*, December 1986, *40*(2), pp. 338–48.

Baumol, William J. Applied Fairness Theory and Rationing Policy. **In** *Baumol, W. J.*, 1986, *1982*, pp. 130–42.

Baumol, William J. Quasi Optimality: The Price We Must Pay for a Price System. **In** *Baumol, W. J.*, 1986, *1979*, pp. 62–83.

Benveniste, Lawrence M. and Cass, David. On the Existence of Optimal Stationary Equilibria with a Fixed Supply of Fiat Money: I. The Case of a Single Consumer. *J. Polit. Econ.*, April 1986, *94*(2), pp. 402–17.

Bernheim, B. Douglas and Ray, Debraj. On the Existence of Markov-Consistent Plans under Production Uncertainty. *Rev. Econ. Stud.*, October 1986, *53*(5), pp. 877–82.

Brander, J. R. G. and Cook, B. A. The Market as a Commons: A Further Comment [The Market as an Open Access Commons: A Neglected Aspect of Excess Capacity]. *De Economist*, 1986, *134*(2), pp. 214–24.

Buchanan, James M. Rights, Efficiency, and Exchange: The Irrelevance of Transactions Cost. **In** *Buchanan, J. M.*, 1986, *1984*, pp. 92–107.

Buchholz, Wolfgang. Kie Elastizitä t des Grenznutzens als Determinante optimaler Allokation. (The Elasticity of Marginal Utility as a Determinant of Optimal Allocation. With English summary.) *Jahr. Nationalökon. Statist.*, January 1986, *201*(1), pp. 66–80.

Cauley, Jon; Sandler, Todd and Cornes, Richard. Nonmarket Institutional Structures: Conjectures, Distribution, and Allocative Efficiency. *Public Finance*, 1986, *41*(2), pp. 153–72.

Chander, Parkash. The Design of Efficient Resource Allocation Mechanisms. **In** *Samuelson, L., ed.*, 1986, pp. 139–57.

Chavas, Jean-Paul; Bishop, Richard C. and Segerson, Kathleen. Ex Ante Consumer Welfare Evaluation in Cost–Benefit Analysis. *J. Environ. Econ. Manage.*, September 1986, *13*(3), pp. 255–68.

Coleman, James S. Collective Decisions in a Social System. **In** *Coleman, J. S.*, 1986, pp. 144–60.

Cornes, Richard; Mason, Charles F. and Sandler, Todd. The Commons and the Optimal Number of Firms. *Quart. J. Econ.*, August 1986, *101*(3), pp. 641–46.

Costrell, Robert M. Equilibrium and Optimality in a Mean-Variance Model. *Rand J. Econ.*,

Spring 1986, *17*(1), pp. 122–32.
Coughlin, Peter J. Rights and the Private Pareto Principle. *Economica*, August 1986, *53*(211), pp. 303–20.
Cox, Louis Anthony, Jr. Theory of Regulatory Benefits Assessment: Econometric and Expressed Preference Approaches. **In** *Bentkover, J. D.; Covello, V. T. and Jeryl, M., eds.*, 1986, pp. 85–159. **[G: U.S.]**
Crocker, Keith J. A Reexamination of the "Lemons" Market When Warranties Are Not Prepurchase Quality Signals. *Info. Econ. Policy*, June 1986, *2*(2), pp. 147–62.
Cummings, Ronald G. and Pearse, Spencer R. The Intertemporal Problem: Comment. **In** *Bromley, D. W., ed.*, 1986, pp. 21–28.
Darvish, Tikva and Eckstein, Shlomo. Evaluation of an Energy Project under Uncertainty: The Case of the Mediterranean–Dead Sea Project. *J. Policy Modeling*, Fall 1986, *8*(3), pp. 391–413. **[G: Israel]**
Diamond, Peter A. Intertemporal Aspects of Learning New Techniques: Implications for Efficiency and Distribution: Comment. *Scand. J. Econ.*, 1986, *88*(1), pp. 189–94.
Dierker, Egbert. When Does Marginal Cost Pricing Lead to Pareto Efficiency? *J. Econ. (Z. Nationalöokon.)*, Supplementum 5, 1986, pp. 41–66.
Dixon, John A. and Meister, Anton D. Time Horizons, Discounting, and Computational Aids. **In** *Dixon, J. A. and Hufschmidt, M. M., eds.*, 1986, pp. 39–55.
Ebert, Udo. Equity and Distribution in Cost–Benefit Analysis. *J. Econ. (Z. Nationalöokon.)*, Supplementum 5, 1986, pp. 67–78.
Eckalbar, John C. Bilateral Trade in a Monetized Pure Exchange Economy. *Econ. Modelling*, April 1986, *3*(2), pp. 135–39.
Epstein, Larry G. Intergenerational Consumption Rules: An Axiomatization of Utilitarianism and Egalitarianism. *J. Econ. Theory*, April 1986, *38*(2), pp. 280–97.
Esteban, Joan M. A Characterization of the Core in Overlapping-Generations Economies [An Exact Consumption-Loan Model of Interest with or without the Social Contrivance of Money]. *J. Econ. Theory*, August 1986, *39*(2), pp. 439–56.
Fink, Gary M. Historical Analysis: Industrial Relations Eras: Discussion. **In** *Dennis, B. D., ed.*, 1986, pp. 246–49. **[G: U.S.]**
Fisher, Ann. Valuation in a Policy Context: Comment. **In** *Bromley, D. W., ed.*, 1986, pp. 201–09.
Forsythe, Robert. The Application of Laboratory Methods to Testing Theories of Resource Allocation under Uncertainty. **In** *Gilad, B. and Kaish, S., eds., Vol. A*, 1986, pp. 19–60. **[G: U.S.]**
Freeman, A. Myrick, III. The Valuation Problem: Comment. **In** *Bromley, D. W., ed.*, 1986, pp. 139–49.
Gibbard, Allan. Risk and Value. **In** *MacLean, D., ed.*, 1986, pp. 94–112.
Greenberg, Joseph and Shitovitz, Benyamin. A Simple Proof of the Equivalence Theorem for Oligopolistic Mixed Markets. *J. Math. Econ.*, 1986, *15*(2), pp. 79–83.
Greenwald, Bruce C. and Stiglitz, Joseph E. Externalities in Economies with Imperfect Information and Incomplete Markets. *Quart. J. Econ.*, May 1986, *101*(2), pp. 229–64.
Hansmann, Henry B. The Rationale for Exempting Nonprofit Organizations from Corporate Income Taxation. **In** *Rose-Ackerman, S., ed.*, 1986, *1981*, pp. 367–93. **[G: U.S.]**
Hassin, Refael. Consumer Information in Markets with Random Product Quality: The Case of Queues and Balking. *Econometrica*, September 1986, *54*(5), pp. 1185–95.
Hau, Timothy D. Distributional Cost–Benefit Analysis in Discrete Choice. *J. Transp. Econ. Policy*, September 1986, *20*(3), pp. 313–38. **[G: U.S.]**
Heal, Geoffrey. The Intertemporal Problem. **In** *Bromley, D. W., ed.*, 1986, pp. 1–20.
Holcombe, Randall G. Non-optimal Unanimous Agreement. *Public Choice*, 1986, *48*(3), pp. 229–44.
Hurwicz, Leonid. On Informationally Decentralized Systems. **In** *[Marschak, J.]*, 1986, *1972*, pp. 297–336.
Jacoby, Sanford M. Historical Analysis: Industrial Relations Eras: Discussion. **In** *Dennis, B. D., ed.*, 1986, pp. 243–45. **[G: U.S.]**
Jones, Larry E. Special Problems Arising in the Study of Economies with Infinitely Many Commodities. **In** *Sonnenschein, H. F., ed.*, 1986, pp. 184–205.
Jungenfelt, Karl G. Intertemporal Aspects of Learning New Techniques: Implications for Efficiency and Distribution. *Scand. J. Econ.*, 1986, *88*(1), pp. 157–87.
Kemp, Murray C. and Wan, Henry Y., Jr. The Comparison of Second-Best Equilibria: The Case of Customs Unions. *J. Econ. (Z. Nationalöokon.)*, Supplementum 5, 1986, pp. 161–67.
Kunreuther, Howard. Behavioral Insights for Public Policy: Ex Ante/Ex Post Considerations. **In** *Gilad, B. and Kaish, S., eds., Vol. B*, 1986, pp. 87–109.
Lacaze, Dominique. Théorie des prix et sélection de techniques ou de projets. (Price Theory and Selection of Techniques or Projects. With English summary.) *Revue Écon.*, July 1986, *37*(4), pp. 677–95.
Lane, John and Leininger, Wolfgang. On Price Characterization and Pareto-Efficiency of Game Equilibrium Growth. *J. Econ. (Z. Nationalöokon.)*, 1986, *46*(4), pp. 347–67.
Lee, Kye Sik. Pareto Optimal Redistribution: A Public Good Approach. *Public Finance*, 1986, *41*(2), pp. 200–217.
Lemche, S. Q. Remarks on Non-paternalism and the Second Theorem of Welfare Economics. *Can. J. Econ.*, May 1986, *19*(2), pp. 270–80.
Lemche, S. Q. The Direct Social Preference Relation in the Theory of Public Expenditure. *Soc. Choice Welfare*, June 1986, *3*(1), pp. 51–59.
Leonard, Herman B. and Zeckhauser, Richard. Cost–Benefit Analysis Applied to Risks: Its Phi-

losophy and Legitimacy. **In** *MacLean, D., ed.*, 1986, pp. 31–48.

López García, Miguel Angel. Pensiones de la Seguridad Social y bienestar. Un análisis de los períodos transitorios. (With English summary.) *Invest. Ecón.*, January 1986, *10*(1), pp. 65–95.

Lyons, Bruce R. The Welfare Loss Due to Strategic Investment in Excess Capacity. *Int. J. Ind. Organ.*, March 1986, *4*(1), pp. 109–19.

MacLean, Douglas. Social Values and the Distribution of Risk. **In** *MacLean, D., ed.*, 1986, pp. 75–93.

Mankiw, N. Gregory and Whinston, Michael D. Free Entry and Social Inefficiency. *Rand J. Econ.*, Spring 1986, *17*(1), pp. 48–58.

Masarani, F. and Sadik Gokturk, S. A Pareto Optimal Characterization of Rawls' Social Choice Mechanism. *J. Math. Econ.*, 1986, *15*(2), pp. 157–70.

McConnell, Kenneth E. The Valuation Problem: Comment. **In** *Bromley, D. W., ed.*, 1986, pp. 151–61.

Mishan, Ezra J. The Limits to Freedom of Choice. **In** *Mishan, E. J.*, 1986, *1982*, pp. 57–77.

Montet, Christian. Échange inégal, gain de l'échange et justice distributive internationale. (Unequal Exchange, Gain from Trade and International Distributive Justice. With English summary.) *Revue Écon.*, July 1986, *37*(4), pp. 659–75.

Mookherjee, Dilip. Shadow Pricing with Suboptimal Policy Rules. *J. Public Econ.*, December 1986, *31*(3), pp. 287–305.

Musgrave, Richard A. Cost–Benefit Analysis and the Theory of Public Finance. **In** *Musgrave, R. A., Vol. 1*, 1986, *1969*, pp. 59–70.

Musgrave, Richard A. Pareto-Optimal Redistribution: Comment. **In** *Musgrave, R. A., Vol. 1*, 1986, *1970*, pp. 71–75.

Nevitte, Neil and Kennedy, Charles H. The Analysis of Policies of Ethnic Preference in Developing States. **In** *Nevitte, N. and Kennedy, C. H., eds.*, 1986, pp. 1–13.

O'Flaherty, Brendan. Potential Pareto Optimality of Risky Projects. *Quart. J. Econ.*, August 1986, *101*(3), pp. 647–51.

Orosel, Gerhard O. Tentative Notes on Prestige Seeking and Pareto-Efficiency. *J. Econ. (Z. Nationalökon.)*, Supplementum 5, 1986, pp. 169–94.

Pithyachariyakul, Pipat. Exchange Markets: A Welfare Comparison of Market Maker and Walrasian Systems. *Quart. J. Econ.*, February 1986, *101*(1), pp. 69–84.

Plummer, Mark L. and Hartman, Richard C. Option Value: A General Approach. *Econ. Inquiry*, July 1986, *24*(3), pp. 455–71.

Quirk, James P. The Intertemporal Problem: Comment. **In** *Bromley, D. W., ed.*, 1986, pp. 29–36.

Randall, Alan. Valuation in a Policy Context. **In** *Bromley, D. W., ed.*, 1986, pp. 163–99.

Roemer, John E. Equality of Resources Implies Equality of Welfare. *Quart. J. Econ.*, November 1986, *101*(4), pp. 751–84.

Rothchild, Donald. State and Ethnicity in Africa: A Policy Perspective. **In** *Nevitte, N. and Kennedy, C. H., eds.*, 1986, pp. 15–61. **[G: Africa]**

Samuelson, Paul A. A Chapter in the History of Ramsey's Optimal Feasible Taxation and Optimal Public Utility Prices. **In** *Samuelson, P. A.*, 1986, *1982*, pp. 76–100.

Scarf, Herbert E. Testing for Optimality in the Absence of Convexity. **In** *[Arrow, K. J.], Vol. 1*, 1986, pp. 117–34.

Scotchmer, Suzanne. Corrigendum [Profit Maximizing Clubs]. *J. Public Econ.*, April 1986, *29*(3), pp. 389.

Seidl, Christian. The Impossibility of Nondictatorial Tolerance. *J. Econ. (Z. Nationalökon.)*, Supplementum 5, 1986, pp. 211–25.

Smith, V. Kerry. A Conceptual Overview of the Foundations of Benefit–Cost Analysis. **In** *Bentkover, J. D.; Covello, V. T. and Jeryl, M., eds.*, 1986, pp. 13–34.

Smith, V. Kerry. Valuation in a Policy Context: Comment. **In** *Bromley, D. W., ed.*, 1986, pp. 211–29.

Sonstelie, Jon C. and Portney, Paul R. Profit Maximizing Communities and the Theory of Local Public Expenditure: Reply. *J. Urban Econ.*, September 1986, *20*(2), pp. 250–55.

Spulber, Daniel F. Second-Best Pricing and Cooperation. *Rand J. Econ.*, Summer 1986, *17*(2), pp. 239–50.

Stephan, Gunter. Competitive Finite Value Prices: A Complete Characterization. **In** *Faber, M., ed.*, 1986, *1985*, pp. 173–83.

Streissler, Erich and Neudeck, Werner. Are There Intellectual Precursors to the Idea of Second Best Optimization? *J. Econ. (Z. Nationalökon.)*, Supplementum 5, 1986, pp. 227–42.

Suda, Shinichi. Pareto Optimality and Monetary Competitive Equilibrium in the Overlapping Generations Model. *Keio Econ. Stud.*, 1986, *23*(1), pp. 79–96.

Suzumura, K. and Suga, K. Gibbardian Libertarian Claims Revisited. *Soc. Choice Welfare*, June 1986, *3*(1), pp. 61–73.

Tesfatsion, Leigh. Time Inconsistency of Benevolent Government Economies. *J. Public Econ.*, October 1986, *31*(1), pp. 25–52.

Thompson, Michael. To Hell with the Turkeys! A Diatribe Directed at the Pernicious Trepidity of the Current Intellectual Debate on Risk. **In** *MacLean, D., ed.*, 1986, pp. 113–35.

Tietzel, Manfred. Moral und Wirtschaftstheorie. (Morals and Economic Theory. With English summary.) *Z. Wirtschaft. Sozialwissen.*, 1986, *106*(2), pp. 113–37.

Tisdell, Clem A. Cost–Benefit Analysis, the Environment and Informational Constraints in LDCs. *J. Econ. Devel.*, December 1986, *11*(2), pp. 63–81. **[G: LDCs]**

Tzur, Joseph. An Agency Model of Search for Alternatives. *J. Econ. Behav. Organ.*, September 1986, *7*(3), pp. 317–27.

Veall, Michael R. Public Pensions as Optimal Social Contracts. *J. Public Econ.*, November 1986, *31*(2), pp. 237–51.

Whittington, Dale and MacRae, Duncan, Jr. The Issue of Standing in Cost–Benefit Analysis. *J. Policy Anal. Manage.*, Summer 1986, *5*(4), pp. 665–82.

Yu, Eden S. H. and Ingene, Charles A. Resource Allocation in a General Equilibrium Model of Production under Uncertainty: The Case of Variable Supply of Labor. *J. Econ. Theory*, December 1986, *40*(2), pp. 329–37.

0243 Redistribution Analyses

Bernheim, B. Douglas; Shleifer, Andrei and Summers, Lawrence H. The Strategic Bequest Motive. *J. Lab. Econ.*, Part 2, July 1986, *4*(3), pp. S151–82. **[G: U.S.]**

Bohanon, Cecil E. and McClure, James E. Taxes, Welfare Costs, and Public Consumption: The Case of the Unwitting Monopsonist. *Public Choice*, 1986, *49*(3), pp. 235–47.

Browning, Edgar K. On the Welfare Cost of Transfers. **In** *Tullock, G.*, 1986, *1974*, pp. 102–06.

Buchanan, James M. Distributive and Redistributive Norms: A Note of Clarification. **In** *Buchanan, J. M.*, 1986, pp. 159–64.

Buchanan, James M. Justice and Equal Treatment. **In** *Buchanan, J. M.*, 1986, *1983*, pp. 140–58.

Coleman, James S. Inequality, Sociology, and Moral Philosophy. **In** *Coleman, J. S.*, 1986, *1974*, pp. 319–47.

Coleman, James S. Rawls, Nozick, and Educational Equality. **In** *Coleman, J. S.*, 1986, *1976*, pp. 365–74.

Cordes, Joseph J.; Goldfarb, Robert S. and Watson, Harry S. The Relative Efficiency of Private and Public Transfers. *Public Choice*, 1986, *49*(1), pp. 29–45.

Daly, George and Mayor, Thomas. Equity, Efficiency and Environmental Quality. *Public Choice*, 1986, *51*(2), pp. 141–59. **[G: U.S.]**

Davies, James B. Does Redistribution Reduce Inequality? *J. Lab. Econ.*, October 1986, *4*(4), pp. 538–59.

Dinkel, Reiner. Social Security and Intergenerational Equity. **In** *von der Schulenburg, J.-M. G., ed.*, 1986, pp. 77–107. **[G: W. Germany]**

Hochman, Harold M. and Rodgers, James D. The Optimal Tax Treatment of Charitable Contributions. **In** *Rose-Ackerman, S., ed.*, 1986, *1977*, pp. 224–45. **[G: U.S.]**

Ioannides, Yannis M. Heritability of Ability, Intergenerational Transfers and the Distribution of Wealth. *Int. Econ. Rev.*, October 1986, *27*(3), pp. 611–23.

Karelis, Charles. Distributive Justice and the Public Good. *Econ. Philos.*, April 1986, *2*(1), pp. 101–25.

Kelman, Steven. A Case for In-Kind Transfers. *Econ. Philos.*, April 1986, *2*(1), pp. 55–73.

Kleindorfer, Paul R. and von der Schulenburg, J.-Matthias Graf. Intergenerational Equity and Fund Balances for Statutory Health Insurance. **In** *von der Schulenburg, J.-M. G., ed.*, 1986, pp. 108–29.

Malfliet, Katlijn. The Economic Function and Purpose of Personal Property and Its Legal Implementation. **In** *Ioffe, O. S. and Janis, M. W., eds.*, 1986, pp. 79–101. **[G: U.S.S.R.]**

Musgrave, Richard A. A Further Note on the Double Taxation of Savings. **In** *Musgrave, R. A., Vol. 1*, 1986, *1939*, pp. 105–07.

Musgrave, Richard A. ET, OT and SBT. **In** *Musgrave, R. A., Vol. 1*, 1986, *1976*, pp. 260–73.

Musgrave, Richard A. Fiscal Functions: Order and Politics. **In** *Musgrave, R. A., Vol. 1*, 1986, *1981*, pp. 76–88.

Musgrave, Richard A. Growth with Equity. **In** *Musgrave, R. A., Vol. 1*, 1986, *1963*, pp. 198–208.

Musgrave, Richard A. In Defence of an Income Concept. **In** *Musgrave, R. A., Vol. 1*, 1986, *1967*, pp. 222–37.

Musgrave, Richard A. Maximin, Uncertainty and the Leisure Trade-off. **In** *Musgrave, R. A., Vol. 2*, 1986, *1974*, pp. 246–53.

Musgrave, Richard A. On Incidence. **In** *Musgrave, R. A., Vol. 1*, 1986, *1953*, pp. 155–77.

Musgrave, Richard A. Private Labour and Common Land. **In** *Musgrave, R. A., Vol. 2*, 1986, *1983*, pp. 304–18.

Musgrave, Richard A. Public Finance, Now and Then. **In** *Musgrave, R. A., Vol. 1*, 1986, *1983*, pp. 89–101.

Musgrave, Richard A. The Nature of Horizontal Equity and the Principle of Broad-Based Taxation: A Friendly Critique. **In** *Musgrave, R. A., Vol. 1*, 1986, *1983*, pp. 301–15.

Musgrave, Richard A. and Musgrave, Peggy B. Inter-nation Equity. **In** *Musgrave, R. A., Vol. 2*, 1986, *1972*, pp. 43–63.

Peck, Richard M. Power and Linear Income Taxes: An Example. *Econometrica*, January 1986, *54*(1), pp. 87–94.

Plotnick, Robert D. An Interest Group Model of Direct Income Redistribution. *Rev. Econ. Statist.*, November 1986, *68*(4), pp. 594–602. **[G: U.S.]**

Plotnick, Robert D. Redistribution to the Poor: An Overheard Conversation. *Public Finance Quart.*, April 1986, *14*(2), pp. 223–28.

Posnett, John and Sandler, Todd. Joint Supply and the Finance of Charitable Activity. *Public Finance Quart.*, April 1986, *14*(2), pp. 209–22. **[G: U.K.]**

Rogers, Carol Ann. The Effect of Distributive Goals on the Time Inconsistency of Optimal Taxes. *J. Monet. Econ.*, March 1986, *17*(2), pp. 251–69.

Scafuri, Allen J. Measurable Welfare Change with Optimal Commodity Taxation [Optimal Taxation, the Compensation Principle and the Measurement of Changes in Economic Welfare]. *J. Public Econ.*, April 1986, *29*(3), pp. 383–87.

Scott, Anthony. Catch Quotas and Shares in the

Fishstock as Property Rights. **In** *[Crutchfield, J. A.]*, 1986, pp. 61–96.

Toumanoff, Peter. Exclusion Costs and the In-Kind Transfer. *Kyklos*, 1986, *39*(3), pp. 443–47.

Tullock, Gordon. Aid in Kind. **In** *Tullock, G.*, 1986, pp. 128–35.

Tullock, Gordon. Demand Revealing, Transfers, and Rent Seeking. **In** *Tullock, G.*, 1986, pp. 136–42.

Tullock, Gordon. Giving Life [Avoiding Difficult Decisions]. **In** *Tullock, G.*, 1986, *1979*, pp. 158–69.

Tullock, Gordon. Information without Profit. **In** *Tullock, G.*, 1986, *1966*, pp. 73–88.

Tullock, Gordon. Inheritance Justified. **In** *Tullock, G.*, 1986, *1971*, pp. 170–79.

Tullock, Gordon. Local Redistribution. **In** *Tullock, G.*, 1986, pp. 113–27.

Tullock, Gordon. More on the Welfare Cost of Transfers. **In** *Tullock, G.*, 1986, *1974*, pp. 107–10.

Tullock, Gordon. Objectives of Income Redistribution. **In** *Tullock, G.*, 1986, *1979*, pp. 42–56.

Tullock, Gordon. Reasons for Redistribution. **In** *Tullock, G.*, 1986, *1981*, pp. 15–41.

Tullock, Gordon. The Charity of the Uncharitable. **In** *Tullock, G.*, 1986, *1971*, pp. 57–69.

Tullock, Gordon. The Cost of Transfers. **In** *Tullock, G.*, 1986, *1971*, pp. 89–101.

Tullock, Gordon. The Economics of Wealth and Poverty: Epilogue—The Grating People. **In** *Tullock, G.*, 1986, pp. 205–06.

Tullock, Gordon. The Economics of Wealth and Poverty: Introduction. **In** *Tullock, G.*, 1986, pp. 1–11.

Wagner, Richard E. The Welfare State, Capital Formation, and Tax-Transfer Politics. **In** *Lee, D. R., ed.*, 1986, pp. 241–73. **[G: U.S.]**

Wagner, Richard E. Wealth Transfers in a Rent-Seeking Polity. *Cato J.*, Spring/Summer 1986, *6*(1), pp. 155–71.

Wickström, Bengt-Arne. Transfers, Collective Goods, and Redistribution. *J. Econ. (Z. Nationalökon.)*, Supplementum 5, 1986, pp. 243–58.

Yunker, James A. In Defense of Utilitarianism: An Economist's Viewpoint. *Rev. Soc. Econ.*, April 1986, *44*(1), pp. 57–79.

0244 Externalities

Anderson, Terry L. and Hill, Peter J. Privatizing the Commons: Reply. *Southern Econ. J.*, April 1986, *52*(4), pp. 1165–67.

Arnold, Roger A. Marriage, Divorce, and Property Rights: A Natural Rights Framework. **In** *Peden, J. R. and Glahe, F. R., eds.*, 1986, pp. 195–227.

Bromley, Daniel W. Markets and Externalities. **In** *Bromley, D. W., ed.*, 1986, pp. 37–68.

Burrows, Paul. Nonconvexity Induced by External Costs on Production: Theoretical Curio or Policy Dilemma? *J. Environ. Econ. Manage.*, June 1986, *13*(2), pp. 101–28.

Butler, Richard V. and Maher, Michael D. The Control of Externalities: Abatement vs. Damage Prevention. *Southern Econ. J.*, April 1986, *52*(4), pp. 1088–1102.

Carlton, Dennis W. and Loury, Glenn C. The Limitation of Pigouvian Taxes as a Long-run Remedy for Externalities: An Extension of Results. *Quart. J. Econ.*, August 1986, *101*(3), pp. 631–34.

Ekelund, Robert B., Jr. and Saba, Richard P. Establishing Property Rights in Utility Franchises. **In** *Moorhouse, J. C., ed.*, 1986, pp. 425–45.

Ellerman, David P. Property Appropriation and Economic Theory. **In** *Mirowski, P., ed.*, 1986, pp. 41–92.

Greenwald, Bruce C. and Stiglitz, Joseph E. Externalities in Economies with Imperfect Information and Incomplete Markets. *Quart. J. Econ.*, May 1986, *101*(2), pp. 229–64.

Izac, A.-M. N. Resource Policies, Property Rights and Conflicts of Interest. *Australian J. Agr. Econ.*, April 1986, *30*(1), pp. 23–37.

Katz, Michael L. and Shapiro, Carl. Technology Adoption in the Presence of Network Externalities. *J. Polit. Econ.*, August 1986, *94*(4), pp. 822–41.

Kohn, Robert E. A Note on the Dolbear Theorem. *Public Finance*, 1986, *41*(2), pp. 285–88.

Kohn, Robert E. The Limitations of Pigouvian Taxes as a Long-run Remedy for Externalities: Comment. *Quart. J. Econ.*, August 1986, *101*(3), pp. 625–30.

Lee, Dwight R. and Kreutzer, David. Privatizing the Commons: Comment. *Southern Econ. J.*, April 1986, *52*(4), pp. 1162–64.

Magnan de Bornier, Jean. The Coase Theorem and the Empty Core: A Reexamination. *Int. Rev. Law Econ.*, December 1986, *6*(2), pp. 265–71.

Martin, Robert E. Externality Regulation and the Monopoly Firm. *J. Public Econ.*, April 1986, *29*(3), pp. 347–62.

Mendelsohn, Robert. Regulating Heterogeneous Emissions. *J. Environ. Econ. Manage.*, December 1986, *13*(4), pp. 301–12.

Mestelman, Stuart. General Equilibrium Modelling of Industries with Production Externalities. *Can. J. Econ.*, August 1986, *19*(3), pp. 522–25.

Oates, Wallace E. Markets and Externalities: Comment. **In** *Bromley, D. W., ed.*, 1986, pp. 69–78.

Pillet, Gonzague. From External Effects to Energy Externality: New Proposals in Environmental Economics. *Hitotsubashi J. Econ.*, June 1986, *27*(1), pp. 77–97.

Tietenberg, Thomas H. Markets and Externalities: Comment. **In** *Bromley, D. W., ed.*, 1986, pp. 79–88.

Tietzel, Manfred. Zur Entstehung des Privateigentums. (On the Evolution of Private Property. With English summary.) **In** *Eucken, W. and Böhm, F., eds.*, 1986, pp. 105–24.

Tullock, Gordon. Local Redistribution. **In** *Tullock, G.*, 1986, pp. 113–27.

025 Social Choice

0250 General

Acheson, Keith and Chant, John F. Bureaucratic Theory and the Choice of Central Bank Goals: The Case of the Bank of Canada. **In** *Toma, E. F. and Toma, M., eds.*, 1986, *1973*, pp. 129–50. **[G: Canada]**

Alt, James E. Party Strategies, World Demand, and Unemployment: The Political Economy of Economic Activity in Western Industrial Nations. *Amer. Econ. Rev.*, May 1986, *76*(2), pp. 57–61.

Bartlett, Bruce. Supply-Side Economics, Industrial Policy, and Rational Ignorance: Comment. **In** *Barfield, C. E. and Schambra, W. A., eds.*, 1986, pp. 272–74.

Baumgarth, William. The Family and the State in Modern Political Theory. **In** *Peden, J. R. and Glahe, F. R., eds.*, 1986, pp. 19–47.

Blumenthal, Sidney. Supply-Side Economics, Industrial Policy, and Rational Ignorance: Comment. **In** *Barfield, C. E. and Schambra, W. A., eds.*, 1986, pp. 270–72.

Boulding, Kenneth E. System Breaks and Positive Feedback as Sources of Catastrophe. **In** *[Rapoport, A.]*, 1986, pp. 47–54.

Buchanan, James M. Can Policy Activism Succeed? A Public Choice Perspective. **In** *Hafer, R. W., ed. (II)*, 1986, pp. 139–50.

Buchanan, James M. From Redistributive Churning to the Plantation State: Review Article. *Public Choice*, 1986, *51*(2), pp. 241–43.

Buchanan, James M. Liberty, Market, and State. **In** *Buchanan, J. M.*, 1986, pp. 3–7.

Buchanan, James M. Notes on Politics as Process. **In** *Buchanan, J. M.*, 1986, pp. 87–91.

Buchanan, James M. The Public Choice Perspective. **In** *Buchanan, J. M.*, 1986, *1983*, pp. 19–27.

Buchanan, James M. The Related but Distinct 'Sciences' of Economics and of Political Economy. **In** *Buchanan, J. M.*, 1986, *1982*, pp. 28–39.

Chant, John F. and Acheson, Keith. The Choice of Monetary Instruments and the Theory of Bureaucracy. **In** *Toma, E. F. and Toma, M., eds.*, 1986, *1972*, pp. 107–28. **[G: Canada]**

Coleman, James S. Individual Interests and Collective Action. **In** *Coleman, J. S.*, 1986, *1966*, pp. 305–18.

Coleman, James S. Processes of Concentration and Dispersal of Power in Social Systems. **In** *Coleman, J. S.*, 1986, *1974*, pp. 267–80.

Elster, Jon. The Market and the Forum: Three Varieties of Political Theory. **In** *Elster, J. and Hylland, A., eds.*, 1986, pp. 103–32.

Elster, Jon and Hylland, Aanund. Foundations of Social Choice Theory: Introduction. **In** *Elster, J. and Hylland, A., eds.*, 1986, pp. 1–10.

Imperato, Isabella. La politica monetaria ottima in presenza di shock esogeni: "Monetary Targeting" e "Nominal Income Targeting." (Optimal Monetary Policy in Presence of Exogenous Shocks: Monetary Targeting and Nominal Income Targeting. With English summary.) *Giorn. Econ.*, Sept.-Oct. 1986, *45*(9–10), pp. 563–78.

Jaarsma, Bert; Schram, Arthur and van Winden, Frans. On the Voting Participation of Public Bureaucrats. *Public Choice*, 1986, *48*(2), pp. 183–87. **[G: Netherlands]**

Jones, Philip R. and Cullis, John G. Fiscal Preferences: Some Theory for Some Evidence. *Scot. J. Polit. Econ.*, February 1986, *33*(1), pp. 86–92.

Lagerspetz, Eerik. Pufendorf on Collective Decisions. *Public Choice*, 1986, *49*(2), pp. 179–82.

Lindenberg, Siegwart. Individual Economic Ignorance versus Social Production Functions and Precarious Enlightenment: Comment on Tullock's View of Rent Seeking in Dictatorships. *J. Inst. Theoretical Econ.*, March 1986, *142*(1), pp. 20–26.

Maasoumi, Esfandiar. The Measurement and Decomposition of Multi-dimensional Inequality. *Econometrica*, July 1986, *54*(4), pp. 991–97.

MacLean, Douglas. Social Values and the Distribution of Risk. **In** *MacLean, D., ed.*, 1986, pp. 75–93.

Manne, Henry G. Industrial Organization and Rent Seeking in Dictatorships: Comment. *J. Inst. Theoretical Econ.*, March 1986, *142*(1), pp. 16–19.

McCaleb, Thomas S. Ideology as the Ultimate Enforcement Mechanism [Constraining the Transfer Society: Constitutional and Moral Dimensions]. *Cato J.*, Spring/Summer 1986, *6*(1), pp. 341–45.

McKenzie, Richard B. Tax/Compensation Schemes: Misleading Advice in a Rent-seeking Society. *Public Choice*, 1986, *48*(2), pp. 189–94.

Mishan, Ezra J. The Road to Repression. **In** *Mishan, E. J.*, 1986, *1976*, pp. 131–68. **[G: MDCs]**

Muris, Timothy J. Regulatory Policymaking at the Federal Trade Commission: The Extent of Congressional Control. *J. Polit. Econ.*, August 1986, *94*(4), pp. 884–89. **[G: U.S.]**

Ng, Yew-Kwang. Social Criteria for Evaluating Population Change: An Alternative to the Blackorby–Donaldson Criterion. *J. Public Econ.*, April 1986, *29*(3), pp. 375–81.

Nisbet, Robert. The American Family and the State: Foreword. **In** *Peden, J. R. and Glahe, F. R., eds.*, 1986, pp. xix–xxvi.

O'Driscoll, Lyla H. Toward a New Theory of the Family. **In** *Peden, J. R. and Glahe, F. R., eds.*, 1986, pp. 81–101.

Olson, Mancur. Supply-Side Economics, Industrial Policy, and Rational Ignorance. **In** *Barfield, C. E. and Schambra, W. A., eds.*, 1986, pp. 245–69.

Peck, Richard M. Power and Linear Income Taxes: An Example. *Econometrica*, January 1986, *54*(1), pp. 87–94.

Peden, Joseph R. and Glahe, Fred R. The American Family in a Free Society. **In** *Peden, J. R. and Glahe, F. R., eds.*, 1986, pp. 1–16.

025 Social Choice

Pizzorno, Alessandro. Some Other Kinds of Otherness: A Critique of "Rational Choice" Theories. **In** *[Hirshman, A. O.]*, 1986, pp. 355–73.

Poulson, Barry W. The Family and the State: A Theoretical Framework. **In** *Peden, J. R. and Glahe, F. R., eds.*, 1986, pp. 49–80.

Roemer, John E. An Historical Materialist Alternative to Welfarism. **In** *Elster, J. and Hylland, A., eds.*, 1986, pp. 133–64.

Ross, H. Laurence and LaFree, Gary D. Deterrence in Criminology and Social Policy. **In** *Smelser, N. J. and Gerstein, D. R., eds.*, 1986, pp. 129–52.

Rowley, Charles K. Ode to a Rent Seeker. *Public Choice*, 1986, *48*(3), pp. 271–72.

Rowley, Charles K. Review Article [The Spatial Theory of Voting]. *Public Choice*, 1986, *48*(1), pp. 93–99.

Rubinstein, Ariel and Fishburn, Peter C. Algebraic Aggregation Theory. *J. Econ. Theory*, February 1986, *38*(1), pp. 63–77.

Schneider, William. Supply-Side Economics, Industrial Policy, and Rational Ignorance: Comment. **In** *Barfield, C. E. and Schambra, W. A., eds.*, 1986, pp. 274–79.

Scotchmer, Suzanne. Corrigendum [Profit Maximizing Clubs]. *J. Public Econ.*, April 1986, *29*(3), pp. 389.

Sen, Amartya K. Rationality, Interest, and Identity. **In** *[Hirshman, A. O.]*, 1986, pp. 343–53.

Shughart, William F., II and Tollison, Robert D. Preliminary Evidence on the Use of Inputs by the Federal Reserve System. **In** *Toma, E. F. and Toma, M., eds.*, 1986, *1983*, pp. 67–90. **[G: U.S.]**

Stigler, George J. Economic Competition and Political Competition. **In** *Stigler, G. J.*, 1986, *1972*, pp. 117–33.

Stigler, George J. Free Riders and Collective Action: An Appendix to Theories of Economic Regulation. **In** *Stigler, G. J.*, 1986, *1974*, pp. 67–75. **[G: U.S.]**

Toma, Eugenia Froedge and Toma, Mark. Central Bankers, Bureaucratic Incentives, and Monetary Policy: An Introduction. **In** *Toma, E. F. and Toma, M., eds.*, 1986, pp. 1–7.

Toma, Eugenia Froedge and Toma, Mark. Research Activities and Budget Allocations among Federal Reserve Banks. **In** *Toma, E. F. and Toma, M., eds.*, 1986, *1985*, pp. 151–68. **[G: U.S.]**

Tullock, Gordon. Industrial Organization and Rent Seeking in Dictatorships. *J. Inst. Theoretical Econ.*, March 1986, *142*(1), pp. 4–15.

Tullock, Gordon. Wanted: New Public-Choice Theories. **In** *[Seldon, A.]*, 1986, pp. 15–27.

Vanberg, Viktor and Buchanan, James M. Organization Theory and Fiscal Economics: Society, State, and Public Debt. *J. Law, Econ., Organ.*, Fall 1986, *2*(2), pp. 215–27.

Weingast, Barry R. and Moran, Mark J. Congress and Regulatory Agency Choice: Reply [Bureaucratic Discretion or Congressional Control? Regulatory Policymaking by the Federal Trade Commission]. *J. Polit. Econ.*, August 1986, *94*(4), pp. 890–94. **[G: U.S.]**

Wellisz, Stanislaw and Wilson, John D. Lobbying and Tariff Formation: A Deadweight Loss Consideration. *J. Int. Econ.*, May 1986, *20*(3/4), pp. 367–75.

0251 Social Choice Theory

Aizerman, M. A. and Aleskerov, F. T. Voting Operators in the Space of Choice Functions. *Math. Soc. Sci.*, June 1986, *11*(3), pp. 201–42.

Appelbaum, Elie and Katz, Eliakim. Transfer Seeking and Avoidance: On the Full Social Costs of Rent Seeking. *Public Choice*, 1986, *48*(2), pp. 175–81.

Austin-Smith, David. Legislative Coalitions and Electoral Equilibrium. *Public Choice*, 1986, *50*(1–3), pp. 185–210.

Axelrod, Robert. An Evolutionary Approach to Norms. *Amer. Polit. Sci. Rev.*, December 1986, *80*(4), pp. 1095–1111.

Bandelt, H. J. and Labbé, M. How Bad Can a Voting Location Be. *Soc. Choice Welfare*, July 1986, *3*(2), pp. 125–45.

Bandyopadhyay, Taradas. Rationality, Path Independence, and the Power Structure. *J. Econ. Theory*, December 1986, *40*(2), pp. 338–48.

Bandyopadhyay, Taradas. Resolution of Paradoxes in Social Choice. **In** *Samuelson, L., ed.*, 1986, pp. 99–120.

Bandyopadhyay, Taradas and Denicolò, Vincenzo. Teoremi di impossibilità per funzioni di scelta sociale debolmente coerenti. (Impossibility Theorems for Weakly Consistent Social Choice Functions. With English summary.) *Econ. Polít.*, August 1986, *3*(2), pp. 207–31.

Barberá, Salvador and Dutta, Bhaskar. General, Direct and Self-implementation of Social Choice Functions via Protective Equilibria. *Math. Soc. Sci.*, April 1986, *11*(2), pp. 109–27.

Barry, Brian. Lady Chatterley's Lover and Doctor Fischer's Bomb Party: Liberalism, Pareto Optimality, and the Problem of Objectionable Preferences. **In** *Elster, J. and Hylland, A., eds.*, 1986, pp. 11–43.

Becker, Gilbert. The Public Interest Hypothesis Revisited: A New Test of Peltzman's Theory of Regulation. *Public Choice*, 1986, *49*(3), pp. 223–34.

Bendor, Jonathan and Moe, Terry M. Agenda Control, Committee Capture, and the Dynamics of Institutional Politics. *Amer. Polit. Sci. Rev.*, December 1986, *80*(4), pp. 1187–1207.

Benson, Bruce L. and Faminow, Merle D. The Incentives to Organize and Demand Regulation: Two Ends against the Middle. *Econ. Inquiry*, July 1986, *24*(3), pp. 473–84.

Bernholz, Peter. A General Constitutional Possibility Theorem. *Public Choice*, 1986, *51*(3), pp. 249–65.

Bhagwati, Jagdish N. and Srinivasan, T. N. Religion as DUP Activity. *Public Choice*, 1986, *48*(1), pp. 49–54

Black, Dan A. and Parker, Darrell F. Unions, Seniority, and Public Choice. *J. Lab. Res.*, Fall 1986, *7*(4), pp. 337–48.

Blair, Douglas H. and Pollak, Robert A. Rationality and Social Choice. **In** *Samuelson, L., ed.*, 1986, pp. 79–98.

Bloch, Peter C. The Politico-Economic Behavior of Authoritarian Governments. *Public Choice*, 1986, *51*(2), pp. 117–28.

Bolger, E. M. Power Indices for Multicandidate Voting Games. *Int. J. Game Theory*, 1986, *15*(3), pp. 175–86.

Born, Richard. Strategic Politicians and Unresponsive Voters. *Amer. Polit. Sci. Rev.*, June 1986, *80*(2), pp. 599–612. **[G: U.S.]**

Brams, Steven J.; Felsenthal, Dan S. and Maoz, Zeev. New Chairman Paradoxes. **In** *[Rapoport, A.]*, 1986, pp. 243–56.

Brough, Wayne T. and Kimenyi, Mwangi S. On the Inefficient Extraction of Rents by Dictators. *Public Choice*, 1986, *48*(1), pp. 37–48.

Browning, Edgar K. On the Welfare Cost of Transfers. **In** *Tullock, G.*, 1986, *1974*, pp. 102–06.

Brubaker, Earl R. Efficient Allocation and Unanimous Consent with Incomplete Demand Disclosures? *Public Choice*, 1986, *48*(3), pp. 217–27.

Brümel, Wolfgang; Pethig, Rüdiger and von dem Hagen, Oskar. The Theory of Public Goods: A Survey of Recent Issues. *J. Inst. Theoretical Econ.*, June 1986, *142*(2), pp. 241–309.

Buchanan, James M. Constitutional Democracy, Individual Liberty, and Political Equality. **In** *Buchanan, J. M.*, 1986, *1985*, pp. 248–60.

Buchanan, James M. Contractarianism and Democracy. **In** *Buchanan, J. M.*, 1986, pp. 240–47.

Buchanan, James M. Distributive and Redistributive Norms: A Note of Clarification. **In** *Buchanan, J. M.*, 1986, pp. 159–64.

Buchanan, James M. Individual Choice in Private, Agency, and Collective Decisions. **In** *Buchanan, J. M.*, 1986, pp. 229–39.

Buchanan, James M. Moral Community, Moral Order, or Moral Anarchy. **In** *Buchanan, J. M.*, 1986, *1981*, pp. 108–20. **[G: U.S.; Japan]**

Buchanan, James M. Political Economy and Social Philosophy. **In** *Buchanan, J. M.*, 1986, *1985*, pp. 261–74.

Buchanan, James M. Rights, Efficiency, and Exchange: The Irrelevance of Transactions Cost. **In** *Buchanan, J. M.*, 1986, *1984*, pp. 92–107.

Buchanan, James M. Rules for a Fair Game: Contractarian Notes on Distributive Justice. **In** *Buchanan, J. M.*, 1986, *1983*, pp. 123–39.

Buchanan, James M. Sources of Opposition to Constitutional Reform. **In** *Buchanan, J. M.*, 1986, *1984*, pp. 55–69.

Buchanan, James M. and Lee, Dwight R. Vote Buying in a Stylized Setting. *Public Choice*, 1986, *49*(1), pp. 3–15.

Budziszewski, J. Persuading Caesar: A New Interpretation of Farquharson's Problem. *Public Choice*, 1986, *51*(2), pp. 129–40.

Camacho, Antonio. Individual Cardinal Utility, Interpersonal Comparisons, and Social Choice. **In** *Daboni, L.; Montesano, A. and Lines, M., eds.*, 1986, pp. 185–200.

Campbell, D. E. and Nitzan, Shmuel I. Social Compromise and Social Metrics. *Soc. Choice Welfare*, June 1986, *3*(1), pp. 1–16.

Campbell, Donald T. Rationality and Utility from the Standpoint of Evolutionary Biology. **In** *Hogarth, R. M. and Reder, M. W., eds.*, 1986, pp. 171–80.

Campbell, Donald T. Rationality and Utility from the Standpoint of Evolutionary Biology. *J. Bus.*, Part 2, October 1986, *59*(4), pp. S355–64.

Cassing, James H. and Hillman, Arye L. Shifting Comparative Advantage and Senescent Industry Collapse. *Amer. Econ. Rev.*, June 1986, *76*(3), pp. 516–23.

Cassing, James H.; Hillman, Arye L. and Long, Ngo Van. Risk Aversion, Terms of Trade Uncertainty and Social-Consensus Trade Policy. *Oxford Econ. Pap.*, July 1986, *38*(2), pp. 234–42.

Cauley, Jon; Sandler, Todd and Cornes, Richard. Nonmarket Institutional Structures: Conjectures, Distribution, and Allocative Efficiency. *Public Finance*, 1986, *41*(2), pp. 153–72.

Chamberlin, John R. Discovering Manipulated Social Choices: The Coincidence of Cycles and Manipulated Outcomes. *Public Choice*, 1986, *51*(3), pp. 295–313.

Chappell, Henry W., Jr. and Keech, William R. Policy Motivation and Party Differences in a Dynamic Spatial Model of Party Competition. *Amer. Polit. Sci. Rev.*, September 1986, *80*(3), pp. 881–99.

Chaudhuri, A. Some Implications of an Intensity Measure of Envy. *Soc. Choice Welfare*, December 1986, *3*(4), pp. 255–70.

Chun, Y. The Solidarity Axiom for Quasi-linear Social Choice Problems. *Soc. Choice Welfare*, December 1986, *3*(4), pp. 297–310.

Cohen, Susan I. Truth-Telling, Dominant Strategies, and Iterative Groves Mechanisms. *Public Choice*, 1986, *51*(3), pp. 333–43.

Coleman, James S. Beyond Pareto Optimality. **In** *Coleman, J. S.*, 1986, *1969*, pp. 33–62.

Coleman, James S. Collective Decisions. **In** *Coleman, J. S.*, 1986, *1964*, pp. 15–32.

Coleman, James S. Collective Decisions in a Social System. **In** *Coleman, J. S.*, 1986, pp. 144–60.

Coleman, James S. Control of Collectivities and the Power of a Collectivity to Act. **In** *Coleman, J. S.*, 1986, *1971*, pp. 192–225.

Coleman, James S. Individual Interests and Collective Action: Selected Essays: Introduction. **In** *Coleman, J. S.*, 1986, pp. 1–11.

Coleman, James S. Legitimate and Illegitimate Use of Power. **In** *Coleman, J. S.*, 1986, *1975*, pp. 247–66.

Coleman, James S. Social Action Systems. **In** *Coleman, J. S.*, 1986, *1977*, pp. 85–136. **[G: U.S.]**

Coleman, James S. The Possibility of a Social Welfare Function. **In** *Coleman, J. S.*, 1986, *1966*, pp. 63–84.

Coleman, James S. Why So Much Stability? Recontracting, Trustworthiness and the Stability of Vote Exchanges. **In** *Coleman, J. S.*, 1986, *1983*, pp. 137–43.

Congleton, Roger D. Rent-Seeking Aspects of Political Advertising. *Public Choice,* 1986, *49*(3), pp. 249–63.

Cook, Wade D. and Kress, Moshe. Ordinal Ranking and Preference Strength. *Math. Soc. Sci.*, June 1986, *11*(3), pp. 295–306.

Coughlin, Peter J. Elections and Income Redistribution. *Public Choice,* 1986, *50*(1–3), pp. 27–91.

Coughlin, Peter J. Elections and Income Redistribution: Reply. *Public Choice,* 1986, *50*(1–3), pp. 131–33.

Coughlin, Peter J. Elections and Income Redistribution: Reply. *Public Choice,* 1986, *50*(1–3), pp. 101–03.

Coughlin, Peter J. Special Majority Rules and the Existence of Voting Equilibria. *Soc. Choice Welfare,* June 1986, *3*(1), pp. 31–35.

Cukierman, Alex and Meltzer, Allan H. A Positive Theory of Discretionary Policy, the Cost of Democratic Government and the Benefits of a Constitution. *Econ. Inquiry,* July 1986, *24*(3), pp. 367–88.

Dawes, Robyn M., et al. Organizing Groups for Collective Action. *Amer. Polit. Sci. Rev.*, December 1986, *80*(4), pp. 1171–85. **[G: U.S.]**

Delbono, Flavio. Giustizia distributiva e decisioni collettive: una nota su un recente saggio di Ackerman. (Distributive Justice and Collective Decisions: A Note on a Recent Book by Ackerman. With English summary.) *Econ. Polit.*, December 1986, *3*(3), pp. 397–408.

Denzau, Arthur T. and Munger, Michael C. Legislators and Interest Groups: How Unorganized Interests Get Represented. *Amer. Polit. Sci. Rev.*, March 1986, *80*(1), pp. 89–106.

Dudley, Leonard. Implicit Labor Contracts and Public Choice: A General Equilibrium Approach. *J. Law Econ.*, April 1986, *29*(1), pp. 61–82. **[G: OECD; LDCs]**

Dunn, John. Defining a Defensible Socialism for Britain Today. **In** *Nolan, P. and Paine, S., eds.*, 1986, pp. 35–52. **[G: U.K.]**

Enelow, James M. The Stability of Logrolling: An Expectations Approach. *Public Choice,* 1986, *51*(3), pp. 285–94.

Feiwel, George R. Shafts from Arrow's Bow: Advance in and beyond Economic Theory. *Economia (Portugal),* May 1986, *10*(2), pp. 229–75.

Feld, Scott L. and Grofman, Bernard. On the Possibility of Faithfully Representative Committees. *Amer. Polit. Sci. Rev.*, September 1986, *80*(3), pp. 863–79. **[G: U.S.]**

Feld, Scott L. and Grofman, Bernard. Partial Single-Peakedness: An Extension and Clarification. *Public Choice,* 1986, *51*(1), pp. 71–80.

Ferejohn, John. Incumbent Performance and Electoral Control. *Public Choice,* 1986, *50*(1–3), pp. 5–25.

Findlay, Ronald and Wellisz, Stanislaw. Tariffs, Quotas and Domestic-Content Protection: Some Political Economy Considerations. *Public Choice,* 1986, *50*(1–3), pp. 221–42.

Findlay, Ronald and Wellisz, Stanislaw. Tariffs, Quotas and Domestic-Content Protection: Some Political Economy Considerations: Response to Comments. *Public Choice,* 1986, *50*(1–3), pp. 247–48.

Finger, J. Michael. Tariffs, Quotas and Domestic-Content Protection: Some Political Economy Considerations: Comment. *Public Choice,* 1986, *50*(1–3), pp. 243–46.

Fiorina, Morris P. Legislator Uncertainty, Legislative Control, and the Delegation of Legislative Power. *J. Law, Econ., Organ.*, Spring 1986, *2*(1), pp. 33–51. **[G: U.S.]**

Frey, Bruno S. and Ramser, Hans J. Where Are the Limits of Regulation? *J. Inst. Theoretical Econ.*, September 1986, *142*(3), pp. 571–80.

Fuchs-Seliger, Susanne. Rational Budgeters in the Theory of Social Choice. *Soc. Choice Welfare,* 1986, *3*(3), pp. 161–76.

Gaertner, Wulf. Pareto, Interdependent Rights Exercising and Strategic Behaviour. *J. Econ. (Z. Nationalökon.),* Supplementum 5, 1986, pp. 79–98.

Galeotti, Gianluigi and Breton, Albert. An Economic Theory of Political Parties. *Kyklos,* 1986, *39*(1), pp. 47–65.

Gehrlein, W. V. and Fishburn, Peter C. Division of Power in Legislatures with Two Cohesive Subgroups. *Soc. Choice Welfare,* July 1986, *3*(2), pp. 119–24.

Gevers, Louis. Walrasian Social Choice: Some Simple Axiomatic Approaches. **In** *[Arrow, K. J.], Vol. 1,* 1986, pp. 97–114.

Goodin, Robert E. Laundering Preferences. **In** *Elster, J. and Hylland, A., eds.*, 1986, pp. 75–101.

Gradstein, Mark and Nitzan, Shmuel I. Performance Evaluation of Some Special Classes of Weighted Majority Rules. *Math. Soc. Sci.*, August 1986, *12*(1), pp. 31–46.

Grier, Kevin B. Monetary Policy as a Political Equilibrium [Central Banking and the Fed: A Public Choice Perspective]. *Cato J.*, Fall 1986, *6*(2), pp. 539–43. **[G: U.S.]**

Hammond, Peter J. Consequentialist Social Norms for Public Decisions. **In** *[Arrow, K. J.], Vol. 1,* 1986, pp. 3–27.

Hansmann, Henry B. A Theory of Status Organizations. *J. Law, Econ., Organ.*, Spring 1986, *2*(1), pp. 119–30.

Harsanyi, John C. Utilitarian Morality in a World of Very Half-hearted Altruists. **In** *[Arrow, K. J.], Vol. 1,* 1986, pp. 57–73.

Hill, Stuart. Lumpy Preference Structures. *Policy Sci.*, July 1986, *19*(1), pp. 5–32.

Hinich, Melvin J. The Positive Theory of Legislative Institutions: Discussion. *Public Choice,* 1986, *50*(1–3), pp. 179–83.

Holcombe, Randall G. Non-optimal Unanimous Agreement. *Public Choice,* 1986, *48*(3), pp. 229–44.

Holler, Manfred J. Intergeneration Solutions to

the Social Security Dilemma. **In** *von der Schulenburg, J.-M. G., ed.*, 1986, pp. 54–74.

Holzman, Ron. On Strong Representations of Games by Social Choice Functions. *J. Math. Econ.*, 1986, *15*(1), pp. 39–57.

Holzman, Ron. The Capacity of a Committee. *Math. Soc. Sci.*, October 1986, *12*(2), pp. 139–57.

Hurwicz, Leonid. On the Implementation of Social Choice Rules in Irrational Societies. **In** *[Arrow, K. J.], Vol. 1*, 1986, pp. 75–96.

Hylland, Aanund. The Purpose and Significance of Social Choice Theory: Some General Remarks and an Application to the 'Lady Chatterley Problem.' **In** *Elster, J. and Hylland, A., eds.*, 1986, pp. 45–73.

Ichiishi, Tatsuro. Stable Extensive Game Forms with Perfect Information. *Int. J. Game Theory*, 1986, *15*(3), pp. 163–74.

Jain, S. K. Special Majority Rules Necessary and Sufficient Condition for Quasi-Transitivity with Quasi-Transitive Individual Preferences. *Soc. Choice Welfare*, July 1986, *3*(2), pp. 99–106.

Johansson, Börje and Leonardi, Giorgio. Public Facility Location: A Multiregional and Multiauthority Decision Context. **In** *Nijkamp, P., ed. (I)*, 1986, pp. 133–70.

Kelly, J. S. Condorcet Winner Proportions. *Soc. Choice Welfare*, December 1986, *3*(4), pp. 311–14.

Kern, Lucian and Räder, Hans-Georg. On Explaining the Rise of the New Social Movements in Germany. **In** *[Rapoport, A.]*, 1986, pp. 169–85. **[G: W. Germany]**

Köhler, Eckehart. Guidelines for Solving Sen's Paradox. **In** *[Rapoport, A.]*, 1986, pp. 37–46.

Kohn, Robert E. Optimal Quantity of a Controversial Good or Service. *Public Choice*, 1986, *51*(1), pp. 81–86.

Ledyard, John O. Elections and Reputations [Incumbent Performance and Electoral Control] [Elections and Income Redistribution]. *Public Choice*, 1986, *50*(1–3), pp. 93–99.

Lemche, S. Q. The Direct Social Preference Relation in the Theory of Public Expenditure. *Soc. Choice Welfare*, June 1986, *3*(1), pp. 51–59.

Lind, Robert C. The Shadow Price of Capital: Implications for the Opportunity Cost of Public Programs, the Burden of the Debt, and Tax Reform. **In** *[Arrow, K. J.], Vol. 1*, 1986, pp. 189–212.

Lindenberg, Siegwart. The Paradox of Privatization in Consumption. **In** *[Rapoport, A.]*, 1986, pp. 297–310.

Littlechild, S. C. and Wiseman, Jack. The Political Economy of Restriction of Choice. *Public Choice*, 1986, *51*(2), pp. 161–72.

Lott, John R., Jr. Brand Names and Barriers to Entry in Political Markets. *Public Choice*, 1986, *51*(1), pp. 87–92.

Masarani, F. and Sadik Gokturk, S. A Pareto Optimal Characterization of Rawls' Social Choice Mechanism. *J. Math. Econ.*, 1986, *15*(2), pp. 157–70.

Mathis, Edward J. and Zech, Charles E. An Examination into the Relevance of the Median Voter Model: Empirical Evidence Offers Support for the Model and Certain Uses. *Amer. J. Econ. Soc.*, October 1986, *45*(4), pp. 403–12. **[G: U.S.]**

McCubbins, Mathew D. and Page, Talbot. The Congressional Foundations of Agency Performance. *Public Choice*, 1986, *51*(2), pp. 173–90. **[G: U.S.]**

McKelvey, Richard D. and Ordeshook, P. C. Sequential Elections with Limited Information: A Formal Analysis. *Soc. Choice Welfare*, 1986, *3*(3), pp. 199–211.

McKelvey, Richard D. and Schofield, Norman. Structural Instability of the Core. *J. Math. Econ.*, 1986, *15*(3), pp. 179–98.

Mezzetti, Claudio. Libertà personale e principio paretiano sono compatibili? Un dilemma di teoria delle scelte sociali. (Is the Pareto Principles Compatible with Personal Liberty? A Dilemma in Social Choice Theory. With English summary.) *Econ. Polit.*, April 1986, *3*(1), pp. 61–91.

Mitchell, Douglas W. A Nash Equilibrium Model of Campaign Spending. *Atlantic Econ. J.*, July 1986, *14*(2), pp. 76–78.

Moene, Karl O. Types of Bureaucratic Interaction. *J. Public Econ.*, April 1986, *29*(3), pp. 333–45.

Moulin, Hervé. Choosing from a Tournament. *Soc. Choice Welfare*, December 1986, *3*(4), pp. 271–91.

Mueller, Dennis C. Rational Egoism versus Adaptive Egoism as Fundamental Postulate for a Descriptive Theory of Human Behavior. *Public Choice*, 1986, *51*(1), pp. 3–23.

Muris, Timothy J. Regulatory Policymaking at the Federal Trade Commission: The Extent of Congressional Control. *J. Polit. Econ.*, August 1986, *94*(4), pp. 884–89. **[G: U.S.]**

Nas, Tevfik F.; Price, Albert C. and Weber, Charles T. A Policy-oriented Theory of Corruption. *Amer. Polit. Sci. Rev.*, March 1986, *80*(1), pp. 107–19.

Ng, Yew-Kwang. A Final Rejoinder [Beyond Pareto Optimality]. *J. Econ. (Z. Nationalökon.)*, 1986, *46*(3), pp. 317–18.

Ng, Yew-Kwang. Beyond Pareto Optimality! A Response. *J. Econ. (Z. Nationalökon.)*, 1986, *46*(3), pp. 311–15.

Nicolaides, Phedon. Political Coalitions and Issues: A Contribution to the Political Economy of Induced Distortions. *Aussenwirtschaft*, December 1986, *41*(4), pp. 497–510.

Nitzan, Shmuel I. and Procaccia, Uriel. Optimal Voting Procedures for Profit Maximizing Firms. *Public Choice*, 1986, *51*(2), pp. 191–208. **[G: U.S.]**

Ostrom, Elinor. An Agenda for the Study of Institutions. *Public Choice*, 1986, *48*(1), pp. 3–25.

Palfrey, Thomas R. Comments on the Papers by Austen-Smith and Shepsle [Legislative Coalitions and Electoral Equilibrium] [The Positive Theory of Legislative Institutions: An Enrichment of Social Choice and Spatial Models]. *Public Choice*, 1986, *50*(1–3), pp. 211–19.

Panda, Santosh C. Some Impossibility Results

with Domain Restrictions. *J. Econ. Theory,* February 1986, *38*(1), pp. 21–34.

Pattanaik, Prasanta K. and Peleg, Bezalel. Distribution of Power under Stochastic Social Choice Rules. *Econometrica,* July 1986, *54*(4), pp. 909–21.

Plotnick, Robert D. Redistribution to the Poor: An Overheard Conversation. *Public Finance Quart.,* April 1986, *14*(2), pp. 223–28.

Porta, Pier Luigi. Deontologia e apriorismo etico. (Deontology and Ethical Apriorism. With English summary.) *Rivista Int. Sci. Econ. Com.,* February 1986, *33*(2), pp. 165–84.

Postlewaite, Andrew and Schmeidler, David. Implementation in Differential Information Economies. *J. Econ. Theory,* June 1986, *39*(1), pp. 14–33.

Postlewaite, Andrew and Schmeidler, David. Strategic Behaviour and a Notion of Ex Ante Efficiency in a Voting Model. *Soc. Choice Welfare,* June 1986, *3*(1), pp. 37–49.

Ray, Depankar. On the Practical Possibility of a 'No Show Paradox' under the Single Transferable Vote. *Math. Soc. Sci.,* April 1986, *11*(2), pp. 183–89.

Riley, J. M. Generalized Social Welfare Functionals: Welfarism, Morality and Liberty. *Soc. Choice Welfare,* December 1986, *3*(4), pp. 233–54.

Ritz, Zvi. A Note on Nondictatorial Conditions for Choice Mechanisms. *Math. Soc. Sci.,* February 1986, *11*(1), pp. 89–92.

Rob, Rafael. The Demand Revealing Mechanism. **In** *Samuelson, L., ed.,* 1986, pp. 121–38.

Rowley, Charles K. and Tollison, Robert D. Rent-Seeking and Trade Protection. *Aussenwirtschaft,* September 1986, *41*(2/3), pp. 303–28.

Rowley, Charles K. and Tollison, Robert D. Rent-Seeking and Trade Protection. **In** *Hauser, H., ed. (II),* 1986, pp. 141–66.

Schofield, Norman. Existence of a 'Structurally Stable' Equilibrium for a Non-collegial Voting Rule. *Public Choice,* 1986, *51*(3), pp. 267–84.

Schofield, Norman. Permutation Cycles and Manipulation of Choice Functions. *Soc. Choice Welfare,* July 1986, *3*(2), pp. 107–17.

Segal, Uzi and Spivak, Avia. On the Single Membership Constituency and the Law of Large Numbers: A Note: Why So Much Stability? *Public Choice,* 1986, *49*(2), pp. 183–90.

Seidl, Christian. A Final Note [Beyond Pareto Optimality]. *J. Econ. (Z. Nationalökon.),* 1986, *46*(3), pp. 317.

Seidl, Christian. Beyond Pareto Optimality? A Comment. *J. Econ. (Z. Nationalökon.),* 1986, *46*(3), pp. 305–10.

Seidl, Christian. The Impossibility of Nondictatorial Tolerance. *J. Econ. (Z. Nationalökon.),* Supplementum 5, 1986, pp. 211–25.

Sen, Amartya K. Foundations of Social Choice Theory: An Epilogue. **In** *Elster, J. and Hylland, A., eds.,* 1986, pp. 213–48.

Sen, Amartya K. Information and Invariance in Normative Choice. **In** *[Arrow, K. J.], Vol. 1,* 1986, pp. 29–55.

Sen, Amartya K. The Right to Take Personal Risks. **In** *MacLean, D., ed.,* 1986, pp. 155–69.

Shepsle, Kenneth A. The Positive Theory of Legislative Institutions: An Enrichment of Social Choice and Spatial Models. *Public Choice,* 1986, *50*(1–3), pp. 135–78.

Silver, Brian D.; Anderson, Barbara A. and Abramson, Paul R. Who Overreports Voting? *Amer. Polit. Sci. Rev.,* June 1986, *80*(2), pp. 613–24. **[G: U.S.]**

Slutsky, Steven M. Elections with Incomplete Information: Comments [Incumbent Performance and Electoral Control] [Elections and Income Redistribution]. *Public Choice,* 1986, *50*(1–3), pp. 105–29.

Starrett, David A. On the Social Risk Premium. **In** *[Arrow, K. J.], Vol. 1,* 1986, pp. 159–76.

Steedman, Ian and Krause, Ulrich. Goethe's *Faust,* Arrow's Possibility Theorem and the Individual Decision-taker. **In** *Elster, J., ed.,* 1986, pp. 197–231.

Stigler, George J. Economic Competition and Political Competition. **In** *Stigler, G. J.,* 1986, *1972,* pp. 117–33.

Stigler, George J. Free Riders and Collective Action: An Appendix to Theories of Economic Regulation. **In** *Stigler, G. J.,* 1986, *1974,* pp. 67–75. **[G: U.S.]**

Suzumura, K. and Suga, K. Gibbardian Libertarian Claims Revisited. *Soc. Choice Welfare,* June 1986, *3*(1), pp. 61–73.

Tideman, T. N. A Majority-Rule Characterization with Multiple Extensions. *Soc. Choice Welfare,* June 1986, *3*(1), pp. 17–30.

Tullock, Gordon. Demand Revealing, Transfers, and Rent Seeking. **In** *Tullock, G.,* 1986, pp. 136–42.

Tullock, Gordon. Giving Life [Avoiding Difficult Decisions]. **In** *Tullock, G.,* 1986, *1979,* pp. 158–69.

Tullock, Gordon. More on the Welfare Cost of Transfers. **In** *Tullock, G.,* 1986, *1974,* pp. 107–10.

Tullock, Gordon. Optimal Majorities for Decisions of Varying Importance: Comment. *Public Choice,* 1986, *48*(3), pp. 291–94.

Vanberg, Viktor. Spontaneous Market Order and Social Rules: A Critical Examination of F. A. Hayek's Theory of Cultural Evolution. *Econ. Philos.,* April 1986, *2*(1), pp. 75–100.

van Velthoven, Ben and van Winden, Frans. Social Classes and State Behavior. *J. Inst. Theoretical Econ.,* September 1986, *142*(3), pp. 542–70. **[G: Netherlands]**

Verbon, Harrie A. A. and van Winden, Frans. Public Pensions and Political Decision-Making. **In** *von der Schulenburg, J.-M. G., ed.,* 1986, pp. 32–53. **[G: Netherlands]**

Wagner, Richard E. Central Banking and the Fed: A Public Choice Perspective. *Cato J.,* Fall 1986, *6*(2), pp. 519–38. **[G: U.S.]**

Weesie, Jeroen and Wippler, Reinhard. Cumulative Effects of Sequential Decisions in Organizations. **In** *[Rapoport, A.],* 1986, pp. 257–79.

Weingast, Barry R. and Moran, Mark J. Congress and Regulatory Agency Choice: Reply [Bureaucratic Discretion or Congressional Control? Regulatory Policymaking by the Federal Trade Commission]. *J. Polit. Econ.*, August 1986, *94*(4), pp. 890–94. **[G: U.S.]**

Wickström, Bengt-Arne. Optimal Majorities for Decisions of Varying Importance: Comment on a Comment. *Public Choice*, 1986, *48*(3), pp. 295–98.

Wickström, Bengt-Arne. Optimal Majorities for Decisions of Varying Importance. *Public Choice*, 1986, *48*(3), pp. 273–90.

Wright, Randall. The Redistributive Roles of Unemployment Insurance and the Dynamics of Voting. *J. Public Econ.*, December 1986, *31*(3), pp. 377–99.

Wriglesworth, J. L. Two Simple Single-Profile Impossibilities. *Soc. Choice Welfare*, July 1986, *3*(2), pp. 89–97.

Yandle, Bruce. Rentless Rent-Seeking and Abnormal Returns. *Public Choice*, 1986, *48*(3), pp. 265–70.

Young, Leslie and Magee, Stephen P. Endogenous Protection, Factor Returns and Resource Allocation. *Rev. Econ. Stud.*, July 1986, *53*(3), pp. 407–19.

Zorn, Thomas S. and Martin, Dolores T. Optimism and Pessimism in Political and Market Institutions. *Public Choice*, 1986, *49*(2), pp. 165–78.

0252 Social Choice Studies: Voting, Committees, etc.

Abrams, Burton A. and Dougan, William R. The Effects of Constitutional Restraints on Government Spending. *Public Choice*, 1986, *49*(2), pp. 101–16. **[G: U.S.]**

Adams, James D. and Kenny, Lawrence W. Optimal Tenure of Elected Public Officials. *J. Law Econ.*, October 1986, *29*(2), pp. 303–28. **[G: U.S.]**

Adams, Richard H., Jr. Bureaucrats, Peasants and the Dominant Coalition: An Egyptian Case Study. *J. Devel. Stud.*, January 1986, *22*(2), pp. 336–54. **[G: Egypt]**

Allen, Stuart D. The Federal Reserve and the Electoral Cycle: A Note. *J. Money, Credit, Banking*, February 1986, *18*(1), pp. 88–94. **[G: U.S.]**

Allen, Stuart D.; Sulock, Joseph M. and Sabo, William A. The Political Business Cycle: How Significant? *Public Finance Quart.*, January 1986, *14*(1), pp. 107–12. **[G: U.S.]**

Anderson, Terry L. and Hill, Peter J. Constraining the Transfer Society: Constitutional and Moral Dimensions. *Cato J.*, Spring/Summer 1986, *6*(1), pp. 317–39.

Baber, William R. and Sen, Pradyot Kumar. The Political Process and the Use of Debt Financing by State Governments. *Public Choice*, 1986, *48*(3), pp. 201–15. **[G: U.S.]**

Banks, Gary and Tumlir, Jan. The Political Problem of Adjustment. *World Econ.*, June 1986, *9*(2), pp. 141–52. **[G: EEC; Canada]**

Bender, Bruce. The Determinants of Relative Political Campaign Expenditures. *Econ. Inquiry*, April 1986, *24*(2), pp. 231–56. **[G: U.S.]**

Benson, Bruce L. and Greenhut, Melvin L. Special Interests, Bureaucrats, and Antitrust: An Explanation of the Antitrust Paradox. **In** *Grieson, R. E., ed.*, 1986, pp. 53–90. **[G: U.S.]**

Benson, Bruce L. and Johnson, Ronald N. The Lagged Impact of State and Local Taxes on Economic Activity and Political Behavior. *Econ. Inquiry*, July 1986, *24*(3), pp. 389–401. **[G: U.S.]**

Berman, David R. Voters, Candidates, and Issues in the Progressive Era: An Analysis of the 1912 Presidential Election in Arizona. *Soc. Sci. Quart.*, June 1986, *67*(2), pp. 255–66. **[G: U.S.]**

Bernholz, Peter. Growth of Government, Economic Growth and Individual Freedom. *J. Inst. Theoretical Econ.*, December 1986, *142*(4), pp. 661–83. **[G: OECD]**

Blomqvist, Ake G. and Mohammad, Sharif. Controls, Corruption, and Competitive Rent-Seeking in LDCs. *J. Devel. Econ.*, April 1986, *21*(1), pp. 161–80. **[G: India]**

Brady, David W. Electoral Realignment in the U.S. House of Representatives. **In** *Wright, G. C., Jr.; Rieselbach, L. N. and Dodd, L. C., eds.*, 1986, pp. 47–69. **[G: U.S.]**

Breton, Albert and Wintrobe, Ronald. The Bureaucracy of Murder Revisited. *J. Polit. Econ.*, October 1986, *94*(5), pp. 905–26.

Brown, Philip J. and Payne, Clive D. Aggregate Data, Ecological Regression, and Voting Transitions. *J. Amer. Statist. Assoc.*, June 1986, *81*(394), pp. 452–60. **[G: U.K.]**

Buchanan, James M. Cultural Evolution and Institutional Reform. **In** *Buchanan, J. M.*, 1986, pp. 75–85.

Buchanan, James M. Moral Community, Moral Order, or Moral Anarchy. **In** *Buchanan, J. M.*, 1986, *1981*, pp. 108–20. **[G: U.S.; Japan]**

Capron, Henri. Préférences idéologiques, contrainte électorale et résultats macroéconomiques. (With English summary.) *Cah. Écon. Bruxelles*, First Trimester 1986, (109), pp. 51–83. **[G: Belgium]**

Carmines, Edward G. and Stimson, James A. The Politics and Policy of Race in Congress. **In** *Wright, G. C., Jr.; Rieselbach, L. N. and Dodd, L. C., eds.*, 1986, pp. 70–93. **[G: U.S.]**

Cassing, James H.; McKeown, Timothy J. and Ochs, Jack. The Political Economy of the Tariff Cycle. *Amer. Polit. Sci. Rev.*, September 1986, *80*(3), pp. 843–62. **[G: U.S.]**

Cebula, Richard J. and Kafoglis, Milton Z. A Note on the Tiebout–Tullock Hypothesis: The Period 1975–1980. *Public Choice*, 1986, *48*(1), pp. 65–69. **[G: U.S.]**

Chappell, Henry W., Jr. and Keech, William R. Party Differences in Macroeconomic Policies and Outcomes. *Amer. Econ. Rev.*, May 1986, *76*(2), pp. 71–74. **[G: U.S.]**

Coleman, James S. Individual Rights and the State. **In** *Coleman, J. S.*, 1986, *1976*, pp. 348–64.

Coleman, James S. Legitimate and Illegitimate Use of Power. **In** *Coleman, J. S.*, 1986, *1975*, pp. 247–66.

Coleman, James S. Political Money. **In** *Coleman, J. S.*, 1986, *1970*, pp. 163–91.

Coleman, James S. Rawls, Nozick, and Educational Equality. **In** *Coleman, J. S.*, 1986, *1976*, pp. 365–74.

Coleman, James S. and Babinec, Anthony. The Corporate Structure of the Economy and Its Effects on Income. **In** *Coleman, J. S.*, 1986, *1978*, pp. 281–301. **[G: U.S.]**

Coleman, James S.; Wu, Shi-Chang and Feld, Scott L. Constitutional Power in Experimental Health Service and Delivery Systems. **In** *Coleman, J. S.*, 1986, *1977*, pp. 226–46. **[G: U.S.]**

Correa, Hector and Vassar, W. F., Jr. United States Policy toward Latin America: A Study of Proactive versus Reactive Hypotheses. *Math. Soc. Sci.*, October 1986, *12*(2), pp. 191–98. **[G: U.S.; Latin America]**

Crain, W. Mark and Goff, Brian L. Televising Legislatures: An Economic Analysis. *J. Law Econ.*, October 1986, *29*(2), pp. 405–21. **[G: U.S.]**

Crain, W. Mark; Leavens, Donald R. and Tollison, Robert D. Final Voting in Legislatures. *Amer. Econ. Rev.*, September 1986, *76*(4), pp. 833–41.

DeLorme, Charles D., Jr.; Kamerschen, David R. and Mbaku, John M. Rent Seeking in the Cameroon Economy: Krueger's Analytic Technique Helps to Account for Development Lag in Colonial States. *Amer. J. Econ. Soc.*, October 1986, *45*(4), pp. 413–23. **[G: Cameroon]**

Dodd, Lawrence C. A Theory of Congressional Cycles: Solving the Puzzle of Change. **In** *Wright, G. C., Jr.; Rieselbach, L. N. and Dodd, L. C., eds.*, 1986, pp. 1–44. **[G: U.S.]**

Fand, David I. Federal Reserve Hegemony and Monetary Surprises [Is There a Political Monetary Cycle?]. *Cato J.*, Fall 1986, *6*(2), pp. 581–86. **[G: U.S.]**

Fleischmann, Arnold. The Politics of Annexation: A Preliminary Assessment of Competing Paradigms. *Soc. Sci. Quart.*, March 1986, *67*(1), pp. 128–42. **[G: U.S.]**

Frey, Bruno S. and Buhofer, Heinz. Integration and Protectionism: A Comparative Institutional Analysis. *Aussenwirtschaft*, September 1986, *41*(2/3), pp. 329–50. **[G: EEC]**

Gandenberger, Otto. On Government Borrowing and False Political Feedback. **In** *Herber, B. P., ed.*, 1986, pp. 205–16.

Gifford, Adam, Jr. and Kenney, Roy W. On Nationalizing Private Property and the Present Value of Dictators: Reply [Socialism and the Revenue Maximizing Leviathan]. *Public Choice*, 1986, *48*(1), pp. 89–91.

Gowa, Joanne. Anarchy, Egoism, and Third Images: *The Evolution of Cooperation* and International Relations. *Int. Organ.*, Winter 1986, *40*(1), pp. 167–86.

Greene, Kenneth V. The Public Choice of Differing Degrees of Tax Progressivity. *Public Choice*, 1986, *49*(3), pp. 265–82. **[G: U.S.]**

Grier, Kevin B. and Munger, Michael C. The Impact of Legislator Attributes on Interest-Group Campaign Contributions. *J. Lab. Res.*, Fall 1986, *7*(4), pp. 349–61. **[G: U.S.]**

Grofman, Bernard; Migalski, Michael and Noviello, Nicholas. Effects of Multimember Districts on Black Representation in State Legislatures. *Rev. Black Polit. Econ.*, Spring 1986, *14*(4), pp. 64–78. **[G: U.S.]**

Hauser, Heinz. Domestic Policy Foundation and Domestic Policy Function of International Trade Rules. *Aussenwirtschaft*, September 1986, *41*(2/3), pp. 171–84. **[G: OECD]**

Hibbs, Douglas A., Jr. Political Parties and Macroeconomic Policies and Outcomes in the United States. *Amer. Econ. Rev.*, May 1986, *76*(2), pp. 66–70. **[G: U.S.]**

Hillman, Arye L. and Schnytzer, Adi. Illegal Economic Activities and Purges in a Soviet-Type Economy: A Rent-Seeking Perspective. *Int. Rev. Law Econ.*, June 1986, *6*(1), pp. 87–99.

Jacobson, Gary C. and Kernell, Samuel. Interpreting the 1974 Congressional Election. *Amer. Polit. Sci. Rev.*, June 1986, *80*(2), pp. 591–93. **[G: U.S.]**

Jagannathan, N. Vijay. Corruption, Delivery Systems, and Property Rights. *World Devel.*, January 1986, *14*(1), pp. 127–32. **[G: India; LDCs]**

Jones, Philip R. and Cullis, John G. Is Democracy Regressive? A Comment on Political Participation [Why Do High Income People Participate More in Politics]. *Public Choice*, 1986, *51*(1), pp. 101–07.

Jorrat, Jorge Raúl. Las elecciones de 1983: "desviación" o "realineamiento"? (With English summary.) *Desarrollo Econ.*, Apr.-June 1986, *26*(101), pp. 89–120. **[G: Argentina]**

Kaempfer, William H. and Lowenberg, Anton D. A Model of the Political Economy of International Investment Sanctions: The Case of South Africa. *Kyklos*, 1986, *39*(3), pp. 377–96. **[G: S. Africa]**

Kane, Edward J. Politics and Fed Policymaking: The More Things Change the More They Remain the Same. **In** *Toma, E. F. and Toma, M., eds.*, 1986, *1980*, pp. 185–98. **[G: U.S.]**

Kemp, Kathleen A. Race, Ethnicity, Class and Urban Spatial Conflict: Chicago as a Crucial Test Case. *Urban Stud.*, June 1986, *23*(3), pp. 197–208. **[G: U.S.]**

Kennedy, Charles H. Policies of Redistributional Preference in Pakistan. **In** *Nevitte, N. and Kennedy, C. H., eds.*, 1986, pp. 63–93. **[G: Pakistan]**

Kern, Lucian and Räder, Hans-Georg. On Explaining the Rise of the New Social Movements in Germany. **In** *[Rapoport, A.]*, 1986, pp. 169–85. **[G: W. Germany]**

Kirchgässner, Gebhard. Überprüfung der Hypothese rationaler Erwartungen anhand von Popularitätsdaten. Eine Untersuchung für die Bundesrepublik Deutschland, 1971–1982. (Testing the Rational Expectations Hypothesis Using Popularity Data. Empirical Investigation for the Federal Republic of Germany, 1971–1982. With English summary.) *Z. Wirtschaft. Sozialwissen.*, 1986, *106*(4), pp. 363–86. [G: W. Germany]

Kitschelt, Herbert. Four Theories of Public Policy Making and Fast Breeder Reactor Development. *Int. Organ.*, Winter 1986, *40*(1), pp. 65–104. [G: France; W. Germany; U.S.]

Krumm, Ronald; Tolley, George and Kelly, Austin. Voter Participation and Voter Choice: An Empirical Examination of Massachusetts' Proposition 2½ **In** *Grieson, R. E., ed.*, 1986, pp. 135–51. [G: U.S.]

Laband, David N. Congressional Junketeering: Public Sector X-Inefficiency. *J. Econ. Bus.*, May 1986, *38*(2), pp. 131–40. [G: U.S.]

Laband, David N. The Private Interest in Public Redistribution: A Public Choice View of the Geographic Distribution of Federal Funds. *Public Choice*, 1986, *49*(2), pp. 117–25.

Landa, Janet T. The Political Economy of Swarming in Honeybees: Voting-with-the-Wings, Decision-Making Costs, and the Unanimity Rule. *Public Choice*, 1986, *51*(1), pp. 25–38.

Laver, Michael. Ireland: Politics with *Some* Social Bases: An Interpretation Based on Survey Data. *Econ. Soc. Rev.*, April 1986, *17*(3), pp. 193–213. [G: Ireland]

Laver, Michael. Ireland: Politics with Some Social Bases on Interpretation Based on Aggregate Data. *Econ. Soc. Rev.*, January 1986, *17*(2), pp. 107–31. [G: Ireland]

Lehmbruch, Gerhard. Interest Groups, Government, and the Politics of Protectionism. **In** *Hauser, H., ed. (II)*, 1986, pp. 111–40.

Lehmbruch, Gerhard. Interest Groups, Government, and the Politics of Protectionism. *Aussenwirtschaft*, September 1986, *41*(2/3), pp. 273–302. [G: OECD]

Lewis, Alan. Fiscal Policy: The Importance of Perceptions and Attitudes. **In** *Gilad, B. and Kaish, S., eds., Vol. B*, 1986, pp. 111–22. [G: U.K.; U.S.]

Lott, John R., Jr. and Reiffen, David. On Nationalizing Private Property and the Present Value of Dictators. *Public Choice*, 1986, *48*(1), pp. 81–87. [G: E. Europe]

Lynn, Laurence E., Jr. The Behavioral Foundations of Public Policy-Making. **In** *Hogarth, R. M. and Reder, M. W., eds.*, 1986, pp. 195–200.

Lynn, Laurence E., Jr. The Behavioral Foundations of Public Policy-Making. *J. Bus.*, Part 2, October 1986, *59*(4), pp. S379–84.

McGuire, Robert A. and Ohsfeldt, Robert L. An Economic Model of Voting Behavior over Specific Issues at the Constitutional Convention of 1787. *J. Econ. Hist.*, March 1986, *46*(1), pp. 79–111. [G: U.S.]

Means, Gordon P. Ethnic Preference Policies in Malaysia. **In** *Nevitte, N. and Kennedy, C. H., eds.*, 1986, pp. 95–118. [G: Malaysia]

Medoff, Marshall H. Determinants of the Political Participation of Women. *Public Choice*, 1986, *48*(3), pp. 245–53. [G: U.S.]

Mehay, Stephen L. and Seiden, Kenneth P. Municipal Residency Laws and Local Public Budgets. *Public Choice*, 1986, *48*(1), pp. 27–35. [G: U.S.]

Meiselman, David I. Is There a Political Monetary Cycle? *Cato J.*, Fall 1986, *6*(2), pp. 563–79. [G: U.S.]

Michaels, Robert. Reinterpreting the Role of Inflation in Politico-Economic Model. *Public Choice*, 1986, *48*(2), pp. 113–24. [G: U.S.]

Morrison, William G. and West, Edwin G. Subsidies for the Performing Arts: Evidence on Voter Preference. *J. Behav. Econ.*, Fall 1986, *15*, pp. 57–72. [G: Canada]

Mueller, Dennis C. Power and Profit in Hierarchical Organizations. **In** *Mueller, D. C.*, 1986, *1980*, pp. 37–51.

Mueller, Dennis C. and Murrell, Peter. Interest Groups and the Size of Government. *Public Choice*, 1986, *48*(2), pp. 125–45. [G: OECD]

Muller, Edward N. and Opp, Karl-Dieter. Rational Choice and Rebellious Collective Action. *Amer. Polit. Sci. Rev.*, June 1986, *80*(2), pp. 471–87. [G: U.S.]

Nevitte, Neil and Kennedy, Charles H. The Analysis of Policies of Ethnic Preference in Developing States. **In** *Nevitte, N. and Kennedy, C. H., eds.*, 1986, pp. 1–13.

Nove, Alec. Some Aspects of Soviet Constitutional Theory. **In** *Nove, A.*, 1986, *1949*, pp. 193–219. [G: U.S.S.R.]

Oberst, Robert. Policies of Ethnic Preference in Sri Lanka. **In** *Nevitte, N. and Kennedy, C. H., eds.*, 1986, pp. 135–54. [G: Sri Lanka]

Pasour, E. C., Jr. Information, Incentives, and Regulation. **In** *Moorhouse, J. C., ed.*, 1986, pp. 359–79.

Premdas, Ralph R. Politics of Preference in the Caribbean: The Case of Guyana. **In** *Nevitte, N. and Kennedy, C. H., eds.*, 1986, pp. 155–87. [G: Guyana]

Pridham, Geoffrey. European Elections, Political Parties and Trends of Internalization in Community Affairs. *J. Common Market Stud.*, June 1986, *24*(4), pp. 279–96. [G: EEC]

Richards, Daniel J. A Note on the Importance of Cost Structures for the Behavior of Political Action Committees. *Public Choice*, 1986, *48*(1), pp. 71–79. [G: U.S.]

Riker, W. H. The First Power Index. *Soc. Choice Welfare*, December 1986, *3*(4), pp. 293–95. [G: U.S.]

Rothchild, Donald. State and Ethnicity in Africa: A Policy Perspective. **In** *Nevitte, N. and Kennedy, C. H., eds.*, 1986, pp. 15–61. [G: Africa]

Rothschild, Kurt W. 'Left' and 'Right' in 'Federal Europe.' *Kyklos*, 1986, *39*(3), pp. 359–76. [G: W. Europe]

Russell, Robert W. Congress and the Proposed Industrial Policy Structures. **In** *Barfield, C. E. and Schambra, W. A., eds.*, 1986, pp. 318–32. [G: U.S.]

Sampson, Anthony A. Voting in Unions with Seniority Rules. *Bull. Econ. Res.*, September 1986, *38*(3), pp. 271–76.

Santerre, Rexford E. Representative versus Direct Democracy: A Tiebout Test of Relative Performance. *Public Choice,* 1986, *48*(1), pp. 55–63. **[G: U.S.]**

Schmidt, Christian. Esquisse d'un modèle de dynamique des dépenses militaires franç aises construit en forme de je de Nash. With English summary.) *Revue Écon. Polit.*, Jan.-Feb. 1986, *96*(1), pp. 1–12. **[G: France]**

Schneider, Friedrich. The Influence of Political Institutions on Social Security Policies: A Public Choice View. **In** *von der Schulenburg, J.-M. G., ed.*, 1986, pp. 13–31. **[G: OECD]**

Scholz, John T. and Wei, Feng Heng. Regulatory Enforcement in a Federalist System. *Amer. Polit. Sci. Rev.*, December 1986, *80*(4), pp. 1249–70. **[G: U.S.]**

Shughart, William F., II; Tollison, Robert D. and Goff, Brian L. Bureaucratic Structure and Congressional Control. *Southern Econ. J.*, April 1986, *52*(4), pp. 962–72. **[G: U.S.]**

Sigelman, Lee and Yanarella, Ernest J. Public Information on Public Issues: A Multivariate Analysis. *Soc. Sci. Quart.*, June 1986, *67*(2), pp. 402–10. **[G: U.S.]**

Skaggs, Neil T. and Wasserkrug, Cheryl L. Banking Sector Influence on the Relationship of Congress to the Federal Reserve System. **In** *Toma, E. F. and Toma, M., eds.*, 1986, *1983*, pp. 169–82. **[G: U.S.]**

Soh, Byung Hee. Political Business Cycles in Industrialized Democratic Countries. *Kyklos*, 1986, *39*(1), pp. 31–46. **[G: OECD]**

Stolz, Peter. Parteienwettbewerb, politisches Kartell und Tausch zwischen sozioökonomischen Gruppen. (Party Competition, Political Cartel and Exchange between Socio-economic Groups. With English summary.) *Schweiz. Z. Volkswirtsch. Statist.*, December 1986, *122*(4), pp. 657–75. **[G: Switzerland]**

Taagepera, Rein. Reformulating the Cube Law for Proportional Representation Elections. *Amer. Polit. Sci. Rev.*, June 1986, *80*(2), pp. 489–504. **[G: W. Europe; U.S.; Canada; Japan]**

Theilmann, John and Wilhite, Allen. Differences in Campaign Funds: A Racial Explanation. *Rev. Black Polit. Econ.*, Summer 1986, *15*(1), pp. 45–58. **[G: U.S.]**

Thies, Clifford F. A Note on the Role of Knowledge in Direct Voting on Milk Price Decontrol. *Public Choice,* 1986, *49*(2), pp. 191–94. **[G: U.S.]**

Toma, Eugenia Froedge. Rent Seeking, Federal Mandates, and the Quality of Public Education. *Atlantic Econ. J.*, July 1986, *14*(2), pp. 37–45. **[G: U.S.]**

Toma, Eugenia Froedge. State University Boards of Trustees: A Principal-Agent Perspective. *Public Choice,* 1986, *49*(2), pp. 155–63. **[G: U.S.]**

Uslaner, Eric M. and Conway, M. Margaret. Interpreting the 1974 Congressional Election. *Amer. Polit. Sci. Rev.*, June 1986, *80*(2), pp. 593–95. **[G: U.S.]**

Vaubel, Roland. A Public Choice Approach to International Organization. *Public Choice,* 1986, *51*(1), pp. 39–57.

Vedder, Richard and Gallaway, Lowell. Rent-Seeking, Distributional Coalitions, Taxes, Relative Prices and Economic Growth. *Public Choice,* 1986, *51*(1), pp. 93–100. **[G: U.S.]**

Wagner, Richard E. Wealth Transfers in a Rent-Seeking Polity. *Cato J.*, Spring/Summer 1986, *6*(1), pp. 155–71.

Weck-Hannemann, Hannelore. The Politics of Protectionism: Discussion to Section II. *Aussenwirtschaft*, September 1986, *41*(2/3), pp. 351–58.

Whicker, Marcia Lynn. Direct Democracy Devices: A Computer-Simulation Analysis. *J. Policy Modeling,* Summer 1986, *8*(2), pp. 255–71. **[G: U.S.]**

Wilhite, Allen and Theilmann, John. Unions, Corporations, and Political Campaign Contributions: The 1982 House Elections. *J. Lab. Res.*, Spring 1986, *7*(2), pp. 175–85. **[G: U.S.]**

Wilhite, Allen and Theilmann, John. Women, Blacks, and PAC Discrimination. *Soc. Sci. Quart.*, June 1986, *67*(2), pp. 283–98. **[G: U.S.]**

Wright, Gerald C., Jr. Elections and the Potential for Policy Change in Congress: The House of Representatives. **In** *Wright, G. C., Jr.; Rieselbach, L. N. and Dodd, L. C., eds.*, 1986, pp. 94–119. **[G: U.S.]**

Yandle, Bruce and Young, Elizabeth. Regulating the Function, Not the Industry. *Public Choice,* 1986, *51*(1), pp. 59–70.

026 Economics of Uncertainty and Information; Game Theory and Bargaining Theory

0260 General

Blume, Lawrence and Jordan, James S. Introduction to Expectations Equilibrium. **In** *Sonnenschein, H. F., ed.*, 1986, pp. 206–12.

Chen, Wen-chen and DeGroot, Morris H. Optimal Search for New Types. **In** *[de Finetti, B.]*, 1986, pp. 443–58.

Deneckere, Raymond J. On the Existence of Random Measure Preserving Bijections. *J. Math. Econ.*, 1986, *15*(3), pp. 267–74.

Gal-Or, Esther. Information Transmission—Cournot and Bertrand Equilibria. *Rev. Econ. Stud.*, January 1986, *53*(1), pp. 85–92.

Grossman, Sanford J. and Perry, Motty. Sequential Bargaining under Asymmetric Information. *J. Econ. Theory,* June 1986, *39*(1), pp. 120–54.

Heiner, Ronald A. Uncertainty, Signal-Detection Experiments, and Modeling Behavior. **In** *Langlois, R. N., ed.*, 1986, pp. 59–115.

Hughes Hallett, A. J. Autonomy and the Choice of Policy in Asymmetrically Dependent Economies: An Investigation of the Gains from International Policy Co-ordination. *Oxford Econ. Pap.*, November 1986, *38*(3), pp. 516–44. **[G: OECD]**

Hurwicz, Leonid. On Informationally Decentralized Systems. **In** *[Marschak, J.]*, 1986, *1972*, pp. 297–336.

Lahiri, Somdeb. Feasibility and Stability in Intertemporal Information Flows. *Econ. Planning*, 1986, *20*(2), pp. 104–30.

Langlois, Richard N. Coherence and Flexibility: Social Institutions in a World of Radical Uncertainty. **In** *[Lachmann, L. M.]*, 1986, pp. 171–91.

Marion, Nancy Peregrim and Svensson, Lars E. O. Adjustment to Expected and Unexpected Oil Price Changes: Corrigendum. *Can. J. Econ.*, November 1986, *19*(4), pp. 816–17.

Marschak, Thomas A. Computation in Organizations: The Comparison of Price Mechanisms and Other Adjustment Processes. **In** *[Marschak, J.]*, 1986, *1972*, pp. 237–81.

McGuire, C. B. and Radner, Roy. Decision and Organization: Preface to the Second Edition. **In** *[Marschak, J.]*, 1986, pp. vii–xxiv.

Muto, Shigeo. An Information Good Market with Symmetric Externalities. *Econometrica*, March 1986, *54*(2), pp. 295–312.

Porter, Robert H. A Note on Tacit Collusion under Demand Uncertainty. *Can. J. Econ.*, August 1986, *19*(3), pp. 556–58.

Postlewaite, Andrew and Schmeidler, David. Implementation in Differential Information Economies. *J. Econ. Theory*, June 1986, *39*(1), pp. 14–33.

Radner, Roy. Normative Theory of Individual Decision: An Introduction. **In** *[Marschak, J.]*, 1986, *1972*, pp. 1–18.

Radner, Roy. Teams. **In** *[Marschak, J.]*, 1986, *1972*, pp. 189–215.

Strydom, P. D. F. The Economics of Information: A Subjectivist View. **In** *[Lachmann, L. M.]*, 1986, pp. 288–94.

White, Harry. Uncertainty and Factor Proportions [Factor Price Uncertainty with Variable Proportions]. *Can. J. Econ.*, November 1986, *19*(4), pp. 814–15.

0261 Theory of Uncertainty and Information

Abel, Andrew B. Capital Accumulation and Uncertain Lifetimes with Adverse Selection. *Econometrica*, September 1986, *54*(5), pp. 1079–97.

Admati, Anat R. and Pfleiderer, Paul. A Monopolistic Market for Information. *J. Econ. Theory*, August 1986, *39*(2), pp. 400–438.

Aiginger, Karl. The Impact of Uncertainty on the Optimal Decision of Risk Neutral Firms. **In** *Daboni, L.; Montesano, A. and Lines, M., eds.*, 1986, pp. 355–73.

Aizenman, Joshua. Stabilization Policies and the Information Content of Real Wages. *Economica*, May 1986, *53*(210), pp. 181–90.

Albrecht, James W.; Axell, Bo and Lang, Harald. General Equilibrium Wage and Price Distributions. *Quart. J. Econ.*, November 1986, *101*(4), pp. 687–706.

Albrecht, James W. and Jovanovic, Boyan. The Efficiency of Search under Competition and Monopsony. *J. Polit. Econ.*, December 1986, *94*(6), pp. 1246–57.

Alchian, Armen A. Uncertainty, Evolution, and Economic Theory. **In** *Barney, J. B. and Ouchi, W. G., eds.*, 1986, *1950*, pp. 305–19.

Allen, Beth. The Demand for (Differentiated) Information. *Rev. Econ. Stud.*, July 1986, *53*(3), pp. 311–23.

Andersen, Torben M. Differential Information and the Role for an Active Stabilization Policy. *Economica*, August 1986, *53*(211), pp. 321–38.

Andersen, Torben M. Speculation, Optimum and Differential Information. *Southern Econ. J.*, July 1986, *53*(1), pp. 170–86.

Antonovitz, Frances and Roe, Terry. A Theoretical and Empirical Approach to the Value of Information in Risky Markets. *Rev. Econ. Statist.*, February 1986, *68*(1), pp. 105–14. **[G: U.S.]**

Aoki, Masahiko. Horizontal vs. Vertical Information Structure of the Firm. *Amer. Econ. Rev.*, December 1986, *76*(5), pp. 971–83.

Appelbaum, Elie and Katz, Eliakim. Measures of Risk Aversion and Comparative Statics of Industry Equilibrium. *Amer. Econ. Rev.*, June 1986, *76*(3), pp. 524–29.

Arai, Kazuhiro. Demand for and Supply of Price Information in Markets for Consumer Goods. *Hitotsubashi J. Econ.*, June 1986, *27*(1), pp. 35–47.

Arigoni, Anio O. Information Utility—Statistical and Semantical Features. **In** *Daboni, L.; Montesano, A. and Lines, M., eds.*, 1986, pp. 277–88.

Arrow, Kenneth J. Exposition of the Theory of Choice under Uncertainty. **In** *[Marschak, J.]*, 1986, *1972*, pp. 19–55.

Arrow, Kenneth J. The Value of and Demand for Information. **In** *[Marschak, J.]*, 1986, *1972*, pp. 131–39.

Baier, Annette. Poisoning the Wells. **In** *MacLean, D., ed.*, 1986, pp. 49–74.

Barberá, Salvador and Pattanaik, Prasanta K. Falmagne and the Rationalizability of Stochastic Choices in Terms of Random Orderings. *Econometrica*, May 1986, *54*(3), pp. 707–15.

Beckmann, Martin J. Decisions over Time. **In** *[Marschak, J.]*, 1986, *1972*, pp. 141–59.

Beladi, Hamid and Lyon, Kenneth S. The Effects of Risk Aversion When an Input Is Random: A Note. *Quart. J. Bus. Econ.*, Spring 1986, *25*(2), pp. 71–83.

Belloc, Bernard. Quelques aspects normatifs du problème d'akerlof. Un exemple. (Some Normative Aspects of Akerlof's Problem. An Example. With English summary.) *Revue Écon.*, September 1986, *37*(5), pp. 783–803.

Berg, Joyce E., et al. Controlling Preferences for Lotteries on Units of Experimental Exchange. *Quart. J. Econ.*, May 1986, *101*(2), pp. 281–306.

Bernheim, B. Douglas and Ray, Debraj. On the Existence of Markov-Consistent Plans under Production Uncertainty. *Rev. Econ. Stud.*, October 1986, *53*(5), pp. 877–82.

Berninghaus, Siegfried; Lippman, Steven A. and

McCall, John J. An Equilibrium Model of Turnover with Belated Information. *Info. Econ. Policy,* September 1986, *2*(3), pp. 221–39.

Black, Max. Some Questions about Bayesian Decision Theory. **In** *Daboni, L.; Montesano, A. and Lines, M., eds.,* 1986, pp. 57–66.

Borio, C. E. V. Do Contingent Rules Really Dominate Fixed Rules? *Econ. J.,* December 1986, *96*(384), pp. 1000–1010.

Bradley, Michael G. and Lehman, Dale E. Comparative Equilibrium versus Comparative Statics. *Can. J. Econ.,* August 1986, *19*(3), pp. 526–38.

Bradley, Michael G. and Lehman, Dale E. Instrument-Dependent Randomness and Increases in Risk. *J. Econ. (Z. Nationalökon.),* 1986, *46*(1), pp. 17–29.

Bray, Margaret M. and Savin, Nathan E. Rational Expectations Equilibria, Learning, and Model Specification. *Econometrica,* September 1986, *54*(5), pp. 1129–60.

Brock, William A. and Rothschild, Michael. Comparative Statics for Multidimensional Optimal Stopping Problems. **In** *Sonnenschein, H. F., ed.,* 1986, pp. 124–38.

Broze, L.; Gouriéroux, Christian and Szafarz, A. Bulles spéculatives et transmission d'information sur le marché d'un bien stockable. (Speculative Bubbles and on the Transmission of Information on the Stockable Commodity Market. With English summary.) *L'Actual. Econ.,* June 1986, *62*(2), pp. 166–84.

Calcoen, F.; Eeckhoudt, L. and Outreville, J.- François. Indemnisation du chômage et revenus de remplacement: Une approche par la théorie de l'assurance. (Unemployment Insurance and Damage Insurance: An Approach through the Theory of Insurance. With English summary.) *Schweiz. Z. Volkswirtsch. Statist.,* September 1986, *122*(3), pp. 323–37.

Carlson, Severin and Lord, Blair. Unisex Retirement Benefits and the Market for Annuity "Lemons." *J. Risk Ins.,* September 1986, *53*(3), pp. 409–18.

Cassing, James H.; Hillman, Arye L. and Long, Ngo Van. Risk Aversion, Terms of Trade Uncertainty and Social-Consensus Trade Policy. *Oxford Econ. Pap.,* July 1986, *38*(2), pp. 234–42.

Chan, Yuk-Shee and Leland, Hayne E. Prices and Qualities: A Search Model. *Southern Econ. J.,* April 1986, *52*(4), pp. 1115–30.

Chen, Yu-Min. An Extension to the Implementability of Reduced Form Auctions. *Econometrica,* September 1986, *54*(5), pp. 1249–51.

Chesney, Marc and Loubergé, Henri. Risk Aversion and the Composition of Wealth in the Demand for Full Insurance Coverage. *Schweiz. Z. Volkswirtsch. Statist.,* September 1986, *122*(3), pp. 359–70.

Cohen, Jacob. Fritz Machlup's Swan Song. *Econ. Educ. Rev.,* 1986, *5*(3), pp. 319–23.

Cotter, Kevin D. Similarity of Information and Behavior with a Pointwise Convergence Topology. *J. Math. Econ.,* 1986, *15*(1), pp. 25–38.

Crocker, Keith J. A Reexamination of the "Lemons" Market When Warranties Are Not Prepurchase Quality Signals. *Info. Econ. Policy,* June 1986, *2*(2), pp. 147–62.

Crocker, Keith J. and Snow, Arthur. The Efficiency Effects of Categorical Discrimination in the Insurance Industry. *J. Polit. Econ.,* April 1986, *94*(2), pp. 321–44.

Dardanoni, Valentino. Consumption Decisions with Income Uncertainty and a Kinked Budget Constraint. *Metroecon.,* October 1986, *38*(3), pp. 317–22.

Davidson, Donald. A New Basis for Decision Theory. **In** *Daboni, L.; Montesano, A. and Lines, M., eds.,* 1986, pp. 43–56.

Davis, Steve J. Does Search Theory Provide a Micro Foundation for Keynesian Models and a Rationale for Policy Activism? A Review of Peter Diamond's Wicksell Lectures. *J. Monet. Econ.,* September 1986, *18*(2), pp. 209–16.

DeGroot, Morris H. Concepts of Information Based on Utility. **In** *Daboni, L.; Montesano, A. and Lines, M., eds.,* 1986, pp. 265–75.

Dekel, Eddie. An Axiomatic Characterization of Preferences under Uncertainty: Weakening the Independence Axiom. *J. Econ. Theory,* December 1986, *40*(2), pp. 304–18.

Demski, Joel S. and Sappington, David E. M. On the Timing of Information Release. *Info. Econ. Policy,* December 1986, *2*(4), pp. 307–16.

Detemple, Jérôme B. A General Equilibrium Model of Asset Pricing with Partial or Heterogeneous Information. *Finance,* December 1986, *7*(2), pp. 183–201.

Dixon, Robert J. Uncertainty, Unobstructedness, and Power. *J. Post Keynesian Econ.,* Summer 1986, *8*(4), pp. 585–90.

Donzelli, Franco. Temporary Equilibrium, Intertemporal Equilibrium and the "Complete Markets" Hypothesis. *Ricerche Econ.,* Apr.-Sept. 1986, *40*(2–3), pp. 214–48.

Dowell, Richard S. and McLaren, Keith R. An Intertemporal Analysis of the Interdependence between Risk Preference, Retirement, and Work Rate Decisions. *J. Polit. Econ.,* Part 1, June 1986, *94*(3), pp. 667–82.

Drynan, Ross G. A Note on Optimal Rules for Stochastic Efficiency Analysis. *Australian J. Agr. Econ.,* April 1986, *30*(1), pp. 53–62.

Duffie, Darrell. Stochastic Equilibria: Existence, Spanning Number, and the 'No Expected Financial Gain from Trade' Hypothesis. *Econometrica,* September 1986, *54*(5), pp. 1161–83.

Duffie, Darrell and Huang, Chi-fu. Multiperiod Security Markets with Differential Information: Martingales and Resolution Times. *J. Math. Econ.,* 1986, *15*(3), pp. 283–303.

Duffie, Darrell and Shafer, Wayne J. Equilibrium in Incomplete Markets: II; Generic Existence in Stochastic Economies. *J. Math. Econ.,* 1986, *15*(3), pp. 199–216.

Dyckhoff, Harald. Informationsverdichtung zur Alternativenbewertung. (With English summary.) *Z. Betriebswirtshaft,* September 1986, *56*(9), pp. 848–72.

Einhorn, Hillel J. and Hogarth, Robin M. Decision Making under Ambiguity. **In** *Hogarth, R. M. and Reder, M. W., eds.*, 1986, pp. 41–66.

Einhorn, Hillel J. and Hogarth, Robin M. Decision Making under Ambiguity. *J. Bus.*, Part 2, October 1986, *59*(4), pp. S225–50.

Eisen, Roland. Wettbewerb und Regulierung in der Versicherung Die Rolle asymmetrischer Information. (Competition and Regulation in Insurance: The Role of Asymmetrical Information. With English summary.) *Schweiz. Z. Volkswirtsch. Statist.*, September 1986, *122*(3), pp. 339–58.

Faxén, Karl-Olof. Perceived Models and Measurable Uncertainty. **In** *Day, R. H. and Eliasson, G., eds.*, 1986, pp. 449–53.

Findlay, M. Chapman, III and Williams, Edward E. Better Betas Didn't Help the Boat People. *J. Portfol. Manage.*, Fall 1986, *13*(1), pp. 4–9.

Fishburn, Peter C. Alternatives to Expected Utility Theory for Risky Decisions. **In** *Samuelson, L., ed.*, 1986, pp. 31–52.

Fooladi, Iraj. The Effect of Proportional Profit Tax on the Level of Output, under Uncertainty. *Atlantic Econ. J.*, December 1986, *14*(4), pp. 90–94.

Fourgeaud, Claude; Gouriéroux, Christian and Pradel, Jacqueline. Learning Procedures and Convergence to Rationality. *Econometrica*, July 1986, *54*(4), pp. 845–68.

Fraser, R. W. Uncertainty and Production Quotas. *Econ. Rec.*, September 1986, *62*(178), pp. 338–42.

Garcia, René. La théorie économique de l'information: exposé synthétique de la littérature. (The Economic Theory of Information: A Synthesis of the Literature. With English summary.) *L'Actual. Econ.*, March 1986, *62*(1), pp. 88–109.

Geanakoplos, John D. and Polemarchakis, Herakles M. Existence, Regularity, and Constrained Suboptimality of Competitive Allocations When the Asset Market Is Incomplete. **In** *[Arrow, K. J.], Vol. 3*, 1986, pp. 65–95.

Gorman, W. M. Assembling Efficient Organizations? **In** *[Arrow, K. J.], Vol. 3*, 1986, pp. 213–28.

Gowdy, John M. Rational Expectations and Predictability. *J. Post Keynesian Econ.*, Winter 1985-86, *8*(2), pp. 192–200.

Gravelle, Hugh S. E. Insurance and Corrective Taxes in the Health Care Market. *J. Econ. (Z. Nationalökon.)*, Supplementum 5, 1986, pp. 99–120.

Green, Jerry R. and Laffont, Jean-Jacques. Alternative Limited Communication Systems: Centralization versus Interchange of Information. **In** *[Arrow, K. J.], Vol. 3*, 1986, pp. 255–70.

Green, Jerry R. and Laffont, Jean-Jacques. Incentive Theory with Data Compression. **In** *[Arrow, K. J.], Vol. 3*, 1986, pp. 239–53.

Green, Jerry R. and Laffont, Jean-Jacques. Partially Verifiable Information and Mechanism Design. *Rev. Econ. Stud.*, July 1986, *53*(3), pp. 447–56.

Hacking, Ian. Culpable Ignorance of Interference Effects. **In** *MacLean, D., ed.*, 1986, pp. 136–54.

Hall, Christopher D. Market Enforced Information Asymmetry: A Study of Claiming Races. *Econ. Inquiry*, April 1986, *24*(2), pp. 271–91. **[G: U.S.]**

Haneda, Toru. Multiperiod Insurance Contracts under Asymmetric Information. *Keio Econ. Stud.*, 1986, *23*(2), pp. 61–76.

Harpaz, Giora. Optimal Risk-Sharing Policies. *Amer. Econ.*, Fall 1986, *30*(2), pp. 37–40.

Harpaz, Giora and Mesznik, Roger. Optimal Government Policy with Imperfect Information. *Amer. Econ.*, Spring 1986, *30*(1), pp. 28–31.

Harsanyi, John C. Practical Certainty and the Acceptance of Empirical Statements. **In** *Daboni, L.; Montesano, A. and Lines, M., eds.*, 1986, pp. 27–41.

Hassin, Refael. Consumer Information in Markets with Random Product Quality: The Case of Queues and Balking. *Econometrica*, September 1986, *54*(5), pp. 1185–95.

Hawawini, Gabriel. The Geometry of Risk Aversion: A Pedagogic Note. *J. Econ. Bus.*, May 1986, *38*(2), pp. 93–104.

Heiner, Ronald A. Rational Expectations When Agents Imperfectly Use Information. *J. Post Keynesian Econ.*, Winter 1985-86, *8*(2), pp. 201–07.

Heiner, Ronald A. The Economics of Information When Decisions Are Imperfect. **In** *MacFadyen, A. J. and MacFadyen, H. W., eds.*, 1986, pp. 293–350.

Hellwig, Martin. Risikoallokation in einem Marktsystem. (The Allocation of Risks in the Markets. With English summary.) *Schweiz. Z. Volkswirtsch. Statist.*, September 1986, *122*(3), pp. 231–51.

Holt, Charles A. Preference Reversals and the Independence Axiom. *Amer. Econ. Rev.*, June 1986, *76*(3), pp. 508–15.

Hughes, Patricia J. Signalling by Direct Disclosure under Asymmetric Information. *J. Acc. Econ.*, June 1986, *8*(2), pp. 119–42.

Hutter, Josef. Ein Modell zur kalkulatorischen Bewältigung von Änderungsrisiken im Schadenbereich eines Versicherungsunternehmens. (A Model with Consideration of Permanent Changes of the Global Risk Situation. With English summary.) *Schweiz. Z. Volkswirtsch. Statist.*, September 1986, *122*(3), pp. 261–91.

Ito, Takatoshi. Implicit Contracts and Risk Aversion. **In** *[Arrow, K. J.], Vol. 2*, 1986, pp. 265–87.

Jewitt, Ian. A Note on Comparative Statics and Stochastic Dominance. *J. Math. Econ.*, 1986, *15*(3), pp. 249–54.

Kagel, John H. and Levin, Dan. The Winner's Curse and Public Information in Common Value Auctions. *Amer. Econ. Rev.*, December 1986, *76*(5), pp. 894–920. **[G: U.S.]**

Karni, Edi and Schmeidler, David. Self-preservation as a Foundation of Rational Behavior under Risk. *J. Econ. Behav. Organ.*, March 1986, *7*(1), pp. 71–81.

Katzner, Donald W. Potential Surprise, Potential Confirmation, and Probability. *J. Post Keynesian Econ.*, Fall 1986, *9*(1), pp. 58–78.

Kirman, Alan P.; Oddou, Claude and Weber, Shlomo. Stochastic Communication and Coalition Formation. *Econometrica*, January 1986, *54*(1), pp. 129–38.

Konakayama, Akira; Mitsui, Toshihide and Watanabe, Shinichi. Efficient Contracting with Reliance and a Damaged Measure. *Rand J. Econ.*, Autumn 1986, *17*(3), pp. 450–57.

Kurz, Mordecai. On Asymmetric Information, Unemployment, and Inflexible Wages. **In** *[Arrow, K. J.], Vol. 2*, 1986, pp. 219–49.

Labadie, Pamela. Comparative Dynamics and Risk Premia in an Overlapping Generations Model. *Rev. Econ. Stud.*, January 1986, *53*(1), pp. 139–52.

Laffont, Jean-Jacques and Tirole, Jean. Une théorie normative des contrats État-entreprises. (A Normative Theory of State-Firms Contracts. With English summary.) *Ann. Écon. Statist.*, Jan./Mar. 1986, (1), pp. 107–32.

Langlois, Richard N. Rationality, Institutions, and Explanation. **In** *Langlois, R. N., ed.*, 1986, pp. 225–55.

Lavoie, Donald C. The Market as a Procedure for Discovery and Conveyance of Inarticulate Knowledge. *Comp. Econ. Stud.*, Spring 1986, *28*(1), pp. 1–19.

Leonardi, Giorgio; Arcangeli, E. F. and Reggiani, A. Aggregate Revealed Preferences and Random Utility Theory. **In** *Daboni, L.; Montesano, A. and Lines, M., eds.*, 1986, pp. 231–48.

Levi, Isaac. The Paradoxes of Allais and Ellsberg. *Econ. Philos.*, April 1986, *2*(1), pp. 23–53.

Lippman, Steven A. and McCall, John J. An Operational Measure of Liquidity. *Amer. Econ. Rev.*, March 1986, *76*(1), pp. 43–55.

Loasby, Brian J. Organisation, Competition, and the Growth of Knowledge. **In** *Langlois, R. N., ed.*, 1986, pp. 41–57.

Loomes, Graham and Sugden, Robert. Disappointment and Dynamic Consistency in Choice under Uncertainty. *Rev. Econ. Stud.*, April 1986, *53*(2), pp. 271–82.

Lopes, Lola. What Naive Decision Makers Can Tell Us about Risk. **In** *Daboni, L.; Montesano, A. and Lines, M., eds.*, 1986, pp. 311–26.

Luton, Richard A. and McAfee, R. Preston. Sequential Procurement Auctions. *J. Public Econ.*, November 1986, *31*(2), pp. 181–95.

MacCrimmon, Kenneth R. and Wehrung, Donald A. Assessing Risk Propensity. **In** *Daboni, L.; Montesano, A. and Lines, M., eds.*, 1986, pp. 291–309.

MacLean, Douglas. Risk and Consent: Philosophical Issues for Centralized Decisions. **In** *MacLean, D., ed.*, 1986, pp. 17–30.

MacLean, Douglas. Values at Risk: Introduction. **In** *MacLean, D., ed.*, 1986, pp. 1–15.

MacMinn, Richard D. Search and the Market for Lemons. *Info. Econ. Policy*, June 1986, *2*(2), pp. 137–46.

Magill, Michael J. P. and Nermuth, Manfred. On the Qualitative Properties of Futures Market Equilibrium. *J. Econ. (Z. Nationalökon.)*, 1986, *46*(3), pp. 233–52.

Malcomson, James M. Rank–Order Contracts for a Principal with Many Agents. *Rev. Econ. Stud.*, October 1986, *53*(5), pp. 807–17.

Manning, Alan. The Profitability of Private Information in Unionised Capitalist Enterprises. *Econ. J.*, Supplement 1986, *96*, pp. 122–33.

Marschak, Thomas A. Independence versus Dominance in Personal Probability Axioms. **In** *[Arrow, K. J.], Vol. 3*, 1986, pp. 129–71.

Maskin, Eric. Optimal Bayesian Mechanisms. **In** *[Arrow, K. J.], Vol. 3*, 1986, pp. 229–38.

McGuire, C. B. Comparisons of Information Structures. **In** *[Marschak, J.]*, 1986, *1972*, pp. 101–30.

McKelvey, Richard D. and Ordeshook, P. C. Sequential Elections with Limited Information: A Formal Analysis. *Soc. Choice Welfare*, 1986, *3*(3), pp. 199–211.

McKelvey, Richard D. and Page, Talbot. Common Knowledge, Consensus, and Aggregate Information. *Econometrica*, January 1986, *54*(1), pp. 109–27.

McKenna, Christopher J. Theories of Individual Search Behaviour. *Bull. Econ. Res.*, September 1986, *38*(3), pp. 189–207.

Milgrom, Paul and Roberts, John. Price and Advertising Signals of Product Quality. *J. Polit. Econ.*, August 1986, *94*(4), pp. 796–821.

Milgrom, Paul and Roberts, John. Relying on the Information of Interested Parties. *Rand J. Econ.*, Spring 1986, *17*(1), pp. 18–32.

Montesano, Aldo. A Measure of Risk Aversion in Terms of Preferences. **In** *Daboni, L.; Montesano, A. and Lines, M., eds.*, 1986, pp. 327–35.

Morgan, Peter B. A Note on "Job Search: The Choice of Intensity." *J. Polit. Econ.*, April 1986, *94*(2), pp. 439–42.

Mueller, Dennis C. Information, Mobility and Profit. **In** *Mueller, D. C.*, 1986, *1976*, pp. 15–36.

Munera, Hector A. The Generalized Means Model (GMM) for Non-deterministic Decision Making: A Unified Treatment for the Two Contending Theories. **In** *Daboni, L.; Montesano, A. and Lines, M., eds.*, 1986, pp. 161–84.

Nishimura, Kiyohiko G. Rational Expectations and Price Rigidity in a Monopolistically Competitive Market. *Rev. Econ. Stud.*, April 1986, *53*(2), pp. 283–92.

Nordquist, Gerald L. State-Dependent Utility and Risk Aversion. **In** *Daboni, L.; Montesano, A. and Lines, M., eds.*, 1986, pp. 337–51.

O'Driscoll, Gerald P., Jr. and Rizzo, Mario J. Subjectivism, Uncertainty, and Rules. **In** *[Lachmann, L. M.]*, 1986, pp. 252–67.

O'Flaherty, Brendan. Potential Pareto Optimality of Risky Projects. *Quart. J. Econ.*, August 1986, *101*(3), pp. 647–51.

Oniki, Hajime. The Cost of Communication in Economic Organization: II. **In** *[Arrow, K. J.], Vol. 3,* 1986, pp. 191–212.

Palfrey, Thomas R. and Srivastava, Sanjay. Private Information in Large Economies. *J. Econ. Theory,* June 1986, *39*(1), pp. 34–58.

Park, Keehwan. A Note on Optimal Hedging under Price and Output Uncertainty. *Atlantic Econ. J.,* December 1986, *14*(4), pp. 99.

Paroush, Jacob. Inflation, Search Costs and Price Dispersion. *J. Macroecon.,* Summer 1986, *8*(3), pp. 329–36.

Pearlman, Joseph; Currie, David and Levine, Paul. Rational Expectations Models with Partial Information. *Econ. Modelling,* April 1986, *3*(2), pp. 90–105.

Peck, Richard M. and Srinagesh, Padmanabhan. Time Preference and Uncertain Lifetime. *Amer. Econ.,* Fall 1986, *30*(2), pp. 41–45.

Perloff, Jeffrey M. and Salop, Steven C. Firm-Specific Information, Product Differentiation, and Industry Equilibrium. *Oxford Econ. Pap.,* Suppl. Nov. 1986, *38,* pp. 184–202.

Perloff, Jeffrey M. and Salop, Steven C. Firm-Specific Information, Product Differentiation, and Industry Equilibrium. **In** *Morris, D. J., et al., eds.,* 1986, pp. 184–202.

Perrakis, Stylianos and Warskett, George. Uncertainty, Economies of Scale, and Barrier to Entry. *Oxford Econ. Pap.,* Suppl. Nov. 1986, *38,* pp. 58–74.

Perry, Motty and Wigderson, Avi. Search in a Known Pattern. *J. Polit. Econ.,* February 1986, *94*(1), pp. 225–30.

Piccinato, Ludovico. De Finetti's Logic of Uncertainty and Its Impact on Statistical Thinking and Practice. **In** *[de Finetti, B.],* 1986, pp. 13–30.

Plummer, Mark L. and Hartman, Richard C. Option Value: A General Approach. *Econ. Inquiry,* July 1986, *24*(3), pp. 455–71.

Polemarchakis, Herakles M., et al. Approximate Aggregation under Uncertainty. *J. Econ. Theory,* April 1986, *38*(2), pp. 189–210.

Pope, Robin. Consistency and Expected Utility Theory. **In** *Daboni, L.; Montesano, A. and Lines, M., eds.,* 1986, pp. 215–29.

Quandt, Richard E. Betting and Equilibrium. *Quart. J. Econ.,* February 1986, *101*(1), pp. 201–07.

Radner, Roy. Allocation of a Scarce Resource under Uncertainty: An Example of a Team. **In** *[Marschak, J.],* 1986, *1972,* pp. 217–36.

Raskin, Rob and Cochran, Mark J. Interpretations and Transformations of Scale for the Pratt–Arrow Absolute Risk Aversion Coefficient: Implications for Generalized Stochastic Dominance. *Western J. Agr. Econ.,* December 1986, *11*(2), pp. 204–10.

Reilly, Robert J. The Markowitz Utility Function and Some Experimental Evidence for Small Speculative Risks. *J. Risk Ins.,* December 1986, *53*(4), pp. 724–33.

Riordan, Michael H. A Note on Optimal Procurement Contracts. *Info. Econ. Policy,* September 1986, *2*(3), pp. 211–19.

Roberts, John. A Signaling Model of Predatory Pricing. *Oxford Econ. Pap.,* Suppl. Nov. 1986, *38,* pp. 75–93.

Rudel, Sylvie. Une gestion particulière des risques dans la toute petite entreprise. (Special Risks Management in Small Firms. With English summary.) *Schweiz. Z. Volkswirtsch. Statist.,* September 1986, *122*(3), pp. 389–403.

Saari, Donald G. and Williams, Steven R. On the Local Convergence of Economic Mechanisms. *J. Econ. Theory,* October 1986, *40*(1), pp. 152–67.

Sakai, Yasuhiro. Cournot and Bertrand Equilibria under Imperfect Information. *J. Econ. (Z. Nationalökon.),* 1986, *46*(3), pp. 213–32.

Sakakibara, Kenichi. A Fisher–Brown Proposition for Speculative Bubbles. *J. Macroecon.,* Fall 1986, *8*(4), pp. 485–90.

Samuelson, Paul A. St. Petersburg Paradoxes: Defanged, Dissected, and Historically Described. **In** *Samuelson, P. A.,* 1986, *1977,* pp. 133–64.

Samuelson, Paul A. Stochastic Land Valuation: Total Return as Martingale Implying Price Changes—A Negatively Correlated Walk. **In** *Samuelson, P. A.,* 1986, pp. 527–36.

Samuelson, Paul A. Why We Should Not Make Mean Log of Wealth Big Though Years to Act Are Long. **In** *Samuelson, P. A.,* 1986, *1979,* pp. 554–56.

Schotter, Andrew. On the Economic Virtues of Incompetency and Dishonesty. **In** *[Rapoport, A.],* 1986, pp. 235–41.

Schultz, Reinhart. Ordinale Wahrscheinlichkeitsurteile, Wahrscheinlichkeitsdominanz und die Anzahl verschiedener Umweltszenarien. (With English summary.) *Z. Betriebswirtschaft,* October 1986, *56*(10), pp. 989–1001.

Schwab, Stewart. Is Statistical Discrimination Efficient? *Amer. Econ. Rev.,* March 1986, *76*(1), pp. 228–34.

Sen, Amartya K. Information and Invariance in Normative Choice. **In** *[Arrow, K. J.], Vol. 1,* 1986, pp. 29–55.

Sen, Amartya K. Rationality and Uncertainty. **In** *Daboni, L.; Montesano, A. and Lines, M., eds.,* 1986, pp. 3–25.

Shackle, George L. S. Decision. *J. Econ. Stud.,* 1986, *13*(5), pp. 58–62.

Shapiro, Carl. Exchange of Cost Information in Oligopoly. *Rev. Econ. Stud.,* July 1986, *53*(3), pp. 433–46.

Singh, Harinder. When Are Expectations Rational? Some Vexing Questions and Behavioral Clues. *J. Behav. Econ.,* Spring/Summer 1986, *15*(1/2), pp. 191–209.

Singh, Nirvikar. Equilibrium Price Dispersion with Sequential Search. *J. Quant. Econ.,* July 1986, *2*(2), pp. 163–71.

Starrett, David A. On the Social Risk Premium. **In** *[Arrow, K. J.], Vol. 1,* 1986, pp. 159–76.

Stein, Jerome L. Real Effects of Futures Speculation: Asymptotically Rational Expectations. *Economica,* May 1986, *53*(210), pp. 159–80.

Stephen, Frank H. Decision Making under Uncertainty: In Defence of Shackle. *J. Econ.*

Stud., 1986, *13*(5), pp. 45–57.

Stigler, George J. The Economics of Information. **In** *Stigler, G. J.*, 1986, *1961*, pp. 46–66.

Stiglitz, Joseph E. The New Development Economics. *World Devel.*, Special Issue, Feb. 1986, *14*(2), pp. 257–65.

Stokey, Nancy L. The Dynamics of Industrywide Learning. **In** *[Arrow, K. J.], Vol. 2*, 1986, pp. 81–104.

Strassl, Wolfgang. Keynes on Expectations and Uncertainty: Rational Expectations Equilibria with Asymmetric Information. *Bull. Econ. Res.*, May 1986, *38*(2), pp. 137–59.

Sugden, Robert. New Developments in the Theory of Choice under Uncertainty. *Bull. Econ. Res.*, January 1986, *38*(1), pp. 1–24.

Sugden, Robert. Regret, Recrimination and Rationality. **In** *Daboni, L.; Montesano, A. and Lines, M., eds.*, 1986, pp. 67–80.

Szpiro, George G. Measuring Risk Aversion: An Alternative Approach. *Rev. Econ. Statist.*, February 1986, *68*(1), pp. 156–59. **[G: U.S.]**

Talpaz, Hovav; Penson, John B., Jr. and Harpaz, Avraham. Activity Selection under Conditions of Risk and Instability: Consideration of Frequency. *J. Agr. Econ.*, January 1986, *37*(1), pp. 59–67.

Taylor, C. Robert. Risk Aversion versus Expected Profit Maximization with a Progressive Income Tax. *Amer. J. Agr. Econ.*, February 1986, *68*(1), pp. 137–43. **[G: U.S.]**

Thaler, Richard H. The Psychology and Economics Conference Handbook: Comments. *J. Bus.*, Part 2, October 1986, *59*(4), pp. S279–84.

Thaler, Richard H. The Psychology and Economics Conference Handbook: Comments. **In** *Hogarth, R. M. and Reder, M. W., eds.*, 1986, pp. 95–100.

Toulet, Claude. Complete Ignorance and Independence Axiom: Optimism, Pessimism, Indecisiveness. *Math. Soc. Sci.*, February 1986, *11*(1), pp. 33–51.

Tversky, Amos and Kahneman, Daniel. Rational Choice and the Framing of Decisions. *J. Bus.*, Part 2, October 1986, *59*(4), pp. S251–78.

Tversky, Amos and Kahneman, Daniel. Rational Choice and the Framing of Decisions. **In** *Hogarth, R. M. and Reder, M. W., eds.*, 1986, pp. 67–94.

Tzur, Joseph. An Agency Model of Search for Alternatives. *J. Econ. Behav. Organ.*, September 1986, *7*(3), pp. 317–27.

Urbany, Joel E. An Experimental Examination of the Economics of Information. *J. Cons. Res.*, September 1986, *13*(2), pp. 257–71.

Vickers, Douglas. Time, Ignorance, Surprise, and Economic Decisions: A Comment on Williams and Findlay's "Risk and the Role of Failed Expectations in an Uncertain World." *J. Post Keynesian Econ.*, Fall 1986, *9*(1), pp. 48–57.

Vickers, John S. Signalling in a Model of Monetary Policy with Incomplete Information. *Oxford Econ. Pap.*, November 1986, *38*(3), pp. 443–55.

Wakker, Peter. Concave Additively Decomposable Representing Functions and Risk Aversion. **In** *Daboni, L.; Montesano, A. and Lines, M., eds.*, 1986, pp. 249–62.

Williams, Edward E. and Findlay, M. Chapman, III. Risk and the Role of Failed Expectations in an Uncertain World. *J. Post Keynesian Econ.*, Fall 1986, *9*(1), pp. 32–47.

Williams, Steven R. Realization and Nash Implementation: Two Aspects of Mechanism Design. *Econometrica*, January 1986, *54*(1), pp. 139–51.

Williamson, Stephen D. Costly Monitoring, Financial Intermediation, and Equilibrium Credit Rationing. *J. Monet. Econ.*, September 1986, *18*(2), pp. 159–79.

Windsperger, Josef. Wettbewerb als dynamischer Prozess. (Competition as a Dynamic Process. With English summary.) **In** *Eucken, W. and Böhm, F., eds.*, 1986, pp. 125–40.

Witt, Ulrich. Firms' Market Behavior under Imperfect Information and Economic Natural Selection. *J. Econ. Behav. Organ.*, September 1986, *7*(3), pp. 265–90.

Wolinsky, Asher. True Monopolistic Competition as a Result of Imperfect Information. *Quart. J. Econ.*, August 1986, *101*(3), pp. 493–511.

Yaari, Menahem E. Univariate and Multivariate Comparisons of Risk Aversion: A New Approach. **In** *[Arrow, K. J.], Vol. 3*, 1986, pp. 173–87.

Yoon, Chang-Ho. Rational Expectations Equilibrium in a Sequence of Asset Markets. *Int. Econ. Rev.*, October 1986, *27*(3), pp. 553–64.

Yu, Eden S. H. and Ingene, Charles A. Resource Allocation in a General Equilibrium Model of Production under Uncertainty: The Case of Variable Supply of Labor. *J. Econ. Theory*, December 1986, *40*(2), pp. 329–37.

Zabel, Edward. Price Smoothing and Equilibrium in a Monopolistic Market. *Int. Econ. Rev.*, June 1986, *27*(2), pp. 349–63.

Zinn, Karl Georg. Does Uncertainy Imply a Bias in Favour of Unemployment and Stagnation? A Question to Bartmann, John and Others. *Jahr. Nationalökon. Statist.*, September 1986, *201*(5), pp. 531–34.

0262 Game Theory and Bargaining Theory

Abreu, Dilip. Extremal Equilibria of Oligopolistic Supergames. *J. Econ. Theory*, June 1986, *39*(1), pp. 191–225.

Abreu, Dilip; Pearce, David and Stacchetti, Ennio. Optimal Cartel Equilibria with Imperfect Monitoring. *J. Econ. Theory*, June 1986, *39*(1), pp. 251–69.

Allen, Beth and Hellwig, Martin. Bertrand–Edgeworth Oligopoly in Large Markets. *Rev. Econ. Stud.*, April 1986, *53*(2), pp. 175–204.

Arvan, Lanny. Sunk Capacity Costs, Long-run Fixed Costs, and Entry Deterrence under Complete and Incomplete Information. *Rand J. Econ.*, Spring 1986, *17*(1), pp. 105–21.

Aumann, Robert J. Rejoinder [Values for Games without Sidepayments: Some Difficulties with Current Concepts]. *Econometrica*, July 1986, *54*(4), pp. 985–89.

Aumann, Robert J. and Drèze, Jacques H. Values of Markets with Satiation or Fixed Prices. *Econometrica,* November 1986, *54*(6), pp. 1271–1318.

Axelrod, Robert. An Evolutionary Approach to Norms. *Amer. Polit. Sci. Rev.,* December 1986, *80*(4), pp. 1095–1111.

Bagchi, Arunabha. Some Economic Applications of Dynamic Stackelberg Games. **In** *Başar, T., ed.,* 1986, pp. 88–102.

Barberá, Salvador and Dutta, Bhaskar. General, Direct and Self-implementation of Social Choice Functions via Protective Equilibria. *Math. Soc. Sci.,* April 1986, *11*(2), pp. 109–27.

Başar, Tamer. A Tutorial on Dynamic and Differential Games. **In** *Başar, T., ed.,* 1986, pp. 1–25.

Bernheim, B. Douglas. Axiomatic Characterizations of Rational Choice in Strategic Environments. *Scand. J. Econ.,* 1986, *88*(3), pp. 473–88.

Bernheim, B. Douglas and Whinston, Michael D. Menu Auctions, Resource Allocation, and Economic Influence. *Quart. J. Econ.,* February 1986, *101*(1), pp. 1–31.

Binmore, Ken; Rubinstein, Ariel and Wolinsky, Asher. The Nash Bargaining Solution in Economic Modelling. *Rand J. Econ.,* Summer 1986, *17*(2), pp. 176–88.

Böge, Werner. Remarks on a Dynamic Game with Macroeconomic Investment. **In** *Faber, M., ed.,* 1986, pp. 259–66.

Böge, Werner; Faber, Malte and Güth, Werner. A Dynamic Game with Macroeconomic Investment Decisions under Alternative Market Structures. **In** *Faber, M., ed.,* 1986, *1982,* pp. 229–58.

Bolger, E. M. Power Indices for Multicandidate Voting Games. *Int. J. Game Theory,* 1986, *15*(3), pp. 175–86.

Bonanno, Giacomo. Vertical Differentiation with Cournot Competition. *Econ. Notes,* 1986, (2), pp. 68–91.

Boyd, John H. and Prescott, Edward C. Financial Intermediary-Coalitions. *J. Econ. Theory,* April 1986, *38*(2), pp. 211–32.

Breton, Michèle; Haurie, Alain and Filar, Jerzy A. On the Computation of Equilibria in Discounted Stochastic Dynamic Games. *J. Econ. Dynam. Control,* June 1986, *10*(1/2), pp. 33–36.

Breton, Michèle, et al. On the Computation of Equilibria in Discounted Stochastic Dynamic Games. **In** *Başar, T., ed.,* 1986, pp. 64–87.

Champlin, Frederic C. and Bognanno, Mario F. A Model of Arbitration and the Incentive to Bargain. **In** *Lipsky, D. B. and Lewin, D., eds.,* 1986, pp. 153–90.

Chatterjee, Kalyan. The Theory of Bargaining. **In** *Samuelson, L., ed.,* 1986, pp. 159–94.

Cohen, Susan I. Truth-Telling, Dominant Strategies, and Iterative Groves Mechanisms. *Public Choice,* 1986, *51*(3), pp. 333–43.

Coleman, James S. Social Structure and the Emergence of Norms among Rational Actors. **In** *[Rapoport, A.],* 1986, pp. 55–83.

Coleman, James S. Why So Much Stability? Recontracting, Trustworthiness and the Stability of Vote Exchanges. **In** *Coleman, J. S.,* 1986, *1983,* pp. 137–43.

Cossutta, Dario and Grillo, Michele. Excess Capacity, Sunk Costs and Collusion: A Non-cooperative Bargaining Game: Some Considerations on the European Car Industry. *Int. J. Ind. Organ.,* September 1986, *4*(3), pp. 251–70. **[G: W. Europe]**

Crawford, Vincent P. and Rochford, Sharon C. Bargaining and Competition in Matching Markets. *Int. Econ. Rev.,* June 1986, *27*(2), pp. 329–48.

Crémer, Jacques. Cooperation in Ongoing Organizations. *Quart. J. Econ.,* February 1986, *101*(1), pp. 33–49.

Cubitt, R. P. Two Perspectives on the Time Inconsistency Problem. *Greek Econ. Rev.,* June 1986, *8*(1), pp. 1–20.

van Damme, Eric E. C. The Nash Bargaining Solution Is Optimal. *J. Econ. Theory,* February 1986, *38*(1), pp. 78–100.

Dana, Rose-Anne and Montrucchio, Luigi. Dynamic Complexity in Duopoly Games. *J. Econ. Theory,* October 1986, *40*(1), pp. 40–56.

Dasgupta, Partha and Maskin, Eric. The Existence of Equilibrium in Discontinuous Economic Games, II: Applications. *Rev. Econ. Stud.,* January 1986, *53*(1), pp. 27–41.

Dasgupta, Partha and Maskin, Eric. The Existence of Equilibrium in Discontinuous Economic Games, I: Theory. *Rev. Econ. Stud.,* January 1986, *53*(1), pp. 1–26.

Demange, Gabrielle and Ponssard, Jean-Pierre. Barrière de mobilité et concurrence dans un duopole. Essai de formalisation dans le cadre de la théorie des jeux. (Barriers to Mobility and Competition in a Duopoly: An Attempt to Formalize within the Context of Game Theory. With English summary.) *Ann. Écon. Statist.,* Jan./Mar. 1986, (1), pp. 35–53.

Diekmann, Andreas. Volunteer's Dilemma. A Social Trap without a Dominant Strategy and Some Empirical Results. **In** *[Rapoport, A.],* 1986, pp. 187–97.

Dixon, Huw. The Cournot and Bertrand Outcomes as Equilibria in a Strategic Metagame. *Econ. J.,* Supplement 1986, *96,* pp. 59–70.

Dockner, Engelbert and Feichtinger, Gustav. Dynamic Advertising and Pricing in an Oligopoly: A Nash Equilibrium Approach. *J. Econ. Dynam. Control,* June 1986, *10*(1/2), pp. 37–39.

Donninger, Christian. Is It Always Efficient to Be Nice? A Computer Simulation of Axelrod's Computer Tournament. **In** *[Rapoport, A.],* 1986, pp. 123–34.

Dubey, Pradeep and Shubik, Martin. General Equilibrium and the Foundations of the Theory of Monopolistic Competition. *Rivista Int. Sci. Econ. Com.,* March 1986, *33*(3), pp. 207–19.

Eaton, Jonathan and Grossman, Gene M. The Provision of Information as Marketing Strategy. *Oxford Econ. Pap.*, Suppl. Nov. 1986, *38*, pp. 166–83.

Ehtamo, Harri and Hämäläinen, Raimo P. On Affine Incentives for Dynamic Decision Problems. **In** *Başar, T., ed.*, 1986, pp. 47–63.

Ehtamo, Harri and Hämäläinen, Raimo P. On Incentive Design for Dynamic Decision Problems. *J. Econ. Dynam. Control*, June 1986, *10*(1/2), pp. 41–43.

Encaoua, David; Geroski, Paul A. and Jacquemin, Alexis. Strategic Competition and the Persistence of Dominant Firms: A Survey. **In** *Stiglitz, J. E. and Mathewson, G. F., eds.*, 1986, pp. 55–86.

Enos, J. L. Public Policy in an Economy with Different Types of Agents. **In** *Hall, P., ed.*, 1986, *1984*, pp. 172–200.

Faber, Malte, et al. On the Methodology of Strategic Interaction in Time. **In** *Faber, M., ed.*, 1986, pp. 210–28.

Fershtman, Chaim and Muller, Eitan. Capital Investments and Price Agreements in Semicollusive Markets. *Rand J. Econ.*, Summer 1986, *17*(2), pp. 214–26.

Fershtman, Chaim and Muller, Eitan. Turnpike Properties of Capital Accumulation Games [Capital Accumulation Games of Infinite Duration]. *J. Econ. Theory*, February 1986, *38*(1), pp. 167–77.

Fishburn, Peter C. and Rosenthal, Robert W. Noncooperative Games and Nontransitive Preferences. *Math. Soc. Sci.*, August 1986, *12*(1), pp. 1–7.

Forges, Françoise M. An Approach to Communication Equilibria. *Econometrica*, November 1986, *54*(6), pp. 1375–85.

Friedman, James W. and Rosenthal, Robert W. A Positive Approach to Non-cooperative Games. *J. Econ. Behav. Organ.*, September 1986, *7*(3), pp. 235–51.

Fudenberg, Drew and Levine, David K. Limit Games and Limit Equilibria. *J. Econ. Theory*, April 1986, *38*(2), pp. 261–79.

Fudenberg, Drew and Maskin, Eric. The Folk Theorem in Repeated Games with Discounting or with Incomplete Information. *Econometrica*, May 1986, *54*(3), pp. 533–54.

Gaertner, Wulf. Pareto, Interdependent Rights Exercising and Strategic Behaviour. *J. Econ. (Z. Nationalökon.)*, Supplementum 5, 1986, pp. 79–98.

Gale, Douglas M. Bargaining and Competition Part II: Existence. *Econometrica*, July 1986, *54*(4), pp. 807–18.

Gale, Douglas M. Bargaining and Competition Part I: Characterization. *Econometrica*, July 1986, *54*(4), pp. 785–806.

Gilbert, Richard J. and Vives, Xavier. Entry Deterrence and the Free Rider Problem. *Rev. Econ. Stud.*, January 1986, *53*(1), pp. 71–83.

Grossman, Sanford J. and Perry, Motty. Perfect Sequential Equilibrium. *J. Econ. Theory*, June 1986, *39*(1), pp. 97–119.

Gul, Faruk; Sonnenschein, Hugo and Wilson, Robert B. Foundations of Dynamic Monopoly and the Coase Conjecture. *J. Econ. Theory*, June 1986, *39*(1), pp. 155–90.

Güth, Werner. Auctions, Public Tenders, and Fair Division Games: An Axiomatic Approach. *Math. Soc. Sci.*, June 1986, *11*(3), pp. 283–94.

Güth, Werner and van Damme, Eric E. C. A Comparison of Pricing Rules for Auctions and Fair Division Games. *Soc. Choice Welfare*, 1986, *3*(3), pp. 177–98.

Hagen, Ole. Some Paradoxes in Economics. **In** *[Rapoport, A.]*, 1986, pp. 13–25.

Hardin, Russell. Pragmatic Intuitions and Rational Choice. **In** *[Rapoport, A.]*, 1986, pp. 27–36.

Harsanyi, John C. Utilitarian Morality in a World of Very Half-hearted Altruists. **In** *[Arrow, K. J.], Vol. 1*, 1986, pp. 57–73.

Hoel, Michael. Perfect Equilibria in Sequential Bargaining Games with Nonlinear Utility Functions. *Scand. J. Econ.*, 1986, *88*(2), pp. 383–400.

Holler, Manfred J. Moral Sentiments and Self-interest Reconsidered. **In** *[Rapoport, A.]*, 1986, pp. 223–33.

Holly, Sean. Games, Expectations, and Optimal Policy for Open Economies. *J. Econ. Dynam. Control*, June 1986, *10*(1/2), pp. 45–49.

Holzman, Ron. On Strong Representations of Games by Social Choice Functions. *J. Math. Econ.*, 1986, *15*(1), pp. 39–57.

Holzman, Ron. The Capacity of a Committee. *Math. Soc. Sci.*, October 1986, *12*(2), pp. 139–57.

Hubbard, R. Glenn and Weiner, Robert J. Oil Supply Shocks and International Policy Coordination. *Europ. Econ. Rev.*, February 1986, *30*(1), pp. 91–106.

Hughes Hallett, A. J. Policy Design in Asymmetrically Dependent Economies. *J. Econ. Dynam. Control*, June 1986, *10*(1/2), pp. 51–57. **[G: U.S.; EEC]**

Ichiishi, Tatsuro. Stable Extensive Game Forms with Perfect Information. *Int. J. Game Theory*, 1986, *15*(3), pp. 163–74.

Imai, Haruo. Bilateral Price-Setting in a Bilateral Monopoly Model. *Math. Soc. Sci.*, December 1986, *12*(3), pp. 279–301.

Jordan, James S. Instability in the Implementation of Walrasian Allocations. *J. Econ. Theory*, August 1986, *39*(2), pp. 301–28.

Justman, Moshe. Intertemporal Dependence of Demand in an Imperfectly Competitive Market: A Differential Game Analysis. *Int. J. Ind. Organ.*, September 1986, *4*(3), pp. 271–86.

Kalai, Ehud. Strategic Behavior and Competition: An Overview. *J. Econ. Theory*, June 1986, *39*(1), pp. 1–13.

Kamien, Morton I. and Tauman, Yair. Fees versus Royalties and the Private Value of a Patent. *Quart. J. Econ.*, August 1986, *101*(3), pp. 471–91.

Kaneko, Mamoru and Wooders, Myrna Holtz. The Core of a Game with a Continuum of Players and Finite Coalitions: The Model and Some Results. *Math. Soc. Sci.*, October 1986, *12*(2), pp. 105–37.

Kennan, John. The Economics of Strikes. In *Ashenfelter, O. and Layard, R., eds., Vol. 2,* 1986, pp. 1091–1137. [G: U.S.]

Kirman, Alan P.; Oddou, Claude and Weber, Shlomo. Stochastic Communication and Coalition Formation. *Econometrica,* January 1986, *54*(1), pp. 129–38.

Kleinberg, Norman L. and Weiss, Jeffrey H. Weak Values, the Core, and New Axioms for the Shapley Value. *Math. Soc. Sci.,* August 1986, *12*(1), pp. 21–30.

Kohlberg, Elon and Mertens, Jean-Francois. On the Strategic Stability of Equilibria. *Econometrica,* September 1986, *54*(5), pp. 1003–37.

Köhler, Eckehart. Guidelines for Solving Sen's Paradox. In *[Rapoport, A.],* 1986, pp. 37–46.

Lane, John and Leininger, Wolfgang. On Price Characterization and Pareto-Efficiency of Game Equilibrium Growth. *J. Econ. (Z. Nationalökon.),* 1986, *46*(4), pp. 347–67.

Lawler, Edward J. Bilateral Deterrence and Conflict Spiral: A Theoretical Analysis. In *Lawler, E. J., ed.,* 1986, pp. 107–30.

Ledyard, John O. The Scope of the Hypothesis of Bayesian Equilibrium. *J. Econ. Theory,* June 1986, *39*(1), pp. 59–82.

Leinfellner, Werner. The Prisoner's Dilemma and Its Evolutionary Iteration. In *[Rapoport, A.],* 1986, pp. 135–48.

Leininger, Wolfgang. The Existence of Perfect Equilibria in a Model of Growth with Altruism between Generations. *Rev. Econ. Stud.,* July 1986, *53*(3), pp. 349–67.

Lewis, Tracy R. Reputation and Contractual Performance in Long-term Projects. *Rand J. Econ.,* Summer 1986, *17*(2), pp. 141–57.

Lipman, Barton L. Cooperation among Egoists in Prisoners' Dilemma and Chicken Games. *Public Choice,* 1986, *51*(3), pp. 315–31.

Malueg, David A. Efficient Outcomes in a Repeated Agency Model without Discounting. *J. Math. Econ.,* 1986, *15*(3), pp. 217–30.

McCain, Roger A. Game Theory and Cultivation of Taste. *J. Cult. Econ.,* June 1986, *10*(1), pp. 1–16.

McClendon, J. F. Existence of Solutions of Games with Some Non-convexity. *Int. J. Game Theory,* 1986, *15*(3), pp. 155–62.

McKelvey, Richard D. and Schofield, Norman. Structural Instability of the Core. *J. Math. Econ.,* 1986, *15*(3), pp. 179–98.

Meijdam, A. C. and de Zeeuw, Aart J. On Expectations, Information and Dynamic Game Equilibria. *J. Econ. Dynam. Control,* June 1986, *10*(1/2), pp. 63–66.

Meijdam, A. C. and de Zeeuw, Aart J. On Expectations, Information and Dynamic Game Equilibria. In *Başar, T., ed.,* 1986, pp. 26–46.

Mercik, Jacek W. and Kołodziejczyk, Waldemar. Taxonomy Approach to a Cabinet Formation Problem. *Math. Soc. Sci.,* October 1986, *12*(2), pp. 159–67.

Michener, H. Andrew; Choi, Young C. and Dettman, David C. Stability by Deterrence in Cooperative Non-sidepayment *n*-Person Games. *J. Econ. Behav. Organ.,* December 1986, *7*(4), pp. 375–402.

Mirowski, Philip. Insitutions as a Solution Concept in a Game Theory Context. In *Samuelson, L., ed.,* 1986, pp. 243–64.

Mirowski, Philip. Institutions as a Solution Concept in a Game Theory Context. In *Mirowski, P., ed.,* 1986, pp. 241–63.

Mitter, Peter. Take-Some Games: The Commons Dilemma and a Land of Cockaigne. In *[Rapoport, A.],* 1986, pp. 199–208.

Morkeliunas, Algis. Generalized Nash's Choice. *Math. Soc. Sci.,* April 1986, *11*(2), pp. 101–07.

Morrow, James D. A Spatial Model of International Conflict. *Amer. Polit. Sci. Rev.,* December 1986, *80*(4), pp. 1131–50.

Myerson, Roger B. Acceptable and Predominant Correlated Equilibria. *Int. J. Game Theory,* 1986, *15*(3), pp. 133–54.

Myerson, Roger B. Multistage Games with Communication. *Econometrica,* March 1986, *54*(2), pp. 323–58.

Myerson, Roger B. Negotiation in Games: A Theoretical Overview. In *[Arrow, K. J.], Vol. 3,* 1986, pp. 3–24.

Ordover, Janusz A. and Rubinstein, Ariel. A Sequential Concession Game with Asymmetric Information. *Quart. J. Econ.,* November 1986, *101*(4), pp. 879–88.

Osborne, Martin J. and Pitchik, Carolyn. Price Competition in a Capacity-Constrained Duopoly. *J. Econ. Theory,* April 1986, *38*(2), pp. 238–60.

Peleg, Bezalel. A Proof That the Core of an Ordinal Convex Game Is a von Neumann–Morgenstern Solution. *Math. Soc. Sci.,* February 1986, *11*(1), pp. 83–87.

Peleg, Bezalel. On the Reduced Game Property and Its Converse. *Int. J. Game Theory,* 1986, *15*(3), pp. 187–200.

Perry, Motty. An Example of Price Formation in Bilateral Situations: A Bargaining Model with Incomplete Information. *Econometrica,* March 1986, *54*(2), pp. 313–21.

Peters, Hans J. M. Simultaneity of Issues and Additivity in Bargaining. *Econometrica,* January 1986, *54*(1), pp. 153–69.

Pohjola, Matti. Applications of Dynamic Game Theory to Macroeconomics. In *Başar, T., ed.,* 1986, pp. 103–33.

Radner, Roy. Normative Theories of Organization: An Introduction. In *[Marschak, J.],* 1986, *1972,* pp. 177–88.

Radner, Roy. Repeated Moral Hazard with Low Discount Rates. In *[Arrow, K. J.], Vol. 3,* 1986, pp. 25–63.

Radner, Roy. Repeated Partnership Games with Imperfect Monitoring and No Discounting. *Rev. Econ. Stud.,* January 1986, *53*(1), pp. 43–57.

Radner, Roy; Myerson, Roger B. and Maskin, Eric. An Example of a Repeated Partnership Game with Discounting and with Uniformly Inefficient Equilibria. *Rev. Econ. Stud.,* January 1986, *53*(1), pp. 59–69.

Ratinova, E. S. A Game Approach to Coordinating Branch and Regional Plans. *Matekon*, Fall 1986, *23*(1), pp. 47–63.

Raub, Werner and Voss, Thomas. Conditions for Cooperation in Problematic Social Situations. **In** *[Rapoport, A.]*, 1986, pp. 85–103.

Ricketts, Martin and Peacock, Alan. Bargaining and the Regulatory System. *Int. Rev. Law Econ.*, June 1986, *6*(1), pp. 3–16.

Robson, Arthur J. The Existence of Nash Equilibria in Reaction Functions for Dynamic Models of Oligopoly. *Int. Econ. Rev.*, October 1986, *27*(3), pp. 539–44.

Roemer, John E. Equality of Resources Implies Equality of Welfare. *Quart. J. Econ.*, November 1986, *101*(4), pp. 751–84.

Rogawski, J. and Shubik, Martin. A Strategic Market Game with Transactions Costs. *Math. Soc. Sci.*, April 1986, *11*(2), pp. 139–60.

Rosen, Sherwin. Prizes and Incentives in Elimination Tournaments. *Amer. Econ. Rev.*, September 1986, *76*(4), pp. 701–15.

Rotemberg, Julio J. and Saloner, Garth. A Supergame-Theoretic Model of Price Wars during Booms. *Amer. Econ. Rev.*, June 1986, *76*(3), pp. 390–407. **[G: U.S.]**

Roth, Alvin E. On the Allocation of Residents to Rural Hospitals: A General Property of Two-Sided Matching Markets. *Econometrica*, March 1986, *54*(2), pp. 425–27.

Roth, Alvin E. On the Non-transferable Utility Value: A Reply [Values for Games without Sidepayments: Some Difficulties with Current Concepts]. *Econometrica*, July 1986, *54*(4), pp. 981–84.

Rubinstein, Ariel. Finite Automata Play Repeated Prisoner's Dilemma. *J. Econ. Theory*, June 1986, *39*(1), pp. 83–96.

Schleicher, Heinz. Classes of Core Configurations of Convex Cost Games and Equivalent One-Point Solution Concepts. *Écon. Soc.*, November 1986, *20*(11), pp. 101–21.

Schleifer, Andrei and Vishny, Robert W. Greenmail, White Knights, and Shareholders' Interest. *Rand J. Econ.*, Autumn 1986, *17*(3), pp. 293–309.

Schotter, Andrew. The Evolution of Rules. **In** *Langlois, R. N., ed.*, 1986, pp. 117–33.

Schüssler, Rudolf A. The Evolution of Reciprocal Cooperation. **In** *[Rapoport, A.]*, 1986, pp. 105–21.

Scotchmer, Suzanne. Corrigendum [Profit Maximizing Clubs]. *J. Public Econ.*, April 1986, *29*(3), pp. 389.

Selten, Reinhard and Stoecker, Rolf. End Behavior in Sequences of Finite Prisoner's Dilemma Supergames: A Learning Theory Approach. *J. Econ. Behav. Organ.*, March 1986, *7*(1), pp. 47–70.

Shubik, Martin. Games with Perceptive Commanders but with Indoctrinated or Less Perceptive Subordinates. **In** *[Rapoport, A.]*, 1986, pp. 209–22.

Shubik, Martin. Strategic Market Game: A Dynamic Programming Application to Money, Banking and Insurance. *Math. Soc. Sci.*, December 1986, *12*(3), pp. 265–78.

Shubik, Martin and Wooders, Myrna Holtz. Near-Markets and Market Games. *Econ. Stud. Quart.*, December 1986, *37*(4), pp. 289–99.

Soldatos, Gerasimos T. On the Stability of Temporal Collusions. *Indian Econ. J.*, Oct.-Dec. 1986, *34*(2), pp. 65–70.

Stanford, William G. On Continuous Reaction Function Equilibria in Duopoly Supergames with Mean Payoffs. *J. Econ. Theory*, June 1986, *39*(1), pp. 233–50.

Stanford, William G. Subgame Perfect Reaction Function Equilibria in Discounted Duopoly Supergames Are Trivial. *J. Econ. Theory*, June 1986, *39*(1), pp. 226–32.

Sutton, John. Non-cooperative Bargaining Theory: An Introduction. *Rev. Econ. Stud.*, October 1986, *53*(5), pp. 709–24.

Svejnar, Jan. Bargaining Power, Fear of Disagreement, and Wage Settlements: Theory and Evidence from U.S. Industry. *Econometrica*, September 1986, *54*(5), pp. 1055–78. **[G: U.S.]**

Tabellini, Guido. Money, Debt and Deficits in a Dynamic Game. *J. Econ. Dynam. Control*, December 1986, *10*(4), pp. 427–42.

von Thadden, Ernst-Ludwig. A Dynamic Macroeconomic Investment Game with Non-linear Saving Behaviour. **In** *Faber, M., ed.*, 1986, pp. 267–91.

Tijs, Stef H. and Driessen, S. H. Extensions of Solution Concepts by Means of Multiplicative ϵ-Tax Games. *Math. Soc. Sci.*, August 1986, *12*(1), pp. 9–20.

Tirole, Jean. Procurement and Renegotiation. *J. Polit. Econ.*, April 1986, *94*(2), pp. 235–59.

Vannucci, Stefano. Effectivity Functions, Indices of Power, and Implementation. *Econ. Notes*, 1986, (2), pp. 92–105.

Walliser, Bernard. Une typologie des jeux à deux joueurs. (A Taxonomy of Two-Person Games. With English summary.) *Écon. Soc.*, November 1986, *20*(11), pp. 123–47.

Wan, Yieh-Hei. The Cournot Problem with Bounded Memory Strategies. **In** *Sonnenschein, H. F., ed.*, 1986, pp. 139–47.

Winckler, Georg and Amann, Erwin. Exchange Rate Policy in the Presence of a Strong Trade Union. *J. Econ. (Z. Nationalökon.)*, Supplementum 5, 1986, pp. 259–80.

Witt, Ulrich. Evolution and Stability of Cooperation without Enforceable Contracts. *Kyklos*, 1986, *39*(2), pp. 245–66.

027 Economics of Centrally Planned Economies

0270 General

Barsky, A. D. and Belagurova, E. A. Toward an Analysis of the Principles Governing the Formation of Material Incentive Funds. *Matekon*, Spring 1986, *22*(3), pp. 91–110. **[G: U.S.S.R.]**

Bergson, Abram. The Politics of Socialist Efficiency. **In** *Szenberg, M., ed.*, 1986, *1980*, pp. 69–81.

Chiancone, Aldo. On the Contents of Public Finance in the Soviet Union. *Ricerche Econ.*, Apr.-Sept. 1986, *40*(2–3), pp. 463–77. **[G: U.S.S.R.]**

Dietrich, Michael. Organisational Requirements of a Socialist Economy: Theoretical and Practical Suggestions. *Cambridge J. Econ.*, December 1986, *10*(4), pp. 319–32.

Evistigneeva, L. and Perlamutrov, V. Intensification and Financial–Credit Relations. *Prob. Econ.*, November 1986, *29*(7), pp. 55–73.

Eysymontt, Jerzy and Maciejewski, Wojciech. Socioeconomic Crises in Poland: A Model Approach. *Eastern Europ. Econ.*, Spring 1986, *24*(3), pp. 6–23. **[G: Poland]**

Grebnev, L. The Application of Contractual Relationships in the Production Planning System. *Prob. Econ.*, August 1986, *29*(4), pp. 18–31. **[G: U.S.S.R.]**

Hillman, Arye L. and Schnytzer, Adi. Illegal Economic Activities and Purges in a Soviet-Type Economy: A Rent-Seeking Perspective. *Int. Rev. Law Econ.*, June 1986, *6*(1), pp. 87–99.

Kazakevich, D. M. Improving Consumer Prices. *Prob. Econ.*, December 1986, *29*(8), pp. 3–14. **[G: U.S.S.R.]**

Kornai, János. The Soft Budget Constraint. *Kyklos*, 1986, *39*(1), pp. 3–30. **[G: Hungary; Yugoslavia; China; U.S.]**

Niculescu-Mizil, E. Anatomic and Physiological Characteristics of the Social and Economic Systems. *Econ. Computat. Cybern. Stud. Res.*, 1986, *21*(1), pp. 25–31.

Pugachev, V. F. The Theoretical Construction of a Set of Optimizing Economic Mechanisms. *Matekon*, Summer 1986, *22*(4), pp. 3–32. **[G: U.S.S.R.]**

Ruccio, David F. Planning and Class in Transitional Societies. **In** *Zarembka, P., ed.*, 1986, pp. 235–52.

Ţigănescu, E. and Oprescu, G. Optimal Dynamic Control Processes of Material Production System. *Econ. Computat. Cybern. Stud. Res.*, 1986, *21*(1), pp. 15–24.

Trzeciakowski, Witold. Problems of Achieving Efficiency and Equilibrium. *Eastern Europ. Econ.*, Summer 1986, *24*(4), pp. 51–66. **[G: Poland]**

Vintrová, Ružena. Reproduction Proportions of Intensive Development. *Czech. Econ. Digest.*, January 1986, (1), pp. 33–57. **[G: Czechoslovakia]**

Winiecki, Jan. Central Planning and Export Orientation. *Eastern Europ. Econ.*, Summer 1986, *24*(4), pp. 67–89.

Zaikov, G. Political and Economic Problems of Accounting for Ecological Factors in Social Production. *Prob. Econ.*, January 1986, *28*(9), pp. 3–17. **[G: U.S.S.R.]**

Zotova, T. Economic Effectiveness of the Production Infrastructure. *Prob. Econ.*, June 1986, *29*(2), pp. 79–96. **[G: U.S.S.R.]**

0271 Microeconomic Theory

Bajt, Aleksander. Post-Keynesian Theory of the Labour-Managed Firm: Some Comments. *Econ. Anal. Workers' Manage.*, 1986, *20*(4), pp. 385–93.

Bon, Ranko. Secrecy and Publicity in the Marshallian Planned Economy. *Econ. Anal. Workers' Manage.*, 1986, *20*(4), pp. 357–74.

Bonin, John P. and Fukuda, Wataru. The Multifactor Illyrian Firm Revisited. *J. Compar. Econ.*, June 1986, *10*(2), pp. 171–80.

Burkett, John P. Search, Selection, and Shortage in an Industry Composed of Labor-Managed Firms. *J. Compar. Econ.*, March 1986, *10*(1), pp. 26–40.

Charemza, Wojciech and Gronicki, Miroslaw. A Model for Investment in Poland: A Disequilibrium Econometrics Approach. *Econ. Modelling*, April 1986, *3*(2), pp. 106–16. **[G: Poland]**

Chilosi, Alberto. Self-Managed Market Socialism with "Free Mobility of Labor." *J. Compar. Econ.*, September 1986, *10*(3), pp. 237–54.

Darbinian, M. The Population's Demand and Ways of Satisfying It. *Prob. Econ.*, March 1986, *28*(11), pp. 76–91. **[G: U.S.S.R.]**

Deriabin, A. Price and Scientific–Technical Progress. *Prob. Econ.*, July 1986, *29*(3), pp. 3–20. **[G: U.S.S.R.]**

Ershov, E. B. and Sadykov, I. S. A Study of Substitution Possibilities between Inputs and Their Relationship over Time in Soviet Industry. *Matekon*, Winter 1986-87, *23*(2), pp. 32–56. **[G: U.S.S.R.]**

Estrin, Saul. Long-run Supply Responses under Self-Management: Reply. *J. Compar. Econ.*, September 1986, *10*(3), pp. 342–45.

Gomulka, Stanislaw. Kornai's Soft Budget Constraint and the Shortage Phenomenon: A Criticism and Restatement. **In** *Gomulka, S.*, 1986, pp. 73–90.

Haruna, Shoji. Long-run Supply Responses under Self-Management: Comment. *J. Compar. Econ.*, September 1986, *10*(3), pp. 338–41.

Horvat, Branko. A Rejoinder [The Theory of the Worker-Managed Firm Revisited]. *Econ. Anal. Workers' Manage.*, 1986, *20*(4), pp. 417–18.

Horvat, Branko. Farewell to the Illyrian Firm. *Econ. Anal. Workers' Manage.*, 1986, *20*(1), pp. 23–29.

Horvat, Branko. The Illyrian Firm: An Alternative View: A Rejoinder. *Econ. Anal. Workers' Manage.*, 1986, *20*(4), pp. 411–16.

Horvat, Branko. The Theory of the Worker-Managed Firm Revisited. *J. Compar. Econ.*, March 1986, *10*(1), pp. 9–25.

Horvat, Branko. Workers' Management and the Market. **In** *Stiglitz, J. E. and Mathewson, G. F., eds.*, 1986, pp. 297–309. **[G: Yugoslavia]**

Ickes, Barry W. On the Economics of Taut Plans. *J. Compar. Econ.*, December 1986, *10*(4), pp. 388–99.

Jossa, Bruno. Considerazioni su di un "tipo

ideale" di cooperativi di produzione. (With English summary.) *Stud. Econ.*, 1986, *41*(28), pp. 3–22.

Kalecki, Michal. Central Price Determination as an Essential Feature of a Socialist Economy. **In** *Kalecki, M.*, 1986, *1958*, pp. 48–53.

Kalecki, Michal. Outline of a New System of Incentives and Directives. **In** *Kalecki, M.*, 1986, *1959*, pp. 41–47.

Kornai, János. "Hard" and "Soft" Budget Constraint. **In** *Kornai, J.*, 1986, *1980*, pp. 33–51.

Kornai, János. The Reproduction of Shortage. **In** *Kornai, J.*, 1986, *1979*, pp. 6–32.

Liu, Pak-Wai. Moral Hazard and Incentives in a Decentralized Planning Environment. *J. Compar. Econ.*, June 1986, *10*(2), pp. 91–105.

Madžar, Ljubomir. The Illyrian Firm: An Alternative View. *Econ. Anal. Workers' Manage.*, 1986, *20*(4), pp. 401–10.

Matlin, A. The Law of Value and Planned Price Formation. *Prob. Econ.*, August 1986, *29*(4), pp. 32–51.

Meško, Ivan. Analysis of Business Process by Opportunity Costs. *Econ. Anal. Workers' Manage.*, 1986, *20*(3), pp. 307–10.

Mihaljek, Dubravko. Financing of Public Services in Yugoslavia: A Lindahl Equilibrium Model for the Labour-Managed Economy. *Econ. Anal. Workers' Manage.*, 1986, *20*(2), pp. 135–68. **[G: Yugoslavia]**

Montias, J. Michael. On the Centralization and Decentralization of Economic Activities. **In** *Adelman, I. and Taylor, J. E., eds.*, 1986, pp. 171–89.

Nove, Alec. Marx, the Market and 'Feasible Socialism.' **In** *Nove, A.*, 1986, *1979*, pp. 51–62.

Nuti, Domenico Mario. Merger Conditions and the Measurement of Disequilibrium in Labour-Managed Economies. *Ann. Pub. Co-op. Econ.*, Jan.-March 1986, *57*(1), pp. 47–53.

Ostojić, Slobodan. Decentralization without Hierarchy: Experience of Yugoslav Enterprises. *Econ. Anal. Workers' Manage.*, 1986, *20*(2), pp. 119–34. **[G: Yugoslavia]**

Pfouts, Ralph W. and Rosefielde, Steven. The Firm in Illyria: Market Syndicalism Reconsidered. *J. Compar. Econ.*, June 1986, *10*(2), pp. 160–70.

Raţiu-Sucio, Camelia and Oprescu, G. Adjusting the Supply Process with Stocking Stochastic Models. *Econ. Computat. Cybern. Stud. Res.*, 1986, *21*(3), pp. 13–22.

Rosefielde, Steven. Behavioral Uncertainty and the Optimal Public Regulation of ELMF Systems: Comments on the State of Worker-Management Theory. *J. Compar. Econ.*, March 1986, *10*(1), pp. 88–90.

Sikdar, Soumyen. Technological Change and the Labour-Managed Firm. *J. Quant. Econ.*, January 1986, *2*(1), pp. 111–18.

Tajnikar, Maks. Post-Keynesian Theory of the Labour-Managed Firm: A Rejoinder. *Econ. Anal. Workers' Manage.*, 1986, *20*(4), pp. 395–400.

Tarasov, V. The Price of New Machinery. *Prob. Econ.*, August 1986, *29*(4), pp. 3–17.

Wong, David C. A Two-Period Model of the Competitive Socialist Labor-Managed Firm. *J. Compar. Econ.*, September 1986, *10*(3), pp. 313–24.

0272 Macroeconomic Theory

Blomqvist, Ake G. The Economics of Price Scissors: Comment. *Amer. Econ. Rev.*, December 1986, *76*(5), pp. 1188–91.

Brada, Josef C. and King, Arthur E. Taut Plans, Repressed Inflation and the Supply of Effort in Centrally Planned Economies. *Econ. Planning*, 1986, *20*(3), pp. 162–78. **[G: Czechoslovakia; E. Germany; Poland; Hungary]**

Carter, Michael R. The Economics of Price Scissors: Comment. *Amer. Econ. Rev.*, December 1986, *76*(5), pp. 1192–94.

Charemza, Wojciech and Gronicki, Miroslaw. A Model for Investment in Poland: A Disequilibrium Econometrics Approach. *Econ. Modelling*, April 1986, *3*(2), pp. 106–16. **[G: Poland]**

Guo, Baoping. Macroeconomic Price Adjustment-Control and Price System Equation. *Econ. Computat. Cybern. Stud. Res.*, 1986, *21*(4), pp. 81–84.

Harrison, Mark. Lessons of Soviet Planning for Full Employment. **In** *Lane, D., ed.*, 1986, pp. 69–82. **[G: U.S.S.R.]**

Henin, Pierre-Yves. Équilibres avec rationnement d'une économie à planification centralisée et secteur parallèle: une analyse macroéconomique. (With English summary.) *Revue Écon. Polit.*, May-June 1986, *96*(3), pp. 217–38.

Kalecki, Michal. On the Coefficient of Capital Tied Up in Construction. **In** *Kalecki, M.*, 1986, *1958*, pp. 109–17.

Kalecki, Michal. Problems in the Theory of Growth of a Socialist Economy. **In** *Kalecki, M.*, 1986, *1959*, pp. 70–96.

Kalecki, Michal. The Influence of the Construction Period on the Relationship between Investment and National Income. **In** *Kalecki, M.*, 1986, *1957*, pp. 97–108.

Kornai, János. The Reproduction of Shortage. **In** *Kornai, J.*, 1986, *1979*, pp. 6–32.

Lane, David. Marxist-Leninism: An Ideology for Full Employment in Socialist States? **In** *Lane, D., ed.*, 1986, pp. 1–16. **[G: U.S.S.R.]**

Matlin, I. S. Macroeconomic Models in a System of Planning Models. *Matekon*, Winter 1986-87, *23*(2), pp. 74–93. **[G: U.S.S.R.]**

Nuti, Domenico Mario. Michal Kalecki's Contribution to the Theory and Practice of Socialist Planning. *Cambridge J. Econ.*, December 1986, *10*(4), pp. 333–53.

Nuti, Domenico Mario. Systemic Aspects of Employment and Investment in Soviet-Type Economies. **In** *Lane, D., ed.*, 1986, pp. 112–21. **[G: U.S.S.R.]**

Peebles, Gavin. On the Importance of Establishing the Inverse Relationship between Open Inflation and Household Liquidity Growth under Socialism: A Critique of Jan Winiecki's Savings Deposit Data. *Comp. Econ. Stud.*, Winter 1986, *28*(4), pp. 85–91. **[G: Cent. Planned Econ.]**

Podkaminer, Leon. Persistent Disequilibrium in Poland's Consumer Markets: Some Hypothetical Explanations. *Comp. Econ. Stud.*, Fall 1986, *28*(3), pp. 1–16. **[G: Poland]**

Rogovskii, E. A. and Rutkovskaia, E. A. A Method of Analyzing the Economic Return to Capital Investment. *Matekon*, Summer 1986, *22*(4), pp. 33–53. **[G: U.S.S.R.]**

Sah, Raaj Kumar and Stiglitz, Joseph E. The Economics of Price Scissors: Reply. *Amer. Econ. Rev.*, December 1986, *76*(5), pp. 1195–99.

Simonovits, András. Growth, Control and Tensions in an Open Socialist Economy. *Econ. Planning*, 1986, *20*(3), pp. 145–61.

Suba-Varga, Judit. "Foreign Trade Constraint" and Cyclical Development. *Acta Oecon.*, 1986, *36*(3–4), pp. 251–70. **[G: Hungary]**

Tajnikar, Maks. Reconstruction of the Theory of Distribution in the Labour-Managed Economy Following the Example of Post-Keynesian Economic Theory. *Econ. Anal. Workers' Manage.*, 1986, *20*(1), pp. 45–63.

Todorov, Wassil. Methodological Principles and Technology for Compilation of Input–Output Tables in Labour Units. **In** *Franz, A. and Rainer, N., eds.*, 1986, pp. 415–25.

Wellisz, Stanislaw and Findlay, Ronald. Central Planning and the 'Second Economy' in Soviet-Type Systems. *Econ. J.*, September 1986, *96*(383), pp. 646–58.

Winiecki, Jan. Distorted Macroeconomics of Central Planning. *Banca Naz. Lavoro Quart. Rev.*, June 1986, (157), pp. 197–223.

Yang, Jinbai, et al. Some Theoretical Problems of Socialist National Income. *Chinese Econ. Stud.*, Fall 1986, *20*(1), pp. 3–99.

Zamkov, O. O. Mathematical Analysis of Extended Reproduction Schemata with a Changing Rate of Surplus Value. *Matekon*, Fall 1986, *23*(1), pp. 25–46.

030 History of Thought; Methodology

031 History of Economic Thought

0310 General

Arrow, Kenneth J. History: The View from Economics. **In** *Parker, W. N., ed.*, 1986, pp. 13–20.

Blaug, Mark. Economic History and the History of Economics: Introduction. **In** *Blaug, M.*, 1986, pp. vii–xx.

Blaug, Mark. Kuhn versus Lakatos, or Paradigms versus Research Programmes in the History of Economics. **In** *Blaug, M.*, 1986, *1976*, pp. 233–64.

David, Paul A. Understanding the Economics of QWERTY: The Necessity of History. **In** *Parker, W. N., ed.*, 1986, pp. 30–49.

Ellig, Jerome R. Do We Walk with Walras? *Atlantic Econ. J.*, July 1986, *14*(2), pp. 82.

Harcourt, Geoffrey C. Reflections on the Development of Economics as a Discipline. **In** *[Harcourt, G. C.]*, 1986, *1984*, pp. 9–45.

Kindleberger, Charles P. Economic History and the Modern Economist: A Further Comment. **In** *Parker, W. N., ed.*, 1986, pp. 83–92.

McCloskey, Donald N. Economics as an Historical Science. **In** *Parker, W. N., ed.*, 1986, pp. 63–69.

Parker, William N. An Historical Introduction. **In** *Parker, W. N., ed.*, 1986, pp. 1–10.

Parker, William N. Economic History and the Modern Economist: Afterword. **In** *Parker, W. N., ed.*, 1986, pp. 93–99.

Quadrio-Curzio, Alberto and Scazzieri, Roberto. The Exchange–Production Duality and the Dynamics of Economic Knowledge. **In** *Baranzini, M. and Scazzieri, R., eds.*, 1986, pp. 377–407.

Rostow, Walt W. Professor Arrow on Economic Analysis and Economic History. **In** *Parker, W. N., ed.*, 1986, pp. 70–76.

Solow, Robert E. Economics: Is Something Missing? **In** *Parker, W. N., ed.*, 1986, pp. 21–29.

Stigler, George J. Perfect Competition, Historically Contemplated. **In** *Stigler, G. J.*, 1986, *1983*, pp. 265–88.

Temin, Peter. Is History Stranger Than Theory? The Origin of Telephone Separations. **In** *Parker, W. N., ed.*, 1986, pp. 50–59.

Wagener, Hans-Jürgen and Drukker, Jan W. The Economic Law of Motion of Modern Society: A Marx–Keynes–Schumpeter Centennial: Introduction. **In** *Wagener, H.-J. and Drukker, J. W., eds.*, 1986, pp. 1–13.

Wright, Gavin. History and the Future of Economics. **In** *Parker, W. N., ed.*, 1986, pp. 77–82.

0311 Ancient, Medieval

Kent, Calvin A. A Christian Approach to Social Economics. *Int. J. Soc. Econ.*, 1986, *13*(3), pp. 80–92.

Ohrenstein, Roman A. Value Analysis in Talmudic Literature in the Light of Modern Economics. *Int. J. Soc. Econ.*, 1986, *13*(3), pp. 34–52.

Temple-Smith, Richard. Aristotle as a Welfare Economist: A Comment. *Hist. Polit. Econ.*, Fall 1986, *18*(3), pp. 523–28.

Worland, Stephen T. Aristotle and Welfare Economics: A Reply. *Hist. Polit. Econ.*, Fall 1986, *18*(3), pp. 528–29.

0312 Preclassical

Marsh, James Barney. Jacob Vanderlint and the Roots of Supply-Side Economics. *Eastern Econ. J.*, Jan.-Mar. 1986, *12*(1), pp. 63–72.

Popescu, Oreste. El Pensamiento Económico en la Escolástica Hispanoamericana. (The Economic Thought in the Hispanoamerican Scholastic. With English summary.) *Económica (La Plata)*, July-December 1986, *32*(2), pp. 227–60. **[G: Spain; Latin America]**

Samuelson, Paul A. Quesnay's 'Tableau Economique' as a Theorist Would Formulate It Today. **In** *Samuelson, P. A.*, 1986, *1982*, pp. 630–63.

Zinn, Karl Georg. Zur Frühgeschichte des "theoretischen Interventionismus." Zugleich eine Erinnerung an Heinrich Ludwig Lambert Gall (1794–1863). (On the Early History of Theoretical Interventionism. The Socialist Underconsumption Theory of the German Ludwig Gall [1794–1863]. With English summary.) *Z. Wirtschaft. Sozialwissen.*, 1986, *106*(2), pp. 139–65.

0313 Mercantilist

Anderson, Gary M. and Tollison, Robert D. Smith, Steuart, and Mercantilism: Reply [Sir James Steuart as the Apothesis of Mercantilism and His Relation to Adam Smith]. *Southern Econ. J.*, January 1986, *52*(3), pp. 853–56.

Giacomin, Alberto. Un modello economico dell'*ancien regime:* il "saggio sulla natura del commercio in generale" di Richard Cantillon. (An Economic Model of the the *Ancient Regime:* Richard Cantillon's "Essay on the Nature of Trade in General." With English summary.) *Ricerche Econ.*, Jan.-Mar. 1986, *40*(1), pp. 96–129.

Guerrieri, Paolo and Padoan, Pier Carlo. Neomercantilism and International Economic Stability. *Int. Organ.*, Winter 1986, *40*(1), pp. 29–42.

McCraw, Thomas K. Mercantilism and the Market: Antecedents of American Industrial Policy. **In** *Barfield, C. E. and Schambra, W. A., eds.*, 1986, pp. 33–62. **[G: U.S.]**

Perlman, Morris. The Bullionist Controversy Revisited. *J. Polit. Econ.*, August 1986, *94*(4), pp. 745–62.

Rashid, Salim. Smith, Steuart, and Mercantilism: Comment [Sir James Steuart as the Apothesis of Mercantilism and His Relation to Adam Smith]. *Southern Econ. J.*, January 1986, *52*(3), pp. 843–52.

Stein, Herbert. Cultural and Historical Perspectives on Industrial Policy: Comment. **In** *Barfield, C. E. and Schambra, W. A., eds.*, 1986, pp. 90–92. **[G: U.S.]**

0314 Classical

Aspromourgos, Tony. Political Economy and the Social Division of Labour: The Economics of Sir William Petty. *Scot. J. Polit. Econ.*, February 1986, *33*(1), pp. 28–45.

Barkai, Haim. Ricardo's Volte-Face on Machinery. *J. Polit. Econ.*, Part 1, June 1986, *94*(3), pp. 595–613.

Baumol, William J. Marx and the Iron Law of Wages. **In** *Baumol, W. J.*, 1986, *1983*, pp. 259–64.

Baumol, William J. Say's (at Least) Eight Laws, or What Say and James Mill May Really Have Meant. **In** *Baumol, W. J.*, 1986, *1977*, pp. 265–81.

Becattini, Giacomo. Conflitto di classe e contrasto di interessi nella teoria economica. (Class Conflict and Clashing Interests in Economic Theory. With English summary.) *Rivista Int. Sci. Econ. Com.*, March 1986, *33*(3), pp. 193–205.

Beretta, Carlo. Una recente ricostruzione della storia del pensiero economico: una nota. (A Recent Reconstruction of the History of Economic Thought: A Note. With English summary.) *Econ. Polít.*, April 1986, *3*(1), pp. 117–27.

Blaug, Mark. Ricardo and the Problem of Public Policy. **In** *Blaug, M.*, 1986, pp. 115–27.

Blaug, Mark. Technical Change and Marxian Economics. **In** *Blaug, M.*, 1986, *1960*, pp. 184–96.

Blaug, Mark. The Classical Economists and the Factory Acts: A Re-examination. **In** *Blaug, M.*, 1986, *1959*, pp. 135–49. **[G: U.K.]**

Blaug, Mark. The Economics of Education in English Classical Political Economy: A Re-examination. **In** *Blaug, M.*, 1986, *1975*, pp. 150–83.

Blaug, Mark. The Empirical Content of Ricardian Economics. **In** *Blaug, M.*, 1986, *1956*, pp. 91–114.

Blaug, Mark. The Myth of the Old Poor Law and the Making of the New. **In** *Blaug, M.*, 1986, *1963*, pp. 3–35. **[G: U.K.]**

Blaug, Mark. The Poor Law Report Re-examined. **In** *Blaug, M.*, 1986, *1964*, pp. 36–50. **[G: U.K.]**

Blaug, Mark. Welfare Indices in *The Wealth of Nations*. **In** *Blaug, M.*, 1986, *1959*, pp. 128–34.

Breton, Yves. La place de la statistique et de l'arithmétique politique dans la méthodologie économique de Jean-Baptiste Say le temps des ruptures. (The Role of Statistics and Political Arithmetic in the Economic Methodology of Jean-Baptiste Say at the Time of the Ruptures. With English summary.) *Revue Écon.*, November 1986, *37*(6), pp. 1033–62.

De Long, James Bradford. Senior's 'Last Hour': Suggested Explanation of a Famous Blunder. *Hist. Polit. Econ.*, Summer 1986, *18*(2), pp. 325–33.

Demeny, Paul. Population and the Invisible Hand. *Demography*, November 1986, *23*(4), pp. 473–87.

Eltis, Walter. Sir James Steuart's Corporate State. **In** *Black, R. D. C., ed.*, 1986, pp. 43–73.

Faccarello, Gilbert. Sraffa versus Ricardo: The Historical Irrelevance of the 'Corn-Profit' Model. **In** *Fine, B., ed.*, 1986, *1982*, pp. 188–203.

Faucci, Riccardo. Note su positivismo e pensiero economico in Italia tra Otto e Novecento. (Positivism and Economic Thought in Italy between 1800 and 1900. With English summary.) *Rivista Int. Sci. Econ. Com.*, January 1986, *33*(1), pp. 75–94. **[G: Italy]**

Fine, Ben. Note: A Dissenting Note on the Transformation Problem. **In** *Fine, B., ed.*, 1986, *1983*, pp. 209–14.

Fine, Ben. On the Economics of Ricardo and Sraffa [Sraffa versus Ricardo: The Historical Irrelevance of the 'Corn-Profit' Model]. **In** *Fine, B., ed.*, 1986, *1983*, pp. 204–08.

Fontana, Biancamaria. Democracy and Civilization: John Stuart Mill and the Critique of Political Economy. *Écon. Soc.*, March 1986, *20*(3), pp. 3–24.

Gerstein, Ira. Production, Circulation and Value: The Significance of the 'Transformation Problem' in Marx's Critique of Political Economy. **In** *Fine, B., ed.*, 1986, *1976*, pp. 45–93.

Hollander, Samuel. On a 'New Interpretation' of Ricardo's Early Treatment of Profitability. *Econ. J.*, December 1986, *96*(384), pp. 1091–97.

Hollander, Samuel. On Malthus's Population Principle and Social Reform. *Hist. Polit. Econ.*, Summer 1986, *18*(2), pp. 187–235.

Hollander, Samuel. The Relevance of John Stuart Mill: Some Implications for Modern Economics. **In** *Black, R. D. C., ed.*, 1986, pp. 129–59.

Humphrey, Thomas M. Adam Smith and the Monetary Approach to the Balance of Payments. **In** *Humphreys, T. M.*, 1986, *1981*, pp. 180–87.

Humphrey, Thomas M. Can the Central Bank Peg Real Interest Rates? A Survey of Classical and Neoclassical Opinion. **In** *Humphreys, T. M.*, 1986, *1983*, pp. 160–69.

Humphrey, Thomas M. Cumulative Process Models from Thornton to Wicksell. *Fed. Res. Bank Richmond Econ. Rev.*, May/June 1986, 72(3), pp. 18–25.

Humphrey, Thomas M. Of Hume, Thornton, the Quantity Theory, and the Phillips Curve. **In** *Humphreys, T. M.*, 1986, *1982*, pp. 128–33.

Humphrey, Thomas M. The Classical Concept of the Lender of Last Resort. **In** *Humphreys, T. M.*, 1986, *1975*, pp. 304–11.

Humphrey, Thomas M. The Dismal Science Revisited. **In** *Humphreys, T. M.*, 1986, *1973*, pp. 312–23.

Humphrey, Thomas M. The Early History of the Real/Nominal Interest Rate Relationship. **In** *Humphreys, T. M.*, 1986, *1983*, pp. 151–59.

Humphrey, Thomas M. The Quantity Theory of Money: Its Historical Evolution and Role in Policy Debates. **In** *Humphreys, T. M.*, 1986, *1974*, pp. 1–18.

Humphrey, Thomas M. The Real Bills Doctrine. **In** *Humphreys, T. M.*, 1986, *1982*, pp. 80–90.

Humphrey, Thomas M. Two Views of Monetary Policy: The Attwood–Mill Debate Revisited. **In** *Humphreys, T. M.*, 1986, *1977*, pp. 242–50.

Kalmbach, Peter and Kurz, Heinz D. Economic Dynamics and Innovation: Ricardo, Marx and Schumpeter on Technological Change and Unemployment. **In** *Wagener, H.-J. and Drukker, J. W., eds.*, 1986, pp. 71–92.

Keleher, Robert E. Of Money and Prices: Some Historical Perspectives. **In** *Putnam, B. H. and Wilford, D. S., eds.*, 1986, *1978*, pp. 27–58.

Kurz, Heinz D. Classical and Early Neoclassical Economists on Joint Production. *Metroecon.*, February 1986, *38*(1), pp. 1–37.

Levine, David P. Reconceptualizing Classical Economics. **In** *Mirowski, P., ed.*, 1986, pp. 13–40.

Mumy, Gene E. Silences in Ricardo: Comparative Advantage and the Class Distribution of Free Trade Benefits. *Rev. Soc. Econ.*, December 1986, *44*(3), pp. 294–305.

Negishi, Takashi. Thornton's Criticism of Equilibrium Theory and Mill. *Hist. Polit. Econ.*, Winter 1986, *18*(4), pp. 567–77.

Peach, Terry. David Ricardo's Treatment of Wages. **In** *Black, R. D. C., ed.*, 1986, pp. 104–28.

Peach, Terry. Ricardo's Early Treatment of Profitability: Reply. *Econ. J.*, December 1986, *96*(384), pp. 1105–12.

Perlman, Morris. The Bullionist Controversy Revisited. *J. Polit. Econ.*, August 1986, *94*(4), pp. 745–62.

Pesciarelli, Enzo. On Adam Smith's Lectures on Jurisprudence. *Scot. J. Polit. Econ.*, February 1986, *33*(1), pp. 74–85.

Pilling, Geoffrey. The Law of Value in Ricardo and Marx. **In** *Fine, B., ed.*, 1986, *1972*, pp. 18–44.

Prendergast, Renée. David Ricardo's Early Treatment of Profitability: A New Interpretation: A Comment. *Econ. J.*, December 1986, *96*(384), pp. 1098–1104.

Prendergast, Renée. Malthus's Discussion of the Corn Ratio Theory of Profits. *Cambridge J. Econ.*, June 1986, *10*(2), pp. 187–89.

Pullen, John M. Correspondence between Malthus and His Parents. *Hist. Polit. Econ.*, Spring 1986, *18*(1), pp. 133–54.

Rashid, Salim. Historical Notes on the Origins of Supply-Side Economics and Its Ethical Roots: Say's Law, Smith's Law, or Moral Law? *Quart. Rev. Econ. Bus.*, Winter 1986, *26*(4), pp. 22–34.

Rutherford, Robert P. Ricardo's Mantle. *Australian Econ. Pap.*, December 1986, *25*(47), pp. 206–21.

Samuelson, Paul A. Noise and Signal in Debates among Classical Economists: A Reply. **In** *Samuelson, P. A.*, 1986, *1980*, pp. 618–21.

Samuelson, Paul A. The Canonical Classical Model of Political Economy. **In** *Samuelson, P. A.*, 1986, *1978*, pp. 598–617.

Sandilands, Roger J. Natural Law and the Political Economy of Henry George. *J. Econ. Stud.*, 1986, *13*(5), pp. 4–15.

Schwartz, Pedro. Jeremy Bentham's Democratic Despotism. **In** *Black, R. D. C., ed.*, 1986, pp. 74–103.

Skinner, Andrew S. Adam Smith: Then and Now. **In** *Black, R. D. C., ed.*, 1986, pp. 16–42.

Skourtos, M. Market Processes in a Ricardian Framework: The Case of V. K. Dmitriev. *Metroecon.*, October 1986, *38*(3), pp. 229–55. **[G: U.K.]**

Steiner, Philippe. J. B. Say et l'enseignement de l'économie politique en France (1816–1832). (J. B. Say and the Teaching of Political Economy in France. With English summary.) *Écon. Soc.*, October 1986, *20*(10), pp. 63–95.

Stigler, George J. Economics or Ethics? **In** *Stig-*

ler, G. J., 1986, *1981*, pp. 303–36.

Stigler, George J. The Economist and the State. **In** *Stigler, G. J.*, 1986, *1965*, pp. 99–116.

Tonsor, Stephen. Christian Political Economy: Malthus to Margaret Thatcher: Comment. **In** *Block, W. and Hexham, I., eds.*, 1986, pp. 118–23.

Waterman, A. M. C. Christian Political Economy: Malthus to Margaret Thatcher: Reply. **In** *Block, W. and Hexham, I., eds.*, 1986, pp. 123–24.

Waterman, A. M. C. Christian Political Economy: Malthus to Margaret Thatcher. **In** *Block, W. and Hexham, I., eds.*, 1986, pp. 99–117.

Young, Jeffrey T. The Impartial Spectator and Natural Jurisprudence: An Interpretation of Adam Smith's Theory of the Natural Price. *Hist. Polit. Econ.*, Fall 1986, *18*(3), pp. 365–82.

0315 Austrian, Marshallian, Neoclassical

Addleson, Mark. "Radical Subjectivism" and the Language of Austrian Economics. **In** *[Lachmann, L. M.]*, 1986, pp. 1–15.

Aspromourgos, Tony. On the Origins of the Term 'Neoclassical.' *Cambridge J. Econ.*, September 1986, *10*(3), pp. 265–70.

Awan, Akhtar A. Marshallian and Schumpeterian Theories of Economic Evolution: Gradualism versus Punctualism. *Atlantic Econ. J.*, December 1986, *14*(4), pp. 37–49.

Beretta, Carlo. Una recente ricostruzione della storia del pensiero economico: una nota. (A Recent Reconstruction of the History of Economic Thought: A Note. With English summary.) *Econ. Polít.*, April 1986, *3*(1), pp. 117–27.

Blaug, Mark. Was There a Marginal Revolution? **In** *Blaug, M.*, 1986, *1972*, pp. 209–18.

Bostaph, Samuel and Shieh, Yeung-Nan. W. S. Jevons and Lardner's *Railway Economy. Hist. Polit. Econ.*, Spring 1986, *18*(1), pp. 49–64.

Chisholm, Roderick M. Brentano on Preference, Desire and Intrinsic Value. **In** *Grassl, W. and Smith, B., eds.*, 1986, pp. 182–95.

Craver, Earlene. The Emigration of the Austrian Economists. *Hist. Polit. Econ.*, Spring 1986, *18*(1), pp. 1–32. **[G: Austria]**

Dahmén, Erik. Rights and Relations in Modern Economic Theory: Comment. **In** *Day, R. H. and Eliasson, G., eds.*, 1986, pp. 342–43.

Egger, John B. A Sympathetic Critic of the Austrian Business-Cycle Theory. **In** *[Lachmann, L. M.]*, 1986, pp. 56–71.

Eliasson, Gunnar. Rights and Relations in Modern Economic Theory: Comment. **In** *Day, R. H. and Eliasson, G., eds.*, 1986, pp. 346–50.

Faber, Malte. On the Development of Austrian Capital Theory. **In** *Faber, M., ed.*, 1986, pp. 12–43.

Fabian, Reinhard and Simons, Peter M. The Second Austrian School of Value Theory. **In** *Grassl, W. and Smith, B., eds.*, 1986, pp. 37–101.

Fehl, Ulrich. Spontaneous Order and the Subjectivity of Expectations: A Contribution to the Lachmann–O'Driscoll Problem. **In** *[Lachmann, L. M.]*, 1986, pp. 72–86.

Feiwel, George R. Schumpeter on Walras, Marshall, and Beyond. *Rivista Int. Sci. Econ. Com.*, August 1986, *33*(8), pp. 763–75.

Garrison, Roger W. From Lachmann to Lucas: On Institutions, Expectations, and Equilibrating Tendencies. **In** *[Lachmann, L. M.]*, 1986, pp. 87–101.

Grassl, Wolfgang. Markets and Morality: Austrian Perspectives on the Economic Approach to Human Behaviour. **In** *Grassl, W. and Smith, B., eds.*, 1986, pp. 139–81.

Gunning, J. Patrick. The Methodology of Austrian Economics and Its Relevance to Institutionalism. *Amer. J. Econ. Soc.*, January 1986, *45*(1), pp. 78–91.

Haller, Rudolf. Emanuel Herrmann: On an Almost Forgotten Chapter of Austrian Intellectual History. **In** *Grassl, W. and Smith, B., eds.*, 1986, pp. 196–209.

Hennings, Klaus H. The Exchange Paradigm and the Theory of Production and Distribution. **In** *Baranzini, M. and Scazzieri, R., eds.*, 1986, pp. 221–43.

Humphrey, Thomas M. Can the Central Bank Peg Real Interest Rates? A Survey of Classical and Neoclassical Opinion. **In** *Humphreys, T. M.*, 1986, *1983*, pp. 160–69.

Humphrey, Thomas M. The Early History of the Real/Nominal Interest Rate Relationship. **In** *Humphreys, T. M.*, 1986, *1983*, pp. 151–59.

Kirzner, Israel M. Roundaboutness, Opportunity and Austrian Economics. **In** *[Seldon, A.]*, 1986, pp. 93–103.

Kurz, Heinz D. Classical and Early Neoclassical Economists on Joint Production. *Metroecon.*, February 1986, *38*(1), pp. 1–37.

Lavoie, Donald C. Euclideanism versus Hermeneutics: A Reinterpretation of Misesian Apriorism. **In** *[Lachmann, L. M.]*, 1986, pp. 192–210.

Loasby, Brian J. Marshall's Economics of Progress. *J. Econ. Stud.*, 1986, *13*(5), pp. 16–26.

Mongin, Philippe. La controverse sur l'entreprise (1940–1950) et la formation de l'"irréalisme méthodologique." (The Controversy over the Enterprise (1940–1950) and the Building-Up of a "Lack of Methodological Realism." With English summary.) *Écon. Soc.*, March 1986, *20*(3), pp. 95–151.

Negishi, Takashi. Marx and Böhm-Bawerk. *Econ. Stud. Quart.*, March 1986, *37*(1), pp. 2–10.

Nyíri, J. C. Intellectual Foundations of Austrian Liberalism. **In** *Grassl, W. and Smith, B., eds.*, 1986, pp. 102–38.

O'Driscoll, Gerald P., Jr. Money: Menger's Evolutionary Theory. *Hist. Polit. Econ.*, Winter 1986, *18*(4), pp. 601–16.

O'Driscoll, Gerald P., Jr. and Rizzo, Mario J. Subjectivism, Uncertainty, and Rules. **In** *[Lachmann, L. M.]*, 1986, pp. 252–67.

Pellengahr, Ingo. Austrians versus Austrians II: Functionalist versus Essentialist Theories of Interest. **In** *Faber, M., ed.*, 1986, pp. 78–95.

Pellengahr, Ingo. Austrians versus Austrians I: A Subjectivist View of Interest. **In** *Faber, M., ed.*, 1986, pp. 60–77.

Perlman, Mark. Subjectivism and American Institutionalism. **In** *[Lachmann, L. M.]*, 1986, pp. 268–80.

Presley, John R. Modern Monetarist Ideas: A British Connection? **In** *Black, R. D. C., ed.*, 1986, pp. 191–210.

Riha, Tomas J. F. The Marxian Law of Value under Socialism: Faith and Reality. **In** *Dowdy, E., ed.*, 1986, pp. 127–44. **[G: U.S.S.R.; China]**

Rima, Ingrid H. The Peculiarities of Labor Markets and the Residuum. *Eastern Econ. J.*, Apr.-June 1986, *12*(2), pp. 158–74.

Samuelson, Larry and Wolfson, Murray. Expository Marxism and Comparative Economic Dynamics. *Hist. Polit. Econ.*, Spring 1986, *18*(1), pp. 65–85.

Shearmur, Jeremy. The Austrian Connection: Hayek's Liberalism and the Thought of Carl Menger. **In** *Grassl, W. and Smith, B., eds.*, 1986, pp. 210–24.

Silber, Jacques G. Rationality, Self Interest and Coordination: On Some Current Controversies in Economics. *Econ. Notes,* 1986, (3), pp. 47–64.

Sinn, Hans-Werner. Risiko als Produktionsfaktor. (Risk as a Factor of Production. With English summary.) *Jahr. Nationalökon. Statist.*, November 1986, *201*(6), pp. 557–71.

Skinner, Andrew S. Edward Chamberlin: The Theory of Monopolistic Competition: A Re-orientation of the Theory of Value. *J. Econ. Stud.*, 1986, *13*(5), pp. 27–44.

Smith, Barry. Austrian Economics and Austrian Philosophy. **In** *Grassl, W. and Smith, B., eds.*, 1986, pp. 1–36.

Smith, Barry. Austrian Economics from Menger to Hayek. **In** *Grassl, W. and Smith, B., eds.*, 1986, pp. vii–x.

Stigler, George J. Perfect Competition, Historically Contemplated. **In** *Stigler, G. J.*, 1986, *1983*, pp. 265–88.

Temple-Smith, Richard. Aristotle as a Welfare Economist: A Comment. *Hist. Polit. Econ.*, Fall 1986, *18*(3), pp. 523–28.

von Weizsäcker, Carl Christian. Rights and Relations in Modern Economic Theory. **In** *Day, R. H. and Eliasson, G., eds.*, 1986, *1984*, pp. 317–41.

Whitaker, John K. The Continuing Relevance of Alfred Marshall. **In** *Black, R. D. C., ed.*, 1986, pp. 176–90.

Williams, Philip L. A Reconstruction of Marshall's Temporary Equilibrium Pricing Model. *Hist. Polit. Econ.*, Winter 1986, *18*(4), pp. 639–53.

Worland, Stephen T. Aristotle and Welfare Economics: A Reply. *Hist. Polit. Econ.*, Fall 1986, *18*(3), pp. 528–29.

Ysander, Bengt-Christer. Rights and Relations in Modern Economic Theory: Comment. **In** *Day, R. H. and Eliasson, G., eds.*, 1986, pp. 344–45.

0316 General Equilibrium until 1945

Dorfman, Robert. Thünen at Two Hundred: Comment. *J. Econ. Lit.*, December 1986, *24*(4), pp. 1773–76.

Olsem, Jean-Pierre. Lat rationalité de l'équilibre concurrentiel général. (With English summary.) *Revue Écon. Polit.*, Nov.-Dec. 1986, *96*(6), pp. 625–41.

Rugina, Anghel N. *Principia Oeconomica:* New and Old Foundations of Economic Analysis. *Int. J. Soc. Econ.*, 1986, *13*(7/8), pp. 1–67.

Samuelson, Paul A. Thünen at Two Hundred. **In** *Samuelson, P. A.*, 1986, *1983*, pp. 575–97.

Samuelson, Paul A. Yes to Robert Dorfman's Vindication of Thünen's Natural-Wage Derivation [Thünen at Two Hundred]. *J. Econ. Lit.*, December 1986, *24*(4), pp. 1777–85.

0317 Socialist and Marxian until 1945

Abeysinghe, Tilak. Rising Needs and Falling Family Size: Implications from Marx on Demographic Transition. *Rev. Soc. Econ.*, December 1986, *44*(3), pp. 281–93.

Amariglio, Jack and Callari, Antonio. Marxian Economics and Freedom: A Comment. *Eastern Econ. J.*, Jan.-Mar. 1986, *12*(1), pp. 73–78.

Bengelsdorf, Carollee. State and Society in the Transition to Socialism: The Theoretical Legacy. **In** *Fagen, R. R.; Deere, C. D. and Coraggio, J. L., eds.*, 1986, pp. 192–211.

Bharadwaj, Krishna. Production and Exchange in Theories of Price Formation and Economic Transition. **In** *Baranzini, M. and Scazzieri, R., eds.*, 1986, pp. 339–60.

Brewer, Anthony. Marx's *Capital* Today. **In** *Black, R. D. C., ed.*, 1986, pp. 160–75.

Bukharin, Nikolai. Notes of an Economist (the Beginning of the New Economic Year). **In** *Smith, K., ed.*, 1986, *1979*, pp. 50–77. **[G: U.S.S.R.]**

Burkett, Paul. Dillard on Keynes and Marx: Comment. *J. Post Keynesian Econ.*, Summer 1986, *8*(4), pp. 623–31.

Callari, Antonio. History, Epistemology, and Marx's Theory of Value. **In** *Zarembka, P., ed.*, 1986, pp. 69–93.

Carling, Alan. Forms of Value and the Logic of Capital. *Sci. Soc.*, Spring 1986, *50*(1), pp. 52–80.

Chesnais, Francois. Marx's Crisis Theory Today. **In** *Freeman, C., ed.*, 1986, pp. 186–93.

Cleaver, Harry. Karl Marx: Economist or Revolutionary? **In** *Helburn, S. W. and Bramhall, D. F., eds.*, 1986, pp. 121–46.

Cohen, G. A. Historical Inevitability and Human Agency in Marxism. **In** *Mason, J.; Mathias, P. and Westcott, J. H., eds.*, 1986, pp. 65–83.

Delabre, Guy and Gautier, Jean-Marie. Quelques réflexions sur l'ambiguïté réformisme—Révolution dans l'"utopie" de Saint-Simon, Owen et Fourier. (Some Thoughts on the Ambiguity "Reformism-Revolution" in the Utopia of Saint-Simon, Owen and Fourier. With English summary.) *Écon. Soc.*, March 1986, *20*(3), pp. 65–94.

Devine, James N. Empirical Studies in Marxian Crisis Theory: Introduction. *Rev. Radical Polit. Econ.*, Spring/Summer 1986, *18*(1/2), pp. 1–12.

Dillard, Dudley. Dillard on Keynes and Marx: Rejoinder. *J. Post Keynesian Econ.*, Summer 1986, *8*(4), pp. 632–37.

Dostaler, Giles. Understanding the Significance of Piero Sraffa's Standard Commodity: A Note on the Marxian Notion of Surplus: "From Marx to Sraffa": Comments. *Hist. Polit. Econ.*, Fall 1986, *18*(3), pp. 463–69.

Dutton, H. I. and King, J. E. "A Private, Perhaps, but Not a Major...": The Reception of C. H. Douglas's Social Credit Ideas in Britain, 1919–1939. *Hist. Polit. Econ.*, Summer 1986, *18*(2), pp. 259–79.

Ehrbar, Hans and Glick, Mark. The Labor Theory of Value and Its Critics. *Sci. Soc.*, Winter 1986-1987, *50*(4), pp. 464–78.

Elliott, John E. On the Possibility of Marx's Moral Critique of Capitalism. *Rev. Soc. Econ.*, October 1986, *44*(2), pp. 130–45.

Faccarello, Gilbert. Understanding the Significance of Piero Sraffa's Standard Commodity: A Note on the Marxian Notion of Surplus: "Understanding Sraffa's Standard Commodity": A Comment. *Hist. Polit. Econ.*, Fall 1986, *18*(3), pp. 471–78.

Fatton, Robert, Jr. Hegel and the Riddle of Poverty: The Limits of Bourgeois Political Economy. *Hist. Polit. Econ.*, Winter 1986, *18*(4), pp. 579–600.

Feiner, Susan F. Property Relations and Class Relations in Genovese and the Modes of Production Controversy. *Cambridge J. Econ.*, March 1986, *10*(1), pp. 61–75.

Gottheil, Fred M. Marx versus Marxists on the Role of Military Production in Capitalist Economies. *J. Post Keynesian Econ.*, Summer 1986, *8*(4), pp. 563–73.

Gottheil, Fred M. Marxism and Military Spending: A Reply. *J. Post Keynesian Econ.*, Summer 1986, *8*(4), pp. 581–84.

Groenewegen, Peter. Professor Porta on the Significance of Understanding Sraffa's Standard Commodity and the Marxian Theory of Surplus: A Comment. *Hist. Polit. Econ.*, Fall 1986, *18*(3), pp. 455–62.

Haupt, Georges. From Marx to Marxism. **In** *Haupt, G.*, 1986, *1978*, pp. 1–22.

Haupt, Georges. The Commune as Symbol and Example. **In** *Haupt, G.*, 1986, *1972*, pp. 23–47. **[G: France]**

Helburn, Suzanne W. Marx's Research Program. **In** *Helburn, S. W. and Bramhall, D. F., eds.*, 1986, pp. 67–94.

Higgins, Winton. Policy Formation and Marxist Reformism. **In** *Dowdy, E., ed.*, 1986, pp. 48–66.

Hollander, Samuel. Marx and Malthusianism: Reply. *Amer. Econ. Rev.*, June 1986, *76*(3), pp. 548–50.

Hunt, E. K. The Putative Defects of Socialist Economic Planning: Reply [Was Marx a Utopian Socialist?]. *Sci. Soc.*, Spring 1986, *50*(1), pp. 102–07.

Jamieson, Dale. Reflections on Economics and Morality: Hegel, Marx, and the Neoclassical Tradition. **In** *Helburn, S. W. and Bramhall, D. F., eds.*, 1986, pp. 336–43.

Kamenka, Eugene. The Rise and Fall of Marxist Ideology in Communist Countries. **In** *Dowdy, E., ed.*, 1986, pp. 67–92. **[G: U.S.S.R.; China]**

Lavoie, Donald C. Marx, the Quantity Theory, and the Theory of Value. *Hist. Polit. Econ.*, Spring 1986, *18*(1), pp. 155–70.

Littlejohn, Gary. State, Plan and Market in the Transition to Socialism: The Legacy of Bukharin. **In** *Smith, K., ed.*, 1986, *1979*, pp. 78–111. **[G: U.S.S.R.]**

Matthaei, Julie A. Reply [Freedom and Unfreedom in Marxian Economics]. *Eastern Econ. J.*, Jan.-Mar. 1986, *12*(1), pp. 78–80.

McLennan, George. Marxist Theory and Historical Research: Between the Hard and Soft Options. *Sci. Soc.*, Spring 1986, *50*(1), pp. 85–95.

Miyao, Takahiro. Marx's Transformation Problem and Sraffa's Standard Commodity. *Econ. Stud. Quart.*, September 1986, *37*(3), pp. 193–98.

Musgrave, Richard A. Theories of Fiscal Crises: An Essay in Fiscal Sociology. **In** *Musgrave, R. A., Vol. 2*, 1986, *1980*, pp. 175–99. **[G: U.S.]**

Negishi, Takashi. Marx and Böhm-Bawerk. *Econ. Stud. Quart.*, March 1986, *37*(1), pp. 2–10.

Nove, Alec. Marx, the Market and 'Feasible Socialism.' **In** *Nove, A.*, 1986, *1979*, pp. 51–62.

Porta, Pier Luigi. Understanding the Significance of Piero Sraffa's Standard Commodity: A Rejoinder. *Hist. Polit. Econ.*, Fall 1986, *18*(3), pp. 479–84.

Porta, Pier Luigi. Understanding the Significance of Piero Sraffa's Standard Commodity: A Note on the Marxian Notion of Surplus. *Hist. Polit. Econ.*, Fall 1986, *18*(3), pp. 443–54.

Ramirez, Miguel D. Marx and Malthusianism: Comment. *Amer. Econ. Rev.*, June 1986, *76*(3), pp. 543–47.

Rattansi, Ali. Marxian Socialism, Division of Labor and Exchange [Was Marx a Utopian Socialist?]. *Sci. Soc.*, Spring 1986, *50*(1), pp. 96–101.

Riddell, Tom. Marxism and Military Spending. *J. Post Keynesian Econ.*, Summer 1986, *8*(4), pp. 574–80.

Rothschild, Kurt W. Capitalists and Entrepreneurs: Prototypes and Roles. **In** *Wagener, H.-J. and Drukker, J. W., eds.*, 1986, pp. 186–96.

Ruccio, David F. and Simon, Lawrence H. Methodological Aspects of a Marxian Approach to Development: An Analysis of the Modes of Production School. *World Devel.*, Special Issue, Feb. 1986, *14*(2), pp. 211–22.

Samuelson, Larry and Wolfson, Murray. Expository Marxism and Comparative Economic Dynamics. *Hist. Polit. Econ.*, Spring 1986, *18*(1), pp. 65–85.

Samuelson, Paul A. Marx without Matrices: Understanding the Rate of Profit. **In** *Samuelson, P. A.*, 1986, *1983*, pp. 359–74.

Stigler, George J. Bernard Shaw, Sidney Webb and the Theory of Fabian Socialism. **In** *Stigler, G. J.*, 1986, *1983*, pp. 289–302.

Swanson, Paul A. The Labor Theory of Value and Fixed Capital. *Rev. Radical Polit. Econ.*, Fall 1986, *18*(3), pp. 44–64.

Tilly, Richard H. Financing Industrial Enterprise in Great Britain and Germany in the Nineteenth Century: Testing Grounds for Marxist and Schumpeterian Theories? **In** *Wagener, H.-J. and Drukker, J. W., eds.*, 1986, pp. 123–55. **[G: U.K.; Germany]**

Wolff, Richard and Resnick, Stephen. What Are Class Analyses? **In** *Zarembka, P., ed.*, 1986, pp. 1–32.

Zagari, Eugenio. Schumpeter Marx: Note in margine ad un convegno. (With English summary.) *Stud. Econ.*, 1986, *41*(29), pp. 29–52.

Zamkov, O. O. Mathematical Analysis of Extended Reproduction Schemata with a Changing Rate of Surplus Value. *Matekon*, Fall 1986, *23*(1), pp. 25–46.

0318 Historical and Institutional

Arrow, Kenneth J. Thorstein Veblen as an Economic Theorist. **In** *Szenberg, M., ed.*, 1986, *1975*, pp. 47–56.

Claeys, George. Ecology and Technology in Early Nineteenth Century American Utopianism: A Note on John Adolphus Etzler. *Sci. Soc.*, Summer 1986, *50*(2), pp. 219–25.

Dillard, Dudley. The Institutional Principle of the Principles of Economics. *J. Econ. Issues*, June 1986, *20*(2), pp. 355–63.

Dopfer, Kurt. Causality and Consciousness in Economics: Concepts of Change in Orthodox and Heterodox Economics. *J. Econ. Issues*, June 1986, *20*(2), pp. 509–23.

Dyer, Alan W. Semiotics, Economic Development, and the Deconstruction of Economic Man. *J. Econ. Issues*, June 1986, *20*(2), pp. 541–49.

Fischer, Charles C. Institutionalism versus Orthodoxy: The Articulation of Methodological Alternatives. *Amer. J. Econ. Soc.*, July 1986, *45*(3), pp. 359–72.

Gordon, Wendell. Thresholds of Change and Core Policy. *J. Econ. Issues*, June 1986, *20*(2), pp. 489–98.

Griffin, Robert. Thorstein Veblen: The Theory of Evolutionary Economics as a Social Science. *Rivista Int. Sci. Econ. Com.*, December 1986, *33*(12), pp. 1145–65.

Gruchy, Allan G. The Cremona Foundation and the St. Mary's College Conference on Institutional Economics. *J. Econ. Issues*, September 1986, *20*(3), pp. 805–23.

Gunning, J. Patrick. The Methodology of Austrian Economics and Its Relevance to Institutionalism. *Amer. J. Econ. Soc.*, January 1986, *45*(1), pp. 78–91.

Hamilton, David. Technology and Institutions Are Neither. *J. Econ. Issues*, June 1986, *20*(2), pp. 525–32.

Hayden, F. Gregory. Defining and Articulating Social Change through the Social Fabric Matrix and System Digraph. *J. Econ. Issues*, June 1986, *20*(2), pp. 383–92.

Jones, Lamar B. The Institutionalist and *On the Origin of Species*: A Case of Mistaken Identity. *Southern Econ. J.*, April 1986, *52*(4), pp. 1043–55.

Langlois, Richard N. The New Institutional Economics: An Introductory Essay. **In** *Langlois, R. N., ed.*, 1986, pp. 1–25.

Leathers, Charles G. Bellamy and Veblen's "Christian Morals." *J. Econ. Issues*, December 1986, *20*(4), pp. 1107–19.

Lee, Han Yu and Hayden, F. Gregory. DeGregori's *A Theory of Technology:* A Review Article. *J. Econ. Issues*, September 1986, *20*(3), pp. 799–804.

Liebhafsky, Herbert H. Peirce on the *Summum Bonum* and the Unlimited Community; Ayres on "The Criterion of Value." *J. Econ. Issues*, March 1986, *20*(1), pp. 5–20.

Matthews, R. C. O. The Economics of Institutions and the Sources of Growth. *Econ. J.*, December 1986, *96*(384), pp. 903–18.

McCormick, Ken. Towards a Definition of Waste in Economics: A Neoinstitutional Approach. *Rev. Soc. Econ.*, April 1986, *44*(1), pp. 80–92.

McFarland, Floyd B. Clarence Ayres and His Gospel of Technology. *Hist. Polit. Econ.*, Winter 1986, *18*(4), pp. 617–37.

McLoughlin, Peter F. M. A Theory of Technology—Continuity and Change in Human Development: A Review Article. *J. Econ. Issues*, September 1986, *20*(3), pp. 785–98.

Mirowski, Philip. Institutions as a Solution Concept in a Game Theory Context. **In** *Mirowski, P., ed.*, 1986, pp. 241–63.

North, Douglass C. The New Institutional Economics. *J. Inst. Theoretical Econ.*, March 1986, *142*(1), pp. 230–37.

Nowotny, Kenneth. Material Stress and Institutional Change. *J. Econ. Issues*, June 1986, *20*(2), pp. 413–19.

Parsons, Kenneth H. The Relevance of the Ideas of John R. Commons for the Formulation of Agricultural Development Policies: Remarks upon Receipt of the Veblen–Commons Award. *J. Econ. Issues*, June 1986, *20*(2), pp. 281–95. **[G: U.S.]**

Perlman, Mark. Subjectivism and American Institutionalism. **In** *[Lachmann, L. M.]*, 1986, pp. 268–80.

Ramstad, Yngve. A Pragmatist's Quest for Holistic Knowledge: The Scientific Methdology of John R. Commons. *J. Econ. Issues*, December 1986, *20*(4), pp. 1067–1105.

Schotter, Andrew. The Evolution of Rules. **In** *Langlois, R. N., ed.*, 1986, pp. 117–33.

Silber, Jacques G. Rationality, Self Interest and Coordination: On Some Current Controversies in Economics. *Econ. Notes,* 1986, (3), pp. 47–64.

Sobel, Irvin. The Decline of Institutionalism: A Retrospective Appraisal. *Rivista Int. Sci. Econ. Com.*, April 1986, *33*(4), pp. 333–52.

Stabile, Donald R. Veblen and the Political Economy of the Engineer: The Radical Thinker and Engineering Leaders Came to Technocratic Ideas at the Same Time. *Amer. J. Econ. Soc.*, January 1986, *45*(1), pp. 41–52.

Stanković, Fuada. The Relevance of the Phenomenon of "Conspicuous Consumption" for the General Theory of Consumption. *Econ. Anal. Workers' Manage.*, 1986, *20*(4), pp. 375–83.

Swaney, James A. A Coevolutionary Model of Structural Change. *J. Econ. Issues,* June 1986, *20*(2), pp. 393–401.

Williamson, Oliver E. Transaction-Cost Economics: The Governance of Contractual Relations. **In** *Barney, J. B. and Ouchi, W. G., eds.*, 1986, *1979,* pp. 98–129.

Williamson, Oliver E. Transaction-Cost Economics: The Governance of Contractual Relations. **In** *Williamson, O. E.*, 1986, *1979,* pp. 101–30.

032 History of Economic Thought (continued)

0321 Other Schools Since 1800

Hill, Lewis E. Pragmatism, Instrumental Value Theory and Social Economics: Comment. *Rev. Soc. Econ.*, October 1986, *44*(2), pp. 193–95. **[G: U.S.]**

Humphrey, Thomas M. Bullionists' Exchange Rate Doctrines and Current Policy Debates. **In** *Humphreys, T. M.*, 1986, *1980,* pp. 251–54. **[G: U.K.]**

Humphrey, Thomas M. On Cost-Push Theories of Inflation in the Pre-war Monetary Literature. **In** *Humphreys, T. M.*, 1986, *1976,* pp. 19–25.

Humphrey, Thomas M. The Monetarist–Nonmonetarist Debate: Some 19th Century Controversies Revisited. **In** *Humphreys, T. M.*, 1986, *1970,* pp. 299–303. **[G: U.K.]**

Lutz, Mark A. Instrumental Value Theory and Social Economics: A Rejoinder. *Rev. Soc. Econ.*, October 1986, *44*(2), pp. 196–200. **[G: U.S.]**

Mott, Tracy. Marx, Keynes, and Schumpeter: A Synthesis with Special Emphasis on the Contributions of Michal Kalecki. **In** *Helburn, S. W. and Bramhall, D. F., eds.*, 1986, pp. 327–35.

Mueller, Franz H. Catholic Social Doctrine between Scylla and Charybdis? Some Comments on Two Books. *Rev. Soc. Econ.*, April 1986, *44*(1), pp. 40–56.

Popescu, Oreste. El Pensamiento Económico en la Escolástica Hispanoamericana. (The Economic Thought in the Hispanoamerican Scholastic. With English summary.) *Económica (La Plata),* July-December 1986, *32*(2), pp. 227–60. **[G: Spain; Latin America]**

Rostow, Walt W. My Life Philosophy. *Amer. Econ.*, Fall 1986, *30*(2), pp. 3–13.

Siven, Claes-Henric. Errata: The End of the Stockholm School. *Scand. J. Econ.*, 1986, *88*(3), pp. 571.

Stigler, George J. The Process and Progress of Economics. **In** *Stigler, G. J.*, 1986, *1983,* pp. 134–49.

Vandewalle, Gaston. Romanticism and Neo-romanticism in Political Economy. *Hist. Polit. Econ.*, Spring 1986, *18*(1), pp. 33–47.

0322 Individuals

Aftalion, Albert

Rainelli, Michel. Loi du prix unique et théorie de la parité des pouvoirs d'achat: un retour à G. Cassal, A. Aftalion et J. Viner. (With English summary.) *Revue Écon. Polit.*, Jan.-Feb. 1986, *96*(1), pp. 25–38.

Andrews, P. W. S.

Lee, Fred S., et al. P. W. S. Andrews' Theory of Competitive Oligopoly: A New Interpretation. *Brit. Rev. Econ. Issues,* Autumn 1986, *8*(19), pp. 13–39.

Aristotle

Temple-Smith, Richard. Aristotle as a Welfare Economist: A Comment. *Hist. Polit. Econ.*, Fall 1986, *18*(3), pp. 523–28.

Worland, Stephen T. Aristotle and Welfare Economics: A Reply. *Hist. Polit. Econ.*, Fall 1986, *18*(3), pp. 528–29.

Arndt, H. W.

Swan, T. W. Perceptions in Kaleidoscope. *Australian Econ. Rev.*, 4th Quarter 1986, (76), pp. 45–47.

Arrow, Kenneth J.

Arrow, Kenneth J. Lives of the Laureates: Kenneth J. Arrow. **In** *Breit, W. and Spencer, R. W., eds.*, 1986, pp. 43–58.

Feiwel, George R. Shafts from Arrow's Bow: Advance in and beyond Economic Theory. *Economia (Portugal),* May 1986, *10*(2), pp. 229–75.

Ayres, Clarence

Liebhafsky, Herbert H. Peirce on the *Summum Bonum* and the Unlimited Community; Ayres on "The Criterion of Value." *J. Econ. Issues,* March 1986, *20*(1), pp. 5–20.

McFarland, Floyd B. Clarence Ayres and His Gospel of Technology. *Hist. Polit. Econ.*, Winter 1986, *18*(4), pp. 617–37.

Bagehot, Walter

Fforde, John Standish. Walter Bagehot and the Theory of Central Banking: Comment. **In** *Capie, F. and Wood, G. E., eds.*, 1986, pp. 185–89.

Rockoff, Hugh. Walter Bagehot and the Theory of Central Banking. **In** *Capie, F. and Wood, G. E., eds.*, 1986, pp. 160–80.

Schiltknecht, Kurt. Walter Bagehot and the Theory of Central Banking: Comment. **In** *Capie, F. and Wood, G. E., eds.*, 1986, pp. 181–84.

Bagiotti, Tullio

Gasparini, Innocenzo. Unità di visione e di cultura nel pensiero di Tullio Bagiotti. (Unity of Vision and Culture in Tullio Bagiotti's Thought. With English summary.) *Rivista Int. Sci. Econ. Com.*, February 1986, *33*(2), pp. 97–103.

Landenna, Giampiero. Profilo scientifico e umano di Tullio Bagiotti. (Tullio Bagiotti: The Man and the Scholar. With English summary.) *Rivista Int. Sci. Econ. Com.*, January 1986, *33*(1), pp. 1–5.

Bauer, Otto

Bauer, Otto. Otto Bauer's 'Accumulation of Capital' (1913). *Hist. Polit. Econ.*, Spring 1986, *18*(1), pp. 87–110.

Samuelson, Larry and Wolfson, Murray. Expository Marxism and Comparative Economic Dynamics. *Hist. Polit. Econ.*, Spring 1986, *18*(1), pp. 65–85.

Baumol, William J.

Baumol, William J. Microtheory: Applications and Origins: Introduction. **In** *Baumol, W. J.*, 1986, pp. viii–xxvii.

Bellamy, Edward

Leathers, Charles G. Bellamy and Veblen's "Christian Morals." *J. Econ. Issues*, December 1986, *20*(4), pp. 1107–19.

Bentham, Jeremy

Schwartz, Pedro. Jeremy Bentham's Democratic Despotism. **In** *Black, R. D. C., ed.*, 1986, pp. 74–103.

Bergson, Abram

Samuelson, Paul A. Bergsonian Welfare Economics. **In** *Samuelson, P. A.*, 1986, *1981*, pp. 3–46.

von Böhm-Bawerk, Eugen

Dahmén, Erik. Rights and Relations in Modern Economic Theory: Comment. **In** *Day, R. H. and Eliasson, G., eds.*, 1986, pp. 342–43.

Eliasson, Gunnar. Rights and Relations in Modern Economic Theory: Comment. **In** *Day, R. H. and Eliasson, G., eds.*, 1986, pp. 346–50.

Negishi, Takashi. Marx and Böhm-Bawerk. *Econ. Stud. Quart.*, March 1986, *37*(1), pp. 2–10.

von Weizsäcker, Carl Christian. Rights and Relations in Modern Economic Theory. **In** *Day, R. H. and Eliasson, G., eds.*, 1986, *1984*, pp. 317–41.

Ysander, Bengt-Christer. Rights and Relations in Modern Economic Theory: Comment. **In** *Day, R. H. and Eliasson, G., eds.*, 1986, pp. 344–45.

Boulding, Kenneth

Harcourt, Geoffrey C. A Man for All Systems: Talking with Kenneth Boulding. **In** *[Harcourt, G. C.]*, 1986, *1983*, pp. 46–59.

Brentano, F.

Chisholm, Roderick M. Brentano on Preference, Desire and Intrinsic Value. **In** *Grassl, W. and Smith, B., eds.*, 1986, pp. 182–95.

Bresciani Turroni, Costantino

Arcelli, Mario. The Relevance of Costantino Bresciani Turroni. *Rev. Econ. Cond. Italy*, Sept.-Dec. 1986, (3), pp. 413–16.

Dornbusch, Rudiger. Money, Interest Rates and Stabilization. *Rev. Econ. Cond. Italy*, Sept.-Dec. 1986, (3), pp. 439–53. **[G: W. Germany]**

de Rosa, Luigi. Bresciani Turroni and the Devaluation of the German Mark. *Rev. Econ. Cond. Italy*, Sept.-Dec. 1986, (3), pp. 425–38. **[G: W. Germany]**

Talamona, Mario. Bresciani Turroni, Keynes and the Problem of Unemployment in Italy. *Rev. Econ. Cond. Italy*, Sept.-Dec. 1986, (3), pp. 541–57. **[G: Italy]**

Cantillon, Richard

Giacomin, Alberto. Un modello economico dell'*ancien regime:* il "saggio sulla natura del commercio in generale" di Richard Cantillon. (An Economic Model of the the *Ancient Regime:* Richard Cantillon's "Essay on the Nature of Trade in General." With English summary.) *Ricerche Econ.*, Jan.-Mar. 1986, *40*(1), pp. 96–129.

Carey, Henry

Perelman, Michael. Political Economy and the Press: Karl Marx and Henry Carey at the New York Tribune. *Econ. Forum*, Winter 1986-1987, *16*(1), pp. 111–28.

Cassal, Gustav

Rainelli, Michel. Loi du prix unique et théorie de la parité des pouvoirs d'achat: un retour à G. Cassal, A. Aftalion et J. Viner. (With English summary.) *Revue Écon. Polit.*, Jan.-Feb. 1986, *96*(1), pp. 25–38.

de Celis, Manuel Rubín

Street, Donald R. The Authorship of Campomanes' *Discurso sobre el fomento de la industria popular:* A Note. *Hist. Polit. Econ.*, Winter 1986, *18*(4), pp. 655–60.

Chamberlin, Edward

Skinner, Andrew S. Edward Chamberlin: The Theory of Monopolistic Competition: A Reorientation of the Theory of Value. *J. Econ. Stud.*, 1986, *13*(5), pp. 27–44.

Chevalier, Michel

Vinokur, Annie. Political Economy between Faith and Works: Saint-Simonism and the Case of Michel Chevalier. *Écon. Soc.*, October 1986, *20*(10), pp. 175–202.

Cheysson, Émile

Hébert, Robert F. Émile Cheysson and the Birth of Econometrics. *Écon. Soc.*, October 1986, *20*(10), pp. 203–22.

Commons, John R.

Chasse, John Dennis. John R. Commons and the Democratic State. *J. Econ. Issues*, September 1986, *20*(3), pp. 759–84.

Ramstad, Yngve. A Pragmatist's Quest for Holistic Knowledge: The Scientific Methodology of John R. Commons. *J. Econ. Issues*, December 1986, *20*(4), pp. 1067–1105.

Cootner, Paul

Samuelson, Paul A. Paul Cootner's Reconciliation of Economic Law with Chance. **In** *Samuelson, P. A.*, 1986, *1982*, pp. 537–53.

Daniels, G. N.

Ashton, Thomas Southcliffe. Recollections of Four British Economic Historians. *Banca Naz. Lavoro Quart. Rev.*, September 1986, (158), pp. 337–52.

Davenant, Charles

Creedy, John. On the King–Davenant "Law" of Demand. *Scot. J. Polit. Econ.*, August 1986, *33*(3), pp. 193–212.

Debreu, Gerard

Samuelson, Paul A. The 1983 Nobel Prize in Economics. **In** *Samuelson, P. A.*, 1986, *1983*, pp. 838–40.

Dmitriev, V. K.

Skourtos, M. Market Processes in a Ricardian Framework: The Case of V. K. Dmitriev. *Metroecon.*, October 1986, *38*(3), pp. 229–55. **[G: U.K.]**

Domar, Evsey D.

Asimakopulos, Athanasios. Harrod and Domar on Dynamic Economics. *Banca Naz. Lavoro Quart. Rev.*, September 1986, (158), pp. 275–98.

Douglas, Clifford Hugh

Dutton, H. I. and King, J. E. "A Private, Perhaps, but Not a Major...": The Reception of C. H. Douglas's Social Credit Ideas in Britain, 1919–1939. *Hist. Polit. Econ.*, Summer 1986, *18*(2), pp. 259–79.

Douglas, Paul

Samuelson, Paul A. Paul Douglas's Measurement of Production Functions and Marginal Productivities. **In** *Samuelson, P. A.*, 1986, *1979*, pp. 203–19.

Dupuit, Jules

Ekelund, Robert B., Jr. and Shieh, Yeung-Nan. Dupuit, Spatial Economics and Optimal Resource Allocation: A French Tradition. *Economica*, November 1986, *53*(212), pp. 483–96.

Eckstein, Otto

Sinai, Allen. Tribute to Otto Eckstein. **In** *Gordon, R. J., ed.*, 1986, pp. 35–36.

Ellet, Charles, Jr.

Bell, Christopher Ross. Charles Ellet, Jr., and the Theory of Optimal Input Choice. *Hist. Polit. Econ.*, Fall 1986, *18*(3), pp. 485–95.

Etzler, John Adolphus

Claeys, George. Ecology and Technology in Early Nineteenth Century American Utopianism: A Note on John Adolphus Etzler. *Sci. Soc.*, Summer 1986, *50*(2), pp. 219–25.

de Finetti, Bruno

Goel, Prem K. Bayesian Inference and Decision Techniques: Essays in Honor of Bruno de Finetti: Introduction. **In** *[de Finetti, B.]*, 1986, pp. 1–9.

Hill, Bruce M. and Lane, David. Conglomerability and Countable Additivity. **In** *[de Finetti, B.]*, 1986, pp. 45–57.

Jaynes, Edwin T. Some Applications and Extensions of the de Finetti Representation Theorem. **In** *[de Finetti, B.]*, 1986, pp. 31–42.

Kadane, Joseph B.; Schervish, Mark J. and Seidenfeld, Teddy. Statistical Implications of Finitely Additive Probability. **In** *[de Finetti, B.]*, 1986, pp. 59–76.

Piccinato, Ludovico. De Finetti's Logic of Uncertainty and Its Impact on Statistical Thinking and Practice. **In** *[de Finetti, B.]*, 1986, pp. 13–30.

Fisher, Ronald A.

Samuelson, Paul A. Generalizing Fisher's "Reproductive Value": "Incipient" and "Penultimate" Reproductive-Value Functions When Environment Limits Growth; Linear Approximants for Nonlinear Mendelian Mating Models. **In** *Samuelson, P. A.*, 1986, *1978*, pp. 782–86.

Samuelson, Paul A. Generalizing Fisher's "Reproductive Value": Overlapping and Nonoverlapping Generations with Competing Genotypes. **In** *Samuelson, P. A.*, 1986, *1978*, pp. 777–81.

Samuelson, Paul A. Generalizing Fisher's "Reproductive Value": Linear Differential and Difference Equations of "Dilute" Biological Systems. **In** *Samuelson, P. A.*, 1986, *1977*, pp. 769–72.

Samuelson, Paul A. Generalizing Fisher's "Reproductive Value": Nonlinear, Homogeneous, Biparental Systems. **In** *Samuelson, P. A.*, 1986, *1978*, pp. 773–76.

Fourier, Charles

Delabre, Guy and Gautier, Jean-Marie. Quelques réflexions sur l'ambiguïté réformisme—Révolution dans l'"utopie" de Saint-Simon, Owen et Fourier. (Some Thoughts on the Ambiguity "Reformism-Revolution" in the Utopia of Saint-Simon, Owen and Fourier. With English summary.) *Écon. Soc.*, March 1986, *20*(3), pp. 65–94.

Fox, Karl A.

Fox, Karl A. A Scientific Autobiography. *J. Behav. Econ.*, Winter 1986, *15*, pp. 105–29.

Frank, Andre Gunder

Simon, Lawrence H. and Ruccio, David F. A Methodological Analysis of Dependency Theory: Explanation in Andre Gunder Frank. *World Devel.*, Special Issue, Feb. 1986, *14*(2), pp. 195–209.

Friedman, Milton

Friedman, Milton. Lives of the Laureates: Milton Friedman. **In** *Breit, W. and Spencer, R. W., eds.*, 1986, pp. 77–92.

Hirsch, Abraham and de Marchi, Neil. Making a Case When Theory Is Unfalsifiable: Friedman's Monetary History. *Econ. Philos.*, April 1986, *2*(1), pp. 1–21.

Galbraith, John Kenneth

Stigler, George J. A Certain Galbraith in an Uncertain Age. **In** *Stigler, G. J.*, 1986, *1985*, pp. 352–59.

Gall, Ludwig Lambert

Zinn, Karl Georg. Zur Frühgeschichte des "theoretischen Interventionismus." Zugleich eine Erinnerung an Heinrich Ludwig Lambert Gall (1794–1863). (On the Early History of Theoretical Interventionism. The Socialist Underconsumption Theory of the German Ludwig Gall [1794–1863]. With English summary.) *Z. Wirtschaft. Sozialwissen.*, 1986, *106*(2), pp. 139–65.

Genovese, Eugene

Feiner, Susan F. Property Relations and Class Relations in Genovese and the Modes of Production Controversy. *Cambridge J. Econ.*, March 1986, *10*(1), pp. 61–75.

George, Henry

Benestad, J. Brian. Henry George and the Catholic Views of Morality and the Common Good, II: George's Proposals in the Context of Perennial Philosophy. *Amer. J. Econ. Soc.*, January 1986, *45*(1), pp. 115–23. **[G: George, Henry]**

Buurman, Gary B. Henry George and the Institution of Private Property in Land: A Property Rights Approach. *Amer. J. Econ. Soc.*, October 1986, *45*(4), pp. 489–502. **[G: U.S.]**

Sandilands, Roger J. Natural Law and the Political Economy of Henry George. *J. Econ. Stud.*, 1986, *13*(5), pp. 4–15.

Schwartzman, Jack. Henry George and the Ethics of Economics. *Amer. J. Econ. Soc.*, January 1986, *45*(1), pp. 101–14.

Silagi, Michael. Henry George and Europe: As Social Philosopher, He Was Seen as Synthesizing Jefferson, the Enlightenment and Mother Earth. *Amer. J. Econ. Soc.*, July 1986, *45*(3), pp. 373–84.

Silagi, Michael. Henry George and Europe: The Far-reaching Effect of the Ideas of the American Social Philosopher at the Turn of the Century. *Amer. J. Econ. Soc.*, April 1986, *45*(2), pp. 201–13.

Giffen, Robert

Kohli, Ulrich. Robert Giffen and the Irish Potato: Note. *Amer. Econ. Rev.*, June 1986, *76*(3), pp. 539–42. **[G: Ireland]**

Goodwin, Richard

Harcourt, Geoffrey C. A Twentieth-Century Eclectic: Richard Goodwin. **In** *[Harcourt, G. C.]*, 1986, *1985*, pp. 60–72.

Gray, Lewis C.

Crabbé, Philippe. Gray and Hotelling: A Reply [The Contribution of L. C. Gray to the Economic Theory of Exhaustible Natural Resources and Its Roots in the History of Economic Thought]. *J. Environ. Econ. Manage.*, September 1986, *13*(3), pp. 295–300.

Smith, Gerald Alonzo. Gray and Hotelling: A Comment [The Contribution of L. C. Gray to the Economic Theory of Exhaustible Natural Resources and Its Roots in the History of Economic Thought]. *J. Environ. Econ. Manage.*, September 1986, *13*(3), pp. 292–94.

Gutenberg, Erich

Albach, Horst. Allgemeine Betriebswirtschaftslehre Zum Gedenken an Erich Gutenberg. (With English summary.) *Z. Betriebswirtshaft*, July 1986, *56*(7), pp. 578–613.

Harrod, Roy Forbes

Asimakopulos, Athanasios. Harrod and Domar on Dynamic Economics. *Banca Naz. Lavoro Quart. Rev.*, September 1986, (158), pp. 275–98.

von Hayek, Friedrich A.

Boehm, Stephan. Time and Equilibrium: Hayek's Notion of Intertemporal Equilibrium Reconsidered. **In** *[Lachmann, L. M.]*, 1986, pp. 16–29.

Boland, Lawrence A. Methodology and the Individual Decision Maker. **In** *[Lachmann, L. M.]*, 1986, pp. 30–38.

Fischer, Stanley. Friedman versus Hayek on Private Money: Review Essay. *J. Monet. Econ.*, May 1986, *17*(3), pp. 433–39.

Klausinger, Hansjörg. "Hayek Re-Analyzed": A Note [F. A. Hayek's "Prices and Production" Re-Analyzed]. *Jahr. Nationalökon. Statist.*, July 1986, *201*(4), pp. 422–28.

Lachmann, Ludwig M. Austrian Economics under Fire: The Hayek–Sraffa Duel in Retrospect. **In** *Grassl, W. and Smith, B., eds.*, 1986, pp. 225–42.

Moss, Laurence S. and Vaughn, Karen I. Hayek's Ricardo Effect: A Second Look. *Hist. Polit. Econ.*, Winter 1986, *18*(4), pp. 545–65.

Shearmur, Jeremy. The Austrian Connection: Hayek's Liberalism and the Thought of Carl Menger. **In** *Grassl, W. and Smith, B., eds.*, 1986, pp. 210–24.

Vanberg, Viktor. Spontaneous Market Order and Social Rules: A Critical Examination of F. A. Hayek's Theory of Cultural Evolution. *Econ. Philos.*, April 1986, *2*(1), pp. 75–100.

Hegel, G. W. F.

Fatton, Robert, Jr. Hegel and the Riddle of Poverty: The Limits of Bourgeois Political Economy. *Hist. Polit. Econ.*, Winter 1986, *18*(4), pp. 579–600.

Herrmann, Emanuel

Haller, Rudolf. Emanuel Herrmann: On an Almost Forgotten Chapter of Austrian Intellectual History. **In** *Grassl, W. and Smith, B., eds.*, 1986, pp. 196–209.

Hicks, John

Maes, Ivo. Did the Keynesian Revolution Retard the Development of Portfolio Theory? *Banca Naz. Lavoro Quart. Rev.*, December 1986, (159), pp. 407–21.

Malinvaud, Edmond. Reflecting on the Theory of Capital and Growth. *Oxford Econ. Pap.*, November 1986, *38*(3), pp. 367–85.

Pekkarinen, Jukka. Early Hicks and Keynesian Monetary Theory: Different Views on Liquidity Preference. *Hist. Polit. Econ.*, Summer 1986, *18*(2), pp. 335–49.

Hirschman, Albert O.

McPherson, Michael S. The Social Scientist as Constructive Skeptic: On Hirschman's Role. **In** *[Hirshman, A. O.]*, 1986, pp. 305–15.

Wilber, Charles K. and Francis, Steven. The Methodological Basis of Hirschman's Development Economics: Pattern Model vs. General Laws. **In** *[Hirshman, A. O.]*, 1986, pp. 317–42.

Wilber, Charles K. and Francis, Steven. The Methodological Basis of Hirschman's Development Economics: Pattern Model vs General

eral Laws. *World Devel.*, Special Issue, Feb. 1986, *14*(2), pp. 181–94.

Hume, David

Samuelson, Paul A. A Corrected Version of Hume's Equilibrating Mechanisms for International Trade. **In** *Samuelson, P. A.*, 1986, *1980*, pp. 397–414.

Hutchison, Terence W.

Meoli, Umberto. Aspetti della metodologia della scienza economica nel pensiero di T. W. Hutchison. (Aspects of the Methodology of Economic Theory in the Thought of T. W. Hutchison. With English summary.) *Ricerche Econ.*, Apr.-Sept. 1986, *40*(2–3), pp. 249–65.

Hutt, William H.

Hazlett, Thomas W. Razing Keynes: An Economist for the Long Run. **In** *[Hutt, W. H.]*, 1986, *1983*, pp. 11–16.

Horwitz, Ralph. Collective Bargaining or Economic Pluralism. **In** *[Hutt, W. H.]*, 1986, pp. 105–24.

Reynolds, Morgan O. An Introduction to W. H. Hutt: An Economist for the Long Run. **In** *[Hutt, W. H.]*, 1986, pp. 7–10.

Reynolds, Morgan O. On *The Economics of the Colour Bar.* **In** *[Hutt, W. H.]*, 1986, pp. 125–52.

Shenfield, Arthur A. *Economists and the Public* Revisited. **In** *[Hutt, W. H.]*, 1986, pp. 87–104.

Jannaccone, Pasquale

Molesti, Romano. La teoria del costo di produzione in Pasquale Jannaccone. (Pasquale Jannaccone's Theory of the Cost of Production. With English summary.) *Rivista Int. Sci. Econ. Com.*, March 1986, *33*(3), pp. 261–80.

Jevons, William Stanley

Bostaph, Samuel and Shieh, Yeung-Nan. W. S. Jevons and Lardner's *Railway Economy. Hist. Polit. Econ.*, Spring 1986, *18*(1), pp. 49–64.

Steedman, Ian. Trade Interest versus Class Interest. *Econ. Polít.*, August 1986, *3*(2), pp. 187–206.

Johannsen, N. A. L. J.

Allsbrook, Ogden O., Jr. N. A. L. J. Johannsen: An Early Monetarist. *J. Inst. Theoretical Econ.*, June 1986, *142*(2), pp. 431–37.

Johnson, Harry G.

Samuelson, Paul A. Correcting the Ricardo Error Spotted in Harry Johnson's Maiden Paper. **In** *Samuelson, P. A.*, 1986, *1977*, pp. 683–94.

Kaldor, Nicholas

Kaldor, Nicholas. Recollections of an Economist. *Banca Naz. Lavoro Quart. Rev.*, March 1986, (156), pp. 3–26.

Pasinetti, Luigi L. Nicholas Kaldor—An Appreciation. *Cambridge J. Econ.*, December 1986, *10*(4), pp. 301–03.

Targetti, Ferdinando. Kaldor. (With English summary.) *Stud. Econ.*, 1986, *41*(30), pp. 3–70.

Kalecki, Michal

Asimakopulos, A. Finance, Investment and Saving: A Reply. *Cambridge J. Econ.*, March 1986, *10*(1), pp. 81–82.

Basile, Liliana and Salvadori, Neri. Kalecki's Pricing Theory: A Reply. *J. Post Keynesian Econ.*, Fall 1986, *9*(1), pp. 159–60.

Lee, Fred S. Reply: [Kalecki's Pricing Theory: Two Comments]. *J. Post Keynesian Econ.*, Fall 1986, *9*(1), pp. 161–62.

Levine, A. L. Reply [Sraffa's *Production of Commodities by Means of Commodities*, Returns to Scale, Relevance, and Other Matters: A Note]. *J. Post Keynesian Econ.*, Fall 1986, *9*(1), pp. 166–68.

Nuti, Domenico Mario. Michal Kalecki's Contribution to the Theory and Practice of Socialist Planning. *Cambridge J. Econ.*, December 1986, *10*(4), pp. 333–53.

Terzi, Andrea. Finance, Investment and Saving: A Comment. *Cambridge J. Econ.*, March 1986, *10*(1), pp. 77–80.

Kerekes, Gabriel T.

Genovese, Frank C. In Memoriam: G. T. Kerekes, 1908–1985. *Amer. J. Econ. Soc.*, January 1986, *45*(1), pp. 125–26.

Keynes, John Maynard

Asimakopulos, A. Finance, Investment and Saving: A Reply. *Cambridge J. Econ.*, March 1986, *10*(1), pp. 81–82.

Asimakopulos, A. Richardson on Asimakopulos on Finance: A Reply [Kalecki and Keynes on Finance, Investment and Saving]. *Cambridge J. Econ.*, June 1986, *10*(2), pp. 199–201.

Beenstock, Michael. The General Theory, Secular Stagnation and the World Economy. **In** *Burton, J., et al.*, 1986, pp. 121–35.

Brems, Hans. Fünfzig Jahre General Theory. (General Theory at Fifty. With English summary.) *Jahr. Nationalökon. Statist.*, May 1986, *201*(3), pp. 213–21.

Bronfenbrenner, Martin. Schumpeter and Keynes as 'Rich Man's Karl Marxes.' **In** *Wagener, H.-J. and Drukker, J. W., eds.*, 1986, pp. 22–30.

Brothwell, John F. *The General Theory* after Fifty Years: Why Are We Not All Keynesians Now? *J. Post Keynesian Econ.*, Summer 1986, *8*(4), pp. 531–47.

Brunner, Karl. Keynes's Intellectual Legacy. **In** *Burton, J., et al.*, 1986, pp. 59–67.

Budd, Alan P. On Keynesian Unemployment and the Unemployment of Keynes. **In** *Burton, J., et al.*, 1986, pp. 139–52.

Burkett, Paul. Dillard on Keynes and Marx: Comment. *J. Post Keynesian Econ.*, Summer 1986, *8*(4), pp. 623–31.

Burton, John. Fifty Years On: Background and Foreground. **In** *Burton, J., et al.*, 1986, pp. 3–24.

Cairncross, Alec. Keynes and the Planned Economy. **In** *Cairncross, A.*, 1986, *1978*, pp. 58–77.

Corry, Bernard. Keynes's Economics: A Revolution in Economic Theory or in Economic

Policy? **In** *Black, R. D. C., ed.*, 1986, pp. 211–37.

Darby, Michael R. and Lothian, James R. Economic Events and Keynesian Ideas: The 1930s and the 1970s. **In** *Burton, J., et al.*, 1986, pp. 71–86.

Dillard, Dudley. Dillard on Keynes and Marx: Rejoinder. *J. Post Keynesian Econ.*, Summer 1986, *8*(4), pp. 632–37.

Dimand, Robert W. Keynes on Inflation and Exchange Rates. *Atlantic Econ. J.*, September 1986, *14*(3), pp. 81–82.

Dimand, Robert W. The Macroeconomics of the *Treatise on Money*. *Eastern Econ. J.*, Oct.-Dec. 1986, *12*(4), pp. 431–50.

Flex, David. The Early Keynes: Logician and Applied Economist. *Challenge*, Sept./Oct. 1986, *29*(4), pp. 51–54.

Foster, Gladys Parker. The Endogeneity of Money and Keynes's *General Theory*. *J. Econ. Issues*, December 1986, *20*(4), pp. 953–68.

Friedman, Milton. Keynes's Political Legacy. **In** *Burton, J., et al.*, 1986, pp. 47–55.

Graziani, Augusto. Keynes' Finance Motive: A Reply. *Econ. Notes*, 1986, (1), pp. 5–9.

Heilbroner, Robert L. Economics and Political Economy: Marx, Keynes, and Schumpeter. **In** *Helburn, S. W. and Bramhall, D. F., eds.*, 1986, pp. 13–26.

Helburn, Suzanne W. Keynes's Research Program. **In** *Helburn, S. W. and Bramhall, D. F., eds.*, 1986, pp. 199–231.

Hicks, John R. Towards a More "General Theory." *Econ. Polít.*, April 1986, *3*(1), pp. 7–19.

Hixson, William F. Keynes's Policies for Financing Recovery from the Great Depression and for Financing World War II. *Écon. Soc.*, Aug.-Sept. 1986, *20*(8–9), pp. 203–17.

Hodgson, Geoff. The Limits to Keynes. **In** *Nolan, P. and Paine, S., eds.*, 1986, pp. 150–64.

Humphrey, Thomas M. Keynes on Inflation. **In** *Humphreys, T. M.*, 1986, *1981*, pp. 38–48.

Kohn, Meir. Monetary Analysis, the Equilibrium Method, and Keynes's "General Theory." *J. Polit. Econ.*, December 1986, *94*(6), pp. 1191–1224.

Kregel, J. A. Laws of the Market and Laws of Motion: An Essay in Comparative Social History. **In** *Wagener, H.-J. and Drukker, J. W., eds.*, 1986, pp. 31–48. **[G: U.S.; U.K.]**

Kregel, J. A. Shylock and Hamlet or Are There Bulls and Bears in the Circuit? *Écon. Soc.*, Aug.-Sept. 1986, *20*(8–9), pp. 11–22.

McCombie, John S. L. Why Cutting Real Wages Will Not Necessarily Reduce Unemployment—Keynes and the "Postulates of the Classical Economics." *J. Post Keynesian Econ.*, Winter 1985-86, *8*(2), pp. 233–48.

Middleton, Elliott. A Behavioral Model of "Animal Spirits." *Metroecon.*, February 1986, *38*(1), pp. 39–51.

Minsky, Hyman P. Money and Crisis in Schumpeter and Keynes. **In** *Wagener, H.-J. and Drukker, J. W., eds.*, 1986, pp. 112–22.

Moggridge, D. E. Keynes and the International Monetary System 1909–46. **In** *[Tarshis, L.]*, 1986, pp. 56–83.

Moggridge, D. E. Keynes and Our Current Discontents. **In** *Helburn, S.W. and Bramhall, D. F., eds.*, 1986, pp. 232–49.

Pekkarinen, Jukka. Early Hicks and Keynesian Monetary Theory: Different Views on Liquidity Preference. *Hist. Polit. Econ.*, Summer 1986, *18*(2), pp. 335–49.

Presley, John R. J. M. Keynes and the Real Balance Effect. *Manchester Sch. Econ. Soc. Stud.*, March 1986, *54*(1), pp. 22–30.

Richardson, David R. Asimakopulos on Kalecki and Keynes on Finance, Investment and Saving. *Cambridge J. Econ.*, June 1986, *10*(2), pp. 191–98.

Riese, Hajo. Keynes, Schumpeter und die Krise. (Keynes, Schumpeter and the Crisis. With English summary.) *Konjunkturpolitik*, 1986, *32*(1/2), pp. 1–26.

Rothschild, Kurt W. Capitalists and Entrepreneurs: Prototypes and Roles. **In** *Wagener, H.-J. and Drukker, J. W., eds.*, 1986, pp. 186–96.

Salant, Walter S. Response: On Rereading Keynes Today. **In** *Helburn, S. W. and Bramhall, D. F., eds.*, 1986, pp. 250–57.

Samuels, Warren J. What Aspects of Keynes's Economic Theories Merit Continued or Renewed Interest? One Interpretation. *J. Post Keynesian Econ.*, Fall 1986, *9*(1), pp. 3–16.

Samuelson, Paul A. The House That Keynes Built. **In** *Samuelson, P. A.*, 1986, *1983*, pp. 279–82.

Samuelson, Paul A. The Keynes Centenary: Sympathy from the Other Cambridge. **In** *Samuelson, P. A.*, 1986, *1983*, pp. 275–78.

Samuelson, Paul A. What Would Keynes Have Thought of Rational Expectation? Comment. **In** *Samuelson, P. A.*, 1986, *1983*, pp. 291–300.

Samuelson, Paul A. 1983: Marx, Keynes and Schumpeter. **In** *Samuelson, P. A.*, 1986, *1983*, pp. 261–74.

Sardoni, Claudio. Marx and Keynes on Effective Demand and Unemployment. *Hist. Polit. Econ.*, Fall 1986, *18*(3), pp. 419–41.

Schefold, Bertram. Schumpeter as a Walrasian Austrian and Keynes as a Classical Marshallian. **In** *Wagener, H.-J. and Drukker, J. W., eds.*, 1986, pp. 93–111.

Smith, Cheryl. Response: Keynes, Capital, and Current Discontents. **In** *Helburn, S. W. and Bramhall, D. F., eds.*, 1986, pp. 258–63.

Snippe, Jan. Finance, Saving and Investment in Keynes's Economics: A Reply. *Cambridge J. Econ.*, December 1986, *10*(4), pp. 373–77.

Talamona, Mario. Bresciani Turroni, Keynes and the Problem of Unemployment in Italy.

Rev. Econ. Cond. Italy, Sept.-Dec. 1986, (3), pp. 541–57. **[G: Italy]**

Terzi, Andrea. Finance, Investment and Saving: A Comment. *Cambridge J. Econ.*, March 1986, *10*(1), pp. 77–80.

Vallageas, Bernard. Le problèmme de la nature du profit et de son agrégation dans le traité sur la monnaie et la théorie généale. (A Restatement of the Theory of Profit in Keynes's Treatise of Money and General Theory. With English summary.) *Écon. Soc.*, Aug.-Sept. 1986, *20*(8–9), pp. 171–88.

Walker, Donald A. Why Keynes's General Theory Was a Success. *Econ. Notes*, 1986, (3), pp. 5–29.

Walters, Alan. Consumption, Savings and the Multiplier. **In** *Burton, J., et al.*, 1986, pp. 89–100.

Wells, Paul. 'Mr Churchill' and the *General Theory*. **In** *[Tarshis, L.]*, 1986, pp. 8–27. **[G: U.K.]**

Yeager, Leland B. The Keynesian Heritage in Economics. **In** *Burton, J., et al.*, 1986, pp. 27–44.

Kindleberger, Charles P.

Kindleberger, Charles P. My Working Philosophy. *Amer. Econ.*, Spring 1986, *30*(1), pp. 13–20.

King, Gregory

Creedy, John. On the King–Davenant "Law" of Demand. *Scot. J. Polit. Econ.*, August 1986, *33*(3), pp. 193–212.

Klein, Lawrence R.

Klein, Lawrence R. Lives of the Laureates: Lawrence R. Klein. **In** *Breit, W. and Spencer, R. W., eds.*, 1986, pp. 21–41.

Samuelson, Paul A. Rigorous Observational Positivism: Klein's Envelope Aggregation; Thermodynamics and Economic Isomorphisms. **In** *Samuelson, P. A.*, 1986, *1983*, pp. 220–57.

Knight, Frank H.

Raines, J. Patrick and Jung, Clarence R. Knight on Religion and Ethics as Agents of Social Change: An Essay to Commemorate the Centennial of Frank H. Knight's Birth. *Amer. J. Econ. Soc.*, October 1986, *45*(4), pp. 429–39.

Krebs, Frederick

Petersen, Jørn Henrik. Three Precursors of Modern Theories of Old-Age Pensions: A Contribution to the History of Social-Policy Doctrines. *Hist. Polit. Econ.*, Fall 1986, *18*(3), pp. 405–17.

Lachmann, Ludwig

Boland, Lawrence A. Methodology and the Individual Decision Maker. **In** *[Lachmann, L. M.]*, 1986, pp. 30–38.

Egger, John B. A Sympathetic Critic of the Austrian Business-Cycle Theory. **In** *[Lachmann, L. M.]*, 1986, pp. 56–71.

Lange, Oscar

Rosefielde, Steven. Competitive Market Socialism Revisited: Impediments to Efficient Price-Fixing. *Comp. Econ. Stud.*, Fall 1986, *28*(3), pp. 17–23.

Laslett, Peter

Wachter, Kenneth W. and Hammel, Eugene A. The Genesis of Experimental History. **In** *[Laslett, P.]*, 1986, pp. 388–406.

Leggett, William

White, Lawrence H. William Leggett: Jacksonian Editorialist as Classical Liberal Political Economist. *Hist. Polit. Econ.*, Summer 1986, *18*(2), pp. 307–24.

Lewis, W. Arthur

Lewis, W. Arthur. Lives of the Laureates: W. Arthur Lewis. **In** *Breit, W. and Spencer, R. W., eds.*, 1986, pp. 1–19.

Wisman, Jon D. The Methodology of W. Arthur Lewis's Development Economics: Economics as Pedagogy. *World Devel.*, Special Issue, Feb. 1986, *14*(2), pp. 165–80.

Lindblom, Charles

Plant, Jeremy F. Charles E. Lindblom's "Decision-Making in Taxation and Expenditures." *Public Budg. Finance*, Summer 1986, *6*(2), pp. 76–86.

Lloyd, William Foster

Gilbert, Geoffrey N. W. F. Lloyd and Socialism: A Note. *Australian Econ. Pap.*, June 1986, *25*(46), pp. 144–46.

Locke, John

Mitchell, Neil J. John Locke and the Rise of Capitalism. *Hist. Polit. Econ.*, Summer 1986, *18*(2), pp. 291–305.

Lösch, August

Batten, David F. Technical Progress and the Implicit Dynamics of Löschian Spatial Demand. **In** *[Lösch, A.]*, 1986, pp. 177–202.

Beckmann, Martin J. From Lösch to Continuous Flow Models. **In** *[Lösch, A.]*, 1986, pp. 123–31.

Chatterji, Manas. August Lösch and Spatial Regularities in the Developing Countries. **In** *[Lösch, A.]*, 1986, pp. 203–17. **[G: India]**

Dziewoński, Kazimierz. The Reception and Influence of Löschian Ideas in Poland. **In** *[Lösch, A.]*, 1986, pp. 67–73. **[G: Poland]**

Felderer, Bernhard. August Lösch on Population Waves. **In** *[Lösch, A.]*, 1986, pp. 47–53.

Funck, Rolf H. August Lösch and the Concept of Region. **In** *[Lösch, A.]*, 1986, pp. 55–66.

Funck, Rolf H. Space–Structure–Economy: A Tribute to August Lösch: Concluding Remarks. **In** *[Lösch, A.]*, 1986, pp. 285–88.

Gould, Peter. August Lösch as a Child of His Time. **In** *[Lösch, A.]*, 1986, pp. 7–19.

Granberg, Alexander. August Lösch's Ideas in the USSR: The Past and the Future. **In** *[Lösch, A.]*, 1986, pp. 75–89. **[G: U.S.S.R.]**

Komorowski, Stanislaw M. Lösch Revisited. **In** *[Lösch, A.]*, 1986, pp. 21–34.

Kuklinski, Antoni. August Lösch—The Prominent Classic of Regional Studies. **In** *[Lösch, A.]*, 1986, pp. 275–83.

Orishimo, Isao. Reception of the Löschian Theory in Japan, and Consideration of Its

Implications for Japanese Regional Planning Policy. **In** *[Lösch, A.]*, 1986, pp. 91–100. **[G: Japan]**

Parr, John B. Economic Flows in Lösch's Modified Urban System. **In** *[Lösch, A.]*, 1986, pp. 103–22.

Ponsard, Claude. August Lösch: A Famous, but Ignored Economist. **In** *[Lösch, A.]*, 1986, pp. 35–45.

Stolper, Wolfgang F. August Lösch: The Record of a Friendship. **In** *[Lösch, A.]*, 1986, pp. 259–73.

Lubbock, John W.

Henderson, James P. Sir John William Lubbock's *On Currency*—"An Interesting Book by a Still More Interesting Man." *Hist. Polit. Econ.*, Fall 1986, *18*(3), pp. 383–404.

Machlup, Fritz

Cohen, Jacob. Fritz Machlup's Swan Song. *Econ. Educ. Rev.*, 1986, *5*(3), pp. 319–23.

Malthus, Thomas Robert

Cocks, Edmond. Malthus on Population in a War-Based Industrial Economy. **In** *Turner, M., ed.*, 1986, pp. 222–35. **[G: France]**

Demeny, Paul. Population and the Invisible Hand. *Demography*, November 1986, *23*(4), pp. 473–87.

Digby, Anne. Malthus and Reform of the English Poor Law. **In** *Turner, M., ed.*, 1986, pp. 157–69. **[G: U.K.]**

Eccleston, Bernard. Malthus, Wages and the Labour Market in England, 1790–1830. **In** *Turner, M., ed.*, 1986, pp. 143–56.

Hollander, Samuel. On Malthus's Population Principle and Social Reform. *Hist. Polit. Econ.*, Summer 1986, *18*(2), pp. 187–235.

Magnusson, Lars. Malthus in Scandinavia, 1799. **In** *Turner, M., ed.*, 1986, pp. 60–70. **[G: Sweden]**

Polkinghorn, Bette A. An Unpublished Letter from Malthus to Jane Marcet, January 22, 1833. *Amer. Econ. Rev.*, September 1986, *76*(4), pp. 845–47.

Prendergast, Renée. Malthus's Discussion of the Corn Ratio Theory of Profits. *Cambridge J. Econ.*, June 1986, *10*(2), pp. 187–89.

Pullen, John M. Correspondence between Malthus and His Parents. *Hist. Polit. Econ.*, Spring 1986, *18*(1), pp. 133–54.

Stapleton, B. Malthus: The Origins of the Principle of Population? **In** *Turner, M., ed.*, 1986, pp. 19–39. **[G: U.K.]**

Vinokur, Annie. Malthusian Ideology and the Crises of the Welfare State. **In** *Turner, M., ed.*, 1986, pp. 170–86. **[G: U.K.]**

Wrigley, E. A. Malthus's Model of a Pre-industrial Economy. **In** *Turner, M., ed.*, 1986, pp. 3–18. **[G: U.K.]**

Marschak, Jacob

Arrow, Kenneth J. Biography of Jacob Marschak. **In** *[Marschak, J.]*, 1986, pp. 337–46.

Marshall, Alfred

Loasby, Brian J. Marshall's Economics of Progress. *J. Econ. Stud.*, 1986, *13*(5), pp. 16–26.

Rima, Ingrid H. The Peculiarities of Labor Markets and the Residuum. *Eastern Econ. J.*, Apr.-June 1986, *12*(2), pp. 158–74.

Whitaker, John K. The Continuing Relevance of Alfred Marshall. **In** *Black, R. D. C., ed.*, 1986, pp. 176–90.

Williams, Philip L. The Place of *Industry and Trade* in the Analysis of Alfred Marshall. **In** *[Yamey, B.]*, 1986, pp. 227–56.

Marx, Karl

Amariglio, Jack and Callari, Antonio. Marxian Economics and Freedom: A Comment. *Eastern Econ. J.*, Jan.-Mar. 1986, *12*(1), pp. 73–78.

Andrews, Marcellus. Response: Is Schumpeter Compatible with Neoclassical Economics? [The Entrepreneur in Marx and Schumpeter]. **In** *Helburn, S. W. and Bramhall, D. F., eds.*, 1986, pp. 179–82.

Ball, Michael. On Marx's Theory of Agricultural Rent: A Reply. **In** *Fine, B., ed.*, 1986, *1980*, pp. 152–74.

Baumol, William J. Marx and the Iron Law of Wages. **In** *Baumol, W. J.*, 1986, *1983*, pp. 259–64.

Baumol, William J. On Marx, the Transformation Problem and Opacity. **In** *Baumol, W. J.*, 1986, *1974*, pp. 247–58.

Baumol, William J. Smith versus Marx on Business Morality and the Social Interest. **In** *Szenberg, M., ed.*, 1986, *1976*, pp. 83–93.

Baumol, William J. Smith vs. Marx on Business Morality and the Social Interest. **In** *Baumol, W. J.*, 1986, *1976*, pp. 241–46.

Bidard, Christian. Baisse tendancielle du taux de profit et marchandise-étalon. (Falling Rate of Profit and the Standard Commodity. With English summary.) *Écon. Appl.*, 1986, *39*(1), pp. 139–54.

Blaug, Mark. Technical Change and Marxian Economics. **In** *Blaug, M.*, 1986, *1960*, pp. 184–96.

Blaug, Mark. The Entrepreneur in Marx and Schumpeter. **In** *Helburn, S. W. and Bramhall, D. F., eds.*, 1986, pp. 167–78.

Brewer, Anthony. Marx's *Capital* Today. **In** *Black, R. D. C., ed.*, 1986, pp. 160–75.

Burkett, Paul. Dillard on Keynes and Marx: Comment. *J. Post Keynesian Econ.*, Summer 1986, *8*(4), pp. 623–31.

Callari, Antonio. History, Epistemology, and Marx's Theory of Value. **In** *Zarembka, P., ed.*, 1986, pp. 69–93.

Catephores, George. The Historical Transformation Problem—A Reply. **In** *Fine, B., ed.*, 1986, *1980*, pp. 180–84.

Collier, Irwin L., Jr. On Marxian Value, Exploitation, and the Transformation Problem: A Geometric Approach. *J. Compar. Econ.*, September 1986, *10*(3), pp. 325–37.

Coram, B. T. Marx, Roemer and the Theory

of the Falling Rate of Profit. *Australian Econ. Pap.*, December 1986, *25*(47), pp. 265–71.

Dillard, Dudley. Dillard on Keynes and Marx: Rejoinder. *J. Post Keynesian Econ.*, Summer 1986, *8*(4), pp. 632–37.

Dostaler, Giles. Understanding the Significance of Piero Sraffa's Standard Commodity: A Note on the Marxian Notion of Surplus: "From Marx to Sraffa": Comments. *Hist. Polit. Econ.*, Fall 1986, *18*(3), pp. 463–69.

Elliott, John E. On the Possibility of Marx's Moral Critique of Capitalism. *Rev. Soc. Econ.*, October 1986, *44*(2), pp. 130–45.

Faccarello, Gilbert. Understanding the Significance of Piero Sraffa's Standard Commodity: A Note on the Marxian Notion of Surplus: "Understanding Sraffa's Standard Commodity": A Comment. *Hist. Polit. Econ.*, Fall 1986, *18*(3), pp. 471–78.

Fine, Ben. Note: A Dissenting Note on the Transformation Problem. **In** *Fine, B., ed.*, 1986, *1983*, pp. 209–14.

Fine, Ben. On the Historical Transformation Problem. **In** *Fine, B., ed.*, 1986, *1980*, pp. 185–87.

Fine, Ben. On Marx's Theory of Agricultural Rent. **In** *Fine, B., ed.*, 1986, *1979*, pp. 114–51.

Fine, Ben. On Marx's Theory of Agricultural Rent: A Rejoinder. **In** *Fine, B., ed.*, 1986, *1980*, pp. 175–79.

Fine, Ben. The Value Dimension: Marx versus Ricardo and Sraffa: Introduction. **In** *Fine, B., ed.*, 1986, pp. 1–17.

Gerstein, Ira. Production, Circulation and Value: The Significance of the 'Transformation Problem' in Marx's Critique of Political Economy. **In** *Fine, B., ed.*, 1986, *1976*, pp. 45–93.

Gottheil, Fred M. Marx versus Marxists on the Role of Military Production in Capitalist Economies. *J. Post Keynesian Econ.*, Summer 1986, *8*(4), pp. 563–73.

Gottheil, Fred M. Marxism and Military Spending: A Reply. *J. Post Keynesian Econ.*, Summer 1986, *8*(4), pp. 581–84.

Groenewegen, Peter. Professor Porta on the Significance of Understanding Sraffa's Standard Commodity and the Marxian Theory of Surplus: A Comment. *Hist. Polit. Econ.*, Fall 1986, *18*(3), pp. 455–62.

Heilbroner, Robert L. Economics and Political Economy: Marx, Keynes, and Schumpeter. **In** *Helburn, S. W. and Bramhall, D. F., eds.*, 1986, pp. 13–26.

Helburn, Suzanne W. Marx's Research Program. **In** *Helburn, S. W. and Bramhall, D. F., eds.*, 1986, pp. 67–94.

Hollander, Samuel. Marx and Malthusianism: Reply. *Amer. Econ. Rev.*, June 1986, *76*(3), pp. 548–50.

Hunt, E. K. Philosophy and Economics in the Writings of Karl Marx. **In** *Helburn, S. W. and Bramhall, D. F., eds.*, 1986, pp. 95–120.

Hunt, E. K. The Putative Defects of Socialist Economic Planning: Reply [Was Marx a Utopian Socialist?]. *Sci. Soc.*, Spring 1986, *50*(1), pp. 102–07.

Lombardini, Siro. L'innovazione. (Innovation. With English summary.) *Rivista Int. Sci. Econ. Com.*, April 1986, *33*(4), pp. 319–32.

Markusen, Ann Roell. Empirical Research in the Marxist and Schumpeterian Traditions: Reflections on Explaining Spatial Change. **In** *Helburn, S. W. and Bramhall, D. F., eds.*, 1986, pp. 267–83.

Matthaei, Julie A. Reply [Freedom and Unfreedom in Marxian Economics]. *Eastern Econ. J.*, Jan.-Mar. 1986, *12*(1), pp. 78–80.

Minkler, Alanson P. In Defense of Marx on the Length of the Working Day. *Econ. Forum*, Winter 1986-1987, *16*(1), pp. 105–10.

Negishi, Takashi. Marx and Böhm-Bawerk. *Econ. Stud. Quart.*, March 1986, *37*(1), pp. 2–10.

Perelman, Michael. Political Economy and the Press: Karl Marx and Henry Carey at the New York Tribune. *Econ. Forum*, Winter 1986-1987, *16*(1), pp. 111–28.

Phillips, Ronnie J. Marx, the Classical Firm, and Economic Planning. *J. Post Keynesian Econ.*, Winter 1985-86, *8*(2), pp. 266–76.

Pilling, Geoffrey. The Law of Value in Ricardo and Marx. **In** *Fine, B., ed.*, 1986, *1972*, pp. 18–44.

Porta, Pier Luigi. Understanding the Significance of Piero Sraffa's Standard Commodity: A Rejoinder. *Hist. Polit. Econ.*, Fall 1986, *18*(3), pp. 479–84.

Porta, Pier Luigi. Understanding the Significance of Piero Sraffa's Standard Commodity: A Note on the Marxian Notion of Surplus. *Hist. Polit. Econ.*, Fall 1986, *18*(3), pp. 443–54.

Ramirez, Miguel D. Marx and Malthusianism: Comment. *Amer. Econ. Rev.*, June 1986, *76*(3), pp. 543–47.

Rattansi, Ali. Marxian Socialism, Division of Labor and Exchange [Was Marx a Utopian Socialist?]. *Sci. Soc.*, Spring 1986, *50*(1), pp. 96–101.

Riddell, Tom. Marxism and Military Spending. *J. Post Keynesian Econ.*, Summer 1986, *8*(4), pp. 574–80.

Samuelson, Paul A. Marx without Matrices: Understanding the Rate of Profit. **In** *Samuelson, P. A.*, 1986, *1983*, pp. 359–74.

Samuelson, Paul A. The Normative and Positivistic Inferiority of Marx's *Values* Paradigm. **In** *Samuelson, P. A.*, 1986, *1982*, pp. 351–58.

Samuelson, Paul A. 1983: Marx, Keynes and Schumpeter. **In** *Samuelson, P. A.*, 1986, *1983*, pp. 261–74.

Sardoni, Claudio. Marx and Keynes on Effective Demand and Unemployment. *Hist. Polit. Econ.*, Fall 1986, *18*(3), pp. 419–41.

Shamsavari, Ali. On the Foundations of Marx's Theory of Money. *Brit. Rev. Econ. Issues*, Spring 1986, *8*(18), pp. 75–98.

Tilly, Richard H. Financing Industrial Enterprise in Great Britain and Germany in the Nineteenth Century: Testing Grounds for Marxist and Schumpeterian Theories? **In** *Wagener, H.-J. and Drukker, J. W., eds.*, 1986, pp. 123–55. **[G: U.K.; Germany]**

Wolfson, Murray; Orzech, Ze'ev B. and Hanna, Susan S. Karl Marx and the Depletion of Human Capital as Open-Access Resource. *Hist. Polit. Econ.*, Fall 1986, *18*(3), pp. 497–514.

Young, Jeffrey T. The Entrepreneur in Marx and Schumpeter: A Post-Keynesian Perspective. **In** *Helburn, S. W. and Bramhall, D. F., eds.*, 1986, pp. 183–95.

Zagari, Eugenio. Schumpeter Marx: Note in margine ad un convegno. (With English summary.) *Stud. Econ.*, 1986, *41*(29), pp. 29–52.

Menger, Carl

O'Driscoll, Gerald P., Jr. Money: Menger's Evolutionary Theory. *Hist. Polit. Econ.*, Winter 1986, *18*(4), pp. 601–16.

Metzler, Lloyd

Samuelson, Paul A. Lloyd Metzler (April 3, 1913–October 26, 1980). **In** *Samuelson, P. A.*, 1986, pp. 827–30.

Mill, James

Baumol, William J. Say's (at Least) Eight Laws, or What Say and James Mill May Really Have Meant. **In** *Baumol, W. J.*, 1986, *1977*, pp. 265–81.

Mill, John Stuart

Fontana, Biancamaria. Democracy and Civilization: John Stuart Mill and the Critique of Political Economy. *Écon. Soc.*, March 1986, *20*(3), pp. 3–24.

Hollander, Samuel. The Relevance of John Stuart Mill: Some Implications for Modern Economics. **In** *Black, R. D. C., ed.*, 1986, pp. 129–59.

Staley, Charles E. Hollander on Mill's Economics and Thomas on Mill's Biography: Review Article. *Scot. J. Polit. Econ.*, August 1986, *33*(3), pp. 298–302.

von Mises, Ludwig Edler

Caldwell, Bruce J. Towards a Broader Conception of Criticism [Praxeology and Its Critics: An Appraisal]. *Hist. Polit. Econ.*, Winter 1986, *18*(4), pp. 675–81.

Hirsch, Abraham. Caldwell on Praxeology and Its Critics: A Reappraisal. *Hist. Polit. Econ.*, Winter 1986, *18*(4), pp. 661–68.

Lavoie, Donald C. Euclideanism versus Hermeneutics: A Reinterpretation of Misesian Apriorism. **In** *[Lachmann, L. M.]*, 1986, pp. 192–210.

Rotwein, Eugene. Flirting with Apriorism: Caldwell on Mises [Praxeology and Its Critics: An Appraisal]. *Hist. Polit. Econ.*, Winter 1986, *18*(4), pp. 669–73.

Modigliani, Franco

Kouri, Pentti J. K. Franco Modigliani's Contributions to Economics. *Scand. J. Econ.*, 1986, *88*(2), pp. 311–34.

Myrdal, Gunnar

Angresano, James. Gunnar Myrdal as a Social Economist. *Rev. Soc. Econ.*, October 1986, *44*(2), pp. 144–58.

Dykema, Eugene R. No View without a Viewpoint: Gunnar Myrdal. *World Devel.*, Special Issue, Feb. 1986, *14*(2), pp. 147–63.

Ohlin, Bertil

Flanders, M. June. The Balance-of-Payments Adjustment Mechanism: The Doctrine According to Ohlin. *Hist. Polit. Econ.*, Summer 1986, *18*(2), pp. 237–57.

Samuelson, Paul A. Bertil Ohlin (1899–1979). **In** *Samuelson, P. A.*, 1986, *1982*, pp. 809–25.

Owen, Robert

Delabre, Guy and Gautier, Jean-Marie. Quelques réflexions sur l'ambiguïté réformisme—Révolution dans l'"utopie" de Saint-Simon, Owen et Fourier. (Some Thoughts on the Ambiguity "Reformism-Revolution" in the Utopia of Saint-Simon, Owen and Fourier. With English summary.) *Écon. Soc.*, March 1986, *20*(3), pp. 65–94.

Parsons, Kenneth H.

Kanel, Don. The Veblen–Commons Award: Kenneth H. Parsons. *J. Econ. Issues*, June 1986, *20*(2), pp. 275–79.

Parsons, Talcott

Holton, Robert J. Talcott Parsons and the Theory of Economy and Society. **In** *Holton, R. J. and Turner, B. S.*, 1986, pp. 25–105.

Peirce, Charles S.

Dyer, Alan W. Veblen on Scientific Creativity: The Influence of Charles S. Peirce. *J. Econ. Issues*, March 1986, *20*(1), pp. 21–41.

Liebhafsky, Herbert H. Peirce on the *Summum Bonum* and the Unlimited Community; Ayres on "The Criterion of Value." *J. Econ. Issues*, March 1986, *20*(1), pp. 5–20.

Peterson, Julius

Petersen, Jørn Henrik. Three Precursors of Modern Theories of Old-Age Pensions: A Contribution to the History of Social-Policy Doctrines. *Hist. Polit. Econ.*, Fall 1986, *18*(3), pp. 405–17.

Petty, William [Sir]

Aspromourgos, Tony. Political Economy and the Social Division of Labour: The Economics of Sir William Petty. *Scot. J. Polit. Econ.*, February 1986, *33*(1), pp. 28–45.

Plant, Arnold

Coase, Ronald H. Professor Sir Arnold Plant: His Ideas and Influence. **In** *[Seldon, A.]*, 1986, pp. 81–90.

Polanyi, Karl

Bugra, Ayşe. Karl Polanyi and the Boundaries of Economics. *METU*, 1986, *13*(3–4), pp. 217–38.

Quesnay, François

Samuelson, Paul A. Quesnay's 'Tableau Economique' as a Theorist Would Formulate It Today. **In** *Samuelson, P. A.*, 1986, *1982*, pp. 630–63.

Ramsey, Frank

Samuelson, Paul A. A Chapter in the History of Ramsey's Optimal Feasible Taxation and Optimal Public Utility Prices. **In** *Samuelson, P. A.*, 1986, *1982*, pp. 76–100.

Redford, Arthur

Ashton, Thomas Southcliffe. Recollections of Four British Economic Historians. *Banca Naz. Lavoro Quart. Rev.*, September 1986, (158), pp. 337–52.

Ricardo, David

Barkai, Haim. Ricardo's Volte-Face on Machinery. *J. Polit. Econ.*, Part 1, June 1986, *94*(3), pp. 595–613.

Blaug, Mark. Ricardo and the Problem of Public Policy. **In** *Blaug, M.*, 1986, pp. 115–27.

Blaug, Mark. The Empirical Content of Ricardian Economics. **In** *Blaug, M.*, 1986, *1956*, pp. 91–114.

Burgstaller, André. Unifying Ricardo's Theories of Growth and Comparative Advantage. *Economica*, November 1986, *53*(212), pp. 467–81.

Faccarello, Gilbert. Sraffa versus Ricardo: The Historical Irrelevance of the 'Corn-Profit' Model. **In** *Fine, B., ed.*, 1986, *1982*, pp. 188–203.

Fine, Ben. On the Economics of Ricardo and Sraffa [Sraffa versus Ricardo: The Historical Irrelevance of the 'Corn-Profit' Model]. **In** *Fine, B., ed.*, 1986, *1983*, pp. 204–08.

Hollander, Samuel. On a 'New Interpretation' of Ricardo's Early Treatment of Profitability. *Econ. J.*, December 1986, *96*(384), pp. 1091–97.

Peach, Terry. David Ricardo's Treatment of Wages. **In** *Black, R. D. C., ed.*, 1986, pp. 104–28.

Peach, Terry. Ricardo's Early Treatment of Profitability: Reply. *Econ. J.*, December 1986, *96*(384), pp. 1105–12.

Pilling, Geoffrey. The Law of Value in Ricardo and Marx. **In** *Fine, B., ed.*, 1986, *1972*, pp. 18–44.

Prendergast, Renée. David Ricardo's Early Treatment of Profitability: A New Interpretation: A Comment. *Econ. J.*, December 1986, *96*(384), pp. 1098–1104.

Prendergast, Renée. Malthus's Discussion of the Corn Ratio Theory of Profits. *Cambridge J. Econ.*, June 1986, *10*(2), pp. 187–89.

Rutherford, Robert P. Ricardo's Mantle. *Australian Econ. Pap.*, December 1986, *25*(47), pp. 206–21.

Samuelson, Paul A. Correcting the Ricardo Error Spotted in Harry Johnson's Maiden Paper. **In** *Samuelson, P. A.*, 1986, *1977*, pp. 683–94.

Samuelson, Paul A. Noise and Signal in Debates among Classical Economists: A Reply. **In** *Samuelson, P. A.*, 1986, *1980*, pp. 618–21.

Richardson, G. B.

Loasby, Brian J. Competition and Imperfect Knowledge: The Contribution of G. B. Richardson. *Scot. J. Polit. Econ.*, May 1986, *33*(2), pp. 145–58.

Roberts, Benjamin Charles

Gennard, John. Ben Roberts: An Appreciation. *Brit. J. Ind. Relat.*, March 1986, *24*(1), pp. 3–23.

Robertson, Dennis H.

Humphrey, Thomas M. Dennis H. Robertson and the Monetary Approach to Exchange Rates. **In** *Humphreys, T. M.*, 1986, *1980*, pp. 220–27.

Robinson, Joan

Harcourt, Geoffrey C. On the Contributions of Joan Robinson and Piero Sraffa to Economic Theory. **In** *[Harcourt, G. C.]*, 1986, *1986*, pp. 90–110.

Harcourt, Geoffrey C. On the Influence of Piero Sraffa on the Contributions of Joan Robinson to Economic Theory. *Econ. J.*, Supplement 1986, *96*, pp. 96–108.

Roemer, John

Coram, B. T. Marx, Roemer and the Theory of the Falling Rate of Profit. *Australian Econ. Pap.*, December 1986, *25*(47), pp. 265–71.

Saint Simon, Claude Henri de Rouvay

Delabre, Guy and Gautier, Jean-Marie. Quelques réflexions sur l'ambiguïté réformisme—Révolution dans l'"utopie" de Saint-Simon, Owen et Fourier. (Some Thoughts on the Ambiguity "Reformism-Revolution" in the Utopia of Saint-Simon, Owen and Fourier. With English summary.) *Écon. Soc.*, March 1986, *20*(3), pp. 65–94.

Samuelson, Paul A.

Samuelson, Paul A. Economics in My Time. **In** *Samuelson, P. A.*, 1986, pp. 797–808.

Samuelson, Paul A. Forewords to the Japanese Edition of *The Collected Scientific Papers of Paul A. Samuelson*. **In** *Samuelson, P. A.*, 1986, *1982*, pp. 858–75.

Samuelson, Paul A. Foundations of Economic Analysis: Introduction to the Enlarged Edition. **In** *Samuelson, P. A.*, 1986, *1983*, pp. 846–57.

Samuelson, Paul A. Lives of the Laureates: Paul A. Samuelson. **In** *Breit, W. and Spencer, R. W., eds.*, 1986, pp. 59–76.

Samuelson, Paul A. My Life Philosophy. **In** *Samuelson, P. A.*, 1986, *1983*, pp. 789–96.

Samuelson, Paul A. Seventieth Birthday Remarks. **In** *Samuelson, P. A.*, 1986, pp. 844–45.

Say, J. B.

Baumol, William J. Say's (at Least) Eight Laws, or What Say and James Mill May Really Have Meant. **In** *Baumol, W. J.*, 1986, *1977*, pp. 265–81.

Breton, Yves. La place de la statistique et de l'arithmétique politique dans la méthodologie économique de Jean-Baptiste Say le temps des ruptures. (The Role of Statistics and Political Arithmetic in the Economic Methodology of Jean-Baptiste Say at the Time of the Ruptures. With English summary.) *Revue Écon.*, November 1986, *37*(6), pp. 1033–62.

Steiner, Philippe. J. B. Say et l'enseignement de l'économie politique en France (1816–1832). (J. B. Say and the Teaching of Political Economy in France. With English summary.) *Écon. Soc.*, October 1986, *20*(10), pp. 63–95.

Schneider, Erich

Brems, Hans. General Equilibrium after Schneider. *Weltwirtsch. Arch.*, 1986, *122*(2), pp. 213–22.

Schumacher, Ernst F.

Hession, Charles H. E. F. Schumacher as Heir to Keynes' Mantle. *Rev. Soc. Econ.*, April 1986, *44*(1), pp. 1–12.

Schumpeter, Joseph A.

Andrews, Marcellus. Response: Is Schumpeter Compatible with Neoclassical Economics? [The Entrepreneur in Marx and Schumpeter]. **In** *Helburn, S. W. and Bramhall, D. F., eds.*, 1986, pp. 179–82.

Blaug, Mark. Entrepreneurship before and after Schumpeter. **In** *Blaug, M.*, 1986, pp. 219–30.

Blaug, Mark. The Entrepreneur in Marx and Schumpeter. **In** *Helburn, S. W. and Bramhall, D. F., eds.*, 1986, pp. 167–78.

Bronfenbrenner, Martin. Schumpeter and Keynes as 'Rich Man's Karl Marxes.' **In** *Wagener, H.-J. and Drukker, J. W., eds.*, 1986, pp. 22–30.

Costabile, Lilia. Metodo della scienza e teoria economica in Schumpeter. Note su "l'essenza e i principi dell'economia teorica." (With English summary.) *Stud. Econ.*, 1986, *41*(29), pp. 147–68.

Feiwel, George R. Schumpeter on Walras, Marshall, and Beyond. *Rivista Int. Sci. Econ. Com.*, August 1986, *33*(8), pp. 763–75.

Heilbroner, Robert L. Economics and Political Economy: Marx, Keynes, and Schumpeter. **In** *Helburn, S. W. and Bramhall, D. F., eds.*, 1986, pp. 13–26.

Helburn, Suzanne W. Schumpeter's Research Program. **In** *Helburn, S. W. and Bramhall, D. F., eds.*, 1986, pp. 149–66.

Lombardini, Siro. L'innovazione. (Innovation. With English summary.) *Rivista Int. Sci. Econ. Com.*, April 1986, *33*(4), pp. 319–32.

Markusen, Ann Roell. Empirical Research in the Marxist and Schumpeterian Traditions: Reflections on Explaining Spatial Change. **In** *Helburn, S. W. and Bramhall, D. F., eds.*, 1986, pp. 267–83.

Minsky, Hyman P. Money and Crisis in Schumpeter and Keynes. **In** *Wagener, H.-J. and Drukker, J. W., eds.*, 1986, pp. 112–22.

Riese, Hajo. Keynes, Schumpeter und die Krise. (Keynes, Schumpeter and the Crisis. With English summary.) *Konjunkturpolitik*, 1986, *32*(1/2), pp. 1–26.

Rothschild, Kurt W. Capitalists and Entrepreneurs: Prototypes and Roles. **In** *Wagener, H.-J. and Drukker, J. W., eds.*, 1986, pp. 186–96.

Samuelson, Paul A. Schumpeter as an Economic Theorist. **In** *Samuelson, P. A.*, 1986, *1982*, pp. 301–27.

Samuelson, Paul A. Schumpeter's *Capitalism, Socialism and Democracy*. **In** *Samuelson, P. A.*, 1986, *1981*, pp. 328–48.

Samuelson, Paul A. The World Economy at Century's End. **In** *Samuelson, P. A.*, 1986, *1983*, pp. 881–900.

Samuelson, Paul A. 1983: Marx, Keynes and Schumpeter. **In** *Samuelson, P. A.*, 1986, *1983*, pp. 261–74.

Schefold, Bertram. Schumpeter as a Walrasian Austrian and Keynes as a Classical Marshallian. **In** *Wagener, H.-J. and Drukker, J. W., eds.*, 1986, pp. 93–111.

Shionoya, Yuichi. The Science and Ideology of Schumpeter. *Rivista Int. Sci. Econ. Com.*, August 1986, *33*(8), pp. 729–62.

Tilly, Richard H. Financing Industrial Enterprise in Great Britain and Germany in the Nineteenth Century: Testing Grounds for Marxist and Schumpeterian Theories? **In** *Wagener, H.-J. and Drukker, J. W., eds.*, 1986, pp. 123–55. **[G: U.K.; Germany]**

Young, Jeffrey T. The Entrepreneur in Marx and Schumpeter: A Post-Keynesian Perspective. **In** *Helburn, S. W. and Bramhall, D. F., eds.*, 1986, pp. 183–95.

Zagari, Eugenio. Schumpeter Marx: Note in margine ad un convegno. (With English summary.) *Stud. Econ.*, 1986, *41*(29), pp. 29–52.

Scitovsky, Tibor

Scitovsky, Tibor. Human Desire and Economic Satisfaction: Preface. **In** *Scitovsky, T.*, 1986, pp. vii–xii.

Seldon, Arthur

Harris, Ralph. The Unfinished Agenda: Essays on the Political Economy of Government Policy in Honour of Arthur Seldon: Prologue: Seldon Man. **In** *[Seldon, A.]*, 1986, pp. 3–11.

Senior, Nassau

De Long, James Bradford. Senior's 'Last Hour': Suggested Explanation of a Famous Blunder. *Hist. Polit. Econ.*, Summer 1986, *18*(2), pp. 325–33.

Shackle, G. L. S.

Dixon, Robert J. Uncertainty, Unobstructedness, and Power. *J. Post Keynesian Econ.*, Summer 1986, *8*(4), pp. 585–90.

Stephen, Frank H. Decision Making under Uncertainty: In Defence of Shackle. *J. Econ. Stud.*, 1986, *13*(5), pp. 45–57.

de Sismondi, Simonde

Vandewalle, Gaston. Romanticism and Neoromanticism in Political Economy. *Hist. Polit. Econ.*, Spring 1986, *18*(1), pp. 33–47.

Smith, Adam

Anderson, Gary M. and Tollison, Robert D. Smith, Steuart, and Mercantilism: Reply [Sir James Steuart as the Apothesis of Mercantilism and His Relation to Adam Smith].

Southern Econ. J., January 1986, *52*(3), pp. 853–56.

Baumol, William J. Smith versus Marx on Business Morality and the Social Interest. **In** *Szenberg, M., ed.*, 1986, *1976*, pp. 83–93.

Baumol, William J. Smith vs. Marx on Business Morality and the Social Interest. **In** *Baumol, W. J.*, 1986, *1976*, pp. 241–46.

Blaug, Mark. Welfare Indices in *The Wealth of Nations*. **In** *Blaug, M.*, 1986, *1959*, pp. 128–34.

Bowles, Paul. Adam Smith and the 'Natural Progress of Opulence.' *Economica*, February 1986, *53*(209), pp. 109–18.

Demeny, Paul. Population and the Invisible Hand. *Demography*, November 1986, *23*(4), pp. 473–87.

Diamond, Arthur M., Jr. The Impact of Smith's Philosophy of Science on His Economics. *Amer. Econ.*, Spring 1986, *30*(1), pp. 60–65.

Henderson, James P. Agency or Alienation? Smith, Mill, and Marx on the Joint-Stock Company. *Hist. Polit. Econ.*, Spring 1986, *18*(1), pp. 111–31.

Letiche, John M. and Dmytryshyn, Basil. The Adam Smith Russian Angle: Student Years of Ivan A. Tretiakov and Simeon E. Desnitskii. *Rivista Int. Sci. Econ. Com.*, January 1986, *33*(1), pp. 7–22.

Musgrave, Richard A. Adam Smith on Public Finance and Distribution. **In** *Musgrave, R. A., Vol. 2*, 1986, *1976*, pp. 254–73.
[G: U.K.; U.S.]

Pesciarelli, Enzo. On Adam Smith's Lectures on Jurisprudence. *Scot. J. Polit. Econ.*, February 1986, *33*(1), pp. 74–85.

Rashid, Salim. Adam Smith and the Division of Labour: A Historical View. *Scot. J. Polit. Econ.*, August 1986, *33*(3), pp. 292–97.

Rashid, Salim. Smith, Steuart, and Mercantilism: Comment [Sir James Steuart as the Apothesis of Mercantilism and His Relation to Adam Smith]. *Southern Econ. J.*, January 1986, *52*(3), pp. 843–52.

Samuelson, Paul A. A Modern Theorist's Vindication of Adam Smith. **In** *Samuelson, P. A.*, 1986, *1977*, pp. 622–29.

Samuelson, Paul A. Noise and Signal in Debates among Classical Economists: A Reply. **In** *Samuelson, P. A.*, 1986, *1980*, pp. 618–21.

Sen, Amartya K. Adam Smith's Prudence. **In** *[Streeten, P.]*, 1986, pp. 28–37.

Skinner, Andrew S. Adam Smith: Then and Now. **In** *Black, R. D. C., ed.*, 1986, pp. 16–42.

Stull, William J. The Urban Economics of Adam Smith. *J. Urban Econ.*, November 1986, *20*(3), pp. 291–311.

Young, Jeffrey T. The Impartial Spectator and Natural Jurisprudence: An Interpretation of Adam Smith's Theory of the Natural Price. *Hist. Polit. Econ.*, Fall 1986, *18*(3), pp. 365–82.

Sraffa, Piero

Bidard, Christian. Production de marchandises, Corrigendum. (Production of Commodities, Corrigendum. With English summary.) *Écon. Appl.*, 1986, *39*(1), pp. 113–38.

Bidard, Christian. The Maximum Rate of Profits in Joint Production. *Metroecon.*, February 1986, *38*(1), pp. 53–66.

Di Ruzza, Renato. Sraffa et la notion d'équilibre. (Sraffa and the Equilibrium Concept. With English summary.) *Écon. Appl.*, 1986, *39*(1), pp. 11–33.

Dostaler, Giles. Understanding the Significance of Piero Sraffa's Standard Commodity: A Note on the Marxian Notion of Surplus: "From Marx to Sraffa": Comments. *Hist. Polit. Econ.*, Fall 1986, *18*(3), pp. 463–69.

Faccarello, Gilbert. Sraffa versus Ricardo: The Historical Irrelevance of the 'Corn-Profit' Model. **In** *Fine, B., ed.*, 1986, *1982*, pp. 188–203.

Faccarello, Gilbert. Understanding the Significance of Piero Sraffa's Standard Commodity: A Note on the Marxian Notion of Surplus: "Understanding Sraffa's Standard Commodity": A Comment. *Hist. Polit. Econ.*, Fall 1986, *18*(3), pp. 471–78.

Fine, Ben. On the Economics of Ricardo and Sraffa [Sraffa versus Ricardo: The Historical Irrelevance of the 'Corn-Profit' Model]. **In** *Fine, B., ed.*, 1986, *1983*, pp. 204–08.

Groenewegen, Peter. Professor Porta on the Significance of Understanding Sraffa's Standard Commodity and the Marxian Theory of Surplus: A Comment. *Hist. Polit. Econ.*, Fall 1986, *18*(3), pp. 455–62.

Harcourt, Geoffrey C. On the Contributions of Joan Robinson and Piero Sraffa to Economic Theory. **In** *[Harcourt, G. C.]*, 1986, *1986*, pp. 90–110.

Harcourt, Geoffrey C. On the Influence of Piero Sraffa on the Contributions of Joan Robinson to Economic Theory. *Econ. J.*, Supplement 1986, *96*, pp. 96–108.

Harcourt, Geoffrey C. On Piero Sraffa's Contributions to Economics. **In** *[Harcourt, G. C.]*, 1986, *1983*, pp. 75–89.

Kurz, Heinz D. and Salvadori, Neri. A Comment on Levine [Sraffa's *Production of Commodities by Means of Commodities*, Returns to Scale, Relevance, and Other Matters: A Note]. *J. Post Keynesian Econ.*, Fall 1986, *9*(1), pp. 163–65.

Lachmann, Ludwig M. Austrian Economics under Fire: The Hayek–Sraffa Duel in Retrospect. **In** *Grassl, W. and Smith, B., eds.*, 1986, pp. 225–42.

Maneschi, Andrea. A Comparative Evaluation of Sraffa's 'The Laws of Returns under Competitive Conditions' and Its Italian Precursor. *Cambridge J. Econ.*, March 1986, *10*(1), pp. 1–12.

Porta, Pier Luigi. Understanding the Significance of Piero Sraffa's Standard Commodity: A Note on the Marxian Notion of Surplus.

Hist. Polit. Econ., Fall 1986, *18*(3), pp. 443–54.

Porta, Pier Luigi. Understanding the Significance of Piero Sraffa's Standard Commodity: A Rejoinder. *Hist. Polit. Econ.*, Fall 1986, *18*(3), pp. 479–84.

Samuelson, Paul A. Durable Capital Inputs: Conditions for Price Ratios to Be Invariant to Profit-Rate Changes. **In** *Samuelson, P. A.*, 1986, *1983*, pp. 375–94.

Sau, Ranjit. Ground Rent and Super Profit in the Sraffa System. *Indian Econ. Rev.*, Jan.-June 1986, *21*(1), pp. 51–60.

Steenge, Albert E. On the Wage–Profit Relation in a Sraffa System with Joint Production. *Revue Écon.*, September 1986, *37*(5), pp. 925–32.

Steuart, James

Anderson, Gary M. and Tollison, Robert D. Smith, Steuart, and Mercantilism: Reply [Sir James Steuart as the Apothesis of Mercantilism and His Relation to Adam Smith]. *Southern Econ. J.*, January 1986, *52*(3), pp. 853–56.

Eltis, Walter. Sir James Steuart's Corporate State. **In** *Black, R. D. C., ed.*, 1986, pp. 43–73.

Rashid, Salim. Smith, Steuart, and Mercantilism: Comment [Sir James Steuart as the Apothesis of Mercantilism and His Relation to Adam Smith]. *Southern Econ. J.*, January 1986, *52*(3), pp. 843–52.

Stigler, George J.

Moore, Thomas Gale. The Essence of Stigler: Introduction. **In** *Stigler, G. J.*, 1986, pp. xxi–xxviii.

Stigler, George J. Lives of the Laureates: George J. Stigler. **In** *Breit, W. and Spencer, R. W., eds.*, 1986, pp. 93–111.

Stone, Richard

Aukrust, Odd. On the Occasion of a Nobel Prize. *Rev. Income Wealth*, March 1986, *32*(1), pp. 109–12.

Samuelson, Paul A. The 1984 Nobel Prize in Economics. **In** *Samuelson, P. A.*, 1986, *1985*, pp. 841–43.

Stöpel, Franz

Schulz, Frank. Die Arbeiten von Franz Stöpel zur Beschäftigungspolitik durch produktive Geldschöpfung—Ein dogmengeschichtlicher Beitrag zur "Functional Finance." (The Works of Franz Stöpel to Employment Policy through Productive Creation of Money—A Contribution to the History of the Idea of "Functional Finance." With English summary.) *Jahr. Nationalökon. Statist.*, November 1986, *201*(6), pp. 642–51.

Streeten, Paul P.

Streeten, Paul. Aerial Roots. *Banca Naz. Lavoro Quart. Rev.*, June 1986, (157), pp. 135–59.

Stretton, Hugh. Paul Streeten: An Appreciation. **In** *[Streeten, P.]*, 1986, pp. 1–27.

Sutch, William Ball

Endres, Anthony M. The Political Economy of W. B. Sutch: Toward a Critical Appreciation. *New Zealand Econ. Pap.*, 1986, *20*, pp. 17–39. **[G: New Zealand]**

Taylor, Frederick W.

Wrege, Charles D. and Greenwood, Ronald G. Frederick W. Taylor and Industrial Espionage: 1895–1897. **In** *Atack, J., ed.*, 1986, pp. 183–93.

Thornton, Henry

Humphrey, Thomas M. Cumulative Process Models from Thornton to Wicksell. *Fed. Res. Bank Richmond Econ. Rev.*, May/June 1986, *72*(3), pp. 18–25.

Thornton, William Thomas

Negishi, Takashi. Thornton's Criticism of Equilibrium Theory and Mill. *Hist. Polit. Econ.*, Winter 1986, *18*(4), pp. 567–77.

von Thünen, Johann Heinrich

Dorfman, Robert. Thünen at Two Hundred: Comment. *J. Econ. Lit.*, December 1986, *24*(4), pp. 1773–76.

Manz, Peter. Forestry Economics in the Steady State: The Contribution of J. H. von Thünen. *Hist. Polit. Econ.*, Summer 1986, *18*(2), pp. 281–90.

Samuelson, Paul A. Thünen at Two Hundred. **In** *Samuelson, P. A.*, 1986, *1983*, pp. 575–97.

Samuelson, Paul A. Yes to Robert Dorfman's Vindication of Thünen's Natural-Wage Derivation [Thünen at Two Hundred]. *J. Econ. Lit.*, December 1986, *24*(4), pp. 1777–85.

Ťiele, Thorvald N.

Petersen, Jørn Henrik. Three Precursors of Modern Theories of Old-Age Pensions: A Contribution to the History of Social-Policy Doctrines. *Hist. Polit. Econ.*, Fall 1986, *18*(3), pp. 405–17.

Tobin, James

Samuelson, Paul A. 1981 Nobel Prize in Economics. **In** *Samuelson, P. A.*, 1986, *1981*, pp. 834–37.

Tobin, James. Lives of the Laureates: James Tobin. **In** *Breit, W. and Spencer, R. W., eds.*, 1986, pp. 113–35.

Vanderlint, Jacob

Marsh, James Barney. Jacob Vanderlint and the Roots of Supply-Side Economics. *Eastern Econ. J.*, Jan.-Mar. 1986, *12*(1), pp. 63–72.

de Vauban, Sébastien le Presto

Steiner, Philippe. Les peuples et l'impôt dans la *'Dixme royalle'* de Vauban. (Peoples and Taxes in Vauban's "Dixme royale." With English summary.) *Écon. Soc.*, March 1986, *20*(3), pp. 153–79.

Veblen, Thorstein

Arrow, Kenneth J. Thorstein Veblen as an Economic Theorist. **In** *Szenberg, M., ed.*, 1986, *1975*, pp. 47–56.

Dyer, Alan W. Veblen on Scientific Creativity: The Influence of Charles S. Peirce. *J. Econ. Issues*, March 1986, *20*(1), pp. 21–41.

Griffin, Robert. Thorstein Veblen: The Theory of Evolutionary Economics as a Social Science. *Rivista Int. Sci. Econ. Com.*, December 1986, *33*(12), pp. 1145–65.

Leathers, Charles G. Bellamy and Veblen's "Christian Morals." *J. Econ. Issues,* December 1986, *20*(4), pp. 1107–19.

Stabile, Donald R. Veblen and the Political Economy of the Engineer: The Radical Thinker and Engineering Leaders Came to Technocratic Ideas at the Same Time. *Amer. J. Econ. Soc.,* January 1986, *45*(1), pp. 41–52.

Stanković, Fuada. The Relevance of the Phenomenon of "Conspicuous Consumption" for the General Theory of Consumption. *Econ. Anal. Workers' Manage.,* 1986, *20*(4), pp. 375–83.

Viner, Jacob

Rainelli, Michel. Loi du prix unique et théorie de la parité des pouvoirs d'achat: un retour à G. Cassal, A. Aftalion et J. Viner. (With English summary.) *Revue Écon. Polit.,* Jan.-Feb. 1986, *96*(1), pp. 25–38.

Walras, Leon

Cirillo, Renato. Leon Walras' Theory of Money. *Amer. J. Econ. Soc.,* April 1986, *45*(2), pp. 215–21.

Walker, Donald A. Walras's Theory of the Entrepreneur. *De Economist,* 1986, *134*(1), pp. 1–24.

Wayland, Francis

Heyne, Paul. Clerical Laissez-Faire: A Study in Theological Economics. **In** *Block, W. and Hexham, I., eds.,* 1986, pp. 125–52.

Heyne, Paul. Clerical Laissez-Faire: A Study in Theological Economics: Reply. **In** *Block, W. and Hexham, I., eds.,* 1986, pp. 160–63.

Marty, Martin E. Clerical Laissez-Faire: A Study in Theological Economics: Comment. **In** *Block, W. and Hexham, I., eds.,* 1986, pp. 153–59.

Weber, Max

Martinelli, Alberto. Economia e società nell'analisi di Max Weber. (Economy and Society in Max Weber's Analysis. With English summary.) *Rivista Int. Sci. Econ. Com.,* February 1986, *33*(2), pp. 139–64.

Wicksell, Knut

Humphrey, Thomas M. Cumulative Process Models from Thornton to Wicksell. *Fed. Res. Bank Richmond Econ. Rev.,* May/June 1986, *72*(3), pp. 18–25.

Humphrey, Thomas M. Interest Rates, Expectations, and the Wicksellian Policy Rule. **In** *Humphreys, T. M.,* 1986, *1976,* pp. 134–42.

Humphrey, Thomas M. The Interest Cost-Push Controversy. **In** *Humphreys, T. M.,* 1986, *1979,* pp. 143–50.

0329 Other Special Topics

Andel, Norbert. Changing Concepts of Public Debt in the History of Economic Thought. **In** *Herber, B. P., ed.,* 1986, pp. 1–13.

Awan, Akhtar A. Marshallian and Schumpeterian Theories of Economic Evolution: Gradualism versus Punctualism. *Atlantic Econ. J.,* December 1986, *14*(4), pp. 37–49.

Baranzini, Mauro and Scazzieri, Roberto. Knowledge in Economics: A Framework. **In** *Baranzini, M. and Scazzieri, R., eds.,* 1986, pp. 1–87.

Baumol, William J. Smith vs. Marx on Business Morality and the Social Interest. **In** *Baumol, W. J.,* 1986, *1976,* pp. 241–46.

Becattini, Giacomo. Conflitto di classe e contrasto di interessi nella teoria economica. (Class Conflict and Clashing Interests in Economic Theory. With English summary.) *Rivista Int. Sci. Econ. Com.,* March 1986, *33*(3), pp. 193–205.

Black, R. D. Collison. Dentists and Preachers. **In** *Black, R. D. C., ed.,* 1986, pp. 1–15.

Bosworth, Barry P. What Would Keynes Have Thought of Rational Expectations? Comment. **In** *Butkiewicz, J. L.; Koford, K. J. and Miller, J. B., eds.,* 1986, pp. 52–55.

Breton, Yves. Les économistes libéraux français et l'emploi des mathématiques en économie politique. 1800–1914. (The French Liberal Economists and the Use of Mathematics in Political Economy, 1800–1914. With English summary.) *Écon. Soc.,* March 1986, *20*(3), pp. 25–63. **[G: France]**

Brewer, Anthony. Marx's *Capital* Today. **In** *Black, R. D. C., ed.,* 1986, pp. 160–75.

Brunner, Karl. Financial Markets and Macroeconomic Fluctuations: Rejoinder. **In** *Butkiewicz, J. L.; Koford, K. J. and Miller, J. B., eds.,* 1986, pp. 108–09. **[G: U.S.]**

Brunner, Karl. Financial Markets and Macroeconomic Fluctuations: Comment. **In** *Butkiewicz, J. L.; Koford, K. J. and Miller, J. B., eds.,* 1986, pp. 88–94. **[G: U.S.]**

Brunner, Karl. What Would Keynes Have Thought of Rational Expectations? Comment. **In** *Butkiewicz, J. L.; Koford, K. J. and Miller, J. B., eds.,* 1986, pp. 59–61.

Bugra, Ayşe. Karl Polanyi and the Boundaries of Economics. *METU,* 1986, *13*(3–4), pp. 217–38.

Caldwell, Bruce J. Economic Methodology and Behavioral Economics: An Interpretive History. **In** *Gilad, B. and Kaish, S., eds., Vol. A,* 1986, pp. 5–17.

Charbit, Yves. L'institution statistique l'économie politique et la démographie entre 1840 et 1870: pour une approche épistémologique. (The Statistical Institution, Political Economy and Demography. An Epistemological View. With English summary.) *Écon. Soc.,* October 1986, *20*(10), pp. 143–57.

Chilosi, Alberto. Self-Managed Market Socialism with "Free Mobility of Labor." *J. Compar. Econ.,* September 1986, *10*(3), pp. 237–54.

Costa, Paolo. Regional Science *Ante Litteram:* Some Early Italian Contributions to Regional Economics. *Ricerche Econ.,* Apr.-Sept. 1986, *40*(2–3), pp. 525–36. **[G: Italy]**

Creedy, John. On the King–Davenant "Law" of Demand. *Scot. J. Polit. Econ.,* August 1986, *33*(3), pp. 193–212.

Cuddington, John T. and Viñals, José M. Budget

Deficits and the Current Account: An Intertemporal Disequilibrium Approach. *J. Int. Econ.*, August 1986, *21* (1/2), pp. 1–24.

Damamme, D. L'économie politique sous le consulat et l'empire. Misère de l'économie, science de la richesse. (Political Economy under the "Consulat" and "Empire," Misery of Economy, Science of Wealth. With English summary.) *Écon. Soc.*, October 1986, *20*(10), pp. 49–62.

Davidsen, Thorkild. Westergaard, Edgeworth and the Use of Lagrange Multipliers in Economics [The Early Use of Lagrange Multipliers in Economics]. *Econ. J.*, September 1986, *96*(383), pp. 808–11.

Davidson, Paul. Financial Markets and Macroeconomic Fluctuations: Comment. **In** *Butkiewicz, J. L.; Koford, K. J. and Miller, J. B., eds.*, 1986, pp. 94–102. **[G: U.S.]**

Davidson, Paul. What Would Keynes Have Thought of Rational Expectations? Comment. **In** *Butkiewicz, J. L.; Koford, K. J. and Miller, J. B., eds.*, 1986, pp. 58–59.

De Long, James Bradford. Senior's 'Last Hour': Suggested Explanation of a Famous Blunder. *Hist. Polit. Econ.*, Summer 1986, *18*(2), pp. 325–33.

Demier, Francis. Avant gardes économiques et diffusion de l'économie politique en France de 1815 à 1914. (Economic Vanguards and the Diffusion of Political Economy in France [1815–1914]. With English summary.) *Écon. Soc.*, October 1986, *20*(10), pp. 103–42.

Dostaler, Giles. Understanding the Significance of Piero Sraffa's Standard Commodity: A Note on the Marxian Notion of Surplus: "From Marx to Sraffa": Comments. *Hist. Polit. Econ.*, Fall 1986, *18*(3), pp. 463–69.

Dunning, John H.; Cantwell, John A. and Corley, T. A. B. The Theory of International Production: Some Historical Antecedents. **In** *Hertner, P. and Jones, G., eds.*, 1986, pp. 19–41.

Dutton, H. I. and King, J. E. "A Private, Perhaps, but Not a Major...": The Reception of C. H. Douglas's Social Credit Ideas in Britain, 1919–1939. *Hist. Polit. Econ.*, Summer 1986, *18*(2), pp. 259–79.

Dykema, Eugene R. No View without a Viewpoint: Gunnar Myrdal. *World Devel.*, Special Issue, Feb. 1986, *14*(2), pp. 147–63.

Etner, F. L'enseignement économique dans les grandes écoles au XIXe siècle en France. (Economic Teaching in the French "grandes écoles" in the 19th Century. With English summary.) *Écon. Soc.*, October 1986, *20*(10), pp. 159–74.

Faccarello, Gilbert. Understanding the Significance of Piero Sraffa's Standard Commodity: A Note on the Marxian Notion of Surplus: "Understanding Sraffa's Standard Commodity": A Comment. *Hist. Polit. Econ.*, Fall 1986, *18*(3), pp. 471–78.

Flanders, M. June. The Balance-of-Payments Adjustment Mechanism: The Doctrine According to Ohlin. *Hist. Polit. Econ.*, Summer 1986, *18*(2), pp. 237–57.

Gershfield, Edward M. Business Regulation and Price Control in Talmudic Economics. *Int. J. Soc. Econ.*, 1986, *13*(9), pp. 45–51.

Godschalk, Hugo. The Moneyless Economy—From Temple Exchange to the Barter Club. **In** *Pohl, H. and Rudolph, B., eds.*, 1986, pp. 57–78. **[G: W. Germany; U.S.]**

Goodwin, Richard M. Swinging along the Turnpike with von Neumann and Sraffa. *Cambridge J. Econ.*, September 1986, *10*(3), pp. 203–10.

Groenewegen, Peter. Professor Porta on the Significance of Understanding Sraffa's Standard Commodity and the Marxian Theory of Surplus: A Comment. *Hist. Polit. Econ.*, Fall 1986, *18*(3), pp. 455–62.

Hahn, Frank H. "Of Marx and Keynes and Many Things." *Oxford Econ. Pap.*, July 1986, *38*(2), pp. 354–61.

Hamada, Koichi. The Impact of the General Theory in Japan. *Eastern Econ. J.*, Oct.-Dec. 1986, *12*(4), pp. 451–66. **[G: Japan]**

Hecht, Jacqueline. Une Héritière des Lumières, de la Physiocratie et de l'Idéologie: La première chaire française d'économie politique (1795). (An Offspring of Enlightenment, Physiocracies and Ideology: The First French Chair of Political Economy [1795]. With English summary.) *Écon. Soc.*, October 1986, *20*(10), pp. 5–48.

Hennings, Klaus H. The State of Microeconomics: An Historical Perspective. **In** *Samuelson, L., ed.*, 1986, pp. 265–71.

Hollander, Samuel. On a 'New Interpretation' of Ricardo's Early Treatment of Profitability. *Econ. J.*, December 1986, *96*(384), pp. 1091–97.

Hollander, Samuel. The Relevance of John Stuart Mill: Some Implications for Modern Economics. **In** *Black, R. D. C., ed.*, 1986, pp. 129–59.

Humphrey, Thomas M. Algebraic Quantity Equations before Fisher and Pigou. **In** *Humphreys, T. M.*, 1986, *1984*, pp. 278–87.

Humphrey, Thomas M. Bullionists' Exchange Rate Doctrines and Current Policy Debates. **In** *Humphreys, T. M.*, 1986, *1980*, pp. 251–54. **[G: U.K.]**

Humphrey, Thomas M. Evolution of the Concept of the Demand for Money. **In** *Humphreys, T. M.*, 1986, *1973*, pp. 288–98.

Humphrey, Thomas M. On Nonneutral Relative Price Effects in Monetarist Thought: Some Austrian Misconceptions. **In** *Humphreys, T. M.*, 1986, *1984*, pp. 73–79.

Humphrey, Thomas M. The Concept of Indexation in the History of Economic Thought. **In** *Humphreys, T. M.*, 1986, *1974*, pp. 264–77.

Humphrey, Thomas M. The Early History of the Phillips Curve. **In** *Humphreys, T. M.*, 1986, *1985*, pp. 91–98.

Humphrey, Thomas M. The Monetarist–Nonmonetarist Debate: Some 19th Century Controversies Revisited. **In** *Humphreys, T. M.*, 1986, *1970*, pp. 299–303. **[G: U.K.]**

Humphrey, Thomas M. The Monetary Approach to Exchange Rates: Its Historical Evolution and Role in Policy Debates. **In** *Putnam, B. H. and*

Wilford, D. S., eds., 1986, *1978*, pp. 152–67. **[G: U.K.; Sweden; Germany]**

Jameson, Kenneth P. Latin American Structuralism: A Methodological Perspective. *World Devel.*, Special Issue, Feb. 1986, *14*(2), pp. 223–32. **[G: Latin America]**

Kaldor, Nicholas. Limits on Growth. *Oxford Econ. Pap.*, July 1986, *38*(2), pp. 187–98.

Katzner, Donald W. The Role of Formalism in Economic Thought, with Illustration Drawn from the Analysis of Social Interaction in the Firm. **In** *Mirowski, P., ed.*, 1986, pp. 137–77.

Keleher, Robert E. Of Money and Prices: Some Historical Perspectives. **In** *Putnam, B. H. and Wilford, D. S., eds.*, 1986, *1978*, pp. 27–58.

Lavoie, Donald C. Marx, the Quantity Theory, and the Theory of Value. *Hist. Polit. Econ.*, Spring 1986, *18*(1), pp. 155–70.

Leijonhufvud, Axel. What Would Keynes Have Thought of Rational Expectations? **In** *Butkiewicz, J. L.; Koford, K. J. and Miller, J. B., eds.*, 1986, pp. 25–52.

Leijonhufvud, Axel. What Would Keynes Have Thought of Rational Expectations? Reply. **In** *Butkiewicz, J. L.; Koford, K. J. and Miller, J. B., eds.*, 1986, pp. 61–63.

Levan-Lemesle, Lucette. De la société d'économie politique aux Facultés de Droit: Caractères et paradoxes de l'institutionnalisation de l'économie politique en France au XIXe siècle. (From "Société d'Économie Politique" to Law Schools: Characterizations and Paradoxes of the Institutionalization of Political Economy in France [19th Century]. With English summary.) *Écon. Soc.*, October 1986, *20*(10), pp. 223–37.

Loasby, Brian J. Organisation, Competition, and the Growth of Knowledge. **In** *Langlois, R. N., ed.*, 1986, pp. 41–57.

Lombardini, Siro. L'innovazione. (Innovation. With English summary.) *Rivista Int. Sci. Econ. Com.*, April 1986, *33*(4), pp. 319–32.

Malinvaud, Edmond. Reflecting on the Theory of Capital and Growth. *Oxford Econ. Pap.*, November 1986, *38*(3), pp. 367–85.

Minkler, Alanson P. In Defense of Marx on the Length of the Working Day. *Econ. Forum*, Winter 1986-1987, *16*(1), pp. 105–10.

Musgrave, Richard A. A Brief History of Fiscal Doctrine. **In** *Musgrave, R. A., Vol. 2*, 1986, *1985*, pp. 338–93.

Musgrave, Richard A. Private Labour and Common Land. **In** *Musgrave, R. A., Vol. 2*, 1986, *1983*, pp. 304–18.

Nitsch, Thomas O. Social Catholicism, Marxism and Liberation Theology: From Antithesis to Coexistence, Coalescence and Synthesis. *Int. J. Soc. Econ.*, 1986, *13*(9), pp. 52–74.

O'Driscoll, Gerald P., Jr. Money: Menger's Evolutionary Theory. *Hist. Polit. Econ.*, Winter 1986, *18*(4), pp. 601–16.

Parkin, Michael. Essays on and in the Chicago Tradition: A Review Essay. *J. Money, Credit, Banking*, February 1986, *18*(1), pp. 104–16.

Pasinetti, Luigi L. Theory of Value—A Source of Alternative Paradigms in Economic Analysis. **In** *Baranzini, M. and Scazzieri, R., eds.*, 1986, pp. 409–31.

Patinkin, Don. Essay on and in the Chicago Tradition: A Reply. *J. Money, Credit, Banking*, February 1986, *18*(1), pp. 116–21.

Peach, Terry. David Ricardo's Treatment of Wages. **In** *Black, R. D. C., ed.*, 1986, pp. 104–28.

Peach, Terry. Ricardo's Early Treatment of Profitability: Reply. *Econ. J.*, December 1986, *96*(384), pp. 1105–12.

Perlman, Morris. The Bullionist Controversy Revisited. *J. Polit. Econ.*, August 1986, *94*(4), pp. 745–62.

Pissarides, Christopher A. What Would Keynes Have Thought of Rational Expectations? Comment. **In** *Butkiewicz, J. L.; Koford, K. J. and Miller, J. B., eds.*, 1986, pp. 55–57.

Porta, Pier Luigi. Understanding the Significance of Piero Sraffa's Standard Commodity: A Note on the Marxian Notion of Surplus. *Hist. Polit. Econ.*, Fall 1986, *18*(3), pp. 443–54.

Porta, Pier Luigi. Understanding the Significance of Piero Sraffa's Standard Commodity: A Rejoinder. *Hist. Polit. Econ.*, Fall 1986, *18*(3), pp. 479–84.

Potestio, Paola. Equilibrium and Employment in "The General Theory." *Giorn. Econ.*, July-Aug. 1986, *45*(7–8), pp. 363–88.

Prendergast, Renée. David Ricardo's Early Treatment of Profitability: A New Interpretation: A Comment. *Econ. J.*, December 1986, *96*(384), pp. 1098–1104.

Prendergast, Renée. Malthus's Discussion of the Corn Ratio Theory of Profits. *Cambridge J. Econ.*, June 1986, *10*(2), pp. 187–89.

Presley, John R. J. M. Keynes and the Real Balance Effect. *Manchester Sch. Econ. Soc. Stud.*, March 1986, *54*(1), pp. 22–30.

Presley, John R. Modern Monetarist Ideas: A British Connection? **In** *Black, R. D. C., ed.*, 1986, pp. 191–210.

Rainelli, Michel. Loi du prix unique et théorie de la parité des pouvoirs d'achat: un retour à G. Cassal, A. Aftalion et J. Viner. (With English summary.) *Revue Écon. Polit.*, Jan.-Feb. 1986, *96*(1), pp. 25–38.

Rashid, Salim. Adam Smith and the Division of Labour: A Historical View. *Scot. J. Polit. Econ.*, August 1986, *33*(3), pp. 292–97.

Rima, Ingrid H. The Pigou–Keynes Controversy about Involuntary Unemployment: A Half-Century Reinterpretation. *Eastern Econ. J.*, Oct.-Dec. 1986, *12*(4), pp. 467–77.

Samuelson, Paul A. A Corrected Version of Hume's Equilibrating Mechanisms for International Trade. **In** *Samuelson, P. A.*, 1986, *1980*, pp. 397–414.

Samuelson, Paul A. St. Petersburg Paradoxes: Defanged, Dissected, and Historically Described. **In** *Samuelson, P. A.*, 1986, *1977*, pp. 133–64.

Samuelson, Paul A. Summing Up on the Australian Case for Protection. **In** *Samuelson, P. A.*, 1986, *1981*, pp. 454–67. **[G: Australia]**

Samuelson, Paul A. The Normative and Positivistic Inferiority of Marx's *Values* Paradigm. **In** *Samuelson, P. A.*, 1986, *1982*, pp. 351–58.

Samuelson, Paul A. The Role of Profits in a Mixed Economy: Changes in the Perceived Reality. **In** *Samuelson, P. A.*, 1986, *1978*, pp. 929–45.

Samuelson, Paul A. 1983: Marx, Keynes and Schumpeter. **In** *Samuelson, P. A.*, 1986, *1983*, pp. 261–74.

Samuelson, Paul A. 1983: Marx, Keynes and Schumpeter. **In** *Samuelson, P. A.*, 1986, *1983*, pp. 261–74.

Sardoni, Claudio. Marx and Keynes on Effective Demand and Unemployment. *Hist. Polit. Econ.*, Fall 1986, *18*(3), pp. 419–41.

Scitovsky, Tibor. Psychologizing by Economists. **In** *MacFadyen, A. J. and MacFadyen, H. W., eds.*, 1986, pp. 165–80.

Shiller, Robert J. Financial Markets and Macroeconomic Fluctuations. **In** *Butkiewicz, J. L.; Koford, K. J. and Miller, J. B., eds.*, 1986, pp. 65–88. **[G: U.S.]**

Shiller, Robert J. Financial Markets and Macroeconomic Fluctuations: Reply. **In** *Butkiewicz, J. L.; Koford, K. J. and Miller, J. B., eds.*, 1986, pp. 105–08. **[G: U.S.]**

Snippe, Jan. Finance, Saving and Investment in Keynes's Economics: A Reply. *Cambridge J. Econ.*, December 1986, *10*(4), pp. 373–77.

Snippe, Jan. Hines on LF versus LP: Reply [Loanable Funds Theory Versus Liquidity Preference Theory]. *De Economist*, 1986, *134*(1), pp. 111.

Stanković, Fuada. The Relevance of the Phenomenon of "Conspicuous Consumption" for the General Theory of Consumption. *Econ. Anal. Workers' Manage.*, 1986, *20*(4), pp. 375–83.

Steedman, Ian. Trade Interest versus Class Interest. *Econ. Polít.*, August 1986, *3*(2), pp. 187–206.

Stigler, George J. Economics or Ethics? **In** *Stigler, G. J.*, 1986, *1981*, pp. 303–36.

Stigler, George J. Perfect Competition, Historically Contemplated. **In** *Stigler, G. J.*, 1986, *1983*, pp. 265–88.

Stiglitz, Joseph E. Financial Markets and Macroeconomic Fluctuations: Comment. **In** *Butkiewicz, J. L.; Koford, K. J. and Miller, J. B., eds.*, 1986, pp. 102–05. **[G: U.S.]**

Streissler, Erich and Neudeck, Werner. Are There Intellectual Precursors to the Idea of Second Best Optimization? *J. Econ. (Z. Nationalökon.)*, Supplementum 5, 1986, pp. 227–42.

Throsby, C. D. Agriculture in the Economy: The Evolution of Economists' Perceptions over Three Centuries. *Rev. Marketing Agr. Econ.*, December 1986, *54*(3), pp. 5–48.

Tollison, Robert D. Economists as the Subject of Economic Inquiry. *Southern Econ. J.*, April 1986, *52*(4), pp. 909–22.

Tullock, Gordon. Wanted: New Public-Choice Theories. **In** *[Seldon, A.]*, 1986, pp. 15–27.

Ventre-Denis, Madeleine. La première tentative en France d'un enseignement de l'économie politique dans une faculté. (The First Chair of Political Economy in the French University. With English summary.) *Écon. Soc.*, October 1986, *20*(10), pp. 97–102.

Vinokur, Annie. Political Economy between Faith and Works: Saint-Simonism and the Case of Michel Chevalier. *Écon. Soc.*, October 1986, *20*(10), pp. 175–202.

Visser, H. Loanable Funds Theory versus Liquidity Preference Theory: A Comment. *De Economist*, 1986, *134*(1), pp. 109–10.

Williams, Philip L. A Reconstruction of Marshall's Temporary Equilibrium Pricing Model. *Hist. Polit. Econ.*, Winter 1986, *18*(4), pp. 639–53.

Wisman, Jon D. The Methodology of W. Arthur Lewis's Development Economics: Economics as Pedagogy. *World Devel.*, Special Issue, Feb. 1986, *14*(2), pp. 165–80.

Wolfson, Murray; Orzech, Ze'ev B. and Hanna, Susan S. Karl Marx and the Depletion of Human Capital as Open-Access Resource. *Hist. Polit. Econ.*, Fall 1986, *18*(3), pp. 497–514.

Zagari, Eugenio. Schumpeter Marx: Note in margine ad un convegno. (With English summary.) *Stud. Econ.*, 1986, *41*(29), pp. 29–52.

036 Economic Methodology

0360 Economic Methodology

Baranzini, Mauro and Scazzieri, Roberto. Knowledge in Economics: A Framework. **In** *Baranzini, M. and Scazzieri, R., eds.*, 1986, pp. 1–87.

Bartoli, Henri. Au-delà des confusions. Propositions hérétiques. (Beyond Confusion, Heretic Propositions. With English summary.) *Écon. Soc.*, April 1986, *20*(4), pp. 3–56.

Basile, Liliana. Causalità ed economia. (Causality and Economics. With English summary.) *Econ. Polít.*, August 1986, *3*(2), pp. 233–58.

Bausor, Randall. Time and Equilibrium. **In** *Mirowski, P., ed.*, 1986, pp. 93–135.

Blaug, Mark. Economic Methodology in One Easy Lesson. **In** *Blaug, M.*, 1986, *1980*, pp. 265–79.

Blaug, Mark. Kuhn versus Lakatos, or Paradigms versus Research Programmes in the History of Economics. **In** *Blaug, M.*, 1986, *1976*, pp. 233–64.

Bliss, Christopher. Progress and Anti-progress in Economic Science. **In** *Baranzini, M. and Scazzieri, R., eds.*, 1986, pp. 363–76.

Boland, Lawrence A. Methodology and the Individual Decision Maker. **In** *[Lachmann, L. M.]*, 1986, pp. 30–38.

Bordo, Michael D. and Landau, Daniel. Advocacy and Neo Classical Economics. *Eastern Econ. J.*, Apr.-June 1986, *12*(2), pp. 94–102.

Brady, Michael Emmett. A Note on Milton Friedman's Application of His "Methodology of Positive Economics." *J. Econ. Issues*, September 1986, *20*(3), pp. 845–51.

Bramhall, David. Economics and Cartesian Science. **In** *Helburn, S. W. and Bramhall, D. F., eds.*, 1986, pp. 45–64.

Bugra, Ayşe. Karl Polanyi and the Boundaries of Economics. *METU*, 1986, *13*(3–4), pp. 217–38.

036 Economic Methodology

Caldwell, Bruce J. Economic Methodology and Behavioral Economics: An Interpretive History. **In** *Gilad, B. and Kaish, S., eds., Vol. A,* 1986, pp. 5–17.

Caldwell, Bruce J. Towards a Broader Conception of Criticism [Praxeology and Its Critics: An Appraisal]. *Hist. Polit. Econ.,* Winter 1986, *18*(4), pp. 675–81.

Coats, A. W. Economic Methodology: Theory, Practice, and the Current State of Economics. *Kyklos,* 1986, *39*(1), pp. 109–15.

Costabile, Lilia. Metodo della scienza e teoria economica in Schumpeter. Note su "l'essenza e i principi dell'economia teorica." (With English summary.) *Stud. Econ.,* 1986, *41*(29), pp. 147–68.

Dagum, Camilo. Economic Model, System and Structure, Philosophy of Science and Lakatos' Methodology of Scientific Research Programs. *Rivista Int. Sci. Econ. Com.,* September 1986, *33*(9), pp. 859–86.

Dahmén, Erik. Schumpeterian Dynamics: Some Methodological Notes. **In** *Day, R. H. and Eliasson, G., eds.,* 1986, *1984,* pp. 181–90.

Demaria, Giovanni. Sul fondamento eurostico di alcuni strumenti analitici impiegati nelle logiche naturali dell'economia. (On the Heuristic Capacity of Some Analytical Tools Employed by the Natural Logic of Economics. With English summary.) *Rivista Int. Sci. Econ. Com.,* June-July 1986, *33*(6–7), pp. 529–44.

Dennis, Kenneth G. Boland on Friedman: A Rebuttal. *J. Econ. Issues,* September 1986, *20*(3), pp. 633–60.

Dnes, Antony W. Individualism in Contemporary Political Economy: A Review Article. *Scot. J. Polit. Econ.,* November 1986, *33*(4), pp. 391–95.

Dopfer, Kurt. The Histonomic Approach to Economics: Beyond Pure Theory and Pure Experience. *J. Econ. Issues,* December 1986, *20*(4), pp. 989–1010.

Dyer, Alan W. Veblen on Scientific Creativity: The Influence of Charles S. Peirce. *J. Econ. Issues,* March 1986, *20*(1), pp. 21–41.

Dykema, Eugene R. No View without a Viewpoint: Gunnar Myrdal. *World Devel.,* Special Issue, Feb. 1986, *14*(2), pp. 147–63.

Eichner, Alfred S. Can Economics Become a Science? *Challenge,* Nov./Dec. 1986, *29*(5), pp. 4–12.

Ellig, Jerome R. Do We Walk with Walras? *Atlantic Econ. J.,* July 1986, *14*(2), pp. 82.

Faber, Malte and Proops, John L. R. Time Irreversibilities in Economics: Some Lessons from the Natural Sciences. **In** *Faber, M., ed.,* 1986, pp. 294–316.

Faucci, Riccardo. Note su positivismo e pensiero economico in Italia tra Otto e Novecento. (Positivism and Economic Thought in Italy between 1800 and 1900. With English summary.) *Rivista Int. Sci. Econ. Com.,* January 1986, *33*(1), pp. 75–94. **[G: Italy]**

Fischer, Charles C. Institutionalism versus Orthodoxy: The Articulation of Methodological Alternatives. *Amer. J. Econ. Soc.,* July 1986, *45*(3), pp. 359–72.

Goldstein, Jonathan P. The Micro–Macro Dialectic: A Concept of a Marxian Microfoundation. **In** *Zarembka, P., ed.,* 1986, pp. 127–55.

Helburn, Suzanne W. Evaluation of Scientific Research Programs in Economics. **In** *Helburn, S. W. and Bramhall, D. F., eds.,* 1986, pp. 27–44.

Helburn, Suzanne W. Keynes's Research Program. **In** *Helburn, S. W. and Bramhall, D. F., eds.,* 1986, pp. 199–231.

Helburn, Suzanne W. Marx's Research Program. **In** *Helburn, S. W. and Bramhall, D. F., eds.,* 1986, pp. 67–94.

Helburn, Suzanne W. Schumpeter's Research Program. **In** *Helburn, S. W. and Bramhall, D. F., eds.,* 1986, pp. 149–66.

Henderson, James P. Sir John William Lubbock's *On Currency*—"An Interesting Book by a Still More Interesting Man." *Hist. Polit. Econ.,* Fall 1986, *18*(3), pp. 383–404.

Henry, John F. On Economic Theory and the Question of Solvability. *J. Post Keynesian Econ.,* Spring 1986, *8*(3), pp. 371–86.

Hicks, John R. Is Economics a Science? **In** *Baranzini, M. and Scazzieri, R., eds.,* 1986, pp. 91–101.

Hirsch, Abraham. Caldwell on Praxeology and Its Critics: A Reappraisal. *Hist. Polit. Econ.,* Winter 1986, *18*(4), pp. 661–68.

Hirsch, Abraham and de Marchi, Neil. Making a Case When Theory Is Unfalsifiable: Friedman's Monetary History. *Econ. Philos.,* April 1986, *2*(1), pp. 1–21.

Hirschman, Alberto O. En contra de la parsimonia: tres formas fáciles para complicar alguans categorías del discurso económico. (Against Parsimony. With English summary.) *Colección Estud. CIEPLAN,* June 1986, (19), pp. 135–47.

Hodgson, Geoff. Behind Methodological Individualism. *Cambridge J. Econ.,* September 1986, *10*(3), pp. 211–24.

Howitt, Peter. Conversations with Economists: A Review Essay. *J. Monet. Econ.,* July 1986, *18*(1), pp. 103–18.

Hutchison, Terence W. Philosophical Issues that Divide Liberals: Omniscience or Omni-nescience about the Future? **In** *[Lachmann, L. M.],* 1986, pp. 122–39.

Jameson, Kenneth P. Latin American Structuralism: A Methodological Perspective. *World Devel.,* Special Issue, Feb. 1986, *14*(2), pp. 223–32. **[G: Latin America]**

Jones, Lamar B. The Institutionalist and *On the Origin of Species*: A Case of Mistaken Identity. *Southern Econ. J.,* April 1986, *52*(4), pp. 1043–55.

Katzner, Donald W. The Role of Formalism in Economic Thought, with Illustration Drawn from the Analysis of Social Interaction in the Firm. **In** *Mirowski, P., ed.,* 1986, pp. 137–77.

Kohn, Meir. Monetary Analysis, the Equilibrium Method, and Keynes's "General Theory." *J.*

Polit. Econ., December 1986, *94*(6), pp. 1191–1224.

Kornai, János. The Health of Nations: Reflections on the Analogy between the Medical Sciences and Economics. **In** *Kornai, J.*, 1986, *1983*, pp. 139–60.

Langlois, Richard N. Coherence and Flexibility: Social Institutions in a World of Radical Uncertainty. **In** *[Lachmann, L. M.]*, 1986, pp. 171–91.

Lavoie, Donald C. Euclideanism versus Hermeneutics: A Reinterpretation of Misesian Apriorism. **In** *[Lachmann, L. M.]*, 1986, pp. 192–210.

Loasby, Brian J. Organisation, Competition, and the Growth of Knowledge. **In** *Langlois, R. N., ed.*, 1986, pp. 41–57.

Lutz, Mark A. and Lux, Kenneth. Neo-Humanistic Economics: A Comment [Is Neo-Humanistic Economics the New Paradigm for Social Economists?]. *Rev. Soc. Econ.*, October 1986, *44*(2), pp. 183–87.

MacFadyen, Alan J. Rational Economic Man: An Introduction Survey. **In** *MacFadyen, A. J. and MacFadyen, H. W., eds.*, 1986, pp. 25–66.

Maes, Ivo and Schokkaert, Erik. On Positivism and the Keynesian Revolution. *Tijdschrift Econ. Manage.*, 1986, *31*(1), pp. 81–91.

McPherson, Michael S. The Social Scientist as Constructive Skeptic: On Hirschman's Role. **In** *[Hirshman, A. O.]*, 1986, pp. 305–15.

Mensch, Gerhard. Schumpeterian Dynamics: Some Methodological Notes: Comment. **In** *Day, R. H. and Eliasson, G., eds.*, 1986, pp. 194–97.

Meoli, Umberto. Aspetti della metodologia della scienza economica nel pensiero di T. W. Hutchison. (Aspects of the Methodology of Economic Theory in the Thought of T. W. Hutchison. With English summary.) *Ricerche Econ.*, Apr.-Sept. 1986, *40*(2–3), pp. 249–65.

Meyer, Willi. Beyond Choice. **In** *[Lachmann, L. M.]*, 1986, pp. 221–35.

Mirowski, Philip. Mathematical Formalism and Economic Explanation. **In** *Mirowski, P., ed.*, 1986, pp. 179–240.

Mirowski, Philip. Paradigms, Hard Cores, and Fuglemen in Modern Economic Theory. **In** *Mirowski, P., ed.*, 1986, pp. 1–11.

Mittermaier, Karl. Mechanomorphism. **In** *[Lachmann, L. M.]*, 1986, pp. 236–51.

Mongin, Philippe. Are "All-and-Some" Statements Falsifiable after All? The Example of Utility Theory. *Econ. Philos.*, October 1986, *2*(2), pp. 185–95.

Mongin, Philippe. La controverse sur l'entreprise (1940–1950) et la formation de l'"irréalisme méthodologique." (The Controversy over the Enterprise (1940–1950) and the Building-Up of a "Lack of Methodological Realism." With English summary.) *Écon. Soc.*, March 1986, *20*(3), pp. 95–151.

Nelson, Richard R. Schumpeterian Dynamics: Some Methodological Notes: Comment. **In** *Day, R. H. and Eliasson, G., eds.*, 1986, pp. 191–93.

Nelson, Richard R. The Tension between Process Stories and Equilibrium Models: Analyzing the Productivity-Growth Slowdown of the 1970s. **In** *Langlois, R. N., ed.*, 1986, pp. 135–51.

Nooteboom, Bart. Plausibility in Economics. *Econ. Philos.*, October 1986, *2*(2), pp. 197–224.

O'Driscoll, Gerald P., Jr. Competition as a Process: A Law and Economics Perspective. **In** *Langlois, R. N., ed.*, 1986, pp. 153–69. **[G: U.S.]**

Olson, Mancur. On the Nature of Disequilibrium: Introduction. **In** *Day, R. H. and Eliasson, G., eds.*, 1986, pp. 475–81.

Pugh, Cedric. Housing Theory and Policy. *Int. J. Soc. Econ.*, 1986, *13*(4/5), pp. 1–104. **[G: Singapore; Norway; China]**

Ramstad, Yngve. A Pragmatist's Quest for Holistic Knowledge: The Scientific Methdology of John R. Commons. *J. Econ. Issues*, December 1986, *20*(4), pp. 1067–1105.

Rosenberg, Alexander. Lakatosian Consolations for Economics. *Econ. Philos.*, April 1986, *2*(1), pp. 127–39.

Rotwein, Eugene. Flirting with Apriorism: Caldwell on Mises [Praxeology and Its Critics: An Appraisal]. *Hist. Polit. Econ.*, Winter 1986, *18*(4), pp. 669–73.

Roy, Paul-Martel. L-approche structuraliste-institutionnaliste nord-américaine: Une forme de réalisme en économie. (The North American Structuralist-Institutional Approach: A Form of Realism in Economics. With English summary.) *Écon. Soc.*, April 1986, *20*(4), pp. 57–75.

Ruccio, David F. and Simon, Lawrence H. Methodological Aspects of a Marxian Approach to Development: An Analysis of the Modes of Production School. *World Devel.*, Special Issue, Feb. 1986, *14*(2), pp. 211–22.

Rugina, Anghel N. *Principia Oeconomica:* New and Old Foundations of Economic Analysis. *Int. J. Soc. Econ.*, 1986, *13*(7/8), pp. 1–67.

Rugina, Anghel N. New Frontiers of a *Principia Oeconomica*: The Development of an Orientation Table and Its Significance. *Rivista Int. Sci. Econ. Com.*, February 1986, *33*(2), pp. 105–22.

Salanti, Andrea. Strumentalismo e fallibilismo in economia: una nota su alcune recenti interpretazioni. (Instrumentalism versus Fallibilism in Economics: A Note on Some Recent Interpretations. With English summary.) *Rivista Int. Sci. Econ. Com.*, June-July 1986, *33*(6–7), pp. 603–20.

Samuelson, Paul A. Maximizing and Biology. **In** *Samuelson, P. A.*, 1986, *1978*, pp. 697–709.

Scaperlanda, Anthony. Neo-Humanistic Economics and Social Economics, Revisited [Is Neo-Humanistic Economics the New Paradigm for Social Economists?]. *Rev. Soc. Econ.*, October 1986, *44*(2), pp. 188–92.

Schefold, Bertram. Schumpeter as a Walrasian Austrian and Keynes as a Classical Marshallian. **In** *Wagener, H.-J. and Drukker, J. W., eds.*, 1986, pp. 93–111.

036 Economic Methodology

Schmitt, Bernard. The Process of Formation of Economics in Relation to Other Sciences. **In** *Baranzini, M. and Scazzieri, R., eds.*, 1986, pp. 103–32.

Sen, Amartya K. Prediction and Economic Theory. **In** *Mason, J.; Mathias, P. and Westcott, J. H., eds.*, 1986, pp. 3–22.

Shackle, George L. S. Decision. *J. Econ. Stud.*, 1986, *13*(5), pp. 58–62.

Shionoya, Yuichi. The Science and Ideology of Schumpeter. *Rivista Int. Sci. Econ. Com.*, August 1986, *33*(8), pp. 729–62.

Simon, Herbert A. The Failure of Armchair Economics. *Challenge*, Nov./Dec. 1986, *29*(5), pp. 18–25.

Simon, Lawrence H. and Ruccio, David F. A Methodological Analysis of Dependency Theory: Explanation in Andre Gunder Frank. *World Devel.*, Special Issue, Feb. 1986, *14*(2), pp. 195–209.

Smith, Barry. Austrian Economics and Austrian Philosophy. **In** *Grassl, W. and Smith, B., eds.*, 1986, pp. 1–36.

Stanley, T. D. Recursive Economic Knowledge: Hierarchy, Maximization and Behavioral Economics. *J. Behav. Econ.*, Winter 1986, *15*, pp. 85–99.

Stigler, George J. The Process and Progress of Economics. **In** *Stigler, G. J.*, 1986, *1983*, pp. 134–49.

Tintner, Gerhard and Licari, Joseph A. The Stochastic View of Economics. **In** *Szenberg, M., ed.*, 1986, *1970*, pp. 23–32.

Wilber, Charles K. Methodological Debate in Economics: Editor's Introduction. *World Devel.*, Special Issue, Feb. 1986, *14*(2), pp. 143–45.

Wilber, Charles K. and Francis, Steven. The Methodological Basis of Hirschman's Development Economics: Pattern Model vs. General Laws. **In** *[Hirshman, A. O.]*, 1986, pp. 317–42.

Wilber, Charles K. and Francis, Steven. The Methodological Basis of Hirschman's Development Economics: Pattern Model vs General Laws. *World Devel.*, Special Issue, Feb. 1986, *14*(2), pp. 181–94.

Wisman, Jon D. The Methodology of W. Arthur Lewis's Development Economics: Economics as Pedagogy. *World Devel.*, Special Issue, Feb. 1986, *14*(2), pp. 165–80.

Yunker, James A. In Defense of Utilitarianism: An Economist's Viewpoint. *Rev. Soc. Econ.*, April 1986, *44*(1), pp. 57–79.

040 Economic History

041 Economic History: General

0410 General

Berend, Iván T. The Great Economic Shocks of the 20th Century in the General Processes of History: Similarities and Differences between the 1930s and the 1970s–1980s. **In** *Berend, I. T. and Borchardt, K., eds.*, 1986, pp. 545–59. **[G: Global]**

Blaug, Mark. Economic History and the History of Economics: Introduction. **In** *Blaug, M.*, 1986, pp. vii–xx.

Borchardt, Knut. The Impact of the Depression of the 1930s and Its Relevance for the Contemporary World: Introductory Report. **In** *Berend, I. T. and Borchardt, K., eds.*, 1986, pp. 5–32.

Bordo, Michael D. Explorations in Monetary History: A Survey of the Literature. *Exploration Econ. Hist.*, October 1986, *23*(4), pp. 339–415. **[G: OECD]**

Bordo, Michael D. Financial Crises, Banking Crises, Stock Market Crashes and the Money Supply: Some International Evidence, 1870–1933. **In** *Capie, F. and Wood, G. E., eds.*, 1986, pp. 190–248.

Braun, Hanne. A Review of the New Literature on Banking History. **In** *Pohl, H. and Rudolph, B., eds.*, 1986, pp. 143–50.

Brüninghaus, Beate. A Reivew of the New Literature on Business History. **In** *Pohl, H. and Rudolph, B., eds.*, 1986, pp. 125–42.

Carlsson, Bo. The Development and Use of Machine Tools in Historical Perspective. **In** *Day, R. H. and Eliasson, G., eds.*, 1986, *1984*, pp. 247–70. **[G: U.K.]**

Claydon, Tim; Partridge, Michael and Ville, Simon. List of Publications on the Economic and Social History of Great Britain and Ireland. *Econ. Hist. Rev., 2nd Ser.*, November 1986, *39*(4), pp. 612–51.

Ford, Alec G. Financial Crises, Banking Crises, Stock Market Crashes and the Money Supply: Some International Evidence, 1870–1933: Comment. **In** *Capie, F. and Wood, G. E., eds.*, 1986, pp. 249–53.

Godschalk, Hugo. The Moneyless Economy—From Temple Exchange to the Barter Club. **In** *Pohl, H. and Rudolph, B., eds.*, 1986, pp. 57–78. **[G: W. Germany; U.S.]**

Jonung, Lars. International Financial Crisis and the Swedish Economy 1857–1933. **In** *Capie, F. and Wood, G. E., eds.*, 1986, pp. 254–64. **[G: Sweden]**

Parker, William N. Capitalistic Organization and National Response: Social Dynamics in the Age of Schumpeter. **In** *Day, R. H. and Eliasson, G., eds.*, 1986, *1984*, pp. 351–71. **[G: Germany; U.S.; France; England]**

Parker, William N. Capitalistic Organization and National Response: Social Dynamics in the Age of Schumpeter: Reply. **In** *Day, R. H. and Eliasson, G., eds.*, 1986, pp. 378–83. **[G: Germany; U.S.; France; England]**

Parker, William N. The Development and Use of Machine Tools in Historical Perspective: Comment. **In** *Day, R. H. and Eliasson, G., eds.*, 1986, pp. 271–76. **[G: U.K.]**

Ross, Steven J. and Perkins, Edwin J. Integrating Business History and Labor History. **In** *Atack, J., ed.*, 1986, pp. 43–52.

Rybczynski, Tad M. Capitalistic Organization and National Response: Social Dynamics in the Age of Schumpeter: Comment. **In** *Day, R. H. and*

Eliasson, G., eds., 1986, pp. 372–77.
[G: Germany; U.S.; France; England]

Schneider, Dieter. Management Mistakes—Do We Need More History in Business Economics? **In** *Pohl, H. and Rudolph, B., eds.*, 1986, pp. 27–40.

Simon, Julian L. Some Theory of Population Growth's Effect on Technical Change in an Industrial Context. *Australian Econ. Hist. Rev.*, September 1986, *26*(2), pp. 148–58.

Solomou, Solomos. Non-balanced Growth and Kondratieff Waves in the World Economy, 1850–1913. *J. Econ. Hist.*, March 1986, *46*(1), pp. 165–69. **[G: Global]**

Sweezy, Paul M. The Historical Materialism Discussion. *Sci. Soc.*, Spring 1986, *50*(1), pp. 81–84.

Wilkins, Mira. Defining a Firm: History and Theory. **In** *Hertner, P. and Jones, G., eds.*, 1986, pp. 80–95.

0411 Development of the Discipline

Ashton, Thomas Southcliffe. Recollections of Four British Economic Historians. *Banca Naz. Lavoro Quart. Rev.*, September 1986, (158), pp. 337–52.

Depelchin, Jacques. For History, but against His-Story: Review Essay. *African Econ. Hist.*, 1986, (15), pp. 173–82.

Meiners, Roger E. and Nardinelli, Clark. What Has Happened to the New Economic History? *J. Inst. Theoretical Econ.*, September 1986, *142*(3), pp. 510–27.

O'Brien, Patrick K. Do We Have a Typology for the Study of European Industrialization in the XIXth Century? *J. Europ. Econ. Hist.*, Fall 1986, *15*(2), pp. 291–333. **[G: Europe]**

Sexton, Robert L. Regional Choice and Economic History. *Econ. Forum*, Winter 1986-1987, *16*(1), pp. 159–66. **[G: U.S.]**

0412 Comparative Intercountry or Intertemporal Economic History

Andersen, Søren Munk. The Need of Central Water Management in Irrigation Systems. **In** *Nørlund, I.; Cederroth, S. and Gerdin, I., eds.*, 1986, pp. 307–21.

Auerbach, Alan J. Major Changes in Cyclical Behavior: Comment. **In** *Gordon, R. J., ed.*, 1986, pp. 573–75. **[G: U.S.; U.K.; France; W. Germany]**

Bairoch, Paul and Goertz, Gary. Factors of Urbanisation in the Nineteenth Century Developed Countries: A Descriptive and Econometric Analysis. *Urban Stud.*, August 1986, *23*(4), pp. 285–305. **[G: MDCs]**

Basevi, Giorgio and Toniolo, Gianni. Debt and Default in the 1930s: Causes and Consequences: Comments. *Europ. Econ. Rev.*, June 1986, *30*(3), pp. 641–47.

Ben-Porat, A. Formation of the Working Class in the U.S.A. and Palestine, 1881–1920: A Comparative Study. *Sci. Soc.*, Winter 1986-1987, *50*(4), pp. 440–63.

Cameron, Ronald. Was England Really Superior to France? Review Article. *J. Econ. Hist.*, December 1986, *46*(4), pp. 1031–39. **[G: U.K.; France]**

Capie, Forrest H. Conditions in Which Very Rapid Inflation Has Appeared. *Carnegie-Rochester Conf. Ser. Public Policy*, Spring 1986, *24*, pp. 115–68. **[G: Global]**

Collet, Pierre; Le Goff, Denis and de Penanros, Roland. The Economic Basis of Social Organization. *J. Compar. Econ.*, June 1986, *10*(2), pp. 106–37.

Davis, Kingsley. Low Fertility in Evolutionary Perspective. *Population Devel. Rev.*, Supp. 1986, *12*, pp. 48–65. **[G: OECD]**

Davis, Lance E. and Huttenback, Robert A. Imperialism and Social Class (Apologies to Marx and Schumpeter): Imperial Investors in the Age of High Imperialism. **In** *Wagener, H.-J. and Drukker, J. W., eds.*, 1986, pp. 156–85. **[G: U.K.]**

Demeny, Paul. The World Demographic Situation. **In** *Menken, J., ed.*, 1986, pp. 27–66. **[G: Global]**

Eichengreen, Barry and Portes, Richard. Debt and Default in the 1930s: Causes and Consequences. *Europ. Econ. Rev.*, June 1986, *30*(3), pp. 599–640. **[G: U.S.; U.K.; Latin America; Australia]**

Fabricant, Solomon. Major Changes in Cyclical Behavior: Comment. **In** *Gordon, R. J., ed.*, 1986, pp. 575–78. **[G: U.S.; U.K.; W. Germany; France]**

Fishlow, Albert. Lessons from the Past: Capital Markets during the 19th Century and the Interwar Period. **In** *Kahler, M., ed.*, 1986, pp. 37–93. **[G: LDCs; MDCs]**

Fratianni, Michele. Conditions in Which Very Rapid Inflation Has Appeared: A Comment. *Carnegie-Rochester Conf. Ser. Public Policy*, Spring 1986, *24*, pp. 169–77. **[G: Global]**

Galloway, Patrick R. Long-term Fluctuations in Climate and Population in the Preindustrial Era. *Population Devel. Rev.*, March 1986, *12*(1), pp. 1–24. **[G: China; Europe]**

Gardella, Robert P. The Boom Years of the Fukien Tea Trade, 1842–1888. **In** *May, E. R. and Fairbank, J. K., eds.*, 1986, pp. 33–75. **[G: U.S.; U.K.; China; Australia]**

Good, David F. Uneven Development in the Nineteenth Century: A Comparison of the Habsburg Empire and the United States. *J. Econ. Hist.*, March 1986, *46*(1), pp. 137–51. **[G: Europe; U.S.]**

Gospel, Howard F. Comparative Patterns of Labor–Management Relations: Great Britain, the U.S., and Japan. **In** *Atack, J., ed.*, 1986, pp. 119–31. **[G: U.S.; U.K.; Japan]**

Herlitz, Lars. Private Consumption and Development of Industrial Production: The 1930s Compared with Post-war Tendencies. **In** *Berend, I. T. and Borchardt, K., eds.*, 1986, pp. 497–515. **[G: U.K.; U.S.; Germany; Sweden; France]**

Hertner, Peter and Jones, Geoffrey. Multinationals: Theory and History. **In** *Hertner, P. and*

Jones, G., eds., 1986, pp. 1–18.

Humphrey, Thomas M. The Monetary Approach to Exchange Rates: Its Historical Evolution and Role in Policy Debates. **In** *Putnam, B. H. and Wilford, D. S., eds.*, 1986, *1978*, pp. 152–67. **[G: U.K.; Sweden; Germany]**

Kaser, Michael and Nötel, R. The East European Economies in Two World Crises. **In** *Berend, I. T. and Borchardt, K., eds.*, 1986, pp. 215–47. **[G: E. Europe]**

Kawagoe, Toshihiko; Otsuka, Keijiro and Hayami, Yujiro. Induced Bias of Technical Change in Agriculture: The United States and Japan, 1880–1980. *J. Polit. Econ.*, Part 1, June 1986, *94*(3), pp. 523–44. **[G: U.S.; Japan]**

Killingsworth, Mark R. and Heckman, James J. Female Labor Supply: A Survey. **In** *Ashenfelter, O. and Layard, R., eds., Vol. 1*, 1986, pp. 103–204. **[G: U.S.; U.K.; Canada; Germany]**

Kranzberg, Melvin. The Technical Elements in International Technology Transfer: Historical Perspectives. **In** *McIntyre, J. R. and Papp, D. S., eds.*, 1986, pp. 31–45. **[G: U.S.; Japan; U.S.S.R.]**

Kuczynski, Thomas. The Development of Foreign Trade during the "Greatest Depression"—An Exceptional Case. Some Statistical Observations Concerning the Structure of World Production of Material Goods. **In** *Berend, I. T. and Borchardt, K., eds.*, 1986, pp. 456–83. **[G: Global]**

Landes, David S. European Expansion: The History of Innovation and Performance. **In** *Gondolf, E. W.; Marcus, I. M. and Dougherty, J. P., eds.*, 1986, pp. 25–41.

Maddison, Angus. Developing Countries in the 1930s: Possible Lessons for the 1980s. **In** *Lal, D. and Wolf, M., eds.*, 1986, pp. 15–47. **[G: LDCs; MDCs]**

Marcus, Irwin M. The Global Economy: Divergent Perspectives on Economic Change: Introduction: A Historical Overview of the Global Economy. **In** *Gondolf, E. W.; Marcus, I. M. and Dougherty, J. P., eds.*, 1986, pp. 1–12.

Michie, Ranald C. The London and New York Stock Exchanges, 1850–1914. *J. Econ. Hist.*, March 1986, *46*(1), pp. 171–87. **[G: U.S.; U.K.]**

Moore, Geoffrey H. and Zarnowitz, Victor. The Development and Role of the National Bureau of Economic Research's Business Cycle Chronologies. **In** *Gordon, R. J., ed.*, 1986, pp. 735–79. **[G: OECD]**

Pencavel, John H. Labor Supply of Men: A Survey. **In** *Ashenfelter, O. and Layard, R., eds., Vol. 1*, 1986, pp. 3–102. **[G: U.S.; U.K.; Canada; Germany]**

Reynolds, Bruce L. The East Asian "Textile Cluster" Trade, 1868–1973: A Comparative-Advantage Interpretation. **In** *May, E. R. and Fairbank, J. K., eds.*, 1986, pp. 129–50. **[G: U.S.; U.K.; China; India; Japan]**

Schmitz, Christopher. The Rise of Big Business in the World Copper Industry 1870–1930. *Econ. Hist. Rev., 2nd Ser.*, August 1986, *39*(3), pp. 392–410. **[G: OECD]**

Schwartz, Anna J. Alternative Monetary Regimes: The Gold Standard. **In** *Campbell, C. D. and Dougan, W. R., eds.*, 1986, pp. 44–72. **[G: U.S.; U.K.; W. Germany; France]**

Servet, J.-Michel. Pièces, billets et monnaies primitives. (Coins, Notes and Primitive Money. With English summary.) *Écon. Soc.*, February 1986, *20*(2), pp. 7–18.

Trebilcock, Clive. The City, Entrepreneurship and Insurance: Two Pioneers in Invisible Exports—The Phoenix Fire Office and the Royal of Liverpool, 1800–90. **In** *[Coleman, D. C.]*, 1986, pp. 137–72. **[G: Selected Countries]**

Zarnowitz, Victor and Moore, Geoffrey H. Major Changes in Cyclical Behavior. **In** *Gordon, R. J., ed.*, 1986, pp. 519–72. **[G: U.S.; W. Germany; U.K.; France]**

042 Economic History: United States and Canada

0420 General

Altman, Morris. Resource Endowments and Location Theory in Economic History: A Case Study of Quebec and Ontario at the Turn of the Twentieth Century. *J. Econ. Hist.*, December 1986, *46*(4), pp. 999–1009. **[G: Canada]**

Auerbach, Alan J. Major Changes in Cyclical Behavior: Comment. **In** *Gordon, R. J., ed.*, 1986, pp. 573–75. **[G: U.S.; U.K.; France; W. Germany]**

Balke, Nathan S. and Gordon, Robert J. The American Business Cycle: Historical Data. **In** *Gordon, R. J., ed.*, 1986, pp. 781–850. **[G: U.S.]**

Bernstein, Michael A. Economic Instability in the United States in the 1930s and the 1970s: An Essay in Historical Homology. **In** *Berend, I. T. and Borchardt, K., eds.*, 1986, pp. 35–61. **[G: U.S.]**

Cain, Louis P. From Mud to Metropolis: Chicago before the Fire. **In** *Uselding, P., ed.*, 1986, pp. 93–129. **[G: U.S.]**

Crew, Spencer R. and Fleckner, John A. Archival Sources for Business History at the National Museum of American History. *Bus. Hist. Rev.*, Autumn 1986, *60*(3), pp. 474–86. **[G: U.S.]**

Dales, J. H. New Estimates of Gross National Product, Canada, 1870–1926: Some Implications for Canadian Development: Comment. **In** *Engerman, S. L. and Gallman, R. E., eds.*, 1986, pp. 89–93. **[G: Canada]**

De Long, James Bradford and Summers, Lawrence H. The Changing Cyclical Variability of Economic Activity in the United States. **In** *Gordon, R. J., ed.*, 1986, pp. 679–719. **[G: U.S.]**

DiMaggio, Paul J. Cultural Entrepreneurship in Nineteenth-Century Boston. **In** *DiMaggio, P. J., ed.*, 1986, pp. 41–61. **[G: U.S.]**

Duménil, Gérard; Glick, Mark and Rangel, José.

La grande dépression énigme d'hier ou d'aujourd'hui? (The Great Depression: Yesterday's Riddle for Today. With English summary.) *Revue Écon.*, May 1986, *37*(3), pp. 381–427. **[G: U.S.]**

Edgerly, Linda. The Present and Future of Corporate Archives: A Golden Age? **In** *Atack, J., ed.*, 1986, pp. 197–203. **[G: U.S.]**

Eisner, Robert. The Changing Cyclical Variability of Economic Activity in the United States: Comment. **In** *Gordon, R. J., ed.*, 1986, pp. 719–27. **[G: U.S.]**

Engelbourg, Saul. John Stewart Kennedy and the City of Glasgow Bank. **In** *Atack, J., ed.*, 1986, pp. 69–82. **[G: U.S.]**

Engelbourg, Saul and Schachter, Gustav. Two "Souths": The United States and Italy since the 1860's. *J. Europ. Econ. Hist.*, Winter 1986, *15*(3), pp. 563–89. **[G: U.S.; Italy]**

Fabricant, Solomon. Major Changes in Cyclical Behavior: Comment. **In** *Gordon, R. J., ed.*, 1986, pp. 575–78. **[G: U.S.; U.K.; W. Germany; France]**

Gallaway, Lowell and Vedder, Richard. Inflation, Migration, and Divorce in Contemporary America. **In** *Peden, J. R. and Glahe, F. R., eds.*, 1986, pp. 285–307. **[G: U.S.]**

Grossman, Herschel I. The Changing Cyclical Variability of Economic Activity in the United States: Comment. **In** *Gordon, R. J., ed.*, 1986, pp. 728–31. **[G: U.S.]**

Hotopp, Susan. Business Location 1860 and 1870: Evidence from the Manufacturing Censuses. **In** *Atack, J., ed.*, 1986, pp. 85–91. **[G: U.S.]**

Huertas, Thomas F. and Silverman, Joan L. Charles E. Mitchell: Scapegoat of the Crash? *Bus. Hist. Rev.*, Spring 1986, *60*(1), pp. 81–103. **[G: U.S.]**

Hutchinson, William K. Regional Exports of the United States to Foreign Countries: A Structural Analysis, 1870–1910. **In** *Uselding, P., ed.*, 1986, pp. 131–54. **[G: U.S.]**

Kahan, Arcadius. The First Wave of Jewish Immigration from Eastern Europe to the United States. **In** *Kahan, A.*, 1986, pp. 118–27. **[G: U.S.]**

Klein, Maury. Jay Gould: A Revisionist Interpretation. **In** *Atack, J., ed.*, 1986, pp. 55–68. **[G: U.S.]**

Kregel, J. A. Laws of the Market and Laws of Motion: An Essay in Comparative Social History. **In** *Wagener, H.-J. and Drukker, J. W., eds.*, 1986, pp. 31–48. **[G: U.S.; U.K.]**

Lebergott, Stanley. Discussion [New Estimates of Prewar Gross National Product and Unemployment] [The Reliability of Historical Macroeconomic Data for Comparing Cyclical Stability]. *J. Econ. Hist.*, June 1986, *46*(2), pp. 367–71. **[G: U.S.]**

Lomnitz, Larissa and Perez-Lizaur, Marisol. Family Enterprise and the Process of Industrialization in Mexico. **In** *Greenfield, S. M. and Strickon, A., eds.*, 1986, pp. 124–37. **[G: Mexico]**

Martin, Albro. The Good That Men Do: A Review Essay. *Bus. Hist. Rev.*, Autumn 1986, *60*(3), pp. 469–73. **[G: U.S.]**

Miranti, Paul J., Jr. From Conflict to Concensus: The American Institute of Accountants and the Professionalization of Public Accountancy, 1886–1940. **In** *Atack, J., ed.*, 1986, pp. 93–100. **[G: U.S.]**

Nash, Michael. Business History at the Hagley Museum and Library. *Bus. Hist. Rev.*, Spring 1986, *60*(1), pp. 104–20. **[G: U.S.]**

Norton, Roger D. Industrial Policy and American Renewal. *J. Econ. Lit.*, March 1986, *24*(1), pp. 1–40. **[G: U.S.]**

Parker, William N. Capitalistic Organization and National Response: Social Dynamics in the Age of Schumpeter: Reply. **In** *Day, R. H. and Eliasson, G., eds.*, 1986, pp. 378–83. **[G: Germany; U.S.; France; England]**

Parker, William N. Capitalistic Organization and National Response: Social Dynamics in the Age of Schumpeter. **In** *Day, R. H. and Eliasson, G., eds.*, 1986, *1984*, pp. 351–71. **[G: Germany; U.S.; France; England]**

Poulson, Barry W. Education and the Family during the Industrial Revolution. **In** *Peden, J. R. and Glahe, F. R., eds.*, 1986, pp. 135–58. **[G: U.S.]**

Pugno, Maurizio. L'"ottima distribuzione del reddito" di Sylos Labini: una nota. (Sylos Labini's "Optimal Distribution of Incomes": A Note. With English summary.) *Econ. Polít.*, August 1986, *3*(2), pp. 259–75. **[G: U.S.]**

Rolnick, Arthur J. and Weber, Warren E. Gresham's Law or Gresham's Fallacy? *J. Polit. Econ.*, February 1986, *94*(1), pp. 185–99. **[G: U.S.]**

Romer, Christina D. New Estimates of Prewar Gross National Product and Unemployment. *J. Econ. Hist.*, June 1986, *46*(2), pp. 341–52. **[G: U.S.]**

Rybczynski, Tad M. Capitalistic Organization and National Response: Social Dynamics in the Age of Schumpeter: Comment. **In** *Day, R. H. and Eliasson, G., eds.*, 1986, pp. 372–77. **[G: Germany; U.S.; France; England]**

Steen, Robert C. Nonubiquitous Transportation and Urban Population Density Gradients. *J. Urban Econ.*, July 1986, *20*(1), pp. 97–106. **[G: U.S.]**

Truman, Dorothy. The Museum of American Textile History: Archival Sources for Business History. *Bus. Hist. Rev.*, Winter 1986, *60*(4), pp. 641–50. **[G: U.S.]**

Urquhart, M. C. New Estimates of Gross National Product, Canada, 1870–1926: Some Implications for Canadian Development. **In** *Engerman, S. L. and Gallman, R. E., eds.*, 1986, pp. 9–88. **[G: Canada]**

Vecoli, Rudolph J. The Formation of Chicago's "Little Italies." **In** *Glazier, I. A. and De Rosa, L., eds.*, 1986, pp. 287–301. **[G: U.S.]**

Walker, Juliet E. K. Racism, Slavery, and Free Enterprise: Black Entrepreneurship in the United States before the Civil War. *Bus. Hist. Rev.*, Autumn 1986, *60*(3), pp. 343–82. **[G: U.S.]**

042 Economic History: United States and Canada

Weir, David R. The Reliability of Historical Macroeconomic Data for Comparing Cyclical Stability. *J. Econ. Hist.*, June 1986, *46*(2), pp. 353–65. **[G: U.S.]**

White, Eugene Nelson. Latin America's Debt Crisis of the 1930s: Lessons for the 1980s. **In** *Berend, I. T. and Borchardt, K., eds.*, 1986, pp. 484–96. **[G: Latin America; U.S.]**

Wrege, Charles D. and Greenwood, Ronald G. Frederick W. Taylor and Industrial Espionage: 1895–1897. **In** *Atack, J., ed.*, 1986, pp. 183–93.

Zarnowitz, Victor and Moore, Geoffrey H. Major Changes in Cyclical Behavior. **In** *Gordon, R. J., ed.*, 1986, pp. 519–72. **[G: U.S.; W. Germany; U.K.; France]**

0421 History of Product Prices and Markets

Abramovitz, Moses. Inventory Fluctuations in the United States since 1929: Comment. **In** *Gordon, R. J., ed.*, 1986, pp. 214–23. **[G: U.S.]**

Adams, Donald R., Jr. Prices and Wages in Maryland, 1750–1850. *J. Econ. Hist.*, September 1986, *46*(3), pp. 625–45. **[G: U.S.]**

Adams, Walter and Brock, James W. The Automobile Industry. **In** *Adams, W., ed.*, 1986, pp. 126–71. **[G: U.S.]**

Atack, Jeremy. Firm Size and Industrial Structure in the United States during the Nineteenth Century. *J. Econ. Hist.*, June 1986, *46*(2), pp. 463–75. **[G: U.S.]**

Barthold, Thomas A. and Dougan, William R. The Fisher Hypothesis under Different Monetary Regimes. *Rev. Econ. Statist.*, November 1986, *68*(4), pp. 674–79. **[G: U.S.]**

Berlan, Jean-Pierre. From the United States to a World System: Technological Change, International Trade, Agricultural Policy in the Twentieth Century. **In** *Maunder, A. and Renborg, U., eds.*, 1986, pp. 343–52. **[G: U.S.]**

Blinder, Alan S. and Holtz-Eakin, Douglas. Inventory Fluctuations in the United States since 1929: Reply. **In** *Gordon, R. J., ed.*, 1986, pp. 231–33. **[G: U.S.]**

Blinder, Alan S. and Holtz-Eakin, Douglas. Inventory Fluctuations in the United States since 1929. **In** *Gordon, R. J., ed.*, 1986, pp. 183–214. **[G: U.S.]**

Brown, Martin and Philips, Peter. Craft Labor and Mechanization in Nineteenth-Century American Canning. *J. Econ. Hist.*, September 1986, *46*(3), pp. 743–56. **[G: U.S.]**

Cain, Louis P. How Public Works Saved Private Enterprise: The Thomas & Betts Company in the Great Depression. **In** *Atack, J., ed.*, 1986, pp. 29–40. **[G: U.S.]**

Cain, Louis P. and Paterson, Donald G. Biased Technical Change, Scale, and Factor Substitution in American Industry, 1850–1919. *J. Econ. Hist.*, March 1986, *46*(1), pp. 153–64. **[G: U.S.]**

Carlos, Ann M. and Hoffman, Elizabeth. The North American Fur Trade: Bargaining to a Joint Profit Maximum under Incomplete Information, 1804–1821. *J. Econ. Hist.*, December 1986, *46*(4), pp. 967–86. **[G: Canada]**

Chao, Kang. The Chinese–American Cotton-Textile Trade, 1830–1930. **In** *May, E. R. and Fairbank, J. K., eds.*, 1986, pp. 103–27. **[G: China; Japan; U.S.; U.K.]**

Cheng, Chu-yuan. The United States Petroleum Trade with China, 1876–1949. **In** *May, E. R. and Fairbank, J. K., eds.*, 1986, pp. 205–33. **[G: U.S.; China]**

Dornbusch, Rudiger. Como deter a hiperinflação: lições da experiência inflacionária alemã da década de 20. (With English summary.) *Pesquisa Planejamento Econ.*, April 1986, *16*(1), pp. 61–85. **[G: U.S.; France; U.K.; W. Germany]**

Drollas, Leonidas P. The Search for Oil in the USA: An Econometric Approach. *Energy Econ.*, July 1986, *8*(3), pp. 155–64. **[G: U.S.]**

Elbaum, Bernard. The Steel Industry before World War I. **In** *Elbaum, B. and Lazonick, W., eds.*, 1986, pp. 51–81. **[G: U.K.; U.S.]**

Esbitt, Milton. Bank Portfolios and Bank Failures during the Great Depression: Chicago. *J. Econ. Hist.*, June 1986, *46*(2), pp. 455–62. **[G: U.S.]**

Fairbank, John K. America's China Trade in Historical Perspective: The Chinese and American Performance: Patterns and Problems. **In** *May, E. R. and Fairbank, J. K., eds.*, 1986, pp. 1–7.

Forbes, Kevin F. Limited Liability and the Development of the Business Corporation. *J. Law, Econ., Organ.*, Spring 1986, *2*(1), pp. 163–77. **[G: U.S.]**

French, Michael. Structural Change and Competition in the United States Tire Industry, 1920–1937. *Bus. Hist. Rev.*, Spring 1986, *60*(1), pp. 28–54. **[G: U.S.]**

Friedman, Benjamin M. Money, Credit, and Interest Rates in the Business Cycle: Reply. **In** *Gordon, R. J., ed.*, 1986, pp. 450–55. **[G: U.S.]**

Friedman, Benjamin M. Money, Credit, and Interest Rates in the Business Cycle. **In** *Gordon, R. J., ed.*, 1986, pp. 395–438. **[G: U.S.]**

Friedman, Milton and Schwartz, Anna J. The Failure of the Bank of United States: A Reappraisal: A Reply [A Monetary History]. *Exploration Econ. Hist.*, April 1986, *23*(2), pp. 199–204. **[G: U.S.]**

Gahvari, Firouz. Demand and Supply of Housing in the U.S.: 1929–1978. *Econ. Inquiry*, April 1986, *24*(2), pp. 333–47. **[G: U.S.]**

Geweke, John. Fixed Investment in the American Business Cycle, 1919–83: Comment. **In** *Gordon, R. J., ed.*, 1986, pp. 336–40. **[G: U.S.]**

Goldfeld, Stephen M. Money, Credit, and Interest Rates in the Business Cycle: Comment. **In** *Gordon, R. J., ed.*, 1986, pp. 438–41. **[G: U.S.]**

González-Vega, Claudio. Human Capital, Technology and Institutions: Discussion. **In** *Maunder, A. and Renborg, U., eds.*, 1986, pp. 360–63. **[G: U.S.]**

Gordon, Robert J. and Veitch, John M. Fixed Investment in the American Business Cycle,

1919–83. **In** *Gordon, R. J., ed.*, 1986, pp. 267–335. **[G: U.S.]**

Gordon, Robert J. and Veitch, John M. Fixed Investment in the American Business Cycle, 1919–83: Reply. **In** *Gordon, R. J., ed.*, 1986, pp. 348–51. **[G: U.S.]**

Hao, Yen-p'ing. Chinese Teas to America—A Synopsis. **In** *May, E. R. and Fairbank, J. K., eds.*, 1986, pp. 11–31. **[G: U.S.; China]**

Hausman, William J.; Kemme, David M. and Neufeld, John L. The Relative Economic Efficiency of Private versus Municipal Waterworks in the 1890s. **In** *Atack, J., ed.*, 1986, pp. 13–27. **[G: U.S.]**

Holtfrerich, Carl-Ludwig. U.S. Capital Exports to Germany 1919–1923 Compared to 1924–1929. *Exploration Econ. Hist.*, January 1986, *23*(1), pp. 1–32. **[G: U.S.; W. Germany]**

Hyclak, Thomas J. Productivity and City Size: Some Historical Evidence. *Eastern Econ. J.*, Jan.-Mar. 1986, *12*(1), pp. 45–51. **[G: U.S.]**

John, Richard R., Jr. Private Mail Delivery in the United States during the Nineteenth Century: A Sketch. **In** *Atack, J., ed.*, 1986, pp. 135–47. **[G: U.S.]**

Lamoreaux, Naomi R. Banks, Kinship, and Economic Development: The New England Case. *J. Econ. Hist.*, September 1986, *46*(3), pp. 647–67. **[G: U.S.]**

Lee, Chi-wen Jevons and Petruzzi, Christopher R. The Gibson Paradox and the Monetary Standard. *Rev. Econ. Statist.*, May 1986, *68*(2), pp. 189–96. **[G: U.K.; U.S.]**

Lewchuk, W. The Motor Vehicle Industry. **In** *Elbaum, B. and Lazonick, W., eds.*, 1986, pp. 135–61. **[G: U.K.; U.S.]**

Mankiw, N. Gregory and Miron, Jeffrey A. The Changing Behavior of the Term Structure of Interest Rates. *Quart. J. Econ.*, May 1986, *101*(2), pp. 211–28. **[G: U.S.]**

Markusen, Ann Roell. Neither Ore, nor Coal, nor Markets: A Policy-Oriented View of Steel Sites in the USA. *Reg. Stud.*, October 1986, *20*(5), pp. 449–61. **[G: U.S.]**

Martin, W. J. Human Capital, Technology and Institutions: Discussion. **In** *Maunder, A. and Renborg, U., eds.*, 1986, pp. 363–65.

McCallum, Bennett T. Inventory Fluctuations in the United States since 1929: Comment. **In** *Gordon, R. J., ed.*, 1986, pp. 223–31. **[G: U.S.]**

Meltzer, Allan H. Money, Credit, and Interest Rates in the Business Cycle: Comment. **In** *Gordon, R. J., ed.*, 1986, pp. 441–50. **[G: U.S.]**

Petrik, Paula. The House That Parcheesi Built: Selchow & Righter Company. *Bus. Hist. Rev.*, Autumn 1986, *60*(3), pp. 410–37. **[G: U.S.]**

Pontecorvo, Giulio. Supply, Demand, and Common Property: The Historical Dynamics of the Fisheries of Georges Bank—Some Preliminary Observations. **In** *[Crutchfield, J. A.]*, 1986, pp. 97–117. **[G: U.S.]**

Puth, Robert C. Human Mobility as a Source of American Economic Growth. *Quart. Rev. Econ. Bus.*, Spring 1986, *26*(1), pp. 57–73. **[G: U.S.]**

Rockoff, Hugh. Institutional Requirements for Stable Free Banking. *Cato J.*, Fall 1986, *6*(2), pp. 617–34. **[G: U.S.]**

Romer, Christina D. Is the Stabilization of the Postwar Economy a Figment of the Data? *Amer. Econ. Rev.*, June 1986, *76*(3), pp. 314–34. **[G: U.S.]**

Schran, Peter. The Minor Significance of Commercial Relations between the United States and China, 1850–1931. **In** *May, E. R. and Fairbank, J. K., eds.*, 1986, pp. 237–58. **[G: China; U.S.; Japan]**

Shaw, Douglas V. Making Leisure Pay: Street Railway Owned Amusement Parks in the United States, 1900–1925. *J. Cult. Econ.*, December 1986, *10*(2), pp. 67–79. **[G: U.S.]**

Shmanske, Stephen. News as a Public Good: Cooperative Ownership, Price Commitments, and the Success of the Associated Press. *Bus. Hist. Rev.*, Spring 1986, *60*(1), pp. 55–80. **[G: U.S.]**

Sims, Christopher A. Fixed Investment in the American Business Cycle, 1919–83: Comment. **In** *Gordon, R. J., ed.*, 1986, pp. 340–48. **[G: U.S.]**

Steckel, Richard H. Birth Weights and Infant Mortality among American Slaves. *Exploration Econ. Hist.*, April 1986, *23*(2), pp. 173–98. **[G: U.S.]**

Trebilcock, Clive. The City, Entrepreneurship and Insurance: Two Pioneers in Invisible Exports—The Phoenix Fire Office and the Royal of Liverpool, 1800–90. **In** *[Coleman, D. C.]*, 1986, pp. 137–72. **[G: Selected Countries]**

Trimble, William F. The Naval Aircraft Factory, the American Aviation Industry, and Government Competition, 1919–1928. *Bus. Hist. Rev.*, Summer 1986, *60*(2), pp. 175–98. **[G: U.S.]**

Vietor, Richard H. K. Perspectives on the Bell System: Strategy, Structure, Technology, and Unionism. *Bus. Hist. Rev.*, Winter 1986, *60*(4), pp. 633–40. **[G: U.S.]**

Wallis, John Joseph and North, Douglass C. Measuring the Transaction Sector in the American Economy, 1870–1970. **In** *Engerman, S. L. and Gallman, R. E., eds.*, 1986, pp. 95–148. **[G: U.S.]**

White, Eugene Nelson. Before the Glass–Steagall Act: An Analysis of the Investment Banking Activities of National Banks. *Exploration Econ. Hist.*, January 1986, *23*(1), pp. 33–55. **[G: U.S.]**

Yates, JoAnne. The Telegraph's Effect on Nineteenth Century Markets and Firms. **In** *Atack, J., ed.*, 1986, pp. 149–63. **[G: U.S.]**

0422 History of Factor Prices and Markets

Adams, Donald R., Jr. Prices and Wages in Maryland, 1750–1850. *J. Econ. Hist.*, September 1986, *46*(3), pp. 625–45. **[G: U.S.]**

Alston, Lee J. Race Etiquette in the South: The Role of Tenancy. **In** *Uselding, P., ed.*, 1986, pp. 199–211. **[G: U.S.]**

Baily, Martin Neil. The Cyclical Behavior of Industrial Labor Markets: A Comparison of the Prewar and Postwar Eras: Comment. **In** *Gordon, R. J., ed.*, 1986, pp. 621–66. **[G: U.S.]**

Barnard, John. Rebirth of the United Automobile Workers: The General Motors Tool and Diemakers' Strike of 1939. *Labor Hist.*, Spring 1986, *27*(2), pp. 165–87. **[G: U.S.]**

Baumol, William J. Productivity Growth, Convergence, and Welfare: What the Long-run Data Show. *Amer. Econ. Rev.*, December 1986, *76*(5), pp. 1072–85. **[G: OECD; U.S.S.R.; China]**

Benston, George J. and Kaufman, George G. Risks and Failures in Banking: Overview, History, and Evaluation. **In** *Kaufman, G. G. and Kormendi, R. C., eds.*, 1986, pp. 49–77. **[G: U.S.]**

Bernanke, Ben S. Employment, Hours, and Earnings in the Depression: An Analysis of Eight Manufacturing Industries. *Amer. Econ. Rev.*, March 1986, *76*(1), pp. 82–109. **[G: U.S.]**

Bernanke, Ben S. and Powell, James L. The Cyclical Behavior of Industrial Labor Markets: A Comparison of the Prewar and Postwar Eras. **In** *Gordon, R. J., ed.*, 1986, pp. 583–621. **[G: U.S.]**

Bernstein, Irving. The Emergence of the American Welfare State: The New Deal and the New Frontier–Great Society. **In** *Dennis, B. D., ed.*, 1986, pp. 237–42. **[G: U.S.]**

Bode, Frederick A. and Ginter, Donald E. Regional Patterns of Intercounty Farm Investment in Antebellum Georgia. **In** *Uselding, P., ed.*, 1986, pp. 241–69. **[G: U.S.]**

Boyle, Kevin. Rite of Passage: The 1939 General Motors Tool and Die Strike. *Labor Hist.*, Spring 1986, *27*(2), pp. 188–203. **[G: U.S.]**

Briggs, John W. Fertility and Cultural Change among Families in Italy and America. *Amer. Hist. Rev.*, December 1986, *91*(5), pp. 1129–45. **[G: U.S.]**

Brown, Edwin L. "...to Make a Man Feel Good": John Henry Mealing, Railroad Caller. *Labor Hist.*, Spring 1986, *27*(2), pp. 257–64. **[G: U.S.]**

Brown, Martin and Philips, Peter. Competition, Racism, and Hiring Practices among California Manufacturers, 1860–1882. *Ind. Lab. Relat. Rev.*, October 1986, *40*(1), pp. 61–74. **[G: U.S.]**

Brown, Martin and Philips, Peter. Craft Labor and Mechanization in Nineteenth-Century American Canning. *J. Econ. Hist.*, September 1986, *46*(3), pp. 743–56. **[G: U.S.]**

Brown, Martin and Philips, Peter. The Decline of the Piece-Rate System in California Canning: Technological Innovation, Labor Management, and Union Pressure, 1890–1947. *Bus. Hist. Rev.*, Winter 1986, *60*(4), pp. 564–601. **[G: U.S.]**

Brown, Martin and Philips, Peter. The Decline of Piece Rates in California Canneries: 1890–1960. *Ind. Relat.*, Winter 1986, *25*(1), pp. 81–91. **[G: U.S.]**

Brown, Martin and Philips, Peter. The Historical Origin of Job Ladders in the U.S. Canning Industry and Their Effects on the Gender Division of Labour. *Cambridge J. Econ.*, June 1986, *10*(2), pp. 129–45. **[G: U.S.]**

Carter, Susan B. Occupational Segregation, Teachers' Wages, and American Economic Growth. *J. Econ. Hist.*, June 1986, *46*(2), pp. 373–83. **[G: U.S.]**

Carter, Susan B. The Female Labor Force and American Economic Growth, 1890–1980: Comment. **In** *Engerman, S. L. and Gallman, R. E., eds.*, 1986, pp. 594–99. **[G: U.S.]**

Cohen, Lizabeth and Chapman, Herrick. Recent Dissertations: In American and European Labor History. *Labor Hist.*, Fall 1986, *27*(4), pp. 545–48. **[G: W. Europe; U.S.]**

David, Paul A. and Sanderson, Warren C. Rudimentary Contraceptive Methods and the American Transition to Marital Fertility Control, 1855–1915. **In** *Engerman, S. L. and Gallman, R. E., eds.*, 1986, pp. 307–79. **[G: U.S.]**

Davis, Lance E. Measuring the Transaction Sector in the American Economy, 1870–1970: Comment. **In** *Engerman, S. L. and Gallman, R. E., eds.*, 1986, pp. 149–59. **[G: U.S.]**

Dick, Trevor J. O. Consumer Behavior in the Nineteenth Century and Ontario Workers, 1885–1889. *J. Econ. Hist.*, June 1986, *46*(2), pp. 477–88. **[G: Canada]**

Dubofsky, Melvyn. Industrial Relations: Comparing the 1980s with the 1920s. **In** *Dennis, B. D., ed.*, 1986, pp. 227–36. **[G: U.S.]**

Eichengreen, Barry and Gemery, Henry A. The Earnings of Skilled and Unskilled Immigrants at the End of the Nineteenth Century. *J. Econ. Hist.*, June 1986, *46*(2), pp. 441–54. **[G: U.S.]**

Engerman, Stanley L. Slavery and Emancipation in Comparative Perspective: A Look at Some Recent Debates. *J. Econ. Hist.*, June 1986, *46*(2), pp. 317–39. **[G: U.S.; Caribbean]**

Evans, M. D. R. American Fertility Pattern: A Comparison of White and Nonwhite Cohorts Born 1903–56. *Population Devel. Rev.*, June 1986, *12*(2), pp. 267–93. **[G: U.S.]**

Fenstermaker, J. Van and Filer, John E. Impact of the First and Second Banks of the United States and the Suffolk System on New England Bank Money: 1791–1837. *J. Money, Credit, Banking*, February 1986, *18*(1), pp. 28–40. **[G: U.S.]**

Fishback, Price V. Did Coal Miners "Owe Their Souls to the Company Store"? Theory and Evidence from the Early 1900s. *J. Econ. Hist.*, December 1986, *46*(4), pp. 1011–29. **[G: U.S.]**

Fishback, Price V. Workplace Safety during the Progressive Era: Fatal Accidents in Bituminous Coal Mining, 1912–1923. *Exploration Econ. Hist.*, July 1986, *23*(3), pp. 269–98. **[G: U.S.]**

Fishlow, Albert. Growth and Productivity Change in the Canadian Railway Sector, 1871–1926: Comment. **In** *Engerman, S. L. and Gallman, R. E., eds.*, 1986, pp. 812–16. **[G: Canada]**

Fogel, Robert William. Nutrition and the Decline in Mortality since 1700: Some Preliminary Findings. **In** *Engerman, S. L. and Gallman, R. E., eds.*, 1986, pp. 439–527. **[G: U.S.]**

Fones-Wolf, Elizabeth. Industrial Recreation, the Second World War, and the Revival of Welfare Capitalism, 1934–1960. *Bus. Hist. Rev.*, Summer 1986, *60*(2), pp. 232–57. **[G: U.S.]**

Galenson, Walter. The Historical Role of American Trade Unionism. **In** *Lipset, S. M., ed.*, 1986, pp. 39–73. **[G: U.S.]**

Gallman, Robert E. The United States Capital Stock in the Nineteenth Century. **In** *Engerman, S. L. and Gallman, R. E., eds.*, 1986, pp. 165–206. **[G: U.S.]**

Gifford, Adam, Jr. and Kenney, Roy W. Contracting and Sharecropping: An Empirical Test. *Atlantic Econ. J.*, July 1986, *14*(2), pp. 81. **[G: U.S.]**

Goldin, Claudia. Monitoring Costs and Occupational Segregation by Sex: A Historical Analysis. *J. Lab. Econ.*, January 1986, *4*(1), pp. 1–27. **[G: U.S.]**

Goldin, Claudia. The Female Labor Force and American Economic Growth, 1890–1980. **In** *Engerman, S. L. and Gallman, R. E., eds.*, 1986, pp. 557–94. **[G: U.S.]**

Goldsmith, Raymond W. The United States Capital Stock in the Nineteenth Century: Comment. **In** *Engerman, S. L. and Gallman, R. E., eds.*, 1986, pp. 206–10. **[G: U.S.]**

Gowaskie, Joe. John Mitchell and the Anthracite Mine Workers: Leadership Conservatism and Rank-and-File Militancy. *Labor Hist.*, Winter 1985-86, *27*(1), pp. 54–83. **[G: U.S.]**

Graves, Philip E. and Sexton, Robert L. Development, Mobility and Slavery: Real Income and Spatial Equilibration in the Postbellum South. *Amer. Econ.*, Spring 1986, *30*(1), pp. 36–39. **[G: U.S.]**

Green, Alan G. Growth and Productivity Change in the Canadian Railway Sector, 1871–1926. **In** *Engerman, S. L. and Gallman, R. E., eds.*, 1986, pp. 779–812. **[G: Canada]**

Grubb, Farley. Redemptioner Immigration to Pennsylvania: Evidence on Contract Choice and Profitability. *J. Econ. Hist.*, June 1986, *46*(2), pp. 407–18. **[G: U.S.]**

Haines, Michael R. New Results on the Decline in Household Fertility in the United States from 1750 to 1900: Comment. **In** *Engerman, S. L. and Gallman, R. E., eds.*, 1986, pp. 426–33. **[G: U.S.]**

Haines, Michael R. Rudimentary Contraceptive Methods and the American Transition to Marital Fertility Control, 1855–1915: Comment. **In** *Engerman, S. L. and Gallman, R. E., eds.*, 1986, pp. 379–83. **[G: U.S.]**

Hall, Jacquelyn Dowd; Korstad, Robert and Leloudis, James. Cotton Mill People: Work, Community, and Protest in the Textile South, 1880–1940. *Amer. Hist. Rev.*, April 1986, *91*(2), pp. 245–86. **[G: U.S.]**

Halpern, Martin. Taft–Hartley and the Defeat of the Progressive Alternative in the United Auto Workers. *Labor Hist.*, Spring 1986, *27*(2), pp. 204–26. **[G: U.S.]**

Huxley, Christopher; Kettler, David and Struthers, James. Is Canada's Experience "Especially Instructive"? **In** *Lipset, S. M., ed.*, 1986, pp. 113–32. **[G: Canada; U.S.]**

Jacoby, Sanford M. Employee Attitude Testing at Sears, Roebuck and Company, 1938–1960. *Bus. Hist. Rev.*, Winter 1986, *60*(4), pp. 602–32. **[G: U.S.]**

Jacoby, Sanford M. Progressive Discipline in American Industry: Its Origins, Development, and Consequences. **In** *Lipsky, D. B. and Lewin, D., eds.*, 1986, pp. 213–60. **[G: U.K.; U.S.]**

Johnson, Michael P. Work, Culture, and the Slave Community: Slave Occupations in the Cotton Belt in 1860. *Labor Hist.*, Summer 1986, *27*(3), pp. 325–55. **[G: U.S.]**

Kahan, Arcadius. Economic Opportunities and Some Pilgrims' Progress: Jewish Immigrants from Eastern Europe in the United States, 1890–1914. **In** *Kahan, A.*, 1986, *1978*, pp. 101–17. **[G: U.S.]**

Kahan, Arcadius. Jewish Life in the United States: Perspectives from Economics. **In** *Kahan, A.*, 1986, *1981*, pp. 128–48. **[G: U.S.]**

Kearl, J. R. and Pope, Clayne L. Choices, Rents, and Luck: Economic Mobility of Nineteenth-Century Utah Households. **In** *Engerman, S. L. and Gallman, R. E., eds.*, 1986, pp. 215–56. **[G: U.S.]**

Lause, Mark A. The "Unwashed Infidelity": Thomas Paine and Early New York City Labor History. *Labor Hist.*, Summer 1986, *27*(3), pp. 385–409. **[G: U.S.]**

Lazear, Edward P. The Cyclical Behavior of Industrial Labor Markets: A Comparison of the Prewar and Postwar Eras: Comment. **In** *Gordon, R. J., ed.*, 1986, pp. 626–32. **[G: U.S.]**

Leahey, Philip J. Skilled Labor and the Rise of the Modern Corporation: The Case of the Electrical Industry. *Labor Hist.*, Winter 1985-86, *27*(1), pp. 31–53. **[G: U.S.]**

Lebergott, Stanley. Revised Estimates of the United States Workforce, 1800–1860: Comment. **In** *Engerman, S. L. and Gallman, R. E., eds.*, 1986, pp. 671–73. **[G: U.S.]**

Lindert, Peter H. Nutrition and the Decline in Mortality since 1700: Some Preliminary Findings: Comment. **In** *Engerman, S. L. and Gallman, R. E., eds.*, 1986, pp. 527–37. **[G: U.S.]**

Margo, Robert A. Race and Human Capital: Comment. *Amer. Econ. Rev.*, December 1986, *76*(5), pp. 1221–24. **[G: U.S.]**

Margo, Robert A. Race, Educational Attainment, and the 1940 Census. *J. Econ. Hist.*, March 1986, *46*(1), pp. 189–98. **[G: U.S.]**

McInnis, R. M. Output and Productivity in Canadian Agriculture, 1870–71 to 1926–27. **In** *Engerman, S. L. and Gallman, R. E., eds.*, 1986, pp. 737–70. **[G: Canada]**

McLewin, Philip J. The Cockroaches of Paterson: A Study of Labor Conflict and Technological

Change. *Rev. Radical Polit. Econ.*, Fall 1986, *18*(3), pp. 23–43. [G: U.S.]

McTighe, Michael J. "True Philanthropy" and the Limits of the Female Sphere: Poor Relief and Labor Organizations in Ante-Bellum Cleveland. *Labor Hist.*, Spring 1986, *27*(2), pp. 227–56. [G: U.S.]

Miller, Ann R. Internal Migration and the Changing Structure of Employment in the United States in 1900: Machine Readable Census Samples as a New Source for Historical Research. **In** *Glazier, I. A. and De Rosa, L., eds.*, 1986, pp. 336–55. [G: U.S.]

Newell, William H. Inheritance on the Maturing Frontier: Butler County, Ohio, 1803–1865: Reply. **In** *Engerman, S. L. and Gallman, R. E., eds.*, 1986, pp. 300–301. [G: U.S.]

Newell, William H. Inheritance on the Maturing Frontier: Butler County, Ohio, 1803–1865. **In** *Engerman, S. L. and Gallman, R. E., eds.*, 1986, pp. 261–97. [G: U.S.]

Ó Gráda, Cormac. Across the Briny Ocean: Some Thoughts on Irish Emigration to America, 1800–1850. **In** *Glazier, I. A. and De Rosa, L., eds.*, 1986, pp. 79–94. [G: U.S.; Ireland]

Oberly, James W. Westward Who? Estimates of Native White Interstate Migration after the War of 1812. *J. Econ. Hist.*, June 1986, *46*(2), pp. 431–40. [G: U.S.]

Ostergren, Robert C. Swedish Migration to North America in Transatlantic Perspective. **In** *Glazier, I. A. and De Rosa, L., eds.*, 1986, pp. 125–47. [G: Sweden; U.S.]

Pastré, Olivier and Rowley, Anthony. The Multinationalisation of British and American Banks. **In** *Teichova, A.; Lévy-Leboyer, M. and Nussbaum, H., eds.*, 1986, pp. 232–38. [G: U.K.; U.S.]

Peterson, Willis and Kislev, Yoav. The Cotton Harvester in Retrospect: Labor Displacement or Replacement? *J. Econ. Hist.*, March 1986, *46*(1), pp. 199–216. [G: U.S.]

Phillips, William H. The Labor Market of Southern Textile Mill Villages: Some Micro Evidence. *Exploration Econ. Hist.*, April 1986, *23*(2), pp. 103–23. [G: U.S.]

Pretzer, William S. "The British, Duff Green, the Rats and the Devil": Custom, Capitalism, and Conflict in the Washington Printing Trade, 1834–36. *Labor Hist.*, Winter 1985-86, *27*(1), pp. 5–30. [G: U.S.]

Ransom, Roger L. and Sutch, Richard. The Labor of Older Americans: Retirement of Men on and off the Job, 1870–1937. *J. Econ. Hist.*, March 1986, *46*(1), pp. 1–30. [G: U.S.]

Roediger, David. Ira Steward and the Anti-Slavery Origins of American Eight-Hour Theory. *Labor Hist.*, Summer 1986, *27*(3), pp. 410–26. [G: U.S.]

Rogin, Lawrence. Historical Analysis: Industrial Relations Eras: Discussion. **In** *Dennis, B. D., ed.*, 1986, pp. 250–53. [G: U.S.]

Romer, Christina D. Spurious Volatility in Historical Unemployment Data. *J. Polit. Econ.*, February 1986, *94*(1), pp. 1–37. [G: U.S.]

Ryder, Norman B. Observations on the History of Cohort Fertility in the United States. *Population Devel. Rev.*, December 1986, *12*(4), pp. 617–43. [G: U.S.]

Schröter, Harm. A Typical Factor of German International Market Strategy: Agreements between the U.S. and German Electrotechnical Industries Up to 1939. **In** *Teichova, A.; Lévy-Leboyer, M. and Nussbaum, H., eds.*, 1986, pp. 160–70. [G: U.S.; Germany]

Schwartz, Stephen. Holdings on the 1934 West Coast Maritime Strike in the San Francisco Headquarters Archive, Sailors' Union of the Pacific: A Descriptive Summary. *Labor Hist.*, Summer 1986, *27*(3), pp. 427–30. [G: U.S.]

Smith, James P. Race and Human Capital: Reply. *Amer. Econ. Rev.*, December 1986, *76*(5), pp. 1225–29. [G: U.S.]

Sokoloff, Kenneth L. Productivity Growth in Manufacturing during Early Industrialization: Evidence from the American Northeast, 1820–1860. **In** *Engerman, S. L. and Gallman, R. E., eds.*, 1986, pp. 679–729. [G: U.S.]

Soltow, Lee. Choices, Rents, and Luck: Economic Mobility of Nineteenth-Century Utah Households: Comment. **In** *Engerman, S. L. and Gallman, R. E., eds.*, 1986, pp. 256–58. [G: U.S.]

Soltow, Lee. Inheritance on the Maturing Frontier: Butler County, Ohio, 1803–1865: Comment. **In** *Engerman, S. L. and Gallman, R. E., eds.*, 1986, pp. 297–300. [G: U.S.]

Steckel, Richard H. A Peculiar Population: The Nutrition, Health, and Mortality of American Slaves from Childhood to Maturity. *J. Econ. Hist.*, September 1986, *46*(3), pp. 721–41. [G: U.S.]

Swanson, Dorothy. Annual Bibliography on American Labor History, 1985: Periodicals, Dissertations, and Research in Progress. *Labor Hist.*, Fall 1986, *27*(4), pp. 529–41. [G: U.S.]

Troy, Leo. The Rise and Fall of American Trade Unions: The Labor Movement from FDR to RR. **In** *Lipset, S. M., ed.*, 1986, pp. 75–109. [G: OECD]

Urry, John. Capitalist Production, Scientific Management and the Service Class. **In** *Scott, A. J. and Storper, M., eds.*, 1986, pp. 43–66. [G: U.S.; U.K.]

Vedder, Richard, et al. Demonstrating Their Freedom: The Post-emancipation Migration of Black Americans. **In** *Uselding, P., ed.*, 1986, pp. 213–39. [G: U.S.]

Wahl, Jenny Bourne. New Results on the Decline in Household Fertility in the United States from 1750 to 1900. **In** *Engerman, S. L. and Gallman, R. E., eds.*, 1986, pp. 391–425. [G: U.S.]

Weiss, Thomas. Revised Estimates of the United States Workforce, 1800–1860: Reply. **In** *Engerman, S. L. and Gallman, R. E., eds.*, 1986, pp. 673–74. [G: U.S.]

Weiss, Thomas. Revised Estimates of the United States Workforce, 1800–1860. **In** *Engerman, S. L. and Gallman, R. E., eds.*, 1986, pp. 641–71. [G: U.S.]

Weitz, Eric D. Class Formation and Labor Protest

in the Mining Communities of Southern Illinois and the Ruhr, 1890–1925. *Labor Hist.*, Winter 1985-86, *27*(1), pp. 85–105. **[G: U.S.; Germany]**

Wilkins, Mira. European Multinationals in the United States: 1875–1914. **In** *Teichova, A.; Lévy-Leboyer, M. and Nussbaum, H., eds.*, 1986, pp. 55–64. **[G: U.S.]**

Wilkins, Mira. The Impacts of American Multinational Enterprise on American–Chinese Economic Relations, 1786–1949. **In** *May, E. R. and Fairbank, J. K., eds.*, 1986, pp. 259–92. **[G: U.S.; China]**

Williamson, Jeffrey G. Productivity Growth in Manufacturing during Early Industrialization: Evidence from the American Northeast, 1820–1860: Comment. **In** *Engerman, S. L. and Gallman, R. E., eds.*, 1986, pp. 729–33. **[G: U.S.]**

Wright, Gavin. Output and Productivity in Canadian Agriculture, 1870–71 to 1926–27: Comment. **In** *Engerman, S. L. and Gallman, R. E., eds.*, 1986, pp. 771–76. **[G: Canada]**

Zonderman, David A. From Mill Village to Industrial City: Letters from Vermont Factory Operatives. *Labor Hist.*, Spring 1986, *27*(2), pp. 265–85. **[G: U.S.]**

0423 History of Public Economic Policy (all levels)

Allen, Andrew T. Private Sector Response to Stabilization Policy: A Case Study. *Exploration Econ. Hist.*, July 1986, *23*(3), pp. 253–68. **[G: U.S.]**

Anderson, Terry L. and Hill, Peter J. Privatizing the Commons: Reply. *Southern Econ. J.*, April 1986, *52*(4), pp. 1165–67.

Arnold, Roger A. Marriage, Divorce, and Property Rights: A Natural Rights Framework. **In** *Peden, J. R. and Glahe, F. R., eds.*, 1986, pp. 195–227.

Bailey, Martin J. The Behavior of United States Deficits: Comment. **In** *Gordon, R. J., ed.*, 1986, pp. 387–89. **[G: U.S.]**

Barro, Robert J. The Behavior of United States Deficits. **In** *Gordon, R. J., ed.*, 1986, pp. 361–87. **[G: U.S.]**

Barro, Robert J. U.S. Deficits since World War I. *Scand. J. Econ.*, 1986, *88*(1), pp. 195–22. **[G: U.S.]**

Barroux, Yves. The Belmont–Morgan Syndicate as an Optimal Investment Banking Contract: Comment. *Europ. Econ. Rev.*, June 1986, *30*(3), pp. 679–80. **[G: U.S.]**

Barth, James R.; Iden, George R. and Russek, Frank S. The Economic Consequences of Federal Deficits: An Examination of the Net Wealth and Instability Issues. *Southern Econ. J.*, July 1986, *53*(1), pp. 27–50. **[G: U.S.]**

Benston, George J. Federal Regulation of Banking: Historical Overview. **In** *Kaufman, G. G. and Kormendi, R. C., eds.*, 1986, pp. 1–47. **[G: U.S.]**

Berman, David R. Voters, Candidates, and Issues in the Progressive Era: An Analysis of the 1912 Presidential Election in Arizona. *Soc. Sci. Quart.*, June 1986, *67*(2), pp. 255–66. **[G: U.S.]**

Black, Stanley W. The Open Economy: Implications for Monetary and Fiscal Policy: Comment. **In** *Gordon, R. J., ed.*, 1986, pp. 501–04. **[G: U.S.]**

Brady, David W. Electoral Realignment in the U.S. House of Representatives. **In** *Wright, G. C., Jr.; Rieselbach, L. N. and Dodd, L. C., eds.*, 1986, pp. 47–69. **[G: U.S.]**

Brooks, Neil. Taxation of Closely-Held Corporations: The Partnership Option and the Lower Rate of Tax. *Australian Tax Forum*, 1986, *3*(4), pp. 381–509. **[G: Australia; U.S.; U.K.; Canada]**

Buurman, Gary B. Henry George and the Institution of Private Property in Land: A Property Rights Approach. *Amer. J. Econ. Soc.*, October 1986, *45*(4), pp. 489–502. **[G: U.S.]**

Cain, Louis P. How Public Works Saved Private Enterprise: The Thomas & Betts Company in the Great Depression. **In** *Atack, J., ed.*, 1986, pp. 29–40. **[G: U.S.]**

de Cecco, Marcello. Modes of Financial Development: American Banking Dynamics and World Financial Crises. **In** *[Hirshman, A. O.]*, 1986, pp. 115–32. **[G: U.S.]**

Christ, Carl F. Accuracy of Forecasting as a Measure of Economic Uncertainty. **In** *Campbell, C. D. and Dougan, W. R., eds.*, 1986, pp. 154–60. **[G: U.S.]**

Clark, Truman A. Interest Rate Seasonals and the Federal Reserve. *J. Polit. Econ.*, February 1986, *94*(1), pp. 76–125. **[G: U.S.]**

Cox, W. Michael and Haslag, Joseph. The Market Value of Government of Canada Debt, Monthly, 1937–84. *Can. J. Econ.*, August 1986, *19*(3), pp. 469–97. **[G: Canada; U.S.]**

Darby, Michael R. and Lothian, James R. Economic Events and Keynesian Ideas: The 1930s and the 1970s. **In** *Burton, J., et al.*, 1986, pp. 71–86.

Davis, Lance E. Long-term Trends in State and Local Finance: Sources and Uses of Funds in North Carolina, 1800–1977: Comment. **In** *Engerman, S. L. and Gallman, R. E., eds.*, 1986, pp. 862–66. **[G: U.S.]**

Domínguez, Jorge I. Seeking Permission to Build a Nation: Cuban Nationalism and U.S. Response under the First Machado Presidency. **In** *Mesa-Lago, C., ed.*, 1986, pp. 33–48. **[G: U.S.; Cuba]**

Dornbusch, Rudiger and Fischer, Stanley. The Open Economy: Implications for Monetary and Fiscal Policy. **In** *Gordon, R. J., ed.*, 1986, pp. 459–501. **[G: U.S.]**

Duprey, James N. and Nelson, Clarence W. A Visible Hand: The Fed's Involvement in the Check Payments System. *Fed. Res. Bank Minn. Rev.*, Spring 1986, *10*(2), pp. 18–29. **[G: U.S.]**

Economopoulos, Andrew J. The Impact of Reserve Requirements on Free Bank Failures. *Atlantic Econ. J.*, December 1986, *14*(4), pp. 76–84. **[G: U.S.]**

Eichengreen, Barry. The Belmont–Morgan Syndicate as an Optimal Investment Banking Contract: Comment. *Europ. Econ. Rev.*, June 1986, *30*(3), pp. 681–82. **[G: U.S.]**

Ekelund, Robert B., Jr. and Thornton, Mark. Schumpeterian Analysis, Supply-Side Economics and Macroeconomic Policy in the 1920s. *Rev. Soc. Econ.*, December 1986, *44*(3), pp. 221–37. **[G: U.S.]**

Eliasson, Gunnar. U.S. Deficits since World War I: Comment. *Scand. J. Econ.*, 1986, *88*(1), pp. 235–38. **[G: U.S.; Sweden]**

Falvey, Rodney E. Why Have U.S. Tariffs Fallen since 1930? Comment. **In** *Snape, R. H., ed.*, 1986, pp. 254–56. **[G: U.S.]**

Fischer, Stanley. Meltzer on Uncertainty under Different Monetary Regimes. **In** *Campbell, C. D. and Dougan, W. R., eds.*, 1986, pp. 161–67. **[G: U.S.]**

Fishback, Price V. Workplace Safety during the Progressive Era: Fatal Accidents in Bituminous Coal Mining, 1912–1923. *Exploration Econ. Hist.*, July 1986, *23*(3), pp. 269–98. **[G: U.S.]**

Flesher, Dale L. and Flesher, Tonya K. Ivar Kreuger's Contribution to U.S. Financial Reporting. *Accounting Rev.*, July 1986, *61*(3), pp. 421–34. **[G: U.S.]**

Garber, Peter M. Interwar Movements of Dollars to Europe and the U.S. Currency Supply. *J. Int. Money Finance*, Supp. March 1986, *5*, pp. S135–56. **[G: U.S.]**

Garber, Peter M. and Grilli, Vittorio U. The Belmont–Morgan Syndicate as an Optimal Investment Banking Contract. *Europ. Econ. Rev.*, June 1986, *30*(3), pp. 649–77. **[G: U.S.]**

George, Peter and Sworden, Philip. The Courts and the Development of Trade in Upper Canada, 1830–1860. *Bus. Hist. Rev.*, Summer 1986, *60*(2), pp. 258–80. **[G: Canada]**

Green, Steven L. The Abrogation of Gold Clauses in 1933 and Its Relation to Current Controversies in Monetary Economics. *Fed. Res. Bank Dallas Econ. Rev.*, July 1986, pp. 1–17. **[G: U.S.]**

Hausman, William J.; Kemme, David M. and Neufeld, John L. The Relative Economic Efficiency of Private versus Municipal Waterworks in the 1890s. **In** *Atack, J., ed.*, 1986, pp. 13–27. **[G: U.S.]**

Hawley, Ellis W. "Industrial Policy" in the 1920s and 1930s. **In** *Barfield, C. E. and Schambra, W. A., eds.*, 1986, pp. 63–86. **[G: U.S.]**

Holtfrerich, Carl-Ludwig. U.S. Economic (Policy) Development and World Trade during the Interwar Period Compared to the Last Twenty Years. **In** *Berend, I. T. and Borchardt, K., eds.*, 1986, pp. 61–81. **[G: U.S.]**

Horton, Paul and Alexander, Lawrence. Freedom of Contract and the Family: A Skeptical Appraisal. **In** *Peden, J. R. and Glahe, F. R., eds.*, 1986, pp. 229–55. **[G: U.S.]**

Kareken, John H. Federal Bank Regulatory Policy: A Description and Some Observations. *J. Bus.*, January 1986, *59*(1), pp. 3–48. **[G: U.S.]**

Kindleberger, Charles P. Reversible and Irreversible Processes in Economics. *Challenge*, Sept./Oct. 1986, *29*(4), pp. 4–10. **[G: U.S.]**

Landau, Ralph. Technology, Economics, and Public Policy. **In** *Landau, R. and Jorgenson, D. W., eds.*, 1986, pp. 1–74. **[G: OECD]**

Lee, Dwight R. and Kreutzer, David. Privatizing the Commons: Comment. *Southern Econ. J.*, April 1986, *52*(4), pp. 1162–64.

Libecap, Gary D. Property Rights in Economic History: Implications for Research. *Exploration Econ. Hist.*, July 1986, *23*(3), pp. 227–52. **[G: U.S.]**

Lipsey, Richard G. Will There Be a Canadian–American Free Trade Association? *World Econ.*, September 1986, *9*(3), pp. 217–38. **[G: U.S.; Canada]**

Mayer, Thomas. Regulating Banks: Comment. *J. Bus.*, January 1986, *59*(1), pp. 87–96. **[G: U.S.]**

McCafferty, Stephen. Interwar Movements of Dollars to Europe and the U.S. Currency Supply: Comments. *J. Int. Money Finance*, Supp. March 1986, *5*, pp. S157–59. **[G: U.S.]**

McCraw, Thomas K. American Society: Public and Private Responsibilities: The Historical Background. **In** *Knowlton, W. and Zeckhauser, R., eds.*, 1986, pp. 15–42. **[G: U.S.]**

McCraw, Thomas K. Mercantilism and the Market: Antecedents of American Industrial Policy. **In** *Barfield, C. E. and Schambra, W. A., eds.*, 1986, pp. 33–62. **[G: U.S.]**

McGuire, Robert A. and Ohsfeldt, Robert L. An Economic Model of Voting Behavior over Specific Issues at the Constitutional Convention of 1787. *J. Econ. Hist.*, March 1986, *46*(1), pp. 79–111. **[G: U.S.]**

Meltzer, Allan H. Real and Psuedo-financial Crises: Comment. **In** *Capie, F. and Wood, G. E., eds.*, 1986, pp. 32–37. **[G: U.S.; U.K.]**

Meltzer, Allan H. Some Evidence on the Comparative Uncertainty Experienced under Different Monetary Regimes. **In** *Campbell, C. D. and Dougan, W. R., eds.*, 1986, pp. 122–53. **[G: U.S.]**

Miranti, Paul J., Jr. Associationalism, Statism, and Professional Regulation: Public Accountants and the Reform of the Financial Markets, 1896–1940. *Bus. Hist. Rev.*, Autumn 1986, *60*(3), pp. 438–68. **[G: U.S.]**

Modigliani, Franco. U.S. Deficits since World War I: Comment. *Scand. J. Econ.*, 1986, *88*(1), pp. 223–34. **[G: U.S.]**

Moggridge, D. E. Real and Pseudo-financial Crises: Comment. **In** *Capie, F. and Wood, G. E., eds.*, 1986, pp. 38–40. **[G: U.S.; U.K.]**

Musgrave, Richard A. Theories of Fiscal Crises: An Essay in Fiscal Sociology. **In** *Musgrave, R. A., Vol. 2*, 1986, *1980*, pp. 175–99. **[G: U.S.]**

Musgrave, Richard A. and Thin, Tun. Income Tax Progression, 1929–48. **In** *Musgrave, R. A., Vol. 1*, 1986, *1948*, pp. 132–54. **[G: U.S.]**

Officer, Lawrence H. The Efficiency of the Dollar–Sterling Gold Standard, 1890–1908. *J. Polit. Econ.*, October 1986, *94*(5), pp. 1038–73. **[G: U.S.; U.K.]**

Parsons, Kenneth H. The Relevance of the Ideas of John R. Commons for the Formulation of Agricultural Development Policies: Remarks upon Receipt of the Veblen–Commons Award. *J. Econ. Issues*, June 1986, *20*(2), pp. 281–95. **[G: U.S.]**

Patterson, James T. Cultural and Historical Perspectives on Industrial Policy: Comment. **In** *Barfield, C. E. and Schambra, W. A., eds.*, 1986, pp. 93–94. **[G: U.S.]**

Paulsen, George E. Ghost of the NRA: Drafting National Wage and Hour Legislation in 1937. *Soc. Sci. Quart.*, June 1986, *67*(2), pp. 241–54. **[G: U.S.]**

Pincus, J. J. Why Have U.S. Tariffs Fallen since 1930? **In** *Snape, R. H., ed.*, 1986, pp. 238–53. **[G: U.S.]**

Pratt, Joseph A. Business and Public Policy: The Uses and Limits of Strategic–Structural Analysis. **In** *Atack, J., ed.*, 1986, pp. 103–18.

Reed, Merl E. Black Workers, Defense Industries, and Federal Agencies in Pennsylvania, 1941–1945. *Labor Hist.*, Summer 1986, *27*(3), pp. 356–84. **[G: U.S.]**

Roback, Jennifer. The Political Economy of Segregation: The Case of Segregated Streetcars. *J. Econ. Hist.*, December 1986, *46*(4), pp. 893–917. **[G: U.S.]**

Rolnick, Arthur J. and Weber, Warren E. Gresham's Law or Gresham's Fallacy? *Fed. Res. Bank Minn. Rev.*, Winter 1986, *10*(1), pp. 17–24. **[G: U.S.]**

Ross, Thomas W. Store Wars: The Chain Tax Movement. *J. Law Econ.*, April 1986, *29*(1), pp. 125–37. **[G: U.S.]**

Rothbard, Murray N. The Progressive Era and the Family. **In** *Peden, J. R. and Glahe, F. R., eds.*, 1986, pp. 109–34. **[G: U.S.]**

Rush, Mark. Unexpected Money and Unemployment, 1920 to 1983. *J. Money, Credit, Banking*, August 1986, *18*(3), pp. 259–74. **[G: U.S.]**

Schwartz, Anna J. Real and Pseudo-financial Crises. **In** *Capie, F. and Wood, G. E., eds.*, 1986, pp. 11–40. **[G: U.S.; U.K.]**

Schwartz, Anna J. The Open Economy: Implications for Monetary and Fiscal Policy: Comment. **In** *Gordon, R. J., ed.*, 1986, pp. 504–10. **[G: U.S.]**

Shoven, John B. The Behavior of United States Deficits: Comment. **In** *Gordon, R. J., ed.*, 1986, pp. 389–91. **[G: U.S.]**

Shughart, William F., II and Tollison, Robert D. On the Growth of Government and the Political Economy of Legislation. **In** *Zerbe, R. O., Jr., ed.*, 1986, pp. 111–27. **[G: U.S.]**

Smolensky, Eugene. Municipal Financing of the U.S. Fine Arts Museum: A Historical Rationale. *J. Econ. Hist.*, September 1986, *46*(3), pp. 757–68. **[G: U.S.]**

Stein, Herbert. Cultural and Historical Perspectives on Industrial Policy: Comment. **In** *Barfield, C. E. and Schambra, W. A., eds.*, 1986, pp. 90–92. **[G: U.S.]**

Stephens, Carlene and Lubar, Steven. A Place for Public Business: The Material Culture of the Nineteenth-Century Federal Office. **In** *Atack, J., ed.*, 1986, pp. 165–79. **[G: U.S.]**

Sylla, Richard. Long-term Trends in State and Local Finance: Sources and Uses of Funds in North Carolina, 1800–1977. **In** *Engerman, S. L. and Gallman, R. E., eds.*, 1986, pp. 819–62. **[G: U.S.]**

Thorson, Douglas Y. The Growth and Failure of the Income Tax. **In** *Lindholm, R. W., ed.*, 1986, pp. 1–32. **[G: U.S.]**

Weinstein, Michael M. Industrial Planning and Economic Policy-Making: Lessons from the 1930s. **In** *[Tarshis, L.]*, 1986, pp. 135–57. **[G: U.S.]**

White, Eugene Nelson. Before the Glass–Steagall Act: An Analysis of the Investment Banking Activities of National Banks. *Exploration Econ. Hist.*, January 1986, *23*(1), pp. 33–55. **[G: U.S.]**

Wildavsky, Aaron. Industrial Policies in American Political Cultures. **In** *Barfield, C. E. and Schambra, W. A., eds.*, 1986, pp. 15–32. **[G: U.S.]**

Zecher, J. Richard. Market Discipline of the Monetary System. **In** *Campbell, C. D. and Dougan, W. R., eds.*, 1986, pp. 82–84. **[G: U.S.]**

043 Economic History: Ancient and Medieval (until 1453)

0430 General

Beauroy, Jacques. Family Patterns and Relations of Bishop's Lynn Will-Makers in the Fourteenth Century. **In** *[Laslett, P.]*, 1986, pp. 23–42. **[G: U.K.]**

Franklin, Peter. Peasant Widows' "Liberation" and Remarriage before the Black Death. *Econ. Hist. Rev., 2nd Ser.*, May 1986, *39*(2), pp. 186–204. **[G: U.K.]**

Poos, L. R. Population Turnover in Medieval Essex: The Evidence of Some Early–Fourteenth-Century Tithing Lists. **In** *[Laslett, P.]*, 1986, pp. 1–22. **[G: U.K.]**

Roehl, Richard. The Ecclesiastical Economy of Medieval Europe. *J. Econ. Hist.*, March 1986, *46*(1), pp. 227–31. **[G: Europe]**

Smith, R. M. Marriage Processes in the English Past: Some Continuities. **In** *[Laslett, P.]*, 1986, pp. 43–99. **[G: U.K.]**

Sørensen, Per. On the Problem of Early Rice in Southeast Asia. **In** *Nørlund, I.; Cederroth, S. and Gerdin, I., eds.*, 1986, pp. 267–79. **[G: S. E. Asia]**

Toch, Michael. Lords and Peasants: A Reappraisal of Medieval Economic Relationships. *J. Europ. Econ. Hist.*, Spring 1986, *15*(1), pp. 163–82. **[G: Germany]**

Veitch, John M. Repudiations and Confiscations by the Medieval State. *J. Econ. Hist.*, March 1986, *46*(1), pp. 31–36. **[G: Europe]**

0431 History of Product Prices and Markets

Stacey, Robert C. Agricultural Investment and the Management of the Royal Demesne Manors, 1236–1240. *J. Econ. Hist.*, December 1986, *46*(4), pp. 919–34.

0432 History of Factor Prices and Markets

Fox, H. S. A. The Alleged Transformation from Two-field to Three-field Systems in Medieval England. *Econ. Hist. Rev., 2nd Ser.*, November 1986, *39*(4), pp. 526–48. **[G: U.K.]**

0433 History of Public Economic Policy (all levels)

Bordo, Michael D. Money, Deflation and Seigniorage in the Fifteenth Century: A Review Essay. *J. Monet. Econ.*, November 1986, *18*(3), pp. 337–46.

044 Economic History: Europe

0440 General

Alter, George and Riley, James C. How to Bet on Lives: A Guide to Life Contingent Contracts in Early Modern Europe. **In** *Uselding, P., ed.*, 1986, pp. 1–53. **[G: Europe]**

Aricanli, Tosun. Agrarian Relations in Turkey: A Historical Sketch. **In** *Richards, A., ed.*, 1986, pp. 23–67. **[G: Turkey]**

Baber, Colin. Canals and the Economic Development of South Wales. **In** *Baber, C. and Williams, L. J., eds.*, 1986, pp. 24–42. **[G: U.K.]**

Barkai, Avraham. German-Jewish Migration in the Nineteenth Century, 1830–1910. **In** *Glazier, I. A. and De Rosa, L., eds.*, 1986, pp. 202–19. **[G: Germany]**

Berend, Iván T. The Historical Evolution of Eastern Europe as a Region. *Int. Organ.*, Spring 1986, *40*(2), pp. 329–46. **[G: CMEA]**

Berend, Iván T. The Historical Evolution of Eastern Europe as a Region. **In** *Comisso, E. and Tyson, L., eds.*, 1986, pp. 153–70. **[G: E. Europe]**

Bićanić, Ivo. Some General Comparisons of the Impact of the Two World Crises of the Twentieth Century on the Yugoslav Economy and Changes in the Well-Being of the Population Caused by the Crises. **In** *Berend, I. T. and Borchardt, K., eds.*, 1986, pp. 248–74. **[G: Yugoslavia]**

Bonfield, Lloyd. Normative Rules and Property Transmission: Reflections on the Link between Marriage and Inheritance in Early Modern England. **In** *[Laslett, P.]*, 1986, pp. 155–76. **[G: U.K.]**

Bonin, Serge. A Cartographic Approach to the Problem of Internal Migration in Sardinia in the Eighteenth Century: Part 2. **In** *Glazier, I. A. and De Rosa, L., eds.*, 1986, pp. 371–78. **[G: Italy]**

Brodsky, Vivien. Widows in Late Elizabethan London: Remarriage, Economic Opportunity and Family Orientations. **In** *[Laslett, P.]*, 1986, pp. 122–54. **[G: U.K.]**

Brus, Włodzimierz. Postwar Reconstruction and Socio-economic Transformation. **In** *Kaser, M. C. and Radice, E. A., eds.*, 1986, pp. 564–641. **[G: E. Europe]**

Bukharin, Nikolai. Notes of an Economist (the Beginning of the New Economic Year). **In** *Smith, K., ed.*, 1986, *1979*, pp. 50–77. **[G: U.S.S.R.]**

Cain, P. J. and Hopkins, Antony G. Gentlemanly Capitalism and British Expansion Overseas. I. The Old Colonial System, 1688–1850. *Econ. Hist. Rev., 2nd Ser.*, November 1986, *39*(4), pp. 501–25. **[G: U.K.]**

Cannadine, David. Conspicuous Consumption by the Landed Classes, 1790–1830. **In** *Turner, M., ed.*, 1986, pp. 96–111. **[G: U.K.]**

Čizmić, Ivan. Emigration from Yugoslavia prior to World War II. **In** *Glazier, I. A. and De Rosa, L., eds.*, 1986, pp. 255–67. **[G: Yugoslavia]**

Cocks, Edmond. Malthus on Population in a War-Based Industrial Economy. **In** *Turner, M., ed.*, 1986, pp. 222–35. **[G: France]**

Craig, Robin. Trade and Shipping in South Wales—The Radcliffe Company, 1882–1921. **In** *Baber, C. and Williams, L. J., eds.*, 1986, pp. 171–91. **[G: U.K.]**

Cuvillier, Jean-Pierre. Economic Change, Taxation and Social Mobility in German Towns in the Late Middle Ages. *J. Europ. Econ. Hist.*, Winter 1986, *15*(3), pp. 535–48. **[G: Germany]**

Day, John. A Cartographic Approach to the Problem of Internal Migration in Sardinia in the Eighteenth Century: Part 1. **In** *Glazier, I. A. and De Rosa, L., eds.*, 1986, pp. 365–70. **[G: Italy]**

Di Comité, Luigi. Aspects of Italian Emigration, 1881–1915. **In** *Glazier, I. A. and De Rosa, L., eds.*, 1986, pp. 148–59. **[G: Italy]**

Dornbusch, Rudiger and Fischer, Stanley. Stopping Hyperinflations Past and Present. *Weltwirtsch. Arch.*, 1986, *122*(1), pp. 1–47. **[G: Europe; Israel; Argentina]**

Dupâquier, Jacques. Geographic and Social Mobility in France in the Nineteenth and Twentieth Centuries. **In** *Glazier, I. A. and De Rosa, L., eds.*, 1986, pp. 356–64. **[G: France]**

Earle, Peter. Age and Accumulation in the London Business Community, 1665–1720. **In** *[Coleman, D. C.]*, 1986, pp. 38–63. **[G: U.K.]**

Elbaum, Bernard and Lazonick, William. An Institutional Perspective on British Decline. **In** *Elbaum, B. and Lazonick, W., eds.*, 1986, pp. 1–17. **[G: U.K.]**

Engelbourg, Saul and Schachter, Gustav. Two "Souths": The United States and Italy since the 1860's. *J. Europ. Econ. Hist.*, Winter 1986, *15*(3), pp. 563–89. **[G: U.S.; Italy]**

Englová, Jana. The Effects of Migration on the Demarcation of Industrial Areas. **In** *Glazier, I. A. and De Rosa, L., eds.*, 1986, pp. 271–75. **[G: Austria]**

Erickson, Charlotte. The Uses of Passenger Lists for the Study of British and Irish Emigration. **In** *Glazier, I. A. and De Rosa, L., eds.*, 1986, pp. 318–35. **[G: U.S.; U.K.; Ireland]**

Faroqhi, Suraiya. The Venetian Presence in the Ottoman Empire (1600–1630). *J. Europ. Econ.*

Hist., Fall 1986, *15*(2), pp. 345–84. **[G: Ottoman Empire; Italy]**

Goldstone, J. A. The Demographic Revolution in England: A Re-examination. *Population Stud.*, March 1986, *40*(1), pp. 5–33. **[G: U.K.]**

Goose, N. R. In Search of the Urban Variable: Towns and the English Economy, 1500–1650. *Econ. Hist. Rev., 2nd Ser.*, May 1986, *39*(2), pp. 165–85. **[G: U.K.]**

Goudzwaard, Bob. Christian Social Thought in the Dutch Neo-Calvinist Tradition. **In** *Block, W. and Hexham, I., eds.*, 1986, pp. 251–65. **[G: Netherlands]**

Goudzwaard, Bob. Christian Social Thought in the Dutch Neo-Calvinist Tradition: Reply. **In** *Block, W. and Hexham, I., eds.*, 1986, pp. 275–79. **[G: Netherlands]**

Greasley, David. British Economic Growth: The Paradox of the 1880s and the Timing of the Climacteric. *Exploration Econ. Hist.*, October 1986, *23*(4), pp. 416–44. **[G: U.K.]**

Haupt, Georges. The Commune as Symbol and Example. **In** *Haupt, G.*, 1986, *1972*, pp. 23–47. **[G: France]**

Heim, Carol E. Interwar Responses to Regional Decline. **In** *Elbaum, B. and Lazonick, W., eds.*, 1986, pp. 240–65. **[G: U.K.]**

Hexham, Irving. Christian Social Thought in the Dutch Neo-Calvinist Tradition: Comment. **In** *Block, W. and Hexham, I., eds.*, 1986, pp. 265–75. **[G: Netherlands]**

Hoffman, Philip T. Taxes and Agrarian Life in Early Modern France: Land Sales, 1550–1730. *J. Econ. Hist.*, March 1986, *46*(1), pp. 37–55. **[G: France]**

Hoppit, Julian. Financial Crises in Eighteenth-century England. *Econ. Hist. Rev., 2nd Ser.*, February 1986, *39*(1), pp. 39–58. **[G: U.K.]**

Kahan, Arcadius. A Day in the Ghetto. **In** *Kahan, A.*, 1986, pp. 170–84. **[G: Poland]**

Kahan, Arcadius. Notes on Jewish Entrepreneurship in Tsarist Russia. **In** *Kahan, A.*, 1986, *1983*, pp. 82–100. **[G: U.S.S.R.]**

Kahan, Arcadius. The Impact of Industrialization in Tsarist Russia on the Socioeconomic Conditions of the Jewish Population. **In** *Kahan, A.*, 1986, pp. 1–69. **[G: U.S.S.R.]**

Kahan, Arcadius. The Urbanization Process of the Jews in Nineteenth-Century Europe. **In** *Kahan, A.*, 1986, pp. 70–81. **[G: Europe]**

Kamphoefner, Walter D. At the Crossroads of Economic Development: Background Factors Affecting Emigration from Nineteenth-Century Germany. **In** *Glazier, I. A. and De Rosa, L., eds.*, 1986, pp. 174–201. **[G: Germany]**

Kaser, Michael and Nötel, R. The East European Economies in Two World Crises. **In** *Berend, I. T. and Borchardt, K., eds.*, 1986, pp. 215–47. **[G: E. Europe]**

Kenwood, A. G. Fixed Capital Formation in the Ports of the South Wales Coalfield, 1850–1913. **In** *Baber, C. and Williams, L. J., eds.*, 1986, pp. 117–27. **[G: U.K.]**

Kregel, J. A. Laws of the Market and Laws of Motion: An Essay in Comparative Social History. **In** *Wagener, H.-J. and Drukker, J. W., eds.*, 1986, pp. 31–48. **[G: U.S.; U.K.]**

Krejči, Jeroslav. The Bohemian–Moravian War Economy. **In** *Kaser, M. C. and Radice, E. A., eds.*, 1986, pp. 452–92. **[G: Bohemia; Moravia]**

Landes, David S. What Do Bosses Really Do? *J. Econ. Hist.*, September 1986, *46*(3), pp. 585–623. **[G: U.K.]**

Langton, John. Atlas of Industrializing Britain 1780–1914: The Physical Environment. **In** *Langton, J. and Morris, R. J., eds.*, 1986, pp. 2–9. **[G: U.K.]**

Langton, John and Morris, R. J. Atlas of Industrializing Britain 1780–1914: Introduction. **In** *Langton, J. and Morris, R. J., eds.*, 1986, pp. xxii–xxx. **[G: U.K.]**

Le Bras, Hervé and Todd, Emmanuel. Mountains, Rivers and the Family: Comments on a Map from the 1975 French Census. **In** *[Laslett, P.]*, 1986, pp. 379–87. **[G: France]**

Lee, Clive. Atlas of Industrializing Britain 1780–1914: Regional Structure and Change. **In** *Langton, J. and Morris, R. J., eds.*, 1986, pp. 30–33. **[G: U.K.]**

Mageean, Deirdre. Ulster Emigration to Philadelphia, 1847–1865: A Preliminary Analysis Using Passenger Lists. **In** *Glazier, I. A. and De Rosa, L., eds.*, 1986, pp. 276–86. **[G: Ireland; U.S.]**

Maier, Charles S. The Economics of Fascism and Nazism: Premises and Performance. **In** *[Hirshman, A. O.]*, 1986, pp. 57–88. **[G: Germany; Italy]**

McKendrick, Neil. 'Gentlemen and Players' Revisited: The Gentlemanly Ideal, the Business Ideal and the Professional Ideal in English Literary Culture. **In** *[Coleman, D. C.]*, 1986, pp. 98–136. **[G: U.K.]**

Mercer, A. J. Relative Trends in Mortality from Related Respiratory and Airborne Infectious Diseases. *Population Stud.*, March 1986, *40*(1), pp. 129–45. **[G: U.K.]**

Mistral, Jacques. 125 ans de contrainte extérieure: l'expérience française. (125 Years of External Constraint: The French Case. With English summary.) *Écon. Soc.*, January 1986, *20*(1), pp. 91–115. **[G: France]**

Montanari, Armando. Planning and Urban Growth in Southern Europe. *J. Europ. Econ. Hist.*, Spring 1986, *15*(1), pp. 183–95. **[G: Greece; Italy; Portugal; Spain; Turkey]**

Morris, R. J. Atlas of Industrializing Britain 1780–1914: Urbanization. **In** *Langton, J. and Morris, R. J., eds.*, 1986, pp. 164–79. **[G: U.K.]**

Mowery, David C. Industry Research, 1900–1950. **In** *Elbaum, B. and Lazonick, W., eds.*, 1986, pp. 189–222. **[G: U.K.]**

Nötel, R. International Credit and Finance. **In** *Kaser, M. C. and Radice, E. A., eds.*, 1986, pp. 170–295. **[G: E. Europe]**

Nove, Alec. History, Political Culture, and Economics in the Soviet Union. **In** *Höhmann, H.-H.; Nove, A. and Vogel, H., eds.*, 1986, pp. 1–16. **[G: U.S.S.R.]**

O'Brien, Patrick K. Do We Have a Typology for

the Study of European Industrialization in the XIXth Century? *J. Europ. Econ. Hist.*, Fall 1986, *15*(2), pp. 291–333. **[G: Europe]**

Outhwaite, R. B. Marriage as Business: Opinions on the Rise in Aristocratic Bridal Portions in Early Modern England. **In** *[Coleman, D. C.]*, 1986, pp. 21–37. **[G: U.K.]**

Parker, William N. Capitalistic Organization and National Response: Social Dynamics in the Age of Schumpeter. **In** *Day, R. H. and Eliasson, G., eds.*, 1986, *1984*, pp. 351–71. **[G: Germany; U.S.; France; England]**

Parker, William N. Capitalistic Organization and National Response: Social Dynamics in the Age of Schumpeter: Reply. **In** *Day, R. H. and Eliasson, G., eds.*, 1986, pp. 378–83. **[G: Germany; U.S.; France; England]**

Pradel de Lamaze, François. Malthusianism in South-west France in the Nineteenth and Twentieth Centuries. **In** *Turner, M., ed.*, 1986, pp. 71–81. **[G: France]**

Preston, Ronald H. The Legacy of the Christian Socialist Movement in England: Reply. **In** *Block, W. and Hexham, I., eds.*, 1986, pp. 208–12. **[G: U.K.]**

Preston, Ronald H. The Legacy of the Christian Socialist Movement in England. **In** *Block, W. and Hexham, I., eds.*, 1986, pp. 181–201. **[G: U.K.]**

Purvis, Martin. Atlas of Industrializing Britain 1780–1914: Popular Institutions. **In** *Langton, J. and Morris, R. J., eds.*, 1986, pp. 194–97. **[G: U.K.]**

Puskás, Julianna. Hungarian Migration Patterns, 1880–1930: From Macroanalysis to Microanalysis. **In** *Glazier, I. A. and De Rosa, L., eds.*, 1986, pp. 231–54. **[G: Hungary; U.S.]**

Radice, E. A. Changes in Property Relationships and Financial Arrangements. **In** *Kaser, M. C. and Radice, E. A., eds.*, 1986, pp. 329–65. **[G: Germany; E. Europe]**

Radice, E. A. The Collapse of German Hegemony and Its Economic Consequences. **In** *Kaser, M. C. and Radice, E. A., eds.*, 1986, pp. 495–519. **[G: Germany; E. Europe]**

Radice, E. A. The Development of Industry. **In** *Kaser, M. C. and Radice, E. A., eds.*, 1986, pp. 416–51. **[G: E. Europe; Germany]**

Radice, E. A. The German Economic Programme in Eastern Europe. **In** *Kaser, M. C. and Radice, E. A., eds.*, 1986, pp. 299–308. **[G: E. Europe; Germany]**

Riley, James C. Insects and the European Mortality Decline. *Amer. Hist. Rev.*, October 1986, *91*(4), pp. 833–58. **[G: Europe]**

Roberts, Brian. Atlas of Industrializing Britain 1780–1914: Rural Settlements. **In** *Langton, J. and Morris, R. J., eds.*, 1986, pp. 54–59. **[G: U.K.]**

Ruggiero, Kristin. Social and Psychological Factors in Migration from Italy to Argentina: From the Waldensian Valleys to San Gustavo. **In** *Glazier, I. A. and De Rosa, L., eds.*, 1986, pp. 160–73. **[G: Italy; Argentina]**

Rybczynski, Tad M. Capitalistic Organization and National Response: Social Dynamics in the Age of Schumpeter: Comment. **In** *Day, R. H. and Eliasson, G., eds.*, 1986, pp. 372–77. **[G: Germany; U.S.; France; England]**

Schofield, Roger. Did the Mothers Really Die? Three Centuries of Maternal Mortality in 'The World We Have Lost.' **In** *[Laslett, P.]*, 1986, pp. 231–60. **[G: Sweden; U.K.]**

Shenfield, Arthur A. The Legacy of the Christian Socialist Movement in England: Comment. **In** *Block, W. and Hexham, I., eds.*, 1986, pp. 202–08. **[G: U.K.]**

Stampfer, Shaul. The Geographic Background of East European Jewish Migration to the United States before World War I. **In** *Glazier, I. A. and De Rosa, L., eds.*, 1986, pp. 220–30. **[G: E. Europe; U.S.]**

Stapleton, B. Malthus: The Origins of the Principle of Population? **In** *Turner, M., ed.*, 1986, pp. 19–39. **[G: U.K.]**

Stiefel, Dieter. The Great Depression in a Small Country: Austria, the World Economic Crisis of the 1930s and Its Significance for the Present Day. **In** *Berend, I. T. and Borchardt, K., eds.*, 1986, pp. 195–214. **[G: Austria]**

Stone, Richard. Nobel Memorial Lecture 1984: The Accounts of Society. *J. Appl. Economet-rics*, January 1986, *1*(1), pp. 5–28. **[G: U.K.; France; Netherlands]**

Szreter, S. R. S. The First Scientific Social Structure of Modern Britain, 1875–1883. **In** *[Laslett, P.]*, 1986, pp. 337–54. **[G: U.K.]**

Taylor, Tom. Capital Formation by Railways in South Wales, 1836–1914. **In** *Baber, C. and Williams, L. J., eds.*, 1986, pp. 97–116. **[G: U.K.]**

Thomas, Brinley. The Industrial Revolution and the Welsh Language. **In** *Baber, C. and Williams, L. J., eds.*, 1986, pp. 6–21. **[G: U.K.]**

Thomas, D. A. War and the Economy: The South Wales Experience. **In** *Baber, C. and Williams, L. J., eds.*, 1986, pp. 251–77. **[G: U.K.]**

Tilly, Richard H. Financing Industrial Enterprise in Great Britain and Germany in the Nineteenth Century: Testing Grounds for Marxist and Schumpeterian Theories? **In** *Wagener, H.-J. and Drukker, J. W., eds.*, 1986, pp. 123–55. **[G: U.K.; Germany]**

Tilly, Richard H. German Banking, 1850–1914: Development Assistance for the Strong. *J. Europ. Econ. Hist.*, Spring 1986, *15*(1), pp. 113–52. **[G: Germany]**

Viazzo, Pier Paolo. Illegitimacy and the European Marriage Pattern: Comparative Evidence from the Alpine Area. **In** *[Laslett, P.]*, 1986, pp. 100–121. **[G: Switzerland]**

Wall, Richard A. Work, Welfare and the Family: An Illustration of the Adaptive Family Economy. **In** *[Laslett, P.]*, 1986, pp. 261–94. **[G: U.K.]**

Williams, L. John. The Climacteric of the 1890s. **In** *Baber, C. and Williams, L. J., eds.*, 1986, pp. 192–203. **[G: U.K.]**

Wilson, Chris. The Proximate Determinants of Marital Fertility in England 1600–1799. **In** *[Laslett, P.]*, 1986, pp. 203–30. **[G: U.K.]**

Winter, J. M. Bernard Shaw, Bertold Brecht and

the Businessman in Literature. **In** *[Coleman, D. C.]*, 1986, pp. 185–204. **[G: U.K.]**

Wrigley, E. A. Malthus's Model of a Pre-industrial Economy. **In** *Turner, M., ed.*, 1986, pp. 3–18. **[G: U.K.]**

0441 History of Product Prices and Markets

Alford, B. W. E. Lost Opportunities: British Business and Businessmen during the First World War. **In** *[Coleman, D. C.]*, 1986, pp. 205–27. **[G: U.K.]**

Atkinson, Michael. The Supply of Raw Materials to the South Wales Iron Industry, 1800–60. **In** *Baber, C. and Williams, L. J., eds.*, 1986, pp. 43–52. **[G: U.K.]**

Blanchard, Ian. The Continental European Cattle Trade, 1400–1600. *Econ. Hist. Rev., 2nd Ser.*, August 1986, *39*(3), pp. 427–60. **[G: Europe]**

Boyns, Trevor. Growth in the Coal Industry: The Cases of Powell Duffryn and the Ocean Coal Company, 1864–1913. **In** *Baber, C. and Williams, L. J., eds.*, 1986, pp. 153–70. **[G: U.K.]**

Broadberry, S. N. Aggregate Supply in Interwar Britain. *Econ. J.*, June 1986, *96*(382), pp. 467–81. **[G: U.K.]**

Broder, Albert. The Multinationalisation of the French Electrical Industry 1880–1914: Dependence and Its Causes. **In** *Hertner, P. and Jones, G., eds.*, 1986, pp. 169–91. **[G: France]**

Buchheim, Christoph. Germany on the World Market at the End of the 19th Century: Successful Supplier of Consumer Related Manufactures. **In** *Pohl, H. and Rudolph, B., eds.*, 1986, pp. 41–55. **[G: Germany]**

Butler, Henry N. General Incorporation in Nineteenth Century England: Interaction of Common Law and Legislative Processes. *Int. Rev. Law Econ.*, December 1986, *6*(2), pp. 169–88. **[G: U.K.]**

Cadieux, François. Western Technology and Early Russian Pipelines, 1877–1917. *J. Europ. Econ. Hist.*, Fall 1986, *15*(2), pp. 335–44. **[G: U.S.S.R.]**

Church, Roy. The Effects of American Multinationals on the British Motor Industry: 1911–83. **In** *Teichova, A.; Lévy-Leboyer, M. and Nussbaum, H., eds.*, 1986, pp. 116–30. **[G: U.K.]**

Collins, Michael. Sterling Exchange Rates, 1847–80. *J. Europ. Econ. Hist.*, Winter 1986, *15*(3), pp. 511–33. **[G: U.K.]**

Crafts, N. F. R. and Thomas, Mark. Comparative Advantage in UK Manufacturing Trade, 1910–1935. *Econ. J.*, September 1986, *96*(383), pp. 629–45. **[G: U.K.]**

Crouzet, François. The Growth of British Exports 1783–1820. **In** *Turner, M., ed.*, 1986, pp. 189–200. **[G: U.K.]**

Dornbusch, Rudiger. Como deter a hiperinflação: lições da experiência inflacionária alemã da década de 20. (With English summary.) *Pesquisa Planejamento Econ.*, April 1986, *16*(1), pp. 61–85. **[G: U.S.; France; U.K.; W. Germany]**

Elbaum, Bernard. The Steel Industry before World War I. **In** *Elbaum, B. and Lazonick, W., eds.*, 1986, pp. 51–81. **[G: U.K.; U.S.]**

Feldbæk, Ole. The Danish Trading Companies of the Seventeenth and Eighteenth Centuries. *Scand. Econ. Hist. Rev.*, 1986, *34*(3), pp. 204–18. **[G: Denmark]**

Foust, C. M. Customs 3 and Russian Rhubarb: A Note on Reliability. *J. Europ. Econ. Hist.*, Winter 1986, *15*(3), pp. 549–62. **[G: U.K.]**

Freeman, Michael. Atlas of Industrializing Britain 1780–1914: Transport. **In** *Langton, J. and Morris, R. J., eds.*, 1986, pp. 80–93. **[G: U.K.]**

Fridenson, Patrick. The Growth of Multinational Activities in the French Motor Industry, 1890–1979. **In** *Hertner, P. and Jones, G., eds.*, 1986, pp. 157–68. **[G: France]**

Gebauer, Wolfgang. Kondratieff's Long Waves. *Konjunkturpolitik*, 1986, *32*(4), pp. 235–55. **[G: W. Europe; U.S.]**

Hanson, John R., II. Export Shares in the European Periphery and the Third World before World War I: Questionable Data, Facile Analogies. *Exploration Econ. Hist.*, January 1986, *23*(1), pp. 85–99. **[G: Europe; LDCs]**

Hertner, Peter. German Multinational Enterprise before 1914: Some Case Studies. **In** *Hertner, P. and Jones, G., eds.*, 1986, pp. 113–34. **[G: Germany]**

Holtfrerich, Carl-Ludwig. U.S. Capital Exports to Germany 1919–1923 Compared to 1924–1929. *Exploration Econ. Hist.*, January 1986, *23*(1), pp. 1–32. **[G: U.S.; W. Germany]**

Howell, David. Farming in South-east Wales c.1840–80. **In** *Baber, C. and Williams, L. J., eds.*, 1986, pp. 82–96. **[G: U.K.]**

Hume, John R. and Oglethorpe, Miles. Atlas of Industrializing Britain 1780–1914: Engineering. **In** *Langton, J. and Morris, R. J., eds.*, 1986, pp. 136–39. **[G: U.K.]**

Jackson, Gordon. Atlas of Industrializing Britain 1780–1914: Sea Trade. **In** *Langton, J. and Morris, R. J., eds.*, 1986, pp. 94–105. **[G: U.K.]**

Jackson, Marvin R. Industrial Output in Romania and Its Historical Regions, 1880 to 1930: Part I—1880 to 1915. *J. Europ. Econ. Hist.*, Spring 1986, *15*(1), pp. 59–111. **[G: Romania]**

Jackson, Marvin R. Industrial Output in Romania and Its Historical Regions, 1880 to 1930, Part II, 1913 to 1930. *J. Europ. Econ. Hist.*, Fall 1986, *15*(2), pp. 231–57. **[G: Romania]**

Jones, Geoffrey. The Performance of British Multinational Enterprise, 1890–1945. **In** *Hertner, P. and Jones, G., eds.*, 1986, pp. 96–112. **[G: U.K.]**

Jonsson, Sigfus. International Saltfish Markets and the Icelandic Economy ca. 1900–1940. *Scand. Econ. Hist. Rev.*, 1986, *34*(1), pp. 20–40. **[G: Iceland]**

Kjaergaard, Thorkild. Origins of Economic Growth in European Societies since the XVIth Century: The Case of Agriculture. *J. Europ. Econ. Hist.*, Winter 1986, *15*(3), pp. 591–98. **[G: Europe]**

Kohli, Ulrich. Robert Giffen and the Irish Potato:

Note. *Amer. Econ. Rev.*, June 1986, *76*(3), pp. 539–42. **[G: Ireland]**

Kriedte, Peter. Demographic and Economic Rhythms: The Rise of the Silk Industry in Krefeld in the Eighteenth Century. *J. Europ. Econ. Hist.*, Fall 1986, *15*(2), pp. 259–89. **[G: Germany]**

Lawton, Richard. Atlas of Industrializing Britain 1780–1914: Population. **In** *Langton, J. and Morris, R. J., eds.*, 1986, pp. 10–29. **[G: U.K.]**

Laxton, Paul. Atlas of Industrializing Britain 1780–1914: Textiles. **In** *Langton, J. and Morris, R. J., eds.*, 1986, pp. 106–13. **[G: U.K.]**

Laxton, Paul. Atlas of Industrializing Britain 1780–1914: Wind and Water Power. **In** *Langton, J. and Morris, R. J., eds.*, 1986, pp. 69–71. **[G: U.K.]**

Lazonick, William. The Cotton Industry. **In** *Elbaum, B. and Lazonick, W., eds.*, 1986, pp. 18–50. **[G: U.K.]**

Lee, Chi-wen Jevons and Petruzzi, Christopher R. The Gibson Paradox and the Monetary Standard. *Rev. Econ. Statist.*, May 1986, *68*(2), pp. 189–96. **[G: U.K.; U.S.]**

Lee, Clive. Atlas of Industrializing Britain 1780–1914: Services. **In** *Langton, J. and Morris, R. J., eds.*, 1986, pp. 140–43. **[G: U.K.]**

Lewchuk, W. The Motor Vehicle Industry. **In** *Elbaum, B. and Lazonick, W., eds.*, 1986, pp. 135–61. **[G: U.K.; U.S.]**

Lorenz, Edward and Wilkinson, Frank. The Shipbuilding Industry 1880–1965. **In** *Elbaum, B. and Lazonick, W., eds.*, 1986, pp. 109–34. **[G: U.K.; OECD]**

Lundström, Ragnhild. Swedish Multinational Growth before 1930. **In** *Hertner, P. and Jones, G., eds.*, 1986, pp. 135–56. **[G: Sweden]**

Makinen, Gail E. The Greek Hyperinflation and Stabilization of 1943–1946. *J. Econ. Hist.*, September 1986, *46*(3), pp. 795–805. **[G: Greece]**

Messerlin, Patrick A. and Becuwe, Stephane. Intra-industry Trade in the Long Run: The French Case, 1850–1913. **In** *Greenaway, D. and Tharakan, P. K. M., eds.*, 1986, pp. 191–215. **[G: France]**

Morgan, R. H. The Development of the Electricity Supply Industry in South Wales to 1939. **In** *Baber, C. and Williams, L. J., eds.*, 1986, pp. 222–36. **[G: U.K.]**

Mounfield, P. R. Atlas of Industrializing Britain 1780–1914: Leather Footwear. **In** *Langton, J. and Morris, R. J., eds.*, 1986, pp. 124–26. **[G: U.K.]**

Nötel, R. International Finance and Monetary Reforms. **In** *Kaser, M. C. and Radice, E. A., eds.*, 1986, pp. 520–63. **[G: E. Europe]**

Outhwaite, R. B. Progress and Backwardness in English Agriculture, 1500–1650. *Econ. Hist. Rev., 2nd Ser.*, February 1986, *39*(1), pp. 1–18. **[G: U.K.]**

Overton, Mark. Atlas of Industrializing Britain 1780–1914: Agriculture. **In** *Langton, J. and Morris, R. J., eds.*, 1986, pp. 34–53. **[G: U.K.]**

Pamuk, Şevket. The Decline and Resistance of Ottoman Cotton Textiles, 1820–1913. *Exploration Econ. Hist.*, April 1986, *23*(2), pp. 205–25. **[G: Turkey]**

Radice, E. A. Agriculture and Food. **In** *Kaser, M. C. and Radice, E. A., eds.*, 1986, pp. 366–97. **[G: E. Europe; Germany]**

Riden, Philip. Atlas of Industrializing Britain 1780–1914: Iron and Steel. **In** *Langton, J. and Morris, R. J., eds.*, 1986, pp. 127–31. **[G: U.K.]**

Sarkar, Prabirjit. The Terms of Trade Experience of Britain since the Nineteenth Century. *J. Devel. Stud.*, October 1986, *23*(1), pp. 20–39. **[G: U.K.]**

Šaskolskij, I. P. New Phenomena in the Baltic Trade of Russia in the Seventeenth Century. *Scand. Econ. Hist. Rev.*, 1986, *34*(1), pp. 41–53. **[G: U.S.S.R.]**

Shaw, Gareth. Atlas of Industrializing Britain 1780–1914: Retail Patterns. **In** *Langton, J. and Morris, R. J., eds.*, 1986, pp. 180–84. **[G: U.K.]**

Slaven, Anthony. Atlas of Industrializing Britain 1780–1914: Shipbuilding. **In** *Langton, J. and Morris, R. J., eds.*, 1986, pp. 132–35. **[G: U.K.]**

Symons, M. V. Coal-Mining in the Llanelli Area—Years of Growth, 1800–64. **In** *Baber, C. and Williams, L. J., eds.*, 1986, pp. 53–64. **[G: U.K.]**

Thomas, Brinley. Was There an Energy Crisis in Great Britain in the 17th Century? *Exploration Econ. Hist.*, April 1986, *23*(2), pp. 124–52. **[G: U.K.]**

Tolliday, Steven. Steel and Rationalization Policies, 1918–1950. **In** *Elbaum, B. and Lazonick, W., eds.*, 1986, pp. 82–108. **[G: U.K.]**

Trebilcock, Clive. The City, Entrepreneurship and Insurance: Two Pioneers in Invisible Exports—The Phoenix Fire Office and the Royal of Liverpool, 1800–90. **In** *[Coleman, D. C.]*, 1986, pp. 137–72. **[G: Selected Countries]**

von Tunzelmann, Nick. Atlas of Industrializing Britain 1780–1914: Coal and Steam Power. **In** *Langton, J. and Morris, R. J., eds.*, 1986, pp. 72–79. **[G: U.K.]**

Turner, Michael. Corn Crises in Britain in the Age of Malthus. **In** *Turner, M., ed.*, 1986, pp. 112–28. **[G: U.K.]**

Turner, Michael. English Open Fields and Enclosures: Retardation or Productivity Improvements. *J. Econ. Hist.*, September 1986, *46*(3), pp. 669–92. **[G: U.K.]**

Ville, Simon. Total Factor Productivity in the English Shipping Industry: The North-east Coal Trade, 1700–1850. *Econ. Hist. Rev., 2nd Ser.*, August 1986, *39*(3), pp. 355–70. **[G: U.K.]**

Wake, C. H. H. The Volume of European Spice Imports at the Beginning and End of the Fifteenth Century. *J. Europ. Econ. Hist.*, Winter 1986, *15*(3), pp. 621–35. **[G: Europe]**

Walton, Whitney. "To Triumph before Feminine Taste": Bourgeois Women's Consumption and Hand Methods of Production in Mid-Nineteenth-Century Paris. *Bus. Hist. Rev.*, Winter

1986, *60*(4), pp. 541–63. **[G: France]**

Warren, Kenneth. Atlas of Industrializing Britain 1780–1914: Chemicals. **In** *Langton, J. and Morris, R. J., eds.*, 1986, pp. 114–18. **[G: U.K.]**

Webb, Steven B. Fiscal News and Inflationary Expectations in Germany after World War I. *J. Econ. Hist.*, September 1986, *46*(3), pp. 769–94. **[G: Germany]**

Weir, R. B. Atlas of Industrializing Britain 1780–1914: Brewing and Distilling. **In** *Langton, J. and Morris, R. J., eds.*, 1986, pp. 119–23. **[G: U.K.]**

Wheatcroft, S. G.; Davies, R. W. and Cooper, Julian. Soviet Industrialization Reconsidered: Some Preliminary Conclusions about Economic Development between 1926 and 1941. *Econ. Hist. Rev., 2nd Ser.*, May 1986, *39*(2), pp. 264–94. **[G: U.S.S.R.]**

0442 History of Factor Prices and Markets

Aldcroft, Derek H. Great Britain—The Constraints to Full Employment in the 1930s and 1980s. **In** *Berend, I. T. and Borchardt, K., eds.*, 1986, pp. 106–24. **[G: U.K.]**

Anderson, B. L. Trends in Capital Accumulation in the Age of Malthus. **In** *Turner, M., ed.*, 1986, pp. 201–21. **[G: U.K.]**

Anderson, Gary M. and Tollison, Robert D. Luddism as Cartel Enforcement. *J. Inst. Theoretical Econ.*, December 1986, *142*(4), pp. 727–38. **[G: U.K.]**

Batchelor, Roy A. The Avoidance of Catastrophe: Two Nineteenth-Century Banking Crises. **In** *Capie, F. and Wood, G. E., eds.*, 1986, pp. 41–73. **[G: U.K.]**

Beaud, Claude Ph. Investments and Profits of the Multinational Schneider Group: 1894–1943. **In** *Teichova, A.; Lévy-Leboyer, M. and Nussbaum, H., eds.*, 1986, pp. 87–102. **[G: Europe]**

Beenstock, Michael and Warburton, Peter. Wages and Unemployment in Interwar Britain. *Exploration Econ. Hist.*, April 1986, *23*(2), pp. 153–72. **[G: U.K.]**

Best, Michael H. and Humphries, Jane. The City and Industrial Decline. **In** *Elbaum, B. and Lazonick, W., eds.*, 1986, pp. 223–39. **[G: U.K.]**

Blaug, Mark. The Productivity of Capital in the Lancashire Cotton Industry during the Nineteenth Century. **In** *Blaug, M.*, 1986, *1961*, pp. 51–87. **[G: U.K.]**

Boje, Per. The Standard of Living in Scandinavia 1750–1914. *Scand. Econ. Hist. Rev.*, 1986, *34*(2), pp. 73–75. **[G: Scandinavia]**

Boje, Per. The Standard of Living in Denmark 1750–1914. *Scand. Econ. Hist. Rev.*, 1986, *34*(2), pp. 171–79. **[G: Denmark]**

Bonfield, Lloyd. Affective Families, Open Elites and Strict Family Settlements in Early Modern England. *Econ. Hist. Rev., 2nd Ser.*, August 1986, *39*(3), pp. 341–54. **[G: U.K.]**

Boyer, George R. The Old Poor Law and the Agricultural Labor Market in Southern England: An Empirical Analysis. *J. Econ. Hist.*, March 1986, *46*(1), pp. 113–35. **[G: U.K.]**

Capie, Forrest H.; Mills, Terence C. and Wood, Geoffrey E. What Happened in 1931? **In** *Capie, F. and Wood, G. E., eds.*, 1986, pp. 120–48. **[G: U.K.]**

Chalmin, Ph. The Strategy of a Multinational in the World Sugar Economy: The Case of Tate and Lyle: 1870–1980. **In** *Teichova, A.; Lévy-Leboyer, M. and Nussbaum, H., eds.*, 1986, pp. 103–15. **[G: Selected Countries]**

Charlesworth, Andrew. Atlas of Industrializing Britain 1780–1914: Labour Protest 1780–1850. **In** *Langton, J. and Morris, R. J., eds.*, 1986, pp. 185–89. **[G: U.K.]**

Cohen, Lizabeth and Chapman, Herrick. Recent Dissertations: In American and European Labor History. *Labor Hist.*, Fall 1986, *27*(4), pp. 545–48. **[G: W. Europe; U.S.]**

Coleman, D. C. and MacLeod, Christine. Attitudes to New Techniques: British Businessmen, 1800–1950. *Econ. Hist. Rev., 2nd Ser.*, November 1986, *39*(4), pp. 588–611. **[G: U.K.]**

Congdon, Tim. What Happened in 1931? Comment. **In** *Capie, F. and Wood, G. E., eds.*, 1986, pp. 149–56. **[G: U.K.]**

Cottrell, P. L. Atlas of Industrializing Britain 1780–1914: Banking and Finance. **In** *Langton, J. and Morris, R. J., eds.*, 1986, pp. 144–55. **[G: U.K.]**

Daunton, M. J. Labour and Technology in South Wales, 1870–1914. **In** *Baber, C. and Williams, L. J., eds.*, 1986, pp. 140–52. **[G: U.K.]**

Davis, Lance E. and Huttenback, Robert A. Imperialism and Social Class (Apologies to Marx and Schumpeter): Imperial Investors in the Age of High Imperialism. **In** *Wagener, H.-J. and Drukker, J. W., eds.*, 1986, pp. 156–85. **[G: U.K.]**

Delbeke, Jos. A Comparison of Price and Money Behaviour between the 1920s–30s and 1970s–80s in Belgium. **In** *Berend, I. T. and Borchardt, K., eds.*, 1986, pp. 149–70. **[G: Belgium]**

Eccleston, Bernard. Malthus, Wages and the Labour Market in England, 1790–1830. **In** *Turner, M., ed.*, 1986, pp. 143–56.

Engelen, Th. L. M. and Hillebrand, J. H. A. Fertility and Nuptiality in the Netherlands, 1850–1960. *Population Stud.*, November 1986, *40*(3), pp. 487–503. **[G: Netherlands]**

Essemyr, Mats. Food, Fare and Nutrition. Some Reflections on the Historical Development of Food Consumption. *Scand. Econ. Hist. Rev.*, 1986, *34*(2), pp. 76–89. **[G: Sweden]**

Frey, Bruno S. and Buhofer, Heinz. A Market for Men, Or: There Is No Such Thing as a Free Lynch. *J. Inst. Theoretical Econ.*, December 1986, *142*(4), pp. 739–44. **[G: Europe]**

Friedlander, Dov and Moshe, Eliahu Ben. Occupations, Migration, Sex Ratios, and Nuptiality in Nineteenth Century English Communities: A Model of Relationships. *Demography*, February 1986, *23*(1), pp. 1–12. **[G: U.K.]**

Girardin, Eric. Estimation en longue période d'une fonction d'investissement pour le Royaume-Uni: 1881–1979. (Estimation of an Investment Function for the United Kingdom in the Long Run: 1881–1979. With English summary.) *Econ. Appl.*, 1986, *39*(2), pp. 297–336. **[G: U.K.]**

Goodhart, Charles. The Summer of 1914: Comment. **In** *Capie, F. and Wood, G. E., eds.*, 1986, pp. 117–19. **[G: U.K.; Europe]**

Harris, John R. Michael Alcock and the Transfer of Birmingham Technology to France before the Revolution. *J. Europ. Econ. Hist.*, Spring 1986, *15*(1), pp. 7–57. **[G: France]**

Hatcher, John. Mortality in the Fifteenth Century: Some New Evidence. *Econ. Hist. Rev., 2nd Ser.*, February 1986, *39*(1), pp. 19–38. **[G: U.K.]**

Hatton, T. J. Rational Expectations and Labour Market Equilibrium in Britain 1855–1913. *Oxford Econ. Pap.*, March 1986, *38*(1), pp. 160–73. **[G: U.K.]**

Hatton, T. J. Structural Aspects of Unemployment in Britain between the World Wars. **In** *Uselding, P., ed.*, 1986, pp. 54–92. **[G: U.K.]**

Heikkinen, Sakari. On Private Consumption and the Standard of Living in Finland, 1860–1912. *Scand. Econ. Hist. Rev.*, 1986, *34*(2), pp. 122–34. **[G: Finland]**

Hertner, Peter. Financial Strategies and Adaptation to Foreign Markets: The German Electrotechnical Industry and Its Multinational Activities: 1890s to 1939. **In** *Teichova, A.; Lévy-Leboyer, M. and Nussbaum, H., eds.*, 1986, pp. 145–59. **[G: Germany]**

Holden, Kenneth and Peel, David A. The Impact of Benefits on Unemployment in Britain in the Interwar Period: Some Further Empirical Evidence. *J. Macroecon.*, Spring 1986, *8*(2), pp. 227–32. **[G: U.K.]**

Hoppit, Julian. The Use and Abuse of Credit in Eighteenth-Century England. **In** *[Coleman, D. C.]*, 1986, pp. 64–78. **[G: U.K.]**

Huberman, Michael. Invisible Handshakes in Lancashire: Cotton Spinning in the First Half of the Nineteenth Century. *J. Econ. Hist.*, December 1986, *46*(4), pp. 987–98. **[G: U.K.]**

Hunt, E. H. Atlas of Industrializing Britain 1780–1914: Wages. **In** *Langton, J. and Morris, R. J., eds.*, 1986, pp. 60–68. **[G: U.K.]**

Hunt, E. H. Industrialization and Regional Inequality: Wages in Britain, 1760–1914. *J. Econ. Hist.*, December 1986, *46*(4), pp. 935–66. **[G: U.K.]**

Hyde, Charles K. Undercover and Underground: Labor Spies and Mine Management in the Early Twentieth Century. *Bus. Hist. Rev.*, Spring 1986, *60*(1), pp. 1–27. **[G: U.S.]**

Johansen, Hans Chr. and Boje, Per. Working Class Housing in Odense 1750–1914. *Scand. Econ. Hist. Rev.*, 1986, *34*(2), pp. 135–52. **[G: Denmark]**

Jones, Geoffrey. British Overseas Banks in the Middle East 1920–70: A Study in Multinational Middle Age. **In** *Teichova, A.; Lévy-Leboyer, M. and Nussbaum, H., eds.*, 1986, pp. 218–31. **[G: U.K.; Middle East]**

Jonung, Lars. International Financial Crisis and the Swedish Economy 1857–1933. **In** *Capie, F. and Wood, G. E., eds.*, 1986, pp. 254–64. **[G: Sweden]**

Kernbauer, Hans and Weber, Fritz. Multinational Banking in the Danube Basin: The Business Strategy of the Viennese Banks after the Collapse of the Habsburg Monarchy. **In** *Teichova, A.; Lévy-Leboyer, M. and Nussbaum, H., eds.*, 1986, pp. 185–99. **[G: Europe]**

Kurgan-van Hentenryk, Ginette. The Groupe Philippart: An Experience of Multinational Enterprise in Railway and Banking Business in Western Europe: 1865–80. **In** *Teichova, A.; Lévy-Leboyer, M. and Nussbaum, H., eds.*, 1986, pp. 65–73. **[G: W. Europe]**

Lindert, Peter H. Unequal English Wealth since 1670. *J. Polit. Econ.*, December 1986, *94*(6), pp. 1127–62. **[G: U.K.]**

Lundström, Ragnhild. Banks and Early Swedish Multinationals. **In** *Teichova, A.; Lévy-Leboyer, M. and Nussbaum, H., eds.*, 1986, pp. 200–217. **[G: Sweden]**

MacKinnon, Mary. Poor Law Policy, Unemployment, and Pauperism. *Exploration Econ. Hist.*, July 1986, *23*(3), pp. 299–336. **[G: U.K.]**

MacLeod, Christine. The 1690s Patents Boom: Invention or Stock-Jobbing? *Econ. Hist. Rev., 2nd Ser.*, November 1986, *39*(4), pp. 549–71. **[G: U.K.]**

Magnusson, Lars. Drinking and the Verlag System 1820–1850: The Significance of Taverns and Drink in Eskilstuna before Industrialisation. *Scand. Econ. Hist. Rev.*, 1986, *34*(1), pp. 1–19. **[G: Sweden]**

Marsden, W. E. Atlas of Industrializing Britain 1780–1914: Education. **In** *Langton, J. and Morris, R. J., eds.*, 1986, pp. 206–11. **[G: U.K.]**

Matthews, K. G. P. Was Sterling Overvalued in 1925? *Econ. Hist. Rev., 2nd Ser.*, November 1986, *39*(4), pp. 572–87. **[G: U.K.]**

McKay, John. The House of Rothschild (Paris) as a Multinational Industrial Enterprise: 1875–1914. **In** *Teichova, A.; Lévy-Leboyer, M. and Nussbaum, H., eds.*, 1986, pp. 74–86. **[G: Europe]**

Minde, Kjell Bjørn and Ramstad, Jan. The Development of Real Wages in Norway about 1730–1910. *Scand. Econ. Hist. Rev.*, 1986, *34*(2), pp. 90–121. **[G: Norway]**

Mingay, G. E. The Course of Rents in the Age of Malthus. **In** *Turner, M., ed.*, 1986, pp. 85–95. **[G: U.K.]**

Myhre, Jan Eivind. Research into Norwegian Living Conditions in the Period 1750–1914. *Scand. Econ. Hist. Rev.*, 1986, *34*(2), pp. 159–66. **[G: Norway]**

Nardinelli, Clark. Technology and Unemployment: The Case of the Handloom Weavers. *Southern Econ. J.*, July 1986, *53*(1), pp. 87–94. **[G: U.K.]**

Nicholas, Stephen. The Hierarchical Division of

Labour and the Growth of British Manufacturing Multinationals: 1870–1939. **In** *Teichova, A.; Lévy-Leboyer, M. and Nussbaum, H., eds.*, 1986, pp. 241–56. **[G: U.K.]**

O'Brien, Patrick K. and Toniolo, Gianni. Sull'arretratezza dell'agricoltura italiana rispetto a quella del regno unito attorno al 1910. (On the Backwardness of Italian Agriculture Relative to the United Kingdom C.A. 1910. With English summary.) *Ricerche Econ.*, Apr.-Sept. 1986, *40*(2–3), pp. 266–85. **[G: U.K.; Italy]**

Ó Gráda, Cormac. Across the Briny Ocean: Some Thoughts on Irish Emigration to America, 1800–1850. **In** *Glazier, I. A. and De Rosa, L., eds.*, 1986, pp. 79–94. **[G: U.S.; Ireland]**

Oakley, Stewart P. Reconstructing Scandinavian Farms 1660–1860: Sources in Denmark, Iceland, Norway and Sweden. *Scand. Econ. Hist. Rev.*, 1986, *34*(3), pp. 181–203. **[G: Denmark; Iceland; Norway; Sweden]**

Olsson, Ulf. Recent Research in Sweden on the Standard of Living during the Eighteenth and Nineteenth Centuries. *Scand. Econ. Hist. Rev.*, 1986, *34*(2), pp. 153–58. **[G: Sweden]**

Ostergren, Robert C. Swedish Migration to North America in Transatlantic Perspective. **In** *Glazier, I. A. and De Rosa, L., eds.*, 1986, pp. 125–47. **[G: Sweden; U.S.]**

Pastré, Olivier and Rowley, Anthony. The Multinationalisation of British and American Banks. **In** *Teichova, A.; Lévy-Leboyer, M. and Nussbaum, H., eds.*, 1986, pp. 232–38. **[G: U.K.; U.S.]**

Plumpe, Gottfried. Industry, Technical Progress and State: The Synthesis of Rubber in Germany 1906–1944/45. **In** *Pohl, H. and Rudolph, B., eds.*, 1986, pp. 97–124. **[G: Germany]**

Pressnell, L. S. The Avoidance of Catastrophe: Two Nineteenth-Century Banking Crises: Comment. **In** *Capie, F. and Wood, G. E., eds.*, 1986, pp. 74–76. **[G: U.K.]**

Radice, E. A. Energy and Materials. **In** *Kaser, M. C. and Radice, E. A., eds.*, 1986, pp. 398–415. **[G: E. Europe; Germany]**

Radice, E. A. Territorial Changes, Population Movements and Labour Supplies. **In** *Kaser, M. C. and Radice, E. A., eds.*, 1986, pp. 309–28. **[G: E. Europe]**

Reader, W. J. 'At the Head of All the New Professions': The Engineer in Victorian Society. **In** *[Coleman, D. C.]*, 1986, pp. 173–84. **[G: U.K.]**

Roberts, R. O. Banks and the Economic Development of South Wales before 1914. **In** *Baber, C. and Williams, L. J., eds.*, 1986, pp. 65–80. **[G: U.K.]**

Rubinstein, W. D. Atlas of Industrializing Britain 1780–1914: Wealth and the Wealthy. **In** *Langton, J. and Morris, R. J., eds.*, 1986, pp. 156–59. **[G: U.K.]**

Schröter, Harm. A Typical Factor of German International Market Strategy: Agreements between the U.S. and German Electrotechnical Industries Up to 1939. **In** *Teichova, A.; Lévy-Leboyer, M. and Nussbaum, H., eds.*, 1986, pp. 160–70. **[G: U.S.; Germany]**

Schröter, Verena. Participation in Market Control through Foreign Investment: IG Farbenindustrie AG in the United States: 1920–38. **In** *Teichova, A.; Lévy-Leboyer, M. and Nussbaum, H., eds.*, 1986, pp. 171–84. **[G: U.S.; Germany]**

Seabourne, Teresa. The Summer of 1914. **In** *Capie, F. and Wood, G. E., eds.*, 1986, pp. 77–116. **[G: U.K.; Europe]**

Soikkanen, Hannu. Finnish Research on Changes in the Standard of Living. *Scand. Econ. Hist. Rev.*, 1986, *34*(2), pp. 167–70. **[G: Finland]**

Southall, Humphrey. Atlas of Industrializing Britain 1780–1914: Unionization. **In** *Langton, J. and Morris, R. J., eds.*, 1986, pp. 189–93. **[G: U.K.]**

Stiefel, Dieter. Austrian Banks at the Zenith of Power and Influence: System and Problems of the Austrian Finance Capital from the 1890s to the International Economic Crisis of the 1930s. **In** *Pohl, H. and Rudolph, B., eds.*, 1986, pp. 79–95. **[G: Austria]**

Swierenga, Robert P. Dutch International Migration and Occupational Change: A Structural Analysis of Multinational Linked Files. **In** *Glazier, I. A. and De Rosa, L., eds.*, 1986, pp. 95–124. **[G: Netherlands; U.S.]**

Urry, John. Capitalist Production, Scientific Management and the Service Class. **In** *Scott, A. J. and Storper, M., eds.*, 1986, pp. 43–66. **[G: U.S.; U.K.]**

Wagner, Michael. What Happened in 1931? Comment. **In** *Capie, F. and Wood, G. E., eds.*, 1986, pp. 157–59. **[G: U.K.]**

Wilkins, Mira. The History of European Multinationals: A New Look. *J. Europ. Econ. Hist.*, Winter 1986, *15*(3), pp. 483–510. **[G: Europe]**

Williamson, Jeffrey G. The Impact of the Irish on British Labor Markets during the Industrial Revolution. *J. Econ. Hist.*, September 1986, *46*(3), pp. 693–720. **[G: U.K.; Ireland]**

Wrigley, E. A. Men on the Land and Men in the Countryside: Employment in Agriculture in Early-Nineteenth-Century England. **In** *[Laslett, P.]*, 1986, pp. 295–336. **[G: U.K.]**

Wrigley, Julia. Technical Education and Industry in the Nineteenth Century. **In** *Elbaum, B. and Lazonick, W., eds.*, 1986, pp. 162–88. **[G: U.K.]**

0443 History of Public Economic Policy (all levels)

Barber, John. The Development of Soviet Employment and Labour Policy, 1930–41. **In** *Lane, D., ed.*, 1986, pp. 50–65. **[G: U.S.S.R.]**

Batchelor, Roy A. The Avoidance of Catastrophe: Two Nineteenth-Century Banking Crises. **In** *Capie, F. and Wood, G. E., eds.*, 1986, pp. 41–73. **[G: U.K.]**

Blaug, Mark. The Classical Economists and the Factory Acts: A Re-examination. **In** *Blaug, M.*, 1986, *1959*, pp. 135–49. **[G: U.K.]**

Blaug, Mark. The Myth of the Old Poor Law and the Making of the New. **In** *Blaug, M.*, 1986, *1963*, pp. 3–35. **[G: U.K.]**

Blaug, Mark. The Poor Law Report Re-examined. **In** *Blaug, M.*, 1986, *1964*, pp. 36–50. **[G: U.K.]**

Boyer, George R. The Old Poor Law and the Agricultural Labor Market in Southern England: An Empirical Analysis. *J. Econ. Hist.*, March 1986, *46*(1), pp. 113–35. **[G: U.K.]**

Boyer, George R. The Poor Law, Migration, and Economic Growth. *J. Econ. Hist.*, June 1986, *46*(2), pp. 419–30. **[G: U.K.]**

Bridbury, A. R. Dr. Rigby's Comment: A Reply [English Provincial Towns in the Later Middle Ages]. *Econ. Hist. Rev., 2nd Ser.*, August 1986, *39*(3), pp. 417–22. **[G: U.K.]**

Brooks, Neil. Taxation of Closely-Held Corporations: The Partnership Option and the Lower Rate of Tax. *Australian Tax Forum*, 1986, *3*(4), pp. 381–509. **[G: Australia; U.S.; U.K.; Canada]**

Buchanan, B. J. The Evolution of the English Turnpike Trusts: Lessons from a Case Study. *Econ. Hist. Rev., 2nd Ser.*, May 1986, *39*(2), pp. 223–43. **[G: U.K.]**

Butler, Henry N. General Incorporation in Nineteenth Century England: Interaction of Common Law and Legislative Processes. *Int. Rev. Law Econ.*, December 1986, *6*(2), pp. 169–88. **[G: U.K.]**

Capie, Forrest H.; Mills, Terence C. and Wood, Geoffrey E. Debt Management and Interest Rates: The British Stock Conversion of 1932. *Appl. Econ.*, October 1986, *18*(10), pp. 1111–26. **[G: U.K.]**

Cavendish, Elizabeth A. Public Provision of the Performing Arts: A Case Study of the Federal Theatre Project in Connecticut. **In** *DiMaggio, P. J., ed.*, 1986, pp. 140–58. **[G: U.S.]**

Cohen, Stephen S.; Halimi, Serge and Zysman, John. Institutions, Politics, and Industrial Policy in France. **In** *Barfield, C. E. and Schambra, W. A., eds.*, 1986, pp. 106–27. **[G: France]**

Coomans, Géry. Système productif et petites nations. (Productive System and Small Nations. With English summary.) *Écon. Soc.*, May 1986, *20*(5), pp. 49–67. **[G: Belgium]**

Davies, R. W. The Ending of Mass Unemployment in the USSR. **In** *Lane, D., ed.*, 1986, pp. 19–35. **[G: U.S.S.R.]**

Digby, Anne. Malthus and Reform of the English Poor Law. **In** *Turner, M., ed.*, 1986, pp. 157–69. **[G: U.K.]**

Dufour, Jean-Marie. Recursive Stability Analysis: The Demand for Money during the German Hyperinflation. **In** *Belsley, D. A. and Kuh, E., eds.*, 1986, pp. 18–61. **[G: Germany]**

Eichengreen, Barry. The Bank of France and the Sterilization of Gold, 1926–1932. *Exploration Econ. Hist.*, January 1986, *23*(1), pp. 56–84. **[G: France]**

Elton, G. R. Piscatorial Politics in the Early Parliaments of Elizabeth I. **In** *[Coleman, D. C.]*, 1986, pp. 1–20. **[G: U.K.]**

Gerchunoff, Pablo. Gasto pblico, tasa de cambio e impulso capitalista después de la hiperinflación. (With English summary.) *Desarrollo Econ.*, Jan.-Mar. 1986, *25*(100), pp. 623–57. **[G: Germany; Hungary; Argentina]**

Giovannini, Alberto. 'Rules of the Game' during the International Gold Standard: England and Germany. *J. Int. Money Finance*, December 1986, *5*(4), pp. 467–83. **[G: U.K.; W. Germany]**

Hadwin, J. F. From Dissonance to Harmony on the Late Medieval Town? *Econ. Hist. Rev., 2nd Ser.*, August 1986, *39*(3), pp. 423–26. **[G: U.K.]**

Hall, Peter A. The State and Economic Decline. **In** *Elbaum, B. and Lazonick, W., eds.*, 1986, pp. 266–302. **[G: U.K.]**

Hauner, M. Military Budgets and the Armaments Industry. **In** *Kaser, M. C. and Radice, E. A., eds.*, 1986, pp. 49–116. **[G: E. Europe; Germany]**

Hedlund, Stefan and Lundahl, Mats. Emergency Considerations in Swedish Agriculture: A Retrospective Look. *Europ. Rev. Agr. Econ.*, 1986, *13*(1), pp. 89–105. **[G: Sweden]**

Hicks, John R. The Abdication of Money. *Hong Kong Econ. Pap.*, 1986, (17), pp. 1–10. **[G: Global]**

Hjerppe, Riitta and Ahvenainen, Jorma. Foreign Enterprises and Nationalistic Control: The Case of Finland since the End of the Nineteenth Century. **In** *Teichova, A.; Lévy-Leboyer, M. and Nussbaum, H., eds.*, 1986, pp. 286–98. **[G: Finland]**

Holmes, Graeme. The First World War and Government Coal Control. **In** *Baber, C. and Williams, L. J., eds.*, 1986, pp. 206–21. **[G: U.K.]**

Humphrey, Thomas M. Eliminating Runaway Inflation: Lessons from the German Hyperinflation. **In** *Humphreys, T. M.*, 1986, *1980*, pp. 237–41. **[G: Germany]**

Huzel, J. P. The Demographic Impact of the Old Poor Laws: More Reflections on Malthus. **In** *Turner, M., ed.*, 1986, pp. 40–59. **[G: U.K.]**

Komlos, John. Institutional Change under Pressure: Enlightened Government Policy in the Eighteenth-Century Habsburg Monarchy. *J. Europ. Econ. Hist.*, Winter 1986, *15*(3), pp. 427–82. **[G: Germany]**

Krejčí, Jan. German Reparations after the Second World War. *Czech. Econ. Digest.*, Oct./Nov. 1986, (7), pp. 44–63. **[G: W. Germany]**

Lagergren, Stina. The Influence of ILO Standards on Swedish Law and Practice. *Int. Lab. Rev.*, May-June 1986, *125*(3), pp. 305–28. **[G: Sweden]**

Landau, Zbigniew and Tomaszewski, Jerzy. Foreign Policy and International Business in Poland: 1918–39. **In** *Teichova, A.; Lévy-Leboyer, M. and Nussbaum, H., eds.*, 1986, pp. 270–85. **[G: Poland]**

Laureyssens, Julienne M. Growth of Central Banking. The *Société Générale* and Its Impact on the Development of Belgium's Monetary System during the United Kingdom of the Netherlands (1815–1830). *J. Europ. Econ. Hist.*, Winter 1986, *15*(3), pp. 599–616. **[G: Netherlands; U.K.; Belgium]**

Leathers, Charles G. Gladstonian Finance and the Virginia School of Public Finance: Comment ["Chaining Leviathan": The Case of Gladstonian Finance]. *Hist. Polit. Econ.*, Fall 1986, *18*(3), pp. 515–21. **[G: U.K.]**

Levitt, Ian. Atlas of Industrializing Britain 1780–1914: Poor Law and Pauperism. **In** *Langton, J. and Morris, R. J., eds.*, 1986, pp. 160–63. **[G: U.K.]**

MacKinnon, Mary. Poor Law Policy, Unemployment, and Pauperism. *Exploration Econ. Hist.*, July 1986, *23*(3), pp. 299–336. **[G: U.K.]**

Makinen, Gail E. and Woodward, G. Thomas. Some Anecdotal Evidence Relating to the Legal Restrictions Theory of the Demand for Money. *J. Polit. Econ.*, April 1986, *94*(2), pp. 260–65. **[G: France]**

Matthews, Derek. Laissez-faire and the London Gas Industry in the Nineteenth Century: Another Look. *Econ. Hist. Rev., 2nd Ser.*, May 1986, *39*(2), pp. 244–63. **[G: U.K.]**

Meltzer, Allan H. Real and Psuedo-financial Crises: Comment. **In** *Capie, F. and Wood, G. E., eds.*, 1986, pp. 32–37. **[G: U.S.; U.K.]**

Mitch, David F. The Impact of Subsidies to Elementary Schooling on Enrolment Rates in Nineteenth-century England. *Econ. Hist. Rev., 2nd Ser.*, August 1986, *39*(3), pp. 371–91. **[G: U.K.]**

Moggridge, D. E. Real and Pseudo-financial Crises: Comment. **In** *Capie, F. and Wood, G. E., eds.*, 1986, pp. 38–40. **[G: U.S.; U.K.]**

Nove, Alec. Trotsky, Collectivization and the Five-Year Plan. **In** *Nove, A.*, 1986, *1982*, pp. 88–103. **[G: U.S.S.R.]**

Nussbaum, Helga. International Cartels and Multinational Enterprises. **In** *Teichova, A.; Lévy-Leboyer, M. and Nussbaum, H., eds.*, 1986, pp. 131–44. **[G: Global]**

Overy, Richard J. German Multinationals and the Nazi State in Occupied Europe. **In** *Teichova, A.; Lévy-Leboyer, M. and Nussbaum, H., eds.*, 1986, pp. 299–325. **[G: Germany]**

Pressnell, L. S. The Avoidance of Catastrophe: Two Nineteenth-Century Banking Crises: Comment. **In** *Capie, F. and Wood, G. E., eds.*, 1986, pp. 74–76. **[G: U.K.]**

Radice, E. A. Agriculture and Food. **In** *Kaser, M. C. and Radice, E. A., eds.*, 1986, pp. 366–97. **[G: E. Europe; Germany]**

Radice, E. A. Energy and Materials. **In** *Kaser, M. C. and Radice, E. A., eds.*, 1986, pp. 398–415. **[G: E. Europe; Germany]**

Ránki, Gy. and Tomaszewski, Jerzy. The Role of the State in Industry, Banking and Trade. **In** *Kaser, M. C. and Radice, E. A., eds.*, 1986, pp. 3–48. **[G: E. Europe]**

Richards, Hamish. Investment in Public Health Provision in the Mining Valleys of South Wales, 1860–1914. **In** *Baber, C. and Williams, L. J., eds.*, 1986, pp. 128–39. **[G: U.K.]**

Rigby, S. H. Late Medieval Urban Prosperity: The Evidence of the Lay Subsidies [English Provincial Towns in the Later Middle Ages] [The Medieval Lay Subsidies and Economic History]. *Econ. Hist. Rev., 2nd Ser.*, August 1986, *39*(3), pp. 411–16. **[G: U.K.]**

Santoni, Gary J. A Private Central Bank: Some Olde English Lessons. **In** *Toma, E. F. and Toma, M., eds.*, 1986, *1984*, pp. 219–39. **[G: U.K.]**

Schwartz, Anna J. Real and Pseudo-financial Crises. **In** *Capie, F. and Wood, G. E., eds.*, 1986, pp. 11–40. **[G: U.S.; U.K.]**

Smith, Keith. Economic Theory and the Closure of the Soviet Industrialisation Debate. **In** *Smith, K., ed.*, 1986, *1979*, pp. 23–49. **[G: U.S.S.R.]**

Spigler, I. Public Finance. **In** *Kaser, M. C. and Radice, E. A., eds.*, 1986, pp. 117–69. **[G: E. Europe]**

Staines, Brian. The Movement of Population from South Wales with Specific Reference to the Effects of the Industrial Transference Scheme, 1928–37. **In** *Baber, C. and Williams, L. J., eds.*, 1986, pp. 237–50. **[G: U.K.]**

Supple, Barry. Ideology or Pragmatism? The Nationalization of Coal, 1916–46. **In** *[Coleman, D. C.]*, 1986, pp. 228–50. **[G: U.K.]**

Thomson, David. Welfare and the Historians. **In** *[Laslett, P.]*, 1986, pp. 355–78.

Vamplew, Wray. Malthus and the Corn Laws. **In** *Turner, M., ed.*, 1986, pp. 129–39. **[G: U.K.]**

Vinokur, Annie. Malthusian Ideology and the Crises of the Welfare State. **In** *Turner, M., ed.*, 1986, pp. 170–86. **[G: U.K.]**

Webb, Steven B. Fiscal News and Inflationary Expectations in Germany after World War I. *J. Econ. Hist.*, September 1986, *46*(3), pp. 769–94. **[G: Germany]**

Wells, Paul. 'Mr Churchill' and the *General Theory*. **In** *[Tarshis, L.]*, 1986, pp. 8–27. **[G: U.K.]**

045 Economic History: Asia

0450 General

Aspengren, Evald. Java and the World: A Study in the Relationship between the Rice Agriculture of Java and the World Economy in the 1930s. **In** *Nørlund, I.; Cederroth, S. and Gerdin, I., eds.*, 1986, pp. 230–63. **[G: Indonesia]**

Bhooshan, B. S. Bangalore, Mandya and Mysore Districts, Karnataka State, South India. **In** *Hardoy, J. E. and Satterthwaite, D., eds.*, 1986, pp. 131–84. **[G: India]**

Grabowski, Richard and Sivan, David. The Supply of Labor in Agriculture and Food Prices: The Cases of Japan and Egypt. *World Devel.*, March 1986, *14*(3), pp. 441–47. **[G: Japan; Egypt]**

Gravers, Mikael. On the Systematic Character of the Thai State: The Properties of Precapitalist Class Relations and the Effects of Capitalist Penetration. **In** *Nørlund, I.; Cederroth, S. and Gerdin, I., eds.*, 1986, pp. 280–306. **[G: Thailand]**

Hanley, Susan B. Standard of Living in Nineteenth-Century Japan: Reply to Yasuba. *J. Econ. Hist.*, March 1986, *46*(1), pp. 225–26. **[G: Japan]**

Latham, A. J. H. Southeast Asia: A Preliminary Survey, 1800–1914. **In** *Glazier, I. A. and De Rosa, L., eds.*, 1986, pp. 11–29. **[G: S. E. Asia]**

Misra, H. N. Rae Bareli, Sultanpur and Pratapgarh Districts, Uttar Pradesh State, North India. **In** *Hardoy, J. E. and Satterthwaite, D., eds.*, 1986, pp. 185–227. **[G: India]**

Nørlund, Irene. Social and Economic Studies on Vietnam: An Overview. **In** *Nørlund, I.; Cederroth, S. and Gerdin, I., eds.*, 1986, pp. 176–202. **[G: Vietnam]**

Prakash, Shri. The Nineteen Thirties Depression and the Indian Agrarian Economy before and after 1947. **In** *Berend, I. T. and Borchardt, K., eds.*, 1986, pp. 275–303. **[G: India]**

Rao, M. S. A. Migration, Agricultural Development, and Deprivation: A Case Study of a Tribal Situation in India. **In** *Glazier, I. A. and De Rosa, L., eds.*, 1986, pp. 58–75. **[G: India]**

Sörbom, Per. The Reception of Western Technology in China and Japan. **In** *Baark, E. and Jamison, A., eds.*, 1986, pp. 35–56. **[G: China; Japan]**

Spooner, Frank. Batavia, 1673–1790: A City of Colonial Growth and Migration. **In** *Glazier, I. A. and De Rosa, L., eds.*, 1986, pp. 30–57. **[G: Indonesia]**

Yasuba, Yasukichi. Standard of Living in Japan before Industrialization: From What Level Did Japan Begin? A Comment. *J. Econ. Hist.*, March 1986, *46*(1), pp. 217–24. **[G: Japan]**

0451 History of Product Prices and Markets

Baladouni, Vahé. Armenian Trade with the English East India Company: An Aperçu. *J. Europ. Econ. Hist.*, Spring 1986, *15*(1), pp. 153–62. **[G: Persia]**

Chao, Kang. The Chinese–American Cotton-Textile Trade, 1830–1930. **In** *May, E. R. and Fairbank, J. K., eds.*, 1986, pp. 103–27. **[G: China; Japan; U.S.; U.K.]**

Cheng, Chu-yuan. The United States Petroleum Trade with China, 1876–1949. **In** *May, E. R. and Fairbank, J. K., eds.*, 1986, pp. 205–33. **[G: U.S.; China]**

Cochran, Sherman. Commercial Penetration and Economic Imperialism in China: An American Cigarette Company's Entrance into the Market. **In** *May, E. R. and Fairbank, J. K., eds.*, 1986, pp. 151–203. **[G: China]**

Fairbank, John K. America's China Trade in Historical Perspective: The Chinese and American Performance: Patterns and Problems. **In** *May, E. R. and Fairbank, J. K., eds.*, 1986, pp. 1–7.

Godley, Michael R. Bacchus in the East: The Chinese Grape Wine Industry, 1892–1938. *Bus. Hist. Rev.*, Autumn 1986, *60*(3), pp. 383–409. **[G: China]**

Hao, Yen-p'ing. Chinese Teas to America—A Synopsis. **In** *May, E. R. and Fairbank, J. K., eds.*, 1986, pp. 11–31. **[G: U.S.; China]**

Li, Lillian M. The Silk Export Trade and Economic Modernization in China and Japan. **In** *May, E. R. and Fairbank, J. K., eds.*, 1986, pp. 77–99. **[G: China; Japan]**

Minami, Ryoshin and Makino, Fumio. Choice of Technology: A Case Study of the Japanese Cotton Weaving Industry 1902–1938. *Hitotsubashi J. Econ.*, December 1986, *27*(2), pp. 111–32. **[G: Japan]**

Murota, Takeshi. History and Present of the Helical Waterwheel: Its Unique Position in the Modern Technology of Japan: Part I/Investigations for the Period of 1920–1942. *Hitotsubashi J. Econ.*, June 1986, *27*(1), pp. 11–33. **[G: Japan]**

Nørlund, Irene. Rice Production in Colonial Vietnam, 1900–1930: Production, Consumption, Market Relations and Social Differentiation. **In** *Nørlund, I.; Cederroth, S. and Gerdin, I., eds.*, 1986, pp. 203–29. **[G: China]**

Ono, Akira. Technical Progress in Silk Industry in Prewar Japan—The Types of Borrowed Technology. *Hitotsubashi J. Econ.*, June 1986, *27*(1), pp. 1–10. **[G: Japan]**

Reynolds, Bruce L. The East Asian "Textile Cluster" Trade, 1868–1973: A Comparative-Advantage Interpretation. **In** *May, E. R. and Fairbank, J. K., eds.*, 1986, pp. 129–50. **[G: U.S.; U.K.; China; India; Japan]**

Schran, Peter. The Minor Significance of Commercial Relations between the United States and China, 1850–1931. **In** *May, E. R. and Fairbank, J. K., eds.*, 1986, pp. 237–58. **[G: China; U.S.; Japan]**

Wilkins, Mira. Japanese Multinational Enterprise before 1914. *Bus. Hist. Rev.*, Summer 1986, *60*(2), pp. 199–231. **[G: Japan]**

0452 History of Factor Prices and Markets

Chokki, Toshiaki. A History of the Machine Tool Industry in Japan. **In** *Fransman, M., ed.*, 1986, pp. 124–52. **[G: Japan]**

Michaelis, Dolf. One Hundred Years of Banking and Currency in Palestine. **In** *Uselding, P., ed.*, 1986, pp. 155–97. **[G: Palestine; Middle East]**

Mosk, Carl and Johansson, S. Ryan. Income and Mortality: Evidence from Modern Japan. *Population Devel. Rev.*, September 1986, *12*(3), pp. 415–40. **[G: Japan]**

Taira, Koji. Diverse Entrepreneurial Traditions and Implications for Internal and External Labor Markets. **In** *Dennis, B. D., ed.*, 1986, pp. 336–45. **[G: Japan]**

Wilkins, Mira. The Impacts of American Multinational Enterprise on American–Chinese Economic Relations, 1786–1949. **In** *May, E. R. and Fairbank, J. K., eds.*, 1986, pp. 259–92. **[G: U.S.; China]**

0453 History of Public Economic Policy (all levels)

Frykenberg, Robert Eric. Modern Education in South India, 1784–1854: Its Roots and Its Role as a Vehicle of Integration under Company Raj. *Amer. Hist. Rev.*, February 1986, *91*(1), pp. 37–65. [G: India]

046 Economic History: Africa

0460 General

Aradeon, David; Aina, Tade Akin and Umo, Joe. South-west Nigeria. **In** *Hardoy, J. E. and Satterthwaite, D., eds.*, 1986, pp. 228–78. [G: Nigeria]

Bucht, Birgitta and El-Badry, M. A. Reflections on Recent Levels and Trends of Fertility and Mortality in Egypt. *Population Stud.*, March 1986, *40*(1), pp. 101–13. [G: Egypt]

Chevillard, Nicole and Leconte, Sébastien. Slavery and Women. **In** *Coontz, S. and Henderson, P., eds.*, 1986, pp. 156–68. [G: Africa]

DeLorme, Charles D., Jr.; Kamerschen, David R. and Mbaku, John M. Rent Seeking in the Cameroon Economy: Krueger's Analytic Technique Helps to Account for Development Lag in Colonial States. *Amer. J. Econ. Soc.*, October 1986, *45*(4), pp. 413–23. [G: Cameroon]

El Agraa, Omer M. A., et al. The Gezira Region, the Sudan. **In** *Hardoy, J. E. and Satterthwaite, D., eds.*, 1986, pp. 80–130. [G: Sudan]

Giblin, James. Famine and Social Change during the Transition to Colonial Rule in Northeastern Tanzania, 1880–1986. *African Econ. Hist.*, 1986, (15), pp. 85–105. [G: Tanzania]

Koponen, Juhani. Population Growth in Historical Perspective: The Key Role of Changing Fertility. **In** *Boesen, J., et al., eds.*, 1986, pp. 31–57. [G: Tanzania]

O'Hear, Ann. Political and Commercial Clientage in Nineteenth-Century Ilorin. *African Econ. Hist.*, 1986, (15), pp. 69–83. [G: Africa]

Pfeifer, Karen. The Development of Commercial Agriculture in Algeria, 1830–1970. **In** *Uselding, P., ed.*, 1986, pp. 271–308. [G: Algeria]

0461 History of Product Prices and Markets

Maier, D. J. E. Colonial Distortion of the Volta River Salt Trade. *African Econ. Hist.*, 1986, (15), pp. 13–37. [G: Africa]

Martin, Phyllis M. Power, Cloth and Currency on the Loango Coast. *African Econ. Hist.*, 1986, (15), pp. 1–12. [G: Africa]

Pangeti, Evelyn. Agribusiness in Colonial Zimbabwe: The Case of the Lowveld. **In** *Teichova, A.; Lévy-Leboyer, M. and Nussbaum, H., eds.*, 1986, pp. 326–38. [G: Zimbabwe]

0462 History of Factor Prices and Markets

Abedian, Iraj and Standish, B. Market Imperfections and Unemployment: A Model of the South African Labour Market 1900–1940. *S. Afr. J. Econ.*, December 1986, *54*(4), pp. 406–17. [G: S. Africa]

Eltis, David. Slave Departures from Africa, 1811–1867: An Annual Time Series. *African Econ. Hist.*, 1986, (15), pp. 143–71. [G: Africa]

Jones, Stuart. The History of Black Involvement in the South African Economy. **In** *Smollan, R., ed.*, 1986, pp. 1–22. [G: S. Africa]

Lever, Jeffrey. The Trade Unions and Black Advancement. **In** *Smollan, R., ed.*, 1986, pp. 52–70. [G: S. Africa]

Mbilinyi, Marjorie. Agribusiness and Casual Labor in Tanzania. *African Econ. Hist.*, 1986, (15), pp. 107–41. [G: Tanzania]

Owen, Roger. Large Landowners, Agricultural Progress and the State in Egypt, 1800–1970: An Overview with Many Questions. **In** *Richards, A., ed.*, 1986, pp. 69–95. [G: Egypt]

Steckel, Richard H. and Jensen, Richard A. New Evidence on the Causes of Slave and Crew Mortality in the Atlantic Slave Trade. *J. Econ. Hist.*, March 1986, *46*(1), pp. 57–77. [G: W. Africa; Caribbean]

0463 History of Public Economic Policy (all levels)

Hartshorne, Ken. The Role of the State in Education and Training. **In** *Smollan, R., ed.*, 1986, pp. 117–37. [G: S. Africa]

McLane, Margaret O. Commercial Rivalries and French Policy on the Senegal River, 1831–1858. *African Econ. Hist.*, 1986, (15), pp. 39–67. [G: Africa]

Young, Crawford. Africa's Colonial Legacy. **In** *Berg, R. J. and Whitaker, J. S., eds.*, 1986, pp. 25–51. [G: Africa]

047 Economic History: Latin America and Caribbean

0470 General

Alhadeff, Peter. The Economic Formulae of the 1930s: A Reassessment. **In** *di Tella, G. and Platt, D. C. M., eds.*, 1986, pp. 95–119. [G: Argentina]

Díaz-Alejandro, Carlos F. The Early 1980s in Latin America: The 1930s One More Time? **In** *[Streeten, P.]*, 1986, pp. 154–64. [G: Latin America]

Kuethe, Allan J. Guns, Subsidies, and Commercial Privilege: Some Historical Factors in the Emergence of the Cuban National Character, 1763–1815. **In** *Mesa-Lago, C., ed.*, 1986, pp. 123–38. [G: Cuba]

Manzanal, Mabel and Vapnarsky, Cesar A. The Development of the Upper Valley of the Rio Negro and Its Periphery within the Comahue Region, Argentina. **In** *Hardoy, J. E. and Satterthwaite, D., eds.*, 1986, pp. 18–79. [G: Argentina]

Rock, David. The Argentine Economy, 1890–1914: Some Salient Features. **In** *di Tella, G. and Platt, D. C. M., eds.*, 1986, pp. 60–73. [G: Argentina]

Rojo, Antonio Benítez. Power/Sugar/Literature: Toward a Reinterpretation of Cubanness. **In** *Mesa-Lago, C., ed.*, 1986, pp. 9–31. [G: Cuba]

Stemplowski, Ryszard and Szlajfer, Henryk. Political Responses to the Economic Crises in El

Salvador: 1930 and 1980. **In** *Berend, I. T. and Borchardt, K., eds.*, 1986, pp. 304–29. **[G: El Salvador]**

di Tella, Guido. Economic Controversies in Argentina from the 1920s to the 1940s. **In** *di Tella, G. and Platt, D. C. M., eds.*, 1986, pp. 120–32. **[G: Argentina]**

di Tella, Guido and Platt, D. C. M. The Political Economy of Argentina, 1880–1946: Postscript and Conclusions. **In** *di Tella, G. and Platt, D. C. M., eds.*, 1986, pp. 201–12. **[G: Argentina]**

White, Eugene Nelson. Latin America's Debt Crisis of the 1930s: Lessons for the 1980s. **In** *Berend, I. T. and Borchardt, K., eds.*, 1986, pp. 484–96. **[G: Latin America; U.S.]**

0471 History of Product Prices and Markets

Halperín, Tulio. The Argentine Export Economy: Intimations of Mortality, 1894–1930. **In** *di Tella, G. and Platt, D. C. M., eds.*, 1986, pp. 39–59. **[G: Argentina]**

O'Connell, Arturo A. Free Trade in One (Primary Producing) Country: The Case of Argentina in the 1920s. **In** *di Tella, G. and Platt, D. C. M., eds.*, 1986, pp. 74–94. **[G: Argentina]**

O'Connell, Arturo A. La fiebre aftosa, el embargo sanitario norteamericano contra las importaciones de carne y el triángulo Argentina–Gran Bretaña–Estados Unidos en el Periodo entre las dos guerras mundiales. (With English summary.) *Desarrollo Econ.*, Apr.-June 1986, *26*(101), pp. 21–50. **[G: Argentina]**

Zahedieh, Nuala. Trade, Plunder, and Economic Development in Early English Jamaica, 1655–89. *Econ. Hist. Rev., 2nd Ser.*, May 1986, *39*(2), pp. 205–22. **[G: Jamaica]**

0472 History of Factor Prices and Markets

Brown, Jonathan C. Foreign Oil Companies, Oil Workers, and the Mexican Revolutionary State in the 1920s. **In** *Teichova, A.; Lévy-Leboyer, M. and Nussbaum, H., eds.*, 1986, pp. 257–69. **[G: Mexico]**

Engerman, Stanley L. Population and Labor in the British Caribbean in the Early Nineteenth Century: Comment. **In** *Engerman, S. L. and Gallman, R. E., eds.*, 1986, pp. 625–29. **[G: Caribbean]**

Engerman, Stanley L. Slavery and Emancipation in Comparative Perspective: A Look at Some Recent Debates. *J. Econ. Hist.*, June 1986, *46*(2), pp. 317–39. **[G: U.S.; Caribbean]**

Fodor, Jorge. The Origin of Argentina's Sterling Balances, 1939–43. **In** *di Tella, G. and Platt, D. C. M., eds.*, 1986, pp. 154–82. **[G: Argentina]**

Friedman, Gerald. Population and Labor in the British Caribbean in the Early Nineteenth Century: Comment. **In** *Engerman, S. L. and Gallman, R. E., eds.*, 1986, pp. 629–37. **[G: Caribbean]**

Higman, B. W. Population and Labor in the British Caribbean in the Early Nineteenth Century. **In** *Engerman, S. L. and Gallman, R. E., eds.*, 1986, pp. 605–25. **[G: Caribbean]**

Pérez, Louis A., Jr. Aspects of Hegemony: Labor, State, and Capital in Plattist Cuba. **In** *Mesa-Lago, C., ed.*, 1986, pp. 49–69. **[G: Cuba]**

Platt, D. C. M. Domestic Finance in the Growth of Buenos Aires, 1880–1914. **In** *di Tella, G. and Platt, D. C. M., eds.*, 1986, pp. 1–14. **[G: Argentina]**

Salvatore, Ricardo D. Control del trabajo y discriminación: el sistema de contratistas en Mendoza, Argentina, 1880–1920. (With English summary.) *Desarrollo Econ.*, July-Sept. 1986, *26*(102), pp. 229–53. **[G: Argentina]**

Scott, Rebecca J. Dismantling Repressive Systems: The Abolition of Slavery in Cuba as a Case Study. **In** *[Hirshman, A. O.]*, 1986, pp. 269–81. **[G: Cuba]**

Steckel, Richard H. and Jensen, Richard A. New Evidence on the Causes of Slave and Crew Mortality in the Atlantic Slave Trade. *J. Econ. Hist.*, March 1986, *46*(1), pp. 57–77. **[G: W. Africa; Caribbean]**

Tulchin, Joseph S. The Relationship between Labour and Capital in Rural Argentina, 1880–1914. **In** *di Tella, G. and Platt, D. C. M., eds.*, 1986, pp. 15–38. **[G: Argentina]**

0473 History of Public Economic Policy (all levels)

Chiaramonte, José Carlos. Legalidad constitucional o caudillismo: el problema del orden social en el surgimiento de los estados autónomos del litoral argentino en la primera mitad del siglo XIX. (With English summary.) *Desarrollo Econ.*, July-Sept. 1986, *26*(102), pp. 175–96. **[G: Argentina]**

Domínguez, Jorge I. Seeking Permission to Build a Nation: Cuban Nationalism and U.S. Response under the First Machado Presidency. **In** *Mesa-Lago, C., ed.*, 1986, pp. 33–48. **[G: U.S.; Cuba]**

Dornbusch, Rudiger. Inflação, taxas de câmbio e estabilização. (With English summary.) *Pesquisa Planejamento Econ.*, August 1986, *16*(2), pp. 321–49. **[G: Brazil; U.S.; Germany]**

Mann, Arthur J. and Schulthess, Walter E. Long-run Expenditure Constraints in Argentina. *Public Finance Quart.*, January 1986, *14*(1), pp. 28–47. **[G: Argentina]**

O'Connell, Arturo A. Free Trade in One (Primary Producing) Country: The Case of Argentina in the 1920s. **In** *di Tella, G. and Platt, D. C. M., eds.*, 1986, pp. 74–94. **[G: Argentina]**

Pérez, Louis A., Jr. Aspects of Hegemony: Labor, State, and Capital in Plattist Cuba. **In** *Mesa-Lago, C., ed.*, 1986, pp. 49–69. **[G: Cuba]**

Prebisch, Raúl. Argentine Economic Policies since the 1930s: Recollections. **In** *di Tella, G. and Platt, D. C. M., eds.*, 1986, pp. 133–53. **[G: Argentina]**

048 Economic History: Oceania

0480 General

Butlin, N. G. Contours of the Australian Economy 1788–1860. *Australian Econ. Hist. Rev.*, September 1986, *26*(2), pp. 96–125. [G: Australia]

Butlin, N. G. and Sinclair, W. A. Australian Gross Domestic Product 1788–1860: Estimates, Sources and Methods. *Australian Econ. Hist. Rev.*, September 1986, *26*(2), pp. 126–47. [G: Australia]

Endres, Anthony M. The Political Economy of W. B. Sutch: Toward a Critical Appreciation. *New Zealand Econ. Pap.*, 1986, *20*, pp. 17–39. [G: New Zealand]

Wilson, C. H. Convicts, Commerce and Sovereignty: The Forces behind the Early Settlement of Australia. **In** *[Coleman, D. C.]*, 1986, pp. 79–97. [G: U.K.; Australia]

0481 History of Product Prices and Markets

Frost, L. E. A Reinterpretation of Victoria's Railway Construction Boom of the 1880s. *Australian Econ. Hist. Rev.*, March 1986, *26*(1), pp. 40–55. [G: Australia]

Pope, David H. Protection and Australian Manufacturers' International Competitiveness, 1901–1930. *Australian Econ. Hist. Rev.*, March 1986, *26*(1), pp. 21–39. [G: Australia]

0482 History of Factor Prices and Markets

Arnold, R. The Dynamics and Quality of Trans-Tasman Migration, 1885–1910. *Australian Econ. Hist. Rev.*, March 1986, *26*(1), pp. 1–20. [G: Australia]

McKenzie, Ian M. Australia's Real Exchange Rate during the Twentieth Century. *Econ. Rec.*, Supplement 1986, pp. 69–78. [G: Australia]

Shann, Edward W. Australia's Real Exchange Rate during the Twentieth Century: Comment. *Econ. Rec.*, Supplement 1986, pp. 79–81. [G: Australia]

0483 History of Public Economic Policy (all levels)

Craigie, Rowen; Cumpston, Richard and Sams, Dennis. Accident Compensation Reform. *Australian Econ. Rev.*, 3rd Quarter 1986, (75), pp. 9–30. [G: Australia]

Endres, Anthony M. and Cook, Malcolm. Administering 'The Unemployed Difficulty': The N.S.W. Government Labour Bureau 1892–1912. *Australian Econ. Hist. Rev.*, March 1986, *26*(1), pp. 56–70. [G: Australia]

Norman, N. R. Accident Compensation Reform: Comment. *Australian Econ. Rev.*, 3rd Quarter 1986, (75), pp. 31–32. [G: Australia]

Spenceley, G. F. R. Responses to Unemployment in Australia: The 1930s and Now. **In** *Berend, I. T. and Borchardt, K., eds.*, 1986, pp. 82–105. [G: Australia]

050 Economic Systems

0500 General

Bennett, John C. Religion, Economics and Social Thought: Overview. **In** *Block, W. and Hexham, I., eds.*, 1986, pp. 543–60.

Bohnet, Armin. Elemente einer allgemeinen Theorie der Wirtschaftsordnung. (An Analytical Framework for a General Theory of Economic Systems. With English summary.) *Jahr. Nationalökon. Statist.*, July 1986, *201*(4), pp. 378–403.

Boulding, Kenneth E. System Breaks and Positive Feedback as Sources of Catastrophe. **In** *[Rapoport, A.]*, 1986, pp. 47–54.

Brown, Alan A. and Neuberger, Egon. Grants and Exchange from a Comparative Systems Perspective. *Amer. Econ.*, Fall 1986, *30*(2), pp. 14–21.

Brown, Lester R. Redefining National Security. *Challenge*, July/Aug. 1986, *29*(3), pp. 25–32.

Desai, Meghnad. Men and Things. *Economica*, February 1986, *53*(209), pp. 1–10.

Fagen, Richard R.; Deere, Carmen Diana and Coraggio, José Luis. Transition and Development: Introduction. **In** *Fagen, R. R.; Deere, C. D. and Coraggio, J. L., eds.*, 1986, pp. 9–27.

Feigenbaum, Susan. Judaism's Historical Response to Economic, Social and Political Systems: Comment. **In** *Block, W. and Hexham, I., eds.*, 1986, pp. 387–92.

Hayden, F. Gregory. Defining and Articulating Social Change through the Social Fabric Matrix and System Digraph. *J. Econ. Issues*, June 1986, *20*(2), pp. 383–92.

Hurwicz, Leonid. On Informationally Decentralized Systems. **In** *[Marschak, J.]*, 1986, *1972*, pp. 297–336.

Kornai, János. Contradictions and Dilemmas: Studies on the Socialist Economy and Society: Introduction. **In** *Kornai, J.*, 1986, pp. 1–5.

Libecap, Gary D. Property Rights in Economic History: Implications for Research. *Exploration Econ. Hist.*, July 1986, *23*(3), pp. 227–52. [G: U.S.]

Novak, Michael. Religion, Economics and Social Thought: Overview. **In** *Block, W. and Hexham, I., eds.*, 1986, pp. 524–43.

Rivkin, Ellis. Judaism's Historical Response to Economic, Social and Political Systems. **In** *Block, W. and Hexham, I., eds.*, 1986, pp. 375–87.

Sah, Raaj Kumar and Stiglitz, Joseph E. The Architecture of Economic Systems: Hierarchies and Polyarchies. *Amer. Econ. Rev.*, September 1986, *76*(4), pp. 716–27.

Tibbitt, Andrew. Teaching Economics to the 16–19 Age Range: Comparative Economics. **In** *Whitehead, D. J., ed.*, 1986, pp. 197–205.

Trivedi, Prajapati. Explaining Public versus Private Partitioning of the Economy. *Indian Econ. J.*, Oct.-Dec. 1986, *34*(2), pp. 112–24.

051 Capitalist Economic Systems: Market Economies

0510 Capitalist Economic Systems: Market Economies

Abdul-Rauf, Muhammad. Islamic Social Thought: Comment. **In** *Block, W. and Hexham, I., eds.*, 1986, pp. 500–508.

051 Capitalist Economic Systems: Market Economies

Abromeit, Heidrun. Privatisation in Great Britain. *Ann. Pub. Co-op. Econ.*, Apr.-June 1986, *57*(2), pp. 153–79. **[G: U.K.]**

Acheson, James M. Constraints on Entrepreneurship: Transaction Costs and Market Efficiency. **In** *Greenfield, S. M. and Strickon, A., eds.*, 1986, pp. 45–53.

Ahmad, Imad. Islamic Social Thought. **In** *Block, W. and Hexham, I., eds.*, 1986, pp. 465–91.

Ahmad, Imad. Islamic Social Thought: Reply. **In** *Block, W. and Hexham, I., eds.*, 1986, pp. 509–12.

Alberro-Semerena, José Luis and Nieto-Ituarte, Marií Dolores. Empirical Estimates of Marxian Categories in Mexico: 1970–1975. *Rev. Radical Polit. Econ.*, Winter 1986, *18*(4), pp. 32–46. **[G: Mexico]**

Alexander, Robert J. Is the United States Substituting a Speculative Economy for a Productive One? *J. Econ. Issues*, June 1986, *20*(2), pp. 365–74. **[G: U.S.]**

Alvi, Eskander. The Production Process in a Competitive Economy: Comment. *Amer. Econ. Rev.*, December 1986, *76*(5), pp. 1200–1202.

Amariglio, Jack and Callari, Antonio. Marxian Economics and Freedom: A Comment. *Eastern Econ. J.*, Jan.-Mar. 1986, *12*(1), pp. 73–78.

Anderson, Terry L. and Hill, Peter J. Constraining the Transfer Society: Constitutional and Moral Dimensions. *Cato J.*, Spring/Summer 1986, *6*(1), pp. 317–39.

Anderson, Terry L. and Hill, Peter J. Privatizing the Commons: Reply. *Southern Econ. J.*, April 1986, *52*(4), pp. 1165–67.

Andrews, Marcellus. Response: Is Schumpeter Compatible with Neoclassical Economics? [The Entrepreneur in Marx and Schumpeter]. **In** *Helburn, S. W. and Bramhall, D. F., eds.*, 1986, pp. 179–82.

Appelbaum, Eileen. Speiser's SuperStock Solution: A Dissent [Can Effective Demand and the Movement toward Further Income Equity Be Maintained in the Face of Robotics? An Introduction]. *J. Post Keynesian Econ.*, Summer 1986, *8*(4), pp. 637–41. **[G: U.S.]**

Arena, Richard and Froeschle, Claude. Formes de progrès technique, séquences d'équilibres temporaires et stabilité économique. (Forms of Technical Progress, Sequences of Temporary Equilibrium and Economic Stability. With English summary.) *Écon. Appl.*, 1986, *39*(3), pp. 415–47.

Bance, Philippe and Monnier, Lionel. The Privatization of Public Enterprises in France. *Ann. Pub. Co-op. Econ.*, Apr.-June 1986, *57*(2), pp. 181–203. **[G: France]**

Barzelay, Michael and Thomas, Lee R., III. Is Capitalism Necessary? A Critique of the Neoclassical Economics of Organization. *J. Econ. Behav. Organ.*, September 1986, *7*(3), pp. 225–33.

Bauer, Otto. Otto Bauer's 'Accumulation of Capital' (1913). *Hist. Polit. Econ.*, Spring 1986, *18*(1), pp. 87–110.

Baum, Gregory. Recent Roman Catholic Social Teaching: A Shift to the Left. **In** *Block, W. and Hexham, I., eds.*, 1986, pp. 47–72. **[G: Canada]**

Baumeister, Eduardo and Neira Cuadra, Oscar. The Making of a Mixed Economy: Class Struggle and State Policy in the Nicaragua Transition. **In** *Fagen, R. R.; Deere, C. D. and Coraggio, J. L., eds.*, 1986, pp. 171–91. **[G: Nicaragua]**

Baumol, William J. Smith versus Marx on Business Morality and the Social Interest. **In** *Szenberg, M., ed.*, 1986, *1976*, pp. 83–93.

Benne, Robert. Recent Roman Catholic Social Teaching: A Shift to the Left: Comment. **In** *Block, W. and Hexham, I., eds.*, 1986, pp. 72–81.

Bernstein, Irving. The Emergence of the American Welfare State: The New Deal and the New Frontier–Great Society. **In** *Dennis, B. D., ed.*, 1986, pp. 237–42. **[G: U.S.]**

Bewley, Truman F. The Share Economy in General Equilibrium. *J. Compar. Econ.*, December 1986, *10*(4), pp. 457–59.

Blaug, Mark. Entrepreneurship before and after Schumpeter. **In** *Blaug, M.*, 1986, 219–30.

Blaug, Mark. The Entrepreneur in Marx and Schumpeter. **In** *Helburn, S. W. and Bramhall, D. F., eds.*, 1986, pp. 167–78.

Blinder, Alan S. On the Share Economy . . . A Bottle Half Full. *Challenge*, Nov./Dec. 1986, *29*(5), pp. 51–52.

Block, Walter. Judaism and the Market Mechanism: Comment. **In** *Block, W. and Hexham, I., eds.*, 1986, pp. 430–49.

Bonus, Holger. The Cooperative Association as a Business Enterprise: A Study in the Economics of Transactions. *J. Inst. Theoretical Econ.*, June 1986, *142*(2), pp. 310–39.

Bowles, Samuel. The Production Process in a Competitive Economy: Walrasian, Neo-Hobbesian, and Marxian Models. **In** *Putterman, L., ed.*, 1986, *1985*, pp. 329–55.

Bowles, Samuel. The Production Process in a Competitive Economy: Reply. *Amer. Econ. Rev.*, December 1986, *76*(5), pp. 1203–04.

Bowles, Samuel; Gordon, David M. and Weisskopf, Thomas E. Power and Profits: The Social Structure of Accumulation and the Profitability of the Postwar U.S. Economy. *Rev. Radical Polit. Econ.*, Spring/Summer 1986, *18*(1/2), pp. 132–67. **[G: U.S.]**

Brede, Helmut and Hoppe, Ulrich. Outline of the Present Status of the Privatization Debate in the Federal German Republic. *Ann. Pub. Co-op. Econ.*, Apr.-June 1986, *57*(2), pp. 205–29. **[G: W. Germany]**

Bronfenbrenner, Martin. Income Distribution and "Economic Justice." *J. Econ. Educ.*, Winter 1986, *17*(1), pp. 35–51. **[G: U.S.]**

Brown, Donald J. Increasing Returns and the Share Economy. *J. Compar. Econ.*, December 1986, *10*(4), pp. 454–56.

Buchanan, James M. Dismantling the Welfare State. **In** *Buchanan, J. M.*, 1986, pp. 178–85.

Buchanan, James M. From Redistributive Churning to the Plantation State: Review Article. *Public Choice,* 1986, *51*(2), pp. 241–43.

Buchanan, James M. Liberty, Market, and State. **In** *Buchanan, J. M.,* 1986, pp. 3–7.

Butler, Stuart. Free-Market Entrepreneurship: Political Realism within American Democracy. **In** *Gondolf, E. W.; Marcus, I. M. and Dougherty, J. P., eds.,* 1986, pp. 182–90. **[G: U.S.]**

Cain, P. J. and Hopkins, Antony G. Gentlemanly Capitalism and British Expansion Overseas. I. The Old Colonial System, 1688–1850. *Econ. Hist. Rev., 2nd Ser.,* November 1986, *39*(4), pp. 501–25. **[G: U.K.]**

Cairncross, Alec. The Market and the State. **In** *Cairncross, A.,* 1986, *1976,* pp. 37–57.

Carrica, J. L. Just Wages: The Law and Morality. *Int. J. Soc. Econ.,* 1986, *13*(9), pp. 17–24.

Cassel, Dieter. Funktionen der Schattenwirtschaft im Koordinationsmechanismus von Markt- und Planwirtschaften. (The Role of the Shadow Economy in Market Economies and in Centrally Planned Economies. With English summary.) **In** *Eucken, W. and Böhm, F., eds.,* 1986, pp. 73–104.

Chesnais, Francois. Marx's Crisis Theory Today. **In** *Freeman, C., ed.,* 1986, pp. 186–93.

Choudhury, Masudul Alam and Rahman, A. N. M. Azizur. Macroeconomic Relations in the Islamic Economic Order. *Int. J. Soc. Econ.,* 1986, *13*(6), pp. 60–78.

Cleaver, Harry. Karl Marx: Economist or Revolutionary? **In** *Helburn, S. W. and Bramhall, D. F., eds.,* 1986, pp. 121–46.

Clunies Ross, Anthony. Wages and Shares: Review Article. *J. Econ. Stud.,* 1986, *13*(2), pp. 65–70.

Conte, Michael A. Entry of Worker Cooperatives in Capitalist Economies. *J. Compar. Econ.,* March 1986, *10*(1), pp. 41–47.

Cook, Scott. The 'Managerial' vs. the 'Labor' Function, Capital Accumulation, and the Dynamics of Simple Commodity Production in Rural Oaxaca, Mexico. **In** *Greenfield, S. M. and Strickon, A., eds.,* 1986, pp. 54–95. **[G: Mexico]**

Cook, Scott and Binford, Leigh. Petty Commodity Production, Capital Accumulation, and Peasant Differentiation: Lenin vs. Chayanov in Rural Mexico. *Rev. Radical Polit. Econ.,* Winter 1986, *18*(4), pp. 1–31. **[G: Mexico]**

Cooper, Russell. Share Contracts and Macroeconomic Externalities. *J. Compar. Econ.,* December 1986, *10*(4), pp. 421–26.

Coram, B. T. Marx, Roemer and the Theory of the Falling Rate of Profit. *Australian Econ. Pap.,* December 1986, *25*(47), pp. 265–71.

Corona, Leonel. Long Waves and the International Diffusion of the Automated Labour Process: The Role of the Semi-industrialized Countries. **In** *Freeman, C., ed.,* 1986, pp. 194–213. **[G: LDCs]**

Curtis, Fred. Understanding the Current Crisis in South Africa—Class, Race and Marxist Analysis: A Review Essay. *Rev. Radical Polit. Econ.,* Winter 1986, *18*(4), pp. 109–19. **[G: S. Africa]**

Dahmén, Erik. Rights and Relations in Modern Economic Theory: Comment. **In** *Day, R. H. and Eliasson, G., eds.,* 1986, pp. 342–43.

Dahmén, Erik. Schumpeterian Dynamics: Some Methodological Notes. **In** *Day, R. H. and Eliasson, G., eds.,* 1986, *1984,* pp. 181–90.

Darity, William A., Jr. The Managerial Class and Industrial Policy. *Ind. Relat.,* Spring 1986, *25*(2), pp. 212–27. **[G: U.S.]**

Dasgupta, Partha. Positive Freedom, Markets and the Welfare State. *Oxford Rev. Econ. Policy,* Summer 1986, *2*(2), pp. 25–36.

Davis, William G. Class, Political Constraints, and Entrepreneurial Strategies: Elites and Petty Market Traders in Northern Luzon. **In** *Greenfield, S. M. and Strickon, A., eds.,* 1986, pp. 166–94. **[G: Philippines]**

Day, Richard H. Disequilibrium Economic Dynamics: A Post-Schumpeterian Contribution: Reply. **In** *Day, R. H. and Eliasson, G., eds.,* 1986, pp. 77.

Deans, Robert H. Macroeconomic Conflicts and Economic and Social Policies. *Rev. Soc. Econ.,* October 1986, *44*(2), pp. 113–29. **[G: OECD]**

Defourny, Jacques. The Economic Performance of Self-Managed Firms: A Comparative Perspective. *Ann. Pub. Co-op. Econ.,* Jan.-March 1986, *57*(1), pp. 3–9.

Defourny, Jacques. Une analyse financière comparée des coopératives de travailleurs et des entreprises capitalistes en France. (A Comparative Financial Analysis of Workers' Cooperatives and Capitalist Firms in France. With English summary.) *Ann. Pub. Co-op. Econ.,* Jan.-March 1986, *57*(1), pp. 55–78. **[G: France]**

Devine, James N. Empirical Studies in Marxian Crisis Theory: Introduction. *Rev. Radical Polit. Econ.,* Spring/Summer 1986, *18*(1/2), pp. 1–12.

Dow, Gregory K. Control Rights, Competitive Markets, and the Labor Management Debate. *J. Compar. Econ.,* March 1986, *10*(1), pp. 48–61.

Downe, Ed. The Behavior of Postwar Rates of Return in Capitalist Countries. *Rev. Radical Polit. Econ.,* Fall 1986, *18*(3), pp. 101–10. **[G: OECD]**

Drago, Robert. Capitalism and Efficiency: A Review and Appraisal of the Recent Discussion. *Rev. Radical Polit. Econ.,* Winter 1986, *18*(4), pp. 71–92.

Drago, Robert. Quality Circles: Lessons from the United States. *Australian Bull. Lab.,* September 1986, *12*(4), pp. 244–51. **[G: U.S.]**

Dugger, William M. The Last Gasp of Liberal Capitalism in America. *J. Econ. Issues,* June 1986, *20*(2), pp. 325–33. **[G: U.S.]**

Duménil, Gérard and Lévy, D. Real and Financial Stability in Capitalism: The Law of the Tendency toward Increasing Instability. *Econ. Forum,* Winter 1986-1987, *16*(1), pp. 1–27.

Dunn, John. Defining a Defensible Socialism for Britain Today. **In** *Nolan, P. and Paine, S., eds.,* 1986, pp. 35–52. **[G: U.K.]**

Eliasson, Gunnar. On the Stability of Economic

Organizational Forms and the Importance of Human Capital: A Proposition about the Endogenous, Market Induced Disintegration of the Non-market Sector. **In** *Day, R. H. and Eliasson, G., eds.*, 1986, pp. 454–67.

Eliasson, Gunnar. Rights and Relations in Modern Economic Theory: Comment. **In** *Day, R. H. and Eliasson, G., eds.*, 1986, pp. 346–50.

Ellerman, David P. The Employment Contract and Liberal Thought. *Rev. Soc. Econ.*, April 1986, *44*(1), pp. 13–39.

Elliott, John E. Modeling Technological and Institutional Change in Karl Marx's Theory of Capitalism. *J. Econ. Issues*, June 1986, *20*(2), pp. 403–12.

Engelbourg, Saul. John Stewart Kennedy and the City of Glasgow Bank. **In** *Atack, J., ed.*, 1986, pp. 69–82. **[G: U.S.]**

Epstein, Eugene. The Share Economy: An Idea Whose Time Came Long Ago. *Challenge*, Jan./Feb. 1986, *28*(6), pp. 62–64.

Escarmelle, Jean-François and Hujoel, Luc. Privatization and Deregulation. Its Implementation in Belgium. *Ann. Pub. Co-op. Econ.*, Apr.-June 1986, *57*(2), pp. 253–73. **[G: Belgium]**

Fardeheb, A. and Hamel, B. Algérie: système productif et choix économiques et sociaux alternatifs. (Algeria: The Productive System and Alternative Economic and Social Choices. With English summary.) *Écon. Soc.*, May 1986, *20*(5), pp. 171–207. **[G: Algeria]**

Faxén, Karl-Olof. Perceived Models and Measurable Uncertainty. **In** *Day, R. H. and Eliasson, G., eds.*, 1986, pp. 449–53.

Feiner, Susan F. Property Relations and Class Relations in Genovese and the Modes of Production Controversy. *Cambridge J. Econ.*, March 1986, *10*(1), pp. 61–75.

Fels, Gerhard. Incentives for Entrepreneurship and Supporting Institutions: Comment. **In** *Balassa, B. and Giersch, H., eds.*, 1986, pp. 188–91.

Fink, Gary M. Historical Analysis: Industrial Relations Eras: Discussion. **In** *Dennis, B. D., ed.*, 1986, pp. 246–49. **[G: U.S.]**

Flisfisch, Angel. Reflexiones algo oblicuas sobre el tema de la concertación. (With English summary.) *Desarrollo Econ.*, Apr.-June 1986, *26*(101), pp. 3–20. **[G: Latin America]**

Fones-Wolf, Elizabeth. Industrial Recreation, the Second World War, and the Revival of Welfare Capitalism, 1934–1960. *Bus. Hist. Rev.*, Summer 1986, *60*(2), pp. 232–57. **[G: U.S.]**

Friedman, Marilyn A. Judaism and the Market Mechanism: Comment. **In** *Block, W. and Hexham, I., eds.*, 1986, pp. 421–30.

Friedman, Milton. Has Liberalism Failed? **In** *[Seldon, A.]*, 1986, pp. 127–39.

Gilad, Benjamin. Entrepreneurial Decision Making: Some Behavioral Considerations. **In** *Gilad, B. and Kaish, S., eds., Vol. A*, 1986, pp. 189–208.

Goffee, Robert and Scase, Richard. Women, Business Start-up and Economic Recession. **In** *Donckels, R. and Meijer, J. N., eds.*, 1986, pp. 21–32. **[G: U.K.]**

Goldstein, Jonathan P. The Micro–Macro Dialectic: A Concept of a Marxian Microfoundation. **In** *Zarembka, P., ed.*, 1986, pp. 127–55.

Goodwin, Richard M. The Economy as an Evolutionary Pulsator. *J. Econ. Behav. Organ.*, December 1986, *7*(4), pp. 341–49.

Goodwin, Richard M. The M–K–S System: The Functioning and Evolution of Capitalism. **In** *Wagener, H.-J. and Drukker, J. W., eds.*, 1986, pp. 14–21.

Gottheil, Fred M. Marx versus Marxists on the Role of Military Production in Capitalist Economies. *J. Post Keynesian Econ.*, Summer 1986, *8*(4), pp. 563–73.

Gottheil, Fred M. Marxism and Military Spending: A Reply. *J. Post Keynesian Econ.*, Summer 1986, *8*(4), pp. 581–84.

Goudzwaard, Bob. Christian Social Thought in the Dutch Neo-Calvinist Tradition: Reply. **In** *Block, W. and Hexham, I., eds.*, 1986, pp. 275–79. **[G: Netherlands]**

Goudzwaard, Bob. Christian Social Thought in the Dutch Neo-Calvinist Tradition. **In** *Block, W. and Hexham, I., eds.*, 1986, pp. 251–65. **[G: Netherlands]**

Gowdy, John M. Neoclassical and Neo-Marxian Views of Scarcity: There Is a Free Lunch. *Rev. Radical Polit. Econ.*, Winter 1986, *18*(4), pp. 102–05.

Grau, Joseph A. Corporate Management and Orthopraxis—Is Synergy Possible? *Int. J. Soc. Econ.*, 1986, *13*(1/2), pp. 7–19.

Graziosi, Andrea. Alla scoperta della produttivita' del capitale. Note a margine del *Discorso sull'economia politica* di Claudio Napoleoni. (With English summary.) *Stud. Econ.*, 1986, *41*(30), pp. 107–29.

Greenfield, Sidney M. and Strickon, Arnold. Entrepreneurship and Social Change: Introduction. **In** *Greenfield, S. M. and Strickon, A., eds.*, 1986, pp. 4–18.

Guimarães, Roberto P. Co-operativism and Popular Participation: New Considerations Regarding an Old Subject. *CEPAL Rev.*, April 1986, (28), pp. 187–201. **[G: Latin America]**

Hajba, Sirpa. Male and Female Entrepreneurs: Similarities and Differences. **In** *Donckels, R. and Meijer, J. N., eds.*, 1986, pp. 16–20.

Hart, Gillian. Interlocking Transactions: Obstacles, Precursors or Instruments of Agrarian Capitalism. *J. Devel. Econ.*, September 1986, *23*(1), pp. 177–203.

von Hayek, Friedrich A. The Moral Imperative of the Market. **In** *[Seldon, A.]*, 1986, pp. 143–49.

Heilbroner, Robert L. Economics and Political Economy: Marx, Keynes, and Schumpeter. **In** *Helburn, S. W. and Bramhall, D. F., eds.*, 1986, pp. 13–26.

Helm, Dieter R. The Assessment: The Economic Borders of the State. *Oxford Rev. Econ. Policy*, Summer 1986, *2*(2), pp. i–xxiv. **[G: U.K.]**

Henderson, James P. Agency or Alienation? Smith, Mill, and Marx on the Joint-Stock Company. *Hist. Polit. Econ.*, Spring 1986, *18*(1), pp. 111–31.

Hewlett, William R. Making the Transition from Entrepreneur to Large Company. **In** *Landau, R. and Rosenberg, N., eds.*, 1986, pp. 441–42.

Hexham, Irving. Christian Social Thought in the Dutch Neo-Calvinist Tradition: Comment. **In** *Block, W. and Hexham, I., eds.*, 1986, pp. 265–75. **[G: Netherlands]**

Heyne, Paul. Clerical Laissez-Faire: A Study in Theological Economics: Reply. **In** *Block, W. and Hexham, I., eds.*, 1986, pp. 160–63.

Heyne, Paul. Clerical Laissez-Faire: A Study in Theological Economics. **In** *Block, W. and Hexham, I., eds.*, 1986, pp. 125–52.

Holmquist, Carin and Sundin, Elisabeth. Female Entrepreneurs: A Newly Discovered Group. **In** *Donckels, R. and Meijer, J. N., eds.*, 1986, pp. 33–44. **[G: Sweden]**

Howe, Carolyn. The Politics of Class Compromise in an International Context: Considerations for a New Strategy for Labor. *Rev. Radical Polit. Econ.*, Fall 1986, *18*(3), pp. 1–22. **[G: U.S.]**

Hoy, Terry. Gustavo Gutierrez: Latin American Liberation Theology. *Int. J. Soc. Econ.*, 1986, *13*(9), pp. 3–16. **[G: Latin America]**

Hunt, E. K. Philosophy and Economics in the Writings of Karl Marx. **In** *Helburn, S. W. and Bramhall, D. F., eds.*, 1986, pp. 95–120.

Jacoby, Sanford M. Historical Analysis: Industrial Relations Eras: Discussion. **In** *Dennis, B. D., ed.*, 1986, pp. 243–45. **[G: U.S.]**

Janeway, William H. Doing Capitalism: Notes on the Practice of Venture Capitalism. *J. Econ. Issues*, June 1986, *20*(2), pp. 431–41.

Jansson, Sune. Swedish Labour-Owned Industrial Firms: Some Empirical Observations. *Ann. Pub. Co-op. Econ.*, Jan.-March 1986, *57*(1), pp. 103–16. **[G: Sweden]**

Jefferis, Keith and Thomas, Alan. Conditions for Financial Viability in Workers' Co-operatives: The Case of UK Clothing and Printing Co-ops. *Ann. Pub. Co-op. Econ.*, Jan.-March 1986, *57*(1), pp. 79–102. **[G: U.K.]**

Jessop, Bob. The Prospects for the Corporatisation of Monetarism in Britain. **In** *Jacobi, O., et al., eds. (II)*, 1986, pp. 105–30. **[G: U.K.]**

Jessop, Bob; Jacobi, Otto and Kastendiek, Hans. Corporatist and Liberal Responses to the Crisis of Postwar Capitalism. **In** *Jacobi, O., et al., eds. (II)*, 1986, pp. 1–13.

Johnson, Erwin H. The Impressario as Entrepreneur. **In** *Greenfield, S. M. and Strickon, A., eds.*, 1986, pp. 138–57.

Johnston, R. J. The State, the Region, and the Division of Labor. **In** *Scott, A. J. and Storper, M., eds.*, 1986, pp. 265–80.

Jones, Derek C. The Scope and Nature of Feasible Initiatives in Workplace Democratization and Participation. **In** *Nolan, P. and Paine, S., eds.*, 1986, pp. 270–83. **[G: U.K.]**

Jossa, Bruno. Considerazioni su di un "tipo ideale" di cooperativi di produzione. (With English summary.) *Stud. Econ.*, 1986, *41*(28), pp. 3–22.

Kahan, Arcadius. Notes on Jewish Entrepreneurship in Tsarist Russia. **In** *Kahan, A.*, 1986, *1983*, pp. 82–100. **[G: U.S.S.R.]**

Kassis, Hanna E. Islamic Social Thought: Comment. **In** *Block, W. and Hexham, I., eds.*, 1986, pp. 492–500.

Khan, Mohsin S. and Mirakhor, Abbas. The Framework and Practice of Islamic Banking. *Finance Develop.*, September 1986, *23*(3), pp. 32–36.

Kirzner, Israel M. Taxes and Discovery: An Entrepreneurial Perspective. **In** *Lee, D. R., ed.*, 1986, pp. 359–80.

Klein, Maury. Jay Gould: A Revisionist Interpretation. **In** *Atack, J., ed.*, 1986, pp. 55–68. **[G: U.S.]**

Kornai, János. The Hungarian Reform Process: Visions, Hopes, and Reality. *J. Econ. Lit.*, December 1986, *24*(4), pp. 1687–1737. **[G: Hungary]**

Kucheman, Clark A. Classical Social Doctrine in the Roman Catholic Church: Comment. **In** *Block, W. and Hexham, I., eds.*, 1986, pp. 23–31.

Landes, David S. What Do Bosses Really Do? *J. Econ. Hist.*, September 1986, *46*(3), pp. 585–623. **[G: U.K.]**

Lane, Robert E. Market Justice, Political Justice. *Amer. Polit. Sci. Rev.*, June 1986, *80*(2), pp. 383–402. **[G: U.S.]**

Lavoie, Marc. Minsky's Law or the Theorem of Systemic Financial Fragility. *Stud. Econ.*, 1986, *41*(29), pp. 3–28.

Lee, Dwight R. and Kreutzer, David. Privatizing the Commons: Comment. *Southern Econ. J.*, April 1986, *52*(4), pp. 1162–64.

Lehmann, David. Sharecropping and the Capitalist Transition in Agriculture: Some Evidence from the Highlands of Ecuador. *J. Devel. Econ.*, October 1986, *23*(2), pp. 333–54. **[G: Ecuador]**

Leijonhufvud, Axel. Capitalism and the Factory System. **In** *Langlois, R. N., ed.*, 1986, pp. 203–23.

Lenel, Hans Otto. Alexander Rüstows wirtschafts- und sozialpolitische Konzeption. (Alexander Rüstow's Conception of Economic and Social Policy. With English summary.) **In** *Eucken, W. and Böhm, F., eds.*, 1986, pp. 45–58.

Lindbeck, Assar. Limits to the Welfare State. *Challenge*, Jan./Feb. 1986, *28*(6), pp. 31–36.

Lipietz, Alain. Behind the Crisis: The Exhaustion of a Regime of Accumulation. A "Regulation School" Perspective on Some French Empirical Works. *Rev. Radical Polit. Econ.*, Spring/Summer 1986, *18*(1/2), pp. 13–32.

von Loesch, Achim. Die unternehmen der arbeiterselbsthilfe in Deutschland. (Self-Managed Firms in Germany. With English summary.) *Ann. Pub. Co-op. Econ.*, September 1986, *57*(3), pp. 373–95. **[G: W. Germany]**

Logue, John. The Welfare State: The Implications of Sweden's Democratic Socialism. **In** *Gondolf, E. W.; Marcus, I. M. and Dougherty, J. P., eds.*, 1986, pp. 161–71. **[G: Sweden]**

Lomnitz, Larissa and Perez-Lizaur, Marisol.

Family Enterprise and the Process of Industrialization in Mexico. **In** *Greenfield, S. M. and Strickon, A., eds.*, 1986, pp. 124–37. **[G: Mexico]**

Lower, Milton D. The Industrial Economy and International Price Shocks. *J. Econ. Issues*, June 1986, *20*(2), pp. 297–312. **[G: U.S.]**

Maddison, Angus. Marx and Bismarck: Capitalism and Government 1883–1983. **In** *Wagener, H.-J. and Drukker, J. W., eds.*, 1986, pp. 196–213. **[G: OECD]**

Maier, Charles S. The Economics of Fascism and Nazism: Premises and Performance. **In** *[Hirshman, A. O.]*, 1986, pp. 57–88. **[G: Germany; Italy]**

Markusen, Ann Roell. Empirical Research in the Marxist and Schumpeterian Traditions: Reflections on Explaining Spatial Change. **In** *Helburn, S. W. and Bramhall, D. F., eds.*, 1986, pp. 267–83.

Marris, Robin and Mueller, Dennis C. The Corporation, Competition, and the Invisible Hand. **In** *Mueller, D. C.*, 1986, *1980*, pp. 261–97.

Marsh, Robert M. and Mannari, Hiroshi. Entrepreneurship in Medium- and Large-scale Japanese Firms. **In** *Greenfield, S. M. and Strickon, A., eds.*, 1986, pp. 19–44.

Marty, Martin E. Clerical Laissez-Faire: A Study in Theological Economics: Comment. **In** *Block, W. and Hexham, I., eds.*, 1986, pp. 153–59.

Masten, Scott E. The Economic Institutions of Capitalism: A Review Article. *J. Inst. Theoretical Econ.*, June 1986, *142*(2), pp. 445–51.

Matejko, Alexander J. The Marxist Response to Current Issues. **In** *Jain, A. and Matejko, A., eds.*, 1986, pp. 1–36. **[G: Poland; Israel]**

Matthaei, Julie A. "Neoclassical and Neo-Marxian Views of Scarcity: There Is a Free Lunch": A Response. *Rev. Radical Polit. Econ.*, Winter 1986, *18*(4), pp. 106–08.

Matthaei, Julie A. Reply [Freedom and Unfreedom in Marxian Economics]. *Eastern Econ. J.*, Jan.-Mar. 1986, *12*(1), pp. 78–80.

McCaleb, Thomas S. Ideology as the Ultimate Enforcement Mechanism [Constraining the Transfer Society: Constitutional and Moral Dimensions]. *Cato J.*, Spring/Summer 1986, *6*(1), pp. 341–45.

Mehrling, Perry G. A Classical Model of the Class Struggle: A Game-Theoretic Approach. *J. Polit. Econ.*, December 1986, *94*(6), pp. 1280–1303.

Mensch, Gerhard. Schumpeterian Dynamics: Some Methodological Notes: Comment. **In** *Day, R. H. and Eliasson, G., eds.*, 1986, pp. 194–97.

Metcalfe, J. S. and Gibbons, Michael. Technological Variety and the Process of Competition. *Écon. Appl.*, 1986, *39*(3), pp. 493–520.

Miettinen, Asko. Contributing Spouses and the Dynamics of Entrepreneurial Families. **In** *Donckels, R. and Meijer, J. N., eds.*, 1986, pp. 78–86.

Minsky, Hyman P. Money and Crisis in Schumpeter and Keynes. **In** *Wagener, H.-J. and Drukker, J. W., eds.*, 1986, pp. 112–22.

Mishan, Ezra J. Religion, Capitalism and Technology. **In** *Mishan, E. J.*, 1986, *1983*, pp. 194–224.

Mishan, Ezra J. The Limits to Freedom of Choice. **In** *Mishan, E. J.*, 1986, *1982*, pp. 57–77.

Mishan, Ezra J. The Road to Repression. **In** *Mishan, E. J.*, 1986, *1976*, pp. 131–68. **[G: MDCs]**

Mitchell, Neil J. John Locke and the Rise of Capitalism. *Hist. Polit. Econ.*, Summer 1986, *18*(2), pp. 291–305.

Molitor, Bruno. Sozialpolitik in der Marktwirtschaft. (Social Policy in the Market Economy. With English summary.) **In** *Eucken, W. and Böhm, F., eds.*, 1986, pp. 59–71.

Moore, Gordon E. Entrepreneurship and Innovation: The Electronics Industry. **In** *Landau, R. and Rosenberg, N., eds.*, 1986, pp. 423–27. **[G: U.S.]**

Moseley, Fred. Estimates of the Rate of Surplus-Value in the Postwar United States Economy. *Rev. Radical Polit. Econ.*, Spring/Summer 1986, *18*(1/2), pp. 169–89. **[G: U.S.]**

Moseley, Fred. The Intensity of Labor and the Productivity Slowdown [Productivity Growth and Capitalist Stagnation]. *Sci. Soc.*, Summer 1986, *50*(2), pp. 210–18.

Muñoz G., Oscar. El papel de los empresarios en el desarrollo: enfoques, problemas y experiencías. (The Role of Business in Development: Approaches, Problems, and Experiences. With English summary.) *Colección Estud. CIEPLAN*, December 1986, (20), pp. 95–120. **[G: Chile]**

Musgrave, Richard A. Leviathan Cometh—Or Does He? **In** *Musgrave, R. A., Vol. 2*, 1986, *1981*, pp. 200–232.

Nelson, Richard R. Incentives for Entrepreneurship and Supporting Institutions. **In** *Balassa, B. and Giersch, H., eds.*, 1986, pp. 173–87.

Nelson, Richard R. Schumpeterian Dynamics: Some Methodological Notes: Comment. **In** *Day, R. H. and Eliasson, G., eds.*, 1986, pp. 191–93.

Nitsch, Thomas O. Social Catholicism, Marxism and Liberation Theology: From Antithesis to Coexistence, Coalescence and Synthesis. *Int. J. Soc. Econ.*, 1986, *13*(9), pp. 52–74.

Nordhaus, William D. Can the Share Economy Cure Our Macroeconomic Woes? Probably Not. *J. Compar. Econ.*, December 1986, *10*(4), pp. 448–53.

Nordhaus, William D. Introduction to the Share Economy. *J. Compar. Econ.*, December 1986, *10*(4), pp. 416–20. **[G: U.S.]**

Nove, Alec. Planning and Markets. **In** *Nolan, P. and Paine, S., eds.*, 1986, pp. 72–82. **[G: U.K.]**

Nuti, Domenico Mario. Economic Planning in Market Economies: Scope, Instruments, Institutions. **In** *Nolan, P. and Paine, S., eds.*, 1986, pp. 83–98.

Paine, Suzanne. Notes on Late Twentieth-Century Socialism for an Advanced Industrial

Mixed Economy. **In** *Nolan, P. and Paine, S., eds.*, 1986, pp. 52–66. **[G: U.K.]**

Panitch, Leo. Ideology and Integration: The Case of the British Labour Party. **In** *Panitch, L.*, 1986, *1971*, pp. 56–77. **[G: U.K.]**

Panitch, Leo. Profits and Politics: Labour and the Crisis of British Capitalism. **In** *Panitch, L.*, 1986, *1977*, pp. 78–108. **[G: U.K.]**

Panitch, Leo. Socialists and the Labour Party: A Reappraisal. **In** *Panitch, L.*, 1986, *1979*, pp. 109–31. **[G: U.K.]**

Panitch, Leo. The Development of Corporatism in Liberal Democracies. **In** *Panitch, L.*, 1986, *1977*, pp. 132–59.

Panitch, Leo. The Impasse of Social Democratic Politics. **In** *Panitch, L.*, 1986, *1985*, pp. 1–55. **[G: U.K.]**

Panitch, Leo. The Importance of Workers' Control for Revolutionary Change. **In** *Panitch, L.*, 1986, *1977*, pp. 215–24.

Panitch, Leo. The State and the Future of Socialism. **In** *Panitch, L.*, 1986, *1980*, pp. 225–44. **[G: Europe]**

Panitch, Leo. Theories of Corporatism: Reflections on a Growth Industry. **In** *Panitch, L.*, 1986, *1980*, pp. 160–86.

Panitch, Leo. Trade Unions and the Capitalist State. **In** *Panitch, L.*, 1986, *1981*, pp. 187–214.

Parker, William N. Capitalistic Organization and National Response: Social Dynamics in the Age of Schumpeter: Reply. **In** *Day, R. H. and Eliasson, G., eds.*, 1986, pp. 378–83. **[G: Germany; U.S.; France; England]**

Parker, William N. Capitalistic Organization and National Response: Social Dynamics in the Age of Schumpeter. **In** *Day, R. H. and Eliasson, G., eds.*, 1986, *1984*, pp. 351–71. **[G: Germany; U.S.; France; England]**

Pasour, E. C., Jr. Monopoly Power, Taxation, and Entrepreneurship. **In** *Lee, D. R., ed.*, 1986, pp. 381–405.

Peck, Merton J. Is Japan Really a Share Economy? *J. Compar. Econ.*, December 1986, *10*(4), pp. 427–32. **[G: Japan]**

Perez, Carlota. Structural Change and Assimilation of New Technologies in the Economic and Social System. **In** *Freeman, C., ed.*, 1986, pp. 27–47.

Pfeifer, Karen. The Development of Commercial Agriculture in Algeria, 1830–1970. **In** *Uselding, P., ed.*, 1986, pp. 271–308. **[G: Algeria]**

Phillips, Ronnie J. Marx, the Classical Firm, and Economic Planning. *J. Post Keynesian Econ.*, Winter 1985-86, *8*(2), pp. 266–76.

Pienkos, Andrew. Organizational Contradiction and Policy Inertia in Yugoslav Institutional Evolution. *J. Econ. Issues*, June 1986, *20*(2), pp. 583–92. **[G: Yugoslavia]**

Platzer, Renate. The Privatisation Debate in Austria. *Ann. Pub. Co-op. Econ.*, Apr.-June 1986, *57*(2), pp. 275–91. **[G: Austria]**

Purg, Danica. Workers' Participation in Management of Enterprises in the Netherlands—Achievements and Problems. *Econ. Anal. Workers' Manage.*, 1986, *20*(1), pp. 89–100. **[G: Netherlands]**

Ribhegge, Hermann. Genossenschaftsgesinnung in entscheidungslogischer Perspektive. (The "Cooperative Spirit" Viewed in Terms of Economic Decision Theory. With English summary.) *Kyklos*, 1986, *39*(4), pp. 574–95.

Riddell, Tom. Marxism and Military Spending. *J. Post Keynesian Econ.*, Summer 1986, *8*(4), pp. 574–80.

Riha, Tomas J. F. Ordo—The German Neoliberal Model of Economic Order. *Econ. Int.*, February 1986, *39*(1), pp. 31–47. **[G: W. Germany]**

Roberti, Paolo. Equità e politiche sociali. (Equity and Social Policy. With English summary.) *Econ. Lavoro*, Apr.-June 1986, *20*(2), pp. 51–68. **[G: U.S.]**

Robinson, Austin. Incentives for Entrepreneurship and Supporting Institutions: Comment. **In** *Balassa, B. and Giersch, H., eds.*, 1986, pp. 192–96.

Rogin, Lawrence. Historical Analysis: Industrial Relations Eras: Discussion. **In** *Dennis, B. D., ed.*, 1986, pp. 250–53. **[G: U.S.]**

Rose-Ackerman, Susan. Efficiency, Equity and Inalienability. **In** *von der Schulenburg, J.-M. G. and Skogh, G., eds.*, 1986, pp. 11–37.

Rostow, Walt W. Economic Growth and the Diffusion of Power. *Challenge*, Sept./Oct. 1986, *29*(4), pp. 29–37.

Rothschild, Kurt W. Capitalists and Entrepreneurs: Prototypes and Roles. **In** *Wagener, H.-J. and Drukker, J. W., eds.*, 1986, pp. 186–96.

Rybczynski, Tad M. Capitalistic Organization and National Response: Social Dynamics in the Age of Schumpeter: Comment. **In** *Day, R. H. and Eliasson, G., eds.*, 1986, pp. 372–77. **[G: Germany; U.S.; France; England]**

Sadowsky, James A. Classical Social Doctrine in the Roman Catholic Church. **In** *Block, W. and Hexham, I., eds.*, 1986, pp. 3–23.

Samuelson, Paul A. Afternoon of the Mixed Economy? **In** *Samuelson, P. A.*, 1986, *1981*, pp. 998–1001.

Samuelson, Paul A. Government and Business. **In** *Samuelson, P. A.*, 1986, *1977*, pp. 973–79.

Samuelson, Paul A. Inequality of Incomes and Wealth Can Lesson amid Competition. **In** *Samuelson, P. A.*, 1986, *1980*, pp. 995–97.

Samuelson, Paul A. Lofty Aims Alone Cannot Create Efficiency, Growth and Equity. **In** *Samuelson, P. A.*, 1986, *1980*, pp. 992–94.

Samuelson, Paul A. Schumpeter's *Capitalism, Socialism and Democracy*. **In** *Samuelson, P. A.*, 1986, *1981*, pp. 328–48.

Samuelson, Paul A. Succumbing to Keynesianism. **In** *Samuelson, P. A.*, 1986, *1985*, pp. 283–90. **[G: U.S.]**

Samuelson, Paul A. The Role of Profits in a Mixed Economy: Changes in the Perceived Reality. **In** *Samuelson, P. A.*, 1986, *1978*, pp. 929–45.

Samuelson, Paul A. Thoughts on Profit-Sharing. **In** *Samuelson, P. A.*, 1986, *1977*, pp. 953–62.

Saulniers, Alfred H. Entrepreneurs in Public Enterprises. **In** *Greenfield, S. M. and Strickon, A., eds.*, 1986, pp. 158–65.

Schenk, Robert. Radical Analyses of Imperialism, the Third World, and the Transition to Socialism: A Survey Article: A Comment. *J. Econ. Lit.*, June 1986, *24*(2), pp. 676. **[G: Global]**

Schildkrout, Enid. Children as Entrepreneurs: Case Studies from Kano, Nigeria. **In** *Greenfield, S. M. and Strickon, A., eds.*, 1986, pp. 195–223. **[G: Nigeria]**

Scitovsky, Tibor. Can Capitalism Survive?—An Old Question in a New Setting. **In** *Scitovsky, T.*, 1986, *1980*, pp. 85–96.

Scitovsky, Tibor. Price Takers' Plenty: A Neglected Benefit of Monopoly Capitalism. **In** *Scitovsky, T.*, 1986, pp. 97–113.

Scott, Allen J. and Storper, Michael. Industrial Change and Territorial Organization: A Summing Up. **In** *Scott, A. J. and Storper, M., eds.*, 1986, pp. 301–11.

Shapiro, Matthew D. Capital and Saving in a Share Economy. *J. Compar. Econ.*, December 1986, *10*(4), pp. 444–47.

Silber, Jacques G. Rationality, Self Interest and Coordination: On Some Current Controversies in Economics. *Econ. Notes*, 1986, (3), pp. 47–64.

Skok, Charles D. The Social Economics of *Guadium et Spes (The Constitution on the Church in the Modern World)* of the Second Vatican Council. *Int. J. Soc. Econ.*, 1986, *13*(9), pp. 25–44.

Smith, Barry. Austrian Economics and Austrian Philosophy. **In** *Grassl, W. and Smith, B., eds.*, 1986, pp. 1–36.

Smith, Sheldon. Entrepreneurial Agriculture and the Involution of Agricultural Dynamics in the Americas. **In** *Greenfield, S. M. and Strickon, A., eds.*, 1986, pp. 96–123. **[G: Central America]**

Speiser, Stuart M. "Speiser's SuperStock Solution": Reply [Can Effective Demand and the Movement toward Further Income Equity Be Maintained in the Face of Robotics? An Introduction]. *J. Post Keynesian Econ.*, Summer 1986, *8*(4), pp. 642–46. **[G: U.S.]**

Stauffer, Robert B. Philippine Corporatism: A Note on the "New Society." **In** *Stauffer, R. B.*, 1986, *1977*, pp. 44–58. **[G: Philippines]**

Stauffer, Robert B. The Philippine Political Economy: (Dependent) State Capitalism in the Corporatist Mode. **In** *Stauffer, R. B.*, 1986, *1985*, pp. 79–102. **[G: Philippines]**

Stefani, Giorgio. Privatizing Public Enterprises in Italy: The Case of State Holdings. *Ann. Pub. Co-op. Econ.*, Apr.-June 1986, *57*(2), pp. 231–51.

Stigler, George J. The Economist and the State. **In** *Stigler, G. J.*, 1986, *1965*, pp. 99–116.

Stigler, George J. The Goals of Economic Policy. **In** *Stigler, G. J.*, 1986, *1975*, pp. 89–98. **[G: U.S.]**

Storper, Michael and Scott, Allen J. Production, Work, Territory: Contemporary Realities and Theoretical Tasks. **In** *Scott, A. J. and Storper, M., eds.*, 1986, pp. 3–15.

Summers, Lawrence H. On the Share Economy: Prospects and Problems . . . *Challenge*, Nov./Dec. 1986, *29*(5), pp. 47–50.

Sun, Li-teh. Confucianism and the Economic Order of Taiwan. *Int. J. Soc. Econ.*, 1986, *13*(6), pp. 3–53. **[G: Taiwan]**

Sweezy, Paul M. The Historical Materialism Discussion. *Sci. Soc.*, Spring 1986, *50*(1), pp. 81–84.

Tamari, Meir. Judaism and the Market Mechanism. **In** *Block, W. and Hexham, I., eds.*, 1986, pp. 393–421.

Thiemeyer, Theo. Privatization: On the Many Senses in Which This Word Is Used in an International Discussion on Economic Theory. *Ann. Pub. Co-op. Econ.*, Apr.-June 1986, *57*(2), pp. 141–52.

Tobin, James. Inflation and Unemployment in the Share Economy. *J. Compar. Econ.*, December 1986, *10*(4), pp. 460–63.

Tonsor, Stephen. Christian Political Economy: Malthus to Margaret Thatcher: Comment. **In** *Block, W. and Hexham, I., eds.*, 1986, pp. 118–23.

Tracy, Joseph S. Unions and the Share Economy. *J. Compar. Econ.*, December 1986, *10*(4), pp. 433–37.

Urry, John. Capitalist Production, Scientific Management and the Service Class. **In** *Scott, A. J. and Storper, M., eds.*, 1986, pp. 43–66. **[G: U.S.; U.K.]**

Vanberg, Viktor. Spontaneous Market Order and Social Rules: A Critical Examination of F. A. Hayek's Theory of Cultural Evolution. *Econ. Philos.*, April 1986, *2*(1), pp. 75–100.

van Velthoven, Ben and van Winden, Frans. Social Classes and State Behavior. *J. Inst. Theoretical Econ.*, September 1986, *142*(3), pp. 542–70. **[G: Netherlands]**

Vercelli, Alessandro. Stagflation and the Recent Revival of Schumpeterian Entrepreneurship. **In** *Frisch, H. and Gahlen, B., eds.*, 1986, pp. 159–85.

Wagener, Hans-Jürgen and Drukker, Jan W. The Economic Law of Motion of Modern Society: A Marx–Keynes–Schumpeter Centennial: Introduction. **In** *Wagener, H.-J. and Drukker, J. W., eds.*, 1986, pp. 1–13.

Walker, Donald A. Walras's Theory of the Entrepreneur. *De Economist*, 1986, *134*(1), pp. 1–24.

Walker, Juliet E. K. Racism, Slavery, and Free Enterprise: Black Entrepreneurship in the United States before the Civil War. *Bus. Hist. Rev.*, Autumn 1986, *60*(3), pp. 343–82. **[G: U.S.]**

Waterman, A. M. C. Christian Political Economy: Malthus to Margaret Thatcher: Reply. **In** *Block, W. and Hexham, I., eds.*, 1986, pp. 123–24.

Waterman, A. M. C. Christian Political Economy: Malthus to Margaret Thatcher. **In** *Block, W. and Hexham, I., eds.*, 1986, pp. 99–117.

Weiermair, Klaus. On the Economics of Institutional Change: An Institutional Change in Economics? *J. Econ. Issues*, June 1986, *20*(2), pp. 571–82. **[G: U.S.]**

Weitzman, Martin L. The Share Economy Symposium: A Reply. *J. Compar. Econ.*, December 1986, *10*(4), pp. 469–73.

von Weizsäcker, Carl Christian. Rights and Relations in Modern Economic Theory. **In** *Day, R. H. and Eliasson, G., eds.*, 1986, *1984*, pp. 317–41.

Wheelwright, E. L. Marxist Analysis of Capitalism in Australia: Past, Present, and Future. **In** *Dowdy, E., ed.*, 1986, pp. 1–23. **[G: Australia]**

Whitt, J. Allen and Rothschild-Whitt, Joyce. Workers' Cooperatives: The Marxian and Non-Marxian Heritage. **In** *Jain, A. and Matejko, A., eds.*, 1986, pp. 228–44.

Williams, L. John. The Climacteric of the 1890s. **In** *Baber, C. and Williams, L. J., eds.*, 1986, pp. 192–203. **[G: U.K.]**

Williamson, Oliver E. Transaction-Cost Economics: The Governance of Contractual Relations. **In** *Barney, J. B. and Ouchi, W. G., eds.*, 1986, *1979*, pp. 98–129.

Wolff, Edward N. The Productivity Slowdown and the Fall in the U.S. Rate of Profit, 1947–76. *Rev. Radical Polit. Econ.*, Spring/Summer 1986, *18*(1/2), pp. 87–109. **[G: U.S.]**

Wolff, Richard and Resnick, Stephen. What Are Class Analyses? **In** *Zarembka, P., ed.*, 1986, pp. 1–32.

Wörgötter, Andreas. Who's Who in Goodwin's Growth Cycle. *Jahr. Nationalökon. Statist.*, May 1986, *201*(3), pp. 222–28.

Young, Crawford. Africa's Colonial Legacy. **In** *Berg, R. J. and Whitaker, J. S., eds.*, 1986, pp. 25–51. **[G: Africa]**

Young, Jeffrey T. The Entrepreneur in Marx and Schumpeter: A Post-Keynesian Perspective. **In** *Helburn, S. W. and Bramhall, D. F., eds.*, 1986, pp. 183–95.

Ysander, Bengt-Christer. Rights and Relations in Modern Economic Theory: Comment. **In** *Day, R. H. and Eliasson, G., eds.*, 1986, pp. 344–45.

Yunker, James A. A Market Socialist Critique of Capitalism's Dynamic Performance. *J. Econ. Issues*, March 1986, *20*(1), pp. 63–86.

Zafiris, Nicos. The Sharing of the Firm's Risks between Capital and Labour. *Ann. Pub. Co-op. Econ.*, Jan.-March 1986, *57*(1), pp. 35–46.

052 Socialist and Communist Economic Systems

0520 Socialist and Communist Economic Systems

Abalkin, L. The Interaction of the Productive Forces and Production Relations. *Prob. Econ.*, April 1986, *28*(12), pp. 23–41. **[G: U.S.S.R.]**

Adams, Richard H., Jr. Corrigenda [Bureaucrats, Peasants and the Dominant Coalition: An Egyptian Case Study]. *J. Devel. Stud.*, October 1986, *23*(1), pp. 4. **[G: Egypt]**

Amann, Ronald. The Political and Social Implications of Economic Reform in the USSR. **In** *Höhmann, H.-H.; Nove, A. and Vogel, H., eds.*, 1986, pp. 125–45. **[G: U.S.S.R.]**

An, Xi-Ji. Pricing System Reform for Agricultural Products and Price Policy Adjustment in China (1979–1984). **In** *Maunder, A. and Renborg, U., eds.*, 1986, pp. 449–60. **[G: China]**

Angyal, Ádám. The Large Enterprise Syndrome. *Eastern Europ. Econ.*, Fall 1986, *25*(1), pp. 61–83. **[G: Hungary]**

Apró, Éva. Collective Responsibility or Collective Scapegoat? *Eastern Europ. Econ.*, Fall 1986, *25*(1), pp. 39–60. **[G: Hungary]**

Assenmacher, Marianne and Dobias, Peter. Zur Methodologie der Analyse Sozialistischer Wirtschaftssysteme. (With English summary.) **In** *Altmann, F.-L., ed.*, 1986, pp. 9–36.

Bakos, Zsigmond. Remarks Concerning the "Thoughts" of András Hegedüs Concerning "Large Enterprises and Socialism." *Eastern Europ. Econ.*, Fall 1986, *25*(1), pp. 18–25. **[G: Hungary]**

Baldwin, Robert E. Rent-Seeking and Trade Policy: An Industry Approach. **In** *Balassa, B. and Giersch, H., eds.*, 1986, pp. 429–43.

Barnett, A. Doak. Ten Years after Mao. *Foreign Aff.*, Fall 1986, *65*(1), pp. 37–65. **[G: China]**

Barsky, A. D. and Belagurova, E. A. Toward an Analysis of the Principles Governing the Formation of Material Incentive Funds. *Matekon*, Spring 1986, *22*(3), pp. 91–110. **[G: U.S.S.R.]**

Baylis, Thomas A. Explaining the GDR's Economic Strategy. **In** *Comisso, E. and Tyson, L., eds.*, 1986, pp. 205–44. **[G: E. Germany]**

Bengelsdorf, Carollee. State and Society in the Transition to Socialism: The Theoretical Legacy. **In** *Fagen, R. R.; Deere, C. D. and Coraggio, J. L., eds.*, 1986, pp. 192–211.

Berend, Iván T. The Historical Evolution of Eastern Europe as a Region. *Int. Organ.*, Spring 1986, *40*(2), pp. 329–46. **[G: CMEA]**

van den Berg, Ger P. Labor Law as a Restraint on the Soviet Economy. **In** *Ioffe, O. S. and Janis, M. W., eds.*, 1986, pp. 41–56. **[G: U.S.S.R.]**

Bergson, Abram. The Politics of Socialist Efficiency. **In** *Szenberg, M., ed.*, 1986, *1980*, pp. 69–81.

Berman, Harold J. The Possibilities and Limits of Soviet Economic Reform. **In** *Ioffe, O. S. and Janis, M. W., eds.*, 1986, pp. 29–38.

Bialer, Seweryn and Afferica, Joan. The Genesis of Gorbachev's World. *Foreign Aff.*, 1986, *64*(3), pp. 605–44. **[G: U.S.S.R.]**

Bossányi, Katalin. Economy on the Way to Democratization: The Switch-Over to Collective Management in Hungarian Industry. *Acta Oecon.*, 1986, *37*(3–4), pp. 285–304. **[G: Hungary]**

Breimyer, Harold F. Human Capital, Technology and Institutions: Discussion. **In** *Maunder, A. and Renborg, U., eds.*, 1986, pp. 460–62. **[G: China]**

Bronshtein, M. Toward a Conception of the Economic Mechanism of the AIC [Agro-Industrial Complex]. *Prob. Econ.*, December 1986, *29*(8), pp. 73–87. **[G: U.S.S.R.]**

Brown, Doug. The Budapest School Model of Eastern European Societies. *Rev. Soc. Econ.*, December 1986, *44*(3), pp. 306–18. **[G: E. Europe]**

Brunner, Georg. Economic Institutions as Instruments of Political Rule. **In** *Höhmann, H.-H.; Nove, A. and Vogel, H., eds.*, 1986, pp. 58–76. **[G: U.S.S.R.]**

Brus, Włodzimierz. Political System and Economic Efficiency: The East European Context. **In** *Gomulka, S.*, 1986, *1980*, pp. 24–41. **[G: E. Europe]**

Brus, Włodzimierz. 1950 to 1953: The Peak of Stalinism. **In** *Kaser, M. C., ed.*, 1986, pp. 3–39. **[G: E. Europe]**

Brus, Włodzimierz. 1957 to 1965: In Search of Balanced Development. **In** *Kaser, M. C., ed.*, 1986, pp. 70–138. **[G: E. Europe]**

Brus, Włodzimierz. 1966 to 1975: Normalization and Conflict. **In** *Kaser, M. C., ed.*, 1986, pp. 139–249. **[G: E. Europe]**

Bunich, P. Centralized Management and the Independence of Production Collectives. *Prob. Econ.*, July 1986, *29*(3), pp. 21–38. **[G: U.S.S.R.]**

Butler, W. E. COMECON and Economic Law. **In** *Ioffe, O. S. and Janis, M. W., eds.*, 1986, pp. 283–97. **[G: CMEA]**

Buzgalin, A. Centralism in a Planned Economy: Boundaries and Methods. *Prob. Econ.*, October 1986, *29*(6), pp. 63–76. **[G: U.S.S.R.]**

Cassel, Dieter. Funktionen der Schattenwirtschaft im Koordinationsmechanismus von Markt- und Planwirtschaften. (The Role of the Shadow Economy in Market Economies and in Centrally Planned Economies. With English summary.) **In** *Eucken, W. and Böhm, F., eds.*, 1986, pp. 73–104.

Chai, C. H. The Economic System of a Special Economic Zone under Socialism. **In** *Jao, Y. C. and Leung, C. K., eds.*, 1986, pp. 141–59. **[G: China]**

Chase, William. Workers' Control and Socialist Democracy. *Sci. Soc.*, Summer 1986, *50*(2), pp. 226–38. **[G: U.S.S.R.]**

Cheung, Steven N. S. China in Transition: Where Is She Heading Now? *Contemp. Policy Issues*, October 1986, *4*(4), pp. 1–11. **[G: China]**

Chilosi, Alberto. Self-Managed Market Socialism with "Free Mobility of Labor." *J. Compar. Econ.*, September 1986, *10*(3), pp. 237–54.

Collier, Irwin L., Jr. Effective Purchasing Power in a Quantity Constrained Economy: An Estimate for the German Democratic Republic. *Rev. Econ. Statist.*, February 1986, *68*(1), pp. 24–32. **[G: E. Germany]**

Colton, Timothy J. The Military and Economic Reform: A Comment [The Soviet Military–Industrial Complex and Economic Reform]. *Soviet Econ.*, July-Sept. 1986, *2*(3), pp. 228–32.

Comisso, Ellen. Introduction: State Structures, Political Processes, and Collective Choice in CMEA States. *Int. Organ.*, Spring 1986, *40*(2), pp. 195–238. **[G: CMEA]**

Comisso, Ellen and Marer, Paul. The Economics and Politics of Reform in Hungary. **In** *Comisso, E. and Tyson, L., eds.*, 1986, pp. 245–78. **[G: Hungary]**

Cooper, Julian. The Soviet Military–Industrial Complex and Economic Reform: Comments. *Soviet Econ.*, July-Sept. 1986, *2*(3), pp. 221–27. **[G: U.S.S.R.]**

Csikós-Nagy, Béla. Restructuring Incentives in Hungary. **In** *Balassa, B. and Giersch, H., eds.*, 1986, pp. 258–68.

Dahm, Helmut. The Role of Economics in Soviet Political Ideology. **In** *Höhmann, H.-H.; Nove, A. and Vogel, H., eds.*, 1986, pp. 17–40. **[G: U.S.S.R.]**

Davies, R. W. The Ending of Mass Unemployment in the USSR. **In** *Lane, D., ed.*, 1986, pp. 19–35. **[G: U.S.S.R.]**

Deere, Carmen Diana. Agrarian Reform, Peasant and Rural Production, and the Organization of Production in the Transition to Socialism. **In** *Fagen, R. R.; Deere, C. D. and Coraggio, J. L., eds.*, 1986, pp. 97–142. **[G: Selected LDCs]**

Dietrich, Michael. Organisational Requirements of a Socialist Economy: Theoretical and Practical Suggestions. *Cambridge J. Econ.*, December 1986, *10*(4), pp. 319–32.

Domínguez, Jorge I. Cuba in the 1980s. *Foreign Aff.*, Fall 1986, *65*(1), pp. 118–35. **[G: Cuba]**

Ellerman, David P. Horizon Problems and Property Rights in Labor-Managed Firms. *J. Compar. Econ.*, March 1986, *10*(1), pp. 62–78.

Elliott, John E. and Scott, Joanna V. Marx, Yugoslavia, and Self-governing Socialism: A Social and Political Economy Approach. **In** *Zarembka, P., ed.*, 1986, pp. 157–217. **[G: Yugoslavia]**

Evistigneeva, L. and Perlamutrov, V. Intensification and Financial–Credit Relations. *Prob. Econ.*, November 1986, *29*(7), pp. 55–73.

Eysymontt, Jerzy and Maciejewski, Wojciech. Socioeconomic Crises in Poland: A Model Approach. *Eastern Europ. Econ.*, Spring 1986, *24*(3), pp. 6–23. **[G: Poland]**

FitzGerald, E. V. K. Notes on the Analysis of the Small Underdeveloped Economy in Transition. **In** *Fagen, R. R.; Deere, C. D. and Coraggio, J. L., eds.*, 1986, pp. 28–53.

Frank, Peter. Economic Activities and the Intermediate and Lower Levels of Party Organisation. **In** *Höhmann, H.-H.; Nove, A. and Vogel, H., eds.*, 1986, pp. 77–91. **[G: U.S.S.R.]**

Frease, Dean. Yugoslav Marxism. **In** *Jain, A. and Matejko, A., eds.*, 1986, pp. 77–92. **[G: Yugoslavia]**

Gitelman, Zvi. Doing Business with the USSR and Eastern Europe: The Political Setting. **In** *Raddock, D. M., et al.*, 1986, pp. 55–70. **[G: E. Europe; U.S.S.R.]**

Gomulka, Stanislaw. Kornai's Soft Budget Constraint and the Shortage Phenomenon: A Criticism and Restatement. **In** *Gomulka, S.*, 1986, pp. 73–90.

Gomulka, Stanislaw. The Incompatibility of Socialism and Rapid Innovation. **In** *Gomulka, S.*, 1986, *1984*, pp. 42–61. **[G: U.S.S.R.; E. Europe]**

Gorbunov, E. and Bulatova, I. Raising the Effectiveness of a "Small-Scale Economy." *Prob. Econ.*, October 1986, *29*(6), pp. 77–87.

Gulácsi, Gábor and Juhász, Pál. Development of Settlements, Decentralization and Communal Management in Hungary. *Acta Oecon.*, 1986, *37*(1–2), pp. 31–46. **[G: Hungary]**

Gutowski, Armin and Merklein, Renate. Restructuring Incentives in the People's Republic of China. **In** *Balassa, B. and Giersch, H., eds.*, 1986, pp. 329–42.

Hall, John B. Plan Bargaining in the Hungarian Economy: An Interview with Dr. Laszlo Antal. *Comp. Econ. Stud.*, Summer 1986, *28*(2), pp. 49–58. **[G: Hungary]**

Hanson, Philip. The Shape of Gorbachev's Economic Reform. *Soviet Econ.*, Oct.-Dec. 1986, *2*(4), pp. 313–26. **[G: U.S.S.R.]**

Hegedüs, András. Large Enterprises and Socialism (Thoughts While Reading Erzsébet Szalai's Book). *Eastern Europ. Econ.*, Fall 1986, *25*(1), pp. 3–17. **[G: Hungary]**

Hegedüs, András. Questions Waiting for Answers (In the Aftermath of a Debate). *Eastern Europ. Econ.*, Fall 1986, *25*(1), pp. 113–27. **[G: Hungary]**

Héthy, Lajos. New Developments in Collective Forms of Work Organisation in Socialist Countries. *Int. Lab. Rev.*, Nov.-Dec. 1986, *125*(6), pp. 659–74. **[G: E. Europe]**

Hewett, Ed. A. Gorbachev at Two Years: Perspective on Economic Reforms. *Soviet Econ.*, Oct.-Dec. 1986, *2*(4), pp. 283–88. **[G: U.S.S.R.]**

Higgins, Winton. Policy Formation and Marxist Reformism. **In** *Dowdy, E., ed.*, 1986, pp. 48–66.

Hoch, Róbert. The Maxi and the Mini (Thoughts on the Large Enterprise Debate). *Eastern Europ. Econ.*, Fall 1986, *25*(1), pp. 84–105. **[G: Hungary]**

Höhmann, Hans-Hermann. The Place of Economic Policy Objectives on the List of Soviet Political Priorities. **In** *Höhmann, H.-H.; Nove, A. and Vogel, H., eds.*, 1986, pp. 41–57. **[G: U.S.S.R.]**

Hough, Jerry F. The Gorbachev Reform: A Maximal Case. *Soviet Econ.*, Oct.-Dec. 1986, *2*(4), pp. 302–12. **[G: U.S.S.R.]**

Hussain, Athar. Money and Socialism: Comment. **In** *Smith, K., ed.*, 1986, *1978*, pp. 139–43. **[G: U.S.S.R.]**

Ickes, Barry W. On the Economics of Taut Plans. *J. Compar. Econ.*, December 1986, *10*(4), pp. 388–99.

Ioffe, Olimpiad S. Soviet Law and the New Economic Experiment. **In** *Ioffe, O. S. and Janis, M. W., eds.*, 1986, pp. 3–28. **[G: U.S.S.R.]**

Iun', O. Developing Management's Planning Mechanism. *Prob. Econ.*, November 1986, *29*(7), pp. 3–19. **[G: U.S.S.R.]**

Jain, Ajit. Class Struggle or Modernization? Post-Mao Era in the People's Republic of China. **In** *Jain, A. and Matejko, A., eds.*, 1986, pp. 37–76. **[G: China]**

Janis, Mark W. The Soviet Theory of International Law and International Economic Relations. **In** *Ioffe, O. S. and Janis, M. W., eds.*, 1986, pp. 235–41. **[G: U.S.S.R.]**

Kachanovskii, Iu. V. Indicators and Their Functions. *Prob. Econ.*, January 1986, *28*(9), pp. 37–49. **[G: U.S.S.R.]**

Kalecki, Michal. Central Price Determination as an Essential Feature of a Socialist Economy. **In** *Kalecki, M.*, 1986, *1958*, pp. 48–53.

Kalecki, Michal. Observations on Labour Productivity. **In** *Kalecki, M.*, 1986, *1960*, pp. 54–59.

Kalecki, Michal. Outline of a New System of Incentives and Directives. **In** *Kalecki, M.*, 1986, *1959*, pp. 41–47.

Kalecki, Michal. Problems in the Theory of Growth of a Socialist Economy. **In** *Kalecki, M.*, 1986, *1959*, pp. 70–96.

Kalecki, Michal. The Essentials for Democratic Planning. **In** *Kalecki, M.*, 1986, *1942*, pp. 19–24.

Kalecki, Michal. The Influence of the Construction Period on the Relationship between Investment and National Income. **In** *Kalecki, M.*, 1986, *1957*, pp. 97–108.

Kamenka, Eugene. The Rise and Fall of Marxist Ideology in Communist Countries. **In** *Dowdy, E., ed.*, 1986, pp. 67–92. **[G: U.S.S.R.; China]**

Kazakevich, D. M. Improving Consumer Prices. *Prob. Econ.*, December 1986, *29*(8), pp. 3–14. **[G: U.S.S.R.]**

Khachaturov, Tigran S. Incentives in the Soviet Economy. **In** *Balassa, B. and Giersch, H., eds.*, 1986, pp. 241–49.

Kletskii, V. I. What Should Be Included in the Economic Mechanism of the Twelfth Five-Year Plan? *Prob. Econ.*, January 1986, *28*(9), pp. 73–88. **[G: U.S.S.R.]**

Kolosi, Tamás. Structural Groups and Reform. *Acta Oecon.*, 1986, *37*(1–2), pp. 15–30. **[G: Hungary]**

Kornai, János. Comments on the Present State and the Prospects of the Hungarian Economic Reform. **In** *Kornai, J.*, 1986, *1983*, pp. 81–123.

Kornai, János. Efficiency and the Principles of Socialist Ethics. **In** *Kornai, J.*, 1986, *1980*, pp. 124–38. **[G: Hungary]**

Kornai, János. The Hungarian Reform Process: Visions, Hopes, and Reality. *J. Econ. Lit.*, December 1986, *24*(4), pp. 1687–1737. **[G: Hungary]**

Kornai, János. The Reproduction of Shortage. **In** *Kornai, J.*, 1986, *1979*, pp. 6–32.

Kornai, János and Dániel, Zsuzsa. The Chinese Economic Reform—as Seen by Hungarian Economists (Marginal Notes to Our Travel Diary). *Acta Oecon.*, 1986, *36*(3–4), pp. 289–305. **[G: China]**

Kroiher, Jaroslav and Vlček, Jiří. Tendencies in the Improvements of the National Economic Mechanisms of the CMEA Countries. *Czech. Econ. Digest.*, Sept./Oct. 1986, (6), pp. 3–19. **[G: CMEA]**

Kroll, Heidi. Decentralization and the Precontract Dispute in Soviet Industry. *Soviet Econ.*,

Jan.-Mar. 1986, *2*(1), pp. 51–71. **[G: U.S.S.R.]**

Kulagin, G. A. Product Mix, Price, Profit. *Prob. Econ.*, September 1986, *29*(5), pp. 3–20. **[G: U.S.S.R.]**

Lane, David. Marxist-Leninism: An Ideology for Full Employment in Socialist States? **In** *Lane, D., ed.*, 1986, pp. 1–16. **[G: U.S.S.R.]**

Lasok, D. Polish Economic Law. **In** *Ioffe, O. S. and Janis, M. W., eds.*, 1986, pp. 299–315. **[G: Poland]**

Lavigne, Marie. Advanced Socialist Society. **In** *Smith, K., ed.*, 1986, *1978*, pp. 179–206. **[G: U.S.S.R.]**

Lavigne, Marie. The Creation of Money by the State Bank of the USSR. **In** *Smith, K., ed.*, 1986, *1978*, pp. 112–38. **[G: U.S.S.R.]**

Linden, Ronald H. Socialist Patrimonialism and the Global Economy: The Case of Romania. **In** *Comisso, E. and Tyson, L., eds.*, 1986, pp. 171–204. **[G: Romania]**

Lipson, Leon. Soviet Law and Foreign Scholarship. **In** *Ioffe, O. S. and Janis, M. W., eds.*, 1986, pp. 317–23. **[G: U.S.S.R.]**

Littlejohn, Gary. State, Plan and Market in the Transition to Socialism: The Legacy of Bukharin. **In** *Smith, K., ed.*, 1986, *1979*, pp. 78–111. **[G: U.S.S.R.]**

Lyons, Thomas P. Explaining Economic Fragmentation in China: A Systems Approach. *J. Compar. Econ.*, September 1986, *10*(3), pp. 209–36. **[G: China]**

Mackerras, Colin. Chinese Marxist Thinking since 1978. **In** *Dowdy, E., ed.*, 1986, pp. 93–126. **[G: China]**

Malfliet, Katlijn. The Economic Function and Purpose of Personal Property and Its Legal Implementation. **In** *Ioffe, O. S. and Janis, M. W., eds.*, 1986, pp. 79–101. **[G: U.S.S.R.]**

Mar'ianovskii, V. Cooperative Forms of Management under Socialism. *Prob. Econ.*, May 1986, *29*(1), pp. 33–49. **[G: U.S.S.R.]**

Marrese, Michael. CMEA: Effective but Cumbersome Political Economy. **In** *Comisso, E. and Tyson, L., eds.*, 1986, pp. 111–51. **[G: CMEA]**

Marrese, Michael. CMEA: Effective but Cumbersome Political Economy. *Int. Organ.*, Spring 1986, *40*(2), pp. 287–327. **[G: CMEA]**

Matejko, Alexander J. Marxists against a Polish Anarchosyndicalist: The Case of Jan Wolski. **In** *Jain, A. and Matejko, A., eds.*, 1986, pp. 178–227. **[G: Poland]**

Matejko, Alexander J. The Marxist Response to Current Issues. **In** *Jain, A. and Matejko, A., eds.*, 1986, pp. 1–36. **[G: Poland; Israel]**

Mencinger, Jože. The Yugoslav Economic Systems and Their Efficiency. *Econ. Anal. Workers' Manage.*, 1986, *20*(1), pp. 31–43. **[G: Yugoslavia]**

Mesa-Lago, Carmelo. On the Objectives and Objectivity of Cubanology: A Response to a Critic from Cuba. **In** *Mesa-Lago, C., ed.*, 1986, pp. 225–34.

Milánovics, Szvetozár. The (Large) Enterprises and Socialism (Thoughts about András Hegedüs's Thoughts). *Eastern Europ. Econ.*, Fall 1986, *25*(1), pp. 26–38. **[G: Hungary]**

Nørlund, Irene. Social and Economic Studies on Vietnam: An Overview. **In** *Nørlund, I.; Cederroth, S. and Gerdin, I., eds.*, 1986, pp. 176–202. **[G: Vietnam]**

Nove, Alec. History, Political Culture, and Economics in the Soviet Union. **In** *Höhmann, H.-H.; Nove, A. and Vogel, H., eds.*, 1986, pp. 1–16. **[G: U.S.S.R.]**

Nove, Alec. Marx, the Market and 'Feasible Socialism.' **In** *Nove, A.*, 1986, *1979*, pp. 51–62.

Nove, Alec. Some Aspects of Soviet Constitutional Theory. **In** *Nove, A.*, 1986, *1949*, pp. 193–219. **[G: U.S.S.R.]**

Nove, Alec. The Economy of the U.S.S.R. and Marxism: What Socialist Model? **In** *Nove, A.*, 1986, *1980*, pp. 63–87. **[G: U.S.S.R.]**

Nove, Alec. The Soviet Industrial Enterprise. **In** *Nove, A.*, 1986, *1981*, pp. 169–79. **[G: U.S.S.R.]**

Nove, Alec. Trotsky, Collectivization and the Five-Year Plan. **In** *Nove, A.*, 1986, *1982*, pp. 88–103. **[G: U.S.S.R.]**

Nyers, Reszö. Efficiency and Socialist Democracy. *Acta Oecon.*, 1986, *37*(1–2), pp. 1–13. **[G: EEC]**

Panitch, Leo. The Importance of Workers' Control for Revolutionary Change. **In** *Panitch, L.*, 1986, *1977*, pp. 215–24.

Panitch, Leo. The State and the Future of Socialism. **In** *Panitch, L.*, 1986, *1980*, pp. 225–44. **[G: Europe]**

Park, Henry. Postrevolutionary China and the Soviet NEP. **In** *Zarembka, P., ed.*, 1986, pp. 219–33. **[G: U.S.S.R.; China]**

Pekhlivanov, Vasil. Problems of Import Pricing in the CMEA. *Soviet E. Europ. Foreign Trade*, Summer 1986, *22*(2), pp. 39–51. **[G: CMEA]**

Peters, G. H. Human Capital, Technology and Institutions: Discussion. **In** *Maunder, A. and Renborg, U., eds.*, 1986, pp. 462–63.

Plyshevskii, B. Socialist Accumulation in the Present Stage. *Prob. Econ.*, December 1986, *29*(8), pp. 15–35. **[G: U.S.S.R.]**

Popov, G. On Improving Centralized Economic Management. *Prob. Econ.*, February 1986, *28*(10), pp. 60–78. **[G: U.S.S.R.]**

Portes, Richard. Restructuring Incentives in Hungary: Comment. **In** *Balassa, B. and Giersch, H., eds.*, 1986, pp. 269–73.

Poznanski, Kazimierz. Economic Adjustment and Political Forces: Poland since 1970. **In** *Comisso, E. and Tyson, L., eds.*, 1986, pp. 279–312. **[G: Poland]**

Preston, Ronald H. The Legacy of the Christian Socialist Movement in England. **In** *Block, W. and Hexham, I., eds.*, 1986, pp. 181–201. **[G: U.K.]**

Preston, Ronald H. The Legacy of the Christian Socialist Movement in England: Reply. **In** *Block, W. and Hexham, I., eds.*, 1986, pp. 208–12. **[G: U.K.]**

Riha, Tomas J. F. The Marxian Law of Value under Socialism: Faith and Reality. **In** *Dowdy,*

E., ed., 1986, pp. 127–44. **[G: U.S.S.R.; China]**

Roca, Sergio G. State Enterprises in Cuba under the New System of Planning and Management (SDPE). **In** *Mesa-Lago, C., ed.*, 1986, pp. 153–79. **[G: Cuba]**

Rodríguez, José Luis. The So-Called Cubanology and Cuban Economic Development. **In** *Mesa-Lago, C., ed.*, 1986, pp. 211–24. **[G: Cuba]**

Rosefielde, Steven. Competitive Market Socialism Revisited: Impediments to Efficient Price-Fixing. *Comp. Econ. Stud.*, Fall 1986, *28*(3), pp. 17–23.

Rzhanitsyna, L. Intensifying the Stimulation of the Effectiveness of Labor. *Prob. Econ.*, May 1986, *29*(1), pp. 50–62. **[G: U.S.S.R.]**

Salgó, István. Economic Mechanism and Foreign Trade Organization in Hungary. *Acta Oecon.*, 1986, *36*(3–4), pp. 271–87. **[G: Hungary]**

Schenk, Robert. Radical Analyses of Imperialism, the Third World, and the Transition to Socialism: A Survey Article: A Comment. *J. Econ. Lit.*, June 1986, *24*(2), pp. 676. **[G: Global]**

Schroeder, Gertrude E. Gorbachev: "Radically" Implementing Brezhnev's Reforms. *Soviet Econ.*, Oct.-Dec. 1986, *2*(4), pp. 289–301. **[G: U.S.S.R.]**

Senchagov, V. Improving the Economic Mechanism under Conditions of Intensification of Production. *Prob. Econ.*, June 1986, *29*(2), pp. 43–63. **[G: U.S.S.R.]**

Shenfield, Arthur A. The Legacy of the Christian Socialist Movement in England: Comment. **In** *Block, W. and Hexham, I., eds.*, 1986, pp. 202–08. **[G: U.K.]**

Shi, Xiulin. Is the Economy of China's Special Economic Zones State Capitalist in Nature? *Chinese Econ. Stud.*, Winter 1985-86, *19*(2), pp. 25–40. **[G: China]**

Simonovits, András. Growth, Control and Tensions in an Open Socialist Economy. *Econ. Planning*, 1986, *20*(3), pp. 145–61.

Sipos, Aladár and Tardos, Márton. Economic Control and the Structural Interdependence of Organizations in Hungary at the End of the Second Decade of Reform. *Acta Oecon.*, 1986, *37*(3–4), pp. 241–65. **[G: Hungary]**

Smith, Keith. Economic Theory and the Closure of the Soviet Industrialisation Debate. **In** *Smith, K., ed.*, 1986, *1979*, pp. 23–49. **[G: U.S.S.R.]**

Stephan, Paul B., III. Comrades' Courts and Labor Discipline since Brezhnev. **In** *Ioffe, O. S. and Janis, M. W., eds.*, 1986, pp. 213–32. **[G: U.S.S.R.]**

Stigler, George J. Why Have the Socialists Been Winning? **In** *Stigler, G. J.*, 1986, *1979*, pp. 337–46.

Su, Yanhan. A Brief Discussion of the Economic Nature of China's Special Economic Zones. *Chinese Econ. Stud.*, Winter 1985-86, *19*(2), pp. 41–58. **[G: China]**

Szalai, Erzsébet. The Structural Reasons for Anti-reform Attitudes (Comments on András Hegedüs's Article and the Subsequent Debate). *Eastern Europ. Econ.*, Fall 1986, *25*(1), pp. 106–12. **[G: Hungary]**

Szamuely, László. An Important Book on the Reform of Soviet Economy. *Acta Oecon.*, 1986, *36*(3–4), pp. 329–37. **[G: U.S.S.R.]**

Szamuely, László. Prospects of Economic Reforms in the European CMEA Countries in the 80s. *Acta Oecon.*, 1986, *36*(1–2), pp. 55–65. **[G: CMEA]**

Tardos, Márton. The Conditions of Developing a Regulated Market. *Acta Oecon.*, 1986, *36*(1–2), pp. 67–89. **[G: Hungary]**

Teague, Elizabeth. The USSR Law on Work Collectives: Workers' Control or Workers Controlled? **In** *Lane, D., ed.*, 1986, pp. 239–55. **[G: U.S.S.R.]**

Teng, Mao-tung. Restructuring Incentives in the People's Republic of China: Comment. **In** *Balassa, B. and Giersch, H., eds.*, 1986, pp. 343–44.

Toporowski, Jan. Selected Essays on Economic Planning: Introduction. **In** *Kalecki, M.*, 1986, pp. 1–18.

Trzeciakowski, Witold. Problems of Achieving Efficiency and Equilibrium. *Eastern Europ. Econ.*, Summer 1986, *24*(4), pp. 51–66. **[G: Poland]**

Vacić, Aleksandar M. Why the Development of Yugoslavia Deviated from the Socialist Self-management Market Economy. *Eastern Europ. Econ.*, Winter 1986-87, *25*(2), pp. 3–21. **[G: Yugoslavia]**

Vági, Gábor. Freedom of Decision-Making and Security of Development. *Acta Oecon.*, 1986, *37*(1–2), pp. 47–58. **[G: Hungary]**

Vintrová, Ružena. Reproduction Proportions of Intensive Development. *Czech. Econ. Digest.*, January 1986, (1), pp. 33–57. **[G: Czechoslovakia]**

Waelbroeck, Jean. Rent-Seeking and Trade Policy: An Industry Approach: Comment. **In** *Balassa, B. and Giersch, H., eds.*, 1986, pp. 444–47.

Weickhardt, George G. The Soviet Military–Industrial Complex and Economic Reform. *Soviet Econ.*, July-Sept. 1986, *2*(3), pp. 193–220. **[G: U.S.S.R.]**

Weiss, Frank D. Incentives in the Soviet Economy: Comment. **In** *Balassa, B. and Giersch, H., eds.*, 1986, pp. 250–52.

Whitt, J. Allen and Rothschild-Whitt, Joyce. Workers' Cooperatives: The Marxian and Non-Marxian Heritage. **In** *Jain, A. and Matejko, A., eds.*, 1986, pp. 228–44.

Wong, Christine P. W. The Economics of Shortage and Problems of Reform in Chinese Industry. *J. Compar. Econ.*, December 1986, *10*(4), pp. 363–87. **[G: China]**

Woodard, Kim. Political Risk in China. **In** *Raddock, D. M., et al.*, 1986, pp. 71–93. **[G: China]**

Woodward, Susan L. Orthodoxy and Solidarity: Competing Claims and International Adjustment in Yugoslavia. **In** *Comisso, E. and Tyson, L., eds.*, 1986, pp. 329–69. **[G: Yugoslavia]**

Yan, Rui-Zhen. Economic Reform in Rural China.

In *Maunder, A. and Renborg, U., eds.*, 1986, pp. 440–48. [G: China]

Yang, Jinbai, et al. Some Theoretical Problems of Socialist National Income. *Chinese Econ. Stud.*, Fall 1986, *20*(1), pp. 3–99.

Yang, Jinbai, et al. Some Theoretical Problems of Socialist National Income. *Chinese Econ. Stud.*, Spring-Summer 1986, *19*(3–4), pp. 7–169. [G: China]

Zou, Erkang. Special Economic Zone Typifies Open Policy. *Chinese Econ. Stud.*, Winter 1985-86, *19*(2), pp. 79–85. [G: China]

053 Comparative Economic Systems

0530 Comparative Economic Systems

Balassa, Bela. Prices, Incentives, and Economic Growth. **In** *Balassa, B. and Giersch, H., eds.*, 1986, pp. 3–21.

Belkaoui, Ahmed and Maksy, Mostafa M. Basic Needs and Economic Systems: A Sensitivity Analysis. *Rev. Soc. Econ.*, October 1986, *44*(2), pp. 178–82. [G: Global]

Bergson, Abram. The Politics of Socialist Efficiency. **In** *Szenberg, M., ed.*, 1986, *1980*, pp. 69–81.

Botos, Katalin. The Impact of the Depression of the 1930s and Its Relevance for the Contemporary World: 1929/33 vs. 1979/83. **In** *Berend, I. T. and Borchardt, K., eds.*, 1986, pp. 333–54.

Brada, Josef C. The Variability of Crop Production in Private and Socialized Agriculture: Evidence from Eastern Europe. *J. Polit. Econ.*, Part 1, June 1986, *94*(3), pp. 545–63. [G: Bulgaria; Czechoslovakia; Hungary; Poland; Romania]

Burkett, John P. PQLI as a Measure of Comparative Performance: Comment. *Comp. Econ. Stud.*, Summer 1986, *28*(2), pp. 59–68.

Cassel, Dieter and Cichy, E. Ulrich. Explaining the Growing Shadow Economy in East and West: A Comparative Systems Approach. *Comp. Econ. Stud.*, Spring 1986, *28*(1), pp. 20–41. [G: OECD; E. Germany; Poland; U.S.S.R.]

Collet, Pierre; Le Goff, Denis and de Penanros, Roland. The Economic Basis of Social Organization. *J. Compar. Econ.*, June 1986, *10*(2), pp. 106–37.

Comisso, Ellen. Introduction: State Structures, Political Processes, and Collective Choice in CMEA States. *Int. Organ.*, Spring 1986, *40*(2), pp. 195–238. [G: CMEA]

Comisso, Ellen. State Structures and Political Processes Outside the CMEA: A Comparison. *Int. Organ.*, Spring 1986, *40*(2), pp. 577–98. [G: CMEA]

Dallago, Bruno. Economic System and the Causes of Irregular Economy: Some Preliminary Questions for East–West Comparison. *Rivista Int. Sci. Econ. Com.*, August 1986, *33*(8), pp. 777–96.

Ka, Chih-Ming and Selden, Mark. Original Accumulation, Equity and Late Industrialization: The Cases of Socialist China and Capitalist Taiwan. *World Devel.*, Oct./Nov. 1986, *14*(10/11), pp. 1293–1310. [G: Taiwan; China]

Kornai, János. The Soft Budget Constraint. *Kyklos*, 1986, *39*(1), pp. 3–30. [G: Hungary; Yugoslavia; China; U.S.]

Lavoie, Donald C. The Market as a Procedure for Discovery and Conveyance of Inarticulate Knowledge. *Comp. Econ. Stud.*, Spring 1986, *28*(1), pp. 1–19.

Malinvaud, Edmond. Prices, Incentives, and Economic Growth: Comment. **In** *Balassa, B. and Giersch, H., eds.*, 1986, pp. 22–27.

Montias, J. Michael. On the Labor-Managed Firm in a Competitive Environment. *J. Compar. Econ.*, March 1986, *10*(1), pp. 2–8.

Ostojić, Slobodan. Decentralization without Hierarchy: Experience of Yugoslav Enterprises. *Econ. Anal. Workers' Manage.*, 1986, *20*(2), pp. 119–34. [G: Yugoslavia]

Pasinetti, Luigi L. Prices, Incentives, and Economic Growth: Comment. **In** *Balassa, B. and Giersch, H., eds.*, 1986, pp. 28–31.

Petr, Jerry L. Comparative Analysis of Thresholds of Non-Revolutionary Institutional Change: China and the United States in the 1980s. *J. Econ. Issues*, June 1986, *20*(2), pp. 561–69. [G: U.S.; China]

Rimler, Judit. Economic Obsolescence and Employment (A Comparative Analysis of the Hungarian and Dutch Economies). *Acta Oecon.*, 1986, *36*(1–2), pp. 123–40. [G: Hungary; Netherlands]

Rostowski, Jacek and Auerbach, Paul. Storming Cycles and Economic Systems. *J. Compar. Econ.*, September 1986, *10*(3), pp. 293–312. [G: OECD; CMEA]

100 Economic Growth; Development; Planning; Fluctuations

110 Economic Growth; Development; Planning Theory and Policy

111 Economic Growth Theory and Models

1110 Growth Theories

Amadeo, Edward J. Crescimento, distribuição e utilização capacidade: um modelo neo-steindliano. (With English summary.) *Pesquisa Planejamento Econ.*, December 1986, *16*(3), pp. 689–711.

Amendola, Mario and Gaffard, J. L. Technology as an Environment: A Suggested Interpretation. *Écon. Appl.*, 1986, *39*(3), pp. 473–92.

Arena, Richard and Froeschle, Claude. Formes de progrès technique, séquences d'équilibres temporaires et stabilité économique. (Forms of Technical Progress, Sequences of Temporary Equilibrium and Economic Stability. With English summary.) *Écon. Appl.*, 1986, *39*(3), pp. 415–47.

Arrow, Kenneth J. Incentives and Growth: An

Appraisal. **In** *Balassa, B. and Giersch, H., eds.*, 1986, pp. 481–85.

Balassa, Bela. Prices, Incentives, and Economic Growth. **In** *Balassa, B. and Giersch, H., eds.*, 1986, pp. 3–21.

Barry, Frank G. Profitability, Investment and Employment: A Survey of Recent Developments in Medium-term Growth Theory. *Econ. Soc. Rev.*, April 1986, *17*(3), pp. 159–73. **[G: OECD]**

Bewley, Truman F. Dynamic Implications of the Form of the Budget Constraint. **In** *Sonnenschein, H. F., ed.*, 1986, pp. 117–23.

Burgstaller, André. Unifying Ricardo's Theories of Growth and Comparative Advantage. *Economica*, November 1986, *53*(212), pp. 467–81.

Chang, Winston W. and Chiang, Shin-Hwan. A Model of Growth and Trade in Time-phased Economies. *Int. Econ. Rev.*, October 1986, *27*(3), pp. 783–802.

Dahmén, Erik. Schumpeterian Dynamics: Some Methodological Notes. **In** *Day, R. H. and Eliasson, G., eds.*, 1986, *1984*, pp. 181–90.

Day, Richard H. Unscrambling the Concept of Chaos through Thick and Thin: Reply [The Emergence of Chaos from Classical Economic Growth]. *Quart. J. Econ.*, May 1986, *101*(2), pp. 425–26.

Diamond, Peter A. Intertemporal Aspects of Learning New Techniques: Implications for Efficiency and Distribution: Comment. *Scand. J. Econ.*, 1986, *88*(1), pp. 189–94.

Donges, Juergen B. Incentives and Growth: A Summary Appraisal. **In** *Balassa, B. and Giersch, H., eds.*, 1986, pp. 486–90.

Eliasson, Gunnar. Micro Heterogeneity of Firms and the Stability of Industrial Growth. **In** *Day, R. H. and Eliasson, G., eds.*, 1986, *1984*, pp. 79–104. **[G: Sweden]**

Eliasson, Gunnar. Micro Heterogeneity of Firms and the Stability of Industrial Growth: Reply. **In** *Day, R. H. and Eliasson, G., eds.*, 1986, pp. 112–14. **[G: Sweden]**

Falkinger, Josef. Konjunkturelle Unsicherheit, längerfristiges Wachstumsklima und Investitionsverhalten. (Short-run Uncertainty, Long-run Growth-Climate, and Investment Behavior. With English summary.) *Jahr. Nationalökon. Statist.*, September 1986, *201*(5), pp. 469–79.

Fisunoglu, H. Mahir. Two Alternative Models for Explaining Capital Accumulation. *METU*, 1986, *13*(3–4), pp. 275–86.

Hahn, Frank H. "Of Marx and Keynes and Many Things." *Oxford Econ. Pap.*, July 1986, *38*(2), pp. 354–61.

Harcourt, Geoffrey C. The Rate of Profits in Equilibrium Growth Models: A Review Article. **In** *[Harcourt, G. C.]*, 1986, *1973*, pp. 207–28.

Hochstein, Alan. GNE and Domar's Theory of Economic Growth. *Atlantic Econ. J.*, July 1986, *14*(2), pp. 83.

Jungenfelt, Karl G. Intertemporal Aspects of Learning New Techniques: Implications for Efficiency and Distribution. *Scand. J. Econ.*, 1986, *88*(1), pp. 157–87.

Kaldor, Nicholas. Limits on Growth. *Oxford Econ. Pap.*, July 1986, *38*(2), pp. 187–98.

Kemp, Murray C. and Kondo, Hitoshi. Overlapping Generations, Competitive Efficiency and Optimal Population. *J. Public Econ.*, July 1986, *30*(2), pp. 237–47.

Lane, John and Leininger, Wolfgang. On Price Characterization and Pareto-Efficiency of Game Equilibrium Growth. *J. Econ. (Z. Nationalökon.)*, 1986, *46*(4), pp. 347–67.

Malinvaud, Edmond. Prices, Incentives, and Economic Growth: Comment. **In** *Balassa, B. and Giersch, H., eds.*, 1986, pp. 22–27.

Malinvaud, Edmond. Reflecting on the Theory of Capital and Growth. *Oxford Econ. Pap.*, November 1986, *38*(3), pp. 367–85.

Marris, Robin and Mueller, Dennis C. The Corporation, Competition, and the Invisible Hand. **In** *Mueller, D. C.*, 1986, *1980*, pp. 261–97.

Melese, Francois and Transue, William. Unscrambling Chaos through Thick and Thin [The Emergence of Chaos from Classical Economic Growth]. *Quart. J. Econ.*, May 1986, *101*(2), pp. 419–23.

Mensch, Gerhard. Schumpeterian Dynamics: Some Methodological Notes: Comment. **In** *Day, R. H. and Eliasson, G., eds.*, 1986, pp. 194–97.

Nelson, Richard R. Schumpeterian Dynamics: Some Methodological Notes: Comment. **In** *Day, R. H. and Eliasson, G., eds.*, 1986, pp. 191–93.

Nishimura, Osamu and Nakao, Takeo. A Note on the Golden-Rule Condition in the Overlapping Generations Growth Model. *Manchester Sch. Econ. Soc. Stud.*, December 1986, *54*(4), pp. 420–24.

Pasinetti, Luigi L. Prices, Incentives, and Economic Growth: Comment. **In** *Balassa, B. and Giersch, H., eds.*, 1986, pp. 28–31.

Samuelson, Larry and Wolfson, Murray. Expository Marxism and Comparative Economic Dynamics. *Hist. Polit. Econ.*, Spring 1986, *18*(1), pp. 65–85.

Simon, Julian L. and Steinmann, Gunter. A Model of Supply, Demand and Technical Progress [Phelps's Technical Progress Model Generalized]. **In** *Simon, J. L.*, 1986, *1981*, pp. 102–14.

Simon, Julian L. and Steinmann, Gunter. The Effects of Population Size and Growth through Learning-by-Doing [The Economic Implications of Learning-by-Doing for Population Size and Growth]. **In** *Simon, J. L.*, 1986, *1984*, pp. 83–101.

Sinclair, P. J. N. Faster Technical Progress Need Not Imply Lower Optimal Savings. *Greek Econ. Rev.*, June 1986, *8*(1), pp. 60–65.

Solow, Robert M. Resources and Economic Growth. **In** *Szenberg, M., ed.*, 1986, *1978*, pp. 57–68.

Tanaka, Yasuhito. The Optimum Interest Rate under Uncertain Life Time. *Econ. Rev. (Keizai Kenkyu)*, January 1986, *37*(1), pp. 79–83.

Thirlwall, A. P. A General Model of Growth and Development on Kaldorian Lines. *Oxford Econ. Pap.*, July 1986, *38*(2), pp. 199–219.

Winter, Sidney G. Micro Heterogeneity of Firms and the Stability of Industrial Growth: Comment. **In** *Day, R. H. and Eliasson, G., eds.*, 1986, pp. 105–11. **[G: Sweden]**

Wörgötter, Andreas. Who's Who in Goodwin's Growth Cycle. *Jahr. Nationalökon. Statist.*, May 1986, *201*(3), pp. 222–28.

1112 One and Two Sector Growth Models and Related Topics

Ahmad, Syed. A Pasinetti Theory of Relative Profit Share for the Anti-Pasinetti Case. *J. Post Keynesian Econ.*, Fall 1986, *9*(1), pp. 149–58.

Anderson, B. L. Trends in Capital Accumulation in the Age of Malthus. **In** *Turner, M., ed.*, 1986, pp. 201–21. **[G: U.K.]**

Asimakopulos, Athanasios. Harrod and Domar on Dynamic Economics. *Banca Naz. Lavoro Quart. Rev.*, September 1986, (158), pp. 275–98.

Boldrin, Michele and Montrucchio, Luigi. On the Indeterminacy of Capital Accumulation Paths. *J. Econ. Theory*, October 1986, *40*(1), pp. 26–39.

Bradley, John and Prendergast, Canice. Verdoorn's Law: A Retrospective View. *Econ. Soc. Rev.*, January 1986, *17*(2), pp. 75–86. **[G: Ireland]**

Deneckere, Raymond J. and Pelikan, Steve. Competitive Chaos. *J. Econ. Theory*, October 1986, *40*(1), pp. 13–25.

Dutt, Amitava Krishna. Growth, Distribution and Technological Change. *Metroecon.*, June 1986, *38*(2), pp. 113–34.

Elbers, C. and Weddepohl, H. N. Steady State Equilibria with Saving for Retirement in a Continuous Time Overlapping Generations Model. *J. Econ. (Z. Nationalökon.)*, 1986, *46*(3), pp. 253–82.

Faber, Malte and Stephan, Gunter. Neo-Austrian Characterization of Proportional Prices with Positive Rate of Interest Relative to the Growth Rate. **In** *Faber, M., ed.*, 1986, pp. 144–53.

Kalecki, Michal. On the Coefficient of Capital Tied Up in Construction. **In** *Kalecki, M.*, 1986, *1958*, pp. 109–17.

Kalecki, Michal. Problems in the Theory of Growth of a Socialist Economy. **In** *Kalecki, M.*, 1986, *1959*, pp. 70–96.

Kalecki, Michal. The Influence of the Construction Period on the Relationship between Investment and National Income. **In** *Kalecki, M.*, 1986, *1957*, pp. 97–108.

Kymn, Kern O. The Steady State Impact of a Declining Saving Rate on Great Ratios of Economics in a Cobb–Douglas Growth Model. *Rivista Int. Sci. Econ. Com.*, June-July 1986, *33*(6–7), pp. 657–66.

Lipton, Michael. Recession, Rent and Debt: Quasi-Ricardian and Quasi-Keynesian Components of Non-recovery. **In** *[Streeten, P.]*, 1986, pp. 58–86.

Nell, Edward J. Cyclical Growth: The Interdependent Dynamics of Industry and Agriculture. **In** *Semmler, W., ed.*, 1986, pp. 289–303.

Prescott, Edward C. Theory Ahead of Business-Cycle Measurement. *Carnegie-Rochester Conf. Ser. Public Policy*, Autumn 1986, *25*, pp. 11–44. **[G: U.S.]**

Struckmeyer, Charles S. The Impact of Energy Price Shocks on Capital Formation and Economic Growth in a Putty–Clay Technology. *Southern Econ. J.*, July 1986, *53*(1), pp. 127–40.

1113 Multisector Growth Models and Related Topics

Arushanian, I. I.; Belen'kii, V. Z. and Biriukova, E. S. A Closed Dynamic Model of Stationary Growth for Variant Analysis of the Interrelations between the Energy System and the Economy of the USSR. *Matekon*, Spring 1986, *22*(3), pp. 35–66. **[G: U.S.S.R.]**

Benveniste, Lawrence M. Pricing Optimal Distributions to Overlapping Generations: A Corollary to Efficiency Pricing [A Complete Characterization of Efficiency in a General Capital Accumulation Model]. *Rev. Econ. Stud.*, April 1986, *53*(2), pp. 301–06.

Bernholz, Peter; Faber, Malte and Reiss, Winfried. A Neo-Austrian Two-Period Multisector Model of Capital. **In** *Faber, M., ed.*, 1986, *1978*, pp. 98–112.

Birolo, Adriano. Crescita e mutamento strutturale: un'analisi preliminare. (Growth and Structural Change: A Preliminary Analysis. With English summary.) *Ricerche Econ.*, Apr.-Sept. 1986, *40*(2–3), pp. 286–302.

Chenery, Hollis B. Growth and Transformation. **In** *Chenery, H.; Robinson, S. and Syrquin, M.*, 1986, pp. 13–36.

Chenery, Hollis B. and Syrquin, Moshe. Typical Patterns of Transformation. **In** *Chenery, H.; Robinson, S. and Syrquin, M.*, 1986, pp. 37–83.

Coles, Jeffrey L. Equilibrium Turnpike Theory with Time-Separable Utility. *J. Econ. Dynam. Control*, September 1986, *10*(3), pp. 367–94.

Dos Santos Ferreira, Rodolphe. Is a Wider Choice Conducive to Stability? A Comment [Money, National Debt, and Economic Growth]. *J. Econ. Theory*, August 1986, *39*(2), pp. 457–63.

Epstein, Larry G. Implicitly Additive Utility and the Nature of Optimal Economic Growth. *J. Math. Econ.*, 1986, *15*(2), pp. 111–28.

Feder, Gershon. Growth in Semi-industrial Countries: A Statistical Analysis. **In** *Chenery, H.; Robinson, S. and Syrquin, M.*, 1986, pp. 263–82. **[G: LDCs]**

Goodwin, Richard M. Swinging along the Turnpike with von Neumann and Sraffa. *Cambridge J. Econ.*, September 1986, *10*(3), pp. 203–10.

Groth, C. Different Indecomposability Concepts for a von Neumann Technology: A Note. *Metroecon.*, June 1986, *38*(2), pp. 157–66.

Khan, M. Ali and Mitra, Tapan. On the Existence of a Stationary Optimal Stock for a Multi-sector Economy: A Primal Approach. *J. Econ. Theory,* December 1986, *40*(2), pp. 319–28.

Kubo, Yuji; Robinson, Sherman and Syrquin, Moshe. The Methodology of Multisector Comparative Analysis. **In** *Chenery, H.; Robinson, S. and Syrquin, M.*, 1986, pp. 121–47. **[G: Mexico; Turkey; Japan; S. Korea]**

Kubo, Yuji, et al. Interdependence and Industrial Structure. **In** *Chenery, H.; Robinson, S. and Syrquin, M.*, 1986, pp. 188–225. **[G: LDCs]**

Lacaze, Dominique. Théorie des prix et sélection de techniques ou de projets. (Price Theory and Selection of Techniques or Projects. With English summary.) *Revue Écon.*, July 1986, *37*(4), pp. 677–95.

Nishimizu, Mieko and Robinson, Sherman. Productivity Growth in Manufacturing. **In** *Chenery, H.; Robinson, S. and Syrquin, M.*, 1986, pp. 283–308. **[G: Japan; S. Korea; Yugoslavia; Turkey]**

Read, Thomas T. Balanced Growth without Constant Returns to Scale. *J. Math. Econ.*, 1986, *15*(2), pp. 171–78.

Reiss, Winfried and Faber, Malte. Own Rates of Interest in a General Multisector Model of Capital. **In** *Faber, M., ed.*, 1986, *1982*, pp. 113–31.

Romer, Paul M. Increasing Returns and Long-run Growth. *J. Polit. Econ.*, October 1986, *94*(5), pp. 1002–37. **[G: OECD]**

Samuelson, Paul A. Balanced-Growth Equilibrium in the General Multi-class Saving Model (Macroeconomic Distribution Theory/Neoclassical Imputation/NeoKeynesian Identities). **In** *Samuelson, P. A.*, 1986, *1977*, pp. 194–202.

Stephan, Gunter. Roundaboutness, Nontightness and Malinvaud Prices in Multisector Models with Infinite Horizon. **In** *Faber, M., ed.*, 1986, pp. 154–72.

Syrquin, Moshe. Productivity Growth and Factor Reallocation. **In** *Chenery, H.; Robinson, S. and Syrquin, M.*, 1986, pp. 229–62. **[G: Latin America; Europe; Asia; Canada]**

1114 Monetary Growth Models

Hayakawa, Hiroaki. Intertemporal Optimization and Neutrality of Money in Growth Models. *J. Monet. Econ.*, November 1986, *18*(3), pp. 323–28.

Kapur, Basant K. Money as a Medium of Exchange and Monetary Growth in an Underdevelopment Context. **In** *Kapur, B. K.*, 1986, *1975*, pp. 1–18.

Kapur, Basant K. The Role of Financial Institutions in Economic Development—A Theoretical Analysis. **In** *Kapur, B. K.*, 1986, pp. 34–48.

Yoo, Jang H. and Pyo, Hak K. Inflationary Expectations, "Endogenous Money," and Economic Growth. *J. Macroecon.*, Summer 1986, *8*(3), pp. 337–53.

112 Economic Development Models and Theories

1120 Economic Development Models and Theories

Abbott, George C. Private Capital and the Proposal for a South Bank. *World Econ.*, September 1986, *9*(3), pp. 275–94. **[G: LDCs]**

Adelman, Irma. A Poverty-Focused Approach to Development Policy. **In** *Lewis, J. P. and Kallab, V., eds.*, 1986, pp. 49–65. **[G: LDCs]**

Adelman, Irma. Beyond Export-Led Growth. **In** *Adelman, I. and Taylor, J. E., eds.*, 1986, *1984*, pp. 242–62. **[G: S. Korea]**

Adelman, Irma. Education and Economic Development: A Comparative Perspective. **In** *Adelman, I. and Taylor, J. E., eds.*, 1986, pp. 296–318. **[G: LDCs; China]**

Agu, C. C. Financial Institutions and Economic Development: The Experience of Nigeria. *S. Afr. J. Econ.*, September 1986, *54*(3), pp. 319–31. **[G: Nigeria]**

Ahmed, Salehuddin. Rural–Urban Migration: Policy Simulations in a Dual Economy Model of Bangladesh. *Devel. Econ.*, March 1986, *24*(1), pp. 26–43. **[G: Bangladesh]**

Amin, Samir. Is an Endogenous Development Strategy Possible in Africa? **In** *[Patel, S.]*, 1986, pp. 159–72. **[G: Africa]**

Anandalingam, G. Incentive Compatibility in Mixed Economy Planning: Results of a Simple Model. *J. Econ. Dynam. Control*, June 1986, *10*(1/2), pp. 9–13.

Arida, Persio. Macroeconomic Issues for Latin America. *J. Devel. Econ.*, June 1986, *22*(1), pp. 171–208. **[G: Latin America]**

Arnott, Richard J. and Gersovitz, Mark. Social Welfare Underpinnings of Urban Bias and Unemployment. *Econ. J.*, June 1986, *96*(382), pp. 413–24.

Bacha, Edmar L. Terms of Reference for the Country Studies. *World Devel.*, Special Issue, August 1986, *14*(8), pp. 909–18. **[G: LDCs]**

Bakalis, Steve and Hazari, Bharat R. A Note on Underutilization of Capital and Unemployment in a Harris–Todaro Framework. *Devel. Econ.*, September 1986, *24*(3), pp. 288–98. **[G: LDCs]**

Balassa, Bela. Dependency and Trade Orientation. *World Econ.*, September 1986, *9*(3), pp. 259–73. **[G: U.S.; LDCs]**

Balassa, Bela. Economic Development in Small Countries. *Acta Oecon.*, 1986, *37*(3–4), pp. 325–40. **[G: Hungary]**

Balassa, Bela. Prices, Incentives, and Economic Growth. **In** *Balassa, B. and Giersch, H., eds.*, 1986, pp. 3–21.

Batra, Raveendra N. A General Equilibrium Model of Multinational Corporations in Developing Economies. *Oxford Econ. Pap.*, July 1986, *38*(2), pp. 342–53.

Bautista, Romeo M. Domestic Price Distortions and Agricultural Income in Developing Countries. *J. Devel. Econ.*, September 1986, *23*(1), pp. 19–39. **[G: Philippines]**

Behrman, Jere R. Shadow Prices and Subsidies in Botswana. *J. Devel. Econ.*, July-Aug. 1986, *22*(2), pp. 351–92. **[G: Botswana]**

Bengelsdorf, Carollee. State and Society in the Transition to Socialism: The Theoretical Legacy. **In** *Fagen, R. R.; Deere, C. D. and Coraggio, J. L., eds.*, 1986, pp. 192–211.

Bhaduri, Amit. Forced Commerce and Agrarian Growth. *World Devel.*, Special Issue, Feb. 1986, *14*(2), pp. 267–72.

Bhaduri, Amit. Hacia un crecimiento con endeudamiento externo. (The Indebted Growth Process. With English summary.) *Estud. Econ.*, January-June 1986, *1*(1), pp. 115–25.

Bhagwati, Jagdish N. Development Economics: What Have We Learnt? **In** *[Patel, S.]*, 1986, pp. 11–27.

Bhagwati, Jagdish N. Rethinking Trade Strategy. **In** *Lewis, J. P. and Kallab, V., eds.*, 1986, pp. 91–104.

Bhalla, Surjit S. and Glewwe, Paul. Growth and Equity in Developing Countries: A Reinterpretation of the Sri Lankan Experience. *World Bank Econ. Rev.*, September 1986, *1*(1), pp. 35–63. **[G: Sri Lanka; LDCs]**

Biswas, Basudeb and Ram, Rati. Military Expenditures and Economic Growth in Less Developed Countries: An Augmented Model and Further Evidence. *Econ. Develop. Cult. Change*, January 1986, *34*(2), pp. 361–72. **[G: LDCs]**

Blomqvist, Ake G. The Economics of Price Scissors: Comment. *Amer. Econ. Rev.*, December 1986, *76*(5), pp. 1188–91.

Blomqvist, Ake G. and McMahon, Gary. Simulating Commercial Policy in a Small, Open Dual Economy with Urban Unemployment: A General Equilibrium Approach. *J. Devel. Stud.*, January 1986, *22*(2), pp. 443–63. **[G: Kenya]**

Blomqvist, Ake G. and Mohammad, Sharif. Controls, Corruption, and Competitive Rent-Seeking in LDCs. *J. Devel. Econ.*, April 1986, *21*(1), pp. 161–80. **[G: India]**

Buffie, Edward F. Devaluation and Imported Inputs: The Large Economy Case. *Int. Econ. Rev.*, February 1986, *27*(1), pp. 123–40.

Buffie, Edward F. Devaluation, Investment and Growth in LDCs. *J. Devel. Econ.*, March 1986, *20*(2), pp. 361–79. **[G: LDCs]**

Bumb, Balu. A Note on Variables and Observations in Factor Analysis: A Reply. *J. Devel. Econ.*, November 1986, *24*(1), pp. 197–200.

Cairncross, Alec. Is There a General Theory of Economic Development? **In** *Cairncross, A.*, 1986, pp. 136–50.

Cairncross, Alec. The Role of Technology and Natural Resources in the Development Process. **In** *Cairncross, A.*, 1986, *1979*, pp. 124–35. **[G: Japan]**

Carter, Michael R. The Economics of Price Scissors: Comment. *Amer. Econ. Rev.*, December 1986, *76*(5), pp. 1192–94.

Chaubey, P. K. A Review of Models in Indian Plans. *Indian Econ. J.*, Apr.-June 1986, *33*(4), pp. 84–91. **[G: India]**

Chazan, Naomi. Ethnicity in Economic Crisis: Development Strategies and Patterns of Ethnicity in Africa. **In** *Thompson, D. L. and Ronen, D., eds.*, 1986, pp. 137–58. **[G: Africa]**

Chenery, Hollis B. Growth and Transformation. **In** *Chenery, H.; Robinson, S. and Syrquin, M.*, 1986, pp. 13–36.

Chenery, Hollis B.; Robinson, Sherman and Syrquin, Moshe. Growth and Structure: A Synthesis. **In** *Chenery, H.; Robinson, S. and Syrquin, M.*, 1986, pp. 348–59.

Chenery, Hollis B. and Syrquin, Moshe. The Semi-industrial Countries. **In** *Chenery, H.; Robinson, S. and Syrquin, M.*, 1986, pp. 84–118. **[G: LDCs]**

Chenery, Hollis B. and Syrquin, Moshe. Typical Patterns of Transformation. **In** *Chenery, H.; Robinson, S. and Syrquin, M.*, 1986, pp. 37–83.

Chenery, Hollis B., et al. Alternative Routes to Development. **In** *Chenery, H.; Robinson, S. and Syrquin, M.*, 1986, pp. 311–47. **[G: S. Korea]**

Chichilnisky, Graciela. A General Equilibrium Theory of North–South Trade. **In** *[Arrow, K. J.], Vol. 2*, 1986, pp. 3–56.

Chiswick, Carmel U. The Efficiency-Wage Hypothesis: Applying a General Model of the Interactions between Labor Quantity and Quality. *J. Devel. Econ.*, March 1986, *20*(2), pp. 311–23.

Chu, Yun-peng. Changes in Income Distribution over Time in a One-Sector Neoclassical Setting. *J. Devel. Econ.*, December 1986, *24*(2), pp. 359–70.

Chu, Yun-peng, et al. Exchange Rates Intervention and Capital Mobility Control: Comparisons and Simultaneous Optimization. *J. Devel. Econ.*, September 1986, *23*(1), pp. 119–34. **[G: LDCs]**

Clausen, A. W. Accelerating Growth and Reducing Poverty: A Multilateral Strategy for Development: Address to the Atlantik-Brücke and the Deutsche Gesellschaft für Auswärtige Politik: Bonn, Federal Republic of Germany: April 18, 1983. **In** *Clausen, A. W.*, 1986, pp. 157–75.

Clausen, A. W. Promoting the Private Sector in Developing Countries: A Multilateral Approach: Address to the Institute of Directors: London, England: February 26, 1985. **In** *Clausen, A. W.*, 1986, pp. 361–80.

Cole, William E. and Sanders, Richard D. Internal Migration and Urban Employment: Reply. *Amer. Econ. Rev.*, June 1986, *76*(3), pp. 570–72. **[G: Mexico; India; Colombia; Nigeria]**

Conyers, Diana. Future Directions in Development Studies: The Case of Decentralization. *World Devel.*, May 1986, *14*(5), pp. 593–603. **[G: Zambia]**

Coraggio, José Luis. Economics and Politics in the Transition to Socialism: Reflections on the Nicaragua Experience. **In** *Fagen, R. R.; Deere,*

C. D. and Coraggio, J. L., eds., 1986, pp. 143–70. **[G: Nicaragua]**

Corea, Gamani. The Crisis: Some Reflections. **In** *[Patel, S.]*, 1986, pp. 29–35.

Crozier, Michel. Strategies for Change in View of Societal Learning Processes. **In** *[Hirshman, A. O.]*, 1986, pp. 219–32.

Dahlman, Carl J. and Westphal, Larry E. The Acquisition of Technological Mastery in Industry. **In** *Adelman, I. and Taylor, J. E., eds.*, 1986, pp. 263–95. **[G: S. Korea]**

Darrat, Ali F. Trade and Development: The Asian Experience. *Cato J.*, Fall 1986, *6*(2), pp. 695–99. **[G: Asia]**

Deere, Carmen Diana. Agrarian Reform, Peasant and Rural Production, and the Organization of Production in the Transition to Socialism. **In** *Fagen, R. R.; Deere, C. D. and Coraggio, J. L., eds.*, 1986, pp. 97–142. **[G: Selected LDCs]**

Diwan, Romesh and Hu, Grace. Country Objectives and IMF Conditionality: An Empirical Analysis of Sudan Economy. *Indian J. Quant. Econ.*, 1986, *2*(2), pp. 83–100. **[G: Sudan]**

Domar, Evsey D. Reflections on Economic Development. **In** *Szenberg, M., ed.*, 1986, pp. 1–12.

Dornbusch, Rudiger. Stabilization Policies in Developing Countries: What Have We Learned? **In** *Dornbusch, R.*, 1986, *1982*, pp. 151–65. **[G: Chile; Argentina; Brazil]**

Dubiel, Ivo. Changes of Social Relevance in the Transplantation of Theories: The Examples of Economics and Agronomics. *CEPAL Rev.*, April 1986, (28), pp. 151–69.

Dutt, Amitava Krishna. Stock Equilibrium in Flexprice Markets in Macromodels for Less Developed Economies: The Case of Food Speculation. *J. Devel. Econ.*, April 1986, *21*(1), pp. 89–109. **[G: LDCs]**

Dutt, Amitava Krishna. Vertical Trading and Uneven Development. *J. Devel. Econ.*, March 1986, *20*(2), pp. 339–59.

Dykema, Eugene R. No View without a Viewpoint: Gunnar Myrdal. *World Devel.*, Special Issue, Feb. 1986, *14*(2), pp. 147–63.

Eaton, Jonathan and Taylor, Lance. Developing Country Finance and Debt. *J. Devel. Econ.*, June 1986, *22*(1), pp. 209–65. **[G: LDCs]**

Edwards, Sebastian. Country Risk, Foreign Borrowing, and the Social Discount Rate in an Open Developing Economy. *J. Int. Money Finance*, Supp. March 1986, *5*, pp. S79–96. **[G: LDCs; Chile; Costa Rica]**

Edwards, Sebastian and van Wijnbergen, Sweder J. G. The Welfare Effects of Trade and Capital Market Liberalization. *Int. Econ. Rev.*, February 1986, *27*(1), pp. 141–48.

Egan, Mary Lou and Bendick, Marc, Jr. The Urban–Rural Dimension in National Economic Development. *J. Devel. Areas*, January 1986, *20*(2), pp. 203–21. **[G: LDCs]**

Emmerij, Louis. Alternative Development Strategies Based on the Experience of the World Employment Programme. **In** *Adelman, I. and Taylor, J. E., eds.*, 1986, pp. 8–26.

Enos, J. L. Public Policy in an Economy with Different Types of Agents. **In** *Hall, P., ed.*, 1986, *1984*, pp. 172–200.

Evans, Peter B. State, Capital, and the Transformation of Dependence: The Brazilian Computer Case. *World Devel.*, July 1986, *14*(7), pp. 791–808. **[G: Brazil]**

Ewing, Arthur F. Agriculture, Trade and Growth: Review Article. *J. World Trade Law*, Nov.:Dec. 1986, *20*(6), pp. 665–89. **[G: Global]**

Fagen, Richard R.; Deere, Carmen Diana and Coraggio, José Luis. Transition and Development: Introduction. **In** *Fagen, R. R.; Deere, C. D. and Coraggio, J. L., eds.*, 1986, pp. 9–27.

Feder, Gershon. Growth in Semi-industrial Countries: A Statistical Analysis. **In** *Chenery, H.; Robinson, S. and Syrquin, M.*, 1986, pp. 263–82. **[G: LDCs]**

FitzGerald, E. V. K. Notes on the Analysis of the Small Underdeveloped Economy in Transition. **In** *Fagen, R. R.; Deere, C. D. and Coraggio, J. L., eds.*, 1986, pp. 28–53.

Folbre, Nancy. Cleaning House: New Perspectives on Households and Economic Development. *J. Devel. Econ.*, June 1986, *22*(1), pp. 5–40.

Foxley, Alejandro. After Authoritarianism: Political Alternatives. **In** *[Hirshman, A. O.]*, 1986, pp. 191–216. **[G: Chile]**

Gangopadhyay, Shubhashis. Choice of Techniques, Employment and Poverty. *J. Quant. Econ.*, July 1986, *2*(2), pp. 199–212.

Ganiatsos, Tom. Transfer of Technology: Theory and Policy. **In** *[Patel, S.]*, 1986, pp. 229–51.

Ghosh, Dipak. Fix Price–Flex Price in Development Economics. *Australian Econ. Pap.*, June 1986, *25*(46), pp. 122–27. **[G: India]**

Ghosh, Dipak. Monetary Dualism and Economic Development. *Indian J. Quant. Econ.*, 1986, *2*(2), pp. 121–31.

Ghosh, Dipak. Monetary Dualism in Developing Economies. *Écon. Soc.*, February 1986, *20*(2), pp. 19–30. **[G: LDCs]**

Glick, Reuven and Kharas, Homi J. The Costs and Benefits of Foreign Borrowing: A Survey of Multi-Period Models. *J. Devel. Stud.*, January 1986, *22*(2), pp. 279–99. **[G: LDCs]**

Goulet, Denis. Three Rationalities in Development Decision-making. *World Devel.*, Special Issue, Feb. 1986, *14*(2), pp. 301–17. **[G: Brazil]**

Green, Sebastian. The Contribution of Anthropology to Economic Growth and Development. **In** *Gilad, B. and Kaish, S., eds., Vol. B*, 1986, pp. 201–13.

Green, Steven L. Monetary Policy in Developing Countries and the New Monetary Economics. *J. Econ. Devel.*, December 1986, *11*(2), pp. 7–23. **[G: LDCs]**

Grieco, Joseph M. Foreign Investment and Development: Theories and Evidence. **In** *Moran, T. H., ed.*, 1986, pp. 35–60.

Gsänger, Hans. Entwicklungspotential und Entwicklungserfolg. Versuch einer typisierenden

Gruppenbildung schwarzafrikanischer Länder. (Socio-Economic Performance and Potentials for Development. An Attempt to Group Sub-Saharan African Countries. With English summary.) *Konjunkturpolitik,* 1986, *32*(1/2), pp. 52–79. **[G: Africa]**

Guha, Ashok. The Less Developed Economy in Fantasy and Myth: A Review Article. *Indian Econ. Rev.*, Jan.-June 1986, *21*(1), pp. 61–69.

Gupta, Kanhaya L. Financial Development and Economic Growth in India and South Korea. *J. Econ. Devel.*, December 1986, *11*(2), pp. 41–62. **[G: India; S. Korea]**

Gupta, M. R. Shadow Wage Rate in a Dynamic Harris–Todaro Model. *Oxford Econ. Pap.*, March 1986, *38*(1), pp. 131–40.

Hagen, Everett E. More on the Employment Effects of Innovation: A Correction. *J. Devel. Econ.*, November 1986, *24*(1), pp. 201.

Harriss, C. Lowell. Tax Policy for Economic Progress: Developing Countries as Well as Developed Ones Should Tax to Promote Production and Jobs. *Amer. J. Econ. Soc.*, July 1986, *45*(3), pp. 257–76.

Herander, Mark G. and Thomas, Christopher R. Export Performance and Export–Import Linkage Requirements. *Quart. J. Econ.*, August 1986, *101*(3), pp. 591–607.

Hoksbergen, Roland. Approaches to Evaluation of Development Interventions: The Importance of World and Life Views. *World Devel.*, Special Issue, Feb. 1986, *14*(2), pp. 283–300.

Hong, Wontack. Institutionalized Monopsonistic Capital Markets in a Developing Economy. *J. Devel. Econ.*, May 1986, *21*(2), pp. 353–59. **[G: LDCs]**

Hyden, Goran. African Social Structure and Economic Development. **In** *Berg, R. J. and Whitaker, J. S., eds.*, 1986, pp. 52–80. **[G: Africa]**

Islam, Nurul. Reflections on Development Perspectives since the 1950s. **In** *[Patel, S.]*, 1986, pp. 213–17.

Jameson, Kenneth P. Latin American Structuralism: A Methodological Perspective. *World Devel.*, Special Issue, Feb. 1986, *14*(2), pp. 223–32. **[G: Latin America]**

Johnson, Chalmers. The Nonsocialist NICs: East Asia. *Int. Organ.*, Spring 1986, *40*(2), pp. 557–65. **[G: Asia]**

Jung, Woo S. Financial Development and Economic Growth: International Evidence. *Econ. Develop. Cult. Change*, January 1986, *34*(2), pp. 333–46. **[G: LDCs; MDCs]**

Jung, Woo S. and Lee, Gyu. The Effectiveness of Export Promotion Policies: The Case of Korea. *Weltwirtsch. Arch.*, 1986, *122*(2), pp. 340–57. **[G: S. Korea]**

Jung, Woo S. and Marshall, Peyton J. Inflation and Economic Growth: Some International Evidence on Structuralist and Distortionist Positions: A Note. *J. Money, Credit, Banking*, May 1986, *18*(2), pp. 227–32.

Ka, Chih-Ming and Selden, Mark. Original Accumulation, Equity and Late Industrialization: The Cases of Socialist China and Capitalist Taiwan. *World Devel.*, Oct./Nov. 1986, *14*(10/11), pp. 1293–1310. **[G: Taiwan; China]**

Kapur, Basant K. Money as a Medium of Exchange and Monetary Growth in an Underdevelopment Context. **In** *Kapur, B. K.*, 1986, *1975*, pp. 1–18.

Kapur, Basant K. Optimal Financial and Foreign-Exchange Liberalization of Less-developed Economies. **In** *Kapur, B. K.*, 1986, *1983*, pp. 92–122.

Katz, Eliakim and Stark, Oded. Labor Migration and Risk Aversion in Less Developed Countries. *J. Lab. Econ.*, January 1986, *4*(1), pp. 134–49.

Katz, Eliakim and Stark, Oded. On the Shadow Wage of Urban Jobs in Less-Developed Countries. *J. Urban Econ.*, September 1986, *20*(2), pp. 121–27. **[G: LDCs]**

Kennedy, Joseph V. and Ruttan, Vernon W. A Reexamination of Professional and Popular Thought on Assistance for Economic Development: 1949–1952. *J. Devel. Areas*, April 1986, *20*(3), pp. 297–326. **[G: LDCs]**

Kiljunen, Kimmo. The International Division of Industrial Labour and the Core–Periphery Concept. *CEPAL Rev.*, December 1986, (30), pp. 97–115.

Kirsch, Henry. University Youth as Social Protagonist in Latin America. *CEPAL Rev.*, August 1986, (29), pp. 191–202. **[G: Latin America]**

Krueger, Anne O. Aid in the Development Process. *World Bank Res. Observer*, January 1986, *1*(1), pp. 57–78. **[G: LDCs]**

Kubo, Yuji; de Melo, Jaime and Robinson, Sherman. Trade Strategies and Growth Episodes. **In** *Chenery, H.; Robinson, S. and Syrquin, M.*, 1986, pp. 148–87. **[G: LDCs]**

Kubo, Yuji; Robinson, Sherman and Urata, Shujiro. The Impact of Alternative Development Strategies: Simulations with a Dynamic Input–Output Model. *J. Policy Modeling*, Winter 1986, *8*(4), pp. 503–29. **[G: Turkey; Korea]**

Kubo, Yuji, et al. Interdependence and Industrial Structure. **In** *Chenery, H.; Robinson, S. and Syrquin, M.*, 1986, pp. 188–225. **[G: LDCs]**

Lewis, John P. Development Promotion: A Time for Regrouping. **In** *Lewis, J. P. and Kallab, V., eds.*, 1986, pp. 3–33.

Lewis, W. Arthur. The Design of Alternative Development Strategies: Final Reflections. **In** *Adelman, I. and Taylor, J. E., eds.*, 1986, pp. 321–30.

Livingstone, Ian. The Common Property Problem and Pastoralist Economic Behaviour. *J. Devel. Stud.*, October 1986, *23*(1), pp. 5–19.

Lundahl, Mats. U-ländernas jordbruk: dualism eller bristande jämlikhet? (Agriculture in Developing Countries: Dualism or Lacking Equality? With English summary.) *Ekon. Samfundets Tidskr.*, 1986, *39*(4), pp. 180–200. **[G: LDCs]**

MacIntyre, Arnold. Finance, Growth and the Balance of Trade in OECS Countries. *Soc. Econ. Stud.*, December 1986, *35*(4), pp. 176–212. **[G: Caribbean]**

Malinvaud, Edmond. Prices, Incentives, and

Economic Growth: Comment. In *Balassa, B. and Giersch, H., eds.*, 1986, pp. 22–27.

Martínez, Javier and Valenzuela, Eduardo. Working-class Youth and Anomy. *CEPAL Rev.*, August 1986, (29), pp. 171–81. **[G: Latin America]**

McIntosh, James. North–South Trade: Export-led Growth with Abundant Labour. *J. Devel. Econ.*, November 1986, *24*(1), pp. 141–52.

Mehretu, Assefa. Towards a Framework for Spatial Resolution of Structural Polarity in African Development. *Econ. Geogr.*, January 1986, *62*(1), pp. 30–51. **[G: Africa]**

Mellor, John W. Agriculture on the Road to Industrialization. In *Lewis, J. P. and Kallab, V., eds.*, 1986, pp. 67–89.

Menken, Jane. World Population and U.S. Policy: The Choices Ahead: Introduction and Overview. In *Menken, J., ed.*, 1986, pp. 6–26. **[G: U.S.]**

Molho, Lazaros E. Interest Rates, Saving, and Investment in Developing Countries: A Re-examination of the McKinnon–Shaw Hypotheses. *Int. Monet. Fund Staff Pap.*, March 1986, *33*(1), pp. 90–116. **[G: LDCs]**

Moore, Basil J. Inflation and Financial Deepening. *J. Devel. Econ.*, Jan.-Feb. 1986, *20*(1), pp. 125–33. **[G: S. Korea]**

Morrison, Barrie M. and Waxler, Nancy E. Three Patterns of Basic Needs Distribution with in Sri Lanka: 1971–73. *World Devel.*, January 1986, *14*(1), pp. 97–114. **[G: Sri Lanka]**

Muñoz G., Oscar. El papel de los empresarios en el desarrollo: enfoques, problemas y experiencías. (The Role of Business in Development: Approaches, Problems, and Experiences. With English summary.) *Colección Estud. CIEPLAN*, December 1986, (20), pp. 95–120. **[G: Chile]**

Murrell, Peter. A Note on Variables and Observations in Factor Analysis. *J. Devel. Econ.*, May 1986, *21*(2), pp. 319–25.

Musgrave, Richard A. Expenditure Policy for Development. In *Musgrave, R. A., Vol. 2*, 1986, *1974*, pp. 158–72. **[G: Latin America]**

Naqvi, Syed Nawab Haider. A Tale of Two Hands. *Pakistan Devel. Rev.*, Autumn 1986, *25*(3), pp. 225–45.

Nishimizu, Mieko and Robinson, Sherman. Productivity Growth in Manufacturing. In *Chenery, H.; Robinson, S. and Syrquin, M.*, 1986, pp. 283–308. **[G: Japan; S. Korea; Yugoslavia; Turkey]**

Nordhaus, William D. Resources, Technology, and Development: Will the Table Be Bare When Poor Countries Get There? *Indian Econ. Rev.*, July-Dec. 1986, *21*(2), pp. 81–94.

Nove, Alec. The Explosive Model. In *Nove, A.*, 1986, *1966*, pp. 30–38.

O'Donnell, Guillermo. On the Fruitful Convergences of Hirschman's *Exit, Voice, and Loyalty* and *Shifting Involvements:* Reflections from the Recent Argentine Experience. In *[Hirshman, A. O.]*, 1986, pp. 249–68. **[G: Argentina]**

Ocampo, José Antonio. New Developments in Trade Theory and LDCs. *J. Devel. Econ.*, June 1986, *22*(1), pp. 129–70. **[G: LDCs]**

Paauw, Douglas S. and Islam, Muhammad M. Leisure-Income Choice and the Development of a Dual Economy. *J. Econ. Devel.*, July 1986, *11*(1), pp. 7–25.

Pack, Howard and Westphal, Larry E. Industrial Strategy and Technological Change: Theory versus Reality. *J. Devel. Econ.*, June 1986, *22*(1), pp. 87–128. **[G: S. Korea]**

Panagariya, Arvind and Succar, Patricia. The Harris–Todaro Model and Economies of Scale. *Southern Econ. J.*, April 1986, *52*(4), pp. 984–98.

Papanek, Gustav F. and Kyn, Oldrich. The Effect on Income Distribution of Development, the Growth Rate and Economic Strategy. *J. Devel. Econ.*, September 1986, *23*(1), pp. 55–65.

Pasinetti, Luigi L. Prices, Incentives, and Economic Growth: Comment. In *Balassa, B. and Giersch, H., eds.*, 1986, pp. 28–31.

Patel, I. G. Employment, Growth and Basic Needs. In *Patel, I. G.*, 1986, pp. 149–55.

Patel, I. G. Social Justice and Economic Development. In *Patel, I. G.*, 1986, pp. 128–37. **[G: India]**

Patel, I. G. Some Reflections on Trade and Development. In *Patel, I. G.*, 1986, *1973*, pp. 35–47.

Paul, M. Thomas and Bhattacharyay, Biswa N. Can Money Matter in a Developing Economy? *J. Monet. Econ.*, September 1986, *18*(2), pp. 205–07. **[G: India; Pakistan]**

Perrings, Charles. Income Redistribution and Labour Surplus in the Classical Theory of Labour Migration. *Manchester Sch. Econ. Soc. Stud.*, September 1986, *54*(3), pp. 283–97.

Please, Stanley and Amoako, K. Y. OAU, ECA and the World Bank: Do They Really Disagree? In *Ravenhill, J., ed.*, 1986, pp. 127–48. **[G: Africa]**

Prebisch, Raúl. Notes on Trade from the Standpoint of the Periphery. *CEPAL Rev.*, April 1986, (28), pp. 203–14.

Prebisch, Raúl. The Dynamic Role of the Periphery. In *[Patel, S.]*, 1986, pp. 3–9. **[G: Latin America]**

Preston, Samuel H. Are the Economic Consequences of Population Growth a Sound Basis for Population Policy? In *Menken, J., ed.*, 1986, pp. 67–95.

Quibria, M. G. A Note on Foreign Investment, the Savings Function and Immiserization of National Welfare. *J. Devel. Econ.*, May 1986, *21*(2), pp. 361–72.

Rana, Pradumna B. Exports and Economic Growth: Further Evidence from Asian LDCs. *Pakistan J. Appl. Econ.*, Winter 1986, *5*(2), pp. 163–78. **[G: Asia]**

Ranis, Gustav. The Dual Economy Framework and Its Application to Asian Development Experience. In *Adelman, I. and Taylor, J. E., eds.*, 1986, pp. 199–215. **[G: India; Philippines; Taiwan]**

Rao, J. Mohan. Agriculture in Recent Development Theory. *J. Devel. Econ.*, June 1986, *22*(1), pp. 41–86.

Rao, V. K. R. V. Balance between Agriculture and Industry in Economic Development. *Indian Econ. J.*, Oct.-Dec. 1986, *34*(2), pp. 1–8. **[G: Global]**

Rattsø, Jørn. A Note on Social Articulation. *J. Devel. Econ.*, May 1986, *21*(2), pp. 347–52. **[G: LDCs]**

Rauch, James E. The Transfer of Production from Rich to Poor Countries. *J. Devel. Econ.*, September 1986, *23*(1), pp. 41–53.

Richardson, Harry W. and Townroe, Peter M. Regional Policies in Developing Countries. **In** *Nijkamp, P., ed. (I)*, 1986, pp. 647–78.

Rodrik, Dani. 'Disequilibrium' Exchange Rates as Industrialization Policy. *J. Devel. Econ.*, September 1986, *23*(1), pp. 89–106. **[G: LDCs]**

Rohrer, Wayne C. Developing Third World Farming: Conflict between Modern Imperatives and Traditional Ways. *Econ. Develop. Cult. Change*, January 1986, *34*(2), pp. 299–314. **[G: Philippines; LDCs]**

Ronen, Dov. Ethnicity, Politics, and Development: An Introduction. **In** *Thompson, D. L. and Ronen, D., eds.*, 1986, pp. 1–10.

Ruccio, David F. and Simon, Lawrence H. Methodological Aspects of a Marxian Approach to Development: An Analysis of the Modes of Production School. *World Devel.*, Special Issue, Feb. 1986, *14*(2), pp. 211–22.

Runge, Carlisle Ford. Common Property and Collective Action in Economic Development. *World Devel.*, May 1986, *14*(5), pp. 623–35. **[G: LDCs]**

Sabel, Charles F. Changing Models of Economic Efficiency and Their Implications for Industrialization in the Third World. **In** *[Hirshman, A. O.]*, 1986, pp. 27–55. **[G: Selected Countries]**

Sah, Raaj Kumar and Stiglitz, Joseph E. The Economics of Price Scissors: Reply. *Amer. Econ. Rev.*, December 1986, *76*(5), pp. 1195–99.

Salehi-Isfahani, Djavad. Oil Supply and Economic Development Strategy: A Dynamic Planning Approach. *J. Devel. Econ.*, April 1986, *21*(1), pp. 1–23. **[G: Algeria]**

Sapsford, David. A New Contribution in the Statistical Debate Over Trends in the Net Barter Terms of Trade Between Primary Commodities and Manufactures. *J. Econ. Soc. Meas.*, December 1986, *14*(4), pp. 277–88. **[G: U.K.]**

Schelling, Thomas C. Against Backsliding. **In** *[Hirshman, A. O.]*, 1986, pp. 233–38.

Schenk, Robert. Radical Analyses of Imperialism, the Third World, and the Transition to Socialism: A Survey Article: A Comment. *J. Econ. Lit.*, June 1986, *24*(2), pp. 676. **[G: Global]**

Schramm, Gunter. Regional Cooperation and Economic Development. *Ann. Reg. Sci.*, July 1986, *20*(2), pp. 1–16. **[G: Africa]**

Scott, Alison MacEwen. Women and Industrialisation: Examining the 'Female Marginalisation' Thesis. *J. Devel. Stud.*, July 1986, *22*(4), pp. 649–80. **[G: Peru; Brazil]**

Shackleton, J. R. Privatising the Third World. *Banca Naz. Lavoro Quart. Rev.*, December 1986, (159), pp. 429–39. **[G: LDCs]**

Sharif, Mohammed. The Concept and Measurement of Subsistence: A Survey of the Literature. *World Devel.*, May 1986, *14*(5), pp. 555–77.

Shaw, Timothy M. The African Crisis: Debates and Dialectics over Alternative Development Strategies for the Continent. **In** *Ravenhill, J., ed.*, 1986, pp. 108–26. **[G: Africa]**

Sheahan, John. The Elusive Balance between Stimulation and Constraint in Analysis of Development. **In** *[Hirshman, A. O.]*, 1986, pp. 169–90. **[G: Latin America]**

Simon, Lawrence H. and Ruccio, David F. A Methodological Analysis of Dependency Theory: Explanation in Andre Gunder Frank. *World Devel.*, Special Issue, Feb. 1986, *14*(2), pp. 195–209.

Singh, Manmohan. Development, Social Justice and Modernisation. *Indian Econ. J.*, Apr.-June 1986, *33*(4), pp. 5–15.

Sirageldin, Ismail. The Potential for Economic–Demographic Development: Whither Theory? *Pakistan Devel. Rev.*, Spring 1986, *25*(1), pp. 1–42. **[G: LDCs]**

Sklair, Leslie. Free Zones, Development and the New International Division of Labour: Review Article. *J. Devel. Stud.*, July 1986, *22*(4), pp. 753–59. **[G: LDCs]**

Skorov, George. Science, Society and Endogenous Development. **In** *[Patel, S.]*, 1986, pp. 253–65.

Solís, Leopoldo and Montemayor, Aurelio. A Mexican View of the Choice between Outward and Inward Orientation. **In** *Lewis, J. P. and Kallab, V., eds.*, 1986, pp. 105–13. **[G: Mexico]**

Solow, Robert M. Resources and Economic Growth. **In** *Szenberg, M., ed.*, 1986, *1978*, pp. 57–68.

Standaert, Stan. Social Articulation as a Condition for Equitable Growth: A Comment. *J. Devel. Econ.*, September 1986, *23*(1), pp. 153–59. **[G: Brazil; Mexico; LDCs]**

Stark, Oded. Migration, Markets, Clusters and Cooperation. **In** *Stark, O., ed.*, 1986, pp. xi–xiv.

Stiglitz, Joseph E. The New Development Economics. *World Devel.*, Special Issue, Feb. 1986, *14*(2), pp. 257–65.

Streeten, Paul. Basic Needs: The Lessons. **In** *Adelman, I. and Taylor, J. E., eds.*, 1986, pp. 27–37.

Streeten, Paul. Suffering from Success. **In** *[Hirshman, A. O.]*, 1986, pp. 239–46.

Swaney, James A. A Coevolutionary Model of Structural Change. *J. Econ. Issues*, June 1986, *20*(2), pp. 393–401.

Syrquin, Moshe. Productivity Growth and Factor Reallocation. **In** *Chenery, H.; Robinson, S. and Syrquin, M.*, 1986, pp. 229–62. **[G: Latin America; Europe; Asia; Canada]**

Takagi, Yasuoki. Inflation and Cumulative Debt Outstanding of Less-Developed Countries. *J.*

Int. Econ., August 1986, *21*(1/2), pp. 61–80. **[G: LDCs]**

Taylor, Lance. Trade and Growth. *Rev. Black Polit. Econ.*, Spring 1986, *14*(4), pp. 17–36. **[G: LDCs]**

Teitel, Simón and Thoumi, Francisco E. Da substituição de importações às exportações: as experiências argentina e brasileira no campo das exportaçoes de manufaturados. (With English summary.) *Pesquisa Planejamento Econ.*, April 1986, *16*(1), pp. 129–66. **[G: Argentina; Brazil]**

Thirlwall, A. P. A General Model of Growth and Development on Kaldorian Lines. *Oxford Econ. Pap.*, July 1986, *38*(2), pp. 199–219.

Todaro, Michael P. Internal Migration and Urban Employment: Comment. *Amer. Econ. Rev.*, June 1986, *76*(3), pp. 566–69. **[G: Mexico; India; Colombia; Nigeria]**

Tourinho, Octávio A. F. Endividamento externo ótimo em um modelo de equilíbrio dinâmico multissetorial: um estudo de caso para o Brasil. (With English summary.) *Pesquisa Planejamento Econ.*, December 1986, *16*(3), pp. 647–87. **[G: Brazil]**

Vogel, Ronald J. and Christianson, Jon B. The Evaluation of Economic Development Projects Where Military Conflict Is Present: Investing in Health Care in El Salvador. *J. Policy Anal. Manage.*, Winter 1986, *5*(2), pp. 292–310. **[G: El Salvador]**

Warr, Peter G. and Jayasuriya, S. K. Welfare Effects of Mechanization: Monopoly and Indivisibility. *Pakistan Devel. Rev.*, Spring 1986, *25*(1), pp. 85–90.

Weigel, Van B. The Basic Needs Approach: Overcoming the Poverty of *Homo oeconomicus*. *World Devel.*, December 1986, *14*(12), pp. 1423–34.

Weiss, John. Japan's Post-War Protection Policy: Some Implications for Less Developed Countries. *J. Devel. Stud.*, January 1986, *22*(2), pp. 385–406. **[G: Japan]**

Wheelwright, Ted. Transnational Corporations and Dependent Development in Asia and the Pacific. **In** *Wheelwright, T., ed.*, 1986, pp. 15–44. **[G: Asia]**

van Wijnbergen, Sweder J. G. Exchange Rate Management and Stabilization Policies in Developing Countries. *J. Devel. Econ.*, October 1986, *23*(2), pp. 227–47. **[G: LDCs]**

van Wijnbergen, Sweder J. G. Macroeconomic Aspects of the Effectiveness of Foreign Aid: On the Two-Gap Model, Home Goods Disequilibrium and Real Exchange Rate Misalignment. *J. Int. Econ.*, August 1986, *21*(1/2), pp. 123–36.

Wilber, Charles K. Methodological Debate in Economics: Editor's Introduction. *World Devel.*, Special Issue, Feb. 1986, *14*(2), pp. 143–45.

Wilber, Charles K. and Francis, Steven. The Methodological Basis of Hirschman's Development Economics: Pattern Model vs General Laws. *World Devel.*, Special Issue, Feb. 1986, *14*(2), pp. 181–94.

Wilford, Walton T. The Monetary Approach to Balance of Payments and Developing Nations: A Review of the Literature. **In** *Putnam, B. H. and Wilford, D. S., eds.*, 1986, pp. 81–106. **[G: LDCs]**

van der Willigen, Tessa A. Cash Crop Production and the Balance of Trade in a Less Developed Economy: A Model of Temporary Equilibrium with Rationing. *Oxford Econ. Pap.*, November 1986, *38*(3), pp. 424–42.

Wisman, Jon D. The Methodology of W. Arthur Lewis's Development Economics: Economics as Pedagogy. *World Devel.*, Special Issue, Feb. 1986, *14*(2), pp. 165–80.

Worrell, Keith. Looking Again at Economic Development: Review Article. *Soc. Econ. Stud.*, March 1986, *35*(1), pp. 215–25.

Yamaguchi, Mitoshi. Some Critical Analyses of Japanese Economic Development. *Kobe Univ. Econ.*, 1986, (32), pp. 41–68. **[G: Japan]**

Yankson, P. W. K. Small-Scale Industries in the Implementation of a Growth Centre Strategy of Regional Development: A Case-Study in Ghana. *Industry Devel.*, 1986, (17), pp. 65–89. **[G: Ghana]**

Zaidi, Iqbal M. Currency Depreciation and Non-clearing Markets in Developing Economies. *Int. Monet. Fund Staff Pap.*, June 1986, *33*(2), pp. 276–303. **[G: LDCs]**

Zaman, Asad. Microfoundations for the Basic Needs Approach to Development: The Lexicographic Utility Function. *Pakistan J. Appl. Econ.*, Summer 1986, *5*(1), pp. 1–11.

Zehender, Wolfgang. Industrialisierung und regionale Kooperation in Schwarzafrika. (Industrialization and Regional Cooperation in Sub-Saharan Africa. With English summary.) *Konjunkturpolitik*, 1986, *32*(4), pp. 218–35. **[G: Africa]**

113 Economic Planning Theory and Policy

1130 General

Brandsma, Andries S. The Implications of Risk Sensitive Decision Making for Macroeconomic Planning in the Netherlands. *De Economist*, 1986, *134*(1), pp. 61–83. **[G: Netherlands]**

Bronshtein, M. Toward a Conception of the Economic Mechanism of the AIC [Agro-Industrial Complex]. *Prob. Econ.*, December 1986, *29*(8), pp. 73–87. **[G: U.S.S.R.]**

Brus, Włodzimierz. 1966 to 1975: Normalization and Conflict. **In** *Kaser, M. C., ed.*, 1986, pp. 139–249. **[G: E. Europe]**

Buzgalin, A. Centralism in a Planned Economy: Boundaries and Methods. *Prob. Econ.*, October 1986, *29*(6), pp. 63–76. **[G: U.S.S.R.]**

Glushkov, N. Improving Pricing in the Agro–Industrial Complex (AIC). *Prob. Econ.*, August 1986, *29*(4), pp. 52–70. **[G: U.S.S.R.]**

Guillaume, Henri. Implications of the New Indicative Planning. **In** *Adams, W. J. and Stoffaës, C., eds.*, 1986, pp. 119–26. **[G: France]**

Hall, John B. Hungary's 'Third' Model. *Econ. Planning*, 1986, *20*(2), pp. 131–36. **[G: Hungary]**

113 Economic Planning Theory and Policy

Iun', O. Developing Management's Planning Mechanism. *Prob. Econ.*, November 1986, *29*(7), pp. 3–19. **[G: U.S.S.R.]**

Kadekodi, Gopal K. Derived Demand Elasticities in a Multi-sectoral Production Framework. *J. Quant. Econ.*, January 1986, *2*(1), pp. 33–41. **[G: India]**

Kletskii, V. I. What Should Be Included in the Economic Mechanism of the Twelfth Five-Year Plan? *Prob. Econ.*, January 1986, *28*(9), pp. 73–88. **[G: U.S.S.R.]**

Manevich, E. L. The Economic Mechanism and the Use of Labor Resources. *Prob. Econ.*, September 1986, *29*(5), pp. 41–56. **[G: U.S.S.R.]**

Nove, Alec. Planning and Markets. **In** *Nolan, P. and Paine, S., eds.*, 1986, pp. 72–82. **[G: U.K.]**

Nove, Alec. The Economy of the U.S.S.R. and Marxism: What Socialist Model? **In** *Nove, A.*, 1986, *1980*, pp. 63–87. **[G: U.S.S.R.]**

Nuti, Domenico Mario. Economic Planning in Market Economies: Scope, Instruments, Institutions. **In** *Nolan, P. and Paine, S., eds.*, 1986, pp. 83–98.

Nuti, Domenico Mario. Michal Kalecki's Contribution to the Theory and Practice of Socialist Planning. *Cambridge J. Econ.*, December 1986, *10*(4), pp. 333–53.

Popov, G. On Improving Centralized Economic Management. *Prob. Econ.*, February 1986, *28*(10), pp. 60–78. **[G: U.S.S.R.]**

Ruccio, David F. Planning and Class in Transitional Societies. **In** *Zarembka, P., ed.*, 1986, pp. 235–52.

Scherer, Alf. Intersectoral Efficiency between Agriculture and Industry in Six C.M.E.A. Countries: Introducing a Simple Equilibrium Model. *Econ. Planning*, 1986, *20*(1), pp. 1–27. **[G: CMEA]**

Sipos, Aladár and Tardos, Márton. Economic Control and the Structural Interdependence of Organizations in Hungary at the End of the Second Decade of Reform. *Acta Oecon.*, 1986, *37*(3–4), pp. 241–65. **[G: Hungary]**

1132 Economic Planning Theory

Amann, Ronald. The Political and Social Implications of Economic Reform in the USSR. **In** *Höhmann, H.-H.; Nove, A. and Vogel, H., eds.*, 1986, pp. 125–45. **[G: U.S.S.R.]**

Anandalingam, G. Incentive Compatibility in Mixed Economy Planning: Results of a Simple Model. *J. Econ. Dynam. Control*, June 1986, *10*(1/2), pp. 9–13.

Arrow, Kenneth J. Planning and Uncertainty. **In** *Adelman, I. and Taylor, J. E., eds.*, 1986, pp. 161–70.

Assenmacher, Marianne and Dobias, Peter. Zur Methodologie der Analyse Sozialistischer Wirtschaftssysteme. (With English summary.) **In** *Altmann, F.-L., ed.*, 1986, pp. 9–36.

Bon, Ranko. Secrecy and Publicity in the Marshallian Planned Economy. *Econ. Anal. Workers' Manage.*, 1986, *20*(4), pp. 357–74.

Brada, Josef C. and King, Arthur E. Taut Plans, Repressed Inflation and the Supply of Effort in Centrally Planned Economies. *Econ. Planning*, 1986, *20*(3), pp. 162–78. **[G: Czechoslovakia; E. Germany; Poland; Hungary]**

Bukharin, Nikolai. Notes of an Economist (the Beginning of the New Economic Year). **In** *Smith, K., ed.*, 1986, *1979*, pp. 50–77. **[G: U.S.S.R.]**

Cairncross, Alec. Planning and Decision Taking under Conditions of Uncertainty. **In** *Cairncross, A.*, 1986, pp. 78–95.

Cella, Guido. The Input–Output Measurement of Interindustry Linkages: A Reply. *Oxford Bull. Econ. Statist.*, November 1986, *48*(4), pp. 379–84.

Grebnev, L. The Application of Contractual Relationships in the Production Planning System. *Prob. Econ.*, August 1986, *29*(4), pp. 18–31. **[G: U.S.S.R.]**

Grosfeld, Irena. Endogenous Planners and the Investment Cycle in the Centrally Planned Economies. *Comp. Econ. Stud.*, Spring 1986, *28*(1), pp. 42–53. **[G: CMEA]**

Guccione, Antonio. The Input–Output Measurement of Interindustry Linkages: A Comment. *Oxford Bull. Econ. Statist.*, November 1986, *48*(4), pp. 373–77.

Heal, Geoffrey. Some Analytical Issues in Long-run Planning. **In** *Adelman, I. and Taylor, J. E., eds.*, 1986, pp. 86–102.

Hoch, Róbert. Open Economy and Domestic Consumption. *Acta Oecon.*, 1986, *37*(3–4), pp. 189–203. **[G: Hungary]**

Ickes, Barry W. On the Economics of Taut Plans. *J. Compar. Econ.*, December 1986, *10*(4), pp. 388–99.

Intriligator, Michael D. and Sheshinski, Eytan. Toward a Theory of Planning. **In** *[Arrow, K. J.], Vol. 1*, 1986, pp. 135–58.

Kachanovskii, Iu. V. Indicators and Their Functions. *Prob. Econ.*, January 1986, *28*(9), pp. 37–49. **[G: U.S.S.R.]**

Kalecki, Michal. Central Price Determination as an Essential Feature of a Socialist Economy. **In** *Kalecki, M.*, 1986, *1958*, pp. 48–53.

Kalecki, Michal. Observations on Labour Productivity. **In** *Kalecki, M.*, 1986, *1960*, pp. 54–59.

Kalecki, Michal. On the Basic Principles of Long-term Planning. **In** *Kalecki, M.*, 1986, *1963*, pp. 60–69.

Kalecki, Michal. On the Coefficient of Capital Tied Up in Construction. **In** *Kalecki, M.*, 1986, *1958*, pp. 109–17.

Kalecki, Michal. Outline of a New System of Incentives and Directives. **In** *Kalecki, M.*, 1986, *1959*, pp. 41–47.

Kalecki, Michal. Problems in the Theory of Growth of a Socialist Economy. **In** *Kalecki, M.*, 1986, *1959*, pp. 70–96.

Kalecki, Michal. The Essentials for Democratic Planning. **In** *Kalecki, M.*, 1986, *1942*, pp. 19–24.

Kalecki, Michal. The Influence of the Construction Period on the Relationship between Investment and National Income. **In** *Kalecki, M.*, 1986, *1957*, pp. 97–108.

Kalecki, Michal. The Vertically Integrated Firm as an Element in the New Economic Model. **In** *Kalecki, M.*, 1986, *1957*, pp. 38–40.

Kalecki, Michal. Workers' Councils and Central Planning. **In** *Kalecki, M.*, 1986, *1956*, pp. 25–37.

Klvačová, Eva. Scientific–Technological Progress and the System of Management of the National Economy. *Czech. Econ. Digest.*, June/July 1986, (4), pp. 71–89. **[G: Czechoslovakia]**

Lahiri, Sajal. Empty Sectors in a Multisectoral Planning Model: An Analytical Note. *Econ. Modelling*, July 1986, *3*(3), pp. 237–39.

Littlejohn, Gary. State, Plan and Market in the Transition to Socialism: The Legacy of Bukharin. **In** *Smith, K., ed.*, 1986, *1979*, pp. 78–111. **[G: U.S.S.R.]**

Liu, Pak-Wai. Moral Hazard and Incentives in a Decentralized Planning Environment. *J. Compar. Econ.*, June 1986, *10*(2), pp. 91–105.

Marsenić, Dragutin V. The Guidance System for Economic and Social Development and the Unity of the Yugoslav Market. *Eastern Europ. Econ.*, Winter 1986-87, *25*(2), pp. 75–99. **[G: Yugoslavia]**

Matlin, I. S. Macroeconomic Models in a System of Planning Models. *Matekon*, Winter 1986-87, *23*(2), pp. 74–93. **[G: U.S.S.R.]**

Montias, J. Michael. On the Centralization and Decentralization of Economic Activities. **In** *Adelman, I. and Taylor, J. E., eds.*, 1986, pp. 171–89.

Patel, I. G. The Strategy of Indian Planning. **In** *Patel, I. G.*, 1986, *1964*, pp. 119–27. **[G: India]**

Ratinova, E. S. A Game Approach to Coordinating Branch and Regional Plans. *Matekon*, Fall 1986, *23*(1), pp. 47–63.

Simai, Mihály. The Socio-economic Issues of Growth-Oriented Strategic Adjustment Programs. *Acta Oecon.*, 1986, *37*(3–4), pp. 155–67.

Smith, Keith. Economic Theory and the Closure of the Soviet Industrialisation Debate. **In** *Smith, K., ed.*, 1986, *1979*, pp. 23–49. **[G: U.S.S.R.]**

Toporowski, Jan. Selected Essays on Economic Planning: Introduction. **In** *Kalecki, M.*, 1986, pp. 1–18.

Whitaker, John K. Markets, Information and the Theory of Indicative Planning: The Case of the Individual Industry. *Rivista Int. Sci. Econ. Com.*, February 1986, *33*(2), pp. 123–38.

Winiecki, Jan. Central Planning and Export Orientation. *Eastern Europ. Econ.*, Summer 1986, *24*(4), pp. 67–89.

1136 Economic Planning Policy

Baylis, Thomas A. Explaining the GDR's Economic Strategy. **In** *Comisso, E. and Tyson, L., eds.*, 1986, pp. 205–44. **[G: E. Germany]**

Brahmananda, P. R. The Seventh Five-Year Plan. *Indian Econ. J.*, Apr.-June 1986, *33*(4), pp. 16–20. **[G: India]**

Brandsma, Andries S. Implications of Risk-Sensitive Decision-Making for the Design of Economic Policies. *J. Econ. Dynam. Control*, June 1986, *10*(1/2), pp. 301–06. **[G: Netherlands]**

Brunner, Georg. Economic Institutions as Instruments of Political Rule. **In** *Höhmann, H.-H.; Nove, A. and Vogel, H., eds.*, 1986, pp. 58–76. **[G: U.S.S.R.]**

Brus, Włodzimierz. 1953 to 1956: The 'Thaw' and the 'New Course.' **In** *Kaser, M. C., ed.*, 1986, pp. 40–69. **[G: E. Europe]**

Brus, Włodzimierz. 1957 to 1965: In Search of Balanced Development. **In** *Kaser, M. C., ed.*, 1986, pp. 70–138. **[G: E. Europe]**

Čerňa, Peter. Change in the System of Plan-Based Management of Agriculture. *Czech. Econ. Digest.*, June/July 1986, (4), pp. 31–38. **[G: Czechoslovakia]**

Chan, Thomas; Chen, E. K. Y. and Chin, Steve. China's Special Economic Zones: Ideology, Policy and Practice. **In** *Jao, Y. C. and Leung, C. K., eds.*, 1986, pp. 87–104. **[G: China]**

Chaubey, P. K. A Review of Models in Indian Plans. *Indian Econ. J.*, Apr.-June 1986, *33*(4), pp. 84–91. **[G: India]**

Chowdhury, Anisuzzaman. A More Generalized Planning Model of Bangladesh: Some Preliminary Observations. *Econ. Planning*, 1986, *20*(1), pp. 68–84. **[G: Bangladesh]**

Clark, G. Regional Planning in Developing Countries: A Consultant's Perspective. *Reg. Stud.*, October 1986, *20*(6), pp. 584–90. **[G: LDCs]**

Comisso, Ellen and Marer, Paul. The Economics and Politics of Reform in Hungary. **In** *Comisso, E. and Tyson, L., eds.*, 1986, pp. 245–78. **[G: Hungary]**

da Costa, G. C. India's Commodity Trade Balance: Retrospect and Prospect over Seventh Plan. *Indian Econ. J.*, Apr.-June 1986, *33*(4), pp. 136–48. **[G: India]**

Davies, R. W. The Ending of Mass Unemployment in the USSR. **In** *Lane, D., ed.*, 1986, pp. 19–35. **[G: U.S.S.R.]**

Deshpande, L. K. The Seventh Plan and Some Aspects of Employment. *Indian Econ. J.*, Apr.-June 1986, *33*(4), pp. 98–105. **[G: India]**

Dholakia, Ravindra H. Sources of Economic Growth in India Implied by the Seventh Five Year Plan 1985–90. *Indian Econ. J.*, Apr.-June 1986, *33*(4), pp. 161–67. **[G: India]**

Dyker, David A. Soviet Planning Reforms from Andropov to Gorbachev. **In** *Amann, R. and Cooper, J., eds.*, 1986, pp. 153–69. **[G: U.S.S.R.]**

Faluvégi, Lajos. The Seventh Five-Year Plan of the Hungarian Economy (1986–1990). *Acta Oecon.*, 1986, *36*(1–2), pp. 3–19. **[G: Hungary]**

Gerken, Egbert. From Bankruptcy to Revival: The Turkish Experience with Restructuring Economic Incentives, 1980–1984: Comment. **In** *Balassa, B. and Giersch, H., eds.*, 1986, pp. 369–72. **[G: Turkey]**

Gomulka, Stanislaw and Rostowski, Jacek. The Reformed Polish Economic System 1982–83. **In** *Gomulka, S.*, 1986, *1984*, pp. 271–98. **[G: Poland]**

Gönensay, Emre. From Bankruptcy to Revival: The Turkish Experience with Restructuring Economic Incentives, 1980–1984. **In** *Balassa, B. and Giersch, H., eds.*, 1986, pp. 348–68. **[G: Turkey]**

Hall, John B. Plan Bargaining in the Hungarian Economy: An Interview with Dr. Laszlo Antal. *Comp. Econ. Stud.*, Summer 1986, *28*(2), pp. 49–58. **[G: Hungary]**

Harrison, Mark. Lessons of Soviet Planning for Full Employment. **In** *Lane, D., ed.*, 1986, pp. 69–82. **[G: U.S.S.R.]**

Harrison, Mark. Why Did NEP Fail? **In** *Smith, K., ed.*, 1986, *1980*, pp. 8–22. **[G: U.S.S.R.]**

Helmstadter, Ernst. Evolution et efficacité des interventions économiques des collectivités territoriales: Comments. *Econ. Int.*, May-Aug.-Nov. 1986, *39*(2–3–4), pp. 151–52. **[G: France]**

Hewett, Ed. A., et al. 1986 Panel on the Soviet Economic Outlook. *Soviet Econ.*, Jan.-Mar. 1986, *2*(1), pp. 3–18. **[G: U.S.S.R.]**

Höhmann, Hans-Hermann. The Place of Economic Policy Objectives on the List of Soviet Political Priorities. **In** *Höhmann, H.-H.; Nove, A. and Vogel, H., eds.*, 1986, pp. 41–57. **[G: U.S.S.R.]**

Hough, Jerry F. Economic Reform and Soviet Foreign Policy. **In** *Höhmann, H.-H.; Nove, A. and Vogel, H., eds.*, 1986, pp. 232–51. **[G: U.S.S.R.]**

Hrivnák, Pavel. Effectiveness and Intensification. *Czech. Econ. Digest.*, June/July 1986, (4), pp. 3–11. **[G: Czechoslovakia]**

Hsu, Robert C. The Political Economy of Guidance Planning in Post-Mao China. *Weltwirtsch. Arch.*, 1986, *122*(2), pp. 382–94. **[G: China]**

Ioffe, Olimpiad S. Soviet Law and the New Economic Experiment. **In** *Ioffe, O. S. and Janis, M. W., eds.*, 1986, pp. 3–28. **[G: U.S.S.R.]**

Iyengar, N. S. and Suryanarayana, M. H. On Growth and Equity in Indian Planning during 1962–62 to 1973–74. *Indian Econ. J.*, Apr.-June 1986, *33*(4), pp. 53–83. **[G: India]**

Komárek, Vlatr. A Large-Scale Programme. *Czech. Econ. Digest.*, May 1986, (3), pp. 59–75. **[G: Czechoslovakia]**

Krasovskii, V. Current Priorities in the Investment Complex. *Prob. Econ.*, February 1986, *28*(10), pp. 26–42. **[G: U.S.S.R.]**

Kubát, Milan. At the Turn of Five-Year Plans. *Czech. Econ. Digest.*, January 1986, (1), pp. 13–21. **[G: Czechoslovakia]**

Kukushkin, G. Planning the Rational Utilization of Natural Resources. *Prob. Econ.*, January 1986, *28*(9), pp. 50–61. **[G: U.S.S.R.]**

Laxminarayan, H. Programmes for Agricultural Development in the Seventh Five-Year Plan. *Indian Econ. J.*, Apr.-June 1986, *33*(4), pp. 21–36. **[G: India]**

Linden, Ronald H. Socialist Patrimonialism and the Global Economy: The Case of Romania. **In** *Comisso, E. and Tyson, L., eds.*, 1986, pp. 171–204. **[G: Romania]**

Lyons, Thomas P. Explaining Economic Fragmentation in China: A Systems Approach. *J. Compar. Econ.*, September 1986, *10*(3), pp. 209–36. **[G: China]**

Marciniak, Stefan and Zawadzka, Zofia. Planning and Spontaneity in Economic Development. *Eastern Europ. Econ.*, Spring 1986, *24*(3), pp. 24–34. **[G: Poland]**

McNeill, D. Regional Planners—Without Power or Purpose? *Reg. Stud.*, October 1986, *20*(6), pp. 575–79. **[G: LDCs]**

Means, Gordon P. Ethnic Preference Policies in Malaysia. **In** *Nevitte, N. and Kennedy, C. H., eds.*, 1986, pp. 95–118. **[G: Malaysia]**

Milne, R. S. Ethnic Aspects of Privatization in Malaysia. **In** *Nevitte, N. and Kennedy, C. H., eds.*, 1986, pp. 119–34. **[G: Malaysia]**

Nove, Alec. The Soviet Industrial Enterprise. **In** *Nove, A.*, 1986, *1981*, pp. 169–79. **[G: U.S.S.R.]**

Nove, Alec. Trotsky, Collectivization and the Five-Year Plan. **In** *Nove, A.*, 1986, *1982*, pp. 88–103. **[G: U.S.S.R.]**

Nuti, Domenico Mario. Systemic Aspects of Employment and Investment in Soviet-Type Economies. **In** *Lane, D., ed.*, 1986, pp. 112–21. **[G: U.S.S.R.]**

O'Relley, Z. Edward. Economic Reform, the Search for Economic Efficiency, and the Expansion of the Second Economy in Hungary. **In** *Altmann, F.-L., ed.*, 1986, pp. 218–37. **[G: Hungary]**

Onoe, Hisao. Indicative Type Plan as an Instrument of Governmental Intervention in Japan. *Rivista Int. Sci. Econ. Com.*, January 1986, *33*(1), pp. 23–40. **[G: Japan]**

Oreshin, V. Problems of Method in Planning the Production Infrastructure. *Prob. Econ.*, July 1986, *29*(3), pp. 81–93. **[G: U.S.S.R.]**

Orlov, A. and Rubval'ter, D. Reforming Consumer Goods Production. *Prob. Econ.*, December 1986, *29*(8), pp. 54–72. **[G: U.S.S.R.]**

Parsons, John E. Credit Contracts in the G.D.R.: Decentralized Investment Decisions in a Planned Economy. *Econ. Planning*, 1986, *20*(1), pp. 28–51. **[G: E. Germany]**

Poznanski, Kazimierz. Economic Adjustment and Political Forces: Poland since 1970. **In** *Comisso, E. and Tyson, L., eds.*, 1986, pp. 279–312. **[G: Poland]**

Raipuria, Kalyan M. Self-reliance: Concept, Measurement and Indicators. **In** *Panchamukhi, V. R., et al.*, 1986, pp. 215–42. **[G: India]**

Rattsø, Jørn. The Macroeconomics of India's 6th Five Year Plan. *Econ. Modelling*, October 1986, *3*(4), pp. 269–82. **[G: India]**

Ravenhill, John. Collective Self-reliance or Collective Self-delusion: Is the Lagos Plan a Viable Alternative? **In** *Ravenhill, J., ed.*, 1986, pp. 85–107. **[G: Africa]**

Robinson, Warren C. and Yamazaki, Fumiko. Agriculture, Population, and Economic Planning in Ethiopia, 1953–1980. *J. Devel. Areas*, April 1986, *20*(3), pp. 327–38. **[G: Ethiopia]**

Roca, Sergio G. State Enterprises in Cuba under the New System of Planning and Management (SDPE). **In** *Mesa-Lago, C., ed.*, 1986, pp. 153–79. **[G: Cuba]**

Rothchild, Donald and Gyimah-Boadi, E. Ghana's Economic Decline and Development Strategies. **In** *Ravenhill, J., ed.*, 1986, pp. 254–85. **[G: Ghana]**

Sandesara, J. C. Industrial Production and Employment in the Seventh Plan—Two Quick Comments. *Indian Econ. J.*, Apr.-June 1986, *33*(4), pp. 92–97. **[G: India]**

Sawant, S. D. and Achuthan, C. V. Agriculture in Seventh Five Year Plan. *Indian Econ. J.*, Apr.-June 1986, *33*(4), pp. 37–52. **[G: India]**

Sicular, Terry. Agricultural Planning in China: The Case of Lee Willow Team No. 4. *Food Res. Inst. Stud.*, 1986, *20*(1), pp. 1–24. **[G: China]**

Singh, Tarlok. Some Suggestions for Reorienting Planning for the Year 2000: An Introductory Discussion Note. *Indian Econ. J.*, Apr.-June 1986, *33*(4), pp. 168–73. **[G: India]**

Sobotka, Luboš. Evaluation of the Performance of Economic Organizations by Means of the So-called Financial Contributions. *Czech. Econ. Digest.*, June/July 1986, (4), pp. 19–30.

Šourek, Stanislav. Modifications in the System of Financial Mangement of Economic Production Units and Enterprises for the 8th Five-Year Plan. *Czech. Econ. Digest.*, May 1986, (3), pp. 11–23. **[G: Czechoslovakia]**

Svendsen, Knud Erik. The Creation of Macroeconomic Imbalances and a Structural Crisis. **In** *Boesen, J., et al., eds.*, 1986, pp. 59–78. **[G: Tanzania]**

Thorner, Alice. India: Development of the Idea of Development. **In** *[Patel, S.]*, 1986, pp. 123–31. **[G: India]**

Žabić, Milan. The Self-management Agreement in Social Reproduction. *Eastern Europ. Econ.*, Winter 1986-87, *25*(2), pp. 60–74. **[G: Yugoslavia]**

114 Economics of War, Defense, and Disarmament

1140 Economics of War, Defense, and Disarmament

Aglietta, Michel. Politics, Trade and Money: Comment. **In** *Tsoukalis, L., ed.*, 1986, pp. 260–64. **[G: U.S.; EEC]**

Albright, David E. East–West Tensions in Africa. **In** *Shulman, M. D., ed.*, 1986, pp. 116–57. **[G: Africa; U.S.; U.S.S.R.]**

Alford, B. W. E. Lost Opportunities: British Business and Businessmen during the First World War. **In** *[Coleman, D. C.]*, 1986, pp. 205–27. **[G: U.K.]**

Anderton, Charles H. Optimality and the Ineffectiveness of the Strategic Defense Initiative. *Conflict Manage. Peace Sci.*, Spring 1986, *9*(2), pp. 31–43. **[G: U.S.]**

Aspin, Les. A Nation without a Defense Policy: Interview. *Challenge*, July/Aug. 1986, *29*(3), pp. 18–24. **[G: U.S.]**

Ayanian, Robert. Nuclear Consequences of the Welfare State. *Public Choice*, 1986, *49*(3), pp. 201–22. **[G: U.S.; U.S.S.R.]**

Ball, Nicole. Converting the Workforce: Defence Industry Conversion in the Industrialised Countries. *Int. Lab. Rev.*, July-Aug. 1986, *125*(4), pp. 401–22. **[G: OECD]**

Barney, L. Dwayne, Jr. Inflation and Risk in Naval Shipbuilding Contracts. *Atlantic Econ. J.*, December 1986, *14*(4), pp. 30–36.

Baumol, William J. Unpredictability, Pseudorandomness and Military–Civilian Budget Interactions. *Rivista Int. Sci. Econ. Com.*, April 1986, *33*(4), pp. 297–318.

Berglas, Eitan. Defense and the Economy. **In** *Ben-Porath, Y., ed.*, 1986, pp. 173–91. **[G: Israel]**

Bergstrom, Theodore. Soldiers of Fortune? **In** *[Arrow, K. J.], Vol. 2*, 1986, pp. 57–80.

Biswas, Basudeb and Ram, Rati. Military Expenditures and Economic Growth in Less Developed Countries: An Augmented Model and Further Evidence. *Econ. Develop. Cult. Change*, January 1986, *34*(2), pp. 361–72. **[G: LDCs]**

Black, Matthew and Fraker, Thomas. First-Term Attrition of High School Graduates in the Military. **In** *Gilroy, C. L., ed.*, 1986, pp. 261–91. **[G: U.S.]**

Boddy, Martin and Lovering, John. High Technology Industry in the Bristol Sub-Region: The Aerospace/Defence Nexus. *Reg. Stud.*, June 1986, *20*(3), pp. 217–31. **[G: U.K.]**

Boulding, Kenneth E. The Economics and the Noneconomics of the World War Industry. *Contemp. Policy Issues*, October 1986, *4*(4), pp. 12–21.

Brown, Charles. Recruiting Goals, Enlistment Supply, and Enlistments in the U.S. Army: Comment. **In** *Gilroy, C. L., ed.*, 1986, pp. 124–26. **[G: U.S.]**

Brown, Lester R. Redefining National Security. *Challenge*, July/Aug. 1986, *29*(3), pp. 25–32.

Brus, Włodzimierz. Postwar Reconstruction and Socio-economic Transformation. **In** *Kaser, M. C. and Radice, E. A., eds.*, 1986, pp. 564–641. **[G: E. Europe]**

Cocks, Edmond. Malthus on Population in a War-Based Industrial Economy. **In** *Turner, M., ed.*, 1986, pp. 222–35. **[G: France]**

Cohen, Benjamin J. Politics, Trade and Money: Comment. **In** *Tsoukalis, L., ed.*, 1986, pp. 256–59. **[G: U.S.; EEC]**

Colton, Timothy J. The Military and Economic Reform: A Comment [The Soviet Military–Industrial Complex and Economic Reform]. *Soviet Econ.*, July-Sept. 1986, *2*(3), pp. 228–32.

Cooper, Julian. The Civilian Production of the Soviet Defence Industry. **In** *Amann, R. and Cooper, J., eds.*, 1986, pp. 31–50. **[G: U.S.S.R.]**

Cooper, Julian. The Soviet Military–Industrial Complex and Economic Reform: Comments.

Soviet Econ., July-Sept. 1986, *2*(3), pp. 221–27. **[G: U.S.S.R.]**

Dale, Charles. The Changing Structure of the U.S. Economy: Its Effects on Army Enlistments. **In** *Gilroy, C. L., ed.*, 1986, pp. 149–65. **[G: U.S.]**

Daula, Thomas V. and Baldwin, Robert H. Reenlistment Decision Models: Implications for Policy Making. **In** *Gilroy, C. L., ed.*, 1986, pp. 203–21. **[G: U.S.]**

Daula, Thomas V. and Smith, D. Alton. Recruiting Goals, Enlistment Supply, and Enlistments in the U.S. Army. **In** *Gilroy, C. L., ed.*, 1986, pp. 101–23. **[G: U.S.]**

Davis, Christopher. Economic and Political Aspects of the Military-Industrial Complex in the USSR. **In** *Höhmann, H.-H.; Nove, A. and Vogel, H., eds.*, 1986, pp. 92–124. **[G: U.S.S.R.]**

Decker, Wayne R. Critical Paths: Broadening the Japanese–American Security Debate. **In** *Finn, R. B., ed.*, 1986, pp. 133–48. **[G: Japan; U.S.]**

Deger, Saadet. Economic Development and Defense Expenditure. *Econ. Develop. Cult. Change*, October 1986, *35*(1), pp. 179–96. **[G: LDCs]**

Denoon, David B. H. Conclusions: Economic Constraints and U.S. Defense Policy in the 1980s. **In** *Denoon, D. B. H., ed.*, 1986, pp. 195–221. **[G: U.S.]**

Denoon, David B. H. Constraints on Strategy: The Economics of Western Security: The Context. **In** *Denoon, D. B. H., ed.*, 1986, pp. 1–26. **[G: U.S.; W. Europe]**

Dertouzos, James N. Microeconomic Foundations of Recruiter Behavior: Implications for Aggregate Enlistment Models. **In** *Gilroy, C. L., ed.*, 1986, pp. 127–45. **[G: U.S.]**

Dinkel, Reiner. Declining Life Expectancy in a Highly Developed Nation: Paradox or Statistical Artifact? **In** *[Rapoport, A.]*, 1986, pp. 311–21. **[G: U.S.S.R.; W. Germany; Sweden]**

Dobson, Alan P. The Export White Paper, 10 September, 1941. *Econ. Hist. Rev., 2nd Ser.*, February 1986, *39*(1), pp. 59–76. **[G: U.K.]**

Doering, Zahava D. Attrition and Retention in the Army Reserve and National Guard: An Empirical Analysis: Comment. **In** *Gilroy, C. L., ed.*, 1986, pp. 198–201. **[G: U.S.]**

Domínguez, Jorge I. U.S., Soviet, and Cuban Policies toward Latin America. **In** *Shulman, M. D., ed.*, 1986, pp. 44–77. **[G: U.S.; U.S.S.R.; Latin America]**

Dumas, Lloyd J. Commanding Resources: The Military Sector and Capital Formation. **In** *Lee, D. R., ed.*, 1986, pp. 323–52. **[G: U.S.]**

Fagan, Thomas W. Comparative Costs of Alternative Forces in the U.S. Army. **In** *Gilroy, C. L., ed.*, 1986, pp. 347–60. **[G: U.S.]**

Forbes, Kevin F.; Korsun, George and McGuire, Martin C. Defense, Growth, and Allocation Behavior in the Alliance: The Southern Tier of NATO. **In** *Denoon, D. B. H., ed.*, 1986, pp. 114–51. **[G: Greece; Turkey; Spain; Portugal]**

Friedlander, Robert A. The Middle East Today: Problems and Portents. **In** *Roukis, G. S. and Montana, P. J., eds.*, 1986, pp. 1–20. **[G: U.S.; Middle East]**

Fukuyama, Francis. Military Aspects of U.S.–Soviet Competition in the Third World. **In** *Shulman, M. D., ed.*, 1986, pp. 181–211. **[G: U.S.; LDCs; U.S.S.R.]**

Galenson, Walter and Galenson, David W. Constraints on Strategy: The Economics of Western Security: Japan and South Korea. **In** *Denoon, D. B. H., ed.*, 1986, pp. 152–94. **[G: U.S.; Japan; S. Korea; W. Germany]**

Gilroy, Curtis L. Army Manpower Economics: Introduction. **In** *Gilroy, C. L., ed.*, 1986, pp. xi–xvii. **[G: U.S.]**

Goldberg, Lawrence and Greenston, Peter. Economic Analysis of Army Enlistments: Policy Implications: Reply. **In** *Gilroy, C. L., ed.*, 1986, pp. 97–99. **[G: U.S.]**

Goldberg, Lawrence and Greenston, Peter. Economic Analysis of Army Enlistments: Policy Implications. **In** *Gilroy, C. L., ed.*, 1986, pp. 61–94. **[G: U.S.]**

Goldberg, Matthew S. Microeconomic Foundations of Recruiter Behavior: Implications for Aggregate Enlistment Models: Comment. **In** *Gilroy, C. L., ed.*, 1986, pp. 146–47. **[G: U.S.]**

Goodhart, Charles. The Summer of 1914: Comment. **In** *Capie, F. and Wood, G. E., eds.*, 1986, pp. 117–19. **[G: U.K.; Europe]**

Gottheil, Fred M. Marx versus Marxists on the Role of Military Production in Capitalist Economies. *J. Post Keynesian Econ.*, Summer 1986, *8*(4), pp. 563–73.

Gottheil, Fred M. Marxism and Military Spending: A Reply. *J. Post Keynesian Econ.*, Summer 1986, *8*(4), pp. 581–84.

Grissmer, David W. and Fernandez, Judith C. Meeting Occupational and Total Manpower Requirements at Least Cost: A Nonlinear Programing Approach. **In** *Gilroy, C. L., ed.*, 1986, pp. 361–83. **[G: U.S.]**

Grissmer, David W. and Kirby, Sheila Nataraj. Attrition and Retention in the Army Reserve and National Guard: An Empirical Analysis. **In** *Gilroy, C. L., ed.*, 1986, pp. 169–97. **[G: U.S.]**

Hale, Robert. The Changing Structure of the U.S. Economy: Its Effects on Army Enlistments: Comment. **In** *Gilroy, C. L., ed.*, 1986, pp. 166–68. **[G: U.S.]**

Hartley, Keith. Defence, Industry and Technology: Problems and Possibilities for European Collaboration. **In** *Hall, G., ed.*, 1986, pp. 245–60. **[G: EEC]**

Hauner, M. Military Budgets and the Armaments Industry. **In** *Kaser, M. C. and Radice, E. A., eds.*, 1986, pp. 49–116. **[G: E. Europe; Germany]**

Hogan, Paul F. Army Reenlistment and Extension Decisions by Occupation: Comment. **In** *Gilroy, C. L., ed.*, 1986, pp. 257–60.

Holmes, Graeme. The First World War and Government Coal Control. **In** *Baber, C. and Wil-*

liams, L. J., eds., 1986, pp. 206–21. **[G: U.K.]**

Holsti, Kal J. Politics in Command: Foreign Trade as National Security Policy. *Int. Organ.*, Summer 1986, *40*(3), pp. 643–71. **[G: Japan; Finland]**

Horne, David K. and Weltin, Mary M. Motivation and Career Intentions. *J. Behav. Econ.*, Fall 1986, *15*, pp. 29–42. **[G: U.S.]**

Hosek, James R. and Peterson, Christine E. Enlistment Decisions of Young Men. **In** *Gilroy, C. L., ed.*, 1986, pp. 1–56. **[G: U.S.]**

Jackson, John L. Long-run Effects of Military Service during the Vietnam War. **In** *Hills, S. M., ed.*, 1986, pp. 113–32. **[G: U.S.]**

Joerding, Wayne. Economic Growth and Defense Spending: Granger Causality. *J. Devel. Econ.*, April 1986, *21*(1), pp. 35–40. **[G: LDCs]**

Kahan, Arcadius. A Day in the Ghetto. **In** *Kahan, A.*, 1986, pp. 170–84. **[G: Poland]**

Kaldor, Mary; Sharp, Margaret and Walker, William. Industrial Competitiveness and Britain's Defence. *Lloyds Bank Rev.*, October 1986, (162), pp. 31–49. **[G: U.K.]**

Kanet, Roger E. The Politics and Economics of Soviet Arms Exports. **In** *Höhmann, H.-H.; Nove, A. and Vogel, H., eds.*, 1986, pp. 274–301. **[G: U.S.S.R.; LDCs]**

Kieval, Gershon R. U.S. Policies in the Persian Gulf. **In** *Roukis, G. S. and Montana, P. J., eds.*, 1986, pp. 21–46. **[G: U.S.; Middle East]**

Krejči, Jeroslav. The Bohemian–Moravian War Economy. **In** *Kaser, M. C. and Radice, E. A., eds.*, 1986, pp. 452–92. **[G: Bohemia; Moravia]**

Laird, Robbin F. Soviet Arms Trade with the Noncommunist Third World. **In** *Laird, R. F. and Hoffmann, E. P., eds.*, 1986, *1984*, pp. 713–30. **[G: U.S.S.R.; LDCs]**

Lakhani, Hyder and Gilroy, Curtis L. Army Reenlistment and Extension Decisions by Occupation. **In** *Gilroy, C. L., ed.*, 1986, pp. 225–56. **[G: U.S.]**

Lambelet, Jean-Christian. The Formal ('Economic') Analysis of Arms Races: What—If Anything—Have We Learned since Richardson? *Conflict Manage. Peace Sci.*, Spring 1986, *9*(2), pp. 1–17.

Lee, Dwight R. Arms Negotiations, the Soviet Economy, and Democratically Induced Delusions. *Contemp. Policy Issues*, October 1986, *4*(4), pp. 22–37. **[G: U.S.S.R.; U.S.]**

Lehman, James and Willett, Thomas D. National Security and Industrial Policy: The Need for a Public Choice Perspective. *Contemp. Policy Issues*, January 1986, *4*(1), pp. 36–47. **[G: U.S.]**

Leontief, Wassily. The Economic Impact—Industrial and Regional—of an Arms Cut. **In** *Leontief, W.*, 1986, *1965*, pp. 204–40. **[G: U.S.]**

Leontief, Wassily and Hoffenberg, Marvin. The Economic Effects of Disarmament. **In** *Leontief, W.*, 1986, *1961*, pp. 188–203. **[G: U.S.]**

Looney, Robert E. Military Expenditures in Latin America: Patterns of Budgetary Tradeoffs. *J. Econ. Devel.*, July 1986, *11*(1), pp. 69–103. **[G: Latin America]**

Looney, Robert E. and Frederiksen, Peter C. Profiles of Current Latin American Arms Producers. *Int. Organ.*, Summer 1986, *40*(3), pp. 745–52. **[G: Latin America]**

Maizels, Alfred and Nissanke, Machiko K. The Determinants of Military Expenditures in Developing Countries. *World Devel.*, September 1986, *14*(9), pp. 1125–40. **[G: LDCs]**

Malpas, Robert. Harnessing Technology for Growth. **In** *Landau, R. and Rosenberg, N., eds.*, 1986, pp. 105–13. **[G: OECD]**

Mangum, Stephen L. and Ball, David. Skill Transfer and Military Occupational Training. **In** *Hills, S. M., ed.*, 1986, pp. 133–47. **[G: U.S.]**

Maynes, Charles William. Lost Opportunities. *Foreign Aff.*, 1986, *64*(3), pp. 413–34. **[G: U.S.]**

Morrow, James D. A Spatial Model of International Conflict. *Amer. Polit. Sci. Rev.*, December 1986, *80*(4), pp. 1131–50.

Murdoch, James C. and Sandler, Todd. The Political Economy of Scandinavian Neutrality. *Scand. J. Econ.*, 1986, *88*(4), pp. 583–603. **[G: Sweden; Finland; Switzerland]**

Nadiri, M. Ishaq. Increase in Defense Expenditure and Its Impact on the U.S. Economy. **In** *Denoon, D. B. H., ed.*, 1986, pp. 27–58. **[G: U.S.]**

Nalebuff, Barry J. Brinkmanship and Nuclear Deterrence: The Neutrality of Escalation. *Conflict Manage. Peace Sci.*, Spring 1986, *9*(2), pp. 19–30. **[G: U.S.]**

Nash, June. Deunionization: Economic Dislocation in an American Community. **In** *Gondolf, E. W.; Marcus, I. M. and Dougherty, J. P., eds.*, 1986, pp. 132–41. **[G: U.S.]**

Nelson, Gary R. Compensation and Force Structure: A Comment. **In** *Gilroy, C. L., ed.*, 1986, pp. 385–91. **[G: U.S.]**

Ostrom, Charles W., Jr. and Marra, Robin F. U.S. Defense Spending and the Soviet Estimate. *Amer. Polit. Sci. Rev.*, September 1986, *80*(3), pp. 819–42. **[G: U.S.; U.S.S.R.]**

Pownall, Grace. An Empirical Analysis of the Regulation of the Defense Contracting Industry: The Cost Accounting Standards Board. *J. Acc. Res.*, Autumn 1986, *24*(2), pp. 291–315. **[G: U.S.]**

Pugliaresi, Lucian. The Iran–Iraq War: A Way Out. **In** *Preeg, E. H. and Bendahmane, D. B., eds.*, 1986, pp. 32–34. **[G: U.S.; Middle East]**

Quandt, William B. U.S.–Soviet Rivalry in the Middle East. **In** *Shulman, M. D., ed.*, 1986, pp. 18–43. **[G: Middle East; U.S.; U.S.S.R.]**

Radice, E. A. Agriculture and Food. **In** *Kaser, M. C. and Radice, E. A., eds.*, 1986, pp. 366–97. **[G: E. Europe; Germany]**

Radice, E. A. Changes in Property Relationships and Financial Arrangements. **In** *Kaser, M. C. and Radice, E. A., eds.*, 1986, pp. 329–65. **[G: Germany; E. Europe]**

Radice, E. A. Energy and Materials. **In** *Kaser,*

M. C. and Radice, E. A., eds., 1986, pp. 398–415. **[G: E. Europe; Germany]**

Radice, E. A. The Collapse of German Hegemony and Its Economic Consequences. **In** *Kaser, M. C. and Radice, E. A., eds.*, 1986, pp. 495–519. **[G: Germany; E. Europe]**

Radice, E. A. The Development of Industry. **In** *Kaser, M. C. and Radice, E. A., eds.*, 1986, pp. 416–51. **[G: E. Europe; Germany]**

Riddell, Tom. Marxism and Military Spending. *J. Post Keynesian Econ.*, Summer 1986, *8*(4), pp. 574–80.

Rizzo, Robert. Nuclear Warfare: The Psychological Effects and Their Impact on Moral Reasoning. *Int. J. Soc. Econ.*, 1986, *13*(1/2), pp. 40–54.

Rob, Rafael. The Design of Procurement Contracts. *Amer. Econ. Rev.*, June 1986, *76*(3), pp. 378–89.

Robinson, Austin. The Economic Problems of the Transition from War to Peace: 1945–49. *Cambridge J. Econ.*, June 1986, *10*(2), pp. 165–85. **[G: U.K.]**

Rohrlich, George F. The Dual Nature of the Nuclear Arms Quandary. *Int. J. Soc. Econ.*, 1986, *13*(1/2), pp. 55–61.

Root, William A. U.S. Policy on East–West Technology Trade: Past, Present, and Future. **In** *McIntyre, J. R. and Papp, D. S., eds.*, 1986, pp. 207–20. **[G: U.S.]**

Rostker, Bernard. Economic Analysis of Army Enlistments: Policy Implications: Comment. **In** *Gilroy, C. L., ed.*, 1986, pp. 95–96. **[G: U.S.]**

Royer, Jacques. The Long-term Employment Impact of Disarmament Policies: Some Findings from an Econometric Model. *Int. Lab. Rev.*, May-June 1986, *125*(3), pp. 279–303. **[G: Global]**

Ryan, James E. Defense Procurement and the Reindustrialization of New York State. **In** *Schoolman, M. and Magid, A., eds.*, 1986, pp. 315–29. **[G: U.S.]**

Sandler, Todd and Murdoch, James C. Defense Burdens and Prospects for the Northern European Allies. **In** *Denoon, D. B. H., ed.*, 1986, pp. 59–113. **[G: W. Europe]**

Saxonhouse, Gary R. The National Security Clause of the Trade Expansion Act of 1962: Import Competition and the Machine Tool Industry. **In** *Saxonhouse, G. R. and Yamamura, K., eds.*, 1986, pp. 218–37. **[G: U.S.]**

Schelling, Thomas C. What Went Wrong with Arms Control? *Foreign Aff.*, Winter 1985/86, *64*(2), pp. 219–33. **[G: U.S.; U.S.S.R.]**

Schmidt, Christian. Esquisse d'un modèle de dynamique des dépenses militaires franç aises construit en forme de je de Nash. With English summary.) *Revue Écon. Polit.*, Jan.-Feb. 1986, *96*(1), pp. 1–12. **[G: France]**

Schubert, Walt. Defence Policy: Objectives, Weapons and Ethics. *Int. J. Soc. Econ.*, 1986, *13*(1/2), pp. 62–67.

Schwartz, Saul. The Relative Earnings of Vietnam and Korean-Era Veterans. *Ind. Lab. Relat. Rev.*, July 1986, *39*(4), pp. 564–72. **[G: U.S.]**

Seabourne, Teresa. The Summer of 1914. **In** *Capie, F. and Wood, G. E., eds.*, 1986, pp. 77–116. **[G: U.K.; Europe]**

Shulman, Marshall D. East–West Tensions in the Third World: Overview. **In** *Shulman, M. D., ed.*, 1986, pp. 5–17. **[G: Global]**

Story, Jonathan. Politics, Trade and Money: Comment. **In** *Tsoukalis, L., ed.*, 1986, pp. 265–69. **[G: U.S.; EEC]**

Strange, Susan. Politics, Trade and Money. **In** *Tsoukalis, L., ed.*, 1986, pp. 243–55. **[G: U.S.; EEC]**

Stromsdorfer, Ernst W. Enlistment Decisions of Young Men: Comment. **In** *Gilroy, C. L., ed.*, 1986, pp. 57–60. **[G: U.S.]**

Thomas, D. A. War and the Economy: The South Wales Experience. **In** *Baber, C. and Williams, L. J., eds.*, 1986, pp. 251–77. **[G: U.K.]**

Utgoff, Kathleen P. First-Term Attrition of High School Graduates in the Military: Comment. **In** *Gilroy, C. L., ed.*, 1986, pp. 292–93. **[G: U.S.]**

Warner, John T. Reenlistment Decision Models: Implications for Policy Making: Comment. **In** *Gilroy, C. L., ed.*, 1986, pp. 222–24. **[G: U.S.]**

Weickhardt, George G. The Soviet Military–Industrial Complex and Economic Reform. *Soviet Econ.*, July-Sept. 1986, *2*(3), pp. 193–220. **[G: U.S.S.R.]**

Weida, William J. and Gertcher, Franklin L. Military Weapon Systems Expenditures and Risk: Theory and Evidence. *Int. J. Soc. Econ.*, 1986, *13*(10), pp. 3–16.

Weida, William J. and Gertcher, Franklin L. The Ethics and Economics of Foreign Sales of U.S.-Made Military Weapons. *Int. J. Soc. Econ.*, 1986, *13*(1/2), pp. 20–39. **[G: U.S.]**

Whatley, Edwin. Realism in "Burden-Sharing": American Interests and Japanese Military Policy. **In** *Finn, R. B., ed.*, 1986, pp. 117–31. **[G: U.S.; Japan]**

Worcester, Dean A., Jr. Economics, Ethics, and the Problem of Building Peace. *Contemp. Policy Issues*, October 1986, *4*(4), pp. 38–51.

Zagoria, Donald S. The Soviet–American Rivalry in Asia. **In** *Shulman, M. D., ed.*, 1986, pp. 78–115. **[G: Asia; U.S.; U.S.S.R.]**

Zycher, Benjamin. Soviet Incentives in Arms Control. *Contemp. Policy Issues*, October 1986, *4*(4), pp. 52–59. **[G: U.S.S.R.]**

120 Country Studies

121 Economic Studies of Developing Countries

1210 General

Adelman, Irma. Education and Economic Development: A Comparative Perspective. **In** *Adelman, I. and Taylor, J. E., eds.*, 1986, pp. 296–318. **[G: LDCs; China]**

Balassa, Bela. Policy Responses to Exogenous Shocks in Developing Countries. *Amer. Econ. Rev.*, May 1986, *76*(2), pp. 75–78. **[G: LDCs]**

Biswas, Basudeb and Ram, Rati. Military Expenditures and Economic Growth in Less Developed Countries: An Augmented Model and Further Evidence. *Econ. Develop. Cult. Change,* January 1986, *34*(2), pp. 361–72. **[G: LDCs]**

Chhibber, Ajay and Wilton, John. Macroeconomic Policies and Agricultural Performance in Developing Countries. *Finance Develop.*, September 1986, *23*(3), pp. 6–9. **[G: LDCs]**

Deger, Saadet. Economic Development and Defense Expenditure. *Econ. Develop. Cult. Change,* October 1986, *35*(1), pp. 179–96. **[G: LDCs]**

Duncan, Alex. Aid Effectiveness in Raising Adaptive Capacity in the Low-income Countries. **In** *Lewis, J. P. and Kallab, V., eds.*, 1986, pp. 129–52. **[G: Selected LDCs]**

Fischer, Bernhard and Langhammer, Rolf J. Determinanten der Sparkapitalbildung in Entwicklungsländern. (Determinants of Savings Mobilization in Developing Countries. With English summary.) *Konjunkturpolitik,* 1986, *32*(5), pp. 282–307. **[G: LDCs]**

Fischer, Stanley. Issues in Medium-term Macroeconomic Adjustment. *World Bank Res. Observer,* July 1986, *1*(2), pp. 163–82. **[G: LDCs]**

Forte, Francesco. Ten Paradoxes Facing African Countries. *Atlantic Econ. J.*, March 1986, *14*(1), pp. 1–7. **[G: LDCs; Africa]**

Hagen, Everett E. More on the Employment Effects of Innovation: A Correction. *J. Devel. Econ.*, November 1986, *24*(1), pp. 201.

Helleiner, Gerald K. Balance-of-Payments Experience and Growth Prospects of Developing Countries: A Synthesis. *World Devel.*, Special Issue, August 1986, *14*(8), pp. 877–908. **[G: LDCs]**

Kapur, Basant K. Alternative Stabilization Policies for Less-developed Economies. **In** *Kapur, B. K.*, 1986, *1976*, pp. 49–68.

Kapur, Basant K. Problems of Indexation in Financially Liberalized Less-developed Economies. **In** *Kapur, B. K.*, 1986, *1982*, pp. 123–41.

Karunaratne, Neil Dias. A Holistic Analysis of Trade versus Aid Issues: World and Australian Insights. *Devel. Econ.*, March 1986, *24*(1), pp. 44–55. **[G: Global; Australia]**

Kohli, Atul. Democracy and Development. **In** *Lewis, J. P. and Kallab, V., eds.*, 1986, pp. 153–82. **[G: Selected LDCs]**

Krueger, Anne O. Developing Countries' Debt Problems and Growth Prospects. *Atlantic Econ. J.*, March 1986, *14*(1), pp. 8–19. **[G: LDCs]**

Landau, Daniel. Government and Economic Growth in the Less Developed Countries: An Empirical Study for 1960–1980. *Econ. Develop. Cult. Change,* October 1986, *35*(1), pp. 35–75. **[G: LDCs]**

Lele, Uma. Women and Structural Transformation. *Econ. Develop. Cult. Change,* January 1986, *34*(2), pp. 195–221. **[G: LDCs]**

Leontief, Wassily. The Structure of Development. **In** *Leontief, W.*, 1986, *1963*, pp. 162–87. **[G: Israel; U.S.; Peru; Egypt]**

Rodrique, André. La contribution de l'amélioration du bien-être au processus de croissance dans les pays en développement. (The Contribution of Welfare to Economic Growth. With English summary.) *L'Actual. Econ.*, March 1986, *62*(1), pp. 64–87. **[G: LDCs]**

Selowsky, Marcelo and van der Tak, Herman G. The Debt Problem and Growth. *World Devel.*, September 1986, *14*(9), pp. 1107–24. **[G: LDCs]**

Shackleton, J. R. Privatising the Third World. *Banca Naz. Lavoro Quart. Rev.*, December 1986, (159), pp. 429–39. **[G: LDCs]**

Singh, Manmohan. Development, Social Justice and Modernisation. *Indian Econ. J.*, Apr.-June 1986, *33*(4), pp. 5–15.

Singh, Manmohan. Sustaining Development in an Uncertain International Environment. *Indian Econ. J.*, Jan.-Mar. 1986, *33*(3), pp. 1–14. **[G: LDCs]**

Wong, Chung Ming. Models of Export Instability and Empirical Tests for Less-Developed Countries. *J. Devel. Econ.*, March 1986, *20*(2), pp. 263–85. **[G: LDCs]**

1211 Comparative Country Studies

Balassa, Bela. Adjustment Policies in Socialist and Private Market Economies. *J. Compar. Econ.*, June 1986, *10*(2), pp. 138–59. **[G: LDCs; Hungary; Yugoslavia]**

Edwards, Sebastian. Adjustment to Windfall Gains: A Comparative Analysis of Oil-Exporting Countries: Comment. **In** *Neary, J. P. and van Wijnbergen, S., eds.*, 1986, pp. 93–95. **[G: OPEC]**

Fry, Maxwell J. National Saving, Financial Saving and Interest Rate Policy in Asian Developing Economies. **In** *U.N., Dept. of International Econ. and Social Affairs,* 1986, pp. 29–46. **[G: Asia] [G: Selected Countries]**

Gelb, Alan. Adjustment to Windfall Gains: A Comparative Analysis of Oil-Exporting Countries. **In** *Neary, J. P. and van Wijnbergen, S., eds.*, 1986, pp. 54–93. **[G: OPEC]**

Gelb, Alan. The Oil Syndrome: Adjustment to Windfall Gains in Oil-Exporting Countries. **In** *Lal, D. and Wolf, M., eds.*, 1986, pp. 115–30.

Hartlyn, Jonathan and Morley, Samuel A. Bureaucratic-Authoritarian Regimes in Comparative Perspective. **In** *Hartlyn, J. and Morley, S. A., eds.*, 1986, pp. 38–53. **[G: Latin America]**

Helleiner, Gerald K. Outward Orientation, Import Instability and African Economic Growth: An Empirical Investigation. **In** *[Streeten, P.],* 1986, pp. 139–53. **[G: Africa; LDCs]**

Islam, Iyanatul and Khan, Habibullah. Income Inequality, Poverty and Socioeconomic Development in Bangladesh: An Empirical Investigation. *Bangladesh Devel. Stud.*, June 1986, *14*(2), pp. 75–92. **[G: Bangladesh]**

Love, James. Commodity Concentration and Export Earnings Instability: A Shift from Cross-section to Time Series Analysis. *J. Devel. Econ.*, December 1986, *24*(2), pp. 239–48. **[G: LDCs]**

Maizels, Alfred and Nissanke, Machiko K. The Determinants of Military Expenditures in Developing Countries. *World Devel.*, September 1986, *14*(9), pp. 1125–40. **[G: LDCs]**

Rittenberg, Libby. Export Growth Performance of Less-Developed Countries. *J. Devel. Econ.*, November 1986, *24*(1), pp. 167–77. **[G: LDCs]**

Srinivasan, T. N. The Costs and Benefits of Being a Small, Remote, Island, Landlocked, or Ministate Economy. *World Bank Res. Observer*, July 1986, *1*(2), pp. 205–18.

1213 European Countries

Bajt, Aleksander. Economic Growth and Factor Substitution: What Happened to the Yugoslav Miracle? Some Comments. *Econ. J.*, December 1986, *96*(384), pp. 1084–88. **[G: Yugoslavia]**

Celasun, Merih. Income Distribution and Domestic Terms of Trade in Turkey, 1978–1983: Estimated Measures of Inequality and Poverty. *METU*, 1986, *13*(1/2), pp. 193–216. **[G: Turkey]**

Chenery, Hollis B. and Syrquin, Moshe. The Semi-industrial Countries. **In** *Chenery, H.; Robinson, S. and Syrquin, M.*, 1986, pp. 84–118. **[G: LDCs]**

Conway, Patrick. Decomposing the Determinants of Trade Deficits: Turkey in the 1970s. *J. Devel. Econ.*, May 1986, *21*(2), pp. 235–58. **[G: Turkey]**

Dauderstädt, Michael. Internationale Konkurrenz und Wohlfahrtsstaat. Überlegungen am Beispiel Portugal. (International Competition and the Welfare State—The Case of Portugal. With English summary.) *Konjunkturpolitik*, 1986, *32*(6), pp. 349–80. **[G: Portugal]**

Diamandouros, P. Nikiforos. The Southern European NICs. *Int. Organ.*, Spring 1986, *40*(2), pp. 546–56. **[G: Greece; Portugal; Spain]**

Elliott, John E. and Scott, Joanna V. Marx, Yugoslavia, and Self-governing Socialism: A Social and Political Economy Approach. **In** *Zarembka, P., ed.*, 1986, pp. 157–217. **[G: Yugoslavia]**

Feder, Gershon. Growth in Semi-industrial Countries: A Statistical Analysis. **In** *Chenery, H.; Robinson, S. and Syrquin, M.*, 1986, pp. 263–82. **[G: LDCs]**

Kubo, Yuji; de Melo, Jaime and Robinson, Sherman. Trade Strategies and Growth Episodes. **In** *Chenery, H.; Robinson, S. and Syrquin, M.*, 1986, pp. 148–87. **[G: LDCs]**

Kubo, Yuji; Robinson, Sherman and Syrquin, Moshe. The Methodology of Multisector Comparative Analysis. **In** *Chenery, H.; Robinson, S. and Syrquin, M.*, 1986, pp. 121–47. **[G: Mexico; Turkey; Japan; S. Korea]**

Kubo, Yuji, et al. Interdependence and Industrial Structure. **In** *Chenery, H.; Robinson, S. and Syrquin, M.*, 1986, pp. 188–225. **[G: LDCs]**

Lianos, Theodore P. Political Stability and Economic Development: The Case of Greece, 1948–1966. *J. Europ. Econ. Hist.*, Winter 1986, *15*(3), pp. 617–19. **[G: Greece]**

Mencinger, Jože. The Yugoslav Economic Systems and Their Efficiency. *Econ. Anal. Workers' Manage.*, 1986, *20*(1), pp. 31–43. **[G: Yugoslavia]**

Norton, Roger D.; Scandizzo, Pasquale L. and Zimmerman, Linda W. Portugal's Entry into the EEC: Aggregate and Distributional Effects Determined by Means of a General Equilibrium Model. *J. Policy Modeling*, Summer 1986, *8*(2), pp. 149–80. **[G: Portugal]**

Öniş, Ziya. Stabilisation and Growth in a Semi-industrial Economy: An Evaluation of the Recent Turkish Experiment, 1977–1984. *METU*, 1986, *13*(1/2), pp. 7–28. **[G: Turkey]**

Petitbó, Amadeu. Notas sobre desindustrializacion y crisis en la economia española. (Note on the De-industrialization and the Crisis in the Spanish Economy. With English summary.) *Écon. Soc.*, May 1986, *20*(5), pp. 69–99. **[G: Spain]**

Sapir, André. Economic Growth and Factor Substitution: What Happened to the Yugoslav Miracle? Further Comments. *Econ. J.*, December 1986, *96*(384), pp. 1089–90. **[G: Yugoslavia]**

Vacić, Aleksandar M. Why the Development of Yugoslavia Deviated from the Socialist Self-management Market Economy. *Eastern Europ. Econ.*, Winter 1986-87, *25*(2), pp. 3–21. **[G: Yugoslavia]**

Woodward, Susan L. Orthodoxy and Solidarity: Competing Claims and International Adjustment in Yugoslavia. *Int. Organ.*, Spring 1986, *40*(2), pp. 505–45. **[G: Yugoslavia]**

Woodward, Susan L. Orthodoxy and Solidarity: Competing Claims and International Adjustment in Yugoslavia. **In** *Comisso, E. and Tyson, L., eds.*, 1986, pp. 329–69. **[G: Yugoslavia]**

1214 Asian Countries

Adelman, Irma. Beyond Export-Led Growth. **In** *Adelman, I. and Taylor, J. E., eds.*, 1986, *1984*, pp. 242–62. **[G: S. Korea]**

Adhikari, Ramesh. Efficiency and Social Analysis of Projects in the Nepalese Economy. *Industry Devel.*, 1986, (17), pp. 91–109. **[G: Nepal]**

Ahluwalia, Montek Singh. Balance-of-Payments Adjustment in India, 1970–71 to 1983–84. *World Devel.*, Special Issue, August 1986, *14*(8), pp. 937–62. **[G: India]**

Ahmad, Shamsuddin. Domestic Saving and Foreign Capital Inflow: The Case of Bangladesh. *Bangladesh Devel. Stud.*, March 1986, *14*(1), pp. 75–91. **[G: Bangladesh]**

Ahmad, Shamsuddin. The Growth Pattern of Bangladesh: 1959–60 to 1979–80. *Pakistan J. Appl. Econ.*, Winter 1986, *5*(2), pp. 179–206. **[G: Bangladesh]**

Alauddin, Mohammad. Erratum [Identification of Key Sectors in the Bangladesh Economy: A Linkage Analysis Approach]. *Appl. Econ.*, October 1986, *18*(10), pp. 1148. **[G: Bangladesh]**

Alauddin, Mohammad. Identification of Key Sectors in the Bangladesh Economy: A Linkage Analysis Approach. *Appl. Econ.*, April 1986, *18*(4), pp. 421–42. **[G: Bangladesh]**

Ben-Porath, Yoram. The Israeli Economy: Maturing through Crises: Introduction. **In** *Ben-Porath, Y., ed.*, 1986, pp. 1–23. **[G: Israel]**

Bhalla, Surjit S. and Glewwe, Paul. Growth and Equity in Developing Countries: A Reinterpretation of the Sri Lankan Experience. *World Bank Econ. Rev.*, September 1986, *1*(1), pp. 35–63. **[G: Sri Lanka; LDCs]**

Blitzer, Charles R. and Eckaus, Richard S. Modeling Energy–Economy Interactions in Small Developing Countries: A Case Study of Sri Lanka. *J. Policy Modeling*, Winter 1986, *8*(4), pp. 471–501. **[G: Sri Lanka]**

Booth, Anne. Survey of Recent Developments. *Bull. Indonesian Econ. Stud.*, December 1986, *22*(3), pp. 1–26. **[G: Indonesia]**

Bradford, Colin I., Jr. East Asian "Models": Myths and Lessons. **In** *Lewis, J. P. and Kallab, V., eds.*, 1986, pp. 115–28. **[G: Hong Kong; S. Korea; Taiwan; Singapore]**

Chenery, Hollis B., et al. Alternative Routes to Development. **In** *Chenery, H.; Robinson, S. and Syrquin, M.*, 1986, pp. 311–47. **[G: S. Korea]**

Engelbrecht, Hans-Jürgen. From Newly Industrialising to Newly Informatising Country: The Primary Information Sector of the Republic of Korea 1975–1980. *Info. Econ. Policy*, September 1986, *2*(3), pp. 169–94. **[G: S. Korea]**

Fischer, Stanley. Israeli Inflation and Indexation. **In** *Fischer, S.*, 1986, *1985*, pp. 453–85. **[G: Israel]**

Fry, Maxwell J. Terms-of-Trade Dynamics in Asia: An Analysis of National Saving and Domestic Investment Responses to Terms-of-Trade Changes in 14 Asian LDCs. *J. Int. Money Finance*, March 1986, *5*(1), pp. 57–73. **[G: Asia]**

Gerken, Egbert. From Bankruptcy to Revival: The Turkish Experience with Restructuring Economic Incentives, 1980–1984: Comment. **In** *Balassa, B. and Giersch, H., eds.*, 1986, pp. 369–72. **[G: Turkey]**

Glassburner, Bruce. Survey of Recent Developments. *Bull. Indonesian Econ. Stud.*, April 1986, *22*(1), pp. 1–33. **[G: Indonesia]**

Gönensay, Emre. From Bankruptcy to Revival: The Turkish Experience with Restructuring Economic Incentives, 1980–1984. **In** *Balassa, B. and Giersch, H., eds.*, 1986, pp. 348–68. **[G: Turkey]**

Gunatilleke, Godfrey. The Cultural Dimension in Asian Development. **In** *[Patel, S.]*, 1986, pp. 195–212. **[G: Asia]**

Gupta, Kanhaya L. Financial Development and Economic Growth in India and South Korea. *J. Econ. Devel.*, December 1986, *11*(2), pp. 41–62. **[G: India; S. Korea]**

Hamilton, Clive. A General Equilibrium Model of Structural Change and Economic Growth, with Application to South Korea. *J. Devel. Econ.*, September 1986, *23*(1), pp. 67–88. **[G: S. Korea]**

Heng, Toh Mun. Income Redistribution and Trade Policy Effects on Macroeconomic Aggregates: A Simulation Study of the Singapore Economy Based on an Extended Input–Output Model. *J. Econ. Devel.*, July 1986, *11*(1), pp. 157–90. **[G: Singapore]**

Iqbal, Badar A. Trade and Development in Asia: Regional and Inter-regional Disparities. *J. World Trade Law*, Mar.:Apr. 1986, *20*(2), pp. 236–41. **[G: Asia]**

Islam, Iyanatul and Kirkpatrick, Colin. Export-Led Development, Labour-Market Conditions and the Distribution of Income: The Case of Singapore. *Cambridge J. Econ.*, June 1986, *10*(2), pp. 113–27. **[G: Singapore]**

Johnson, Chalmers. The Nonsocialist NICs: East Asia. *Int. Organ.*, Spring 1986, *40*(2), pp. 557–65. **[G: Asia]**

Kim, W. Chan and Tschoegl, Adrian E. The Regional Balance of Industrialization: An Empirical Investigation of the Asian Pacific Area. *J. Devel. Areas*, January 1986, *20*(2), pp. 173–83. **[G: Asia; LDCs]**

Kirkpatrick, Colin. Singapore at the Crossroads: The Economic Challenges Ahead. *Nat. Westminster Bank Quart. Rev.*, May 1986, pp. 43–51. **[G: Singapore]**

Klein, Lawrence R. Models of Development: A Comparative Study of Economic Growth in South Korea and Taiwan: Foreword. **In** *Lau, L. J., ed.*, 1986, pp. xi–xv. **[G: Taiwan; S. Korea]**

Klinov, Ruth. Changes in the Industrial Structure. **In** *Ben-Porath, Y., ed.*, 1986, pp. 119–36. **[G: Israel]**

Kubo, Yuji, et al. General Equilibrium Models for the Analysis of Alternative Foreign Trade Strategies: An Application to Korea. **In** *Adelman, I. and Taylor, J. E., eds.*, 1986, pp. 124–60. **[G: S. Korea]**

Kwack, Sung Yeung. The Economic Development of the Republic of Korea, 1965–1981. **In** *Lau, L. J., ed.*, 1986, pp. 65–133. **[G: S. Korea]**

Lal, Deepak. Stolper–Samuleson–Rybczynski in the Pacific: Real Wages and Real Exchange Rates in the Philippines, 1956–1978. *J. Devel. Econ.*, April 1986, *21*(1), pp. 181–204. **[G: Philippines]**

Lau, Lawrence J. Models of Development: A Comparative Study of Economic Growth in South Korea and Taiwan: Introduction. **In** *Lau, L. J., ed.*, 1986, pp. 1–11. **[G: S. Korea; Taiwan]**

Lim, Teck Ghee. Nationalism and Development in Asia. **In** *Wheelwright, T., ed.*, 1986, pp. 45–66. **[G: Asia]**

Manasan, Rosario G. and Buenaventura, Corazon R. A Macroeconomic Overview of Public Enterprise in the Philippines, 1975–84. *Philippine Econ. J.*, 1986, *25*(1–2), pp. 24–50. **[G: Philippines]**

McGee, T. G. and Yeung, Y. M. Participatory Urban Services in Asia. **In** *Yeung, Y. M. and*

McGee, T. G., eds., 1986, pp. 9–27. [G: Asia]

Metzer, Jacob. The Slowdown of Economic Growth: A Passing Phase or the End of the Big Spurt? **In** *Ben-Porath, Y., ed.*, 1986, pp. 75–100. [G: Israel]

Muir, Ross. Survey of Recent Developments. *Bull. Indonesian Econ. Stud.*, August 1986, *22*(2), pp. 1–27. [G: Indonesia]

Myers, Ramon H. The Economic Development of the Republic of China on Taiwan, 1965–1981. **In** *Lau, L. J., ed.*, 1986, pp. 13–64. [G: Taiwan]

Oshima, Harry T. East Asia's High Growth. *Singapore Econ. Rev.*, October 1986, *31*(2), pp. 1–22. [G: Asia]

Oshima, Harry T. The Construction Boom of the 1970s: The End of High Growth in the NICs and ASEAN? *Devel. Econ.*, September 1986, *24*(3), pp. 207–28. [G: LDCs; Asia]

Oshima, Harry T. The Transition from an Agricultural to an Industrial Economy in East Asia. *Econ. Develop. Cult. Change*, July 1986, *34*(4), pp.783–809. [G: Japan;Taiwan; S. Korea]

Pack, Howard and Westphal, Larry E. Industrial Strategy and Technological Change: Theory versus Reality. *J. Devel. Econ.*, June 1986, *22*(1), pp. 87–128. [G: S. Korea]

Park, Yung Chul. Foreign Debt, Balance of Payments, and Growth Prospects: The Case of the Republic of Korea, 1965–88. *World Devel.*, Special Issue, August 1986, *14*(8), pp. 1019–58. [G: S. Korea]

Prakash, Shri. The Nineteen Thirties Depression and the Indian Agrarian Economy before and after 1947. **In** *Berend, I. T. and Borchardt, K., eds.*, 1986, pp. 275–303. [G: India]

Purvis, Douglas D. Indonesia's Other Dutch Disease: Economic Effects of the Petroleum Boom: Comment. **In** *Neary, J. P. and van Wijnbergen, S., eds.*, 1986, pp. 321–23. [G: Indonesia]

Raipuria, Kalyan M. Self-reliance: Concept, Measurement and Indicators. **In** *Panchamukhi, V. R., et al.*, 1986, pp. 215–42. [G: India]

Ranis, Gustav. The Dual Economy Framework and Its Application to Asian Development Experience. **In** *Adelman, I. and Taylor, J. E., eds.*, 1986, pp. 199–215. [G: India; Philippines; Taiwan]

Remolona, Eli M.; Mangahas, Mahar and Pante, Filologo, Jr. Foreign Debt, Balance of Payments, and the Economic Crisis of the Philippines in 1983–84. *World Devel.*, Special Issue, August 1986, *14*(8), pp. 993–1018. [G: Philippines]

Roberts, John. The Effect of the Oil Price Collapse on the Gulf Cooperation Council Economies. *J. Energy Devel.*, Autumn 1986, *12*(1), pp. 103–14. [G: Middle East]

Saxena, Pradeep Kumar. Inter-relationship between Socio-economic Development and Economic Structure: Indian Experience. *Margin*, July 1986, *18*(4), pp. 76–87. [G: India]

Scitovsky, Tibor. Economic Development in Taiwan and South Korea, 1965–81. **In** *Lau, L. J., ed.*, 1986, pp. 135–95. [G: S. Korea; Taiwan]

Shome, Parthasarathi. Fiscal Issues in South-east Asia: Comparative Studies of Selected Economies: A Comparison of Economic Structures. **In** *Shome, P., ed.*, 1986, pp. 3–8. [G: ASEAN]

Stoever, William A. Foreign Investment as an Aid in Moving from Least Developed to Newly Industrializing: A Study in Korea. *J. Devel. Areas*, January 1986, *20*(2), pp. 223–47. [G: S. Korea]

Sun, Li-teh. Confucianism and the Economic Order of Taiwan. *Int. J. Soc. Econ.*, 1986, *13*(6), pp. 3–53. [G: Taiwan]

Sundrum, R. M. Indonesia's Rapid Economic Growth: 1968–81. *Bull. Indonesian Econ. Stud.*, December 1986, *22*(3), pp. 40–69. [G: Indonesia]

Syrquin, Moshe. Economic Growth and Structural Change: An International Perspective. **In** *Ben-Porath, Y., ed.*, 1986, pp. 42–74. [G: Selected Countries; Israel]

Tanzi, Vito. Economic Development and Tax Structure. **In** *Shome, P., ed.*, 1986, pp. 9–24. [G: ASEAN]

Thorner, Alice. India: Development of the Idea of Development. **In** *[Patel, S.]*, 1986, pp. 123–31. [G: India]

Uppal, J. S. Hinduism and Economic Development in South Asia. *Int. J. Soc. Econ.*, 1986, *13*(3), pp. 20–33. [G: Asia]

Valencia, Mark J. and Marsh, James Barney. Southeast Asia: Marine Resources, Extended Maritime Jurisdiction, and Development. *Marine Resource Econ.*, 1986, *3*(1), pp. 3–27. [G: S.E. Asia]

Warr, Peter G. Indonesia's Other Dutch Disease: Economic Effects of the Petroleum Boom. **In** *Neary, J. P. and van Wijnbergen, S., eds.*, 1986, pp. 288–320.

Wilkens, Bodo. Sri Lanka: Exportdiversifizierung und weltwirtschaftliche Rezession. (Sri Lanka: Export Diversification and World Economic Recession. With English summary.) *Konjunkturpolitik*, 1986, *32*(1/2), pp. 80–99. [G: Sri Lanka]

Yamazawa, Ippei; Nohara, Takashi and Osada, Hiroshi. Economic Interdependence in Pacific Asia: An International Input–Output Analysis. *Devel. Econ.*, June 1986, *24*(2), pp. 95–108. [G: Asia]

1215 African Countries

Amin, Samir. Is an Endogenous Development Strategy Possible in Africa? **In** *[Patel, S.]*, 1986, pp. 159–72. [G: Africa]

de Azcarate, Luis. The World Bank in Adjustment and Economic Growth in Africa. **In** *Helleiner, G. K, ed.*, 1986, pp. 184–219. [G: Africa]

de Azcarate, Luis. The World Bank in Adjustment and Economic Growth in Africa: Reply. **In** *Helleiner, G. K, ed.*, 1986, pp. 228–34. [G: Africa]

Bigsten, Arne. Welfare and Economic Growth in Kenya, 1914–76. *World Devel.*, September 1986, *14*(9), pp. 1151–60. **[G: Kenya]**

Blomqvist, Ake G. and McMahon, Gary. Simulating Commercial Policy in a Small, Open Dual Economy with Urban Unemployment: A General Equilibrium Approach. *J. Devel. Stud.*, January 1986, *22*(2), pp. 443–63. **[G: Kenya]**

Boesen, Jannik, et al. Tanzania: Crisis and Struggle for Survival: Introduction. **In** *Boesen, J., et al., eds.*, 1986, pp. 19–29. **[G: Tanzania]**

Clapham, Christopher. Politics and Government in African States, 1960–1985: The Horn of Africa. **In** *Duignan, P. and Jackson, R. H., eds.*, 1986, pp. 253–82. **[G: Ethiopia; Somalia]**

Cowen, Michael. Change in State Power, International Conditions and Peasant Producers: The Case of Kenya. *J. Devel. Stud.*, January 1986, *22*(2), pp. 355–84. **[G: Kenya]**

Curry, Robert L., Jr. Adaptation of Botswana's Development Strategy to Meet Its Peoples' Needs for Land, Jobs: The Southern Africa Capitalist Democracy Can Maintain Its Growth by a New Problem-Oriented Policy. *Amer. J. Econ. Soc.*, July 1986, *45*(3), pp. 297–312. **[G: Botswana]**

Diwan, Romesh and Hu, Grace. Country Objectives and IMF Conditionality: An Empirical Analysis of Sudan Economy. *Indian J. Quant. Econ.*, 1986, *2*(2), pp. 83–100. **[G: Sudan]**

Dreyer, J. P. and Brand, S. S. 'n Sectorale Beskouing van die Suid-Afrikaanse Ekonomie in 'n Veranderende Omgewing. (With English summary.) *S. Afr. J. Econ.*, June 1986, *54*(2), pp. 131–50. **[G: S. Africa]**

Duignan, Peter. Politics and Government in African States, 1960–1985: Introduction. **In** *Duignan, P. and Jackson, R. H., eds.*, 1986, pp. 1–29. **[G: Africa]**

Duignan, Peter and Gann, L. H. Politics and Government in African States, 1960–1985: South Africa. **In** *Duignan, P. and Jackson, R. H., eds.*, 1986, pp. 283–344. **[G: S. Africa]**

Fardeheb, A. and Hamel, B. Algérie: système productif et choix économiques et sociaux alternatifs. (Algeria: The Productive System and Alternative Economic and Social Choices. With English summary.) *Écon. Soc.*, May 1986, *20*(5), pp. 171–207. **[G: Algeria]**

Gann, L. H. Politics and Government in African States, 1960–1985: Malawi, Zambia and Zimbabwe. **In** *Duignan, P. and Jackson, R. H., eds.*, 1986, pp. 162–201. **[G: Malawi; Zambia; Zimbabwe]**

Gann, L. H. and Duignan, Peter. Politics and Government in African States, 1960–1985: Namibia, Botswana, Lesotho, and Swaziland. **In** *Duignan, P. and Jackson, R. H., eds.*, 1986, pp. 345–76. **[G: Namibia; Botswana; Lesotho; Swaziland]**

Green, Reginald Herbold. Africa in the 1980s: Some Key Political Economic Issues, Problems and Prospects. **In** *[Patel, S.]*, 1986, pp. 173–94. **[G: Africa]**

Green, Reginald Herbold and Kadhani, Xavier. Zimbabwe: Transition to Economic Crises, 1981–83: Retrospect and Prospect. *World Devel.*, Special Issue, August 1986, *14*(8), pp. 1059–83. **[G: Zimbabwe]**

Gsänger, Hans. Entwicklungspotential und Entwicklungserfolg. Versuch einer typisierenden Gruppenbildung schwarzafrikanischer Länder. (Socio-Economic Performance and Potentials for Development. An Attempt to Group Sub-Saharan African Countries. With English summary.) *Konjunkturpolitik*, 1986, *32*(1/2), pp. 52–79. **[G: Africa]**

Henriksen, Thomas H. Politics and Government in African States, 1960–1985: Lusophone Africa: Angola, Mozambique, and Guinea-Bissau. **In** *Duignan, P. and Jackson, R. H., eds.*, 1986, pp. 377–407. **[G: Angola; Mozambique; Guinea-Bissau]**

Hopkins, Antony G. The World Bank in Africa: Historical Reflections on the African Present. *World Devel.*, December 1986, *14*(12), pp. 1473–87. **[G: Africa]**

Jabber, Paul. Egypt's Crisis, America's Dilemma. *Foreign Aff.*, Summer 1986, *64*(5), pp. 960–80. **[G: Egypt]**

Jackson, Robert H. Politics and Government in African States, 1960–1985: Conclusion. **In** *Duignan, P. and Jackson, R. H., eds.*, 1986, pp. 408–29. **[G: Sub-Saharan Africa]**

Jackson, Robert H. and Rosberg, Carl G. Politics and Government in African States, 1960–1985: The States of East Africa: Tanzania, Uganda, and Kenya. **In** *Duignan, P. and Jackson, R. H., eds.*, 1986, pp. 202–52. **[G: Tanzania; Uganda; Kenya]**

Jennings, Anthony. Measures to Assist the Least Developed Countries: The Case of Malawi. *World Devel.*, December 1986, *14*(12), pp. 1463–68. **[G: Malawi]**

Jones, Barclay Gibbs. Urban Support for Rural Development in Kenya. *Econ. Geogr.*, July 1986, *62*(3), pp. 201–14. **[G: Kenya]**

Kirk-Greene, A. H. M. Politics and Government in African States, 1960–1985: West Africa: Nigeria and Ghana. **In** *Duignan, P. and Jackson, R. H., eds.*, 1986, pp. 30–77. **[G: Nigeria; Ghana]**

Kydd, J. and Hewitt, A. The Effectiveness of Structural Adjustment Lending: Initial Evidence from Malawi. *World Devel.*, March 1986, *14*(3), pp. 347–65. **[G: Malawi]**

Le Vine, Victor T. Politics and Government in African States, 1960–1985: Cameroon, Togo, and the States of Formerly French West Africa. **In** *Duignan, P. and Jackson, R. H., eds.*, 1986, pp. 78–119. **[G: W. Africa]**

Livingstone, Ian. International Transport Costs and Industrial Development in the Least Developed African Countries. *Industry Devel.*, 1986, (19), pp. 1–54. **[G: Africa]**

Mtei, E. I. M. Design, Implementation, and Adequacy of Fund Programs in Africa: Comments. **In** *Helleiner, G. K, ed.*, 1986, pp. 96–99. **[G: Africa]**

Ndegwa, Philip. The World Bank in Adjustment and Economic Growth in Africa: Comments. In *Helleiner, G. K, ed.*, 1986, pp. 220–26. **[G: Africa]**

Oliver, H. B. B. Design, Implementation, and Adequacy of Fund Programs in Africa: Comments. In *Helleiner, G. K, ed.*, 1986, pp. 99–100. **[G: Africa]**

Ouattara, Alassane D. Design, Implementation, and Adequacy of Fund Programs in Africa: Reply. In *Helleiner, G. K, ed.*, 1986, pp. 100–103. **[G: Africa]**

Ouattara, Alassane D. Design, Implementation, and Adequacy of Fund Programs in Africa. In *Helleiner, G. K, ed.*, 1986, pp. 68–92. **[G: Africa]**

Ouattara, Alassane D. The Balance-of-Payments Adjustment Process in Developing Countries: The Experience of the Ivory Coast. *World Devel.*, Special Issue, August 1986, *14*(8), pp. 1085–1105. **[G: Ivory Coast]**

Phiri, David. Design, Implementation, and Adequacy of Fund Programs in Africa: Comments. In *Helleiner, G. K, ed.*, 1986, pp. 93–96. **[G: Africa; Zambia]**

Ravenhill, John. Africa's Continuing Crises: The Elusiveness of Development. In *Ravenhill, J., ed.*, 1986, pp. 1–43. **[G: Africa]**

Ravenhill, John. Collective Self-reliance or Collective Self-delusion: Is the Lagos Plan a Viable Alternative? In *Ravenhill, J., ed.*, 1986, pp. 85–107. **[G: Africa]**

Robinson, Warren C. and Yamazaki, Fumiko. Agriculture, Population, and Economic Planning in Ethiopia, 1953–1980. *J. Devel. Areas*, April 1986, *20*(3), pp. 327–38. **[G: Ethiopia]**

Rothchild, Donald and Gyimah-Boadi, E. Ghana's Economic Decline and Development Strategies. In *Ravenhill, J., ed.*, 1986, pp. 254–85. **[G: Ghana]**

Salehi-Isfahani, Djavad. Oil Supply and Economic Development Strategy: A Dynamic Planning Approach. *J. Devel. Econ.*, April 1986, *21*(1), pp. 1–23. **[G: Algeria]**

Sandbrook, Richard. The State and Economic Stagnation in Tropical Africa. *World Devel.*, March 1986, *14*(3), pp. 319–32. **[G: Africa]**

Svendsen, Knud Erik. The Creation of Macroeconomic Imbalances and a Structural Crisis. In *Boesen, J., et al., eds.*, 1986, pp. 59–78. **[G: Tanzania]**

Williamson, John. The World Bank in Adjustment and Economic Growth in Africa: Comments. In *Helleiner, G. K, ed.*, 1986, pp. 226–28. **[G: Africa]**

Young, Crawford. Politics and Government in African States, 1960–1985: Zaire and Cameroon. In *Duignan, P. and Jackson, R. H., eds.*, 1986, pp. 120–61. **[G: Zaire; Cameroon]**

Zehender, Wolfgang. Industrialisierung und regionale Kooperation in Schwarzafrika. (Industrialization and Regional Cooperation in Sub-Saharan Africa. With English summary.) *Konjunkturpolitik*, 1986, *32*(4), pp. 218–35. **[G: Africa]**

1216 Latin American and Caribbean Countries

Alberro-Semerena, José Luis and Nieto-Ituarte, Marií Dolores. Empirical Estimates of Marxian Categories in Mexico: 1970–1975. *Rev. Radical Polit. Econ.*, Winter 1986, *18*(4), pp. 32–46. **[G: Mexico]**

Arellano, José Pablo and Cortázar, Rene. Inflación, conflictos macroeconómicos y democratización en Chile. (Inflation, Macroeconomic Conflicts, and Democratization in Chile. With English summary.) *Colección Estud. CIEPLAN*, June 1986, (19), pp. 57–81. **[G: Chile]**

Arellano, José Pablo and Marfán, Manuel. Ahorro-inversión y relaciones financieras en la actual crisis económica chilena. (Savings, Investment, and Financial Relations in the Present Chilean Economic Crisis. With English summary.) *Colección Estud. CIEPLAN*, December 1986, (20), pp. 61–93. **[G: Chile]**

Arida, Persio. Macroeconomic Issues for Latin America. *J. Devel. Econ.*, June 1986, *22*(1), pp. 171–208. **[G: Latin America]**

Auty, Richard and Gelb, Alan. Oil Windfalls in a Small Parliamentary Democracy: Their Impact on Trinidad and Tobago. *World Devel.*, September 1986, *14*(9), pp. 1161–75. **[G: Trinidad and Tobago]**

Ayala, José and Durán, Clemente Ruiz. Development and Crisis in Mexico: A Structuralist Approach. In *Hartlyn, J. and Morley, S. A., eds.*, 1986, pp. 243–64. **[G: Mexico]**

Bacha, Edmar L. External Shocks and Growth Prospects: The Case of Brazil, 1973–89. *World Devel.*, Special Issue, August 1986, *14*(8), pp. 919–36. **[G: Brazil]**

Baumeister, Eduardo and Neira Cuadra, Oscar. The Making of a Mixed Economy: Class Struggle and State Policy in the Nicaragua Transition. In *Fagen, R. R.; Deere, C. D. and Coraggio, J. L., eds.*, 1986, pp. 171–91. **[G: Nicaragua]**

Blitzer, Charles R. and Eckaus, Richard S. Energy–Economy Interactions in Mexico: A Multiperiod General Equilibrium Model. *J. Devel. Econ.*, May 1986, *21*(2), pp. 259–81. **[G: Mexico]**

Bullock, Colin. IMF Conditionality and Jamaica's Economic Policy in the 1980s. *Soc. Econ. Stud.*, December 1986, *35*(4), pp. 129–76. **[G: Jamaica]**

Calvo, Guillermo A. Fractured Liberalism: Argentina under Martínez de Hoz. *Econ. Develop. Cult. Change*, April 1986, *34*(3), pp. 511–33. **[G: Argentina]**

Canitrot, Adolfo and Rozenwurcel, Guillermo. A relação entre a taxa de câmbio e os salários em uma economia semi-industrializada de dois setores. (With English summary.) *Pesquisa Planejamento Econ.*, August 1986, *16*(2), pp. 351–79. **[G: Latin America]**

Cardoso, Eliana A. What Policymakers Can Learn from Brazil and Mexico. *Challenge,* Sept./Oct. 1986, *29*(4), pp. 19–28. **[G: Brazil; Mexico]**

Corbo, Vittorio; de Melo, Jaime and Tybout, James. What Went Wrong with the Recent Reforms in the Southern Cone. *Econ. Develop. Cult. Change,* April 1986, *34*(3), pp. 607–40. **[G: Uruguay; Chile; Argentina]**

Davies, Omar. An Analysis of the Management of the Jamaican Economy: 1972–1985. *Soc. Econ. Stud.,* March 1986, *35*(1), pp. 73–109. **[G: Jamaica]**

Dore, Elizabeth. Nicaragua: The Experience of the Mixed Economy. **In** *Hartlyn, J. and Morley, S. A., eds.,* 1986, pp. 319–50. **[G: Nicaragua]**

Dornbusch, Rudiger. A New Chance for Argentina. *Challenge,* Jan./Feb. 1986, *28*(6), pp. 15–20. **[G: Argentina]**

ECLAC Secretariat, Port of Spain. A View of the Caribbean. **In** *Maddison, A., ed.,* 1986, pp. 91–115. **[G: Caribbean]**

ECLAC Secretariat, Santiago. Central America: Bases for Reactivation and Development. **In** *Maddison, A., ed.,* 1986, pp. 116–29. **[G: Central America]**

ECLAC Secretariat, Santiago. Development and Crisis in Latin America: 1950–84. **In** *Maddison, A., ed.,* 1986, pp. 28–66. **[G: Latin America]**

Edwards, Sebastian. Monetarism in Chile, 1973–1983: Some Economic Puzzles. *Econ. Develop. Cult. Change,* April 1986, *34*(3), pp. 535–59. **[G: Chile]**

Edwards, Sebastian and Teitel, Simón. Introduction to Growth, Reform, and Adjustment: Latin America's Trade and Macroeconomic Policies in the 1970s and 1980s. *Econ. Develop. Cult. Change,* April 1986, *34*(3), pp. 423–31. **[G: Latin America]**

Fischer, Bernhard and Trapp, Peter. Geld- und Finanzpolitik in Argentinien: Der Weg in die finanzielle Repression. (Financial Policies and Financial Repression in Argentina. With English summary.) *Kredit Kapital,* 1986, *19*(1), pp. 122–43. **[G: Argentina]**

Fishlow, Albert. A economia política do ajustamento brasileiro aos choques do petróleo: uma nota sobre o período 1974/84. (With English summary.) *Pesquisa Planejamento Econ.,* December 1986, *16*(3), pp. 507–50. **[G: Brazil]**

Geiger, Pedro P. and Davidovich, Fany R. The Spatial Strategies of the State in the Political-Economic Development of Brazil. **In** *Scott, A. J. and Storper, M., eds.,* 1986, pp. 281–98. **[G: Brazil]**

Geller, Lucio and Tokman, Víctor E. From Austerity Measures to Structural Adjustment. *CEPAL Rev.,* December 1986, (30), pp. 35–50. **[G: Latin America]**

Gibson, Bill; Lustig, Nora and Taylor, Lance. Terms of Trade and Class Conflict in a Computable General Equilibrium Model for Mexico. *J. Devel. Stud.,* October 1986, *23*(1), pp. 40–59. **[G: Mexico]**

González, Norberto. Reactivation and Development: The Great Commitment of Latin America and the Caribbean. *CEPAL Rev.,* December 1986, (30), pp. 7–16. **[G: Latin America]**

Ground, Richard L. Origin and Magnitude of Recessionary Adjustment in Latin America. *CEPAL Rev.,* December 1986, (30), pp. 67–85. **[G: Latin America]**

Guillen, Arturo. Mexico: crisis, industria y restructuracion del sistema productivo. (Mexico: Crisis, Industry and Restructuring of the Productive System. With English summary.) *Écon. Soc.,* May 1986, *20*(5), pp. 155–69. **[G: Mexico]**

Hartlyn, Jonathan and Morley, Samuel A. Bureaucratic-Authoritarian Regimes in Comparative Perspective. **In** *Hartlyn, J. and Morley, S. A., eds.,* 1986, pp. 38–53. **[G: Latin America]**

Hartlyn, Jonathan and Morley, Samuel A. Political Regimes and Economic Performance in Latin America. **In** *Hartlyn, J. and Morley, S. A., eds.,* 1986, pp. 15–37. **[G: Latin America]**

Hiemenz, Ulrich. Economic Reforms in Chile, 1973–9181: Comment. **In** *Balassa, B. and Giersch, H., eds.,* 1986, pp. 321–25. **[G: Chile]**

Kamas, Linda. Dutch Disease Economics and the Colombian Export Boom. *World Devel.,* September 1986, *14*(9), pp. 1177–98. **[G: Colombia]**

Lamounier, Bolivar and Moura, Alkimar R. Economic Policy and Political Opening in Brazil. **In** *Hartlyn, J. and Morley, S. A., eds.,* 1986, pp. 165–96. **[G: Brazil]**

MacIntyre, Arnold. Finance, Growth and the Balance of Trade in OECS Countries. *Soc. Econ. Stud.,* December 1986, *35*(4), pp. 176–212. **[G: Caribbean]**

de Melo, Jaime and Tybout, James. The Effects of Financial Liberalization on Savings and Investment in Uruguay. *Econ. Develop. Cult. Change,* April 1986, *34*(3), pp. 561–87. **[G: Uruguay]**

Mesa-Lago, Carmelo. Social Security and Development in Latin America. *CEPAL Rev.,* April 1986, (28), pp. 135–50. **[G: Latin America]**

Moore, Richard. U.S. Virgin Islands Industrial Ambitions in the Context of a Maturing Caribbean Basin Initiative. *Atlantic Econ. J.,* September 1986, *14*(3), pp. 14–17. **[G: U.S.; Caribbean]**

Nove, Alec. The Political Economy of the Allende Regime. **In** *Nove, A.,* 1986, *1976,* pp. 3–29. **[G: Chile]**

Orlando, Frank and Teitel, Simón. Latin America's External Debt Problem: Debt-Servicing Strategies Compatible with Long-term Economic Growth. *Econ. Develop. Cult. Change,* April 1986, *34*(3), pp. 641–71. **[G: Latin America]**

Roett, Riordan. Peru: The Message from García. *Foreign Aff.,* Winter 1985/86, *64*(2), pp. 274–86. **[G: Peru]**

Saieh, Alvaro and Sjaastad, Larry A. Economic Reforms in Chile, 1973–9181. **In** *Balassa, B. and Giersch, H., eds.*, 1986, pp. 305–20. **[G: Chile]**

Sanchez-Arnau, Juan C. Medium-term Scenarios for the Future of Latin America. **In** *Maddison, A., ed.*, 1986, pp. 67–84. **[G: Latin America]**

Sarney, José. Brazil: A President's Story. *Foreign Aff.*, Fall 1986, *65*(1), pp. 101–17. **[G: Brazil]**

Schloss, Miguel and Thomas, Vinod. Adjustment with Growth: Colombia's Experience. *Finance Develop.*, December 1986, *23*(4), pp. 10–13. **[G: Colombia]**

Schydlowsky, Daniel M. The Macroeconomic Effect of Nontraditional Exports in Peru. *Econ. Develop. Cult. Change*, April 1986, *34*(3), pp. 491–509. **[G: Peru]**

Sheehey, Edmund J. Unanticipated Inflation, Devaluation and Output in Latin America. *World Devel.*, May 1986, *14*(5), pp. 665–71. **[G: Latin America]**

Singh, Ajit. Crisis and Recovery in the Mexican Economy: The Role of the Capital Goods Sector. **In** *Fransman, M., ed.*, 1986, pp. 246–68. **[G: Mexico]**

Syrquin, Moshe. Growth and Structural Change in Latin America since 1960: A Comparative Analysis. *Econ. Develop. Cult. Change*, April 1986, *34*(3), pp. 433–54. **[G: Latin America]**

di Tella, Guido. La estrategia del desarrollo indirecto veinte años después. (With English summary.) *Desarrollo Econ.*, Apr.-June 1986, *26*(101), pp. 51–70. **[G: Argentina]**

di Tella, Guido and Platt, D. C. M. The Political Economy of Argentina, 1880–1946: Postscript and Conclusions. **In** *di Tella, G. and Platt, D. C. M., eds.*, 1986, pp. 201–12. **[G: Argentina]**

Vilas, Carlos M. Sobre la estrategia económica de la Revolución Sandinista. (With English summary.) *Desarrollo Econ.*, Apr.-June 1986, *26*(101), pp. 121–42. **[G: Nicaragua]**

Weisskoff, Richard and Wolff, Edward N. Development and Trade Dependence: The Case of Puerto Rico, 1948–1963. **In** *Sohn, I., ed.*, 1986, *1975*, pp. 406–16. **[G: Puerto Rico]**

Werneck, Rogério L. F. Poupança estatal, dívida externa e crise financeira do sector público. (With English summary.) *Pesquisa Planejamento Econ.*, December 1986, *16*(3), pp. 551–74. **[G: Brazil]**

White, Averille. Profiles: Women in the Caribbean Project. *Soc. Econ. Stud.*, June 1986, *35*(2), pp. 59–81. **[G: Barbados; Antigua; St. Vincent]**

Witter, M. and Ramjeesingh, D. An Analysis of the Internal Sectoral Structure of the Jamaican Economy: 1969–1974. *Soc. Econ. Stud.*, March 1986, *35*(1), pp. 1–72. **[G: Jamaica]**

Zedillo Ponce de Leon, Ernesto. Mexico's Recent Balance-of-Payments Experience and Prospects for Growth. *World Devel.*, Special Issue, August 1986, *14*(8), pp. 963–91. **[G: Mexico]**

1217 Oceanic Countries

Ahlburg, Dennis A. Population and Economic Development in the Island Nations of the South Pacific. **In** *Cole, R. V. and Parry, T. G., eds.*, 1986, pp. 21–70. **[G: S. Pacific]**

Bertram, Geoffrey. "Sustainable Development" in Pacific Micro-economies. *World Devel.*, July 1986, *14*(7), pp. 809–22. **[G: New Zealand; Tuvalu; Tokelou; Kiribati]**

Cole, Rodney V. and Parry, T. G. Key Issues in Pacific Island Development. **In** *Cole, R. V. and Parry, T. G., eds.*, 1986, pp. 1–20. **[G: S. Pacific]**

Guest, James. Macroeconomic Stabilization Policy with Special Reference to Fiscal Policy. **In** *Cole, R. V. and Parry, T. G., eds.*, 1986, pp. 71–110. **[G: S. Pacific]**

Roucek, Joseph S. The Geopolitics of the Antarctic: The Land Is Free for Scientific Work but Its Wealth of Minerals Has Excited Imperialist Claims. *Amer. J. Econ. Soc.*, January 1986, *45*(1), pp. 69–77. **[G: Antarctica]**

122 Economic Studies of Developed Countries

1221 Comparative Country Studies

Abramovitz, Moses. Catching Up, Forging Ahead, and Falling Behind. *J. Econ. Hist.*, June 1986, *46*(2), pp. 385–406. **[G: OECD]**

Britton, Andrew; Eastwood, Fiona and Major, Robin L. Macroeconomic Policy in Italy and Britain. *Nat. Inst. Econ. Rev.*, November 1986, (118), pp. 38–52. **[G: Italy; U.K.]**

De Long, James Bradford and Summers, Lawrence H. Are Business Cycles Symmetrical? Additional Contribution. **In** *Gordon, R. J., ed.*, 1986, pp. 166–78. **[G: OECD]**

Flemming, John S. Booming Sectors and Structural Change in Australia and Britain: A Comparison: Comment. **In** *Neary, J. P. and van Wijnbergen, S., eds.*, 1986, pp. 284–87. **[G: U.K.; Australia]**

Forsyth, Peter J. Booming Sectors and Structural Change in Australia and Britain: A Comparison. **In** *Neary, J. P. and van Wijnbergen, S., eds.*, 1986, pp. 251–84. **[G: Australia; U.K.]**

Kosters, Marvin H. Free Markets Bring Change and Growth. *Challenge*, Mar./Apr. 1986, *29*(1), pp. 55–64. **[G: U.S.; U.K.; Italy; France; W. Germany]**

Mentré, Paul. The French Economy Should Be Deregulated. **In** *Adams, W. J. and Stoffaës, C., eds.*, 1986, pp. 143–55. **[G: OECD; France]**

Panchamukhi, V. R. Tinbergen Fourasite Thesis and the Lima Target. **In** *Panchamukhi, V. R., et al.*, 1986, pp. 94–111. **[G: OECD]**

Peterson, Richard E. and Seo, K. K. Crime Trends—East and West. *Int. J. Soc. Econ.*, 1986, *13*(1/2), pp. 68–76. **[G: U.S.; Japan; U.K.]**

Reynolds, Morgan O. Taxation, Saving, and Investment: A Look at the Evidence. **In** *Lee, D. R., ed.*, 1986, pp. 49–85. **[G: OECD]**

Virén, Matti. Estimating the Output Effects of Energy Price and Real Interest Rate Shocks: A Cross-Country Study. *Schweiz. Z. Volkswirtsch. Statist.*, December 1986, *122*(4), pp. 627–39. **[G: OECD]**

Winiecki, Jan. Macroeconomic Policies and Economic Slowdown: In Search of Linkages in 1972–1982 Period. *Econ. Notes*, 1986, (1), pp. 118–33. **[G: OECD]**

1223 European Countries

Arestis, Philip. Post-Keynesian Economic Policies: The Case of Sweden. *J. Econ. Issues*, September 1986, *20*(3), pp. 709–23. **[G: Sweden]**

Bergman, Lars. ELIAS—A Model of Multisectoral Economic Growth in a Small Open Economy. **In** *Ysander, B.-C., ed.*, 1986, pp. 25–70. **[G: Sweden]**

Brera, Paolo. Austro-Keynesism in a Monetarist Decade: Or, Will Austria's 'Social Partnership' Live through the 1980s? (With a Game Theory Postscript). *Rivista Int. Sci. Econ. Com.*, June-July 1986, *33*(6–7), pp. 667–84. **[G: Austria]**

Britton, Andrew. Seasonal Patterns in the British Economy. *Nat. Inst. Econ. Rev.*, August 1986, (117), pp. 33–42. **[G: U.K.]**

Fitoussi, Jean-Paul and Phelps, Edmund S. Causes of the 1980s Slump in Europe. *Brookings Pap. Econ. Act.*, 1986, (2), pp. 487–513. **[G: W. Europe; U.S.]**

Frijns, Jean M. G. The Dutch Disease in the Netherlands: Comment. **In** *Neary, J. P. and van Wijnbergen, S., eds.*, 1986, pp. 136–41. **[G: Netherlands]**

Genosko, Joachim. Der wechselnde Einfluss des Subsidiaritätsprinzips auf die wirtschafts- und sozialpolitische Praxis in der Bundesrepublik Deutschland. (The Changing Influence of the So-called "Subsidiaritätsprinzip" on the Economic and Social Policies in the Federal Republic of Germany. With English summary.) *Jahr. Nationalökon. Statist.*, July 1986, *201*(4), pp. 404–21. **[G: W. Germany]**

Giovannetti, G. and Siniscalco, D. Structural Change, Foreign Trade and Income Multipliers in the Italian Economy. *Banca Naz. Lavoro Quart. Rev.*, September 1986, (158), pp. 319–35. **[G: Italy]**

Hadjimatheou, George. Why Has Britain Not Had Full Employment since the Early 1970s? *J. Post Keynesian Econ.*, Spring 1986, *8*(3), pp. 359–70. **[G: U.K.]**

Hughes, Alan. Investment Finance, Industrial Strategy and Economic Recovery. **In** *Nolan, P. and Paine, S., eds.*, 1986, pp. 198–233. **[G: U.K.; Selected OECD]**

Kremers, Jeroen J. M. The Dutch Disease in the Netherlands. **In** *Neary, J. P. and van Wijnbergen, S., eds.*, 1986, pp. 96–136. **[G: Netherlands]**

Layard, Richard, et al. Europe: The Case for Unsustainable Growth. **In** *Blanchard, O.; Dornbusch, R. and Layard, R., eds.*, 1986, pp. 33–94. **[G: W. Europe; EEC]**

Mairate, Andréa; Tourres, Pascal and Troisvallets, Marc. La déformation de léconomie française: déstructuration et rupture d'un système productif dans la crise (1960–1980). (The Distortion of the French Economy: Destructuring and Breaking of Productive System in the Crisis. With English summary.) *Écon. Soc.*, May 1986, *20*(5), pp. 9–47. **[G: France]**

Masera, Rainer Stefano. Europe's Economic Problems in an International Perspective. *Banca Naz. Lavoro Quart. Rev.*, December 1986, (159), pp. 391–406. **[G: W. Europe]**

Ølgaard, Anders. Finansierings- og fordelingsproblemer i lys af balanceproblemerne. (Saving, Investment and Functional Income Distribution in the Danish Economy. With English summary.) *Nationaløkon. Tidsskr.*, 1986, *124*(2), pp. 179–88. **[G: Denmark]**

Poscetti, Marcello. Highlights of the 19th Report of the Centre for Research on Social Investment—CENSIS. *Rev. Econ. Cond. Italy*, Jan.-Apr. 1986, (1), pp. 87–98. **[G: Italy]**

Posner, Michael. The State of the Economy. *Scot. J. Polit. Econ.*, November 1986, *33*(4), pp. 305–16. **[G: U.K.]**

Robinson, Austin. The Economic Problems of the Transition from War to Peace: 1945–49. *Cambridge J. Econ.*, June 1986, *10*(2), pp. 165–85. **[G: U.K.]**

Rothschild, Kurt W. 'Left' and 'Right' in 'Federal Europe.' *Kyklos*, 1986, *39*(3), pp. 359–76. **[G: W. Europe]**

Sachs, Jeffrey. Causes of the 1980s Slump in Europe: Comments. *Brookings Pap. Econ. Act.*, 1986, (2), pp. 514–19. **[G: W. Europe; U.S.]**

Saville, I. D. and Gardiner, K. L. Stagflation in the UK since 1970: A Model-based Explanation. *Nat. Inst. Econ. Rev.*, August 1986, (117), pp. 52–69. **[G: U.K.]**

Shepherd, Geoffrey. A Comparison of the Three Economies. **In** *Morgan, R. and Bray, C., eds.*, 1986, pp. 24–53. **[G: U.K.; France; W. Germany]**

Sneessens, Henri R. and Drèze, Jacques H. A Discussion of Belgian Unemployment, Combining Traditional Concepts and Disequilibrium Econometrics. **In** *Bean, C. R.; Layard, P. R. G. and Nickell, S. J., eds.*, 1986, pp. 89–119. **[G: Belgium]**

Walker, John and Clements, Michael. The UK Economy: Analysis and Prospects. *Oxford Rev. Econ. Policy*, Autumn 1986, *2*(3), pp. xxvii–xxxix. **[G: U.K.]**

Ysander, Bengt-Christer. Structural Change as an Equilibrium or Disequilibrium Process—An Introduction. **In** *Ysander, B.-C., ed.*, 1986, pp. 9–24. **[G: Sweden]**

Ysander, Bengt-Christer; Nordström, Tomas and Jansson, Leif. ISAC—A Model of Stabilization and Structural Change in a Small Open Economy. **In** *Ysander, B.-C., ed.*, 1986, pp. 71–161. **[G: Sweden]**

Zeuthen, Hans E. De senere års omvurderinger af centrale økonomiske sammenhænge. (Shifts in the Conceptions of How the Danish Economy Works. With English summary.) *Nationaløkon. Tidsskr.*, 1986, *124*(3), pp. 274–83. **[G: Denmark]**

1224 Asian Countries

Fodella, Gianni. Eliminare l'avanzo rivalutando lo yen? (Yen Revaluation to Offset the Surplus? With English summary.) *Rivista Int. Sci. Econ. Com.*, May 1986, *33*(5), pp. 401–07. **[G: Japan]**

Nato, Takatsugu. The Influence of Confucianism and Buddhism on Life-Innovators in the Japanese Socio-Economic Order. *Int. J. Soc. Econ.*, 1986, *13*(3), pp. 53–63. **[G: Japan]**

Weiss, John. Japan's Post-War Protection Policy: Some Implications for Less Developed Countries. *J. Devel. Stud.*, January 1986, *22*(2), pp. 385–406. **[G: Japan]**

Yamaguchi, Mitoshi. Some Critical Analyses of Japanese Economic Development. *Kobe Univ. Econ.*, 1986, (32), pp. 41–68. **[G: Japan]**

1227 Oceanic Countries

Butlin, N. G. Contours of the Australian Economy 1788–1860. *Australian Econ. Hist. Rev.*, September 1986, *26*(2), pp. 96–125. **[G: Australia]**

Dixon, Peter B. and McDonald, Daina. The Australian Economy in 1985–86 and 1986–87. *Australian Econ. Rev.*, 2nd Quarter 1986, (74), pp. 3–21. **[G: Australia]**

Endres, Anthony M. The Political Economy of W. B. Sutch: Toward a Critical Appreciation. *New Zealand Econ. Pap.*, 1986, *20*, pp. 17–39. **[G: New Zealand]**

Gruen, Fred H. How Bad Is Australia's Economic Performance and Why? *Econ. Rec.*, June 1986, *62*(177), pp. 180–93. **[G: Australia]**

Harcourt, Geoffrey C. Making Socialism in Your Own Country. **In** *[Harcourt, G. C.]*, 1986, pp. 250–72. **[G: Australia]**

McDonald, Daina and Dixon, Peter B. Macroeconomic Developments in 1986–87 and 1987–88. *Australian Econ. Rev.*, 4th Quarter 1986, (76), pp. 3–24. **[G: Australia]**

Pitchford, J. D. The Australian Economy: 1985 and Prospects for 1986. *Econ. Rec.*, March 1986, *62*(176), pp. 1–21. **[G: Australia]**

1228 North American Countries

Barbera, Anthony J.; Pollock, Stephen H. and Meade, Douglas S. Tax Simplification and the Performance of the U.S. Economy. *J. Policy Modeling*, Fall 1986, *8*(3), pp. 415–31. **[G: U.S.]**

Blanchard, Olivier J. and Watson, Mark W. Are Business Cycles All Alike? **In** *Gordon, R. J., ed.*, 1986, pp. 123–56. **[G: U.S.]**

Butlin, N. G. and Sinclair, W. A. Australian Gross Domestic Product 1788–1860: Estimates, Sources and Methods. *Australian Econ. Hist. Rev.*, September 1986, *26*(2), pp. 126–47. **[G: Australia]**

Carmichael, Edward A.; Dobson, Wendy and Lipsey, Richard G. The Macdonald Report: Signpost or Shopping Basket? *Can. Public Policy*, Supp. February 1986, *12*, pp. 23–39. **[G: Canada]**

Chimerine, Lawrence and Young, Richard M. Economic Surprises and Messages of the 1980's. *Amer. Econ. Rev.*, May 1986, *76*(2), pp. 31–36. **[G: U.S.]**

Cooper, Richard N. The United States as an Open Economy. **In** *Hafer, R. W., ed. (I)*, 1986, pp. 3–24. **[G: U.S.]**

De Long, James Bradford and Summers, Lawrence H. The Changing Cyclical Variability of Economic Activity in the United States. **In** *Gordon, R. J., ed.*, 1986, pp. 679–719. **[G: U.S.]**

Dugger, William M. The Last Gasp of Liberal Capitalism in America. *J. Econ. Issues*, June 1986, *20*(2), pp. 325–33. **[G: U.S.]**

Eckstein, Otto and Sinai, Allen. The Mechanisms of the Business Cycle in the Postwar Era. **In** *Gordon, R. J., ed.*, 1986, pp. 39–105. **[G: U.S.]**

Eisner, Robert. The Changing Cyclical Variability of Economic Activity in the United States: Comment. **In** *Gordon, R. J., ed.*, 1986, pp. 719–27. **[G: U.S.]**

Epstein, Gerald. What Hath Conservative Economics Wrought? *Challenge*, July/Aug. 1986, *29*(3), pp. 40–46. **[G: U.S.]**

Feldstein, Martin S. Supply Side Economics: Old Truths and New Claims. *Amer. Econ. Rev.*, May 1986, *76*(2), pp. 26–30. **[G: U.S.]**

Gisser, Micha and Goodwin, Thomas H. Crude Oil and the Macroeconomy: Tests of Some Popular Notions: A Note. *J. Money, Credit, Banking*, February 1986, *18*(1), pp. 95–103. **[G: U.S.]**

Gould, Brian W. The Impact of Structural Change within an Economy on Resource Use: An Input–Output Analysis. *Appl. Econ.*, May 1986, *18*(5), pp. 457–77. **[G: Canada]**

Grossman, Herschel I. The Changing Cyclical Variability of Economic Activity in the United States: Comment. **In** *Gordon, R. J., ed.*, 1986, pp. 728–31. **[G: U.S.]**

Kenen, Peter B. The United States as an Open Economy: Comments. **In** *Hafer, R. W., ed. (I)*, 1986, pp. 25–31. **[G: U.S.]**

Lovell, Michael C. The Mechanisms of the Business Cycle in the Postwar Era: Comment. **In** *Gordon, R. J., ed.*, 1986, pp. 105–10. **[G: U.S.]**

Puth, Robert C. Human Mobility as a Source of American Economic Growth. *Quart. Rev. Econ. Bus.*, Spring 1986, *26*(1), pp. 57–73. **[G: U.S.]**

Shiller, Robert J. Are Business Cycles All Alike? Comment. **In** *Gordon, R. J., ed.*, 1986, pp. 156–60. **[G: U.S.]**

Singleton, Kenneth J. The Mechanisms of the Business Cycle in the Postwar Era: Comment. **In** *Gordon, R. J., ed.*, 1986, pp. 110–18. **[G: U.S.]**

Temin, Peter. Are Business Cycles All Alike? Comment. **In** *Gordon, R. J., ed.*, 1986, pp. 160–65. **[G: U.S.]**

123 Comparative Studies of Developing, Developed, and/or Centrally Planned Economies

1230 Comparative Studies of Developing, Developed, and/or Centrally Planned Economies

Addison, John T.; Chappell, Henry W., Jr. and Castro, Alberto C. Output–Inflation Tradeoffs in 34 Selected Countries. *J. Econ. Bus.*, December 1986, *38*(4), pp. 353–60. **[G: Selected Countries]**

Beckerman, Wilfred. Stagflation and the Third World. **In** *[Streeten, P.]*, 1986, pp. 38–57. **[G: LDCs; MDCs]**

Bruno, Michael. External Shocks and Domestic Response: Macroeconomic Performance, 1965–1982. **In** *Ben-Porath, Y., ed.*, 1986, pp. 276–301. **[G: Israel; OECD]**

Burkett, John P. PQLI as a Measure of Comparative Performance: Comment. *Comp. Econ. Stud.*, Summer 1986, *28*(2), pp. 59–68.

Clague, Christopher. Short-Cut Estimates of Real Income. *Rev. Income Wealth*, September 1986, *32*(3), pp. 313–31.

Diejomaoh, Vremudia P. Impact of Different Types of Foreign Investments on Capital Formation in Africa. **In** *Association of African Central Banks*, 1986, pp. 123–50. **[G: Africa]**

Dornbusch, Rudiger. Unemployment: Europe's Challenge of the '80s. *Challenge*, Sept./Oct. 1986, *29*(4), pp. 11–18. **[G: Europe; U.S.]**

Goldsbrough, David and Zaidi, Iqbal M. Transmission of Economic Influences from Industrial to Developing Countries. **In** *International Monetary Fund, Research Department*, 1986, pp. 150–95. **[G: OECD; LDCs]**

Griffin, Keith. Communal Land Tenure Systems and Their Role in Rural Development. **In** *[Streeten, P.]*, 1986, pp. 165–91. **[G: Selected Countries]**

Hakim, Leonardo and Wallich, Christine. OECD Deficits, Debt, and Savings Structure and Trends, 1965–81: A Survey of the Evidence. **In** *Lal, D. and Wolf, M., eds.*, 1986, pp. 292–360. **[G: OECD]**

Hopkins, Michael. Basic Needs Performance in the Past. **In** *Adelman, I. and Taylor, J. E., eds.*, 1986, pp. 38–73. **[G: Global]**

Jauković, Radovan. Structural Problems of East–West Economic Relations. *Eastern Europ. Econ.*, Winter 1986-87, *25*(2), pp. 22–59. **[G: E. Europe]**

Jung, Woo S. Financial Development and Economic Growth: International Evidence. *Econ. Develop. Cult. Change*, January 1986, *34*(2), pp. 333–46. **[G: LDCs; MDCs]**

Jung, Woo S. and Marshall, Peyton J. Inflation and Economic Growth: Some International Evidence on Structuralist and Distortionist Positions: A Note. *J. Money, Credit, Banking*, May 1986, *18*(2), pp. 227–32.

Koskela, Erkki and Virén, Matti. Testing the Direct Substitutability Hypotheses of Saving. *Appl. Econ.*, February 1986, *18*(2), pp. 143–55. **[G: OECD]**

Kravis, Irving B. The Three Faces of the International Comparison Project. *World Bank Res. Observer*, January 1986, *1*(1), pp. 3–26. **[G: Global]**

Lal, Deepak and Wolf, Martin. Debt, Deficits, and Distortions. **In** *Lal, D. and Wolf, M., eds.*, 1986, pp. 239–91. **[G: Global]**

Leontief, Wassily. Population Growth and Economic Development: Illustrative Projections. **In** *Leontief, W.*, 1986, *1979*, pp. 338–62. **[G: Global]**

Leontief, Wassily. The Structure of Development. **In** *Leontief, W.*, 1986, *1963*, pp. 162–87. **[G: Israel; U.S.; Peru; Egypt]**

Looney, Robert E. and Frederiksen, Peter C. Profiles of Current Latin American Arms Producers. *Int. Organ.*, Summer 1986, *40*(3), pp. 745–52. **[G: Latin America]**

MacDonald, C. A. The United States, Britain and Argentina in the Years Immediately after the Second World War. **In** *di Tella, G. and Platt, D. C. M., eds.*, 1986, pp. 183–200. **[G: U.S.; U.K.; Argentina]**

Maddison, Angus. Economic Performance and Policy in Latin American and OECD Countries 1938–85: A Comparative Analysis. **In** *Maddison, A., ed.*, 1986, pp. 11–27. **[G: OECD; Latin America]**

McGregor, Peter G. and Swales, J. K. Balance of Payments Constrained Growth: A Rejoinder. *Appl. Econ.*, December 1986, *18*(12), pp. 1265–74. **[G: OECD]**

Moreno, Ramon. Monetary Control without a Central Bank: The Case of Hong Kong. *Fed. Res. Bank San Francisco Econ. Rev.*, Spring 1986, (2), pp. 17–37. **[G: Hong Kong]**

Nemetz, Peter N. The Pacific Rim: Investment, Development and Trade: Introduction and Overview. **In** *Nemetz, P. N., ed.*, 1986, pp. 1–52. **[G: Pacific Basin]**

Nishimura, Hiroyuki. The Rural–Urban Balance in Rural Development. **In** *Maunder, A. and Renborg, U., eds.*, 1986, pp. 513–25. **[G: LDCs; MDCs]**

Oshima, Harry T. East Asia's High Growth. *Singapore Econ. Rev.*, October 1986, *31*(2), pp. 1–22. **[G: Asia]**

Pandit, Kavita. Sectoral Allocation of Labor Force with Development and the Effect of Trade Activity. *Econ. Geogr.*, April 1986, *62*(2), pp. 144–54.

Papanek, Gustav F. and Kyn, Oldrich. The Effect on Income Distribution of Development, the Growth Rate and Economic Strategy. *J. Devel. Econ.*, September 1986, *23*(1), pp. 55–65.

Ram, Rati. Comparison of Rates of Growth of GDP Based on International and Domestic Prices for 104 Countries over the Period 1960–80. *Indian Econ. J.*, Apr.-June 1986, *33*(4), pp. 149–60. **[G: Global]**

Ram, Rati. Government Size and Economic Growth: A New Framework and Some Evidence from Cross-Section and Time-Series Data. *Amer. Econ. Rev.*, March 1986, *76*(1), pp. 191–203.

123 Comparative Studies of Developing, Developed, and/or Centrally Planned Economies

Rimler, Judit. Economic Obsolescence and Employment (A Comparative Analysis of the Hungarian and Dutch Economies). *Acta Oecon.*, 1986, *36*(1–2), pp. 123–40. **[G: Hungary; Netherlands]**

Rostowski, Jacek and Auerbach, Paul. Storming Cycles and Economic Systems. *J. Compar. Econ.*, September 1986, *10*(3), pp. 293–312. **[G: OECD; CMEA]**

Samuelson, Paul A. Second Thoughts on Analytical Income Comparisons. **In** *Samuelson, P. A.*, 1986, *1984*, pp. 165–76.

Sen, Amartya K. Economic Distance and the Living Standard. **In** *[Patel, S.]*, 1986, pp. 63–74. **[G: India; China; Mexico; Sri Lanka; Brazil]**

Sevilla Guzman, E. Structure of Agriculture and People in Rural Societies: Discussion. **In** *Maunder, A. and Renborg, U., eds.*, 1986, pp. 527–29.

Sláma, Jiří. An International Comparison of Sulphur Dioxide Emissions. *J. Compar. Econ.*, September 1986, *10*(3), pp. 277–92. **[G: Europe]**

Swanson, Earl R. Structure of Agriculture and People in Rural Societies: Discussion. **In** *Maunder, A. and Renborg, U., eds.*, 1986, pp. 526–27.

Syrquin, Moshe. Economic Growth and Structural Change: An International Perspective. **In** *Ben-Porath, Y., ed.*, 1986, pp. 42–74. **[G: Selected Countries; Israel]**

Thirlwall, A. P. Balance of Payments Constrained Growth: A Reply. *Appl. Econ.*, December 1986, *18*(12), pp. 1259–63. **[G: OECD]**

Winiecki, Jan. Distorted Macroeconomics of Central Planning. *Banca Naz. Lavoro Quart. Rev.*, June 1986, (157), pp. 197–223.

Winiecki, Jan. The Overgrown Industrial Sector in Soviet-Type Economies: Explanations, Evidence, Consequences. *Comp. Econ. Stud.*, Winter 1986, *28*(4), pp. 13–36. **[G: Cent. Planned Econ.]**

124 Economic Studies of Centrally Planned Economies

1241 Comparative Country Studies

Marrese, Michael. CMEA: Effective but Cumbersome Political Economy. *Int. Organ.*, Spring 1986, *40*(2), pp. 287–327. **[G: CMEA]**

1243 European Countries

Abalkin, L. The Acceleration of Socioeconomic Development: Its Essence and Sources. *Prob. Econ.*, October 1986, *29*(6), pp. 50–62. **[G: U.S.S.R.]**

Abalkin, L. The Interaction of the Productive Forces and Production Relations. *Prob. Econ.*, April 1986, *28*(12), pp. 23–41. **[G: U.S.S.R.]**

Balassa, Bela. Adjustment Policies in Socialist and Private Market Economies. *J. Compar. Econ.*, June 1986, *10*(2), pp. 138–59. **[G: LDCs; Hungary; Yugoslavia]**

Baylis, Thomas A. Explaining the GDR's Economic Strategy. *Int. Organ.*, Spring 1986, *40*(2), pp. 381–420. **[G: E. Germany]**

Baylis, Thomas A. Explaining the GDR's Economic Strategy. **In** *Comisso, E. and Tyson, L., eds.*, 1986, pp. 205–44. **[G: E. Germany]**

Bekker, Zsuzsa. Adjustment Processes in Hungary, 1973–1983: Policy Options, Intentions, Facts. *Acta Oecon.*, 1986, *37*(3–4), pp. 169–88. **[G: Hungary]**

Bond, Daniel L. Prospects for the Soviet Economy. **In** *Amann, R. and Cooper, J., eds.*, 1986, pp. 170–81. **[G: U.S.S.R.]**

Brus, Włodzimierz. 1950 to 1953: The Peak of Stalinism. **In** *Kaser, M. C., ed.*, 1986, pp. 3–39. **[G: E. Europe]**

Brus, Włodzimierz. 1953 to 1956: The 'Thaw' and the 'New Course.' **In** *Kaser, M. C., ed.*, 1986, pp. 40–69. **[G: E. Europe]**

Brus, Włodzimierz. 1957 to 1965: In Search of Balanced Development. **In** *Kaser, M. C., ed.*, 1986, pp. 70–138. **[G: E. Europe]**

Brus, Włodzimierz. 1966 to 1975: Normalization and Conflict. **In** *Kaser, M. C., ed.*, 1986, pp. 139–249. **[G: E. Europe]**

Bukhval'd, E. and Pogrebinskaia, V. V. I. Lenin on the Dynamics of Reproduction and the Rates of the USSR's Economic Development. *Prob. Econ.*, April 1986, *28*(12), pp. 59–77. **[G: U.S.S.R.]**

Comisso, Ellen and Marer, Paul. The Economics and Politics of Reform in Hungary. **In** *Comisso, E. and Tyson, L., eds.*, 1986, pp. 245–78. **[G: Hungary]**

Comisso, Ellen and Marer, Paul. The Economics and Politics of Reform in Hungary. *Int. Organ.*, Spring 1986, *40*(2), pp. 421–54. **[G: Hungary]**

Eysymontt, Jerzy and Maciejewski, Wojciech. Socioeconomic Crises in Poland: A Model Approach. *Eastern Europ. Econ.*, Spring 1986, *24*(3), pp. 6–23. **[G: Poland]**

Farrell, John P. On Polish Disequilibria: Comment [Estimates of the Disequilibria in Poland's Consumer Markets]. *Rev. Econ. Statist.*, May 1986, *68*(2), pp. 355–57. **[G: Poland]**

Gomulka, Stanislaw. Industrialisation and the Rate of Growth: Eastern Europe 1955–75. **In** *Gomulka, S.*, 1986, *1983*, pp. 92–102. **[G: E. Europe]**

Gomulka, Stanislaw. Poland's Industrialisation. **In** *Gomulka, S.*, 1986, pp. 154–94. **[G: Poland]**

Gomulka, Stanislaw. Slowdown in Soviet Industrial Growth: 1947–75 Reconsidered. **In** *Gomulka, S.*, 1986, *1977*, pp. 138–49. **[G: U.S.S.R.]**

Gomulka, Stanislaw. Slowdown in Soviet Industrial Growth: 1947–75 Reconsidered: Afterword. **In** *Gomulka, S.*, 1986, pp. 150–53. **[G: U.S.S.R.]**

Gomulka, Stanislaw. Soviet Growth Slowdown: Duality, Maturity, and Innovation. *Amer. Econ. Rev.*, May 1986, *76*(2), pp. 170–74. **[G: U.S.S.R.]**

Gulácsi, Gábor and Juhász, Pál. Development of Settlements, Decentralization and Communal Management in Hungary. *Acta Oecon.*, 1986, *37*(1–2), pp. 31–46. **[G: Hungary]**

Hall, John B. Reform-Bargaining in Hungary: An Interview with Dr. János Mátyás Kovács. *Comp. Econ. Stud.*, Fall 1986, *28*(3), pp. 25–42. **[G: Hungary]**

Hanson, Philip. The Shape of Gorbachev's Economic Reform. *Soviet Econ.*, Oct.-Dec. 1986, *2*(4), pp. 313–26. **[G: U.S.S.R.]**

Harrison, Mark. The USSR State Budget under Late Stalinism (1945–55): Capital Formation, Government Borrowing and Monetary Growth. *Econ. Planning*, 1986, *20*(3), pp. 179–205. **[G: U.S.S.R.]**

Harrison, Mark. Why Did NEP Fail? **In** *Smith, K., ed.*, 1986, *1980*, pp. 8–22. **[G: U.S.S.R.]**

Hewett, Ed. A. Gorbachev at Two Years: Perspective on Economic Reforms. *Soviet Econ.*, Oct.-Dec. 1986, *2*(4), pp. 283–88. **[G: U.S.S.R.]**

Hoch, Róbert. Open Economy and Domestic Consumption. *Acta Oecon.*, 1986, *37*(3–4), pp. 189–203. **[G: Hungary]**

Hough, Jerry F. The Gorbachev Reform: A Maximal Case. *Soviet Econ.*, Oct.-Dec. 1986, *2*(4), pp. 302–12. **[G: U.S.S.R.]**

Hrnčíř, Miroslav. External Criteria and the Mechanism of the Czechoslovak Economy. *Czech. Econ. Digest.*, January 1986, (1), pp. 58–89. **[G: Czechoslovakia]**

Illés, Iván. Structural Changes in the Hungarian Economy (1979–1985). *Acta Oecon.*, 1986, *36*(1–2), pp. 21–33. **[G: Hungary]**

Janza, Vladimír. The First Year of the 8th Five-Year Plan. *Czech. Econ. Digest.*, March 1986, (2), pp. 3–12. **[G: Czechoslovakia]**

Kontorovich, Vladimir. Soviet Growth Slowdown: Econometric vs. Direct Evidence. *Amer. Econ. Rev.*, May 1986, *76*(2), pp. 181–85. **[G: U.S.S.R.]**

Kornai, János. Comments on the Present State and the Prospects of the Hungarian Economic Reform. **In** *Kornai, J.*, 1986, *1983*, pp. 81–123.

Kornai, János. The Hungarian Reform Process: Visions, Hopes, and Reality. *J. Econ. Lit.*, December 1986, *24*(4), pp. 1687–1737. **[G: Hungary]**

Kroll, Heidi. Decentralization and the Precontract Dispute in Soviet Industry. *Soviet Econ.*, Jan.-Mar. 1986, *2*(1), pp. 51–71. **[G: U.S.S.R.]**

Linden, Ronald H. Socialist Patrimonialism and the Global Economy: The Case of Romania. *Int. Organ.*, Spring 1986, *40*(2), pp. 347–80. **[G: Romania]**

Linden, Ronald H. Socialist Patrimonialism and the Global Economy: The Case of Romania. **In** *Comisso, E. and Tyson, L., eds.*, 1986, pp. 171–204. **[G: Romania]**

Marciniak, Stefan and Zawadzka, Zofia. Planning and Spontaneity in Economic Development. *Eastern Europ. Econ.*, Spring 1986, *24*(3), pp. 24–34. **[G: Poland]**

Nishimizu, Mieko and Robinson, Sherman. Productivity Growth in Manufacturing. **In** *Chenery, H.; Robinson, S. and Syrquin, M.*, 1986, pp. 283–308. **[G: Japan; S. Korea; Yugoslavia; Turkey]**

Nove, Alec. The Class Nature of the Soviet Union Revisited. **In** *Nove, A.*, 1986, *1983*, pp. 220–38. **[G: U.S.S.R.]**

Nove, Alec. The Soviet Economy: Problems and Prospects. **In** *Nove, A.*, 1986, *1980*, pp. 131–49. **[G: U.S.S.R.]**

Park, Henry. Postrevolutionary China and the Soviet NEP. **In** *Zarembka, P., ed.*, 1986, pp. 219–33. **[G: U.S.S.R.; China]**

Peebles, Gavin. On the Importance of Establishing the Inverse Relationship between Open Inflation and Household Liquidity Growth under Socialism: A Critique of Jan Winiecki's Savings Deposit Data. *Comp. Econ. Stud.*, Winter 1986, *28*(4), pp. 85–91. **[G: Cent. Planned Econ.]**

Plyshevskii, B. Socialist Accumulation in the Present Stage. *Prob. Econ.*, December 1986, *29*(8), pp. 15–35. **[G: U.S.S.R.]**

Podkaminer, Leon. On Polish Disequilbria: Reply [Estimates of the Disequilibria in Poland's Consumer Markets]. *Rev. Econ. Statist.*, May 1986, *68*(2), pp. 358. **[G: Poland]**

Poznanski, Kazimierz. Economic Adjustment and Political Forces: Poland since 1970. **In** *Comisso, E. and Tyson, L., eds.*, 1986, pp. 279–312. **[G: Poland]**

Poznanski, Kazimierz. Economic Adjustment and Political Forces: Poland since 1970. *Int. Organ.*, Spring 1986, *40*(2), pp. 455–88. **[G: Poland]**

Rába, András. Hungarian Development—with Bottlenecks. *Acta Oecon.*, 1986, *36*(3–4), pp. 181–96. **[G: Hungary]**

Radice, E. A. The Collapse of German Hegemony and Its Economic Consequences. **In** *Kaser, M. C. and Radice, E. A., eds.*, 1986, pp. 495–519. **[G: Germany; E. Europe]**

Schroeder, Gertrude E. Gorbachev: "Radically" Implementing Brezhnev's Reforms. *Soviet Econ.*, Oct.-Dec. 1986, *2*(4), pp. 289–301. **[G: U.S.S.R.]**

Sipos, Aladár and Tardos, Márton. Economic Control and the Structural Interdependence of Organizations in Hungary at the End of the Second Decade of Reform. *Acta Oecon.*, 1986, *37*(3–4), pp. 241–65. **[G: Hungary]**

Šujan, Ivan. Simulations of Restoring the External Economic Equilibrium of Czechoslovakia. *Comp. Econ. Stud.*, Winter 1986, *28*(4), pp. 61–83. **[G: Czechoslovakia]**

Syrquin, Moshe. Productivity Growth and Factor Reallocation. **In** *Chenery, H.; Robinson, S. and Syrquin, M.*, 1986, pp. 229–62. **[G: Latin America; Europe; Asia; Canada]**

Szamuely, László. Prospects of Economic Reforms in the European CMEA Countries in the 80s. *Acta Oecon.*, 1986, *36*(1–2), pp. 55–65. **[G: CMEA]**

Vintrová, Ružena. Reproduction Proportions of Intensive Development. *Czech. Econ. Digest.*, January 1986, (1), pp. 33–57. **[G: Czechoslovakia]**

Walkowiak, Witold. Investment Processes in

1976–1981. *Eastern Europ. Econ.*, Spring 1986, *24*(3), pp. 35–52. **[G: Poland]**

Wernik, Andrzej. Inflationary Processes during the Seventies. *Eastern Europ. Econ.*, Spring 1986, *24*(3), pp. 74–98. **[G: Poland]**

Winiecki, Jan. Distorted Macroeconomics of Central Planning. *Banca Naz. Lavoro Quart. Rev.*, June 1986, (157), pp. 197–223.

Winiecki, Jan. The Overgrown Industrial Sector in Soviet-Type Economies: Explanations, Evidence, Consequences. *Comp. Econ. Stud.*, Winter 1986, *28*(4), pp. 13–36. **[G: Cent. Planned Econ.]**

1244 Asian Countries

Barnett, A. Doak. Ten Years after Mao. *Foreign Aff.*, Fall 1986, *65*(1), pp. 37–65. **[G: China]**

Cheung, Steven N. S. China in Transition: Where Is She Heading Now? *Contemp. Policy Issues*, October 1986, *4*(4), pp. 1–11. **[G: China]**

Fureng, Dong. China's Price Reform. *Cambridge J. Econ.*, September 1986, *10*(3), pp. 291–300. **[G: China]**

Hsu, Robert C. The Political Economy of Guidance Planning in Post-Mao China. *Weltwirtsch. Arch.*, 1986, *122*(2), pp. 382–94. **[G: China]**

Jain, Ajit. Class Struggle or Modernization? Post-Mao Era in the People's Republic of China. **In** *Jain, A. and Matejko, A., eds.*, 1986, pp. 37–76. **[G: China]**

Kornai, János and Dániel, Zsuzsa. The Chinese Economic Reform—as Seen by Hungarian Economists (Marginal Notes to Our Travel Diary). *Acta Oecon.*, 1986, *36*(3–4), pp. 289–305. **[G: China]**

Lyons, Thomas P. Explaining Economic Fragmentation in China: A Systems Approach. *J. Compar. Econ.*, September 1986, *10*(3), pp. 209–36. **[G: China]**

Martellaro, Joseph A. Two Economies, One China: Hong Kong's Return to China. *Econ. Notes*, 1986, (1), pp. 149–66. **[G: China; Hong Kong]**

Park, Henry. Postrevolutionary China and the Soviet NEP. **In** *Zarembka, P., ed.*, 1986, pp. 219–33. **[G: U.S.S.R.; China]**

Wong, Christine P. W. The Economics of Shortage and Problems of Reform in Chinese Industry. *J. Compar. Econ.*, December 1986, *10*(4), pp. 363–87. **[G: China]**

1246 Latin American and Caribbean Countries

Alcalde, Oscar E. and López Paz, Ernesto. Comments on the Development of the Savings Stimulation Policy in Cuba. **In** *U.N., Dept. of International Econ. and Social Affairs*, 1986, pp. 71–77. **[G: CMEA]**

Domínguez, Jorge I. Cuba in the 1980s. *Foreign Aff.*, Fall 1986, *65*(1), pp. 118–35. **[G: Cuba]**

Eckstein, Susan. Cuba's Centrally Planned Economy: An Equity Trade-off for Growth: Comment. **In** *Hartlyn, J. and Morley, S. A., eds.*, 1986, pp. 367–73. **[G: Cuba]**

Mesa-Lago, Carmelo. Cuba's Centrally Planned Economy: An Equity Trade-off for Growth. **In** *Hartlyn, J. and Morley, S. A., eds.*, 1986, pp. 292–318. **[G: Cuba]**

Pérez-López, Jorge F. Real Economic Growth in Cuba, 1965–1982. *J. Devel. Areas*, January 1986, *20*(2), pp. 151–72. **[G: Cuba]**

130 Economic Fluctuations; Forecasting; Stabilization; Inflation

131 Economic Fluctuations

1310 Economic Fluctuations: General

Benassy, Jean-Pascal. A Non-Walrasian Model of the Business Cycle. **In** *Day, R. H. and Eliasson, G., eds.*, 1986, *1984*, pp. 133–45.

Benassy, Jean-Pascal. A Non-Walrasian Model of the Business Cycle: Reply. **In** *Day, R. H. and Eliasson, G., eds.*, 1986, pp. 150–51.

Bernanke, Ben S. Employment, Hours, and Earnings in the Depression: An Analysis of Eight Manufacturing Industries. *Amer. Econ. Rev.*, March 1986, *76*(1), pp. 82–109. **[G: U.S.]**

Brunner, Karl and Meltzer, Allan H. The National Bureau Method, International Capital Mobility, and Other Essays. *Carnegie-Rochester Conf. Ser. Public Policy*, Spring 1986, *24*, pp. 1–10.

Candela, G. and Gardini, A. Estimation of a Non-linear Discrete-Time Macro Model. *J. Econ. Dynam. Control*, June 1986, *10*(1/2), pp. 249–54. **[G: Italy]**

Clower, Robert W. On the Behavioral and Rational Foundations of Economic Dynamics: Comment. **In** *Day, R. H. and Eliasson, G., eds.*, 1986, pp. 42–44.

Cozier, Barry V. A Model of Output Fluctuations in a Small, Specialized Economy. *J. Money, Credit, Banking*, May 1986, *18*(2), pp. 179–90. **[G: LDCs]**

Crotty, James R. Marx, Keynes, and Minsky on the Instability of the Capitalist Growth Process and the Nature of Government Economic Policy. **In** *Helburn, S. W. and Bramhall, D. F., eds.*, 1986, pp. 297–324. **[G: U.S.]**

Day, Richard H. A Non-Walrasian Model of the Business Cycle: Comment. **In** *Day, R. H. and Eliasson, G., eds.*, 1986, pp. 148–49.

Day, Richard H. Unscrambling the Concept of Chaos through Thick and Thin: Reply [The Emergence of Chaos from Classical Economic Growth]. *Quart. J. Econ.*, May 1986, *101*(2), pp. 425–26.

Dorn, James A. Money, Politics, and the Business Cycle. *Cato J.*, Fall 1986, *6*(2), pp. 353–64. **[G: U.S.]**

Eysymontt, Jerzy and Maciejewski, Wojciech. Socioeconomic Crises in Poland: A Model Approach. *Eastern Europ. Econ.*, Spring 1986, *24*(3), pp. 6–23. **[G: Poland]**

Fand, David I. Federal Reserve Hegemony and Monetary Surprises [Is There a Political Monetary Cycle?]. *Cato J.*, Fall 1986, *6*(2), pp. 581–86. **[G: U.S.]**

Freeman, Christopher. Design, Innovation and

Long Cycles in Economic Development: Introduction. **In** *Freeman, C., ed.*, 1986, pp. 1–4.

Gordon, Robert J. The American Business Cycle: Introduction: Continuity and Change in Theory, Behavior, and Methodology. **In** *Gordon, R. J., ed.*, 1986, pp. 1–33. **[G: U.S.]**

Grosfeld, Irena. Endogenous Planners and the Investment Cycle in the Centrally Planned Economies. *Comp. Econ. Stud.*, Spring 1986, *28*(1), pp. 42–53. **[G: CMEA]**

Kuczynski, M. G. Recent Developments in Business Cycle Theory. *J. Econ. Dynam. Control*, June 1986, *10*(1/2), pp. 255–60.

Lipton, Michael. Recession, Rent and Debt: Quasi-Ricardian and Quasi-Keynesian Components of Non-recovery. **In** *[Streeten, P.]*, 1986, pp. 58–86.

Markusen, Ann Roell. Empirical Research in the Marxist and Schumpeterian Traditions: Reflections on Explaining Spatial Change. **In** *Helburn, S. W. and Bramhall, D. F., eds.*, 1986, pp. 267–83.

Meiselman, David I. Is There a Political Monetary Cycle? *Cato J.*, Fall 1986, *6*(2), pp. 563–79. **[G: U.S.]**

Melese, Francois and Transue, William. Unscrambling Chaos through Thick and Thin [The Emergence of Chaos from Classical Economic Growth]. *Quart. J. Econ.*, May 1986, *101*(2), pp. 419–23.

Meltzer, Allan H. Size, Persistence and Interrelation of Nominal and Real Shocks: Some Evidence from Four Countries. *J. Monet. Econ.*, January 1986, *17*(1), pp. 161–94. **[G: U.S.; U.K.; Canada; W. Germany]**

Minsky, Hyman P. The Crises of 1983 and the Prospects for Advanced Capitalist Economies. **In** *Helburn, S. W. and Bramhall, D. F., eds.*, 1986, pp. 284–96. **[G: U.S.]**

Miron, Jeffrey A. Financial Panics, the Seasonality of the Nominal Interest Rate, and the Founding of the Fed. *Amer. Econ. Rev.*, March 1986, *76*(1), pp. 125–40. **[G: U.S.]**

Modigliani, Franco. A Non-Walrasian Model of the Business Cycle: Comment. **In** *Day, R. H. and Eliasson, G., eds.*, 1986, pp. 146–47.

Moss, Laurence S. and Vaughn, Karen I. Hayek's Ricardo Effect: A Second Look. *Hist. Polit. Econ.*, Winter 1986, *18*(4), pp. 545–65.

Nijkamp, Peter. The Triangle of Industrial Dynamics, Labour Markets and Spatial Systems. **In** *Nijkamp, P., ed. (II)*, 1986, pp. 1–17.

Riese, Hajo. Keynes, Schumpeter und die Krise. (Keynes, Schumpeter and the Crisis. With English summary.) *Konjunkturpolitik*, 1986, *32*(1/2), pp. 1–26.

Rosende R., Francisco. Institucionalidad financiera y estabilidad económica. (With English summary.) *Cuadernos Econ.*, April 1986, *23*(68), pp. 77–99. **[G: Argentina; Chile]**

Samuelson, Paul A. Myths and Realities about the Crash and Depression. **In** *Samuelson, P. A.*, 1986, *1979*, pp. 921–24. **[G: U.S.]**

Sharefkin, Mark F. On the Behavioral and Rational Foundations of Economic Dynamics: Comment. **In** *Day, R. H. and Eliasson, G., eds.*, 1986, pp. 45–47.

Simon, Herbert A. On the Behavioral and Rational Foundations of Economic Dynamics: Reply. **In** *Day, R. H. and Eliasson, G., eds.*, 1986, pp. 48–49.

Simon, Herbert A. On the Behavioral and Rational Foundations of Economic Dynamics. **In** *Day, R. H. and Eliasson, G., eds.*, 1986, *1984*, pp. 21–41.

Sordi, Serena. Dynamical Systems in Macroeconomics: Alternative Approaches to the Analysis of Macroeconomic Fluctuations. *J. Econ. Dynam. Control*, June 1986, *10*(1/2), pp. 261–67.

Sørensen, Peter Birch. Errata: Countercyclical versus Passive Monetary Policy in a Medium-run Macro Model. *Scand. J. Econ.*, 1986, *88*(2), pp. 453.

Sprinkel, Beryl W. Monetary Policy and the Business Cycle. *Cato J.*, Fall 1986, *6*(2), pp. 365–67.

Velupillai, K. From the Fractals of Micro to the Chaos of Macro. *J. Econ. Dynam. Control*, June 1986, *10*(1/2), pp. 269–72.

Wörgötter, Andreas. Who's Who in Goodwin's Growth Cycle. *Jahr. Nationalökon. Statist.*, May 1986, *201*(3), pp. 222–28.

1312 Economic Fluctuations: Theory

Abraham, Katharine G. and Katz, Lawrence F. Cyclical Unemployment: Sectoral Shifts or Aggregate Disturbances? *J. Polit. Econ.*, Part 1, June 1986, *94*(3), pp. 507–22.

Abramovitz, Moses. Inventory Fluctuations in the United States since 1929: Comment. **In** *Gordon, R. J., ed.*, 1986, pp. 214–23. **[G: U.S.]**

Akashi, Shigeo and Asada, Toichiro. Money in Kaldorian Cycle Theory. *Econ. Rev. (Keizai Kenkyu)*, April 1986, *37*(2), pp. 169–77.

Andersen, Torben M. Fagforeninger, lønudvikling og arbejdsløshed. (Trade Unions and the Wage–Employment Nexus. With English summary.) *Nationaløkon. Tidsskr.*, 1986, *124*(3), pp. 241–58. **[G: Denmark]**

Azariadis, Costas and Guesnerie, Roger. Sunspots and Cycles. *Rev. Econ. Stud.*, October 1986, *53*(5), pp. 725–37.

Bailey, Martin J. The Behavior of United States Deficits: Comment. **In** *Gordon, R. J., ed.*, 1986, pp. 387–89. **[G: U.S.]**

Barro, Robert J. Do Equilibrium Real Business Cycle Theories Explain Postwar U.S. Business Cycles? Comment. **In** *Fischer, S., ed.*, 1986, pp. 135–39. **[G: U.S.]**

Barro, Robert J. The Behavior of United States Deficits. **In** *Gordon, R. J., ed.*, 1986, pp. 361–87. **[G: U.S.]**

Beenstock, Michael. The General Theory, Secular Stagnation and the World Economy. **In** *Burton, J., et al.*, 1986, pp. 121–35.

Bernanke, Ben S. Alternative Explanations of the Money–Income Correlation. *Carnegie-Rochester Conf. Ser. Public Policy*, Autumn 1986, 25, pp. 49–99. **[G: U.S.]**

Bernard, Victor L. Unanticipated Inflation and the Value of the Firm. *J. Finan. Econ.*, March 1986, *15*(3), pp. 285–321. **[G: U.S.]**

Blanchard, Olivier J. Market Structure and Macroeconomic Fluctuations: Comments. *Brookings Pap. Econ. Act.*, 1986, (2), pp. 323–28.

Boddy, Raford and Alwan, Rami. Work Shifts and the Cyclical Behavior of Productivity and Real Wages. *J. Macroecon.*, Summer 1986, *8*(3), pp. 355–63.

Bordo, Michael D. Austrian Influence on Business Cycle Theory [Hayekian Trade Cycle Theory: A Reappraisal]. *Cato J.*, Fall 1986, *6*(2), pp. 455–59.

Boschen, John F. The Information Content of Indexed Bonds. *J. Money, Credit, Banking*, February 1986, *18*(1), pp. 76–87.

Brock, William A. Distinguishing Random and Deterministic Systems: Abridged Version. *J. Econ. Theory*, October 1986, *40*(1), pp. 168–95. **[G: U.S.]**

Brunner, Karl and Meltzer, Allan H. Real Business Cycles, Real Exchange Rates, and Actual Policies. *Carnegie-Rochester Conf. Ser. Public Policy*, Autumn 1986, *25*, pp. 1–10.

Bruno, Sergio. Incertezza, complesità e crisi della "economia del controllo." (Uncertainty, Complexity and Crisis of the "Economics of Control." With English summary.) *Econ. Lavoro*, July-Sept. 1986, *20*(3), pp. 39–61.

Buffie, Edward F. Input Price Shocks in the Small Open Economy. *Oxford Econ. Pap.*, November 1986, *38*(3), pp. 551–65.

Businaro, Ugo L. Applying the Biological Evolution Metaphor to Technological Innovation. **In** *Freeman, C., ed.*, 1986, pp. 104–20.

Day, Richard H. A Non-Walrasian Model of the Business Cycle: Comment. **In** *Day, R. H. and Eliasson, G., eds.*, 1986, pp. 148–49.

De Long, James Bradford and Summers, Lawrence H. Is Increased Price Flexibility Stabilizing? *Amer. Econ. Rev.*, December 1986, *76*(5), pp. 1031–44.

Del Vecchio, Vincenzo and Garonna, Paolo. L'aggiustamento alla recessione in condizioni di incertezza: riduzione di orario, Part-Time e disoccupazione. (Adjustment to the Recession under Uncertainty. With English summary.) *Econ. Lavoro*, Apr.-June 1986, *20*(2), pp. 31–49.

Dellas, Harris. A Real Model of the World Business Cycle. *J. Int. Money Finance*, September 1986, *5*(3), pp. 381–94. **[G: Japan; U.K.; U.S.; W. Germany]**

Devine, James N. Empirical Studies in Marxian Crisis Theory: Introduction. *Rev. Radical Polit. Econ.*, Spring/Summer 1986, *18*(1/2), pp. 1–12.

Di Matteo, Massimo. Long Waves in Relative Prices: An Interpretation. **In** *Frisch, H. and Gahlen, B., eds.*, 1986, pp. 126–44.

Diamand, Marcelo. Overcoming Argentina's Stop-and-Go Economic Cycles. **In** *Hartlyn, J. and Morley, S. A., eds.*, 1986, pp. 129–64. **[G: Argentina]**

Dosi, Giovanni. Technology and Conditions of Macroeconomic Development. **In** *Freeman, C., ed.*, 1986, pp. 60–77.

Dotsey, Michael. Wealth Effects of Open Market Operations and Optimal Monetary Policy. *J. Monet. Econ.*, March 1986, *17*(2), pp. 225–38.

Duménil, Gérard and Lévy, D. Real and Financial Stability in Capitalism: The Law of the Tendency toward Increasing Instability. *Econ. Forum*, Winter 1986-1987, *16*(1), pp. 1–27.

Egger, John B. A Sympathetic Critic of the Austrian Business-Cycle Theory. **In** *[Lachmann, L. M.]*, 1986, pp. 56–71.

Eichenbaum, Martin and Singleton, Kenneth J. Do Equilibrium Real Business Cycle Theories Explain Postwar U.S. Business Cycles? **In** *Fischer, S., ed.*, 1986, pp. 91–135. **[G: U.S.]**

Farmer, Roger E. A. Deficits and Cycles. *J. Econ. Theory*, October 1986, *40*(1), pp. 77–88.

Foley, Duncan K. Stabilization Policy in a Nonlinear Business Cycle Model. **In** *Semmler, W., ed.*, 1986, pp. 200–211.

Freeman, Scott. Inside Money, Monetary Contractions, and Welfare. *Can. J. Econ.*, February 1986, *19*(1), pp. 87–98.

Friedman, Benjamin M. Money, Credit, and Interest Rates in the Business Cycle. **In** *Gordon, R. J., ed.*, 1986, pp. 395–438. **[G: U.S.]**

Garrison, Roger W. Hayekian Trade Cycle Theory: A Reappraisal. *Cato J.*, Fall 1986, *6*(2), pp. 437–53.

Gebauer, Wolfgang. Kondratieff's Long Waves. *Konjunkturpolitik*, 1986, *32*(4), pp. 235–55. **[G: W. Europe; U.S.]**

Glombowski, Jörg and Krüger, Michael. Some Extensions of a Classical Growth Cycle Model. **In** *Semmler, W., ed.*, 1986, pp. 212–51.

Goldstein, Jonathan P. Mark-Up Pricing over the Business Cycle: The Microfoundations of the Variable Mark-Up. *Southern Econ. J.*, July 1986, *53*(1), pp. 233–46.

Goodwin, Richard M. The Economy as an Evolutionary Pulsator. *J. Econ. Behav. Organ.*, December 1986, *7*(4), pp. 341–49.

Goodwin, Richard M. The M–K–S System: The Functioning and Evolution of Capitalism. **In** *Wagener, H.-J. and Drukker, J. W., eds.*, 1986, pp. 14–21.

Goroff, Daniel. On Endogenous Competitive Business Cycles: Comment. **In** *Sonnenschein, H. F., ed.*, 1986, pp. 35–36.

Grandmont, Jean-Michel. On Endogenous Competitive Business Cycles. **In** *Sonnenschein, H. F., ed.*, 1986, pp. 25–34.

Grandmont, Jean-Michel. Stabilizing Competitive Business Cycles. *J. Econ. Theory*, October 1986, *40*(1), pp. 57–76.

Grandmont, Jean-Michel and Laroque, Guy. Stability of Cycles and Expectations. *J. Econ. Theory*, October 1986, *40*(1), pp. 138–51.

Grandmont, Jean-Michel and Malgrange, Pierre. Nonlinear Economic Dynamics: Introduction. *J. Econ. Theory*, October 1986, *40*(1), pp. 3–12.

Grossman, Herschel I. Money, Real Activity, and Rationality [The Significance of Monetary Disequilibrium]. *Cato J.*, Fall 1986, *6*(2), pp. 401–08.

Guesnerie, Roger. Stationary Sunspot Equilibria

in an *N* Commodity World. *J. Econ. Theory*, October 1986, *40*(1), pp. 103–27.

Haberler, Gottfried. Reflections on Hayek's Business Cycle Theory. *Cato J.*, Fall 1986, *6*(2), pp. 421–35. **[G: U.S.]**

Hall, Robert E. Market Structure and Macroeconomic Fluctuations. *Brookings Pap. Econ. Act.*, 1986, (2), pp. 285–322. **[G: U.S.]**

Hillinger, Claude. Theorie und Empirie der Konjunkturzyklen. (Business Cycles—Theory and Empirical Results. With English summary.) *Konjunkturpolitik*, 1986, *32*(3), pp. 101–29. **[G: W. Germany]**

Hubbard, R. Glenn. Market Structure and Macroeconomic Fluctuations: Comments. *Brookings Pap. Econ. Act.*, 1986, (2), pp. 328–36.

Jarsulic, Marc. Growth Cycles in a Classical-Keynesian Model. **In** *Semmler, W., ed.*, 1986, pp. 252–68.

Kaish, Stanley. Behavioral Economics in the Theory of the Business Cycle. **In** *Gilad, B. and Kaish, S., eds., Vol. B*, 1986, pp. 31–49.

King, Robert G. Money and Business Cycle: Comments on Bernanke and Related Literature. *Carnegie-Rochester Conf. Ser. Public Policy*, Autumn 1986, *25*, pp. 101–15. **[G: U.S.]**

Kleinknecht, Alfred. Post–World War II Growth as a Schumpeter Boom. **In** *Berend, I. T. and Borchardt, K., eds.*, 1986, pp. 371–92.

Kraft, Manfred and Weise, Peter. Grundzüge einer mikroökonomischen Konjunkturtheorie. (Outline of a Microeconomic Theory of Business Cycles. With English summary.) *Jahr. Nationalökon. Statist.*, July 1986, *201*(4), pp. 370–77.

Kromphardt, Jürgen. The Contribution of Business Cycle Theories to the Explanation of the Actual Economic Slowdown. **In** *Frisch, H. and Gahlen, B., eds.*, 1986, pp. 70–85. **[G: W. Germany]**

Lakshmanan, T. R. and Chatterjee, Lata. Technical Change, Employment and Metropolitan Adjustment. **In** *Nijkamp, P., ed. (II)*, 1986, pp. 21–45.

Leijonhufvud, Axel. Real and Monetary Factors in Business Fluctuations [The Significance of Monetary Disequilibrium]. *Cato J.*, Fall 1986, *6*(2), pp. 409–20.

Lewin, Peter. Economic Policy and the Capital Structure. **In** *[Lachmann, L. M.]*, 1986, pp. 211–20.

Lipietz, Alain. Behind the Crisis: The Exhaustion of a Regime of Accumulation. A "Regulation School" Perspective on Some French Empirical Works. *Rev. Radical Polit. Econ.*, Spring/Summer 1986, *18*(1/2), pp. 13–32.

Lorenz, Hans-Walter. On the Uniqueness of Limit Cycles in Business Cycle Theory. *Metroecon.*, October 1986, *38*(3), pp. 281–93.

Mankiw, N. Gregory. Do Equilibrium Real Business Cycle Theories Explain Postwar U.S. Business Cycles? Comment. **In** *Fischer, S., ed.*, 1986, pp. 139–45. **[G: U.S.]**

Manuelli, Rodolfo E. Modern Business Cycle Analysis: A Guide to the Prescott–Summers Debate. *Fed. Res. Bank Minn. Rev.*, Fall 1986, *10*(4), pp. 3–8.

Maravall, Agustin and Bentolila, Samuel. Una medida de volatilidad en series temporales con una Aplicación al control monetario en España. (With English summary.) *Invest. Ecón.*, January 1986, *10*(1), pp. 185–99. **[G: Spain]**

McCallum, Bennett T. Issues Concerning the Nonpecuniary Yield of Money [Money, Deregulation, and the Business Cycle]. *Cato J.*, Fall 1986, *6*(2), pp. 607–11. **[G: U.S.]**

McCallum, Bennett T. On "Real" and "Sticky-Price" Theories of the Business Cycle. *J. Money, Credit, Banking*, November 1986, *18*(4), pp. 397–414.

Mengarelli, Gianluigi. Business Cycle Theory and Structural Changes in the 1970s. *Rev. Econ. Cond. Italy*, Sept.-Dec. 1986, (3), pp. 455–84. **[G: OECD]**

Minsky, Hyman P. Money and Crisis in Schumpeter and Keynes. **In** *Wagener, H.-J. and Drukker, J. W., eds.*, 1986, pp. 112–22.

Musgrave, Richard A. Fiscal Policy in Prosperity and Depression. **In** *Musgrave, R. A., Vol. 1*, 1986, *1948*, pp. 359–69.

Neftci, Salih N. Testing Non-linearity in Business Cycles. **In** *Semmler, W., ed.*, 1986, pp. 324–40.

Nell, Edward J. Cyclical Growth: The Interdependent Dynamics of Industry and Agriculture. **In** *Semmler, W., ed.*, 1986, pp. 289–303.

O'Donnell, Guillermo. Overcoming Argentina's Stop-and-Go Economic Cycles: Comment. **In** *Hartlyn, J. and Morley, S. A., eds.*, 1986, pp. 356–59. **[G: Argentina]**

O'Driscoll, Gerald P., Jr. Money, Deregulation, and the Business Cycle. *Cato J.*, Fall 1986, *6*(2), pp. 587–605. **[G: U.S.]**

Parguez, Alain. Au cœur du circuit ou quelques réponses aux énigmes du circuit. (Inside the Core or the First Principles of the General Theory of Circuit. With English summary.) *Écon. Soc.*, Aug.-Sept. 1986, *20*(8–9), pp. 23–39.

Perez, Carlota. Structural Change and Assimilation of New Technologies in the Economic and Social System. **In** *Freeman, C., ed.*, 1986, pp. 27–47.

Phaneuf, Louis. Approche d'équilibre général stochastique du cycle économique: problèmes et réalisations. (The Stochastic General Equilibrium Approach to Business Cycles: Results and Problems. With English summary.) *L'Actual. Econ.*, March 1986, *62*(1), pp. 110–46.

Poterba, James M.; Rotemberg, Julio J. and Summers, Lawrence H. A Tax-Based Test for Nominal Rigidities. *Amer. Econ. Rev.*, September 1986, *76*(4), pp. 659–75. **[G: U.S.; U.K.]**

Prescott, Edward C. Response to a Skeptic. *Fed. Res. Bank Minn. Rev.*, Fall 1986, *10*(4), pp. 28–33. **[G: U.S.]**

Prescott, Edward C. Theory Ahead of Business Cycle Measurement. *Fed. Res. Bank Minn. Rev.*, Fall 1986, *10*(4), pp. 9–22. **[G: U.S.]**

Prescott, Edward C. Theory Ahead of Business-

Cycle Measurement. *Carnegie-Rochester Conf. Ser. Public Policy,* Autumn 1986, *25,* pp. 11–44. **[G: U.S.]**

Puu, Tönu. Multiplier-Accelerator Models Revisited. *Reg. Sci. Urban Econ.,* February 1986, *16*(1), pp. 81–95.

Reichlin, Pietro. Equilibrium Cycles in an Overlapping Generations Economy with Production. *J. Econ. Theory,* October 1986, *40*(1), pp. 89–102.

Rogoff, Kenneth. Theory Ahead of Business Cycle Measurement: A Comment. *Carnegie-Rochester Conf. Ser. Public Policy,* Autumn 1986, *25,* pp. 45–48.

Rosenberg, Nathan and Frischtak, Claudio R. Technological Innovation and Long Waves. **In** *Freeman, C., ed.,* 1986, pp. 5–26.

Scheide, Joachim. New Classical and Austrian Business Cycle Theory: Is There a Difference? *Weltwirtsch. Arch.,* 1986, *122*(3), pp. 575–98.

Scheinkman, Jose A. On Endogenous Competitive Business Cycles: Comment. **In** *Sonnenschein, H. F., ed.,* 1986, pp. 36–37.

Scheinkman, Jose A. and Weiss, Laurence. Borrowing Constraints and Aggregate Economic Activity. *Econometrica,* January 1986, *54*(1), pp. 23–45.

Schlieper, Ulrich. Real Wages, Business Cycles and Unemployment. **In** *Frisch, H. and Gahlen, B., eds.,* 1986, pp. 145–58.

Semmler, Willi. On a Microdynamics of a Nonlinear Macrocycle Model. **In** *Semmler, W., ed.,* 1986, pp. 170–99.

Semmler, Willi. On Nonlinear Theories of Economic Cycles and the Persistence of Business Cycles. *Math. Soc. Sci.,* August 1986, *12*(1), pp. 47–76.

Shleifer, Andrei. Implementation Cycles. *J. Polit. Econ.,* December 1986, *94*(6), pp. 1163–90.

Siegenthaler, Hansjörg. The State of Confidence and Economic Behaviour in the 30s and 70s: Theoretical Framework—Historical Evidence. **In** *Berend, I. T. and Borchardt, K., eds.,* 1986, pp. 409–36.

Sims, Christopher A. On Endogenous Competitive Business Cycles: Comment. **In** *Sonnenschein, H. F., ed.,* 1986, pp. 37–39.

Soete, Luc L. G. Long Cycles and the International Diffusion of Technology. **In** *Freeman, C., ed.,* 1986, pp. 214–30.

Steindl, Alois, et al. On the Optimality of Cyclical Employment Policies: A Numerical Investigation. *J. Econ. Dynam. Control,* December 1986, *10*(4), pp. 457–66.

Stockman, Alan C. and Koh, Ai Tee. Open-Economy Implications of Two Models of Business Fluctuations. *Can. J. Econ.,* February 1986, *19*(1), pp. 23–34.

Summers, Lawrence H. Some Skeptical Observations on Real Business Cycle Theory. *Fed. Res. Bank Minn. Rev.,* Fall 1986, *10*(4), pp. 23–27. **[G: U.S.]**

Taub, Bart. The Tradeoff between Social Insurance and Aggregate Fluctuations. *Info. Econ. Policy,* December 1986, *2*(4), pp. 259–76.

Tullock, Gordon. The Macro Instability of the Market. **In** *Tullock, G.,* 1986, pp. 193–203.

Vercelli, Alessandro. Stagflation and the Recent Revival of Schumpeterian Entrepreneurship. **In** *Frisch, H. and Gahlen, B., eds.,* 1986, pp. 159–85.

Wallace, Neil. On Endogenous Competitive Business Cycles: Comment. **In** *Sonnenschein, H. F., ed.,* 1986, pp. 40.

Wallace, Neil. The Relevance of Legal Restrictions Theory [Money, Deregulation, and the Business Cycle]. *Cato J.,* Fall 1986, *6*(2), pp. 613–16. **[G: U.S.]**

Weiss, Laurence. Asymmetric Adjustment Costs and Sectoral Shifts. **In** *[Arrow, K. J.], Vol. 2,* 1986, pp. 251–64.

Winckler, Georg and Kunst, Robert. The Influence of Wage Rate Variations on the Level of Employment with and without an Exogenous Interest Rate. **In** *Frisch, H. and Gahlen, B., eds.,* 1986, pp. 186–200.

Woodford, Michael. On Endogenous Competitive Business Cycles: Comment. **In** *Sonnenschein, H. F., ed.,* 1986, pp. 41–44.

Woodford, Michael. Stationary Sunspot Equilibria in a Finance Constrained Economy. *J. Econ. Theory,* October 1986, *40*(1), pp. 128–37.

Wörgötter, Andreas. Asymmetric Adjustment Costs and Price Stickiness. **In** *Frisch, H. and Gahlen, B., eds.,* 1986, pp. 201–16.

Wright, Randall. Job Search and Cyclical Unemployment. *J. Polit. Econ.,* February 1986, *94*(1), pp. 38–55.

Yeager, Leland B. The Significance of Monetary Disequilibrium. *Cato J.,* Fall 1986, *6*(2), pp. 369–99.

Yunker, James A. A Market Socialist Critique of Capitalism's Dynamic Performance. *J. Econ. Issues,* March 1986, *20*(1), pp. 63–86.

1313 Economic Fluctuations: Studies

Abel, Andrew B. and Blanchard, Olivier J. The Present Value of Profits and Cyclical Movements in Investment. *Econometrica,* March 1986, *54*(2), pp. 249–73. **[G: U.S.]**

Adnett, N. J. On the Job Search in a Recession. *Appl. Econ.,* March 1986, *18*(3), pp. 333–45. **[G: U.K.]**

Akhtar, M. A. and Harris, Ethan S. Monetary Policy Influence on the Economy—An Empirical Analysis. *Fed. Res. Bank New York Quart. Rev.,* Winter 1986-87, *11*(4), pp. 19–34. **[G: U.S.]**

Allen, Stuart D. The Federal Reserve and the Electoral Cycle: A Note. *J. Money, Credit, Banking,* February 1986, *18*(1), pp. 88–94. **[G: U.S.]**

Allen, Stuart D.; Sulock, Joseph M. and Sabo, William A. The Political Business Cycle: How Significant? *Public Finance Quart.,* January 1986, *14*(1), pp. 107–12. **[G: U.S.]**

Andersen, P. S. Keynesian and Classical Unemployment: Evidence from the Current Cycle. *Eastern Econ. J.,* July-Sept. 1986, *12*(3), pp. 223–36. **[G: OECD]**

Apeloig, Shalom. Graphoscopy: A New Method for Business Cycle Forecasting. *J. Stud. Econ. Econometrics,* April 1986, (24), pp. 43–80.

Auerbach, Alan J. Major Changes in Cyclical Behavior: Comment. **In** *Gordon, R. J., ed.,* 1986, pp. 573–75. **[G: U.S.; U.K.; France; W. Germany]**

Baily, Martin Neil. The Cyclical Behavior of Industrial Labor Markets: A Comparison of the Prewar and Postwar Eras: Comment. **In** *Gordon, R. J., ed.,* 1986, pp. 621–66. **[G: U.S.]**

Balke, Nathan S. and Gordon, Robert J. The American Business Cycle: Historical Data. **In** *Gordon, R. J., ed.,* 1986, pp. 781–850. **[G: U.S.]**

Barnard, Jerald R. and Kennedy, James E. A Method for Analyzing the Changing Impact of the Business Cycle on Regional Economies. **In** *Perryman, M. R. and Schmidt, J. R., eds.,* 1986, pp. 159–78. **[G: U.S.]**

Berend, Iván T. The Great Economic Shocks of the 20th Century in the General Processes of History: Similarities and Differences between the 1930s and the 1970s–1980s. **In** *Berend, I. T. and Borchardt, K., eds.,* 1986, pp. 545–59. **[G: Global]**

Bernanke, Ben S. and Powell, James L. The Cyclical Behavior of Industrial Labor Markets: A Comparison of the Prewar and Postwar Eras. **In** *Gordon, R. J., ed.,* 1986, pp. 583–621. **[G: U.S.]**

Bernstein, Michael A. Economic Instability in the United States in the 1930s and the 1970s: An Essay in Historical Homology. **In** *Berend, I. T. and Borchardt, K., eds.,* 1986, pp. 35–61. **[G: U.S.]**

Bićanić, Ivo. Some General Comparisons of the Impact of the Two World Crises of the Twentieth Century on the Yugoslav Economy and Changes in the Well-Being of the Population Caused by the Crises. **In** *Berend, I. T. and Borchardt, K., eds.,* 1986, pp. 248–74. **[G: Yugoslavia]**

Bieshaar, Hans and Kleinknecht, Alfred. Kondratieff Long Waves? Reply. *Konjunkturpolitik,* 1986, *32*(3), pp. 185–94. **[G: OECD]**

Black, Stanley W. The Open Economy: Implications for Monetary and Fiscal Policy: Comment. **In** *Gordon, R. J., ed.,* 1986, pp. 501–04. **[G: U.S.]**

Blanchard, Olivier J. and Melino, Angelo. The Cyclical Behavior of Prices and Quantities: The Case of the Automobile Market. *J. Monet. Econ.,* May 1986, *17*(3), pp. 379–407.

Blanchard, Olivier J. and Watson, Mark W. Are Business Cycles All Alike? **In** *Gordon, R. J., ed.,* 1986, pp. 123–56. **[G: U.S.]**

Blinder, Alan S. and Holtz-Eakin, Douglas. Inventory Fluctuations in the United States since 1929. **In** *Gordon, R. J., ed.,* 1986, pp. 183–214. **[G: U.S.]**

Blinder, Alan S. and Holtz-Eakin, Douglas. Inventory Fluctuations in the United States since 1929: Reply. **In** *Gordon, R. J., ed.,* 1986, pp. 231–33. **[G: U.S.]**

Bluestone, Barry; Harrison, Bennett and Clayton-Matthews, Alan. Structure vs. Cycle in U.S. Manufacturing Job Growth. *Ind. Relat.,* Spring 1986, *25*(2), pp. 101–17. **[G: U.S.]**

Booth, Douglas E. Long Waves and Uneven Regional Growth. *Southern Econ. J.,* October 1986, *53*(2), pp. 448–60. **[G: U.S.]**

Borchardt, Knut. The Impact of the Depression of the 1930s and Its Relevance for the Contemporary World: Introductory Report. **In** *Berend, I. T. and Borchardt, K., eds.,* 1986, pp. 5–32.

Bordo, Michael D. Financial Crises, Banking Crises, Stock Market Crashes and the Money Supply: Some International Evidence, 1870–1933. **In** *Capie, F. and Wood, G. E., eds.,* 1986, pp. 190–248.

Botos, Katalin. The Impact of the Depression of the 1930s and Its Relevance for the Contemporary World: 1929/33 vs. 1979/83. **In** *Berend, I. T. and Borchardt, K., eds.,* 1986, pp. 333–54.

Britton, Andrew; Eastwood, Fiona and Major, Robin L. Macroeconomic Policy in Italy and Britain. *Nat. Inst. Econ. Rev.,* November 1986, (118), pp. 38–52. **[G: Italy; U.K.]**

Broadberry, S. N. Aggregate Supply in Interwar Britain. *Econ. J.,* June 1986, *96*(382), pp. 467–81. **[G: U.K.]**

Bronfenbrenner, Martin. Causes of Contemporary Stagnation: What Should We Have Done? **In** *Frisch, H. and Gahlen, B., eds.,* 1986, pp. 1–12. **[G: U.S.]**

Bruno, Michael. Stagflation in the Industrial Countries: An Updated Overview. *Hitotsubashi J. Econ.,* Spec. Iss. Oct. 1986, *27,* pp. 57–74. **[G: OECD]**

Calzolari, Michele and Somaini, Eugenio. Ciclicitá del mark-up in un modello di oligopolio. Costi e prezzi nel settore manifatturiero italiano (1970–1982). (Mark-up Cycles in an Oligopoly Model. Costs and Prices in the Italian Manufacturing Industry [1970–1982]. With English summary.) *Polit. Econ.,* April 1986, *2*(1), pp. 81–120. **[G: Italy]**

Chimerine, Lawrence and Young, Richard M. Economic Surprises and Messages of the 1980's. *Amer. Econ. Rev.,* May 1986, *76*(2), pp. 31–36. **[G: U.S.]**

Cholette, Pierre A. and Lamy, Robert. Multivariate ARIMA Forecasting of Irregular Time Series. *Int. J. Forecasting,* 1986, *2*(2), pp. 201–16. **[G: Canada]**

Connaughton, John E. and Madsen, Ronald A. Recession and Recovery: A State and Regional Analysis. *Rev. Reg. Stud.,* Spring 1986, *16*(2), pp. 1–10. **[G: U.S.]**

Coombs, Rod and Kleinknecht, Alfred. New Evidence on the Shift toward Process Innovation during the Long-Wave Upswing. **In** *Freeman, C., ed.,* 1986, pp. 78–103. **[G: OECD]**

Corona, Leonel. Long Waves and the International Diffusion of the Automated Labour Process: The Role of the Semi-industrialized Countries. **In** *Freeman, C., ed.,* 1986, pp. 194–213. **[G: LDCs]**

De Long, James Bradford and Summers, Law-

rence H. Are Business Cycles Symmetrical? Additional Contribution. **In** *Gordon, R. J., ed.*, 1986, pp. 166–78. **[G: OECD]**

De Long, James Bradford and Summers, Lawrence H. Improvements in Macroeconomic Stability: The Role of Wages and Prices: Comment. **In** *Gordon, R. J., ed.*, 1986, pp. 669–72. **[G: U.S.]**

De Long, James Bradford and Summers, Lawrence H. The Changing Cyclical Variability of Economic Activity in the United States. **In** *Gordon, R. J., ed.*, 1986, pp. 679–719. **[G: U.S.]**

Deaton, Angus S. The Role of Consumption in Economic Fluctuations: Comment. **In** *Gordon, R. J., ed.*, 1986, pp. 255–59. **[G: U.S.]**

Defris, Lorraine V.; Layton, Allan P. and Zehnwirth, Ben. The Impact of Economic Cycles on the Demand for International Telecommunications in Australia. *Info. Econ. Policy*, June 1986, *2*(2), pp. 105–17. **[G: Australia]**

Dirkson, Erik and Klopper, Marcel. Is There an Economic Crisis in the USSR? *Comp. Econ. Stud.*, Spring 1986, *28*(1), pp. 66–74. **[G: U.S.S.R.]**

Domowitz, Ian; Hubbard, R. Glenn and Petersen, Bruce C. Business Cycles and the Relationship between Concentration and Price–Cost Margins. *Rand J. Econ.*, Spring 1986, *17*(1), pp. 1–17. **[G: U.S.]**

Dornbusch, Rudiger and Fischer, Stanley. The Open Economy: Implications for Monetary and Fiscal Policy. **In** *Gordon, R. J., ed.*, 1986, pp. 459–501. **[G: U.S.]**

Duménil, Gérard; Glick, Mark and Rangel, José. La grande dépression énigme d'hier ou d'aujourd'hui? (The Great Depression: Yesterday's Riddle for Today. With English summary.) *Revue Écon.*, May 1986, *37*(3), pp. 381–427. **[G: U.S.]**

Eckstein, Otto and Sinai, Allen. The Mechanisms of the Business Cycle in the Postwar Era. **In** *Gordon, R. J., ed.*, 1986, pp. 39–105. **[G: U.S.]**

ECLAC Secretariat, Santiago. Development and Crisis in Latin America: 1950–84. **In** *Maddison, A., ed.*, 1986, pp. 28–66. **[G: Latin America]**

Eisner, Robert. The Changing Cyclical Variability of Economic Activity in the United States: Comment. **In** *Gordon, R. J., ed.*, 1986, pp. 719–27. **[G: U.S.]**

Eliasson, Gunnar. Micro Heterogeneity of Firms and the Stability of Industrial Growth. **In** *Day, R. H. and Eliasson, G., eds.*, 1986, *1984*, pp. 79–104. **[G: Sweden]**

Eliasson, Gunnar. Micro Heterogeneity of Firms and the Stability of Industrial Growth: Reply. **In** *Day, R. H. and Eliasson, G., eds.*, 1986, pp. 112–14. **[G: Sweden]**

Erić, Milan, et al. Identification of Cycles in Yugoslav Industry during the Period 1953–1982. *Eastern Europ. Econ.*, Winter 1986-87, *25*(2), pp. 100–123. **[G: Yugoslavia]**

Fabricant, Solomon. Major Changes in Cyclical Behavior: Comment. **In** *Gordon, R. J., ed.*, 1986, pp. 575–78. **[G: U.S.; U.K.; W. Germany; France]**

Falk, Barry. Further Evidence on the Asymmetric Behavior of Economic Time Series over the Business Cycle. *J. Polit. Econ.*, October 1986, *94*(5), pp. 1096–1109. **[G: U.S.]**

Feldstein, Martin S. Supply Side Economics: Old Truths and New Claims. *Amer. Econ. Rev.*, May 1986, *76*(2), pp. 26–30. **[G: U.S.]**

Fitoussi, Jean-Paul and Phelps, Edmund S. Causes of the 1980s Slump in Europe. *Brookings Pap. Econ. Act.*, 1986, (2), pp. 487–513. **[G: W. Europe; U.S.]**

Ford, Alec G. Financial Crises, Banking Crises, Stock Market Crashes and the Money Supply: Some International Evidence, 1870–1933: Comment. **In** *Capie, F. and Wood, G. E., eds.*, 1986, pp. 249–53.

Fraile, Pedro and Andreu, Juan Hernández. The Twentieth Century's Two Big Crises: Origins and Similarities. **In** *Berend, I. T. and Borchardt, K., eds.*, 1986, pp. 355–70.

Friedman, Benjamin M. Money, Credit, and Interest Rates in the Business Cycle: Reply. **In** *Gordon, R. J., ed.*, 1986, pp. 450–55. **[G: U.S.]**

Gabriel, Stuart A. and Maoz, Ilan. Cyclical Fluctuations in the Israeli Housing Markets. *J. Urban Econ.*, May 1986, *19*(3), pp. 249–63. **[G: Israel]**

Gahlen, Bernhard. Price and Quantity Variability under Stagflation. **In** *Frisch, H. and Gahlen, B., eds.*, 1986, pp. 45–69. **[G: W. Germany]**

Gandolfo, Giancarlo, et al. The Election and the Economy: A Systemic Analysis of the Italian Case. *J. Econ. Dynam. Control*, June 1986, *10*(1/2), pp. 213–18. **[G: Italy]**

Garraty, John A. Agriculture in the Great Depression and in the 1970s. **In** *Berend, I. T. and Borchardt, K., eds.*, 1986, pp. 516–44. **[G: Global]**

Geweke, John. Fixed Investment in the American Business Cycle, 1919–83: Comment. **In** *Gordon, R. J., ed.*, 1986, pp. 336–40. **[G: U.S.]**

Goldfeld, Stephen M. Money, Credit, and Interest Rates in the Business Cycle: Comment. **In** *Gordon, R. J., ed.*, 1986, pp. 438–41. **[G: U.S.]**

Goldstein, Harvey A. The Changing International Division of Labor and Regional Employment Cycles in the U.S. *Rev. Reg. Stud.*, Winter 1986, *16*(1), pp. 31–43. **[G: U.S.]**

Gomulka, Stanislaw. Specific and Systemic Causes of the Polish Crisis, 1980–82. **In** *Gomulka, S.*, 1986, *1983*, pp. 227–50. **[G: Poland]**

Gordon, Robert J. and Veitch, John M. Fixed Investment in the American Business Cycle, 1919–83: Reply. **In** *Gordon, R. J., ed.*, 1986, pp. 348–51. **[G: U.S.]**

Gordon, Robert J. and Veitch, John M. Fixed Investment in the American Business Cycle, 1919–83. **In** *Gordon, R. J., ed.*, 1986, pp. 267–335. **[G: U.S.]**

Grossman, Gregory. Inflationary, Political, and

Social Implications of the Current Economic Slowdown. **In** *Höhmann, H.-H.; Nove, A. and Vogel, H., eds.*, 1986, pp. 172–97. **[G: U.S.S.R.]**

Grossman, Herschel I. The Changing Cyclical Variability of Economic Activity in the United States: Comment. **In** *Gordon, R. J., ed.*, 1986, pp. 728–31. **[G: U.S.]**

Hadjimatheou, George. Why Has Britain Not Had Full Employment since the Early 1970s? *J. Post Keynesian Econ.*, Spring 1986, *8*(3), pp. 359–70. **[G: U.K.]**

Hall, Robert E. The Role of Consumption in Economic Fluctuations. **In** *Gordon, R. J., ed.*, 1986, pp. 237–55. **[G: U.S.]**

Hansen, Gerd. Der konjunkturelle Einfluss der Geld- und Fiskalpolitik in der Bundesrepublik 1972–1982. Eine ökonometrische Analyse unter rationalen Erwartungen. (The Effect of Monetary and Fiscal Policy on Business Cycles in the Federal Republic of Germany 1972–1982. With English summary.) *Kyklos*, 1986, *39*(2), pp. 180–208. **[G: W. Germany]**

Harrison, Bennett; Tilly, Chris and Bluestone, Barry. Wage Inequality Takes a Great U-Turn. *Challenge*, Mar./Apr. 1986, *29*(1), pp. 26–32. **[G: U.S.]**

Heller, Walter W. A Distinction *with* a Difference. *Challenge*, July/Aug. 1986, *29*(3), pp. 59. **[G: U.S.]**

Heller, Walter W. Activist Government: Key to Growth. *Challenge*, Mar./Apr. 1986, *29*(1), pp. 4–10. **[G: U.S.]**

Howland, Marie. Cyclical Startups and Closures in Key Industries of America's Cities and Suburbs. **In** *Bergman, E. M., ed.*, 1986, pp. 111–28. **[G: U.S.]**

Jonung, Lars. International Financial Crisis and the Swedish Economy 1857–1933. **In** *Capie, F. and Wood, G. E., eds.*, 1986, pp. 254–64. **[G: Sweden]**

Kaser, Michael and Nötel, R. The East European Economies in Two World Crises. **In** *Berend, I. T. and Borchardt, K., eds.*, 1986, pp. 215–47. **[G: E. Europe]**

Keyserling, Leon H. Let's Get This Straight [Activist Government: Key to Growth]. *Challenge*, Nov./Dec. 1986, *29*(5), pp. 56–58. **[G: U.S.]**

Kindleberger, Charles P. International Capital Movements and Foreign-Exchange Markets in Crisis: The 1930s and the 1980s. **In** *Berend, I. T. and Borchardt, K., eds.*, 1986, pp. 437–55.

King, Robert G. The Role of Consumption in Economic Fluctuations: Comment. **In** *Gordon, R. J., ed.*, 1986, pp. 259–63. **[G: U.S.]**

King, Stephen R. Improvements in Macroeconomic Stability: The Role of Wages and Prices: Comment. **In** *Gordon, R. J., ed.*, 1986, pp. 665–69. **[G: U.S.]**

King, Stephen R. Monetary Transmission: Through Bank Loans or Bank Liabilities? *J. Money, Credit, Banking*, August 1986, *18*(3), pp. 290–303. **[G: U.S.]**

Kleiman, Ephraim and Pincus, J. J. Incremental Export Subsidies: A Rejoinder [The Cyclical Effects of Incremental Export Subsidies]. *Econ. Rec.*, March 1986, *62*(176), pp. 93–94. **[G: Australia]**

Klein, Philip A. Leading Indicators of Inflation in Market Economies. *Int. J. Forecasting*, 1986, *2*(4), pp. 403–12. **[G: OECD]**

Kleinknecht, Alfred. Long Waves, Depression and Innovation. *De Economist*, 1986, *134*(1), pp. 84–108. **[G: Global]**

Kleinknecht, Alfred. Post–World War II Growth as a Schumpeter Boom. **In** *Berend, I. T. and Borchardt, K., eds.*, 1986, pp. 371–92.

de Koning, Jaap. The Expected Industrial Production Volume Estimated with the Help of Data from the Business-Cycle Test. *De Economist*, 1986, *134*(4), pp. 479–91. **[G: Netherlands]**

Kuczynski, Thomas. The Development of Foreign Trade during the "Greatest Depression"—An Exceptional Case. Some Statistical Observations Concerning the Structure of World Production of Material Goods. **In** *Berend, I. T. and Borchardt, K., eds.*, 1986, pp. 456–83. **[G: Global]**

Kuntjoro-Jakti, Dorodjatun. The Global Crisis of the 1980s and Indonesia's Response. *Hitotsubashi J. Econ.*, Spec. Iss. Oct. 1986, *27*, pp. 101–13.

Kuszczak, John and Murray, John D. A VAR Analysis of Economic Interdependence: Canada, the United States, and the Rest of the World. **In** *Hafer, R. W., ed. (I)*, 1986, pp. 77–131. **[G: Canada; U.S.]**

Layard, Richard and Nickell, Stephen J. Unemployment in Britain. *Economica*, Supplement 1986, *53*(210(S)), pp. S121–69. **[G: U.K.]**

Layton, Allan P. A Causality Analysis of Australia's Growth Cycle and the Composite Index of Leading Indicators. *Australian Econ. Pap.*, June 1986, *25*(46), pp. 57–66. **[G: Australia]**

Layton, Allan P.; Defris, Lorraine V. and Zehnwirth, Ben. An International Comparison of Economic Leading Indicators of Telecommunications Traffic. *Int. J. Forecasting*, 1986, *2*(4), pp. 413–25. **[G: Australia; U.S.]**

Lazear, Edward P. The Cyclical Behavior of Industrial Labor Markets: A Comparison of the Prewar and Postwar Eras: Comment. **In** *Gordon, R. J., ed.*, 1986, pp. 626–32. **[G: U.S.]**

Lebergott, Stanley. Discussion [New Estimates of Prewar Gross National Product and Unemployment] [The Reliability of Historical Macroeconomic Data for Comparing Cyclical Stability]. *J. Econ. Hist.*, June 1986, *46*(2), pp. 367–71. **[G: U.S.]**

Lilien, David M. and Hall, Robert E. Cyclical Fluctuations in the Labor Market. **In** *Ashenfelter, O. and Layard, R., eds., Vol. 2*, 1986, pp. 1001–35. **[G: U.S.]**

Liu, Tai-Ying and Hsu, Shuh-Tzy. The Validity of TIER's Business Climate Indicator. *Ifo-Studien*, 1986, *32*(1–3), pp. 71–80. **[G: Taiwan]**

Lluch, Constantino. ICORS, Savings Rates, and the Determinants of Public Expenditure in Developing Countries. **In** *Lal, D. and Wolf, M., eds.*, 1986, pp. 361–95. **[G: LDCs]**

Lovell, Michael C. The Mechanisms of the Business Cycle in the Postwar Era: Comment. **In** *Gordon, R. J., ed.*, 1986, pp. 105–10. **[G: U.S.]**

Maddison, Angus. Developing Countries in the 1930s: Possible Lessons for the 1980s. **In** *Lal, D. and Wolf, M., eds.*, 1986, pp. 15–47. **[G: LDCs; MDCs]**

Martin, Ronald L. Industrial Restructuring, Labour Shake-Out and the Geography of Recession. **In** *Danson, M., ed.*, 1986, pp. 1–22. **[G: U.K.]**

McCallum, Bennett T. Inventory Fluctuations in the United States since 1929: Comment. **In** *Gordon, R. J., ed.*, 1986, pp. 223–31. **[G: U.S.]**

Meiselman, David I. Avoidable Uncertainty and the Effects of Monetary Policy: Why Even Experts Can't Forecast [Monetary Control and the Political Business Cycle]. *Cato J.*, Winter 1986, *5*(3), pp. 701–07. **[G: U.S.]**

Meltzer, Allan H. Money, Credit, and Interest Rates in the Business Cycle: Comment. **In** *Gordon, R. J., ed.*, 1986, pp. 441–50. **[G: U.S.]**

Meltzer, Allan H. Real and Psuedo-financial Crises: Comment. **In** *Capie, F. and Wood, G. E., eds.*, 1986, pp. 32–37. **[G: U.S.; U.K.]**

Mills, Geofrey and Rockoff, Hugh. A Study of the End of the Depression in the United States and the United Kingdom Compared to the 1970s: Lessons for the Contemporary World. **In** *Berend, I. T. and Borchardt, K., eds.*, 1986, pp. 393–408. **[G: U.K.; U.S.]**

Mistral, Jacques. 125 ans de contrainte extérieure: l'expérience française. (125 Years of External Constraint: The French Case. With English summary.) *Écon. Soc.*, January 1986, *20*(1), pp. 91–115. **[G: France]**

Moggridge, D. E. Real and Pseudo-financial Crises: Comment. **In** *Capie, F. and Wood, G. E., eds.*, 1986, pp. 38–40. **[G: U.S.; U.K.]**

Moore, Geoffrey H. and Zarnowitz, Victor. The Development and Role of the National Bureau of Economic Research's Business Cycle Chronologies. **In** *Gordon, R. J., ed.*, 1986, pp. 735–79. **[G: OECD]**

Naples, Michele I. The Unraveling of the Union–Capital Truce and the U.S. Industrial Productivity Crisis. *Rev. Radical Polit. Econ.*, Spring/Summer 1986, *18*(1/2), pp. 110–31. **[G: U.S.]**

Neftci, Salih N. Is There a Cyclical Time Unit? *Carnegie-Rochester Conf. Ser. Public Policy*, Spring 1986, *24*, pp. 11–48. **[G: U.S.]**

Oshima, Harry T. The Construction Boom of the 1970s: The End of High Growth in the NICs and ASEAN? *Devel. Econ.*, September 1986, *24*(3), pp. 207–28. **[G: LDCs; Asia]**

Ott, Mack and Tatom, John A. Are Energy Prices Cyclical? *Energy Econ.*, October 1986, *8*(4), pp. 227–36. **[G: U.S.]**

Pauly, R. and Tosstorff, G. Lead- und Lag-Beziehungen zwischen makroökonomischen Aggregaten. (Lead and Lag Relationships between Macroeconomic Aggregates. With English summary.) *Jahr. Nationalökon. Statist.*, January 1986, *201*(1), pp. 12–31. **[G: W. Germany]**

Perryman, M. Ray and Perryman, Nancy S. The Regional Business Cycle: A Theoretical Exposition with Time Series, Cross Sectional, and Predictive Applications. **In** *Perryman, M. R. and Schmidt, J. R., eds.*, 1986, pp. 125–58. **[G: U.S.]**

Persson, B. A. On the Relationship between Qualitative and Quantitative Indicators: Outline of an Explanatory Model. *J. Stud. Econ. Econometrics*, April 1986, (24), pp. 99–132.

Peterson, George E. Urban Policy and the Cyclical Behavior of Cities. **In** *Peterson, G. E. and Lewis, C. W., eds.*, 1986, pp. 11–35. **[G: U.S.]**

Petzina, Dietmar. Krisen und Krisenstrategien: Die deutschen Erfahrungen der Zwischenkriegszeit und die Gegenwart. (With English summary.) **In** *Berend, I. T. and Borchardt, K., eds.*, 1986, pp. 171–94. **[G: W. Germany]**

Pikkarainen, Pentti and Virén, Matti. New Evidence on Long Swings. *Kyklos*, 1986, *39*(4), pp. 596–602. **[G: OECD]**

Poole, William. Monetary Control and the Political Business Cycle. *Cato J.*, Winter 1986, *5*(3), pp. 685–99. **[G: U.S.]**

Prakash, Shri. The Nineteen Thirties Depression and the Indian Agrarian Economy before and after 1947. **In** *Berend, I. T. and Borchardt, K., eds.*, 1986, pp. 275–303. **[G: India]**

Rich, Georg. A VAR Analysis of Economic Interdependence: Canada, the United States, and the Rest of the World: Comments. **In** *Hafer, R. W., ed. (I)*, 1986, pp. 133–36. **[G: U.S.; Canada]**

Richards, Daniel J. Unanticipated Money and the Political Business Cycle. *J. Money, Credit, Banking*, November 1986, *18*(4), pp. 447–57. **[G: U.S.]**

Richardson, Martin and Wilkie, Simon. Incremental Export Subsidies [The Cyclical Effects of Incremental Export Subsidies]. *Econ. Rec.*, March 1986, *62*(176), pp. 88–92. **[G: Australia]**

Riefler, Roger F. Comparative Cyclic Behavior of an Agricultural Economy: Nebraska in the 70s and 80s. *Rev. Reg. Stud.*, Winter 1986, *16*(1), pp. 24–30. **[G: U.S.]**

Rohwer, Bernd. Der Konjunkturaufschwung 1983–1986—Ein Erfolg des wirtschaftspolitischen Kurswechsels der christlich-liberalen Koaltion? Einige Anmerkungen zur konjunkturtheoretischen Beurteilung des gegenwätigen Aufschwungs. (The Business Revival 1983–1986 in West Germany—A Success of the CDU/CSU–FDP Coalition's Change of Policy?—Some Remarks on the Causes of the Present Business Upswing. With English summary.) *Konjunkturpolitik*, 1986, *32*(6), pp. 325–48. **[G: W. Germany]**

Romer, Christina D. Is the Stabilization of the Postwar Economy a Figment of the Data?

Amer. Econ. Rev., June 1986, *76*(3), pp. 314–34. **[G: U.S.]**

Romer, Christina D. New Estimates of Prewar Gross National Product and Unemployment. *J. Econ. Hist.*, June 1986, *46*(2), pp. 341–52. **[G: U.S.]**

van Roon, Ger. Cycles, Turning Phases and Societal Structures: Historical Perspective and Current Problems. **In** *Freeman, C., ed.*, 1986, pp. 48–59. **[G: U.K.; U.S.; W. Europe]**

Rostowski, Jacek and Auerbach, Paul. Storming Cycles and Economic Systems. *J. Compar. Econ.*, September 1986, *10*(3), pp. 293–312. **[G: OECD; CMEA]**

Rotemberg, Julio J. Is There a Cyclical Time Unit? A Comment. *Carnegie-Rochester Conf. Ser. Public Policy*, Spring 1986, *24*, pp. 49–53.

Rush, Mark. Unexpected Money and Unemployment, 1920 to 1983. *J. Money, Credit, Banking*, August 1986, *18*(3), pp. 259–74. **[G: U.S.]**

Sachs, Jeffrey. Causes of the 1980s Slump in Europe: Comments. *Brookings Pap. Econ. Act.*, 1986, (2), pp. 514–19. **[G: W. Europe; U.S.]**

Salant, Walter S. Was Kennedy Always First? *Challenge*, July/Aug. 1986, *29*(3), pp. 56–59. **[G: U.S.]**

Samuelson, Paul A. Has Economic Science Improved the System? **In** *Knowlton, W. and Zeckhauser, R., eds.*, 1986, pp. 299–315. **[G: U.S.]**

Samuelson, Paul A. The Crash of '29: Lessons for '79. **In** *Samuelson, P. A.*, 1986, *1979*, pp. 925–28. **[G: U.S.]**

Samuelson, Paul A. and Samuelson, William F. Recession: Causes and Consequences. **In** *Samuelson, P. A.*, 1986, *1980*, pp. 968–71.

Santoni, Gary J. The Employment Act of 1946: Some History Notes. *Fed. Res. Bank St. Louis Rev.*, November 1986, *68*(9), pp. 5–16. **[G: U.S.]**

Schultze, Charles L. The Cyclical Flexibility of Wages. *Amer. Econ. Rev.*, December 1986, *76*(5), pp. 1152–53. **[G: U.S.]**

Schwartz, Anna J. Real and Pseudo-financial Crises. **In** *Capie, F. and Wood, G. E., eds.*, 1986, pp. 11–40. **[G: U.S.; U.K.]**

Schwartz, Anna J. The Open Economy: Implications for Monetary and Fiscal Policy: Comment. **In** *Gordon, R. J., ed.*, 1986, pp. 504–10. **[G: U.S.]**

Sherman, Howard J. Changes in the Character of the U.S. Business Cycle. *Rev. Radical Polit. Econ.*, Spring/Summer 1986, *18*(1/2), pp. 190–204. **[G: U.S.]**

Shiller, Robert J. Are Business Cycles All Alike? Comment. **In** *Gordon, R. J., ed.*, 1986, pp. 156–60. **[G: U.S.]**

Shoven, John B. The Behavior of United States Deficits: Comment. **In** *Gordon, R. J., ed.*, 1986, pp. 389–91. **[G: U.S.]**

Siegenthaler, Hansjörg. The State of Confidence and Economic Behaviour in the 30s and 70s: Theoretical Framework—Historical Evidence. **In** *Berend, I. T. and Borchardt, K., eds.*, 1986, pp. 409–36.

Šik, Ota. Zuar Problematik kurzfristiger Zyklen. (On the Problems of Shortterm Cycles. With English summary.) *Jahr. Nationalökon. Statist.*, January 1986, *201*(1), pp. 32–53. **[G: W. Germany]**

Sims, Christopher A. Fixed Investment in the American Business Cycle, 1919–83: Comment. **In** *Gordon, R. J., ed.*, 1986, pp. 340–48. **[G: U.S.]**

Singleton, Kenneth J. The Mechanisms of the Business Cycle in the Postwar Era: Comment. **In** *Gordon, R. J., ed.*, 1986, pp. 110–18. **[G: U.S.]**

Soh, Byung Hee. Political Business Cycles in Industrialized Democratic Countries. *Kyklos*, 1986, *39*(1), pp. 31–46. **[G: OECD]**

Solomon, Ezra. Economic Prospects for the Balance of the Decade—Toward a New Continuity. *Bus. Econ.*, January 1986, *21*(1), pp. 22–27. **[G: U.S.]**

Solomou, Solomos. Innovation Clusters and Kondratieff Long Waves in Economic Growth. *Cambridge J. Econ.*, June 1986, *10*(2), pp. 101–12. **[G: U.S.]**

Solomou, Solomos. Kondratieff Long Waves in Aggregate Output? A Comment. *Konjunkturpolitik*, 1986, *32*(3), pp. 179–84. **[G: OECD]**

Solomou, Solomos. Non-balanced Growth and Kondratieff Waves in the World Economy, 1850–1913. *J. Econ. Hist.*, March 1986, *46*(1), pp. 165–69. **[G: Global]**

Spröndli, E. Construction of Business Cycle Indicators from Qualitative Survey Data by Means of Multivariate Methods. *J. Stud. Econ. Econometrics*, April 1986, (24), pp. 3–41.

Stemplowski, Ryszard and Szlajfer, Henryk. Political Responses to the Economic Crises in El Salvador: 1930 and 1980. **In** *Berend, I. T. and Borchardt, K., eds.*, 1986, pp. 304–29. **[G: El Salvador]**

Stiefel, Dieter. The Great Depression in a Small Country: Austria, the World Economic Crisis of the 1930s and Its Significance for the Present Day. **In** *Berend, I. T. and Borchardt, K., eds.*, 1986, pp. 195–214. **[G: Austria]**

Suba-Varga, Judit. "Foreign Trade Constraint" and Cyclical Development. *Acta Oecon.*, 1986, *36*(3–4), pp. 251–70. **[G: Hungary]**

Summers, Lawrence H. Government Policy and Economic Performance. **In** *Knowlton, W. and Zeckhauser, R., eds.*, 1986, pp. 317–22. **[G: U.S.]**

Svindland, Eirik. Über Konjunturpronosen auf der Grundlage einer monetären Schätzgleichung. Ein Fallsudie. (On Trade Cycle Forecasts Based on a Monetary Estimating Equation. With English summary.) *Kredit Kapital*, 1986, *19*(1), pp. 25–57.

Taylor, John B. Improvements in Macroeconomic Stability: The Role of Wages and Prices. **In** *Gordon, R. J., ed.*, 1986, pp. 639–65. **[G: U.S.]**

Taylor, John B. Improvements in Macroeconomic Stability: The Role of Wages and Prices: Reply.

In *Gordon, R. J., ed.*, 1986, pp. 672–75. **[G: U.S.]**

Temin, Peter. Are Business Cycles All Alike? Comment. **In** *Gordon, R. J., ed.*, 1986, pp. 160–65. **[G: U.S.]**

Tichy, Gunther. Die Amplitude der Österreichischen Konjunkturschwankungen im internationalen Vergleich. (With English summary.) *Empirica*, 1986, *13*(1), pp. 69–96. **[G: Austria; OECD]**

Tucker, Paul W. The Natural Gas Market: The Cyclical Process. **In** *Stevens, P., ed.*, 1986, pp. 5–13.

Walker, John F. and Vatter, Harold G. Stagnation—Performance and Policy: A Comparison of the Depression Decade with 1973–1984. *J. Post Keynesian Econ.*, Summer 1986, *8*(4), pp. 515–30. **[G: U.S.]**

Weir, David R. The Reliability of Historical Macroeconomic Data for Comparing Cyclical Stability. *J. Econ. Hist.*, June 1986, *46*(2), pp. 353–65. **[G: U.S.]**

Werneck, Rogério L. F. Poupança estatal, dívida externa e crise financeira do sector público. (With English summary.) *Pesquisa Planejamento Econ.*, December 1986, *16*(3), pp. 551–74. **[G: Brazil]**

Winer, Stanley L. Money and Politics in a Small Open Economy. *Public Choice*, 1986, *51*(2), pp. 221–39. **[G: Canada]**

Winiecki, Jan. Macroeconomic Policies and Economic Slowdown: In Search of Linkages in 1972–1982 Period. *Econ. Notes*, 1986, (1), pp. 118–33. **[G: OECD]**

Winter, Sidney G. Micro Heterogeneity of Firms and the Stability of Industrial Growth: Comment. **In** *Day, R. H. and Eliasson, G., eds.*, 1986, pp. 105–11. **[G: Sweden]**

Zarnowitz, Victor and Moore, Geoffrey H. Major Changes in Cyclical Behavior. **In** *Gordon, R. J., ed.*, 1986, pp. 519–72. **[G: U.S.; W. Germany; U.K.; France]**

132 Forecasting; Econometric Models

1320 General

Chatfield, Chris. Simple Is Best? Editorial. *Int. J. Forecasting*, 1986, *2*(4), pp. 401–02.

Grunberg, Emile. Predictability and Reflexivity. *Amer. J. Econ. Soc.*, October 1986, *45*(4), pp. 475–88.

Henry, Ken R., et al. Implementing Computable General Equilibrium Models: Data Preparation, Calibration, and Replication. *New Zealand Econ. Pap.*, 1986, *20*, pp. 101–20. **[G: New Zealand]**

Hughes Hallett, A. J. Dynamic Policy Games and the Gains from Cooperation in Interdependent Economies: An Example from U.S.–EEC Policy Making. **In** *Pau, L. F., ed.*, 1986, pp. 147–55. **[G: U.S.; EEC]**

Klein, Lawrence R. Macroeconomic Modeling and Forecasting. **In** *Smelser, N. J. and Gerstein, D. R., eds.*, 1986, pp. 95–110.

Naik, Gopal and Leuthold, Raymond M. A Note on Qualitative Forecast Evaluation. *Amer. J. Agr. Econ.*, August 1986, *68*(3), pp. 721–26. **[G: U.S.]**

Nowzad, Bahram. The Perils of Prescription: Economics and the Macroeconomic Policy Adviser. *World Devel.*, Oct./Nov. 1986, *14*(10/11), pp. 1361–73.

Pecci-Boriani, Marco. International Comparability of the Input–Output Tables. **In** *Franz, A. and Rainer, N., eds.*, 1986, pp. 313–23.

Simmons, LeRoy F. M-Competition—A Closer Look at NAIVE2 and Median *APE:* A Note. *Int. J. Forecasting*, 1986, *2*(4), pp. 457–60.

Walters, Alan. The Rise and Fall of Econometrics. **In** *[Seldon, A.]*, 1986, pp. 117–24.

1322 General Forecasts and Models

Alauddin, Mohammad. Erratum [Identification of Key Sectors in the Bangladesh Economy: A Linkage Analysis Approach]. *Appl. Econ.*, October 1986, *18*(10), pp. 1148. **[G: Bangladesh]**

Alauddin, Mohammad. Identification of Key Sectors in the Bangladesh Economy: A Linkage Analysis Approach. *Appl. Econ.*, April 1986, *18*(4), pp. 421–42. **[G: Bangladesh]**

Amano, Akihiro. Exchange Rate Simulations: A Comparative Study. *Europ. Econ. Rev.*, February 1986, *30*(1), pp. 137–48. **[G: W. Germany; Japan; U.S.]**

Amano, Akihiro, et al. Comparative Exchange Rate Simulations. *Europ. Econ. Rev.*, February 1986, *30*(1), pp. 131–35.

Andersen, Leonall C. and Carlson, Keith M. A Monetarist Model for Economic Stabilization. *Fed. Res. Bank St. Louis Rev.*, October 1986, *68*(8), pp. 45–66. **[G: U.S.]**

Andersen, Leonall C. and Jordan, Jerry L. Monetary and Fiscal Actions: A Test of Their Relative Importance in Economic Stabilization. *Fed. Res. Bank St. Louis Rev.*, October 1986, *68*(8), pp. 29–44. **[G: U.S.]**

Aoki, Masanao and Havenner, Arthur. Approximate State Space Models of Some Vector-Valued Macroeconomic Time Series for Cross-Country Comparisons. *J. Econ. Dynam. Control*, June 1986, *10*(1/2), pp. 149–55. **[G: U.K.; W. Germany; Japan]**

Apeloig, Shalom. Graphoscopy: A New Method for Business Cycle Forecasting. *J. Stud. Econ. Econometrics*, April 1986, (24), pp. 43–80.

Arestis, Philip; Driver, Ciaran and Rooney, J. The Real Segment of a UK Post Keynesian Model. *J. Post Keynesian Econ.*, Winter 1985-86, *8*(2), pp. 163–81. **[G: U.K.]**

Artus, Patrick. An Aggregate Model of the World Economy. **In** *Artus, P. and Guvenen, O., eds.*, 1986, pp. 105–27. **[G: Global]**

Askari, Mostafa. A Non-nested Test of the New Classical Neutrality Proposition for Canada. *Appl. Econ.*, December 1986, *18*(12), pp. 1349–57. **[G: Canada]**

Batten, Dallas S. and Thornton, Daniel L. The Monetary–Fiscal Policy Debate and the Andersen–Jordan Equation. *Fed. Res. Bank St. Louis*

Rev., October 1986, *68*(8), pp. 9–17. [G: U.S.]

Becker, Robin G., et al. Rival Models in Policy Optimization. *J. Econ. Dynam. Control,* June 1986, *10*(1/2), pp. 75–81. [G: U.K.]

Becker, Robin G., et al. The Simultaneous Use of Rival Models in Public Optimisation. *Econ. J.*, June 1986, *96*(382), pp. 425–48. [G: U.K.]

Beenstock, Michael, et al. A Macroeconomic Model of Aggregate Supply and Demand for the UK. *Econ. Modelling,* October 1986, *3*(4), pp. 242–68. [G: U.K.]

Bergman, Lars. ELIAS—A Model of Multisectoral Economic Growth in a Small Open Economy. **In** *Ysander, B.-C., ed.*, 1986, pp. 25–70. [G: Sweden]

Blitzer, Charles R. and Eckaus, Richard S. Modeling Energy–Economy Interactions in Small Developing Countries: A Case Study of Sri Lanka. *J. Policy Modeling,* Winter 1986, *8*(4), pp. 471–501. [G: Sri Lanka]

Bosi, Paolo. Modelli macroeconometrici e valutazione della politica fiscale in Italia. (Econometric Models and the Evaluation of Fiscal Policy in Italy. With English summary.) *Polit. Econ.*, April 1986, *2*(1), pp. 3–43. [G: Italy]

Boutillier, Michel and Durand, Bruno. Investigations in the Causal Structure of the Yearly OFCE Model. *J. Econ. Dynam. Control,* June 1986, *10*(1/2), pp. 131–37.

Bradley, John. Unemployment and Fiscal Activism in a Small Open Economy. *Rech. Écon. Louvain,* 1986, *52*(3–4), pp. 339–72. [G: Ireland]

Brandsma, Andries S. The Implications of Risk Sensitive Decision Making for Macroeconomic Planning in the Netherlands. *De Economist,* 1986, *134*(1), pp. 61–83. [G: Netherlands]

Brandsma, Andries S. and Hughes Hallett, A. J. The Coordination Approach to Policymaking in Interdependent Economies. **In** *Artus, P. and Guvenen, O., eds.*, 1986, pp. 209–28. [G: OECD]

Britton, Andrew. Can Fiscal Expansion Cut Unemployment? *Nat. Inst. Econ. Rev.*, February 1986, (115), pp. 83–99. [G: U.K.]

Bureau, Dominique and Norotte, Michel. Ralentir la substitution capital-travail. Une analyse critique. (Shift in the Factor Demands to Reduce Unemployment: A Review. With English summary.) *Revue Écon.*, September 1986, *37*(5), pp. 833–56. [G: France]

Carlson, Keith M. A Monetarist Model for Economic Stabilization: Review and Update. *Fed. Res. Bank St. Louis Rev.*, October 1986, *68*(8), pp. 18–28. [G: U.S.]

Carnazza, Paulo. Measuring the Effects of Fiscal Policy: The Case of Italy (1964–1984). *Econ. Notes,* 1986, (1), pp. 98–117. [G: Italy]

Catinat, Michel; Maurice, Joël and Zagamé, Paul. Stratégie du taux de change et mesures d'accompagnement. Une analyse des coûts et avantages à partir d'exercises quantitatifs. (Rate of Exchange Strategy and Accompanying Measures of Economic Policy. With English summary.) *Revue Écon.*, September 1986, *37*(5), pp. 857–84. [G: France]

Celasun, Merih. A General Equilibrium Model of the Turkish Economy, SIMLOG-1: Validation Results (1978–83) and Counterfactual Experiments with Trade Liberalization, External Borrowing and Wage Policies (1981–83). *METU,* 1986, *13*(1/2), pp. 29–94. [G: Turkey]

Chiarini, B. Optimal Control of Econometric Models. Problems Developments and an Application with a Model of the Italian Economy. *Metroecon.*, October 1986, *38*(3), pp. 295–315. [G: Italy]

Clemen, Robert T. and Winkler, Robert L. Combining Economic Forecasts. *J. Bus. Econ. Statist.*, January 1986, *4*(1), pp. 39–46. [G: U.S.]

Conrad, Klaus and Henseler-Unger, Iris. Applied General Equilibrium Modeling for Long-term Energy Policy in Germany. *J. Policy Modeling,* Winter 1986, *8*(4), pp. 531–49. [G: W. Germany]

Cortés, Rosalía and Marshall, Adriana. Salario real, composición del consumo y balanza comercial. (With English summary.) *Desarrollo Econ.*, Apr.-June 1986, *26*(101), pp. 71–88. [G: Argentina]

Dadkhah, Kamran M. and Zahedi, Fatemeh. Simultaneous Estimation of Production Functions and Capital Stocks for Developing Countries. *Rev. Econ. Statist.*, August 1986, *68*(3), pp. 443–51. [G: LDCs]

Deardorff, Alan V. and Stern, Robert M. The Structure and Sample Results of the Michigan Computational Model of World Production and Trade. **In** *Srinivasan, T. N. and Whalley, J., eds.*, 1986, pp. 151–88. [G: LDCs; MDCs]

van Dijk, Herman K. and Kloek, Teun. Posterior Moments of the Klein–Goldberger Model. **In** *[de Finetti, B.]*, 1986, pp. 95–108. [G: U.S.]

Diwan, Romesh and Hu, Grace. Country Objectives and IMF Conditionality: An Empirical Analysis of Sudan Economy. *Indian J. Quant. Econ.*, 1986, *2*(2), pp. 83–100. [G: Sudan]

Drud, Arne; Grais, Wafik and Pyatt, Graham. Macroeconomic Modeling Based on Social-Accounting Principles. *J. Policy Modeling,* Spring 1986, *8*(1), pp. 111–45. [G: Thailand]

Edison, Hali J. The U.K. Sector of the Federal Reserve's Multicountry Model: The Effects of Monetary and Fiscal Policies. *Manchester Sch. Econ. Soc. Stud.*, December 1986, *54*(4), pp. 403–19. [G: U.K.]

Feroldi, Mathieu and Sterdyniak, Henri. Maximiser l'emploi: la réponse de modèles macro-économiques. (Maximizing the Employment: The Macroeconomics Models Response. With English summary.) *Écon. Soc.*, January 1986, *20*(1), pp. 235–63. [G: France]

Fisher, Paul G.; Holly, Sean and Hughes Hallett, A. J. Efficient Solution Techniques for Dynamic Non-Linear Rational Expectations Models. *J. Econ. Dynam. Control,* June 1986, *10*(1/2), pp. 139–45. [G: U.K.]

Gaburro, Giuseppe. A Small Quarterly Model of

the Italian Economy. *Rivista Int. Sci. Econ. Com.*, January 1986, *33*(1), pp. 59–73. **[G: Italy]**

Gibson, Bill; Lustig, Nora and Taylor, Lance. Terms of Trade and Class Conflict in a Computable General Equilibrium Model for Mexico. *J. Devel. Stud.*, October 1986, *23*(1), pp. 40–59. **[G: Mexico]**

Giovannetti, G. and Siniscalco, D. Structural Change, Foreign Trade and Income Multipliers in the Italian Economy. *Banca Naz. Lavoro Quart. Rev.*, September 1986, (158), pp. 319–35. **[G: Italy]**

Glattfelder, P.; Cser, I. and Magyar, E. The Structure of the Hungarian Economy in 2000. **In** *Franz, A. and Rainer, N., eds.*, 1986, pp. 295–312. **[G: Hungary]**

Grais, Wafik. Comments [A General Equilibrium Analysis of Tariff Reductions] [Trade Liberalization through Tariff Cuts and the European Economic Community: A General Equilibrium Evaluation]. **In** *Srinivasan, T. N. and Whalley, J., eds.*, 1986, pp. 145–48. **[G: EEC]**

Granger, Clive W. J. Forecasting Accuracy of Alternative Techniques: A Comparison of U.S. Macroeconomic Forecasts: Comment. *J. Bus. Econ. Statist.*, January 1986, *4*(1), pp. 16–17. **[G: U.S.]**

Grant, James H. and Nichols, Len M. On the Existence of a Market for Second Hand Physical Capital: An Empirical Test of the Keynesian and Neoclassical Assumptions. *J. Macroecon.*, Spring 1986, *8*(2), pp. 131–57. **[G: U.S.]**

Greene, Mark N.; Howrey, E. Philip and Hymans, Saul H. The Use of Outside Information in Econometric Forecasting. **In** *Belsley, D. A. and Kuh, E., eds.*, 1986, pp. 90–116. **[G: U.S.]**

Haas, Richard D. and Masson, Paul R. MINIMOD: Specification and Simulation Results. *Int. Monet. Fund Staff Pap.*, December 1986, *33*(4), pp. 722–67. **[G: U.S.]**

Hafkamp, Wim and Nijkamp, Peter. Integrated Economic–Environmental–Energy Policy and Conflict Analysis. *J. Policy Modeling,* Winter 1986, *8*(4), pp. 551–76. **[G: Netherlands]**

Hall, Stephen G. Estimating the Uncertainty of the Simulation Properties of Large Nonlinear Econometric Models. *Appl. Econ.*, September 1986, *18*(9), pp. 985–93. **[G: U.K.]**

Hall, Stephen G. The Application of Stochastic Simulation Techniques to the National Institute's Model 7. *Manchester Sch. Econ. Soc. Stud.*, June 1986, *54*(2), pp. 180–201.

Hall, Stephen G. and Henry, S. G. B. A Dynamic Econometric Model of the UK with Rational Expectations. *J. Econ. Dynam. Control,* June 1986, *10*(1/2), pp. 219–23. **[G: U.K.]**

Hall, Stephen G.; Henry, S. G. B. and Herbert, Rhys. Oil Prices and the Economy. *Nat. Inst. Econ. Rev.*, May 1986, (116), pp. 38–44. **[G: U.K.]**

Hall, Stephen G.; Henry, S. G. B. and Johns, C. B. Forecasting with an Econometric Model: Some Recent Results Using the National Institute Model. *J. Appl. Econometrics*, April 1986, *1*(2), pp. 163–83. **[G: U.K.]**

Hall, Stephen G. and Herbert, Rhys. Consistent Simulations and the National Institute Model 8. *Nat. Inst. Econ. Rev.*, February 1986, (115), pp. 64–73. **[G: U.K.]**

Hamilton, Clive. A General Equilibrium Model of Structural Change and Economic Growth, with Application to South Korea. *J. Devel. Econ.*, September 1986, *23*(1), pp. 67–88. **[G: S. Korea]**

Hansen, Gerd. Der konjunkturelle Einfluss der Geld- und Fiskalpolitik in der Bundesrepublik 1972–1982. Eine ökonometrische Analyse unter rationalen Erwartungen. (The Effect of Monetary and Fiscal Policy on Business Cycles in the Federal Republic of Germany 1972–1982. With English summary.) *Kyklos*, 1986, *39*(2), pp. 180–208. **[G: W. Germany]**

Harris, Richard G. Market Structure and Trade Liberalization: A General Equilibrium Assessment. **In** *Srinivasan, T. N. and Whalley, J., eds.*, 1986, pp. 231–50. **[G: Canada]**

Harrison, Glenn W. A General Equilibrium Analysis of Tariff Reductions. **In** *Srinivasan, T. N. and Whalley, J., eds.*, 1986, pp. 101–23. **[G: Selected Countries]**

Havlicek, Joseph, Jr. Food Demand Analysis: Implications for Future Consumption: Discussion. **In** *Capps, O., Jr. and Senauer, B., eds.*, 1986, pp. 87–90. **[G: U.S.]**

Helliwell, John F., et al. The Supply Side in the OECD's Macroeconomic Model. *OECD Econ. Stud.*, Spring 1986, (6), pp. 75–131. **[G: OECD]**

Holtham, Gerald. Exchange Rates in the OECD INTERLINK Model: Specification and Simulation Properties. *Europ. Econ. Rev.*, February 1986, *30*(1), pp. 199–235. **[G: OECD]**

Hooper, Peter. Exchange Rate Simulation Properties of the MCM. *Europ. Econ. Rev.*, February 1986, *30*(1), pp. 171–98. **[G: U.S.; W. Germany; Japan]**

Huot, Guy, et al. Analysis of Revisions in the Seasonal Adjustment of Data Using X-11-ARIMA Model-Based Filters. *Int. J. Forecasting*, 1986, *2*(2), pp. 217–29. **[G: Canada]**

Ishii, Naoko. Scope for Macroeconomic Policy Coordination between the U.S. and Japan. **In** *Finn, R. B., ed.*, 1986, pp. 211–23. **[G: Japan; U.S.]**

Jahnke, Wilfried. Simulation verschiedener Strategien zur Verringerung der Arbeitslosigkeit. (Simulation of Alternative Policies to Reduce Unemployment. With English summary.) *Z. Wirtschaft. Sozialwissen.*, 1986, *106*(6), pp. 557–78. **[G: W. Germany]**

Jaksch, Hans Jürgen. Simulaciones de políticas antiinflacionarias en Argentina, 1983/87. (Simulation of Anti-inflationary Policies in Argentina, 1983–87. With English summary.) *Económica (La Plata)*, Jan.-June 1986, *32*(1), pp. 21–56. **[G: Argentina]**

Jordan, Jerry L. Economic Outlook. **In** *Shadow Open Market Committee (II)*, 1986, pp. 9–36. **[G: U.S.]**

Jordan, Jerry L. Economic Outlook. **In** *Shadow Open Market Committee (I),* 1986, pp. 9–18. **[G: U.S.]**

Jordan, Jerry L. The Anderson–Jordan Approach after Nearly 20 Years. *Fed. Res. Bank St. Louis Rev.*, October 1986, *68*(8), pp. 5–8. **[G: U.S.]**

Jorgenson, Dale W. and Yun, Kun-Young. The Efficiency of Capital Allocation. *Scand. J. Econ.*, 1986, *88*(1), pp. 85–107. **[G: U.S.]**

Kaneko, Takafumi and Yasuhara, Norikazu. Exchange Rate Simulations with the EPA World Economic Model. *Europ. Econ. Rev.*, February 1986, *30*(1), pp. 237–59. **[G: W. Europe; U.S.; Japan; Canada]**

Kharas, Homi J. and Shishido, Hisanobu. A Dynamic-Optimization Model of Foreign Borrowing: A Case Study of Thailand. *J. Policy Modeling*, Spring 1986, *8*(1), pp. 1–26. **[G: Thailand]**

Kirkpatrick, Grant. A Globus OECD/COMECON Simulation Model. **In** *Artus, P. and Guvenen, O., eds.*, 1986, pp. 129–58. **[G: Global]**

Kremp, E. and Le Dem, J. Competitiveness and Employment in the Large Industrialized Countries. **In** *Artus, P. and Guvenen, O., eds.*, 1986, pp. 159–80. **[G: U.S.; France; W. Germany; Japan]**

Kunst, Robert and Neusser, Klaus. Forecasting with Vector Autoregressive Models: An Empirical Investigation for Austria. *Empirica*, 1986, *13*(2), pp. 187–202. **[G: Austria]**

Kwack, Sung Y. Policy Analysis with a Macroeconomic Model of Korea. *Econ. Modelling*, July 1986, *3*(3), pp. 175–96. **[G: S. Korea]**

Laffargue, Jean-Pierre. Decomposition of the International Consequences of Policies into World and Difference Effects: Application to the Fair Multi-Country Model. *J. Econ. Dynam. Control*, June 1986, *10*(1/2), pp. 291–95. **[G: U.S.; W. Germany; Italy; Belgium]**

Lenjosek, Gordon and Whalley, John. A Small Open Economy Model Applied to an Evaluation of Canadian Energy Policies Using 1980 Data. *J. Policy Modeling*, Spring 1986, *8*(1), pp. 89–110. **[G: Canada]**

Leontief, Wassily. Population Growth and Economic Development: Illustrative Projections. **In** *Leontief, W.*, 1986, *1979*, pp. 338–62. **[G: Global]**

Leontief, Wassily. Structure of the World Economy: Outline of a Simple Input–Output Formulation. **In** *Leontief, W.*, 1986, *1974*, pp. 321–37. **[G: Global]**

Levine, Paul. The Formulation of Robust Policies for Rival Rational Expectations Models of the Economy. *J. Econ. Dynam. Control*, June 1986, *10*(1/2), pp. 93–97.

Litterman, Robert B. Forecasting with Bayesian Vector Autoregressions—Five Years of Experience. *J. Bus. Econ. Statist.*, January 1986, *4*(1), pp. 25–38. **[G: U.S.]**

Litterman, Robert B. Forecasting Accuracy of Alternative Techniques: A Comparison of U.S. Macroeconomic Forecasts: Comment. *J. Bus. Econ. Statist.*, January 1986, *4*(1), pp. 17–19. **[G: U.S.]**

Liu, Tai-Ying and Hsu, Shuh-Tzy. The Validity of TIER's Business Climate Indicator. *Ifo-Studien*, 1986, *32*(1–3), pp. 71–80. **[G: Taiwan]**

Livesey, D. A. New Perspectives from the Complex Plane. *J. Econ. Dynam. Control*, June 1986, *10*(1/2), pp. 99–107.

Loue, Jean-François and Morin, Pierre. La boucle prix-salaires des modèles de l'économie française. Structure et robustesse. (The Wage-Price Spiral of the Models of the French Economy: Structure and Robustness. With English summary.) *Revue Écon.*, November 1986, *37*(6), pp. 1067–92. **[G: France]**

Lupoletti, William M. and Webb, Roy H. Defining and Improving the Accuracy of Macroeconomic Forecasts: Contributions from a VAR Model. *J. Bus.*, Part 1, April 1986, *59*(2), pp. 263–85. **[G: U.S.]**

MacIntyre, Arnold. Finance, Growth and the Balance of Trade in OECS Countries. *Soc. Econ. Stud.*, December 1986, *35*(4), pp. 176–212. **[G: Caribbean]**

Marquez, Jaime and Pauly, Peter. Cooperative Policies among the North, the South, and OPEC: An Optimal Control Application. *Econ. Modelling*, July 1986, *3*(3), pp. 213–36. **[G: Global]**

Marquez, Jaime and Pauly, Peter. Policy Coordination among the North, the South, and OPEC. *J. Econ. Dynam. Control*, June 1986, *10*(1/2), pp. 59–62. **[G: Global]**

Masson, Paul R. and Knight, Malcolm D. International Transmission of Fiscal Policies in Major Industrial Countries. *Int. Monet. Fund Staff Pap.*, September 1986, *33*(3), pp. 387–438. **[G: U.S.; W. Germany; Japan]**

Matlin, I. S. Macroeconomic Models in a System of Planning Models. *Matekon*, Winter 1986-87, *23*(2), pp. 74–93. **[G: U.S.S.R.]**

McNees, Stephen K. Forecasting Accuracy of Alternative Techniques: A Comparison of U.S. Macroeconomic Forecasts. *J. Bus. Econ. Statist.*, January 1986, *4*(1), pp. 5–15. **[G: U.S.]**

McNees, Stephen K. Forecasting Accuracy of Alternative Techniques: A Comparison of U.S. Macroeconomic Forecasts: Reply. *J. Bus. Econ. Statist.*, January 1986, *4*(1), pp. 23. **[G: U.S.]**

McNown, Robert. On the Uses of Econometric Models: A Guide for Policy Makers. *Policy Sci.*, December 1986, *19*(4), pp. 359–80. **[G: U.S.]**

de Melo, Jaime. Comments [The Structure and Sample Results of the Michigan Computational Model of World Production and Trade] [Impacts of a 50 Percent Tariff Reduction in an Eight-Region Global Trade Model]. **In** *Srinivasan, T. N. and Whalley, J., eds.*, 1986, pp. 215–23. **[G: Global]**

Mercenier, Jean and Waelbroeck, Jean. Effect of a 50 Percent Tariff Cut in the Varuna Model. **In** *Srinivasan, T. N. and Whalley, J., eds.*, 1986, pp. 283–310. **[G: Global]**

Minford, Patrick; Agénor, Pierre-Richard and

Nowell, Eric. A New Classical Econometric Model of the World Economy. *Econ. Modelling,* July 1986, *3*(3), pp. 154–74. **[G: Selected OECD]**

Naggl, W. The Forecasting Record of the Anticipations Model, since 1983. *J. Stud. Econ. Econometrics,* April 1986, (24), pp. 81–98. **[G: W. Germany]**

Nakamura, Shinichiro. A Flexible Dynamic Model of Multiproduct Technology for the West German Economy. *J. Appl. Econometrics,* October 1986, *1*(4), pp. 333–44. **[G: W. Germany]**

Nallari, Raj. An Application of Stochastic Control on a Small Macroeconometric Model of the Indian Economy. *Indian J. Quant. Econ.,* 1986, *2*(2), pp. 1–14. **[G: India]**

Neftci, Salih N. Is There a Cyclical Time Unit? *Carnegie-Rochester Conf. Ser. Public Policy,* Spring 1986, *24,* pp. 11–48. **[G: U.S.]**

Norton, Roger D.; Scandizzo, Pasquale L. and Zimmerman, Linda W. Portugal's Entry into the EEC: Aggregate and Distributional Effects Determined by Means of a General Equilibrium Model. *J. Policy Modeling,* Summer 1986, *8*(2), pp. 149–80. **[G: Portugal]**

Onishi, Akira. North–South Interdependence: Protections of the World Economy, 1985–2000. *J. Policy Modeling,* Summer 1986, *8*(2), pp. 181–98. **[G: Global]**

Panchamukhi, V. R. and Mehta, Rajesh. Structural Changes, Inter-country Disparities and the Lima Target. **In** *Panchamukhi, V. R., et al.,* 1986, pp. 55–75. **[G: LDCs]**

Pauly, Peter and Petersen, Christian E. Exchange Rate Responses in the LINK System. *Europ. Econ. Rev.,* February 1986, *30*(1), pp. 149–70. **[G: W. Europe; Canada; U.S.; Japan]**

Pesaran, M. Hashem. A Macro Model of an Oil Exporter: Nigeria: Comment. **In** *Neary, J. P. and van Wijnbergen, S., eds.,* 1986, pp. 225–28. **[G: Nigeria]**

Petri, Peter. Comments [The Structure and Sample Results of the Michigan Computational Model of World Production and Trade] [Impacts of a 50 Percent Tariff Reduction in an Eight-Region Global Trade Model]. **In** *Srinivasan, T. N. and Whalley, J., eds.,* 1986, pp. 225–28. **[G: Global]**

Pylkkänen, Eero and Vartia, Pentti. Some Comments on Fine-Tuning Macro-Model Forecasts. *Liiketaloudellinen Aikak.,* 1986, *35*(1), pp. 58–70. **[G: Finland]**

Raj, Baldev and Siklos, Pierre L. The Role of Fiscal Policy in the St. Louis Model: An Evaluation and Some New Evidence. *J. Appl. Econometrics,* July 1986, *1*(3), pp. 287–94. **[G: U.S.]**

Rattsø, Jørn. The Macroeconomics of India's 6th Five Year Plan. *Econ. Modelling,* October 1986, *3*(4), pp. 269–82. **[G: India]**

Rausser, Gordon C., et al. Macroeconomic Linkages, Taxes, and Subsidies in the U.S. Agricultural Sector. *Amer. J. Agr. Econ.,* May 1986, *68*(2), pp. 399–412. **[G: U.S.]**

Rocherieux, François. La dynamique macro-économique de l'internationalisation et des caractéristiques de l'emploi. (The Macroeconomic Dynamics of Internationalization and Employment Characteristics. With English summary.) *Écon. Soc.,* January 1986, *20*(1), pp. 169–209. **[G: France]**

Rotemberg, Julio J. Is There a Cyclical Time Unit? A Comment. *Carnegie-Rochester Conf. Ser. Public Policy,* Spring 1986, *24,* pp. 49–53.

Sarkar, Hiren and Panda, Manoj Kumar. Quantity–Price–Money Interaction in a CGE Model with Applications to Fiscal Policy. *Margin,* April 1986, *18*(3), pp. 31–52. **[G: India]**

Saunders, Norman C. Sensitivity of BLS Economic Projections to Exogenous Variables. *Mon. Lab. Rev.,* December 1986, *109*(12), pp. 23–29. **[G: U.S.]**

Siebrand, Jan C. and Swank, Job. An Evaluation of the Morkmon Model. *De Economist,* 1986, *134*(3), pp. 289–300. **[G: Netherlands]**

Sneessens, Henri R. and Drèze, Jacques H. What, If Anything, Have We Learned from the Rise of Unemployment in Belgium, 1974–1983. *Cah. Écon. Bruxelles,* 2nd/3rd Trimester 1986, (110/111), pp. 21–66. **[G: Belgium]**

Spencer, John E. Trade Liberalization through Tariff Cuts and the European Economic Community: A General Equilibrium Evaluation. **In** *Srinivasan, T. N. and Whalley, J., eds.,* 1986, pp. 125–44. **[G: EEC]**

Spivey, W. Allen. Forecasting Accuracy of Alternative Techniques: A Comparison of U.S. Macroeconomic Forecasts: Comment. *J. Bus. Econ. Statist.,* January 1986, *4*(1), pp. 19–22. **[G: U.S.]**

Stahmer, Carsten. Integration of Input–Output Statistics with the International Systems of National Accounts. **In** *Franz, A. and Rainer, N., eds.,* 1986, pp. 501–24.

Šujan, Ivan. Simulations of Restoring the External Economic Equilibrium of Czechoslovakia. *Comp. Econ. Stud.,* Winter 1986, *28*(4), pp. 61–83. **[G: Czechoslovakia]**

Sundararajan, V. Exchange Rate versus Credit Policy: Analysis with a Monetary Model of Trade and Inflation in India. *J. Devel. Econ.,* Jan.-Feb. 1986, *20*(1), pp. 75–105. **[G: India]**

Suttle, Phil. Debt Projection Models: A Survey. *Oxford Rev. Econ. Policy,* Spring 1986, *2*(1), pp. 62–77. **[G: LDCs]**

Taylor, Lance; Yurukoglu, Kadir T. and Chaudhry, Shahid A. A Macro Model of an Oil Exporter: Nigeria. **In** *Neary, J. P. and van Wijnbergen, S., eds.,* 1986, pp. 201–24. **[G: Nigeria]**

Thury, Gerhard. Macroeconomic Forecasting in Austria: An Agnostic Viewpoint. *Empirica,* 1986, *13*(2), pp. 173–86. **[G: Austria]**

Tourinho, Octávio A. F. Endividamento externo ótimo em um modelo de equilíbrio dinâmico multissetorial: um estudo de caso para o Brasil. (With English summary.) *Pesquisa Planejamento Econ.,* December 1986, *16*(3), pp. 647–87. **[G: Brazil]**

Virén, Matti. Estimating the Output Effects of Energy Price and Real Interest Rate Shocks: A Cross-Country Study. *Schweiz. Z. Volkswirtsch. Statist.*, December 1986, *122*(4), pp. 627–39. **[G: OECD]**

Vuchelen, Jef. Voorspellingen voor de Belgische Economie in de Jaren Tachtig. (With English summary.) *Cah. Écon. Bruxelles*, First Trimester 1986, (109), pp. 85–122. **[G: Belgium]**

Weidenbaum, Murray L. The Case for Making Economic Forecasts. *Challenge*, July/Aug. 1986, *29*(3), pp. 54–56. **[G: U.S.]**

Whalley, John. Impacts of a 50 Percent Tariff Reduction in an Eight-Region Global Trade Model. **In** *Srinivasan, T. N. and Whalley, J., eds.*, 1986, pp. 189–214. **[G: Global]**

Wigle, Randall. General Equilibrium Trade Policy Modeling: Summary of the Panel and Floor Discussion. **In** *Srinivasan, T. N. and Whalley, J., eds.*, 1986, pp. 323–54. **[G: Selected Countries]**

Yoshino, Toshihiko. A New YRI Business Index: Based on Microeconomic Data. *Ifo-Studien*, 1986, *32*(1–3), pp. 91–104.

Ysander, Bengt-Christer. Structural Change as an Equilibrium or Disequilibrium Process—An Introduction. **In** *Ysander, B.-C., ed.*, 1986, pp. 9–24. **[G: Sweden]**

Ysander, Bengt-Christer; Nordström, Tomas and Jansson, Leif. ISAC—A Model of Stabilization and Structural Change in a Small Open Economy. **In** *Ysander, B.-C., ed.*, 1986, pp. 71–161. **[G: Sweden]**

Zeineldin, Aly. The Egyptian Economy in 1999: An Input–Output Study. *Econ. Modelling*, April 1986, *3*(2), pp. 140–46. **[G: Egypt]**

1323 Specific Forecasts and Models

Al-Osh, Mohamed. Birth Forecasting Based on Birth Order Probabilities, with Application to U.S. Data. *J. Amer. Statist. Assoc.*, September 1986, *81*(395), pp. 645–56. **[G: U.S.]**

Alam, A. K. M. Shamsul and Kamath, Shyam J. Models and Forecasts of Inflation in a Developing Economy. *J. Econ. Stud.*, 1986, *13*(4), pp. 3–29. **[G: India]**

Almon, Clopper. Investment in Input–Output Models and the Treatment of Secondary Products. **In** *Sohn, I., ed.*, 1986, *1970*, pp. 285–94. **[G: U.S.]**

Arnaudo, A. A., et al. Tipología del Desempleo en la Argentina 1950–84. (Typology of Argentine Unemployment 1950–84. With English summary.) *Económica (La Plata)*, July-December 1986, *32*(2), pp. 143–63. **[G: Argentina]**

Arregui, Jorge H. A Quarterly Model for the EEC Beef Sector. *J. Agr. Econ.*, May 1986, *37*(2), pp. 221–32. **[G: EEC]**

Aslaksen, Iulie and Bjerkholt, Olav. Certainty Equivalence Methods in the Macroeconomic Management of Petroleum Resources. **In** *Neary, J. P. and van Wijnbergen, S., eds.*, 1986, pp. 170–95. **[G: Norway]**

Bacha, Edmar L. Terms of Reference for the Country Studies. *World Devel.*, Special Issue, August 1986, *14*(8), pp. 909–18. **[G: LDCs]**

Barten, A. P. and d'Alcantara, G. Simulating Economic Policy with the COMET Model. **In** *Artus, P. and Guvenen, O., eds.*, 1986, pp. 229–37. **[G: EEC]**

Beaumont, Paul, et al. The ECESIS Economic–Demographic Model of the United States. **In** *Isserman, A. M., ed.*, 1986, pp. 203–38. **[G: U.S.]**

Bennett, Robert J. and Hordijk, Leen. Regional Econometric and Dynamic Models. **In** *Nijkamp, P., ed. (I)*, 1986, pp. 407–41.

Bera, Anil K. and Kannan, Srinivasan. An Adjustment Procedure for Predicting Systematic Risk. *J. Appl. Econometrics*, October 1986, *1*(4), pp. 317–32.

Bezdek, Roger H. Long-Range U.S. Manpower Forecasts in Retrospect: How Accurate Were We? *Econ. Planning*, 1986, *20*(1), pp. 52–67. **[G: U.S.]**

Blake, David; Beenstock, Michael and Brasse, Valerie G. The Performance of UK Exchange Rate Forecasters. *Econ. J.*, December 1986, *96*(384), pp. 986–99. **[G: U.K.]**

Breen, William J.; Jagannathan, Ravi and Ofer, Aharon R. Correcting for Heteroscedasticity in Tests for Market Timing Ability. *J. Bus.*, Part 1, October 1986, *59*(4), pp. 585–98. **[G: U.S.]**

Brown, Mark G. and Lee, Jong-Ying. Orange and Grapefruit Juice Demand Forecasts. **In** *Capps, O., Jr. and Senauer, B., eds.*, 1986, pp. 215–32. **[G: U.S.]**

Bruni, Michele and Franciosi, Franco B. Scenari alternativi di domanda e di offerta di lavoro. (Alternative Scenarios of Labour Demand and Supply. With English summary.) *Econ. Lavoro*, July-Sept. 1986, *20*(3), pp. 113–36. **[G: U.S.; Italy]**

Brunner, E. and Schubert, U. Capital Mobility, Labour Demand and R&D Investment in Austria in a Multiregional Context: A First Attempt at Econometric Modelling. **In** *Nijkamp, P., ed. (II)*, 1986, pp. 429–53. **[G: Austria]**

Bryan, Michael F. and Gavin, William T. Models of Inflation Expectations Formation: A Comparison of Household and Economist Forecasts: A Comment. *J. Money, Credit, Banking*, November 1986, *18*(4), pp. 539–44. **[G: U.S.]**

Burt, Oscar R. Econometric Modeling of the Capitalization Formula for Farmland Prices. *Amer. J. Agr. Econ.*, February 1986, *68*(1), pp. 10–26. **[G: U.S.]**

Caballero, Ricardo and Corbo, Vittorio. Análisis de la Balanza Comercial: Un Enfoque de Equilibrio General. (With English summary.) *Cuadernos Econ.*, December 1986, *23*(70), pp. 285–313. **[G: Chile]**

Capps, Oral, Jr. and Pearson, Joanne M. Analysis of Convenience and Nonconvenience Food Expenditures by U.S. Households with Projections to the Year 2000. **In** *Capps, O., Jr. and Senauer, B., eds.*, 1986, pp. 233–50. **[G: U.S.]**

Carter, Lawrence R. and Lee, Ronald D. Joint

Forecasts of U.S. Marital Fertility, Nuptiality, Births, and Marriages Using Time Series Models. *J. Amer. Statist. Assoc.*, December 1986, *81*(396), pp. 902–11. **[G: U.S.]**

Caselles-Moncho, Antonio. An Empirical Comparison of Cross-Impact Models for Forecasting Sales. *Int. J. Forecasting*, 1986, *2*(3), pp. 295–303. **[G: Spain]**

Charemza, Wojciech and Gronicki, Miroslaw. A Model for Investment in Poland: A Disequilibrium Econometrics Approach. *Econ. Modelling*, April 1986, *3*(2), pp. 106–16. **[G: Poland]**

Chen, Chia-Yon. The Optimal Adjustment to Mineral-supply Disruptions: The Case of Aluminum in Taiwan. *J. Policy Modeling*, Summer 1986, *8*(2), pp. 199–221. **[G: Taiwan]**

Cholette, Pierre A. and Lamy, Robert. Multivariate ARIMA Forecasting of Irregular Time Series. *Int. J. Forecasting*, 1986, *2*(2), pp. 201–16. **[G: Canada]**

van Clark, W. A. V. and Lierop, Wal F. J. Residential Mobility and Household Location Modelling. **In** *Nijkamp, P., ed. (I)*, 1986, pp. 97–132.

Cohen, Joel E. Population Forecasts and Confidence Intervals for Sweden: A Comparison of Model-based and Empirical Approaches. *Demography*, February 1986, *23*(1), pp. 105–26. **[G: Sweden]**

Coplin, William and O'Leary, Michael. The Frost and Sullivan Method: Applying the "Prince." **In** *Raddock, D. M., et al.*, 1986, pp. 163–75.

Cordier, J. and Indjehagopian, J. P. Multidimensional Analysis of a Commodity Price System. *Int. J. Forecasting*, 1986, *2*(2), pp. 153–89. **[G: France]**

Costanza, Robert. Embodied Energy and Economic Valuation. **In** *Sohn, I., ed.*, 1986, *1980*, pp. 432–44. **[G: U.S.]**

Deardorff, Alan V. Comments [Market Structure and Trade Liberalization: A General Equilibrium Assessment] [Short-run Impact of Trade Liberalization Measures on the Economy of Bangladesh: Exercises in Comparative Statics for the Year 1977]. **In** *Srinivasan, T. N. and Whalley, J., eds.*, 1986, pp. 311–17. **[G: Canada; Bangladesh]**

Demeny, Paul. The World Demographic Situation. **In** *Menken, J., ed.*, 1986, pp. 27–66. **[G: Global]**

Desormeaux, Jorge and Bravo, Luis Eduardo. Modelo agregado de la Balanza Comercial: Chile 1974–1982. (With English summary.) *Cuadernos Econ.*, December 1986, *23*(70), pp. 315–42. **[G: Chile]**

Dixon, Peter B.; Parmenter, B. R. and Rimmer, Russell J. ORANI Projections of the Short-run Effects of a 50 Percent Across-the-Board Cut in Protection Using Alternative Data Bases. **In** *Srinivasan, T. N. and Whalley, J., eds.*, 1986, pp. 33–60. **[G: Australia]**

Dormont, Brigitte and Sevestre, Patrick. Modèles dynamiques de demande de travail: spécification et estimation sur données de panel. (Dynamic Labor Demand Models: Specification and Estimation Using Panel Data. With English summary.) *Revue Écon.*, May 1986, *37*(3), pp. 455–87. **[G: France]**

Dunkelberg, William C. The Use of Survey Data in Forecasting. *Bus. Econ.*, January 1986, *21*(1), pp. 44–49. **[G: U.S.]**

Dzhikiia, I. Ia. An Integrated Econometric Model for Forecasting Agricultural Production. *Matekon*, Spring 1986, *22*(3), pp. 67–90. **[G: U.S.S.R.]**

Eliasson, Gunnar. Micro Heterogeneity of Firms and the Stability of Industrial Growth: Reply. **In** *Day, R. H. and Eliasson, G., eds.*, 1986, pp. 112–14. **[G: Sweden]**

Eliasson, Gunnar. Micro Heterogeneity of Firms and the Stability of Industrial Growth. **In** *Day, R. H. and Eliasson, G., eds.*, 1986, *1984*, pp. 79–104. **[G: Sweden]**

Fair, Ray C. and Alexander, Lewis S. A Comparison of the Michigan and Fair Models: Further Results. **In** *Belsley, D. A. and Kuh, E., eds.*, 1986, pp. 191–212. **[G: U.S.]**

Feenstra, Robert C. ORANI Projections of the Short-run Effects of a 50 Percent Across-the-Board Cut in Protection Using Alternative Data Bases: Comments. **In** *Srinivasan, T. N. and Whalley, J., eds.*, 1986, pp. 89–90. **[G: Australia]**

Fomby, Thomas B. A Comparison of Forecasting Accuracies of Alternative Regional Production Index Methodologies. *J. Bus. Econ. Statist.*, April 1986, *4*(2), pp. 177–86. **[G: U.S.]**

Fretz, Deborah; Srinivasan, T. N. and Whalley, John. General Equilibrium Trade Policy Modeling: Introduction. **In** *Srinivasan, T. N. and Whalley, J., eds.*, 1986, pp. 1–29.

Gerster, Hans J. Kritische Beurteilung der Arbeitsmarktinterpretationen auf der Grundlage saisonbereinigter Daten. (A Statistical Evaluation of the Labor Market—Interpretations Based on Seasonally Adjusted Data. With English summary.) *Jahr. Nationalökon. Statist.*, March 1986, *201*(2), pp. 152–74. **[G: W. Germany]**

Geurts, Michael D. and Kelly, J. Patrick. Forecasting Retail Sales Using Alternative Models. *Int. J. Forecasting*, 1986, *2*(3), pp. 261–72. **[G: U.S.]**

Grais, Wafik; de Melo, Jaime and Urata, Shujiro. A General Equilibrium Estimation of the Effects of Reductions in Tariffs and Quantitative Restrictions in Turkey in 1978. **In** *Srinivasan, T. N. and Whalley, J., eds.*, 1986, pp. 61–88. **[G: Turkey]**

Greenberg, Carol and Renfro, Charles. An Econometric–Demographic Model of New York State. **In** *Isserman, A. M., ed.*, 1986, pp. 105–25. **[G: U.S.]**

Guay, Richard and Raynauld, Jacques. L'hypothèse du revenu permanent avec attentes rationnelles: une évaluation économétrique canadienne. (The Rational Expectations–Permanent Income Hypothesis: A Canadian Econometric Evaluation. With English summary.) *L'Actual. Econ.*, March 1986, *62*(1), pp. 43–63. **[G: Canada]**

Guinn, Charles R. New York Electricity and Energy Forecasts. **In** *Saltzman, S. and Schuler, R. E., eds.*, 1986, pp. 52–66. **[G: U.S.]**

Hall, Stephen G.; Henry, S. G. B. and Wren-Lewis, Simon. Manufacturing Stocks and Forward-Looking Expectations in the UK. *Economica*, November 1986, *53*(212), pp. 447–65. **[G: U.K.]**

Hall, Stephen G., et al. Forecasting Employment: The Role of Forward-Looking Behaviour. *Int. J. Forecasting*, 1986, *2*(4), pp. 435–45. **[G: U.K.]**

Harris, Richard G. Comments [ORANI Projections of the Short-run Effects of a 50 Percent Across-the-Board Cut in Protection Using Alternative Data Bases] [A General Equilibrium Estimation of the Effects of Reductions in Tariffs and Quantitative Restrictions in Turkey in 1978]. **In** *Srinivasan, T. N. and Whalley, J., eds.*, 1986, pp. 91–97. **[G: Australia; Turkey]**

Hassell, John M. and Jennings, Robert H. Relative Forecast Accuracy and the Timing of Earnings Forecast Announcements. *Accounting Rev.*, January 1986, *61*(1), pp. 58–75. **[G: U.S.]**

Hewings, Geoffrey J. D. and Jensen, Rodney C. Regional Interregional and Multiregional Input–Output Analysis. **In** *Nijkamp, P., ed. (I)*, 1986, pp. 295–355.

Holden, Kenneth and Peel, David A. Expectations Formation, Public Forecasts and the Wage Equation. *Econ. Modelling*, April 1986, *3*(2), pp. 129–34. **[G: U.K.]**

Hooper, Peter and Tryon, Ralph. The Current Account of the United States, Japan, and Germany: A Cyclical Analysis. **In** *Artus, P. and Guvenen, O., eds.*, 1986, pp. 181–205. **[G: U.S.; U.K.; W. Germany; Japan; Canada]**

Huang, Kuo S. and Haidacher, Richard C. Projecting Aggregate Food Expenditures to the Year 2000. **In** *Capps, O., Jr. and Senauer, B., eds.*, 1986, pp. 67–85. **[G: U.S.]**

Isserman, Andrew. Forecasting Birth and Migration Rates: The Theoretical Foundation. **In** *Isserman, A. M., ed.*, 1986, pp. 3–30. **[G: U.S.]**

Italianer, A. and d'Alcantara, G. Modelling Bilateral Sectoral Trade Flows. **In** *Artus, P. and Guvenen, O., eds.*, 1986, pp. 3–38. **[G: OECD]**

Jaksch, Hans Jürgen. Kleine ökonometrische Modelle für sich rasch entwertende Währungen: Deutschland 1920/23 und Argentinien 1977/81. (Small Econometric Models for Rapidly Depreciating Currencies: Germany 1920/23 and Argentina 1977/81. With English summary.) *Ifo-Studien*, 1986, *32*(4), pp. 241–74. **[G: Germany; Argentina]**

Johnson, Stan R., et al. Market Demand Functions. **In** *Capps, O., Jr. and Senauer, B., eds.*, 1986, pp. 1–33. **[G: Canada; U.S.]**

Kawasaki, Seiichi and Zimmermann, Klaus F. Testing the Rationality of Price Expectations for Manufacturing Firms. *Appl. Econ.*, December 1986, *18*(12), pp. 1335–47. **[G: W. Germany]**

Kelly, J. Patrick and Geurts, Michael D. Increasing the Efficiency of Forecasting Seasonal Demand for Individual Products. **In** *Pellegrini, L. and Reddy, S. K., eds.*, 1986, pp. 183–95. **[G: U.S.]**

Keyzer, Michiel A. Short-run Impact of Trade Liberalization Measures on the Economy of Bangladesh: Exercises in Comparative Statics for the Year 1977. **In** *Srinivasan, T. N. and Whalley, J., eds.*, 1986, pp. 251–82. **[G: Bangladesh]**

Klein, Lawrence R. The Energy Crisis Ten Years Later. **In** *Saltzman, S. and Schuler, R. E., eds.*, 1986, pp. 18–31. **[G: U.S.]**

Klein, Philip A. Leading Indicators of Inflation in Market Economies. *Int. J. Forecasting*, 1986, *2*(4), pp. 403–12. **[G: OECD]**

Koskela, Erkki and Virén, Matti. Endogenous Policy, Structural Shift, and Demand for Money. *Weltwirtsch. Arch.*, 1986, *122*(4), pp. 647–56. **[G: U.S.]**

Kuh, Edwin; Neese, John and Hollinger, Peter. Linear Analysis of Large Nonlinear Models and Model Simplification. **In** *Belsley, D. A. and Kuh, E., eds.*, 1986, pp. 213–38. **[G: U.S.]**

Kunisawa, Kiyonori and Horibe, Yasuichi. Forecasting International Telecommunications Traffic by the Data Translation Method. *Int. J. Forecasting*, 1986, *2*(4), pp. 427–34.

Landefeld, J. Steven and Seskin, Eugene P. A Comparison of Anticipatory Surveys and Econometric Models in Forecasting U.S. Business Investment. *J. Econ. Soc. Meas.*, April 1986, *14*(1), pp. 77–85. **[G: U.S.]**

Lane, William R.; Looney, Stephen W. and Wansley, James W. An Application of the Cox Proportional Hazards Model to Bank Failure. *J. Banking Finance*, December 1986, *10*(4), pp. 511–31. **[G: U.S.]**

Layton, Allan P.; Defris, Lorraine V. and Zehnwirth, Ben. An International Comparison of Economic Leading Indicators of Telecommunications Traffic. *Int. J. Forecasting*, 1986, *2*(4), pp. 413–25. **[G: Australia; U.S.]**

Leamer, Edward E. A Bayesian Analysis of the Determinants of Inflation. **In** *Belsley, D. A. and Kuh, E., eds.*, 1986, pp. 62–89. **[G: U.S.]**

Lefebvre, Bruno and Mouillart, Michel. Logement et épargne des ménages: le modèle Fanie. (Housing Markets and Saving of Households: The Fanie Model. With English summary.) *Revue Écon.*, May 1986, *37*(3), pp. 521–70. **[G: France]**

Lin, Winston T. Modeling and Forecasting U.S. Public Construction. *Int. J. Forecasting*, 1986, *2*(3), pp. 319–31. **[G: U.S.]**

Loeb, Peter D. Specification Error Tests and the Jorgenson–Stephenson Investment Functions. *Appl. Econ.*, August 1986, *18*(8), pp. 851–61.

Lönnqvist, Åke. Forecasting Power of Entrepreneurs Expectations. *Ifo-Studien*, 1986, *32*(1–3), pp. 181–99. **[G: Sweden]**

Lorentsen, Lorents and Roland, Kjell. The World

Oil Market (WOM) Model: An Assessment of the Crude Oil Market through 2000. *Energy J.*, January 1986, *7*(1), pp. 23–34. **[G: Global]**

Lovell, Michael C. On Forecast Rationality: The Case of Gas Mileage Estimates. *J. Post Keynesian Econ.*, Summer 1986, *8*(4), pp. 548–62. **[G: U.S.]**

Maravall, Agustin. An Application of Model-Based Estimation of Unobserved Components. *Int. J. Forecasting*, 1986, *2*(3), pp. 305–18. **[G: Spain]**

Marshall R., Pablo. Predicción de inflación con modelos de series de tiempo múltiples. (With English summary.) *Cuadernos Econ.*, April 1986, *23*(68), pp. 101–17. **[G: Chile]**

Martin, Ricardo and van Wijnbergen, Sweder J. G. Shadow Prices and the Intertemporal Aspects of Remittances and Oil Revenues in Egypt. **In** *Neary, J. P. and van Wijnbergen, S., eds.*, 1986, pp. 142–68. **[G: Egypt]**

Masson, Paul R. and Richardson, Peter. Exchange Rate Expectations and Current Balances in the OECD Interlink System. **In** *Artus, P. and Guvenen, O., eds.*, 1986, pp. 53–77. **[G: OECD]**

Meiners, Nancy. New York State Economic and Demographic Forecasts to 2003. **In** *Saltzman, S. and Schuler, R. E., eds.*, 1986, pp. 45–51. **[G: U.S.]**

Motley, Brian and Rasche, Robert H. Predicting the Money Stock: A Comparison of Alternative Approaches. *Fed. Res. Bank San Francisco Econ. Rev.*, Spring 1986, (2), pp. 38–54. **[G: U.S.]**

Mount, Timothy D. and Deehan, William J. Determinants of the Demand for Electricity in New York: Economic Conditions, Nuclear Power Costs, and Primary Fuel Prices. **In** *Saltzman, S. and Schuler, R. E., eds.*, 1986, pp. 77–96. **[G: U.S.]**

Murfin, Andy and Ormerod, Paul. The Sterling–Dollar Exchange Market 1973–1982: Surprises and Expectations. **In** *Artus, P. and Guvenen, O., eds.*, 1986, pp. 79–102. **[G: U.K.; U.S.]**

Naik, Gopal and Dixon, Bruce L. A Monte Carlo Comparison of Alternative Estimators of Autocorrelated Simultaneous Systems Using A U.S. Pork Sector Model as the True Structure. *Western J. Agr. Econ.*, December 1986, *11*(2), pp. 134–45. **[G: U.S.]**

Newbery, David M. G. Certainty Equivalence Methods in the Macroeconomic Management of Petroleum Resources: Comment. **In** *Neary, J. P. and van Wijnbergen, S., eds.*, 1986, pp. 195–200. **[G: Norway]**

Nijkamp, Peter; Rietveld, Piet and Snickars, Folke. Regional and Multiregional Economic Models: A Survey. **In** *Nijkamp, P., ed. (I)*, 1986, pp. 257–94.

Nyankori, James C. O. A Systematic Analysis of Household Food Consumption Behavior with Specific Emphasis on Predicting Aggregate Food Expenditures. **In** *Capps, O., Jr. and Senauer, B., eds.*, 1986, pp. 251–68. **[G: U.S.]**

Palm, F. C. and Vogelvang, E. A Short-run Econometric Analysis of the International Coffee Market. *Europ. Rev. Agr. Econ.*, 1986, *13*(4), pp. 451–76. **[G: Global]**

Panchamukhi, V. R. and Raipuria, Kalyan M. South–South Trade in Manufactures and the Lima Target: Projections through 1900 and 2000 under Alternative Scenarios. **In** *Panchamukhi, V. R., et al.*, 1986, pp. 76–93. **[G: Global]**

Park, Hun Y. Changes in Expectations and the Forecasting Error of Interest Rates: An Error Learning Model of Treasury Bill Futures. *Quart. J. Bus. Econ.*, Spring 1986, *25*(2), pp. 22–31. **[G: U.S.]**

Plaut, Thomas. Economic–Demographic Interactions in the Growth of Texas. **In** *Isserman, A. M., ed.*, 1986, pp. 81–104. **[G: U.S.]**

Price, D. H. R. and Sharp, J. A. A Comparison of the Performance of Different Univariate Forecasting Methods in a Model of Capacity Acquisition in UK Electricity Supply. *Int. J. Forecasting*, 1986, *2*(3), pp. 333–48. **[G: U.K.]**

Quiggin, John; Gargett, D. and Barrett, G. Exits from the Australian Dairy Industry: Causes and Predictions. *J. Agr. Econ.*, May 1986, *37*(2), pp. 233–42. **[G: Australia]**

Rasche, Robert H. Multiplier Forecasts and the Velocities of Various M's. **In** *Shadow Open Market Committee (I)*, 1986, pp. 43–50. **[G: U.S.]**

Robison, H. David and Silver, Stephen J. The Impact of Changing Oil Prices on Interfuel Substitution: Ethanol's Prospects in the United States to 1995. *J. Policy Modeling*, Summer 1986, *8*(2), pp. 241–53. **[G: U.S.]**

Royer, Jacques. The Long-term Employment Impact of Disarmament Policies: Some Findings from an Econometric Model. *Int. Lab. Rev.*, May-June 1986, *125*(3), pp. 279–303. **[G: Global]**

Schroeter, John R. and Smith, Scott L. A Reexamination of the Rationality of the Livingston Price Expectations: A Note. *J. Money, Credit, Banking*, May 1986, *18*(2), pp. 239–46.

Simos, Evangelos O. and Triantis, John E. The Effect of Structural Instability on the Demand for Money Forecast. *Econ. Notes*, 1986, (2), pp. 43–61. **[G: U.S.]**

Slater, Paul B. World Population Distribution: Smoothed Representations. **In** *Slater, P. B.*, 1986, pp. 77–106. **[G: Global]**

Smith, Alasdair. Shadow Prices and the Intertemporal Aspects of Remittances and Oil Revenues in Egypt: Comment. **In** *Neary, J. P. and van Wijnbergen, S., eds.*, 1986, pp. 168–69. **[G: Egypt]**

Smith, Kenneth L. Real, Nominal, and Price Adjustment in Generalized Models of Money Demand: Can We Improve Stability and Forecasts? *Quart. J. Bus. Econ.*, Summer 1986, *25*(3), pp. 72–86. **[G: U.S.]**

Smith, P. N. and Wickens, M. R. An Empirical Investigation into the Causes of Failure of the Monetary Model of the Exchange Rate. *J.*

Appl. Econometrics, April 1986, *1*(2), pp. 143–62. **[G: U.S.]**

Sneessens, Henri R. and Drèze, Jacques H. A Discussion of Belgian Unemployment, Combining Traditional Concepts and Disequilibrium Econometrics. *Economica*, Supplement 1986, *53*(210(S)), pp. S89–119. **[G: Belgium]**

Solimano, Andrés. Salarios Reales y Empleo Bajo Distintos Regímenes Macroeconómicos. Una Aplicación para Chile y Brasil. (With English summary.) *Cuadernos Econ.*, December 1986, *23*(70), pp. 343–71. **[G: Chile; Brazil]**

Svindland, Eirik. Über Konjunturpronosen auf der Grundlage einer monetären Schätzgleichung. Ein Fallsudie. (On Trade Cycle Forecasts Based on a Monetary Estimating Equation. With English summary.) *Kredit Kapital*, 1986, *19*(1), pp. 25–57.

Swartz, Stephen and Welsch, Roy E. Applications of Bounded-Influence and Diagnostic Methods in Energy Modeling. **In** *Belsley, D. A. and Kuh, E., eds.*, 1986, pp. 154–90. **[G: U.S.]**

Takayama, T. and Labys, Walter C. Spatial Equilibrium Analysis. **In** *Nijkamp, P., ed. (I)*, 1986, pp. 171–99.

Taylor, Mark P. From the General to the Specific: The Demand for M2 in Three European Countries. *Empirical Econ.*, 1986, *11*(4), pp. 243–61. **[G: W. Germany; Netherlands; France]**

Teräsvirta, Timo. Model Selection Using Business Survey Data: Forecasting the Output of the Finnish Metal and Engineering Industries. *Int. J. Forecasting*, 1986, *2*(2), pp. 191–200. **[G: Finland]**

Tourinho, Octávio A. F. A expansão de longa prazo do sistema elétrico brasileiro: uma análise com o modelo PSE. (With English summary.) *Pesquisa Planejamento Econ.*, April 1986, *16*(1), pp. 87–127. **[G: Brazil]**

Veall, Michael R. and Zimmermann, Klaus F. A Monthly Dynamic Consumer Expenditure System for Germany with Different Kinds of Households. *Rev. Econ. Statist.*, May 1986, *68*(2), pp. 256–64. **[G: W. Germany]**

Viaene, Jean-Marie. Product Availability, Price Discrimination and Interdependent Import Flows. **In** *Artus, P. and Guvenen, O., eds.*, 1986, pp. 39–51. **[G: OECD]**

Waymire, Gregory. Additional Evidence on the Accuracy of Analyst Forecasts before and after Voluntary Management Earnings Forecasts. *Accounting Rev.*, January 1986, *61*(1), pp. 129–42. **[G: U.S.]**

Weinberg, Charles B. Arts Plan: Implementation, Evolution, and Usage. *Marketing Sci.*, Spring 1986, *5*(2), pp. 143–58. **[G: U.S.]**

Westaway, P. F. Some Experiments with Simple Feedback Rules on the Treasury Model. *J. Econ. Dynam. Control*, June 1986, *10*(1/2), pp. 239–46. **[G: U.K.]**

Winter, Sidney G. Micro Heterogeneity of Firms and the Stability of Industrial Growth: Comment. **In** *Day, R. H. and Eliasson, G., eds.*, 1986, pp. 105–11. **[G: Sweden]**

Wohlgenant, Michael K. Global Behavior of Demand Elasticities for Food: Implications for Demand Projections. **In** *Capps, O., Jr. and Senauer, B., eds.*, 1986, pp. 35–48.

Wren-Lewis, Simon. An Econometric Model of U.K. Manufacturing Employment Using Survey Data on Expected Output. *J. Appl. Econometrics*, October 1986, *1*(4), pp. 297–316. **[G: U.K.]**

Wright, D. J., et al. Evaluation of Forecasting Methods for Decision Support. *Int. J. Forecasting*, 1986, *2*(2), pp. 139–52.

Zimmermann, Klaus F. On Rationality of Business Expectations: A Micro Analysis of Qualitative Responses. *Empirical Econ.*, 1986, *11*(1), pp. 23–40. **[G: W. Germany]**

1324 Forecasting and Econometric Models: Theory and Methodology

Arminger, Gerhard. Fallacies and Paradoxes Caused by Heterogeneity. **In** *[Rapoport, A.]*, 1986, pp. 323–36.

Ashley, Richard A. and Vaughan, David. Measuring Measurement Error in Economic Time Series. *J. Bus. Econ. Statist.*, January 1986, *4*(1), pp. 95–103. **[G: U.S.]**

Bikker, J. A.; Boeschoten, W. C. and Fase, M. M. G. Diagnostic Checking of Macroeconomic Models: A Specification Analysis of Morkmon. *De Economist*, 1986, *134*(3), pp. 301–50. **[G: Netherlands]**

Borges, Antonio M. Applied General Equilibrium Models: An Assessment of Their Usefulness for Policy Analysis. *OECD Econ. Stud.*, Autumn 1986, (7), pp. 7–43.

Boyce, James K. Kinked Exponential Models for Growth Rate Estimation. *Oxford Bull. Econ. Statist.*, November 1986, *48*(4), pp. 385–91. **[G: India; Bangladesh]**

Bretschneider, Stuart. Estimating Forecast Variance with Exponential Smoothing: Some New Results. *Int. J. Forecasting*, 1986, *2*(3), pp. 349–55.

Burmeister, Edwin; Wall, Kent D. and Hamilton, James D. Estimation of Unobserved Expected Monthly Inflation Using Kalman Filtering. *J. Bus. Econ. Statist.*, April 1986, *4*(2), pp. 147–60. **[G: U.S.]**

Burns, Terence [Sir]. The Interpretation and Use of Economic Predictions. **In** *Mason, J.; Mathias, P. and Westcott, J. H., eds.*, 1986, pp. 103–23. **[G: U.K.; U.S.]**

Chong, Yock Y. and Hendry, David F. Econometric Evaluation of Linear Macro-Economic Models. *Rev. Econ. Stud.*, August 1986, *53*(4), pp. 671–90.

Clemen, Robert T. and Winkler, Robert L. Combining Economic Forecasts. *J. Bus. Econ. Statist.*, January 1986, *4*(1), pp. 39–46. **[G: U.S.]**

Decaluwe, Bernard; Martens, André and Monette, Marcel. Comment contruire un modèle calculable d'équilibre général? Une illustration. (How to Construct a Computable General-equilibrium Model? With English summary.) *L'Actual. Econ.*, September 1986, *62*(3), pp. 442–73.

Drud, Arne; Grais, Wafik and Pyatt, Graham. Macroeconomic Modeling Based on Social-Accounting Principles. *J. Policy Modeling,* Spring 1986, *8*(1), pp. 111–45. **[G: Thailand]**

Dunkelberg, William C. The Use of Survey Data in Forecasting. *Bus. Econ.,* January 1986, *21*(1), pp. 44–49. **[G: U.S.]**

Fackler, James S. and Krieger, Sandra C. An Application of Vector Time Series Techniques to Macroeconomic Forecasting. *J. Bus. Econ. Statist.,* January 1986, *4*(1), pp. 71–80. **[G: U.S.]**

Fisher, Paul G. and Salmon, Mark. On Evaluating the Importance of Nonlinearity in Large Macroeconometric Models. *Int. Econ. Rev.,* October 1986, *27*(3), pp. 625–46.

Flores, Benito E. Use of the Sign Test to Supplement the Percentage Better Statistic. *Int. J. Forecasting,* 1986, *2*(4), pp. 477–89.

Fourie, F. C. v. N. Second Thoughts on Economic Forecasting. *S. Afr. J. Econ.,* September 1986, *54*(3), pp. 307–18.

Granger, Clive W. J. Forecasting Accuracy of Alternative Techniques: A Comparison of U.S. Macroeconomic Forecasts: Comment. *J. Bus. Econ. Statist.,* January 1986, *4*(1), pp. 16–17. **[G: U.S.]**

Guvenen, Orhan. International Macroeconomic Modelling for Policy Decisions: Some Proposals. **In** *Artus, P. and Guvenen, O., eds.,* 1986, pp. 259–65.

Hall, Stephen G.; Henry, S. G. B. and Johns, C. B. Forecasting with an Econometric Model: Some Recent Results Using the National Institute Model. *J. Appl. Econometrics,* April 1986, *1*(2), pp. 163–83. **[G: U.K.]**

Hendry, David F. The Role of Prediction in Evaluating Econometric Models. **In** *Mason, J.; Mathias, P. and Westcott, J. H., eds.,* 1986, pp. 25–33.

Hsu, Wu-ron and Murphy, Allan H. The Attributes Diagram: A Geometrical Framework for Assessing the Quality of Probability Forecasts. *Int. J. Forecasting,* 1986, *2*(3), pp. 285–93.

Jajuga, Krzysztof. On Pattern Recognition Methods in Econometric Regression Model. **In** *Pau, L. F., ed.,* 1986, pp. 167–71.

Johnson, Stan R. Future Challenges for Modeling in Agricultural Economics. *Amer. J. Agr. Econ.,* May 1986, *68*(2), pp. 387–94.

Kang, Heejoon. Univariate ARIMA Forecasts of Defined Variables. *J. Bus. Econ. Statist.,* January 1986, *4*(1), pp. 81–86. **[G: U.S.]**

Kimbell, Larry J. and Harrison, Glenn W. On the Solution of General Equilibrium Models. *Econ. Modelling,* July 1986, *3*(3), pp. 197–212.

Kunst, Robert and Neusser, Klaus. A Forecasting Comparison of Some VAR Techniques. *Int. J. Forecasting,* 1986, *2*(4), pp. 447–56. **[G: Austria]**

Land, Kenneth C. Methods for National Population Forecasts: A Review. *J. Amer. Statist. Assoc.,* December 1986, *81*(396), pp. 888–901. **[G: U.S.]**

Leonard, David C. and Solt, Michael E. Recent Evidence on the Accuracy and Rationality of Popular Inflation Forecasts. *J. Finan. Res.,* Winter 1986, *9*(4), pp. 281–90. **[G: U.S.]**

Leontief, Wassily. An Information System for Policy Decisions in a Modern Economy. **In** *Leontief, W.,* 1986, *1979,* pp. 418–28.

Litterman, Robert B. A Statistical Approach to Economic Forecasting. *J. Bus. Econ. Statist.,* January 1986, *4*(1), pp. 1–4. **[G: U.S.]**

Litterman, Robert B. Forecasting Accuracy of Alternative Techniques: A Comparison of U.S. Macroeconomic Forecasts: Comment. *J. Bus. Econ. Statist.,* January 1986, *4*(1), pp. 17–19. **[G: U.S.]**

Litterman, Robert B. Specifying Vector Autoregressions for Macroeconomic Forecasting. **In** *[de Finetti, B.],* 1986, pp. 79–94. **[G: U.S.]**

Llewellyn, John; Samuelson, Lee and Vanston, Nick. Making International Economic Forecasts. **In** *Artus, P. and Guvenen, O., eds.,* 1986, pp. 241–57. **[G: Global]**

Lupoletti, William M. and Webb, Roy H. Defining and Improving the Accuracy of Macroeconomic Forecasts: Contributions from a VAR Model. *J. Bus.,* Part 1, April 1986, *59*(2), pp. 263–85. **[G: U.S.]**

Lütkepohl, Helmut. Comparison of Predictors for Temporally and Contemporaneously Aggregated Time Series. *Int. J. Forecasting,* 1986, *2*(4), pp. 461–75. **[G: U.S.]**

McKenzie, Ed. Error Analysis for Winters' Additive Seasonal Forecasting System. *Int. J. Forecasting,* 1986, *2*(3), pp. 373–82.

McNees, Stephen K. Forecasting Accuracy of Alternative Techniques: A Comparison of U.S. Macroeconomic Forecasts: Reply. *J. Bus. Econ. Statist.,* January 1986, *4*(1), pp. 23. **[G: U.S.]**

McNees, Stephen K. Forecasting Accuracy of Alternative Techniques: A Comparison of U.S. Macroeconomic Forecasts. *J. Bus. Econ. Statist.,* January 1986, *4*(1), pp. 5–15. **[G: U.S.]**

McNees, Stephen K. The Accuracy of Two Forecasting Techniques: Some Evidence and an Interpretation. *New Eng. Econ. Rev.,* Mar./Apr. 1986, pp. 20–31.

Neftci, Salih N. Testing Non-linearity in Business Cycles. **In** *Semmler, W., ed.,* 1986, pp. 324–40.

Peel, David A.; Walters, K. and Pope, P. F. Public Forecasts and Their Impact on Expectation Formation. *Econ. Modelling,* April 1986, *3*(2), pp. 126–28. **[G: U.K.]**

Persson, B. A. On the Relationship between Qualitative and Quantitative Indicators: Outline of an Explanatory Model. *J. Stud. Econ. Econometrics,* April 1986, (24), pp. 99–132.

Sen, Amartya K. Prediction and Economic Theory. **In** *Mason, J.; Mathias, P. and Westcott, J. H., eds.,* 1986, pp. 3–22.

Sims, Christopher A. Are Forecasting Models Usable for Policy Analysis? *Fed. Res. Bank Minn. Rev.,* Winter 1986, *10*(1), pp. 2–16.

Smallwood, David M. and Blaylock, James R. Forecasting Performance of Models Using the Box–Cox Transformation. *Agr. Econ. Res.,* Fall 1986, *38*(4), pp. 14–24.

Spivey, W. Allen. Forecasting Accuracy of Alternative Techniques: A Comparison of U.S. Macroeconomic Forecasts: Comment. *J. Bus. Econ. Statist.*, January 1986, *4*(1), pp. 19–22. **[G: U.S.]**

Taylor, Stephen J. Conjectured Models for Trends in Financial Prices, Tests and Forecasts. **In** *Goss, B. A., ed.*, 1986, *1980*, pp. 209–46. **[G: U.K.]**

Trivellato, Ugo and Rettore, Enrico. Preliminary Data Errors and Their Impact on the Forecast Error of Simultaneous-Equations Models. *J. Bus. Econ. Statist.*, October 1986, *4*(4), pp. 445–53. **[G: Italy]**

Weiss, Andrew A. ARCH and Bilinear Time Series Models: Comparison and Combination. *J. Bus. Econ. Statist.*, January 1986, *4*(1), pp. 59–70.

Weitz, Rob R. NOSTRADAMUS: A Knowledge-Based Forecasting Advisor. *Int. J. Forecasting*, 1986, *2*(3), pp. 273–83.

West, Mike and Harrison, P. Jeff. Monitoring and Adaptation in Bayesian Forecasting Models. *J. Amer. Statist. Assoc.*, September 1986, *81*(395), pp. 741–50.

Zellner, Arnold. A Tale of Forecasting 1001 Series: The Bayesian Knight Strikes Again. *Int. J. Forecasting*, 1986, *2*(4), pp. 491–94.

133 General Outlook and Stabilization Theories and Policies

1330 General Outlook and General Economic Policy Discussions

Abalkin, L. The Acceleration of Socioeconomic Development: Its Essence and Sources. *Prob. Econ.*, October 1986, *29*(6), pp. 50–62. **[G: U.S.S.R.]**

Aganbegian, A. G. The General Course of Economic Policy. *Prob. Econ.*, October 1986, *29*(6), pp. 3–35.

Amann, Ronald. The Political and Social Implications of Economic Reform in the USSR. **In** *Höhmann, H.-H.; Nove, A. and Vogel, H., eds.*, 1986, pp. 125–45. **[G: U.S.S.R.]**

Axilrod, Stephen H. Statement to the Subcommittee on Domestic Monetary Policy of the House Committee on Banking, Finance and Urban Affairs, November 7, 1985. *Fed. Res. Bull.*, January 1986, *72*(1), pp. 15–19. **[G: U.S.]**

Balassa, Bela. Adjustment Policies in Socialist and Private Market Economies. *J. Compar. Econ.*, June 1986, *10*(2), pp. 138–59. **[G: LDCs; Hungary; Yugoslavia]**

Balassa, Bela. Prices, Incentives, and Economic Growth. **In** *Balassa, B. and Giersch, H., eds.*, 1986, pp. 3–21.

Ben-Porath, Yoram. The Israeli Economy: Maturing through Crises: Introduction. **In** *Ben-Porath, Y., ed.*, 1986, pp. 1–23. **[G: Israel]**

Berg, Elliot. The World Bank's Strategy. **In** *Ravenhill, J., ed.*, 1986, pp. 44–59. **[G: Africa]**

Bergsten, C. Fred. Gearing Up World Growth. *Challenge*, May/June 1986, *29*(2), pp. 35–40. **[G: Global]**

Berman, Harold J. The Possibilities and Limits of Soviet Economic Reform. **In** *Ioffe, O. S. and Janis, M. W., eds.*, 1986, pp. 29–38.

Bilger, François. Frankreich vor der ordnungspolitischen Wende? Die wirtschaftspolitischen Wahlprogramme der französischen Parteien. (France at the Economic Turning Point? Economic Policy in the Election Platforms of the French Political Parties. With English summary.) **In** *Eucken, W. and Böhm, F., eds.*, 1986, pp. 3–43. **[G: France]**

Boesen, Jannik, et al. Tanzania: Crisis and Struggle for Survival: Introduction. **In** *Boesen, J., et al., eds.*, 1986, pp. 19–29. **[G: Tanzania]**

Bond, Daniel L. Prospects for the Soviet Economy. **In** *Amann, R. and Cooper, J., eds.*, 1986, pp. 170–81. **[G: U.S.S.R.]**

Bootle, Roger. Budget Strategy and the Exchange Rate. *Fisc. Stud.*, May 1986, *7*(2), pp. 1–10. **[G: U.K.]**

Bradley, Michael D. and Potter, Susan M. The State of the Federal Budget and the State of the Economy: Further Evidence. *Econ. Inquiry*, January 1986, *24*(1), pp. 143–53. **[G: U.S.]**

Britton, Andrew; Eastwood, Fiona and Major, Robin L. Macroeconomic Policy in Italy and Britain. *Nat. Inst. Econ. Rev.*, November 1986, (118), pp. 38–52. **[G: Italy; U.K.]**

Bronfenbrenner, Martin. Causes of Contemporary Stagnation: What Should We Have Done? **In** *Frisch, H. and Gahlen, B., eds.*, 1986, pp. 1–12. **[G: U.S.]**

Bruno, Michael. Aggregate Supply and Demand Factors in OECD Unemployment: An Update. *Economica*, Supplement 1986, *53*(210(S)), pp. S35–52. **[G: OECD]**

Bruno, Michael. Stagflation in the Industrial Countries: An Updated Overview. *Hitotsubashi J. Econ.*, Spec. Iss. Oct. 1986, *27*, pp. 57–74. **[G: OECD]**

Buchanan, James M. Ideas, Institutions, and Political Economy: A Plea for Disestablishment. *Carnegie-Rochester Conf. Ser. Public Policy*, Autumn 1986, *25*, pp. 245–57. **[G: U.S.]**

Buchanan, James M. Our Times: Past, Present and Future. **In** *[Seldon, A.]*, 1986, pp. 31–38.

Budd, Alan P. The 1986 Budget and Macroeconomic Policy. *Fisc. Stud.*, May 1986, *7*(2), pp. 21–32. **[G: U.K.]**

Bullock, Colin. IMF Conditionality and Jamaica's Economic Policy in the 1980s. *Soc. Econ. Stud.*, December 1986, *35*(4), pp. 129–76. **[G: Jamaica]**

Capron, Henri. Préférences idéologiques, contrainte électorale et résultats macroéconomiques. (With English summary.) *Cah. Écon. Bruxelles*, First Trimester 1986, (109), pp. 51–83. **[G: Belgium]**

Carmichael, Edward A.; Dobson, Wendy and Lipsey, Richard G. The Macdonald Report: Signpost or Shopping Basket? *Can. Public Policy*, Supp. February 1986, *12*, pp. 23–39. **[G: Canada]**

Castañeda, Jorge G. Mexico at the Brink. *Foreign*

Aff., Winter 1985/86, *64*(2), pp. 287–303. **[G: Mexico]**

Chakravarthy, Nikhil. India: What's Missing? **In** *[Patel, S.]*, 1986, pp. 133–38. **[G: India]**

Chakravarty, Sukhamoy. A Few Remarks on Economic Policy. *Indian Econ. J.*, Apr.-June 1986, *33*(4), pp. 1–4. **[G: India]**

Chimerine, Lawrence and Young, Richard M. Economic Surprises and Messages of the 1980's. *Amer. Econ. Rev.*, May 1986, *76*(2), pp. 31–36. **[G: U.S.]**

Chowdhury, Abdur R. A Note on the Relative Impact of Monetary and Fiscal Actions in India. *Indian Econ. J.*, July-Sept. 1986, *34*(1), pp. 89–93. **[G: India]**

Clausen, A. W. Address to the Board of Governors: Washington, D.C.: September 27, 1983. **In** *Clausen, A. W.*, 1986, pp. 191–216.

Clausen, A. W. Address to the Business Council: Hot Springs, Virginia: October 8, 1983. **In** *Clausen, A. W.*, 1986, pp. 217–28.

Clausen, A. W. Address to the Overseas Press Club of America Annual Awards Dinner: New York, New York: April 24, 1985. **In** *Clausen, A. W.*, 1986, pp. 381–90.

Clausen, A. W. Economic Growth: The Path to the Alleviation of Debt and Poverty: Address at the Central Bank of Argentina: Buenos Aires, Argentina: December 9, 1985. **In** *Clausen, A. W.*, 1986, pp. 425–39.

Clausen, A. W. Poverty in the Developing Countries, 1985: Address at the Martin Luther King, Jr., Center: Atlanta, Georgia: January 11, 1985. **In** *Clausen, A. W.*, 1986, pp. 347–60.

Clausen, A. W. The Challenge of Development in Sub-Saharan Africa: Address to the Nigerian Institute of International Affairs: Lagos, Nigeria: April 15, 1982. **In** *Clausen, A. W.*, 1986, pp. 67–78. **[G: Sub-Saharan Africa]**

Cole, Rodney V. and Parry, T. G. Key Issues in Pacific Island Development. **In** *Cole, R. V. and Parry, T. G., eds.*, 1986, pp. 1–20. **[G: S. Pacific]**

Cooper, Richard N. The United States as an Open Economy. **In** *Hafer, R. W., ed. (I)*, 1986, pp. 3–24. **[G: U.S.]**

Corbo, Vittorio; de Melo, Jaime and Tybout, James. What Went Wrong with the Recent Reforms in the Southern Cone. *Econ. Develop. Cult. Change*, April 1986, *34*(3), pp. 607–40. **[G: Uruguay; Chile; Argentina]**

Corrigan, E. Gerald. Reducing International Imbalances in an Interdependent World. *Fed. Res. Bank New York Quart. Rev.*, Spring 1986, *11*(1), pp. 1–5. **[G: U.S.; LDCs]**

Crotty, James R. Marx, Keynes, and Minsky on the Instability of the Capitalist Growth Process and the Nature of Government Economic Policy. **In** *Helburn, S. W. and Bramhall, D. F., eds.*, 1986, pp. 297–324. **[G: U.S.]**

Dalziel, Paul C. The 1984 Economic Summit Conference: A Search for Policy Objectives. *New Zealand Econ. Pap.*, 1986, *20*, pp. 41–51. **[G: New Zealand]**

Deans, Robert H. Macroeconomic Conflicts and Economic and Social Policies. *Rev. Soc. Econ.*, October 1986, *44*(2), pp. 113–29. **[G: OECD]**

Diamandouros, P. Nikiforos. The Southern European NICs. **In** *Comisso, E. and Tyson, L., eds.*, 1986, pp. 371–80. **[G: Greece; Portugal; Spain]**

Domínguez, Jorge I. Cuba in the 1980s. *Foreign Aff.*, Fall 1986, *65*(1), pp. 118–35. **[G: Cuba]**

Dornbusch, Rudiger. A New Chance for Argentina. *Challenge*, Jan./Feb. 1986, *28*(6), pp. 15–20. **[G: Argentina]**

Dornbusch, Rudiger. Sound Currency and Full Employment. **In** *Dornbusch, R.*, 1986, *1985*, pp. 205–31. **[G: U.K.]**

Dornbusch, Rudiger. The World Debt Problem: 1980–84 and Beyond. **In** *Dornbusch, R.*, 1986, *1985*, pp. 131–50.

Dornbusch, Rudiger, et al. Macroeconomic Prospects and Policies for the European Community. **In** *Blanchard, O.; Dornbusch, R. and Layard, R., eds.*, 1986, pp. 1–32. **[G: EEC]**

Drucker, Peter F. The Changed World Economy. *Foreign Aff.*, Spring 1986, *64*(4), pp. 768–91.

Dugger, William M. The Last Gasp of Liberal Capitalism in America. *J. Econ. Issues*, June 1986, *20*(2), pp. 325–33. **[G: U.S.]**

Dürr, Ernst. Growth, Technical Progress, and Unemployment in the Federal Republic of Germany. **In** *Hax, H.; Kraus, W. and Tsuchiya, K., eds.*, 1986, pp. 145–62. **[G: W. Germany; OECD]**

Dyker, David A. Soviet Planning Reforms from Andropov to Gorbachev. **In** *Amann, R. and Cooper, J., eds.*, 1986, pp. 153–69. **[G: U.S.S.R.]**

ECLAC Secretariat, Port of Spain. A View of the Caribbean. **In** *Maddison, A., ed.*, 1986, pp. 91–115. **[G: Caribbean]**

ECLAC Secretariat, Santiago. Central America: Bases for Reactivation and Development. **In** *Maddison, A., ed.*, 1986, pp. 116–29. **[G: Central America]**

ECLAC Secretariat, Santiago. Development and Crisis in Latin America: 1950–84. **In** *Maddison, A., ed.*, 1986, pp. 28–66. **[G: Latin America]**

Edwards, Sebastian and Teitel, Simón. Introduction to Growth, Reform, and Adjustment: Latin America's Trade and Macroeconomic Policies in the 1970s and 1980s. *Econ. Develop. Cult. Change*, April 1986, *34*(3), pp. 423–31. **[G: Latin America]**

Epstein, Gerald. What Hath Conservative Economics Wrought? *Challenge*, July/Aug. 1986, *29*(3), pp. 40–46. **[G: U.S.]**

Feldstein, Martin S. Supply Side Economics: Old Truths and New Claims. *Amer. Econ. Rev.*, May 1986, *76*(2), pp. 26–30. **[G: U.S.]**

Feldstein, Martin S. U.S. Budget Deficits and the European Economies: Resolving the Political Economy Puzzle. *Amer. Econ. Rev.*, May 1986, *76*(2), pp. 342–46. **[G: U.S.; W. Europe]**

Fishlow, Albert. A economia política do ajustamento brasileiro aos choques do petróleo: uma nota sobre o período 1974/84. (With English summary.) *Pesquisa Planejamento Econ.*, December 1986, *16*(3), pp. 507–50. **[G: Brazil]**

Fitoussi, Jean-Paul and Phelps, Edmund S. Causes of the 1980s Slump in Europe. *Brookings Pap. Econ. Act.*, 1986, (2), pp. 487–513. **[G: W. Europe; U.S.]**

Forte, Francesco. Ten Paradoxes Facing African Countries. *Atlantic Econ. J.*, March 1986, *14*(1), pp. 1–7. **[G: LDCs; Africa]**

Franz, Wolfgang. Towards an Evaluation of the Costs and Benefits of a (Dis-) Inflationary Policy in the Federal Republic of Germany. **In** *Frisch, H. and Gahlen, B., eds.*, 1986, pp. 13–44. **[G: W. Germany]**

Fuchs, Peter. Past, Present, and Future Perfect? Casing Japan's Competitive Strategy. **In** *Finn, R. B., ed.*, 1986, pp. 17–37. **[G: Japan]**

von Furstenberg, George M. and Green, R. Jeffrey. Supply-Side Modeling from Bits and Pieces. *Amer. Econ. Rev.*, May 1986, *76*(2), pp. 37–42. **[G: U.S.]**

Giersch, Herbert. Weltwirtschaftliches Wachstum durch Liberalisierung. (Global Economic Growth by Liberalization. With English summary.) *Kyklos*, 1986, *39*(4), pp. 518–36. **[G: W. Europe]**

Glassburner, Bruce. Survey of Recent Developments. *Bull. Indonesian Econ. Stud.*, April 1986, *22*(1), pp. 1–33. **[G: Indonesia]**

González, Norberto. Meeting on Growth, Adjustment and the Debt in Latin America: Opening Address. *CEPAL Rev.*, April 1986, (28), pp. 7–10. **[G: Latin America]**

González, Norberto. Reactivation and Development: The Great Commitment of Latin America and the Caribbean. *CEPAL Rev.*, December 1986, (30), pp. 7–16. **[G: Latin America]**

Gordon, Robert J. U.S. Fiscal Deficits and the World Imbalance of Payments. *Hitotsubashi J. Econ.*, Spec. Iss. Oct. 1986, *27*, pp. 7–41. **[G: U.S.]**

Gordon, Wendell. Thresholds of Change and Core Policy. *J. Econ. Issues*, June 1986, *20*(2), pp. 489–98.

Green, Reginald Herbold. Africa in the 1980s: Some Key Political Economic Issues, Problems and Prospects. **In** *[Patel, S.]*, 1986, pp. 173–94. **[G: Africa]**

Green, Reginald Herbold and Allison, Caroline. The World Bank's Agenda for Accelerated Development: Dialectics, Doubts and Dialogues. **In** *Ravenhill, J., ed.*, 1986, pp. 60–84. **[G: Africa]**

Grjebine, André. France and Its External Constraints. **In** *Sjöstedt, G. and Sundelius, B., eds.*, 1986, pp. 127–37. **[G: France]**

Guglielmi, Jean-Louis. Incertitudes conjoncturelles et évolution des espaces des économies industrielles. (With English summary.) *Revue Écon. Polit.*, Sept.-Oct. 1986, *96*(5), pp. 551–59. **[G: OECD]**

Haberler, Gottfried. The Slowdown of the World Economy and the Problem of Stagflation. **In** *Lal, D. and Wolf, M., eds.*, 1986, pp. 48–90. **[G: Global]**

Hafer, R. W. How Open Is the U.S. Economy? Preface. **In** *Hafer, R. W., ed. (I)*, 1986, pp. xiii–xviii.

Hale, David D. The Economy to 1990. *Bus. Econ.*, January 1986, *21*(1), pp. 34–38. **[G: U.S.]**

Hall, John B. Reform-Bargaining in Hungary: An Interview with Dr. János Mátyás Kovács. *Comp. Econ. Stud.*, Fall 1986, *28*(3), pp. 25–42. **[G: Hungary]**

Harcourt, Geoffrey C. Making Socialism in Your Own Country. **In** *[Harcourt, G. C.]*, 1986, pp. 250–72. **[G: Australia]**

Hartland-Thunberg, Penelope. Brazil's Interrupted Economic Miracle. **In** *Hartland-Thunberg, P. and Ebinger, C. K., eds.*, 1986, pp. 99–130. **[G: Brazil]**

Hartland-Thunberg, Penelope and Ebinger, Charles K. Mexico's Economic Anguish. **In** *Hartland-Thunberg, P. and Ebinger, C. K., eds.*, 1986, pp. 55–98. **[G: Mexico]**

Hartlyn, Jonathan and Morley, Samuel A. Bureaucratic-Authoritarian Regimes in Comparative Perspective. **In** *Hartlyn, J. and Morley, S. A., eds.*, 1986, pp. 38–53. **[G: Latin America]**

Hartlyn, Jonathan and Morley, Samuel A. Latin American Political Economy: Financial Crisis and Political Change: Introduction. **In** *Hartlyn, J. and Morley, S. A., eds.*, 1986, pp. 1–12. **[G: Latin America]**

Held, David. Liberalism, Marxism and the Future Direction of Public Policy. **In** *Nolan, P. and Paine, S., eds.*, 1986, pp. 13–34. **[G: U.K.]**

Heller, Walter W. A Distinction *with* a Difference. *Challenge*, July/Aug. 1986, *29*(3), pp. 59. **[G: U.S.]**

Heller, Walter W. Activist Government: Key to Growth. *Challenge*, Mar./Apr. 1986, *29*(1), pp. 4–10. **[G: U.S.]**

Hewett, Ed. A., et al. 1986 Panel on the Soviet Economic Outlook. *Soviet Econ.*, Jan.-Mar. 1986, *2*(1), pp. 3–18. **[G: U.S.S.R.]**

Hoch, Róbert. Open Economy and Domestic Consumption. *Acta Oecon.*, 1986, *37*(3–4), pp. 189–203. **[G: Hungary]**

Hormats, Robert D. The World Economy under Stress. *Foreign Aff.*, 1986, *64*(3), pp. 455–78. **[G: Global]**

Hrivnák, Pavel. Effectiveness and Intensification. *Czech. Econ. Digest.*, June/July 1986, (4), pp. 3–11. **[G: Czechoslovakia]**

Jaycox, Edward V. K. Africa: Development Challenges and the World Bank's Response. *Finance Develop.*, March 1986, *23*(1), pp. 21–22. **[G: Africa]**

Johnson, Chalmers. The Nonsocialist NICs: East Asia. **In** *Comisso, E. and Tyson, L., eds.*, 1986, pp. 381–89. **[G: E. Asia]**

Jordan, Jerry L. Economic Outlook. **In** *Shadow Open Market Committee (II)*, 1986, pp. 9–36. **[G: U.S.]**

Jordan, Jerry L. Economic Outlook. **In** *Shadow Open Market Committee (I)*, 1986, pp. 9–18. **[G: U.S.]**

Jung, Aleksander. Exporting, Refinancing, Restructuring. *Eastern Europ. Econ.*, Summer 1986, *24*(4), pp. 40–50. **[G: Poland]**

Kaufman, Henry. In the Shadow of Financial Exhilaration. *Challenge,* July/Aug. 1986, *29*(3), pp. 4–10. **[G: U.S.]**

Kenen, Peter B. The United States as an Open Economy: Comments. **In** *Hafer, R. W., ed. (I),* 1986, pp. 25–31. **[G: U.S.]**

Keyserling, Leon H. Let's Get This Straight [Activist Government: Key to Growth]. *Challenge,* Nov./Dec. 1986, *29*(5), pp. 56–58. **[G: U.S.]**

Kolosi, Tamás. Structural Groups and Reform. *Acta Oecon.*, 1986, *37*(1–2), pp. 15–30. **[G: Hungary]**

Köves, András. Foreign Economic Equilibrium, Economic Development and Economic Policy in the CMEA Countries. *Acta Oecon.*, 1986, *36*(1–2), pp. 35–53. **[G: CMEA]**

Köves, András. Is Opening Still Topical? *Acta Oecon.*, 1986, *37*(3–4), pp. 205–18. **[G: CMEA; Hungary]**

Kuntjoro-Jakti, Dorodjatun. The Global Crisis of the 1980s and Indonesia's Response. *Hitotsubashi J. Econ.*, Spec. Iss. Oct. 1986, *27*, pp. 101–13.

Kuttner, Robert L. A Great American Tradition: Government Opening Opportunity. *Challenge,* Mar./Apr. 1986, *29*(1), pp. 18–25. **[G: U.S.]**

Lal, Deepak and Wolf, Martin. Stagflation, Savings, and the State: Perspectives on the Global Economy: Introduction. **In** *Lal, D. and Wolf, M., eds.*, 1986, pp. 3–13.

Langr, František. From His Address at the 28th International Engineering Fair in Brno, September 1986. *Czech. Econ. Digest.*, December 1986, (8), pp. 26–35. **[G: Czechoslovakia]**

Lér, Ondřej and Urban, Ludck. European CMEA Countries in 1985–1986. *Czech. Econ. Digest.*, Oct./Nov. 1986, (7), pp. 3–20. **[G: CMEA]**

Livshits, A. Criticism of Supply-Side Economics. *Prob. Econ.*, September 1986, *29*(5), pp. 76–94. **[G: U.S.]**

Lombardi, Mauro. Anni '70: il governo della moneta tra economia e politica. (With English summary.) *Stud. Econ.*, 1986, *41*(29), pp. 99–146. **[G: Italy]**

Lowenthal, Abraham F. Threat and Opportunity in the Americas. *Foreign Aff.*, 1986, *64*(3), pp. 539–61. **[G: Latin America]**

Lower, Milton D. The Industrial Economy and International Price Shocks. *J. Econ. Issues,* June 1986, *20*(2), pp. 297–312. **[G: U.S.]**

Malinvaud, Edmond. Prices, Incentives, and Economic Growth: Comment. **In** *Balassa, B. and Giersch, H., eds.*, 1986, pp. 22–27.

Maramba, Felix K., Jr. Privatization: Imperative for Sustained Economic Development. *Philippine Econ. J.*, 1986, *25*(1–2), pp. 17–23. **[G: Philippines]**

Masera, Rainer Stefano. Europe's Economic Problems in an International Perspective. *Banca Naz. Lavoro Quart. Rev.*, December 1986, (159), pp. 391–406. **[G: W. Europe]**

Maynes, Charles William. Lost Opportunities. *Foreign Aff.*, 1986, *64*(3), pp. 413–34. **[G: U.S.]**

McNown, Robert. On the Uses of Econometric Models: A Guide for Policy Makers. *Policy Sci.*, December 1986, *19*(4), pp. 359–80. **[G: U.S.]**

Meier, Alfred and Mettler, Daniel. Einfluss und Macht in der Wirtschaftspolitik. (Influence and Power in Economic Policy. With English summary.) *Schweiz. Z. Volkswirtsch. Statist.*, March 1986, *122*(1), pp. 37–59.

Merhaut, Josef. Strengthening the Integration Activity of CMEA. *Soviet E. Europ. Foreign Trade,* Summer 1986, *22*(2), pp. 67–77. **[G: CMEA]**

Mickwitz, Gösta. Internationaliseringens konsekvenser. (Consequences of Internationalization. With English summary.) *Ekon. Samfundets Tidskr.*, 1986, *39*(3), pp. 117–18.

Minsky, Hyman P. The Crises of 1983 and the Prospects for Advanced Capitalist Economies. **In** *Helburn, S. W. and Bramhall, D. F., eds.*, 1986, pp. 284–96. **[G: U.S.]**

Mishan, Ezra J. The Future Is Worse Than It Was. **In** *Mishan, E. J.*, 1986, *1983*, pp. 169–93.

de Montbrial, Thierry. The European Dimension. *Foreign Aff.*, 1986, *64*(3), pp. 499–514. **[G: EEC]**

Morgan, Roger. Partners and Rivals in Western Europe: The Historical Background, 1955–85. **In** *Morgan, R. and Bray, C., eds.*, 1986, pp. 7–23. **[G: U.K.; France; W. Germany]**

Morris, Frank E. Statement to the U.S. House Subcommittee on Domestic Monetary Policy of the Committee on Banking, Finance and Urban Affairs, March 19, 1986. *Fed. Res. Bull.*, May 1986, *72*(5), pp. 315–16. **[G: U.S.]**

Morse, Edward L. After the Fall: The Politics of Oil. *Foreign Aff.*, Spring 1986, *64*(4), pp. 792–811.

Nagy, András. Open We Must! *Acta Oecon.*, 1986, *37*(3–4), pp. 219–39. **[G: Hungary]**

Nakamura, Takafusa. The World Economy and Japan since the 1970's. **In** *Hax, H.; Kraus, W. and Tsuchiya, K., eds.*, 1986, pp. 1–14. **[G: Japan; OECD]**

Ndulu, Benno J. Governance and Economic Management. **In** *Berg, R. J. and Whitaker, J. S., eds.*, 1986, pp. 81–107. **[G: Sub-Saharan Africa]**

Niskanen, William A. A Reflection on the Role of the Council of Economic Advisers. *Carnegie-Rochester Conf. Ser. Public Policy,* Autumn 1986, *25*, pp. 259–63. **[G: U.S.]**

Nordhaus, William D. The Council of Economic Advisers: Conscience or Advocate? *Carnegie-Rochester Conf. Ser. Public Policy,* Autumn 1986, *25*, pp. 265–77. **[G: U.S.]**

Nove, Alec. The Economic Problems of Brezhnev's Successors. **In** *Nove, A.*, 1986, *1978*, pp. 180–90. **[G: U.S.S.R.]**

Nove, Alec. The Soviet Economy: Problems and Prospects. **In** *Nove, A.*, 1986, *1980*, pp. 131–49. **[G: U.S.S.R.]**

Nyirabu, C. M. A View from Africa: 2. **In** *Hel-*

leiner, G. K, ed., 1986, pp. 32–42. **[G: Africa]**

Öniş, Ziya. Stabilisation and Growth in a Semi-industrial Economy: An Evaluation of the Recent Turkish Experiment, 1977–1984. *METU*, 1986, *13*(1/2), pp. 7–28. **[G: Turkey]**

Page, S. A. B. Prospects for Non-oil Developing Countries. *Nat. Inst. Econ. Rev.*, May 1986, (116), pp. 31–37. **[G: LDCs]**

Pasinetti, Luigi L. Prices, Incentives, and Economic Growth: Comment. **In** *Balassa, B. and Giersch, H., eds.*, 1986, pp. 28–31.

Patel, I. G. Economic Theory and Economic Policy. **In** *Patel, I. G.*, 1986, pp. 101–16. **[G: India]**

Patel, I. G. Free Enterprise in the Nehru Era. **In** *Patel, I. G.*, 1986, *1984*, pp. 165–81. **[G: India]**

Patel, I. G. The Limits of Economic Policy. **In** *Patel, I. G.*, 1986, *1966*, pp. 17–34. **[G: India]**

Pesaran, M. Hashem. A Macro Model of an Oil Exporter: Nigeria: Comment. **In** *Neary, J. P. and van Wijnbergen, S., eds.*, 1986, pp. 225–28. **[G: Nigeria]**

Pfouts, Ralph W. Is the Outlook for the U.S. Economy Even Murkier Than Usual? *Atlantic Econ. J.*, September 1986, *14*(3), pp. 1–5. **[G: U.S.]**

Pitchford, J. D. The Australian Economy: 1985 and Prospects for 1986. *Econ. Rec.*, March 1986, *62*(176), pp. 1–21. **[G: Australia]**

Pollard, Sidney. Stagflation, Fiscal Deficits and Balance of Payments—Great Britain and Germany. *Hitotsubashi J. Econ.*, Spec. Iss. Oct. 1986, *27*, pp. 42–56. **[G: U.K.; W. Germany]**

Posner, Michael. The State of the Economy. *Scot. J. Polit. Econ.*, November 1986, *33*(4), pp. 305–16. **[G: U.K.]**

Prebisch, Raúl. Address Delivered to the Twenty-first Session of ECLAC (Mexico City, 24 April 1986). *CEPAL Rev.*, August 1986, (29), pp. 13–16. **[G: Latin America]**

Rába, András. Hungarian Development—with Bottlenecks. *Acta Oecon.*, 1986, *36*(3–4), pp. 181–96. **[G: Hungary]**

Ravenhill, John. Africa's Continuing Crises: The Elusiveness of Development. **In** *Ravenhill, J., ed.*, 1986, pp. 1–43. **[G: Africa]**

Regini, Marino. Political Bargaining in Western Europe during the Economic Crisis of the 1980s. **In** *Jacobi, O., et al., eds. (II)*, 1986, pp. 61–76.

Rohwer, Bernd. Der Konjunkturaufschwung 1983–1986—Ein Erfolg des wirtschaftspolitischen Kurswechsels der christlich-liberalen Koaltion? Einige Anmerkungen zur konjunkturtheoretischen Beurteilung des gegenwätigen Aufschwungs. (The Business Revival 1983–1986 in West Germany—A Success of the CDU/CSU–FDP Coalition's Change of Policy?—Some Remarks on the Causes of the Present Business Upswing. With English summary.) *Konjunkturpolitik*, 1986, *32*(6), pp. 325–48. **[G: W. Germany]**

Romberg, Alan D. New Stirrings in Asia. *Foreign Aff.*, 1986, *64*(3), pp. 515–38. **[G: E. Asia]**

Rossi, Vanessa and Clements, Michael. The World Economy: Analysis and Prospects. *Oxford Rev. Econ. Policy*, Spring 1986, *2*(1), pp. xxxiv–li. **[G: Global]**

Sachs, Jeffrey. Causes of the 1980s Slump in Europe: Comments. *Brookings Pap. Econ. Act.*, 1986, (2), pp. 514–19. **[G: W. Europe; U.S.]**

Saitoti, G. A View from Africa: 1. **In** *Helleiner, G. K, ed.*, 1986, pp. 26–31. **[G: Africa]**

Salant, Walter S. Was Kennedy Always First? *Challenge*, July/Aug. 1986, *29*(3), pp. 56–59. **[G: U.S.]**

Samuelson, Paul A. Afternoon of the Mixed Economy? **In** *Samuelson, P. A.*, 1986, *1981*, pp. 998–1001.

Samuelson, Paul A. Evaluating Reaganomics. **In** *Samuelson, P. A.*, 1986, *1984*, pp. 901–08. **[G: U.S.]**

Samuelson, Paul A. Japan and the World at the Century's End. **In** *Samuelson, P. A.*, 1986, *1984*, pp. 496–509. **[G: Japan]**

Samuelson, Paul A. Lofty Aims Alone Cannot Create Efficiency, Growth and Equity. **In** *Samuelson, P. A.*, 1986, *1980*, pp. 992–94.

Samuelson, Paul A. The Crash of '29: Lessons for '79. **In** *Samuelson, P. A.*, 1986, *1979*, pp. 925–28. **[G: U.S.]**

Samuelson, Paul A. The World Economy at Century's End. **In** *Samuelson, P. A.*, 1986, *1983*, pp. 881–900.

Samuelson, Paul A. World Economy of the Eighties. **In** *Samuelson, P. A.*, 1986, pp. 1002–04.

Sanchez-Arnau, Juan C. Medium-term Scenarios for the Future of Latin America. **In** *Maddison, A., ed.*, 1986, pp. 67–84. **[G: Latin America]**

Sarney, José. Brazil: A President's Story. *Foreign Aff.*, Fall 1986, *65*(1), pp. 101–17. **[G: Brazil]**

Saulnier, Raymond J. The President's Economic Report: A Critique. *J. Portfol. Manage.*, Summer 1986, *12*(4), pp. 72–73. **[G: U.S.]**

Scott, Anthony. The Macdonald Report: The Reviews in Review. *Can. Public Policy*, Supp. February 1986, *12*, pp. 1–22. **[G: Canada]**

Simonsen, Palle. Finans- og pengepolitikkens muligheder under nye internationale vilkår. (Danish Fiscal and Monetary Policy and the Deregulation of International Capital Movements. With English summary.) *Nationaløkon. Tidsskr.*, 1986, *124*(1), pp. 51–61. **[G: Denmark]**

Singh, Manmohan. Sustaining Development in an Uncertain International Environment. *Indian Econ. J.*, Jan.-Mar. 1986, *33*(3), pp. 1–14. **[G: LDCs]**

Solomon, Anthony. Economics, Ideology, and Public Policy. *Challenge*, July/Aug. 1986, *29*(3), pp. 11–17. **[G: U.S.]**

Solomon, Ezra. Economic Prospects for the Balance of the Decade—Toward a New Continuity. *Bus. Econ.*, January 1986, *21*(1), pp. 22–27. **[G: U.S.]**

Solow, Robert M. The Unemployment of Nations.

Bus. Econ., January 1986, *21*(1), pp. 5–12. [G: U.S.; EEC]

Sørensen, Christen. Dansk økonomi: Udsigter og økonomisk politik. (The Main Problems of Danish Economic Policy. With English summary.) *Nationaløkon. Tidsskr.*, 1986, *124*(2), pp. 132–38. [G: Denmark]

Spechler, Martin C. Big Inflations Need Potent Cures. *Challenge*, Nov./Dec. 1986, *29*(5), pp. 26–32. [G: OECD]

Starr, Joyce R. Israel: From Dream to Reality. **In** *Hartland-Thunberg, P. and Ebinger, C. K., eds.*, 1986, pp. 155–79. [G: Israel]

Stauffer, Robert B. Philippine Authoritarianism: Framework for Peripheral "Development." **In** *Stauffer, R. B.*, 1986, *1977*, pp. 59–78. [G: Philippines]

Steger, Debra. The Impact of U.S. Trade Laws on Canadian Economic Policies. **In** *C. D. Howe Institute*, 1986, pp. 73–100. [G: Canada; U.S.]

Stein, Herbert. Should Growth Be a Priority of National Policy? *Challenge*, Mar./Apr. 1986, *29*(1), pp. 11–17. [G: U.S.]

Stewart, Ian A. Consensus, Flexibility and Equity. *Can. Public Policy*, June 1986, *12*(2), pp. 307–13. [G: Canada]

Stigler, George J. The Goals of Economic Policy. **In** *Stigler, G. J.*, 1986, *1975*, pp. 89–98. [G: U.S.]

Street, James H. Can Mexico Break the Vicious Circle of "Stop–Go" Policy? An Institutional Overview. *J. Econ. Issues*, June 1986, *20*(2), pp. 601–12. [G: Mexico]

Summers, Lawrence H. Government Policy and Economic Performance. **In** *Knowlton, W. and Zeckhauser, R., eds.*, 1986, pp. 317–22. [G: U.S.]

Sylos Labini, Paolo. Some Reflections on the Austral Plan and Argentine Economic Policy. *Rev. Econ. Cond. Italy*, Sept.-Dec. 1986, (3), pp. 511–40. [G: Argentina]

Tarantelli, Ezio. Erratum [The Regulation of Inflation and Unemployment]. *Ind. Relat.*, Spring 1986, *25*(2), pp. 94. [G: OECD]

Tarantelli, Ezio. The Regulation of Inflation and Unemployment. *Ind. Relat.*, Winter 1986, *25*(1), pp. 1–15. [G: OECD]

Tobin, James. High Time to Restore the Employment Act of 1946. *Challenge*, May/June 1986, *29*(2), pp. 4–12. [G: U.S.]

Truu, M. L. Economics and Politics in South Africa Today. *S. Afr. J. Econ.*, December 1986, *54*(4), pp. 343–61. [G: S. Africa]

Tyson, Laura D'Andrea. The Debt Crisis and Adjustment Responses in Eastern Europe: A Comparative Perspective. *Int. Organ.*, Spring 1986, *40*(2), pp. 239–85. [G: CMEA; LDCs]

Vesperini, Jean-Pierre. La conjoncture de la France en 1985–1986 succès et echecs de la politique de rigueur. (With English summary.) *Revue Écon. Polit.*, Sept.-Oct. 1986, *96*(5), pp. 560–74. [G: France]

Vogel, Ezra F. Pax Nipponica? *Foreign Aff.*, Spring 1986, *64*(4), pp. 752–67. [G: Japan]

Volcker, Paul A. Statement to the U.S. House Committee on the Budget, February 26, 1986. *Fed. Res. Bull.*, April 1986, *72*(4), pp. 241–43. [G: U.S.]

Volcker, Paul A. Statement to the U.S. House Committee on Banking, Finance and Urban Affairs, February 19, 1986. *Fed. Res. Bull.*, April 1986, *72*(4), pp. 233–41. [G: U.S.]

Volcker, Paul A. Statement to the U.S. Senate Committee on Banking, Housing, and Urban Affairs, July 23, 1986. *Fed. Res. Bull.*, September 1986, *72*(9), pp. 635–42. [G: U.S.]

Walker, John and Clements, Michael. The UK Economy: Analysis and Prospects. *Oxford Rev. Econ. Policy*, Autumn 1986, *2*(3), pp. xxvii–xxxix. [G: U.K.]

Walker, John and Clements, Michael. The UK Economy: Analysis and Prospects. *Oxford Rev. Econ. Policy*, Summer 1986, *2*(2), pp. xxv–xliii. [G: U.K.]

Walker, John and Clements, Michael. The UK Economy: Analysis and Prospects. *Oxford Rev. Econ. Policy*, Winter 1986, *2*(4), pp. xx–xxxii. [G: U.K.]

Wasserfallen, Walter. On the Way to More Employment: A Comment to the 1985/1986 Report of the German Council of Economic Experts. *J. Inst. Theoretical Econ.*, June 1986, *142*(2), pp. 452–59. [G: W. Germany]

Weitzman, Martin L. The Share Economy Symposium: A Reply. *J. Compar. Econ.*, December 1986, *10*(4), pp. 469–73.

Wells, John. Economic Recovery and Industrial Expansion in the U.K. **In** *Nolan, P. and Paine, S., eds.*, 1986, pp. 135–44. [G: U.K.]

Wheelwright, E. L. Marxist Analysis of Capitalism in Australia: Past, Present, and Future. **In** *Dowdy, E., ed.*, 1986, pp. 1–23. [G: Australia]

Young, Soogil. A Global Outlook from the Old Hermit Kingdom. *World Econ.*, March 1986, *9*(1), pp. 51–64. [G: S. Korea]

Zeuthen, Hans E. De senere års omvurderinger af centrale økonomiske sammenhænge. (Shifts in the Conceptions of How the Danish Economy Works. With English summary.) *Nationaløkon. Tidsskr.*, 1986, *124*(3), pp. 274–83. [G: Denmark]

1331 Stabilization Theories and Policies

Addo, J. S. Alternative Approaches to Stabilization in Africa: Comments. **In** *Helleiner, G. K, ed.*, 1986, pp. 153–56. [G: Sub-Saharan Africa]

Ahamed, Liaquat. Stabilization Policies in Developing Countries. *World Bank Res. Observer*, January 1986, *1*(1), pp. 79–110. [G: Peru; Mexico; Portugal; Bangladesh]

Ahmadian, Majid. Oil Pricing Policies and Macroeconomy for an Oil-Based Economy. *Energy Econ.*, October 1986, *8*(4), pp. 251–56.

Aizenman, Joshua. Stabilization Policies and the Information Content of Real Wages. *Economica*, May 1986, *53*(210), pp. 181–90.

Allen, Larry and Price, Don. The Short-run Impact of Monetary and Fiscal Policy in a Two

Sector Keynesian Model. *Amer. Econ.*, Spring 1986, *30*(1), pp. 40–50.

Altvater, Elmar; Huebner, Kurt and Stanger, Michael. The End of the Keynesian Consensus. **In** *Jacobi, O., et al., eds. (II),* 1986, pp. 17–31.

Andersen, Leonall C. and Carlson, Keith M. A Monetarist Model for Economic Stabilization. *Fed. Res. Bank St. Louis Rev.*, October 1986, *68*(8), pp. 45–66. **[G: U.S.]**

Andersen, Leonall C. and Jordan, Jerry L. Monetary and Fiscal Actions: A Test of Their Relative Importance in Economic Stabilization. *Fed. Res. Bank St. Louis Rev.*, October 1986, *68*(8), pp. 29–44. **[G: U.S.]**

Andersen, Torben M. Pre-set Prices, Differential Information and Monetary Policy. *Oxford Econ. Pap.*, November 1986, *38*(3), pp. 456–80.

Arestis, Philip. Post-Keynesian Economic Policies: The Case of Sweden. *J. Econ. Issues*, September 1986, *20*(3), pp. 709–23. **[G: Sweden]**

Axilrod, Stephen H. Debt, Financial Stability, and Public Policy: Overview. **In** *Axilrod, S. H., et al.*, 1986, pp. 209–17.

Balassa, Bela. Policy Responses to Exogenous Shocks in Developing Countries. *Amer. Econ. Rev.*, May 1986, *76*(2), pp. 75–78. **[G: LDCs]**

Barro, Robert J. Recent Developments in the Theory of Rules versus Discretion. *Econ. J.*, Supplement 1986, *96*, pp. 23–37.

Barro, Robert J. Reputation in a Model of Monetary Policy with Incomplete Information. *J. Monet. Econ.*, January 1986, *17*(1), pp. 3–20.

Barten, A. P. and d'Alcantara, G. Simulating Economic Policy with the COMET Model. **In** *Artus, P. and Guvenen, O., eds.*, 1986, pp. 229–37. **[G: EEC]**

Basevi, Giorgio and Giavazzi, Francesco. Stabilization Policies in an Explosive Economy: Announcements and Expectations. *Europ. Econ. Rev.*, February 1986, *30*(1), pp. 43–55.

Batten, Dallas S. and Thornton, Daniel L. The Monetary–Fiscal Policy Debate and the Andersen–Jordan Equation. *Fed. Res. Bank St. Louis Rev.*, October 1986, *68*(8), pp. 9–17. **[G: U.S.]**

Baum, Christopher F. Coordination of Large Macroeconomies' Policies and the Stability of Small Economies. *J. Econ. Dynam. Control,* June 1986, *10*(1/2), pp. 21–25. **[G: U.S.; Austria; Australia; Canada]**

Beare, John B. Automatic Stabilizers? *J. Macroecon.*, Winter 1986, *8*(1), pp. 43–54.

Becker, Robin G., et al. Optimal Policy Design with Non-Linear Models: The Multi-Agent Case. *J. Econ. Dynam. Control,* June 1986, *10*(1/2), pp. 27–31. **[G: U.S.; France; Italy; W. Germany; U.K.]**

Becker, Robin G., et al. Rival Models in Policy Optimization. *J. Econ. Dynam. Control,* June 1986, *10*(1/2), pp. 75–81. **[G: U.K.]**

Becker, Robin G., et al. The Simultaneous Use of Rival Models in Public Optimisation. *Econ. J.*, June 1986, *96*(382), pp. 425–48. **[G: U.K.]**

Bellemare, Diane and Poulin-Simon, Lise. Le plein emploi: objectif et stratégie économique. (Full Employment: An Objective and an Economic Strategy. With English summary.) *Écon. Soc.*, April 1986, *20*(4), pp. 345–90. **[G: Canada]**

Bhandari, Jagdeep S. and Hanson, Donald A. Optimal Fiscal Policy in an Open Economy with Time-varying Elasticities. *Southern Econ. J.*, January 1986, *52*(3), pp. 763–76.

Black, Stanley W. The Open Economy: Implications for Monetary and Fiscal Policy: Comment. **In** *Gordon, R. J., ed.*, 1986, pp. 501–04. **[G: U.S.]**

Blinder, Alan S. Ruminations on Karl Brunner's Reflections [Fiscal Policy in Macro Theory: A Survey and Evaluation]. **In** *Hafer, R. W., ed. (II),* 1986, pp. 117–26.

Bluestone, Barry and Havens, John. The Microeconomic Impacts of Macroeconomic Fiscal Policy, 1981–85. *J. Post Keynesian Econ.*, Summer 1986, *8*(4), pp. 499–514. **[G: U.S.]**

Borio, C. E. V. Do Contingent Rules Really Dominate Fixed Rules? *Econ. J.*, December 1986, *96*(384), pp. 1000–1010.

Botos, Katalin. The Impact of the Depression of the 1930s and Its Relevance for the Contemporary World: 1929/33 vs. 1979/83. **In** *Berend, I. T. and Borchardt, K., eds.*, 1986, pp. 333–54.

Boughton, James M., et al. Effects of Exchange Rate Changes in Industrial Countries. **In** *International Monetary Fund, Research Department,* 1986, pp. 115–49. **[G: OECD]**

Boyer, Robert and Coriat, Benjamin. Technical Flexibility and Macro Stabilisation. *Ricerche Econ.*, Oct.-Dec. 1986, *40*(4), pp. 771–835. **[G: U.S.]**

Brandsma, Andries S. Implications of Risk-Sensitive Decision-Making for the Design of Economic Policies. *J. Econ. Dynam. Control,* June 1986, *10*(1/2), pp. 301–06. **[G: Netherlands]**

Brandsma, Andries S. The Implications of Risk Sensitive Decision Making for Macroeconomic Planning in the Netherlands. *De Economist,* 1986, *134*(1), pp. 61–83. **[G: Netherlands]**

Brandsma, Andries S. and Hughes Hallett, A. J. The Coordination Approach to Policymaking in Interdependent Economies. **In** *Artus, P. and Guvenen, O., eds.*, 1986, pp. 209–28. **[G: OECD]**

Brera, Paolo. Austro-Keynesism in a Monetarist Decade: Or, Will Austria's 'Social Partnership' Live through the 1980s? (With a Game Theory Postscript). *Rivista Int. Sci. Econ. Com.*, June-July 1986, *33*(6–7), pp. 667–84. **[G: Austria]**

Brimmer, Andrew F. and Sinai, Allen. The Monetary–Fiscal Policy Mix: Implications for the Short Run. *Amer. Econ. Rev.*, May 1986, *76*(2), pp. 203–08. **[G: U.S.]**

Brunner, Karl. Deficits, Interest Rates, and Monetary Policy. *Cato J.*, Winter 1986, *5*(3), pp. 709–26. **[G: U.S.]**

Brunner, Karl. Fiscal Policy in Macro Theory:

A Survey and Evaluation. **In** *Hafer, R. W., ed. (II),* 1986, pp. 33–116.

Bruno, Sergio. Incertezza, complesità e crisi della "economia del controllo." (Uncertainty, Complexity and Crisis of the "Economics of Control." With English summary.) *Econ. Lavoro,* July-Sept. 1986, *20*(3), pp. 39–61.

Buchanan, James M. Can Policy Activism Succeed? A Public Choice Perspective. **In** *Hafer, R. W., ed. (II),* 1986, pp. 139–50.

Buiter, Willem H. Macroeconomic Policy Design in an Interdependent World Economy: An Analysis of Three Contingencies. *Int. Monet. Fund Staff Pap.,* September 1986, *33*(3), pp. 541–82. **[G: U.S.]**

Burchardt, Andrew. Jobs for All: A Comment. *Econ. J.,* September 1986, *96*(383), pp. 812–13.

Bureau, Dominique and Norotte, Michel. Ralentir la substitution capital-travail. Une analyse critique. (Shift in the Factor Demands to Reduce Unemployment: A Review. With English summary.) *Revue Écon.,* September 1986, *37*(5), pp. 833–56. **[G: France]**

Cairncross, Alec. Is Employment Policy a Thing of the Past? **In** *Cairncross, A.,* 1986, *1983,* pp. 208–23. **[G: U.K.]**

Cairncross, Alec. Keynes and the Planned Economy. **In** *Cairncross, A.,* 1986, *1978,* pp. 58–77.

Cairncross, Alec. The Limitations of Shadow Rates. **In** *Cairncross, A.,* 1986, *1976,* pp. 96–107.

Cairncross, Alec. The Market and the State. **In** *Cairncross, A.,* 1986, *1976,* pp. 37–57.

Cairncross, Alec. The Relationship between Monetary and Fiscal Policy. **In** *Cairncross, A.,* 1986, pp. 151–68.

Cairncross, Alec. The Rise and Fall of Employment Policy. **In** *Cairncross, A.,* 1986, pp. 193–207. **[G: U.K.]**

Calmfors, Lars and Horn, Henrik. Employment Policies and Centralized Wage-Setting. *Economica,* August 1986, *53*(211), pp. 281–302.

Calvo, Guillermo A. Temporary Stabilization: Predetermined Exchange Rates. *J. Polit. Econ.,* December 1986, *94*(6), pp. 1319–29.

Canitrot, Adolfo and Rozenwurcel, Guillermo. A relação entre a taxa de câmbio e os salários em uma economia semi-industrializada de dois setores. (With English summary.) *Pesquisa Planejamento Econ.,* August 1986, *16*(2), pp. 351–79. **[G: Latin America]**

Caravani, P. On Extending Linear Quadratic Control Theory to Non-symmetric Risky Objectives. *J. Econ. Dynam. Control,* June 1986, *10*(1/2), pp. 83–88.

Cardoso, Eliana A. What Policymakers Can Learn from Brazil and Mexico. *Challenge,* Sept./Oct. 1986, *29*(4), pp. 19–28. **[G: Brazil; Mexico]**

Cardoso, Eliana A. and Reis, Eustáquio J. *Deficits,* dívidas e inflação no Brasil. (With English summary.) *Pesquisa Planejamento Econ.,* December 1986, *16*(3), pp. 575–97.

Carlson, Keith M. A Monetarist Model for Economic Stabilization: Review and Update. *Fed. Res. Bank St. Louis Rev.,* October 1986, *68*(8), pp. 18–28. **[G: U.S.]**

Carraro, Carlo. Indicatori sintetici della politica economica: teoria e applicazioni. (Synthetic Indicators of Macro Policy Goals: Theory and Applications. With English summary.) *Rivista Int. Sci. Econ. Com.,* June-July 1986, *33*(6–7), pp. 629–56. **[G: Italy]**

Carraro, Carlo. Teoria dei giochi e il problema della coordinazione tra politica monetaria e fiscale. (Game Theory and the Coordination of Monetary and Fiscal Policy. With English summary.) *Ricerche Econ.,* Apr.-Sept. 1986, *40*(2–3), pp. 377–99.

Catinat, Michel; Maurice, Joël and Zagamé, Paul. Stratégie du taux de change et mesures d'accompagnement. Une analyse des coûts et avantages à partir d'exercises quantitatifs. (Rate of Exchange Strategy and Accompanying Measures of Economic Policy. With English summary.) *Revue Écon.,* September 1986, *37*(5), pp. 857–84. **[G: France]**

Cayton, J. Michael. The U.S. Policy Mix, Foreign Financing, and the Consequences. *J. Econ. Issues,* September 1986, *20*(3), pp. 743–58.

Chand, Sheetal K. and Otani, Ichiro. Aggregate Demand and the Coordination of Monetary and Fiscal Action. **In** *Shome, P., ed.,* 1986, pp. 173–97. **[G: Malaysia; Thailand; Philippines; S. Korea; Japan]**

Chappell, Henry W., Jr. and Keech, William R. Party Differences in Macroeconomic Policies and Outcomes. *Amer. Econ. Rev.,* May 1986, *76*(2), pp. 71–74. **[G: U.S.]**

Chowdhury, Abdur R. A Note on the Dominant Influence of Fiscal Actions. *Eastern Econ. J.,* Jan.-Mar. 1986, *12*(1), pp. 61–62. **[G: India]**

Christodoulakis, Nicos; Vines, David and Weale, Martin. Developments in New Keynesian Policy Formation. *J. Econ. Dynam. Control,* June 1986, *10*(1/2), pp. 185–89.

Chung, Pham. A Note on Policy Evaluation and Rational Expectations. *Public Finance,* 1986, *41*(1), pp. 139–46.

Cloete, J. J. Recent Exchange Rate Policy in South Africa—A Critique. *S. Afr. J. Econ.,* September 1986, *54*(3), pp. 239–49. **[G: S. Africa]**

Cloete, J. J. The Failure of Anti-cyclical Policy in South Africa in Recent Years and the Need for a Medium-term Strategy. *J. Stud. Econ. Econometrics,* November 1986, (26), pp. 3–33. **[G: S. Africa]**

Condon, Timothy J. Flujo de comercio y la política del tipo de cambio reptante: Un Modelo de Predicción Perfecta de Largo Plaza. (With English summary.) *Cuadernos Econ.,* April 1986, *23*(68), pp. 25–47.

Cooper, Richard N. Economic Interdependence and Coordination of Economic Policies. **In** *Cooper, R. N.,* 1986, *1985,* pp. 289–331.

Cooper, Richard N. Economic Mobility and National Economic Policy. **In** *Cooper, R. N.,* 1986, *1974,* pp. 71–121.

Corden, W. Max. Fiscal Policies, Current Accounts and Real Exchange Rates: In Search of a Logic of International Policy Coordination. *Weltwirtsch. Arch.*, 1986, *122*(3), pp. 423–38.

Cover, James Peery. A Note on the Empirical Evidence for the Role of Credit in Macroeconomic Policy and Analysis. *Southern Econ. J.*, April 1986, *52*(4), pp. 1145–50.

Cubitt, R. P. Two Perspectives on the Time Inconsistency Problem. *Greek Econ. Rev.*, June 1986, *8*(1), pp. 1–20.

Cukierman, Alex and Meltzer, Allan H. A Positive Theory of Discretionary Policy, the Cost of Democratic Government and the Benefits of a Constitution. *Econ. Inquiry*, July 1986, *24*(3), pp. 367–88.

Cukierman, Alex and Meltzer, Allan H. A Theory of Ambiguity, Credibility, and Inflation under Discretion and Asymmetric Information. *Econometrica*, September 1986, *54*(5), pp. 1099–1128.

Currie, David and Levine, Paul. Time Inconsistency and Optimal Policies in Deterministic and Stochastic Worlds. *J. Econ. Dynam. Control*, June 1986, *10*(1/2), pp. 191–99.

Curry, Robert L., Jr. Adaptation of Botswana's Development Strategy to Meet Its Peoples' Needs for Land, Jobs: The Southern Africa Capitalist Democracy Can Maintain Its Growth by a New Problem-Oriented Policy. *Amer. J. Econ. Soc.*, July 1986, *45*(3), pp. 297–312. **[G: Botswana]**

Darby, Michael R. International Economic Policy Coordination and Transmission: A Review. *Oxford Econ. Pap.*, November 1986, *38*(3), pp. 545–50.

Darby, Michael R. Optimal Monetary Institutions and Policy: Comments. **In** *Campbell, C. D. and Dougan, W. R., eds.*, 1986, pp. 244–47. **[G: U.S.]**

Darrat, Ali F. The Economic Impact of Taxes in the U.S.: Some Tests Based on the St. Louis Model. *J. Econ. Stud.*, 1986, *13*(2), pp. 3–13. **[G: U.S.]**

Davies, Omar. An Analysis of the Management of the Jamaican Economy: 1972–1985. *Soc. Econ. Stud.*, March 1986, *35*(1), pp. 73–109. **[G: Jamaica]**

Diamand, Marcelo. Overcoming Argentina's Stop-and-Go Economic Cycles. **In** *Hartlyn, J. and Morley, S. A., eds.*, 1986, pp. 129–64. **[G: Argentina]**

Dornbusch, Rudiger. Flexible Exchange Rates and Interdependence. **In** *Dornbusch, R.*, 1986, *1983*, pp. 58–85. **[G: U.S.]**

Dornbusch, Rudiger. Inflação, taxas de câmbio e estabilização. (With English summary.) *Pesquisa Planejamento Econ.*, August 1986, *16*(2), pp. 321–49. **[G: Brazil; U.S.; Germany]**

Dornbusch, Rudiger. Money, Interest Rates and Stabilization. *Rev. Econ. Cond. Italy*, Sept.-Dec. 1986, (3), pp. 439–53. **[G: W. Germany]**

Dornbusch, Rudiger. Stabilization Policies in Developing Countries: What Have We Learned? **In** *Dornbusch, R.*, 1986, *1982*, pp. 151–65. **[G: Chile; Argentina; Brazil]**

Dornbusch, Rudiger and Fischer, Stanley. Stopping Hyperinflations Past and Present. *Weltwirtsch. Arch.*, 1986, *122*(1), pp. 1–47. **[G: Europe; Israel; Argentina]**

Dornbusch, Rudiger and Fischer, Stanley. The Open Economy: Implications for Monetary and Fiscal Policy. **In** *Gordon, R. J., ed.*, 1986, pp. 459–501. **[G: U.S.]**

Doron, Gideon. Telling the Big Stories—Policy Responses to Analytical Complexity: A Comment [Big Decisions and a Culture of Decision Making] [The Narrative Structure of Policy Analysis]. *J. Policy Anal. Manage.*, Summer 1986, *5*(4), pp. 798–802.

Edward, Sebastian. Are Devaluations Contractionary? *Rev. Econ. Statist.*, August 1986, *68*(3), pp. 501–08. **[G: LDCs]**

Ellman, Michael. Images of a Socialist Economy: The End of the Statist Model. **In** *Nolan, P. and Paine, S., eds.*, 1986, pp. 359–73. **[G: U.K.]**

Erbas, S. Nuri. Inflationary Finance of Budget Deficits as an Automatic Stabilizer. *J. Monet. Econ.*, September 1986, *18*(2), pp. 197–204.

Felix, David. On Financial Blowups and Authoritarian Regimes in Latin America. **In** *Hartlyn, J. and Morley, S. A., eds.*, 1986, pp. 85–125. **[G: Latin America]**

Feroldi, Mathieu and Sterdyniak, Henri. Maximiser l'emploi: la réponse de modèles macroéconomiques. (Maximizing the Employment: The Macroeconomics Models Response. With English summary.) *Écon. Soc.*, January 1986, *20*(1), pp. 235–63. **[G: France]**

Fischer, Stanley. Wage Indexation and Macroeconomic Stability. **In** *Fischer, S.*, 1986, *1977*, pp. 159–91.

Foley, Duncan K. Stabilization Policy in a Nonlinear Business Cycle Model. **In** *Semmler, W., ed.*, 1986, pp. 200–211.

Fourgeaud, Claude; Lenclud, B. and Picard, P. Shadow Prices and Public Policies in a Disequilibrium Model of an Open Economy. *Europ. Econ. Rev.*, October 1986, *30*(5), pp. 991–1012. **[G: France]**

Frenkel, Jacob A. International Interdependence and the Constraints on Macroeconomic Policies. **In** *Hafer, R. W., ed. (I)*, 1986, pp. 171–205.

Frenkel, Jacob A. International Interdependence and the Constraints on Macroeconomic Policies. *Weltwirtsch. Arch.*, 1986, *122*(4), pp. 615–46.

Friend, Irwin. The Policy Options for Stimulating National Saving. **In** *Adams, F. G. and Wachter, S. M., eds.*, 1986, pp. 45–63.

Fry, Maxwell J. and Lilien, David M. Monetary Policy Responses to Exogenous Shocks. *Amer. Econ. Rev.*, May 1986, *76*(2), pp. 79–83. **[G: Global]**

Gagey, Frédéric; Laroque, Guy and Lollivier, Stefan. Monetary and Fiscal Policies in a General Equilibrium Model. *J. Econ. Theory*, August 1986, *39*(2), pp. 329–57.

Geanakoplos, John D. and Polemarchakis, Herakles M. Walrasian Indeterminacy and Keynesian Macroeconomics. *Rev. Econ. Stud.*,

October 1986, *53*(5), pp. 755–79.

Geller, Lucio and Tokman, Víctor E. From Austerity Measures to Structural Adjustment. *CEPAL Rev.*, December 1986, (30), pp. 35–50. **[G: Latin America]**

Gerchunoff, Pablo. Gasto pblico, tasa de cambio e impulso capitalista después de la hiperinflación. (With English summary.) *Desarrollo Econ.*, Jan.-Mar. 1986, *25*(100), pp. 623–57. **[G: Germany; Hungary; Argentina]**

Goldstein, Morris. Global Effects of Fund-Supported Programs. *Finance Develop.*, March 1986, *23*(1), pp. 24–27.

Goldstein, Morris and Montiel, Peter J. Evaluating Fund Stabilization Programs with Multicountry Data: Some Methodological Pitfalls. *Int. Monet. Fund Staff Pap.*, June 1986, *33*(2), pp. 304–44.

Gordon, Robert J. Fiscal Policy in Macro Theory: A Survey and Evaluation: Comment. **In** *Hafer, R. W., ed. (II)*, 1986, pp. 127–36. **[G: U.S.]**

Grant, John. The Macdonald Commission on Stabilization Policy. *Can. Public Policy*, Supp. February 1986, *12*, pp. 76–83. **[G: Canada]**

Green, Steven L. and Grossman, Herschel I. The Illusion of Stabilization Policy? *Carnegie-Rochester Conf. Ser. Public Policy*, Autumn 1986, *25*, pp. 221–35. **[G: W. Europe; U.S.; Canada]**

Ground, Richard L. A Survey and Critique of IMF Adjustment Programs in Latin America. **In** *Economic Commission for Latin America and the Caribbean*, 1986, pp. 101–58. **[G: Latin America]**

Guest, James. Macroeconomic Stabilization Policy with Special Reference to Fiscal Policy. **In** *Cole, R. V. and Parry, T. G., eds.*, 1986, pp. 71–110. **[G: S. Pacific]**

Guvenen, Orhan. International Macroeconomic Modelling for Policy Decisions: Some Proposals. **In** *Artus, P. and Guvenen, O., eds.*, 1986, pp. 259–65.

Hafer, R. W. The Monetary versus Fiscal Policy Debate: Lessons from Two Decades: Introduction. **In** *Hafer, R. W., ed. (II)*, 1986, pp. 1–6. **[G: U.S.]**

Hall, Stephen G. Time Inconsistency and Optimal Policy Formulation in the Presence of Rational Expectations. *J. Econ. Dynam. Control*, June 1986, *10*(1/2), pp. 323–26.

Hallwood, C. Paul. External Economy Arguments for Commodity Stockpiling: A Review. *Bull. Econ. Res.*, January 1986, *38*(1), pp. 25–41.

Hansen, Gerd. Der konjunkturelle Einfluss der Geld- und Fiskalpolitik in der Bundesrepublik 1972–1982. Eine ökonometrische Analyse unter rationalen Erwartungen. (The Effect of Monetary and Fiscal Policy on Business Cycles in the Federal Republic of Germany 1972–1982. With English summary.) *Kyklos*, 1986, *39*(2), pp. 180–208. **[G: W. Germany]**

Harpaz, Giora and Mesznik, Roger. Optimal Government Policy with Imperfect Information. *Amer. Econ.*, Spring 1986, *30*(1), pp. 28–31.

Hegji, Charles. Optimal Monetary Policy and the Lag Structure of Disturbances. *J. Macroecon.*, Summer 1986, *8*(3), pp. 297–312.

Heimann, John G. Debt, Financial Stability, and Public Policy: Overview. **In** *Axilrod, S. H., et al.*, 1986, pp. 219–22.

Henry, John F. On Economic Theory and the Question of Solvability. *J. Post Keynesian Econ.*, Spring 1986, *8*(3), pp. 371–86.

Heymann, Daniel. Inflation and Stabilization Policies. *CEPAL Rev.*, April 1986, (28), pp. 67–97. **[G: Argentina]**

Higgins, Bryon. Debt, Financial Stability, and Public Policy: Symposium Overview. **In** *Axilrod, S. H., et al.*, 1986, pp. 1–14.

Hoffmeyer, Erik. Beskæftigelse, betalingsbalance og økonomisk politik. (Employment, Balance of Payments and Economic Policy. With English summary.) *Nationaløkon. Tidsskr.*, 1986, *124*(3), pp. 259–64. **[G: Denmark; Sweden]**

Holly, Sean. Games, Expectations, and Optimal Policy for Open Economies. *J. Econ. Dynam. Control*, June 1986, *10*(1/2), pp. 45–49.

Holmlund, Bertil. Centralized Wage Setting, Wage Drift and Stabilization Policies under Trade Unionism. *Oxford Econ. Pap.*, July 1986, *38*(2), pp. 243–58. **[G: Sweden]**

Horn, Gustav-Adolf. Preisstabilisierende Geldpolitik. (Price-stabilizing Monetary Policy. With English summary.) *Kredit Kapital*, 1986, *19*(1), pp. 58–75.

Hughes Hallett, A. J. Autonomy and the Choice of Policy in Asymmetrically Dependent Economies: An Investigation of the Gains from International Policy Co-ordination. *Oxford Econ. Pap.*, November 1986, *38*(3), pp. 516–44. **[G: OECD]**

Hughes Hallett, A. J. Dynamic Policy Games and the Gains from Cooperation in Interdependent Economies: An Example from U.S.–EEC Policy Making. **In** *Pau, L. F., ed.*, 1986, pp. 147–55. **[G: U.S.; EEC]**

Hughes Hallett, A. J. International Policy Design and the Sustainability of Policy Bargains. *J. Econ. Dynam. Control*, December 1986, *10*(4), pp. 467–94. **[G: U.S.; EEC]**

Hughes Hallett, A. J. Policy Design in Asymmetrically Dependent Economies. *J. Econ. Dynam. Control*, June 1986, *10*(1/2), pp. 51–57. **[G: U.S.; EEC]**

Ishii, Naoko. Scope for Macroeconomic Policy Coordination between the U.S. and Japan. **In** *Finn, R. B., ed.*, 1986, pp. 211–23. **[G: Japan; U.S.]**

Jespersen, Jesper. "Wage Fixing" and "Demand Management": The Cures for Stagflation—New Keynesianism. *Econ. Lavoro*, Apr.-June 1986, *20*(2), pp. 125–33. **[G: OECD]**

Jimenez, Julio. Alternative Approaches to Stabilization in Africa: Comments. **In** *Helleiner, G. K, ed.*, 1986, pp. 151–53. **[G: Sub-Saharan Africa]**

Jordan, Jerry L. The Anderson–Jordan Approach after Nearly 20 Years. *Fed. Res. Bank St. Louis Rev.*, October 1986, *68*(8), pp. 5–8. **[G: U.S.]**

Joyce, Joseph P. On the Specification and Estimation of Macroeconomic Policy Functions. *Quart. J. Bus. Econ.*, Winter 1986, *25*(1), pp. 16–37. **[G: OECD]**

Jung, Woo S. Optimal Stabilization Policies under Rational Expectations. *Econ. Modelling*, April 1986, *3*(2), pp. 117–25.

Kaplan, Thomas J. The Narrative Structure of Policy Analysis. *J. Policy Anal. Manage.*, Summer 1986, *5*(4), pp. 761–78.

Kapur, Basant K. Alternative Stabilization Policies for Less-developed Economies. **In** *Kapur, B. K.*, 1986, *1976*, pp. 49–68.

Kapur, Basant K. Optimal Stabilization Policies for Less-developed Economies with Rational Expectations. **In** *Kapur, B. K.*, 1986, *1982*, pp. 69–91.

Kaufman, Henry. Debt: The Threat to Economic and Financial Stability. **In** *Axilrod, S. H., et al.*, 1986, pp. 15–26. **[G: U.S.]**

Kaufman, Herbert M. and Lombra, Raymond E. The Effect of Changes in the Federal Reserve's Policy Rule on the Stochastic Structure Linking Reserves, Interest Rates, and Money. *Southern Econ. J.*, April 1986, *52*(4), pp. 1080–87. **[G: U.S.]**

Kempf, Hubert. Sur le rôle stabilisateur des politiques monétaires et budgétaires dans un modèle avec anticipations rationnelles et dette publique. (With English summary.) *Revue Écon. Polit.*, Nov.-Dec. 1986, *96*(6), pp. 642–65.

Khan, Mohsin S. and Knight, Malcolm D. Do Fund-Supported Adjustment Programs Retard Growth? *Finance Develop.*, March 1986, *23*(1), pp. 30–32.

Kimbrough, Kent P. Monetary Procedures and Monetary Policy. **In** *Campbell, C. D. and Dougan, W. R., eds.*, 1986, pp. 215–23. **[G: U.S.]**

Knight, Peter T.; McCarthy, F. Desmond and van Wijnbergen, Sweder J. G. Escaping Hyperinflation. *Finance Develop.*, December 1986, *23*(4), pp. 14–17. **[G: Argentina; Brazil; Israel]**

Kwack, Sung Y. Policy Analysis with a Macroeconomic Model of Korea. *Econ. Modelling*, July 1986, *3*(3), pp. 175–96. **[G: S. Korea]**

Laden, Ben E. The Implications of Budget Deficits [Deficits, Interest Rates, and Monetary Policy]. *Cato J.*, Winter 1986, *5*(3), pp. 727–31. **[G: U.S.]**

Lamounier, Bolivar and Moura, Alkimar R. Economic Policy and Political Opening in Brazil. **In** *Hartlyn, J. and Morley, S. A., eds.*, 1986, pp. 165–96. **[G: Brazil]**

Lavoie, Marc. Chômage classique et chômage keynésien: un prétexte aux politiques d'austérité. (Classical Unemployment and Keynesian Unemployment: A Pretext for Policies of Austerity. With English summary.) *Écon. Appl.*, 1986, *39*(2), pp. 203–38.

Levin, Jay H. Monetary–Fiscal Policy Assignment under Floating Exchange Rates. *De Economist*, 1986, *134*(4), pp. 467–78.

Levine, Paul. The Formulation of Robust Policies for Rival Rational Expectations Models of the Economy. *J. Econ. Dynam. Control*, June 1986, *10*(1/2), pp. 93–97.

Lewin, Peter. Economic Policy and the Capital Structure. **In** *[Lachmann, L. M.]*, 1986, pp. 211–20.

Lii, Sheng-Yann. An Interpretation of the Optimal Control Rules: The Case of Taiwan for the First Oil Shock Period. *Appl. Econ.*, January 1986, *18*(1), pp. 71–85. **[G: Taiwan]**

Lipsey, Richard G. and Smith, Murray G. An Overview of Harmonization Issues. **In** *C. D. Howe Institute*, 1986, pp. 1–41. **[G: Canada; U.S.]**

Lombra, Raymond E. Shocks and Stabilization Policy: Illusions and Issues: A Comment. *Carnegie-Rochester Conf. Ser. Public Policy*, Autumn 1986, *25*, pp. 237–43.

Lovell, Michael C. Tests of the Rational Expectations Hypothesis. *Amer. Econ. Rev.*, March 1986, *76*(1), pp. 110–24. **[G: U.S.]**

Loxley, John. Alternative Approaches to Stabilization in Africa. **In** *Helleiner, G. K, ed.*, 1986, pp. 117–47. **[G: Sub-Saharan Africa]**

Loxley, John. Alternative Approaches to Stabilization in Africa: Reply. **In** *Helleiner, G. K, ed.*, 1986, pp. 156–59. **[G: Sub-Saharan Africa]**

Lucas, Robert E., Jr. Principles of Fiscal and Monetary Policy. *J. Monet. Econ.*, January 1986, *17*(1), pp. 117–34.

Marini, Giancarlo. Employment Fluctuations and Demand Management. *Economica*, May 1986, *53*(210), pp. 209–18.

Marini, Giancarlo. Information Structure and Policy Effectiveness. *Econ. Notes*, 1986, (2), pp. 5–16.

Markose, S. M. A Theory of Policy-Induced Structural Change: An Application of the Bismut Stochastic Maximum Principle. *J. Econ. Dynam. Control*, June 1986, *10*(1/2), pp. 109–14.

Marquez, Jaime. Oil-Price Effects in Theory and Practice. *J. Devel. Econ.*, November 1986, *24*(1), pp. 1–27. **[G: Global]**

Marquez, Jaime and Pauly, Peter. Cooperative Policies among the North, the South, and OPEC: An Optimal Control Application. *Econ. Modelling*, July 1986, *3*(3), pp. 213–36. **[G: Global]**

Marquez, Jaime and Pauly, Peter. Policy Coordination among the North, the South, and OPEC. *J. Econ. Dynam. Control*, June 1986, *10*(1/2), pp. 59–62. **[G: Global]**

McCallum, Bennett T. Monetary versus Fiscal Policy Effects: A Review of the Debate. **In** *Hafer, R. W., ed. (II)*, 1986, pp. 9–29. **[G: U.S.]**

McClintock, Cynthia. The Tragedy of Lost Opportunity in Peru: Comment. **In** *Hartlyn, J. and Morley, S. A., eds.*, 1986, pp. 360–66. **[G: Peru]**

Meller, Patricio. Keynesianismo y monetarismo: discrepancias metodológicas. (With English summary.) *Desarrollo Econ.*, Oct.-Dec. 1986, *26*(103), pp. 389–422.

Miles, Marc A. Refocusing Monetary Theory and Policy. **In** *Putnam, B. H. and Wilford, D. S., eds.*, 1986, pp. 307–24. **[G: U.S.]**

Minford, Patrick. Expectations and the Economy. In *Burton, J., et al.*, 1986, pp. 103–17.

Minford, Patrick. Rational Expectations and Monetary Policy. *Scot. J. Polit. Econ.*, November 1986, *33*(4), pp. 317–33.

Minsky, Hyman P. Stabilizing and Unstable Economy: The Lessons for Industry, Finance and Government. In *Aiginger, K., ed.*, 1986, pp. 31–44. **[G: U.S.]**

Mohammed, Azizali F. Alternative Approaches to Stabilization in Africa: Comments. In *Helleiner, G. K, ed.*, 1986, pp. 148–51. **[G: Sub-Saharan Africa]**

Morgan, Peter B.; McDonald, John and Woodfield, A. Affordability and Some Welfare Aspects of Indexation. *Econ. Rec.*, March 1986, *62*(176), pp. 37–48.

Musgrave, Richard A. and Gillis, Malcolm. Objectives: Report of Colombia Tax Mission. In *Musgrave, R. A., Vol. 2*, 1986, *1971*, pp. 149–57. **[G: Colombia]**

Neck, Reinhard. Kann Stabilisierungspolitik unter Unsicherheit und Risiko "Optimal" sein? (Can Stabilization Policy Be "Optimal" under Uncertainty? With English summary.) *Schweiz. Z. Volkswirtsch. Statist.*, September 1986, *122*(3), pp. 509–34.

Nove, Alec. The Political Economy of the Allende Regime. In *Nove, A.*, 1986, *1976*, pp. 3–29. **[G: Chile]**

O'Donnell, Guillermo. Overcoming Argentina's Stop-and-Go Economic Cycles: Comment. In *Hartlyn, J. and Morley, S. A., eds.*, 1986, pp. 356–59. **[G: Argentina]**

Oudiz, Gilles. Stratégies économiques européennes: coordination ou confrontation? (European Economic Stategies. Cooperation versus Conflict. With English summary.) *Écon. Soc.*, January 1986, *20*(1), pp. 265–96.

Pesaran, M. Hashem. Structural Keynesianism as an Alternative to Monetarism. In *Nolan, P. and Paine, S., eds.*, 1986, pp. 165–75. **[G: U.K.]**

Peterson, William. Keynesian Policies for Voluntary Unemployment. *Rech. Écon. Louvain*, 1986, *52*(3–4), pp. 399–411. **[G: U.K.]**

Petzina, Dietmar. Krisen und Krisenstrategien: Die deutschen Erfahrungen der Zwischenkriegszeit und die Gegenwart. (With English summary.) In *Berend, I. T. and Borchardt, K., eds.*, 1986, pp. 171–94. **[G: W. Germany]**

Poole, William. Fiscal and Monetary Policy Overkills. In *Shadow Open Market Committee (I)*, 1986, pp. 19–30. **[G: U.S.]**

Poole, William. International Interdependence and the Constraints on Macroeconomic Policies: Comments. In *Hafer, R. W., ed. (I)*, 1986, pp. 207–10.

Prebisch, Raúl. Argentine Economic Policies since the 1930s: Recollections. In *di Tella, G. and Platt, D. C. M., eds.*, 1986, pp. 133–53. **[G: Argentina]**

Putnam, Bluford H. and Wilford, D. Sykes. The Policy Consequences of Interdependence. In *Putnam, B. H. and Wilford, D. S., eds.*, 1986, pp. 287–97.

Rabeau, Yves. Le statu quo est-il préférable à la régionalisation de la politique de stabilisation? (With English summary.) *Can. Public Policy*, June 1986, *12*(2), pp. 329–40. **[G: Canada]**

Raj, Baldev and Siklos, Pierre L. The Role of Fiscal Policy in the St. Louis Model: An Evaluation and Some New Evidence. *J. Appl. Econometrics*, July 1986, *1*(3), pp. 287–94. **[G: U.S.]**

Ramanathan, Ramu. Government Policy with Deficit Financing, Imperfect Capital Mobility and Exchange Rate Effects on the Supply Side. *Econ. Modelling*, April 1986, *3*(2), pp. 147–52.

Ramos, Joseph. Stabilization and Adjustment Policies in the Southern Cone, 1974–1983. In *Economic Commission for Latin America and the Caribbean*, 1986, pp. 65–99. **[G: Argentina; Chile; Uruguay]**

Reichlin, Pietro. Equilibrium Cycles in an Overlapping Generations Economy with Production. *J. Econ. Theory*, October 1986, *40*(1), pp. 89–102.

Reither, Franco. The Dynamics of Financial Adjustments in an Open Economy and the Effects of Stabilization Policy: Comment. *J. Inst. Theoretical Econ.*, June 1986, *142*(2), pp. 438–41.

Revéiz, Edgar and Pérez, María José. Columbia: Moderate Economic Growth, Political Stability, and Social Welfare. In *Hartlyn, J. and Morley, S. A., eds.*, 1986, pp. 265–91. **[G: Columbia]**

Ribe, Frederick C. and Beeman, William J. The Monetary–Fiscal Mix and Long-run Growth in an Open Economy. *Amer. Econ. Rev.*, May 1986, *76*(2), pp. 209–12. **[G: U.S.]**

Richards, Peter J. Preserving Jobs under Economic Stabilisation Programmes: Can There Be an Employment Target? *Int. Lab. Rev.*, July-Aug. 1986, *125*(4), pp. 423–34. **[G: LDCs]**

Roberts, Paul Craig. In Defense of Savings. In *Adams, F. G. and Wachter, S. M., eds.*, 1986, pp. 189–94. **[G: U.S.]**

Rothengatter, Werner. The Dynamics of Financial Adjustments in an Open Economy and the Effects of Stabilization Policy: Reply. *J. Inst. Theoretical Econ.*, June 1986, *142*(2), pp. 442–44.

Santoni, Gary J. The Employment Act of 1946: Some History Notes. *Fed. Res. Bank St. Louis Rev.*, November 1986, *68*(9), pp. 5–16. **[G: U.S.]**

Schiller, Karl. Die Grenzen der Wirtschaftspolitik (neu betrachtet). (Limits to Economic Policy Revisited. With English summary.) *Jahr. Nationalökon. Statist.*, January 1986, *201*(1), pp. 1–11.

Schwartz, Anna J. The Open Economy: Implications for Monetary and Fiscal Policy: Comment. In *Gordon, R. J., ed.*, 1986, pp. 504–10. **[G: U.S.]**

Schydlowsky, Daniel M. The Tragedy of Lost Opportunity in Peru. In *Hartlyn, J. and Morley, S. A., eds.*, 1986, pp. 217–42. **[G: Peru]**

Seidman, L. William. Debt, Financial Stability, and Public Policy: Overview. **In** *Axilrod, S. H., et al.*, 1986, pp. 223–30. **[G: U.S.]**

Shleifer, Andrei. Implementation Cycles. *J. Polit. Econ.*, December 1986, *94*(6), pp. 1163–90.

Sigmund, Paul. On Financial Blowups and Authoritarian Regimes in Latin America: Comment. **In** *Hartlyn, J. and Morley, S. A., eds.*, 1986, pp. 353–55. **[G: Latin America]**

Simai, Mihály. The Socio-economic Issues of Growth-Oriented Strategic Adjustment Programs. *Acta Oecon.*, 1986, *37*(3–4), pp. 155–67.

Smithin, John N. The Length of the Production Period and Effective Stabilization Policy. *J. Macroecon.*, Winter 1986, *8*(1), pp. 55–62.

Solow, Robert M. Macroeconomic Theory and Government Action. **In** *Aiginger, K., ed.*, 1986, pp. 19–30.

Svendsen, Knud Erik. The Creation of Macroeconomic Imbalances and a Structural Crisis. **In** *Boesen, J., et al., eds.*, 1986, pp. 59–78. **[G: Tanzania]**

Tabellini, Guido. Money, Debt and Deficits in a Dynamic Game. *J. Econ. Dynam. Control*, December 1986, *10*(4), pp. 427–42.

Tabellini, Guido. Rules, Discretion and the Provision of Employment Incentives. *Giorn. Econ.*, May-June 1986, *45*(5–6), pp. 243–50.

Tanzi, Vito. Fiscal Policy Responses to Exogenous Shocks in Developing Countries. *Amer. Econ. Rev.*, May 1986, *76*(2), pp. 88–91. **[G: LDCs]**

Taylor, John B. An Appeal for Rationality in the Policy Activism Debate. **In** *Hafer, R. W., ed. (II)*, 1986, pp. 151–63.

Tichy, Gunther. Die Amplitude der Österreichischen Konjunkturschwankungen im internationalen Vergleich. (With English summary.) *Empirica*, 1986, *13*(1), pp. 69–96. **[G: Austria; OECD]**

Tobin, James. The Monetary–Fiscal Mix: Long-run Implications. *Amer. Econ. Rev.*, May 1986, *76*(2), pp. 213–18.

Travaglini, Guido. Quattro modelli macroeconomici a confronto. Somiglianze e divergenze in merito alla struttura, alle implicazioni di politica economica e alla stabilita' asintotica. (With English summary.) *Econ. Int.*, February 1986, *39*(1), pp. 60–91.

Tweedie, A. J. Monetary Policy in New Zealand. **In** *Reserve Bank of New Zealand*, 1986, pp. 47–62. **[G: New Zealand]**

Vastrup, Claus. Beskæftigelse, betalingsbalance og dansk økonomisk politik. (Employment, Balance of Payments and Danish Economic Policy. With English summary.) *Nationaløkon. Tidsskr.*, 1986, *124*(3), pp. 265–73. **[G: Denmark]**

Vilas, Carlos M. Sobre la estrategia económica de la Revolución Sandinista. (With English summary.) *Desarrollo Econ.*, Apr.-June 1986, *26*(101), pp. 121–42. **[G: Nicaragua]**

Walker, John F. and Vatter, Harold G. Stagnation—Performance and Policy: A Comparison of the Depression Decade with 1973–1984. *J. Post Keynesian Econ.*, Summer 1986, *8*(4), pp. 515–30. **[G: U.S.]**

West, Kenneth D. Targeting Nominal Income: A Note. *Econ. J.*, December 1986, *96*(384), pp. 1077–83.

Whiteman, Charles H. An Analytical Policy Design under Rational Expectations. *Econometrica*, November 1986, *54*(6), pp. 1387–1405.

Whittaker, Rod, et al. Alternative Financial Policy Rules in an Open Economy under Rational and Adaptive Expectations. *Econ. J.*, September 1986, *96*(383), pp. 680–95. **[G: U.K.]**

Wicker, Elmus R. Terminating Hyperinflation in the Dismembered Habsburg Monarchy. *Amer. Econ. Rev.*, June 1986, *76*(3), pp. 350–64. **[G: Poland; Austria; Hungary]**

van Wijnbergen, Sweder J. G. Exchange Rate Management and Stabilization Policies in Developing Countries. *J. Devel. Econ.*, October 1986, *23*(2), pp. 227–47. **[G: LDCs]**

Wilford, D. Sykes and Krieger, Ronald A. Discretionary Monetary Policy and the Gold Standard. **In** *Putnam, B. H. and Wilford, D. S., eds.*, 1986, pp. 298–306.

1332 Wage and Price Controls

Balbino, L. R. and Monteiro Marques, M. Fertilizer Pricing Policy in Portugal. **In** *Segura, E. L.; Shetty, Y. T. and Nishimizu, M., eds.*, 1986, pp. 102–08. **[G: Portugal]**

Bawa, H. S. The Pricing of Fertilizers in India. **In** *Segura, E. L.; Shetty, Y. T. and Nishimizu, M., eds.*, 1986, pp. 156–63. **[G: India]**

Bosworth, Barry P. Financial Markets and Macroeconomic Fluctuations: Comment. **In** *Butkiewicz, J. L.; Koford, K. J. and Miller, J. B., eds.*, 1986, pp. 133–35.

Brown, William. Facing Up to Incomes Policy. **In** *Nolan, P. and Paine, S., eds.*, 1986, pp. 341–55. **[G: U.K.]**

Chand, Sheetal K. European Experiences with Tax-Based Income Policies. **In** *Colander, D. C., ed.*, 1986, pp. 211–22. **[G: W. Europe]**

Chatterji, Monojit. Unions, Employment and the Inflation Tax. *Econ. J.*, June 1986, *96*(382), pp. 342–51.

Cling, Jean-Pierre and Meunier, François. La désinflation en France: Le point de vue de l'économètre. (The French Disinflation. With English summary.) *Revue Écon.*, November 1986, *37*(6), pp. 1093–1125. **[G: France]**

Colander, David C. Financial Markets and Macroeconomic Fluctuations: Comment. **In** *Butkiewicz, J. L.; Koford, K. J. and Miller, J. B., eds.*, 1986, pp. 145–49.

Colander, David C. In Defense of Incentive Anti-inflation Plans. **In** *Colander, D. C., ed.*, 1986, pp. 237–43.

Colander, David C. Incentive-Based Incomes Policies: Advances in TIP and MAP: Introduction. **In** *Colander, D. C., ed.*, 1986, pp. 1–12. **[G: U.S.]**

Colander, David C. On the Theory of Incentive Anti-inflation Plans. **In** *Colander, D. C., ed.*, 1986, pp. 129–38.

Davidson, Paul. Financial Markets and Macroeconomic Fluctuations: Comment. **In** *Butkiewicz, J. L.; Koford, K. J. and Miller, J. B., eds.*, 1986, pp. 135–43.

De Luca, Paolo. Punto unico, politica dei redditi, struttura del salario. (Income Policies and Wage Indexing in Italy. With English summary.) *Econ. Lavoro*, Oct.-Dec. 1986, *20*(4), pp. 21–37. **[G: Italy]**

Desai, Gunvant M. Growth in Indian Fertilizer Consumption: Price and Non-price Policies. **In** *Segura, E. L.; Shetty, Y. T. and Nishimizu, M., eds.*, 1986, pp. 109–36. **[G: India]**

Fischer, Stanley. Indexing and Inflation. **In** *Fischer, S.*, 1986, *1983*, pp. 193–219. **[G: Selected Countries]**

Galbraith, James K. Political Problems of Incentive Anti-inflation Plans. **In** *Colander, D. C., ed.*, 1986, pp. 231–35.

Galbraith, James K. The Continuing Importance of Price Stabilization. **In** *Colander, D. C., ed.*, 1986, pp. 15–26. **[G: U.S.]**

Gapinski, James H. TIP and Tradition as Tools against Inflation. *J. Post Keynesian Econ.*, Summer 1986, *8*(4), pp. 591–606.

Gilbert, Christopher L. Commodity Price Stabilization: The Massell Model and Multiplicative Disturbances. *Quart. J. Econ.*, August 1986, *101*(3), pp. 635–40.

Gros, Daniel. Wage Indexation and the Real Exchange Rate in Small Open Economies: A Study of the Effects of Fluctuations in Export Earnings. *Int. Monet. Fund Staff Pap.*, March 1986, *33*(1), pp. 117–38.

Humphrey, Thomas M. The Economics of Incomes Policies. **In** *Humphreys, T. M.*, 1986, *1972*, pp. 255–63.

Jackman, Richard and Layard, Richard. Is TIP Administratively Feasible? **In** *Colander, D. C., ed.*, 1986, pp. 141–48.

Jackman, Richard and Layard, Richard. The Economic Effects of Tax-Based Incomes Policy. **In** *Colander, D. C., ed.*, 1986, pp. 95–109.

Jackman, Richard; Layard, Richard and Pissarides, Christopher A. Policies for Reducing the Natural Rate of Unemployment. **In** *Butkiewicz, J. L.; Koford, K. J. and Miller, J. B., eds.*, 1986, pp. 111–33.

Jaeger, Klaus. Stabilisierungspolitik in kurzfristigen Einkommens- und Beschäftigungsmodellen mit rationalen Erwartungen. (Stabilization Policy in Short-run Income and Employment Models with Rational Expectations. With English summary.) *Jahr. Nationalökon. Statist.*, July 1986, *201*(4), pp. 329–49.

Kehoe, Timothy J. and Serra-Puche, Jaime. A General Equilibrium Analysis of Price Controls and Subsidies on Food in Mexico. *J. Devel. Econ.*, April 1986, *21*(1), pp. 65–87. **[G: Mexico]**

Kenyon, Peter. The Australian Labour Market, June 1986. *Australian Bull. Lab.*, June 1986, *12*(3), pp. 131–53. **[G: Australia]**

Koford, Kenneth J. Innovation and Adaptation under Incentive Anti-inflation Plans. *Public Finance*, 1986, *41*(2), pp. 218–31.

Koford, Kenneth J. and Miller, Jeffrey B. Incentive Anti-inflation Policies in a Model of Market Disequilibrium. **In** *Colander, D. C., ed.*, 1986, pp. 71–93.

Kymn, Kern O. and Cushing, Brian J. TIP, Wage–Price Controls and Profit-Based Incomes Policies. *Atlantic Econ. J.*, September 1986, *14*(3), pp. 79–80.

Layard, Richard. Financial Markets and Macroeconomic Fluctuations: Reply. **In** *Butkiewicz, J. L.; Koford, K. J. and Miller, J. B., eds.*, 1986, pp. 149–52.

Lerda, Juan Carlos. A política salarial do período 1979/85: alguns aspectos dinâmicos. (With English summary.) *Pesquisa Planejamento Econ.*, August 1986, *16*(2), pp. 467–92. **[G: Brazil]**

McCallum, John. Two Cheers for the Anti-Inflation Board. *Can. Public Policy*, March 1986, *12*(1), pp. 133–47. **[G: Canada]**

Miller, Jeffrey B.; Koford, Kenneth J. and Schneider, Jerrold E. Plans for Fighting Inflation with Microeconomic Incentives. **In** *Colander, D. C., ed.*, 1986, pp. 35–53. **[G: U.S.]**

Narayan, Pratap. Fertilizer Pricing in India. **In** *Segura, E. L.; Shetty, Y. T. and Nishimizu, M., eds.*, 1986, pp. 137–55. **[G: India]**

Neale, Walter C. Tax-Based Incomes Policies: A Commentary for the Future. *J. Econ. Issues*, December 1986, *20*(4), pp. 969–87. **[G: U.S.]**

Nguyen, Trien T. and Whalley, John. Equilibrium under Price Controls with Endogenous Transactions Costs. *J. Econ. Theory*, August 1986, *39*(2), pp. 290–300.

Niaz, M. Shafi. The Fertilizer Pricing System in Pakistan. **In** *Segura, E. L.; Shetty, Y. T. and Nishimizu, M., eds.*, 1986, pp. 164–84. **[G: Pakistan]**

Peston, Maurice H. Incomes Policy. **In** *Nolan, P. and Paine, S., eds.*, 1986, pp. 315–25.

Pissarides, Christopher A. Equilibrium Effects of Tax-Based Incomes Policies. **In** *Colander, D. C., ed.*, 1986, pp. 111–27.

van der Ploeg, Frederick. The Effects of a Tax and Incomes Policy on Government Finance, Employment and Capital Formation. *De Economist*, 1986, *134*(3), pp. 269–88.

Russell, R. Robert. Tax-Based Incomes Policies: Some Skeptical Remarks. **In** *Colander, D. C., ed.*, 1986, pp. 159–75.

Salant, Walter S. Effects of Price Control on Output and the Price Level. **In** *Colander, D. C., ed.*, 1986, pp. 58–70. **[G: U.S.]**

Schneider, Jerrold E. U.S. Politics and Anti-inflation Policy. **In** *Colander, D. C., ed.*, 1986, pp. 223–30. **[G: U.S.]**

Schultz, Knud H. and Mattos, Jorge A. S. Fertilizer Pricing in Brazil. **In** *Segura, E. L.; Shetty, Y. T. and Nishimizu, M., eds.*, 1986, pp. 185–95. **[G: Brazil]**

Seidman, Laurence S. Financial Markets and Macroeconomic Fluctuations: Comment. **In** *Butkiewicz, J. L.; Koford, K. J. and Miller, J. B., eds.*, 1986, pp. 143–44.

Seidman, Laurence S. Why an Incentive Anti-inflation Plan Should Be Implemented. **In**

Colander, D. C., ed., 1986, pp. 201–07. **[G: U.S.]**

Shiffer, Zalman F. Adjusting to High Inflation: The Israeli Experience. *Fed. Res. Bank St. Louis Rev.*, May 1986, *68*(5), pp. 18–29. **[G: Israel]**

Smith, Russell E. Indexación salarial, rotación de personal y variaciones de los salarios nominales en la industria monufacturera brasileña, 1966–1976. (With English summary.) *Desarrollo Econ.*, July-Sept. 1986, *26*(102), pp. 269–87. **[G: Brazil]**

Srinivasan, T. N. Fertilizer Pricing in Developing Countries: A Market-Based Approach. **In** *Segura, E. L.; Shetty, Y. T. and Nishimizu, M., eds.*, 1986, pp. 48–68. **[G: LDCs]**

Stiglitz, Joseph E. Financial Markets and Macroeconomic Fluctuations: Comment. **In** *Butkiewicz, J. L.; Koford, K. J. and Miller, J. B., eds.*, 1986, pp. 144–45.

Triplett, Jack E. Can TIP–MIP–MAP Proposals Work? Lessons from the Council on Wage and Price Stability. **In** *Colander, D. C., ed.*, 1986, pp. 177–200. **[G: U.S.]**

Vickrey, William. Design of a Market Anti-inflation Program. **In** *Colander, D. C., ed.*, 1986, pp. 149–58.

Vickrey, William. The Need for a Direct Anti-inflation Program. **In** *Colander, D. C., ed.*, 1986, pp. 27–34. **[G: U.S.]**

Whitley, J. D. A Model of Incomes Policy in the U.K., 1963–79. *Manchester Sch. Econ. Soc. Stud.*, March 1986, *54*(1), pp. 31–64. **[G: U.K.]**

Zaidi, Mahmood A. Do Incomes Policies Restrain Wage Inflation? Some Evidence from Australia, Canada, and the United States. *Econ. Rec.*, December 1986, *62*(179), pp. 468–84. **[G: Australia; Canada; U.S.]**

134 Inflation and Deflation

1340 General

Arestis, Philip. Wages and Prices in the UK: The Post Keynesian View. *J. Post Keynesian Econ.*, Spring 1986, *8*(3), pp. 339–58. **[G: U.K.]**

Barrère, Alain. Price System and Money-Wage System. *J. Post Keynesian Econ.*, Winter 1985-86, *8*(2), pp. 315–35.

Barro, Robert J. Futures Markets and the Fluctuations in Inflation, Monetary Growth, and Asset Returns. *J. Bus.*, Part 2, April 1986, *59*(2), pp. S21–38.

Beckerman, Wilfred. Stagflation and the Third World. **In** *[Streeten, P.]*, 1986, pp. 38–57. **[G: LDCs; MDCs]**

Berglas, Eitan. Taxes and Transfers in an Inflationary Decade. **In** *Ben-Porath, Y., ed.*, 1986, pp. 221–38. **[G: Israel]**

Bernholz, Peter. The Implementation and Maintenance of a Monetary Constitution. *Cato J.*, Fall 1986, *6*(2), pp. 477–511. **[G: OECD]**

Boinet, Thierry. La liaison taux d'intérêt-taux d'inflation. Une analyse historique de longue période. (The Interest–Inflation Rates Relationship: A Long Term Historical Analysis. With English summary.) *Écon. Soc.*, June 1986, *20*(6), pp. 101–45. **[G: France]**

Boschen, John F. The Information Content of Indexed Bonds. *J. Money, Credit, Banking*, February 1986, *18*(1), pp. 76–87.

Bronfenbrenner, Martin. Causes of Contemporary Stagnation: What Should We Have Done? **In** *Frisch, H. and Gahlen, B., eds.*, 1986, pp. 1–12. **[G: U.S.]**

Brunner, Karl and Meltzer, Allan H. The National Bureau Method, International Capital Mobility, and Other Essays. *Carnegie-Rochester Conf. Ser. Public Policy*, Spring 1986, *24*, pp. 1–10.

Buchanan, James M. The Relevance of Constitutional Strategy [The Implementation and Maintenance of a Monetary Constitution]. *Cato J.*, Fall 1986, *6*(2), pp. 513–17.

Caffè, Federico. Hyperinflation and the Quantity Theory of Money: A Historical View. *Rev. Econ. Cond. Italy*, Sept.-Dec. 1986, (3), pp. 417–23.

Cagan, Phillip. Containing Inflation. **In** *Cagan, P., ed.*, 1986, pp. 247–74. **[G: U.S.]**

Coate, Douglas and VanderHoff, James. Stock Returns, Inflation, and Real Output. *Econ. Inquiry*, October 1986, *24*(4), pp. 555–61. **[G: U.S.]**

Colander, David C. In Defense of Incentive Anti-inflation Plans. **In** *Colander, D. C., ed.*, 1986, pp. 237–43.

Dimand, Robert W. Keynes on Inflation and Exchange Rates. *Atlantic Econ. J.*, September 1986, *14*(3), pp. 81–82.

Dutkowsky, Donald H. and Gianturco, David J. On the Inflation-Unit Labor Cost Relation. *J. Econ. Bus.*, May 1986, *38*(2), pp. 173–81. **[G: U.S.]**

Early, John F.; Lane, Walter and Sturm, Philip. A Half-Year Pause in Inflation: Its Antecedents and Structure. *Mon. Lab. Rev.*, October 1986, *109*(10), pp. 3–14. **[G: U.S.]**

Edwards, Edgar O. The State of Current Value Accounting. **In** *Parker, R. H.; Harcourt, G. C. and Whittington, G., eds.*, 1986, *1975*, pp. 264–77.

Fischer, Stanley. Israeli Inflation and Indexation. **In** *Fischer, S.*, 1986, *1985*, pp. 453–85. **[G: Israel]**

Fischer, Stanley. On the Nonexistence of Privately Issued Index Bonds in the U.S. Capital Market. **In** *Fischer, S.*, 1986, *1983*, pp. 301–20. **[G: U.S.]**

Fischer, Stanley. The Demand for Index Bonds. **In** *Fischer, S.*, 1986, *1975*, pp. 271–99.

Fischer, Stanley and Modigliani, Franco. Toward an Understanding of the Real Effects and Costs of Inflation. **In** *Fischer, S.*, 1986, *1978*, pp. 7–33. **[G: U.S.]**

Fry, Maxwell J. Turkey's Great Inflation. *METU*, 1986, *13*(1/2), pp. 95–116. **[G: Turkey]**

Galbraith, James K. The Continuing Importance of Price Stabilization. **In** *Colander, D. C., ed.*, 1986, pp. 15–26. **[G: U.S.]**

Gallaway, Lowell and Vedder, Richard. Inflation,

Migration, and Divorce in Contemporary America. **In** *Peden, J. R. and Glahe, F. R., eds.*, 1986, pp. 285–307. **[G: U.S.]**

Gazioğlu, Şaziye. Government Deficits, Consumption and Inflation in Turkey. *METU*, 1986, *13*(1/2), pp. 117–34. **[G: Turkey]**

Gynther, Reg S. Why Use General Purchasing Power? **In** *Parker, R. H.; Harcourt, G. C. and Whittington, G., eds.*, 1986, *1974*, pp. 314–43.

Haberler, Gottfried. The Slowdown of the World Economy and the Problem of Stagflation. **In** *Lal, D. and Wolf, M., eds.*, 1986, pp. 48–90. **[G: Global]**

Hafer, R. W. and Thornton, Daniel L. Price Expectations and the Demand for Money: A Comment. *Rev. Econ. Statist.*, August 1986, *68*(3), pp. 539–42. **[G: U.S.]**

Holland, A. Steven. Wage Indexation and the Effect of Inflation Uncertainty on Employment: An Empirical Analysis. *Amer. Econ. Rev.*, March 1986, *76*(1), pp. 235–43. **[G: U.S.]**

Hua, Mingshu. The Inflationary Effect on the Structure of Trade. *Weltwirtsch. Arch.*, 1986, *122*(2), pp. 254–69. **[G: U.S.]**

Kennedy, Charles. Inflation Accounting: Retrospect and Prospect. **In** *Parker, R. H.; Harcourt, G. C. and Whittington, G., eds.*, 1986, *1978*, pp. 179–99. **[G: U.K.]**

Kim, Moon K.; Booth, G. Geoffrey and Wu, Chunchi. Stock Returns, Inflation, and the Phillips Curve. *Southern Econ. J.*, April 1986, *52*(4), pp. 973–83. **[G: U.S.]**

Kimbrough, Kent P. Inflation, Employment, and Welfare in the Presence of Transactions Costs. *J. Money, Credit, Banking*, May 1986, *18*(2), pp. 127–40.

Kleiman, Ephraim. Indexation in the Labor Market. **In** *Ben-Porath, Y., ed.*, 1986, pp. 302–19. **[G: Israel]**

Kleiman, Ephraim. The Indexation of Public Debt in Israel. **In** *Herber, B. P., ed.*, 1986, pp. 193–204. **[G: Israel]**

Koford, Kenneth J. and Miller, Jeffrey B. Incentive Anti-inflation Policies in a Model of Market Disequilibrium. **In** *Colander, D. C., ed.*, 1986, pp. 71–93.

Leonard, David C. and Solt, Michael E. Recent Evidence on the Accuracy and Rationality of Popular Inflation Forecasts. *J. Finan. Res.*, Winter 1986, *9*(4), pp. 281–90. **[G: U.S.]**

Liviatan, Nissan and Piterman, Sylvia. Accelerating Inflation and Balance-of-Payments Crises, 1973–1984. **In** *Ben-Porath, Y., ed.*, 1986, pp. 320–46. **[G: Israel]**

McClure, J. Harold, Jr. Welfare-Maximizing Inflation Rates under Fractional Reserve Banking with and without Deposit Rate Ceilings: A Note. *J. Money, Credit, Banking*, May 1986, *18*(2), pp. 233–38.

McCormick, Robert E. Inflation, Regulation, and Financial Adequacy. **In** *Moorhouse, J. C., ed.*, 1986, pp. 135–61. **[G: U.S.]**

McKinnon, Ronald I. The Case for Internationalizing American Monetary Policy. **In** *Tsoukalis, L., ed.*, 1986, pp. 199–226. **[G: OECD]**

Milbourne, Ross. Price Expectations and the Demand for Money: Reply. *Rev. Econ. Statist.*, August 1986, *68*(3), pp. 543–44. **[G: U.S.]**

Monti, Mario. Indexation of Government Debt and Its Alternatives. **In** *Herber, B. P., ed.*, 1986, pp. 181–92. **[G: Italy; U.S.; LDCs]**

Myatt, Anthony E. Money Supply Endogeneity: An Empirical Test for the United States, 1954-84. *J. Econ. Issues*, March 1986, *20*(1), pp. 133–44. **[G: U.S.]**

Nötel, R. International Finance and Monetary Reforms. **In** *Kaser, M. C. and Radice, E. A., eds.*, 1986, pp. 520–63. **[G: E. Europe]**

Okun, Arthur M. The Invisible Handshake and the Inflationary Process. **In** *Reynolds, L. G.; Masters, S. H. and Moser, C. H., eds.*, 1986, *1980*, pp. 99–107.

Padoa-Schioppa, Tommaso. The Case for Internationalizing American Monetary Policy: Comment. **In** *Tsoukalis, L., ed.*, 1986, pp. 227–31. **[G: OECD]**

Parkin, Michael. The Output–Inflation Trade-off When Prices Are Costly to Change. *J. Polit. Econ.*, February 1986, *94*(1), pp. 200–224.

Patel, I. G. Inflation—Should It Be Cured or Endured? **In** *Patel, I. G.*, 1986, *1983*, pp. 83–100.

Penati, Alessandro. The Sources of the Movements in Interest Rates: An Empirical Investigation. *J. Banking Finance*, October 1986, *10*(3), pp. 343–60. **[G: Italy]**

Ramos, Joseph. Stabilization and Adjustment Policies in the Southern Cone, 1974–1983. **In** *Economic Commission for Latin America and the Caribbean*, 1986, pp. 65–99. **[G: Argentina; Chile; Uruguay]**

Rubery, Jill and Wilkinson, Frank. Inflation and Income Distribution. **In** *Nolan, P. and Paine, S., eds.*, 1986, pp. 326–40. **[G: U.K.]**

Salant, Walter S. Effects of Price Control on Output and the Price Level. **In** *Colander, D. C., ed.*, 1986, pp. 58–70. **[G: U.S.]**

Salin, Pascal. The Case for Internationalizing American Monetary Policy: Comment. **In** *Tsoukalis, L., ed.*, 1986, pp. 232–37. **[G: OECD]**

Samuelson, Paul A. The Roots of Inflation. **In** *Samuelson, P. A.*, 1986, *1979*, pp. 963–67.

Schneider, Jerrold E. U.S. Politics and Anti-inflation Policy. **In** *Colander, D. C., ed.*, 1986, pp. 223–30. **[G: U.S.]**

Silver, Mick. The Economic Implications of Rising Food Prices: Friedman and the Price of Steaks. *J. Agr. Econ.*, September 1986, *37*(3), pp. 377–83. **[G: U.K.]**

Tanzi, Vito. Is There a Limit to the Size of Fiscal Deficits in Developing Countries? **In** *Herber, B. P., ed.*, 1986, pp. 139–52. **[G: LDCs]**

Toma, Mark. Inflationary Bias of the Federal Reserve System: A Bureaucratic Perspective. **In** *Toma, E. F. and Toma, M., eds.*, 1986, *1982*, pp. 37–66. **[G: U.S.]**

Vaubel, Roland. The Case for Internationalizing American Monetary Policy: Comment. **In** *Tsoukalis, L., ed.*, 1986, pp. 238–42. **[G: OECD]**

Vickrey, William. Design of a Market Anti-inflation Program. **In** *Colander, D. C., ed.*, 1986, pp. 149–58.

Vickrey, William. The Need for a Direct Anti-inflation Program. **In** *Colander, D. C., ed.*, 1986, pp. 27–34. **[G: U.S.]**

1342 Inflation Theories; Studies Illustrating Inflation Theories

Adams, Charles and Gros, Daniel. The Consequences of Real Exchange Rate Rules for Inflation: Some Illustrative Examples. *Int. Monet. Fund Staff Pap.*, September 1986, *33*(3), pp. 439–76.

Addison, John T.; Chappell, Henry W., Jr. and Castro, Alberto C. Output–Inflation Tradeoffs in 34 Selected Countries. *J. Econ. Bus.*, December 1986, *38*(4), pp. 353–60. **[G: Selected Countries]**

Ahamed, Liaquat. Stabilization Policies in Developing Countries. *World Bank Res. Observer*, January 1986, *1*(1), pp. 79–110. **[G: Peru; Mexico; Portugal; Bangladesh]**

Aizenman, Joshua and Frenkel, Jacob A. Supply Shocks, Wage Indexation and Monetary Accommodation. *J. Money, Credit, Banking*, August 1986, *18*(3), pp. 304–22.

Aizenman, Joshua and Frenkel, Jacob A. Wage Indexation, Supply Shocks, and Monetary Policy in a Small, Open Economy. **In** *Edwards, S. and Ahamed, L., eds.*, 1986, pp. 89–131.

Alam, A. K. M. Shamsul and Kamath, Shyam J. Models and Forecasts of Inflation in a Developing Economy. *J. Econ. Stud.*, 1986, *13*(4), pp. 3–29. **[G: India]**

Alogoskoufis, George S. On the Determinants of Consumer Price Inflation in Greece. *Greek Econ. Rev.*, December 1986, *8*(2), pp. 245–66. **[G: Greece]**

Andersen, P. S. Keynesian and Classical Unemployment: Evidence from the Current Cycle. *Eastern Econ. J.*, July-Sept. 1986, *12*(3), pp. 223–36. **[G: OECD]**

Andersen, Torben M. Pre-set Prices, Differential Information and Monetary Policy. *Oxford Econ. Pap.*, November 1986, *38*(3), pp. 456–80.

Arellano, José Pablo and Cortázar, Rene. Inflación, conflictos macroeconómicos y democratización en Chile. (Inflation, Macroeconomic Conflicts, and Democratization in Chile. With English summary.) *Colección Estud. CIEPLAN*, June 1986, (19), pp. 57–81. **[G: Chile]**

Arnould, Daniel and Lavaux, Robert. La violence par la monnaie: l'hyperinflation dans les pays en développement. (Violence by Money: Hyperinflation in the Developing Countries. With English summary.) *Écon. Soc.*, February 1986, *20*(2), pp. 169–95. **[G: LDCs]**

Artus, Patrick and Bismut, Claude. Exchange Rate and Wage–Price Dynamics: A Theoretical Analysis and an Econometric Investigation. *Europ. Econ. Rev.*, February 1986, *30*(1), pp. 57–90. **[G: U.S.; Japan; W. Germany; France; U.K.]**

Ashley, Richard A. and Vaughan, David. Measuring Measurement Error in Economic Time Series. *J. Bus. Econ. Statist.*, January 1986, *4*(1), pp. 95–103. **[G: U.S.]**

Assarsson, Bengt. Inflation and Relative-Price Variability—A Model for an Open Economy Applied to Sweden. *J. Macroecon.*, Fall 1986, *8*(4), pp. 455–69. **[G: Sweden]**

Assenmacher, Walter. Die Dynamik der Inflations- und Beschäftigungsentwicklung. Eine theoretische und ökonometrische Analyse. (The Dynamism of Inflationary and Employment Trends: A Theoretical and Econometric Analysis. With English summary.) *Kredit Kapital*, 1986, *19*(4), pp. 540–68.

Banaian, King; Laney, Leroy O. and Willett, Thomas D. Central Bank Independence: An International Comparison. **In** *Toma, E. F. and Toma, M., eds.*, 1986, *1983*, pp. 199–217. **[G: OECD]**

Barro, Robert J. Reputation in a Model of Monetary Policy with Incomplete Information. *J. Monet. Econ.*, January 1986, *17*(1), pp. 3–20.

Barro, Robert J. U.S. Deficits since World War I. *Scand. J. Econ.*, 1986, *88*(1), pp. 195–22. **[G: U.S.]**

Barthold, Thomas A. and Dougan, William R. The Fisher Hypothesis under Different Monetary Regimes. *Rev. Econ. Statist.*, November 1986, *68*(4), pp. 674–79. **[G: U.S.]**

Basevi, Giorgio and Giavazzi, Francesco. Stabilization Policies in an Explosive Economy: Announcements and Expectations. *Europ. Econ. Rev.*, February 1986, *30*(1), pp. 43–55.

Batavia, Bala; Lash, Nicholas A. and Malliaris, A. G. The Dynamics of Inflation and Economy Policy: The Case of Greece, 1953–83. *Greek Econ. Rev.*, December 1986, *8*(2), pp. 200–217. **[G: Greece]**

Batchelor, Roy A. Quantitative v. Qualitative Measures of Inflation Expectations. *Oxford Bull. Econ. Statist.*, May 1986, *48*(2), pp. 99–120. **[G: U.S.]**

Batten, Dallas S. and Hafer, R. W. The Impact of International Factors on U.S. Inflation: An Empirical Test of the Currency Substitution Hypothesis. *Southern Econ. J.*, October 1986, *53*(2), pp. 400–412. **[G: U.S.]**

Baumol, William J. On the Stochastic Unemployment Distribution Model and the Long-run Phillips Curve. **In** *Baumol, W. J.*, 1986, *1978*, pp. 206–23.

Beckerman, Wilfred and Jenkinson, Tim. What Stopped the Inflation? Unemployment of Commodity Prices? *Econ. J.*, March 1986, *96*(381), pp. 39–54. **[G: OECD]**

Bernard, Victor L. Unanticipated Inflation and the Value of the Firm. *J. Finan. Econ.*, March 1986, *15*(3), pp. 285–321. **[G: U.S.]**

Bernard, Victor L. and Hayn, Carla. Inflation and the Distribution of the Corporate Income Tax Burden. *Nat. Tax J.*, June 1986, *39*(2), pp. 171–87. **[G: U.S.]**

Bhattacharya, Anand K. The Joint Effect of Housing Start and Inflation Announcements on GNMA Futures Prices. *J. Futures Markets*,

Winter 1986, *6*(4), pp. 645–57. **[G: U.S.]**

Blanchard, Olivier J. The Wage Price Spiral. *Quart. J. Econ.*, August 1986, *101*(3), pp. 543–65.

Bordo, Michael D. and Stuart, Charles. Optimal Inflation and Labor Taxes. *Quart. Rev. Econ. Bus.*, Summer 1986, *26*(2), pp. 6–13.

Breeden, Douglas T. Consumption, Production, Inflation and Interest Rates: A Synthesis. *J. Finan. Econ.*, May 1986, *16*(1), pp. 3–39.

Broniatowski, M. and Kebabdjian, G. Inflation et dynamique des prix: un traitement non paramétrique de données françaises. (Inflation and the Dynamic of Prices: A Non Parametric Study of French Series. With English summary.) *Écon. Appl.*, 1986, *39*(2), pp. 337–68. **[G: France]**

Bruno, Michael. Stagflation in the Industrial Countries: An Updated Overview. *Hitotsubashi J. Econ.*, Spec. Iss. Oct. 1986, *27*, pp. 57–74. **[G: OECD]**

Bruno, Michael and Fischer, Stanley. The Inflationary Process: Shocks and Accommodation. **In** *Ben-Porath, Y., ed.*, 1986, pp. 347–71. **[G: Israel]**

Bryan, Michael F. and Gavin, William T. Models of Inflation Expectations Formation: A Comparison of Household and Economist Forecasts: A Comment. *J. Money, Credit, Banking*, November 1986, *18*(4), pp. 539–44. **[G: U.S.]**

Buisán, Ana C. and Restoy, Fernando. Inflación y variabilidad de los precios relativos en España (1976–1983). (With English summary.) *Invest. Ecón.*, May 1986, *10*(2), pp. 327–55. **[G: Spain]**

Burmeister, Edwin; Wall, Kent D. and Hamilton, James D. Estimation of Unobserved Expected Monthly Inflation Using Kalman Filtering. *J. Bus. Econ. Statist.*, April 1986, *4*(2), pp. 147–60. **[G: U.S.]**

Calvo, Guillermo A. Fractured Liberalism: Argentina under Martínez de Hoz. *Econ. Develop. Cult. Change*, April 1986, *34*(3), pp. 511–33. **[G: Argentina]**

Capie, Forrest H. Conditions in Which Very Rapid Inflation Has Appeared. *Carnegie-Rochester Conf. Ser. Public Policy*, Spring 1986, *24*, pp. 115–68. **[G: Global]**

Card, David. An Empirical Model of Wage Indexation Provisions in Union Contracts. *J. Polit. Econ.*, Part 2, June 1986, *94*(3), pp. S144–75. **[G: Canada]**

Cardoso, Eliana A. What Policymakers Can Learn from Brazil and Mexico. *Challenge*, Sept./Oct. 1986, *29*(4), pp. 19–28. **[G: Brazil; Mexico]**

Cardoso, Eliana A. and Reis, Eustáquio J. *Deficits*, dívidas e inflação no Brasil. (With English summary.) *Pesquisa Planejamento Econ.*, December 1986, *16*(3), pp. 575–97.

Chappell, David. The Optimal Rate of Inflation When the Rate of Growth of the Money Supply Is Stochastic. *Manchester Sch. Econ. Soc. Stud.*, September 1986, *54*(3), pp. 314–21.

Cheema, Aftab Ahmad and Malik, Muhammad Hussain. Income-Specific Inflation Rates in Pakistan. *Pakistan Devel. Rev.*, Spring 1986, *25*(1), pp. 73–84. **[G: Pakistan]**

Chen, Nai-Ruenn and Hou, Chi-ming. China's Inflation, 1979–1983: Measurement and Analysis. *Econ. Develop. Cult. Change*, July 1986, *34*(4), pp. 811–35. **[G: China]**

Chen, Son-Nan and Aggarwal, Reena. Optimal Portfolio Selection and Uncertain Inflation. *J. Portfol. Manage.*, Fall 1986, *13*(1), pp. 44–49.

Cho, Dong W. Formation of Inflationary Expectations by Business Economists. *Bus. Econ.*, April 1986, *21*(2), pp. 34–39. **[G: U.S.]**

Christiano, Lawrence J. Money and the U.S. Economy in the 1980s: A Break from the Past? *Fed. Res. Bank Minn. Rev.*, Summer 1986, *10*(3), pp. 2–13. **[G: U.S.]**

Chung, Jae Wan and Kim, Dookyung. An Interactive Causal Analysis of Price Dynamics: A Case Study of Korea. *Econ. Develop. Cult. Change*, July 1986, *34*(4), pp. 837–53. **[G: S. Korea]**

Cling, Jean-Pierre and Meunier, François. La désinflation en France: Le point de vue de l'économètre. (The French Disinflation. With English summary.) *Revue Écon.*, November 1986, *37*(6), pp. 1093–1125. **[G: France]**

Colander, David C. On the Theory of Incentive Anti-inflation Plans. **In** *Colander, D. C., ed.*, 1986, pp. 129–38.

Contini, B.; Galeotti, Marcello and Cugno, F. Inflation and the Irregular Economy: A Dynamic Analysis. *Metroecon.*, February 1986, *38*(1), pp. 67–84.

Cukierman, Alex. Measuring Inflation Expectations: A Review Essay. *J. Monet. Econ.*, March 1986, *17*(2), pp. 315–24.

Cukierman, Alex and Meltzer, Allan H. A Theory of Ambiguity, Credibility, and Inflation under Discretion and Asymmetric Information. *Econometrica*, September 1986, *54*(5), pp. 1099–1128.

Danthine, Jean-Pierre and Donaldson, John B. Inflation and Asset Prices in an Exchange Economy. *Econometrica*, May 1986, *54*(3), pp. 585–605.

Darrat, Ali F. Money, Inflation, and Causality in the North African Countries: An Empirical Investigation. *J. Macroecon.*, Winter 1986, *8*(1), pp. 87–103. **[G: Morocco; Libya; Tunisia]**

De Long, James Bradford and Summers, Lawrence H. Improvements in Macroeconomic Stability: The Role of Wages and Prices: Comment. **In** *Gordon, R. J., ed.*, 1986, pp. 669–72. **[G: U.S.]**

Dehez, Pierre and Fitoussi, Jean-Paul. Indexation des salaires et fluctuations macroéconomiques. (With English summary.) *Revue Écon. Polit.*, May-June 1986, *96*(3), pp. 239–55.

Dehez, Pierre and Fitoussi, Jean-Paul. Wage Indexation and Macroeconomic Fluctuations. **In** *Beckerman, W., ed.*, 1986, pp. 201–17.

Delbeke, Jos. A Comparison of Price and Money Behaviour between the 1920s–30s and 1970s–80s in Belgium. **In** *Berend, I. T. and Borchardt, K., eds.*, 1986, pp. 149–70. **[G: Belgium]**

Di Matteo, Massimo. Long Waves in Relative Prices: An Interpretation. **In** *Frisch, H. and Gahlen, B., eds.*, 1986, pp. 126–44.

Dolado, Juan J.; Malo de Molina, José Luis and Ortega, Eloísa. Respuesta en el deflactor del valor añadido en la industria ante variaciones en los costes laborales unitarios. (With English summary.) *Invest. Ecón.*, January 1986, *10*(1), pp. 163–72. **[G: Spain]**

Dornbusch, Rudiger. Como deter a hiperinflação: lições da experiência inflacionária alemã da década de 20. (With English summary.) *Pesquisa Planejamento Econ.*, April 1986, *16*(1), pp. 61–85. **[G: U.S.; France; U.K.; W. Germany]**

Dornbusch, Rudiger. Inflação, taxas de câmbio e estabilização. (With English summary.) *Pesquisa Planejamento Econ.*, August 1986, *16*(2), pp. 321–49. **[G: Brazil; U.S.; Germany]**

Dornbusch, Rudiger. Money, Interest Rates and Stabilization. *Rev. Econ. Cond. Italy,* Sept.-Dec. 1986, (3), pp. 439–53. **[G: W. Germany]**

Dornbusch, Rudiger. Sound Currency and Full Employment. **In** *Dornbusch, R.*, 1986, *1985*, pp. 205–31. **[G: U.K.]**

Dornbusch, Rudiger and Fischer, Stanley. Stopping Hyperinflations Past and Present. *Weltwirtsch. Arch.*, 1986, *122*(1), pp. 1–47. **[G: Europe; Israel; Argentina]**

Dow, Christopher. Trade Unions and Inflation. *Lloyds Bank Rev.*, January 1986, (159), pp. 1–21. **[G: U.K.]**

Dunson, Bruce H. and Jackson, Peter. The Distributional Aspects of Inflation. *Quart. Rev. Econ. Bus.*, Winter 1986, *26*(4), pp. 62–73.

Eisner, Robert. The Revolution Restored: Keynesian Unemployment, Inflation and Budget Deficits. *Eastern Econ. J.*, July-Sept. 1986, *12*(3), pp. 217–21.

Eliasson, Gunnar. U.S. Deficits since World War I: Comment. *Scand. J. Econ.*, 1986, *88*(1), pp. 235–38. **[G: U.S.; Sweden]**

Encaoua, David and Geroski, Paul A. Price Dynamics and Competition in Five OECD Countries. *OECD Econ. Stud.*, Spring 1986, (6), pp. 47–74. **[G: Canada; Japan; U.K.; U.S.; Sweden]**

Faustini, Gino. A New Method of Indexing Wages. *Rev. Econ. Cond. Italy,* Jan.-Apr. 1986, (1), pp. 65–84. **[G: Italy]**

Ferris, Stephen P. and Kumar, Raman. A Time Series Analysis of Real Interest Rates. *Indian Econ. J.*, July-Sept. 1986, *34*(1), pp. 79–88. **[G: India]**

Fischer, Bernhard and Trapp, Peter. Public Sector Deficits and the Dynamics of the Inflation Tax in Argentina. *Rivista Int. Sci. Econ. Com.*, Oct.-Nov. 1986, *33*(10–11), pp. 1107–27. **[G: Argentina]**

Fischer, Edwin O. and Jammernegg, Werner. Empirical Investigation of a Catastrophe Theory Extension of the Phillips Curve. *Rev. Econ. Statist.*, February 1986, *68*(1), pp. 9–17. **[G: U.S.]**

Fischer, Georges and Kern, Anita. Zur Problematik der Indexbindung: Fragwürdige Diktatur des Konsumentenpreisindexes? (With English summary.) *Aussenwirtschaft*, December 1986, *41*(4), pp. 483–96.

Fischer, Stanley. Contracts, Credibility, and Disinflation. **In** *Fischer, S.*, 1986, *1985*, pp. 221–45. **[G: U.S.]**

Fischer, Stanley. Exchange Rate versus Money Targets in Disinflation. **In** *Fischer, S.*, 1986, pp. 247–62.

Fischer, Stanley. Indexing and Inflation. **In** *Fischer, S.*, 1986, *1983*, pp. 193–219. **[G: Selected Countries]**

Fischer, Stanley. On Activist Monetary Policy with Rational Expectations. **In** *Fischer, S.*, 1986, *1980*, pp. 383–412. **[G: U.S.]**

Fischer, Stanley. Relative Shocks, Relative Price Variability, and Inflation. **In** *Fischer, S.*, 1986, *1981*, pp. 71–122. **[G: U.S.]**

Fischer, Stanley. Toward an Understanding of the Costs of Inflation: II. **In** *Fischer, S.*, 1986, *1983*, pp. 35–69. **[G: U.S.]**

Fischer, Stanley. Wage Indexation and Macroeconomic Stability. **In** *Fischer, S.*, 1986, *1977*, pp. 159–91.

Fischer, Stanley. Wage Indexation, Supply Shocks, and Monetary Policy in a Small, Open Economy: Comment. **In** *Edwards, S. and Ahamed, L., eds.*, 1986, pp. 132–39.

Fischer, Stanley. Welfare Aspects of Government Issue of Indexed Bonds. **In** *Fischer, S.*, 1986, *1983*, pp. 333–55.

Franz, Wolfgang. Towards an Evaluation of the Costs and Benefits of a (Dis-) Inflationary Policy in the Federal Republic of Germany. **In** *Frisch, H. and Gahlen, B., eds.*, 1986, pp. 13–44. **[G: W. Germany]**

Fratianni, Michele. Conditions in Which Very Rapid Inflation Has Appeared: A Comment. *Carnegie-Rochester Conf. Ser. Public Policy,* Spring 1986, *24*, pp. 169–77. **[G: Global]**

Frenkel, Roberto. Salários e inflação na América Latina: resultados de pesquisas recentes na Argentina, Brasil, Chile, Colômbia e Costa Rica. (With English summary.) *Pesquisa Planejamento Econ.*, April 1986, *16*(1), pp. 21–59. **[G: Argentina; Brazil; Chile; Colombia; Costa Rica]**

Frenkel, Roberto. Salarios e inflación en América Latina. Resultados de investigaciones recientes en la Argentina, Brasil, Colombia, Costa Rica y Chile. (With English summary.) *Desarrollo Econ.*, Jan.-Mar. 1986, *25*(100), pp. 587–622. **[G: Argentina; Brazil; Colombia; Costa Rica; Chile]**

Gahlen, Bernhard. Price and Quantity Variability under Stagflation. **In** *Frisch, H. and Gahlen, B., eds.*, 1986, pp. 45–69. **[G: W. Germany]**

Gapinski, James H. TIP and Tradition as Tools against Inflation. *J. Post Keynesian Econ.*, Summer 1986, *8*(4), pp. 591–606.

Gerchunoff, Pablo. Gasto pblico, tasa de cambio e impulso capitalista después de la hiperinflación. (With English summary.) *Desarrollo Econ.*, Jan.-Mar. 1986, *25*(100), pp. 623–57. **[G: Germany; Hungary; Argentina]**

Gil Díaz, Francisco. Government Budget Measurement under Inflation in LDCs. **In** *Herber, B. P., ed.*, 1986, pp. 123–37. **[G: Mexico]**

Gisser, Micha and Goodwin, Thomas H. Crude Oil and the Macroeconomy: Tests of Some Popular Notions: A Note. *J. Money, Credit, Banking,* February 1986, *18*(1), pp. 95–103. **[G: U.S.]**

Glezakos, Constantine and Nugent, Jeffrey B. A Confirmation of the Relation between Inflation and Relative Price Variability. *J. Polit. Econ.*, August 1986, *94*(4), pp. 895–99. **[G: U.S.]**

Glezakos, Constantine and Nugent, Jeffrey B. Inflation and Relative Price Variability once Again. *J. Post Keynesian Econ.*, Summer 1986, *8*(4), pp. 607–13. **[G: U.S.]**

Goodwin, Thomas H. Inflation, Risk, Taxes, and the Demand for Owner-Occupied Housing. *Rev. Econ. Statist.*, May 1986, *68*(2), pp. 197–206. **[G: U.S.]**

Green, Steven L. and Grossman, Herschel I. The Illusion of Stabilization Policy? *Carnegie-Rochester Conf. Ser. Public Policy,* Autumn 1986, *25,* pp. 221–35. **[G: W. Europe; U.S.; Canada]**

Gros, Daniel. Wage Indexation and the Real Exchange Rate in Small Open Economies: A Study of the Effects of Fluctuations in Export Earnings. *Int. Monet. Fund Staff Pap.*, March 1986, *33*(1), pp. 117–38.

Grossman, Herschel I. and Van Huyck, John B. Seigniorage, Inflation, and Reputation. *J. Monet. Econ.*, July 1986, *18*(1), pp. 21–31.

Grubb, David B. Topics in the OECD Phillips Curve. *Econ. J.*, March 1986, *96*(381), pp. 55–79. **[G: OECD]**

Hafer, R. W. Inflation Uncertainty and a Test of the Friedman Hypothesis. *J. Macroecon.*, Summer 1986, *8*(3), pp. 365–72. **[G: U.S.]**

Hamermesh, Daniel S. Inflation and Labour Market Adjustment. *Economica,* February 1986, *53*(209), pp. 63–73. **[G: U.S.]**

Hamilton, James D. On Testing for Self-fulfilling Speculative Price Bubbles. *Int. Econ. Rev.*, October 1986, *27*(3), pp. 545–52.

Harcourt, Geoffrey C. The Social Consequences of Inflation. **In** *[Harcourt, G. C.],* 1986, *1974,* pp. 231–49.

Heri, Erwin W. Irrationales rational gesehen: Eine Übersicht über die Theorie der "Bubbles." (The Irrational Seen Rationally: A Review of the Theory of "Bubbles." With English summary.) *Schweiz. Z. Volkswirtsch. Statist.*, June 1986, *122*(2), pp. 163–86.

Heymann, Daniel. Inflation and Stabilization Policies. *CEPAL Rev.*, April 1986, (28), pp. 67–97. **[G: Argentina]**

Hibbs, Douglas A., Jr. Political Parties and Macroeconomic Policies and Outcomes in the United States. *Amer. Econ. Rev.*, May 1986, *76*(2), pp. 66–70. **[G: U.S.]**

Hill, G. P. and Seagraves, J. A. Agricultural Finance and Inflation: An Examination of Alternative Methods with Reference to British Experience. *J. Agr. Econ.*, May 1986, *37*(2), pp. 173–83. **[G: U.K.]**

Holden, Kenneth and Peel, David A. Expectations Formation, Public Forecasts and the Wage Equation. *Econ. Modelling,* April 1986, *3*(2), pp. 129–34. **[G: U.K.]**

Holloway, Thomas M. Simple Methods to Measure the Automatic Responsiveness of the Federal Budget to Inflation. *J. Econ. Soc. Meas.*, October 1986, *14*(3), pp. 219–31. **[G: U.S.]**

Honohan, Patrick and Flynn, John. Irish Inflation in EMS. *Econ. Soc. Rev.*, April 1986, *17*(3), pp. 175–91. **[G: Ireland]**

Hossain, Md. Akhtar. Monetary Disequilibrium and Inflation: A Monetary Model of Inflation in Pakistan, 1963–82. *Pakistan Devel. Rev.*, Summer 1986, *25*(2), pp. 141–62. **[G: Pakistan]**

Howell, Craig and Clem, Andrew. Inflation Remained Mild Again during 1985. *Mon. Lab. Rev.*, April 1986, *109*(4), pp. 17–21. **[G: U.S.]**

Humphrey, Thomas M. A Monetarist Model of the Inflationary Process. **In** *Humphreys, T. M.*, 1986, *1975,* pp. 49–59.

Humphrey, Thomas M. A Monetarist Model of World Inflation and the Balance of Payments. **In** *Humphreys, T. M.*, 1986, *1976,* pp. 170–79.

Humphrey, Thomas M. Eliminating Runaway Inflation: Lessons from the German Hyperinflation. **In** *Humphreys, T. M.*, 1986, *1980,* pp. 237–41. **[G: Germany]**

Humphrey, Thomas M. Interest Rates, Expectations, and the Wicksellian Policy Rule. **In** *Humphreys, T. M.*, 1986, *1976,* pp. 134–42.

Humphrey, Thomas M. Keynes on Inflation. **In** *Humphreys, T. M.*, 1986, *1981,* pp. 38–48.

Humphrey, Thomas M. On Cost-Push Theories of Inflation in the Pre-war Monetary Literature. **In** *Humphreys, T. M.*, 1986, *1976,* pp. 19–25.

Humphrey, Thomas M. Some Current Controversies in the Theory of Inflation. **In** *Humphreys, T. M.*, 1986, *1976,* pp. 26–37.

Humphrey, Thomas M. Some Recent Developments in Phillips Curve Analysis. **In** *Humphreys, T. M.*, 1986, *1978,* pp. 119–27.

Humphrey, Thomas M. The Concept of Indexation in the History of Economic Thought. **In** *Humphreys, T. M.*, 1986, *1974,* pp. 264–77.

Humphrey, Thomas M. The Early History of the Real/Nominal Interest Rate Relationship. **In** *Humphreys, T. M.*, 1986, *1983,* pp. 151–59.

Humphrey, Thomas M. The Early History of the Phillips Curve. **In** *Humphreys, T. M.*, 1986, *1985,* pp. 91–98.

Humphrey, Thomas M. The Evolution and Policy Implications of Phillips Curve Analysis. **In** *Humphreys, T. M.*, 1986, *1985,* pp. 99–118.

Humphrey, Thomas M. The Interest Cost-Push Controversy. **In** *Humphreys, T. M.*, 1986, *1979,* pp. 143–50.

Humphrey, Thomas M. The Persistence of Inflation. **In** *Humphreys, T. M.*, 1986, *1979,* pp. 60–72.

Huszti, Ernö. Changes in the Purchasing Power of the Hungarian Forint between 1946–1984.

Acta Oecon., 1986, *37*(1–2), pp. 87–101. **[G: Hungary]**

Irvine, Ian. Inflation, Taxation, Capital Markets and the Demand for Housing in Ireland. *Econ. Soc. Rev.*, July 1986, *17*(4), pp. 277–92. **[G: Ireland]**

Isaac, Alan G. Bursting Bubbles: Further Results. *J. Monet. Econ.*, May 1986, *17*(3), pp. 425–31.

Isaac, Alan G. Reversing the Phillips' Curve: A Microfoundation. *J. Macroecon.*, Spring 1986, *8*(2), pp. 221–26.

Jaksch, Hans Jürgen. Kleine ökonometrische Modelle für sich rasch entwertende Währungen: Deutschland 1920/23 und Argentinien 1977/81. (Small Econometric Models for Rapidly Depreciating Currencies: Germany 1920/23 and Argentina 1977/81. With English summary.) *Ifo-Studien*, 1986, *32*(4), pp. 241–74. **[G: Germany; Argentina]**

Jaksch, Hans Jürgen. Simulaciones de políticas antiinflacionarias en Argentina, 1983/87. (Simulation of Anti-inflationary Policies in Argentina, 1983–87. With English summary.) *Económica (La Plata)*, Jan.-June 1986, *32*(1), pp. 21–56. **[G: Argentina]**

Jung, Woo S. and Marshall, Peyton J. Inflation and Economic Growth: Some International Evidence on Structuralist and Distortionist Positions: A Note. *J. Money, Credit, Banking*, May 1986, *18*(2), pp. 227–32.

Kantor, Brian S. and Barr, G. D. I. The Impact of a Change in the Price of Petrol on the South African Rate of Inflation. *J. Stud. Econ. Econometrics*, November 1986, (26), pp. 35–57. **[G: S. Africa]**

Kantor, Laurence G. Inflation Uncertainty and Real Economic Activity: An Alternative Approach. *Rev. Econ. Statist.*, August 1986, *68*(3), pp. 493–500. **[G: U.S.]**

Kapur, Basant K. Problems of Indexation in Financially Liberalized Less-developed Economies. **In** *Kapur, B. K.*, 1986, *1982*, pp. 123–41.

Kaufman, Roger T. and Woglom, Geoffrey. The Degree of Indexation in Major U.S. Union Contracts. *Ind. Lab. Relat. Rev.*, April 1986, *39*(3), pp. 439–48. **[G: U.S.]**

Kiguel, Miguel A. Déficit fiscal e inflación. (With English summary.) *Desarrollo Econ.*, July-Sept. 1986, *26*(102), pp. 255–68.

King, Stephen R. Improvements in Macroeconomic Stability: The Role of Wages and Prices: Comment. **In** *Gordon, R. J., ed.*, 1986, pp. 665–69. **[G: U.S.]**

Klein, Philip A. Leading Indicators of Inflation in Market Economies. *Int. J. Forecasting*, 1986, *2*(4), pp. 403–12. **[G: OECD]**

Klein, Philip A. Reinventing the Square Wheel: A Behavioral Assessment of Inflation. **In** *Gilad, B. and Kaish, S., eds., Vol. B*, 1986, pp. 5–30.

Knight, Peter T.; McCarthy, F. Desmond and van Wijnbergen, Sweder J. G. Escaping Hyperinflation. *Finance Develop.*, December 1986, *23*(4), pp. 14–17. **[G: Argentina; Brazil; Israel]**

Koford, Kenneth J. Innovation and Adaptation under Incentive Anti-inflation Plans. *Public Finance*, 1986, *41*(2), pp. 218–31.

Kryzanowski, Lawrence and Jalilvand, Abolhassan. Statistical Tests of the Accuracy of Alternative Forecasts: Some Results for U.S. Utility Betas. *Financial Rev.*, May 1986, *21*(2), pp. 319–35. **[G: U.S.]**

Kuran, Timur. Anticipated Inflation and Aggregate Employment: The Case of Costly Price Adjustment. *Econ. Inquiry*, April 1986, *24*(2), pp. 293–311.

Kuran, Timur. Price Adjustment Costs, Anticipated Inflation, and Output. *Quart. J. Econ.*, May 1986, *101*(2), pp. 407–18.

Landmann, Oliver. International Portfolio-Shifts and the Choice of a Monetary Rule. **In** *Frisch, H. and Gahlen, B., eds.*, 1986, pp. 86–125.

Leamer, Edward E. A Bayesian Analysis of the Determinants of Inflation. **In** *Belsley, D. A. and Kuh, E., eds.*, 1986, pp. 62–89. **[G: U.S.]**

Lerda, Juan Carlos. A política salarial do período 1979/85: alguns aspectos dinâmicos. (With English summary.) *Pesquisa Planejamento Econ.*, August 1986, *16*(2), pp. 467–92. **[G: Brazil]**

Lluch, Constantino. Wage Indexation, Supply Shocks, and Monetary Policy in a Small, Open Economy: Comment. **In** *Edwards, S. and Ahamed, L., eds.*, 1986, pp. 139–42.

Loderer, Claudio; Lys, Thomas and Schweizer, Urs. Daily Monetary Impulses and Security Prices. *J. Monet. Econ.*, July 1986, *18*(1), pp. 33–47. **[G: Switzerland]**

Lombra, Raymond E. Shocks and Stabilization Policy: Illusions and Issues: A Comment. *Carnegie-Rochester Conf. Ser. Public Policy*, Autumn 1986, *25*, pp. 237–43.

Loranger, Jean-Guy and Halévi, Joseph. La théorie du "Markup" comme explication de l'inflation: une critique kaleckienne de certains post-keynésiens. (The Markup Theory as an Explanation of Inflation. With English summary.) *L'Actual. Econ.*, September 1986, *62*(3), pp. 385–408. **[G: Canada]**

Loue, Jean-François and Morin, Pierre. La boucle prix-salaires des modèles de l'économie française. Structure et robustesse. (The Wage-Price Spiral of the Models of the French Economy: Structure and Robustness. With English summary.) *Revue Écon.*, November 1986, *37*(6), pp. 1067–92. **[G: France]**

Makinen, Gail E. The Greek Hyperinflation and Stabilization of 1943–1946. *J. Econ. Hist.*, September 1986, *46*(3), pp. 795–805. **[G: Greece]**

Marshall R., Pablo. Predicción de inflación con modelos de series de tiempo múltiples. (With English summary.) *Cuadernos Econ.*, April 1986, *23*(68), pp. 101–17. **[G: Chile]**

McCallum, Bennett T. Estimating the Long-run Relationship between Interest Rates and Inflation: A Reply. *J. Monet. Econ.*, July 1986, *18*(1), pp. 87–90.

McCallum, John. Two Cheers for the Anti-Inflation Board. *Can. Public Policy,* March 1986, *12*(1), pp. 133–47. **[G: Canada]**

McDonald, John. An Econometric Test of Inflation Neutrality Using Observable Variables Only. *J. Macroecon.,* Spring 1986, *8*(2), pp. 193–99. **[G: U.S.]**

Michaels, Robert. Reinterpreting the Role of Inflation in Politico-Economic Model. *Public Choice,* 1986, *48*(2), pp. 113–24. **[G: U.S.]**

Miller, Jeffrey B.; Koford, Kenneth J. and Schneider, Jerrold E. Plans for Fighting Inflation with Microeconomic Incentives. **In** *Colander, D. C., ed.,* 1986, pp. 35–53. **[G: U.S.]**

Minczeles, Alain and Sicsic, Pierre. La désinflation: 1982–1985. Une analyse variantielle. (Disinflation in France: 1982–1985. With English summary.) *Revue Écon.,* November 1986, *37*(6), pp. 1127–46. **[G: France]**

Mishan, Ezra J. Demand-Pull and Wage-Push: Inflation—Causes, Consequences, Cures. **In** *Mishan, E. J.,* 1986, *1975,* pp. 7–17.

Mishan, Ezra J. The New Inflation: Its Theory and Practice. **In** *Mishan, E. J.,* 1986, *1974,* pp. 18–49. **[G: U.K.]**

Modiano, Eduardo M. A inflação e a moeda indexada. (With English summary.) *Pesquisa Planejamento Econ.,* April 1986, *16*(1), pp. 1–19. **[G: Brazil]**

Modigliani, Franco. U.S. Deficits since World War I: Comment. *Scand. J. Econ.,* 1986, *88*(1), pp. 223–34. **[G: U.S.]**

Mohr, P. J. The De Kock Commission and Inflation. *S. Afr. J. Econ.,* March 1986, *54*(1), pp. 22–40. **[G: S. Africa]**

Montesano, Aldo. Debito pubblico e tasso di inflazione. (Public Debt and Inflation Rate. With English summary.) *Ricerche Econ.,* Apr.-Sept. 1986, *40*(2–3), pp. 400–408.

Moore, Basil J. Inflation and Financial Deepening. *J. Devel. Econ.,* Jan.-Feb. 1986, *20*(1), pp. 125–33. **[G: S. Korea]**

Moore, Basil J. and Smit, B. W. Wages, Money and Inflation. *S. Afr. J. Econ.,* March 1986, *54*(1), pp. 80–93. **[G: S. Africa]**

Moore, Geoffrey H. Inflation Forecasts: Businessmen vs. Economists. *Ifo-Studien,* 1986, *32*(1–3), pp. 229–38.

Moosa, S. A. Inflation, Non-neutral Growth, Equity Yields and the Fisher Hypothesis. *Appl. Econ.,* March 1986, *18*(3), pp. 237–47. **[G: U.S.]**

Murphy, Robert G. The Expectations Theory of the Term Structure: Evidence from Inflation Forecasts. *J. Macroecon.,* Fall 1986, *8*(4), pp. 423–34. **[G: U.S.]**

Myatt, Anthony E. and Young, Gregory. Interest Rates and Inflation: Uncertainty Cushions, Threshold and "Patman" Effects. *Eastern Econ. J.,* Apr.-June 1986, *12*(2), pp. 103–14. **[G: U.S.]**

Naish, Howard F. Price Adjustment Costs and the Output–Inflation Trade-off. *Economica,* May 1986, *53*(210), pp. 219–30.

Navarro, Alfredo Martin. Precios relativos, dinero e inflación en la Argentina. (Relative Prices, Money and Inflation in Argentina. With English summary.) *Económica (La Plata),* Jan.-June 1986, *32*(1), pp. 119–33. **[G: Argentina]**

Nicoletti, G. Unsustainability of Public Debt Dynamics and Inflation. *Metroecon.,* June 1986, *38*(2), pp. 181–204.

Paleologos, John. Unanticipated Money, Output, and Inflation in Greece. *Public Finance,* December 1986, *41*(3), pp. 415–29. **[G: Greece]**

Paroush, Jacob. Inflation, Search Costs and Price Dispersion. *J. Macroecon.,* Summer 1986, *8*(3), pp. 329–36.

Peebles, Gavin. On the Importance of Establishing the Inverse Relationship between Open Inflation and Household Liquidity Growth under Socialism: A Critique of Jan Winiecki's Savings Deposit Data. *Comp. Econ. Stud.,* Winter 1986, *28*(4), pp. 85–91. **[G: Cent. Planned Econ.]**

Peel, David A. and Chappell, David. On Stylized Learning and Hyper-inflations. *Metroecon.,* June 1986, *38*(2), pp. 205–12.

Peel, David A.; Walters, K. and Pope, P. F. Public Forecasts and Their Impact on Expectation Formation. *Econ. Modelling,* April 1986, *3*(2), pp. 126–28. **[G: U.K.]**

Perry, George L. Policy Lessons from the Postwar Period. **In** *Beckerman, W., ed.,* 1986, pp. 127–51. **[G: OECD]**

Persico, Pasquale. Inflazione e prezzi relativi in Italia: Commento alla replica. *Stud. Econ.,* 1986, *41*(29), pp. 185–86.

Pietra, Tito. Inflazione e prezzi relativi in Italia: Replica a persico. (With English summary.) *Stud. Econ.,* 1986, *41*(29), pp. 169–83.

Plessner, Yakir and Shalit, Haim. Inflation, the Level of Investment, and Interest Rates. *Europ. Econ. Rev.,* December 1986, *30*(6), pp. 1169–87.

Rampa, Lorenzo. Commercio e inflazione. Un'analisi dinamica dei prezzi in sistemi con intermediazione dei prodotti. (Commerce and Inflation. A Dynamic Analysis of Prices in Systems with Commercial Firms. With English summary.) *Ricerche Econ.,* Apr.-Sept. 1986, *40*(2–3), pp. 303–16.

Rappoport, Peter. Inflation in the Service Sector. *Fed. Res. Bank New York Quart. Rev.,* Winter 1986-87, *11*(4), pp. 35–45. **[G: U.S.]**

Richards, Daniel J. The Macroeconomic Models and Expectations of Corporate Executives. *J. Post Keynesian Econ.,* Spring 1986, *8*(3), pp. 438–46. **[G: U.S.]**

Romer, David. A Simple General Equilibrium Version of the Baumol–Tobin Model. *Quart. J. Econ.,* November 1986, *101*(4), pp. 663–85.

Rose, Louis A. A Respecified Tax-Adjusted Fisher Relation. *Econ. Inquiry,* April 1986, *24*(2), pp. 319–31. **[G: U.S.]**

Salvatore, Dominick. Oil Import Costs and Domestic Inflation in Industrial Countries. *Weltwirtsch. Arch.,* 1986, *122*(2), pp. 281–91. **[G: OECD; LDCs]**

Samanta, Subarna K. Price Surprises and Real

Output: The Indian Evidence. *Indian Econ. J.*, Oct.-Dec. 1986, *34*(2), pp. 49–58. **[G: India]**

Saville, I. D. and Gardiner, K. L. Stagflation in the UK since 1970: A Model-based Explanation. *Nat. Inst. Econ. Rev.*, August 1986, (117), pp. 52–69. **[G: U.K.]**

Savona, Paolo. Money Supply, Wages and Prices: Reflections with Hindsight. *Rev. Econ. Cond. Italy*, Sept.-Dec. 1986, (3), pp. 485–510. **[G: Italy]**

Schlieper, Ulrich. Real Wages, Business Cycles and Unemployment. **In** *Frisch, H. and Gahlen, B., eds.*, 1986, pp. 145–58.

Schöler, Klaus. Preisniveaustabilität durch kompetitive Geldsysteme? (Price Level Stability by Means of Competitive Monetary System? With English summary.) *Kredit Kapital*, 1986, *19*(3), pp. 351–65.

Schroeter, John R. and Smith, Scott L. A Reexamination of the Rationality of the Livingston Price Expectations: A Note. *J. Money, Credit, Banking*, May 1986, *18*(2), pp. 239–46.

Sekkat, Khalid. Inflation et Monnaie en Belgique: une analyse de causalité. (With English summary.) *Cah. Écon. Bruxelles*, 4th Trimester 1986, (112), pp. 3–31. **[G: Belgium]**

Sellekaerts, Brigitte H. and Sellekaerts, Willy. Unanticipated Inflation and Relative Price Variability. *Atlantic Econ. J.*, July 1986, *14*(2), pp. 31–36. **[G: U.S.]**

Sellekaerts, Willy and Sellekaerts, Brigitte H. The Impact of Anticipated and Unanticipated Inflation on Relative Price Variability: Further Results. *J. Post Keynesian Econ.*, Summer 1986, *8*(4), pp. 614–22.

Shannon, Russell and Wallace, Myles S. Wages and Inflation: An Investigation into Causality. *J. Post Keynesian Econ.*, Winter 1985-86, *8*(2), pp. 182–91. **[G: U.S.]**

Sheehey, Edmund J. Unanticipated Inflation, Devaluation and Output in Latin America. *World Devel.*, May 1986, *14*(5), pp. 665–71. **[G: Latin America]**

Shiffer, Zalman F. Adjusting to High Inflation: The Israeli Experience. *Fed. Res. Bank St. Louis Rev.*, May 1986, *68*(5), pp. 18–29. **[G: Israel]**

Shorrocks, Anthony. The Measurement of Inflation Experienced by the Poor, 1970–80: A Reply. *Can. Public Policy*, December 1986, *12*(4), pp. 640–44. **[G: Canada]**

Silber, Jacques G. Variability in the Experienced Rates of Inflation and Price Index Linkage to Social Welfare. *Appl. Econ.*, January 1986, *18*(1), pp. 49–58. **[G: Israel]**

Smirlock, Michael. Inflation Announcements and Financial Market Reaction: Evidence from the Long-term Bond Market. *Rev. Econ. Statist.*, May 1986, *68*(2), pp. 329–33. **[G: U.S.]**

Smith, Russell E. Indexación salarial, rotación de personal y variaciones de los salarios nominales en la industria monufacturera brasileña, 1966–1976. (With English summary.) *Desarrollo Econ.*, July-Sept. 1986, *26*(102), pp. 269–87. **[G: Brazil]**

Sørensen, Peter Birch. Taxation, Inflation, and Asset Accumulation in a Small Open Economy. *Europ. Econ. Rev.*, October 1986, *30*(5), pp. 1025–41.

Spechler, Martin C. Big Inflations Need Potent Cures. *Challenge*, Nov./Dec. 1986, *29*(5), pp. 26–32. **[G: OECD]**

Starck, Christian C. Indexation and Household Saving Behavior: Some Empirical Evidence from Finnish Data. *Weltwirtsch. Arch.*, 1986, *122*(4), pp. 713–27. **[G: Finland]**

Steindl, Frank G. General Equilibrium Models of Inflation and Interest Rates: Specification Considerations. *Kredit Kapital*, 1986, *19*(2), pp. 252–70.

Stenius, Marianne. Separating Short-term and Long-term Inflation Expectations Using Observations from Financial Markets. *Empirical Econ.*, 1986, *11*(1), pp. 57–63. **[G: U.S.]**

Stiglitz, Joseph E. Financial Markets and Macroeconomic Fluctuations: Comment. **In** *Butkiewicz, J. L.; Koford, K. J. and Miller, J. B., eds.*, 1986, pp. 144–45.

Summers, Lawrence H. Estimating the Long-run Relationship between Interest Rates and Inflation: A Response. *J. Monet. Econ.*, July 1986, *18*(1), pp. 77–86.

Sumner, Michael T. and Ward, Robert. Nonlinear Estimates of the UK Phillips Curve. *Econ. Notes*, 1986, (2), pp. 62–67. **[G: U.K.]**

Sundararajan, V. Exchange Rate versus Credit Policy: Analysis with a Monetary Model of Trade and Inflation in India. *J. Devel. Econ.*, Jan.-Feb. 1986, *20*(1), pp. 75–105. **[G: India]**

Takagi, Yasuoki. Inflation and Cumulative Debt Outstanding of Less-Developed Countries. *J. Int. Econ.*, August 1986, *21*(1/2), pp. 61–80. **[G: LDCs]**

Tarantelli, Ezio. Erratum [The Regulation of Inflation and Unemployment]. *Ind. Relat.*, Spring 1986, *25*(2), pp. 94. **[G: OECD]**

Tarantelli, Ezio. The Regulation of Inflation and Unemployment. *Ind. Relat.*, Winter 1986, *25*(1), pp. 1–15. **[G: OECD]**

Taylor, John B. Improvements in Macroeconomic Stability: The Role of Wages and Prices: Reply. **In** *Gordon, R. J., ed.*, 1986, pp. 672–75. **[G: U.S.]**

Taylor, John B. Improvements in Macroeconomic Stability: The Role of Wages and Prices. **In** *Gordon, R. J., ed.*, 1986, pp. 639–65. **[G: U.S.]**

Thies, Clifford F. Business Price Expectations: 1947–83. *J. Money, Credit, Banking*, August 1986, *18*(3), pp. 336–54. **[G: U.S.]**

Tobin, James. On the Welfare Macroeconomics of Government Financial Policy. *Scand. J. Econ.*, 1986, *88*(1), pp. 9–24.

von Ungern-Sternberg, Thomas. Inflation and the Consumption Function. *Weltwirtsch. Arch.*, 1986, *122*(4), pp. 741–44. **[G: U.K.]**

VanderHoff, James. Endogenous Expectation Formation Methods: Evidence from Consumers' Inflation Expectations. *J. Macroecon.*, Winter 1986, *8*(1), pp. 63–74. **[G: U.S.]**

Vercelli, Alessandro. Stagflation and the Recent Revival of Schumpeterian Entrepreneurship. **In** *Frisch, H. and Gahlen, B., eds.*, 1986, pp. 159–85.

Wadhwani, Sushil B. Inflation, Bankruptcy, Default Premia and the Stock Market. *Econ. J.*, March 1986, *96*(381), pp. 120–38. **[G: U.K.]**

Wahlroos, Björn and Berglund, Tom. Stock Returns, Inflationary Expectations and Real Activity: New Evidence. *J. Banking Finance*, October 1986, *10*(3), pp. 377–89. **[G: Finland]**

Walz, Daniel T. and Spencer, Roger W. Expectations and the Phillips Curve: An Ex-Ante Approach. *Atlantic Econ. J.*, July 1986, *14*(2), pp. 26–30. **[G: U.S.]**

Webb, Steven B. Fiscal News and Inflationary Expectations in Germany after World War I. *J. Econ. Hist.*, September 1986, *46*(3), pp. 769–94. **[G: Germany]**

Wernik, Andrzej. Inflationary Processes during the Seventies. *Eastern Europ. Econ.*, Spring 1986, *24*(3), pp. 74–98. **[G: Poland]**

Whitley, J. D. A Model of Incomes Policy in the U.K., 1963–79. *Manchester Sch. Econ. Soc. Stud.*, March 1986, *54*(1), pp. 31–64. **[G: U.K.]**

Wicker, Elmus R. Terminating Hyperinflation in the Dismembered Habsburg Monarchy. *Amer. Econ. Rev.*, June 1986, *76*(3), pp. 350–64. **[G: Poland; Austria; Hungary]**

Winer, Stanley L. The Role of Exchange Rate Flexibility in the International Transmission of Inflation in Long and Shorter Runs: Canada, 1953 to 1981. *Can. J. Econ.*, February 1986, *19*(1), pp. 62–86. **[G: Canada]**

Winiecki, Jan. Open, Hidden and Repressed Inflation under Central Planning: An Overview. *Rivista Int. Sci. Econ. Com.*, Oct.-Nov. 1986, *33*(10–11), pp. 969–94. **[G: CMEA]**

Winiecki, Jan. Sources and Symptoms of Inflation in the Planned Economy. *Eastern Europ. Econ.*, Spring 1986, *24*(3), pp. 53–73. **[G: Selected Countries]**

Wolters, Jürgen. Preiserwartungen der Unternehmer. Eine empirische Untersuchung anhand der Ifo-Salden. (Price Expectations of Firms. An Empirical Analysis on the Basis of the Ifo-Business Test. With English summary.) *Z. Wirtschaft. Sozialwissen.*, 1986, *106*(6), pp. 579–604. **[G: W. Germany]**

Zenezini, Maurizio. I salari e la curva di Phillips: alcune considerazioni sull'esperienza italiana e un commento ad un articolo di onofri e salituro. (Wages and Phillips Curve: A Comment. With English summary.) *Polit. Econ.*, December 1986, *2*(3), pp. 401–34. **[G: Italy]**

Zinn, Karl Georg. Geldvermögen, Zinseinkommensquote und Inflation. (Financial Capital, Share of Interest Income and Inflation. With English summary.) *Jahr. Nationalökon. Statist.*, July 1986, *201*(4), pp. 350–69. **[G: W. Germany]**

200 Quantitative Economic Methods and Data

210 Econometric, Statistical, and Mathematical Methods and Models

211 Econometric and Statistical Methods and Models

2110 General

Andrews, Donald W. K. Complete Consistency: A Testing Analogue of Estimator Consistency. *Rev. Econ. Stud.*, April 1986, *53*(2), pp. 263–69.

Bruno, Vincenzo. L'entropia e la variabilità paretiana dei redditi. (The Entropy in a Pareto Distribution of Incomes. With English summary.) *Giorn. Econ.*, Sept.-Oct. 1986, *45*(9–10), pp. 515–25.

Chen, Wen-chen and DeGroot, Morris H. Optimal Search for New Types. **In** *[de Finetti, B.]*, 1986, pp. 443–58.

Collender, Robert Neil and Chalfant, James A. An Alternative Approach to Decisions under Uncertainty Using the Empirical Moment-Generating Function. *Amer. J. Agr. Econ.*, August 1986, *68*(3), pp. 727–31.

Cox, D. R. Statistics and Causal Inference: Comment. *J. Amer. Statist. Assoc.*, December 1986, *81*(396), pp. 963–64.

Dawid, A. Philip. A Bayesian View of Statistical Modelling. **In** *[de Finetti, B.]*, 1986, pp. 391–404.

Dickey, J. M.; Dawid, A. Philip and Kadane, Joseph B. Subjective-Probability Assessment Methods for Multivariate-*t* and Matrix-*t* Models. **In** *[de Finetti, B.]*, 1986, pp. 177–95.

Don, F. J. Henk. The Specification of Least Informative Error Distributions. *J. Econometrics*, February 1986, *31*(1), pp. 81–91.

Esteban, Joan M. Income-Share Elasticity and the Size Distribution of Income. *Int. Econ. Rev.*, June 1986, *27*(2), pp. 439–44.

Fisher, Franklin M. Statisticians, Econometricians, and Adversary Proceedings. *J. Amer. Statist. Assoc.*, June 1986, *81*(394), pp. 277–86. **[G: U.S.]**

Gastwirth, Joseph L.; Nayak, Tapan K. and Krieger, Abba M. Large Sample Theory for the Bounds on the Gini and Related Indices of Inequality Estimated from Grouped Data. *J. Bus. Econ. Statist.*, April 1986, *4*(2), pp. 269–73. **[G: U.S.]**

Glymour, Clark. Statistics and Causal Inference: Comment: Statistics and Metaphysics. *J. Amer. Statist. Assoc.*, December 1986, *81*(396), pp. 964–66.

Goldstein, Michael. Separating Beliefs. **In** *[de Finetti, B.]*, 1986, pp. 197–215.

Gouriéroux, Christian and Pradel, Jacqueline. Direct Test of the Rational Expectations Hypothesis. *Europ. Econ. Rev.*, April 1986, *30*(2), pp. 265–84.

Granger, Clive W. J. Statistics and Causal Inference: Comment. *J. Amer. Statist. Assoc.*, December 1986, *81*(396), pp. 967–68.

Heckman, James J. and Singer, Burton. Econometric Analysis of Longitudinal Data. **In** *Griliches, Z. and Intriligator, M. D., eds.*, 1986, pp. 1689–1763.

Hill, Bruce M. and Lane, David. Conglomerability and Countable Additivity. **In** *[de Finetti, B.]*, 1986, pp. 45–57.

Holland, Paul W. Statistics and Causal Inference: Rejoinder. *J. Amer. Statist. Assoc.*, December 1986, *81*(396), pp. 968–70.

Holland, Paul W. Statistics and Causal Inference. *J. Amer. Statist. Assoc.*, December 1986, *81*(396), pp. 945–60.

Holt, Charles A. Scoring-Rule Procedures for Eliciting Subjective Probability and Utility Functions. **In** *[de Finetti, B.]*, 1986, pp. 279–90.

Jaynes, Edwin T. Some Applications and Extensions of the de Finetti Representation Theorem. **In** *[de Finetti, B.]*, 1986, pp. 31–42.

Kadane, Joseph B.; Schervish, Mark J. and Seidenfeld, Teddy. Statistical Implications of Finitely Additive Probability. **In** *[de Finetti, B.]*, 1986, pp. 59–76.

Katzner, Donald W. Potential Surprise, Potential Confirmation, and Probability. *J. Post Keynesian Econ.*, Fall 1986, *9*(1), pp. 58–78.

Klein, Gary, et al. Simplified Assessment of Single and Multi-attribute Utility Functions. **In** *[de Finetti, B.]*, 1986, pp. 319–34.

Kodde, David A. and Palm, F. C. Wald Criteria for Jointly Testing Equality and Inequality Restrictions. *Econometrica*, September 1986, *54*(5), pp. 1243–48.

Leamer, Edward E. Bid–Ask Spreads for Subjective Probabilities. **In** *[de Finetti, B.]*, 1986, pp. 217–32.

Leserer, Michael. Kognitive Inferenz als ökonometrische Aufgabe. Einige Bemerkungen zur ökonometrischen Grundsatzdiskussion. Cognitive Inference as an Econometric Problem: Some Remarks on the Fundamentals of Econometrics. With English summary.) *Jahr. Nationalökon. Statist.*, March 1986, *201*(2), pp. 97–106.

Lindley, Dennis V. The Relationship between the Number of Factors and Size of an Experiment. **In** *[de Finetti, B.]*, 1986, pp. 459–70.

Mazzarino, Giuseppe. Fitting of Distribution Curves to Grouped Data. *Oxford Bull. Econ. Statist.*, May 1986, *48*(2), pp. 189–200.

McAleer, Michael and Deistler, Manfred. Some Recent Developments in Econometrics. **In** *Bittanti, S., ed.*, 1986, pp. 222–43.

Mizon, Grayham E. and Richard, Jean-Francois. The Encompassing Principle and Its Application to Testing Non-nested Hypotheses. *Econometrica*, May 1986, *54*(3), pp. 657–78.

Nelder, J. A. Statistics, Science and Technology. *J. Roy. Statist. Soc.*, 1986, *149*(2), pp. 109–21.

Novàk, M. Catastrophe Theory as a Tool for Statistical Analysis of Systems. **In** *De Antoni, F.; Lauro, N. and Rizzi, A., eds.*, 1986, pp. 10–14.

Rogers, Alan J. Modified Lagrange Multiplier Tests for Problems with One-Sided Alternatives. *J. Econometrics*, April 1986, *31*(3), pp. 341–61.

Rubin, Donald B. Statistical Matching Using File Concatenation with Adjusted Weights and Multiple Imputations. *J. Bus. Econ. Statist.*, January 1986, *4*(1), pp. 87–94.

Rubin, Donald B. Statistics and Causal Inference: Comment: Which Ifs Have Causal Answers. *J. Amer. Statist. Assoc.*, December 1986, *81*(396), pp. 961–62.

Sargan, J. D. and Satchell, Stephen E. A Theorem of Validity for Edgeworth Expansions. *Econometrica*, January 1986, *54*(1), pp. 189–213.

Segal, Uzi. On Lexicographic Probability Relations. *Math. Soc. Sci.*, April 1986, *11*(2), pp. 195–99.

Sen, Ashish. Maximum Likelihood Estimation of Gravity Model Parameters. *J. Reg. Sci.*, August 1986, *26*(3), pp. 461–74.

Singh, Chatter. Random Number Generation and Some Econometric Applications. *J. Quant. Econ.*, July 1986, *2*(2), pp. 309–18.

Solon, Gary. Effects of Rotation Group Bias on Estimation of Unemployment. *J. Bus. Econ. Statist.*, January 1986, *4*(1), pp. 105–09. **[G: U.S.]**

Tsay, Ruey S. Time Series Model Specification in the Presence of Outliers. *J. Amer. Statist. Assoc.*, March 1986, *81*(393), pp. 132–41. **[G: U.K.]**

Winkler, Robert L. On "Good Probability Appraisers." **In** *[de Finetti, B.]*, 1986, pp. 265–78.

Zellner, Arnold. Basic Issues in Econometrics: Past and Present. **In** *Szenberg, M., ed.*, 1986, *1982*, pp. 95–103.

Zellner, Arnold. Bayesian Estimation and Prediction Using Asymmetric Loss Functions. *J. Amer. Statist. Assoc.*, June 1986, *81*(394), pp. 446–51.

2112 Inferential Problems in Simultaneous Equation Systems

Amemiya, Takeshi and MaCurdy, Thomas E. Instrumental-Variable Estimation of an Error-Components Model. *Econometrica*, July 1986, *54*(4), pp. 869–80.

Andrews, Donald W. K. Stability Comparisons of Estimators. *Econometrica*, September 1986, *54*(5), pp. 1207–35.

Bekker, Paul A. and Pollock, D. S. G. Identification of Linear Stochastic Models with Covariance Restrictions. *J. Econometrics*, March 1986, *31*(2), pp. 179–208.

Breusch, Trevor S. Hypothesis Testing in Unidentified Models. *Rev. Econ. Stud.*, August 1986, *53*(4), pp. 635–51.

Calzolari, Giorgio and Sterbenz, Frederic P. Control Variates to Estimate the Reduced Form Variances in Econometric Models. *Eco-*

nometrica, November 1986, *54*(6), pp. 1483–90.

Campos, Julia. Finite-Sample Properties of the Instrumental-Variables Estimator for Dynamic Simultaneous-Equation Subsystems with ARMA Disturbances. *J. Econometrics,* August 1986, *32*(3), pp. 333–66.

Erlat, Haluk. Testing for Exogeneity in Underidentified Models and Its Implication for Testing Recursiveness in Triangular Systems: A Note in Clarification. *METU,* 1986, *13*(3–4), pp. 299–305.

Evans, Lewis and Wells, Graeme. Confidence Regions for Multipliers in Linear Dynamic Models. *Econometrica,* May 1986, *54*(3), pp. 699–706.

Giannini, Carlo. Sul concetto di variabile esogena e sulla previsione condizionale. (On the Meaning of Exogenous Variables and Conditional Prediction. With English summary.) *Polit. Econ.,* August 1986, *2*(2), pp. 273–80.

Hamilton, James D. A Standard Error for the Estimated State Vector of a State-Space Model. *J. Econometrics,* December 1986, *33*(3), pp. 387–97. **[G: U.S.]**

Hensher, David A. Sequential and Full Information Maximum Likelihood Estimation of a Nested Logit Model. *Rev. Econ. Statist.,* November 1986, *68*(4), pp. 657–67. **[G: Australia]**

Jajuga, Krzysztof. On Pattern Recognition Methods in Econometric Regression Model. **In** *Pau, L. F., ed.,* 1986, pp. 167–71.

Krasker, William S. Two-Stage Bounded-Influence Estimators for Simultaneous-Equations Models. *J. Bus. Econ. Statist.,* October 1986, *4*(4), pp. 437–44. **[G: U.S.]**

Lanning, Steven G. Missing Observations: A Simultaneous Approach versus Interpolation by Related Series. *J. Econ. Soc. Meas.,* July 1986, *14*(2), pp. 155–63. **[G: U.S.]**

Maasoumi, Esfandiar. Reduced Form Estimation and Prediction from Uncertain Structural Models: A Generic Approach. *J. Econometrics,* February 1986, *31*(1), pp. 3–29.

Maddala, G. S. Disequilibrium, Self-selection, and Switching Models. **In** *Griliches, Z. and Intriligator, M. D., eds.,* 1986, pp. 1633–88.

Magnus, Jan R. The Exact Moments of a Ratio of Quadratic Forms in Normal Variables. *Ann. Écon. Statist.,* Oct./Dec. 1986, (4), pp. 95–109.

Mayer, Lawrence S. On Cross-Lagged Panel Models with Serially Correlated Errors. *J. Bus. Econ. Statist.,* July 1986, *4*(3), pp. 347–57.

Naik, Gopal and Dixon, Bruce L. A Monte Carlo Comparison of Alternative Estimators of Autocorrelated Simultaneous Systems Using A U.S. Pork Sector Model as the True Structure. *Western J. Agr. Econ.,* December 1986, *11*(2), pp. 134–45. **[G: U.S.]**

Newey, Whitney K. Linear Instrumental Variable Estimation of Limited Dependent Variable Models with Endogenous Explanatory Variables. *J. Econometrics,* June 1986, *32*(1), pp. 127–41.

Pagan, Adrian. Two Stage and Related Estimators and Their Applications. *Rev. Econ. Stud.,* August 1986, *53*(4), pp. 517–38.

Parke, William R. Two Modified FIML Estimators for Use in Small Samples. *Int. Econ. Rev.,* June 1986, *27*(2), pp. 465–81.

Phillips, P. C. B. The Distribution of FIML in the Leading Case. *Int. Econ. Rev.,* February 1986, *27*(1), pp. 239–43.

Phillips, P. C. B. The Exact Distribution of the Wald Statistic. *Econometrica,* July 1986, *54*(4), pp. 881–95.

Phillips, P. C. B. and Durlauf, S. N. Multiple Time Series Regression with Integrated Processes. *Rev. Econ. Stud.,* August 1986, *53*(4), pp. 473–95.

Quandt, Richard E. A Note on Estimating Disequilibrium Models with Aggregation. *Empirical Econ.,* 1986, *11*(4), pp. 223–42.

Ruud, Paul A. Consistent Estimation of Limited Dependent Variable Models Despite Misspecification of Distribution. *J. Econometrics,* June 1986, *32*(1), pp. 157–87.

Salemi, Michael K. Solution and Estimation of Linear Rational Expectations Models. *J. Econometrics,* February 1986, *31*(1), pp. 41–66.

Smith, Richard J. and Blundell, Richard. An Exogeneity Test for a Simultaneous Equation Tobit Model with an Application to Labor Supply. *Econometrica,* May 1986, *54*(3), pp. 679–85. **[G: U.K.]**

Stoker, Thomas M. Aggregation, Efficiency, and Cross-section Regression. *Econometrica,* January 1986, *54*(1), pp. 171–88.

Thurman, Walter N. Endogeneity Testing in a Supply and Demand Framework. *Rev. Econ. Statist.,* November 1986, *68*(4), pp. 638–46. **[G: U.S.]**

Toyoda, Toshihisa and Ohtani, Kazuhiro. Testing Equality between Sets of Coefficients after a Preliminary Test for Equality of Disturbance Variances in Two Linear Regressions. *J. Econometrics,* February 1986, *31*(1), pp. 67–80. **[G: Japan]**

Trivellato, Ugo and Rettore, Enrico. Preliminary Data Errors and Their Impact on the Forecast Error of Simultaneous-Equations Models. *J. Bus. Econ. Statist.,* October 1986, *4*(4), pp. 445–53. **[G: Italy]**

Tsurumi, Hiroki; Wago, Hajime and Ilmakunnas, Pekka. Gradual Switching Multivariate Regression Models with Stochastic Cross-Equational Constraints and an Application to the *KLEM* Translog Production Model. *J. Econometrics,* April 1986, *31*(3), pp. 235–53. **[G: Japan]**

West, Kenneth D. Full- versus Limited-Information Estimation of a Rational-Expectations Model: Some Numerical Comparisons. *J. Econometrics,* December 1986, *33*(3), pp. 367–85.

2113 Distributed Lags and Serially Correlated Disturbance Terms; Inferential Problems in Single Equation Models

Akaike, Hirotugu. The Selection of Smoothness Priors for Distributed Lag Estimation. **In** *[de*

Finetti, B.], 1986, pp. 109–18.

Anderson, Gordon J. Empirical Assessment of Present Value Relations: Comment. *Econometric Rev.*, 1986, *5*(2), pp. 235–39. **[G: U.S.]**

Anderson, Richard G. and Thursby, Jerry G. Confidence Intervals for Elasticity Estimators in Translog Models. *Rev. Econ. Statist.*, November 1986, *68*(4), pp. 647–56.

Andrews, Donald W. K. A Note on the Unbiasedness of Feasible GLS, Quasi-maximum Likelihood, Robust, Adaptive, and Spectral Estimators of the Linear Model. *Econometrica*, May 1986, *54*(3), pp. 687–98.

Andrews, Donald W. K. Stability Comparisons of Estimators. *Econometrica*, September 1986, *54*(5), pp. 1207–35.

Anselin, Luc. Non-nested Tests on the Weight Structure in Spatial Autoregressive Models: Some Monte Carlo Results. *J. Reg. Sci.*, May 1986, *26*(2), pp. 267–84.

Anselin, Luc. Some Further Notes on Spatial Models and Regional Science [Non-nested Tests on the Weight Structure in Spatial Autoregressive Models: Some Monte-Carlo Results]. *J. Reg. Sci.*, November 1986, *26*(4), pp. 799–802.

Antoch, J. Algorithmic Development in Variable Selection Procedures. **In** *De Antoni, F.; Lauro, N. and Rizzi, A., eds.*, 1986, pp. 83–90.

Arnold, Barry C. and Press, S. James. Bayesian Analysis of Censored or Grouped Data from Pareto Populations. **In** *[de Finetti, B.]*, 1986, pp. 157–73.

Baldessari, B. and Bellacicco, A. Identification of Linear Regression Models by a Clustering Algorithm. **In** *De Antoni, F.; Lauro, N. and Rizzi, A., eds.*, 1986, pp. 157–62.

Banerjee, Anindya, et al. Exploring Equilibrium Relationships in Econometrics through Static Models: Some Monte Carlo Evidence. *Oxford Bull. Econ. Statist.*, August 1986, *48*(3), pp. 253–77.

Bekker, Paul A. Identification in the Linear Errors in Variables Model: Comment. *Econometrica*, January 1986, *54*(1), pp. 215–17.

Belsley, David A. Centering, the Constant, First-Differencing, and Assessing Conditioning. **In** *Belsley, D. A. and Kuh, E., eds.*, 1986, pp. 117–53. **[G: U.S.]**

Boomsma, A. On the Use of Bootstrap and Jackknife in Covariance Structure Analysis. **In** *De Antoni, F.; Lauro, N. and Rizzi, A., eds.*, 1986, pp. 205–10.

Boothe, Paul M. and MacKinnon, James G. A Specification Test for Models Estimated by GLS. *Rev. Econ. Statist.*, November 1986, *68*(4), pp. 711–14.

Breusch, Trevor S. Hypothesis Testing in Unidentified Models. *Rev. Econ. Stud.*, August 1986, *53*(4), pp. 635–51.

Breusch, Trevor S. and Godfrey, L. G. Data Transformation Tests. *Econ. J.*, Supplement 1986, *96*, pp. 47–58.

Cameron, A. Colin and Trivedi, Pravin K. Econometric Models Based on Count Data: Comparisons and Applications of Some Estimators and Tests. *J. Appl. Econometrics*, January 1986, *1*(1), pp. 29–53.

Campbell, John Y. Empirical Assessment of Present Value Relations: Comment. *Econometric Rev.*, 1986, *5*(2), pp. 241–45.

Campos, Julia. Erratum [Instrumental Variables Estimation of Dynamic Simultaneous Systems with ARMA Errors]. *Rev. Econ. Stud.*, October 1986, *53*(5), pp. 885.

Campos, Julia. Instrumental Variables Estimation of Dynamic Simultaneous Systems with ARMA Errors. *Rev. Econ. Stud.*, January 1986, *53*(1), pp. 125–38.

Chamberlain, Gary. Asymptotic Efficiency in Semi-Parametric Models with Censoring. *J. Econometrics*, July 1986, *32*(2), pp. 189–218.

Chambers, Raymond L. Outlier Robust Finite Population Estimation. *J. Amer. Statist. Assoc.*, December 1986, *81*(396), pp. 1063–69.

Chavas, Jean-Paul and Segerson, Kathleen. Singularity and Auotregressive Disturbances in Linear Logit Models. *J. Bus. Econ. Statist.*, April 1986, *4*(2), pp. 161–69. **[G: U.S.]**

Claverie, Pierre; Szpiro, Daniel and Topol, Richard. Distributed Lag Analysis: The 'Padé z-Transform' Method. *J. Econ. Dynam. Control*, June 1986, *10*(1/2), pp. 157–61.

Conley, W. C. Comparison of Least Squares with Least Absolute Deviation Forecasting Using Simulation Techniques. **In** *De Antoni, F.; Lauro, N. and Rizzi, A., eds.*, 1986, pp. 31–36.

Cooley, Thomas F. and LeRoy, Stephen F. What Will Take the Con Out of Econometrics? A Reply [Identification and Estimation of Money Demand]. *Amer. Econ. Rev.*, June 1986, *76*(3), pp. 504–07. **[G: U.S.]**

Deistler, Manfred. Linear Errors-in-Variables Models. **In** *Bittanti, S., ed.*, 1986, pp. 37–68.

Delaney, Nancy Jo and Chatterjee, Sangit. Use of the Bootstrap and Cross-validation in Ridge Regression. *J. Bus. Econ. Statist.*, April 1986, *4*(2), pp. 255–62.

Delong, David M. Statistical Properties of Generalized Method-of-Moments Estimators of Structural Parameters Obtained from Financial Market Data: Comment. *J. Bus. Econ. Statist.*, October 1986, *4*(4), pp. 417–18.

Denteneer, D. Linear Models of Categorical Variables. **In** *De Antoni, F.; Lauro, N. and Rizzi, A., eds.*, 1986, pp. 91–96.

Dhrymes, Phoebus J. Limited Dependent Variables. **In** *Griliches, Z. and Intriligator, M. D., eds.*, 1986, pp. 1567–1631.

Doran, Howard E. and Kmenta, Jan. A Lack-of-Fit Test for Econometric Applications to Cross-Section Data. *Rev. Econ. Statist.*, May 1986, *68*(2), pp. 346–50.

Duncan, Gregory M. A Semi-parametric Censored Regression Estimator. *J. Econometrics*, June 1986, *32*(1), pp. 5–34.

Ericsson, Neil R. Post-simulation Analysis of Monte Carlo Experiments: Interpreting Pesaran's (1974) Study of Non-nested Hypothesis Test Statistics. *Rev. Econ. Stud.*, August 1986, *53*(4), pp. 691–707.

Evans, Merran Anderson. BLUF Disturbance Estimators with Quarterly Seasonal Economic Data. *J. Quant. Econ.*, January 1986, *2*(1), pp. 19–32.

Fernandez, Luis. Non-parametric Maximum Likelihood Estimation of Censored Regression Models. *J. Econometrics*, June 1986, *32*(1), pp. 35–57.

Flavin, Marjorie A. Empirical Assessment of Present Value Relations: Comment. *Econometric Rev.*, 1986, *5*(2), pp. 247–52.

Fourgeaud, Claude; Gouriéroux, Christian and Pradel, Jacqueline. Learning Procedures and Convergence to Rationality. *Econometrica*, July 1986, *54*(4), pp. 845–68.

George, Edward I. Combining Minimax Shrinkage Estimators. *J. Amer. Statist. Assoc.*, June 1986, *81*(394), pp. 437–45.

Geweke, John. Exact Inference in the Inequality Constrained Normal Linear Regression Model. *J. Appl. Econometrics*, April 1986, *1*(2), pp. 127–41.

Gilbert, Christopher L. Professor Hendry's Econometric Methodology. *Oxford Bull. Econ. Statist.*, August 1986, *48*(3), pp. 283–307.

Giles, David E. A. Missing Measurements and Estimator Inefficiency in Linear Regression: A Generalization. *J. Quant. Econ.*, January 1986, *2*(1), pp. 87–91.

Granger, Clive W. J. Developments in the Study of Cointegrated Economic Variables. *Oxford Bull. Econ. Statist.*, August 1986, *48*(3), pp. 213–28.

Granger, Clive W. J.; Robins, R. P. and Engle, Robert F. Wholesale and Retail Prices: Bivariate Time-Series Modeling with Forecastable Error Variances. **In** *Belsley, D. A. and Kuh, E., eds.*, 1986, pp. 1–17. **[G: U.S.]**

Green, M. Generalized Multiplicative Models. **In** *De Antoni, F.; Lauro, N. and Rizzi, A., eds.*, 1986, pp. 102–07.

Griffiths, William E. and Surekha, K. A Monte Carlo Evaluation of the Power of Some Tests for Heteroscedasticity. *J. Econometrics*, March 1986, *31*(2), pp. 219–31.

Griliches, Zvi. Economic Data Issues. **In** *Griliches, Z. and Intriligator, M. D., eds.*, 1986, pp. 1466–1514.

Griliches, Zvi and Hausman, Jerry A. Errors in Variables in Panel Data. *J. Econometrics*, February 1986, *31*(1), pp. 93–118. **[G: U.S.]**

Haber, Michael and Brown, Morton B. Maximum Likelihood Methods for Log-Linear Models When Expected Frequencies Are Subject to Linear Constraints. *J. Amer. Statist. Assoc.*, June 1986, *81*(394), pp. 477–82.

Haining, Robert. Spatial Models and Regional Science: A Comment on Anselin's Paper and Research Directions [Non-nested Tests on the Weight Structure in Spatial Autoregressive Models: Some Monte-Carlo Results]. *J. Reg. Sci.*, November 1986, *26*(4), pp. 793–98.

Haitovsky, Yoel. The Linear Hierarchical Model and Its Applications in Econometric Analysis. **In** *[de Finetti, B.]*, 1986, pp. 119–38.

Hansen, Lars Peter. Statistical Properties of Generalized Method-of-Moments Estimators of Structural Parameters Obtained from Financial Market Data: Comment. *J. Bus. Econ. Statist.*, October 1986, *4*(4), pp. 418–21.

Hart, Jeffrey D. and Wehrly, Thomas E. Kernel Regression Estimation Using Repeated Measurements Data. *J. Amer. Statist. Assoc.*, December 1986, *81*(396), pp. 1080–88.

Heijmans, Risto D. H. and Magnus, Jan R. Consistent Maximum-Likelihood Estimation with Dependent Observations: The General (Non-Normal) Case and the Normal Case. *J. Econometrics*, July 1986, *32*(2), pp. 253–85.

Hendry, David F. Econometric Modelling with Cointegrated Variables: An Overview. *Oxford Bull. Econ. Statist.*, August 1986, *48*(3), pp. 201–12.

Honda, Yuzo and Ohtani, Kazuhiro. Modified Wald Tests in Tests of Equality between Sets of Coefficients in Two Linear Regressions under Heteroscedasticity. *Manchester Sch. Econ. Soc. Stud.*, June 1986, *54*(2), pp. 208–18.

Hoque, Asraul; Kataoka, Yusaku and Miyashita, Hiroshi. The Exact Moments of Ordinary Least Squares Estimators for Koyck Distributed Lag Models. *Int. Econ. Rev.*, February 1986, *27*(1), pp. 245–60.

Horowitz, Joel L. A Distribution-Free Least Squares Estimator for Censored Linear Regression Models. *J. Econometrics*, June 1986, *32*(1), pp. 59–84.

Huet, S. and Messéan, A. NL: A Statistical Package for General Nonlinear Regression Problems. **In** *De Antoni, F.; Lauro, N. and Rizzi, A., eds.*, 1986, pp. 326–31.

Hwang, Jiunn T. Multiplicative Errors-in-Variables Models with Applications to Recent Data Released by the U.S. Department of Energy. *J. Amer. Statist. Assoc.*, September 1986, *81*(395), pp. 680–88. **[G: U.S.]**

Kadiyala, Krishna. MSE Properties of Operational Weighted Average Estimator. *J. Quant. Econ.*, January 1986, *2*(1), pp. 77–86.

Kennedy, Peter. Interpreting Dummy Variables. *Rev. Econ. Statist.*, February 1986, *68*(1), pp. 174–75.

King, Maxwell L. Efficient Estimation and Testing of Regressions with a Serially Correlated Error Component. *J. Quant. Econ.*, July 1986, *2*(2), pp. 231–47.

King, Maxwell L. and Evans, Merran Anderson. Testing for Block Effects in Regression Models Based on Survey Data. *J. Amer. Statist. Assoc.*, September 1986, *81*(395), pp. 677–79.

King, Maxwell L. and Smith, Murray D. Joint One-Sided Tests of Linear Regression Coefficients. *J. Econometrics*, August 1986, *32*(3), pp. 367–83.

Kiviet, Jan F. On the Rigour of Some Misspecification Tests for Modelling Dynamic Relationships. *Rev. Econ. Stud.*, April 1986, *53*(2), pp. 241–61.

Kobayashi, Masahito. A Bounds Test of Equality between Sets of Coefficients in Two Linear Regressions When Disturbance Variances Are

Unequal. *J. Amer. Statist. Assoc.*, June 1986, *81*(394), pp. 510–13.

Krämer, Walter. Least Squares Regression When the Independent Variable Follows an ARIMA Process. *J. Amer. Statist. Assoc.*, March 1986, *81*(393), pp. 150–54.

Krämer, Walter and Sonnberger, Harald. Computational Pitfalls of the Hausman Test. *J. Econ. Dynam. Control*, June 1986, *10*(1/2), pp. 163–65.

Krasker, William S. and Pratt, John W. Bounding the Effects of Proxy Variables on Regression Coefficients. *Econometrica*, May 1986, *54*(3), pp. 641–55.

Kredler, C. and Kowarschick, W. A Convenient Way of Computing ML-Estimates: Use of Automatic Differentiation. **In** *De Antoni, F.; Lauro, N. and Rizzi, A., eds.*, 1986, pp. 108–13.

Kuh, Edwin and Samarov, A. Robust Recursive Estimation and Detection of Shifts in Regression. **In** *De Antoni, F.; Lauro, N. and Rizzi, A., eds.*, 1986, pp. 217–22.

Lancaster, Tony and Chesher, Andrew. Erratum [Residuals Tests and Plots with a Job Matching Illustration]. *Ann. Écon. Statist.*, Apr./June 1986, (2), pp. 171.

Lanning, Steven G. Missing Observations: A Simultaneous Approach versus Interpolation by Related Series. *J. Econ. Soc. Meas.*, July 1986, *14*(2), pp. 155–63. **[G: U.S.]**

Lee, Lung-Fei. Specification Test for Poisson Regression Models. *Int. Econ. Rev.*, October 1986, *27*(3), pp. 689–706.

Lee, Lung-Fei and Chesher, Andrew. Specification Testing When Score Test Statistics Are Identically Zero. *J. Econometrics*, March 1986, *31*(2), pp. 121–49.

Levine, David K. Reverse Regressions for Latent-Variable Models. *J. Econometrics*, July 1986, *32*(2), pp. 291–92.

Lo, Andrew W. Logit versus Discriminant Analysis: A Specification Test and Application to Corporate Bankruptcies. *J. Econometrics*, March 1986, *31*(2), pp. 151–78. **[G: U.S.]**

Longford, N. Variance Components as a Method for Routine Regression Analysis of Survey Data. **In** *De Antoni, F.; Lauro, N. and Rizzi, A., eds.*, 1986, pp. 69–74.

Maasoumi, Esfandiar. Reduced Form Estimation and Prediction from Uncertain Structural Models: A Generic Approach. *J. Econometrics*, February 1986, *31*(1), pp. 3–29.

Maddala, G. S. Disequilibrium, Self-selection, and Switching Models. **In** *Griliches, Z. and Intriligator, M. D., eds.*, 1986, pp. 1633–88.

Magnus, Jan R. The Exact Moments of a Ratio of Quadratic Forms in Normal Variables. *Ann. Écon. Statist.*, Oct./Dec. 1986, (4), pp. 95–109.

Manski, Charles F. Semiparametric Analysis of Binary Response from Response-Based Samples. *J. Econometrics*, February 1986, *31*(1), pp. 31–40.

Manski, Charles F. and Thompson, T. Scott. Operational Characteristics of Maximum Score Estimation. *J. Econometrics*, June 1986, *32*(1), pp. 85–108.

Marazzi, A. On the Numerical Solutions of Bounded Influence Regression Problems. **In** *De Antoni, F.; Lauro, N. and Rizzi, A., eds.*, 1986, pp. 114–19.

Mattey, Joe and Meese, Richard. Empirical Assessment of Present Value Relations: Rejoinder. *Econometric Rev.*, 1986, *5*(2), pp. 279–85. **[G: U.S.]**

Mattey, Joe and Meese, Richard. Empirical Assessment of Present Value Relations. *Econometric Rev.*, 1986, *5*(2), pp. 171–234. **[G: U.S.]**

McAleer, Michael; Pagan, Adrian and Visco, Ignazio. A Further Result on the Sign of Restricted Least-Squares Estimates. *J. Econometrics*, July 1986, *32*(2), pp. 287–90.

Mitchell, Douglas W. and Speaker, Paul J. A Simple, Flexible Distributed Lag Technique: The Polynomial Inverse Lag. *J. Econometrics*, April 1986, *31*(3), pp. 329–40.

Miyashita, Hiroshi. Monte Carlo Studies on a Linear Model with Autocorrelated Error Terms. *Econ. Stud. Quart.*, September 1986, *37*(3), pp. 248–58.

Miyazaki, Shigetaka; Judge, George and Yancey, Thomas. Estimation of Location Parameters under Nonnormal Errors and Quadratic Loss. *J. Bus. Econ. Statist.*, April 1986, *4*(2), pp. 263–68. **[G: U.S.]**

Modica, Salvatore. Linear Approximation and Test of Linearity for a Particular Regression Model. *Statistica*, Jan.-Mar. 1986, *46*(1), pp. 93–97.

Montmarquette, Claude and Houle, Rachel. An Empirical Note on Selectivity Bias in Educational Production Functions. *J. Econ. Educ.*, Spring 1986, *17*(2), pp. 99–105. **[G: Canada]**

Morgenthaler, S. and Vardi, Y. Choice-Based Samples: A Non-parametric Approach. *J. Econometrics*, June 1986, *32*(1), pp. 109–25.

Moulton, Brent R. Random Group Effects and the Precision of Regression Estimates. *J. Econometrics*, August 1986, *32*(3), pp. 385–97. **[G: U.S.]**

Mullahy, John. Specification and Testing of Some Modified Count Data Models. *J. Econometrics*, December 1986, *33*(3), pp. 341–65. **[G: U.S.]**

Newey, Whitney K. Linear Instrumental Variable Estimation of Limited Dependent Variable Models with Endogenous Explanatory Variables. *J. Econometrics*, June 1986, *32*(1), pp. 127–41.

Ohtani, Kazuhiro. The Compatibility Bounds Test in Mixed Regression. *Econ. Stud. Quart.*, September 1986, *37*(3), pp. 242–47.

Onukogu, Ike B. Analysis of Nonlinear Regression Models with Cubic Spline Functions: A Systematic Approach. *Statistica*, Jan.-Mar. 1986, *46*(1), pp. 83–91.

Orme, Chris. A Simple Correction for Local Misspecification. *Bull. Econ. Res.*, May 1986, *38*(2), pp. 177–81.

Peixoto, Julio L. and Harville, David A. Comparisons of Alternative Predictors under the Balanced One-Way Random Model. *J. Amer. Statist. Assoc.*, June 1986, *81*(394), pp. 431–36.

Phillips, P. C. B. The Exact Distribution of the Wald Statistic. *Econometrica*, July 1986, *54*(4), pp. 881–95.

Phillips, P. C. B. Understanding Spurious Regressions in Econometrics. *J. Econometrics*, December 1986, *33*(3), pp. 311–40.

Pierce, Donald A. and Schafer, Daniel W. Residuals in Generalized Linear Models. *J. Amer. Statist. Assoc.*, December 1986, *81*(396), pp. 977–86.

Pinckney, Thomas C. and Gnaegy, Suzanne. Exponential versus Linear Trends: Which Is the Best Fit? *Pakistan Econ. Soc. Rev.*, Winter 1986, *24*(2), pp. 77–81.

Poirier, Dale J.; Tello, Mario D. and Zin, Stanley E. A Diagnostic Test for Normality within the Power Exponential Family. *J. Bus. Econ. Statist.*, July 1986, *4*(3), pp. 359–53.

Pötscher, Benedikt M. and Prucha, Ingmar R. A Class of Partially Adaptive One-Step *M*-Estimators for the Non-linear Regression Model with Dependent Observations. *J. Econometrics*, July 1986, *32*(2), pp. 219–51.

Powell, James L. Censored Regression Quantiles. *J. Econometrics*, June 1986, *32*(1), pp. 143–55.

Powell, James L. Symmetrically Trimmed Least Squares Estimation for Tobit Models. *Econometrica*, November 1986, *54*(6), pp. 1435–60.

Reichert, Alan K. and Moore, James S. Using Latent Root Regression to Identify Nonpredictive Collinearity in Statistical Appraisal Models. *Amer. Real Estate Urban Econ. Assoc. J.*, Spring 1986, *14*(1), pp. 136–52. **[G: U.S.]**

Robinson, P. M. Nonparametric Methods in Specification. *Econ. J.*, Supplement 1986, *96*, pp. 134–41.

Rossi, Peter E. Statistical Properties of Generalized Method-of-Moments Estimators of Structural Parameters Obtained from Financial Market Data: Comment. *J. Bus. Econ. Statist.*, October 1986, *4*(4), pp. 421–22.

Rukhin, Andrew L. Improved Estimation in Lognormal Models. *J. Amer. Statist. Assoc.*, December 1986, *81*(396), pp. 1046–49.

Ruud, Paul A. Consistent Estimation of Limited Dependent Variable Models Despite Misspecification of Distribution. *J. Econometrics*, June 1986, *32*(1), pp. 157–87.

San Martini, Aristide and Spezzaferri, Fulvio. Selection of Variables in Multiple Regression for Prediction and Control. *Statistica*, Jan.-Mar. 1986, *46*(1), pp. 117–28.

Schafer, Daniel W. Combining Information on Measurement Error in the Errors-in-Variables Model. *J. Amer. Statist. Assoc.*, March 1986, *81*(393), pp. 181–85.

Simon, Gary A. and Simonoff, Jeffrey S. Diagnostic Plots for Missing Data in Least Squares Regression. *J. Amer. Statist. Assoc.*, June 1986, *81*(394), pp. 501–09.

Srivastava, V. K. and Misra, G. D. Efficiency of an OGLS Estimator in Seemingly Unrelated Regression Equations with Constrained Covariance Structures. *J. Quant. Econ.*, July 1986, *2*(2), pp. 221–30.

Stoker, Thomas M. Aggregation, Efficiency, and Cross-section Regression. *Econometrica*, January 1986, *54*(1), pp. 171–88.

Stoker, Thomas M. Consistent Estimation of Scaled Coefficients. *Econometrica*, November 1986, *54*(6), pp. 1461–81.

Tauchen, George. Statistical Properties of Generalized Method-of-Moments Estimators of Structural Parameters Obtained from Financial Market Data: Reply. *J. Bus. Econ. Statist.*, October 1986, *4*(4), pp. 423–25.

Tauchen, George. Statistical Properties of Generalized Method-of-Moments Estimators of Structural Parameters Obtained from Financial Market Data. *J. Bus. Econ. Statist.*, October 1986, *4*(4), pp. 397–416. **[G: U.S.]**

Toyoda, Toshihisa and Ohtani, Kazuhiro. Testing Equality between Sets of Coefficients after a Preliminary Test for Equality of Disturbance Variances in Two Linear Regressions. *J. Econometrics*, February 1986, *31*(1), pp. 67–80. **[G: Japan]**

Ullah, A.; Vinod, H. D. and Singh, R. S. Estimation of Linear Models with Moving Average Disturbances. *J. Quant. Econ.*, January 1986, *2*(1), pp. 137–52.

West, Kenneth D. Empirical Assessment of Present Value Relations: Comment. *Econometric Rev.*, 1986, *5*(2), pp. 273–78. **[G: U.S.]**

Williams, Michael A. An Economic Application of Bootstrap Statistical Methods: *Addyston Pipe* Revisited. *Amer. Econ.*, Fall 1986, *30*(2), pp. 52–58. **[G: U.S.]**

2114 Multivariate Analysis, Statistical Information Theory, and Other Special Inferential Problems; Queuing Theory; Markov Chains

Boley, Daniel and Bittanti, Sergio. Numerical Problems in Linear System Theory. **In** *Bittanti, S., ed.*, 1986, pp. 183–221.

Bouissou, Michel B.; Laffont, Jean-Jacques and Vuong, Quang H. Tests of Noncausality under Markov Assumptions for Qualitative Panel Data. *Econometrica*, March 1986, *54*(2), pp. 395–414. **[G: France]**

Brown, Philip J. and Payne, Clive D. Aggregate Data, Ecological Regression, and Voting Transitions. *J. Amer. Statist. Assoc.*, June 1986, *81*(394), pp. 452–60. **[G: U.K.]**

Bumb, Balu. A Note on Variables and Observations in Factor Analysis: A Reply. *J. Devel. Econ.*, November 1986, *24*(1), pp. 197–200.

Celeux, G. Validity Tests in Cluster Analysis Using a Probabilistic Teacher Algorithm. **In** *De Antoni, F.; Lauro, N. and Rizzi, A., eds.*, 1986, pp. 163–68.

Dambroise, E. and Massotte, P. MUSE: An Expert System in Statistics. **In** *De Antoni, F.; Lauro, N. and Rizzi, A., eds.*, 1986, pp. 271–76.

Diday, E. New Kinds of Graphical Representation

in Clustering. **In** *De Antoni, F.; Lauro, N. and Rizzi, A., eds.*, 1986, pp. 169–75.

Dobrić, V. On a Class of Robust Methods for Multivariate Data Analysis. **In** *De Antoni, F.; Lauro, N. and Rizzi, A., eds.*, 1986, pp. 211–16.

Geweke, John; Marshall, Robert C. and Zarkin, Gary A. Exact Inference for Continuous Time Markov Chain Models. *Rev. Econ. Stud.*, August 1986, *53*(4), pp. 653–69.

Geweke, John; Marshall, Robert C. and Zarkin, Gary A. Mobility Indices in Continuous Time Markov Chains. *Econometrica*, November 1986, *54*(6), pp. 1407–23.

Gilula, Zvi and Haberman, Shelby J. Canonical Analysis of Contingency Tables by Maximum Likelihood. *J. Amer. Statist. Assoc.*, September 1986, *81*(395), pp. 780–88.

Lbov, G. S. Algorithm and Software of Multivariate Statistical Analysis of Heterogeneous Data. **In** *De Antoni, F.; Lauro, N. and Rizzi, A., eds.*, 1986, pp. 498–503.

Lo, Andrew W. Logit versus Discriminant Analysis: A Specification Test and Application to Corporate Bankruptcies. *J. Econometrics*, March 1986, *31*(2), pp. 151–78. **[G: U.S.]**

Marcotorchino, F. Cross Association Measures and Optimal Clustering. **In** *De Antoni, F.; Lauro, N. and Rizzi, A., eds.*, 1986, pp. 188–94.

Mayer, Lawrence S. On Cross-Lagged Panel Models with Serially Correlated Errors. *J. Bus. Econ. Statist.*, July 1986, *4*(3), pp. 347–57.

Murrell, Peter. A Note on Variables and Observations in Factor Analysis. *J. Devel. Econ.*, May 1986, *21*(2), pp. 319–25.

Shapiro, Alexander. Asymptotic Theory of Overparameterized Structural Models. *J. Amer. Statist. Assoc.*, March 1986, *81*(393), pp. 142–49.

Skinner, C. J.; Holmes, D. J. and Smith, T. M. F. The Effect of Sample Design on Principal Component Analysis. *J. Amer. Statist. Assoc.*, September 1986, *81*(395), pp. 789–98. **[G: U.K.]**

Srivastava, M. S. and Worsley, K. J. Likelihood Ratio Tests for a Change in the Multivariate Normal Mean. *J. Amer. Statist. Assoc.*, March 1986, *81*(393), pp. 199–204.

Tarumi, T. and Tanaka, Y. Statistical Software SAM—Sensitivity Analysis in Multivariate Methods. **In** *De Antoni, F.; Lauro, N. and Rizzi, A., eds.*, 1986, pp. 351–56.

2115 Bayesian Statistics and Bayesian Econometrics

Akaike, Hirotugu. The Selection of Smoothness Priors for Distributed Lag Estimation. **In** *[de Finetti, B.]*, 1986, pp. 109–18.

Arnold, Barry C. and Press, S. James. Bayesian Analysis of Censored or Grouped Data from Pareto Populations. **In** *[de Finetti, B.]*, 1986, pp. 157–73.

Berger, James. Bayesian Salesmanship. **In** *[de Finetti, B.]*, 1986, pp. 473–88.

Broemeling, Lyle D. and Shaarawy, Samir. A Bayesian Analysis of Time Series. **In** *[de Finetti, B.]*, 1986, pp. 337–54.

Chen, Chan-fu. A Bayesian Approach to Nested Missing-Data Problems. **In** *[de Finetti, B.]*, 1986, pp. 355–61.

Chiu, H. Y. and Sedransk, J. A Bayesian Procedure for Imputing Missing Values in Sample Surveys. *J. Amer. Statist. Assoc.*, September 1986, *81*(395), pp. 667–76.

Florens, Jean-Pierre and Mouchart, Michel. Exhaustivité, ancillarité et identification en statistique bayesienne. (Sufficiency, Ancillarity and Identification in Bayesian Statistics. With English summary.) *Ann. Écon. Statist.*, Oct./Dec. 1986, (4), pp. 63–93.

Geweke, John; Marshall, Robert C. and Zarkin, Gary A. Exact Inference for Continuous Time Markov Chain Models. *Rev. Econ. Stud.*, August 1986, *53*(4), pp. 653–69.

Goel, Prem K. Bayesian Inference and Decision Techniques: Essays in Honor of Bruno de Finetti: Introduction. **In** *[de Finetti, B.]*, 1986, pp. 1–9.

Kadiyala, K. Rao and Oberhelman, H. Dennis. Estimation of Actual Realizations in Stochastic Parameter Models. **In** *[de Finetti, B.]*, 1986, pp. 363–73. **[G: U.S.]**

Piccinato, Ludovico. De Finetti's Logic of Uncertainty and Its Impact on Statistical Thinking and Practice. **In** *[de Finetti, B.]*, 1986, pp. 13–30.

Polasek, Wolfgang. Local Sensitivity Analysis and Bayesian Regression Diagnostics. **In** *[de Finetti, B.]*, 1986, pp. 375–87. **[G: Austria; U.S.]**

Rust, Roland T. and Schmittlein, David. A Bayesian Cross-validated Likelihood Method for Comparing Alternative Specifications of Quantitative Models. *Marketing Sci.*, Winter 1986, *5*(1), pp. 89.

Shubik, Martin. Games with Perceptive Commanders but with Indoctrinated or Less Perceptive Subordinates. **In** *[Rapoport, A.]*, 1986, pp. 209–22.

Thompson, Patrick A. and Miller, Robert B. Sampling the Future: A Bayesian Approach to Forecasting from Univariate Time Series Models. *J. Bus. Econ. Statist.*, October 1986, *4*(4), pp. 427–36. **[G: U.S.]**

Zellner, Arnold. A Tale of Forecasting 1001 Series: The Bayesian Knight Strikes Again. *Int. J. Forecasting*, 1986, *2*(4), pp. 491–94.

Zellner, Arnold. Bayesian Estimation and Prediction Using Asymmetric Loss Functions. *J. Amer. Statist. Assoc.*, June 1986, *81*(394), pp. 446–51.

Zellner, Arnold. On Assessing Prior Distributions and Bayesian Regression Analysis with *g*-Prior Distributions. **In** *[de Finetti, B.]*, 1986, pp. 233–43.

2116 Time Series and Spectral Analysis

Aoki, Masanao and Havenner, Arthur. Approximate State Space Models of Some Vector-

Valued Macroeconomic Time Series for Cross-Country Comparisons. *J. Econ. Dynam. Control,* June 1986, *10*(1/2), pp. 149–55. **[G: U.K.; W. Germany; Japan]**

Ashley, Richard A. and Vaughan, David. Measuring Measurement Error in Economic Time Series. *J. Bus. Econ. Statist.*, January 1986, *4*(1), pp. 95–103. **[G: U.S.]**

Balacco, Hugo Roberto. Algunas Consideraciones Sobre la Definición de Causalidad de Granger en el Analisis Econométrico. (Some Considerations on the Limits of Granger's Definition of Causality. With English summary.) *Económica (La Plata),* July-December 1986, *32*(2), pp. 207–25.

Banerjee, Anindya, et al. Exploring Equilibrium Relationships in Econometrics through Static Models: Some Monte Carlo Evidence. *Oxford Bull. Econ. Statist.*, August 1986, *48*(3), pp. 253–77.

Battaglia, Francesco. Recursive Estimation of the Inverse Correlation Function. *Statistica,* Jan.-Mar. 1986, *46*(1), pp. 75–82.

Bhargava, Alok. On the Theory of Testing for Unit Roots in Observed Time Series. *Rev. Econ. Stud.*, July 1986, *53*(3), pp. 369–84.

Bittanti, Sergio. Deterministic and Stochastic Linear Periodic Systems. **In** *Bittanti, S., ed.*, 1986, pp. 141–82.

Bollerslev, Tim. Generalized Autoregressive Conditional Heteroskedasticity. *J. Econometrics,* April 1986, *31*(3), pp. 307–27.

Brock, William A. Distinguishing Random and Deterministic Systems: Abridged Version. *J. Econ. Theory,* October 1986, *40*(1), pp. 168–95. **[G: U.S.]**

Broemeling, Lyle D. and Shaarawy, Samir. A Bayesian Analysis of Time Series. **In** *[de Finetti, B.],* 1986, pp. 337–54.

Bustos, Oscar H. and Yohai, Victor J. Robust Estimates for ARMA Models. *J. Amer. Statist. Assoc.*, March 1986, *81*(393), pp. 155–68.

Campos, Julia. Erratum [Instrumental Variables Estimation of Dynamic Simultaneous Systems with ARMA Errors]. *Rev. Econ. Stud.*, October 1986, *53*(5), pp. 885.

Campos, Julia. Finite-Sample Properties of the Instrumental-Variables Estimator for Dynamic Simultaneous-Equation Subsystems with ARMA Disturbances. *J. Econometrics,* August 1986, *32*(3), pp. 333–66.

Campos, Julia. Instrumental Variables Estimation of Dynamic Simultaneous Systems with ARMA Errors. *Rev. Econ. Stud.*, January 1986, *53*(1), pp. 125–38.

Cholette, Pierre A. and Lamy, Robert. Multivariate ARIMA Forecasting of Irregular Time Series. *Int. J. Forecasting,* 1986, *2*(2), pp. 201–16. **[G: Canada]**

Chowdhury, Abdur R. Vector Autoregression as an Alternative Macro-Modelling Technique. *Bangladesh Devel. Stud.*, June 1986, *14*(2), pp. 21–32.

Cupingood, Leonard A. and Wei, William W. S. Seasonal Adjustment of Time Series Using One-Sided Filters. *J. Bus. Econ. Statist.*, October 1986, *4*(4), pp. 473–84. **[G: U.S.]**

Deistler, Manfred. Linear Errors-in-Variables Models. **In** *Bittanti, S., ed.*, 1986, pp. 37–68.

Diebold, Francis X. Modeling the Persistence of Conditional Variances: A Comment. *Econometric Rev.*, 1986, *5*(1), pp. 51–56.

Engle, Robert F. and Bollerslev, Tim. Modelling the Persistence of Conditional Variances. *Econometric Rev.*, 1986, *5*(1), pp. 1–50. **[G: U.S.; Switzerland]**

Engle, Robert F. and Bollerslev, Tim. Modelling the Persistence of Conditional Variances: Reply. *Econometric Rev.*, 1986, *5*(1), pp. 81–87.

Evans, George W. and Honkapohja, Seppo. A Complete Characterization of ARMA Solutions to Linear Rational Expectations Models. *Rev. Econ. Stud.*, April 1986, *53*(2), pp. 227–39.

Evans, Lewis and Wells, Graeme. Confidence Regions for Multipliers in Linear Dynamic Models. *Econometrica,* May 1986, *54*(3), pp. 699–706.

Evans, Merran Anderson. BLUF Disturbance Estimators with Quarterly Seasonal Economic Data. *J. Quant. Econ.*, January 1986, *2*(1), pp. 19–32.

Fackler, James S. and Krieger, Sandra C. An Application of Vector Time Series Techniques to Macroeconomic Forecasting. *J. Bus. Econ. Statist.*, January 1986, *4*(1), pp. 71–80. **[G: U.S.]**

Findley, David F. and Monsell, Brian C. New Techniques for Determining if a Time Series Can Be Seasonally Adjusted Reliably. **In** *Perryman, M. R. and Schmidt, J. R., eds.*, 1986, pp. 195–228. **[G: U.S.]**

Geweke, John. Modelling the Persistence of Conditional Variances: Comment. *Econometric Rev.*, 1986, *5*(1), pp. 57–61.

Geweke, John. The Superneutrality of Money in the United States: An Interpretation of the Evidence. *Econometrica,* January 1986, *54*(1), pp. 1–21. **[G: U.S.]**

Gilbert, Christopher L. Professor Hendry's Econometric Methodology. *Oxford Bull. Econ. Statist.*, August 1986, *48*(3), pp. 283–307.

Granger, Clive W. J. Developments in the Study of Cointegrated Economic Variables. *Oxford Bull. Econ. Statist.*, August 1986, *48*(3), pp. 213–28.

Granger, Clive W. J.; Robins, R. P. and Engle, Robert F. Wholesale and Retail Prices: Bivariate Time-Series Modeling with Forecastable Error Variances. **In** *Belsley, D. A. and Kuh, E., eds.*, 1986, pp. 1–17. **[G: U.S.]**

Gray, H. L. and Woodward, Wayne A. A New ARMA Spectral Estimator. *J. Amer. Statist. Assoc.*, December 1986, *81*(396), pp. 1100–1108.

Hamilton, James D. A Standard Error for the Estimated State Vector of a State-Space Model. *J. Econometrics,* December 1986, *33*(3), pp. 387–97. **[G: U.S.]**

Hamilton, James D. On Testing for Self-fulfilling Speculative Price Bubbles. *Int. Econ. Rev.*, October 1986, *27*(3), pp. 545–52.

Hannan, E. J. Time Series and Stochastic Models.

In *Bittanti, S., ed.*, 1986, pp. 1–36.

Hendry, David F. An Excursion into Conditional Varianceland [Modelling the Persistence of Conditional Variances]. *Econometric Rev.*, 1986, *5*(1), pp. 63–69.

Hendry, David F. Econometric Modelling with Cointegrated Variables: An Overview. *Oxford Bull. Econ. Statist.*, August 1986, *48*(3), pp. 201–12.

Hietala, P. How to Assist an Inexperienced User in the Preliminary Analysis of Time Series: First Version of the ESTES Expert System. **In** *De Antoni, F.; Lauro, N. and Rizzi, A., eds.*, 1986, pp. 295–300.

van der Hoeven, W. H. M. and Hundepool, A. J. A Method for Seasonally Adjusted Time Series with Variation in the Seasonal Amplitude. *J. Bus. Econ. Statist.*, October 1986, *4*(4), pp. 455–71. **[G: Netherlands]**

Huot, Guy, et al. Analysis of Revisions in the Seasonal Adjustment of Data Using X-11-ARIMA Model-Based Filters. *Int. J. Forecasting*, 1986, *2*(2), pp. 217–29. **[G: Canada]**

Kaergård, Niels and Milhøj, Anders. Årsag og virkning i økonomien—en oversigt. (Causality and Exogeneity in Economics—A Survey Article. With English summary.) *Nationaløkon. Tidsskr.*, 1986, *124*(1), pp. 1–14.

Kang, Heejoon. Univariate ARIMA Forecasts of Defined Variables. *J. Bus. Econ. Statist.*, January 1986, *4*(1), pp. 81–86. **[G: U.S.]**

Kinal, Terrence and Ratner, Jonathan. A VAR Forecasting Model of a Regional Economy: Its Construction and Comparative Accuracy. *Int. Reg. Sci. Rev.*, August 1986, *10*(2), pp. 113–26. **[G: U.S.]**

Koch, Paul D. and Yang, Shie-Shien. A Method for Testing the Independence of Two Time Series That Accounts for a Potential Pattern in the Cross-Correlation Function. *J. Amer. Statist. Assoc.*, June 1986, *81*(394), pp. 533–44.

Kohn, Robert and Ansley, Craig F. Estimation, Prediction, and Interpolation for ARIMA Models with Missing Data. *J. Amer. Statist. Assoc.*, September 1986, *81*(395), pp. 751–61.

Krämer, Walter. Least Squares Regression When the Independent Variable Follows an ARIMA Process. *J. Amer. Statist. Assoc.*, March 1986, *81*(393), pp. 150–54.

Kunst, Robert and Neusser, Klaus. A Forecasting Comparison of Some VAR Techniques. *Int. J. Forecasting*, 1986, *2*(4), pp. 447–56. **[G: Austria]**

Kunst, Robert and Neusser, Klaus. Forecasting with Vector Autoregressive Models: An Empirical Investigation for Austria. *Empirica*, 1986, *13*(2), pp. 187–202. **[G: Austria]**

Layton, Allan P.; Defris, Lorraine V. and Zehnwirth, Ben. An International Comparison of Economic Leading Indicators of Telecommunications Traffic. *Int. J. Forecasting*, 1986, *2*(4), pp. 413–25. **[G: Australia; U.S.]**

Le Van, Cuong. Stationary Uncertainty Frontiers in Macroeconometric Models: An Approach for Solving Matrix Riccati Equations. *J. Econ. Dynam. Control*, June 1986, *10*(1/2), pp. 225–29.

Levy, E. and Nobay, A. R. The Speculative Efficiency Hypothesis: A Bivariate Analysis. *Econ. J.*, Supplement 1986, *96*, pp. 109–21.

Litterman, Robert B. Forecasting with Bayesian Vector Autoregressions—Five Years of Experience. *J. Bus. Econ. Statist.*, January 1986, *4*(1), pp. 25–38. **[G: U.S.]**

Litterman, Robert B. Specifying Vector Autoregressions for Macroeconomic Forecasting. **In** *[de Finetti, B.]*, 1986, pp. 79–94. **[G: U.S.]**

Liu, Lon-Mu. Identification of Time Series Models in the Presence of Calender Variation. *Int. J. Forecasting*, 1986, *2*(3), pp. 357–72. **[G: U.S.; Taiwan]**

Lupoletti, William M. and Webb, Roy H. Defining and Improving the Accuracy of Macroeconomic Forecasts: Contributions from a VAR Model. *J. Bus.*, Part 1, April 1986, *59*(2), pp. 263–85. **[G: U.S.]**

Lütkepohl, Helmut. Forecasting Vector ARMA Processes with Systematically Missing Observations. *J. Bus. Econ. Statist.*, July 1986, *4*(3), pp. 375–90.

Mack, Michael E. Efficiencies of Weighted Averages in Stationary Autoregressive Processes. *J. Amer. Statist. Assoc.*, September 1986, *81*(395), pp. 730–35.

Maravall, Agustin. An Application of Model-Based Estimation of Unobserved Components. *Int. J. Forecasting*, 1986, *2*(3), pp. 305–18. **[G: Spain]**

Maravall, Agustin. Revisions in ARIMA Signal Extraction. *J. Amer. Statist. Assoc.*, September 1986, *81*(395), pp. 736–40.

Maravall, Agustin and Pierce, David A. The Transmission of Data Noise into Policy Noise in U.S. Monetary Control. *Econometrica*, July 1986, *54*(4), pp. 961–79. **[G: U.S.]**

McCallum, Bennett T. Estimating the Long-run Relationship between Interest Rates and Inflation: A Reply. *J. Monet. Econ.*, July 1986, *18*(1), pp. 87–90.

McKenzie, Ed. Error Analysis for Winters' Additive Seasonal Forecasting System. *Int. J. Forecasting*, 1986, *2*(3), pp. 373–82.

Miyashita, Hiroshi. Monte Carlo Studies on a Linear Model with Autocorrelated Error Terms. *Econ. Stud. Quart.*, September 1986, *37*(3), pp. 248–58.

Molinas, César. A Note on Spurious Regressions with Integrated Moving Average Errors. *Oxford Bull. Econ. Statist.*, August 1986, *48*(3), pp. 379–82.

Nijman, T. E. and Palm, F. C. The Construction and Use of Approximations for Missing Quarterly Observations: A Model-based Approach. *J. Bus. Econ. Statist.*, January 1986, *4*(1), pp. 47–58. **[G: Netherlands]**

Nyblom, Jukka. Testing for Deterministic Linear Trend in Time Series. *J. Amer. Statist. Assoc.*, June 1986, *81*(394), pp. 545–49.

Öller, Lars-Erik. A Note on Exponentially Smoothed Seasonal Differences. *J. Bus. Econ. Statist.*, October 1986, *4*(4), pp. 485–89. **[G: U.S.]**

Pagan, Adrian. Two Stage and Related Estimators

and Their Applications. *Rev. Econ. Stud.*, August 1986, *53*(4), pp. 517–38.

Pantula, Sastry G. Modelling the Persistence of Conditional Variances: Comment. *Econometric Rev.*, 1986, *5*(1), pp. 71–74.

Phillips, P. C. B. Understanding Spurious Regressions in Econometrics. *J. Econometrics*, December 1986, *33*(3), pp. 311–40.

Phillips, P. C. B. and Durlauf, S. N. Multiple Time Series Regression with Integrated Processes. *Rev. Econ. Stud.*, August 1986, *53*(4), pp. 473–95.

Picci, Giorgio and Pinzoni, Stefano. A New Class of Dynamic Models for Stationary Time Series. **In** *Bittanti, S., ed.*, 1986, pp. 69–114.

Pikkarainen, Pentti and Virén, Matti. Mitä erilaiset kokonaistuotannon trendipoikkeamat kuvaavat? (How to Interpret Various Trend Models. With English summary.) *Liiketaloudellinen Aikak.*, 1986, *35*(3), pp. 236–49. **[G: Selected Countries]**

Rissanen, Jorma. Predictive and Nonpredictive Minimum Description Length Principles. **In** *Bittanti, S., ed.*, 1986, pp. 115–40.

Rowley, Robin and Jain, Renuka. Sims on Causality: An Illustration of Soft Econometrics. *Scot. J. Polit. Econ.*, May 1986, *33*(2), pp. 171–81.

Salemi, Michael K. Solution and Estimation of Linear Rational Expectations Models. *J. Econometrics*, February 1986, *31*(1), pp. 41–66.

Scarani, C. An Efficient Algorithm for Time Series Decomposition. **In** *De Antoni, F.; Lauro, N. and Rizzi, A., eds.*, 1986, pp. 399–404.

Schmidt, James R. A General Framework for Interpolation, Distribution, and Extrapolation of a Time Series by Related Series. **In** *Perryman, M. R. and Schmidt, J. R., eds.*, 1986, pp. 181–94. **[G: U.S.]**

Silver, J. Lew. Two Results Useful for Implementing Litterman's Procedure for Interpolating a Time Series [A Random Walk, Markov Model for the Distribution of Time Series]. *J. Bus. Econ. Statist.*, January 1986, *4*(1), pp. 129–30. **[G: U.K.]**

Simmons, LeRoy F. M-Competition—A Closer Look at NAIVE2 and Median *APE:* A Note. *Int. J. Forecasting*, 1986, *2*(4), pp. 457–60.

Stoffer, David S. Estimation and Identification of Space-Time ARMAX Models in the Presence of Missing Data. *J. Amer. Statist. Assoc.*, September 1986, *81*(395), pp. 762–62. **[G: U.S.; France; Ivory Coast; Senegal; Morocco]**

Summers, Lawrence H. Estimating the Long-run Relationship between Interest Rates and Inflation: A Response. *J. Monet. Econ.*, July 1986, *18*(1), pp. 77–86.

Taylor, Stephen J. Conjectured Models for Trends in Financial Prices, Tests and Forecasts. **In** *Goss, B. A., ed.*, 1986, *1980*, pp. 209–46. **[G: U.K.]**

Thompson, Patrick A. and Miller, Robert B. Sampling the Future: A Bayesian Approach to Forecasting from Univariate Time Series Models. *J. Bus. Econ. Statist.*, October 1986, *4*(4), pp. 427–36. **[G: U.S.]**

Thury, Gerhard. The Consequences of Trading Day Variation and Calendar Effects for ARIMA Model Building and Seasonal Adjustment. *Empirica*, 1986, *13*(1), pp. 3–25. **[G: Austria]**

Tintner, Gerhard and Licari, Joseph A. The Stochastic View of Economics. **In** *Szenberg, M., ed.*, 1986, *1970*, pp. 23–32.

Ullah, A.; Vinod, H. D. and Singh, R. S. Estimation of Linear Models with Moving Average Disturbances. *J. Quant. Econ.*, January 1986, *2*(1), pp. 137–52.

Wasserfallen, Walter. Non-stationarities in Macro-economic Time Series—Further Evidence and Implications. *Can. J. Econ.*, August 1986, *19*(3), pp. 498–510. **[G: W. Europe; U.S.]**

Watson, Mark W. Univariate Detrending Methods with Stochastic Trends. *J. Monet. Econ.*, July 1986, *18*(1), pp. 49–75. **[G: U.S.]**

Weiss, Andrew A. ARCH and Bilinear Time Series Models: Comparison and Combination. *J. Bus. Econ. Statist.*, January 1986, *4*(1), pp. 59–70.

Zeger, Scott L. and Brookmeyer, Ron. Regression Analysis with Censored Autocorrelated Data. *J. Amer. Statist. Assoc.*, September 1986, *81*(395), pp. 722–29.

Zin, Stanley E. Modelling the Persistence of Conditional Variances: Comment. *Econometric Rev.*, 1986, *5*(1), pp. 75–80.

2117 Survey Methods; Sampling Methods

Banks, Martha J. The Sample Design and Its Effect on the Data. **In** *Fleming, G. V. and Andersen, R. M., eds.*, 1986, pp. 228–49. **[G: U.S.]**

Chiu, H. Y. and Sedransk, J. A Bayesian Procedure for Imputing Missing Values in Sample Surveys. *J. Amer. Statist. Assoc.*, September 1986, *81*(395), pp. 667–76.

DeStavola, Bianca L. Sampling Designs for Short Panel Data. *Econometrica*, March 1986, *54*(2), pp. 415–24.

Ford, Barry L.; Nealon, Jack and Tortora, Robert D. Area Frame Estimators in Agricultural Surveys: Sampling versus Nonsampling Errors. *Agr. Econ. Res.*, Spring 1986, *38*(2), pp. 1–10. **[G: U.S.]**

Freedman, David A. A Case Study in Nonresponse: Plaintiff vs. California State Board of Equalization. *J. Bus. Econ. Statist.*, January 1986, *4*(1), pp. 123–24. **[G: U.S.]**

Freedman, David A. A Case Study in Nonresponse: Plaintiff vs. California State Board of Equalization: Reply. *J. Bus. Econ. Statist.*, January 1986, *4*(1), pp. 126–27.

Grossman, Jean Baldwin. Optimal Sample Designs with Preliminary Tests of Significance. *J. Bus. Econ. Statist.*, April 1986, *4*(2), pp. 171–76.

Hill, Bruce M. A Bayesian Approach to the Nonresponse Problem, Using Covariates à la

Freedman: Comment [A Case Study in Nonresponse: Plaintiff vs. California State Board of Equalization]. *J. Bus. Econ. Statist.*, January 1986, *4*(1), pp. 125–26. **[G: U.S.]**

Juster, F. Thomas. Response Errors in the Measurement of Time Use. *J. Amer. Statist. Assoc.*, June 1986, *81*(394), pp. 390–402. **[G: U.S.]**

Lee, Eun Sul, et al. Complex Survey Data Analysis: Estimation of Standard Errors Using Pseudostrata. *J. Econ. Soc. Meas.*, July 1986, *14*(2), pp. 135–44. **[G: U.S.]**

Lyttle, Christopher. Methodology for Imputing Missing Values, MHSP. **In** *Fleming, G. V. and Andersen, R. M., eds.*, 1986, pp. 250–62. **[G: U.S.]**

Marquis, Kent H.; Marquis, M. Susan and Polich, J. Michael. Response Bias and Reliability in Sensitive Topic Surveys. *J. Amer. Statist. Assoc.*, June 1986, *81*(394), pp. 381–89. **[G: U.S.]**

Marton, Adam. Synthetic Estimates for Small Areas: Problems and Results of a Simulation Experiment. *Statist. J.*, May 1986, *4*(1), pp. 71–80.

Morgenthaler, S. and Vardi, Y. Choice-Based Samples: A Non-parametric Approach. *J. Econometrics*, June 1986, *32*(1), pp. 109–25.

Poterba, James M. and Summers, Lawrence H. Reporting Errors and Labor Market Dynamics. *Econometrica*, November 1986, *54*(6), pp. 1319–38. **[G: U.S.]**

Rouault, Jacques and Capy, Pierre. Comment évaluer un nombre de catégories par échantillonnage. (Estimating the Number of Categories of Sampling. With English summary.) *Ann. Écon. Statist.*, Oct./Dec. 1986, (4), pp. 111–24.

Shack-Marquez, Janice. Effects of Repeated Interviewing on Estimation of Labor Force Status. *J. Econ. Soc. Meas.*, December 1986, *14*(4), pp. 379–98. **[G: U.S.]**

Smith, V. Kerry. To Keep or Toss the Contingent Valuation Method. **In** *Cummings, R. G.; Brookshire, D. S. and Schulze, W. D., eds.*, 1986, pp. 162–79.

Stasny, Elizabeth A. Estimating Gross Flows Using Panel Data with Nonresponse: An Example from the Canadian Labour Force Survey. *J. Amer. Statist. Assoc.*, March 1986, *81*(393), pp. 42–47. **[G: Canada]**

2118 Theory of Index Numbers and Aggregation

Ara, Kenjiro. Condition for the Aggregation of Industrial Sectors into the Capital-Goods Sector and the Consumption-Goods Sector. *Hitotsubashi J. Econ.*, December 1986, *27*(2), pp. 99–109.

Balk, B. M. and Kersten, H. M. P. On the Precision of Consumer Price Indices Caused by the Sampling Variability of Budget Surveys. *J. Econ. Soc. Meas.*, April 1986, *14*(1), pp. 19–35. **[G: U.S.]**

Blankmeyer, Eric. Inference for Multiperiod Price and Quantity Indices. *Atlantic Econ. J.*, July 1986, *14*(2), pp. 84.

Danziger, Leif. Relative-Price Seasonality, Wage Indexation and the Perfect Price Index. *Europ. Econ. Rev.*, December 1986, *30*(6), pp. 1145–67.

Fuchs-Seliger, Susanne and Pfingsten, Andreas. Cost of Living Indices Based on Demand Functions. *J. Econ. (Z. Nationalökon.)*, 1986, *46*(1), pp. 49–64.

Gorman, W. M. Compatible Indices. *Econ. J.*, Supplement 1986, *96*, pp. 83–95.

Kohli, Ulrich. Direct Index Numbers and Demand Theory. *Australian Econ. Pap.*, June 1986, *25*(46), pp. 17–32.

Layton, Allan P. A Causality Analysis of Australia's Growth Cycle and the Composite Index of Leading Indicators. *Australian Econ. Pap.*, June 1986, *25*(46), pp. 57–66. **[G: Australia]**

Samuelson, Paul A. Rigorous Observational Positivism: Klein's Envelope Aggregation; Thermodynamics and Economic Isomorphisms. **In** *Samuelson, P. A.*, 1986, *1983*, pp. 220–57.

Samuelson, Paul A. Second Thoughts on Analytical Income Comparisons. **In** *Samuelson, P. A.*, 1986, *1984*, pp. 165–76.

Stoker, Thomas M. Aggregation, Efficiency, and Cross-section Regression. *Econometrica*, January 1986, *54*(1), pp. 171–88.

Triplett, Jack E. The Economic Interpretation of Hedonic Methods. *Surv. Curr. Bus.*, January 1986, *66*(1), pp. 36–40. **[G: U.S.]**

Zanardi, Giampaolo. Concordance–Discordance between Values Assumed by Pairs of Measures of Variability or Concentration of Characteristics. *Ricerche Econ.*, Apr.-Sept. 1986, *40*(2–3), pp. 317–27.

2119 Experimental Design; Social Experiments

Burtless, Gary and Orr, Larry L. Are Classical Experiments Needed for Manpower Policy? *J. Human Res.*, Fall 1986, *21*(4), pp. 606–39. **[G: U.S.]**

Chambers, R. L. Design-adjusted Parameter Estimation. *J. Roy. Statist. Soc.*, 1986, *149*(2), pp. 161–73.

Conlisk, John. Design Model Issues in *Social Experimentation:* Review Article. *J. Human Res.*, Fall 1986, *21*(4), pp. 564–85.

Freeman, A. Myrick, III. On Assessing the State of the Arts of the Contingent Valuation Method of Valuing Environmental Changes. **In** *Cummings, R. G.; Brookshire, D. S. and Schulze, W. D., eds.*, 1986, pp. 148–61.

Grossman, Jean Baldwin. Optimal Sample Designs with Preliminary Tests of Significance. *J. Bus. Econ. Statist.*, April 1986, *4*(2), pp. 171–76.

Haveman, Robert H. Social Experimentation and *Social Experimentation:* Review Article. *J. Human Res.*, Fall 1986, *21*(4), pp. 586–605.

LaLonde, Robert J. Evaluating the Econometric Evaluations of Training Programs with Experimental Data. *Amer. Econ. Rev.*, September 1986, *76*(4), pp. 604–20. **[G: U.S.]**

212 Construction, Analysis, and Use of Econometric Models

2120 Construction, Analysis, and Use of Econometric Models

Altonji, Joseph G. Econometric Approaches to the Specification of Life-Cycle Labour Supply and Commodity Demand Behaviour: Comment. *Econometric Rev.*, 1986, *5*(1), pp. 147–51.

Anderson, Gordon J. Empirical Assessment of Present Value Relations: Comment. *Econometric Rev.*, 1986, *5*(2), pp. 235–39. **[G: U.S.]**

Anderson, Richard G. and Thursby, Jerry G. Confidence Intervals for Elasticity Estimators in Translog Models. *Rev. Econ. Statist.*, November 1986, *68*(4), pp. 647–56.

Andrews, Donald W. K. Stability Comparisons of Estimators. *Econometrica*, September 1986, *54*(5), pp. 1207–35.

Antle, John M. Aggregation, Expectations, and the Explanation of Technological Change. *J. Econometrics*, Oct./Nov. 1986, *33*(1/2), pp. 213–36. **[G: U.S.]**

Antle, John M. and Hatchett, Stephen A. Dynamic Input Decisions in Econometric Product Models. *Amer. J. Agr. Econ.*, November 1986, *68*(4), pp. 939–49. **[G: U.S.]**

Atkinson, Scott E. and Tschirhart, John. Flexible Modelling of Time to Failure in Risky Careers. *Rev. Econ. Statist.*, November 1986, *68*(4), pp. 558–66. **[G: U.S.]**

Auger, Pierre. Production nationale et productions sectorielles. (National Production and Sectorial Productions. With English summary.) *Écon. Soc.*, November 1986, *20*(11), pp. 65–75.

Banerjee, Anindya, et al. Exploring Equilibrium Relationships in Econometrics through Static Models: Some Monte Carlo Evidence. *Oxford Bull. Econ. Statist.*, August 1986, *48*(3), pp. 253–77.

Barmby, Tim. Estimating Labour Supply Functions in a Linear Expenditure System Framework. *Bull. Econ. Res.*, May 1986, *38*(2), pp. 183–87. **[G: U.K.]**

Basemann, R. L., et al. Correction [On Deviations between Neoclassical and GFT-Based True Cost-of-Living Indexes Derived from the Same Demand Function System]. *J. Econometrics*, July 1986, *32*(2), pp. 293.

Bean, Charles R. The Estimation of "Surprise" Models and the "Surprise" Consumption Function. *Rev. Econ. Stud.*, August 1986, *53*(4), pp. 497–516. **[G: U.S.]**

Becker, Robin G., et al. Rival Models in Policy Optimization. *J. Econ. Dynam. Control*, June 1986, *10*(1/2), pp. 75–81. **[G: U.K.]**

Becker, Robin G., et al. The Simultaneous Use of Rival Models in Public Optimisation. *Econ. J.*, June 1986, *96*(382), pp. 425–48. **[G: U.K.]**

Belsley, David A. Centering, the Constant, First-Differencing, and Assessing Conditioning. **In** *Belsley, D. A. and Kuh, E., eds.*, 1986, pp. 117–53. **[G: U.S.]**

Bessler, David A. and Kling, John L. Forecasting Vector Autoregressions with Bayesian Priors. *Amer. J. Agr. Econ.*, February 1986, *68*(1), pp. 144–51. **[G: U.S.]**

Blinder, Alan S. More on the Speed of Adjustment in Inventory Models. *J. Money, Credit, Banking*, August 1986, *18*(3), pp. 355–65.

Blommestein, Hans and Nijkamp, Peter. Testing the Spatial Scale and the Dynamic Structure in Regional Models (A Contribution to Spatial Econometric Specification Analysis.) *J. Reg. Sci.*, February 1986, *26*(1), pp. 1–17. **[G: Netherlands]**

Blundell, Richard. Econometric Approaches to the Specification of Life-Cycle Labour Supply and Commodity Demand Behaviour: Reply. *Econometric Rev.*, 1986, *5*(1), pp. 163–70.

Blundell, Richard. Econometric Approaches to the Specification of Life-Cycle Labour Supply and Commodity Demand Behaviour. *Econometric Rev.*, 1986, *5*(1), pp. 89–146.

Blundell, Richard and Meghir, Costas. Selection Criteria for a Microeconometric Model of Labour Supply. *J. Appl. Econometrics*, January 1986, *1*(1), pp. 55–80. **[G: U.K.]**

Borges, Antonio M. Applied General Equilibrium Models: An Assessment of Their Usefulness for Policy Analysis. *OECD Econ. Stud.*, Autumn 1986, (7), pp. 7–43.

Borio, C. E. V. Do Contingent Rules Really Dominate Fixed Rules? *Econ. J.*, December 1986, *96*(384), pp. 1000–1010.

Borjas, George J. The Sensitivity of Labor Demand Functions to Choice of Dependent Variable. *Rev. Econ. Statist.*, February 1986, *68*(1), pp. 58–66. **[G: U.S.]**

Bouissou, Michel B.; Laffont, Jean-Jacques and Vuong, Quang H. Disequilibrium Econometrics on Micro Data. *Rev. Econ. Stud.*, January 1986, *53*(1), pp. 113–24. **[G: France]**

Boutillier, Michel. Causalités et bouclages dans les modèles macroéconomiques. (Causalities and Loops in Macroeconomic Models. With English summary.) *Écon. Soc.*, November 1986, *20*(11), pp. 41–64.

Boutillier, Michel and Durand, Bruno. Investigations in the Causal Structure of the Yearly OFCE Model. *J. Econ. Dynam. Control*, June 1986, *10*(1/2), pp. 131–37.

Brandsma, Andries S. Implications of Risk-Sensitive Decision-Making for the Design of Economic Policies. *J. Econ. Dynam. Control*, June 1986, *10*(1/2), pp. 301–06. **[G: Netherlands]**

Bray, Margaret M. and Savin, Nathan E. Rational Expectations Equilibria, Learning, and Model Specification. *Econometrica*, September 1986, *54*(5), pp. 1129–60.

Brewer, A. C. and Mead, R. Continuous Second Order Models of Spatial Variation with Application to the Efficiency of Field Crop Experiments. *J. Roy. Statist. Soc.*, 1986, *149*(4), pp. 314–36.

Bronsard, Camille and Salvas-Bronsard, Lise. Commodity and Asset Demands with and without Quantity Constraints in the Labour Market. *J. Appl. Econometrics,* April 1986, *1*(2), pp. 185–208. **[G: U.S.; Canada]**

Brouwer, Floor and Nijkamp, Peter. Mixed Qualitative Calculus as a Tool in Policy Modeling: A Dynamic Simulation Model of Urban Decline. *J. Policy Modeling,* Spring 1986, *8*(1), pp. 69–88.

Brown, Stephen J. and Klein, Roger W. Model Selection in the Federal Courts: An Application of the Posterior Odds Ratio Criterion. **In** *[de Finetti, B.],* 1986, pp. 141–56. **[G: U.S.]**

Browning, Martin. Econometric Approaches to the Specification of Life-Cycle Labour Supply and Commodity Demand Behaviour: Comment. *Econometric Rev.,* 1986, *5*(1), pp. 153–58.

Buccola, Steven T. Testing for Nonnormality in Farm Net Returns. *Amer. J. Agr. Econ.,* May 1986, *68*(2), pp. 334–43. **[G: U.S.]**

Buccola, Steven T. and McCarl, Bruce A. Small-Sample Evaluation of Mean-Variance Production Function Estimators. *Amer. J. Agr. Econ.,* August 1986, *68*(3), pp. 732–38.

Butler, J. S. and Schachter, Barry. Unbiased Estimation of the Black/Scholes Formula. *J. Finan. Econ.,* March 1986, *15*(3), pp. 341–57.

Calzolari, Giorgio and Sterbenz, Frederic P. Control Variates to Estimate the Reduced Form Variances in Econometric Models. *Econometrica,* November 1986, *54*(6), pp. 1483–90.

Cameron, A. Colin and Trivedi, Pravin K. Econometric Models Based on Count Data: Comparisons and Applications of Some Estimators and Tests. *J. Appl. Econometrics,* January 1986, *1*(1), pp. 29–53.

Campbell, John Y. Empirical Assessment of Present Value Relations: Comment. *Econometric Rev.,* 1986, *5*(2), pp. 241–45.

Candela, G. and Gardini, A. Estimation of a Non-linear Discrete-Time Macro Model. *J. Econ. Dynam. Control,* June 1986, *10*(1/2), pp. 249–54. **[G: Italy]**

Capalbo, Susan M. Temporary Equilibrium Production Models for a Common-Property Renewable-Resource Sector. *J. Econometrics,* Oct./Nov. 1986, *33*(1/2), pp. 263–84.

Caravani, P. On Extending Linear Quadratic Control Theory to Non-symmetric Risky Objectives. *J. Econ. Dynam. Control,* June 1986, *10*(1/2), pp. 83–88.

Carraro, Carlo. Indicatori sintetici della politica economica: teoria e applicazioni. (Synthetic Indicators of Macro Policy Goals: Theory and Applications. With English summary.) *Rivista Int. Sci. Econ. Com.,* June-July 1986, *33*(6–7), pp. 629–56. **[G: Italy]**

Chamberlain, Gary. Asymptotic Efficiency in Semi-Parametric Models with Censoring. *J. Econometrics,* July 1986, *32*(2), pp. 189–218.

Chavas, Jean-Paul and Segerson, Kathleen. Singularity and Auotregressive Disturbances in Linear Logit Models. *J. Bus. Econ. Statist.,* April 1986, *4*(2), pp. 161–69. **[G: U.S.]**

Chetty, V. K. and Heckman, James J. A Dynamic Model of Aggregate Output Supply, Factor Demand and Entry and Exit for a Competitive Industry with Heterogeneous Plants. *J. Econometrics,* Oct./Nov. 1986, *33*(1/2), pp. 237–62. **[G: U.S.]**

Chiarella, Carl. Perfect Foresight Models and the Dynamic Instability Problem from a Higher Viewpoint. *Econ. Modelling,* October 1986, *3*(4), pp. 283–92.

Chong, Yock Y. and Hendry, David F. Econometric Evaluation of Linear Macro-Economic Models. *Rev. Econ. Stud.,* August 1986, *53*(4), pp. 671–90.

Chowdhury, Abdur R. Vector Autoregression as an Alternative Macro-Modelling Technique. *Bangladesh Devel. Stud.,* June 1986, *14*(2), pp. 21–32.

Clark, Jeffrey A. Single-Equation, Multiple-Regression Methodology: Is It an Appropriate Methodology for the Estimation of the Structure–Performance Relationship in Banking? *J. Monet. Econ.,* November 1986, *18*(3), pp. 295–312. **[G: U.S.]**

Claverie, Pierre; Szpiro, Daniel and Topol, Richard. Distributed Lag Analysis: The 'Padé z-Transform' Method. *J. Econ. Dynam. Control,* June 1986, *10*(1/2), pp. 157–61.

Clayton, Murray K.; Geisser, Seymour and Jennings, Dennis E. A Comparison of Several Model Selection Procedures. **In** *[de Finetti, B.],* 1986, pp. 425–39.

Conley, W. C. Comparison of Least Squares with Least Absolute Deviation Forecasting Using Simulation Techniques. **In** *De Antoni, F.; Lauro, N. and Rizzi, A., eds.,* 1986, pp. 31–36.

Currie, David and Levine, Paul. Time Inconsistency and Optimal Policies in Deterministic and Stochastic Worlds. *J. Econ. Dynam. Control,* June 1986, *10*(1/2), pp. 191–99.

Dadkhah, Kamran M. and Zahedi, Fatemeh. Simultaneous Estimation of Production Functions and Capital Stocks for Developing Countries. *Rev. Econ. Statist.,* August 1986, *68*(3), pp. 443–51. **[G: LDCs]**

Dagum, Camilo. Analyzing Rational and Adaptive Expectations Hypotheses and Model Specifications. *Écon. Soc.,* November 1986, *20*(11), pp. 15–34.

Dagum, Camilo. Economic Model, System and Structure, Philosophy of Science and Lakatos' Methodology of Scientific Research Programs. *Rivista Int. Sci. Econ. Com.,* September 1986, *33*(9), pp. 859–86.

Dawid, A. Philip. A Bayesian View of Statistical Modelling. **In** *[de Finetti, B.],* 1986, pp. 391–404.

Deaton, Angus S. Demand Analysis. **In** *Griliches, Z. and Intriligator, M. D., eds.,* 1986, pp. 1767–1839.

DeGroot, Morris H. and Fienberg, Stephen E. Comparing Probability Forecasters: Basic Binary Concepts and Multivariate Extensions. **In** *[de Finetti, B.],* 1986, pp. 247–64.

Delong, David M. Statistical Properties of Generalized Method-of-Moments Estimators of Structural Parameters Obtained from Financial

Market Data: Comment. *J. Bus. Econ. Statist.*, October 1986, *4*(4), pp. 417–18.

Despotakis, Kostas A. Economic Performance of Flexible Functional Forms: Implications for Equilibrium Modeling. *Europ. Econ. Rev.*, December 1986, *30*(6), pp. 1107–43.

Diebold, Francis X. Modeling the Persistence of Conditional Variances: A Comment. *Econometric Rev.*, 1986, *5*(1), pp. 51–56.

van Dijk, Herman K. and Kloek, Teun. Posterior Moments of the Klein–Goldberger Model. **In** *[de Finetti, B.]*, 1986, pp. 95–108. **[G: U.S.]**

Dufour, Jean-Marie. Recursive Stability Analysis: The Demand for Money during the German Hyperinflation. **In** *Belsley, D. A. and Kuh, E., eds.*, 1986, pp. 18–61. **[G: Germany]**

Engle, Robert F. and Bollerslev, Tim. Modelling the Persistence of Conditional Variances: Reply. *Econometric Rev.*, 1986, *5*(1), pp. 81–87.

Engle, Robert F. and Bollerslev, Tim. Modelling the Persistence of Conditional Variances. *Econometric Rev.*, 1986, *5*(1), pp. 1–50. **[G: U.S.; Switzerland]**

Engle, Robert F., et al. Semiparametric Estimates of the Relation between Weather and Electricity Sales. *J. Amer. Statist. Assoc.*, June 1986, *81*(394), pp. 310–20. **[G: U.S.]**

Eriksson, Erik Anders. Generalized Extreme Value Discrete Choice Demand Models: Existence and Uniqueness of Market Equilibria. *Reg. Sci. Urban Econ.*, November 1986, *16*(4), pp. 547–72.

Ershov, E. B. and Sadykov, I. S. A Study of Substitution Possibilities between Inputs and Their Relationship over Time in Soviet Industry. *Matekon*, Winter 1986-87, *23*(2), pp. 32–56. **[G: U.S.S.R.]**

Evans, George W. and Honkapohja, Seppo. A Complete Characterization of ARMA Solutions to Linear Rational Expectations Models. *Rev. Econ. Stud.*, April 1986, *53*(2), pp. 227–39.

Fair, Ray C. Evaluating the Predictive Accuracy of Models. **In** *Griliches, Z. and Intriligator, M. D., eds.*, 1986, pp. 1979–95.

Fisher, Paul G. and Salmon, Mark. On Evaluating the Importance of Nonlinearity in Large Macroeconometric Models. *Int. Econ. Rev.*, October 1986, *27*(3), pp. 625–46.

Flavin, Marjorie A. Empirical Assessment of Present Value Relations: Comment. *Econometric Rev.*, 1986, *5*(2), pp. 247–52.

Flinn, Christopher J. Econometric Analysis of CPS-Type Unemployment Data. *J. Human Res.*, Fall 1986, *21*(4), pp. 456–84. **[G: Italy]**

Fourgeaud, Claude; Gouriéroux, Christian and Pradel, Jacqueline. Learning Procedures and Convergence to Rationality. *Econometrica*, July 1986, *54*(4), pp. 845–68.

Garrod, Peter V. and Roberts, Roland K. Prices as Proxies for Prices. *Amer. J. Agr. Econ.*, August 1986, *68*(3), pp. 626–33. **[G: U.S.]**

Geweke, John. Exact Inference in the Inequality Constrained Normal Linear Regression Model. *J. Appl. Econometrics*, April 1986, *1*(2), pp. 127–41.

Geweke, John. Modelling the Persistence of Conditional Variances: Comment. *Econometric Rev.*, 1986, *5*(1), pp. 57–61.

Gilbert, Christopher L. Professor Hendry's Econometric Methodology. *Oxford Bull. Econ. Statist.*, August 1986, *48*(3), pp. 283–307.

Gilbert, Christopher L. Testing the Efficient Markets Hypothesis on Averaged Data. *Appl. Econ.*, November 1986, *18*(11), pp. 1149–66. **[G: U.K.]**

Goldstein, Morris and Montiel, Peter J. Evaluating Fund Stabilization Programs with Multicountry Data: Some Methodological Pitfalls. *Int. Monet. Fund Staff Pap.*, June 1986, *33*(2), pp. 304–44.

Goodwin, Thomas H. The Impact of Credit Rationing on Housing Investment: A Multi-Market Disequilibrium Approach. *Int. Econ. Rev.*, June 1986, *27*(2), pp. 445–64. **[G: U.S.]**

Goss, Barry A. Rejection of Unbiasedness Is Not Rejection of Market Efficiency: Reply. *Appl. Econ.*, November 1986, *18*(11), pp. 1167–78. **[G: U.K.]**

Gouriéroux, Christian and Pradel, Jacqueline. Direct Test of the Rational Expectations Hypothesis. *Europ. Econ. Rev.*, April 1986, *30*(2), pp. 265–84.

Granger, Clive W. J. Developments in the Study of Cointegrated Economic Variables. *Oxford Bull. Econ. Statist.*, August 1986, *48*(3), pp. 213–28.

Greenberg, Marshall G. The Cost of Simplifying Preference Models: Commentary. *Marketing Sci.*, Fall 1986, *5*(4), pp. 320–21.

Greene, Mark N.; Howrey, E. Philip and Hymans, Saul H. The Use of Outside Information in Econometric Forecasting. **In** *Belsley, D. A. and Kuh, E., eds.*, 1986, pp. 90–116. **[G: U.S.]**

Grosskopf, Shawna and Hayes, Kathy J. The Demand for Local Public Goods: Choosing an Appropriate Functional Form. *Appl. Econ.*, November 1986, *18*(11), pp. 1179–92. **[G: U.S.]**

Grunberg, Emile. Predictability and Reflexivity. *Amer. J. Econ. Soc.*, October 1986, *45*(4), pp. 475–88.

Hagerty, Michael R. Reflections on the Cost of Simplifying Preference Models: Reply. *Marketing Sci.*, Fall 1986, *5*(4), pp. 323–24.

Hagerty, Michael R. The Cost of Simplifying Preference Models. *Marketing Sci.*, Fall 1986, *5*(4), pp. 298–319.

Haitovsky, Yoel. The Linear Hierarchical Model and Its Applications in Econometric Analysis. **In** *[de Finetti, B.]*, 1986, pp. 119–38.

Hall, Stephen G. An Application of the Granger & Engle Two-Step Estimation Procedure to United Kingdom Aggregate Wage Data. *Oxford Bull. Econ. Statist.*, August 1986, *48*(3), pp. 229–39. **[G: U.K.]**

Hall, Stephen G. Estimating the Uncertainty of the Simulation Properties of Large Nonlinear Econometric Models. *Appl. Econ.*, September 1986, *18*(9), pp. 985–93. **[G: U.K.]**

Hall, Stephen G. Time Inconsistency and Optimal Policy Formulation in the Presence of Rational Expectations. *J. Econ. Dynam. Control*, June 1986, *10*(1/2), pp. 323–26.

Hall, Stephen G.; Henry, S. G. B. and Wren-Lewis, Simon. Manufacturing Stocks and Forward-Looking Expectations in the UK. *Economica,* November 1986, *53*(212), pp. 447–65. **[G: U.K.]**

Hall, Stephen G. and Herbert, Rhys. Consistent Simulations and the National Institute Model 8. *Nat. Inst. Econ. Rev.,* February 1986, (115), pp. 64–73. **[G: U.K.]**

Hamilton, James D. A Standard Error for the Estimated State Vector of a State-Space Model. *J. Econometrics,* December 1986, *33*(3), pp. 387–97. **[G: U.S.]**

Hamilton, James D. On Testing for Self-fulfilling Speculative Price Bubbles. *Int. Econ. Rev.,* October 1986, *27*(3), pp. 545–52.

Hammond, Christopher J. Estimating the Statistical Cost Curve: An Application of the Stochastic Frontier Technique. *Appl. Econ.,* September 1986, *18*(9), pp. 971–84. **[G: U.K.]**

Hansen, Lars Peter. Statistical Properties of Generalized Method-of-Moments Estimators of Structural Parameters Obtained from Financial Market Data: Comment. *J. Bus. Econ. Statist.,* October 1986, *4*(4), pp. 418–21.

Harvey, A. C. and Durbin, J. The Effects of Seat Belt Legislation on British Road Casualties: A Case Study in Structural Time Series Modelling. *J. Roy. Statist. Soc.,* 1986, *149*(3), pp. 187–210. **[G: U.S.]**

Harvey, A. C., et al. Stochastic Trends in Dynamic Regression Models: An Application to the Employment–Output Equations. *Econ. J.,* December 1986, *96*(384), pp. 975–85. **[G: U.K.]**

Hayes, Kathy J. Third-Order Translog Utility Functions. *J. Bus. Econ. Statist.,* July 1986, *4*(3), pp. 339–46. **[G: U.S.]**

Hazilla, Michael and Kopp, Raymond J. Systematic Effects of Capital Service Price Definition on Perceptions of Input Substitution. *J. Bus. Econ. Statist.,* April 1986, *4*(2), pp. 209–24. **[G: U.S.]**

Hazilla, Michael and Kopp, Raymond J. Testing for Separable Functional Structure Using Temporary Equilibrium Models. *J. Econometrics,* Oct./Nov. 1986, *33*(1/2), pp. 119–41. **[G: U.S.]**

Heckman, James J. and MaCurdy, Thomas E. Labor Econometrics. **In** *Griliches, Z. and Intriligator, M. D., eds.,* 1986, pp. 1917–77.

Heckman, James J. and Singer, Burton. Econometric Analysis of Longitudinal Data. **In** *Griliches, Z. and Intriligator, M. D., eds.,* 1986, pp. 1689–1763.

Helliwell, John F. and Chung, Alan. Aggregate Output with Variable Rates of Utilization of Employed Factors. *J. Econometrics,* Oct./Nov. 1986, *33*(1/2), pp. 285–310. **[G: Canada]**

Helliwell, John F., et al. The Supply Side in the OECD's Macroeconomic Model. *OECD Econ. Stud.,* Spring 1986, (6), pp. 75–131. **[G: OECD]**

Hendry, David F. An Excursion into Conditional Varianceland [Modelling the Persistence of Conditional Variances]. *Econometric Rev.,* 1986, *5*(1), pp. 63–69.

Hendry, David F. Econometric Modelling with Cointegrated Variables: An Overview. *Oxford Bull. Econ. Statist.,* August 1986, *48*(3), pp. 201–12.

Hendry, David F. The Role of Prediction in Evaluating Econometric Models. **In** *Mason, J.; Mathias, P. and Westcott, J. H., eds.,* 1986, pp. 25–33.

Hensher, David A. Sequential and Full Information Maximum Likelihood Estimation of a Nested Logit Model. *Rev. Econ. Statist.,* November 1986, *68*(4), pp. 657–67. **[G: Australia]**

Hjorth-Andersen, Chr. Hedoniske regressioner: Hvad koster en meter bil? (Hedonic Regressions. With English summary.) *Nationaløkon. Tidsskr.,* 1986, *124*(1), pp. 89–106. **[G: Denmark]**

Hodrick, Robert J. Empirical Assessment of Present Value Relations: Comment. *Econometric Rev.,* 1986, *5*(2), pp. 253–60.

Holly, Sean. Games, Expectations, and Optimal Policy for Open Economies. *J. Econ. Dynam. Control,* June 1986, *10*(1/2), pp. 45–49.

Hujer, Reinhard. Ökonometrische "Switch"-Modelle: Methodische Ansätze und empirische Analysen. (Econometric Switch-Models: Methodical and Empirical Analysis. With English summary.) *Jahr. Nationalökon. Statist.,* May 1986, *201*(3), pp. 229–56. **[G: W. Germany]**

Ilmakunnas, Pekka. Stochastic Constraints on Cost Function Parameters: Mixed and Hierarchical Approaches. *Empirical Econ.,* 1986, *11*(2), pp. 69–80.

Jenkinson, Tim. Testing Neo-Classical Theories of Labour Demand: An Application of Cointegration Techniques. *Oxford Bull. Econ. Statist.,* August 1986, *48*(3), pp. 241–51. **[G: U.K.]**

Johnson, Richard M. The Cost of Simplifying Preference Models: Commentary. *Marketing Sci.,* Fall 1986, *5*(4), pp. 322.

Jorgenson, Dale W. Econometric Methods for Modeling Producer Behavior. **In** *Griliches, Z. and Intriligator, M. D., eds.,* 1986, pp. 1841–1915.

Kamakura, Wagner A. and Srivastava, Rajendra K. An Ideal-Point Probabilistic Choice Model for Heterogeneous Preference. *Marketing Sci.,* Summer 1986, *5*(3), pp. 199–218.

Keen, Michael. Zero Expenditures and the Estimation of Engel Curves. *J. Appl. Econometrics,* July 1986, *1*(3), pp. 277–86. **[G: U.K.]**

Kiefer, Nicholas M. Econometric Approaches to the Specification of Life-Cycle Labour Supply and Commodity Demand Behaviour: Comment. *Econometric Rev.,* 1986, *5*(1), pp. 159–62.

Kiviet, Jan F. On the Rigour of Some Misspecification Tests for Modelling Dynamic Relationships. *Rev. Econ. Stud.,* April 1986, *53*(2), pp. 241–61.

Kleidon, Allan W. Empirical Assessment of Present Value Relations: Comment. *Econometric Rev.,* 1986, *5*(2), pp. 261–65.

Klein, Lawrence R. Economic Policy Formation: Theory and Implementation (Applied Econometrics in the Public Sector). **In** *Griliches, Z. and Intriligator, M. D., eds.*, 1986, pp. 2057–93.

Knudson, Daniel C. and Fotheringham, A. Stewart. Matrix Comparison, Goodness-of-Fit, and Spatial Interaction Modeling. *Int. Reg. Sci. Rev.*, August 1986, *10*(2), pp. 127–47.

Kokkelenberg, Edward C. and Bischoff, Charles W. Expectations and Factor Demand. *Rev. Econ. Statist.*, August 1986, *68*(3), pp. 423–31. **[G: U.S.]**

Kollintzas, Tryphon. A Non-recursive Solution for the Linear Rational Expectations Model. *J. Econ. Dynam. Control*, June 1986, *10*(1/2), pp. 327–32.

Kondo, Hitoshi. On Pitfalls in the Construction of Family-based Models of Population Growth: A Note. *Europ. Econ. Rev.*, April 1986, *30*(2), pp. 439–47.

de Koning, Jaap. The Expected Industrial Production Volume Estimated with the Help of Data from the Business-Cycle Test. *De Economist*, 1986, *134*(4), pp. 479–91. **[G: Netherlands]**

Krinsky, Itzhak and Robb, A. Leslie. On Approximating the Statistical Properties of Elasticities. *Rev. Econ. Statist.*, November 1986, *68*(4), pp. 715–19.

Kuh, Edwin; Neese, John and Hollinger, Peter. Linear Analysis of Large Nonlinear Models and Model Simplification. **In** *Belsley, D. A. and Kuh, E., eds.*, 1986, pp. 213–38. **[G: U.S.]**

LaFrance, Jeffrey T. The Structure of Constant Elasticity Demand Models. *Amer. J. Agr. Econ.*, August 1986, *68*(3), pp. 543–52.

LaLonde, Robert J. Evaluating the Econometric Evaluations of Training Programs with Experimental Data. *Amer. Econ. Rev.*, September 1986, *76*(4), pp. 604–20. **[G: U.S.]**

Lanning, Steven G. Missing Observations: A Simultaneous Approach versus Interpolation by Related Series. *J. Econ. Soc. Meas.*, July 1986, *14*(2), pp. 155–63. **[G: U.S.]**

Lau, Lawrence J. Functional Forms in Econometric Model Building. **In** *Griliches, Z. and Intriligator, M. D., eds.*, 1986, pp. 1515–66.

Le Van, Cuong. Stationary Uncertainty Frontiers in Macroeconometric Models: An Approach for Solving Matrix Riccati Equations. *J. Econ. Dynam. Control*, June 1986, *10*(1/2), pp. 225–29.

Lee, Lung-Fei. The Specification of Multi-market Disequilibrium Econometric Models. *J. Econometrics*, August 1986, *32*(3), pp. 297–332.

Lee, Lung-Fei and Pitt, Mark M. Microeconometric Demand Systems with Binding Nonnegativity Constraints: The Dual Approach. *Econometrica*, September 1986, *54*(5), pp. 1237–42.

Legendre, François and Vidal, Denis. Processus d'ajustement et croissance: un commentaire. (The Adjust Process and Growth: A Comment. With English summary.) *Ann. Écon. Statist.*, Apr./June 1986, (2), pp. 165–70.

Leontief, Wassily. An Information System for Policy Decisions in a Modern Economy. **In** *Leontief, W.*, 1986, *1979*, pp. 418–28.

LeRoy, Stephen F. Empirical Assessment of Present Value Relations: Comment. *Econometric Rev.*, 1986, *5*(2), pp. 267–71.

Leserer, Michael. Kognitive Inferenz als ökonometrische Aufgabe. Einige Bemerkungen zur ökonometrischen Grundsatzdiskussion. Cognitive Inference as an Econometric Problem: Some Remarks on the Fundamentals of Econometrics. With English summary.) *Jahr. Nationalökon. Statist.*, March 1986, *201*(2), pp. 97–106.

Lighthill, James [Sir]. The Recently Recognized Failure of Predictability in Newtonian Dynamics. **In** *Mason, J.; Mathias, P. and Westcott, J. H., eds.*, 1986, pp. 35–48.

Lin, Winston T. Analysis of Lumber and Pulpwood Production in a Partial Adjustment Model with Dynamic and Variable Speeds of Adjustment. *J. Bus. Econ. Statist.*, July 1986, *4*(3), pp. 305–16. **[G: U.S.]**

Livesey, D. A. New Perspectives from the Complex Plane. *J. Econ. Dynam. Control*, June 1986, *10*(1/2), pp. 99–107.

Lo, Andrew W. Statistical Tests of Contingent-Claims Asset-Pricing Models: A New Methodology. *J. Finan. Econ.*, September 1986, *17*(1), pp. 143–73.

Löflund, Anders. Tasapainomallin merkitys osakemarkkinoiden tehokkuustesteissä. (The Effect of Using Different Market Model Specifications in Tests of the Efficient Market Hypothesis [EMH] on the Finnish Stock Market. With English summary.) *Liiketaloudellinen Aikak.*, 1986, *35*(3), pp. 218–35. **[G: Finland]**

Lubrano, Michel; Pierse, R. G. and Richard, Jean-Francois. Stability of a U.K. Money Demand Equation: A Bayesian Approach to Testing Exogeneity. *Rev. Econ. Stud.*, August 1986, *53*(4), pp. 603–24. **[G: U.K.]**

Luger, Michael I. and Stahl, Dale O., II. Specification Errors in Models of Aggregate Labor Supply. *Rev. Econ. Statist.*, May 1986, *68*(2), pp. 274–83. **[G: U.S.]**

Lupoletti, William M. and Webb, Roy H. Defining and Improving the Accuracy of Macroeconomic Forecasts: Contributions from a VAR Model. *J. Bus.*, Part 1, April 1986, *59*(2), pp. 263–85. **[G: U.S.]**

Maddala, G. S. Disequilibrium, Self-selection, and Switching Models. **In** *Griliches, Z. and Intriligator, M. D., eds.*, 1986, pp. 1633–88.

Malatesta, Paul H. Measuring Abnormal Performance: The Event Parameter Approach Using Joint Generalized Least Squares. *J. Finan. Quant. Anal.*, March 1986, *21*(1), pp. 27–38.

Manski, Charles F. Semiparametric Analysis of Binary Response from Response-Based Samples. *J. Econometrics*, February 1986, *31*(1), pp. 31–40.

Markose, S. M. A Theory of Policy-Induced Structural Change: An Application of the Bismut Stochastic Maximum Principle. *J. Econ. Dynam. Control*, June 1986, *10*(1/2), pp. 109–14.

Marsden, James R. and Pingry, David E. Engineering Production Functions and the Testing of Quantitative Economic Hypotheses. *Economica,* November 1986, *53*(212), pp. 533–34.

Mattey, Joe and Meese, Richard. Empirical Assessment of Present Value Relations: Rejoinder. *Econometric Rev.,* 1986, *5*(2), pp. 279–85. **[G: U.S.]**

Mattey, Joe and Meese, Richard. Empirical Assessment of Present Value Relations. *Econometric Rev.,* 1986, *5*(2), pp. 171–234. **[G: U.S.]**

Mayer, Lawrence S. On Cross-Lagged Panel Models with Serially Correlated Errors. *J. Bus. Econ. Statist.,* July 1986, *4*(3), pp. 347–57.

McAleer, Michael and Deistler, Manfred. Some Recent Developments in Econometrics. In *Bittanti, S., ed.,* 1986, pp. 222–43.

McFadden, Daniel. The Choice Theory Approach to Market Research. *Marketing Sci.,* Fall 1986, *5*(4), pp. 275–97.

Mitchell, Douglas W. and Speaker, Paul J. A Simple, Flexible Distributed Lag Technique: The Polynomial Inverse Lag. *J. Econometrics,* April 1986, *31*(3), pp. 329–40.

Moffitt, Robert. The Econometrics of Piecewise-Linear Budget Constraints: A Survey and Exposition of the Maximum Likelihood Method. *J. Bus. Econ. Statist.,* July 1986, *4*(3), pp. 317–28. **[G: U.K.; U.S.; Sweden]**

Morey, Edward R. An Introduction to Checking, Testing, and Imposing Curvature Properties: The True Function and the Estimated Function. *Can. J. Econ.,* May 1986, *19*(2), pp. 207–35.

Morgenthaler, S. and Vardi, Y. Choice-Based Samples: A Non-parametric Approach. *J. Econometrics,* June 1986, *32*(1), pp. 109–25.

Mouchart, Michel and Orsi, R. A Note on Price Adjustment Models in Disequilibrium Econometrics. *J. Econometrics,* March 1986, *31*(2), pp. 209–17.

Moulton, Brent R. Random Group Effects and the Precision of Regression Estimates. *J. Econometrics,* August 1986, *32*(3), pp. 385–97. **[G: U.S.]**

Mountain, Dean C. Economies of Scale versus Technological Change: An Aggregate Production Function for Switzerland. *Rev. Econ. Statist.,* November 1986, *68*(4), pp. 707–11. **[G: Switzerland]**

Mullahy, John. Specification and Testing of Some Modified Count Data Models. *J. Econometrics,* December 1986, *33*(3), pp. 341–65. **[G: U.S.]**

Naik, Gopal and Leuthold, Raymond M. A Note on Qualitative Forecast Evaluation. *Amer. J. Agr. Econ.,* August 1986, *68*(3), pp. 721–26. **[G: U.S.]**

Nakamura, Shinichiro. A Flexible Dynamic Model of Multiproduct Technology for the West German Economy. *J. Appl. Econometrics,* October 1986, *1*(4), pp. 333–44. **[G: W. Germany]**

Nakhaeizadeh, Gholamreza. The Effects of Various Treatments of Truncation Remainders in the Estimation of the Consumption Function: A Bayesian Approach. *Bull. Econ. Res.,* May 1986, *38*(2), pp. 119–36. **[G: W. Germany]**

Nijman, T. E. and Palm, F. C. The Construction and Use of Approximations for Missing Quarterly Observations: A Model-based Approach. *J. Bus. Econ. Statist.,* January 1986, *4*(1), pp. 47–58. **[G: Netherlands]**

Norton, Roger D.; Scandizzo, Pasquale L. and Zimmerman, Linda W. Portugal's Entry into the EEC: Aggregate and Distributional Effects Determined by Means of a General Equilibrium Model. *J. Policy Modeling,* Summer 1986, *8*(2), pp. 149–80. **[G: Portugal]**

Olsen, Randall J.; Smith, D. Alton and Farkas, George. Structural and Reduced-Form Models of Choice among Alternatives in Continuous Time: Youth Employment under a Guaranteed Jobs Program. *Econometrica,* March 1986, *54*(2), pp. 375–94. **[G: U.S.]**

Orazem, Peter F. and Miranowski, John. An Indirect Test for the Specification of Expectation Regimes. *Rev. Econ. Statist.,* November 1986, *68*(4), pp. 603–09. **[G: U.S.]**

Osborn, Denise R. A Note on Error Correction Mechanisms and Steady-State Error. *Econ. J.,* March 1986, *96*(381), pp. 208–11.

Owusu-Gyapong, Anthony. Alternative Estimating Techniques for Panel Data on Strike Activity. *Rev. Econ. Statist.,* August 1986, *68*(3), pp. 526–31. **[G: Canada]**

Pantula, Sastry G. Modelling the Persistence of Conditional Variances: Comment. *Econometric Rev.,* 1986, *5*(1), pp. 71–74.

Patterson, K. D. The Stability of Some Annual Consumption Functions. *Oxford Econ. Pap.,* March 1986, *38*(1), pp. 1–30. **[G: U.K.]**

Pau, L. F. Inference of Functional Economic Model Relations from Natural Language Analysis. In *Pau, L. F., ed.,* 1986, pp. 173–83.

Pearlman, Joseph. Diverse Information and Rational Expectations Models. *J. Econ. Dynam. Control,* June 1986, *10*(1/2), pp. 333–38.

Pearlman, Joseph; Currie, David and Levine, Paul. Rational Expectations Models with Partial Information. *Econ. Modelling,* April 1986, *3*(2), pp. 90–105.

Picci, Giorgio and Pinzoni, Stefano. A New Class of Dynamic Models for Stationary Time Series. In *Bittanti, S., ed.,* 1986, pp. 69–114.

Prescott, Edward C. Theory Ahead of Business Cycle Measurement. *Fed. Res. Bank Minn. Rev.,* Fall 1986, *10*(4), pp. 9–22. **[G: U.S.]**

Prucha, Ingmar R. and Nadiri, M. Ishaq. A Comparison of Alternative Methods for the Estimation of Dynamic Factor Demand Models under Non-static Expectations. *J. Econometrics,* Oct./Nov. 1986, *33*(1/2), pp. 187–211.

Quandt, Richard E. A Note on Estimating Disequilibrium Models with Aggregation. *Empirical Econ.,* 1986, *11*(4), pp. 223–42.

Quandt, Richard E. and Rosen, Harvey S. Unemployment, Disequilibrium and the Short Run Phillips Curve: An Econometric Approach. *J. Appl. Econometrics,* July 1986, *1*(3), pp. 235–53. **[G: U.S.]**

Ray, Ranjan. Flexibility in Dynamic Demand Modelling and Its Implications for Testing Restrictions. *Manchester Sch. Econ. Soc. Stud.*, March 1986, *54*(1), pp. 1–21. **[G: U.K.]**

Rissanen, Jorma. Predictive and Nonpredictive Minimum Description Length Principles. **In** *Bittanti, S., ed.*, 1986, pp. 115–40.

Robins, Philip K. and West, Richard W. Sample Attrition and Labor Supply Response in Experimental Panel Data: A Study of Alternative Correction Procedures. *J. Bus. Econ. Statist.*, July 1986, *4*(3), pp. 329–38. **[G: U.S.]**

Ronning, Gerd. Ökonometrische Analyse dynamischer Anteilsgleichungen. (Econometric and Statistical Methods and Models. With English summary.) *Z. Wirtschaft. Sozialwissen.*, 1986, *106*(6), pp. 605–21.

Rowley, Robin and Jain, Renuka. Sims on Causality: An Illustration of Soft Econometrics. *Scot. J. Polit. Econ.*, May 1986, *33*(2), pp. 171–81.

Rust, Roland T. and Schmittlein, David. A Bayesian Cross-validated Likelihood Method for Comparing Alternative Specifications of Quantitative Models. *Marketing Sci.*, Winter 1986, *5*(1), pp. 89.

Rustem, B. and Velupillai, K. On Rationalizing Expectations Using Rank-One Updates of the Kalman Filter. *J. Econ. Dynam. Control*, June 1986, *10*(1/2), pp. 119–24.

Salemi, Michael K. Solution and Estimation of Linear Rational Expectations Models. *J. Econometrics*, February 1986, *31*(1), pp. 41–66.

Schankerman, Mark and Nadiri, M. Ishaq. A Test of Static Equilibrium Models and Rates of Return to Quasi-fixed Factors, with an Application to the Bell System. *J. Econometrics*, Oct./Nov. 1986, *33*(1/2), pp. 97–118.

Schmalensee, Richard and Joskow, Paul L. Estimated Parameters as Independent Variables: An Application to the Costs of Electric Generating Units. *J. Econometrics*, April 1986, *31*(3), pp. 275–305. **[G: U.S.]**

Sefcik, Stephan E. and Thompson, Rex. An Approach to Statistical Inference in Cross-Sectional Models with Security Abnormal Returns as Dependent Variable. *J. Acc. Res.*, Autumn 1986, *24*(2), pp. 316–34. **[G: U.S.]**

Sellar, Christine; Chavas, Jean-Paul and Stoll, John R. Specification of the Logit Model: The Case of Valuation of Nonmarket Goods. *J. Environ. Econ. Manage.*, December 1986, *13*(4), pp. 382–90. **[G: U.S.]**

Sickles, Robin C.; Good, David H. and Johnson, Richard L. Allocative Distortions and the Regulatory Transition of the U.S. Airline Industry. *J. Econometrics*, Oct./Nov. 1986, *33*(1/2), pp. 143–63. **[G: U.S.]**

Sims, Christopher A. Are Forecasting Models Usable for Policy Analysis? *Fed. Res. Bank Minn. Rev.*, Winter 1986, *10*(1), pp. 2–16.

Smallwood, David M. and Blaylock, James R. Forecasting Performance of Models Using the Box–Cox Transformation. *Agr. Econ. Res.*, Fall 1986, *38*(4), pp. 14–24.

Smith, James Q. and Gathercole, R. B. Principles of Interactive Forecasting. **In** *[de Finetti, B.]*, 1986, pp. 405–23.

Smith, Richard J. and Blundell, Richard. An Exogeneity Test for a Simultaneous Equation Tobit Model with an Application to Labor Supply. *Econometrica*, May 1986, *54*(3), pp. 679–85. **[G: U.K.]**

Smith, V. Kerry. Another View of the State of Engineering Production Functions. *Economica*, November 1986, *53*(212), pp. 529–32.

Stoker, Thomas M. Simple Tests of Distributional Effects on Macroeconomic Equations. *J. Polit. Econ.*, August 1986, *94*(4), pp. 763–95.

Swartz, Stephen and Welsch, Roy E. Applications of Bounded-Influence and Diagnostic Methods in Energy Modeling. **In** *Belsley, D. A. and Kuh, E., eds.*, 1986, pp. 154–90. **[G: U.S.]**

Tauchen, George. Statistical Properties of Generalized Method-of-Moments Estimators of Structural Parameters Obtained from Financial Market Data: Reply. *J. Bus. Econ. Statist.*, October 1986, *4*(4), pp. 423–25.

Tauchen, George. Statistical Properties of Generalized Method-of-Moments Estimators of Structural Parameters Obtained from Financial Market Data. *J. Bus. Econ. Statist.*, October 1986, *4*(4), pp. 397–416. **[G: U.S.]**

Taylor, John B. New Econometric Approaches to Stabilization Policy in Stochastic Models of Macroeconomic Fluctuations. **In** *Griliches, Z. and Intriligator, M. D., eds.*, 1986, pp. 1997–2055.

Thurman, Walter N. Endogeneity Testing in a Supply and Demand Framework. *Rev. Econ. Statist.*, November 1986, *68*(4), pp. 638–46. **[G: U.S.]**

Tinbergen, Jan. Some Extensions and Refinements of Gottschalk's Estimation of Production Functions. **In** *Perryman, M. R. and Schmidt, J. R., eds.*, 1986, pp. 3–12. **[G: U.S.]**

Veall, Michael R. On Estimating the Effects of Peak Demand Pricing. *J. Appl. Econometrics*, January 1986, *1*(1), pp. 81–93. **[G: Canada]**

van Velthoven, Ben and van Winden, Frans. Social Classes and State Behavior. *J. Inst. Theoretical Econ.*, September 1986, *142*(3), pp. 542–70. **[G: Netherlands]**

Vijverberg, Wim P. M. Consistent Estimates of the Wage Equation When Individuals Choose among Income-Earning Activities. *Southern Econ. J.*, April 1986, *52*(4), pp. 1028–42. **[G: Malaysia]**

Weissenberger, Edgar; Müller-Brockhausen, Gerd and Welsch, Heinz. A Factor Demand Model with Quasi-fixed Factors and Rational Expectations. *J. Econ. (Z. Nationalökon.)*, 1986, *46*(2), pp. 123–42. **[G: U.S.]**

West, Kenneth D. Empirical Assessment of Present Value Relations: Comment. *Econometric Rev.*, 1986, *5*(2), pp. 273–78. **[G: U.S.]**

West, Mike and Harrison, P. Jeff. Monitoring and Adaptation in Bayesian Forecasting Models. *J. Amer. Statist. Assoc.*, September 1986, *81*(395), pp. 741–50.

Westcott, J. H. Application of Control Theory to Macro-economic Models. **In** *Mason, J.; Ma-*

thias, P. and Westcott, J. H., eds., 1986, pp. 89–99. **[G: U.K.]**

Whiteman, Charles H. An Analytical Policy Design under Rational Expectations. *Econometrica,* November 1986, *54*(6), pp. 1387–1405.

Wibe, Sören. Observable and Non-observable Data: A Reply [Engineering Production Functions—A Survey]. *Economica,* November 1986, *53*(212), pp. 535–36.

de Witte, M. A. C. and Cramer, J. S. Functional Form of Engel Curve for Foodstuffs. *Europ. Econ. Rev.*, August 1986, *30*(4), pp. 909–13. **[G: Netherlands]**

Zellner, Arnold. Basic Issues in Econometrics: Past and Present. **In** *Szenberg, M., ed.*, 1986, *1982*, pp. 95–103.

Zin, Stanley E. Modelling the Persistence of Conditional Variances: Comment. *Econometric Rev.*, 1986, *5*(1), pp. 75–80.

213 Mathematical Methods and Models

2130 General

Artzner, Philippe; Simon, Carl P. and Sonnenschein, Hugo. Convergence of Myopic Firms to Long-run Equilibrium via the Method of Characteristics. **In** *Sonnenschein, H. F., ed.*, 1986, pp. 157–83.

Aulin, Arvid. Cybernetic Causality II: Causal Recursion in Goal-Directed Systems, with Applications to Evolution Dynamics and Economics. *Math. Soc. Sci.*, December 1986, *12*(3), pp. 227–64.

Debreu, Gerard. Theoretical Models: Mathematical Forms and Economic Content. *Econometrica,* November 1986, *54*(6), pp. 1259–70.

Fishburn, Peter C. Implicit Mean Value and Certainty Equivalence. *Econometrica,* September 1986, *54*(5), pp. 1197–1205.

Grubel, Herbert G. and Boland, Lawrence A. On the Efficient Use of Mathematics in Economics: Some Theory, Facts and Results of an Opinion Survey. *Kyklos,* 1986, *39*(3), pp. 419–42.

Hirschhorn, Eric. A Note on the Use (and Misuse) of Log-Linear Approximations in Economics. *Amer. Econ.*, Spring 1986, *30*(1), pp. 75–77.

Mak, King-Tim. On Separability: Functional Structure. *J. Econ. Theory,* December 1986, *40*(2), pp. 250–82.

Rubinstein, Ariel and Fishburn, Peter C. Algebraic Aggregation Theory. *J. Econ. Theory,* February 1986, *38*(1), pp. 63–77.

Saari, Donald G. Dynamical Systems and Mathematical Economics. **In** *Sonnenschein, H. F., ed.*, 1986, pp. 1–24.

Semmler, Willi. Competition, Instability, and Nonlinear Cycles: Introduction. **In** *Semmler, W., ed.*, 1986, pp. v–xii.

Vallée, Robert. Extension de la transformation de Laplace et de la transformation $\mathfrak{z}$ au cas d'un argument matriciel, application à la théorie des systèmes dynamiques. (Extension of Laplace Transform and $\mathfrak{z}$ Transform to the Case of a Matrix Argument, Application to the Theory of Dynamic Systems. With English summary.) *Écon. Soc.*, November 1986, *20*(11), pp. 35–40.

2132 Optimization Techniques

Brock, William A. A Revised Version of Samuelson's Correspondence Principle: Applications of Recent Results on the Asymptotic Stability of Optimal Control to the Problem of Comparing Long Run Equilibria. **In** *Sonnenschein, H. F., ed.*, 1986, pp. 86–116.

Brock, William A. and Rothschild, Michael. Comparative Statics for Multidimensional Optimal Stopping Problems. **In** *Sonnenschein, H. F., ed.*, 1986, pp. 124–38.

Caravani, P. On Extending Linear Quadratic Control Theory to Non-symmetric Risky Objectives. *J. Econ. Dynam. Control,* June 1986, *10*(1/2), pp. 83–88.

Chen, Zhao-Ying. Decision Support System for Management of Oil Pipeline. **In** *Pau, L. F., ed.*, 1986, pp. 103–06.

Cheng, Leonard. The Impact of Changes in Relative Weights on the Optimal Solution of a Maximization Problem. *J. Math. Econ.*, 1986, *15*(2), pp. 143–50.

Davidsen, Thorkild. Westergaard, Edgeworth and the Use of Lagrange Multipliers in Economics [The Early Use of Lagrange Multipliers in Economics]. *Econ. J.*, September 1986, *96*(383), pp. 808–11.

Galeotti, Marcello and Gori, Franco. Global Analysis and Controls of an Irregular Economy Model. *J. Econ. Dynam. Control,* June 1986, *10*(1/2), pp. 205–12.

Ivović, Miodrag. Intervalna optimalnost. (Intervallic Optimality. With English summary.) *Econ. Anal. Workers' Manage.*, 1986, *20*(1), pp. 77–88.

Jewitt, Ian. A Note on Comparative Statics and Stochastic Dominance. *J. Math. Econ.*, 1986, *15*(3), pp. 249–54.

Livesey, D. A. New Perspectives from the Complex Plane. *J. Econ. Dynam. Control,* June 1986, *10*(1/2), pp. 99–107.

Markose, S. M. A Theory of Policy-Induced Structural Change: An Application of the Bismut Stochastic Maximum Principle. *J. Econ. Dynam. Control,* June 1986, *10*(1/2), pp. 109–14.

Pereira, F. and Vinter, R. B. Necessary Conditions for Optimal Control Problems with Discontinuous Trajectories. *J. Econ. Dynam. Control,* June 1986, *10*(1/2), pp. 115–18.

Romer, Paul M. Cake Eating, Chattering, and Jumps: Existence Results for Variational Problems. *Econometrica,* July 1986, *54*(4), pp. 897–908.

2133 Existence and Stability Conditions of Equilibrium

Back, Kerry. Concepts of Similarity for Utility Functions. *J. Math. Econ.*, 1986, *15*(2), pp. 129–42.

Boggio, Luciano. Stability of Production Prices

in a Model of General Interdependence. **In** *Semmler, W., ed.*, 1986, pp. 83–114.

Brock, William A. A Revised Version of Samuelson's Correspondence Principle: Applications of Recent Results on the Asymptotic Stability of Optimal Control to the Problem of Comparing Long Run Equilibria. **In** *Sonnenschein, H. F., ed.*, 1986, pp. 86–116.

Debreu, Gerard and Herstein, I. N. Nonnegative Square Matrices. **In** *Sohn, I., ed.*, 1986, *1953*, pp. 200–209.

Duménil, Gérard and Lévy, D. Stability and Instability in a Dynamic Model of Capitalist Production. **In** *Semmler, W., ed.*, 1986, pp. 132–69.

Evans, George W. Selection Criteria for Models with Non-uniqueness. *J. Monet. Econ.*, September 1986, *18*(2), pp. 147–57.

Flaschel, Peter and Semmler, Willi. The Dynamic Equalization of Profit Rates for Input–Output Models with Fixed Capital. **In** *Semmler, W., ed.*, 1986, pp. 1–34.

Fujimoto, Takao and Indelli, Paola. A Note on Quick Stability Checks for Linear Difference Equations. *Econ. Stud. Quart.*, March 1986, *37*(1), pp. 81–86.

Fujimoto, Takao and Krause, Ulrich. Ergodic Price Setting with Technical Progress. **In** *Semmler, W., ed.*, 1986, pp. 115–24.

Furth, Dave. Stability and Instability of Oligopoly. *J. Econ. Theory*, December 1986, *40*(2), pp. 197–228.

Hawkins, David and Simon, Herbert A. Some Conditions of Macroeconomic Stability: Note. **In** *Sohn, I., ed.*, 1986, *1949*, pp. 196–99.

Honda, Nakaji and Mimaki, Tadashi. Multiobjective Decision Method Using Heuristic Rules. **In** *Pau, L. F., ed.*, 1986, pp. 157–65.

Krause, Ulrich. Perron's Stability Theorem for Non-linear Mappings. *J. Math. Econ.*, 1986, *15*(3), pp. 275–82.

Luenberger, David G. Control of Linear Dynamic Market Systems. *J. Econ. Dynam. Control*, September 1986, *10*(3), pp. 339–51.

Matsuyama, Keisuke; Kojina, Mitsuhiro and Koken, Junichiro. Revisiting Phillips' Model by Applying the Root Locus Method. *Econ. Computat. Cybern. Stud. Res.*, 1986, *21*(3), pp. 43–68.

Pereira, F. and Vinter, R. B. Necessary Conditions for Optimal Control Problems with Discontinuous Trajectories. *J. Econ. Dynam. Control*, June 1986, *10*(1/2), pp. 115–18.

Rath, Kali. On Non-linear Extensions of the Perron–Frobenius Theorem. *J. Math. Econ.*, 1986, *15*(1), pp. 59–62.

2134 Computational Techniques

Amman, Hans M. Are Supercomputers Useful for Optimal Control Experiments? *J. Econ. Dynam. Control*, June 1986, *10*(1/2), pp. 127–30.

Amman, Hans M. Corrigendum: Supercomputers for Optimal Control Experiments? *J. Econ. Dynam. Control*, September 1986, *10*(3), pp. 425.

Boley, Daniel and Bittanti, Sergio. Numerical Problems in Linear System Theory. **In** *Bittanti, S., ed.*, 1986, pp. 183–221.

Fisher, Paul G.; Holly, Sean and Hughes Hallett, A. J. Efficient Solution Techniques for Dynamic Non-Linear Rational Expectations Models. *J. Econ. Dynam. Control*, June 1986, *10*(1/2), pp. 139–45. **[G: U.K.]**

Gelders, Ludo F.; Maes, Johan and Van Wassenhove, Luk N. A Branch and Bound Algorithm for the Multi Item Single Level Capacitated Dynamic Lotsizing Problem. **In** *Axsäter, S.; Schneeweiss, C. and Silver, E., eds.*, 1986, pp. 92–108.

Kimbell, Larry J. and Harrison, Glenn W. On the Solution of General Equilibrium Models. *Econ. Modelling*, July 1986, *3*(3), pp. 197–212.

Kollintzas, Tryphon. A Non-recursive Solution for the Linear Rational Expectations Model. *J. Econ. Dynam. Control*, June 1986, *10*(1/2), pp. 327–32.

Kosko, Bart. Optimal Fuzzy Hierarchical Decisions. **In** *Pau, L. F., ed.*, 1986, pp. 51–56.

Le Van, Cuong. Stationary Uncertainty Frontiers in Macroeconometric Models: An Approach for Solving Matrix Riccati Equations. *J. Econ. Dynam. Control*, June 1986, *10*(1/2), pp. 225–29.

Muckstadt, John A. Planning Component Delivery Intervals in Constrained Assembly Systems. **In** *Axsäter, S.; Schneeweiss, C. and Silver, E., eds.*, 1986, pp. 132–49.

Pearlman, Joseph. Diverse Information and Rational Expectations Models. *J. Econ. Dynam. Control*, June 1986, *10*(1/2), pp. 333–38.

2135 Construction, Analysis, and Use of Mathematical Programming Models

Baumol, William J. Planning and Dual Values of Linearized Nonlinear Problems: A Gothic Tale. **In** *Baumol, W. J.*, 1986, *1982*, pp. 224–33.

Breton, Michèle, et al. On the Computation of Equilibria in Discounted Stochastic Dynamic Games. **In** *Başar, T., ed.*, 1986, pp. 64–87.

Carvalhais, Z. and Davis, M. H. A. Optimal Timing of Capacity Expansion. *J. Econ. Dynam. Control*, June 1986, *10*(1/2), pp. 89–91.

Drezner, Z.; Thisse, Jacques-François and Wesolowsky, George O. The Minimax-Min Location Problem. *J. Reg. Sci.*, February 1986, *26*(1), pp. 87–101.

Drynan, Ross G. On Resolving Multiple Optima in Linear Programming: Forum. *Rev. Marketing Agr. Econ.*, August 1986, *54*(2), pp. 31–35.

Gol'shtein, E. G. Decomposition Methods for Linear and Convex Programming Problems. *Matekon*, Summer 1986, *22*(4), pp. 75–101.

Hoffman, Elizabeth, et al. Artificial Intelligence in Economics—Expert Systems Modelling of Microeconomic Systems. **In** *Pau, L. F., ed.*, 1986, pp. 1–9.

McCamley, Francis and Kliebenstein, James B. Two Simple Stochastic Efficiency Tests for MOTAD Solutions. *Can. J. Agr. Econ.*, July 1986, *34*(2), pp. 177–94.

McCarl, Bruce A. and Apland, Jeffrey. Validation

of Linear Programming Models. *Southern J. Agr. Econ.*, December 1986, *18*(2), pp. 155–64.

Meško, Ivan. Solution of Some Programming Problems by the Use of Piecewise Linear Approximation. *Econ. Anal. Workers' Manage.*, 1986, *20*(1), pp. 65–75.

Niculescu, I. and Boconcios, Rodica. Mathematical Model for Optimizing the Functioning of the National Energy System. *Econ. Computat. Cybern. Stud. Res.*, 1986, *21*(2), pp. 27–32.

Nijkamp, Peter and Rietveld, Piet. Multiple Objective Decision Analysis in Regional Economics. **In** *Nijkamp, P., ed. (I),* 1986, pp. 493–541.

Scarf, Herbert E. Neighborhood Systems for Production Sets with Indivisibilities. *Econometrica,* May 1986, *54*(3), pp. 507–32.

214 Computer Programs

2140 Computer Programs

Amman, Hans M. Are Supercomputers Useful for Optimal Control Experiments? *J. Econ. Dynam. Control*, June 1986, *10*(1/2), pp. 127–30.

Amman, Hans M. Corrigendum: Supercomputers for Optimal Control Experiments? *J. Econ. Dynam. Control*, September 1986, *10*(3), pp. 425.

Baines, A. and Clithero, D. T. Interactive User-Friendly Package for Design and Analysis of Experiments. **In** *De Antoni, F.; Lauro, N. and Rizzi, A., eds.*, 1986, pp. 320–25.

Beilock, Richard P., et al. A Microcomputer Package to Teach the Simplex Algorithm. *Southern J. Agr. Econ.*, December 1986, *18*(2), pp. 267–71.

Ben-David, Arie and Sterling, Leon. A Prototype Expert System for Credit Evaluation. **In** *Pau, L. F., ed.*, 1986, pp. 121–28.

Berzuini, C.; Ross, G. and Larizza, C. Developing Intelligent Software for Non-linear Model Fitting as an Expert System. **In** *De Antoni, F.; Lauro, N. and Rizzi, A., eds.*, 1986, pp. 259–64.

Carlsen, F. and Heuch, I. EXPRESS—An Expert System Utilizing Standard Statistical Packages. **In** *De Antoni, F.; Lauro, N. and Rizzi, A., eds.*, 1986, pp. 265–70.

Coles, Charles. Use of a Lotus 1-2-3 Spreadsheet Program in Farm Management Extension. *Can. J. Agr. Econ.*, June 1986, *33*, pp. 100–106.

Darius, P. L. Building Expert Systems with the Help of Existing Statistical Software: An Example. **In** *De Antoni, F.; Lauro, N. and Rizzi, A., eds.*, 1986, pp. 277–82.

Di Battista, G. and Tamassia, R. An Interactive Graphic System for Designing and Accessing Statistical Data Bases. **In** *De Antoni, F.; Lauro, N. and Rizzi, A., eds.*, 1986, pp. 231–36.

Dickson, J. M. and Talbot, M. Statistical Data Validation and Expert Systems. **In** *De Antoni, F.; Lauro, N. and Rizzi, A., eds.*, 1986, pp. 283–88.

Dumitrescu, Vl.; Somnea, D. and Garboan, I. Graphical Systems Using the BASIC Interpreter: A Simple Graphical Noninteractive System. *Econ. Computat. Cybern. Stud. Res.*, 1986, *21*(1), pp. 81–91.

Dumitrescu, Vl., et al. Graphical Systems Using the BASIC Interpreter—A Simple Interactive Graphical System. *Econ. Computat. Cybern. Stud. Res.*, 1986, *21*(2), pp. 91–98.

Dumitrescu, Vl., et al. Using GBASIC in the 2D and 3D Applications. *Econ. Computat. Cybern. Stud. Res.*, 1986, *21*(3), pp. 27–41.

Dumitrescu, Vl., et al. 3D Graphics with GBASIC. *Econ. Computat. Cybern. Stud. Res.*, 1986, *21*(4), pp. 63–79.

Fordyce, Kenneth J. and Sullivan, Gerald A. Decision Simulation (DSIM)—One Outcome of Combining Expert Systems and Decision Support Systems. **In** *Pau, L. F., ed.*, 1986, pp. 31–40.

Froeschl, K. A. and Grossmann, W. Knowledge Base Supported Analysis of Longitudinal Data. **In** *De Antoni, F.; Lauro, N. and Rizzi, A., eds.*, 1986, pp. 289–94.

Georgiev, A. A. A Fast Algorithm for Curve Fitting. **In** *De Antoni, F.; Lauro, N. and Rizzi, A., eds.*, 1986, pp. 97–101.

Gervais, Paul E. Innovations in Spreadsheet Analysis: 1. A Design Methodology 2. Spreadsheet Limitations. *Can. J. Agr. Econ.*, June 1986, *33*, pp. 86–99.

Gordesch, J. Non-standard Graphical Presentation. **In** *De Antoni, F.; Lauro, N. and Rizzi, A., eds.*, 1986, pp. 237–42.

Hall, H. Keith; Moore, James C. and Whinston, Andrew B. A Theoretical Basis for Expert Systems. **In** *Pau, L. F., ed.*, 1986, pp. 11–19.

Hendry, David F. Using PC-GIVE in Econometrics Teaching. *Oxford Bull. Econ. Statist.*, February 1986, *48*(1), pp. 87–98.

Hoffman, Elizabeth, et al. Artificial Intelligence in Economics—Expert Systems Modelling of Microeconomic Systems. **In** *Pau, L. F., ed.*, 1986, pp. 1–9.

Honda, Nakaji, et al. Decision Support System Using Fuzzy Reasoning and Evaluation. **In** *Pau, L. F., ed.*, 1986, pp. 41–49.

Huet, S. and Messéan, A. NL: A Statistical Package for General Nonlinear Regression Problems. **In** *De Antoni, F.; Lauro, N. and Rizzi, A., eds.*, 1986, pp. 326–31.

Iwasieczko, B., et al. Expert System in Financial Analysis. **In** *Pau, L. F., ed.*, 1986, pp. 113–20.

Jasiński, P. J.; Butlewski, B. and Paradowski, S. Towards Natural Integration of Database Management System and Statistical Software. **In** *De Antoni, F.; Lauro, N. and Rizzi, A., eds.*, 1986, pp. 437–41.

Jida, J. and Lemaire, J. Expert Systems and Data Analysis Package Management. **In** *De Antoni, F.; Lauro, N. and Rizzi, A., eds.*, 1986, pp. 251–58.

de Jong, V. J. A Multilingual Specification System for Statistical Software. **In** *De Antoni, F.; Lauro, N. and Rizzi, A., eds.*, 1986, pp. 393–98.

Keller, W. J. Statistical Software for Personal Computers. **In** *De Antoni, F.; Lauro, N. and Rizzi, A., eds.*, 1986, pp. 332–37.

Kosy, Donald W. and Wise, Ben P. Overview of Rome: A Reason-Oriented Modeling Environment. **In** *Pau, L. F., ed.*, 1986, pp. 21–30.

Kredler, C. and Kowarschick, W. A Convenient Way of Computing ML-Estimates: Use of Automatic Differentiation. **In** *De Antoni, F.; Lauro, N. and Rizzi, A., eds.*, 1986, pp. 108–13.

Lbov, G. S. Algorithm and Software of Multivariate Statistical Analysis of Heterogeneous Data. **In** *De Antoni, F.; Lauro, N. and Rizzi, A., eds.*, 1986, pp. 498–503.

MacRae, C. Duncan. User Control Knowledge in a Tax Consulting System. **In** *Pau, L. F., ed.*, 1986, pp. 194–203.

Maes, R. and van Dijk, J. E. M. A User-Friendly Propositional Formalism for a Managerial DSS-Generator. **In** *Pau, L. F., ed.*, 1986, pp. 65–76.

McGrann, James M., et al. Microcomputer Budget Management System. *Southern J. Agr. Econ.*, July 1986, *18*(1), pp. 151–56.

Miller, Ross M. Markets as Logic Programs. **In** *Pau, L. F., ed.*, 1986, pp. 129–36.

Molenaar, W. Computer Graphics and Data Presentation, a First Step toward a Cognitive and Ergonomic Analysis. **In** *De Antoni, F.; Lauro, N. and Rizzi, A., eds.*, 1986, pp. 243–48.

Morabito, A. AMS—A Computer Program for Survival Analysis, General Linear Models and a Stochastic Survival Model. **In** *De Antoni, F.; Lauro, N. and Rizzi, A., eds.*, 1986, pp. 384–89.

Murphy, B. P.; Rohl, J. S. and Cribb, R. L. Recursive Techniques in Statistical Programming. **In** *De Antoni, F.; Lauro, N. and Rizzi, A., eds.*, 1986, pp. 338–44.

Nagel, Stuart and Long, John. P/G Percent Analysis: A Decision-Aiding Program. **In** *Pau, L. F., ed.*, 1986, pp. 137–45.

Pau, L. F. An Expert System Kernel for the Analysis of Strategies over Time. **In** *Pau, L. F., ed.*, 1986, pp. 107–12.

Pau, L. F. Artificial Intelligence in Economics and Management: Why? **In** *Pau, L. F., ed.*, 1986, pp. v–ix.

Payne, R. W. and Lane, P. W. Design Criteria for a Flexible Statistical Language. **In** *De Antoni, F.; Lauro, N. and Rizzi, A., eds.*, 1986, pp. 345–50.

Posten, H. O. Algorithms for the Beta Distribution Function. **In** *De Antoni, F.; Lauro, N. and Rizzi, A., eds.*, 1986, pp. 309–19.

Ross, Randolph W. Innovation in Spreadsheet Analysis and Farm Management. *Can. J. Agr. Econ.*, June 1986, *33*, pp. 80–85.

Rossi, Peter E. Statistical Properties of Generalized Method-of-Moments Estimators of Structural Parameters Obtained from Financial Market Data: Comment. *J. Bus. Econ. Statist.*, October 1986, *4*(4), pp. 421–22.

Scarani, C. An Efficient Algorithm for Time Series Decomposition. **In** *De Antoni, F.; Lauro, N. and Rizzi, A., eds.*, 1986, pp. 399–404.

Scheraga, Joel D. Instruction in Economics through Simulated Computer Programming. *J. Econ. Educ.*, Spring 1986, *17*(2), pp. 129–39.

Sposito, V. A. and English, Burton C. Reliability of Linear Programming Software: An Experience with the IBM Mathematical Programming System Series: Comment. *Amer. J. Agr. Econ.*, May 1986, *68*(2), pp. 370–72.

Spriggs, John and Van Kooten, G. C. Estimating Systems of Nonlinear Equations in a Single Equation Framework. *Can. J. Agr. Econ.*, March 1986, *34*(1), pp. 105–11. **[G: Canada]**

Straszak, A., et al. Computer Aided Learning in a Two-level Economy with Nonlinear Economic Regulators. **In** *Pau, L. F., ed.*, 1986, pp. 185–91.

Tarumi, T. and Tanaka, Y. Statistical Software SAM—Sensitivity Analysis in Multivariate Methods. **In** *De Antoni, F.; Lauro, N. and Rizzi, A., eds.*, 1986, pp. 351–56.

Tice, Thomas F. and Kletke, Marilyn G. Reliability of Linear Programming Software: An Experience with the IBM Mathematical Programming System Series: Reply. *Amer. J. Agr. Econ.*, May 1986, *68*(2), pp. 373–74.

215 Experimental Economic Methods

2150 Experimental Economic Methods

Alhadeff, David A. Microeconomics and the Experimental Analysis of Behavior. **In** *MacFadyen, A. J. and MacFadyen, H. W., eds.*, 1986, pp. 183–215.

Allison, James. Economic Interpretations of Animal Experiments. **In** *MacFadyen, A. J. and MacFadyen, H. W., eds.*, 1986, pp. 219–45.

Arrow, Kenneth J. Valuing Environmental Goods: An Assessment of the Contingent Valuation Method: The Review Panel's Assessment: Comments. **In** *Cummings, R. G.; Brookshire, D. S. and Schulze, W. D., eds.*, 1986, pp. 180–85.

Battalio, Raymond C.; Kagel, John H. and Phillips, Owen R. Optimal Prices and Animal Consumers in Congested Markets. *Econ. Inquiry*, April 1986, *24*(2), pp. 181–93.

Berg, Joyce E., et al. Controlling Preferences for Lotteries on Units of Experimental Exchange. *Quart. J. Econ.*, May 1986, *101*(2), pp. 281–306.

Bishop, Richard C. and Heberlein, Thomas A. Does Contingent Valuation Work? **In** *Cummings, R. G.; Brookshire, D. S. and Schulze, W. D., eds.*, 1986, pp. 123–47.

Brown, James N. and Ashenfelter, Orley. Testing the Efficiency of Employment Contracts. *J. Polit. Econ.*, Part 2, June 1986, *94*(3), pp. S40–S87. **[G: U.S.]**

Coursey, Don L. and Schulze, William D. The Application of Laboratory Experimental Economics to the Contingent Valuation of Public Goods. *Public Choice*, 1986, *49*(1), pp. 47–68. **[G: U.S.]**

Cox, James C. and Isaac, R. Mark. Experimental Economics and Experimental Psychology: Ever the Twain Shall Meet? **In** *MacFadyen, A. J. and MacFadyen, H. W., eds.*, 1986, pp. 647–69.

Davis, Douglas D. and Williams, Arlington W. The Effects of Rent Asymmetries in Posted Offer Markets. *J. Econ. Behav. Organ.*, September 1986, *7*(3), pp. 303–16.

Dawes, Robyn M., et al. Organizing Groups for Collective Action. *Amer. Polit. Sci. Rev.*, December 1986, *80*(4), pp. 1171–85. **[G: U.S.]**

Diekmann, Andreas. Volunteer's Dilemma. A Social Trap without a Dominant Strategy and Some Empirical Results. **In** *[Rapoport, A.]*, 1986, pp. 187–97.

Forsythe, Robert. The Application of Laboratory Methods to Testing Theories of Resource Allocation under Uncertainty. **In** *Gilad, B. and Kaish, S., eds., Vol. A*, 1986, pp. 19–60. **[G: U.S.]**

Freeman, A. Myrick, III. On Assessing the State of the Arts of the Contingent Valuation Method of Valuing Environmental Changes. **In** *Cummings, R. G.; Brookshire, D. S. and Schulze, W. D., eds.*, 1986, pp. 148–61.

Gagey, Frédéric and Rey, Patrick. L'économie expérimentale comme outil pédagogique: Élaboration d'un jeu d'initiation à la microéconomie. (Experimental Economics Applied to Teaching: Elaboration of a Microeconomic Game. With English summary.) *Revue Écon.*, January 1986, *37*(1), pp. 5–30.

Guttman, Joel M. Matching Behavior and Collective Action: Some Experimental Evidence. *J. Econ. Behav. Organ.*, June 1986, *7*(2), pp. 171–98.

Harrison, Glenn W. Experimental Futures Markets. **In** *Goss, B. A., ed.*, 1986, pp. 43–76.

Hoffman, Elizabeth; Marsden, James R. and Whinston, Andrew B. Using Different Economic Data Forms [Microeconomic Systems as an Experimental Science]. *J. Behav. Econ.*, Winter 1986, *15*, pp. 67–84.

Holt, Charles A.; Langan, Loren W. and Villamil, Anne P. Market Power in Oral Double Auctions. *Econ. Inquiry*, January 1986, *24*(1), pp. 107–23.

Holt, Charles A. and Sherman, Roger. Quality Uncertainty and Bundling. **In** *Ippolito, P. M. and Scheffman, D. T., eds.*, 1986, pp. 221–50.

Holt, Charles A. and Villamil, Anne P. A Laboratory Experiment with a Single-Person Cobweb. *Atlantic Econ. J.*, July 1986, *14*(2), pp. 51–54.

Kagel, John H. and Levin, Dan. The Winner's Curse and Public Information in Common Value Auctions. *Amer. Econ. Rev.*, December 1986, *76*(5), pp. 894–920. **[G: U.S.]**

Kahneman, Daniel. Valuing Environmental Goods: An Assessment of the Contingent Valuation Method: The Review Panel's Assessment: Comments. **In** *Cummings, R. G.; Brookshire, D. S. and Schulze, W. D., eds.*, 1986, pp. 185–94.

Kahneman, Daniel; Knetsch, Jack L. and Thaler, Richard H. Fairness and the Assumptions of Economics. *J. Bus.*, Part 2, October 1986, *59*(4), pp. S285–300.

Kahneman, Daniel; Knetsch, Jack L. and Thaler, Richard H. Fairness and the Assumptions of Economics. **In** *Hogarth, R. M. and Reder, M. W., eds.*, 1986, pp. 101–16.

Kunreuther, Howard. Comments [Fairness and the Assumptions of Economics] [Rational Choice in Experimental Markets]. **In** *Hogarth, R. M. and Reder, M. W., eds.*, 1986, pp. 145–51.

Kunreuther, Howard. Comments [Rational Choice in Experimental Markets] [Fairness and the Assumptions of Economics]. *J. Bus.*, Part 2, October 1986, *59*(4), pp. S329–35.

Lucas, Robert E., Jr. Adaptive Behavior and Economic Theory. **In** *Hogarth, R. M. and Reder, M. W., eds.*, 1986, pp. 217–42.

Lucas, Robert E., Jr. Adoptive Behavior and Economic Theory. *J. Bus.*, Part 2, October 1986, *59*(4), pp. S401–26.

Luce, R. Duncan. Comments [Fairness and the Assumptions of Economics] [Rational Choice in Experimental Markets]. **In** *Hogarth, R. M. and Reder, M. W., eds.*, 1986, pp. 153–59.

Luce, R. Duncan. Comments [Rational Choice in Experimental Markets] [Fairness and the Assumptions of Economics]. *J. Bus.*, Part 2, October 1986, *59*(4), pp. S337–45.

Lynch, Michael, et al. Product Quality, Consumer Information and "Lemons" in Experimental Markets. **In** *Ippolito, P. M. and Scheffman, D. T., eds.*, 1986, pp. 251–306.

Mackay, Robert J. Comments [Quality Uncertainty and Bundling] [Product Quality, Consumer Information and "Lemons" in Experimental Markets] [An Experimental Study of Warranty Coverage and Dispute Resolution in Competitive Markets]. **In** *Ippolito, P. M. and Scheffman, D. T., eds.*, 1986, pp. 373–74. **[G: U.S.]**

Maital, Sharone L.; Maital, Shlomo and Pollak, Nava. Economic Behavior and Social Learning. **In** *MacFadyen, A. J. and MacFadyen, H. W., eds.*, 1986, pp. 271–90.

Miller, Ross M. Comments [Quality Uncertainty and Bundling] [Product Quality, Consumer Information and "Lemons" in Experimental Markets] [An Experimental Study of Warranty Coverage and Dispute Resolution in Competitive Markets]. **In** *Ippolito, P. M. and Scheffman, D. T., eds.*, 1986, pp. 375–76. **[G: U.S.]**

Mitchell, Robert Cameron and Carson, Richard T. Some Comments on the State of the Arts Assessment of the Contigent Valuation Method Draft Report: Appendix. **In** *Cummings, R. G.; Brookshire, D. S. and Schulze, W. D., eds.*, 1986, pp. 237–45.

Palfrey, Thomas R. and Romer, Thomas. An Experimental Study of Warranty Coverage and Dispute Resolution in Competitive Markets. **In** *Ippolito, P. M. and Scheffman, D. T., eds.*, 1986, pp. 307–72. **[G: U.S.]**

215 Experimental Economic Methods

Plott, Charles R. Rational Choice in Experimental Markets. *J. Bus.*, Part 2, October 1986, *59*(4), pp. S301–27.

Plott, Charles R. Rational Choice in Experimental Markets. **In** *Hogarth, R. M. and Reder, M. W., eds.*, 1986, pp. 117–43.

Randall, Alan. The Possibility of Satisfactory Benefit Estimation with Contingent Markets. **In** *Cummings, R. G.; Brookshire, D. S. and Schulze, W. D., eds.*, 1986, pp. 114–22.

Rosen, Sherwin. Valuing Environmental Goods: An Assessment of the Contingent Valuation Method: The Review Panel's Assessment: Comments. **In** *Cummings, R. G.; Brookshire, D. S. and Schulze, W. D., eds.*, 1986, pp. 194–97.

Roth, Alvin E. Laboratory Experimentation in Economics. *Econ. Philos.*, October 1986, *2*(2), pp. 245–73.

Schoumaker, Françoise. Tour d'horizon des méthodes expérimentales en sciences économiques et de leurs résultats. (Methods of Experiments in Economics. With English summary.) *L'Actual. Econ.*, September 1986, *62*(3), pp. 474–85.

Selten, Reinhard and Stoecker, Rolf. End Behavior in Sequences of Finite Prisoner's Dilemma Supergames: A Learning Theory Approach. *J. Econ. Behav. Organ.*, March 1986, *7*(1), pp. 47–70.

Shweder, Richard A. Comments [Fairness and the Assumptions of Economics] [Rational Choice in Experimental Markets]. **In** *Hogarth, R. M. and Reder, M. W., eds.*, 1986, pp. 161–70.

Shweder, Richard A. Comments [Rational Choice in Experimental Markets] [Fairness and the Assumptions of Economics]. *J. Bus.*, Part 2, October 1986, *59*(4), pp. S345–54.

Smith, V. Kerry. To Keep or Toss the Contingent Valuation Method. **In** *Cummings, R. G.; Brookshire, D. S. and Schulze, W. D., eds.*, 1986, pp. 162–79.

Smith, Vernon L. Valuing Environmental Goods: An Assessment of the Contingent Valuation Method: The Review Panel's Assessment: Comments. **In** *Cummings, R. G.; Brookshire, D. S. and Schulze, W. D., eds.*, 1986, pp. 197–204.

Sugden, Robert. New Developments in the Theory of Choice under Uncertainty. *Bull. Econ. Res.*, January 1986, *38*(1), pp. 1–24.

Urbany, Joel E. An Experimental Examination of the Economics of Information. *J. Cons. Res.*, September 1986, *13*(2), pp. 257–71.

220 Economic and Social Statistical Data and Analysis

2200 General

Archer, David. The New Zealand Department of Statistics Business Directory. *Statist. J.*, October 1986, *4*(2), pp. 113–25. **[G: New Zealand]**

Barnes, Robert. Use of Registers and Population Censuses as Sampling Frames in Great Britain. *Statist. J.*, May 1986, *4*(1), pp. 81–92. **[G: U.K.]**

Blades, Derek. International Statistics: An OECD View. *Bus. Econ.*, July 1986, *21*(3), pp. 37–42. **[G: OECD]**

Butler, Richard J. and McDonald, James B. Trends in Unemployment Duration Data. *Rev. Econ. Statist.*, November 1986, *68*(4), pp. 545–57. **[G: U.S.]**

Cohen, Steven B. Data Collection Organization Effect in the National Medical Care Utilization and Expenditure Survey. *J. Econ. Soc. Meas.*, December 1986, *14*(4), pp. 367–78. **[G: U.S.]**

Davies, R. W. and Wheatcroft, S. G. A Note on the Sources of Unemployment Statistics. **In** *Lane, D., ed.*, 1986, pp. 36–49. **[G: U.S.S.R.]**

Duncan, Joseph W. Federal Statistics and Business Economists. *Bus. Econ.*, July 1986, *21*(3), pp. 26–30. **[G: U.S.]**

Fischer, Stanley and Huizinga, John. Inflation, Unemployment, and Public Opinion Polls. **In** *Fischer, S.*, 1986, *1982*, pp. 123–48.

Freedman, Audrey and Goldstein, Kenneth. Labor Market Data from the Conference Board. **In** *Dennis, B. D., ed.*, 1986, pp. 34–41. **[G: U.S.]**

Griliches, Zvi. Economic Data Issues. **In** *Griliches, Z. and Intriligator, M. D., eds.*, 1986, pp. 1466–1514.

Jacoby, Sanford M. and Mitchell, Daniel J. B. Alternative Sources of Labor Market Data. **In** *Dennis, B. D., ed.*, 1986, pp. 42–49. **[G: U.S.]**

Jasiński, P. J.; Butlewski, B. and Paradowski, S. Towards Natural Integration of Database Management System and Statistical Software. **In** *De Antoni, F.; Lauro, N. and Rizzi, A., eds.*, 1986, pp. 437–41.

Jones, Sidney L. The Status of Federal Economic Statistics. *Bus. Econ.*, July 1986, *21*(3), pp. 31–36. **[G: U.S.]**

Lella, G.; Pavan, S. and Bucci, P. EASY-LINK: An Expert Natural Language Interface to a Statistical Data Bank. **In** *De Antoni, F.; Lauro, N. and Rizzi, A., eds.*, 1986, pp. 442–47.

Leontief, Wassily. An Information System for Policy Decisions in a Modern Economy. **In** *Leontief, W.*, 1986, *1979*, pp. 418–28.

Maunder, W. F. and Fleming, M. C. Reviews of United Kingdom Statistical Sources. *J. Econ. Soc. Meas.*, December 1986, *14*(4), pp. 271–75. **[G: U.K.]**

Moore, Geoffrey H. Needed Improvements in Economic Statistics. *Bus. Econ.*, July 1986, *21*(3), pp. 21–25. **[G: U.S.]**

Nilsson, Björn. Microcomputers in the Statistical Environment of Developed and Developing Countries. *Statist. J.*, October 1986, *4*(2), pp. 127–43.

Oleński, Józef. Meta-information Systems—An Efficient Tool for Integration and Co-ordination of Statistical Surveys. *Statist. J.*, May 1986, *4*(1), pp. 31–45. **[G: Poland]**

Prewitt, Kenneth. Public Statistics and Democratic Politics. **In** *Smelser, N. J. and Gerstein, D. R., eds.*, 1986, pp. 113–28. **[G: U.S.]**

Reisman, A., et. al. On the Voids in U.S. National Education Statistics. *J. Econ. Soc. Meas.*, December 1986, *14*(4), pp. 357–65. **[G: U.S.]**

Ryten, Jacob. Registers as a Tool for Statistical Integration—The Large Enterprise Components. *Statist. J.*, May 1986, *4*(1), pp. 47–58. **[G: Canada]**

Stone, Richard. Social Accounting: The State of Play. *Scand. J. Econ.*, 1986, *88*(3), pp. 453–72.

Treml, Vladimir G. A Turning Point in Availability of Soviet Economic Statistics? *Soviet Econ.*, July-Sept. 1986, *2*(3), pp. 277–82. **[G: U.S.S.R.]**

Vişinoiu, N. Analysis of the System of Socio-economic Statistics. *Econ. Computat. Cybern. Stud. Res.*, 1986, *21*(4), pp. 37–45.

Waite, Charles A. Recent Developments in Economic Statistics at the Census Bureau. *Bus. Econ.*, July 1986, *21*(3), pp. 10–15. **[G: U.S.]**

Walsh, John M. Sources of Labor Market Data from BNA. **In** *Dennis, B. D., ed.*, 1986, pp. 26–33. **[G: U.S.]**

Weinstein, Paul. Sources of Labor Statistics in an Era of Budget Cutbacks: What Are Alternative Sources for I.R. Data? Discussion. **In** *Dennis, B. D., ed.*, 1986, pp. 50–51. **[G: U.S.]**

Worrall, Leslie. The Analysis and Management of Urban Change: The Role of Local Information Systems. *J. Econ. Soc. Meas.*, December 1986, *14*(4), pp. 257–70. **[G: U.K.]**

Wright, Charlotte J. and Groff, James E. Uses of Indexes and Data Bases for Information Release Analysis. *Accounting Rev.*, January 1986, *61*(1), pp. 91–100. **[G: U.S.]**

221 National Income Accounting

2210 National Income Accounting Theory and Procedures

Abouchar, Alan. The Treatment of Intermediate Goods in Cuban National Income Accounts: Parallels and Differences with Soviet Methodology. *Comp. Econ. Stud.*, Summer 1986, *28*(2), pp. 37–48. **[G: Cuba]**

Aukrust, Odd. On the Occasion of a Nobel Prize. *Rev. Income Wealth*, March 1986, *32*(1), pp. 109–12.

Aukrust, Odd. Special Issue on the Review of the United Nations System of National Accounts: Comments on the Overall Program. *Rev. Income Wealth*, June 1986, *32*(2), pp. 118–22.

Bandu, I. and Vârlan, G. Considerations on the Mathematical-Economic Modelling of the National Income per Head of the Population. *Econ. Computat. Cybern. Stud. Res.*, 1986, *21*(4), pp. 59–61.

Beaver, William H. and Demski, Joel S. The Nature of Income Measurement. **In** *Parker, R. H.; Harcourt, G. C. and Whittington, G., eds.*, 1986, *1979*, pp. 167–78.

van Bochave, C. A. and van Tuinen, H. K. Flexibility in the Next SNA: The Case for an Institutional Core. *Rev. Income Wealth*, June 1986, *32*(2), pp. 127–54.

Chadeau, Ann and Roy, Caroline. Relating Households' Final Consumption to Household Activities: Substitutability or Complementarity between Market and Non-market Production. *Rev. Income Wealth*, December 1986, *32*(4), pp. 387–407. **[G: France]**

Choudhury, Uma Datta Roy. Special Issue on the Review of the United Nations System of National Accounts: Comments on the Overall Program. *Rev. Income Wealth*, June 1986, *32*(2), pp. 122–26.

Dallago, Bruno. Economic System and the Causes of Irregular Economy: Some Preliminary Questions for East–West Comparison. *Rivista Int. Sci. Econ. Com.*, August 1986, *33*(8), pp. 777–96.

David, Martin, et al. Alternative Methods for CPS Income Imputation. *J. Amer. Statist. Assoc.*, March 1986, *81*(393), pp. 29–41. **[G: U.S.]**

Diewert, W. Erwin and Morrison, Catherine J. Adjusting Output and Productivity Indexes for Changes in the Terms of Trade. *Econ. J.*, September 1986, *96*(383), pp. 659–79.

Fergie, Ron. Statistical Units Standards and Central Register Systems: Key to the Development of Economic Accounting. *Rev. Income Wealth*, March 1986, *32*(1), pp. 49–68. **[G: Australia]**

Fisher, Irving. The Economics of Accountancy. **In** *Parker, R. H.; Harcourt, G. C. and Whittington, G., eds.*, 1986, *1930*, pp. 66–81.

Gligo, Nicolo. The Preparation of Natural and Cultural Heritage Inventories and Accounts. *CEPAL Rev.*, April 1986, (28), pp. 171–86.

Gynther, Reg S. Why Use General Purchasing Power? **In** *Parker, R. H.; Harcourt, G. C. and Whittington, G., eds.*, 1986, *1974*, pp. 314–43.

von Hayek, Friedrich A. Maintaining Capital Intact: A Reply. **In** *Parker, R. H.; Harcourt, G. C. and Whittington, G., eds.*, 1986, *1941*, pp. 139–43.

Hicks, John R. Maintaining Capital Intact: A Further Suggestion. **In** *Parker, R. H.; Harcourt, G. C. and Whittington, G., eds.*, 1986, *1942*, pp. 144–50.

Jaszi, George. An Economic Accountant's Audit. *Amer. Econ. Rev.*, May 1986, *76*(2), pp. 411–17. **[G: U.S.]**

Karunaratne, Neil Dias. Issues in Measuring the Information Economy. *J. Econ. Stud.*, 1986, *13*(3), pp. 51–68. **[G: Australia]**

Lal, Kishori. Canadian Input–Output Tables and Their Integration with Other Sub-systems of the National Accounts. **In** *Franz, A. and Rainer, N., eds.*, 1986, pp. 147–63. **[G: Canada]**

Leipert, Christian. Social Costs of Economic Growth. *J. Econ. Issues*, March 1986, *20*(1), pp. 109–31. **[G: W. Germany]**

Leontief, Wassily. Input–Output Analysis. **In**

Leontief, W., 1986, 1985, pp. 19–40. [G: U.S.]

Leontief, Wassily. National Income, Economic Structure, and Environmental Externalities. **In** *Leontief, W.*, 1986, *1973*, pp. 261–72.

Lindahl, Erik. The Concept of Income. **In** *Parker, R. H.; Harcourt, G. C. and Whittington, G., eds.*, 1986, *1933*, pp. 82–90.

Littlejohn, Gary. Economic Calculation in the USSR. **In** *Smith, K., ed.*, 1986, *1980*, pp. 144–78. **[G: U.S.S.R.]**

Lützel, Heinrich. Market Transactions in the National Accounts. *Rev. Income Wealth*, June 1986, *32*(2), pp. 201–12. **[G: W. Germany]**

Malaguerra, Carlo. Towards a New Statistical Data Dissemination Policy. *Statist. J.*, October 1986, *4*(2), pp. 101–12. **[G: Switzerland]**

Marczewski, Jean. The Concept of Macroeconomic Cost and Its Utility. *Rev. Income Wealth*, March 1986, *32*(1), pp. 1–24. **[G: France; W. Germany]**

Milot, Jean-Paul and Teillet, Pierre. Financial Operations and Monetary Statistics: Improved Concordance in the French National Accounts. *Rev. Income Wealth*, December 1986, *32*(4), pp. 371–85. **[G: France]**

Mishan, Ezra J. GNP: Measurement or Mirage? **In** *Mishan, E. J.*, 1986, *1984*, pp. 108–23.

Pigou, Arthur C. Maintaining Capital Intact. **In** *Parker, R. H.; Harcourt, G. C. and Whittington, G., eds.*, 1986, *1941*, pp. 135–38.

Portier, Jean-Michel. Procedures for Making the Input–Output Tables Consistent with the French National Accounts by Institutional Sectors. **In** *Franz, A. and Rainer, N., eds.*, 1986, pp. 165–78. **[G: France]**

Postner, Harry H. Microbusiness Accounting and Macroeconomic Accounting: The Limits to Consistency. *Rev. Income Wealth*, September 1986, *32*(3), pp. 217–44.

Riech, Utz P. Treatment of Government Activity on the Production Account. *Rev. Income Wealth*, March 1986, *32*(1), pp. 69–85. **[G: OECD]**

Ruggles, Nancy D. Special Issue on the Review of the United Nations System of National Accounts: Comment. *Rev. Income Wealth*, June 1986, *32*(2), pp. 213–16.

Ruggles, Richard. Special Issue on the Review of the United Nations System of National Accounts. *Rev. Income Wealth*, June 1986, *32*(2), pp. 109–15.

Ruggles, Richard and Ruggles, Nancy D. The Integration of Macro and Micro Data for the Household Sector. *Rev. Income Wealth*, September 1986, *32*(3), pp. 245–76. **[G: U.S.]**

Rymes, Thomas K. Further Thoughts on the Banking Imputation in the National Accounts. *Rev. Income Wealth*, December 1986, *32*(4), pp. 425–41.

Scitovsky, Tibor. The Place of Economic Welfare in Human Welfare. **In** *Scitovsky, T.*, 1986, *1973*, pp. 13–25.

Scitovsky, Tibor. Why the U.S. Saving Rate Is Low—A Conflict between the National Accountant's and the Individual Saver's Perceptions. **In** *[Tarshis, L.]*, 1986, pp. 125–34. **[G: U.S.]**

Solomons, David. Economic and Accounting Concepts of Income. **In** *Parker, R. H.; Harcourt, G. C. and Whittington, G., eds.*, 1986, *1961*, pp. 153–66.

Stone, Richard. Nobel Memorial Lecture 1984: The Accounts of Society. *J. Appl. Econometrics*, January 1986, *1*(1), pp. 5–28. **[G: U.K.; France; Netherlands]**

Stone, Richard. Special Issue on the Review of the United Nations System of National Accounts: Comments on the Overall Programme. *Rev. Income Wealth*, June 1986, *32*(2), pp. 117–18.

Szilágyi, György. Procedures for Linking International Comparisons. *Statist. J.*, October 1986, *4*(2), pp. 165–81.

Tighe, Michael. Teaching Economics to the 16–19 Age Range: National Income: An Introduction to Macroeconomics. **In** *Whitehead, D. J., ed.*, 1986, pp. 211–17.

van Tongeren, Jan W. Development of an Algorithm for the Compilation of National Accounts and Related Systems of Statistics. *Rev. Income Wealth*, March 1986, *32*(1), pp. 25–47. **[G: Suriname]**

Vanoli, André. Sur la structure générale du SCN à partir de l'expérience du système élargi de comptabilité nationale français. (With English summary.) *Rev. Income Wealth*, June 1986, *32*(2), pp. 155–99. **[G: France]**

Webb, Roy H. The National Income and Product Accounts. *Fed. Res. Bank Richmond Econ. Rev.*, May/June 1986, *72*(3), pp. 11–17. **[G: U.S.]**

Wiles, Peter. Political and Moral Aspects of the Two Economies. **In** *Höhmann, H.-H.; Nove, A. and Vogel, H., eds.*, 1986, pp. 198–213. **[G: U.S.S.R.]**

Yang, Jinbai, et al. Some Theoretical Problems of Socialist National Income. *Chinese Econ. Stud.*, Spring-Summer 1986, *19*(3–4), pp. 7–169. **[G: China]**

2212 National Income Accounts

Abramovitz, Moses. Inventory Fluctuations in the United States since 1929: Comment. **In** *Gordon, R. J., ed.*, 1986, pp. 214–23. **[G: U.S.]**

Alcalde, Oscar E. and López Paz, Ernesto. Comments on the Development of the Savings Stimulation Policy in Cuba. **In** *U.N., Dept. of International Econ. and Social Affairs*, 1986, pp. 71–77. **[G: CMEA]**

Ando, Albert. Why Is Japan's Saving Rate So Apparently High? Comment. **In** *Fischer, S., ed.*, 1986, pp. 211–20. **[G: Japan; U.S.]**

Auerbach, Alan J. Tax Reform and Capital Formation: Discussion. **In** *Federal Reserve Bank of Boston*, 1986, pp. 145–48. **[G: U.S.]**

Ayala, José and Durán, Clemente Ruiz. Development and Crisis in Mexico: A Structuralist Approach. **In** *Hartlyn, J. and Morley, S. A., eds.*, 1986, pp. 243–64. **[G: Mexico]**

de Azcarate, Luis. The World Bank in Adjustment

and Economic Growth in Africa. **In** *Helleiner, G. K, ed.*, 1986, pp. 184–219. **[G: Africa]**

de Azcarate, Luis. The World Bank in Adjustment and Economic Growth in Africa: Reply. **In** *Helleiner, G. K, ed.*, 1986, pp. 228–34. **[G: Africa]**

Balke, Nathan S. and Gordon, Robert J. The American Business Cycle: Historical Data. **In** *Gordon, R. J., ed.*, 1986, pp. 781–850. **[G: U.S.]**

Ben-Porath, Yoram. The Entwined Growth of Population and Product, 1922–1982. **In** *Ben-Porath, Y., ed.*, 1986, pp. 27–41. **[G: Israel]**

Bhatt, V. V. Resource Mobilization in Developing Countries: Financial Institutions and Policies. **In** *U.N., Dept. of Tech. Co-op. for Devel., Devel. Admin. Div.*, 1986, pp. 99–121. **[G: LDCs]**

Bivens, Gordon E. and Volker, Carol B. A Value-Added Approach to Household Production: The Special Case of Meal Preparation. *J. Cons. Res.*, September 1986, *13*(2), pp. 272–79. **[G: U.S.]**

Blanchard, Olivier J. and Watson, Mark W. Are Business Cycles All Alike? **In** *Gordon, R. J., ed.*, 1986, pp. 123–56. **[G: U.S.]**

Blinder, Alan S. and Holtz-Eakin, Douglas. Inventory Fluctuations in the United States since 1929: Reply. **In** *Gordon, R. J., ed.*, 1986, pp. 231–33. **[G: U.S.]**

Blinder, Alan S. and Holtz-Eakin, Douglas. Inventory Fluctuations in the United States since 1929. **In** *Gordon, R. J., ed.*, 1986, pp. 183–214. **[G: U.S.]**

Britton, Andrew. Seasonal Patterns in the British Economy. *Nat. Inst. Econ. Rev.*, August 1986, (117), pp. 33–42. **[G: U.K.]**

Britton, Andrew. The British Economy in the Long Term: Output Growth and Unemployment. *Nat. Inst. Econ. Rev.*, November 1986, (118), pp. 89–104. **[G: U.K.]**

Browne, F. X. Loan Market Price and Quantity Effects in a Production Smoothing Model of Inventory Investment. *Appl. Econ.*, June 1986, *18*(6), pp. 691–707. **[G: Ireland]**

Buchanan, James M. Cultural Evolution and Institutional Reform. **In** *Buchanan, J. M.*, 1986, pp. 75–85.

Bukhval'd, E. and Pogrebinskaia, V. V. I. Lenin on the Dynamics of Reproduction and the Rates of the USSR's Economic Development. *Prob. Econ.*, April 1986, *28*(12), pp. 59–77. **[G: U.S.S.R.]**

Butlin, N. G. and Sinclair, W. A. Australian Gross Domestic Product 1788–1860: Estimates, Sources and Methods. *Australian Econ. Hist. Rev.*, September 1986, *26*(2), pp. 126–47. **[G: Australia]**

Carlson, Keith M. Recent Revisions of GNP Data. *Fed. Res. Bank St. Louis Rev.*, January 1986, *68*(1), pp. 17–24. **[G: U.S.]**

Cassel, Dieter. Funktionen der Schattenwirtschaft im Koordinationsmechanismus von Markt- und Planwirtschaften. (The Role of the Shadow Economy in Market Economies and in Centrally Planned Economies. With English summary.) **In** *Eucken, W. and Böhm, F., eds.*, 1986, pp. 73–104.

Cassel, Dieter and Cichy, E. Ulrich. Explaining the Growing Shadow Economy in East and West: A Comparative Systems Approach. *Comp. Econ. Stud.*, Spring 1986, *28*(1), pp. 20–41. **[G: OECD; E. Germany; Poland; U.S.S.R.]**

Chandavarkar, Anand G. The Non-institutional Financial Sector in Developing Countries: Macro-economic Implications for Savings Policies. **In** *U.N., Dept. of International Econ. and Social Affairs*, 1986, pp. 81–86. **[G: LDCs]**

Clague, Christopher. Short-Cut Estimates of Real Income. *Rev. Income Wealth*, September 1986, *32*(3), pp. 313–31.

Dales, J. H. New Estimates of Gross National Product, Canada, 1870–1926: Some Implications for Canadian Development: Comment. **In** *Engerman, S. L. and Gallman, R. E., eds.*, 1986, pp. 89–93. **[G: Canada]**

Davis, Lance E. Measuring the Transaction Sector in the American Economy, 1870–1970: Comment. **In** *Engerman, S. L. and Gallman, R. E., eds.*, 1986, pp. 149–59. **[G: U.S.]**

De Long, James Bradford and Summers, Lawrence H. Are Business Cycles Symmetrical? Additional Contribution. **In** *Gordon, R. J., ed.*, 1986, pp. 166–78. **[G: OECD]**

De Long, James Bradford and Summers, Lawrence H. The Changing Cyclical Variability of Economic Activity in the United States. **In** *Gordon, R. J., ed.*, 1986, pp. 679–719. **[G: U.S.]**

Deaton, Angus S. The Role of Consumption in Economic Fluctuations: Comment. **In** *Gordon, R. J., ed.*, 1986, pp. 255–59. **[G: U.S.]**

Delaunay, Jean-Claude. Comptes à prix constants et mesure du taux de la plus-value. (National Accountings at Constant Prices and Evaluation of the Rate of Surplus-Value. With English summary.) *Écon. Appl.*, 1986, *39*(2), pp. 263–95.

Dore, Elizabeth. Nicaragua: The Experience of the Mixed Economy. **In** *Hartlyn, J. and Morley, S. A., eds.*, 1986, pp. 319–50. **[G: Nicaragua]**

Eckstein, Otto and Sinai, Allen. The Mechanisms of the Business Cycle in the Postwar Era. **In** *Gordon, R. J., ed.*, 1986, pp. 39–105. **[G: U.S.]**

Eisner, Robert. Tax Reform and Capital Formation: Discussion. **In** *Federal Reserve Bank of Boston*, 1986, pp. 149–52. **[G: U.S.]**

Eisner, Robert. The Changing Cyclical Variability of Economic Activity in the United States: Comment. **In** *Gordon, R. J., ed.*, 1986, pp. 719–27. **[G: U.S.]**

Ercolani, Paolo. Decline in the Share of the Agricultural Product: Measurements and Explanations. *Banca Naz. Lavoro Quart. Rev.*, March 1986, (156), pp. 103–28. **[G: Global]**

Feige, Edgar L. A Re-examination of the "Underground Economy" in the United States: A Comment. *Int. Monet. Fund Staff Pap.*, December 1986, *33*(4), pp. 768–81. **[G: Selected Countries]**

Fry, Maxwell J. National Saving, Financial Saving and Interest Rate Policy in Asian Developing Economies. **In** *U.N., Dept. of International Econ. and Social Affairs,* 1986, pp. 29–46. **[G: Asia]**

Gomulka, Stanislaw. East–West Trade and the Polish Experience, 1970–82. **In** *Gomulka, S.,* 1986, pp. 251–70. **[G: CMEA; Poland]**

Greasley, David. British Economic Growth: The Paradox of the 1880s and the Timing of the Climacteric. *Exploration Econ. Hist.*, October 1986, *23*(4), pp. 416–44. **[G: U.K.]**

Grossman, Herschel I. The Changing Cyclical Variability of Economic Activity in the United States: Comment. **In** *Gordon, R. J., ed.*, 1986, pp. 728–31. **[G: U.S.]**

Haig, Bryan. The Treatment of Interest and Financial Intermediaries in the National Accounts of Australia. *Rev. Income Wealth,* December 1986, *32*(4), pp. 409–24. **[G: Australia]**

Hall, Robert E. The Role of Consumption in Economic Fluctuations. **In** *Gordon, R. J., ed.*, 1986, pp. 237–55. **[G: U.S.]**

Hamilton, Clive. A Technique for Calculating Capital Coefficients in Newly Industrializing Countries, with Application to the Republic of Korea. *Devel. Econ.*, March 1986, *24*(1), pp. 56–70. **[G: S. Korea]**

Hartlyn, Jonathan and Morley, Samuel A. Political Regimes and Economic Performance in Latin America. **In** *Hartlyn, J. and Morley, S. A., eds.*, 1986, pp. 15–37. **[G: Latin America]**

Hatsopoulos, George N. Tax Reform and Capital Formation: Discussion. **In** *Federal Reserve Bank of Boston,* 1986, pp. 140–44. **[G: U.S.]**

Hayashi, Fumio. Why Is Japan's Saving Rate So Apparently High? **In** *Fischer, S., ed.*, 1986, pp. 147–210. **[G: U.S.; Japan]**

Heien, Dale and Nuckton, Carole. A Note on the Savings Rate [National Savings in the U.S.]. *J. Econ. Soc. Meas.*, April 1986, *14*(1), pp. 87–89. **[G: U.S.]**

Herr, Ellen M. Capital Expenditures by Majority-Owned Foreign Affiliates of U.S. Companies, 1986 and 1987. *Surv. Curr. Bus.*, October 1986, *66*(10), pp. 21–30. **[G: U.S.]**

Hill, Peter. International Price Levels and Purchasing Power Parities. *OECD Econ. Stud.*, Spring 1986, (6), pp. 133–59. **[G: OECD]**

Hilzenbecher, Manfred. Die (schattenwirtschaftliche) Wertschöpfung der Hausarbeit. Eine empirische Untersuchung für die Bundesrepublik Deutschland. (The [Hidden] Value Added of Household Work: An Empirical Study for the Federal Republic of Germany. With English summary.) *Jahr. Nationalökon. Statist.*, March 1986, *201*(2), pp. 107–30. **[G: W. Germany]**

Hussain, Irtiza. Role of Financial Institutions in the Financing of Public Enterprises. **In** *U.N., Dept. of Technical Co-operation for Development,* 1986, pp. 65–83. **[G: Pakistan]**

Joines, Douglas H. Government Spending, Tax Rates, and Private Investment in Plant and Equipment. **In** *Canto, V. A.; Kadlec, C. W. and Laffer, A. B., eds.*, 1986, pp. 36–53. **[G: U.S.]**

Karmann, Alexander J. Monetäre Schätzansätze zur Erfassung der Schattenwirtschaft. Ein Vergleich verschiedener Messmethoden. (Monetary Estimation Approaches to Assessing the "Shadow Economy." A Comparison of Various Methods. With English summary.) *Kredit Kapital,* 1986, *19*(2), pp. 233–47. **[G: OECD]**

Katz, Arnold J. An Analysis of Trends in the Intensity of U.S. Capital Formation and Their Determinants. *J. Policy Modeling,* Fall 1986, *8*(3), pp. 433–69. **[G: U.S.]**

Khanna, Kailash C. India: Aspects of the Black Economy: Report of a Study. *Bull. Int. Fiscal Doc.*, February 1986, *40*(2), pp. 61–65. **[G: India]**

King, Robert G. The Role of Consumption in Economic Fluctuations: Comment. **In** *Gordon, R. J., ed.*, 1986, pp. 259–63. **[G: U.S.]**

Klinov, Ruth. Changes in the Industrial Structure. **In** *Ben-Porath, Y., ed.*, 1986, pp. 119–36. **[G: Israel]**

Kopcke, Richard W. Tax Reform and Capital Formation. **In** *Federal Reserve Bank of Boston,* 1986, pp. 103–39. **[G: U.S.]**

Kravis, Irving B. The Three Faces of the International Comparison Project. *World Bank Res. Observer,* January 1986, *1*(1), pp. 3–26. **[G: Global]**

Krejči, Jeroslav. The Bohemian–Moravian War Economy. **In** *Kaser, M. C. and Radice, E. A., eds.*, 1986, pp. 452–92. **[G: Bohemia; Moravia]**

Lebergott, Stanley. Discussion [New Estimates of Prewar Gross National Product and Unemployment] [The Reliability of Historical Macroeconomic Data for Comparing Cyclical Stability]. *J. Econ. Hist.*, June 1986, *46*(2), pp. 367–71. **[G: U.S.]**

Lee, Eddy. Domestic Resource Mobilisation and Self-reliance. **In** *Islam, R. and Muqtada, M., eds.*, 1986, pp. 279–89. **[G: Bangladesh]**

de Leeuw, Frank. An Indirect Technique for Measuring the Underground Economy: A Note on Revised Data. *Surv. Curr. Bus.*, September 1986, *66*(9), pp. 21–22. **[G: U.S.]**

Leontief, Wassily. An Alternative to Aggregation in Input–Output Analysis and National Accounts. **In** *Leontief, W.*, 1986, *1967*, pp. 41–54. **[G: U.S.]**

Levitt, M. S. and Joyce, M. A. S. Government Output in the National Accounts. *Nat. Inst. Econ. Rev.*, February 1986, (115), pp. 48–51. **[G: U.K.]**

Lluch, Constantino. ICORS, Savings Rates, and the Determinants of Public Expenditure in Developing Countries. **In** *Lal, D. and Wolf, M., eds.*, 1986, pp. 361–95. **[G: LDCs]**

Lovell, Michael C. The Mechanisms of the Business Cycle in the Postwar Era: Comment. **In**

Gordon, R. J., ed., 1986, pp. 105–10. [G: U.S.]

Lundager, Jens and Schneider, Friedrich. En sammenligning af udviklingen i den sorte økonomi for Danmark, Norge og Sverige. (The Shadow Economics in Demark, Norway and Sweden. With English summary.) *Nationaløkon. Tidsskr.*, 1986, *124*(3), pp. 362–79. [G: Denmark; Sweden; Norway]

Lütkepohl, Helmut. Comparison of Predictors for Temporally and Contemporaneously Aggregated Time Series. *Int. J. Forecasting*, 1986, *2*(4), pp. 461–75. [G: U.S.]

Mankiw, N. Gregory and Shapiro, Matthew D. News or Noise: An Analysis of GNP Revisions. *Surv. Curr. Bus.*, May 1986, *66*(5), pp. 20–25. [G: U.S.]

Marcel, Mario and Meller, Patricio. Empalme de las Cuentas Nacionales de Chile 1960–1985. Metodos alternativos y resultados. (Splicing the Chilean National Accounts 1960–1985: Alternative Methods and Results. With English summary.) *Colección Estud. CIEPLAN*, December 1986, (20), pp. 121–46. [G: Chile]

Mayshar, Joram. Investment Patterns. **In** *Ben-Porath, Y., ed.*, 1986, pp. 101–18. [G: Israel]

McCallum, Bennett T. Inventory Fluctuations in the United States since 1929: Comment. **In** *Gordon, R. J., ed.*, 1986, pp. 223–31. [G: U.S.]

McClintock, Cynthia. The Tragedy of Lost Opportunity in Peru: Comment. **In** *Hartlyn, J. and Morley, S. A., eds.*, 1986, pp. 360–66. [G: Peru]

McCrohan, Kevin F. The Revenue Loss Due to Undocumented Alien Earnings: Estimates for 1980. *J. Econ. Soc. Meas.*, December 1986, *14*(4), pp. 311–24. [G: U.S.]

McDonald, Daina and Dixon, Peter B. Macroeconomic Developments in 1986–87 and 1987–88. *Australian Econ. Rev.*, 4th Quarter 1986, (76), pp. 3–24. [G: Australia]

McNees, Stephen K. Estimating GNP: The Trade-off between Timeliness and Accuracy. *New Eng. Econ. Rev.*, Jan./Feb. 1986, pp. 3–10. [G: U.S.]

Monza, Alfredo, et al. Algunas limitaciones de un cociente clásico. (With English summary.) *Desarrollo Econ.*, July-Sept. 1986, *26*(102), pp. 197–227. [G: Argentina]

Nakamura, Takafusa. The World Economy and Japan since the 1970's. **In** *Hax, H.; Kraus, W. and Tsuchiya, K., eds.*, 1986, pp. 1–14. [G: Japan; OECD]

Ndegwa, Philip. The World Bank in Adjustment and Economic Growth in Africa: Comments. **In** *Helleiner, G. K, ed.*, 1986, pp. 220–26. [G: Africa]

O'Relley, Z. Edward. Economic Reform, the Search for Economic Efficiency, and the Expansion of the Second Economy in Hungary. **In** *Altmann, F.-L., ed.*, 1986, pp. 218–37. [G: Hungary]

Ølgaard, Anders. Finansierings- og fordelingsproblemer i lys af balanceproblemerne. (Saving, Investment and Functional Income Distribution in the Danish Economy. With English summary.) *Nationaløkon. Tidsskr.*, 1986, *124*(2), pp. 179–88. [G: Denmark]

Park, Thae S. Relationship between Personal Income and Adjusted Gross Income: Revised Estimates, 1947–83. *Surv. Curr. Bus.*, May 1986, *66*(5), pp. 34–40. [G: U.S.]

Parker, Robert P. National Income and Product Accounts: The Comprehensive Revision. *Bus. Econ.*, July 1986, *21*(3), pp. 5–9. [G: U.S.]

Pérez-López, Jorge F. Real Economic Growth in Cuba, 1965–1982. *J. Devel. Areas*, January 1986, *20*(2), pp. 151–72. [G: Cuba]

Peterson, Milo O. Gross Product by Industry: Revised and Updated Estimates, 1947–85. *Surv. Curr. Bus.*, April 1986, *66*(4), pp. 24–25. [G: U.S.]

Pikkarainen, Pentti and Virén, Matti. Mitä erilaiset kokonaistuotannon trendipoikkeamat kuvaavat? (How to Interpret Various Trend Models. With English summary.) *Liiketaloudellinen Aikak.*, 1986, *35*(3), pp. 236–49. [G: Selected Countries]

Reynolds, Morgan O. Taxation, Saving, and Investment: A Look at the Evidence. **In** *Lee, D. R., ed.*, 1986, pp. 49–85. [G: OECD]

Romer, Christina D. New Estimates of Prewar Gross National Product and Unemployment. *J. Econ. Hist.*, June 1986, *46*(2), pp. 341–52. [G: U.S.]

Romer, Paul M. Why Is Japan's Saving Rate So Apparently High? Comment. **In** *Fischer, S., ed.*, 1986, pp. 220–33. [G: Japan; U.S.]

Ruggles, Richard and Ruggles, Nancy D. The Integration of Macro and Micro Data for the Household Sector. *Rev. Income Wealth*, September 1986, *32*(3), pp. 245–76. [G: U.S.]

Rutledge, Gary L. and Stergioulas, Nikolaos A. Plant and Equipment Expenditures by Business for Pollution Abatement, 1985 and 1986. *Surv. Curr. Bus.*, December 1986, *66*(12), pp. 20–22. [G: U.S.]

Ryscavage, Paul. Reconciling Divergent Trends in Real Income. *Mon. Lab. Rev.*, July 1986, *109*(7), pp. 24–29. [G: U.S.]

Savage, David and Biswas, Rajiv. The British Economy in the Long Term: Use of Resources. *Nat. Inst. Econ. Rev.*, November 1986, (118), pp. 70–81. [G: U.K.]

Saxena, Pradeep Kumar. Inter-relationship between Socio-economic Development and Economic Structure: Indian Experience. *Margin*, July 1986, *18*(4), pp. 76–87. [G: India]

Schneider, Friedrich. Estimating the Size of the Danish Shadow Economy Using the Currency Demand Approach: An Attempt. *Scand. J. Econ.*, 1986, *88*(4), pp. 643–68. [G: Denmark]

Schydlowsky, Daniel M. The Tragedy of Lost Opportunity in Peru. **In** *Hartlyn, J. and Morley, S. A., eds.*, 1986, pp. 217–42. [G: Peru]

Sen, Amartya K. Economic Distance and the Living Standard. **In** *[Patel, S.]*, 1986, pp. 63–74. [G: India; China; Mexico; Sri Lanka; Brazil]

Seskin, Eugene P. and Sullivan, David F. Plant

and Equipment Expenditures, the Four Quarters of 1986. *Surv. Curr. Bus.*, June 1986, *66*(6), pp. 17–20. **[G: U.S.]**

Seskin, Eugene P. and Sullivan, David F. Plant and Equipment Expenditures: Quarters of 1986, First and Second Quarters of 1987, Year 1987. *Surv. Curr. Bus.*, December 1986, *66*(12), pp. 17–19. **[G: U.S.]**

Seskin, Eugene P. and Sullivan, David F. Plant and Equipment Expenditures, the Four Quarters of 1986. *Surv. Curr. Bus.*, September 1986, *66*(9), pp. 23–26. **[G: U.S.]**

Seskin, Eugene P. and Sullivan, David F. Plant and Equipment Expenditures, First and Second Quarters and Second Half of 1986. *Surv. Curr. Bus.*, April 1986, *66*(4), pp. 26–30. **[G: U.S.]**

Shiller, Robert J. Are Business Cycles All Alike? Comment. **In** *Gordon, R. J., ed.*, 1986, pp. 156–60. **[G: U.S.]**

Shriver, Keith A. A Statistical Test of the Stability Assumption Inherent in Empirical Estimates of Economic Depreciation. *J. Econ. Soc. Meas.*, July 1986, *14*(2), pp. 145–53. **[G: U.S.]**

Singleton, Kenneth J. The Mechanisms of the Business Cycle in the Postwar Era: Comment. **In** *Gordon, R. J., ed.*, 1986, pp. 110–18. **[G: U.S.]**

Skarstein, Rune. Growth and Crisis in the Manufacturing Sector. **In** *Boesen, J., et al., eds.*, 1986, pp. 79–104. **[G: Tanzania]**

Summers, Lawrence H. Issues in National Savings Policy. **In** *Adams, F. G. and Wachter, S. M., eds.*, 1986, pp. 65–88. **[G: OECD]**

Tanzi, Vito. The Underground Economy in the United States: Reply to Comments. *Int. Monet. Fund Staff Pap.*, December 1986, *33*(4), pp. 799–811. **[G: Selected Countries; U.S.]**

Tatom, John A. How Federal Farm Spending Distorts Measures of Economic Activity. *Fed. Res. Bank St. Louis Rev.*, June/July 1986, *68*(6), pp. 16–22. **[G: U.S.]**

Temin, Peter. Are Business Cycles All Alike? Comment. **In** *Gordon, R. J., ed.*, 1986, pp. 160–65. **[G: U.S.]**

Thomas, J. J. The Underground Economy in the United States: A Comment. *Int. Monet. Fund Staff Pap.*, December 1986, *33*(4), pp. 782–89. **[G: U.S.; Selected Countries]**

Tice, Helen Stone and Moczar, Louis J. Foreign Transactions in the National Income and Product Accounts: An Overview. *Surv. Curr. Bus.*, November 1986, *66*(11), pp. 23–36. **[G: U.S.]**

Urquhart, M. C. New Estimates of Gross National Product, Canada, 1870–1926: Some Implications for Canadian Development. **In** *Engerman, S. L. and Gallman, R. E., eds.*, 1986, pp. 9–88. **[G: Canada]**

Walkowiak, Witold. Investment Processes in 1976–1981. *Eastern Europ. Econ.*, Spring 1986, *24*(3), pp. 35–52. **[G: Poland]**

Wallis, John Joseph and North, Douglass C. Measuring the Transaction Sector in the American Economy, 1870–1970. **In** *Engerman, S. L. and Gallman, R. E., eds.*, 1986, pp. 95–148. **[G: U.S.]**

Watson, Mark W. Univariate Detrending Methods with Stochastic Trends. *J. Monet. Econ.*, July 1986, *18*(1), pp. 49–75. **[G: U.S.]**

Weir, David R. The Reliability of Historical Macroeconomic Data for Comparing Cyclical Stability. *J. Econ. Hist.*, June 1986, *46*(2), pp. 353–65. **[G: U.S.]**

Williamson, John. The World Bank in Adjustment and Economic Growth in Africa: Comments. **In** *Helleiner, G. K, ed.*, 1986, pp. 226–28. **[G: Africa]**

Wiśniewski, Marian. The Economy and Its Shadow. *Eastern Europ. Econ.*, Summer 1986, *24*(4), pp. 29–39. **[G: Poland]**

Witte, Ann D. The Underground Economy in the United States and Western Europe. **In** *Lindholm, R. W., ed.*, 1986, pp. 204–29. **[G: U.S.; W. Europe]**

Wolff, Edward N. The Productivity Slowdown and the Fall in the U.S. Rate of Profit, 1947–76. *Rev. Radical Polit. Econ.*, Spring/Summer 1986, *18*(1/2), pp. 87–109. **[G: U.S.]**

Zilberfarb, Ben-Zion. Estimates of the Underground Economy in the United States, 1930–80: A Comment. *Int. Monet. Fund Staff Pap.*, December 1986, *33*(4), pp. 790–98. **[G: Selected Countries; U.S.]**

Zinn, Karl Georg. Geldvermögen, Zinseinkommensquote und Inflation. (Financial Capital, Share of Interest Income and Inflation. With English summary.) *Jahr. Nationalökon. Statist.*, July 1986, *201*(4), pp. 350–69. **[G: W. Germany]**

2213 Income Distribution

Abegaz, Berhanu. Mass Poverty, Demography, and Development Strategy: A Selective Survey. **In** *Abegaz, B., ed.*, 1986, pp. 1–54. **[G: LDCs]**

Adelman, Irma. A Poverty-Focused Approach to Development Policy. **In** *Lewis, J. P. and Kallab, V., eds.*, 1986, pp. 49–65. **[G: LDCs]**

Adelman, Irma and Levy, Amnon. Decomposing Theil's Index of Income Inequality: A Reply. *Rev. Income Wealth*, March 1986, *32*(1), pp. 107–08. **[G: Israel]**

Altimir, Oscar. Estimaciones de la distribución del ingreso en la Argentina, 1953–1980. (With English summary.) *Desarrollo Econ.*, Jan.-Mar. 1986, *25*(100), pp. 521–66. **[G: Argentina]**

Amos, Orley M., Jr. Substate and SMSA Personal Income Inequality and Regional Development. *Rev. Reg. Stud.*, Spring 1986, *16*(2), pp. 23–30. **[G: U.S.]**

Apps, Patricia. Taxation Reform and Income Distribution in Australia: Comment. *Australian Econ. Rev.*, 3rd Quarter 1986, (75), pp. 57–59. **[G: Australia]**

Bentham, Graham. Socio-Tenurial Polarization in the United Kingdom, 1953–83: The Income Evidence. *Urban Stud.*, April 1986, *23*(2), pp. 157–62. **[G: U.K.]**

Birdsall, Nancy and Meesook, Oey Astra. Children's Education and the Intergenerational Transmission of Inequality: A Simulation. *Econ. Educ. Rev.*, 1986, *5*(3), pp. 239–56. **[G: Brazil]**

Blank, Rebecca M. and Blinder, Alan S. Macroeconomics, Income Distribution, and Poverty. **In** *Danziger, S. H. and Weinberg, D. H., eds.*, 1986, pp. 180–208. **[G: U.S.]**

Borooah, V. K. and Sharpe, D. R. Aggregate Consumption and the Distribution of Income in the United Kingdom: An Econometric Analysis. *Econ. J.*, June 1986, *96*(382), pp. 449–66. **[G: U.K.]**

Bradbury, Katharine L. The Shrinking Middle Class. *New Eng. Econ. Rev.*, Sept./Oct. 1986, pp. 41–55. **[G: U.S.]**

Brimmer, Andrew F. Trends, Prospects, and Strategies for Black Economic Progress. *Rev. Black Polit. Econ.*, Spring 1986, *14*(4), pp. 91–97. **[G: U.S.]**

Bronfenbrenner, Martin. Income Distribution and "Economic Justice." *J. Econ. Educ.*, Winter 1986, *17*(1), pp. 35–51. **[G: U.S.]**

Bruno, Vincenzo. L'entropia e la variabilità paretiana dei redditi. (The Entropy in a Pareto Distribution of Incomes. With English summary.) *Giorn. Econ.*, Sept.-Oct. 1986, *45*(9–10), pp. 515–25.

Burkhauser, Richard V. Social Security in Panama: A Multiperiod Analysis of Income Distribution. *J. Devel. Econ.*, April 1986, *21*(1), pp. 53–64. **[G: Panama]**

Butler, Richard J. and McDonald, James B. Income Inequality in the United States, 1948–1980. **In** *Ehrenberg, R. G., ed., Pt. A*, 1986, pp. 85–140. **[G: U.S.]**

Celasun, Merih. Income Distribution and Domestic Terms of Trade in Turkey, 1978–1983: Estimated Measures of Inequality and Poverty. *METU*, 1986, *13*(1/2), pp. 193–216. **[G: Turkey]**

Clark, Don P. and Thompson, Henry. Immigration, International Capital Flows, and Long Run Income Distribution in Canada. *Atlantic Econ. J.*, December 1986, *14*(4), pp. 24–29. **[G: Canada]**

Curtis, Fred. Class, Race, and Income Distribution: Analyzing "White South Africa." **In** *Zarembka, P., ed.*, 1986, pp. 33–67. **[G: S. Africa]**

Dagum, Camilo; Grenier, Gilles and Bédard, Mario. Répartition du revenu selon le sexe dans quatre agglomérations urbaines du Canada: Exemple d'application de données des déclarations de revenus des particuliers. (An Analysis of Income Distribution by Sex in Four Canadian Metropolitan Areas, Using Personal Income Tax Records. With English summary.) *L'Actual. Econ.*, March 1986, *62*(1), pp. 23–42. **[G: Canada]**

Debroy, B. Decomposing Welfare Measures According to Groups of the Economy. *Margin*, July 1986, *18*(4), pp. 69–75. **[G: India]**

Dilnot, Andrew W. and Stark, Graham K. The Distributional Consequences of Mrs. Thatcher. *Fisc. Stud.*, May 1986, *7*(2), pp. 48–53. **[G: U.K.]**

Dreyer, J. P. and Brand, S. S. 'n Sectorale Beskouing van die Suid-Afrikaanse Ekonomie in 'n Veranderende Omgewing. (With English summary.) *S. Afr. J. Econ.*, June 1986, *54*(2), pp. 131–50. **[G: S. Africa]**

Esteban, Joan M. Income-Share Elasticity and the Size Distribution of Income. *Int. Econ. Rev.*, June 1986, *27*(2), pp. 439–44.

Even-Shoshan, Orit and Gabbay, Yoram. Distribution of Family Income and Taxes. **In** *Kop, Y., ed.*, 1986, pp. 169–98. **[G: Israel]**

Friesen, Peter H. Distortion of the Trend of Inequality by the Life-Cycle Profile of Incomes. *Rev. Econ. Statist.*, February 1986, *68*(1), pp. 170–74. **[G: U.S.]**

Gastwirth, Joseph L.; Nayak, Tapan K. and Krieger, Abba M. Large Sample Theory for the Bounds on the Gini and Related Indices of Inequality Estimated from Grouped Data. *J. Bus. Econ. Statist.*, April 1986, *4*(2), pp. 269–73. **[G: U.S.]**

Geva, Yehuda and Habib, Jack. The Development of the Transfer System and the Redistribution of Income. **In** *Ben-Porath, Y., ed.*, 1986, pp. 209–20. **[G: Israel]**

Glewwe, Paul. The Distribution of Income in Sri Lanka in 1969–70 and 1980–81: A Decomposition Analysis. *J. Devel. Econ.*, December 1986, *24*(2), pp. 255–74. **[G: Sri Lanka]**

Grosh, Margaret E. and Nafziger, E. Wayne. The Computation of World Income Distribution. *Econ. Develop. Cult. Change*, January 1986, *34*(2), pp. 347–59. **[G: Global]**

Heng, Toh Mun. Income Redistribution and Trade Policy Effects on Macroeconomic Aggregates: A Simulation Study of the Singapore Economy Based on an Extended Input–Output Model. *J. Econ. Devel.*, July 1986, *11*(1), pp. 157–90. **[G: Singapore]**

Higgins, James. The Distribution of Income on Irish Farms. *Irish J. Agr. Econ. Rural Soc.*, 1986, *11*, pp. 73–91. **[G: Ireland]**

Hoehn, Thomas and Reichle, Marc. Einkommensdisparitä ten im Zentren-Peripherie-Kontext in der Schweiz. (Income Inequalities in Switzerland: A Centre-Periphery Approach. With English summary.) *Schweiz. Z. Volkswirtsch. Statist.*, June 1986, *122*(2), pp. 143–61. **[G: Switzerland]**

Holcombe, Randall G. The Effects of the Tax Structure on the Distribution of Disposable Income. *Rivista Int. Sci. Econ. Com.*, June-July 1986, *33*(6–7), pp. 585–602. **[G: U.S.]**

Islam, Iyanatul and Khan, Habibullah. Income Inequality, Poverty and Socioeconomic Development in Bangladesh: An Empirical Investigation. *Bangladesh Devel. Stud.*, June 1986, *14*(2), pp. 75–92. **[G: Bangladesh]**

Iyengar, N. S. and Suryanarayana, M. H. On Growth and Equity in Indian Planning during 1962–62 to 1973–74. *Indian Econ. J.*, Apr.-June 1986, *33*(4), pp. 53–83. **[G: India]**

Katz, Claudio J.; Mahler, Vincent A. and Franz, Michael G. The Impact of Taxes in Developed

Capitalist Countries [Reply]. *Amer. Polit. Sci. Rev.*, March 1986, *80*(1), pp. 254–57. **[G: OECD]**

Kearl, J. R. and Pope, Clayne L. Choices, Rents, and Luck: Economic Mobility of Nineteenth-Century Utah Households. **In** *Engerman, S. L. and Gallman, R. E., eds.*, 1986, pp. 215–56. **[G: U.S.]**

King, Ronald F., et al. The Impact of Taxes in Developed Capitalist Countries [Comment]. *Amer. Polit. Sci. Rev.*, March 1986, *80*(1), pp. 251–54. **[G: OECD]**

Kusnic, Michael W. and DaVanzo, Julie. Accounting for Non-market Activities in the Distribution of Income: An Empirical Investigation. *J. Devel. Econ.*, May 1986, *21*(2), pp. 211–27. **[G: Malaysia]**

Lazear, Edward P. and Michael, Robert T. Estimating the Personal Distribution of Income with Adjustment for Within-Family Variation. *J. Lab. Econ.*, Part 2, July 1986, *4*(3), pp. S216–39. **[G: U.S.]**

Lerman, Donald L. and Lerman, Robert I. Imputed Incomes from Owner-Occupied Housing and Income Inequality. *Urban Stud.*, August 1986, *23*(4), pp. 323–31. **[G: U.S.]**

Leu, Robert E.; Buhmann, Brigitte and Frey, René L. Die personelle Einkommens- und Vermögensverteilung der Schweiz 1982. (The Size Distribution of Income and Wealth in Switzerland. With English summary.) *Schweiz. Z. Volkswirtsch. Statist.*, June 1986, *122*(2), pp. 111–42. **[G: Switzerland]**

Levy, Frank S. and Michel, Richard C. An Economic Bust for the Baby Boom. *Challenge*, Mar./Apr. 1986, *29*(1), pp. 33–39. **[G: U.S.]**

Lim, Joseph and Bautista, Carlos. The Impact of Income Redistribution on the Composition of Output Demand. *Philippine Rev. Econ. Bus.*, Sept.-Dec. 1986, *23*(3–4), pp. 243–73. **[G: Philippines]**

McLean, Ian and Richardson, Sue. More or Less Equal? Australian Income Distribution in 1933 and 1980. *Econ. Rec.*, March 1986, *62*(176), pp. 67–81. **[G: Australia]**

McMahon, Patrick J. and Tschetter, John H. The Declining Middle Class: A Further Analysis. *Mon. Lab. Rev.*, September 1986, *109*(9), pp. 22–27. **[G: U.S.]**

Meagher, G. A. and Agrawal, Nisha. Taxation Reform and Income Distribution in Australia. *Australian Econ. Rev.*, 3rd Quarter 1986, (75), pp. 33–56. **[G: Australia]**

Meagher, G. A. and Dixon, Peter B. Analyzing Income Distribution in Australia. *Econ. Rec.*, December 1986, *62*(179), pp. 427–41. **[G: Australia]**

Means, Gordon P. Ethnic Preference Policies in Malaysia. **In** *Nevitte, N. and Kennedy, C. H., eds.*, 1986, pp. 95–118. **[G: Malaysia]**

Mittar, Vishwa. Income Distribution and Poverty in the Urban Informal Sector. *Margin*, January 1986, *18*(2), pp. 29–41. **[G: India]**

Monza, Alfredo, et al. Algunas limitaciones de un cociente clásico. (With English summary.) *Desarrollo Econ.*, July-Sept. 1986, *26*(102), pp. 197–227. **[G: Argentina]**

Morris, C. Nick and Preston, Ian. Taxes, Benefits and the Distribution of Income 1968–83. *Fisc. Stud.*, November 1986, *7*(4), pp. 18–27. **[G: U.K.]**

Morris, Nick and Preston, Ian. Inequality, Poverty and the Redistribution of Income. *Bull. Econ. Res.*, November 1986, *38*(4), pp. 275–344. **[G: U.K.]**

Muqtada, M. Poverty and Inequality: Trends and Causes. **In** *Islam, R. and Muqtada, M., eds.*, 1986, pp. 41–60. **[G: Bangladesh]**

Musgrove, Philip. Desigualdad en la distribución del ingreso en diez ciudades sudamericanas: descomposición e interpretación del coeficiente de gini. (With English summary.) *Cuadernos Econ.*, August 1986, *23*(69), pp. 201–27. **[G: Latin America]**

Nolan, Brian. Comment on 'Cyclical and Secular Influences on the Size Distribution of Personal Income in the UK: Some Econometric Tests.' *Appl. Econ.*, October 1986, *18*(10), pp. 1103–07. **[G: U.K.]**

Nolan, Brian. Unemployment and the Size Distribution of Income. *Economica*, November 1986, *53*(212), pp. 421–45. **[G: U.K.]**

Oshima, Harry T.; de Borja, Elizabeth and Paz, Wilhelmina. Rising National Income per Worker and Falling Real Wages in the Philippines in the 1970s. *Philippine Rev. Econ. Bus.*, Sept.-Dec. 1986, *23*(3–4), pp. 151–90. **[G: Philippines]**

Panitch, Leo. Profits and Politics: Labour and the Crisis of British Capitalism. **In** *Panitch, L.*, 1986, *1977*, pp. 78–108. **[G: U.K.]**

Papanek, Gustav F. and Kyn, Oldrich. The Effect on Income Distribution of Development, the Growth Rate and Economic Strategy. *J. Devel. Econ.*, September 1986, *23*(1), pp. 55–65.

Quizón, Jaime and Binswanger, Hans P. Modeling the Impact of Agricultural Growth and Government Policy on Income Distribution in India. *World Bank Econ. Rev.*, September 1986, *1*(1), pp. 103–48. **[G: India]**

Rao, T. Divakara. Urban Income and Wealth Distribution by Size in Andhra Pradesh. *Margin*, April 1986, *18*(3), pp. 53–60. **[G: India]**

Rattsø, Jørn. A Note on Social Articulation. *J. Devel. Econ.*, May 1986, *21*(2), pp. 347–52. **[G: LDCs]**

Rubery, Jill and Wilkinson, Frank. Inflation and Income Distribution. **In** *Nolan, P. and Paine, S., eds.*, 1986, pp. 326–40. **[G: U.K.]**

Rubin, Marc. Occupation and Earnings Inequality: Some Contrasts between Workers and Management in Soviet Industry. *Econ. Planning*, 1986, *20*(3), pp. 206–30. **[G: U.S.S.R.]**

Samuelson, Paul A. Inequality of Incomes and Wealth Can Lesson amid Competition. **In** *Samuelson, P. A.*, 1986, *1980*, pp. 995–97.

Scitovsky, Tibor. Inequalities: Open and Hidden, Measured and Unmeasurable. **In** *Scitovsky, T.*, 1986, *1973*, pp. 26–34.

Sen, Pranab Kumar. The Gini Coefficient and Poverty Indexes: Some Reconciliations. *J.*

Amer. Statist. Assoc., December 1986, *81*(396), pp. 1050–57.

Simon, Owen. Investing in the Infrastructure. *Nat. Westminster Bank Quart. Rev.*, May 1986, pp. 2–16. **[G: U.K.]**

Smith, James D. Estimating the Personal Distribution of Income with Adjustment for Within-Family Variation: Comment. *J. Lab. Econ.*, Part 2, July 1986, *4*(3), pp. S239–44. **[G: U.S.]**

Soltow, Lee. Choices, Rents, and Luck: Economic Mobility of Nineteenth-Century Utah Households: Comment. **In** *Engerman, S. L. and Gallman, R. E., eds.*, 1986, pp. 256–58. **[G: U.S.]**

Standaert, Stan. Social Articulation as a Condition for Equitable Growth: A Comment. *J. Devel. Econ.*, September 1986, *23*(1), pp. 153–59. **[G: Brazil; Mexico; LDCs]**

Stark, Oded; Taylor, J. Edward and Yitzhaki, Shlomo. Remittances and Inequality. *Econ. J.*, September 1986, *96*(383), pp. 722–40. **[G: Mexico]**

Sun, Li-teh. Confucianism and the Economic Order of Taiwan. *Int. J. Soc. Econ.*, 1986, *13*(6), pp. 3–53. **[G: Taiwan]**

Uppal, J. S. Income Distribution and Poverty in Indonesia. *J. Econ. Devel.*, December 1986, *11*(2), pp. 177–96. **[G: Indonesia]**

Weil, Gordon. Reply [Cyclical and Secular Influences on the Size Distribution of Personal Income in the UK: Some Econometric Tests]. *Appl. Econ.*, October 1986, *18*(10), pp. 1109–10. **[G: U.K.]**

Wolfson, Michael. Stasis amid Change—Income Inequality in Canada, 1965–1983. *Rev. Income Wealth*, December 1986, *32*(4), pp. 337–69. **[G: Canada]**

Wüger, Michael. The Influence of the Personal Income Distribution on Private Demand in Austria. *Empirica*, 1986, *13*(2), pp. 155–72. **[G: Austria]**

222 Input–Output

2220 Input–Output

Aidenoff, Abraham. Input–Output Data in the United Nations System of National Accounts. **In** *Sohn, I., ed.*, 1986, *1970*, pp. 130–50.

Al, Pieter and Broesterhuizen, Guus. Comparability of Input–Output Tables in Time. **In** *Franz, A. and Rainer, N., eds.*, 1986, pp. 263–83.

Almon, Clopper. Investment in Input–Output Models and the Treatment of Secondary Products. **In** *Sohn, I., ed.*, 1986, *1970*, pp. 285–94. **[G: U.S.]**

Antille, Gabrielle and Gilli, Daisy. Establishing Input–Output Tables: The Swiss Experience. **In** *Franz, A. and Rainer, N., eds.*, 1986, pp. 201–19. **[G: Switzerland]**

Ara, Kenjiro. Condition for the Aggregation of Industrial Sectors into the Capital-Goods Sector and the Consumption-Goods Sector. *Hitotsubashi J. Econ.*, December 1986, *27*(2), pp. 99–109.

Bar-Eliezer, Simcha. The Role of Input–Output Tables as an Implement to Reconcile Basic Economic Statistics—The Case of Israel. **In** *Franz, A. and Rainer, N., eds.*, 1986, pp. 87–99. **[G: Israel]**

Bivin, David G. Input and Output Inventories in a Disaggregated Macro-model. *J. Post Keynesian Econ.*, Spring 1986, *8*(3), pp. 478–96. **[G: U.S.]**

Bjerkholt, Olav. Experiences in Using Input–Output Techniques for Price Calculations. **In** *Sohn, I., ed.*, 1986, *1982*, pp. 35–48. **[G: Norway]**

Bon, Ranko. Comparative Stability Analysis of Demand-Side and Supply-Side Input–Output Models. *Int. J. Forecasting*, 1986, *2*(2), pp. 231–35. **[G: U.S.]**

Bruno, Roberto. Problems of Comparability of Input–Output Tables over a Period of Time. **In** *Franz, A. and Rainer, N., eds.*, 1986, pp. 285–93.

Buckler, Margaret B.; Gilmartin, David and Reimbold, Thomas C. The INFORUM Model. **In** *Sohn, I., ed.*, 1986, *1976*, pp. 49–80. **[G: U.S.]**

Bulmer-Thomas, Victor. Application of Input–Output Analysis for Less Developed Countries (LDCs). **In** *Sohn, I., ed.*, 1986, *1982*, pp. 108–29. **[G: LDCs]**

Cekota, Jaromir. Technological Change in the USSR (1959–72), Poland (1962–77), and Czechoslovakia (1962–77): An Application of the Contemporary Production Model to National Input–Output Data. **In** *Altmann, F.-L., ed.*, 1986, pp. 58–81. **[G: U.S.S.R.; Poland; Czechoslovakia]**

Cella, Guido. The Input–Output Measurement of Interindustry Linkages: A Reply. *Oxford Bull. Econ. Statist.*, November 1986, *48*(4), pp. 379–84.

Chowdhury, Anisuzzaman. A More Generalized Planning Model of Bangladesh: Some Preliminary Observations. *Econ. Planning*, 1986, *20*(1), pp. 68–84. **[G: Bangladesh]**

Conrad, Klaus and Henseler-Unger, Iris. Applied General Equilibrium Modeling for Long-term Energy Policy in Germany. *J. Policy Modeling*, Winter 1986, *8*(4), pp. 531–49. **[G: W. Germany]**

Csepinszky, Andor. Some Principles Established in Compiling Input–Ouput Tables of Hungary. **In** *Franz, A. and Rainer, N., eds.*, 1986, pp. 101–09. **[G: Hungary]**

Curry, Steve. The Economic Impact of the Tourist Industry in the United Republic of Tanzania: An Input–Output Analysis. *Industry Devel.*, 1986, (19), pp. 55–75. **[G: Tanzania]**

Debreu, Gerard and Herstein, I. N. Nonnegative Square Matrices. **In** *Sohn, I., ed.*, 1986, *1953*, pp. 200–209.

Delarue, Antoine. Circulation des marchandises et création de valeur: Une approche néoricardienne de la fonction distribution. (Commodity Flows andd Value Creation: A Neoricardian Approach to Trade. With English summary.) *Écon. Appl.*, 1986, *39*(1), pp. 87–111.

Donkers, H. W. J. and van der Zwan, A. C.

Analysing Consumer Price Changes by Using Input–Output Tables. *Statist. J.*, October 1986, *4*(2), pp. 195–211. **[G: Netherlands]**

Driver, Ciaran; Kilpatrick, Andrew and Naisbitt, Barry. The Employment Effects of UK Manufacturing Trade Expansion with the EEC and the Newly Industrialising Countries. *Europ. Econ. Rev.*, April 1986, *30*(2), pp. 427–38. **[G: U.K.]**

Dubgaard, Alex. Disaggregation of the Farm Sector in the Danish Input–Output Table. **In** *Franz, A. and Rainer, N., eds.*, 1986, pp. 427–45. **[G: Denmark]**

Duchin, Faye. Computers, Input–Output, and the Future. *J. Econ. Issues*, June 1986, *20*(2), pp. 499–507. **[G: U.S.]**

Fisher, W. Halder and Chilton, Cecil H. Developing Ex Ante Input–Output Flow and Capital Coefficients. **In** *Sohn, I., ed.*, 1986, *1972*, pp. 314–24. **[G: U.S.]**

Fisher, Walter D. Criteria for Aggregation in Input–Output Analysis. **In** *Sohn, I., ed.*, 1986, *1958*, pp. 210–25. **[G: U.S.]**

Flaschel, Peter and Semmler, Willi. The Dynamic Equalization of Profit Rates for Input–Output Models with Fixed Capital. **In** *Semmler, W., ed.*, 1986, pp. 1–34.

Fleischmann, Eduard and Rainer, Norbert. How to Define Gross Output? A Review of Borderline Cases. **In** *Franz, A. and Rainer, N., eds.*, 1986, pp. 447–59. **[G: Austria]**

Franz, Alfred. Supplementary Breakdown of Activity and Commodity Classifications for Input–Output Purposes. **In** *Franz, A. and Rainer, N., eds.*, 1986, pp. 461–69.

Fukui, Yukio. A More Powerful Method for Triangularizing Input–Output Matrices and the Similarity of Production Structures. *Econometrica*, November 1986, *54*(6), pp. 1425–33. **[G: U.S.; Japan; Norway; Italy]**

Glattfelder, P.; Cser, I. and Magyar, E. The Structure of the Hungarian Economy in 2000. **In** *Franz, A. and Rainer, N., eds.*, 1986, pp. 295–312. **[G: Hungary]**

Guccione, Antonio. The Input–Output Measurement of Interindustry Linkages: A Comment. *Oxford Bull. Econ. Statist.*, November 1986, *48*(4), pp. 373–77.

Hamilton, Clive. A General Equilibrium Model of Structural Change and Economic Growth, with Application to South Korea. *J. Devel. Econ.*, September 1986, *23*(1), pp. 67–88. **[G: S. Korea]**

Heller, Peter S. Factor Endowment Change and Comparative Advantage: The Case of Japan, 1956–1969. **In** *Sohn, I., ed.*, 1986, *1976*, pp. 327–39. **[G: Japan]**

Heng, Toh Mun. Income Redistribution and Trade Policy Effects on Macroeconomic Aggregates: A Simulation Study of the Singapore Economy Based on an Extended Input–Output Model. *J. Econ. Devel.*, July 1986, *11*(1), pp. 157–90. **[G: Singapore]**

Jackson, Randall W. The Full-Distribution Approach to Aggregate Representation in the Input–Output Modeling Framework. *J. Reg. Sci.*, August 1986, *26*(3), pp. 515–31. **[G: U.S.]**

Johansen, Leif. On the Theory of Dynamic Input–Output Models with Different Time Profiles of Capital Construction and Finite Lifetime of Capital Equipment. **In** *Sohn, I., ed.*, 1986, *1978*, pp. 295–313.

Johnson, Thomas G. A Dynamic Input–Output Model for Small Regions. *Rev. Reg. Stud.*, Winter 1986, *16*(1), pp. 14–23.

Juillard, Michel. The Stability of the Reproduction Scheme: Theoretical Discussion and Empirical Evidence for the United States, 1948–1980. **In** *Semmler, W., ed.*, 1986, pp. 304–23. **[G: U.S.]**

Karbstein, Werner; Ludwig, Udo and Siehndel, Karl-Heinz. On the Data Basis for the Compilation of Inter-industry Balances of Gross Output: Some Experiences of the GDR. **In** *Franz, A. and Rainer, N., eds.*, 1986, pp. 471–84. **[G: E. Germany]**

Karunaratne, Neil Dias. An Input–Output Approach to the Measurement of the Information Economy. *Econ. Planning*, 1986, *20*(2), pp. 87–103. **[G: Australia]**

Karunaratne, Neil Dias. Issues in Measuring the Information Economy. *J. Econ. Stud.*, 1986, *13*(3), pp. 51–68. **[G: Australia]**

Kubo, Yuji; Robinson, Sherman and Urata, Shujiro. The Impact of Alternative Development Strategies: Simulations with a Dynamic Input–Output Model. *J. Policy Modeling*, Winter 1986, *8*(4), pp. 503–29. **[G: Turkey; Korea]**

Kuboniwa, Masaaki; Matsue, Yumiko and Arita, Fumiko. Derivation of U.S. Commodity-by-Commodity Input–Output Tables from SNA Use and Make Tables. *Hitotsubashi J. Econ.*, June 1986, *27*(1), pp. 49–75. **[G: U.S.]**

Kuyvenhoven, Arie and Poot, Huib. The Structure of Indonesian Manufacturing Industry: An Input–Output Approach. *Bull. Indonesian Econ. Stud.*, August 1986, *22*(2), pp. 54–79. **[G: Indonesia]**

Lahiri, Sajal and Satchell, Steven E. Properties of the Expected Value of the Leontief Inverse: Some Further Results. *Math. Soc. Sci.*, February 1986, *11*(1), pp. 69–82.

Lal, Kishori. Canadian Input–Output Tables and Their Integration with Other Sub-systems of the National Accounts. **In** *Franz, A. and Rainer, N., eds.*, 1986, pp. 147–63. **[G: Canada]**

Leontief, Wassily. Air Pollution and the Economic Structure: Empirical Results of Input–Output Computations. **In** *Leontief, W.*, 1986, *1972*, pp. 273–93. **[G: U.S.]**

Leontief, Wassily. An Alternative to Aggregation in Input–Output Analysis and National Accounts. **In** *Leontief, W.*, 1986, *1967*, pp. 41–54. **[G: U.S.]**

Leontief, Wassily. Domestic Production and Foreign Trade: The American Capital Position Reexamined. **In** *Leontief, W.*, 1986, *1953*, pp. 65–93. **[G: U.S.]**

Leontief, Wassily. Environmental Repercussions and the Economic Structure: An Input–Output

Approach. **In** *Leontief, W.*, 1986, *1970*, pp. 241–60.

Leontief, Wassily. Factor Proportions and the Structure of American Trade: Further Theoretical and Empirical Analysis. **In** *Leontief, W.*, 1986, *1956*, pp. 94–128. **[G: U.S.]**

Leontief, Wassily. Input–Output Economics. **In** *Leontief, W.*, 1986, *1951*, pp. 3–18. **[G: U.S.]**

Leontief, Wassily. Structure of the World Economy: Outline of a Simple Input–Output Formulation. **In** *Leontief, W.*, 1986, *1974*, pp. 321–37. **[G: Global]**

Leontief, Wassily. The Dynamic Inverse. **In** *Leontief, W.*, 1986, *1970*, pp. 294–320.

Leontief, Wassily. The Growth of Maritime Traffic and the Future of World Ports. **In** *Leontief, W.*, 1986, *1979*, pp. 379–91. **[G: Global]**

Leontief, Wassily. The Structure of Development. **In** *Leontief, W.*, 1986, *1963*, pp. 162–87. **[G: Israel; U.S.; Peru; Egypt]**

Leontief, Wassily. Wages, Profits, Prices, and Taxes. **In** *Leontief, W.*, 1986, *1947*, pp. 55–64. **[G: U.S.]**

Leontief, Wassily and Hoffenberg, Marvin. The Economic Effects of Disarmament. **In** *Leontief, W.*, 1986, *1961*, pp. 188–203. **[G: U.S.]**

Lim, Joseph and Bautista, Carlos. The Impact of Income Redistribution on the Composition of Output Demand. *Philippine Rev. Econ. Bus.*, Sept.-Dec. 1986, *23*(3–4), pp. 243–73. **[G: Philippines]**

Lorigny, Jacques. Une approche théorique du coût de l'information dans la régulation du modèle linéaire d'entrée-sortie. (A Theoretical Approach to Information Cost in the Linear Input–Output Model Regulation. With English summary.) *Écon. Soc.*, November 1986, *20*(11), pp. 77–99.

Luptáčik, M. and Schmoranz, I. Economic Consequences of a Change in Demographic Patterns: An Integrated Approach. **In** *Batey, P. W. and Madden, M., eds.*, 1986, pp. 107–21. **[G: Austria]**

Lynch, R. G. An Assessment of the RAS Method for Updating Input–Output Tables. **In** *Sohn, I., ed.*, 1986, *1985*, pp. 271–84. **[G: U.K.]**

Martinez Lopez, Antonio and Anton Valero, Vicente. Feedback of Basic Statistics in the Case of the Spanish Input–Output Table. **In** *Franz, A. and Rainer, N., eds.*, 1986, pp. 111–19. **[G: Spain]**

Maruya, Reishi. Structural Change in the German Economy in the 1970's. *Kobe Univ. Econ.*, 1986, (32), pp. 69–86. **[G: W. Germany]**

Miller, Ronald E. Upper Bounds on the Sizes of Interregional Feedbacks in Multiregional Input–Output Models. *J. Reg. Sci.*, May 1986, *26*(2), pp. 285–306.

Münzenmaier, Werner. Some Notes on the Appropriate Definition of Sectors in Regional Input–Output Tables, Especially for the Federal Republic of Germany. **In** *Franz, A. and Rainer, N., eds.*, 1986, pp. 23–46. **[G: W. Germany]**

Mürdter, Heinz. The Compilation of an Input–Output Table with Disaggregated Steel-Sectors—Framework and First Experience. **In** *Franz, A. and Rainer, N., eds.*, 1986, pp. 325–31. **[G: W. Germany]**

Ochoa, Eduardo M. An Input–Output Study of Labor Productivity in the U.S. Economy, 1947–72. *J. Post Keynesian Econ.*, Fall 1986, *9*(1), pp. 111–37. **[G: U.S.]**

Pagoulatos, A.; Mattas, K. and Debertin, D. L. A Comparison of Some Alternatives to Input–Output Multipliers. *Land Econ.*, November 1986, *62*(4), pp. 371–77. **[G: U.S.]**

Pecci-Boriani, Marco. International Comparability of the Input–Output Tables. **In** *Franz, A. and Rainer, N., eds.*, 1986, pp. 313–23.

Polenske, Karen R. The Implementation of a Multiregional Input–Output Model for the United States. **In** *Sohn, I., ed.*, 1986, *1972*, pp. 93–107. **[G: U.S.]**

Portier, Jean-Michel. Procedures for Making the Input–Output Tables Consistent with the French National Accounts by Institutional Sectors. **In** *Franz, A. and Rainer, N., eds.*, 1986, pp. 165–78. **[G: France]**

Postner, Harry H. The 'Division' as Statistical Unit for Input–Output Compilation: A Proposal. **In** *Franz, A. and Rainer, N., eds.*, 1986, pp. 485–99.

ten Raa, Thijs. Applied Dynamic Input–Output with Distributed Activities. *Europ. Econ. Rev.*, August 1986, *30*(4), pp. 805–31. **[G: Poland]**

ten Raa, Thijs. Dynamic Input–Output Analysis with Distributed Activities. *Rev. Econ. Statist.*, May 1986, *68*(2), pp. 300–310.

Rainer, Norbert. The Set of Trade and Transport Margin Matrices in the Austrian IO-System. **In** *Franz, A. and Rainer, N., eds.*, 1986, pp. 47–67. **[G: Austria]**

Reich, Utz-Peter. Treatment of Trade and Valuation of Flows in Input–Output Tables. **In** *Franz, A. and Rainer, N., eds.*, 1986, pp. 333–53.

Richter, Josef. The Role of Import-Matrices in Compiling Constant Price Input–Output Tables. **In** *Franz, A. and Rainer, N., eds.*, 1986, pp. 355–71. **[G: Austria]**

Riedel, James. Factor Proportions, Linkages, and the Open Developing Economy. **In** *Sohn, I., ed.*, 1986, *1975*, pp. 340–53. **[G: Taiwan]**

Ritvanen, Kari. Input–Output and Its Balancing in Finland. **In** *Franz, A. and Rainer, N., eds.*, 1986, pp. 221–31. **[G: Finland]**

Rymes, Thomas K. The Measurement of Multifactor Productivity in an Input–Output Framework: New Canadian Estimates. **In** *Franz, A. and Rainer, N., eds.*, 1986, pp. 373–401. **[G: Canada]**

Sarkar, Hiren and Panda, Manoj Kumar. Quantity–Price–Money Interaction in a CGE Model with Applications to Fiscal Policy. *Margin*, April 1986, *18*(3), pp. 31–52. **[G: India]**

Sevaldson, Per. The Stability of Input–Output Coefficients. **In** *Sohn, I., ed.*, 1986, *1970*, pp. 226–52. **[G: Norway]**

Silva, J. A. Equivalent Conditions on Solvability

for Non-linear Leontief Models. *Metroecon.*, June 1986, *38*(2), pp. 167–79.

Simpson, David and Tsukui, Jinkichi. The Fundamental Structure of Input–Output Tables: An International Comparison. **In** *Sohn, I., ed.*, 1986, pp. 372–91. **[G: U.S.; Japan]**

Slater, Paul B. The Determination of Groups of Functionally Integrated Industries in the United States Using a 1967 Interindustry Flow Table. **In** *Slater, P. B.*, 1986, *1977*, pp. 13–17. **[G: U.S.]**

Slater, Paul B. The Network Structure of the United States Input–Output Table. **In** *Slater, P. B.*, 1986, *1978*, pp. 18–28. **[G: U.S.]**

Sohn, Ira. Readings in Input–Output Analysis: Theory and Applications: Introduction. **In** *Sohn, I., ed.*, 1986, pp. 3–10.

Soofi, Abdollah S. and Parvin, Kumars. The Import Leakage Effect and the Effectiveness of Fiscal Policy: An Input–Output Analysis. *Public Finance*, December 1986, *41*(3), pp. 430–39. **[G: Iran]**

Stäglin, Reiner and Stahmer, Carsten. Towards a Consistent System of Input–Output Tables for the Federal Republic of Germany. **In** *Franz, A. and Rainer, N., eds.*, 1986, pp. 179–200. **[G: W. Germany]**

Stahmer, Carsten. Integration of Input–Output Statistics with the International Systems of National Accounts. **In** *Franz, A. and Rainer, N., eds.*, 1986, pp. 501–24.

Stone, Richard. Demographic Input–Output: An Extension of Social Accounting. **In** *Sohn, I., ed.*, 1986, *1970*, pp. 151–72. **[G: U.K.]**

Stone, Richard. Where Are We Now? A Short Account of the Development of Input–Output Studies and Their Present Trends. **In** *Sohn, I., ed.*, 1986, pp. 13–31.

Szybisz, Boguslaw. An Integrated Quantity and Price Indices System Based on Input–Output Tables. **In** *Franz, A. and Rainer, N., eds.*, 1986, pp. 403–13. **[G: Poland]**

Taniura, Taeko. Economic Development Effects of an Integrated Iron and Steel Works: A Case Study of Minas Gerais Steel in Brazil. *Devel. Econ.*, June 1986, *24*(2), pp. 169–93. **[G: Brazil]**

Tate, D. M. Structural Change Implications for Industrial Water Use. *Water Resources Res.*, October 1986, *22*(11), pp. 1526–30. **[G: Canada]**

Thage, Bent. Balancing Procedures in the Detailed Commodity Flow System Used as a Basis for Annual Input–Output Tables in Denmark. **In** *Franz, A. and Rainer, N., eds.*, 1986, pp. 233–62. **[G: Denmark]**

Todorov, Wassil. Methodological Principles and Technology for Compilation of Input–Output Tables in Labour Units. **In** *Franz, A. and Rainer, N., eds.*, 1986, pp. 415–25.

United Nations Statistical Office. Input–Output Standards in the SNA Framework. **In** *Franz, A. and Rainer, N., eds.*, 1986, pp. 525–66.

Uno, Kimio. Resource Allocation by Social Purpose and the Input–Output Framework. **In** *Franz, A. and Rainer, N., eds.*, 1986, pp. 69–86. **[G: Japan]**

Vaccara, Beatrice N. Changes over Time in Input–Output Coefficients for the United States. **In** *Sohn, I., ed.*, 1986, *1970*, pp. 253–70. **[G: U.S.]**

Ville, Jean A. Extension de l'usage des matrices technologiques. (Extension of the Use of Technological Matrices. With English summary.) *Écon. Soc.*, November 1986, *20*(11), pp. 5–13.

West, Guy R. A Stochastic Analysis of an Input–Output Model. *Econometrica*, March 1986, *54*(2), pp. 363–74. **[G: Australia]**

Witter, M. and Ramjeesingh, D. An Analysis of the Internal Sectoral Structure of the Jamaican Economy: 1969–1974. *Soc. Econ. Stud.*, March 1986, *35*(1), pp. 1–72. **[G: Jamaica]**

Yamazawa, Ippei; Nohara, Takashi and Osada, Hiroshi. Economic Interdependence in Pacific Asia: An International Input–Output Analysis. *Devel. Econ.*, June 1986, *24*(2), pp. 95–108. **[G: Asia]**

Yan, Chiou-Shuang and Ames, Edward. Economic Interrelatedness. **In** *Sohn, I., ed.*, 1986, *1965*, pp. 392–405. **[G: U.S.]**

Young, Paula C. The U.S. Input–Output Experience—Present Status and Future Prospects. **In** *Franz, A. and Rainer, N., eds.*, 1986, pp. 121–45. **[G: U.S.]**

Zeineldin, Aly. The Egyptian Economy in 1999: An Input–Output Study. *Econ. Modelling*, April 1986, *3*(2), pp. 140–46. **[G: Egypt]**

223 Financial Accounts

2230 Financial Accounts; Financial Statistics; Empirical Analyses of Capital Adequacy

Adelberger, Otto L. Financing Corporations in Major European Capital Markets. **In** *Macharzina, K. and Staehle, W. H., eds.*, 1986, pp. 295–315. **[G: OECD]**

Barnett, William A.; Hinich, Melvin J. and Weber, Warren E. The Regulatory Wedge between the Demand-Side and Supply-Side Aggregation-Theoretic Monetary Aggregates. *J. Econometrics*, Oct./Nov. 1986, *33*(1/2), pp. 165–85. **[G: U.S.]**

Blanchard, Olivier J. Investment, Output, and the Cost of Capital: Comments. *Brookings Pap. Econ. Act.*, 1986, (1), pp. 153–58. **[G: U.S.]**

Boskin, Michael J. Theoretical and Empirical Issues in the Measurement, Evaluation, and Interpretation of Postwar U.S. Saving. **In** *Adams, F. G. and Wachter, S. M., eds.*, 1986, pp. 11–43. **[G: U.S.]**

Bosworth, Barry P. Savings and Government Policy. **In** *Adams, F. G. and Wachter, S. M., eds.*, 1986, pp. 173–87. **[G: U.S.; Japan]**

Cargill, Thomas F. Japanese Monetary Policy, Flow of Funds, and Domestic Financial Liberalization. *Fed. Res. Bank San Francisco Econ. Rev.*, Summer 1986, (3), pp. 21–32. **[G: Japan]**

Carter, R. L.; Chiplin, B. and Lewis, M. K. Personal Saving and Finance. **In** *Carter, R. L.; Chiplin, B. and Lewis, M. K., eds.*, 1986, pp. 1–26. **[G: U.K.]**

Cebrecos Revilla, Felipe. Savings for Development: The Case of Peru. **In** *U.N., Dept. of International Econ. and Social Affairs*, 1986, pp. 65–70. **[G: Peru]**

Cheng, Hang-Sheng. Financial Policy and Reform in Taiwan, China. **In** *Cheng, H.-S., ed.*, 1986, pp. 143–59. **[G: Taiwan]**

De Wulf, Luc and Goldsbrough, David. The Evolving Role of Monetary Policy in China. *Int. Monet. Fund Staff Pap.*, June 1986, *33*(2), pp. 209–42. **[G: China]**

Diejomaoh, Vremudia P. Impact of Different Types of Foreign Investments on Capital Formation in Africa. **In** *Association of African Central Banks*, 1986, pp. 123–50. **[G: Africa]**

Foxley R., Juan. Determinantes económicos del ahorro nacional: Chile 1963–1983. (With English summary.) *Cuadernos Econ.*, April 1986, *23*(68), pp. 119–27. **[G: Chile]**

Friedman, Benjamin M. Financing American Investment in New Technology. **In** *Landau, R. and Jorgenson, D. W., eds.*, 1986, pp. 205–19. **[G: U.S.]**

Friedman, Benjamin M. Financing Corporate Capital Formation: An Introduction and Overview. **In** *Friedman, B. M., ed.*, 1986, pp. 1–11.

Grebler, Leo. Household Saving in an Era of Financial Turmoil, 1975–1984. *J. Econ. Soc. Meas.*, July 1986, *14*(2), pp. 91–105. **[G: U.S.]**

Hakim, Leonardo and Wallich, Christine. OECD Deficits, Debt, and Savings Structure and Trends, 1965–81: A Survey of the Evidence. **In** *Lal, D. and Wolf, M., eds.*, 1986, pp. 292–360. **[G: OECD]**

Hart, Jeffrey A. British Industrial Policy. **In** *Barfield, C. E. and Schambra, W. A., eds.*, 1986, pp. 128–60. **[G: U.K.]**

Horioka, Charles Yuji. Why Is Japan's Private Savings Rate So High? *Finance Develop.*, December 1986, *23*(4), pp. 22–25. **[G: Japan]**

Klein, Lawrence R. International Aspects of Saving. **In** *Adams, F. G. and Wachter, S. M., eds.*, 1986, pp. 195–204. **[G: OECD]**

Landau, Ralph and Hatsopoulos, George N. Capital Formation in the United States and Japan. **In** *Landau, R. and Rosenberg, N., eds.*, 1986, pp. 583–606. **[G: U.S.; Japan]**

Lluch, Constantino. ICORS, Savings Rates, and the Determinants of Public Expenditure in Developing Countries. **In** *Lal, D. and Wolf, M., eds.*, 1986, pp. 361–95. **[G: LDCs]**

Lovell, Michael C. Investment, Output, and the Cost of Capital: Comments. *Brookings Pap. Econ. Act.*, 1986, (1), pp. 158–61. **[G: U.S.]**

Mayshar, Joram. Investment Patterns. **In** *Ben-Porath, Y., ed.*, 1986, pp. 101–18. **[G: Israel]**

Milot, Jean-Paul and Teillet, Pierre. Financial Operations and Monetary Statistics: Improved Concordance in the French National Accounts. *Rev. Income Wealth*, December 1986, *32*(4), pp. 371–85. **[G: France]**

Muser, Alexander. Mobilization of Personal Savings through Self-help Promotion Institutions. **In** *U.N., Dept. of International Econ. and Social Affairs*, 1986, pp. 101–06. **[G: LDCs]**

Petschnig, Mária. The Changing Role of Private Savings. *Acta Oecon.*, 1986, *37*(1–2), pp. 103–21. **[G: Hungary]**

Pollin, Robert. Alternative Perspectives on the Rise of Corporate Debt Dependency: The U.S. Postwar Experience. *Rev. Radical Polit. Econ.*, Spring/Summer 1986, *18*(1/2), pp. 205–35. **[G: U.S.]**

de Rezende Rocha, Roberto. Costs of Intermediation in Developing Countries: A Preliminary Investigation. **In** *Hanson, J. A. and Rocha, R.*, 1986, pp. 17–82. **[G: MDCs; LDCs]**

Roach, Stephen S. Macrorealities of the Information Economy. **In** *Landau, R. and Rosenberg, N., eds.*, 1986, pp. 93–103. **[G: U.S.]**

Shapiro, Matthew D. Investment, Output, and the Cost of Capital. *Brookings Pap. Econ. Act.*, 1986, (1), pp. 111–52. **[G: U.S.]**

Taggart, Robert A., Jr. Have U.S. Corporations Grown Financially Weak? **In** *Friedman, B. M., ed.*, 1986, pp. 13–33. **[G: U.S.]**

Taylor, Alwyn Beresford. National Financial Policies and Capital Formation in Africa: Summation of the Symposium. **In** *Association of African Central Banks*, 1986, pp. 151–69. **[G: Africa]**

Wagner, Richard E. The Welfare State, Capital Formation, and Tax-Transfer Politics. **In** *Lee, D. R., ed.*, 1986, pp. 241–73. **[G: U.S.]**

Wilson, John F., et al. Major Borrowing and Lending Trends in the U.S. Economy, 1981–85. *Fed. Res. Bull.*, August 1986, *72*(8), pp. 511–24. **[G: U.S.]**

224 National Wealth and Balance Sheets

2240 National Wealth and Balance Sheets

Abalkin, L. The Interaction of the Productive Forces and Production Relations. *Prob. Econ.*, April 1986, *28*(12), pp. 23–41. **[G: U.S.S.R.]**

Ando, Albert. Why Is Japan's Saving Rate So Apparently High? Comment. **In** *Fischer, S., ed.*, 1986, pp. 211–20. **[G: Japan; U.S.]**

Arellano, José Pablo and Marfán, Manuel. Ahorro-inversión y relaciones financieras en la actual crisis económica chilena. (Savings, Investment, and Financial Relations in the Present Chilean Economic Crisis. With English summary.) *Colección Estud. CIEPLAN*, December 1986, (20), pp. 61–93. **[G: Chile]**

Avery, Robert B.; Elliehausen, Gregory E. and Gustafson, Thomas A. Pensions and Social Security in Household Portfolios: Evidence from the *1983 Survey of Consumer Finances.* **In** *Adams, F. G. and Wachter, S. M., eds.*, 1986, pp. 127–60. **[G: U.S.]**

Carter, R. L.; Chiplin, B. and Lewis, M. K. Personal Saving and Finance. **In** *Carter, R. L.; Chiplin, B. and Lewis, M. K., eds.*, 1986, pp. 1–26. **[G: U.K.]**

Carter, R. L. and Diacon, S. R. Personal Investment Markets. **In** *Carter, R. L.; Chiplin, B. and Lewis, M. K., eds.*, 1986, pp. 196–228. **[G: U.K.]**

Downe, Ed. The Behavior of Postwar Rates of Return in Capitalist Countries. *Rev. Radical Polit. Econ.*, Fall 1986, *18*(3), pp. 101–10. **[G: OECD]**

Drèze, Jacques H., et al. Per una minore disoccupazione in Europa: il ruolo della formazione di capitale. (For a Reduction of Unemployment in Europe: The Role of the Capital Formation. With English summary.) *Giorn. Econ.*, Sept.-Oct. 1986, *45*(9–10), pp. 479–514. **[G: EEC]**

Dumas, Lloyd J. Commanding Resources: The Military Sector and Capital Formation. **In** *Lee, D. R., ed.*, 1986, pp. 323–52. **[G: U.S.]**

Friedman, Benjamin M. Financing Corporate Capital Formation: An Introduction and Overview. **In** *Friedman, B. M., ed.*, 1986, pp. 1–11.

Friedman, Benjamin M. Implications of Government Deficits for Interest Rates, Equity Returns, and Corporate Financing. **In** *Friedman, B. M., ed.*, 1986, pp. 67–89. **[G: U.S.]**

Gallman, Robert E. The United States Capital Stock in the Nineteenth Century. **In** *Engerman, S. L. and Gallman, R. E., eds.*, 1986, pp. 165–206. **[G: U.S.]**

Girardin, Eric. Estimation en longue période d'une fonction d'investissement pour le Royaume-Uni: 1881–1979. (Estimation of an Investment Function for the United Kingdom in the Long Run: 1881–1979. With English summary.) *Écon. Appl.*, 1986, *39*(2), pp. 297–336. **[G: U.K.]**

Goldsmith, Raymond W. The United States Capital Stock in the Nineteenth Century: Comment. **In** *Engerman, S. L. and Gallman, R. E., eds.*, 1986, pp. 206–10. **[G: U.S.]**

Hamilton, Clive. A Technique for Calculating Capital Coefficients in Newly Industrializing Countries, with Application to the Republic of Korea. *Devel. Econ.*, March 1986, *24*(1), pp. 56–70. **[G: S. Korea]**

Hayashi, Fumio. Why Is Japan's Saving Rate So Apparently High? **In** *Fischer, S., ed.*, 1986, pp. 147–210. **[G: U.S.; Japan]**

Hendershott, Patric H. Tax Reform, Interest Rates, and Capital Allocation. **In** *Follain, J. R., ed.*, 1986, pp. 27–57. **[G: U.S.]**

Jorgenson, Dale W. and Yun, Kun-Young. Tax Policy and Capital Allocation. *Scand. J. Econ.*, 1986, *88*(2), pp. 355–77. **[G: U.S.]**

Jorgenson, Dale W. and Yun, Kun-Young. The Efficiency of Capital Allocation. *Scand. J. Econ.*, 1986, *88*(1), pp. 85–107. **[G: U.S.]**

Jungenfelt, Karl G. Comment [The Efficiency of Capital Allocation] [Tax Policy and Capital Allocation]. *Scand. J. Econ.*, 1986, *88*(2), pp. 379–82. **[G: U.S.]**

Kane, Edward J. Wealth-Based Engels Curves for Financial and Real Estate Assets. **In** *Chen, A. H., ed.*, 1986, pp. 233–45. **[G: U.S.]**

Katz, Arnold J. An Analysis of Trends in the Intensity of U.S. Capital Formation and Their Determinants. *J. Policy Modeling*, Fall 1986, *8*(3), pp. 433–69. **[G: U.S.]**

Kearl, J. R. and Pope, Clayne L. Choices, Rents, and Luck: Economic Mobility of Nineteenth-Century Utah Households. **In** *Engerman, S. L. and Gallman, R. E., eds.*, 1986, pp. 215–56. **[G: U.S.]**

Kearl, J. R. and Pope, Clayne L. Unobservable Family and Individual Contributions to the Distributions of Income and Wealth. *J. Lab. Econ.*, Part 2, July 1986, *4*(3), pp. S48–79. **[G: U.S.]**

Kenwood, A. G. Fixed Capital Formation in the Ports of the South Wales Coalfield, 1850–1913. **In** *Baber, C. and Williams, L. J., eds.*, 1986, pp. 117–27. **[G: U.K.]**

Kohn, Martin J. and Leggett, Robert E. A Look at Soviet Capital Retirement Statistics: Unraveling Some Mysteries? *Comp. Econ. Stud.*, Summer 1986, *28*(2), pp. 21–35. **[G: U.S.S.R.]**

Krasovskii, V. and Fridman, L. Accumulation and Technical Progress in the USSR Economy. *Prob. Econ.*, March 1986, *28*(11), pp. 3–18. **[G: U.S.S.R.]**

Leontief, Wassily. The Distribution of Work and Income. **In** *Leontief, W.*, 1986, *1982*, pp. 363–78. **[G: U.S.; Austria]**

Leu, Robert E.; Buhmann, Brigitte and Frey, René L. Die personelle Einkommens- und Vermögensverteilung der Schweiz 1982. (The Size Distribution of Income and Wealth in Switzerland. With English summary.) *Schweiz. Z. Volkswirtsch. Statist.*, June 1986, *122*(2), pp. 111–42. **[G: Switzerland]**

Lindert, Peter H. Unequal English Wealth since 1670. *J. Polit. Econ.*, December 1986, *94*(6), pp. 1127–62. **[G: U.K.]**

Masson, André. A Cohort Analysis of Wealth–Age Profiles Generated by a Simulation Model in France (1949–75). *Econ. J.*, March 1986, *96*(381), pp. 173–90. **[G: France]**

Musgrave, John C. Fixed Reproducible Tangible Wealth in the United States, 1982–85. *Surv. Curr. Bus.*, August 1986, *66*(8), pp. 36–39. **[G: U.S.]**

Musgrave, John C. Fixed Reproducible Tangible Wealth in the United States: Revised Estimates. *Surv. Curr. Bus.*, January 1986, *66*(1), pp. 51–76. **[G: U.S.]**

Newell, William H. Inheritance on the Maturing Frontier: Butler County, Ohio, 1803–1865: Reply. **In** *Engerman, S. L. and Gallman, R. E., eds.*, 1986, pp. 300–301. **[G: U.S.]**

Newell, William H. Inheritance on the Maturing Frontier: Butler County, Ohio, 1803–1865. **In** *Engerman, S. L. and Gallman, R. E., eds.*, 1986, pp. 261–97. **[G: U.S.]**

Ortmeyer, David L. and Peek, Joe. An Ex Ante View of Household Portfolio Choice: The Role of Expected Capital Gains. *Rev. Econ. Statist.*, May 1986, *68*(2), pp. 207–16. **[G: U.S.]**

Peek, Joe. Household Wealth Composition: The Impact of Capital Gains. *New Eng. Econ. Rev.*, Nov./Dec. 1986, pp. 26–39. **[G: U.S.]**

Prais, S. J. Some International Comparisons of

the Age of the Machine-Stock. *J. Ind. Econ.*, March 1986, *34*(3), pp. 261–77. **[G: France; Japan; U.K.; U.S.; W. Germany]**

Rao, T. Divakara. Urban Income and Wealth Distribution by Size in Andhra Pradesh. *Margin*, April 1986, *18*(3), pp. 53–60. **[G: India]**

Reynolds, Morgan O. Taxation, Saving, and Investment: A Look at the Evidence. **In** *Lee, D. R., ed.*, 1986, pp. 49–85. **[G: OECD]**

Romer, Paul M. Why Is Japan's Saving Rate So Apparently High? Comment. **In** *Fischer, S., ed.*, 1986, pp. 220–33. **[G: Japan; U.S.]**

Rosen, Sherwin. Unobservable Family and Individual Contributions to the Distributions of Income and Wealth: Comment. *J. Lab. Econ.*, Part 2, July 1986, *4*(3), pp. S80–82.

Rubinstein, W. D. Atlas of Industrializing Britain 1780–1914: Wealth and the Wealthy. **In** *Langton, J. and Morris, R. J., eds.*, 1986, pp. 156–59. **[G: U.K.]**

Sato, Kazuo. Economic Laws and the Household Economy in Japan: Lags in Policy Response to Economic Changes. **In** *Saxonhouse, G. R. and Yamamura, K., eds.*, 1986, pp. 3–55. **[G: Japan]**

Soltow, Lee. Choices, Rents, and Luck: Economic Mobility of Nineteenth-Century Utah Households: Comment. **In** *Engerman, S. L. and Gallman, R. E., eds.*, 1986, pp. 256–58. **[G: U.S.]**

Soltow, Lee. Inheritance on the Maturing Frontier: Butler County, Ohio, 1803–1865: Comment. **In** *Engerman, S. L. and Gallman, R. E., eds.*, 1986, pp. 297–300. **[G: U.S.]**

Taylor, Tom. Capital Formation by Railways in South Wales, 1836–1914. **In** *Baber, C. and Williams, L. J., eds.*, 1986, pp. 97–116. **[G: U.K.]**

Wadhwani, Sushil B. and Wall, Martin. The UK Capital Stock—New Estimates of Premature Scrapping. *Oxford Rev. Econ. Policy*, Autumn 1986, *2*(3), pp. 44–55. **[G: U.K.]**

Zotov, M. Improving the Investment Process. *Prob. Econ.*, March 1986, *28*(11), pp. 57–75. **[G: U.S.S.R.]**

Zotova, T. Economic Effectiveness of the Production Infrastructure. *Prob. Econ.*, June 1986, *29*(2), pp. 79–96. **[G: U.S.S.R.]**

225 Social Indicators: Data and Analysis

2250 Social Indicators: Data and Analysis

Belkaoui, Ahmed and Maksy, Mostafa M. Basic Needs and Economic Systems: A Sensitivity Analysis. *Rev. Soc. Econ.*, October 1986, *44*(2), pp. 178–82. **[G: Global]**

Burkett, John P. PQLI as a Measure of Comparative Performance: Comment. *Comp. Econ. Stud.*, Summer 1986, *28*(2), pp. 59–68.

Carr-Hill, Roy A. An Approach to Monitoring Social Welfare. **In** *Nolan, P. and Paine, S., eds.*, 1986, pp. 291–309.

Eckstein, Susan. Cuba's Centrally Planned Economy: An Equity Trade-off for Growth: Comment. **In** *Hartlyn, J. and Morley, S. A., eds.*, 1986, pp. 367–73. **[G: Cuba]**

Fox, Karl A. An Eco-behavioral Approach to Social Systems Accounting, Time-Allocation Matrices, and Measures of the Quality of Life. **In** *MacFadyen, A. J. and MacFadyen, H. W., eds.*, 1986, pp. 549–81. **[G: U.S.]**

Fried, Marc. The Neighborhood in Metropolitan Life: Its Psychosocial Significance. **In** *Taylor, R. B., ed.*, 1986, pp. 331–63. **[G: U.S.]**

Karamoy, Amir and Dias, Gillian. Delivery of Urban Services in Kampungs in Jakarta and Ujung Pandang. **In** *Yeung, Y. M. and McGee, T. G., eds.*, 1986, pp. 191–210. **[G: Indonesia]**

Lau, Siu-kai; Kuan, Hsin-chi and Ho, Kam-fai. Leaders, Officials, and Citizens in Urban Service Delivery: A Comparative Study of Four Localities in Hong Kong. **In** *Yeung, Y. M. and McGee, T. G., eds.*, 1986, pp. 211–37. **[G: Hong Kong]**

Leipert, Christian. Social Costs of Economic Growth. *J. Econ. Issues*, March 1986, *20*(1), pp. 109–31. **[G: W. Germany]**

Levy, Shlomit. Psycho-economic Wellbeing: The Case of Israel. **In** *MacFadyen, A. J. and MacFadyen, H. W., eds.*, 1986, pp. 585–617. **[G: Israel]**

Liu, Ben-chieh; Mulvey, Thomas and Hsieh, Chang-Tzeh. Effects of Educational Expenditures on Regional Inequality in the Social Quality of Life. *Amer. J. Econ. Soc.*, April 1986, *45*(2), pp. 131–44. **[G: U.S.]**

Mesa-Lago, Carmelo. Cuba's Centrally Planned Economy: An Equity Trade-off for Growth. **In** *Hartlyn, J. and Morley, S. A., eds.*, 1986, pp. 292–318. **[G: Cuba]**

van Moeseke, Paul. Time and Cost Budgets. *Math. Soc. Sci.*, April 1986, *11*(2), pp. 129–38.

Morrison, Barrie M. and Waxler, Nancy E. Three Patterns of Basic Needs Distribution with in Sri Lanka: 1971–73. *World Devel.*, January 1986, *14*(1), pp. 97–114. **[G: Sri Lanka]**

Park, Soo-Young; Kim, Yong-Woong and Yang, Ok-Hyee. Urban Services and the Poor: The Case of Korea. **In** *Yeung, Y. M. and McGee, T. G., eds.*, 1986, pp. 29–57. **[G: S. Korea]**

Ramos, Exaltacion and Roman, Ma. A. A. Participatory Urban Services in the Philippines. **In** *Yeung, Y. M. and McGee, T. G., eds.*, 1986, pp. 73–96. **[G: Philippines]**

Reiss, Albert J., Jr. Measuring Social Change. **In** *Smelser, N. J. and Gerstein, D. R., eds.*, 1986, pp. 36–72.

Revéiz, Edgar and Pérez, María José. Columbia: Moderate Economic Growth, Political Stability, and Social Welfare. **In** *Hartlyn, J. and Morley, S. A., eds.*, 1986, pp. 265–91. **[G: Columbia]**

Saxena, Pradeep Kumar. Inter-relationship between Socio-economic Development and Economic Structure: Indian Experience. *Margin*, July 1986, *18*(4), pp. 76–87. **[G: India]**

Sen, Amartya K. Economic Distance and the Living Standard. **In** *[Patel, S.]*, 1986, pp. 63–74. **[G: India; China; Mexico; Sri Lanka; Brazil]**

Sengupta, Jati K. Modeling Eco-behavioral Systems. *Math. Soc. Sci.*, February 1986, *11*(1), pp. 1–31.

Shiratori, Rei. The Future of the Welfare State. **In** *Rose, R. and Shiratori, R., eds.*, 1986, pp. 193–206. **[G: OECD]**

Smelser, Neil J. The Ogburn Vision Fifty Years Later. **In** *Smelser, N. J. and Gerstein, D. R., eds.*, 1986, pp. 21–35.

Warren, Donald I. The Helping Roles of Neighbors: Some Empirical Patterns. **In** *Taylor, R. B., ed.*, 1986, pp. 310–30. **[G: U.S.]**

Wish, Naomi Bailin. Some Issues about the "Quality" of Sunbelt/Frostbelt Life: Factor Analysis of the Better Data Demonstrates That This Dichotomy Is Hopelessly Biased. *Amer. J. Econ. Soc.*, July 1986, *45*(3), pp. 343–57. **[G: U.S.]**

Wood, Charles H. and McCracken, Stephen D. Underdevelopment, Urban Growth and Collective Social Action in Sao Paulo, Brazil. **In** *Abegaz, B., ed.*, 1986, pp. 101–40. **[G: Brazil]**

Zinam, Oleg. Impact of Ideology and Organizational Structures on Technology and Quality of Life. *Rivista Int. Sci. Econ. Com.*, January 1986, *33*(1), pp. 41–58. **[G: Global]**

226 Productivity and Growth: Theory and Data

2260 Productivity and Growth: Theory and Data

Abalkin, L. Intensification and Economic Growth. *Prob. Econ.*, June 1986, *29*(2), pp. 64–78. **[G: U.S.S.R.]**

Abouchar, Alan. The Treatment of Intermediate Goods in Cuban National Income Accounts: Parallels and Differences with Soviet Methodology. *Comp. Econ. Stud.*, Summer 1986, *28*(2), pp. 37–48. **[G: Cuba]**

Abramovitz, Moses. Catching Up, Forging Ahead, and Falling Behind. *J. Econ. Hist.*, June 1986, *46*(2), pp. 385–406. **[G: OECD]**

Adams, Charles; Fenton, Paul R. and Larsen, Flemming. Differences in Employment Behavior among Industrial Countries. **In** *International Monetary Fund, Research Department*, 1986, pp. 1–50. **[G: OECD]**

Amann, Ronald. Technical Progress and Soviet Economic Development: Setting the Scene. **In** *Amann, R. and Cooper, J., eds.*, 1986, pp. 5–30. **[G: U.S.S.R.]**

Anderson, B. L. Trends in Capital Accumulation in the Age of Malthus. **In** *Turner, M., ed.*, 1986, pp. 201–21. **[G: U.K.]**

Anderson, Kym. Economic Growth, Structural Change and the Political Economy of Protection. **In** *Anderson, K. and Hayami, Y.*, 1986, pp. 7–16. **[G: E. Asia]**

Aron, Paul H. Industrial Policy in Japan: Implications for Technological Catch-up and Leadership: Comment. **In** *Pugel, T. A., ed.*, 1986, pp. 233–35. **[G: U.S.; Japan]**

Arrow, Kenneth J. Incentives and Growth: An Appraisal. **In** *Balassa, B. and Giersch, H., eds.*, 1986, pp. 481–85.

Auerbach, Alan J. Major Changes in Cyclical Behavior: Comment. **In** *Gordon, R. J., ed.*, 1986, pp. 573–75. **[G: U.S.; U.K.; France; W. Germany]**

Ayala, José and Durán, Clemente Ruiz. Development and Crisis in Mexico: A Structuralist Approach. **In** *Hartlyn, J. and Morley, S. A., eds.*, 1986, pp. 243–64. **[G: Mexico]**

Baily, Martin Neil. Productivity Growth and Materials Use in U.S. Manufacturing [Productivity and the Services of Capital and Labor]. *Quart. J. Econ.*, February 1986, *101*(1), pp. 185–95. **[G: U.S.]**

Barras, Richard. A Comparison of Embodied Technical Change in Services and Manufacturing Industry. *Appl. Econ.*, September 1986, *18*(9), pp. 941–58. **[G: U.K.]**

Barro, Robert J. Do Equilibrium Real Business Cycle Theories Explain Postwar U.S. Business Cycles? Comment. **In** *Fischer, S., ed.*, 1986, pp. 135–39. **[G: U.S.]**

Barry, Frank G. Profitability, Investment and Employment: A Survey of Recent Developments in Medium-term Growth Theory. *Econ. Soc. Rev.*, April 1986, *17*(3), pp. 159–73. **[G: OECD]**

Baumol, William J. Productivity Growth, Convergence, and Welfare: What the Long-run Data Show. *Amer. Econ. Rev.*, December 1986, *76*(5), pp. 1072–85. **[G: OECD; U.S.S.R.; China]**

Beckerman, Wilfred. Stagflation and the Third World. **In** *[Streeten, P.]*, 1986, pp. 38–57. **[G: LDCs; MDCs]**

Bergés Lobera, Angel; Maravall, Fernando and Pérez Simarro, Ramón. Eficiencia técnica en las grandes empresas industriales de España y Europa. (With English summary.) *Invest. Ecón.*, September 1986, *10*(3), pp. 449–66. **[G: EEC]**

Berndt, Ernst R. and Fuss, Melvyn A. Productivity Measurement with Adjustments for Variations in Capacity Utilization and Other Forms of Temporary Equilibrium. *J. Econometrics*, Oct./Nov. 1986, *33*(1/2), pp. 7–29. **[G: U.S.]**

Bićanić, Ivo. Some General Comparisons of the Impact of the Two World Crises of the Twentieth Century on the Yugoslav Economy and Changes in the Well-Being of the Population Caused by the Crises. **In** *Berend, I. T. and Borchardt, K., eds.*, 1986, pp. 248–74. **[G: Yugoslavia]**

Blanchard, Olivier J., et al. Employment and Growth in Europe: A Two-Handed Approach. **In** *Blanchard, O.; Dornbusch, R. and Layard, R., eds.*, 1986, pp. 95–124. **[G: W. Europe]**

Bond, Daniel L. Prospects for the Soviet Economy. **In** *Amann, R. and Cooper, J., eds.*, 1986, pp. 170–81. **[G: U.S.S.R.]**

Boskin, Michael J. Budgets, Deficits, Technology and Economic Growth. **In** *Landau, R. and Jorgenson, D. W., eds.*, 1986, pp. 191–204. **[G: U.S.]**

Boskin, Michael J. Macroeconomics, Technology, and Economic Growth: An Introduction to

Some Important Issues. **In** *Landau, R. and Rosenberg, N., eds.*, 1986, pp. 33–56. **[G: U.S.]**

Bowers, Albert. The Need for National Consensus to Improve Competitiveness. **In** *Landau, R. and Rosenberg, N., eds.*, 1986, pp. 511–15. **[G: U.S.]**

Boyce, James K. Kinked Exponential Models for Growth Rate Estimation. *Oxford Bull. Econ. Statist.*, November 1986, *48*(4), pp. 385–91. **[G: India; Bangladesh]**

Boyer, Robert and Ralle, Pierre. Croissances nationales et contrainte extérieure avant et après 1973. (National Growth and External Trade Share after and before 1973. With English summary.) *Écon. Soc.*, January 1986, *20*(1), pp. 117–44. **[G: EEC]**

Boyer, Robert and Ralle, Pierre. L'insertion internationale conditionne-t-elle les formes nationales d'emploi? Convergences ou différenciations des pays européens. (Are Jobs Dependent on International Openness? Similarities and Differences between European Countries. With English summary.) *Écon. Soc.*, January 1986, *20*(1), pp. 145–68. **[G: EEC]**

Bradley, John and Prendergast, Canice. Verdoorn's Law: A Retrospective View. *Econ. Soc. Rev.*, January 1986, *17*(2), pp. 75–86. **[G: Ireland]**

Brotchie, John F. Industrial Interdependence via Information Technology and Transport Interaction—Employment Impacts. **In** *Nijkamp, P., ed. (II)*, 1986, pp. 115–30.

Bruno, Michael. External Shocks and Domestic Response: Macroeconomic Performance, 1965–1982. **In** *Ben-Porath, Y., ed.*, 1986, pp. 276–301. **[G: Israel; OECD]**

Bruno, Michael. Raw Materials, Profits, and the Productivity Slowdown: A Complementary Note [Productivity and the Services of Capital and Labor]. *Quart. J. Econ.*, February 1986, *101*(1), pp. 197–200. **[G: U.S.]**

Bruno, Michael. Stagflation in the Industrial Countries: An Updated Overview. *Hitotsubashi J. Econ.*, Spec. Iss. Oct. 1986, *27*, pp. 57–74. **[G: OECD]**

Brus, Włodzimierz. Postwar Reconstruction and Socio-economic Transformation. **In** *Kaser, M. C. and Radice, E. A., eds.*, 1986, pp. 564–641. **[G: E. Europe]**

Carter, Anne P. Energy, Environment, and Economic Growth. **In** *Sohn, I., ed.*, 1986, *1974*, pp. 417–31. **[G: U.S.]**

Chenery, Hollis B. Growth and Transformation. **In** *Chenery, H.; Robinson, S. and Syrquin, M.*, 1986, pp. 13–36.

Chenery, Hollis B.; Robinson, Sherman and Syrquin, Moshe. Growth and Structure: A Synthesis. **In** *Chenery, H.; Robinson, S. and Syrquin, M.*, 1986, pp. 348–59.

Chenery, Hollis B. and Syrquin, Moshe. The Semi-industrial Countries. **In** *Chenery, H.; Robinson, S. and Syrquin, M.*, 1986, pp. 84–118. **[G: LDCs]**

Chenery, Hollis B. and Syrquin, Moshe. Typical Patterns of Transformation. **In** *Chenery, H.; Robinson, S. and Syrquin, M.*, 1986, pp. 37–83.

Coale, Ansley J. Population Trends and Economic Development. **In** *Menken, J., ed.*, 1986, pp. 96–104. **[G: LDCs]**

Coombs, Rod and Kleinknecht, Alfred. New Evidence on the Shift toward Process Innovation during the Long-Wave Upswing. **In** *Freeman, C., ed.*, 1986, pp. 78–103. **[G: OECD]**

Currie, Lauchlin. Sources of Growth. *World Devel.*, April 1986, *14*(4), pp. 541–47.

Datta, Samar K. and Nugent, Jeffrey B. Adversary Activities and Per Capita Income Growth. *World Devel.*, December 1986, *14*(12), pp. 1457–61.

Dendrinos, Dimitrios S. On the Incongruous Spatial Employment Dynamics. **In** *Nijkamp, P., ed. (II)*, 1986, pp. 321–39.

Desai, Padma. Soviet Growth Retardation. *Amer. Econ. Rev.*, May 1986, *76*(2), pp. 175–80. **[G: U.S.S.R.]**

Dholakia, Ravindra H. Sources of Economic Growth in India Implied by the Seventh Five Year Plan 1985–90. *Indian Econ. J.*, Apr.-June 1986, *33*(4), pp. 161–67. **[G: India]**

Donges, Juergen B. Incentives and Growth: A Summary Appraisal. **In** *Balassa, B. and Giersch, H., eds.*, 1986, pp. 486–90.

Dore, Elizabeth. Nicaragua: The Experience of the Mixed Economy. **In** *Hartlyn, J. and Morley, S. A., eds.*, 1986, pp. 319–50. **[G: Nicaragua]**

Dosi, Giovanni. Technology and Conditions of Macroeconomic Development. **In** *Freeman, C., ed.*, 1986, pp. 60–77.

Dürr, Ernst. Growth, Technical Progress, and Unemployment in the Federal Republic of Germany. **In** *Hax, H.; Kraus, W. and Tsuchiya, K., eds.*, 1986, pp. 145–62. **[G: W. Germany; OECD]**

Eads, George C. Dangers in U.S. Efforts to Promote International Competitiveness. **In** *Landau, R. and Rosenberg, N., eds.*, 1986, pp. 527–33. **[G: U.S.]**

Eckstein, Susan. Cuba's Centrally Planned Economy: An Equity Trade-off for Growth: Comment. **In** *Hartlyn, J. and Morley, S. A., eds.*, 1986, pp. 367–73. **[G: Cuba]**

ECLAC Secretariat, Santiago. Central America: Bases for Reactivation and Development. **In** *Maddison, A., ed.*, 1986, pp. 116–29. **[G: Central America]**

Eichenbaum, Martin and Singleton, Kenneth J. Do Equilibrium Real Business Cycle Theories Explain Postwar U.S. Business Cycles? **In** *Fischer, S., ed.*, 1986, pp. 91–135. **[G: U.S.]**

Elbaum, Bernard and Lazonick, William. An Institutional Perspective on British Decline. **In** *Elbaum, B. and Lazonick, W., eds.*, 1986, pp. 1–17. **[G: U.K.]**

Etzioni, Amitai. The Reindustrialization of the United States of America. **In** *Redburn, F. S.; Buss, T. F. and Ledebur, L. C., eds.*, 1986, pp. 6–27. **[G: U.S.]**

Fabricant, Solomon. Major Changes in Cyclical

Behavior: Comment. **In** *Gordon, R. J., ed.*, 1986, pp. 575–78. **[G: U.S.; U.K.; W. Germany; France]**

Fal'tsman, F. Increasing the Return on Industry's Fixed Capital. *Prob. Econ.*, January 1986, *28*(9), pp. 18–36. **[G: U.S.S.R.]**

Feder, Gershon. Growth in Semi-industrial Countries: A Statistical Analysis. **In** *Chenery, H.; Robinson, S. and Syrquin, M.*, 1986, pp. 263–82. **[G: LDCs]**

Flemming, John S. Booming Sectors and Structural Change in Australia and Britain: A Comparison: Comment. **In** *Neary, J. P. and van Wijnbergen, S., eds.*, 1986, pp. 284–87. **[G: U.K.; Australia]**

Forbes, Kevin F.; Korsun, George and McGuire, Martin C. Defense, Growth, and Allocation Behavior in the Alliance: The Southern Tier of NATO. **In** *Denoon, D. B. H., ed.*, 1986, pp. 114–51. **[G: Greece; Turkey; Spain; Portugal]**

Forsyth, Peter J. Booming Sectors and Structural Change in Australia and Britain: A Comparison. **In** *Neary, J. P. and van Wijnbergen, S., eds.*, 1986, pp. 251–84. **[G: Australia; U.K.]**

Fransman, Martin. Machinery in Economic Development. **In** *Fransman, M., ed.*, 1986, pp. 1–53.

Friedlaender, Ann F. Macroeconomics and Microeconomics of Innovation: The Role of the Technological Environment. **In** *Landau, R. and Rosenberg, N., eds.*, 1986, pp. 327–32.

Galenson, Walter and Galenson, David W. Constraints on Strategy: The Economics of Western Security: Japan and South Korea. **In** *Denoon, D. B. H., ed.*, 1986, pp. 152–94. **[G: U.S.; Japan; S. Korea; W. Germany]**

Gelb, Alan. The Oil Syndrome: Adjustment to Windfall Gains in Oil-Exporting Countries. **In** *Lal, D. and Wolf, M., eds.*, 1986, pp. 115–30. **[G: Selected Countries]**

Goldar, Bishwanath. Import Substitution, Industrial Concentration and Productivity Growth in Indian Manufacturing. *Oxford Bull. Econ. Statist.*, May 1986, *48*(2), pp. 143–64. **[G: India]**

Goldsbrough, David and Zaidi, Iqbal M. Transmission of Economic Influences from Industrial to Developing Countries. **In** *International Monetary Fund, Research Department*, 1986, pp. 150–95. **[G: OECD; LDCs]**

Gomulka, Stanislaw. Poland's Industrialisation. **In** *Gomulka, S.*, 1986, pp. 154–94. **[G: Poland]**

Gomulka, Stanislaw. Slowdown in Soviet Industrial Growth: 1947–75 Reconsidered. **In** *Gomulka, S.*, 1986, *1977*, pp. 138–49. **[G: U.S.S.R.]**

Gomulka, Stanislaw. Slowdown in Soviet Industrial Growth: 1947–75 Reconsidered: Afterword. **In** *Gomulka, S.*, 1986, pp. 150–53. **[G: U.S.S.R.]**

Gomulka, Stanislaw. Soviet Growth Slowdown: Duality, Maturity, and Innovation. *Amer. Econ. Rev.*, May 1986, *76*(2), pp. 170–74. **[G: U.S.S.R.]**

Gomulka, Stanislaw. Specific and Systemic Causes of the Polish Crisis, 1980–82. **In** *Gomulka, S.*, 1986, *1983*, pp. 227–50. **[G: Poland]**

Greasley, David. British Economic Growth: The Paradox of the 1880s and the Timing of the Climacteric. *Exploration Econ. Hist.*, October 1986, *23*(4), pp. 416–44. **[G: U.K.]**

Grubb, David B. Raw Materials, Profits, and the Productivity Slowdown: Some Doubts. *Quart. J. Econ.*, February 1986, *101*(1), pp. 175–84. **[G: U.S.; W. Europe; Japan]**

Haberler, Gottfried. The Slowdown of the World Economy and the Problem of Stagflation. **In** *Lal, D. and Wolf, M., eds.*, 1986, pp. 48–90. **[G: Global]**

Hahn, Frank H. "Of Marx and Keynes and Many Things." *Oxford Econ. Pap.*, July 1986, *38*(2), pp. 354–61.

Hall, Stephen G., et al. Forecasting Employment: The Role of Forward-Looking Behaviour. *Int. J. Forecasting*, 1986, *2*(4), pp. 435–45. **[G: U.K.]**

Hamilton, Clive. A General Equilibrium Model of Structural Change and Economic Growth, with Application to South Korea. *J. Devel. Econ.*, September 1986, *23*(1), pp. 67–88. **[G: S. Korea]**

Harcourt, Geoffrey C. Notes on the Social Limits to Growth. **In** *[Harcourt, G. C.]*, 1986, *1981*, pp. 273–81.

Hartlyn, Jonathan and Morley, Samuel A. Political Regimes and Economic Performance in Latin America. **In** *Hartlyn, J. and Morley, S. A., eds.*, 1986, pp. 15–37. **[G: Latin America]**

Heierli, U. Division of Labour and Appropriate Technology—From Adam Smith to E. F. Schumacher. **In** *Bassand, M., et al., eds.*, 1986, pp. 9–37.

Herlitz, Lars. Private Consumption and Development of Industrial Production: The 1930s Compared with Post-war Tendencies. **In** *Berend, I. T. and Borchardt, K., eds.*, 1986, pp. 497–515. **[G: U.K.; U.S.; Germany; Sweden; France]**

Hong, Wontack. Trade, Growth and Economic Problems of Asian NICs. *Hitotsubashi J. Econ.*, Spec. Iss. Oct. 1986, *27*, pp. 79–100. **[G: Asian NICs]**

Hopkins, Michael. Basic Needs Performance in the Past. **In** *Adelman, I. and Taylor, J. E., eds.*, 1986, pp. 38–73. **[G: Global]**

Hughes, Alan. Investment Finance, Industrial Strategy and Economic Recovery. **In** *Nolan, P. and Paine, S., eds.*, 1986, pp. 198–233. **[G: U.K.; Selected OECD]**

Hulten, Charles R. Productivity Change, Capacity Utilization, and the Sources of Efficiency Growth. *J. Econometrics*, Oct./Nov. 1986, *33*(1/2), pp. 31–50.

Ikemoto, Yukio. Technical Progress and Level of Technology in Asian Countries, 1970–80: A Translog Index Approach. *Devel. Econ.*, December 1986, *24*(4), pp. 368–90. **[G: Selected Asian]**

Jorgenson, Dale W. Microeconomics and Pro-

ductivity. **In** *Landau, R. and Rosenberg, N., eds.*, 1986, pp. 57–76. **[G: U.S.]**
Jorgenson, Dale W. The Oil Price Decline and Economic Growth in Japan and the United States. *Keio Econ. Stud.*, 1986, *23*(1), pp. 1–19. **[G: Japan; U.S.]**
Jung, Woo S. Financial Development and Economic Growth: International Evidence. *Econ. Develop. Cult. Change*, January 1986, *34*(2), pp. 333–46. **[G: LDCs; MDCs]**
Kaldor, Nicholas. Limits on Growth. *Oxford Econ. Pap.*, July 1986, *38*(2), pp. 187–98.
Kamaev, V. Intensification and the Quality of Economic Growth. *Prob. Econ.*, March 1986, *28*(11), pp. 19–38. **[G: U.S.S.R.]**
Kamal, Salih, et al. Young Workers and Urban Services in Penang. **In** *Yeung, Y. M. and McGee, T. G., eds.*, 1986, pp. 119–63. **[G: Malaysia]**
Karunaratne, Neil Dias. A Holistic Analysis of Trade versus Aid Issues: World and Australian Insights. *Devel. Econ.*, March 1986, *24*(1), pp. 44–55. **[G: Global; Australia]**
Klein, Burton H. Dynamic Competition and Productivity Advances. **In** *Landau, R. and Rosenberg, N., eds.*, 1986, pp. 77–88. **[G: U.S.]**
Klinov, Ruth. Changes in the Industrial Structure. **In** *Ben-Porath, Y., ed.*, 1986, pp. 119–36. **[G: Israel]**
Kontorovich, Vladimir. Soviet Growth Slowdown: Econometric vs. Direct Evidence. *Amer. Econ. Rev.*, May 1986, *76*(2), pp. 181–85. **[G: U.S.S.R.]**
Krejči, Jeroslav. The Bohemian–Moravian War Economy. **In** *Kaser, M. C. and Radice, E. A., eds.*, 1986, pp. 452–92. **[G: Bohemia; Moravia]**
Kubo, Yuji; de Melo, Jaime and Robinson, Sherman. Trade Strategies and Growth Episodes. **In** *Chenery, H.; Robinson, S. and Syrquin, M.*, 1986, pp. 148–87. **[G: LDCs]**
Kubo, Yuji; Robinson, Sherman and Syrquin, Moshe. The Methodology of Multisector Comparative Analysis. **In** *Chenery, H.; Robinson, S. and Syrquin, M.*, 1986, pp. 121–47. **[G: Mexico; Turkey; Japan; S. Korea]**
Kubo, Yuji, et al. Interdependence and Industrial Structure. **In** *Chenery, H.; Robinson, S. and Syrquin, M.*, 1986, pp. 188–225. **[G: LDCs]**
Kuczynski, Thomas. The Development of Foreign Trade during the "Greatest Depression"—An Exceptional Case. Some Statistical Observations Concerning the Structure of World Production of Material Goods. **In** *Berend, I. T. and Borchardt, K., eds.*, 1986, pp. 456–83. **[G: Global]**
Kwack, Sung Yeung. The Economic Development of the Republic of Korea, 1965–1981. **In** *Lau, L. J., ed.*, 1986, pp. 65–133. **[G: S. Korea]**
Lakshmanan, T. R. and Chatterjee, Lata. Technical Change, Employment and Metropolitan Adjustment. **In** *Nijkamp, P., ed. (II)*, 1986, pp. 21–45.
Lal, Deepak and Wolf, Martin. Debt, Deficits, and Distortions. **In** *Lal, D. and Wolf, M., eds.*, 1986, pp. 239–91. **[G: Global]**
Landau, Ralph. Technology, Economics, and Public Policy. **In** *Landau, R. and Jorgenson, D. W., eds.*, 1986, pp. 1–74. **[G: OECD]**
Landau, Ralph and Rosenberg, Nathan. The Positive Sum Strategy: Harnessing Technology for Economic Growth: Editors' Overview. **In** *Landau, R. and Rosenberg, N., eds.*, 1986, pp. 1–16.
Layard, Richard, et al. Europe: The Case for Unsustainable Growth. **In** *Blanchard, O.; Dornbusch, R. and Layard, R., eds.*, 1986, pp. 33–94. **[G: W. Europe; EEC]**
Leontief, Wassily. Population Growth and Economic Development: Illustrative Projections. **In** *Leontief, W.*, 1986, *1979*, pp. 338–62. **[G: Global]**
Loginov, V. and Novitskii, N. Factors and Trends in the Intensification of Socialist Reproduction. *Prob. Econ.*, June 1986, *29*(2), pp. 3–23. **[G: U.S.S.R.]**
Maddison, Angus. Economic Performance and Policy in Latin American and OECD Countries 1938–85: A Comparative Analysis. **In** *Maddison, A., ed.*, 1986, pp. 11–27. **[G: OECD; Latin America]**
Mankiw, N. Gregory. Do Equilibrium Real Business Cycle Theories Explain Postwar U.S. Business Cycles? Comment. **In** *Fischer, S., ed.*, 1986, pp. 139–45. **[G: U.S.]**
Mansfield, Edwin. Microeconomics of Technological Innovation. **In** *Landau, R. and Rosenberg, N., eds.*, 1986, pp. 307–25. **[G: U.S.]**
Marques Mendes, A. J. The Contribution of the European Community to Economic Growth: An Assessment of the First 25 Years. *J. Common Market Stud.*, June 1986, *24*(4), pp. 261–77. **[G: EEC]**
McGregor, Peter G. and Swales, J. K. Balance of Payments Constrained Growth: A Rejoinder. *Appl. Econ.*, December 1986, *18*(12), pp. 1265–74. **[G: OECD]**
McIntosh, James. Economic Growth and Technical Change in Britain 1950–1978. *Europ. Econ. Rev.*, February 1986, *30*(1), pp. 117–28. **[G: U.K.]**
McLennan, Kenneth. The Case for a Non-targeted Approach to Industrial Strategy. **In** *Redburn, F. S.; Buss, T. F. and Ledebur, L. C., eds.*, 1986, pp. 45–63. **[G: U.S.; OECD]**
Mesa-Lago, Carmelo. Cuba's Centrally Planned Economy: An Equity Trade-off for Growth. **In** *Hartlyn, J. and Morley, S. A., eds.*, 1986, pp. 292–318. **[G: Cuba]**
Metzer, Jacob. The Slowdown of Economic Growth: A Passing Phase or the End of the Big Spurt? **In** *Ben-Porath, Y., ed.*, 1986, pp. 75–100. **[G: Israel]**
Morrison, Catherine J. Productivity Measurement with Non-static Expectations and Varying Capacity Utilization: An Integrated Approach. *J. Econometrics*, Oct./Nov. 1986, *33*(1/2), pp. 51–74. **[G: U.S.]**
Myers, Ramon H. The Economic Development of the Republic of China on Taiwan, 1965–1981. **In** *Lau, L. J., ed.*, 1986, pp. 13–64. **[G: Taiwan]**

Nelson, Richard R. The Tension between Process Stories and Equilibrium Models: Analyzing the Productivity-Growth Slowdown of the 1970s. **In** *Langlois, R. N., ed.*, 1986, pp. 135–51.

Nemetz, Peter N. The Pacific Rim: Investment, Development and Trade: Introduction and Overview. **In** *Nemetz, P. N., ed.*, 1986, pp. 1–52. **[G: Pacific Basin]**

Nishimizu, Mieko and Robinson, Sherman. Productivity Growth in Manufacturing. **In** *Chenery, H.; Robinson, S. and Syrquin, M.*, 1986, pp. 283–308. **[G: Japan; S. Korea; Yugoslavia; Turkey]**

Okimoto, Daniel I. The Japanese Challenge in High Technology. **In** *Landau, R. and Rosenberg, N., eds.*, 1986, pp. 541–67. **[G: Japan]**

Oshima, Harry T. The Transition from an Agricultural to an Industrial Economy in East Asia. *Econ. Develop. Cult. Change*, July 1986, *34*(4), pp. 783–809. **[G: Japan; Taiwan; S. Korea]**

Panayotou, Theodore. Investment, Growth and Employment in Thailand: From Agriculture to Rural Industry. **In** *Nemetz, P. N., ed.*, 1986, pp. 117–58. **[G: Thailand]**

Panchamukhi, V. R. Tinbergen Fourasite Thesis and the Lima Target. **In** *Panchamukhi, V. R., et al.*, 1986, pp. 94–111. **[G: OECD]**

Panchamukhi, V. R. and Mehta, Rajesh. Structural Changes, Inter-country Disparities and the Lima Target. **In** *Panchamukhi, V. R., et al.*, 1986, pp. 55–75. **[G: LDCs]**

Patel, I. G. Productivity and Economic Growth. **In** *Patel, I. G.*, 1986, *1970*, pp. 138–48.

Pauly, R. and Tosstorff, G. Lead- und Lag-Beziehungen zwischen makroökonomischen Aggregaten. (Lead and Lag Relationships between Macroeconomic Aggregates. With English summary.) *Jahr. Nationalökon. Statist.*, January 1986, *201*(1), pp. 12–31. **[G: W. Germany]**

Pepper, Thomas. Industrial Policy in Japan: Implications for Technological Catch-up and Leadership: Comment. **In** *Pugel, T. A., ed.*, 1986, pp. 229–32. **[G: U.S.; Japan]**

Pérez-López, Jorge F. Real Economic Growth in Cuba, 1965–1982. *J. Devel. Areas*, January 1986, *20*(2), pp. 151–72. **[G: Cuba]**

Pugel, Thomas A. Industrial Policy in Japan: Implications for Technological Catch-up and Leadership. **In** *Pugel, T. A., ed.*, 1986, pp. 209–27. **[G: U.S.; Japan]**

Pugno, Maurizio. L'"ottima distribuzione del reddito" di Sylos Labini: una nota. (Sylos Labini's "Optimal Distribution of Incomes": A Note. With English summary.) *Econ. Polít.*, August 1986, *3*(2), pp. 259–75. **[G: U.S.]**

Purvis, Douglas D. Indonesia's Other Dutch Disease: Economic Effects of the Petroleum Boom: Comment. **In** *Neary, J. P. and van Wijnbergen, S., eds.*, 1986, pp. 321–23. **[G: Indonesia]**

Radice, E. A. The Collapse of German Hegemony and Its Economic Consequences. **In** *Kaser, M. C. and Radice, E. A., eds.*, 1986, pp. 495–519. **[G: Germany; E. Europe]**

Radice, E. A. The Development of Industry. **In** *Kaser, M. C. and Radice, E. A., eds.*, 1986, pp. 416–51. **[G: E. Europe; Germany]**

Ram, Rati. Comparison of Rates of Growth of GDP Based on International and Domestic Prices for 104 Countries over the Period 1960–80. *Indian Econ. J.*, Apr.-June 1986, *33*(4), pp. 149–60. **[G: Global]**

Ram, Rati. Government Size and Economic Growth: A New Framework and Some Evidence from Cross-Section and Time-Series Data. *Amer. Econ. Rev.*, March 1986, *76*(1), pp. 191–203.

Reeder, Charles B. The Effect of Recent Macroeconomic Policies on Innovation and Productivity. **In** *Landau, R. and Rosenberg, N., eds.*, 1986, pp. 89–91. **[G: U.S.]**

Reynolds, Morgan O. Taxation, Saving, and Investment: A Look at the Evidence. **In** *Lee, D. R., ed.*, 1986, pp. 49–85. **[G: OECD]**

Rodrique, André. La contribution de l'amélioration du bien-être au processus de croissance dans les pays en développement. (The Contribution of Welfare to Economic Growth. With English summary.) *L'Actual. Econ.*, March 1986, *62*(1), pp. 64–87. **[G: LDCs]**

Romer, Paul M. Increasing Returns and Long-run Growth. *J. Polit. Econ.*, October 1986, *94*(5), pp. 1002–37. **[G: OECD]**

Rostow, Walt W. Economic Growth and the Diffusion of Power. *Challenge*, Sept./Oct. 1986, *29*(4), pp. 29–37.

Rothschild, Emma. A Divergence Hypothesis. *J. Devel. Econ.*, October 1986, *23*(2), pp. 205–26. **[G: U.S.]**

Royer, Jacques. The Long-term Employment Impact of Disarmament Policies: Some Findings from an Econometric Model. *Int. Lab. Rev.*, May-June 1986, *125*(3), pp. 279–303. **[G: Global]**

Rymes, Thomas K. The Measurement of Multifactor Productivity in an Input–Output Framework: New Canadian Estimates. **In** *Franz, A. and Rainer, N., eds.*, 1986, pp. 373–401. **[G: Canada]**

Sabel, Charles F. Changing Models of Economic Efficiency and Their Implications for Industrialization in the Third World. **In** *[Hirshman, A. O.]*, 1986, pp. 27–55. **[G: Selected Countries]**

Sandler, Todd and Murdoch, James C. Defense Burdens and Prospects for the Northern European Allies. **In** *Denoon, D. B. H., ed.*, 1986, pp. 59–113. **[G: W. Europe]**

Savage, David and Biswas, Rajiv. The British Economy in the Long Term: An Analysis of Post-War Growth Rates and an Illustrative Long-Term Projection. *Nat. Inst. Econ. Rev.*, November 1986, (118), pp. 59–69. **[G: U.K.]**

Scitovsky, Tibor. Economic Development in Taiwan and South Korea, 1965–81. **In** *Lau, L. J., ed.*, 1986, pp. 135–95. **[G: S. Korea; Taiwan]**

Simon, Julian L. and Steinmann, Gunter. A Model of Supply, Demand and Technical Progress [Phelps's Technical Progress Model Generalized]. **In** *Simon, J. L.*, 1986, *1981*, pp. 102–14.

Singh, Ajit. The Interrupted Industrial Revolution of the Third World: Prospects and Policies for Resumption. **In** *Sjöstedt, G. and Sundelius, B., eds.*, 1986, pp. 139–82. **[G: LDCs]**

Soete, Luc L. G. Long Cycles and the International Diffusion of Technology. **In** *Freeman, C., ed.*, 1986, pp. 214–30.

Sokoloff, Kenneth L. Productivity Growth in Manufacturing during Early Industrialization: Evidence from the American Northeast, 1820–1860. **In** *Engerman, S. L. and Gallman, R. E., eds.*, 1986, pp. 679–729. **[G: U.S.]**

Solow, Robert M. Resources and Economic Growth. **In** *Szenberg, M., ed.*, 1986, *1978*, pp. 57–68.

Sorokin, G. Growth Rates of the Soviet Economy. *Prob. Econ.*, December 1986, *29*(8), pp. 36–53. **[G: U.S.S.R.]**

Spechler, Martin C. Social Influences on Growth and Productivity in the West, 1965–1984. **In** *Gilad, B. and Kaish, S., eds., Vol. B*, 1986, pp. 163–200. **[G: OECD]**

Sundrum, R. M. Indonesia's Rapid Economic Growth: 1968–81. *Bull. Indonesian Econ. Stud.*, December 1986, *22*(3), pp. 40–69. **[G: Indonesia]**

Syrquin, Moshe. Economic Growth and Structural Change: An International Perspective. **In** *Ben-Porath, Y., ed.*, 1986, pp. 42–74. **[G: Selected Countries; Israel]**

Syrquin, Moshe. Growth and Structural Change in Latin America since 1960: A Comparative Analysis. *Econ. Develop. Cult. Change*, April 1986, *34*(3), pp. 433–54. **[G: Latin America]**

Syrquin, Moshe. Productivity Growth and Factor Reallocation. **In** *Chenery, H.; Robinson, S. and Syrquin, M.*, 1986, pp. 229–62. **[G: Latin America; Europe; Asia; Canada]**

Thirlwall, A. P. Balance of Payments Constrained Growth: A Reply. *Appl. Econ.*, December 1986, *18*(12), pp. 1259–63. **[G: OECD]**

Vuchelen, Jef. Voorspellingen voor de Belgische Economie in de Jaren Tachtig. (With English summary.) *Cah. Écon. Bruxelles*, First Trimester 1986, (109), pp. 85–122. **[G: Belgium]**

Walkowiak, Witold. Investment Processes in 1976–1981. *Eastern Europ. Econ.*, Spring 1986, *24*(3), pp. 35–52. **[G: Poland]**

Warr, Peter G. Indonesia's Other Dutch Disease: Economic Effects of the Petroleum Boom. **In** *Neary, J. P. and van Wijnbergen, S., eds.*, 1986, pp. 288–320.

Williamson, Jeffrey G. Productivity Growth in Manufacturing during Early Industrialization: Evidence from the American Northeast, 1820–1860: Comment. **In** *Engerman, S. L. and Gallman, R. E., eds.*, 1986, pp. 729–33. **[G: U.S.]**

Young, John A. Global Competition—The New Reality: Results of the President's Commission on Industrial Competitiveness. **In** *Landau, R. and Rosenberg, N., eds.*, 1986, pp. 501–09. **[G: U.S.]**

Zarnowitz, Victor and Moore, Geoffrey H. Major Changes in Cyclical Behavior. **In** *Gordon, R. J., ed.*, 1986, pp. 519–72. **[G: U.S.; W. Germany; U.K.; France]**

Zhuravlev, S. N. Structural Shifts in the Economy: Techniques for Evaluating Their Impact on Efficiency and Growth. *Matekon*, Winter 1986-87, *23*(2), pp. 3–31. **[G: U.S.S.R.]**

227 Prices

2270 Prices

Adams, Donald R., Jr. Prices and Wages in Maryland, 1750–1850. *J. Econ. Hist.*, September 1986, *46*(3), pp. 625–45. **[G: U.S.]**

Aurikko, Esko. A Dynamic Analysis of Finnish Export Prices. *Liiketaloudellinen Aikak.*, 1986, *35*(1), pp. 23–38. **[G: Finland]**

Balk, B. M. and Kersten, H. M. P. On the Precision of Consumer Price Indices Caused by the Sampling Variability of Budget Surveys. *J. Econ. Soc. Meas.*, April 1986, *14*(1), pp. 19–35. **[G: U.S.]**

Bernholz, Peter. The Implementation and Maintenance of a Monetary Constitution. *Cato J.*, Fall 1986, *6*(2), pp. 477–511. **[G: OECD]**

Bjerkholt, Olav. Experiences in Using Input–Output Techniques for Price Calculations. **In** *Sohn, I., ed.*, 1986, *1982*, pp. 35–48. **[G: Norway]**

Black, Stanley W. Discrete Devaluation as a Signal to Price Setters: Suggested Evidence from Greece: Comment. **In** *Edwards, S. and Ahamed, L., eds.*, 1986, pp. 326–29. **[G: Greece]**

Blackley, Dixie M.; Follain, James R. and Lee, Haeduck. Evaluation of Hedonic Price Indexes for Thirty-four Large SMSAs. *Amer. Real Estate Urban Econ. Assoc. J.*, Summer 1986, *14*(2), pp. 179–205. **[G: U.S.]**

Blankmeyer, Eric. Inference for Multiperiod Price and Quantity Indices. *Atlantic Econ. J.*, July 1986, *14*(2), pp. 84.

Broniatowski, M. and Kebabdjian, G. Inflation et dynamique des prix: un traitement non paramétrique de données françaises. (Inflation and the Dynamic of Prices: A Non Parametric Study of French Series. With English summary.) *Écon. Appl.*, 1986, *39*(2), pp. 337–68. **[G: France]**

Bryan, Michael F. and Gavin, William T. Models of Inflation Expectations Formation: A Comparison of Household and Economist Forecasts: A Comment. *J. Money, Credit, Banking*, November 1986, *18*(4), pp. 539–44. **[G: U.S.]**

Buchanan, James M. The Relevance of Constitutional Strategy [The Implementation and Maintenance of a Monetary Constitution]. *Cato J.*, Fall 1986, *6*(2), pp. 513–17.

Buisán, Ana C. and Restoy, Fernando. Inflación y variabilidad de los precios relativos en España (1976–1983). (With English summary.) *Invest. Ecón.*, May 1986, *10*(2), pp. 327–55. **[G: Spain]**

Bushe, Dennis M.; Kravis, Irving B. and Lipsey, Robert E. Prices, Activity, and Machinery Exports: An Analysis Based on New Price Data. *Rev. Econ. Statist.*, May 1986, *68*(2), pp. 248–55. **[G: U.S.; W. Germany; Japan]**

Carlton, Dennis W. The Rigidity of Prices. *Amer. Econ. Rev.*, September 1986, *76*(4), pp. 637–58. **[G: U.S.]**

Cartwright, David W. Improved Deflation of Purchases of Computers. *Surv. Curr. Bus.*, March 1986, *66*(3), pp. 7–10. **[G: U.S.]**

Cebula, Richard J. A Living Cost Index for SMSAs. *Soc. Sci. Quart.*, December 1986, *67*(4), pp. 887–91. **[G: U.S.]**

Cebula, Richard J. On the Impact of Right-to-Work Laws: A Reply. *Urban Stud.*, February 1986, *23*(1), pp. 69. **[G: U.S.]**

Cebula, Richard J. Right-to-Work Laws and Geographic Differences in Living Costs: Reply. *Amer. J. Econ. Soc.*, April 1986, *45*(2), pp. 252–54. **[G: U.S.]**

Cecchetti, Stephen G. The Frequency of Price Adjustment: A Study of the Newsstand Prices of Magazines. *J. Econometrics*, April 1986, *31*(3), pp. 255–74. **[G: U.S.]**

Chang, Rosita P. and Rhee, S. Ghon. Does the Stock Market React to Announcements of the Producer Price Index? *Financial Rev.*, February 1986, *21*(1), pp. 125–34. **[G: U.S.]**

Cheema, Aftab Ahmad and Malik, Muhammad Hussain. Income-Specific Inflation Rates in Pakistan. *Pakistan Devel. Rev.*, Spring 1986, *25*(1), pp. 73–84. **[G: Pakistan]**

Chen, Nai-Ruenn and Hou, Chi-ming. China's Inflation, 1979–1983: Measurement and Analysis. *Econ. Develop. Cult. Change,* July 1986, *34*(4), pp. 811–35. **[G: China]**

Chu, Ke-young and Morrison, Thomas K. World Non-Oil Primary Commodity Markets: A Medium-term Framework of Analysis. *Int. Monet. Fund Staff Pap.*, March 1986, *33*(1), pp. 139–84.

Chung, Jae Wan and Kim, Dookyung. An Interactive Causal Analysis of Price Dynamics: A Case Study of Korea. *Econ. Develop. Cult. Change,* July 1986, *34*(4), pp. 837–53. **[G: S. Korea]**

Clague, Christopher. Determinants of the National Price Level: Some Empirical Results. *Rev. Econ. Statist.*, May 1986, *68*(2), pp. 320–23. **[G: Global]**

Cole, Rosanne, et al. Quality-adjusted Price Indexes for Computer Processors and Selected Peripheral Equipment. *Surv. Curr. Bus.*, January 1986, *66*(1), pp. 41–50. **[G: U.S.]**

Collier, Irwin L., Jr. Effective Purchasing Power in a Quantity Constrained Economy: An Estimate for the German Democratic Republic. *Rev. Econ. Statist.*, February 1986, *68*(1), pp. 24–32. **[G: E. Germany]**

Cuthbertson, Keith. The Behaviour of U.K. Export Prices of Manufactured Goods 1970–1983. *J. Appl. Econometrics,* July 1986, *1*(3), pp. 255–75. **[G: U.K.]**

Danziger, Leif. Relative-Price Seasonality, Wage Indexation and the Perfect Price Index. *Europ. Econ. Rev.*, December 1986, *30*(6), pp. 1145–67.

Di Matteo, Massimo. Long Waves in Relative Prices: An Interpretation. **In** *Frisch, H. and Gahlen, B., eds.*, 1986, pp. 126–44.

Donkers, H. W. J. and van der Zwan, A. C. Analysing Consumer Price Changes by Using Input–Output Tables. *Statist. J.*, October 1986, *4*(2), pp. 195–211. **[G: Netherlands]**

Early, John F.; Lane, Walter and Sturm, Philip. A Half-Year Pause in Inflation: Its Antecedents and Structure. *Mon. Lab. Rev.*, October 1986, *109*(10), pp. 3–14. **[G: U.S.]**

Encaoua, David and Geroski, Paul A. Price Dynamics and Competition in Five OECD Countries. *OECD Econ. Stud.*, Spring 1986, (6), pp. 47–74. **[G: Canada; Japan; U.K.; U.S.; Sweden]**

Feinberg, Robert M. The Interaction of Foreign Exchange and Market Power Effects on German Domestic Prices. *J. Ind. Econ.*, September 1986, *35*(1), pp. 61–70. **[G: W. Germany]**

Fischer, Georges and Kern, Anita. Zur Problematik der Indexbindung: Fragwürdige Diktatur des Konsumentenpreisindexes? (With English summary.) *Aussenwirtschaft,* December 1986, *41*(4), pp. 483–96.

Fischer, Stanley. Relative Shocks, Relative Price Variability, and Inflation. **In** *Fischer, S.*, 1986, *1981*, pp. 71–122. **[G: U.S.]**

Frantzen, Dirk J. The Cyclical Behaviour of Manufacturing Prices in a Small Open Economy. *J. Ind. Econ.*, June 1986, *34*(4), pp. 389–408. **[G: Belgium]**

Fureng, Dong. China's Price Reform. *Cambridge J. Econ.*, September 1986, *10*(3), pp. 291–300. **[G: China]**

Garber, Steven and Klepper, Steven. Relative Price Changes in Recession: A Microeconometric Analysis of U.S. Manufacturing. *Int. Econ. Rev.*, February 1986, *27*(1), pp. 187–208. **[G: U.S.]**

Garrod, Peter V. and Roberts, Roland K. Prices as Proxies for Prices. *Amer. J. Agr. Econ.*, August 1986, *68*(3), pp. 626–33. **[G: U.S.]**

Glezakos, Constantine and Nugent, Jeffrey B. A Confirmation of the Relation between Inflation and Relative Price Variability. *J. Polit. Econ.*, August 1986, *94*(4), pp. 895–99. **[G: U.S.]**

Glezakos, Constantine and Nugent, Jeffrey B. Inflation and Relative Price Variability once Again. *J. Post Keynesian Econ.*, Summer 1986, *8*(4), pp. 607–13. **[G: U.S.]**

Gorman, W. M. Compatible Indices. *Econ. J.*, Supplement 1986, *96*, pp. 83–95.

Gorodetskii, A. Cost Accounting and Wholesale Prices. *Prob. Econ.*, August 1986, *29*(4), pp. 71–89. **[G: U.S.S.R.]**

Granger, Clive W. J.; Robins, R. P. and Engle, Robert F. Wholesale and Retail Prices: Bivariate Time-Series Modeling with Forecastable Error Variances. **In** *Belsley, D. A. and Kuh, E., eds.*, 1986, pp. 1–17. **[G: U.S.]**

Herlitz, Lars. Private Consumption and Development of Industrial Production: The 1930s Compared with Post-war Tendencies. **In** *Berend,*

I. T. and Borchardt, K., eds., 1986, pp. 497–515. [G: U.K.; U.S.; Germany; Sweden; France]

Heytens, Paul J. Testing Market Integration. *Food Res. Inst. Stud.*, 1986, *20*(1), pp. 25–41. [G: Nigeria]

Hill, Peter. International Price Levels and Purchasing Power Parities. *OECD Econ. Stud.*, Spring 1986, (6), pp. 133–59. [G: OECD]

Honohan, Patrick and Flynn, John. Irish Inflation in EMS. *Econ. Soc. Rev.*, April 1986, *17*(3), pp. 175–91. [G: Ireland]

Hughes, Gordon A. A New Method for Estimating the Effects of Fuel Taxes: An Application to Thailand. *World Bank Econ. Rev.*, September 1986, *1*(1), pp. 65–101. [G: Thailand]

Huszti, Ernö. Changes in the Purchasing Power of the Hungarian Forint between 1946–1984. *Acta Oecon.*, 1986, *37*(1–2), pp. 87–101. [G: Hungary]

Jackson, Marvin R. When Is a Price a Price? The Level and Patterns of Price in the CMEA. *Soviet E. Europ. Foreign Trade*, Spring 1986, *22*(1), pp. 100–112. [G: CMEA]

Jerala, Tomislav. Fertilizer Pricing in Yugoslavia. In *Segura, E. L.; Shetty, Y. T. and Nishimizu, M., eds.*, 1986, pp. 204–18. [G: Yugoslavia]

Jones, Jonathan D. Consumer Prices, Wholesale Prices, and Causality (More Empirical Evidence for the U.S., 1947–1983). *Empirical Econ.*, 1986, *11*(1), pp. 41–55. [G: U.S.]

Kantor, Brian S. and Barr, G. D. I. The Impact of a Change in the Price of Petrol on the South African Rate of Inflation. *J. Stud. Econ. Econometrics*, November 1986, (26), pp. 35–57. [G: S. Africa]

Katseli, Louka T. Discrete Devaluation as a Signal to Price Setters: Suggested Evidence from Greece. In *Edwards, S. and Ahamed, L., eds.*, 1986, pp. 295–326. [G: Greece]

Klein, Philip A. Leading Indicators of Inflation in Market Economies. *Int. J. Forecasting*, 1986, *2*(4), pp. 403–12. [G: OECD]

Kravis, Irving B. The Three Faces of the International Comparison Project. *World Bank Res. Observer*, January 1986, *1*(1), pp. 3–26. [G: Global]

Lee, Chi-wen Jevons and Petruzzi, Christopher R. The Gibson Paradox and the Monetary Standard. *Rev. Econ. Statist.*, May 1986, *68*(2), pp. 189–96. [G: U.K.; U.S.]

Leonard, David C. and Solt, Michael E. Recent Evidence on the Accuracy and Rationality of Popular Inflation Forecasts. *J. Finan. Res.*, Winter 1986, *9*(4), pp. 281–90. [G: U.S.]

Leontief, Wassily. Wages, Profits, Prices, and Taxes. In *Leontief, W.*, 1986, *1947*, pp. 55–64. [G: U.S.]

Madhur, Srinivasa and Roy, Prannoy. Price Setting in Indian Industry. *J. Devel. Econ.*, March 1986, *20*(2), pp. 205–24. [G: India]

Marcoot, John L. and Bahr, Richard C. The Revised Consumer Price Index: Changes in Definitions and Availability. *Mon. Lab. Rev.*, July 1986, *109*(7), pp. 15–23. [G: U.S.]

Marshall R., Pablo. Predicción de inflación con modelos de series de tiempo múltiples. (With English summary.) *Cuadernos Econ.*, April 1986, *23*(68), pp. 101–17. [G: Chile]

Meister, Shelley and Sherman, Thomas A. Import, Export Prices Reflect Declining Dollar and Oversupply in 1985. *Mon. Lab. Rev.*, April 1986, *109*(4), pp. 3–16. [G: U.S.]

Minde, Kjell Bjørn and Ramstad, Jan. The Development of Real Wages in Norway about 1730–1910. *Scand. Econ. Hist. Rev.*, 1986, *34*(2), pp. 90–121. [G: Norway]

Mittnik, Stefan. Modelling Price Inflation Using Polynomial Distributed Lags: The Almon Lag Technique and Its Pitfalls [Die Determinanten der Preisentwicklung in der Bundesrepublik Deutschland]. *Jahr. Nationalökon. Statist.*, September 1986, *201*(5), pp. 518–26. [G: W. Germany]

Mornande, Felipe G. Domestic Prices of Importable Goods in Chile and the Law of One Price: 1975–1982. *J. Devel. Econ.*, April 1986, *21*(1), pp. 131–47. [G: Chile]

Morrow, Anne M. M. The Measurement of Inflation Experienced by the Poor, 1970–80. *Can. Public Policy*, March 1986, *12*(1), pp. 245–52. [G: Canada]

Navarro, Alfredo Martin. Precios relativos, dinero e inflación en la Argentina. (Relative Prices, Money and Inflation in Argentina. With English summary.) *Económica (La Plata)*, Jan.-June 1986, *32*(1), pp. 119–33. [G: Argentina]

Niron, Suna. Fertilizer Pricing in Turkey. In *Segura, E. L.; Shetty, Y. T. and Nishimizu, M., eds.*, 1986, pp. 219–35. [G: Turkey]

Officer, Lawrence H. The Law of One Price Cannot Be Rejected: Two Tests Based on the Tradable/Nontradable Price Ratio. *J. Macroecon.*, Spring 1986, *8*(2), pp. 159–82. [G: Global]

Ostrosky, Anthony L. The Impact of Right-to-Work Laws on the Cost of Living in the United States: A Comment. *Urban Stud.*, February 1986, *23*(1), pp. 67. [G: U.S.]

Persico, Pasquale. Inflazione e prezzi relativi in Italia: Commento alla replica. *Stud. Econ.*, 1986, *41*(29), pp. 185–86.

Pietra, Tito. Inflazione e prezzi relativi in Italia: Replica a persico. (With English summary.) *Stud. Econ.*, 1986, *41*(29), pp. 169–83.

Rączkowski, Stanisław. The Influence of International Movements of Prices and Inflation on the Economies of the Socialist Countries. *Eastern Europ. Econ.*, Summer 1986, *24*(4), pp. 3–28. [G: CMEA]

Rappoport, Peter. Inflation in the Service Sector. *Fed. Res. Bank New York Quart. Rev.*, Winter 1986-87, *11*(4), pp. 35–45. [G: U.S.]

Reynolds, Morgan O. and Edwards, Mary. Right-to-Work Laws and Geographic Differences in Living Costs: Comment. *Amer. J. Econ. Soc.*, April 1986, *45*(2), pp. 247–52. [G: U.S.]

Ross, Howard N. and Krausz, Joshua. Buyers' and Sellers' Prices and Administered Behavior.

Rev. Econ. Statist., August 1986, *68*(3), pp. 369–78. **[G: U.S.]**

Schroeter, John R. and Smith, Scott L. A Reexamination of the Rationality of the Livingston Price Expectations: A Note. *J. Money, Credit, Banking*, May 1986, *18*(2), pp. 239–46.

Schultz, Knud H. and Mattos, Jorge A. S. Fertilizer Pricing in Brazil. **In** *Segura, E. L.; Shetty, Y. T. and Nishimizu, M., eds.*, 1986, pp. 185–95. **[G: Brazil]**

Seitz, H. Firms Responses to Changes in Demand: Some Insight from Survey-Data. *Empirical Econ.*, 1986, *11*(2), pp. 111–23. **[G: W. Germany]**

Sellekaerts, Brigitte H. and Sellekaerts, Willy. Unanticipated Inflation and Relative Price Variability. *Atlantic Econ. J.*, July 1986, *14*(2), pp. 31–36. **[G: U.S.]**

Sellekaerts, Willy and Sellekaerts, Brigitte H. The Impact of Anticipated and Unanticipated Inflation on Relative Price Variability: Further Results. *J. Post Keynesian Econ.*, Summer 1986, *8*(4), pp. 614–22.

Shannon, Russell and Wallace, Myles S. Wages and Inflation: An Investigation into Causality. *J. Post Keynesian Econ.*, Winter 1985-86, *8*(2), pp. 182–91. **[G: U.S.]**

Shorrocks, Anthony. The Measurement of Inflation Experienced by the Poor, 1970–80: A Reply. *Can. Public Policy*, December 1986, *12*(4), pp. 640–44. **[G: Canada]**

Shriver, Keith A. Further Evidence on the Marginal Gains in Accuracy of Alternative Levels of Specificity of the Producer Price Indexes. *J. Acc. Res.*, Spring 1986, *24*(1), pp. 151–65. **[G: U.S.]**

Stoker, Thomas M. The Distributional Welfare Effects of Rising Prices in the United States: The 1970's Experience. *Amer. Econ. Rev.*, June 1986, *76*(3), pp. 335–49. **[G: U.S.]**

Szybisz, Boguslaw. An Integrated Quantity and Price Indices System Based on Input–Output Tables. **In** *Franz, A. and Rainer, N., eds.*, 1986, pp. 403–13. **[G: Poland]**

Thies, Clifford F. Business Price Expectations: 1947–83. *J. Money, Credit, Banking*, August 1986, *18*(3), pp. 336–54. **[G: U.S.]**

Triplett, Jack E. The Economic Interpretation of Hedonic Methods. *Surv. Curr. Bus.*, January 1986, *66*(1), pp. 36–40. **[G: U.S.]**

Turvey, Ralph. Consumer Price Indices—What Is the Question? *Statist. J.*, October 1986, *4*(2), pp. 145–63. **[G: U.K.]**

VanderHoff, James. Endogenous Expectation Formation Methods: Evidence from Consumers' Inflation Expectations. *J. Macroecon.*, Winter 1986, *8*(1), pp. 63–74. **[G: U.S.]**

Wolters, Jürgen. Preiserwartungen der Unternehmer. Eine empirische Untersuchung anhand der Ifo-Salden. (Price Expectations of Firms. An Empirical Analysis on the Basis of the Ifo-Business Test. With English summary.) *Z. Wirtschaft. Sozialwissen.*, 1986, *106*(6), pp. 579–604. **[G: W. Germany]**

228 Regional Statistics

2280 Regional Statistics

Friedenberg, Howard L. and DePass, Rudolph E. Regional Nonfarm Wages and Salaries: Three Years of Expansion. *Surv. Curr. Bus.*, April 1986, *66*(4), pp. 37–38. **[G: U.S.]**

Wagener, Hans-Jürgen. The Political Economy of Soviet Nationalities and Regions. **In** *Höhmann, H.-H.; Nove, A. and Vogel, H., eds.*, 1986, pp. 146–71. **[G: U.S.S.R.]**

229 Microdata and Database Analysis

2290 Microdata and Database Analysis

Stafford, Frank. Forestalling the Demise of Empirical Economics: The Role of Microdata in Labor Economics Research. **In** *Ashenfelter, O. and Layard, R., eds., Vol. 1*, 1986, pp. 387–423.

300 Domestic Monetary and Fiscal Theory and Institutions

310 Domestic Monetary and Financial Theory and Institutions

3100 General

Agu, C. C. Financial Institutions and Economic Development: The Experience of Nigeria. *S. Afr. J. Econ.*, September 1986, *54*(3), pp. 319–31. **[G: Nigeria]**

Avery, Robert B., et al. The Use of Cash and Transaction Accounts by American Families. *Fed. Res. Bull.*, February 1986, *72*(2), pp. 87–108. **[G: U.S.]**

Best, Michael H. and Humphries, Jane. The City and Industrial Decline. **In** *Elbaum, B. and Lazonick, W., eds.*, 1986, pp. 223–39. **[G: U.K.]**

Bhatt, V. V. Improving the Financial Structure in Developing Countries. *Finance Develop.*, June 1986, *23*(2), pp. 20–22. **[G: LDCs]**

de Boissieu, Christian. Les innovations financières en France. (With English summary.) *Revue Écon. Polit.*, Sept.-Oct. 1986, *96*(5), pp. 585–600. **[G: France]**

de Boissieu, Christian. Quelques réflexions sur l'analyse économique des innovations financières. (Some Reflections on the Economics Analysis of Financial Innovation. With English summary.) *Écon. Appl.*, 1986, *39*(3), pp. 449–72.

Bresolin, Ferruccio. L'evoluzione della struttura finanziaria italiana: Un'applicazione dell'analisi Shift-and-Share. (The Evolution of Italian Financial Structure: An Application of Shift-and-Share Analysis. With English summary.) *Ricerche Econ.*, Apr.-Sept. 1986, *40*(2–3), pp. 360–76. **[G: Italy]**

Brown, William H. Opening Japanese Financial Markets: What Has Changed, What Will

Change? **In** *Pugel, T. A., ed.*, 1986, pp. 117–35. **[G: Japan]**

Budd, Alan P. Do We Need a National Investment Bank? *Nat. Westminster Bank Quart. Rev.*, August 1986, pp. 36–48. **[G: U.K.]**

Butler, David R. Teaching Economics to the 16–19 Age Range: Money and Banking. **In** *Whitehead, D. J., ed.*, 1986, pp. 206–08.

Butler, David R. Teaching Economics to the 13–16 Age Range: Money and Banking. **In** *Whitehead, D. J., ed.*, 1986, pp. 99–102.

Buxton, Andrew. Financial Deregulation: The Opportunities and Some of the Dangers. **In** *Dale, R., ed.*, 1986, pp. 13–17. **[G: U.K.]**

Cargill, Thomas F. Background and Causes of Financial Innovation: An International Comparison: Comments. **In** *Suzuki, Y. and Yomo, H., eds.*, 1986, pp. 107–11.

Cargill, Thomas F. Japanese Monetary Policy, Flow of Funds, and Domestic Financial Liberalization. *Fed. Res. Bank San Francisco Econ. Rev.*, Summer 1986, (3), pp. 21–32. **[G: Japan]**

de Cecco, Marcello. Modes of Financial Development: American Banking Dynamics and World Financial Crises. **In** *[Hirshman, A. O.]*, 1986, pp. 115–32. **[G: U.S.]**

Chatelus, Michel. Les monnaies des pays arabes pétroliers du golfe. (The Currencies of the Gulf Arab Oil Countries. With English summary.) *Écon. Soc.*, February 1986, *20*(2), pp. 61–94. **[G: OPEC]**

Conklin, David W. and Courchene, Thomas J. New Institutions for a Market Economy. *Can. Public Policy*, Supp. February 1986, *12*, pp. 40–50. **[G: Canada]**

Corrigan, E. Gerald. Coping with Globally Integrated Financial Markets. *Fed. Res. Bank New York Quart. Rev.*, Winter 1986-87, *11*(4), pp. 1–5. **[G: U.S.]**

De Wulf, Luc and Goldsbrough, David. The Evolving Role of Monetary Policy in China. *Int. Monet. Fund Staff Pap.*, June 1986, *33*(2), pp. 209–42. **[G: China]**

Dini, Lamberto. Towards a European Integrated Financial Market. *Banca Naz. Lavoro Quart. Rev.*, December 1986, (159), pp. 377–89. **[G: EEC]**

Dudler, Hermann-Josef. Geldmengenpolitik und Finanzinnovationen. (Money Supply Policy and Financial Innovations. With English summary.) *Kredit Kapital*, 1986, *19*(4), pp. 472–95. **[G: W. Germany]**

Fry, Maxwell J. Financial Innovation and Monetary Policy: Asia and the West: Summing-up: Three Issues of Financial Reform and Innovation. **In** *Suzuki, Y. and Yomo, H., eds.*, 1986, pp. 319–27.

Galpin, Rodney. A Supervisor's Perspective on Deregulation. **In** *Dale, R., ed.*, 1986, pp. 28–35. **[G: U.K.]**

Godschalk, Hugo. The Moneyless Economy—From Temple Exchange to the Barter Club. **In** *Pohl, H. and Rudolph, B., eds.*, 1986, pp. 57–78. **[G: W. Germany; U.S.]**

Gupta, Kanhaya L. Financial Development and Economic Growth in India and South Korea. *J. Econ. Devel.*, December 1986, *11*(2), pp. 41–62. **[G: India; S. Korea]**

Harper, Ian R. Why Financial Deregulation? *Australian Econ. Rev.*, 1st Quarter 1986, (73), pp. 37–49. **[G: Australia]**

Henni, Ahmed. Les théories économiques de la monnaie à l'épreuve dans les sociétés en développement planifié: le cas de l'Algérie. (The Economic Theories of Money on Trial in Planned Developing Societies: The Case of Algeria. With English summary.) *Écon. Soc.*, February 1986, *20*(2), pp. 49–60. **[G: Algeria]**

Hoppit, Julian. Financial Crises in Eighteenth-century England. *Econ. Hist. Rev., 2nd Ser.*, February 1986, *39*(1), pp. 39–58. **[G: U.K.]**

Jack, R. B. A Review of the Legal Problems. **In** *Dale, R., ed.*, 1986, pp. 48–63. **[G: U.K.]**

Jung, Woo S. Financial Development and Economic Growth: International Evidence. *Econ. Develop. Cult. Change*, January 1986, *34*(2), pp. 333–46. **[G: LDCs; MDCs]**

Kajiyama, Naoki. Deregulating Interest Rates on Deposits: Lessons from the U.S. Experience. **In** *Finn, R. B., ed.*, 1986, pp. 187–202. **[G: U.S.]**

Kaufman, Henry. In the Shadow of Financial Exhilaration. *Challenge*, July/Aug. 1986, *29*(3), pp. 4–10. **[G: U.S.]**

Lachmann, Ludwig M. The Monetary System of a Market Economy. *S. Afr. J. Econ.*, March 1986, *54*(1), pp. 1–7. **[G: S. Africa]**

Lewis, M. K. Financial Services in the United States. **In** *Carter, R. L.; Chiplin, B. and Lewis, M. K., eds.*, 1986, pp. 106–36. **[G: U.S.]**

Lewis, M. K. and Chiplin, B. Characteristics of Markets for Personal Financial Services. **In** *Carter, R. L.; Chiplin, B. and Lewis, M. K., eds.*, 1986, pp. 27–47. **[G: U.S.; U.K.]**

Mauri, Arnaldo. Improvement of the Savings Mobilization Process through Institutional and Procedural Innovations. **In** *U.N., Dept. of International Econ. and Social Affairs*, 1986, pp. 47–49.

Mayer, Colin. The Assessment: Financial Innovation: Curse or Blessing? *Oxford Rev. Econ. Policy*, Winter 1986, *2*(4), pp. i–xix. **[G: U.K.]**

McClam, Warren D. Background and Causes of Financial Innovation: An International Comparison: Comments. **In** *Suzuki, Y. and Yomo, H., eds.*, 1986, pp. 113–19. **[G: OECD]**

McLeod, Alex N. Better Late Than Never. *Can. Public Policy*, September 1986, *12*(3), pp. 484–98. **[G: Canada]**

de Melo, Jaime and Tybout, James. The Effects of Financial Liberalization on Savings and Investment in Uruguay. *Econ. Develop. Cult. Change*, April 1986, *34*(3), pp. 561–87. **[G: Uruguay]**

Meyerson, Per-Martin. Industrial Finance System in Europe, U.S. and Japan: Comment. **In** *Day, R. H. and Eliasson, G., eds.*, 1986, pp. 401–03. **[G: Europe; U.S.; Japan]**

Miller, Merton H. Financial Innovation: The Last

Twenty Years and the Next. *J. Finan. Quant. Anal.*, December 1986, *21*(4), pp. 459–71. **[G: U.S.]**

Parker, William N. Industrial Finance System in Europe, U.S. and Japan: Comment. **In** *Day, R. H. and Eliasson, G., eds.*, 1986, pp. 397–400. **[G: Europe; U.S.; Japan]**

Remolona, Eli M. and Lamberte, Mario B. Financial Reforms and Balance-of-Payments Crisis: The Case of the Philippines: 1980–83. *Philippine Rev. Econ. Bus.*, Mar./June 1986, *23* (1/2), pp. 101–41. **[G: Philippines]**

Rivallain, Josette. Paléomonnaies africaines: moyens d'approche et fonctionnement: un exemple en pays SARA, sud du Tchad. (African Palaeomonies: Means of Access and Functioning: An Example Taken from the Sara Country, in Southern Chad. With English summary.) *Écon. Soc.*, February 1986, *20*(2), pp. 31–48. **[G: Chad]**

Rosende R., Francisco and Vergara M., Rodrigo. Opciones de Política para el Sector Financiero. (With English summary.) *Cuadernos Econ.*, December 1986, *23*(70), pp. 373–97. **[G: Chile]**

Rybczynski, Tad M. Industrial Finance System in Europe, U.S. and Japan: Reply. **In** *Day, R. H. and Eliasson, G., eds.*, 1986, pp. 408–09. **[G: Europe; U.S.; Japan]**

Rybczynski, Tad M. Industrial Finance System in Europe, U.S. and Japan. **In** *Day, R. H. and Eliasson, G., eds.*, 1986, *1984*, pp. 385–96. **[G: Europe; U.S.; Japan]**

Schulze, David L. Monetization in ASEAN: 1970–1984. *Singapore Econ. Rev.*, October 1986, *31*(2), pp. 57–66. **[G: Asia]**

Serletis, Apostolos and Robb, A. Leslie. Divisia Aggregation and Substitutability among Monetary Assets. *J. Money, Credit, Banking*, November 1986, *18*(4), pp. 430–46. **[G: Canada]**

Spinanger, Dean. Industrial Finance System in Europe, U.S. and Japan: Comment. **In** *Day, R. H. and Eliasson, G., eds.*, 1986, pp. 404–07. **[G: Europe; U.S.; Japan]**

Stigler, George J. The Regularities of Regulation. **In** *Dale, R., ed.*, 1986, pp. 1–12. **[G: U.S.]**

Teranishi, Juro. Economic Growth and Regulation of Financial Markets: Japanese Experience during Postwar High Growth Period. *Hitotsubashi J. Econ.*, December 1986, *27*(2), pp. 145–65. **[G: Japan]**

Teranishi, Juro. The "Catch-up" Process, Financial System, and Japan's Rise as a Capital Exporter. *Hitotsubashi J. Econ.*, Spec. Iss. Oct. 1986, *27*, pp. 133–46. **[G: Japan]**

Thygesen, Niels. Financial Innovation and Monetary Policy: Asia and the West: Concluding Remarks. **In** *Suzuki, Y. and Yomo, H., eds.*, 1986, pp. 307–18. **[G: U.S.]**

Vaciago, Giacomo. Financial Innovation in Italy and Its Implications for Monetary Policy. *Greek Econ. Rev.*, December 1986, *8*(2), pp. 176–86. **[G: Italy]**

Van Horne, James C. An Inquiry into Recent Financial Innovation. *Kredit Kapital*, 1986, *19*(4), pp. 453–71.

Vogel, Robert C. and Burkett, Paul. Deposit Mobilization in Developing Countries: The Importance of Reciprocity in Lending. *J. Devel. Areas*, July 1986, *20*(4), pp. 425–37. **[G: LDCs]**

Wahlroos, Björn. Informationsteknologi, risk och nya finansiella instrument. (Information Technology, Risk and New Financial Instruments. With English summary.) *Ekon. Samfundets Tidskr.*, 1986, *39*(2), pp. 91–98. **[G: Finland]**

Wallace, Neil. The Impact of New Payment Technologies: A Macro View. **In** *Lawrence, C. and Shay, R. P., eds.*, 1986, pp. 201–06. **[G: U.S.]**

Wilson, J. S. G. A Money Market for Thailand? *Banca Naz. Lavoro Quart. Rev.*, September 1986, (158), pp. 299–317. **[G: Thailand]**

Yumoto, Masashi, et al. Financial Innovation in Major Industrial Countries. **In** *Suzuki, Y. and Yomo, H, eds.*, 1986, pp. 45–78. **[G: OECD]**

311 Domestic Monetary and Financial Theory and Policy

3110 Domestic Monetary Theory and Policy

Abbott, Graham J. The Political Economy of Financial Reform in Developing Economies. **In** *Cheng, H.-S., ed.*, 1986, pp. 343–44.

Arnould, Daniel and Lavaux, Robert. La violence par la monnaie: l'hyperinflation dans les pays en développement. (Violence by Money: Hyperinflation in the Developing Countries. With English summary.) *Écon. Soc.*, February 1986, *20*(2), pp. 169–95. **[G: LDCs]**

Beard, Thomas R. and McMillin, W. Douglas. Government Budgets and Money: How Are They Related? *J. Econ. Educ.*, Spring 1986, *17*(2), pp. 107–19. **[G: U.S.]**

Bernholz, Peter. The Implementation and Maintenance of a Monetary Constitution. *Cato J.*, Fall 1986, *6*(2), pp. 477–511. **[G: OECD]**

Bofinger, Peter. Wechselkurstheorien und Wirtschaftspolitik. (Exchange Rate Theories and Economic Policy. With English summary.) *Kredit Kapital*, 1986, *19*(2), pp. 184–212. **[G: OECD]**

Borio, C. E. V. Income–Financial Aggregates Interactions and Policy Design: The Case of Italy. *Metroecon.*, February 1986, *38*(1), pp. 85–111. **[G: Italy]**

Botha, D. J. J. Interest Rates as an Instrument of Monetary Policy in South Africa. *S. Afr. J. Econ.*, March 1986, *54*(1), pp. 41–54. **[G: S. Africa]**

Brown, William Walter and Santoni, Gary J. Rational Optimizing, Monetary Theory, and Welfare. *Cato J.*, Winter 1986, *5*(3), pp. 949–55.

Brunner, Karl. Deficits, Interest Rates, and Monetary Policy. *Cato J.*, Winter 1986, *5*(3), pp. 709–26. **[G: U.S.]**

Brunner, Karl and Meltzer, Allan H. The National Bureau Method, International Capital

Mobility, and Other Essays. *Carnegie-Rochester Conf. Ser. Public Policy,* Spring 1986, *24,* pp. 1–10.

Buchanan, James M. The Relevance of Constitutional Strategy [The Implementation and Maintenance of a Monetary Constitution]. *Cato J.*, Fall 1986, *6*(2), pp. 513–17.

Caskey, John and Fazzari, Steven M. Macroeconomics and Credit Markets. *J. Econ. Issues,* June 1986, *20*(2), pp. 421–29.

Cayton, J. Michael. Commodity and Gold Targeting. *Bus. Econ.*, October 1986, *21*(4), pp. 21–25.

Chishti, Salim U. The Case for an Indexed Financial Instrument in an Interest-Free Economy. *Pakistan J. Appl. Econ.*, Summer 1986, *5*(1), pp. 47–61. **[G: Pakistan]**

Christiano, Lawrence J. Money and the U.S. Economy in the 1980s: A Break from the Past? *Fed. Res. Bank Minn. Rev.*, Summer 1986, *10*(3), pp. 2–13. **[G: U.S.]**

Chrystal, K. Alec and Peel, David A. What Can Economics Learn from Political Science, and Vice Versa? *Amer. Econ. Rev.*, May 1986, *76*(2), pp. 62–65. **[G: U.K.]**

Connolly, Michael. The Speculative Attack on the Peso and the Real Exchange Rate: Argentina, 1979–81. *J. Int. Money Finance,* Supp. March 1986, *5,* pp. S117–30. **[G: Argentina]**

Cooper, Richard N. Macroeconomic Policy Adjustment in Interdependent Economies. **In** *Cooper, R. N.*, 1986, *1969,* pp. 155–78.

Cooper, Richard N. Monetary Theory and Policy in an Open Economy. **In** *Cooper, R. N.*, 1986, *1976,* pp. 179–98.

Day, A. Edward. Reserve Ratios: A Proposal for Change. *J. Macroecon.*, Fall 1986, *8*(4), pp. 479–84. **[G: U.S.]**

De Wet, G. L. Monetary Control as Seen by the De Kock Commission: An Assessment. *S. Afr. J. Econ.*, March 1986, *54*(1), pp. 8–21. **[G: S. Africa]**

Dorn, James A. Money, Politics, and the Business Cycle. *Cato J.*, Fall 1986, *6*(2), pp. 353–64. **[G: U.S.]**

Duesenberry, James S. Financial Deregulation: Micro and Macroeconomic Effects. **In** *Cheng, H.-S., ed.*, 1986, pp. 353–56.

Edwards, Sebastian. Monetarism in Chile, 1973–1983: Some Economic Puzzles. *Econ. Develop. Cult. Change,* April 1986, *34*(3), pp. 535–59. **[G: Chile]**

Friedman, Milton. The Resource Cost of Irredeemable Paper Money. *J. Polit. Econ.*, Part 1, June 1986, *94*(3), pp. 642–47.

Friedman, Milton and Schwartz, Anna J. Has Government Any Role in Money? *J. Monet. Econ.*, January 1986, *17*(1), pp. 37–62.

Garber, Peter M. Interwar Movements of Dollars to Europe and the U.S. Currency Supply. *J. Int. Money Finance,* Supp. March 1986, *5,* pp. S135–56. **[G: U.S.]**

Giovannini, Alberto. 'Rules of the Game' during the International Gold Standard: England and Germany. *J. Int. Money Finance,* December 1986, *5*(4), pp. 467–83. **[G: U.K.; W. Germany]**

Gray, Jo Anna. The Speculative Attack on the Peso and the Real Exchange Rate: Argentina, 1979–81: Comments. *J. Int. Money Finance,* Supp. March 1986, *5,* pp. S131–33.

Green, Steven L. The Abrogation of Gold Clauses in 1933 and Its Relation to Current Controversies in Monetary Economics. *Fed. Res. Bank Dallas Econ. Rev.*, July 1986, pp. 1–17. **[G: U.S.]**

Greenfield, Robert L. and Yeager, Leland B. Competitive Payments Systems: Comment. *Amer. Econ. Rev.*, September 1986, *76*(4), pp. 848–49.

Hicks, John R. The Abdication of Money. *Hong Kong Econ. Pap.*, 1986, (17), pp. 1–10. **[G: Global]**

Humphrey, Thomas M. Can the Central Bank Peg Real Interest Rates? A Survey of Classical and Neoclassical Opinion. **In** *Humphreys, T. M.*, 1986, *1983,* pp. 160–69.

Humphrey, Thomas M. The Early History of the Real/Nominal Interest Rate Relationship. **In** *Humphreys, T. M.*, 1986, *1983,* pp. 151–59.

Jaksch, Hans Jürgen. Simulaciones de políticas antiinflacionarias en Argentina, 1983/87. (Simulation of Anti-inflationary Policies in Argentina, 1983–87. With English summary.) *Económica (La Plata),* Jan.-June 1986, *32*(1), pp. 21–56. **[G: Argentina]**

Kane, Edward J. Politics and Fed Policymaking: The More Things Change the More They Remain the Same. **In** *Toma, E. F. and Toma, M., eds.*, 1986, *1980,* pp. 185–98. **[G: U.S.]**

Kantor, Brian S. The De Kock Commission Report: A Monetarist Perspective. *S. Afr. J. Econ.*, March 1986, *54*(1), pp. 94–107. **[G: S. Africa]**

Kapur, Basant K. Optimal Financial and Foreign-Exchange Liberalization of Less-developed Economies. **In** *Kapur, B. K.*, 1986, *1983,* pp. 92–122.

Kapur, Basant K. The Concepts of "Financial Repression" and "Financial Liberalization." **In** *Kapur, B. K.*, 1986, pp. xi–xviii.

Kopcke, Richard W. How Erratic Is Money Growth? *New Eng. Econ. Rev.*, May/June 1986, pp. 3–20. **[G: U.S.]**

Kwaczek, Adrienne S. and Kerr, William A. A Note on the Current Chinese Experience with Gresham's Law. *Econ. Notes,* 1986, (1), pp. 134–48. **[G: China]**

Laden, Ben E. The Implications of Budget Deficits [Deficits, Interest Rates, and Monetary Policy]. *Cato J.*, Winter 1986, *5*(3), pp. 727–31. **[G: U.S.]**

Lal, Deepak and van Wijnbergen, Sweder J. G. Government Deficits, the Real Interest Rate, and Developing Country Debt: On Global Crowding Out. **In** *Lal, D. and Wolf, M., eds.*, 1986, pp. 182–238. **[G: OECD]**

Lavoie, Marc. Minsky's Law or the Theorem of Systemic Financial Fragility. *Stud. Econ.*, 1986, *41*(29), pp. 3–28.

Ledesma, Rodolfo G. Testing the Information

Content of U.S. Monetary Components. *Atlantic Econ. J.*, March 1986, *14*(1), pp. 123. **[G: U.S.]**

Lehrman, Lewis E. Back to Gold: Giving Up the "Order of the Jungle." *Challenge*, Jan./Feb. 1986, *28*(6), pp. 21–30. **[G: U.S.]**

Lovell, Michael C. Tests of the Rational Expectations Hypothesis. *Amer. Econ. Rev.*, March 1986, *76*(1), pp. 110–24. **[G: U.S.]**

McCafferty, Stephen. Interwar Movements of Dollars to Europe and the U.S. Currency Supply: Comments. *J. Int. Money Finance*, Supp. March 1986, *5*, pp. S157–59. **[G: U.S.]**

McKinnon, Ronald I. Currency Substitution and Instability in the World Dollar Standard [Dollar Stabilization and American Monetary Policy]. **In** *Putnam, B. H. and Wilford, D. S., eds.*, 1986, *1980*, pp. 249–71. **[G: U.S.]**

Meltzer, Allan H. Monetary and Exchange Rate Regimes: A Comparison of Japan and the United States. *Cato J.*, Fall 1986, *6*(2), pp. 667–83. **[G: U.S.; Japan]**

Merrick, John J., Jr. and Saunders, Anthony. International Expected Real Interest Rates: New Tests of the Parity Hypothesis and U.S. Fiscal Policy Effects. *J. Monet. Econ.*, November 1986, *18*(3), pp. 313–22. **[G: OECD]**

Minsky, Hyman P. The Evolution of Financial Institutions and the Performance of the Economy. *J. Econ. Issues*, June 1986, *20*(2), pp. 345–53. **[G: U.S.]**

Mitchell, George W. It's the Old Time Religion, but Is It Good Enough Today? *J. Bank Res.*, 1986, *16*(4), pp. 258–60. **[G: U.S.]**

Molho, Lazaros E. Selective Credit Controls in Greece: A Test of Their Effectiveness. *Int. Monet. Fund Staff Pap.*, September 1986, *33*(3), pp. 477–508. **[G: Greece]**

Moore, Basil J. Inflation and Financial Deepening. *J. Devel. Econ.*, Jan.-Feb. 1986, *20*(1), pp. 125–33. **[G: S. Korea]**

Moore, Basil J. and Smit, B. W. Wages, Money and Inflation. *S. Afr. J. Econ.*, March 1986, *54*(1), pp. 80–93. **[G: S. Africa]**

Orden, David. Money and Agriculture: The Dynamics of Money–Financial Market–Agricultural Trade Linkages. *Agr. Econ. Res.*, Summer 1986, *38*(3), pp. 14–28. **[G: U.S.]**

Plane, Patrick. Politique monétaire et options sur le régime de change dans les pays utilisant le dollar comme monnaie nationale. (Monetary Policy and the Choice of a Foreign Exchange System in Countries Using the Dollar as Their National Currency. With English summary.) *Écon. Soc.*, February 1986, *20*(2), pp. 197–214. **[G: Liberia; Panama]**

Prescott, Edward C. Financial Structures as Communication Systems: Commentary. **In** *Lawrence, C. and Shay, R. P., eds.*, 1986, pp. 179–83.

Rockoff, Hugh. Institutional Requirements for Stable Free Banking. *Cato J.*, Fall 1986, *6*(2), pp. 617–34. **[G: U.S.]**

Rogers, C. The De Kock Report: A Critical Assessment of the Theoretical Issues. *S. Afr. J. Econ.*, March 1986, *54*(1), pp. 66–79. **[G: S. Africa]**

Rolnick, Arthur J. and Weber, Warren E. Gresham's Law or Gresham's Fallacy? *Fed. Res. Bank Minn. Rev.*, Winter 1986, *10*(1), pp. 17–24. **[G: U.S.]**

Rolnick, Arthur J. and Weber, Warren E. Gresham's Law or Gresham's Fallacy? *J. Polit. Econ.*, February 1986, *94*(1), pp. 185–99. **[G: U.S.]**

Rosende R., Francisco. Institucionalidad financiera y estabilidad económica. (With English summary.) *Cuadernos Econ.*, April 1986, *23*(68), pp. 77–99. **[G: Argentina; Chile]**

Sargent, Thomas J. Financial Structures as Communication Systems. **In** *Lawrence, C. and Shay, R. P., eds.*, 1986, pp. 184–88.

Servet, J.-Michel. Pièces, billets et monnaies primitives. (Coins, Notes and Primitive Money. With English summary.) *Écon. Soc.*, February 1986, *20*(2), pp. 7–18.

Sprinkel, Beryl W. Monetary Policy and the Business Cycle. *Cato J.*, Fall 1986, *6*(2), pp. 365–67.

Svindland, Eirik. Über Konjunturpronosen auf der Grundlage einer monetären Schätzgleichung. Ein Fallsudie. (On Trade Cycle Forecasts Based on a Monetary Estimating Equation. With English summary.) *Kredit Kapital*, 1986, *19*(1), pp. 25–57.

Timberlake, Richard H., Jr. The Feasibility of Free Banking Institutions. *Cato J.*, Fall 1986, *6*(2), pp. 635–39.

Townsend, Robert M. Financial Structures as Communication Systems. **In** *Lawrence, C. and Shay, R. P., eds.*, 1986, pp. 163–78.

Wenninger, John. Responsiveness of Interest Rate Spreads and Deposit Flows to Changes in Market Rates. *Fed. Res. Bank New York Quart. Rev.*, Autumn 1986, *11*(3), pp. 1–10. **[G: U.S.]**

Wenninger, John and Radecki, Lawrence J. Financial Transactions and the Demand for M1. *Fed. Res. Bank New York Quart. Rev.*, Summer 1986, *11*(2), pp. 24–29. **[G: U.S.]**

White, Lawrence H. Competitive Payments Systems: Reply. *Amer. Econ. Rev.*, September 1986, *76*(4), pp. 850–53.

3112 Monetary Theory; Empirical Studies Illustrating Theory

Adolph, Brigitte. Die Existenz einer wirksamen Geldpolitik bei rationalen Erwartungen und starren Güterpreisen. (The Existence of an Effective Monetary Policy under Rational Expectations and Rigid Goods Prices. With English summary.) *Kredit Kapital*, 1986, *19*(3), pp. 340–50.

Aizenman, Joshua and Frenkel, Jacob A. Supply Shocks, Wage Indexation and Monetary Accommodation. *J. Money, Credit, Banking*, August 1986, *18*(3), pp. 304–22.

Aizenman, Joshua and Frenkel, Jacob A. Wage Indexation, Supply Shocks, and Monetary Policy in a Small, Open Economy. **In** *Edwards,*

S. and Ahamed, L., eds., 1986, pp. 89–131.

Akashi, Shigeo and Asada, Toichiro. Money in Kaldorian Cycle Theory. *Econ. Rev. (Keizai Kenkyu),* April 1986, *37*(2), pp. 169–77.

Akhand, Hafiz and Milbourne, Ross. Credit Cards and Aggregate Money Demand. *J. Macroecon.*, Fall 1986, *8*(4), pp. 471–78.

Akhtar, M. A. Some Common Misconceptions about the Monetary Approach to International Adjustment. **In** *Putnam, B. H. and Wilford, D. S., eds.*, 1986, *1978*, pp. 107–19.

Allen, Larry and Price, Don. The Short-run Impact of Monetary and Fiscal Policy in a Two Sector Keynesian Model. *Amer. Econ.*, Spring 1986, *30*(1), pp. 40–50.

Allsbrook, Ogden O., Jr. Rational Expectations and Crowding-Out. *Kredit Kapital,* 1986, *19*(2), pp. 248–51.

Allsbrook, Ogden O., Jr. Real Velocity and Crowding-In. *S. Afr. J. Econ.*, June 1986, *54*(2), pp. 222–25.

Amsler, Christine E. The Fisher Effect: Sometimes Inverted, Sometimes Not? [Fisher's Paradox and the Theory of Interest]. *Southern Econ. J.*, January 1986, *52*(3), pp. 832–35.

Anderlini, Luca. Competitive Banking in a Simple Model. **In** *Edwards, J., et al., eds.*, 1986, pp. 144–77.

Andersen, Leonall C. and Carlson, Keith M. A Monetarist Model for Economic Stabilization. *Fed. Res. Bank St. Louis Rev.*, October 1986, *68*(8), pp. 45–66. **[G: U.S.]**

Andersen, Leonall C. and Jordan, Jerry L. Monetary and Fiscal Actions: A Test of Their Relative Importance in Economic Stabilization. *Fed. Res. Bank St. Louis Rev.*, October 1986, *68*(8), pp. 29–44. **[G: U.S.]**

Andersen, Torben M. Differential Information and the Role for an Active Stabilization Policy. *Economica,* August 1986, *53*(211), pp. 321–38.

Andersen, Torben M. Pre-set Prices, Differential Information and Monetary Policy. *Oxford Econ. Pap.*, November 1986, *38*(3), pp. 456–80.

Andersen, Torben M. Rules versus Discretion in Monetary Policy: The Case of Asymmetric Information. *J. Econ. Dynam. Control,* June 1986, *10*(1/2), pp. 169–74.

Anderson, William A. Payments Indivisibilities and the Demand for Money: Some Empirical Evidence. *Atlantic Econ. J.*, September 1986, *14*(3), pp. 45–50. **[G: U.S.]**

Aoki, Masanao. Effects of Anticipated Central Bank Actions on Tobin's *Q*, Share Prices and Economy Rate in a Small Open Economy. *Europ. Econ. Rev.*, April 1986, *30*(2), pp. 285–304.

Aoki, Masanao. Effects of Anticipated Real Supply Shocks and Coordinated Monetary Accommodation. *Econ. Stud. Quart.*, June 1986, *37*(2), pp. 134–50.

Artus, Patrick. Crises de balance des paiements, politique monétaire, controle des changes. (Balance of Payment Crisis, Monetary Policy and Capital Control. With English summary.) *Revue Écon.*, July 1986, *37*(4), pp. 637–58.

Arvan, Lanny and Brueckner, Jan K. Efficient Contracts in Credit Markets Subject to Interest Rate Risk: An Application of Raviv's Insurance Model. *Amer. Econ. Rev.*, March 1986, *76*(1), pp. 259–63.

Asimakopulos, Athanasios. Finance, Liquidity, Saving, and Investment. *J. Post Keynesian Econ.*, Fall 1986, *9*(1), pp. 79–90.

Askari, Mostafa. A Non-nested Test of the New Classical Neutrality Proposition for Canada. *Appl. Econ.*, December 1986, *18*(12), pp. 1349–57. **[G: Canada]**

Auld, Douglas. A Note on the Price Effects of Indirect Taxes. *Econ. Notes,* 1986, (2), pp. 152–57.

d'Autume, Antoine. Les anticipations rationnelles dans l'analyse macro-Économique. (Rational Expectations and Macroeconomic Analysis. With English summary.) *Revue Écon.*, March 1986, *37*(2), pp. 243–83. **[G: U.S.]**

Barnett, William A.; Hinich, Melvin J. and Weber, Warren E. The Regulatory Wedge between the Demand-Side and Supply-Side Aggregation-Theoretic Monetary Aggregates. *J. Econometrics,* Oct./Nov. 1986, *33*(1/2), pp. 165–85. **[G: U.S.]**

Barrère, Alain. Price System and Money-Wage System. *J. Post Keynesian Econ.*, Winter 1985-86, *8*(2), pp. 315–35.

Barro, Robert J. Recent Developments in the Theory of Rules versus Discretion. *Econ. J.*, Supplement 1986, *96,* pp. 23–37.

Barro, Robert J. Reputation in a Model of Monetary Policy with Incomplete Information. *J. Monet. Econ.*, January 1986, *17*(1), pp. 3–20.

Barro, Robert J. Rules versus Discretion. **In** *Campbell, C. D. and Dougan, W. R., eds.*, 1986, pp. 16–30.

Barth, James R.; Russek, Frank S. and Wang, George H. K. A Time Series Analysis of the Relationship between the Capital Stock and Federal Debt: A Comment. *J. Money, Credit, Banking,* November 1986, *18*(4), pp. 527–38. **[G: U.S.]**

Barthold, Thomas A. and Dougan, William R. The Fisher Hypothesis under Different Monetary Regimes. *Rev. Econ. Statist.*, November 1986, *68*(4), pp. 674–79. **[G: U.S.]**

Başar, Tamer; Turnovsky, Stephen J. and d'Orey, Vasco. Optimal Strategic Monetary Policies in Dynamic Interdependent Economies. **In** *Başar, T., ed.*, 1986, pp. 134–78. **[G: U.S.]**

Başar, Tamer; Turnovsky, Stephen J. and d'Orey, Vasco. Optimal Strategic Monetary Policies in Dynamic Interdependent Economies: A Summary Paper. *J. Econ. Dynam. Control,* June 1986, *10*(1/2), pp. 15–19.

Batten, Dallas S. and Thornton, Daniel L. The Monetary–Fiscal Policy Debate and the Andersen–Jordan Equation. *Fed. Res. Bank St. Louis Rev.*, October 1986, *68*(8), pp. 9–17. **[G: U.S.]**

Baye, Michael R. and Cosimano, Thomas F. Erratic Monetary Policy and the Dispersion of Commodity Prices. *J. Macroecon.*, Spring

1986, *8*(2), pp. 201–12.

Beladi, Hamid; Biswas, Basudeb and Tribedy, Gopal. Growth of Income and the Balance of Payments: Keynesian and Monetary Theories. *J. Econ. Stud.*, 1986, *13*(4), pp. 44–55.

Benninga, Simon and Protopapadakis, Aris A. General Equilibrium Properties of the Term Structure of Interest Rates. *J. Finan. Econ.*, July 1986, *16*(3), pp. 389–410.

Bernanke, Ben S. Alternative Explanations of the Money–Income Correlation. *Carnegie-Rochester Conf. Ser. Public Policy*, Autumn 1986, *25*, pp. 49–99. **[G: U.S.]**

Biswas, Basudeb and Saunders, Peter J. Money-Income Casuality: Further Empirical Evidence. *Atlantic Econ. J.*, December 1986, *14*(4), pp. 65–75. **[G: U.S.]**

Blanchard, Olivier J. and Summers, Lawrence H. Pourquoi les taux d'intérêts sont-ils aussi élevés. (Perspectives on High World Real Interest Rates. With English summary.) *Ann. Écon. Statist.*, July-Sept. 1986, (3), pp. 53–100. **[G: OECD]**

Blejer, Mario I. and Díaz, José Gil. Domestic and External Factors in the Determination of the Real Interest Rate: The Case of Uruguay. *Econ. Develop. Cult. Change*, April 1986, *34*(3), pp. 589–606. **[G: Uruguay]**

Boinet, Thierry. La liaison taux d'intérêt-taux d'inflation. Une analyse historique de longue période. (The Interest–Inflation Rates Relationship: A Long Term Historical Analysis. With English summary.) *Écon. Soc.*, June 1986, *20*(6), pp. 101–45. **[G: France]**

de Boissieu, Christian. Quelques réflexions sur l'analyse économique des innovations financières. (Some Reflections on the Economics Analysis of Financial Innovation. With English summary.) *Écon. Appl.*, 1986, *39*(3), pp. 449–72.

Bordo, Michael D. Explorations in Monetary History: A Survey of the Literature. *Exploration Econ. Hist.*, October 1986, *23*(4), pp. 339–415. **[G: OECD]**

Bordo, Michael D. Financial Crises, Banking Crises, Stock Market Crashes and the Money Supply: Some International Evidence, 1870–1933. **In** *Capie, F. and Wood, G. E., eds.*, 1986, pp. 190–248.

Bordo, Michael D. Money, Deflation and Seigniorage in the Fifteenth Century: A Review Essay. *J. Monet. Econ.*, November 1986, *18*(3), pp. 337–46.

Boschen, John F. The Information Content of Indexed Bonds. *J. Money, Credit, Banking*, February 1986, *18*(1), pp. 76–87.

Boyd, John H. and Prescott, Edward C. Financial Intermediary-Coalitions. *J. Econ. Theory*, April 1986, *38*(2), pp. 211–32.

Bradley, Michael D. Government Spending or Deficit Financing: Which Causes Crowding Out? *J. Econ. Bus.*, August 1986, *38*(3), pp. 203–14. **[G: U.S.]**

Branson, William H. The Limits of Monetary Coordination as Exchange Rate Policy. *Brookings Pap. Econ. Act.*, 1986, (1), pp. 175–94. **[G: U.S.]**

Breeden, Douglas T. Consumption, Production, Inflation and Interest Rates: A Synthesis. *J. Finan. Econ.*, May 1986, *16*(1), pp. 3–39.

Broll, Udo and Gilroy, Michael B. Collateral in Banking Policy and Adverse Selection. *Manchester Sch. Econ. Soc. Stud.*, December 1986, *54*(4), pp. 357–66.

Browne, F. X. Loan Market Price and Quantity Effects in a Production Smoothing Model of Inventory Investment. *Appl. Econ.*, June 1986, *18*(6), pp. 691–707. **[G: Ireland]**

Browne, F. X. Multilateral Currency Substitution and Capital Flows as Sources of Instability in the Soe Demand for Money Function—A Case Study. *Empirical Econ.*, 1986, *11*(3), pp. 181–96. **[G: Ireland]**

Burkett, Paul. Dillard on Keynes and Marx: Comment. *J. Post Keynesian Econ.*, Summer 1986, *8*(4), pp. 623–31.

Burkett, Paul. Interest Rate Restrictions and Deposit Opportunities for Small Savers in Developing Countries: An Analytical View. *J. Devel. Stud.*, October 1986, *23*(1), pp. 77–92. **[G: LDCs]**

Caffè, Federico. Hyperinflation and the Quantity Theory of Money: A Historical View. *Rev. Econ. Cond. Italy*, Sept.-Dec. 1986, (3), pp. 417–23.

Cagan, Phillip. Competitive Monies: Some Unanswered Questions [Currency Competition versus Governmental Money Monopolies]. *Cato J.*, Winter 1986, *5*(3), pp. 943–47.

Cagan, Phillip. Regulation and the Monetary Economy. **In** *Lawrence, C. and Shay, R. P., eds.*, 1986, pp. 196–200. **[G: U.S.]**

Cagan, Phillip. The Conflict between Short-run and Long-run Objectives. **In** *Campbell, C. D. and Dougan, W. R., eds.*, 1986, pp. 31–37.

Calliari, S.; Carraro, Carlo and Sartore, D. Intermediate Targets and Instruments of Monetary Policy. *J. Econ. Dynam. Control*, June 1986, *10*(1/2), pp. 175–84.

Campbell, Colin D. and Dougan, William R. Alternative Monetary Regimes: Introduction. **In** *Campbell, C. D. and Dougan, W. R., eds.*, 1986, pp. 1–15.

Cantor, Richard. A Macroeconomic Model with Auction Markets and Nominal Contracts. *Amer. Econ. Rev.*, March 1986, *76*(1), pp. 204–11.

Carlson, Keith M. A Monetarist Model for Economic Stabilization: Review and Update. *Fed. Res. Bank St. Louis Rev.*, October 1986, *68*(8), pp. 18–28. **[G: U.S.]**

Carraro, Carlo. Teoria dei giochi e il problema della coordinazione tra politica monetaria e fiscale. (Game Theory and the Coordination of Monetary and Fiscal Policy. With English summary.) *Ricerche Econ.*, Apr.-Sept. 1986, *40*(2–3), pp. 377–99.

Cecchetti, Stephen G. Testing Short-run Neutrality. *J. Monet. Econ.*, May 1986, *17*(3), pp. 409–23. **[G: U.S.]**

Chant, John F. and Acheson, Keith. The Choice

of Monetary Instruments and the Theory of Bureaucracy. **In** *Toma, E. F. and Toma, M., eds.*, 1986, *1972*, pp. 107–28. **[G: Canada]**

Chappell, David. The Optimal Rate of Inflation When the Rate of Growth of the Money Supply Is Stochastic. *Manchester Sch. Econ. Soc. Stud.*, September 1986, *54*(3), pp. 314–21.

Chiarella, Carl. Perfect Foresight Models and the Dynamic Instability Problem from a Higher Viewpoint. *Econ. Modelling*, October 1986, *3*(4), pp. 283–92.

Chick, Victoria. The Evolution of the Banking System and the Theory of Saving, Investment and Interest. *Écon. Soc.*, Aug.-Sept. 1986, *20*(8–9), pp. 111–26.

Cho, Yoon Je. Inefficiencies from Financial Liberalization in the Absence of Well-Functioning Equity Markets. *J. Money, Credit, Banking*, May 1986, *18*(2), pp. 191–99.

Chowdhury, Abdur R. A Note on the Dominant Influence of Fiscal Actions. *Eastern Econ. J.*, Jan.-Mar. 1986, *12*(1), pp. 61–62. **[G: India]**

Chowdhury, Abdur R. A Note on the Relative Impact of Monetary and Fiscal Actions in India. *Indian Econ. J.*, July-Sept. 1986, *34*(1), pp. 89–93. **[G: India]**

Chowdhury, Abdur R. Monetary and Fiscal Impacts on Economic Activities in Bangladesh: A Note. *Bangladesh Devel. Stud.*, March 1986, *14*(1), pp. 101–06. **[G: Bangladesh]**

Chowdhury, Abdur R.; Fackler, James S. and McMillin, W. Douglas. Monetary Policy, Fiscal Policy, and Investment Spending: An Empirical Analysis. *Southern Econ. J.*, January 1986, *52*(3), pp. 794–806. **[G: U.S.]**

Christ, Carl F. Accuracy of Forecasting as a Measure of Economic Uncertainty. **In** *Campbell, C. D. and Dougan, W. R., eds.*, 1986, pp. 154–60. **[G: U.S.]**

Cirillo, Renato. Leon Walras' Theory of Money. *Amer. J. Econ. Soc.*, April 1986, *45*(2), pp. 215–21.

Clower, Robert W. and Friedman, Daniel. Trade Specialists and Money in an Ongoing Exchange Economy. **In** *Day, R. H. and Eliasson, G., eds.*, 1986, pp. 115–29.

Colangelo, Giuseppe. Alcune riflessioni sulla questione dell'indeterminazione del livello dei prezzi nel caso di una politica del tasso d'interesse nei modelli con aspettative razionali. (Some Reflections on the Price Level Indeterminacy under an Interest Rate Policy Rule in Models with Rational Expectations. With English summary.) *Giorn. Econ.*, Jan.-Feb. 1986, *45*(1–2), pp. 79–89.

Coleman, James S. Political Money. **In** *Coleman, J. S.*, 1986, *1970*, pp. 163–91.

Colletaz, Gilbert. Prévisions explicites de taux d'intérêt en France: une étude empirique sur la période 1981–1985. (Explicit Forecasting of Interest Rates in France: An Empirical Study over the Period 1981–1985. With English summary.) *Finance*, December 1986, *7*(2), pp. 111–34. **[G: France]**

Cooley, Thomas F. and LeRoy, Stephen F. What Will Take the Con Out of Econometrics? A Reply [Identification and Estimation of Money Demand]. *Amer. Econ. Rev.*, June 1986, *76*(3), pp. 504–07. **[G: U.S.]**

Cornell, Bradford and French, Kenneth R. Commodity Own Rates, Real Interest Rates, and Money Supply Announcements. *J. Monet. Econ.*, July 1986, *18*(1), pp. 3–20. **[G: U.S.]**

Corrado, Charles J. and Taylor, Dean. The Cost of a Central Bank Leaning against a Random Walk. *J. Int. Money Finance*, September 1986, *5*(3), pp. 303–14.

Cottrell, Allin F. The Endogeneity of Money and Money–Income Causality. *Scot. J. Polit. Econ.*, February 1986, *33*(1), pp. 2–27.

Cover, James Peery. A Note on the Empirical Evidence for the Role of Credit in Macroeconomic Policy and Analysis. *Southern Econ. J.*, April 1986, *52*(4), pp. 1145–50.

Cramer, J. S. The Volume of Transactions and the Circulation of Money in the United States, 1950–1979. *J. Bus. Econ. Statist.*, April 1986, *4*(2), pp. 225–32. **[G: U.S.]**

Cuddington, John T. and Viñals, José M. Budget Deficits and the Current Account in the Presence of Classical Unemployment. *Econ. J.*, March 1986, *96*(381), pp. 101–19.

Cukierman, Alex. Central Bank Behavior and Credibility: Some Recent Theoretical Developments. *Fed. Res. Bank St. Louis Rev.*, May 1986, *68*(5), pp. 5–17.

Cukierman, Alex and Meltzer, Allan H. A Theory of Ambiguity, Credibility, and Inflation under Discretion and Asymmetric Information. *Econometrica*, September 1986, *54*(5), pp. 1099–1128.

Culbertson, W. Patton, Jr. and Koray, Faik. Interest Rates, the Forward Premium, and Unanticipated Money. *Southern Econ. J.*, October 1986, *53*(2), pp. 393–99. **[G: U.S.]**

Cumby, Robert E. and Mishkin, Frederic S. The International Linkage of Real Interest Rates: The European–U.S. Connection. *J. Int. Money Finance*, March 1986, *5*(1), pp. 5–23. **[G: OECD]**

Cuthbertson, Keith. Monetary Anticipations and the Demand for Money: Some UK Evidence. *Bull. Econ. Res.*, September 1986, *38*(3), pp. 257–70. **[G: U.K.]**

Cuthbertson, Keith. Price Expectations and Lags in the Demand for Money. *Scot. J. Polit. Econ.*, November 1986, *33*(4), pp. 334–54. **[G: Australia]**

Cuthbertson, Keith and Taylor, Mark P. Monetary Anticipation and the Demand for Money in the U.K.: Testing Rationality in the Shock-Absorber Hypothesis. *J. Appl. Econometrics*, October 1986, *1*(4), pp. 355–65. **[G: U.K.]**

Daniel, Betty C. Monetary Aggregate versus Interest Rate Rules. *J. Macroecon.*, Winter 1986, *8*(1), pp. 75–86.

Daniel, Betty C. The Transactions Demand for Money in a Two-Currency Economy: A Note. *J. Monet. Econ.*, July 1986, *18*(1), pp. 91–94.

Darby, Michael R. Optimal Monetary Institutions and Policy: Comments. **In** *Campbell, C. D.*

and Dougan, W. R., eds., 1986, pp. 244–47. **[G: U.S.]**

Darrat, Ali F. Money, Inflation, and Causality in the North African Countries: An Empirical Investigation. *J. Macroecon.*, Winter 1986, *8*(1), pp. 87–103. **[G: Morocco; Libya; Tunisia]**

Darrat, Ali F. and Webb, Michael A. Financial Changes and Interest Elasticity of Money Demand: Further Tests of the Gurley and Shaw Thesis. *J. Devel. Stud.*, July 1986, *22*(4), pp. 724–30. **[G: U.S.]**

Davidson, Paul. Finance, Funding, Saving, and Investment. *J. Post Keynesian Econ.*, Fall 1986, *9*(1), pp. 101–10.

Day, Richard H. Trade Specialists and Money in an Ongoing Exchange Economy: Comment. In *Day, R. H. and Eliasson, G., eds.*, 1986, pp. 130–31.

Day, Theodore E. Information, Production, and the Term Structure. *J. Polit. Econ.*, February 1986, *94*(1), pp. 167–84.

De Fraja, Giovanni. Il tasso reale di interesse in presenza di inflazione perfettamente prevista. (The Real Rate of Interest with Perfectly Expected Inflation. With English summary.) *Econ. Polít.*, April 1986, *3*(1), pp. 39–60.

Debroy, B. Patinkin's Neutral Shift in Liquidity Preference: A Second Note. *Indian Econ. J.*, July-Sept. 1986, *34*(1), pp. 94–97.

Dermine, J. Deposit Rates, Credit Rates and Bank Capital: The Klein–Monti Model Revisited. *J. Banking Finance,* March 1986, *10*(1), pp. 99–114.

Dewald, William G. Government Deficits in a Generalized Fisherian Credit Market: Theory with an Application to Indexing Interest Taxation. *Int. Monet. Fund Staff Pap.*, June 1986, *33*(2), pp. 243–75.

Dillard, Dudley. Dillard on Keynes and Marx: Rejoinder. *J. Post Keynesian Econ.*, Summer 1986, *8*(4), pp. 632–37.

Dimand, Robert W. The Macroeconomics of the *Treatise on Money*. *Eastern Econ. J.*, Oct.-Dec. 1986, *12*(4), pp. 431–50.

Dornbusch, Rudiger. Equilibrium and Disequilibrium Exchange Rates. In *Dornbusch, R.*, 1986, *1982*, pp. 31–57.

Dornbusch, Rudiger. Flexible Exchange Rates and Excess Capital Mobility. *Brookings Pap. Econ. Act.*, 1986, (1), pp. 209–26. **[G: U.S.]**

Dornbusch, Rudiger. Money, Interest Rates and Stabilization. *Rev. Econ. Cond. Italy*, Sept.-Dec. 1986, (3), pp. 439–53. **[G: W. Germany]**

Dornbusch, Rudiger and Fischer, Stanley. Stopping Hyperinflations Past and Present. *Weltwirtsch. Arch.*, 1986, *122*(1), pp. 1–47. **[G: Europe; Israel; Argentina]**

Dos Santos Ferreira, Rodolphe. Is a Wider Choice Conducive to Stability? A Comment [Money, National Debt, and Economic Growth]. *J. Econ. Theory*, August 1986, *39*(2), pp. 457–63.

Dotsey, Michael. Japanese Monetary Policy, a Comparative Analysis. *Fed. Res. Bank Richmond Econ. Rev.*, Nov./Dec. 1986, *72*(6), pp. 12–24. **[G: Japan; U.S.]**

Dotsey, Michael. Wealth Effects of Open Market Operations and Optimal Monetary Policy. *J. Monet. Econ.*, March 1986, *17*(2), pp. 225–38.

Dotsey, Michael and King, Robert G. Informational Implications of Interest Rate Rules. *Amer. Econ. Rev.*, March 1986, *76*(1), pp. 33–42.

Doukas, John and Melhem, Melhem. The Reaction of Spot and Forward Rates to New Information. *Europ. Econ. Rev.*, April 1986, *30*(2), pp. 305–24. **[G: U.S.; Canada]**

Dow, Sheila C. Speculation and the Monetary Circuit with Particular Attention to the Eurocurrency Market. *Écon. Soc.*, Aug.-Sept. 1986, *20*(8–9), pp. 95–109.

Driscoll, Michael, et al. Testing for Monetary Policy Effectiveness in Austria: Reply. *Empirica*, 1986, *13*(1), pp. 105–08. **[G: Austria]**

Duck, Nigel W. The Influence of Lagged Unanticipated Money on Real Variables: A Simple Illustrative Model. *J. Macroecon.*, Spring 1986, *8*(2), pp. 183–92.

Dufour, Jean-Marie. Recursive Stability Analysis: The Demand for Money during the German Hyperinflation. In *Belsley, D. A. and Kuh, E., eds.*, 1986, pp. 18–61. **[G: Germany]**

Dutkowsky, Donald H. and Atesoglu, H. Sonmez. Unanticipated Money Growth and Unemployment: Post-Sample Forecasts. *Southern Econ. J.*, October 1986, *53*(2), pp. 413–21. **[G: U.S.]**

Dwyer, Gerald P., Jr. and Saving, Thomas R. Government Revenue from Money Creation with Government and Private Money. *J. Monet. Econ.*, March 1986, *17*(2), pp. 239–49.

Eden, Benjamin. Trading Uncertainty and the Cash-in-Advance Constraint. *J. Monet. Econ.*, November 1986, *18*(3), pp. 285–93.

El-Sheikh, S. A Time Series Analysis of Financial Asset Holdings for a Developing Country: Egypt, 1952–1973. *Empirical Econ.*, 1986, *11*(3), pp. 125–51. **[G: Egypt]**

Engel, Charles M. On the Correlation of Exchange Rates and Interest Rates. *J. Int. Money Finance*, March 1986, *5*(1), pp. 125–28.

Evans, David J. UK Companies' Demand for Money: An Empirical Study, 1974–1983. *J. Econ. Stud.*, 1986, *13*(4), pp. 30–43. **[G: U.K.]**

Evans, Paul. Does the Potency of Monetary Policy Vary with Capacity Utilization? *Carnegie-Rochester Conf. Ser. Public Policy*, Spring 1986, *24*, pp. 303–31. **[G: U.S.]**

Falk, Barry. Unanticipated Money-Supply Growth and Single-Family Housing Starts in the U.S.: 1964–1983. *Housing Finance Rev.*, Summer 1986, *5*(1), pp. 15–23. **[G: U.S.]**

Fasano-Filho, Ugo. Currency Substitution and the Demand for Money: The Argentine Case, 1960–1976. *Weltwirtsch. Arch.*, 1986, *122*(2), pp. 327–39. **[G: Argentina]**

Fayyad, Salam K. A Microeconomic System-Wide Approach to the Estimation of the Demand for Money. *Fed. Res. Bank St. Louis*

Rev., Aug./Sept. 1986, *68*(7), pp. 22–33. **[G: U.S.]**

Feenstra, Robert C. Functional Equivalence between Liquidity Costs and the Utility of Money. *J. Monet. Econ.*, March 1986, *17*(2), pp. 271–91.

Fender, John. Monetary and Exchange Rate Policies in an Open Macroeconomic Model with Unemployment and Rational Expectations. *Oxford Econ. Pap.*, November 1986, *38*(3), pp. 501–15.

Ferris, Stephen P. and Kumar, Raman. A Time Series Analysis of Real Interest Rates. *Indian Econ. J.*, July-Sept. 1986, *34*(1), pp. 79–88. **[G: India]**

Ferris, Stephen P. and Kumar, Raman. Evidence Regarding the Non-stationarity of Real Interest Rates. *Rivista Int. Sci. Econ. Com.*, Oct.-Nov. 1986, *33*(10–11), pp. 957–67. **[G: U.S.]**

Fforde, John Standish. Walter Bagehot and the Theory of Central Banking: Comment. **In** *Capie, F. and Wood, G. E., eds.*, 1986, pp. 185–89.

Fischer, Bernhard and Langhammer, Rolf J. Determinanten der Sparkapitalbildung in Entwicklungsländern. (Determinants of Savings Mobilization in Developing Countries. With English summary.) *Konjunkturpolitik*, 1986, *32*(5), pp. 282–307. **[G: LDCs]**

Fischer, Stanley. Contracts, Credibility, and Disinflation. **In** *Fischer, S.*, 1986, *1985*, pp. 221–45. **[G: U.S.]**

Fischer, Stanley. Exchange Rate versus Money Targets in Disinflation. **In** *Fischer, S.*, 1986, pp. 247–62.

Fischer, Stanley. Friedman versus Hayek on Private Money: Review Essay. *J. Monet. Econ.*, May 1986, *17*(3), pp. 433–39.

Fischer, Stanley. Indexing and Inflation. **In** *Fischer, S.*, 1986, *1983*, pp. 193–219. **[G: Selected Countries]**

Fischer, Stanley. Long-term Contracts, Rational Expectations, and the Optimal Money Supply Rule. **In** *Fischer, S.*, 1986, *1977*, pp. 365–81.

Fischer, Stanley. Meltzer on Uncertainty under Different Monetary Regimes. **In** *Campbell, C. D. and Dougan, W. R., eds.*, 1986, pp. 161–67. **[G: U.S.]**

Fischer, Stanley. Monetary Rules and Commodity Money Schemes under Uncertainty. *J. Monet. Econ.*, January 1986, *17*(1), pp. 21–35.

Fischer, Stanley. On Activist Monetary Policy with Rational Expectations. **In** *Fischer, S.*, 1986, *1980*, pp. 383–412. **[G: U.S.]**

Fischer, Stanley. Seigniorage and the Case for a National Money. **In** *Fischer, S.*, 1986, *1982*, pp. 431–52.

Fischer, Stanley. Toward an Understanding of the Costs of Inflation: II. **In** *Fischer, S.*, 1986, *1983*, pp. 35–69. **[G: U.S.]**

Fischer, Stanley. Wage Indexation, Supply Shocks, and Monetary Policy in a Small, Open Economy: Comment. **In** *Edwards, S. and Ahamed, L., eds.*, 1986, pp. 132–39.

Fischer, Stanley. Welfare Aspects of Government Issue of Indexed Bonds. **In** *Fischer, S.*, 1986, *1983*, pp. 333–55.

Flaig, Gebhard. Staatsverschuldung und langfristiger Zinssatz in einem Modell effizienter Märkte und rationaler Erwartungen. Eine empirische Untersuchung für die Bundesrepublik Deutschland. (Public Debt and Long-term Interest Rate in a Model of Efficient Markets and Rational Expectations. An Empirical Study for the Federal Republic of Germany. With English summary.) *Kredit Kapital*, 1986, *19*(3), pp. 366–85. **[G: W. Germany]**

Flemming, John S. Implications for Monetary Policy: Comments. **In** *Suzuki, Y. and Yomo, H., eds.*, 1986, pp. 287–90. **[G: U.S.; U.K.]**

Ford, Alec G. Financial Crises, Banking Crises, Stock Market Crashes and the Money Supply: Some International Evidence, 1870–1933: Comment. **In** *Capie, F. and Wood, G. E., eds.*, 1986, pp. 249–53.

Foster, Gladys Parker. The Endogeneity of Money and Keynes's *General Theory. J. Econ. Issues*, December 1986, *20*(4), pp. 953–68.

Frankel, Jeffrey A. Expectations and Commodity Price Dynamics: The Overshooting Model. *Amer. J. Agr. Econ.*, May 1986, *68*(2), pp. 344–48.

Freeman, Scott. Inside Money, Monetary Contractions, and Welfare. *Can. J. Econ.*, February 1986, *19*(1), pp. 87–98.

Fremling, Gertrud Margareta. A Specie-Flow Model of the Gold Standard. *J. Int. Money Finance*, March 1986, *5*(1), pp. 37–55.

Frenkel, Jacob A. and Razin, Assaf. Real Exchange Rates, Interest Rates and Fiscal Policies. *Econ. Stud. Quart.*, June 1986, *37*(2), pp. 99–113. **[G: U.S.; Japan; Europe]**

Friedman, Benjamin M. Implications of Government Deficits for Interest Rates, Equity Returns, and Corporate Financing. **In** *Friedman, B. M., ed.*, 1986, pp. 67–89. **[G: U.S.]**

Friedman, Benjamin M. Money, Credit, and Interest Rates in the Business Cycle. **In** *Gordon, R. J., ed.*, 1986, pp. 395–438. **[G: U.S.]**

Friedman, Benjamin M. Money, Credit, and Interest Rates in the Business Cycle: Reply. **In** *Gordon, R. J., ed.*, 1986, pp. 450–55. **[G: U.S.]**

Friedman, Milton. Monetary Policy in a Fiat World. **In** *Suzuki, Y. and Yomo, H., eds.*, 1986, pp. 21–29.

Friedman, Milton. Monetary Policy: Theory and Practice. **In** *Toma, E. F. and Toma, M., eds.*, 1986, *1982*, pp. 11–35. **[G: U.S.]**

Friedman, Milton. Monetary Trends in the United States and the United Kingdom. **In** *Szenberg, M., ed.*, 1986, *1972*, pp. 33–46. **[G: U.S.; U.K.]**

Fumagalli, Andrea. Elementi per la costruzione di uno schema monetario di circuito economico. (With English summary.) *Stud. Econ.*, 1986, *41*(29), pp. 53–98.

Gagey, Frédéric; Laroque, Guy and Lollivier, Stefan. Monetary and Fiscal Policies in a General Equilibrium Model. *J. Econ. Theory*, August 1986, *39*(2), pp. 329–57.

Gallagher, Martin. The Inverted Fisher Hypothesis: Additional Evidence [Fisher's Paradox and the Theory of Interest]. *Amer. Econ. Rev.*, March 1986, *76*(1), pp. 247–49.

Gardner, Grant W. Currency Substitution, Money Growth Rules, and the Interdependence of Monetary Policy. *J. Econ. Bus.*, May 1986, *38*(2), pp. 165–72.

Garofalo, Giuseppe. Interdipendenza e processi causali nell'analisi monetaria. (With English summary.) *Stud. Econ.*, 1986, *41*(28), pp. 101–40.

Gedeon, Shirley J. The Post Keynesian Theory of Money: Summary and an Eastern European Example. *J. Post Keynesian Econ.*, Winter 1985-86, *8*(2), pp. 208–21. **[G: Yugoslavia]**

Gedeon, Shirley J. and Flaherty, Diane P. Yugoslav Monetary Theory and Its Implications for Self-management. **In** *Altmann, F.-L., ed.*, 1986, pp. 82–100. **[G: Yugoslavia]**

Geisler, Klaus-Dieter. Zur "Kausalität" von Geldmenge und Sozialprodukt. (On the "Causality" of Money Supply and National Product. With English summary.) *Kredit Kapital*, 1986, *19*(3), pp. 325–39. **[G: W. Germany]**

Gerdes, William D. Mr. Fisher and the Classics. *Amer. Econ.*, Spring 1986, *30*(1), pp. 66–72.

Geweke, John. The Superneutrality of Money in the United States: An Interpretation of the Evidence. *Econometrica*, January 1986, *54*(1), pp. 1–21. **[G: U.S.]**

Giaccotto, Carmelo. Stochastic Modelling of Interest Rates: Actuarial vs. Equilibrium Approach. *J. Risk Ins.*, September 1986, *53*(3), pp. 435–53. **[G: U.S.]**

Giannini, Curzio. Determinazione del livello dei prezzi e politica "monetaria" in un'economia senza moneta. (The Determinancy of Price Level and Monetary Policy in an Economy without Money. With English summary.) *Giorn. Econ.*, Sept.-Oct. 1986, *45*(9–10), pp. 545–62.

Gilles, Christian and LeRoy, Stephen F. A Note on the Local Expectations Hypothesis: A Discrete-Time Exposition. *J. Finance*, September 1986, *41*(4), pp. 975–79.

Girton, Lance and Roper, Don. Theory and Implications of Currency Substitution. **In** *Putnam, B. H. and Wilford, D. S., eds.*, 1986, *1981*, pp. 212–35.

Gochoco, Maria S. Tests of the Money Neutrality and Rationality Hypotheses: The Case of Japan 1973–1985. *J. Money, Credit, Banking*, November 1986, *18*(4), pp. 458–66. **[G: Japan]**

Goldfeld, Stephen M. Money, Credit, and Interest Rates in the Business Cycle: Comment. **In** *Gordon, R. J., ed.*, 1986, pp. 438–41. **[G: U.S.]**

Goldfeld, Stephen M. The Term Structure of Interest Rates Revisited: Comments. *Brookings Pap. Econ. Act.*, 1986, (1), pp. 97–100. **[G: U.S.; U.K.; W. Germany; Canada]**

Goodfriend, Marvin, et al. A Weekly Rational Expectations Model of the Nonborrowed Reserve Operating Procedure. *Fed. Res. Bank Richmond Econ. Rev.*, Jan./Feb. 1986, *72*(1), pp. 11–28. **[G: U.S.]**

Goodhart, Charles. How Can Non-interest-bearing Assets Co-exist with Safe Interest-Bearing Assets? *Brit. Rev. Econ. Issues*, Autumn 1986, *8*(19), pp. 1–12.

Gottardi, Piero. Decisioni di risparmio, scelte di portafoglio e politiche di finanziamento del disavanzo. (Saving Decisions, Portfolio Choices and Government Financial Policies. With English summary.) *Giorn. Econ.*, May-June 1986, *45*(5–6), pp. 263–93.

Goudswaard, Kees P. and Halberstadt, Victor. Aspects of Debt Management and Monetary Policy in Small Open Economies. **In** *Herber, B. P., ed.*, 1986, pp. 343–60. **[G: OECD; Netherlands]**

Graham, Fred C. A Note on the Vanishing Liquidity Effect of Money on Interest. *Econ. Inquiry*, July 1986, *24*(3), pp. 497–503. **[G: U.S.]**

Graziani, Augusto. Keynes' Finance Motive: A Reply. *Econ. Notes*, 1986, (1), pp. 5–9.

Green, Steven L. Monetary Policy in Developing Countries and the New Monetary Economics. *J. Econ. Devel.*, December 1986, *11*(2), pp. 7–23. **[G: LDCs]**

Green, Steven L. and Grossman, Herschel I. The Illusion of Stabilization Policy? *Carnegie-Rochester Conf. Ser. Public Policy*, Autumn 1986, *25*, pp. 221–35. **[G: W. Europe; U.S.; Canada]**

Greenfield, Robert L. and Yeager, Leland B. Money and Credit Confused: An Appraisal of Economic Doctrine and Federal Reserve Procedure. *Southern Econ. J.*, October 1986, *53*(2), pp. 364–73. **[G: U.S.]**

Grier, Kevin B. A Note on Unanticipated Money Growth and Interest Rate Surprises: Mishkin and Makin Revisited. *J. Finance*, September 1986, *41*(4), pp. 981–85. **[G: U.S.]**

Grossman, Herschel I. Money, Real Activity, and Rationality [The Significance of Monetary Disequilibrium]. *Cato J.*, Fall 1986, *6*(2), pp. 401–08.

Grossman, Herschel I. and Van Huyck, John B. Seigniorage, Inflation, and Reputation. *J. Monet. Econ.*, July 1986, *18*(1), pp. 21–31.

Hafer, R. W. and Thornton, Daniel L. Price Expectations and the Demand for Money: A Comment. *Rev. Econ. Statist.*, August 1986, *68*(3), pp. 539–42. **[G: U.S.]**

Hahn, Franz. Zur strukturellen Stabilität eines nichtlinearen Kreditmarktmodells bei Unsicherhiet: Eine einfache Anwendung der elementaren Katastrophentheorie. (On Structural Stability of a Nonlinear Credit Market Model under Uncertainty: A Simple Application of the Elementary Catastrophe Theory. With English summary.) *Jahr. Nationalökon. Statist.*, November 1986, *201*(6), pp. 572–88.

Hakkio, Craig S. and Leiderman, Leonardo. Intertemporal Asset Pricing and the Term Structures of Exchange Rates and Interest Rates: The Eurocurrency Market. *Europ. Econ. Rev.*, April 1986, *30*(2), pp. 325–44. **[G: OECD]**

Hall, Robert E. Monetary Policy under Financial Innovation and Deregulation. **In** *Suzuki, Y. and Yomo, H., eds.*, 1986, pp. 227–39. **[G: U.S.]**

Hall, Robert E. Optimal Monetary Institutions and Policy. **In** *Campbell, C. D. and Dougan, W. R., eds.*, 1986, pp. 224–39. **[G: U.S.]**

Hancock, Diana. A Model of the Financial Firm with Imperfect Asset and Deposit Elasticities. *J. Banking Finance*, March 1986, *10*(1), pp. 37–54. **[G: U.S.]**

Hanson, James A. High Real Interest Rates and Spreads: An Introduction. **In** *Hanson, J. A. and Rocha, R.*, 1986, pp. 1–16. **[G: Selected Countries]**

Hansson, Ingemar and Stuart, Charles. The Fisher Hypothesis and International Capital Markets. *J. Polit. Econ.*, December 1986, *94*(6), pp. 1330–37.

Hart, Oliver D. Credit Rationing and Collateral: Comment. **In** *Edwards, J., et al., eds.*, 1986, pp. 136–43.

Haubrich, Joseph G. Does the Potency of Monetary Policy Vary with Capacity Utilization? A Comment. *Carnegie-Rochester Conf. Ser. Public Policy,* Spring 1986, *24,* pp. 333–37.

Havrilesky, Thomas. Innovation in Monetary Policy: A Comment. *J. Banking Finance,* December 1986, *10*(4), pp. 611–13.

Hayakawa, Hiroaki. Intertemporal Optimization and Neutrality of Money in Growth Models. *J. Monet. Econ.*, November 1986, *18*(3), pp. 323–28.

Hegji, Charles. Optimal Monetary Policy and the Lag Structure of Disturbances. *J. Macroecon.*, Summer 1986, *8*(3), pp. 297–312.

Henderson, James P. Sir John William Lubbock's *On Currency*—"An Interesting Book by a Still More Interesting Man." *Hist. Polit. Econ.*, Fall 1986, *18*(3), pp. 383–404.

Henin, Pierre-Yves and Zylberberg, André. Contrats indexés dans une économie monétaire. (Indexed Contracts in a Monetary Economy. With English summary.) *Ann. Écon. Statist.*, Apr./June 1986, (2), pp. 147–63.

le Héron, Edwin. Généralisation de la préférence pour la liquidité et financement de l'investissement. (Generalizing the Liquidity Preference and the Theory of Investment Financing. With English summary.) *Écon. Soc.*, Aug.-Sept. 1986, *20*(8–9), pp. 67–93.

Hester, Donald D. Monetary Policy in an Evolutionary Disequilibrium. **In** *Suzuki, Y. and Yomo, H., eds.*, 1986, pp. 241–86. **[G: U.S.]**

Hicks, John R. Loanable Funds and Liquidity Preference. *Greek Econ. Rev.*, December 1986, *8*(2), pp. 125–31.

Himarios, Daniel. Administered Interest Rates and the Demand for Money in Greece under Rational Expectations. *Weltwirtsch. Arch.*, 1986, *122*(1), pp. 173–88. **[G: Greece]**

Hirsch, Abraham and de Marchi, Neil. Making a Case When Theory Is Unfalsifiable: Friedman's Monetary History. *Econ. Philos.*, April 1986, *2*(1), pp. 1–21.

Hoelscher, Gregory. New Evidence on Deficits and Interest Rates. *J. Money, Credit, Banking,* February 1986, *18*(1), pp. 1–17.

Hong, Wontack. Institutionalized Monopsonistic Capital Markets in a Developing Economy. *J. Devel. Econ.*, May 1986, *21*(2), pp. 353–59. **[G: LDCs]**

Horn, Gustav-Adolf. Preisstabilisierende Geldpolitik. (Price-stabilizing Monetary Policy. With English summary.) *Kredit Kapital,* 1986, *19*(1), pp. 58–75.

Horne, Jocelyn; Martin, Vance and Bonetti, Shane. Asset Substitution and Aggregate Liquidity in Australia: 1969–1983. *Econ. Rec.*, March 1986, *62*(176), pp. 22–36. **[G: Australia]**

Hossain, Md. Akhtar. Monetary Disequilibrium and Inflation: A Monetary Model of Inflation in Pakistan, 1963–82. *Pakistan Devel. Rev.*, Summer 1986, *25*(2), pp. 141–62. **[G: Pakistan]**

Huizinga, John and Mishkin, Frederic S. How Robust Are the Results? A Reply. *Carnegie-Rochester Conf. Ser. Public Policy,* Spring 1986, *24*, pp. 289–302. **[G: U.S.]**

Huizinga, John and Mishkin, Frederic S. Monetary Policy Regime Shifts and the Unusual Behavior of Real Interest Rates. *Carnegie-Rochester Conf. Ser. Public Policy*, Spring 1986, *24*, pp. 231–74. **[G: U.S.]**

Humphrey, Thomas M. A Monetarist Model of the Inflationary Process. **In** *Humphreys, T. M.*, 1986, *1975*, pp. 49–59.

Humphrey, Thomas M. A Monetarist Model of Exchange Rate Determination. **In** *Humphreys, T. M.*, 1986, *1977*, pp. 188–94.

Humphrey, Thomas M. Algebraic Quantity Equations before Fisher and Pigou. **In** *Humphreys, T. M.*, 1986, *1984*, pp. 278–87.

Humphrey, Thomas M. Cumulative Process Models from Thornton to Wicksell. *Fed. Res. Bank Richmond Econ. Rev.*, May/June 1986, *72*(3), pp. 18–25.

Humphrey, Thomas M. Dennis H. Robertson and the Monetary Approach to Exchange Rates. **In** *Humphreys, T. M.*, 1986, *1980*, pp. 220–27.

Humphrey, Thomas M. Evolution of the Concept of the Demand for Money. **In** *Humphreys, T. M.*, 1986, *1973*, pp. 288–98.

Humphrey, Thomas M. Explaining Exchange Rate Behavior: An Augmented Version of the Monetary Approach. **In** *Humphreys, T. M.*, 1986, *1981*, pp. 228–36.

Humphrey, Thomas M. Factors Determining Exchange Rates: A Simple Model and Empirical Tests. **In** *Humphreys, T. M.*, 1986, *1977*, pp. 195–200. **[G: U.K.; U.S.; Italy]**

Humphrey, Thomas M. Interest Rates, Expectations, and the Wicksellian Policy Rule. **In** *Humphreys, T. M.*, 1986, *1976*, pp. 134–42.

Humphrey, Thomas M. On Nonneutral Relative Price Effects in Monetarist Thought: Some Austrian Misconceptions. **In** *Humphreys, T. M.*, 1986, *1984*, pp. 73–79.

Humphrey, Thomas M. The Classical Concept of the Lender of Last Resort. **In** *Humphreys,*

T. M., 1986, *1975*, pp. 304–11.

Humphrey, Thomas M. The Interest Cost-Push Controversy. **In** *Humphreys, T. M.*, 1986, *1979*, pp. 143–50.

Humphrey, Thomas M. The Monetarist–Nonmonetarist Debate: Some 19th Century Controversies Revisited. **In** *Humphreys, T. M.*, 1986, *1970*, pp. 299–303. **[G: U.K.]**

Humphrey, Thomas M. The Monetary Approach to Exchange Rates: Its Historical Evolution and Role in Policy Debates. **In** *Humphreys, T. M.*, 1986, *1978*, pp. 201–08.

Humphrey, Thomas M. The Monetary Approach to Exchange Rates: Its Historical Evolution and Role in Policy Debates. **In** *Putnam, B. H. and Wilford, D. S., eds.*, 1986, *1978*, pp. 152–67. **[G: U.K.; Sweden; Germany]**

Humphrey, Thomas M. The Quantity Theory of Money: Its Historical Evolution and Role in Policy Debates. **In** *Humphreys, T. M.*, 1986, *1974*, pp. 1–18.

Humphrey, Thomas M. The Real Bills Doctrine. **In** *Humphreys, T. M.*, 1986, *1982*, pp. 80–90.

Humphrey, Thomas M. Two Views of Monetary Policy: The Attwood–Mill Debate Revisited. **In** *Humphreys, T. M.*, 1986, *1977*, pp. 242–50.

Huq, Shamsul and Majumdar, Badiul A. Stability of the Demand for Money Function: Evidence from a Developing Country. *Pakistan Econ. Soc. Rev.*, Summer 1986, *24*(1), pp. 45–55. **[G: Pakistan]**

Hussain, Athar. Money and Socialism: Comment. **In** *Smith, K., ed.*, 1986, *1978*, pp. 139–43. **[G: U.S.S.R.]**

Imperato, Isabella. La politica monetaria ottima in presenza di shock esogeni: "Monetary Targeting" e "Nominal Income Targeting." (Optimal Monetary Policy in Presence of Exogenous Shocks: Monetary Targeting and Nominal Income Targeting. With English summary.) *Giorn. Econ.*, Sept.-Oct. 1986, *45*(9–10), pp. 563–78.

Isaac, Alan G. Bursting Bubbles: Further Results. *J. Monet. Econ.*, May 1986, *17*(3), pp. 425–31.

Isard, Peter and Rojas-Suarez, Liliana. Velocity of Money and the Practice of Monetary Targeting: Experience, Theory, and the Policy Debate. **In** *International Monetary Fund, Research Department*, 1986, pp. 73–114. **[G: OECD]**

Ize, Alain. Dynamic Model of Financial Intermediation with Perfect Foresight. *Int. Econ. Rev.*, February 1986, *27*(1), pp. 209–22.

Jarchow, Hans-Joachim. Ein Geldangebots/Geldnachfrage-Modell für flexible Wechselkurse und Zentrallbankpolitik. (A Money Supply/Money Demand Model for Flexible Exchange Rates and Central Bank Policy. With English summary.) *Kredit Kapital*, 1986, *19*(1), pp. 1–24.

Johansson, Peter. Kapitalrörelser och penningpolitik i Finland. (Capital Flow and Monetary Policy in Finland. With English summary.) *Ekon. Samfundets Tidskr.*, 1986, *39*(1), pp. 35–49. **[G: Finland]**

Jones, Jonathan D. and Sattar, Zaidi. Validating the Conventional Paradigm about Budget Deficits and Interest Rates. *Atlantic Econ. J.*, September 1986, *14*(3), pp. 83. **[G: U.S.]**

Jonson, P. D. and Rankin, R. W. On Some Recent Developments in Monetary Economics. *Econ. Rec.*, September 1986, *62*(178), pp. 257–67.

Jordan, Jerry L. The Anderson–Jordan Approach after Nearly 20 Years. *Fed. Res. Bank St. Louis Rev.*, October 1986, *68*(8), pp. 5–8. **[G: U.S.]**

Kanatas, George. Deposit Insurance and the Discount Window: Pricing under Asymmetric Information. *J. Finance*, June 1986, *41*(2), pp. 437–50.

Kanniainen, Vesa and Tarkka, Juha. On the Shock-Absorption View of Money: International Evidence from the 1960s and 1970s. *Appl. Econ.*, October 1986, *18*(10), pp. 1085–1101. **[G: W. Germany; U.S.; Australia; Finland; Sweden]**

Kapur, Basant K. Alternative Stabilization Policies for Less-developed Economies. **In** *Kapur, B. K.*, 1986, *1976*, pp. 49–68.

Kapur, Basant K. Monetary Growth in Less-developed Economies—The Self-finance Case. **In** *Kapur, B. K.*, 1986, pp. 19–33.

Kapur, Basant K. Problems of Indexation in Financially Liberalized Less-developed Economies. **In** *Kapur, B. K.*, 1986, *1982*, pp. 123–41.

Karakitsos, Elias. Monetary Policy, Exchange Rate Dynamics and the Labour Market. *J. Econ. Dynam. Control*, June 1986, *10*(1/2), pp. 281–89.

Karmann, Alexander J. Monetäre Schätzansätze zur Erfassung der Schattenwirtschaft. Ein Vergleich verschiedener Messmethoden. (Monetary Estimation Approaches to Assessing the "Shadow Economy." A Comparison of Various Methods. With English summary.) *Kredit Kapital*, 1986, *19*(2), pp. 233–47. **[G: OECD]**

Kaufman, Herbert M. and Lombra, Raymond E. The Effect of Changes in the Federal Reserve's Policy Rule on the Stochastic Structure Linking Reserves, Interest Rates, and Money. *Southern Econ. J.*, April 1986, *52*(4), pp. 1080–87. **[G: U.S.]**

Kearney, Colm and MacDonald, Ronald. Intervention and Sterilisation under Floating Exchange Rates: The UK 1973–1983. *Europ. Econ. Rev.*, April 1986, *30*(2), pp. 345–64. **[G: U.K.]**

Keeley, Michael C. and Zimmerman, Gary C. Deposit Rate Deregulation and the Demand for Transactions Media. *Fed. Res. Bank San Francisco Econ. Rev.*, Summer 1986, (3), pp. 47–62. **[G: U.S.]**

Keleher, Robert E. Of Money and Prices: Some Historical Perspectives. **In** *Putnam, B. H. and Wilford, D. S., eds.*, 1986, *1978*, pp. 27–58.

Kempf, Hubert. Sur le rôle stabilisateur des politiques monétaires et budgétaires dans un modèle avec anticipations rationnelles et dette publique. (With English summary.) *Revue Écon. Polit.*, Nov.-Dec. 1986, *96*(6), pp. 642–65.

Khan, Mohsin S. Islamic Interest-Free Banking: A Theoretical Analysis. *Int. Monet. Fund Staff Pap.*, March 1986, *33*(1), pp. 1–27. **[G: Islamic Countries]**

Khatkhate, Deena R. Estimating Real Interest Rates in LDCs. *Finance Develop.*, June 1986, *23*(2), pp. 45–48. **[G: LDCs]**

Kiguel, Miguel A. Déficit fiscal e inflación. (With English summary.) *Desarrollo Econ.*, July-Sept. 1986, *26*(102), pp. 255–68.

Kimbrough, Kent P. Inflation, Employment, and Welfare in the Presence of Transactions Costs. *J. Money, Credit, Banking*, May 1986, *18*(2), pp. 127–40.

Kimbrough, Kent P. Monetary Procedures and Monetary Policy. **In** *Campbell, C. D. and Dougan, W. R., eds.*, 1986, pp. 215–23. **[G: U.S.]**

Kimbrough, Kent P. The Optimum Quantity of Money Rule in the Theory of Public Finance. *J. Monet. Econ.*, November 1986, *18*(3), pp. 277–84.

King, David T.; Putnam, Bluford H. and Wilford, D. Sykes. A Currency Portfolio Approach to Exchange Rate Determination: Exchange Rate Stability and the Independence of Monetary Policy. **In** *Putnam, B. H. and Wilford, D. S., eds.*, 1986, *1978*, pp. 179–96.

King, Robert G. Money and Business Cycle: Comments on Bernanke and Related Literature. *Carnegie-Rochester Conf. Ser. Public Policy*, Autumn 1986, *25*, pp. 101–15. **[G: U.S.]**

King, Robert G. and Plosser, Charles I. Money as the Mechanism of Exchange. *J. Monet. Econ.*, January 1986, *17*(1), pp. 93–115.

King, Stephen R. Monetary Transmission: Through Bank Loans or Bank Liabilities? *J. Money, Credit, Banking*, August 1986, *18*(3), pp. 290–303. **[G: U.S.]**

Klotz, Ben P. and Meinster, David R. An Integration of CAPM with IS–LM Analysis into a Unified Theory of Aggregate Demand. *Southern Econ. J.*, January 1986, *52*(3), pp. 718–34.

Kohn, Meir. Monetary Analysis, the Equilibrium Method, and Keynes's "General Theory." *J. Polit. Econ.*, December 1986, *94*(6), pp. 1191–1224.

Kohn, Robert E. The Rate of Interest in a Stationary Economy. *J. Macroecon.*, Summer 1986, *8*(3), pp. 373–80.

Koskela, Erkki and Virén, Matti. Endogenous Policy, Structural Shift, and Demand for Money. *Weltwirtsch. Arch.*, 1986, *122*(4), pp. 647–56. **[G: U.S.]**

Kregel, J. A. A Note on Finance, Liquidity, Saving, and Investment. *J. Post Keynesian Econ.*, Fall 1986, *9*(1), pp. 91–100.

Kregel, J. A. Shylock and Hamlet or Are There Bulls and Bears in the Circuit? *Écon. Soc.*, Aug.-Sept. 1986, *20*(8–9), pp. 11–22.

Krol, Robert. The Interdependence of the Term Structure of Eurocurrency Interest Rates. *J. Int. Money Finance*, June 1986, *5*(2), pp. 245–53. **[G: Switzerland; W. Germany]**

Kulkarni, Vijayalakshmi C. and Miller, Stephen M. The Money-Supply Process in India: Does It Have Operational Significance? *Indian Econ. J.*, July-Sept. 1986, *34*(1), pp. 1–22. **[G: India]**

Lai, Ching-chong. Flexible Exchange Rates and Monetary Policy. *Atlantic Econ. J.*, December 1986, *14*(4), pp. 103.

Laidler, David. Money in Crisis: A Review Essay. *J. Monet. Econ.*, March 1986, *17*(2), pp. 305–13.

Laidler, David. What Do We Really Know about Monetary Policy? *Australian Econ. Pap.*, June 1986, *25*(46), pp. 1–16.

Landmann, Oliver. International Portfolio-Shifts and the Choice of a Monetary Rule. **In** *Frisch, H. and Gahlen, B., eds.*, 1986, pp. 86–125.

Langohr, Herwig M. and Santomero, Anthony M. The Impact of Equity in Bank Portfolios. *Finance*, June 1986, *7*(1), pp. 23–39.

Lardaro, Leonard. Interest Rate Volatility and the Level of Long-term Interest Rates. *Bus. Econ.*, January 1986, *21*(1), pp. 39–43. **[G: U.S.]**

Laumas, Prem S. and Porter-Hudak, Susan. Monetization, Economic Development and the Exogeneity of Money. *J. Devel. Econ.*, April 1986, *21*(1), pp. 25–34. **[G: India]**

Lavigne, Marie. The Creation of Money by the State Bank of the USSR. **In** *Smith, K., ed.*, 1986, *1978*, pp. 112–38. **[G: U.S.S.R.]**

Lavoie, Donald C. Marx, the Quantity Theory, and the Theory of Value. *Hist. Polit. Econ.*, Spring 1986, *18*(1), pp. 155–70.

Leamer, Edward E. A Bayesian Analysis of the Determinants of Inflation. **In** *Belsley, D. A. and Kuh, E., eds.*, 1986, pp. 62–89. **[G: U.S.]**

Lee, Chi-wen Jevons and Petruzzi, Christopher R. The Gibson Paradox and the Monetary Standard. *Rev. Econ. Statist.*, May 1986, *68*(2), pp. 189–96. **[G: U.K.; U.S.]**

Leijonhufvud, Axel. Real and Monetary Factors in Business Fluctuations [The Significance of Monetary Disequilibrium]. *Cato J.*, Fall 1986, *6*(2), pp. 409–20.

Leijonhufvud, Axel. Rules with Some Discretion. **In** *Campbell, C. D. and Dougan, W. R., eds.*, 1986, pp. 38–43.

Liang, Ming-Yih. Bank Float, Mail Float and the Definition of Money. *J. Banking Finance*, December 1986, *10*(4), pp. 533–48. **[G: U.S.]**

Lippman, Steven A. and McCall, John J. An Operational Measure of Liquidity. *Amer. Econ. Rev.*, March 1986, *76*(1), pp. 43–55.

Littlejohn, Gary. Economic Calculation in the USSR. **In** *Smith, K., ed.*, 1986, *1980*, pp. 144–78. **[G: U.S.S.R.]**

Liviatan, Nissan. The Tight Money Paradox—An Alternative View. *J. Macroecon.*, Winter 1986, *8*(1), pp. 105–12.

Lluch, Constantino. Wage Indexation, Supply Shocks, and Monetary Policy in a Small, Open Economy: Comment. **In** *Edwards, S. and*

Ahamed, L., eds., 1986, pp. 139–42.

Loderer, Claudio; Lys, Thomas and Schweizer, Urs. Daily Monetary Impulses and Security Prices. *J. Monet. Econ.*, July 1986, *18*(1), pp. 33–47. **[G: Switzerland]**

Lombra, Raymond E. Shocks and Stabilization Policy: Illusions and Issues: A Comment. *Carnegie-Rochester Conf. Ser. Public Policy*, Autumn 1986, *25*, pp. 237–43.

Lubrano, Michel; Pierse, R. G. and Richard, Jean-Francois. Stability of a U.K. Money Demand Equation: A Bayesian Approach to Testing Exogeneity. *Rev. Econ. Stud.*, August 1986, *53*(4), pp. 603–24. **[G: U.K.]**

Lucas, Robert E., Jr. Adaptive Behavior and Economic Theory. **In** *Hogarth, R. M. and Reder, M. W., eds.*, 1986, pp. 217–42.

Lucas, Robert E., Jr. Adoptive Behavior and Economic Theory. *J. Bus.*, Part 2, October 1986, *59*(4), pp. S401–26.

Lucas, Robert E., Jr. Principles of Fiscal and Monetary Policy. *J. Monet. Econ.*, January 1986, *17*(1), pp. 117–34.

Luciano, Elisa. Un modello di affidamento in condizioni di incertezza. (A Model of Borrowing and Lending under Conditions of Uncertainty. With English summary.) *Giorn. Econ.*, Sept.-Oct. 1986, *45*(9–10), pp. 527–44.

MacDonald, Ronald and Peel, David A. On Lagged Adjustment, Permanent Income, Expectations Formation and the Demand for Money. *Oxford Bull. Econ. Statist.*, February 1986, *48*(1), pp. 61–72. **[G: U.K.]**

Maes, Ivo. Did the Keynesian Revolution Retard the Development of Portfolio Theory? *Banca Naz. Lavoro Quart. Rev.*, December 1986, (159), pp. 407–21.

Makinen, Gail E. and Woodward, G. Thomas. Some Anecdotal Evidence Relating to the Legal Restrictions Theory of the Demand for Money. *J. Polit. Econ.*, April 1986, *94*(2), pp. 260–65. **[G: France]**

Mankiw, N. Gregory. Issues in Keynesian Macroeconomics: A Review Essay. *J. Monet. Econ.*, September 1986, *18*(2), pp. 217–23.

Mankiw, N. Gregory. The Allocation of Credit and Financial Collapse. *Quart. J. Econ.*, August 1986, *101*(3), pp. 455–70.

Mankiw, N. Gregory. The Term Structure of Interest Rates Revisited. *Brookings Pap. Econ. Act.*, 1986, (1), pp. 61–96. **[G: U.S.; U.K.; W. Germany; Canada]**

Mankiw, N. Gregory and Miron, Jeffrey A. The Changing Behavior of the Term Structure of Interest Rates. *Quart. J. Econ.*, May 1986, *101*(2), pp. 211–28. **[G: U.S.]**

Mankiw, N. Gregory and Summers, Lawrence H. Money Demand and the Effects of Fiscal Policies. *J. Money, Credit, Banking*, November 1986, *18*(4), pp. 415–29.

Maravall, Agustin and Bentolila, Samuel. Una medida de volatilidad en series temporales con una Aplicación al control monetario en España. (With English summary.) *Invest. Ecón.*, January 1986, *10*(1), pp. 185–99. **[G: Spain]**

Marini, Giancarlo. Information Structure and Policy Effectiveness. *Econ. Notes*, 1986, (2), pp. 5–16.

Matsukawa, Shigeru. The Equilibrium Distribution of Wage Settlements and Economic Stability. *Int. Econ. Rev.*, June 1986, *27*(2), pp. 415–37.

McCafferty, Stephen. Aggregate Demand and Interest Rates: A Macroeconomic Approach to the Term Structure. *Econ. Inquiry*, October 1986, *24*(4), pp. 521–33.

McCallum, Bennett T. Estimating the Long-run Relationship between Interest Rates and Inflation: A Reply. *J. Monet. Econ.*, July 1986, *18*(1), pp. 87–90.

McCallum, Bennett T. Issues Concerning the Nonpecuniary Yield of Money [Money, Deregulation, and the Business Cycle]. *Cato J.*, Fall 1986, *6*(2), pp. 607–11. **[G: U.S.]**

McCallum, Bennett T. On "Real" and "Sticky-Price" Theories of the Business Cycle. *J. Money, Credit, Banking*, November 1986, *18*(4), pp. 397–414.

McCallum, Bennett T. Some Issues Concerning Interest Rate Pegging, Price Level Determinancy, and the Real Bills Doctrine. *J. Monet. Econ.*, January 1986, *17*(1), pp. 135–60.

McCandless, George T., Jr. Tenencia de una segunda moneda durante períodos de inflación. (With English summary.) *Cuadernos Econ.*, August 1986, *23*(69), pp. 265–74.

McClure, J. Harold, Jr. Welfare-Maximizing Inflation Rates under Fractional Reserve Banking with and without Deposit Rate Ceilings: A Note. *J. Money, Credit, Banking*, May 1986, *18*(2), pp. 233–38.

McGibany, James M. and Nourzad, Farrokh. Interest Rate Volatility and the Demand for Money. *Quart. Rev. Econ. Bus.*, Autumn 1986, *26*(3), pp. 73–83. **[G: U.S.]**

McKinnon, Ronald I. The Case for Internationalizing American Monetary Policy. **In** *Tsoukalis, L., ed.*, 1986, pp. 199–226. **[G: OECD]**

McLeod, Alex N. Credit Aggregates: Some Suggestions. *Banca Naz. Lavoro Quart. Rev.*, June 1986, (157), pp. 186–95. **[G: U.S.]**

McMillin, W. Douglas. Federal Deficits, Macrostabilization Goals, and Federal Reserve Behavior. *Econ. Inquiry*, April 1986, *24*(2), pp. 257–69. **[G: U.S.]**

McMillin, W. Douglas. Federal Deficits and Short-term Interest Rates. *J. Macroecon.*, Fall 1986, *8*(4), pp. 403–22. **[G: U.S.]**

Mehra, Yash. Recent Financial Deregulation and the Interest Elasticity of M1 Demand. *Fed. Res. Bank Richmond Econ. Rev.*, July/Aug. 1986, *72*(4), pp. 13–24. **[G: U.S.]**

Meltzer, Allan H. Money, Credit, and Interest Rates in the Business Cycle: Comment. **In** *Gordon, R. J., ed.*, 1986, pp. 441–50. **[G: U.S.]**

Meltzer, Allan H. Size, Persistence and Interrelation of Nominal and Real Shocks: Some Evidence from Four Countries. *J. Monet. Econ.*, January 1986, *17*(1), pp. 161–94. **[G: U.S.; U.K.; Canada; W. Germany]**

Meltzer, Allan H. Some Evidence on the Comparative Uncertainty Experienced under Different Monetary Regimes. **In** *Campbell, C. D. and Dougan, W. R., eds.*, 1986, pp. 122–53. **[G: U.S.]**

Messori, Marcello. Financement bancaire et décisions de production. (Banking Finance and Production Decisions. With English summary.) *Écon. Soc.*, Aug.-Sept. 1986, *20*(8–9), pp. 127–58.

Milbourne, Ross. Financial Innovation and the Demand for Liquid Assets: A Note. *J. Money, Credit, Banking*, November 1986, *18*(4), pp. 506–11. **[G: U.S.]**

Milbourne, Ross. Price Expectations and the Demand for Money: Reply. *Rev. Econ. Statist.*, August 1986, *68*(3), pp. 543–44. **[G: U.S.]**

Milbourne, Ross and Moore, H. Alec. Some Statistical Evidence on the Effects of Financial Innovation. *Rev. Econ. Statist.*, August 1986, *68*(3), pp. 521–25. **[G: Canada]**

Miles, Marc A. Currency Substitution, Flexible Exchange Rates, and Monetary Independence. **In** *Putnam, B. H. and Wilford, D. S., eds.*, 1986, *1978*, pp. 237–48. **[G: Canada]**

Miles, Marc A. Refocusing Monetary Theory and Policy. **In** *Putnam, B. H. and Wilford, D. S., eds.*, 1986, pp. 307–24. **[G: U.S.]**

Miller, Edward M. Implications of Multiple Motives for Holding Bank Money. *Quart. Rev. Econ. Bus.*, Autumn 1986, *26*(3), pp. 84–104. **[G: U.S.]**

Miller, Edward M. Liquidity, Its Origins and Effects: Its Implications for Corporations, Deposit Institutions and Security Markets. *Amer. J. Econ. Soc.*, January 1986, *45*(1), pp. 27–39.

Miller, Stephen M. Financial Innovation, Depository–Institution Deregulation, and the Demand for Money. *J. Macroecon.*, Summer 1986, *8*(3), pp. 279–96. **[G: U.S.]**

Mills, Terence C. and Stephenson, Michael J. Modelling Real Returns on UK Government Stock. *Bull. Econ. Res.*, September 1986, *38*(3), pp. 237–56. **[G: U.K.]**

Minford, Patrick. Rational Expectations and Monetary Policy. *Scot. J. Polit. Econ.*, November 1986, *33*(4), pp. 317–33.

Minsky, Hyman P. Money and Crisis in Schumpeter and Keynes. **In** *Wagener, H.-J. and Drukker, J. W., eds.*, 1986, pp. 112–22.

Miron, Jeffrey A. Financial Panics, the Seasonality of the Nominal Interest Rate, and the Founding of the Fed. *Amer. Econ. Rev.*, March 1986, *76*(1), pp. 125–40. **[G: U.S.]**

Mishan, Ezra J. Demand-Pull and Wage-Push: Inflation—Causes, Consequences, Cures. **In** *Mishan, E. J.*, 1986, *1975*, pp. 7–17.

Mitchell, Douglas W. Some Regulatory Determinants of Bank Risk Behavior: A Note. *J. Money, Credit, Banking*, August 1986, *18*(3), pp. 374–82.

Mizrach, Bruce and Santomero, Anthony M. The Stability of Money Demand and Forecasting through Changes in Regimes [The Demand for Money Revisited] [The Case of the Missing Money]. *Rev. Econ. Statist.*, May 1986, *68*(2), pp. 324–28. **[G: U.S.]**

Modica, Salvatore. Temporary Equilibrium with Money, Unit-Elastic Price Expectations and Production Lags. *Econ. Notes*, 1986, (3), pp. 65–69.

Molho, Lazaros E. Interest Rates, Saving, and Investment in Developing Countries: A Re-examination of the McKinnon–Shaw Hypotheses. *Int. Monet. Fund Staff Pap.*, March 1986, *33*(1), pp. 90–116. **[G: LDCs]**

Montesano, Aldo. Una riformulazione della teoria monetaria di Walras. (A Restatement of Walras' Theory of Money. With English summary.) *Rivista Int. Sci. Econ. Com.*, September 1986, *33*(9), pp. 901–38.

Monticelli, Carlo. Tasso di interesse reale e politica monetaria: una applicazione del metodo dell'autoregressione vettoriale al caso Italiano. (Real Interest Rate and Monetary Policy: An Application of the Method Vector Autoregression: The Case of Italy. With English summary.) *Giorn. Econ.*, May-June 1986, *45*(5–6), pp. 295–316. **[G: Italy]**

Montiel, Peter J. An Optimizing Model of Household Behavior under Credit Rationing. *Int. Monet. Fund Staff Pap.*, September 1986, *33*(3), pp. 583–615.

Moore, Basil J. How Credit Drives the Money Supply: The Significance of Institutional Developments. *J. Econ. Issues*, June 1986, *20*(2), pp. 443–52. **[G: U.S.]**

Morgan, George Emir, III and Smith, Stephen D. Basic Risk, Partial Takedown and Hedging by Financial Intermediaries. *J. Banking Finance*, December 1986, *10*(4), pp. 467–90.

Mott, Tracy. Towards a Post-Keynesian Formulation of Liquidity Preference. *J. Post Keynesian Econ.*, Winter 1985-86, *8*(2), pp. 222–32.

Murphy, Robert G. The Expectations Theory of the Term Structure: Evidence from Inflation Forecasts. *J. Macroecon.*, Fall 1986, *8*(4), pp. 423–34. **[G: U.S.]**

Myatt, Anthony E. Money Supply Endogeneity: An Empirical Test for the United States, 1954-84. *J. Econ. Issues*, March 1986, *20*(1), pp. 133–44. **[G: U.S.]**

Myatt, Anthony E. and Young, Gregory. Interest Rates and Inflation: Uncertainty Cushions, Threshold and "Patman" Effects. *Eastern Econ. J.*, Apr.-June 1986, *12*(2), pp. 103–14. **[G: U.S.]**

Naish, Howard F. Price Adjustment Costs and the Output–Inflation Trade-off. *Economica*, May 1986, *53*(210), pp. 219–30.

Navarro, Alfredo Martin. Precios relativos, dinero e inflación en la Argentina. (Relative Prices, Money and Inflation in Argentina. With English summary.) *Económica (La Plata)*, Jan.-June 1986, *32*(1), pp. 119–33. **[G: Argentina]**

Nguyen, Hong V. Money in the Aggregate Production Function: Reexamination and Further Evidence. *J. Money, Credit, Banking*, May 1986, *18*(2), pp. 141–51. **[G: U.S.]**

Niehans, Jürg. Innovation in Monetary Policy: Further Comment. *J. Banking Finance*, December 1986, *10*(4), pp. 615–16.

O'Driscoll, Gerald P., Jr. Deregulation and Monetary Reform. *Fed. Res. Bank Dallas Econ. Rev.*, July 1986, pp. 19–31. **[G: U.S.]**

O'Driscoll, Gerald P., Jr. Money, Deregulation, and the Business Cycle. *Cato J.*, Fall 1986, *6*(2), pp. 587–605. **[G: U.S.]**

O'Driscoll, Gerald P., Jr. Money: Menger's Evolutionary Theory. *Hist. Polit. Econ.*, Winter 1986, *18*(4), pp. 601–16.

Obstfeld, Maurice. Rational and Self-fulfilling Balance-of-Payments Crises. *Amer. Econ. Rev.*, March 1986, *76*(1), pp. 72–81.

Obstfeld, Maurice. Speculative Attack and the External Constraint in a Maximizing Model of the Balance of Payments. *Can. J. Econ.*, February 1986, *19*(1), pp. 1–22.

Obstfeld, Maurice and Rogoff, Kenneth. Ruling Out Divergent Speculative Bubbles. *J. Monet. Econ.*, May 1986, *17*(3), pp. 349–62.

Olivera, Julio H. G. Inflexibilidad descendente de los precios monetarios. (With English summary.) *Desarrollo Econ.*, Jan.-Mar. 1986, *25*(100), pp. 567–70.

Olsen, Leif H. Is Monetarism Dead? [Hayekian Trade Cycle Theory: A Reappraisal]. *Cato J.*, Fall 1986, *6*(2), pp. 461–76. **[G: U.S.]**

Osano, Hiroshi and Tsutsui, Yoshiro. Credit Rationing and Implicit Contract Theory: An Empirical Study. *Int. J. Ind. Organ.*, December 1986, *4*(4), pp. 419–38. **[G: Japan]**

Osborne, Dale K. Velocities of M1 and the Monetary Base: A Correction of Standard Formulas. *Fed. Res. Bank Dallas Econ. Rev.*, January 1986, pp. 10–24.

Padoa-Schioppa, Tommaso. The Case for Internationalizing American Monetary Policy: Comment. **In** *Tsoukalis, L., ed.*, 1986, pp. 227–31. **[G: OECD]**

Paleologos, John. Unanticipated Money, Output, and Inflation in Greece. *Public Finance,* December 1986, *41*(3), pp. 415–29. **[G: Greece]**

Parguez, Alain. Au cæur du circuit ou quelques réponses aux énigmes du circuit. (Inside the Core or the First Principles of the General Theory of Circuit. With English summary.) *Écon. Soc.*, Aug.-Sept. 1986, *20*(8–9), pp. 23–39.

Parkin, Michael. Essays on and in the Chicago Tradition: A Review Essay. *J. Money, Credit, Banking,* February 1986, *18*(1), pp. 104–16.

Parkin, Michael. The Output–Inflation Trade-off When Prices Are Costly to Change. *J. Polit. Econ.*, February 1986, *94*(1), pp. 200–224.

Paroush, Jacob and Ruthenberg, David. Automated Teller Machines and the Share of Demand Deposits in the Money Supply: The Israeli Experience. *Europ. Econ. Rev.*, December 1986, *30*(6), pp. 1207–15. **[G: Israel]**

Patinkin, Don. Essay on and in the Chicago Tradition: A Reply. *J. Money, Credit, Banking,* February 1986, *18*(1), pp. 116–21.

Paul, M. Thomas and Bhattacharyay, Biswa N. Can Money Matter in a Developing Economy? *J. Monet. Econ.*, September 1986, *18*(2), pp. 205–07. **[G: India; Pakistan]**

Pekkarinen, Jukka. Early Hicks and Keynesian Monetary Theory: Different Views on Liquidity Preference. *Hist. Polit. Econ.*, Summer 1986, *18*(2), pp. 335–49.

Pellengahr, Ingo. Austrians versus Austrians II: Functionalist versus Essentialist Theories of Interest. **In** *Faber, M., ed.*, 1986, pp. 78–95.

Pellengahr, Ingo. Austrians versus Austrians I: A Subjectivist View of Interest. **In** *Faber, M., ed.*, 1986, pp. 60–77.

Penati, Alessandro. The Sources of the Movements in Interest Rates: An Empirical Investigation. *J. Banking Finance,* October 1986, *10*(3), pp. 343–60. **[G: Italy]**

Pesaran, M. Hashem. Structural Keynesianism as an Alternative to Monetarism. **In** *Nolan, P. and Paine, S., eds.*, 1986, pp. 165–75. **[G: U.K.]**

Pesek, Boris P. Microeconomics of Money. *Giorn. Econ.*, Nov.-Dec. 1986, *45*(11–12), pp. 595–616.

Phaneuf, Louis. Approche d'équilibre général stochastique du cycle économique: problèmes et réalisations. (The Stochastic General Equilibrium Approach to Business Cycles: Results and Problems. With English summary.) *L'Actual. Econ.*, March 1986, *62*(1), pp. 110–46.

Poloz, Stephen S. Currency Substitution and the Precautionary Demand for Money. *J. Int. Money Finance,* March 1986, *5*(1), pp. 115–24.

Poole, William. Deposit Deregulation and Monetary Policy: A Comment. *Carnegie-Rochester Conf. Ser. Public Policy,* Spring 1986, *24,* pp. 225–30. **[G: U.S.]**

Poole, William. Fiscal and Monetary Policy Overkills. **In** *Shadow Open Market Committee (I),* 1986, pp. 19–30. **[G: U.S.]**

Presley, John R. J. M. Keynes and the Real Balance Effect. *Manchester Sch. Econ. Soc. Stud.*, March 1986, *54*(1), pp. 22–30.

Presley, John R. Modern Monetarist Ideas: A British Connection? **In** *Black, R. D. C., ed.*, 1986, pp. 191–210.

Putnam, Bluford H. Monetary Policy, Interest Rate Targets, and Foreign Exchange Markets. **In** *Putnam, B. H. and Wilford, D. S., eds.*, 1986, *1978*, pp. 168–75.

Putnam, Bluford H. and Wilford, D. Sykes. Money, Income, and Causality in the United States and the United Kingdom. **In** *Putnam, B. H. and Wilford, D. S., eds.*, 1986, *1978*, pp. 59–65. **[G: U.S.; U.K.]**

Putnam, Bluford H. and Wilford, D. Sykes. The Policy Consequences of Interdependence. **In** *Putnam, B. H. and Wilford, D. S., eds.*, 1986, pp. 287–97.

Raga, José T. Public Debt, Margin of Financial Intermediation and the Rates of Interest: Is There Any Link? **In** *Herber, B. P., ed.*, 1986, pp. 167–79.

Ramachandra, V. Sree. Direction of Causation between Monetary and Real Variable in India: An Extended Result. *Indian Econ. J.*, July-Sept. 1986, *34*(1), pp. 98–102. **[G: India]**

Rasche, Robert H. Multiplier Forecasts and the Velocities of Various M's. **In** *Shadow Open*

Market Committee (I), 1986, pp. 43–50. [G: U.S.]

Rasche, Robert H. Time Series Analysis of "Velocity" Concepts. **In** *Shadow Open Market Committee (II)*, 1986, pp. 47–62. [G: U.S.]

Raymond, Robert. Implications for Monetary Policy: Comments. **In** *Suzuki, Y. and Yomo, H., eds.*, 1986, pp. 295–99.

Reiss, Winfried and Faber, Malte. Own Rates of Interest in a General Multisector Model of Capital. **In** *Faber, M., ed.*, 1986, *1982*, pp. 113–31.

Richards, Daniel J. Unanticipated Money and the Political Business Cycle. *J. Money, Credit, Banking*, November 1986, *18*(4), pp. 447–57. [G: U.S.]

Rockoff, Hugh. Walter Bagehot and the Theory of Central Banking. **In** *Capie, F. and Wood, G. E., eds.*, 1986, pp. 160–80.

Rogers, C. The Theory of Monetary Policy Reconsidered. *J. Stud. Econ. Econometrics*, August 1986, (25), pp. 13–50.

Romer, David. A Simple General Equilibrium Version of the Baumol–Tobin Model. *Quart. J. Econ.*, November 1986, *101*(4), pp. 663–85.

Rosati, Furio Camillo. La domanda di moneta e di credito per transazioni. (The Transaction Demand for Credit and Money. With English summary.) *Econ. Polít.*, April 1986, *3*(1), pp. 93–115.

Rose, Louis A. A Respecified Tax-Adjusted Fisher Relation. *Econ. Inquiry*, April 1986, *24*(2), pp. 319–31. [G: U.S.]

Rossini, Gianpaolo. Alcune teorie della diffusione della moneta a confronto. (Money and Microeconomic Foundations: Some Comments. With English summary.) *Econ. Polít.*, August 1986, *3*(2), pp. 277–98.

Rousseas, Stephen. The Finance Motive, Keynes, and Post Keynesians. *Écon. Soc.*, Aug.-Sept. 1986, *20*(8–9), pp. 189–201.

Rowe, Timothy D.; Lawler, Thomas A. and Cook, Timothy Q. Treasury Bill versus Private Money Market Yield Curves. *Fed. Res. Bank Richmond Econ. Rev.*, July/Aug. 1986, *72*(4), pp. 3–12. [G: U.S.]

Rush, Mark. Unexpected Money and Unemployment, 1920 to 1983. *J. Money, Credit, Banking*, August 1986, *18*(3), pp. 259–74. [G: U.S.]

Salin, Pascal. The Case for Internationalizing American Monetary Policy: Comment. **In** *Tsoukalis, L., ed.*, 1986, pp. 232–37. [G: OECD]

Samuelson, Paul A. and Sato, Ryuzo. Unattainability of Integrability and Definiteness Conditions in the General Case of Demand for Money and Goods. **In** *Samuelson, P. A.*, 1986, *1984*, pp. 177–93.

Sanni, T. A. Vector Autoregression on Nigerian Money and Agricultural Aggregates. *Can. J. Agr. Econ.*, March 1986, *34*(1), pp. 67–85. [G: Nigeria]

Santomero, Anthony M. and Siegel, Jeremy J. Deposit Deregulation and Monetary Policy. *Carnegie-Rochester Conf. Ser. Public Policy*, Spring 1986, *24*, pp. 179–224. [G: U.S.]

Saurman, David S. Currency Substitution, the Exchange Rate, and the Real Interest Rate (Non)Differential: Shipping the Bad Money In: A Note. *J. Money, Credit, Banking*, November 1986, *18*(4), pp. 512–18.

Scheinkman, Jose A. and Weiss, Laurence. Borrowing Constraints and Aggregate Economic Activity. *Econometrica*, January 1986, *54*(1), pp. 23–45.

Schiltknecht, Kurt. Walter Bagehot and the Theory of Central Banking: Comment. **In** *Capie, F. and Wood, G. E., eds.*, 1986, pp. 181–84.

Schöler, Klaus. Preisniveaustabilität durch kompetitive Geldsysteme? (Price Level Stability by Means of Competitive Monetary System? With English summary.) *Kredit Kapital*, 1986, *19*(3), pp. 351–65.

Schulz, Frank. Die Arbeiten von Franz Stöpel zur Beschäftigungspolitik durch produktive Geldschöpfung—Ein dogmengeschichtlicher Beitrag zur "Functional Finance." (The Works of Franz Stöpel to Employment Policy through Productive Creation of Money—A Contribution to the History of the Idea of "Functional Finance." With English summary.) *Jahr. Nationalökon. Statist.*, November 1986, *201*(6), pp. 642–51.

Schwert, G. William. The Time Series Behavior of Real Interest Rates: A Comment. *Carnegie-Rochester Conf. Ser. Public Policy*, Spring 1986, *24*, pp. 275–87. [G: U.S.]

Sekkat, Khalid. Inflation et Monnaie en Belgique: une analyse de causalité. (With English summary.) *Cah. Écon. Bruxelles*, 4th Trimester 1986, (112), pp. 3–31. [G: Belgium]

Shamsavari, Ali. On the Foundations of Marx's Theory of Money. *Brit. Rev. Econ. Issues*, Spring 1986, *8*(18), pp. 75–98.

Shiller, Robert J. The Term Structure of Interest Rates Revisited: Comments. *Brookings Pap. Econ. Act.*, 1986, (1), pp. 100–107. [G: U.S.]

Shubik, Martin. Strategic Market Game: A Dynamic Programming Application to Money, Banking and Insurance. *Math. Soc. Sci.*, December 1986, *12*(3), pp. 265–78.

Silva Torres, Francisco and de Teles, Pedro Pinho. O desvio deflacionista na ausência de cooperação internacional em contexto de incerteza. (With English summary.) *Economia (Portugal)*, May 1986, *10*(2), pp. 277–92.

Simos, Evangelos O. and Triantis, John E. The Effect of Structural Instability on the Demand for Money Forecast. *Econ. Notes*, 1986, (2), pp. 43–61. [G: U.S.]

Sinclair, P. J. N. Interest, Employment and Money: An Editorial Note. *Oxford Econ. Pap.*, November 1986, *38*(3), pp. 363–66.

Smith, Bruce. Limited Information, Money, and Competitive Equilibrium. *Can. J. Econ.*, November 1986, *19*(4), pp. 780–97.

Smith, Gregor W. A Dynamic Baumol–Tobin Model of Money Demand. *Rev. Econ. Stud.*, July 1986, *53*(3), pp. 465–69.

Smith, Kenneth L. Real, Nominal, and Price Adjustment in Generalized Models of Money Demand: Can We Improve Stability and Forecasts? *Quart. J. Bus. Econ.*, Summer 1986, *25*(3), pp. 72–86. **[G: U.S.]**

Snippe, Jan. Finance, Saving and Investment in Keynes's Economics: A Reply. *Cambridge J. Econ.*, December 1986, *10*(4), pp. 373–77.

Snippe, Jan. Hines on LF versus LP: Reply [Loanable Funds Theory Versus Liquidity Preference Theory]. *De Economist*, 1986, *134*(1), pp. 111.

Sørensen, Peter Birch. Errata: Countercyclical versus Passive Monetary Policy in a Medium-run Macro Model. *Scand. J. Econ.*, 1986, *88*(2), pp. 453.

Sprenkle, Case M. and Stanhouse, Bryan E. A Framework for Evaluating Operating Targets. *J. Macroecon.*, Winter 1986, *8*(1), pp. 1–29.

Starr, Ross M. Decentralized Trade in a Credit Economy. **In** *[Arrow, K. J.], Vol. 2*, 1986, pp. 105–20.

Steindl, Frank G. General Equilibrium Models of Inflation and Interest Rates: Specification Considerations. *Kredit Kapital*, 1986, *19*(2), pp. 252–70.

Sterdyniak, Henri and Villa, Pierre. Des conséquences conjoncturelles de la régulation monétaire. (The Choice of the Intermediate Target in an Overdraft Economy. With English summary.) *Revue Écon.*, November 1986, *37*(6), pp. 963–98.

Stiglitz, Joseph E. and Weiss, Andrew M. Credit Rationing and Collateral. **In** *Edwards, J., et al., eds.*, 1986, pp. 101–36.

Stulz, René M. Interest Rates and Monetary Policy Uncertainty. *J. Monet. Econ.*, May 1986, *17*(3), pp. 331–47.

Suda, Shinichi. Pareto Optimality and Monetary Competitive Equilibrium in the Overlapping Generations Model. *Keio Econ. Stud.*, 1986, *23*(1), pp. 79–96.

Summers, Lawrence H. Estimating the Long-run Relationship between Interest Rates and Inflation: A Response. *J. Monet. Econ.*, July 1986, *18*(1), pp. 77–86.

Sundararajan, V. Exchange Rate versus Credit Policy: Analysis with a Monetary Model of Trade and Inflation in India. *J. Devel. Econ.*, Jan.-Feb. 1986, *20*(1), pp. 75–105. **[G: India]**

Svensson, Lars E. O. Sticky Goods Prices, Flexible Asset Prices, Monopolistic Competition, and Monetary Policy. *Rev. Econ. Stud.*, July 1986, *53*(3), pp. 385–405.

Swofford, James L. and Whitney, Gerald A. Flexible Functional Forms and the Utility Approach to the Demand for Money: A Nonparametric Analysis: A Note. *J. Money, Credit, Banking*, August 1986, *18*(3), pp. 383–89. **[G: U.S.]**

Tabellini, Guido. Money, Debt and Deficits in a Dynamic Game. *J. Econ. Dynam. Control*, December 1986, *10*(4), pp. 427–42.

Takigawa, Yoshio. Deregulation of Interest Rate and Bank Rate Policy. *Kobe Univ. Econ.*, 1986, (32), pp. 121–37.

Tanaka, Yasuhito. The Optimum Interest Rate under Uncertain Life Time. *Econ. Rev. (Keizai Kenkyu)*, January 1986, *37*(1), pp. 79–83.

Taub, Bart. Asymptotic Properties of Pipeline Control of the Money Supply. *Int. Econ. Rev.*, October 1986, *27*(3), pp. 647–65.

Taurand, Francis. Le troc en économie monétaire. (Barter in Monetary Economies. With English summary.) *L'Actual. Econ.*, June 1986, *62*(2), pp. 236–56.

Taylor, Mark P. From the General to the Specific: The Demand for M2 in Three European Countries. *Empirical Econ.*, 1986, *11*(4), pp. 243–61. **[G: W. Germany; Netherlands; France]**

Teh, Kok Peng. Monetary Policy in an Evolutionary Disequilibrium: Comments. **In** *Suzuki, Y. and Yomo, H., eds.*, 1986, pp. 301–04. **[G: U.S.]**

Teixeira dos Santos, Fernando. The Portuguese Demand for Money Function. *Economia (Portugal)*, October 1986, *10*(3), pp. 377–413. **[G: Portugal]**

Telser, Lester G. Futures and Actual Markets: How They Are Related. *J. Bus.*, Part 2, April 1986, *59*(2), pp. S5–20.

Teranishi, Juro. Economic Growth and Regulation of Financial Markets: Japanese Experience during Postwar High Growth Period. *Hitotsubashi J. Econ.*, December 1986, *27*(2), pp. 145–65. **[G: Japan]**

Thornton, Daniel L. The Discount Rate and Market Interest Rates: Theory and Evidence. *Fed. Res. Bank St. Louis Rev.*, Aug./Sept. 1986, *68*(7), pp. 5–21. **[G: U.S.]**

Thornton, J. Bank Rediscounting at the Central Bank: A Survey of Alternative Theories and Some Evidence. *S. Afr. J. Econ.*, June 1986, *54*(2), pp. 194–206. **[G: W. Germany]**

Tiwari, Kashi Nath. The Money Supply Process under Deregulation. *Financial Rev.*, February 1986, *21*(1), pp. 111–23.

Tobin, James. Monetary Control in a Brave New World. **In** *Lawrence, C. and Shay, R. P., eds.*, 1986, pp. 190–95. **[G: U.S.]**

Tobin, James. Monetary Policy Symposium: Closing Comments. **In** *Lawrence, C. and Shay, R. P., eds.*, 1986, pp. 207–08. **[G: U.S.]**

Tobin, James. On the Welfare Macroeconomics of Government Financial Policy. *Scand. J. Econ.*, 1986, *88*(1), pp. 9–24.

Toma, Mark. Inflationary Bias of the Federal Reserve System: A Bureaucratic Perspective. **In** *Toma, E. F. and Toma, M., eds.*, 1986, *1982*, pp. 37–66. **[G: U.S.]**

Tsang, Shu-Ki. Testing Money–Income Causality in South Korea. *Hong Kong Econ. Pap.*, 1986, (17), pp. 34–50. **[G: S. Korea]**

Turnovsky, Stephen J. Monetary and Fiscal Policy under Perfect Foresight: A Symmetric Two-country Analysis. *Economica*, May 1986, *53*(210), pp. 139–57.

Turnovsky, Stephen J. Short-term and Long-term Interest Rates in a Monetary Model of a Small Open Economy. *J. Int. Econ.*, May 1986, *20* (3/4), pp. 291–311.

Turnovsky, Stephen J. and d'Orey, Vasco. Monetary Polices in Interdependent Economies: A Strategic Approach. *Econ. Stud. Quart.*, June

1986, *37*(2), pp. 114–33.

Turnovsky, Stephen J. and d'Orey, Vasco. Monetary Policies in Interdependent Economies with Stochastic Disturbances: A Strategic Approach. *Econ. J.*, September 1986, *96*(383), pp. 696–721.

Vallageas, Bernard. Le problèmme de la nature du profit et de son agrégation dans le traité sur la monnaie et la théorie généale. (A Restatement of the Theory of Profit in Keynes's Treatise of Money and General Theory. With English summary.) *Écon. Soc.*, Aug.-Sept. 1986, *20*(8–9), pp. 171–88.

Van Hoose, David D. A Note on Interest on Required Reserves as an Instrument of Monetary Control. *J. Banking Finance,* March 1986, *10*(1), pp. 147–56.

Vandevelde, Franck. La thésaurisation dans le circuit de l'économie monétaire de production. (Hoarding in the Circuit of the Monetary Production Economy. With English summary.) *Écon. Soc.*, Aug.-Sept. 1986, *20*(8–9), pp. 41–66.

Vaubel, Roland. Competing Currencies: The Case for Free Entry: Reply. *Z. Wirtschaft. Sozialwissen.*, 1986 , *106*(6), pp. 623–27.

Vaubel, Roland. Currency Competition versus Governmental Money Monopolies. *Cato J.*, Winter 1986, *5*(3), pp. 927–42.

Vaubel, Roland. The Case for Internationalizing American Monetary Policy: Comment. **In** *Tsoukalis, L., ed.*, 1986, pp. 238–42. **[G: OECD]**

Vickers, John S. Signalling in a Model of Monetary Policy with Incomplete Information. *Oxford Econ. Pap.*, November 1986, *38*(3), pp. 443–55.

Virén, Matti. Examining the Long-run Relationship between Interest Rates and Inflation: Some Cross-country Evidence. *Econ. Notes*, 1986, (3), pp. 122–33. **[G: OECD]**

Visser, H. Loanable Funds Theory versus Liquidity Preference Theory: A Comment. *De Economist*, 1986, *134*(1), pp. 109–10.

Wahlroos, Björn and Berglund, Tom. Stock Returns, Inflationary Expectations and Real Activity: New Evidence. *J. Banking Finance*, October 1986, *10*(3), pp. 377–89. **[G: Finland]**

Wallace, Neil. The Relevance of Legal Restrictions Theory [Money, Deregulation, and the Business Cycle]. *Cato J.*, Fall 1986, *6*(2), pp. 613–16. **[G: U.S.]**

Walsh, Carl E. In Defense of Base Drift. *Amer. Econ. Rev.*, September 1986, *76*(4), pp. 692–700. **[G: U.S.]**

Weale, Martin. The Structure of Personal Sector Short-term Asset Holdings. *Manchester Sch. Econ. Soc. Stud.*, June 1986, *54*(2), pp. 141–61. **[G: U.K.]**

Webb, David C. Competitive Banking in a Simple Model: Comment. **In** *Edwards, J., et al., eds.*, 1986, pp. 177–81.

Wenninger, John. Implications for Monetary Policy: Comments. **In** *Suzuki, Y. and Yomo, H., eds.*, 1986, pp. 291–93. **[G: U.S.]**

West, Kenneth D. Targeting Nominal Income: A Note. *Econ. J.*, December 1986, *96*(384), pp. 1077–83.

White, Lawrence H. A Subjectivist Perspective on the Definition and Identification of Money. **In** *[Lachmann, L. M.]*, 1986, pp. 301–14.

Whittaker, Rod, et al. Alternative Financial Policy Rules in an Open Economy under Rational and Adaptive Expectations. *Econ. J.*, September 1986, *96*(383), pp. 680–95. **[G: U.K.]**

Wilford, D. Sykes and Krieger, Ronald A. Discretionary Monetary Policy and the Gold Standard. **In** *Putnam, B. H. and Wilford, D. S., eds.*, 1986, pp. 298–306.

Wilford, Walton T. The Monetary Approach to Balance of Payments and Developing Nations: A Review of the Literature. **In** *Putnam, B. H. and Wilford, D. S., eds.*, 1986, pp. 81–106. **[G: LDCs]**

Williamson, Stephen D. Costly Monitoring, Financial Intermediation, and Equilibrium Credit Rationing. *J. Monet. Econ.*, September 1986, *18*(2), pp. 159–79.

Williamson, Stephen D. Increasing Returns to Scale in Financial Intermediation and the Non-neuturality of Government Policy. *Rev. Econ. Stud.*, October 1986, *53*(5), pp. 863–75.

Winckler, Georg and Kunst, Robert. The Influence of Wage Rate Variations on the Level of Employment with and without an Exogenous Interest Rate. **In** *Frisch, H. and Gahlen, B., eds.*, 1986, pp. 186–200.

Winer, Stanley L. Money and Politics in a Small Open Economy. *Public Choice*, 1986, *51*(2), pp. 221–39. **[G: Canada]**

Wright, D. J., et al. Evaluation of Forecasting Methods for Decision Support. *Int. J. Forecasting*, 1986, *2*(2), pp. 139–52.

Yeager, Leland B. Hall's Proposals for Monetary Reform [Optimal Monetary Institutions and Policy]. **In** *Campbell, C. D. and Dougan, W. R., eds.*, 1986, pp. 240–43. **[G: U.S.]**

Yeager, Leland B. The Significance of Monetary Disequilibrium. *Cato J.*, Fall 1986, *6*(2), pp. 369–99.

Yoo, Jang H. and Pyo, Hak K. Inflationary Expectations, "Endogenous Money," and Economic Growth. *J. Macroecon.*, Summer 1986, *8*(3), pp. 337–53.

3116 Monetary Policy, Including All Central Banking Topics

Acheson, Keith and Chant, John F. Bureaucratic Theory and the Choice of Central Bank Goals: The Case of the Bank of Canada. **In** *Toma, E. F. and Toma, M., eds.*, 1986, *1973*, pp. 129–50. **[G: Canada]**

Achwan. Financial Reform in Indonesia. **In** *Cheng, H.-S., ed.*, 1986, pp. 221–23. **[G: Indonesia]**

Aharony, Joseph; Saunders, Anthony and Swary, Ithzak. The Effects of a Shift in Monetary Policy Regime on the Profitability and Risk of Commercial Banks. *J. Monet. Econ.*, May 1986, *17*(3), pp. 363–77. **[G: U.S.]**

Akhtar, M. A. and Harris, Ethan S. Monetary

Policy Influence on the Economy—An Empirical Analysis. *Fed. Res. Bank New York Quart. Rev.*, Winter 1986-87, *11*(4), pp. 19–34. **[G: U.S.]**

Allen, Andrew T. Private Sector Response to Stabilization Policy: A Case Study. *Exploration Econ. Hist.*, July 1986, *23*(3), pp. 253–68. **[G: U.S.]**

Allen, Stuart D. The Federal Reserve and the Electoral Cycle: A Note. *J. Money, Credit, Banking*, February 1986, *18*(1), pp. 88–94. **[G: U.S.]**

Antoncic, Madelyn. High and Volatile Real Interest Rates: Where Does the Fed Fit In? *J. Money, Credit, Banking*, February 1986, *18*(1), pp. 18–27. **[G: U.S.]**

Apel, Emmanuel. The Administered Bank Rate and the Canada–U.S. Spot Exchange Rate: 1975–1979. *Empirical Econ.*, 1986, *11*(3), pp. 169–79. **[G: U.S.; Canada]**

Baliño, Tómas J. T. and Sundararajan, V. Financial Reform in Indonesia: Causes, Consequences, and Prospects. **In** *Cheng, H.-S., ed.*, 1986, pp. 191–219. **[G: Indonesia]**

Banaian, King; Laney, Leroy O. and Willett, Thomas D. Central Bank Independence: An International Comparison. **In** *Toma, E. F. and Toma, M., eds.*, 1986, *1983*, pp. 199–217. **[G: OECD]**

Batchelor, Roy A. The Avoidance of Catastrophe: Two Nineteenth-Century Banking Crises. **In** *Capie, F. and Wood, G. E., eds.*, 1986, pp. 41–73. **[G: U.K.]**

Batten, Dallas S. and Belongia, Michael T. Monetary Policy, Real Exchange Rates, and U.S. Agricultural Exports. *Amer. J. Agr. Econ.*, May 1986, *68*(2), pp. 422–27. **[G: U.S.]**

Beenstock, Michael and Dadashi, Saiid. The Profitability of Forward Currency Speculation by Central Banks. *Europ. Econ. Rev.*, April 1986, *30*(2), pp. 449–56. **[G: Canada]**

Benston, George J. Federal Regulation of Banking: Historical Overview. **In** *Kaufman, G. G. and Kormendi, R. C., eds.*, 1986, pp. 1–47. **[G: U.S.]**

Biacabe, Pierre. La politique monétaire en 1985: une transition avant la rupture. (With English summary.) *Revue Écon. Polit.*, Sept.-Oct. 1986, *96*(5), pp. 575–84. **[G: France]**

Bisignano, Joseph. The Process of Financial Deregulation, Monetary Reform, and the Financial System of the Future: Comments. **In** *Suzuki, Y. and Yomo, H., eds.*, 1986, pp. 207–15. **[G: U.S.]**

Black, Robert P. A Proposal to Clarify the Fed's Policy Mandate. *Cato J.*, Winter 1986, *5*(3), pp. 787–95. **[G: U.S.]**

Black, Stanley W. Flexible Exchange Rates and National Monetary Policies: Comment. **In** *Tsoukalis, L., ed.*, 1986, pp. 186–88. **[G: OECD]**

Bordo, Michael D. Explorations in Monetary History: A Survey of the Literature. *Exploration Econ. Hist.*, October 1986, *23*(4), pp. 339–415. **[G: OECD]**

Bordo, Michael D. Financial Crises, Banking Crises, Stock Market Crashes and the Money Supply: Some International Evidence, 1870–1933. **In** *Capie, F. and Wood, G. E., eds.*, 1986, pp. 190–248.

Bradley, Michael D. and Jansen, Dennis W. Deposit Market Deregulation and Interest Rates. *Southern Econ. J.*, October 1986, *53*(2), pp. 478–89.

Bradley, Michael D. and Jansen, Dennis W. Federal Reserve Operating Procedure in the Eighties: A Dynamic Analysis. *J. Money, Credit, Banking*, August 1986, *18*(3), pp. 323–35. **[G: U.S.]**

Bradley, Michael D. and Potter, Susan M. The State of the Federal Budget and the State of the Economy: Further Evidence. *Econ. Inquiry*, January 1986, *24*(1), pp. 143–53. **[G: U.S.]**

Brocato, Joe. The October 1979 Federal Reserve Policy Shift: An Analysis Using Variance Decomposition. *Atlantic Econ. J.*, December 1986, *14*(4), pp. 85–89. **[G: U.S.]**

Bruno, Michael and Fischer, Stanley. The Inflationary Process: Shocks and Accommodation. **In** *Ben-Porath, Y., ed.*, 1986, pp. 347–71. **[G: Israel]**

Bub, Norbert. Background and Causes of Financial Innovation: An International Comparison: Comments. **In** *Suzuki, Y. and Yomo, H., eds.*, 1986, pp. 121–24. **[G: W. Germany]**

Butos, William N. The Knowledge Problem under Alternative Monetary Regimes. *Cato J.*, Winter 1986, *5*(3), pp. 849–71. **[G: U.S.]**

Cagan, Phillip. Regulation and the Monetary Economy. **In** *Lawrence, C. and Shay, R. P., eds.*, 1986, pp. 196–200. **[G: U.S.]**

Canlas, Dante B. Monetary Policy and Economic Activity in a Low-Income Country: An Empirical Investigation. *Philippine Rev. Econ. Bus.*, Mar./June 1986, *23*(1/2), pp. 83–99. **[G: Philippines]**

Capie, Forrest H.; Mills, Terence C. and Wood, Geoffrey E. What Happened in 1931? **In** *Capie, F. and Wood, G. E., eds.*, 1986, pp. 120–48. **[G: U.K.]**

Cargill, Thomas F. Japanese Monetary Policy, Flow of Funds, and Domestic Financial Liberalization. *Fed. Res. Bank San Francisco Econ. Rev.*, Summer 1986, (3), pp. 21–32. **[G: Japan]**

Chant, John F. and Acheson, Keith. The Choice of Monetary Instruments and the Theory of Bureaucracy. **In** *Toma, E. F. and Toma, M., eds.*, 1986, *1972*, pp. 107–28. **[G: Canada]**

Chatelus, Michel. Les monnaies des pays arabes pétroliers du golfe. (The Currencies of the Gulf Arab Oil Countries. With English summary.) *Écon. Soc.*, February 1986, *20*(2), pp. 61–94. **[G: OPEC]**

Cheng, Hang-Sheng. Financial Policy and Reform in Taiwan, China. **In** *Cheng, H.-S., ed.*, 1986, pp. 143–59. **[G: Taiwan]**

Clark, Truman A. Interest Rate Seasonals and the Federal Reserve. *J. Polit. Econ.*, February 1986, *94*(1), pp. 76–125. **[G: U.S.]**

Congdon, Tim. What Happened in 1931? Comment. In *Capie, F. and Wood, G. E., eds.*, 1986, pp. 149–56. **[G: U.K.]**

Corrigan, E. Gerald. Statement to the U.S. House Subcommittee on Domestic Monetary Policy of the Committee on Banking, Finance and Urban Affairs, December 12, 1985. *Fed. Res. Bull.*, February 1986, *72*(2), pp. 117–25. **[G: U.S.]**

Cross, Sam Y. Treasury and Federal Reserve Foreign Exchange Operations: Interim Report. *Fed. Res. Bull.*, February 1986, *72*(2), pp. 109–12. **[G: U.S.]**

Cross, Sam Y. Treasury and Federal Reserve Foreign Exchange Operations. *Fed. Res. Bull.*, May 1986, *72*(5), pp. 298–302. **[G: U.S.]**

Cross, Sam Y. Treasury and Federal Reserve Foreign Exchange Operations, August–October 1986. *Fed. Res. Bank New York Quart. Rev.*, Autumn 1986, *11*(3), pp. 36–42. **[G: U.S.]**

Cross, Sam Y. Treasury and Federal Reserve Foreign Exchange Operations. *Fed. Res. Bull.*, November 1986, *72*(11), pp. 766–69.

Cross, Sam Y. Treasury and Federal Reserve Foreign Exchange Operations. *Fed. Res. Bull.*, August 1986, *72*(8), pp. 525–28. **[G: U.S.]**

Cross, Sam Y. Treasury and Federal Reserve Foreign Exchange Operations, May–July 1986. *Fed. Res. Bank New York Quart. Rev.*, Autumn 1986, *11*(3), pp. 43–47. **[G: U.S.]**

Cross, Sam Y. Treasury and Federal Reserve Foreign Exchange Operations. *Fed. Res. Bank New York Quart. Rev.*, Summer 1986, *11*(2), pp. 47–51. **[G: U.S.]**

Cross, Sam Y. Treasury and Federal Reserve Foreign Exchange Operations. *Fed. Res. Bank New York Quart. Rev.*, Spring 1986, *11*(1), pp. 54–60. **[G: U.S.]**

Cyrnak, Anthony W. Chain Banks and Competition: The Effectiveness of Federal Reserve Policy in 1977. *Fed. Res. Bank San Francisco Econ. Rev.*, Spring 1986, (2), pp. 5–15. **[G: U.S.]**

Cyrnak, Anthony W. and Canner, Glenn B. Consumer Experiences with Credit Insurance: Some New Evidence. *Fed. Res. Bank San Francisco Econ. Rev.*, Summer 1986, (3), pp. 5–20. **[G: U.S.]**

Dahl, Frederick R. Statement to the U.S. House Subcommittee on Commerce, Consumer, and Monetary Affairs of the Committee on Government Operations, March 4, 1986. *Fed. Res. Bull.*, May 1986, *72*(5), pp. 307–12. **[G: U.S.]**

Dahl, Frederick R. Statement to the U.S. House Subcommittee on International Economic Policy and Trade of the Committee on Foreign Affairs, April 22, 1986. *Fed. Res. Bull.*, June 1986, *72*(6), pp. 393–98. **[G: U.S.]**

Darby, Michael R. The Internationalization of American Banking and Finance: Structure, Risk, and World Interest Rates. *J. Int. Money Finance*, December 1986, *5*(4), pp. 403–28. **[G: U.S.]**

Darby, Michael R. and Lothian, James R. Economic Events and Keynesian Ideas: The 1930s and the 1970s. In *Burton, J., et al.*, 1986, pp. 71–86.

Davis, Richard G. and Korobow, Leon. The Pricing of Consumer Deposit Products—The Nonrate Dimensions. *Fed. Res. Bank New York Quart. Rev.*, Winter 1986-87, *11*(4), pp. 14–18. **[G: U.S.]**

De Grauwe, Paul. Flexible Exchange Rates and National Monetary Policies: Comment. In *Tsoukalis, L., ed.*, 1986, pp. 189–91. **[G: OECD]**

De Wulf, Luc and Goldsbrough, David. The Evolving Role of Monetary Policy in China. *Int. Monet. Fund Staff Pap.*, June 1986, *33*(2), pp. 209–42. **[G: China]**

Deane, Roderick S. Financial Sector Policy Reform. In *Reserve Bank of New Zealand*, 1986, pp. 11–29. **[G: New Zealand]**

Deane, Roderick S. Financial Sector Policy Reform: The Case of New Zealand. In *Cheng, H.-S., ed.*, 1986, pp. 89–104. **[G: New Zealand]**

Deane, Roderick S. Reflections on the New Zealand Financial Sector. In *Reserve Bank of New Zealand*, 1986, pp. 99–108. **[G: New Zealand]**

Delbeke, Jos. A Comparison of Price and Money Behaviour between the 1920s–30s and 1970s–80s in Belgium. In *Berend, I. T. and Borchardt, K., eds.*, 1986, pp. 149–70. **[G: Belgium]**

Dingle, James F. The Role of the Bank of Canada in the Canadian Payments System. *J. Bank Res.*, 1986, *16*(4), pp. 194–97. **[G: Canada]**

Dorn, James A. Reforming the Monetary Regime: Introduction. *Cato J.*, Winter 1986, *5*(3), pp. 675–84. **[G: U.S.]**

Dornbusch, Rudiger. Sound Currency and Full Employment. In *Dornbusch, R.*, 1986, *1985*, pp. 205–31. **[G: U.K.]**

Dornbusch, Rudiger, et al. Macroeconomic Prospects and Policies for the European Community. In *Blanchard, O.; Dornbusch, R. and Layard, R., eds.*, 1986, pp. 1–32. **[G: EEC]**

Dotsey, Michael. Japanese Monetary Policy, a Comparative Analysis. *Fed. Res. Bank Richmond Econ. Rev.*, Nov./Dec. 1986, *72*(6), pp. 12–24. **[G: Japan; U.S.]**

Doughty, A. J. New Banks and Financial Structure Reform. In *Reserve Bank of New Zealand*, 1986, pp. 111–23. **[G: New Zealand]**

Doukas, John and Rahman, Abdul H. Foreign Currency Futures and Monetary Policy Announcements: An Intervention Analysis. *J. Futures Markets*, Fall 1986, *6*(3), pp. 343–73. **[G: W. Europe; U.S.; Canada; Japan]**

Dudley, William C. Controlling Risk on Large-Dollar Wire Transfer Systems. In *Saunders, A. and White, L. J., eds.*, 1986, pp. 121–35. **[G: U.S.]**

Duprey, James N. and Nelson, Clarence W. A Visible Hand: The Fed's Involvement in the Check Payments System. *Fed. Res. Bank Minn. Rev.*, Spring 1986, *10*(2), pp. 18–29. **[G: U.S.]**

Economopoulos, Andrew J. The Impact of Reserve Requirements on Free Bank Failures. *Atlantic Econ. J.*, December 1986, *14*(4), pp. 76–84. **[G: U.S.]**

Eichengreen, Barry. The Bank of France and the Sterilization of Gold, 1926–1932. *Exploration Econ. Hist.*, January 1986, *23*(1), pp. 56–84. **[G: France]**

Fand, David I. A Monetarist View of the Federal Reserve System. **In** *Campbell, C. D. and Dougan, W. R., eds.*, 1986, pp. 209–14. **[G: U.S.]**

Fand, David I. Federal Reserve Hegemony and Monetary Surprises [Is There a Political Monetary Cycle?]. *Cato J.*, Fall 1986, *6*(2), pp. 581–86. **[G: U.S.]**

Fand, David I. The Fed as an Institution [Institutional Evolution of Federal Reserve Hegemony]. *Cato J.*, Winter 1986, *5*(3), pp. 765–69. **[G: U.S.]**

Fenstermaker, J. Van and Filer, John E. Impact of the First and Second Banks of the United States and the Suffolk System on New England Bank Money: 1791–1837. *J. Money, Credit, Banking*, February 1986, *18*(1), pp. 28–40. **[G: U.S.]**

Fforde, John Standish. Walter Bagehot and the Theory of Central Banking: Comment. **In** *Capie, F. and Wood, G. E., eds.*, 1986, pp. 185–89.

Fischer, Bernhard and Trapp, Peter. Geld- und Finanzpolitik in Argentinien: Der Weg in die finanzielle Repression. (Financial Policies and Financial Repression in Argentina. With English summary.) *Kredit Kapital*, 1986, *19*(1), pp. 122–43. **[G: Argentina]**

Flemming, John S. Implications for Monetary Policy: Comments. **In** *Suzuki, Y. and Yomo, H., eds.*, 1986, pp. 287–90. **[G: U.S.; U.K.]**

Ford, Alec G. Financial Crises, Banking Crises, Stock Market Crashes and the Money Supply: Some International Evidence, 1870–1933: Comment. **In** *Capie, F. and Wood, G. E., eds.*, 1986, pp. 249–53.

Francis, Carlene. Monetary Policy in a Small, Open, Dependent Economy: The Case of the Bahamas. *Soc. Econ. Stud.*, December 1986, *35*(4), pp. 111–28. **[G: Bahamas]**

Friedman, Milton. Monetary Policy in a Fiat World. *Contemp. Policy Issues*, January 1986, *4*(1), pp. 1–9. **[G: U.K.; U.S.]**

Friedman, Milton. Monetary Policy: Theory and Practice. **In** *Toma, E. F. and Toma, M., eds.*, 1986, *1982*, pp. 11–35. **[G: U.S.]**

Fry, Maxwell J. and Lilien, David M. Monetary Policy Responses to Exogenous Shocks. *Amer. Econ. Rev.*, May 1986, *76*(2), pp. 79–83. **[G: Global]**

Ganjarerndee, Siri. Financial Reform in Thailand. **In** *Cheng, H.-S., ed.*, 1986, pp. 185–89. **[G: Thailand]**

Gérardin, Hubert. Intégration monétaire et création de monnaie: le cas de la zone franc. (Monetary Integration and the Creation of Money: The Case of the Franc Zone. With English summary.) *Écon. Soc.*, February 1986, *20*(2), pp. 95–133. **[G: Africa]**

Gidlow, R. M. Intervention in the Forward Market by the Reserve Bank under the Spot–Swap System. *S. Afr. J. Econ.*, September 1986, *54*(3), pp. 250–62. **[G: S. Africa]**

Gilbert, R. Alton. Requiem for Regulation Q: What It Did and Why It Passed Away. *Fed. Res. Bank St. Louis Rev.*, February 1986, *68*(2), pp. 22–37. **[G: U.S.]**

Gilbert, R. Alton and Wood, Geoffrey E. Coping with Bank Failures: Some Lessons from the United States and the United Kingdom. *Fed. Res. Bank St. Louis Rev.*, December 1986, *68*(10), pp. 5–14. **[G: U.S.; U.K.]**

Goodfriend, Marvin. Fed Secrecy and the Choice of a Rule [Fed Watching and the Monetary Regime]. *Cato J.*, Fall 1986, *6*(2), pp. 557–62. **[G: U.S.]**

Goodfriend, Marvin. Monetary Mystique: Secrecy and Central Banking. *J. Monet. Econ.*, January 1986, *17*(1), pp. 63–92.

Goodfriend, Marvin and Whelpley, William. Federal Funds: Instrument of Federal Reserve Policy. *Fed. Res. Bank Richmond Econ. Rev.*, Sept./Oct. 1986, *72*(5), pp. 3–11. **[G: U.S.]**

Goodhart, Charles. Financial Innovation and Monetary Control. *Oxford Rev. Econ. Policy*, Winter 1986, *2*(4), pp. 79–102. **[G: U.K.]**

Goodhart, Charles. The Summer of 1914: Comment. **In** *Capie, F. and Wood, G. E., eds.*, 1986, pp. 117–19. **[G: U.K.; Europe]**

Goodlet, Clyde. Themes in Financial Reform: The Canadian Perspective. **In** *Cheng, H.-S., ed.*, 1986, pp. 345–51. **[G: Canada]**

Gramley, Lyle E. The Federal Reserve's Current Policy Dilemma. *Bus. Econ.*, October 1986, *21*(4), pp. 5–9. **[G: U.S.]**

Green, Edward J. The Problem of Monetary Control: Another Viewpoint [The Knowledge Problem under Alternative Monetary Regimes]. *Cato J.*, Winter 1986, *5*(3), pp. 873–76. **[G: U.S.]**

Greenbaum, Stuart I. Deregulation of the Thrift Industry: A Prologue to Transitional Problems and Risks. **In** *Federal Home Loan Bank of San Francisco*, 1986, pp. 15–39. **[G: U.S.]**

Greenwood, John G. Financial Liberalization and Innovation in Seven East Asian Economies. **In** *Suzuki, Y. and Yomo, H., eds.*, 1986, pp. 79–105. **[G: E. Asia]**

Grier, Kevin B. Monetary Policy as a Political Equilibrium [Central Banking and the Fed: A Public Choice Perspective]. *Cato J.*, Fall 1986, *6*(2), pp. 539–43. **[G: U.S.]**

Grubel, Herbert G. Government Deposit Insurance, Moral Hazard and the International Debt Crisis. **In** *Giersch, H., ed.*, 1986, pp. 172–86. **[G: U.S.]**

Hafer, R. W. The FOMC in 1985: Reacting to Declining M1 Velocity. *Fed. Res. Bank St. Louis Rev.*, February 1986, *68*(2), pp. 5–21. **[G: U.S.]**

Hafer, R. W. The Response of Stock Prices to Changes in Weekly Money and the Discount Rate. *Fed. Res. Bank St. Louis Rev.*, March 1986, *68*(3), pp. 5–14. **[G: U.S.]**

Hall, Robert E. Monetary Policy under Financial

Innovation and Deregulation. **In** *Suzuki, Y. and Yomo, H., eds.*, 1986, pp. 227–39. **[G: U.S.]**

Hammer, Frederick S. Banking Markets: Comment. **In** *Saunders, A. and White, L. J., eds.*, 1986, pp. 161–63. **[G: U.S.]**

Hanson, James A. High Real Interest Rates and Spreads: An Introduction. **In** *Hanson, J. A. and Rocha, R.*, 1986, pp. 1–16. **[G: Selected Countries]**

Happ, Scott. The Behavior of Rates on Federal Funds and Repurchase Agreements. *Amer. Econ.*, Fall 1986, *30*(2), pp. 22–32. **[G: U.S.]**

Haraf, William S. Monetary Velocity and Monetary Rules. *Cato J.*, Fall 1986, *6*(2), pp. 641–62. **[G: U.S.]**

Hartmann, Wendelin. Deutsche Bundesbank and Payment System Risk in the Federal Republic of Germany. *J. Bank Res.*, 1986, *16*(4), pp. 214–17. **[G: W. Germany]**

Havrilesky, Thomas. The Effect of the Federal Reserve Reform Act on the Economic Affiliations of Directors of Federal Reserve Banks. *Soc. Sci. Quart.*, June 1986, *67*(2), pp. 393–401. **[G: U.S.]**

Heebner, A. Gilbert. Issues in the Conduct of Monetary Policy. *Bus. Econ.*, October 1986, *21*(4), pp. 26–31. **[G: U.S.]**

Heldring, Frederick. Payment System Risk in the United States. *J. Bank Res.*, 1986, *16*(4), pp. 209–13. **[G: U.S.]**

Henderson, Dan F. Access to the Japanese Market: Some Aspects of Foreign Exchange Controls and Banking Law. **In** *Saxonhouse, G. R. and Yamamura, K., eds.*, 1986, pp. 131–56. **[G: Japan]**

Hester, Donald D. Monetary Policy in an Evolutionary Disequilibrium. **In** *Suzuki, Y. and Yomo, H., eds.*, 1986, pp. 241–86. **[G: U.S.]**

Hetzel, Robert L. A Congressional Mandate for Monetary Policy. *Cato J.*, Winter 1986, *5*(3), pp. 797–20. **[G: U.S.]**

Hetzel, Robert L. Monetary Policy in the Early 1980s. *Fed. Res. Bank Richmond Econ. Rev.*, Mar./Apr. 1986, *72*(2), pp. 20–32. **[G: U.S.]**

Humphrey, David B. Payments Finality and Risk of Settlement Failure. **In** *Saunders, A. and White, L. J., eds.*, 1986, pp. 97–120. **[G: U.S.]**

Humphrey, Thomas M. Eliminating Runaway Inflation: Lessons from the German Hyperinflation. **In** *Humphreys, T. M.*, 1986, *1980*, pp. 237–41. **[G: Germany]**

Hussain, Athar. Money and Socialism: Comment. **In** *Smith, K., ed.*, 1986, *1978*, pp. 139–43. **[G: U.S.S.R.]**

Hutchison, Michael M. Japan's "Money Focused" Monetary Policy. *Fed. Res. Bank San Francisco Econ. Rev.*, Summer 1986, (3), pp. 33–46. **[G: Japan]**

Ingram, James C. Central Bank Intervention: To Sterilize or Not? *Banca Naz. Lavoro Quart. Rev.*, June 1986, (157), pp. 179–86.

Isard, Peter and Rojas-Suarez, Liliana. Velocity of Money and the Practice of Monetary Targeting: Experience, Theory, and the Policy Debate. **In** *International Monetary Fund, Research Department*, 1986, pp. 73–114. **[G: OECD]**

Islam, Shafiqul. The Dollar: Fickle Fundamentals or Misguided Markets? *World Econ.*, December 1986, *9*(4), pp. 365–83. **[G: U.S.; OECD]**

Jager, Henk. Flexible Exchange Rates and National Monetary Policies: Comment. **In** *Tsoukalis, L., ed.*, 1986, pp. 192–98. **[G: OECD]**

Jao, Y. C. Financial Liberalization and Innovation in Seven East Asian Economies: Comments. **In** *Suzuki, Y. and Yomo, H., eds.*, 1986, pp. 125–31. **[G: E. Asia]**

Jessop, Bob. The Prospects for the Corporatisation of Monetarism in Britain. **In** *Jacobi, O., et al., eds. (II)*, 1986, pp. 105–30. **[G: U.K.]**

Johnson, Manuel H. Statement to the U.S. House Subcommittee on Financial Institutions Supervision, Regulation and Insurance of the Committee on Banking, Finance and Urban Affairs, June 4, 1986. *Fed. Res. Bull.*, August 1986, *72*(8), pp. 531–34. **[G: U.S.]**

Jones, Robert A. U.S. Monetary Policy Responses to the Debt Crisis. **In** *Claudon, M. P., ed.*, 1986, pp. 85–98. **[G: U.S.]**

Jonung, Lars. International Financial Crisis and the Swedish Economy 1857–1933. **In** *Capie, F. and Wood, G. E., eds.*, 1986, pp. 254–64. **[G: Sweden]**

Jordan, Jerry L. Economic Outlook. **In** *Shadow Open Market Committee (I)*, 1986, pp. 9–18. **[G: U.S.]**

Jordan, Jerry L. Monetary Policy as a Fiscal Instrument. *Cato J.*, Winter 1986, *5*(3), pp. 733–41. **[G: U.S.]**

Joyce, Joseph P. Canadian Exchange Market Intervention and Domestic Monetary Operations. *Quart. Rev. Econ. Bus.*, Summer 1986, *26*(2), pp. 94–105. **[G: Canada]**

Kallberg, Jarl G. and Parkinson, Kenneth L. Banking Markets: Comment. **In** *Saunders, A. and White, L. J., eds.*, 1986, pp. 155–59. **[G: U.S.]**

Kamas, Linda. The Balance of Payments Offset to Monetary Policy: Monetarist, Portfolio Balance, and Keynesian Estimates for Mexico and Venezuela. *J. Money, Credit, Banking*, November 1986, *18*(4), pp. 467–81. **[G: Mexico; Venezuela]**

Kane, Edward J. Confronting Incentive Problems in U.S. Deposit Insurance: The Range of Alternative Solutions. **In** *Kaufman, G. G. and Kormendi, R. C., eds.*, 1986, pp. 97–120. **[G: U.S.]**

Katz, Samuel I. Government Deposit Insurance, Moral Hazard and the International Debt Crisis: Comment. **In** *Giersch, H., ed.*, 1986, pp. 187–91. **[G: U.S.]**

Kaufman, Herbert M. and Lombra, Raymond E. The Effect of Changes in the Federal Reserve's Policy Rule on the Stochastic Structure Linking Reserves, Interest Rates, and Money. *Southern Econ. J.*, April 1986, *52*(4), pp. 1080–87. **[G: U.S.]**

Keeley, Michael C. and Zimmerman, Gary C. Deposit Rate Deregulation and the Demand for Transactions Media. *Fed. Res. Bank San Francisco Econ. Rev.*, Summer 1986, (3), pp. 47–62. [G: U.S.]

Kimbrough, Kent P. Monetary Procedures and Monetary Policy. **In** *Campbell, C. D. and Dougan, W. R., eds.*, 1986, pp. 215–23. [G: U.S.]

Kohli, Ulrich and Rich, Georg. Monetary Control: The Swiss Experience. *Cato J.*, Winter 1986, *5*(3), pp. 911–26. [G: Switzerland]

Krejča, František. Principles of Domestic and External Monetary Bank Policy after 1985. *Czech. Econ. Digest.*, May 1986, (3), pp. 24–46. [G: Czechoslovakia]

Kuprianov, Anatoli. An Analysis of Federal Reserve Pricing. *Fed. Res. Bank Richmond Econ. Rev.*, Mar./Apr. 1986, *72*(2), pp. 3–19. [G: U.S.]

Lavigne, Marie. The Creation of Money by the State Bank of the USSR. **In** *Smith, K., ed.*, 1986, *1978*, pp. 112–38. [G: U.S.S.R.]

Layton, Allan P. A Second Look at the U.S.–Australian Monetary Growth Causal Nexus. *Appl. Econ.*, April 1986, *18*(4), pp. 443–51. [G: U.S.; Australia]

Leddin, Anthony. Portfolio Equilibrium and Monetary Policy in Ireland. *Econ. Soc. Rev.*, January 1986, *17*(2), pp. 133–46. [G: Ireland]

Ledingham, P. J. Liquidity Management Policy. **In** *Reserve Bank of New Zealand*, 1986, pp. 65–85. [G: New Zealand]

Leite, Sergio Pereira and Vaez-Zadeh, Reza. Credit Allocation and Investment Decisions: The Case of the Manufacturing Sector in Korea. *World Devel.*, January 1986, *14*(1), pp. 115–26. [G: S. Korea]

Lelart, Michel. Zone monétaire et convertibilité: l'expérience africaine. (Currency Zone and Convertibility: The African Experience. With English summary.) *Écon. Soc.*, February 1986, *20*(2), pp. 135–67. [G: Africa]

Levy, Aviram. Tasso di cambio e interventi delle banche centrali: Schemi teorici ed esperienza italiana. (Exchange Rate and Central Banks' Exchange Market Intervention: Theoretical Issues and the Italian Experience. With English summary.) *Giorn. Econ.*, July-Aug. 1986, *45*(7–8), pp. 407–31. [G: Italy]

Liang, Ming-Yih. Bank Float, Mail Float and the Definition of Money. *J. Banking Finance*, December 1986, *10*(4), pp. 533–48. [G: U.S.]

Lindsey, David E. The Monetary Regime of the Federal Reserve System. **In** *Campbell, C. D. and Dougan, W. R., eds.*, 1986, pp. 168–208. [G: U.S.]

Lombardi, Mauro. Anni '70: il governo della moneta tra economia e politica. (With English summary.) *Stud. Econ.*, 1986, *41*(29), pp. 99–146. [G: Italy]

Mallyon, Jim S. The Process of Financial Deregulation, Monetary Reform, and the Financial System of the Future: Comments. **In** *Suzuki, Y. and Yomo, H., eds.*, 1986, pp. 203–06. [G: U.S.]

Maravall, Agustin and Pierce, David A. The Transmission of Data Noise into Policy Noise in U.S. Monetary Control. *Econometrica*, July 1986, *54*(4), pp. 961–79. [G: U.S.]

Martin, Preston. Savings Banking in the Next Decade. **In** *Federal Home Loan Bank of San Francisco*, 1986, pp. 5–11. [G: U.S.]

Mauri, Arnaldo and Caselli, Clara. Financial Evolution and the Role of Central Banks in Africa. **In** *Association of African Central Banks*, 1986, pp. 60–110. [G: Africa]

McLeod, Alex N. Credit Aggregates: Some Suggestions. *Banca Naz. Lavoro Quart. Rev.*, June 1986, (157), pp. 186–95. [G: U.S.]

McNees, Stephen K. Modeling the Fed: A Forward-Looking Monetary Policy Reaction Functions. *New Eng. Econ. Rev.*, Nov./Dec. 1986, pp. 3–8. [G: U.S.]

Meiselman, David I. Avoidable Uncertainty and the Effects of Monetary Policy: Why Even Experts Can't Forecast [Monetary Control and the Political Business Cycle]. *Cato J.*, Winter 1986, *5*(3), pp. 701–07. [G: U.S.]

Meiselman, David I. Is There a Political Monetary Cycle? *Cato J.*, Fall 1986, *6*(2), pp. 563–79. [G: U.S.]

Meltzer, Allan H. Financial Failures and Financial Policies. **In** *Kaufman, G. G. and Kormendi, R. C., eds.*, 1986, pp. 79–96. [G: U.S.]

Meltzer, Allan H. Real and Psuedo-financial Crises: Comment. **In** *Capie, F. and Wood, G. E., eds.*, 1986, pp. 32–37. [G: U.S.; U.K.]

Mengle, David L. The Discount Window. *Fed. Res. Bank Richmond Econ. Rev.*, May/June 1986, *72*(3), pp. 2–10. [G: U.S.]

Meyer, Hans. The Role of the Swiss National Bank in the Payment System. *J. Bank Res.*, 1986, *16*(4), pp. 190–93. [G: Switzerland]

Michaelis, Dolf. One Hundred Years of Banking and Currency in Palestine. **In** *Uselding, P., ed.*, 1986, pp. 155–97. [G: Palestine; Middle East]

Miles, Marc A. Stabilizing the Dollar in a Global Economy. *Cato J.*, Winter 1986, *5*(3), pp. 825–41. [G: U.S.]

Miller, Stephen M. Financial Innovation, Depository–Institution Deregulation, and the Demand for Money. *J. Macroecon.*, Summer 1986, *8*(3), pp. 279–96. [G: U.S.]

Miron, Jeffrey A. Financial Panics, the Seasonality of the Nominal Interest Rate, and the Founding of the Fed. *Amer. Econ. Rev.*, March 1986, *76*(1), pp. 125–40. [G: U.S.]

Moggridge, D. E. Real and Pseudo-financial Crises: Comment. **In** *Capie, F. and Wood, G. E., eds.*, 1986, pp. 38–40. [G: U.S.; U.K.]

Mohanty, Subhransu Sekhar. An Empirical Evaluation of Public Deposits as a Source of Finance in the Corporate Sector. *Indian Econ. J.*, July-Sept. 1986, *34*(1), pp. 59–78. [G: India]

Moreno, Ramon. Monetary Control without a Central Bank: The Case of Hong Kong. *Fed. Res. Bank San Francisco Econ. Rev.*, Spring 1986, (2), pp. 17–37. [G: Hong Kong]

Morris, Frank E. The Changing World of Central

Banking. *New Eng. Econ. Rev.*, Mar./Apr. 1986, pp. 3–6. **[G: U.S.]**

Motley, Brian and Rasche, Robert H. Predicting the Money Stock: A Comparison of Alternative Approaches. *Fed. Res. Bank San Francisco Econ. Rev.*, Spring 1986, (2), pp. 38–54. **[G: U.S.]**

Mounts, Wm. Stewart, Jr. and Sowell, Clifford. The Structure and Use of Inputs by the Federal Reserve: Reconsidered: The Monetary Constitution, Human Capital, and Property Rights. **In** *Toma, E. F. and Toma, M., eds.*, 1986, pp. 91–104. **[G: U.S.]**

Muth, Richard F. Financial Deregulation and the Cost of Mortgage Funds. **In** *Grieson, R. E., ed.*, 1986, pp. 153–64. **[G: U.S.]**

Nambara, Akira. Financial Reform in Japan: A Central Banker's View. **In** *Cheng, H.-S., ed.*, 1986, pp. 65–67. **[G: Japan]**

Neumann, Manfred J. M. Die Grundgeldmenge—Ein neuer Indikator der Geldpolitik. (The Base Money Stock—A New Indictor of Monetary Policy. With English summary.) *Weltwirtsch. Arch.*, 1986, *122*(3), pp. 520–32. **[G: W. Germany]**

Nickelsburg, Gerald. Rediscounting Private Dollar Debt and Capital Flight in Ecuador. *J. Int. Money Finance*, December 1986, *5*(4), pp. 497–503. **[G: Ecuador]**

Nielsen, Peter Erling. Dansk pengepolitik under forvandling. (Monetary Policy in Denmark. With English summary.) *Nationaløkon. Tidsskr.*, 1986, *124*(1), pp. 40–50. **[G: Denmark]**

Nötel, R. International Finance and Monetary Reforms. **In** *Kaser, M. C. and Radice, E. A., eds.*, 1986, pp. 520–63. **[G: E. Europe]**

Officer, Lawrence H. The Efficiency of the Dollar–Sterling Gold Standard, 1890–1908. *J. Polit. Econ.*, October 1986, *94*(5), pp. 1038–73. **[G: U.S.; U.K.]**

Owens, John E. The State Regulation and Deregulation of Financial Institutions and Services in the United States. **In** *Cox, A., ed.*, 1986, pp. 172–230. **[G: U.S.]**

Parsons, R. W. K. The Reserve Bank and the Treasury. *S. Afr. J. Econ.*, March 1986, *54*(1), pp. 108–14. **[G: S. Africa]**

Partee, J. Charles. The Status of Banking Deregulation in the United States. **In** *Cheng, H.-S., ed.*, 1986, pp. 59–63. **[G: U.S.]**

Partlan, John C.; Hamdani, Kausar and Camilli, Kathleen M. Reserves Forecasting for Open Market Operations. *Fed. Res. Bank New York Quart. Rev.*, Spring 1986, *11*(1), pp. 19–33. **[G: U.S.]**

Petrovich, Giuliano. Politiche di contenimento e diversione del sistema dei *Factors*. (Credit Restrictions and Factoring Diversion. With English summary.) *Ricerche Econ.*, Apr.-Sept. 1986, *40*(2–3), pp. 447–62. **[G: Italy]**

Phillips, M. John. Financial Reform: The Australian Experience. **In** *Cheng, H.-S., ed.*, 1986, pp. 105–12. **[G: Australia]**

Pierce, James L. Financial Reform in the United States and the Financial System of the Future. **In** *Suzuki, Y. and Yomo, H., eds.*, 1986, pp. 183–201. **[G: U.S.]**

Poole, William. Is Monetarism Dead? *Bus. Econ.*, October 1986, *21*(4), pp. 10–15. **[G: U.S.]**

Poole, William. Monetary Control and the Political Business Cycle. *Cato J.*, Winter 1986, *5*(3), pp. 685–99. **[G: U.S.]**

Pressnell, L. S. The Avoidance of Catastrophe: Two Nineteenth-Century Banking Crises: Comment. **In** *Capie, F. and Wood, G. E., eds.*, 1986, pp. 74–76. **[G: U.K.]**

Pyle, David H. Financial Deregulation. **In** *Cagan, P., ed.*, 1986, pp. 147–90. **[G: U.S.]**

Rasche, Robert H. Velocity and the Choice of Policy Regimes [Monetary Velocity and Monetary Rules]. *Cato J.*, Fall 1986, *6*(2), pp. 663–66. **[G: U.S.]**

Raymond, Robert. Implications for Monetary Policy: Comments. **In** *Suzuki, Y. and Yomo, H., eds.*, 1986, pp. 295–99.

Reynolds, Alan. Fed Watching and the Monetary Regime. *Cato J.*, Fall 1986, *6*(2), pp. 545–55. **[G: U.S.]**

Rice, Emmett J. Statement to the U.S. Senate Subcommittee on Financial Institutions and Consumer Affairs of the Committee on Banking, Housing, and Urban Affairs, January 28, 1986. *Fed. Res. Bull.*, March 1986, *72*(3), pp. 180–84. **[G: U.S.]**

Rice, Emmett J. Statement to the U.S. Senate Subcommittee on Financial Institutions and Consumer Affairs of the Committee on Banking, Housing, and Urban Affairs, May 21, 1986. *Fed. Res. Bull.*, July 1986, *72*(7), pp. 472–75. **[G: U.S.]**

Roberts, Paul Craig. How the Fed Crowded Out Reagan's Economic Policy. *Cato J.*, Winter 1986, *5*(3), pp. 777–85. **[G: U.S.]**

Roberts, Paul Craig. Problems with Monetary Policy. *Bus. Econ.*, October 1986, *21*(4), pp. 16–20. **[G: U.S.]**

Rockoff, Hugh. Walter Bagehot and the Theory of Central Banking. **In** *Capie, F. and Wood, G. E., eds.*, 1986, pp. 160–80.

Roos, Lawrence K. Inherent Conflicts of U.S. Monetary Policymaking. *Cato J.*, Winter 1986, *5*(3), pp. 771–76. **[G: U.S.]**

Rōyama, Shōichi. The Process of Financial Deregulation, Monetary Reform, and the Financial System of the Future: Comments. **In** *Suzuki, Y. and Yomo, H., eds.*, 1986, pp. 217–20.

Salop, Joanne. Monetary Targeting in the United Kingdom. *Finance Develop.*, December 1986, *23*(4), pp. 33–35. **[G: U.K.]**

Santoni, Gary J. A Private Central Bank: Some Olde English Lessons. **In** *Toma, E. F. and Toma, M., eds.*, 1986, *1984*, pp. 219–39. **[G: U.K.]**

Savona, Paolo. Money Supply, Wages and Prices: Reflections with Hindsight. *Rev. Econ. Cond. Italy*, Sept.-Dec. 1986, (3), pp. 485–510. **[G: Italy]**

Schiltknecht, Kurt. Walter Bagehot and the Theory of Central Banking: Comment. **In** *Capie, F. and Wood, G. E., eds.*, 1986, pp. 181–84.

Schwartz, Anna J. Assessing the Fed's Control of Domestic Monetary Policy [Stabilizing the Dollar in a Global Economy]. *Cato J.*, Winter 1986, *5*(3), pp. 843–48. **[G: U.S.]**

Schwartz, Anna J. Real and Pseudo-financial Crises. **In** *Capie, F. and Wood, G. E., eds.*, 1986, pp. 11–40. **[G: U.S.; U.K.]**

Seabourne, Teresa. The Summer of 1914. **In** *Capie, F. and Wood, G. E., eds.*, 1986, pp. 77–116. **[G: U.K.; Europe]**

Seidman, L. William. Equitably Allocating Federal Insurance Premiums. **In** *Federal Home Loan Bank of San Francisco*, 1986, pp. 71–75. **[G: U.S.]**

Shughart, William F., II and Tollison, Robert D. Preliminary Evidence on the Use of Inputs by the Federal Reserve System. **In** *Toma, E. F. and Toma, M., eds.*, 1986, *1983*, pp. 67–90. **[G: U.S.]**

Sinkey, Joseph F., Jr. Can Regulation and Supervision Ensure Financial Stability? **In** *Federal Home Loan Bank of San Francisco*, 1986, pp. 133–48. **[G: U.S.]**

Skaggs, Neil T. and Wasserkrug, Cheryl L. Banking Sector Influence on the Relationship of Congress to the Federal Reserve System. **In** *Toma, E. F. and Toma, M., eds.*, 1986, *1983*, pp. 169–82. **[G: U.S.]**

Stammer, Donald. Interest Rates, Money and the Availability of Credit. **In** *Bruce, R., et al., eds.*, 1986, pp. 33–48. **[G: Australia]**

Sternlight, Peter D. and Meulendyke, Ann-Marie. Monetary Policy and Open Market Operations in 1985. *Fed. Res. Bank New York Quart. Rev.*, Spring 1986, *11*(1), pp. 34–53. **[G: U.S.]**

Takagi, Shinji. Rediscount Policy and Official Capital Flows: A Study of Monetary Control in Central America in the 1950s. *J. Money, Credit, Banking*, May 1986, *18*(2), pp. 200–210. **[G: Costa Rica; El Salvador; Nicaragua]**

Taylor, Herb. Deposit Market Deregulation and the Recent Behavior of M1. *Eastern Econ. J.*, July-Sept. 1986, *12*(3), pp. 307–12. **[G: U.S.]**

Teh, Kok Peng. Monetary Policy in an Evolutionary Disequilibrium: Comments. **In** *Suzuki, Y. and Yomo, H., eds.*, 1986, pp. 301–04. **[G: U.S.]**

Thornton, J. A Note on Repurchase Agreements, Bank Behaviour and Monetary Policy. *S. Afr. J. Econ.*, December 1986, *54*(4), pp. 437–39. **[G: W. Germany]**

Thygesen, Niels. Flexible Exchange Rates and National Monetary Policies. **In** *Tsoukalis, L., ed.*, 1986, pp. 163–85. **[G: OECD]**

Timberlake, Richard H., Jr. Institutional Evolution of Federal Reserve Hegemony. *Cato J.*, Winter 1986, *5*(3), pp. 743–63. **[G: U.S.]**

Tobin, James. Financial Innovation and Deregulation in Perspective. **In** *Suzuki, Y. and Yomo, H., eds.*, 1986, pp. 31–42.

Tobin, James. Monetary Control in a Brave New World. **In** *Lawrence, C. and Shay, R. P., eds.*, 1986, pp. 190–95. **[G: U.S.]**

Tobin, James. Monetary Policy Symposium: Closing Comments. **In** *Lawrence, C. and Shay, R. P., eds.*, 1986, pp. 207–08. **[G: U.S.]**

Toma, Eugenia Froedge and Toma, Mark. Central Bankers and the Issue of Independence. **In** *Toma, E. F. and Toma, M., eds.*, 1986, pp. 243–49.

Toma, Eugenia Froedge and Toma, Mark. Central Bankers, Bureaucratic Incentives, and Monetary Policy: An Introduction. **In** *Toma, E. F. and Toma, M., eds.*, 1986, pp. 1–7.

Toma, Eugenia Froedge and Toma, Mark. Research Activities and Budget Allocations among Federal Reserve Banks. **In** *Toma, E. F. and Toma, M., eds.*, 1986, *1985*, pp. 151–68. **[G: U.S.]**

Toma, Mark. Inflationary Bias of the Federal Reserve System: A Bureaucratic Perspective. **In** *Toma, E. F. and Toma, M., eds.*, 1986, *1982*, pp. 37–66. **[G: U.S.]**

Tweedie, A. J. Monetary Policy in New Zealand. **In** *Reserve Bank of New Zealand*, 1986, pp. 47–62. **[G: New Zealand]**

Udell, Gregory F. Technology and Bank Monitoring. **In** *Saunders, A. and White, L. J., eds.*, 1986, pp. 137–54. **[G: U.S.]**

Uppal, J. S. Public Financial Institutions and Economic Concentration in India. *J. Devel. Econ.*, Jan.-Feb. 1986, *20*(1), pp. 135–44. **[G: India]**

Urkowitz, Michael. Paper-Based Payments—A System in Transition. *J. Bank Res.*, 1986, *16*(4), pp. 241–43. **[G: U.S.]**

Vaez-Zadeh, Reza and Leite, Sergio Pereira. Effectiveness of Selective Credit Controls: An Empirical Test Applied to India. *J. Devel. Stud.*, April 1986, *22*(3), pp. 558–72. **[G: India]**

Verma, Satish. Controlling the Borrowed Reserves of Scheduled Commercial Banks in India. *Indian Econ. J.*, July-Sept. 1986, *34*(1), pp. 23–33. **[G: India]**

Volcker, Paul A. Statement to the U.S. House Subcommittee on Domestic Monetary Policy of the Committee on Banking, Finance and Urban Affairs, January 29, 1986. *Fed. Res. Bull.*, March 1986, *72*(3), pp. 184–90. **[G: U.S.]**

Volcker, Paul A. Statement to the U.S. House Subcommittee on Financial Institutions Supervision, Regulation and Insurance of the Committee on Banking, Finance and Urban Affairs, May 7, 1986. *Fed. Res. Bull.*, July 1986, *72*(7), pp. 463–67. **[G: U.S.]**

Volcker, Paul A. Statement to the U.S. House Subcommittee on Domestic Monetary Policy of the Committee on Banking, Finance and Urban Affairs, December 12, 1985. *Fed. Res. Bull.*, February 1986, *72*(2), pp. 115–16. **[G: U.S.]**

Volcker, Paul A. Statement to the U.S. House Committee on Banking, Finance and Urban Affairs, February 19, 1986. *Fed. Res. Bull.*, April 1986, *72*(4), pp. 233–41. **[G: U.S.]**

Volcker, Paul A. Statement to the U.S. House Committee on the Budget, February 26, 1986. *Fed. Res. Bull.*, April 1986, *72*(4), pp. 241–43. **[G: U.S.]**

Volcker, Paul A. Statement to the U.S. House Subcommittee on Domestic Monetary Policy of the Committee on Banking, Finance and Urban Affairs, June 5, 1986. *Fed. Res. Bull.*, August 1986, *72*(8), pp. 534–41. **[G: U.S.]**

Volcker, Paul A. Statement to the U.S. Senate Committee on Banking, Housing, and Urban Affairs, July 23, 1986. *Fed. Res. Bull.*, September 1986, *72*(9), pp. 635–42. **[G: U.S.]**

Wagner, Michael. What Happened in 1931? Comment. **In** *Capie, F. and Wood, G. E., eds.*, 1986, pp. 157–59. **[G: U.K.]**

Wagner, Richard E. Central Banking and the Fed: A Public Choice Perspective. *Cato J.*, Fall 1986, *6*(2), pp. 519–38. **[G: U.S.]**

Wallich, Henry C. A Broad View of Deregulation. **In** *Cheng, H.-S., ed.*, 1986, pp. 3–12.

Wang, Weicai. China's Economic and Financial Reform. **In** *Cheng, H.-S., ed.*, 1986, pp. 227–34. **[G: China]**

Weber, Warren E. Do Sterilized Interventions Affect Exchange Rates? *Fed. Res. Bank Minn. Rev.*, Summer 1986, *10*(3), pp. 14–23. **[G: U.S.]**

Wenninger, John. Implications for Monetary Policy: Comments. **In** *Suzuki, Y. and Yomo, H., eds.*, 1986, pp. 291–93. **[G: U.S.]**

Wesierski, Brigitte. Konflikte der monetären Steuerung bei flexiblen Wechselkursen. (Conflicts on Monetary Control under Flexible Exchange Rates. With English summary.) *Kredit Kapital*, 1986, *19*(2), pp. 213–32. **[G: W. Germany]**

Westaway, P. F. Some Experiments with Simple Feedback Rules on the Treasury Model. *J. Econ. Dynam. Control*, June 1986, *10*(1/2), pp. 239–46. **[G: U.K.]**

White, Lawrence J. The Partial Deregulation of Banks and Other Depository Institutions. **In** *Weiss, L. W. and Klass, M. W., eds.*, 1986, pp. 169–209. **[G: U.S.]**

Wong, Shee Q. The Contribution of Inflation Uncertainty to the Variable Impacts of Money on Stock Prices. *J. Finan. Res.*, Spring 1986, *9*(1), pp. 97–101. **[G: U.S.]**

Woodward, R. S. The Effect of Monetary Surprises on Financial Futures Prices. *J. Futures Markets*, Fall 1986, *6*(3), pp. 375–83. **[G: U.S.]**

Yeager, Leland B. Price-Level Stability as the Goal of Monetary Reform [A Congressional Mandate for Monetary Policy]. *Cato J.*, Winter 1986, *5*(3), pp. 821–24. **[G: U.S.]**

312 Commercial Banking

3120 Commercial Banking

Abidin, Abang Zainal. Financial Reform and the Role of Foreign Banks in Malaysia. **In** *Cheng, H.-S., ed.*, 1986, pp. 305–09. **[G: Malaysia]**

Aharony, Joseph; Saunders, Anthony and Swary, Ithzak. The Effects of a Shift in Monetary Policy Regime on the Profitability and Risk of Commercial Banks. *J. Monet. Econ.*, May 1986, *17*(3), pp. 363–77. **[G: U.S.]**

Allen, Linda and Saunders, Anthony. The Large–Small Bank Dichotomy in the Federal Funds Market. *J. Banking Finance*, June 1986, *10*(2), pp. 219–30.

Anderlini, Luca. Competitive Banking in a Simple Model. **In** *Edwards, J., et al., eds.*, 1986, pp. 144–77.

Anderson, Richard G.; McCarthy, E. Jayne and Patten, Leslie A. Valuing the Core Deposits of Financial Institutions: A Statistical Analysis. *J. Bank Res.*, Spring 1986, *17*(1), pp. 9–17. **[G: U.S.]**

Andrikopoulos, Andreas A. and Brox, James A. The Demand for Deposits and Risk Sensitivity: The Case for Greece, 1955–1980. *Empirical Econ.*, 1986, *11*(4), pp. 197–206. **[G: Greece]**

Antiporda, Tirso D., Jr. Privatization in the Philippine Banking Sector. *Philippine Econ. J.*, 1986, *25*(1–2), pp. 7–16. **[G: Philippines]**

Aoki, Tatsuo. ATMs, POS and Home Banking Developments in Japan. *J. Bank Res.*, 1986, *16*(4), pp. 218–20. **[G: Japan]**

Appleman, Norman. Payment System Needs of Corporations. *J. Bank Res.*, 1986, *16*(4), pp. 252–53. **[G: U.S.]**

Ashenfelter, Orley and Hannan, Timothy. Sex Discrimination and Product Market Competition: The Case of the Banking Industry. *Quart. J. Econ.*, February 1986, *101*(1), pp. 149–73. **[G: U.S.]**

Assunção, João and Lucas, Maria da Conceição. Decision Support Systems for Dimensioning Branch Cashiers. *Economia (Portugal)*, January 1986, *10*(1), pp. 99–108.

Baliño, Tómas J. T. and Sundararajan, V. Financial Reform in Indonesia: Causes, Consequences, and Prospects. **In** *Cheng, H.-S., ed.*, 1986, pp. 191–219. **[G: Indonesia]**

Barbé, Henri-Jean. Cheque Truncation in Belgium. *J. Bank Res.*, 1986, *16*(4), pp. 235–40. **[G: Belgium]**

Batchelor, Roy A. The Avoidance of Catastrophe: Two Nineteenth-Century Banking Crises. **In** *Capie, F. and Wood, G. E., eds.*, 1986, pp. 41–73. **[G: U.K.]**

Ben-David, Arie and Sterling, Leon. A Prototype Expert System for Credit Evaluation. **In** *Pau, L. F., ed.*, 1986, pp. 121–28.

Bennett, Barbara. Off Balance Sheet Risk in Banking: The Case of Standby Letters of Credit. *Fed. Res. Bank San Francisco Econ. Rev.*, Winter 1986, (1), pp. 19–29. **[G: U.S.]**

Benston, George J. Federal Regulation of Banking: Historical Overview. **In** *Kaufman, G. G. and Kormendi, R. C., eds.*, 1986, pp. 1–47. **[G: U.S.]**

Benston, George J. Regulatory Policies and Financial Stability: Commentary. **In** *Axilrod, S. H., et al.*, 1986, pp. 137–51. **[G: U.S.]**

Benston, George J. and Kaufman, George G. Risks and Failures in Banking: Overview, History, and Evaluation. **In** *Kaufman, G. G. and Kormendi, R. C., eds.*, 1986, pp. 49–77. **[G: U.S.]**

Berger, Allen N. The Role of Interstate Banking

in the Diffusion of Electronic Payments Technology: Rejoinder. **In** *Lawrence, C. and Shay, R. P., eds.*, 1986, pp. 105. **[G: U.S.]**

Berger, Allen N. and Humphrey, David B. The Role of Interstate Banking in the Diffusion of Electronic Payments Technology. **In** *Lawrence, C. and Shay, R. P., eds.*, 1986, pp. 13–52. **[G: U.S.]**

Bertoni, Alberto. Major Banks in Italy: New Objectives and Strategies. *Rev. Econ. Cond. Italy*, May-Aug. 1986, (2), pp. 169–209. **[G: Italy]**

Bhat, N. S. The Banking System as the Financial Infrastructure of the Economy. *Indian Econ. J.*, July-Sept. 1986, *34*(1), pp. 34–40. **[G: India]**

Bisignano, Joseph. The Process of Financial Deregulation, Monetary Reform, and the Financial System of the Future: Comments. **In** *Suzuki, Y. and Yomo, H., eds.*, 1986, pp. 207–15. **[G: U.S.]**

Booth, G. Geoffrey and Koveos, Peter E. A Programming Model for Bank Hedging Decisions. *J. Finan. Res.*, Fall 1986, *9*(3), pp. 271–79.

Born, Jeffrey A. and Anderson, Seth Copeland. A Comparison of Intervention and Residual Analysis. *J. Finan. Res.*, Fall 1986, *9*(3), pp. 261–70. **[G: U.S.]**

Boyd, John H. and Graham, Stanley L. Risk, Regulation, and Bank Holding Company Expansion into Nonbanking. *Fed. Res. Bank Minn. Rev.*, Spring 1986, *10*(2), pp. 2–17. **[G: U.S.]**

Bradley, Michael D. and Jansen, Dennis W. Deposit Market Deregulation and Interest Rates. *Southern Econ. J.*, October 1986, *53*(2), pp. 478–89.

Braun, Hanne. A Review of the New Literature on Banking History. **In** *Pohl, H. and Rudolph, B., eds.*, 1986, pp. 143–50.

Brickley, James A. Returns and Risks of U.S. Bank Foreign Currency Activities: Discussion. *J. Finance*, July 1986, *41*(3), pp. 682–83. **[G: U.S.]**

Brobeck, Stephen. Corporate and Consumer Issues. *J. Bank Res.*, 1986, *16*(4), pp. 248–51. **[G: U.S.]**

Broll, Udo and Gilroy, Michael B. Collateral in Banking Policy and Adverse Selection. *Manchester Sch. Econ. Soc. Stud.*, December 1986, *54*(4), pp. 357–66.

Brunetti, Giorgio. Il controllo direzionale nel processo di cambiamento strategico–organizzativo delle aziende di credito. (The Role of Management Control in Banking's Strategic and Organizational Change. With English summary.) *Ricerche Econ.*, Apr.-Sept. 1986, *40*(2–3), pp. 478–88. **[G: Italy]**

Buswell, David. The Development of a Quality Measurement System for a UK Bank. **In** *Moores, B., ed.*, 1986, pp. 141–55. **[G: U.K.]**

Cagan, Phillip. Financial Regulation: Comment. *J. Bus.*, January 1986, *59*(1), pp. 49–54. **[G: U.S.]**

Cargill, Thomas F. Financial Reform in the United States and Japan: A Comparative Overview. **In** *Cheng, H.-S., ed.*, 1986, pp. 39–57. **[G: U.S.; Japan]**

Cargill, Thomas F.; Cheng, Hang-Sheng and Hutchison, Michael M. Financial Market Changes and Regulatory Reforms in Pacific Basin Countries: An Overview. **In** *Cheng, H.-S., ed.*, 1986, pp. 13–36. **[G: Pacific Basin]**

Carraro, Kenneth C. and Thornton, Daniel L. The Cost of Checkable Deposits in the United States. *Fed. Res. Bank St. Louis Rev.*, April 1986, *68*(4), pp. 19–27. **[G: U.S.]**

Carron, Andrew S. Financial Reform in Australia. **In** *Cheng, H.-S., ed.*, 1986, pp. 69–87. **[G: Australia]**

Carstensen, Erik. Den fremtidige arbejdsdeling på penge- og kapitalmarkedet. (The Future Structure of Financial Markets in Denmark. With English summary.) *Nationaløkon. Tidsskr.*, 1986, *124*(1), pp. 62–76. **[G: Denmark]**

Carter, R. L.; Chiplin, B. and Lewis, M. K. Markets, Regulation, and the Financial Firm. **In** *Carter, R. L.; Chiplin, B. and Lewis, M. K., eds.*, 1986, pp. 248–71. **[G: U.K.]**

Cassese, Sabino. Banks of National Interest and Changes in the Banking System. *Rev. Econ. Cond. Italy*, May-Aug. 1986, (2), pp. 237–49. **[G: Italy]**

Cebrecos Revilla, Felipe. Savings for Development: The Case of Peru. **In** *U.N., Dept. of International Econ. and Social Affairs*, 1986, pp. 65–70. **[G: Peru]**

Cesarini, Francesco. Equity Financing by Banks in the Italian Market: The 1980–1984 Experience and the New Trends. *J. Bank Res.*, Spring 1986, *17*(1), pp. 28–39. **[G: Italy]**

Chan, Yuk-Shee; Greenbaum, Stuart I. and Thakor, Anjan V. Information Reusability, Competition and Bank Asset Quality. *J. Banking Finance*, June 1986, *10*(2), pp. 243–53.

Chick, Victoria. The Evolution of the Banking System and the Theory of Saving, Investment and Interest. *Écon. Soc.*, Aug.-Sept. 1986, *20*(8–9), pp. 111–26.

Child, Denis M. Payments Issues in the United Kingdom. *J. Bank Res.*, 1986, *16*(4), pp. 198–201. **[G: U.K.]**

Chiplin, B. Information Technology and Personal Financial Services. **In** *Carter, R. L.; Chiplin, B. and Lewis, M. K., eds.*, 1986, pp. 75–105. **[G: U.K.]**

Choi, Sang-Rim; Tschoegl, Adrian E. and Yu, Chwo-Ming. Banks and the World's Major Financial Centers, 1970–1980. *Weltwirtsch. Arch.*, 1986, *122*(1), pp. 48–64. **[G: Global]**

Clark, Jeffrey A. Market Structure, Risk, and Profitability: The Quiet Life Hypothesis Revisited. *Quart. Rev. Econ. Bus.*, Spring 1986, *26*(1), pp. 45–56. **[G: U.S.]**

Clark, Jeffrey A. Single-Equation, Multiple-Regression Methodology: Is It an Appropriate Methodology for the Estimation of the Structure–Performance Relationship in Banking? *J. Monet. Econ.*, November 1986, *18*(3), pp. 295–312. **[G: U.S.]**

Cole, John A. and Reuben, Lucy J. Linkages between Minority Business Characteristics an Minority Banks' Locations. *Rev. Black Polit. Econ.*, Fall 1986, *15*(2), pp. 73–92. **[G: U.S.]**

Cooke, William Peter. Regulatory Policies and Financial Stability: Commentary. **In** *Axilrod, S. H., et al.*, 1986, pp. 153–63. **[G: U.S.]**

Cornell, Bradford and Shapiro, Alan C. The Reaction of Bank Stock Price to the International Debt Crisis. *J. Banking Finance*, March 1986, *10*(1), pp. 55–73. **[G: U.S.]**

Corrigan, E. Gerald. Statement to the U.S. House Subcommittee on Domestic Monetary Policy of the Committee on Banking, Finance and Urban Affairs, December 12, 1985. *Fed. Res. Bull.*, February 1986, *72*(2), pp. 117–25. **[G: U.S.]**

Cottrell, P. L. Atlas of Industrializing Britain 1780–1914: Banking and Finance. **In** *Langton, J. and Morris, R. J., eds.*, 1986, pp. 144–55. **[G: U.K.]**

Crouhy, Michel and Galai, Dan. An Economic Assessment of Capital Requirements in the Banking Industry. *J. Banking Finance*, June 1986, *10*(2), pp. 231–41.

Cyrnak, Anthony W. Chain Banks and Competition: The Effectiveness of Federal Reserve Policy in 1977. *Fed. Res. Bank San Francisco Econ. Rev.*, Spring 1986, (2), pp. 5–15. **[G: U.S.]**

Danker, Deborah J. and McLaughlin, Mary M. Profitability of U.S.-Chartered Insured Commercial Banks in 1985. *Fed. Res. Bull.*, September 1986, *72*(9), pp. 618–32. **[G: U.S.]**

Darby, Michael R. The Internationalization of American Banking and Finance: Structure, Risk, and World Interest Rates. *J. Int. Money Finance*, December 1986, *5*(4), pp. 403–28. **[G: U.S.]**

Davis, Richard G. The Recent Performance of the Commercial Banking Industry. *Fed. Res. Bank New York Quart. Rev.*, Summer 1986, *11*(2), pp. 1–11. **[G: U.S.]**

Davis, Richard G. and Korobow, Leon. The Pricing of Consumer Deposit Products—The Nonrate Dimensions. *Fed. Res. Bank New York Quart. Rev.*, Winter 1986-87, *11*(4), pp. 14–18. **[G: U.S.]**

Davis, Richard G.; Korobow, Leon and Wenninger, John. Bankers on Pricing Consumer Deposits. *Fed. Res. Bank New York Quart. Rev.*, Winter 1986-87, *11*(4), pp. 6–13. **[G: U.S.]**

Deane, Roderick S. Financial Sector Policy Reform: The Case of New Zealand. **In** *Cheng, H.-S., ed.*, 1986, pp. 89–104. **[G: New Zealand]**

Dermine, J. Deposit Rates, Credit Rates and Bank Capital: The Klein–Monti Model Revisited. *J. Banking Finance*, March 1986, *10*(1), pp. 99–114.

Devlin, Robert. La estructura y comportamiento de la banca international en los años setenta y su impacto en la crísis de América Latina. (The Structure and Behavior of the International Banking System in the Seventies and Its Impact on the Crisis of Latin America. With English summary.) *Colección Estud. CIEPLAN*, June 1986, (19), pp. 5–55. **[G: Latin America]**

Diamond, Douglas W. and Dybvig, Philip H. Banking Theory, Deposit Insurance, and Bank Regulation. *J. Bus.*, January 1986, *59*(1), pp. 55–68. **[G: U.S.]**

Díaz-Alejandro, Carlos F. Some Unintended Consequences of Financial Laissez-Faire. **In** *[Hirshman, A. O.]*, 1986, pp. 91–113. **[G: Chile]**

Dingle, James F. The Role of the Bank of Canada in the Canadian Payments System. *J. Bank Res.*, 1986, *16*(4), pp. 194–97. **[G: Canada]**

Doughty, A. J. New Banks and Financial Structure Reform. **In** *Reserve Bank of New Zealand*, 1986, pp. 111–23. **[G: New Zealand]**

Douglas, William E. Evolution of Electronic Payments and Collections in the U.S. Government. *J. Bank Res.*, 1986, *16*(4), pp. 206–08. **[G: U.S.]**

Doukas, John. Bankers versus Bankruptcy Prediction Models: An Empirical Investigation, 1979–82. *Appl. Econ.*, May 1986, *18*(5), pp. 479–93. **[G: Canada]**

Dudley, William C. Controlling Risk on Large-Dollar Wire Transfer Systems. **In** *Saunders, A. and White, L. J., eds.*, 1986, pp. 121–35. **[G: U.S.]**

Dunham, Constance R. Interstate Banking and the Outflow of Local Funds. *New Eng. Econ. Rev.*, Mar./Apr. 1986, pp. 7–19. **[G: U.S.]**

Dunham, Constance R. Regional Banking Competition. *New Eng. Econ. Rev.*, July/Aug. 1986, pp. 3–19. **[G: U.S.]**

Dyson, Kenneth. The State, Banks and Industry: The West German Case. **In** *Cox, A., ed.*, 1986, pp. 118–41. **[G: W. Germany]**

Eaton, Jonathan. Lending with Costly Enforcement of Repayment and Potential Fraud. *J. Banking Finance*, June 1986, *10*(2), pp. 281–93.

Economopoulos, Andrew J. The Impact of Reserve Requirements on Free Bank Failures. *Atlantic Econ. J.*, December 1986, *14*(4), pp. 76–84. **[G: U.S.]**

Edwards, Franklin R. Concentration in Banking: Problem or Solution? **In** *Kaufman, G. G. and Kormendi, R. C., eds.*, 1986, pp. 145–68. **[G: U.S.]**

Edwards, Franklin R. Technology and Regulation: Commentary. **In** *Lawrence, C. and Shay, R. P., eds.*, 1986, pp. 144–48. **[G: U.S.]**

Eisenbeis, Robert A. Regulatory Policies and Financial Stability. **In** *Axilrod, S. H., et al.*, 1986, pp. 107–35. **[G: U.S.]**

Eisenbeis, Robert A. Risk as a Criterion for Expanding Banking Activities. **In** *Kaufman, G. G. and Kormendi, R. C., eds.*, 1986, pp. 169–89. **[G: U.S.]**

Esbitt, Milton. Bank Portfolios and Bank Failures during the Great Depression: Chicago. *J. Econ. Hist.*, June 1986, *46*(2), pp. 455–62. **[G: U.S.]**

Estanislao, Jesus P. Privatization in the Financial

Sector. *Philippine Econ. J.*, 1986, *25*(1–2), pp. 1–6. **[G: Philippines]**

Evans, John J. Commercial Banks and the Consumer Services Revolution. *J. Bank Res.*, 1986, *16*(4), pp. 182–85. **[G: U.S.]**

Felgran, Steven D. and Ferguson, R. Edward. The Evolution of Retail EFT Networks. *New Eng. Econ. Rev.*, July/Aug. 1986, pp. 42–56. **[G: U.S.]**

Fenstermaker, J. Van and Filer, John E. Impact of the First and Second Banks of the United States and the Suffolk System on New England Bank Money: 1791–1837. *J. Money, Credit, Banking*, February 1986, *18*(1), pp. 28–40. **[G: U.S.]**

Flannery, Mark J. Technology and Banking: Commentary. **In** *Lawrence, C. and Shay, R. P., eds.*, 1986, pp. 93–97. **[G: U.S.]**

Flemming, John S. Implications for Monetary Policy: Comments. **In** *Suzuki, Y. and Yomo, H., eds.*, 1986, pp. 287–90. **[G: U.S.; U.K.]**

Friedman, Milton and Schwartz, Anna J. The Failure of the Bank of United States: A Reappraisal: A Reply [A Monetary History]. *Exploration Econ. Hist.*, April 1986, *23*(2), pp. 199–204. **[G: U.S.]**

Fry, Maxwell J. Financial Structure, Financial Regulation, and Financial Reform in the Philippines and Thailand, 1960–1984. **In** *Cheng, H.-S., ed.*, 1986, pp. 161–84. **[G: Philippines; Thailand]**

Garten, Helen A. Banking On the Market: Relying On Depositors to Control Bank Risks. *Yale J. Regul.*, Fall 1986, *4*(1), pp. 129–72. **[G: U.S.]**

Gentili, Matteo Mattei. Strategy Options, Human Resources and Organization of Major Banks. *Rev. Econ. Cond. Italy*, May-Aug. 1986, (2), pp. 225–36. **[G: Italy]**

Gilbert, R. Alton. Requiem for Regulation Q: What It Did and Why It Passed Away. *Fed. Res. Bank St. Louis Rev.*, February 1986, *68*(2), pp. 22–37. **[G: U.S.]**

Gilbert, R. Alton and Wood, Geoffrey E. Coping with Bank Failures: Some Lessons from the United States and the United Kingdom. *Fed. Res. Bank St. Louis Rev.*, December 1986, *68*(10), pp. 5–14. **[G: U.S.; U.K.]**

Goodfriend, Marvin and Whelpley, William. Federal Funds: Instrument of Federal Reserve Policy. *Fed. Res. Bank Richmond Econ. Rev.*, Sept./Oct. 1986, *72*(5), pp. 3–11. **[G: U.S.]**

Goodhart, Charles. How Can Non-interest-bearing Assets Co-exist with Safe Interest-Bearing Assets? *Brit. Rev. Econ. Issues*, Autumn 1986, *8*(19), pp. 1–12.

Goodman, Laurie S. The Interface between Technology and Regulation in Banking. **In** *Saunders, A. and White, L. J., eds.*, 1986, pp. 181–86.

Goodman, Laurie S. and Santomero, Anthony M. Variable-Rate Deposit Insurance: A Re-examination. *J. Banking Finance*, June 1986, *10*(2), pp. 203–18.

Göppl, Hermann. Operating-Leverage als weiteres Bankrisiko? (With English summary.) *Z. Betriebswirtshaft*, November 1986, *56*(11), pp. 1117–28. **[G: W. Germany]**

Gori, Enrico; Pastacaldi, Andrea and Vitali, Letizia. Models of Spatial Choice: The Case of Banking Services in Urban Areas. *Econ. Notes*, 1986, (2), pp. 129–39.

Graddy, Duane B. and Karna, Adi S. Dividend Policy and the Return of Bank Holding Company Stock. *Quart. J. Bus. Econ.*, Spring 1986, *25*(2), pp. 3–21. **[G: U.S.]**

Grammatikos, Theoharry; Saunders, Anthony and Swary, Itzhak. Returns and Risks of U.S. Bank Foreign Currency Activities. *J. Finance*, July 1986, *41*(3), pp. 671–82. **[G: U.S.]**

Green, Gary P. Capital Flows in Rural Areas: An Analysis of the Impact of Banking Centralization on Lending Policies. *Soc. Sci. Quart.*, June 1986, *67*(2), pp. 365–78. **[G: U.S.]**

Greenwood, John G. Financial Liberalization and Innovation in Seven East Asian Economies. **In** *Suzuki, Y. and Yomo, H., eds.*, 1986, pp. 79–105. **[G: E. Asia]**

Gualandri, Elisabetta. Italian Banks and Interest Rate Risk. *J. Bank Res.*, Spring 1986, *17*(1), pp. 40–44. **[G: Italy]**

Guttentag, Jack M. and Herring, Richard. Disclosure Policy and International Banking. *J. Banking Finance*, March 1986, *10*(1), pp. 75–97. **[G: U.S.]**

Häger, Karl Erik. The Swedish Postal Giro and Its Progress. *J. Bank Res.*, 1986, *16*(4), pp. 227–31. **[G: Sweden]**

Hammer, Frederick S. Banking Markets: Comment. **In** *Saunders, A. and White, L. J., eds.*, 1986, pp. 161–63. **[G: U.S.]**

Hancock, Diana. A Model of the Financial Firm with Imperfect Asset and Deposit Elasticities. *J. Banking Finance*, March 1986, *10*(1), pp. 37–54. **[G: U.S.]**

Hancock, Diana. Testing Price Taking in Loan and Deposit Markets by Financial Firms. *Financial Rev.*, May 1986, *21*(2), pp. 239–57. **[G: U.S.]**

Happ, Scott. The Behavior of Rates on Federal Funds and Repurchase Agreements. *Amer. Econ.*, Fall 1986, *30*(2), pp. 22–32. **[G: U.S.]**

Hartmann, Wendelin. Deutsche Bundesbank and Payment System Risk in the Federal Republic of Germany. *J. Bank Res.*, 1986, *16*(4), pp. 214–17. **[G: W. Germany]**

Hefron, Barry and Gloster, Geoffrey. Trading Bank Finance. **In** *Bruce, R., et al., eds.*, 1986, pp. 147–60. **[G: Australia]**

Heggestad, Arnold A. and Shepherd, William G. The "Banking" Industry. **In** *Adams, W., ed.*, 1986, pp. 290–324. **[G: U.S.]**

Heldring, Frederick. Payment System Risk in the United States. *J. Bank Res.*, 1986, *16*(4), pp. 209–13. **[G: U.S.]**

Henderson, Dan F. Access to the Japanese Market: Some Aspects of Foreign Exchange Controls and Banking Law. **In** *Saxonhouse, G. R. and Yamamura, K., eds.*, 1986, pp. 131–56. **[G: Japan]**

le Héron, Edwin. Généralisation de la préférence pour la liquidité et financement de l'investissement. (Generalizing the Liquidity Preference and the Theory of Investment Financing. With English summary.) *Écon. Soc.*, Aug.-Sept. 1986, *20*(8–9), pp. 67–93.

Hester, Donald D. Monetary Policy in an Evolutionary Disequilibrium. **In** *Suzuki, Y. and Yomo, H., eds.*, 1986, pp. 241–86. **[G: U.S.]**

Hopper, Max. Strategies for the Development of Electronic Systems. *J. Bank Res.*, 1986, *16*(4), pp. 202–05.

Horvitz, Paul M. Technological Innovation: Implications for Regulation of Financial Institutions. **In** *Lawrence, C. and Shay, R. P., eds.*, 1986, pp. 111–23. **[G: U.S.]**

Huertas, Thomas F. and Silverman, Joan L. Charles E. Mitchell: Scapegoat of the Crash? *Bus. Hist. Rev.*, Spring 1986, *60*(1), pp. 81–103. **[G: U.S.]**

Hultman, Charles W. Foreign Bank Offices in the U.S. since the International Banking Act of 1978. *Rivista Int. Sci. Econ. Com.*, Oct.-Nov. 1986, *33*(10–11), pp. 1129–44. **[G: U.S.]**

Humphrey, David B. Payments Finality and Risk of Settlement Failure. **In** *Saunders, A. and White, L. J., eds.*, 1986, pp. 97–120. **[G: U.S.]**

Hunter, William C. and Timme, Stephen G. Technical Change, Organizational Form, and the Structure of Bank Production. *J. Money, Credit, Banking*, May 1986, *18*(2), pp. 152–66. **[G: U.S.]**

Jaffee, Dwight M. Term Structure Intermediation by Depository Institutions. *J. Banking Finance*, June 1986, *10*(2), pp. 309–25. **[G: U.S.]**

Jahera, John S. and Modani, Naval K. An Examination of the Stationarity of Selected Risk Measures in Commercial Banking. *Quart. J. Bus. Econ.*, Winter 1986, *25*(1), pp. 3–15. **[G: U.S.]**

Jao, Y. C. Financial Liberalization and Innovation in Seven East Asian Economies: Comments. **In** *Suzuki, Y. and Yomo, H., eds.*, 1986, pp. 125–31. **[G: E. Asia]**

Jappelli, Tullio. The Estimation of the Degree of Oligopoly of the Italian Banking Sector. *Stud. Econ.*, 1986, *41*(30), pp. 91–105. **[G: Italy]**

Jehle, Geoffrey A. Regulation and the Public Interest in Banking. *J. Banking Finance*, December 1986, *10*(4), pp. 549–73. **[G: U.S.]**

Jensen, Frederick H. and Parkinson, Patrick M. Recent Developments in the Bankers Acceptance Market. *Fed. Res. Bull.*, January 1986, *72*(1), pp. 1–12. **[G: U.S.]**

Kadiyala, K. Rao and Oberhelman, H. Dennis. Estimation of Actual Realizations in Stochastic Parameter Models. **In** *[de Finetti, B.]*, 1986, pp. 363–73. **[G: U.S.]**

Kallberg, Jarl G. and Parkinson, Kenneth L. Banking Markets: Comment. **In** *Saunders, A. and White, L. J., eds.*, 1986, pp. 155–59. **[G: U.S.]**

Kanatas, George. Deposit Insurance and the Discount Window: Pricing under Asymmetric Information. *J. Finance*, June 1986, *41*(2), pp. 437–50.

Kane, Edward J. Appearance and Reality in Deposit Insurance: The Case for Reform. *J. Banking Finance*, June 1986, *10*(2), pp. 175–88. **[G: U.S.]**

Kane, Edward J. Confronting Incentive Problems in U.S. Deposit Insurance: The Range of Alternative Solutions. **In** *Kaufman, G. G. and Kormendi, R. C., eds.*, 1986, pp. 97–120. **[G: U.S.]**

Kane, Edward J. Regulatory Policy for a Changing Financial Services Industry: Rejoinder. **In** *Lawrence, C. and Shay, R. P., eds.*, 1986, pp. 156–60. **[G: U.S.]**

Kane, Edward J. Regulatory Policy for a Changing Financial Services Industry. **In** *Lawrence, C. and Shay, R. P., eds.*, 1986, pp. 125–43. **[G: U.S.]**

Kareken, John H. Federal Bank Regulatory Policy: A Description and Some Observations. *J. Bus.*, January 1986, *59*(1), pp. 3–48. **[G: U.S.]**

Kareken, John H. Technology and Regulation: Commentary. **In** *Lawrence, C. and Shay, R. P., eds.*, 1986, pp. 149–55. **[G: U.S.]**

Kaufman, George G. Federal Bank Regulatory Policy: Comment. *J. Bus.*, January 1986, *59*(1), pp. 69–77. **[G: U.S.]**

Keeley, Michael C. and Furlong, Frederick T. Bank Regulation and the Public Interest. *Fed. Res. Bank San Francisco Econ. Rev.*, Spring 1986, (2), pp. 55–71.

Kernbauer, Hans and Weber, Fritz. Multinational Banking in the Danube Basin: The Business Strategy of the Viennese Banks after the Collapse of the Habsburg Monarchy. **In** *Teichova, A.; Lévy-Leboyer, M. and Nussbaum, H., eds.*, 1986, pp. 185–99. **[G: Europe]**

Khan, Mohsin S. Islamic Interest-Free Banking: A Theoretical Analysis. *Int. Monet. Fund Staff Pap.*, March 1986, *33*(1), pp. 1–27. **[G: Islamic Countries]**

Khan, Mohsin S. and Mirakhor, Abbas. The Framework and Practice of Islamic Banking. *Finance Develop.*, September 1986, *23*(3), pp. 32–36.

Kilbride, Bernard J.; McDonald, Bill and Miller, Robert E. A Reexamination of Economies of Scale in Banking Using a Generalized Functional Form: A Note. *J. Money, Credit, Banking*, November 1986, *18*(4), pp. 519–26. **[G: U.S.]**

Kim, Moshe. Banking Technology and the Existence of a Consistent Output Aggregate. *J. Monet. Econ.*, September 1986, *18*(2), pp. 181–95. **[G: Israel]**

King, Stephen R. Monetary Transmission: Through Bank Loans or Bank Liabilities? *J. Money, Credit, Banking*, August 1986, *18*(3), pp. 290–303. **[G: U.S.]**

Kulshreshta, U. C. Role of Lead Banks in Branch Expansion—A Case Study. *Indian Econ. J.*, July-Sept. 1986, *34*(1), pp. 52–58. **[G: India]**

Kwack, Sung Y. and Chung, Un Chan. The Role of Financial Policies and Institutions in Korea's

Economic Development Process. In *Cheng, H.-S., ed.*, 1986, pp. 115–35. [G: S. Korea]

Ladenson, Mark L. and Bombara, Kenneth J. Entry in Commercial Banking: 1962–78: A Reply. *J. Money, Credit, Banking,* August 1986, *18*(3), pp. 390–91. [G: U.S.]

Lamoreaux, Naomi R. Banks, Kinship, and Economic Development: The New England Case. *J. Econ. Hist.*, September 1986, *46*(3), pp. 647–67. [G: U.S.]

Lamy, Robert E. and Thompson, G. Rodney. Penn Square, Problem Loans, and Insolvency Risk. *J. Finan. Res.*, Summer 1986, *9*(2), pp. 103–11. [G: U.S.]

Lane, William R.; Looney, Stephen W. and Wansley, James W. An Application of the Cox Proportional Hazards Model to Bank Failure. *J. Banking Finance,* December 1986, *10*(4), pp. 511–31. [G: U.S.]

Langohr, Herwig M. and Santomero, Anthony M. The Impact of Equity in Bank Portfolios. *Finance,* June 1986, *7*(1), pp. 23–39.

Lawrence, Colin and Shay, Robert P. Money and Technology. In *Lawrence, C. and Shay, R. P., eds.*, 1986, pp. 1–10. [G: U.S.]

Lawrence, Colin and Shay, Robert P. Technology and Financial Intermediation in Multiproduct Banking Firms: An Econometric Study of U.S. Banks, 1979–1982: Rejoinder. In *Lawrence, C. and Shay, R. P., eds.*, 1986, pp. 106–07. [G: U.S.]

Lawrence, Colin and Shay, Robert P. Technology and Financial Intermediation in Multiproduct Banking Firms: An Econometric Study of U.S. Banks, 1979–1982. In *Lawrence, C. and Shay, R. P., eds.*, 1986, pp. 53–92. [G: U.S.]

Lawrence, David B. and Watkins, Thomas G. Rural Banking Markets and Holding Company Entry. *J. Econ. Bus.*, May 1986, *38*(2), pp. 123–30. [G: U.S.]

Lee, Chang-Kyu. Financial Reform Experiences in Korea. In *Cheng, H.-S., ed.*, 1986, pp. 137–42. [G: S. Korea]

Level, Leon J. Meeting the Needs of Multinational Corporations. *J. Bank Res.*, 1986, *16*(4), pp. 254–57. [G: U.S.]

Lewis, M. K. and Wright, D. M. Banking and Deposit Services. In *Carter, R. L.; Chiplin, B. and Lewis, M. K., eds.*, 1986, pp. 137–68. [G: U.K.]

Lieber, Zvi and Orgler, Yair E. Optimal Borrowing and Bank Lending Policies: An Interactive Approach. *J. Banking Finance,* June 1986, *10*(2), pp. 255–65.

Linneman, Peter. Technology and Financial Services: Regulatory Problems in a Deregulated Environment: Discussion. In *Faulhaber, G.; Noam, E. and Tasley, R., eds.*, 1986, pp. 73–75. [G: U.S.]

Lundström, Ragnhild. Banks and Early Swedish Multinationals. In *Teichova, A.; Lévy-Leboyer, M. and Nussbaum, H., eds.*, 1986, pp. 200–217. [G: Sweden]

Mahajan, Arvind and Mehta, Dileep. Swaps, Expectations, and Exchange Rates. *J. Banking Finance,* March 1986, *10*(1), pp. 7–20. [G: U.S.]

Mallyon, Jim S. The Process of Financial Deregulation, Monetary Reform, and the Financial System of the Future: Comments. In *Suzuki, Y. and Yomo, H., eds.*, 1986, pp. 203–06. [G: U.S.]

Marsan, Veniero Ajmone. Public Enterprise: Studies in Organisational Structure: Instituto per la Ricostruzione Industriale. In *Ramanadham, V. V., ed.*, 1986, pp. 83–113. [G: Italy]

Martin, Preston. Statement to the U.S. House Subcommittee on Financial Institutions Supervision, Regulation and Insurance of the Committee on Banking, Finance and Urban Affairs, April 9, 1986. *Fed. Res. Bull.*, June 1986, *72*(6), pp. 382–89. [G: U.S.]

Martinengo, Giancarlo. Rischio da leverage, finanziamento esterno ed interno: un contributo allo studio degli equilibri tra banca e impresa. (Leverage Risk, External and Internal Financing: An Integration of Banks and Firms Decisions. With English summary.) *Polit. Econ.*, August 1986, *2*(2), pp. 243–71.

Mayer, Colin. The Assessment: Financial Innovation: Curse or Blessing? *Oxford Rev. Econ. Policy,* Winter 1986, *2*(4), pp. i–xix. [G: U.K.]

Mayer, Thomas. Regulating Banks: Comment. *J. Bus.*, January 1986, *59*(1), pp. 87–96. [G: U.S.]

McCauley, Robert N. Are Large U.S. Banks Moving International Activity Off Their Balance Sheets? *Fed. Res. Bank New York Quart. Rev.*, Summer 1986, *11*(2), pp. 42–44. [G: U.S.]

McCulloch, J. Huston. Bank Regulation and Deposit Insurance. *J. Bus.*, January 1986, *59*(1), pp. 79–85. [G: U.S.]

McKinnon, Ronald I. Financial Liberalization and Economic Development. In *Cheng, H.-S., ed.*, 1986, pp. 337–42. [G: LDCs]

Melnik, Arie and Plaut, Steven E. The Economics of Loan Commitment Contracts: Credit Pricing and Utilization. *J. Banking Finance,* June 1986, *10*(2), pp. 267–80.

Meltzer, Allan H. Financial Failures and Financial Policies. In *Kaufman, G. G. and Kormendi, R. C., eds.*, 1986, pp. 79–96. [G: U.S.]

Mengle, David L. and Walter, John R. A Review of Bank Performance in the Fifth District, 1985. *Fed. Res. Bank Richmond Econ. Rev.*, July/Aug. 1986, *72*(4), pp. 25–33. [G: U.S.]

Meyer, Hans. The Role of the Swiss National Bank in the Payment System. *J. Bank Res.*, 1986, *16*(4), pp. 190–93. [G: Switzerland]

Michaelis, Dolf. One Hundred Years of Banking and Currency in Palestine. In *Uselding, P., ed.*, 1986, pp. 155–97. [G: Palestine; Middle East]

Mickwitz, Gösta. Socialisera bankledningarna? (Should Bank Management Be Socialized? With English summary.) *Ekon. Samfundets Tidskr.*, 1986, *39*(1), pp. 3–5.

Mills, Rodney H. Foreign Lending by Banks: A Guide to International and U.S. Statistics. *Fed.*

Res. Bull., October 1986, *72*(10), pp. 683–94. **[G: U.S.]**

Miron, Jeffrey A. Financial Panics, the Seasonality of the Nominal Interest Rate, and the Founding of the Fed. *Amer. Econ. Rev.*, March 1986, *76*(1), pp. 125–40. **[G: U.S.]**

Mitchell, Douglas W. Some Regulatory Determinants of Bank Risk Behavior: A Note. *J. Money, Credit, Banking*, August 1986, *18*(3), pp. 374–82.

Mitchell, George W. It's the Old Time Religion, but Is It Good Enough Today? *J. Bank Res.*, 1986, *16*(4), pp. 258–60. **[G: U.S.]**

Mitchell, George W. Similarities and Contrasts in Payment Systems. *J. Bank Res.*, 1986, *16*(4), pp. 175–77. **[G: W. Europe; Canada; U.S.; Japan]**

Moniez, Jean-Claude. The Smart Card in France. *J. Bank Res.*, 1986, *16*(4), pp. 221–22. **[G: France]**

Montel, Jean. Risque, financement et rentabilité. (Risk, Financing and Profitability. With English summary.) *Écon. Soc.*, July 1986, *20*(7), pp. 115–28.

Moore, W. Robert. Large Value Payment Systems. *J. Bank Res.*, 1986, *16*(4), pp. 232–34. **[G: U.S.]**

Morelli, G. Payment Systems in Eleven Developed Countries. *J. Bank Res.*, 1986, *16*(4), pp. 173–74.

Müller, Albert. Risikoeinschätzung und Bankverhalten. (Risk Preferences and the Behavior of Bank Management. With English summary.) *Schweiz. Z. Volkswirtsch. Statist.*, September 1986, *122*(3), pp. 371–87.

Murphy, Neil B. and Rogers, Ronald C. Life Cycle and the Adoption of Consumer Financial Innovation: An Empirical Study of the Adoption Process. *J. Bank Res.*, Spring 1986, *17*(1), pp. 3–8. **[G: U.S.]**

Mussa, Michael. Competition, Efficiency, and Fairness in the Financial Services Industry. **In** *Kaufman, G. G. and Kormendi, R. C., eds.*, 1986, pp. 121–44. **[G: U.S.]**

Mussa, Michael. Safety and Soundness as an Objective of Regulation of Depository Institutions: Comment. *J. Bus.*, January 1986, *59*(1), pp. 97–117. **[G: U.S.]**

Noma, Toshikatsu. "Scale-Maximizing Behavior" of the Japanese Banks: An Empirical Analysis. (In Japanese. With English summary.) *Econ. Stud. Quart.*, December 1986, *37*(4), pp. 336–50. **[G: Japan]**

Nunnenkamp, Peter. Liberalisierung der Finanzmärkte und Ersparnisbildung in Indonesien. (Liberalization of the Financial Markets and Savings in Indonesia. With English summary.) *Kredit Kapital*, 1986, *19*(3), pp. 417–40. **[G: Indonesia]**

O'Driscoll, Gerald P., Jr. Deregulation and Monetary Reform. *Fed. Res. Bank Dallas Econ. Rev.*, July 1986, pp. 19–31. **[G: U.S.]**

Osano, Hiroshi and Tsutsui, Yoshiro. Credit Rationing and Implicit Contract Theory: An Empirical Study. *Int. J. Ind. Organ.*, December 1986, *4*(4), pp. 419–38. **[G: Japan]**

Overdahl, James A. and Starleaf, Dennis R. The Hedging Performance of the CD Futures Market. *J. Futures Markets*, Spring 1986, *6*(1), pp. 71–81. **[G: U.S.]**

Owens, John E. The State Regulation and Deregulation of Financial Institutions and Services in the United States. **In** *Cox, A., ed.*, 1986, pp. 172–230. **[G: U.S.]**

Partee, J. Charles. The Status of Banking Deregulation in the United States. **In** *Cheng, H.-S., ed.*, 1986, pp. 59–63. **[G: U.S.]**

Pascoe, Anthony. Case Studies of Black Advancement: Barclays National Bank. **In** *Smollan, R., ed.*, 1986, pp. 211–17. **[G: S. Africa]**

Petrovich, Giuliano. Politiche di contenimento e diversione del sistema dei *Factors*. (Credit Restrictions and Factoring Diversion. With English summary.) *Ricerche Econ.*, Apr.-Sept. 1986, *40*(2–3), pp. 447–62. **[G: Italy]**

Phillips, Almarin and Berlin, Mitchell. Technology and Financial Services: Regulatory Problems in a Deregulated Environment. **In** *Faulhaber, G.; Noam, E. and Tasley, R., eds.*, 1986, pp. 49–72. **[G: U.S.]**

Pierce, James L. Financial Reform in the United States and the Financial System of the Future. **In** *Suzuki, Y. and Yomo, H., eds.*, 1986, pp. 183–201. **[G: U.S.]**

Pollack, Elliott D. The Business Economist at Work: Valley National Bank. *Bus. Econ.*, October 1986, *21*(4), pp. 48–50. **[G: U.S.]**

Poole, William. Deposit Deregulation and Monetary Policy: A Comment. *Carnegie-Rochester Conf. Ser. Public Policy*, Spring 1986, *24*, pp. 225–30. **[G: U.S.]**

Poulsen, Annette B. Japanese Bank Regulation and the Activities of U.S. Offices of Japanese Banks: A Note. *J. Money, Credit, Banking*, August 1986, *18*(3), pp. 366–73. **[G: Japan]**

Pozdena, Randall J. Structure and Performance: Some Evidence from California Banking. *Fed. Res. Bank San Francisco Econ. Rev.*, Winter 1986, (1), pp. 5–17. **[G: U.S.]**

Pressnell, L. S. The Avoidance of Catastrophe: Two Nineteenth-Century Banking Crises: Comment. **In** *Capie, F. and Wood, G. E., eds.*, 1986, pp. 74–76. **[G: U.K.]**

Prisman, Eliezer Z.; Slovin, Myron B. and Sushka, Marie E. A General Model of the Banking Firm under Conditions of Monopoly, Uncertainty, and Recourse. *J. Monet. Econ.*, March 1986, *17*(2), pp. 293–304.

Pyle, David H. Capital Regulation and Deposit Insurance. *J. Banking Finance*, June 1986, *10*(2), pp. 189–201.

Pyle, David H. Financial Deregulation. **In** *Cagan, P., ed.*, 1986, pp. 147–90. **[G: U.S.]**

Rajan, Amin and Cooke, Geoffrey. The Impact of Information Technology on Employment in the Financial Services Industry. *Nat. Westminster Bank Quart. Rev.*, August 1986, pp. 21–35. **[G: U.K.]**

Ránki, Gy. and Tomaszewski, Jerzy. The Role of the State in Industry, Banking and Trade. **In** *Kaser, M. C. and Radice, E. A., eds.*, 1986, pp. 3–48. **[G: E. Europe]**

Ranuzzi, Paolo. Internationalisation of the Lira and the Italian Banking System. *Econ. Notes,* 1986, (3), pp. 85–100. **[G: Italy]**

Raymond, Robert. Implications for Monetary Policy: Comments. **In** *Suzuki, Y. and Yomo, H., eds.,* 1986, pp. 295–99.

Reed, John S. and Moreno, Glen R. The Role of Large Banks in Financing Innovation. **In** *Landau, R. and Rosenberg, N., eds.,* 1986, pp. 443–65. **[G: U.S.]**

Reidenbach, R. Eric; Moak, Donald L. and Pitts, Robert E. The Impact of Marketing Operations on Bank Performance: A Structural Investigation. *J. Bank Res.,* Spring 1986, *17*(1), pp. 18–27. **[G: U.S.]**

de Rezende Rocha, Roberto. Costs of Intermediation in Developing Countries: A Preliminary Investigation. **In** *Hanson, J. A. and Rocha, R.,* 1986, pp. 17–82. **[G: MDCs; LDCs]**

Roberts, R. O. Banks and the Economic Development of South Wales before 1914. **In** *Baber, C. and Williams, L. J., eds.,* 1986, pp. 65–80. **[G: U.K.]**

Rolnick, Arthur J. and Weber, Warren E. Inherent Instability in Banking: The Free Banking Experience. *Cato J.,* Winter 1986, *5*(3), pp. 877–90. **[G: U.S.]**

Ronn, Ehud I. and Verma, Avinash K. Pricing Risk-Adjusted Deposit Insurance: An Option-Based Model. *J. Finance,* September 1986, *41*(4), pp. 871–95. **[G: U.S.]**

Rose, Harold. Change in Financial Intermediation in the UK. *Oxford Rev. Econ. Policy,* Winter 1986, *2*(4), pp. 18–40. **[G: U.K.]**

Rose, John T. Entry in Commercial Banking, 1962–78: A Comment. *J. Money, Credit, Banking,* May 1986, *18*(2), pp. 247–49. **[G: U.S.]**

Rose, John T. and Savage, Donald T. Bank Holding Company De Novo Entry and Banking Market Performance. *J. Bank Res.,* Spring 1986, *17*(1), pp. 45–50. **[G: U.S.]**

Rōyama, Shōichi. The Process of Financial Deregulation, Monetary Reform, and the Financial System of the Future: Comments. **In** *Suzuki, Y. and Yomo, H., eds.,* 1986, pp. 217–20.

Rymes, Thomas K. Further Thoughts on the Banking Imputation in the National Accounts. *Rev. Income Wealth,* December 1986, *32*(4), pp. 425–41.

Sandhu, H. S. and Goswami, R. K. Determinants of Commercial Bank Deposits in India. *Indian Econ. J.,* July-Sept. 1986, *34*(1), pp. 41–51. **[G: India]**

Santomero, Anthony M. and Siegel, Jeremy J. Deposit Deregulation and Monetary Policy. *Carnegie-Rochester Conf. Ser. Public Policy,* Spring 1986, *24,* pp. 179–224. **[G: U.S.]**

Santoni, Gary J. The Effects of Inflation on Commercial Banks. *Fed. Res. Bank St. Louis Rev.,* March 1986, *68*(3), pp. 15–26. **[G: U.S.]**

Sarcinelli, Mario. The Evolution of the International Framework: The Constraints on Major Banks and Their Operations. *Rev. Econ. Cond. Italy,* May-Aug. 1986, (2), pp. 137–67. **[G: OECD]**

Savona, Paolo. The Strategy Options Open to Italian Banks in International Markets. *Rev. Econ. Cond. Italy,* May-Aug. 1986, (2), pp. 211–24. **[G: Italy]**

Schuster, Leo. Concentration and Competition in Banking. *J. Bank Res.,* Spring 1986, *17*(1), pp. 51–53. **[G: N. America; Japan; U.K.; W. Germany; France]**

Scott, Jonathan A. and Smith, Terence C. The Effect of the Bankruptcy Reform Act of 1978 on Small Business Loan Pricing. *J. Finan. Econ.,* May 1986, *16*(1), pp. 119–40. **[G: U.S.]**

Scott, William L. and Peterson, Richard L. Interest Rate Risk and Equity Values of Hedged and Unhedged Financial Intermediaries. *J. Finan. Res.,* Winter 1986, *9*(4), pp. 325–29. **[G: U.S.]**

Seger, Martha R. Statement to the U.S. House Subcommittee on Financial Institutions Supervision, Regulation and Insurance of the Committee on Banking, Finance and Urban Affairs, May 14, 1986. *Fed. Res. Bull.,* July 1986, *72*(7), pp. 467–72. **[G: U.S.]**

Seidman, L. William. Debt, Financial Stability, and Public Policy: Overview. **In** *Axilrod, S. H., et al.,* 1986, pp. 223–30. **[G: U.S.]**

Seidman, L. William. The American Experience: Bank Supervision in the United States. **In** *Dale, R., ed.,* 1986, pp. 64–80. **[G: U.S.]**

Shay, Robert P. Technology and Financial Services: Regulatory Problems in a Deregulated Environment: Discussion. **In** *Faulhaber, G.; Noam, E. and Tasley, R., eds.,* 1986, pp. 76–79. **[G: U.S.]**

Sherbiny, Naiem A. Oil and International Activities of Arab Banks. *World Econ.,* June 1986, *9*(2), pp. 193–210. **[G: OPEC]**

Shome, Dilip K.; Smith, Stephen D. and Heggestad, Arnold A. Capital Adequacy and the Valuation of Large Commercial Banking Organizations. *J. Finan. Res.,* Winter 1986, *9*(4), pp. 331–41. **[G: U.S.]**

Skully, Michael. Banks and Financial Institutions. **In** *Bruce, R., et al., eds.,* 1986, pp. 13–32. **[G: Australia]**

Smirlock, Michael. Technology and Banking: Commentary. **In** *Lawrence, C. and Shay, R. P., eds.,* 1986, pp. 98–104. **[G: U.S.]**

Smirlock, Michael and Brown, David. Collusion, Efficiency and Pricing Behavior: Evidence from the Banking Industry. *Econ. Inquiry,* January 1986, *24*(1), pp. 85–96. **[G: U.S.]**

St Germain, Fernand J. Consumer Banking Issues. *J. Bank Res.,* 1986, *16*(4), pp. 244–47. **[G: U.S.]**

Stanhouse, Bryan E. Commercial Bank Portfolio Behavior and Endogenous Uncertainty. *J. Finance,* December 1986, *41*(5), pp. 1103–14.

Starke, Wolfgang. Efficiencies in Credit-Based Transfer Systems. *J. Bank Res.,* 1986, *16*(4), pp. 223–26. **[G: W. Germany]**

Stiefel, Dieter. Austrian Banks at the Zenith of Power and Influence: System and Problems of the Austrian Finance Capital from the 1890s to the International Economic Crisis of the

1930s. **In** *Pohl, H. and Rudolph, B., eds.*, 1986, pp. 79–95. **[G: Austria]**

Strøm, Trygve. Project Financing in the North Sea. *Écon. Soc.*, July 1986, *20*(7), pp. 145–57.

Sullivan, Barry F. Meeting the Challenge of Controlling Bank Costs and Developing Pricing Strategies. *J. Bank Res.*, 1986, *16*(4), pp. 178–81. **[G: U.S.]**

Swary, Itzhak. Stock Market Reaction to Regulatory Action in the Continental Illinois Crisis. *J. Bus.*, July 1986, *59*(3), pp. 451–73. **[G: U.S.]**

Szegö, Giorgio. Bank Asset Management and Financial Insurance. *J. Banking Finance*, June 1986, *10*(2), pp. 295–307.

Takigawa, Yoshio. Deregulation of Interest Rate and Bank Rate Policy. *Kobe Univ. Econ.*, 1986, (32), pp. 121–37.

Tam, On-Kit. Reform of China's Banking System. *World Econ.*, December 1986, *9*(4), pp. 427–40. **[G: China]**

Taylor, William. Statement to the U.S. House Subcommittee on Commerce, Consumer, and Monetary Affairs of the Committee on Government Operations, December 12, 1985. *Fed. Res. Bull.*, February 1986, *72*(2), pp. 125–27. **[G: U.S.]**

Taylor, William. Statement to the U.S. House Subcommittee on Conservation, Credit, and Rural Development of the Committee on Agriculture, April 9, 1986. *Fed. Res. Bull.*, June 1986, *72*(6), pp. 389–93. **[G: U.S.]**

Taylor, William. Statement to the U.S. Senate Subcommittee on International Finance and Monetary Policy of the Committee on Banking, Housing, and Urban Affairs, June 25, 1986. *Fed. Res. Bull.*, August 1986, *72*(8), pp. 565–68. **[G: U.S.]**

Teh, Kok Peng. Monetary Policy in an Evolutionary Disequilibrium: Comments. **In** *Suzuki, Y. and Yomo, H., eds.*, 1986, pp. 301–04. **[G: U.S.]**

Terrell, Henry S. The Role of Foreign Banks in Domestic Banking Markets. **In** *Cheng, H.-S., ed.*, 1986, pp. 297–304. **[G: U.S.]**

Thore, Sten. Regional Lending Risk in Eurodollar Markets. *Scand. J. Econ.*, 1986, *88*(2), pp. 437–51.

Thornton, J. A Note on Repurchase Agreements, Bank Behaviour and Monetary Policy. *S. Afr. J. Econ.*, December 1986, *54*(4), pp. 437–39. **[G: W. Germany]**

Tilly, Richard H. German Banking, 1850–1914: Development Assistance for the Strong. *J. Europ. Econ. Hist.*, Spring 1986, *15*(1), pp. 113–52. **[G: Germany]**

Tiwari, Kashi Nath. The Money Supply Process under Deregulation. *Financial Rev.*, February 1986, *21*(1), pp. 111–23.

Tobin, James. Financial Innovation and Deregulation in Perspective. **In** *Suzuki, Y. and Yomo, H., eds.*, 1986, pp. 31–42.

Todhanakasem, Warapatr, et al. Economies of Scale and Organization Efficiency in Banking. *Managerial Dec. Econ.*, December 1986, *7*(4), pp. 255–61. **[G: U.S.]**

Udell, Gregory F. Pricing Returned Check Charges under Asymmetric Information. *J. Money, Credit, Banking*, November 1986, *18*(4), pp. 495–505. **[G: U.S.]**

Udell, Gregory F. Technology and Bank Monitoring. **In** *Saunders, A. and White, L. J., eds.*, 1986, pp. 137–54. **[G: U.S.]**

Urkowitz, Michael. Paper-Based Payments—A System in Transition. *J. Bank Res.*, 1986, *16*(4), pp. 241–43. **[G: U.S.]**

Verma, Satish. Controlling the Borrowed Reserves of Scheduled Commercial Banks in India. *Indian Econ. J.*, July-Sept. 1986, *34*(1), pp. 23–33. **[G: India]**

Visentini, Gustavo. Guidelines for Changing Banking Law. *Rev. Econ. Cond. Italy*, May-Aug. 1986, (2), pp. 251–69. **[G: Italy]**

Vittas, Dimitri. Banks' Relations with Industry: An International Survey. *Nat. Westminster Bank Quart. Rev.*, February 1986, pp. 2–14. **[G: U.K.; France; W. Germany; U.S.; Japan]**

Volcker, Paul A. Statement to the U.S. House Subcommittee on Commerce, Consumer, and Monetary Affairs of the Committee on Government Operations, June 11, 1986. *Fed. Res. Bull.*, August 1986, 72(8), pp. 541–54. **[G: U.S.]**

Volcker, Paul A. Statement to the U.S. House Subcommittee on Financial Institutions Supervision, Regulation and Insurance of the Committee on Banking, Finance and Urban Affairs, May 7, 1986. *Fed. Res. Bull.*, July 1986, *72*(7), pp. 463–67. **[G: U.S.]**

Volcker, Paul A. Statement to the U.S. House Subcommittee on Domestic Monetary Policy of the Committee on Banking, Finance and Urban Affairs, December 12, 1985. *Fed. Res. Bull.*, February 1986, *72*(2), pp. 115–16. **[G: U.S.]**

Wallich, Henry C. A Broad View of Deregulation. **In** *Cheng, H.-S., ed.*, 1986, pp. 3–12.

Watkins, Thomas G. The Marketing of Personal Financial Services. **In** *Carter, R. L.; Chiplin, B. and Lewis, M. K., eds.*, 1986, pp. 48–74. **[G: U.K.; U.S.]**

Webb, David C. Competitive Banking in a Simple Model: Comment. **In** *Edwards, J., et al., eds.*, 1986, pp. 177–81.

Welker, Donald L. Thrift Competition: Does It Matter? *Fed. Res. Bank Richmond Econ. Rev.*, Jan./Feb. 1986, *72*(1), pp. 2–10. **[G: U.S.]**

Wells, Donald R. and Scruggs, L. S. Historical Insights into the Deregulation of Money and Banking. *Cato J.*, Winter 1986, *5*(3), pp. 899–910. **[G: U.S.]**

Wenninger, John. Implications for Monetary Policy: Comments. **In** *Suzuki, Y. and Yomo, H., eds.*, 1986, pp. 291–93. **[G: U.S.]**

White, Bob and Vittas, Dimitri. Barriers in International Banking. *Lloyds Bank Rev.*, July 1986, (161), pp. 19–31. **[G: OECD]**

White, Eugene Nelson. Before the Glass–Steagall Act: An Analysis of the Investment Banking Activities of National Banks. *Exploration Econ.*

Hist., January 1986, *23*(1), pp. 33–55. **[G: U.S.]**

White, Lawrence H. Regulatory Sources of Instability in Banking [Inherent Instability in Banking: The Free Banking Experience]. *Cato J.*, Winter 1986, *5*(3), pp. 891–97. **[G: U.S.]**

White, Lawrence J. The Partial Deregulation of Banks and Other Depository Institutions. **In** *Weiss, L. W. and Klass, M. W., eds.*, 1986, pp. 169–209. **[G: U.S.]**

Wilson, Gene and Sullivan, Gene D. Agricultural Banks in the Southeast and Nation: A Study in Contrasts. *Southern J. Agr. Econ.*, July 1986, *18*(1), pp. 93–101. **[G: U.S.]**

Witt, Horst J. The Cost of Developing and Implementing Electronic Payment Systems. *J. Bank Res.*, 1986, *16*(4), pp. 186–89.

Wondrak, Bernhard. Zur Steuerung des Zinsänderungsrisikos in Kreditinstituten. (On Control of the Risk of Interest-Rate Changes in Banks. With English summary.) *Kredit Kapital*, 1986, *19*(3), pp. 401–16.

Zardkoohi, Asghar; Rangan, Nanda and Kolari, James. Homogeneity Restrictions on the Translog Cost Model: A Note [Scale Economies in Banking: A Restructuring and Reassessment]. *J. Finance*, December 1986, *41*(5), pp. 1153–55. **[G: U.S.]**

313 Capital Markets

3130 General

Anderson, Ronald W. Regulation of Futures Trading in the United States and the United Kingdom. *Oxford Rev. Econ. Policy*, Winter 1986, *2*(4), pp. 41–57. **[G: U.S.; U.K.]**

Baliño, Tómas J. T. and Sundararajan, V. Financial Reform in Indonesia: Causes, Consequences, and Prospects. **In** *Cheng, H.-S., ed.*, 1986, pp. 191–219. **[G: Indonesia]**

Bamberg, Günter and Spremann, Klaus. Capital Market Equilibria: Prologue. **In** *Bamberg, G. and Spremann, K., eds.*, 1986, pp. 1–5.

Bellante, Don and Saba, Richard P. Human Capital and Life-Cycle Effects on Risk Aversion. *J. Finan. Res.*, Spring 1986, *9*(1), pp. 41–51. **[G: U.S.]**

Benston, George J. Regulatory Policies and Financial Stability: Commentary. **In** *Axilrod, S. H., et al.*, 1986, pp. 137–51. **[G: U.S.]**

Black, Fischer. Noise. *J. Finance*, July 1986, *41*(3), pp. 529–43.

Burkett, Paul. Interest Rate Restrictions and Deposit Opportunities for Small Savers in Developing Countries: An Analytical View. *J. Devel. Stud.*, October 1986, *23*(1), pp. 77–92. **[G: LDCs]**

Büschgen, Hans E. Finanzinnovationen—Neuerungen und Entwicklungen an nationalen und internationalen Finanzmärkten. (With English summary.) *Z. Betriebswirtshaft*, Apr.-May 1986, *56*(4/5), pp. 301–36. **[G: W. Germany]**

Cargill, Thomas F. Financial Reform in the United States and Japan: A Comparative Overview. **In** *Cheng, H.-S., ed.*, 1986, pp. 39–57. **[G: U.S.; Japan]**

Cargill, Thomas F.; Cheng, Hang-Sheng and Hutchison, Michael M. Financial Market Changes and Regulatory Reforms in Pacific Basin Countries: An Overview. **In** *Cheng, H.-S., ed.*, 1986, pp. 13–36. **[G: Pacific Basin]**

Cheng, Hang-Sheng. Financial Policy and Reform in Taiwan, China. **In** *Cheng, H.-S., ed.*, 1986, pp. 143–59. **[G: Taiwan]**

Cho, Yoon Je. Inefficiencies from Financial Liberalization in the Absence of Well-Functioning Equity Markets. *J. Money, Credit, Banking*, May 1986, *18*(2), pp. 191–99.

Cooke, William Peter. Regulatory Policies and Financial Stability: Commentary. **In** *Axilrod, S. H., et al.*, 1986, pp. 153–63. **[G: U.S.]**

Dinehart, Stephen J. Insider Trading in Futures Markets: A Discussion. *J. Futures Markets*, Summer 1986, *6*(2), pp. 325–33. **[G: U.S.]**

Easterbrook, Frank H. Monopoly, Manipulation, and the Regulation of Futures Markets. *J. Bus.*, Part 2, April 1986, *59*(2), pp. S103–27. **[G: U.S.]**

Eisenbeis, Robert A. Regulatory Policies and Financial Stability. **In** *Axilrod, S. H., et al.*, 1986, pp. 107–35. **[G: U.S.]**

Engberg, Holger L. Capital Formation and Economic Development: The Role of Financial Institutions and Markets. **In** *Wasow, B. and Hill, R. D., eds.*, 1986, pp. 107–19.

Engle, Robert F. and Bollerslev, Tim. Modelling the Persistence of Conditional Variances. *Econometric Rev.*, 1986, *5*(1), pp. 1–50. **[G: U.S.; Switzerland]**

Firth, Michael. The Efficient Markets Theory. **In** *Firth, M. and Keane, S. M., eds.*, 1986, pp. 1–15.

Gillis, Kevin. A Note on the Definition of Basis. *Can. J. Agr. Econ.*, July 1986, *34*(2), pp. 253–56.

Goss, Barry A. Feasibility and the Consequences of Using Information in Futures Markets. **In** *Goss, B. A., ed.*, 1986, pp. 1–11.

Grier, Kevin B. A Note on Unanticipated Money Growth and Interest Rate Surprises: Mishkin and Makin Revisited. *J. Finance*, September 1986, *41*(4), pp. 981–85. **[G: U.S.]**

Grossman, Sanford J. An Analysis of the Role of "Insider Trading" on Futures Markets. *J. Bus.*, Part 2, April 1986, *59*(2), pp. S129–46. **[G: U.S.]**

Huertas, Thomas F. and Silverman, Joan L. Charles E. Mitchell: Scapegoat of the Crash? *Bus. Hist. Rev.*, Spring 1986, *60*(1), pp. 81–103. **[G: U.S.]**

Joy, O. Maurice and Jones, Charles P. Should We Believe the Tests of Market Efficiency? *J. Portfol. Manage.*, Summer 1986, *12*(4), pp. 49–54.

Kane, Edward J. Technology and the Regulation of Financial Markets. **In** *Saunders, A. and White, L. J., eds.*, 1986, pp. 187–93.

Kemp, Jack F. Industrial Policy and the Major U.S. Parties. **In** *Barfield, C. E. and Schambra, W. A., eds.*, 1986, pp. 217–21. **[G: U.S.]**

Lee, Chang-Kyu. Financial Reform Experiences

in Korea. In *Cheng, H.-S., ed.*, 1986, pp. 137–42. [G: S. Korea]

Malatesta, Paul H. Measuring Abnormal Performance: The Event Parameter Approach Using Joint Generalized Least Squares. *J. Finan. Quant. Anal.*, March 1986, *21*(1), pp. 27–38.

Mann, Michael D. International Legal Assistance in Securities Law Enforcement—Status and Perspectives. *Wirtsch. Recht*, 1986, *38*(2), pp. 157–92. [G: U.S.]

Marver, James D. Trends in Financing Innovation. In *Landau, R. and Rosenberg, N., eds.*, 1986, pp. 473–78.

Miller, Merton H. The Academic Field of Finance: Some Observations on Its History and Prospects. *Tijdschrift Econ. Manage.*, 1986, *31*(4), pp. 395–408. [G: U.S.]

Moore, Basil J. Inflation and Financial Deepening. *J. Devel. Econ.*, Jan.-Feb. 1986, *20*(1), pp. 125–33. [G: S. Korea]

Moylan, James J. and Ukman, Laren. Dispute Resolution Systems in the Commodity Futures Industry. *J. Futures Markets*, Winter 1986, *6*(4), pp. 659–70. [G: U.S.]

Munnell, Alicia H. and Grolnic, Joseph B. Should the U.S. Government Issue Index Bonds? *New Eng. Econ. Rev.*, Sept./Oct. 1986, pp. 3–21. [G: U.S.; U.K.]

Nambara, Akira. Financial Reform in Japan: A Central Banker's View. In *Cheng, H.-S., ed.*, 1986, pp. 65–67. [G: Japan]

Rosende R., Francisco and Vergara M., Rodrigo. Opciones de Política para el Sector Financiero. (With English summary.) *Cuadernos Econ.*, December 1986, *23*(70), pp. 373–97. [G: Chile]

Rosengren, Eric S. Is There a Need for Regulation in the Government Securities Market? *New Eng. Econ. Rev.*, Sept./Oct. 1986, pp. 29–40. [G: U.S.]

Samuelson, Paul A. Myths and Realities about the Crash and Depression. In *Samuelson, P. A.*, 1986, *1979*, pp. 921–24. [G: U.S.]

Schreiber, Paul S. and Schwartz, Robert A. Price Discovery in Securities Markets. *J. Portfol. Manage.*, Summer 1986, *12*(4), pp. 43–48. [G: U.S.]

Tilly, Richard H. German Banking, 1850–1914: Development Assistance for the Strong. *J. Europ. Econ. Hist.*, Spring 1986, *15*(1), pp. 113–52. [G: Germany]

Vermaelen, Theo. Encouraging Information Disclosure. *Tijdschrift Econ. Manage.*, 1986, *31*(4), pp. 435–49. [G: Belgium]

White, Frederick L. and Stein, William. Legal and Regulatory Developments. *J. Futures Markets*, Fall 1986, *6*(3), pp. 503–04. [G: U.S.]

3131 Capital Markets: Theory, Including Portfolio Selection, and Empirical Studies Illustrating Theory

Admati, Anat R. and Ross, Stephen A. Corrigendum [Measuring Investment Performance in a Rational Expectations Equilibrium Model]. *J. Bus.*, Part 1, April 1986, *59*(2), pp. 367.

Admati, Anat R., et al. On Timing and Selectivity. *J. Finance*, July 1986, *41*(3), pp. 715–30.

Albrecht, Peter. Zinsimmunisierung mehrfacher Verpflichtungen bei Arbitragemodellen für die Zinsstruktur, insbesondere im Versicherungsfall. (With English summary.) *Z. Betriebswirtshaft*, October 1986, *56*(10), pp. 1002–28.

Amihud, Yakov; Dodd, Peter and Weinstein, Mark. Conglomerate Mergers, Managerial Motives and Stockholder Wealth. *J. Banking Finance*, October 1986, *10*(3), pp. 401–10.

Amihud, Yakov and Mendelson, Haim. Asset Pricing and the Bid–Ask Spread. *J. Finan. Econ.*, December 1986, *17*(2), pp. 223–49.

Amsler, Christine E. The Fisher Effect: Sometimes Inverted, Sometimes Not? [Fisher's Paradox and the Theory of Interest]. *Southern Econ. J.*, January 1986, *52*(3), pp. 832–35.

Andersen, Torben M. Speculation, Optimum and Differential Information. *Southern Econ. J.*, July 1986, *53*(1), pp. 170–86.

Antonovitz, Frances and Roe, Terry. Effects of Expected Cash and Futures Prices on Hedging and Production. *J. Futures Markets*, Summer 1986, *6*(2), pp. 187–205. [G: U.S.]

Arak, Marcelle; Goodman, Laurie S. and Silver, Andrew. Premium and Discount Securities: Relative Tax Advantage under the Deficit Reduction Act of 1984. *Nat. Tax J.*, March 1986, *39*(1), pp. 65–77. [G: U.S.]

Asquith, Paul and Mullins, David W., Jr. Equity Issues and Offering Dilution. In *Edwards, J., et al., eds.*, 1986, pp. 51–82. [G: U.S.]

Ball, Clifford A. and Torous, Walter N. Futures Options and the Volatility of Futures Prices. *J. Finance*, September 1986, *41*(4), pp. 857–70. [G: U.S.; Europe]

Bamberg, Günter. The Hybrid Model and Related Approaches to Capital Market Equilibria. In *Bamberg, G. and Spremann, K., eds.*, 1986, pp. 7–54.

Batchelor, Roy A. The Avoidance of Catastrophe: Two Nineteenth-Century Banking Crises. In *Capie, F. and Wood, G. E., eds.*, 1986, pp. 41–73. [G: U.K.]

Beatty, Randolph P. and Ritter, Jay R. Investment Banking, Reputation, and the Underpricing of Initial Public Offerings. *J. Finan. Econ.*, Jan./Feb. 1986, *15*(1/2), pp. 213–32. [G: U.S.]

Beenstock, Michael. A Theory of Home Currency Preference. *Weltwirtsch. Arch.*, 1986, *122*(2), pp. 223–32. [G: U.K.]

Beenstock, Michael and Chan, Kam-Fai. Testing the Arbitrage Pricing Theory in the United Kingdom. *Oxford Bull. Econ. Statist.*, May 1986, *48*(2), pp. 121–41. [G: U.S.]

Benninga, Simon and Protopapadakis, Aris A. General Equilibrium Properties of the Term Structure of Interest Rates. *J. Finan. Econ.*, July 1986, *16*(3), pp. 389–410.

Billingsley, Randall S.; Lamy, Robert E. and Thompson, G. Rodney. Valuation of Primary Issue Convertible Bonds. *J. Finan. Res.*, Fall 1986, *9*(3), pp. 251–59. [G: U.S.]

Blomeyer, Edward C. An Analytic Approximation for the American Put Price for Options on Stocks with Dividends. *J. Finan. Quant. Anal.*, June 1986, *21*(2), pp. 229–33.

Bodurtha, James N., Jr. and Courtadon, Georges R. Efficiency Tests of the Foreign Currency Options Market. *J. Finance*, March 1986, *41*(1), pp. 151–62. **[G: U.S.]**

Bosch, Jean-Claude. Portfolio Choices, Consumption, and Prices in a Market with Durable Assets. *J. Finan. Res.*, Fall 1986, *9*(3), pp. 239–50.

Boschen, John F. The Information Content of Indexed Bonds. *J. Money, Credit, Banking*, February 1986, *18*(1), pp. 76–87.

Boughton, James M., et al. Effects of Exchange Rate Changes in Industrial Countries. **In** *International Monetary Fund, Research Department*, 1986, pp. 115–49. **[G: OECD]**

Bradley, Michael G. and Graham, John W. Inflation Risk and Consumer Portfolio Behavior. *Quart. Rev. Econ. Bus.*, Spring 1986, *26*(1), pp. 88–94.

Brasse, Valerie G. Testing the Efficiency of the Tin Futures Market on the London Metal Exchange. **In** *[Yamey, B.]*, 1986, pp. 43–60. **[G: U.K.]**

Brauer, Greggory A. Using Jump-Diffusion Return Models to Measure Differential Information by Firm Size. *J. Finan. Quant. Anal.*, December 1986, *21*(4), pp. 447–58. **[G: U.S.]**

Brealey, Richard A. Do We Really Know That Financial Markets Are Efficient? Comment. **In** *Edwards, J., et al., eds.*, 1986, pp. 24–29. **[G: U.S.]**

Brealey, Richard A. How To Combine Active Management with Index Funds. *J. Portfol. Manage.*, Winter 1986, *12*(2), pp. 4–10. **[G: U.S.]**

Breeden, Douglas T. Consumption, Production, Inflation and Interest Rates: A Synthesis. *J. Finan. Econ.*, May 1986, *16*(1), pp. 3–39.

Brennan, Michael J. A Theory of Price Limits in Futures Markets. *J. Finan. Econ.*, June 1986, *16*(2), pp. 213–33. **[G: U.S.]**

Bresnahan, Timothy F. and Spiller, Pablo T. Futures Market Backwardation under Risk Neutrality. *Econ. Inquiry*, July 1986, *24*(3), pp. 429–41.

Brown, Stewart L. A Reformulation of the Portfolio Model of Hedging: Reply. *Amer. J. Agr. Econ.*, November 1986, *68*(4), pp. 1010–12. **[G: U.S.]**

Broze, L.; Gouriéroux, Christian and Szafarz, A. Bulles spéculatives et transmission d'information sur le marché d'un bien stockable. (Speculative Bubbles and on the Transmission of Information on the Stockable Commodity Market. With English summary.) *L'Actual. Econ.*, June 1986, *62*(2), pp. 166–84.

Brunner, Karl. Financial Markets and Macroeconomic Fluctuations: Comment. **In** *Butkiewicz, J. L.; Koford, K. J. and Miller, J. B., eds.*, 1986, pp. 88–94. **[G: U.S.]**

Brunner, Karl. Financial Markets and Macroeconomic Fluctuations: Rejoinder. **In** *Butkiewicz, J. L.; Koford, K. J. and Miller, J. B., eds.*, 1986, pp. 108–09. **[G: U.S.]**

Burgstahler, David and Noreen, Eric W. Detecting Contemporaneous Security Market Reactions to a Sequence of Related Events. *J. Acc. Res.*, Spring 1986, *24*(1), pp. 170–86. **[G: U.S.]**

Burmeister, Edwin and Wall, Kent D. The Arbitrage Pricing Theory and Macroeconomic Factor Measures. *Financial Rev.*, February 1986, *21*(1), pp. 1–20. **[G: U.S.]**

Cadsby, Charles Bram. Performance Hypothesis Testing with the Sharpe and Treynor Measures: A Comment. *J. Finance*, December 1986, *41*(5), pp. 1175–76.

Campbell, John Y. A Defense of Traditional Hypotheses about the Term Structure of Interest Rates. *J. Finance*, March 1986, *41*(1), pp. 183–93. **[G: U.S.]**

Campbell, John Y. Bond and Stock Returns in a Simple Exchange Model. *Quart. J. Econ.*, November 1986, *101*(4), pp. 785–803.

Cannaday, Roger E. and Colwell, Peter F. Real Estate Valuation Models: Lender and Equity Investor Criteria. *Amer. Real Estate Urban Econ. Assoc. J.*, Summer 1986, *14*(2), pp. 316–37.

Capie, Forrest H.; Mills, Terence C. and Wood, Geoffrey E. What Happened in 1931? **In** *Capie, F. and Wood, G. E., eds.*, 1986, pp. 120–48. **[G: U.K.]**

Chen, Andrew H.; Chen, K. C. and Sears, R. Stephen. The Value of Loan Guarantees: The Case of Chrysler Corporation. **In** *Chen, A. H., ed.*, 1986, pp. 101–17. **[G: U.S.]**

Chen, K. C.; Cheng, David C. and Hite, Gailen L. Systematic Risk and Market Power: An Application of Tobin's *q*. *Quart. Rev. Econ. Bus.*, Autumn 1986, *26*(3), pp. 58–72. **[G: U.S.]**

Chen, Nai-Fu; Roll, Richard and Ross, Stephen A. Economic Forces and the Stock Market. *J. Bus.*, July 1986, *59*(3), pp. 383–403.

Chen, Son-Nan. An Intertemporal Capital Asset Pricing Model under Heterogeneous Beliefs. *J. Econ. Bus.*, December 1986, *38*(4), pp. 317–30.

Chen, Son-Nan. Optimal Portfolio Selection under Differential Taxation: Simple Rules. *Quart. Rev. Econ. Bus.*, Spring 1986, *26*(1), pp. 6–16.

Chen, Son-Nan and Aggarwal, Reena. Optimal Portfolio Selection and Uncertain Inflation. *J. Portfol. Manage.*, Fall 1986, *13*(1), pp. 44–49.

Cheng, David C. and Lee, Cheng F. Ramsey's Specification Error Test and Alternative Specifications of the Market Model: Methods and Applications. *Quart. Rev. Econ. Bus.*, Autumn 1986, *26*(3), pp. 6–24. **[G: U.S.]**

Chiang, Raymond and Kolb, Robert W. An Analytical Model of the Relationship between Maturity and Bonds Risk Differentials. *Financial Rev.*, May 1986, *21*(2), pp. 191–209.

Chua, Jess H. and Schnabel, Jacques A. Nonpecuniary Benefits and Asset Market Equilibrium. *Financial Rev.*, May 1986, *21*(2), pp. 185–90.

Congdon, Tim. What Happened in 1931? Comment. **In** *Capie, F. and Wood, G. E., eds.*, 1986, pp. 149–56. **[G: U.K.]**

Connor, Gregory and Korajczyk, Robert A. Performance Measurement with the Arbitrage Pricing Theory: A New Framework for Analysis. *J. Finan. Econ.*, March 1986, *15*(3), pp. 373–94.

Conroy, Robert M. and Winkler, Robert L. Market Structure: The Specialist as Dealer and Broker. *J. Banking Finance*, March 1986, *10*(1), pp. 21–36.

Constantinides, George M. Capital Market Equilibrium with Transaction Costs. *J. Polit. Econ.*, August 1986, *94*(4), pp. 842–62.

Cooper, Ian and Kaplanis, Evi. Costs to Cross-border Investment and International Equity Market Equilibrium. **In** *Edwards, J., et al., eds.*, 1986, pp. 209–40. **[G: OECD]**

Cornell, Bradford. Inflation Measurement, Inflation Risk, and the Pricing of Treasury Bills. *J. Finan. Res.*, Fall 1986, *9*(3), pp. 193–202. **[G: U.S.]**

Danthine, Jean-Pierre and Donaldson, John B. Inflation and Asset Prices in an Exchange Economy. *Econometrica*, May 1986, *54*(3), pp. 585–605.

Davidson, Paul. Financial Markets and Macroeconomic Fluctuations: Comment. **In** *Butkiewicz, J. L.; Koford, K. J. and Miller, J. B., eds.*, 1986, pp. 94–102. **[G: U.S.]**

Davies, J. R. Valuation of Shares. **In** *Firth, M. and Keane, S. M., eds.*, 1986, pp. 193–206.

DeGennaro, Ramon P. and Kim, Sangphill. The CAPM and Beta in an Imperfect Market: Comment. *J. Portfol. Manage.*, Summer 1986, *12*(4), pp. 78–79.

Denny, J. L. and Suchanek, Gerry L. On the Use of Semimartingales and Stochastic Integrals to Model Continuous Trading. *J. Math. Econ.*, 1986, *15*(3), pp. 255–66.

Detemple, Jérôme B. A General Equilibrium Model of Asset Pricing with Partial or Heterogeneous Information. *Finance*, December 1986, *7*(2), pp. 183–201.

Detemple, Jérôme B. Asset Pricing in a Production Economy with Incomplete Information. *J. Finance*, June 1986, *41*(2), pp. 383–91.

Dickinson, J. Portfolio Theory. **In** *Firth, M. and Keane, S. M., eds.*, 1986, pp. 16–27.

Dietrich-Campbell, Bruce and Schwartz, Eduardo S. Valuing Debt Options: Empirical Evidence. *J. Finan. Econ.*, July 1986, *16*(3), pp. 321–43. **[G: U.S.]**

Dixon, Bruce L. Optimum Multi-period Portfolios with Imperfectly Elastic Assets and Parameter Uncertainty. *J. Econ. Dynam. Control*, June 1986, *10*(1/2), pp. 307–08.

Dothan, Michael U. and Feldman, David. Equilibrium Interest Rates and Multiperiod Bonds in a Partially Observable Economy. *J. Finance*, June 1986, *41*(2), pp. 369–82.

Duffie, Darrell and Huang, Chi-fu. Multiperiod Security Markets with Differential Information: Martingales and Resolution Times. *J. Math. Econ.*, 1986, *15*(3), pp. 283–303.

Dybvig, Philip H. and Ross, Stephen A. Tax Clienteles and Asset Pricing. *J. Finance*, July 1986, *41*(3), pp. 751–62.

Elton, Edwin J.; Gruber, Martin J. and Koo, Suk Mo. Effect of Quarterly Earnings Announcements on Analysts' Forecasts. **In** *Chen, A. H., ed.*, 1986, pp. 247–59. **[G: U.S.]**

Eun, Cheol S. and Janakiramanan, S. A Model of International Asset Pricing with a Constraint on the Foreign Equity Ownership. *J. Finance*, September 1986, *41*(4), pp. 897–914.

Eytan, T. Hanan and Harpaz, Giora. The Pricing of Futures and Options Contracts on the Value Line Index. *J. Finance*, September 1986, *41*(4), pp. 843–55. **[G: U.S.]**

Feldman, David. Optimal Portfolio Choice under Incomplete Information: Discussion. *J. Finance*, July 1986, *41*(3), pp. 747–49.

Ferguson, Robert. The Trouble with Performance Measurement. *J. Portfol. Manage.*, Spring 1986, *12*(3), pp. 4–9.

Findlay, M. Chapman, III and Williams, Edward E. Better Betas Didn't Help the Boat People. *J. Portfol. Manage.*, Fall 1986, *13*(1), pp. 4–9.

Firchau, Volker. Portfolio Decisions and Capital Market Equilibria under Incomplete Information. **In** *Bamberg, G. and Spremann, K., eds.*, 1986, pp. 55–78.

Flannery, Mark J. Asymmetric Information and Risky Debt Maturity Choice. *J. Finance*, March 1986, *41*(1), pp. 19–37.

Flood, Robert P. and Hodrick, Robert J. Asset Price Volatility, Bubbles, and Process Switching. *J. Finance*, September 1986, *41*(4), pp. 831–42.

Fluet, Claude. Stockage spéculatif et effets redistributifs de l'information prospective. (Speculative Stockpiling and Redistributive Impact of Prospective Information. With English summary.) *Can. J. Econ.*, August 1986, *19*(3), pp. 559–67.

Forsythe, Robert. The Application of Laboratory Methods to Testing Theories of Resource Allocation under Uncertainty. **In** *Gilad, B. and Kaish, S., eds., Vol. A*, 1986, pp. 19–60. **[G: U.S.]**

French, Kenneth R. Detecting Spot Price Forecasts in Futures Prices. *J. Bus.*, Part 2, April 1986, *59*(2), pp. S39–54. **[G: U.S.]**

Frost, Peter A. and Savarino, James E. An Empirical Bayes Approach to Efficient Portfolio Selection. *J. Finan. Quant. Anal.*, September 1986, *21*(3), pp. 293–305.

Frost, Peter A. and Savarino, James E. Portfolio Size and Estimation Risk. *J. Portfol. Manage.*, Summer 1986, *12*(4), pp. 60–64.

Gallagher, Martin. The Inverted Fisher Hypothesis: Additional Evidence [Fisher's Paradox and the Theory of Interest]. *Amer. Econ. Rev.*, March 1986, *76*(1), pp. 247–49.

Garven, James R. A Pedagogic Note on the Derivation of the Black–Scholes Option Pricing Formula. *Financial Rev.*, May 1986, *21*(2), pp. 337–44.

Gay, Gerald D. and Manaster, Steven. Implicit

Delivery Options and Optimal Delivery Strategies for Financial Futures Contracts. *J. Finan. Econ.*, May 1986, *16*(1), pp. 41–72. [G: U.S.]

Geanakoplos, John D. and Polemarchakis, Herakles M. Existence, Regularity, and Constrained Suboptimality of Competitive Allocations When the Asset Market Is Incomplete. **In** *[Arrow, K. J.], Vol. 3*, 1986, pp. 65–95.

Gennotte, Gerard. Optimal Portfolio Choice under Incomplete Information. *J. Finance*, July 1986, *41*(3), pp. 733–46.

Geske, Robert and Trautmann, Siegfried. Option Valuation: Theory and Empirical Evidence. **In** *Bamberg, G. and Spremann, K., eds.*, 1986, pp. 79–133. [G: U.S.]

Giaccotto, Carmelo. Stochastic Modelling of Interest Rates: Actuarial vs. Equilibrium Approach. *J. Risk Ins.*, September 1986, *53*(3), pp. 435–53. [G: U.S.]

Gilbert, Christopher L. Commodity Price Stabilization: The Massell Model and Multiplicative Disturbances. *Quart. J. Econ.*, August 1986, *101*(3), pp. 635–40.

Gilles, Christian and LeRoy, Stephen F. A Note on the Local Expectations Hypothesis: A Discrete-Time Exposition. *J. Finance*, September 1986, *41*(4), pp. 975–79.

Goldenberg, David H. Sample Path Properties of Futures Prices. *J. Futures Markets*, Spring 1986, *6*(1), pp. 127–40.

Goldfeld, Stephen M. The Term Structure of Interest Rates Revisited: Comments. *Brookings Pap. Econ. Act.*, 1986, (1), pp. 97–100. [G: U.S.; U.K.; W. Germany; Canada]

Gordon, Roger H. Taxation of Investment and Savings in a World Economy. *Amer. Econ. Rev.*, December 1986, *76*(5), pp. 1086–1102.

Goss, Barry A. and Giles, David E. A. Intertemporal Allocation in the Australian Wool Market. **In** *Goss, B. A., ed.*, 1986, pp. 93–118. [G: Australia]

Goss, Barry A. and Giles, David E. A. Price Determination and Storage in Commodity Markets: Soybeans and Wool. **In** *[Yamey, B.]*, 1986, pp. 3–41. [G: U.S.; Australia]

Granito, Michael R. Investment Rules and the Ergodic Hypothesis. *J. Portfol. Manage.*, Fall 1986, *13*(1), pp. 50–58.

Grauer, Robert R. Normality, Solvency, and Portfolio Choice. *J. Finan. Quant. Anal.*, September 1986, *21*(3), pp. 265–78.

Grauer, Robert R. and Hakansson, Nils H. A Half Century of Returns on Levered and Unlevered Portfolios of Stocks, Bonds, and Bills, with and without Small Stocks. *J. Bus.*, Part 1, April 1986, *59*(2), pp. 287–318. [G: U.S.]

Green, Richard C. Benchmark Portfolio Inefficiency and Deviations from the Security Market Line. *J. Finance*, June 1986, *41*(2), pp. 295–312. [G: U.S.]

Green, Richard C. Positively Weighted Portfolios on the Minimum-Variance Frontier. *J. Finance*, December 1986, *41*(5), pp. 1051–68.

Green, Richard C. and Talmor, Eli. Asset Substitution and the Agency Costs of Debt Financing. *J. Banking Finance*, October 1986, *10*(3), pp. 391–99.

Gressis, Nicholas; Philippatos, George C. and Vlahos, George. Net Selectivity as a Component Measure of Investment Performance. *Financial Rev.*, February 1986, *21*(1), pp. 103–10.

Haber, Lawrence J. Production Theory under Uncertain Inflation. *Atlantic Econ. J.*, September 1986, *14*(3), pp. 24–33.

Hagen, Ole. Some Paradoxes in Economics. **In** *[Rapoport, A.]*, 1986, pp. 13–25.

Hamilton, James D. On Testing for Self-fulfilling Speculative Price Bubbles. *Int. Econ. Rev.*, October 1986, *27*(3), pp. 545–52.

Harrison, Glenn W. Experimental Futures Markets. **In** *Goss, B. A., ed.*, 1986, pp. 43–76.

Hartley, Peter. Portfolio Theory and Foreign Investment—The Role of Non-marketed Assets. *Econ. Rec.*, September 1986, *62*(178), pp. 286–95.

Hartzmark, Michael L. The Effects of Changing Margin Levels on Futures Market Activity, the Composition of Traders in the Market, and Price Performance. *J. Bus.*, Part 2, April 1986, *59*(2), pp. S147–80. [G: U.S.]

Hawawini, Gabriel. The Geometry of Risk Aversion: A Pedagogic Note. *J. Econ. Bus.*, May 1986, *38*(2), pp. 93–104.

Heaton, Hal. The Relative Yields on Taxable and Tax-Exempt Debt. *J. Money, Credit, Banking*, November 1986, *18*(4), pp. 482–94. [G: U.S.]

Ho, Thomas S. Y. and Lee, Sang-bin. Term Structure Movements and Pricing Interest Rate Contingent Claims. *J. Finance*, December 1986, *41*(5), pp. 1011–29.

Holtz-Eakin, Douglas. Explaining the Yield Spread between Taxable and Tax-Exempt Bonds: The Role of Expected Tax Policy: Comment. **In** *Rosen, H. S., ed.*, 1986, pp. 49–51. [G: U.S.]

Horner, Melchior. Ein Portfolio-Modell zur Erklärung des Preisabschlages der Namenaktien gegenü ber den Inhaberaktien und Partizipationsscheinen. (A Portfolio Model Explaining the Price Discount of Registered Relative to Bearer and Non-voting Shares in Switzerland. With English summary.) *Schweiz. Z. Volkswirtsch. Statist.*, March 1986, *122*(1), pp. 61–79. [G: Switzerland]

Howard, Charles T. and D'Antonio, Louis J. Treasury Bill Futures as a Hedging Tool: A Risk-Return Approach. *J. Finan. Res.*, Spring 1986, *9*(1), pp. 25–39. [G: U.S.]

Huffman, Gregory W. Asset Pricing with Capital Accumulation. *Int. Econ. Rev.*, October 1986, *27*(3), pp. 565–82. [G: U.S.]

Hughes, Patricia J. Signalling by Direct Disclosure under Asymmetric Information. *J. Acc. Econ.*, June 1986, *8*(2), pp. 119–42.

Jagannathan, Ravi and Korajczyk, Robert A. Assessing the Market Timing Performance of Managed Portfolios. *J. Bus.*, Part 1, April 1986, *59*(2), pp. 217–35. [G: U.S.]

Jain, Prem C. Relation between Market Model Prediction Errors and Omitted Variables: A Methodological Note. *J. Acc. Res.*, Spring 1986, *24*(1), pp. 187–93.

Jarrow, Robert. The Relationship between Arbitrage and First Order Stochastic Dominance. *J. Finance*, September 1986, *41*(4), pp. 915–21.

Jean, William H. and Helms, Billy P. Stochastic Dominance as a Decision Model. *Quart. J. Bus. Econ.*, Winter 1986, *25*(1), pp. 65–101.

Joerding, Wayne. The Model Dependence of Relative Mean-Square Error Tests for Market Efficiency. *J. Econ. Bus.*, August 1986, *38*(3), pp. 227–36.

Kaen, Fred R. and Rosenman, Robert E. Predictable Behavior in Financial Markets: Some Evidence in Support of Heiner's Hypothesis. *Amer. Econ. Rev.*, March 1986, *76*(1), pp. 212–20.

Kahl, Kandice H. A Reformulation of the Portfolio Model of Hedging: Comment. *Amer. J. Agr. Econ.*, November 1986, *68*(4), pp. 1007–09. **[G: U.S.]**

Kandel, Shmuel. The Geometry of the Maximum Likelihood Estimator of the Zero-Beta Return. *J. Finance*, June 1986, *41*(2), pp. 339–46.

Karpoff, Jonathan M. A Theory of Trading Volume. *J. Finance*, December 1986, *41*(5), pp. 1069–87.

Keim, Donald B. Dividend Yields and the January Effect. *J. Portfol. Manage.*, Winter 1986, *12*(2), pp. 54–60. **[G: U.S.]**

Kennedy, Brian A. How to Measure Fixed-Income Performance *Correctly* : Comment. *J. Portfol. Manage.*, Winter 1986, *12*(2), pp. 84–86. **[G: U.S.]**

Kihlstrom, Richard E. The Informational Role of Mergers in the Context of a Complete Securities Market. **In** *[Dean, J.]*, 1986, pp. 171–85.

Kleidon, Allan W. Anomalies in Financial Economics: Blueprint for Change? **In** *Hogarth, R. M. and Reder, M. W., eds.*, 1986, pp. 285–315.

Kleidon, Allan W. Anomalies in Financial Economics: Blueprint for Change? *J. Bus.*, Part 2, October 1986, *59*(4), pp. S469–99.

Kleidon, Allan W. Bias in Small Sample Tests of Stock Price Rationality. *J. Bus.*, Part 1, April 1986, *59*(2), pp. 237–61.

Kleidon, Allan W. Variance Bounds Tests and Stock Price Valuation Models. *J. Polit. Econ.*, October 1986, *94*(5), pp. 953–1001. **[G: U.S.]**

Klotz, Ben P. and Meinster, David R. An Integration of CAPM with IS–LM Analysis into a Unified Theory of Aggregate Demand. *Southern Econ. J.*, January 1986, *52*(3), pp. 718–34.

Korkie, Bob. Market Line Deviations and Market Anomalies with Reference to Small and Large Firms. *J. Finan. Quant. Anal.*, June 1986, *21*(2), pp. 161–80. **[G: U.S.]**

Kosmicke, Ralph. The Limited Relevance of Volatility to Risk. *J. Portfol. Manage.*, Fall 1986, *13*(1), pp. 18–20.

Kouri, Pentti J. K. Franco Modigliani's Contributions to Economics. *Scand. J. Econ.*, 1986, *88*(2), pp. 311–34.

Krasker, William S. Stock Price Movements in Response to Stock Issues under Asymmetric Information. *J. Finance*, March 1986, *41*(1), pp. 93–105.

Krushwitz, Lutz. Bezugsrechtsemissionen in optionspreistheoretischer Sicht. (Rights Issues from the Standpoint of Option Price Theory. With English summary.) *Kredit Kapital*, 1986, *19*(1), pp. 110–21.

Kumar, Raman and Makhija, Anil K. Volatility of Stock Prices and Market Efficiency. *Managerial Dec. Econ.*, June 1986, *7*(2), pp. 119–22.

Labadie, Pamela. Comparative Dynamics and Risk Premia in an Overlapping Generations Model. *Rev. Econ. Stud.*, January 1986, *53*(1), pp. 139–52.

Langetieg, Terence C. Stochastic Control of Corporate Investment When Output Affects Future Prices. *J. Finan. Quant. Anal.*, September 1986, *21*(3), pp. 239–63.

Latham, Mark. Informational Efficiency and Information Subsets. *J. Finance*, March 1986, *41*(1), pp. 39–52.

Lee, Cheng F., et al. On Accounting-based, Market-based and Composite-based Beta Predictions: Methods and Implications. *Financial Rev.*, February 1986, *21*(1), pp. 51–68. **[G: U.S.]**

Levy, Haim. Upper and Lower Bounds of Put and Call Option Value: Stochastic Dominance Approach—Erratum. *J. Finance*, December 1986, *41*(5), pp. 1181.

Li, Elizabeth H. Compensating Differentials for Cyclical and Noncyclical Unemployment: The Interaction between Investors' and Employees' Risk Aversion. *J. Lab. Econ.*, April 1986, *4*(2), pp. 277–300. **[G: U.S.]**

Little, Patricia Knain. Financial Futures and Immunization. *J. Finan. Res.*, Spring 1986, *9*(1), pp. 1–12.

Litzenberger, Robert H. and Ronn, Ehud I. A Utility-based Model of Common Stock Price Movements. *J. Finance*, March 1986, *41*(1), pp. 67–92. **[G: U.S.]**

Lo, Andrew W. Statistical Tests of Contingent-Claims Asset-Pricing Models: A New Methodology. *J. Finan. Econ.*, September 1986, *17*(1), pp. 143–73.

Löflund, Anders. Tasapainomallin merkitys osakemarkkinoiden tehokkuustesteissä. (The Effect of Using Different Market Model Specifications in Tests of the Efficient Market Hypothesis [EMH] on the Finnish Stock Market. With English summary.) *Liiketaloudellinen Aikak.*, 1986, *35*(3), pp. 218–35. **[G: Finland]**

Lotruglio, Anthony F. How to Measure Fixed-Income Performance *Correctly*: Comment. *J. Portfol. Manage.*, Winter 1986, *12*(2), pp. 87. **[G: U.S.]**

Madura, Jeff. Model for Financing in International Money Markets. *Rivista Int. Sci. Econ. Com.*, Oct.-Nov. 1986, *33*(10–11), pp. 1049–56.

Magill, Michael J. P. and Nermuth, Manfred.

On the Qualitative Properties of Futures Market Equilibrium. *J. Econ. (Z. Nationalökon.)*, 1986, *46*(3), pp. 233–52.

Mahajan, Arvind and Mehta, Dileep. Efficiency and Speculation in the Foreign Exchange Market. *Indian Econ. J.*, Jan.-Mar. 1986, *33*(3), pp. 85–109.

Malatesta, Paul H. and Thompson, Rex. Stock Price Reactions to Partially Anticipated Events: Evidence on the Economic Impact of Corporate Acquisition Attempts. **In** *Chen, A. H., ed.*, 1986, pp. 119–48. **[G: U.S.]**

Maloney, Kevin J. and Yawitz, Jess B. Interest Rate Risk, Immunization, and Duration. *J. Portfol. Manage.*, Spring 1986, *12*(3), pp. 41–48.

Mankiw, N. Gregory. The Equity Premium and the Concentration of Aggregate Shocks. *J. Finan. Econ.*, September 1986, *17*(1), pp. 211–19.

Mankiw, N. Gregory. The Term Structure of Interest Rates Revisited. *Brookings Pap. Econ. Act.*, 1986, (1), pp. 61–96. **[G: U.S.; U.K.; W. Germany; Canada]**

Marsh, Terry A. and Merton, Robert C. Dividend Variability and Variance Bounds Tests for the Rationality of Stock Market Prices. *Amer. Econ. Rev.*, June 1986, *76*(3), pp. 483–98.

Martinengo, Giancarlo. Rischio da leverage, finanziamento esterno ed interno: un contributo allo studio degli equilibri tra banca e impresa. (Leverage Risk, External and Internal Financing: An Integration of Banks and Firms Decisions. With English summary.) *Polit. Econ.*, August 1986, *2*(2), pp. 243–71.

McCafferty, Stephen. Aggregate Demand and Interest Rates: A Macroeconomic Approach to the Term Structure. *Econ. Inquiry*, October 1986, *24*(4), pp. 521–33.

McDaniel, William R. The Economic Ordering Quantity Problem and Wealth Maximization. *Financial Rev.*, November 1986, *21*(4), pp. 527–36.

McDonald, Robert. Taxes and the Hedging of Forward Commitments. *J. Futures Markets*, Summer 1986, *6*(2), pp. 207–22.

McEnally, Richard W. Latané's Bequest: The Best of Portfolio Strategies. *J. Portfol. Manage.*, Winter 1986, *12*(2), pp. 21–30.

McKenna, Fred W. and Kim, Yong H. Managerial Risk Preferences, Real Pension Costs, and Long-run Corporate Pension Fund Investment Policy. *J. Risk Ins.*, March 1986, *53*(1), pp. 29–48.

McKinnon, Ronald I. Foreign Exchange Dealers, the Domestic Money Market and Stabilising Speculation. **In** *[Tarshis, L.]*, 1986, pp. 28–55.

McLaren, Keith R. and Upcher, Mark R. Testing Further Restrictions on Portfolio Models. *Australian Econ. Pap.*, December 1986, *25*(47), pp. 193–205.

McMillan, Henry M. Nonassignable Pensions and the Price of Risk. *J. Money, Credit, Banking*, February 1986, *18*(1), pp. 60–75.

Miller, Edward M. Liquidity, Its Origins and Effects: Its Implications for Corporations, Deposit Institutions and Security Markets. *Amer. J. Econ. Soc.*, January 1986, *45*(1), pp. 27–39.

Miller, Merton H. Behavioral Rationality in Finance: The Case of Dividends. *J. Bus.*, Part 2, October 1986, *59*(4), pp. S451–68.

Miller, Merton H. Behavioral Rationality in Finance: The Case of Dividends. **In** *Hogarth, R. M. and Reder, M. W., eds.*, 1986, pp. 267–84.

Morgan, George Emir. Floating Rate Securities and Immunization: Some Further Results. *J. Finan. Quant. Anal.*, March 1986, *21*(1), pp. 87–94.

Morgan, George Emir, III and Smith, Stephen D. Basic Risk, Partial Takedown and Hedging by Financial Intermediaries. *J. Banking Finance*, December 1986, *10*(4), pp. 467–90.

Morris, Victor F. Central Value in Review: Reply. *J. Portfol. Manage.*, Summer 1986, *12*(4), pp. 76–77.

Murphy, James M. and Rappaport, Allen. A Multiple Discriminant Analysis of BHC Commercial Paper Ratings: A Comment. *J. Banking Finance*, March 1986, *10*(1), pp. 143–44. **[G: U.S.]**

Myer, Richard L. and Antia, Murad J. A Note on the Calculation of Probabilistic Betas. *Financial Rev.*, February 1986, *21*(1), pp. 151–56.

Näslund, Bertil. Some Views on the Current State of Financial Theory. *Liiketaloudellinen Aikak.*, 1986, *35*(4), pp. 267–74.

Nawrocki, David N. and Harding, William H. State-Value Weighted Entropy as a Measure of Investment Risk. *Appl. Econ.*, April 1986, *18*(4), pp. 411–19. **[G: U.S.]**

O'Brien, Thomas J. A Discrete Time Option Model Dependent on Expected Return: A Note. *J. Finance*, June 1986, *41*(2), pp. 515–20.

O'Brien, Thomas J. and Selby, Michael J. P. Option Pricing Theory and Asset Expectations: A Review and Discussion in Tribute to James Boness. *Financial Rev.*, November 1986, *21*(4), pp. 399–418.

O'Hara, Maureen and Oldfield, George S. The Microeconomics of Market Making. *J. Finan. Quant. Anal.*, December 1986, *21*(4), pp. 361–76.

Opsal, Scott. Time Diversification: The Surest Route to Lower Risk: Comment. *J. Portfol. Manage.*, Summer 1986, *12*(4), pp. 74–75.

Ortmeyer, David L. and Peek, Joe. An Ex Ante View of Household Portfolio Choice: The Role of Expected Capital Gains. *Rev. Econ. Statist.*, May 1986, *68*(2), pp. 207–16. **[G: U.S.]**

Page, Frank H., Jr. and Sanders, Anthony B. A General Derivation of the Jump Process Option Pricing Formula. *J. Finan. Quant. Anal.*, December 1986, *21*(4), pp. 437–46.

Peasnell, K. The Capital Asset Pricing Model. **In** *Firth, M. and Keane, S. M., eds.*, 1986, pp. 28–43.

Peavy, John W., III and Edgar, S. Michael. A

Multiple Discriminant Analysis of BHC Commercial Paper Ratings: A Reply. *J. Banking Finance,* March 1986, *10*(1), pp. 145–46. **[G: U.S.]**

Perrakis, Stylianos. Option Bounds in Discrete Time: Extensions and the Pricing of the American Put. *J. Bus.*, January 1986, *59*(1), pp. 119–41.

Peterson, David R. An Empirical Test of an Exante Model of the Determination of Stock Return Volatility. *J. Finan. Res.*, Fall 1986, *9*(3), pp. 203–14.

Philippatos, George C.; Vlahos, George and Gressis, Nicholas. Portfolio Risk Transference through Trading in Stock-Index Futures. *Rivista Int. Sci. Econ. Com.*, Oct.-Nov. 1986, *33*(10–11), pp. 995–1016.

Pippenger, John. Arbitrage and Efficient Markets Interpretations of Purchasing Power Parity: Theory and Evidence. *Fed. Res. Bank San Francisco Econ. Rev.*, Winter 1986, (1), pp. 31–47. **[G: U.S.; Canada; France; W. Germany]**

van der Ploeg, Frederick. Rational Expectations, Risk and Chaos in Financial Markets. *Econ. J.*, Supplement 1986, *96*, pp. 151–62.

Polemarchakis, Herakles M., et al. Approximate Aggregation under Uncertainty. *J. Econ. Theory,* April 1986, *38*(2), pp. 189–210.

Pope, P. F. Corporate Bonds—Determinants of Yield. **In** *Firth, M. and Keane, S. M., eds.*, 1986, pp. 126–41. **[G: U.K.]**

Poterba, James M. Explaining the Yield Spread between Taxable and Tax-Exempt Bonds: The Role of Expected Tax Policy. **In** *Rosen, H. S., ed.*, 1986, pp. 5–49. **[G: U.S.]**

Prakash, Arun J. and Bear, Robert M. A Simplifying Performance Measure Recognizing Skewness. *Financial Rev.*, February 1986, *21*(1), pp. 135–44.

Pressnell, L. S. The Avoidance of Catastrophe: Two Nineteenth-Century Banking Crises: Comment. **In** *Capie, F. and Wood, G. E., eds.*, 1986, pp. 74–76. **[G: U.K.]**

Prisman, Eliezer Z. Immunization as a Maxmin Strategy: A New Look. *J. Banking Finance,* December 1986, *10*(4), pp. 491–509.

Prisman, Eliezer Z. Valuation of Risky Assets in Arbitrage Free Economies with Frictions. *J. Finance,* July 1986, *41*(3), pp. 545–57.

Ramaswamy, Krishna and Sundaresan, Suresh M. The Valuation of Floating-Rate Instruments: Theory and Evidence. *J. Finan. Econ.*, December 1986, *17*(2), pp. 251–72.

Reagan, Patricia B. and Stulz, René M. Risk-Bearing, Labor Contracts, and Capital Markets. **In** *Chen, A. H., ed.*, 1986, pp. 217–31.

Reid, Donald W. and Tew, Bernard V. Mean-Variance versus Direct Utility Maximization: A Comment. *J. Finance,* December 1986, *41*(5), pp. 1177–79. **[G: U.S.]**

Reinganum, Marc R. Is Time Travel Impossible? A Financial Proof. *J. Portfol. Manage.*, Fall 1986, *13*(1), pp. 10–12.

Rhee, S. Ghon. Stochastic Demand and a Decomposition of Systematic Risk. **In** *Chen, A. H., ed.*, 1986, pp. 197–216.

Roberts, Gordon S. and Viscione, Jerry A. Agency Costs, Bond Covenants, and Bond Yields. **In** *Chen, A. H., ed.*, 1986, pp. 73–99. **[G: U.S.]**

Rock, Kevin. Why New Issues Are Underpriced. *J. Finan. Econ.*, Jan./Feb. 1986, *15*(1/2), pp. 187–212.

Ronn, Ehud I. On the Rationality of Common Stock Return Volatility. *Financial Rev.*, November 1986, *21*(4), pp. 355–81.

Ronn, Ehud I. Valuation of Risky Assets in Arbitrage Free Economies with Frictions: Discussion. *J. Finance,* July 1986, *41*(3), pp. 557–60.

Ronn, Ehud I. and Verma, Avinash K. Pricing Risk-Adjusted Deposit Insurance: An Option-Based Model. *J. Finance,* September 1986, *41*(4), pp. 871–95. **[G: U.S.]**

Rothschild, Michael. Asset Pricing Theories. **In** *[Arrow, K. J.], Vol. 3,* 1986, pp. 97–128.

Rudolph, Bernd. The Value of Security Agreements. **In** *Bamberg, G. and Spremann, K., eds.*, 1986, pp. 135–62.

Rudolph, Bernd and Wondrak, Bernhard. Modelle zur Planung von Zinsänderungsrisiken und Zinsänderungschancen. (Models for Planning Interest Rate Risks and Interest Rate Opportunities. With English summary.) *Z. Wirtschaft. Sozialwissen.*, 1986, *106*(4), pp. 337–61.

Sachdeva, Kanwal. On the Equality of Two Lower Bounds on the Call Price: A Note. *J. Finan. Quant. Anal.*, June 1986, *21*(2), pp. 235–37.

Samuelson, Paul A. Paul Cootner's Reconciliation of Economic Law with Chance. **In** *Samuelson, P. A.*, 1986, *1982*, pp. 537–53.

Samuelson, Paul A. Stochastic Land Valuation: Total Return as Martingale Implying Price Changes—A Negatively Correlated Walk. **In** *Samuelson, P. A.*, 1986, pp. 527–36.

Schachter, Barry. A Note on the Welfare Consequences of New Option Markets. *J. Finance,* March 1986, *41*(1), pp. 263–67.

Schwartz, Eduardo S. and Brennan, Michael J. Asset Pricing in a Small Economy: A Test of the Omitted Assets Model. **In** *Bamberg, G. and Spremann, K., eds.*, 1986, pp. 163–88. **[G: Canada; U.S.]**

Shanken, Jay. On Exclusion of Assets from Tests of the Mean Variance Efficiency of the Market Portfolio: An Extension. *J. Finance,* June 1986, *41*(2), pp. 331–37.

Shiller, Robert J. Comments [Behavioral Rationality in Finance: The Case of Dividends] [Anomalies in Financial Economics: Blueprint for Change?]. *J. Bus.*, Part 2, October 1986, *59*(4), pp. S501–05.

Shiller, Robert J. Comments [Behavioral Rationality in Finance: The Case of Dividends] [Anomalies in Financial Economics: Blueprint for Change?]. **In** *Hogarth, R. M. and Reder, M. W., eds.*, 1986, pp. 317–21.

Shiller, Robert J. Financial Markets and Macroeconomic Fluctuations. **In** *Butkiewicz, J. L.;*

Koford, K. J. and Miller, J. B., eds., 1986, pp. 65–88. **[G: U.S.]**

Shiller, Robert J. Financial Markets and Macroeconomic Fluctuations: Reply. **In** *Butkiewicz, J. L.; Koford, K. J. and Miller, J. B., eds.*, 1986, pp. 105–08. **[G: U.S.]**

Shiller, Robert J. The Marsh–Merton Model of Managers' Smoothing of Dividends. *Amer. Econ. Rev.*, June 1986, *76*(3), pp. 499–503.

Shiller, Robert J. The Term Structure of Interest Rates Revisited: Comments. *Brookings Pap. Econ. Act.*, 1986, (1), pp. 100–107. **[G: U.S.]**

Shleifer, Andrei. Do Demand Curves for Stocks Slope Down? *J. Finance*, July 1986, *41*(3), pp. 579–90. **[G: U.S.]**

Spremann, Klaus. The Simple Analytics of Arbitrage. **In** *Bamberg, G. and Spremann, K., eds.*, 1986, pp. 189–207.

Sproule, Robert A. The Portfolio Effects of Increasing Asset-Return Uncertainty in a Two-Asset, Two-Period Model. *Rivista Int. Sci. Econ. Com.*, Oct.-Nov. 1986, *33*(10–11), pp. 1017–26.

Stambaugh, Robert F. Does the Stock Market Rationally Reflect Fundamental Values? Discussion. *J. Finance*, July 1986, *41*(3), pp. 601–02.

Stanhouse, Bryan E. Commercial Bank Portfolio Behavior and Endogenous Uncertainty. *J. Finance*, December 1986, *41*(5), pp. 1103–14.

Stein, Jerome L. Real Effects of Futures Speculation: Asymptotically Rational Expectations. *Economica*, May 1986, *53*(210), pp. 159–80.

Stickel, Scott E. The Effect of Preferred Stock Rating Changes on Preferred and Common Stock Prices. *J. Acc. Econ.*, October 1986, *8*(3), pp. 197–215. **[G: U.S.]**

Stiglitz, Joseph E. Financial Markets and Macroeconomic Fluctuations: Comment. **In** *Butkiewicz, J. L.; Koford, K. J. and Miller, J. B., eds.*, 1986, pp. 102–05. **[G: U.S.]**

Stock, Duane. The Analytics of Tax Effects in Discount Bond Valuation. *Financial Rev.*, November 1986, *21*(4), pp. 451–62.

Strassl, Wolfgang. Keynes on Expectations and Uncertainty: Rational Expectations Equilibria with Asymmetric Information. *Bull. Econ. Res.*, May 1986, *38*(2), pp. 137–59.

Stulz, René M. Asset Pricing and Expected Inflation. *J. Finance*, March 1986, *41*(1), pp. 209–23.

Sturm, Norbert. Erfolgsbesteuerung und Risikobereitschaft bei unternehmerischen Langfristentscheidungen. (With English summary.) *Z. Betriebswirtshaft*, September 1986, *56*(9), pp. 805–26.

Summers, Lawrence H. Do We Really Know That Financial Markets Are Efficient? **In** *Edwards, J., et al., eds.*, 1986, pp. 13–24. **[G: U.S.]**

Summers, Lawrence H. Does the Stock Market Rationally Reflect Fundamental Values? *J. Finance*, July 1986, *41*(3), pp. 591–601.

Sweeney, Richard J. and Warga, Arthur D. The Possibility of Estimating Risk Premia in Asset Pricing Models. *Financial Rev.*, May 1986, *21*(2), pp. 299–308.

Swidler, Steve. Simultaneous Option Prices and an Implied Risk-Free Rate of Interest: A Test of the Black–Scholes Model. *J. Econ. Bus.*, May 1986, *38*(2), pp. 155–64. **[G: U.S.]**

Tanigawa, Yasuhiko. On Mutual Share Holding by Corporations. *Econ. Stud. Quart.*, December 1986, *37*(4), pp. 319–35. **[G: Japan]**

Tauchen, George. Statistical Properties of Generalized Method-of-Moments Estimators of Structural Parameters Obtained from Financial Market Data: Reply. *J. Bus. Econ. Statist.*, October 1986, *4*(4), pp. 423–25.

Telser, Lester G. Futures and Actual Markets: How They Are Related. *J. Bus.*, Part 2, April 1986, *59*(2), pp. S5–20.

Theobald, M. Empirical Problems in Finance. **In** *Firth, M. and Keane, S. M., eds.*, 1986, pp. 242–53.

Tinic, Seha M. and West, Richard R. Risk, Return, and Equilibrium: A Revisit. *J. Polit. Econ.*, February 1986, *94*(1), pp. 126–47. **[G: U.S.]**

Trzcinka, Charles A. Risk, Segmentation, and the Municipal Term Structure. *Financial Rev.*, November 1986, *21*(4), pp. 501–26. **[G: U.S.]**

Valentine, T. J. A Further Comment on the Zero Row-Sum Property of Mean-Variance Portfolio Allocation Models. *Econ. Rec.*, March 1986, *62*(176), pp. 49–51.

Varaiya, Nikhil P. An Empirical Investigation of the Bidding Firms' Gains from Corporate Takeovers. **In** *Chen, A. H., ed.*, 1986, pp. 149–78. **[G: U.S.]**

Veljanovski, Cento G. An Institutional Analysis of Futures Contracting. **In** *Goss, B. A., ed.*, 1986, pp. 13–41.

Verrecchia, Robert E. On Timing and Selectivity: Discussion. *J. Finance*, July 1986, *41*(3), pp. 730–32.

Vickers, Douglas. Time, Ignorance, Surprise, and Economic Decisions: A Comment on Williams and Findlay's "Risk and the Role of Failed Expectations in an Uncertain World." *J. Post Keynesian Econ.*, Fall 1986, *9*(1), pp. 48–57.

Wagner, Michael. What Happened in 1931? Comment. **In** *Capie, F. and Wood, G. E., eds.*, 1986, pp. 157–59. **[G: U.K.]**

Ward, Charles W. R. Option Pricing. **In** *Firth, M. and Keane, S. M., eds.*, 1986, pp. 158–70.

Whaley, Robert E. Valuation of American Futures Options: Theory and Empirical Tests. *J. Finance*, March 1986, *41*(1), pp. 127–50. **[G: U.S.]**

Williams, Joseph. Tax Clienteles and Asset Pricing: Discussion. *J. Finance*, July 1986, *41*(3), pp. 762–63.

Yamey, Basil. Hedging, Risk and Profits: Notes on Motives for Hedging on Futures Markets. **In** *Goss, B. A., ed.*, 1986, pp. 77–91.

Yoon, Chang-Ho. Rational Expectations Equilibrium in a Sequence of Asset Markets. *Int. Econ. Rev.*, October 1986, *27*(3), pp. 553–64.

Zhu, Yu and Friend, Irwin. The Effects of Different Taxes on Risky and Risk-free Investment and on the Cost of Capital. *J. Finance*, March

1986, *41*(1), pp. 53–66.

Zimmermann, Heinz. The Stochastic Hedge Ratio and Option Pricing. *Schweiz. Z. Volkswirtsch. Statist.*, March 1986, *122*(1), pp. 81–94.

3132 Capital Markets: Empirical Studies, Including Regulation

Abel, U. and Boing, G. An Empirical Law of the Stock Option Market. *Z. Wirtschaft. Sozialwissen.*, 1986, *106*(1), pp. 15–24. **[G: U.S.]**

Adler, Michael and Simon, David. Exchange Risk Surprises in International Portfolios. *J. Portfol. Manage.*, Winter 1986, *12*(2), pp. 44–53. **[G: OECD]**

Aivazian, Varouj A., et al. International Exchange Risk and Asset Substitutability. *J. Int. Money Finance*, December 1986, *5*(4), pp. 449–66. **[G: Selected OECD]**

Aivazian, Varouj A., et al. An Empirical Portfolio Analysis of Financial Asset Substitutability: The Case of the U.S. Household Sector. *Quart. Rev. Econ. Bus.*, Summer 1986, *26*(2), pp. 47–65. **[G: U.S.]**

Akemann, Charles A. Predicting Changes in T-Bond Futures Spreads Using Implied Yields from T-Bill Futures. *J. Futures Markets*, Summer 1986, *6*(2), pp. 223–30. **[G: U.S.]**

Akgiray, Vedat and Booth, G. Geoffrey. Stock Price Processes with Discontinuous Time Paths: An Empirical Examination. *Financial Rev.*, May 1986, *21*(2), pp. 163–84. **[G: U.S.]**

Alderson, Michael J. and Chen, K. C. Excess Asset Reversions and Shareholder Wealth. *J. Finance*, March 1986, *41*(1), pp. 225–41. **[G: U.S.]**

Alexander, Vickie J.; Musser, Wesley N. and Mason, George. Futures Markets and Firm Decisions under Price, Production, and Financial Uncertainty. *Southern J. Agr. Econ.*, December 1986, *18*(2), pp. 39–49. **[G: U.S.]**

Amoako-Adu, Ben and Yagil, Joseph. Stock Price Behavior between the Base, Announcement, and Consummation Dates of the Merger. *J. Econ. Bus.*, May 1986, *38*(2), pp. 105–11. **[G: Canada]**

Anderson, Gordon J. Empirical Assessment of Present Value Relations: Comment. *Econometric Rev.*, 1986, *5*(2), pp. 235–39. **[G: U.S.]**

Anderson, Seth Copeland. Closed-End Funds versus Market Efficiency. *J. Portfol. Manage.*, Fall 1986, *13*(1), pp. 63–65. **[G: U.S.]**

Arak, Marcelle; Goodman, Laurie S. and Snailer, Joseph. Duration Equivalent Bond Swaps: A New Tool. *J. Portfol. Manage.*, Summer 1986, *12*(4), pp. 26–32. **[G: U.S.]**

Arnott, Robert D. and Vincent, Stephen J. S&P Additions and Deletions: A Market Anomaly. *J. Portfol. Manage.*, Fall 1986, *13*(1), pp. 29–33. **[G: U.S.]**

Asay, Michael and Edelsburg, Charles. Can a Dynamic Strategy Replicate the Returns of an Option? *J. Futures Markets*, Spring 1986, *6*(1), pp. 63–70. **[G: U.S.]**

Ashley, Richard A. and Patterson, Douglas M. A Nonparametric, Distribution-Free Test for Serial Independence in Stock Returns. *J. Finan. Quant. Anal.*, June 1986, *21*(2), pp. 221–27. **[G: U.S.]**

Asquith, Paul and Mullins, David W., Jr. Equity Issues and Offering Dilution. In *Edwards, J., et al., eds.*, 1986, pp. 51–82. **[G: U.S.]**

Asquith, Paul and Mullins, David W., Jr. Equity Issues and Offering Dilution. *J. Finan. Econ.*, Jan./Feb. 1986, *15*(1/2), pp. 61–89. **[G: U.S.]**

Atchison, Michael D. Non-representative Trading Frequencies and the Detection of Abnormal Performance. *J. Finan. Res.*, Winter 1986, *9*(4), pp. 343–48.

Baillie, Richard T. and McMahon, Patrick C. Estimation and Testing of the Term Structure of the Forward Premium under Rational Expectations. *J. Macroecon.*, Summer 1986, *8*(3), pp. 387–91. **[G: U.K.; W. Germany; Italy]**

Baldwin, Robert H. B. A View from Wall Street. In *Landau, R. and Rosenberg, N., eds.*, 1986, pp. 467–71. **[G: U.S.]**

Bamber, Linda Smith. The Information Content of Annual Earnings Releases: A Trading Volume Approach. *J. Acc. Res.*, Spring 1986, *24*(1), pp. 40–56. **[G: U.S.]**

Banz, Rolf W. and Breen, William J. Sample-Dependent Results Using Accounting and Market Data: Some Evidence. *J. Finance*, September 1986, *41*(4), pp. 779–93. **[G: U.S.]**

Barone-Adesi, Giovanni and Whaley, Robert E. The Valuation of American Call Options and the Expected Ex-dividend Stock Price Decline. *J. Finan. Econ.*, September 1986, *17*(1), pp. 91–111. **[G: U.S.]**

Barrett, W. Brian; Heuson, Andrea J. and Kolb, Robert W. The Differential Effects of Sinking Funds on Bond Risk Premia. *J. Finan. Res.*, Winter 1986, *9*(4), pp. 303–12. **[G: U.S.]**

Barrett, W. Brian; Heuson, Andrea J. and Kolb, Robert W. The Effect of Three Mile Island on Utility Bond Risk Premia: A Note. *J. Finance*, March 1986, *41*(1), pp. 255–61. **[G: U.S.]**

Barro, Robert J. Futures Markets and the Fluctuations in Inflation, Monetary Growth, and Asset Returns. *J. Bus.*, Part 2, April 1986, *59*(2), pp. S21–38.

Barry, Christopher B. and Brown, Stephen J. Limited Information as a Source of Risk. *J. Portfol. Manage.*, Winter 1986, *12*(2), pp. 66–72. **[G: U.S.]**

Bayley, Molly G. Technology Meets Regulation. In *Saunders, A. and White, L. J., eds.*, 1986, pp. 63–71. **[G: U.S.]**

Becker, Brian E. and Olson, Craig A. The Impact of Strikes on Shareholder Equity. *Ind. Lab. Relat. Rev.*, April 1986, *39*(3), pp. 425–38. **[G: U.S.]**

Bellingham, John. Options. In *Bruce, R., et al., eds.*, 1986, pp. 378–89. **[G: Australia]**

Bera, Anil K. and Kannan, Srinivasan. An Adjustment Procedure for Predicting Systematic Risk. *J. Appl. Econometrics*, October 1986, *1*(4), pp. 317–32.

Berman, Marc L. Technology and the Clearing

Function. In *Saunders, A. and White, L. J., eds.*, 1986, pp. 167–69. [G: U.S.]

Berrill, Kenneth [Sir]. The Securities and Investment Board: Its Objectives and Expectations. In *Dale, R., ed.*, 1986, pp. 18–21. [G: U.K.]

Bhagat, Sanjai. The Effect of Management's Choice between Negotiated and Competitive Equity Offerings on Shareholder Wealth. *J. Finan. Quant. Anal.*, June 1986, *21*(2), pp. 181–96. [G: U.S.]

Bhattacharya, Anand K. The Joint Effect of Housing Start and Inflation Announcements on GNMA Futures Prices. *J. Futures Markets*, Winter 1986, *6*(4), pp. 645–57. [G: U.S.]

Bhattacharya, Anand K.; Ramjee, Anju and Ramjee, Balasubramani. The Causal Relationship between Futures Price Volatility and the Cash Price Volatility of GNMA Securities. *J. Futures Markets*, Spring 1986, *6*(1), pp. 29–39. [G: U.S.]

Bird, Peter J. W. N. Variation in Price Dependency Measures on the London Metal Exchange. *Appl. Econ.*, September 1986, *18*(9), pp. 929–40. [G: U.K.]

Blum, Gerald A.; Kracaw, William A. and Lewellen, Wilbur G. Determinants of the Execution Costs of Common Stock Trades by Individual Investors. *J. Finan. Res.*, Winter 1986, *9*(4), pp. 291–301. [G: U.S.]

Boardman, Anthony; Freedman, Ruth and Eckel, Catherine C. The Price of Government Ownership: A Study of the Domtar Takeover. *J. Public Econ.*, December 1986, *31*(3), pp. 269–85. [G: Canada]

Boardman, Calvin M.; Dark, Frederick H. and Lease, Ronald C. On the Listing of Corporate Debt: A Note. *J. Finan. Quant. Anal.*, March 1986, *21*(1), pp. 107–14. [G: U.S.]

Bodie, Zvi; Kane, Alex and McDonald, Robert. Risk and Required Returns on Debt and Equity. In *Friedman, B. M., ed.*, 1986, pp. 51–66. [G: U.S.]

Bodurtha, James N., Jr. Integration vs. Segmentation in the Canadian Stock Market: Discussion. *J. Finance*, July 1986, *41*(3), pp. 614–16. [G: U.S.; Canada]

Bodurtha, James N., Jr. and Courtadon, Georges R. Efficiency Tests of the Foreign Currency Options Market. *J. Finance*, March 1986, *41*(1), pp. 151–62. [G: U.S.]

Bolten, Steven E. and Long, Susan W. A Note on Cyclical and Dynamic Aspects of Stock Market Price Cycles. *Financial Rev.*, February 1986, *21*(1), pp. 145–59. [G: U.S.]

Bond, Gary E. and Thompson, Stanley R. Optimal Commodity Hedging within the Capital Asset Pricing Model. *J. Futures Markets*, Fall 1986, *6*(3), pp. 421–31. [G: Australia]

Boothe, Paul M. and Longworth, David. Foreign Exchange Market Efficiency Tests: Implications of Recent Empirical Findings. *J. Int. Money Finance*, June 1986, *5*(2), pp. 135–52. [G: U.S.; Canada]

Boothe, Paul M. and Reid, Bradford G. The Market Value and Maturity Structure of Government of Canada Debt, 1967–83. *Can. J. Econ.*, August 1986, *19*(3), pp. 443–68. [G: Canada]

Bordo, Michael D. Financial Crises, Banking Crises, Stock Market Crashes and the Money Supply: Some International Evidence, 1870–1933. In *Capie, F. and Wood, G. E., eds.*, 1986, pp. 190–248.

Born, Jeffrey A. and Anderson, Seth Copeland. A Comparison of Intervention and Residual Analysis. *J. Finan. Res.*, Fall 1986, *9*(3), pp. 261–70. [G: U.S.]

Bosworth, Barry P. Tax Simplification and Financial Markets: Discussion. In *Federal Reserve Bank of Boston*, 1986, pp. 184–86. [G: U.S.]

Brauer, Greggory A. and Ravichandran, R. How Sweet Is Silver? *J. Portfol. Manage.*, Summer 1986, *12*(4), pp. 33–42. [G: U.S.]

Brealey, Richard A. Innovation in the British Securities Markets. *Tijdschrift Econ. Manage.*, 1986, *31*(4), pp. 409–15. [G: U.K.]

Breen, William J.; Jagannathan, Ravi and Ofer, Aharon R. Correcting for Heteroscedasticity in Tests for Market Timing Ability. *J. Bus.*, Part 1, October 1986, *59*(4), pp. 585–98. [G: U.S.]

Brenner, Menachem and Galai, Dan. Implied Interest Rates. *J. Bus.*, July 1986, *59*(3), pp. 493–507. [G: U.S.]

Brickley, James A. Interpreting Common Stock Returns around Proxy Statement Disclosures and Annual Shareholder Meetings. *J. Finan. Quant. Anal.*, September 1986, *21*(3), pp. 343–49. [G: U.S.]

Brown, Stephen J. and Dybvig, Philip H. The Empirical Implications of the Cox, Ingersoll, Ross Theory of the Term Structure of Interest Rates. *J. Finance*, July 1986, *41*(3), pp. 617–30. [G: U.S.]

Brox, James A. and Maclean, Wendy A. The Financial Behaviour of Canadian Private Corporations and Government Enterprise: A Flow of Funds Analysis. *Bull. Econ. Res.*, January 1986, *38*(1), pp. 49–66. [G: Canada]

Brush, John S. Eight Relative Strength Models Compared. *J. Portfol. Manage.*, Fall 1986, *13*(1), pp. 21–28. [G: U.S.]

Buchholz, H. E. Agriculture in a Turbulent World Economy: Theoretical Developments: Discussion. In *Maunder, A. and Renborg, U., eds.*, 1986, pp. 604–06.

Bullock, John. The Audit Role in the Context of Financial Deregulation. In *Dale, R., ed.*, 1986, pp. 36–47. [G: U.K.]

Buser, Stephen A. and Hess, Patrick J. Empirical Determinants of the Relative Yields on Taxable and Tax-Exempt Securities. *J. Finan. Econ.*, December 1986, *17*(2), pp. 335–55. [G: U.S.]

Butler, J. S. and Schachter, Barry. Unbiased Estimation of the Black/Scholes Formula. *J. Finan. Econ.*, March 1986, *15*(3), pp. 341–57.

Callier, Philippe. "Professional Trading," Exchange Rate Risk and the Growth of International Banking: A Note. *Banca Naz. Lavoro Quart. Rev.*, December 1986, (159), pp. 423–28.

Campbell, John Y. Empirical Assessment of Present Value Relations: Comment. *Econometric Rev.*, 1986, *5*(2), pp. 241–45.

Canarella, Giorgio and Pollard, Stephen K. The 'Efficiency' of the London Metal Exchange: A Test with Overlapping and Non-overlapping Data. *J. Banking Finance,* December 1986, *10*(4), pp. 575–93. **[G: U.K.]**

Canzoneri, Matthew B. The Implications of Mean-Variance Optimization for Four Questions in International Macroeconomics: Comments. *J. Int. Money Finance,* Supp. March 1986, *5*, pp. S77–78.

Carleton, Willard T. and Lakonishok, Josef. The Size Anomaly: Does Industry Group Matter? *J. Portfol. Manage.*, Spring 1986, *12*(3), pp. 36–40. **[G: U.S.]**

Carter, R. L.; Chiplin, B. and Lewis, M. K. Markets, Regulation, and the Financial Firm. **In** *Carter, R. L.; Chiplin, B. and Lewis, M. K., eds.*, 1986, pp. 248–71. **[G: U.K.]**

Carter, R. L. and Diacon, S. R. Personal Investment Markets. **In** *Carter, R. L.; Chiplin, B. and Lewis, M. K., eds.*, 1986, pp. 196–228. **[G: U.K.]**

Cebrecos Revilla, Felipe. Savings for Development: The Case of Peru. **In** *U.N., Dept. of International Econ. and Social Affairs,* 1986, pp. 65–70. **[G: Peru]**

Cesarini, Francesco. Equity Financing by Banks in the Italian Market: The 1980–1984 Experience and the New Trends. *J. Bank Res.*, Spring 1986, *17*(1), pp. 28–39. **[G: Italy]**

Chalk, Andrew. Market Forces and Aircraft Safety: The Case of the DC-10. *Econ. Inquiry,* January 1986, *24*(1), pp. 43–60. **[G: U.S.]**

Chan, K. C. Can Tax-Loss Selling Explain the January Seasonal in Stock Returns? *J. Finance,* December 1986, *41*(5), pp. 1115–28. **[G: U.S.]**

Chance, Don M.; Marr, M. Wayne and Thompson, G. Rodney. Hedging Shelf Registrations. *J. Futures Markets,* Spring 1986, *6*(1), pp. 11–27. **[G: U.S.]**

Chang, Eric C. and Pinegar, J. Michael. Return Seasonality and Tax-Loss Selling in the Market for Long-term Government and Corporate Bonds. *J. Finan. Econ.*, December 1986, *17*(2), pp. 391–415. **[G: U.S.]**

Chang, Jack S. K. and Shanker, Latha. Hedging Effectiveness of Currency Options and Currency Futures. *J. Futures Markets,* Summer 1986, *6*(2), pp. 289–305. **[G: W. Europe; U.S.; Japan; Canada]**

Chang, Rosita P. and Rhee, S. Ghon. Does the Stock Market React to Announcements of the Producer Price Index? *Financial Rev.*, February 1986, *21*(1), pp. 125–34. **[G: U.S.]**

Chen, Andrew H. and Merville, Larry J. An Analysis of Divestiture Effects Resulting from Deregulation. *J. Finance,* December 1986, *41*(5), pp. 997–1010. **[G: U.S.]**

Chen, Carl R. and Stockum, Steve. Selectivity, Market Timing, and Random Beta Behavior of Mutual Funds: A Generalized Model. *J. Finan. Res.*, Spring 1986, *9*(1), pp. 87–96. **[G: U.S.]**

Chesney, Marc. Prix d'équilibre et efficience sur le marché suisse des options sur devises: analyse théorique et tests empiriques. (Equilibrium Value and the Efficiency of the Swiss Market for Foreign Exchange Options: Theoretical Analysis and Empirical Tests. With English summary.) *Finance,* December 1986, *7*(2), pp. 149–67. **[G: Switzerland]**

Chiang, Thomas C. On the Predictors of the Future Spot Rates—A Multi-currency Analysis. *Financial Rev.*, February 1986, *21*(1), pp. 69–83. **[G: U.S.; U.K.; France; W. Germany; Canada]**

Cho, D. Chinhyung; Eun, Cheol S. and Senbet, Lemma W. International Arbitrage Pricing Theory: An Empirical Investigation. *J. Finance,* June 1986, *41*(2), pp. 313–29. **[G: OECD; Singapore; Hong Kong]**

Cholerton, Kenneth; Pieraerts, Pierre and Solnick, Bruno. Why Invest in Foreign Currency Bonds? *J. Portfol. Manage.*, Summer 1986, *12*(4), pp. 4–8. **[G: W. Europe; U.S.; Japan]**

Coate, Douglas and VanderHoff, James. Stock Returns, Inflation, and Real Output. *Econ. Inquiry,* October 1986, *24*(4), pp. 555–61. **[G: U.S.]**

Colletaz, Gilbert. Prévisions explicites de taux d'intérêt en France: une étude empirique sur la période 1981–1985. (Explicit Forecasting of Interest Rates in France: An Empirical Study over the Period 1981–1985. With English summary.) *Finance,* December 1986, *7*(2), pp. 111–34. **[G: France]**

Contzen Fuentes, Patricia and Parada Daza, José Rigoberto. Rentabilidad y riesgo para el propietario de una empresa: un nuevo enfoque. (With English summary.) *Cuadernos Econ.*, August 1986, *23*(69), pp. 237–63. **[G: Chile]**

Cooper, Ian. Innovations: New Market Instruments. *Oxford Rev. Econ. Policy,* Winter 1986, *2*(4), pp. 1–17. **[G: U.K.]**

Cooper, Richard N. Towards an International Capital Market? **In** *Cooper, R. N.*, 1986, *1971*, pp. 137–54. **[G: OECD]**

Cordier, J. and Indjehagopian, J. P. Multidimensional Analysis of a Commodity Price System. *Int. J. Forecasting,* 1986, *2*(2), pp. 153–89. **[G: France]**

Cornell, Bradford and Shapiro, Alan C. The Reaction of Bank Stock Price to the International Debt Crisis. *J. Banking Finance,* March 1986, *10*(1), pp. 55–73. **[G: U.S.]**

Cornew, Ronald W. Note on Initial Margin to Net Asset Value: Average Values for the Commodity Pool Industry. *J. Futures Markets,* Fall 1986, *6*(3), pp. 495–501. **[G: U.S.]**

Cornew, Ronald W. Stable Distributions, Futures Prices, and the Measurement of Trading Performance: Response. *J. Futures Markets,* Winter 1986, *6*(4), pp. 677–80. **[G: U.S.]**

Cox, Charles C. and Kohn, Bruce A. Regulatory Implications of Computerized Communications in Securities Markets. **In** *Saunders, A. and White, L. J., eds.*, 1986, pp. 7–18. **[G: U.S.]**

Cox, W. Michael and Haslag, Joseph. The Market

Value of Government of Canada Debt, Monthly, 1937–84. *Can. J. Econ.*, August 1986, *19*(3), pp. 469–97. **[G: Canada; U.S.]**

Cumby, Robert E. and Mishkin, Frederic S. The International Linkage of Real Interest Rates: The European–U.S. Connection. *J. Int. Money Finance*, March 1986, *5*(1), pp. 5–23. **[G: OECD]**

D'Souza, Rudolph E.; Oberhelman, H. Dennis and Brooks, LeRoy D. A Stationary Stochastic Parameter Model and OLS Estimation of Beta: A Simulation Study. *J. Econ. Bus.*, December 1986, *38*(4), pp. 283–96.

Dale, Richard. Financial Deregulation: The Proceedings of a Conference Held by the David Hume Institute in May 1986: Introduction. **In** *Dale, R., ed.*, 1986, pp. ix–xiii. **[G: Global]**

Davis, Lance E. and Huttenback, Robert A. Imperialism and Social Class (Apologies to Marx and Schumpeter): Imperial Investors in the Age of High Imperialism. **In** *Wagener, H.-J. and Drukker, J. W., eds.*, 1986, pp. 156–85. **[G: U.K.]**

Defeo, Victor J. An Empirical Investigation of the Speed of the Market Reaction to Earnings Announcements. *J. Acc. Res.*, Autumn 1986, *24*(2), pp. 349–63. **[G: U.S.]**

Delong, David M. Statistical Properties of Generalized Method-of-Moments Estimators of Structural Parameters Obtained from Financial Market Data: Comment. *J. Bus. Econ. Statist.*, October 1986, *4*(4), pp. 417–18.

Dennis, Debra K. and McConnell, John J. Corporate Mergers and Security Returns. *J. Finan. Econ.*, June 1986, *16*(2), pp. 143–87. **[G: U.S.]**

Dimson, Elroy and Fraletti, Paulo. Brokers' Recommendations: The Value of a Telephone Tip. *Econ. J.*, March 1986, *96*(381), pp. 139–59. **[G: U.K.]**

Dimson, Elroy and Marsh, Paul. Event Study Methodologies and the Size Effect: The Case of UK Press Recommendations. *J. Finan. Econ.*, September 1986, *17*(1), pp. 113–42. **[G: U.S.]**

Dopuch, Nicholas; Holthausen, Robert W. and Leftwich, Richard W. Abnormal Stock Returns Associated with Media Disclosures of 'Subject to' Qualified Audit Opinions. *J. Acc. Econ.*, June 1986, *8*(2), pp. 93–117. **[G: U.S.]**

Doukas, John and Rahman, Abdul H. Foreign Currency Futures and Monetary Policy Announcements: An Intervention Analysis. *J. Futures Markets*, Fall 1986, *6*(3), pp. 343–73. **[G: W. Europe; U.S.; Canada; Japan]**

Doukas, John and Rahman, Abdul H. Stable Distributions, Futures Prices, and the Measurement of Trading Performance: A Comment. *J. Futures Markets*, Fall 1986, *6*(3), pp. 505–06. **[G: U.S.]**

Dowen, Richard J. and Bauman, W. Scott. The Relative Importance of Size, P/E, and Neglect. *J. Portfol. Manage.*, Spring 1986, *12*(3), pp. 30–34. **[G: U.S.]**

Draper, Paul. Unit Trust Objectives and Investor Choice. *Appl. Econ.*, February 1986, *18*(2), pp. 157–72. **[G: U.K.]**

Drèze, Jacques H., et al. Per una minore disoccupazione in Europa: il ruolo della formazione di capitale. (For a Reduction of Unemployment in Europe: The Role of the Capital Formation. With English summary.) *Giorn. Econ.*, Sept.-Oct. 1986, *45*(9–10), pp. 479–514. **[G: EEC]**

Dubofsky, David A. and Groth, John C. An Examination of Asked-Bid Spreads for Two Over-the-Counter Market Segments. *Financial Rev.*, May 1986, *21*(2), pp. 289–98. **[G: U.S.]**

Dubofsky, David A. and Groth, John C. Relative Information Accessibility for OTC Stocks and Security Returns. *Financial Rev.*, February 1986, *21*(1), pp. 85–102. **[G: U.S.]**

Dukász, A. Trade in Securities in Hungary. *Acta Oecon.*, 1986, *36*(3–4), pp. 339–48. **[G: Hungary]**

Dullum, Kåre B. Børsreform—i dansk og internationalt perspektiv. (The Danish Stock Exchange Reform in International Perspective. With English summary.) *Nationaløkon. Tidsskr.*, 1986, *124*(1), pp. 77–88. **[G: Denmark; U.S.; U.K.]**

Dumontier, Pascal. Le modèle d'évaluation par arbitrage des actifs financiers: une étude empirique sur le marché financier parisien. (The Arbitrage Pricing Theory: An Empirical Study on the French Stock Exchange. With English summary.) *Finance*, June 1986, *7*(1), pp. 7–21. **[G: France]**

Dunn, Kenneth B. and Singleton, Kenneth J. Modeling the Term Structure of Interest Rates under Non-separable Utility and Durability of Goods. *J. Finan. Econ.*, September 1986, *17*(1), pp. 27–55. **[G: U.S.]**

Dyl, Edward A. and Maberly, Edwin D. The Daily Distribution of Changes in the Price of Stock Index Futures. *J. Futures Markets*, Winter 1986, *6*(4), pp. 513–21. **[G: U.S.]**

Dyl, Edward A. and Maberly, Edwin D. The Weekly Pattern in Stock Index Futures: A Further Note. *J. Finance*, December 1986, *41*(5), pp. 1149–52. **[G: U.S.]**

Dyl, Edward A. and Martin, Stanley A., Jr. Another Look at Barbells versus Ladders. *J. Portfol. Manage.*, Spring 1986, *12*(3), pp. 54–59. **[G: U.S.]**

Dymits, Lee and Murray, Michael L. Another Look at Implied Tax Rates. *J. Banking Finance*, March 1986, *10*(1), pp. 133–41. **[G: U.S.]**

Easterwood, John C. and Senchack, A. J., Jr. Arbitrage Opportunities with T-Bill/T-Bond Futures Combinations. *J. Futures Markets*, Fall 1986, *6*(3), pp. 433–42. **[G: U.S.]**

Echchihab, Slimane. L'évaluation des contrats à terme sur le sucre à la Bourse de commerce de Paris. (The Pricing of Sugar Futures Contracts on the Paris Commodity Exchange. With English summary.) *Finance*, June 1986, *7*(1), pp. 41–56. **[G: France]**

Eckbo, B. Espen. Mergers and the Market for Corporate Control: The Canadian Evidence. *Can. J. Econ.*, May 1986, *19*(2), pp. 236–60. **[G: Canada]**

Eckbo, B. Espen. Valuation Effects of Corporate Debt Offerings. *J. Finan. Econ.*, Jan./Feb. 1986, *15*(1/2), pp. 119–51. **[G: U.S.]**

Eckel, Catherine C. and Vermaelen, Theo. Internal Regulation: The Effects of Government Ownership on the Value of the Firm. *J. Law Econ.*, October 1986, *29*(2), pp. 381–403. **[G: Canada]**

Eddy, Albert and Seifert, Bruce. Dividend Changes of Financially Weak Firms. *Financial Rev.*, November 1986, *21*(4), pp. 419–31. **[G: U.S.]**

Edwards, Franklin R. Technology and New Regulatory Challenges in Futures Markets. **In** *Saunders, A. and White, L. J., eds.*, 1986, pp. 171–79. **[G: U.S.]**

El-Sheikh, S. A Time Series Analysis of Financial Asset Holdings for a Developing Country: Egypt, 1952–1973. *Empirical Econ.*, 1986, *11*(3), pp. 125–51. **[G: Egypt]**

Elam, Emmett W.; Miller, Stephen E. and Holder, Shelby H. Simple and Multiple Cross-Hedging of Rice Bran. *Southern J. Agr. Econ.*, July 1986, *18*(1), pp. 123–28. **[G: U.S.]**

Elmer, Peter J. Preferred Stock Arbitrage of Municipal Bond Market Segmentation. *Financial Rev.*, November 1986, *21*(4), pp. 383–98.

Elton, Edwin J.; Gruber, Martin J. and Grossman, Seth. Discrete Expectational Data and Portfolio Performance. *J. Finance,* July 1986, *41*(3), pp. 699–713. **[G: U.S.]**

Etzioni, Ethan S. Rebalance Disciplines for Portfolio Insurance. *J. Portfol. Manage.*, Fall 1986, *13*(1), pp. 59–62.

Evans, George W. A Test for Speculative Bubbles in the Sterling–Dollar Exchange Rate: 1981–84. *Amer. Econ. Rev.*, September 1986, *76*(4), pp. 621–36. **[G: U.S.; U.K.]**

Fabozzi, Frank J. and Thurston, Thom B. State Taxes and Reserve Requirements as Major Determinants of Yield Spreads among Money Market Instruments. *J. Finan. Quant. Anal.*, December 1986, *21*(4), pp. 427–36. **[G: U.S.]**

Fama, Eugene F. Term Premiums and Default Premiums in Money Markets. *J. Finan. Econ.*, September 1986, *17*(1), pp. 175–96. **[G: U.S.]**

Ferris, Stephen P.; Johnson, Dana J. and Shome, Dilip K. Regulatory Environment and Market Response to Public Utility Rate Decisions. *J. Finan. Res.*, Winter 1986, *9*(4), pp. 313–18. **[G: U.S.]**

Ferris, Stephen P. and Kumar, Raman. Evidence Regarding the Non-stationarity of Real Interest Rates. *Rivista Int. Sci. Econ. Com.*, Oct.-Nov. 1986, *33*(10–11), pp. 957–67. **[G: U.S.]**

Ferson, Wayne E. The Empirical Implications of the Cox, Ingersoll, Ross Theory of the Term Structure of Interest Rates: Discussion. *J. Finance,* July 1986, *41*(3), pp. 630–32. **[G: U.S.]**

Fielitz, Bruce D. and Gay, Gerald D. Managing Cash Flow Risks in Stock Index Futures. *J. Portfol. Manage.*, Winter 1986, *12*(2), pp. 74–78. **[G: U.S.]**

Figlewski, Stephen. Futures Markets: Comment. **In** *Saunders, A. and White, L. J., eds.*, 1986, pp. 91–94. **[G: U.S.]**

Fischel, Daniel R. Regulatory Conflict and Entry Regulation of New Futures Contracts. *J. Bus.*, Part 2, April 1986, *59*(2), pp. S85–102. **[G: U.S.]**

Fischer, Stanley. Call Option Pricing When the Exercise Price Is Uncertain, and the Valuation of Index Bonds. **In** *Fischer, S.*, 1986, *1978*, pp. 321–31.

Fischer, Stanley. On the Nonexistence of Privately Issued Index Bonds in the U.S. Capital Market. **In** *Fischer, S.*, 1986, *1983*, pp. 301–20. **[G: U.S.]**

Fishe, Raymond P. H. and Goldberg, Lawrence G. The Effects of Margins on Trading in Futures Markets. *J. Futures Markets,* Summer 1986, *6*(2), pp. 261–71. **[G: U.S.]**

Fisher, Brian S. Agriculture in a Turbulent World Economy: Theoretical Developments: Discussion. **In** *Maunder, A. and Renborg, U., eds.*, 1986, pp. 606–09.

Flesher, Dale L. and Flesher, Tonya K. Ivar Kreuger's Contribution to U.S. Financial Reporting. *Accounting Rev.*, July 1986, *61*(3), pp. 421–34. **[G: U.S.]**

Ford, Alec G. Financial Crises, Banking Crises, Stock Market Crashes and the Money Supply: Some International Evidence, 1870–1933: Comment. **In** *Capie, F. and Wood, G. E., eds.*, 1986, pp. 249–53.

Frankel, Jeffrey A. The Implications of Mean–Variance Optimization for Four Questions in International Macroeconomics. *J. Int. Money Finance,* Supp. March 1986, *5*, pp. S53–75.

Franks, Julian R. and Harris, Robert S. The Role of the Mergers and Monopolies Commission in Merger Policy: Costs and Alternatives. *Oxford Rev. Econ. Policy,* Winter 1986, *2*(4), pp. 58–78. **[G: U.K.]**

Fredrickson, E. Bruce and Kim, Moon K. Projections and Implications of Equity Holdings by Institutional Investors in the Year 2000. *Quart. J. Bus. Econ.*, Summer 1986, *25*(3), pp. 34–54. **[G: U.S.]**

French, Dan W. and Dubofsky, David A. Stock Splits and Implied Stock Price Volatility. *J. Portfol. Manage.*, Summer 1986, *12*(4), pp. 55–59. **[G: U.S.]**

French, Dan W. and Fraser, Donald R. A Note on Interest Rates and the Risk of Bank and Savings and Loan Stock. *Financial Rev.*, November 1986, *21*(4), pp. 551–58. **[G: U.S.]**

French, Kenneth R. and Roll, Richard. Stock Return Variances: The Arrival of Information and the Reaction of Traders. *J. Finan. Econ.*, September 1986, *17*(1), pp. 5–26. **[G: U.S.]**

Frenkel, Jacob A. The Covariation of Risk Premiums and Expected Future Spot Exchange Rates: Comments. *J. Int. Money Finance,* Supp. March 1986, *5*, pp. S23–30.

Fung, W. K. H. and Rudd, Andrew. Pricing New Corporate Bond Issues: An Analysis of Issue Cost and Seasoning Effects. *J. Finance,* July 1986, *41*(3), pp. 633–43. **[G: U.S.]**

Garber, Peter M. Nominal Contracts in a Bimetallic Standard. *Amer. Econ. Rev.*, December 1986, *76*(5), pp. 1012–30. **[G: U.S.]**

Garcia, Philip; Leuthold, Raymond M. and Zapata, Hector. Lead-Lag Relationships between Trading Volume and Price Variability: New Evidence. *J. Futures Markets,* Spring 1986, *6*(1), pp. 1–10. **[G: U.S.]**

Gay, Gerald D.; Hunter, William C. and Kolb, Robert W. A Comparative Analysis of Futures Contract Margins. *J. Futures Markets,* Summer 1986, *6*(2), pp. 307–24. **[G: U.S.]**

Gay, Gerald D. and Manaster, Steven. Implicit Delivery Options and Optimal Delivery Strategies for Financial Futures Contracts. *J. Finan. Econ.*, May 1986, *16*(1), pp. 41–72. **[G: U.S.]**

Gemmill, Gordon and Dickins, Paul. An Examination of the Efficiency of the London Traded Options Market. *Appl. Econ.*, September 1986, *18*(9), pp. 995–1010. **[G: U.K.]**

Gilbert, Christopher L. Testing the Efficient Markets Hypothesis on Averaged Data. *Appl. Econ.*, November 1986, *18*(11), pp. 1149–66. **[G: U.K.]**

Goodhart, Charles. The Summer of 1914: Comment. **In** *Capie, F. and Wood, G. E., eds.*, 1986, pp. 117–19. **[G: U.K.; Europe]**

Goss, Barry A. Rejection of Unbiasedness Is Not Rejection of Market Efficiency: Reply. *Appl. Econ.*, November 1986, *18*(11), pp. 1167–78. **[G: U.K.]**

Goss, Barry A. The Forward Pricing Function of the London Metal Exchange. **In** *Goss, B. A., ed.*, 1986, pp. 157–73. **[G: U.K.]**

Goss, Barry A. and Giles, David E. A. Intertemporal Allocation in the Australian Wool Market. **In** *Goss, B. A., ed.*, 1986, pp. 93–118. **[G: Australia]**

Gould, J. B. and Sorensen, Eric H. Duration: A Factor in Equity Pricing. *J. Portfol. Manage.*, Fall 1986, *13*(1), pp. 38–43. **[G: U.S.]**

Gowland, D. H. Rationality, Efficiency and News in the Gilt-Edged Market: Some Results. *Greek Econ. Rev.*, December 1986, *8*(2), pp. 132–54. **[G: U.K.]**

Graddy, Duane B. and Karna, Adi S. Dividend Policy and the Return of Bank Holding Company Stock. *Quart. J. Bus. Econ.*, Spring 1986, *25*(2), pp. 3–21. **[G: U.S.]**

Grammatikos, Theoharry. Intervalling Effects and the Hedging Performance of Foreign Currency Futures. *Financial Rev.*, February 1986, *21*(1), pp. 21–36. **[G: U.K.; Japan; W. Germany; Canada; Switzerland]**

Grammatikos, Theoharry and Papaioannou, George. Market Reaction to NYSE Listings: Tests of the Marketability Gains Hypothesis. *J. Finan. Res.*, Fall 1986, *9*(3), pp. 215–27. **[G: U.S.]**

Grammatikos, Theoharry and Saunders, Anthony. Futures Price Variability: A Test of Maturity and Volume Effects. *J. Bus.*, Part 1, April 1986, *59*(2), pp. 319–30. **[G: U.S.]**

Grammatikos, Theoharry and Papaioannou, George. The Information Value of Listing on the New York Stock Exchange. *Financial Rev.*, November 1986, *21*(4), pp. 485–99. **[G: U.S.]**

Grantham, Jerry. "You Can't Fool All of the People All of the Time." *J. Portfol. Manage.*, Winter 1986, *12*(2), pp. 11–15. **[G: U.S.]**

Grauer, Robert R. and Hakansson, Nils H. A Half Century of Returns on Levered and Unlevered Portfolios of Stocks, Bonds, and Bills, with and without Small Stocks. *J. Bus.*, Part 1, April 1986, *59*(2), pp. 287–318. **[G: U.S.]**

Gregory, Allan W. and McCurdy, Thomas H. The Unbiasedness Hypothesis in the Forward Foreign Exchange Market: A Specification Analysis with Application to France, Italy, Japan, the United Kingdom and West Germany. *Europ. Econ. Rev.*, April 1986, *30*(2), pp. 365–81. **[G: France; Italy; Japan; U.K.; W. Germany]**

Grieves, Robin. Hedging Corporate Bond Portfolios. *J. Portfol. Manage.*, Summer 1986, *12*(4), pp. 23–25. **[G: U.S.]**

Grossman, Sanford J. and Miller, Merton H. Economic Costs and Benefits of the Proposed One-Minute Time Bracketing Regulation. *J. Futures Markets,* Spring 1986, *6*(1), pp. 141–66. **[G: U.S.]**

Haddad, Kamal M. The Treasury's Constant-Maturity Yield Curves: A Test for Systematic Measurement Errors. *Quart. J. Bus. Econ.*, Autumn 1986, *25*(4), pp. 3–13. **[G: U.S.]**

Haddock, David D. and Macey, Jonathan R. Controlling Insider Trading in Europe and America: The Economics of the Politics. **In** *von der Schulenburg, J.-M. G. and Skogh, G., eds.*, 1986, pp. 149–67. **[G: W. Europe; U.S.]**

Hafer, R. W. The Response of Stock Prices to Changes in Weekly Money and the Discount Rate. *Fed. Res. Bank St. Louis Rev.*, March 1986, *68*(3), pp. 5–14. **[G: U.S.]**

Hamon, Jacques. La caractère saisonnier des rentabilités mensuelles à la Bourse de Paris. (Monthly Return Seasonality on the Paris Stock Exchange. With English summary.) *Finance,* June 1986, *7*(1), pp. 57–74. **[G: France]**

Hansen, Lars Peter. Statistical Properties of Generalized Method-of-Moments Estimators of Structural Parameters Obtained from Financial Market Data: Comment. *J. Bus. Econ. Statist.*, October 1986, *4*(4), pp. 418–21.

Harris, Frederick H. deB. Market Structure and Price–Cost Performance under Endogenous Profit Risk. *J. Ind. Econ.*, September 1986, *35*(1), pp. 35–59. **[G: U.S.]**

Harris, Lawrence E. A Transaction Data Study of Weekly and Intradaily Patterns in Stock Returns. *J. Finan. Econ.*, May 1986, *16*(1), pp. 99–117. **[G: U.S.]**

Harris, Lawrence E. Cross-Security Tests of the Mixture of Distributions Hypothesis. *J. Finan. Quant. Anal.*, March 1986, *21*(1), pp. 39–46. **[G: U.S.]**

Harris, Lawrence E. How to Profit from Intradaily Stock Returns. *J. Portfol. Manage.*, Winter 1986, *12*(2), pp. 61–64. **[G: U.S.]**

Harris, Lawrence E. and Gurel, Eitan. Price and

Volume Effects Associated with Changes in the S&P 500 List: New Evidence for the Existence of Price Pressures. *J. Finance,* September 1986, *41*(4), pp. 815–29. **[G: U.S.]**

Hart, Oliver D. and Kreps, David M. Price Destabilizing Speculation. *J. Polit. Econ.,* October 1986, *94*(5), pp. 927–52.

Hartigan, James C.; Perry, Philip R. and Kamma, Sreenivas. The Value of Administered Protection: A Capital Market Approach. *Rev. Econ. Statist.,* November 1986, *68*(4), pp. 610–17. **[G: U.S.]**

Hartzell, David; Hekman, John and Miles, Mike. Diversification Categories in Investment Real Estate. *Amer. Real Estate Urban Econ. Assoc. J.,* Summer 1986, *14*(2), pp. 230–54. **[G: U.S.]**

Hartzmark, Michael L. The Effects of Changing Margin Levels on Futures Market Activity, the Composition of Traders in the Market, and Price Performance. *J. Bus.,* Part 2, April 1986, *59*(2), pp. S147–80. **[G: U.S.]**

Hauser, Robert J. and Eales, James S. On Marketing Strategies with Options: A Technique to Measure Risk and Return. *J. Futures Markets,* Summer 1986, *6*(2), pp. 273–88. **[G: U.S.]**

Hays, Patrick A. and Upton, David E. A Shifting Regimes Approach to the Stationarity of the Market Model Parameters of Individual Securities. *J. Finan. Quant. Anal.,* September 1986, *21*(3), pp. 307–21. **[G: U.S.]**

Heaton, Hal. Volatilities Implied by Options Premia: A Test of Market Efficiency. *Financial Rev.,* February 1986, *21*(1), pp. 37–49. **[G: U.S.]**

Heck, J. Louis. Market Efficiency and Investors' Adjustments to Asset Valuation Errors. *Appl. Econ.,* August 1986, *18*(8), pp. 837–50. **[G: U.S.]**

Hegde, Shantaram P. and McDonald, Bill. On the Informational Role of Treasury Bill Futures. *J. Futures Markets,* Winter 1986, *6*(4), pp. 629–43. **[G: U.S.]**

Hendershott, Patric H. Debt and Equity Returns Revisited. **In** *Friedman, B. M., ed.,* 1986, pp. 35–50. **[G: U.S.]**

Hendershott, Patric H. Tax Simplification and Financial Markets. **In** *Federal Reserve Bank of Boston,* 1986, pp. 153–77. **[G: U.S.]**

Hendershott, Patric H. and Ling, David C. Likely Impacts of the Administration's Tax Proposals and H.R. 3838. **In** *Follain, J. R., ed.,* 1986, pp. 87–112. **[G: U.S.]**

Hess, Alan C. and Bhagat, Sanjai. Size Effects of Seasoned Stock Issues: Empirical Evidence. *J. Bus.,* Part 1, October 1986, *59*(4), pp. 567–84. **[G: U.S.]**

Hilke, John C. Early Mandatory Disclosure Regulations. *Int. Rev. Law Econ.,* December 1986, *6*(2), pp. 229–39. **[G: U.S.]**

Hite, Gailen L. The Timing and Substance of Divestiture Announcements: Individual, Simultaneous and Cumulative Effects: Discussion. *J. Finance,* July 1986, *41*(3), pp. 696–97. **[G: U.S.]**

Hodrick, Robert J. Empirical Assessment of Present Value Relations: Comment. *Econometric Rev.,* 1986, *5*(2), pp. 253–60.

Hodrick, Robert J. and Srivastava, Sanjay. The Covariation of Risk Premiums and Expected Future Spot Exchange Rates. *J. Int. Money Finance,* Supp. March 1986, *5*, pp. S5–21. **[G: U.S.]**

Holthausen, Robert W. and Leftwich, Richard W. The Effect of Bond Rating Changes on Common Stock Prices. *J. Finan. Econ.,* September 1986, *17*(1), pp. 57–89. **[G: U.S.]**

Holtz-Eakin, Douglas. Explaining the Yield Spread between Taxable and Tax-Exempt Bonds: The Role of Expected Tax Policy: Comment. **In** *Rosen, H. S., ed.,* 1986, pp. 49–51. **[G: U.S.]**

Howe, John S. and Schlarbaum, Gary G. SEC Trading Suspensions: Empirical Evidence. *J. Finan. Quant. Anal.,* September 1986, *21*(3), pp. 323–33. **[G: U.S.]**

Hsia, Chi-Cheng. Comparative Efficiency of Market Indices: An Empirical Study. *J. Finan. Res.,* Summer 1986, *9*(2), pp. 123–35. **[G: U.S.]**

Hsieh, David A. and Leiderman, Leonardo. Portfolio Implications of Empirical Rejections of the Expectations Hypothesis. *Rev. Econ. Statist.,* November 1986, *68*(4), pp. 680–84. **[G: U.S.]**

Huang, Roger D. Does Monitization of Federal Debt Matter? Evidence from the Financial Markets. *J. Money, Credit, Banking,* August 1986, *18*(3), pp. 275–89. **[G: U.S.]**

Hughes, John S.; Magat, Wesley A. and Ricks, William E. The Economic Consequences of the OSHA Cotton Dust Standards: An Analysis of Stock Price Behavior. *J. Law Econ.,* April 1986, *29*(1), pp. 29–59. **[G: U.S.]**

Humphrey, Nancy P. and Maurice, Diane Rausa. Infrastructure Bond Bank Initiatives: Policy Implications and Credit Concerns. *Public Budg. Finance,* Autumn 1986, *6*(3), pp. 38–56. **[G: U.S.]**

Ioannidis, Chris and Thompson, R. S. Political Opinion Polls and the Stock Market. *Managerial Dec. Econ.,* December 1986, *7*(4), pp. 267–71. **[G: U.S.; U.K.]**

Ito, Takatoshi. Capital Controls and Covered Interest Parity between the Yen and the Dollar. *Econ. Stud. Quart.,* September 1986, *37*(3), pp. 223–41. **[G: U.S.; Japan; W. Europe]**

Jahera, John S. and Modani, Naval K. An Examination of the Stationarity of Selected Risk Measures in Commercial Banking. *Quart. J. Bus. Econ.,* Winter 1986, *25*(1), pp. 3–15. **[G: U.S.]**

Jain, Prem C. Analyses of the Distribution of Security Market Model Prediction Errors for Daily Returns Data. *J. Acc. Res.,* Spring 1986, *24*(1), pp. 76–96. **[G: U.S.]**

Jennings, Robert H. and Starks, Laura. Earnings Announcements, Stock Price Adjustment, and the Existence of Option Markets. *J. Finance,* March 1986, *41*(1), pp. 107–25. **[G: U.S.]**

Johnson, Larry J. Foreign-Currency Options, Ex

Ante Exchange-Rate Volatility, and Market Efficiency: An Empirical Test. *Financial Rev.*, November 1986, *21*(4), pp. 433–50. [G: U.S.]

Johnson, Lewis D. Dividend Yields Are Equity Risk Premiums: Comment. *J. Portfol. Manage.*, Winter 1986, *12*(2), pp. 81–83. [G: U.S.]

Johnson, R. Stafford; Zuber, Richard A. and Loy, David. An Investigation into Currency Options and Market Efficiency. *Rivista Int. Sci. Econ. Com.*, Oct.-Nov. 1986, *33*(10–11), pp. 1077–93. [G: U.S.; Canada; U.K.; W. Germany]

Jorion, Philippe. Bayes–Stein Estimation for Portfolio Analysis. *J. Finan. Quant. Anal.*, September 1986, *21*(3), pp. 279–92.

Jorion, Philippe and Schwartz, Eduardo S. Integration vs. Segmentation in the Canadian Stock Market. *J. Finance*, July 1986, *41*(3), pp. 603–14. [G: Canada; U.S.]

Junkus, Joan C. Weekend and Day of the Week Effects in Returns on Stock Index Futures. *J. Futures Markets*, Fall 1986, *6*(3), pp. 397–407. [G: U.S.]

Jüttner, Johannes. Public Debt and Asset Preferences. *Kredit Kapital*, 1986, *19*(3), pp. 386–400. [G: Australia]

Kahl, Kandice H. and Tomek, William G. Forward-Pricing Models for Futures Markets: Some Statistical and Interpretive Issues. *Food Res. Inst. Stud.*, 1986, *20*(1), pp. 71–85. [G: U.S.]

Kalay, Avner and Loewenstein, Uri. The Informational Content of the Timing of Dividend Announcements. *J. Finan. Econ.*, July 1986, *16*(3), pp. 373–88. [G: U.S.]

Kane, Alex and Marcus, Alan J. The Quality Option in the Treasury Bond Futures Market: An Empirical Assessment. *J. Futures Markets*, Summer 1986, *6*(2), pp. 231–48. [G: U.S.]

Kane, Alex and Marcus, Alan J. Valuation and Optimal Exercise of the Wild Card Option in the Treasury Bond Futures Market. *J. Finance*, March 1986, *41*(1), pp. 195–207. [G: U.S.]

Kantor, Laurence G. Inflation Uncertainty and Real Economic Activity: An Alternative Approach. *Rev. Econ. Statist.*, August 1986, *68*(3), pp. 493–500. [G: U.S.]

Kaplanis, Costas P. Options, Taxes, and Ex-Dividend Day Behavior. *J. Finance*, June 1986, *41*(2), pp. 411–24. [G: U.K.]

Keim, Donald B. and Stambaugh, Robert F. Predicting Returns in the Stock and Bond Markets. *J. Finan. Econ.*, December 1986, *17*(2), pp. 357–90. [G: U.S.]

Khan, Arshad M. Conformity with Large Speculators: A Test of Efficiency in the Grain Futures Market. *Atlantic Econ. J.*, September 1986, *14*(3), pp. 51–55.

Kidwell, David S. and Marr, M. Wayne. Preferred Stock: The Impact of Credit Market Conditions on Competitive versus Negotiated Sale. *Quart. Rev. Econ. Bus.*, Winter 1986, *26*(4), pp. 35–50. [G: U.S.]

Kim, Moon K.; Booth, G. Geoffrey and Wu, Chunchi. Stock Returns, Inflation, and the Phillips Curve. *Southern Econ. J.*, April 1986, *52*(4), pp. 973–83. [G: U.S.]

King, Raymond D. Convertible Bond Valuation: An Empirical Test. *J. Finan. Res.*, Spring 1986, *9*(1), pp. 53–69. [G: U.S.]

King, Raymond D. and O'Keefe, Terrence B. Lobbying Activities and Insider Trading. *Accounting Rev.*, January 1986, *61*(1), pp. 76–90. [G: U.S.]

Kleidon, Allan W. Empirical Assessment of Present Value Relations: Comment. *Econometric Rev.*, 1986, *5*(2), pp. 261–65.

Klein, April. The Timing and Substance of Divestiture Announcements: Individual, Simultaneous and Cumulative Effects. *J. Finance*, July 1986, *41*(3), pp. 685–96. [G: U.S.]

Korkie, Bob. Market Line Deviations and Market Anomalies with Reference to Small and Large Firms. *J. Finan. Quant. Anal.*, June 1986, *21*(2), pp. 161–80. [G: U.S.]

Koveos, Peter E. and Seifert, Bruce. Market Efficiency, Purchasing Power Parity, and Black Markets: Evidence from Latin American Countries. *Weltwirtsch. Arch.*, 1986, *122*(2), pp. 313–26. [G: Latin America]

Krause, David S. Ownership Control and Stock Market Performance. *J. Behav. Econ.*, Spring/Summer 1986, *15*(1/2), pp. 113–21. [G: U.S.]

Kritzman, Mark. How to Detect Skill in Management Performance. *J. Portfol. Manage.*, Winter 1986, *12*(2), pp. 16–20. [G: U.S.]

Kritzman, Mark. What's Wrong with Portfolio Insurance? *J. Portfol. Manage.*, Fall 1986, *13*(1), pp. 13–16.

Kryzanowski, Lawrence and Jalilvand, Abolhassan. Statistical Tests of the Accuracy of Alternative Forecasts: Some Results for U.S. Utility Betas. *Financial Rev.*, May 1986, *21*(2), pp. 319–35. [G: U.S.]

Kuprianov, Anatoli. Options on Short-term Interest Rate Futures. *Fed. Res. Bank Richmond Econ. Rev.*, Nov./Dec. 1986, *72*(6), pp. 3–11. [G: U.S.]

Kuprianov, Anatoli. Short-term Interest Rate Futures. *Fed. Res. Bank Richmond Econ. Rev.*, Sept./Oct. 1986, *72*(5), pp. 12–26. [G: U.S.]

Lakonishok, Josef and Shapiro, Alan C. Systematic Risk, Total Risk and Size as Determinants of Stock Market Returns. *J. Banking Finance*, March 1986, *10*(1), pp. 115–32. [G: U.S.]

Lakonishok, Josef and Smidt, Seymour. Trading Bargains in Small Firms at Year-end. *J. Portfol. Manage.*, Spring 1986, *12*(3), pp. 24–29. [G: U.S.]

Lakonishok, Josef and Smidt, Seymour. Volume for Winners and Losers: Taxation and Other Motives for Stock Trading. *J. Finance*, September 1986, *41*(4), pp. 951–74. [G: U.S.]

Lakonishok, Josef and Vermaelen, Theo. Tax-Induced Trading around Ex-dividend Days. *J. Finan. Econ.*, July 1986, *16*(3), pp. 287–319. [G: U.S.]

Lamy, Robert E. and Thompson, G. Rodney. Penn Square, Problem Loans, and Insolvency Risk. *J. Finan. Res.*, Summer 1986, 9(2), pp. 103–11. [G: U.S.]

Landsman, Wayne. An Empirical Investigation of Pension Fund Property Rights. *Accounting Rev.*, October 1986, *61*(4), pp. 662–91. **[G: U.S.]**

Langohr, Herwig M. and Viallet, Claude J. Compensation and Wealth Transfers in the French Nationalizations: 1981–1982. *J. Finan. Econ.*, December 1986, *17*(2), pp. 273–312. **[G: France]**

Larrain, Maurice R. Portfolio Stock Adjustment and the Real Exchange Rate: The Dollar–Mark (DM) and Mark–Sterling. *J. Policy Modeling*, Winter 1986, *8*(4), pp. 577–96. **[G: U.S.; U.K.; W. Germany]**

Lashgari, Malek. Gold Investing Behavior over the Phases of the Business Cycle. *Atlantic Econ. J.*, December 1986, *14*(4), pp. 104. **[G: U.S.]**

Laurence, Martin M. Weak-Form Efficiency in the Kuala Lumpur and Singapore Stock Markets. *J. Banking Finance*, October 1986, *10*(3), pp. 431–45. **[G: Singapore; Malaysia]**

Lee, Cheng F. and Leuthold, Raymond M. An Analysis of Investment Horizon and Alternative Risk-Return Measures for Commodity Futures Markets. **In** *Goss, B. A., ed.*, 1986, pp. 119–36. **[G: U.S.]**

Lee, Chi-wen Jevons. Information Content of Financial Columns. *J. Econ. Bus.*, February 1986, *38*(1), pp. 27–39. **[G: U.S.]**

Lee, Wayne Y. and Solt, Michael E. Insider Trading: A Poor Guide to Market Timing. *J. Portfol. Manage.*, Summer 1986, *12*(4), pp. 65–71. **[G: U.S.]**

Lien, Da-Hsiang Donald. Asymmetric Arbitrage in Futures Markets: An Empirical Study. *J. Futures Markets*, Winter 1986, *6*(4), pp. 575–91. **[G: U.S.]**

Lloyd, William P.; Jahera, John S. and Goldstein, Steven J. The Relation between Returns, Ownership Structure, and Market Value. *J. Finan. Res.*, Summer 1986, *9*(2), pp. 171–77. **[G: U.S.]**

Loderer, Claudio; Lys, Thomas and Schweizer, Urs. Daily Monetary Impulses and Security Prices. *J. Monet. Econ.*, July 1986, *18*(1), pp. 33–47. **[G: Switzerland]**

Logue, Dennis E. Discrete Expectational Data and Portfolio Performance: Discussion. *J. Finance*, July 1986, *41*(3), pp. 713–14. **[G: U.S.]**

Luft, Carl F. and Fielitz, Bruce D. An Empirical Test of the Commodity Option Pricing Model Using Ginnie Mae Call Options. *J. Finan. Res.*, Summer 1986, *9*(2), pp. 137–51. **[G: U.S.]**

Ma, Christopher K. A Further Investigation of the Day-of-the-Week Effect in the Gold Market. *J. Futures Markets*, Fall 1986, *6*(3), pp. 409–19. **[G: U.S.; U.K.]**

Ma, Christopher K. and Weed, Garry M. Fact and Fancy of Takeover Junk Bonds. *J. Portfol. Manage.*, Fall 1986, *13*(1), pp. 34–37. **[G: U.S.]**

Maberly, Edwin D. The Informational Content of the Interday Price Change with Respect to Stock Index Futures. *J. Futures Markets*, Fall 1986, *6*(3), pp. 385–95. **[G: U.S.]**

Mahajan, Arvind and Mehta, Dileep. Swaps, Expectations, and Exchange Rates. *J. Banking Finance*, March 1986, *10*(1), pp. 7–20. **[G: U.S.]**

Maital, Shlomo; Filer, Randall K. and Simon, Julian L. What Do People Bring to the Stock Market (Besides Money)? The Economic Psychology of Stock Market Behavior. **In** *Gilad, B. and Kaish, S., eds., Vol. B*, 1986, pp. 273–307. **[G: U.S.]**

Mankiw, N. Gregory and Shapiro, Matthew D. Risk and Return: Consumption Beta versus Market Beta. *Rev. Econ. Statist.*, August 1986, *68*(3), pp. 452–59. **[G: U.S.]**

Marcus, Alan J. and Modest, David M. The Valuation of a Random Number of Put Options: An Application to Agricultural Price Supports. *J. Finan. Quant. Anal.*, March 1986, *21*(1), pp. 73–86. **[G: U.S.]**

Marmer, Harry S. Portfolio Model Hedging with Canadian Dollar Futures: A Framework for Analysis. *J. Futures Markets*, Spring 1986, *6*(1), pp. 83–92. **[G: Canada]**

Marsh, Terry A. and Rosenfeld, Eric R. Nontrading, Market Making, and Estimates of Stock Price Volatility. *J. Finan. Econ.*, March 1986, *15*(3), pp. 359–72. **[G: U.S.]**

Marshman, Peter and Davies, Peter. The Role of the Stock Exchange and the Financial Characteristics of Australian Companies. **In** *Bruce, R., et al., eds.*, 1986, pp. 51–84. **[G: Australia]**

Mason, Scott P. LYON Taming: Discussion. *J. Finance*, July 1986, *41*(3), pp. 576–77. **[G: U.S.]**

Mason, Scott P. Valuing Financial Flexibility. **In** *Friedman, B. M., ed.*, 1986, pp. 91–106. **[G: U.S.]**

Masulis, Ronald W. and Korwar, Ashok N. Seasoned Equity Offerings: An Empirical Investigation. *J. Finan. Econ.*, Jan./Feb. 1986, *15*(1/2), pp. 91–118. **[G: U.S.]**

Matolcsy, Z. P. The Distributive Nominal and Real Micro Effects of Inflation on Security Returns: Some Australian Evidence. *J. Banking Finance*, October 1986, *10*(3), pp. 361–76. **[G: Australia]**

Mattey, Joe and Meese, Richard. Empirical Assessment of Present Value Relations: Rejoinder. *Econometric Rev.*, 1986, *5*(2), pp. 279–85. **[G: U.S.]**

Mattey, Joe and Meese, Richard. Empirical Assessment of Present Value Relations. *Econometric Rev.*, 1986, *5*(2), pp. 171–234. **[G: U.S.]**

Mazzocco, Gian Nereo. L'indicizzazione finanziaria e le scelte di composizione del portafoglio titoli. (Variable Interest Rate Securities and Bond Portfolio Selection. With English summary.) *Ricerche Econ.*, Apr.-Sept. 1986, *40*(2–3), pp. 431–46. **[G: Italy]**

McConnell, John J. and Schwartz, Eduardo S. LYON Taming. *J. Finance*, July 1986, *41*(3), pp. 561–76. **[G: U.S.]**

McGee, Robert T. The Cycle in Property/Casualty Insurance. *Fed. Res. Bank New York Quart. Rev.*, Autumn 1986, *11*(3), pp. 22–30. **[G: U.S.]**

McInish, Thomas H. and Wood, Robert A. Adjusting for Beta Bias: An Assessment of Alternative Techniques: A Note. *J. Finance*, March 1986, *41*(1), pp. 277–86. **[G: U.S.]**

Meese, Richard. Testing for Bubbles in Exchange Markets: A Case of Sparkling Rates? *J. Polit. Econ.*, April 1986, *94*(2), pp. 345–73. **[G: U.S.]**

Michas, Nicholas A. The Performance Measurement and Evaluation of a Corporate Retirement Plan: A Case Study. *Financial Rev.*, November 1986, *21*(4), pp. 537–49.

Michie, Ranald C. The London and New York Stock Exchanges, 1850–1914. *J. Econ. Hist.*, March 1986, *46*(1), pp. 171–87. **[G: U.S.; U.K.]**

Mikkelson, Wayne H. and Partch, M. Megan. Valuation Effects of Security Offerings and the Issuance Process. *J. Finan. Econ.*, Jan./Feb. 1986, *15*(1/2), pp. 31–60. **[G: U.S.]**

Miller, Ross M. Markets as Logic Programs. **In** *Pau, L. F., ed.*, 1986, pp. 129–36.

Miller, Stephen E. Forward Cash Contracting of Cotton. *J. Futures Markets*, Summer 1986, *6*(2), pp. 249–59. **[G: U.S.]**

Miller, Stephen E. Forward Contracting versus Hedging under Price and Yield Uncertainty. *Southern J. Agr. Econ.*, December 1986, *18*(2), pp. 139–46. **[G: U.S.]**

Mills, Terence C. and Stephenson, Michael J. Modelling Real Returns on UK Government Stock. *Bull. Econ. Res.*, September 1986, *38*(3), pp. 237–56. **[G: U.K.]**

Milonas, Nikolaos T. A Note on Agricultural Options and the Variance of Futures Prices. *J. Futures Markets*, Winter 1986, *6*(4), pp. 671–76. **[G: U.S.]**

Milonas, Nikolaos T. Liquidity and Price Variability in Futures Markets. *Financial Rev.*, May 1986, *21*(2), pp. 211–37. **[G: U.S.]**

Milonas, Nikolaos T. Price Variability and the Maturity Effect in Futures Markets. *J. Futures Markets*, Fall 1986, *6*(3), pp. 443–60. **[G: U.S.]**

Milonas, Nikolaos T. and Papaioannou, George. Thinness and Portfolio Diversification Benefits: The Case of the Greek Stock Exchange. *Rivista Int. Sci. Econ. Com.*, Oct.-Nov. 1986, *33*(10–11), pp. 1027–40. **[G: Greece]**

Minnerop, Henry F. and Stoll, Hans R. Technological Change in the Back Office: Implications for Structure and Regulation of the Securities Industry. **In** *Saunders, A. and White, L. J., eds.*, 1986, pp. 31–51. **[G: U.S.]**

Mitchell, William E. and Sorensen, Robert L. Pricing, Price Dispersion, and Information: The Discount Brokerage Industry. *J. Econ. Bus.*, December 1986, *38*(4), pp. 273–82. **[G: U.S.]**

Monroe, Margaret A. and Cohn, Richard A. The Relative Efficiency of the Gold and Treasury Bill Futures Markets. *J. Futures Markets*, Fall 1986, *6*(3), pp. 477–93. **[G: U.S.]**

Moore, Norman H.; Peterson, David R. and Peterson, Pamela P. Shelf Registrations and Shareholder Wealth: A Comparison of Shelf and Traditional Equity Offerings. *J. Finance*, June 1986, *41*(2), pp. 451–63. **[G: U.S.]**

Moosa, S. A. Inflation, Non-neutral Growth, Equity Yields and the Fisher Hypothesis. *Appl. Econ.*, March 1986, *18*(3), pp. 237–47. **[G: U.S.]**

Murphy, J. Austin. Futures Fund Performance: A Test of the Effectiveness of Technical Analysis. *J. Futures Markets*, Summer 1986, *6*(2), pp. 175–85. **[G: U.S.]**

Nieswiadomy, Michael and Smith, Kenneth L. Insurance Stock Returns and Unanticipated Money. *Atlantic Econ. J.*, December 1986, *14*(4), pp. 100–101. **[G: U.S.]**

Nunn, Kenneth P., Jr.; Hill, Joanne and Schneeweis, Thomas. Corporate Bond Price Data Sources and Return/Risk Measurement. *J. Finan. Quant. Anal.*, June 1986, *21*(2), pp. 197–208. **[G: U.S.]**

O'Hanlon, John and Ward, Charles W. R. How to Lose at Winning Strategies. *J. Portfol. Manage.*, Spring 1986, *12*(3), pp. 20–23. **[G: U.S.]**

Obstfeld, Maurice. Capital Mobility in the World Economy: Theory and Measurement. *Carnegie-Rochester Conf. Ser. Public Policy*, Spring 1986, *24*, pp. 55–103. **[G: OECD]**

Oellermann, Charles M. and Farris, Paul L. Trader Concentration Effects in Live Cattle Futures. *J. Futures Markets*, Winter 1986, *6*(4), pp. 565–74. **[G: U.S.]**

Officer, Dennis T. and Smith, Richard L., II. Announcement Effects of Withdrawn Security Offerings: Evidence on the Wealth Redistribution Hypothesis. *J. Finan. Res.*, Fall 1986, *9*(3), pp. 229–38. **[G: U.S.]**

Overdahl, James A. and Starleaf, Dennis R. The Hedging Performance of the CD Futures Market. *J. Futures Markets*, Spring 1986, *6*(1), pp. 71–81. **[G: U.S.]**

Overturf, Stephen Frank. Interest Rate Expectations and Interest Parity. *J. Int. Money Finance*, March 1986, *5*(1), pp. 91–98. **[G: U.S.; U.K.]**

Palepu, Krishna G. Predicting Takeover Targets: A Methodological and Empirical Analysis. *J. Acc. Econ.*, March 1986, *8*(1), pp. 3–35. **[G: U.S.]**

Pantalone, Coleen C. and Welch, Jonathon B. The Usefulness of Public Information about Corporate Goals. *Quart. J. Bus. Econ.*, Autumn 1986, *25*(4), pp. 29–40.

Park, Hun Y. Changes in Expectations and the Forecasting Error of Interest Rates: An Error Learning Model of Treasury Bill Futures. *Quart. J. Bus. Econ.*, Spring 1986, *25*(2), pp. 22–31. **[G: U.S.]**

Park, Sang Yong and Reinganum, Marc R. The Puzzling Price Behavior of Treasury Bills That Mature at the Turn of Calendar Months. *J. Finan. Econ.*, June 1986, *16*(2), pp. 267–83. **[G: U.S.]**

Pashigian, B. Peter. The Political Economy of

Futures Market Regulation. *J. Bus.*, Part 2, April 1986, *59*(2), pp. S55–84. **[G: U.S.]**

Patterson, Douglas M. The Speed of Adjustment of Warrant Prices to Changes in Stock Prices. *J. Bus. Econ. Statist.*, April 1986, *4*(2), pp. 233–41. **[G: U.S.]**

Paul, Allen B. Liquidation Bias in Futures Price Spreads. *Amer. J. Agr. Econ.*, May 1986, *68*(2), pp. 313–21. **[G: U.S.]**

Peavy, John W., III and Scott, Jonathan A. The AT&T Divestiture: Effect of Rating Changes on Bond Returns. *J. Econ. Bus.*, August 1986, *38*(3), pp. 255–71. **[G: U.S.]**

Peek, Joe and Wilcox, James A. Tax Rates and Interest Rates on Tax-Exempt Securities. *New Eng. Econ. Rev.*, Jan./Feb. 1986, pp. 29–41. **[G: U.S.]**

Peel, David A.; Walters, K. and Pope, P. F. Public Forecasts and Their Impact on Expectation Formation. *Econ. Modelling*, April 1986, *3*(2), pp. 126–28. **[G: U.K.]**

Perry, Larry G. and Cronan, Timothy P. A Note on Rank Transformation Discriminant Analysis: An Alternative Procedure for Classifying Bank Holding Company Commercial Paper Ratings. *J. Banking Finance*, December 1986, *10*(4), pp. 605–10.

Petersen, John E. Innovative Approaches to the Capital Markets for Public Borrowers. **In** *Walzer, N. and Chicoine, D. L., eds.*, 1986, pp. 139–61. **[G: U.S.]**

Pettengill, Glenn N. A Non-Tax Cause for the January Effect? Evidence from Early Data. *Quart. J. Bus. Econ.*, Summer 1986, *25*(3), pp. 15–33.

Petzel, Todd E. Self-regulation and Futures Markets: Benefits from Technology Gains. **In** *Saunders, A. and White, L. J., eds.*, 1986, pp. 73–77. **[G: U.S.]**

Piga, Francesco. The CONSOB and the Transparency of Markets. *Rev. Econ. Cond. Italy*, May-Aug. 1986, (2), pp. 317–41. **[G: Italy]**

Pinegar, J. Michael and Lease, Ronald C. The Impact of Preferred-for-Common Exchange Offers on Firm Value. *J. Finance*, September 1986, *41*(4), pp. 795–814. **[G: U.S.]**

Pinkus, Scott M. and Chandoha, Marie A. The Relative Price Volatility of Mortgage Securities. *J. Portfol. Manage.*, Summer 1986, *12*(4), pp. 9–22. **[G: U.S.]**

Poitras, G. Futures Hedging Policies for the South African Gold Mining Industry. *S. Afr. J. Econ.*, December 1986, *54*(4), pp. 395–405. **[G: S. Africa]**

Pollock, Oscar S. Gunning for Capital Gains Again. **In** *Landau, R. and Jorgenson, D. W., eds.*, 1986, pp. 153–57. **[G: U.S.]**

Polonchek, John A.; Slovin, Myron B. and Sushka, Marie E. Tender-Offer Premia as a Management Signal. *Managerial Dec. Econ.*, March 1986, *7*(1), pp. 69–76. **[G: U.S.]**

Poterba, James M. Explaining the Yield Spread between Taxable and Tax-Exempt Bonds: The Role of Expected Tax Policy. **In** *Rosen, H. S., ed.*, 1986, pp. 5–49. **[G: U.S.]**

Poterba, James M. and Summers, Lawrence H. The Persistence of Volatility and Stock Market Fluctuations. *Amer. Econ. Rev.*, December 1986, *76*(5), pp. 1142–51. **[G: U.S.]**

Protopapadakis, Aris A. and Stoll, Hans R. The Law of One Price in International Commodity Markets: A Reformulation and Some Formal Tests. *J. Int. Money Finance*, September 1986, *5*(3), pp. 335–60. **[G: U.S.]**

Pruitt, Stephen W. and Peterson, David R. Security Price Reactions around Product Recall Announcements. *J. Finan. Res.*, Summer 1986, *9*(2), pp. 113–22. **[G: U.S.]**

Pruitt, Stephen W.; Reilly, Robert J. and Hoffer, George E. Security Market Anticipation of Consumer Preference Shifts: The Case of Automotive Recalls. *Quart. J. Bus. Econ.*, Autumn 1986, *25*(4), pp. 14–28. **[G: U.S.]**

Purcell, Wayne D. and Hudson, Michael A. The Certificate System for Delivery in Live Cattle: Conceptual Issues and Measures of Performance. *J. Futures Markets*, Fall 1986, *6*(3), pp. 461–75. **[G: U.S.]**

Quirk, Anthony and van Zijl, Tony. The Impact of Variation in Share Market and/or Business Conditions on the Parameters of the Market Model. *New Zealand Econ. Pap.*, 1986, *20*, pp. 93–99. **[G: New Zealand]**

Rainbow, Keven and Praetz, Peter D. The Distribution of Returns in Sydney Wool Futures. **In** *Goss, B. A., ed.*, 1986, pp. 191–207. **[G: Australia]**

Rajaraman, Indira. Testing the Rationality of Futures Prices for Selected LDC Agricultural Exports. *J. Futures Markets*, Winter 1986, *6*(4), pp. 523–40. **[G: U.S.; LDCs]**

Rausser, Gordon C.; Chalfant, James A. and Stamoulis, Kostas G. Instability in Agricultural Markets: The U.S. Experience. **In** *Maunder, A. and Renborg, U., eds.*, 1986, pp. 595–604. **[G: U.S.]**

Redfield, Corey B. A Theoretical Analysis of the Volatility Premium in the Dollar Index Contract. *J. Futures Markets*, Winter 1986, *6*(4), pp. 619–27. **[G: U.S.]**

Redwood, John. How to Protect the Investor. *Lloyds Bank Rev.*, April 1986, (160), pp. 21–35. **[G: U.K.]**

Reeve, James M. and Herring, Hartwell C. An Examination of Nonrated Municipal Bonds. *J. Econ. Bus.*, February 1986, *38*(1), pp. 65–76. **[G: U.S.]**

Rentzler, Joel C. Trading Treasury Bond Spreads against Treasury Bill Futures— A Model and Empirical Test of the Turtle Trade. *J. Futures Markets*, Spring 1986, *6*(1), pp. 41–61. **[G: U.S.]**

Richardson, Gordon; Sefcik, Stephan E. and Thompson, Rex. A Test of Dividend Irrelevance Using Volume Reactions to a Change in Dividend Policy. *J. Finan. Econ.*, December 1986, *17*(2), pp. 313–33. **[G: U.S.]**

Richardson, Ray and Nejad, Aaron. Employee Share Ownership Schemes in the UK—An Evaluation. *Brit. J. Ind. Relat.*, July 1986, *24*(2), pp. 233–50. **[G: U.K.]**

Ricks, William E. Firm Size Effects and the Association between Excess Returns and LIFO Tax Savings. *J. Acc. Res.*, Spring 1986, *24*(1), pp. 206–16. **[G: U.S.]**

Riley, William B., Jr. and Montgomery, Austin H., Jr. The Tax Reform Act of 1984 and Market Discount Bonds. *Nat. Tax J.*, March 1986, *39*(1), pp. 79–83. **[G: U.S.]**

Ritchey, Robert J. An Application of the Chi-squared Goodness-of-Fit Test to Discrete Common Stock Returns. *J. Bus. Econ. Statist.*, April 1986, *4*(2), pp. 243–54. **[G: U.S.]**

Roden, Peyton Foster and Bland, Robert L. Issuer Sophistication and Underpricing in the Negotiated Municipal Bond Market. *J. Finan. Res.*, Summer 1986, *9*(2), pp. 163–70. **[G: U.S.]**

Rohatyn, Felix G. Needed: Restraints on the Takeover Mania. *Challenge*, May/June 1986, *29*(2), pp. 30–34. **[G: U.S.]**

Rossi, Peter E. Statistical Properties of Generalized Method-of-Moments Estimators of Structural Parameters Obtained from Financial Market Data: Comment. *J. Bus. Econ. Statist.*, October 1986, *4*(4), pp. 421–22.

Rowe, Timothy D.; Lawler, Thomas A. and Cook, Timothy Q. Treasury Bill versus Private Money Market Yield Curves. *Fed. Res. Bank Richmond Econ. Rev.*, July/Aug. 1986, *72*(4), pp. 3–12. **[G: U.S.]**

Ruhm, Thomas F. Capital Gains Taxation: Incentive to Growth. **In** *Landau, R. and Jorgenson, D. W., eds.*, 1986, pp. 159–69. **[G: U.S.]**

Rutledge, David J. S. The Futures Markets. **In** *Bruce, R., et al., eds.*, 1986, pp. 357–77. **[G: Australia]**

Rutledge, David J. S. Trading Volume and Price Variability: New Evidence on the Price Effects of Speculation. **In** *Goss, B. A., ed.*, 1986, *1978*, pp. 137–56. **[G: U.S.]**

Rutz, Roger D. Futures Markets: Comment. **In** *Saunders, A. and White, L. J., eds.*, 1986, pp. 85–90. **[G: U.S.]**

Samuelson, Paul A. Canny Investing. **In** *Samuelson, P. A.*, 1986, *1981*, pp. 565–69.

Samuelson, Paul A. Economics of Futures Contracts on Basic Macroeconomic Indexes: An Economist's Appraisal. **In** *Samuelson, P. A.*, 1986, *1983*, pp. 557–58.

Sanger, Gary C. and McConnell, John J. Stock Exchange Listings, Firm Value, and Security Market Efficiency: The Impact of NASDAQ. *J. Finan. Quant. Anal.*, March 1986, *21*(1), pp. 1–25. **[G: U.S.]**

Schachter, Stanley, et al. Aggregate Variables in Psychology and Economics: Dependence and the Stock Market. **In** *Gilad, B. and Kaish, S., eds., Vol. B*, 1986, pp. 237–72. **[G: U.S.]**

Schipper, Katherine and Smith, Abbie. A Comparison of Equity Carve-outs and Seasoned Equity Offerings: Share Price Effects and Corporate Restructuring. *J. Finan. Econ.*, Jan./Feb. 1986, *15*(1/2), pp. 153–86. **[G: U.S.]**

Schneider, Dieter. Ausweichhandlungen vor Regulierungen auf Finanzmärkten als Prüfstein wettbewerbspolitischer Konzepte. (Evasions of Regulations in Financial Markets as a Test of Concepts of Competition Policy. With English summary.) **In** *Eucken, W. and Böhm, F., eds.*, 1986, pp. 155–81.

Schulman, Evan. A Parable of Tulips. *J. Portfol. Manage.*, Spring 1986, *12*(3), pp. 10–11.

Schwartz, Robert A. Securities Markets: Comment. **In** *Saunders, A. and White, L. J., eds.*, 1986, pp. 57–59. **[G: U.S.]**

Scott, William L. and Peterson, Richard L. Interest Rate Risk and Equity Values of Hedged and Unhedged Financial Intermediaries. *J. Finan. Res.*, Winter 1986, *9*(4), pp. 325–29. **[G: U.S.]**

Scribner, Richard O. The Technological Revolution in Securities Trading: Can Regulation Keep Up? **In** *Saunders, A. and White, L. J., eds.*, 1986, pp. 19–29. **[G: U.S.]**

Seabourne, Teresa. The Summer of 1914. **In** *Capie, F. and Wood, G. E., eds.*, 1986, pp. 77–116. **[G: U.K.; Europe]**

Sears, R. Stephen and Trennepohl, Gary L. Skewness, Sampling Risk, and the Importance of Diversification. *J. Econ. Bus.*, February 1986, *38*(1), pp. 77–91. **[G: U.S.]**

Sefcik, Stephan E. and Thompson, Rex. An Approach to Statistical Inference in Cross-Sectional Models with Security Abnormal Returns as Dependent Variable. *J. Acc. Res.*, Autumn 1986, *24*(2), pp. 316–34. **[G: U.S.]**

Seix, Christina and Akhoury, Ravi. Bond Indexation: The Optimal Quantitative Approach. *J. Portfol. Manage.*, Spring 1986, *12*(3), pp. 50–53.

Seyhun, H. Nejat. Insiders' Profits, Costs of Trading, and Market Efficiency. *J. Finan. Econ.*, June 1986, *16*(2), pp. 189–212. **[G: U.S.]**

Shaaf, Mohammad. An Investment Portfolio for OPEC: The Lagrangian Approach. *Atlantic Econ. J.*, July 1986, *14*(2), pp. 65–70. **[G: OPEC]**

Shanken, Jay. Testing Portfolio Efficiency When the Zero-Beta Rate Is Unknown: A Note. *J. Finance*, March 1986, *41*(1), pp. 269–76. **[G: U.S.]**

Shastri, Kuldeep and Tandon, Kishore. An Empirical Test of a Valuation Model for American Options of Futures Contracts. *J. Finan. Quant. Anal.*, December 1986, *21*(4), pp. 377–92. **[G: U.S.; W. Germany]**

Shastri, Kuldeep and Tandon, Kishore. On the Use of European Models to Price American Options on Foreign Currency. *J. Futures Markets*, Spring 1986, *6*(1), pp. 93–108. **[G: U.S.]**

Shastri, Kuldeep and Tandon, Kishore. Options on Futures Contracts: A Comparison of European and American Pricing Models. *J. Futures Markets*, Winter 1986, *6*(4), pp. 593–618. **[G: U.S.; W. Europe]**

Shastri, Kuldeep and Tandon, Kishore. Valuation of Foreign Currency Options: Some Empirical Tests. *J. Finan. Quant. Anal.*, June 1986, *21*(2), pp. 145–60. **[G: U.S.]**

Shonkwiler, J. Scott. Are Livestock Futures Prices Rational Forecasts? *Western J. Agr.*

Econ., December 1986, *11*(2), pp. 123–28. [G: U.S.]

Simonds, Richard R. Mutual Fund Strategies for IRA Investors. *J. Portfol. Manage.*, Winter 1986, *12*(2), pp. 40–43. [G: U.S.]

Simonds, Richard R.; LaMotte, Lynn Roy and McWhorter, Archer, Jr. Testing for Nonstationarity of Market Risk: An Exact Test and Power Considerations. *J. Finan. Quant. Anal.*, June 1986, *21*(2), pp. 209–20. [G: U.S.]

Singleton, J. Clay and Wingender, John. Skewness Persistence in Common Stock Returns. *J. Finan. Quant. Anal.*, September 1986, *21*(3), pp. 335–41. [G: U.S.]

Skomp, Stephen E.; Cronan, Timothy P. and Seaver, William L. On Application of the Rank Transformation Discrimination Method to Financial Problems. *Financial Rev.*, November 1986, *21*(4), pp. 473–83. [G: U.S.]

Smidt, Seymour. Productivity, Technological Change, and Futures Trading. **In** *Saunders, A. and White, L. J., eds.*, 1986, pp. 79–84. [G: U.S.]

Smirlock, Michael. Inflation Announcements and Financial Market Reaction: Evidence from the Long-term Bond Market. *Rev. Econ. Statist.*, May 1986, *68*(2), pp. 329–33. [G: U.S.]

Smirlock, Michael and Starks, Laura. Day-of-the-Week and Intraday Effects in Stock Returns. *J. Finan. Econ.*, September 1986, *17*(1), pp. 197–210. [G: U.S.]

Smith, Clifford W., Jr. Investment Banking and the Capital Acquisition Process. *J. Finan. Econ.*, Jan./Feb. 1986, *15*(1/2), pp. 3–29. [G: U.S.]

Spencer, Lee B., Jr. Securities Markets: Comment. **In** *Saunders, A. and White, L. J., eds.*, 1986, pp. 53–55. [G: U.S.]

Streit, M. E. and Graw, E. 'Halbstrenge' Effizienz des Terminkontraktmarktes für Währungen. Ein an Mustervorhersagen orientierter Test. (With English summary.) *Z. Wirtschaft. Sozialwissen.*, 1986, *106*(1), pp. 25–39. [G: U.S.; W. Germany; Switzerland]

Stulz, René M. Capital Mobility in the World Economy: Theory and Measurement: A Comment. *Carnegie-Rochester Conf. Ser. Public Policy*, Spring 1986, *24*, pp. 105–13.

Swanson, Peggy E. and How, William S. Y. Portfolio Diversification by Currency Denomination: An Approach to International Cash Management with Implications for Foreign Exchange Markets. *Quart. Rev. Econ. Bus.*, Spring 1986, *26*(1), pp. 95–103. [G: U.S.; W. Germany; U.K.]

Swary, Itzhak. Stock Market Reaction to Regulatory Action in the Continental Illinois Crisis. *J. Bus.*, July 1986, *59*(3), pp. 451–73. [G: U.S.]

Sweeney, Richard J. Beating the Foreign Exchange Market. *J. Finance*, March 1986, *41*(1), pp. 163–82. [G: U.S.; W. Germany; Selected Countries]

Sweeney, Richard J. and Warga, Arthur D. The Pricing of Interest-Rate Risk: Evidence from the Stock Market. *J. Finance*, June 1986, *41*(2), pp. 393–410. [G: U.S.]

Taggart, Robert A., Jr. Pricing New Corporate Bond Issues: An Analysis of Issue Cost and Seasoning Effects: Discussion. *J. Finance*, July 1986, *41*(3), pp. 643–44. [G: U.S.]

Tauchen, George. Statistical Properties of Generalized Method-of-Moments Estimators of Structural Parameters Obtained from Financial Market Data. *J. Bus. Econ. Statist.*, October 1986, *4*(4), pp. 397–416. [G: U.S.]

Taylor, Stephen J. Conjectured Models for Trends in Financial Prices, Tests and Forecasts. **In** *Goss, B. A., ed.*, 1986, *1980*, pp. 209–46. [G: U.K.]

Tehranian, Hassan and Waegelein, James F. Short-term Bonus Plan Adoption and Stock Market Performance—Proxy and Industry Effects: A Note. *Financial Rev.*, May 1986, *21*(2), pp. 345–53. [G: U.S.]

Terasawa, Yoshio. Opening Japanese Financial Markets: What Has Changed, What Will Change? Comment. **In** *Pugel, T. A., ed.*, 1986, pp. 137–39. [G: Japan]

Thomas, Lee R., III. Random Walk Profits in Currency Futures Trading. *J. Futures Markets*, Spring 1986, *6*(1), pp. 109–25. [G: U.S.]

Thompson, Sarahelen. Returns to Storage in Coffee and Cocoa Futures Markets. *J. Futures Markets*, Winter 1986, *6*(4), pp. 541–64. [G: U.S.; U.K.; LDCs]

Tilly, Richard H. Financing Industrial Enterprise in Great Britain and Germany in the Nineteenth Century: Testing Grounds for Marxist and Schumpeterian Theories? **In** *Wagener, H.-J. and Drukker, J. W., eds.*, 1986, pp. 123–55. [G: U.K.; Germany]

Titman, Sheridan and Warga, Arthur D. Risk and the Performance of Real Estate Investment Trusts: A Multiple Index Approach. *Amer. Real Estate Urban Econ. Assoc. J.*, Fall 1986, *14*(3), pp. 414–31. [G: U.S.]

Tobin, James. Tax Simplification and Financial Markets: Discussion. **In** *Federal Reserve Bank of Boston*, 1986, pp. 178–83. [G: U.S.]

Toevs, Alden L. and Jacob, David P. Futures and Alternative Hedge Ratio Methodologies. *J. Portfol. Manage.*, Spring 1986, *12*(3), pp. 60–70. [G: U.S.]

Trzcinka, Charles A. On the Number of Factors in the Arbitrage Pricing Model. *J. Finance*, June 1986, *41*(2), pp. 347–68. [G: U.S.]

Tse, Senyo. Intra-Year Trends in the Degree of Association between Accounting Numbers and Security Prices. *Accounting Rev.*, July 1986, *61*(3), pp. 475–97. [G: U.S.]

Tse, Y. K. The Spot and Forward Exchange Rates: Some Empirical Evidence of Singapore. *Appl. Econ.*, March 1986, *18*(3), pp. 319–31. [G: Singapore]

Vandell, Robert F. and Parrino, Robert. A Purposeful Stride down Wall Street. *J. Portfol. Manage.*, Winter 1986, *12*(2), pp. 31–39. [G: U.S.]

VanderHoff, James and VanderHoff, Mary. Inflation and Stock Returns: An Industry Analysis. *J. Econ. Bus.*, December 1986, *38*(4), pp. 341–52. **[G: U.S.]**

Vanthienen, L. and Vermaelen, Theo. The Effect of Royal Decree 15 on Security Prices and Financing Decisions. *Tijdschrift Econ. Manage.*, 1986, *31*(4), pp. 541–82. **[G: Netherlands]**

Venkatesh, P. C. and Chiang, Raymond. Information Asymmetry and the Dealer's Bid–Ask Spread: A Case Study of Earnings and Dividend Announcements. *J. Finance,* December 1986, *41*(5), pp. 1089–1102. **[G: U.S.]**

Vu, Joseph D. An Empirical Investigation of Calls of Non-Convertible Bonds. *J. Finan. Econ.*, June 1986, *16*(2), pp. 235–65. **[G: U.S.]**

Wadhwani, Sushil B. Inflation, Bankruptcy, Default Premia and the Stock Market. *Econ. J.*, March 1986, *96*(381), pp. 120–38. **[G: U.K.]**

Walter, John R. Short-term Municipal Securities. *Fed. Res. Bank Richmond Econ. Rev.*, Nov./Dec. 1986, *72*(6), pp. 25–34. **[G: U.S.]**

Wansley, James W. and Fayez, Elayan. Stock Repurchases and Securityholder Returns: A Case Study of Teledyne. *J. Finan. Res.*, Summer 1986, *9*(2), pp. 179–91. **[G: U.S.]**

Wassermann, Ursula. Tin and Other Commodities in Crisis. *J. World Trade Law,* Mar.:Apr. 1986, *20*(2), pp. 232–35. **[G: Global]**

Weale, Martin. The Structure of Personal Sector Short-term Asset Holdings. *Manchester Sch. Econ. Soc. Stud.*, June 1986, *54*(2), pp. 141–61. **[G: U.K.]**

Wenninger, John. Responsiveness of Interest Rate Spreads and Deposit Flows to Changes in Market Rates. *Fed. Res. Bank New York Quart. Rev.*, Autumn 1986, *11*(3), pp. 1–10. **[G: U.S.]**

West, Kenneth D. Empirical Assessment of Present Value Relations: Comment. *Econometric Rev.*, 1986, *5*(2), pp. 273–78. **[G: U.S.]**

Weston, C. Rae and McDonnell, Ross. An Analysis of Gold Futures Prices in Large and Small Markets. **In** *Goss, B. A., ed.*, 1986, pp. 175–89. **[G: U.S.; Australia; Canada]**

Whaley, Robert E. Valuation of American Futures Options: Theory and Empirical Tests. *J. Finance,* March 1986, *41*(1), pp. 127–50. **[G: U.S.]**

White, Bob and Vittas, Dimitri. Barriers in International Banking. *Lloyds Bank Rev.*, July 1986, (161), pp. 19–31. **[G: OECD]**

Wilkinson, Philip. Preparing for the Big Bang. **In** *Dale, R., ed.*, 1986, pp. 22–27. **[G: U.K.]**

Wong, Shee Q. The Contribution of Inflation Uncertainty to the Variable Impacts of Money on Stock Prices. *J. Finan. Res.*, Spring 1986, *9*(1), pp. 97–101. **[G: U.S.]**

Woodward, R. S. The Effect of Monetary Surprises on Financial Futures Prices. *J. Futures Markets,* Fall 1986, *6*(3), pp. 375–83. **[G: U.S.]**

Woolridge, J. Randall and Ghosh, Chinmoy. Institutional Trading and Security Prices: The Case of Changes in the Composition of the S&P 500 Index. *J. Finan. Res.*, Spring 1986, *9*(1), pp. 13–24. **[G: U.S.]**

Wright, Charlotte J. and Groff, James E. Uses of Indexes and Data Bases for Information Release Analysis. *Accounting Rev.*, January 1986, *61*(1), pp. 91–100. **[G: U.S.]**

Zorn, C. Kurt and Towfighi, Shah. Not All Bond Banks Are Created Equal. *Public Budg. Finance,* Autumn 1986, *6*(3), pp. 57–69. **[G: U.S.]**

314 Financial Intermediaries

3140 Financial Intermediaries

Alderson, Michael J. and Chen, K. C. Excess Asset Reversions and Shareholder Wealth. *J. Finance,* March 1986, *41*(1), pp. 225–41. **[G: U.S.]**

Amougou, Thomas Balla and Ottou, Jean. The Phenomenon of Thrift and Loan Societies. **In** *U.N., Dept. of International Econ. and Social Affairs,* 1986, pp. 95–100. **[G: Cameroon]**

Anderson, Richard G.; McCarthy, E. Jayne and Patten, Leslie A. Valuing the Core Deposits of Financial Institutions: A Statistical Analysis. *J. Bank Res.*, Spring 1986, *17*(1), pp. 9–17. **[G: U.S.]**

Andrikopoulos, Andreas A. and Brox, James A. The Demand for Deposits and Risk Sensitivity: The Case for Greece, 1955–1980. *Empirical Econ.*, 1986, *11*(4), pp. 197–206. **[G: Greece]**

Barth, James R., et al. The Thrift Industry's Rough Road Ahead. *Challenge,* Sept./Oct. 1986, *29*(4), pp. 38–43. **[G: U.S.]**

Beatty, Randolph P. and Ritter, Jay R. Investment Banking, Reputation, and the Underpricing of Initial Public Offerings. *J. Finan. Econ.*, Jan./Feb. 1986, *15*(1/2), pp. 213–32. **[G: U.S.]**

Bertoni, Alberto. Industrial Credit Institutions and Patterns of Corporate Finance. *Rev. Econ. Cond. Italy,* Jan.-Apr. 1986, (1), pp. 27–41. **[G: Italy]**

Booth, James R. and Smith, Richard L., II. Capital Raising, Underwriting and the Certification Hypothesis. *J. Finan. Econ.*, Jan./Feb. 1986, *15*(1/2), pp. 261–81.

Bowyer, Linda E.; Thompson, A. Frank and Srinivasan, Venkat. The Ohio Banking Crisis: A Lesson in Consumer Finance. *J. Cons. Aff.*, Winter 1986, *20*(2), pp. 290–99. **[G: U.S.]**

Boyd, John H. and Graham, Stanley L. Risk, Regulation, and Bank Holding Company Expansion into Nonbanking. *Fed. Res. Bank Minn. Rev.*, Spring 1986, *10*(2), pp. 2–17. **[G: U.S.]**

Boyd, John H. and Prescott, Edward C. Financial Intermediary-Coalitions. *J. Econ. Theory,* April 1986, *38*(2), pp. 211–32.

Bresnahan, Timothy F. Measuring the Spillovers from Technical Advance: Mainframe Computers in Financial Services. *Amer. Econ. Rev.*, September 1986, *76*(4), pp. 742–55. **[G: U.S.]**

Brickley, James A. and James, Christopher M. Access to Deposit Insurance, Insolvency Rules and the Stock Returns of Financial Institutions. *J. Finan. Econ.*, July 1986, *16*(3), pp. 345–71. **[G: U.S.]**

Cammarano, Guido. The Contribution of Investment Funds to the Development of the Financial Market in Italy. *Rev. Econ. Cond. Italy*, Jan.-Apr. 1986, (1), pp. 43–62. **[G: Italy]**

Cargill, Thomas F. Financial Reform in the United States and Japan: A Comparative Overview. **In** *Cheng, H.-S., ed.*, 1986, pp. 39–57. **[G: U.S.; Japan]**

Carraro, Kenneth C. and Thornton, Daniel L. The Cost of Checkable Deposits in the United States. *Fed. Res. Bank St. Louis Rev.*, April 1986, *68*(4), pp. 19–27. **[G: U.S.]**

Carron, Andrew S. Financial Reform in Australia. **In** *Cheng, H.-S., ed.*, 1986, pp. 69–87. **[G: Australia]**

Carstensen, Erik. Den fremtidige arbejdsdeling på penge- og kapitalmarkedet. (The Future Structure of Financial Markets in Denmark. With English summary.) *Nationaløkon. Tidsskr.*, 1986, *124*(1), pp. 62–76. **[G: Denmark]**

Carter, R. L.; Chiplin, B. and Lewis, M. K. Markets, Regulation, and the Financial Firm. **In** *Carter, R. L.; Chiplin, B. and Lewis, M. K., eds.*, 1986, pp. 248–71. **[G: U.K.]**

Carter, R. L. and Diacon, S. R. Personal Investment Markets. **In** *Carter, R. L.; Chiplin, B. and Lewis, M. K., eds.*, 1986, pp. 196–228. **[G: U.K.]**

Cebrecos Revilla, Felipe. Savings for Development: The Case of Peru. **In** *U.N., Dept. of International Econ. and Social Affairs*, 1986, pp. 65–70. **[G: Peru]**

Chan, M. W. Luke and Mountain, Dean C. Measuring Returns to Scale and Technological Change in Co-operative Banks: A Provincial Analysis of Canadian Credit Unions and Caisses Populaires. *Empirical Econ.*, 1986, *11*(4), pp. 207–22. **[G: Canada]**

Chen, K. C. and D'Arcy, Stephen P. Market Sensitivity to Interest Rate Assumptions in Corporate Pension Plans. *J. Risk Ins.*, June 1986, *53*(2), pp. 209–25. **[G: U.S.]**

Chiplin, B. Information Technology and Personal Financial Services. **In** *Carter, R. L.; Chiplin, B. and Lewis, M. K., eds.*, 1986, pp. 75–105. **[G: U.K.]**

Christensen, Hans Skov. Opsparing og balance. (The Socio-economic Balance Problem and the Need of Increased Private Saving. With English summary.) *Nationaløkon. Tidsskr.*, 1986, *124*(2), pp. 219–22. **[G: Denmark]**

Clarke, David. Merchant Bank Finance. **In** *Bruce, R., et al., eds.*, 1986, pp. 161–79. **[G: Australia]**

Curry, Timothy and Warshawsky, Mark. Life Insurance Companies in a Changing Environment. *Fed. Res. Bull.*, July 1986, *72*(7), pp. 449–60. **[G: U.S.]**

Cyrnak, Anthony W. Chain Banks and Competition: The Effectiveness of Federal Reserve Policy in 1977. *Fed. Res. Bank San Francisco Econ. Rev.*, Spring 1986, (2), pp. 5–15. **[G: U.S.]**

Dahl, Frederick R. Statement to the U.S. House Subcommittee on International Economic Policy and Trade of the Committee on Foreign Affairs, April 22, 1986. *Fed. Res. Bull.*, June 1986, *72*(6), pp. 393–98. **[G: U.S.]**

Draper, Paul. Unit Trust Objectives and Investor Choice. *Appl. Econ.*, February 1986, *18*(2), pp. 157–72. **[G: U.K.]**

Edwards, Franklin R. Concentration in Banking: Problem or Solution? **In** *Kaufman, G. G. and Kormendi, R. C., eds.*, 1986, pp. 145–68. **[G: U.S.]**

Edwards, Franklin R. Technology and Regulation: Commentary. **In** *Lawrence, C. and Shay, R. P., eds.*, 1986, pp. 144–48. **[G: U.S.]**

Eisenbeis, Robert A. Risk as a Criterion for Expanding Banking Activities. **In** *Kaufman, G. G. and Kormendi, R. C., eds.*, 1986, pp. 169–89. **[G: U.S.]**

Erikson, Walter E. Credible Accounting and Disclosure. **In** *Federal Home Loan Bank of San Francisco*, 1986, pp. 119–27. **[G: U.S.]**

Flannery, Mark J. Recapitalizing the Thrift Industry. **In** *Federal Home Loan Bank of San Francisco*, 1986, pp. 91–114. **[G: U.S.]**

Flannery, Mark J. Technology and Banking: Commentary. **In** *Lawrence, C. and Shay, R. P., eds.*, 1986, pp. 93–97. **[G: U.S.]**

French, Dan W. and Fraser, Donald R. A Note on Interest Rates and the Risk of Bank and Savings and Loan Stock. *Financial Rev.*, November 1986, *21*(4), pp. 551–58. **[G: U.S.]**

Fry, Maxwell J. Financial Structure, Financial Regulation, and Financial Reform in the Philippines and Thailand, 1960–1984. **In** *Cheng, H.-S., ed.*, 1986, pp. 161–84. **[G: Philippines; Thailand]**

Gilbert, R. Alton. Requiem for Regulation Q: What It Did and Why It Passed Away. *Fed. Res. Bank St. Louis Rev.*, February 1986, *68*(2), pp. 22–37. **[G: U.S.]**

Gray, Edwin J. Remarks from the Chairman: Bank Board Progress in 1985. **In** *Federal Home Loan Bank of San Francisco*, 1986, pp. 81–88. **[G: U.S.]**

Green, Jerry R. and Shoven, John B. The Effects of Interest Rates on Mortgage Prepayments. *J. Money, Credit, Banking*, February 1986, *18*(1), pp. 41–59. **[G: U.S.]**

Greenbaum, Stuart I. Deregulation of the Thrift Industry: A Prologue to Transitional Problems and Risks. **In** *Federal Home Loan Bank of San Francisco*, 1986, pp. 15–39. **[G: U.S.]**

Hancock, Diana. Testing Price Taking in Loan and Deposit Markets by Financial Firms. *Financial Rev.*, May 1986, *21*(2), pp. 239–57. **[G: U.S.]**

Hashi, Iraj and Hussain, Athar. The Employee Investment Funds in Sweden. *Nat. Westminster Bank Quart. Rev.*, May 1986, pp. 17–27. **[G: Sweden]**

Heggestad, Arnold A. and Shepherd, William G. The "Banking" Industry. **In** *Adams, W., ed.*, 1986, pp. 290–324. **[G: U.S.]**

Horvitz, Paul M. Technological Innovation: Implications for Regulation of Financial Institutions. **In** *Lawrence, C. and Shay, R. P., eds.*, 1986, pp. 111–23. **[G: U.S.]**

Jaffee, Dwight M. Term Structure Intermediation by Depository Institutions. *J. Banking Finance*, June 1986, *10*(2), pp. 309–25. **[G: U.S.]**

Jensen, Holger. Lønmodtagerfondes rolle som formidlere af risikovillig kapital. (The Role of Wage-Owners Funds on the Danish Capital Market. With English summary.) *Nationaløkon. Tidsskr.*, 1986, *124*(2), pp. 196–201. **[G: Denmark]**

Kanatas, George and Schouppe, Jacques. Subordinated Debt and Net Worth in the Savings and Loan Industry. *Housing Finance Rev.*, Winter 1986, *5*(3), pp. 219–30. **[G: U.S.]**

Kane, Edward J. Confronting Incentive Problems in U.S. Deposit Insurance: The Range of Alternative Solutions. **In** *Kaufman, G. G. and Kormendi, R. C., eds.*, 1986, pp. 97–120. **[G: U.S.]**

Kane, Edward J. Regulatory Policy for a Changing Financial Services Industry: Rejoinder. **In** *Lawrence, C. and Shay, R. P., eds.*, 1986, pp. 156–60. **[G: U.S.]**

Kane, Edward J. Regulatory Policy for a Changing Financial Services Industry. **In** *Lawrence, C. and Shay, R. P., eds.*, 1986, pp. 125–43. **[G: U.S.]**

Kaplan, Donald M. Managerial Excellence at Thrift Institutions. **In** *Federal Home Loan Bank of San Francisco*, 1986, pp. 151–57. **[G: U.S.]**

Kareken, John H. Technology and Regulation: Commentary. **In** *Lawrence, C. and Shay, R. P., eds.*, 1986, pp. 149–55. **[G: U.S.]**

Kim, H. Youn. Economies of Scale and Economies of Scope in Multiproduct Financial Institutions: Further Evidence from Credit Unions: A Note. *J. Money, Credit, Banking*, May 1986, *18*(2), pp. 220–26. **[G: Canada]**

Kohers, Theodor and Mullis, David. The Effects of Parent Company Business on Occupational Credit Union Behaviour. *Appl. Econ.*, December 1986, *18*(12), pp. 1311–21. **[G: U.S.]**

Kwack, Sung Y. and Chung, Un Chan. The Role of Financial Policies and Institutions in Korea's Economic Development Process. **In** *Cheng, H.-S., ed.*, 1986, pp. 115–35. **[G: S. Korea]**

Lawrence, Colin and Shay, Robert P. Technology and Financial Intermediation in Multiproduct Banking Firms: An Econometric Study of U.S. Banks, 1979–1982. **In** *Lawrence, C. and Shay, R. P., eds.*, 1986, pp. 53–92. **[G: U.S.]**

Lawrence, Colin and Shay, Robert P. Technology and Financial Intermediation in Multiproduct Banking Firms: An Econometric Study of U.S. Banks, 1979–1982: Rejoinder. **In** *Lawrence, C. and Shay, R. P., eds.*, 1986, pp. 106–07. **[G: U.S.]**

Lawrence, John F. Media Relations and Public Confidence: Panel Presentation. **In** *Federal Home Loan Bank of San Francisco*, 1986, pp. 201–03. **[G: U.S.]**

Lelart, Michel. Informal Savings in Africa. **In** *Association of African Central Banks*, 1986, pp. 13–59. **[G: Africa]**

Lewis, M. K. and Wright, D. M. Banking and Deposit Services. **In** *Carter, R. L.; Chiplin, B. and Lewis, M. K., eds.*, 1986, pp. 137–68. **[G: U.K.]**

Linneman, Peter. Technology and Financial Services: Regulatory Problems in a Deregulated Environment: Discussion. **In** *Faulhaber, G.; Noam, E. and Tasley, R., eds.*, 1986, pp. 73–75. **[G: U.S.]**

Martin, Preston. Savings Banking in the Next Decade. **In** *Federal Home Loan Bank of San Francisco*, 1986, pp. 5–11. **[G: U.S.]**

Mayer, Colin. The Assessment: Financial Innovation: Curse or Blessing? *Oxford Rev. Econ. Policy*, Winter 1986, *2*(4), pp. i–xix. **[G: U.K.]**

McGee, Robert T. The Cycle in Property/Casualty Insurance. *Fed. Res. Bank New York Quart. Rev.*, Autumn 1986, *11*(3), pp. 22–30. **[G: U.S.]**

McKenna, Fred W. and Kim, Yong H. Managerial Risk Preferences, Real Pension Costs, and Long-run Corporate Pension Fund Investment Policy. *J. Risk Ins.*, March 1986, *53*(1), pp. 29–48.

Meltzer, Allan H. Financial Failures and Financial Policies. **In** *Kaufman, G. G. and Kormendi, R. C., eds.*, 1986, pp. 79–96. **[G: U.S.]**

Michas, Nicholas A. The Performance Measurement and Evaluation of a Corporate Retirement Plan: A Case Study. *Financial Rev.*, November 1986, *21*(4), pp. 537–49.

Minnerop, Henry F. and Stoll, Hans R. Technological Change in the Back Office: Implications for Structure and Regulation of the Securities Industry. **In** *Saunders, A. and White, L. J., eds.*, 1986, pp. 31–51. **[G: U.S.]**

Murphy, Neil B. and Rogers, Ronald C. Life Cycle and the Adoption of Consumer Financial Innovation: An Empirical Study of the Adoption Process. *J. Bank Res.*, Spring 1986, *17*(1), pp. 3–8. **[G: U.S.]**

Mussa, Michael. Competition, Efficiency, and Fairness in the Financial Services Industry. **In** *Kaufman, G. G. and Kormendi, R. C., eds.*, 1986, pp. 121–44. **[G: U.S.]**

Mussa, Michael. Safety and Soundness as an Objective of Regulation of Depository Institutions: Comment. *J. Bus.*, January 1986, *59*(1), pp. 97–117. **[G: U.S.]**

Muth, Richard F. Financial Deregulation and the Cost of Mortgage Funds. **In** *Grieson, R. E., ed.*, 1986, pp. 153–64. **[G: U.S.]**

Nielsen, Niels Chr. Opsparing, investering og fordeling. (The Saving and Investment Problems and the Role of Profit Sharing Systems and Pension Funds in the Danish Economy. With English summary.) *Nationaløkon. Tidsskr.*, 1986, *124*(2), pp. 202–18. **[G: Denmark]**

O'Connell, William B. The Role of Trade Associations in Promoting Financial Stability: Panel Presentation. **In** *Federal Home Loan Bank of*

San Francisco, 1986, pp. 53–57. [G: U.S.]

Perry, Larry G. and Cronan, Timothy P. A Note on Rank Transformation Discriminant Analysis: An Alternative Procedure for Classifying Bank Holding Company Commercial Paper Ratings. *J. Banking Finance,* December 1986, *10*(4), pp. 605–10.

Phillips, Almarin and Berlin, Mitchell. Technology and Financial Services: Regulatory Problems in a Deregulated Environment. **In** *Faulhaber, G.; Noam, E. and Tasley, R., eds.*, 1986, pp. 49–72. [G: U.S.]

Pitelis, Christos N. The Pension Funds "Revolution" and the Managerialist Saving Function. *Scot. J. Polit. Econ.*, November 1986, *33*(4), pp. 383–90.

Pyle, David H. Financial Deregulation. **In** *Cagan, P., ed.*, 1986, pp. 147–90. [G: U.S.]

Rajan, Amin and Cooke, Geoffrey. The Impact of Information Technology on Employment in the Financial Services Industry. *Nat. Westminster Bank Quart. Rev.*, August 1986, pp. 21–35. [G: U.K.]

de Rezende Rocha, Roberto. Costs of Intermediation in Developing Countries: A Preliminary Investigation. **In** *Hanson, J. A. and Rocha, R.*, 1986, pp. 17–82. [G: MDCs; LDCs]

Rice, Gene E. Retrospective Survival Lessons: Panel Presentation. **In** *Federal Home Loan Bank of San Francisco*, 1986, pp. 169–72. [G: U.S.]

Rose, Harold. Change in Financial Intermediation in the UK. *Oxford Rev. Econ. Policy*, Winter 1986, *2*(4), pp. 18–40. [G: U.K.]

Rose, Sanford. Reviewing the Solution to the Thrift Problem: Panel Presentation. **In** *Federal Home Loan Bank of San Francisco*, 1986, pp. 187–91. [G: U.S.]

Rousselot, John H. The Role of Trade Associations in Promoting Financial Stability: Panel Presentation. **In** *Federal Home Loan Bank of San Francisco*, 1986, pp. 59–65. [G: U.S.]

Rowen, Hobart. Media Relations and Public Confidence: Panel Presentation. **In** *Federal Home Loan Bank of San Francisco*, 1986, pp. 193–98. [G: U.S.]

Salvemini, Maria Teresa. Medium-term Credit Institutions' Liquidity Management: Trends and Problems. *Rev. Econ. Cond. Italy*, Jan.-Apr. 1986, (1), pp. 9–25. [G: Italy]

Scott, William L. and Peterson, Richard L. Interest Rate Risk and Equity Values of Hedged and Unhedged Financial Intermediaries. *J. Finan. Res.*, Winter 1986, *9*(4), pp. 325–29. [G: U.S.]

Seibel, Hans Dieter and Marx, Michael. Mobilization of Personal Savings through Co-operative Societies or Indigenous Savings and Credit Associations: Case Studies from Nigeria. **In** *U.N., Dept. of International Econ. and Social Affairs*, 1986, pp. 107–12. [G: Nigeria]

Seidman, L. William. Equitably Allocating Federal Insurance Premiums. **In** *Federal Home Loan Bank of San Francisco*, 1986, pp. 71–75. [G: U.S.]

Shay, Robert P. Technology and Financial Services: Regulatory Problems in a Deregulated Environment: Discussion. **In** *Faulhaber, G.; Noam, E. and Tasley, R., eds.*, 1986, pp. 76–79. [G: U.S.]

Sinkey, Joseph F., Jr. Can Regulation and Supervision Ensure Financial Stability? **In** *Federal Home Loan Bank of San Francisco*, 1986, pp. 133–48. [G: U.S.]

Skully, Michael. Banks and Financial Institutions. **In** *Bruce, R., et al., eds.*, 1986, pp. 13–32. [G: Australia]

Smirlock, Michael. Technology and Banking: Commentary. **In** *Lawrence, C. and Shay, R. P., eds.*, 1986, pp. 98–104. [G: U.S.]

Smith, Donald J. A Test for Variant Objective Functions in Credit Unions. *Appl. Econ.*, September 1986, *18*(9), pp. 959–70. [G: U.S.]

Smith, Stanley D.; Sirmans, G. Stacy and Sirmans, C. F. Valuation of Creative Financing: An Empirical Test of Financed Fee Valuation Adjustment versus Cash Equivalence. *Housing Finance Rev.*, Fall 1986, *5*(2), pp. 151–58. [G: U.S.]

Starck, Christian C. Penningmarknadsindexering och hushållens sparande. (Financial Market Indexation and Household Savings Behaviour. With English summary.) *Ekon. Samfundets Tidskr.*, 1986, *39*(4), pp. 229–37. [G: Finland]

Strachan, Stan. Media Relations and Public Confidence: Panel Presentation. **In** *Federal Home Loan Bank of San Francisco*, 1986, pp. 205–07. [G: U.S.]

Taylor, R. G. Retrospective Survival Lessons: Panel Presentation. **In** *Federal Home Loan Bank of San Francisco*, 1986, pp. 175–79. [G: U.S.]

Throop, Adrian W. Financial Deregulation, Interest Rates, and the Housing Cycle. *Fed. Res. Bank San Francisco Econ. Rev.*, Summer 1986, (3), pp. 63–78. [G: U.S.]

U.N. Food and Agricultural Organization. Savings Mobilization for Agricultural and Rural Development in Africa. **In** *U.N., Dept. of International Econ. and Social Affairs*, 1986, pp. 87–94. [G: Africa]

Van Order, Robert. Deregulation, Thrifts, and Secondary Markets or Will Thrifts Diversify Out of Mortgages? *Housing Finance Rev.*, Summer 1986, *5*(1), pp. 1–14. [G: U.S.]

Vogel, Robert C. and Burkett, Paul. Deposit Mobilization in Developing Countries: The Importance of Reciprocity in Lending. *J. Devel. Areas*, July 1986, *20*(4), pp. 425–37. [G: LDCs]

Volcker, Paul A. Statement to the U.S. House Subcommittee on Financial Institutions Supervision, Regulation and Insurance of the Committee on Banking, Finance and Urban Affairs, May 7, 1986. *Fed. Res. Bull.*, July 1986, *72*(7), pp. 463–67. [G: U.S.]

Volcker, Paul A. Statement to the U.S. House Subcommittee on Commerce, Consumer, and Monetary Affairs of the Committee on Government Operations, June 11, 1986. *Fed. Res. Bull.*, August 1986, *72*(8), pp. 541–54. [G: U.S.]

Watkins, Thomas G. The Marketing of Personal Financial Services. **In** *Carter, R. L.; Chiplin, B. and Lewis, M. K., eds.*, 1986, pp. 48–74. **[G: U.K.; U.S.]**

Welker, Donald L. Thrift Competition: Does It Matter? *Fed. Res. Bank Richmond Econ. Rev.*, Jan./Feb. 1986, *72*(1), pp. 2–10. **[G: U.S.]**

Wenninger, John. Responsiveness of Interest Rate Spreads and Deposit Flows to Changes in Market Rates. *Fed. Res. Bank New York Quart. Rev.*, Autumn 1986, *11*(3), pp. 1–10. **[G: U.S.]**

White, Lawrence J. The Partial Deregulation of Banks and Other Depository Institutions. **In** *Weiss, L. W. and Klass, M. W., eds.*, 1986, pp. 169–209. **[G: U.S.]**

Whitehead, C. The Structure and Behaviour of the British Building Society Movement. **In** *[Yamey, B.]*, 1986, pp. 83–106. **[G: U.K.]**

Wright, D. M. Housing Finance and Consumer Credit. **In** *Carter, R. L.; Chiplin, B. and Lewis, M. K., eds.*, 1986, pp. 169–95. **[G: U.K.]**

315 Credit to Business, Consumer, etc. (including mortgages)

3150 General

Arvan, Lanny and Brueckner, Jan K. Efficient Contracts in Credit Markets Subject to Interest Rate Risk: An Application of Raviv's Insurance Model. *Amer. Econ. Rev.*, March 1986, *76*(1), pp. 259–63.

Bennett, James T. and DiLorenzo, Thomas J. Credit Allocation and Capital Formation: The Political Economy of Indirect Taxation. **In** *Lee, D. R., ed.*, 1986, pp. 275–96. **[G: U.S.]**

Benston, George J. Regulatory Policies and Financial Stability: Commentary. **In** *Axilrod, S. H., et al.*, 1986, pp. 137–51. **[G: U.S.]**

Cooke, William Peter. Regulatory Policies and Financial Stability: Commentary. **In** *Axilrod, S. H., et al.*, 1986, pp. 153–63. **[G: U.S.]**

Cover, James Peery. A Note on the Empirical Evidence for the Role of Credit in Macroeconomic Policy and Analysis. *Southern Econ. J.*, April 1986, *52*(4), pp. 1145–50.

Edwards, Franklin R. Technology and Regulation: Commentary. **In** *Lawrence, C. and Shay, R. P., eds.*, 1986, pp. 144–48. **[G: U.S.]**

Eisenbeis, Robert A. Regulatory Policies and Financial Stability. **In** *Axilrod, S. H., et al.*, 1986, pp. 107–35. **[G: U.S.]**

Evistigneeva, L. and Perlamutrov, V. Intensification and Financial–Credit Relations. *Prob. Econ.*, November 1986, *29*(7), pp. 55–73.

Gravelle, Hugh S. E. Default Risk and the Optimal Pricing of Court Enforcement Services. **In** *von der Schulenburg, J.-M. G. and Skogh, G., eds.*, 1986, pp. 85–112.

Hetzel, Robert L. Monetary Policy in the Early 1980s. *Fed. Res. Bank Richmond Econ. Rev.*, Mar./Apr. 1986, *72*(2), pp. 20–32. **[G: U.S.]**

Kane, Edward J. Regulatory Policy for a Changing Financial Services Industry. **In** *Lawrence, C. and Shay, R. P., eds.*, 1986, pp. 125–43. **[G: U.S.]**

Kane, Edward J. Regulatory Policy for a Changing Financial Services Industry: Rejoinder. **In** *Lawrence, C. and Shay, R. P., eds.*, 1986, pp. 156–60. **[G: U.S.]**

Kareken, John H. Technology and Regulation: Commentary. **In** *Lawrence, C. and Shay, R. P., eds.*, 1986, pp. 149–55. **[G: U.S.]**

King, Stephen R. Monetary Transmission: Through Bank Loans or Bank Liabilities? *J. Money, Credit, Banking*, August 1986, *18*(3), pp. 290–303. **[G: U.S.]**

Mankiw, N. Gregory. The Allocation of Credit and Financial Collapse. *Quart. J. Econ.*, August 1986, *101*(3), pp. 455–70.

Melnik, Arie and Plaut, Steven E. Loan Commitment Contracts, Terms of Lending, and Credit Allocation. *J. Finance*, June 1986, *41*(2), pp. 425–35. **[G: U.S.]**

Parsons, John E. Credit Contracts in the G.D.R.: Decentralized Investment Decisions in a Planned Economy. *Econ. Planning*, 1986, *20*(1), pp. 28–51. **[G: E. Germany]**

Ramaswamy, Krishna and Sundaresan, Suresh M. The Valuation of Floating-Rate Instruments: Theory and Evidence. *J. Finan. Econ.*, December 1986, *17*(2), pp. 251–72.

Stammer, Donald. Interest Rates, Money and the Availability of Credit. **In** *Bruce, R., et al., eds.*, 1986, pp. 33–48. **[G: Australia]**

Volcker, Paul A. Statement to the U.S. House Subcommittee on Telecommunications, Consumer Protection, and Finance of the Committee on Energy and Commerce, April 23, 1986. *Fed. Res. Bull.*, June 1986, *72*(6), pp. 398–403. **[G: U.S.]**

Wilson, John F., et al. Major Borrowing and Lending Trends in the U.S. Economy, 1981–85. *Fed. Res. Bull.*, August 1986, *72*(8), pp. 511–24. **[G: U.S.]**

3151 Consumer Finance

Barth, James R.; Cordes, Joseph J. and Yezer, Anthony M. J. Benefits and Costs of Legal Restrictions on Personal Loan Markets. *J. Law Econ.*, October 1986, *29*(2), pp. 357–80. **[G: U.S.]**

Blinder, Alan S. Debt Problems and Macroeconomic Policies: Commentary. **In** *Axilrod, S. H., et al.*, 1986, pp. 193–201. **[G: U.S.]**

Boyes, William J.; Hoffman, Dennis and Low, Stuart A. Lender Reactions to Information Restrictions: The Case of Banks and ECOA. *J. Money, Credit, Banking*, May 1986, *18*(2), pp. 211–19. **[G: U.S.]**

Bray, Ann Marie and Smith, Dolores S. The Consumer Advisory Council in Its First Decade: An Overview. *Fed. Res. Bull.*, November 1986, *72*(11), pp. 757–65. **[G: U.S.]**

Cagan, Phillip. Debt Problems and Macroeconomic Policies: Commentary. **In** *Axilrod, S. H., et al.*, 1986, pp. 203–08. **[G: U.S.]**

Cyrnak, Anthony W. and Canner, Glenn B. Consumer Experiences with Credit Insurance: Some New Evidence. *Fed. Res. Bank San Francisco Econ. Rev.*, Summer 1986, (3), pp. 5–20. **[G: U.S.]**

DeMuth, Christopher C. The Case against Credit Card Interest Rate Regulation. *Yale J. Regul.*, Spring 1986, *3*(2), pp. 201–42. **[G: U.S.]**

Friedman, Benjamin M. Increasing Indebtedness and Financial Stability in the United States. **In** *Axilrod, S. H., et al.*, 1986, pp. 27–53. **[G: U.S.]**

Higgins, Bryon. Debt, Financial Stability, and Public Policy: Symposium Overview. **In** *Axilrod, S. H., et al.*, 1986, pp. 1–14.

Kaufman, Henry. Debt: The Threat to Economic and Financial Stability. **In** *Axilrod, S. H., et al.*, 1986, pp. 15–26. **[G: U.S.]**

King, Mervyn A. Capital Market "Imperfections" and the Consumption Function. *Scand. J. Econ.*, 1986, *88*(1), pp. 59–80. **[G: U.K.]**

Luckett, Charles A. Recent Developments in Automobile Finance. *Fed. Res. Bull.*, June 1986, *72*(6), pp. 355–65. **[G: U.S.]**

Meltzer, Allan H. Increasing Indebtedness and Financial Stability in the United States: Commentary. **In** *Axilrod, S. H., et al.*, 1986, pp. 55–61. **[G: U.S.]**

Paquette, Lynn. Estimating Household Debt Service Payments. *Fed. Res. Bank New York Quart. Rev.*, Summer 1986, *11*(2), pp. 12–23. **[G: U.S.]**

Persson, Torsten. Capital Market "Imperfections" and the Consumption Function: Comment. *Scand. J. Econ.*, 1986, *88*(1), pp. 81–83. **[G: U.K.]**

Peterson, Richard L. Creditors' Use of Collection Remedies. *J. Finan. Res.*, Spring 1986, *9*(1), pp. 71–86. **[G: U.S.]**

Rice, Emmett J. Statement to the U.S. Senate Subcommittee on Financial Institutions and Consumer Affairs of the Committee on Banking, Housing, and Urban Affairs, January 28, 1986. *Fed. Res. Bull.*, March 1986, *72*(3), pp. 180–84. **[G: U.S.]**

Rice, Emmett J. Statement to the U.S. Senate Subcommittee on Financial Institutions and Consumer Affairs of the Committee on Banking, Housing, and Urban Affairs, May 21, 1986. *Fed. Res. Bull.*, July 1986, *72*(7), pp. 472–75. **[G: U.S.]**

Summers, Lawrence H. Debt Problems and Macroeconomic Policies. **In** *Axilrod, S. H., et al.*, 1986, pp. 165–91. **[G: U.S.]**

Wright, D. M. Housing Finance and Consumer Credit. **In** *Carter, R. L.; Chiplin, B. and Lewis, M. K., eds.*, 1986, pp. 169–95. **[G: U.K.]**

3152 Mortgage Market

Anderson, Dan R. and Weinrobe, Maurice. Insurance Issues Related to Mortgage Default Risks Associated with Natural Disasters. *J. Risk Ins.*, September 1986, *53*(3), pp. 501–13. **[G: U.S.]**

Anderson, Dan R. and Weinrobe, Maurice. Mortgage Default Risks and the 1971 San Fernando Earthquake. *Amer. Real Estate Urban Econ. Assoc. J.*, Spring 1986, *14*(1), pp. 110–35. **[G: U.S.]**

Askari, Mostafa. A Disequilibrium Econometric Study of the Canadian Mortgage Market. *Appl. Econ.*, April 1986, *18*(4), pp. 399–410. **[G: Canada]**

Barney, L. Dwayne and White, Harry. The Optimal Mortgage Payment Path under Price Uncertainty. *Amer. Real Estate Urban Econ. Assoc. J.*, Fall 1986, *14*(3), pp. 406–13.

Barry, Robert and Pollard, Ian. Domestic Sources of Long Term Corporate Debt. **In** *Bruce, R., et al., eds.*, 1986, pp. 180–204. **[G: Australia]**

Bhattacharya, Anand K.; Ramjee, Anju and Ramjee, Balasubramani. The Causal Relationship between Futures Price Volatility and the Cash Price Volatility of GNMA Securities. *J. Futures Markets*, Spring 1986, *6*(1), pp. 29–39. **[G: U.S.]**

Brueckner, Jan K. Reply [Creative Financing and House Prices: A Theoretical Inquiry into the Capitalization Issue]. *Amer. Real Estate Urban Econ. Assoc. J.*, Spring 1986, *14*(1), pp. 158–62.

Brueckner, Jan K. The Pricing of Interest Rate Caps and Consumer Choice in the Market for Adjustable-Rate Mortgages. *Housing Finance Rev.*, Fall 1986, *5*(2), pp. 119–36.

Clauretie, Terrence M.; Sirmans, C. F. and Merkle, Paul E. The Effect of Bond Issues on Housing Markets. *Housing Finance Rev.*, Winter 1986, *5*(3), pp. 207–17. **[G: U.S.]**

Dale-Johnson, David and Findlay, M. Chapman, III. Creative Financing and Housing Prices: On a Theoretical Inquiry into the Capitalization Issue: Comment. *Amer. Real Estate Urban Econ. Assoc. J.*, Spring 1986, *14*(1), pp. 153–57.

Falk, Barry. The Impact of Federally Sponsored Credit Agencies' Policy Instruments on Housing and Credit Markets. *Housing Finance Rev.*, Fall 1986, *5*(2), pp. 99–118. **[G: U.S.]**

Gabriel, Stuart A. Housing Policy. **In** *Kop, Y., ed.*, 1986, pp. 227–59. **[G: Israel]**

Goodwin, Thomas H. The Impact of Credit Rationing on Housing Investment: A Multi-Market Disequilibrium Approach. *Int. Econ. Rev.*, June 1986, *27*(2), pp. 445–64. **[G: U.S.]**

Green, Jerry R. and Shoven, John B. The Effects of Interest Rates on Mortgage Prepayments. *J. Money, Credit, Banking*, February 1986, *18*(1), pp. 41–59. **[G: U.S.]**

Guttentag, Jack M. Home Equity Conversion in 1986: Some Perspectives on a New Approach. *Housing Finance Rev.*, Summer 1986, *5*(1), pp. 61–64.

Guttentag, Jack M. Measuring Imperfections in the Primary Home Mortgage Market. *Housing Finance Rev.*, Winter 1986, *5*(3), pp. 233–37. **[G: U.S.]**

Haurin, Donald R. and Hendershott, Patric H. Affordability and the Value of Creative Finance: An Application to Seller Financed

Transactions. *Housing Finance Rev.*, Winter 1986, *5*(3), pp. 189–206. **[G: U.S.]**

Hendershott, Patric H. Mortgage Pricing: What Have We Learned So Far? *Amer. Real Estate Urban Econ. Assoc. J.*, Winter 1986, *14*(4), pp. 497–509. **[G: U.S.]**

Jessell, Kenneth A.; McCarty, Daniel E. and McDaniel, William R. An Empirical Examination of the Bias in the APR and the Need for Annual Percentage Rate Schedules. *Housing Finance Rev.*, Fall 1986, *5*(2), pp. 137–47.

Kau, J. B., et al. Corrigendum to "Rational Pricing of Adjustable Rate Mortgages." *Amer. Real Estate Urban Econ. Assoc. J.*, Fall 1986, *14*(3), pp. 499.

Lea, Michael J. and Zorn, Peter M. Adjustable-Rate Mortgages, Economic Fluctuations, and Lender Portfolio Change. *Amer. Real Estate Urban Econ. Assoc. J.*, Fall 1986, *14*(3), pp. 432–47. **[G: U.S.]**

Malatesta, Paul H. and Hess, Alan C. Discount Mortgage Financing and Housing Prices. *Housing Finance Rev.*, Summer 1986, *5*(1), pp. 25–41. **[G: U.S.]**

McCulloch, J. Huston. Risk Characteristics and Underwriting Standards for Price Level Adjusted Mortgages versus Other Mortgage Instruments. *Housing Finance Rev.*, Fall 1986, *5*(2), pp. 65–97. **[G: U.S.]**

Mills, Dixie L. and Gardner, Mona J. Consumer Response to Adjustable Rate Mortgages: Implications of the Evidence from Illinois and Wisconsin. *J. Cons. Aff.*, Summer 1986, *20*(1), pp. 77–105. **[G: U.S.]**

Muth, Richard F. Financial Deregulation and the Cost of Mortgage Funds. **In** *Grieson, R. E., ed.*, 1986, pp. 153–64. **[G: U.S.]**

Muth, Richard F. The Supply of Mortgage Lending. *J. Urban Econ.*, January 1986, *19*(1), pp. 88–106. **[G: U.S.]**

Nellis, Joseph G. and Thom, Rodney. The Nature of Credit Rationing in the United Kingdom Mortgage Market. *J. Urban Econ.*, July 1986, *20*(1), pp. 39–54. **[G: U.K.]**

Ott, Robert A., Jr. The Duration of an Adjustable-Rate Mortgage and the Impact of the Index. *J. Finance*, September 1986, *41*(4), pp. 923–33. **[G: U.S.]**

Page, Frank H., Jr. and Sanders, Anthony B. On the Pricing of Shared-Appreciation Mortgages. *Housing Finance Rev.*, Summer 1986, *5*(1), pp. 49–57.

Paquette, Lynn. Estimating Household Debt Service Payments. *Fed. Res. Bank New York Quart. Rev.*, Summer 1986, *11*(2), pp. 12–23. **[G: U.S.]**

Pinkus, Scott M. and Chandoha, Marie A. The Relative Price Volatility of Mortgage Securities. *J. Portfol. Manage.*, Summer 1986, *12*(4), pp. 9–22. **[G: U.S.]**

Plaut, Steven E. Mortgage Design in Imperfect Capital Markets. *J. Urban Econ.*, July 1986, *20*(1), pp. 107–19.

Rice, Gene E. Retrospective Survival Lessons: Panel Presentation. **In** *Federal Home Loan Bank of San Francisco*, 1986, pp. 169–72. **[G: U.S.]**

Sanders, Anthony B. Spot-Rate Uncertainty and Mortgage Pricing. *Housing Finance Rev.*, Summer 1986, *5*(1), pp. 43–48. **[G: U.S.]**

Schnitzel, Paul. Do Deposit Rates Cause Mortgage Loan Rates? The Evidence from Causality Tests. *Amer. Real Estate Urban Econ. Assoc. J.*, Fall 1986, *14*(3), pp. 448–64. **[G: U.S.]**

Sharp, Keith P. Mortgage Rate Insurance in Canada. *Can. Public Policy*, September 1986, *12*(3), pp. 432–37. **[G: Canada]**

Smith, Stanley D.; Sirmans, G. Stacy and Sirmans, C. F. Valuation of Creative Financing: An Empirical Test of Financed Fee Valuation Adjustment versus Cash Equivalence. *Housing Finance Rev.*, Fall 1986, *5*(2), pp. 151–58. **[G: U.S.]**

Spahr, Ronald W. and Escolas, Edmond L. Mortgage Guaranty Insurance: A Unique Style of Insurance. *J. Risk Ins.*, June 1986, *53*(2), pp. 308–19. **[G: U.S.]**

Taylor, William. Statement to the U.S. House Subcommittee on Commerce, Consumer, and Monetary Affairs of the Committee on Government Operations, December 12, 1985. *Fed. Res. Bull.*, February 1986, *72*(2), pp. 125–27. **[G: U.S.]**

Throop, Adrian W. Financial Deregulation, Interest Rates, and the Housing Cycle. *Fed. Res. Bank San Francisco Econ. Rev.*, Summer 1986, (3), pp. 63–78. **[G: U.S.]**

Van Order, Robert. Deregulation, Thrifts, and Secondary Markets or Will Thrifts Diversify Out of Mortgages? *Housing Finance Rev.*, Summer 1986, *5*(1), pp. 1–14. **[G: U.S.]**

Whitehead, C. The Structure and Behaviour of the British Building Society Movement. **In** *[Yamey, B.]*, 1986, pp. 83–106. **[G: U.K.]**

Wright, D. M. Housing Finance and Consumer Credit. **In** *Carter, R. L.; Chiplin, B. and Lewis, M. K., eds.*, 1986, pp. 169–95. **[G: U.K.]**

Zumpano, Leonard V.; Rudolph, Patricia M. and Cheng, David C. The Demand and Supply of Mortgage Funds and Mortgage Loan Terms. *Amer. Real Estate Urban Econ. Assoc. J.*, Spring 1986, *14*(1), pp. 91–109. **[G: U.S.]**

3153 Business Credit

Barry, Robert and Pollard, Ian. Domestic Sources of Long Term Corporate Debt. **In** *Bruce, R., et al., eds.*, 1986, pp. 180–204. **[G: Australia]**

Ben-David, Arie and Sterling, Leon. A Prototype Expert System for Credit Evaluation. **In** *Pau, L. F., ed.*, 1986, pp. 121–28.

Bertoni, Alberto. Industrial Credit Institutions and Patterns of Corporate Finance. *Rev. Econ. Cond. Italy*, Jan.-Apr. 1986, (1), pp. 27–41. **[G: Italy]**

Binks, M. R. and Coyne, John. Entrepreneurial Finance for Small Business. **In** *Carter, R. L.; Chiplin, B. and Lewis, M. K., eds.*, 1986, pp. 229–47. **[G: U.K.]**

Braverman, Avishay and Guasch, J. Luis. Rural Credit Markets and Institutions in Developing Countries: Lessons for Policy Analysis from Practice and Modern Theory. *World Devel.*, Oct./Nov. 1986, *14*(10/11), pp. 1253–67. **[G: LDCs]**

Broll, Udo and Gilroy, Michael B. Collateral in Banking Policy and Adverse Selection. *Manchester Sch. Econ. Soc. Stud.*, December 1986, *54*(4), pp. 357–66.

Clark, Telfred and Bruce, Robert. International Trade Finance. **In** *Bruce, R., et al., eds.*, 1986, pp. 321–38.

Clarke, David. Merchant Bank Finance. **In** *Bruce, R., et al., eds.*, 1986, pp. 161–79. **[G: Australia]**

Cox, Andrew. The State, Finance and Industry Relationship in Comparative Perspective. **In** *Cox, A., ed.*, 1986, pp. 1–59. **[G: OECD]**

Dyson, Kenneth. The State, Banks and Industry: The West German Case. **In** *Cox, A., ed.*, 1986, pp. 118–41. **[G: W. Germany]**

Eccleston, Bernard. The State, Finance and Industry in Japan. **In** *Cox, A., ed.*, 1986, pp. 60–79. **[G: Japan]**

Farrell, Terrence; Najjar, Annette and Marcelle, Hazel. Corporate Financing and Use of Bank Credit in Trinidad and Tobago. *Soc. Econ. Stud.*, December 1986, *35*(4), pp. 1–65. **[G: Trinidad and Tobago]**

Furlong, Paul. State, Finance and Industry in Italy. **In** *Cox, A., ed.*, 1986, pp. 142–71. **[G: Italy]**

Green, Diana. The State, Finance and Industry in France. **In** *Cox, A., ed.*, 1986, pp. 80–117. **[G: France]**

Grossman, Gregory. Inflationary, Political, and Social Implications of the Current Economic Slowdown. **In** *Höhmann, H.-H.; Nove, A. and Vogel, H., eds.*, 1986, pp. 172–97. **[G: U.S.S.R.]**

Harrison, Richard T. and Mason, Colin M. The Regional Impact of the Small Firms Loan Guarantee Scheme in the United Kingdom. *Reg. Stud.*, October 1986, *20*(6), pp. 535–49. **[G: U.K.]**

Hart, Oliver D. Credit Rationing and Collateral: Comment. **In** *Edwards, J., et al., eds.*, 1986, pp. 136–43.

Hefron, Barry and Gloster, Geoffrey. Trading Bank Finance. **In** *Bruce, R., et al., eds.*, 1986, pp. 147–60. **[G: Australia]**

Hong, Wontack. Institutionalized Monopsonistic Capital Markets in a Developing Economy. *J. Devel. Econ.*, May 1986, *21*(2), pp. 353–59. **[G: LDCs]**

Hoppit, Julian. The Use and Abuse of Credit in Eighteenth-Century England. **In** *[Coleman, D. C.]*, 1986, pp. 64–78. **[G: U.K.]**

Hudson, John. An Analysis of Company Liquidations. *Appl. Econ.*, February 1986, *18*(2), pp. 219–35. **[G: U.K.]**

Hussain, Irtiza. Role of Financial Institutions in the Financing of Public Enterprises. **In** *U.N., Dept. of Technical Co-operation for Development*, 1986, pp. 65–83. **[G: Pakistan]**

Iwasieczko, B., et al. Expert System in Financial Analysis. **In** *Pau, L. F., ed.*, 1986, pp. 113–20.

Jensen, Frederick H. and Parkinson, Patrick M. Recent Developments in the Bankers Acceptance Market. *Fed. Res. Bull.*, January 1986, *72*(1), pp. 1–12. **[G: U.S.]**

Leite, Sergio Pereira and Vaez-Zadeh, Reza. Credit Allocation and Investment Decisions: The Case of the Manufacturing Sector in Korea. *World Devel.*, January 1986, *14*(1), pp. 115–26. **[G: S. Korea]**

Lisle-Williams, Michael. The State, Finance and Industry in Britain. **In** *Cox, A., ed.*, 1986, pp. 231–81. **[G: U.K.]**

Martin, John. Project Finance. **In** *Bruce, R., et al., eds.*, 1986, pp. 247–76. **[G: Australia]**

Mato Leal, Gonzalo and Ríos Rull, José V. Efectos de los créditos participativos públicos en la financiación de las empresas. (With English summary.) *Invest. Ecón.*, January 1986, *10*(1), pp. 173–84.

Melnik, Arie and Plaut, Steven E. The Economics of Loan Commitment Contracts: Credit Pricing and Utilization. *J. Banking Finance*, June 1986, *10*(2), pp. 267–80.

Osano, Hiroshi and Tsutsui, Yoshiro. Credit Rationing and Implicit Contract Theory: An Empirical Study. *Int. J. Ind. Organ.*, December 1986, *4*(4), pp. 419–38. **[G: Japan]**

Pinder, D. A. Small Firms, Regional Development and the European Investment Bank. *J. Common Market Stud.*, March 1986, *24*(3), pp. 171–86. **[G: EEC]**

Poulsen, Annette B. Japanese Bank Regulation and the Activities of U.S. Offices of Japanese Banks: A Note. *J. Money, Credit, Banking*, August 1986, *18*(3), pp. 366–73. **[G: Japan]**

Roberts, R. O. Banks and the Economic Development of South Wales before 1914. **In** *Baber, C. and Williams, L. J., eds.*, 1986, pp. 65–80. **[G: U.K.]**

Schierenbeck, Henner. Zur Integration von Betriebsergebnis- und Effektivzinsrechnung bei Disagiokrediten mit Festzinsvereinbarung. (On the Integration of Operating Statement and Effective Interest Statement for Loans at a Discount with Fixed-rate Agreement. With English summary.) *Kredit Kapital*, 1986, *19*(1), pp. 76–109.

Scott, Jonathan A. and Smith, Terence C. The Effect of the Bankruptcy Reform Act of 1978 on Small Business Loan Pricing. *J. Finan. Econ.*, May 1986, *16*(1), pp. 119–40. **[G: U.S.]**

Seger, Martha R. Statement to the U.S. House Subcommittee on Consumer Affairs and Coinage of the Committee on Banking, Finance and Urban Affairs, August 12, 1986. *Fed. Res. Bull.*, October 1986, *72*(10), pp. 697–700. **[G: U.S.]**

Stiefel, Dieter. Austrian Banks at the Zenith of Power and Influence: System and Problems of the Austrian Finance Capital from the 1890s to the International Economic Crisis of the

1930s. In *Pohl, H. and Rudolph, B., eds.*, 1986, pp. 79–95. [G: Austria]

Stiglitz, Joseph E. and Weiss, Andrew M. Credit Rationing and Collateral. In *Edwards, J., et al., eds.*, 1986, pp. 101–36.

Vaez-Zadeh, Reza and Leite, Sergio Pereira. Effectiveness of Selective Credit Controls: An Empirical Test Applied to India. *J. Devel. Stud.*, April 1986, *22*(3), pp. 558–72. [G: India]

Vittas, Dimitri. Banks' Relations with Industry: An International Survey. *Nat. Westminster Bank Quart. Rev.*, February 1986, pp. 2–14. [G: U.K.; France; W. Germany; U.S.; Japan]

320 Fiscal Theory and Policy; Public Finance

3200 General

Abromeit, Heidrun. Privatisation in Great Britain. *Ann. Pub. Co-op. Econ.*, Apr.-June 1986, *57*(2), pp. 153–79. [G: U.K.]

Bance, Philippe and Monnier, Lionel. The Privatization of Public Enterprises in France. *Ann. Pub. Co-op. Econ.*, Apr.-June 1986, *57*(2), pp. 181–203. [G: France]

Beckerman, Wilfred. How Large a Public Sector? *Oxford Rev. Econ. Policy*, Summer 1986, *2*(2), pp. 7–24. [G: EEC; OECD]

Berry, William D. and Lowery, David. Authors' Erratum [The Growing Cost of Government: A Test of Two Explanations]. *Soc. Sci. Quart.*, March 1986, *67*(1), pp. 214–15. [G: U.S.]

Berry, William D. and Lowery, David. Testing the Right Hypothesis with the Right Specification: A Reply [The Growing Cost of Government: A Test of Two Explanations]. *Soc. Sci. Quart.*, March 1986, *67*(1), pp. 218–21. [G: U.S.]

Brede, Helmut and Hoppe, Ulrich. Outline of the Present Status of the Privatization Debate in the Federal German Republic. *Ann. Pub. Co-op. Econ.*, Apr.-June 1986, *57*(2), pp. 205–29. [G: W. Germany]

Buchanan, James M. The Moral Dimension of Debt Financing. In *Buchanan, J. M.*, 1986, *1985*, pp. 189–94.

Escarmelle, Jean-François and Hujoel, Luc. Privatization and Deregulation. Its Implementation in Belgium. *Ann. Pub. Co-op. Econ.*, Apr.-June 1986, *57*(2), pp. 253–73. [G: Belgium]

Hensher, David A. Privatisation: An Interpretative Essay. *Australian Econ. Pap.*, December 1986, *25*(47), pp. 147–74. [G: Global]

Kirkpatrick, Colin. The World Bank's Views on State Owned Enterprises in Less Developed Countries: A Critical Comment. *Rivista Int. Sci. Econ. Com.*, June-July 1986, *33*(6–7), pp. 685–96. [G: LDCs]

Knowlton, Winthrop and Zeckhauser, Richard. American Society: Public and Private Responsibilities: Overview. In *Knowlton, W. and Zeckhauser, R., eds.*, 1986, pp. 3–14. [G: U.S.]

Landau, Daniel. Government and Economic Growth in the Less Developed Countries: An Empirical Study for 1960–1980. *Econ. Develop. Cult. Change*, October 1986, *35*(1), pp. 35–75. [G: LDCs]

Le Pen, Claude. La productivité des services publics non marchands: quelques réflexions méthodologiques. (With English summary.) *Revue Écon. Polit.*, Sept.-Oct. 1986, *96*(5), pp. 476–89. [G: France]

Luker, Stuart. Teaching Economics to the 16–19 Age Range: Teaching the Economics of the Public Sector. In *Whitehead, D. J., ed.*, 1986, pp. 231–36.

Lynn, Laurence E., Jr. The Behavioral Foundations of Public Policy-Making. In *Hogarth, R. M. and Reder, M. W., eds.*, 1986, pp. 195–200.

Lynn, Laurence E., Jr. The Behavioral Foundations of Public Policy-Making. *J. Bus.*, Part 2, October 1986, *59*(4), pp. S379–84.

McCraw, Thomas K. American Society: Public and Private Responsibilities: The Historical Background. In *Knowlton, W. and Zeckhauser, R., eds.*, 1986, pp. 15–42. [G: U.S.]

Miller, John A. The Fiscal Crisis of the State Reconsidered: Two Views of the State and the Accumulation of Capital in the Postwar Economy. *Rev. Radical Polit. Econ.*, Spring/Summer 1986, *18*(1/2), pp. 236–60. [G: U.S.]

Mueller, Dennis C. and Murrell, Peter. Interest Groups and the Size of Government. *Public Choice*, 1986, *48*(2), pp. 125–45. [G: OECD]

Musgrave, Richard A. A Brief History of Fiscal Doctrine. In *Musgrave, R. A., Vol.* 2, 1986, *1985*, pp. 338–93.

Musgrave, Richard A. Leviathan Cometh—Or Does He? In *Musgrave, R. A., Vol.* 2, 1986, *1981*, pp. 200–232.

Pillai, Vel and Sopchokchai, Orapin. Budgeting, Financing, and Planning in Thailand: Study of a Trichotomous Process. *Public Budg. Finance*, Winter 1986, *6*(4), pp. 34–42. [G: Thailand]

Platzer, Renate. The Privatisation Debate in Austria. *Ann. Pub. Co-op. Econ.*, Apr.-June 1986, *57*(2), pp. 275–91. [G: Austria]

Roper, Brian A. Market Forces, Privatisation and Prisons: A Polar Case for Government Policy. *Int. J. Soc. Econ.*, 1986, *13*(1/2), pp. 77–92. [G: U.K.]

Rose-Ackerman, Susan. Reforming Public Bureaucracy through Economic Incentives? *J. Law, Econ., Organ.*, Spring 1986, *2*(1), pp. 131–61.

Samuelson, Paul A. Government and Business. In *Samuelson, P. A.*, 1986, *1977*, pp. 973–79.

Samuelson, Paul A. The Public Role in the Modern American Economy. In *Samuelson, P. A.*, 1986, *1980*, pp. 946–52. [G: U.S.]

Savoie, Donald J. Le programme federal de decentralisation: Un reexamen. (With English summary.) *Can. Public Policy*, September 1986, *12*(3), pp. 413–23. [G: Canada]

Shughart, William F., II and Tollison, Robert D. On the Growth of Government and the Political Economy of Legislation. In *Zerbe, R.*

O., Jr., ed., 1986, pp. 111–27. **[G: U.S.]**

Stefani, Giorgio. Privatizing Public Enterprises in Italy: The Case of State Holdings. *Ann. Pub. Co-op. Econ.*, Apr.-June 1986, *57*(2), pp. 231–51.

Steve, Sergio. Riflessioni sulla mia esperienza di studioso di scienza delle finanze. (Some Reflections on My Experience as a Scholar of Public Finance. With English summary.) *Giorn. Econ.*, Jan.-Feb. 1986, *45*(1–2), pp. 3–16.

Stigler, George J. Why Have the Socialists Been Winning? **In** *Stigler, G. J.*, 1986, *1979*, pp. 337–46.

Summers, Lawrence H. Government Policy and Economic Performance. **In** *Knowlton, W. and Zeckhauser, R., eds.*, 1986, pp. 317–22. **[G: U.S.]**

Taylor, Alwyn Beresford. National Financial Policies and Capital Formation in Africa: Summation of the Symposium. **In** *Association of African Central Banks*, 1986, pp. 151–69. **[G: Africa]**

Thiemeyer, Theo. Privatization: On the Many Senses in Which This Word Is Used in an International Discussion on Economic Theory. *Ann. Pub. Co-op. Econ.*, Apr.-June 1986, *57*(2), pp. 141–52.

Thorne, Richard. Teaching Economics to the 13–16 Age Range: Public Finance. **In** *Whitehead, D. J., ed.*, 1986, pp. 119–21.

Tullock, Gordon. Explaining the Growing Cost of Government: A Comment [The Expanding Public Sector: Wagner Squared]. *Soc. Sci. Quart.*, March 1986, *67*(1), pp. 216–18. **[G: U.S.]**

Vatter, Harold G. and Walker, John F. Real Public Sector Employment Growth, Wagner's Law, and Economic Growth in the United States. *Public Finance*, 1986, *41*(1), pp. 116–38. **[G: U.S.]**

Vedder, Richard. Tithing for Leviathan: The Case for a True Flat-Rate Tax. **In** *Lee, D. R., ed.*, 1986, pp. 141–69. **[G: U.S.]**

Venkateswarlu, Tadiboyina. Public Finance: Survey of Course Reading Materials in Academic Institutions. *Amer. Econ.*, Fall 1986, *30*(2), pp. 62–93.

Walzer, Michael. Toward a Theory of Social Assignments. **In** *Knowlton, W. and Zeckhauser, R., eds.*, 1986, pp. 79–96. **[G: U.S.]**

Zeckhauser, Richard. The Muddled Responsibilities of Public and Private America. **In** *Knowlton, W. and Zeckhauser, R., eds.*, 1986, pp. 45–77. **[G: U.S.]**

321 Fiscal Theory and Policy

3210 General

Adhikari, Ramesh. Efficiency and Social Analysis of Projects in the Nepalese Economy. *Industry Devel.*, 1986, (17), pp. 91–109. **[G: Nepal]**

Behrman, Jere R. Shadow Prices and Subsidies in Botswana. *J. Devel. Econ.*, July-Aug. 1986, *22*(2), pp. 351–92. **[G: Botswana]**

Blackorby, Charles and Donaldson, David. Can Risk–Benefit Analysis Provide Consistent Policy Evaluations of Projects Involving Loss of Life? *Econ. J.*, September 1986, *96*(383), pp. 758–73.

Blomqvist, Ake G. International Migration of Educated Manpower and Social Rates of Return to Education in LDCs. *Int. Econ. Rev.*, February 1986, *27*(1), pp. 165–74. **[G: LDCs]**

Brean, Donald J. S. Fiscal Policy Harmonization and Negotiation of a Free-Trade Area. **In** *C. D. Howe Institute*, 1986, pp. 43–71. **[G: Canada; U.S.]**

Cairncross, Alec. The Relationship between Monetary and Fiscal Policy. **In** *Cairncross, A.*, 1986, pp. 151–68.

Canto, Victor A. and Rapp, Donald. The "Crowding Out" Myth. **In** *Canto, V. A.; Kadlec, C. W. and Laffer, A. B., eds.*, 1986, pp. 75–86. **[G: U.S.]**

Dinwiddy, Caroline L. and Teal, Francis J. Project Appraisal Procedures and the Evaluation of Foreign Exchange. *Economica*, February 1986, *53*(209), pp. 97–107.

Dufour, Jean-Marie and Racette, Daniel. Une évaluation économique du financement public des exportations. (With English summary.) *Can. Public Policy*, December 1986, *12*(4), pp. 584–95. **[G: Canada]**

Edwards, Sebastian. Country Risk, Foreign Borrowing, and the Social Discount Rate in an Open Developing Economy. *J. Int. Money Finance*, Supp. March 1986, *5*, pp. S79–96. **[G: LDCs; Chile; Costa Rica]**

Eisner, Robert. The Real Federal Deficit: What It Is, How It Matters, and What It Should Be. *Quart. Rev. Econ. Bus.*, Winter 1986, *26*(4), pp. 6–21. **[G: U.S.]**

Eisner, Robert and Pieper, Paul J. A New View of the Federal Debt and Budget Deficits: Reply. *Amer. Econ. Rev.*, December 1986, *76*(5), pp. 1156–57. **[G: U.S.]**

Fischer, Stanley. Dynamic Inconsistency, Cooperation, and the Benevolent Dissembling Government. **In** *Fischer, S.*, 1986, *1980*, pp. 413–29.

Fitoussi, Jean-Paul and Muet, Pierre-Alain. Avant-Propos. Numéro spécial "déficit public." (Special Issue on Public Deficit: Forward.) *Ann. Écon. Statist.*, July-Sept. 1986, (3), pp. 3–25.

Fourgeaud, Claude; Lenclud, B. and Picard, P. Shadow Prices and Public Policies in a Disequilibrium Model of an Open Economy. *Europ. Econ. Rev.*, October 1986, *30*(5), pp. 991–1012. **[G: France]**

Gibson, Richard E. Selection and Evaluation of Small Scale Rural Infrastructure Projects. *Bull. Indonesian Econ. Stud.*, April 1986, *22*(1), pp. 113–22. **[G: Indonesia]**

Hamilton, Joel R. and Gardner, Richard L. Value Added and Secondary Benefits in Regional Projection Evaluation: Irrigation Development in the Snake River Basin. *Ann. Reg. Sci.*, March 1986, *20*(1), pp. 1–11. **[G: U.S.]**

Hammond, Peter J. Project Evaluation by Potential Tax Reform. *J. Public Econ.*, June 1986, *30*(1), pp. 1–36.

Henderson, Dale W. Country Risk, Foreign Borrowing, and the Social Discount Rate in an Open Developing Economy: Comments. *J. Int. Money Finance*, Supp. March 1986, *5*, pp. 97–99. **[G: LDCs; Chile; Costa Rica]**

Hill, Stuart. Lumpy Preference Structures. *Policy Sci.*, July 1986, *19*(1), pp. 5–32.

Hoksbergen, Roland. Approaches to Evaluation of Development Interventions: The Importance of World and Life Views. *World Devel.*, Special Issue, Feb. 1986, *14*(2), pp. 283–300.

Kula, Erhun. The Analysis of Social Interest Rate in Trinidad and Tobago. *J. Devel. Stud.*, July 1986, *22*(4), pp. 731–39. **[G: Trinidad and Tobago]**

Leathers, Charles G. Gladstonian Finance and the Virginia School of Public Finance: Comment ["Chaining Leviathan": The Case of Gladstonian Finance]. *Hist. Polit. Econ.*, Fall 1986, *18*(3), pp. 515–21. **[G: U.K.]**

McCain, Roger A. Costs of Transaction and a Theory of Public Policy. *Rev. Soc. Econ.*, December 1986, *44*(3), pp. 238–50.

Milbourne, Ross and Richards, Daniel J. A New View of the Federal Debt and Budget Deficits: Comment. *Amer. Econ. Rev.*, December 1986, *76*(5), pp. 1154–55. **[G: U.S.]**

Mookherjee, Dilip. Shadow Pricing with Suboptimal Policy Rules. *J. Public Econ.*, December 1986, *31*(3), pp. 287–305.

Musgrave, Richard A. Expenditure Policy for Development. **In** *Musgrave, R. A., Vol. 2*, 1986, *1974*, pp. 158–72. **[G: Latin America]**

Musgrave, Richard A. Pareto-Optimal Redistribution: Comment. **In** *Musgrave, R. A., Vol. 1*, 1986, *1970*, pp. 71–75.

Musgrave, Richard A. Public Finance, Now and Then. **In** *Musgrave, R. A., Vol. 1*, 1986, *1983*, pp. 89–101.

Musgrave, Richard A. and Peacock, Alan. Classics in the Theory of Public Finance. **In** *Musgrave, R. A., Vol. 2*, 1986, *1958*, pp. 235–45.

Norgaard, Richard B. and Dixon, John A. Pluralistic Project Design: An Argument for Combining Economic and Coevolutionary Methodologies. *Policy Sci.*, October 1986, *19*(3), pp. 297–317.

O'Flaherty, Brendan. Potential Pareto Optimality of Risky Projects. *Quart. J. Econ.*, August 1986, *101*(3), pp. 647–51.

Olson, Mancur. Toward a More General Theory of Governmental Structure. *Amer. Econ. Rev.*, May 1986, *76*(2), pp. 120–25. **[G: U.S.; U.K.; Canada]**

Paté-Cornell, M. Elisabeth and Tagaras, George. Risk Costs for New Dams: Economic Analysis and Effects of Monitoring. *Water Resources Res.*, January 1986, *22*(1), pp. 5–14. **[G: U.S.]**

Rees, Ray. Incentive Compatible Discount Rates for Public Investment. *J. Public Econ.*, July 1986, *30*(2), pp. 249–57.

Richardson, David H. The St. Lawrence Seaway and Power Project: An *Ex Post* Evaluation. *Public Finance*, 1986, *41*(1), pp. 8–41. **[G: U.S.; Canada]**

Roberts, Paul Craig. How the Fed Crowded Out Reagan's Economic Policy. *Cato J.*, Winter 1986, *5*(3), pp. 777–85. **[G: U.S.]**

Schleicher, Heinz. Classes of Core Configurations of Convex Cost Games and Equivalent One-Point Solution Concepts. *Écon. Soc.*, November 1986, *20*(11), pp. 101–21.

Smithies, Arthur. The Planning–Programming–Budgeting System. **In** *Szenberg, M., ed.*, 1986, pp. 13–21. **[G: U.S.]**

Starrett, David A. On the Social Risk Premium. **In** *[Arrow, K. J.], Vol. 1*, 1986, pp. 159–76.

Steiner, Philippe. Les peuples et l'impôt dans la *'Dixme royalle'* de Vauban. (Peoples and Taxes in Vauban's "Dixme royale." With English summary.) *Écon. Soc.*, March 1986, *20*(3), pp. 153–79.

Tisdell, Clem A. Cost–Benefit Analysis, the Environment and Informational Constraints in LDCs. *J. Econ. Devel.*, December 1986, *11*(2), pp. 63–81. **[G: LDCs]**

Torrance, George W. Measurement of Health State Utilities for Economic Appraisal: A Review. *J. Health Econ.*, March 1986, *5*(1), pp. 1–30.

Tullock, Gordon. Transitional Gains and Transfers. *Cato J.*, Spring/Summer 1986, *6*(1), pp. 143–54.

Ulrich, Alvin; Furtan, Hartley and Schmitz, Andrew. Public and Private Returns from Joint Venture Research: An Example from Agriculture. *Quart. J. Econ.*, February 1986, *101*(1), pp. 103–29. **[G: Canada]**

Wu, C. L. Government Land Sales in Hong Kong: Auctions and a Proposed Alternative. *Hong Kong Econ. Pap.*, 1986, (17), pp. 51–63. **[G: Hong Kong]**

Yang, Jinbai, et al. Some Theoretical Problems of Socialist National Income. *Chinese Econ. Stud.*, Fall 1986, *20*(1), pp. 3–99.

Zotova, T. Economic Effectiveness of the Production Infrastructure. *Prob. Econ.*, June 1986, *29*(2), pp. 79–96. **[G: U.S.S.R.]**

3212 Fiscal Theory; Empirical Studies Illustrating Fiscal Theory

Abel, Andrew B. The Failure of Ricardian Equivalence under Progressive Wealth Taxation. *J. Public Econ.*, June 1986, *30*(1), pp. 117–28.

Abrams, Burton A. and Dougan, William R. The Effects of Constitutional Restraints on Government Spending. *Public Choice*, 1986, *49*(2), pp. 101–16. **[G: U.S.]**

Adams, James D. Equilibrium Taxation and Experience Rating in a Federal System of Unemployment Insurance. *J. Public Econ.*, February 1986, *29*(1), pp. 51–77.

Agell, Jonas Nils. Subsidy to Capital through Tax Incentives. **In** *Shome, P., ed.*, 1986, pp. 48–79. **[G: ASEAN]**

Ahmed, Shaghil. Temporary and Permanent Government Spending in an Open Economy: Some Evidence for the United Kingdom. *J. Monet.*

Econ., March 1986, *17*(2), pp. 197–224. **[G: U.K.]**

Aizenman, Joshua. On the Complementarity of Commercial Policy, Capital Controls, and Inflation Tax. *Can. J. Econ.*, February 1986, *19*(1), pp. 114–33.

Allen, Larry and Price, Don. The Short-run Impact of Monetary and Fiscal Policy in a Two Sector Keynesian Model. *Amer. Econ.*, Spring 1986, *30*(1), pp. 40–50.

Anandalingam, G. Incentive Compatibility in Mixed Economy Planning: Results of a Simple Model. *J. Econ. Dynam. Control*, June 1986, *10*(1/2), pp. 9–13.

Andel, Norbert. Changing Concepts of Public Debt in the History of Economic Thought. **In** *Herber, B. P., ed.*, 1986, pp. 1–13.

Anderson, John E. Property Taxes and the Timing of Urban Land Development. *Reg. Sci. Urban Econ.*, November 1986, *16*(4), pp. 483–92.

Apps, Patricia and Jones, Glenn. Selective Taxation of Couples. *J. Econ. (Z. Nationalökon.)*, Supplementum 5, 1986, pp. 1–15.

Arnott, Richard J. and Stiglitz, Joseph E. Moral Hazard and Optimal Commodity Taxation. *J. Public Econ.*, February 1986, *29*(1), pp. 1–24.

Artus, Patrick. Les dépenses publiques et leur mode de financement en économie ouverte avec changes flexibles: efficacité et stabilité de l'économie. (Public Expenditures and Deficit Financing in an Open Economy with Flexible Exchange Rates: Efficiency and Stability of the Economy. With English summary.) *Ann. Écon. Statist.*, July-Sept. 1986, (3), pp. 119–40.

Atkinson, Glen W. Concept of Income Realization and Deductible Costs. **In** *Lindholm, R. W., ed.*, 1986, pp. 251–79.

Auerbach, Alan J. The Dynamic Effects of Tax Law Asymmetries. *Rev. Econ. Stud.*, April 1986, *53*(2), pp. 205–25.

Bach, George Leland and Musgrave, Richard A. A Stable Purchasing Power Bond. **In** *Musgrave, R. A., Vol. 1*, 1986, *1941*, pp. 332–35.

Balasko, Yves and Shell, Karl. Lump-sum Taxes and Transfers: Public Debt in the Overlapping-Generations Model. **In** *[Arrow, K. J.], Vol. 2*, 1986, pp. 121–53.

Balcer, Yves and Sadka, Efraim. Equivalence Scales, Horizontal Equity and Optimal Taxation under Utilitarianism. *J. Public Econ.*, February 1986, *29*(1), pp. 79–97.

Baltensperger, Ernst. The Public Debt, Uncertainty, and Government Credibility. *J. Econ. Bus.*, August 1986, *38*(3), pp. 183–92.

Barro, Robert J. Payroll-Tax Financed Social Insurance with Variable Retirement: Comment. *Scand. J. Econ.*, 1986, *88*(1), pp. 55–58.

Barsky, Robert B.; Mankiw, N. Gregory and Zeldes, Stephen P. Ricardian Consumers with Keynesian Propensities. *Amer. Econ. Rev.*, September 1986, *76*(4), pp. 676–91.

Barth, James R.; Iden, George R. and Russek, Frank S. Government Debt, Government Spending, and Private Sector Behavior: Comment. *Amer. Econ. Rev.*, December 1986, *76*(5), pp. 1158–67. **[G: U.S.]**

Barth, James R.; Iden, George R. and Russek, Frank S. The Economic Consequences of Federal Deficits: An Examination of the Net Wealth and Instability Issues. *Southern Econ. J.*, July 1986, *53*(1), pp. 27–50. **[G: U.S.]**

Barth, James R.; Russek, Frank S. and Wang, George H. K. A Time Series Analysis of the Relationship between the Capital Stock and Federal Debt: A Comment. *J. Money, Credit, Banking*, November 1986, *18*(4), pp. 527–38. **[G: U.S.]**

Basevi, Giorgio and Giavazzi, Francesco. Stabilization Policies in an Explosive Economy: Announcements and Expectations. *Europ. Econ. Rev.*, February 1986, *30*(1), pp. 43–55.

Bates, Jim and Gerrie, Dave. Withholding on All Incomes. **In** *Lindholm, R. W., ed.*, 1986, pp. 104–39. **[G: U.S.]**

Batina, Raymond G. The Optimal Linear Income Tax with Tax Credits Contingent on Fertility. *J. Public Econ.*, July 1986, *30*(2), pp. 219–35.

Baumol, William J. The Public-Good Attribute as Independent Justification for Subsidy. **In** *Baumol, W. J.*, 1986, *1977*, pp. 101–10.

Baumol, William J. and Ordover, Janusz A. On the Optimality of Public-Goods Pricing with Exclusionary Devices. **In** *Baumol, W. J.*, 1986, *1977*, pp. 84–100.

Beare, John B. Automatic Stabilizers? *J. Macroecon.*, Winter 1986, *8*(1), pp. 43–54.

Benavie, Arthur and Froyen, Richard I. A Balanced-Budget Constraint in Modern Stochastic Macromodels. *Southern Econ. J.*, July 1986, *53*(1), pp. 247–58.

Bentzel, Ragnar. Payroll-Tax Financed Social Insurance with Variable Retirement: Comment. *Scand. J. Econ.*, 1986, *88*(1), pp. 51–54.

Bergstrom, Theodore; Blume, Lawrence and Varian, Hal. On the Private Provision of Public Goods. *J. Public Econ.*, February 1986, 29(1), pp. 25–49.

Bernheim, B. Douglas. On the Voluntary and Involuntary Provision of Public Goods. *Amer. Econ. Rev.*, September 1986, *76*(4), pp. 789–93.

Bhandari, Jagdeep S. and Hanson, Donald A. Optimal Fiscal Policy in an Open Economy with Time-varying Elasticities. *Southern Econ. J.*, January 1986, *52*(3), pp. 763–76.

Bhatia, Kul B. Taxes, Intermediate Goods, and Relative Prices: The Case of Variable Coefficients. *J. Public Econ.*, November 1986, *31*(2), pp. 197–213.

Blinder, Alan S. Ruminations on Karl Brunner's Reflections [Fiscal Policy in Macro Theory: A Survey and Evaluation]. **In** *Hafer, R. W., ed. (II)*, 1986, pp. 117–26.

Blomquist, N. Sören. Nonlinear Taxes and the Intertemporal Allocation of Hours of Work. **In** *Blundell, R. and Walker, I., eds.*, 1986, pp. 318–34.

Blomqvist, Ake G. The Economics of Price Scissors: Comment. *Amer. Econ. Rev.*, December 1986, *76*(5), pp. 1188–91.

Blundell, Richard, et al. A Labour Supply Model for the Simulation of Tax and Benefit Reforms. **In** *Blundell, R. and Walker, I., eds.*, 1986, pp. 267–93. **[G: U.K.]**

Bohanon, Cecil E. and McClure, James E. Taxes, Welfare Costs, and Public Consumption: The Case of the Unwitting Monopsonist. *Public Choice*, 1986, *49*(3), pp. 235–47.

Bordo, Michael D. and Stuart, Charles. Optimal Inflation and Labor Taxes. *Quart. Rev. Econ. Bus.*, Summer 1986, *26*(2), pp. 6–13.

Bosanquet, Nick. Inconsistencies of the NHS: Buchanan Revisited. **In** *Culyer, A. J. and Jönsson, B., eds.*, 1986, pp. 101–11. **[G: U.K.]**

Bossons, John. Measuring the Viability of Implicit Intergenerational Social Contracts. **In** *Herber, B. P., ed.*, 1986, pp. 265–75.

Bosworth, Barry P. Tax Simplification and Financial Markets: Discussion. **In** *Federal Reserve Bank of Boston*, 1986, pp. 184–86. **[G: U.S.]**

Bourguignon, François. Female Participation and Taxation in France. **In** *Blundell, R. and Walker, I., eds.*, 1986, pp. 243–66. **[G: France]**

Bradford, David F. A Problem of Financial Market Equilibrium When the Timing of Tax Payments Is Indeterminate. **In** *[Arrow, K. J.], Vol. 1*, 1986, pp. 177–88.

Bradley, Michael D. Government Spending or Deficit Financing: Which Causes Crowding Out? *J. Econ. Bus.*, August 1986, *38*(3), pp. 203–14. **[G: U.S.]**

Browning, Edgar K. Reply [Tax Incidence, Indirect Taxes, and Transfers]. *Nat. Tax J.*, December 1986, *39*(4), pp. 541–42.

Brueckner, Jan K. A Modern Analysis of the Effects of Site Value Taxation. *Nat. Tax J.*, March 1986, *39*(1), pp. 49–58.

Brümel, Wolfgang; Pethig, Rüdiger and von dem Hagen, Oskar. The Theory of Public Goods: A Survey of Recent Issues. *J. Inst. Theoretical Econ.*, June 1986, *142*(2), pp. 241–309.

Brunner, Johann K. A Two-Period Model on Optimal Taxation with Learning Incentives. *J. Econ. (Z. Nationalökon.)*, 1986, *46*(1), pp. 31–47.

Brunner, Karl. Fiscal Policy in Macro Theory: A Survey and Evaluation. **In** *Hafer, R. W., ed. (II)*, 1986, pp. 33–116.

Buchanan, James M. Debt, Demos, and the Welfare State. **In** *Buchanan, J. M.*, 1986, pp. 210–21.

Buchanan, James M. Economists on the Deficit. **In** *Buchanan, J. M.*, 1986, pp. 222–26.

Buchanan, James M. Public Debt and Capital Formation. **In** *Lee, D. R., ed.*, 1986, pp. 177–94.

Buchanan, James M. The Ethical Limits of Taxation. **In** *Buchanan, J. M.*, 1986, *1984*, pp. 165–77.

Cabral, Luís M. B. Nota Sobre a Hipótese de Laffer e o Sistema Fiscal Português. (With English summary.) *Economia (Portugal)*, May 1986, *10*(2), pp. 293–300. **[G: Portugal]**

Calmus, Thomas W. Intersecting Tax Concentration Curves and the Measurement of Tax Progressivity: A Comment. *Nat. Tax J.*, March 1986, *39*(1), pp. 119–21.

Caniglia, Alan S. A Common Fallacy about In-Kind Subsidies: A Housing Program Application. *Eastern Econ. J.*, Apr.-June 1986, *12*(2), pp. 149–57.

Caniglia, Alan S. Variable versus Fixed Rate Subsidies: Are the Latter Necessarily Less Efficient? *Public Finance Quart.*, January 1986, *14*(1), pp. 100–106.

Carlton, Dennis W. and Loury, Glenn C. The Limitation of Pigouvian Taxes as a Long-run Remedy for Externalities: An Extension of Results. *Quart. J. Econ.*, August 1986, *101*(3), pp. 631–34.

Carnazza, Paulo. Measuring the Effects of Fiscal Policy: The Case of Italy (1964–1984). *Econ. Notes*, 1986, (1), pp. 98–117. **[G: Italy]**

Carraro, Carlo. Teoria dei giochi e il problema della coordinazione tra politica monetaria e fiscale. (Game Theory and the Coordination of Monetary and Fiscal Policy. With English summary.) *Ricerche Econ.*, Apr.-Sept. 1986, *40*(2–3), pp. 377–99.

Carter, Michael R. The Economics of Price Scissors: Comment. *Amer. Econ. Rev.*, December 1986, *76*(5), pp. 1192–94.

Casarosa, Carlo. Il significato economico del rapporto fra debito pubblico e pil: un'analisi critica. (Meaning of the Ratio Public Data/GPD. With English summary.) *Polit. Econ.*, August 1986, *2*(2), pp. 167–80.

Cassel, Dieter and Cichy, E. Ulrich. Explaining the Growing Shadow Economy in East and West: A Comparative Systems Approach. *Comp. Econ. Stud.*, Spring 1986, *28*(1), pp. 20–41. **[G: OECD; E. Germany; Poland; U.S.S.R.]**

Cauley, Jon; Sandler, Todd and Cornes, Richard. Nonmarket Institutional Structures: Conjectures, Distribution, and Allocative Efficiency. *Public Finance*, 1986, *41*(2), pp. 153–72.

Cavaco Silva, Anibal A. Macroeconomic Impact of Debt Financed Fiscal Deficits: Non-sceptical Considerations. **In** *Herber, B. P., ed.*, 1986, pp. 69–80.

Chamley, Christophe. Optimal Taxation of Capital Income in General Equilibrium with Infinite Lives. *Econometrica*, May 1986, *54*(3), pp. 607–22.

Chang, F. R. and Wildasin, David E. Randomization of Commodity Taxes: An Expenditure Minimization Approach. *J. Public Econ.*, December 1986, *31*(3), pp. 329–45.

Chatterji, Monojit and Junankar, P. N. Agricultural Taxation in Less Developed Countries: Effects of a Tax on Inefficiency. *J. Quant. Econ.*, July 1986, *2*(2), pp. 275–90.

Chiesa, Gabriella. Disavanzo pubblico, cambio reale e trasmissione internazionale. (Public Deficit, Real Exchange and International Transmission. With English summary.) *Polit. Econ.*, April 1986, *2*(1), pp. 121–44.

Chowdhury, Abdur R. A Note on the Dominant Influence of Fiscal Actions. *Eastern Econ. J.*, Jan.-Mar. 1986, *12*(1), pp. 61–62. **[G: India]**

Chowdhury, Abdur R. A Note on the Relative Impact of Monetary and Fiscal Actions in India. *Indian Econ. J.*, July-Sept. 1986, *34*(1), pp. 89–93. **[G: India]**

Chowdhury, Abdur R. Monetary and Fiscal Impacts on Economic Activities in Bangladesh: A Note. *Bangladesh Devel. Stud.*, March 1986, *14*(1), pp. 101–06. **[G: Bangladesh]**

Chowdhury, Abdur R.; Fackler, James S. and McMillin, W. Douglas. Monetary Policy, Fiscal Policy, and Investment Spending: An Empirical Analysis. *Southern Econ. J.*, January 1986, *52*(3), pp. 794–806. **[G: U.S.]**

Cigno, Alessandro. Fertility and the Tax–Benefit System: A Reconsideration of the Theory of Family Taxation. *Econ. J.*, December 1986, *96*(384), pp. 1035–51.

Coleman, James S. Individual Interests and Collective Action. **In** *Coleman, J. S.*, 1986, *1966*, pp. 305–18.

Cordes, Joseph J.; Goldfarb, Robert S. and Watson, Harry S. The Relative Efficiency of Private and Public Transfers. *Public Choice*, 1986, *49*(1), pp. 29–45.

Courant, Paul N. Welfare Effects of Marginal-Cost Taxation of Motor Freight Transportation: A Study of Infrastructure Pricing: Comment. **In** *Rosen, H. S., ed.*, 1986, pp. 128–34. **[G: U.S.]**

Coursey, Don L. and Schulze, William D. The Application of Laboratory Experimental Economics to the Contingent Valuation of Public Goods. *Public Choice*, 1986, *49*(1), pp. 47–68. **[G: U.S.]**

Cuddington, John T. and Viñals, José M. Budget Deficits and the Current Account in the Presence of Classical Unemployment. *Econ. J.*, March 1986, *96*(381), pp. 101–19.

Cuddington, John T. and Viñals, José M. Budget Deficits and the Current Account: An Intertemporal Disequilibrium Approach. *J. Int. Econ.*, August 1986, *21*(1/2), pp. 1–24.

Darrat, Ali F. On the Neutrality of Fiscal Policy. *J. Econ. Bus.*, August 1986, *38*(3), pp. 193–201. **[G: U.K.]**

Darrat, Ali F. The Demand for Money in Some Major OPEC Members: Regression Estimates and Stability Results. *Appl. Econ.*, February 1986, *18*(2), pp. 127–42. **[G: Saudi Arabia; Libya; Nigeria]**

Davies, James B. Does Redistribution Reduce Inequality? *J. Lab. Econ.*, October 1986, *4*(4), pp. 538–59.

Demopoulos, George D.; Katsimbris, George M. and Miller, Stephen M. Ex Ante Crowding Out? A Cross-country Comparison of Direct-Substitutability Hypotheses. *J. Policy Modeling*, Fall 1986, *8*(3), pp. 351–70. **[G: OECD]**

Deravajan, Shantayanan; Fullerton, Don and Musgrave, Richard A. Estimating the Distribution of Tax Burdens: A Comparison of Different Approaches. **In** *Musgrave, R. A., Vol. 1*, 1986, *1980*, pp. 274–300. **[G: U.S.]**

Dewald, William G. Government Deficits in a Generalized Fisherian Credit Market: Theory with an Application to Indexing Interest Taxation. *Int. Monet. Fund Staff Pap.*, June 1986, *33*(2), pp. 243–75.

Diamond, Peter A. and Mirrlees, James A. Payroll-Tax Financed Social Insurance with Variable Retirement. *Scand. J. Econ.*, 1986, *88*(1), pp. 25–50.

Domar, Evsey D. and Musgrave, Richard A. Proportional Income Taxation and Risk-Taking. **In** *Musgrave, R. A., Vol. 1*, 1986, *1944*, pp. 108–31.

Dornbusch, Rudiger; Blanchard, Olivier J. and Buiter, Willem H. Public Debt and Fiscal Responsibility. **In** *Dornbusch, R.*, 1986, pp. 179–204. **[G: U.S.; Europe]**

Due, John F. Tax Incidence, Indirect Taxes, and Transfers—A Comment. *Nat. Tax J.*, December 1986, *39*(4), pp. 539–40.

Dutton, John. Optimal Taxes on Foreign Investment in an Overlapping Generation Model. *Public Finance Quart.*, July 1986, *14*(3), pp. 289–311.

Dwyer, Gerald P., Jr. and Saving, Thomas R. Government Revenue from Money Creation with Government and Private Money. *J. Monet. Econ.*, March 1986, *17*(2), pp. 239–49.

Dye, Ronald A. and Antle, Rick. Cost-Minimizing Welfare Programs. *J. Public Econ.*, July 1986, *30*(2), pp. 259–65.

Eichberger, Jürgen. On the Efficacy of Fiscal Policy. *Ann. Écon. Statist.*, July-Sept. 1986, (3), pp. 151–68.

Epple, Dennis and Spatt, Chester. State Restrictions on Local Debt: Their Role in Preventing Default. *J. Public Econ.*, March 1986, *29*(2), pp. 199–221. **[G: U.S.]**

Erbas, S. Nuri. Inflationary Finance of Budget Deficits as an Automatic Stabilizer. *J. Monet. Econ.*, September 1986, *18*(2), pp. 197–204.

van Ewijk, Casper. Interest Payments and the Stability of the Government Budget Deficit in an Open and Growing Economy. *De Economist*, 1986, *134*(2), pp. 143–64.

Feltenstein, Andrew. An Intertemporal General Equilibrium Analysis of Financial Crowding Out: A Policy Model and an Application to Australia. *J. Public Econ.*, October 1986, *31*(1), pp. 79–104. **[G: Australia]**

Feltenstein, Andrew. Financial Crowding Out: Theory with an Application to Australia. *Int. Monet. Fund Staff Pap.*, March 1986, *33*(1), pp. 60–89. **[G: Australia]**

Findlay, Christopher C. Optimal Taxation of International Income Flows. *Econ. Rec.*, June 1986, *62*(177), pp. 208–14.

Fischer, Stanley. Dynamic Inconsistency, Cooperation, and the Benevolent Dissembling Government. **In** *Fischer, S.*, 1986, *1980*, pp. 413–29.

Fischer, Stanley. Welfare Aspects of Government Issue of Indexed Bonds. **In** *Fischer, S.*, 1986, *1983*, pp. 333–55.

Formby, John P.; Smith, W. James and Sykes, David. Income Redistribution and Local Tax Progressivity: A Reconsideration. *Can. J. Econ.*, November 1986, *19*(4), pp. 807–11.

Formby, John P.; Smith, W. James and Sykes,

David. Intersecting Tax Concentration Curves and the Measurement of Tax Progressivity. *Nat. Tax J.*, March 1986, *39*(1), pp. 115–18.

Frank, Richard G. and Kamlet, Mark S. Quality, Quantity and Total Expenditures on Publicly Provided Goods: The Case of Public Mental Hospitals. *J. Public Econ.*, April 1986, *29*(3), pp. 295–316. **[G: U.S.]**

Frenkel, Jacob A. and Razin, Assaf. Fiscal Policies in the World Economy. *J. Polit. Econ.*, Part 1, June 1986, *94*(3), pp. 564–94.

Frenkel, Jacob A. and Razin, Assaf. Government Spending, Debt, and International Economic Interdependence: Errata. *Econ. J.*, September 1986, *96*(383), pp. 814.

Frenkel, Jacob A. and Razin, Assaf. Real Exchange Rates, Interest Rates and Fiscal Policies. *Econ. Stud. Quart.*, June 1986, *37*(2), pp. 99–113. **[G: U.S.; Japan; Europe]**

Frenkel, Jacob A. and Razin, Assaf. The International Transmission and Effects of Fiscal Policies. *Amer. Econ. Rev.*, May 1986, *76*(2), pp. 330–35. **[G: U.S.; Japan; Europe]**

Funaki, Yukihiko and Kaneko, Mamoru. Economies with Labor Indivisibilities: Part II: Competitive Equilibria under Tax Schedules. *Econ. Stud. Quart.*, September 1986, *37*(3), pp. 199–222.

Funaki, Yukihiko and Kaneko, Mamoru. Economies with Labor Indivisibilities—Part I: Optimal Tax Schedules. *Econ. Stud. Quart.*, March 1986, *37*(1), pp. 11–29.

Gagey, Frédéric; Laroque, Guy and Lollivier, Stefan. Monetary and Fiscal Policies in a General Equilibrium Model. *J. Econ. Theory*, August 1986, *39*(2), pp. 329–57.

Gandenberger, Otto. On Government Borrowing and False Political Feedback. **In** *Herber, B. P., ed.*, 1986, pp. 205–16.

Gang, Ira N. and Khan, Haider. Foreign Aid and Public Expenditures in LDC's. *Atlantic Econ. J.*, September 1986, *14*(3), pp. 56–58. **[G: LDCs]**

García Alba, Pascual. Resultados en imposición indirecta con independencia de los parámetros de demanda: el caso de México. (Results of Indirect Taxation with Independence of Demand Parameters: The Mexican Case. With English summary.) *Estud. Econ.*, January-June 1986, *1*(1), pp. 147–70. **[G: Mexico]**

Garfinkel, Irwin; Moreland, Kemper and Sadka, Efraim. Budget Size Effects on the Optimal Linear Income Tax. *Southern Econ. J.*, July 1986, *53*(1), pp. 187–200.

Gaudet, Gérard and Lasserre, Pierre. Capital Income Taxation, Depletion Allowances, and Nonrenewable Resource Extraction. *J. Public Econ.*, March 1986, *29*(2), pp. 241–53.

Gordon, Robert J. Fiscal Policy in Macro Theory: A Survey and Evaluation: Comment. **In** *Hafer, R. W., ed. (II)*, 1986, pp. 127–36. **[G: U.S.]**

Gordon, Roger H. Taxation of Investment and Savings in a World Economy. *Amer. Econ. Rev.*, December 1986, *76*(5), pp. 1086–1102.

Gordon, Roger H. and Wilson, John D. An Examination of Multijurisdictional Corporate Income Taxation under Formula Apportionment. *Econometrica*, November 1986, *54*(6), pp. 1357–73.

Gottardi, Piero. Risparmio e finanziamento del disavanzo pubblico in un'economia con generazioni sovrapposte. (Saving and Deficit-Financing in an Overlapping Generations Model. With English summary.) *Econ. Polít.*, December 1986, *3*(3), pp. 355–78.

Grandmont, Jean-Michel. Stabilizing Competitive Business Cycles. *J. Econ. Theory*, October 1986, *40*(1), pp. 57–76.

Gravelle, Hugh S. E. Insurance and Corrective Taxes in the Health Care Market. *J. Econ. (Z. Nationalökon.)*, Supplementum 5, 1986, pp. 99–120.

Greene, Leonard M. and Fishbein, Bette K. The VAT Alternative. **In** *Lindholm, R. W., ed.*, 1986, pp. 72–103.

Greenhut, Melvin L. and Norman, George. Spatial Pricing with a General Cost Function; the Effects of Taxes on Imports. *Int. Econ. Rev.*, October 1986, *27*(3), pp. 761–76.

Greenwald, Bruce C. and Stiglitz, Joseph E. Externalities in Economies with Imperfect Information and Incomplete Markets. *Quart. J. Econ.*, May 1986, *101*(2), pp. 229–64.

Gregory, Robin. Interpreting Measures of Economic Loss: Evidence from Contingent Valuation and Experimental Studies. *J. Environ. Econ. Manage.*, December 1986, *13*(4), pp. 325–37.

Guttman, Joel M. Matching Behavior and Collective Action: Some Experimental Evidence. *J. Econ. Behav. Organ.*, June 1986, *7*(2), pp. 171–98.

Gylfason, Thorvaldur and Lindbeck, Assar. Endogenous Unions and Governments: A Game-Theoretic Approach. *Europ. Econ. Rev.*, February 1986, *30*(1), pp. 5–26.

Hamada, Fumimasa. A Macroeconomic Model with the Rate of Unemployment as a Risk Probability under the Government Budget Restraint. *Keio Econ. Stud.*, 1986, *23*(1), pp. 49–62.

Hamada, Koichi. Strategic Aspects of International Fiscal Interdependence. *Econ. Stud. Quart.*, June 1986, *37*(2), pp. 165–80.

Hamilton, Jonathan H. The Flypaper Effect and the Deadweight Loss from Taxation. *J. Urban Econ.*, March 1986, *19*(2), pp. 148–55.

Hatta, Tatsuo. Welfare Effects on Changing Commodity Tax Rates toward Uniformity. *J. Public Econ.*, February 1986, *29*(1), pp. 99–112.

Hatta, Tatsuo and Haltiwanger, John. Tax Reform and Strong Substitutes. *Int. Econ. Rev.*, June 1986, *27*(2), pp. 303–15.

Haugen, Robert A.; Senbet, Lemma W. and Talmor, Eli. Debt, Dividends, and Taxes: Equilibrium Conditions for Simultaneous Tax Neutrality of Debt and Dividend Policies. **In** *Chen, A. H., ed.*, 1986, pp. 1–27. **[G: U.S.]**

Heady, Christopher J. and Mitra, Pradeep K. Optimal Taxation and Public Production in an Open Dual Economy. *J. Public Econ.*, August 1986, *30*(3), pp. 293–316.

Hellwig, Martin. The Optimal Linear Income Tax Revisited. *J. Public Econ.*, November 1986, *31*(2), pp. 163–79.

Hendershott, Patric H. Tax Simplification and Financial Markets. **In** *Federal Reserve Bank of Boston*, 1986, pp. 153–77. **[G: U.S.]**

Hettich, Walter and Winer, Stanley L. Vertical Imbalance in the Fiscal Systems of Federal States. *Can. J. Econ.*, November 1986, *19*(4), pp. 745–65.

Hewett, Roger S. and Stephenson, Susan C. Estimating Tax Interdependence: A Reply [State Tax Revenues under Competition]. *Nat. Tax J.*, June 1986, *39*(2), pp. 249.

Hixson, William F. Keynes's Policies for Financing Recovery from the Great Depression and for Financing World War II. *Écon. Soc.*, Aug.-Sept. 1986, *20*(8–9), pp. 203–17.

Hobson, Paul A. R. The Incidence of Heterogeneous Residential Property Taxes. *J. Public Econ.*, April 1986, *29*(3), pp. 363–73.

Hochman, Harold M. The Charitable Deduction: Comments. **In** *Rose-Ackerman, S., ed.*, 1986, pp. 297–99.

Hochman, Harold M. and Rodgers, James D. The Optimal Tax Treatment of Charitable Contributions. **In** *Rose-Ackerman, S., ed.*, 1986, *1977*, pp. 224–45. **[G: U.S.]**

Honkapohja, Seppo. Intergenerational Aspects of Public Transfers, Borrowing and Debt: Comment. *Scand. J. Econ.*, 1986, *88*(1), pp. 269–72.

Horrigan, Brian R. The Determinants of the Public Debt in the United States, 1953–1978. *Econ. Inquiry*, January 1986, *24*(1), pp. 11–23. **[G: U.S.]**

Huang, Roger D. Does Monitization of Federal Debt Matter? Evidence from the Financial Markets. *J. Money, Credit, Banking*, August 1986, *18*(3), pp. 275–89. **[G: U.S.]**

Jackman, Richard and Layard, Richard. A Wage-Tax, Worker-Subsidy Policy for Reducing the 'Natural' Rate of Unemployment. **In** *Beckerman, W., ed.*, 1986, pp. 153–69.

Jackman, Richard and Layard, Richard. Is TIP Administratively Feasible? **In** *Colander, D. C., ed.*, 1986, pp. 141–48.

Jackman, Richard and Layard, Richard. The Economic Effects of Tax-Based Incomes Policy. **In** *Colander, D. C., ed.*, 1986, pp. 95–109.

Jha, Raghbendra and Murty, M. N. Optimal Non-linear Taxation with Interdependent Utilities. *J. Quant. Econ.*, July 1986, *2*(2), pp. 213–20.

Johnson, David. Are Government Bonds Net Wealth? Intertemporal Optimization and the Government Budget Constraint. *J. Macroecon.*, Fall 1986, *8*(4), pp. 435–53. **[G: Canada]**

Jones, Philip R. and Cullis, John G. Fiscal Preferences: Some Theory for Some Evidence. *Scot. J. Polit. Econ.*, February 1986, *33*(1), pp. 86–92.

Karelis, Charles. Distributive Justice and the Public Good. *Econ. Philos.*, April 1986, *2*(1), pp. 101–25.

Kempf, Hubert. Sur le rôle stabilisateur des politiques monétaires et budgétaires dans un modèle avec anticipations rationnelles et dette publique. (With English summary.) *Revue Écon. Polit.*, Nov.-Dec. 1986, *96*(6), pp. 642–65.

Kessler, Denis; Perelman, Sergio and Pestieau, Pierre. L'hypothèse d'équivalence entre impôt et emprunt: un test sur les pays de l'OCDE. (With English summary.) *Ann. Écon. Statist.*, July-Sept. 1986, (3), pp. 141–49. **[G: OECD]**

Kessler, Denis; Perelman, Sergio and Pestieau, Pierre. Public Debt, Tax, and Consumption: A Test on O.E.C.D. Countries. *Public Finance*, 1986, *41*(1), pp. 63–70. **[G: OECD]**

Kimbrough, Kent P. Foreign Aid and Optimal Fiscal Policy. *Can. J. Econ.*, February 1986, *19*(1), pp. 35–61.

Kimbrough, Kent P. The Optimum Quantity of Money Rule in the Theory of Public Finance. *J. Monet. Econ.*, November 1986, *18*(3), pp. 277–84.

Kindleberger, Charles P. International Public Good without International Government. *Amer. Econ. Rev.*, March 1986, *76*(1), pp. 1–13.

King, Mervyn A. A Pigovian Rule for the Optimum Provision of Public Goods. *J. Public Econ.*, August 1986, *30*(3), pp. 273–91.

Kingston, Geoffrey H. and Layton, Allan P. The Tax Smoothing Hypothesis: Some Australian Empirical Results. *Australian Econ. Pap.*, December 1986, *25*(47), pp. 247–51. **[G: Australia]**

Kirzner, Israel M. Taxes and Discovery: An Entrepreneurial Perspective. **In** *Lee, D. R., ed.*, 1986, pp. 359–80.

Kitterer, Wolfgang. Sind Steuern und Staatsverschuldung äquivalente Instrumente zur Finanzierung der Staatsausgaben? (Are Taxes and Public Debt Equivalent Instruments for Financing Government Expenditures? With English summary.) *Kredit Kapital*, 1986, *19*(2), pp. 271–91. **[G: W. Germany]**

van de Klundert, Theo. C. and Peters, Peter J. Tax Incidence in a Model with Perfect Foresight of Agents and Rationing in Markets. *J. Public Econ.*, June 1986, *30*(1), pp. 37–59.

Koford, Kenneth J. Innovation and Adaptation under Incentive Anti-inflation Plans. *Public Finance*, 1986, *41*(2), pp. 218–31.

Kofuji, Yasuo. Wealth Effects and Fiscal Policy in the Context of a Flexible Price Level. *Public Finance*, 1986, *41*(2), pp. 232–43.

Kohn, Robert E. Optimal Quantity of a Controversial Good or Service. *Public Choice*, 1986, *51*(1), pp. 81–86.

Kohn, Robert E. The Limitations of Pigouvian Taxes as a Long-run Remedy for Externalities: Comment. *Quart. J. Econ.*, August 1986, *101*(3), pp. 625–30.

Kollintzas, Tryphon. Tax Policy under Nongeometric Physical Depreciation. *Public Finance Quart.*, July 1986, *14*(3), pp. 263–88.

Kormendi, Roger C. and Meguire, Philip. Government Debt, Government Spending, and Private Sector Behavior: Reply. *Amer. Econ.*

Rev., December 1986, *76*(5), pp. 1180–87. **[G: U.S.]**

Kovenock, Dan. Property and Income Taxation in an Economy with an Austrian Sector. *Land Econ.*, May 1986, *62*(2), pp. 201–09.

Kreutzer, David and Lee, Dwight R. On Taxation and Understated Monopoly Profits. *Nat. Tax J.*, June 1986, *39*(2), pp. 241–43.

Laffer, Arthur B. The Complete Flat Tax. **In** *Canto, V. A.; Kadlec, C. W. and Laffer, A. B., eds.*, 1986, pp. 108–40. **[G: U.S.]**

Laffer, Arthur B. The Ellipse: An Explication of the Laffer Curve in a Two-Factor Model. **In** *Canto, V. A.; Kadlec, C. W. and Laffer, A. B., eds.*, 1986, pp. 1–35. **[G: U.S.]**

Laffont, Jean-Jacques and Tirole, Jean. Une théorie normative des contrats État-entreprises. (A Normative Theory of State-Firms Contracts. With English summary.) *Ann. Écon. Statist.*, Jan./Mar. 1986, (1), pp. 107–32.

Latham, Roger W. and Naisbitt, Barry. A Note on Progression and Leisure. *Public Finance*, December 1986, *41*(3), pp. 440–46.

Latham, Roger W. and Naisbitt, Barry. Balanced Budget Tax Incidence. *Public Finance*, 1986, *41*(2), pp. 244–59.

Lee, Kye Sik. Pareto Optimal Redistribution: A Public Good Approach. *Public Finance*, 1986, *41*(2), pp. 200–217.

Lemche, S. Q. Benevolent Preferences and Pure Public Goods. *J. Public Econ.*, June 1986, *30*(1), pp. 129–34.

Lemche, S. Q. The Direct Social Preference Relation in the Theory of Public Expenditure. *Soc. Choice Welfare*, June 1986, *3*(1), pp. 51–59.

Lin, Chuan. A General Equilibrium Analysis of Property Tax Incidence. *J. Public Econ.*, February 1986, *29*(1), pp. 113–32.

Lind, Robert C. The Shadow Price of Capital: Implications for the Opportunity Cost of Public Programs, the Burden of the Debt, and Tax Reform. **In** *[Arrow, K. J.], Vol. 1*, 1986, pp. 189–212.

Lindbeck, Assar and Weibull, Jörgen W. Intergenerational Aspects of Public Transfers, Borrowing and Debt. *Scand. J. Econ.*, 1986, *88*(1), pp. 239–67.

Liu, Pak-Wai. Lorenz Domination and Global Tax Progressivity: A Reply [Income Redistribution and Local Tax Progressivity: A Reconsideration]. *Can. J. Econ.*, November 1986, *19*(4), pp. 812–13.

Logan, Robert R. Fiscal Illusion and the Grantor Government. *J. Polit. Econ.*, December 1986, *94*(6), pp. 1304–18.

Lucas, Robert E., Jr. Principles of Fiscal and Monetary Policy. *J. Monet. Econ.*, January 1986, *17*(1), pp. 117–34.

Lund, Diderik. Less Than Single Dividend Taxation: A Note. *J. Public Econ.*, March 1986, *29*(2), pp. 255–61.

Mack, Eric. The Ethics of Taxation: Rights versus Public Goods. **In** *Lee, D. R., ed.*, 1986, pp. 487–514.

Malcomson, James M. Some Analytics of the Laffer Curve. *J. Public Econ.*, April 1986, *29*(3), pp. 263–79.

Malinvaud, Edmond. International Borrowing and Time-Consistent Fiscal Policy: Comment. *Scand. J. Econ.*, 1986, *88*(1), pp. 297–303.

Mankiw, N. Gregory and Summers, Lawrence H. Money Demand and the Effects of Fiscal Policies. *J. Money, Credit, Banking*, November 1986, *18*(4), pp. 415–29.

Marcus, Matityahu; Palmon, Dan and Yaari, Uzi. Growth and the Decision to Incorporate: A Financial Theory of the U.S. Tax System. **In** *Chen, A. H., ed.*, 1986, pp. 29–50. **[G: U.S.]**

Mato Leal, Gonzalo and Ríos Rull, José V. Efectos de los créditos participativos públicos en la financiación de las empresas. (With English summary.) *Invest. Ecón*, January 1986, *10*(1), pp. 173–84.

Mayer, Colin. Corporation Tax, Finance and the Cost of Capital. *Rev. Econ. Stud.*, January 1986, *53*(1), pp. 93–112.

McCaleb, Thomas S. Tax Deductions and Credits, Direct Subsidies, and Efficiency in Public Expenditure. *Public Choice*, 1986, *49*(2), pp. 127–41.

McKenzie, Richard B. Capital Taxation and Industrial Policy. **In** *Lee, D. R., ed.*, 1986, pp. 459–75.

McKenzie, Richard B. Tax/Compensation Schemes: Misleading Advice in a Rent-seeking Society. *Public Choice*, 1986, *48*(2), pp. 189–94.

Mihaljek, Dubravko. Financing of Public Services in Yugoslavia: A Lindahl Equilibrium Model for the Labour-Managed Economy. *Econ. Anal. Workers' Manage.*, 1986, *20*(2), pp. 135–68. **[G: Yugoslavia]**

Mintz, Jack M. and Tulkens, Henry. Commodity Tax Competition between Member States of a Federation: Equilibrium and Efficiency. *J. Public Econ.*, March 1986, *29*(2), pp. 133–72.

Mixon, J. Wilson, Jr. On the Incidence of Excise Taxes on a Monopolist's Price: A Pedagogical Note. *J. Econ. Educ.*, Summer 1986, *17*(3), pp. 201–03.

Modigliani, Franco; Jappelli, Tullio and Pagano, M. Errata corrige [The Impact of Fiscal Policy and Inflation on National Saving: The Italian Case]. *Banca Naz. Lavoro Quart. Rev.*, March 1986, (156), pp. 129. **[G: Italy]**

Modigliani, Franco and Sterling, Arlie. Government Debt, Government Spending and Private Sector Behavior: Comment. *Amer. Econ. Rev.*, December 1986, *76*(5), pp. 1168–79. **[G: U.S.]**

Moene, Karl O. Types of Bureaucratic Interaction. *J. Public Econ.*, April 1986, *29*(3), pp. 333–45.

Montesano, Aldo. Debito pubblico e tasso di inflazione. (Public Debt and Inflation Rate. With English summary.) *Ricerche Econ.*, Apr.-Sept. 1986, *40*(2–3), pp. 400–408.

Moulin, Hervé. Characterizations of the Pivotal Mechanism. *J. Public Econ.*, October 1986, *31*(1), pp. 53–78.

Musgrave, Peggy B. Public Debt and Cost–Benefit Analysis. **In** *Herber, B. P., ed.*, 1986, pp. 81–96.

Musgrave, Richard A. A Further Note on the Double Taxation of Savings. **In** *Musgrave, R. A., Vol. 1*, 1986, *1939*, pp. 105–07.

Musgrave, Richard A. A Multiple Theory of Budget Determination. **In** *Musgrave, R. A., Vol. 1*, 1986, *1957*, pp. 23–33.

Musgrave, Richard A. Alternative Budget Policies for Full Employment. **In** *Musgrave, R. A., Vol. 1*, 1986, *1945*, pp. 336–50.

Musgrave, Richard A. Cost–Benefit Analysis and the Theory of Public Finance. **In** *Musgrave, R. A., Vol. 1*, 1986, *1969*, pp. 59–70.

Musgrave, Richard A. ET, OT and SBT. **In** *Musgrave, R. A., Vol. 1*, 1986, *1976*, pp. 260–73.

Musgrave, Richard A. Fiscal Functions: Order and Politics. **In** *Musgrave, R. A., Vol. 1*, 1986, *1981*, pp. 76–88.

Musgrave, Richard A. Fiscal Policy in Prosperity and Depression. **In** *Musgrave, R. A., Vol. 1*, 1986, *1948*, pp. 359–69.

Musgrave, Richard A. Growth with Equity. **In** *Musgrave, R. A., Vol. 1*, 1986, *1963*, pp. 198–208.

Musgrave, Richard A. In Defence of an Income Concept. **In** *Musgrave, R. A., Vol. 1*, 1986, *1967*, pp. 222–37.

Musgrave, Richard A. On Incidence. **In** *Musgrave, R. A., Vol. 1*, 1986, *1953*, pp. 155–77.

Musgrave, Richard A. Private Labour and Common Land. **In** *Musgrave, R. A., Vol. 2*, 1986, *1983*, pp. 304–18.

Musgrave, Richard A. Provision for Social Goods. **In** *Musgrave, R. A., Vol. 1*, 1986, *1969*, pp. 41–58.

Musgrave, Richard A. Public Debt and Future Generations. **In** *Musgrave, R. A., Vol. 1*, 1986, *1965*, pp. 374–76.

Musgrave, Richard A. Revenue Requirements for Growth. **In** *Musgrave, R. A., Vol. 2*, 1986, *1965*, pp. 125–26.

Musgrave, Richard A. Samuelson on Public Goods. **In** *Musgrave, R. A., Vol. 2*, 1986, *1983*, pp. 319–34.

Musgrave, Richard A. Should We Have a Capital Budget? **In** *Musgrave, R. A., Vol. 1*, 1986, *1963*, pp. 370–73.

Musgrave, Richard A. The Nature of Budgetary Balance and the Case for the Capital Budget. **In** *Musgrave, R. A., Vol. 1*, 1986, *1939*, pp. 319–31.

Musgrave, Richard A. The Nature of Horizontal Equity and the Principle of Broad-Based Taxation: A Friendly Critique. **In** *Musgrave, R. A., Vol. 1*, 1986, *1983*, pp. 301–15.

Musgrave, Richard A. The Voluntary Exchange Theory of Public Economy. **In** *Musgrave, R. A., Vol. 1*, 1986, *1939*, pp. 3–22.

Musgrave, Richard A. Theories of Fiscal Crises: An Essay in Fiscal Sociology. **In** *Musgrave, R. A., Vol. 2*, 1986, *1980*, pp. 175–99. **[G: U.S.]**

Musgrave, Richard A. and Miller, Merton H. Built-in Flexibility. **In** *Musgrave, R. A., Vol. 1*, 1986, *1948*, pp. 351–58.

Musgrave, Richard A. and Musgrave, Peggy B. Inter-nation Equity. **In** *Musgrave, R. A., Vol. 2*, 1986, *1972*, pp. 43–63.

Navajas, Fernando H. Bonos, incentivos gerenciales, eficiencia y control en la empresa pública. (Bonds, Managerial Incentives, Efficiency and Control in the Public Enterprise. With English summary.) *Económica (La Plata)*, Jan.-June 1986, *32*(1), pp. 81–118.

Nicoletti, G. Unsustainability of Public Debt Dynamics and Inflation. *Metroecon.*, June 1986, *38*(2), pp. 181–204.

Okuno, Nobuhiro. Public Investment and Unegalitarian Equilibrium. *Public Finance*, 1986, *41*(2), pp. 260–66.

Parai, Amar K. Tax Incidence in an Open Economy with Unemployment of Labor. *Atlantic Econ. J.*, September 1986, *14*(3), pp. 84.

Park, Wankyu. A Theoretical Analysis of the Efficient Provision of a Public Good. *J. Econ. Devel.*, July 1986, *11*(1), pp. 191–209.

Pasour, E. C., Jr. Monopoly Power, Taxation, and Entrepreneurship. **In** *Lee, D. R., ed.*, 1986, pp. 381–405.

Pauwels, Wilfried. Correct and Incorrect Measures of the Deadweight Loss of Taxation. *Public Finance*, 1986, *41*(2), pp. 267–76.

Peck, Richard M. Power and Linear Income Taxes: An Example. *Econometrica*, January 1986, *54*(1), pp. 87–94.

Penati, Alessandro. Budget Deficit, External Official Borrowing, and Sterilized Intervention Policy in Foreign Exchange Markets. *J. Int. Money Finance*, March 1986, *5*(1), pp. 99–113.

Persson, Torsten and Svensson, Lars E. O. International Borrowing and Time-Consistent Fiscal Policy. *Scand. J. Econ.*, 1986, *88*(1), pp. 273–95.

Pfingsten, Andreas. Distributionally-Neutral Tax Changes for Different Inequality Concepts ['Linear' Income Tax Cuts: Distributional Effects, Social Preferences, and Revenue Elasticities]. *J. Public Econ.*, August 1986, *30*(3), pp. 385–93.

Phelps, Edmund S. Profits Theory and Profits Taxation. *Int. Monet. Fund Staff Pap.*, December 1986, *33*(4), pp. 674–96. **[G: OECD]**

Phelps, Edmund S. The Significance of Customer Markets for the Effects of Budgetary Policy in Open Economies. *Ann. Écon. Statist.*, July-Sept. 1986, (3), pp. 101–17.

Philpotts, Geoffrey. Public Good Benefit Attribution. *Public Finance Quart.*, July 1986, *14*(3), pp. 313–28.

Pissarides, Christopher A. Equilibrium Effects of Tax-Based Incomes Policies. **In** *Colander, D. C., ed.*, 1986, pp. 111–27.

Plant, Jeremy F. Charles E. Lindblom's "Decision-Making in Taxation and Expenditures." *Public Budg. Finance*, Summer 1986, *6*(2), pp. 76–86.

van der Ploeg, Frederick. The Effects of a Tax and Incomes Policy on Government Finance, Employment and Capital Formation. *De Economist*, 1986, *134*(3), pp. 269–88.

Plotnick, Robert D. Redistribution to the Poor:

An Overheard Conversation. *Public Finance Quart.*, April 1986, *14*(2), pp. 223–28.

Plummer, Mark L. Supply Uncertainty, Option Price, and Option Value: An Extension. *Land Econ.*, August 1986, *62*(3), pp. 313–18.

Pointon, J. UK Taxation and Financial Decision Making. **In** *Firth, M. and Keane, S. M., eds.*, 1986, pp. 182–92. **[G: U.K.]**

Pöll, Günther. On the Graphical Analysis of the Ramsey-Problem. *Public Finance*, 1986, *41*(1), pp. 71–77.

Posnett, John and Sandler, Todd. Joint Supply and the Finance of Charitable Activity. *Public Finance Quart.*, April 1986, *14*(2), pp. 209–22. **[G: U.K.]**

Poterba, James M.; Rotemberg, Julio J. and Summers, Lawrence H. A Tax-Based Test for Nominal Rigidities. *Amer. Econ. Rev.*, September 1986, *76*(4), pp. 659–75. **[G: U.S.; U.K.]**

Quigley, John M. and Rubinfeld, Daniel L. Budget Reform and the Theory of Fiscal Federalism. *Amer. Econ. Rev.*, May 1986, *76*(2), pp. 132–37.

Quintieri, Beniamino and Rosati, Furio Camillo. Changes in Tax Structure and Individual Behaviour. *Econ. Notes*, 1986, (3), pp. 30–46.

Raga, José T. Public Debt, Margin of Financial Intermediation and the Rates of Interest: Is There Any Link? **In** *Herber, B. P., ed.*, 1986, pp. 167–79.

Ramirez, Miguel D. The Composition of Government Spending as an Additional Policy Instrument. *J. Econ. Bus.*, August 1986, *38*(3), pp. 215–25.

Rankin, N. Debt Policy under Fixed and Flexible Prices. *Oxford Econ. Pap.*, November 1986, *38*(3), pp. 481–500.

Rapanos, Vassilis. Variable Returns to Scale and Tax Incidence: An Extension of Harberger's Model. *J. Econ. (Z. Nationalökon.)*, 1986, *46*(4), pp. 397–406.

Ray, Ranjan. Redistribution through Commodity Taxes: The Nonlinear Engel Curve Case. *Public Finance*, 1986, *41*(2), pp. 277–84. **[G: India]**

Reinganum, Jennifer F. and Wilde, Louis L. Equilibrium Verification and Reporting Policies in a Model of Tax Compliance. *Int. Econ. Rev.*, October 1986, *27*(3), pp. 739–60.

Revesz, John T. On Some Advantages of Progressive Indirect Taxation. *Public Finance*, 1986, *41*(2), pp. 182–99.

Ring, Raymond J., Jr. Tax Interdependence and the Importance of Using a Correctly Specified Estimating Equation [State Tax Revenues under Competition]. *Nat. Tax J.*, June 1986, *39*(2), pp. 245–48. **[G: U.S.]**

Rob, Rafael. The Demand Revealing Mechanism. **In** *Samuelson, L., ed.*, 1986, pp. 121–38.

Rogers, Carol Ann. The Effect of Distributive Goals on the Time Inconsistency of Optimal Taxes. *J. Monet. Econ.*, March 1986, *17*(2), pp. 251–69.

Rose-Ackerman, Susan. Do Government Grants to Charity Reduce Private Donations? **In** *Rose-Ackerman, S., ed.*, 1986, *1981*, pp. 313–29.

Rose-Ackerman, Susan. Unfair Competition and Corporate Income Taxation. **In** *Rose-Ackerman, S., ed.*, 1986, *1982*, pp. 394–414.

Roskamp, Karl W. Optimal Life Time Consumption Paths under Income and Property Taxes: Effects of Tax Structure Changes. *Public Finance*, 1986, *41*(1), pp. 1–7.

Sah, Raaj Kumar and Stiglitz, Joseph E. The Economics of Price Scissors: Reply. *Amer. Econ. Rev.*, December 1986, *76*(5), pp. 1195–99.

Salant, Walter S. A Critical Look at Supply-Side Theory and a Brief Look at Some of Its International Aspects. **In** *[Tarshis, L.]*, 1986, pp. 108–24.

Samuelson, Paul A. A Chapter in the History of Ramsey's Optimal Feasible Taxation and Optimal Public Utility Prices. **In** *Samuelson, P. A.*, 1986, *1982*, pp. 76–100.

Samuelson, Paul A. Theory of Optimal Taxation. *J. Public Econ.*, July 1986, *30*(2), pp. 137–43.

Sargent, Thomas J. Interpreting the Reagan Deficits. *Fed. Res. Bank San Francisco Econ. Rev.*, Fall 1986, (4), pp. 5–12. **[G: U.S.]**

Sarkar, Hiren and Panda, Manoj Kumar. Quantity–Price–Money Interaction in a CGE Model with Applications to Fiscal Policy. *Margin*, April 1986, *18*(3), pp. 31–52. **[G: India]**

Scafuri, Allen J. Measurable Welfare Change with Optimal Commodity Taxation [Optimal Taxation, the Compensation Principle and the Measurement of Changes in Economic Welfare]. *J. Public Econ.*, April 1986, *29*(3), pp. 383–87.

Schokkaert, Erik and Van Rompuy, Victor. Intergenerational Distribution of the Burden of Debt: The Case of Belgium. **In** *Herber, B. P., ed.*, 1986, pp. 255–64. **[G: Belgium]**

Schweizer, Urs. Suburbanisierung als Folge fiskalischer Inäquivalenz. (Suburbanisation Caused by Fiscal Inequivalence. With English summary.) *Schweiz. Z. Volkswirtsch. Statist.*, March 1986, *122*(1), pp. 1–15.

Scotchmer, Suzanne. Local Public Goods in an Equilibrium: How Pecuniary Externalities Matter. *Reg. Sci. Urban Econ.*, November 1986, *16*(4), pp. 463–81.

Seidman, Laurence S. Why an Incentive Anti-inflation Plan Should Be Implemented. **In** *Colander, D. C., ed.*, 1986, pp. 201–07. **[G: U.S.]**

Sgontz, L. G. and Pogue, Thomas F. Non-monetary Returns to Human Capital: Implications for Inter-temporal Tax Neutrality. *Nat. Tax J.*, June 1986, *39*(2), pp. 201–09.

Shibata, Hirofumi and Kimura, Yoko. Are Budget Deficits the Cause of Growth in Government Expenditures? **In** *Herber, B. P., ed.*, 1986, pp. 229–42. **[G: U.S.; Japan]**

Shieh, Yeung-Nan. Wealth Effects, Treasury Bill Financing, Perpetuity Financing, and Stability. *J. Public Econ.*, August 1986, *30*(3), pp. 395–98.

Shome, Parthasarathi. Empirical Evidence on the Incidence of the Corporate Income Tax. **In**

Shome, P., ed., 1986, pp. 93–113. [G: ASEAN]

Singh, Balvir and Sahni, Balbir S. Patterns and Directions of Causality between Government Expenditure and National Income in the United States. *J. Quant. Econ.*, July 1986, *2*(2), pp. 291–308. [G: U.S.]

Singh, Nirvikar and Thomas, Ravi. User Charges as a Delegation Mechanism. *Nat. Tax J.*, March 1986, *39*(1), pp. 109–13.

Sinn, Hans-Werner. Sufficient Conditions for a Vanishing Clarke Tax—A Note. *J. Econ. (Z. Nationalökon.)*, 1986, *46*(1), pp. 65–72.

Slade, Margaret E. Taxation of Non-renewable Resources at Various Stages of Production. *Can. J. Econ.*, May 1986, *19*(2), pp. 281–97.

Small, Kenneth A. and Winston, Clifford. Welfare Effects of Marginal-Cost Taxation of Motor Freight Transportation: A Study of Infrastructure Pricing. **In** *Rosen, H. S., ed.*, 1986, pp. 113–28. [G: U.S.]

Sørensen, Peter Birch. Taxation, Inflation, and Asset Accumulation in a Small Open Economy. *Europ. Econ. Rev.*, October 1986, *30*(5), pp. 1025–41.

Steedman, Ian. Produced Inputs and Tax Incidence Theory. *Public Finance*, December 1986, *41*(3), pp. 331–49.

Stern, Nicholas. A Note on Commodity Taxation: The Choice of Variable and the Slutsky, Hessian and Antonelli Matrices (SHAM). *Rev. Econ. Stud.*, April 1986, *53*(2), pp. 293–99.

Stewart, Marion B. U.S. Tax Policy, Intrafirm Transfers, and the Allocative Efficiency of Transnational Corporations. *Public Finance*, December 1986, *41*(3), pp. 350–71. [G: U.S.]

Stiglitz, Joseph E. Financial Markets and Macroeconomic Fluctuations: Comment. **In** *Butkiewicz, J. L.; Koford, K. J. and Miller, J. B., eds.*, 1986, pp. 144–45.

Strnad, Jeff. The Charitable Contribution Deduction: A Politico-Economic Analysis. **In** *Rose-Ackerman, S., ed.*, 1986, pp. 265–96.

Suits, Daniel B. and Musgrave, Richard A. *Ad Valorem* and Unit Taxes Compared. **In** *Musgrave, R. A., Vol. 1*, 1986, *1953*, pp. 191–97.

Svensson, Lars-Gunnar. National Income and Marginal Taxes. *Scand. J. Econ.*, 1986, *88*(4), pp. 565–81.

Svensson, Lars-Gunnar. Taxation of Savings. *J. Econ. (Z. Nationalökon.)*, 1986, *46*(4), pp. 421–26.

Svensson, Lars-Gunnar and Weibull, Jörgen W. An Upper Bound on Optimal Income Taxes. *J. Public Econ.*, July 1986, *30*(2), pp. 165–81.

Tabellini, Guido. Money, Debt and Deficits in a Dynamic Game. *J. Econ. Dynam. Control*, December 1986, *10*(4), pp. 427–42.

Taub, Bart. The Tradeoff between Social Insurance and Aggregate Fluctuations. *Info. Econ. Policy*, December 1986, *2*(4), pp. 259–76.

Tesfatsion, Leigh. Time Inconsistency of Benevolent Government Economies. *J. Public Econ.*, October 1986, *31*(1), pp. 25–52.

Throsby, C. D. and Withers, Glenn A. Strategic Bias and Demand for Public Goods: Theory and an Application to the Arts. *J. Public Econ.*, December 1986, *31*(3), pp. 307–27. [G: Australia]

Tobin, James. On the Welfare Macroeconomics of Government Financial Policy. *Scand. J. Econ.*, 1986, *88*(1), pp. 9–24.

Tobin, James. Tax Simplification and Financial Markets: Discussion. **In** *Federal Reserve Bank of Boston*, 1986, pp. 178–83. [G: U.S.]

Toma, Eugenia Froedge and Toma, Mark. A Congressional Control Model of Treasury Revenue Collection. *Southern Econ. J.*, July 1986, *53*(1), pp. 141–54. [G: U.S.]

Toumanoff, Peter. Exclusion Costs and the In-Kind Transfer. *Kyklos*, 1986, *39*(3), pp. 443–47.

Tullock, Gordon. Reasons for Redistribution. **In** *Tullock, G.*, 1986, *1981*, pp. 15–41.

Tuomala, Matti. On the Optimal Income Taxation and Educational Decisions. *J. Public Econ.*, July 1986, *30*(2), pp. 183–98.

Turnbull, Geoffrey Keith and Niho, Yoshio. The Optimal Property Tax with Mobile Nonresidential Capital. *J. Public Econ.*, March 1986, *29*(2), pp. 223–39.

Turnovsky, Stephen J. Monetary and Fiscal Policy under Perfect Foresight: A Symmetric Two-country Analysis. *Economica*, May 1986, *53*(210), pp. 139–57.

Usher, Dan. Police, Punishment, and Public Goods. *Public Finance*, 1986, *41*(1), pp. 96–115.

Usher, Dan. Tax Evasion and the Marginal Cost of Public Funds. *Econ. Inquiry*, October 1986, *24*(4), pp. 563–86.

Vanberg, Viktor and Buchanan, James M. Organization Theory and Fiscal Economics: Society, State, and Public Debt. *J. Law, Econ., Organ.*, Fall 1986, *2*(2), pp. 215–27.

Vedder, Richard. Tithing for Leviathan: The Case for a True Flat-Rate Tax. **In** *Lee, D. R., ed.*, 1986, pp. 141–69. [G: U.S.]

Venables, Anthony J. Production Subsidies, Import Tariffs, and Imperfectly Competitive Trade. **In** *Greenaway, D. and Tharakan, P. K. M., eds.*, 1986, pp. 68–87.

Vickrey, William. Budget-Smudget. Why Balance What, How, and When? *Atlantic Econ. J.*, September 1986, *14*(3), pp. 6–13. [G: U.S.]

Vickrey, William. Design of a Market Anti-inflation Program. **In** *Colander, D. C., ed.*, 1986, pp. 149–58.

Wagner, Richard E. The Welfare State, Capital Formation, and Tax-Transfer Politics. **In** *Lee, D. R., ed.*, 1986, pp. 241–73. [G: U.S.]

Waud, Roger N. Tax Aversion and the Laffer Curve. *Scot. J. Polit. Econ.*, August 1986, *33*(3), pp. 213–27.

Wenzel, H.-Dieter. Öffentliche Kreditaufnahme und Öffentliche Investitionen im Wachstumsgleichgewicht. (Deficit Spending, Public Investment and Growth Equilibrium. With English summary.) *Kredit Kapital*, 1986, *19*(4), pp. 496–521.

Weymark, John A. A Reduced-Form Optimal

Nonlinear Income Tax Problem. *J. Public Econ.*, July 1986, *30*(2), pp. 199–217.

Weymark, John A. Bunching Properties of Optimal Nonlinear Income Taxes. *Soc. Choice Welfare*, 1986, *3*(3), pp. 213–32.

Wickström, Bengt-Arne. Transfers, Collective Goods, and Redistribution. *J. Econ. (Z. Nationalökon.)*, Supplementum 5, 1986, pp. 243–58.

van Wijnbergen, Sweder J. G. On Fiscal Deficits, the Real Exchange Rate and the World Rate of Interest. *Europ. Econ. Rev.*, October 1986, *30*(5), pp. 1013–23.

Yoshida, Masatoshi. Public Investment Criterion in an Overlapping Generations Economy. *Economica*, May 1986, *53*(210), pp. 247–63.

Yunker, James A. A Supply Side Analysis of the Laffer Hypothesis. *Public Finance*, December 1986, *41*(3), pp. 372–92.

Zodrow, George R. Implementing Tax Reform: The Intergenerational Carryover Problem. *Nat. Tax J.*, December 1986, *39*(4), pp. 419–33.

Zodrow, George R. and Mieszkowski, Peter M. Pigou, Tiebout, Property Taxation, and the Underprovision of Local Public Goods. *J. Urban Econ.*, May 1986, *19*(3), pp. 356–70.

Zodrow, George R. and Mieszkowski, Peter M. The New View of the Property Tax: A Reformulation. *Reg. Sci. Urban Econ.*, August 1986, *16*(3), pp. 309–27.

3216 Fiscal Policy

Aaron, Henry J. Rationale Underlying the Treasury Proposals: Discussion. **In** *Federal Reserve Bank of Boston*, 1986, pp. 49–54. **[G: U.S.]**

Ahmad, Ehtisham and Stern, Nicholas. Tax Reform for Pakistan: Overview and Effective Taxes for 1975–76. *Pakistan Devel. Rev.*, Spring 1986, *25*(1), pp. 43–72. **[G: Pakistan]**

Alhadeff, Peter. The Economic Formulae of the 1930s: A Reassessment. **In** *di Tella, G. and Platt, D. C. M., eds.*, 1986, pp. 95–119. **[G: Argentina]**

Auerbach, Alan J. Tax Reform and Capital Formation: Discussion. **In** *Federal Reserve Bank of Boston*, 1986, pp. 145–48. **[G: U.S.]**

Blanchard, Olivier J. and Dornbusch, Rudiger. U.S. Deficits, the Dollar, and Europe. **In** *Blanchard, O.; Dornbusch, R. and Layard, R., eds.*, 1986, pp. 155–79. **[G: U.S.; W. Europe]**

Blanchard, Olivier J.; Dornbusch, Rudiger and Buiter, Willem. Public Debt and Fiscal Responsibility. **In** *Blanchard, O.; Dornbusch, R. and Layard, R., eds.*, 1986, pp. 125–53. **[G: EEC]**

Blejer, Mario I. and Cheasty, Adrienne. Budgetary Policy and the Mobilization of Domestic Financial Resources. **In** *U.N., Dept. of Tech. Co-op. for Devel., Devel. Admin. Div.*, 1986, pp. 83–98.

Blejer, Mario I. and Cheasty, Adrienne. Using Fiscal Measures to Stimulate Savings in Developing Countries. *Finance Develop.*, June 1986, *23*(2), pp. 16–19. **[G: LDCs]**

Blinder, Alan S. The Effect of Tax Simplification on Individuals: Discussion. **In** *Federal Reserve Bank of Boston*, 1986, pp. 92–98. **[G: U.S.]**

Bluestone, Barry and Havens, John. How to Cut the Deficit and Rebuild America. *Challenge*, May/June 1986, *29*(2), pp. 22–29. **[G: U.S.]**

Bluestone, Barry and Havens, John. The Microeconomic Impacts of Macroeconomic Fiscal Policy, 1981–85. *J. Post Keynesian Econ.*, Summer 1986, *8*(4), pp. 499–514. **[G: U.S.]**

Boadway, Robin W. Sales Tax Reform Options and the BTT. **In** *Boadway, R. W. and Mintz, J. M., eds.*, 1986, pp. 14–23. **[G: Canada]**

Boadway, Robin W. and Mintz, Jack M. The Business Transfer Tax: An Overview of the Issues. **In** *Boadway, R. W. and Mintz, J. M., eds.*, 1986, pp. 1–7. **[G: U.S.; Canada]**

Bosi, Paolo. Modelli macroeconometrici e valutazione della politica fiscale in Italia. (Econometric Models and the Evaluation of Fiscal Policy in Italy. With English summary.) *Polit. Econ.*, April 1986, *2*(1), pp. 3–43. **[G: Italy]**

Boskin, Michael J. Taxation and the Deficit Economy: Fiscal Policy and Capital Formation in the United States: Foreword. **In** *Lee, D. R., ed.*, 1986, pp. xxi–xxvii. **[G: U.S.]**

Bosworth, Barry P. Savings and Government Policy. **In** *Adams, F. G. and Wachter, S. M., eds.*, 1986, pp. 173–87. **[G: U.S.; Japan]**

Bosworth, Barry P. Tax Simplification and Financial Markets: Discussion. **In** *Federal Reserve Bank of Boston*, 1986, pp. 184–86. **[G: U.S.]**

Bradford, David F. Policy Forum on the Business Transfer Tax: Wrap-Up. **In** *Boadway, R. W. and Mintz, J. M., eds.*, 1986, pp. 62–68.

Bradford, David F. The Effect of Tax Simplification on Individuals: Discussion. **In** *Federal Reserve Bank of Boston*, 1986, pp. 99–102. **[G: U.S.]**

Bradley, Michael D. and Potter, Susan M. The State of the Federal Budget and the State of the Economy: Further Evidence. *Econ. Inquiry*, January 1986, *24*(1), pp. 143–53. **[G: U.S.]**

Brean, Donald J. S. and Bird, Richard M. Fiscal Risk of State-Owned Enterprise. **In** *Herber, B. P., ed.*, 1986, pp. 333–42. **[G: LDCs; MDCs]**

Britton, Andrew. Can Fiscal Expansion Cut Unemployment? *Nat. Inst. Econ. Rev.*, February 1986, (115), pp. 83–99. **[G: U.K.]**

Buckley, Robert M. and Schnare, Ann B. The Uncertain and Variable Costs of Efficiency Gains. **In** *Follain, J. R., ed.*, 1986, pp. 187–204. **[G: U.S.]**

Burdekin, Richard C. K. Fiscal Pressure and Central Bank Policy Objectives. *Fed. Res. Bank Dallas Econ. Rev.*, May 1986, pp. 1–9. **[G: U.S.]**

Cagan, Phillip. Essays in Contemporary Economic Problems, 1986: The Impact of the Reagan Program: Introduction. **In** *Cagan, P., ed.*, 1986, pp. 1–5. **[G: U.S.]**

Canlas, Dante B. Some Preliminary Evidence on the Short-Run Aggregate Demand Effects of Fiscal Policy. *Philippine Rev. Econ. Bus.*,

Mar./June 1986, *23*(1/2), pp. 143–50. **[G: Philippines]**

Carliner, Michael S. The Impact of Tax Reform on Housing Demand and Residential Construction Activity. **In** *Follain, J. R., ed.*, 1986, pp. 113–33. **[G: U.S.]**

Chand, Sheetal K. European Experiences with Tax-Based Income Policies. **In** *Colander, D. C., ed.*, 1986, pp. 211–22. **[G: W. Europe]**

Chernick, Howard and Reschovsky, Andrew. Effects of the Reagan Proposal in Massachusetts and New York. **In** *Gold, S. D., ed.*, 1986, pp. 143–59. **[G: U.S.]**

Clotfelter, Charles T. The Effect of Tax Simplification on Educational and Charitable Organizations. **In** *Federal Reserve Bank of Boston*, 1986, pp. 187–215. **[G: U.S.]**

Currie, David and Hall, Stephen G. The Exchange Rate and the Balance of Payments. *Nat. Inst. Econ. Rev.*, February 1986, (115), pp. 74–82. **[G: U.K.]**

Darrat, Ali F. Fiscal Impulse and the Real Economy. *Public Finance*, December 1986, *41*(3), pp. 316–30. **[G: W. Germany]**

David, Paul A. Technology Diffusion, Public Policy, and Industrial Competitiveness. **In** *Landau, R. and Rosenberg, N., eds.*, 1986, pp. 373–91.

Davies, James B. Equity and Efficiency Aspects of a Business Transfer Tax. **In** *Boadway, R. W. and Mintz, J. M., eds.*, 1986, pp. 31–41. **[G: Canada]**

Davis, Albert. Implications of Federal Reform for State and Local Governments. **In** *Gold, S. D., ed.*, 1986, pp. 161–75. **[G: U.S.]**

Diokno, Benjamin E. Revenue Mobilization and Responsiveness of Philippine Income Taxes: Implications for Fiscal Policy. *Philippine Rev. Econ. Bus.*, Sept.-Dec. 1986, *23*(3–4), pp. 323–39. **[G: Philippines]**

Dornbusch, Rudiger. Sound Currency and Full Employment. **In** *Dornbusch, R.*, 1986, *1985*, pp. 205–31. **[G: U.K.]**

Dornbusch, Rudiger, et al. Macroeconomic Prospects and Policies for the European Community. **In** *Blanchard, O.; Dornbusch, R. and Layard, R., eds.*, 1986, pp. 1–32. **[G: EEC]**

Easson, Alex. Designing a Business Transfer Tax: Some Basic Considerations. **In** *Boadway, R. W. and Mintz, J. M., eds.*, 1986, pp. 42–46. **[G: Canada]**

Eisner, Robert. Tax Reform and Capital Formation: Discussion. **In** *Federal Reserve Bank of Boston*, 1986, pp. 149–52. **[G: U.S.]**

Ekelund, Robert B., Jr. and Thornton, Mark. Schumpeterian Analysis, Supply-Side Economics and Macroeconomic Policy in the 1920s. *Rev. Soc. Econ.*, December 1986, *44*(3), pp. 221–37. **[G: U.S.]**

Even-Shoshan, Orit and Gabbay, Yoram. Distribution of Family Income and Taxes. **In** *Kop, Y., ed.*, 1986, pp. 169–98. **[G: Israel]**

Feldstein, Martin S. U.S. Budget Deficits and the European Economies: Resolving the Political Economy Puzzle. *Amer. Econ. Rev.*, May 1986, *76*(2), pp. 342–46. **[G: U.S.; W. Europe]**

Follain, James R. The Impact of the President's Proposals and H.R. 3838 on the Housing Market. **In** *Follain, J. R., ed.*, 1986, pp. 61–85. **[G: U.S.]**

Follain, James R. What Are the Issues and What Is at Stake? **In** *Follain, J. R., ed.*, 1986, pp. 3–8. **[G: U.S.]**

Follain, James R. and Brueckner, Jan K. Federal Income Taxation and Real Estate: Tax Distortions and Their Impacts. **In** *Follain, J. R., ed.*, 1986, pp. 9–25. **[G: U.S.]**

Fox, Alan, et al. The Effects of Tax Reform on Metropolitan Housing. **In** *Follain, J. R., ed.*, 1986, pp. 165–85. **[G: U.S.]**

von Furstenberg, George M. and Green, R. Jeffrey. Supply-Side Modeling from Bits and Pieces. *Amer. Econ. Rev.*, May 1986, *76*(2), pp. 37–42. **[G: U.S.]**

Gabbay, Yoram. Fiscal Policy. **In** *Kop, Y., ed.*, 1986, pp. 147–58. **[G: Israel]**

Gandhi, Ved P. Effects of Tax Incentives on Investment and Employment. **In** *Shome, P., ed.*, 1986, pp. 27–42.

Gensler, Howard. Complexity, Verbosity, and Progressivity. **In** *Lindholm, R. W., ed.*, 1986, pp. 50–71. **[G: U.S.]**

Gold, Steven D. Themes of Federal Tax Reform for State Tax Policy. **In** *Gold, S. D., ed.*, 1986, pp. 177–83. **[G: U.S.]**

Gramlich, Edward M. The Effect of Tax Simplification on State and Local Governments: Discussion. **In** *Federal Reserve Bank of Boston*, 1986, pp. 252–58. **[G: U.S.]**

Greenaway, David and Tharakan, P. K. Mathew. Imperfect Competition, Adjustment Policy, and Commercial Policy. **In** *Greenaway, D. and Tharakan, P. K. M., eds.*, 1986, pp. 7–33.

Guenther, Robert. Tax Reform and Its Role in the Emerging Dual Market for Housing. **In** *Follain, J. R., ed.*, 1986, pp. 233–36. **[G: U.S.]**

Guest, James. Macroeconomic Stabilization Policy with Special Reference to Fiscal Policy. **In** *Cole, R. V. and Parry, T. G., eds.*, 1986, pp. 71–110. **[G: S. Pacific]**

Hall, Robert E. Liquidity Constraints, Fiscal Policy, and Consumption: Comments. *Brookings Pap. Econ. Act.*, 1986, (1), pp. 51–53. **[G: U.S.]**

Hatsopoulos, George N. Tax Reform and Capital Formation: Discussion. **In** *Federal Reserve Bank of Boston*, 1986, pp. 140–44. **[G: U.S.]**

Heclo, Hugh. Industrial Policy and the Executive Capacities of Government. **In** *Barfield, C. E. and Schambra, W. A., eds.*, 1986, pp. 292–317. **[G: U.S.]**

Hendershott, Patric H. Tax Reform, Interest Rates, and Capital Allocation. **In** *Follain, J. R., ed.*, 1986, pp. 27–57. **[G: U.S.]**

Hendershott, Patric H. Tax Simplification and Financial Markets. **In** *Federal Reserve Bank of Boston*, 1986, pp. 153–77. **[G: U.S.]**

Hendershott, Patric H. and Ling, David C. Likely Impacts of the Administration's Tax Proposals and H.R. 3838. **In** *Follain, J. R., ed.*, 1986, pp. 87–112. **[G: U.S.]**

Hubbard, R. Glenn and Judd, Kenneth L. Liquidity Constraints, Fiscal Policy, and Consumption. *Brookings Pap. Econ. Act.*, 1986, (1), pp. 1–50. **[G: U.S.]**

Ishi, Hiromitsu. Overview of Fiscal Deficits in Japan with Special Reference to the Fiscal Policy Debate. *Hitotsubashi J. Econ.*, December 1986, *27*(2), pp. 133–48. **[G: Japan]**

Jenkins, Glenn. The Evolution of Sales Tax Reform in Canada. **In** *Boadway, R. W. and Mintz, J. M., eds.*, 1986, pp. 9–13. **[G: Canada]**

Joines, Douglas H. Government Deficits and the Fiscal Policy Debate. **In** *Canto, V. A.; Kadlec, C. W. and Laffer, A. B., eds.*, 1986, pp. 87–107. **[G: U.S.]**

Jorgenson, Dale W. and Yun, Kun-Young. Tax Policy and Capital Allocation. *Scand. J. Econ.*, 1986, *88*(2), pp. 355–77. **[G: U.S.]**

Jungenfelt, Karl G. Comment [The Efficiency of Capital Allocation] [Tax Policy and Capital Allocation]. *Scand. J. Econ.*, 1986, *88*(2), pp. 379–82. **[G: U.S.]**

Kopcke, Richard W. Tax Reform and Capital Formation. **In** *Federal Reserve Bank of Boston*, 1986, pp. 103–39. **[G: U.S.]**

Laffer, Arthur B. The Ellipse: An Explication of the Laffer Curve in a Two-Factor Model. **In** *Canto, V. A.; Kadlec, C. W. and Laffer, A. B., eds.*, 1986, pp. 1–35. **[G: U.S.]**

Lee, Dwight R. Taxation and the Deficit Economy: Fiscal Policy and Capital Formation in the United States: Introduction. **In** *Lee, D. R., ed.*, 1986, pp. 1–15. **[G: U.S.]**

Levin, Henry M. Are Block Grants the Answer to the Federal Role in Education? **In** *Cohn, E., ed.*, 1986, pp. 261–69. **[G: U.S.]**

Mair, Douglas. Industrial De-rating: Panacea or Palliative? *Scot. J. Polit. Econ.*, May 1986, *33*(2), pp. 159–70. **[G: U.K.]**

Makin, John H. Savings Rates in Japan and the United States: The Roles of Tax Policy and Other Factors. **In** *Adams, F. G. and Wachter, S. M., eds.*, 1986, pp. 91–126. **[G: OECD]**

Masson, Paul R. and Knight, Malcolm D. International Transmission of Fiscal Policies in Major Industrial Countries. *Int. Monet. Fund Staff Pap.*, September 1986, *33*(3), pp. 387–438. **[G: U.S.; W. Germany; Japan]**

Mauer, Jay. The President's 1985 Tax Reform Proposal: An Economic Assessment. **In** *Lindholm, R. W., ed.*, 1986, pp. 230–50. **[G: U.S.]**

McKenna, William F. Tax Reform Must Consider the Realities of Housing. **In** *Follain, J. R., ed.*, 1986, pp. 213–17. **[G: U.S.]**

McLure, Charles E., Jr. Rationale Underlying the Treasury Proposals. **In** *Federal Reserve Bank of Boston*, 1986, pp. 29–48. **[G: U.S.]**

McLure, Charles E., Jr. The Tax Treatment of Owner-Occupied Housing: The Achilles' Heel of Tax Reform? **In** *Follain, J. R., ed.*, 1986, pp. 219–32. **[G: U.S.]**

Melck, Antony. On Subsidizing Education with Block Grants. **In** *Cohn, E., ed.*, 1986, *1985*, pp. 253–59. **[G: U.S.]**

Merrick, John J., Jr. and Saunders, Anthony. International Expected Real Interest Rates: New Tests of the Parity Hypothesis and U.S. Fiscal Policy Effects. *J. Monet. Econ.*, November 1986, *18*(3), pp. 313–22. **[G: OECD]**

Mikesell, John L. Federal Individual Income Tax Collection Costs: The Burden of Compliance and Administration. **In** *Lindholm, R. W., ed.*, 1986, pp. 33–49. **[G: U.S.]**

Mills, Edwin S. and Rosen, Harvey S. Tax Reform and Commercial Real Estate. **In** *Follain, J. R., ed.*, 1986, pp. 151–61. **[G: U.S.]**

Mintz, Jack M. Issues Arising from the Design of the BTT. **In** *Boadway, R. W. and Mintz, J. M., eds.*, 1986, pp. 49–61.

Moffitt, Robert. Work Incentives in Transfer Programs (Revisited): A Study of the AFDC Program. **In** *Ehrenberg, R. G., ed., Pt. B*, 1986, pp. 389–439. **[G: U.S.]**

Munnell, Alicia H. Economic Consequences of Tax Simplification: An Overview. **In** *Federal Reserve Bank of Boston*, 1986, pp. 1–28. **[G: U.S.]**

Musgrave, Richard A. Economic Consequences of Tax Simplification: An Overall Assessment—Is It Worth It? **In** *Federal Reserve Bank of Boston*, 1986, pp. 259–84. **[G: U.S.]**

Musgrave, Richard A. Effects of Business Taxes on International Commodity Flows. **In** *Musgrave, R. A., Vol. 1*, 1986, *1966*, pp. 209–21. **[G: France; U.K.; U.S.; W. Germany; Italy]**

Musgrave, Richard A. How Progressive Is the Income Tax? **In** *Musgrave, R. A., Vol. 1*, 1986, *1959*, pp. 178–90. **[G: U.S.]**

Musgrave, Richard A. Pathway to Tax Reform. **In** *Musgrave, R. A., Vol. 2*, 1986, *1984*, pp. 335–37. **[G: U.S.]**

Musgrave, Richard A. The Role of Social Insurance in an Overall Programme for Social Welfare. **In** *Musgrave, R. A., Vol. 2*, 1986, *1967*, pp. 67–81. **[G: U.S.]**

Musgrave, Richard A.; Case, Karl E. and Leonard, Herman B. The Distribution of Fiscal Burdens and Benefits. **In** *Musgrave, R. A., Vol. 1*, 1986, *1974*, pp. 238–59. **[G: U.S.]**

Musgrave, Richard A. and Gillis, Malcolm. Objectives: Report of Colombia Tax Mission. **In** *Musgrave, R. A., Vol. 2*, 1986, *1971*, pp. 149–57. **[G: Colombia]**

Musgrave, Richard A. and Thin, Tun. Income Tax Progression, 1929–48. **In** *Musgrave, R. A., Vol. 1*, 1986, *1948*, pp. 132–54. **[G: U.S.]**

Netzer, Dick. The Effect of Tax Simplification on State and Local Governments. **In** *Federal Reserve Bank of Boston*, 1986, pp. 222–51. **[G: U.S.]**

Pavitt, Keith L. R. Determinants of Innovative Activity. **In** *Landau, R. and Rosenberg, N., eds.*, 1986, pp. 393–97.

Pechman, Joseph A. Economic Consequences of Tax Simplification: An Overall Assessment—Is It Worth It? Discussion. **In** *Federal Reserve Bank of Boston*, 1986, pp. 285–89. **[G: U.S.]**

Perry, David. Designing a Business Transfer Tax:

Some Basic Considerations: Comment. **In** *Boadway, R. W. and Mintz, J. M., eds.*, 1986, pp. 47–48. **[G: Canada]**

Poole, William. Fiscal and Monetary Policy Overkills. **In** *Shadow Open Market Committee (I)*, 1986, pp. 19–30. **[G: U.S.]**

Roberts, Paul Craig. Problems with Monetary Policy. *Bus. Econ.*, October 1986, *21*(4), pp. 16–20. **[G: U.S.]**

Roberts, Paul Craig. The Revolution in U.S. Tax Policy. *Nat. Westminster Bank Quart. Rev.*, November 1986, pp. 2–7. **[G: U.S.]**

Sack, Paul. Winners and Losers in Commercial Real Estate from the President's Proposals. **In** *Follain, J. R., ed.*, 1986, pp. 137–49. **[G: U.S.]**

Samuelson, Paul A. That Constitutional Budget Amendment—'Tremendous Potential for Harm.' **In** *Samuelson, P. A.*, 1986, *1979*, pp. 1005–08.

Samuelson, Paul A. The U.S. Fiscal Crisis of the 1980s. **In** *Samuelson, P. A.*, 1986, *1984*, pp. 909–20.

Seiders, David F. Should Tax Laws Be Used to Stimulate Investment in Housing? **In** *Follain, J. R., ed.*, 1986, pp. 207–12. **[G: U.S.]**

Shome, Parthasarathi. Effects of Tax Incentives on Investment and Employment: Appendix: The Broad Goals of Tax Incentives. **In** *Shome, P., ed.*, 1986, pp. 43–47. **[G: Thailand; Malaysia; Philippines]**

Shoven, John B. Rationale Underlying the Treasury Proposals: Discussion. **In** *Federal Reserve Bank of Boston*, 1986, pp. 55–59. **[G: U.S.]**

Silkman, Richard H. Old Federalism and New Federalism in New York State. **In** *Schoolman, M. and Magid, A., eds.*, 1986, pp. 331–55. **[G: U.S.]**

Slemrod, Joel. The Effect of Tax Simplification on Individuals. **In** *Federal Reserve Bank of Boston*, 1986, pp. 64–91. **[G: U.S.]**

Soofi, Abdollah S. and Parvin, Kumars. The Import Leakage Effect and the Effectiveness of Fiscal Policy: An Input–Output Analysis. *Public Finance*, December 1986, *41*(3), pp. 430–39. **[G: Iran]**

Spigler, I. Public Finance. **In** *Kaser, M. C. and Radice, E. A., eds.*, 1986, pp. 117–69. **[G: E. Europe]**

Steuerle, C. Eugene. The Effect of Tax Simplification on Educational and Charitable Organizations: Discussion. **In** *Federal Reserve Bank of Boston*, 1986, pp. 216–21. **[G: U.S.]**

Summers, Lawrence H. Economic Consequences of Tax Simplification: An Overall Assessment—Is It Worth It? Discussion. **In** *Federal Reserve Bank of Boston*, 1986, pp. 290–94. **[G: U.S.]**

Summers, Lawrence H. Liquidity Constraints, Fiscal Policy, and Consumption: Comments. *Brookings Pap. Econ. Act.*, 1986, (1), pp. 53–57. **[G: U.S.]**

Sunley, Emil M. Rationale Underlying the Treasury Proposals: Discussion. **In** *Federal Reserve Bank of Boston*, 1986, pp. 60–63. **[G: U.S.]**

Tanzi, Vito. Fiscal Policy Responses to Exogenous Shocks in Developing Countries. *Amer. Econ. Rev.*, May 1986, *76*(2), pp. 88–91. **[G: LDCs]**

Thorson, Douglas Y. The Growth and Failure of the Income Tax. **In** *Lindholm, R. W., ed.*, 1986, pp. 1–32. **[G: U.S.]**

Tobin, James. Tax Simplification and Financial Markets: Discussion. **In** *Federal Reserve Bank of Boston*, 1986, pp. 178–83. **[G: U.S.]**

Wiseman, Jack. Public Debt and Public Policy: An Evaluation of Recent History. **In** *Herber, B. P., ed.*, 1986, pp. 243–53.

322 National Government Expenditures and Budgeting

3220 General

Beard, Thomas R. and McMillin, W. Douglas. Government Budgets and Money: How Are They Related? *J. Econ. Educ.*, Spring 1986, *17*(2), pp. 107–19. **[G: U.S.]**

Berglas, Eitan. Taxes and Transfers in an Inflationary Decade. **In** *Ben-Porath, Y., ed.*, 1986, pp. 221–38. **[G: Israel]**

Bernholz, Peter. Growth of Government, Economic Growth and Individual Freedom. *J. Inst. Theoretical Econ.*, December 1986, *142*(4), pp. 661–83. **[G: OECD]**

Boskin, Michael J. Macroeconomics, Technology, and Economic Growth: An Introduction to Some Important Issues. **In** *Landau, R. and Rosenberg, N., eds.*, 1986, pp. 33–56. **[G: U.S.]**

Boskin, Michael J., et al. New Estimates of the Value of Federal Mineral Rights and Land: Erratum. *Amer. Econ. Rev.*, September 1986, *76*(4), pp. 859. **[G: U.S.]**

Bruno, Michael and Fischer, Stanley. The Inflationary Process: Shocks and Accommodation. **In** *Ben-Porath, Y., ed.*, 1986, pp. 347–71. **[G: Israel]**

Buchanan, James M. The Moral Dimension of Debt Financing. **In** *Buchanan, J. M.*, 1986, *1985*, pp. 189–94.

Der Hovanessian, Aida. Economic Forces Affecting the Middle East. **In** *Roukis, G. S. and Montana, P. J., eds.*, 1986, pp. 47–70. **[G: OPEC]**

Forbes, Kevin F.; Korsun, George and McGuire, Martin C. Defense, Growth, and Allocation Behavior in the Alliance: The Southern Tier of NATO. **In** *Denoon, D. B. H., ed.*, 1986, pp. 114–51. **[G: Greece; Turkey; Spain; Portugal]**

Hakim, Leonardo and Wallich, Christine. OECD Deficits, Debt, and Savings Structure and Trends, 1965–81: A Survey of the Evidence. **In** *Lal, D. and Wolf, M., eds.*, 1986, pp. 292–360. **[G: OECD]**

Heclo, Hugh. Industrial Policy and the Executive Capacities of Government. **In** *Barfield, C. E. and Schambra, W. A., eds.*, 1986, pp. 292–317. **[G: U.S.]**

Levitt, M. S. and Joyce, M. A. S. Government Output in the National Accounts. *Nat. Inst.*

Econ. Rev., February 1986, (115), pp. 48–51. **[G: U.K.]**

Marlow, Michael L. Private Sector Shrinkage and the Growth of Industrialized Economies. *Public Choice*, 1986, *49*(2), pp. 143–54. **[G: OECD]**

Mera, Koichi. Population Stabilization and National Spatial Policy of Public Investment: The Japanese Experience. *Int. Reg. Sci. Rev.*, April 1986, *10*(1), pp. 47–65. **[G: Japan]**

Musgrave, Richard A. A Multiple Theory of Budget Determination. **In** *Musgrave, R. A., Vol. 1*, 1986, *1957*, pp. 23–33.

Pfouts, Ralph W. Is the Outlook for the U.S. Economy Even Murkier Than Usual? *Atlantic Econ. J.*, September 1986, *14*(3), pp. 1–5. **[G: U.S.]**

Pliatzky, Leo. Can Government Be Efficient? *Lloyds Bank Rev.*, January 1986, (159), pp. 22–32. **[G: U.K.]**

Ram, Rati. Causality between Income and Government Expenditure: A Broad International Perspective. *Public Finance*, December 1986, *41*(3), pp. 393–414. **[G: Global]**

Ram, Rati. Government Size and Economic Growth: A New Framework and Some Evidence from Cross-Section and Time-Series Data. *Amer. Econ. Rev.*, March 1986, *76*(1), pp. 191–203.

Riech, Utz P. Treatment of Government Activity on the Production Account. *Rev. Income Wealth*, March 1986, *32*(1), pp. 69–85. **[G: OECD]**

Sandler, Todd and Murdoch, James C. Defense Burdens and Prospects for the Northern European Allies. **In** *Denoon, D. B. H., ed.*, 1986, pp. 59–113. **[G: W. Europe]**

Sjaastad, Larry A.; Almansi, Aquiles and Hurtado, Carlos. The Debt Crisis in Latin America. **In** *Lal, D. and Wolf, M., eds.*, 1986, pp. 131–81. **[G: Argentina; Brazil; Chile; Mexico; Venezuela]**

Spigler, I. Public Finance. **In** *Kaser, M. C. and Radice, E. A., eds.*, 1986, pp. 117–69. **[G: E. Europe]**

Stewart, Ian A. Consensus, Flexibility and Equity. *Can. Public Policy*, June 1986, *12*(2), pp. 307–13. **[G: Canada]**

Tavitian, M. Robert. Politiques sociales et interdépendance économique. Les dangers da la notion de contrainte extérieure. (The Impact of Economic Interdependence on Social Policies—Constraints or Opportunities. With English summary.) *Écon. Soc.*, January 1986, *20*(1), pp. 45–68. **[G: W. Europe]**

Thimmaiah, G. India: Long-term Fiscal Policy—A Critique. *Bull. Int. Fiscal Doc.*, June 1986, *40*(6), pp. 231–34. **[G: India]**

3221 National Government Expenditures

Abrams, Burton A. and Dougan, William R. The Effects of Constitutional Restraints on Government Spending. *Public Choice*, 1986, *49*(2), pp. 101–16. **[G: U.S.]**

Abrams, Burton A. and Schmitz, Mark D. The Crowding-out Effect of Governmental Transfers on Private Charitable Contributions. **In** *Rose-Ackerman, S., ed.*, 1986, *1978*, pp. 303–12. **[G: U.S.]**

Allardt, Erik. The Civic Conception of the Welfare State in Scandinavia. **In** *Rose, R. and Shiratori, R., eds.*, 1986, pp. 107–25. **[G: Scandinavia]**

Anderson, William; Wallace, Myles S. and Warner, John T. Government Spending and Taxation: What Causes What? *Southern Econ. J.*, January 1986, *52*(3), pp. 630–39. **[G: U.S.]**

Bach, George Leland and Musgrave, Richard A. A Stable Purchasing Power Bond. **In** *Musgrave, R. A., Vol. 1*, 1986, *1941*, pp. 332–35.

Blackley, Paul R. Causality between Revenues and Expenditures and the Size of the Federal Budget. *Public Finance Quart.*, April 1986, *14*(2), pp. 139–56. **[G: U.S.]**

Brooks, Harvey. National Science Policy and Technological Innovation. **In** *Landau, R. and Rosenberg, N., eds.*, 1986, pp. 119–67. **[G: U.S.; U.K.; Japan; France; W. Germany]**

Castells, Antoni. Una nota sobre la descentralización del gasto público entre los distintos niveles de gobierno en España. (With English summary.) *Invest. Ecón.*, September 1986, *10*(3), pp. 529–43. **[G: OECD]**

Chiancone, Aldo. On the Contents of Public Finance in the Soviet Union. *Ricerche Econ.*, Apr.-Sept. 1986, *40*(2–3), pp. 463–77. **[G: U.S.S.R.]**

Douglas, William E. Evolution of Electronic Payments and Collections in the U.S. Government. *J. Bank Res.*, 1986, *16*(4), pp. 206–08. **[G: U.S.]**

van't Eind, Gerrit Jan, et al. Evaluating the Distribution of Public Expenditure. *Rev. Income Wealth*, September 1986, *32*(3), pp. 299–312. **[G: Netherlands]**

von Furstenberg, George M.; Green, R. Jeffrey and Jeong, Jin-Ho. Tax and Spend, or Spend and Tax? *Rev. Econ. Statist.*, May 1986, *68*(2), pp. 179–88. **[G: U.S.]**

Galenson, Walter and Galenson, David W. Constraints on Strategy: The Economics of Western Security: Japan and South Korea. **In** *Denoon, D. B. H., ed.*, 1986, pp. 152–94. **[G: U.S.; Japan; S. Korea; W. Germany]**

Gerchunoff, Pablo. Gasto pblico, tasa de cambio e impulso capitalista después de la hiperinflación. (With English summary.) *Desarrollo Econ.*, Jan.-Mar. 1986, *25*(100), pp. 623–57. **[G: Germany; Hungary; Argentina]**

Gifford, Adam, Jr. and Kenney, Roy W. On Nationalizing Private Property and the Present Value of Dictators: Reply [Socialism and the Revenue Maximizing Leviathan]. *Public Choice*, 1986, *48*(1), pp. 89–91.

Glazer, Nathan. Welfare and "Welfare" in America. **In** *Rose, R. and Shiratori, R., eds.*, 1986, pp. 40–63. **[G: U.S.]**

Hauner, M. Military Budgets and the Armaments Industry. **In** *Kaser, M. C. and Radice, E. A., eds.*, 1986, pp. 49–116. **[G: E. Europe; Germany]**

Heller, Peter S. and Hemming, Richard. Aging and Social Expenditure in Major Industrial Countries. *Finance Develop.*, December 1986, *23*(4), pp. 18–21. **[G: OECD]**

Jefferson, Edward G. Tax Policy for the Eighties. **In** *Landau, R. and Jorgenson, D. W., eds.*, 1986, pp. 75–84. **[G: U.S.]**

Joines, Douglas H. Government Spending, Tax Rates, and Private Investment in Plant and Equipment. **In** *Canto, V. A.; Kadlec, C. W. and Laffer, A. B., eds.*, 1986, pp. 36–53. **[G: U.S.]**

Kavalsky, Basil. Reviewing Public Investment Programs. *Finance Develop.*, March 1986, *23*(1), pp. 37–40.

Kop, Yaakov; Blankett, Joel and Sharon, Dalit. Government Expenditure on Social Services. **In** *Kop, Y., ed.*, 1986, pp. 1–107. **[G: Israel]**

Laband, David N. The Private Interest in Public Redistribution: A Public Choice View of the Geographic Distribution of Federal Funds. *Public Choice*, 1986, *49*(2), pp. 117–25.

Landau, Daniel. Government and Economic Growth in the Less Developed Countries: An Empirical Study for 1960–1980. *Econ. Develop. Cult. Change*, October 1986, *35*(1), pp. 35–75. **[G: LDCs]**

Leontief, Wassily and Hoffenberg, Marvin. The Economic Effects of Disarmament. **In** *Leontief, W.*, 1986, *1961*, pp. 188–203. **[G: U.S.]**

Levy, Mickey D. A Positive Trend in the Federal Budget Outlook. **In** *Shadow Open Market Committee (I)*, 1986, pp. 31–42. **[G: U.S.]**

Lin, Winston T. Modeling and Forecasting U.S. Public Construction. *Int. J. Forecasting*, 1986, *2*(3), pp. 319–31. **[G: U.S.]**

Lluch, Constantino. ICORS, Savings Rates, and the Determinants of Public Expenditure in Developing Countries. **In** *Lal, D. and Wolf, M., eds.*, 1986, pp. 361–95. **[G: LDCs]**

Lott, John R., Jr. and Reiffen, David. On Nationalizing Private Property and the Present Value of Dictators. *Public Choice*, 1986, *48*(1), pp. 81–87. **[G: E. Europe]**

Lowery, David; Brunn, Stanley D. and Webster, Gerald. From Stable Disparity to Dynamic Equity: The Spatial Distribution of Federal Expenditures, 1971–1983. *Soc. Sci. Quart.*, March 1986, *67*(1), pp. 98–107. **[G: U.S.]**

Maddison, Angus. Marx and Bismarck: Capitalism and Government 1883–1983. **In** *Wagener, H.-J. and Drukker, J. W., eds.*, 1986, pp. 196–213. **[G: OECD]**

Malpas, Robert. Harnessing Technology for Growth. **In** *Landau, R. and Rosenberg, N., eds.*, 1986, pp. 105–13. **[G: OECD]**

Manage, Neela and Marlow, Michael L. The Causal Relation between Federal Expenditures and Receipts. *Southern Econ. J.*, January 1986, *52*(3), pp. 617–29. **[G: U.S.]**

Mann, Arthur J. and Schulthess, Walter E. Long-run Expenditure Constraints in Argentina. *Public Finance Quart.*, January 1986, *14*(1), pp. 28–47. **[G: Argentina]**

Marnata, Françoise and Sarrazin, Chantal. Les pays nordiques: protection sociale et contrainte extérieure. (Nordic Countries: Social Welfare and External Constraint. With English summary.) *Écon. Soc.*, January 1986, *20*(1), pp. 211–34. **[G: Denmark; Sweden; Norway; Finland]**

Musgrave, Richard A. Expenditure Policy for Development. **In** *Musgrave, R. A., Vol. 2*, 1986, *1974*, pp. 158–72. **[G: Latin America]**

Musgrave, Richard A. Theories of Fiscal Crises: An Essay in Fiscal Sociology. **In** *Musgrave, R. A., Vol. 2*, 1986, *1980*, pp. 175–99. **[G: U.S.]**

Musgrave, Richard A.; Heller, Peter S. and Peterson, George E. Cost-Effectiveness of Alternative Income Maintenance Schemes. **In** *Musgrave, R. A., Vol. 2*, 1986, *1970*, pp. 82–102. **[G: U.S.]**

Nadiri, M. Ishaq. Increase in Defense Expenditure and Its Impact on the U.S. Economy. **In** *Denoon, D. B. H., ed.*, 1986, pp. 27–58. **[G: U.S.]**

Noguchi, Yukio. Overcommitment in Pensions: The Japanese Experience. **In** *Rose, R. and Shiratori, R., eds.*, 1986, pp. 173–92. **[G: Japan]**

Ofer, Gur. National Expenditure on Education and Health. **In** *Kop, Y., ed.*, 1986, pp. 111–34. **[G: Israel]**

Ofer, Gur. Public Spending on Civilian Services. **In** *Ben-Porath, Y., ed.*, 1986, pp. 192–208. **[G: Israel]**

Rose-Ackerman, Susan. Do Government Grants to Charity Reduce Private Donations? **In** *Rose-Ackerman, S., ed.*, 1986, *1981*, pp. 313–29.

Rose, Richard. Common Goals but Different Roles: The State's Contribution to the Welfare Mix. **In** *Rose, R. and Shiratori, R., eds.*, 1986, pp. 13–39. **[G: OECD]**

Ryan, James E. Defense Procurement and the Reindustrialization of New York State. **In** *Schoolman, M. and Magid, A., eds.*, 1986, pp. 315–29. **[G: U.S.]**

Schick, Allen. Controlling Nonconventional Expenditure: Tax Expenditures and Loans. *Public Budg. Finance*, Spring 1986, *6*(1), pp. 3–19. **[G: OECD]**

Schick, Allen. The Evolution of Congressional Budgeting. **In** *Schick, A., et al.*, 1986, pp. 3–54. **[G: U.S.]**

Shibata, Hirofumi and Kimura, Yoko. Are Budget Deficits the Cause of Growth in Government Expenditures? **In** *Herber, B. P., ed.*, 1986, pp. 229–42. **[G: U.S.; Japan]**

Simon, Owen. Investing in the Infrastructure. *Nat. Westminster Bank Quart. Rev.*, May 1986, pp. 2–16. **[G: U.K.]**

Singh, Balvir and Sahni, Balbir S. Patterns and Directions of Causality between Government Expenditure and National Income in the United States. *J. Quant. Econ.*, July 1986, *2*(2), pp. 291–308. **[G: U.S.]**

Wakefield, Joseph C. Federal Fiscal Programs. *Surv. Curr. Bus.*, February 1986, *66*(2), pp. 26–31. **[G: U.S.]**

Weicher, John C. The Reagan Domestic Budget Cuts: Proposals, Outcomes, and Effects. **In** *Ca-*

gan, P., ed., 1986, pp. 7–44. **[G: U.S.]**

Zapf, Wolfgang. Development, Structure, and Prospects of the German Social State. **In** *Rose, R. and Shiratori, R., eds.*, 1986, pp. 126–55. **[G: W. Germany]**

3226 National Government Budgeting and Deficits

Afxentiou, Panayiotis C. Wagner's Law: The Experience of Cyprus. *Econ. Notes*, 1986, (2), pp. 158–72. **[G: Cyprus]**

Bailey, Martin J. The Behavior of United States Deficits: Comment. **In** *Gordon, R. J., ed.*, 1986, pp. 387–89. **[G: U.S.]**

Barro, Robert J. The Behavior of United States Deficits. **In** *Gordon, R. J., ed.*, 1986, pp. 361–87. **[G: U.S.]**

Barro, Robert J. U.S. Deficits since World War I. *Scand. J. Econ.*, 1986, *88*(1), pp. 195–22. **[G: U.S.]**

Barth, James R.; Iden, George R. and Russek, Frank S. The Economic Consequences of Federal Deficits: An Examination of the Net Wealth and Instability Issues. *Southern Econ. J.*, July 1986, *53*(1), pp. 27–50. **[G: U.S.]**

Barth, James R.; Russek, Frank S. and Wang, George H. K. A Time Series Analysis of the Relationship between the Capital Stock and Federal Debt: A Comment. *J. Money, Credit, Banking*, November 1986, *18*(4), pp. 527–38. **[G: U.S.]**

Bennett, James T. and DiLorenzo, Thomas J. Credit Allocation and Capital Formation: The Political Economy of Indirect Taxation. **In** *Lee, D. R., ed.*, 1986, pp. 275–96. **[G: U.S.]**

Bispham, John. Growing Public-Sector Debt: A Policy Dilemma. *Nat. Westminster Bank Quart. Rev.*, May 1986, pp. 52–67. **[G: OECD]**

Blackley, Paul R. Causality between Revenues and Expenditures and the Size of the Federal Budget. *Public Finance Quart.*, April 1986, *14*(2), pp. 139–56. **[G: U.S.]**

Blanchard, Olivier J. and Dornbusch, Rudiger. U.S. Deficits, the Dollar, and Europe. **In** *Blanchard, O.; Dornbusch, R. and Layard, R., eds.*, 1986, pp. 155–79. **[G: U.S.; W. Europe]**

Blanchard, Olivier J.; Dornbusch, Rudiger and Buiter, Willem. Public Debt and Fiscal Responsibility. **In** *Blanchard, O.; Dornbusch, R. and Layard, R., eds.*, 1986, pp. 125–53. **[G: EEC]**

Blanchard, Olivier J. and Summers, Lawrence H. Pourquoi les taux d'intérêts sont-ils aussi élevés. (Perspectives on High World Real Interest Rates. With English summary.) *Ann. Écon. Statist.*, July-Sept. 1986, (3), pp. 53–100. **[G: OECD]**

Blandy, Richard and Kain, Peter. The Australian Labour Market, September 1986. *Australian Bull. Lab.*, September 1986, *12*(4), pp. 199–220. **[G: Australia]**

Bluestone, Barry and Havens, John. How to Cut the Deficit and Rebuild America. *Challenge*, May/June 1986, *29*(2), pp. 22–29. **[G: U.S.]**

Bootle, Roger. Budget Strategy and the Exchange Rate. *Fisc. Stud.*, May 1986, *7*(2), pp. 1–10. **[G: U.K.]**

Boskin, Michael J. Budgets, Deficits, Technology and Economic Growth. **In** *Landau, R. and Jorgenson, D. W., eds.*, 1986, pp. 191–204. **[G: U.S.]**

Boskin, Michael J. Taxation and the Deficit Economy: Fiscal Policy and Capital Formation in the United States: Foreword. **In** *Lee, D. R., ed.*, 1986, pp. xxi–xxvii. **[G: U.S.]**

Bossons, John. Measuring the Viability of Implicit Intergenerational Social Contracts. **In** *Herber, B. P., ed.*, 1986, pp. 265–75.

Brean, Donald J. S. and Bird, Richard M. Fiscal Risk of State-Owned Enterprise. **In** *Herber, B. P., ed.*, 1986, pp. 333–42. **[G: LDCs; MDCs]**

Britton, Andrew. The Budget and Unemployment. *Fisc. Stud.*, May 1986, *7*(2), pp. 11–20. **[G: U.K.]**

Brunner, Karl. Deficits, Interest Rates, and Monetary Policy. *Cato J.*, Winter 1986, *5*(3), pp. 709–26. **[G: U.S.]**

Bryson, Phillip J. and Perry, Philip J. *Sozialpolitik:* East German Social Welfare Policies. *Comp. Econ. Stud.*, Summer 1986, *28*(2), pp. 1–20. **[G: E. Germany]**

Buchanan, James M. Economists on the Deficit. **In** *Buchanan, J. M.*, 1986, pp. 222–26.

Budd, Alan P. The 1986 Budget and Macroeconomic Policy. *Fisc. Stud.*, May 1986, *7*(2), pp. 21–32. **[G: U.K.]**

Canto, Victor A. and Rapp, Donald. The "Crowding Out" Myth. **In** *Canto, V. A.; Kadlec, C. W. and Laffer, A. B., eds.*, 1986, pp. 75–86. **[G: U.S.]**

Canziani, Arnaldo. Di alcuni effetti dei deficit pubblici. (On the General Consequences of Uninterrupted Public Deficits. With English summary.) *Ricerche Econ.*, Apr.-Sept. 1986, *40*(2–3), pp. 409–30. **[G: Italy]**

Cavaco Silva, Anibal A. Macroeconomic Impact of Debt Financed Fiscal Deficits: Non-sceptical Considerations. **In** *Herber, B. P., ed.*, 1986, pp. 69–80.

Chiancone, Aldo. On the Contents of Public Finance in the Soviet Union. *Ricerche Econ.*, Apr.-Sept. 1986, *40*(2–3), pp. 463–77. **[G: U.S.S.R.]**

Cox-George, N. A. The Budget as a Tool for the Mobilization of Domestic Resources for Capital Formation. **In** *Association of African Central Banks*, 1986, pp. 111–22.

Cox, W. Michael. Government Debt and the Stock Market. *Fed. Res. Bank Dallas Econ. Rev.*, September 1986, pp. 1–9.

De Ionna, Paolo. Governo e amministrazione nel processo di bilancio: Linee evolutive. (Government and Bureaucracy in the Italian Budgetary System. With English summary.) *Polit. Econ.*, April 1986, *2*(1), pp. 145–63. **[G: Italy]**

Dean, Peter N. Performance Budgeting in Sri Lanka. *Public Budg. Finance*, Summer 1986, *6*(2), pp. 63–75. **[G: Sri Lanka]**

Dewald, William G. Real Budget Deficit Implications of Gramm–Rudman–Hollings. *Fed. Res. Bank Richmond Econ. Rev.*, Mar./Apr. 1986, *72*(2), pp. 33–34. **[G: U.S.]**

Diller, Klaus Dieter. Die mittelfristigen Zinserwartungen des Bundes. (Medium Term Interest Rate Expectation of the Federal Government. With English summary.) *Kredit Kapital*, 1986, *19*(4), pp. 522–39. **[G: W. Germany]**

Dixon, Daryl A. Suggested Refinements of the Treasury Costings of the Occupational Superannuation Tax Expenditures. *Australian Tax Forum*, 1986, *3*(2), pp. 223–32. **[G: Australia]**

Dornbusch, Rudiger. Overborrowing: Three Case Studies. **In** *Dornbusch, R.*, 1986, *1985*, pp. 97–130. **[G: Chile; Brazil; Argentina]**

Dornbusch, Rudiger. The Budget Deficit and the Dollar: Comment. **In** *Fischer, S., ed.*, 1986, pp. 393–402. **[G: U.S.; W. Germany; Japan]**

Dornbusch, Rudiger; Blanchard, Olivier J. and Buiter, Willem H. Public Debt and Fiscal Responsibility. **In** *Dornbusch, R.*, 1986, pp. 179–204. **[G: U.S.; Europe]**

Eisner, Robert. Real vs. Nominal Debt. *Challenge*, Nov./Dec. 1986, *29*(5), pp. 58. **[G: U.S.]**

Eisner, Robert. The Real Federal Deficit: What It Is, How It Matters, and What It Should Be. *Quart. Rev. Econ. Bus.*, Winter 1986, *26*(4), pp. 6–21. **[G: U.S.]**

Eisner, Robert. Will the Real Federal Deficit Stand Up? *Challenge*, May/June 1986, *29*(2), pp. 13–21. **[G: U.S.]**

Eisner, Robert and Pieper, Paul J. A New View of the Federal Debt and Budget Deficits: Reply. *Amer. Econ. Rev.*, December 1986, *76*(5), pp. 1156–57. **[G: U.S.]**

Eisner, Robert and Pieper, Paul J. Dette et déficit gouvernementaux: mesures et effets. (Measurement and Effects of Government Debt and Deficits. With English summary.) *Ann. Écon. Statist.*, July-Sept. 1986, (3), pp. 27–52. **[G: U.S.; W. Europe; Japan]**

Eliasson, Gunnar. U.S. Deficits since World War I: Comment. *Scand. J. Econ.*, 1986, *88*(1), pp. 235–38. **[G: U.S.; Sweden]**

Elkind, Avi; Spiegel, Menahem and Sheshinski, Eytan. Tax Expenditure. **In** *Kop, Y., ed.*, 1986, pp. 199–225. **[G: Israel]**

Evans, Paul. Is the Dollar High because of Large Budget Deficits? *J. Monet. Econ.*, November 1986, *18*(3), pp. 227–49. **[G: U.S.]**

Feldstein, Martin S. The Budget Deficit and the Dollar. **In** *Fischer, S., ed.*, 1986, pp. 355–92. **[G: U.S.; W. Germany]**

Feldstein, Martin S. U.S. Budget Deficits and the European Economies: Resolving the Political Economy Puzzle. *Amer. Econ. Rev.*, May 1986, *76*(2), pp. 342–46. **[G: U.S.; W. Europe]**

Fischer, Bernhard and Trapp, Peter. Public Sector Deficits and the Dynamics of the Inflation Tax in Argentina. *Rivista Int. Sci. Econ. Com.*, Oct.-Nov. 1986, *33*(10–11), pp. 1107–27. **[G: Argentina]**

Flaig, Gebhard. Staatsverschuldung und langfristiger Zinssatz in einem Modell effizienter Märkte und rationaler Erwartungen. Eine empirische Untersuchung für die Bundesrepublik Deutschland. (Public Debt and Long-term Interest Rate in a Model of Efficient Markets and Rational Expectations. An Empirical Study for the Federal Republic of Germany. With English summary.) *Kredit Kapital*, 1986, *19*(3), pp. 366–85. **[G: W. Germany]**

Gazioğlu, Şaziye. Government Deficits, Consumption and Inflation in Turkey. *METU*, 1986, *13*(1/2), pp. 117–34. **[G: Turkey]**

Gil Díaz, Francisco. Government Budget Measurement under Inflation in LDCs. **In** *Herber, B. P., ed.*, 1986, pp. 123–37. **[G: Mexico]**

Gordon, Robert J. U.S. Fiscal Deficits and the World Imbalance of Payments. *Hitotsubashi J. Econ.*, Spec. Iss. Oct. 1986, *27*, pp. 7–41. **[G: U.S.]**

Hamilton, James D. and Flavin, Marjorie A. On the Limitations of Government Borrowing: A Framework for Empirical Testing. *Amer. Econ. Rev.*, September 1986, *76*(4), pp. 808–19. **[G: U.S.]**

Hanushek, Eric A. Formula Budgeting: The Economics and Analytics of Fiscal Policy under Rules. *J. Policy Anal. Manage.*, Fall 1986, *6*(1), pp. 3–19. **[G: U.S.]**

Harrison, Mark. The USSR State Budget under Late Stalinism (1945–55): Capital Formation, Government Borrowing and Monetary Growth. *Econ. Planning*, 1986, *20*(3), pp. 179–205. **[G: U.S.S.R.]**

Havens, Harry S. Gramm–Rudman–Hollings: Origins and Implementation. *Public Budg. Finance*, Autumn 1986, *6*(3), pp. 4–24. **[G: U.S.]**

Hoelscher, Gregory. New Evidence on Deficits and Interest Rates. *J. Money, Credit, Banking*, February 1986, *18*(1), pp. 1–17.

Holloway, Thomas M. Simple Methods to Measure the Automatic Responsiveness of the Federal Budget to Inflation. *J. Econ. Soc. Meas.*, October 1986, *14*(3), pp. 219–31. **[G: U.S.]**

Holloway, Thomas M. The Cyclically Adjusted Federal Budget and Federal Debt: Revised and Updated Estimates. *Surv. Curr. Bus.*, March 1986, *66*(3), pp. 11–17. **[G: U.S.]**

Hong, Lee Fook. A Summary of Singapore's 1986 Budget. *Bull. Int. Fiscal Doc.*, July 1986, *40*(7), pp. 319–25. **[G: Singapore]**

Hutchens, Robert M. The Effects of the Omnibus Budget Reconciliation Act of 1981 on AFDC Recipients: A Review of Studies. **In** *Ehrenberg, R. G., ed., Pt. B*, 1986, pp. 351–87. **[G: U.S.]**

Hutchison, Michael M. Financial Effects of Budget Deficits in the Pacific Basin. **In** *Cheng, H.-S., ed.*, 1986, pp. 311–33. **[G: Pacific Basin]**

Ishi, Hiromitsu. Overview of Fiscal Deficits in Japan with Special Reference to the Fiscal Policy Debate. *Hitotsubashi J. Econ.*, December 1986, *27*(2), pp. 133–48. **[G: Japan]**

Jaksch, Hans Jürgen. Simulaciones de políticas

antiinflacionarias en Argentina, 1983/87. (Simulation of Anti-inflationary Policies in Argentina, 1983–87. With English summary.) *Económica (La Plata)*, Jan.-June 1986, *32*(1), pp. 21–56. **[G: Argentina]**

Jao, Y. C. Hong Kong: Return to Balanced Budget. *Bull. Int. Fiscal Doc.*, July 1986, *40*(7), pp. 326–29. **[G: Hong Kong]**

Joines, Douglas H. Government Deficits and the Fiscal Policy Debate. **In** *Canto, V. A.; Kadlec, C. W. and Laffer, A. B., eds.*, 1986, pp. 87–107. **[G: U.S.]**

Jones, Jonathan D. and Sattar, Zaidi. Validating the Conventional Paradigm about Budget Deficits and Interest Rates. *Atlantic Econ. J.*, September 1986, *14*(3), pp. 83. **[G: U.S.]**

Jones, L. R. and Thompson, Fred. Reform of Budget Execution Control. *Public Budg. Finance*, Spring 1986, *6*(1), pp. 33–49.

Kessler, Denis; Perelman, Sergio and Pestieau, Pierre. L'hypothèse d'équivalence entre impôt et emprunt: un test sur les pays de l'OCDE. (With English summary.) *Ann. Écon. Statist.*, July-Sept. 1986, (3), pp. 141–49. **[G: OECD]**

Kjellstrom, Sven B. and d'Almeida, Ayité-Fily. Aid Coordination: A Recipient's Perspective. *Finance Develop.*, September 1986, *23*(3), pp. 37–40. **[G: Togo]**

Laden, Ben E. The Implications of Budget Deficits [Deficits, Interest Rates, and Monetary Policy]. *Cato J.*, Winter 1986, *5*(3), pp. 727–31. **[G: U.S.]**

Lal, Deepak and van Wijnbergen, Sweder J. G. Government Deficits, the Real Interest Rate, and Developing Country Debt: On Global Crowding Out. **In** *Lal, D. and Wolf, M., eds.*, 1986, pp. 182–238. **[G: OECD]**

Laney, Leroy O. Twin Deficits in the 1980s; What Are the Linkages? *Bus. Econ.*, April 1986, *21*(2), pp. 40–45. **[G: U.S.]**

Levy, Mickey D. A Positive Trend in the Federal Budget Outlook. **In** *Shadow Open Market Committee (I)*, 1986, pp. 31–42. **[G: U.S.]**

Levy, Mickey D. Circumventing the Intent of Gramm–Rudman–Hollings. **In** *Shadow Open Market Committee (II)*, 1986, pp. 37–46. **[G: U.S.]**

Looney, Robert E. Military Expenditures in Latin America: Patterns of Budgetary Tradeoffs. *J. Econ. Devel.*, July 1986, *11*(1), pp. 69–103. **[G: Latin America]**

Lott, Trent. The Need to Improve the Budget Process: A Republican's View. **In** *Schick, A., et al.*, 1986, pp. 72–77. **[G: U.S.]**

Manage, Neela and Marlow, Michael L. The Causal Relation between Federal Expenditures and Receipts. *Southern Econ. J.*, January 1986, *52*(3), pp. 617–29. **[G: U.S.]**

Mauleón, Iñaki. El déficit público y el mercado de trabajo en España: algunas conexiones e implicaciones. (With English summary.) *Invest. Écon.*, September 1986, *10*(3), pp. 483–504. **[G: Spain]**

McMillin, W. Douglas. Federal Deficits, Macrostabilization Goals, and Federal Reserve Behavior. *Econ. Inquiry*, April 1986, *24*(2), pp. 257–69. **[G: U.S.]**

McMillin, W. Douglas. Federal Deficits and Short-term Interest Rates. *J. Macroecon.*, Fall 1986, *8*(4), pp. 403–22. **[G: U.S.]**

Medgyessy, Peter. Debt Policy of the Socialist State. **In** *Herber, B. P., ed.*, 1986, pp. 43–52. **[G: Hungary]**

Meyer, Annette. Financing the Federal Budget: Sources and Structure. *Public Budg. Finance*, Winter 1986, *6*(4), pp. 56–73. **[G: U.S.]**

Milbourne, Ross and Richards, Daniel J. A New View of the Federal Debt and Budget Deficits: Comment. *Amer. Econ. Rev.*, December 1986, *76*(5), pp. 1154–55. **[G: U.S.]**

Miller, John A. The Fiscal Crisis of the State Reconsidered: Two Views of the State and the Accumulation of Capital in the Postwar Economy. *Rev. Radical Polit. Econ.*, Spring/Summer 1986, *18*(1/2), pp. 236–60. **[G: U.S.]**

Modigliani, Franco. U.S. Deficits since World War I: Comment. *Scand. J. Econ.*, 1986, *88*(1), pp. 223–34. **[G: U.S.]**

Modigliani, Franco; Jappelli, Tullio and Pagano, M. Errata corrige [The Impact of Fiscal Policy and Inflation on National Saving: The Italian Case]. *Banca Naz. Lavoro Quart. Rev.*, March 1986, (156), pp. 129. **[G: Italy]**

Morrison, Rodney J. Fiscal Marksmanship in the United States: 1950–83. *Manchester Sch. Econ. Soc. Stud.*, September 1986, *54*(3), pp. 322–33. **[G: U.S.]**

Musgrave, Richard A. Alternative Budget Policies for Full Employment. **In** *Musgrave, R. A., Vol. 1*, 1986, *1945*, pp. 336–50.

Musgrave, Richard A. Should We Have a Capital Budget? **In** *Musgrave, R. A., Vol. 1*, 1986, *1963*, pp. 370–73.

Musgrave, Richard A. The Nature of Budgetary Balance and the Case for the Capital Budget. **In** *Musgrave, R. A., Vol. 1*, 1986, *1939*, pp. 319–31.

Nicoletti, G. Unsustainability of Public Debt Dynamics and Inflation. *Metroecon.*, June 1986, *38*(2), pp. 181–204.

Ornstein, Norman. Crisis in the Budget Process: Exercising Political Choice: Comment. **In** *Schick, A., et al.*, 1986, pp. 86–88. **[G: U.S.]**

Panetta, Leon. The Need to Improve the Budget Process: A Democrat's View. **In** *Schick, A., et al.*, 1986, pp. 78–85. **[G: U.S.]**

Pantalone, Coleen C. and Platt, Marjorie B. The Federal Financing Bank: Harbinger of the Federal Deficit. *Bus. Econ.*, April 1986, *21*(2), pp. 46–51. **[G: U.S.]**

Penner, Rudolph G. An Appraisal of the Congressional Budget Process. **In** *Schick, A., et al.*, 1986, pp. 67–71. **[G: U.S.]**

Pillai, Vel and Sopchokchai, Orapin. Budgeting, Financing, and Planning in Thailand: Study of a Trichotomous Process. *Public Budg. Finance*, Winter 1986, *6*(4), pp. 34–42. **[G: Thailand]**

Pollard, Sidney. Stagflation, Fiscal Deficits and Balance of Payments—Great Britain and Germany. *Hitotsubashi J. Econ.*, Spec. Iss. Oct. 1986, 27, pp. 42–56. **[G: U.K.; W. Germany]**

Roe, Emery M. The Ceiling as Base: National Budgeting in Kenya. *Public Budg. Finance*, Summer 1986, *6*(2), pp. 87–103. **[G: Kenya]**

Rossi, José W. Considerações sobre a questão da dívida pública. (With English summary.) *Pesquisa Planejamento Econ.*, August 1986, *16*(2), pp. 413–24. **[G: Brazil]**

Samuelson, Paul A. That Constitutional Budget Amendment—'Tremendous Potential for Harm.' **In** *Samuelson, P. A.*, 1986, *1979*, pp. 1005–08.

Sargent, Thomas J. Interpreting the Reagan Deficits. *Fed. Res. Bank San Francisco Econ. Rev.*, Fall 1986, (4), pp. 5–12. **[G: U.S.]**

Schick, Allen. The Evolution of Congressional Budgeting. **In** *Schick, A., et al.*, 1986, pp. 3–54. **[G: U.S.]**

Seguiti, Maria Laura. Toward Comprehensive Budgeting under Fiscal Limitations: A Comparison of Reforms in the U.S. and Italy. *Public Budg. Finance*, Winter 1986, *6*(4), pp. 43–55. **[G: U.S.; Italy]**

Seidman, Laurence S. Gramm–Rudman–Hollings: Can It Be Improved? *Challenge*, July/Aug. 1986, *29*(3), pp. 51–54. **[G: U.S.]**

Shibata, Hirofumi and Kimura, Yoko. Are Budget Deficits the Cause of Growth in Government Expenditures? **In** *Herber, B. P., ed.*, 1986, pp. 229–42. **[G: U.S.; Japan]**

Shoven, John B. The Behavior of United States Deficits: Comment. **In** *Gordon, R. J., ed.*, 1986, pp. 389–91. **[G: U.S.]**

Sigelman, Lee. The Bureaucrat as Budget Maximizer: An Assumption Examined. *Public Budg. Finance*, Spring 1986, *6*(1), pp. 50–59. **[G: U.S.]**

Stockman, Alan C. The Budget Deficit and the Dollar: Comment. **In** *Fischer, S., ed.*, 1986, pp. 402–07. **[G: U.S.; W. Germany]**

Stockman, David. The Crisis in Federal Budgeting. **In** *Schick, A., et al.*, 1986, pp. 57–66. **[G: U.S.]**

Sunley, Emil M. Federal Tax Policy and the Budget. **In** *Landau, R. and Jorgenson, D. W., eds.*, 1986, pp. 85–96. **[G: U.S.]**

Tanzi, Vito. Is There a Limit to the Size of Fiscal Deficits in Developing Countries? **In** *Herber, B. P., ed.*, 1986, pp. 139–52. **[G: LDCs]**

Tarschys, Daniel. From Expansion to Restraint: Recent Developments in Budgeting. *Public Budg. Finance*, Autumn 1986, *6*(3), pp. 25–37. **[G: OECD]**

Vickrey, William. Budget-Smudget. Why Balance What, How, and When? *Atlantic Econ. J.*, September 1986, *14*(3), pp. 6–13. **[G: U.S.]**

Wakefield, Joseph C. Federal Fiscal Programs. *Surv. Curr. Bus.*, February 1986, *66*(2), pp. 26–31. **[G: U.S.]**

Wakefield, Joseph C. Reducing the Federal Government Deficit: An Update. *Surv. Curr. Bus.*, February 1986, *66*(2), pp. 32–34. **[G: U.S.]**

Washington, Charles W. The President's Budget for Fiscal Year 1987. *Public Budg. Finance*, Summer 1986, *6*(2), pp. 3–26. **[G: U.S.]**

Weicher, John C. The Reagan Domestic Budget Cuts: Proposals, Outcomes, and Effects. **In** *Cagan, P., ed.*, 1986, pp. 7–44. **[G: U.S.]**

Wonnacott, Paul. The Nominal Deficit Really Matters. *Challenge*, Sept./Oct. 1986, *29*(4), pp. 48–51. **[G: U.S.]**

3228 National Government Debt Management

Alter, George and Riley, James C. How to Bet on Lives: A Guide to Life Contingent Contracts in Early Modern Europe. **In** *Uselding, P., ed.*, 1986, pp. 1–53. **[G: Europe]**

Andel, Norbert. Changing Concepts of Public Debt in the History of Economic Thought. **In** *Herber, B. P., ed.*, 1986, pp. 1–13.

Axilrod, Stephen H. Debt, Financial Stability, and Public Policy: Overview. **In** *Axilrod, S. H., et al.*, 1986, pp. 209–17.

Balassa, Bela. The Problem of the Debt in Developing Countries. **In** *Herber, B. P., ed.*, 1986, pp. 153–66. **[G: LDCs]**

Baltensperger, Ernst. The Public Debt, Uncertainty, and Government Credibility. *J. Econ. Bus.*, August 1986, *38*(3), pp. 183–92.

Barth, James R.; Iden, George R. and Russek, Frank S. The Economic Consequences of Federal Deficits: An Examination of the Net Wealth and Instability Issues. *Southern Econ. J.*, July 1986, *53*(1), pp. 27–50. **[G: U.S.]**

Barth, James R.; Russek, Frank S. and Wang, George H. K. A Time Series Analysis of the Relationship between the Capital Stock and Federal Debt: A Comment. *J. Money, Credit, Banking*, November 1986, *18*(4), pp. 527–38. **[G: U.S.]**

Bispham, John. Growing Public-Sector Debt: A Policy Dilemma. *Nat. Westminster Bank Quart. Rev.*, May 1986, pp. 52–67. **[G: OECD]**

Blanchard, Olivier J.; Dornbusch, Rudiger and Buiter, Willem. Public Debt and Fiscal Responsibility. **In** *Blanchard, O.; Dornbusch, R. and Layard, R., eds.*, 1986, pp. 125–53. **[G: EEC]**

Blinder, Alan S. Debt Problems and Macroeconomic Policies: Commentary. **In** *Axilrod, S. H., et al.*, 1986, pp. 193–201. **[G: U.S.]**

Boothe, Paul M. and Reid, Bradford G. The Market Value and Maturity Structure of Government of Canada Debt, 1967–83. *Can. J. Econ.*, August 1986, *19*(3), pp. 443–68. **[G: Canada]**

Boskin, Michael J. Budgets, Deficits, Technology and Economic Growth. **In** *Landau, R. and Jorgenson, D. W., eds.*, 1986, pp. 191–204. **[G: U.S.]**

Bosworth, Barry P. Savings and Government Policy. **In** *Adams, F. G. and Wachter, S. M., eds.*, 1986, pp. 173–87. **[G: U.S.; Japan]**

Boyer, André. Dette Publique et Choix Public: Retrouver le Lien. (With English summary.) **In** *Herber, B. P., ed.*, 1986, pp. 217–28. **[G: France]**

Buchanan, James M. Debt, Demos, and the Welfare State. **In** *Buchanan, J. M.*, 1986, pp. 210–21.

Buchanan, James M. Public Debt and Capital Formation. **In** *Lee, D. R., ed.*, 1986, pp. 177–94.

Buchanan, James M. Public Debt and Capital Formation. **In** *Buchanan, J. M.*, 1986, *1985*, pp. 195–209.

Byatt, I. C. R. Public Debt in the U.K.: Trends, Composition and Economic Performance. **In** *Herber, B. P., ed.*, 1986, pp. 97–110. **[G: U.K.]**

Cagan, Phillip. Debt Problems and Macroeconomic Policies: Commentary. **In** *Axilrod, S. H., et al.*, 1986, pp. 203–08. **[G: U.S.]**

Canziani, Arnaldo. Di alcuni effetti dei deficit pubblici. (On the General Consequences of Uninterrupted Public Deficits. With English summary.) *Ricerche Econ.*, Apr.-Sept. 1986, *40*(2–3), pp. 409–30. **[G: Italy]**

Capie, Forrest H.; Mills, Terence C. and Wood, Geoffrey E. Debt Management and Interest Rates: The British Stock Conversion of 1932. *Appl. Econ.*, October 1986, *18*(10), pp. 1111–26. **[G: U.K.]**

Casarosa, Carlo. Il significato economico del rapporto fra debito pubblico e pil: un'analisi critica. (Meaning of the Ratio Public Data/GPD. With English summary.) *Polit. Econ.*, August 1986, *2*(2), pp. 167–80.

Cavaco Silva, Anibal A. Macroeconomic Impact of Debt Financed Fiscal Deficits: Non-sceptical Considerations. **In** *Herber, B. P., ed.*, 1986, pp. 69–80.

Chouraqui, Jean-Claude; Jones, Brian and Montador, Robert Bruce. Public Debt in a Medium-term Perspective. *OECD Econ. Stud.*, Autumn 1986, (7), pp. 103–53. **[G: OECD]**

Cox, W. Michael. Government Debt and the Stock Market. *Fed. Res. Bank Dallas Econ. Rev.*, September 1986, pp. 1–9.

Cox, W. Michael and Haslag, Joseph. The Market Value of Government of Canada Debt, Monthly, 1937–84. *Can. J. Econ.*, August 1986, *19*(3), pp. 469–97. **[G: Canada; U.S.]**

Csikós-Nagy, Béla and Gadó, Ottó. Public Enterprises and Off-Budget Debt. **In** *Herber, B. P., ed.*, 1986, pp. 321–31. **[G: Hungary]**

Dornbusch, Rudiger; Blanchard, Olivier J. and Buiter, Willem H. Public Debt and Fiscal Responsibility. **In** *Dornbusch, R.*, 1986, pp. 179–204. **[G: U.S.; Europe]**

Eisner, Robert and Pieper, Paul J. A New View of the Federal Debt and Budget Deficits: Reply. *Amer. Econ. Rev.*, December 1986, *76*(5), pp. 1156–57. **[G: U.S.]**

Eisner, Robert and Pieper, Paul J. Dette et déficit gouvernementaux: mesures et effets. (Measurement and Effects of Government Debt and Deficits. With English summary.) *Ann. Écon. Statist.*, July-Sept. 1986, (3), pp. 27–52. **[G: U.S.; W. Europe; Japan]**

van Ewijk, Casper. Interest Payments and the Stability of the Government Budget Deficit in an Open and Growing Economy. *De Economist*, 1986, *134*(2), pp. 143–64.

Friedman, Benjamin M. Financing American Investment in New Technology. **In** *Landau, R. and Jorgenson, D. W., eds.*, 1986, pp. 205–19. **[G: U.S.]**

Friedman, Benjamin M. Implications of Government Deficits for Interest Rates, Equity Returns, and Corporate Financing. **In** *Friedman, B. M., ed.*, 1986, pp. 67–89. **[G: U.S.]**

Friedman, Benjamin M. Increasing Indebtedness and Financial Stability in the United States. **In** *Axilrod, S. H., et al.*, 1986, pp. 27–53. **[G: U.S.]**

Gandenberger, Otto. On Government Borrowing and False Political Feedback. **In** *Herber, B. P., ed.*, 1986, pp. 205–16.

Goudswaard, Kees P. and Halberstadt, Victor. Aspects of Debt Management and Monetary Policy in Small Open Economies. **In** *Herber, B. P., ed.*, 1986, pp. 343–60. **[G: OECD; Netherlands]**

Hamilton, James D. and Flavin, Marjorie A. On the Limitations of Government Borrowing: A Framework for Empirical Testing. *Amer. Econ. Rev.*, September 1986, *76*(4), pp. 808–19. **[G: U.S.]**

Heimann, John G. Debt, Financial Stability, and Public Policy: Overview. **In** *Axilrod, S. H., et al.*, 1986, pp. 219–22.

Higgins, Bryon. Debt, Financial Stability, and Public Policy: Symposium Overview. **In** *Axilrod, S. H., et al.*, 1986, pp. 1–14.

Holloway, Thomas M. The Cyclically Adjusted Federal Budget and Federal Debt: Revised and Updated Estimates. *Surv. Curr. Bus.*, March 1986, *66*(3), pp. 11–17. **[G: U.S.]**

Horrigan, Brian R. The Determinants of the Public Debt in the United States, 1953–1978. *Econ. Inquiry*, January 1986, *24*(1), pp. 11–23. **[G: U.S.]**

Hutchison, Michael M. Financial Effects of Budget Deficits in the Pacific Basin. **In** *Cheng, H.-S., ed.*, 1986, pp. 311–33. **[G: Pacific Basin]**

Jüttner, Johannes. Public Debt and Asset Preferences. *Kredit Kapital*, 1986, *19*(3), pp. 386–400. **[G: Australia]**

Kaufman, Henry. Debt: The Threat to Economic and Financial Stability. **In** *Axilrod, S. H., et al.*, 1986, pp. 15–26. **[G: U.S.]**

Kessler, Denis; Perelman, Sergio and Pestieau, Pierre. Public Debt, Tax, and Consumption: A¯Test on O.E.C.D. Countries. *Public Finance*, 1986, *41*(1), pp. 63–70. **[G: OECD]**

Kleiman, Ephraim. The Indexation of Public Debt in Israel. **In** *Herber, B. P., ed.*, 1986, pp. 193–204. **[G: Israel]**

Koneczny, Walter. Problems Relating to the Increasing Debt of Off-Budget Public Corporations. *Ann. Pub. Co-op. Econ.*, September 1986, *57*(3), pp. 359–72. **[G: Austria]**

de Larosière, J. The Growth of Public Debt and the Need for Fiscal Discipline. **In** *Herber, B. P., ed.*, 1986, pp. 15–27. **[G: OECD]**

Levy, Mickey D. Circumventing the Intent of Gramm–Rudman–Hollings. **In** *Shadow Open Market Committee (II)*, 1986, pp. 37–46. **[G: U.S.]**

Mathews, Russell. The Australian Loan Council:

Co-ordination of Public Debt Policies in a Federation. **In** *Herber, B. P., ed.*, 1986, pp. 307–19. **[G: Australia]**

Medgyessy, Peter. Debt Policy of the Socialist State. **In** *Herber, B. P., ed.*, 1986, pp. 43–52. **[G: Hungary]**

Meltzer, Allan H. Increasing Indebtedness and Financial Stability in the United States: Commentary. **In** *Axilrod, S. H., et al.*, 1986, pp. 55–61. **[G: U.S.]**

Meyer, Annette. Financing the Federal Budget: Sources and Structure. *Public Budg. Finance*, Winter 1986, *6*(4), pp. 56–73. **[G: U.S.]**

Milbourne, Ross and Richards, Daniel J. A New View of the Federal Debt and Budget Deficits: Comment. *Amer. Econ. Rev.*, December 1986, *76*(5), pp. 1154–55. **[G: U.S.]**

Monti, Mario. Indexation of Government Debt and Its Alternatives. **In** *Herber, B. P., ed.*, 1986, pp. 181–92. **[G: Italy; U.S.; LDCs]**

Munnell, Alicia H. and Grolnic, Joseph B. Should the U.S. Government Issue Index Bonds? *New Eng. Econ. Rev.*, Sept./Oct. 1986, pp. 3–21. **[G: U.S.; U.K.]**

Musgrave, Peggy B. Public Debt and Cost–Benefit Analysis. **In** *Herber, B. P., ed.*, 1986, pp. 81–96.

Musgrave, Richard A. Public Debt and Future Generations. **In** *Musgrave, R. A., Vol. 1*, 1986, *1965*, pp. 374–76.

Ortner, Robert. Savings and Government Deficits. **In** *Adams, F. G. and Wachter, S. M., eds.*, 1986, pp. 163–71. **[G: U.S.]**

Peacock, Alan. Is There a Public Debt "Problem" in Developed Countries? **In** *Herber, B. P., ed.*, 1986, pp. 29–41.

Penati, Alessandro. Budget Deficit, External Official Borrowing, and Sterilized Intervention Policy in Foreign Exchange Markets. *J. Int. Money Finance*, March 1986, *5*(1), pp. 99–113.

Raga, José T. Public Debt, Margin of Financial Intermediation and the Rates of Interest: Is There Any Link? **In** *Herber, B. P., ed.*, 1986, pp. 167–79.

Rossi, José W. Considerações sobre a questão da dívida pública. (With English summary.) *Pesquisa Planejamento Econ.*, August 1986, *16*(2), pp. 413–24. **[G: Brazil]**

Schokkaert, Erik and Van Rompuy, Victor. Intergenerational Distribution of the Burden of Debt: The Case of Belgium. **In** *Herber, B. P., ed.*, 1986, pp. 255–64. **[G: Belgium]**

Seidman, L. William. Debt, Financial Stability, and Public Policy: Overview. **In** *Axilrod, S. H., et al.*, 1986, pp. 223–30. **[G: U.S.]**

Sishev, Nikolai. Public Debt Trends and Problems in the USSR. **In** *Herber, B. P., ed.*, 1986, pp. 111–22. **[G: U.S.S.R.]**

Stockman, David. The Crisis in Federal Budgeting. **In** *Schick, A., et al.*, 1986, pp. 57–66. **[G: U.S.]**

Summers, Lawrence H. Debt Problems and Macroeconomic Policies. **In** *Axilrod, S. H., et al.*, 1986, pp. 165–91. **[G: U.S.]**

Summers, Lawrence H. Issues in National Savings Policy. **In** *Adams, F. G. and Wachter, S. M., eds.*, 1986, pp. 65–88. **[G: OECD]**

Tait, Alan A. Public Debt Statistics: Some Problems of Definition and Measurement. **In** *Herber, B. P., ed.*, 1986, pp. 53–68. **[G: LDCs; MDCs]**

Tanzi, Vito. Is There a Limit to the Size of Fiscal Deficits in Developing Countries? **In** *Herber, B. P., ed.*, 1986, pp. 139–52. **[G: LDCs]**

Tweedie, A. J. Monetary Policy in New Zealand. **In** *Reserve Bank of New Zealand*, 1986, pp. 47–62. **[G: New Zealand]**

Volcker, Paul A. Statement to the U.S. House Subcommittee on Telecommunications, Consumer Protection, and Finance of the Committee on Energy and Commerce, April 23, 1986. *Fed. Res. Bull.*, June 1986, *72*(6), pp. 398–403. **[G: U.S.]**

Wiseman, Jack. Public Debt and Public Policy: An Evaluation of Recent History. **In** *Herber, B. P., ed.*, 1986, pp. 243–53.

323 National Taxation, Revenue, and Subsidies

3230 National Taxation, Revenue, and Subsidies

Aaron, Henry J. Rationale Underlying the Treasury Proposals: Discussion. **In** *Federal Reserve Bank of Boston*, 1986, pp. 49–54. **[G: U.S.]**

Abel, Andrew B. The Failure of Ricardian Equivalence under Progressive Wealth Taxation. *J. Public Econ.*, June 1986, *30*(1), pp. 117–28.

Abrams, Burton A. and Schmitz, Mark D. The Crowding-out Effect of Governmental Transfers on Private Charitable Contributions. **In** *Rose-Ackerman, S., ed.*, 1986, *1978*, pp. 303–12. **[G: U.S.]**

Adams, Richard H., Jr. Taxation, Control, and Agrarian Transition in Rural Egypt: A Local-Level View. **In** *Richards, A., ed.*, 1986, pp. 159–82. **[G: Egypt]**

Afxentiou, Panayiotis C. Tax Revenue Performance of Cyprus, 1960–1982. *Can. J. Devel. Stud.*, 1986, *7*(1), pp. 47–63. **[G: Cyprus]**

Agell, Jonas Nils. Subsidy to Capital through Tax Incentives. **In** *Shome, P., ed.*, 1986, pp. 48–79. **[G: ASEAN]**

Ahmad, Ehtisham and Stern, Nicholas. Tax Reform for Pakistan: Overview and Effective Taxes for 1975–76. *Pakistan Devel. Rev.*, Spring 1986, *25*(1), pp. 43–72. **[G: Pakistan]**

Alderman, Harold. Food Subsidies and State Policies in Egypt. **In** *Richards, A., ed.*, 1986, pp. 183–200. **[G: Egypt]**

Alworth, Julian. A Cost of Capital Approach to the Taxation of Foreign Direct Investment Income. **In** *Edwards, J., et al., eds.*, 1986, pp. 185–208.

Anderson, Eric E. Taxes vs. Quotas for Regulating Fisheries under Uncertainty: A Hybrid Discrete-Time Continuous-Time Model. *Marine Resource Econ.*, 1986, *3*(3), pp. 183–207.

Anderson, William; Wallace, Myles S. and Warner, John T. Government Spending and Taxation: What Causes What? *Southern Econ. J.*, January 1986, *52*(3), pp. 630–39. **[G: U.S.]**

323 National Taxation, Revenue, and Subsidies

Apostolakis, Bobby E. Labor Subsidies in a Neoclassical Framework and an Empirical Extension. *Ricerche Econ.*, Jan.-Mar. 1986, *40*(1), pp. 31–49. **[G: Greece]**

Apps, Patricia. Taxation Reform and Income Distribution in Australia: Comment. *Australian Econ. Rev.*, 3rd Quarter 1986, (75), pp. 57–59. **[G: Australia]**

Apps, Patricia and Jones, Glenn. Selective Taxation of Couples. *J. Econ. (Z. Nationalökon.)*, Supplementum 5, 1986, pp. 1–15.

Arak, Marcelle; Goodman, Laurie S. and Silver, Andrew. Premium and Discount Securities: Relative Tax Advantage under the Deficit Reduction Act of 1984. *Nat. Tax J.*, March 1986, *39*(1), pp. 65–77. **[G: U.S.]**

Arrufat, Jose Luis and Zabalza, Antonio. Female Labor Supply with Taxation, Random Preferences, and Optimization Errors. *Econometrica*, January 1986, *54*(1), pp. 47–63. **[G: U.K.]**

Asher, Mukul G. Issues in Corporate Tax Design. **In** *Shome, P., ed.*, 1986, pp. 83–92.

Atkinson, Glen W. Concept of Income Realization and Deductible Costs. **In** *Lindholm, R. W., ed.*, 1986, pp. 251–79.

Auerbach, Alan J. Incentives and Windfalls in Corporate Tax Reform. **In** *Landau, R. and Jorgenson, D. W., eds.*, 1986, pp. 119–35. **[G: U.S.]**

Auerbach, Alan J. Tax Reform and Capital Formation: Discussion. **In** *Federal Reserve Bank of Boston*, 1986, pp. 145–48. **[G: U.S.]**

Auerbach, Alan J. The Dynamic Effects of Tax Law Asymmetries. *Rev. Econ. Stud.*, April 1986, *53*(2), pp. 205–25.

Auerbach, Alan J. The Economic Effects of the Corporate Income Tax: Changing Revenues and Changing Views. **In** *Friedman, B. M., ed.*, 1986, pp. 107–21. **[G: U.S.]**

Auld, Douglas. A Note on the Price Effects of Indirect Taxes. *Econ. Notes*, 1986, (2), pp. 152–57.

Auten, Gerald E. and Rudney, Gabriel G. Tax Reform and Individual Giving to Higher Education. *Econ. Educ. Rev.*, 1986, *5*(2), pp. 167–78. **[G: U.S.]**

Baccouche, Rafiq and Laisney, François. Analyse microéconomique de la réforme de la TVA de juillet 1982 en France. (Microeconomic Analysis of the French VAT Reform of July 1982. With English summary.) *Ann. Écon. Statist.*, Apr./June 1986, (2), pp. 37–74. **[G: France]**

Baden, John; Blood, Tom and Stroup, Richard L. America's Version of the Melanesian Cargo Cults: The New Industrial Policy. **In** *Lee, D. R., ed.*, 1986, pp. 437–58. **[G: U.S.]**

Baker, James A., III. Some Reflections on Tax Reform in the U.S.A. *Bull. Int. Fiscal Doc.*, Aug./Sept. 1986, *40*(8/9), pp. 348–49. **[G: U.S.]**

Balbino, L. R. and Monteiro Marques, M. Fertilizer Pricing Policy in Portugal. **In** *Segura, E. L.; Shetty, Y. T. and Nishimizu, M., eds.*, 1986, pp. 102–08. **[G: Portugal]**

Baqai, Moin. The Question of Subsidies in the Pricing Policy of Public Enterprises. **In** *U.N., Dept. of Technical Co-operation for Development*, 1986, pp. 107–15. **[G: Pakistan]**

Barbera, Anthony J.; Pollock, Stephen H. and Meade, Douglas S. Tax Simplification and the Performance of the U.S. Economy. *J. Policy Modeling*, Fall 1986, *8*(3), pp. 415–31. **[G: U.S.]**

Barkai, Haim. The Energy Sector in the 1960s and 1970s. **In** *Ben-Porath, Y., ed.*, 1986, pp. 264–75. **[G: Israel]**

Barro, Robert J. Payroll-Tax Financed Social Insurance with Variable Retirement: Comment. *Scand. J. Econ.*, 1986, *88*(1), pp. 55–58.

Barro, Robert J. and Sahasakul, Chaipat. Average Marginal Tax Rates from Social Security and the Individual Income Tax. *J. Bus.*, Part 1, October 1986, *59*(4), pp. 555–66. **[G: U.S.]**

Barrow, Michael and Robinson, Ray. Housing and Tax Capitalisation. *Urban Stud.*, February 1986, *23*(1), pp. 61–66. **[G: U.K.]**

Bassoco, Luz María; Cartas, Celso and Norton, Roger D. Sectoral Analysis of the Benefits of Subsidized Insurance in Mexico. **In** *Hazell, P.; Pomareda, C. and Valdés, A., eds.*, 1986, pp. 126–42. **[G: Mexico]**

Bates, Jim and Gerrie, Dave. Withholding on All Incomes. **In** *Lindholm, R. W., ed.*, 1986, pp. 104–39. **[G: U.S.]**

Batina, Raymond G. The Optimal Linear Income Tax with Tax Credits Contingent on Fertility. *J. Public Econ.*, July 1986, *30*(2), pp. 219–35.

Bayar, Ali. L'impôt sur le revnu élargi: Analyse théorique et étude quantitative pour la Belgique. (With English summary.) *Cah. Écon. Bruxelles*, 4th Trimester 1986, (112), pp. 67–108. **[G: Belgium]**

Benker, Karen M. Tax Expenditure Reporting: Closing the Loophole in State Budget Oversight. *Nat. Tax J.*, December 1986, *39*(4), pp. 403–17. **[G: U.S.]**

Bennett, Robert J. The Impact of Non-Domestic Rates on Profitability and Investment. *Fisc. Stud.*, February 1986, *7*(1), pp. 34–50. **[G: U.K.]**

Bentzel, Ragnar. Incentives in the United Kingdom: Comment. **In** *Balassa, B. and Giersch, H., eds.*, 1986, pp. 296–300. **[G: U.K.]**

Bentzel, Ragnar. Payroll-Tax Financed Social Insurance with Variable Retirement: Comment. *Scand. J. Econ.*, 1986, *88*(1), pp. 51–54.

Berglas, Eitan. Taxes and Transfers in an Inflationary Decade. **In** *Ben-Porath, Y., ed.*, 1986, pp. 221–38. **[G: Israel]**

Bernard, Victor L. and Hayn, Carla. Inflation and the Distribution of the Corporate Income Tax Burden. *Nat. Tax J.*, June 1986, *39*(2), pp. 171–87. **[G: U.S.]**

Bernstein, Jeffrey I. The Effect of Direct and Indirect Tax Incentives on Canadian Industrial R&D Expenditures. *Can. Public Policy*, September 1986, *12*(3), pp. 438–48. **[G: Canada]**

Betson, David M. and Greenberg, David H. Labor Supply and Tax Rates: Comment. *Amer. Econ. Rev.*, June 1986, *76*(3), pp. 551–56.

Betten, Rijkele. OECD Report: Trends in International Taxation: Taxation Issues Relating to International Hiring-out of Labor. *Bull. Int. Fiscal Doc.*, July 1986, *40*(7), pp. 330–34. **[G: OECD]**

Bhatia, Kul B. Taxes, Intermediate Goods, and Relative Prices: The Case of Variable Coefficients. *J. Public Econ.*, November 1986, *31*(2), pp. 197–213.

Biger, Nahum and Pepe, Michael F. G. The Inhibiting Effect of Bilateral Tax Treaties on Domestic Tax Incentives. *Can. Public Policy*, September 1986, *12*(3), pp. 424–31. **[G: Canada; Italy]**

Bird, Richard M. The Interjurisdictional Allocation of Income. *Australian Tax Forum*, 1986, *3*(3), pp. 333–54.

Black, Andrew P. Industrial Policy in W. Germany. Policy in Search of a Goal? **In** *Hall, G., ed.*, 1986, pp. 84–127. **[G: W. Germany]**

Blackley, Paul R. Causality between Revenues and Expenditures and the Size of the Federal Budget. *Public Finance Quart.*, April 1986, *14*(2), pp. 139–56. **[G: U.S.]**

Blank, Rebecca M. and Blinder, Alan S. Macroeconomics, Income Distribution, and Poverty. **In** *Danziger, S. H. and Weinberg, D. H., eds.*, 1986, pp. 180–208. **[G: U.S.]**

Blau, Francine D. Immigration and the U.S. Taxpayer. **In** *Pozo, S., ed.*, 1986, pp. 89–110. **[G: U.S.]**

Blejer, Mario I. and Cheasty, Adrienne. Budgetary Policy and the Mobilization of Domestic Financial Resources. **In** *U.N., Dept. of Tech. Co-op. for Devel., Devel. Admin. Div.*, 1986, pp. 83–98.

Blejer, Mario I. and Cheasty, Adrienne. Using Fiscal Measures to Stimulate Savings in Developing Countries. *Finance Develop.*, June 1986, *23*(2), pp. 16–19. **[G: LDCs]**

Blinder, Alan S. The Effect of Tax Simplification on Individuals: Discussion. **In** *Federal Reserve Bank of Boston*, 1986, pp. 92–98. **[G: U.S.]**

Blomqvist, Ake G. and McKee, Michael J. Eliminating the 'Married Exemption' in the Canadian Income Tax: The Erola Proposal. *Can. J. Econ.*, May 1986, *19*(2), pp. 309–18. **[G: Canada]**

Blumstein, James F. Providing Hospital Care to Indigent Patients: Hill–Burton as a Case Study and a Paradigm. **In** *Sloan, F. A.; Blumstein, J. F. and Perrin, J. M., eds.*, 1986, pp. 94–107. **[G: U.S.]**

Boadway, Robin W. Sales Tax Reform Options and the BTT. **In** *Boadway, R. W. and Mintz, J. M., eds.*, 1986, pp. 14–23. **[G: Canada]**

Boadway, Robin W. and Mintz, Jack M. The Business Transfer Tax: An Overview of the Issues. **In** *Boadway, R. W. and Mintz, J. M., eds.*, 1986, pp. 1–7. **[G: U.S.; Canada]**

Bohanon, Cecil E. and McClure, James E. Taxes, Welfare Costs, and Public Consumption: The Case of the Unwitting Monopsonist. *Public Choice*, 1986, *49*(3), pp. 235–47.

Bohanon, Cecil E. and Van Cott, T. Norman. Labor Supply and Tax Rates: Comment. *Amer. Econ. Rev.*, March 1986, *76*(1), pp. 277–79.

Boidman, Nathan. The Peripatetic Alien: His/Her Tax Problems in the United States and Abroad. *Bull. Int. Fiscal Doc.*, Aug./Sept. 1986, *40*(8/9), pp. 385–400. **[G: W. Europe; Colombia; U.S.; Canada]**

Bond, Eric W. and Samuelson, Larry. Tax Holidays as Signals. *Amer. Econ. Rev.*, September 1986, *76*(4), pp. 820–26.

Booth, Anne. Agricultural Taxation: A Survey of Issues and Evidence. **In** *Shome, P., ed.*, 1986, pp. 117–40. **[G: S. Asia; S. E. Asia]**

Borsu-Bilande, A.; Glejser, Herbert and Louveaux, F. Behaviour under Uncertainty: How 94 Belgian Individuals and Firms Prepay Their Incometax over a Sixteen Quarter Period. *Cah. Écon. Bruxelles*, First Trimester 1986, (109), pp. 33–50. **[G: Belgium]**

Bosanquet, Nick. Inconsistencies of the NHS: Buchanan Revisited. **In** *Culyer, A. J. and Jönsson, B., eds.*, 1986, pp. 101–11. **[G: U.K.]**

Boskin, Michael J. Macroeconomics, Technology, and Economic Growth: An Introduction to Some Important Issues. **In** *Landau, R. and Rosenberg, N., eds.*, 1986, pp. 33–56. **[G: U.S.]**

Bosworth, Barry P. Tax Simplification and Financial Markets: Discussion. **In** *Federal Reserve Bank of Boston*, 1986, pp. 184–86. **[G: U.S.]**

Boucher, Trevor. Self-Assessment of Income Tax. *Australian Tax Forum*, 1986, *3*(1), pp. 45–53. **[G: Australia]**

Bovenberg, Arij Lans. Capital Income Taxation in Growing Open Economies. *J. Public Econ.*, December 1986, *31*(3), pp. 347–76. **[G: U.S.]**

Boyd, Roy and Daniels, Barbara J. Errata [Capital Gains Treatment of Timber Income: Incidence and Welfare Implications]. *Land Econ.*, February 1986, *62*(1), pp. ii. **[G: U.S.]**

Bradford, David F. Policy Forum on the Business Transfer Tax: Wrap-Up. **In** *Boadway, R. W. and Mintz, J. M., eds.*, 1986, pp. 62–68.

Bradford, David F. The Effect of Tax Simplification on Individuals: Discussion. **In** *Federal Reserve Bank of Boston*, 1986, pp. 99–102. **[G: U.S.]**

Bradford, David F. and Stuart, Charles. Issues in the Measurement and Interpretation of Effective Tax Rates. *Nat. Tax J.*, September 1986, *39*(3), pp. 307–16. **[G: U.S.]**

Braendgaard, Asger. Danish Industrial Policy: Liberalism Revised or Revisited. **In** *Hall, G., ed.*, 1986, pp. 165–82. **[G: Denmark]**

Brannon, Gerard M. Some Economics of Tax Reform, 1986. *Nat. Tax J.*, September 1986, *39*(3), pp. 277–79. **[G: U.S.]**

Break, George F. Tax Competition and Federal Tax Deductibility. *Nat. Tax J.*, September 1986, *39*(3), pp. 349–52. **[G: U.S.]**

Brean, Donald J. S. Fiscal Policy Harmonization and Negotiation of a Free-Trade Area. **In** *C. D. Howe Institute*, 1986, pp. 43–71. **[G: Canada; U.S.]**

Brent, Robert J. Lagged Reactions in Short-run Estimates of Tax Shifting of Company Income and Sales Taxes in Kenya. *J. Devel. Econ.*, Jan.-Feb. 1986, *20*(1), pp. 15–32. **[G: Kenya]**

Bridbury, A. R. Dr. Rigby's Comment: A Reply [English Provincial Towns in the Later Middle Ages]. *Econ. Hist. Rev., 2nd Ser.*, August 1986, *39*(3), pp. 417–22. **[G: U.K.]**

Brooks, Neil. Taxation of Closely-Held Corporations: The Partnership Option and the Lower Rate of Tax. *Australian Tax Forum*, 1986, *3*(4), pp. 381–509. **[G: Australia; U.S.; U.K.; Canada]**

Brown, Eleanor P. Unemployment Insurance Taxes and Cyclical Layoff Incentives. *J. Lab. Econ.*, January 1986, *4*(1), pp. 50–65. **[G: U.S.]**

Browning, Edgar K. Pechman's Tax Incidence Study: A Note on the Data. *Amer. Econ. Rev.*, December 1986, *76*(5), pp. 1214–18. **[G: U.S.]**

Browning, Edgar K. Reply [Tax Incidence, Indirect Taxes, and Transfers]. *Nat. Tax J.*, December 1986, *39*(4), pp. 541–42.

Browning, Edgar K. Taxation, Capital Accumulation, and Equity. **In** *Lee, D. R., ed.*, 1986, pp. 19–47. **[G: OECD]**

Browning, Edgar K. The Marginal Cost of Raising Tax Revenue. **In** *Cagan, P., ed.*, 1986, pp. 73–103. **[G: U.S.]**

Browning, Edgar K. and Johnson, William R. The Cost of Reducing Economic Inequality. *Cato J.*, Spring/Summer 1986, *6*(1), pp. 85–109. **[G: U.S.]**

Brunner, Johann K. A Two-Period Model on Optimal Taxation with Learning Incentives. *J. Econ. (Z. Nationalökon.)*, 1986, *46*(1), pp. 31–47.

Bryson, Phillip J. and Perry, Philip J. *Sozialpolitik:* East German Social Welfare Policies. *Comp. Econ. Stud.*, Summer 1986, *28*(2), pp. 1–20. **[G: E. Germany]**

Buchanan, James M. Cultural Evolution and Institutional Reform. **In** *Buchanan, J. M.*, 1986, pp. 75–85.

Buchanan, James M. The Ethical Limits of Taxation. **In** *Buchanan, J. M.*, 1986, *1984*, pp. 165–77.

Buckley, Robert M. and Schnare, Ann B. The Uncertain and Variable Costs of Efficiency Gains. **In** *Follain, J. R., ed.*, 1986, pp. 187–204. **[G: U.S.]**

Buurman, Gary B. Henry George and the Institution of Private Property in Land: A Property Rights Approach. *Amer. J. Econ. Soc.*, October 1986, *45*(4), pp. 489–502. **[G: U.S.]**

Caballero, M. Ga. Argentina: Compulsory Loan Based on Savings Capacity. *Bull. Int. Fiscal Doc.*, February 1986, *40*(2), pp. 71–74. **[G: Argentina]**

Cabral, Luís M. B. Nota Sobre a Hipótese de Laffer e o Sistema Fiscal Português. (With English summary.) *Economia (Portugal)*, May 1986, *10*(2), pp. 293–300. **[G: Portugal]**

Calmus, Thomas W. Intersecting Tax Concentration Curves and the Measurement of Tax Progressivity: A Comment. *Nat. Tax J.*, March 1986, *39*(1), pp. 119–21.

Caniglia, Alan S. Variable versus Fixed Rate Subsidies: Are the Latter Necessarily Less Efficient? *Public Finance Quart.*, January 1986, *14*(1), pp. 100–106.

Canto, Victor A.; Joines, Douglas H. and Webb, Robert I. The Revenue Effects of the Kennedy and Reagan Tax Cuts: Some Time Series Estimates. *J. Bus. Econ. Statist.*, July 1986, *4*(3), pp. 281–88. **[G: U.S.]**

Carliner, Michael S. The Impact of Tax Reform on Housing Demand and Residential Construction Activity. **In** *Follain, J. R., ed.*, 1986, pp. 113–33. **[G: U.S.]**

del Castillo, Gustavo and Barajas de Vega, Rosario. U.S.–Mexican Agricultural Relations: The Upper Limits of Linkage Formation. **In** *Browne, W. P. and Hadwiger, D. F., eds.*, 1986, pp. 153–68. **[G: U.S.; Mexico]**

Cavendish, Elizabeth A. Public Provision of the Performing Arts: A Case Study of the Federal Theatre Project in Connecticut. **In** *DiMaggio, P. J., ed.*, 1986, pp. 140–58. **[G: U.S.]**

Caves, Richard E. and Petersen, Bruce C. Cooperatives' Tax "Advantages": Growth, Retained Earnings, and Equity Rotation. *Amer. J. Agr. Econ.*, May 1986, *68*(2), pp. 207–13. **[G: U.S.]**

Chang, Eric C. and Pinegar, J. Michael. Return Seasonality and Tax-Loss Selling in the Market for Long-term Government and Corporate Bonds. *J. Finan. Econ.*, December 1986, *17*(2), pp. 391–415. **[G: U.S.]**

Chang, F. R. and Wildasin, David E. Randomization of Commodity Taxes: An Expenditure Minimization Approach. *J. Public Econ.*, December 1986, *31*(3), pp. 329–45.

Chatterji, Monojit. Unions, Employment and the Inflation Tax. *Econ. J.*, June 1986, *96*(382), pp. 342–51.

Chatterji, Monojit and Junankar, P. N. Agricultural Taxation in Less Developed Countries: Effects of a Tax on Inefficiency. *J. Quant. Econ.*, July 1986, *2*(2), pp. 275–90.

Chen, Andrew H.; Chen, K. C. and Sears, R. Stephen. The Value of Loan Guarantees: The Case of Chrysler Corporation. **In** *Chen, A. H., ed.*, 1986, pp. 101–17. **[G: U.S.]**

Chen, Tain-Jy and Tang, De-Piao. The Production Characteristics of Multinational Firms and the Effects of Tax Incentives: The Case of Taiwan's Electronics Industry. *J. Devel. Econ.*, November 1986, *24*(1), pp. 119–29. **[G: Taiwan]**

Chernick, Howard and Reschovsky, Andrew. Effects of the Reagan Proposal in Massachusetts and New York. **In** *Gold, S. D., ed.*, 1986, pp. 143–59. **[G: U.S.]**

Chernick, Howard and Reschovsky, Andrew. Federal Tax Reform and the Financing of State and Local Government. *J. Policy Anal. Manage.*, Summer 1986, *5*(4), pp. 683–706. **[G: U.S.]**

Chiancone, Aldo. On the Contents of Public Finance in the Soviet Union. *Ricerche Econ.*, Apr.-Sept. 1986, *40*(2–3), pp. 463–77. **[G: U.S.S.R.]**

Chirinko, Robert S. Business Investment and Tax Policy: A Perspective on Existing Models and Empirical Results. *Nat. Tax J.*, June 1986, *39*(2), pp. 137–55. **[G: U.S.]**

Clotfelter, Charles T. The Effect of Tax Simplification on Educational and Charitable Organizations. **In** *Federal Reserve Bank of Boston*, 1986, pp. 187–215. **[G: U.S.]**

Clotfelter, Charles T. and Salamon, Lester M. The Impact of the 1981 Tax Act on Individual Charitable Giving. **In** *Rose-Ackerman, S., ed.*, 1986, *1982*, pp. 207–23. **[G: U.S.]**

Cnossen, Sijbren. Tax Harmonization in the European Community. *Bull. Int. Fiscal Doc.*, December 1986, *40*(12), pp. 545–63. **[G: EEC]**

Conely, William S. and Dodge, William G. U.S.A.: New Delaware Law Facilitates Failsafe Planning. *Bull. Int. Fiscal Doc.*, January 1986, *40*(1), pp. 3–4. **[G: U.S.]**

Cooper, Graeme S. Income Tax Law and Contributive Justice: Some Thoughts on Defining and Expressing a Consistent Theory of Tax Justice and Its Limitations. *Australian Tax Forum*, 1986, *3*(3), pp. 297–332.

Corry, John A. and Decelles, Robert K. The Proposed Branch Level Tax in the U.S.A. *Bull. Int. Fiscal Doc.*, June 1986, *40*(6), pp. 268–71. **[G: U.S.]**

Courant, Paul N. Welfare Effects of Marginal-Cost Taxation of Motor Freight Transportation: A Study of Infrastructure Pricing: Comment. **In** *Rosen, H. S., ed.*, 1986, pp. 128–34. **[G: U.S.]**

Coyne, John and Wright, Mike. The Small Firm, Government Policy and Industrial Change. **In** *Hall, G., ed.*, 1986, pp. 284–306. **[G: U.K.]**

Crane, Steven E. and Nourzad, Farrokh. Federal Income Tax Evasion. **In** *Lindholm, R. W., ed.*, 1986, pp. 140–62. **[G: U.S.]**

Crane, Steven E. and Nourzad, Farrokh. Inflation and Tax Evasion: An Empirical Analysis. *Rev. Econ. Statist.*, May 1986, *68*(2), pp. 217–23. **[G: U.S.]**

Crawford, Roy E. Currency Exchange Problems in California's Worldwide Unitary Taxation. *Bull. Int. Fiscal Doc.*, Aug./Sept. 1986, *40*(8/9), pp. 378–84. **[G: U.S.]**

Dalvi, M. Q. and Ansari, M. M. Measuring Fiscal Performance of the Central and the State Governments in India: A Study in Resource Mobilization. *Indian Econ. J.*, Apr.-June 1986, *33*(4), pp. 106–22. **[G: India]**

Darrat, Ali F. The Economic Impact of Taxes in the U.S.: Some Tests Based on the St. Louis Model. *J. Econ. Stud.*, 1986, *13*(2), pp. 3–13. **[G: U.S.]**

Davies, James B. Equity and Efficiency Aspects of a Business Transfer Tax. **In** *Boadway, R. W. and Mintz, J. M., eds.*, 1986, pp. 31–41. **[G: Canada]**

Davis, Albert. Implications of Federal Reform for State and Local Governments. **In** *Gold, S. D., ed.*, 1986, pp. 161–75. **[G: U.S.]**

Davis, J. Ronnie. Capital Subsidies, Capital Allocation, and Economic Welfare [Targeted Capital Subsidies and Economic Welfare]. *Cato J.*, Spring/Summer 1986, *6*(1), pp. 313–15.

DeBoer, Larry. Lottery Taxes May Be Too High. *J. Policy Anal. Manage.*, Spring 1986, *5*(3), pp. 594–96. **[G: U.S.]**

Dekker, Peter. Transfer Pricing: The Netherlands. *Bull. Int. Fiscal Doc.*, November 1986, *40*(11), pp. 502–05. **[G: Netherlands]**

Del Monte, Alfredo. The Impact of Italian Industrial Policy, 1960–1980. **In** *Hall, G., ed.*, 1986, pp. 128–64. **[G: Italy]**

Der Hovanessian, Aida. Economic Forces Affecting the Middle East. **In** *Roukis, G. S. and Montana, P. J., eds.*, 1986, pp. 47–70. **[G: OPEC]**

Deravajan, Shantayanan; Fullerton, Don and Musgrave, Richard A. Estimating the Distribution of Tax Burdens: A Comparison of Different Approaches. **In** *Musgrave, R. A., Vol. 1*, 1986, *1980*, pp. 274–300. **[G: U.S.]**

Desai, Gunvant M. Growth in Indian Fertilizer Consumption: Price and Non-price Policies. **In** *Segura, E. L.; Shetty, Y. T. and Nishimizu, M., eds.*, 1986, pp. 109–36. **[G: India]**

Diamond, Peter A. and Mirrlees, James A. Payroll-Tax Financed Social Insurance with Variable Retirement. *Scand. J. Econ.*, 1986, *88*(1), pp. 25–50.

Dilnot, Andrew W. and Stark, Graham K. The Distributional Consequences of Mrs. Thatcher. *Fisc. Stud.*, May 1986, *7*(2), pp. 48–53. **[G: U.K.]**

Dilnot, Andrew W. and Stark, Graham K. The Poverty Trap, Tax Cuts, and the Reform of Social Security. *Fisc. Stud.*, February 1986, *7*(1), pp. 1–10. **[G: U.K.]**

DiMaggio, Paul J. Can Culture Survive the Marketplace? **In** *DiMaggio, P. J., ed.*, 1986, pp. 65–92. **[G: U.S.]**

Diokno, Benjamin E. Revenue Mobilization and Responsiveness of Philippine Income Taxes: Implications for Fiscal Policy. *Philippine Rev. Econ. Bus.*, Sept.-Dec. 1986, *23*(3–4), pp. 323–39. **[G: Philippines]**

Dixon, Daryl A. Suggested Refinements of the Treasury Costings of the Occupational Superannuation Tax Expenditures. *Australian Tax Forum*, 1986, *3*(2), pp. 223–32. **[G: Australia]**

Dorgan, Byron L. National Tax Association—Tax Institute of America Symposium: Reform or Revenue? Luncheon Speech. *Nat. Tax J.*, September 1986, *39*(3), pp. 281–84. **[G: U.S.]**

Dresch, Stephen P. The Educational Credit Trust: A Proposal for Reconstitution and Reform of the Student Loan System. *Econ. Educ. Rev.*, 1986, *5*(1), pp. 1–16. **[G: U.S.]**

Due, John F. Tax Incidence, Indirect Taxes, and Transfers—A Comment. *Nat. Tax J.*, December 1986, *39*(4), pp. 539–40.

Duncan, James A. International Financing by U.S. Borrowers: Questions Remain Open after Repeal. *Bull. Int. Fiscal Doc.*, Aug./Sept. 1986, *40*(8/9), pp. 358–62. **[G: U.S.; W. Europe]**

Durán Heras, Almudena. Características de la población y equilibrio financiero del sistema de pensiones. (With English summary.) *Invest. Ecón.*, January 1986, *10*(1), pp. 97–126. **[G: Spain]**

Dutton, John. Optimal Taxes on Foreign Investment in an Overlapping Generation Model. *Public Finance Quart.*, July 1986, *14*(3), pp. 289–311.

Dybvig, Philip H. and Ross, Stephen A. Tax Clienteles and Asset Pricing. *J. Finance*, July 1986, *41*(3), pp. 751–62.

Dye, Richard F. Aid Sources for Higher Education: Taxes and Other Determinants. *Econ. Educ. Rev.*, 1986, *5*(2), pp. 191–95.

Dymits, Lee and Murray, Michael L. Another Look at Implied Tax Rates. *J. Banking Finance*, March 1986, *10*(1), pp. 133–41. **[G: U.S.]**

Easson, Alex. Designing a Business Transfer Tax: Some Basic Considerations. **In** *Boadway, R. W. and Mintz, J. M., eds.*, 1986, pp. 42–46. **[G: Canada]**

Eisner, Robert. Tax Reform and Capital Formation: Discussion. **In** *Federal Reserve Bank of Boston*, 1986, pp. 149–52. **[G: U.S.]**

Elkind, Avi; Spiegel, Menahem and Sheshinski, Eytan. Tax Expenditure. **In** *Kop, Y., ed.*, 1986, pp. 199–225. **[G: Israel]**

Elmer, Peter J. Preferred Stock Arbitrage of Municipal Bond Market Segmentation. *Financial Rev.*, November 1986, *21*(4), pp. 383–98.

Emerson, Craig. Fiscal Arrangements for Mineral Development. **In** *Shome, P., ed.*, 1986, pp. 141–59. **[G: Indonesia; Philippines; Papua New Guinea; Australia]**

Englund, Peter. Transaction Costs, Capital-Gains Taxes, and Housing Demand. *J. Urban Econ.*, November 1986, *20*(3), pp. 274–90.

Etuk, O. E. U. Fertilizer Pricing in Nigeria. **In** *Segura, E. L.; Shetty, Y. T. and Nishimizu, M., eds.*, 1986, pp. 95–101. **[G: Nigeria]**

Evans, Paul and Joines, Douglas H. The Resolution of the Tax Debate. **In** *Canto, V. A.; Kadlec, C. W. and Laffer, A. B., eds.*, 1986, pp. 54–74. **[G: U.S.]**

Even-Shoshan, Orit and Gabbay, Yoram. Distribution of Family Income and Taxes. **In** *Kop, Y., ed.*, 1986, pp. 169–98. **[G: Israel]**

Ezejelue, A. C. Nigeria's Petroleum Profits Tax. *Bull. Int. Fiscal Doc.*, Aug./Sept. 1986, *40*(8/9), pp. 406–12. **[G: Nigeria]**

Fagan, G. and Murphy, A. Employers' Social Insurance Contributions and Employment. *Econ. Soc. Rev.*, October 1986, *18*(1), pp. 43–56. **[G: Ireland]**

Fawthrop, R. Equipment Leasing. **In** *Firth, M. and Keane, S. M., eds.*, 1986, pp. 103–14. **[G: U.K.]**

Feenberg, Daniel R. and Rosen, Harvey S. The Deductibility of State and Local Taxes: Impact Effects by State and Income Class. *Growth Change*, April 1986, *17*(2), pp. 11–31. **[G: U.S.]**

Feenberg, Daniel R. and Rosen, Harvey S. The Interaction of State and Federal Tax Systems: The Impact of State and Local Tax Deductibility. *Amer. Econ. Rev.*, May 1986, *76*(2), pp. 126–31. **[G: U.S.]**

Ferron, Mark J. Issues in Excise Taxation. **In** *Shome, P., ed.*, 1986, pp. 160–70. **[G: ASEAN]**

Findlay, Christopher C. Optimal Taxation of International Income Flows. *Econ. Rec.*, June 1986, *62*(177), pp. 208–14.

Finnerty, John D. Refunding Discounted Debt: A Clarifying Analysis. *J. Finan. Quant. Anal.*, March 1986, *21*(1), pp. 95–106.

Fishelson, Gideon. Allocation for Services and Equity. **In** *Kop, Y., ed.*, 1986, pp. 159–66. **[G: Israel]**

Fisher, Jeffrey D. and Lentz, George H. Tax Reform and the Value of Real Estate Income Property. *Amer. Real Estate Urban Econ. Assoc. J.*, Summer 1986, *14*(2), pp. 287–315. **[G: U.S.]**

Follain, James R. The Impact of the President's Proposals and H.R. 3838 on the Housing Market. **In** *Follain, J. R., ed.*, 1986, pp. 61–85. **[G: U.S.]**

Follain, James R. What Are the Issues and What Is at Stake? **In** *Follain, J. R., ed.*, 1986, pp. 3–8. **[G: U.S.]**

Follain, James R. and Brueckner, Jan K. Federal Income Taxation and Real Estate: Tax Distortions and Their Impacts. **In** *Follain, J. R., ed.*, 1986, pp. 9–25. **[G: U.S.]**

Follain, James R. and Miyake, Tamar Emi. Land versus Capital Value Taxation: A General Equilibrium Analysis. *Nat. Tax J.*, December 1986, *39*(4), pp. 451–70. **[G: Jamaica]**

Fooladi, Iraj. The Effect of Proportional Profit Tax on the Level of Output, under Uncertainty. *Atlantic Econ. J.*, December 1986, *14*(4), pp. 90–94.

Fooladi, Iraj and Roberts, Gordon S. On Preferred Stock. *J. Finan. Res.*, Winter 1986, *9*(4), pp. 319–24. **[G: Canada; U.S.]**

Formby, John P.; Smith, W. James and Sykes, David. Income Redistribution and Local Tax Progressivity: A Reconsideration. *Can. J. Econ.*, November 1986, *19*(4), pp. 807–11.

Formby, John P.; Smith, W. James and Sykes, David. Intersecting Tax Concentration Curves and the Measurement of Tax Progressivity. *Nat. Tax J.*, March 1986, *39*(1), pp. 115–18.

Fournier, Gary M. and Rasmussen, David W. Targeted Capital Subsidies and Economic Welfare. *Cato J.*, Spring/Summer 1986, *6*(1), pp. 295–312.

Fox, Alan, et al. The Effects of Tax Reform on Metropolitan Housing. **In** *Follain, J. R., ed.*, 1986, pp. 165–85. **[G: U.S.]**

Freiberg, Arie. Enforcement Discretion and Taxation Offences. *Australian Tax Forum*, 1986, *3*(1), pp. 55–91. **[G: Australia]**

Freud, Nicholas S. Caveat Vendor: Without Requirements for Transfers of United States Real Property Interests. *Bull. Int. Fiscal Doc.*, Aug./Sept. 1986, *40*(8/9), pp. 363–68. **[G: U.S.]**

Fry, Gene R. Heinze. The Economics of Home Solar Water Heating and the Role of Solar Tax Credits. *Land Econ.*, May 1986, *62*(2), pp. 134–44. **[G: U.S.]**

Fuchs, Victor R. From Bismarck to Woodcock. **In** *Fuchs, V. R.*, 1986, *1976*, pp. 257–71. **[G: U.S.]**

Fuller, James P. U.S.A.: International Tax Aspects of the Transfer or Use of Intangibles. *Bull. Int. Fiscal Doc.*, Apr./May 1986, *40*(4/5), pp. 182–209. **[G: U.S.]**

Fullerton, Don. The Use of Effective Tax Rates in Tax Policy. *Nat. Tax J.*, September 1986, *39*(3), pp. 285–92. **[G: U.S.]**

Fullerton, Don and Lyon, Andrew B. Does the Tax System Favor Investment in High-Tech or Smoke-Stack Industries? *Econ. Inquiry*, July 1986, *24*(3), pp. 403–16. **[G: U.S.]**

Fullerton, Don and Lyon, Andrew B. Uncertain Parameter Values and the Choice among Policy Options. *J. Public Econ.*, June 1986, *30*(1), pp. 109–16.

von Furstenberg, George M. and Green, R. Jeffrey. Supply-Side Modeling from Bits and Pieces. *Amer. Econ. Rev.*, May 1986, *76*(2), pp. 37–42. **[G: U.S.]**

von Furstenberg, George M.; Green, R. Jeffrey and Jeong, Jin-Ho. Tax and Spend, or Spend and Tax? *Rev. Econ. Statist.*, May 1986, *68*(2), pp. 179–88. **[G: U.S.]**

G-Yohannes, Arefaine. The IRA and the Withdrawal Penalty. *J. Cons. Aff.*, Winter 1986, *20*(2), pp. 280–89. **[G: U.S.]**

Gabbay, Yoram. Fiscal Policy. **In** *Kop, Y., ed.*, 1986, pp. 147–58. **[G: Israel]**

Gahvari, Firouz. Labor Supply and Tax Rates: Comment. *Amer. Econ. Rev.*, March 1986, *76*(1), pp. 280–83.

Gandhi, Ved P. Effects of Tax Incentives on Investment and Employment. **In** *Shome, P., ed.*, 1986, pp. 27–42.

García Alba, Pascual. Resultados en imposición indirecta con independencia de los parámetros de demanda: el caso de México. (Results of Indirect Taxation with Independence of Demand Parameters: The Mexican Case. With English summary.) *Estud. Econ.*, January-June 1986, *1*(1), pp. 147–70. **[G: Mexico]**

García Alvarez-Coque, José María. La política de precios agrarios y el bienestar. (With English summary.) *Invest. Ecón.*, May 1986, *10*(2), pp. 227–50. **[G: Spain]**

Gardner, Bruce L. Farm Commodity Programs as Income Transfers. *Cato J.*, Spring/Summer 1986, *6*(1), pp. 251–61.

Gardner, Bruce L. Farm Policy and the Farm Problem. **In** *Cagan, P., ed.*, 1986, pp. 223–46. **[G: U.S.]**

Gardner, Bruce L. and Kramer, Randall A. Experience with Crop Insurance Programs in the United States. **In** *Hazell, P.; Pomareda, C. and Valdés, A., eds.*, 1986, pp. 195–222. **[G: U.S.]**

Garfinkel, Irwin; Moreland, Kemper and Sadka, Efraim. Budget Size Effects on the Optimal Linear Income Tax. *Southern Econ. J.*, July 1986, *53*(1), pp. 187–200.

Gaudet, Gérard and Lasserre, Pierre. Capital Income Taxation, Depletion Allowances, and Nonrenewable Resource Extraction. *J. Public Econ.*, March 1986, *29*(2), pp. 241–53.

Gensler, Howard. Complexity, Verbosity, and Progressivity. **In** *Lindholm, R. W., ed.*, 1986, pp. 50–71. **[G: U.S.]**

Gerken, Egbert; Gross, Martin and Lächler, Ulrich. The Causes and Consequences of Steel Subsidization in Germany. *Europ. Econ. Rev.*, August 1986, *30*(4), pp. 773–804. **[G: W. Germany]**

Geva, Yehuda and Habib, Jack. The Development of the Transfer System and the Redistribution of Income. **In** *Ben-Porath, Y., ed.*, 1986, pp. 209–20. **[G: Israel]**

Gillani, Syeda Fizza. Elasticity and Buoyancy of Federal Taxes in Pakistan. *Pakistan Devel. Rev.*, Summer 1986, *25*(2), pp. 163–74. **[G: Pakistan]**

Gillis, Malcolm. Worldwide Experience in Sales Taxation: Lessons for North America. *Policy Sci.*, September 1986, *19*(2), pp. 125–42. **[G: EEC; U.S.; Canada]**

Gillis, Malcolm; Jenkins, Glenn and Leitzel, Jim. Financing Universal Access in the Telephone Network. *Nat. Tax J.*, March 1986, *39*(1), pp. 35–48. **[G: U.S.]**

Glenday, Graham; Gupta, Anil K. and Pawlak, Henry. Tax Incentives for Personal Charitable Contributions. *Rev. Econ. Statist.*, November 1986, *68*(4), pp. 688–93. **[G: Canada]**

Glickman, David. A Long View of Tax Reform: Remarks. *Nat. Tax J.*, September 1986, *39*(3), pp. 269–72. **[G: U.S.]**

Gofran, K. A. Bangladesh: Depreciation Allowances under the Income-Tax Ordinance, 1984—A Summary. *Bull. Int. Fiscal Doc.*, January 1986, *40*(1), pp. 20–22. **[G: Bangladesh]**

Gold, Steven D. Themes of Federal Tax Reform for State Tax Policy. **In** *Gold, S. D., ed.*, 1986, pp. 177–83. **[G: U.S.]**

Goldberg, Sanford H. Competent Authority: USA. *Bull. Int. Fiscal Doc.*, October 1986, *40*(10), pp. 431–51. **[G: U.S.; OECD]**

Goldsmith, J. C. Summary of Rules Applicable to Transfer Pricing in France. *Bull. Int. Fiscal Doc.*, December 1986, *40*(12), pp. 564–68. **[G: France]**

Goodwin, Thomas H. Inflation, Risk, Taxes, and the Demand for Owner-Occupied Housing. *Rev. Econ. Statist.*, May 1986, *68*(2), pp. 197–206. **[G: U.S.]**

Gordon, Roger H. Taxation of Investment and Savings in a World Economy. *Amer. Econ. Rev.*, December 1986, *76*(5), pp. 1086–1102.

Govind, Har. India: Measures against Tax Avoidance by Multinationals. *Bull. Int. Fiscal Doc.*, July 1986, *40*(7), pp. 302–09. **[G: India]**

Graetz, Michael J.; Reinganum, Jennifer F. and Wilde, Louis L. The Tax Compliance Game: Toward an Interactive Theory of Law Enforcement. *J. Law, Econ., Organ.*, Spring 1986, *2*(1), pp. 1–32. **[G: U.S.]**

Gramlich, Edward M. The Effect of Tax Simplification on State and Local Governments: Discussion. **In** *Federal Reserve Bank of Boston*, 1986, pp. 252–58. **[G: U.S.]**

Granwell, A. W. U.S.A.: Life after Rev. Rul. 84-

152: Treaty Shopping: Recent U.S. Developments. *Bull. Int. Fiscal Doc.*, Apr./May 1986, *40*(4/5), pp. 215–23. **[G: U.S.]**

Gravelle, Hugh S. E. Insurance and Corrective Taxes in the Health Care Market. *J. Econ. (Z. Nationalökon.)*, Supplementum 5, 1986, pp. 99–120.

Gravelle, Jane G. International Tax Competition: Does It Make a Difference for Tax Policy? *Nat. Tax J.*, September 1986, *39*(3), pp. 375–84. **[G: U.S.]**

Grbich, Yuri. Putting Zero Tax Threshold Proposals Back on the Agenda. *Australian Tax Forum*, 1986, *3*(1), pp. 105–13. **[G: Australia]**

Green, Richard C. and Talmor, Eli. Effects of Asymmetric Taxation on the Scale of Corporate Investment. **In** *Edwards, J., et al., eds.*, 1986, pp. 83–97.

Greene, Kenneth V. The Public Choice of Differing Degrees of Tax Progressivity. *Public Choice*, 1986, *49*(3), pp. 265–82. **[G: U.S.]**

Greene, Leonard M. and Fishbein, Bette K. The VAT Alternative. **In** *Lindholm, R. W., ed.*, 1986, pp. 72–103.

Grossman, Philip J. and Chan, Yoke-Fong. The Impact of CPF Savings on Charitable Contributions in Singapore: A Note. *Singapore Econ. Rev.*, October 1986, *31*(2), pp. 79–84. **[G: Singapore]**

Guenther, Robert. Tax Reform and Its Role in the Emerging Dual Market for Housing. **In** *Follain, J. R., ed.*, 1986, pp. 233–36. **[G: U.S.]**

Gupta, Anand P. Taxation and Subsidies. **In** *Dantwala, M. L., et al.*, 1986, pp. 385–99. **[G: India]**

Guttentag, Joseph H. and Misback, Ann E. Resolving Tax Treaty Issues: A Novel Solution. *Bull. Int. Fiscal Doc.*, Aug./Sept. 1986, *40*(8/9), pp. 350–57. **[G: OECD]**

Gwartney, James and Long, James. Tax Rates, Tax Shelters, and the Efficiency of Capital Formation. **In** *Lee, D. R., ed.*, 1986, pp. 107–39. **[G: U.S.]**

Gwartney, James and Stroup, Richard L. Labor Supply and Tax Rates: Reply. *Amer. Econ. Rev.*, March 1986, *76*(1), pp. 284–85.

Gwartney, James and Stroup, Richard L. Labor Supply and Tax Rates: Reply. *Amer. Econ. Rev.*, June 1986, *76*(3), pp. 557–58.

Hadwin, J. F. From Dissonance to Harmony on the Late Medieval Town? *Econ. Hist. Rev., 2nd Ser.*, August 1986, *39*(3), pp. 423–26. **[G: U.K.]**

Hakim, Leonardo and Wallich, Christine. OECD Deficits, Debt, and Savings Structure and Trends, 1965–81: A Survey of the Evidence. **In** *Lal, D. and Wolf, M., eds.*, 1986, pp. 292–360. **[G: OECD]**

Hale, David D. Are the U.S. and Japan Swapping Tax Systems? *Challenge*, Nov./Dec. 1986, *29*(5), pp. 52–56. **[G: U.S.; Japan]**

Hall, Robert E. Liquidity Constraints, Fiscal Policy, and Consumption: Comments. *Brookings Pap. Econ. Act.*, 1986, (1), pp. 51–53. **[G: U.S.]**

Halperin, Daniel I. Interest in Disguise: Taxing the "Time Value of Money." *Yale Law J.*, January 1986, *95*(3), pp. 506–52. **[G: U.S.]**

Halphen, Christine. U.S.A.: Effect of the 1985–1986 U.S. Tax Reform Bill on Foreign Investments in U.S. Real Estate. *Bull. Int. Fiscal Doc.*, March 1986, *40*(3), pp. 115–24. **[G: U.S.]**

Hamaekers, H. M. A. L. Multilateral Instruments on the Avoidance of Double Taxation. *Bull. Int. Fiscal Doc.*, March 1986, *40*(3), pp. 99–104. **[G: OECD; CMEA]**

Hamson, Don and Ziegler, Peter. The Implications of Negative Gearing Restrictions and Capital Gains Taxation on Investment. *Australian Tax Forum*, 1986, *3*(4), pp. 369–80. **[G: Australia]**

Hansmann, Henry B. The Rationale for Exempting Nonprofit Organizations from Corporate Income Taxation. **In** *Rose-Ackerman, S., ed.*, 1986, *1981*, pp. 367–93. **[G: U.S.]**

Harriss, C. Lowell. Tax Policy for Economic Progress: Developing Countries as Well as Developed Ones Should Tax to Promote Production and Jobs. *Amer. J. Econ. Soc.*, July 1986, *45*(3), pp. 257–76.

Hart, Jeffrey A. British Industrial Policy. **In** *Barfield, C. E. and Schambra, W. A., eds.*, 1986, pp. 128–60. **[G: U.K.]**

Hart, Jeffrey A. West German Industrial Policy. **In** *Barfield, C. E. and Schambra, W. A., eds.*, 1986, pp. 161–86. **[G: W. Germany]**

Hart, Peter E. and Trinder, C. Employment Protection, National Insurance, Income Tax and Youth Unemployment. **In** *Hart, P. E., ed.*, 1986, pp. 29–44. **[G: U.K.]**

Hatsopoulos, George N. Tax Reform and Capital Formation: Discussion. **In** *Federal Reserve Bank of Boston*, 1986, pp. 140–44. **[G: U.S.]**

Hatta, Tatsuo and Haltiwanger, John. Tax Reform and Strong Substitutes. *Int. Econ. Rev.*, June 1986, *27*(2), pp. 303–15.

Head, John G. The Australian Tax Debate: Some Myths and Misconceptions. *Australian Tax Forum*, 1986, *3*(1), pp. 31–44. **[G: Australia]**

Heady, Christopher J. and Mitra, Pradeep K. Optimal Taxation and Public Production in an Open Dual Economy. *J. Public Econ.*, August 1986, *30*(3), pp. 293–316.

Heaton, Hal. Corporate Taxation and Leasing. *J. Finan. Quant. Anal.*, September 1986, *21*(3), pp. 351–59.

Heaton, Hal. The Relative Yields on Taxable and Tax-Exempt Debt. *J. Money, Credit, Banking*, November 1986, *18*(4), pp. 482–94. **[G: U.S.]**

Helfrich-Laubrock, Jacoba. Review of Activities of the ICC Tax Commission. *Bull. Int. Fiscal Doc.*, Aug./Sept. 1986, *40*(8/9), pp. 401–03. **[G: OECD]**

Helliwell, John F., et al. The Western Accord and Lower World Oil Prices. *Can. Public Policy*, June 1986, *12*(2), pp. 341–55. **[G: Canada]**

Hellwig, Martin. The Optimal Linear Income Tax

Revisited. *J. Public Econ.*, November 1986, *31*(2), pp. 163–79.

Hendershott, Patric H. Tax Reform, Interest Rates, and Capital Allocation. **In** *Follain, J. R., ed.*, 1986, pp. 27–57. **[G: U.S.]**

Hendershott, Patric H. Tax Simplification and Financial Markets. **In** *Federal Reserve Bank of Boston*, 1986, pp. 153–77. **[G: U.S.]**

Hendershott, Patric H. and Ling, David C. Likely Impacts of the Administration's Tax Proposals and H.R. 3838. **In** *Follain, J. R., ed.*, 1986, pp. 87–112. **[G: U.S.]**

Henderson, Yolanda K. Lessons from Federal Reform of Business Taxes. *New Eng. Econ. Rev.*, Nov./Dec. 1986, pp. 9–25. **[G: U.S.]**

Herzog, Henry W., Jr. and Schlottmann, Alan M. State and Local Tax Deductibility and Metropolitan Migration. *Nat. Tax J.*, June 1986, *39*(2), pp. 189–200. **[G: U.S.]**

Hochman, Harold M. The Charitable Deduction: Comments. **In** *Rose-Ackerman, S., ed.*, 1986, pp. 297–99.

Hochman, Harold M. and Rodgers, James D. The Optimal Tax Treatment of Charitable Contributions. **In** *Rose-Ackerman, S., ed.*, 1986, *1977*, pp. 224–45. **[G: U.S.]**

Hodes, Daniel A. and Mauer, Laurence J. U.S. Tax Reform: Capital Recovery and International Direct Investment. *Bus. Econ.*, January 1986, *21*(1), pp. 50–54. **[G: U.S.]**

Hoffman, Philip T. Taxes and Agrarian Life in Early Modern France: Land Sales, 1550–1730. *J. Econ. Hist.*, March 1986, *46*(1), pp. 37–55. **[G: France]**

Holloway, Thomas M. and Reeb, Jane S. Sources of Change in Federal Transfer Payments to Persons: An Update. *Surv. Curr. Bus.*, June 1986, *66*(6), pp. 21–25. **[G: U.S.]**

Hongskrailers, Montri and Jap, Kim Siong. Thailand: Recent Tax Package to Boost the Economy. *Bull. Int. Fiscal Doc.*, Aug./Sept. 1986, *40*(8/9), pp. 417–20. **[G: Thailand]**

Hongskrailers, Montri and Jap, Kim Siong. Transfer Pricing Provisions, Rulings and Case Law: Thailand. *Bull. Int. Fiscal Doc.*, November 1986, *40*(11), pp. 514–20. **[G: Thailand]**

Honkapohja, Seppo. Intergenerational Aspects of Public Transfers, Borrowing and Debt: Comment. *Scand. J. Econ.*, 1986, *88*(1), pp. 269–72.

Hrubovcak, James. Measuring Implicit Rental Rates for Farm Capital. *Agr. Econ. Res.*, Winter 1986, *38*(1), pp. 19–33. **[G: U.S.]**

Hubbard, R. Glenn and Judd, Kenneth L. Liquidity Constraints, Fiscal Policy, and Consumption. *Brookings Pap. Econ. Act.*, 1986, (1), pp. 1–50. **[G: U.S.]**

Hughes, Gerard. Employers' Social Insurance Contributions and Employment: Reply. *Econ. Soc. Rev.*, October 1986, *18*(1), pp. 57–68. **[G: Ireland]**

Hughes, Gordon A. A New Method for Estimating the Effects of Fuel Taxes: An Application to Thailand. *World Bank Econ. Rev.*, September 1986, *1*(1), pp. 65–101. **[G: Thailand]**

Hutchens, Robert M. The Effects of the Omnibus Budget Reconciliation Act of 1981 on AFDC Recipients: A Review of Studies. **In** *Ehrenberg, R. G., ed., Pt. B*, 1986, pp. 351–87. **[G: U.S.]**

Ingberg, Mikael. Reformen av företagsbeskattningen. Nuläge och framtidsutsikter. (The Reform of Business Taxation. With English summary.) *Ekon. Samfundets Tidskr.*, 1986, *39*(3), pp. 131–48. **[G: Finland]**

Jackman, Richard and Layard, Richard. A Wage-Tax, Worker-Subsidy Policy for Reducing the 'Natural' Rate of Unemployment. **In** *Beckerman, W., ed.*, 1986, pp. 153–69.

Jackson, Ira A. Amnesty and Creative Tax Administration. *Nat. Tax J.*, September 1986, *39*(3), pp. 317–23. **[G: U.S.]**

Jap, Kim Siong. Indonesia: Overhaul of an Inherited Tax System: New Tax on Land, Buildings and New Stamp Duties. *Bull. Int. Fiscal Doc.*, Apr./May 1986, *40*(4/5), pp. 165–67. **[G: Indonesia]**

Jap, Kim Siong. Taiwan: An Outline of the Proposed Value Added Tax System. *Bull. Int. Fiscal Doc.*, January 1986, *40*(1), pp. 18–19.

Jap, Kim Siong. Taiwan: Tax Changes for 1986. *Bull. Int. Fiscal Doc.*, February 1986, *40*(2), pp. 66. **[G: Taiwan]**

Jap, Kim Siong. Taiwan: The Value Added Tax Law in Force. *Bull. Int. Fiscal Doc.*, July 1986, *40*(7), pp. 315–18. **[G: Taiwan]**

Jefferson, Edward G. Tax Policy for the Eighties. **In** *Landau, R. and Jorgenson, D. W., eds.*, 1986, pp. 75–84. **[G: U.S.]**

Jenkins, Glenn. The Evolution of Sales Tax Reform in Canada. **In** *Boadway, R. W. and Mintz, J. M., eds.*, 1986, pp. 9–13. **[G: Canada]**

Jha, Raghbendra and Murty, M. N. Optimal Non-linear Taxation with Interdependent Utilities. *J. Quant. Econ.*, July 1986, *2*(2), pp. 213–20.

Jimenez, Emmanuel. The Public Subsidization of Education and Health in Developing Countries: A Review of Equity and Efficiency. *World Bank Res. Observer*, January 1986, *1*(1), pp. 111–29. **[G: LDCs]**

Johnson, Chalmers. The Institutional Foundations of Japanese Industrial Policy. **In** *Barfield, C. E. and Schambra, W. A., eds.*, 1986, pp. 187–205. **[G: Japan]**

Joines, Douglas H. Government Spending, Tax Rates, and Private Investment in Plant and Equipment. **In** *Canto, V. A.; Kadlec, C. W. and Laffer, A. B., eds.*, 1986, pp. 36–53. **[G: U.S.]**

Jorgenson, Dale W. and Yun, Kun-Young. Tax Policy and Capital Allocation. *Scand. J. Econ.*, 1986, *88*(2), pp. 355–77. **[G: U.S.]**

Jorgenson, Dale W. and Yun, Kun-Young. The Efficiency of Capital Allocation. *Scand. J. Econ.*, 1986, *88*(1), pp. 85–107. **[G: U.S.]**

Junge, G. and Zarinnejadan, Milad. A Rate-of-Return Model of Investment Behavior for Switzerland. *Empirical Econ.*, 1986, *11*(3), pp. 153–67. **[G: Switzerland]**

Jungenfelt, Karl G. Comment [The Efficiency of Capital Allocation] [Tax Policy and Capital Allocation]. *Scand. J. Econ.*, 1986, *88*(2), pp. 379–82. **[G: U.S.]**

Kafoglis, Milton Z. Tax Policy and Public Utility Regulation. **In** *Moorhouse, J. C., ed.*, 1986, pp. 97–133. **[G: U.S.]**

Kaneko, Hiroshi. Basic Structure of the Foreign Tax Credit System of Japan. *Bull. Int. Fiscal Doc.*, Apr./May 1986, *40*(4/5), pp. 148–53. **[G: Japan]**

Karlinger, Janos. Fertilizer Pricing in Hungary. **In** *Segura, E. L.; Shetty, Y. T. and Nishimizu, M., eds.*, 1986, pp. 201–03. **[G: Hungary]**

Katz, Claudio J.; Mahler, Vincent A. and Franz, Michael G. The Impact of Taxes in Developed Capitalist Countries [Reply]. *Amer. Polit. Sci. Rev.*, March 1986, *80*(1), pp. 254–57. **[G: OECD]**

Kay, John A. Approaching an Expenditure Tax? *Fisc. Stud.*, May 1986, *7*(2), pp. 33–37. **[G: U.K.]**

Kay, John A. Tax Reform in Context: A Strategy for the 1990s. *Fisc. Stud.*, November 1986, *7*(4), pp. 1–17. **[G: U.K.]**

Kay, John A. The Rationale of Taxation. *Oxford Rev. Econ. Policy*, Summer 1986, *2*(2), pp. 1–6. **[G: U.K.]**

Kehoe, Timothy J. and Serra-Puche, Jaime. A General Equilibrium Analysis of Price Controls and Subsidies on Food in Mexico. *J. Devel. Econ.*, April 1986, *21*(1), pp. 65–87. **[G: Mexico]**

Kemp, Robert; Reckers, Philip M. J. and Arrington, C. Edward. U.S. Tax Reform: Tax Evasion Concerns. *Bus. Econ.*, January 1986, *21*(1), pp. 55–57. **[G: U.S.]**

Kesselman, Jonathan R. Pros and Cons of a Business Transfer Tax in Canada. **In** *Boadway, R. W. and Mintz, J. M., eds.*, 1986, pp. 24–30. **[G: Canada]**

Kesselman, Jonathan R. The Royal Commission's Proposals for Income Security Reform. *Can. Public Policy*, Supp. February 1986, *12*, pp. 101–12. **[G: Canada]**

Kessler, Denis; Perelman, Sergio and Pestieau, Pierre. L'hypothèse d'équivalence entre impôt et emprunt: un test sur les pays de l'OCDE. (With English summary.) *Ann. Écon. Statist.*, July-Sept. 1986, (3), pp. 141–49. **[G: OECD]**

Kessler, Denis; Perelman, Sergio and Pestieau, Pierre. Public Debt, Tax, and Consumption: A Test on O.E.C.D. Countries. *Public Finance*, 1986, *41*(1), pp. 63–70. **[G: OECD]**

Khanna, Kailash C. India: Aspects of the Black Economy: Report of a Study. *Bull. Int. Fiscal Doc.*, February 1986, *40*(2), pp. 61–65. **[G: India]**

King, John R. On the Revenue Effects of Tax Changes. *Fisc. Stud.*, February 1986, *7*(1), pp. 51–60. **[G: U.K.]**

King, Ronald F., et al. The Impact of Taxes in Developed Capitalist Countries [Comment]. *Amer. Polit. Sci. Rev.*, March 1986, *80*(1), pp. 251–54. **[G: OECD]**

Kingston, Geoffrey H. and Layton, Allan P. The Tax Smoothing Hypothesis: Some Australian Empirical Results. *Australian Econ. Pap.*, December 1986, *25*(47), pp. 247–51. **[G: Australia]**

Kinnucan, Henry; Cacho, Oscar and Hanson, Gregory D. Effects of Selected Tax Policies on Management and Growth of a Catfish Enterprise. *Southern J. Agr. Econ.*, December 1986, *18*(2), pp. 215–25.

Kleiman, Ephraim and Pincus, J. J. Incremental Export Subsidies: A Rejoinder [The Cyclical Effects of Incremental Export Subsidies]. *Econ. Rec.*, March 1986, *62*(176), pp. 93–94. **[G: Australia]**

van de Klundert, Theo. C. and Peters, Peter J. Tax Incidence in a Model with Perfect Foresight of Agents and Rationing in Markets. *J. Public Econ.*, June 1986, *30*(1), pp. 37–59.

Knapp, Martin. The Relative Cost-Effectiveness of Public, Voluntary and Private Providers of Residential Child Care. **In** *Culyer, A. J. and Jönsson, B., eds.*, 1986, pp. 171–99. **[G: U.S.]**

Knowlton, Winthrop. Members of the Audience: Public and Private Responsibilities to the Arts. **In** *Knowlton, W. and Zeckhauser, R., eds.*, 1986, pp. 137–51. **[G: U.S.]**

Kollintzas, Tryphon. Tax Policy under Nongeometric Physical Depreciation. *Public Finance Quart.*, July 1986, *14*(3), pp. 263–88.

Kopcke, Richard W. Tax Reform and Capital Formation. **In** *Federal Reserve Bank of Boston*, 1986, pp. 103–39. **[G: U.S.]**

Kostecki, Apoloniusz. The Trends in Taxation of Foreign Enterprises (1945–1986): Poland. *Bull. Int. Fiscal Doc.*, December 1986, *40*(12), pp. 569–73. **[G: Poland]**

Kovenock, Dan. Property and Income Taxation in an Economy with an Austrian Sector. *Land Econ.*, May 1986, *62*(2), pp. 201–09.

Krever, Richard. Companies, Shareholders and Capital Gains Taxation. *Australian Tax Forum*, 1986, *3*(3), pp. 267–96. **[G: Australia]**

Kwon, O. Yul. A Critique of Korea's Foreign Capital Inducement Policy in the Light of Neutral Taxation. *J. Econ. Devel.*, July 1986, *11*(1), pp. 47–67. **[G: S. Korea]**

Laffer, Arthur B. The Complete Flat Tax. **In** *Canto, V. A.; Kadlec, C. W. and Laffer, A. B., eds.*, 1986, pp. 108–40. **[G: U.S.]**

Laffer, Arthur B. The Ellipse: An Explication of the Laffer Curve in a Two-Factor Model. **In** *Canto, V. A.; Kadlec, C. W. and Laffer, A. B., eds.*, 1986, pp. 1–35. **[G: U.S.]**

Laffer, Arthur B. The Tightening Grip of the Poverty Trap. **In** *Canto, V. A.; Kadlec, C. W. and Laffer, A. B., eds.*, 1986, pp. 141–59. **[G: U.S.]**

Lakonishok, Josef and Smidt, Seymour. Volume for Winners and Losers: Taxation and Other Motives for Stock Trading. *J. Finance*, September 1986, *41*(4), pp. 951–74. **[G: U.S.]**

Lanthier, Allan R. Draft Guidelines on International Transfer Pricing: Canada. *Bull. Int. Fiscal Doc.*, November 1986, *40*(11), pp. 487–96. **[G: Canada]**

Lapidoth, Arye. The Israeli Experience of an Inflation Adjusted Tax Base with Special Reference to Income Tax Law (Adjustment for Inflation) Provisional Measure, 5755-1985. *Bull. Int. Fiscal Doc.*, March 1986, *40*(3), pp. 125–28. **[G: Israel]**

Lapidoth, Arye. The Territorial Scope of Income Tax with Special Reference to the 1984 Amendment: Israel. *Bull. Int. Fiscal Doc.*, November 1986, *40*(11), pp. 521–25. **[G: Israel]**

Latham, Roger W. and Naisbitt, Barry. Balanced Budget Tax Incidence. *Public Finance,* 1986, *41*(2), pp. 244–59.

LeBlanc, Michael and Hrubovcak, James. The Effects of Tax Policy on Aggregate Agricultural Investment. *Amer. J. Agr. Econ.*, November 1986, *68*(4), pp. 767–77. **[G: U.S.]**

Lee, Dwight R. and Misiolek, Walter S. Substituting Pollution Taxation for General Taxation: Some Implications for Efficiency in Pollutions Taxation. *J. Environ. Econ. Manage.*, December 1986, *13*(4), pp. 338–47.

Lehmann, Geoffrey. Tax Shelters and Anti-shelters—Economic and Legal Analysis of Tax Proposals. *Australian Tax Forum,* 1986, *3*(2), pp. 115–30.

Lerman, Allen H. Tax Amnesty: The Federal Perspective. *Nat. Tax J.*, September 1986, *39*(3), pp. 325–32. **[G: U.S.]**

Lerman, Paul. The Effect of Marginal Tax Rates on the Advantage of Tax-Sheltered Savings Plans. *J. Cons. Aff.*, Summer 1986, *20*(1), pp. 106–17. **[G: U.S.]**

Levis, Mario. The 1984 Budget: The Impact on Corporate Tax Payments. *Nat. Westminster Bank Quart. Rev.*, May 1986, pp. 28–42. **[G: U.K.]**

Lewis, Alan. Fiscal Policy: The Importance of Perceptions and Attitudes. **In** *Gilad, B. and Kaish, S., eds., Vol. B,* 1986, pp. 111–22. **[G: U.K.; U.S.]**

Lind, Stephen A. Current Proposals for Tax Reform in the United States. *Australian Tax Forum,* 1986, *3*(1), pp. 93–104. **[G: U.S.]**

Lindbeck, Assar and Weibull, Jörgen W. Intergenerational Aspects of Public Transfers, Borrowing and Debt. *Scand. J. Econ.*, 1986, *88*(1), pp. 239–67.

Lindley, Robert. Labour Demand: Microeconomic Aspects of State Intervention. **In** *Hart, P. E., ed.*, 1986, pp. 154–75. **[G: U.K.]**

Lindsey, Lawrence B. The Effect of the President's Tax Reform Proposal on Charitable Giving. *Nat. Tax J.*, March 1986, *39*(1), pp. 1–12. **[G: U.S.]**

Liu, Pak-Wai. Lorenz Domination and Global Tax Progressivity: A Reply [Income Redistribution and Local Tax Progressivity: A Reconsideration]. *Can. J. Econ.*, November 1986, *19*(4), pp. 812–13.

Lloyd, Alan G. and Mauldon, Roger G. Agricultural Instability and Alternative Government Policies: The Australian Experience. **In** *Hazell, P.; Pomareda, C. and Valdés, A., eds.*, 1986, pp. 156–77. **[G: Australia]**

Lloyd, Peter J. and McDonald, Ian M. The FBT—Does It Matter Who Pays? *Australian Econ. Rev.*, 4th Quarter 1986, (76), pp. 34–38. **[G: Australia]**

Loizides, Ioannis. On Income Tax Progression: A Decomposition Analysis. *Greek Econ. Rev.*, June 1986, *8*(1), pp. 79–94. **[G: Greece]**

Lopes, Mauro de Rezende and Dias, Guilherme Leite da Silva. The Brazilian Experience with Crop Insurance Programs. **In** *Hazell, P.; Pomareda, C. and Valdés, A., eds.*, 1986, pp. 240–62. **[G: Brazil]**

Luger, Michael I. Depreciation Profiles and Depreciation Policy in a Spatial Context. *J. Reg. Sci.*, February 1986, *26*(1), pp. 141–59. **[G: U.S.]**

Lund, Diderik. Less Than Single Dividend Taxation: A Note. *J. Public Econ.*, March 1986, *29*(2), pp. 255–61.

Luskin, David. The Case for Subsidising Extra Jobs: A Comment. *Econ. J.*, March 1986, *96*(381), pp. 212–15. **[G: U.K.]**

Lüthi, D. Survey of the Swiss Treaty Practice. *Bull. Int. Fiscal Doc.*, June 1986, *40*(6), pp. 272–74. **[G: Switzerland]**

Lynk, Edward L. and Webb, Michael G. An Unintended Consequence of the Taxation System for U.K. North Sea Oil. *Scot. J. Polit. Econ.*, February 1986, *33*(1), pp. 58–73. **[G: U.K.]**

Makin, John H. Savings Rates in Japan and the United States: The Roles of Tax Policy and Other Factors. **In** *Adams, F. G. and Wachter, S. M., eds.*, 1986, pp. 91–126. **[G: OECD]**

Malanga, Frank. The Relationship between IRS Enforcement and Tax Yield. *Nat. Tax J.*, September 1986, *39*(3), pp. 333–37. **[G: U.S.]**

Malcomson, James M. Some Analytics of the Laffer Curve. *J. Public Econ.*, April 1986, *29*(3), pp. 263–79.

Mallon, Richard. Public Enterprise Pricing Policies. **In** *U.N., Dept. of Technical Co-operation for Development*, 1986, pp. 84–99.

Manage, Neela and Marlow, Michael L. The Causal Relation between Federal Expenditures and Receipts. *Southern Econ. J.*, January 1986, *52*(3), pp. 617–29. **[G: U.S.]**

Mansfield, Charles Y. Taxation of International Tourism in Developing Countries. *Bull. Int. Fiscal Doc.*, October 1986, *40*(10), pp. 452–61. **[G: LDCs]**

Mansfield, Edwin. The R&D Tax Credit and Other Technology Policy Issues. *Amer. Econ. Rev.*, May 1986, *76*(2), pp. 190–94. **[G: U.S.; Canada; Sweden]**

Mansury, R. The Measurement of Business Income. *Bull. Int. Fiscal Doc.*, March 1986, *40*(3), pp. 129–36. **[G: Indonesia]**

Marcel, Mario. Diez años del IVA en Chile. (Ten Years of VAT in Chile. With English summary.) *Colección Estud. CIEPLAN*, June 1986, (19), pp. 83–134. **[G: Chile]**

Marks, Bernard. Structure and Design of the Fringe Benefits Tax. *Australian Econ. Rev.*, 4th Quarter 1986, (76), pp. 25–29. **[G: Australia]**

Martini, Christine; Collins, Brett and Rickard, John A. FBT: How to Structure Remuneration

Packages for 1986–87. *Australian Econ. Rev.*, 4th Quarter 1986, (76), pp. 39–44. **[G: Australia]**

Massone, Pedro. The Argentine Income Tax Reform. *Bull. Int. Fiscal Doc.*, June 1986, *40*(6), pp. 237–59. **[G: Argentina]**

Mauer, Jay. The President's 1985 Tax Reform Proposal: An Economic Assessment. **In** *Lindholm, R. W., ed.*, 1986, pp. 230–50. **[G: U.S.]**

Mayer, Colin. Corporation Tax, Finance and the Cost of Capital. *Rev. Econ. Stud.*, January 1986, *53*(1), pp. 93–112.

Mayo, Stephen K. Sources of Inefficiency in Subsidized Housing Programs: A Comparison of U.S. and German Experience. *J. Urban Econ.*, September 1986, *20*(2), pp. 229–49. **[G: U.S.; W. Germany]**

McCaleb, Thomas S. Tax Deductions and Credits, Direct Subsidies, and Efficiency in Public Expenditure. *Public Choice*, 1986, *49*(2), pp. 127–41.

McConaghy, Mark. A Long View of Tax Reform. *Nat. Tax J.*, September 1986, *39*(3), pp. 265–67. **[G: U.S.]**

McDonald, Robert. Taxes and the Hedging of Forward Commitments. *J. Futures Markets*, Summer 1986, *6*(2), pp. 207–22.

McKee, Michael J.; Visser, Jacob J. C. and Saunders, Peter G. Marginal Tax Rates on the Use of Labour and Capital in OECD Countries. *OECD Econ. Stud.*, Autumn 1986, (7), pp. 45–101. **[G: OECD]**

McKenna, William F. Tax Reform Must Consider the Realities of Housing. **In** *Follain, J. R., ed.*, 1986, pp. 213–17. **[G: U.S.]**

McKeown, Mary P. Issues in Higher Education Budgeting Policy [An Adult Life Cycle Perspective on Public Subsidies to Higher Education in Three Countries] [Reform of Budget Control in Higher Education]. *Econ. Educ. Rev.*, 1986, *5*(2), pp. 159–63. **[G: U.S.]**

McLure, Charles E., Jr. Rationale Underlying the Treasury Proposals. **In** *Federal Reserve Bank of Boston*, 1986, pp. 29–48. **[G: U.S.]**

McLure, Charles E., Jr. Tax Competition: Is What's Good for the Private Goose Also Good for the Public Gander? *Nat. Tax J.*, September 1986, *39*(3), pp. 341–48. **[G: U.S.]**

McLure, Charles E., Jr. The Tax Treatment of Owner-Occupied Housing: The Achilles' Heel of Tax Reform? **In** *Follain, J. R., ed.*, 1986, pp. 219–32. **[G: U.S.]**

McMurtry, Burton J. Tax Policy Influence on Venture Capital. **In** *Landau, R. and Jorgenson, D. W., eds.*, 1986, pp. 137–51. **[G: U.S.]**

Meagher, G. A. An Empirical Analysis of the Effects of a Change in the Mix of Direct and Indirect Taxation. *Australian Econ. Pap.*, June 1986, *25*(46), pp. 47–56. **[G: Australia]**

Meagher, G. A. and Agrawal, Nisha. Taxation Reform and Income Distribution in Australia. *Australian Econ. Rev.*, 3rd Quarter 1986, (75), pp. 33–56. **[G: Australia]**

Mikesell, John L. Federal Individual Income Tax Collection Costs: The Burden of Compliance and Administration. **In** *Lindholm, R. W., ed.*, 1986, pp. 33–49. **[G: U.S.]**

Mills, Edwin S. and Rosen, Harvey S. Tax Reform and Commercial Real Estate. **In** *Follain, J. R., ed.*, 1986, pp. 151–61. **[G: U.S.]**

Mills, J. E. A. Ghana's Wealth Tax: Some Issues and Problems. *Bull. Int. Fiscal Doc.*, February 1986, *40*(2), pp. 49–54. **[G: Ghana]**

Minarik, Joseph J. Tax Reform: Up from the Ashes. *Challenge*, July/Aug. 1986, *29*(3), pp. 33–39. **[G: U.S.]**

Minford, Patrick. Incentives in the United Kingdom. **In** *Balassa, B. and Giersch, H., eds.*, 1986, pp. 279–95. **[G: U.K.]**

Mintz, Jack M. Issues Arising from the Design of the BTT. **In** *Boadway, R. W. and Mintz, J. M., eds.*, 1986, pp. 49–61.

Mintz, Jack M. and Tulkens, Henry. Commodity Tax Competition between Member States of a Federation: Equilibrium and Efficiency. *J. Public Econ.*, March 1986, *29*(2), pp. 133–72.

Moffitt, Robert. Work Incentives in Transfer Programs (Revisited): A Study of the AFDC Program. **In** *Ehrenberg, R. G., ed., Pt. B*, 1986, pp. 389–439. **[G: U.S.]**

Montias, J. Michael. Public Support for the Performing Arts in Europe and the United States. **In** *DiMaggio, P. J., ed.*, 1986, pp. 287–319. **[G: OECD]**

Moran, Patrick J. U.S.A.: Recent Developments Relating to the Taxation of International Technology Transfers in the Pharmaceutical Industry. *Bull. Int. Fiscal Doc.*, Apr./May 1986, *40*(4/5), pp. 210–14. **[G: U.S.]**

Morgan, David R. The Government's Tax Reform Package: An Overview. *Australian Tax Forum*, 1986, *3*(1), pp. 3–30. **[G: Australia]**

Morgan, Eleanor. Stimulating Investment—Government Incentives and the Financial Leasing Industry. **In** *Hall, G., ed.*, 1986, pp. 261–83. **[G: W. Europe; U.K.]**

Morris, C. Nick and Preston, Ian. Taxes, Benefits and the Distribution of Income 1968–83. *Fisc. Stud.*, November 1986, *7*(4), pp. 18–27. **[G: U.K.]**

Morris, Michael H. and McDonald, Bill. Income Averaging Benefits from Income Growth: The Gradual Elimination of an Inequity. *Public Finance Quart.*, April 1986, *14*(2), pp. 199–208. **[G: U.S.]**

Morris, Nick and Preston, Ian. Inequality, Poverty and the Redistribution of Income. *Bull. Econ. Res.*, November 1986, *38*(4), pp. 275–344. **[G: U.K.]**

Munnell, Alicia H. Economic Consequences of Tax Simplification: An Overview. **In** *Federal Reserve Bank of Boston*, 1986, pp. 1–28. **[G: U.S.]**

Munnell, Alicia H. The Economics of Tax Simplification: An Overview. *New Eng. Econ. Rev.*, Jan./Feb. 1986, pp. 11–27. **[G: U.S.]**

Murphy, D. G. The Zimbabwe 1985 Budget. *Bull. Int. Fiscal Doc.*, January 1986, *40*(1), pp. 23–25. **[G: Zimbabwe]**

Musgrave, Richard A. A Further Note on the Double Taxation of Savings. **In** *Musgrave,*

R. A., Vol. 1, 1986, *1939,* pp. 105–07.

Musgrave, Richard A. Economic Consequences of Tax Simplification: An Overall Assessment—Is It Worth It? **In** *Federal Reserve Bank of Boston,* 1986, pp. 259–84. **[G: U.S.]**

Musgrave, Richard A. Effects of Business Taxes on International Commodity Flows. **In** *Musgrave, R. A., Vol. 1,* 1986, *1966,* pp. 209–21. **[G: France; U.K.; U.S.; W. Germany; Italy]**

Musgrave, Richard A. Growth with Equity. **In** *Musgrave, R. A., Vol. 1,* 1986, *1963,* pp. 198–208.

Musgrave, Richard A. How Progressive Is the Income Tax? **In** *Musgrave, R. A., Vol. 1,* 1986, *1959,* pp. 178–90. **[G: U.S.]**

Musgrave, Richard A. In Defence of an Income Concept. **In** *Musgrave, R. A., Vol. 1,* 1986, *1967,* pp. 222–37.

Musgrave, Richard A. On Incidence. **In** *Musgrave, R. A., Vol. 1,* 1986, *1953,* pp. 155–77.

Musgrave, Richard A. Pathway to Tax Reform. **In** *Musgrave, R. A., Vol. 2,* 1986, *1984,* pp. 335–37. **[G: U.S.]**

Musgrave, Richard A. The Nature of Horizontal Equity and the Principle of Broad-Based Taxation: A Friendly Critique. **In** *Musgrave, R. A., Vol. 1,* 1986, *1983,* pp. 301–15.

Musgrave, Richard A.; Case, Karl E. and Leonard, Herman B. The Distribution of Fiscal Burdens and Benefits. **In** *Musgrave, R. A., Vol. 1,* 1986, *1974,* pp. 238–59. **[G: U.S.]**

Musgrave, Richard A. and Gillis, Malcolm. Objectives: Report of Colombia Tax Mission. **In** *Musgrave, R. A., Vol. 2,* 1986, *1971,* pp. 149–57. **[G: Colombia]**

Musgrave, Richard A.; Heller, Peter S. and Peterson, George E. Cost-Effectiveness of Alternative Income Maintenance Schemes. **In** *Musgrave, R. A., Vol. 2,* 1986, *1970,* pp. 82–102. **[G: U.S.]**

Musgrave, Richard A. and Musgrave, Peggy B. Inter-nation Equity. **In** *Musgrave, R. A., Vol. 2,* 1986, *1972,* pp. 43–63.

Musgrave, Richard A. and Thin, Tun. Income Tax Progression, 1929–48. **In** *Musgrave, R. A., Vol. 1,* 1986, *1948,* pp. 132–54. **[G: U.S.]**

Neale, Walter C. Tax-Based Incomes Policies: A Commentary for the Future. *J. Econ. Issues,* December 1986, *20*(4), pp. 969–87. **[G: U.S.]**

Nelson, Michael A. An Empirical Analysis of State and Local Tax Structure in the Context of the Leviathan Model of Government. *Public Choice,* 1986, *49*(3), pp. 283–94. **[G: U.S.]**

Netzer, Dick. The Effect of Tax Simplification on State and Local Governments. **In** *Federal Reserve Bank of Boston,* 1986, pp. 222–51. **[G: U.S.]**

Niaz, M. Shafi. The Fertilizer Pricing System in Pakistan. **In** *Segura, E. L.; Shetty, Y. T. and Nishimizu, M., eds.,* 1986, pp. 164–84. **[G: Pakistan]**

Niron, Suna. Fertilizer Pricing in Turkey. **In** *Segura, E. L.; Shetty, Y. T. and Nishimizu, M., eds.,* 1986, pp. 219–35. **[G: Turkey]**

Niskanen, William A. A Constitutional Approach to Taxes and Transfers. *Cato J.,* Spring/Summer 1986, *6*(1), pp. 347–52. **[G: U.S.]**

Nolan, Brian. An Administrator's Overview of Tax Reform. *Australian Tax Forum,* 1986, *3*(4), pp. 355–67. **[G: Australia]**

O'Faircheallaigh, Ciaran. Mineral Taxation in Less Developed Countries: Papua New Guinea's Balanced System. *Amer. J. Econ. Soc.,* July 1986, *45*(3), pp. 291–95.

O'Faircheallaigh, Ciaran. Mineral Taxation, Mineral Revenues and Mine Investment in Zambia, 1964–83. *Amer. J. Econ. Soc.,* January 1986, *45*(1), pp. 53–67. **[G: Zambia]**

Odling-Smee, John. Labour Demand: Microeconomic Aspects of State Intervention: Comment. **In** *Hart, P. E., ed.,* 1986, pp. 176–79. **[G: U.K.]**

Oestreich, Nathan; Summer, Jeinie and Walker, John F. Roots of the Existing Federal Corporate Income Taxes. **In** *Lindholm, R. W., ed.,* 1986, pp. 280–314. **[G: U.S.]**

Okimoto, Daniel I. The Japanese Challenge in High Technology. **In** *Landau, R. and Rosenberg, N., eds.,* 1986, pp. 541–67. **[G: Japan]**

Olmstead, Dennis J. Fiji: An Outline of the Budget Tax Proposals for 1986. *Bull. Int. Fiscal Doc.,* February 1986, *40*(2), pp. 66–68. **[G: Fiji]**

Olmstead, Dennis J. Malaysia: An Outline of the 1985 Budget Tax Proposals. *Bull. Int. Fiscal Doc.,* February 1986, *40*(2), pp. 68–70. **[G: Malaysia]**

Olson, Mancur. The Exploitation and Subsidization of Agriculture in Developing and Developed Countries. **In** *Maunder, A. and Renborg, U., eds.,* 1986, pp. 49–59.

Oner, Erhan. Ex-factory Pricing in Turkey. **In** *Segura, E. L.; Shetty, Y. T. and Nishimizu, M., eds.,* 1986, pp. 236–46. **[G: Turkey]**

Oosterhuis, Paul W. A Long View of Tax Reform: Remarks. *Nat. Tax J.,* September 1986, *39*(3), pp. 261–63. **[G: U.S.]**

Orrock, Don C. Australia: Foreign Exchange Gains and Losses. *Bull. Int. Fiscal Doc.,* Aug./Sept. 1986, *40*(8/9), pp. 404–05. **[G: Australia]**

Orrock, Don C. Foreign Tax Credits: Australia. *Bull. Int. Fiscal Doc.,* November 1986, *40*(11), pp. 508–11. **[G: Australia]**

Paqué, Karl-Heinz. The Efficiency of Tax Incentives to Private Charitable Giving—Some Econometric Evidence for the Federal Republic of Germany. *Weltwirtsch. Arch.,* 1986, *122*(4), pp. 690–712. **[G: W. Germany]**

Parikh, Parimal M. India: Is Tax Avoidance Merging into Tax Evasion? A Change in the Judiciaries' Approach to Tax Avoidance. *Bull. Int. Fiscal Doc.,* January 1986, *40*(1), pp. 11–14. **[G: India]**

Parikh, Parimal M. Long-term Fiscal Policy 1985: Its Bearing on Direct Taxes in India. *Bull. Int. Fiscal Doc.,* June 1986, *40*(6), pp. 235–36. **[G: India]**

Park, Thae S. Federal Personal Income Taxes: Revised and Updated Estimates of Liabilities and Payments, 1949–84. *Surv. Curr. Bus.,*

May 1986, *66*(5), pp. 41. **[G: U.S.]**

Parmenter, B. R. Taxation of Non-cash Fringe Benefits. *Australian Econ. Rev.*, 4th Quarter 1986, (76), pp. 30–33. **[G: Australia]**

Parsons, Ross W. Income Taxation—An Institution in Decay? *Australian Tax Forum*, 1986, *3*(3), pp. 233–66.

Pasour, E. C., Jr. Rent Seeking and Farm Commodity Programs: Is Education the Solution? [Farm Commodity Programs as Income Transfers]. *Cato J.*, Spring/Summer 1986, *6*(1), pp. 263–70.

Pauly, Mark V. Taxation, Health Insurance, and Market Failure in the Medical Economy. *J. Econ. Lit.*, June 1986, *24*(2), pp. 629–75. **[G: U.S.]**

Pauwels, Wilfried. Correct and Incorrect Measures of the Deadweight Loss of Taxation. *Public Finance*, 1986, *41*(2), pp. 267–76.

Pechman, Joseph A. Economic Consequences of Tax Simplification: An Overall Assessment—Is It Worth It? Discussion. **In** *Federal Reserve Bank of Boston*, 1986, pp. 285–89. **[G: U.S.]**

Pechman, Joseph A. Pechman's Tax Incidence Study: A Response. *Amer. Econ. Rev.*, December 1986, *76*(5), pp. 1219–20.

Peek, Joe and Wilcox, James A. Tax Rates and Interest Rates on Tax-Exempt Securities. *New Eng. Econ. Rev.*, Jan./Feb. 1986, pp. 29–41. **[G: U.S.]**

Perry, David. Designing a Business Transfer Tax: Some Basic Considerations: Comment. **In** *Boadway, R. W. and Mintz, J. M., eds.*, 1986, pp. 47–48. **[G: Canada]**

Petersen, John E. The Impacts of the President's Tax Proposal on State and Local Government Capital Financing. **In** *Walzer, N. and Chicoine, D. L., eds.*, 1986, pp. 162–78. **[G: U.S.]**

Pfingsten, Andreas. Distributionally-Neutral Tax Changes for Different Inequality Concepts ['Linear' Income Tax Cuts: Distributional Effects, Social Preferences, and Revenue Elasticities]. *J. Public Econ.*, August 1986, *30*(3), pp. 385–93.

Phelps, Charles E. Cross-Subsidies and Charge-Shifting in American Hospitals. **In** *Sloan, F. A.; Blumstein, J. F. and Perrin, J. M., eds.*, 1986, pp. 108–25. **[G: U.S.]**

Pollock, Oscar S. Gunning for Capital Gains Again. **In** *Landau, R. and Jorgenson, D. W., eds.*, 1986, pp. 153–57. **[G: U.S.]**

Pomareda, Carlos. The Financial Viability of Agricultural Insurance. **In** *Hazell, P.; Pomareda, C. and Valdés, A., eds.*, 1986, pp. 281–91. **[G: Selected Countries]**

Poterba, James M.; Rotemberg, Julio J. and Summers, Lawrence H. A Tax-Based Test for Nominal Rigidities. *Amer. Econ. Rev.*, September 1986, *76*(4), pp. 659–75. **[G: U.S.; U.K.]**

Prisman, Eliezer Z. Immunization as a Maxmin Strategy: A New Look. *J. Banking Finance*, December 1986, *10*(4), pp. 491–509.

Purohit, Mahesh C. Nigeria: Reforming Sales Tax in Developing Countries: A Study of the Nigerian Sales Tax System. *Bull. Int. Fiscal Doc.*, January 1986, *40*(1), pp. 5–10. **[G: Nigeria]**

Quintieri, Beniamino and Rosati, Furio Camillo. Changes in Tax Structure and Individual Behaviour. *Econ. Notes*, 1986, (3), pp. 30–46.

Rapanos, Vassilis. Variable Returns to Scale and Tax Incidence: An Extension of Harberger's Model. *J. Econ. (Z. Nationalökon.)*, 1986, *46*(4), pp. 397–406.

Rashid, Muhammad and Gandhi, Devinder K. Tax and Savings Implications of the Canadian Registered Retirement Savings Plans. *Financial Rev.*, November 1986, *21*(4), pp. 463–71. **[G: Canada]**

Rausser, Gordon C., et al. Macroeconomic Linkages, Taxes, and Subsidies in the U.S. Agricultural Sector. *Amer. J. Agr. Econ.*, May 1986, *68*(2), pp. 399–412. **[G: U.S.]**

Ray, Ranjan. On Setting Indirect Taxes in India Using the Ramsey Approach: Evidence from Household Budget Data. *J. Quant. Econ.*, July 1986, *2*(2), pp. 249–62. **[G: India]**

Ray, Ranjan. Redistribution through Commodity Taxes: The Nonlinear Engel Curve Case. *Public Finance*, 1986, *41*(2), pp. 277–84. **[G: India]**

Ray, Ranjan. Sensitivity of 'Optimal' Commodity Tax Rates to Alternative Demand Functional Forms: An Econometric Case Study of India. *J. Public Econ.*, November 1986, *31*(2), pp. 253–68. **[G: India]**

Rebelo, Sérgio. Optimização do controlo da evasao fiscal: O caso do imposto sobre o lucro das empresas. (With English summary.) *Economia (Portugal)*, October 1986, *10*(3), pp. 415–45.

Reese, Thomas J. Miracles or Incrementalism. *Nat. Tax J.*, September 1986, *39*(3), pp. 273–76. **[G: U.S.]**

Revesz, John T. On Some Advantages of Progressive Indirect Taxation. *Public Finance*, 1986, *41*(2), pp. 182–99.

Richardson, Martin and Wilkie, Simon. Incremental Export Subsidies [The Cyclical Effects of Incremental Export Subsidies]. *Econ. Rec.*, March 1986, *62*(176), pp. 88–92. **[G: Australia]**

Rigby, S. H. Late Medieval Urban Prosperity: The Evidence of the Lay Subsidies [English Provincial Towns in the Later Middle Ages] [The Medieval Lay Subsidies and Economic History]. *Econ. Hist. Rev., 2nd Ser.*, August 1986, *39*(3), pp. 411–16. **[G: U.K.]**

Riley, William B., Jr. and Montgomery, Austin H., Jr. The Tax Reform Act of 1984 and Market Discount Bonds. *Nat. Tax J.*, March 1986, *39*(1), pp. 79–83. **[G: U.S.]**

Robbins, Aldona E.; Robbins, Gary A. and Roberts, Paul Craig. The Relative Impact of Taxation and Interest Rates on the Cost of Capital. **In** *Landau, R. and Jorgenson, D. W., eds.*, 1986, pp. 281–316. **[G: U.S.]**

Roberts, Paul Craig. Taxation, Relative Prices, and Capital Formation. **In** *Lee, D. R., ed.*, 1986, pp. 87–106. **[G: U.S.]**

Roberts, Paul Craig. The Revolution in U.S. Tax Policy. *Nat. Westminster Bank Quart. Rev.*, November 1986, pp. 2–7. **[G: U.S.]**

Robinson, Olive. Employment Protection, National Insurance, Income Tax and Youth Unemployment: Comment. **In** *Hart, P. E., ed.*, 1986, pp. 45–49. **[G: U.K.]**

Roglin, Otto. Zur Steuerbilanzoptimierung von Personengesellschaften. (With English summary.) *Z. Betriebswirtshaft*, February 1986, *56*(2), pp. 152–77.

Rose, Louis A. Inflation, Tax Rules, and the Price of Land Relative to Capital. *Nat. Tax J.*, March 1986, *39*(1), pp. 59–64.

Rosenman, Robert E. The Optimal Tax for Maximum Economic Yield: Fishery Regulation under Rational Expectations. *J. Environ. Econ. Manage.*, December 1986, *13*(4), pp. 348–62.

Roskamp, Karl W. Optimal Life Time Consumption Paths under Income and Property Taxes: Effects of Tax Structure Changes. *Public Finance*, 1986, *41*(1), pp. 1–7.

Roth, Allan. Legal Environment. **In** *Gray, H. P., ed.*, 1986, pp. 43–69. **[G: U.S.]**

Rothschild, Leonard W., Jr. Worldwide Combined Reporting—The End Is in Sight. *Bull. Int. Fiscal Doc.*, Aug./Sept. 1986, *40*(8/9), pp. 374–77. **[G: U.S.]**

Ruback, Richard S. Calculating the Market Value of Riskless Cash Flows. *J. Finan. Econ.*, March 1986, *15*(3), pp. 323–39.

Ruhm, Thomas F. Capital Gains Taxation: Incentive to Growth. **In** *Landau, R. and Jorgenson, D. W., eds.*, 1986, pp. 159–69. **[G: U.S.]**

Sack, Paul. Winners and Losers in Commercial Real Estate from the President's Proposals. **In** *Follain, J. R., ed.*, 1986, pp. 137–49. **[G: U.S.]**

Sahasakul, Chaipat. The U.S. Evidence on Optimal Taxation over Time. *J. Monet. Econ.*, November 1986, *18*(3), pp. 251–75. **[G: U.S.]**

Salant, Walter S. A Critical Look at Supply-Side Theory and a Brief Look at Some of Its International Aspects. **In** *[Tarshis, L.]*, 1986, pp. 108–24.

Sampson, Anthony A. The Shift to Indirect Taxation in a Unionized Economy. *Bull. Econ. Res.*, January 1986, *38*(1), pp. 87–91.

Samuelson, Paul A. Theory of Optimal Taxation. *J. Public Econ.*, July 1986, *30*(2), pp. 137–43.

Sappington, David E. M. Designing Incentives for Efficient Production in Large-scale Enterprises: The Case of Fertilizer Manufacturers. **In** *Segura, E. L.; Shetty, Y. T. and Nishimizu, M., eds.*, 1986, pp. 69–89. **[G: Egypt; India]**

Sato, Kazuo. Economic Laws and the Household Economy in Japan: Lags in Policy Response to Economic Changes. **In** *Saxonhouse, G. R. and Yamamura, K., eds.*, 1986, pp. 3–55. **[G: Japan]**

Sav, G. Thomas. On Subsidies for Energy-Saving Durables. *Amer. Econ.*, Spring 1986, *30*(1), pp. 56–59.

Sav, G. Thomas. The Failure of Solar Tax Incentives: A Dynamic Analysis. *Energy J.*, July 1986, *7*(3), pp. 51–66. **[G: U.S.]**

Saxonhouse, Gary R. Industrial Policy and Factor Markets: Biotechnology in Japan and the United States. **In** *Patrick, H., ed.*, 1986, pp. 97–135. **[G: U.S.; Japan]**

Scafuri, Allen J. Measurable Welfare Change with Optimal Commodity Taxation [Optimal Taxation, the Compensation Principle and the Measurement of Changes in Economic Welfare]. *J. Public Econ.*, April 1986, *29*(3), pp. 383–87.

van Schijndel, Geert-Jan C. Th. Dynamic Behaviour of a Value Maximizing Firm under Personal Taxation. *Europ. Econ. Rev.*, October 1986, *30*(5), pp. 1043–62.

Schindler, Guenter. Taxation of Intercorporate Transfer Pricing: A Management Responsibility: U.S.A. *Bull. Int. Fiscal Doc.*, November 1986, *40*(11), pp. 497–501. **[G: U.S.]**

Schneider, Friedrich. Estimating the Size of the Danish Shadow Economy Using the Currency Demand Approach: An Attempt. *Scand. J. Econ.*, 1986, *88*(4), pp. 643–68. **[G: Denmark]**

Schroeder, Edward A. and Lindbeck, Rudolph. A Problem with Marginal Analysis. *Atlantic Econ. J.*, March 1986, *14*(1), pp. 122. **[G: U.S.]**

Schuck, Peter H. Designing Hospital Care Subsidies for the Poor. **In** *Sloan, F. A.; Blumstein, J. F. and Perrin, J. M., eds.*, 1986, pp. 72–93. **[G: U.S.]**

Schuster, J. Mark Davidson. Tax Incentives as Arts Policy in Western Europe. **In** *DiMaggio, P. J., ed.*, 1986, pp. 320–60. **[G: W. Europe]**

Schwartz, J. Brad. Wealth Neutrality in Higher Education: The Effects of Student Grants. *Econ. Educ. Rev.*, 1986, *5*(2), pp. 107–17. **[G: U.S.]**

Scitovsky, Tibor. Subsidies for the Arts: The Economic Argument. **In** *Scitovsky, T.*, 1986, *1983*, pp. 149–59.

Seiders, David F. Should Tax Laws Be Used to Stimulate Investment in Housing? **In** *Follain, J. R., ed.*, 1986, pp. 207–12. **[G: U.S.]**

Sergiovanni, B. A. and Mills, J. E. A. A Survey of Taxes on the Individual in Ghana. *Bull. Int. Fiscal Doc.*, February 1986, *40*(2), pp. 47–48. **[G: Ghana]**

Severn, Alan K. Taxation of Federal Land Banks: Competitive Effects. *Quart. J. Bus. Econ.*, Autumn 1986, *25*(4), pp. 41–55. **[G: U.S.]**

Shannon, John. Interstate Tax Competition—The Need for a New Look. *Nat. Tax J.*, September 1986, *39*(3), pp. 339–40. **[G: U.S.]**

Sharda, N. K. Tax Structure in a Transitional Provincial Economy: A Study of Himachal Pradesh. *Margin*, January 1986, *18*(2), pp. 42–50. **[G: India]**

Shome, Parthasarathi. Effects of Tax Incentives on Investment and Employment: Appendix: The Broad Goals of Tax Incentives. **In** *Shome, P., ed.*, 1986, pp. 43–47. **[G: Thailand; Malaysia; Philippines]**

Shome, Parthasarathi. Empirical Evidence on the Incidence of the Corporate Income Tax. **In** *Shome, P., ed.*, 1986, pp. 93–113. **[G: ASEAN]**

Shome, Parthasarathi and Dalton, Alfred H. Why Rate Reductions Are Not a Substitute for Inflation Adjustment of the Personal Income Tax Base: Botswana. *Bull. Int. Fiscal Doc.*, November 1986, *40*(11), pp. 529–31. **[G: Botswana]**

Short, Cameron. Reducing the Cost of the Dairy Program. *Can. J. Agr. Econ.*, November 1986, *34*(3), pp. 379–97. **[G: Canada]**

Shoven, John B. Rationale Underlying the Treasury Proposals: Discussion. **In** *Federal Reserve Bank of Boston*, 1986, pp. 55–59. **[G: U.S.]**

Siegfried, John J. The Effects of Student Higher Education Grants. *Econ. Educ. Rev.*, 1986, *5*(2), pp. 129–33. **[G: U.S.]**

Siggel, Eckhard. Protection, Distortions and Investment Incentives in Zaire: A Quantitative Analysis. *J. Devel. Econ.*, July-Aug. 1986, *22*(2), pp. 295–319. **[G: Zaire]**

de Silva, R. G. L. Sri Lanka: Witholding Tax on Interest—Operation of the Law. *Bull. Int. Fiscal Doc.*, July 1986, *40*(7), pp. 310–11. **[G: Sri Lanka]**

Simon, John G. Charity and Dynasty under the Federal Tax System. **In** *Rose-Ackerman, S., ed.*, 1986, *1978*, pp. 246–64. **[G: U.S.]**

Simonds, Richard R. Mutual Fund Strategies for IRA Investors. *J. Portfol. Manage.*, Winter 1986, *12*(2), pp. 40–43. **[G: U.S.]**

Sjaastad, Larry A.; Almansi, Aquiles and Hurtado, Carlos. The Debt Crisis in Latin America. **In** *Lal, D. and Wolf, M., eds.*, 1986, pp. 131–81. **[G: Argentina; Brazil; Chile; Mexico; Venezuela]**

Slade, Margaret E. Taxation of Non-renewable Resources at Various Stages of Production. *Can. J. Econ.*, May 1986, *19*(2), pp. 281–97.

Slemrod, Joel. Taxation and Business Investment. **In** *Cagan, P., ed.*, 1986, pp. 45–72. **[G: U.S.]**

Slemrod, Joel. The Effect of Tax Simplification on Individuals. **In** *Federal Reserve Bank of Boston*, 1986, pp. 64–91. **[G: U.S.]**

Slesnick, Daniel T. The Measurement of Effective Commodity Tax Progressivity. *Rev. Econ. Statist.*, May 1986, *68*(2), pp. 224–31. **[G: U.S.]**

Sloan, Frank A. and Adamache, Killard W. Taxation and the Growth of Nonwage Compensation. *Public Finance Quart.*, April 1986, *14*(2), pp. 115–37. **[G: U.S.]**

Small, Kenneth A. and Winston, Clifford. Welfare Effects of Marginal-Cost Taxation of Motor Freight Transportation: A Study of Infrastructure Pricing. **In** *Rosen, H. S., ed.*, 1986, pp. 113–28. **[G: U.S.]**

Solow, John L. Interindustry Flows and the Incidence of the Corporate Income Tax. *J. Public Econ.*, August 1986, *30*(3), pp. 359–68. **[G: U.S.]**

Somel, Kutlu. Agricultural Support Policies in Turkey, 1950–1980: An Overview. **In** *Richards, A., ed.*, 1986, pp. 97–130. **[G: Turkey]**

Sommers, Paul M. Measurement of Tax Progressivity: A Further Application. *Atlantic Econ. J.*, March 1986, *14*(1), pp. 59–62. **[G: U.S.]**

Spencer, Nicola S. Taxation of Husband and Wife: Lessons from Europe. *Fisc. Stud.*, August 1986, *7*(3), pp. 83–90. **[G: U.K.]**

Spicer, Michael W. Civilization at a Discount: The Problem of Tax Evasion. *Nat. Tax J.*, March 1986, *39*(1), pp. 13–20. **[G: U.S.]**

Spigler, I. Public Finance. **In** *Kaser, M. C. and Radice, E. A., eds.*, 1986, pp. 117–69. **[G: E. Europe]**

Spiro, Erwin. Republic of South Africa: The 1986 Income Tax Changes. *Bull. Int. Fiscal Doc.*, July 1986, *40*(7), pp. 312–14. **[G: S. Africa]**

Spiro, Erwin. The Income Tax Law since the Second World War: Republic of South Africa. *Bull. Int. Fiscal Doc.*, December 1986, *40*(12), pp. 574–78. **[G: S. Africa]**

Spooner, Gillian M. Effective Tax Rates from Financial Statements. *Nat. Tax J.*, September 1986, *39*(3), pp. 293–306.

Starr, Paul. Health Care for the Poor: The Past Twenty Years. **In** *Danziger, S. H. and Weinberg, D. H., eds.*, 1986, pp. 106–32. **[G: U.S.]**

Steedman, Ian. Produced Inputs and Tax Incidence Theory. *Public Finance*, December 1986, *41*(3), pp. 331–49.

Steindel, Charles. Tax Reform and the Merger and Acquisition Market: The Repeal of *General Utilities*. *Fed. Res. Bank New York Quart. Rev.*, Autumn 1986, *11*(3), pp. 31–35. **[G: U.S.]**

Steinmo, Sven. So What's Wrong with Tax Expenditures? A Reevaluation Based on Swedish Experience. *Public Budg. Finance*, Summer 1986, *6*(2), pp. 27–44. **[G: Sweden]**

Steuerle, C. Eugene. The Effect of Tax Simplification on Educational and Charitable Organizations: Discussion. **In** *Federal Reserve Bank of Boston*, 1986, pp. 216–21. **[G: U.S.]**

Stewart, Ian A. Consensus, Flexibility and Equity. *Can. Public Policy*, June 1986, *12*(2), pp. 307–13. **[G: Canada]**

Stewart, Marion B. U.S. Tax Policy, Intrafirm Transfers, and the Allocative Efficiency of Transnational Corporations. *Public Finance*, December 1986, *41*(3), pp. 350–71. **[G: U.S.]**

Stikeman, Heward. *Furniss* v *Dawson*: The Canadian Approach. *Fisc. Stud.*, February 1986, *7*(1), pp. 82–94. **[G: Canada]**

Stock, Duane. The Analytics of Tax Effects in Discount Bond Valuation. *Financial Rev.*, November 1986, *21*(4), pp. 451–62.

Stoddart, Greg L., et al. Tobacco Taxes and Health Care Costs: Do Canadian Smokers Pay Their Way? *J. Health Econ.*, March 1986, *5*(1), pp. 63–80. **[G: Canada]**

Strauss, Robert P. and Harkins, Peter B. The Net Fiscal Impact of Selected Federal Block Grant Programs. *J. Reg. Sci.*, February 1986, *26*(1), pp. 63–85. **[G: U.S.]**

Strnad, Jeff. The Charitable Contribution Deduction: A Politico-Economic Analysis. **In** *Rose-Ackerman, S., ed.*, 1986, pp. 265–96.

Sturm, Norbert. Erfolgsbesteuerung und Risikobereitschaft bei unternehmerischen Langfristentscheidungen. (With English summary.) Z. *Betriebswirtshaft*, September 1986, *56*(9), pp. 805–26.

Suits, Daniel B. and Musgrave, Richard A. *Ad Valorem* and Unit Taxes Compared. **In** *Musgrave, R. A., Vol. 1*, 1986, *1953*, pp. 191–97.

Summers, Lawrence H. Economic Consequences of Tax Simplification: An Overall Assessment—Is It Worth It? Discussion. **In** *Federal Reserve Bank of Boston*, 1986, pp. 290–94. **[G: U.S.]**

Summers, Lawrence H. Liquidity Constraints, Fiscal Policy, and Consumption: Comments. *Brookings Pap. Econ. Act.*, 1986, (1), pp. 53–57. **[G: U.S.]**

Sumner, Michael T. Investment and the 1984 Budget: An Interim Assessment. *Oxford Bull. Econ. Statist.*, November 1986, *48*(4), pp. 331–38. **[G: U.K.]**

Sunley, Emil M. Federal Tax Policy and the Budget. **In** *Landau, R. and Jorgenson, D. W., eds.*, 1986, pp. 85–96. **[G: U.S.]**

Sunley, Emil M. Rationale Underlying the Treasury Proposals: Discussion. **In** *Federal Reserve Bank of Boston*, 1986, pp. 60–63. **[G: U.S.]**

Svensson, Lars-Gunnar. National Income and Marginal Taxes. *Scand. J. Econ.*, 1986, *88*(4), pp. 565–81.

Svensson, Lars-Gunnar. Taxation of Savings. *J. Econ. (Z. Nationalökon.)*, 1986, *46*(4), pp. 421–26.

Svensson, Lars-Gunnar and Weibull, Jörgen W. An Upper Bound on Optimal Income Taxes. *J. Public Econ.*, July 1986, *30*(2), pp. 165–81.

Symons, Elizabeth and Walker, Ian. The Reform of Personal Taxation: A Brief Analysis. *Fisc. Stud.*, May 1986, *7*(2), pp. 38–47. **[G: U.K.]**

Tanzi, Vito. Economic Development and Tax Structure. **In** *Shome, P., ed.*, 1986, pp. 9–24. **[G: ASEAN]**

Tatom, John A. The Adjustableness of the Federal Income Tax System. **In** *Lindholm, R. W., ed.*, 1986, pp. 163–203. **[G: U.S.]**

Taylor, C. Robert. Risk Aversion versus Expected Profit Maximization with a Progressive Income Tax. *Amer. J. Agr. Econ.*, February 1986, *68*(1), pp. 137–43. **[G: U.S.]**

van Thiel, Servaas. Ghana: Tax Incentives for Investment: Ghana's More Realistic Approach. *Bull. Int. Fiscal Doc.*, Apr./May 1986, *40*(4/5), pp. 168–75. **[G: Ghana]**

Thimmaiah, G. India: Long-term Fiscal Policy—A Critique. *Bull. Int. Fiscal Doc.*, June 1986, *40*(6), pp. 231–34. **[G: India]**

Thirsk, Wayne R. The Marginal Welfare Cost of Corporate Taxation in Canada. *Public Finance*, 1986, *41*(1), pp. 78–95. **[G: Canada]**

Thorson, Douglas Y. The Growth and Failure of the Income Tax. **In** *Lindholm, R. W., ed.*, 1986, pp. 1–32. **[G: U.S.]**

Tobin, James. Tax Simplification and Financial Markets: Discussion. **In** *Federal Reserve Bank of Boston*, 1986, pp. 178–83. **[G: U.S.]**

Toma, Eugenia Froedge and Toma, Mark. A Congressional Control Model of Treasury Revenue Collection. *Southern Econ. J.*, July 1986, *53*(1), pp. 141–54. **[G: U.S.]**

Tridimas, G. Effective Demand and the Switch from Direct to Indirect Taxes in South Africa. *S. Afr. J. Econ.*, September 1986, *54*(3), pp. 263–72. **[G: S. Africa]**

Tsujii, Hiroshi. An Economic Analysis of Rice Insurance in Japan. **In** *Hazell, P.; Pomareda, C. and Valdés, A., eds.*, 1986, pp. 143–55. **[G: Japan]**

Tuomala, Matti. On the Optimal Income Taxation and Educational Decisions. *J. Public Econ.*, July 1986, *30*(2), pp. 183–98.

Ture, Norman B. and Bonilla, Carlos E. ACRS-ITC, CCRS, and NCRS Cost Recovery in an Inflationary Economy. **In** *Landau, R. and Jorgenson, D. W., eds.*, 1986, pp. 171–89. **[G: U.S.]**

Utton, Michael. Developments in British Industrial and Competition Policies. **In** *Hall, G., ed.*, 1986, pp. 59–83. **[G: U.K.]**

Vann, Richard J. and Parsons, Ross W. The Foreign Tax Credit and Reform of International Taxation. *Australian Tax Forum*, 1986, *3*(2), pp. 131–221. **[G: Australia]**

Vedder, Richard. Tithing for Leviathan: The Case for a True Flat-Rate Tax. **In** *Lee, D. R., ed.*, 1986, pp. 141–69. **[G: U.S.]**

Vella, Edwin A. Malta: The Merchant Shipping Act, 1973—Tax Concessions. *Bull. Int. Fiscal Doc.*, Aug./Sept. 1986, *40*(8/9), pp. 413–16.

Venables, Anthony J. Production Subsidies, Import Tariffs, and Imperfectly Competitive Trade. **In** *Greenaway, D. and Tharakan, P. K. M., eds.*, 1986, pp. 68–87.

Vennamo, Pekka. Finlands skattepolitik nu och i framtiden. (Finnish Taxation Policy Now and in the Future. With English summary.) *Ekon. Samfundets Tidskr.*, 1986, *39*(2), pp. 77–89. **[G: Finland]**

Venti, Steven F. and Wise, David A. Tax-Deferred Accounts, Constrained Choice and Estimation of Individual Saving. *Rev. Econ. Stud.*, August 1986, *53*(4), pp. 579–601. **[G: U.S.]**

Verbon, Harrie A. A. Altruism, Political Power and Public Pensions. *Kyklos*, 1986, *39*(3), pp. 343–58.

Wakefield, Joseph C. Federal Fiscal Programs. *Surv. Curr. Bus.*, February 1986, *66*(2), pp. 26–31. **[G: U.S.]**

Walker, Charls E. The Treasury Tax Reform Plan. **In** *Landau, R. and Jorgenson, D. W., eds.*, 1986, pp. 317–24. **[G: U.S.]**

Walter, John R. Short-term Municipal Securities. *Fed. Res. Bank Richmond Econ. Rev.*, Nov./Dec. 1986, *72*(6), pp. 25–34. **[G: U.S.]**

Warren, Alvin C., Jr. Taxation of Corporations. **In** *Knowlton, W. and Zeckhauser, R., eds.*, 1986, pp. 281–97. **[G: U.S.]**

Warren, Alvin C., Jr. The Timing of Taxes. *Nat. Tax J.*, December 1986, *39*(4), pp. 499–505.

Waud, Roger N. Tax Aversion and the Laffer Curve. *Scot. J. Polit. Econ.*, August 1986, *33*(3), pp. 213–27.

Wenders, John T. Efficiency, Subsidy, and Cross-Subsidy in Electric Utility Pricing. **In** *Moorhouse, J. C., ed.*, 1986, pp. 307–36. **[G: U.S.]**

Wenger, Ekkehard. Einkommensteuerliche Periodisierungsregeln, Unternehmenserhaltung und optimale Einkommensbesteuerung. Teil II: Einkommensteuerliche Periodisierungregeln, neutrale und optimale Besteuerung. (With English summary.) *Z. Betriebswirtshaft,* February 1986, *56*(2), pp. 132–51.

Wetzler, James W. Corporate Income Tax Reform. **In** *Landau, R. and Jorgenson, D. W., eds.,* 1986, pp. 97–117. **[G: U.S.]**

Weymark, John A. A Reduced-Form Optimal Nonlinear Income Tax Problem. *J. Public Econ.,* July 1986, *30*(2), pp. 199–217.

Wheeler, James E. and Outslay, Edmund. The Phantom Federal Income Taxes of General Dynamics Corporation. *Accounting Rev.,* October 1986, *61*(4), pp. 760–74. **[G: U.S.]**

Wildasin, David E. Interstate Tax Competition: A Comment [Tax Competition: Is What's Good for the Private Goose Also Good for the Public Gander?]. *Nat. Tax J.,* September 1986, *39*(3), pp. 353–56. **[G: U.S.]**

Wilensky, Gail R. Underwriting the Uninsured: Targeting Providers or Individuals. **In** *Sloan, F. A.; Blumstein, J. F. and Perrin, J. M., eds.,* 1986, pp. 148–66. **[G: U.S.]**

Williams, Joseph. Tax Clienteles and Asset Pricing: Discussion. *J. Finance,* July 1986, *41*(3), pp. 762–63.

Witte, Ann D. The Underground Economy in the United States and Western Europe. **In** *Lindholm, R. W., ed.,* 1986, pp. 204–29. **[G: U.S.; W. Europe]**

Witte, John F. A Long View of Tax Reform. *Nat. Tax J.,* September 1986, *39*(3), pp. 255–60. **[G: U.S.]**

Yamauchi, Toyoji. Evolution of the Crop Insurance Program in Japan. **In** *Hazell, P.; Pomareda, C. and Valdés, A., eds.,* 1986, pp. 223–39. **[G: Japan]**

Yang, James T. Y. Collaboration between Nonprofit Universities and Commercial Enterprises: The Rationale for Exempting Nonprofit Universities from Federal Income Taxation. *Yale Law J.,* July 1986, *95*(8), pp. 1857–81. **[G: U.S.]**

Yoost, Dean A.; Watanabe, Takashi and Fox-Moore, Nancy. The New Intercompany Pricing Rules: Japan. *Bull. Int. Fiscal Doc.,* November 1986, *40*(11), pp. 506–07. **[G: Japan]**

Yunker, James A. A Supply Side Analysis of the Laffer Hypothesis. *Public Finance,* December 1986, *41*(3), pp. 372–92.

Zak, Barbara M. Determination of Residency of Alien Individuals for U.S. Federal Income Tax Purposes. *Bull. Int. Fiscal Doc.,* Aug./Sept. 1986, *40*(8/9), pp. 369–73. **[G: U.S.]**

Zechner, Josef and Swoboda, Peter. The Critical Implicit Tax Rate and Capital Structure. *J. Banking Finance,* October 1986, *10*(3), pp. 327–41.

Zhu, Yu and Friend, Irwin. The Effects of Different Taxes on Risky and Risk-free Investment and on the Cost of Capital. *J. Finance,* March 1986, *41*(1), pp. 53–66.

Zschau, Ed. Government Policies for Innovation and Growth. **In** *Landau, R. and Rosenberg, N., eds.,* 1986, pp. 535–39. **[G: U.S.]**

324 State and Local Government Finance

3240 General

Adams, James D. Equilibrium Taxation and Experience Rating in a Federal System of Unemployment Insurance. *J. Public Econ.,* February 1986, *29*(1), pp. 51–77.

Bramley, Glen. Defining Equal Standards in Local Public Services. *Urban Stud.,* October 1986, *23*(5), pp. 391–412. **[G: U.K.]**

Breen, Eleanor; Costa, Frank J. and Hendon, William S. Annexation: An Economic Analysis: Whether a Small Village or Town Should Annex Adjacent Land Is a Cost/Revenue Problem. *Amer. J. Econ. Soc.,* April 1986, *45*(2), pp. 159–72. **[G: U.S.]**

Caniglia, Alan S. Variable versus Fixed Rate Subsidies: Are the Latter Necessarily Less Efficient? *Public Finance Quart.,* January 1986, *14*(1), pp. 100–106.

Canto, Victor A.; Kadlec, Charles W. and Laffer, Arthur B. The State Competitive Environment. **In** *Canto, V. A.; Kadlec, C. W. and Laffer, A. B., eds.,* 1986, pp. 189–218. **[G: U.S.]**

Chicoine, David L. and Walzer, Norman. Financing Local Infrastructure in Nonmetropolitan Areas: Introduction. **In** *Chicoine, D. L. and Walzer, N., eds.,* 1986, pp. 1–15. **[G: U.S.]**

Davis, Lance E. Long-term Trends in State and Local Finance: Sources and Uses of Funds in North Carolina, 1800–1977: Comment. **In** *Engerman, S. L. and Gallman, R. E., eds.,* 1986, pp. 862–66. **[G: U.S.]**

DeBoer, Larry. State and Local Government Utility Maximization According to GARP. *Public Finance Quart.,* January 1986, *14*(1), pp. 87–99. **[G: U.S.]**

Domberger, Simon; Meadowcroft, Shirley A. and Thompson, David J. Competitive Tendering and Efficiency: The Case of Refuse Collection. *Fisc. Stud.,* November 1986, *7*(4), pp. 69–87. **[G: U.K.]**

Goldberg, Kalman and Scott, Robert C. Intrametropolitan Fiscal Relations: Special Taxing Districts. *J. Urban Econ.,* November 1986, *20*(3), pp. 341–55. **[G: U.S.]**

Goldstein, Gerald S. and Gronberg, Timothy J. Local Public Goods and Private Suppliers: Musical Suburbs Replayed. *J. Urban Econ.,* May 1986, *19*(3), pp. 338–55.

Gramlich, Edward M. The Effect of Tax Simplification on State and Local Governments: Discussion. **In** *Federal Reserve Bank of Boston,* 1986, pp. 252–58. **[G: U.S.]**

Greenberg, Joseph and Weber, Shlomo. Strong Tiebout Equilibrium under Restricted Preferences Domain. *J. Econ. Theory,* February 1986, *38*(1), pp. 101–17.

Grosskopf, Shawna and Hayes, Kathy J. The Demand for Local Public Goods: Choosing an Appropriate Functional Form. *Appl. Econ.*, November 1986, *18*(11), pp. 1179–92. **[G: U.S.]**

Hall, John Stuart. Retrenchment in Phoenix, Arizona. **In** *Peterson, G. E. and Lewis, C. W., eds.*, 1986, pp. 185–207. **[G: U.S.]**

Hamilton, Jonathan H. The Flypaper Effect and the Deadweight Loss from Taxation. *J. Urban Econ.*, March 1986, *19*(2), pp. 148–55.

Hardoy, Jorge E. and Satterthwaite, David. Government Policies and Small and Intermediate Urban Centres. **In** *Hardoy, J. E. and Satterthwaite, D., eds.*, 1986, pp. 335–97. **[G: LDCs]**

Hayes, Kathy J. Local Public Goods Demands and Demographic Effects. *Appl. Econ.*, October 1986, *18*(10), pp. 1039–45. **[G: U.S.]**

Johansson, Börje and Leonardi, Giorgio. Public Facility Location: A Multiregional and Multi-authority Decision Context. **In** *Nijkamp, P., ed. (I)*, 1986, pp. 133–70.

Levin, David J. Alternative Measure of the State and Local Government Fiscal Position: Revised and Updated Estimates. *Surv. Curr. Bus.*, April 1986, *66*(4), pp. 36. **[G: U.S.]**

Levin, David J. State and Local Government Fiscal Position in 1985. *Surv. Curr. Bus.*, February 1986, *66*(2), pp. 35–38. **[G: U.S.]**

Levin, David J. and Peters, Donald L. Receipts and Expenditures of State Governments and of Local Governments: Revised and Updated Estimates, 1959–84. *Surv. Curr. Bus.*, May 1986, *66*(5), pp. 26–33. **[G: U.S.]**

Lowery, David. After the Tax Revolt: Some Positive, If Unintended, Consequences. *Soc. Sci. Quart.*, December 1986, *67*(4), pp. 736–50. **[G: U.S.]**

Mathis, Stephen A. and Posatko, Robert C. Local Government Expenditures and Private Sector Output: Theory and Evidence on Crowding Out at the Regional Level. *Quart. Rev. Econ. Bus.*, Autumn 1986, *26*(3), pp. 105–15. **[G: U.S.]**

McGuire, Martin C. Private Production, Collective Consumption, and Regional Population Structure: The Interactions between Public and Private Good Provision as Determinants of Community Composition. *J. Reg. Sci.*, November 1986, *26*(4), pp. 677–705.

Moor, G. and Parnell, R. Private Sector Involvement in Local Authority Service Delivery. *Reg. Stud.*, June 1986, *20*(3), pp. 253–57. **[G: U.K.]**

Netzer, Dick. The Effect of Tax Simplification on State and Local Governments. **In** *Federal Reserve Bank of Boston*, 1986, pp. 222–51. **[G: U.S.]**

Penny, P. E. An Opposing View on Site Rating [The Site Value Tax: An Evaluation]. *S. Afr. J. Econ.*, December 1986, *54*(4), pp. 430–31. **[G: S. Africa]**

Plaut, Thomas. State and Local Fiscal Analysis with an Econometric Model of Texas. **In** *Batey, P. W. and Madden, M., eds.*, 1986, pp. 187–200. **[G: U.S.]**

Poister, Theodore H. A HUD Capacity Sharing Effort: The Financial Trend Monitoring System. *Public Budg. Finance*, Spring 1986, *6*(1), pp. 20–32. **[G: U.S.]**

Pollock, Richard and Suyderhoud, Jack P. The Role of Rainy Day Funds in Achieving Fiscal Stability. *Nat. Tax J.*, December 1986, *39*(4), pp. 485–97. **[G: U.S.]**

Pope, Ralph A. Economies of Scale in Large State and Municipal Retirement Systems. *Public Budg. Finance*, Autumn 1986, *6*(3), pp. 70–80.

Raimondo, Henry J. and Stuart, Robert C. Variations in Soviet City Finance. *Growth Change*, April 1986, *17*(2), pp. 56–67. **[G: U.S.S.R.]**

Reid, J. Norman and Sullivan, Patrick J. The Rural Infrastructure Problem: A National Perspective. **In** *Chicoine, D. L. and Walzer, N., eds.*, 1986, pp. 17–32. **[G: U.S.]**

Renshaw, Edward F. Trends in Manufacturing Employment and Reflections on Infrastructure Investment, Tax and Expenditure Policy in New York State. **In** *Schoolman, M. and Magid, A., eds.*, 1986, pp. 91–114. **[G: U.S.]**

Schmitt, Robert P. State and Federal Management Assistance. **In** *Chicoine, D. L. and Walzer, N., eds.*, 1986, pp. 127–41. **[G: U.S.]**

Schneider, Mark. Fragmentation and the Growth of Local Government. *Public Choice*, 1986, *48*(3), pp. 255–63. **[G: U.S.]**

Scholer, Charles. Cost-Saving Techniques. **In** *Chicoine, D. L. and Walzer, N., eds.*, 1986, pp. 185–97. **[G: U.S.]**

Schoolman, Morton. Solving the Dilemma of Statesmanship: Reindustrialization through an Evolving Democratic Plan. **In** *Schoolman, M. and Magid, A., eds.*, 1986, pp. 3–49. **[G: U.S.]**

Schweizer, Urs. Suburbanisierung als Folge fiskalischer Inäquivalenz. (Suburbanisation Caused by Fiscal Inequivalence. With English summary.) *Schweiz. Z. Volkswirtsch. Statist.*, March 1986, *122*(1), pp. 1–15.

Scotchmer, Suzanne. Local Public Goods in an Equilibrium: How Pecuniary Externalities Matter. *Reg. Sci. Urban Econ.*, November 1986, *16*(4), pp. 463–81.

Silkman, Richard H. Old Federalism and New Federalism in New York State. **In** *Schoolman, M. and Magid, A., eds.*, 1986, pp. 331–55. **[G: U.S.]**

Singh, Nirvikar and Thomas, Ravi. User Charges as a Delegation Mechanism. *Nat. Tax J.*, March 1986, *39*(1), pp. 109–13.

Solomon, D. The Site Value Tax: A Reply [The Site Value Tax: An Evaluation]. *S. Afr. J. Econ.*, December 1986, *54*(4), pp. 432–36. **[G: S. Africa]**

Southwick, Lawrence, Jr. Local Economic Development and the State. **In** *Schoolman, M. and Magid, A., eds.*, 1986, pp. 147–64. **[G: U.S.]**

Sylla, Richard. Long-term Trends in State and Local Finance: Sources and Uses of Funds in North Carolina, 1800–1977. **In** *Engerman, S. L. and Gallman, R. E., eds.*, 1986, pp. 819–62. **[G: U.S.]**

Vavouras, Ioannis S. Local Government Investment Planning: A Proposed Approach Applied to Greece. *Comp. Econ. Stud.*, Winter 1986, *28*(4), pp. 1–11. [G: Greece]

Walzer, Norman and Chicoine, David L. Financing Economic Development in the 1980s: Issues and Trends: Introduction. **In** *Walzer, N. and Chicoine, D. L., eds.*, 1986, pp. xv–xxvii.

Watson, William G. An Estimate of the Welfare Gain from Fiscal Equalization. *Can. J. Econ.*, May 1986, *19*(2), pp. 298–308. [G: Canada]

Wheat, Leonard F. State Industrial Growth: Comment [Business Climate, Taxes and Expenditures, and State Industrial Growth in the United States]. *Southern Econ. J.*, April 1986, *52*(4), pp. 1179–84. [G: U.S.]

Wilson, John D. A Theory of Interregional Tax Competition. *J. Urban Econ.*, May 1986, *19*(3), pp. 296–315.

Yinger, John. On Fiscal Disparities across Cities. *J. Urban Econ.*, May 1986, *19*(3), pp. 316–37.

Zodrow, George R. and Mieszkowski, Peter M. Pigou, Tiebout, Property Taxation, and the Underprovision of Local Public Goods. *J. Urban Econ.*, May 1986, *19*(3), pp. 356–70.

3241 State and Local Government Expenditures and Budgeting

Arcelus, F. J. and Levine, A. L. Merit Goods and Public Choice: The Case of Higher Education. *Public Finance*, December 1986, *41*(3), pp. 303–15.

Banham, John M. M. Paying for Local Government. *Lloyds Bank Rev.*, July 1986, (161), pp. 1–18. [G: U.K.]

Baum, Donald N. A Simultaneous Equations Model of the Demand for and Production of Local Public Services: The Case of Education. *Public Finance Quart.*, April 1986, *14*(2), pp. 157–78. [G: U.S.]

Benker, Karen M. Tax Expenditure Reporting: Closing the Loophole in State Budget Oversight. *Nat. Tax J.*, December 1986, *39*(4), pp. 403–17. [G: U.S.]

Bezdek, Roger H. and Zampelli, Ernest M. State and Local Government Tax Expenditures Relating to the Federal Government. *Nat. Tax J.*, December 1986, *39*(4), pp. 533–38. [G: U.S.]

Blazar, William A. Minnesota's Approach to Budgeting: Executive and Legislative Responsibilities. **In** *Minnesota Tax Study Commission*, 1986, pp. 75–97. [G: U.S.]

Brazer, Harvey E. and McCarty, Therese A. Municipal Overburden: An Empirical Analysis. *Econ. Educ. Rev.*, 1986, *5*(4), pp. 353–61. [G: U.S.]

Bryson, John. State Government Conservation Programs: Comments. **In** *Sawhill, J. C. and Cotton, R., eds.*, 1986, pp. 234–35. [G: U.S.]

Castells, Antoni. Una nota sobre la descentralización del gasto público entre los distintos niveles de gobierno en España. (With English summary.) *Invest. Ecón.*, September 1986, *10*(3), pp. 529–43. [G: OECD]

Cebula, Richard J. Tax-Expenditure Limitation in the United States: Two Alternative Evaluations. *Econ. Notes*, 1986, (2), pp. 140–51. [G: U.S.]

Cebula, Richard J. and Kafoglis, Milton Z. A Note on the Tiebout–Tullock Hypothesis: The Period 1975–1980. *Public Choice*, 1986, *48*(1), pp. 65–69. [G: U.S.]

Cothran, Dan A. Some Sources of "Budgetary Uncontrollability": The Interaction of Automatic Funding and Program Flexibility. *Public Budg. Finance*, Summer 1986, *6*(2), pp. 45–62. [G: U.S.]

Craig, Steven G. and Inman, Robert P. Education, Welfare and the "New" Federalism: State Budgeting in a Federalist Public Economy. **In** *Rosen, H. S., ed.*, 1986, pp. 187–222. [G: U.S.]

Cummings, Ronald G., et al. Measuring the Elasticity of Substitution of Wages for Municipal Infrastructure: A Comparison of the Survey and Wage Hedonic Approaches. *J. Environ. Econ. Manage.*, September 1986, *13*(3), pp. 269–76. [G: U.S.]

Edwards, John H. Y. A Note on the Publicness of Local Goods: Evidence from New York State Municipalities. *Can. J. Econ.*, August 1986, *19*(3), pp. 568–73. [G: U.S.]

Fleischman, Richard K. and Marquette, R. Penny. The Origins of Public Budgeting: Municipal Reformers during the Progressive Era. *Public Budg. Finance*, Spring 1986, *6*(1), pp. 71–77. [G: U.S.]

Folkman, Gordon and Asmussen, John. Analysis of State Budget Policy. **In** *Minnesota Tax Study Commission*, 1986, pp. 23–49. [G: U.S.]

Fournier, Gary M. and Rasmussen, David W. Salaries in Public Education: The Impact of Geographic Cost-of-Living Differentials. *Public Finance Quart.*, April 1986, *14*(2), pp. 179–98. [G: U.S.]

Frank, Richard G. and Kamlet, Mark S. Quality, Quantity and Total Expenditures on Publicly Provided Goods: The Case of Public Mental Hospitals. *J. Public Econ.*, April 1986, *29*(3), pp. 295–316. [G: U.S.]

Greiner, John M. and Peterson, George E. Do Budget Reductions Stimulate Public Sector Productivity? Evidence from Proposition 2½ in Massachusetts. **In** *Peterson, G. E. and Lewis, C. W., eds.*, 1986, pp. 63–95. [G: U.S.]

Griffin, Karen. State Government Conservation Programs. **In** *Sawhill, J. C. and Cotton, R., eds.*, 1986, pp. 205–32. [G: U.S.]

Grizzle, Gloria A. Does Budget Format Really Govern the Actions of Budgetmakers? *Public Budg. Finance*, Spring 1986, *6*(1), pp. 60–70. [G: U.S.]

Hall, John Stuart. Retrenchment in Phoenix, Arizona. **In** *Peterson, G. E. and Lewis, C. W., eds.*, 1986, pp. 185–207. [G: U.S.]

Hirst, Eric. State Government Conservation Programs: Comments. **In** *Sawhill, J. C. and Cotton, R., eds.*, 1986, pp. 232–34. [G: U.S.]

Holtz-Eakin, Douglas. Unobserved Tastes and

the Determination of Municipal Services. *Nat. Tax J.*, December 1986, *39*(4), pp. 527–32. [G: U.S.]

Hough, J. R. and Warburton, S. J. U.K. Research into School Costs and Resources. *Econ. Educ. Rev.*, 1986, *5*(4), pp. 383–94. [G: U.K.]

Hughes, Jesse W. and Laverdiere, Raymond. Comparative Local Government Financial Analysis. *Public Budg. Finance*, Winter 1986, *6*(4), pp. 23–33. [G: U.S.]

Inman, Robert P. Appraising the Funding Status of Teacher Pensions: An Econometric Approach. *Nat. Tax J.*, March 1986, *39*(1), pp. 21–33. [G: U.S.]

Ladd, Helen F. Education, Welfare and the "New" Federalism: State Budgeting in a Federalist Public Economy: Comment. **In** *Rosen, H. S., ed.*, 1986, pp. 222–27. [G: U.S.]

Lines, Jon J.; Parker, Ellen L. and Perry, David C. Building the Twentieth-Century Public Works Machine: Robert Moses and the Public Authority. **In** *Schoolman, M. and Magid, A., eds.*, 1986, pp. 231–55. [G: U.S.]

Mathis, Edward J. and Zech, Charles E. An Examination into the Relevance of the Median Voter Model: Empirical Evidence Offers Support for the Model and Certain Uses. *Amer. J. Econ. Soc.*, October 1986, *45*(4), pp. 403–12. [G: U.S.]

Megdal, Sharon Bernstein. Estimating a Public School Expenditure Model under Binding Spending Limitations. *J. Urban Econ.*, May 1986, *19*(3), pp. 277–95. [G: U.S.]

Mehay, Stephen L. and Seiden, Kenneth P. Municipal Residency Laws and Local Public Budgets. *Public Choice*, 1986, *48*(1), pp. 27–35. [G: U.S.]

Merriman, David. The Distributional Effects of New Jersey's Tax and Expenditure Limitation. *Land Econ.*, November 1986, *62*(4), pp. 353–61. [G: U.S.]

Moore, Chris and Booth, Simon. Unlocking Enterprise: The Search for Synergy. **In** *Lever, W. and Moore, C., eds.*, 1986, pp. 107–19. [G: U.K.]

Myers, Beverlee A. Public Subsidies for Hospital Care of the Poor: Medicaid and Other Myths of Equity. **In** *Sloan, F. A.; Blumstein, J. F. and Perrin, J. M., eds.*, 1986, pp. 126–47. [G: U.S.]

Nelson, Michael A. Voter Perceptions of the Cost of Government: The Case of Local School Expenditures in Louisiana. *Public Finance Quart.*, January 1986, *14*(1), pp. 48–68. [G: U.S.]

Payette, Micheline and Vaillancourt, François. L'incidence des recettes et dépenses gouvernementales au Québec en 1981. (The Incidence of Governmental Revenues and Expenditures in Quebec 1981. With English summary.) *L'Actual. Econ.*, September 1986, *62*(3), pp. 409–41. [G: Canada]

Richards, Hamish. Investment in Public Health Provision in the Mining Valleys of South Wales, 1860–1914. **In** *Baber, C. and Williams, L. J., eds.*, 1986, pp. 128–39. [G: U.K.]

Santerre, Rexford E. Representative versus Direct Democracy: A Tiebout Test of Relative Performance. *Public Choice*, 1986, *48*(1), pp. 55–63. [G: U.S.]

Sonstelie, Jon C. and Portney, Paul R. Profit Maximizing Communities and the Theory of Local Public Expenditure: Reply. *J. Urban Econ.*, September 1986, *20*(2), pp. 250–55.

Windham, Susan R. The Massachusetts Medicaid Case Management Program. **In** *Kern, R. G. and Windham, S. R.*, 1986, pp. 3–17. [G: U.S.]

Zampelli, Ernest M. Resource Fungibility, the Flypaper Effect, and the Expenditure Impact of Grants-in-Aid. *Rev. Econ. Statist.*, February 1986, *68*(1), pp. 33–40. [G: U.S.]

3242 State and Local Government Taxation, Subsidies, and Revenue

Anderson, John E. Property Taxes and the Timing of Urban Land Development. *Reg. Sci. Urban Econ.*, November 1986, *16*(4), pp. 483–92.

Baum, Donald N. A Simultaneous Equations Model of the Demand for and Production of Local Public Services: The Case of Education. *Public Finance Quart.*, April 1986, *14*(2), pp. 157–78. [G: U.S.]

Bell, Michael E. and Bowman, John H. Property Tax Differences among Minnesota Cities: The Effect of Property Tax Relief Programs. **In** *Minnesota Tax Study Commission*, 1986, pp. 349–59. [G: U.S.]

Benson, Bruce L. and Johnson, Ronald N. Capital Formation and Interstate Tax Competition. **In** *Lee, D. R., ed.*, 1986, pp. 407–36. [G: U.S.]

Benson, Bruce L. and Johnson, Ronald N. The Lagged Impact of State and Local Taxes on Economic Activity and Political Behavior. *Econ. Inquiry*, July 1986, *24*(3), pp. 389–401. [G: U.S.]

Bivens, W. E., III. Rural Highway Finance: State and Local Innovation. **In** *Chicoine, D. L. and Walzer, N., eds.*, 1986, pp. 199–217. [G: U.S.]

Bowman, John H. Direct Property Tax Relief in Minnesota: An Analysis. **In** *Minnesota Tax Study Commission*, 1986, pp. 281–332. [G: U.S.]

Bowman, John H. and Butcher, William A. Institutional Remedies and the Uniform Assessment of Property: An Update and Extension. *Nat. Tax J.*, June 1986, *39*(2), pp. 157–69. [G: U.S.]

Boyd, Roy and Daniels, Barbara J. Errata [Capital Gains Treatment of Timber Income: Incidence and Welfare Implications]. *Land Econ.*, February 1986, *62*(1), pp. ii. [G: U.S.]

Brueckner, Jan K. A Modern Analysis of the Effects of Site Value Taxation. *Nat. Tax J.*, March 1986, *39*(1), pp. 49–58.

Cebula, Richard J. Tax-Expenditure Limitation in the United States: Two Alternative Evaluations. *Econ. Notes*, 1986, (2), pp. 140–51. [G: U.S.]

Chernick, Howard and Reschovsky, Andrew. Effects of the Reagan Proposal in Massachusetts and New York. **In** *Gold, S. D., ed.*, 1986, pp. 143–59. **[G: U.S.]**

Chernick, Howard and Reschovsky, Andrew. Federal Tax Reform and the Financing of State and Local Government. *J. Policy Anal. Manage.*, Summer 1986, *5*(4), pp. 683–706. **[G: U.S.]**

Chicoine, David L. Farm Taxes. **In** *Gold, S. D., ed.*, 1986, pp. 307–31. **[G: U.S.]**

Chicoine, David L. and Walzer, Norman. Factors Affecting Property Tax Reliance: Additional Evidence. *Public Choice*, 1986, *49*(1), pp. 17–28. **[G: U.S.]**

Chicoine, David L. and Walzer, Norman. Financing Rural Roads in the Midwest. **In** *Chicoine, D. L. and Walzer, N., eds.*, 1986, pp. 33–51. **[G: U.S.]**

Cline, Robert J. Personal Income Tax. **In** *Gold, S. D., ed.*, 1986, pp. 185–210. **[G: U.S.]**

Cline, Robert J. and Shannon, John. Characteristics of a Balanced and Moderate State–Local Revenue System. **In** *Gold, S. D., ed.*, 1986, pp. 31–54. **[G: U.S.]**

Coughlin, Cletus C. and Erekson, O. Homer. Determinants of State Aid and Voluntary Support of Higher Education. *Econ. Educ. Rev.*, 1986, *5*(2), pp. 179–90. **[G: U.S.]**

Crawford, Roy E. Currency Exchange Problems in California's Worldwide Unitary Taxation. *Bull. Int. Fiscal Doc.*, Aug./Sept. 1986, *40*(8/9), pp. 378–84. **[G: U.S.]**

Crawford, Roy E. and Thomas, W. Scott. The New California Unitary Tax Law: U.S.A. *Bull. Int. Fiscal Doc.*, November 1986, *40*(11), pp. 526–28. **[G: U.S.]**

Dalvi, M. Q. and Ansari, M. M. Measuring Fiscal Performance of the Central and the State Governments in India: A Study in Resource Mobilization. *Indian Econ. J.*, Apr.-June 1986, *33*(4), pp. 106–22. **[G: India]**

Damania, D. The Impact of Non-domestic Property Taxes on Employment: A Comment [The Effect of Business Rates on the Location of Employment] [The Determinants of Employment in Counties: Some Evidence on the Importance of Local Authority Fiscal Policy and Government Regional Policy in England and Wales]. *Urban Stud.*, October 1986, *23*(5), pp. 413–18. **[G: U.K.]**

Daniels, Thomas L.; Daniels, Robert H. and Lapping, Mark B. The Vermont Land Gains Tax: Experience with It Provides a Useful Lesson in the Design of Modern Land Policy. *Amer. J. Econ. Soc.*, October 1986, *45*(4), pp. 441–55. **[G: U.S.]**

Davis, Albert. Implications of Federal Reform for State and Local Governments. **In** *Gold, S. D., ed.*, 1986, pp. 161–75. **[G: U.S.]**

De Tray, Dennis and Fernandez, Judith. Distributional Impacts of the Property Tax Revolt. *Nat. Tax J.*, December 1986, *39*(4), pp. 435–50. **[G: U.S.]**

DeBoer, Larry. When Will State Lottery Sales Growth Slow? *Growth Change*, January 1986, *17*(1), pp. 28–36. **[G: U.S.]**

Dwivedi, D. N. On Measurement of Tax Effort of Indian State Governments. *Indian Econ. J.*, Apr.-June 1986, *33*(4), pp. 123–35. **[G: India]**

Ebel, Robert D. The Role of Research in Formulating State Tax Policy. **In** *Gold, S. D., ed.*, 1986, pp. 55–66. **[G: U.S.]**

Eckl, Corina. Death Taxes. **In** *Gold, S. D., ed.*, 1986, pp. 291–306. **[G: U.S.]**

Elegido, J. M. Nigeria: The Sales Tax Decree 1986. *Bull. Int. Fiscal Doc.*, July 1986, *40*(7), pp. 300–301. **[G: Nigeria]**

Feenberg, Daniel R. and Rosen, Harvey S. State Personal Income and Sales Taxes, 1977–1983. **In** *Rosen, H. S., ed.*, 1986, pp. 135–79. **[G: U.S.]**

Feenberg, Daniel R. and Rosen, Harvey S. The Deductibility of State and Local Taxes: Impact Effects by State and Income Class. *Growth Change*, April 1986, *17*(2), pp. 11–31. **[G: U.S.]**

Feenberg, Daniel R. and Rosen, Harvey S. The Interaction of State and Federal Tax Systems: The Impact of State and Local Tax Deductibility. *Amer. Econ. Rev.*, May 1986, *76*(2), pp. 126–31. **[G: U.S.]**

Fender, John. Local Taxation and Housing Finance: A Proposal for Reform. *Lloyds Bank Rev.*, October 1986, (162), pp. 17–30. **[G: U.K.]**

Fisher, Ronald and Martin, Lawrence. Taxes and Telecommunications in an Era of Change. **In** *Minnesota Tax Study Commission*, 1986, pp. 223–49. **[G: U.S.]**

Folkman, Gordon and Asmussen, John. Analysis of State Budget Policy. **In** *Minnesota Tax Study Commission*, 1986, pp. 23–49. **[G: U.S.]**

Follain, James R. and Miyake, Tamar Emi. Land versus Capital Value Taxation: A General Equilibrium Analysis. *Nat. Tax J.*, December 1986, *39*(4), pp. 451–70. **[G: Jamaica]**

Fox, William F. Insurance Taxation in Minnesota. **In** *Minnesota Tax Study Commission*, 1986, pp. 251–78. **[G: U.S.]**

Fox, William F. Tax Structure and the Location of Economic Activity along State Borders. *Nat. Tax J.*, December 1986, *39*(4), pp. 387–401. **[G: U.S.]**

Friedman, Julia Mason. Taxation of Timberland. **In** *Minnesota Tax Study Commission*, 1986, pp. 399–410. **[G: U.S.]**

Gillis, Malcolm; Jenkins, Glenn and Leitzel, Jim. Financing Universal Access in the Telephone Network. *Nat. Tax J.*, March 1986, *39*(1), pp. 35–48. **[G: U.S.]**

Gold, Steven D. Minnesota's Farm Sector and the Taxation of Agriculture. **In** *Minnesota Tax Study Commission*, 1986, pp. 411–60. **[G: U.S.]**

Gold, Steven D. Reforming State Tax Systems: Introduction. **In** *Gold, S. D., ed.*, 1986, pp. 1–10.

Gold, Steven D. State Tax Policy: Recent Trends and Future Directions. **In** *Gold, S. D., ed.*, 1986, pp. 11–30. **[G: U.S.]**

Gold, Steven D. Themes of Federal Tax Reform

for State Tax Policy. In *Gold, S. D., ed.*, 1986, pp. 177–83. [G: U.S.]

Gordon, Roger H. A Critical Look at Formula Apportionment. In *Minnesota Tax Study Commission*, 1986, pp. 209–22. [G: U.S.]

Gordon, Roger H. and Slemrod, Joel. An Empirical Examination of Municipal Financial Policy. In *Rosen, H. S., ed.*, 1986, pp. 53–78. [G: U.S.]

Gordon, Roger H. and Wilson, John D. An Examination of Multijurisdictional Corporate Income Taxation under Formula Apportionment. *Econometrica*, November 1986, *54*(6), pp. 1357–73.

Greiner, John M. and Peterson, George E. Do Budget Reductions Stimulate Public Sector Productivity? Evidence from Proposition 2½ in Massachusetts. In *Peterson, G. E. and Lewis, C. W., eds.*, 1986, pp. 63–95. [G: U.S.]

Hart, Jeffrey A. West German Industrial Policy. In *Barfield, C. E. and Schambra, W. A., eds.*, 1986, pp. 161–86. [G: W. Germany]

Hellerstein, Walter. Legal Perspectives on the Interstate Incidence and Shifting of State and Local Taxes. *Int. Reg. Sci. Rev.*, April 1986, *10*(1), pp. 67–87. [G: U.S.]

Herzog, Henry W., Jr. and Schlottmann, Alan M. State and Local Tax Deductibility and Metropolitan Migration. *Nat. Tax J.*, June 1986, *39*(2), pp. 189–200. [G: U.S.]

Hewett, Roger S. and Stephenson, Susan C. Estimating Tax Interdependence: A Reply [State Tax Revenues under Competition]. *Nat. Tax J.*, June 1986, *39*(2), pp. 249.

Hildred, William M. and Pinto, James V. Passive Tax Expenditures: Estimates of States' Revenue Losses Attributable to Federal Tax Expenditures. *J. Econ. Issues*, December 1986, *20*(4), pp. 941–52. [G: U.S.]

Hirsch, Werner Z. Revenue Limitation Measures and Their Effects on Municipal Bonds: The Case of California Municipalities. In *Herber, B. P., ed.*, 1986, pp. 293–305. [G: U.S.]

Hirsch, Werner Z. and Rufolo, Anthony M. Effects of State Income Taxes on Fringe Benefits Demand of Policeman and Firemen. *Nat. Tax J.*, June 1986, *39*(2), pp. 211–19. [G: U.S.]

Hobson, Paul A. R. The Incidence of Heterogeneous Residential Property Taxes. *J. Public Econ.*, April 1986, *29*(3), pp. 363–73.

Hoggart, Keith. Property Tax Resources and Political Party Control in England 1974–1984. *Urban Stud.*, February 1986, *23*(1), pp. 33–46. [G: U.K.]

Holcombe, Randall G. The Effects of the Tax Structure on the Distribution of Disposable Income. *Rivista Int. Sci. Econ. Com.*, June-July 1986, *33*(6–7), pp. 585–602. [G: U.S.]

Holtz-Eakin, Douglas. Explaining the Yield Spread between Taxable and Tax-Exempt Bonds: The Role of Expected Tax Policy: Comment. In *Rosen, H. S., ed.*, 1986, pp. 49–51. [G: U.S.]

Hovey, Harold A. Interstate Tax Competition and Economic Development. In *Gold, S. D., ed.*, 1986, pp. 89–100. [G: U.S.]

Huddleston, Jack R. Intrametropolitan Financial Flows under Tax Increment Financing. *Policy Sci.*, September 1986, *19*(2), pp. 143–61. [G: U.S.]

Hunter, William J. and Scott, Charles E. Interstate Differences in Individual Income Taxes. *Public Finance Quart.*, January 1986, *14*(1), pp. 69–85. [G: U.S.]

Ihlanfeldt, Keith R. and Jackson, John D. Systematic Assessment Error and Intrajurisdiction Property Tax Capitalization: Reply. *Southern Econ. J.*, January 1986, *52*(3), pp. 836–42. [G: U.S.]

Jackson, Ira A. Tax Administration. In *Gold, S. D., ed.*, 1986, pp. 333–46. [G: U.S.]

James, Estelle. The Private Nonprofit Provision of Education: A Theoretical Model and Application to Japan. *J. Compar. Econ.*, September 1986, *10*(3), pp. 255–76. [G: Japan]

Jani, B. M. Impact of Development Finance on Small Scale Industries in Saurashtra. *Indian Econ. J.*, Oct.-Dec. 1986, *34*(2), pp. 106–11. [G: India]

Kovenock, Dan. Property and Income Taxation in an Economy with an Austrian Sector. *Land Econ.*, May 1986, *62*(2), pp. 201–09.

Krumm, Ronald; Tolley, George and Kelly, Austin. Voter Participation and Voter Choice: An Empirical Examination of Massachusetts' Proposition 2½ In *Grieson, R. E., ed.*, 1986, pp. 135–51. [G: U.S.]

Lankford, R. Hamilton. Property Taxes, Tax-Cost Illusion and Desired Education Expenditures. *Public Choice*, 1986, *49*(1), pp. 79–97. [G: U.S.]

Ledebur, Larry C. and Hamilton, William W. Cost-Effective Development Finance. In *Walzer, N. and Chicoine, D. L., eds.*, 1986, pp. 103–21. [G: U.S.]

Ledebur, Larry C. and Hamilton, William W. The Failure of Tax Concessions as Economic Development Incentives. In *Gold, S. D., ed.*, 1986, pp. 101–17. [G: U.S.]

Livernois, John R. The Taxing Game of Lotteries in Canada. *Can. Public Policy*, December 1986, *12*(4), pp. 622–27. [G: Canada]

Mair, Douglas. Industrial De-rating: Panacea or Palliative? *Scot. J. Polit. Econ.*, May 1986, *33*(2), pp. 159–70. [G: U.K.]

Mason, Colin M. and Harrison, Richard T. The Regional Impact of Public Policy towards Small Firms in the United Kingdom. In *Keeble, D. and Wever, E., eds.*, 1986, pp. 224–55. [G: U.K.]

Matz, Deborah and Ledebur, Larry C. The State Role in Economic Development. In *Walzer, N. and Chicoine, D. L., eds.*, 1986, pp. 85–102. [G: U.S.]

Mayo, Stephen K. Sources of Inefficiency in Subsidized Housing Programs: A Comparison of U.S. and German Experience. *J. Urban Econ.*, September 1986, *20*(2), pp. 229–49. [G: U.S.; W. Germany]

McGuire, Therese J. Interstate Tax Differentials,

Tax Competition, and Tax Policy. *Nat. Tax J.*, September 1986, *39*(3), pp. 367–73. **[G: U.S.]**

Megdal, Sharon Bernstein. Property Taxes and Firm Location: Evidence from Proposition 13: Comment. **In** *Rosen, H. S., ed.*, 1986, pp. 108–12. **[G: U.S.]**

Meng, Ronald and Gillespie, W. Irwin. Horizontal Equity and Property Taxation in Canada. *Nat. Tax J.*, June 1986, *39*(2), pp. 221–28. **[G: Canada]**

Merriman, David. The Distributional Effects of New Jersey's Tax and Expenditure Limitation. *Land Econ.*, November 1986, *62*(4), pp. 353–61. **[G: U.S.]**

Mieszkowski, Peter M. An Empirical Examination of Municipal Financial Policy: Comment. **In** *Rosen, H. S., ed.*, 1986, pp. 79–81. **[G: U.S.]**

Mikesell, John L. Amnesties for State Tax Evaders: The Nature of and Response to Recent Programs. *Nat. Tax J.*, December 1986, *39*(4), pp. 507–25. **[G: U.S.]**

Mikesell, John L. General Sales Tax. **In** *Gold, S. D., ed.*, 1986, pp. 211–30. **[G: U.S.]**

Mikesell, John L. Retail Sales and Use Taxation in Minnesota. **In** *Minnesota Tax Study Commission*, 1986, pp. 155–87. **[G: U.S.]**

Mikesell, John L. and Zorn, C. Kurt. Impact of the Sales Tax Rate on Its Base: Evidence from a Small Town. *Public Finance Quart.*, July 1986, *14*(3), pp. 329–38. **[G: U.S.]**

Mintz, Jack M. and Tulkens, Henry. Commodity Tax Competition between Member States of a Federation: Equilibrium and Efficiency. *J. Public Econ.*, March 1986, *29*(2), pp. 133–72.

Morse, George W. and Farmer, Michael C. Location and Investment Effects of a Tax Abatement Program. *Nat. Tax J.*, June 1986, *39*(2), pp. 229–36. **[G: U.S.]**

Mutti, John H. and Morgan, William E. Interstate Tax Exportation within the United States: An Appraisal of the Literature. *Int. Reg. Sci. Rev.*, August 1986, *10*(2), pp. 89–112. **[G: U.S.]**

Nelson, Glenn and Sigalla, Fiona. An Income–Wealth Alternative to the Property Tax Circuit Breaker. **In** *Minnesota Tax Study Commission*, 1986, pp. 375–98. **[G: U.S.]**

Nelson, Michael A. An Empirical Analysis of State and Local Tax Structure in the Context of the Leviathan Model of Government. *Public Choice*, 1986, *49*(3), pp. 283–94. **[G: U.S.]**

Nelson, Michael A. Voter Perceptions of the Cost of Government: The Case of Local School Expenditures in Louisiana. *Public Finance Quart.*, January 1986, *14*(1), pp. 48–68. **[G: U.S.]**

Niskanen, Esko. The Choice between Income Tax and Land Tax in Danish Municipalities: Another Comment. *Public Finance*, December 1986, *41*(3), pp. 447–49. **[G: Denmark]**

Papke, James A. and Papke, Leslie E. Measuring Differential State–Local Tax Liabilities and Their Implications for Business Investment Location. *Nat. Tax J.*, September 1986, *39*(3), pp. 357–66. **[G: U.S.]**

Payette, Micheline and Vaillancourt, François. L'incidence des recettes et dépenses gouvernementales au Québec en 1981. (The Incidence of Governmental Revenues and Expenditures in Quebec 1981. With English summary.) *L'Actual. Econ.*, September 1986, *62*(3), pp. 409–41. **[G: Canada]**

Petersen, John E. The Impacts of the President's Tax Proposal on State and Local Government Capital Financing. **In** *Walzer, N. and Chicoine, D. L., eds.*, 1986, pp. 162–78. **[G: U.S.]**

Phares, Donald. The Role of Tax Burden Studies in State Tax Policy. **In** *Gold, S. D., ed.*, 1986, pp. 67–88. **[G: U.S.]**

Pogue, Thomas F. Excise Taxes. **In** *Gold, S. D., ed.*, 1986, pp. 259–75. **[G: U.S.]**

Pogue, Thomas F. Minnesota Highway User Taxes: Issues and Alternatives. **In** *Minnesota Tax Study Commission*, 1986, pp. 189–205. **[G: U.S.]**

Pomp, Richard D. Simplicity and Complexity in the Context of a State Tax System. **In** *Gold, S. D., ed.*, 1986, pp. 119–41. **[G: U.S.]**

Poterba, James M. Explaining the Yield Spread between Taxable and Tax-Exempt Bonds: The Role of Expected Tax Policy. **In** *Rosen, H. S., ed.*, 1986, pp. 5–49. **[G: U.S.]**

Premus, Robert. Attracting High-Tech Industry and Jobs: An Assessment of State Practices. **In** *Walzer, N. and Chicoine, D. L., eds.*, 1986, pp. 55–71. **[G: U.S.]**

Proctor, Allen J. Short-Term Borrowing by Local School Districts. *Fed. Res. Bank New York Quart. Rev.*, Summer 1986, *11*(2), pp. 30–41. **[G: U.S.]**

Rao, M. Govinda and Tulasidhar, V. B. Economic Analysis of Sales Taxation in India. *Bull. Int. Fiscal Doc.*, July 1986, *40*(7), pp. 288–99. **[G: India]**

Reister, Raymond A. Minnesota Transfer Taxes. **In** *Minnesota Tax Study Commission*, 1986, pp. 139–52. **[G: U.S.]**

Richardson, James A. Severance Tax Reform. **In** *Gold, S. D., ed.*, 1986, pp. 277–90. **[G: U.S.]**

Ring, Raymond J., Jr. Tax Interdependence and the Importance of Using a Correctly Specified Estimating Equation [State Tax Revenues under Competition]. *Nat. Tax J.*, June 1986, *39*(2), pp. 245–48. **[G: U.S.]**

Roden, Lisa A. Long-term and Cyclical Change in the Minnesota Economy. **In** *Minnesota Tax Study Commission*, 1986, pp. 3–22. **[G: U.S.]**

Rose, Louis A. Inflation, Tax Rules, and the Price of Land Relative to Capital. *Nat. Tax J.*, March 1986, *39*(1), pp. 59–64.

Ross, Thomas W. Store Wars: The Chain Tax Movement. *J. Law Econ.*, April 1986, *29*(1), pp. 125–37. **[G: U.S.]**

Rupley, Lawrence A. Taxation of Rental Property Income in Burkina Faso. *Bull. Int. Fiscal Doc.*, July 1986, *40*(7), pp. 299, 309. **[G: Burkina Faso]**

Sander, William and Giertz, J. Fred. The Political Economy of State Level Welfare Benefits.

Public Choice, 1986, *51*(2), pp. 209–19. **[G: U.S.]**

Senge, Stephen V. Local Government User Charges and Cost–Volume–Profit Analysis. *Public Budg. Finance*, Autumn 1986, *6*(3), pp. 92–105.

Sexton, Terri Erickson and Sexton, Richard J. Re-evaluating the Income Elasticity of the Property Tax Base. *Land Econ.*, May 1986, *62*(2), pp. 182–91. **[G: U.S.]**

Shannon, John. Fiscal Federalism: Past Trends, Future Prospects. **In** *Walzer, N. and Chicoine, D. L., eds.*, 1986, pp. 198–213. **[G: U.S.]**

Sharda, N. K. Tax Structure in a Transitional Provincial Economy: A Study of Himachal Pradesh. *Margin*, January 1986, *18*(2), pp. 42–50. **[G: India]**

Sharp, Elaine B. The Politics and Economics of the New City Debt. *Amer. Polit. Sci. Rev.*, December 1986, *80*(4), pp. 1271–88. **[G: U.S.]**

Sinn, Hans-Werner. Vacant Land and the Role of Government Intervention. *Reg. Sci. Urban Econ.*, August 1986, *16*(3), pp. 353–85.

Slemrod, Joel. The Optimal Progressivity of the Minnesota Tax System. **In** *Minnesota Tax Study Commission*, 1986, pp. 127–37. **[G: U.S.]**

Smith, Stephen R. and Squire, Duncan L. The Local Government Green Paper. *Fisc. Stud.*, May 1986, *7*(2), pp. 63–71. **[G: U.K.]**

Stinson, Thomas F. and Vanderwall, Kathleen M. The Impact of Existing Property Tax Relief Programs on Taxes Paid on Owner-Occupied Housing in Minnesota. **In** *Minnesota Tax Study Commission*, 1986, pp. 361–74. **[G: U.S.]**

Strauss, Robert P. Business Taxes. **In** *Gold, S. D., ed.*, 1986, pp. 231–58. **[G: U.S.]**

Subrahmanyam, Ganti; Kamaiah, Bandi and Swami, Sooraj B. Tax Buoyancies and Elasticities. *Margin*, October 1986, *19*(1), pp. 42–49. **[G: India]**

Sunley, Emil M. and Walz, Mary M. Simplification of Minnesota's Personal Income Tax. **In** *Minnesota Tax Study Commission*, 1986, pp. 101–26. **[G: U.S.]**

Turnbull, Geoffrey Keith and Niho, Yoshio. The Optimal Property Tax with Mobile Nonresidential Capital. *J. Public Econ.*, March 1986, *29*(2), pp. 223–39.

Wheaton, William C. The Impact of State Taxation on Life Insurance Company Growth. *Nat. Tax J.*, March 1986, *39*(1), pp. 85–95. **[G: U.S.]**

White, Michelle J. Property Taxes and Firm Location: Evidence from Proposition 13. **In** *Rosen, H. S., ed.*, 1986, pp. 83–107. **[G: U.S.]**

White, Michelle J. Property Taxes and Urban Housing Abandonment. *J. Urban Econ.*, November 1986, *20*(3), pp. 312–30. **[G: U.S.]**

Zodrow, George R. State Personal Income and Sales Taxes, 1977–1983: Comment. **In** *Rosen, H. S., ed.*, 1986, pp. 179–85. **[G: U.S.]**

Zodrow, George R. and Mieszkowski, Peter M. The New View of the Property Tax: A Reformulation. *Reg. Sci. Urban Econ.*, August 1986, *16*(3), pp. 309–27.

3243 State and Local Government Borrowing

Baber, William R. and Sen, Pradyot Kumar. The Political Process and the Use of Debt Financing by State Governments. *Public Choice*, 1986, *48*(3), pp. 201–15. **[G: U.S.]**

Buser, Stephen A. and Hess, Patrick J. Empirical Determinants of the Relative Yields on Taxable and Tax-Exempt Securities. *J. Finan. Econ.*, December 1986, *17*(2), pp. 335–55. **[G: U.S.]**

Epple, Dennis and Spatt, Chester. State Restrictions on Local Debt: Their Role in Preventing Default. *J. Public Econ.*, March 1986, *29*(2), pp. 199–221. **[G: U.S.]**

Hewitt, Daniel P. Fiscal Illusion from Grants and the Level of State and Federal Expenditures. *Nat. Tax J.*, December 1986, *39*(4), pp. 471–83. **[G: U.S.]**

Hirsch, Werner Z. Revenue Limitation Measures and Their Effects on Municipal Bonds: The Case of California Municipalities. **In** *Herber, B. P., ed.*, 1986, pp. 293–305. **[G: U.S.]**

Humphrey, Nancy P. and Maurice, Diane Rausa. Infrastructure Bond Bank Initiatives: Policy Implications and Credit Concerns. *Public Budg. Finance*, Autumn 1986, *6*(3), pp. 38–56. **[G: U.S.]**

Peek, Joe and Wilcox, James A. Tax Rates and Interest Rates on Tax-Exempt Securities. *New Eng. Econ. Rev.*, Jan./Feb. 1986, pp. 29–41. **[G: U.S.]**

Petersen, John E. Innovative Approaches to the Capital Markets for Public Borrowers. **In** *Walzer, N. and Chicoine, D. L., eds.*, 1986, pp. 139–61. **[G: U.S.]**

Roden, Peyton Foster and Bland, Robert L. Issuer Sophistication and Underpricing in the Negotiated Municipal Bond Market. *J. Finan. Res.*, Summer 1986, *9*(2), pp. 163–70. **[G: U.S.]**

Sharp, Elaine B. The Politics and Economics of the New City Debt. *Amer. Polit. Sci. Rev.*, December 1986, *80*(4), pp. 1271–88. **[G: U.S.]**

Smekal, Christian. Institutional Debt Restriction Rules at the Level of Local Government and Their Allocational and Stabilising Effects in Switzerland, FR Germany and Austria. **In** *Herber, B. P., ed.*, 1986, pp. 277–92. **[G: W. Germany; Switzerland; Austria]**

Squires, Gregory D. Inequality in Metropolitan Industrial Revenue Bond Programs. *Rev. Black Polit. Econ.*, Spring 1986, *14*(4), pp. 37–50. **[G: U.S.]**

Walter, John R. Short-term Municipal Securities. *Fed. Res. Bank Richmond Econ. Rev.*, Nov./Dec. 1986, *72*(6), pp. 25–34. **[G: U.S.]**

Zorn, C. Kurt and Towfighi, Shah. Not All Bond Banks Are Created Equal. *Public Budg. Finance*, Autumn 1986, *6*(3), pp. 57–69. **[G: U.S.]**

325 Intergovernmental Financial Relationships

3250 Intergovernmental Financial Relationships

Bahl, Roy. The Design of Intergovernmental Transfers in Industrialized Countries. *Public Budg. Finance,* Winter 1986, *6*(4), pp. 3–22. **[G: OECD]**

Banham, John M. M. Paying for Local Government. *Lloyds Bank Rev.*, July 1986, (161), pp. 1–18. **[G: U.K.]**

Bell, Michael E. Minnesota's Local Government Aids Program. **In** *Minnesota Tax Study Commission,* 1986, pp. 333–48. **[G: U.S.]**

Blazar, William A. Minnesota's Approach to Budgeting: Executive and Legislative Responsibilities. **In** *Minnesota Tax Study Commission,* 1986, pp. 75–97. **[G: U.S.]**

Castells, Antoni. Una nota sobre la descentralización del gasto público entre los distintos niveles de gobierno en España. (With English summary.) *Invest. Ecón.*, September 1986, *10*(3), pp. 529–43. **[G: OECD]**

Chicoine, David L. and Walzer, Norman. Financing Local Infrastructure in Nonmetropolitan Areas: Introduction. **In** *Chicoine, D. L. and Walzer, N., eds.*, 1986, pp. 1–15. **[G: U.S.]**

Cline, Robert J. and Shannon, John. Characteristics of a Balanced and Moderate State–Local Revenue System. **In** *Gold, S. D., ed.*, 1986, pp. 31–54. **[G: U.S.]**

Cohn, Elchanan. Implementation of Federal Chapter 2 Block Grants to Education in South Carolina. **In** *Cohn, E., ed.*, 1986, *1985*, pp. 215–25. **[G: U.S.]**

Cohn, Elchanan and Costa, José da Silva. Equity and Efficiency Effects of Intergovernmental Aid: The Case of Portugal. *Public Finance,* 1986, *41*(1), pp. 42–62. **[G: Portugal]**

Craig, Steven G. and Inman, Robert P. Education, Welfare and the "New" Federalism: State Budgeting in a Federalist Public Economy. **In** *Rosen, H. S., ed.*, 1986, pp. 187–222. **[G: U.S.]**

Egbert, Robert L.; Kluender, Mary M. and Roach, James L. Rural Elementary School Districts in Nebraska: Their Application for ECIA Funds as Related to Demographic and Economic Issues. **In** *Cohn, E., ed.*, 1986, *1985*, pp. 189–95. **[G: U.S.]**

Elmore, Richard F. Implementation of Chapter 2 in Washington State. **In** *Cohn, E., ed.*, 1986, *1985*, pp. 245–52. **[G: U.S.]**

Epple, Dennis and Spatt, Chester. State Restrictions on Local Debt: Their Role in Preventing Default. *J. Public Econ.*, March 1986, *29*(2), pp. 199–221. **[G: U.S.]**

Evans, Diana Yiannakis. Sunbelt versus Frostbelt: The Evolution of Regional Conflict over Federal Aid to Cities in the House of Representatives. *Soc. Sci. Quart.*, March 1986, *67*(1), pp. 108–17. **[G: U.S.]**

Eyler, Janet. Implementation of Chapter 2 in Tennessee. **In** *Cohn, E., ed.*, 1986, *1985*, pp. 227–35. **[G: U.S.]**

Florida, Richard L. The Distribution of Transfers to Various Types of Cities. *Public Budg. Finance,* Autumn 1986, *6*(3), pp. 81–91. **[G: U.S.]**

Gramlich, Edward M. The Effect of Tax Simplification on State and Local Governments: Discussion. **In** *Federal Reserve Bank of Boston,* 1986, pp. 252–58. **[G: U.S.]**

Grasso, Patrick G. Distributive Policies and the Politics of Economic Development. **In** *Redburn, F. S.; Buss, T. F. and Ledebur, L. C., eds.*, 1986, pp. 83–98. **[G: U.S.]**

Hettich, Walter and Winer, Stanley L. Vertical Imbalance in the Fiscal Systems of Federal States. *Can. J. Econ.*, November 1986, *19*(4), pp. 745–65.

Hewitt, Daniel P. Fiscal Illusion from Grants and the Level of State and Federal Expenditures. *Nat. Tax J.*, December 1986, *39*(4), pp. 471–83. **[G: U.S.]**

Kasoff, Mark J. and Soskin, Mark D. Economic Development Prospects for New York's St. Lawrence River Basin. **In** *Schoolman, M. and Magid, A., eds.*, 1986, pp. 131–46. **[G: U.S.]**

Katzman, Martin T. Implementation of Chapter 2 of ECIA in Texas. **In** *Cohn, E., ed.*, 1986, *1985*, pp. 237–43. **[G: U.S.]**

Kearney, C. Philip. Michigan's Experiences with the Federal Education Block Grant. **In** *Cohn, E., ed.*, 1986, *1985*, pp. 181–88. **[G: U.S.]**

Kern, Rosemary Gibson. The Unfinished Agenda for Medicaid Reform. **In** *Kern, R. G. and Windham, S. R.*, 1986, pp. 51–66. **[G: U.S.]**

Kuriloff, Peter J. The Distributive and Educational Consequences of Chapter 2 Block Grants in Pennsylvania. **In** *Cohn, E., ed.*, 1986, *1985*, pp. 197–214. **[G: U.S.]**

Ladd, Helen F. Education, Welfare and the "New" Federalism: State Budgeting in a Federalist Public Economy: Comment. **In** *Rosen, H. S., ed.*, 1986, pp. 222–27. **[G: U.S.]**

Lever, William. Old Policies in a New Role. **In** *Lever, W. and Moore, C., eds.*, 1986, pp. 44–61. **[G: U.K.]**

Levin, Henry M. Are Block Grants the Answer to the Federal Role in Education? **In** *Cohn, E., ed.*, 1986, pp. 261–69. **[G: U.S.]**

Liebschutz, Sarah F. and Taddiken, Alan J. The Effects of Reagan Administration Budget Cuts on Human Services in Rochester, New York. **In** *Peterson, G. E. and Lewis, C. W., eds.*, 1986, pp. 131–54. **[G: U.S.]**

Logan, Robert R. Fiscal Illusion and the Grantor Government. *J. Polit. Econ.*, December 1986, *94*(6), pp. 1304–18.

Mathews, Russell. The Australian Loan Council: Co-ordination of Public Debt Policies in a Federation. **In** *Herber, B. P., ed.*, 1986, pp. 307–19. **[G: Australia]**

Melck, Antony. On Subsidizing Education with Block Grants. **In** *Cohn, E., ed.*, 1986, *1985*, pp. 253–59. **[G: U.S.]**

Musgrave, Richard A. Economics of Fiscal Federalism. **In** *Musgrave, R. A., Vol. 2*, 1986, *1971*, pp. 33–42. **[G: U.S.]**

Netzer, Dick. The Effect of Tax Simplification on State and Local Governments. **In** *Federal Reserve Bank of Boston*, 1986, pp. 222–51. **[G: U.S.]**

Petersen, John E. The Impacts of the President's Tax Proposal on State and Local Government Capital Financing. **In** *Walzer, N. and Chicoine, D. L., eds.*, 1986, pp. 162–78. **[G: U.S.]**

Quigley, John M. and Rubinfeld, Daniel L. Budget Reform and the Theory of Fiscal Federalism. *Amer. Econ. Rev.*, May 1986, *76*(2), pp. 132–37.

Reid, J. Norman and Sullivan, Patrick J. The Rural Infrastructure Problem: A National Perspective. **In** *Chicoine, D. L. and Walzer, N., eds.*, 1986, pp. 17–32. **[G: U.S.]**

Rose, James. Implementation of Federal ECIA Block Grants to Education in Colorado. **In** *Cohn, E., ed.*, 1986, *1985*, pp. 171–79. **[G: U.S.]**

Schmitt, Robert P. State and Federal Management Assistance. **In** *Chicoine, D. L. and Walzer, N., eds.*, 1986, pp. 127–41. **[G: U.S.]**

Shannon, John. Fiscal Federalism: Past Trends, Future Prospects. **In** *Walzer, N. and Chicoine, D. L., eds.*, 1986, pp. 198–213. **[G: U.S.]**

Shannon, W. Wayne, et al. The Public Sector in Stamford, Connecticut: Responses to a Changing Federal Role. **In** *Peterson, G. E. and Lewis, C. W., eds.*, 1986, pp. 155–83. **[G: U.S.]**

Silkman, Richard H. Old Federalism and New Federalism in New York State. **In** *Schoolman, M. and Magid, A., eds.*, 1986, pp. 331–55. **[G: U.S.]**

Southwick, Lawrence, Jr. Local Economic Development and the State. **In** *Schoolman, M. and Magid, A., eds.*, 1986, pp. 147–64. **[G: U.S.]**

Strauss, Robert P. and Harkins, Peter B. The Net Fiscal Impact of Selected Federal Block Grant Programs. *J. Reg. Sci.*, February 1986, *26*(1), pp. 63–85. **[G: U.S.]**

Turnbull, Geoffrey Keith and Niho, Yoshio. The Optimal Property Tax with Mobile Nonresidential Capital. *J. Public Econ.*, March 1986, *29*(2), pp. 223–39.

Watson, William G. An Estimate of the Welfare Gain from Fiscal Equalization. *Can. J. Econ.*, May 1986, *19*(2), pp. 298–308. **[G: Canada]**

Wedeman, Sara Capen; Passman, Vicki Fay and Day, James Meredith. Education Block Grants: Introduction to the Debate. **In** *Cohn, E., ed.*, 1986, *1985*, pp. 163–70. **[G: U.S.]**

Weicher, John C. The Reagan Domestic Budget Cuts: Proposals, Outcomes, and Effects. **In** *Cagan, P., ed.*, 1986, pp. 7–44. **[G: U.S.]**

Yinger, John. On Fiscal Disparities across Cities. *J. Urban Econ.*, May 1986, *19*(3), pp. 316–37.

Zampelli, Ernest M. Resource Fungibility, the Flypaper Effect, and the Expenditure Impact of Grants-in-Aid. *Rev. Econ. Statist.*, February 1986, *68*(1), pp. 33–40. **[G: U.S.]**

400 International Economics

4000 General

Adeniran, Tunde. Africa, the United Nations and the NIEO. **In** *Onwuka, R. I. and Aluko, O., eds.*, 1986, pp. 115–31. **[G: Africa]**

Akinsanya, Adeoye. The United Nations Charter of Economic Rights and Duties of States: The International Protection of the Economic Independence of Third World Countries—A New International Economic Order. **In** *Onwuka, R. I. and Aluko, O., eds.*, 1986, pp. 64–104.

Albright, David E. East–West Tensions in Africa. **In** *Shulman, M. D., ed.*, 1986, pp. 116–57. **[G: Africa; U.S.; U.S.S.R.]**

Asante, S. K. B. The New International Economic Order and the Problem of Controlling Multinational Corporations in Africa. **In** *Onwuka, R. I. and Aluko, O., eds.*, 1986, pp. 17–34. **[G: Africa]**

Bhagwati, Jagdish N. Ideology and North–South Relations. *World Devel.*, June 1986, *14*(6), pp. 767–74. **[G: Global]**

Bulajic, Milan. Indebtedness of the Developing Countries and the New International Economic Order. **In** *Dicke, D. C., ed.*, 1986, pp. 43–73.

Clausen, A. W. Adjustment with Growth in the Developing Countries: A Challenge for the International Community: Address to the Commonwealth Secretariat: London, England: March 14, 1986. **In** *Clausen, A. W.*, 1986, pp. 453–70.

Clausen, A. W. Global Interdependence in the 1980s: Address to the Yomiuri International Economic Society: Tokyo, Japan: January 13, 1982. **In** *Clausen, A. W.*, 1986, pp. 37–54.

Clausen, A. W. Priority Issues for 1984: Address to the European Management Forum: Davos, Switzerland: January 26, 1984. **In** *Clausen, A. W.*, 1986, pp. 229–45.

Clausen, A. W. The Pacific Asian Countries: A Force for Growth in the Global Economy: Address to the Los Angeles World Affairs Council: Los Angeles, California: April 25, 1984. **In** *Clausen, A. W.*, 1986, pp. 247–60.

Coats, A. W. Economists in International Agencies: An Exploratory Study: Conclusions. **In** *Coats, A. W., ed.*, 1986, pp. 165–71.

Coats, A. W. Economists in International Agencies: An Exploratory Study: Introduction. **In** *Coats, A. W., ed.*, 1986, pp. 1–35.

Comisso, Ellen. State Structures and Political Processes outside the CMEA: A Comparison. **In** *Comisso, E. and Tyson, L., eds.*, 1986, pp. 401–22. **[G: CMEA; LDCs]**

Domínguez, Jorge I. U.S., Soviet, and Cuban Policies toward Latin America. **In** *Shulman, M. D., ed.*, 1986, pp. 44–77. **[G: U.S.; U.S.S.R.; Latin America]**

Dougherty, James P. The Global Economy: Divergent Perspectives on Economic Change: Epilogue: Seeking an Alternative to the Global Economy. **In** *Gondolf, E. W.; Marcus, I. M. and Dougherty, J. P., eds.*, 1986, pp. 199–208.

Ewing, Arthur F. Reform of the United Nations. *J. World Trade Law,* Mar.:Apr. 1986, *20*(2), pp. 131–41. **[G: Global]**

Fujino, Shozaburo. International Symposium on World Economy and Japan: Introduction. *Hitotsubashi J. Econ.*, Spec. Iss. Oct. 1986, 27, pp. 1–3. **[G: Global]**

Fukuyama, Francis. Military Aspects of U.S.–Soviet Competition in the Third World. **In** *Shulman, M. D., ed.*, 1986, pp. 181–211. **[G: U.S.; LDCs; U.S.S.R.]**

Galtung, Johan. The Winners and the Losers: The Rise of the South-east, the Decline of the North-west. **In** *[Patel, S.]*, 1986, pp. 37–46.

Gondolf, Edward W. The Global Economy: Divergent Perspectives on Economic Change: Conclusion: A Sociological Assessment of Divergent Perspectives. **In** *Gondolf, E. W.; Marcus, I. M. and Dougherty, J. P., eds.*, 1986, pp. 191–98.

Gruhn, Isebill V. The New International Economic Order and the United Nations. **In** *Onwuka, R. I. and Aluko, O., eds.*, 1986, pp. 42–63.

Heininger, Horst. Transnational Corporations and the Struggle for the Establishment of a New International Economic Order. **In** *Teichova, A.; Lévy-Leboyer, M. and Nussbaum, H., eds.*, 1986, pp. 351–61.

Higgott, Richard. Africa and the New International Division of Labour. **In** *Ravenhill, J., ed.*, 1986, pp. 286–306. **[G: Africa]**

Horne, J. Paul. Structural Changes in the International Economy. *Bus. Econ.*, January 1986, *21*(1), pp. 28–33. **[G: Global]**

Hossain, Kamal. Foreign Debts in the Present and a New International Economic Order: Introduction to the Symposium. **In** *Dicke, D. C., ed.*, 1986, pp. 5–9.

Jones, Graham. Teaching Economics to the 16–19 Age Range: International Trade. **In** *Whitehead, D. J., ed.*, 1986, pp. 222–27.

Kindleberger, Charles P. Hierarchy versus Inertial Cooperation. *Int. Organ.*, Autumn 1986, *40*(4), pp. 841–47.

Kindleberger, Charles P. International Public Good without International Government. *Amer. Econ. Rev.*, March 1986, *76*(1), pp. 1–13.

Kitamura, Hiroshi. A Requiem for the Global Negotiations or a New Beginning of North–South Dialogues? A Review Article. *Devel. Econ.*, June 1986, *24*(2), pp. 194–200.

Layton, Christopher. One Europe: One World: A First Exploration of Europe's Potential Contribution to World Order. *J. World Trade Law*, Supp. No. 4, 1986, *20*, pp. 1–70. **[G: Europe]**

Lipietz, Alain. New Tendencies in the International Division of Labor: Regimes of Accumulation and Modes of Regulation. **In** *Scott, A. J. and Storper, M., eds.*, 1986, pp. 16–40.

Marcus, Irwin M. The Global Economy: Divergent Perspectives on Economic Change: Introduction: A Historical Overview of the Global Economy. **In** *Gondolf, E. W.; Marcus, I. M. and Dougherty, J. P., eds.*, 1986, pp. 1–12.

de Montbrial, Thierry. The European Dimension. *Foreign Aff.*, 1986, *64*(3), pp. 499–514. **[G: EEC]**

Ndekwu, E. C. International Financial Organisations and the NIEO. **In** *Onwuka, R. I. and Aluko, O., eds.*, 1986, pp. 132–49.

Nerfin, Marc. Neither Prince nor Merchant: Citizen—An Introduction to the Third System. **In** *[Patel, S.]*, 1986, pp. 47–59.

Nweke, G. Aforka. From Old to New World Economic Order: The Nigerian Initiative of 1961. **In** *Onwuka, R. I. and Aluko, O., eds.*, 1986, pp. 272–95.

Ojo, M. A. United Nations and Related Agencies' Attempts at a New International Economic Order. **In** *Onwuka, R. I. and Aluko, O., eds.*, 1986, pp. 105–14.

Onwuka, Ralph I. The Illusions of the New International Economic Order. **In** *Onwuka, R. I. and Aluko, O., eds.*, 1986, pp. 1–16.

Paisley, Robert. Teaching Economics to the 13–16 Age Range: International Trade and the Balance of Payments. **In** *Whitehead, D. J., ed.*, 1986, pp. 109–18. **[G: U.K.]**

Panchamukhi, V. R. Inter-dependence and Dependence in the World Economic System: Some Reflections. *Indian J. Quant. Econ.*, 1986, *2*(1), pp. 57–66. **[G: Global]**

Panchamukhi, V. R. Interdependence and Dependence in the World Economic System: Some Reflections. **In** *Panchamukhi, V. R., et al.*, 1986, pp. 3–14.

Patel, I. G. Next Steps in International Economic Co-operation. **In** *Patel, I. G.*, 1986, *1985*, pp. 233–52.

Patel, I. G. The Current Crisis in International Economic Co-operation. **In** *Patel, I. G.*, 1986, *1984*, pp. 212–32.

Pfaller, Alfred. The Changing North–South Division of Labour: Promises, Threats and EC Policy Options. *Kyklos*, 1986, *39*(1), pp. 85–108. **[G: Global]**

Quandt, William B. U.S.–Soviet Rivalry in the Middle East. **In** *Shulman, M. D., ed.*, 1986, pp. 18–43. **[G: Middle East; U.S.; U.S.S.R.]**

Robinson, James D., III. Redefining Global Security in the Face of Threats on the Economic Front. *World Econ.*, September 1986, *9*(3), pp. 311–13. **[G: Global]**

Romberg, Alan D. New Stirrings in Asia. *Foreign Aff.*, 1986, *64*(3), pp. 515–38. **[G: E. Asia]**

Shulman, Marshall D. East–West Tensions in the Third World: Overview. **In** *Shulman, M. D., ed.*, 1986, pp. 5–17. **[G: Global]**

Theodoropoulos, Christos. NIEO and African Relations with the Centrally-Planned Economies. **In** *Onwuka, R. I. and Aluko, O., eds.*, 1986, pp. 209–28. **[G: Africa; CMEA]**

Udokang, Okon. The Energy Question and Africa's Role in a NIEO. **In** *Onwuka, R. I. and Aluko, O., eds.*, 1986, pp. 165–86. **[G: Africa]**

Wallerstein, Immanuel. The World-System: Myths and Historical Shifts. **In** *Gondolf, E.*

W.; Marcus, I. M. and Dougherty, J. P., eds., 1986, pp. 15–24.

Zagoria, Donald S. The Soviet–American Rivalry in Asia. **In** *Shulman, M. D., ed.*, 1986, pp. 78–115. **[G: Asia; U.S.; U.S.S.R.]**

410 International Trade Theory

411 International Trade Theory

4110 General

Bovenberg, Arij Lans. Capital Income Taxation in Growing Open Economies. *J. Public Econ.*, December 1986, *31* (3), pp. 347–76. **[G: U.S.]**

Galor, Oded. Global Dynamic Inefficiency in the Absence of International Policy Coordination: A North–South Case. *J. Int. Econ.*, August 1986, *21* (1/2), pp. 137–49.

Hillman, Arye L. and Katz, Eliakim. Domestic Uncertainty and Foreign Dumping. *Can. J. Econ.*, August 1986, *19* (3), pp. 403–16.

Officer, Lawrence H. The Law of One Price Cannot Be Rejected: Two Tests Based on the Tradable/Nontradable Price Ratio. *J. Macroecon.*, Spring 1986, *8* (2), pp. 159–82. **[G: Global]**

4112 Theory of International Trade

Anderson, F. J. Trade with Transfer Costs in a Sraffa-Type System. *Int. J. Transport Econ.*, June 1986, *13* (2), pp. 135–52.

Artus, Patrick. Comment fonctionne le marché des exportations? (How Does the Export Market Operate? With English summary.) *Ann. Écon. Statist.*, Apr./June 1986, (2), pp. 3–36. **[G: France]**

Artus, Patrick. Demande intérieure et commerce extérieur de produits industriels. Une approche par le déséquilibre. (A Disequilibrium Approach to the Domestic Demand and the Foreign Trade of Manufactured Goods. With English summary.) *Revue Écon.*, January 1986, *37* (1), pp. 31–66. **[G: France]**

Asheim, Geir B. Hartwick's Rule in Open Economies. *Can. J. Econ.*, August 1986, *19* (3), pp. 395–402.

Balassa, Bela. Comparative Advantage in Manufactured Goods: A Reappraisal. *Rev. Econ. Statist.*, May 1986, *68* (2), pp. 315–19. **[G: U.S.]**

Balassa, Bela. Intra-industry Trade among Exporters of Manufactured Goods. **In** *Greenaway, D. and Tharakan, P. K. M., eds.*, 1986, pp. 108–28. **[G: LDCs; MDCs]**

Ballance, Robert; Forstner, Helmut and Murray, Tracy. More on Measuring Comparative Advantage: A Reply. *Weltwirtsch. Arch.*, 1986, *122* (2), pp. 375–78.

Batra, Raveendra N. A General Equilibrium Model of Multinational Corporations in Developing Economies. *Oxford Econ. Pap.*, July 1986, *38* (2), pp. 342–53.

Bean, Charles R. The Terms of Trade, Labour Supply and the Current Account. *Econ. J.*, Supplement 1986, *96*, pp. 38–46.

Bhagwati, Jagdish N. Incentives and Disincentives: International Migration. **In** *Balassa, B. and Giersch, H., eds.*, 1986, pp. 89–111. **[G: U.S.; W. Germany]**

Bhagwati, Jagdish N. and Brecher, Richard A. Extending Free Trade to Include International Investment: A Welfare-Theoretic Analysis. **In** *[Streeten, P.]*, 1986, pp. 115–21.

Bond, Eric W. Entrepreneurial Ability, Income Distribution, and International Trade. *J. Int. Econ.*, May 1986, *20* (3/4), pp. 343–56.

Bowden, Roger J. An Empirical Model of Bilateral Trade (or Its Absence) in Manufactured Commodities. *Manchester Sch. Econ. Soc. Stud.*, September 1986, *54* (3), pp. 255–82.

Bowen, Harry P. On Measuring Comparative Advantage: Further Comments. *Weltwirtsch. Arch.*, 1986, *122* (2), pp. 379–81.

Branson, William H. Natural Resources and the Macroeconomy: A Theoretical Framework: Discussion: An International Macroeconomic Perspective. **In** *Neary, J. P. and van Wijnbergen, S., eds.*, 1986, pp. 50–52.

Buffie, Edward F. and Spiller, Pablo T. Trade Liberalization in Oligopolistic Industries: The Quota Case. *J. Int. Econ.*, February 1986, *20* (1/2), pp. 65–81.

Burgstaller, André. Unifying Ricardo's Theories of Growth and Comparative Advantage. *Economica*, November 1986, *53* (212), pp. 467–81.

Cassing, James H. A Wicksellian Model of International Freights and Prices. *Int. J. Transport Econ.*, February 1986, *13* (1), pp. 7–19.

Cassing, James H.; Hillman, Arye L. and Long, Ngo Van. Risk Aversion, Terms of Trade Uncertainty and Social-Consensus Trade Policy. *Oxford Econ. Pap.*, July 1986, *38* (2), pp. 234–42.

Casson, Mark. The International Division of Labour. **In** *Casson, M., et al.*, 1986, pp. 63–102.

Casson, Mark. Vertical Integration and Intra-firm Trade. **In** *Casson, M., et al.*, 1986, pp. 103–37.

Chang, Winston W. and Chiang, Shin-Hwan. A Model of Growth and Trade in Time-phased Economies. *Int. Econ. Rev.*, October 1986, *27* (3), pp. 783–802.

Chaudhuri, T. Datta and Khan, M. Ali. Commercial Policy in an Asymmetric World Economy. *J. Econ. (Z. Nationalökon.)*, 1986, *46* (2), pp. 143–61.

Cima, Lawrence R. The Excess Supply–Pure Demand Approach to International Commodity Trade: The Case of Japanese Steel Exports to the United States. *Econ. Inquiry*, October 1986, *24* (4), pp. 645–56. **[G: U.S.; Japan]**

Clague, Christopher. Tariffs, Transfers and the Real Exchange Rate. *Southern Econ. J.*, July 1986, *53* (1), pp. 155–69.

Clark, Don P. and Thompson, Henry. Immigration, International Capital Flows, and Long Run Income Distribution in Canada. *Atlantic Econ. J.*, December 1986, *14* (4), pp. 24–29. **[G: Canada]**

Coloma C., Fernando and Lagos M., Luis Felipe. Los efectos de una desgravación arancelaria en el contexto de una economiá con movilidad imperfecta de trabajo. (With English summary.) *Cuadernos Econ.*, August 1986, *23*(69), pp. 145–72.

Comolli, Paul M. Exhaustible Resources and International Trade. *Eastern Econ. J.*, July-Sept. 1986, *12*(3), pp. 291–96.

Das, Satya P. Optimal Taxation of Foreign Capital When Its Movements Are Sluggish. *J. Int. Econ.*, November 1986, *21*(3/4), pp. 351–60.

Dasgupta, Partha. Natural Resources and the Macroeconomy: A Theoretical Framework: Discussion: A Natural Resources Perspective. **In** *Neary, J. P. and van Wijnbergen, S., eds.*, 1986, pp. 53.

Deardorff, Alan V. FIRless FIRwoes: How Preferences Can Interfere with the Theorems of International Trade. *J. Int. Econ.*, February 1986, *20*(1/2), pp. 131–42.

Dinopoulos, Elias and Wooton, Ian. A North–South Model of International Justice. *Can. J. Econ.*, November 1986, *19*(4), pp. 766–79.

Dixit, Avinash K. and Grossman, Gene M. Targeted Export Promotion with Several Oligopolistic Industries. *J. Int. Econ.*, November 1986, *21*(3/4), pp. 233–49.

Dixit, Avinash K. and Norman, Victor. Gains from Trade without Lump-Sum Compensation. *J. Int. Econ.*, August 1986, *21*(1/2), pp. 111–22.

Djajić, Slobodan. International Migration, Remittances and Welfare in a Dependent Economy. *J. Devel. Econ.*, May 1986, *21*(2), pp. 229–34.

Dollar, David. Technological Innovations, Capital Mobility, and the Product Cycle in North–South Trade. *Amer. Econ. Rev.*, March 1986, *76*(1), pp. 177–90.

Donnenfeld, Shabtai. Intra-industry Trade and Imperfect Information about Product Quality. *Europ. Econ. Rev.*, April 1986, *30*(2), pp. 401–17.

Dornbusch, Rudiger; Fischer, Stanley and Samuelson, Paul A. Comparative Advantage, Trade, and Payments in a Ricardian Model with a Continuum of Goods. **In** *Samuelson, P. A.*, 1986, *1977*, pp. 415–31.

Dornbusch, Rudiger; Fischer, Stanley and Samuelson, Paul A. Heckscher–Ohlin Trade Theory with a Continuum of Goods. **In** *Samuelson, P. A.*, 1986, *1980*, pp. 432–53.

Dung, Tran Huu. International Commodity Transfers and Capital Movements. *Greek Econ. Rev.*, December 1986, *8*(2), pp. 155–66.

Dutt, Amitava Krishna. Vertical Trading and Uneven Development. *J. Devel. Econ.*, March 1986, *20*(2), pp. 339–59.

Eaton, Jonathan and Grossman, Gene M. Optimal Trade and Industrial Policy under Oligopoly. *Quart. J. Econ.*, May 1986, *101*(2), pp. 383–406.

Ethier, Wilfred J. Illegal Immigration: The Host-Country Problem. *Amer. Econ. Rev.*, March 1986, *76*(1), pp. 56–71.

Ethier, Wilfred J. International Trade Theory and International Migration. **In** *Stark, O., ed.*, 1986, pp. 27–74.

Ethier, Wilfred J. The Multinational Firm. *Quart. J. Econ.*, November 1986, *101*(4), pp. 805–33.

Ethier, Wilfred J. and Svensson, Lars E. O. The Theorems of International Trade with Factor Mobility. *J. Int. Econ.*, February 1986, *20*(1/2), pp. 21–42.

Feldman, David H. and Tower, Edward. The Welfare Economics of an Unstable Real Exchange Rate. *Southern Econ. J.*, January 1986, *52*(3), pp. 607–16.

Flückiger, Yves. Effets de la croissance factorielle sur la structure de production d'un pays: le cas des termes de l'échange variables. (With English summary.) *Revue Écon. Polit.*, July-Aug. 1986, *96*(4), pp. 398–411.

Flug, Karnit and Galor, Oded. Minimum Wage in a General Equilibrium Model of International Trade and Human Capital. *Int. Econ. Rev.*, February 1986, *27*(1), pp. 149–64.

Francesco, Drudi. Effetti redistributivi e di benessere di un'apertura a movimenti di capitale. (Effects of Capital Flows on Income Distribution and Welfare. A Review Article. With English summary.) *Giorn. Econ.*, July-Aug. 1986, *45*(7–8), pp. 433–62.

Frijns, Jean M. G. The Dutch Disease in the Netherlands: Comment. **In** *Neary, J. P. and van Wijnbergen, S., eds.*, 1986, pp. 136–41. **[G: Netherlands]**

Fry, Maxwell J. Terms-of-Trade Dynamics in Asia: An Analysis of National Saving and Domestic Investment Responses to Terms-of-Trade Changes in 14 Asian LDCs. *J. Int. Money Finance*, March 1986, *5*(1), pp. 57–73. **[G: Asia]**

Galor, Oded. Time Preference and International Labor Migration. *J. Econ. Theory*, February 1986, *38*(1), pp. 1–20.

Geldner, Marian. Integrating the Theories of International Trade and Foreign Direct Investment. **In** *Gray, H. P., ed.*, 1986, pp. 95–107.

Gottfries, Nils. Price Dynamics of Exporting and Import-Competing Firms. *Scand. J. Econ.*, 1986, *88*(2), pp. 417–36.

Greenaway, David and Tharakan, P. K. Mathew. Imperfect Competition, Adjustment Policy, and Commercial Policy. **In** *Greenaway, D. and Tharakan, P. K. M., eds.*, 1986, pp. 7–33.

Hahne, Ulf. Changes in the International Division of Labour and Prospects for Endogenous Development. **In** *Bassand, M., et al., eds.*, 1986, pp. 90–102. **[G: W. Germany]**

Hartigan, James C. and Tower, Edward. The Leontief Question: A Cobb–Douglas Approach to Simulating the U.S. Income Distribution in Autarky. *Weltwirtsch. Arch.*, 1986, *122*(4), pp. 677–89. **[G: U.S.]**

Hazari, Bharat R. and Sgro, Pasquale M. Factor Accumulation, Unemployment and Welfare in a Model with Non-traded Goods and Specific Factors. *Greek Econ. Rev.*, December 1986, *8*(2), pp. 187–99.

Hazari, Bharat R. and Sgro, Pasquale M. International Trade Theory in a Two Country General Equilibrium Model with Traded Intermediate Goods. *J. Quant. Econ.*, January 1986, *2*(1), pp. 1–18.

Heierli, U. Division of Labour and Appropriate Technology—From Adam Smith to E. F. Schumacher. **In** *Bassand, M., et al., eds.*, 1986, pp. 9–37.

Heller, Peter S. Factor Endowment Change and Comparative Advantage: The Case of Japan, 1956–1969. **In** *Sohn, I., ed.*, 1986, *1976*, pp. 327–39. **[G: Japan]**

Herander, Mark G. and Thomas, Christopher R. Export Performance and Export–Import Linkage Requirements. *Quart. J. Econ.*, August 1986, *101*(3), pp. 591–607.

Heravi, Iraj. The Leontief Paradox, Reconsidered: Correction. *J. Polit. Econ.*, October 1986, *94*(5), pp. 1120. **[G: U.S.]**

Inoue, Tadashi. On the Shape of the World Production Possibility Frontier with Three Goods and Two Primary Factors with and without Capital Mobility. *Int. Econ. Rev.*, October 1986, *27*(3), pp. 707–26.

Ishii, Yasunori. Asymmetric Technological Uncertainty and International Trade in the Presence of Risk-Sharing Arrangements. *J. Econ. (Z. Nationalökon.)*, 1986, *46*(1), pp. 1–16.

Jensen, Richard A. and Thursby, Marie C. A Strategic Approach to the Product Life Cycle. *J. Int. Econ.*, November 1986, *21*(3/4), pp. 269–84.

Jones, Ronald W. Natural Resources and the Macroeconomy: A Theoretical Framework: Discussion: A Trade Theoretic Perspective. **In** *Neary, J. P. and van Wijnbergen, S., eds.*, 1986, pp. 46–50.

Jones, Ronald W.; Coelho, Isaias and Easton, Stephen T. The Theory of International Factor Flows: The Basic Model. *J. Int. Econ.*, May 1986, *20*(3/4), pp. 313–27.

Jones, Ronald W. and Kierzkowski, Henryk. Neighborhood Production Structures, with an Application to the Theory of International Trade. *Oxford Econ. Pap.*, March 1986, *38*(1), pp. 59–76.

Jones, Ronald W. and Neary, J. Peter. The Positive Theory of International Trade. **In** *Jones, R. W., ed.*, 1986, *1984*, pp. 1–62.

Kakimoto, Sumio and Yabuuchi, Shigemi. The Rybczynski Theorem in a Model with Non-traded Goods and Indecomposable Interindustry Flows: Revisited. *J. Int. Econ.*, February 1986, *20*(1/2), pp. 157–69.

Kanbur, S. M. Ravi and Vines, David. North–South Interaction and Commod Control. *J. Devel. Econ.*, October 1986, *23*(2), pp. 371–87.

Kawai, Masahiro and Zilcha, Itzhak. International Trade with Forward-Futures Markets under Exchange Rate and Price Uncertainty. *J. Int. Econ.*, February 1986, *20*(1/2), pp. 83–98.

Kemp, Murray C. and Tawada, Makoto. The World Production Frontier under Variable Returns to Scale. *J. Int. Econ.*, November 1986, *21*(3/4), pp. 251–68.

Kemp, Murray C. and Wan, Henry Y., Jr. Gains from Trade with and without Lump-Sum Compensation. *J. Int. Econ.*, August 1986, *21*(1/2), pp. 99–110.

Khan, M. Ali and Lin, Po-Sheng. Two-Way Capital Flows in an Asymmetric World Economy. *Manchester Sch. Econ. Soc. Stud.*, June 1986, *54*(2), pp. 219–24.

Kiljunen, Kimmo. The International Division of Industrial Labour and the Core–Periphery Concept. *CEPAL Rev.*, December 1986, (30), pp. 97–115.

Kirwan, Frank and Holden, Darryl. Emigrants' Remittances, Non-traded Goods and Economic Welfare in the Source Country. *J. Econ. Stud.*, 1986, *13*(2), pp. 52–58.

Kremers, Jeroen J. M. The Dutch Disease in the Netherlands. **In** *Neary, J. P. and van Wijnbergen, S., eds.*, 1986, pp. 96–136. **[G: Netherlands]**

Lal, Deepak. Stolper–Samuleson–Rybczynski in the Pacific: Real Wages and Real Exchange Rates in the Philippines, 1956–1978. *J. Devel. Econ.*, April 1986, *21*(1), pp. 181–204. **[G: Philippines]**

Lall, Sanjaya. The Third World and Comparative Advantage in Trade Services. **In** *[Streeten, P.]*, 1986, pp. 122–38.

Lee, Young Sun. Changing Export Patterns in Korea, Taiwan and Japan. *Weltwirtsch. Arch.*, 1986, *122*(1), pp. 150–63. **[G: S. Korea; Taiwan; Japan]**

Leontief, Wassily. Factor Proportions and the Structure of American Trade: Further Theoretical and Empirical Analysis. **In** *Leontief, W.*, 1986, *1956*, pp. 94–128. **[G: U.S.]**

Levy, Santiago. Un modelo clásico de comercio internacional. (A Classical-type Model of International Trade. With English summary.) *Estud. Econ.*, July-Dec. 1986, *1*(2), pp. 281–303.

Lundberg, Lars and Hansson, Pär. Intra-industry Trade and Its Consequences for Adjustment. **In** *Greenaway, D. and Tharakan, P. K. M., eds.*, 1986, pp. 129–47. **[G: Sweden]**

Mainardi, Stefano. A Theoretical Interpretation of Intra-firm Trade in the Presence of Intra-industry Trade. **In** *Greenaway, D. and Tharakan, P. K. M., eds.*, 1986, pp. 88–107.

Mainwaring, Lynn. International Trade in New and Used Machines. *Cambridge J. Econ.*, September 1986, *10*(3), pp. 247–63.

Mainwaring, Lynn. The Theory of International Transport Costs with Tradeable Intermediate Goods. *Scot. J. Polit. Econ.*, May 1986, *33*(2), pp. 111–23.

Marion, Nancy Peregrim and Svensson, Lars E. O. The Terms of Trade between Oil Importers . *J. Int. Econ.*, February 1986, *20*(1/2), pp. 99–113.

Markusen, James R. Explaining the Volume of Trade: An Eclectic Approach. *Amer. Econ. Rev.*, December 1986, *76*(5), pp. 1002–11.

Marquez, Jaime. Oil-Price Effects in Theory and

Practice. *J. Devel. Econ.*, November 1986, *24*(1), pp. 1–27. **[G: Global]**

Matusz, Steven J. Implicit Contracts, Unemployment and International Trade. *Econ. J.*, June 1986, *96*(382), pp. 307–22.

Maurisson, Patrick. Réflexions sur les théories sraffaienne et post-sraffaienne du commerce international: à propos de la notion de "branche fictive." (Consideration about the Sraffian and Post-Sraffian Theories of International Trade with Regard to the Notion of "Fictitious Branch." With English summary.) *Écon. Appl.*, 1986, *39*(1), pp. 35–60.

McIntosh, James. North–South Trade: Export-led Growth with Abundant Labour. *J. Devel. Econ.*, November 1986, *24*(1), pp. 141–52.

Melvin, James R. The Nonequivalence of Tariffs and Import Quotas. *Amer. Econ. Rev.*, December 1986, *76*(5), pp. 1131–34.

Milner, Chris. Optimal Intervention and Intra-industry Trade: The Case of Horizontally Differentiated Goods and Monopolistically Competitive Industries. **In** *Greenaway, D. and Tharakan, P. K. M., eds.*, 1986, pp. 47–67.

Miyagiwa, Kaz F. A Reconsideration of the Welfare Economics of a Free-Trade Zone. *J. Int. Econ.*, November 1986, *21*(3/4), pp. 337–50.

Montet, Christian. Échange inégal, gain de l'échange et justice distributive internationale. (Unequal Exchange, Gain from Trade and International Distributive Justice. With English summary.) *Revue Écon.*, July 1986, *37*(4), pp. 659–75.

Morgan, Peter B.; McDonald, John and Woodfield, A. Affordability and Some Welfare Aspects of Indexation. *Econ. Rec.*, March 1986, *62*(176), pp. 37–48.

Mumy, Gene E. Silences in Ricardo: Comparative Advantage and the Class Distribution of Free Trade Benefits. *Rev. Soc. Econ.*, December 1986, *44*(3), pp. 294–305.

Nakao, Takeo. Industrial Organization in an International Framework. **In** *de Jong, H. W. and Shepherd, W. G., eds., Bk. 1*, 1986, pp. 159–87. **[G: OECD]**

Naqvi, Nadeem. International Debt, Investment and the Currency Account: An Intertemporal Analysis. *Indian Econ. J.*, Jan.-Mar. 1986, *33*(3), pp. 53–64.

Neary, J. Peter and Schweinberger, Albert G. Factor Content Functions and the Theory of International Trade. *Rev. Econ. Stud.*, July 1986, *53*(3), pp. 421–32.

Neary, J. Peter and van Wijnbergen, Sweder J. G. Natural Resources and the Macroeconomy: A Theoretical Framework. **In** *Neary, J. P. and van Wijnbergen, S., eds.*, 1986, pp. 13–45.

Niehans, Jürg. The International Division of Assets as Determined by Comparative Advantage. *J. Int. Money Finance*, June 1986, *5*(2), pp. 153–65.

Nielsen, Søren Bo. Handelsskatter i en råvareimporterende økonomi. (Trade Taxes in a Small Open Economy. With English summary.) *Nationaløkon. Tidsskr.*, 1986, *124*(3), pp. 380–95.

Ocampo, José Antonio. New Developments in Trade Theory and LDCs. *J. Devel. Econ.*, June 1986, *22*(1), pp. 129–70. **[G: LDCs]**

Opocher, A. The Terms of Trade in the Presence of Re-export Trade: Some Further Developments. *Metroecon.*, October 1986, *38*(3), pp. 215–27.

Panagariya, Arvind. Increasing Returns and the Specific Factors Model. *Southern Econ. J.*, July 1986, *53*(1), pp. 1–17.

Panagariya, Arvind. Increasing Returns, Dynamic Stability, and International Trade. *J. Int. Econ.*, February 1986, *20*(1/2), pp. 43–63.

Panagariya, Arvind and Succar, Patricia. The Harris–Todaro Model and Economies of Scale. *Southern Econ. J.*, April 1986, *52*(4), pp. 984–98.

Pinto, Brian R. Repeated Games and the 'Reciprocal Dumping' Model of Trade. *J. Int. Econ.*, May 1986, *20*(3/4), pp. 357–66.

Pomfret, Richard. On the Division of Labour and International Trade: Or, Adam Smith's Explanation of Intra-industry Trade. *J. Econ. Stud.*, 1986, *13*(4), pp. 56–63.

Rauch, James E. The Transfer of Production from Rich to Poor Countries. *J. Devel. Econ.*, September 1986, *23*(1), pp. 41–53.

Rieber, William J. Domestic Monopoly and Customs Union Formation. *Amer. Econ.*, Spring 1986, *30*(1), pp. 32–35.

Rivera-Batiz, Francisco L. International Migration, Remittances and Economic Welfare in the Source Country. *J. Econ. Stud.*, 1986, *13*(3), pp. 3–19.

Rodrik, Dani. Tariffs, Subsidies, and Welfare with Endogenous Policy. *J. Int. Econ.*, November 1986, *21*(3/4), pp. 285–99.

Samuelson, Paul A. A Corrected Version of Hume's Equilibrating Mechanisms for International Trade. **In** *Samuelson, P. A.*, 1986, *1980*, pp. 397–414.

Samuelson, Paul A. Bertil Ohlin (1899–1979). **In** *Samuelson, P. A.*, 1986, *1982*, pp. 809–25.

Samuelson, Paul A. Free Trade's Intertemporal Pareto-Optimality. **In** *Samuelson, P. A.*, 1986, *1978*, pp. 477–79.

Samuelson, Paul A. Interest Rate Equalization and Nonequalization by Trade in Leontief–Sraffa Models. **In** *Samuelson, P. A.*, 1986, *1978*, pp. 470–76.

Schatz, Klaus-Werner. Incentives and Disincentives: International Migration: Comment. **In** *Balassa, B. and Giersch, H., eds.*, 1986, pp. 112–17. **[G: U.S.; W. Germany]**

Sieber, René. Accumulation de capital, propriété étrangère et bien-être national en présence de facteurs de production spécifiques et de biens non-échangeables. (Capital Accumulation, Foreign Ownership and National Welfare with Specific Factors of Production and Non-tradable Goods. With English summary.) *Écon. Appl.*, 1986, *39*(2), pp. 239–62.

Sieber, René and Wetterwald, Paul. Environmental Protection and Direct Foreign Investment with Specific Factors of Production: The Case of the Small Open Economy. *Schweiz.*

Z. Volkswirtsch. Statist., December 1986, *122*(4), pp. 611–25.

Simons, William B. Soviet Foreign Trade: Economic, Legal, and Political Aspects. **In** *Ioffe, O. S. and Janis, M. W., eds.*, 1986, pp. 243–81. **[G: U.S.S.R.]**

Siroën, Jean-Marc. Discrimination des prix différenciation des produits et échange international. (Price Discrimination, Product Differentiation and International Trade. With English summary.) *Revue Écon.*, May 1986, *37*(3), pp. 489–520.

Sjöstedt, Gunnar and Sundelius, Bengt. International Trade Theory and the Crisis of Knowledge. **In** *Sjöstedt, G. and Sundelius, B., eds.*, 1986, pp. 1–39.

Staiger, Robert W. Measurement of the Factor Content of Foreign Trade with Traded Intermediate Goods. *J. Int. Econ.*, November 1986, *21*(3/4), pp. 361–68.

Stockman, Alan C. and Dellas, Harris. Asset Markets, Tariffs, and Political Risk. *J. Int. Econ.*, November 1986, *21*(3/4), pp. 199–213.

Syrquin, Moshe and Urata, Shujiro. Sources of Changes in Factor Intensity of Trade. *J. Devel. Econ.*, December 1986, *24*(2), pp. 225–37. **[G: Mexico; Japan; S. Korea; Taiwan; Israel]**

Tapvong, Churai. Duality in Factor Endowments, International Trade, and Factor Prices: An Analysis of Labour Migration. *Indian Econ. J.*, Jan.-Mar. 1986, *33*(3), pp. 46–52.

Teck, Hoon Hian. Effects of Technical Progress and Foreign Labour Importation on Shifting Comparative Advantage: A Geometrical Note. *S. Afr. J. Econ.*, December 1986, *54*(4), pp. 442–45.

Thompson, Henry. Free Trade and Factor-Price Polarization. *Europ. Econ. Rev.*, April 1986, *30*(2), pp. 419–25.

Trannoy, Alain. Paradoxe global des transferts et multiplicité des équilibres: deux résultats. (Global Transfer Paradox and Multiplicity of Equilibria: Two Results. With English summary.) *Ann. Écon. Statist.*, Oct./Dec. 1986, (4), pp. 53–61.

Wong, Kar-yiu. Are International Trade and Factor Mobility Substitutes? *J. Int. Econ.*, August 1986, *21*(1/2), pp. 25–43.

Wong, Kar-yiu. International Factor Movements, Repatriation and Welfare. *J. Int. Econ.*, November 1986, *21*(3/4), pp. 327–35.

Wong, Kar-yiu. The Economic Analysis of International Migration: A Generalization. *Can. J. Econ.*, May 1986, *19*(2), pp. 357–62.

Young, Leslie. A Note on 'Secular Specific Capital, Interconnectedness in Production, and Welfare.' *Can. J. Econ.*, November 1986, *19*(4), pp. 678–84.

Young, Leslie and Miyagiwa, Kaz F. International Investment and Immiserizing Growth. *J. Int. Econ.*, February 1986, *20*(1/2), pp. 171–78.

4113 Theory of Protection

Aizenman, Joshua. On the Complementarity of Commercial Policy, Capital Controls, and Inflation Tax. *Can. J. Econ.*, February 1986, *19*(1), pp. 114–33.

Baldwin, Robert E. Rent-Seeking and Trade Policy: An Industry Approach. **In** *Balassa, B. and Giersch, H., eds.*, 1986, pp. 429–43.

Baldwin, Robert E. Trade Policies in Developed Countries. **In** *Jones, R. W., ed.*, 1986, *1984*, pp. 183–231. **[G: MDCs]**

Blomqvist, Ake G. and McMahon, Gary. Simulating Commercial Policy in a Small, Open Dual Economy with Urban Unemployment: A General Equilibrium Approach. *J. Devel. Stud.*, January 1986, *22*(2), pp. 443–63. **[G: Kenya]**

Brander, James A. Rationales for Strategic Trade and Industrial Policy. **In** *Krugman, P. R., ed.*, 1986, pp. 23–46.

Buffie, Edward F. and Spiller, Pablo T. Trade Liberalization in Oligopolistic Industries: The Quota Case. *J. Int. Econ.*, February 1986, *20*(1/2), pp. 65–81.

Cassing, James H. A Note on the Welfare Cost of a Tariff. *Eastern Econ. J.*, Apr.-June 1986, *12*(2), pp. 145–48.

Cassing, James H. and Hillman, Arye L. Shifting Comparative Advantage and Senescent Industry Collapse. *Amer. Econ. Rev.*, June 1986, *76*(3), pp. 516–23.

Chambers, Robert G. Domestic and International Agricultural Policy Interfaces. *Southern J. Agr. Econ.*, July 1986, *18*(1), pp. 61–66.

Clague, Christopher. Tariffs, Transfers and the Real Exchange Rate. *Southern Econ. J.*, July 1986, *53*(1), pp. 155–69.

Coloma C., Fernando and Lagos M., Luis Felipe. Los efectos de una desgravación arancelaria en el contexto de una economiá con movilidad imperfecta de trabajo. (With English summary.) *Cuadernos Econ.*, August 1986, *23*(69), pp. 145–72.

Cooper, H. The Welfare Effects of Sanctions. *J. Stud. Econ. Econometrics*, August 1986, (25), pp. 2–11.

Cooper, Richard N. Economic Interdependence and Coordination of Economic Policies. **In** *Cooper, R. N.*, 1986, *1985*, pp. 289–331.

Corden, W. Max. Policies towards Market Disturbance. **In** *Snape, R. H., ed.*, 1986, pp. 121–39.

Corden, W. Max. The Normative Theory of International Trade. **In** *Jones, R. W., ed.*, 1986, *1984*, pp. 63–130.

Das, Satya P. and Niho, Yoshio. A Dynamic Analysis of Protection, Market Structure, and Welfare. *Int. Econ. Rev.*, June 1986, *27*(2), pp. 513–23.

Deardorff, Alan V. and Stern, Robert M. Neighborhood Effects of Developing Country Protection. *J. Devel. Econ.*, May 1986, *21*(2), pp. 327–46. **[G: LDCs]**

Dixit, Avinash K. Trade Policy: An Agenda for Research. **In** *Krugman, P. R., ed.*, 1986, pp. 283–304.

Donnenfeld, Shabtai. Intra-industry Trade and Imperfect Information about Product Quality. *Europ. Econ. Rev.*, April 1986, *30*(2), pp. 401–17.

Eaton, Jonathan and Grossman, Gene M. Optimal Trade and Industrial Policy under Oligopoly. *Quart. J. Econ.*, May 1986, *101*(2), pp. 383–406.

Edwards, Sebastian and van Wijnbergen, Sweder J. G. The Welfare Effects of Trade and Capital Market Liberalization. *Int. Econ. Rev.*, February 1986, *27*(1), pp. 141–48.

Eldor, Rafael. The Effective Protection Rate under Uncertainty: A Note. *Econ. Rec.*, December 1986, *62*(179), pp. 485–89.

Fausten, Dietrich. The Choice of Instrument for Industry Protection: Comment. **In** *Snape, R. H., ed.*, 1986, pp. 171–74.

Feenstra, Robert C. Trade Policy with Several Goods and 'Market Linkages.' *J. Int. Econ.*, May 1986, *20*(3/4), pp. 249–67.

Felder, Joseph. Protectionism, Domestic Monopoly, and the Levels of Domestic Production and Consumption. *Quart. J. Bus. Econ.*, Autumn 1986, *25*(4), pp. 77–100. **[G: LDCs]**

Feldman, David H. and Tower, Edward. Optimal Destabilizing Speculation or Why the Optimum Tariff May Oscillate. *De Economist*, 1986, *134*(3), pp. 368–77.

Findlay, Roland and Wellisz, Stanislaw. Tariffs, Quotas and Domestic-Content Protection: Some Political Economy Considerations: Response to Comments. *Public Choice*, 1986, *50*(1–3), pp. 247–48.

Findlay, Ronald and Wellisz, Stanislaw. Tariffs, Quotas and Domestic-Content Protection: Some Political Economy Considerations. *Public Choice*, 1986, *50*(1–3), pp. 221–42.

Finger, J. Michael. Tariffs, Quotas and Domestic-Content Protection: Some Political Economy Considerations: Comment. *Public Choice*, 1986, *50*(1–3), pp. 243–46.

Fourgeaud, Claude; Lenclud, B. and Picard, P. Shadow Prices and Public Policies in a Disequilibrium Model of an Open Economy. *Europ. Econ. Rev.*, October 1986, *30*(5), pp. 991–1012. **[G: France]**

Frey, Bruno S. and Buhofer, Heinz. Integration and Protectionism: A Comparative Institutional Analysis. **In** *Hauser, H., ed. (II)*, 1986, pp. 167–88.

Gray, H. Peter. "Natural Resource Pricing," Allocative Efficiency and Protection. *Weltwirtsch. Arch.*, 1986, *122*(2), pp. 365–70.

Greenaway, David and Tharakan, P. K. Mathew. Imperfect Competition, Adjustment Policy, and Commercial Policy. **In** *Greenaway, D. and Tharakan, P. K. M., eds.*, 1986, pp. 7–33.

Greenhut, Melvin L. and Norman, George. Spatial Pricing with a General Cost Function; the Effects of Taxes on Imports. *Int. Econ. Rev.*, October 1986, *27*(3), pp. 761–76.

Hamilton, Carl. ASEAN Systems for Allocation of Export Licences under VERs. **In** *Findlay, C. and Garnaut, R., eds.*, 1986, pp. 235–47. **[G: ASEAN]**

Hamilton, Carl. Import Quotas and Voluntary Export Restraints: Focusing on Exporting Countries. **In** *Findlay, C. and Garnaut, R., eds.*, 1986, pp. 214–34.

Hamilton, Carl. The Upgrading Effect of Voluntary Export Restraints. *Weltwirtsch. Arch.*, 1986, *122*(2), pp. 358–64.

Herander, Mark G. Export Drawback and the Structure of Protection. *Bull. Econ. Res.*, January 1986, *38*(1), pp. 43–48.

Herander, Mark G. The (Non-) Equivalence of Quantitative Restrictions. *J. Econ. Stud.*, 1986, *13*(4), pp. 64–73.

Horstmann, Ignatius J. and Markusen, James R. Up the Average Cost Curve: Inefficient Entry and the New Protectionism. *J. Int. Econ.*, May 1986, *20*(3/4), pp. 225–47.

Janis, Mark W. The Soviet Theory of International Law and International Economic Relations. **In** *Ioffe, O. S. and Janis, M. W., eds.*, 1986, pp. 235–41. **[G: U.S.S.R.]**

Jeon, Bang Nam and von Furstenberg, George M. Techniques for Measuring the Welfare Effects of Protection: Appraising the Choices. *J. Policy Modeling*, Summer 1986, *8*(2), pp. 273–303.

Krueger, Anne O. Trade Policies in Developing Countries. **In** *Jones, R. W., ed.*, 1986, pp. 131–81. **[G: LDCs]**

Lloyd, Peter J. and Falvey, Rodney E. The Choice of Instrument for Industry Protection. **In** *Snape, R. H., ed.*, 1986, pp. 152–70.

Mantel, Rolf R. and Martirena-Mantel, Ana M. On the Uniformity of Optimal Tariffs. *J. Devel. Econ.*, April 1986, *21*(1), pp. 41–52. **[G: Argentina]**

McKeown, Timothy J. The Limitations of "Structural" Theories of Commercial Policy. *Int. Organ.*, Winter 1986, *40*(1), pp. 43–64.

Melvin, James R. The Nonequivalence of Tariffs and Import Quotas. *Amer. Econ. Rev.*, December 1986, *76*(5), pp. 1131–34.

de Meza, David. Export Subsidies and High Productivity: Cause or Effect? *Can. J. Econ.*, May 1986, *19*(2), pp. 347–50.

Milner, Chris. Optimal Intervention and Intraindustry Trade: The Case of Horizontally Differentiated Goods and Monopolistically Competitive Industries. **In** *Greenaway, D. and Tharakan, P. K. M., eds.*, 1986, pp. 47–67.

Miyagiwa, Kaz F. and Young, Leslie. International Capital Mobility and Commercial Policy in an Economic Region. *J. Int. Econ.*, May 1986, *20*(3/4), pp. 329–41.

Nicolaides, Phedon. Political Coalitions and Issues: A Contribution to the Political Economy of Induced Distortions. *Aussenwirtschaft*, December 1986, *41*(4), pp. 497–510.

Ohyama, Michihiro. Protection and Factor Mobility. *Keio Econ. Stud.*, 1986, *23*(2), pp. 57–60.

Ordover, Janusz A. and Willig, Robert D. Perspectives on Mergers and World Competition. **In** *Grieson, R. E., ed.*, 1986, pp. 201–18.

Pomfret, Richard. The Effects of Trade Preferences for Developing Countries. *Southern Econ. J.*, July 1986, *53*(1), pp. 18–26. **[G: LDCs]**

Pomfret, Richard. The Theory of Preferential Trading Arrangements. *Weltwirtsch. Arch.*, 1986, *122*(3), pp. 439–65.

Reiber, William J. Trade Liberalization and Monopoly. *Indian Econ. J.*, Jan.-Mar. 1986, *33*(3), pp. 15–22.

Rodrik, Dani. Tariffs, Subsidies, and Welfare with Endogenous Policy. *J. Int. Econ.*, November 1986, *21*(3/4), pp. 285–99.

Rothschild, R. Raising Rivals' Costs: Regulation as a Competitive Strategy in Intra-industry Trade. **In** *Greenaway, D. and Tharakan, P. K. M., eds.*, 1986, pp. 34–46.

Rowley, Charles K. and Tollison, Robert D. Rent-Seeking and Trade Protection. **In** *Hauser, H., ed. (II)*, 1986, pp. 141–66.

Samuelson, Paul A. Justice to the Australians. **In** *Samuelson, P. A.*, 1986, *1981*, pp. 468–69.

Samuelson, Paul A. Summing Up on the Australian Case for Protection. **In** *Samuelson, P. A.*, 1986, *1981*, pp. 454–67. **[G: Australia]**

Samuelson, Paul A. To Protect Manufacturing? **In** *Samuelson, P. A.*, 1986, *1981*, pp. 510–17.

Sauernheimer, Karlhans. Tariffs, Imported Inputs and Employment. *Economica*, August 1986, *53*(211), pp. 393–99.

Siebert, Horst. Allokationseffekte von Importbeschränkungen. Eine Anmerkung. (Allocative Effects of Quotas. With English summary.) *Z. Wirtschaft. Sozialwissen.*, 1986, *106*(5), pp. 509–16.

Snape, Richard H. The Impact on Exporters of Import Restrictions. **In** *[Yamey, B.]*, 1986, pp. 201–24.

Spencer, Barbara J. What Should Trade Policy Target? **In** *Krugman, P. R., ed.*, 1986, pp. 69–89.

Stockman, Alan C. and Dellas, Harris. Asset Markets, Tariffs, and Political Risk. *J. Int. Econ.*, November 1986, *21*(3/4), pp. 199–213.

Turnovsky, Stephen J. Optimal Tariffs in Consistent Conjectural Variations Equilibrium. *J. Int. Econ.*, November 1986, *21*(3/4), pp. 301–12.

Venables, Anthony J. Production Subsidies, Import Tariffs, and Imperfectly Competitive Trade. **In** *Greenaway, D. and Tharakan, P. K. M., eds.*, 1986, pp. 68–87.

Waelbroeck, Jean. Rent-Seeking and Trade Policy: An Industry Approach: Comment. **In** *Balassa, B. and Giersch, H., eds.*, 1986, pp. 444–47.

Warr, Peter G. and Parmenter, B. R. Protection through Government Procurement. **In** *Snape, R. H., ed.*, 1986, pp. 175–90. **[G: Australia]**

Wellisz, Stanislaw and Wilson, John D. Lobbying and Tariff Formation: A Deadweight Loss Consideration. *J. Int. Econ.*, May 1986, *20*(3/4), pp. 367–75.

Wooton, Ian. Comments [Market Structure and Trade Liberalization: A General Equilibrium Assessment] [Short-run Impact of Trade Liberalization Measures on the Economy of Bangladesh: Exercises in Comparative Statics for the Year 1977]. **In** *Srinivasan, T. N. and Whalley, J., eds.*, 1986, pp. 319–21. **[G: Canada; Bangladesh]**

Wooton, Ian. Preferential Trading Agreements: An Investigation. *J. Int. Econ.*, August 1986, *21*(1/2), pp. 81–97.

Yeh, Yeong-Her. Export Subsidies vs. Production Subsidies. *Atlantic Econ. J.*, July 1986, *14*(2), pp. 71–75.

Yeh, Yeong-Her. The Maximum Revenue Tariff vs. Transfer Payments. *Eastern Econ. J.*, Apr.-June 1986, *12*(2), pp. 142–44.

Young, Leslie and Magee, Stephen P. Endogenous Protection, Factor Returns and Resource Allocation. *Rev. Econ. Stud.*, July 1986, *53*(3), pp. 407–19.

4114 Theory of International Trade and Economic Development

Adelman, Irma. Beyond Export-Led Growth. **In** *Adelman, I. and Taylor, J. E., eds.*, 1986, *1984*, pp. 242–62. **[G: S. Korea]**

Amsden, Alice H. The Direction of Trade—Past and Present—And the 'Learning Effects' of Exports to Different Directions. *J. Devel. Econ.*, October 1986, *23*(2), pp. 249–74. **[G: Japan; LDCs]**

Bakalis, Steve and Hazari, Bharat R. A Note on Underutilization of Capital and Unemployment in a Harris–Todaro Framework. *Devel. Econ.*, September 1986, *24*(3), pp. 288–98. **[G: LDCs]**

Balassa, Bela. Economic Development in Small Countries. *Acta Oecon.*, 1986, *37*(3–4), pp. 325–40. **[G: Hungary]**

Balassa, Bela. The Process of Industrial Development and Alternative Development Strategies. **In** *Adelman, I. and Taylor, J. E., eds.*, 1986, pp. 216–41.

Bhagwati, Jagdish N. Rethinking Trade Strategy. **In** *Lewis, J. P. and Kallab, V., eds.*, 1986, pp. 91–104.

Chenery, Hollis B., et al. Alternative Routes to Development. **In** *Chenery, H.; Robinson, S. and Syrquin, M.*, 1986, pp. 311–47. **[G: S. Korea]**

Chichilnisky, Graciela. A General Equilibrium Theory of North–South Trade. **In** *[Arrow, K. J.], Vol. 2*, 1986, pp. 3–56.

Deardorff, Alan V. and Stern, Robert M. Neighborhood Effects of Developing Country Protection. *J. Devel. Econ.*, May 1986, *21*(2), pp. 327–46. **[G: LDCs]**

Edwards, Sebastian. A Commodity Export Boom and the Real Exchange Rate: The Money–Inflation Link. **In** *Neary, J. P. and van Wijnbergen, S., eds.*, 1986, pp. 229–48. **[G: Colombia]**

Felder, Joseph. Protectionism, Domestic Monopoly, and the Levels of Domestic Production and Consumption. *Quart. J. Bus. Econ.*, Autumn 1986, *25*(4), pp. 77–100. **[G: LDCs]**

Grieco, Joseph M. Foreign Investment and Development: Theories and Evidence. **In** *Moran, T. H., ed.*, 1986, pp. 35–60.

Grinols, Earl L. Foreign Investment and Economic Growth: Characterization of a Second-Best Policy for Welfare Gains. *J. Int. Econ.*, August 1986, *21*(1/2), pp. 165–71.

Hawkins, A. M. Can Africa Industrialize? **In** *Berg, R. J. and Whitaker, J. S., eds.*, 1986, pp. 279–307. **[G: Africa]**

411 International Trade Theory

Heierli, U. Division of Labour and Appropriate Technology—From Adam Smith to E. F. Schumacher. **In** *Bassand, M., et al., eds.*, 1986, pp. 9–37.

Helleiner, Gerald K. Outward Orientation, Import Instability and African Economic Growth: An Empirical Investigation. **In** *[Streeten, P.]*, 1986, pp. 139–53. **[G: Africa; LDCs]**

Honohan, Patrick. A Commodity Export Boom and the Real Exchange Rate: The Money–Inflation Link: Comment. **In** *Neary, J. P. and van Wijnbergen, S., eds.*, 1986, pp. 249–50. **[G: Colombia]**

Kiljunen, Kimmo. The International Division of Industrial Labour and the Core–Periphery Concept. *CEPAL Rev.*, December 1986, (30), pp. 97–115.

Krueger, Anne O. Trade Policies in Developing Countries. **In** *Jones, R. W., ed.*, 1986, pp. 131–81. **[G: LDCs]**

Kubo, Yuji; de Melo, Jaime and Robinson, Sherman. Trade Strategies and Growth Episodes. **In** *Chenery, H.; Robinson, S. and Syrquin, M.*, 1986, pp. 148–87. **[G: LDCs]**

Kubo, Yuji, et al. General Equilibrium Models for the Analysis of Alternative Foreign Trade Strategies: An Application to Korea. **In** *Adelman, I. and Taylor, J. E., eds.*, 1986, pp. 124–60. **[G: S. Korea]**

Kuttner, Robert L. Some Keynesian Reflections on Free Trade. **In** *Sjöstedt, G. and Sundelius, B., eds.*, 1986, pp. 41–50.

Lall, Sanjaya. The Third World and Comparative Advantage in Trade Services. **In** *[Streeten, P.]*, 1986, pp. 122–38.

McIntosh, James. North–South Trade: Export-led Growth with Abundant Labour. *J. Devel. Econ.*, November 1986, *24*(1), pp. 141–52.

Ocampo, José Antonio. New Developments in Trade Theory and LDCs. *J. Devel. Econ.*, June 1986, *22*(1), pp. 129–70. **[G: LDCs]**

Panchamukhi, V. R. Complementarity and Economic Cooperation among Developing Countries (ECDC). **In** *Panchamukhi, V. R., et al.*, 1986, *1983*, pp. 15–24.

Panchamukhi, V. R. Trade and International Finance: Some Issues and Dilemmas of the Developing Countries. **In** *Panchamukhi, V. R., et al.*, 1986, pp. 27–54. **[G: LDCs]**

Patel, I. G. Some Reflections on Trade and Development. **In** *Patel, I. G.*, 1986, *1973*, pp. 35–47.

Prebisch, Raúl. The Dynamic Role of the Periphery. **In** *[Patel, S.]*, 1986, pp. 3–9. **[G: Latin America]**

Quibria, M. G. A Note on Foreign Investment, the Savings Function and Immiserization of National Welfare. *J. Devel. Econ.*, May 1986, *21*(2), pp. 361–72.

Raipuria, Kalyan M. Self-reliance: Concept, Measurement and Indicators. **In** *Panchamukhi, V. R., et al.*, 1986, pp. 215–42. **[G: India]**

Riedel, James. Factor Proportions, Linkages, and the Open Developing Economy. **In** *Sohn, I., ed.*, 1986, *1975*, pp. 340–53. **[G: Taiwan]**

Rodrik, Dani. 'Disequilibrium' Exchange Rates as Industrialization Policy. *J. Devel. Econ.*, September 1986, *23*(1), pp. 89–106. **[G: LDCs]**

Sapsford, David. A New Contribution in the Statistical Debate Over Trends in the Net Barter Terms of Trade Between Primary Commodities and Manufactures. *J. Econ. Soc. Meas.*, December 1986, *14*(4), pp. 277–88. **[G: U.K.]**

Solís, Leopoldo and Montemayor, Aurelio. A Mexican View of the Choice between Outward and Inward Orientation. **In** *Lewis, J. P. and Kallab, V., eds.*, 1986, pp. 105–13. **[G: Mexico]**

Stallings, Barbara. External Finance and the Transition to Socialism in Small Peripheral Societies. **In** *Fagen, R. R.; Deere, C. D. and Coraggio, J. L., eds.*, 1986, pp. 54–78. **[G: Cuba; Tanzania; Chile; Mozambique; Nicaragua]**

Taylor, Lance. Trade and Growth. *Rev. Black Polit. Econ.*, Spring 1986, *14*(4), pp. 17–36. **[G: LDCs]**

Winiecki, Jan. Central Planning and Export Orientation. *Eastern Europ. Econ.*, Summer 1986, *24*(4), pp. 67–89.

420 Trade Relations; Commercial Policy; International Economic Integration

4200 General

Bergsten, C. Fred. Gearing Up World Growth. *Challenge*, May/June 1986, *29*(2), pp. 35–40. **[G: Global]**

Berthelot, Yves; Kessler, Véronique and Pisani-Ferry, Jean. The Dynamics of World Trade: A Perspective View. **In** *Maddison, A., ed.*, 1986, pp. 135–47. **[G: Global]**

Clausen, A. W. International Trade and Global Economic Growth: The Critical Relationship: Address to the Economic Club of Detroit: Detroit, Michigan: May 23, 1984. **In** *Clausen, A. W.*, 1986, pp. 261–80.

Cooper, Richard N. The United States as an Open Economy. **In** *Hafer, R. W., ed. (I)*, 1986, pp. 3–24. **[G: U.S.]**

Corea, Gamani. The Crisis: Some Reflections. **In** *[Patel, S.]*, 1986, pp. 29–35.

Dauderstädt, Michael. Societal Consequences and Conditions of a Free Trade Regime. **In** *Sjöstedt, G. and Sundelius, B., eds.*, 1986, pp. 99–125. **[G: Selected Countries]**

Goldsbrough, David and Zaidi, Iqbal M. Transmission of Economic Influences from Industrial to Developing Countries. **In** *International Monetary Fund, Research Department*, 1986, pp. 150–95. **[G: OECD; LDCs]**

Gowa, Joanne. Anarchy, Egoism, and Third Images: *The Evolution of Cooperation* and International Relations. *Int. Organ.*, Winter 1986, *40*(1), pp. 167–86.

Hafer, R. W. How Open Is the U.S. Economy? Preface. **In** *Hafer, R. W., ed. (I)*, 1986, pp. xiii–xviii.

Hager, Wolfgang. Free Trade: A Threat to World

Economic Stability and Socio-economic Autonomy. **In** *Sjöstedt, G. and Sundelius, B., eds.*, 1986, pp. 81–98.

Kenen, Peter B. The United States as an Open Economy: Comments. **In** *Hafer, R. W., ed. (I)*, 1986, pp. 25–31. **[G: U.S.]**

Marer, Paul. The Political Economy of Soviet Relations with Eastern Europe. **In** *Laird, R. F. and Hoffmann, E. P., eds.*, 1986, *1984*, pp. 570–600. **[G: U.S.S.R.; CMEA]**

Okolo, Amechi. Dependency: The Highest Stage of Capitalist Domination in Africa. **In** *Onwuka, R. I. and Aluko, O., eds.*, 1986, pp. 296–320. **[G: Africa]**

Panchamukhi, V. R. Lima Target and the Interdependencies. **In** *Panchamukhi, V. R., et al.*, 1986, pp. 112–36. **[G: LDCs; MDCs]**

Raipuria, Kalyan M. Researching Long-term Issues of International Development Relations. **In** *Panchamukhi, V. R., et al.*, 1986, pp. 294–309.

Rothschild, Kurt W. Economic Theory: U.S.–European Linkages: A Journal Analysis. *Weltwirtsch. Arch.*, 1986, *122*(3), pp. 566–74. **[G: U.S.; EEC]**

Stewart, Frances. Alternative Approaches to North–South Negotiations. **In** *[Streeten, P.]*, 1986, pp. 95–114.

421 Trade Relations

4210 Trade Relations

Abd-El-Rahman, K. S. La "différence" et la "similitude" dans l'analyse de la composition du commerce international. (Difference and Similarity Elements in International Trade Composition Analysis. With English summary.) *Revue Écon.*, March 1986, *37*(2), pp. 307–40. **[G: France]**

Abd-El-Rahman, K. S. Réexamen de la définition et de la mesure des échanges croisés de produits similaires entre les nations. (Definition and Measurements of Two-way Trade in Similar Products: A Re-examination. With English summary.) *Revue Écon.*, January 1986, *37*(1), pp. 89–115. **[G: EEC]**

Adams, Walter and Mueller, Hans. The Steel Industry. **In** *Adams, W., ed.*, 1986, pp. 74–125. **[G: U.S.; OECD]**

Ahluwalia, Montek Singh. Balance-of-Payments Adjustment in India, 1970–71 to 1983–84. *World Devel.*, Special Issue, August 1986, *14*(8), pp. 937–62. **[G: India]**

Aizenman, Joshua. Testing Deviations from Purchasing Power Parity. *J. Int. Money Finance*, March 1986, *5*(1), pp. 25–35.

Albinski, Henry S. Assessing Corporate Political Risk: A Guide for International Businessmen: Country Studies: Australia. **In** *Raddock, D. M., et al.*, 1986, pp. 127–45. **[G: Australia]**

von Alvensleben, Reimar; Behr, Hans-Christoph and Jahn, Hans-Harald. Fruits and Vegetables in the European Community. **In** *Bale, M. D., ed.*, 1986, pp. 5–93. **[G: EEC]**

Amsden, Alice H. The Direction of Trade—Past and Present—and the "Learning Effects" of Exports to Different Directions. **In** *Sjöstedt, G. and Sundelius, B., eds.*, 1986, pp. 183–222. **[G: Selected Countries]**

Amsden, Alice H. The Direction of Trade—Past and Present—And the 'Learning Effects' of Exports to Different Directions. *J. Devel. Econ.*, October 1986, *23*(2), pp. 249–74. **[G: Japan; LDCs]**

Anderson, Kym and Tyers, Rodney. Agricultural Policies of Industrial Countries and Their Effects on Traditional Food Exporters. *Econ. Rec.*, December 1986, *62*(179), pp. 385–99. **[G: Global]**

Antonelli, Cristiano. The International Diffusion of Process Innovations and the Neotechnology Theory of International Trade. *Econ. Notes*, 1986, (1), pp. 60–83. **[G: Global]**

Arize, Augustine. The Supply and Demand for Imports and Exports in a Simultaneous Model. *Pakistan Econ. Soc. Rev.*, Winter 1986, *24*(2), pp. 57–76. **[G: African LDCs]**

Arndt, Sven W. Government Policy and the Decline in U.S. Trade Competitiveness. **In** *Cagan, P., ed.*, 1986, pp. 307–23. **[G: U.S.]**

Artus, Patrick. Comment fonctionne le marché des exportations? (How Does the Export Market Operate? With English summary.) *Ann. Écon. Statist.*, Apr./June 1986, (2), pp. 3–36. **[G: France]**

Artus, Patrick. Demande intérieure et commerce extérieur de produits industriels. Une approche par le déséquilibre. (A Disequilibrium Approach to the Domestic Demand and the Foreign Trade of Manufactured Goods. With English summary.) *Revue Écon.*, January 1986, *37*(1), pp. 31–66. **[G: France]**

Aurikko, Esko. A Dynamic Analysis of Finnish Export Prices. *Liiketaloudellinen Aikak.*, 1986, *35*(1), pp. 23–38. **[G: Finland]**

Auty, Richard and Gelb, Alan. Oil Windfalls in a Small Parliamentary Democracy: Their Impact on Trinidad and Tobago. *World Devel.*, September 1986, *14*(9), pp. 1161–75. **[G: Trinidad and Tobago]**

Aw, Bee Yan and Roberts, Mark J. Measuring Quality Change in Quota-Constrained Import Markets: The Case of U.S. Footwear. *J. Int. Econ.*, August 1986, *21*(1/2), pp. 45–60. **[G: U.S.]**

Bach, Christopher L. U.S. International Transactions, Fourth Quarter and Year 1985. *Surv. Curr. Bus.*, March 1986, *66*(3), pp. 24–54. **[G: U.S.]**

Bacha, Edmar L. External Shocks and Growth Prospects: The Case of Brazil, 1973–89. *World Devel.*, Special Issue, August 1986, *14*(8), pp. 919–36. **[G: Brazil]**

Baer, Werner. Brazil: Diversifying Exports. **In** *Preeg, E. H. and Bendahmane, D. B., eds.*, 1986, pp. 101–07. **[G: Brazil]**

Bahmani-Oskooee, Mohsen. Determinants of International Trade Flows: The Case of Developing Countries. *J. Devel. Econ.*, Jan.-Feb. 1986, *20*(1), pp. 107–23. **[G: LDCs]**

Bailey, Martin J.; Tavlas, George S. and Ulan,

Michael. Exchange-Rate Variability and Trade Performance: Evidence for the Big Seven Industrial Countries. *Weltwirtsch. Arch.*, 1986, *122*(3), pp. 466–77. **[G: Selected OECD]**

Balassa, Bela. Adjustment Policies in Socialist and Private Market Economies. *J. Compar. Econ.*, June 1986, *10*(2), pp. 138–59. **[G: LDCs; Hungary; Yugoslavia]**

Balassa, Bela. Comparative Advantage in Manufactured Goods: A Reappraisal. *Rev. Econ. Statist.*, May 1986, *68*(2), pp. 315–19. **[G: U.S.]**

Balassa, Bela. Dependency and Trade Orientation. *World Econ.*, September 1986, 9(3), pp. 259–73. **[G: U.S.; LDCs]**

Balassa, Bela. Developing Country Debt: Policies and Prospects. **In** *Giersch, H., ed.*, 1986, pp. 103–22. **[G: LDCs]**

Balassa, Bela. Intra-industry Specialization: A Cross-Country Analysis. *Europ. Econ. Rev.*, February 1986, *30*(1), pp. 27–42. **[G: LDCs; MDCs]**

Balassa, Bela. Intra-industry Trade among Exporters of Manufactured Goods. **In** *Greenaway, D. and Tharakan, P. K. M., eds.*, 1986, pp. 108–28. **[G: LDCs; MDCs]**

Balassa, Bela. The Determinants of Intra-industry Specialization in United States Trade. *Oxford Econ. Pap.*, July 1986, *38*(2), pp. 220–33. **[G: U.S.]**

Balassa, Bela. The Employment Effects of Trade in Manufactured Products between Developed and Developing Countries. *J. Policy Modeling*, Fall 1986, *8*(3), pp. 371–90.

Baldinelli, Elvio. Turning Page in Relations between Latin America and the European Communities. *CEPAL Rev.*, December 1986, (30), pp. 87–96. **[G: EEC; Latin America]**

Baldwin, John R.; Gorecki, Paul K. and McVey, John S. International Trade, Secondary Output and Concentration in Canadian Manufacturing Industries, 1979. *Appl. Econ.*, May 1986, *18*(5), pp. 529–43. **[G: Canada]**

Baldwin, Robert E. and Murray, Tracy. MFN Tariff Reductions and Developing Country Trade Benefits under the GSP: A Reply. *Econ. J.*, June 1986, *96*(382), pp. 537–39.

Bale, Malcolm D. Horticultural Trade of the Expanded European Community: Implications for Mediterranean Countries: Overview. **In** *Bale, M. D., ed.*, 1986, pp. 1–3. **[G: EEC]**

Barker, Betty L. U.S. Merchandise Trade Associated with U.S. Multinational Companies. *Surv. Curr. Bus.*, May 1986, *66*(5), pp. 55–72. **[G: U.S.]**

Baruh, Joseph. Factor Proportions in Israel's Manufacturing Trade: 1965–1982. *J. Devel. Econ.*, November 1986, *24*(1), pp. 131–39. **[G: Israel]**

Becker, Abraham S. Soviet Union and the Third World: The Economic Dimension. *Soviet Econ.*, July-Sept. 1986, *2*(3), pp. 233–60. **[G: U.S.S.R.]**

Beckerman, Wilfred and Jenkinson, Tim. What Stopped the Inflation? Unemployment of Commodity Prices? *Econ. J.*, March 1986, *96*(381), pp. 39–54. **[G: OECD]**

Bekker, Zsuzsa. Adjustment Processes in Hungary, 1973–1983: Policy Options, Intentions, Facts. *Acta Oecon.*, 1986, *37*(3–4), pp. 169–88. **[G: Hungary]**

Bellégo, Alain and Beer, Barbro. Legal Aspects of Trade Data Interchange. *J. World Trade Law*, Nov.:Dec. 1986, *20*(6), pp. 690–99. **[G: Global]**

Belongia, Michael T. Estimating Exchange Rate Effects on Exports: A Cautionary Note. *Fed. Res. Bank St. Louis Rev.*, January 1986, *68*(1), pp. 5–16. **[G: U.S.]**

Beltramo, Mark A.; Manne, Alan S. and Weyant, John P. A North American Gas Trade Model (GTM). *Energy J.*, July 1986, *7*(3), pp. 15–32. **[G: U.S.; Canada; Mexico]**

Benyon, Frank S. The EC–U.S. Steel Trade Crisis: Comment. **In** *Tsoukalis, L., ed.*, 1986, pp. 45–49. **[G: EEC; U.S.]**

Bergstrand, Jeffrey H. United States–Japanese Trade: Predictions Using Selected Economic Models. *New Eng. Econ. Rev.*, May/June 1986, pp. 26–37. **[G: U.S.; Japan]**

Bertsch, Gary K. Technology Transfers and Technology Controls: A Synthesis of the Western–Soviet Relationship. **In** *Amann, R. and Cooper, J., eds.*, 1986, pp. 115–34. **[G: U.S.S.R.; OECD]**

von Beyme, Klaus. Economic Relations as an Instrument of Soviet Hegemony over Eastern Europe? **In** *Höhmann, H.-H.; Nove, A. and Vogel, H., eds.*, 1986, pp. 214–31. **[G: CMEA]**

Biersteker, Thomas J. Self-reliance in Theory and Practice in Tanzanian Trade Relations. **In** *Ravenhill, J., ed.*, 1986, pp. 213–53. **[G: Tanzania]**

Black, Stanley W. The Open Economy: Implications for Monetary and Fiscal Policy: Comment. **In** *Gordon, R. J., ed.*, 1986, pp. 501–04. **[G: U.S.]**

Blanchard, Ian. The Continental European Cattle Trade, 1400–1600. *Econ. Hist. Rev., 2nd Ser.*, August 1986, *39*(3), pp. 427–60. **[G: Europe]**

Bodde, David L.; Quasebarth, Mollie V. and Thomasian, John B. The Economics of Strategic Choice: U.S. Uranium Enrichment in the World Market. *Energy J.*, October 1986, *7*(4), pp. 95–107. **[G: U.S.]**

Booth, Anne. Survey of Recent Developments. *Bull. Indonesian Econ. Stud.*, December 1986, *22*(3), pp. 1–26. **[G: Indonesia]**

Botos, Balázs. Changes in the Structure of Hungarian Industrial Foreign Trade: Review Article. *Acta Oecon.*, 1986, *37*(1–2), pp. 129–42. **[G: Hungary]**

Bowden, Roger J. An Empirical Model of Bilateral Trade (or Its Absence) in Manufactured Commodities. *Manchester Sch. Econ. Soc. Stud.*, September 1986, *54*(3), pp. 255–82.

Boyer, Robert. Industrial Policy in Macroeconomic Perspective. **In** *Adams, W. J. and Stoffaës, C., eds.*, 1986, pp. 88–96. **[G: France]**

Boyer, Robert and Ralle, Pierre. Croissances nationales et contrainte extérieure avant et après 1973. (National Growth and External Trade Share after and before 1973. With English summary.) *Écon. Soc.*, January 1986, *20*(1), pp. 117–44. **[G: EEC]**

Boyer, Robert and Ralle, Pierre. L'insertion internationale conditionne-t-elle les formes nationales d'emploi? Convergences ou différenciations des pays européens. (Are Jobs Dependent on International Openness? Similarities and Differences between European Countries. With English summary.) *Écon. Soc.*, January 1986, *20*(1), pp. 145–68. **[G: EEC]**

Braga, Helson C. and Guimarães, Edson P. Estrutura industrial e exportação de manufaturados no Brasil: 1978. (With English summary.) *Pesquisa Planejamento Econ.*, April 1986, *16*(1), pp. 167–88. **[G: Brazil]**

Branson, William H. Trade Deficits: The Evidence against the Reagan Fiscal Policy. **In** *Gondolf, E. W.; Marcus, I. M. and Dougherty, J. P., eds.*, 1986, pp. 87–95. **[G: U.S.]**

Brickman, Ronald. National Policies for Developing High Technology Industries: International Comparisons: France. **In** *Rushing, F. W. and Brown, C. G., eds.*, 1986, pp. 71–87. **[G: France; OECD]**

Bronfenbrenner, Martin. Japan-Bashing: A View from "Over There." *Challenge*, Jan./Feb. 1986, *28*(6), pp. 58–61. **[G: U.S.; Japan]**

Browne, Lynn E. High Technology Industry in the World Marketplace. *New Eng. Econ. Rev.*, May/June 1986, pp. 21–25. **[G: U.S.]**

Browne, William P. Issues of World Food and Trade: Perspectives and Projections. **In** *Browne, W. P. and Hadwiger, D. F., eds.*, 1986, pp. 1–13.

Brus, Włodzimierz. Postwar Reconstruction and Socio-economic Transformation. **In** *Kaser, M. C. and Radice, E. A., eds.*, 1986, pp. 564–641. **[G: E. Europe]**

Buchheim, Christoph. Germany on the World Market at the End of the 19th Century: Successful Supplier of Consumer Related Manufactures. **In** *Pohl, H. and Rudolph, B., eds.*, 1986, pp. 41–55. **[G: Germany]**

Burian, Gustav. Czechoslovak Economic Law and External Economic Relations. *Soviet E. Europ. Foreign Trade*, Summer 1986, *22*(2), pp. 6–27. **[G: Czechoslovakia]**

Bushe, Dennis M.; Kravis, Irving B. and Lipsey, Robert E. Prices, Activity, and Machinery Exports: An Analysis Based on New Price Data. *Rev. Econ. Statist.*, May 1986, *68*(2), pp. 248–55. **[G: U.S.; W. Germany; Japan]**

Caballero, Ricardo and Corbo, Vittorio. Análisis de la Balanza Comercial: Un Enfoque de Equilibrio General. (With English summary.) *Cuadernos Econ.*, December 1986, *23*(70), pp. 285–313. **[G: Chile]**

Camps, Miriam. The Bickering Bigemony: GATT as an Instrument in Atlantic Trade Policy: Comment. **In** *Tsoukalis, L., ed.*, 1986, pp. 107–12. **[G: U.S.; EEC]**

Carey, Sarah C. and McLean, Sheila Avrin. The United States, Countertrade and Third World Trade. *J. World Trade Law*, July:Aug. 1986, *20*(4), pp. 441–73. **[G: U.S.; LDCs]**

Carter, C. A.; Loyns, R. M. A. and Ahmadi-Esfahani, Z. F. Varietal Licensing Standards and Canadian Wheat Exports. *Can. J. Agr. Econ.*, November 1986, *34*(3), pp. 361–77. **[G: Canada]**

Casson, Mark. Multinationals and World Trade: Introduction and Summary. **In** *Casson, M., et al.*, 1986, pp. 1–59. **[G: U.S.]**

Caves, Richard E. Exporting Behavior and Market Structure: Evidence from the United States. **In** *de Jong, H. W. and Shepherd, W. G., eds., Bk. 1*, 1986, pp. 189–210. **[G: U.S.]**

Chambers, Robert G. and Just, Richard E. A Critique of Exchange Rate Treatment in Agricultural Trade Models: Reply. *Amer. J. Agr. Econ.*, November 1986, *68*(4), pp. 994–97.

Chao, Kang. The Chinese–American Cotton-Textile Trade, 1830–1930. **In** *May, E. R. and Fairbank, J. K., eds.*, 1986, pp. 103–27. **[G: China; Japan; U.S.; U.K.]**

Chen, Chia-Yon. The Optimal Adjustment to Mineral-supply Disruptions: The Case of Aluminum in Taiwan. *J. Policy Modeling*, Summer 1986, *8*(2), pp. 199–221. **[G: Taiwan]**

Cheng, Chu-yuan. The United States Petroleum Trade with China, 1876–1949. **In** *May, E. R. and Fairbank, J. K., eds.*, 1986, pp. 205–33. **[G: U.S.; China]**

Chishti, Sumitra. Third World Multinationals and Trade Expansion among the Countries of the South. **In** *Khan, K. M., ed.*, 1986, pp. 88–112. **[G: LDCs; OPEC]**

Chou, Tein-Chen. Concentration, Profitability and Trade in a Simultaneous Equation Analysis: The Case of Taiwan. *J. Ind. Econ.*, June 1986, *34*(4), pp. 429–43. **[G: Taiwan]**

Chu, Ke-young and Morrison, Thomas K. World Non-Oil Primary Commodity Markets: A Medium-term Framework of Analysis. *Int. Monet. Fund Staff Pap.*, March 1986, *33*(1), pp. 139–84.

Chung, Joseph S. National Policies for Developing High Technology Industries: International Comparisons: Korea. **In** *Rushing, F. W. and Brown, C. G., eds.*, 1986, pp. 143–72. **[G: S. Korea]**

Cima, Lawrence R. The Excess Supply–Pure Demand Approach to International Commodity Trade: The Case of Japanese Steel Exports to the United States. *Econ. Inquiry*, October 1986, *24*(4), pp. 645–56. **[G: U.S.; Japan]**

Cohen, Stephen S. and Zysman, John. Can America Compete? *Challenge*, May/June 1986, *29*(2), pp. 56–64. **[G: U.S.]**

Conway, Patrick. Decomposing the Determinants of Trade Deficits: Turkey in the 1970s. *J. Devel. Econ.*, May 1986, *21*(2), pp. 235–58. **[G: Turkey]**

Coomans, Géry. Système productif et petites nations. (Productive System and Small Nations. With English summary.) *Écon. Soc.*, May 1986, *20*(5), pp. 49–67. **[G: Belgium]**

Cornelisse, Peter A. and Akin, Bahadir. An Economic Appraisal of the Association Agreement between the European Community and Turkey. *METU*, 1986, *13*(3–4), pp. 259–73. **[G: EEC; Turkey]**

Cortés, Rosalía and Marshall, Adriana. Salario real, composición del consumo y balanza comercial. (With English summary.) *Desarrollo Econ.*, Apr.-June 1986, *26*(101), pp. 71–88. **[G: Argentina]**

da Costa, G. C. India's Commodity Trade Balance: Retrospect and Prospect over Seventh Plan. *Indian Econ. J.*, Apr.-June 1986, *33*(4), pp. 136–48. **[G: India]**

Côté, Agathe. Les effets de la variablilité des taux de change sur le commerce international. Une analyse pour le Canada. (The Effects of Exchange Rate Variability on International Trade. An Analysis for Canada. With English summary.) *L'Actual. Econ.*, December 1986, *62*(4), pp. 501–20. **[G: Canada]**

Cowen, Michael. Change in State Power, International Conditions and Peasant Producers: The Case of Kenya. *J. Devel. Stud.*, January 1986, *22*(2), pp. 355–84. **[G: Kenya]**

Cox, David and Harris, Richard G. A Quantitative Assessment of the Economic Impact on Canada of Sectoral Free Trade with the United States. *Can. J. Econ.*, August 1986, *19*(3), pp. 377–94. **[G: U.S.; Canada]**

Crafts, N. F. R. and Thomas, Mark. Comparative Advantage in UK Manufacturing Trade, 1910–1935. *Econ. J.*, September 1986, *96*(383), pp. 629–45. **[G: U.K.]**

Crandall, Robert W. The EC–U.S. Steel Trade Crisis. **In** *Tsoukalis, L., ed.*, 1986, pp. 17–35. **[G: U.S.; EEC]**

Crouzet, François. The Growth of British Exports 1783–1820. **In** *Turner, M., ed.*, 1986, pp. 189–200. **[G: U.K.]**

Culem, Claudy and Lundberg, Lars. The Product Pattern of Intra-Industry Trade: Stability among Countries and over Time. *Weltwirtsch. Arch.*, 1986, *122*(1), pp. 113–30. **[G: Global]**

Cushman, David O. Has Exchange Risk Depressed International Trade? The Impact of Third-Country Exchange Risk. *J. Int. Money Finance*, September 1986, *5*(3), pp. 361–79. **[G: U.S.; Selected OECD]**

Cuthbertson, Keith. The Behaviour of U.K. Export Prices of Manufactured Goods 1970–1983. *J. Appl. Econometrics*, July 1986, *1*(3), pp. 255–75. **[G: U.K.]**

Daly, Michael J. and Rao, P. Someshwar. Free Trade, Scale Economies and Productivity Growth in Canadian Manufacturing. *Manchester Sch. Econ. Soc. Stud.*, December 1986, *54*(4), pp. 391–402. **[G: Canada]**

Darrat, Ali F. Trade and Development: The Asian Experience. *Cato J.*, Fall 1986, *6*(2), pp. 695–99. **[G: Asia]**

Dauderstädt, Michael. Internationale Konkurrenz und Wohlfahrtsstaat. Überlegungen am Beispiel Portugal. (International Competition and the Welfare State—The Case of Portugal. With English summary.) *Konjunkturpolitik*, 1986, *32*(6), pp. 349–80. **[G: Portugal]**

David, Frédéric. Le commerce international de produits pétroliers. (International Trade of Petroleum Products. With English summary.) *Écon. Soc.*, July 1986, *20*(7), pp. 95–113.

Dearden, Stephen. EEC Membership and the United Kingdom's Trade in Manufactured Goods. *Nat. Westminster Bank Quart. Rev.*, February 1986, pp. 15–25. **[G: U.K.; EEC]**

Dell, Edmund. Of Free Trade and Reciprocity. *World Econ.*, June 1986, *9*(2), pp. 125–39. **[G: U.S.; EEC]**

Desormeaux, Jorge and Bravo, Luis Eduardo. Modelo agregado de la Balanza Comercial: Chile 1974–1982. (With English summary.) *Cuadernos Econ.*, December 1986, *23*(70), pp. 315–42. **[G: Chile]**

Dichtl, Erwin; Köglmayr, Hans-Georg and Müller, Stefan. Die Auslandsorientierung als Voraussetzung für Exporterfolge. (With English summary.) *Z. Betriebswirtshaft*, November 1986, *56*(11), pp. 1064–76. **[G: W. Germany]**

Dilullo, Anthony J. U.S. International Transactions, Second Quarter 1986. *Surv. Curr. Bus.*, September 1986, *66*(9), pp. 40–63. **[G: U.S.]**

Dilullo, Anthony J. U.S. International Transactions, Third Quarter 1986. *Surv. Curr. Bus.*, December 1986, *66*(12), pp. 23–46. **[G: U.S.]**

Dixon, Peter B. and Johnson, David. Competitiveness Indices and Trade Performance. *Australian Bull. Lab.*, June 1986, *12*(3), pp. 154–72. **[G: Australia]**

Dockner, Engelbert and Sitz, Alfred. An Investigation into Austrian Export Pricing: Price Taking or Price Setting of a Small Open Economy? *Empirica*, 1986, *13*(2), pp. 221–41. **[G: Austria]**

Dominique, C.-René. A Practical Way of Assessing Firms' X-Efficiency and Ability to Compete in Mature Good Industries: The Case of Textiles and Apparel. *J. Econ. Devel.*, December 1986, *11*(2), pp. 25–40. **[G: Selected Countries]**

Dominique, C.-René and Oral, Muhittin. Exporting to Northern Markets: The Making of an Industrial Competitiveness Index. *Industry Devel.*, 1986, (18), pp. 1–17. **[G: Global]**

Dornbusch, Rudiger. Flexible Exchange Rates and Interdependence. **In** *Dornbusch, R.*, 1986, *1983*, pp. 58–85. **[G: U.S.]**

Dornbusch, Rudiger. The Overvalued Dollar. **In** *Dornbusch, R.*, 1986, pp. 17–30. **[G: U.S.; Global]**

Dornbusch, Rudiger and Fischer, Stanley. The Open Economy: Implications for Monetary and Fiscal Policy. **In** *Gordon, R. J., ed.*, 1986, pp. 459–501. **[G: U.S.]**

Douglas, Susan P. Selling in Japan: Consumer Behavior and Distribution as Barriers to Imports: Comment. **In** *Pugel, T. A., ed.*, 1986, pp. 107–13. **[G: U.S.; Japan; W. Germany]**

Dreyer, P. Importations gaziéres et commerce extérieur. (Gas Imports and Foreign Trade. With English summary.) *Écon. Soc.*, July 1986, *20*(7), pp. 63–76. **[G: France]**

Driver, Ciaran; Kilpatrick, Andrew and Naisbitt, Barry. The Employment Effects of UK Manufacturing Trade Expansion with the EEC and the Newly Industrialising Countries. *Europ. Econ. Rev.*, April 1986, *30*(2), pp. 427–38. **[G: U.K.]**

Drucker, Peter F. The Changed World Economy. *Foreign Aff.*, Spring 1986, *64*(4), pp. 768–91.

Drysdale, Peter, et al. Australia and the Pacific Economy. *Econ. Rec.*, March 1986, *62*(176), pp. 60–66. **[G: Australia; ASEAN]**

Dunn, Malcolm H. and Körner, Heiko. Third World Multinationals and Trade Expansion among the Countries of the South: Comment. **In** *Khan, K. M., ed.*, 1986, pp. 113–29. **[G: LDCs; OPEC]**

Ebinger, Charles K. The Brazilian Energy Sector. **In** *Hartland-Thunberg, P. and Ebinger, C. K., eds.*, 1986, pp. 131–53. **[G: Brazil]**

Eilts, Hermann Frederick. Assessing Corporate Political Risk: A Guide for International Businessmen: Country Studies: Saudi Arabia. **In** *Raddock, D. M., et al.*, 1986, pp. 110–26. **[G: Saudi Arabia]**

Erber, Fabio Stefano. The Capital Goods Industry and the Dynamics of Economic Development in LDCs: The Case of Brazil. **In** *Fransman, M., ed.*, 1986, pp. 215–45. **[G: Brazil]**

Eriksson, Bo Göran. EFTA och EG: aktuella utvecklingslinjer i europeisk integration. (EFTA and EC: Current Trends in the Development of European Integration. With English summary.) *Ekon. Samfundets Tidskr.*, 1986, *39*(4), pp. 201–16. **[G: EEC; Finland]**

Etuk, O. E. U. Fertilizer Pricing in Nigeria. **In** *Segura, E. L.; Shetty, Y. T. and Nishimizu, M., eds.*, 1986, pp. 95–101. **[G: Nigeria]**

Ewing, Arthur F. Agriculture, Trade and Growth: Review Article. *J. World Trade Law*, Nov.:Dec. 1986, *20*(6), pp. 665–89. **[G: Global]**

Ewing, Arthur F. East–West Trade. *J. World Trade Law*, Mar.:Apr. 1986, *20*(2), pp. 241–43. **[G: Global]**

Fairbank, John K. America's China Trade in Historical Perspective: The Chinese and American Performance: Patterns and Problems. **In** *May, E. R. and Fairbank, J. K., eds.*, 1986, pp. 1–7.

Falgon, Claude. The Effect of Enlargement of the EC on Tunisian Fruits and Vegetables. **In** *Bale, M. D., ed.*, 1986, pp. 95–130. **[G: EEC; Tunisia]**

Falvey, Rodney E. Trade Problems and Policies of Pacific Island Economies. **In** *Cole, R. V. and Parry, T. G., eds.*, 1986, pp. 111–46. **[G: S. Pacific]**

Feketekuty, Geza and Hauser, Kathryn. The Impact of Information Technology on Trade in Services. **In** *Faulhaber, G.; Noam, E. and Tasley, R., eds.*, 1986, pp. 81–97. **[G: U.S.]**

Feldbaek, Ole. The Danish Trading Companies of the Seventeenth and Eighteenth Centuries. *Scand. Econ. Hist. Rev.*, 1986, *34*(3), pp. 204–18. **[G: Denmark]**

Felmingham, B. S. and Divisekera, Sarath. The Response of Australia's Trade Balance under Different Exchange Rate Regimes. *Australian Econ. Pap.*, June 1986, *25*(46), pp. 33–46. **[G: Australia]**

Fieleke, Norman S. New England Manufacturing and International Trade. *New Eng. Econ. Rev.*, Sept./Oct. 1986, pp. 22–28. **[G: U.S.]**

Findley, David F. and Monsell, Brian C. New Techniques for Determining if a Time Series Can Be Seasonally Adjusted Reliably. **In** *Perryman, M. R. and Schmidt, J. R., eds.*, 1986, pp. 195–228. **[G: U.S.]**

Fink, Gerhard. Settlement System and Hard Currency Trade in the CMEA. *Soviet E. Europ. Foreign Trade*, Spring 1986, *22*(1), pp. 68–82. **[G: CMEA]**

Fitzgibbon, C. H. Rethinking Australia's International Competitiveness. *Australian Bull. Lab.*, September 1986, *12*(4), pp. 221–33. **[G: Australia]**

Foreman-Peck, James. The Motor Industry. **In** *Casson, M., et al.*, 1986, pp. 141–73. **[G: Selected Countries]**

Foroutan, Faezeh. Determinants of European Community Imports of Steel Mill Products. *Appl. Econ.*, August 1986, *18*(8), pp. 863–73. **[G: EEC]**

Foust, C. M. Customs 3 and Russian Rhubarb: A Note on Reliability. *J. Europ. Econ. Hist.*, Winter 1986, *15*(3), pp. 549–62. **[G: U.K.]**

Fransman, Martin. International Competitiveness, International Diffusion of Technology and the State: A Case Study from Taiwan and Japan. **In** *Fransman, M., ed.*, 1986, pp. 153–214. **[G: Taiwan; Japan]**

Fransman, Martin. International Competitiveness, Technical Change and the State: The Machine Tool Industry in Taiwan and Japan. *World Devel.*, December 1986, *14*(12), pp. 1375–96. **[G: Taiwan; Japan]**

Frantzen, Dirk J. The Cyclical Behaviour of Manufacturing Prices in a Small Open Economy. *J. Ind. Econ.*, June 1986, *34*(4), pp. 389–408. **[G: Belgium]**

Freebairn, John W. The Exchange Rate and the Trade Account: Comment. *Econ. Rec.*, Supplement 1986, pp. 108–10. **[G: Australia]**

Friedman, Benjamin M. Implications of the U.S. Net Capital Inflow. **In** *Hafer, R. W., ed. (1)*, 1986, pp. 137–61. **[G: U.S.]**

Fry, Maxwell J. Terms-of-Trade Dynamics in Asia: An Analysis of National Saving and Domestic Investment Responses to Terms-of-Trade Changes in 14 Asian LDCs. *J. Int. Money Finance*, March 1986, *5*(1), pp. 57–73. **[G: Asia]**

Fryar, Edward O., Jr. Residual Supplier Model of Coarse Grains Trade: Comment. *Amer. J. Agr. Econ.*, November 1986, *68*(4), pp. 1028–29. **[G: Selected Countries]**

Fuchs, Peter. Past, Present, and Future Perfect? Casing Japan's Competitive Strategy. **In** *Finn, R. B., ed.*, 1986, pp. 17–37. **[G: Japan]**

Gafar, John S. The Impact of External Factors on the Debt Burden and Import Capacity of Developing Countries. *Indian Econ. J.*, Jan.-

Mar. 1986, *33*(3), pp. 35–45. [G: LDCs]

Gahlen, Bernhard; Rahmeyer, Fritz and Stadler, Manfred. Zur internationalen Wettbewerbsfähigkeit der deutschen Wirtschaft. (The International Competitiveness of the German Economy. With English summary.) *Konjunkturpolitik*, 1986, *32*(3), pp. 130–50. [G: W. Germany]

Garčár, Ján. Broad Possibilities of Economic Co-operation. *Czech. Econ. Digest.*, June 1986, (5), pp. 50–54. [G: Czechoslovakia]

Garcia, Philip and Anderson, Margot. The U.S. Trade Deficit and International Competition. **In** *Walzer, N. and Chicoine, D. L., eds.*, 1986, pp. 179–97. [G: U.S.]

Gardella, Robert P. The Boom Years of the Fukien Tea Trade, 1842–1888. **In** *May, E. R. and Fairbank, J. K., eds.*, 1986, pp. 33–75. [G: U.S.; U.K.; China; Australia]

Gaussens, O. and Phan, D. L. Avantage comparatif et performance dans le commerce international des produits différenciés. (Comparative Advantage and Performance in the International Trade in Differentiated Products. With English summary.) *L'Actual. Econ.*, December 1986, *62*(4), pp. 535–56. [G: OECD]

Gewen, Barry. Imports and Apparel: From Riches to Rags. **In** *Schoolman, M. and Magid, A., eds.*, 1986, pp. 53–73. [G: U.S.]

Ghose, Devajyoti; Lahiri, Ashok K. and Wadhwa, Wilima. Quantitative Restrictions and Indian Imports. *J. Devel. Econ.*, March 1986, *20*(2), pp. 247–62. [G: India]

Ginzburg, Andrea. Dependency and the Political Solution of Balance of Payments Crises: The Italian Case. **In** *[Hirshman, A. O.]*, 1986, pp. 133–66. [G: Italy; W. Germany]

Giovannetti, G. and Siniscalco, D. Structural Change, Foreign Trade and Income Multipliers in the Italian Economy. *Banca Naz. Lavoro Quart. Rev.*, September 1986, (158), pp. 319–35. [G: Italy]

Gitelman, Zvi. Doing Business with the USSR and Eastern Europe: The Political Setting. **In** *Raddock, D. M., et al.*, 1986, pp. 55–70. [G: E. Europe; U.S.S.R.]

Goldar, Bishwanath. Import Substitution, Industrial Concentration and Productivity Growth in Indian Manufacturing. *Oxford Bull. Econ. Statist.*, May 1986, *48*(2), pp. 143–64. [G: India]

Goldsbrough, David and Zaidi, Iqbal M. How Performance in Industrial Economies Affects Developing Economies. *Finance Develop.*, December 1986, *23*(4), pp. 6–9. [G: LDCs]

Goldstein, Judith. The Political Economy of Trade: Institutions of Protection. *Amer. Polit. Sci. Rev.*, March 1986, *80*(1), pp. 161–84. [G: U.S.]

Goldstein, Walter. The Changing Impact of International Trade on the Economy of New York State. **In** *Schoolman, M. and Magid, A., eds.*, 1986, pp. 167–203. [G: U.S.]

Gordon, J. M. The J-Curve Effects. *Econ. Rec.*, Supplement 1986, pp. 82–88. [G: Australia; U.S.]

Green, Reginald Herbold and Kadhani, Xavier. Zimbabwe: Transition to Economic Crises, 1981–83: Retrospect and Prospect. *World Devel.*, Special Issue, August 1986, *14*(8), pp. 1059–83. [G: Zimbabwe]

Gremmen, Hans J. and Vollebergh, Ad H. J. An Input Approach to European Comparative Advantage in Advanced Products: A Study with Special Emphasis on the Netherlands. *Weltwirtsch. Arch.*, 1986, *122*(2), pp. 270–80. [G: Netherlands; Global]

Grennes, Thomas J. and Lapp, John S. Neutrality of Inflation in the Agricultural Sector. *J. Int. Money Finance*, June 1986, *5*(2), pp. 231–43. [G: U.S.]

Griffin, Keith. Communal Land Tenure Systems and Their Role in Rural Development. **In** *[Streeten, P.]*, 1986, pp. 165–91. [G: Selected Countries]

Grinberg, R. and Liubskii, M. Prices and Currency Relations in the Cooperation of CMEA Countries. *Prob. Econ.*, May 1986, *29*(1), pp. 17–32. [G: CMEA]

Groenewegen, John R. A Perspective on Canadian Wheat Board Exports, Price Pooling, and West Coast Capacity Constraints. *Can. J. Agr. Econ.*, November 1986, *34*(3), pp. 331–46. [G: Canada]

Grossman, Gene M. Strategic Export Promotion: A Critique. **In** *Krugman, P. R., ed.*, 1986, pp. 47–68. [G: U.S.]

Guerci, Carlo Maria and Treichler, Sergio. Crisis, Adjustment and Outlook of the Steel Industry. **In** *Goldberg, W. H., ed.*, 1986, pp. 53–93. [G: Selected Countries]

Gwiazda, Adam. Poland's Trade with the West: Chances for Improvement. **In** *Altmann, F.-L., ed.*, 1986, pp. 165–78. [G: Poland]

Hager, Wolfgang. The Bickering Bigemony: GATT as an Instrument in Atlantic Trade Policy: Comment. **In** *Tsoukalis, L., ed.*, 1986, pp. 113–16. [G: U.S.; EEC]

Halevi, Nadav. Perspectives on the Balance of Payments. **In** *Ben-Porath, Y., ed.*, 1986, pp. 241–63. [G: Israel]

Halperín, Tulio. The Argentine Export Economy: Intimations of Mortality, 1894–1930. **In** *di Tella, G. and Platt, D. C. M., eds.*, 1986, pp. 39–59. [G: Argentina]

Halvorson, Harold. The British Columbia Coal Industry. **In** *Nemetz, P. N., ed.*, 1986, pp. 293–306. [G: Canada; Pacific Basin]

Hamilton, Carl. An Assessment of Voluntary Restraints on Hong Kong Exports to Europe and the USA. *Economica*, August 1986, *53*(211), pp. 339–50. [G: Hong Kong; U.S.; W. Europe]

Hanna, David R. Petroleum Product Trade East of Suez. **In** *El Mallakh, R., ed.*, 1986, pp. 37–45. [G: Middle East]

Hanson, John R., II. Export Shares in the European Periphery and the Third World before World War I: Questionable Data, Facile Analogies. *Exploration Econ. Hist.*, January 1986, *23*(1), pp. 85–99. [G: Europe; LDCs]

Hao, Yen-p'ing. Chinese Teas to America—A Synopsis. In *May, E. R. and Fairbank, J. K., eds.*, 1986, pp. 11–31. **[G: U.S.; China]**

Hartigan, James C. and Tower, Edward. The Leontief Question: A Cobb–Douglas Approach to Simulating the U.S. Income Distribution in Autarky. *Weltwirtsch. Arch.*, 1986, *122*(4), pp. 677–89. **[G: U.S.]**

Hauner, M. Military Budgets and the Armaments Industry. In *Kaser, M. C. and Radice, E. A., eds.*, 1986, pp. 49–116. **[G: E. Europe; Germany]**

Hawdon, David. The Economics of the Natural Gas Market and Its Competitiveness. In *Stevens, P., ed.*, 1986, pp. 14–33. **[G: Selected Countries]**

Haynes, Stephen E.; Hutchison, Michael M. and Mikesell, Raymond F. U.S.–Japanese Bilateral Trade and the Yen–Dollar Exchange Rate: An Empirical Analysis. *Southern Econ. J.*, April 1986, *52*(4), pp. 923–32. **[G: U.S.; Japan]**

Helleiner, Gerald K. Balance-of-Payments Experience and Growth Prospects of Developing Countries: A Synthesis. *World Devel.*, Special Issue, August 1986, *14*(8), pp. 877–908. **[G: LDCs]**

Heller, Peter S. Factor Endowment Change and Comparative Advantage: The Case of Japan, 1956–1969. In *Sohn, I., ed.*, 1986, *1976*, pp. 327–39. **[G: Japan]**

Heravi, Iraj. The Leontief Paradox, Reconsidered: Correction. *J. Polit. Econ.*, October 1986, *94*(5), pp. 1120. **[G: U.S.]**

Herrmann, Roland. Free Riders and the Redistributive Effects of International Commodity Agreements: The Case of Coffee. *J. Policy Modeling*, Winter 1986, *8*(4), pp. 597–621. **[G: Global]**

Hersztajn-Moldau, Juan and Pelin, Eli Roberto. O custo dos recursos domésticos das exportações brasileiras em 1980. (With English summary.) *Pesquisa Planejamento Econ.*, April 1986, *16*(1), pp. 189–222. **[G: Brazil]**

Hicks, Donald A. The Impact of Information Technology on Trade in Services: Discussion. In *Faulhaber, G.; Noam, E. and Tasley, R., eds.*, 1986, pp. 98–105. **[G: U.S.]**

Hill, Hal. On the Transferability of United States Factor Intensity Classifications to LDC Manufacturing: Indonesia and Singapore Compared. *Singapore Econ. Rev.*, October 1986, *31*(2), pp. 67–78. **[G: Indonesia; Singapore]**

Hindley, Brian and MacBean, Alasdair. Edmund Dell's Manifesto for Mercantilist Liberation. *World Econ.*, December 1986, *9*(4), pp. 359–64. **[G: U.S.; EEC]**

Hiney, Robert A. Importing Canadian Electricity. In *Saltzman, S. and Schuler, R. E., eds.*, 1986, pp. 123–25. **[G: U.S.; Canada]**

Hogan, William T. The EC–U.S. Steel Trade Crisis: Comment. In *Tsoukalis, L., ed.*, 1986, pp. 42–44. **[G: U.S.; EEC]**

Holbik, Karel. Progress in the Internationalization of the Japanese Yen. *Rivista Int. Sci. Econ. Com.*, May 1986, *33*(5), pp. 409–24. **[G: Japan; U.S.]**

Holtzman, Franklyn D. The Significance of Soviet Subsidies to Eastern Europe. *Comp. Econ. Stud.*, Spring 1986, *28*(1), pp. 54–65. **[G: CMEA]**

Holzman, Franklyn D. Further Thoughts on the Significance of Soviet Subsidies to Eastern Europe. *Comp. Econ. Stud.*, Fall 1986, *28*(3), pp. 59–64. **[G: CMEA]**

Hong, Wontack. Trade, Growth and Economic Problems of Asian NICs. *Hitotsubashi J. Econ.*, Spec. Iss. Oct. 1986, *27*, pp. 79–100. **[G: Asian NICs]**

Horák, Vladimír. Czechoslovakia–Latin America: Interest in Broader Relations. *Czech. Econ. Digest.*, December 1986, (8), pp. 36–39. **[G: Czechoslovakia; Latin America]**

Horn, Ernst-Jürgen; Klodt, Henning and Saunders, Christopher. Advanced Machine Tools: Production, Diffusion and Trade. In *Sharp, M., ed.*, 1986, pp. 46–86. **[G: OECD]**

Hotta, Kazuyoshi. Historische Entwicklungslinien der Wettbewerbsdynamik im japanischen Markt. (With English summary.) *Z. Betriebswirtshaft*, June 1986, *56*(6), pp. 500–508. **[G: Japan]**

Hrnčíř, Miroslav. External Criteria and the Mechanism of the Czechoslovak Economy. *Czech. Econ. Digest.*, January 1986, (1), pp. 58–89. **[G: Czechoslovakia]**

Hrnčíř, Miroslav. Ways of Achieving External Equilibrium in the Czechoslovak Economy. *Czech. Econ. Digest.*, June/July 1986, (4), pp. 39–70. **[G: Czechoslovakia]**

Hua, Mingshu. The Inflationary Effect on the Structure of Trade. *Weltwirtsch. Arch.*, 1986, *122*(2), pp. 254–69. **[G: U.S.]**

Hughes Hallett, A. J. Commodity Market Stabilisation and "North–South" Income Transfers: An Empirical Investigation. *J. Devel. Econ.*, December 1986, *24*(2), pp. 293–316.

Hughes Hallett, A. J. International Policy Design and the Sustainability of Policy Bargains. *J. Econ. Dynam. Control*, December 1986, *10*(4), pp. 467–94. **[G: U.S.; EEC]**

Hughes, Helen. The Political Economy of Protection in Eleven Industrial Countries. In *Snape, R. H., ed.*, 1986, pp. 222–37. **[G: OECD]**

Hughes, Kirsty S. Exports and Innovation: A Simultaneous Model. *Europ. Econ. Rev.*, April 1986, *30*(2), pp. 383–99. **[G: U.K.]**

Hughes, Warren R. A Risk Appraisal of New Zealand's Export Industries Using Asset Pricing Models. *New Zealand Econ. Pap.*, 1986, *20*, pp. 61–75. **[G: New Zealand]**

Huizinga, John. Implications of the U.S. Net Capital Inflow: Comments. In *Hafer, R. W., ed. (I)*, 1986, pp. 163–67. **[G: U.S.]**

Hurni, Bettina. EFTA–EC Relations: Aftermath of the Luxembourg Declaration. *J. World Trade Law*, Sept.:Oct. 1986, *20*(5), pp. 497–506. **[G: W. Europe]**

Hussain, M. Nureldin and Thirlwall, A. P. The IMF Supply-Side Approach to Devaluation: A Reply. *Oxford Bull. Econ. Statist.*, February 1986, *48*(1), pp. 83–86. **[G: Sudan]**

Hutchinson, William K. Regional Exports of the United States to Foreign Countries: A Structural Analysis, 1870–1910. **In** *Uselding, P., ed.*, 1986, pp. 131–54. **[G: U.S.]**

Inotai, András. Economic Relations between the CMEA and the EEC: Facts, Trends, Prospects. *Acta Oecon.*, 1986, *36*(3–4), pp. 307–27. **[G: CMEA; EEC]**

Ionescu, V., et al. Model for Establishing the Competitiveness of the "SPOT" Lots in Crude Oil Imports. *Econ. Computat. Cybern. Stud. Res.*, 1986, *21*(3), pp. 23–25.

Iqbal, Badar A. Trade and Development in Asia: Regional and Inter-regional Disparities. *J. World Trade Law*, Mar.:Apr. 1986, *20*(2), pp. 236–41. **[G: Asia]**

Italianer, A. and d'Alcantara, G. Modelling Bilateral Sectoral Trade Flows. **In** *Artus, P. and Guvenen, O., eds.*, 1986, pp. 3–38. **[G: OECD]**

Ivanov, N. and Loshchakov, A. Foreign Economic Relations of CMEA Countries. *Prob. Econ.*, May 1986, *29*(1), pp. 3–16. **[G: CMEA; LDCs; OECD]**

Jackson, Gordon. Atlas of Industrializing Britain 1780–1914: Sea Trade. **In** *Langton, J. and Morris, R. J., eds.*, 1986, pp. 94–105. **[G: U.K.]**

Jauković, Radovan. Structural Problems of East–West Economic Relations. *Eastern Europ. Econ.*, Winter 1986-87, *25*(2), pp. 22–59. **[G: E. Europe]**

Jensen, Flemming Skov. Industriens og arbejdskraftens vilkår. (Production Strategies and Labour Market Requirements of Increasing Danish Export. With English summary.) *Nationaløkon. Tidsskr.*, 1986, *124*(2), pp. 175–78. **[G: Denmark]**

Jerala, Tomislav. Fertilizer Pricing in Yugoslavia. **In** *Segura, E. L.; Shetty, Y. T. and Nishimizu, M., eds.*, 1986, pp. 204–18. **[G: Yugoslavia]**

Johnson, Manuel H. Statement to the U.S. Senate Subcommittee on International Finance and Monetary Policy of the Committee on Banking, Housing, and Urban Affairs, June 17, 1986. *Fed. Res. Bull.*, August 1986, *72*(8), pp. 554–59. **[G: U.S.]**

Johnson, Robert A. U.S. International Transactions in 1985. *Fed. Res. Bull.*, May 1986, *72*(5), pp. 287–97. **[G: U.S.]**

Johnston, Felton McC. Political Risk Insurance. **In** *Raddock, D. M., et al.*, 1986, pp. 186–96.

Jonsson, Sigfus. International Saltfish Markets and the Icelandic Economy ca. 1900–1940. *Scand. Econ. Hist. Rev.*, 1986, *34*(1), pp. 20–40. **[G: Iceland]**

Jung, Aleksander. Exporting, Refinancing, Restructuring. *Eastern Europ. Econ.*, Summer 1986, *24*(4), pp. 40–50. **[G: Poland]**

Jung, Zdeněk. From Possibilities to Concrete Practice. *Czech. Econ. Digest.*, June 1986, (5), pp. 33–41. **[G: CMEA]**

Kabir, M. and Ridler, Neil B. The Market for Atlantic Salmon. *Atlantic Econ. J.*, March 1986, *14*(1), pp. 125. **[G: Canada]**

Kádár, Béla. Hungary's External Economic Strategy in the Second Half of the 1980s. *Acta Oecon.*, 1986, *36*(3–4), pp. 209–29. **[G: Hungary]**

Kamas, Linda. Dutch Disease Economics and the Colombian Export Boom. *World Devel.*, September 1986, *14*(9), pp. 1177–98. **[G: Colombia]**

Kanbur, S. M. Ravi and Vines, David. North–South Interaction and Commod Control. *J. Devel. Econ.*, October 1986, *23*(2), pp. 371–87.

Kanet, Roger E. Economic Aspects of Soviet Policy in the Third World: A Comment. *Soviet Econ.*, July-Sept. 1986, *2*(3), pp. 261–68. **[G: U.S.S.R.]**

Kanet, Roger E. The Politics and Economics of Soviet Arms Exports. **In** *Höhmann, H.-H.; Nove, A. and Vogel, H., eds.*, 1986, pp. 274–301. **[G: U.S.S.R.; LDCs]**

Karunaratne, Neil Dias. A Holistic Analysis of Trade versus Aid Issues: World and Australian Insights. *Devel. Econ.*, March 1986, *24*(1), pp. 44–55. **[G: Global; Australia]**

Kaser, Michael. Soviet Gas Supplies. **In** *Stevens, P., ed.*, 1986, pp. 71–88. **[G: U.S.S.R.]**

Kaser, Michael and Nötel, R. The East European Economies in Two World Crises. **In** *Berend, I. T. and Borchardt, K., eds.*, 1986, pp. 215–47. **[G: E. Europe]**

Kasman, Bruce. Prospects for the U.S. International Travel Deficit. *Fed. Res. Bank New York Quart. Rev.*, Summer 1986, *11*(2), pp. 44–46. **[G: U.S.]**

Keil, Stanley R. and Mack, Richard S. Identifying Export Potential in the Service Sector. *Growth Change*, April 1986, *17*(2), pp. 1–10. **[G: U.S.]**

Kelkar, Vijay L. A View from the South: Growth of World Trade in Manufactures. **In** *[Patel, S.]*, 1986, pp. 105–21. **[G: MDCs; LDCs]**

Kenen, Peter B. and Rodrik, Dani. Measuring and Analyzing the Effects of Short-term Volatility in Real Exchange Rates. *Rev. Econ. Statist.*, May 1986, *68*(2), pp. 311–15. **[G: W. Europe; U.S.; Canada; Japan]**

Keohane, Robert O. Reciprocity in International Relations. *Int. Organ.*, Winter 1986, *40*(1), pp. 1–27.

Khan, Mahmud Jameel and Chowdhury, Nuimuddin. Trade, Industrialisation and Employment. **In** *Islam, R. and Muqtada, M., eds.*, 1986, pp. 89–117. **[G: Bangladesh]**

Kiljunen, Kimmo. The International Division of Industrial Labour and the Core–Periphery Concept. *CEPAL Rev.*, December 1986, (30), pp. 97–115.

Kim, W. Chan and Tschoegl, Adrian E. The Regional Balance of Industrialization: An Empirical Investigation of the Asian Pacific Area. *J. Devel. Areas*, January 1986, *20*(2), pp. 173–83. **[G: Asia; LDCs]**

Kimura, Yui. Japanese Policy toward Foreign Multinationals: Implications for Trade and Competitiveness: Comment. **In** *Pugel, T. A., ed.*, 1986, pp. 169–74. **[G: Japan]**

Kinoshita, Toshihiko. Japanese Investment in Indonesia: Problems and Prospects. *Bull. Indonesian Econ. Stud.*, April 1986, *22*(1), pp. 34–56. **[G: Indonesia; Japan]**

Kirkpatrick, Colin and Diakosavvas, Dimitris. Food Insecurity and the Foreign Exchange Constraint in Sub-Saharan Africa. **In** *Maunder, A. and Renborg, U., eds.*, 1986, pp. 230–39. **[G: Sub-Saharan Africa]**

Kleiman, Ephraim and Pincus, J. J. Incremental Export Subsidies: A Rejoinder [The Cyclical Effects of Incremental Export Subsidies]. *Econ. Rec.*, March 1986, *62*(176), pp. 93–94. **[G: Australia]**

Kohama, Hirohisa and Kajiwara, Hirokazu. Structural Change in Steel Trade and International Industrial Adjustments. *Devel. Econ.*, June 1986, *24*(2), pp. 109–30. **[G: Global]**

Kohli, Ulrich and Morey, Edward R. The U.S. Demand for Foreign Crude Oil: A Translog Approach. *J. Energy Devel.*, Autumn 1986, *12*(1), pp. 115–33. **[G: U.S.]**

Kol, Jacob and Mennes, Loet B. M. Intra-industry Specialization: Some Observations on Concepts and Measurement. *J. Int. Econ.*, August 1986, *21*(1/2), pp. 173–81. **[G: EEC]**

Kolstad, Charles D. and Burris, Anthony E. Imperfectly Competitive Equilibria in International Commodity Markets. *Amer. J. Agr. Econ.*, February 1986, *68*(1), pp. 27–36. **[G: Global]**

Köves, András. Foreign Economic Equilibrium, Economic Development and Economic Policy in the CMEA Countries. *Acta Oecon.*, 1986, *36*(1–2), pp. 35–53. **[G: CMEA]**

Krayenbühl, Thomas E. Comecon as a Debtor of the Western Financial System. **In** *Dicke, D. C., ed.*, 1986, pp. 231–47. **[G: OECD; Comecon]**

Krommenacker, Raymond J. The Impact of Information Technology on Trade Interdependence. *J. World Trade Law,* July:Aug. 1986, *20*(4), pp. 381–400. **[G: Global]**

Krueger, Russell C. U.S. International Transactions, First Quarter 1986. *Surv. Curr. Bus.*, June 1986, *66*(6), pp. 36–73. **[G: U.S.]**

Krugman, Paul R. New Thinking about Trade Policy. **In** *Krugman, P. R., ed.*, 1986, pp. 1–22.

Kubo, Yuji; de Melo, Jaime and Robinson, Sherman. Trade Strategies and Growth Episodes. **In** *Chenery, H.; Robinson, S. and Syrquin, M.*, 1986, pp. 148–87. **[G: LDCs]**

Kuehn, John A. and Braschler, Curtis. Technology and Foreign Trade Impacts on U.S. Manufacturing Employment 1975–80. *Growth Change,* October 1986, *17*(4), pp. 46–60. **[G: U.S.]**

Kuyvenhoven, Arie and Poot, Huib. The Structure of Indonesian Manufacturing Industry: An Input–Output Approach. *Bull. Indonesian Econ. Stud.*, August 1986, *22*(2), pp. 54–79. **[G: Indonesia]**

Lagrange, François. Industrial Policy Should Be Conducted at the Supranational Level. **In** *Adams, W. J. and Stoffaës, C., eds.*, 1986, pp. 133–42. **[G: France]**

Lall, Sanjaya. Technological Development and Export Performance in LDCs: Leading Engineering and Chemical Firms in India. *Weltwirtsch. Arch.*, 1986, *122*(1), pp. 80–92. **[G: India]**

Langdon, Steven. Industrial Dependence and Export Manufacturing in Kenya. **In** *Ravenhill, J., ed.*, 1986, pp. 181–212. **[G: Kenya]**

Lavigne, Marie. Comment on the Economic Dimension of Soviet Interaction with the Third World. *Soviet Econ.*, July-Sept. 1986, *2*(3), pp. 269–76. **[G: U.S.S.R.]**

Łebkowski, Maciej and Monkiewicz, Jan. Information Industries in the CMEA Countries: A Foreign Trade Dimension. *Konjunkturpolitik,* 1986, *32*(5), pp. 308–24. **[G: CMEA]**

Lecaillon, Jean-Didier. Un modèle explicatif de l'évolution du taux de couverture des échanges franco-allemands. (With English summary.) *Revue Écon. Polit.*, Mar.-Apr. 1986, *96*(2), pp. 118–46. **[G: France; W. Germany]**

Ledić, Michèle and Silberston, Aubrey. The Technological Balance of Payments in Perspective. **In** *Hall, P., ed.*, 1986, *1984*, pp. 104–34. **[G: OECD]**

Lee, Jaymin. Determinants of Offshore Production in Developing Countries. *J. Devel. Econ.*, Jan.-Feb. 1986, *20*(1), pp. 1–13. **[G: LDCs]**

Lee, Young Sun. Changing Export Patterns in Korea, Taiwan and Japan. *Weltwirtsch. Arch.*, 1986, *122*(1), pp. 150–63. **[G: S. Korea; Taiwan; Japan]**

Lehto, Sakari T. Företagens internationalisering. (The Internationalization of Business. With English summary.) *Ekon. Samfundets Tidskr.*, 1986, *39*(1), pp. 21–33. **[G: Finland]**

Leontief, Wassily. Domestic Production and Foreign Trade: The American Capital Position Reexamined. **In** *Leontief, W.*, 1986, *1953*, pp. 65–93. **[G: U.S.]**

Leontief, Wassily. Factor Proportions and the Structure of American Trade: Further Theoretical and Empirical Analysis. **In** *Leontief, W.*, 1986, *1956*, pp. 94–128. **[G: U.S.]**

Leontief, Wassily. The Growth of Maritime Traffic and the Future of World Ports. **In** *Leontief, W.*, 1986, *1979*, pp. 379–91. **[G: Global]**

Lewis, Stephen R., Jr. Africa's Trade and the World Economy. **In** *Berg, R. J. and Whitaker, J. S., eds.*, 1986, pp. 476–504. **[G: Africa]**

Li, Lillian M. The Silk Export Trade and Economic Modernization in China and Japan. **In** *May, E. R. and Fairbank, J. K., eds.*, 1986, pp. 77–99. **[G: China; Japan]**

Lincoln, Edward J. Japanese Policy toward Foreign Multinationals: Implications for Trade and Competitiveness: Comment. **In** *Pugel, T. A., ed.*, 1986, pp. 163–68. **[G: Japan]**

Lipsey, Richard G. Will There Be a Canadian–American Free Trade Association? *World Econ.*, September 1986, *9*(3), pp. 217–38. **[G: U.S.; Canada]**

Little, Jane Sneddon. Intra-firm Trade and U.S. Protectionism: Thoughts Based on a Small Survey. *New Eng. Econ. Rev.*, Jan./Feb. 1986, pp. 42–51. **[G: U.S.]**

Love, James. Commodity Concentration and Export Instability: The Choice of Concentration Measure and Analytical Framework. *J. Devel.*

Areas, October 1986, *21*(1), pp. 63–73. **[G: LDCs]**

Love, James. Commodity Concentration and Export Earnings Instability: A Shift from Cross-section to Time Series Analysis. *J. Devel. Econ.*, December 1986, *24*(2), pp. 239–48. **[G: LDCs]**

Love, James. Currency of Denomination and the Measurement of Export Instability. *J. Devel. Stud.*, October 1986, *23*(1), pp. 106–13. **[G: LDCs]**

Lukman, Nasrun and McGlinchey, James M. The Indonesian Petroleum Industry: Current Problems and Future Prospects. *Bull. Indonesian Econ. Stud.*, December 1986, *22*(3), pp. 70–92. **[G: Indonesia]**

Lumsden, George Quincey, Jr. International Oil Trade through the Strait of of Hormuz. *J. Energy Devel.*, Autumn 1986, *12*(1), pp. 43–48. **[G: Global]**

Lundberg, Lars and Hansson, Pär. Intra-industry Trade and Its Consequences for Adjustment. **In** *Greenaway, D. and Tharakan, P. K. M., eds.*, 1986, pp. 129–47. **[G: Sweden]**

MacCharles, Donald C. Canadian International Intra-industry Trade. **In** *Greenaway, D. and Tharakan, P. K. M., eds.*, 1986, pp. 148–73. **[G: Canada]**

Machowski, Heinrich A. Developing Countries in the Foreign Economic Relations and Foreign Policy of the USSR. **In** *Höhmann, H.-H.; Nove, A. and Vogel, H., eds.*, 1986, pp. 252–73. **[G: U.S.S.R.; LDCs]**

Maddison, Angus. Developing Countries in the 1930s: Possible Lessons for the 1980s. **In** *Lal, D. and Wolf, M., eds.*, 1986, pp. 15–47. **[G: LDCs; MDCs]**

Maki, Dennis R. and Meredith, Lindsay N. The Effect of U.S. and Canadian Wage and Productivity Differentials and FDI Status on the Canadian Propensity to Import U.S. Sourced Products. *Weltwirtsch. Arch.*, 1986, *122*(1), pp. 164–72. **[G: U.S.; Canada]**

Mann, Catherine L. Prices, Profit Margins, and Exchange Rates. *Fed. Res. Bull.*, June 1986, *72*(6), pp. 366–79. **[G: U.S.]**

Maravall, Agustin. An Application of Model-Based Estimation of Unobserved Components. *Int. J. Forecasting*, 1986, *2*(3), pp. 305–18. **[G: Spain]**

Marin, Dalia. Exchange Rate and Industrial Profits: Austria's Revaluation Policy in the 1970s. *Appl. Econ.*, June 1986, *18*(6), pp. 675–89. **[G: Austria]**

Marnata, Françoise and Sarrazin, Chantal. Les pays nordiques: protection sociale et contrainte extérieure. (Nordic Countries: Social Welfare and External Constraint. With English summary.) *Écon. Soc.*, January 1986, *20*(1), pp. 211–34. **[G: Denmark; Sweden; Norway; Finland]**

Marquez, Jaime. Oil-Price Effects in Theory and Practice. *J. Devel. Econ.*, November 1986, *24*(1), pp. 1–27. **[G: Global]**

Marrese, Michael. CMEA: Effective but Cumbersome Political Economy. **In** *Comisso, E. and Tyson, L., eds.*, 1986, pp. 111–51. **[G: CMEA]**

Martin, Ricardo and van Wijnbergen, Sweder J. G. Shadow Prices and the Intertemporal Aspects of Remittances and Oil Revenues in Egypt. **In** *Neary, J. P. and van Wijnbergen, S., eds.*, 1986, pp. 142–68. **[G: Egypt]**

Martin, W. and Shaw, I. The Effect of Exchange Rate Changes on the Value of Australia's Major Agricultural Exports. *Econ. Rec.*, Supplement 1986, pp. 101–07. **[G: Australia]**

Massad, Carlos. Relieving the Debt Burden: Past Experience and Present Needs. *CEPAL Rev.*, December 1986, (30), pp. 17–34. **[G: Latin America]**

Matejka, Harriet. The Foreign Trade System. **In** *Kaser, M. C., ed.*, 1986, pp. 250–88. **[G: E. Europe]**

Matthews, Ron. Technological Dynamism in India and Japan: The Case of Machine-Tool Manufacture. **In** *Baark, E. and Jamison, A., eds.*, 1986, pp. 142–204. **[G: India; Japan]**

Mauleón, Iñaki. Una función de exportación para la economía española. (With English summary.) *Invest. Econ.*, May 1986, *10*(2), pp. 357–78. **[G: Spain]**

Mayer, Helmut. Developing Country Debt: Policies and Prospects: Comment. **In** *Giersch, H., ed.*, 1986, pp. 123–26. **[G: LDCs]**

Mayer, Leo V. Farm Exports and the Farm Economy: Economic and Political Interdependence. **In** *Browne, W. P. and Hadwiger, D. F., eds.*, 1986, pp. 17–27. **[G: U.S.]**

McKinnon, Ronald I. Exchange-Rate Volatility, International Trade, and Resource Allocation: A Perspective on Recent Research: Comments. *J. Int. Money Finance*, Supp. March 1986, *5*, pp. S113–15.

Measday, Walter S. and Martin, Stephen. The Petroleum Industry. **In** *Adams, W., ed.*, 1986, pp. 38–73. **[G: U.S.; OPEC]**

Meister, Shelley and Sherman, Thomas A. Import, Export Prices Reflect Declining Dollar and Oversupply in 1985. *Mon. Lab. Rev.*, April 1986, *109*(4), pp. 3–16. **[G: U.S.]**

Meller, Patricio. Un enfoque analítico-empirico de las causas del actual endeudamiento externo chileno. (Causes of Present Chilean Foreign Debt: An Analytical–Empirical Approach. With English summary.) *Colección Estud. CIEPLAN*, December 1986, (20), pp. 19–60. **[G: Chile]**

de Melo, Jaime and Urata, Shujiro. The Influence of Increased Foreign Competition on Industrial Concentration and Profitability. *Int. J. Ind. Organ.*, September 1986, *4*(3), pp. 287–304. **[G: Chile]**

Menda, Jean-Luc. La spécialisation internationale de la France dans les échanges de services. (With English summary.) *Revue Écon. Polit.*, Sept.-Oct. 1986, *96*(5), pp. 527–40. **[G: France]**

Mendel, Julius S. The Effect of Exchange Rate Depreciation on the Metal and Engineering Industry. *Econ. Rec.*, Supplement 1986, pp. 89–93. **[G: Australia]**

Méndez, José A. The Short-run Trade and Employment Effects of Steel Import Restraints. *J. World Trade Law*, Sept.:Oct. 1986, *20*(5), pp. 554–66. [G: U.S.]

Meredith, David. State Controlled Marketing and Economic "Development": The Case of West African Produce during the Second World War. *Econ. Hist. Rev., 2nd Ser.*, February 1986, *39*(1), pp. 77–91. [G: W. Africa]

Messerlin, Patrick A. The EC–U.S. Steel Trade Crisis: Comment. In *Tsoukalis, L., ed.*, 1986, pp. 36–41. [G: U.S.; EEC]

Messerlin, Patrick A. and Becuwe, Stephane. Intra-industry Trade in the Long Run: The French Case, 1850–1913. In *Greenaway, D. and Tharakan, P. K. M., eds.*, 1986, pp. 191–215. [G: France]

Milone, Luciano Marcello. The Law of One Price: Further Empirical Evidence Concerning Italy and the United Kingdom. *Appl. Econ.*, June 1986, *18*(6), pp. 645–61. [G: Italy; U.K.]

Mirus, Rolf and Yeung, Bernard. "Buy-Back" in International Trade: A Rationale. *Weltwirtsch. Arch.*, 1986, *122*(2), pp. 371–74.

Misala, Jozef. East–West Relations in the Seventies. In *Altmann, F.-L., ed.*, 1986, pp. 179–217. [G: CMEA; OECD]

Mistral, Jacques. 125 ans de contrainte extérieure: l'expérience française. (125 Years of External Constraint: The French Case. With English summary.) *Écon. Soc.*, January 1986, *20*(1), pp. 91–115. [G: France]

Monza, Alfredo, et al. Algunas limitaciones de un cociente clásico. (With English summary.) *Desarrollo Econ.*, July-Sept. 1986, *26*(102), pp. 197–227. [G: Argentina]

Mornande, Felipe G. Domestic Prices of Importable Goods in Chile and the Law of One Price: 1975–1982. *J. Devel. Econ.*, April 1986, *21*(1), pp. 131–47. [G: Chile]

Msambichaka, L. A. Balancing Overproduction and Malnutrition: Discussion. In *Maunder, A. and Renborg, U., eds.*, 1986, pp. 239–42. [G: Sub-Saharan Africa]

Nakatani, Iwao. Towards the New International Economic Order—The Role of Japan in the World Economy. *Hitotsubashi J. Econ.*, Spec. Iss. Oct. 1986, *27*, pp. 121–32. [G: Japan; U.S.]

Naray, Peter. Hungarian Foreign Trade Reform. *J. World Trade Law*, May:June 1986, *20*(3), pp. 274–86. [G: Hungary]

Nashashibi, Karim and Clawson, Patrick. The IMF Supply-Side Approach to Devaluation: A Response. *Oxford Bull. Econ. Statist.*, February 1986, *48*(1), pp. 73–82. [G: Sudan]

Nau, Henry R. National Policies for High Technology Development and Trade: An International and Comparative Assessment. In *Rushing, F. W. and Brown, C. G., eds.*, 1986, pp. 9–29. [G: India; Brazil; Mexico; S. Korea; Argentina]

Nayyar, Deepak. East–South Trade. In *[Streeten, P.]*, 1986, pp. 240–69. [G: E. Europe; LDCs]

Niron, Suna. Fertilizer Pricing in Turkey. In *Segura, E. L.; Shetty, Y. T. and Nishimizu, M., eds.*, 1986, pp. 219–35. [G: Turkey]

Nishimizu, Mieko and Page, John M., Jr. Productivity Change and Dynamic Comparative Advantage. *Rev. Econ. Statist.*, May 1986, *68*(2), pp. 241–47. [G: Thailand]

Nolle, Daniel E. and Pigott, Charles. The Changing Commodity Composition of U.S. Imports from Japan. *Fed. Res. Bank New York Quart. Rev.*, Spring 1986, *11*(1), pp. 12–18. [G: U.S.]

Nötel, R. International Credit and Finance. In *Kaser, M. C. and Radice, E. A., eds.*, 1986, pp. 170–295. [G: E. Europe]

O'Connell, Arturo A. Free Trade in One (Primary Producing) Country: The Case of Argentina in the 1920s. In *di Tella, G. and Platt, D. C. M., eds.*, 1986, pp. 74–94. [G: Argentina]

Oliveira, Joao do Carmo. Trade Policy, Market 'Distortions,' and Agriculture in the Process of Economic Development: Brazil, 1950–1974. *J. Devel. Econ.*, November 1986, *24*(1), pp. 91–109. [G: Brazil]

Orden, David. A Critique of Exchange Rate Treatment in Agricultural Trade Models: Comment. *Amer. J. Agr. Econ.*, November 1986, *68*(4), pp. 990–93.

Orden, David. Agriculture, Trade, and Macroeconomics: The U.S. Case. *J. Policy Modeling*, Spring 1986, *8*(1), pp. 27–51. [G: U.S.]

Oshima, Harry T. The Construction Boom of the 1970s: The End of High Growth in the NICs and ASEAN? *Devel. Econ.*, September 1986, *24*(3), pp. 207–28. [G: LDCs; Asia]

Ouattara, Alassane D. The Balance-of-Payments Adjustment Process in Developing Countries: The Experience of the Ivory Coast. *World Devel.*, Special Issue, August 1986, *14*(8), pp. 1085–1105. [G: Ivory Coast]

Owen, Robert F. Developing Country Debt: Policies and Prospects: Comment. In *Giersch, H., ed.*, 1986, pp. 127–32. [G: LDCs]

Ozawa, Terutomo. Japanese Policy toward Foreign Multinationals: Implications for Trade and Competitiveness. In *Pugel, T. A., ed.*, 1986, pp. 141–62. [G: Japan]

Paarlberg, Philip L. and Webb, Alan J. Public Policy and the Reemergence of International Economic Influences on U.S. Agriculture. *Agr. Econ. Res.*, Winter 1986, *38*(1), pp. 45–56. [G: U.S.]

Padevct, Zdenck. Trade with Advanced Capitalist States. *Czech. Econ. Digest.*, Oct./Nov. 1986, (7), pp. 35–39. [G: Czechoslovakia]

Page, S. A. B. Prospects for Non-oil Developing Countries. *Nat. Inst. Econ. Rev.*, May 1986, (116), pp. 31–37. [G: LDCs]

Panchamukhi, V. R. Trade in Agricultural Commodities—A Profile of Two Decades: 1960–80. In *Dantwala, M. L., et al.*, 1986, pp. 432–59. [G: India]

Panchamukhi, V. R. and Raipuria, Kalyan M. South–South Trade in Manufactures and the Lima Target: Projections through 1900 and 2000 under Alternative Scenarios. In *Pancha-*

mukhi, V. R., et al., 1986, pp. 76–93. **[G: Global]**

Pandit, Kavita. Sectoral Allocation of Labor Force with Development and the Effect of Trade Activity. *Econ. Geogr.*, April 1986, *62*(2), pp. 144–54.

Park, Yung Chul. Foreign Debt, Balance of Payments, and Growth Prospects: The Case of the Republic of Korea, 1965–88. *World Devel.*, Special Issue, August 1986, *14*(8), pp. 1019–58. **[G: S. Korea]**

Patel, I. G. The Balance of Payments Problem. **In** *Patel, I. G.*, 1986, pp. 48–60. **[G: India]**

Pekhlivanov, Vasil. Problems of Import Pricing in the CMEA. *Soviet E. Europ. Foreign Trade*, Summer 1986, *22*(2), pp. 39–51. **[G: CMEA]**

Pelkmans, Jacques. The Bickering Bigemony: GATT as an Instrument in Atlantic Trade Policy. **In** *Tsoukalis, L., ed.*, 1986, pp. 83–106. **[G: U.S.; EEC]**

Perdikis, Nicholas. An Assessment of Cyprus' Association with the EEC. *J. Econ. Stud.*, 1986, *13*(2), pp. 38–51. **[G: Cyprus; EEC]**

Pfaller, Alfred. The Changing North–South Division of Labour: Promises, Threats and EC Policy Options. *Kyklos*, 1986, *39*(1), pp. 85–108. **[G: Global]**

Pinder, John. The Bickering Bigemony: GATT as an Instrument in Atlantic Trade Policy: Comment. **In** *Tsoukalis, L., ed.*, 1986, pp. 117–18. **[G: U.S.; EEC]**

Pogorel, Gérard. The Impact of Information Technology on Trade in Services: Discussion. **In** *Faulhaber, G.; Noam, E. and Tasley, R., eds.*, 1986, pp. 106–09. **[G: U.S.]**

Polopolus, Leo C. The Competitive Position of Southern Commodities in International Markets: A Synopsis. *Southern J. Agr. Econ.*, July 1986, *18*(1), pp. 75–78. **[G: U.S.]**

Pomfret, Richard. MFN Tariff Reductions and Developing Country Trade Benefits under the GSP: A Comment. *Econ. J.*, June 1986, *96*(382), pp. 534–36.

Pomfret, Richard. On the Division of Labour and International Trade: Or, Adam Smith's Explanation of Intra-industry Trade. *J. Econ. Stud.*, 1986, *13*(4), pp. 56–63.

Popa, Ioan. Correlation of Prices and the Measurement of Efficiency in the Foreign Trade of the Socialist Countries. *Soviet E. Europ. Foreign Trade*, Summer 1986, *22*(2), pp. 52–66. **[G: Romania]**

Pope, David H. Australian Capital Inflow, Sectional Prices and the Terms of Trade: 1870–1939. *Australian Econ. Pap.*, June 1986, *25*(46), pp. 67–82. **[G: Australia]**

Pope, David H. Protection and Australian Manufacturers' International Competitiveness, 1901–1930. *Australian Econ. Hist. Rev.*, March 1986, *26*(1), pp. 21–39. **[G: Australia]**

Poznanski, Kazimierz. Patterns of Technology Imports: Interregional Comparison. *World Devel.*, June 1986, *14*(6), pp. 743–56. **[G: E. Europe; Latin America]**

Prebisch, Raúl. Notes on Trade from the Standpoint of the Periphery. *CEPAL Rev.*, April 1986, (28), pp. 203–14.

Price, Robert S. Government Policy and International Natural Gas Trade. *J. Energy Devel.*, Spring 1986, *11*(2), pp. 189–211. **[G: OECD]**

Prieto, Francisco Javier. Services: A Disquieting Link between Latin America and the World Economy. *CEPAL Rev.*, December 1986, (30), pp. 17–36.

Pugel, Thomas A. Fragile Interdependence: Introduction. **In** *Pugel, T. A., ed.*, 1986, pp. 1–18. **[G: U.S.; Japan]**

Rączkowski, Stanisław. The Influence of International Movements of Prices and Inflation on the Economies of the Socialist Countries. *Eastern Europ. Econ.*, Summer 1986, *24*(4), pp. 3–28. **[G: CMEA]**

Radice, E. A. Changes in Property Relationships and Financial Arrangements. **In** *Kaser, M. C. and Radice, E. A., eds.*, 1986, pp. 329–65. **[G: Germany; E. Europe]**

Raikes, Phil. Eating the Carrot and Wielding the Stick: The Agricultural Sector in Tanzania. **In** *Boesen, J., et al., eds.*, 1986, pp. 105–41. **[G: Tanzania]**

Raipuria, Kalyan M. Third World in the 'Third Wave': Imperative of South–South Cooperation in Science and Technology. **In** *Panchamukhi, V. R., et al.*, 1986, pp. 166–214. **[G: Global]**

Ramstetter, Eric D. Interaction between Japanese Policy Priorities: Energy and Trade in the 1980s. *J. Energy Devel.*, Spring 1986, *11*(2), pp. 285–300. **[G: Japan]**

Rana, Pradumna B. Exports and Economic Growth: Further Evidence from Asian LDCs. *Pakistan J. Appl. Econ.*, Winter 1986, *5*(2), pp. 163–78. **[G: Asia]**

Redmond, John and Lan, Zou. The European Community and China: New Horizons. *J. Common Market Stud.*, December 1986, *25*(2), pp. 133–55. **[G: EEC; China]**

Reilly, Barry. A Note on Demand Elasticities for Energy Imports. *Econ. Soc. Rev.*, January 1986, *17*(2), pp. 147–58. **[G: Ireland]**

Reinhart, Vincent. Macroeconomic Influences on the U.S.–Japan Trade Imbalance. *Fed. Res. Bank New York Quart. Rev.*, Spring 1986, *11*(1), pp. 6–11. **[G: U.S.]**

Remolona, Eli M.; Mangahas, Mahar and Pante, Filologo, Jr. Foreign Debt, Balance of Payments, and the Economic Crisis of the Philippines in 1983–84. *World Devel.*, Special Issue, August 1986, *14*(8), pp. 993–1018. **[G: Philippines]**

Renard, François. La place des échanges de services dans la balance des paiements française. (With English summary.) *Revue Écon. Polit.*, Sept.-Oct. 1986, *96*(5), pp. 513–26. **[G: France]**

Reynolds, Bruce L. The East Asian "Textile Cluster" Trade, 1868–1973: A Comparative-Advantage Interpretation. **In** *May, E. R. and Fairbank, J. K., eds.*, 1986, pp. 129–50. **[G: U.S.; U.K.; China; India; Japan]**

Richardson, J. David. The New Political Economy of Trade Policy. **In** *Krugman, P. R., ed.*, 1986, pp. 257–82. **[G: U.S.]**

Richardson, Martin and Wilkie, Simon. Incremental Export Subsidies [The Cyclical Effects of Incremental Export Subsidies]. *Econ. Rec.*, March 1986, *62*(176), pp. 88–92. **[G: Australia]**

Riethmuller, Paul and Roe, Terry. Government Intervention in Commodity Markets: The Case of Japanese Rice and Wheat Policy. *J. Policy Modeling*, Fall 1986, *8*(3), pp. 327–49. **[G: Japan]**

Riethmuller, Paul, et al. Survey Evidence on the Effects of the 1985 Depreciation on Importers and Import-Competing Manufacturers. *Econ. Rec.*, Supplement 1986, pp. 94–100. **[G: Australia]**

Rittenberg, Libby. Export Growth Performance of Less-Developed Countries. *J. Devel. Econ.*, November 1986, *24*(1), pp. 167–77. **[G: LDCs]**

Robertson, Max. The South Pacific Regional Trade and Economic Cooperation Agreement: A Critique. **In** *Cole, R. V. and Parry, T. G., eds.*, 1986, pp. 147–75. **[G: Australia; S. Pacific]**

Root, William A. U.S. Policy on East–West Technology Trade: Past, Present, and Future. **In** *McIntyre, J. R. and Papp, D. S., eds.*, 1986, pp. 207–20. **[G: U.S.]**

Rooth, T. J. T. Tariffs and Trade Bargaining: Anglo–Scandinavian Economic Relations in the 1930s. *Scand. Econ. Hist. Rev.*, 1986, *34*(1), pp. 54–71. **[G: U.K.; Denmark; Finland; Norway; Sweden]**

Rosensweig, Jeffrey A. Exchange Rates and Competition for Tourists. *New Eng. Econ. Rev.*, July/Aug. 1986, pp. 57–67. **[G: U.S.]**

Rossi, Vanessa, et al. Exchange Rates, Productivity and International Competitiveness. *Oxford Rev. Econ. Policy*, Autumn 1986, *2*(3), pp. 56–73. **[G: U.K.; U.S.]**

Rothchild, Donald and Gyimah-Boadi, E. Ghana's Economic Decline and Development Strategies. **In** *Ravenhill, J., ed.*, 1986, pp. 254–85. **[G: Ghana]**

Rowse, John. Allocation of Canadian Natural Gas to Domestic and Export Markets. *Can. J. Econ.*, August 1986, *19*(3), pp. 417–42. **[G: Canada]**

Salathe, Larry and Langley, Suchada. An Empirical Analysis of Alternative Export Subsidy Programs for U.S. Wheat. *Agr. Econ. Res.*, Winter 1986, *38*(1), pp. 1–18. **[G: U.S.]**

Samuelson, Paul A. America's Interest in International Trade. **In** *Samuelson, P. A.*, 1986, *1979*, pp. 518–19.

Samuelson, Paul A. Free Trade's Intertemporal Pareto-Optimality. **In** *Samuelson, P. A.*, 1986, *1978*, pp. 477–79.

Sandilands, Roger J. and Ling-Hui, Tan. Comparative Advantage in a Re-export Economy: The Case of Singapore. *Singapore Econ. Rev.*, October 1986, *31*(2), pp. 34–56. **[G: Singapore]**

Sanz Guerrero, Rolando. New Objectives for the Development of Mining Resources. *CEPAL Rev.*, December 1986, (30), pp. 173–200. **[G: Latin America]**

Sapir, André. Trade in Investment-Related Technological Studies. *World Devel.*, May 1986, *14*(5), pp. 605–22. **[G: India]**

Sapsford, David. A New Contribution in the Statistical Debate Over Trends in the Net Barter Terms of Trade Between Primary Commodities and Manufactures. *J. Econ. Soc. Meas.*, December 1986, *14*(4), pp. 277–88. **[G: U.K.]**

Sarkar, Prabirjit. The Singer–Prebisch Hypothesis: A Statistical Evaluation. *Cambridge J. Econ.*, December 1986, *10*(4), pp. 355–71. **[G: Global]**

Sarkar, Prabirjit. The Terms of Trade Experience of Britain since the Nineteenth Century. *J. Devel. Stud.*, October 1986, *23*(1), pp. 20–39. **[G: U.K.]**

Šaskolskij, I. P. New Phenomena in the Baltic Trade of Russia in the Seventeenth Century. *Scand. Econ. Hist. Rev.*, 1986, *34*(1), pp. 41–53. **[G: U.S.S.R.]**

Sawant, S. D. Balancing Overproduction and Malnutrition: Discussion. **In** *Maunder, A. and Renborg, U., eds.*, 1986, pp. 243–45. **[G: Sub-Saharan Africa]**

Sawyer, W. Charles and Sprinkle, Richard L. U.S.–Israel Free Trade Area: Trade Expansion Effects of the Agreement. *J. World Trade Law*, Sept.:Oct. 1986, *20*(5), pp. 526–39. **[G: U.S.; Israel]**

Saxonhouse, Gary R. Japan's Intractable Trade Surpluses in a New Era. *World Econ.*, September 1986, *9*(3), pp. 239–58. **[G: Japan; U.S.]**

Saxonhouse, Gary R. The National Security Clause of the Trade Expansion Act of 1962: Import Competition and the Machine Tool Industry. **In** *Saxonhouse, G. R. and Yamamura, K., eds.*, 1986, pp. 218–37. **[G: U.S.]**

Sayer, Andrew. Industrial Location on a World Scale: The Case of the Semiconductor Industry. **In** *Scott, A. J. and Storper, M., eds.*, 1986, pp. 107–23. **[G: Selected Countries]**

Sazanami, Yoko. Japanese Trade in the Pacific Rim: The Relationship between Trade and Investment. **In** *Nemetz, P. N., ed.*, 1986, pp. 53–73. **[G: ASEAN; Japan; New Zealand; Australia]**

Sazanami, Yoko. Some Policy Implications of Intra-industry Trade for Japan. **In** *Greenaway, D. and Tharakan, P. K. M., eds.*, 1986, pp. 174–90. **[G: Selected Countries; Japan]**

Schadler, Susan M. Effect of a Slowdown in Industrial Economies on Selected Asian Countries. *Int. Monet. Fund Staff Pap.*, June 1986, *33*(2), pp. 345–72. **[G: OECD; Asia]**

Schatán, Claudia. Destino de las importaciones y política comercial en México (1975–1980). (Import Destination and Trade Policy in Mexico. With English summary.) *Estud. Econ.*, July-Dec. 1986, *1*(2), pp. 255–80. **[G: Mexico]**

Schlegelmilch, B. B. Can Export Performance Be Explained by Attitudinal Differences? *Manage-*

rial Dec. Econ., December 1986, *7*(4), pp. 249–54. **[G: U.K.; W. Germany]**

Schmitz, Andrew. Marketing Institutions in International Commodity Markets. *Southern J. Agr. Econ.*, July 1986, *18*(1), pp. 41–48. **[G: U.S.]**

Schoo, E. M. European Community's Trade Relations with Developing Countries. *World Econ.*, September 1986, *9*(3), pp. 313–18. **[G: EEC; LDCs]**

Schott, Jeffrey J. and Mazza, Jacqueline. Trade in Services and Developing Countries. *J. World Trade Law*, May:June 1986, *20*(3), pp. 253–73. **[G: Global]**

Schran, Peter. The Minor Significance of Commercial Relations between the United States and China, 1850–1931. **In** *May, E. R. and Fairbank, J. K., eds.*, 1986, pp. 237–58. **[G: China; U.S.; Japan]**

Schuh, G. Edward. Maximizing U.S. Benefits from Agricultural Interdependence. **In** *Browne, W. P. and Hadwiger, D. F., eds.*, 1986, pp. 29–41. **[G: U.S.]**

Schwartz, Anna J. The Open Economy: Implications for Monetary and Fiscal Policy: Comment. **In** *Gordon, R. J., ed.*, 1986, pp. 504–10. **[G: U.S.]**

Schydlowsky, Daniel M. The Macroeconomic Effect of Nontraditional Exports in Peru. *Econ. Develop. Cult. Change*, April 1986, *34*(3), pp. 491–509. **[G: Peru]**

Sennholz, Hans. Protectionism and Unemployment. *Rivista Int. Sci. Econ. Com.*, March 1986, *33*(3), pp. 247–60. **[G: U.S.; Japan]**

Seringhaus, F. H. Rolf. Market Entry and the Impact of Export Marketing Assistance: A Conceptual Approach to Causal Modelling. *Liiketaloudellinen Aikak.*, 1986, *35*(4), pp. 275–85.

Shelp, Ronald Kent. The Impact of Information Technology on Trade in Services: Discussion. **In** *Faulhaber, G.; Noam, E. and Tasley, R., eds.*, 1986, pp. 110–17. **[G: U.S.]**

Shiells, Clinton R.; Stern, Robert M. and Deardorff, Alan V. Estimates of the Elasticities of Substitution between Imports and Home Goods for the United States. *Weltwirtsch. Arch.*, 1986, *122*(3), pp. 497–519. **[G: U.S.]**

Siddiqi, Toufiq A. Factors Affecting Steam Coal Trade in Asia and the Pacific. **In** *Nemetz, P. N., ed.*, 1986, pp. 275–92. **[G: Asia; Pacific Basin]**

Simon, Denis Fred and Schive, Chi. National Policies for Developing High Technology Industries: International Comparisons: Taiwan. **In** *Rushing, F. W. and Brown, C. G., eds.*, 1986, pp. 201–26.

Simons, William B. Soviet Foreign Trade: Economic, Legal, and Political Aspects. **In** *Ioffe, O. S. and Janis, M. W., eds.*, 1986, pp. 243–81. **[G: U.S.S.R.]**

Singhal, K. C. and Kaur, Narinder. Destination-wise Export Instability in India. *Margin*, April 1986, *18*(3), pp. 61–71. **[G: India]**

Singleton, John. Lancashire's Last Stand: Declining Employment in the British Cotton Industry, 1950–70. *Econ. Hist. Rev., 2nd Ser.*, February 1986, *39*(1), pp. 92–107. **[G: U.K.]**

Sinha, Dipendra. Export Demand for Indian Jute Goods. *Atlantic Econ. J.*, December 1986, *14*(4), pp. 102. **[G: India]**

Skarstein, Rune. Growth and Crisis in the Manufacturing Sector. **In** *Boesen, J., et al., eds.*, 1986, pp. 79–104. **[G: Tanzania]**

Slater, Paul B. Petroleum Trade in 1970: An Exploratory Analysis. **In** *Slater, P. B.*, 1986, *1975*, pp. 7–12. **[G: Global]**

Slater, Paul B. and Schwarz, Wolfgang. Global Trade Patterns: Scaling and Clustering Analyses. **In** *Slater, P. B.*, 1986, *1979*, pp. 37–42. **[G: Global]**

Smith, Alasdair. Shadow Prices and the Intertemporal Aspects of Remittances and Oil Revenues in Egypt: Comment. **In** *Neary, J. P. and van Wijnbergen, S., eds.*, 1986, pp. 168–69. **[G: Egypt]**

Sobell, Vladimir. Technology Flows within COMECON and Channels of Communication. **In** *Amann, R. and Cooper, J., eds.*, 1986, pp. 135–52. **[G: CMEA]**

Solimano, Andrés. Contractionary Devaluation in the Southern Cone: The Case of Chile. *J. Devel. Econ.*, September 1986, *23*(1), pp. 135–51. **[G: Chile]**

Soofi, Abdollah S. and Parvin, Kumars. The Import Leakage Effect and the Effectiveness of Fiscal Policy: An Input–Output Analysis. *Public Finance*, December 1986, *41*(3), pp. 430–39. **[G: Iran]**

Spinanger, Dean and Zietz, Joachim. Managing Trade but Mangling the Consumer: Reflections on the EEC's and West Germany's Experience with the Multifiber Arrangement. *Aussenwirtschaft*, December 1986, *41*(4), pp. 511–31. **[G: EEC]**

Srinivasan, T. N. Fertilizer Pricing in Developing Countries: A Market-Based Approach. **In** *Segura, E. L.; Shetty, Y. T. and Nishimizu, M., eds.*, 1986, pp. 48–68. **[G: LDCs]**

Srivastava, Rajendra K. and Green, Robert T. Determinants of Bilateral Trade Flows. *J. Bus.*, Part 1, October 1986, *59*(4), pp. 623–40.

Stopford, John M. International Competitiveness of European Industry. **In** *Macharzina, K. and Staehle, W. H., eds.*, 1986, pp. 5–14. **[G: W. Europe]**

Štouračová, Judita. External Economic Relations: The Only Way Forward: Intensification. *Czech. Econ. Digest.*, Sept./Oct. 1986, (6), pp. 43–50. **[G: Czechoslovakia]**

Suissa, A. Le nouveau marché international du charbon. (The New International Market for Coal. With English summary.) *Écon. Soc.*, July 1986, *20*(7), pp. 77–93.

Sumner, Daniel A. The Competitive Position of Southern Commodities: Some Trends and Underlying Forces. *Southern J. Agr. Econ.*, July 1986, *18*(1), pp. 49–59. **[G: U.S.]**

van Suntum, Ulrich. Internationale Wettbewerbsfähigkeit einer Volkswirtschaft. Ein sinnvolles wirtschaftspolitisches Ziel? (International Competitiveness of an Economy—Does It Make Sense as an Economic Goal? With English summary.) *Z. Wirtschaft. Sozialwis-*

sen., 1986, *106*(5), pp. 495–507.

Sutherland, William Morrison. Microstates and Unequal Trade in the South Pacific: The Sparteca Agreement of 1980. *J. World Trade Law,* May:June 1986, *20*(3), pp. 313–28. **[G: Oceania]**

Symons, M. V. Coal-Mining in the Llanelli Area—Years of Growth, 1800–64. **In** *Baber, C. and Williams, L. J., eds.*, 1986, pp. 53–64. **[G: U.K.]**

Syrquin, Moshe and Urata, Shujiro. Sources of Changes in Factor Intensity of Trade. *J. Devel. Econ.*, December 1986, *24*(2), pp. 225–37. **[G: Mexico; Japan; S. Korea; Taiwan; Israel]**

Tatom, John A. Domestic vs. International Explanations of Recent U.S. Manufacturing Developments. *Fed. Res. Bank St. Louis Rev.*, April 1986, *68*(4), pp. 5–18. **[G: U.S.]**

Taylor, Lance. Trade and Growth. *Rev. Black Polit. Econ.*, Spring 1986, *14*(4), pp. 17–36. **[G: LDCs]**

Tecson, Gwendolyn R. Export Markets for Philippine Diversified Agriculture and Labor-Intensive Industries. *Philippine Rev. Econ. Bus.*, Mar./June 1986, *23*(1/2), pp. 1–56. **[G: Philippines]**

Tecson, Gwendolyn R. Nontraditional Markets for Philippine Exports. *Philippine Rev. Econ. Bus.*, Sept.-Dec. 1986, *23*(3–4), pp. 191–242. **[G: Philippines]**

Teitel, Simón and Thoumi, Francisco E. Da substituição de importações às exportações: as experiências argentina e brasileira no campo das exportações de manufaturados. (With English summary.) *Pesquisa Planejamento Econ.*, April 1986, *16*(1), pp. 129–66. **[G: Argentina; Brazil]**

Teitel, Simón and Thoumi, Francisco E. From Import Substitution to Exports: The Manufacturing Exports Experience of Argentina and Brazil. *Econ. Develop. Cult. Change,* April 1986, *34*(3), pp. 455–90. **[G: Brazil; Argentina]**

di Tella, Guido. La estrategia del desarrollo indirecto veinte años después. (With English summary.) *Desarrollo Econ.*, Apr.-June 1986, *26*(101), pp. 51–70. **[G: Argentina]**

Teubal, Morris; Halevi, Nadav and Tsiddon, D. Learning and the Rise of Israel's Exports of Sophisticated Products. *World Devel.*, December 1986, *14*(12), pp. 1397–1410. **[G: Israel]**

Tharakan, P. K. Mathew. The Intra-Industry Trade of Benelux with the Developing World. *Weltwirtsch. Arch.*, 1986, *122*(1), pp. 131–49. **[G: Belgium; Netherlands; Luxemburg]**

Thoma, G. A. The Structure of Trade between the U.S. and China. *Bus. Econ.*, October 1986, *21*(4), pp. 32–36. **[G: China; U.S.]**

Thursby, Marie C.; Johnson, Paul R. and Grennes, Thomas J. The Law of One Price and the Modelling of Disaggregated Trade Flows. *Econ. Modelling,* October 1986, *3*(4), pp. 293–302.

Tice, Helen Stone and Moczar, Louis J. Foreign Transactions in the National Income and Product Accounts: An Overview. *Surv. Curr. Bus.*, November 1986, *66*(11), pp. 23–36. **[G: U.S.]**

Tiwari, R. S. Constant–Market-Share Analysis of Export Growth: The Indian Case. *Indian Econ. J.*, Jan.-Mar. 1986, *33*(3), pp. 70–80. **[G: India]**

Torok, Stephen J. and Huffman, Wallace E. U.S.–Mexican Trade in Winter Vegetables and Illegal Immigration. *Amer. J. Agr. Econ.*, May 1986, *68*(2), pp. 246–60. **[G: U.S.; Mexico]**

Trehan, Bharat. Oil Prices, Exchange Rates and the U.S. Economy: An Empirical Investigation. *Fed. Res. Bank San Francisco Econ. Rev.*, Fall 1986, (4), pp. 25–43. **[G: U.S.]**

Treml, Vladimir G. Soviet Foreign Trade in Foodstuffs. *Soviet Econ.*, Jan.-Mar. 1986, *2*(1), pp. 19–50. **[G: U.S.S.R.]**

Tyers, Rodney and Phillips, Prue. ASEAN in Pacific Basin Trade: Export Composition and Performance. **In** *Nemetz, P. N., ed.*, 1986, pp. 74–116. **[G: Pacific Basin; ASEAN]**

Urban, Bohumil. High Criteria for the Fulfilment of Tasks. *Czech. Econ. Digest.*, June 1986, (5), pp. 3–7. **[G: Czechoslovakia; CMEA]**

Valkenier, Elizabeth Kridl. East–West Economic Competition in the Third World. **In** *Shulman, M. D., ed.*, 1986, pp. 158–80. **[G: LDCs; U.S.; U.S.S.R.]**

Viaene, Jean-Marie. Product Availability, Price Discrimination and Interdependent Import Flows. **In** *Artus, P. and Guvenen, O., eds.*, 1986, pp. 39–51. **[G: OECD]**

Vogel, Ezra F. Pax Nipponica? *Foreign Aff.*, Spring 1986, *64*(4), pp. 752–67. **[G: Japan]**

Volcker, Paul A. Statement to the U.S. House Subcommittee on Trade, Committee on Ways and Means, September 24, 1986. *Fed. Res. Bull.*, November 1986, *72*(11), pp. 773–79. **[G: U.S.]**

Vosický, Emilián. Relations between CMEA and the European Economic Community. *Czech. Econ. Digest.*, May 1986, (3), pp. 55–58. **[G: CMEA; EEC]**

Wada, Mitsuo. Selling in Japan: Consumer Behavior and Distribution as Barriers to Imports. **In** *Pugel, T. A., ed.*, 1986, pp. 91–105. **[G: U.S.; Japan; W. Germany]**

Wake, C. H. H. The Volume of European Spice Imports at the Beginning and End of the Fifteenth Century. *J. Europ. Econ. Hist.*, Winter 1986, *15*(3), pp. 621–35. **[G: Europe]**

Wasow, Bernard. Insurance and the Balance of Payments. **In** *Wasow, B. and Hill, R. D., eds.*, 1986, pp. 87–103. **[G: S. Korea; Portugal; India; Brazil; Taiwan]**

Watrin, Christian. Japan, Trade Partner of the European Community and the Federal Republic of Germany. **In** *Hax, H.; Kraus, W. and Tsuchiya, K., eds.*, 1986, pp. 15–28. **[G: Japan; EEC]**

Weida, William J. and Gertcher, Franklin L. The Ethics and Economics of Foreign Sales of U.S.-Made Military Weapons. *Int. J. Soc. Econ.*, 1986, *13*(1/2), pp. 20–39. **[G: U.S.]**

Weisskoff, Richard and Wolff, Edward N. Development and Trade Dependence: The Case of

Puerto Rico, 1948–1963. **In** *Sohn, I., ed.*, 1986, *1975*, pp. 406–16. **[G: Puerto Rico]**

Wilkens, Bodo. Sri Lanka: Exportdiversifizierung und weltwirtschaftliche Rezession. (Sri Lanka: Export Diversification and World Economic Recession. With English summary.) *Konjunkturpolitik*, 1986, *32*(1/2), pp. 80–99. **[G: Sri Lanka]**

Willett, Thomas D. Exchange-Rate Volatility, International Trade, and Resource Allocation: A Perspective on Recent Research. *J. Int. Money Finance*, Supp. March 1986, *5*, pp. S101–12.

Williamson, Peter J. Multinational Enterprise Behaviour and Domestic Industry Adjustment under Import Threat. *Rev. Econ. Statist.*, August 1986, *68*(3), pp. 359–68. **[G: Australia]**

Wolf, Bernard M. The Bearing Industry: Rationalization in Europe. **In** *Casson, M., et al.*, 1986, pp. 175–95. **[G: OECD]**

Wolter, Frank. The Bickering Bigemony: GATT as an Instrument in Atlantic Trade Policy: Comment. **In** *Tsoukalis, L., ed.*, 1986, pp. 119–23. **[G: U.S.; EEC]**

Wong, Chung Ming. Models of Export Instability and Empirical Tests for Less-Developed Countries. *J. Devel. Econ.*, March 1986, *20*(2), pp. 263–85. **[G: LDCs]**

Wood, Van R. The Information Needs of Exporters: Theory, Framework and Empirical Tests. *Liiketaloudellinen Aikak.*, 1986, *35*(1), pp. 3–22. **[G: U.S.]**

Woodard, Kim. Political Risk in China. **In** *Raddock, D. M., et al.*, 1986, pp. 71–93. **[G: China]**

Yamawaki, Hideki. Exports, Foreign Market Structure, and Profitability in Japanese and U.S. Manufacturing. *Rev. Econ. Statist.*, November 1986, *68*(4), pp. 618–27. **[G: Japan; U.S.]**

Yamazawa, Ippei; Nohara, Takashi and Osada, Hiroshi. Economic Interdependence in Pacific Asia: An International Input–Output Analysis. *Devel. Econ.*, June 1986, *24*(2), pp. 95–108. **[G: Asia]**

Yannopoulos, George N. The Impact of the European Economic Community on East–West Trade in Europe. *Comp. Econ. Stud.*, Spring 1986, *28*(1), pp. 75–85. **[G: EEC; CMEA]**

Young, Soogil. A Global Outlook from the Old Hermit Kingdom. *World Econ.*, March 1986, *9*(1), pp. 51–64. **[G: S. Korea]**

Zech, Charles E. Sub-national Foreign Export Development and Its Impact on Productivity. *Growth Change*, July 1986, *17*(3), pp. 1–12. **[G: U.S.]**

Zedillo Ponce de Leon, Ernesto. Mexico's Recent Balance-of-Payments Experience and Prospects for Growth. *World Devel.*, Special Issue, August 1986, *14*(8), pp. 963–91. **[G: Mexico]**

Zevin, L. Z., et al. Cooperation of CMEA Member-Countries and Developing Countries in the Resolution of the Food Problem. *Soviet E. Europ. Foreign Trade*, Fall-Winter 1986-87, *22*(3), pp. 1–209. **[G: CMEA; LDCs]**

Zinn, Eberhard and Kotz, Hans-Helmut. Exportversicherung, Exportfinanzierung und internationaler Wettbewerb. (With English summary.) *Z. Betriebswirtshaft*, November 1986, *56*(11), pp. 1077–94. **[G: W. Germany]**

422 Commercial Policy

4220 Commercial Policy

Abd-El-Rahman, K. S. La "différence" et la "similitude" dans l'analyse de la composition du commerce international. (Difference and Similarity Elements in International Trade Composition Analysis. With English summary.) *Revue Écon.*, March 1986, *37*(2), pp. 307–40. **[G: France]**

Adelman, M. A. Lessons from the 1986 Oil Price Collapse: Comments. *Brookings Pap. Econ. Act.*, 1986, (2), pp. 272–76. **[G: OPEC]**

Agarwal, J. P. Third World Multinationals and Balance-of-Payments Effect on Home Countries: A Case Study of India. **In** *Khan, K. M., ed.*, 1986, pp. 184–95. **[G: India]**

Akrasanee, Narongchai and Ajanant, Juanjai. Manufacturing Industry Protection in Thailand: Issues and Empirical Studies. **In** *Findlay, C. and Garnaut, R., eds.*, 1986, pp. 77–98. **[G: Thailand]**

von Alvensleben, Reimar; Behr, Hans-Christoph and Jahn, Hans-Harald. Fruits and Vegetables in the European Community. **In** *Bale, M. D., ed.*, 1986, pp. 5–93. **[G: EEC]**

Anderson, David L. Marketing Arrangements for Western Canadian Coking Coal. *Can. Public Policy*, September 1986, *12*(3), pp. 473–83. **[G: Canada; Japan]**

Anderson, Kym. The Peculiar Rationality of Beef Import Quotas in Japan and Korea. **In** *Anderson, K. and Hayami, Y.*, 1986, pp. 80–90. **[G: Japan; S. Korea]**

Anderson, Kym and Garnaut, Ross. The Political Economy of Manufacturing Protection in Australia. **In** *Findlay, C. and Garnaut, R., eds.*, 1986, pp. 159–83. **[G: Australia]**

Anderson, Kym and Hayami, Yujiro. Lessons and Implications. **In** *Anderson, K. and Hayami, Y.*, 1986, pp. 111–19. **[G: E. Asia]**

Anderson, Kym and Hayami, Yujiro. The Political Economy of Agricultural Protection: East Asia in International Perspective: Introduction. **In** *Anderson, K. and Hayami, Y.*, 1986, pp. 1–6. **[G: Europe; Asia]**

Anderson, Kym; Hayami, Yujiro and Honma, Masayoshi. The Growth of Agricultural Protection. **In** *Anderson, K. and Hayami, Y.*, 1986, pp. 17–30. **[G: Japan]**

Anderson, Kym and Tyers, Rodney. International Effects of Agricultural Policies. **In** *Snape, R. H., ed.*, 1986, pp. 93–114. **[G: OECD]**

Anderson, Kym, et al. Details of Agricultural Protection Estimates, 1955–82. **In** *Anderson, K. and Hayami, Y.*, 1986, pp. 123–45. **[G: Europe; E. Asia; U.S.]**

Anjaria, Shailendra J. A New Round of Global Trade Negotiations. *Finance Develop.*, June 1986, *23*(2), pp. 2–6.

Arndt, Sven W. Government Policy and the Decline in U.S. Trade Competitiveness. **In** *Cagan, P., ed.*, 1986, pp. 307–23. **[G: U.S.]**

Atsumi, Naoki. Voluntary Restraint Agreements: The Case of Automobiles and Steel. **In** *Finn, R. B., ed.*, 1986, pp. 39–49. **[G: U.S.; Japan]**

Aw, Bee Yan and Roberts, Mark J. Measuring Quality Change in Quota-Constrained Import Markets: The Case of U.S. Footwear. *J. Int. Econ.*, August 1986, *21*(1/2), pp. 45–60. **[G: U.S.]**

Balassa, Bela. Japan's Trade Policies. *Weltwirtsch. Arch.*, 1986, *122*(4), pp. 745–90. **[G: Japan]**

Balassa, Bela and Michalopoulos, Constantine. Liberalizing Trade between Developed and Developing Countries. *J. World Trade Law*, Jan.:Feb. 1986, *20*(1), pp. 3–28. **[G: Global]**

Baldwin, Robert E. Rent-Seeking and Trade Policy: An Industry Approach. **In** *Balassa, B. and Giersch, H., eds.*, 1986, pp. 429–43.

Baldwin, Robert E. Toward More Efficient Procedures for Multilateral Trade Negotiations. **In** *Hauser, H., ed. (II)*, 1986, pp. 217–32.

Baldwin, Robert E. Toward More Efficient Procedures for Multilateral Trade Negotiations. *Aussenwirtschaft*, September 1986, *41*(2/3), pp. 379–94. **[G: U.S.]**

Baldwin, Robert E. Trade Policies in Developed Countries. **In** *Jones, R. W., ed.*, 1986, *1984*, pp. 183–231. **[G: MDCs]**

Baldwin, Robert E. and Murray, Tracy. MFN Tariff Reductions and Developing Country Trade Benefits under the GSP: A Reply. *Econ. J.*, June 1986, *96*(382), pp. 537–39.

Bamossy, Gary J. and Scammon, Debra L. Counterfeiting—A Worldwide Problem: What Is the Role of Channel Members? **In** *Pellegrini, L. and Reddy, S. K., eds.*, 1986, pp. 141–54. **[G: U.S.]**

Banks, Gary and Tumlir, Jan. The Political Problem of Adjustment. *World Econ.*, June 1986, *9*(2), pp. 141–52. **[G: EEC; Canada]**

Barichello, Richard R. and Warley, T. K. Agriculture and Negotiation of a Free-Trade Area: Issues in Policy Harmonization. **In** *C. D. Howe Institute*, 1986, pp. 135–64. **[G: Canada; U.S.]**

Bautista, Romeo M. Domestic Price Distortions and Agricultural Income in Developing Countries. *J. Devel. Econ.*, September 1986, *23*(1), pp. 19–39. **[G: Philippines]**

Bayne, Nicholas. International Economic Policy Coordination. **In** *Morgan, R. and Bray, C., eds.*, 1986, pp. 175–83. **[G: France; U.K.; W. Germany]**

Benedek, Wolfgang. The Caribbean Basin Economic Recovery Act: A New Type of Preference in GATT? *J. World Trade Law*, Jan.:Feb. 1986, *20*(1), pp. 29–46. **[G: U.S.; Caribbean]**

Benyon, Frank S. The EC–U.S. Steel Trade Crisis: Comment. **In** *Tsoukalis, L., ed.*, 1986, pp. 45–49. **[G: EEC; U.S.]**

Benzoni, Laurent. Taux de change, prix du pétrole, déséquilibres monétaires internationaux. (Exchange Rate, Oil Price, International Monetary Disequilibrium. With English summary.) *Écon. Soc.*, July 1986, *20*(7), pp. 27–61. **[G: OPEC]**

Bertsch, Gary K. Technology Transfers and Technology Controls: A Synthesis of the Western–Soviet Relationship. **In** *Amann, R. and Cooper, J., eds.*, 1986, pp. 115–34. **[G: U.S.S.R.; OECD]**

Bertsch, Gary K. The Extraterritoriality Issue in the Transatlantic Context: A Question of Law or Diplomacy? Comment. **In** *Tsoukalis, L., ed.*, 1986, pp. 152–57. **[G: U.S.; EEC]**

Bhagwati, Jagdish N. Ideology and North–South Relations. *World Devel.*, June 1986, *14*(6), pp. 767–74. **[G: Global]**

Blackhurst, Richard. GATT Surveillance of Industrial Policies. *Aussenwirtschaft*, September 1986, *41*(2/3), pp. 361–78. **[G: OECD]**

Blackhurst, Richard. GATT Surveillance of Industrial Policies. **In** *Hauser, H., ed. (II)*, 1986, pp. 199–216. **[G: OECD]**

Blomqvist, Ake G. and Mohammad, Sharif. Controls, Corruption, and Competitive Rent-Seeking in LDCs. *J. Devel. Econ.*, April 1986, *21*(1), pp. 161–80. **[G: India]**

Booth, Anne. Agricultural Taxation: A Survey of Issues and Evidence. **In** *Shome, P., ed.*, 1986, pp. 117–40. **[G: S. Asia; S. E. Asia]**

Borrus, Michael; Tyson, Laura D'Andrea and Zysman, John. Creating Advantage: How Government Policies Shape International Trade in the Semiconductor Industry. **In** *Krugman, P. R., ed.*, 1986, pp. 91–113. **[G: U.S.; Japan]**

Brander, James A. Rationales for Strategic Trade and Industrial Policy. **In** *Krugman, P. R., ed.*, 1986, pp. 23–46.

Branson, William H. and Klevorick, Alvin K. Strategic Behavior and Trade Policy. **In** *Krugman, P. R., ed.*, 1986, pp. 241–55. **[G: U.S.]**

Brean, Donald J. S. Fiscal Policy Harmonization and Negotiation of a Free-Trade Area. **In** *C. D. Howe Institute*, 1986, pp. 43–71. **[G: Canada; U.S.]**

Brinkman, Richard L. The Genesis of a New Industrial Policy: Equity and Efficiency. *J. Econ. Issues*, June 1986, *20*(2), pp. 335–44. **[G: U.S.]**

Bronfenbrenner, Martin. Japan-Bashing: A View from "Over There." *Challenge*, Jan./Feb. 1986, *28*(6), pp. 58–61. **[G: U.S.; Japan]**

Brown, William H. Opening Japanese Financial Markets: What Has Changed, What Will Change? **In** *Pugel, T. A., ed.*, 1986, pp. 117–35. **[G: Japan]**

Bruce, C. J. and Kerr, William A. A Proposed Arbitration Mechanism to Ensure Free Trade in Livestock Products. *Can. J. Agr. Econ.*, November 1986, *34*(3), pp. 347–60. **[G: Canada; U.S.]**

Buffie, Edward F. and Spiller, Pablo T. Trade Liberalization in Oligopolistic Industries: The Quota Case. *J. Int. Econ.*, February 1986, *20*(1/2), pp. 65–81.

Burian, Gustav. Czechoslovak Economic Law and External Economic Relations. *Soviet E. Europ.*

Foreign Trade, Summer 1986, *22*(2), pp. 6–27. **[G: Czechoslovakia]**

Butler, Nicholas. The Common Agricultural Policy and World Food Trade. **In** *Browne, W. P. and Hadwiger, D. F., eds.*, 1986, pp. 45–57. **[G: EEC]**

Butt Philip, Alan. Europe's Industrial Policies: An Overview. **In** *Hall, G., ed.*, 1986, pp. 1–20. **[G: EEC]**

Calvani, Terry and Tritell, Randolph W. Invocation of United States Import Relief Laws as an Antitrust Violation. *Antitrust Bull.*, Summer 1986, *31*(2), pp. 527–50. **[G: U.S.]**

Camps, Miriam. The Bickering Bigemony: GATT as an Instrument in Atlantic Trade Policy: Comment. **In** *Tsoukalis, L., ed.*, 1986, pp. 107–12. **[G: U.S.; EEC]**

Carey, Sarah C. and McLean, Sheila Avrin. The United States, Countertrade and Third World Trade. *J. World Trade Law*, July:Aug. 1986, *20*(4), pp. 441–73. **[G: U.S.; LDCs]**

Carliner, Geoffrey. Industrial Policies for Emerging Industries. **In** *Krugman, P. R., ed.*, 1986, pp. 147–68. **[G: U.S.; France; Japan]**

Carmichael, W. B. National Interest and International Trade Negotiations. *World Econ.*, December 1986, *9*(4), pp. 341–57.

Cassing, James H. A Note on the Welfare Cost of a Tariff. *Eastern Econ. J.*, Apr.-June 1986, *12*(2), pp. 145–48.

Cassing, James H.; McKeown, Timothy J. and Ochs, Jack. The Political Economy of the Tariff Cycle. *Amer. Polit. Sci. Rev.*, September 1986, *80*(3), pp. 843–62. **[G: U.S.]**

Casson, Mark. Multinationals and World Trade: Introduction and Summary. **In** *Casson, M., et al.*, 1986, pp. 1–59. **[G: U.S.]**

Charnovitz, Steve. Fair Labor Standards and International Trade. *J. World Trade Law*, Jan.: Feb. 1986, *20*(1), pp. 61–78. **[G: U.S.]**

Chhibber, Ajay and Wilton, John. Macroeconomic Policies and Agricultural Performance in Developing Countries. *Finance Develop.*, September 1986, *23*(3), pp. 6–9. **[G: LDCs]**

Choi, Kwang-Ho and Cumming, Tracey A. Who Pays for Protection in Australia? *Econ. Rec.*, December 1986, *62*(179), pp. 490–96. **[G: Australia]**

Chung, Joseph S. National Policies for Developing High Technology Industries: International Comparisons: Korea. **In** *Rushing, F. W. and Brown, C. G., eds.*, 1986, pp. 143–72. **[G: S. Korea]**

Clausen, A. W. Corrective Initiatives in International Trade and Finance: Address to the United Nations Conference on Trade and Development: Belgrade, Yugoslavia: June 9, 1983. **In** *Clausen, A. W.*, 1986, pp. 177–90.

Clausen, A. W. Statement before the GATT Ministerial Meeting: Geneva, Switzerland: November 24, 1982. **In** *Clausen, A. W.*, 1986, pp. 125–31.

Cline, William R. U.S. Trade and Industrial Policy: The Experience of Textiles, Steel, and Automobiles. **In** *Krugman, P. R., ed.*, 1986, pp. 211–39. **[G: U.S.]**

Clingan, Thomas A., Jr. The United States and the Law of the Sea Conference. **In** *Pontecorvo, G., ed.*, 1986, pp. 219–37. **[G: U.S.]**

Conway, Patrick. Decomposing the Determinants of Trade Deficits: Turkey in the 1970s. *J. Devel. Econ.*, May 1986, *21*(2), pp. 235–58. **[G: Turkey]**

Coomans, Géry. Système productif et petites nations. (Productive System and Small Nations. With English summary.) *Écon. Soc.*, May 1986, *20*(5), pp. 49–67. **[G: Belgium]**

Cooper, H. The Welfare Effects of Sanctions. *J. Stud. Econ. Econometrics*, August 1986, (25), pp. 2–11.

Cooper, Richard N. Economic Interdependence and Foreign Policy in the Seventies. **In** *Cooper, R. N.*, 1986, *1972*, pp. 1–22.

Cooper, Richard N. Global Economic Policy in a World of Energy Shortage. **In** *Cooper, R. N.*, 1986, *1982*, pp. 53–69.

Corden, W. Max. Policies towards Market Disturbance. **In** *Snape, R. H., ed.*, 1986, pp. 121–39.

Cox, David and Harris, Richard G. A Quantitative Assessment of the Economic Impact on Canada of Sectoral Free Trade with the United States. *Can. J. Econ.*, August 1986, *19*(3), pp. 377–94. **[G: U.S.; Canada]**

Crandall, Robert W. The EC–U.S. Steel Trade Crisis. **In** *Tsoukalis, L., ed.*, 1986, pp. 17–35. **[G: U.S.; EEC]**

Curzon, Gerard and Curzon Price, Victoria. Defusing Conflict between Traders and Non-traders. *World Econ.*, March 1986, *9*(1), pp. 19–35. **[G: Global]**

Curzon Price, Victoria. Industrial and Trade Policy in a Period of Rapid Structural Change. *Aussenwirtschaft*, September 1986, *41*(2/3), pp. 201–23. **[G: EEC]**

Curzon Price, Victoria. Industrial and Trade Policy in a Period of Rapid Structural Change. **In** *Hauser, H., ed. (II)*, 1986, pp. 39–61. **[G: EEC]**

Dahl, Frederick R. Statement to the U.S. House Subcommittee on Commerce, Consumer, and Monetary Affairs of the Committee on Government Operations, March 4, 1986. *Fed. Res. Bull.*, May 1986, *72*(5), pp. 307–12. **[G: U.S.]**

Deardorff, Alan V. Comments [Market Structure and Trade Liberalization: A General Equilibrium Assessment] [Short-run Impact of Trade Liberalization Measures on the Economy of Bangladesh: Exercises in Comparative Statics for the Year 1977]. **In** *Srinivasan, T. N. and Whalley, J., eds.*, 1986, pp. 311–17. **[G: Canada; Bangladesh]**

Deardorff, Alan V. and Stern, Robert M. Neighborhood Effects of Developing Country Protection. *J. Devel. Econ.*, May 1986, *21*(2), pp. 327–46. **[G: LDCs]**

Deardorff, Alan V. and Stern, Robert M. The Structure and Sample Results of the Michigan Computational Model of World Production and Trade. **In** *Srinivasan, T. N. and Whalley, J., eds.*, 1986, pp. 151–88. **[G: LDCs; MDCs]**

Dell, Edmund. Of Free Trade and Reciprocity. *World Econ.*, June 1986, *9*(2), pp. 125–39. **[G: U.S.; EEC]**

Demaret, Paul. The Extraterritoriality Issue in the Transatlantic Context: A Question of Law or Diplomacy? **In** *Tsoukalis, L., ed.*, 1986, pp. 124–48. **[G: U.S.; EEC]**

Diamandouros, P. Nikiforos. The Southern European NICs. **In** *Comisso, E. and Tyson, L., eds.*, 1986, pp. 371–80. **[G: Greece; Portugal; Spain]**

Dias, Guilherme Leite da Silva. Markets and Trade: Discussion. **In** *Maunder, A. and Renborg, U., eds.*, 1986, pp. 577–78.

de Dios, Emmanuel S. Protection, Concentration, and the Direction of Foreign Investments. *Philippine Rev. Econ. Bus.*, Mar./June 1986, *23*(1/2), pp. 57–82. **[G: Philippines]**

Dixit, Avinash K. Trade Policy: An Agenda for Research. **In** *Krugman, P. R., ed.*, 1986, pp. 283–304.

Dixit, Avinash K. and Grossman, Gene M. Targeted Export Promotion with Several Oligopolistic Industries. *J. Int. Econ.*, November 1986, *21*(3/4), pp. 233–49.

Dixon, Peter B.; Parmenter, B. R. and Rimmer, Russell J. ORANI Projections of the Short-run Effects of a 50 Percent Across-the-Board Cut in Protection Using Alternative Data Bases. **In** *Srinivasan, T. N. and Whalley, J., eds.*, 1986, pp. 33–60. **[G: Australia]**

Djalal, Hasjim. A Southeast Asian Perspective. **In** *Pontecorvo, G., ed.*, 1986, pp. 199–216. **[G: S. E. Asia]**

Dobson, Alan P. The Export White Paper, 10 September, 1941. *Econ. Hist. Rev., 2nd Ser.*, February 1986, *39*(1), pp. 59–76. **[G: U.K.]**

Drummond, Ian M. On Disbelieving the Commissioners' Free-Trade Case. *Can. Public Policy*, Supp. February 1986, *12*, pp. 59–67. **[G: Canada]**

Dubey, Muchkund. The North–South Negotiating Process. **In** *[Patel, S.]*, 1986, pp. 85–104.

Dubs, Marne A. Minerals of the Deep Sea: Myth and Reality. **In** *Pontecorvo, G., ed.*, 1986, pp. 85–121. **[G: France; Japan; U.S.S.R.; U.S.; India]**

Dufour, Jean-Marie and Racette, Daniel. Une évaluation économique du financement public des exportations. (With English summary.) *Can. Public Policy*, December 1986, *12*(4), pp. 584–95. **[G: Canada]**

Eads, George C. Dangers in U.S. Efforts to Promote International Competitiveness. **In** *Landau, R. and Rosenberg, N., eds.*, 1986, pp. 527–33. **[G: U.S.]**

Eaton, Jonathan. Credit Policy and International Competition. **In** *Krugman, P. R., ed.*, 1986, pp. 115–45. **[G: U.S.]**

Edwards, Sebastian and Teitel, Simón. Introduction to Growth, Reform, and Adjustment: Latin America's Trade and Macroeconomic Policies in the 1970s and 1980s. *Econ. Develop. Cult. Change*, April 1986, *34*(3), pp. 423–31. **[G: Latin America]**

Encarnation, Dennis J. and Wells, Louis T., Jr. Evaluating Foreign Investment. **In** *Moran, T. H., ed.*, 1986, pp. 61–86.

English, Edward. Canada and the Far West. **In** *Nemetz, P. N., ed.*, 1986, pp. 307–19. **[G: Canada; Pacific Basin]**

Erdilek, Asim. Turkey's New Open-Door Policy of Direct Foreign Investment: A Critical Analysis of Problems and Prospects. *METU*, 1986, *13*(1/2), pp. 171–91. **[G: Turkey]**

Ewing, Arthur F. Agriculture, Trade and Growth: Review Article. *J. World Trade Law*, Nov.:Dec. 1986, *20*(6), pp. 665–89. **[G: Global]**

Fairburn, J. A.; Kay, John A. and Sharpe, T. A. E. The Economics of Article 86. **In** *Hall, G., ed.*, 1986, pp. 21–43. **[G: EEC]**

Falvey, Rodney E. Trade Problems and Policies of Pacific Island Economies. **In** *Cole, R. V. and Parry, T. G., eds.*, 1986, pp. 111–46. **[G: S. Pacific]**

Falvey, Rodney E. Why Have U.S. Tariffs Fallen since 1930? Comment. **In** *Snape, R. H., ed.*, 1986, pp. 254–56. **[G: U.S.]**

Fane, George. International Effects of Agricultural Policies: Comment. **In** *Snape, R. H., ed.*, 1986, pp. 115–18. **[G: OECD]**

Farran, Andrew. The Interplay of Law and Economics in International Trade Regulation. **In** *Snape, R. H., ed.*, 1986, pp. 193–217.

Fausten, Dietrich. The Choice of Instrument for Industry Protection: Comment. **In** *Snape, R. H., ed.*, 1986, pp. 171–74.

Feenstra, Robert C. ORANI Projections of the Short-run Effects of a 50 Percent Across-the-Board Cut in Protection Using Alternative Data Bases: Comments. **In** *Srinivasan, T. N. and Whalley, J., eds.*, 1986, pp. 89–90. **[G: Australia]**

Feenstra, Robert C. Trade Policy with Several Goods and 'Market Linkages.' *J. Int. Econ.*, May 1986, *20*(3/4), pp. 249–67.

Fieleke, Norman S. The Decline of the Oil Cartel. *New Eng. Econ. Rev.*, July/Aug. 1986, pp. 32–41. **[G: OECD; OPEC]**

Findlay, Christopher C. Optimal Taxation of International Income Flows. *Econ. Rec.*, June 1986, *62*(177), pp. 208–14.

Findlay, Christopher C. and Garnaut, Ross. The Political Economy of Manufacturing Protection: Experiences of ASEAN and Australia: Conclusions and Suggestions for Policy Action. **In** *Findlay, C. and Garnaut, R., eds.*, 1986, pp. 264–80. **[G: ASEAN; Australia]**

Findlay, Christopher C. and Garnaut, Ross. The Political Economy of Manufacturing Protection: Experiences of ASEAN and Australia: Introduction. **In** *Findlay, C. and Garnaut, R., eds.*, 1986, pp. xiv–xxiii. **[G: ASEAN; Australia]**

Finger, J. Michael. Ideas Count, Words Inform. **In** *Snape, R. H., ed.*, 1986, pp. 257–80. **[G: U.S.]**

First, Harry. Japan's Antitrust Policy: Impact on Import Competition. **In** *Pugel, T. A., ed.*, 1986, pp. 63–76. **[G: U.S.; Japan]**

Fretz, Deborah; Srinivasan, T. N. and Whalley,

John. General Equilibrium Trade Policy Modeling: Introduction. **In** *Srinivasan, T. N. and Whalley, J., eds.*, 1986, pp. 1–29.

Frey, Bruno S. and Buhofer, Heinz. Integration and Protectionism: A Comparative Institutional Analysis. *Aussenwirtschaft*, September 1986, *41*(2/3), pp. 329–50. **[G: EEC]**

Freyche, Michel. Export Promotion as Industrial Policy. **In** *Adams, W. J. and Stoffaës, C., eds.*, 1986, pp. 82–87. **[G: France]**

Friedlander, Robert A. The Middle East Today: Problems and Portents. **In** *Roukis, G. S. and Montana, P. J., eds.*, 1986, pp. 1–20. **[G: U.S.; Middle East]**

Frignani, Aldo. The GATT Agreement on Government Procurement: ICC Symposium. *J. World Trade Law*, Sept.:Oct. 1986, *20*(5), pp. 567–70. **[G: Global]**

Fuchs, Peter. Past, Present, and Future Perfect? Casing Japan's Competitive Strategy. **In** *Finn, R. B., ed.*, 1986, pp. 17–37. **[G: Japan]**

Funatsu, Hideki. Export Credit Insurance. *J. Risk Ins.*, December 1986, *53*(4), pp. 679–92.

Gács, János. The Conditions, Chances and Predictable Consequences of Implementing a Step-by-Step Liberalization of Imports in the Hungarian Economy. *Acta Oecon.*, 1986, *36*(3–4), pp. 231–50. **[G: Hungary]**

Garčár, Ján. Broad Possibilities of Economic Cooperation. *Czech. Econ. Digest.*, June 1986, (5), pp. 50–54. **[G: Czechoslovakia]**

Gately, Dermot. Lessons from the 1986 Oil Price Collapse. *Brookings Pap. Econ. Act.*, 1986, (2), pp. 237–71. **[G: OPEC]**

George, Aurelia and Saxon, Eric. The Politics of Agricultural Protection in Japan. **In** *Anderson, K. and Hayami, Y.*, 1986, pp. 91–110. **[G: Japan]**

Gerken, Egbert; Gross, Martin and Lächler, Ulrich. The Causes and Consequences of Steel Subsidization in Germany. *Europ. Econ. Rev.*, August 1986, *30*(4), pp. 773–804. **[G: W. Germany]**

Ghose, Devajyoti; Lahiri, Ashok K. and Wadhwa, Wilima. Quantitative Restrictions and Indian Imports. *J. Devel. Econ.*, March 1986, *20*(2), pp. 247–62. **[G: India]**

Giersch, Herbert. Weltwirtschaftliches Wachstum durch Liberalisierung. (Global Economic Growth by Liberalization. With English summary.) *Kyklos*, 1986, *39*(4), pp. 518–36. **[G: W. Europe]**

Globerman, Steven. Potential Implications of Canadian–U.S. Trade Negotiations for Canadian Cultural Support Policies. **In** *C. D. Howe Institute*, 1986, pp. 123–34. **[G: Canada; U.S.]**

Godek, Paul E. The Politically Optimal Tariff: Levels of Trade Restrictions across Developed Countries. *Econ. Inquiry*, October 1986, *24*(4), pp. 587–93. **[G: OECD]**

Goetz, Charles J.; Granet, Lloyd and Schwartz, Warren F. The Meaning of 'Subsidy' and 'Injury' in the Countervailing Duty Law. *Int. Rev. Law Econ.*, June 1986, *6*(1), pp. 17–32. **[G: U.S.]**

Gold, Hyam and Thakur, Ramesh. Australia and New Zealand: The Role of Agriculture in a Closer Economic Relationship. **In** *Browne, W. P. and Hadwiger, D. F., eds.*, 1986, pp. 63–75. **[G: Australia; New Zealand]**

Goldberg, Walter H. Ailing Steel: The Transoceanic Quarrel: The Problems. **In** *Goldberg, W. H., ed.*, 1986, pp. 3–35. **[G: Global]**

Goldberg, Walter H. The European Steel Industry. **In** *Goldberg, W. H., ed.*, 1986, pp. 111–23. **[G: EEC]**

Goldstein, Judith. The Political Economy of Trade: Institutions of Protection. *Amer. Polit. Sci. Rev.*, March 1986, *80*(1), pp. 161–84. **[G: U.S.]**

Gomulka, Stanislaw. East–West Trade and the Polish Experience, 1970–82. **In** *Gomulka, S.*, 1986, pp. 251–70. **[G: CMEA; Poland]**

Grais, Wafik. Comments [A General Equilibrium Analysis of Tariff Reductions] [Trade Liberalization through Tariff Cuts and the European Economic Community: A General Equilibrium Evaluation]. **In** *Srinivasan, T. N. and Whalley, J., eds.*, 1986, pp. 145–48. **[G: EEC]**

Grais, Wafik; de Melo, Jaime and Urata, Shujiro. A General Equilibrium Estimation of the Effects of Reductions in Tariffs and Quantitative Restrictions in Turkey in 1978. **In** *Srinivasan, T. N. and Whalley, J., eds.*, 1986, pp. 61–88. **[G: Turkey]**

Gravelle, Jane G. International Tax Competition: Does It Make a Difference for Tax Policy? *Nat. Tax J.*, September 1986, *39*(3), pp. 375–84. **[G: U.S.]**

Gray, H. Peter. Protection in a Democracy: A Conversation with H. Peter Gray and Roy Licklider. *Eastern Econ. J.*, Apr.-June 1986, *12*(2), pp. 89–93.

Greenaway, David. Estimating the Welfare Effects of Voluntary Export Restraints and Tariffs: An Application to Nonleather Footwear in the UK. *Appl. Econ.*, October 1986, *18*(10), pp. 1065–83. **[G: U.K.]**

Greenaway, David and Milner, Chris. Estimating the Shifting of Protection across Sectors: An Application to Mauritius. *Industry Devel.*, 1986, (16), pp. 1–22. **[G: Mauritius]**

Grey, Rodney de C. The Decay of the Trade Relations System. **In** *Snape, R. H., ed.*, 1986, pp. 17–29.

Griffin, James M. Lessons from the 1986 Oil Price Collapse: Comments. *Brookings Pap. Econ. Act.*, 1986, (2), pp. 276–82. **[G: OPEC]**

Grjebine, André. France and Its External Constraints. **In** *Sjöstedt, G. and Sundelius, B., eds.*, 1986, pp. 127–37. **[G: France]**

Grossman, Gene M. Imports as a Cause of Injury: The Case of the U.S. Steel Industry. *J. Int. Econ.*, May 1986, *20*(3/4), pp. 201–23. **[G: U.S.]**

Grossman, Gene M. Strategic Export Promotion: A Critique. **In** *Krugman, P. R., ed.*, 1986, pp. 47–68. **[G: U.S.]**

Grubel, Herbert G. Free Trade Zones and Their Relation to GATT. **In** *Snape, R. H., ed.*, 1986, pp. 140–51.

Gruen, Fred H. The Decay of the Trade Relations System: Comment. **In** *Snape, R. H., ed.*, 1986, pp. 30–31.

Guerrieri, Paolo and Padoan, Pier Carlo. Neomercantilism and International Economic Stability. *Int. Organ.*, Winter 1986, *40*(1), pp. 29–42.

Guisinger, Stephen. Do Performance Requirements and Investment Incentives Work? *World Econ.*, March 1986, *9*(1), pp. 79–96. **[G: U.S.]**

Haberler, Gottfried. The World Economy: Its Performance and Prospects, with Emphasis on Trade Liberalization and Protection. **In** *Cagan, P., ed.*, 1986, pp. 325–62.

Hadwiger, Don F. Public Policy and Interdependence. **In** *Browne, W. P. and Hadwiger, D. F., eds.*, 1986, pp. 203–09.

Hager, Wolfgang. The Bickering Bigemony: GATT as an Instrument in Atlantic Trade Policy: Comment. **In** *Tsoukalis, L., ed.*, 1986, pp. 113–16. **[G: U.S.; EEC]**

Haglund, David G. Protectionism and National Security: The Case of Canadian Uranium Exports to the United States. *Can. Public Policy*, September 1986, *12*(3), pp. 459–72. **[G: U.S.; Canada]**

Hallwood, C. Paul. External Economy Arguments for Commodity Stockpiling: A Review. *Bull. Econ. Res.*, January 1986, *38*(1), pp. 25–41.

Hamilton, Bob and Whalley, John. Border Tax Adjustments and U.S. Trade. *J. Int. Econ.*, May 1986, *20*(3/4), pp. 377–83. **[G: U.S.]**

Hamilton, Carl. Agricultural Protection in Sweden 1970–1980. *Europ. Rev. Agr. Econ.*, 1986, *13*(1), pp. 75–87. **[G: Sweden]**

Hamilton, Carl. An Assessment of Voluntary Restraints on Hong Kong Exports to Europe and the USA. *Economica*, August 1986, *53*(211), pp. 339–50. **[G: Hong Kong; U.S.; W. Europe]**

Hamilton, Carl. ASEAN Systems for Allocation of Export Licences under VERs. **In** *Findlay, C. and Garnaut, R., eds.*, 1986, pp. 235–47. **[G: ASEAN]**

Hamilton, Carl. Import Quotas and Voluntary Export Restraints: Focusing on Exporting Countries. **In** *Findlay, C. and Garnaut, R., eds.*, 1986, pp. 214–34.

Hamilton, Carl. The Upgrading Effect of Voluntary Export Restraints. *Weltwirtsch. Arch.*, 1986, *122*(2), pp. 358–64.

Hannay, N. Bruce. Technology and Trade: A Study of U.S. Competitiveness in Seven Industries. **In** *Landau, R. and Rosenberg, N., eds.*, 1986, pp. 479–99. **[G: U.S.]**

Harris, Richard G. Comments [ORANI Projections of the Short-run Effects of a 50 Percent Across-the-Board Cut in Protection Using Alternative Data Bases] [A General Equilibrium Estimation of the Effects of Reductions in Tariffs and Quantitative Restrictions in Turkey in 1978]. **In** *Srinivasan, T. N. and Whalley, J., eds.*, 1986, pp. 91–97. **[G: Australia; Turkey]**

Harris, Richard G. Market Structure and Trade Liberalization: A General Equilibrium Assessment. **In** *Srinivasan, T. N. and Whalley, J., eds.*, 1986, pp. 231–50. **[G: Canada]**

Harrison, Glenn W. A General Equilibrium Analysis of Tariff Reductions. **In** *Srinivasan, T. N. and Whalley, J., eds.*, 1986, pp. 101–23. **[G: Selected Countries]**

Hartigan, James C.; Perry, Philip R. and Kamma, Sreenivas. The Value of Administered Protection: A Capital Market Approach. *Rev. Econ. Statist.*, November 1986, *68*(4), pp. 610–17. **[G: U.S.]**

Hauser, Heinz. Domestic Policy Foundation and Domestic Policy Function of International Trade Rules. *Aussenwirtschaft*, September 1986, *41*(2/3), pp. 171–84. **[G: OECD]**

Hauser, Heinz. Domestic Policy Foundation and Domestic Policy Function of International Trade Rules. **In** *Hauser, H., ed. (II)*, 1986, pp. 9–22.

Hauser, Heinz. International Trade Policy: Discussion to Session III. *Aussenwirtschaft*, September 1986, *41*(2/3), pp. 395–401. **[G: OECD]**

Hay, Fenton. Canada's Role in International Negotiations Concerning Intellectual Property Laws. **In** *Palmer, J., ed.*, 1986, pp. 239–63. **[G: Canada]**

Hayami, Yujiro. The Roots of Agricultural Protectionism. **In** *Anderson, K. and Hayami, Y.*, 1986, pp. 31–38. **[G: E. Asia]**

Henderson, Dan F. Access to the Japanese Market: Some Aspects of Foreign Exchange Controls and Banking Law. **In** *Saxonhouse, G. R. and Yamamura, K., eds.*, 1986, pp. 131–56. **[G: Japan]**

Heng, Toh Mun. Income Redistribution and Trade Policy Effects on Macroeconomic Aggregates: A Simulation Study of the Singapore Economy Based on an Extended Input–Output Model. *J. Econ. Devel.*, July 1986, *11*(1), pp. 157–90. **[G: Singapore]**

Herander, Mark G. Discriminatory Government Procurement with a Content Requirement: Its Protective Effects and Welfare Costs. *Atlantic Econ. J.*, March 1986, *14*(1), pp. 20–29.

Herander, Mark G. and Thomas, Christopher R. Export Performance and Export–Import Linkage Requirements. *Quart. J. Econ.*, August 1986, *101*(3), pp. 591–607.

Herrmann, Roland. Free Riders and the Redistributive Effects of International Commodity Agreements: The Case of Coffee. *J. Policy Modeling*, Winter 1986, *8*(4), pp. 597–621. **[G: Global]**

Hilf, Meinhard. International Trade Disputes and the Individual: Private Party Involvement in National and International Procedures Regarding Unfair Foreign Trade Practices. *Aussenwirtschaft*, September 1986, *41*(2/3), pp. 441–66. **[G: Global]**

Hilf, Meinhard. International Trade Disputes and the Individual: Private Party Involvement in National and International Procedures Regarding Unfair Foreign Trade Practices. **In** *Hauser, H., ed. (II)*, 1986, pp. 279–304.

Hill, Malcolm R. Soviet and Eastern European

Company Activity in the United Kingdom and Ireland. In *Hamilton, G., ed.*, 1986, pp. 17–87. **[G: E. Europe; U.K.; Ireland]**

Hillman, Arye L. and Katz, Eliakim. Domestic Uncertainty and Foreign Dumping. *Can. J. Econ.*, August 1986, *19*(3), pp. 403–16.

Hillman, Jimmye S. and Faminow, Merle D. Inconsistencies in U.S. Trade and Agricultural Policies vis-a-vis Its Major Trading Partners. *Keio Econ. Stud.*, 1986, *23*(2), pp. 1–18. **[G: U.S.]**

Hindley, Brian. EC Imports of VCRs from Japan: A Costly Precedent. *J. World Trade Law*, Mar.:Apr. 1986, *20*(2), pp. 168–84. **[G: EEC; Japan]**

Hindley, Brian and MacBean, Alasdair. Edmund Dell's Manifesto for Mercantilist Liberation. *World Econ.*, December 1986, *9*(4), pp. 359–64. **[G: U.S.; EEC]**

Hogan, William T. The EC–U.S. Steel Trade Crisis: Comment. In *Tsoukalis, L., ed.*, 1986, pp. 42–44. **[G: U.S.; EEC]**

Holsti, Kal J. Politics in Command: Foreign Trade as National Security Policy. *Int. Organ.*, Summer 1986, *40*(3), pp. 643–71. **[G: Japan; Finland]**

Holtfrerich, Carl-Ludwig. U.S. Capital Exports to Germany 1919–1923 Compared to 1924–1929. *Exploration Econ. Hist.*, January 1986, *23*(1), pp. 1–32. **[G: U.S.; W. Germany]**

Holtfrerich, Carl-Ludwig. U.S. Economic (Policy) Development and World Trade during the Interwar Period Compared to the Last Twenty Years. In *Berend, I. T. and Borchardt, K., eds.*, 1986, pp. 61–81. **[G: U.S.]**

Honma, Masayoshi and Hayami, Yujiro. Structure of Agricultural Protection in Industrial Countries. *J. Int. Econ.*, February 1986, *20*(1/2), pp. 115–29. **[G: U.S.; EEC; Japan]**

Honma, Masayoshi and Hayami, Yujiro. The Determinants of Agricultural Protection Levels: An Econometric Analysis: Explanatory Variables Used in the Regression Analysis. In *Anderson, K. and Hayami, Y.*, 1986, pp. 146–51. **[G: U.S.; Europe; E. Asia]**

Honma, Masayoshi and Hayami, Yujiro. The Determinants of Agricultural Protection Levels: An Econometric Analysis. In *Anderson, K. and Hayami, Y.*, 1986, pp. 39–49. **[G: Europe; U.S.; E. Asia]**

Horstmann, Ignatius J. and Markusen, James R. Up the Average Cost Curve: Inefficient Entry and the New Protectionism. *J. Int. Econ.*, May 1986, *20*(3/4), pp. 225–47.

Hough, Jerry F. Attack on Protectionism in the Soviet Union? A Comment. *Int. Organ.*, Spring 1986, *40*(2), pp. 489–503. **[G: U.S.; U.S.S.R.]**

Hough, Jerry F. Attack on Protectionism in the Soviet Union? A Comment. In *Comisso, E. and Tyson, L., eds.*, 1986, pp. 313–27. **[G: U.S.S.R.]**

Hough, Jerry F. Economic Reform and Soviet Foreign Policy. In *Höhmann, H.-H.; Nove, A. and Vogel, H., eds.*, 1986, pp. 232–51. **[G: U.S.S.R.]**

Hubbard, R. Glenn and Weiner, Robert J. Oil Supply Shocks and International Policy Coordination. *Europ. Econ. Rev.*, February 1986, *30*(1), pp. 91–106.

Hufbauer, Gary Clyde. Should Unconditional MFN Be Revived, Retired or Recast? In *Snape, R. H., ed.*, 1986, pp. 32–54. **[G: Selected Countries]**

Hufbauer, Gary Clyde; Berliner, Diane T. and Elliott, Kimberly Ann. Trade Protection in the United States. *Aussenwirtschaft*, September 1986, *41*(2/3), pp. 225–58. **[G: U.S.]**

Hufbauer, Gary Clyde; Berliner, Diane T. and Elliott, Kimberly Ann. Trade Protection in the United States. In *Hauser, H., ed. (II)*, 1986, pp. 63–96. **[G: U.S.]**

Hughes Hallett, A. J. Commodity Market Stabilisation and "North–South" Income Transfers: An Empirical Investigation. *J. Devel. Econ.*, December 1986, *24*(2), pp. 293–316.

Hughes, Helen. The Political Economy of Protection in Eleven Industrial Countries. In *Snape, R. H., ed.*, 1986, pp. 222–37. **[G: OECD]**

Hultman, Charles W. G-5 Exchange Market Intervention and Commercial Policy. *J. World Trade Law*, May:June 1986, *20*(3), pp. 287–93. **[G: U.S.]**

Hurni, Bettina. EFTA–EC Relations: Aftermath of the Luxembourg Declaration. *J. World Trade Law*, Sept.:Oct. 1986, *20*(5), pp. 497–506. **[G: W. Europe]**

Hutchinson, P. J. The Effect of the E.E.C. Fourth Directive on Corporate Financial Disclosure by European Industry. In *Hall, G., ed.*, 1986, pp. 44–58. **[G: EEC]**

Jakubec, Jaroslav. Efforts to Establish Mutually Advantageous Relations. *Czech. Econ. Digest.*, June 1986, (5), pp. 42–46. **[G: Czechoslovakia]**

Janis, Mark W. The Soviet Theory of International Law and International Economic Relations. In *Ioffe, O. S. and Janis, M. W., eds.*, 1986, pp. 235–41. **[G: U.S.S.R.]**

Janiszewski, Hubert A. New Rules Concerning Technology Transfer in Poland. *J. World Trade Law*, Sept.:Oct. 1986, *20*(5), pp. 571–74. **[G: Poland]**

Jeon, Bang Nam and von Furstenberg, George M. Techniques for Measuring the Welfare Effects of Protection: Appraising the Choices. *J. Policy Modeling*, Summer 1986, *8*(2), pp. 273–303.

Johnson, D. Gale. Agricultural Policies and World Trade: The U.S. and the European Community at Bay: Comment. In *Tsoukalis, L., ed.*, 1986, pp. 77–80. **[G: U.S.; EEC]**

Johnson, Manuel H. Statement to the U.S. Senate Subcommittee on International Finance and Monetary Policy of the Committee on Banking, Housing, and Urban Affairs, June 17, 1986. *Fed. Res. Bull.*, August 1986, *72*(8), pp. 554–59. **[G: U.S.]**

Josling, Timothy E. Agricultural Policies and World Trade: The U.S. and the European Community at Bay. In *Tsoukalis, L., ed.*, 1986, pp. 50–70. **[G: U.S.; EEC]**

Joson, S. S. Substitutability of "Buy Local" Policy for Tariff Protection in Small Economies. *J. Policy Modeling,* Summer 1986, *8*(2), pp. 223–39. **[G: Australia]**

Jung, Woo S. and Lee, Gyu. The Effectiveness of Export Promotion Policies: The Case of Korea. *Weltwirtsch. Arch.*, 1986, *122*(2), pp. 340–57. **[G: S. Korea]**

Kádár, Béla. Hungary's External Economic Strategy in the Second Half of the 1980s. *Acta Oecon.*, 1986, *36*(3–4), pp. 209–29. **[G: Hungary]**

Kavoussi, Rostam M. Trade Policy and Industrialization in an Oil-Exporting Country: The Case of Iran. *J. Devel. Areas,* July 1986, *20*(4), pp. 453–71. **[G: Iran]**

Kelkar, Vijay L. A View from the South: Growth of World Trade in Manufactures. **In** *[Patel, S.],* 1986, pp. 105–21. **[G: MDCs; LDCs]**

Keohane, Robert O. Reciprocity in International Relations. *Int. Organ.*, Winter 1986, *40*(1), pp. 1–27.

Keyzer, Michiel A. Short-run Impact of Trade Liberalization Measures on the Economy of Bangladesh: Exercises in Comparative Statics for the Year 1977. **In** *Srinivasan, T. N. and Whalley, J., eds.*, 1986, pp. 251–82. **[G: Bangladesh]**

Kimura, Yui. Japanese Policy toward Foreign Multinationals: Implications for Trade and Competitiveness: Comment. **In** *Pugel, T. A., ed.*, 1986, pp. 169–74. **[G: Japan]**

Klett, Daniel. The U.S. Tariff Act: Section 337: Off-Shore Assembly and the "Domestic Industry." *J. World Trade Law,* May:June 1986, *20*(3), pp. 294–312. **[G: U.S.]**

Koekkoek, K. A. and Mennes, Loet B. M. Liberalizing the Multi Fibre Arrangement: Some Aspects for the Netherlands, the EC and the LDCs. *J. World Trade Law,* Mar.:Apr. 1986, *20*(2), pp. 142–67. **[G: EEC; LDCs]**

Koo, Won W. and Uhm, Ihn H. A Spatial Equilibrium Analysis of U.S. Wheat Exports under Alternative Transport Costs and Trade Restrictions. *Logist. Transp. Rev.*, March 1986, *22*(1), pp. 27–41. **[G: OECD]**

Kosugi, Ryoji. Japan's Role in the Coming Pacific Era. **In** *Finn, R. B., ed.*, 1986, pp. 101–16. **[G: Japan]**

Köves, András. Is Opening Still Topical? *Acta Oecon.*, 1986, *37*(3–4), pp. 205–18. **[G: CMEA; Hungary]**

Krueger, Anne O. Issues in World Trade Policy: GATT at the Crossroads: Summary. **In** *Snape, R. H., ed.*, 1986, pp. 283–90.

Krueger, Anne O. Trade Policies in Developing Countries. **In** *Jones, R. W., ed.*, 1986, pp. 131–81. **[G: LDCs]**

Krugman, Paul R. New Thinking about Trade Policy. **In** *Krugman, P. R., ed.*, 1986, pp. 1–22.

Lamo de Espinosa, Jaime. International Markets and Price Policy: The Instability of Agriculture. **In** *Maunder, A. and Renborg, U., eds.*, 1986, pp. 557–65.

ıael A. UK Policy and the International Economy: An Internationalist Perspective. **In** *Nolan, P. and Paine, S., eds.*, 1986, pp. 115–34. **[G: U.K.]**

Lawler, K. A. OPEC: A Moribund Cartel? An Analysis of the Oil Cartel's Problems and Prospects. *Brit. Rev. Econ. Issues,* Autumn 1986, *8*(19), pp. 65–84. **[G: OPEC]**

Layton, Christopher. The High-tech Triangle. **In** *Morgan, R. and Bray, C., eds.*, 1986, pp. 184–204. **[G: U.K.; W. Germany; France]**

Lee, Kiong-Hock. The Structure and Causes of Malaysian Manufacturing Sector Protection. **In** *Findlay, C. and Garnaut, R., eds.*, 1986, pp. 99–134. **[G: Malaysia]**

Lehmbruch, Gerhard. Interest Groups, Government, and the Politics of Protectionism. **In** *Hauser, H., ed. (II),* 1986, pp. 111–40.

Lehmbruch, Gerhard. Interest Groups, Government, and the Politics of Protectionism. *Aussenwirtschaft,* September 1986, *41*(2/3), pp. 273–302. **[G: OECD]**

Levačić, Rosalind. Government Policies towards the Consumer Electronics Industry and Their Effects: A Comparison of Britain and France. **In** *Hall, G., ed.*, 1986, pp. 227–44. **[G: U.K.; France]**

Levačić, Rosalind. Import Penetration and Barriers to Trade: The Case of the UK Television Set Market. *Appl. Econ.*, June 1986, *18*(6), pp. 615–30. **[G: U.K.]**

Liang, Xiang. Shenzhen: Opening to the World. *Chinese Econ. Stud.*, Winter 1985-86, *19*(2), pp. 73–78. **[G: China]**

Liebowitz, S. J. International Policies and Intellectual Property: Comments. **In** *Palmer, J., ed.*, 1986, pp. 285–87.

Lincoln, Edward J. Japanese Policy toward Foreign Multinationals: Implications for Trade and Competitiveness: Comment. **In** *Pugel, T. A., ed.*, 1986, pp. 163–68. **[G: Japan]**

Lipsey, Richard G. Will There Be a Canadian–American Free Trade Association? *World Econ.*, September 1986, *9*(3), pp. 217–38. **[G: U.S.; Canada]**

Lipsey, Richard G. and Smith, Murray G. An Overview of Harmonization Issues. **In** *C. D. Howe Institute,* 1986, pp. 1–41. **[G: Canada; U.S.]**

Lipsey, Richard G. and Smith, Murray G. Policy Harmonization: The Effects of a Canadian–American Free Trade Area: Preface: An Introductory Overview. **In** *C. D. Howe Institute,* 1986, pp. vi–xv. **[G: Canada; U.S.]**

Little, Jane Sneddon. Intra-firm Trade and U.S. Protectionism: Thoughts Based on a Small Survey. *New Eng. Econ. Rev.*, Jan./Feb. 1986, pp. 42–51. **[G: U.S.]**

Lloyd, Peter J. and Falvey, Rodney E. The Choice of Instrument for Industry Protection. **In** *Snape, R. H., ed.*, 1986, pp. 152–70.

Lodwick, Seeley G. The International Trading Environment in Petrochemicals. **In** *El Mallakh, R., ed.*, 1986, pp. 47–54. **[G: U.S.]**

Luyten, Paul. Agricultural Policies and World Trade: The U.S. and the European Community at Bay: Comment. **In** *Tsoukalis, L., ed.*, 1986, pp. 81–82. **[G: U.S.; EEC]**

Machowski, Heinrich A. Developing Countries in the Foreign Economic Relations and Foreign Policy of the USSR. **In** *Höhmann, H.-H.; Nove, A. and Vogel, H., eds.*, 1986, pp. 252–73. **[G: U.S.S.R.; LDCs]**

Marcel, Mario. Diez años del IVA en Chile. (Ten Years of VAT in Chile. With English summary.) *Colección Estud. CIEPLAN*, June 1986, (19), pp. 83–134. **[G: Chile]**

Marquez, Jaime. The International Transmission of Oil-Price Effects and OPEC's Pricing Policy. *J. Econ. Bus.*, August 1986, *38*(3), pp. 237–53.

Marrese, Michael. CMEA: Effective but Cumbersome Political Economy. **In** *Comisso, E. and Tyson, L., eds.*, 1986, pp. 111–51. **[G: CMEA]**

Maule, Christopher J. Trade and Culture in Canada. *J. World Trade Law*, Nov.:Dec. 1986, *20*(6), pp. 615–23. **[G: Canada]**

Mawdsley, Andrés Aguilar. Law of the Sea: The Latin American View. **In** *Pontecorvo, G., ed.*, 1986, pp. 158–98. **[G: Latin America]**

McCulloch, Rachel. Japan's Invisible Barriers to Trade: Comment. **In** *Pugel, T. A., ed.*, 1986, pp. 55–62. **[G: Japan; U.S.]**

McDonnell, John. Should Unconditional MFN Be Revived, Retired or Recast? Comment. **In** *Snape, R. H., ed.*, 1986, pp. 55–57. **[G: Selected Countries]**

McKee, Michael J. You Can't Always Get What You Want: Lessons from the Paris Convention Revision Exercise. **In** *Palmer, J., ed.*, 1986, pp. 265–72.

McKeown, Timothy J. The Limitations of "Structural" Theories of Commercial Policy. *Int. Organ.*, Winter 1986, *40*(1), pp. 43–64.

McKinney, Joseph A. and Rowley, Keith A. The Economic Impact of the Japanese Automobile Export Restraint. *Atlantic Econ. J.*, July 1986, *14*(2), pp. 9–15. **[G: Japan; U.S.]**

Meester, Gerrit. Agriculture in a Turbulent World Economy: Theoretical Developments: Discussion. **In** *Maunder, A. and Renborg, U., eds.*, 1986, pp. 633–35.

de Melo, Jaime. Comments [The Structure and Sample Results of the Michigan Computational Model of World Production and Trade] [Impacts of a 50 Percent Tariff Reduction in an Eight-Region Global Trade Model]. **In** *Srinivasan, T. N. and Whalley, J., eds.*, 1986, pp. 215–23. **[G: Global]**

Meltzer, Ronald I. The U.S. Renewal of the GSP: Implications for North–South Trade. *J. World Trade Law*, Sept.:Oct. 1986, *20*(5), pp. 507–25. **[G: U.S.]**

Méndez, José A. The Short-run Trade and Employment Effects of Steel Import Restraints. *J. World Trade Law*, Sept.:Oct. 1986, *20*(5), pp. 554–66. **[G: U.S.]**

Mercenier, Jean and Waelbroeck, Jean. Effect of a 50 Percent Tariff Cut in the Varuna Model. **In** *Srinivasan, T. N. and Whalley, J., eds.*, 1986, pp. 283–310. **[G: Global]**

Messerlin, Patrick A. Export-Credit Mercantilism à la Française. *World Econ.*, December 1986, *9*(4), pp. 385–408. **[G: France]**

Messerlin, Patrick A. The EC–U.S. Steel Trade Crisis: Comment. **In** *Tsoukalis, L., ed.*, 1986, pp. 36–41. **[G: U.S.; EEC]**

Michalski, Wolfgang. Costs and Benefits of Protection. *Aussenwirtschaft*, September 1986, *41*(2/3), pp. 187–99. **[G: OECD]**

Michalski, Wolfgang. Costs and Benefits of Protection. **In** *Hauser, H., ed. (II)*, 1986, pp. 25–37.

Miller, Debra Lynn. National Policies for Developing High Technology Industries: International Comparisons: Mexico. **In** *Rushing, F. W. and Brown, C. G., eds.*, 1986, pp. 173–99. **[G: Mexico]**

Mishra, S. N. Protection versus Underpricing of Agriculture in the Developing Countries: A Case Study of India. *Devel. Econ.*, June 1986, *24*(2), pp. 131–48. **[G: India]**

Mistral, Jacques. 125 ans de contrainte extérieure: l'expérience française. (125 Years of External Constraint: The French Case. With English summary.) *Écon. Soc.*, January 1986, *20*(1), pp. 91–115. **[G: France]**

Miyagiwa, Kaz F. A Reconsideration of the Welfare Economics of a Free-Trade Zone. *J. Int. Econ.*, November 1986, *21*(3/4), pp. 337–50.

Morse, Edward L. After the Fall: The Politics of Oil. *Foreign Aff.*, Spring 1986, *64*(4), pp. 792–811.

Mulloney, Peter. Unfair Trade and Foreign Subsidies: Steel "Chaos" in the United States. **In** *Gondolf, E. W.; Marcus, I. M. and Dougherty, J. P., eds.*, 1986, pp. 78–85. **[G: U.S.]**

Musgrave, Richard A. Effects of Business Taxes on International Commodity Flows. **In** *Musgrave, R. A., Vol. 1*, 1986, *1966*, pp. 209–21. **[G: France; U.K.; U.S.; W. Germany; Italy]**

Nagy, András. Open We Must! *Acta Oecon.*, 1986, *37*(3–4), pp. 219–39. **[G: Hungary]**

Nakatani, Iwao. Towards the New International Economic Order—The Role of Japan in the World Economy. *Hitotsubashi J. Econ.*, Spec. Iss. Oct. 1986, 27, pp. 121–32. **[G: Japan; U.S.]**

Naray, Peter. Hungarian Foreign Trade Reform. *J. World Trade Law*, May:June 1986, *20*(3), pp. 274–86. **[G: Hungary]**

Nau, Henry R. National Policies for High Technology Development and Trade: An International and Comparative Assessment. **In** *Rushing, F. W. and Brown, C. G., eds.*, 1986, pp. 9–29. **[G: India; Brazil; Mexico; S. Korea; Argentina]**

Nelson, Michael. Technology Transfer in the Mining Sector: Options for the Latin American Mining Organization (OLAMI). *CEPAL Rev.*, December 1986, (30), pp. 137–42. **[G: Latin America]**

Nicolaides, Phedon. Political Coalitions and Issues: A Contribution to the Political Economy of Induced Distortions. *Aussenwirtschaft*, December 1986, *41*(4), pp. 497–510.

Nielsen, Søren Bo. Handelsskatter i en råvareimporterende økonomi. (Trade Taxes in a Small

Open Economy. With English summary.) *Nationaløkon. Tidsskr.*, 1986, *124*(3), pp. 380–95.

Njenga, Frank X. Historical Background of the Evolution of the Exclusive Economic Zone and the Contribution of Africa. **In** *Pontecorvo, G., ed.*, 1986, pp. 125–57. **[G: Africa]**

Nogués, Julio J. Note sobre los casos de aranceles compensatorios de Estados Unidos en contra de México. (Note on United States Countervailing Duty Cases against Mexico. With English summary.) *Estud. Econ.*, July-Dec. 1986, *1*(2), pp. 337–55. **[G: U.S.; Mexico]**

Nogués, Julio J.; Olechowski, Andrzej and Winters, L. Alan. The Extent of Nontariff Barriers to Industrial Countries' Imports. *World Bank Econ. Rev.*, September 1986, *1*(1), pp. 181–99. **[G: OECD]**

Norall, Christopher. New Trends in Anti-dumping Practice in Brussels. *World Econ.*, March 1986, *9*(1), pp. 97–111. **[G: Global]**

Nusbaumer, Jacques. Les négociations internationales sur les services ou la quadrature du cercle. (With English summary.) *Revue Écon. Polit.*, Sept.-Oct. 1986, *96*(5), pp. 541–50.

O'Connell, Arturo A. La fiebre aftosa, el embargo sanitario norteamericano contra las importaciones de carne y el triángulo Argentina–Gran Bretaña–Estados Unidos en el Periodo entre las dos guerras mundiales. (With English summary.) *Desarrollo Econ.*, Apr.-June 1986, *26*(101), pp. 21–50. **[G: Argentina]**

Ohtsuka, Seiichiro. Japan's Invisible Barriers to Trade: Comment. **In** *Pugel, T. A., ed.*, 1986, pp. 47–54. **[G: U.S.; Japan]**

Oliveira, Joao do Carmo. Trade Policy, Market 'Distortions,' and Agriculture in the Process of Economic Development: Brazil, 1950–1974. *J. Devel. Econ.*, November 1986, *24*(1), pp. 91–109. **[G: Brazil]**

Ordover, Janusz A. and Willig, Robert D. Perspectives on Mergers and World Competition. **In** *Grieson, R. E., ed.*, 1986, pp. 201–18.

Ozawa, Terutomo. Japanese Policy toward Foreign Multinationals: Implications for Trade and Competitiveness. **In** *Pugel, T. A., ed.*, 1986, pp. 141–62. **[G: Japan]**

Panchamukhi, V. R. Complementarity and Economic Cooperation among Developing Countries (ECDC). **In** *Panchamukhi, V. R., et al.*, 1986, *1983*, pp. 15–24.

Pangestu, Mari and Boediono. The Structure and Causes of Manufacturing Sector Protection in Indonesia. **In** *Findlay, C. and Garnaut, R., eds.*, 1986, pp. 1–47. **[G: Indonesia]**

Parmenter, B. R. What Does Manufacturing Protection Cost Farmers? A Review of Some Recent Australian Contributions. *Australian J. Agr. Econ.*, August/December 1986, *30*(2–3), pp. 118–27. **[G: Australia]**

Patrick, Hugh. Japanese High Technology Industrial Policy in Comparative Context. **In** *Patrick, H., ed.*, 1986, pp. 3–33. **[G: Japan]**

Patterson, Eliza R. Improving GATT Rules for Nonmarket Economies. *J. World Trade Law*, Mar.:Apr. 1986, *20*(2), pp. 185–205. **[G: U.S.S.R.; China; E. Europe]**

Patterson, Gardner. The Role of Economists in the GATT Secretariat. **In** *Coats, A. W., ed.*, 1986, pp. 91–97.

Patterson, Gardner and Patterson, Eliza R. Importance of a GATT Review in the New Negotiations. *World Econ.*, June 1986, *9*(2), pp. 153–69. **[G: Global]**

Pelkmans, Jacques. The Bickering Bigemony: GATT as an Instrument in Atlantic Trade Policy. **In** *Tsoukalis, L., ed.*, 1986, pp. 83–106. **[G: U.S.; EEC]**

Perlman, Mark. Sustained Recovery and Trade Liberalization: How the Transfer Problem Can Be Solved: Comment. **In** *Giersch, H., ed.*, 1986, pp. 149–51.

Petersmann, Ernst-Ulrich. Trade Policy as a Constitutional Problem. On the "Domestic Policy Functions" of International Trade Rules. *Aussenwirtschaft*, September 1986, *41*(2/3), pp. 405–39. **[G: Global]**

Petersmann, Ernst-Ulrich. Trade Policy as a Constitutional Problem. On the "Domestic Policy Functions" of International Trade Rules. **In** *Hauser, H., ed. (II)*, 1986, pp. 243–77.

Petersmann, Ernst-Ulrich. Trade Restrictions for Balance-of-Payments Purposes and the GATT: Strengthening the Soft International Law of Balance-of-Payments Adjustment Measures. **In** *Dicke, D. C., ed.*, 1986, pp. 181–212.

Petit, Michel. Agricultural Policies and World Trade: The U.S. and the European Community at Bay: Comment. **In** *Tsoukalis, L., ed.*, 1986, pp. 71–76. **[G: U.S.; EEC]**

Petri, Peter. Comments [The Structure and Sample Results of the Michigan Computational Model of World Production and Trade] [Impacts of a 50 Percent Tariff Reduction in an Eight-Region Global Trade Model]. **In** *Srinivasan, T. N. and Whalley, J., eds.*, 1986, pp. 225–28. **[G: Global]**

Petříček, Václav. Open System of Economic Instruments in Foreign Trade. *Czech. Econ. Digest.*, May 1986, (3), pp. 47–54. **[G: Czechoslovakia]**

Pfaller, Alfred. The Changing North–South Division of Labour: Promises, Threats and EC Policy Options. *Kyklos*, 1986, *39*(1), pp. 85–108. **[G: Global]**

Phegan, Colin. The Interplay of Law and Economics in International Trade Regulation: Comment. **In** *Snape, R. H., ed.*, 1986, pp. 218–21.

Phillips, David R. Special Economic Zones in China's Modernization: Changing Policies and Changing Fortunes. *Nat. Westminster Bank Quart. Rev.*, February 1986, pp. 37–49. **[G: China]**

Pincus, J. J. Why Have U.S. Tariffs Fallen since 1930? **In** *Snape, R. H., ed.*, 1986, pp. 238–53. **[G: U.S.]**

Pinder, John. The Bickering Bigemony: GATT as an Instrument in Atlantic Trade Policy: Comment. **In** *Tsoukalis, L., ed.*, 1986, pp. 117–18. **[G: U.S.; EEC]**

Pomfret, Richard. MFN Tariff Reductions and Developing Country Trade Benefits under the

GSP: A Comment. *Econ. J.*, June 1986, *96*(382), pp. 534–36.

Pomfret, Richard. The Effects of Trade Preferences for Developing Countries. *Southern Econ. J.*, July 1986, *53*(1), pp. 18–26. [G: LDCs]

Pomfret, Richard. The Theory of Preferential Trading Arrangements. *Weltwirtsch. Arch.*, 1986, *122*(3), pp. 439–65.

Pomfret, Richard. The Trade-Diverting Bias of Preferential Trading Arrangements. *J. Common Market Stud.*, December 1986, *25*(2), pp. 109–17. [G: EEC]

Pope, David H. Protection and Australian Manufacturers' International Competitiveness, 1901–1930. *Australian Econ. Hist. Rev.*, March 1986, *26*(1), pp. 21–39. [G: Australia]

Prebisch, Raúl. Notes on Trade from the Standpoint of the Periphery. *CEPAL Rev.*, April 1986, (28), pp. 203–14.

Preeg, Ernest H. Implications for U.S. Trade and Aid Policy. **In** *Preeg, E. H. and Bendahmane, D. B., eds.*, 1986, pp. 109–14. [G: U.S.]

Preeg, Ernest H. The New Economic Diplomacy: An Overview. **In** *Preeg, E. H. and Bendahmane, D. B., eds.*, 1986, pp. v–xiii.

Prieto, Francisco Javier. Services: A Disquieting Link between Latin America and the World Economy. *CEPAL Rev.*, December 1986, (30), pp. 17–36.

Pugel, Thomas A. Fragile Interdependence: Introduction. **In** *Pugel, T. A., ed.*, 1986, pp. 1–18. [G: U.S.; Japan]

Quandt, William B. Two Kinds of Threats to U.S. Energy Supplies. **In** *Preeg, E. H. and Bendahmane, D. B., eds.*, 1986, pp. 27–32. [G: U.S.; Middle East]

Ránki, Gy. and Tomaszewski, Jerzy. The Role of the State in Industry, Banking and Trade. **In** *Kaser, M. C. and Radice, E. A., eds.*, 1986, pp. 3–48. [G: E. Europe]

Rapp, William V. Japan's Invisible Barriers to Trade. **In** *Pugel, T. A., ed.*, 1986, pp. 21–45. [G: Japan; U.S.]

Rassekh, Farhad. Employment Effects of the Steel Trigger Price Mechanism on the Steel and Motor Vehicle Industries. *Atlantic Econ. J.*, March 1986, *14*(1), pp. 39–49. [G: U.S.]

Ray, Anandarup. Trade and Pricing Policies in World Agriculture. *Finance Develop.*, September 1986, *23*(3), pp. 2–5. [G: Global]

Ray, John E. The OECD 'Consensus' on Export Credits. *World Econ.*, September 1986, *9*(3), pp. 295–309. [G: OECD]

Richardson, J. David. The New Political Economy of Trade Policy. **In** *Krugman, P. R., ed.*, 1986, pp. 257–82. [G: U.S.]

Rieger, Hans Christoph. Game Theory and the Analysis of Protectionist Trends. *World Econ.*, June 1986, *9*(2), pp. 171–92. [G: OECD]

Robertson, Max. The South Pacific Regional Trade and Economic Cooperation Agreement: A Critique. **In** *Cole, R. V. and Parry, T. G., eds.*, 1986, pp. 147–75. [G: Australia; S. Pacific]

Rodríguez Mendoza, Miguel. Latin America and the U.S. Trade and Tariff Act. *J. World Trade Law*, Jan.:Feb. 1986, *20*(1), pp. 47–60. [G: U.S.; Latin America]

Roessler, Frieder. Competition and Trade Policies. The Constitutional Function of International Economic Law: Discussion to Session IV. *Aussenwirtschaft*, September 1986, *41*(2/3), pp. 467–74. [G: Global]

Rooth, T. J. T. Tariffs and Trade Bargaining: Anglo–Scandinavian Economic Relations in the 1930s. *Scand. Econ. Hist. Rev.*, 1986, *34*(1), pp. 54–71. [G: U.K.; Denmark; Finland; Norway; Sweden]

Rosenthal, Douglas E. The Extraterritoriality Issue in the Transatlantic Context: A Question of Law or Diplomacy? Comment. **In** *Tsoukalis, L., ed.*, 1986, pp. 149–52. [G: U.S.; EEC]

Ross, David A. Ocean Science: Its Place in the New Order of the Oceans. **In** *Pontecorvo, G., ed.*, 1986, pp. 65–84.

Rowley, Charles K. and Tollison, Robert D. Rent-Seeking and Trade Protection. *Aussenwirtschaft*, September 1986, *41*(2/3), pp. 303–28.

Rugman, Alan M. U.S. Protectionism and Canadian Trade Policy. *J. World Trade Law*, July: Aug. 1986, *20*(4), pp. 363–80. [G: U.S.; Canada]

Salgó, István. Economic Mechanism and Foreign Trade Organization in Hungary. *Acta Oecon.*, 1986, *36*(3–4), pp. 271–87. [G: Hungary]

Sampson, Gary P. Market Disturbances and the Multifibre Arrangement. **In** *Snape, R. H., ed.*, 1986, pp. 61–87.

Samuelson, Paul A. Analytics of Free-Trade or Protectionist Response by America to Japan's Growth Spurt. **In** *Samuelson, P. A.*, 1986, *1985*, pp. 480–95. [G: U.S.; Japan]

Samuelson, Paul A. Justice to the Australians. **In** *Samuelson, P. A.*, 1986, *1981*, pp. 468–69.

Samuelson, Paul A. Summing Up on the Australian Case for Protection. **In** *Samuelson, P. A.*, 1986, *1981*, pp. 454–67. [G: Australia]

Samuelson, Paul A. To Protect Manufacturing? **In** *Samuelson, P. A.*, 1986, *1981*, pp. 510–17.

Sanderson, Fred H. The Common Agricultural Policy and World Food Trade: CAP Update. **In** *Browne, W. P. and Hadwiger, D. F., eds.*, 1986, pp. 58–61. [G: EEC]

Sawyer, W. Charles and Sprinkle, Richard L. U.S.–Israel Free Trade Area: Trade Expansion Effects of the Agreement. *J. World Trade Law*, Sept.:Oct. 1986, *20*(5), pp. 526–39. [G: U.S.; Israel]

Saxonhouse, Gary R. Japan's Intractable Trade Surpluses in a New Era. *World Econ.*, September 1986, *9*(3), pp. 239–58. [G: Japan; U.S.]

Saxonhouse, Gary R. The National Security Clause of the Trade Expansion Act of 1962: Import Competition and the Machine Tool Industry. **In** *Saxonhouse, G. R. and Yamamura, K., eds.*, 1986, pp. 218–37. [G: U.S.]

Sazanami, Yoko. Some Policy Implications of Intra-industry Trade for Japan. **In** *Greenaway, D. and Tharakan, P. K. M., eds.*, 1986, pp. 174–90. [G: Selected Countries; Japan]

Schachter, Oscar. Concepts and Realities in the New Law of the Sea. **In** *Pontecorvo, G., ed.*, 1986, pp. 29–59.

Schatán, Claudia. Destino de las importaciones y política comercial en México (1975–1980). (Import Destination and Trade Policy in Mexico. With English summary.) *Estud. Econ.*, July-Dec. 1986, *1* (2), pp. 255–80. **[G: Mexico]**

Schmitz, Andrew; Sigurdson, Dale and Doering, Otto. Domestic Farm Policy and the Gains from Trade. *Amer. J. Agr. Econ.*, November 1986, *68* (4), pp. 820–27. **[G: U.S.]**

Schmitz, Peter M. Markets and Trade: Discussion. **In** *Maunder, A. and Renborg, U., eds.*, 1986, pp. 578–80.

Scholsem, Jean-Claude. The Extraterritoriality Issue in the Transatlantic Context: A Question of Law or Diplomacy? Comment. **In** *Tsoukalis, L., ed.*, 1986, pp. 158–62. **[G: U.S.; EEC]**

Schoo, E. M. European Community's Trade Relations with Developing Countries. *World Econ.*, September 1986, *9* (3), pp. 313–18. **[G: EEC; LDCs]**

Schott, Jeffrey J. and Mazza, Jacqueline. Trade in Services and Developing Countries. *J. World Trade Law*, May:June 1986, *20* (3), pp. 253–73. **[G: Global]**

Schwartz, Anna J. Sustained Recovery and Trade Liberalization: How the Transfer Problem Can Be Solved. **In** *Giersch, H., ed.*, 1986, pp. 133–44.

Sennholz, Hans. Protectionism and Unemployment. *Rivista Int. Sci. Econ. Com.*, March 1986, *33* (3), pp. 247–60. **[G: U.S.; Japan]**

Senti, Richard. Erscheinungsformen und Ursachen des neuen Protektionismus im Aussenhandel. (Forms and Causes of the New Protectionism. With English summary.) **In** *Eucken, W. and Böhm, F., eds.*, 1986, pp. 219–34.

Shearer, Ronald A. The New Face of Canadian Mercantilism: The Macdonald Commission and the Case for Free Trade. *Can. Public Policy*, Supp. February 1986, *12*, pp. 51–58. **[G: Canada]**

Shi, Xiulin. Is the Economy of China's Special Economic Zones State Capitalist in Nature? *Chinese Econ. Stud.*, Winter 1985-86, *19* (2), pp. 25–40. **[G: China]**

Short, Cameron. Reducing the Cost of the Dairy Program. *Can. J. Agr. Econ.*, November 1986, *34* (3), pp. 379–97. **[G: Canada]**

Siggel, Eckhard. Protection, Distortions and Investment Incentives in Zaire: A Quantitative Analysis. *J. Devel. Econ.*, July-Aug. 1986, *22* (2), pp. 295–319. **[G: Zaire]**

Simons, William B. Soviet Foreign Trade: Economic, Legal, and Political Aspects. **In** *Ioffe, O. S. and Janis, M. W., eds.*, 1986, pp. 243–81. **[G: U.S.S.R.]**

Singh, Ajit. The Long-term Structural Disequilibrium of the U.K. Economy: Employment, Trade, and Import Controls. **In** *Sjöstedt, G. and Sundelius, B., eds.*, 1986, pp. 51–80. **[G: U.K.]**

Sklair, Leslie. Free Zones, Development and the New International Division of Labour: Review Article. *J. Devel. Stud.*, July 1986, *22* (4), pp. 753–59. **[G: LDCs]**

Smith, Murray G. Implications for Canadian Commercial Policy of Negotiating a Free-Trade Area with the United States. **In** *C. D. Howe Institute*, 1986, pp. 101–22. **[G: Canada; U.S.]**

Smith, Ron. Britain and the International State Apparatus. **In** *Nolan, P. and Paine, S., eds.*, 1986, pp. 103–14. **[G: U.K.]**

Snape, Richard H. Issues in World Trade Policy: GATT at the Crossroads. **In** *Snape, R. H., ed.*, 1986, pp. 3–14.

Spencer, Barbara J. What Should Trade Policy Target? **In** *Krugman, P. R., ed.*, 1986, pp. 69–89.

Spencer, John E. Trade Liberalization through Tariff Cuts and the European Economic Community: A General Equilibrium Evaluation. **In** *Srinivasan, T. N. and Whalley, J., eds.*, 1986, pp. 125–44. **[G: EEC]**

Spinanger, Dean and Zietz, Joachim. Managing Trade but Mangling the Consumer: Reflections on the EEC's and West Germany's Experience with the Multifiber Arrangement. *Aussenwirtschaft*, December 1986, *41* (4), pp. 511–31. **[G: EEC]**

Steger, Debra. The Impact of U.S. Trade Laws on Canadian Economic Policies. **In** *C. D. Howe Institute*, 1986, pp. 73–100. **[G: Canada; U.S.]**

Stern, Paula and Wechsler, Andrew. Escape Clause Relief and Recessions: An Economic and Legal Look at Section 201. **In** *Saxonhouse, G. R. and Yamamura, K., eds.*, 1986, pp. 195–217. **[G: U.S.]**

Stohl, Michael. Domestic and International Interests and Consequences in U.S. Foreign Economic Policy. **In** *Onwuka, R. I. and Aluko, O., eds.*, 1986, pp. 229–56. **[G: U.S.]**

Su, Yanhan. A Brief Discussion of the Economic Nature of China's Special Economic Zones. *Chinese Econ. Stud.*, Winter 1985-86, *19* (2), pp. 41–58. **[G: China]**

Suarez, Ricardo Acosta. State Trading in International Markets: A Multinational Strategy for Developing Countries. **In** *Khan, K. M., ed.*, 1986, pp. 130–48. **[G: LDCs]**

Sutherland, William Morrison. Microstates and Unequal Trade in the South Pacific: The Sparteca Agreement of 1980. *J. World Trade Law*, May:June 1986, *20* (3), pp. 313–28. **[G: Oceania]**

Tan, Norma A. The Structure and Causes of Manufacturing Sector Protection in the Philippines. **In** *Findlay, C. and Garnaut, R., eds.*, 1986, pp. 48–76. **[G: Philippines]**

Taniura, Taeko. Economic Development Effects of an Integrated Iron and Steel Works: A Case Study of Minas Gerais Steel in Brazil. *Devel. Econ.*, June 1986, *24* (2), pp. 169–93. **[G: Brazil]**

Tay, Boon Nga. The Structure and Causes of Manufacturing Sector Protection in Singapore. **In**

Findlay, C. and Garnaut, R., eds., 1986, pp. 135–58. **[G: Singapore]**

Tecson, Gwendolyn R. Export Markets for Philippine Diversified Agriculture and Labor-Intensive Industries. *Philippine Rev. Econ. Bus.*, Mar./June 1986, *23*(1/2), pp. 1–56. **[G: Philippines]**

Teitel, Simón and Thoumi, Francisco E. From Import Substitution to Exports: The Manufacturing Exports Experience of Argentina and Brazil. *Econ. Develop. Cult. Change*, April 1986, *34*(3), pp. 455–90. **[G: Brazil; Argentina]**

Terasawa, Yoshio. Opening Japanese Financial Markets: What Has Changed, What Will Change? Comment. **In** *Pugel, T. A., ed.*, 1986, pp. 137–39. **[G: Japan]**

Theodoropoulos, Christos. NIEO and African Relations with the Centrally-Planned Economies. **In** *Onwuka, R. I. and Aluko, O., eds.*, 1986, pp. 209–28. **[G: Africa; CMEA]**

Thomson, Graeme. Market Disturbances and the Multifibre Arrangement: Comment. **In** *Snape, R. H., ed.*, 1986, pp. 88–92.

Tsoukalis, Loukas. Euro–American Relations and Global Economic Interdependence. **In** *Tsoukalis, L., ed.*, 1986, pp. 1–16. **[G: EEC; U.S.]**

Turner, J. Michael. New Perspectives on African–Latin American Relations in the 1980s. **In** *Onwuka, R. I. and Aluko, O., eds.*, 1986, pp. 187–208. **[G: Brazil; Africa]**

Tyers, Rodney and Anderson, Kym. The Price, Trade and Welfare Effects of Agricultural Protection. **In** *Anderson, K. and Hayami, Y.*, 1986, pp. 50–62. **[G: U.S.; Europe; E. Asia]**

Utton, Michael. Developments in British Industrial and Competition Policies. **In** *Hall, G., ed.*, 1986, pp. 59–83. **[G: U.K.]**

Valdés, Alberto. Exchange Rates and Trade Policy: Help or Hindrance to Agricultural Growth? **In** *Maunder, A. and Renborg, U., eds.*, 1986, pp. 624–33. **[G: Peru; LDCs]**

Valkenier, Elizabeth Kridl. The USSR and the Third World: Economic Dilemmas. **In** *Laird, R. F. and Hoffmann, E. P., eds.*, 1986, pp. 731–57. **[G: LDCs; U.S.S.R.]**

Vamplew, Wray. Malthus and the Corn Laws. **In** *Turner, M., ed.*, 1986, pp. 129–39. **[G: U.K.]**

Vogel, Ezra F. Observations on U.S.–Japan Relations: Unwritten Letters, Unspoken Words. **In** *Finn, R. B., ed.*, 1986, pp. 77–84. **[G: U.S.; Japan]**

Vogel, Ezra F. Pax Nipponica? *Foreign Aff.*, Spring 1986, *64*(4), pp. 752–67. **[G: Japan]**

Volcker, Paul A. Statement to the U.S. House Subcommittee on Trade, Committee on Ways and Means, September 24, 1986. *Fed. Res. Bull.*, November 1986, *72*(11), pp. 773–79. **[G: U.S.]**

Waelbroeck, Jean. Rent-Seeking and Trade Policy: An Industry Approach: Comment. **In** *Balassa, B. and Giersch, H., eds.*, 1986, pp. 444–47.

Wallace, Helen. Bilateral, Trilateral and Multilateral Negotiations in the European Community. **In** *Morgan, R. and Bray, C., eds.*, 1986, pp. 156–74. **[G: EEC]**

Wang, Jici and Bradbury, John H. The Changing Industrial Geography of the Chinese Special Economic Zones. *Econ. Geogr.*, October 1986, *62*(4), pp. 307–20. **[G: China]**

Wang, Muheng and Chen, Yongshan. On the Nature of Asian Export Processing Zones and China's Special Economic Zones. *Chinese Econ. Stud.*, Winter 1985-86, *19*(2), pp. 8–24. **[G: Asia; China]**

Warr, Peter G. Australian Protection and the ASEAN Countries. **In** *Findlay, C. and Garnaut, R., eds.*, 1986, pp. 248–63. **[G: ASEAN; Australia]**

Warr, Peter G. and Parmenter, B. R. Protection through Government Procurement. **In** *Snape, R. H., ed.*, 1986, pp. 175–90. **[G: Australia]**

Watrin, Christian. Japan, Trade Partner of the European Community and the Federal Republic of Germany. **In** *Hax, H.; Kraus, W. and Tsuchiya, K., eds.*, 1986, pp. 15–28. **[G: Japan; EEC]**

Weck-Hannemann, Hannelore. The Politics of Protectionism: Discussion to Section II. *Aussenwirtschaft*, September 1986, *41*(2/3), pp. 351–58.

Weinstein, Michael M. Industrial Planning and Economic Policy-Making: Lessons from the 1930s. **In** *[Tarshis, L.]*, 1986, pp. 135–57. **[G: U.S.]**

Weintraub, Sidney. A Note on Trade Discrimination. *Rivista Int. Sci. Econ. Com.*, April 1986, *33*(4), pp. 353–70. **[G: U.S.]**

Weiss, John. Japan's Post-War Protection Policy: Some Implications for Less Developed Countries. *J. Devel. Stud.*, January 1986, *22*(2), pp. 385–406. **[G: Japan]**

Wendt, E. Allan. Oil Products: Prospects for an Open Trading Regime. **In** *El Mallakh, R., ed.*, 1986, pp. 123–27.

Whalley, John. Impacts of a 50 Percent Tariff Reduction in an Eight-Region Global Trade Model. **In** *Srinivasan, T. N. and Whalley, J., eds.*, 1986, pp. 189–214. **[G: Global]**

Whalley, John. International Aspects of Copyright Legislation in Canada: Economic Analysis of Policy Options. **In** *Palmer, J., ed.*, 1986, pp. 273–83. **[G: Canada]**

White, Bob and Vittas, Dimitri. Barriers in International Banking. *Lloyds Bank Rev.*, July 1986, (161), pp. 19–31. **[G: OECD]**

Wigle, Randall. General Equilibrium Trade Policy Modeling: Summary of the Panel and Floor Discussion. **In** *Srinivasan, T. N. and Whalley, J., eds.*, 1986, pp. 323–54. **[G: Selected Countries]**

Wijkman, Per Magnus. Informal Systemic Change in the GATT. *World Econ.*, March 1986, *9*(1), pp. 37–49. **[G: Global]**

Winpisinger, William. Surplus Labor: An Appeal for an International Trade Program. **In** *Gondolf, E. W.; Marcus, I. M. and Dougherty, J. P., eds.*, 1986, pp. 111–21. **[G: U.S.]**

Wolf, Martin. Fiddling while the GATT Burns.

World Econ., March 1986, 9(1), pp. 1–18. [G: Global]

Wolf, Martin. Industrial and Trade Policy: Discussion to Session I. *Aussenwirtschaft*, September 1986, *41*(2/3), pp. 259–69.

Wolter, Frank. The Bickering Bigemony: GATT as an Instrument in Atlantic Trade Policy: Comment. **In** *Tsoukalis, L., ed.*, 1986, pp. 119–23. [G: U.S.; EEC]

Wong, Kar-yiu. International Factor Movements, Repatriation and Welfare. *J. Int. Econ.*, November 1986, *21*(3/4), pp. 327–35.

Wonnacott, R. J. On the Employment Effects of Free Trade with the United States. *Can. Public Policy*, March 1986, *12*(1), pp. 258–63. [G: Canada; U.S.]

Wooton, Ian. Comments [Market Structure and Trade Liberalization: A General Equilibrium Assessment] [Short-run Impact of Trade Liberalization Measures on the Economy of Bangladesh: Exercises in Comparative Statics for the Year 1977]. **In** *Srinivasan, T. N. and Whalley, J., eds.*, 1986, pp. 319–21. [G: Canada; Bangladesh]

Yamamura, Kozo. Caveat Emptor: The Industrial Policy of Japan. **In** *Krugman, P. R., ed.*, 1986, pp. 169–209. [G: Japan]

Yamamura, Kozo and Vandenberg, Jan. Japan's Rapid-Growth Policy on Trial: The Television Case. **In** *Saxonhouse, G. R. and Yamamura, K., eds.*, 1986, pp. 238–83. [G: U.S.; Japan]

Yannopoulos, George N. European Development Cooperation Policies and the New Round of Multilateral Trade Negotiations. *Greek Econ. Rev.*, June 1986, *8*(1), pp. 66–78. [G: Global]

Yannopoulos, George N. Patterns of Response to EC Tariff Preferences: An Empirical Investigation of Selected Non-ACP Associates. *J. Common Market Stud.*, September 1986, *25*(1), pp. 15–30. [G: Mediterranean; EEC]

Yannopoulos, George N. The Impact of the European Economic Community on East–West Trade in Europe. *Comp. Econ. Stud.*, Spring 1986, *28*(1), pp. 75–85. [G: EEC; CMEA]

Yeh, Yeong-Her. Export Subsidies vs. Production Subsidies. *Atlantic Econ. J.*, July 1986, *14*(2), pp. 71–75.

Yoshitomi, Masaru. Sustained Recovery and Trade Liberalization: How the Transfer Problem Can Be Solved: Comment. **In** *Giersch, H., ed.*, 1986, pp. 145–48.

Young, Michael K. Japan's Antitrust Policy: Impact on Import Competition: Comment. **In** *Pugel, T. A., ed.*, 1986, pp. 77–90. [G: U.S.; Japan]

Young, Soogil. A Global Outlook from the Old Hermit Kingdom. *World Econ.*, March 1986, *9*(1), pp. 51–64. [G: S. Korea]

Zietz, Joachim. Trade Liberalization in Cereals: Blessing or Curse to Developing Countries? *J. Econ. Devel.*, December 1986, *11*(2), pp. 103–22. [G: LDCs]

Zietz, Joachim and Valdés, Alberto. The Potential Benefits to LDCs of Trade Liberalization in Beef and Sugar by Industrialized Countries. *Weltwirtsch. Arch.*, 1986, *122*(1), pp. 93–112. [G: Global]

Zinn, Eberhard and Kotz, Hans-Helmut. Exportversicherung, Exportfinanzierung und internationaler Wettbewerb. (With English summary.) *Z. Betriebswirtshaft*, November 1986, *56*(11), pp. 1077–94. [G: W. Germany]

Zou, Erkang. Special Economic Zone Typifies Open Policy. *Chinese Econ. Stud.*, Winter 1985-86, *19*(2), pp. 79–85. [G: China]

423 Economic Integration

4230 General

Cooper, Richard N. Worldwide Regional Integration: Is There an Optimal Size of the Integrated Area? **In** *Cooper, R. N.*, 1986, *1976*, pp. 123–36.

Feinberg, Richard E. Between Two Worlds: The World Bank's Next Decade: Overview: An Open Letter to the World Bank's New President. **In** *Feinberg, R. E., et al.*, 1986, pp. 3–30.

Kanno, Ryohei. U.S.–Japan Capital Interaction: Implications of Euroyen and Direct Investment. **In** *Finn, R. B., ed.*, 1986, pp. 173–83. [G: U.S.; Japan; Selected Countries]

4232 Theory of Economic Integration

Bej, Emil. The CMEA's Attempts at Integration: A Survey of Theory and Institutional Organization. **In** *Altmann, F.-L., ed.*, 1986, pp. 37–57. [G: CMEA]

Bruni, Franco and Monti, Mario. Protezionismo valutario e integrazione internazionale. (Foreign Exchange Controls and International Economic Integration. With English summary.) *Rivista Int. Sci. Econ. Com.*, September 1986, *33*(9), pp. 887–900.

Cooper, Richard N. Economic Interdependence and Coordination of Economic Policies. **In** *Cooper, R. N.*, 1986, *1985*, pp. 289–331.

Grinols, Earl L. Foreign Investment and Economic Growth: Characterization of a Second-Best Policy for Welfare Gains. *J. Int. Econ.*, August 1986, *21*(1/2), pp. 165–71.

Kemp, Murray C. and Wan, Henry Y., Jr. The Comparison of Second-Best Equilibria: The Case of Customs Unions. *J. Econ. (Z. Nationalökon.)*, Supplementum 5, 1986, pp. 161–67.

Marston, Richard C. The Effects of Coordinated Foreign Exchange Intervention in an Exchange-Rate Union. *Econ. Stud. Quart.*, June 1986, *37*(2), pp. 151–64.

Panchamukhi, V. R. Complementarity and Economic Cooperation among Developing Countries (ECDC). **In** *Panchamukhi, V. R., et al.*, 1986, *1983*, pp. 15–24.

Pomfret, Richard. The Theory of Preferential Trading Arrangements. *Weltwirtsch. Arch.*, 1986, *122*(3), pp. 439–65.

Rieber, William J. Domestic Monopoly and Customs Union Formation. *Amer. Econ.*, Spring 1986, *30*(1), pp. 32–35.

Wooton, Ian. Preferential Trading Agreements: An Investigation. *J. Int. Econ.*, August 1986, *21*(1/2), pp. 81–97.

4233 Economic Integration: Policy and Empirical Studies

von Alvensleben, Reimar; Behr, Hans-Christoph and Jahn, Hans-Harald. Fruits and Vegetables in the European Community. In *Bale, M. D., ed.*, 1986, pp. 5–93. **[G: EEC]**

Baldinelli, Elvio. Turning Page in Relations between Latin America and the European Communities. *CEPAL Rev.*, December 1986, (30), pp. 87–96. **[G: EEC; Latin America]**

Barichello, Richard R. and Warley, T. K. Agriculture and Negotiation of a Free-Trade Area: Issues in Policy Harmonization. In *C. D. Howe Institute*, 1986, pp. 135–64. **[G: Canada; U.S.]**

Bayne, Nicholas. International Economic Policy Coordination. In *Morgan, R. and Bray, C., eds.*, 1986, pp. 175–83. **[G: France; U.K.; W. Germany]**

Bej, Emil. The CMEA's Attempts at Integration: A Survey of Theory and Institutional Organization. In *Altmann, F.-L., ed.*, 1986, pp. 37–57. **[G: CMEA]**

Berend, Iván T. The Historical Evolution of Eastern Europe as a Region. In *Comisso, E. and Tyson, L., eds.*, 1986, pp. 153–70. **[G: E. Europe]**

von Beyme, Klaus. Economic Relations as an Instrument of Soviet Hegemony over Eastern Europe? In *Höhmann, H.-H.; Nove, A. and Vogel, H., eds.*, 1986, pp. 214–31. **[G: CMEA]**

Bollard, Alan. The Economic Relations Agreement between Australia and New Zealand: A Tentative Appraisal. *J. Common Market Stud.*, December 1986, *25*(2), pp. 89–107. **[G: Australia; New Zealand]**

Brean, Donald J. S. Fiscal Policy Harmonization and Negotiation of a Free-Trade Area. In *C. D. Howe Institute*, 1986, pp. 43–71. **[G: Canada; U.S.]**

Brewin, Christopher and McAllister, Richard. Annual Review of the Activities of the European Communities in 1985. *J. Common Market Stud.*, June 1986, *24*(4), pp. 313–45. **[G: EEC]**

Butler, W. E. COMECON and Economic Law. In *Ioffe, O. S. and Janis, M. W., eds.*, 1986, pp. 283–97. **[G: CMEA]**

Butt Philip, Alan. Europe's Industrial Policies: An Overview. In *Hall, G., ed.*, 1986, pp. 1–20. **[G: EEC]**

Calvet, J. Le développement de l'écu privé pré figure-t-il un système productif européen? (Is the Development of Private Use of the E.C.U. a Prefiguration of a European Productive System? With English summary.) *Écon. Soc.*, May 1986, *20*(5), pp. 101–24. **[G: W. Europe]**

Camargo Barros, Geraldo. Growing Interdependencies and Uncertainties: Discussion. In *Maunder, A. and Renborg, U., eds.*, 1986, pp. 122–23.

Comisso, Ellen. State Structures, Political Processes, and Collective Choice in CMEA States. In *Comisso, E. and Tyson, L., eds.*, 1986, pp. 19–62. **[G: CMEA]**

Corado, Cristina and de Melo, Jaime. An Ex-ante Model for Estimating the Impact on Trade Flows of a Country's Joining a Customs Union. *J. Devel. Econ.*, November 1986, *24*(1), pp. 153–66. **[G: Portugal]**

Cornelisse, Peter A. and Akin, Bahadir. An Economic Appraisal of the Association Agreement between the European Community and Turkey. *METU*, 1986, *13*(3–4), pp. 259–73. **[G: EEC; Turkey]**

Csaba, Lászlá. CMEA and East–West Trade. *Comp. Econ. Stud.*, Fall 1986, *28*(3), pp. 43–57. **[G: CMEA]**

De Visscher, Guy. Growing Interdependencies and Uncertainties: Discussion. In *Maunder, A. and Renborg, U., eds.*, 1986, pp. 123–25.

Desai, Padma. Is the Soviet Union Subsidizing Eastern Europe? *Europ. Econ. Rev.*, February 1986, *30*(1), pp. 107–16. **[G: CMEA]**

Deubner, Christian. Potentials and Forms of Increasing International Regionalism: The Role of Japan as a Dominant Regional Power. In *Sjöstedt, G. and Sundelius, B., eds.*, 1986, pp. 223–61. **[G: Japan; ASEAN]**

Dietz, Raimund. Soviet Foregone Gains in Trade with the CMEA Six: A Reappraisal. *Comp. Econ. Stud.*, Summer 1986, *28*(2), pp. 69–94. **[G: CMEA]**

Dornbusch, Rudiger, et al. Macroeconomic Prospects and Policies for the European Community. In *Blanchard, O.; Dornbusch, R. and Layard, R., eds.*, 1986, pp. 1–32. **[G: EEC]**

Eriksson, Bo Göran. EFTA och EG: aktuella utvecklingslinjer i europeisk integration. (EFTA and EC: Current Trends in the Development of European Integration. With English summary.) *Ekon. Samfundets Tidskr.*, 1986, *39*(4), pp. 201–16. **[G: EEC; Finland]**

Esiemokhai, Emma O. The Role of the Nigerian Chambers of Commerce, Industry, Mines and Agriculture in the Establishment of ECOWAS. In *Onwuka, R. I. and Aluko, O., eds.*, 1986, pp. 257–71. **[G: W. Africa]**

Fairburn, J. A.; Kay, John A. and Sharpe, T. A. E. The Economics of Article 86. In *Hall, G., ed.*, 1986, pp. 21–43. **[G: EEC]**

Fink, Gerhard. Settlement System and Hard Currency Trade in the CMEA. *Soviet E. Europ. Foreign Trade*, Spring 1986, *22*(1), pp. 68–82. **[G: CMEA]**

Foroutan, Faezeh. Determinants of European Community Imports of Steel Mill Products. *Appl. Econ.*, August 1986, *18*(8), pp. 863–73. **[G: EEC]**

Georgakopoulos, Theodore A. Greece in the EC: Inter-country Income Transfers. *J. Common Market Stud.*, December 1986, *25*(2), pp. 119–32. **[G: Greece; EEC]**

Gernant, Paul L. Economic Integration: Trade Creation Effects over Time. *Atlantic Econ. J.*, July 1986, *14*(2), pp. 85. **[G: U.S.; Canada]**

Globerman, Steven. Potential Implications of

Canadian–U.S. Trade Negotiations for Canadian Cultural Support Policies. **In** *C. D. Howe Institute*, 1986, pp. 123–34. **[G: Canada; U.S.]**

Grais, Wafik. Comments [A General Equilibrium Analysis of Tariff Reductions] [Trade Liberalization through Tariff Cuts and the European Economic Community: A General Equilibrium Evaluation]. **In** *Srinivasan, T. N. and Whalley, J., eds.*, 1986, pp. 145–48. **[G: EEC]**

Grinberg, R. and Liubskii, M. Prices and Currency Relations in the Cooperation of CMEA Countries. *Prob. Econ.*, May 1986, *29*(1), pp. 17–32. **[G: CMEA]**

Hloch, Alois. Expansion of Economic Cooperation with the Socialist Countries in the 8th Five-Year Plan Period. *Czech. Econ. Digest.*, June 1986, (5), pp. 16–22. **[G: CMEA]**

Holsti, Kal J. Politics in Command: Foreign Trade as National Security Policy. *Int. Organ.*, Summer 1986, *40*(3), pp. 643–71. **[G: Japan; Finland]**

Holtzman, Franklyn D. The Significance of Soviet Subsidies to Eastern Europe. *Comp. Econ. Stud.*, Spring 1986, *28*(1), pp. 54–65. **[G: CMEA]**

Holzman, Franklyn D. Further Thoughts on the Significance of Soviet Subsidies to Eastern Europe. *Comp. Econ. Stud.*, Fall 1986, *28*(3), pp. 59–64. **[G: CMEA]**

Hughes Hallett, A. J. Dynamic Policy Games and the Gains from Cooperation in Interdependent Economies: An Example from U.S.–EEC Policy Making. **In** *Pau, L. F., ed.*, 1986, pp. 147–55. **[G: U.S.; EEC]**

Hurni, Bettina. EFTA–EC Relations: Aftermath of the Luxembourg Declaration. *J. World Trade Law*, Sept.:Oct. 1986, *20*(5), pp. 497–506. **[G: W. Europe]**

Inotai, András. Economic Relations between the CMEA and the EEC: Facts, Trends, Prospects. *Acta Oecon.*, 1986, *36*(3–4), pp. 307–27. **[G: CMEA; EEC]**

Jackson, Marvin R. When Is a Price a Price? The Level and Patterns of Price in the CMEA. *Soviet E. Europ. Foreign Trade*, Spring 1986, *22*(1), pp. 100–112. **[G: CMEA]**

Johnson, D. Gale. Agricultural Policies and World Trade: The U.S. and the European Community at Bay: Comment. **In** *Tsoukalis, L., ed.*, 1986, pp. 77–80. **[G: U.S.; EEC]**

Josling, Timothy E. Agricultural Policies and World Trade: The U.S. and the European Community at Bay. **In** *Tsoukalis, L., ed.*, 1986, pp. 50–70. **[G: U.S.; EEC]**

Jung, Zdeněk. From Possibilities to Concrete Practice. *Czech. Econ. Digest.*, June 1986, (5), pp. 33–41. **[G: CMEA]**

Koester, Ulrich. Regional Co-operation in the Food Sector among Developing Countries to Improve Food Security. **In** *Maunder, A. and Renborg, U., eds.*, 1986, pp. 100–113. **[G: Africa]**

Kogut, Bruce. Steel and the European Communities. **In** *Macharzina, K. and Staehle, W. H., eds.*, 1986, pp. 185–203. **[G: EEC]**

Kosugi, Ryoji. Japan's Role in the Coming Pacific Era. **In** *Finn, R. B., ed.*, 1986, pp. 101–16. **[G: Japan]**

Krayenbühl, Thomas E. Comecon as a Debtor of the Western Financial System. **In** *Dicke, D. C., ed.*, 1986, pp. 231–47. **[G: OECD; Comecon]**

Lantzke, Ulf. Energy Supply in the European Community. **In** *Hax, H.; Kraus, W. and Tsuchiya, K., eds.*, 1986, pp. 42–48. **[G: EEC]**

Lér, Ondřej. An Important Stage of CMEA Activities. *Czech. Econ. Digest.*, December 1986, (8), pp. 5–9. **[G: CMEA]**

Lipsey, Richard G. Will There Be a Canadian–American Free Trade Association? *World Econ.*, September 1986, *9*(3), pp. 217–38. **[G: U.S.; Canada]**

Lipsey, Richard G. and Smith, Murray G. An Overview of Harmonization Issues. **In** *C. D. Howe Institute*, 1986, pp. 1–41. **[G: Canada; U.S.]**

Lipsey, Richard G. and Smith, Murray G. Policy Harmonization: The Effects of a Canadian–American Free Trade Area: Preface: An Introductory Overview. **In** *C. D. Howe Institute*, 1986, pp. vi–xv. **[G: Canada; U.S.]**

Lodge, Juliet. The Single European Act: Towards a New Euro-Dynamism? *J. Common Market Stud.*, March 1986, *24*(3), pp. 203–23. **[G: EEC]**

Lourenço, Joachim Silva. Origens, evolução e futuro da Política Agrícola Comum. (With English summary.) *Economia (Portugal)*, January 1986, *10*(1), pp. 67–89. **[G: EEC]**

Luyten, Paul. Agricultural Policies and World Trade: The U.S. and the European Community at Bay: Comment. **In** *Tsoukalis, L., ed.*, 1986, pp. 81–82. **[G: U.S.; EEC]**

Maasdorp, G. G. Economic and Political Aspects of Regional Cooperation in Southern Africa. *S. Afr. J. Econ.*, June 1986, *54*(2), pp. 151–71. **[G: S. Africa]**

Marques Mendes, A. J. The Contribution of the European Community to Economic Growth: An Assessment of the First 25 Years. *J. Common Market Stud.*, June 1986, *24*(4), pp. 261–77. **[G: EEC]**

Marrese, Michael. CMEA: Effective but Cumbersome Political Economy. *Int. Organ.*, Spring 1986, *40*(2), pp. 287–327. **[G: CMEA]**

Marrese, Michael. CMEA: Effective but Cumbersome Political Economy. **In** *Comisso, E. and Tyson, L., eds.*, 1986, pp. 111–51. **[G: CMEA]**

Merhaut, Josef. Strengthening the Integration Activity of CMEA. *Soviet E. Europ. Foreign Trade*, Summer 1986, *22*(2), pp. 67–77. **[G: CMEA]**

Morgan, Roger. Partners and Rivals in Western Europe: Conclusion. **In** *Morgan, R. and Bray, C., eds.*, 1986, pp. 245–48. **[G: U.K.; France; W. Germany]**

Morgan, Roger. Partners and Rivals in Western Europe: The Historical Background, 1955–85. **In** *Morgan, R. and Bray, C., eds.*, 1986, pp. 7–23. **[G: U.K.; France; W. Germany]**

Nerfin, Marc. Neither Prince nor Merchant: Citizen—An Introduction to the Third System. **In** *[Patel, S.]*, 1986, pp. 47–59.

Nicoll, William. From Rejection to Repudiation: EC Budgetary Affairs in 1985. *J. Common Market Stud.*, September 1986, *25*(1), pp. 31–49. **[G: EEC]**

Norton, Desmond. Smuggling under the Common Agricultural Policy: Northern Ireland and the Republic of Ireland. *J. Common Market Stud.*, June 1986, *24*(4), pp. 297–312. **[G: Ireland; EEC]**

Norton, Roger D.; Scandizzo, Pasquale L. and Zimmerman, Linda W. Portugal's Entry into the EEC: Aggregate and Distributional Effects Determined by Means of a General Equilibrium Model. *J. Policy Modeling*, Summer 1986, *8*(2), pp. 149–80. **[G: Portugal]**

O'Riordan, William K. An Alternative Measure of Employment Intensity. *Econ. Soc. Rev.*, October 1986, *18*(1), pp. 27–41. **[G: EEC]**

Pekhlivanov, Vasil. Problems of Import Pricing in the CMEA. *Soviet E. Europ. Foreign Trade*, Summer 1986, *22*(2), pp. 39–51. **[G: CMEA]**

Perdikis, Nicholas. An Assessment of Cyprus' Association with the EEC. *J. Econ. Stud.*, 1986, *13*(2), pp. 38–51. **[G: Cyprus; EEC]**

Petit, Michel. Agricultural Policies and World Trade: The U.S. and the European Community at Bay: Comment. **In** *Tsoukalis, L., ed.*, 1986, pp. 71–76. **[G: U.S.; EEC]**

Pinder, D. A. Small Firms, Regional Development and the European Investment Bank. *J. Common Market Stud.*, March 1986, *24*(3), pp. 171–86. **[G: EEC]**

Pinder, John. The Political Economy of Integration in Europe: Policies and Institutions in East and West. *J. Common Market Stud.*, September 1986, *25*(1), pp. 1–14. **[G: EEC]**

Pomfret, Richard. The Trade-Diverting Bias of Preferential Trading Arrangements. *J. Common Market Stud.*, December 1986, *25*(2), pp. 109–17. **[G: EEC]**

Popa, Ioan. Correlation of Prices and the Measurement of Efficiency in the Foreign Trade of the Socialist Countries. *Soviet E. Europ. Foreign Trade*, Summer 1986, *22*(2), pp. 52–66. **[G: Romania]**

Pridham, Geoffrey. European Elections, Political Parties and Trends of Internalization in Community Affairs. *J. Common Market Stud.*, June 1986, *24*(4), pp. 279–96. **[G: EEC]**

Robertson, Max. The South Pacific Regional Trade and Economic Cooperation Agreement: A Critique. **In** *Cole, R. V. and Parry, T. G., eds.*, 1986, pp. 147–75. **[G: Australia; S. Pacific]**

Schotta, Charles. Middle East Economic Cooperation: Energy Product Trade. **In** *El Mallakh, R., ed.*, 1986, pp. 29–36. **[G: Middle East]**

Scott, Andrew. Britain and the E.M.S.: An Appraisal of the Report of the Treasury and Civil Service Committee. *J. Common Market Stud.*, March 1986, *24*(3), pp. 187–201. **[G: EEC]**

Smith, Murray G. Implications for Canadian Commercial Policy of Negotiating a Free-Trade Area with the United States. **In** *C. D. Howe Institute*, 1986, pp. 101–22. **[G: Canada; U.S.]**

Smith, Ron. Britain and the International State Apparatus. **In** *Nolan, P. and Paine, S., eds.*, 1986, pp. 103–14. **[G: U.K.]**

Soremekun, Kayode. Potency and Limitations: The Dilemma of OPEC in the NIEO. **In** *Onwuka, R. I. and Aluko, O., eds.*, 1986, pp. 150–64. **[G: OPEC]**

Spencer, John E. Trade Liberalization through Tariff Cuts and the European Economic Community: A General Equilibrium Evaluation. **In** *Srinivasan, T. N. and Whalley, J., eds.*, 1986, pp. 125–44. **[G: EEC]**

Spinanger, Dean and Zietz, Joachim. Managing Trade but Mangling the Consumer: Reflections on the EEC's and West Germany's Experience with the Multifiber Arrangement. *Aussenwirtschaft*, December 1986, *41*(4), pp. 511–31. **[G: EEC]**

Steger, Debra. The Impact of U.S. Trade Laws on Canadian Economic Policies. **In** *C. D. Howe Institute*, 1986, pp. 73–100. **[G: Canada; U.S.]**

Sutherland, P. D. Europe and the Principle of Convergence. *Reg. Stud.*, August 1986, *20*(4), pp. 371–77. **[G: EEC]**

Taylor, D.; Diprose, G. and Duffy, M. EC Environmental Policy and the Control of Water Pollution: The Implementation of Directive 76/464 in Perspective. *J. Common Market Stud.*, March 1986, *24*(3), pp. 225–46. **[G: EEC]**

Totu, Ioan V. Developing and Perfecting Collaboration among the Socialist CMEA Member Countries. *Soviet E. Europ. Foreign Trade*, Summer 1986, *22*(2), pp. 78–95. **[G: CMEA]**

Voráček, Josef. Cooperation in the Engineering Industry. *Czech. Econ. Digest.*, June 1986, (5), pp. 28–32. **[G: CMEA]**

Wallace, Helen. Bilateral, Trilateral and Multilateral Negotiations in the European Community. **In** *Morgan, R. and Bray, C., eds.*, 1986, pp. 156–74. **[G: EEC]**

Watrin, Christian. Japan, Trade Partner of the European Community and the Federal Republic of Germany. **In** *Hax, H.; Kraus, W. and Tsuchiya, K., eds.*, 1986, pp. 15–28. **[G: Japan; EEC]**

von Witzke, Harald. Endogenous Supranational Policy Decisions: The Common Agricultural Policy of the European Community. *Public Choice*, 1986, *48*(2), pp. 157–74. **[G: EEC]**

Yannopoulos, George N. Patterns of Response to EC Tariff Preferences: An Empirical Investigation of Selected Non-ACP Associates. *J. Common Market Stud.*, September 1986, *25*(1), pp. 15–30. **[G: Mediterranean; EEC]**

Yannopoulos, George N. The Impact of the European Economic Community on East–West Trade in Europe. *Comp. Econ. Stud.*, Spring 1986, *28*(1), pp. 75–85. **[G: EEC; CMEA]**

Young, Stephen. European Car Industry. **In** *Macharzina, K. and Staehle, W. H., eds.*, 1986, pp. 147–62. **[G: W. Europe]**

Zehender, Wolfgang. Industrialisierung und regionale Kooperation in Schwarzafrika. (Industrialization and Regional Cooperation in Sub-Saharan Africa. With English summary.) *Konjunkturpolitik,* 1986, *32*(4), pp. 218–35. **[G: Africa]**

Zevin, L. Z., et al. Cooperation of CMEA Member-Countries and Developing Countries in the Resolution of the Food Problem. *Soviet E. Europ. Foreign Trade,* Fall-Winter 1986-87, 22(3), pp. 1–209. **[G: CMEA; LDCs]**

430 International Finance

431 Open Economy Macroeconomics; Exchange Rates

4310 General

Brunner, Karl and Meltzer, Allan H. The National Bureau Method, International Capital Mobility, and Other Essays. *Carnegie-Rochester Conf. Ser. Public Policy,* Spring 1986, *24,* pp. 1–10.

Cooper, Richard N. Economic Interdependence and Foreign Policy in the Seventies. **In** *Cooper, R. N.,* 1986, *1972,* pp. 1–22.

Corbo, Vittorio; de Melo, Jaime and Tybout, James. What Went Wrong with the Recent Reforms in the Southern Cone. *Econ. Develop. Cult. Change,* April 1986, *34*(3), pp. 607–40. **[G: Uruguay; Chile; Argentina]**

Darby, Michael R. International Economic Policy Coordination and Transmission: A Review. *Oxford Econ. Pap.,* November 1986, *38*(3), pp. 545–50.

Diewert, W. Erwin and Morrison, Catherine J. Adjusting Output and Productivity Indexes for Changes in the Terms of Trade. *Econ. J.,* September 1986, *96*(383), pp. 659–79.

Edwards, Sebastian. Monetarism in Chile, 1973–1983: Some Economic Puzzles. *Econ. Develop. Cult. Change,* April 1986, *34*(3), pp. 535–59. **[G: Chile]**

Fiebig, Denzil G. On Sign Reversals in Restricted Models: Comment [Spurious Tests and Sign Reversals in International Economics]. *Southern Econ. J.,* July 1986, *53*(1), pp. 269–71. **[G: U.S.]**

Frankel, Jeffrey A. International Capital Mobility and Crowding-out in the U.S. Economy: Imperfect Integration of Financial Markets or of Goods Markets? **In** *Hafer, R. W., ed. (I),* 1986, pp. 33–67. **[G: U.S.]**

Hafer, R. W. How Open Is the U.S. Economy? Preface. **In** *Hafer, R. W., ed. (I),* 1986, pp. xiii–xviii.

Kaufman, Robert R. Democratic and Authoritarian Responses to the Debt Issue: Argentina, Brazil, Mexico. **In** *Kahler, M., ed.,* 1986, pp. 187–217. **[G: Argentina; Brazil; Mexico]**

Keleher, Robert E. Of Money and Prices: Some Historical Perspectives. **In** *Putnam, B. H. and Wilford, D. S., eds.,* 1986, *1978,* pp. 27–58.

Khan, Mohsin S. and Knight, Malcolm D. Do Fund-Supported Adjustment Programs Retard Growth? *Finance Develop.,* March 1986, *23*(1), pp. 30–32.

Kuszczak, John and Murray, John D. A VAR Analysis of Economic Interdependence: Canada, the United States, and the Rest of the World. **In** *Hafer, R. W., ed. (I),* 1986, pp. 77–131. **[G: Canada; U.S.]**

Maddison, Angus. Developing Countries in the 1930s: Possible Lessons for the 1980s. **In** *Lal, D. and Wolf, M., eds.,* 1986, pp. 15–47. **[G: LDCs; MDCs]**

Meester, Gerrit. Agriculture in a Turbulent World Economy: Theoretical Developments: Discussion. **In** *Maunder, A. and Renborg, U., eds.,* 1986, pp. 633–35.

Mishkin, Frederic S. International Capital Mobility and Crowding-out in the U.S. Economy: Imperfect Integration of Financial Markets or of Goods Markets? Comments. **In** *Hafer, R. W., ed. (I),* 1986, pp. 69–74. **[G: U.S.; OECD]**

Rich, Georg. A VAR Analysis of Economic Interdependence: Canada, the United States, and the Rest of the World: Comments. **In** *Hafer, R. W., ed. (I),* 1986, pp. 133–36. **[G: U.S.; Canada]**

Williamson, John. Target Zones and the Management of the Dollar. *Brookings Pap. Econ. Act.,* 1986, (1), pp. 165–74. **[G: U.S.; Japan; W. Germany; Switzerland]**

4312 Open Economy Macroeconomic Theory: Balance of Payments and Adjustment Mechanisms

Adams, Charles and Gros, Daniel. The Consequences of Real Exchange Rate Rules for Inflation: Some Illustrative Examples. *Int. Monet. Fund Staff Pap.,* September 1986, *33*(3), pp. 439–76.

Ahmed, Shaghil. Temporary and Permanent Government Spending in an Open Economy: Some Evidence for the United Kingdom. *J. Monet. Econ.,* March 1986, *17*(2), pp. 197–224. **[G: U.K.]**

Aizenman, Joshua and Frenkel, Jacob A. Wage Indexation, Supply Shocks, and Monetary Policy in a Small, Open Economy. **In** *Edwards, S. and Ahamed, L., eds.,* 1986, pp. 89–131.

Akhtar, M. A. Some Common Misconceptions about the Monetary Approach to International Adjustment. **In** *Putnam, B. H. and Wilford, D. S., eds.,* 1986, *1978,* pp. 107–19.

Aoki, Masanao. Dynamic Adjustment Behaviour to Anticipated Supply Shocks in a Two-Country Model. *Econ. J.,* March 1986, *96*(381), pp. 80–100.

Aoki, Masanao. Effects of Anticipated Central Bank Actions on Tobin's *Q,* Share Prices and Economy Rate in a Small Open Economy. *Europ. Econ. Rev.,* April 1986, *30*(2), pp. 285–304.

Aoki, Masanao. Effects of Anticipated Real Supply Shocks and Coordinated Monetary Accommodation. *Econ. Stud. Quart.,* June 1986, *37*(2), pp. 134–50.

Ariga, Kenn. On Variability of Exchange Rates. *Econ. Stud. Quart.,* December 1986, *37*(4), pp. 300–318.

Artus, Jacques R. Stabilization, Stagflation, and Investment Incentives: The Case of Kenya, 1979–1980: Comment. **In** *Edwards, S. and Ahamed, L., eds.*, 1986, pp. 289–92. **[G: Kenya]**

Artus, Patrick. Crises de balance des paiements, politique monétaire, controle des changes. (Balance of Payment Crisis, Monetary Policy and Capital Control. With English summary.) *Revue Écon.*, July 1986, *37*(4), pp. 637–58.

Artus, Patrick. Les dépenses publiques et leur mode de financement en économie ouverte avec changes flexibles: efficacité et stabilité de l'économie. (Public Expenditures and Deficit Financing in an Open Economy with Flexible Exchange Rates: Efficiency and Stability of the Economy. With English summary.) *Ann. Écon. Statist.*, July-Sept. 1986, (3), pp. 119–40.

Artus, Patrick and Bismut, Claude. Exchange Rate and Wage–Price Dynamics: A Theoretical Analysis and an Econometric Investigation. *Europ. Econ. Rev.*, February 1986, *30*(1), pp. 57–90. **[G: U.S.; Japan; W. Germany; France; U.K.]**

Assarsson, Bengt. Inflation and Relative-Price Variability—A Model for an Open Economy Applied to Sweden. *J. Macroecon.*, Fall 1986, *8*(4), pp. 455–69. **[G: Sweden]**

Avila, Jorge C. Reducción del Empleo Público Redundante, Capital Humano y Ajuste en una Economía Abierta. (Reducing Government Overmanning, Human Capital and Open-Economy Adjustment. With English summary.) *Económica (La Plata)*, July-December 1986, *32*(2), pp. 165–205. **[G: Argentina]**

Barten, A. P. and d'Alcantara, G. Simulating Economic Policy with the COMET Model. **In** *Artus, P. and Guvenen, O., eds.*, 1986, pp. 229–37. **[G: EEC]**

Başar, Tamer; Turnovsky, Stephen J. and d'Orey, Vasco. Optimal Strategic Monetary Policies in Dynamic Interdependent Economies: A Summary Paper. *J. Econ. Dynam. Control*, June 1986, *10*(1/2), pp. 15–19.

Başar, Tamer; Turnovsky, Stephen J. and d'Orey, Vasco. Optimal Strategic Monetary Policies in Dynamic Interdependent Economies. **In** *Başar, T., ed.*, 1986, pp. 134–78. **[G: U.S.]**

Batra, Raveendra N. and Naqvi, Nadeem. International Debt, Factor Accumulation, and the Balance of Payments. **In** *Chen, A. H., ed.*, 1986, pp. 261–77.

Bean, Charles R. The Terms of Trade, Labour Supply and the Current Account. *Econ. J.*, Supplement 1986, *96*, pp. 38–46.

Beladi, Hamid; Biswas, Basudeb and Tribedy, Gopal. Growth of Income and the Balance of Payments: Keynesian and Monetary Theories. *J. Econ. Stud.*, 1986, *13*(4), pp. 44–55.

Bhaduri, Amit. Hacia un crecimiento con endeudamiento externo. (The Indebted Growth Process. With English summary.) *Estud. Econ.*, January-June 1986, *1*(1), pp. 115–25.

Bhandari, Jagdeep S. and Decaluwe, Bernard. A Framework for the Analysis of Legal and Fraudulent Trade Transactions in "Parallel" Exchange Markets. *Weltwirtsch. Arch.*, 1986, *122*(2), pp. 233–53. **[G: LDCs]**

Bhandari, Jagdeep S. and Hanson, Donald A. Optimal Fiscal Policy in an Open Economy with Time-varying Elasticities. *Southern Econ. J.*, January 1986, *52*(3), pp. 763–76.

Bhandari, Jagdeep S. and Rahmatian, Morteza. Country Size and 'Insulation' from External Disturbances. *De Economist*, 1986, *134*(4), pp. 438–66. **[G: U.S.; W. Germany; Denmark]**

Blejer, Mario I. Welfare, Banks, and Capital Mobility in Steady State: The Case of Predetermined Exchange Rates: Comment. **In** *Edwards, S. and Ahamed, L., eds.*, 1986, pp. 199–200.

Bordo, Michael D. Explorations in Monetary History: A Survey of the Literature. *Exploration Econ. Hist.*, October 1986, *23*(4), pp. 339–415. **[G: OECD]**

Boyer, Russell S. Currency Mobility and Balance of Payments Adjustment. **In** *Putnam, B. H. and Wilford, D. S., eds.*, 1986, *1978*, pp. 197–211.

Braga de Macedo, Jorge. Small Countries in Monetary Unions: A Two-Tier Model. *J. Econ. Dynam. Control*, June 1986, *10*(1/2), pp. 275–80.

Brandsma, Andries S. and Hughes Hallett, A. J. The Coordination Approach to Policymaking in Interdependent Economies. **In** *Artus, P. and Guvenen, O., eds.*, 1986, pp. 209–28. **[G: OECD]**

Branson, William H. Natural Resources and the Macroeconomy: A Theoretical Framework: Discussion: An International Macroeconomic Perspective. **In** *Neary, J. P. and van Wijnbergen, S., eds.*, 1986, pp. 50–52.

Branson, William H. Stabilization, Stagflation, and Investment Incentives: The Case of Kenya, 1979–1980. **In** *Edwards, S. and Ahamed, L., eds.*, 1986, pp. 267–88. **[G: Kenya]**

Buffie, Edward F. Devaluation and Imported Inputs: The Large Economy Case. *Int. Econ. Rev.*, February 1986, *27*(1), pp. 123–40.

Buffie, Edward F. Devaluation, Investment and Growth in LDCs. *J. Devel. Econ.*, March 1986, *20*(2), pp. 361–79. **[G: LDCs]**

Buffie, Edward F. Input Price Shocks in the Small Open Economy. *Oxford Econ. Pap.*, November 1986, *38*(3), pp. 551–65.

Buiter, Willem H. Macroeconomic Policy Design in an Interdependent World Economy: An Analysis of Three Contingencies. *Int. Monet. Fund Staff Pap.*, September 1986, *33*(3), pp. 541–82. **[G: U.S.]**

Butlin, M. W. and Gray, Malcolm R. Exchange Rate Depreciation, the Current Account and Wages: Comment. *Econ. Rec.*, Supplement 1986, pp. 22–23. **[G: Australia]**

Calvo, Guillermo A. Temporary Stabilization: Predetermined Exchange Rates. *J. Polit. Econ.*, December 1986, *94*(6), pp. 1319–29.

Calvo, Guillermo A. Welfare, Banks, and Capital Mobility in Steady State: The Case of Predetermined Exchange Rates. **In** *Edwards, S. and Ahamed, L., eds.*, 1986, pp. 177–99.

Canzoneri, Matthew B. The Implications of Mean-Variance Optimization for Four Questions in International Macroeconomics: Comments. *J. Int. Money Finance*, Supp. March 1986, *5*, pp. S77–78.

Catinat, Michel; Maurice, Joël and Zagamé, Paul. Stratégie du taux de change et mesures d'accompagnement. Une analyse des coûts et avantages à partir d'exercises quantitatifs. (Rate of Exchange Strategy and Accompanying Measures of Economic Policy. With English summary.) *Revue Écon.*, September 1986, *37*(5), pp. 857–84. **[G: France]**

Chiesa, Gabriella. Disavanzo pubblico, cambio reale e trasmissione internazionale. (Public Deficit, Real Exchange and International Transmission. With English summary.) *Polit. Econ.*, April 1986, *2*(1), pp. 121–44.

Chopra, Ajai and Montiel, Peter J. Output and Unanticipated Money with Imported Intermediate Goods and Foreign Exchange Rationing. *Int. Monet. Fund Staff Pap.*, December 1986, *33*(4), pp. 697–721. **[G: Philippines]**

Chu, Yun-peng, et al. Exchange Rates Intervention and Capital Mobility Control: Comparisons and Simultaneous Optimization. *J. Devel. Econ.*, September 1986, *23*(1), pp. 119–34. **[G: LDCs]**

Cohen, Daniel and Sachs, Jeffrey. Growth and External Debt under Risk of Debt Repudiation. *Europ. Econ. Rev.*, June 1986, *30*(3), pp. 529–60.

Condon, Timothy J. Flujo de comercio y la política del tipo de cambio reptante: Un Modelo de Predicción Perfecta de Largo Plaza. (With English summary.) *Cuadernos Econ.*, April 1986, *23*(68), pp. 25–47.

Connolly, Michael. The Monetary Approach to an Open Economy: The Fundamental Theory Revisited. **In** *Putnam, B. H. and Wilford, D. S., eds.*, 1986, pp. 11–26.

Consiglieri, Isabella. The Perception of Economic Policies and Exchange Rate Dynamics. *Econ. Notes*, 1986, (2), pp. 106–28.

Cooper, Richard N. Macroeconomic Policy Adjustment in Interdependent Economies. **In** *Cooper, R. N.*, 1986, *1969*, pp. 155–78.

Cooper, Richard N. Monetary Theory and Policy in an Open Economy. **In** *Cooper, R. N.*, 1986, *1976*, pp. 179–98.

Cooper, Richard N. and Sachs, Jeffrey. Borrowing Abroad: The Debtor's Perspective. **In** *Cooper, R. N.*, 1986, *1985*, pp. 229–88.

Corden, W. Max. Exchange Rate Depreciation, the Current Account and Wages. *Econ. Rec.*, Supplement 1986, pp. 14–21.

Corden, W. Max. Fiscal Policies, Current Accounts and Real Exchange Rates: In Search of a Logic of International Policy Coordination. *Weltwirtsch. Arch.*, 1986, *122*(3), pp. 423–38.

Cuddington, John T. and Viñals, José M. Budget Deficits and the Current Account: An Intertemporal Disequilibrium Approach. *J. Int. Econ.*, August 1986, *21*(1/2), pp. 1–24.

Cuddington, John T. and Viñals, José M. Budget Deficits and the Current Account in the Presence of Classical Unemployment. *Econ. J.*, March 1986, *96*(381), pp. 101–19.

Daniel, Betty C. Optimal Purchasing Power Parity Deviations. *Int. Econ. Rev.*, June 1986, *27*(2), pp. 483–511.

Daniel, Betty C. Real and Nominal Shocks in a Two-Country Price-Setting World. *J. Int. Econ.*, May 1986, *20*(3/4), pp. 269–89.

Dasgupta, Partha. Natural Resources and the Macroeconomy: A Theoretical Framework: Discussion: A Natural Resources Perspective. **In** *Neary, J. P. and van Wijnbergen, S., eds.*, 1986, pp. 53.

Dellas, Harris. A Real Model of the World Business Cycle. *J. Int. Money Finance*, September 1986, *5*(3), pp. 381–94. **[G: Japan; U.K.; U.S.; W. Germany]**

Di Matteo, Massimo and Ruiz, Maria Laura. Alcuni effetti dell'interdipendenza tra paesi produttori di petrolio e paesi industrializzati: un-'analisi macrodinamica. (Some Effects of the Interdependence between Oil Producing and Oil Consuming Countries: A Macrodynamic Analysis. With English summary.) *Rivista Int. Sci. Econ. Com.*, August 1986, *33*(8), pp. 797–812.

Díaz-Alejandro, Carlos F. Economic Adjustment and the Real Exchange Rate: Comment. **In** *Edwards, S. and Ahamed, L., eds.*, 1986, pp. 414–19.

Dornbusch, Rudiger. Equilibrium and Disequilibrium Exchange Rates. **In** *Dornbusch, R.*, 1986, *1982*, pp. 31–57.

Dornbusch, Rudiger. Flexible Exchange Rates and Interdependence. **In** *Dornbusch, R.*, 1986, *1983*, pp. 58–85. **[G: U.S.]**

Dornbusch, Rudiger. Flexible Exchange Rates and Excess Capital Mobility. *Brookings Pap. Econ. Act.*, 1986, (1), pp. 209–26. **[G: U.S.]**

Dornbusch, Rudiger. Special Exchange Rates for Capital Account Transactions. *World Bank Econ. Rev.*, September 1986, *1*(1), pp. 3–33. **[G: LDCs; Venezuela; Mexico]**

Dornbusch, Rudiger; Fischer, Stanley and Samuelson, Paul A. Comparative Advantage, Trade, and Payments in a Ricardian Model with a Continuum of Goods. **In** *Samuelson, P. A.*, 1986, *1977*, pp. 415–31.

Eaton, Jonathan; Gersovitz, Mark and Stiglitz, Joseph E. The Pure Theory of Country Risk. *Europ. Econ. Rev.*, June 1986, *30*(3), pp. 481–513.

Edwards, Sebastian. A Commodity Export Boom and the Real Exchange Rate: The Money–Inflation Link. **In** *Neary, J. P. and van Wijnbergen, S., eds.*, 1986, pp. 229–48. **[G: Colombia]**

Edwards, Sebastian and van Wijnbergen, Sweder J. G. The Welfare Effects of Trade and Capital Market Liberalization. *Int. Econ. Rev.*, February 1986, *27*(1), pp. 141–48.

Enders, Klaus-Stefan. Langsame Preise und schnelle Finanzmärkte: Wechselkursstabilisierung und seine realen Kosten. (Slow Prices and Fast Financial Markets: Exchange Rate

Stabilization and Its Real Cost. With English summary.) *Jahr. Nationalökon. Statist.*, May 1986, *201*(3), pp. 264–79.

van Ewijk, Casper. Interest Payments and the Stability of the Government Budget Deficit in an Open and Growing Economy. *De Economist*, 1986, *134*(2), pp. 143–64.

Farhadian, Ziba and Dunn, Robert M., Jr. Fiscal Policy and Financial Deepening in a Monetarist Model of the Balance of Payments. *Kyklos*, 1986, *39*(1), pp. 66–84. **[G: LDCs]**

Feldman, David H. and Tower, Edward. The Welfare Economics of an Unstable Real Exchange Rate. *Southern Econ. J.*, January 1986, *52*(3), pp. 607–16.

Fender, John. Monetary and Exchange Rate Policies in an Open Macroeconomic Model with Unemployment and Rational Expectations. *Oxford Econ. Pap.*, November 1986, *38*(3), pp. 501–15.

Fischer, Stanley. Wage Indexation, Supply Shocks, and Monetary Policy in a Small, Open Economy: Comment. **In** *Edwards, S. and Ahamed, L., eds.*, 1986, pp. 132–39.

Flanders, M. June. The Balance-of-Payments Adjustment Mechanism: The Doctrine According to Ohlin. *Hist. Polit. Econ.*, Summer 1986, *18*(2), pp. 237–57.

Flood, Robert P. and Hodrick, Robert J. Real Aspects of Exchange Rate Regime Choice with Collapsing Fixed Rates. *J. Int. Econ.*, November 1986, *21*(3/4), pp. 215–32.

Francesco, Drudi. Effetti redistributivi e di benessere di un'apertura a movimenti di capitale. (Effects of Capital Flows on Income Distribution and Welfare. A Review Article. With English summary.) *Giorn. Econ.*, July-Aug. 1986, *45*(7–8), pp. 433–62.

Frankel, Jeffrey A. The Effects of Commercial, Fiscal, Monetary, and Exchange Rate Policies on the Real Exchange Rate: Comment. **In** *Edwards, S. and Ahamed, L., eds.*, 1986, pp. 86–87.

Frankel, Jeffrey A. The Implications of Mean–Variance Optimization for Four Questions in International Macroeconomics. *J. Int. Money Finance*, Supp. March 1986, *5*, pp. S53–75.

Fremling, Gertrud Margareta. A Specie-Flow Model of the Gold Standard. *J. Int. Money Finance*, March 1986, *5*(1), pp. 37–55.

Frenkel, Jacob A. International Interdependence and the Constraints on Macroeconomic Policies. **In** *Hafer, R. W., ed. (I)*, 1986, pp. 171–205.

Frenkel, Jacob A. International Interdependence and the Constraints on Macroeconomic Policies. *Weltwirtsch. Arch.*, 1986, *122*(4), pp. 615–46.

Frenkel, Jacob A. and Razin, Assaf. Fiscal Policies in the World Economy. *J. Polit. Econ.*, Part 1, June 1986, *94*(3), pp. 564–94.

Frenkel, Jacob A. and Razin, Assaf. Government Spending, Debt, and International Economic Interdependence: Errata. *Econ. J.*, September 1986, *96*(383), pp. 814.

Frenkel, Jacob A. and Razin, Assaf. Real Exchange Rates, Interest Rates and Fiscal Policies. *Econ. Stud. Quart.*, June 1986, *37*(2), pp. 99–113. **[G: U.S.; Japan; Europe]**

Frenkel, Jacob A. and Razin, Assaf. The International Transmission and Effects of Fiscal Policies. *Amer. Econ. Rev.*, May 1986, *76*(2), pp. 330–35. **[G: U.S.; Japan; Europe]**

Fukiharu, Toshitaka. Economic Friction in a Two Country IS–LM Model. *Kobe Univ. Econ.*, 1986, (32), pp. 87–120.

Gardner, Grant W. Currency Substitution, Money Growth Rules, and the Interdependence of Monetary Policy. *J. Econ. Bus.*, May 1986, *38*(2), pp. 165–72.

Gärtner, Manfred. Anticipated Shocks and Exchange Rate Disequilibrium beyond the Short Run. *Z. Wirtschaft. Sozialwissen.*, 1986, *106*(1), pp. 1–13.

Ghosh, Sukesh K. Expectations and Niehans' Exchange Rate Dynamics [Exchange Rate Dynamics with Stock/Flow Interaction]. *Weltwirtsch. Arch.*, 1986, *122*(3), pp. 552–65.

Girton, Lance and Roper, Don. Theory and Implications of Currency Substitution. **In** *Putnam, B. H. and Wilford, D. S., eds.*, 1986, *1981*, pp. 212–35.

Glick, Reuven. Real Exchange Rates, Imperfect Information, and Economic Disturbances. *Fed. Res. Bank San Francisco Econ. Rev.*, Fall 1986, (4), pp. 44–59. **[G: U.S.]**

Glick, Reuven and Wihlborg, Clas. The Role of Information Acquisition and Financial Markets in International Macroeconomic Adjustment. *J. Int. Money Finance*, September 1986, *5*(3), pp. 257–83.

Gordon, Roger H. Taxation of Investment and Savings in a World Economy. *Amer. Econ. Rev.*, December 1986, *76*(5), pp. 1086–1102.

Goudswaard, Kees P. and Halberstadt, Victor. Aspects of Debt Management and Monetary Policy in Small Open Economies. **In** *Herber, B. P., ed.*, 1986, pp. 343–60. **[G: OECD; Netherlands]**

Green, Steven L. Monetary Policy in Developing Countries and the New Monetary Economics. *J. Econ. Devel.*, December 1986, *11*(2), pp. 7–23. **[G: LDCs]**

Guesnerie, Roger. The Pure Theory of Country Risk: Comments. *Europ. Econ. Rev.*, June 1986, *30*(3), pp. 515–19.

Gulhati, Ravi. Stabilization, Stagflation, and Investment Incentives: The Case of Kenya, 1979–1980: Comment. **In** *Edwards, S. and Ahamed, L., eds.*, 1986, pp. 292–93. **[G: Kenya]**

Guvenen, Orhan. International Macroeconomic Modelling for Policy Decisions: Some Proposals. **In** *Artus, P. and Guvenen, O., eds.*, 1986, pp. 259–65.

Haas, Richard D. and Masson, Paul R. MINIMOD: Specification and Simulation Results. *Int. Monet. Fund Staff Pap.*, December 1986, *33*(4), pp. 722–67. **[G: U.S.]**

Hamada, Koichi. Strategic Aspects of International Fiscal Interdependence. *Econ. Stud. Quart.*, June 1986, *37*(2), pp. 165–80.

Hanson, James A. Exchange Rate Management

and Stabilization Policies in Developing Countries: Comment. **In** *Edwards, S. and Ahamed, L., eds.*, 1986, pp. 39–41.

Hansson, Ingemar and Stuart, Charles. The Fisher Hypothesis and International Capital Markets. *J. Polit. Econ.*, December 1986, *94*(6), pp. 1330–37.

Haralambides, Hercules E. Investment in Shipping and the Balance of Payments Short-run Equilibrium Freight Rate. *Int. J. Transport Econ.*, October 1986, *13*(3), pp. 351–57.

Harberger, Arnold C. Economic Adjustment and the Real Exchange Rate. **In** *Edwards, S. and Ahamed, L., eds.*, 1986, pp. 371–414.

Hartley, Peter. Portfolio Theory and Foreign Investment—The Role of Non-marketed Assets. *Econ. Rec.*, September 1986, *62*(178), pp. 286–95.

Honohan, Patrick. A Commodity Export Boom and the Real Exchange Rate: The Money–Inflation Link: Comment. **In** *Neary, J. P. and van Wijnbergen, S., eds.*, 1986, pp. 249–50. **[G: Colombia]**

Howson, Susan. External Financial Markets, Capital Mobility and Monetary Independence. **In** *[Tarshis, L.]*, 1986, pp. 84–107. **[G: U.S.; W. Europe]**

Hughes Hallett, A. J. Autonomy and the Choice of Policy in Asymmetrically Dependent Economies: An Investigation of the Gains from International Policy Co-ordination. *Oxford Econ. Pap.*, November 1986, *38*(3), pp. 516–44. **[G: OECD]**

Hughes Hallett, A. J. Policy Design in Asymmetrically Dependent Economies. *J. Econ. Dynam. Control*, June 1986, *10*(1/2), pp. 51–57. **[G: U.S.; EEC]**

Humphrey, Thomas M. A Monetarist Model of World Inflation and the Balance of Payments. **In** *Humphreys, T. M.*, 1986, *1976*, pp. 170–79.

Humphrey, Thomas M. Adam Smith and the Monetary Approach to the Balance of Payments. **In** *Humphreys, T. M.*, 1986, *1981*, pp. 180–87.

Jarchow, Hans-Joachim. Ein Geldangebots/Geldnachfrage-Modell für flexible Wechselkurse und Zentrallbankpolitik. (A Money Supply/Money Demand Model for Flexible Exchange Rates and Central Bank Policy. With English summary.) *Kredit Kapital*, 1986, *19*(1), pp. 1–24.

Jones, Ronald W. Natural Resources and the Macroeconomy: A Theoretical Framework: Discussion: A Trade Theoretic Perspective. **In** *Neary, J. P. and van Wijnbergen, S., eds.*, 1986, pp. 46–50.

Kaneko, Takafumi and Yasuhara, Norikazu. Exchange Rate Simulations with the EPA World Economic Model. *Europ. Econ. Rev.*, February 1986, *30*(1), pp. 237–59. **[G: W. Europe; U.S.; Japan; Canada]**

Karakitsos, Elias. Monetary Policy, Exchange Rate Dynamics and the Labour Market. *J. Econ. Dynam. Control*, June 1986, *10*(1/2), pp. 281–89.

Kawai, Masahiro and Zilcha, Itzhak. International Trade with Forward-Futures Markets under Exchange Rate and Price Uncertainty. *J. Int. Econ.*, February 1986, *20*(1/2), pp. 83–98.

Khan, Mohsin S. Economic Adjustment and the Real Exchange Rate: Comment. **In** *Edwards, S. and Ahamed, L., eds.*, 1986, pp. 419–23.

Kiguel, Miguel A. Macroeconomic Adjustment under a Sliding Peg Exchange Rate and Imperfect Capital Mobility. *Eastern Econ. J.*, July-Sept. 1986, *12*(3), pp. 297–306.

van de Klundert, Theo C. Economic Resilience: A Two-Country Analysis. *De Economist*, 1986, *134*(1), pp. 25–41.

Krumm, Kathie L. The Effects of Commercial, Fiscal, Monetary, and Exchange Rate Policies on the Real Exchange Rate: Comment. **In** *Edwards, S. and Ahamed, L., eds.*, 1986, pp. 87–88.

Landmann, Oliver. International Portfolio-Shifts and the Choice of a Monetary Rule. **In** *Frisch, H. and Gahlen, B., eds.*, 1986, pp. 86–125.

Larraín, Felipe. Expectativas racionales y dinámica del tipo de cambio: una nota. (With English summary.) *Cuadernos Econ.*, April 1986, *23*(68), pp. 69–76.

Laskar, Daniel. International Cooperation and Exchange Rate Stabilization. *J. Int. Econ.*, August 1986, *21*(1/2), pp. 151–64.

Le Fort, Guillermo. La dinámica de ajuste del tipo de cambio real y la tasa de interés real luego de una devaluación. (With English summary.) *Cuadernos Econ.*, April 1986, *23*(68), pp. 49–67.

Levin, Jay H. Monetary–Fiscal Policy Assignment under Floating Exchange Rates. *De Economist*, 1986, *134*(4), pp. 467–78.

Levin, Jay H. Trade Flow Lags, Monetary and Fiscal Policy, and Exchange-Rate Overshooting. *J. Int. Money Finance*, December 1986, *5*(4), pp. 485–95.

Lluch, Constantino. Wage Indexation, Supply Shocks, and Monetary Policy in a Small, Open Economy: Comment. **In** *Edwards, S. and Ahamed, L., eds.*, 1986, pp. 139–42.

Malinvaud, Edmond. International Borrowing and Time-Consistent Fiscal Policy: Comment. *Scand. J. Econ.*, 1986, *88*(1), pp. 297–303.

Marion, Nancy Peregrim and Svensson, Lars E. O. The Terms of Trade between Oil Importers. *J. Int. Econ.*, February 1986, *20*(1/2), pp. 99–113.

Marois, William. Théorie du déséquilibre et politique économique en économie ouverte. (Disequilibrium Theory and Economic Policy for Open Economies. With English summary.) *L'Actual. Econ.*, June 1986, *62*(2), pp. 257–88.

Marquez, Jaime. The International Transmission of Oil-Price Effects and OPEC's Pricing Policy. *J. Econ. Bus.*, August 1986, *38*(3), pp. 237–53.

Masson, Paul R. and Knight, Malcolm D. International Transmission of Fiscal Policies in Major Industrial Countries. *Int. Monet. Fund*

Staff Pap., September 1986, *33*(3), pp. 387–438. **[G: U.S.; W. Germany; Japan]**

Masson, Paul R. and Richardson, Peter. Exchange Rate Expectations and Current Balances in the OECD Interlink System. **In** *Artus, P. and Guvenen, O., eds.*, 1986, pp. 53–77. **[G: OECD]**

McKinnon, Ronald I. Currency Substitution and Instability in the World Dollar Standard [Dollar Stabilization and American Monetary Policy]. **In** *Putnam, B. H. and Wilford, D. S., eds.*, 1986, *1980*, pp. 249–71. **[G: U.S.]**

Miles, Marc A. Currency Substitution, Flexible Exchange Rates, and Monetary Independence. **In** *Putnam, B. H. and Wilford, D. S., eds.*, 1986, *1978*, pp. 237–48. **[G: Canada]**

Miller, Norman C. The Structure of Open Economy Macro-Models. *J. Int. Money Finance*, March 1986, *5*(1), pp. 75–89.

Montiel, Peter J. Long-run Equilibrium in a Keynesian Model of a Small Open Economy. *Int. Monet. Fund Staff Pap.*, March 1986, *33*(1), pp. 28–59.

Morandé, Felipe G. Volatilidad de los tipos de cambio y contratos traslapados. (With English summary.) *Cuadernos Econ.*, August 1986, *23*(69), pp. 229–36.

Mulder, C. B. and van der Ploeg, Frederick. Trade Unions, Investment and Employment in a Small Open Economy: A Dutch Perspective. *Rech. Écon. Louvain*, 1986, *52*(3–4), pp. 313–38. **[G: Netherlands; OECD]**

Murfin, Andy and Ormerod, Paul. The Sterling–Dollar Exchange Market 1973–1982: Surprises and Expectations. **In** *Artus, P. and Guvenen, O., eds.*, 1986, pp. 79–102. **[G: U.K.; U.S.]**

Murphy, C. W. Exchange Rate Policy and the AMPS Model. *Econ. Rec.*, Supplement 1986, pp. 41–54.

Murphy, Robert G. Productivity Shocks, Non-traded Goods and Optimal Capital Accumulation. *Europ. Econ. Rev.*, October 1986, *30*(5), pp. 1081–95.

Mussa, Michael. The Effects of Commercial, Fiscal, Monetary, and Exchange Rate Policies on the Real Exchange Rate. **In** *Edwards, S. and Ahamed, L., eds.*, 1986, pp. 43–86.

Naqvi, Nadeem. International Debt, Investment and the Currency Account: An Intertemporal Analysis. *Indian Econ. J.*, Jan.-Mar. 1986, *33*(3), pp. 53–64.

Naqvi, Nadeem and Beladi, Hamid. An Analysis of Some Trade Theoretic Aspects of Investment and the Balance of Payments. *J. Econ. Devel.*, December 1986, *11*(2), pp. 197–211. **[G: S. Korea]**

Neary, J. Peter and van Wijnbergen, Sweder J. G. Natural Resources and the Macroeconomy: A Theoretical Framework. **In** *Neary, J. P. and van Wijnbergen, S., eds.*, 1986, pp. 13–45.

das Neves, João César and de Teles, Pedro Pinho. Teoria de desvalorização cambial: A abordagem Keynesiana—Comentário numa perspectiva estrutural. (With English summary.) *Economia (Portugal)*, January 1986, *10*(1), pp. 91–98.

Niehans, Jürg. The International Division of Assets as Determined by Comparative Advantage. *J. Int. Money Finance*, June 1986, *5*(2), pp. 153–65.

Obstfeld, Maurice. Capital Controls, the Dual Exchange Rate, and Devaluation. *J. Int. Econ.*, February 1986, *20*(1/2), pp. 1–20.

Obstfeld, Maurice. Capital Flows, the Current Account, and the Real Exchange Rate: Some Consequences of Stabilization and Liberalization. **In** *Edwards, S. and Ahamed, L., eds.*, 1986, pp. 201–29.

Obstfeld, Maurice. Capital Mobility in the World Economy: Theory and Measurement. *Carnegie-Rochester Conf. Ser. Public Policy*, Spring 1986, *24*, pp. 55–103. **[G: OECD]**

Obstfeld, Maurice. Rational and Self-fulfilling Balance-of-Payments Crises. *Amer. Econ. Rev.*, March 1986, *76*(1), pp. 72–81.

Obstfeld, Maurice. Speculative Attack and the External Constraint in a Maximizing Model of the Balance of Payments. *Can. J. Econ.*, February 1986, *19*(1), pp. 1–22.

Oudiz, Gilles. Stratégies économiques européennes: coordination ou confrontation? (European Economic Stategies. Cooperation versus Conflict. With English summary.) *Écon. Soc.*, January 1986, *20*(1), pp. 265–96.

Papell, David H. Exchange Rate and Current Account Dynamics under Rational Expectations: An Econometric Analysis. *Int. Econ. Rev.*, October 1986, *27*(3), pp. 583–600. **[G: Japan]**

Penati, Alessandro. Budget Deficit, External Official Borrowing, and Sterilized Intervention Policy in Foreign Exchange Markets. *J. Int. Money Finance*, March 1986, *5*(1), pp. 99–113.

Persson, Torsten and Svensson, Lars E. O. International Borrowing and Time-Consistent Fiscal Policy. *Scand. J. Econ.*, 1986, *88*(1), pp. 273–95.

Phelps, Edmund S. Profits Theory and Profits Taxation. *Int. Monet. Fund Staff Pap.*, December 1986, *33*(4), pp. 674–96. **[G: OECD]**

Phelps, Edmund S. The Significance of Customer Markets for the Effects of Budgetary Policy in Open Economies. *Ann. Écon. Statist.*, July-Sept. 1986, (3), pp. 101–17.

Poole, William. International Interdependence and the Constraints on Macroeconomic Policies: Comments. **In** *Hafer, R. W., ed. (1)*, 1986, pp. 207–10.

Prachowny, Martin F. J. Managed Exchange Rates. *Econ. Rec.*, December 1986, *62*(179), pp. 442–50.

Putnam, Bluford H. and Wilford, D. Sykes. Money, Income, and Causality in the United States and the United Kingdom. **In** *Putnam, B. H. and Wilford, D. S., eds.*, 1986, *1978*, pp. 59–65. **[G: U.S.; U.K.]**

Raaum, Oddbjørn. Wage Formation in a Two-Sector Open Economy with Two Strong Unions. *Rech. Écon. Louvain*, 1986, *52*(3–4), pp. 283–311.

Ramanathan, Ramu. Government Policy with Deficit Financing, Imperfect Capital Mobility and Exchange Rate Effects on the Supply Side.

Econ. Modelling, April 1986, *3*(2), pp. 147–52.

Reither, Franco. The Dynamics of Financial Adjustments in an Open Economy and the Effects of Stabilization Policy: Comment. *J. Inst. Theoretical Econ.*, June 1986, *142*(2), pp. 438–41.

Rothengatter, Werner. The Dynamics of Financial Adjustments in an Open Economy and the Effects of Stabilization Policy: Reply. *J. Inst. Theoretical Econ.*, June 1986, *142*(2), pp. 442–44.

Rübel, Gerhard. Arbeitszeit, Ersparnis und Leistungsbilanz—Eine intertemporale Untersuchung. (Working Hours, Savings and the Current Account—An Intertemporal Study. With English summary.) *Jahr. Nationalökon. Statist.*, March 1986, *201*(2), pp. 175–89.

Rübel, Gerhard. Factors Determining External Indebtedness. *Econ. Notes*, 1986, (3), pp. 101–21.

Salant, Walter S. A Critical Look at Supply-Side Theory and a Brief Look at Some of Its International Aspects. **In** *[Tarshis, L.]*, 1986, pp. 108–24.

Samuelson, Paul A. A Corrected Version of Hume's Equilibrating Mechanisms for International Trade. **In** *Samuelson, P. A.*, 1986, *1980*, pp. 397–414.

Sarantis, Nicholas C. The Mundell–Fleming Model with Perfect Capital Mobility and Oligopolistic Pricing. *J. Post Keynesian Econ.*, Fall 1986, *9*(1), pp. 138–48.

Sauernheimer, Karlhans. Tariffs, Imported Inputs and Employment. *Economica*, August 1986, *53*(211), pp. 393–99.

Selowsky, Marcelo. Capital Flows, the Current Account, and the Real Exchange Rate: Some Consequences of Stabilization and Liberalization: Comment. **In** *Edwards, S. and Ahamed, L., eds.*, 1986, pp. 229–31.

Silva Torres, Francisco and de Teles, Pedro Pinho. O desvio deflacionista na ausência de cooperação internacional em contexto de incerteza. (With English summary.) *Economia (Portugal)*, May 1986, *10*(2), pp. 277–92.

Simes, R. M. Exchange Rate Policy and the AMPS Model: Comment. *Econ. Rec.*, Supplement 1986, pp. 55–57.

Sørensen, Peter Birch. Taxation, Inflation, and Asset Accumulation in a Small Open Economy. *Europ. Econ. Rev.*, October 1986, *30*(5), pp. 1025–41.

Stockman, Alan C. and Koh, Ai Tee. Open-Economy Implications of Two Models of Business Fluctuations. *Can. J. Econ.*, February 1986, *19*(1), pp. 23–34.

Stulz, René M. Capital Mobility in the World Economy: Theory and Measurement: A Comment. *Carnegie-Rochester Conf. Ser. Public Policy*, Spring 1986, *24*, pp. 105–13.

Sundararajan, V. Exchange Rate versus Credit Policy: Analysis with a Monetary Model of Trade and Inflation in India. *J. Devel. Econ.*, Jan.-Feb. 1986, *20*(1), pp. 75–105. **[G: India]**

Tamborini, Roberto. Financial Flows, Trade Flows and Income in the Multilateral System. The Transfer Approach. *Stud. Econ.*, 1986, *41*(28), pp. 63–100.

Taylor, Lance; Yurukoglu, Kadir T. and Chaudhry, Shahid A. A Macro Model of an Oil Exporter: Nigeria. **In** *Neary, J. P. and van Wijnbergen, S., eds.*, 1986, pp. 201–24. **[G: Nigeria]**

Turnovsky, Stephen J. Monetary and Fiscal Policy under Perfect Foresight: A Symmetric Two-country Analysis. *Economica*, May 1986, *53*(210), pp. 139–57.

Turnovsky, Stephen J. Short-term and Long-term Interest Rates in a Monetary Model of a Small Open Economy. *J. Int. Econ.*, May 1986, *20*(3/4), pp. 291–311.

Turnovsky, Stephen J. and d'Orey, Vasco. Monetary Polices in Interdependent Economies: A Strategic Approach. *Econ. Stud. Quart.*, June 1986, *37*(2), pp. 114–33.

Turnovsky, Stephen J. and d'Orey, Vasco. Monetary Policies in Interdependent Economies with Stochastic Disturbances: A Strategic Approach. *Econ. J.*, September 1986, *96*(383), pp. 696–721.

Tyson, Laura D'Andrea. The Debt Crisis and Adjustment Responses in Eastern Europe: A Comparative Perspective. **In** *Comisso, E. and Tyson, L., eds.*, 1986, pp. 63–110. **[G: E. Europe; E. Asia; Latin America]**

Whittaker, Rod, et al. Alternative Financial Policy Rules in an Open Economy under Rational and Adaptive Expectations. *Econ. J.*, September 1986, *96*(383), pp. 680–95. **[G: U.K.]**

van Wijnbergen, Sweder J. G. Exchange Rate Management and Stabilization Policies in Developing Countries. *J. Devel. Econ.*, October 1986, *23*(2), pp. 227–47. **[G: LDCs]**

van Wijnbergen, Sweder J. G. Exchange Rate Management and Stabilization Policies in Developing Countries. **In** *Edwards, S. and Ahamed, L., eds.*, 1986, pp. 17–38. **[G: LDCs]**

van Wijnbergen, Sweder J. G. On Fiscal Deficits, the Real Exchange Rate and the World Rate of Interest. *Europ. Econ. Rev.*, October 1986, *30*(5), pp. 1013–23.

Wilford, D. Sykes. Exchange Rates with Substitutable Currencies. **In** *Putnam, B. H. and Wilford, D. S., eds.*, 1986, pp. 272–83. **[G: U.S.; Canada]**

Wilford, Walton T. The Monetary Approach to Balance of Payments and Developing Nations: A Review of the Literature. **In** *Putnam, B. H. and Wilford, D. S., eds.*, 1986, pp. 81–106. **[G: LDCs]**

van der Willigen, Tessa A. Cash Crop Production and the Balance of Trade in a Less Developed Economy: A Model of Temporary Equilibrium with Rationing. *Oxford Econ. Pap.*, November 1986, *38*(3), pp. 424–42.

Winckler, Georg and Amann, Erwin. Exchange Rate Policy in the Presence of a Strong Trade Union. *J. Econ. (Z. Nationalökon.)*, Supplementum 5, 1986, pp. 259–80.

Wyplosz, Charles. Capital Controls and Balance of Payments Crises. *J. Int. Money Finance*,

June 1986, *5*(2), pp. 167–79.

Zaidi, Iqbal M. Currency Depreciation and Nonclearing Markets in Developing Economies. *Int. Monet. Fund Staff Pap.*, June 1986, *33*(2), pp. 276–303. **[G: LDCs]**

4313 Open Economy Macroeconomic Studies: Balance of Payments and Adjustment Mechanisms

Agarwal, J. P. Third World Multinationals and Balance-of-Payments Effect on Home Countries: A Case Study of India. **In** *Khan, K. M., ed.*, 1986, pp. 184–95. **[G: India]**

Ahamed, Liaquat. Stabilization Policies in Developing Countries. *World Bank Res. Observer*, January 1986, *1*(1), pp. 79–110. **[G: Peru; Mexico; Portugal; Bangladesh]**

Ahluwalia, Montek Singh. Balance-of-Payments Adjustment in India, 1970–71 to 1983–84. *World Devel.*, Special Issue, August 1986, *14*(8), pp. 937–62. **[G: India]**

Alburo, Florian and Canlas, Dante B. Balance of Payments, Output, and the IMF. *Philippine Rev. Econ. Bus.*, Sept.-Dec. 1986, *23*(3–4), pp. 275–92. **[G: Philippines]**

Aslaksen, Iulie and Bjerkholt, Olav. Certainty Equivalence Methods in the Macroeconomic Management of Petroleum Resources. **In** *Neary, J. P. and van Wijnbergen, S., eds.*, 1986, pp. 170–95. **[G: Norway]**

Bach, Christopher L. U.S. International Transactions, Fourth Quarter and Year 1985. *Surv. Curr. Bus.*, March 1986, *66*(3), pp. 24–54. **[G: U.S.]**

Bacha, Edmar L. External Shocks and Growth Prospects: The Case of Brazil, 1973–89. *World Devel.*, Special Issue, August 1986, *14*(8), pp. 919–36. **[G: Brazil]**

Bacha, Edmar L. Terms of Reference for the Country Studies. *World Devel.*, Special Issue, August 1986, *14*(8), pp. 909–18. **[G: LDCs]**

Balassa, Bela. Adjustment Policies in Socialist and Private Market Economies. *J. Compar. Econ.*, June 1986, *10*(2), pp. 138–59. **[G: LDCs; Hungary; Yugoslavia]**

Balassa, Bela. Policy Responses to Exogenous Shocks in Developing Countries. *Amer. Econ. Rev.*, May 1986, *76*(2), pp. 75–78. **[G: LDCs]**

Baum, Christopher F. Coordination of Large Macroeconomies' Policies and the Stability of Small Economies. *J. Econ. Dynam. Control*, June 1986, *10*(1/2), pp. 21–25. **[G: U.S.; Austria; Australia; Canada]**

Benzoni, Laurent. Taux de change, prix du pétrole, déséquilibres monétaires internationaux. (Exchange Rate, Oil Price, International Monetary Disequilibrium. With English summary.) *Écon. Soc.*, July 1986, *20*(7), pp. 27–61. **[G: OPEC]**

Black, Stanley W. The Open Economy: Implications for Monetary and Fiscal Policy: Comment. **In** *Gordon, R. J., ed.*, 1986, pp. 501–04. **[G: U.S.]**

Brau, Eduard H. External Debt Management in the African Context. **In** *Helleiner, G. K, ed.*, 1986, pp. 160–80. **[G: Africa]**

Browne, F. X. Multilateral Currency Substitution and Capital Flows as Sources of Instability in the Soe Demand for Money Function—A Case Study. *Empirical Econ.*, 1986, *11*(3), pp. 181–96. **[G: Ireland]**

Bruno, Michael. External Shocks and Domestic Response: Macroeconomic Performance, 1965–1982. **In** *Ben-Porath, Y., ed.*, 1986, pp. 276–301. **[G: Israel; OECD]**

Buiter, Willem H. The Role of Reserves in the International Monetary System: Comment. **In** *Posner, M., ed.*, 1986, pp. 109–12. **[G: Global]**

Bullock, Colin. IMF Conditionality and Jamaica's Economic Policy in the 1980s. *Soc. Econ. Stud.*, December 1986, *35*(4), pp. 129–76. **[G: Jamaica]**

Caballero, Ricardo and Corbo, Vittorio. Análisis de la Balanza Comercial: Un Enfoque de Equilibrio General. (With English summary.) *Cuadernos Econ.*, December 1986, *23*(70), pp. 285–313. **[G: Chile]**

Caire, Guy. Contrainte extérieure et emploi: trois discours. (Foreign Constraint and Employment: Three Approaches. With English summary.) *Écon. Soc.*, January 1986, *20*(1), pp. 11–44. **[G: OECD]**

Cayton, J. Michael. The U.S. Policy Mix, Foreign Financing, and the Consequences. *J. Econ. Issues*, September 1986, *20*(3), pp. 743–58.

Chatterjee, S. and Michelini, C. Balance of Payments Constraints and Feasible Growth Rates: The New Zealand Experience. *New Zealand Econ. Pap.*, 1986, *20*, pp. 121–30. **[G: New Zealand]**

Cheng, Hang-Sheng. International Financial Crises, Past and Present. *Fed. Res. Bank San Francisco Econ. Rev.*, Fall 1986, (4), pp. 13–23. **[G: Global]**

Choucri, Nazli. The Hidden Economy: A New View of Remittances in the Arab World. *World Devel.*, June 1986, *14*(6), pp. 697–712. **[G: Middle East]**

Chrystal, K. Alec and Dowd, Kevin. Two Arguments for the Restriction of International Capital Flows. *Nat. Westminster Bank Quart. Rev.*, November 1986, pp. 8–19. **[G: U.K.]**

Conti, Vittorio and Silvani, Marco. Il moltipliatore del commercio con l'estero: una formulazione Input–Output. (External trade Multiplier: An Input–Output Approach. With English summary.) *Polit. Econ.*, August 1986, *2*(2), pp. 181–202. **[G: W. Europe]**

Conway, Patrick. Decomposing the Determinants of Trade Deficits: Turkey in the 1970s. *J. Devel. Econ.*, May 1986, *21*(2), pp. 235–58. **[G: Turkey]**

Cooper, Richard N. An Analysis of Currency Devaluation in Developing Countries. **In** *Cooper, R. N.*, 1986, *1973*, pp. 199–227. **[G: LDCs]**

Cooper, Richard N. Dealing with the Trade Deficit in a Floating Rate System. *Brookings Pap. Econ. Act.*, 1986, (1), pp. 195–207. **[G: U.S.]**

Cortés, Rosalía and Marshall, Adriana. Salario

real, composición del consumo y balanza comercial. (With English summary.) *Desarrollo Econ.*, Apr.-June 1986, *26*(101), pp. 71–88. **[G: Argentina]**

Cozier, Barry V. A Model of Output Fluctuations in a Small, Specialized Economy. *J. Money, Credit, Banking,* May 1986, *18*(2), pp. 179–90. **[G: LDCs]**

Cumby, Robert E. and Mishkin, Frederic S. The International Linkage of Real Interest Rates: The European–U.S. Connection. *J. Int. Money Finance,* March 1986, *5*(1), pp. 5–23. **[G: OECD]**

Currie, David and Hall, Stephen G. The Exchange Rate and the Balance of Payments. *Nat. Inst. Econ. Rev.*, February 1986, (115), pp. 74–82. **[G: U.K.]**

Deane, Marjorie. The Role and Resources of the Fund: Comment. **In** *Posner, M., ed.*, 1986, pp. 158–63. **[G: Selected LDCs]**

Der Hovanessian, Aida. Economic Forces Affecting the Middle East. **In** *Roukis, G. S. and Montana, P. J., eds.*, 1986, pp. 47–70. **[G: OPEC]**

Díaz-Alejandro, Carlos F. The Early 1980s in Latin America: The 1930s One More Time? **In** *[Streeten, P.]*, 1986, pp. 154–64. **[G: Latin America]**

Dickinson, Gerard M. The Impact of International Insurance and Reinsurance on the Balance of Payments. **In** *Wasow, B. and Hill, R. D., eds.*, 1986, pp. 69–86.

Dilullo, Anthony J. U.S. International Transactions, Third Quarter 1986. *Surv. Curr. Bus.*, December 1986, *66*(12), pp. 23–46. **[G: U.S.]**

Dilullo, Anthony J. U.S. International Transactions, Second Quarter 1986. *Surv. Curr. Bus.*, September 1986, *66*(9), pp. 40–63. **[G: U.S.]**

Dooley, Michael P. The Role of Reserves in the International Monetary System. **In** *Posner, M., ed.*, 1986, pp. 97–109. **[G: Global]**

Dornbusch, Rudiger. International Debt and Economic Instability. **In** *Axilrod, S. H., et al.*, 1986, pp. 63–86. **[G: U.S.; Latin America]**

Dornbusch, Rudiger. Overborrowing: Three Case Studies. **In** *Dornbusch, R.*, 1986, *1985*, pp. 97–130. **[G: Chile; Brazil; Argentina]**

Dornbusch, Rudiger and Fischer, Stanley. The Open Economy: Implications for Monetary and Fiscal Policy. **In** *Gordon, R. J., ed.*, 1986, pp. 459–501. **[G: U.S.]**

Edison, Hali J. The U.K. Sector of the Federal Reserve's Multicountry Model: The Effects of Monetary and Fiscal Policies. *Manchester Sch. Econ. Soc. Stud.*, December 1986, *54*(4), pp. 403–19. **[G: U.K.]**

Edwards, Sebastian. Adjustment to Windfall Gains: A Comparative Analysis of Oil-Exporting Countries: Comment. **In** *Neary, J. P. and van Wijnbergen, S., eds.*, 1986, pp. 93–95. **[G: OPEC]**

Edwards, Sebastian and Ahamed, Liaquat. Economic Adjustment and Exchange Rates in Developing Countries: Introduction. **In** *Edwards, S. and Ahamed, L., eds.*, 1986, pp. 1–14.

Felmingham, B. S. and Divisekera, Sarath. The Response of Australia's Trade Balance under Different Exchange Rate Regimes. *Australian Econ. Pap.*, June 1986, *25*(46), pp. 33–46. **[G: Australia]**

Fischer, Stanley. Issues in Medium-term Macroeconomic Adjustment. *World Bank Res. Observer,* July 1986, *1*(2), pp. 163–82. **[G: LDCs]**

Fishlow, Albert. Latin American Adjustment to the Oil Shocks of 1973 and 1979. **In** *Hartlyn, J. and Morley, S. A., eds.*, 1986, pp. 54–84. **[G: Selected LDCs]**

Fodor, Jorge. The Origin of Argentina's Sterling Balances, 1939–43. **In** *di Tella, G. and Platt, D. C. M., eds.*, 1986, pp. 154–82. **[G: Argentina]**

Fouet, Monique and Aroyo, Philippe. Pétrodollars et marchés financiers internationaux. (Petrodollars and International Financial Markets. With English summary.) *Écon. Soc.*, July 1986, *20*(7), pp. 15–25. **[G: OPEC]**

Frenkel, Jacob A. and Razin, Assaf. Real Exchange Rates, Interest Rates and Fiscal Policies. *Econ. Stud. Quart.*, June 1986, *37*(2), pp. 99–113. **[G: U.S.; Japan; Europe]**

Frenkel, Jacob A. and Razin, Assaf. The International Transmission and Effects of Fiscal Policies. *Amer. Econ. Rev.*, May 1986, *76*(2), pp. 330–35. **[G: U.S.; Japan; Europe]**

Friedman, Benjamin M. Implications of the U.S. Net Capital Inflow. **In** *Hafer, R. W., ed. (I),* 1986, pp. 137–61. **[G: U.S.]**

Frijns, Jean M. G. The Dutch Disease in the Netherlands: Comment. **In** *Neary, J. P. and van Wijnbergen, S., eds.*, 1986, pp. 136–41. **[G: Netherlands]**

Gahlen, Bernhard; Rahmeyer, Fritz and Stadler, Manfred. Zur internationalen Wettbewerbsfähigkeit der deutschen Wirtschaft. (The International Competitiveness of the German Economy. With English summary.) *Konjunkturpolitik*, 1986, *32*(3), pp. 130–50. **[G: W. Germany]**

Garber, Peter M. Interwar Movements of Dollars to Europe and the U.S. Currency Supply. *J. Int. Money Finance,* Supp. March 1986, *5*, pp. S135–56. **[G: U.S.]**

Garcia, Philip and Anderson, Margot. The U.S. Trade Deficit and International Competition. **In** *Walzer, N. and Chicoine, D. L., eds.*, 1986, pp. 179–97. **[G: U.S.]**

Gelb, Alan. Adjustment to Windfall Gains: A Comparative Analysis of Oil-Exporting Countries. **In** *Neary, J. P. and van Wijnbergen, S., eds.*, 1986, pp. 54–93. **[G: OPEC]**

Ginzburg, Andrea. Dependency and the Political Solution of Balance of Payments Crises: The Italian Case. **In** *[Hirshman, A. O.]*, 1986, pp. 133–66. **[G: Italy; W. Germany]**

Gordon, Robert J. U.S. Fiscal Deficits and the World Imbalance of Payments. *Hitotsubashi J. Econ.*, Spec. Iss. Oct. 1986, *27*, pp. 7–41. **[G: U.S.]**

Green, Reginald Herbold and Kadhani, Xavier. Zimbabwe: Transition to Economic Crises,

1981–83: Retrospect and Prospect. *World Devel.*, Special Issue, August 1986, *14*(8), pp. 1059–83. **[G: Zimbabwe]**

Griffith-Jones, Stephany. The Role and Resources of the Fund. **In** *Posner, M., ed.*, 1986, pp. 139–58. **[G: Selected LDCs]**

Ground, Richard L. Origin and Magnitude of Recessionary Adjustment in Latin America. *CEPAL Rev.*, December 1986, (30), pp. 67–85. **[G: Latin America]**

Halevi, Nadav. Perspectives on the Balance of Payments. **In** *Ben-Porath, Y., ed.*, 1986, pp. 241–63. **[G: Israel]**

Helleiner, Gerald K. Balance-of-Payments Experience and Growth Prospects of Developing Countries: A Synthesis. *World Devel.*, Special Issue, August 1986, *14*(8), pp. 877–908. **[G: LDCs]**

Hoffmeyer, Erik. Beskæftigelse, betalingsbalance og økonomisk politik. (Employment, Balance of Payments and Economic Policy. With English summary.) *Nationaløkon. Tidsskr.*, 1986, *124*(3), pp. 259–64. **[G: Denmark; Sweden]**

Holtfrerich, Carl-Ludwig. U.S. Capital Exports to Germany 1919–1923 Compared to 1924–1929. *Exploration Econ. Hist.*, January 1986, *23*(1), pp. 1–32. **[G: U.S.; W. Germany]**

Hooper, Peter. Exchange Rate Simulation Properties of the MCM. *Europ. Econ. Rev.*, February 1986, *30*(1), pp. 171–98. **[G: U.S.; W. Germany; Japan]**

Hooper, Peter and Tryon, Ralph. The Current Account of the United States, Japan, and Germany: A Cyclical Analysis. **In** *Artus, P. and Guvenen, O., eds.*, 1986, pp. 181–205. **[G: U.S.; U.K.; W. Germany; Japan; Canada]**

Hrnčíř, Miroslav. Ways of Achieving External Equilibrium in the Czechoslovak Economy. *Czech. Econ. Digest.*, June/July 1986, (4), pp. 39–70. **[G: Czechoslovakia]**

Huizinga, John. Implications of the U.S. Net Capital Inflow: Comments. **In** *Hafer, R. W., ed. (I)*, 1986, pp. 163–67. **[G: U.S.]**

Ishii, Naoko. Scope for Macroeconomic Policy Coordination between the U.S. and Japan. **In** *Finn, R. B., ed.*, 1986, pp. 211–23. **[G: Japan; U.S.]**

Jao, Y. C. Banking and Currency in the Special Economic Zones: Problems and Prospects. **In** *Jao, Y. C. and Leung, C. K., eds.*, 1986, pp. 160–83. **[G: China]**

Jauković, Radovan. Structural Problems of East–West Economic Relations. *Eastern Europ. Econ.*, Winter 1986-87, *25*(2), pp. 22–59. **[G: E. Europe]**

Johnson, David. Consumption, Permanent Income, and Financial Wealth in Canada: Empirical Evidence on the Intertemporal Approach to the Current Account. *Can. J. Econ.*, May 1986, *19*(2), pp. 189–206. **[G: Canada]**

Johnson, Robert A. U.S. International Transactions in 1985. *Fed. Res. Bull.*, May 1986, *72*(5), pp. 287–97. **[G: U.S.]**

Kamas, Linda. The Balance of Payments Offset to Monetary Policy: Monetarist, Portfolio Balance, and Keynesian Estimates for Mexico and Venezuela. *J. Money, Credit, Banking*, November 1986, *18*(4), pp. 467–81. **[G: Mexico; Venezuela]**

Kenneally, Martin and Nhan, Tai Van. The Strength and Stability of the Relationships between Monetary Variables and Exchange Market Pressure Reconsidered. *Southern Econ. J.*, July 1986, *53*(1), pp. 95–109. **[G: OECD]**

Kharas, Homi J. and Shishido, Hisanobu. A Dynamic-Optimization Model of Foreign Borrowing: A Case Study of Thailand. *J. Policy Modeling*, Spring 1986, *8*(1), pp. 1–26. **[G: Thailand]**

Killick, Tony. Balance of Payments Adjustment and Developing Countries: Some Outstanding Issues. **In** *Posner, M., ed.*, 1986, pp. 64–90.

Klein, Lawrence R. International Aspects of Saving. **In** *Adams, F. G. and Wachter, S. M., eds.*, 1986, pp. 195–204. **[G: OECD]**

Köves, András. Foreign Economic Equilibrium, Economic Development and Economic Policy in the CMEA Countries. *Acta Oecon.*, 1986, *36*(1–2), pp. 35–53. **[G: CMEA]**

Krejča, František. Principles of Domestic and External Monetary Bank Policy after 1985. *Czech. Econ. Digest.*, May 1986, (3), pp. 24–46. **[G: Czechoslovakia]**

Krejčí, Jan. German Reparations after the Second World War. *Czech. Econ. Digest.*, Oct./Nov. 1986, (7), pp. 44–63. **[G: W. Germany]**

Kremers, Jeroen J. M. The Dutch Disease in the Netherlands. **In** *Neary, J. P. and van Wijnbergen, S., eds.*, 1986, pp. 96–136. **[G: Netherlands]**

Krol, Robert. The Interdependence of the Term Structure of Eurocurrency Interest Rates. *J. Int. Money Finance*, June 1986, *5*(2), pp. 245–53. **[G: Switzerland; W. Germany]**

Krueger, Russell C. U.S. International Transactions, First Quarter 1986. *Surv. Curr. Bus.*, June 1986, *66*(6), pp. 36–73. **[G: U.S.]**

Kuntjoro-Jakti, Dorodjatun. The Global Crisis of the 1980s and Indonesia's Response. *Hitotsubashi J. Econ.*, Spec. Iss. Oct. 1986, 27, pp. 101–13.

Laffargue, Jean-Pierre. Decomposition of the International Consequences of Policies into World and Difference Effects: Application to the Fair Multi-Country Model. *J. Econ. Dynam. Control*, June 1986, *10*(1/2), pp. 291–95. **[G: U.S.; W. Germany; Italy; Belgium]**

Lal, Deepak and Wolf, Martin. Debt, Deficits, and Distortions. **In** *Lal, D. and Wolf, M., eds.*, 1986, pp. 239–91. **[G: Global]**

Lancaster, Carol and Williamson, John. African Debt and Financing: Concluding Appraisal. **In** *Lancaster, C. and Williamson, J., eds.*, 1986, pp. 201–15. **[G: Africa]**

Laney, Leroy O. The Case of the World's Missing Money. *Fed. Res. Bank Dallas Econ. Rev.*, January 1986, pp. 1–9. **[G: Global]**

Laney, Leroy O. Twin Deficits in the 1980s; What Are the Linkages? *Bus. Econ.*, April 1986, *21*(2), pp. 40–45. **[G: U.S.]**

Leddin, Anthony. Portfolio Equilibrium and Monetary Policy in Ireland. *Econ. Soc. Rev.*, January 1986, *17*(2), pp. 133–46. **[G: Ireland]**

Lee, Chi-wen Jevons. A Portfolio Equilibrium Approach to Short-term Capital Movements in Developing Countries. *Rivista Int. Sci. Econ. Com.*, Oct.-Nov. 1986, *33*(10–11), pp. 1095–1105. **[G: Taiwan; Korea; Finland; Israel]**

Léonard, Jacques. Les fuites de capitaux hors des pays les plus endettés de l'Amérique latine. (Capital Flights out of the Most Indebted Latino-American Countries. With English summary.) *Écon. Soc.*, January 1986, *20*(1), pp. 297–316. **[G: Argentina; Brazil; Mexico; Venezuela]**

Liviatan, Nissan and Piterman, Sylvia. Accelerating Inflation and Balance-of-Payments Crises, 1973–1984. **In** *Ben-Porath, Y., ed.*, 1986, pp. 320–46. **[G: Israel]**

MacIntyre, Arnold. Finance, Growth and the Balance of Trade in OECS Countries. *Soc. Econ. Stud.*, December 1986, *35*(4), pp. 176–212. **[G: Caribbean]**

Martin, Ricardo and van Wijnbergen, Sweder J. G. Shadow Prices and the Intertemporal Aspects of Remittances and Oil Revenues in Egypt. **In** *Neary, J. P. and van Wijnbergen, S., eds.*, 1986, pp. 142–68. **[G: Egypt]**

McCafferty, Stephen. Interwar Movements of Dollars to Europe and the U.S. Currency Supply: Comments. *J. Int. Money Finance*, Supp. March 1986, *5*, pp. S157–59. **[G: U.S.]**

McGregor, Peter G. and Swales, J. K. Balance of Payments Constrained Growth: A Rejoinder. *Appl. Econ.*, December 1986, *18*(12), pp. 1265–74. **[G: OECD]**

McKenzie, Ian M. Australia's Real Exchange Rate during the Twentieth Century. *Econ. Rec.*, Supplement 1986, pp. 69–78. **[G: Australia]**

Meltzer, Allan H. Size, Persistence and Interrelation of Nominal and Real Shocks: Some Evidence from Four Countries. *J. Monet. Econ.*, January 1986, *17*(1), pp. 161–94. **[G: U.S.; U.K.; Canada; W. Germany]**

Merrick, John J., Jr. and Saunders, Anthony. International Expected Real Interest Rates: New Tests of the Parity Hypothesis and U.S. Fiscal Policy Effects. *J. Monet. Econ.*, November 1986, *18*(3), pp. 313–22. **[G: OECD]**

Mickwitz, Gösta. Internationaliseringens konsekvenser. (Consequences of Internationalization. With English summary.) *Ekon. Samfundets Tidskr.*, 1986, *39*(3), pp. 117–18.

Milone, Luciano Marcello. The Law of One Price: Further Empirical Evidence Concerning Italy and the United Kingdom. *Appl. Econ.*, June 1986, *18*(6), pp. 645–61. **[G: Italy; U.K.]**

Minford, Patrick; Agénor, Pierre-Richard and Nowell, Eric. A New Classical Econometric Model of the World Economy. *Econ. Modelling*, July 1986, *3*(3), pp. 154–74. **[G: Selected OECD]**

Mitra, Pradeep K. A Description of Adjustment to External Shocks: Country Groups. **In** *Lal, D. and Wolf, M., eds.*, 1986, pp. 103–14. **[G: LDCs]**

Newbery, David M. G. Certainty Equivalence Methods in the Macroeconomic Management of Petroleum Resources: Comment. **In** *Neary, J. P. and van Wijnbergen, S., eds.*, 1986, pp. 195–200. **[G: Norway]**

Nickelsburg, Gerald. Rediscounting Private Dollar Debt and Capital Flight in Ecuador. *J. Int. Money Finance*, December 1986, *5*(4), pp. 497–503. **[G: Ecuador]**

Nötel, R. International Credit and Finance. **In** *Kaser, M. C. and Radice, E. A., eds.*, 1986, pp. 170–295. **[G: E. Europe]**

Nyirabu, C. M. External Debt Management in the African Context: Comment. **In** *Helleiner, G. K, ed.*, 1986, pp. 181–83. **[G: Africa]**

Ouattara, Alassane D. The Balance-of-Payments Adjustment Process in Developing Countries: The Experience of the Ivory Coast. *World Devel.*, Special Issue, August 1986, *14*(8), pp. 1085–1105. **[G: Ivory Coast]**

Page, S. A. B. Prospects for Non-oil Developing Countries. *Nat. Inst. Econ. Rev.*, May 1986, (116), pp. 31–37. **[G: LDCs]**

Panchamukhi, V. R. Trade and International Finance: Some Issues and Dilemmas of the Developing Countries. **In** *Panchamukhi, V. R., et al.*, 1986, pp. 27–54. **[G: LDCs]**

Park, Yung Chul. Foreign Debt, Balance of Payments, and Growth Prospects: The Case of the Republic of Korea, 1965–88. *World Devel.*, Special Issue, August 1986, *14*(8), pp. 1019–58. **[G: S. Korea]**

Patel, I. G. The Balance of Payments Problem. **In** *Patel, I. G.*, 1986, pp. 48–60. **[G: India]**

Petersmann, Ernst-Ulrich. Trade Restrictions for Balance-of-Payments Purposes and the GATT: Strengthening the Soft International Law of Balance-of-Payments Adjustment Measures. **In** *Dicke, D. C., ed.*, 1986, pp. 181–212.

Please, Stanley. Balance of Payments Adjustment and Developing Countries: Some Outstanding Issues: Comment. **In** *Posner, M., ed.*, 1986, pp. 90–96.

Pollard, Sidney. Stagflation, Fiscal Deficits and Balance of Payments—Great Britain and Germany. *Hitotsubashi J. Econ.*, Spec. Iss. Oct. 1986, *27*, pp. 42–56. **[G: U.K.; W. Germany]**

Pope, David H. Australian Capital Inflow, Sectional Prices and the Terms of Trade: 1870–1939. *Australian Econ. Pap.*, June 1986, *25*(46), pp. 67–82. **[G: Australia]**

Pope, Mervyn J. Adjustment to What: Do We Really Have a Balance of Payments Problem? *New Zealand Econ. Pap.*, 1986, *20*, pp. 131–47. **[G: New Zealand]**

Purvis, Douglas D. Indonesia's Other Dutch Disease: Economic Effects of the Petroleum Boom: Comment. **In** *Neary, J. P. and van Wijnbergen, S., eds.*, 1986, pp. 321–23. **[G: Indonesia]**

Putnam, Bluford H. and Wilford, D. Sykes. International Reserve Flows: Seemingly Unrelated Regressions. **In** *Putnam, B. H. and Wilford, D. S., eds.*, 1986, *1978*, pp. 66–80. **[G: W. Europe]**

Putnam, Bluford H. and Wilford, D. Sykes. The

Evolution of the Flexible Exchange Rate Debate. **In** *Putnam, B. H. and Wilford, D. S., eds.*, 1986, pp. 123–38. **[G: U.S.; W. Germany]**

Rączkowski, Stanisław. The Influence of International Movements of Prices and Inflation on the Economies of the Socialist Countries. *Eastern Europ. Econ.*, Summer 1986, *24*(4), pp. 3–28. **[G: CMEA]**

Ramos, Joseph. Stabilization and Adjustment Policies in the Southern Cone, 1974–1983. **In** *Economic Commission for Latin America and the Caribbean*, 1986, pp. 65–99. **[G: Argentina; Chile; Uruguay]**

Redfield, Corey B. A Theoretical Analysis of the Volatility Premium in the Dollar Index Contract. *J. Futures Markets*, Winter 1986, *6*(4), pp. 619–27. **[G: U.S.]**

Reinhart, Vincent. Macroeconomic Influences on the U.S.–Japan Trade Imbalance. *Fed. Res. Bank New York Quart. Rev.*, Spring 1986, *11*(1), pp. 6–11. **[G: U.S.]**

Reisen, Helmut. The Latin American Transfer Problem in Historical Perspective. **In** *Maddison, A., ed.*, 1986, pp. 148–54. **[G: Latin America]**

Remolona, Eli M. and Lamberte, Mario B. Financial Reforms and Balance-of-Payments Crisis: The Case of the Philippines: 1980–83. *Philippine Rev. Econ. Bus.*, Mar./June 1986, *23*(1/2), pp. 101–41. **[G: Philippines]**

Remolona, Eli M.; Mangahas, Mahar and Pante, Filologo, Jr. Foreign Debt, Balance of Payments, and the Economic Crisis of the Philippines in 1983–84. *World Devel.*, Special Issue, August 1986, *14*(8), pp. 993–1018. **[G: Philippines]**

Revéiz, Edgar and Pérez, María José. Columbia: Moderate Economic Growth, Political Stability, and Social Welfare. **In** *Hartlyn, J. and Morley, S. A., eds.*, 1986, pp. 265–91. **[G: Columbia]**

Ribe, Frederick C. and Beeman, William J. The Monetary–Fiscal Mix and Long-run Growth in an Open Economy. *Amer. Econ. Rev.*, May 1986, *76*(2), pp. 209–12. **[G: U.S.]**

Ruffin, Roy J. and Rassekh, Farhad. The Role of Foreign Direct Investment in U.S. Capital Outflows. *Amer. Econ. Rev.*, December 1986, *76*(5), pp. 1126–30. **[G: U.S.]**

Russell, Sharon Stanton. Remittances from International Migration: A Review in Perspective. *World Devel.*, June 1986, *14*(6), pp. 677–96. **[G: LDCs]**

Schadler, Susan M. Effect of a Slowdown in Industrial Economies on Selected Asian Countries. *Int. Monet. Fund Staff Pap.*, June 1986, *33*(2), pp. 345–72. **[G: OECD; Asia]**

Schiemann, Jürgen. Der Bedarf an offizieller Währungsreserve als Kriterium für die Bestimmung einer optimalen Währungsunion: Ein theoretischer Ansatz und empirischer Befund für die Länder der Europäischen Gemeinschaft. (The Need of Official Currency Reserves as a Criterion for the Determination of an Optimal Currency Union: A Theoretical Approach and Empirical Evidence for the EEC. With English summary.) *Jahr. Nationalökon. Statist.*, November 1986, *201*(6), pp. 589–604. **[G: EEC]**

Scholl, Russell B. The International Investment Position of the United States in 1985. *Surv. Curr. Bus.*, June 1986, *66*(6), pp. 26–35, 16. **[G: U.S.]**

Schwartz, Anna J. The Open Economy: Implications for Monetary and Fiscal Policy: Comment. **In** *Gordon, R. J., ed.*, 1986, pp. 504–10. **[G: U.S.]**

Sengupta, Arjun. Allocation of SDRs Linked to Reserve Needs. *Finance Develop.*, September 1986, *23*(3), pp. 19–21.

Shann, Edward W. Australia's Real Exchange Rate during the Twentieth Century: Comment. *Econ. Rec.*, Supplement 1986, pp. 79–81. **[G: Australia]**

Sjaastad, Larry A.; Almansi, Aquiles and Hurtado, Carlos. The Debt Crisis in Latin America. **In** *Lal, D. and Wolf, M., eds.*, 1986, pp. 131–81. **[G: Argentina; Brazil; Chile; Mexico; Venezuela]**

Smith, Alasdair. Shadow Prices and the Intertemporal Aspects of Remittances and Oil Revenues in Egypt: Comment. **In** *Neary, J. P. and van Wijnbergen, S., eds.*, 1986, pp. 168–69. **[G: Egypt]**

Solimano, Andrés. Contractionary Devaluation in the Southern Cone: The Case of Chile. *J. Devel. Econ.*, September 1986, *23*(1), pp. 135–51. **[G: Chile]**

Suba-Varga, Judit. "Foreign Trade Constraint" and Cyclical Development. *Acta Oecon.*, 1986, *36*(3–4), pp. 251–70. **[G: Hungary]**

Svendsen, Knud Erik. The Creation of Macroeconomic Imbalances and a Structural Crisis. **In** *Boesen, J., et al., eds.*, 1986, pp. 59–78. **[G: Tanzania]**

Takagi, Shinji. Rediscount Policy and Official Capital Flows: A Study of Monetary Control in Central America in the 1950s. *J. Money, Credit, Banking*, May 1986, *18*(2), pp. 200–210. **[G: Costa Rica; El Salvador; Nicaragua]**

Tandon, Rameshwar. Balance of Payments Adjustment and Financing in Developing Countries: Scenarios for the 1980s. *Econ. Int.*, February 1986, *39*(1), pp. 48–59. **[G: LDCs]**

Taylor, Mark P. A Varying-Parameter Empirical Model of Balance of Payments Determination under Fixed Exchange Rates: Results for the UK and West Germany. *Appl. Econ.*, June 1986, *18*(6), pp. 567–82. **[G: U.K.; W. Germany]**

Thirlwall, A. P. Balance of Payments Constrained Growth: A Reply. *Appl. Econ.*, December 1986, *18*(12), pp. 1259–63. **[G: OECD]**

Tourinho, Octávio A. F. Endividamento externo ótimo em um modelo de equilíbrio dinâmico multissetorial: um estudo de caso para o Brasil. (With English summary.) *Pesquisa Planejamento Econ.*, December 1986, *16*(3), pp. 647–87. **[G: Brazil]**

Toyoda, Toshihisa. Effects of Temporal Aggregation in a Model of Exchange Rate Determination. *Kobe Univ. Econ.*, 1986, (32), pp. 19–39. **[G: Japan; U.S.]**

Triffin, Robert. Correcting the World Monetary Scandal. *Challenge,* Jan./Feb. 1986, *28*(6), pp. 4–14. **[G: Global; U.S.]**

Tyson, Laura D'Andrea. The Debt Crisis and Adjustment Responses in Eastern Europe: A Comparative Perspective. *Int. Organ.*, Spring 1986, *40*(2), pp. 239–85. **[G: CMEA; LDCs]**

Vastrup, Claus. Beskæftigelse, betalingsbalance og dansk økonomisk politik. (Employment, Balance of Payments and Danish Economic Policy. With English summary.) *Nationaløkon. Tidsskr.*, 1986, *124*(3), pp. 265–73. **[G: Denmark]**

Viñals, José M. Deuda exterior y objectivos de balanza de pagos en España: un análisis de largo plazo. (With English summary.) *Invest. Ecón.*, September 1986, *10*(3), pp. 505–28. **[G: Spain]**

de Vries, Rimmer. International Debt and Economic Instability: Commentary. **In** *Axilrod, S. H., et al.*, 1986, pp. 87–97. **[G: U.S.; Latin America]**

Warr, Peter G. Indonesia's Other Dutch Disease: Economic Effects of the Petroleum Boom. **In** *Neary, J. P. and van Wijnbergen, S., eds.*, 1986, pp. 288–320.

Wasow, Bernard. Insurance and the Balance of Payments. **In** *Wasow, B. and Hill, R. D., eds.*, 1986, pp. 87–103. **[G: S. Korea; Portugal; India; Brazil; Taiwan]**

Werneck, Rogério L. F. Poupança estatal, dívida externa e crise financeira do sector público. (With English summary.) *Pesquisa Planejamento Econ.*, December 1986, *16*(3), pp. 551–74. **[G: Brazil]**

Wernerfelt, Karsten. Industriens muligheder for at løse balanceproblemerne. (Suggestions for a Growth-Oriented Industrial Policy. With English summary.) *Nationaløkon. Tidsskr.*, 1986, *124*(2), pp. 147–55. **[G: Denmark]**

Winer, Stanley L. Money and Politics in a Small Open Economy. *Public Choice,* 1986, *51*(2), pp. 221–39. **[G: Canada]**

Zedillo Ponce de Leon, Ernesto. Mexico's Recent Balance-of-Payments Experience and Prospects for Growth. *World Devel.*, Special Issue, August 1986, *14*(8), pp. 963–91. **[G: Mexico]**

4314 Exchange Rates and Markets: Theory and Studies

Adam, Marie-Christine, et al. The Devaluation Controversy: The Integration of Monetary and Real Variables in a Small, Open Economy. *J. Policy Modeling,* Spring 1986, *8*(1), pp. 53–67. **[G: Belgium]**

Adams, Charles and Boyer, Russell S. Efficiency and a Simple Model of Exchange-Rate Determination. *J. Int. Money Finance,* September 1986, *5*(3), pp. 285–302. **[G: Canada; U.S.]**

Adler, Michael and Simon, David. Exchange Risk Surprises in International Portfolios. *J. Portfol. Manage.*, Winter 1986, *12*(2), pp. 44–53. **[G: OECD]**

Ahamed, Liaquat. Collective Pegging to a Single Currency: The West African Monetary Union: Comment. **In** *Edwards, S. and Ahamed, L., eds.*, 1986, pp. 363–65. **[G: W. Africa]**

Ahking, Francis W. A Problem with Estimating the Short-run Monetary Exchange Rate Model. *J. Macroecon.*, Spring 1986, *8*(2), pp. 213–20.

Aivazian, Varouj A., et al. International Exchange Risk and Asset Substitutability. *J. Int. Money Finance,* December 1986, *5*(4), pp. 449–66. **[G: Selected OECD]**

Aizenman, Joshua. Testing Deviations from Purchasing Power Parity. *J. Int. Money Finance,* March 1986, *5*(1), pp. 25–35.

Aliber, Robert Z. Fixed Exchange Rates and the Rate of Inflation. **In** *Campbell, C. D. and Dougan, W. R., eds.*, 1986, pp. 116–21.

Amano, Akihiro. Exchange Rate Simulations: A Comparative Study. *Europ. Econ. Rev.*, February 1986, *30*(1), pp. 137–48. **[G: W. Germany; Japan; U.S.]**

Amano, Akihiro, et al. Comparative Exchange Rate Simulations. *Europ. Econ. Rev.*, February 1986, *30*(1), pp. 131–35.

Apel, Emmanuel. 'News' and Its Impact on Spot Exchange Rates: 1970–1982. *Finance,* December 1986, *7*(2), pp. 135–48. **[G: Canada]**

Apel, Emmanuel. The Administered Bank Rate and the Canada–U.S. Spot Exchange Rate: 1975–1979. *Empirical Econ.*, 1986, *11*(3), pp. 169–79. **[G: U.S.; Canada]**

Argy, Victor. The International Financial System. **In** *Bruce, R., et al., eds.*, 1986, pp. 279–96. **[G: OECD]**

Ariga, Kenn. On Variability of Exchange Rates. *Econ. Stud. Quart.*, December 1986, *37*(4), pp. 300–318.

Arndt, Sven W. Government Policy and the Decline in U.S. Trade Competitiveness. **In** *Cagan, P., ed.*, 1986, pp. 307–23. **[G: U.S.]**

Artus, Jacques R. Stabilization, Stagflation, and Investment Incentives: The Case of Kenya, 1979–1980: Comment. **In** *Edwards, S. and Ahamed, L., eds.*, 1986, pp. 289–92. **[G: Kenya]**

Artus, Patrick. Les dépenses publiques et leur mode de financement en économie ouverte avec changes flexibles: efficacité et stabilité de l'économie. (Public Expenditures and Deficit Financing in an Open Economy with Flexible Exchange Rates: Efficiency and Stability of the Economy. With English summary.) *Ann. Écon. Statist.*, July-Sept. 1986, (3), pp. 119–40.

Artus, Patrick and Bismut, Claude. Exchange Rate and Wage–Price Dynamics: A Theoretical Analysis and an Econometric Investigation. *Europ. Econ. Rev.*, February 1986, *30*(1), pp. 57–90. **[G: Selected OECD]**

Axilrod, Stephen H. Statement to the Subcommittee on Domestic Monetary Policy of the House Committee on Banking, Finance and Urban Affairs, November 7, 1985. *Fed. Res. Bull.*, January 1986, *72*(1), pp. 15–19. **[G: U.S.]**

Backus, David. The Canadian–U.S. Exchange Rate: Evidence from a Vector Autoregression. *Rev. Econ. Statist.*, November 1986, *68*(4), pp. 628–37. **[G: U.S.; Canada]**

Bailey, Martin J.; Tavlas, George S. and Ulan, Michael. Exchange-Rate Variability and Trade Performance: Evidence for the Big Seven Industrial Countries. *Weltwirtsch. Arch.*, 1986, *122*(3), pp. 466–77. **[G: Selected OECD]**

Baillie, Richard T. and McMahon, Patrick C. Estimation and Testing of the Term Structure of the Forward Premium under Rational Expectations. *J. Macroecon.*, Summer 1986, *8*(3), pp. 387–91. **[G: U.K.; W. Germany; Italy]**

Banaian, King; Laney, Leroy O. and Willett, Thomas D. Central Bank Independence: An International Comparison. **In** *Toma, E. F. and Toma, M., eds.*, 1986, *1983*, pp. 199–217. **[G: OECD]**

Barroux, Yves. The Belmont–Morgan Syndicate as an Optimal Investment Banking Contract: Comment. *Europ. Econ. Rev.*, June 1986, *30*(3), pp. 679–80. **[G: U.S.]**

Batten, Dallas S. and Belongia, Michael T. Monetary Policy, Real Exchange Rates, and U.S. Agricultural Exports. *Amer. J. Agr. Econ.*, May 1986, *68*(2), pp. 422–27. **[G: U.S.]**

Beenstock, Michael. A Theory of Home Currency Preference. *Weltwirtsch. Arch.*, 1986, *122*(2), pp. 223–32. **[G: U.K.]**

Beenstock, Michael and Dadashi, Saiid. The Profitability of Forward Currency Speculation by Central Banks. *Europ. Econ. Rev.*, April 1986, *30*(2), pp. 449–56. **[G: Canada]**

Belongia, Michael T. Estimating Exchange Rate Effects on Exports: A Cautionary Note. *Fed. Res. Bank St. Louis Rev.*, January 1986, *68*(1), pp. 5–16. **[G: U.S.]**

Bennett, Karl M. An Analysis of Jamaica's Foreign Exchange Auction. *Soc. Econ. Stud.*, December 1986, *35*(4), pp. 93–110. **[G: Jamaica]**

Benzoni, Laurent. Taux de change, prix du pétrole, déséquilibres monétaires internationaux. (Exchange Rate, Oil Price, International Monetary Disequilibrium. With English summary.) *Écon. Soc.*, July 1986, *20*(7), pp. 27–61. **[G: OPEC]**

Bergsten, C. Fred. Gearing Up World Growth. *Challenge*, May/June 1986, *29*(2), pp. 35–40. **[G: Global]**

Bhandari, Jagdeep S. and Decaluwe, Bernard. A Framework for the Analysis of Legal and Fraudulent Trade Transactions in "Parallel" Exchange Markets. *Weltwirtsch. Arch.*, 1986, *122*(2), pp. 233–53. **[G: LDCs]**

Biswas, Basudeb and Nandi, Sukumar. The Black Market Exchange Rate in a Developing Economy: The Case of India. *Indian Econ. J.*, Jan.-Mar. 1986, *33*(3), pp. 23–34. **[G: India]**

Black, Stanley W. Discrete Devaluation as a Signal to Price Setters: Suggested Evidence from Greece: Comment. **In** *Edwards, S. and Ahamed, L., eds.*, 1986, pp. 326–29. **[G: Greece]**

Black, Stanley W. Flexible Exchange Rates and National Monetary Policies: Comment. **In** *Tsoukalis, L., ed.*, 1986, pp. 186–88. **[G: OECD]**

Black, Stanley W. Real Exchange Rates and Deviations from Purchasing Power Parity under Floating Exchange Rates: A Comment. *Carnegie-Rochester Conf. Ser. Public Policy*, Autumn 1986, *25*, pp. 215–20. **[G: OECD]**

Blades, Derek. International Statistics: An OECD View. *Bus. Econ.*, July 1986, *21*(3), pp. 37–42. **[G: OECD]**

Blake, David; Beenstock, Michael and Brasse, Valerie G. The Performance of UK Exchange Rate Forecasters. *Econ. J.*, December 1986, *96*(384), pp. 986–99. **[G: U.K.]**

Blanchard, Olivier J. and Dornbusch, Rudiger. U.S. Deficits, the Dollar, and Europe. **In** *Blanchard, O.; Dornbusch, R. and Layard, R., eds.*, 1986, pp. 155–79. **[G: U.S.; W. Europe]**

Blanco, Herminio and Garber, Peter M. Recurrent Devaluation and Speculative Attacks on the Mexican Peso. *J. Polit. Econ.*, February 1986, *94*(1), pp. 148–66. **[G: Mexico]**

Blejer, Mario I. Welfare, Banks, and Capital Mobility in Steady State: The Case of Predetermined Exchange Rates: Comment. **In** *Edwards, S. and Ahamed, L., eds.*, 1986, pp. 199–200.

Bliss, Christopher. The Rise and Fall of the Dollar. *Oxford Rev. Econ. Policy*, Spring 1986, *2*(1), pp. 7–24. **[G: U.S.; U.K.; Japan; W. Germany]**

Blundell-Wignall, A. Understanding the U.S. Dollar in the Eighties: Comment. *Econ. Rec.*, Supplement 1986, pp. 39–40. **[G: U.S.]**

Bodurtha, James N., Jr. and Courtadon, Georges R. Efficiency Tests of the Foreign Currency Options Market. *J. Finance*, March 1986, *41*(1), pp. 151–62. **[G: U.S.]**

Bofinger, Peter. Wechselkurstheorien und Wirtschaftspolitik. (Exchange Rate Theories and Economic Policy. With English summary.) *Kredit Kapital*, 1986, *19*(2), pp. 184–212. **[G: OECD]**

Booth, Anne. Survey of Recent Developments. *Bull. Indonesian Econ. Stud.*, December 1986, *22*(3), pp. 1–26. **[G: Indonesia]**

Boothe, Paul M. and Longworth, David. Foreign Exchange Market Efficiency Tests: Implications of Recent Empirical Findings. *J. Int. Money Finance*, June 1986, *5*(2), pp. 135–52. **[G: U.S.; Canada]**

Boughton, James M., et al. Effects of Exchange Rate Changes in Industrial Countries. **In** *International Monetary Fund, Research Department*, 1986, pp. 115–49. **[G: OECD]**

Boyer, Russell S. Currency Mobility and Balance of Payments Adjustment. **In** *Putnam, B. H. and Wilford, D. S., eds.*, 1986, *1978*, pp. 197–211.

Braga de Macedo, Jorge. Collective Pegging to a Single Currency: The West African Monetary Union. **In** *Edwards, S. and Ahamed, L., eds.*, 1986, pp. 333–62. **[G: W. Africa]**

Branson, William H. Stabilization, Stagflation, and Investment Incentives: The Case of Kenya,

1979–1980. **In** *Edwards, S. and Ahamed, L., eds.*, 1986, pp. 267–88. **[G: Kenya]**

Branson, William H. The Limits of Monetary Coordination as Exchange Rate Policy. *Brookings Pap. Econ. Act.*, 1986, (1), pp. 175–94. **[G: U.S.]**

Brickley, James A. Returns and Risks of U.S. Bank Foreign Currency Activities: Discussion. *J. Finance*, July 1986, *41*(3), pp. 682–83. **[G: U.S.]**

Brinner, Roger E. The Dollar Exchange Rate and International Monetary Cooperation: Comments. **In** *Hafer, R. W., ed. (I)*, 1986, pp. 233–35. **[G: OECD]**

Brown, Stephen P. A. and Phillips, Keith R. Exchange Rates and World Oil Prices. *Fed. Res. Bank Dallas Econ. Rev.*, March 1986, pp. 1–10. **[G: U.S.; Global]**

Bruni, Franco and Monti, Mario. Protezionismo valutario e integrazione internazionale. (Foreign Exchange Controls and International Economic Integration. With English summary.) *Rivista Int. Sci. Econ. Com.*, September 1986, *33*(9), pp. 887–900.

Brunner, Karl and Meltzer, Allan H. Real Business Cycles, Real Exchange Rates, and Actual Policies. *Carnegie-Rochester Conf. Ser. Public Policy*, Autumn 1986, *25*, pp. 1–10.

Butlin, M. W. and Gray, Malcolm R. Exchange Rate Depreciation, the Current Account and Wages: Comment. *Econ. Rec.*, Supplement 1986, pp. 22–23. **[G: Australia]**

Cairncross, Alec. The Sterling Rate of Exchange as an Instrument of Policy. **In** *Cairncross, A.*, 1986, pp. 169–92. **[G: U.K.]**

Callier, Philippe. "Professional Trading," Exchange Rate Risk and the Growth of International Banking: A Note. *Banca Naz. Lavoro Quart. Rev.*, December 1986, (159), pp. 423–28.

Calvo, Guillermo A. Welfare, Banks, and Capital Mobility in Steady State: The Case of Predetermined Exchange Rates. **In** *Edwards, S. and Ahamed, L., eds.*, 1986, pp. 177–99.

Canzoneri, Matthew B. The Implications of Mean-Variance Optimization for Four Questions in International Macroeconomics: Comments. *J. Int. Money Finance*, Supp. March 1986, *5*, pp. S77–78.

Capie, Forrest H.; Mills, Terence C. and Wood, Geoffrey E. What Happened in 1931? **In** *Capie, F. and Wood, G. E., eds.*, 1986, pp. 120–48. **[G: U.K.]**

Carey, D. A. and Duggan, K. G. The Abolition of Exchange Controls. **In** *Reserve Bank of New Zealand*, 1986, pp. 153–63. **[G: New Zealand]**

Catinat, Michel; Maurice, Joël and Zagamé, Paul. Stratégie du taux de change et mesures d'accompagnement. Une analyse des coûts et avantages à partir d'exercises quantitatifs. (Rate of Exchange Strategy and Accompanying Measures of Economic Policy. With English summary.) *Revue Écon.*, September 1986, *37*(5), pp. 857–84. **[G: France]**

Chambers, Robert G. and Just, Richard E. A Critique of Exchange Rate Treatment in Agricultural Trade Models: Reply. *Amer. J. Agr. Econ.*, November 1986, *68*(4), pp. 994–97.

Chang, Jack S. K. and Shanker, Latha. Hedging Effectiveness of Currency Options and Currency Futures. *J. Futures Markets*, Summer 1986, *6*(2), pp. 289–305. **[G: W. Europe; U.S.; Japan; Canada]**

Chesney, Marc. Prix d'équilibre et efficience sur le marché suisse des options sur devises: analyse théorique et tests empiriques. (Equilibrium Value and the Efficiency of the Swiss Market for Foreign Exchange Options: Theoretical Analysis and Empirical Tests. With English summary.) *Finance*, December 1986, *7*(2), pp. 149–67. **[G: Switzerland]**

Chiang, Thomas C. Empirical Analysis on the Predictors of Future Spot Rates. *J. Finan. Res.*, Summer 1986, *9*(2), pp. 153–62. **[G: U.K.; Canada; France; W. Germany]**

Chiang, Thomas C. On the Predictors of the Future Spot Rates—A Multi-currency Analysis. *Financial Rev.*, February 1986, *21*(1), pp. 69–83. **[G: U.S.; U.K.; France; W. Germany; Canada]**

Chiesa, Gabriella. Disavanzo pubblico, cambio reale e trasmissione internazionale. (Public Deficit, Real Exchange and International Transmission. With English summary.) *Polit. Econ.*, April 1986, *2*(1), pp. 121–44.

Choksi, Armeane. Commodity Export Prices and the Real Exchange Rate in Developing Countries: Coffee in Colombia: Comment. **In** *Edwards, S. and Ahamed, L., eds.*, 1986, pp. 260–63. **[G: Colombia]**

Christ, Carl F. Accuracy of Forecasting as a Measure of Economic Uncertainty. **In** *Campbell, C. D. and Dougan, W. R., eds.*, 1986, pp. 154–60. **[G: U.S.]**

Clague, Christopher. Determinants of the National Price Level: Some Empirical Results. *Rev. Econ. Statist.*, May 1986, *68*(2), pp. 320–23. **[G: Global]**

Clague, Christopher. Tariffs, Transfers and the Real Exchange Rate. *Southern Econ. J.*, July 1986, *53*(1), pp. 155–69.

Clements, Kenneth W. Perspectives on Exchange Rate Regimes. **In** *Campbell, C. D. and Dougan, W. R., eds.*, 1986, pp. 110–15.

Cloete, J. J. Recent Exchange Rate Policy in South Africa—A Critique. *S. Afr. J. Econ.*, September 1986, *54*(3), pp. 239–49. **[G: S. Africa]**

Coleman, J. R. A Policy Analysis of Exchange Rate Fluctuations on the Rural Sector: The Experience of the Canadian Red Meat Industry. *J. Agr. Econ.*, May 1986, *37*(2), pp. 253–66. **[G: Canada]**

Collins, Michael. Sterling Exchange Rates, 1847–80. *J. Europ. Econ. Hist.*, Winter 1986, *15*(3), pp. 511–33. **[G: U.K.]**

Congdon, Tim. What Happened in 1931? Comment. **In** *Capie, F. and Wood, G. E., eds.*, 1986, pp. 149–56. **[G: U.K.]**

Connolly, Michael. The Speculative Attack on the Peso and the Real Exchange Rate: Argentina,

1979–81. *J. Int. Money Finance,* Supp. March 1986, *5,* pp. S117–30. **[G: Argentina]**

Consiglieri, Isabella. The Perception of Economic Policies and Exchange Rate Dynamics. *Econ. Notes,* 1986, (2), pp. 106–28.

Cooper, Richard N. A Monetary System Based on Fixed Exchange Rates. **In** *Campbell, C. D. and Dougan, W. R., eds.,* 1986, pp. 85–109.

Cooper, Richard N. An Analysis of Currency Devaluation in Developing Countries. **In** *Cooper, R. N.,* 1986, *1973,* pp. 199–227. **[G: LDCs]**

Cooper, Richard N. Dealing with the Trade Deficit in a Floating Rate System. *Brookings Pap. Econ. Act.,* 1986, (1), pp. 195–207. **[G: U.S.]**

Corden, W. Max. Exchange Rate Depreciation, the Current Account and Wages. *Econ. Rec.,* Supplement 1986, pp. 14–21.

Corden, W. Max. Fiscal Policies, Current Accounts and Real Exchange Rates: In Search of a Logic of International Policy Coordination. *Weltwirtsch. Arch.,* 1986, *122*(3), pp. 423–38.

Corrado, Charles J. and Taylor, Dean. The Cost of a Central Bank Leaning against a Random Walk. *J. Int. Money Finance,* September 1986, *5*(3), pp. 303–14.

Côté, Agathe. Les effets de la variablilité des taux de change sur le commerce international. Une analyse pour le Canada. (The Effects of Exchange Rate Variability on International Trade. An Analysis for Canada. With English summary.) *L'Actual. Econ.,* December 1986, *62*(4), pp. 501–20. **[G: Canada]**

Cox, W. Michael. A New Alternative Trade-Weighted Dollar Exchange Rate Index. *Fed. Res. Bank Dallas Econ. Rev.,* September 1986, pp. 20–28. **[G: U.S.]**

Cross, Sam Y. Treasury and Federal Reserve Foreign Exchange Operations. *Fed. Res. Bull.,* August 1986, *72*(8), pp. 525–28. **[G: U.S.]**

Cross, Sam Y. Treasury and Federal Reserve Foreign Exchange Operations. *Fed. Res. Bull.,* May 1986, *72*(5), pp. 298–302. **[G: U.S.]**

Cross, Sam Y. Treasury and Federal Reserve Foreign Exchange Operations. *Fed. Res. Bull.,* November 1986, *72*(11), pp. 766–69.

Cross, Sam Y. Treasury and Federal Reserve Foreign Exchange Operations: Interim Report. *Fed. Res. Bull.,* February 1986, *72*(2), pp. 109–12. **[G: U.S.]**

Cross, Sam Y. Treasury and Federal Reserve Foreign Exchange Operations. *Fed. Res. Bank New York Quart. Rev.,* Spring 1986, *11*(1), pp. 54–60. **[G: U.S.]**

Cross, Sam Y. Treasury and Federal Reserve Foreign Exchange Operations, May–July 1986. *Fed. Res. Bank New York Quart. Rev.,* Autumn 1986, *11*(3), pp. 43–47. **[G: U.S.]**

Cross, Sam Y. Treasury and Federal Reserve Foreign Exchange Operations, August–October 1986. *Fed. Res. Bank New York Quart. Rev.,* Autumn 1986, *11*(3), pp. 36–42. **[G: U.S.]**

Cross, Sam Y. Treasury and Federal Reserve Foreign Exchange Operations. *Fed. Res. Bank New York Quart. Rev.,* Summer 1986, *11*(2), pp. 47–51. **[G: U.S.]**

Culbertson, W. Patton, Jr. and Koray, Faik. Interest Rates, the Forward Premium, and Unanticipated Money. *Southern Econ. J.,* October 1986, *53*(2), pp. 393–99. **[G: U.S.]**

Currie, David and Hall, Stephen G. The Exchange Rate and the Balance of Payments. *Nat. Inst. Econ. Rev.,* February 1986, (115), pp. 74–82. **[G: U.K.]**

Cushman, David O. Has Exchange Risk Depressed International Trade? The Impact of Third-Country Exchange Risk. *J. Int. Money Finance,* September 1986, *5*(3), pp. 361–79. **[G: U.S.; Selected OECD]**

Daniel, Betty C. Empirical Determinants of Purchasing Power Parity Deviations. *J. Int. Econ.,* November 1986, *21*(3/4), pp. 313–26. **[G: U.K.; Japan; U.S.; Canada; W. Germany]**

Daniel, Betty C. Optimal Purchasing Power Parity Deviations. *Int. Econ. Rev.,* June 1986, *27*(2), pp. 483–511.

De Grauwe, Paul. Flexible Exchange Rates and National Monetary Policies: Comment. **In** *Tsoukalis, L., ed.,* 1986, pp. 189–91. **[G: OECD]**

Deane, Roderick S. Financial Sector Policy Reform: The Case of New Zealand. **In** *Cheng, H.-S., ed.,* 1986, pp. 89–104. **[G: New Zealand]**

Díaz-Alejandro, Carlos F. Economic Adjustment and the Real Exchange Rate: Comment. **In** *Edwards, S. and Ahamed, L., eds.,* 1986, pp. 414–19.

Dimand, Robert W. Keynes on Inflation and Exchange Rates. *Atlantic Econ. J.,* September 1986, *14*(3), pp. 81–82.

Dinwiddy, Caroline L. and Teal, Francis J. Project Appraisal Procedures and the Evaluation of Foreign Exchange. *Economica,* February 1986, *53*(209), pp. 97–107.

Dornbusch, Rudiger. Equilibrium and Disequilibrium Exchange Rates. **In** *Dornbusch, R.,* 1986, *1982,* pp. 31–57.

Dornbusch, Rudiger. Flexible Exchange Rates and Excess Capital Mobility. *Brookings Pap. Econ. Act.,* 1986, (1), pp. 209–26. **[G: U.S.]**

Dornbusch, Rudiger. Inflação, taxas de câmbio e estabilização. (With English summary.) *Pesquisa Planejamento Econ.,* August 1986, *16*(2), pp. 321–49. **[G: Brazil; U.S.; Germany]**

Dornbusch, Rudiger. Multiple Exchange Rates for Commercial Transactions. **In** *Edwards, S. and Ahamed, L., eds.,* 1986, pp. 143–65. **[G: Argentina]**

Dornbusch, Rudiger. Overborrowing: Three Case Studies. **In** *Dornbusch, R.,* 1986, *1985,* pp. 97–130. **[G: Chile; Brazil; Argentina]**

Dornbusch, Rudiger. Special Exchange Rates for Capital Account Transactions. *World Bank Econ. Rev.,* September 1986, *1*(1), pp. 3–33. **[G: LDCs; Venezuela; Mexico]**

Dornbusch, Rudiger. The Budget Deficit and the Dollar: Comment. **In** *Fischer, S., ed.,* 1986, pp. 393–402. **[G: U.S.; W. Germany; Japan]**

Dornbusch, Rudiger. The Overvalued Dollar. **In** *Dornbusch, R.,* 1986, pp. 17–30. **[G: U.S.; Global]**

Dornbusch, Rudiger and Fischer, Stanley. Stopping Hyperinflations Past and Present. *Weltwirtsch. Arch.*, 1986, *122*(1), pp. 1–47. **[G: Europe; Israel; Argentina]**

Doukas, John and Melhem, Melhem. The Reaction of Spot and Forward Rates to New Information. *Europ. Econ. Rev.*, April 1986, *30*(2), pp. 305–24. **[G: U.S.; Canada]**

Doukas, John and Rahman, Abdul H. Foreign Currency Futures and Monetary Policy Announcements: An Intervention Analysis. *J. Futures Markets,* Fall 1986, *6*(3), pp. 343–73. **[G: W. Europe; U.S.; Canada; Japan]**

Edison, Hali J. and Marquez, Jaime. Optimal Crawling Peg in Venezuela: An Optimal Control Application. *J. Econ. Dynam. Control,* June 1986, *10*(1/2), pp. 201–04. **[G: Venezuela]**

Edward, Sebastian. Are Devaluations Contractionary? *Rev. Econ. Statist.*, August 1986, *68*(3), pp. 501–08. **[G: LDCs]**

Edwards, Sebastian. A Commodity Export Boom and the Real Exchange Rate: The Money–Inflation Link. **In** *Neary, J. P. and van Wijnbergen, S., eds.*, 1986, pp. 229–48. **[G: Colombia]**

Edwards, Sebastian. Commodity Export Prices and the Real Exchange Rate in Developing Countries: Coffee in Colombia. **In** *Edwards, S. and Ahamed, L., eds.*, 1986, pp. 235–60. **[G: Colombia]**

Edwards, Sebastian and Ahamed, Liaquat. Economic Adjustment and Exchange Rates in Developing Countries: Introduction. **In** *Edwards, S. and Ahamed, L., eds.*, 1986, pp. 1–14.

Eichengreen, Barry. The Belmont–Morgan Syndicate as an Optimal Investment Banking Contract: Comment. *Europ. Econ. Rev.*, June 1986, *30*(3), pp. 681–82. **[G: U.S.]**

Enders, Klaus-Stefan. Langsame Preise und schnelle Finanzmärkte: Wechselkursstabilisierung und seine realen Kosten. (Slow Prices and Fast Financial Markets: Exchange Rate Stabilization and Its Real Cost. With English summary.) *Jahr. Nationalökon. Statist.*, May 1986, *201*(3), pp. 264–79.

Engel, Charles M. On the Correlation of Exchange Rates and Interest Rates. *J. Int. Money Finance,* March 1986, *5*(1), pp. 125–28.

Engel, Charles M. The International Monetary System: Forty Years after Bretton Woods: Review Essay. *J. Monet. Econ.*, May 1986, *17*(3), pp. 441–48.

Engle, Robert F. and Bollerslev, Tim. Modelling the Persistence of Conditional Variances. *Econometric Rev.*, 1986, *5*(1), pp. 1–50. **[G: U.S.; Switzerland]**

Evans, George W. A Test for Speculative Bubbles in the Sterling–Dollar Exchange Rate: 1981–84. *Amer. Econ. Rev.*, September 1986, *76*(4), pp. 621–36. **[G: U.S.; U.K.]**

Evans, Paul. Is the Dollar High because of Large Budget Deficits? *J. Monet. Econ.*, November 1986, *18*(3), pp. 227–49. **[G: U.S.]**

Fasano-Filho, Ugo. Currency Substitution and the Demand for Money: The Argentine Case, 1960–1976. *Weltwirtsch. Arch.*, 1986, *122*(2), pp. 327–39. **[G: Argentina]**

Feinberg, Robert M. The Interaction of Foreign Exchange and Market Power Effects on German Domestic Prices. *J. Ind. Econ.*, September 1986, *35*(1), pp. 61–70. **[G: W. Germany]**

Feldman, David H. and Tower, Edward. The Welfare Economics of an Unstable Real Exchange Rate. *Southern Econ. J.*, January 1986, *52*(3), pp. 607–16.

Feldstein, Martin S. The Budget Deficit and the Dollar. **In** *Fischer, S., ed.*, 1986, pp. 355–92. **[G: U.S.; W. Germany]**

Feldstein, Martin S. U.S. Budget Deficits and the European Economies: Resolving the Political Economy Puzzle. *Amer. Econ. Rev.*, May 1986, *76*(2), pp. 342–46. **[G: U.S.; W. Europe]**

Felmingham, B. S. and Divisekera, Sarath. The Response of Australia's Trade Balance under Different Exchange Rate Regimes. *Australian Econ. Pap.*, June 1986, *25*(46), pp. 33–46. **[G: Australia]**

Fender, John. Monetary and Exchange Rate Policies in an Open Macroeconomic Model with Unemployment and Rational Expectations. *Oxford Econ. Pap.*, November 1986, *38*(3), pp. 501–15.

Finn, Mary G. Forecasting the Exchange Rate: A Monetary or Random Walk Phenomenon? *J. Int. Money Finance,* June 1986, *5*(2), pp. 181–93. **[G: U.S.; U.K.]**

Fiorentini, Riccardo. Parità del potere d'acquisto: un riesame. (Purchasing Power Parity: A Reexamination. With English summary.) *Giorn. Econ.*, Nov.-Dec. 1986, *45*(11–12), pp. 639–51.

Fiorentini, Riccardo. Tasso di cambio e struttura dell'industria: il caso dell'economia periferica negli anni '70. (Exchange Rate and the Structure of Italian Industry in the Seventies. With English summary.) *Econ. Lavoro,* Jan.-Mar. 1986, *20*(1), pp. 87–97. **[G: Italy]**

Fischer, Bernhard and Trapp, Peter. Geld- und Finanzpolitik in Argentinien: Der Weg in die finanzielle Repression. (Financial Policies and Financial Repression in Argentina. With English summary.) *Kredit Kapital,* 1986, *19*(1), pp. 122–43. **[G: Argentina]**

Fischer, Stanley. Exchange Rate versus Money Targets in Disinflation. **In** *Fischer, S.*, 1986, pp. 247–62.

Fischer, Stanley. Meltzer on Uncertainty under Different Monetary Regimes. **In** *Campbell, C. D. and Dougan, W. R., eds.*, 1986, pp. 161–67. **[G: U.S.]**

Fischer, Stanley. Symposium on Exchange Rates, Trade, and Capital Flows: Comments. *Brookings Pap. Econ. Act.*, 1986, (1), pp. 227–32.

Flood, Robert P. and Hodrick, Robert J. Real Aspects of Exchange Rate Regime Choice with Collapsing Fixed Rates. *J. Int. Econ.*, November 1986, *21*(3/4), pp. 215–32.

Fodella, Gianni. Eliminare l'avanzo rivalutando lo yen? (Yen Revaluation to Offset the Surplus?

With English summary.) *Rivista Int. Sci. Econ. Com.*, May 1986, *33*(5), pp. 401–07. **[G: Japan]**

Fraga, Arminio. Price Uncertainty and the Exchange-Rate Risk Premium. *J. Int. Econ.*, February 1986, *20*(1/2), pp. 179–85.

Frankel, Jeffrey A. The Effects of Commercial, Fiscal, Monetary, and Exchange Rate Policies on the Real Exchange Rate: Comment. **In** *Edwards, S. and Ahamed, L., eds.*, 1986, pp. 86–87.

Frankel, Jeffrey A. The Implications of Mean–Variance Optimization for Four Questions in International Macroeconomics. *J. Int. Money Finance,* Supp. March 1986, *5*, pp. S53–75.

Frankel, Jeffrey A. and Froot, Kenneth A. Understanding the U.S. Dollar in the Eighties: The Expectations of Chartists and Fundamentalists. *Econ. Rec.*, Supplement 1986, pp. 24–38. **[G: U.S.]**

Freebairn, John W. The Exchange Rate and the Trade Account: Comment. *Econ. Rec.*, Supplement 1986, pp. 108–10. **[G: Australia]**

Frenkel, Jacob A. International Interdependence and the Constraints on Macroeconomic Policies. *Weltwirtsch. Arch.*, 1986, *122*(4), pp. 615–46.

Frenkel, Jacob A. On Some International Parity Conditions: An Empirical Investigation: Comments. *Europ. Econ. Rev.*, June 1986, *30*(3), pp. 715–22. **[G: U.S.; U.K.; W. Germany; France]**

Frenkel, Jacob A. The Covariation of Risk Premiums and Expected Future Spot Exchange Rates: Comments. *J. Int. Money Finance*, Supp. March 1986, *5*, pp. S23–30.

Frenkel, Jacob A. and Goldstein, Morris. A Guide to Target Zones. *Int. Monet. Fund Staff Pap.*, December 1986, *33*(4), pp. 633–73. **[G: OECD]**

Fry, Maxwell J. Financial Structure, Financial Regulation, and Financial Reform in the Philippines and Thailand, 1960–1984. **In** *Cheng, H.-S., ed.*, 1986, pp. 161–84. **[G: Philippines; Thailand]**

Gaab, W.; Granziol, M. J. and Horner, Melchior. On Some International Parity Conditions: An Empirical Investment. *Europ. Econ. Rev.*, June 1986, *30*(3), pp. 683–713. **[G: U.S.; U.K.; W. Germany; France]**

Galy, M. On Some International Parity Conditions: An Empirical Investigation: Comments. *Europ. Econ. Rev.*, June 1986, *30*(3), pp. 723–26. **[G: U.S.; U.K.; W. Germany; France]**

Garber, Peter M. and Grilli, Vittorio U. The Belmont–Morgan Syndicate as an Optimal Investment Banking Contract. *Europ. Econ. Rev.*, June 1986, *30*(3), pp. 649–77. **[G: U.S.]**

Gärtner, Manfred. Anticipated Shocks and Exchange Rate Disequilibrium beyond the Short Run. *Z. Wirtschaft. Sozialwissen.*, 1986, *106*(1), pp. 1–13.

Ghosh, Sukesh K. Expectations and Niehans' Exchange Rate Dynamics [Exchange Rate Dynamics with Stock/Flow Interaction]. *Weltwirtsch. Arch.*, 1986, *122*(3), pp. 552–65.

Gidlow, R. M. Intervention in the Forward Market by the Reserve Bank under the Spot–Swap System. *S. Afr. J. Econ.*, September 1986, *54*(3), pp. 250–62. **[G: S. Africa]**

Glick, Reuven. Real Exchange Rates, Imperfect Information, and Economic Disturbances. *Fed. Res. Bank San Francisco Econ. Rev.*, Fall 1986, (4), pp. 44–59. **[G: U.S.]**

Gordon, J. M. The J-Curve Effects. *Econ. Rec.*, Supplement 1986, pp. 82–88. **[G: Australia; U.S.]**

Gordon, Robert J. U.S. Fiscal Deficits and the World Imbalance of Payments. *Hitotsubashi J. Econ.*, Spec. Iss. Oct. 1986, *27*, pp. 7–41. **[G: U.S.]**

Grammatikos, Theoharry. Intervalling Effects and the Hedging Performance of Foreign Currency Futures. *Financial Rev.*, February 1986, *21*(1), pp. 21–36. **[G: U.K.; Japan; W. Germany; Canada; Switzerland]**

Grammatikos, Theoharry; Saunders, Anthony and Swary, Itzhak. Returns and Risks of U.S. Bank Foreign Currency Activities. *J. Finance*, July 1986, *41*(3), pp. 671–82. **[G: U.S.]**

Gray, Jo Anna. The Speculative Attack on the Peso and the Real Exchange Rate: Argentina, 1979–81: Comments. *J. Int. Money Finance*, Supp. March 1986, *5*, pp. S131–33.

Gregory, Allan W. and McCurdy, Thomas H. The Unbiasedness Hypothesis in the Forward Foreign Exchange Market: A Specification Analysis with Application to France, Italy, Japan, the United Kingdom and West Germany. *Europ. Econ. Rev.*, April 1986, *30*(2), pp. 365–81. **[G: France; Italy; Japan; U.K.; W. Germany]**

Grigsby, S. Elaine and Arnade, Carlos Anthony. The Effect of Exchange Rate Distortions on Grain Export Markets, the Case of Argentina. *Amer. J. Agr. Econ.*, May 1986, *68*(2), pp. 434–40. **[G: Argentina]**

Grilli, Vittorio U. Buying and Selling Attacks on Fixed Exchange Rate Systems. *J. Int. Econ.*, February 1986, *20*(1/2), pp. 143–56.

Grinberg, R. and Liubskii, M. Prices and Currency Relations in the Cooperation of CMEA Countries. *Prob. Econ.*, May 1986, *29*(1), pp. 17–32. **[G: CMEA]**

Gros, Daniel. Wage Indexation and the Real Exchange Rate in Small Open Economies: A Study of the Effects of Fluctuations in Export Earnings. *Int. Monet. Fund Staff Pap.*, March 1986, *33*(1), pp. 117–38.

Guitián, Manuel. Multiple Exchange Rates for Commercial Transactions: Comment. **In** *Edwards, S. and Ahamed, L., eds.*, 1986, pp. 165–69. **[G: Argentina]**

Gulhati, Ravi. Stabilization, Stagflation, and Investment Incentives: The Case of Kenya, 1979–1980: Comment. **In** *Edwards, S. and Ahamed, L., eds.*, 1986, pp. 292–93. **[G: Kenya]**

Hakkio, Craig S. Does the Exchange Rate Follow a Random Walk? A Monte Carlo Study of Four Tests for a Random Walk. *J. Int. Money Finance*, June 1986, *5*(2), pp. 221–29.

Hakkio, Craig S. and Leiderman, Leonardo. Intertemporal Asset Pricing and the Term Structures of Exchange Rates and Interest Rates: The Eurocurrency Market. *Europ. Econ. Rev.*, April 1986, *30*(2), pp. 325–44. **[G: OECD]**

Hanson, James A. Exchange Rate Management and Stabilization Policies in Developing Countries: Comment. **In** *Edwards, S. and Ahamed, L., eds.*, 1986, pp. 39–41.

Harberger, Arnold C. Economic Adjustment and the Real Exchange Rate. **In** *Edwards, S. and Ahamed, L., eds.*, 1986, pp. 371–414.

Haynes, Stephen E.; Hutchison, Michael M. and Mikesell, Raymond F. U.S.–Japanese Bilateral Trade and the Yen–Dollar Exchange Rate: An Empirical Analysis. *Southern Econ. J.*, April 1986, *52*(4), pp. 923–32. **[G: U.S.; Japan]**

Henderson, Dan F. Access to the Japanese Market: Some Aspects of Foreign Exchange Controls and Banking Law. **In** *Saxonhouse, G. R. and Yamamura, K., eds.*, 1986, pp. 131–56. **[G: Japan]**

Heri, Erwin W. Market Efficiency and Forecasting. An Investigation of Foreign Exchange Markets. *Rivista Int. Sci. Econ. Com.*, Oct.-Nov. 1986, *33*(10–11), pp. 1057–76. **[G: U.S.; W. Europe]**

Hill, Peter. International Price Levels and Purchasing Power Parities. *OECD Econ. Stud.*, Spring 1986, (6), pp. 133–59. **[G: OECD]**

Hodrick, Robert J. and Srivastava, Sanjay. The Covariation of Risk Premiums and Expected Future Spot Exchange Rates. *J. Int. Money Finance*, Supp. March 1986, *5*, pp. S5–21. **[G: U.S.]**

Hogan, Lindsay I. A Comparison of Alternative Exchange Rate Forecasting Models. *Econ. Rec.*, June 1986, *62*(177), pp. 215–23. **[G: Australia; U.S.]**

Holbik, Karel. Progress in the Internationalization of the Japanese Yen. *Rivista Int. Sci. Econ. Com.*, May 1986, *33*(5), pp. 409–24. **[G: Japan; U.S.]**

Holden, Merle. A Note on Purchasing Power Parity in South Africa. *S. Afr. J. Econ.*, September 1986, *54*(3), pp. 332–38. **[G: S. Africa]**

Holtham, Gerald. Exchange Rates in the OECD INTERLINK Model: Specification and Simulation Properties. *Europ. Econ. Rev.*, February 1986, *30*(1), pp. 199–235. **[G: OECD]**

Honohan, Patrick. A Commodity Export Boom and the Real Exchange Rate: The Money–Inflation Link: Comment. **In** *Neary, J. P. and van Wijnbergen, S., eds.*, 1986, pp. 249–50. **[G: Colombia]**

Honohan, Patrick and Peruga, Rodrigo. Exchange Rates Do Not Fail Variance Bounds Tests. *Manchester Sch. Econ. Soc. Stud.*, September 1986, *54*(3), pp. 308–13.

Hooper, Peter. Exchange Rate Simulation Properties of the MCM. *Europ. Econ. Rev.*, February 1986, *30*(1), pp. 171–98. **[G: U.S.; W. Germany; Japan]**

Hultman, Charles W. G-5 Exchange Market Intervention and Commercial Policy. *J. World Trade Law*, May:June 1986, *20*(3), pp. 287–93. **[G: U.S.]**

Humphrey, Thomas M. A Monetarist Model of Exchange Rate Determination. **In** *Humphreys, T. M.*, 1986, *1977*, pp. 188–94.

Humphrey, Thomas M. Bullionists' Exchange Rate Doctrines and Current Policy Debates. **In** *Humphreys, T. M.*, 1986, *1980*, pp. 251–54. **[G: U.K.]**

Humphrey, Thomas M. Dennis H. Robertson and the Monetary Approach to Exchange Rates. **In** *Humphreys, T. M.*, 1986, *1980*, pp. 220–27.

Humphrey, Thomas M. Explaining Exchange Rate Behavior: An Augmented Version of the Monetary Approach. **In** *Humphreys, T. M.*, 1986, *1981*, pp. 228–36.

Humphrey, Thomas M. Factors Determining Exchange Rates: A Simple Model and Empirical Tests. **In** *Humphreys, T. M.*, 1986, *1977*, pp. 195–200. **[G: U.K.; U.S.; Italy]**

Humphrey, Thomas M. The Monetary Approach to Exchange Rates: Its Historical Evolution and Role in Policy Debates. **In** *Humphreys, T. M.*, 1986, *1978*, pp. 201–08.

Humphrey, Thomas M. The Monetary Approach to Exchange Rates: Its Historical Evolution and Role in Policy Debates. **In** *Putnam, B. H. and Wilford, D. S., eds.*, 1986, *1978*, pp. 152–67. **[G: U.K.; Sweden; Germany]**

Humphrey, Thomas M. The Purchasing Power Parity Doctrine. **In** *Humphreys, T. M.*, 1986, *1979*, pp. 209–19.

Humphrey, Thomas M. and Lawler, Thomas A. Factors Determining Exchange Rates: A Simple Model and Empirical Tests. **In** *Putnam, B. H. and Wilford, D. S., eds.*, 1986, *1977*, pp. 139–51. **[G: U.K.; U.S.; Italy]**

Hussain, M. Nureldin and Thirlwall, A. P. The IMF Supply-Side Approach to Devaluation: A Reply. *Oxford Bull. Econ. Statist.*, February 1986, *48*(1), pp. 83–86. **[G: Sudan]**

Ikpi, A. E. Growing Interdependencies and Uncertainties: Discussion. **In** *Maunder, A. and Renborg, U., eds.*, 1986, pp. 90–93. **[G: LDCs]**

Ingram, James C. Central Bank Intervention: To Sterilize or Not? *Banca Naz. Lavoro Quart. Rev.*, June 1986, (157), pp. 179–86.

Islam, Shafiqul. The Dollar: Fickle Fundamentals or Misguided Markets? *World Econ.*, December 1986, *9*(4), pp. 365–83. **[G: U.S.; OECD]**

Ito, Takatoshi. Capital Controls and Covered Interest Parity between the Yen and the Dollar. *Econ. Stud. Quart.*, September 1986, *37*(3), pp. 223–41. **[G: U.S.; Japan; W. Europe]**

Jackson, Louise and Bruce, Robert. Foreign Exchange. **In** *Bruce, R., et al., eds.*, 1986, pp. 339–54. **[G: Australia]**

Jackson, Marvin R. When Is a Price a Price? The Level and Patterns of Price in the CMEA. *Soviet E. Europ. Foreign Trade*, Spring 1986, *22*(1), pp. 100–112. **[G: CMEA]**

Jager, Henk. Flexible Exchange Rates and National Monetary Policies: Comment. **In** *Tsoukalis, L., ed.*, 1986, pp. 192–98. **[G: OECD]**

Johnson, G. G. Exchange Rate Management and

Surveillance since 1972. **In** *Posner, M., ed.*, 1986, pp. 48–61. **[G: OECD]**

Johnson, Larry J. Foreign-Currency Options, Ex Ante Exchange-Rate Volatility, and Market Efficiency: An Empirical Test. *Financial Rev.*, November 1986, *21*(4), pp. 433–50. **[G: U.S.]**

Johnson, R. Stafford; Zuber, Richard A. and Loy, David. An Investigation into Currency Options and Market Efficiency. *Rivista Int. Sci. Econ. Com.*, Oct.-Nov. 1986, *33*(10–11), pp. 1077–93. **[G: U.S.; Canada; U.K.; W. Germany]**

Joyce, Joseph P. Canadian Exchange Market Intervention and Domestic Monetary Operations. *Quart. Rev. Econ. Bus.*, Summer 1986, *26*(2), pp. 94–105. **[G: Canada]**

Jungfer, Joachim. Die Hemmung des Wirtschaftswachstums in Entwicklungsländern durch Devisenbewirtschaftung. (Exchange Control and Economic Growth in Developing Countries. With English summary.) **In** *Eucken, W. and Böhm, F., eds.*, 1986, pp. 235–47. **[G: LDCs]**

Kaminsky, Graciela Laura. Uncertainty, Expectations of Devaluation, and the Real Exchange Rate. *J. Devel. Econ.*, November 1986, *24*(1), pp. 29–57. **[G: Argentina]**

Kamitake, Yoshiro. Darling, Goodenough and McKenna: Economic Thoughts of the City towards British Return to Gold in 1925. *Hitotsubashi J. Econ.*, December 1986, *27*(2), pp. 167–80. **[G: U.K.]**

Kaneko, Takafumi and Yasuhara, Norikazu. Exchange Rate Simulations with the EPA World Economic Model. *Europ. Econ. Rev.*, February 1986, *30*(1), pp. 237–59. **[G: W. Europe; U.S.; Japan; Canada]**

Kanno, Ryohei. U.S.–Japan Capital Interaction: Implications of Euroyen and Direct Investment. **In** *Finn, R. B., ed.*, 1986, pp. 173–83. **[G: U.S.; Japan; Selected Countries]**

Kapur, Basant K. Optimal Financial and Foreign-Exchange Liberalization of Less-developed Economies. **In** *Kapur, B. K.*, 1986, *1983*, pp. 92–122.

Karakitsos, Elias. Monetary Policy, Exchange Rate Dynamics and the Labour Market. *J. Econ. Dynam. Control*, June 1986, *10*(1/2), pp. 281–89.

Katseli, Louka T. Discrete Devaluation as a Signal to Price Setters: Suggested Evidence from Greece. **In** *Edwards, S. and Ahamed, L., eds.*, 1986, pp. 295–326. **[G: Greece]**

Kawai, Masahiro and Zilcha, Itzhak. International Trade with Forward-Futures Markets under Exchange Rate and Price Uncertainty. *J. Int. Econ.*, February 1986, *20*(1/2), pp. 83–98.

Kearney, Colm and MacDonald, Ronald. A Structural Portfolio Balance Model of the Sterling–Dollar Exchange Rate. *Weltwirtsch. Arch.*, 1986, *122*(3), pp. 478–96. **[G: U.S.; U.K.]**

Kearney, Colm and MacDonald, Ronald. Intervention and Sterilisation under Floating Exchange Rates: The UK 1973–1983. *Europ. Econ. Rev.*, April 1986, *30*(2), pp. 345–64. **[G: U.K.]**

Kenen, Peter B. and Rodrik, Dani. Measuring and Analyzing the Effects of Short-term Volatility in Real Exchange Rates. *Rev. Econ. Statist.*, May 1986, *68*(2), pp. 311–15. **[G: W. Europe; U.S.; Canada; Japan]**

Kenneally, Martin and Nhan, Tai Van. The Strength and Stability of the Relationships between Monetary Variables and Exchange Market Pressure Reconsidered. *Southern Econ. J.*, July 1986, *53*(1), pp. 95–109. **[G: OECD]**

Khan, Mohsin S. Developing Country Exchange Rate Policy Responses to Exogenous Shocks. *Amer. Econ. Rev.*, May 1986, *76*(2), pp. 84–87. **[G: LDCs]**

Khan, Mohsin S. Economic Adjustment and the Real Exchange Rate: Comment. **In** *Edwards, S. and Ahamed, L., eds.*, 1986, pp. 419–23.

Khan, Mohsin S. Exchange Rate Policies of Developing Countries in the Context of External Shocks. *Pakistan Devel. Rev.*, Autumn 1986, *25*(3), pp. 403–21. **[G: LDCs]**

Khilji, Nasir M. Exchange Rate Policies of Developing Countries in the Context of External Shocks: Comments. *Pakistan Devel. Rev.*, Autumn 1986, *25*(3), pp. 425–27. **[G: LDCs]**

Kiguel, Miguel A. Macroeconomic Adjustment under a Sliding Peg Exchange Rate and Imperfect Capital Mobility. *Eastern Econ. J.*, July-Sept. 1986, *12*(3), pp. 297–306.

Kindleberger, Charles P. International Capital Movements and Foreign-Exchange Markets in Crisis: The 1930s and the 1980s. **In** *Berend, I. T. and Borchardt, K., eds.*, 1986, pp. 437–55.

King, David T.; Putnam, Bluford H. and Wilford, D. Sykes. A Currency Portfolio Approach to Exchange Rate Determination: Exchange Rate Stability and the Independence of Monetary Policy. **In** *Putnam, B. H. and Wilford, D. S., eds.*, 1986, *1978*, pp. 179–96.

Koveos, Peter E. and Seifert, Bruce. Market Efficiency, Purchasing Power Parity, and Black Markets: Evidence from Latin American Countries. *Weltwirtsch. Arch.*, 1986, *122*(2), pp. 313–26. **[G: Latin America]**

Kravis, Irving B. The Three Faces of the International Comparison Project. *World Bank Res. Observer*, January 1986, *1*(1), pp. 3–26. **[G: Global]**

Krumm, Kathie L. The Effects of Commercial, Fiscal, Monetary, and Exchange Rate Policies on the Real Exchange Rate: Comment. **In** *Edwards, S. and Ahamed, L., eds.*, 1986, pp. 87–88.

Lai, Ching-chong. Flexible Exchange Rates and Monetary Policy. *Atlantic Econ. J.*, December 1986, *14*(4), pp. 103.

Lai, Ching-chong and Chu, Yun-peng. Exchange Rates Dynamics under Dual Floating Exchange Rate Regimes. *Southern Econ. J.*, October 1986, *53*(2), pp. 502–08.

Larraín, Felipe. Expectativas racionales y dinámica del tipo de cambio: una nota. (With English summary.) *Cuadernos Econ.*, April 1986, *23*(68), pp. 69–76.

Larrain, Maurice R. Portfolio Stock Adjustment and the Real Exchange Rate: The Dollar–Mark (DM) and Mark–Sterling. *J. Policy Modeling*, Winter 1986, *8*(4), pp. 577–96. **[G: U.S.; U.K.; W. Germany]**

Laskar, Daniel. International Cooperation and Exchange Rate Stabilization. *J. Int. Econ.*, August 1986, *21*(1/2), pp. 151–64.

Lawrence, Roger. Adjustment in Africa: What Can Be Done? **In** *Helleiner, G. K, ed.*, 1986, pp. 255–58. **[G: Africa]**

Lecaillon, Jean-Didier. Un modèle explicatif de l'évolution du taux de couverture des échanges franco-allemands. (With English summary.) *Revue Écon. Polit.*, Mar.-Apr. 1986, *96*(2), pp. 118–46. **[G: France; W. Germany]**

Leddin, Anthony. Portfolio Equilibrium and Monetary Policy in Ireland. *Econ. Soc. Rev.*, January 1986, *17*(2), pp. 133–46. **[G: Ireland]**

Lehrman, Lewis E. Back to Gold: Giving Up the "Order of the Jungle." *Challenge*, Jan./Feb. 1986, *28*(6), pp. 21–30. **[G: U.S.]**

Levy, Aviram. Tasso di cambio e interventi delle banche centrali: Schemi teorici ed esperienza italiana. (Exchange Rate and Central Banks' Exchange Market Intervention: Theoretical Issues and the Italian Experience. With English summary.) *Giorn. Econ.*, July-Aug. 1986, *45*(7–8), pp. 407–31. **[G: Italy]**

Levy, E. and Nobay, A. R. The Speculative Efficiency Hypothesis: A Bivariate Analysis. *Econ. J.*, Supplement 1986, *96*, pp. 109–21.

Lothian, James R. Real Dollar Exchange Rates under the Bretton-Woods and Floating Exchange-Rate Regimes. *J. Int. Money Finance*, December 1986, *5*(4), pp. 429–48. **[G: U.S.; OECD]**

MacDonald, Ronald and Young, Robert. Decision Rules, Expectations and Efficiency in Two Foreign Exchange Markets. *De Economist*, 1986, *134*(1), pp. 42–60. **[G: W. Germany; U.K.]**

Mahajan, Arvind and Mehta, Dileep. Efficiency and Speculation in the Foreign Exchange Market. *Indian Econ. J.*, Jan.-Mar. 1986, *33*(3), pp. 85–109.

Mahajan, Arvind and Mehta, Dileep. Swaps, Expectations, and Exchange Rates. *J. Banking Finance*, March 1986, *10*(1), pp. 7–20. **[G: U.S.]**

Makin, John H. and Sauer, Raymond D. Exchange Rate Determination with Changes in the Policy Regime: The Yen/Dollar Rate. *Rev. Econ. Statist.*, February 1986, *68*(1), pp. 164–69. **[G: U.S.; Japan]**

Mann, Catherine L. Prices, Profit Margins, and Exchange Rates. *Fed. Res. Bull.*, June 1986, *72*(6), pp. 366–79. **[G: U.S.]**

Marin, Dalia. Exchange Rate and Industrial Profits: Austria's Revaluation Policy in the 1970s. *Appl. Econ.*, June 1986, *18*(6), pp. 675–89. **[G: Austria]**

Marmer, Harry S. Portfolio Model Hedging with Canadian Dollar Futures: A Framework for Analysis. *J. Futures Markets*, Spring 1986, *6*(1), pp. 83–92. **[G: Canada]**

Marston, Richard C. Multiple Exchange Rates for Commercial Transactions: Comment. **In** *Edwards, S. and Ahamed, L., eds.*, 1986, pp. 169–73. **[G: Argentina]**

Marston, Richard C. The Effects of Coordinated Foreign Exchange Intervention in an Exchange-Rate Union. *Econ. Stud. Quart.*, June 1986, *37*(2), pp. 151–64.

Martin, W. and Shaw, I. The Effect of Exchange Rate Changes on the Value of Australia's Major Agricultural Exports. *Econ. Rec.*, Supplement 1986, pp. 101–07. **[G: Australia]**

Masson, Paul R. and Richardson, Peter. Exchange Rate Expectations and Current Balances in the OECD Interlink System. **In** *Artus, P. and Guvenen, O., eds.*, 1986, pp. 53–77. **[G: OECD]**

Matthews, K. and Valentine, T. J. The Australian Foreign Exchange Market 1983–86. *Econ. Rec.*, Supplement 1986, pp. 4–11. **[G: Australia]**

Matthews, K. G. P. Was Sterling Overvalued in 1925? *Econ. Hist. Rev., 2nd Ser.*, November 1986, *39*(4), pp. 572–87. **[G: U.K.]**

McCandless, George T., Jr. Tenencia de una segunda moneda durante períodos de inflación. (With English summary.) *Cuadernos Econ.*, August 1986, *23*(69), pp. 265–74.

McCulloch, J. Huston. Beyond the Historical Gold Standard. **In** *Campbell, C. D. and Dougan, W. R., eds.*, 1986, pp. 73–81.

McKenzie, Ian M. Australia's Real Exchange Rate during the Twentieth Century. *Econ. Rec.*, Supplement 1986, pp. 69–78. **[G: Australia]**

McKinnon, Ronald I. Currency Substitution and Instability in the World Dollar Standard [Dollar Stabilization and American Monetary Policy]. **In** *Putnam, B. H. and Wilford, D. S., eds.*, 1986, *1980*, pp. 249–71. **[G: U.S.]**

McKinnon, Ronald I. Exchange-Rate Volatility, International Trade, and Resource Allocation: A Perspective on Recent Research: Comments. *J. Int. Money Finance*, Supp. March 1986, *5*, pp. S113–15.

McKinnon, Ronald I. Foreign Exchange Dealers, the Domestic Money Market and Stabilising Speculation. **In** *[Tarshis, L.]*, 1986, pp. 28–55.

McKinnon, Ronald I. The Case for Internationalizing American Monetary Policy. **In** *Tsoukalis, L., ed.*, 1986, pp. 199–226. **[G: OECD]**

McKinnon, Ronald I. The Dollar Exchange Rate and International Monetary Cooperation. **In** *Hafer, R. W., ed. (I)*, 1986, pp. 211–31. **[G: OECD]**

Meese, Richard. Testing for Bubbles in Exchange Markets: A Case of Sparkling Rates? *J. Polit. Econ.*, April 1986, *94*(2), pp. 345–73. **[G: U.S.]**

Meese, Richard and Rogoff, Kenneth. Was It Real? The Exchange Rate–Interest Differential Relation: 1973–1984. *J. Econ. Dynam. Control*, June 1986, *10*(1/2), pp. 297–98.

Meister, Shelley and Sherman, Thomas A. Import, Export Prices Reflect Declining Dollar and Oversupply in 1985. *Mon. Lab. Rev.*, April 1986, *109*(4), pp. 3–16. **[G: U.S.]**

Meltzer, Allan H. Monetary and Exchange Rate Regimes: A Comparison of Japan and the United States. *Cato J.*, Fall 1986, *6*(2), pp. 667–83. **[G: U.S.; Japan]**

Meltzer, Allan H. Some Evidence on the Comparative Uncertainty Experienced under Different Monetary Regimes. **In** *Campbell, C. D. and Dougan, W. R., eds.*, 1986, pp. 122–53. **[G: U.S.]**

Mendel, Julius S. The Effect of Exchange Rate Depreciation on the Metal and Engineering Industry. *Econ. Rec.*, Supplement 1986, pp. 89–93. **[G: Australia]**

Metghalchi, Massoud and Im, Eric Iksoon. Purchasing Power Parity: A Spectral Analysis. *Rivista Int. Sci. Econ. Com.*, Oct.-Nov. 1986, *33*(10–11), pp. 1041–47. **[G: EEC]**

Micossi, Stephano and Rossi, Salvatore. Controlli sui movimenti di capitale: il caso italiano. (Foreign-Exchange Controls: The Case of Italy. With English summary.) *Giorn. Econ.*, Jan.-Feb. 1986, *45*(1–2), pp. 17–53. **[G: Italy]**

Minczeles, Alain and Sicsic, Pierre. La désinflation: 1982–1985. Une analyse variantielle. (Disinflation in France: 1982–1985. With English summary.) *Revue Écon.*, November 1986, *37*(6), pp. 1127–46. **[G: France]**

Moggridge, D. E. Keynes and the International Monetary System 1909–46. **In** *[Tarshis, L.]*, 1986, pp. 56–83.

Morandé, Felipe G. Volatilidad de los tipos de cambio y contratos traslapados. (With English summary.) *Cuadernos Econ.*, August 1986, *23*(69), pp. 229–36.

Moreno, Ramon. Monetary Control without a Central Bank: The Case of Hong Kong. *Fed. Res. Bank San Francisco Econ. Rev.*, Spring 1986, (2), pp. 17–37. **[G: Hong Kong]**

Morris, Frank E. The Changing World of Central Banking. *New Eng. Econ. Rev.*, Mar./Apr. 1986, pp. 3–6. **[G: U.S.]**

Murfin, Andy and Ormerod, Paul. The Sterling–Dollar Exchange Market 1973–1982: Surprises and Expectations. **In** *Artus, P. and Guvenen, O., eds.*, 1986, pp. 79–102. **[G: U.K.; U.S.]**

Murphy, C. W. Exchange Rate Policy and the AMPS Model. *Econ. Rec.*, Supplement 1986, pp. 41–54.

Murtfeld, Martin. The Debt Problem and External Shocks: Comment. **In** *Giersch, H., ed.*, 1986, pp. 37–41. **[G: Selected Countries]**

Mussa, Michael. Nominal Exchange Rate Regimes and the Behavior of Real Exchange Rates: Evidence and Implications. *Carnegie-Rochester Conf. Ser. Public Policy*, Autumn 1986, *25*, pp. 117–213. **[G: OECD]**

Mussa, Michael. The Effects of Commercial, Fiscal, Monetary, and Exchange Rate Policies on the Real Exchange Rate. **In** *Edwards, S. and Ahamed, L., eds.*, 1986, pp. 43–86.

Nashashibi, Karim and Clawson, Patrick. The IMF Supply-Side Approach to Devaluation: A Response. *Oxford Bull. Econ. Statist.*, February 1986, *48*(1), pp. 73–82. **[G: Sudan]**

Nguyen, D. T. Exchange Rate Regimes and the Volatility of Financial Prices: Comment. *Econ. Rec.*, Supplement 1986, pp. 67–68. **[G: U.S.; Australia; Japan; W. Germany]**

Nickelsburg, Gerald. Rediscounting Private Dollar Debt and Capital Flight in Ecuador. *J. Int. Money Finance*, December 1986, *5*(4), pp. 497–503. **[G: Ecuador]**

O'Brien, Stephen. Collective Pegging to a Single Currency: The West African Monetary Union: Comment. **In** *Edwards, S. and Ahamed, L., eds.*, 1986, pp. 365–67. **[G: W. Africa]**

Obstfeld, Maurice. Capital Controls, the Dual Exchange Rate, and Devaluation. *J. Int. Econ.*, February 1986, *20*(1/2), pp. 1–20.

Obstfeld, Maurice. Capital Flows, the Current Account, and the Real Exchange Rate: Some Consequences of Stabilization and Liberalization. **In** *Edwards, S. and Ahamed, L., eds.*, 1986, pp. 201–29.

Obstfeld, Maurice. Speculative Attack and the External Constraint in a Maximizing Model of the Balance of Payments. *Can. J. Econ.*, February 1986, *19*(1), pp. 1–22.

Officer, Lawrence H. The Law of One Price Cannot Be Rejected: Two Tests Based on the Tradable/Nontradable Price Ratio. *J. Macroecon.*, Spring 1986, *8*(2), pp. 159–82. **[G: Global]**

Orchard, Freddy. Liberalizing Capital Controls: The Singapore Case. **In** *Cheng, H.-S., ed.*, 1986, pp. 261–63. **[G: Singapore]**

Orden, David. A Critique of Exchange Rate Treatment in Agricultural Trade Models: Comment. *Amer. J. Agr. Econ.*, November 1986, *68*(4), pp. 990–93.

Orden, David. Public Policy, the Exchange Rate, and Agricultural Exports: Discussion [Monetary Policy, Real Exchange Rates, and U.S. Agricultural Exports] [The Consequences of a Floating Exchange Rate for the U.S. Wheat Market] [The Effect of Exchange Rate Distortions on Grain Export Markets, the Case of Argentina]. *Amer. J. Agr. Econ.*, May 1986, *68*(2), pp. 443–44.

Ott, Mack and Veugelers, Paul T. W. M. Forward Exchange Rates in Efficient Markets: The Effects of News and Changes in Monetary Policy Regimes. *Fed. Res. Bank St. Louis Rev.*, June/July 1986, *68*(6), pp. 5–15. **[G: U.S.; Canada; W. Europe]**

Overturf, Stephen Frank. Interest Rate Expectations and Interest Parity. *J. Int. Money Finance*, March 1986, *5*(1), pp. 91–98. **[G: U.S.; U.K.]**

Padoa-Schioppa, Tommaso. The Case for Internationalizing American Monetary Policy: Comment. **In** *Tsoukalis, L., ed.*, 1986, pp. 227–31. **[G: OECD]**

Pagoulatos, Emilio. Public Policy, the Exchange Rate, and Agricultural Exports: Discussion [Monetary Policy, Real Exchange Rates, and U.S. Agricultural Exports] [The Consequences of a Floating Exchange Rate for the U.S. Wheat Market] [The Effect of Exchange Rate Distortions on Grain Export Markets, the Case of

Argentina]. *Amer. J. Agr. Econ.*, May 1986, *68*(2), pp. 441–42. [G: U.S.; Argentina]

Papell, David H. Exchange Rate and Current Account Dynamics under Rational Expectations: An Econometric Analysis. *Int. Econ. Rev.*, October 1986, *27*(3), pp. 583–600. [G: Japan]

Pauly, Peter and Petersen, Christian E. Exchange Rate Responses in the LINK System. *Europ. Econ. Rev.*, February 1986, *30*(1), pp. 149–70. [G: W. Europe; Canada; U.S.; Japan]

Peel, David A. On Incomplete Current Information and Empirical Tests of the Rational Expectations Hypothesis. *J. Econ. Stud.*, 1986, *13*(2), pp. 59–64.

Phillips, M. John. Financial Reform: The Australian Experience. **In** *Cheng, H.-S., ed.*, 1986, pp. 105–12. [G: Australia]

Phillips, R. J. Maxi-devaluations and Black Market Dollars in Wartime South Vietnam. *Quart. Rev. Econ. Bus.*, Summer 1986, *26*(2), pp. 106–10. [G: Vietnam]

Pippenger, John. Arbitrage and Efficient Markets Interpretations of Purchasing Power Parity: Theory and Evidence. *Fed. Res. Bank San Francisco Econ. Rev.*, Winter 1986, (1), pp. 31–47. [G: U.S.; Canada; France; W. Germany]

Pitchford, J. D. The Australian Foreign Exchange Market 1983–86: Comment. *Econ. Rec.*, Supplement 1986, pp. 12–13. [G: Australia]

Plane, Patrick. Politique monétaire et options sur le régime de change dans les pays utilisant le dollar comme monnaie nationale. (Monetary Policy and the Choice of a Foreign Exchange System in Countries Using the Dollar as Their National Currency. With English summary.) *Écon. Soc.*, February 1986, *20*(2), pp. 197–214. [G: Liberia; Panama]

Poloz, Stephen S. Currency Substitution and the Precautionary Demand for Money. *J. Int. Money Finance*, March 1986, *5*(1), pp. 115–24.

Praagman, J. and Soenen, L. A. Stability of Optimal-Currency Cocktails. *J. Econ. Bus.*, February 1986, *38*(1), pp. 1–17. [G: W. Europe; U.S.; Canada; Japan]

Prachowny, Martin F. J. Managed Exchange Rates. *Econ. Rec.*, December 1986, *62*(179), pp. 442–50.

Price, L. D. D. Exchange Rate Management and Surveillance since 1972: Comment. **In** *Posner, M., ed.*, 1986, pp. 61–63. [G: OECD]

Protopapadakis, Aris A. and Stoll, Hans R. The Law of One Price in International Commodity Markets: A Reformulation and Some Formal Tests. *J. Int. Money Finance*, September 1986, *5*(3), pp. 335–60. [G: U.S.]

Putnam, Bluford H. Monetary Policy, Interest Rate Targets, and Foreign Exchange Markets. **In** *Putnam, B. H. and Wilford, D. S., eds.*, 1986, *1978*, pp. 168–75.

Putnam, Bluford H. and Wilford, D. Sykes. The Evolution of the Flexible Exchange Rate Debate. **In** *Putnam, B. H. and Wilford, D. S., eds.*, 1986, pp. 123–38. [G: U.S.; W. Germany]

Putnam, Bluford H. and Wilford, D. Sykes. The Policy Consequences of Interdependence. **In** *Putnam, B. H. and Wilford, D. S., eds.*, 1986, pp. 287–97.

Radice, E. A. Changes in Property Relationships and Financial Arrangements. **In** *Kaser, M. C. and Radice, E. A., eds.*, 1986, pp. 329–65. [G: Germany; E. Europe]

Rainelli, Michel. Loi du prix unique et théorie de la parité des pouvoirs d'achat: un retour à G. Cassal, A. Aftalion et J. Viner. (With English summary.) *Revue Écon. Polit.*, Jan.-Feb. 1986, *96*(1), pp. 25–38.

Rajapatirana, Sarath. Commodity Export Prices and the Real Exchange Rate in Developing Countries: Coffee in Colombia: Comment. **In** *Edwards, S. and Ahamed, L., eds.*, 1986, pp. 263–66. [G: Colombia]

Ramirez-Rojas, C. L. Monetary Substitution in Developing Countries. *Finance Develop.*, June 1986, *23*(2), pp. 35–38. [G: LDCs]

Rapaz, Virgílio José. European Monetary System: An Indicator of Foreign Exchange Fixity/Flexibility. *Economia (Portugal),* October 1986, *10*(3), pp. 513–17. [G: EEC]

Reither, Franco. The Dynamics of Financial Adjustments in an Open Economy and the Effects of Stabilization Policy: Comment. *J. Inst. Theoretical Econ.*, June 1986, *142*(2), pp. 438–41.

Riethmuller, Paul, et al. Survey Evidence on the Effects of the 1985 Depreciation on Importers and Import-Competing Manufacturers. *Econ. Rec.*, Supplement 1986, pp. 94–100. [G: Australia]

Rodrik, Dani. 'Disequilibrium' Exchange Rates as Industrialization Policy. *J. Devel. Econ.*, September 1986, *23*(1), pp. 89–106. [G: LDCs]

Roemer, Michael. Simple Analytics of Segmented Markets: What Case for Liberalization? *World Devel.*, March 1986, *14*(3), pp. 429–39.

Rogers, C. The De Kock Report: A Critical Assessment of the Theoretical Issues. *S. Afr. J. Econ.*, March 1986, *54*(1), pp. 66–79. [G: S. Africa]

de Rosa, Luigi. Bresciani Turroni and the Devaluation of the German Mark. *Rev. Econ. Cond. Italy*, Sept.-Dec. 1986, (3), pp. 425–38. [G: W. Germany]

Rosensweig, Jeffrey A. Exchange Rates and Competition for Tourists. *New Eng. Econ. Rev.*, July/Aug. 1986, pp. 57–67. [G: U.S.]

Rossi, Vanessa, et al. Exchange Rates, Productivity and International Competitiveness. *Oxford Rev. Econ. Policy*, Autumn 1986, *2*(3), pp. 56–73. [G: U.K.; U.S.]

Rothengatter, Werner. The Dynamics of Financial Adjustments in an Open Economy and the Effects of Stabilization Policy: Reply. *J. Inst. Theoretical Econ.*, June 1986, *142*(2), pp. 442–44.

Rousseau, Patrick. Conversion des documents comptables et taux de change: proposition d'une nouvelle approch. (Translating Financial

Statements and Exchange Rate: Proposals for a New Approach. With English summary.) *Écon. Soc.*, December 1986, *20*(12), pp. 83–103.

Sachs, Jeffrey. The Uneasy Case for Greater Exchange Rate Coordination. *Amer. Econ. Rev.*, May 1986, *76*(2), pp. 336–41. **[G: U.S.; U.K.; W. Germany; France; Japan]**

Salin, Pascal. The Case for Internationalizing American Monetary Policy: Comment. **In** *Tsoukalis, L., ed.*, 1986, pp. 232–37. **[G: OECD]**

Saurman, David S. Currency Substitution, the Exchange Rate, and the Real Interest Rate (Non)Differential: Shipping the Bad Money In: A Note. *J. Money, Credit, Banking*, November 1986, *18*(4), pp. 512–18.

Schiemann, Jürgen. Der Bedarf an offizieller Währungsreserve als Kriterium für die Bestimmung einer optimalen Währungsunion: Ein theoretischer Ansatz und empirischer Befund für die Länder der Europäischen Gemeinschaft. (The Need of Official Currency Reserves as a Criterion for the Determination of an Optimal Currency Union: A Theoretical Approach and Empirical Evidence for the EEC. With English summary.) *Jahr. Nationalökon. Statist.*, November 1986, *201*(6), pp. 589–604. **[G: EEC]**

Schiemann, Jürgen. Wechselkursstabilisierung durch internationale geldpolitische Kooperation. Kritische Anmerkungen zum McKinnon-Vosrschlag. (Stabilising Exchange Rates via International Monetary Cooperation. Critical Remarks on the McKinnon Proposal. With English summary.) *Kredit Kapital*, 1986, *19*(4), pp. 569–82.

Schiff, Maurice. Growing Interdependencies and Uncertainties: Discussion. **In** *Maunder, A. and Renborg, U., eds.*, 1986, pp. 94–98.

Schuh, G. Edward. The International Capital Market as a Source of Instability in International Commodity Markets. **In** *Maunder, A. and Renborg, U., eds.*, 1986, pp. 83–90.

Schwartz, Anna J. Alternative Monetary Regimes: The Gold Standard. **In** *Campbell, C. D. and Dougan, W. R., eds.*, 1986, pp. 44–72. **[G: U.S.; U.K.; W. Germany; France]**

Schwartz, Nancy E. The Consequences of a Floating Exchange Rate for the U.S. Wheat Market. *Amer. J. Agr. Econ.*, May 1986, *68*(2), pp. 428–33. **[G: U.S.]**

Seabourne, Teresa. The Summer of 1914. **In** *Capie, F. and Wood, G. E., eds.*, 1986, pp. 77–116. **[G: U.K.; Europe]**

Selowsky, Marcelo. Capital Flows, the Current Account, and the Real Exchange Rate: Some Consequences of Stabilization and Liberalization: Comment. **In** *Edwards, S. and Ahamed, L., eds.*, 1986, pp. 229–31.

Shaaf, Mohammad. An Investment Portfolio for OPEC: The Lagrangian Approach. *Atlantic Econ. J.*, July 1986, *14*(2), pp. 65–70. **[G: OPEC]**

Shann, Edward W. Australia's Real Exchange Rate during the Twentieth Century: Comment. *Econ. Rec.*, Supplement 1986, pp. 79–81. **[G: Australia]**

Shastri, Kuldeep and Tandon, Kishore. On the Use of European Models to Price American Options on Foreign Currency. *J. Futures Markets*, Spring 1986, *6*(1), pp. 93–108. **[G: U.S.]**

Shastri, Kuldeep and Tandon, Kishore. Valuation of Foreign Currency Options: Some Empirical Tests. *J. Finan. Quant. Anal.*, June 1986, *21*(2), pp. 145–60. **[G: U.S.]**

Sherwin, M. A. Exchange Rate Policy Developments. **In** *Reserve Bank of New Zealand*, 1986, pp. 127–34. **[G: New Zealand]**

Siggel, Eckhard. Protection, Distortions and Investment Incentives in Zaire: A Quantitative Analysis. *J. Devel. Econ.*, July-Aug. 1986, *22*(2), pp. 295–319. **[G: Zaire]**

Simes, R. M. Exchange Rate Policy and the AMPS Model: Comment. *Econ. Rec.*, Supplement 1986, pp. 55–57.

Sjaastad, Larry A. The Debt Problem and External Shocks. **In** *Giersch, H., ed.*, 1986, pp. 23–36. **[G: Selected Countries]**

Smith, P. N. and Wickens, M. R. An Empirical Investigation into the Causes of Failure of the Monetary Model of the Exchange Rate. *J. Appl. Econometrics*, April 1986, *1*(2), pp. 143–62. **[G: U.S.]**

Solimano, Andrés. Contractionary Devaluation in the Southern Cone: The Case of Chile. *J. Devel. Econ.*, September 1986, *23*(1), pp. 135–51. **[G: Chile]**

Solomon, Robert. The Report of the Group of Twenty-four: A Comment. *World Devel.*, September 1986, *14*(9), pp. 1233–36.

Somanath, V. S. Efficient Exchange Rate Forecasts: Lagged Models Better than the Random Walk. *J. Int. Money Finance*, June 1986, *5*(2), pp. 195–220. **[G: W. Germany]**

Spencer, G. H. A Comparison of Alternative Exchange Rate Regimes. **In** *Reserve Bank of New Zealand*, 1986, pp. 137–49. **[G: New Zealand]**

Stockman, Alan C. Sterling in Decline: A Review Essay. *J. Monet. Econ.*, July 1986, *18*(1), pp. 95–102. **[G: U.K.]**

Stockman, Alan C. The Budget Deficit and the Dollar: Comment. **In** *Fischer, S., ed.*, 1986, pp. 402–07. **[G: U.S.; W. Germany]**

Strydom, P. D. F. A Critical Assessment of the Equilibrium Approach to the Rate of Exchange. *S. Afr. J. Econ.*, March 1986, *54*(1), pp. 55–65. **[G: S. Africa]**

Swanson, Peggy E. and How, William S. Y. Portfolio Diversification by Currency Denomination: An Approach to International Cash Management with Implications for Foreign Exchange Markets. *Quart. Rev. Econ. Bus.*, Spring 1986, *26*(1), pp. 95–103. **[G: U.S.; W. Germany; U.K.]**

Sweeney, Richard J. Beating the Foreign Exchange Market. *J. Finance*, March 1986, *41*(1), pp. 163–82. **[G: U.S.; W. Germany; Selected Countries]**

Swoboda, Alexander K. Credibility and Viability

in International Monetary Arrangements. *Finance Develop.*, September 1986, *23*(3), pp. 15–18.

Takagi, Shinji. Pegging to a Currency Basket. *Finance Develop.*, September 1986, *23*(3), pp. 41–44.

Tatom, John A. Domestic vs. International Explanations of Recent U.S. Manufacturing Developments. *Fed. Res. Bank St. Louis Rev.*, April 1986, *68*(4), pp. 5–18. **[G: U.S.]**

Thomas, Lee R., III. Random Walk Profits in Currency Futures Trading. *J. Futures Markets*, Spring 1986, *6*(1), pp. 109–25. **[G: U.S.]**

Thygesen, Niels. Flexible Exchange Rates and National Monetary Policies. **In** *Tsoukalis, L., ed.*, 1986, pp. 163–85. **[G: OECD]**

van der Toorn, Frans B. International Trade Credit and Exchange Rates: A Survey among Dutch Firms. *De Economist*, 1986, *134*(4), pp. 492–96. **[G: Netherlands]**

Toyoda, Toshihisa. Effects of Temporal Aggregation in a Model of Exchange Rate Determination. *Kobe Univ. Econ.*, 1986, (32), pp. 19–39. **[G: Japan; U.S.]**

Trehan, Bharat. Oil Prices, Exchange Rates and the U.S. Economy: An Empirical Investigation. *Fed. Res. Bank San Francisco Econ. Rev.*, Fall 1986, (4), pp. 25–43. **[G: U.S.]**

Trevor, Robert G. and Donald, Stephen G. Exchange Rate Regimes and the Volatility of Financial Prices: The Australian Case. *Econ. Rec.*, Supplement 1986, pp. 58–66. **[G: U.S.; W. Germany; Japan; Australia]**

Triffin, Robert. Correcting the World Monetary Scandal. *Challenge*, Jan./Feb. 1986, *28*(6), pp. 4–14. **[G: Global; U.S.]**

Tse, Y. K. The Spot and Forward Exchange Rates: Some Empirical Evidence of Singapore. *Appl. Econ.*, March 1986, *18*(3), pp. 319–31. **[G: Singapore]**

Valdés, Alberto. Exchange Rates and Trade Policy: Help or Hindrance to Agricultural Growth? **In** *Maunder, A. and Renborg, U., eds.*, 1986, pp. 624–33. **[G: Peru; LDCs]**

Vaňous, Jan. Commercial Exchange Rates of East European Countries and Realistic Dollar/Ruble Exchange Rates for Soviet Trade with Eastern Europe. *Soviet E. Europ. Foreign Trade*, Spring 1986, 22(1), pp. 83–99. **[G: CMEA]**

Vaubel, Roland. The Case for Internationalizing American Monetary Policy: Comment. **In** *Tsoukalis, L., ed.*, 1986, pp. 238–42. **[G: OECD]**

de Vries, Margaret Garritsen. The IMF in a Changing World, 1945–85: The Emerging System as of Mid-1975. **In** *de Vries, M. G.*, 1986, *1975*, pp. 126–35.

de Vries, Margaret Garritsen. The IMF in a Changing World, 1945–85: Exchange Crises and Changes in the World Economy. **In** *de Vries, M. G.*, 1986, *1974*, pp. 94–100.

de Vries, Margaret Garritsen. The IMF in a Changing World, 1945–85: Magnitudes of Devaluation, 1948–67. **In** *de Vries, M. G.*, 1986, *1968*, pp. 57–65. **[G: Global]**

de Vries, Margaret Garritsen. The IMF in a Changing World, 1945–85: Fluctuating Rates in the Par Value Era. **In** *de Vries, M. G.*, 1986, *1969*, pp. 49–56. **[G: Canada]**

de Vries, Margaret Garritsen. The IMF in a Changing World, 1945–85: Twenty Years with Par Values, 1946–66. **In** *de Vries, M. G.*, 1986, *1966*, pp. 40–48.

de Vries, Margaret Garritsen. The IMF in a Changing World, 1945–85: Decline of Multiple Rates, 1947–67. **In** *de Vries, M. G.*, 1986, *1967*, pp. 21–29.

de Vries, Margaret Garritsen. The IMF in a Changing World, 1945–85: Decline of Exchange Restrictions, 1945–69. **In** *de Vries, M. G.*, 1986, *1969*, pp. 30–39.

Wagner, Michael. What Happened in 1931? Comment. **In** *Capie, F. and Wood, G. E., eds.*, 1986, pp. 157–59. **[G: U.K.]**

Weber, Warren E. Do Sterilized Interventions Affect Exchange Rates? *Fed. Res. Bank Minn. Rev.*, Summer 1986, *10*(3), pp. 14–23. **[G: U.S.]**

Wesierski, Brigitte. Konflikte der monetären Steuerung bei flexiblen Wechselkursen. (Conflicts on Monetary Control under Flexible Exchange Rates. With English summary.) *Kredit Kapital*, 1986, *19*(2), pp. 213–32. **[G: W. Germany]**

Wihlborg, Clas and Antoncic, Madelyn. Relative Price Changes and Exchange Rate Determination with Slow Price Adjustment: An Empirical Analysis. *Southern Econ. J.*, July 1986, *53*(1), pp. 217–32. **[G: U.S.]**

van Wijnbergen, Sweder J. G. Exchange Rate Management and Stabilization Policies in Developing Countries. **In** *Edwards, S. and Ahamed, L., eds.*, 1986, pp. 17–38. **[G: LDCs]**

Wilford, D. Sykes. Exchange Rates with Substitutable Currencies. **In** *Putnam, B. H. and Wilford, D. S., eds.*, 1986, pp. 272–83. **[G: U.S.; Canada]**

Willett, Thomas D. Exchange-Rate Volatility, International Trade, and Resource Allocation: A Perspective on Recent Research. *J. Int. Money Finance*, Supp. March 1986, *5*, pp. S101–12.

Williamson, John. Discrete Devaluation as a Signal to Price Setters: Suggested Evidence from Greece: Comment. **In** *Edwards, S. and Ahamed, L., eds.*, 1986, pp. 329–31. **[G: Greece]**

Williamson, John. Target Zones and the Management of the Dollar. *Brookings Pap. Econ. Act.*, 1986, (1), pp. 165–74. **[G: U.S.; Japan; W. Germany; Switzerland]**

Winckler, Georg and Amann, Erwin. Exchange Rate Policy in the Presence of a Strong Trade Union. *J. Econ. (Z. Nationalökon.)*, Supplementum 5, 1986, pp. 259–80.

Winer, Stanley L. The Role of Exchange Rate Flexibility in the International Transmission of Inflation in Long and Shorter Runs: Canada, 1953 to 1981. *Can. J. Econ.*, February 1986, *19*(1), pp. 62–86. **[G: Canada]**

Wright, D. J., et al. Evaluation of Forecasting

Methods for Decision Support. *Int. J. Forecasting*, 1986, *2*(2), pp. 139–52.

Wyplosz, Charles. Capital Controls and Balance of Payments Crises. *J. Int. Money Finance*, June 1986, *5*(2), pp. 167–79.

Zandi, Farrokh R. and Rahman, Syed Sajjadur. Real Interest Rate Differentials and Foreign Exchange Markets in Canada. *Atlantic Econ. J.*, July 1986, *14*(2), pp. 55–64. **[G: U.S.; Canada]**

Zecher, J. Richard. Market Discipline of the Monetary System. **In** *Campbell, C. D. and Dougan, W. R., eds.*, 1986, pp. 82–84. **[G: U.S.]**

Zuberi, Habib A. Exchange Rate Policies of Developing Countries in the Context of External Shocks: Comments. *Pakistan Devel. Rev.*, Autumn 1986, *25*(3), pp. 422–24. **[G: LDCs]**

432 International Monetary Arrangements

4320 International Monetary Arrangements

Addo, J. S. Alternative Approaches to Stabilization in Africa: Comments. **In** *Helleiner, G. K, ed.*, 1986, pp. 153–56. **[G: Sub-Saharan Africa]**

Ahamed, Liaquat. Collective Pegging to a Single Currency: The West African Monetary Union: Comment. **In** *Edwards, S. and Ahamed, L., eds.*, 1986, pp. 363–65. **[G: W. Africa]**

Alburo, Florian and Canlas, Dante B. Balance of Payments, Output, and the IMF. *Philippine Rev. Econ. Bus.*, Sept.-Dec. 1986, *23*(3–4), pp. 275–92. **[G: Philippines]**

Aliber, Robert Z. Fixed Exchange Rates and the Rate of Inflation. **In** *Campbell, C. D. and Dougan, W. R., eds.*, 1986, pp. 116–21.

Argy, Victor. The International Financial System. **In** *Bruce, R., et al., eds.*, 1986, pp. 279–96. **[G: OECD]**

Baldwin, George B. Economics and Economists in the World Bank. **In** *Coats, A. W., ed.*, 1986, pp. 67–90.

Barroux, Yves. The Belmont–Morgan Syndicate as an Optimal Investment Banking Contract: Comment. *Europ. Econ. Rev.*, June 1986, *30*(3), pp. 679–80. **[G: U.S.]**

Berg, Elliot. The Question of Conditionality: Comments. **In** *Lancaster, C. and Williamson, J., eds.*, 1986, pp. 95–98. **[G: Africa]**

Bisignano, Joseph. The Process of Financial Deregulation, Monetary Reform, and the Financial System of the Future: Comments. **In** *Suzuki, Y. and Yomo, H., eds.*, 1986, pp. 207–15. **[G: U.S.]**

Blackwell, Michael P. From G-5 to G-77: International Forums for Discussion of Economic Issues. *Finance Develop.*, December 1986, *23*(4), pp. 40–41.

Bofinger, Peter. Über "ECUnomics" zu einer europäischen Geldverfassung. (On ECUnomics for a European Monetary Order? With English summary.) *Kredit Kapital*, 1986, *19*(2), pp. 178–83. **[G: EEC]**

Bordo, Michael D. Explorations in Monetary History: A Survey of the Literature. *Exploration Econ. Hist.*, October 1986, *23*(4), pp. 339–415. **[G: OECD]**

Bosshard, Rudolf. The Relationship between the International Monetary Fund and the Commercial Banks. **In** *Dicke, D. C., ed.*, 1986, pp. 170–74.

Braga de Macedo, Jorge. Collective Pegging to a Single Currency: The West African Monetary Union. **In** *Edwards, S. and Ahamed, L., eds.*, 1986, pp. 333–62. **[G: W. Africa]**

Braga de Macedo, Jorge. Small Countries in Monetary Unions: A Two-Tier Model. *J. Econ. Dynam. Control*, June 1986, *10*(1/2), pp. 275–80.

Branson, William H. The Limits of Monetary Coordination as Exchange Rate Policy. *Brookings Pap. Econ. Act.*, 1986, (1), pp. 175–94. **[G: U.S.]**

Brau, Eduard H. The IMF: Changes Required to Restore Voluntary Lending. **In** *Preeg, E. H. and Bendahmane, D. B., eds.*, 1986, pp. 49–51.

Brinner, Roger E. The Dollar Exchange Rate and International Monetary Cooperation: Comments. **In** *Hafer, R. W., ed. (I)*, 1986, pp. 233–35. **[G: OECD]**

Bronfenbrenner, Martin. Japan-Bashing: A View from "Over There." *Challenge*, Jan./Feb. 1986, *28*(6), pp. 58–61. **[G: U.S.; Japan]**

Bruce, Robert and Murnane, Paul. Borrowing from Overseas. **In** *Bruce, R., et al., eds.*, 1986, pp. 297–320. **[G: Australia]**

Bryant, Ralph C. International Financial Intermediation: Underlying Trends and Implications for Government Policies. **In** *Suzuki, Y. and Yomo, H., eds.*, 1986, pp. 135–81.

Buiter, Willem H. The Role of Reserves in the International Monetary System: Comment. **In** *Posner, M., ed.*, 1986, pp. 109–12. **[G: Global]**

Callaghy, Thomas M. The Political Economy of African Debt: The Case of Zaire. **In** *Ravenhill, J., ed.*, 1986, pp. 307–46. **[G: Zaire]**

Calvet, J. Le développement de l'écu privé pré figure-t-il un système productif européen? (Is the Development of Private Use of the E.C.U. a Prefiguration of a European Productive System? With English summary.) *Écon. Soc.*, May 1986, *20*(5), pp. 101–24. **[G: W. Europe]**

Capie, Forrest H.; Mills, Terence C. and Wood, Geoffrey E. What Happened in 1931? **In** *Capie, F. and Wood, G. E., eds.*, 1986, pp. 120–48. **[G: U.K.]**

Cheng, Hang-Sheng. International Financial Crises, Past and Present. *Fed. Res. Bank San Francisco Econ. Rev.*, Fall 1986, (4), pp. 13–23. **[G: Global]**

Clark, Telfred and Bruce, Robert. International Trade Finance. **In** *Bruce, R., et al., eds.*, 1986, pp. 321–38.

Clements, Kenneth W. Perspectives on Exchange Rate Regimes. **In** *Campbell, C. D. and Dougan, W. R., eds.*, 1986, pp. 110–15.

Conable, Barber B. The Bank's Mission in a Changing World. *Finance Develop.*, December 1986, *23*(4), pp. 2–5.

Congdon, Tim. What Happened in 1931? Comment. **In** *Capie, F. and Wood, G. E., eds.*, 1986, pp. 149–56. **[G: U.K.]**

Cooper, Richard N. A Monetary System Based on Fixed Exchange Rates. **In** *Campbell, C. D. and Dougan, W. R., eds.*, 1986, pp. 85–109.

Cooper, Richard N. Managing Risks to the International Economic System. **In** *Cooper, R. N.*, 1986, *1983*, pp. 23–51.

Dallara, Charles. The Question of Conditionality: Comments. **In** *Lancaster, C. and Williamson, J., eds.*, 1986, pp. 92–95. **[G: Africa]**

Deane, Marjorie. The Role and Resources of the Fund: Comment. **In** *Posner, M., ed.*, 1986, pp. 158–63. **[G: Selected LDCs]**

Dell, Sidney. The History of the IMF. *World Devel.*, September 1986, *14*(9), pp. 1203–12.

Dini, Lamberto. Towards a European Integrated Financial Market. *Banca Naz. Lavoro Quart. Rev.*, December 1986, (159), pp. 377–89. **[G: EEC]**

Dooley, Michael P. The Role of Reserves in the International Monetary System. **In** *Posner, M., ed.*, 1986, pp. 97–109. **[G: Global]**

Dornbusch, Rudiger. The Overvalued Dollar. **In** *Dornbusch, R.*, 1986, pp. 17–30. **[G: U.S.; Global]**

Dow, Sheila C. Speculation and the Monetary Circuit with Particular Attention to the Eurocurrency Market. *Écon. Soc.*, Aug.-Sept. 1986, *20*(8–9), pp. 95–109.

Eichengreen, Barry. The Belmont–Morgan Syndicate as an Optimal Investment Banking Contract: Comment. *Europ. Econ. Rev.*, June 1986, *30*(3), pp. 681–82. **[G: U.S.]**

Engel, Charles M. The International Monetary System: Forty Years after Bretton Woods: Review Essay. *J. Monet. Econ.*, May 1986, *17*(3), pp. 441–48.

Erb, Richard D. A View from the Fund. **In** *Helleiner, G. K, ed.*, 1986, pp. 15–25. **[G: Africa]**

Fischer, Stanley. Friedman versus Hayek on Private Money: Review Essay. *J. Monet. Econ.*, May 1986, *17*(3), pp. 433–39.

Fouet, Monique and Aroyo, Philippe. Pétrodollars et marchés financiers internationaux. (Petrodollars and International Financial Markets. With English summary.) *Écon. Soc.*, July 1986, *20*(7), pp. 15–25. **[G: OPEC]**

Fremling, Gertrud Margareta. A Specie-Flow Model of the Gold Standard. *J. Int. Money Finance*, March 1986, *5*(1), pp. 37–55.

Friedman, Milton. The Resource Cost of Irredeemable Paper Money. *J. Polit. Econ.*, Part 1, June 1986, *94*(3), pp. 642–47.

Garber, Peter M. and Grilli, Vittorio U. The Belmont–Morgan Syndicate as an Optimal Investment Banking Contract. *Europ. Econ. Rev.*, June 1986, *30*(3), pp. 649–77. **[G: U.S.]**

Gebauer, Wolfgang. ECUnomics—Perspektiven einer europäischen Geldverfassung. (ECUnomics—Perspectives of a European Monetary Order. With English summary.) *Kredit Kapital*, 1986, *19*(2), pp. 159–77. **[G: EEC]**

Gérardin, Hubert. Intégration monétaire et création de monnaie: le cas de la zone franc. (Monetary Integration and the Creation of Money: The Case of the Franc Zone. With English summary.) *Écon. Soc.*, February 1986, *20*(2), pp. 95–133. **[G: Africa]**

Giovannini, Alberto. 'Rules of the Game' during the International Gold Standard: England and Germany. *J. Int. Money Finance*, December 1986, *5*(4), pp. 467–83. **[G: U.K.; W. Germany]**

Goodhart, Charles. The Summer of 1914: Comment. **In** *Capie, F. and Wood, G. E., eds.*, 1986, pp. 117–19. **[G: U.K.; Europe]**

Griffith-Jones, Stephany. The Role and Resources of the Fund. **In** *Posner, M., ed.*, 1986, pp. 139–58. **[G: Selected LDCs]**

Ground, Richard L. A Survey and Critique of IMF Adjustment Programs in Latin America. **In** *Economic Commission for Latin America and the Caribbean*, 1986, pp. 101–58. **[G: Latin America]**

Guerrieri, Paolo and Padoan, Pier Carlo. Neomercantilism and International Economic Stability. *Int. Organ.*, Winter 1986, *40*(1), pp. 29–42.

Haggard, Stephan. The Politics of Adjustment: Lessons from the IMF's Extended Fund Facility. **In** *Kahler, M., ed.*, 1986, pp. 157–86.

Hallwood, C. Paul. External Economy Arguments for Commodity Stockpiling: A Review. *Bull. Econ. Res.*, January 1986, *38*(1), pp. 25–41.

ul Haq, Mahbub. Proposal for an IMF Debt Refinancing Subsidiary. **In** *[Streeten, P.]*, 1986, pp. 87–94.

Helleiner, Gerald K. Africa and the International Monetary Fund: Introduction. **In** *Helleiner, G. K, ed.*, 1986, pp. 1–11. **[G: Africa]**

Helleiner, Gerald K. The Question of Conditionality. **In** *Lancaster, C. and Williamson, J., eds.*, 1986, pp. 63–91. **[G: Africa]**

Hicks, John R. The Abdication of Money. *Hong Kong Econ. Pap.*, 1986, (17), pp. 1–10. **[G: Global]**

Hino, Hiroyuki. IMF–World Bank Collaboration. *Finance Develop.*, September 1986, *23*(3), pp. 10–14.

Jager, Henk and de Jong, Eelke. The Perspective of the SDR's Position in Monetary Reserves: On the Robustness of Optimal Portfolio Results. *De Economist*, 1986, *134*(4), pp. 417–37. **[G: Global]**

Jimenez, Julio. Alternative Approaches to Stabilization in Africa: Comments. **In** *Helleiner, G. K, ed.*, 1986, pp. 151–53. **[G: Sub-Saharan Africa]**

Johnson, G. G. Exchange Rate Management and Surveillance since 1972. **In** *Posner, M., ed.*, 1986, pp. 48–61. **[G: OECD]**

Kamitake, Yoshiro. Darling, Goodenough and McKenna: Economic Thoughts of the City towards British Return to Gold in 1925. *Hitotsubashi J. Econ.*, December 1986, *27*(2), pp. 167–80. **[G: U.K.]**

Killick, Tony. Balance of Payments Adjustment and Developing Countries: Some Outstanding

Issues. In *Posner, M., ed.*, 1986, pp. 64–90.

Leddin, Anthony. Portfolio Equilibrium and Monetary Policy in Ireland. *Econ. Soc. Rev.*, January 1986, *17*(2), pp. 133–46. **[G: Ireland]**

Lehrman, Lewis E. Back to Gold: Giving Up the "Order of the Jungle." *Challenge*, Jan./Feb. 1986, *28*(6), pp. 21–30. **[G: U.S.]**

Lelart, Michel. Zone monétaire et convertibilité: l'expérience africaine. (Currency Zone and Convertibility: The African Experience. With English summary.) *Écon. Soc.*, February 1986, *20*(2), pp. 135–67. **[G: Africa]**

Lipson, Charles. International Debt and International Institutions. In *Kahler, M., ed.*, 1986, pp. 219–43.

Llewellyn, David T. The International Monetary System since 1972: Structural Change and Financial Innovation. In *Posner, M., ed.*, 1986, pp. 14–44.

Lodge, Juliet. The Single European Act: Towards a New Euro-Dynamism? *J. Common Market Stud.*, March 1986, *24*(3), pp. 203–23. **[G: EEC]**

Loxley, John. Alternative Approaches to Stabilization in Africa: Reply. In *Helleiner, G. K, ed.*, 1986, pp. 156–59. **[G: Sub-Saharan Africa]**

Loxley, John. Alternative Approaches to Stabilization in Africa. In *Helleiner, G. K, ed.*, 1986, pp. 117–47. **[G: Sub-Saharan Africa]**

de Lusignan, Guy. The Bank's Economic Development Institute. *Finance Develop.*, June 1986, *23*(2), pp. 28–31.

Mallyon, Jim S. The Process of Financial Deregulation, Monetary Reform, and the Financial System of the Future: Comments. In *Suzuki, Y. and Yomo, H., eds.*, 1986, pp. 203–06. **[G: U.S.]**

Mawakani, Samba. Fund Conditionality and the Socioeconomic Situation in Africa. In *Helleiner, G. K, ed.*, 1986, pp. 104–12. **[G: Africa]**

McCauley, Robert N. IMF: Managed Lending. In *Claudon, M. P., ed.*, 1986, pp. 123–45. **[G: LDCs]**

McKinnon, Ronald I. The Dollar Exchange Rate and International Monetary Cooperation. In *Hafer, R. W., ed. (I)*, 1986, pp. 211–31. **[G: OECD]**

Meessen, Karl M. IMF Conditionality and State Sovereignty. In *Dicke, D. C., ed.*, 1986, pp. 117–29.

Miles, Marc A. Refocusing Monetary Theory and Policy. In *Putnam, B. H. and Wilford, D. S., eds.*, 1986, pp. 307–24. **[G: U.S.]**

Moggridge, D. E. Keynes and the International Monetary System 1909–46. In *[Tarshis, L.]*, 1986, pp. 56–83.

Mohammed, Azizali F. Alternative Approaches to Stabilization in Africa: Comments. In *Helleiner, G. K, ed.*, 1986, pp. 148–51. **[G: Sub-Saharan Africa]**

Moyana, Kombo. Fund Conditionality and the Socioeconomic Situation in Africa: Comment. In *Helleiner, G. K, ed.*, 1986, pp. 113–16. **[G: Africa]**

Mtei, E. I. M. Design, Implementation, and Adequacy of Fund Programs in Africa: Comments. In *Helleiner, G. K, ed.*, 1986, pp. 96–99. **[G: Africa]**

Mushin, J. D. Non-symmetry in the European Monetary System: A Comment. *Brit. Rev. Econ. Issues*, Autumn 1986, *8*(19), pp. 85–87. **[G: W. Europe]**

Narasimham, M. International Monetary Arrangements and Future Adaptation: Comment. In *Posner, M., ed.*, 1986, pp. 182–89.

Ndegwa, Philip. The Economic Crisis in Africa. In *Helleiner, G. K, ed.*, 1986, pp. 45–51. **[G: Africa]**

Ndekwu, E. C. International Financial Organisations and the NIEO. In *Onwuka, R. I. and Aluko, O., eds.*, 1986, pp. 132–49.

Nötel, R. International Finance and Monetary Reforms. In *Kaser, M. C. and Radice, E. A., eds.*, 1986, pp. 520–63. **[G: E. Europe]**

Nyirabu, C. M. A View from Africa: 2. In *Helleiner, G. K, ed.*, 1986, pp. 32–42. **[G: Africa]**

O'Brien, Stephen. Collective Pegging to a Single Currency: The West African Monetary Union: Comment. In *Edwards, S. and Ahamed, L., eds.*, 1986, pp. 365–67. **[G: W. Africa]**

O'Connell, Arturo A. External Debt and the Reform of the International Monetary System. *CEPAL Rev.*, December 1986, (30), pp. 51–66.

Officer, Lawrence H. The Efficiency of the Dollar–Sterling Gold Standard, 1890–1908. *J. Polit. Econ.*, October 1986, *94*(5), pp. 1038–73. **[G: U.S.; U.K.]**

Oliver, H. B. B. Design, Implementation, and Adequacy of Fund Programs in Africa: Comments. In *Helleiner, G. K, ed.*, 1986, pp. 99–100. **[G: Africa]**

Ouattara, Alassane D. Design, Implementation, and Adequacy of Fund Programs in Africa: Reply. In *Helleiner, G. K, ed.*, 1986, pp. 100–103. **[G: Africa]**

Ouattara, Alassane D. Design, Implementation, and Adequacy of Fund Programs in Africa. In *Helleiner, G. K, ed.*, 1986, pp. 68–92. **[G: Africa]**

Phiri, David. Design, Implementation, and Adequacy of Fund Programs in Africa: Comments. In *Helleiner, G. K, ed.*, 1986, pp. 93–96. **[G: Africa; Zambia]**

Pinder, John. The Political Economy of Integration in Europe: Policies and Institutions in East and West. *J. Common Market Stud.*, September 1986, *25*(1), pp. 1–14. **[G: EEC]**

Please, Stanley. Balance of Payments Adjustment and Developing Countries: Some Outstanding Issues: Comment. In *Posner, M., ed.*, 1986, pp. 90–96.

Posner, Michael. Problems of International Money, 1972–85: Introduction. In *Posner, M., ed.*, 1986, pp. 1–13.

Potter, Stephen. International Financial Intermediation: Underlying Trends and Implications for Government Policies: Comments. In *Suzuki, Y. and Yomo, H., eds.*, 1986, pp. 221–23.

Price, L. D. D. Exchange Rate Management and Surveillance since 1972: Comment. **In** *Posner, M., ed.*, 1986, pp. 61–63. **[G: OECD]**

Putnam, Bluford H. and Wilford, D. Sykes. The Evolution of the Flexible Exchange Rate Debate. **In** *Putnam, B. H. and Wilford, D. S., eds.*, 1986, pp. 123–38. **[G: U.S.; W. Germany]**

Ranuzzi, Paolo. Internationalisation of the Lira and the Italian Banking System. *Econ. Notes*, 1986, (3), pp. 85–100. **[G: Italy]**

Rapaz, Virgílio José. European Monetary System: An Indicator of Foreign Exchange Fixity/Flexibility. *Economia (Portugal),* October 1986, *10*(3), pp. 513–17. **[G: EEC]**

Rieke, Wolfgang. Jahrestagung von IWF und Weltbank 1986. (Annual Meeting of IMF and the World Bank 1986. With English summary.) *Kredit Kapital*, 1986, *19*(4), pp. 583–93.

Rōyama, Shōichi. The Process of Financial Deregulation, Monetary Reform, and the Financial System of the Future: Comments. **In** *Suzuki, Y. and Yomo, H., eds.*, 1986, pp. 217–20.

Saitoti, G. A View from Africa: 1. **In** *Helleiner, G. K, ed.*, 1986, pp. 26–31. **[G: Africa]**

Sanusi, J. O. African Economic Disequilibria and the International Monetary System. **In** *Helleiner, G. K, ed.*, 1986, pp. 52–67. **[G: Africa]**

Sarcevic, Petar. Two Approaches to the Debt Problem: A) Adjustment of Loan Agreements (De Lege Lata); B) Strengthening of International Monetary Soft Law (De Lege Ferenda). **In** *Dicke, D. C., ed.*, 1986, pp. 130–56.

Sarcinelli, Mario. The EMS and the International Monetary System: Towards Greater Stability. *Banca Naz. Lavoro Quart. Rev.*, March 1986, (156), pp. 57–83. **[G: Global]**

Scott, Andrew. Britain and the E.M.S.: An Appraisal of the Report of the Treasury and Civil Service Committee. *J. Common Market Stud.*, March 1986, *24*(3), pp. 187–201. **[G: EEC]**

Sengupta, Arjun. Allocation of SDRs Linked to Reserve Needs. *Finance Develop.*, September 1986, *23*(3), pp. 19–21.

Sengupta, Arjun. The Functioning of the International Monetary System: A Critique of the Perspective of the Industrial Countries. *World Devel.*, September 1986, *14*(9), pp. 1213–31.

Smits, René J. H. The International Monetary System and Development: General Outlook on the Legal Issues. **In** *Dicke, D. C., ed.*, 1986, pp. 74–96.

Solomon, Robert. The IMF in a Period of Turbulence. *Finance Develop.*, March 1986, *23*(1), pp. 41–43.

Solomon, Robert. The Report of the Group of Twenty-four: A Comment. *World Devel.*, September 1986, *14*(9), pp. 1233–36.

Stockman, Alan C. Sterling in Decline: A Review Essay. *J. Monet. Econ.*, July 1986, *18*(1), pp. 95–102. **[G: U.K.]**

Strange, Susan. The International Monetary System since 1972: Structural Change and Financial Innovation: Comment. **In** *Posner, M., ed.*, 1986, pp. 44–47.

de Strycker, Cecil. A Single Currency: Utopia Today? Reality Tomorrow? *Banca Naz. Lavoro Quart. Rev.*, June 1986, (157), pp. 161–77.

Swoboda, Alexander K. Credibility and Viability in International Monetary Arrangements. *Finance Develop.*, September 1986, *23*(3), pp. 15–18.

Taylor, Alwyn Beresford. The Question of Conditionality: Comments. **In** *Lancaster, C. and Williamson, J., eds.*, 1986, pp. 99–103. **[G: Africa]**

Triffin, Robert. Correcting the World Monetary Scandal. *Challenge,* Jan./Feb. 1986, *28*(6), pp. 4–14. **[G: Global; U.S.]**

Tsoukalis, Loukas. International Monetary Arrangements and Future Adaptation. **In** *Posner, M., ed.*, 1986, pp. 164–82.

Tyler, William G. The Role of International Organizations in the Adjustment Process. **In** *Giersch, H., ed.*, 1986, pp. 152–66. **[G: Selected LDCs]**

Vaňous, Jan. Commercial Exchange Rates of East European Countries and Realistic Dollar/Ruble Exchange Rates for Soviet Trade with Eastern Europe. *Soviet E. Europ. Foreign Trade,* Spring 1986, *22*(1), pp. 83–99. **[G: CMEA]**

Vaubel, Roland. The Role of International Organizations in the Adjustment Process: Comment. **In** *Giersch, H., ed.*, 1986, pp. 167–71. **[G: Selected LDCs]**

de Vries, Margaret Garritsen. Origins of the Debt Crisis and of the Fund's Involvement. **In** *de Vries, M. G.*, 1986, *1985*, pp. 182–90. **[G: LDCs]**

de Vries, Margaret Garritsen. The International Monetary Fund: Economists in Key Roles. **In** *Coats, A. W., ed.*, 1986, pp. 53–66.

de Vries, Margaret Garritsen. The IMF in a Changing World, 1945–85: Highlights of 1966 through 1971. **In** *de Vries, M. G.*, 1986, *1977*, pp. 75–84.

de Vries, Margaret Garritsen. The IMF in a Changing World, 1945–85: Forty Years of Challenge and Change. **In** *de Vries, M. G.*, 1986, *1985*, pp. 217–25.

de Vries, Margaret Garritsen. The IMF in a Changing World, 1945–85: Bretton Woods. **In** *de Vries, M. G.*, 1986, *1984*, pp. 5–13.

de Vries, Margaret Garritsen. The IMF in a Changing World, 1945–85: The Interim Committee. **In** *de Vries, M. G.*, 1986, *1985*, pp. 158–68.

de Vries, Margaret Garritsen. The IMF in a Changing World, 1945–85: The Decade of Pierre-Paul Schweitzer, 1963–73. **In** *de Vries, M. G.*, 1986, *1973*, pp. 85–93.

de Vries, Margaret Garritsen. The IMF in a Changing World, 1945–85: Decline of Exchange Restrictions, 1945–69. **In** *de Vries, M. G.*, 1986, *1969*, pp. 30–39.

de Vries, Margaret Garritsen. The IMF in a Changing World, 1945–85: Economic Turbulence of the 1970s. **In** *de Vries, M. G.*, 1986, *1980*, pp. 149–57.

de Vries, Margaret Garritsen. The IMF in a Changing World, 1945–85: Twenty Years with Par Values, 1946–66. **In** *de Vries, M. G.*, 1986, *1966*, pp. 40–48.

de Vries, Margaret Garritsen. The IMF in a Changing World, 1945–85: The Outlook for World Debt as of 1985. **In** *de Vries, M. G.*, 1986, *1985*, pp. 191–98.

de Vries, Margaret Garritsen. The IMF in a Changing World, 1945–85: Fluctuating Rates in the Par Value Era. **In** *de Vries, M. G.*, 1986, *1969*, pp. 49–56. **[G: Canada]**

de Vries, Margaret Garritsen. The IMF in a Changing World, 1945–85: Highlights of 1972 through 1978. **In** *de Vries, M. G.*, 1986, *1985*, pp. 113–25.

de Vries, Margaret Garritsen. The IMF in a Changing World, 1945–85: Decline of Multiple Rates, 1947–67. **In** *de Vries, M. G.*, 1986, *1967*, pp. 21–29.

de Vries, Margaret Garritsen. The IMF in a Changing World, 1945–85: The H. Johannes Witteveen Years, 1973–78. **In** *de Vries, M. G.*, 1986, *1978*, pp. 136–48.

de Vries, Margaret Garritsen. The IMF in a Changing World, 1945–85: The Emerging System as of Mid-1975. **In** *de Vries, M. G.*, 1986, *1975*, pp. 126–35.

de Vries, Margaret Garritsen. The Role of the International Monetary Fund in the World Debt Problem. **In** *Claudon, M. P., ed.*, 1986, pp. 111–22.

Wagner, Michael. What Happened in 1931? Comment. **In** *Capie, F. and Wood, G. E., eds.*, 1986, pp. 157–59. **[G: U.K.]**

Wilford, D. Sykes and Krieger, Ronald A. Discretionary Monetary Policy and the Gold Standard. **In** *Putnam, B. H. and Wilford, D. S., eds.*, 1986, pp. 298–306.

Williamson, John. Target Zones and the Management of the Dollar. *Brookings Pap. Econ. Act.*, 1986, (1), pp. 165–74. **[G: U.S.; Japan; W. Germany; Switzerland]**

Wood, Geoffrey E. European Monetary Integration? A Review Essay. *J. Monet. Econ.*, November 1986, *18*(3), pp. 329–36. **[G: EEC]**

Wyplosz, Charles. Capital Controls and Balance of Payments Crises. *J. Int. Money Finance*, June 1986, *5*(2), pp. 167–79.

Zis, George. Non-symmetry in the European Monetary System: A Reply. *Brit. Rev. Econ. Issues*, Autumn 1986, *8*(19), pp. 89–92. **[G: W. Europe]**

Zis, George. The European Monetary System and the U.K. *Brit. Rev. Econ. Issues*, Spring 1986, *8*(18), pp. 1–27. **[G: W. Europe]**

433 Private International Lending

4330 Private International Lending

Abidin, Abang Zainal. Financial Reform and the Role of Foreign Banks in Malaysia. **In** *Cheng, H.-S., ed.*, 1986, pp. 305–09. **[G: Malaysia]**

Aglietta, Michel. Politics, Trade and Money: Comment. **In** *Tsoukalis, L., ed.*, 1986, pp. 260–64. **[G: U.S.; EEC]**

Allsopp, Christopher and Joshi, Vijay. The Assessment: The International Debt Crisis. *Oxford Rev. Econ. Policy*, Spring 1986, *2*(1), pp. i–xxxiii. **[G: LDCs; MDCs]**

Amelung, Torsten and Mehltretter, Thorsten. Early-Warning Systems in Light of the International Debt Crisis. *Konjunkturpolitik*, 1986, *32*(5), pp. 257–81. **[G: LDCs]**

Amstutz, Max D. Co-operation with IFC: Experience of a European Investor. *Aussenwirtschaft*, April 1986, *41*(1), pp. 81–87. **[G: LDCs]**

Amstutz, Max D. Co-operation with IFC: Experience of a European Investor. **In** *Hauser, H., ed. (I)*, 1986, pp. 81–87.

Backhaus, Klaus and Meyer, Margit. Country Risk Assessment in International Industrial Marketing. **In** *Backhaus, K. and Wilson, D. T., eds.*, 1986, pp. 245–73. **[G: LDCs]**

Balassa, Bela. Developing Country Debt: Policies and Prospects. **In** *Giersch, H., ed.*, 1986, pp. 103–22. **[G: LDCs]**

Baneth, Jean. Government Policies in Developing Countries: Was Capital Wasted? **In** *Giersch, H., ed.*, 1986, pp. 79–94. **[G: India; Mexico; Ivory Coast; Indonesia]**

Basevi, Giorgio and Toniolo, Gianni. Debt and Default in the 1930s: Causes and Consequences: Comments. *Europ. Econ. Rev.*, June 1986, *30*(3), pp. 641–47.

Bench, Robert R. U.S. Interests and Policy Implications: The Role of Lending Limits. **In** *Preeg, E. H. and Bendahmane, D. B., eds.*, 1986, pp. 65–67. **[G: U.S.]**

Bhaduri, Amit. Hacia un crecimiento con endeudamiento externo. (The Indebted Growth Process. With English summary.) *Estud. Econ.*, January-June 1986, *1*(1), pp. 115–25.

Bird, Graham. New Approaches to Country Risk. *Lloyds Bank Rev.*, October 1986, (162), pp. 1–16. **[G: LDCs]**

Bogdanowicz-Bindert, Christine A. World Debt: The United State Reconsiders. *Foreign Aff.*, Winter 1985/86, *64*(2), pp. 259–73.

Bosshard, Rudolf. The Relationship between the International Monetary Fund and the Commercial Banks. **In** *Dicke, D. C., ed.*, 1986, pp. 170–74.

Brainard, Lawrence J. Prospects for Lending to LDCs: Bankers' Views: The Investment Banking Strategy. **In** *Preeg, E. H. and Bendahmane, D. B., eds.*, 1986, pp. 39–41.

Brau, Eduard H. External Debt Management in the African Context. **In** *Helleiner, G. K, ed.*, 1986, pp. 160–80. **[G: Africa]**

Brau, Eduard H. The IMF: Changes Required to Restore Voluntary Lending. **In** *Preeg, E. H. and Bendahmane, D. B., eds.*, 1986, pp. 49–51.

Bruce, Robert and Murnane, Paul. Borrowing from Overseas. **In** *Bruce, R., et al., eds.*, 1986, pp. 297–320. **[G: Australia]**

Callier, Philippe. "Professional Trading," Exchange Rate Risk and the Growth of International Banking: A Note. *Banca Naz. Lavoro*

Quart. Rev., December 1986, (159), pp. 423–28.

Camdessus, Michel. Debt: Are We at the End of the Crisis? *Europ. Econ. Rev.*, June 1986, *30*(3), pp. 469–75.

Carmichael, Jeffrey. Economic Analysis and the World Debt Problem. *Australian Econ. Rev.*, 1st Quarter 1986, (73), pp. 29–36. **[G: LDCs]**

Choi, Sang-Rim; Tschoegl, Adrian E. and Yu, Chwo-Ming. Banks and the World's Major Financial Centers, 1970–1980. *Weltwirtsch. Arch.*, 1986, *122*(1), pp. 48–64. **[G: Global]**

Clairmonte, Frederick F. Transnational Conglomerates: Reflections on Global Power. **In** *[Patel, S.]*, 1986, pp. 139–56. **[G: Global]**

Clark, George J. Perspectives on Commercial Bank Lending. **In** *Lancaster, C. and Williamson, J., eds.*, 1986, pp. 142–46. **[G: Sub-Saharan Africa]**

Clausen, A. W. The World Bank and International Commercial Banks: Partners for Development: Address to the International Monetary Conference: Vancouver, Canada: May 23, 1982. **In** *Clausen, A. W.*, 1986, pp. 79–95.

Cohen, Benjamin J. Politics, Trade and Money: Comment. **In** *Tsoukalis, L., ed.*, 1986, pp. 256–59. **[G: U.S.; EEC]**

Cornell, Bradford and Shapiro, Alan C. The Reaction of Bank Stock Price to the International Debt Crisis. *J. Banking Finance*, March 1986, *10*(1), pp. 55–73. **[G: U.S.]**

Corrigan, E. Gerald. Coping with Globally Integrated Financial Markets. *Fed. Res. Bank New York Quart. Rev.*, Winter 1986-87, *11*(4), pp. 1–5. **[G: U.S.]**

Corrigan, E. Gerald. Reducing International Imbalances in an Interdependent World. *Fed. Res. Bank New York Quart. Rev.*, Spring 1986, *11*(1), pp. 1–5. **[G: U.S.; LDCs]**

Darby, Michael R. The Internationalization of American Banking and Finance: Structure, Risk, and World Interest Rates. *J. Int. Money Finance*, December 1986, *5*(4), pp. 403–28. **[G: U.S.]**

Darity, William A., Jr. Did the Commercial Banks Push Loans on the LDCs? **In** *Claudon, M. P., ed.*, 1986, pp. 199–25.

Debonneuil, Xavier H. The Pricing of Bonds and Bank Loans in International Markets: An Empirical Analysis of Developing Countries' Foreign Borrowing: Comments. *Europ. Econ. Rev.*, June 1986, *30*(3), pp. 591–93.

von der Decken, Christoph. Bank Lending and Government Intervention in Capital Markets: Has Recycling Gone Too Far? Comment. **In** *Giersch, H., ed.*, 1986, pp. 66–73. **[G: Selected LDCs; OECD]**

Devlin, Robert. La estructura y comportamiento de la banca international en los años setenta y su impacto en la crísis de América Latina. (The Structure and Behavior of the International Banking System in the Seventies and Its Impact on the Crisis of Latin America. With English summary.) *Colección Estud. CIEPLAN*, June 1986, (19), pp. 5–55. **[G: Latin America]**

Devlin, Robert. Private Banks, Debt, and the Bargaining Power of the Periphery: Theory and Practice. **In** *Economic Commission for Latin America and the Caribbean*, 1986, pp. 3–28. **[G: Peru; Bolivia]**

Díaz-Alejandro, Carlos F. Some Unintended Consequences of Financial Laissez-Faire. **In** *[Hirshman, A. O.]*, 1986, pp. 91–113. **[G: Chile]**

Dietz, James L. Debt and Development: The Future of Latin America. *J. Econ. Issues*, December 1986, *20*(4), pp. 1029–51. **[G: Latin America]**

Dixon, Peter B. and McDonald, Daina. Australia's Foreign Debt: 1975 to 1985. *Australian Econ. Rev.*, 2nd Quarter 1986, (74), pp. 22–37. **[G: Australia]**

Dooley, Michael P., et al. An Analysis of External Debt Positions of Eight Developing Countries through 1990. *J. Devel. Econ.*, May 1986, *21*(2), pp. 283–318. **[G: S. Korea; Philippines; Latin America]**

Dornbusch, Rudiger. The World Debt Problem: 1980–84 and Beyond. **In** *Dornbusch, R.*, 1986, *1985*, pp. 131–50.

Duncan, James A. International Financing by U.S. Borrowers: Questions Remain Open after Repeal. *Bull. Int. Fiscal Doc.*, Aug./Sept. 1986, *40*(8/9), pp. 358–62. **[G: U.S.; W. Europe]**

Eaton, Jonathan; Gersovitz, Mark and Stiglitz, Joseph E. The Pure Theory of Country Risk. *Europ. Econ. Rev.*, June 1986, *30*(3), pp. 481–513.

Eaton, Jonathan and Taylor, Lance. Developing Country Finance and Debt. *J. Devel. Econ.*, June 1986, *22*(1), pp. 209–65. **[G: LDCs]**

Edwards, Sebastian. The Pricing of Bonds and Bank Loans in International Markets: An Empirical Analysis of Developing Countries' Foreign Borrowing. *Europ. Econ. Rev.*, June 1986, *30*(3), pp. 565–89. **[G: LDCs]**

Eichengreen, Barry and Portes, Richard. Debt and Default in the 1930s: Causes and Consequences. *Europ. Econ. Rev.*, June 1986, *30*(3), pp. 599–640. **[G: U.S.; U.K.; Latin America; Australia]**

Erdilek, Asim. Government Policies in Developing Countries: Was Capital Wasted? Comment. **In** *Giersch, H., ed.*, 1986, pp. 95–99. **[G: India; Mexico; Ivory Coast; Indonesia]**

Errunza, V. R. and Ghalbouni, J. P. Interest Rates and International Debt Crisis. *Banca Naz. Lavoro Quart. Rev.*, June 1986, (157), pp. 225–45. **[G: LDCs]**

Ffrench-Davis, Ricardo. El financiamiento externo negativo: tendencias, consecuencias y opciones para América Latina. (Negative External Financing: Trends, Implications, and Options for Latin America. With English summary.) *Colección Estud. CIEPLAN*, December 1986, (20), pp. 5–17. **[G: Latin America]**

Ffrench-Davis, Ricardo. Notas sobre el desarrollo económico y la deuda externa en América Latina. (With English summary.) *Desarrollo Econ.*, Jan.-Mar. 1986, *25*(100), pp. 571–85. **[G: Latin America]**

Frimpong-Ansah, Jonathan H. The Supply of External Finance: Comments. **In** *Lancaster, C. and Williamson, J., eds.*, 1986, pp. 162–66. **[G: Sub-Saharan Africa]**

Gemmill, Robert. U.S. Interests and Policy Implications: Differential Treatment of Debts. **In** *Preeg, E. H. and Bendahmane, D. B., eds.*, 1986, pp. 62–65. **[G: U.S.]**

Glick, Reuven and Kharas, Homi J. The Costs and Benefits of Foreign Borrowing: A Survey of Multi-Period Models. *J. Devel. Stud.*, January 1986, *22*(2), pp. 279–99. **[G: LDCs]**

Gluck, Jeremy. International "Middle-Market" Borrowing. *Fed. Res. Bank New York Quart. Rev.*, Winter 1986-87, *11*(4), pp. 46–52.

Goldsbrough, David. Investment Trends and Prospects: The Link with Bank Lending. **In** *Moran, T. H., ed.*, 1986, pp. 173–86. **[G: LDCs]**

Griffith-Jones, Stephany. Ways Forward from the Debt Crisis. *Oxford Rev. Econ. Policy*, Spring 1986, *2*(1), pp. 39–61. **[G: LDCs]**

Grubel, Herbert G. Government Deposit Insurance, Moral Hazard and the International Debt Crisis. **In** *Giersch, H., ed.*, 1986, pp. 172–86. **[G: U.S.]**

Guerguil, Martine. The International Financial Crisis: Diagnoses and Prescriptions. **In** *Economic Commission for Latin America and the Caribbean*, 1986, *1984*, pp. 29–62.

Guesnerie, Roger. The Pure Theory of Country Risk: Comments. *Europ. Econ. Rev.*, June 1986, *30*(3), pp. 515–19.

Guttentag, Jack M. and Herring, Richard. Disclosure Policy and International Banking. *J. Banking Finance*, March 1986, *10*(1), pp. 75–97. **[G: U.S.]**

Hakim, Peter. The Baker Plan: Unfulfilled Promises. *Challenge*, Sept./Oct. 1986, *29*(4), pp. 55–59. **[G: U.S.]**

Hallberg, Kristin. International Debt, 1985: Origins and Issues for the Future. **In** *Claudon, M. P., ed.*, 1986, pp. 3–42. **[G: LDCs]**

Hellwig, Martin. The Pure Theory of Country Risk: Comments. *Europ. Econ. Rev.*, June 1986, *30*(3), pp. 521–27.

Hiemenz, Ulrich. Government Policies in Developing Countries: Was Capital Wasted? Comment. **In** *Giersch, H., ed.*, 1986, pp. 100–102. **[G: India; Mexico; Ivory Coast; Indonesia]**

Hoguet, George R. U.S. Interests and Policy Implications: A Strategy for Dealing with the Debt Crisis. **In** *Preeg, E. H. and Bendahmane, D. B., eds.*, 1986, pp. 57–60. **[G: U.S.]**

Huber, Klaus. Funding Direct Investment through Cofinancing: The Commercial Banker's View. **In** *Hauser, H., ed. (I)*, 1986, pp. 89–96.

Huber, Klaus. Funding Direct Investment through Cofinancing: The Commercial Banker's View. *Aussenwirtschaft*, April 1986, *41*(1), pp. 89–96. **[G: LDCs]**

Jao, Y. C. Banking and Currency in the Special Economic Zones: Problems and Prospects. **In** *Jao, Y. C. and Leung, C. K., eds.*, 1986, pp. 160–83. **[G: China]**

Jaycox, Edward V. K., et al. The Nature of the Debt Problem in Eastern and Southern Africa. **In** *Lancaster, C. and Williamson, J., eds.*, 1986, pp. 47–62. **[G: E. Africa; Southern Africa]**

Jones, Geoffrey. British Overseas Banks in the Middle East 1920–70: A Study in Multinational Middle Age. **In** *Teichova, A.; Lévy-Leboyer, M. and Nussbaum, H., eds.*, 1986, pp. 218–31. **[G: U.K.; Middle East]**

Kahler, Miles. Politics and International Debt: Explaining the Crisis. **In** *Kahler, M., ed.*, 1986, pp. 11–36.

Kahler, Miles. The Politics of International Debt: Conclusion: Politics and Proposals for Reform. **In** *Kahler, M., ed.*, 1986, pp. 245–72.

Katz, Samuel I. Government Deposit Insurance, Moral Hazard and the International Debt Crisis: Comment. **In** *Giersch, H., ed.*, 1986, pp. 187–91. **[G: U.S.]**

Kharas, Homi J. and Shishido, Hisanobu. A Dynamic-Optimization Model of Foreign Borrowing: A Case Study of Thailand. *J. Policy Modeling*, Spring 1986, *8*(1), pp. 1–26. **[G: Thailand]**

Kohler, Daniel F. To Pay or Not to Pay: A Model of International Defaults. *J. Policy Anal. Manage.*, Summer 1986, *5*(4), pp. 742–60.

König, Heinz. The Pricing of Bonds and Bank Loans in International Markets: An Empirical Analysis of Developing Countries' Foreign Borrowing: Comments. *Europ. Econ. Rev.*, June 1986, *30*(3), pp. 595–97.

Krueger, Anne O. Developing Countries' Debt Problems and Growth Prospects. *Atlantic Econ. J.*, March 1986, *14*(1), pp. 8–19. **[G: LDCs]**

Lessard, Donald R. The Supply of External Finance: Comments. **In** *Lancaster, C. and Williamson, J., eds.*, 1986, pp. 166–69. **[G: Africa]**

Lomax, David F. The Debt Problem: A Banking Perspective. **In** *Posner, M., ed.*, 1986, pp. 118–29. **[G: LDCs]**

MacEwan, Arthur. International Debt and Banking: Rising Instability within the General Crisis. *Sci. Soc.*, Summer 1986, *50*(2), pp. 177–209.

Madura, Jeff. Model for Financing in International Money Markets. *Rivista Int. Sci. Econ. Com.*, Oct.-Nov. 1986, *33*(10–11), pp. 1049–56.

Magee, Stephen P. and Brock, William A. Third World Debt and International Capital Market Failure as a Consequence of Redistributive Political Risk Sharing. **In** *Claudon, M. P., ed.*, 1986, pp. 173–98. **[G: OPEC; U.S.; Selected LDCs]**

Martin, Preston. Statement to the U.S. House Subcommittee on Financial Institutions Supervision, Regulation and Insurance of the Committee on Banking, Finance and Urban Affairs, April 9, 1986. *Fed. Res. Bull.*, June 1986, *72*(6), pp. 382–89. **[G: U.S.]**

Mayer, Helmut. Developing Country Debt: Policies and Prospects: Comment. **In** *Giersch, H., ed.*, 1986, pp. 123–26. **[G: LDCs]**

McCauley, Robert N. Are Large U.S. Banks Moving International Activity Off Their Balance Sheets? *Fed. Res. Bank New York Quart. Rev.*, Summer 1986, *11*(2), pp. 42–44. **[G: U.S.]**

Meese, Richard. Risk in International Lending: A Dynamic Factor Analysis Applied to France and Mexico: Comments. *J. Int. Money Finance*, Supp. March 1986, *5*, pp. S49–51. **[G: France; Mexico]**

Meissner, Charles F. Prospects for Lending to LDCs: Bankers' Views: The Need for a New International Banking Structure. **In** *Preeg, E. H. and Bendahmane, D. B., eds.*, 1986, pp. 45–48.

Meller, Patricio. Un enfoque analítico-empirico de las causas del actual endeudamiento externo chileno. (Causes of Present Chilean Foreign Debt: An Analytical–Empirical Approach. With English summary.) *Colección Estud. CIEPLAN*, December 1986, (20), pp. 19–60. **[G: Chile]**

Melvin, Michael and Schlagenhauf, Don. Risk in International Lending: A Dynamic Factor Analysis Applied to France and Mexico. *J. Int. Money Finance*, Supp. March 1986, *5*, pp. S31–48. **[G: France; Mexico]**

Mills, Rodney H. Foreign Lending by Banks: A Guide to International and U.S. Statistics. *Fed. Res. Bull.*, October 1986, *72*(10), pp. 683–94. **[G: U.S.]**

Mrak, Mojmir. Multilateral Finance Institutions of Developing Countries as Promoters of Their Financial Cooperation. **In** *Khan, K. M., ed.*, 1986, pp. 149–64. **[G: LDCs]**

Nunnenkamp, Peter. Bank Lending and Government Intervention in Capital Markets: Has Recycling Gone Too Far? **In** *Giersch, H., ed.*, 1986, pp. 42–65. **[G: Selected LDCs; OECD]**

Nyirabu, C. M. External Debt Management in the African Context: Comment. **In** *Helleiner, G. K, ed.*, 1986, pp. 181–83. **[G: Africa]**

O'Brien, Richard. Banking Perspectives on the Debt Crisis. *Oxford Rev. Econ. Policy*, Spring 1986, *2*(1), pp. 25–38. **[G: LDCs; MDCs]**

O'Connell, Arturo A. External Debt and the Reform of the International Monetary System. *CEPAL Rev.*, December 1986, (30), pp. 51–66.

Ortiz, Guillermo and Serra-Puche, Jaime. A Note on the Burden of the Mexican Foreign Debt. *J. Devel. Econ.*, April 1986, *21*(1), pp. 111–29. **[G: Mexico]**

Owen, Charles T. Prospects for Lending to LDCs: Bankers' Views: The Viewpoint of Regional Banks. **In** *Preeg, E. H. and Bendahmane, D. B., eds.*, 1986, pp. 43–45.

Owen, Robert F. Developing Country Debt: Policies and Prospects: Comment. **In** *Giersch, H., ed.*, 1986, pp. 127–32. **[G: LDCs]**

Pastré, Olivier and Rowley, Anthony. The Multinationalisation of British and American Banks. **In** *Teichova, A.; Lévy-Leboyer, M. and Nussbaum, H., eds.*, 1986, pp. 232–38. **[G: U.K.; U.S.]**

Pigot, Charles. Financial Reform and the Role of Foreign Banks in Pacific Basin Nations. **In** *Cheng, H.-S., ed.*, 1986, pp. 265–95. **[G: Pacific Basin]**

Pollan, Hans. Case Studies: IFC Projects. **In** *Hauser, H., ed. (I)*, 1986, pp. 71–80. **[G: India; Yugoslavia; Central America]**

Preeg, Ernest H. The New Economic Diplomacy: An Overview. **In** *Preeg, E. H. and Bendahmane, D. B., eds.*, 1986, pp. v–xiii.

Purcell, John F. H. and Miller, Michelle B. The World Bank and Private Capital. **In** *Feinberg, R. E., et al.*, 1986, pp. 111–33. **[G: LDCs]**

Raymond, Robert. International Seminar on Macroeconomics: An Overview. *Europ. Econ. Rev.*, June 1986, *30*(3), pp. 477–79.

Rodriguez, Carlos Alfredo. La Deuda Externa Argentina. (The Argentine Foreign Debt. With English summary.) *Económica (La Plata)*, July-December 1986, *32*(2), pp. 261–96. **[G: Argentina]**

Roett, Riordan. Peru: The Message from García. *Foreign Aff.*, Winter 1985/86, *64*(2), pp. 274–86. **[G: Peru]**

Rübel, Gerhard. Factors Determining External Indebtedness. *Econ. Notes*, 1986, (3), pp. 101–21.

Rybczynski, Tad M. Bank Lending and Government Intervention in Capital Markets: Has Recycling Gone Too Far? Comment. **In** *Giersch, H., ed.*, 1986, pp. 74–78. **[G: Selected LDCs; OECD]**

Sachs, Jeffrey. Managing the LDC Debt Crisis. *Brookings Pap. Econ. Act.*, 1986, (2), pp. 397–431. **[G: LDCs]**

Santow, Leonard J. The View from Wall Street. **In** *Claudon, M. P., ed.*, 1986, pp. 99–107. **[G: U.S.]**

Saunders, Paul and Dean, Andrew. The International Debt Situation and Linkages between Developing Countries and the OECD. *OECD Econ. Stud.*, Autumn 1986, (7), pp. 155–203. **[G: OECD; LDCs]**

Schwartz, Anna J. External Debt and the Banking System. **In** *Shadow Open Market Committee (I)*, 1986, pp. 51–58. **[G: U.S.; Mexico]**

Smith, Richard J. U.S. Interests and Policy Implications: Encouraging Private Investment in Developing Countries. **In** *Preeg, E. H. and Bendahmane, D. B., eds.*, 1986, pp. 60–62. **[G: U.S.]**

Solís, Leopoldo. Some Thoughts on Mexico's Foreign Indebtedness. *World Econ.*, March 1986, *9*(1), pp. 65–77. **[G: Mexico]**

Sotirova, Rumiana and Gocheva, Boryiana. Credit Relations in Bulgarian Imports from the Developed Capitalist Countries. *Soviet E. Europ. Foreign Trade*, Spring 1986, *22*(1), pp. 6–18. **[G: Bulgaria]**

Steiner, Manfred. Margin and Risk Management in International Credit Transactions Undertaken by Banks. **In** *Macharzina, K. and Staehle, W. H., eds.*, 1986, pp. 317–34. **[G: U.S.; W. Germany]**

433 Private International Lending

Story, Jonathan. Politics, Trade and Money: Comment. **In** *Tsoukalis, L., ed.*, 1986, pp. 265–69. **[G: U.S.; EEC]**

Strange, Susan. Politics, Trade and Money. **In** *Tsoukalis, L., ed.*, 1986, pp. 243–55. **[G: U.S.; EEC]**

Street, James H. Can Mexico Break the Vicious Circle of "Stop–Go" Policy? An Institutional Overview. *J. Econ. Issues*, June 1986, *20*(2), pp. 601–12. **[G: Mexico]**

Strøm, Trygve. Project Financing in the North Sea. *Écon. Soc.*, July 1986, *20*(7), pp. 145–57.

Taylor, Lance. Debt Crisis: North–South, North–North, and in Between. **In** *Claudon, M. P., ed.*, 1986, pp. 227–47.

Taylor, William. Statement to the U.S. Senate Subcommittee on International Finance and Monetary Policy of the Committee on Banking, Housing, and Urban Affairs, June 25, 1986. *Fed. Res. Bull.*, August 1986, *72*(8), pp. 565–68. **[G: U.S.]**

Teranishi, Juro. The "Catch-up" Process, Financial System, and Japan's Rise as a Capital Exporter. *Hitotsubashi J. Econ.*, Spec. Iss. Oct. 1986, *27*, pp. 133–46. **[G: Japan]**

Terrell, Henry S. The Role of Foreign Banks in Domestic Banking Markets. **In** *Cheng, H.-S., ed.*, 1986, pp. 297–304. **[G: U.S.]**

Thore, Sten. Regional Lending Risk in Eurodollar Markets. *Scand. J. Econ.*, 1986, *88*(2), pp. 437–51.

Tourinho, Octávio A. F. Endividamento externo ótimo em um modelo de equilíbrio dinâmico multissetorial: um estudo de caso para o Brasil. (With English summary.) *Pesquisa Planejamento Econ.*, December 1986, *16*(3), pp. 647–87. **[G: Brazil]**

Trejo Reyes, Saúl. Deuda externa: una alternativa de solución. (Foreign Debt: An Alternative Solution. With English summary.) *Estud. Econ.*, July-Dec. 1986, *1*(2), pp. 357–75. **[G: Mexico]**

Ver Hulst, N. and Laporte, J. M. Le rôle des banques dans les grands projets énergétiques. (The Role of Banks in Big Energetic Projects. With English summary.) *Écon. Soc.*, July 1986, *20*(7), pp. 129–43.

Volcker, Paul A. Statement to the U.S. House Committee on Foreign Affairs, June 18, 1986. *Fed. Res. Bull.*, August 1986, *72*(8), pp. 560–65. **[G: LDCs]**

Wellons, Philip A. International Debt: The Behavior of Banks in a Politicized Environment. **In** *Kahler, M., ed.*, 1986, pp. 95–125. **[G: U.S.; U.K.; W. Germany; France; Japan]**

Wellons, Philip A. Multinational Institutions in the Debt Crisis: National Interest and Long Term Consequences. **In** *Claudon, M. P., ed.*, 1986, pp. 147–69. **[G: LDCs]**

Wessel, Robert H. Solving the Third World Debt Crisis. *Rivista Int. Sci. Econ. Com.*, Oct.-Nov. 1986, *33*(10–11), pp. 949–56. **[G: LDCs]**

White, Eugene Nelson. Latin America's Debt Crisis of the 1930s: Lessons for the 1980s. **In** *Berend, I. T. and Borchardt, K., eds.*, 1986, pp. 484–96. **[G: Latin America; U.S.]**

Williamson, John. Managing the LDC Debt Crisis: Comments. *Brookings Pap. Econ. Act.*, 1986, (2), pp. 432–37.

Williamson, John. The Outlook for Debt Relief or Repudiation in Latin America. *Oxford Rev. Econ. Policy*, Spring 1986, *2*(1), pp. 1–6. **[G: Latin America]**

Zakariya, Hasan S. Financing Petroleum Development in the Third World: The Role of the Public International Sector. *J. World Trade Law*, July:Aug. 1986, *20*(4), pp. 417–40. **[G: LDCs]**

440 International Investment and Foreign Aid

441 International Investment and Long-term Capital Movements

4410 General

Alejo, F. Javier. Investing for Development in a Changing World. **In** *Hauser, H., ed. (I)*, 1986, pp. 57–70.

Balassa, Bela. Dependency and Trade Orientation. *World Econ.*, September 1986, *9*(3), pp. 259–73. **[G: U.S.; LDCs]**

Baneth, Jean. Government Policies in Developing Countries: Was Capital Wasted? **In** *Giersch, H., ed.*, 1986, pp. 79–94. **[G: India; Mexico; Ivory Coast; Indonesia]**

Bergsten, C. Fred. Trade, Debt and Investment: The Importance of Foreign Private Investment for Development. **In** *Hauser, H., ed. (I)*, 1986, pp. 27–36.

Burkhardt, Hans-Martin. Investment Protection Treaties: Recent Trends and Prospects. **In** *Hauser, H., ed. (I)*, 1986, pp. 99–104.

Clausen, A. W. Address to the Board of Governors: Washington, D.C.: September 24, 1984. **In** *Clausen, A. W.*, 1986, pp. 319–45.

Cooper, Richard N. Towards an International Capital Market? **In** *Cooper, R. N.*, 1986, *1971*, pp. 137–54. **[G: OECD]**

Dollar, David. Technological Innovations, Capital Mobility, and the Product Cycle in North–South Trade. *Amer. Econ. Rev.*, March 1986, *76*(1), pp. 177–90.

Dutton, John. Optimal Taxes on Foreign Investment in an Overlapping Generation Model. *Public Finance Quart.*, July 1986, *14*(3), pp. 289–311.

Encarnation, Dennis J. and Wells, Louis T., Jr. Evaluating Foreign Investment. **In** *Moran, T. H., ed.*, 1986, pp. 61–86.

Erdilek, Asim. Government Policies in Developing Countries: Was Capital Wasted? Comment. **In** *Giersch, H., ed.*, 1986, pp. 95–99. **[G: India; Mexico; Ivory Coast; Indonesia]**

Grieco, Joseph M. Foreign Investment and Development: Theories and Evidence. **In** *Moran, T. H., ed.*, 1986, pp. 35–60.

Hegewisch, Adolfo. The Importance of Direct Investment for Developing Countries. **In** *Hauser, H., ed. (I),* 1986, pp. 47–53.

Hiemenz, Ulrich. Government Policies in Developing Countries: Was Capital Wasted? Comment. **In** *Giersch, H., ed.,* 1986, pp. 100–102. **[G: India; Mexico; Ivory Coast; Indonesia]**

Jones, Ronald W.; Coelho, Isaias and Easton, Stephen T. The Theory of International Factor Flows: The Basic Model. *J. Int. Econ.,* May 1986, *20*(3/4), pp. 313–27.

Khan, Ali M. and Lin, Po-Sheng. Two-Way Capital Flows in an Asymmetric World Economy. *Manchester Sch. Econ. Soc. Stud.,* June 1986, *54*(2), pp. 219–24.

Maki, Dennis R. and Meredith, Lindsay N. Production Cost Differentials and Foreign Direct Investment: A Test of Two Models. *Appl. Econ.,* October 1986, *18*(10), pp. 1127–34. **[G: U.S.; Canada]**

Miyagiwa, Kaz F. and Young, Leslie. International Capital Mobility and Commercial Policy in an Economic Region. *J. Int. Econ.,* May 1986, *20*(3/4), pp. 329–41.

Moran, Theodore H. The Future of Foreign Direct Investment in the Third World. **In** *Moran, T. H., ed.,* 1986, pp. 3–19.

Niehans, Jürg. The International Division of Assets as Determined by Comparative Advantage. *J. Int. Money Finance,* June 1986, *5*(2), pp. 153–65.

Nordhaus, William D. A Geometrical Analysis of the Incentives for Default and Credit Rationing: Comment [Growth and External Debt under Risk of Debt Repudiation]. *Europ. Econ. Rev.,* June 1986, *30*(3), pp. 561–64.

Obstfeld, Maurice. Capital Mobility in the World Economy: Theory and Measurement. *Carnegie-Rochester Conf. Ser. Public Policy,* Spring 1986, *24*, pp. 55–103. **[G: OECD]**

Oman, Charles P. New Forms of Investment in Developing Countries. **In** *Moran, T. H., ed.,* 1986, pp. 131–55.

Purcell, John F. H. and Miller, Michelle B. The World Bank and Private Capital. **In** *Feinberg, R. E., et al.,* 1986, pp. 111–33. **[G: LDCs]**

Quibria, M. G. A Note on Foreign Investment, the Savings Function and Immiserization of National Welfare. *J. Devel. Econ.,* May 1986, *21*(2), pp. 361–72.

Radcliffe, Julian G. Y. Coverage of Political Risk by the Private Insurance Industry. **In** *Hauser, H., ed. (I),* 1986, pp. 135–39.

Rauch, James E. The Transfer of Production from Rich to Poor Countries. *J. Devel. Econ.,* September 1986, *23*(1), pp. 41–53.

Rugman, Alan M. New Theories of the Multinational Enterprise: An Assessment of Internationalization Theory. *Bull. Econ. Res.,* May 1986, *38*(2), pp. 101–18.

Shihata, Ibrahim F. I. The Role of ICSID and the Projected Multilateral Investment Guarantee Agency (MIGA). **In** *Hauser, H., ed. (I),* 1986, pp. 105–22.

Stulz, René M. Capital Mobility in the World Economy: Theory and Measurement: A Comment. *Carnegie-Rochester Conf. Ser. Public Policy,* Spring 1986, *24*, pp. 105–13.

Wurmstich, Jörg-Dietrich. Coverage of Political Risk by National Insurance Agencies: The German Investment Guarantee Scheme. **In** *Hauser, H., ed. (I),* 1986, pp. 123–33. **[G: W. Germany]**

Young, Leslie and Miyagiwa, Kaz F. International Investment and Immiserizing Growth. *J. Int. Econ.,* February 1986, *20*(1/2), pp. 171–78.

4411 International Investment and Long-term Capital Movements: Theory

Bhagwati, Jagdish N. and Brecher, Richard A. Extending Free Trade to Include International Investment: A Welfare-Theoretic Analysis. **In** *[Streeten, P.],* 1986, pp. 115–21.

Blejer, Mario I. Welfare, Banks, and Capital Mobility in Steady State: The Case of Predetermined Exchange Rates: Comment. **In** *Edwards, S. and Ahamed, L., eds.,* 1986, pp. 199–200.

Calvo, Guillermo A. Welfare, Banks, and Capital Mobility in Steady State: The Case of Predetermined Exchange Rates. **In** *Edwards, S. and Ahamed, L., eds.,* 1986, pp. 177–99.

Cooper, Ian and Kaplanis, Evi. Costs to Crossborder Investment and International Equity Market Equilibrium. **In** *Edwards, J., et al., eds.,* 1986, pp. 209–40. **[G: OECD]**

Das, Satya P. Optimal Taxation of Foreign Capital When Its Movements Are Sluggish. *J. Int. Econ.,* November 1986, *21*(3/4), pp. 351–60.

Ethier, Wilfred J. The Multinational Firm. *Quart. J. Econ.,* November 1986, *101*(4), pp. 805–33.

Francesco, Drudi. Effetti redistributivi e di benessere di un'apertura a movimenti di capitale. (Effects of Capital Flows on Income Distribution and Welfare. A Review Article. With English summary.) *Giorn. Econ.,* July-Aug. 1986, *45*(7–8), pp. 433–62.

Geldner, Marian. Integrating the Theories of International Trade and Foreign Direct Investment. **In** *Gray, H. P., ed.,* 1986, pp. 95–107.

Grinols, Earl L. Foreign Investment and Economic Growth: Characterization of a Second-Best Policy for Welfare Gains. *J. Int. Econ.,* August 1986, *21*(1/2), pp. 165–71.

Kaempfer, William H. and Lowenberg, Anton D. A Model of the Political Economy of International Investment Sanctions: The Case of South Africa. *Kyklos,* 1986, *39*(3), pp. 377–96. **[G: S. Africa]**

Mathieson, Donald J. International Capital Flows, Capital Controls, and Financial Reform. **In** *Cheng, H.-S., ed.,* 1986, pp. 237–60. **[G: China]**

Obstfeld, Maurice. Capital Flows, the Current Account, and the Real Exchange Rate: Some Consequences of Stabilization and Liberalization. **In** *Edwards, S. and Ahamed, L., eds.,* 1986, pp. 201–29.

Selowsky, Marcelo. Capital Flows, the Current Account, and the Real Exchange Rate: Some Consequences of Stabilization and Liberalization: Comment. **In** *Edwards, S. and Ahamed, L., eds.*, 1986, pp. 229–31.

Sieber, René. Accumulation de capital, propriété étrangère et bien-être national en présence de facteurs de production spécifiques et de biens non-échangeables. (Capital Accumulation, Foreign Ownership and National Welfare with Specific Factors of Production and Non-tradable Goods. With English summary.) *Écon. Appl.*, 1986, *39*(2), pp. 239–62.

Sieber, René and Wetterwald, Paul. Environmental Protection and Direct Foreign Investment with Specific Factors of Production: The Case of the Small Open Economy. *Schweiz. Z. Volkswirtsch. Statist.*, December 1986, *122*(4), pp. 611–25.

Takagi, Yasuoki. Inflation and Cumulative Debt Outstanding of Less-Developed Countries. *J. Int. Econ.*, August 1986, *21*(1/2), pp. 61–80. **[G: LDCs]**

Taylor, Lance. Debt Crisis: North–South, North–North, and in Between. **In** *Claudon, M. P., ed.*, 1986, pp. 227–47.

Wong, Kar-yiu. Are International Trade and Factor Mobility Substitutes? *J. Int. Econ.*, August 1986, *21*(1/2), pp. 25–43.

Wong, Kar-yiu. International Factor Movements, Repatriation and Welfare. *J. Int. Econ.*, November 1986, *21*(3/4), pp. 327–35.

4412 International Investment and Long-term Capital Movements: Studies

Ahiakpor, James C. W. The Profits of Foreign Firms in a Less Developed Country: Ghana. *J. Devel. Econ.*, July-Aug. 1986, *22*(2), pp. 321–35. **[G: Ghana]**

Ahmad, Shamsuddin. Domestic Saving and Foreign Capital Inflow: The Case of Bangladesh. *Bangladesh Devel. Stud.*, March 1986, *14*(1), pp. 75–91. **[G: Bangladesh]**

Alejo, F. Javier. Investment for Development in a Changing World. *Aussenwirtschaft,* April 1986, *41*(1), pp. 57–70. **[G: LDCs]**

Androuais, Anne. Spatialisation du système productif japonais. (Spacialisation of the Japanese Productive System. With English summary.) *Écon. Soc.*, May 1986, *20*(5), pp. 125–53. **[G: Japan; ASEAN]**

Azpiazu, Daniel; Basualdo, Eduardo and Kosacoff, Bernardo. Transnational Corporations in Argentina, 1976–1983. *CEPAL Rev.*, April 1986, (28), pp. 99–133. **[G: Argentina]**

Balasubramanyam, V. N. Incentives and Disincentives for Foreign Direct Investment in Less Developed Countries. **In** *Balassa, B. and Giersch, H., eds.*, 1986, pp. 401–15. **[G: Selected LDCs]**

Belli, R. David. U.S. Multinational Companies: Operations in 1983. *Surv. Curr. Bus.*, January 1986, *66*(1), pp. 23–35. **[G: U.S.]**

Bergsten, C. Fred. Trade, Debt and Investment: The Importance of Foreign Private Investment for Development. *Aussenwirtschaft,* April 1986, *41*(1), pp. 27–36. **[G: LDCs]**

Brereton, Barbara F. U.S. Multinational Companies: Operations in 1984. *Surv. Curr. Bus.*, September 1986, *66*(9), pp. 27–39. **[G: U.S.]**

Burkhardt, Hans-Martin. Investment Protection Treaties: Recent Trends and Prospects. *Aussenwirtschaft,* April 1986, *41*(1), pp. 99–104. **[G: Global]**

Burton, F. N. and Saelens, F. H. Japanese Direct Investment Abroad: The Unfulfilled Promise. *Rivista Int. Sci. Econ. Com.*, May 1986, *33*(5), pp. 493–510. **[G: Japan]**

Cable, Vincent and Mukherjee, Bishakha. Foreign Investment in Low-income Developing Countries. **In** *Moran, T. H., ed.*, 1986, pp. 87–111. **[G: LDCs]**

Chen, Che-Hung. Taiwan's Foreign Direct Investment. *J. World Trade Law,* Nov.:Dec. 1986, *20*(6), pp. 639–64. **[G: Taiwan]**

Chishti, Sumitra. Third World Multinationals and Trade Expansion among the Countries of the South. **In** *Khan, K. M., ed.*, 1986, pp. 88–112. **[G: LDCs; OPEC]**

Chrystal, K. Alec and Dowd, Kevin. Two Arguments for the Restriction of International Capital Flows. *Nat. Westminster Bank Quart. Rev.*, November 1986, pp. 8–19. **[G: U.K.]**

Diejomaoh, Vremudia P. Impact of Different Types of Foreign Investments on Capital Formation in Africa. **In** *Association of African Central Banks,* 1986, pp. 123–50. **[G: Africa]**

Dunn, Malcolm H. and Körner, Heiko. Third World Multinationals and Trade Expansion among the Countries of the South: Comment. **In** *Khan, K. M., ed.*, 1986, pp. 113–29. **[G: LDCs; OPEC]**

Dunning, John H. The Investment Development Cycle and Third World Multinationals. **In** *Khan, K. M., ed.*, 1986, pp. 15–47. **[G: Asia; Latin America]**

Dunning, John H. The Investment Development Cycle Revisited. *Weltwirtsch. Arch.*, 1986, *122*(4), pp. 667–76. **[G: LDCs]**

Dunning, John H. and Norman, George. Intra-industry Investment. **In** *Gray, H. P., ed.*, 1986, pp. 73–94. **[G: U.S.]**

Erdilek, Asim. Turkey's New Open-Door Policy of Direct Foreign Investment: A Critical Analysis of Problems and Prospects. *METU,* 1986, *13*(1/2), pp. 171–91. **[G: Turkey]**

Euh, Yoon-Dae and Min, Sang H. Foreign Direct Investment from Developing Countries: The Case of Korean Firms. *Devel. Econ.*, June 1986, *24*(2), pp. 149–68. **[G: S. Korea]**

Fishlow, Albert. Lessons from the Past: Capital Markets during the 19th Century and the Interwar Period. **In** *Kahler, M., ed.*, 1986, pp. 37–93. **[G: LDCs; MDCs]**

Frankel, Jeffrey A. International Capital Mobility and Crowding-out in the U.S. Economy: Imperfect Integration of Financial Markets or of Goods Markets? **In** *Hafer, R. W., ed. (I),* 1986, pp. 33–67. **[G: U.S.]**

Friedman, Benjamin M. Implications of the U.S. Net Capital Inflow. **In** *Hafer, R. W., ed. (I),* 1986, pp. 137–61. **[G: U.S.]**

Frimpong-Ansah, Jonathan H. The Supply of External Finance: Comments. **In** *Lancaster, C.*

and Williamson, J., eds., 1986, pp. 162–66. **[G: Sub-Saharan Africa]**

Gandhi, Prem. Foreign Direct Investment and Regional Development: The Case of Canadian Investment in New York State. **In** *Schoolman, M. and Magid, A., eds.*, 1986, pp. 205–27. **[G: U.S.; Canada]**

Goldberg, Michael A. Hedging Your Great Grandchildren's Bets: The Case of Overseas Chinese Investment in Real Estate around the Cities of the Pacific Rim. **In** *Nemetz, P. N., ed.*, 1986, pp. 159–98. **[G: S. E. Asia; ASEAN; Hong Kong]**

Goldsbrough, David. Investment Trends and Prospects: The Link with Bank Lending. **In** *Moran, T. H., ed.*, 1986, pp. 173–86. **[G: LDCs]**

von Graffenried, Rudolf. Control of Transborder Movements of Capital. **In** *Dicke, D. C., ed.*, 1986, pp. 214–30.

Graziani, G. Capital Movements within the CMEA. *Soviet E. Europ. Foreign Trade*, Spring 1986, *22*(1), pp. 19–50. **[G: CMEA]**

Guisinger, Stephen. Do Performance Requirements and Investment Incentives Work? *World Econ.*, March 1986, *9*(1), pp. 79–96. **[G: U.S.]**

Harrington, James W., Jr.; Burns, Karen and Cheung, Man. Market-Oriented Foreign Investment and Regional Development: Canadian Companies in Western New York. *Econ. Geogr.*, April 1986, *62*(2), pp. 155–66. **[G: U.S.]**

Hauser, Heinz. Promotion of Foreign Direct Investment to Developing Countries: An Exercise in Cooperation. *Aussenwirtschaft*, April 1986, *41*(1), pp. 9–18. **[G: LDCs]**

Hegewisch, Adolfo. The Importance of Direct Investment for Developing Countries. *Aussenwirtschaft*, April 1986, *41*(1), pp. 47–53. **[G: LDCs]**

Helmboldt, Niles E.; West, Tina and Hardy, Benjamin H. Private Investment and African Economic Policy. **In** *Berg, R. J. and Whitaker, J. S., eds.*, 1986, pp. 331–57. **[G: Africa]**

Herr, Ellen M. Capital Expenditures by Majority-Owned Foreign Affiliates of U.S. Companies, 1986 and 1987. *Surv. Curr. Bus.*, October 1986, *66*(10), pp. 21–30. **[G: U.S.]**

Hodes, Daniel A. and Mauer, Laurence J. U.S. Tax Reform: Capital Recovery and International Direct Investment. *Bus. Econ.*, January 1986, *21*(1), pp. 50–54. **[G: U.S.]**

Huber, Klaus. Funding Direct Investment through Cofinancing: The Commercial Banker's View. *Aussenwirtschaft*, April 1986, *41*(1), pp. 89–96. **[G: LDCs]**

Huizinga, John. Implications of the U.S. Net Capital Inflow: Comments. **In** *Hafer, R. W., ed. (I)*, 1986, pp. 163–67. **[G: U.S.]**

Jao, Y. C. Banking and Currency in the Special Economic Zones: Problems and Prospects. **In** *Jao, Y. C. and Leung, C. K., eds.*, 1986, pp. 160–83. **[G: China]**

Kanno, Ryohei. U.S.–Japan Capital Interaction: Implications of Euroyen and Direct Investment. **In** *Finn, R. B., ed.*, 1986, pp. 173–83. **[G: U.S.; Japan; Selected Countries]**

Kelkar, Vijay L. A View from the South: Growth of World Trade in Manufactures. **In** *[Patel, S.]*, 1986, pp. 105–21. **[G: MDCs; LDCs]**

Kimura, Yui. Japanese Policy toward Foreign Multinationals: Implications for Trade and Competitiveness: Comment. **In** *Pugel, T. A., ed.*, 1986, pp. 169–74. **[G: Japan]**

Kindleberger, Charles P. International Capital Movements and Foreign-Exchange Markets in Crisis: The 1930s and the 1980s. **In** *Berend, I. T. and Borchardt, K., eds.*, 1986, pp. 437–55.

Kinoshita, Toshihiko. Japanese Investment in Indonesia: Problems and Prospects. *Bull. Indonesian Econ. Stud.*, April 1986, *22*(1), pp. 34–56. **[G: Indonesia; Japan]**

Knirsch, Peter. Soviet and Eastern European Firms in the Federal Republic of Germany. **In** *Hamilton, G., ed.*, 1986, pp. 103–30. **[G: W. Germany; E. Europe; CMEA]**

Kumar, Nagesh. Foreign Direct Investments and Technology Transfers among Developing Countries. **In** *Panchamukhi, V. R., et al.*, 1986, pp. 139–65. **[G: LDCs]**

Kwok, R. Y. W. Structure and Policies in Industrial Planning in the Shenzhen Special Economic Zone. **In** *Jao, Y. C. and Leung, C. K., eds.*, 1986, pp. 39–64. **[G: China]**

Kwon, O. Yul. A Critique of Korea's Foreign Capital Inducement Policy in the Light of Neutral Taxation. *J. Econ. Devel.*, July 1986, *11*(1), pp. 47–67. **[G: S. Korea]**

Landau, Zbigniew and Tomaszewski, Jerzy. Foreign Policy and International Business in Poland: 1918–39. **In** *Teichova, A.; Lévy-Leboyer, M. and Nussbaum, H., eds.*, 1986, pp. 270–85. **[G: Poland]**

Łebkowski, Maciej and Monkiewicz, Jan. Western Direct Investment in Centrally Planned Economies. *J. World Trade Law*, Nov.:Dec. 1986, *20*(6), pp. 624–38. **[G: CMEA]**

Lessard, Donald R. The Supply of External Finance: Comments. **In** *Lancaster, C. and Williamson, J., eds.*, 1986, pp. 166–69. **[G: Africa]**

Lincoln, Edward J. Japanese Policy toward Foreign Multinationals: Implications for Trade and Competitiveness: Comment. **In** *Pugel, T. A., ed.*, 1986, pp. 163–68. **[G: Japan]**

Little, Jane Sneddon. Recent Trends in Foreign Direct Investment in the United States: An Overview. **In** *Gray, H. P., ed.*, 1986, pp. 9–41. **[G: U.S.]**

Lowe, Jeffrey H. Capital Expenditures by Majority-Owned Foreign Affiliates of U.S. Companies, 1986. *Surv. Curr. Bus.*, March 1986, *66*(3), pp. 18–23. **[G: U.S.]**

Magee, Stephen P. and Brock, William A. Third World Debt and International Capital Market Failure as a Consequence of Redistributive Political Risk Sharing. **In** *Claudon, M. P., ed.*, 1986, pp. 173–98. **[G: OPEC; U.S.; Selected LDCs]**

Mathieson, Donald J. International Capital

Flows, Capital Controls, and Financial Reform. In *Cheng, H.-S., ed.*, 1986, pp. 237–60. **[G: China]**

McClain, David. Direct Investment in the United States: The European Experience. In *Gray, H. P., ed.*, 1986, pp. 309–43. **[G: Europe; U.S.]**

McKinnon, Ronald I. Financial Liberalization and Economic Development. In *Cheng, H.-S., ed.*, 1986, pp. 337–42. **[G: LDCs]**

Mishkin, Frederic S. International Capital Mobility and Crowding-out in the U.S. Economy: Imperfect Integration of Financial Markets or of Goods Markets? Comments. In *Hafer, R. W., ed. (I)*, 1986, pp. 69–74. **[G: U.S.; OECD]**

Moose, Richard M. Alternative Sources of Capital. In *Lancaster, C. and Williamson, J., eds.*, 1986, pp. 147–61. **[G: LDCs]**

Nigh, Douglas. Political Events and the Foreign Direct Investment Decision: An Empirical Examination. *Managerial Dec. Econ.*, June 1986, *7*(2), pp. 99–106. **[G: U.S.; Latin America]**

Ó Huallacháin, Breandán. The Role of Foreign Direct Investment in the Development of Regional Industrial Systems: Current Knowledge and Suggestions for a Future American Research Agenda. *Reg. Stud.*, April 1986, *20*(2), pp. 151–62. **[G: U.S.]**

Ortner, Robert. Savings and Government Deficits. In *Adams, F. G. and Wachter, S. M., eds.*, 1986, pp. 163–71. **[G: U.S.]**

Owen, Robert F. Incentives and Disincentives for Foreign Direct Investment in Less Developed Countries: Comment. In *Balassa, B. and Giersch, H., eds.*, 1986, pp. 416–25. **[G: Selected LDCs]**

Ozawa, Terutomo. Japanese Policy toward Foreign Multinationals: Implications for Trade and Competitiveness. In *Pugel, T. A., ed.*, 1986, pp. 141–62. **[G: Japan]**

Pollan, Hans. Case Studies: IFC Projects. In *Hauser, H., ed. (I)*, 1986, pp. 71–80. **[G: India; Yugoslavia; Central America]**

Pollan, Hans. Case Studies: IFC Projects. *Aussenwirtschaft*, April 1986, *41*(1), pp. 71–80. **[G: India; Yugoslavia; Central America]**

Radcliffe, Julian G. Y. Coverage of Political Risk by the Private Insurance Industry. *Aussenwirtschaft*, April 1986, *41*(1), pp. 135–39.

Rivera-Batiz, Francisco L. International Migration, Remittances and Economic Welfare in the Source Country. *J. Econ. Stud.*, 1986, *13*(3), pp. 3–19.

Robertson, P. Official Policy on American Direct Investment in Australia, 1945–1952. *Australian Econ. Hist. Rev.*, September 1986, *26*(2), pp. 159–81. **[G: U.S.; U.K.; Australia]**

Rose, Margarita M. Moderating the Investment Debate. *Econ. Forum*, Winter 1986-1987, *16*(1), pp. 147–58. **[G: S. Africa]**

Ruffin, Roy J. and Rassekh, Farhad. The Role of Foreign Direct Investment in U.S. Capital Outflows. *Amer. Econ. Rev.*, December 1986, *76*(5), pp. 1126–30. **[G: U.S.]**

Rugman, Alan M. and McIlveen, John. Canadian Foreign Direct Investment in the United States. In *Gray, H. P., ed.*, 1986, pp. 289–307. **[G: Canada; U.S.]**

Sazanami, Yoko. Japanese Trade in the Pacific Rim: The Relationship between Trade and Investment. In *Nemetz, P. N., ed.*, 1986, pp. 53–73. **[G: ASEAN; Japan; New Zealand; Australia]**

Scholl, Russell B. The International Investment Position of the United States in 1985. *Surv. Curr. Bus.*, June 1986, *66*(6), pp. 26–35, 16. **[G: U.S.]**

Shea, Michael A. U.S. Business Enterprises Acquired or Established by Foreign Direct Investors in 1985. *Surv. Curr. Bus.*, May 1986, *66*(5), pp. 47–54. **[G: U.S.]**

Shihata, Ibrahim F. I. The Role of ICSID and the Projected Multilateral Investment Guarantee Agency (MIGA). *Aussenwirtschaft*, April 1986, *41*(1), pp. 105–22. **[G: Global]**

Siddayao, Corazon Morales. Petroleum Resources in the Pacific Rim: The Roles Played by Governments in Their Development and Trade. In *Nemetz, P. N., ed.*, 1986, pp. 234–74. **[G: Pacific Basin]**

Sit, Victor F. S. Industries in Shenzhen: An Attempt at Open-Door Industrialization. In *Jao, Y. C. and Leung, C. K., eds.*, 1986, pp. 226–46. **[G: China]**

Sommaruga, Cornelio. Promotion of Foreign Direct Investment to Developing Countries: Opening Address. *Aussenwirtschaft*, April 1986, *41*(1), pp. 19–23. **[G: LDCs]**

Sornarajah, M. State Responsibility and Bilateral Investment Treaties. *J. World Trade Law*, Jan.:Feb. 1986, *20*(1), pp. 79–98. **[G: Global]**

Stallings, Barbara. External Finance and the Transition to Socialism in Small Peripheral Societies. In *Fagen, R. R.; Deere, C. D. and Coraggio, J. L., eds.*, 1986, pp. 54–78. **[G: Cuba; Tanzania; Chile; Mozambique; Nicaragua]**

Stoever, William A. Foreign Investment as an Aid in Moving from Least Developed to Newly Industrializing: A Study in Korea. *J. Devel. Areas*, January 1986, *20*(2), pp. 223–47. **[G: S. Korea]**

Triffin, Robert. Correcting the World Monetary Scandal. *Challenge*, Jan./Feb. 1986, *28*(6), pp. 4–14. **[G: Global; U.S.]**

de Vries, Barend A. Future Capital Flows: Critical Improvements and the Role of Coordination. In *Claudon, M. P., ed.*, 1986, pp. 63–77.

Wheeler, J. W. Japanese Foreign Direct Investment in the United States. In *Gray, H. P., ed.*, 1986, pp. 345–75. **[G: U.S.; Japan]**

Wilkins, Mira. Japanese Multinational Enterprise before 1914. *Bus. Hist. Rev.*, Summer 1986, *60*(2), pp. 199–231. **[G: Japan]**

Wilkins, Mira. The Impacts of American Multinational Enterprise on American–Chinese Economic Relations, 1786–1949. In *May, E. R. and Fairbank, J. K., eds.*, 1986, pp. 259–92. **[G: U.S.; China]**

Wurmstich, Jörg-Dietrich. Coverage of Political

Risk by National Insurance Agencies: The German Investment Guarantee Scheme. *Aussenwirtschaft*, April 1986, *41*(1), pp. 123–33.

442 International Business and Multinational Enterprises

4420 International Business and Multinational Enterprises

Aderinto, Adeyemo. Indigenous African Managers and Corporate Social Responsibility. **In** *Damachi, U. G. and Seibel, H. D., eds.*, 1986, pp. 359–84. **[G: Nigeria]**

Agarwal, J. P. Third World Multinationals and Balance-of-Payments Effect on Home Countries: A Case Study of India. **In** *Khan, K. M., ed.*, 1986, pp. 184–95. **[G: India]**

Ahiakpor, James C. W. The Capital Intensity of Foreign, Private Local and State Owned Firms in a Less Developed Country: Ghana. *J. Devel. Econ.*, Jan.-Feb. 1986, *20*(1), pp. 145–62. **[G: Ghana]**

Ahiakpor, James C. W. The Profits of Foreign Firms in a Less Developed Country: Ghana. *J. Devel. Econ.*, July-Aug. 1986, *22*(2), pp. 321–35. **[G: Ghana]**

Albinski, Henry S. Assessing Corporate Political Risk: A Guide for International Businessmen: Country Studies: Australia. **In** *Raddock, D. M., et al.*, 1986, pp. 127–45. **[G: Australia]**

Albrecht, Hellmut K. Success Factors in International Management: The "Turnaround" Case of a Multinational's European Subsidiary. **In** *Macharzina, K. and Staehle, W. H., eds.*, 1986, pp. 285–93. **[G: W. Germany]**

Alworth, Julian. A Cost of Capital Approach to the Taxation of Foreign Direct Investment Income. **In** *Edwards, J., et al., eds.*, 1986, pp. 185–208.

Amstutz, Max D. Co-operation with IFC: Experience of a European Investor. **In** *Hauser, H., ed. (I)*, 1986, pp. 81–87.

Androuais, Anne. Spatialisation du système productif japonais. (Spacialisation of the Japanese Productive System. With English summary.) *Écon. Soc.*, May 1986, *20*(5), pp. 125–53. **[G: Japan; ASEAN]**

Asante, S. K. B. The New International Economic Order and the Problem of Controlling Multinational Corporations in Africa. **In** *Onwuka, R. I. and Aluko, O., eds.*, 1986, pp. 17–34. **[G: Africa]**

Azpiazu, Daniel; Basualdo, Eduardo and Kosacoff, Bernardo. Transnational Corporations in Argentina, 1976–1983. *CEPAL Rev.*, April 1986, (28), pp. 99–133. **[G: Argentina]**

Backhaus, Klaus and Meyer, Margit. Country Risk Assessment in International Industrial Marketing. **In** *Backhaus, K. and Wilson, D. T., eds.*, 1986, pp. 245–73. **[G: LDCs]**

Barker, Betty L. U.S. Merchandise Trade Associated with U.S. Multinational Companies. *Surv. Curr. Bus.*, May 1986, *66*(5), pp. 55–72. **[G: U.S.]**

Barnet, Richard. Multinational Corporations: Profits at What Cost? **In** *Gondolf, E. W.; Marcus, I. M. and Dougherty, J. P., eds.*, 1986, pp. 43–57.

Batra, Raveendra N. A General Equilibrium Model of Multinational Corporations in Developing Economies. *Oxford Econ. Pap.*, July 1986, *38*(2), pp. 342–53.

Beaud, Claude Ph. Investments and Profits of the Multinational Schneider Group: 1894–1943. **In** *Teichova, A.; Lévy-Leboyer, M. and Nussbaum, H., eds.*, 1986, pp. 87–102. **[G: Europe]**

Belli, R. David. U.S. Multinational Companies: Operations in 1983. *Surv. Curr. Bus.*, January 1986, *66*(1), pp. 23–35. **[G: U.S.]**

Bird, Richard M. The Interjurisdictional Allocation of Income. *Australian Tax Forum*, 1986, *3*(3), pp. 333–54.

Blomström, Magnus. Foreign Investment and Productive Efficiency: The Case of Mexico. *J. Ind. Econ.*, September 1986, *35*(1), pp. 97–110. **[G: Mexico]**

Blomström, Magnus. Multinationals and Market Structure in Mexico. *World Devel.*, April 1986, *14*(4), pp. 523–30. **[G: Mexico]**

Boisot, Max. Industrial Policy and Industrial Culture: The Case of European Petrochemical. **In** *Macharzina, K. and Staehle, W. H., eds.*, 1986, pp. 163–84. **[G: W. Europe]**

Bond, Eric W. and Samuelson, Larry. Tax Holidays as Signals. *Amer. Econ. Rev.*, September 1986, *76*(4), pp. 820–26.

Borrmann, Werner A. Strategic Resource Management: Securing International Competitiveness through Competitive Resources. **In** *Macharzina, K. and Staehle, W. H., eds.*, 1986, pp. 275–83.

Brada, Josef C. and Méndez, José A. Foreign Direct Investment in the U.S. Pharmaceutical Industry. **In** *Gray, H. P., ed.*, 1986, pp. 223–60. **[G: U.S.]**

Braithwaite, John. Consumers as Victims of Corporate Crime. **In** *Wheelwright, T., ed.*, 1986, pp. 331–42.

Brauchlin, Emil A. Role and Structure of Swiss Multinationals. **In** *Macharzina, K. and Staehle, W. H., eds.*, 1986, pp. 67–77. **[G: Switzerland]**

Brereton, Barbara F. U.S. Multinational Companies: Operations in 1984. *Surv. Curr. Bus.*, September 1986, *66*(9), pp. 27–39. **[G: U.S.]**

Broder, Albert. The Multinationalisation of the French Electrical Industry 1880–1914: Dependence and Its Causes. **In** *Hertner, P. and Jones, G., eds.*, 1986, pp. 169–91. **[G: France]**

Brown, Jonathan C. Foreign Oil Companies, Oil Workers, and the Mexican Revolutionary State in the 1920s. **In** *Teichova, A.; Lévy-Leboyer, M. and Nussbaum, H., eds.*, 1986, pp. 257–69. **[G: Mexico]**

Burkhardt, Hans-Martin. Investment Protection Treaties: Recent Trends and Prospects. *Aussenwirtschaft*, April 1986, *41*(1), pp. 99–104. **[G: Global]**

Campbell, Duncan C. U.S. Firms and Black Labor in South Africa: Creating a Structure for Change. *J. Lab. Res.*, Winter 1986, *7*(1), pp. 1–18. **[G: S. Africa]**

Casson, Mark. Foreign Divestment and International Rationalisation: The Sale of Chrysler (UK) to Peugeot. **In** *Coyne, J. and Wright, M., eds.*, 1986, pp. 102–39. **[G: U.K.]**

Casson, Mark. General Theories of the Multinational Enterprise: Their Relevance to Business History. **In** *Hertner, P. and Jones, G., eds.*, 1986, pp. 42–63.

Casson, Mark. Multinationals and World Trade: Introduction and Summary. **In** *Casson, M., et al.*, 1986, pp. 1–59. **[G: U.S.]**

Casson, Mark. The International Division of Labour. **In** *Casson, M., et al.*, 1986, pp. 63–102.

Casson, Mark. Vertical Integration and Intra-firm Trade. **In** *Casson, M., et al.*, 1986, pp. 103–37.

Casson, Mark; Barry, David and Horner, Dennis. The Shipping Industry. **In** *Casson, M., et al.*, 1986, pp. 343–71.

Chai, C. H. The Economic System of a Special Economic Zone under Socialism. **In** *Jao, Y. C. and Leung, C. K., eds.*, 1986, pp. 141–59. **[G: China]**

Chalmin, Ph. The Strategy of a Multinational in the World Sugar Economy: The Case of Tate and Lyle: 1870–1980. **In** *Teichova, A.; Lévy-Leboyer, M. and Nussbaum, H., eds.*, 1986, pp. 103–15. **[G: Selected Countries]**

Chandler, Alfred D., Jr. Technological and Organizational Underpinnings of Modern Industrial Multinational Enterprise: The Dynamics of Competitive Advantage. **In** *Teichova, A.; Lévy-Leboyer, M. and Nussbaum, H., eds.*, 1986, pp. 30–54. **[G: OECD]**

Chandler, Alfred D., Jr. Technological and Organizational Underpinnings of Modern Industrial Multinational Enterprise: The Dynamics of Competitive Advantage. *Ricerche Econ.*, Jan.-Mar. 1986, *40*(1), pp. 3–30. **[G: Global]**

Chen, Tain-Jy and Tang, De-Piao. The Production Characteristics of Multinational Firms and the Effects of Tax Incentives: The Case of Taiwan's Electronics Industry. *J. Devel. Econ.*, November 1986, *24*(1), pp. 119–29. **[G: Taiwan]**

Chishti, Sumitra. Third World Multinationals and Trade Expansion among the Countries of the South. **In** *Khan, K. M., ed.*, 1986, pp. 88–112. **[G: LDCs; OPEC]**

Church, Roy. The Effects of American Multinationals on the British Motor Industry: 1911–83. **In** *Teichova, A.; Lévy-Leboyer, M. and Nussbaum, H., eds.*, 1986, pp. 116–30. **[G: U.K.]**

Clairmonte, Frederick F. Transnational Conglomerates: Reflections on Global Power. **In** *[Patel, S.]*, 1986, pp. 139–56. **[G: Global]**

Cochran, Sherman. Commercial Penetration and Economic Imperialism in China: An American Cigarette Company's Entrance into the Market. **In** *May, E. R. and Fairbank, J. K., eds.*, 1986, pp. 151–203. **[G: China]**

Cooper, Ian and Kaplanis, Evi. Costs to Cross-border Investment and International Equity Market Equilibrium. **In** *Edwards, J., et al., eds.*, 1986, pp. 209–40. **[G: OECD]**

Coplin, William and O'Leary, Michael. The Frost and Sullivan Method: Applying the "Prince." **In** *Raddock, D. M., et al.*, 1986, pp. 163–75.

Dekker, Peter. Transfer Pricing: The Netherlands. *Bull. Int. Fiscal Doc.*, November 1986, *40*(11), pp. 502–05. **[G: Netherlands]**

Derakhshani, Shidan. Negotiating Transfer of Technology Agreements. *Finance Develop.*, December 1986, *23*(4), pp. 42–44.

Dias, Guilherme Leite da Silva. Markets and Trade: Discussion. **In** *Maunder, A. and Renborg, U., eds.*, 1986, pp. 577–78.

Dick, H. W. and Rimmer, P. J. Urban Public Transport in Southeast Asia: A Case Study of Technological Imperialism? *Int. J. Transport Econ.*, June 1986, *13*(2), pp. 177–96. **[G: S.E. Asia]**

de Dios, Emmanuel S. Protection, Concentration, and the Direction of Foreign Investments. *Philippine Rev. Econ. Bus.*, Mar./June 1986, *23*(1/2), pp. 57–82. **[G: Philippines]**

Dufour, Jean-Claude; Ghersi, Gérard and Saint-Louis, Robert. New Types of Multinational Firms in the Agribusiness Sector: Implications of Their Emergence in the Least Industrialised World. **In** *Maunder, A. and Renborg, U., eds.*, 1986, pp. 566–77.

Dunn, Malcolm H. and Körner, Heiko. Third World Multinationals and Trade Expansion among the Countries of the South: Comment. **In** *Khan, K. M., ed.*, 1986, pp. 113–29. **[G: LDCs; OPEC]**

Dunning, John H. The Investment Development Cycle and Third World Multinationals. **In** *Khan, K. M., ed.*, 1986, pp. 15–47. **[G: Asia; Latin America]**

Dunning, John H. The Investment Development Cycle Revisited. *Weltwirtsch. Arch.*, 1986, *122*(4), pp. 667–76. **[G: LDCs]**

Dunning, John H.; Cantwell, John A. and Corley, T. A. B. The Theory of International Production: Some Historical Antecedents. **In** *Hertner, P. and Jones, G., eds.*, 1986, pp. 19–41.

Dunning, John H. and Norman, George. Intra-industry Investment. **In** *Gray, H. P., ed.*, 1986, pp. 73–94. **[G: U.S.]**

Eilts, Hermann Frederick. Assessing Corporate Political Risk: A Guide for International Businessmen: Country Studies: Saudi Arabia. **In** *Raddock, D. M., et al.*, 1986, pp. 110–26. **[G: Saudi Arabia]**

Eliasson, Gunnar. International Competition, Productivity Change and the Organization of Production. **In** *de Jong, H. W. and Shepherd, W. G., eds., Bk. 1*, 1986, pp. 127–58. **[G: OECD]**

Encarnation, Dennis J. and Wells, Louis T., Jr. Evaluating Foreign Investment. **In** *Moran, T. H., ed.*, 1986, pp. 61–86.

Ethier, Wilfred J. The Multinational Firm. *Quart. J. Econ.*, November 1986, *101*(4), pp. 805–33.

Euh, Yoon-Dae and Min, Sang H. Foreign Direct

Investment from Developing Countries: The Case of Korean Firms. *Devel. Econ.*, June 1986, *24*(2), pp. 149–68. **[G: S. Korea]**

Eun, Cheol S. and Janakiramanan, S. A Model of International Asset Pricing with a Constraint on the Foreign Equity Ownership. *J. Finance*, September 1986, *41*(4), pp. 897–914.

Evans, Eric S. FMC Corporation: Inflation-Adjusted Performance Evaluation. **In** *Holzer, H. P. and Schoenfeld, H.-M. W., eds.*, 1986, pp. 73–86. **[G: U.S.]**

Evans, Peter B. Generalized Linkages in Industrial Development: A Reexamination of Basic Petrochemicals in Brazil. **In** *[Hirshman, A. O.]*, 1986, pp. 7–26. **[G: Brazil]**

Evans, Peter B. State, Capital, and the Transformation of Dependence: The Brazilian Computer Case. *World Devel.*, July 1986, *14*(7), pp. 791–808. **[G: Brazil]**

Fairchild, Loretta and Sosin, Kim. Evaluating Differences in Technological Activity between Transnational and Domestic Firms in Latin America. *J. Devel. Stud.*, July 1986, *22*(4), pp. 697–708. **[G: Latin America]**

Falvey, Rodney E. and Fried, Harold O. National Ownership Requirements and Transfer Pricing. *J. Devel. Econ.*, December 1986, *24*(2), pp. 249–54.

Fieldhouse, D. K. The Multinational: A Critique of a Concept. **In** *Teichova, A.; Lévy-Leboyer, M. and Nussbaum, H., eds.*, 1986, pp. 9–29.

Filipović, Snežana. Multinational Companies and the CMEA Countries. **In** *Altmann, F.-L., ed.*, 1986, pp. 151–63. **[G: CMEA]**

Filipović, Snežana. Multinational Companies and the COMECON Countries. *Rivista Int. Sci. Econ. Com.*, August 1986, *33*(8), pp. 819–28. **[G: CMEA]**

Fletcher, John C. Management Control and the Internal Auditor: The Borg-Warner Case. **In** *Holzer, H. P. and Schoenfeld, H.-M. W., eds.*, 1986, pp. 87–100.

Foreman-Peck, James. The Motor Industry. **In** *Casson, M., et al.*, 1986, pp. 141–73. **[G: Selected Countries]**

Franko, Lawrence G. Expansion of Japanese Companies Abroad: The Management of Cross-Cultural Interface: Comment. **In** *Pugel, T. A., ed.*, 1986, pp. 201–05. **[G: U.S.; Japan]**

Fridenson, Patrick. The Growth of Multinational Activities in the French Motor Industry, 1890–1979. **In** *Hertner, P. and Jones, G., eds.*, 1986, pp. 157–68. **[G: France]**

Frischtak, Claudio R. National Policies for Developing High Technology Industries: International Comparisons: Brazil. **In** *Rushing, F. W. and Brown, C. G., eds.*, 1986, pp. 31–69. **[G: Brazil]**

Fujimori, Hideo. Industrial Policy and Technology Transfer: A Case Study of Automobile Industry in the Philippines. *Devel. Econ.*, December 1986, *24*(4), pp. 349–67. **[G: Philippines]**

Galbraith, Craig S. and Kay, Neil M. Towards a Theory of Multinational Enterprise. *J. Econ. Behav. Organ.*, March 1986, *7*(1), pp. 3–19.

Gandhi, Prem. Foreign Direct Investment and Regional Development: The Case of Canadian Investment in New York State. **In** *Schoolman, M. and Magid, A., eds.*, 1986, pp. 205–27. **[G: U.S.; Canada]**

Gershenberg, Irving. Labor, Capital, and Management Slack in Multinational and Local Firms in Kenyan Manufacturing. *Econ. Develop. Cult. Change*, October 1986, *35*(1), pp. 163–78. **[G: Kenya]**

Ghader, Fariborz. Managing Financial Risk: Assessing Devaluation, Foreign Exchange Controls, and Debt Repayment. **In** *Raddock, D. M., et al.*, 1986, pp. 179–85.

Ghertman, Michel. New Multinationals in Europe. **In** *Macharzina, K. and Staehle, W. H., eds.*, 1986, pp. 38–50. **[G: W. Europe]**

Glover, David J. Multinational Corporations and Third World Agriculture. **In** *Moran, T. H., ed.*, 1986, pp. 113–29. **[G: LDCs]**

Goldsmith, J. C. Summary of Rules Applicable to Transfer Pricing in France. *Bull. Int. Fiscal Doc.*, December 1986, *40*(12), pp. 564–68. **[G: France]**

Gonçalves, Reinaldo. Technological Spill-Overs and Manpower Training: A Comparative Analysis of Multinational and National Enterprises in Brazilian Manufacturing. *J. Econ. Devel.*, July 1986, *11*(1), pp. 119–32. **[G: Brazil]**

Govind, Har. India: Measures against Tax Avoidance by Multinationals. *Bull. Int. Fiscal Doc.*, July 1986, *40*(7), pp. 302–09. **[G: India]**

Gray, H. Peter. North–South Technology Transfer: Two Neglected Problems. *J. Econ. Devel.*, July 1986, *11*(1), pp. 27–45. **[G: LDCs]**

Gray, H. Peter. Uncle Sam as Host: Introduction. **In** *Gray, H. P., ed.*, 1986, pp. 3–8.

Green, Reginald Herbold. Operational Relevance of Third World Multinationals to Collective Self-reliance: Some Problems, Provocations and Possibilities. **In** *Khan, K. M., ed.*, 1986, pp. 48–66. **[G: Africa]**

Grieco, Joseph M. Foreign Investment and Development: Theories and Evidence. **In** *Moran, T. H., ed.*, 1986, pp. 35–60.

Guisinger, Stephen. Host-Country Policies to Attract and Control Foreign Investment. **In** *Moran, T. H., ed.*, 1986, pp. 157–72.

Günter, Bernd. Risk Management in Industrial Marketing Project-Cooperations—Some Comments on Joint Risk Handling. **In** *Backhaus, K. and Wilson, D. T., eds.*, 1986, pp. 274–93.

Gupta, Amar. National Policies for Developing High Technology Industries: International Comparisons: India. **In** *Rushing, F. W. and Brown, C. G., eds.*, 1986, pp. 89–110. **[G: India]**

Hamilton, Geoffrey. Red Multinationals or Red Herrings? The Activities of Enterprises from Socialist Countries in the West: Conclusion. **In** *Hamilton, G., ed.*, 1986, pp. 185–94. **[G: E. Europe]**

Hamilton, Geoffrey. Red Multinationals or Red Herrings? The Activities of Enterprises from Socialist Countries in the West: Introduction.

In *Hamilton, G., ed.*, 1986, pp. 1–16.

Harrington, James W., Jr.; Burns, Karen and Cheung, Man. Market-Oriented Foreign Investment and Regional Development: Canadian Companies in Western New York. *Econ. Geogr.*, April 1986, *62*(2), pp. 155–66. **[G: U.S.]**

Harrison, Glenn W. and Rutström, E. E. The Effect of Manufacturing Sector Protection on ASEAN and Australia: A General Equilibrium Analysis. **In** *Findlay, C. and Garnaut, R., eds.*, 1986, pp. 184–213. **[G: ASEAN; Australia]**

Hattori, Tamio. Technology Transfer and Management Systems. *Devel. Econ.*, December 1986, *24*(4), pp. 314–25. **[G: Japan]**

Haug, Peter. U.S. High Technology Multinationals and Silicon Glen. *Reg. Stud.*, April 1986, *20*(2), pp. 103–16. **[G: U.S.; U.K.]**

Hauser, Heinz. Promotion of Foreign Direct Investment to Developing Countries: An Exercise in Cooperation. **In** *Hauser, H., ed. (I)*, 1986, pp. 9–18.

Hayashi, Kichiro. Expansion of Japanese Companies Abroad: The Management of Cross-Cultural Interface. **In** *Pugel, T. A., ed.*, 1986, pp. 175–99. **[G: Japan; U.S.]**

Heininger, Horst. Transnational Corporations and the Struggle for the Establishment of a New International Economic Order. **In** *Teichova, A.; Lévy-Leboyer, M. and Nussbaum, H., eds.*, 1986, pp. 351–61.

Helmboldt, Niles E.; West, Tina and Hardy, Benjamin H. Private Investment and African Economic Policy. **In** *Berg, R. J. and Whitaker, J. S., eds.*, 1986, pp. 331–57. **[G: Africa]**

Hennart, Jean-François. The Tin Industry. **In** *Casson, M., et al.*, 1986, pp. 225–73. **[G: Selected Countries]**

Hennart, Jean-François. What Is Internalization? *Weltwirtsch. Arch.*, 1986, *122*(4), pp. 791–804.

Herbst, Karl. The Regulatory Framework for Foreign Investment in the Special Economic Zones. **In** *Jao, Y. C. and Leung, C. K., eds.*, 1986, pp. 124–37. **[G: China]**

Hertner, Peter. Financial Strategies and Adaptation to Foreign Markets: The German Electrotechnical Industry and Its Multinational Activities: 1890s to 1939. **In** *Teichova, A.; Lévy-Leboyer, M. and Nussbaum, H., eds.*, 1986, pp. 145–59. **[G: Germany]**

Hertner, Peter. German Multinational Enterprise before 1914: Some Case Studies. **In** *Hertner, P. and Jones, G., eds.*, 1986, pp. 113–34. **[G: Germany]**

Hertner, Peter and Jones, Geoffrey. Multinationals: Theory and History. **In** *Hertner, P. and Jones, G., eds.*, 1986, pp. 1–18.

Hill, Malcolm R. Soviet and Eastern European Company Activity in Sweden. **In** *Hamilton, G., ed.*, 1986, pp. 88–102. **[G: E. Europe; Sweden]**

Hill, Malcolm R. Soviet and Eastern European Company Activity in the United Kingdom and Ireland. **In** *Hamilton, G., ed.*, 1986, pp. 17–87. **[G: E. Europe; U.K.; Ireland]**

Hjerppe, Riitta and Ahvenainen, Jorma. Foreign Enterprises and Nationalistic Control: The Case of Finland since the End of the Nineteenth Century. **In** *Teichova, A.; Lévy-Leboyer, M. and Nussbaum, H., eds.*, 1986, pp. 286–98. **[G: Finland]**

Hochmuth, Milton S. The European Aerospace Industry. **In** *Macharzina, K. and Staehle, W. H., eds.*, 1986, pp. 205–25. **[G: U.S.; U.K.; France; W. Germany]**

Holland, J. The International Dimensions of Corporate Financial Management. **In** *Firth, M. and Keane, S. M., eds.*, 1986, pp. 207–22.

Holzer, H. Peter. Past Research on Performance Evaluation of International Subsidiaries. **In** *Holzer, H. P. and Schoenfeld, H.-M. W., eds.*, 1986, pp. 1–12.

Hongskrailers, Montri and Jap, Kim Siong. Transfer Pricing Provisions, Rulings and Case Law: Thailand. *Bull. Int. Fiscal Doc.*, November 1986, *40*(11), pp. 514–20. **[G: Thailand]**

Hood, Neil. Role and Structure of British Multinationals. **In** *Macharzina, K. and Staehle, W. H., eds.*, 1986, pp. 79–91. **[G: U.K.]**

Hood, Neil and Young, Stephen. Foreign Direct Investment in the U.S. Automobile Industry. **In** *Gray, H. P., ed.*, 1986, pp. 163–90. **[G: U.S.]**

Hörnell, Erik. Role and Structure of Swedish Multinationals. **In** *Macharzina, K. and Staehle, W. H., eds.*, 1986, pp. 93–103. **[G: Sweden]**

Huber, Klaus. Funding Direct Investment through Cofinancing: The Commercial Banker's View. **In** *Hauser, H., ed. (I)*, 1986, pp. 89–96.

Hultman, Charles W. Foreign Bank Offices in the U.S. since the International Banking Act of 1978. *Rivista Int. Sci. Econ. Com.*, Oct.-Nov. 1986, *33*(10–11), pp. 1129–44. **[G: U.S.]**

Itọ, Shọji. Technology Transfer from Japan to Asian Developing Countries: Introduction. *Devel. Econ.*, December 1986, *24*(4), pp. 309–13. **[G: Japan]**

Jenkins, Barbara. Reexamining the "Obsolescing Bargain": A Study of Canada's National Energy Program. *Int. Organ.*, Winter 1986, *40*(1), pp. 139–65. **[G: Canada]**

Johnson, Douglas A. Confronting Corporate Power: Strategies and Phases of the Nestlé Boycott. **In** *Wheelwright, T., ed.*, 1986, pp. 305–30.

Johnston, Felton McC. Political Risk Insurance. **In** *Raddock, D. M., et al.*, 1986, pp. 186–96.

Jones, Geoffrey. British Overseas Banks in the Middle East 1920–70: A Study in Multinational Middle Age. **In** *Teichova, A.; Lévy-Leboyer, M. and Nussbaum, H., eds.*, 1986, pp. 218–31. **[G: U.K.; Middle East]**

Jones, Geoffrey. The Performance of British Multinational Enterprise, 1890–1945. **In** *Hertner, P. and Jones, G., eds.*, 1986, pp. 96–112. **[G: U.K.]**

Jones, Patricio. Mining Development and the Origin of Capital. *CEPAL Rev.*, December 1986, (30), pp. 163–72. **[G: Latin America]**

Kang, K. Won and Park, Soong H. Managerial

Accounting and Analysis in Multinational Enterprises: GoldStar Electronics. **In** *Holzer, H. P. and Schoenfeld, H.-M. W., eds.*, 1986, pp. 51–71. **[G: S. Korea]**

Kernbauer, Hans and Weber, Fritz. Multinational Banking in the Danube Basin: The Business Strategy of the Viennese Banks after the Collapse of the Habsburg Monarchy. **In** *Teichova, A.; Lévy-Leboyer, M. and Nussbaum, H., eds.*, 1986, pp. 185–99. **[G: Europe]**

Khan, Khushi M. Multinationals from the South: Emergence, Patterns and Issues. **In** *Khan, K. M., ed.*, 1986, pp. 1–14. **[G: LDCs]**

Kimura, Yui. Japanese Policy toward Foreign Multinationals: Implications for Trade and Competitiveness: Comment. **In** *Pugel, T. A., ed.*, 1986, pp. 169–74. **[G: Japan]**

Kirim, Arman S. Transnational Corporations and Local Capital: Comparative Conduct and Performance in the Turkish Pharmaceutical Industry. *World Devel.*, April 1986, *14*(4), pp. 503–21. **[G: Turkey]**

Kñakal, Jan. The Role of the Public Sector and Transnational Corporations in the Mining Development of Latin America. *CEPAL Rev.*, December 1986, (30), pp. 143–62.

Knirsch, Peter. Soviet and East European Firms in Austria. **In** *Hamilton, G., ed.*, 1986, pp. 131–55. **[G: E. Europe; Austria]**

Knirsch, Peter. Soviet and Eastern European Firms in the Federal Republic of Germany. **In** *Hamilton, G., ed.*, 1986, pp. 103–30. **[G: W. Germany; E. Europe; CMEA]**

Kogut, Bruce. Steel and the European Communities. **In** *Macharzina, K. and Staehle, W. H., eds.*, 1986, pp. 185–203. **[G: EEC]**

Komoda, Fumio. Japanese Studies on Technology Transfer to Developing Countries: A Survey. *Devel. Econ.*, December 1986, *24*(4), pp. 405–20. **[G: Japan]**

Kostecki, Apoloniusz. The Trends in Taxation of Foreign Enterprises (1945–1986): Poland. *Bull. Int. Fiscal Doc.*, December 1986, *40*(12), pp. 569–73. **[G: Poland]**

Kumar, Nagesh. Foreign Direct Investments and Technology Transfers among Developing Countries. **In** *Panchamukhi, V. R., et al.*, 1986, pp. 139–65. **[G: LDCs]**

Kurgan-van Hentenryk, Ginette. The Groupe Philippart: An Experience of Multinational Enterprise in Railway and Banking Business in Western Europe: 1865–80. **In** *Teichova, A.; Lévy-Leboyer, M. and Nussbaum, H., eds.*, 1986, pp. 65–73. **[G: W. Europe]**

Lall, Rajiv. Third World Multinationals: The Characteristics of Indian Firms Investing Abroad. *J. Devel. Econ.*, March 1986, *20*(2), pp. 381–97. **[G: India]**

Landau, Zbigniew and Tomaszewski, Jerzy. Foreign Policy and International Business in Poland: 1918–39. **In** *Teichova, A.; Lévy-Leboyer, M. and Nussbaum, H., eds.*, 1986, pp. 270–85. **[G: Poland]**

Lanfermann, Josef. Performance Evaluation of International Subsidiaries in the Case of Acquisition/Disposal and Annual Audits from the Point of View of a German Wirtschaftsprüfer. **In** *Holzer, H. P. and Schoenfeld, H.-M. W., eds.*, 1986, pp. 189–215.

Langdon, Steven. Industrial Dependence and Export Manufacturing in Kenya. **In** *Ravenhill, J., ed.*, 1986, pp. 181–212. **[G: Kenya]**

Lanthier, Allan R. Draft Guidelines on International Transfer Pricing: Canada. *Bull. Int. Fiscal Doc.*, November 1986, *40*(11), pp. 487–96. **[G: Canada]**

Lee, Jaymin. Determinants of Offshore Production in Developing Countries. *J. Devel. Econ.*, Jan.-Feb. 1986, *20*(1), pp. 1–13. **[G: LDCs]**

Lee, Seung-Dong. On the Theory of an Exhaustible Resource Extractive Multinational Firm. *Can. J. Econ.*, November 1986, *19*(4), pp. 716–29.

Lehto, Sakari T. Företagens internationalisering. (The Internationalization of Business. With English summary.) *Ekon. Samfundets Tidskr.*, 1986, *39*(1), pp. 21–33. **[G: Finland]**

Lévy-Leboyer, Maurice. Multinational Enterprise in Historical Perspective: Introduction. **In** *Teichova, A.; Lévy-Leboyer, M. and Nussbaum, H., eds.*, 1986, pp. 1–5.

Liang, Xiang. Shenzhen: Opening to the World. *Chinese Econ. Stud.*, Winter 1985-86, *19*(2), pp. 73–78. **[G: China]**

Lincoln, Edward J. Japanese Policy toward Foreign Multinationals: Implications for Trade and Competitiveness: Comment. **In** *Pugel, T. A., ed.*, 1986, pp. 163–68. **[G: Japan]**

Little, Jane Sneddon. Intra-firm Trade and U.S. Protectionism: Thoughts Based on a Small Survey. *New Eng. Econ. Rev.*, Jan./Feb. 1986, pp. 42–51. **[G: U.S.]**

Little, Jane Sneddon. Recent Trends in Foreign Direct Investment in the United States: An Overview. **In** *Gray, H. P., ed.*, 1986, pp. 9–41. **[G: U.S.]**

Little, Jane Sneddon. The Effects of Foreign Direct Investment on U.S. Employment during Recession and Structural Change. *New Eng. Econ. Rev.*, Nov./Dec. 1986, pp. 40–48. **[G: U.S.]**

Lo, T. W. C. Foreign Investment in the Special Economic Zones: A Management Perspective. **In** *Jao, Y. C. and Leung, C. K., eds.*, 1986, pp. 184–200. **[G: China]**

Lundström, Ragnhild. Banks and Early Swedish Multinationals. **In** *Teichova, A.; Lévy-Leboyer, M. and Nussbaum, H., eds.*, 1986, pp. 200–217. **[G: Sweden]**

Lundström, Ragnhild. Swedish Multinational Growth before 1930. **In** *Hertner, P. and Jones, G., eds.*, 1986, pp. 135–56. **[G: Sweden]**

Mainardi, Stefano. A Theoretical Interpretation of Intra-firm Trade in the Presence of Intra-industry Trade. **In** *Greenaway, D. and Tharakan, P. K. M., eds.*, 1986, pp. 88–107.

Maki, Dennis R. and Meredith, Lindsay N. Production Cost Differentials and Foreign Direct Investment: A Test of Two Models. *Appl. Econ.*, October 1986, *18*(10), pp. 1127–34. **[G: U.S.; Canada]**

Marton, Katherin. Technology Transfer to Developing Countries via Multinationals. *World Econ.*, December 1986, *9*(4), pp. 409–26. **[G: OECD; LDCs]**

Maucher, Helmut. Multinational Enterprise and Host Country Policy: Opportunities for Mutual Benefit. **In** *Hauser, H., ed. (I)*, 1986, pp. 37–46.

Maucher, Helmut. Mutinational Enterprise and Host Country Policy: Opportunities for Mutual Benefit. *Aussenwirtschaft*, April 1986, *41*(1), pp. 37–46.

McClain, David. Direct Investment in the United States: The European Experience. **In** *Gray, H. P., ed.*, 1986, pp. 309–43. **[G: Europe; U.S.]**

McDowell, John M. Foreign Direct Investment in U.S. Natural Resource Industries. **In** *Gray, H. P., ed.*, 1986, pp. 261–86. **[G: U.S.]**

McKay, John. The House of Rothschild (Paris) as a Multinational Industrial Enterprise: 1875–1914. **In** *Teichova, A.; Lévy-Leboyer, M. and Nussbaum, H., eds.*, 1986, pp. 74–86. **[G: Europe]**

Miller, Elwood L. Monsanto Company—Managing Change. **In** *Holzer, H. P. and Schoenfeld, H.-M. W., eds.*, 1986, pp. 31–50. **[G: U.S.]**

Mirus, Rolf and Yeung, Bernard. "Buy-Back" in International Trade: A Rationale. *Weltwirtsch. Arch.*, 1986, *122*(2), pp. 371–74.

Montgomery, David B. Conjoint Calibration of the Customer/Competitor Interface in Industrial Markets. **In** *Backhaus, K. and Wilson, D. T., eds.*, 1986, pp. 297–319.

Moran, Theodore H. The Future of Foreign Direct Investment in the Third World. **In** *Moran, T. H., ed.*, 1986, pp. 3–19.

Moses, Frederick, A. and Pugel, Thomas A. Foreign Direct Investment in the United States: The Electronics Industries. **In** *Gray, H. P., ed.*, 1986, pp. 111–61. **[G: U.S.]**

Musgrave, Richard A. and Musgrave, Peggy B. Inter-nation Equity. **In** *Musgrave, R. A., Vol. 2*, 1986, *1972*, pp. 43–63.

Muzaffar, Chandra. Changing Lifestyles Today for Tomorrow: The Spiritual Basis. **In** *Wheelwright, T., ed.*, 1986, pp. 1–13.

Nambudiri, C. N. S. and Iyanda, O. Multinational Corporate Strategies: The Case of Nigeria. **In** *Damachi, U. G. and Seibel, H. D., eds.*, 1986, pp. 89–100. **[G: Nigeria]**

Nambudiri, C. N. S.; Iyanda, O. and Akinnusi, D. M. Third World Firms in Third World Countries. **In** *Damachi, U. G. and Seibel, H. D., eds.*, 1986, pp. 101–11. **[G: Nigeria]**

Natke, Paul A. Market Imperfections and Import Pricing Behavior by Multinational Enterprises. *J. Econ. Devel.*, July 1986, *11*(1), pp. 105–18. **[G: Brazil]**

Negandhi, Anant R. Role and Structure of German Multinationals: A Comparative Profile. **In** *Macharzina, K. and Staehle, W. H., eds.*, 1986, pp. 51–66. **[G: W. Germany]**

Neuhauser, Lenz. Financial Reporting Systems of Multinational Companies—An External Auditor's Viewpoint. **In** *Holzer, H. P. and Schoenfeld, H.-M. W., eds.*, 1986, pp. 175–88.

Nicholas, Stephen. The Hierarchical Division of Labour and the Growth of British Manufacturing Multinationals: 1870–1939. **In** *Teichova, A.; Lévy-Leboyer, M. and Nussbaum, H., eds.*, 1986, pp. 241–56. **[G: U.K.]**

Nicholas, Stephen. The Theory of Multinational Enterprise as a Transactional Mode. **In** *Hertner, P. and Jones, G., eds.*, 1986, pp. 64–79.

Nugent, Jeffrey B. Arab Multinationals: Problems, Potential and Policies. **In** *Khan, K. M., ed.*, 1986, pp. 165–83. **[G: Arab Countries]**

Nussbaum, Helga. International Cartels and Multinational Enterprises. **In** *Teichova, A.; Lévy-Leboyer, M. and Nussbaum, H., eds.*, 1986, pp. 131–44. **[G: Global]**

Oman, Charles P. New Forms of Investment in Developing Countries. **In** *Moran, T. H., ed.*, 1986, pp. 131–55.

Overy, Richard J. German Multinationals and the Nazi State in Occupied Europe. **In** *Teichova, A.; Lévy-Leboyer, M. and Nussbaum, H., eds.*, 1986, pp. 299–325. **[G: Germany]**

Ozawa, Terutomo. Japan's Largest Financier of Multinationalism: The EXIM Bank. *J. World Trade Law*, Nov.:Dec. 1986, *20*(6), pp. 599–614. **[G: Japan]**

Ozawa, Terutomo. Japanese Policy toward Foreign Multinationals: Implications for Trade and Competitiveness. **In** *Pugel, T. A., ed.*, 1986, pp. 141–62. **[G: Japan]**

Pangeti, Evelyn. Agribusiness in Colonial Zimbabwe: The Case of the Lowveld. **In** *Teichova, A.; Lévy-Leboyer, M. and Nussbaum, H., eds.*, 1986, pp. 326–38. **[G: Zimbabwe]**

Pastré, Olivier and Rowley, Anthony. The Multinationalisation of British and American Banks. **In** *Teichova, A.; Lévy-Leboyer, M. and Nussbaum, H., eds.*, 1986, pp. 232–38. **[G: U.K.; U.S.]**

Pearson, Ruth. Multinational Companies and the Sexual Division of Labour: A Historical Perspective. **In** *Teichova, A.; Lévy-Leboyer, M. and Nussbaum, H., eds.*, 1986, pp. 339–50.

Pérez-López, Jorge F. The Economics of Cuban Joint Ventures. **In** *Mesa-Lago, C., ed.*, 1986, pp. 181–207. **[G: Cuba]**

Perrons, Diane. Unequal Integration in Global Fordism: The Case of Ireland. **In** *Scott, A. J. and Storper, M., eds.*, 1986, pp. 246–64. **[G: Ireland]**

Phillips, David R. Special Economic Zones in China's Modernization: Changing Policies and Changing Fortunes. *Nat. Westminster Bank Quart. Rev.*, February 1986, pp. 37–49. **[G: China]**

Poznanski, Kazimierz. Patterns of Technology Imports: Interregional Comparison. *World Devel.*, June 1986, *14*(6), pp. 743–56. **[G: E. Europe; Latin America]**

Rahman, M. Zubaidur and Finnerty, Joseph E. International Accounting Standards and Transnational Corporations. *Rivista Int. Sci. Econ. Com.*, June-July 1986, *33*(6–7), pp. 697–714.

Read, Robert A. The Banana Industry: Oligopoly and Barriers to Entry. **In** *Casson, M., et al.*, 1986, pp. 317–42. **[G: Selected Countries]**

Read, Robert A. The Copper Industry. **In** *Casson, M., et al.*, 1986, pp. 275–315. **[G: Global]**

Read, Robert A. The Synthetic Fibre Industry: Innovation Integration and Market Structure. **In** *Casson, M., et al.*, 1986, pp. 197–223. **[G: Global]**

Rivera-Batiz, Francisco L. Can Border Industries Be a Substitute for Immigration? *Amer. Econ. Rev.*, May 1986, *76*(2), pp. 263–68. **[G: U.S.; Mexico]**

Roth, Allan. Legal Environment. **In** *Gray, H. P., ed.*, 1986, pp. 43–69. **[G: U.S.]**

Rubino, R. J. Accounting Techniques Utilized for the Evaluation of International Subsidiaries: The IBM Case. **In** *Holzer, H. P. and Schoenfeld, H.-M. W., eds.*, 1986, pp. 13–30. **[G: U.S.]**

Rugman, Alan M. European Multinationals: An International Comparison of Size and Performance. **In** *Macharzina, K. and Staehle, W. H., eds.*, 1986, pp. 15–22. **[G: OECD]**

Rugman, Alan M. New Theories of the Multinational Enterprise: An Assessment of Internationalization Theory. *Bull. Econ. Res.*, May 1986, *38*(2), pp. 101–18.

Rugman, Alan M. and Douglas, Sheila. The Strategic Management of Multinationals and World Product Mandating. *Can. Public Policy*, June 1986, *12*(2), pp. 320–28. **[G: Canada]**

Rugman, Alan M. and McIlveen, John. Canadian Foreign Direct Investment in the United States. **In** *Gray, H. P., ed.*, 1986, pp. 289–307. **[G: Canada; U.S.]**

Samuelson, Larry. The Multinational Firm and Exhaustible Resources. *Economica*, May 1986, *53*(210), pp. 191–207.

Sazanami, Yoko. Japanese Trade in the Pacific Rim: The Relationship between Trade and Investment. **In** *Nemetz, P. N., ed.*, 1986, pp. 53–73. **[G: ASEAN; Japan; New Zealand; Australia]**

Schindler, Guenter. Taxation of Intercorporate Transfer Pricing: A Management Responsibility: U.S.A. *Bull. Int. Fiscal Doc.*, November 1986, *40*(11), pp. 497–501. **[G: U.S.]**

Schmitz, Christopher. The Rise of Big Business in the World Copper Industry 1870–1930. *Econ. Hist. Rev., 2nd Ser.*, August 1986, *39*(3), pp. 392–410. **[G: OECD]**

Schmitz, Peter M. Markets and Trade: Discussion. **In** *Maunder, A. and Renborg, U., eds.*, 1986, pp. 578–80.

Schoenfeld, Hanns-Martin W. Performance Evaluation in Multinational Companies: Two European Examples. **In** *Holzer, H. P. and Schoenfeld, H.-M. W., eds.*, 1986, pp. 101–62. **[G: W. Germany; Netherlands]**

Schoenfeld, Hanns-Martin W. The Present State of Performance Evaluation in Multinational Companies. **In** *Holzer, H. P. and Schoenfeld, H.-M. W., eds.*, 1986, pp. 217–52.

Schröter, Harm. A Typical Factor of German International Market Strategy: Agreements between the U.S. and German Electrotechnical Industries Up to 1939. **In** *Teichova, A.; Lévy-Leboyer, M. and Nussbaum, H., eds.*, 1986, pp. 160–70. **[G: U.S.; Germany]**

Schröter, Verena. Participation in Market Control through Foreign Investment: IG Farbenindustrie AG in the United States: 1920–38. **In** *Teichova, A.; Lévy-Leboyer, M. and Nussbaum, H., eds.*, 1986, pp. 171–84. **[G: U.S.; Germany]**

Seibel, Hans Dieter. Achievement Orientation: A Case Study in Multinational Firms in Africa. **In** *Damachi, U. G. and Seibel, H. D., eds.*, 1986, pp. 215–31. **[G: Liberia]**

Shea, Michael A. U.S. Affiliates of Foreign Companies: Operations in 1984. *Surv. Curr. Bus.*, October 1986, *66*(10), pp. 31–47. **[G: U.S.]**

Shi, Xiulin. Is the Economy of China's Special Economic Zones State Capitalist in Nature? *Chinese Econ. Stud.*, Winter 1985-86, *19*(2), pp. 25–40. **[G: China]**

Shihata, Ibrahim F. I. The Role of ICSID and the Projected Multilateral Investment Guarantee Agency (MIGA). *Aussenwirtschaft*, April 1986, *41*(1), pp. 105–22. **[G: Global]**

Sikkink, Kathryn. Codes of Conduct for Transnational Corporations: The Case of the WHO/UNICEF Code. *Int. Organ.*, Autumn 1986, *40*(4), pp. 815–40.

Sit, Victor F. S. Industries in Shenzhen: An Attempt at Open-Door Industrialization. **In** *Jao, Y. C. and Leung, C. K., eds.*, 1986, pp. 226–46. **[G: China]**

Slater, Robert O. The Bootstrapping Approach: An Alternative to Old Methods Restyled. **In** *Raddock, D. M., et al.*, 1986, pp. 149–62.

Sommaruga, Cornelio. Promotion of Direct Investment in Developing Countries: Opening Address. **In** *Hauser, H., ed. (I)*, 1986, pp. 19–23.

Sornarajah, M. State Responsibility and Bilateral Investment Treaties. *J. World Trade Law*, Jan.:Feb. 1986, *20*(1), pp. 79–98. **[G: Global]**

Staehle, Wolfgang H. Industrial Relations and Europe's Multinationals. **In** *Macharzina, K. and Staehle, W. H., eds.*, 1986, pp. 129–42. **[G: W. Europe]**

Stauffer, Robert B. The Marcos Coup in the Philippines. **In** *Stauffer, R. B.*, 1986, *1973*, pp. 1–7. **[G: Philippines]**

Stauffer, Robert B. The Marcos Legacy. **In** *Stauffer, R. B.*, 1986, pp. 171–99. **[G: Philippines]**

Stauffer, Robert B. The Marcos Regime: Failure of Transnational Developmentalism and Hegemony-Building from Above and Outside. **In** *Stauffer, R. B.*, 1986, *1985*, pp. 135–70. **[G: Philippines]**

Stauffer, Robert B. The Political Economy of Refeudalization. **In** *Stauffer, R. B.*, 1986, *1979*, pp. 8–43. **[G: Philippines]**

Stewart, Marion B. U.S. Tax Policy, Intrafirm Transfers, and the Allocative Efficiency of Transnational Corporations. *Public Finance*, December 1986, *41*(3), pp. 350–71. **[G: U.S.]**

Stoever, William A. Foreign Investment as an Aid in Moving from Least Developed to Newly

Industrializing: A Study in Korea. *J. Devel. Areas*, January 1986, *20*(2), pp. 223–47. **[G: S. Korea]**

Su, Yanhan. A Brief Discussion of the Economic Nature of China's Special Economic Zones. *Chinese Econ. Stud.*, Winter 1985-86, *19*(2), pp. 41–58. **[G: China]**

Suissa, A. Le nouveau marché international du charbon. (The New International Market for Coal. With English summary.) *Écon. Soc.*, July 1986, *20*(7), pp. 77–93.

Svetličič, Marjan. Multinational Production Joint Ventures of Developing Countries, Their Economic Development and Specific Features. **In** *Khan, K. M., ed.*, 1986, pp. 67–87. **[G: LDCs]**

Teece, David J. Transactions Cost Economics and the Multinational Enterprise: An Assessment. *J. Econ. Behav. Organ.*, March 1986, *7*(1), pp. 21–45. **[G: U.K.; U.S.]**

Teichova, Alice. Multinationals in Perspective. **In** *Teichova, A.; Lévy-Leboyer, M. and Nussbaum, H., eds.*, 1986, pp. 362–73.

van der Toorn, Frans B. International Trade Credit and Exchange Rates: A Survey among Dutch Firms. *De Economist*, 1986, *134*(4), pp. 492–96. **[G: Netherlands]**

de la Torre, José. Corporate Adjustment Strategies in the European Clothing Industry. **In** *Macharzina, K. and Staehle, W. H., eds.*, 1986, pp. 227–39. **[G: W. Europe]**

Toy, Charles D. New Provisions Encouraging Foreign Investment: People's Republic of China. *Bull. Int. Fiscal Doc.*, December 1986, *40*(12), pp. 579–80. **[G: China]**

Toy, Charles D. People's Republic of China: New Regulations on Foreign Exchange Balancing in Joint Ventures. *Bull. Int. Fiscal Doc.*, Apr./May 1986, *40*(4/5), pp. 154–56. **[G: China]**

Tsurumi, Yoshi. Japanese and European Multinationals in America: A Case of Flexible Corporate Systems. **In** *Macharzina, K. and Staehle, W. H., eds.*, 1986, pp. 23–37. **[G: U.S.]**

Tufer, Armin C. and Aiken, Leisa B. Performance Evaluation Techniques for International Operations: Impacts on Managerial Incentives and Strategic Planning Considerations. **In** *Holzer, H. P. and Schoenfeld, H.-M. W., eds.*, 1986, pp. 163–73.

Van Den Bulcke, Daniel. Role and Structure of Belgian Multinationals. **In** *Macharzina, K. and Staehle, W. H., eds.*, 1986, pp. 105–27. **[G: Belgium]**

Vernon, Raymond. Multinationals Are Mushrooming. *Challenge*, May/June 1986, 29(2), pp. 41–47.

Wang, Muheng and Chen, Yongshan. On the Nature of Asian Export Processing Zones and China's Special Economic Zones. *Chinese Econ. Stud.*, Winter 1985-86, *19*(2), pp. 8–24. **[G: Asia; China]**

Washio, Hiroaki. The Provision of Manuals and Japanese Private Technology Transfer. *Devel. Econ.*, December 1986, *24*(4), pp. 326–33. **[G: Japan]**

Weiss, John. Japan's Post-War Protection Policy: Some Implications for Less Developed Countries. *J. Devel. Stud.*, January 1986, *22*(2), pp. 385–406. **[G: Japan]**

Wellons, Philip A. Multinational Institutions in the Debt Crisis: National Interest and Long Term Consequences. **In** *Claudon, M. P., ed.*, 1986, pp. 147–69. **[G: LDCs]**

Wells, Louis T., Jr. New and Old Multinationals: Competitors or Partners. **In** *Khan, K. M., ed.*, 1986, pp. 196–210.

Wheeler, J. W. Japanese Foreign Direct Investment in the United States. **In** *Gray, H. P., ed.*, 1986, pp. 345–75. **[G: U.S.; Japan]**

Wheelwright, Ted. The Corporate Response. **In** *Wheelwright, T., ed.*, 1986, pp. 227–304.

Wheelwright, Ted. The World Drug Industry. **In** *Wheelwright, T., ed.*, 1986, pp. 89–125. **[G: LDCs]**

Wheelwright, Ted. The World Food Industry. **In** *Wheelwright, T., ed.*, 1986, pp. 143–82. **[G: Global]**

Wheelwright, Ted. Transnational Corporations and Dependent Development in Asia and the Pacific. **In** *Wheelwright, T., ed.*, 1986, pp. 15–44. **[G: Asia]**

Wilkins, Mira. Defining a Firm: History and Theory. **In** *Hertner, P. and Jones, G., eds.*, 1986, pp. 80–95.

Wilkins, Mira. European Multinationals in the United States: 1875–1914. **In** *Teichova, A.; Lévy-Leboyer, M. and Nussbaum, H., eds.*, 1986, pp. 55–64. **[G: U.S.]**

Wilkins, Mira. Japanese Multinational Enterprise before 1914. *Bus. Hist. Rev.*, Summer 1986, *60*(2), pp. 199–231. **[G: Japan]**

Wilkins, Mira. The History of European Multinationals: A New Look. *J. Europ. Econ. Hist.*, Winter 1986, *15*(3), pp. 483–510. **[G: Europe]**

Wilkins, Mira. The Impacts of American Multinational Enterprise on American–Chinese Economic Relations, 1786–1949. **In** *May, E. R. and Fairbank, J. K., eds.*, 1986, pp. 259–92. **[G: U.S.; China]**

Williams, Mansfield. Petrochemicals and Chemicals. **In** *Gray, H. P., ed.*, 1986, pp. 191–221. **[G: U.S.; OECD]**

Williamson, Peter J. Multinational Enterprise Behaviour and Domestic Industry Adjustment under Import Threat. *Rev. Econ. Statist.*, August 1986, *68*(3), pp. 359–68. **[G: Australia]**

Willmore, Larry N. The Comparative Performance of Foreign and Domestic Firms in Brazil. *World Devel.*, April 1986, *14*(4), pp. 489–502. **[G: Brazil]**

Wohlmuth, Karl. Practices and Policies of Host Countries towards Third World Multinationals: A Competitive Edge against Old Multinationals? **In** *Khan, K. M., ed.*, 1986, pp. 211–39. **[G: LDCs]**

Wolf, Bernard M. The Bearing Industry: Rationalization in Europe. **In** *Casson, M., et al.*, 1986, pp. 175–95. **[G: OECD]**

Wood, Van R. The Information Needs of Exporters: Theory, Framework and Empirical Tests.

Liiketaloudellinen Aikak., 1986, *35*(1), pp. 3–22. **[G: U.S.]**

Wright, Mike. Demergers: The Case of Bowater. **In** *Coyne, J. and Wright, M., eds.*, 1986, pp. 45–72. **[G: U.K.]**

Wurmstich, Jörg-Dietrich. Coverage of Political Risk by National Insurance Agencies: The German Investment Guarantee Scheme. *Aussenwirtschaft*, April 1986, *41*(1), pp. 123–33.

Young, Stephen. European Car Industry. **In** *Macharzina, K. and Staehle, W. H., eds.*, 1986, pp. 147–62. **[G: W. Europe]**

Zaleski, Eugène. Socialist Multinationals in Developing Countries. **In** *Hamilton, G., ed.*, 1986, pp. 156–84. **[G: E. Europe; LDCs]**

Zhang, Zeyu. A Mirror for Urban Economic Reforms. *Chinese Econ. Stud.*, Winter 1985-86, *19*(2), pp. 86–92. **[G: China]**

Zou, Erkang. Special Economic Zone Typifies Open Policy. *Chinese Econ. Stud.*, Winter 1985-86, *19*(2), pp. 79–85. **[G: China]**

443 International Lending and Aid (public)

4430 International Lending and Aid (public)

Abbott, George C. Private Capital and the Proposal for a South Bank. *World Econ.*, September 1986, *9*(3), pp. 275–94. **[G: LDCs]**

Addo, J. S. Alternative Approaches to Stabilization in Africa: Comments. **In** *Helleiner, G. K, ed.*, 1986, pp. 153–56. **[G: Sub-Saharan Africa]**

Agarwala, Ramgopal. Resource Requirements for Restoring Growth. **In** *Lancaster, C. and Williamson, J., eds.*, 1986, pp. 16–19. **[G: Sub-Saharan Africa]**

Alejo, F. Javier. Investment for Development in a Changing World. *Aussenwirtschaft*, April 1986, *41*(1), pp. 57–70. **[G: LDCs]**

Allsopp, Christopher and Joshi, Vijay. The Assessment: The International Debt Crisis. *Oxford Rev. Econ. Policy*, Spring 1986, *2*(1), pp. i–xxxiii. **[G: LDCs; MDCs]**

Amelung, Torsten and Mehltretter, Thorsten. Early-Warning Systems in Light of the International Debt Crisis. *Konjunkturpolitik*, 1986, *32*(5), pp. 257–81. **[G: LDCs]**

Amstutz, Max D. Co-operation with IFC: Experience of a European Investor. *Aussenwirtschaft*, April 1986, *41*(1), pp. 81–87. **[G: LDCs]**

Annis, Sheldon. The Shifting Grounds of Poverty Lending at the World Bank. **In** *Feinberg, R. E., et al.*, 1986, pp. 87–109.

de Azcarate, Luis. The World Bank in Adjustment and Economic Growth in Africa: Reply. **In** *Helleiner, G. K, ed.*, 1986, pp. 228–34. **[G: Africa]**

de Azcarate, Luis. The World Bank in Adjustment and Economic Growth in Africa. **In** *Helleiner, G. K, ed.*, 1986, pp. 184–219. **[G: Africa]**

Bacha, Edmar L. and Feinberg, Richard E. The World Bank and Structural Adjustment in Latin America. *World Devel.*, March 1986, *14*(3), pp. 333–46. **[G: Latin America]**

Bailey, Conner; Cycon, Dean E. and Morris, Michael. Fisheries Development in the Third World: The Role of International Agencies. *World Devel.*, Oct./Nov. 1986, *14*(10/11), pp. 1269–75. **[G: LDCs]**

Baker, James A., III. The Baker Plan. **In** *Dicke, D. C., ed.*, 1986, pp. 291–301.

Balassa, Bela. Developing Country Debt: Policies and Prospects. **In** *Giersch, H., ed.*, 1986, pp. 103–22. **[G: LDCs]**

Balassa, Bela. The Problem of the Debt in Developing Countries. **In** *Herber, B. P., ed.*, 1986, pp. 153–66. **[G: LDCs]**

Baneth, Jean. Government Policies in Developing Countries: Was Capital Wasted? **In** *Giersch, H., ed.*, 1986, pp. 79–94. **[G: India; Mexico; Ivory Coast; Indonesia]**

Batra, Raveendra N. and Naqvi, Nadeem. International Debt, Factor Accumulation, and the Balance of Payments. **In** *Chen, A. H., ed.*, 1986, pp. 261–77.

Becker, Abraham S. Soviet Union and the Third World: The Economic Dimension. *Soviet Econ.*, July-Sept. 1986, *2*(3), pp. 233–60. **[G: U.S.S.R.]**

Beckmann, David. The World Bank and Poverty in the 1980s. *Finance Develop.*, September 1986, *23*(3), pp. 26–29.

Beenstock, Michael. The Role of the World Bank in a Maturing Capital Market. **In** *World Bank*, 1986, pp. 34–46. **[G: LDCs]**

Belaunde-Moreyra, Antonio. Dramatic Action or Muddling through Strategy in the Debt Problem. **In** *Dicke, D. C., ed.*, 1986, pp. 10–25.

Bench, Robert R. U.S. Interests and Policy Implications: The Role of Lending Limits. **In** *Preeg, E. H. and Bendahmane, D. B., eds.*, 1986, pp. 65–67. **[G: U.S.]**

Berg, Elliot. The Question of Conditionality: Comments. **In** *Lancaster, C. and Williamson, J., eds.*, 1986, pp. 95–98. **[G: Africa]**

Berg, Elliot. The World Bank's Strategy. **In** *Ravenhill, J., ed.*, 1986, pp. 44–59. **[G: Africa]**

Berg, Robert J. Foreign Aid in Africa: Here's the Answer—Is It Relevant to the Question? **In** *Berg, R. J. and Whitaker, J. S., eds.*, 1986, pp. 505–43. **[G: Africa]**

Bergsten, C. Fred. Trade, Debt and Investment: The Importance of Foreign Private Investment for Development. *Aussenwirtschaft*, April 1986, *41*(1), pp. 27–36. **[G: LDCs]**

Bhaduri, Amit. Hacia un crecimiento con endeudamiento externo. (The Indebted Growth Process. With English summary.) *Estud. Econ.*, January-June 1986, *1*(1), pp. 115–25.

Bhagwati, Jagdish N. Ideology and North–South Relations. *World Devel.*, June 1986, *14*(6), pp. 767–74. **[G: Global]**

Bird, Graham. New Approaches to Country Risk. *Lloyds Bank Rev.*, October 1986, (162), pp. 1–16. **[G: LDCs]**

Blitzer, Charles R. Financing the World Bank. **In** *Feinberg, R. E., et al.*, 1986, pp. 135–60. **[G: LDCs]**

Bock, David and Michalopoulos, Constantine. The Emerging Role of the Bank in Heavily

Indebted Countries. *Finance Develop.*, September 1986, *23*(3), pp. 22–25.

Bogdanowicz-Bindert, Christine A. World Debt: The United State Reconsiders. *Foreign Aff.*, Winter 1985/86, *64*(2), pp. 259–73.

Brau, Eduard H. External Debt Management in the African Context. **In** *Helleiner, G. K, ed.*, 1986, pp. 160–80. **[G: Africa]**

Brau, Eduard H. The Demand for External Finance. **In** *Lancaster, C. and Williamson, J., eds.*, 1986, pp. 11–15. **[G: Sub-Saharan Africa]**

Brett, E. A. Reaching the Poorest: Does the World Bank Still Believe in "Redistribution with Growth"? **In** *World Bank*, 1986, pp. 74–84.

Buiter, Willem H. The Role of Reserves in the International Monetary System: Comment. **In** *Posner, M., ed.*, 1986, pp. 109–12. **[G: Global]**

Bulajic, Milan. Indebtedness of the Developing Countries and the New International Economic Order. **In** *Dicke, D. C., ed.*, 1986, pp. 43–73.

Bullock, Colin. IMF Conditionality and Jamaica's Economic Policy in the 1980s. *Soc. Econ. Stud.*, December 1986, *35*(4), pp. 129–76. **[G: Jamaica]**

Burki, Shahid Javed and Ayres, Robert L. A Fresh Look at Development Aid. *Finance Develop.*, March 1986, *23*(1), pp. 6–10. **[G: Global]**

Callaghy, Thomas M. The Political Economy of African Debt: The Case of Zaire. **In** *Ravenhill, J., ed.*, 1986, pp. 307–46. **[G: Zaire]**

Camdessus, Michel. Debt: Are We at the End of the Crisis? *Europ. Econ. Rev.*, June 1986, *30*(3), pp. 469–75.

Carey, Richard H. Prospects for Bilateral Aid. **In** *Lancaster, C. and Williamson, J., eds.*, 1986, pp. 107–21. **[G: LDCs; Africa]**

Carmichael, Jeffrey. Economic Analysis and the World Debt Problem. *Australian Econ. Rev.*, 1st Quarter 1986, (73), pp. 29–36. **[G: LDCs]**

Cassen, Robert. The Effectiveness of Aid. *Finance Develop.*, March 1986, *23*(1), pp. 1–14.

Castañeda, Jorge G. Mexico at the Brink. *Foreign Aff.*, Winter 1985/86, *64*(2), pp. 287–303. **[G: Mexico]**

Charlton, Mark W. The Management of Canada's Bilateral Food Aid: An Organizational Perspective. *Can. J. Devel. Stud.*, 1986, 7(1), pp. 7–19. **[G: Canada; LDCs]**

Chowdhury, Subrata Roy. Foreign Debts in the Present and a New International Economic Order: The Indian Point of View. **In** *Dicke, D. C., ed.*, 1986, pp. 311–15. **[G: India]**

Clausen, A. W. Address to the Board of Governors: Toronto, Canada: September 6, 1982. **In** *Clausen, A. W.*, 1986, pp. 97–123.

Clausen, A. W. Address to the Board of Governors: Washington, D.C.: September 29, 1981. **In** *Clausen, A. W.*, 1986, pp. 1–20.

Clausen, A. W. Address to the Board of Governors: Seoul, Korea: October 8, 1985. **In** *Clausen, A. W.*, 1986, pp. 391–423.

Clausen, A. W. Address to the Board of Governors: Washington, D.C.: September 27, 1983. **In** *Clausen, A. W.*, 1986, pp. 191–216.

Clausen, A. W. Address to the Business Council: Hot Springs, Virginia: October 8, 1983. **In** *Clausen, A. W.*, 1986, pp. 217–28.

Clausen, A. W. Adjustment with Growth in the Developing World: A World Bank Perspective: Address to the Deutsche Gesellschaft für Auswärtige Politik: Bonn, Federal Republic of Germany: April 16, 1986. **In** *Clausen, A. W.*, 1986, pp. 479–96.

Clausen, A. W. Economic Growth: The Path to the Alleviation of Debt and Poverty: Address at the Central Bank of Argentina: Buenos Aires, Argentina: December 9, 1985. **In** *Clausen, A. W.*, 1986, pp. 425–39.

Clausen, A. W. International Debt and Public Policy. **In** *Axilrod, S. H., et al.*, 1986, pp. 99–106.

Clausen, A. W. Priority Issues on the World Bank's Agenda: Address to the Bretton Woods Committee: Washington, D.C.: January 22, 1986. **In** *Clausen, A. W.*, 1986, pp. 441–51.

Clausen, A. W. Statement to the Development Committee: Washington, D.C.: April 10, 1986. **In** *Clausen, A. W.*, 1986, pp. 471–77.

Clausen, A. W. Sustainable Development: The Global Imperative: Fairfield Osborn Memorial Lecture in Environmental Science: Washington, D.C.: November 12, 1981. **In** *Clausen, A. W.*, 1986, pp. 21–35.

Clausen, A. W. The World Bank and International Commercial Banks: Partners for Development: Address to the International Monetary Conference: Vancouver, Canada: May 23, 1982. **In** *Clausen, A. W.*, 1986, pp. 79–95.

Clausen, A. W. The World Bank: A Financial Appraisal: Address to Representatives of the Financial Community: New York, New York: February 25, 1982. **In** *Clausen, A. W.*, 1986, pp. 55–66.

Clausen, A. W. Third World Debt and Global Recovery: The 1983 Jodidi Lecture at the Center for International Affairs, Harvard University: Boston, Massachusetts: February 24, 1983. **In** *Clausen, A. W.*, 1986, pp. 133–56.

Cohen, Benjamin J. International Debt and Linkage Strategies: Some Foreign-Policy Implications for the United States. **In** *Kahler, M., ed.*, 1986, pp. 127–55. **[G: U.S.]**

Cohen, Daniel and Sachs, Jeffrey. Growth and External Debt under Risk of Debt Repudiation. *Europ. Econ. Rev.*, June 1986, *30*(3), pp. 529–60.

Conable, Barber B. The Bank's Mission in a Changing World. *Finance Develop.*, December 1986, *23*(4), pp. 2–5.

Cooper, Richard N. Managing Risks to the International Economic System. **In** *Cooper, R. N.*, 1986, *1983*, pp. 23–51.

Cooper, Richard N. and Sachs, Jeffrey. Borrowing Abroad: The Debtor's Perspective. **In** *Cooper, R. N.*, 1986, *1985*, pp. 229–88.

Corrigan, E. Gerald. Reducing International Imbalances in an Interdependent World. *Fed. Res. Bank New York Quart. Rev.*, Spring 1986, *11*(1), pp. 1–5. **[G: U.S.; LDCs]**

Crawford, Malcolm. The Crisis in Aid-Supported Project Finance. *Nat. Westminster Bank Quart. Rev.*, November 1986, pp. 34–44. **[G: LDCs]**

D'Arista, Jane. The International Debt Problem in a Monetary Context. **In** *Hartland-Thunberg, P. and Ebinger, C. K., eds.*, 1986, pp. 39–53.

Dallara, Charles. The Question of Conditionality: Comments. **In** *Lancaster, C. and Williamson, J., eds.*, 1986, pp. 92–95. **[G: Africa]**

Davies, Omar. An Analysis of the Management of the Jamaican Economy: 1972–1985. *Soc. Econ. Stud.*, March 1986, *35*(1), pp. 73–109. **[G: Jamaica]**

von der Decken, Christoph. Bank Lending and Government Intervention in Capital Markets: Has Recycling Gone Too Far? Comment. **In** *Giersch, H., ed.*, 1986, pp. 66–73. **[G: Selected LDCs; OECD]**

Dell, Sidney. The History of the IMF. *World Devel.*, September 1986, *14*(9), pp. 1203–12.

Devlin, Robert. Private Banks, Debt, and the Bargaining Power of the Periphery: Theory and Practice. **In** *Economic Commission for Latin America and the Caribbean*, 1986, pp. 3–28. **[G: Peru; Bolivia]**

Díaz-Alejandro, Carlos F. Some Unintended Consequences of Financial Laissez-Faire. **In** *[Hirshman, A. O.]*, 1986, pp. 91–113. **[G: Chile]**

Dicke, Detlev Chr. Economic Coercion on Heavily Indebted Countries. **In** *Dicke, D. C., ed.*, 1986, pp. 256–63.

Diejomaoh, Vremudia P. Impact of Different Types of Foreign Investments on Capital Formation in Africa. **In** *Association of African Central Banks*, 1986, pp. 123–50. **[G: Africa]**

Dietz, James L. Debt and Development: The Future of Latin America. *J. Econ. Issues*, December 1986, *20*(4), pp. 1029–51. **[G: Latin America]**

Dietz, Raimund. Soviet Foregone Gains in Trade with the CMEA Six: A Reappraisal. *Comp. Econ. Stud.*, Summer 1986, *28*(2), pp. 69–94. **[G: CMEA]**

Diwan, Romesh and Hu, Grace. Country Objectives and IMF Conditionality: An Empirical Analysis of Sudan Economy. *Indian J. Quant. Econ.*, 1986, *2*(2), pp. 83–100. **[G: Sudan]**

Dixon, Peter B. and McDonald, Daina. Australia's Foreign Debt: 1975 to 1985. *Australian Econ. Rev.*, 2nd Quarter 1986, (74), pp. 22–37. **[G: Australia]**

Dobson, Alan P. The Export White Paper, 10 September, 1941. *Econ. Hist. Rev., 2nd Ser.*, February 1986, *39*(1), pp. 59–76. **[G: U.K.]**

Dooley, Michael P., et al. An Analysis of External Debt Positions of Eight Developing Countries through 1990. *J. Devel. Econ.*, May 1986, *21*(2), pp. 283–318. **[G: S. Korea; Philippines; Latin America]**

Dooley, Michael P. The Role of Reserves in the International Monetary System. **In** *Posner, M., ed.*, 1986, pp. 97–109. **[G: Global]**

Dornbusch, Rudiger. International Debt and Economic Instability. **In** *Axilrod, S. H., et al.*, 1986, pp. 63–86. **[G: U.S.; Latin America]**

Dornbusch, Rudiger. Overborrowing: Three Case Studies. **In** *Dornbusch, R.*, 1986, *1985*, pp. 97–130. **[G: Chile; Brazil; Argentina]**

Dornbusch, Rudiger. The World Debt Problem: 1980–84 and Beyond. **In** *Dornbusch, R.*, 1986, *1985*, pp. 131–50.

Duncan, Alex. Aid Effectiveness in Raising Adaptive Capacity in the Low-income Countries. **In** *Lewis, J. P. and Kallab, V., eds.*, 1986, pp. 129–52. **[G: Selected LDCs]**

Eaton, Jonathan; Gersovitz, Mark and Stiglitz, Joseph E. The Pure Theory of Country Risk. *Europ. Econ. Rev.*, June 1986, *30*(3), pp. 481–513.

Eaton, Jonathan and Taylor, Lance. Developing Country Finance and Debt. *J. Devel. Econ.*, June 1986, *22*(1), pp. 209–65. **[G: LDCs]**

Ebinger, Charles K. The Brazilian Energy Sector. **In** *Hartland-Thunberg, P. and Ebinger, C. K., eds.*, 1986, pp. 131–53. **[G: Brazil]**

Eckaus, Richard S. How the IMF Lives with Its Conditionality. *Policy Sci.*, October 1986, *19*(3), pp. 237–52.

Edwards, Sebastian. Country Risk, Foreign Borrowing, and the Social Discount Rate in an Open Developing Economy. *J. Int. Money Finance*, Supp. March 1986, *5*, pp. S79–96. **[G: LDCs; Chile; Costa Rica]**

Eicher, Carl K. Facing Up to Africa's Food Crisis. **In** *Ravenhill, J., ed.*, 1986, pp. 149–80. **[G: Africa]**

Eicher, Carl K. Strategic Issues in Combating Hunger and Poverty in Africa. **In** *Berg, R. J. and Whitaker, J. S., eds.*, 1986, pp. 242–75. **[G: Sub-Saharan Africa]**

Engel, Charles M. The International Monetary System: Forty Years after Bretton Woods: Review Essay. *J. Monet. Econ.*, May 1986, *17*(3), pp. 441–48.

Erb, Richard D. A View from the Fund. **In** *Helleiner, G. K, ed.*, 1986, pp. 15–25. **[G: Africa]**

Erb, Richard D. Adjustment, Growth, and the Fund's Role [Interview]. *Finance Develop.*, March 1986, *23*(1), pp. 2–5.

Erb, Richard D. Collaboration between Aid Agencies and the IMF. *Finance Develop.*, March 1986, *23*(1), pp. 15–16.

Erdilek, Asim. Government Policies in Developing Countries: Was Capital Wasted? Comment. **In** *Giersch, H., ed.*, 1986, pp. 95–99. **[G: India; Mexico; Ivory Coast; Indonesia]**

Errunza, V. R. and Ghalbouni, J. P. Interest Rates and International Debt Crisis. *Banca Naz. Lavoro Quart. Rev.*, June 1986, (157), pp. 225–45. **[G: LDCs]**

Eussner, Ansgar. Agro-Industrial Co-operation between the European Community and the ACP Countries. *J. Common Market Stud.*, September 1986, *25*(1), pp. 51–73. **[G: EEC; Cameroon; Rwanda]**

Faber, Mike. Recovery in the Developing World: Concluding Remarks. **In** *World Bank,* 1986, pp. 118–20.

Fadiga, Abdoulaye. Adjustment in Africa: What Can Be Done? **In** *Helleiner, G. K, ed.,* 1986, pp. 261–64. **[G: Africa]**

Feinberg, Richard E. Between Two Worlds: The World Bank's Next Decade: Overview: An Open Letter to the World Bank's New President. **In** *Feinberg, R. E., et al.,* 1986, pp. 3–30.

Felix, David. On Financial Blowups and Authoritarian Regimes in Latin America. **In** *Hartlyn, J. and Morley, S. A., eds.,* 1986, pp. 85–125. **[G: Latin America]**

Ffrench-Davis, Ricardo. El financiamiento externo negativo: tendencias, consecuencias y opciones para América Latina. (Negative External Financing: Trends, Implications, and Options for Latin America. With English summary.) *Colección Estud. CIEPLAN,* December 1986, (20), pp. 5–17. **[G: Latin America]**

Ffrench-Davis, Ricardo. Notas sobre el desarrollo económico y la deuda externa en América Latina. (With English summary.) *Desarrollo Econ.,* Jan.-Mar. 1986, *25*(100), pp. 571–85. **[G: Latin America]**

Fischer, Bernhard and Langhammer, Rolf J. Determinanten der Sparkapitalbildung in Entwicklungsländern. (Determinants of Savings Mobilization in Developing Countries. With English summary.) *Konjunkturpolitik,* 1986, 32(5), pp. 282–307. **[G: LDCs]**

Fischer, Stanley. Issues in Medium-term Macroeconomic Adjustment. *World Bank Res. Observer,* July 1986, *1*(2), pp. 163–82. **[G: LDCs]**

Fishlow, Albert. Latin American Adjustment to the Oil Shocks of 1973 and 1979. **In** *Hartlyn, J. and Morley, S. A., eds.,* 1986, pp. 54–84. **[G: Selected LDCs]**

Fishlow, Albert. Lessons from the Past: Capital Markets during the 19th Century and the Interwar Period. **In** *Kahler, M., ed.,* 1986, pp. 37–93. **[G: LDCs; MDCs]**

Fishlow, Albert. The East European Debt Crisis in the Latin American Mirror. **In** *Comisso, E. and Tyson, L., eds.,* 1986, pp. 391–99. **[G: Latin America]**

Fishlow, Albert. The East European Debt Crisis in the Latin American Mirror. *Int. Organ.,* Spring 1986, *40*(2), pp. 567–75. **[G: E. Europe]**

Flint, David. Renegotiation and Rescheduling. **In** *Dicke, D. C., ed.,* 1986, pp. 264–90.

Forte, Francesco. Ten Paradoxes Facing African Countries. *Atlantic Econ. J.,* March 1986, *14*(1), pp. 1–7. **[G: LDCs; Africa]**

Frey, Bruno S. The Function of Governments and Intergovernmental Organizations in the International Resource Transfer—The Case of the World Bank. **In** *Balassa, B. and Giersch, H., eds.,* 1986, pp. 454–70.

Frey, Bruno S. and Schneider, Friedrich. Competing Models of International Lending Activity. *J. Devel. Econ.,* March 1986, *20*(2), pp. 225–45. **[G: LDCs]**

Frimpong-Ansah, Jonathan H. The Supply of External Finance: Comments. **In** *Lancaster, C. and Williamson, J., eds.,* 1986, pp. 162–66. **[G: Sub-Saharan Africa]**

Gafar, John S. The Impact of External Factors on the Debt Burden and Import Capacity of Developing Countries. *Indian Econ. J.,* Jan.-Mar. 1986, *33*(3), pp. 35–45. **[G: LDCs]**

Gang, Ira N. and Khan, Haider. Foreign Aid and Public Expenditures in LDC's. *Atlantic Econ. J.,* September 1986, *14*(3), pp. 56–58. **[G: LDCs]**

Ganshev, Gansho T. The Economic Effectiveness of Loans and Credits from the International Bank for Economic Cooperation in Transferable Rubles. *Soviet E. Europ. Foreign Trade,* Spring 1986, 22(1), pp. 51–67. **[G: CMEA]**

Gaudard, Gaston. Le Problème de l'Endettement International: Rupture ou Concertation. (With English summary.) **In** *Dicke, D. C., ed.,* 1986, pp. 26–42.

Gebre-Kidan, A. Tadesse. Adjustment in Africa: What Can Be Done? **In** *Helleiner, G. K, ed.,* 1986, pp. 258–61. **[G: Africa]**

Geller, Lucio and Tokman, Víctor E. From Austerity Measures to Structural Adjustment. *CEPAL Rev.,* December 1986, (30), pp. 35–50. **[G: Latin America]**

Gemmill, Robert. U.S. Interests and Policy Implications: Differential Treatment of Debts. **In** *Preeg, E. H. and Bendahmane, D. B., eds.,* 1986, pp. 62–65. **[G: U.S.]**

Glick, Reuven and Kharas, Homi J. The Costs and Benefits of Foreign Borrowing: A Survey of Multi-Period Models. *J. Devel. Stud.,* January 1986, 22(2), pp. 279–99. **[G: LDCs]**

Goldsbrough, David. Investment Trends and Prospects: The Link with Bank Lending. **In** *Moran, T. H., ed.,* 1986, pp. 173–86. **[G: LDCs]**

Goldstein, Morris. Global Effects of Fund-Supported Programs. *Finance Develop.,* March 1986, 23(1), pp. 24–27.

Goldstein, Morris and Montiel, Peter J. Evaluating Fund Stabilization Programs with Multicountry Data: Some Methodological Pitfalls. *Int. Monet. Fund Staff Pap.,* June 1986, 33(2), pp. 304–44.

Gonzalez del Valle, Jorge. A Possible International Solution to the Foreign Debt Problem. **In** *Maddison, A., ed.,* 1986, pp. 155–60. **[G: Latin America]**

González, Norberto. Meeting on Growth, Adjustment and the Debt in Latin America: Opening Address. *CEPAL Rev.,* April 1986, (28), pp. 7–10. **[G: Latin America]**

Graziani, G. Capital Movements within the CMEA. *Soviet E. Europ. Foreign Trade,* Spring 1986, 22(1), pp. 19–50. **[G: CMEA]**

Green, Reginald Herbold. The Demand for External Finance: Comments. **In** *Lancaster, C. and Williamson, J., eds.,* 1986, pp. 21–27. **[G: Sub-Saharan Africa]**

Green, Reginald Herbold. Third World Sovereign Debt Renegotiation 1980–85 and After: Reflections on Procedures and Paradigms. **In** *Dicke, D. C., ed.*, 1986, pp. 316–38.

Green, Reginald Herbold and Allison, Caroline. The World Bank's Agenda for Accelerated Development: Dialectics, Doubts and Dialogues. **In** *Ravenhill, J., ed.*, 1986, pp. 60–84. **[G: Africa]**

Griffith-Jones, Stephany. Ways Forward from the Debt Crisis. *Oxford Rev. Econ. Policy*, Spring 1986, *2*(1), pp. 39–61. **[G: LDCs]**

Ground, Richard L. Origin and Magnitude of Recessionary Adjustment in Latin America. *CEPAL Rev.*, December 1986, (30), pp. 67–85. **[G: Latin America]**

Grubel, Herbert G. Government Deposit Insurance, Moral Hazard and the International Debt Crisis. **In** *Giersch, H., ed.*, 1986, pp. 172–86. **[G: U.S.]**

Guerguil, Martine. The International Financial Crisis: Diagnoses and Prescriptions. **In** *Economic Commission for Latin America and the Caribbean*, 1986, *1984*, pp. 29–62.

Guesnerie, Roger. The Pure Theory of Country Risk: Comments. *Europ. Econ. Rev.*, June 1986, *30*(3), pp. 515–19.

Gutowski, Armin. From Recycling to Overindebtedness—What Went Wrong? **In** *Giersch, H., ed.*, 1986, pp. 1–14.

Gwiazda, Adam. Poland's Trade with the West: Chances for Improvement. **In** *Altmann, F.-L., ed.*, 1986, pp. 165–78. **[G: Poland]**

Haggard, Stephan. The Politics of Adjustment: Lessons from the IMF's Extended Fund Facility. **In** *Kahler, M., ed.*, 1986, pp. 157–86.

Hahn, Hugo J. The Restructuring of International Debt: Recent Developments. **In** *Dicke, D. C., ed.*, 1986, pp. 97–106.

Hakim, Peter. The Baker Plan: Unfulfilled Promises. *Challenge*, Sept./Oct. 1986, *29*(4), pp. 55–59. **[G: U.S.]**

Hallberg, Kristin. International Debt, 1985: Origins and Issues for the Future. **In** *Claudon, M. P., ed.*, 1986, pp. 3–42. **[G: LDCs]**

ul Haq, Mahbub. Proposal for an IMF Debt Refinancing Subsidiary. **In** *[Streeten, P.]*, 1986, pp. 87–94.

Hardy, Chandra S. Africa's Debt: Structural Adjustment with Stability. **In** *Berg, R. J. and Whitaker, J. S., eds.*, 1986, pp. 453–75. **[G: Africa]**

Hartland-Thunberg, Penelope. Brazil's Interrupted Economic Miracle. **In** *Hartland-Thunberg, P. and Ebinger, C. K., eds.*, 1986, pp. 99–130. **[G: Brazil]**

Hartland-Thunberg, Penelope. Causes and Consequences of the World Debt Crisis. **In** *Hartland-Thunberg, P. and Ebinger, C. K., eds.*, 1986, pp. 1–22.

Hartland-Thunberg, Penelope and Ebinger, Charles K. Mexico's Economic Anguish. **In** *Hartland-Thunberg, P. and Ebinger, C. K., eds.*, 1986, pp. 55–98. **[G: Mexico]**

Helleiner, Gerald K. Africa and the International Monetary Fund: Introduction. **In** *Helleiner, G. K, ed.*, 1986, pp. 1–11. **[G: Africa]**

Helleiner, Gerald K. Policy-Based Program Lending: A Look at the Bank's New Role. **In** *Feinberg, R. E., et al.*, 1986, pp. 47–66.

Helleiner, Gerald K. The Question of Conditionality. **In** *Lancaster, C. and Williamson, J., eds.*, 1986, pp. 63–91. **[G: Africa]**

Hellwig, Martin. The Pure Theory of Country Risk: Comments. *Europ. Econ. Rev.*, June 1986, *30*(3), pp. 521–27.

Henderson, Dale W. Country Risk, Foreign Borrowing, and the Social Discount Rate in an Open Developing Economy: Comments. *J. Int. Money Finance*, Supp. March 1986, *5*, pp. 97–99. **[G: LDCs; Chile; Costa Rica]**

Hercowitz, Zvi. On the Determination of the External Debt: The Case of Israel. *J. Int. Money Finance*, September 1986, *5*(3), pp. 315–34. **[G: Israel]**

Hiemenz, Ulrich. Government Policies in Developing Countries: Was Capital Wasted? Comment. **In** *Giersch, H., ed.*, 1986, pp. 100–102. **[G: India; Mexico; Ivory Coast; Indonesia]**

Higgins, Bryon. Debt, Financial Stability, and Public Policy: Symposium Overview. **In** *Axilrod, S. H., et al.*, 1986, pp. 1–14.

Hino, Hiroyuki. IMF–World Bank Collaboration. *Finance Develop.*, September 1986, *23*(3), pp. 10–14.

Hoguet, George R. U.S. Interests and Policy Implications: A Strategy for Dealing with the Debt Crisis. **In** *Preeg, E. H. and Bendahmane, D. B., eds.*, 1986, pp. 57–60. **[G: U.S.]**

Hoksbergen, Roland. Approaches to Evaluation of Development Interventions: The Importance of World and Life Views. *World Devel.*, Special Issue, Feb. 1986, *14*(2), pp. 283–300.

Holland, Stuart. The World Bank—Where Now? **In** *World Bank*, 1986, pp. 23–31.

Holtzman, Franklyn D. The Significance of Soviet Subsidies to Eastern Europe. *Comp. Econ. Stud.*, Spring 1986, *28*(1), pp. 54–65. **[G: CMEA]**

Holzman, Franklyn D. Further Thoughts on the Significance of Soviet Subsidies to Eastern Europe. *Comp. Econ. Stud.*, Fall 1986, *28*(3), pp. 59–64. **[G: CMEA]**

Hope, Nicholas. The Debt Crisis and Its Impact on Middle-Income and Poor Countries. **In** *World Bank*, 1986, pp. 12–19. **[G: LDCs]**

Hopkins, Antony G. The World Bank in Africa: Historical Reflections on the African Present. *World Devel.*, December 1986, *14*(12), pp. 1473–87. **[G: Africa]**

Hossain, Kamal. Foreign Debts in the Present and a New International Economic Order: Introduction to the Symposium. **In** *Dicke, D. C., ed.*, 1986, pp. 5–9.

Husain, S. Shahid. The World Bank and Economic Policy in Developing Countries. **In** *World Bank*, 1986, pp. 49–55.

Hussain, M. Nureldin and Thirlwall, A. P. The IMF Supply-Side Approach to Devaluation: A Reply. *Oxford Bull. Econ. Statist.*, February 1986, *48*(1), pp. 83–86. **[G: Sudan]**

Ivanov, N. and Loshchakov, A. Foreign Economic Relations of CMEA Countries. *Prob.*

Econ., May 1986, *29*(1), pp. 3–16. [G: CMEA; LDCs; OECD]

Jaycox, Edward V. K. Africa Debt and Financing: What Is to Be Done? A Panel Discussion. **In** *Lancaster, C. and Williamson, J., eds.*, 1986, pp. 179–84. [G: Africa]

Jaycox, Edward V. K. Africa: Development Challenges and the World Bank's Response. *Finance Develop.*, March 1986, *23*(1), pp. 21–22. [G: Africa]

Jaycox, Edward V. K., et al. The Nature of the Debt Problem in Eastern and Southern Africa. **In** *Lancaster, C. and Williamson, J., eds.*, 1986, pp. 47–62. [G: E. Africa; Southern Africa]

Jennings, Anthony. Measures to Assist the Least Developed Countries: The Case of Malawi. *World Devel.*, December 1986, *14*(12), pp. 1463–68. [G: Malawi]

Jimenez, Julio. Alternative Approaches to Stabilization in Africa: Comments. **In** *Helleiner, G. K, ed.*, 1986, pp. 151–53. [G: Sub-Saharan Africa]

Jones, Robert A. U.S. Monetary Policy Responses to the Debt Crisis. **In** *Claudon, M. P., ed.*, 1986, pp. 85–98. [G: U.S.]

Jung, Aleksander. Exporting, Refinancing, Restructuring. *Eastern Europ. Econ.*, Summer 1986, *24*(4), pp. 40–50. [G: Poland]

Kahler, Miles. Politics and International Debt: Explaining the Crisis. **In** *Kahler, M., ed.*, 1986, pp. 11–36.

Kahler, Miles. The Politics of International Debt: Conclusion: Politics and Proposals for Reform. **In** *Kahler, M., ed.*, 1986, pp. 245–72.

Kaibni, Nihad. Evolution of the Compensatory Financing Facility. *Finance Develop.*, June 1986, *23*(2), pp. 24–27.

Kanet, Roger E. Economic Aspects of Soviet Policy in the Third World: A Comment. *Soviet Econ.*, July-Sept. 1986, *2*(3), pp. 261–68. [G: U.S.S.R.]

Karunaratne, Neil Dias. A Holistic Analysis of Trade versus Aid Issues: World and Australian Insights. *Devel. Econ.*, March 1986, *24*(1), pp. 44–55. [G: Global; Australia]

Katz, Samuel I. Government Deposit Insurance, Moral Hazard and the International Debt Crisis: Comment. **In** *Giersch, H., ed.*, 1986, pp. 187–91. [G: U.S.]

Kaufman, Robert R. Democratic and Authoritarian Responses to the Debt Issue: Argentina , Brazil, Mexico. **In** *Kahler, M., ed.*, 1986, pp. 187–217. [G: Argentina; Brazil; Mexico]

Kavalsky, Basil. Reviewing Public Investment Programs. *Finance Develop.*, March 1986, *23*(1), pp. 37–40.

Kennedy, Joseph V. and Ruttan, Vernon W. A Reexamination of Professional and Popular Thought on Assistance for Economic Development: 1949–1952. *J. Devel. Areas*, April 1986, *20*(3), pp. 297–326. [G: LDCs]

Khan, Mohsin S. and Knight, Malcolm D. Do Fund-Supported Adjustment Programs Retard Growth? *Finance Develop.*, March 1986, *23*(1), pp. 30–32.

Kharas, Homi J. and Shishido, Hisanobu. A Dynamic-Optimization Model of Foreign Borrowing: A Case Study of Thailand. *J. Policy Modeling*, Spring 1986, *8*(1), pp. 1–26. [G: Thailand]

Kieval, Gershon R. U.S. Policies in the Persian Gulf. **In** *Roukis, G. S. and Montana, P. J., eds.*, 1986, pp. 21–46. [G: U.S.; Middle East]

Killick, Tony. African Debt and Financing: What Is to Be Done? A Panel Discussion. **In** *Lancaster, C. and Williamson, J., eds.*, 1986, pp. 173–78. [G: Africa]

Kimbrough, Kent P. Foreign Aid and Optimal Fiscal Policy. *Can. J. Econ.*, February 1986, *19*(1), pp. 35–61.

Kirchhof, Paul. The Public Debt, Democratic Principles and the Rule of Law. **In** *Dicke, D. C., ed.*, 1986, pp. 339–60.

Kjellstrom, Sven B. and d'Almeida, Ayité-Fily. Aid Coordination: A Recipient's Perspective. *Finance Develop.*, September 1986, *23*(3), pp. 37–40. [G: Togo]

Kohler, Daniel F. To Pay or Not to Pay: A Model of International Defaults. *J. Policy Anal. Manage.*, Summer 1986, *5*(4), pp. 742–60.

Krayenbühl, Thomas E. Comecon as a Debtor of the Western Financial System. **In** *Dicke, D. C., ed.*, 1986, pp. 231–47. [G: OECD; CMEA]

Krueger, Anne O. Aid in the Development Process. *World Bank Res. Observer*, January 1986, *1*(1), pp. 57–78. [G: LDCs]

Krueger, Anne O. Developing Countries' Debt Problems and Growth Prospects. *Atlantic Econ. J.*, March 1986, *14*(1), pp. 8–19. [G: LDCs]

Kydd, J. and Hewitt, A. The Effectiveness of Structural Adjustment Lending: Initial Evidence from Malawi. *World Devel.*, March 1986, *14*(3), pp. 347–65. [G: Malawi]

Lafay, Jean-Dominique. L'aide au développement: des analyses normatives aux théories politico-économiques. (With English summary.) *Revue Écon. Polit.*, July-Aug. 1986, *96*(4), pp. 384–97. [G: LDCs]

Laird, Robbin F. Soviet Arms Trade with the Noncommunist Third World. **In** *Laird, R. F. and Hoffmann, E. P., eds.*, 1986, *1984*, pp. 713–30. [G: U.S.S.R.; LDCs]

Lal, Deepak and van Wijnbergen, Sweder J. G. Government Deficits, the Real Interest Rate, and Developing Country Debt: On Global Crowding Out. **In** *Lal, D. and Wolf, M., eds.*, 1986, pp. 182–238. [G: OECD]

Lal, Deepak and Wolf, Martin. Debt, Deficits, and Distortions. **In** *Lal, D. and Wolf, M., eds.*, 1986, pp. 239–91. [G: Global]

Lal, Deepak and Wolf, Martin. Stagflation, Savings, and the State: Perspectives on the Global Economy: Introduction. **In** *Lal, D. and Wolf, M., eds.*, 1986, pp. 3–13.

Lancaster, Carol. Multilateral Development Banks and Africa. **In** *Lancaster, C. and Williamson, J., eds.*, 1986, pp. 122–33. [G: Africa]

Lancaster, Carol and Williamson, John. Africa's Economic Predicament. **In** *Lancaster, C. and Williamson, J., eds.*, 1986, pp. 1–9. **[G: Sub-Saharan Africa]**

Lancaster, Carol and Williamson, John. African Debt and Financing: Concluding Appraisal. **In** *Lancaster, C. and Williamson, J., eds.*, 1986, pp. 201–15. **[G: Africa]**

Lavigne, Marie. Comment on the Economic Dimension of Soviet Interaction with the Third World. *Soviet Econ.*, July-Sept. 1986, *2*(3), pp. 269–76. **[G: U.S.S.R.]**

Lawrence, Robert Z. Systemic Risk and Developing Country Debt. **In** *Lal, D. and Wolf, M., eds.*, 1986, pp. 91–102.

Lee, Eddy. Domestic Resource Mobilisation and Self-reliance. **In** *Islam, R. and Muqtada, M., eds.*, 1986, pp. 279–89. **[G: Bangladesh]**

Lee, James and Goodland, Robert. Economic Development and the Environment. *Finance Develop.*, December 1986, *23*(4), pp. 36–39. **[G: LDCs]**

Lessard, Donald R. The Supply of External Finance: Comments. **In** *Lancaster, C. and Williamson, J., eds.*, 1986, pp. 166–69. **[G: Africa]**

Lipson, Charles. International Debt and International Institutions. **In** *Kahler, M., ed.*, 1986, pp. 219–43.

Lomax, David F. The Debt Problem: A Banking Perspective. **In** *Posner, M., ed.*, 1986, pp. 118–29. **[G: LDCs]**

Lowenthal, Abraham F. Threat and Opportunity in the Americas. *Foreign Aff.*, 1986, *64*(3), pp. 539–61. **[G: Latin America]**

Loxley, John. Alternative Approaches to Stabilization in Africa: Reply. **In** *Helleiner, G. K, ed.*, 1986, pp. 156–59. **[G: Sub-Saharan Africa]**

Loxley, John. Alternative Approaches to Stabilization in Africa. **In** *Helleiner, G. K, ed.*, 1986, pp. 117–47. **[G: Sub-Saharan Africa]**

Lyman, Princeton. African Debt and Financing: What Is to Be Done? A Panel Discussion. **In** *Lancaster, C. and Williamson, J., eds.*, 1986, pp. 189–94. **[G: Africa]**

MacEwan, Arthur. International Debt and Banking: Rising Instability within the General Crisis. *Sci. Soc.*, Summer 1986, *50*(2), pp. 177–209.

Maddison, Angus. Developing Countries in the 1930s: Possible Lessons for the 1980s. **In** *Lal, D. and Wolf, M., eds.*, 1986, pp. 15–47. **[G: LDCs; MDCs]**

Magee, Stephen P. and Brock, William A. Third World Debt and International Capital Market Failure as a Consequence of Redistributive Political Risk Sharing. **In** *Claudon, M. P., ed.*, 1986, pp. 173–98. **[G: OPEC; U.S.; Selected LDCs]**

Marer, Paul. The Political Economy of Soviet Relations with Eastern Europe. **In** *Laird, R. F. and Hoffmann, E. P., eds.*, 1986, *1984*, pp. 570–600. **[G: U.S.S.R.; CMEA]**

Massad, Carlos. Adjustment in Africa: What Can Be Done? **In** *Helleiner, G. K, ed.*, 1986, pp. 237–40. **[G: Africa]**

Massad, Carlos. Relieving the Debt Burden: Past Experience and Present Needs. *CEPAL Rev.*, December 1986, (30), pp. 17–34. **[G: Latin America]**

Mattione, Richard P. Managing World Debt: Past Lessons and Future Prospects. **In** *Claudon, M. P., ed.*, 1986, pp. 43–62. **[G: LDCs]**

Mawakani, Samba. Fund Conditionality and the Socioeconomic Situation in Africa. **In** *Helleiner, G. K, ed.*, 1986, pp. 104–12. **[G: Africa]**

Mayer, Helmut. Developing Country Debt: Policies and Prospects: Comment. **In** *Giersch, H., ed.*, 1986, pp. 123–26. **[G: LDCs]**

McCauley, Robert N. IMF: Managed Lending. **In** *Claudon, M. P., ed.*, 1986, pp. 123–45. **[G: LDCs]**

Measham, Anthony R. Health and Development: The Bank's Experience. *Finance Develop.*, December 1986, *23*(4), pp. 26–29. **[G: LDCs]**

Meese, Richard. Risk in International Lending: A Dynamic Factor Analysis Applied to France and Mexico: Comments. *J. Int. Money Finance*, Supp. March 1986, *5*, pp. S49–51. **[G: France; Mexico]**

Meessen, Karl M. IMF Conditionality and State Sovereignty. **In** *Dicke, D. C., ed.*, 1986, pp. 117–29.

Mehran, Hassanali. External Debt Management. *Finance Develop.*, June 1986, *23*(2), pp. 40–41.

Meller, Patricio. Un enfoque analítico-empirico de las causas del actual endeudamiento externo chileno. (Causes of Present Chilean Foreign Debt: An Analytical–Empirical Approach. With English summary.) *Colección Estud. CIEPLAN*, December 1986, (20), pp. 19–60. **[G: Chile]**

Melvin, Michael and Schlagenhauf, Don. Risk in International Lending: A Dynamic Factor Analysis Applied to France and Mexico. *J. Int. Money Finance*, Supp. March 1986, *5*, pp. S31–48. **[G: France; Mexico]**

Mohammed, Azizali F. Alternative Approaches to Stabilization in Africa: Comments. **In** *Helleiner, G. K, ed.*, 1986, pp. 148–51. **[G: Sub-Saharan Africa]**

Mohammed, Azizali F. The Debt Problem. **In** *Posner, M., ed.*, 1986, pp. 113–18. **[G: LDCs]**

Monti, Mario. Indexation of Government Debt and Its Alternatives. **In** *Herber, B. P., ed.*, 1986, pp. 181–92. **[G: Italy; U.S.; LDCs]**

Moore, Richard. U.S. Virgin Islands Industrial Ambitions in the Context of a Maturing Caribbean Basin Initiative. *Atlantic Econ. J.*, September 1986, *14*(3), pp. 14–17. **[G: U.S.; Caribbean]**

Moose, Richard M. Alternative Sources of Capital. **In** *Lancaster, C. and Williamson, J., eds.*, 1986, pp. 147–61. **[G: LDCs]**

Morris, Frank E. Disinflation and the Third World Debt Crisis. **In** *Claudon, M. P., ed.*, 1986, pp. 81–84.

Moyana, Kombo. Fund Conditionality and the Socioeconomic Situation in Africa: Comment.

In *Helleiner, G. K, ed.*, 1986, pp. 113–16. [G: Africa]

Mrak, Mojmir. Multilateral Finance Institutions of Developing Countries as Promoters of Their Financial Cooperation. **In** *Khan, K. M., ed.*, 1986, pp. 149–64. [G: LDCs]

Mtei, E. I. M. Design, Implementation, and Adequacy of Fund Programs in Africa: Comments. **In** *Helleiner, G. K, ed.*, 1986, pp. 96–99. [G: Africa]

Murtfeld, Martin. The Debt Problem and External Shocks: Comment. **In** *Giersch, H., ed.*, 1986, pp. 37–41. [G: Selected Countries]

Narasimham, M. Adjustment in Africa: What Can Be Done? **In** *Helleiner, G. K, ed.*, 1986, pp. 241–49. [G: Africa]

Narasimham, M. International Monetary Arrangements and Future Adaptation: Comment. **In** *Posner, M., ed.*, 1986, pp. 182–89.

Nashashibi, Karim and Clawson, Patrick. The IMF Supply-Side Approach to Devaluation: A Response. *Oxford Bull. Econ. Statist.*, February 1986, *48*(1), pp. 73–82. [G: Sudan]

Ndegwa, Philip. The Economic Crisis in Africa. **In** *Helleiner, G. K, ed.*, 1986, pp. 45–51. [G: Africa]

Ndegwa, Philip. The World Bank in Adjustment and Economic Growth in Africa: Comments. **In** *Helleiner, G. K, ed.*, 1986, pp. 220–26. [G: Africa]

Ndekwu, E. C. International Financial Organisations and the NIEO. **In** *Onwuka, R. I. and Aluko, O., eds.*, 1986, pp. 132–49.

Nelson, Joan M. The Diplomacy of Policy-Based Lending. **In** *Feinberg, R. E., et al.*, 1986, pp. 67–86. [G: LDCs]

Nickelsburg, Gerald. Rediscounting Private Dollar Debt and Capital Flight in Ecuador. *J. Int. Money Finance*, December 1986, *5*(4), pp. 497–503. [G: Ecuador]

Nordhaus, William D. A Geometrical Analysis of the Incentives for Default and Credit Rationing: Comment [Growth and External Debt under Risk of Debt Repudiation]. *Europ. Econ. Rev.*, June 1986, *30*(3), pp. 561–64.

Nötel, R. International Credit and Finance. **In** *Kaser, M. C. and Radice, E. A., eds.*, 1986, pp. 170–295. [G: E. Europe]

Nötel, R. International Finance and Monetary Reforms. **In** *Kaser, M. C. and Radice, E. A., eds.*, 1986, pp. 520–63. [G: E. Europe]

Nunnenkamp, Peter. Bank Lending and Government Intervention in Capital Markets: Has Recycling Gone Too Far? **In** *Giersch, H., ed.*, 1986, pp. 42–65. [G: Selected LDCs; OECD]

Nyirabu, C. M. External Debt Management in the African Context: Comment. **In** *Helleiner, G. K, ed.*, 1986, pp. 181–83. [G: Africa]

O'Connell, Arturo A. External Debt and the Reform of the International Monetary System. *CEPAL Rev.*, December 1986, (30), pp. 51–66.

Okolo, Amechi. Dependency: The Highest Stage of Capitalist Domination in Africa. **In** *Onwuka, R. I. and Aluko, O., eds.*, 1986, pp. 296–320. [G: Africa]

Oliver, H. B. B. Design, Implementation, and Adequacy of Fund Programs in Africa: Comments. **In** *Helleiner, G. K, ed.*, 1986, pp. 99–100. [G: Africa]

Orlando, Frank and Teitel, Simón. Latin America's External Debt Problem: Debt-Servicing Strategies Compatible with Long-term Economic Growth. *Econ. Develop. Cult. Change*, April 1986, *34*(3), pp. 641–71. [G: Latin America]

Ortiz, Guillermo and Serra-Puche, Jaime. A Note on the Burden of the Mexican Foreign Debt. *J. Devel. Econ.*, April 1986, *21*(1), pp. 111–29. [G: Mexico]

Ouattara, Alassane D. Adjustment in Africa: What Can Be Done? **In** *Helleiner, G. K, ed.*, 1986, pp. 264–68. [G: Africa]

Ouattara, Alassane D. African Debt and Financing: What Is to Be Done? A Panel Discussion. **In** *Lancaster, C. and Williamson, J., eds.*, 1986, pp. 185–89. [G: Africa]

Ouattara, Alassane D. Design, Implementation, and Adequacy of Fund Programs in Africa. **In** *Helleiner, G. K, ed.*, 1986, pp. 68–92. [G: Africa]

Ouattara, Alassane D. Design, Implementation, and Adequacy of Fund Programs in Africa: Reply. **In** *Helleiner, G. K, ed.*, 1986, pp. 100–103. [G: Africa]

Owen, Robert F. Developing Country Debt: Policies and Prospects: Comment. **In** *Giersch, H., ed.*, 1986, pp. 127–32. [G: LDCs]

Pack, Howard. The Technological Impact of World Bank Operations. **In** *Feinberg, R. E., et al.*, 1986, pp. 161–75.

Park, Yung Chul. Foreign Debt, Balance of Payments, and Growth Prospects: The Case of the Republic of Korea, 1965–88. *World Devel.*, Special Issue, August 1986, *14*(8), pp. 1019–58. [G: S. Korea]

Patel, I. G. Aid Relationship. **In** *Patel, I. G.*, 1986, *1971*, pp. 195–211.

Patel, I. G. How to Give Aid—A Recipient's Point of View. **In** *Patel, I. G.*, 1986, *1966*, pp. 185–94.

Perlman, Mark. Sustained Recovery and Trade Liberalization: How the Transfer Problem Can Be Solved: Comment. **In** *Giersch, H., ed.*, 1986, pp. 149–51.

Phiri, David. Design, Implementation, and Adequacy of Fund Programs in Africa: Comments. **In** *Helleiner, G. K, ed.*, 1986, pp. 93–96. [G: Africa; Zambia]

Please, Stanley. Development Priorities for Sub-Saharan Africa. **In** *World Bank*, 1986, pp. 107–14. [G: Sub-Saharan Africa]

Pollan, Hans. Case Studies: IFC Projects. **In** *Hauser, H., ed. (I)*, 1986, pp. 71–80. [G: India; Yugoslavia; Central America]

Pollan, Hans. Case Studies: IFC Projects. *Aussenwirtschaft*, April 1986, *41*(1), pp. 71–80. [G: India; Yugoslavia; Central America]

Posner, Michael. Problems of International

Money, 1972–85: Introduction. In *Posner, M., ed.*, 1986, pp. 1–13.

Purcell, John F. H. and Miller, Michelle B. The World Bank and Private Capital. In *Feinberg, R. E., et al.*, 1986, pp. 111–33. **[G: LDCs]**

Raison, Timothy. Challenges to the International Donor Community. In *World Bank*, 1986, pp. 3–10.

Raymond, Robert. International Seminar on Macroeconomics: An Overview. *Europ. Econ. Rev.*, June 1986, *30*(3), pp. 477–79.

Reisen, Helmut. The Latin American Transfer Problem in Historical Perspective. In *Maddison, A., ed.*, 1986, pp. 148–54. **[G: Latin America]**

Remolona, Eli M.; Mangahas, Mahar and Pante, Filologo, Jr. Foreign Debt, Balance of Payments, and the Economic Crisis of the Philippines in 1983–84. *World Devel.*, Special Issue, August 1986, *14*(8), pp. 993–1018. **[G: Philippines]**

Rieke, Wolfgang. Jahrestagung von IWF und Weltbank 1986. (Annual Meeting of IMF and the World Bank 1986. With English summary.) *Kredit Kapital*, 1986, *19*(4), pp. 583–93.

Rodriguez, Carlos Alfredo. La Deuda Externa Argentina. (The Argentine Foreign Debt. With English summary.) *Económica (La Plata)*, July-December 1986, *32*(2), pp. 261–96. **[G: Argentina]**

Roett, Riordan. Peru: The Message from García. *Foreign Aff.*, Winter 1985/86, *64*(2), pp. 274–86. **[G: Peru]**

Rossi, José W. Considerações sobre a questão da dívida pública. (With English summary.) *Pesquisa Planejamento Econ.*, August 1986, *16*(2), pp. 413–24. **[G: Brazil]**

Rostow, Walt W. Economic Growth and the Diffusion of Power. *Challenge*, Sept./Oct. 1986, *29*(4), pp. 29–37.

Ruttan, Vernon W. Assistance to Expand Agricultural Production. *World Devel.*, January 1986, *14*(1), pp. 39–63. **[G: LDCs]**

Rwegasira, Delphin G. The Demand for External Finance: Comments. In *Lancaster, C. and Williamson, J., eds.*, 1986, pp. 20–21. **[G: Sub-Saharan Africa]**

Rybczynski, Tad M. Bank Lending and Government Intervention in Capital Markets: Has Recycling Gone Too Far? Comment. In *Giersch, H., ed.*, 1986, pp. 74–78. **[G: Selected LDCs; OECD]**

Sachs, Jeffrey. Managing the LDC Debt Crisis. *Brookings Pap. Econ. Act.*, 1986, (2), pp. 397–431. **[G: LDCs]**

Samuels, Nathaniel. Dealing with the International Debt Issue. In *Hartland-Thunberg, P. and Ebinger, C. K., eds.*, 1986, pp. 23–38.

Sanson, Carlos E. The Present Strategy to Deal with the Debt Problem. In *Dicke, D. C., ed.*, 1986, pp. 164–69.

Santow, Leonard J. The View from Wall Street. In *Claudon, M. P., ed.*, 1986, pp. 99–107. **[G: U.S.]**

Sanusi, J. O. African Economic Disequilibria and the International Monetary System. In *Helleiner, G. K, ed.*, 1986, pp. 52–67. **[G: Africa]**

Sarcevic, Petar. Two Approaches to the Debt Problem: A) Adjustment of Loan Agreements (De Lege Lata); B) Strengthening of International Monetary Soft Law (De Lege Ferenda). In *Dicke, D. C., ed.*, 1986, pp. 130–56.

Saunders, Paul and Dean, Andrew. The International Debt Situation and Linkages between Developing Countries and the OECD. *OECD Econ. Stud.*, Autumn 1986, (7), pp. 155–203. **[G: OECD; LDCs]**

Schubert, James N. The Social Developmental, and Political Impacts of Food Aid. In *Browne, W. P. and Hadwiger, D. F., eds.*, 1986, pp. 185–201.

Schulmann, Horst. From Recycling to Overindebtedness—What Went Wrong? Comment. In *Giersch, H., ed.*, 1986, pp. 15–18.

Schwartz, Anna J. External Debt and the Banking System. In *Shadow Open Market Committee (I)*, 1986, pp. 51–58. **[G: U.S.; Mexico]**

Schwartz, Anna J. Sustained Recovery and Trade Liberalization: How the Transfer Problem Can Be Solved. In *Giersch, H., ed.*, 1986, pp. 133–44.

Selowsky, Marcelo and van der Tak, Herman G. The Debt Problem and Growth. *World Devel.*, September 1986, *14*(9), pp. 1107–24. **[G: LDCs]**

Shihata, Ibrahim F. I. The Role of ICSID and the Projected Multilateral Investment Guarantee Agency (MIGA). In *Hauser, H., ed. (I)*, 1986, pp. 105–22.

Shihata, Ibrahim F. I. and Sherbiny, Naiem A. A Review of OPEC Aid Efforts. *Finance Develop.*, March 1986, *23*(1), pp. 17–20. **[G: OPEC]**

Sigmund, Paul. On Financial Blowups and Authoritarian Regimes in Latin America: Comment. In *Hartlyn, J. and Morley, S. A., eds.*, 1986, pp. 353–55. **[G: Latin America]**

Sishev, Nikolai. Public Debt Trends and Problems in the USSR. In *Herber, B. P., ed.*, 1986, pp. 111–22. **[G: U.S.S.R.]**

Sisson, Charles A. Fund-Supported Programs and Income Distribution in LDCs. *Finance Develop.*, March 1986, *23*(1), pp. 33–36. **[G: LDCs]**

Sjaastad, Larry A. Causes of and Remedies for the Debt Crisis in Latin America. In *Claudon, M. P., ed.*, 1986, pp. 249–66. **[G: Argentina; Brazil; Chile; Mexico; Venezuela]**

Sjaastad, Larry A. The Debt Problem and External Shocks. In *Giersch, H., ed.*, 1986, pp. 23–36. **[G: Selected Countries]**

Sjaastad, Larry A.; Almansi, Aquiles and Hurtado, Carlos. The Debt Crisis in Latin America. In *Lal, D. and Wolf, M., eds.*, 1986, pp. 131–81. **[G: Argentina; Brazil; Chile; Mexico; Venezuela]**

Smith, Richard J. U.S. Interests and Policy Implications: Encouraging Private Investment in Developing Countries. In *Preeg, E. H. and Bendahmane, D. B., eds.*, 1986, pp. 60–62. **[G: U.S.]**

Solís, Leopoldo. Some Thoughts on Mexico's Foreign Indebtedness. *World Econ.*, March 1986, *9*(1), pp. 65–77. **[G: Mexico]**

Solomon, Robert. The IMF in a Period of Turbulence. *Finance Develop.*, March 1986, *23*(1), pp. 41–43.

Solomon, Robert. The Report of the Group of Twenty-four: A Comment. *World Devel.*, September 1986, *14*(9), pp. 1233–36.

Soremekun, Kayode. Potency and Limitations: The Dilemma of OPEC in the NIEO. **In** *Onwuka, R. I. and Aluko, O., eds.*, 1986, pp. 150–64. **[G: OPEC]**

Sotirova, Rumiana and Gocheva, Boryiana. Credit Relations in Bulgarian Imports from the Developed Capitalist Countries. *Soviet E. Europ. Foreign Trade*, Spring 1986, *22*(1), pp. 6–18. **[G: Bulgaria]**

Stallings, Barbara. External Finance and the Transition to Socialism in Small Peripheral Societies. **In** *Fagen, R. R.; Deere, C. D. and Coraggio, J. L., eds.*, 1986, pp. 54–78. **[G: Cuba; Tanzania; Chile; Mozambique; Nicaragua]**

Starr, Joyce R. Israel: From Dream to Reality. **In** *Hartland-Thunberg, P. and Ebinger, C. K., eds.*, 1986, pp. 155–79. **[G: Israel]**

Stauffer, Robert B. The Manila–Washington Connection: Continuities in the Transnational Political Economy of Philippine Development. **In** *Stauffer, R. B.*, 1986, *1983*, pp. 103–34. **[G: Philippines]**

Stauffer, Robert B. The Marcos Legacy. **In** *Stauffer, R. B.*, 1986, pp. 171–99. **[G: Philippines]**

Street, James H. Can Mexico Break the Vicious Circle of "Stop–Go" Policy? An Institutional Overview. *J. Econ. Issues*, June 1986, *20*(2), pp. 601–12. **[G: Mexico]**

Suttle, Phil. Debt Projection Models: A Survey. *Oxford Rev. Econ. Policy*, Spring 1986, *2*(1), pp. 62–77. **[G: LDCs]**

Takagi, Yasuoki. Inflation and Cumulative Debt Outstanding of Less-Developed Countries. *J. Int. Econ.*, August 1986, *21*(1/2), pp. 61–80. **[G: LDCs]**

Talbot, Ross B. The Role of World Food Organizations. **In** *Browne, W. P. and Hadwiger, D. F., eds.*, 1986, pp. 171–84. **[G: Selected Countries]**

Taylor, Alwyn Beresford. The Question of Conditionality: Comments. **In** *Lancaster, C. and Williamson, J., eds.*, 1986, pp. 99–103. **[G: Africa]**

Taylor, Lance. Debt Crisis: North–South, North–North, and in Between. **In** *Claudon, M. P., ed.*, 1986, pp. 227–47.

Touré, Mamoudou. African Debt and Financing: What Is to Be Done? A Panel Discussion. **In** *Lancaster, C. and Williamson, J., eds.*, 1986, pp. 194–97. **[G: Africa]**

Tourinho, Octávio A. F. Endividamento externo ótimo em um modelo de equilíbrio dinâmico multissetorial: um estudo de caso para o Brasil. (With English summary.) *Pesquisa Planejamento Econ.*, December 1986, *16*(3), pp. 647–87. **[G: Brazil]**

Toye, John. Promoting the Private Sector: Should the World Bank Do More or Less? **In** *World Bank*, 1986, pp. 61–68.

Trejo Reyes, Saúl. Deuda externa: una alternativa de solución. (Foreign Debt: An Alternative Solution. With English summary.) *Estud. Econ.*, July-Dec. 1986, *1*(2), pp. 357–75. **[G: Mexico]**

Tsoukalis, Loukas. International Monetary Arrangements and Future Adaptation. **In** *Posner, M., ed.*, 1986, pp. 164–82.

Tyler, William G. The Role of International Organizations in the Adjustment Process. **In** *Giersch, H., ed.*, 1986, pp. 152–66. **[G: Selected LDCs]**

Tyson, Laura D'Andrea. The Debt Crisis and Adjustment Responses in Eastern Europe: A Comparative Perspective. *Int. Organ.*, Spring 1986, *40*(2), pp. 239–85. **[G: CMEA; LDCs]**

Tyson, Laura D'Andrea. The Debt Crisis and Adjustment Responses in Eastern Europe: A Comparative Perspective. **In** *Comisso, E. and Tyson, L., eds.*, 1986, pp. 63–110. **[G: E. Europe; E. Asia; Latin America]**

Udokang, Okon. The Energy Question and Africa's Role in a NIEO. **In** *Onwuka, R. I. and Aluko, O., eds.*, 1986, pp. 165–86. **[G: Africa]**

Valkenier, Elizabeth Kridl. The USSR and the Third World: Economic Dilemmas. **In** *Laird, R. F. and Hoffmann, E. P., eds.*, 1986, pp. 731–57. **[G: LDCs; U.S.S.R.]**

Vaubel, Roland. The Function of Governments and Intergovernmental Organizations in the International Resource Transfer—The Case of the World Bank: Comment. **In** *Balassa, B. and Giersch, H., eds.*, 1986, pp. 471–75.

Vaubel, Roland. The Role of International Organizations in the Adjustment Process: Comment. **In** *Giersch, H., ed.*, 1986, pp. 167–71. **[G: Selected LDCs]**

Viñals, José M. Deuda exterior y objectivos de balanza de pagos en España: un análisis de largo plazo. (With English summary.) *Invest. Ecón.*, September 1986, *10*(3), pp. 505–28. **[G: Spain]**

Volcker, Paul A. Statement to the U.S. House Subcommittee on Trade, Committee on Ways and Means, September 24, 1986. *Fed. Res. Bull.*, November 1986, *72*(11), pp. 773–79. **[G: U.S.]**

Volcker, Paul A. Statement to the U.S. House Committee on Foreign Affairs, June 18, 1986. *Fed. Res. Bull.*, August 1986, *72*(8), pp. 560–65. **[G: LDCs]**

de Vries, Barend A. Future Capital Flows: Critical Improvements and the Role of Coordination. **In** *Claudon, M. P., ed.*, 1986, pp. 63–77.

de Vries, Margaret Garritsen. Origins of the Debt Crisis and of the Fund's Involvement. **In** *de Vries, M. G.*, 1986, *1985*, pp. 182–90. **[G: LDCs]**

de Vries, Margaret Garritsen. The IMF in a

Changing World, 1945–85: The Outlook for World Debt as of 1985. **In** *de Vries, M. G.,* 1986, *1985,* pp. 191–98.

de Vries, Margaret Garritsen. The Role of the International Monetary Fund in the World Debt Problem. **In** *Claudon, M. P., ed.,* 1986, pp. 111–22.

de Vries, Rimmer. International Debt and Economic Instability: Commentary. **In** *Axilrod, S. H., et al.,* 1986, pp. 87–97. **[G: U.S.; Latin America]**

Wellons, Philip A. International Debt: The Behavior of Banks in a Politicized Environment. **In** *Kahler, M., ed.,* 1986, pp. 95–125. **[G: U.S.; U.K.; W. Germany; France; Japan]**

Wellons, Philip A. Multinational Institutions in the Debt Crisis: National Interest and Long Term Consequences. **In** *Claudon, M. P., ed.,* 1986, pp. 147–69. **[G: LDCs]**

Wessel, Robert H. Solving the Third World Debt Crisis. *Rivista Int. Sci. Econ. Com.,* Oct.-Nov. 1986, *33*(10–11), pp. 949–56. **[G: LDCs]**

Whitaker, Jennifer Seymour. Strategies for African Development: The Policy Setting: Crisis and Consensus. **In** *Berg, R. J. and Whitaker, J. S., eds.,* 1986, pp. 1–22. **[G: Africa]**

White, Eugene Nelson. Latin America's Debt Crisis of the 1930s: Lessons for the 1980s. **In** *Berend, I. T. and Borchardt, K., eds.,* 1986, pp. 484–96. **[G: Latin America; U.S.]**

van Wijnbergen, Sweder J. G. Macroeconomic Aspects of the Effectiveness of Foreign Aid: On the Two-Gap Model, Home Goods Disequilibrium and Real Exchange Rate Misalignment. *J. Int. Econ.,* August 1986, *21*(1/2), pp. 123–36.

Williamson, John. Adjustment in Africa: What Can Be Done? **In** *Helleiner, G. K, ed.,* 1986, pp. 249–55. **[G: Africa]**

Williamson, John. Managing the LDC Debt Crisis: Comments. *Brookings Pap. Econ. Act.,* 1986, (2), pp. 432–37.

Williamson, John. Prospects for the Flow of IMF Finance. **In** *Lancaster, C. and Williamson, J., eds.,* 1986, pp. 134–41. **[G: Sub-Saharan Africa]**

Williamson, John. The Outlook for Debt Relief or Repudiation in Latin America. *Oxford Rev. Econ. Policy,* Spring 1986, *2*(1), pp. 1–6. **[G: Latin America]**

Williamson, John. The World Bank in Adjustment and Economic Growth in Africa: Comments. **In** *Helleiner, G. K, ed.,* 1986, pp. 226–28. **[G: Africa]**

Wolf, Martin. From Recycling to Overindebtedness—What Went Wrong? Comment. **In** *Giersch, H., ed.,* 1986, pp. 19–22.

Wood, D. Joseph. The World Bank of Tomorrow: Policies and Operations. **In** *World Bank,* 1986, pp. 89–99.

Wood, D. Joseph. The World Bank: Restoring Balance—A Task for Both Debtor and Creditor. **In** *Preeg, E. H. and Bendahmane, D. B., eds.,* 1986, pp. 51–56.

Yoshitomi, Masaru. Sustained Recovery and Trade Liberalization: How the Transfer Problem Can Be Solved: Comment. **In** *Giersch, H., ed.,* 1986, pp. 145–48.

Zakariya, Hasan S. Financing Petroleum Development in the Third World: The Role of the Public International Sector. *J. World Trade Law,* July:Aug. 1986, *20*(4), pp. 417–40. **[G: LDCs]**

Zedillo Ponce de Leon, Ernesto. Mexico's Recent Balance-of-Payments Experience and Prospects for Growth. *World Devel.,* Special Issue, August 1986, *14*(8), pp. 963–91. **[G: Mexico]**

Zedillo Ponce de Leon, Ernesto. The Debt Problem: A Borrower's Perspective. **In** *Posner, M., ed.,* 1986, pp. 130–38. **[G: Mexico]**

500 Administration; Business Finance; Marketing; Accounting

5000 General

Heinen, Edmund and Dill, Peter. Unternehmenskultur—Überlegungen aus betriebswirtschaftlicher Sicht. (With English summary.) *Z. Betriebswirtshaft,* March 1986, *56*(3), pp. 202–18.

Moore, Peter G. Positioning Business Schools in the UK. *Lloyds Bank Rev.,* April 1986, (160), pp. 36–51. **[G: U.K.; U.S.]**

510 Administration

511 Organization and Decision Theory

5110 Organization and Decision Theory

Ács, János. Strategic Planning Models and Risk Management. **In** *Daboni, L.; Montesano, A. and Lines, M., eds.,* 1986, pp. 375–91.

Alchian, Armen A. and Demsetz, Harold. Production, Information Costs, and Economic Organization. **In** *Barney, J. B. and Ouchi, W. G., eds.,* 1986, *1972,* pp. 129–55.

Alchian, Armen A. and Demsetz, Harold. Production, Information Costs, and Economic Organization. **In** *Putterman, L., ed.,* 1986, *1972,* pp. 111–34.

Apte, P. G. Aspects of Corporate Decision Making: An Econometric Investigation. *Indian Econ. Rev.,* July-Dec. 1986, *21*(2), pp. 185–215. **[G: India]**

Armour, Henry Ogden and Teece, David J. Organizational Structure and Economic Performance: A Test of the Multidivisional Hypothesis. **In** *Barney, J. B. and Ouchi, W. G., eds.,* 1986, *1978,* pp. 187–204.

Arrow, Kenneth J. Exposition of the Theory of Choice under Uncertainty. **In** *[Marschak, J.],* 1986, *1972,* pp. 19–55.

Axsäter, Sven and Nuttle, Henry L. W. Aggregating Items in Multi-level Lot Sizing. **In** *Axsäter, S.; Schneeweiss, C. and Silver, E., eds.,* 1986, pp. 109–18.

Barney, Jay B. and Ouchi, William G. Learning from Organizational Economics. **In** *Barney,*

J. B. and Ouchi, W. G., eds., 1986, pp. 423–45.

Barney, Jay B. and Ouchi, William G. The Search for New Microeconomic and Organization Theory Paradigms. **In** *Barney, J. B. and Ouchi, W. G., eds.*, 1986, pp. 1–17.

Baysinger, Barry D. and Zardkoohi, Asghar. Technology, Residual Claimants, and Corporate Control. *J. Law, Econ., Organ.*, Fall 1986, *2*(2), pp. 339–49. **[G: U.S.]**

Beck, Paul J. Internal Control Technologies within Industrial Organizations. *Managerial Dec. Econ.*, June 1986, *7*(2), pp. 81–89.

Beckmann, Martin J. Decisions over Time. **In** *[Marschak, J.]*, 1986, *1972*, pp. 141–59.

Bello, Joseph A. Behavioural Problems of Operational Research Implementation in Developing Countries. **In** *Damachi, U. G. and Seibel, H. D., eds.*, 1986, pp. 232–69. **[G: Nigeria]**

Bernheim, B. Douglas. Axiomatic Characterizations of Rational Choice in Strategic Environments. *Scand. J. Econ.*, 1986, *88*(3), pp. 473–88.

Black, Max. Some Questions about Bayesian Decision Theory. **In** *Daboni, L.; Montesano, A. and Lines, M., eds.*, 1986, pp. 57–66.

Blanning, Robert W. A System for Natural Language Communication between a Decision Model and Its Users. **In** *Pau, L. F., ed.*, 1986, pp. 77–85.

Bonus, Holger. The Cooperative Association as a Business Enterprise: A Study in the Economics of Transactions. *J. Inst. Theoretical Econ.*, June 1986, *142*(2), pp. 310–39.

Borrmann, Werner A. Strategic Resource Management: Securing International Competitiveness through Competitive Resources. **In** *Macharzina, K. and Staehle, W. H., eds.*, 1986, pp. 275–83.

Bossányi, Katalin. Economy on the Way to Democratization: The Switch-Over to Collective Management in Hungarian Industry. *Acta Oecon.*, 1986, *37*(3–4), pp. 285–304. **[G: Hungary]**

Boyer, André and Billon, Alain. Promotion de la qualité de la recherche en gestion initiatives et coopération. (Promotion of the Quality and Research in Management Initiatives and Cooperation. With English summary.) *Écon. Soc.*, June 1986, *20*(6), pp. 249–54.

Brauers, Jutta and Weber, Martin. Szenarioanalyse als Hilfsmittel der strategischen Planung: Methodenvergleich und Darstellung einer neuen Methode. (With English summary.) *Z. Betriebswirtschaft*, July 1986, *56*(7), pp. 631–52.

Brockhoff, Klaus. The Incentive Limits of Firms: A Comparative Institutional Assessment of Bureaucracy: Comment. **In** *Balassa, B. and Giersch, H., eds.*, 1986, pp. 231–34.

Brownell, Peter and Hirst, Mark. Reliance on Accounting Information, Budgetary Participation, and Task Uncertainty: Tests of a Three-Way Interaction. *J. Acc. Res.*, Autumn 1986, *24*(2), pp. 241–49. **[G: U.S.]**

Brownell, Peter and McInnes, Morris. Budgetary Participation, Motivation, and Managerial Performance. *Accounting Rev.*, October 1986, *61*(4), pp. 587–600. **[G: U.S.]**

Brunetti, Giorgio. Il controllo direzionale nel processo di cambiamento strategico–organizzativo delle aziende di credito. (The Role of Management Control in Banking's Strategic and Organizational Change. With English summary.) *Ricerche Econ.*, Apr.-Sept. 1986, *40*(2–3), pp. 478–88. **[G: Italy]**

Bühner, Rolf. Rendite, Kosten der Leitungsdelegation und Geschäftsbereichsorganisation. (With English summary.) *Z. Betriebswirtschaft*, Apr.-May 1986, *56*(4/5), pp. 370–84. **[G: W. Germany]**

Casson, Mark. General Theories of the Multinational Enterprise: Their Relevance to Business History. **In** *Hertner, P. and Jones, G., eds.*, 1986, pp. 42–63.

Cave, Martin. Computers in Soviet Management, 1963–1984. **In** *Altmann, F.-L., ed.*, 1986, pp. 133–50. **[G: U.S.S.R.]**

Coase, Ronald H. The Nature of the Firm. **In** *Putterman, L., ed.*, 1986, *1937*, pp. 72–85.

Coffee, John C., Jr. Shareholders versus Managers: The Strain in the Corporate Web. *Mich. Law Rev.*, October 1986, *85*(1), pp. 1–109. **[G: U.S.]**

Cohen, Susan I. Truth-Telling, Dominant Strategies, and Iterative Groves Mechanisms. *Public Choice*, 1986, *51*(3), pp. 333–43.

Collender, Robert Neil and Chalfant, James A. An Alternative Approach to Decisions under Uncertainty Using the Empirical Moment-Generating Function. *Amer. J. Agr. Econ.*, August 1986, *68*(3), pp. 727–31.

Crémer, Jacques. Cooperation in Ongoing Organizations. *Quart. J. Econ.*, February 1986, *101*(1), pp. 33–49.

Crew, Michael A. and Crocker, Keith J. Vertically Integrated Governance Structures and Optimal Institutional Arrangements for Cogeneration. *J. Inst. Theoretical Econ.*, June 1986, *142*(2), pp. 340–59. **[G: U.S.]**

Davidson, Donald. A New Basis for Decision Theory. **In** *Daboni, L.; Montesano, A. and Lines, M., eds.*, 1986, pp. 43–56.

Demski, Joel S. and Sappington, David E. M. Line-Item Reporting, Factor Acquisition, and Subcontracting. *J. Acc. Res.*, Autumn 1986, *24*(2), pp. 250–69.

Desreumaux, Alain. Formation des structures d'entreprise: revue des travaux et quelques hypothèses. (Determinants of Organizational Structures: A Review of Literature and Some Proposals. With English summary.) *Écon. Soc.*, June 1986, *20*(6), pp. 3–41.

Diederich, Helmut. Entwicklung und Stand der Verkehrsbetriebslehre. (With English summary.) *Z. Betriebswirtschaft*, January 1986, *56*(1), pp. 51–88.

van Donselaar, Karel and Wijngaard, Jacob. Practical Application of the Echelon Approach in a System with Divergent Product Structures. **In** *Axsäter, S.; Schneeweiss, C. and Sil-*

ver, E., eds., 1986, pp. 182–96. [G: Netherlands]

Doron, Gideon. Telling the Big Stories—Policy Responses to Analytical Complexity: A Comment [Big Decisions and a Culture of Decision Making] [The Narrative Structure of Policy Analysis]. *J. Policy Anal. Manage.*, Summer 1986, *5*(4), pp. 798–802.

Dyckhoff, Harald. Informationsverdichtung zur Alternativenbewertung. (With English summary.) *Z. Betriebswirtshaft*, September 1986, *56*(9), pp. 848–72.

Fama, Eugene F. and Jensen, Michael C. Separation of Ownership and Control. **In** *Barney, J. B. and Ouchi, W. G., eds.*, 1986, *1983*, pp. 276–98.

Filios, Vassilios P. The Conceptual Framework of a Human Resource Accounting System. *Rivista Int. Sci. Econ. Com.*, March 1986, *33*(3), pp. 281–92.

FitzRoy, Felix R. and Mueller, Dennis C. Cooperation and Conflict in Contractual Organizations. **In** *Mueller, D. C.*, 1986, *1984*, pp. 52–77.

Fordyce, Kenneth J. and Sullivan, Gerald A. Decision Simulation (DSIM)—One Outcome of Combining Expert Systems and Decision Support Systems. **In** *Pau, L. F., ed.*, 1986, pp. 31–40.

Franko, Lawrence G. Expansion of Japanese Companies Abroad: The Management of Cross-Cultural Interface: Comment. **In** *Pugel, T. A., ed.*, 1986, pp. 201–05. [G: U.S.; Japan]

Gaitanides, Michael. Strategic Planning and Structuring of Organization. **In** *Macharzina, K. and Staehle, W. H., eds.*, 1986, pp. 261–74.

Gaitanides, Michael and Wicher, Hans. Strategien und Strukturen innovationsfähiger Organisationen. (With English summary.) *Z. Betriebswirtshaft*, Apr.-May 1986, *56*(4/5), pp. 385–403.

Gaynor, Martin. Misperceptions, Moral Hazard and Incentives in Groups. *Managerial Dec. Econ.*, December 1986, *7*(4), pp. 279–82.

Gibbard, Allan. A Characterization of Decision Matrices That Yield Instrumental Expected Utility. **In** *Daboni, L.; Montesano, A. and Lines, M., eds.*, 1986, pp. 139–48.

Gorman, W. M. Assembling Efficient Organizations? **In** *[Arrow, K. J.], Vol. 3*, 1986, pp. 213–28.

Graves, Stephen C., et al. Two-Stage Production Planning in a Dynamic Environment. **In** *Axsäter, S.; Schneeweiss, C. and Silver, E., eds.*, 1986, pp. 9–43.

Günther, Hans O. The Design of an Hierarchical Model for Production Planning and Scheduling. **In** *Axsäter, S.; Schneeweiss, C. and Silver, E., eds.*, 1986, pp. 227–60.

Gustavsen, Björn. Evolving Patterns of Enterprise Organisation: The Move toward Greater Flexibility. *Int. Lab. Rev.*, July-Aug. 1986, *125*(4), pp. 367–82.

Hagen, Ole. Surviving Implications of Expected Utility Theory. **In** *Daboni, L.; Montesano, A. and Lines, M., eds.*, 1986, pp. 201–14.

Hakuli, Markku and Rouotamaa, Vesa. A Contextual Approach to Research on Managerial Work. *Liiketaloudellinen Aikak.*, 1986, *35*(1), pp. 39–47.

Hall, H. Keith; Moore, James C. and Whinston, Andrew B. A Theoretical Basis for Expert Systems. **In** *Pau, L. F., ed.*, 1986, pp. 11–19.

Hannan, Michael T. Uncertainty, Diversity, and Organizational Change. **In** *Smelser, N. J. and Gerstein, D. R., eds.*, 1986, pp. 73–94.

Hattori, Tamio. Technology Transfer and Management Systems. *Devel. Econ.*, December 1986, *24*(4), pp. 314–25. [G: Japan]

Hayashi, Kichiro. Expansion of Japanese Companies Abroad: The Management of Cross-Cultural Interface. **In** *Pugel, T. A., ed.*, 1986, pp. 175–99. [G: Japan; U.S.]

Hedderich, Rudolf. Die Grundlagen des Handelsbetriebes. (With English summary.) *Z. Betriebswirtshaft*, June 1986, *56*(6), pp. 484–99.

Heinrich, Claus E. and Schneeweiss, Christoph. Multi-stage Lot-Sizing for General Production Systems. **In** *Axsäter, S.; Schneeweiss, C. and Silver, E., eds.*, 1986, pp. 150–81.

Heinrich, Lutz J. Zur Arbeitsteilung zwischen Betriebswirtschaftslehre und Betriebsinformatik—zugleich eine Stellungnahme zu A.-W. Scheer's Beitrag "EDV-orientierte Betriebswirtschaftslehre." (With English summary.) Z. *Betriebswirtshaft*, September 1986, *56*(9), pp. 895–901.

Hill, Stephen and Blyton, Paul. The Practice of Decision-making—Some Further Evidence. *Managerial Dec. Econ.*, March 1986, *7*(1), pp. 25–28.

Himmelstrand, Ulf; Brulin, Göran and Swedberg, Richard. Control, Motivation, and Structure: The "New Managerial Philosophies" vs. Industrial Democracy. *Econ. Anal. Workers' Manage.*, 1986, *20*(1), pp. 1–21. [G: Sweden]

Honda, Nakaji, et al. Decision Support System Using Fuzzy Reasoning and Evaluation. **In** *Pau, L. F., ed.*, 1986, pp. 41–49.

Horváth, Péter, et al. Budgetierung in industriellen Grossunternehmen—Eine vergleichende Fallstudienanalyse. (With English summary.) Z. *Betriebswirtshaft*, January 1986, *56*(1), pp. 24–39. [G: W. Germany]

Intriligator, Michael D. and Sheshinski, Eytan. Toward a Theory of Planning. **In** *[Arrow, K. J.], Vol. 1*, 1986, pp. 135–58.

Janssen, Ron and Nijkamp, Peter. A Typological Approach to Multiple Criteria Conflict Analysis. *Conflict Manage. Peace Sci.*, Spring 1986, *9*(2), pp. 45–53.

Jensen, Michael C. and Meckling, William H. Theory of the Firm: Managerial Behavior, Agency Costs, and Ownership Structure. **In** *Barney, J. B. and Ouchi, W. G., eds.*, 1986, *1976*, pp. 214–75.

Kaplan, Thomas J. The Narrative Structure of Policy Analysis. *J. Policy Anal. Manage.*, Summer 1986, *5*(4), pp. 761–78.

Klein, Benjamin; Crawford, Robert G. and Alchian, Armen A. Vertical Integration, Appropriable Rents, and the Competitive Contracting Process. In *Barney, J. B. and Ouchi, W. G., eds.*, 1986, *1978*, pp. 39–71. [G: U.S.]

Kohlöffel, Klaus and Zietemann, Ulrich. Betriebswirtschaftliche Aspekte von arbeitszeitverkürzenden Massnahmen. (With English summary.) *Z. Betriebswirtshaft*, October 1986, *56*(10), pp. 1030–38.

König, Wolfgang and Niedereichholz, Joachim. Der Fortschritt der Informationstechnik und seine Auswirkungen auf Managementtechniken. (With English summary.) *Z. Betriebswirtshaft*, January 1986, *56*(1), pp. 4–23.

Krieger, Martin H. Big Decisions and a Culture of Decisionmaking. *J. Policy Anal. Manage.*, Summer 1986, *5*(4), pp. 779–97.

Landau, Kurt and Bokranz, Rainer. Istzustands-Analyse in Arbeitssystemen—Methoden und Erkenntnisse zur Erfassung von Istzuständen an Arbeitsplätzen und in Arbeitsfeldern. (With English summary.) *Z. Betriebswirtshaft*, August 1986, *56*(8), pp. 728–54.

Lange, Mark; Luksetich, William and Jacobs, Philip. Managerial Objectives of Symphony Orchestras. *Managerial Dec. Econ.*, December 1986, *7*(4), pp. 273–78. [G: U.S.]

Langlois, Richard N. Rationality, Institutions, and Explanation. In *Langlois, R. N., ed.*, 1986, pp. 225–55.

Leijonhufvud, Axel. Capitalism and the Factory System. In *Langlois, R. N., ed.*, 1986, pp. 203–23.

Linz, Susan J. Emigrants as Expert Informants on Soviet Management Decision-Making: A Methodological Note. *Comp. Econ. Stud.*, Fall 1986, *28*(3), pp. 65–89. [G: U.S.S.R.]

Loasby, Brian J. Organisation, Competition, and the Growth of Knowledge. In *Langlois, R. N., ed.*, 1986, pp. 41–57.

Luyten, Robert. System-Based Heuristics for Multi-echelon Distribution Systems. In *Axsäter, S.; Schneeweiss, C. and Silver, E., eds.*, 1986, pp. 50–91.

Malecki, Edward J. Technological Imperatives and Modern Corporate Strategy. In *Scott, A. J. and Storper, M., eds.*, 1986, pp. 67–79.

Marschak, Thomas A. Computation in Organizations: The Comparison of Price Mechanisms and Other Adjustment Processes. In *[Marschak, J.]*, 1986, *1972*, pp. 237–81.

Martin, Claude. Vers une approche cinématique du fonctionnement de l'entreprise. Une nouvelle typologie des modèles de prévision et de décision. (Towards a Dynamic Approach to the Functioning of the Organisation. A New Typology of Forecast and Decision Models. With English summary.) *Écon. Soc.*, June 1986, *20*(6), pp. 223–47.

Martin, Maryse. Fiabilité et prix de l'information analyse de sensibilité par les arbres de décision. (Sensibility Analysis by Decision-Tree. With English summary.) *Écon. Soc.*, December 1986, *20*(12), pp. 105–20.

Mathé, Jean-Charles and Gontier, Jean-Louis. Gestion de la dimension technologique de l'entreprise. (Management of Technological Dimensions of the Firm. With English summary.) *Écon. Soc.*, December 1986, *20*(12), pp. 3–36.

McGuire, C. B. and Radner, Roy. Decision and Organization: Preface to the Second Edition. In *[Marschak, J.]*, 1986, pp. vii–xxiv.

Mertens, Peter; Allgeyer, Karlheinz and Däs, Harald. Betriebliche Expertensysteme in deutschsprachigen Ländern. Versuch einer Bestandsaufnahme. (With English summary.) *Z. Betriebswirtshaft*, September 1986, *56*(9), pp. 905–41. [G: W. Germany; Switzerland; Austria]

Meško, Ivan. Transformation of Piecewise Linear and Quadratic Functions: A Reply. *Econ. Anal. Workers' Manage.*, 1986, *20*(4), pp. 423–26.

Middleton, Elliott. A Behavioral Model of "Animal Spirits." *Metroecon.*, February 1986, *38*(1), pp. 39–51.

Milgrom, Paul and Roberts, John. Relying on the Information of Interested Parties. *Rand J. Econ.*, Spring 1986, *17*(1), pp. 18–32.

Muckstadt, John A. Planning Component Delivery Intervals in Constrained Assembly Systems. In *Axsäter, S.; Schneeweiss, C. and Silver, E., eds.*, 1986, pp. 132–49.

Mueller, Dennis C. The Modern Corporation: Profits, Power, Growth and Performance: Introduction. In *Mueller, D. C.*, 1986, pp. 1–11.

Munera, Hector A. The Generalized Means Model (GMM) for Non-deterministic Decision Making: A Unified Treatment for the Two Contending Theories. In *Daboni, L.; Montesano, A. and Lines, M., eds.*, 1986, pp. 161–84.

Nagel, Stuart and Long, John. P/G Percent Analysis: A Decision-Aiding Program. In *Pau, L. F., ed.*, 1986, pp. 137–45.

Nan, Zhu. A Comment on Optimization of Business Processes by Mixed Integer Programming. *Econ. Anal. Workers' Manage.*, 1986, *20*(4), pp. 419–22.

Negro, Yves. L'apport de l'analyse de notoriété au positionnement stratégique des P.M.I. (Contribution of Notoriety's Analysis to the Positioning of the Small Venture. With English summary.) *Écon. Soc.*, June 1986, *20*(6), pp. 67–99.

Ostojić, Slobodan. Decentralization without Hierarchy: Experience of Yugoslav Enterprises. *Econ. Anal. Workers' Manage.*, 1986, *20*(2), pp. 119–34. [G: Yugoslavia]

Pau, L. F. An Expert System Kernel for the Analysis of Strategies over Time. In *Pau, L. F., ed.*, 1986, pp. 107–12.

Pienkos, Andrew. Organizational Contradiction and Policy Inertia in Yugoslav Institutional Evolution. *J. Econ. Issues*, June 1986, *20*(2), pp. 583–92. [G: Yugoslavia]

Polonchek, John A.; Slovin, Myron B. and Sushka, Marie E. Tender-Offer Premia as a Management Signal. *Managerial Dec. Econ.*, March 1986, *7*(1), pp. 69–76. [G: U.S.]

Pope, Robin. Consistency and Expected Utility Theory. In *Daboni, L.; Montesano, A. and*

Lines, M., eds., 1986, pp. 215–29.

Porter, Michael E. The Contributions of Industrial Organization to Strategic Management. **In** *Barney, J. B. and Ouchi, W. G., eds.*, 1986, *1981*, pp. 381–96.

Pulkkinen, Kyösti. The Relationship between Corporate Strategies and Knowledge Representation as a Factor to Be Considered in Designing Organizational Structures and Decision Support Systems. *Liiketaloudellinen Aikak.*, 1986, *35*(3), pp. 196–212.

Putterman, Louis G. The Economic Nature of the Firm: Overview. **In** *Putterman, L., ed.*, 1986, pp. 1–29.

Radner, Roy. Allocation of a Scarce Resource under Uncertainty: An Example of a Team. **In** *[Marschak, J.]*, 1986, *1972*, pp. 217–36.

Radner, Roy. Normative Theories of Organization: An Introduction. **In** *[Marschak, J.]*, 1986, *1972*, pp. 177–88.

Radner, Roy. Normative Theory of Individual Decision: An Introduction. **In** *[Marschak, J.]*, 1986, *1972*, pp. 1–18.

Radner, Roy. Teams. **In** *[Marschak, J.]*, 1986, *1972*, pp. 189–215.

Rao, T. V. S. Ramomahan. Welfare Economics of Organizational Decisions and Its Implications for Industrial Economics. *Indian Econ. J.*, Oct.-Dec. 1986, *34*(2), pp. 87–105.

Reix, Robert. Processus d'informatisation et conception de l'organisation. (Computerization Process and Organization Design. With English summary.) *Écon. Soc.*, December 1986, *20*(12), pp. 121–53.

Reuter, Edzard. Wunsch und Wirklichkeit in der Unternehmensführung. (With English summary.) *Z. Betriebswirtschaft*, November 1986, *56*(11), pp. 1052–63.

Ribhegge, Hermann. Genossenschaftsgesinnung in entscheidungslogischer Perspektive. (The "Cooperative Spirit" Viewed in Terms of Economic Decision Theory. With English summary.) *Kyklos*, 1986, *39*(4), pp. 574–95.

Rosling, Kaj. Optimal Lot-Sizing for Dynamic Assembly Systems. **In** *Axsäter, S.; Schneeweiss, C. and Silver, E., eds.*, 1986, pp. 119–31.

Rossi, Guido A. On Utility Functions in a Financial Context. **In** *Daboni, L.; Montesano, A. and Lines, M., eds.*, 1986, pp. 153–60.

Sah, Raaj Kumar and Stiglitz, Joseph E. The Architecture of Economic Systems: Hierarchies and Polyarchies. *Amer. Econ. Rev.*, September 1986, *76*(4), pp. 716–27.

Schneeweiss, Christoph. Some Modelling Theoretic Remarks on Multi-stage Production Planning. **In** *Axsäter, S.; Schneeweiss, C. and Silver, E., eds.*, 1986, pp. 1–8.

Schneider, Dieter. Management Mistakes—Do We Need More History in Business Economics? **In** *Pohl, H. and Rudolph, B., eds.*, 1986, pp. 27–40.

Schreyögg, Georg and Steinmann, Horst. Zur Praxis strategischer Kontrolle—Ergebnisse einer explorativen Studie. (With English summary.) *Z. Betriebswirtschaft*, January 1986, *56*(1), pp. 40–50.

Schultz, Reinhart. Ordinale Wahrscheinlichkeitsurteile, Wahrscheinlichkeitsdominanz und die Anzahl verschiedener Umweltszenarien. (With English summary.) *Z. Betriebswirtschaft*, October 1986, *56*(10), pp. 989–1001.

Souder, H. Ray and Damachi, Nicholas. Introduction of Computers to Management in Developing Countries. **In** *Damachi, U. G. and Seibel, H. D., eds.*, 1986, pp. 333–55.

Stadtler, Hartmut. Hierarchical Production Planning: Tuning Aggregate Planning with Sequencing and Scheduling. **In** *Axsäter, S.; Schneeweiss, C. and Silver, E., eds.*, 1986, pp. 197–226.

Stoica, M. and Hartulari, Carmen. Modalities and Principles to Design Heuristic Algorithms. *Econ. Computat. Cybern. Stud. Res.*, 1986, *21*(4), pp. 31–36.

Sufrin, Sidney C. A Note on Strategic and Synthetic Planning. *Rivista Int. Sci. Econ. Com.*, June-July 1986, *33*(6–7), pp. 612–27.

Sugden, Robert. Regret, Recrimination and Rationality. **In** *Daboni, L.; Montesano, A. and Lines, M., eds.*, 1986, pp. 67–80.

Tirole, Jean. Hierarchies and Bureaucracies: On the Role of Collusion in Organizations. *J. Law, Econ., Organ.*, Fall 1986, *2*(2), pp. 181–214.

Tu, Xu-Yen. Intelligent Control and Intelligent Management for Large Scale Systems. **In** *Pau, L. F., ed.*, 1986, pp. 87–91.

Van Hulle, C. Corporate Restructuring. *Tijdschrift Econ. Manage.*, 1986, *31*(4), pp. 417–33. **[G: Belgium]**

Virtanen, Visa and Laitinen, Erkki K. Vastaperustetun pienyrityksen eloonjäänti/konkurssiprosessin selittäminen. (The Success/Failure Process of a Newly-Founded Business Firm. With English summary.) *Liiketaloudellinen Aikak.*, 1986, *35*(3), pp. 250–63. **[G: Finland]**

Watanabe, Takehiko and Mochizuki, Hiroshi. Perception Gap between the U.S. and Japan: Delegation and Sharing of Authority and Responsibility. **In** *Finn, R. B., ed.*, 1986, pp. 85–100. **[G: U.S.; Japan]**

Wilkins, Mira. Defining a Firm: History and Theory. **In** *Hertner, P. and Jones, G., eds.*, 1986, pp. 80–95.

Williamson, Oliver E. The Economics of Governance: Framework and Implications. **In** *Langlois, R. N., ed.*, 1986, pp. 171–202.

Williamson, Oliver E. The Incentive Limits of Firms: A Comparative Institutional Assessment of Bureaucracy. **In** *Balassa, B. and Giersch, H., eds.*, 1986, pp. 204–30.

Williamson, Oliver E. The Multidivisional Structure. **In** *Barney, J. B. and Ouchi, W. G., eds.*, 1986, *1975*, pp. 163–87.

Williamson, Oliver E. Transaction-Cost Economics: The Governance of Contractual Relations. **In** *Barney, J. B. and Ouchi, W. G., eds.*, 1986, *1979*, pp. 98–129.

Willmer, M. A. P. Can Artificial Intelligence Do Better Than Humans at Leadership? **In** *Pau, L. F., ed.*, 1986, pp. 241–58.

Wintrobe, Ronald and Breton, Albert. Organizational Structure and Productivity. *Amer. Econ.*

Rev., June 1986, *76*(3), pp. 530–38.

Wohlgemuth, André C. Der Aufbau eines modernen Management-Development-Informationssystems (dargestellt am Beispiel einer Schweizer Grossbank). (With English summary.) *Z. Betriebswirtshaft,* June 1986, *56*(6), pp. 538–53.

512 Managerial Economics

5120 Managerial Economics

Albach, Horst. Allgemeine Betriebswirtschaftslehre Zum Gedenken an Erich Gutenberg. (With English summary.) *Z. Betriebswirtshaft,* July 1986, *56*(7), pp. 578–613.

Albrecht, Hellmut K. Success Factors in International Management: The "Turnaround" Case of a Multinational's European Subsidiary. **In** *Macharzina, K. and Staehle, W. H., eds.,* 1986, pp. 285–93. **[G: W. Germany]**

Alchian, Armen A. and Demsetz, Harold. Production, Information Costs, and Economic Organization. **In** *Putterman, L., ed.,* 1986, *1972,* pp. 111–34.

Allen, Ralph C.; Rabianski, Joseph S. and Stone, Jack H. A Managerial Model of the Effect of Product Market Structure on Firm Location. *J. Reg. Sci.,* May 1986, *26*(2), pp. 393–409.

Amihud, Yakov; Dodd, Peter and Weinstein, Mark. Conglomerate Mergers, Managerial Motives and Stockholder Wealth. *J. Banking Finance,* October 1986, *10*(3), pp. 401–10.

Aoki, Masahiko. Horizontal vs. Vertical Information Structure of the Firm. *Amer. Econ. Rev.,* December 1986, *76*(5), pp. 971–83.

Asquith, Paul and Mullins, David W., Jr. Equity Issues and Offering Dilution. *J. Finan. Econ.,* Jan./Feb. 1986, *15*(1/2), pp. 61–89. **[G: U.S.]**

Axsäter, Sven and Nuttle, Henry L. W. Aggregating Items in Multi-level Lot Sizing. **In** *Axsäter, S.; Schneeweiss, C. and Silver, E., eds.,* 1986, pp. 109–18.

Ballantine, John W.; Cleveland, Frederick W. and Koeller, C. Timothy. Profit Differences: A Management Approach. *J. Post Keynesian Econ.,* Winter 1985-86, *8*(2), pp. 277–97. **[G: U.S.]**

Bannon, Bob. Fedwatching. *Bus. Econ.,* October 1986, *21*(4), pp. 43–47.

Beck, Paul J. Internal Control Technologies within Industrial Organizations. *Managerial Dec. Econ.,* June 1986, *7*(2), pp. 81–89.

Bello, Joseph A. Behavioural Problems of Operational Research Implementation in Developing Countries. **In** *Damachi, U. G. and Seibel, H. D., eds.,* 1986, pp. 232–69. **[G: Nigeria]**

Bello, Joseph A. The Changing Dimensions of the Nigerian Business Environment and Their Behavioural Implications. **In** *Damachi, U. G. and Seibel, H. D., eds.,* 1986, pp. 3–29. **[G: Nigeria]**

Bozeman, Barry; Link, Albert N. and Zardkoohi, Asghar. An Economic Analysis of R&D Joint Ventures. *Managerial Dec. Econ.,* December 1986, *7*(4), pp. 263–66.

Brauers, Jutta and Weber, Martin. Szenarioanalyse als Hilfsmittel der strategischen Planung: Methodenvergleich und Darstellung einer neuen Methode. (With English summary.) *Z. Betriebswirtshaft,* July 1986, *56*(7), pp. 631–52.

Brownell, Peter and McInnes, Morris. Budgetary Participation, Motivation, and Managerial Performance. *Accounting Rev.,* October 1986, *61*(4), pp. 587–600. **[G: U.S.]**

Bühner, Rolf. Rendite, Kosten der Leitungsdelegation und Geschäftsbereichsorganisation. (With English summary.) *Z. Betriebswirtshaft,* Apr.-May 1986, *56*(4/5), pp. 370–84. **[G: W. Germany]**

Bulmash, Samuel. An Agency Perspective of the Firm's Life-cycle. *Managerial Dec. Econ.,* June 1986, *7*(2), pp. 107–11.

Cameron, Trudy Ann and White, K. J. The Demand for Computer Services: A Disaggregate Decision Model. *Managerial Dec. Econ.,* March 1986, *7*(1), pp. 37–41.

Chen, Zhao-Ying. Decision Support System for Management of Oil Pipeline. **In** *Pau, L. F., ed.,* 1986, pp. 103–06.

Chiang, Shin-Hwan. Cost Savings, Wages and the Growth of the Firm. *Econ. J.,* September 1986, *96*(383), pp. 798–807.

Clifford, James; Jarke, Matthias and Lucas, Henry C., Jr. Designing Expert Systems in a Business Environment. **In** *Pau, L. F., ed.,* 1986, pp. 221–31.

Coase, Ronald H. The Nature of the Firm. **In** *Barney, J. B. and Ouchi, W. G., eds.,* 1986, *1937,* pp. 80–98.

Coase, Ronald H. The Nature of the Firm. **In** *Putterman, L., ed.,* 1986, *1937,* pp. 72–85.

Coate, Malcolm B. Relative Market Share and Profitability. *J. Behav. Econ.,* Spring/Summer 1986, *15*(1/2), pp. 41–53.

Cubbin, John S. and Leech, Dennis. Growth versus Profit-Maximization: A Simultaneous-Equations Approach to Testing the Marris Model. *Managerial Dec. Econ.,* June 1986, *7*(2), pp. 123–31. **[G: U.K.]**

Dahmén, Erik. Företagarverksamheten och den ekonomiska omvandlingen. (Entrepreneurial Activity and Changing Economic Conditions. With English summary.) *Ekon. Samfundets Tidskr.,* 1986, *39*(3), pp. 119–30.

Dale, Barrie. Experience with Quality Circles and Quality Costs. **In** *Moores, B., ed.,* 1986, pp. 36–49. **[G: U.K.]**

De, Suranjan. Integrated Problem Solving in Manufacturing. **In** *Pau, L. F., ed.,* 1986, pp. 277–82.

DeAngelo, David J. The Business Economist at Work: Pennsylvania Power and Light Co. *Bus. Econ.,* April 1986, *21*(2), pp. 57–59. **[G: U.S.]**

Defourny, Jacques. The Economic Performance of Self-Managed Firms: A Comparative Perspective. *Ann. Pub. Co-op. Econ.,* Jan.-March 1986, *57*(1), pp. 3–9.

Demetrius, David G. Expert Systems and Board

Level Decisions. **In** *Pau, L. F., ed.*, 1986, pp. 233–40.

Demski, Joel S. and Sappington, David E. M. Line-Item Reporting, Factor Acquisition, and Subcontracting. *J. Acc. Res.*, Autumn 1986, *24*(2), pp. 250–69.

DeSarbo, Wayne and Rao, Vithala R. A Constrained Unfolding Methodology for Product Positioning. *Marketing Sci.*, Winter 1986, *5*(1), pp. 1–19. **[G: U.S.]**

Dichtl, Erwin; Köglmayr, Hans-Georg and Müller, Stefan. Die Auslandsorientierung als Voraussetzung für Exporterfolge. (With English summary.) *Z. Betriebswirtshaft*, November 1986, *56*(11), pp. 1064–76. **[G: W. Germany]**

van Donselaar, Karel and Wijngaard, Jacob. Practical Application of the Echelon Approach in a System with Divergent Product Structures. **In** *Axsäter, S.; Schneeweiss, C. and Silver, E., eds.*, 1986, pp. 182–96. **[G: Netherlands]**

Drago, Robert. Participatory Management in Capitalist Firms: An Analysis of "Quality Circles." *Econ. Anal. Workers' Manage.*, 1986, *20*(3), pp. 233–49. **[G: U.S.]**

Drexl, Andreas. Erhebungskosten versus Schätzgenauigkeit bei der Stichprobeninventur—Ein integrierender Ansatz. (With English summary.) *Z. Betriebswirtshaft*, June 1986, *56*(6), pp. 509–24.

Duncan, Joseph W. Federal Statistics and Business Economists. *Bus. Econ.*, July 1986, *21*(3), pp. 26–30. **[G: U.S.]**

Eliashberg, Jehoshua and Jeuland, Abel P. The Impact of Competitive Entry in a Developing Market upon Dynamic Pricing Strategies. *Marketing Sci.*, Winter 1986, *5*(1), pp. 20–36.

Farmer, Roger E. A. and Winter, Ralph A. The Role of Options in the Resolution of Agency Problems: A Comment [Theory of the Firm: Managerial Behaviour, Agency Costs and Ownership Structure]. *J. Finance*, December 1986, *41*(5), pp. 1157–70.

Fershtman, Chaim and Spiegel, Uriel. Learning by Doing, Inventory and Optimal Pricing Policy. *J. Econ. Bus.*, February 1986, *38*(1), pp. 19–26.

FitzRoy, Felix R. and Kraft, Kornelius. Profitability and Profit-Sharing. *J. Ind. Econ.*, December 1986, *35*(2), pp. 113–30. **[G: W. Germany]**

Forbes, Kevin F. Limited Liability and the Development of the Business Corporation. *J. Law, Econ., Organ.*, Spring 1986, *2*(1), pp. 163–77. **[G: U.S.]**

Galbraith, Craig S. and Kay, Neil M. Towards a Theory of Multinational Enterprise. *J. Econ. Behav. Organ.*, March 1986, *7*(1), pp. 3–19.

Gelders, Ludo F.; Maes, Johan and Van Wassenhove, Luk N. A Branch and Bound Algorithm for the Multi Item Single Level Capacitated Dynamic Lotsizing Problem. **In** *Axsäter, S.; Schneeweiss, C. and Silver, E., eds.*, 1986, pp. 92–108.

Ghosh, Dipak. Effect of Fixed Cost under Uncertainty and Access to the Capital Market. *Managerial Dec. Econ.*, September 1986, *7*(3), pp. 211–13.

Gilad, Benjamin. Go Industrial Young Man, and Then Go Behavioral. *Bus. Econ.*, April 1986, *21*(2), pp. 28–33. **[G: U.S.]**

Goering, Patricia A. Consumer Learning and Optimal Pricing Strategies for Products of Unknown Quality. **In** *Samuelson, L., ed.*, 1986, pp. 53–77.

Goldstein, Jonathan P. Markup Variability and Flexibility: Theory and Empirical Evidence. *J. Bus.*, Part 1, October 1986, *59*(4), pp. 599–621.

Grabowski, Henry G. and Mueller, Dennis C. Managerial and Stockholder Welfare Models of Firm Expenditures. **In** *Mueller, D. C.*, 1986, *1972*, pp. 81–107.

Graves, Stephen C., et al. Two-Stage Production Planning in a Dynamic Environment. **In** *Axsäter, S.; Schneeweiss, C. and Silver, E., eds.*, 1986, pp. 9–43.

Günther, Hans O. The Design of an Hierarchical Model for Production Planning and Scheduling. **In** *Axsäter, S.; Schneeweiss, C. and Silver, E., eds.*, 1986, pp. 227–60.

Haller, Hans. Market Power, Objectives of the Firm, and Objectives of Shareholders. *J. Inst. Theoretical Econ.*, December 1986, *142*(4), pp. 716–26.

Haugen, Robert A. and Senbet, Lemma W. The Role of Options in the Resolution of Agency Problems: A Reply. *J. Finance*, December 1986, *41*(5), pp. 1171–73.

Heinrich, Claus E. and Schneeweiss, Christoph. Multi-stage Lot-Sizing for General Production Systems. **In** *Axsäter, S.; Schneeweiss, C. and Silver, E., eds.*, 1986, pp. 150–81.

Hoadley, Walter E. Tomorrow's Business Economist. *Bus. Econ.*, April 1986, *21*(2), pp. 5–10. **[G: U.S.]**

Hodder, James E. and Ilan, Yael A. Declining Prices and Optimality When Costs Follow an Experience Curve. *Managerial Dec. Econ.*, December 1986, *7*(4), pp. 229–34.

Holmes, John. The Organization and Locational Structure of Production Subcontracting. **In** *Scott, A. J. and Storper, M., eds.*, 1986, pp. 80–106.

Hoskins, W. Lee. Professional Certification: An Idea in Search of a Problem. *Bus. Econ.*, April 1986, *21*(2), pp. 15–20. **[G: U.S.]**

Houston, Douglas A. and Howe, John S. An Economic Rationale for Couponing: Reply. *Quart. J. Bus. Econ.*, Autumn 1986, *25*(4), pp. 75–76.

d'Iribarne, Philippe. Régulation sociale vie des entreprises et performances économiques. (Social Regulation, the Activity of Firms and Economic Performances. With English summary.) *Revue Écon.*, May 1986, *37*(3), pp. 429–54. **[G: France; Netherlands; U.S.; Cameroon]**

Janeway, William H. Doing Capitalism: Notes on the Practice of Venture Capitalism. *J. Econ. Issues*, June 1986, *20*(2), pp. 431–41.

Johansson, Börje and Larsson, Jan. Characteristics of the Firm and the Speed of Technology Adoption. *Ricerche Econ.*, Oct.-Dec. 1986, *40*(4), pp. 675–95.

Jönsson, Henrik and Silver, Edward A. Overview of a Stock Allocation Model for a Two-Echelon Push System Having Identical Units at the Lower Echelon. **In** *Axsäter, S.; Schneeweiss, C. and Silver, E., eds.*, 1986, pp. 44–49.

Kacprzyk, Janusz. A "Down-to-Earth" Managerial Decision Making via a Fuzzy-Logic-Based Representation of Commonsense Knowledge. **In** *Pau, L. F., ed.*, 1986, pp. 57–64.

Kahneman, Daniel; Knetsch, Jack L. and Thaler, Richard H. Fairness as a Constraint on Profit Seeking: Entitlements in the Market. *Amer. Econ. Rev.*, September 1986, *76*(4), pp. 728–41.

Knoeber, Charles R. Golden Parachutes, Shark Repellents, and Hostile Tender Offers. *Amer. Econ. Rev.*, March 1986, *76*(1), pp. 155–67. **[G: U.S.]**

Knudsen, Morten. Virksomhederne kan gøre det bedre. (Danish Enterprises Have Unrealized Potentials. With English summary.) *Nationaløkon. Tidsskr.*, 1986, *124*(2), pp. 166–74. **[G: Denmark]**

Kosko, Bart. Optimal Fuzzy Hierarchical Decisions. **In** *Pau, L. F., ed.*, 1986, pp. 51–56.

Kosy, Donald W. and Wise, Ben P. Overview of Rome: A Reason-Oriented Modeling Environment. **In** *Pau, L. F., ed.*, 1986, pp. 21–30.

Kouri, Pentti J. K. Franco Modigliani's Contributions to Economics. *Scand. J. Econ.*, 1986, *88*(2), pp. 311–34.

Kroll, Mark and Johnson, Herb. A Note on Managerial Behavior and the Theory of the Firm. *J. Behav. Econ.*, Spring/Summer 1986, *15* (1/2), pp. 123–34.

Lal, Rajiv. Delegating Pricing Responsibility to the Salesforce. *Marketing Sci.*, Spring 1986, *5*(2), pp. 159–68.

Lall, Sanjaya. Technological Development and Export Performance in LDCs: Leading Engineering and Chemical Firms in India. *Weltwirtsch. Arch.*, 1986, *122*(1), pp. 80–92. **[G: India]**

Lambert, Richard A. Executive Effort and Selection of Risky Projects. *Rand J. Econ.*, Spring 1986, *17*(1), pp. 77–88.

Lazear, Edward P. Retail Pricing and Clearance Sales. *Amer. Econ. Rev.*, March 1986, *76*(1), pp. 14–32.

Lee, Chi-wen Jevons. Information Content of Financial Columns. *J. Econ. Bus.*, February 1986, *38*(1), pp. 27–39. **[G: U.S.]**

Lefebvre, Louis A., et al. L'impact de la technologie informatique sur la main-d'oeuvre dans les organisations. (The Impact of Information Technology on Human Resources in Organizations. With English summary.) *L'Actual. Econ.*, December 1986, *62*(4), pp. 557–78. **[G: Canada]**

Levedahl, J. William. Profit Maximizing Pricing of Cents Off Coupons: Promotion or Price Discrimination? *Quart. J. Bus. Econ.*, Autumn 1986, *25*(4), pp. 56–70. **[G: U.S.]**

Liu, Tai-Ying and Hsu, Shuh-Tzy. The Validity of TIER's Business Climate Indicator. *Ifo-Studien*, 1986, *32*(1–3), pp. 71–80. **[G: Taiwan]**

Lukka, Kari. Taloustieteen metodologiset suuntaukset: liiketaloustieteen ja kansantaloustieteen vertailu. (Methodological Approaches in Economic Sciences: A Comparison between Business Economics and Economics. With English summary.) *Liiketaloudellinen Aikak.*, 1986, *35*(2), pp. 133–49.

Luyten, Robert. System-Based Heuristics for Multi-echelon Distribution Systems. **In** *Axsäter, S.; Schneeweiss, C. and Silver, E., eds.*, 1986, pp. 50–91.

Maes, R. and van Dijk, J. E. M. A User-Friendly Propositional Formalism for a Managerial DSS-Generator. **In** *Pau, L. F., ed.*, 1986, pp. 65–76.

Marmuse, Christian and Baron, Bernard. Faisabilité et risques des projets d'activités nouvelles Propositions méthodologiques. (The Evaluation of the Feasibility of New Activities Projects. Methodological Proposals. With English summary.) *Écon. Soc.*, June 1986, *20*(6), pp. 43–66.

Masten, Scott E. Institutional Choice and the Organization of Production: The Make-or-Buy Decision. *J. Inst. Theoretical Econ.*, September 1986, *142*(3), pp. 493–509.

McMillan, Robert A. The Business Economist at Work: The BFGoodrich Company. *Bus. Econ.*, January 1986, *21*(1), pp. 58–60. **[G: U.S.]**

Mefford, Robert N. Introducing Management into the Production Function. *Rev. Econ. Statist.*, February 1986, *68*(1), pp. 96–104. **[G: U.S.]**

Mirus, Rolf and Yeung, Bernard. "Buy-Back" in International Trade: A Rationale. *Weltwirtsch. Arch.*, 1986, *122*(2), pp. 371–74.

Morgan, George Emir and Martin, John D. A Rationale for Planning: Implications from the Economic Theory of the Firm. *Managerial Dec. Econ.*, December 1986, *7*(4), pp. 219–28.

Mortiboys, Ron. Quality in the Boardroom. **In** *Moores, B., ed.*, 1986, pp. 13–24.

Muckstadt, John A. Planning Component Delivery Intervals in Constrained Assembly Systems. **In** *Axsäter, S.; Schneeweiss, C. and Silver, E., eds.*, 1986, pp. 132–49.

Negro, Yves. L'apport de l'analyse de notoriété au positionnement stratégique des P.M.I. (Contribution of Notoriety's Analysis to the Positioning of the Small Venture. With English summary.) *Écon. Soc.*, June 1986, *20*(6), pp. 67–99.

Neun, Stephen P. and Santerre, Rexford E. Dominant Stockownership and Profitability. *Managerial Dec. Econ.*, September 1986, *7*(3), pp. 207–10. **[G: U.S.]**

O'Neil, Brian F. Information—A Viable Substitute for Inventory. *Logist. Transp. Rev.*, March 1986, *22*(1), pp. 83–89.

Paroush, Jacob. Sales-Optimization under an Unstable Profit-Constraint. *Managerial Dec.*

Econ., June 1986, *7*(2), pp. 145–46.

Peles, Yoram C. A Note on Yield Variance and Mix Variance. *Accounting Rev.*, April 1986, *61*(2), pp. 325–29.

Pitelis, Christos N. and Sugden, Roger. The Separation of Ownership and Control in the Theory of the Firm: A Reappraisal. *Int. J. Ind. Organ.*, March 1986, *4*(1), pp. 69–86.

Pollack, Elliott D. The Business Economist at Work: Valley National Bank. *Bus. Econ.*, October 1986, *21*(4), pp. 48–50. **[G: U.S.]**

Price, Frank. How Does Britain Rate on Quality? **In** *Moores, B., ed.*, 1986, pp. 25–35. **[G: U.K.]**

Putterman, Louis G. The Economic Nature of the Firm: Overview. **In** *Putterman, L., ed.*, 1986, pp. 1–29.

Quirk, James P. and Terasawa, Katsuaki. Sample Selection and Cost Underestimation Bias in Pioneer Projects. *Land Econ.*, May 1986, *62*(2), pp. 192–200. **[G: U.S.]**

Radner, Roy. Allocation of a Scarce Resource under Uncertainty: An Example of a Team. **In** *[Marschak, J.]*, 1986, *1972*, pp. 217–36.

Radner, Roy. The Internal Economy of Large Firms. *Econ. J.*, Supplement 1986, *96*, pp. 1–22.

Rampa, Lorenzo. Commercio e inflazione. Un'analisi dinamica dei prezzi in sistemi con intermediazione dei prodotti. (Commerce and Inflation. A Dynamic Analysis of Prices in Systems with Commercial Firms. With English summary.) *Ricerche Econ.*, Apr.-Sept. 1986, *40*(2–3), pp. 303–16.

Raţiu-Sucio, Camelia and Oprescu, G. Adjusting the Supply Process with Stocking Stochastic Models. *Econ. Computat. Cybern. Stud. Res.*, 1986, *21*(3), pp. 13–22.

Ravid, S. A. and Sudit, E. F. Application of Production Standards in Complex Organizations under Uncertainty. *J. Econ. Bus.*, December 1986, *38*(4), pp. 307–16.

Reekie, W. Duncan. The Economics of Business and the Business of Economics. *S. Afr. J. Econ.*, December 1986, *54*(4), pp. 362–80. **[G: S. Africa]**

Ribhegge, Hermann. Genossenschaftsgesinnung in entscheidungslogischer Perspektive. (The "Cooperative Spirit" Viewed in Terms of Economic Decision Theory. With English summary.) *Kyklos*, 1986, *39*(4), pp. 574–95.

Rieber, William J. An Economic Rationale for Couponing: A Comment. *Quart. J. Bus. Econ.*, Autumn 1986, *25*(4), pp. 71–74.

Riordan, Michael H. A Note on Optimal Procurement Contracts. *Info. Econ. Policy*, September 1986, *2*(3), pp. 211–19.

Rixhon, Philippe. Intelligent Knowledge-Based Systems: A Tool for Manufacturing Planning and Scheduling. **In** *Pau, L. F., ed.*, 1986, pp. 283–88.

Rob, Rafael. The Design of Procurement Contracts. *Amer. Econ. Rev.*, June 1986, *76*(3), pp. 378–89.

Rosling, Kaj. Optimal Lot-Sizing for Dynamic Assembly Systems. **In** *Axsäter, S.; Schneeweiss, C. and Silver, E., eds.*, 1986, pp. 119–31.

Ross, Howard N. and Krausz, Joshua. Buyers' and Sellers' Prices and Administered Behavior. *Rev. Econ. Statist.*, August 1986, *68*(3), pp. 369–78. **[G: U.S.]**

Rudel, Sylvie. Une gestion particulière des risques dans la toute petite entreprise. (Special Risks Management in Small Firms. With English summary.) *Schweiz. Z. Volkswirtsch. Statist.*, September 1986, *122*(3), pp. 389–403.

Savitt, Ronald. Time, Space and Competition: Formulations for the Development of Marketing Strategy. *Managerial Dec. Econ.*, March 1986, *7*(1), pp. 11–18.

Schipper, Katherine and Smith, Abbie. A Comparison of Equity Carve-outs and Seasoned Equity Offerings: Share Price Effects and Corporate Restructuring. *J. Finan. Econ.*, Jan./Feb. 1986, *15*(1/2), pp. 153–86. **[G: U.S.]**

Schneeweiss, Christoph. Some Modelling Theoretic Remarks on Multi-stage Production Planning. **In** *Axsäter, S.; Schneeweiss, C. and Silver, E., eds.*, 1986, pp. 1–8.

Schott, Francis H. Tomorrow's Business Economist—An Alternative View. *Bus. Econ.*, April 1986, *21*(2), pp. 11–14. **[G: U.S.]**

Seitz, H. Firms Responses to Changes in Demand: Some Insight from Survey-Data. *Empirical Econ.*, 1986, *11*(2), pp. 111–23. **[G: W. Germany]**

Shaiken, Harley; Herzenberg, Stephen and Kuhn, Sarah. The Work Process under More Flexible Production. *Ind. Relat.*, Spring 1986, *25*(2), pp. 167–83. **[G: U.S.]**

Shapiro, Matthew D. Capital Utilization and Capital Accumulation: Theory and Evidence. *J. Appl. Econometrics*, July 1986, *1*(3), pp. 211–34. **[G: U.S.]**

Shieh, Yeung-Nan. Industrial Location and the Divorce of Management and Ownership: Comment. *Ann. Reg. Sci.*, March 1986, *20*(1), pp. 81–84.

Shleifer, Andrei and Vishny, Robert W. Large Shareholders and Corporate Control. *J. Polit. Econ.*, Part 1, June 1986, *94*(3), pp. 461–88.

Silver, Mick and Tull, Donald. Pricing and the Flat-maximum Principle. *Managerial Dec. Econ.*, September 1986, *7*(3), pp. 203–06.

Springer, Robert F. and Frech, H. E., III. Deterring Fraud: The Role of Resale Price Maintenance. *J. Bus.*, July 1986, *59*(3), pp. 433–49.

Stadtler, Hartmut. Hierarchical Production Planning: Tuning Aggregate Planning with Sequencing and Scheduling. **In** *Axsäter, S.; Schneeweiss, C. and Silver, E., eds.*, 1986, pp. 197–226.

Straszak, A., et al. Computer Aided Learning in a Two-level Economy with Nonlinear Economic Regulators. **In** *Pau, L. F., ed.*, 1986, pp. 185–91.

Sufrin, Sidney C. A Note on Strategic and Synthetic Planning. *Rivista Int. Sci. Econ. Com.*, June-July 1986, *33*(6–7), pp. 612–27.

Suominen, Seppo I. Dynamisk modell för vertikal integration. (A Dynamic Model of Vertical Integration. With English summary.) *Ekon. Samfundets Tidskr.*, 1986, *39*(4), pp. 239–46.

Swidler, Steve. Consumption and Price Effects of State-run Liquor Monopolies. *Managerial Dec. Econ.*, March 1986, *7*(1), pp. 49–55. **[G: U.S.]**

Teece, David J. Transactions Cost Economics and the Multinational Enterprise: An Assessment. *J. Econ. Behav. Organ.*, March 1986, *7*(1), pp. 21–45. **[G: U.K.; U.S.]**

Templé, Philippe. Le processus d'innovation dans les entreprises. (Innovation Process and Firms. With English summary.) *Écon. Appl.*, 1986, *39*(3), pp. 583–614. **[G: France]**

Trossmann, Ernst. Betriebliche Bedarfsplanung auf der Grundlage einer dynamischen Produktionstheorie. (With English summary.) *Z. Betriebswirtschaft*, September 1986, *56*(9), pp. 827–47.

Trueman, Brett. Why Do Managers Voluntarily Release Earnings Forecasts? *J. Acc. Econ.*, March 1986, *8*(1), pp. 53–71.

Tufer, Armin C. and Aiken, Leisa B. Performance Evaluation Techniques for International Operations: Impacts on Managerial Incentives and Strategic Planning Considerations. **In** *Holzer, H. P. and Schoenfeld, H.-M. W., eds.*, 1986, pp. 163–73.

Tybout, James. A Firm-Level Chronicle of Financial Crises in the Southern Cone. *J. Devel. Econ.*, December 1986, *24*(2), pp. 371–400. **[G: Chile; Argentina; Uruguay]**

Uvalic, Milica. The Investment Behaviour of a Labour-Managed Firm. *Ann. Pub. Co-op. Econ.*, Jan.-March 1986, *57*(1), pp. 11–33.

Văduva, I. A Computer Simulation Model for Estimating the Optimum Renewal Moment of an Equipment. *Econ. Computat. Cybern. Stud. Res.*, 1986, *21*(4), pp. 13–20.

Van Dyke, Daniel T. How to Measure the Performance of a Business Economics Unit. *Bus. Econ.*, April 1986, *21*(2), pp. 21–24. **[G: U.S.]**

Van Hulle, C. Corporate Restructuring. *Tijdschrift Econ. Manage.*, 1986, *31*(4), pp. 417–33. **[G: Belgium]**

Verbeke, A. and Winkelmans, W. The Illusion of Belgian Sea Port Policy Evaluation of Structural Effectiveness and Development of a Policy Alternative. *Int. J. Transport Econ.*, June 1986, *13*(2), pp. 209–20. **[G: Belgium]**

Virtanen, Visa and Laitinen, Erkki K. Vastaperustetun pienyrityksen eloonjäänti/konkurssiprosessin selittäminen. (The Success/Failure Process of a Newly-Founded Business Firm. With English summary.) *Liiketaloudellinen Aikak.*, 1986, *35*(3), pp. 250–63. **[G: Finland]**

Walter, John D., Jr. The Business Economist at Work: Dow Corning Corporation. *Bus. Econ.*, July 1986, *21*(3), pp. 46–48. **[G: U.S.]**

Wegner, Trevor. A Microcomputer-based Decision-support System for Manpower Planning. *Managerial Dec. Econ.*, June 1986, *7*(2), pp. 91–98. **[G: S. Africa; U.K.]**

Wildemann, Horst. Einführungsstrategien für neue Produktionstechnologien—dargestellt an CAD/CAM-Systemen und Flexiblen Fertigungssystemen. (With English summary.) *Z. Betriebswirtschaft*, Apr.-May 1986, *56*(4/5), pp. 337–69. **[G: W. Germany]**

Williamson, Oliver E. Managerial Discretion and Business Behaviour. **In** *Williamson, O. E.*, 1986, *1963*, pp. 6–31.

Wise, Ben P. and Kosy, Donald W. Model-Based Evaluation of Long-range Resource Allocation Plans. **In** *Pau, L. F., ed.*, 1986, pp. 93–102.

Witt, Ulrich. Firms' Market Behavior under Imperfect Information and Economic Natural Selection. *J. Econ. Behav. Organ.*, September 1986, *7*(3), pp. 265–90.

Yoshino, Toshihiko. A New YRI Business Index: Based on Microeconomic Data. *Ifo-Studien*, 1986, *32*(1–3), pp. 91–104.

Young, Richard A. A Note on "Economically Optimal Performance Evaluation and Control Systems": The Optimality of Two-Tailed Investigations. *J. Acc. Res.*, Spring 1986, *24*(1), pp. 231–40.

Zachmann, Roberto. Reduction of Working Time as a Means to Reduce Unemployment: A Micro-economic Perspective. *Int. Lab. Rev.*, Mar.-Apr. 1986, *125*(2), pp. 163–75.

Zafiris, Nicos. Profitability as a Criterion of Enterprise Efficiency. *Ann. Pub. Co-op. Econ.*, September 1986, *57*(3), pp. 345–58.

513 Business and Public Administration

5130 General

Austin, James E. and Ickis, John C. Management, Managers, and Revolution. *World Devel.*, July 1986, *14*(7), pp. 775–90. **[G: Nicaragua]**

Bello, Joseph A. Quality Control in Delegated Administrative Work. **In** *Damachi, U. G. and Seibel, H. D., eds.*, 1986, pp. 273–91. **[G: Nigeria]**

Boyer, André and Billon, Alain. Promotion de la qualité de la recherche en gestion initiatives et coopération. (Promotion of the Quality and Research in Management Initiatives and Cooperation. With English summary.) *Écon. Soc.*, June 1986, *20*(6), pp. 249–54.

Charoux, Eric. The Identification of Black Management Potential. **In** *Smollan, R., ed.*, 1986, pp. 178–88. **[G: S. Africa]**

Ekpo-Ufot, Abel. Personnel Functions, Practices and Productivity in Nigeria. **In** *Damachi, U. G. and Seibel, H. D., eds.*, 1986, pp. 292–314. **[G: Nigeria]**

Freedman, Audrey and Goldstein, Kenneth. Labor Market Data from the Conference Board. **In** *Dennis, B. D., ed.*, 1986, pp. 34–41. **[G: U.S.]**

Freedman, Marc R. The Elusive Promise of Management Cooperation in the Performing Arts. **In** *DiMaggio, P. J., ed.*, 1986, pp. 199–213. **[G: U.S.]**

Gilardi, Jean-Claude. Le détermination des critères de choix utilsés par le travailleur. (The Determination of the Criteria Influencing Worker's Choice. With English summary.)

Écon. Soc., December 1986, *20*(12), pp. 155–86.

Jacoby, Sanford M. and Mitchell, Daniel J. B. Alternative Sources of Labor Market Data. **In** *Dennis, B. D., ed.*, 1986, pp. 42–49. **[G: U.S.]**

Jones, David D. Rejoinder to Brown's Comment and a Reaction to Schilling's "Estimating the Present Value...." [Inflation Rates Implicit in Discounting Personal Injury Economic Losses]. *J. Risk Ins.*, September 1986, *53*(3), pp. 489–500. **[G: U.S.]**

Jones, Ian S. Apprentice Training Costs in British Manufacturing Establishments: Some New Evidence. *Brit. J. Ind. Relat.*, November 1986, *24*(3), pp. 333–62. **[G: U.K.]**

Knudsen, Morten. Virksomhederne kan gøre det bedre. (Danish Enterprises Have Unrealized Potentials. With English summary.) *Nationaløkon. Tidsskr.*, 1986, *124*(2), pp. 166–74. **[G: Denmark]**

Matulovich, Michael. Organisational Programmes of Black Advancement: Training Needs and Techniques. **In** *Smollan, R., ed.*, 1986, pp. 189–202. **[G: S. Africa]**

Peterson, Richard A. From Impresario to Arts Administrator: Formal Accountability in Nonprofit Cultural Organizations. **In** *DiMaggio, P. J., ed.*, 1986, pp. 161–83. **[G: U.S.]**

Souder, H. Ray and Damachi, Nicholas. Introduction of Computers to Management in Developing Countries. **In** *Damachi, U. G. and Seibel, H. D., eds.*, 1986, pp. 333–55.

Watanabe, Takehiko and Mochizuki, Hiroshi. Perception Gap between the U.S. and Japan: Delegation and Sharing of Authority and Responsibility. **In** *Finn, R. B., ed.*, 1986, pp. 85–100. **[G: U.S.; Japan]**

5131 Business Administration

Akhtar, Haq Nawaz. Manpower Development in Public Enterprises. **In** *U.N., Dept. of Technical Co-operation for Development*, 1986, pp. 149–61. **[G: Pakistan]**

Antle, Rick and Smith, Abbie. An Empirical Investigation of the Relative Performance Evaluation of Corporate Executives. *J. Acc. Res.*, Spring 1986, *24*(1), pp. 1–39. **[G: U.S.]**

Baysinger, Barry D. and Zardkoohi, Asghar. Technology, Residual Claimants, and Corporate Control. *J. Law, Econ., Organ.*, Fall 1986, *2*(2), pp. 339–49. **[G: U.S.]**

Bhatt, V. V. Entrepreneurship Development: India's Experience. *Finance Develop.*, March 1986, *23*(1), pp. 48–49. **[G: India]**

Franko, Lawrence G. Expansion of Japanese Companies Abroad: The Management of Cross-Cultural Interface: Comment. **In** *Pugel, T. A., ed.*, 1986, pp. 201–05. **[G: U.S.; Japan]**

Gershenberg, Irving. Labor, Capital, and Management Slack in Multinational and Local Firms in Kenyan Manufacturing. *Econ. Develop. Cult. Change*, October 1986, *35*(1), pp. 163–78. **[G: Kenya]**

Guest, David E. Workers' Participation and Personnel Policy in the United Kingdom: Some Case Studies. *Int. Lab. Rev.*, Nov.-Dec. 1986, *125*(6), pp. 685–702. **[G: U.K.]**

Hakuli, Markku and Rouotamaa, Vesa. A Contextual Approach to Research on Managerial Work. *Liiketaloudellinen Aikak.*, 1986, *35*(1), pp. 39–47.

Hayashi, Kichiro. Expansion of Japanese Companies Abroad: The Management of Cross-Cultural Interface. **In** *Pugel, T. A., ed.*, 1986, pp. 175–99. **[G: Japan; U.S.]**

Himmelstrand, Ulf; Brulin, Göran and Swedberg, Richard. Control, Motivation, and Structure: The "New Managerial Philosophies" vs. Industrial Democracy. *Econ. Anal. Workers' Manage.*, 1986, *20*(1), pp. 1–21. **[G: Sweden]**

Holmstrom, Bengt and Ricart i Costa, Joan. Managerial Incentives and Capital Management. *Quart. J. Econ.*, November 1986, *101*(4), pp. 835–60.

Jensen, Flemming Skov. Industriens og arbejdskraftens vilkår. (Production Strategies and Labour Market Requirements of Increasing Danish Export. With English summary.) *Nationaløkon. Tidsskr.*, 1986, *124*(2), pp. 175–78. **[G: Denmark]**

Kaplan, Donald M. Managerial Excellence at Thrift Institutions. **In** *Federal Home Loan Bank of San Francisco*, 1986, pp. 151–57. **[G: U.S.]**

Kolosova, E. Five Questions to the Manager. *Prob. Econ.*, August 1986, *29*(4), pp. 90–93. **[G: U.S.S.R.]**

Kumar, Brij and Steinmann, Horst. Managementkonflikte zwischen entsandten und lokalen Führungskräften in deutschen und japanischen Unternehmungen. (With English summary.) *Z. Betriebswirtschaft*, December 1986, *56*(12), pp. 1182–96. **[G: W. Germany; Japan]**

Linz, Susan J. Emigrants as Expert Informants on Soviet Management Decision-Making: A Methodological Note. *Comp. Econ. Stud.*, Fall 1986, *28*(3), pp. 65–89. **[G: U.S.S.R.]**

Montgomery, John D. Levels of Managerial Leadership in Southern Africa. *J. Devel. Areas*, October 1986, *21*(1), pp. 15–29. **[G: Southern Africa]**

Murphy, Kevin J. Incentives, Learning, and Compensation: A Theoretical and Empirical Investigation of Managerial Labor Contracts. *Rand J. Econ.*, Spring 1986, *17*(1), pp. 59–76. **[G: U.S.]**

Navajas, Fernando H. Bonos, incentivos gerenciales, eficiencia y control en la empresa pública. (Bonds, Managerial Incentives, Efficiency and Control in the Public Enterprise. With English summary.) *Económica (La Plata)*, Jan.-June 1986, *32*(1), pp. 81–118.

Roos, Poul. Workers' Participation and Personnel Policy in Denmark. *Int. Lab. Rev.*, Nov.-Dec. 1986, *125*(6), pp. 703–13. **[G: Denmark]**

Santerre, Rexford E. and Neun, Stephen P. Stock Dispersion and Executive Compensation. *Rev. Econ. Statist.*, November 1986, *68*(4), pp. 685–87. **[G: U.S.]**

513 Business and Public Administration

Schroeder, Sandra J. and Finlay, William. Internal Labor Markets, Professional Domination, and Gender: A Comparison of Laboratory Employees in Hospitals and Chemical/Oil Firms. *Soc. Sci. Quart.*, December 1986, *67*(4), pp. 827–40. **[G: U.S.]**

Schwartz, Alan. Search Theory and the Tender Offer Auction. *J. Law, Econ., Organ.*, Fall 1986, *2*(2), pp. 229–53.

Shum, K. K. and Sigel, L. T. Managerial Reform and Enterprise Performance: Assessing the Experiment in Shenzhen and Zhuhai. **In** *Jao, Y. C. and Leung, C. K., eds.*, 1986, pp. 201–25. **[G: China]**

Suojanen, Waino W., et al. The Type A Manager as Addict: Can the Behavior Pattern Be Changed? *Liiketaloudellinen Aikak.*, 1986, *35*(2), pp. 91–104. **[G: U.S.]**

Tehranian, Hassan and Waegelein, James F. Short-term Bonus Plan Adoption and Stock Market Performance—Proxy and Industry Effects: A Note. *Financial Rev.*, May 1986, *21*(2), pp. 345–53. **[G: U.S.]**

Tesař, Vladimír. The Role and Problems of an Enterprise Director in the Czechoslovak Automobile Industry. *Int. Lab. Rev.*, July-Aug. 1986, *125*(4), pp. 435–45. **[G: Czechoslovakia]**

Washio, Hiroaki. The Provision of Manuals and Japanese Private Technology Transfer. *Devel. Econ.*, December 1986, *24*(4), pp. 326–33. **[G: Japan]**

Wegner, Trevor. A Microcomputer-based Decision-support System for Manpower Planning. *Managerial Dec. Econ.*, June 1986, *7*(2), pp. 91–98. **[G: S. Africa; U.K.]**

Woo, Jennie Hay. Graduate Degrees and Job Success: Managers in One U.S. Corporation. *Econ. Educ. Rev.*, 1986, *5*(3), pp. 227–37. **[G: U.S.]**

5132 Public Administration

Barrett, Ina. Administrative Problems of Small Island States with Particular Reference to the States of the Eastern Caribbean. *Soc. Econ. Stud.*, March 1986, *35*(1), pp. 199–213. **[G: Caribbean]**

Berkowitz, Monroe. The Administration of Workers' Compensation. **In** *Chelius, J., ed.*, 1986, pp. 237–49. **[G: U.S.]**

Blackburn, Clark Waring, Jr. The Tug Hill Approach: Circuit Riders and Technology. **In** *Chicoine, D. L. and Walzer, N., eds.*, 1986, pp. 143–57. **[G: U.S.]**

Chang, C. Y. Bureaucracy and Modernization: A Case Study of the Special Economic Zones in China. **In** *Jao, Y. C. and Leung, C. K., eds.*, 1986, pp. 105–23. **[G: China]**

Clemens, John K. and Gomillion, Merrilee R. Classical Management Strategies for Public Administrators. *J. Policy Anal. Manage.*, Winter 1986, *5*(2), pp. 373–77.

Elmore, Richard F. Graduate Education in Public Management: Working the Seams of Government. *J. Policy Anal. Manage.*, Fall 1986, *6*(1), pp. 69–83.

Foell, Wesley K. and Siddayao, Corazon Morales. Microcomputers and Energy Policy Analysis: Growth Prospects in Developing Countries. *World Devel.*, Oct./Nov. 1986, *14*(10/11), pp. 1311–27. **[G: Indonesia; Philippines]**

Guzda, Henry P. Ellis Island a Welcome Site? Only after Years of Reform. *Mon. Lab. Rev.*, July 1986, *109*(7), pp. 30–36. **[G: U.S.]**

Iun', O. Developing Management's Planning Mechanism. *Prob. Econ.*, November 1986, *29*(7), pp. 3–19. **[G: U.S.S.R.]**

Jagannathan, N. Vijay. Corruption, Delivery Systems, and Property Rights. *World Devel.*, January 1986, *14*(1), pp. 127–32. **[G: India; LDCs]**

James, Jeffrey. Bureaucratic, Engineering and Economic Men: Decision-Making for Technology in Tanzania's State-Owned Enterprises. **In** *[Streeten, P.]*, 1986, pp. 217–39. **[G: Tanzania]**

Lui, Francis T. A Dynamic Model of Corruption Deterrence. *J. Public Econ.*, November 1986, *31*(2), pp. 215–36.

Montgomery, John D. Levels of Managerial Leadership in Southern Africa. *J. Devel. Areas*, October 1986, *21*(1), pp. 15–29. **[G: Southern Africa]**

Oechsler, Walter A. Public Administration and Civil Service in Europe—Approaches to Reform. **In** *Macharzina, K. and Staehle, W. H., eds.*, 1986, pp. 369–79. **[G: W. Europe]**

Rose-Ackerman, Susan. Reforming Public Bureaucracy through Economic Incentives? *J. Law, Econ., Organ.*, Spring 1986, *2*(1), pp. 131–61.

Shughart, William F., II; Tollison, Robert D. and Goff, Brian L. Bureaucratic Structure and Congressional Control. *Southern Econ. J.*, April 1986, *52*(4), pp. 962–72. **[G: U.S.]**

Thompson, Fred and Jones, L. R. Controllership in the Public Sector. *J. Policy Anal. Manage.*, Spring 1986, *5*(3), pp. 547–71.

Toma, Eugenia Froedge. Rent Seeking, Federal Mandates, and the Quality of Public Education. *Atlantic Econ. J.*, July 1986, *14*(2), pp. 37–45. **[G: U.S.]**

Vaganov, Boris. Fifty Years since the Creation of the All-Union Foreign Trade Academy of the Ministry of Foreign Trade of the USSR. *Soviet E. Europ. Foreign Trade*, Summer 1986, *22*(2), pp. 28–38. **[G: U.S.S.R.]**

514 Goals and Objectives of Firms

5140 Goals and Objectives of Firms

Aderinto, Adeyemo. Indigenous African Managers and Corporate Social Responsibility. **In** *Damachi, U. G. and Seibel, H. D., eds.*, 1986, pp. 359–84. **[G: Nigeria]**

Ballantine, John W.; Cleveland, Frederick W. and Koeller, C. Timothy. Profit Differences: A Management Approach. *J. Post Keynesian Econ.*, Winter 1985-86, *8*(2), pp. 277–97. **[G: U.S.]**

Baumol, William J. Smith versus Marx on Business Morality and the Social Interest. **In** *Szenberg, M., ed.*, 1986, *1976*, pp. 83–93.

Clark, Robert C. Tender Offers and Corporate Governance. **In** *Knowlton, W. and Zeckhauser, R., eds.*, 1986, pp. 251–80. **[G: U.S.]**

Coffee, John C., Jr. Shareholders versus Managers: The Strain in the Corporate Web. *Mich. Law Rev.*, October 1986, *85*(1), pp. 1–109. **[G: U.S.]**

Fama, Eugene F. and Jensen, Michael C. Separation of Ownership and Control. **In** *Barney, J. B. and Ouchi, W. G., eds.*, 1986, *1983*, pp. 276–98.

Farmer, Roger E. A. and Winter, Ralph A. The Role of Options in the Resolution of Agency Problems: A Comment [Theory of the Firm: Managerial Behaviour, Agency Costs and Ownership Structure]. *J. Finance*, December 1986, *41*(5), pp. 1157–70.

FitzRoy, Felix R. and Mueller, Dennis C. Cooperation and Conflict in Contractual Organizations. **In** *Mueller, D. C.*, 1986, *1984*, pp. 52–77.

Gaa, James C. User Primacy in Corporate Financial Reporting: A Social Contract Approach. *Accounting Rev.*, July 1986, *61*(3), pp. 435–54.

Grabowski, Henry G. and Mueller, Dennis C. Managerial and Stockholder Welfare Models of Firm Expenditures. **In** *Mueller, D. C.*, 1986, *1972*, pp. 81–107.

Grau, Joseph A. Corporate Management and Orthopraxis—Is Synergy Possible? *Int. J. Soc. Econ.*, 1986, *13*(1/2), pp. 7–19.

Hattwick, Richard E. The Behavioral Economics of Business Ethics. *J. Behav. Econ.*, Spring/Summer 1986, *15*(1/2), pp. 87–101.

Haugen, Robert A. and Senbet, Lemma W. The Role of Options in the Resolution of Agency Problems: A Reply. *J. Finance*, December 1986, *41*(5), pp. 1171–73.

Jensen, Michael C. and Meckling, William H. Theory of the Firm: Managerial Behavior, Agency Costs, and Ownership Structure. **In** *Barney, J. B. and Ouchi, W. G., eds.*, 1986, *1976*, pp. 214–75.

Kahneman, Daniel; Knetsch, Jack L. and Thaler, Richard H. Fairness as a Constraint on Profit Seeking: Entitlements in the Market. *Amer. Econ. Rev.*, September 1986, *76*(4), pp. 728–41.

Laitinen, Erkki K. Suomalaisten ja ulkomaisten vuosikertomusten välittämä yrityskuva. (Corporate Image as Reflected in the Annual Reports of Finnish and Foreign Firms. With English summary.) *Liiketaloudellinen Aikak.*, 1986, *35*(4), pp. 357–75. **[G: Finland]**

Marris, Robin and Mueller, Dennis C. The Corporation, Competition, and the Invisible Hand. **In** *Mueller, D. C.*, 1986, *1980*, pp. 261–97.

Meyer, Peter B. The Corporate Person and Social Control: Responding to Deregulation. *Rev. Radical Polit. Econ.*, Fall 1986, *18*(3), pp. 65–84. **[G: U.S.]**

Montias, J. Michael. On the Labor-Managed Firm in a Competitive Environment. *J. Compar. Econ.*, March 1986, *10*(1), pp. 2–8.

O'Farrell, Patrick N. Entrepreneurship and Regional Development: Some Conceptual Issues. *Reg. Stud.*, October 1986, *20*(6), pp. 565–74. **[G: U.K.]**

O'Neil, Robert F. Corporate Social Responsibility and Business Ethics: A European Perspective. *Int. J. Soc. Econ.*, 1986, *13*(10), pp. 64–76.

Pantalone, Coleen C. and Welch, Jonathon B. The Usefulness of Public Information about Corporate Goals. *Quart. J. Bus. Econ.*, Autumn 1986, *25*(4), pp. 29–40.

Useem, Michael and Kutner, Stephen I. Corporate Contributions to Culture and the Arts: The Organization of Giving and the Influence of the Chief Executive Officer and of Other Firms on Company Contributions in Massachusetts. **In** *DiMaggio, P. J., ed.*, 1986, pp. 93–112. **[G: U.S.]**

Wheelwright, Ted. The Corporate Response. **In** *Wheelwright, T., ed.*, 1986, pp. 227–304.

Williamson, Oliver E. The Modern Corporation: Origins, Evolution, Attributes. **In** *Williamson, O. E.*, 1986, *1981*, pp. 131–73.

Zafiris, Nicos. Profitability as a Criterion of Enterprise Efficiency. *Ann. Pub. Co-op. Econ.*, September 1986, *57*(3), pp. 345–58.

520 Business Finance and Investment

5200 Business Finance and Investment

Agell, Jonas Nils. Subsidy to Capital through Tax Incentives. **In** *Shome, P., ed.*, 1986, pp. 48–79. **[G: ASEAN]**

Asimakopulos, A. Finance, Investment and Saving: A Reply. *Cambridge J. Econ.*, March 1986, *10*(1), pp. 81–82.

Asimakopulos, A. Richardson on Asimakopulos on Finance: A Reply [Kalecki and Keynes on Finance, Investment and Saving]. *Cambridge J. Econ.*, June 1986, *10*(2), pp. 199–201.

Auerbach, Alan J. The Dynamic Effects of Tax Law Asymmetries. *Rev. Econ. Stud.*, April 1986, *53*(2), pp. 205–25.

Brealey, Richard A. The Future Direction of Finance. **In** *Firth, M. and Keane, S. M., eds.*, 1986, pp. 254–63.

Coffee, John C., Jr. Shareholders versus Managers: The Strain in the Corporate Web. *Mich. Law Rev.*, October 1986, *85*(1), pp. 1–109. **[G: U.S.]**

Davidson, Paul. Finance, Funding, Saving, and Investment. *J. Post Keynesian Econ.*, Fall 1986, *9*(1), pp. 101–10.

Edwards, Jeremy, et al. Recent Developments in Corporate Finance: Introduction. **In** *Edwards, J., et al., eds.*, 1986, pp. 1–10.

Friedman, Benjamin M. Financing Corporate Capital Formation: An Introduction and Overview. **In** *Friedman, B. M., ed.*, 1986, pp. 1–11.

Hamson, Don and Ziegler, Peter. The Implications of Negative Gearing Restrictions and

Capital Gains Taxation on Investment. *Australian Tax Forum,* 1986, *3*(4), pp. 369–80. **[G: Australia]**

Holland, J. The International Dimensions of Corporate Financial Management. **In** *Firth, M. and Keane, S. M., eds.,* 1986, pp. 207–22.

John, Teresa A. Mergers and Investment Incentives. *J. Finan. Quant. Anal.,* December 1986, *21*(4), pp. 393–413.

Marshman, Peter and Davies, Peter. The Role of the Stock Exchange and the Financial Characteristics of Australian Companies. **In** *Bruce, R., et al., eds.,* 1986, pp. 51–84. **[G: Australia]**

Mayer, Colin. Corporation Tax, Finance and the Cost of Capital. *Rev. Econ. Stud.,* January 1986, *53*(1), pp. 93–112.

Niggle, Christopher J. Financial Innovation and the Distinction between Financial and Industrial Capital. *J. Econ. Issues,* June 1986, *20*(2), pp. 375–82. **[G: U.S.]**

Plessner, Yakir and Shalit, Haim. Inflation, the Level of Investment, and Interest Rates. *Europ. Econ. Rev.,* December 1986, *30*(6), pp. 1169–87.

Pollard, Ian. Corporate Reconstructions. **In** *Bruce, R., et al., eds.,* 1986, pp. 413–27. **[G: Australia]**

Richardson, David R. Asimakopulos on Kalecki and Keynes on Finance, Investment and Saving. *Cambridge J. Econ.,* June 1986, *10*(2), pp. 191–98.

Ruhm, Thomas F. Capital Gains Taxation: Incentive to Growth. **In** *Landau, R. and Jorgenson, D. W., eds.,* 1986, pp. 159–69. **[G: U.S.]**

Shum, K. K. and Sigel, L. T. Managerial Reform and Enterprise Performance: Assessing the Experiment in Shenzhen and Zhuhai. **In** *Jao, Y. C. and Leung, C. K., eds.,* 1986, pp. 201–25. **[G: China]**

Terzi, Andrea. Finance, Investment and Saving: A Comment. *Cambridge J. Econ.,* March 1986, *10*(1), pp. 77–80.

Weate, Philip. Raising Equity Capital. **In** *Bruce, R., et al., eds.,* 1986, pp. 85–108. **[G: Australia]**

521 Business Finance

5210 Business Finance

Adjaoud, Fodil. La réticence des firmes à baisser le dividende: le cas canadien. (The Reluctance of Firms to Cut Dividend: The Canadian Case. With English summary.) *Finance,* December 1986, *7*(2), pp. 169–81. **[G: Canada]**

Alderson, Michael J. and Chen, K. C. Excess Asset Reversions and Shareholder Wealth. *J. Finance,* March 1986, *41*(1), pp. 225–41. **[G: U.S.]**

Allsop, Peter and Pollard, Ian. Taxation Aspects of Corporation Finance. **In** *Bruce, R., et al., eds.,* 1986, pp. 390–412. **[G: Australia]**

Alworth, Julian. A Cost of Capital Approach to the Taxation of Foreign Direct Investment Income. **In** *Edwards, J., et al., eds.,* 1986, pp. 185–208.

Ang, James S. and Peterson, David R. Optimal Debt versus Debt Capacity: A Disequilibrium Model of Corporate Debt Behavior. **In** *Chen, A. H., ed.,* 1986, pp. 51–72. **[G: U.S.]**

Apte, P. G. Aspects of Corporate Decision Making: An Econometric Investigation. *Indian Econ. Rev.,* July-Dec. 1986, *21*(2), pp. 185–215. **[G: India]**

Arnott, Robert D. and Clarke, Roger. "Pension Funds and the Bottom Line:" A Review Article. *J. Portfol. Manage.,* Spring 1986, *12*(3), pp. 78–79.

Asher, Mukul G. Issues in Corporate Tax Design. **In** *Shome, P., ed.,* 1986, pp. 83–92.

Asquith, Paul and Mullins, David W., Jr. Equity Issues and Offering Dilution. **In** *Edwards, J., et al., eds.,* 1986, pp. 51–82. **[G: U.S.]**

Auerbach, Alan J. Incentives and Windfalls in Corporate Tax Reform. **In** *Landau, R. and Jorgenson, D. W., eds.,* 1986, pp. 119–35. **[G: U.S.]**

Auerbach, Alan J. The Economic Effects of the Corporate Income Tax: Changing Revenues and Changing Views. **In** *Friedman, B. M., ed.,* 1986, pp. 107–21. **[G: U.S.]**

Bamber, Linda Smith. The Information Content of Annual Earnings Releases: A Trading Volume Approach. *J. Acc. Res.,* Spring 1986, *24*(1), pp. 40–56. **[G: U.S.]**

Bar-Yosef, Sasson and Huffman, Lucy. The Information Content of Dividends: A Signalling Approach. *J. Finan. Quant. Anal.,* March 1986, *21*(1), pp. 47–58.

Barone-Adesi, Giovanni and Whaley, Robert E. The Valuation of American Call Options and the Expected Ex-dividend Stock Price Decline. *J. Finan. Econ.,* September 1986, *17*(1), pp. 91–111. **[G: U.S.]**

Barry, Robert and Pollard, Ian. Domestic Sources of Long Term Corporate Debt. **In** *Bruce, R., et al., eds.,* 1986, pp. 180–204. **[G: Australia]**

Bartley, Jon W. and Boardman, Calvin M. Replacement-Cost–Adjusted Valuation Ratio as a Discriminator among Takeover Target and Nontarget Firms. *J. Econ. Bus.,* February 1986, *38*(1), pp. 41–55. **[G: U.S.]**

Baxter, W. T. Accounting Values: Sale Price versus Replacement Cost. **In** *Parker, R. H.; Harcourt, G. C. and Whittington, G., eds.,* 1986, *1967*, pp. 242–49.

Bebchuk, Lucian Arye. The Case for Facilitating Competing Tender Offers: A Last (?) Reply [The Proper Role of a Target's Management in Responding to a Tender Offer] [Auctions and Sunk Costs in Tender Offers]. *J. Law, Econ., Organ.,* Fall 1986, *2*(2), pp. 253–71.

Becker, Brian E. and Olson, Craig A. The Impact of Strikes on Shareholder Equity. *Ind. Lab. Relat. Rev.,* April 1986, *39*(3), pp. 425–38. **[G: U.S.]**

Bell, Philip W. and Johnson, L. Todd. Current Value Accounting and the Simple Production Case: Edbejo and Other Companies in the Taxi Business. **In** *Parker, R. H.; Harcourt, G. C.*

and Whittington, G., eds., 1986, *1979*, pp. 278–313.

Bennett, John. Equipment Leasing. **In** *Bruce, R., et al., eds.*, 1986, pp. 205–31. **[G: Australia]**

Bennett, Robert J. The Impact of Non-Domestic Rates on Profitability and Investment. *Fisc. Stud.*, February 1986, *7*(1), pp. 34–50. **[G: U.K.]**

Bernard, Victor L. Unanticipated Inflation and the Value of the Firm. *J. Finan. Econ.*, March 1986, *15*(3), pp. 285–321. **[G: U.S.]**

Bertoni, Alberto. Industrial Credit Institutions and Patterns of Corporate Finance. *Rev. Econ. Cond. Italy*, Jan.-Apr. 1986, (1), pp. 27–41. **[G: Italy]**

Bhagat, Sanjai. The Effect of Management's Choice between Negotiated and Competitive Equity Offerings on Shareholder Wealth. *J. Finan. Quant. Anal.*, June 1986, *21*(2), pp. 181–96. **[G: U.S.]**

Bhagat, Sanjai and Frost, Peter A. Issuing Costs to Existing Shareholders in Competitive and Negotiated Underwritten Public Utility Equity Offerings. *J. Finan. Econ.*, Jan./Feb. 1986, *15*(1/2), pp. 233–59. **[G: U.S.]**

Bicksler, James and Chen, Andrew H. An Economic Analysis of Interest Rate Swaps. *J. Finance*, July 1986, *41*(3), pp. 645–55. **[G: U.S.]**

Binks, M. R. and Coyne, John. Entrepreneurial Finance for Small Business. **In** *Carter, R. L.; Chiplin, B. and Lewis, M. K., eds.*, 1986, pp. 229–47. **[G: U.K.]**

Black, Fischer. Noise. *J. Finance*, July 1986, *41*(3), pp. 529–43.

Board, J. Corporate Borrowing Policy. **In** *Firth, M. and Keane, S. M., eds.*, 1986, pp. 59–75.

Boardman, Calvin M.; Dark, Frederick H. and Lease, Ronald C. On the Listing of Corporate Debt: A Note. *J. Finan. Quant. Anal.*, March 1986, *21*(1), pp. 107–14. **[G: U.S.]**

Bodie, Zvi; Kane, Alex and McDonald, Robert. Risk and Required Returns on Debt and Equity. **In** *Friedman, B. M., ed.*, 1986, pp. 51–66. **[G: U.S.]**

Booth, James R. and Smith, Richard L., II. Capital Raising, Underwriting and the Certification Hypothesis. *J. Finan. Econ.*, Jan./Feb. 1986, *15*(1/2), pp. 261–81.

Bourne, Compton. The Propensities to Consume Labour and Property Incomes in the Commonwealth Caribbean. *J. Devel. Stud.*, April 1986, *22*(3), pp. 583–97. **[G: Jamaica; Guyana]**

Bowen, Robert M.; Burgstahler, David and Daley, Lane A. Evidence on the Relationships between Earnings and Various Measures of Cash Flow. *Accounting Rev.*, October 1986, *61*(4), pp. 713–25.

Bowles, Samuel; Gordon, David M. and Weisskopf, Thomas E. Power and Profits: The Social Structure of Accumulation and the Profitability of the Postwar U.S. Economy. *Rev. Radical Polit. Econ.*, Spring/Summer 1986, *18*(1/2), pp. 132–67. **[G: U.S.]**

Boyes, William J. and Faith, Roger L. Some Effects of the Bankruptcy Reform Act of 1978. *J. Law Econ.*, April 1986, *29*(1), pp. 139–49. **[G: U.S.]**

Boyns, Trevor. Growth in the Coal Industry: The Cases of Powell Duffryn and the Ocean Coal Company, 1864–1913. **In** *Baber, C. and Williams, L. J., eds.*, 1986, pp. 153–70. **[G: U.K.]**

Brander, James A. and Lewis, Tracy R. Oligopoly and Financial Structure: The Limited Liability Effect. *Amer. Econ. Rev.*, December 1986, *76*(5), pp. 956–70.

Bromiley, Philip. Corporate Planning and Capital Investment. *J. Econ. Behav. Organ.*, June 1986, *7*(2), pp. 147–70. **[G: U.S.]**

Brooks, LeRoy D. and Buckmaster, Dale. The Impact of Inflation on the Monetary Stocks of the Firm. *J. Econ. Soc. Meas.*, April 1986, *14*(1), pp. 51–63. **[G: U.S.]**

Brox, James A. and Maclean, Wendy A. The Financial Behaviour of Canadian Private Corporations and Government Enterprise: A Flow of Funds Analysis. *Bull. Econ. Res.*, January 1986, *38*(1), pp. 49–66. **[G: Canada]**

Bruce, Robert and Murnane, Paul. Borrowing from Overseas. **In** *Bruce, R., et al., eds.*, 1986, pp. 297–320. **[G: Australia]**

Büschgen, Hans E. Finanzinnovationen—Neuerungen und Entwicklungen an nationalen und internationalen Finanzmärkten. (With English summary.) *Z. Betriebswirtschaft*, Apr.-May 1986, *56*(4/5), pp. 301–36. **[G: W. Germany]**

Buser, Stephen A. LaPlace Transforms as Present Value Rules: A Note. *J. Finance*, March 1986, *41*(1), pp. 243–47.

Cain, Louis P. How Public Works Saved Private Enterprise: The Thomas & Betts Company in the Great Depression. **In** *Atack, J., ed.*, 1986, pp. 29–40. **[G: U.S.]**

Calvet, A. Louis and Lefoll, Jean. Industry and Firm-Specific Factors in Canadian Corporate Acquisitions. *Finance*, December 1986, *7*(2), pp. 203–30. **[G: Canada]**

Casey, Cornelius J.; McGee, Victor E. and Stickney, Clyde P. Discriminating between Reorganized and Liquidated Firms in Bankruptcy. *Accounting Rev.*, April 1986, *61*(2), pp. 249–62. **[G: U.S.]**

Casey, Cornelius J. and Selling, Thomas I. The Effect of Task Predictability and Prior Probability Disclosure on Judgment Quality and Confidence. *Accounting Rev.*, April 1986, *61*(2), pp. 302–17.

Castanias, Richard P., II and Griffin, Paul A. The Effects of Foreign-Currency Translation Accounting on Security Analysts' Forecasts. *Managerial Dec. Econ.*, March 1986, *7*(1), pp. 3–10. **[G: U.S.]**

Chan-Lee, James H. Pure Profits and Tobin's *q* in Nine OECD Countries. *OECD Econ. Stud.*, Autumn 1986, (7), pp. 205–32. **[G: Selected OECD]**

Chen, Andrew H.; Chen, K. C. and Sears, R. Stephen. The Value of Loan Guarantees: The Case of Chrysler Corporation. **In** *Chen, A. H., ed.*, 1986, pp. 101–17. **[G: U.S.]**

Clark, Jeffrey A. and Speaker, Paul J. Compensating Balance Requirements and the Firm's Demand for Transactions Balances. *J. Banking Finance,* October 1986, *10*(3), pp. 411–29.

Connolly, Robert A.; Hirsch, Barry T. and Hirschey, Mark. Union Rent Seeking, Intangible Capital, and Market Value of the Firm. *Rev. Econ. Statist.*, November 1986, *68*(4), pp. 567–77. **[G: U.S.]**

Contzen Fuentes, Patricia and Parada Daza, José Rigoberto. Rentabilidad y riesgo para el propietario de una empresa: un nuevo enfoque. (With English summary.) *Cuadernos Econ.*, August 1986, *23*(69), pp. 237–63. **[G: Chile]**

Cox, W. Michael. Government Debt and the Stock Market. *Fed. Res. Bank Dallas Econ. Rev.*, September 1986, pp. 1–9.

Craig, Robin. Trade and Shipping in South Wales—The Radcliffe Company, 1882–1921. **In** *Baber, C. and Williams, L. J., eds.*, 1986, pp. 171–91. **[G: U.K.]**

Cross, Mark L.; Davidson, Wallace N., III and Thornton, John H. The Impact of Captive Insurer Formation on the Parent Firm's Value. *J. Risk Ins.*, September 1986, *53*(3), pp. 471–83. **[G: U.S.]**

Darrough, Masako N. and Stoughton, Neal M. Moral Hazard and Adverse Selection: The Question of Financial Structure. *J. Finance,* June 1986, *41*(2), pp. 501–13.

Davies, J. R. Valuation of Shares. **In** *Firth, M. and Keane, S. M., eds.*, 1986, pp. 193–206.

DeAngelo, Linda Elizabeth. Accounting Numbers as Market Valuation Substitutes: A Study of Management Buyouts of Public Stockholders. *Accounting Rev.*, July 1986, *61*(3), pp. 400–420. **[G: U.S.]**

Defourny, Jacques. Une analyse financière comparée des coopératives de travailleurs et des entreprises capitalistes en France. (A Comparative Financial Analysis of Workers' Cooperatives and Capitalist Firms in France. With English summary.) *Ann. Pub. Co-op. Econ.*, Jan.-March 1986, *57*(1), pp. 55–78. **[G: France]**

Demsetz, Harold. Corporate Control, Insider Trading, and Rates of Return. *Amer. Econ. Rev.*, May 1986, *76*(2), pp. 313–16. **[G: U.S.]**

Dennis, Debra K. and McConnell, John J. Corporate Mergers and Security Returns. *J. Finan. Econ.*, June 1986, *16*(2), pp. 143–87. **[G: U.S.]**

Dhaliwal, Dan S. Measurement of Financial Leverage in the Presence of Unfunded Pension Obligations. *Accounting Rev.*, October 1986, *61*(4), pp. 651–61.

Doukas, John. Bankers versus Bankruptcy Prediction Models: An Empirical Investigation, 1979–82. *Appl. Econ.*, May 1986, *18*(5), pp. 479–93. **[G: Canada]**

Dow, Sheila C. Speculation and the Monetary Circuit with Particular Attention to the Eurocurrency Market. *Écon. Soc.*, Aug.-Sept. 1986, *20*(8–9), pp. 95–109.

Downs, Thomas W. The User Cost and Capital Budgeting. *Financial Rev.*, May 1986, *21*(2), pp. 277–87.

Eckbo, B. Espen. Valuation Effects of Corporate Debt Offerings. *J. Finan. Econ.*, Jan./Feb. 1986, *15*(1/2), pp. 119–51. **[G: U.S.]**

Eddy, Albert and Seifert, Bruce. Dividend Changes of Financially Weak Firms. *Financial Rev.*, November 1986, *21*(4), pp. 419–31. **[G: U.S.]**

El-Gazzar, Samir; Lilien, Steve and Pastena, Victor. Accounting for Leases by Lessees. *J. Acc. Econ.*, October 1986, *8*(3), pp. 217–37. **[G: U.S.]**

Espitia, Manuel; Salas, Vicente and Vagüe, M. Jesús. Medidas de resultados empresariales: relevancia para los estudios sobre el poder de monopolio. (With English summary.) *Invest. Ecón.*, September 1986, *10*(3), pp. 427–48.

Evans, David J. UK Companies' Demand for Money: An Empirical Study, 1974–1983. *J. Econ. Stud.*, 1986, *13*(4), pp. 30–43. **[G: U.K.]**

Farrell, Terrence; Najjar, Annette and Marcelle, Hazel. Corporate Financing and Use of Bank Credit in Trinidad and Tobago. *Soc. Econ. Stud.*, December 1986, *35*(4), pp. 1–65. **[G: Trinidad and Tobago]**

Fawthrop, R. Equipment Leasing. **In** *Firth, M. and Keane, S. M., eds.*, 1986, pp. 103–14. **[G: U.K.]**

Finnerty, John D. Refunding Discounted Debt: A Clarifying Analysis. *J. Finan. Quant. Anal.*, March 1986, *21*(1), pp. 95–106.

Flannery, Mark J. Asymmetric Information and Risky Debt Maturity Choice. *J. Finance,* March 1986, *41*(1), pp. 19–37.

Flannery, Mark J. Recapitalizing the Thrift Industry. **In** *Federal Home Loan Bank of San Francisco,* 1986, pp. 91–114. **[G: U.S.]**

Fooladi, Iraj and Roberts, Gordon S. On Preferred Stock. *J. Finan. Res.*, Winter 1986, *9*(4), pp. 319–24. **[G: Canada; U.S.]**

Fooladi, Iraj; Roberts, Gordon S. and Viscione, Jerry A. Captive Finance Subsidiaries: Overview and Synthesis. *Financial Rev.*, May 1986, *21*(2), pp. 259–75. **[G: U.S.]**

Forbes, Ronald. Determinants of the Cost of Capital for the New York Power Authority. **In** *Saltzman, S. and Schuler, R. E., eds.*, 1986, pp. 288–307. **[G: U.S.]**

Freeman, Robert N. The Information Contained in the Components of Earnings: Discussion. *J. Acc. Res.*, Supp. 1986, *24*, pp. 65–68. **[G: U.S.]**

Friedman, Benjamin M. Implications of Government Deficits for Interest Rates, Equity Returns, and Corporate Financing. **In** *Friedman, B. M., ed.*, 1986, pp. 67–89. **[G: U.S.]**

Fries, Steven M. Precommitment to Equity Financing Choices in a World of Asymmetric Information: Comment. **In** *Edwards, J., et al., eds.*, 1986, pp. 45–50.

Fung, W. K. H. and Rudd, Andrew. Pricing New Corporate Bond Issues: An Analysis of Issue Cost and Seasoning Effects. *J. Finance,* July 1986, *41*(3), pp. 633–43. **[G: U.S.]**

Gedeon, Shirley J. The Post Keynesian Theory of Money: Summary and an Eastern European

Example. *J. Post Keynesian Econ.*, Winter 1985-86, *8*(2), pp. 208–21. **[G: Yugoslavia]**

Ghemawat, Pankaj and Caves, Richard E. Capital Commitment and Profitability: An Empirical Investigation. *Oxford Econ. Pap.*, Suppl. Nov. 1986, *38*, pp. 94–110. **[G: N. America]**

Ghosh, Dipak. Effect of Fixed Cost under Uncertainty and Access to the Capital Market. *Managerial Dec. Econ.*, September 1986, *7*(3), pp. 211–13.

Gilmer, R. H., Jr. and Lee, Cheng F. Empirical Tests of Granger's Propositions on the Dividend Effect Controversy. *Rev. Econ. Statist.*, May 1986, *68*(2), pp. 351–55. **[G: U.S.]**

Glick, Mark and Ehrbar, Hans. An Econometric Model of Industrial Profit Rate Adjustment in the U.S. *Econ. Forum*, Winter 1986-1987, *16*(1), pp. 29–43. **[G: U.S.]**

Graddy, Duane B. and Karna, Adi S. Dividend Policy and the Return of Bank Holding Company Stock. *Quart. J. Bus. Econ.*, Spring 1986, *25*(2), pp. 3–21. **[G: U.S.]**

Green, Richard C. and Talmor, Eli. Asset Substitution and the Agency Costs of Debt Financing. *J. Banking Finance*, October 1986, *10*(3), pp. 391–99.

Hall, G. and Stark, A. W. Bankruptcy Risk and the Effects of Conservative Policy for 1979–81. *Int. J. Ind. Organ.*, September 1986, *4*(3), pp. 317–32. **[G: U.K.]**

Hall, Lana and Sweeney, Jan. Profitability of Mergers in Food Manufacturing. *Appl. Econ.*, July 1986, *18*(7), pp. 709–27. **[G: U.S.]**

Haller, Hans. Market Power, Objectives of the Firm, and Objectives of Shareholders. *J. Inst. Theoretical Econ.*, December 1986, *142*(4), pp. 716–26.

Hansen, Robert S.; Pinkerton, John M. and Ma, Tai. On the Rightholders' Subscription to the Underwritten Rights Offering. *J. Banking Finance*, December 1986, *10*(4), pp. 595–604. **[G: U.S.]**

Hassell, John M. and Jennings, Robert H. Relative Forecast Accuracy and the Timing of Earnings Forecast Announcements. *Accounting Rev.*, January 1986, *61*(1), pp. 58–75. **[G: U.S.]**

Hatsopoulos, George N. and Brooks, Stephen H. The Gap in the Cost of Capital: Causes, Effects, and Remedies. **In** *Landau, R. and Jorgenson, D. W., eds.*, 1986, pp. 221–80. **[G: U.S.; Japan]**

Haugen, Robert A.; Senbet, Lemma W. and Talmor, Eli. Debt, Dividends, and Taxes: Equilibrium Conditions for Simultaneous Tax Neutrality of Debt and Dividend Policies. **In** *Chen, A. H., ed.*, 1986, pp. 1–27. **[G: U.S.]**

Heaton, Hal. Corporate Taxation and Leasing. *J. Finan. Quant. Anal.*, September 1986, *21*(3), pp. 351–59.

Heinkel, Robert L. and Schwartz, Eduardo S. Precommitment to Equity Financing Choices in a World of Asymmetric Information. **In** *Edwards, J., et al., eds.*, 1986, pp. 33–45.

Heinkel, Robert L. and Schwartz, Eduardo S. Rights versus Underwritten Offerings: An Asymmetric Information Approach. *J. Finance*, March 1986, *41*(1), pp. 1–18.

Hellwig, Martin. Risikoallokation in einem Marktsystem. (The Allocation of Risks in the Markets. With English summary.) *Schweiz. Z. Volkswirtsch. Statist.*, September 1986, *122*(3), pp. 231–51.

Hendershott, Patric H. Debt and Equity Returns Revisited. **In** *Friedman, B. M., ed.*, 1986, pp. 35–50. **[G: U.S.]**

Hess, Alan C. and Bhagat, Sanjai. Size Effects of Seasoned Stock Issues: Empirical Evidence. *J. Bus.*, Part 1, October 1986, *59*(4), pp. 567–84. **[G: U.S.]**

Hirschey, Mark. Mergers, Buyouts and Fakeouts. *Amer. Econ. Rev.*, May 1986, *76*(2), pp. 317–22.

Hite, Gailen L. The Timing and Substance of Divestiture Announcements: Individual, Simultaneous and Cumulative Effects: Discussion. *J. Finance*, July 1986, *41*(3), pp. 696–97. **[G: U.S.]**

Ho, Kwok S. An Empirical Analysis of a Causality Relationship between Corporate Investment and Financing Decisions. **In** *Chen, A. H., ed.*, 1986, pp. 179–96. **[G: U.S.]**

Horváth, Péter, et al. Budgetierung in industriellen Grossunternehmen—Eine vergleichende Fallstudienanalyse. (With English summary.) *Z. Betriebswirtshaft*, January 1986, *56*(1), pp. 24–39. **[G: W. Germany]**

Hudson, John. An Analysis of Company Liquidations. *Appl. Econ.*, February 1986, *18*(2), pp. 219–35. **[G: U.K.]**

Hughes, Patricia J. Signalling by Direct Disclosure under Asymmetric Information. *J. Acc. Econ.*, June 1986, *8*(2), pp. 119–42.

Hyman, Leonard S.; Kelley, Doris A. and Toole, Richard C. Financial Constraints on Electric Utilities in New York State: Technology, Institutional Structure, and Investors' Attitudes. **In** *Saltzman, S. and Schuler, R. E., eds.*, 1986, pp. 275–80. **[G: U.S.]**

Ingberg, Mikael. Reformen av företagsbeskattningen. Nuläge och framtidsutsikter. (The Reform of Business Taxation. With English summary.) *Ekon. Samfundets Tidskr.*, 1986, *39*(3), pp. 131–48. **[G: Finland]**

Jansson, Sune. Swedish Labour-Owned Industrial Firms: Some Empirical Observations. *Ann. Pub. Co-op. Econ.*, Jan.-March 1986, *57*(1), pp. 103–16. **[G: Sweden]**

Jefferis, Keith and Thomas, Alan. Conditions for Financial Viability in Workers' Co-operatives: The Case of UK Clothing and Printing Co-ops. *Ann. Pub. Co-op. Econ.*, Jan.-March 1986, *57*(1), pp. 79–102. **[G: U.K.]**

Jegers, Marc. Le concept d'intérêts cumulés: nécessaire ou suffisant? (The Concept of Cumulated Interests: Necessary or Sufficient? With English summary.) *Écon. Soc.*, December 1986, *20*(12), pp. 37–48.

Jensen, Frederick H. and DeCubellis, Paula J. Recent Developments in Corporate Finance. *Fed. Res. Bull.*, November 1986, *72*(11), pp. 745–56. **[G: U.S.]**

Jensen, Michael C. Agency Costs of Free Cash Flow, Corporate Finance, and Takeovers. *Amer. Econ. Rev.*, May 1986, *76*(2), pp. 323–29. **[G: U.S.]**

Jensen, Michael C. and Meckling, William H. Theory of the Firm: Managerial Behavior, Agency Costs, and Ownership Structure. **In** *Barney, J. B. and Ouchi, W. G., eds.*, 1986, *1976*, pp. 214–75.

Jones, Leroy. Towards Performance Evaluation: Methodology for Public Enterprises, with Particular Reference to Pakistan. **In** *U.N., Dept. of Technical Co-operation for Development*, 1986, pp. 116–38. **[G: Pakistan]**

Kalay, Avner and Loewenstein, Uri. The Informational Content of the Timing of Dividend Announcements. *J. Finan. Econ.*, July 1986, *16*(3), pp. 373–88. **[G: U.S.]**

Kanniainen, Vesa. On the Effects of Inflation: The Debtor–Creditor Hypothesis Reconsidered. *Liiketaloudellinen Aikak.*, 1986, *35*(4), pp. 303–12. **[G: Finland]**

Kaplanis, Costas P. Options, Taxes, and Ex-Dividend Day Behavior. *J. Finance*, June 1986, *41*(2), pp. 411–24. **[G: U.K.]**

Keane, Simon M. Dividend Policy. **In** *Firth, M. and Keane, S. M., eds.*, 1986, pp. 76–88.

Keeley, M. Raising Equity—The Problem of Setting the Issue Price. **In** *Firth, M. and Keane, S. M., eds.*, 1986, pp. 115–25. **[G: U.K.]**

Kim, Wi Saeng and Sorensen, Eric H. Evidence on the Impact of the Agency Costs of Debt on Corporate Dept Policy. *J. Finan. Quant. Anal.*, June 1986, *21*(2), pp. 131–44. **[G: U.S.]**

Kirkman, P. Working Capital Management. **In** *Firth, M. and Keane, S. M., eds.*, 1986, pp. 142–57. **[G: U.K.]**

Klein, April. The Timing and Substance of Divestiture Announcements: Individual, Simultaneous and Cumulative Effects. *J. Finance*, July 1986, *41*(3), pp. 685–96. **[G: U.S.]**

Knoeber, Charles R. Golden Parachutes, Shark Repellents, and Hostile Tender Offers. *Amer. Econ. Rev.*, March 1986, *76*(1), pp. 155–67. **[G: U.S.]**

Koch, Helmut. Zum Problem der optimalen Kapitalstruktur: Der handlungsorientierte Ansatz in der Theorie der Unternehmensfinanzierung. (With English summary.) *Z. Betriebswirtshaft*, December 1986, *56*(12), pp. 1213–29.

Krasker, William S. Stock Price Movements in Response to Stock Issues under Asymmetric Information. *J. Finance*, March 1986, *41*(1), pp. 93–105.

Krever, Richard. Companies, Shareholders and Capital Gains Taxation. *Australian Tax Forum*, 1986, *3*(3), pp. 267–96. **[G: Australia]**

Kron, Philip C. The Electric Utility Financial Crisis from a Banker's Perspective. **In** *Saltzman, S. and Schuler, R. E., eds.*, 1986, pp. 281–87. **[G: U.S.]**

Laitinen, Erkki K. Financial Ratio Model of a Public Enterprise. *Liiketaloudellinen Aikak.*, 1986, *35*(4), pp. 313–32. **[G: Finland]**

Lam, Chun H. and Chen, Andrew H. A Note on Optimal Credit and Pricing Policy under Uncertainty: A Contingent-Claims Approach. *J. Finance*, December 1986, *41*(5), pp. 1141–48.

Landsman, Wayne. An Empirical Investigation of Pension Fund Property Rights. *Accounting Rev.*, October 1986, *61*(4), pp. 662–91. **[G: U.S.]**

Langetieg, Terence C. Stochastic Control of Corporate Investment When Output Affects Future Prices. *J. Finan. Quant. Anal.*, September 1986, *21*(3), pp. 239–63.

Lanser, Howard P. and Halloran, John A. Evaluating Cash Flow Systems under Growth. *Financial Rev.*, May 1986, *21*(2), pp. 309–18.

Ledebur, Larry C. and Hamilton, William W. Cost-Effective Development Finance. **In** *Walzer, N. and Chicoine, D. L., eds.*, 1986, pp. 103–21. **[G: U.S.]**

Lewellen, Wilbur G. and Emery, Douglas R. Corporate Debt Management and the Value of the Firm. *J. Finan. Quant. Anal.*, December 1986, *21*(4), pp. 415–26.

Lipe, Robert C. The Information Contained in the Components of Earnings. *J. Acc. Res.*, Supp. 1986, *24*, pp. 37–64. **[G: U.S.]**

Litzenberger, Robert H. Some Observations on Capital Structure and the Impact of Recent Recapitalizations on Share Prices. *J. Finan. Quant. Anal.*, March 1986, *21*(1), pp. 59–71. **[G: U.S.]**

Lloyd, William P.; Jahera, John S. and Goldstein, Steven J. The Relation between Returns, Ownership Structure, and Market Value. *J. Finan. Res.*, Summer 1986, *9*(2), pp. 171–77. **[G: U.S.]**

Lobez, Frédéric. Décision de crédit-bail et théorie des mandats. (Lease Decision and Agency Theory. With English summary.) *Écon. Soc.*, June 1986, *20*(6), pp. 181–201.

Loistl, Otto and Rosenthal, Harald. Zur Bewertung konkursgefährdeter Finanztitel. (With English summary.) *Z. Betriebswirtshaft*, February 1986, *56*(2), pp. 104–31.

Luciano, Elisa. Un modello di affidamento in condizioni di incertezza. (A Model of Borrowing and Lending under Conditions of Uncertainty. With English summary.) *Giorn. Econ.*, Sept.-Oct. 1986, *45*(9–10), pp. 527–44.

Makhija, Anil K. and Thompson, Howard E. Some Aspects of Equilibrium for a Cross-section of Firms Signalling Profitability with Dividends: A Note. *J. Finance*, March 1986, *41*(1), pp. 249–53.

Malécot, Jean-François. Sait-on vraiment prévoir les défaillances d'entreprises? (Predicting Business Failure: Is It Really Possible? With English summary.) *Écon. Soc.*, December 1986, *20*(12), pp. 55–82. **[G: France]**

Malécot, Jean-François and Hamon, Jean. Contraintes financieères et demande d'investissement des entreprises. (Financial Constraints and Firms' Investment. With English summary.) *Revue Écon.*, September 1986, *37*(5), pp. 885–923. **[G: France]**

Marcus, Matityahu; Palmon, Dan and Yaari, Uzi. Growth and the Decision to Incorporate: A Financial Theory of the U.S. Tax System. **In** *Chen, A. H., ed.*, 1986, pp. 29–50. **[G: U.S.]**

Marsh, Terry A. and Merton, Robert C. Dividend Variability and Variance Bounds Tests for the Rationality of Stock Market Prices. *Amer. Econ. Rev.*, June 1986, *76*(3), pp. 483–98.

Martin, John. Project Finance. **In** *Bruce, R., et al., eds.*, 1986, pp. 247–76. **[G: Australia]**

Martinengo, Giancarlo. Rischio da leverage, finanziamento esterno ed interno: un contributo allo studio degli equilibri tra banca e impresa. (Leverage Risk, External and Internal Financing: An Integration of Banks and Firms Decisions. With English summary.) *Polit. Econ.*, August 1986, *2*(2), pp. 243–71.

Mason, Scott P. Valuing Financial Flexibility. **In** *Friedman, B. M., ed.*, 1986, pp. 91–106. **[G: U.S.]**

Masulis, Ronald W. and Korwar, Ashok N. Seasoned Equity Offerings: An Empirical Investigation. *J. Finan. Econ.*, Jan./Feb. 1986, *15*(1/2), pp. 91–118. **[G: U.S.]**

Mayers, David and Smith, Clifford W., Jr. Ownership Structure and Control: The Mutualization of Stock Life Insurance Companies. *J. Finan. Econ.*, May 1986, *16*(1), pp. 73–98. **[G: U.S.]**

McCormick, Robert E. Inflation, Regulation, and Financial Adequacy. **In** *Moorhouse, J. C., ed.*, 1986, pp. 135–61. **[G: U.S.]**

McDaniel, William R. The Economic Ordering Quantity Problem and Wealth Maximization. *Financial Rev.*, November 1986, *21*(4), pp. 527–36.

McKern, Bruce. The Funding Decision in Corporate Finance. **In** *Bruce, R., et al., eds.*, 1986, pp. 1–10. **[G: Australia]**

McLeay, Stuart. The Ratio of Means, the Mean of Ratios and Other Benchmarks: An Examination of Characteristic Financial Ratios in the French Corporate Sector. *Finance*, June 1986, *7*(1), pp. 75–93. **[G: France]**

McMillan, Henry M. Nonassignable Pensions and the Price of Risk. *J. Money, Credit, Banking*, February 1986, *18*(1), pp. 60–75.

Meyerson, Per-Martin. Industrial Finance System in Europe, U.S. and Japan: Comment. **In** *Day, R. H. and Eliasson, G., eds.*, 1986, pp. 401–03. **[G: Europe; U.S.; Japan]**

Michel, Allen and Shaked, Israel. Industry Influence on Pension Funding. *J. Portfol. Manage.*, Spring 1986, *12*(3), pp. 71–77. **[G: U.S.]**

Mikkelson, Wayne H. and Partch, M. Megan. Valuation Effects of Security Offerings and the Issuance Process. *J. Finan. Econ.*, Jan./Feb. 1986, *15*(1/2), pp. 31–60. **[G: U.S.]**

Miller, Merton H. The Academic Field of Finance: Some Observations on Its History and Prospects. *Tijdschrift Econ. Manage.*, 1986, *31*(4), pp. 395–408. **[G: U.S.]**

Miller, Merton H. Behavioral Rationality in Finance: The Case of Dividends. *J. Bus.*, Part 2, October 1986, *59*(4), pp. S451–68.

Miller, Merton H. Behavioral Rationality in Finance: The Case of Dividends. **In** *Hogarth, R. M. and Reder, M. W., eds.*, 1986, pp. 267–84.

Mohanty, Subhransu Sekhar. An Empirical Evaluation of Public Deposits as a Source of Finance in the Corporate Sector. *Indian Econ. J.*, July-Sept. 1986, *34*(1), pp. 59–78. **[G: India]**

Molho, Lazaros E. Selective Credit Controls in Greece: A Test of Their Effectiveness. *Int. Monet. Fund Staff Pap.*, September 1986, *33*(3), pp. 477–508. **[G: Greece]**

Montel, Jean. Risque, financement et rentabilité. (Risk, Financing and Profitability. With English summary.) *Écon. Soc.*, July 1986, *20*(7), pp. 115–28.

Moore, Norman H.; Peterson, David R. and Peterson, Pamela P. Shelf Registrations and Shareholder Wealth: A Comparison of Shelf and Traditional Equity Offerings. *J. Finance*, June 1986, *41*(2), pp. 451–63. **[G: U.S.]**

Moore, William T. Asset Composition, Bankruptcy Costs, and the Firm's Choice of Capital Structure. *Quart. Rev. Econ. Bus.*, Winter 1986, *26*(4), pp. 51–61.

Moosa, S. A. Inflation, Non-neutral Growth, Equity Yields and the Fisher Hypothesis. *Appl. Econ.*, March 1986, *18*(3), pp. 237–47. **[G: U.S.]**

Morgan, Eleanor. Stimulating Investment—Government Incentives and the Financial Leasing Industry. **In** *Hall, G., ed.*, 1986, pp. 261–83. **[G: W. Europe; U.K.]**

Näslund, Bertil. Some Views on the Current State of Financial Theory. *Liiketaloudellinen Aikak.*, 1986, *35*(4), pp. 267–74.

Neun, Stephen P. and Santerre, Rexford E. Dominant Stockownership and Profitability. *Managerial Dec. Econ.*, September 1986, *7*(3), pp. 207–10. **[G: U.S.]**

Nishina, Kazuhiko. The Effect of Firm's Capital Structure on the Valuation in Financial Markets. *Econ. Stud. Quart.*, March 1986, *37*(1), pp. 67–80. **[G: Japan]**

Oestreich, Nathan; Summer, Jeinie and Walker, John F. Roots of the Existing Federal Corporate Income Taxes. **In** *Lindholm, R. W., ed.*, 1986, pp. 280–314. **[G: U.S.]**

Officer, Dennis T. and Smith, Richard L., II. Announcement Effects of Withdrawn Security Offerings: Evidence on the Wealth Redistribution Hypothesis. *J. Finan. Res.*, Fall 1986, *9*(3), pp. 229–38. **[G: U.S.]**

Okubo, Tatsuo. Response to Liberalization: Changing Corporate Finance Strategies. **In** *Finn, R. B., ed.*, 1986, pp. 203–09. **[G: U.S.; Japan]**

Palepu, Krishna G. Predicting Takeover Targets: A Methodological and Empirical Analysis. *J. Acc. Econ.*, March 1986, *8*(1), pp. 3–35. **[G: U.S.]**

Pantalone, Coleen C. and Welch, Jonathon B. The Usefulness of Public Information about Corporate Goals. *Quart. J. Bus. Econ.*, Autumn 1986, *25*(4), pp. 29–40.

Parker, William N. Industrial Finance System in Europe, U.S. and Japan: Comment. **In** *Day,*

R. H. and Eliasson, G., eds., 1986, pp. 397–400. **[G: Europe; U.S.; Japan]**

Pastena, Victor and Ruland, William. The Merger/Bankruptcy Alternative. *Accounting Rev.*, April 1986, *61*(2), pp. 288–301. **[G: U.S.]**

Pattison, Robert V. Response to Financial Incentives among Investor-Owned and Not-for-Profit Hospitals: An Analysis Based on California Data, 1978–1982. **In** *Gray, B. H., ed.*, 1986, pp. 290–302. **[G: U.S.]**

Peterson, David R. An Empirical Test of an Ex-ante Model of the Determination of Stock Return Volatility. *J. Finan. Res.*, Fall 1986, *9*(3), pp. 203–14.

Petrovich, Giuliano. Politiche di contenimento e diversione del sistema dei *Factors*. (Credit Restrictions and Factoring Diversion. With English summary.) *Ricerche Econ.*, Apr.-Sept. 1986, *40*(2–3), pp. 447–62. **[G: Italy]**

Pike, Richard H. The Design of Capital Budgeting Processes and the Corporate Context. *Managerial Dec. Econ.*, September 1986, *7*(3), pp. 187–95. **[G: U.K.]**

Pincus, Morton. The Incremental Information Content of Financial Statement Disclosures: The Case of LIFO Inventory Liquidations: Discussion. *J. Acc. Res.*, Supp. 1986, *24*, pp. 161–64. **[G: U.S.]**

Pinegar, J. Michael and Lease, Ronald C. The Impact of Preferred-for-Common Exchange Offers on Firm Value. *J. Finance*, September 1986, *41*(4), pp. 795–814. **[G: U.S.]**

Pitelis, Christos N. Corporate Control, Social Choice and Capital Accumulation: An Asymmetrical Choice Approach. *Rev. Radical Polit. Econ.*, Fall 1986, *18*(3), pp. 85–100.

Pointon, J. UK Taxation and Financial Decision Making. **In** *Firth, M. and Keane, S. M., eds.*, 1986, pp. 182–92. **[G: U.K.]**

Pollin, Robert. Alternative Perspectives on the Rise of Corporate Debt Dependency: The U.S. Postwar Experience. *Rev. Radical Polit. Econ.*, Spring/Summer 1986, *18*(1/2), pp. 205–35. **[G: U.S.]**

Pollin, Robert. Corporate Interest Payments and the Falling Rate of Profit in the U.S. Postwar Economy. *Econ. Forum*, Winter 1986-1987, *16*(1), pp. 129–45. **[G: U.S.]**

Polonchek, John A.; Slovin, Myron B. and Sushka, Marie E. Tender-Offer Premia as a Management Signal. *Managerial Dec. Econ.*, March 1986, *7*(1), pp. 69–76. **[G: U.S.]**

Poterba, James M. The Market Valuation of Cash Dividends: The Citizens Utilities Case Reconsidered. *J. Finan. Econ.*, March 1986, *15*(3), pp. 395–405.

Praagman, J. and Soenen, L. A. Stability of Optimal-Currency Cocktails. *J. Econ. Bus.*, February 1986, *38*(1), pp. 1–17. **[G: W. Europe; U.S.; Canada; Japan]**

Ramaswamy, Krishna and Sundaresan, Suresh M. The Valuation of Floating-Rate Instruments: Theory and Evidence. *J. Finan. Econ.*, December 1986, *17*(2), pp. 251–72.

Reinhardt, Uwe E. The Nature of Equity Financing. **In** *Gray, B. H., ed.*, 1986, pp. 67–73. **[G: U.S.]**

Rhee, S. Ghon. Stochastic Demand and a Decomposition of Systematic Risk. **In** *Chen, A. H., ed.*, 1986, pp. 197–216.

Richardson, Gordon; Sefcik, Stephan E. and Thompson, Rex. A Test of Dividend Irrelevance Using Volume Reactions to a Change in Dividend Policy. *J. Finan. Econ.*, December 1986, *17*(2), pp. 313–33. **[G: U.S.]**

Robbins, Edward Henry and Schatzberg, John D. Callable Bonds: A Risk-Reducing Signalling Mechanism. *J. Finance*, September 1986, *41*(4), pp. 935–49.

Roberts, Gordon S. and Viscione, Jerry A. Agency Costs, Bond Covenants, and Bond Yields. **In** *Chen, A. H., ed.*, 1986, pp. 73–99. **[G: U.S.]**

Rock, Kevin. Why New Issues Are Underpriced. *J. Finan. Econ.*, Jan./Feb. 1986, *15*(1/2), pp. 187–212.

Rohatyn, Felix G. Needed: Restraints on the Takeover Mania. *Challenge*, May/June 1986, *29*(2), pp. 30–34. **[G: U.S.]**

Roll, Richard. The Hubris Hypothesis of Corporate Takeovers. *J. Bus.*, Part 1, April 1986, *59*(2), pp. 197–216. **[G: U.S.]**

Ronn, Ehud I. and Verma, Avinash K. Pricing Risk-Adjusted Deposit Insurance: An Option-Based Model. *J. Finance*, September 1986, *41*(4), pp. 871–95. **[G: U.S.]**

Rousseau, Patrick. Conversion des documents comptables et taux de change: proposition d'une nouvelle approch. (Translating Financial Statements and Exchange Rate: Proposals for a New Approach. With English summary.) *Écon. Soc.*, December 1986, *20*(12), pp. 83–103.

Ruback, Richard S. Calculating the Market Value of Riskless Cash Flows. *J. Finan. Econ.*, March 1986, *15*(3), pp. 323–39.

Rudolph, Bernd. The Value of Security Agreements. **In** *Bamberg, G. and Spremann, K., eds.*, 1986, pp. 135–62.

Rybczynski, Tad M. Industrial Finance System in Europe, U.S. and Japan: Reply. **In** *Day, R. H. and Eliasson, G., eds.*, 1986, pp. 408–09. **[G: Europe; U.S.; Japan]**

Rybczynski, Tad M. Industrial Finance System in Europe, U.S. and Japan. **In** *Day, R. H. and Eliasson, G., eds.*, 1986, *1984*, pp. 385–96. **[G: Europe; U.S.; Japan]**

Salmi, Timo, et al. Financial Ratio Variability and Industry Classification. *Liiketaloudellinen Aikak.*, 1986, *35*(4), pp. 333–56. **[G: Finland]**

Samuelson, William F. and Rosenthal, Leonard. Price Movements as Indicators of Tender Offer Success. *J. Finance*, June 1986, *41*(2), pp. 481–99. **[G: U.S.]**

Schaumann, Alexander. Opsparing og finansieringskanaler. (Private Saving, Pension-Schemes and Channels of Business Financing. With English summary.) *Nationaløkon. Tidsskr.*, 1986, *124*(2), pp. 189–95. **[G: Denmark]**

van Schijndel, Geert-Jan C. Th. Dynamic Behaviour of a Value Maximizing Firm under Personal Taxation. *Europ. Econ. Rev.*, October 1986, *30*(5), pp. 1043–62.

Schipper, Katherine and Smith, Abbie. A Comparison of Equity Carve-outs and Seasoned Equity Offerings: Share Price Effects and Corporate Restructuring. *J. Finan. Econ.*, Jan./Feb. 1986, *15*(1/2), pp. 153–86. **[G: U.S.]**

Schleifer, Andrei and Vishny, Robert W. Greenmail, White Knights, and Shareholders' Interest. *Rand J. Econ.*, Autumn 1986, *17*(3), pp. 293–309.

Schwartz, Alan. Bebchuk on Minimum Offer Periods. *J. Law, Econ., Organ.*, Fall 1986, *2*(2), pp. 271–77.

Schwartz, Alan. Search Theory and the Tender Offer Auction. *J. Law, Econ., Organ.*, Fall 1986, *2*(2), pp. 229–53.

Shiller, Robert J. Comments [Behavioral Rationality in Finance: The Case of Dividends] [Anomalies in Financial Economics: Blueprint for Change?]. *J. Bus.*, Part 2, October 1986, *59*(4), pp. S501–05.

Shiller, Robert J. Comments [Behavioral Rationality in Finance: The Case of Dividends] [Anomalies in Financial Economics: Blueprint for Change?]. **In** *Hogarth, R. M. and Reder, M. W., eds.*, 1986, pp. 317–21.

Shiller, Robert J. The Marsh–Merton Model of Managers' Smoothing of Dividends. *Amer. Econ. Rev.*, June 1986, *76*(3), pp. 499–503.

Shleifer, Andrei and Vishny, Robert W. Large Shareholders and Corporate Control. *J. Polit. Econ.*, Part 1, June 1986, *94*(3), pp. 461–88.

Shome, Parthasarathi. Empirical Evidence on the Incidence of the Corporate Income Tax. **In** *Shome, P., ed.*, 1986, pp. 93–113. **[G: ASEAN]**

Smith, Clifford W., Jr. Investment Banking and the Capital Acquisition Process. *J. Finan. Econ.*, Jan./Feb. 1986, *15*(1/2), pp. 3–29. **[G: U.S.]**

Šourek, Stanislav. Modifications in the System of Financial Mangement of Economic Production Units and Enterprises for the 8th Five-Year Plan. *Czech. Econ. Digest.*, May 1986, (3), pp. 11–23. **[G: Czechoslovakia]**

Spinanger, Dean. Industrial Finance System in Europe, U.S. and Japan: Comment. **In** *Day, R. H. and Eliasson, G., eds.*, 1986, pp. 404–07. **[G: Europe; U.S.; Japan]**

Srivastava, Rajendra P. Auditing Functions for Internal Control Systems with Interdependent Documents and Channels. *J. Acc. Res.*, Autumn 1986, *24*(2), pp. 422–26.

Stober, Thomas L. The Incremental Information Content of Financial Statement Disclosures: The Case of LIFO Inventory Liquidations. *J. Acc. Res.*, Supp. 1986, *24*, pp. 138–60. **[G: U.S.]**

Taggart, Robert A., Jr. Have U.S. Corporations Grown Financially Weak? **In** *Friedman, B. M., ed.*, 1986, pp. 13–33. **[G: U.S.]**

Taggart, Robert A., Jr. Pricing New Corporate Bond Issues: An Analysis of Issue Cost and Seasoning Effects: Discussion. *J. Finance*, July 1986, *41*(3), pp. 643–44. **[G: U.S.]**

Tanigawa, Yasuhiko. On Mutual Share Holding by Corporations. *Econ. Stud. Quart.*, December 1986, *37*(4), pp. 319–35. **[G: Japan]**

Thompson, Nancy L. Financially Troubled Museums and the Law. **In** *DiMaggio, P. J., ed.*, 1986, pp. 214–42. **[G: U.S.]**

Titman, Sheridan and Trueman, Brett. Information Quality and the Valuation of New Issues. *J. Acc. Econ.*, June 1986, *8*(2), pp. 159–72.

Trueman, Brett. The Relationship between the Level of Capital Expenditures and Firm Value. *J. Finan. Quant. Anal.*, June 1986, *21*(2), pp. 115–29.

Ture, Norman B. and Bonilla, Carlos E. ACRS-ITC, CCRS, and NCRS Cost Recovery in an Inflationary Economy. **In** *Landau, R. and Jorgenson, D. W., eds.*, 1986, pp. 171–89. **[G: U.S.]**

Tybout, James. A Firm-Level Chronicle of Financial Crises in the Southern Cone. *J. Devel. Econ.*, December 1986, *24*(2), pp. 371–400. **[G: Chile; Argentina; Uruguay]**

Uvalic, Milica. The Investment Behaviour of a Labour-Managed Firm. *Ann. Pub. Co-op. Econ.*, Jan.-March 1986, *57*(1), pp. 11–33.

Vanthienen, L. and Vermaelen, Theo. The Effect of Royal Decree 15 on Security Prices and Financing Decisions. *Tijdschrift Econ. Manage.*, 1986, *31*(4), pp. 541–82. **[G: Netherlands]**

Venkatesh, P. C. and Chiang, Raymond. Information Asymmetry and the Dealer's Bid–Ask Spread: A Case Study of Earnings and Dividend Announcements. *J. Finance*, December 1986, *41*(5), pp. 1089–1102. **[G: U.S.]**

Voszka, Éva. Company Liquidation without a Legal Successor. *Acta Oecon.*, 1986, *37*(1–2), pp. 59–71. **[G: Hungary]**

Vu, Joseph D. An Empirical Investigation of Calls of Non-Convertible Bonds. *J. Finan. Econ.*, June 1986, *16*(2), pp. 235–65. **[G: U.S.]**

Warren, Alvin C., Jr. Taxation of Corporations. **In** *Knowlton, W. and Zeckhauser, R., eds.*, 1986, pp. 281–97. **[G: U.S.]**

Wetzler, James W. Corporate Income Tax Reform. **In** *Landau, R. and Jorgenson, D. W., eds.*, 1986, pp. 97–117. **[G: U.S.]**

Wheeler, James E. and Outslay, Edmund. The Phantom Federal Income Taxes of General Dynamics Corporation. *Accounting Rev.*, October 1986, *61*(4), pp. 760–74. **[G: U.S.]**

Whitehall, Peter. Profit Variation in the Barbados Manufacturing Sector. *Soc. Econ. Stud.*, December 1986, *35*(4), pp. 67–91. **[G: Barbados]**

Woolford, Joseph and Pohl, Rolf. The Financing of Inventory and Accounts Receivable. **In** *Bruce, R., et al., eds.*, 1986, pp. 232–46. **[G: Australia]**

Yli-Olli, Paavo and Virtanen, Ilkka. Classification Pattern of Financial Ratios: A Comparative Analysis between U.S. and Finnish Firms on the Aggregate Level. *Liiketaloudellinen Aikak.*, 1986, *35*(2), pp. 112–32. **[G: U.S.; Finland]**

Zechner, Josef and Swoboda, Peter. The Critical Implicit Tax Rate and Capital Structure. *J.*

Banking Finance, October 1986, *10*(3), pp. 327–41.

Zhu, Yu and Friend, Irwin. The Effects of Different Taxes on Risky and Risk-free Investment and on the Cost of Capital. *J. Finance*, March 1986, *41*(1), pp. 53–66.

522 Business Investment

5220 Business Investment

Abel, Andrew B. and Blanchard, Olivier J. The Present Value of Profits and Cyclical Movements in Investment. *Econometrica*, March 1986, *54*(2), pp. 249–73. **[G: U.S.]**

Alworth, Julian. A Cost of Capital Approach to the Taxation of Foreign Direct Investment Income. **In** *Edwards, J., et al., eds.*, 1986, pp. 185–208.

Anthony, Robert N. Accounting Rates of Return: Note [On the Misuse of Accounting Rates of Return to Infer Monopoly Profits]. *Amer. Econ. Rev.*, March 1986, *76*(1), pp. 244–46.

Apte, P. G. Aspects of Corporate Decision Making: An Econometric Investigation. *Indian Econ. Rev.*, July-Dec. 1986, *21*(2), pp. 185–215. **[G: India]**

Auerbach, Alan J. Inflation, Uncertainty, and Investment: Discussion. *J. Finance*, July 1986, *41*(3), pp. 668–69.

Auerbach, Alan J. Tax Reform and Capital Formation: Discussion. **In** *Federal Reserve Bank of Boston*, 1986, pp. 145–48. **[G: U.S.]**

Auernheimer, Leonardo. Variable Depreciation and Some of Its Implications. *Can. J. Econ.*, February 1986, *19*(1), pp. 99–113.

Baba, Masao. Changes in Industrial Structure and Investment Planning. *Ifo-Studien*, 1986, *32*(1–3), pp. 123–30. **[G: Japan]**

Baldwin, Carliss Y. and Ruback, Richard S. Inflation, Uncertainty, and Investment. *J. Finance*, July 1986, *41*(3), pp. 657–68.

Barbera, Anthony J.; Pollock, Stephen H. and Meade, Douglas S. Tax Simplification and the Performance of the U.S. Economy. *J. Policy Modeling*, Fall 1986, *8*(3), pp. 415–31. **[G: U.S.]**

Baumol, William J. Optimal Depreciation Policy: Pricing the Products of Durable Assets. **In** *Baumol, W. J.*, 1986, pp. 111–29.

Behrman, Jere R. Shadow Prices and Subsidies in Botswana. *J. Devel. Econ.*, July-Aug. 1986, *22*(2), pp. 351–92. **[G: Botswana]**

Bennett, Robert J. The Impact of Non-Domestic Rates on Profitability and Investment. *Fisc. Stud.*, February 1986, *7*(1), pp. 34–50. **[G: U.K.]**

Bivin, David G. Inventories and Interest Rates: A Critique of the Buffer Stock Model. *Amer. Econ. Rev.*, March 1986, *76*(1), pp. 168–76. **[G: U.S.]**

Blanchard, Olivier J. Investment, Output, and the Cost of Capital: Comments. *Brookings Pap. Econ. Act.*, 1986, (1), pp. 153–58. **[G: U.S.]**

Blinder, Alan S. Can the Production Smoothing Model of Inventory Behavior Be Saved? *Quart. J. Econ.*, August 1986, *101*(3), pp. 431–53. **[G: U.S.]**

Blinder, Alan S. More on the Speed of Adjustment in Inventory Models. *J. Money, Credit, Banking*, August 1986, *18*(3), pp. 355–65.

Bromiley, Philip. Corporate Planning and Capital Investment. *J. Econ. Behav. Organ.*, June 1986, *7*(2), pp. 147–70. **[G: U.S.]**

Browne, F. X. Loan Market Price and Quantity Effects in a Production Smoothing Model of Inventory Investment. *Appl. Econ.*, June 1986, *18*(6), pp. 691–707. **[G: Ireland]**

Browning, Edgar K. Taxation, Capital Accumulation, and Equity. **In** *Lee, D. R., ed.*, 1986, pp. 19–47. **[G: OECD]**

Bruce, Alistair. State-to-Private Sector Divestment: The Case of Sealink. **In** *Coyne, J. and Wright, M., eds.*, 1986, pp. 202–44. **[G: U.K.]**

Casson, Mark. Foreign Divestment and International Rationalisation: The Sale of Chrysler (UK) to Peugeot. **In** *Coyne, J. and Wright, M., eds.*, 1986, pp. 102–39. **[G: U.K.]**

Chan-Lee, James H. Pure Profits and Tobin's *q* in Nine OECD Countries. *OECD Econ. Stud.*, Autumn 1986, (7), pp. 205–32. **[G: Selected OECD]**

Chirinko, Robert S. Business Investment and Tax Policy: A Perspective on Existing Models and Empirical Results. *Nat. Tax J.*, June 1986, *39*(2), pp. 137–55. **[G: U.S.]**

Cochran, Neilsen. Divestiture: A Public Service Commissioner's Perspective. **In** *[Dorsey, J. N. and Wiggins, B. T.]*, 1986, pp. 13–15. **[G: U.S.]**

Comiskey, Eugene E. and Mulford, Charles W. Investment Decisions and the Equity Accounting Standard. *Accounting Rev.*, July 1986, *61*(3), pp. 519–25. **[G: U.S.]**

Connolly, Robert A. Assessing the Importance of Measurement Error in Capital Investment Models. *Managerial Dec. Econ.*, September 1986, *7*(3), pp. 177–85.

Coyne, John. Divestment by Management Buy-Out: Variant and Variety. **In** *Coyne, J. and Wright, M., eds.*, 1986, pp. 140–65. **[G: U.K.]**

Coyne, John and Wright, Mike. An Introduction to Divestment: The Conceptual Issues. **In** *Coyne, J. and Wright, M., eds.*, 1986, pp. 1–26.

Davis, Gary. Strategic Trading: Rationalisation in U.S. Brewing. **In** *Coyne, J. and Wright, M., eds.*, 1986, pp. 73–101. **[G: U.S.]**

Day, Richard H. and Hanson, Kenneth A. Adaptive Economising, Technological Change and the Demand for Labour in Disequilibrium. **In** *Nijkamp, P., ed. (II)*, 1986, pp. 301–20.

van Donselaar, Karel and Wijngaard, Jacob. Practical Application of the Echelon Approach in a System with Divergent Product Structures. **In** *Axsäter, S.; Schneeweiss, C. and Silver, E., eds.*, 1986, pp. 182–96. **[G: Netherlands]**

Downe, Ed. The Behavior of Postwar Rates of Return in Capitalist Countries. *Rev. Radical*

Polit. Econ., Fall 1986, *18*(3), pp. 101–10. [G: OECD]

Downs, Thomas W. The User Cost and Capital Budgeting. *Financial Rev.*, May 1986, *21*(2), pp. 277–87.

Downs, Thomas W. Using the User Cost. *J. Econ. Bus.*, December 1986, *38*(4), pp. 297–305.

Driver, Ciaran. The Scrapping Behaviour of Concentrated and Non-concentrated Industries in the UK. *Appl. Econ.*, March 1986, *18*(3), pp. 249–63. [G: U.K.]

Eisner, Robert. Tax Reform and Capital Formation: Discussion. **In** *Federal Reserve Bank of Boston*, 1986, pp. 149–52. [G: U.S.]

Fershtman, Chaim and Muller, Eitan. Capital Investments and Price Agreements in Semicollusive Markets. *Rand J. Econ.*, Summer 1986, *17*(2), pp. 214–26.

Frankel, Jeffrey A. International Capital Mobility and Crowding-out in the U.S. Economy: Imperfect Integration of Financial Markets or of Goods Markets? **In** *Hafer, R. W., ed. (I)*, 1986, pp. 33–67. [G: U.S.]

Friedman, Benjamin M. Financing American Investment in New Technology. **In** *Landau, R. and Jorgenson, D. W., eds.*, 1986, pp. 205–19. [G: U.S.]

Gertler, Meric S. Regional Dynamics of Manufacturing and Non-manufacturing Investment in Canada. *Reg. Stud.*, October 1986, *20*(6), pp. 523–34. [G: Canada]

Geweke, John. Fixed Investment in the American Business Cycle, 1919–83: Comment. **In** *Gordon, R. J., ed.*, 1986, pp. 336–40. [G: U.S.]

Giannaros, Demetrios S. Determinants of Sectoral Investment in a Developing Capital Market Economy. *J. Econ. Devel.*, July 1986, *11*(1), pp. 133–56. [G: Greece]

Girardin, Eric. Estimation en longue période d'une fonction d'investissement pour le Royaume-Uni: 1881–1979. (Estimation of an Investment Function for the United Kingdom in the Long Run: 1881–1979. With English summary.) *Écon. Appl.*, 1986, *39*(2), pp. 297–336. [G: U.K.]

Gofran, K. A. Bangladesh: Depreciation Allowances under the Income-Tax Ordinance, 1984—A Summary. *Bull. Int. Fiscal Doc.*, January 1986, *40*(1), pp. 20–22. [G: Bangladesh]

Gordon, Robert J. and Veitch, John M. Fixed Investment in the American Business Cycle, 1919–83. **In** *Gordon, R. J., ed.*, 1986, pp. 267–335. [G: U.S.]

Gordon, Robert J. and Veitch, John M. Fixed Investment in the American Business Cycle, 1919–83: Reply. **In** *Gordon, R. J., ed.*, 1986, pp. 348–51. [G: U.S.]

Grabowski, Henry G. and Mueller, Dennis C. Life Cycle Effects on Corporate Returns on Retentions. **In** *Mueller, D. C.*, 1986, *1975*, pp. 138–52. [G: U.S.]

Grabowski, Henry G. and Mueller, Dennis C. Managerial and Stockholder Welfare Models of Firm Expenditures. **In** *Mueller, D. C.*, 1986, *1972*, pp. 81–107.

Green, Richard C. and Talmor, Eli. Effects of Asymmetric Taxation on the Scale of Corporate Investment. **In** *Edwards, J., et al., eds.*, 1986, pp. 83–97.

Gronchi, Sandro. A Note on Truncation. *Bull. Econ. Res.*, May 1986, *38*(2), pp. 161–67.

Gronchi, Sandro. On Investment Criteria Based on the Internal Rate of Return. *Oxford Econ. Pap.*, March 1986, *38*(1), pp. 174–80.

Hall, Stephen G.; Henry, S. G. B. and Wren-Lewis, Simon. Manufacturing Stocks and Forward-Looking Expectations in the UK. *Economica*, November 1986, *53*(212), pp. 447–65. [G: U.K.]

Hatsopoulos, George N. Tax Reform and Capital Formation: Discussion. **In** *Federal Reserve Bank of Boston*, 1986, pp. 140–44. [G: U.S.]

Hatsopoulos, George N. and Brooks, Stephen H. The Gap in the Cost of Capital: Causes, Effects, and Remedies. **In** *Landau, R. and Jorgenson, D. W., eds.*, 1986, pp. 221–80. [G: U.S.; Japan]

Hayes, Beth and Siegel, Daniel. Rate of Return Regulation with Price Flexibility. *J. Bus.*, Part 1, October 1986, *59*(4), pp. 537–53.

Heinrich, Claus E. and Schneeweiss, Christoph. Multi-stage Lot-Sizing for General Production Systems. **In** *Axsäter, S.; Schneeweiss, C. and Silver, E., eds.*, 1986, pp. 150–81.

Hendershott, Patric H. Tax Reform, Interest Rates, and Capital Allocation. **In** *Follain, J. R., ed.*, 1986, pp. 27–57. [G: U.S.]

Henderson, Yolanda K. Lessons from Federal Reform of Business Taxes. *New Eng. Econ. Rev.*, Nov./Dec. 1986, pp. 9–25. [G: U.S.]

Hill, Raymond D. Insurance and Financial Intermediation. **In** *Wasow, B. and Hill, R. D., eds.*, 1986, pp. 120–34. [G: U.S.]

Ho, Kwok S. An Empirical Analysis of a Causality Relationship between Corporate Investment and Financing Decisions. **In** *Chen, A. H., ed.*, 1986, pp. 179–96. [G: U.S.]

Holmstrom, Bengt and Ricart i Costa, Joan. Managerial Incentives and Capital Management. *Quart. J. Econ.*, November 1986, *101*(4), pp. 835–60.

Holz, Arnold. Die Ausrüstungsinvestitionen der schweizerischen Industrie. Desaggregierte Hochrechnungen 1969–1985. (Equipment Investment of Swiss Industry. Disaggregated Estimations 1969 to 1985. With English summary.) *Schweiz. Z. Volkswirtsch. Statist.*, December 1986, *122*(4), pp. 677–96. [G: Switzerland]

Jegers, Marc. Le concept d'intérêts cumulés: nécessaire ou suffisant? (The Concept of Cumulated Interests: Necessary or Sufficient? With English summary.) *Écon. Soc.*, December 1986, *20*(12), pp. 37–48.

Johar, R. S. and Singh, Tarlok. Determinants of Investment in Liquor Industry in Punjab. *Margin*, October 1986, *19*(1), pp. 59–65. [G: India]

Jones, Ian S. The Application of Risk Analysis to the Appraisal of Optional Investment in the Electricity Supply Industry. *Appl. Econ.*, May 1986, *18*(5), pp. 509–28. [G: U.K.]

Jönsson, Henrik and Silver, Edward A. Overview of a Stock Allocation Model for a Two-Echelon Push System Having Identical Units at the Lower Echelon. In *Axsäter, S.; Schneeweiss, C. and Silver, E., eds.*, 1986, pp. 44–49.

Junge, G. and Zarinnejadan, Milad. A Rate-of-Return Model of Investment Behavior for Switzerland. *Empirical Econ.*, 1986, *11*(3), pp. 153–67. **[G: Switzerland]**

Kanniainen, Vesa and Hernesniemi, Hannu. Inventories, Cost of Inventory Capital, and Sales Expectations. *Liiketaloudellinen Aikak.*, 1986, *35*(3), pp. 184–95. **[G: Finland]**

Kay, John A. and Mayer, Colin. On the Application of Accounting Rates of Returns. *Econ. J.*, March 1986, *96*(381), pp. 199–207.

Kohli, Ulrich and Ryan, Christopher J. Australian Business Investment: A New Look at the Neoclassical Approach. *Econ. Rec.*, December 1986, *62*(179), pp. 451–67. **[G: Australia]**

Kollintzas, Tryphon. Tax Policy under Nongeometric Physical Depreciation. *Public Finance Quart.*, July 1986, *14*(3), pp. 263–88.

Kopcke, Richard W. Tax Reform and Capital Formation. In *Federal Reserve Bank of Boston*, 1986, pp. 103–39. **[G: U.S.]**

Landefeld, J. Steven and Seskin, Eugene P. A Comparison of Anticipatory Surveys and Econometric Models in Forecasting U.S. Business Investment. *J. Econ. Soc. Meas.*, April 1986, *14*(1), pp. 77–85. **[G: U.S.]**

Langetieg, Terence C. Stochastic Control of Corporate Investment When Output Affects Future Prices. *J. Finan. Quant. Anal.*, September 1986, *21*(3), pp. 239–63.

Leite, Sergio Pereira and Vaez-Zadeh, Reza. Credit Allocation and Investment Decisions: The Case of the Manufacturing Sector in Korea. *World Devel.*, January 1986, *14*(1), pp. 115–26. **[G: S. Korea]**

Leontief, Wassily. Technological Change, Prices, Wages, and Rates of Return on Capital in the U.S. Economy. In *Leontief, W.*, 1986, *1985*, pp. 392–417. **[G: U.S.]**

Lluch, Constantino. ICORS, Savings Rates, and the Determinants of Public Expenditure in Developing Countries. In *Lal, D. and Wolf, M., eds.*, 1986, pp. 361–95. **[G: LDCs]**

Loeb, Peter D. Specification Error Tests and the Jorgenson–Stephenson Investment Functions. *Appl. Econ.*, August 1986, *18*(8), pp. 851–61.

Lönnqvist, Åke. Forecasting Power of Entrepreneurs Expectations. *Ifo-Studien*, 1986, *32*(1–3), pp. 181–99. **[G: Sweden]**

Lovell, Michael C. Investment, Output, and the Cost of Capital: Comments. *Brookings Pap. Econ. Act.*, 1986, (1), pp. 158–61. **[G: U.S.]**

Lowe, Jeffrey H. Capital Expenditures by Majority-Owned Foreign Affiliates of U.S. Companies, 1986. *Surv. Curr. Bus.*, March 1986, *66*(3), pp. 18–23. **[G: U.S.]**

Malécot, Jean-François and Hamon, Jean. Contraintes financieères et demande d'investissement des entreprises. (Financial Constraints and Firms' Investment. With English summary.) *Revue Écon.*, September 1986, *37*(5), pp. 885–923. **[G: France]**

Martin, Ronald L. Industrial Restructuring, Labour Shake-Out and the Geography of Recession. In *Danson, M., ed.*, 1986, pp. 1–22. **[G: U.K.]**

McDonald, Robert and Siegel, Daniel. The Value of Waiting to Invest. *Quart. J. Econ.*, November 1986, *101*(4), pp. 707–27.

McMurtry, Burton J. Tax Policy Influence on Venture Capital. In *Landau, R. and Jorgenson, D. W., eds.*, 1986, pp. 137–51. **[G: U.S.]**

Messori, Marcello. Financement bancaire et décisions de production. (Banking Finance and Production Decisions. With English summary.) *Écon. Soc.*, Aug.-Sept. 1986, *20*(8–9), pp. 127–58.

Mishkin, Frederic S. International Capital Mobility and Crowding-out in the U.S. Economy: Imperfect Integration of Financial Markets or of Goods Markets? Comments. In *Hafer, R. W., ed. (I)*, 1986, pp. 69–74. **[G: U.S.; OECD]**

Mohnen, Pierre A.; Nadiri, M. Ishaq and Prucha, Ingmar R. R&D, Production Structure and Rates of Return in the U.S., Japanese and German Manufacturing Sectors: A Non-separable Dynamic Factor Demand Model. *Europ. Econ. Rev.*, August 1986, *30*(4), pp. 749–71. **[G: U.S.; Japan; W. Germany]**

Molho, Lazaros E. Selective Credit Controls in Greece: A Test of Their Effectiveness. *Int. Monet. Fund Staff Pap.*, September 1986, *33*(3), pp. 477–508. **[G: Greece]**

Montllor, Joan. La sensibilidad de las decisiones de inversión ante variaciones sistemáticas de los flujos de caja. (With English summary.) *Invest. Ecón.*, January 1986, *10*(1), pp. 141–62.

Muckstadt, John A. Planning Component Delivery Intervals in Constrained Assembly Systems. In *Axsäter, S.; Schneeweiss, C. and Silver, E., eds.*, 1986, pp. 132–49.

Naqvi, Nadeem. International Debt, Investment and the Currency Account: An Intertemporal Analysis. *Indian Econ. J.*, Jan.-Mar. 1986, *33*(3), pp. 53–64.

Naqvi, Nadeem and Beladi, Hamid. An Analysis of Some Trade Theoretic Aspects of Investment and the Balance of Payments. *J. Econ. Devel.*, December 1986, *11*(2), pp. 197–211. **[G: S. Korea]**

Nguyen, Sang V. and Andrews, Stephen H. Measuring Service Prices of U.S. Manufacturing Capital Input, Inventories, and Financial Working Capital, 1947–1981. *J. Econ. Soc. Meas.*, December 1986, *14*(4), pp. 325–40. **[G: U.S.]**

O'Brien, D. P. Divestiture: The Case of AT&T. In *Coyne, J. and Wright, M., eds.*, 1986, pp. 166–201. **[G: U.S.]**

O'Neil, Brian F. Information—A Viable Substitute for Inventory. *Logist. Transp. Rev.*, March 1986, *22*(1), pp. 83–89.

Papke, James A. and Papke, Leslie E. Measuring Differential State–Local Tax Liabilities and Their Implications for Business Investment Location. *Nat. Tax J.*, September 1986, *39*(3), pp. 357–66. **[G: U.S.]**

Peck, S. C. Econometric Aspects of Firm Growth Behaviour. **In** *[Yamey, B.]*, 1986, pp. 133–58.

Pereira, Alfredo M. On the Computation of the Users' Cost of Capital in the Presence of Adjustments Costs. *Economia (Portugal)*, October 1986, *10*(3), pp. 447–52.

Petrović, Radivoj and Memedović, Olga. Višekriterijumski pristup rangiranju i izboru investicija. (Multicriteria Ranking and Selection of Investment Projects. With English summary.) *Econ. Anal. Workers' Manage.*, 1986, *20*(3), pp. 311–28.

Pike, Richard H. The Design of Capital Budgeting Processes and the Corporate Context. *Managerial Dec. Econ.*, September 1986, *7*(3), pp. 187–95. **[G: U.K.]**

Pointon, J. UK Taxation and Financial Decision Making. **In** *Firth, M. and Keane, S. M., eds.*, 1986, pp. 182–92. **[G: U.K.]**

Qureshi, D. M. Financing of Investments of Public Enterprises in Developing Countries. **In** *U.N., Dept. of Technical Co-operation for Development*, 1986, pp. 57–64. **[G: Pakistan]**

Reynolds, Stanley S. Strategic Capital Investment in the American Aluminum Industry. *J. Ind. Econ.*, March 1986, *34*(3), pp. 225–45. **[G: U.S.]**

Rieper, Bernd. Die Bestellmengenrechnung als Investitions- und Finanzierungsproblem. (With English summary.) *Z. Betriebswirtshaft*, December 1986, *56*(12), pp. 1230–55.

Robbins, Aldona E.; Robbins, Gary A. and Roberts, Paul Craig. The Relative Impact of Taxation and Interest Rates on the Cost of Capital. **In** *Landau, R. and Jorgenson, D. W., eds.*, 1986, pp. 281–316. **[G: U.S.]**

Robinson, Terence. Depreciation Reserve Assessment. **In** *[Dorsey, J. N. and Wiggins, B. T.]*, 1986, pp. 189–206. **[G: U.S.]**

Ruback, Richard S. Calculating the Market Value of Riskless Cash Flows. *J. Finan. Econ.*, March 1986, *15*(3), pp. 323–39.

Samuels, J. The Required Return on Investment Projects. **In** *Firth, M. and Keane, S. M., eds.*, 1986, pp. 89–102.

Schankerman, Mark and Nadiri, M. Ishaq. A Test of Static Equilibrium Models and Rates of Return to Quasi-fixed Factors, with an Application to the Bell System. *J. Econometrics*, Oct./Nov. 1986, *33*(1/2), pp. 97–118.

van Schijndel, Geert-Jan C. Th. Dynamic Behaviour of a Value Maximizing Firm under Personal Taxation. *Europ. Econ. Rev.*, October 1986, *30*(5), pp. 1043–62.

Seskin, Eugene P. and Sullivan, David F. Plant and Equipment Expenditures, the Four Quarters of 1986. *Surv. Curr. Bus.*, June 1986, *66*(6), pp. 17–20. **[G: U.S.]**

Seskin, Eugene P. and Sullivan, David F. Plant and Equipment Expenditures, the Four Quarters of 1986. *Surv. Curr. Bus.*, September 1986, *66*(9), pp. 23–26. **[G: U.S.]**

Seskin, Eugene P. and Sullivan, David F. Plant and Equipment Expenditures: Quarters of 1986, First and Second Quarters of 1987, Year 1987. *Surv. Curr. Bus.*, December 1986, *66*(12), pp. 17–19. **[G: U.S.]**

Shapiro, Matthew D. Investment, Output, and the Cost of Capital. *Brookings Pap. Econ. Act.*, 1986, (1), pp. 111–52. **[G: U.S.]**

Shapiro, Matthew D. The Dynamic Demand for Capital and Labor. *Quart. J. Econ.*, August 1986, *101*(3), pp. 513–42. **[G: U.S.]**

Shome, Parthasarathi. Effects of Tax Incentives on Investment and Employment: Appendix: The Broad Goals of Tax Incentives. **In** *Shome, P., ed.*, 1986, pp. 43–47. **[G: Thailand; Malaysia; Philippines]**

Shriver, Keith A. A Statistical Test of the Stability Assumption Inherent in Empirical Estimates of Economic Depreciation. *J. Econ. Soc. Meas.*, July 1986, *14*(2), pp. 145–53. **[G: U.S.]**

Shriver, Keith A. The Valuation of Used Capital Assets During Time Periods Exhibiting Alternative Degrees of Demand for Industrial Machinery and Equipment. *J. Econ. Soc. Meas.*, December 1986, *14*(4), pp. 289–310. **[G: U.S.]**

Sims, Christopher A. Fixed Investment in the American Business Cycle, 1919–83: Comment. **In** *Gordon, R. J., ed.*, 1986, pp. 340–48. **[G: U.S.]**

Slemrod, Joel. Taxation and Business Investment. **In** *Cagan, P., ed.*, 1986, pp. 45–72. **[G: U.S.]**

Steinmo, Sven. So What's Wrong with Tax Expenditures? A Reevaluation Based on Swedish Experience. *Public Budg. Finance*, Summer 1986, *6*(2), pp. 27–44. **[G: Sweden]**

Struckmeyer, Charles S. The Impact of Energy Price Shocks on Capital Formation and Economic Growth in a Putty–Clay Technology. *Southern Econ. J.*, July 1986, *53*(1), pp. 127–40.

Sumner, Michael T. Investment and the 1984 Budget: An Interim Assessment. *Oxford Bull. Econ. Statist.*, November 1986, *48*(4), pp. 331–38. **[G: U.K.]**

Sutcliffe, C. and Bromwich, M. Investment Appraisal. **In** *Firth, M. and Keane, S. M., eds.*, 1986, pp. 44–58.

Thomas, R. E. Parent-to-Parent Divestment. **In** *Coyne, J. and Wright, M., eds.*, 1986, pp. 27–44. **[G: U.K.]**

Tirole, Jean. Procurement and Renegotiation. *J. Polit. Econ.*, April 1986, *94*(2), pp. 235–59.

Trueman, Brett. The Relationship between the Level of Capital Expenditures and Firm Value. *J. Finan. Quant. Anal.*, June 1986, *21*(2), pp. 115–29.

Ueda, Kazuo and Yoshikawa, Hiroshi. Financial Volatility and the *q* Theory of Investment. *Economica*, February 1986, *53*(209), pp. 11–27. **[G: Japan]**

Uvalic, Milica. The Investment Behaviour of a Labour-Managed Firm. *Ann. Pub. Co-op. Econ.*, Jan.-March 1986, *57*(1), pp. 11–33.

Vaez-Zadeh, Reza and Leite, Sergio Pereira. Effectiveness of Selective Credit Controls: An

Empirical Test Applied to India. *J. Devel. Stud.*, April 1986, *22*(3), pp. 558–72. **[G: India]**

West, Kenneth D. A Variance Bounds Test of the Linear Quadratic Inventory Model. *J. Polit. Econ.*, April 1986, *94*(2), pp. 374–401. **[G: U.S.]**

Wodopia, Franz-Josef. Flow and Fund Approaches to Irreversible Investment Decisions. **In** *Faber, M., ed.*, 1986, pp. 195–207.

Wright, J. F. On Investment Criteria Based on the Internal Rate of Return: A Response. *Oxford Econ. Pap.*, March 1986, *38*(1), pp. 181–84.

Wright, Mike. Demergers: The Case of Bowater. **In** *Coyne, J. and Wright, M., eds.*, 1986, pp. 45–72. **[G: U.K.]**

Zafiris, Nicos. Profitability as a Criterion of Enterprise Efficiency. *Ann. Pub. Co-op. Econ.*, September 1986, *57*(3), pp. 345–58.

530 Marketing and Advertising

531 Marketing and Advertising

5310 Marketing and Advertising

Aaker, David A.; Stayman, Douglas M. and Hagerty, Michael R. Warmth in Advertising: Measurement, Impact, and Sequence Effects. *J. Cons. Res.*, March 1986, *12*(4), pp. 365–81. **[G: U.S.]**

Akerlof, George A. The Market for "Lemons": Quality Uncertainty and the Market Mechanism. **In** *Barney, J. B. and Ouchi, W. G., eds.*, 1986, *1970*, pp. 27–39. **[G: India]**

Albers, Sönke. Controlling Independent Manufacturer Representatives by Using Commission Rate Functions Depending on Achieved Sales Volume. **In** *Backhaus, K. and Wilson, D. T., eds.*, 1986, pp. 88–112.

Anderson, Evan E. Image Differentiation and Locational Proximity among Retail Firms. *Managerial Dec. Econ.*, March 1986, *7*(1), pp. 63–68.

Anderson, James C. and Narus, James A. Toward a Better Understanding of Distribution Channel Working Relationships. **In** *Backhaus, K. and Wilson, D. T., eds.*, 1986, pp. 320–36.

Anderson, Paul F. On Method in Consumer Research: A Critical Relativist Perspective. *J. Cons. Res.*, September 1986, *13*(2), pp. 155–73.

Apte, P. G. Aspects of Corporate Decision Making: An Econometric Investigation. *Indian Econ. Rev.*, July-Dec. 1986, *21*(2), pp. 185–215. **[G: India]**

Backhaus, Klaus. Industrial Marketing—State of the Art in Germany. **In** *Backhaus, K. and Wilson, D. T., eds.*, 1986, pp. 3–14. **[G: W. Germany]**

Backhaus, Klaus and Meyer, Margit. Country Risk Assessment in International Industrial Marketing. **In** *Backhaus, K. and Wilson, D. T., eds.*, 1986, pp. 245–73. **[G: LDCs]**

Bahn, Kenneth D. How and When Do Brand Perceptions and Preferences First Form? A Cognitive Developmental Investigation. *J. Cons. Res.*, December 1986, *13*(3), pp. 382–93.

Batra, Rajeev and Ray, Michael L. Affective Responses Mediating Acceptance of Advertising. *J. Cons. Res.*, September 1986, *13*(2), pp. 234–49. **[G: U.S.]**

Batra, Rajeev and Ray, Michael L. Situational Effects of Advertising Repetition: The Moderating Influence of Motivation, Ability, and Opportunity to Respond. *J. Cons. Res.*, March 1986, *12*(4), pp. 432–45. **[G: U.S.]**

Beales, J. Howard, III. Comments [The Effects of the Advertising Substantiation Program on Advertising Agencies] [An Economic Analysis of the FTC's Ad Substantiation Program]. **In** *Ippolito, P. M. and Scheffman, D. T., eds.*, 1986, pp. 213–16. **[G: U.S.]**

Bello, Joseph A. The Changing Dimensions of the Nigerian Business Environment and Their Behavioural Implications. **In** *Damachi, U. G. and Seibel, H. D., eds.*, 1986, pp. 3–29. **[G: Nigeria]**

Bender, Horst O. High Technology Marketing. **In** *Backhaus, K. and Wilson, D. T., eds.*, 1986, pp. 191–223.

Bettman, James R.; John, Deborah Roedder and Scott, Carol A. Covariation Assessment by Consumers. *J. Cons. Res.*, December 1986, *13*(3), pp. 316–26.

Biehal, Gabriel and Chakravarti, Dipankar. Consumers' Use of Memory and External Information in Choice: Macro and Micro Perspectives. *J. Cons. Res.*, March 1986, *12*(4), pp. 382–405. **[G: U.S.]**

Bloch, Peter H.; Sherrell, Daniel L. and Ridgway, Nancy M. Consumer Search: An Extended Framework. *J. Cons. Res.*, June 1986, *13*(1), pp. 119–26. **[G: U.S.]**

Böcker, Franz and Hubel, Walter. Individual's Influence within Multi Person Decision Units. **In** *Backhaus, K. and Wilson, D. T., eds.*, 1986, pp. 25–40.

Bonanno, Giacomo. Advertising, Perceived Quality and Strategic Entry Deterrence and Accommodation. *Metroecon.*, October 1986, *38*(3), pp. 257–80.

Boyer, Kenneth D. and Lancaster, Kent M. Are There Scale Economies in Advertising? *J. Bus.*, July 1986, *59*(3), pp. 509–26.

Bresnahan, Timothy F. The Demand for Advertising by Medium: Implications for the Economies of Scale in Advertising. **In** *Ippolito, P. M. and Scheffman, D. T., eds.*, 1986, pp. 135–63. **[G: U.S.]**

Burfoot, Tim. Quality Control in Thomas Cook. **In** *Moores, B., ed.*, 1986, pp. 166–78. **[G: U.K.]**

Burke, Marian C. and Edell, Julie A. Ad Reactions over Time: Capturing Changes in the Real World. *J. Cons. Res.*, June 1986, *13*(1), pp. 114–18.

Busch, Paul and Leong, Siew Meng. A Review of Recent Social Power Research and Its Implications for Industrial Marketing Management.

In *Backhaus, K. and Wilson, D. T., eds.*, 1986, pp. 167–88.

Butters, Gerard R. The Impact of Product Recalls on the Wealth of Sellers: Comments. **In** *Ippolito, P. M. and Scheffman, D. T., eds.*, 1986, pp. 411–13. **[G: U.S.]**

Büyükkurt, B. Kemal. Integration of Serially Sampled Price Information: Modeling and Some Findings. *J. Cons. Res.*, December 1986, *13*(3), pp. 357–73.

Caves, Richard E. Information Structures of Product Markets. *Econ. Inquiry*, April 1986, *24*(2), pp. 195–212. **[G: U.S.]**

Chapman, Simon. The World Tobacco Industry. **In** *Wheelwright, T., ed.*, 1986, pp. 191–227. **[G: LDCs]**

Chard, John S. Economic Effects of Exclusive Purchasing Arrangements in the Distribution of Goods. **In** *Pellegrini, L. and Reddy, S. K., eds.*, 1986, pp. 39–57.

Coate, Malcolm B. Relative Market Share and Profitability. *J. Behav. Econ.*, Spring/Summer 1986, *15*(1/2), pp. 41–53.

Coate, Malcolm B. and Uri, Noel D. A Simultaneous Equations Model of Profitability, Concentration and Marketing Expense. *J. Behav. Econ.*, Fall 1986, *15*, pp. 1–15. **[G: U.S.]**

Corder, Clive. *Adimpact*—A Multi-media Advertising Effectiveness-Measurement Method. *Managerial Dec. Econ.*, December 1986, *7*(4), pp. 243–47. **[G: S. Africa]**

Cox, Steven R.; Schroeter, John R. and Smith, Scott L. Attorney Advertising and the Quality of Routine Legal Services. *Rev. Ind. Organ.*, 1986, *2*(4), pp. 340–54. **[G: U.S.]**

Davis, Harry L.; Hoch, Stephen J. and Ragsdale, E. K. Easton. An Anchoring and Adjustment Model of Spousal Predictions. *J. Cons. Res.*, June 1986, *13*(1), pp. 25–37. **[G: U.S.]**

DeSarbo, Wayne and Rao, Vithala R. A Constrained Unfolding Methodology for Product Positioning. *Marketing Sci.*, Winter 1986, *5*(1), pp. 1–19. **[G: U.S.]**

Dickson, John P. Locational Interdependency: The Impact of Change on Retail Images. **In** *Pellegrini, L. and Reddy, S. K., eds.*, 1986, pp. 171–81. **[G: U.S.]**

Dockner, Engelbert and Feichtinger, Gustav. Dynamic Advertising and Pricing in an Oligopoly: A Nash Equilibrium Approach. *J. Econ. Dynam. Control*, June 1986, *10*(1/2), pp. 37–39.

Dockner, Engelbert and Feichtinger, Gustav. Dynamic Advertising and Pricing in an Oligopoly: A Nash Equilibrium Approach. **In** *Başar, T., ed.*, 1986, pp. 238–51.

Douglas, Susan P. Selling in Japan: Consumer Behavior and Distribution as Barriers to Imports: Comment. **In** *Pugel, T. A., ed.*, 1986, pp. 107–13. **[G: U.S.; Japan; W. Germany]**

Eastlack, Joseph O., Jr. and Rao, Ambar G. Modeling Response to Advertising and Pricing Changes for "V-8" Cocktail Vegetable Juice. *Marketing Sci.*, Summer 1986, *5*(3), pp. 245–59. **[G: U.S.]**

Eaton, Jonathan and Grossman, Gene M. The Provision of Information as Marketing Strategy. **In** *Morris, D. J., et al., eds.*, 1986, pp. 166–83.

Eliashberg, Jehoshua and Jeuland, Abel P. The Impact of Competitive Entry in a Developing Market upon Dynamic Pricing Strategies. *Marketing Sci.*, Winter 1986, *5*(1), pp. 20–36.

Evans, Carolyn. Airline Performance as Rated by Frequent Passengers. **In** *Moores, B., ed.*, 1986, pp. 67–76. **[G: Selected Countries]**

Feick, Lawrence F.; Hermann, Robert O. and Warland, Rex H. Search for Nutrition Information: A Probit Analysis of the Use of Different Information Sources. *J. Cons. Aff.*, Winter 1986, *20*(2), pp. 173–92. **[G: U.S.]**

Feinberg, Richard A. Credit Cards as Spending Facilitating Stimuli: A Conditioning Interpretation. *J. Cons. Res.*, December 1986, *13*(3), pp. 348–56.

Ferguson, James M. The Demand for Advertising by Medium: Implications for the Economies of Scale in Advertising: Comments. **In** *Ippolito, P. M. and Scheffman, D. T., eds.*, 1986, pp. 165–69. **[G: U.S.]**

Friedman, Monroe. Commercial Influences in the Lyrics of Popular American Music of the Postwar Era. *J. Cons. Aff.*, Winter 1986, *20*(2), pp. 193–213. **[G: U.S.]**

Fritz, Wolfgang. Unternehmerische Reaktionen auf vergleichende Warentests—Ein empirischer Vergleich zweier Erklärungsmodelle. (With English summary.) *Z. Betriebswirtshaft*, Apr.-May 1986, *56*(4/5), pp. 404–24.

Fugate, Douglas L. The Effects of Manufacturer Disclosure on Consumer Perceptions of Private Brand Grocery Product Attributes. *J. Cons. Aff.*, Summer 1986, *20*(1), pp. 118–30.

Gemünden, Hans Georg. "Promoters"—Key Persons for the Development and Marketing of Innovative Industrial Products. **In** *Backhaus, K. and Wilson, D. T., eds.*, 1986, pp. 134–66. **[G: W. Germany]**

Gerstner, Eitan and Holthausen, Duncan. Profitable Pricing When Market Segments Overlap. *Marketing Sci.*, Winter 1986, *5*(1), pp. 55–69.

Ghosh, Avijit and McLafferty, Sara. Shopping Behavior and Optimal Store Locations in Multipurpose Trip Environments. **In** *Pellegrini, L. and Reddy, S. K., eds.*, 1986, pp. 157–70.

Giblin, Daniel. Customer Care in British Rail. **In** *Moores, B., ed.*, 1986, pp. 57–66. **[G: U.K.]**

Gomes, Lawrence J. The Competitive and Anticompetitive Theories of Advertising: An Empirical Analysis. *Appl. Econ.*, June 1986, *18*(6), pp. 599–613. **[G: U.K.]**

Gorodetskii, A. Cost Accounting and Wholesale Prices. *Prob. Econ.*, August 1986, *29*(4), pp. 71–89. **[G: U.S.S.R.]**

Greenberg, Marshall G. The Cost of Simplifying Preference Models: Commentary. *Marketing Sci.*, Fall 1986, *5*(4), pp. 320–21.

Günter, Bernd. Risk Management in Industrial Marketing Project-Cooperations—Some Comments on Joint Risk Handling. **In** *Backhaus,*

K. and Wilson, D. T., eds., 1986, pp. 274–93.

Hagerty, Michael R. Reflections on the Cost of Simplifying Preference Models: Reply. *Marketing Sci.*, Fall 1986, *5*(4), pp. 323–24.

Hagerty, Michael R. The Cost of Simplifying Preference Models. *Marketing Sci.*, Fall 1986, *5*(4), pp. 298–319.

Hamill, Brian and Davies, Roger. Quality in British Airways. **In** *Moores, B., ed.*, 1986, pp. 77–87. **[G: U.K.]**

Hammann, Peter and Mittag, Heiko. The Marketing of Industrial Technology through Licensing. **In** *Backhaus, K. and Wilson, D. T., eds.*, 1986, pp. 224–42. **[G: W. Germany]**

Hauser, John. Theory and Application of Defensive Strategy. **In** *[Dean, J.]*, 1986, pp. 114–39. **[G: U.S.]**

Havlena, William J. and Holbrook, Morris B. The Varieties of Consumption Experience: Comparing Two Typologies of Emotion in Consumer Behavior. *J. Cons. Res.*, December 1986, *13*(3), pp. 394–404. **[G: U.S.]**

Heeler, Roger M. On the Awareness Effects of Mere Distribution: Comment. *Marketing Sci.*, Summer 1986, *5*(3), pp. 273.

Hessner, Catherine and Mellor, C. J. An Empirical Analysis of the Relationship between Advertising and Sales: A Case Study of the Liquid Milk Market. *J. Agr. Econ.*, May 1986, *37*(2), pp. 193–206. **[G: U.K.]**

Higgins, Richard S. and McChesney, Fred S. An Economic Analysis of the FTC's Ad Substantiation Program. **In** *Ippolito, P. M. and Scheffman, D. T., eds.*, 1986, pp. 197–211. **[G: U.S.]**

Higgins, Richard S. and McChesney, Fred S. Truth and Consequences: The Federal Trade Commission's Ad Substantiation Program. *Int. Rev. Law Econ.*, December 1986, *6*(2), pp. 151–68. **[G: U.S.]**

Hoch, Stephen J. and Ha, Young-Won. Consumer Learning: Advertising and the Ambiguity of Product Experience. *J. Cons. Res.*, September 1986, *13*(2), pp. 221–33. **[G: U.S.]**

Holbrook, Morris B. Aims, Concepts, and Methods for the Representation of Individual Differences in Esthetic Responses to Design Features. *J. Cons. Res.*, December 1986, *13*(3), pp. 337–47.

Holbrook, Morris B. and Grayson, Mark W. The Semiology of Cinematic Consumption: Symbolic Consumer Behavior in *Out of Africa*. *J. Cons. Res.*, December 1986, *13*(3), pp. 374–81.

Holstius, Karin. Choice of Retailer in Non-equilibrium Competition. *Liiketaloudellinen Aikak.*, 1986, *35*(3), pp. 175–83. **[G: Finland]**

Holstius, Karin. Sales Response to Advertising. *Liiketaloudellinen Aikak.*, 1986, *35*(4), pp. 286–302. **[G: Finland]**

Holt, Charles A. and Sherman, Roger. Quality Uncertainty and Bundling. **In** *Ippolito, P. M. and Scheffman, D. T., eds.*, 1986, pp. 221–50.

Houston, Douglas A. and Howe, John S. An Economic Rationale for Couponing: Reply. *Quart. J. Bus. Econ.*, Autumn 1986, *25*(4), pp. 75–76.

Hutchinson, J. Wesley. Discrete Attribute Models of Brand Switching. *Marketing Sci.*, Fall 1986, *5*(4), pp. 350–71. **[G: U.S.]**

Hutton, R. Bruce, et al. Effects of Cost-Related Feedback on Consumer Knowledge and Consumption Behavior: A Field Experimental Approach. *J. Cons. Res.*, December 1986, *13*(3), pp. 327–36. **[G: U.S.; Canada]**

Infosino, William J. Forecasting New Product Sales from Likelihood of Purchase Ratings: Reply. *Marketing Sci.*, Fall 1986, *5*(4), pp. 389–90. **[G: U.S.]**

Infosino, William J. Forecasting New Product Sales from Likelihood of Purchase Ratings. *Marketing Sci.*, Fall 1986, *5*(4), pp. 372–84. **[G: U.S.]**

Jaccard, James; Brinberg, David and Ackerman, Lee J. Assessing Attribute Importance: A Comparison of Six Methods. *J. Cons. Res.*, March 1986, *12*(4), pp. 463–68. **[G: U.S.]**

Jarrell, Gregg A. and Peltzman, Sam. The Impact of Product Recalls on the Wealth of Sellers. **In** *Ippolito, P. M. and Scheffman, D. T., eds.*, 1986, pp. 377–409. **[G: U.S.]**

John, Deborah Roedder and Cole, Catherine A. Age Differences in Information Processing: Understanding Deficits in Young and Elderly Consumers. *J. Cons. Res.*, December 1986, *13*(3), pp. 297–315.

John, Deborah Roedder; Scott, Carol A. and Bettman, James R. Sampling Data for Covariation Assessment: The Effect of Prior Beliefs on Search Patterns. *J. Cons. Res.*, June 1986, *13*(1), pp. 38–47. **[G: U.S.]**

John, Deborah Roedder and Whitney, John C., Jr. The Development of Consumer Knowledge in Children: A Cognitive Structure Approach. *J. Cons. Res.*, March 1986, *12*(4), pp. 406–17. **[G: U.S.]**

Johnson, Michael D. Modeling Choice Strategies for Noncomparable Alternatives. *Marketing Sci.*, Winter 1986, *5*(1), pp. 37–54.

Johnson, Richard M. The Cost of Simplifying Preference Models: Commentary. *Marketing Sci.*, Fall 1986, *5*(4), pp. 322.

Kahle, Lynn R.; Beatty, Sharon E. and Homer, Pamela. Alternative Measurement Approaches to Consumer Values: The List of Values (LOV) and Values and Life Style (VALS). *J. Cons. Res.*, December 1986, *13*(3), pp. 405–09. **[G: U.S.]**

Kahn, Barbara E.; Morrison, Donald G. and Wright, Gordon P. Aggregating Individual Purchases to the Household Level. *Marketing Sci.*, Summer 1986, *5*(3), pp. 260–68.

Kamakura, Wagner A. and Srivastava, Rajendra K. An Ideal-Point Probabilistic Choice Model for Heterogeneous Preference. *Marketing Sci.*, Summer 1986, *5*(3), pp. 199–218.

Kamann, Dirk-Jan F. Industrial Organisation, Innovation and Employment. **In** *Nijkamp, P., ed. (II)*, 1986, pp. 131–54.

Kardes, Frank R. Effects of Initial Product Judgments on Subsequent Memory-Based Judgments. *J. Cons. Res.*, June 1986, *13*(1), pp. 1–11.

Katz, Michael L. and Shapiro, Carl. Consumer Shopping Behavior in the Retail Coffee Market. **In** *Ippolito, P. M. and Scheffman, D. T., eds.*, 1986, pp. 415–43. **[G: U.S.]**

Kelly, J. Patrick and Geurts, Michael D. Increasing the Efficiency of Forecasting Seasonal Demand for Individual Products. **In** *Pellegrini, L. and Reddy, S. K., eds.*, 1986, pp. 183–95. **[G: U.S.]**

Kessides, Ioannis N. Advertising, Sunk Costs, and Barriers to Entry. *Rev. Econ. Statist.*, February 1986, *68*(1), pp. 84–95. **[G: U.S.]**

Kihlstrom, Richard E. Advertising and Consumer Learning: Comments. **In** *Ippolito, P. M. and Scheffman, D. T., eds.*, 1986, pp. 171–76. **[G: U.S.]**

Kisielius, Jolita and Sternthal, Brian. Examining the Vividness Controversy: An Availability-Valence Interpretation. *J. Cons. Res.*, March 1986, *12*(4), pp. 418–31.

Kotowitz, Y. and Mathewson, G. Frank. Advertising and Consumer Learning. **In** *Ippolito, P. M. and Scheffman, D. T., eds.*, 1986, pp. 109–34. **[G: U.S.]**

Kroll, Robert J. and Stampfl, Ronald W. Orientations toward Consumerism: A Test of a Two-Dimensional Theory. *J. Cons. Aff.*, Winter 1986, *20*(2), pp. 214–30. **[G: U.S.]**

Laband, David N. Advertising as Information: An Empirical Note. *Rev. Econ. Statist.*, August 1986, *68*(3), pp. 517–21. **[G: U.S.]**

Lal, Rajiv. Delegating Pricing Responsibility to the Salesforce. *Marketing Sci.*, Spring 1986, *5*(2), pp. 159–68.

Lal, Rajiv and Staelin, Richard. Salesforce Compensation Plans in Environments with Asymmetric Information. *Marketing Sci.*, Summer 1986, *5*(3), pp. 179–98.

Lane, Chris. Putting People First—A Company-Wide Approach to Good Service. **In** *Moores, B., ed.*, 1986, pp. 50–53.

Lazear, Edward P. Retail Pricing and Clearance Sales. *Amer. Econ. Rev.*, March 1986, *76*(1), pp. 14–32.

Leffler, Keith B. and Sauer, Raymond, Jr. The Effects of the Advertising Substantiation Program on Advertising Agencies. **In** *Ippolito, P. M. and Scheffman, D. T., eds.*, 1986, pp. 177–95. **[G: U.S.]**

Levedahl, J. William. Profit Maximizing Pricing of Cents Off Coupons: Promotion or Price Discrimination? *Quart. J. Bus. Econ.*, Autumn 1986, *25*(4), pp. 56–70. **[G: U.S.]**

Lewis, Barbara and Owtram, Mike. Customer Satisfaction with Package Holidays. **In** *Moores, B., ed.*, 1986, pp. 201–13.

Lichtenstein, Donald R. and Bearden, William O. Measurement and Structure of Kelley's Covariance Theory. *J. Cons. Res.*, September 1986, *13*(2), pp. 290–96. **[G: U.S.]**

Liebermann, Yehoshua. The Advertising-to-Sales Ratio along the Brand Life Cycle: A Critical Review. *Managerial Dec. Econ.*, March 1986, *7*(1), pp. 43–48.

Lilien, Gary L. New Product Success in Business/Industrial Markets: Progress, Problems, and Research Program. **In** *Backhaus, K. and Wilson, D. T., eds.*, 1986, pp. 339–48.

Little, John D. C. Advertising Pulsing Policies for Generating Awareness for New Products: Comments. *Marketing Sci.*, Spring 1986, *5*(2), pp. 107–08. **[G: U.S.]**

Lynch, Michael, et al. Product Quality, Consumer Information and "Lemons" in Experimental Markets. **In** *Ippolito, P. M. and Scheffman, D. T., eds.*, 1986, pp. 251–306.

MacKay, David B. and Zinnes, Joseph L. A Probabilistic Model for the Multidimensional Scaling of Proximity and Preference Data. *Marketing Sci.*, Fall 1986, *5*(4), pp. 325–44. **[G: U.S.]**

MacKay, David B. and Zinnes, Joseph L. Considerations in the Use of Probabilistic Multidimensional Scaling Models: Reply. *Marketing Sci.*, Fall 1986, *5*(4), pp. 348–49. **[G: U.S.]**

Mackay, Robert J. Comments [Quality Uncertainty and Bundling] [Product Quality, Consumer Information and "Lemons" in Experimental Markets] [An Experimental Study of Warranty Coverage and Dispute Resolution in Competitive Markets]. **In** *Ippolito, P. M. and Scheffman, D. T., eds.*, 1986, pp. 373–74. **[G: U.S.]**

MacKenzie, Scott B. The Role of Attention in Mediating the Effect of Advertising on Attribute Importance. *J. Cons. Res.*, September 1986, *13*(2), pp. 174–95.

Mahajan, Vijay and Muller, Eitan. Advertising Pulsing Policies for Generating Awareness for New Products. *Marketing Sci.*, Spring 1986, *5*(2), pp. 89–106. **[G: U.S.]**

Mahajan, Vijay and Muller, Eitan. Reflections on Advertising Pulsing Policies for Generating Awareness for New Products: Reply. *Marketing Sci.*, Spring 1986, *5*(2), pp. 110–11. **[G: U.S.]**

Mason, Charles F. Predation by Noisy Advertising. *Rev. Ind. Organ.*, 1986, *3*(1), pp. 78–93.

McCracken, Grant. Culture and Consumption: A Theoretical Account of the Structure and Movement of the Cultural Meaning of Consumer Goods. *J. Cons. Res.*, June 1986, *13*(1), pp. 71–84. **[G: U.S.]**

McFadden, Daniel. The Choice Theory Approach to Market Research. *Marketing Sci.*, Fall 1986, *5*(4), pp. 275–97.

McMennamin, John L. A Probabilistic Model for the Multidimensional Scaling of Proximity and Preference Data: Commentary. *Marketing Sci.*, Fall 1986, *5*(4), pp. 345. **[G: U.S.]**

Meffert, Heribert. Marketing im Spannungsfeld von weltweitem Wettbewerb und nationalen Bedürfnissen. (With English summary.) *Z. Betriebswirtshaft*, August 1986, *56*(8), pp. 689–712. **[G: W. Germany]**

Menneer, Peter. Broadcasting Research—Necessity or Nicety? **In** *Moores, B., ed.*, 1986, pp. 255–65. **[G: U.K.]**

Mick, David Glen. Consumer Research and Semiotics: Exploring the Morphology of Signs, Symbols, and Significance. *J. Cons. Res.*, September 1986, *13*(2), pp. 196–213.

Milgrom, Paul and Roberts, John. Price and Advertising Signals of Product Quality. *J. Polit. Econ.*, August 1986, *94*(4), pp. 796–821.

Miller, Ross M. Comments [Quality Uncertainty and Bundling] [Product Quality, Consumer Information and "Lemons" in Experimental Markets] [An Experimental Study of Warranty Coverage and Dispute Resolution in Competitive Markets]. **In** *Ippolito, P. M. and Scheffman, D. T., eds.*, 1986, pp. 375–76. **[G: U.S.]**

Mitchell, Andrew A. The Effect of Verbal and Visual Components of Advertisements on Brand Attitudes and Attitude toward the Advertisement. *J. Cons. Res.*, June 1986, *13*(1), pp. 12–24.

Montgomery, David B. Conjoint Calibration of the Customer/Competitor Interface in Industrial Markets. **In** *Backhaus, K. and Wilson, D. T., eds.*, 1986, pp. 297–319.

Moore, Danny L.; Hausknecht, Douglas and Thamodaran, Kanchana. Time Compression, Response Opportunity, and Persuasion. *J. Cons. Res.*, June 1986, *13*(1), pp. 85–99.

Morrison, Donald G. Forecasting New Product Sales from Likelihood of Purchase Ratings: Commentary. *Marketing Sci.*, Fall 1986, *5*(4), pp. 385–86. **[G: U.S.]**

Mortiboys, Ron. Quality in the Boardroom. **In** *Moores, B., ed.*, 1986, pp. 13–24.

Murphy, Patrick E. and Ross, Steven C. Local Consumer Information Systems for Services: A Test. *J. Cons. Aff.*, Winter 1986, *20*(2), pp. 249–66. **[G: U.S.]**

Palfrey, Thomas R. and Romer, Thomas. An Experimental Study of Warranty Coverage and Dispute Resolution in Competitive Markets. **In** *Ippolito, P. M. and Scheffman, D. T., eds.*, 1986, pp. 307–72. **[G: U.S.]**

Paltschik, Mikael. Innovationer och forskningstaktik. (Innovations and Research Strategy. With English summary.) *Ekon. Samfundets Tidskr.*, 1986, *39*(2), pp. 99–104.

Pellegrini, Luca. Sale or Return Agreements versus Outright Sales. **In** *Pellegrini, L. and Reddy, S. K., eds.*, 1986, pp. 59–72.

Plinke, Wulff. Information Processing Behavior in Industrial Selling. **In** *Backhaus, K. and Wilson, D. T., eds.*, 1986, pp. 71–87.

Powelz, Herbert J. H. Gewinnung und Nutzung von Informationen aus den Faktormärkten unter Verwendung des Erlösspaltungskonzeptes. (With English summary.) *Z. Betriebswirtschaft*, March 1986, *56*(3), pp. 244–59.

Pratt, Robert W., Jr. Forecasting New Product Sales from Likelihood of Purchase Ratings: Commentary. *Marketing Sci.*, Fall 1986, *5*(4), pp. 387–88. **[G: U.S.]**

Price, Frank. How Does Britain Rate on Quality? **In** *Moores, B., ed.*, 1986, pp. 25–35. **[G: U.K.]**

Rangan, V. Kasturi. Relationship Management of Distributors: A Proposed Framework. **In** *Pellegrini, L. and Reddy, S. K., eds.*, 1986, pp. 103–17.

Rao, Ram C. Estimating Continuous Time Advertising–Sales Models. *Marketing Sci.*, Spring 1986, *5*(2), pp. 125–42. **[G: U.S.]**

Reekie, W. Duncan. Advertising Intensity and Media Selection. *Appl. Econ.*, May 1986, *18*(5), pp. 557–65. **[G: S. Africa]**

Reekie, W. Duncan. Forecasting South African Advertising Expenditures. *J. Stud. Econ. Econometrics*, November 1986, (26), pp. 59–69. **[G: S. Africa]**

Reidenbach, R. Eric; Moak, Donald L. and Pitts, Robert E. The Impact of Marketing Operations on Bank Performance: A Structural Investigation. *J. Bank Res.*, Spring 1986, *17*(1), pp. 18–27. **[G: U.S.]**

Richins, Marsha L. and Bloch, Peter H. After the New Wears Off: The Temporal Context of Product Involvement. *J. Cons. Res.*, September 1986, *13*(2), pp. 280–85. **[G: U.S.]**

Rieber, William J. An Economic Rationale for Couponing: A Comment. *Quart. J. Bus. Econ.*, Autumn 1986, *25*(4), pp. 71–74.

Rotondo, John. Price as an Aspect of Choice in EBA. *Marketing Sci.*, Fall 1986, *5*(4), pp. 391–402.

Rust, Roland T. and Schmittlein, David. A Bayesian Cross-validated Likelihood Method for Comparing Alternative Specifications of Quantitative Models. *Marketing Sci.*, Winter 1986, *5*(1), pp. 89.

Sappington, David E. M. Consumer Shopping Behavior in the Retail Coffee Market: Comments. **In** *Ippolito, P. M. and Scheffman, D. T., eds.*, 1986, pp. 445–46. **[G: U.S.]**

Savitt, Ronald. Time, Space and Competition: Formulations for the Development of Marketing Strategy. *Managerial Dec. Econ.*, March 1986, *7*(1), pp. 11–18.

Schlegelmilch, B. B. Can Export Performance Be Explained by Attitudinal Differences? *Managerial Dec. Econ.*, December 1986, *7*(4), pp. 249–54. **[G: U.K.; W. Germany]**

Schmalensee, Richard. Advertising and Market Structure. **In** *Stiglitz, J. E. and Mathewson, G. F., eds.*, 1986, pp. 373–96.

Schoenfeld, Hanns-Martin W. The Present State of Performance Evaluation in Multinational Companies. **In** *Holzer, H. P. and Schoenfeld, H.-M. W., eds.*, 1986, pp. 217–52.

Seringhaus, F. H. Rolf. Market Entry and the Impact of Export Marketing Assistance: A Conceptual Approach to Causal Modelling. *Liiketaloudellinen Aikak.*, 1986, *35*(4), pp. 275–85.

Smith, Stephen A. New Product Pricing in Quality Sensitive Markets. *Marketing Sci.*, Winter 1986, *5*(1), pp. 70–87.

Spekman, Robert E. and Strauss, Deborah. An Exploratory Investigation of Strategic Vulnerability and Its Impact on Buyer–Seller Relationships. **In** *Backhaus, K. and Wilson, D. T., eds.*, 1986, pp. 115–33. **[G: U.S.]**

Spiggle, Susan. Measuring Social Values: A Content Analysis of Sunday Comics and Underground Comix. *J. Cons. Res.*, June 1986, *13*(1), pp. 100–113. **[G: U.S.]**

Spiller, Pablo T. Comments [The Effects of the Advertising Substantiation Program on Advertising Agencies] [An Economic Analysis of the FTC's Ad Substantiation Program]. **In** *Ippolito, P. M. and Scheffman, D. T., eds.*, 1986, pp. 217–20. **[G: U.S.]**

Springer, Robert F. and Frech, H. E., III. Deterring Fraud: The Role of Resale Price Maintenance. *J. Bus.*, July 1986, *59*(3), pp. 433–49.

Sproles, George B. and Kendall, Elizabeth L. A Methodology for Profiling Consumers' Decision-Making Styles. *J. Cons. Aff.*, Winter 1986, *20*(2), pp. 267–79. **[G: U.S.]**

Srinivasan, V. and Mason, Charlotte H. Nonlinear Least Squares Estimation of New Product Diffusion Models. *Marketing Sci.*, Spring 1986, *5*(2), pp. 169–78. **[G: U.S.]**

Stone, Merlin. Keeping Customers by Keeping Them Happy—An Example from the Computer Industry. **In** *Moores, B., ed.*, 1986, pp. 266–77. **[G: U.K.]**

Stowe, John D. and Ingene, Charles A. Product Pricing under Risk. *Quart. J. Bus. Econ.*, Spring 1986, *25*(2), pp. 51–70.

Thill, Jean-Claude. A Note on Multipurpose and Multistop Shopping, Sales, and Market Areas of Firms. *J. Reg. Sci.*, November 1986, *26*(4), pp. 775–84.

Thomas, Owen. Ensuring Quality of Service for Sainsbury's Customers. **In** *Moores, B., ed.*, 1986, pp. 156–65. **[G: U.K.]**

Touzin, Mia. The Sheraton Guest Experience. **In** *Moores, B., ed.*, 1986, pp. 181–92.

Ursic, Anthony C.; Ursic, Michael L. and Ursic, Virginia L. A Longitudinal Study of the Use of the Elderly in Magazine Advertising. *J. Cons. Res.*, June 1986, *13*(1), pp. 131–33. **[G: U.S.]**

Vyas, Niren M. and Woodside, Arch G. Micro Analysis of Supplier Choice Strategies: Industrial Packaging Materials. **In** *Backhaus, K. and Wilson, D. T., eds.*, 1986, pp. 41–68.

Wagner, Udo and Taudes, Alfred. A Multivariate Polya Model of Brand Choice and Purchase Incidence. *Marketing Sci.*, Summer 1986, *5*(3), pp. 219–44. **[G: W. Germany]**

Wärneryd, Karl-Erik. Advertising and Consumer Behavior. **In** *Gilad, B. and Kaish, S., eds., Vol. A*, 1986, pp. 89–126.

Weinberg, Charles B. and Weiss, Doyle L. A Simpler Estimation Procedure for a Micromodeling Approach to the Advertising–Sales Relationship. *Marketing Sci.*, Summer 1986, *5*(3), pp. 269–72.

Wilson, David T. Industrial Marketing—State of the Art in the USA. **In** *Backhaus, K. and Wilson, D. T., eds.*, 1986, pp. 15–21. **[G: U.S.]**

Wilson, David T. New Product Success in Business/Industrial Markets: A Buyer–Seller Perspective. **In** *Backhaus, K. and Wilson, D. T., eds.*, 1986, pp. 349–67.

Wilton, Peter C. and Myers, John G. Task, Expectancy, and Information Assessment Effects in Information Utilization Processes. *J. Cons. Res.*, March 1986, *12*(4), pp. 469–86.

Windal, Pierre. A Probabilistic Model for the Multidimensional Scaling of Proximity and Preference Data: Commentary. *Marketing Sci.*, Fall 1986, *5*(4), pp. 346–47. **[G: U.S.]**

Winer, Russell S. A Reference Price Model of Brand Choice for Frequently Purchased Products. *J. Cons. Res.*, September 1986, *13*(2), pp. 250–56. **[G: U.S.]**

Zielske, Hugh A. Advertising Pulsing Policies for Generating Awareness for New Products: Comments. *Marketing Sci.*, Spring 1986, *5*(2), pp. 109. **[G: U.S.]**

Zinkhan, George M. and Shermohamad, Ali. Is Other-Directedness on the Increase? An Empirical Test of Riesman's Theory of Social Character. *J. Cons. Res.*, June 1986, *13*(1), pp. 127–30. **[G: U.S.]**

540 Accounting

541 Accounting

5410 Accounting

Abdel-Khalik, A. Rashad; Graul, Paul R. and Newton, James D. Reporting Uncertainty and Assessment of Risk: Replication and Extension in a Canadian Setting. *J. Acc. Res.*, Autumn 1986, *24*(2), pp. 372–82. **[G: Canada]**

Allsop, Peter and Pollard, Ian. Taxation Aspects of Corporation Finance. **In** *Bruce, R., et al., eds.*, 1986, pp. 390–412. **[G: Australia]**

Anderson, John C. and Kraushaar, James M. Measurement Error and Statistical Sampling in Auditing: The Potential Effects. *Accounting Rev.*, July 1986, *61*(3), pp. 379–99.

Anthony, Robert N. Accounting Rates of Return: Note [On the Misuse of Accounting Rates of Return to Infer Monopoly Profits]. *Amer. Econ. Rev.*, March 1986, *76*(1), pp. 244–46.

Aukes, Robert G. Economic/Accounting Confusion Underlying the Current Farm Financial Crisis. *Can. J. Agr. Econ.*, June 1986, *33*, pp. S43–68.

Ayres, Frances L. A Comment on Corporate Preferences for Foreign Currency Accounting Standards. *J. Acc. Res.*, Spring 1986, *24*(1), pp. 166–69. **[G: U.S.]**

Ayres, Frances L. Characteristics of Firms Electing Early Adoption of SFAS 52. *J. Acc. Econ.*, June 1986, *8*(2), pp. 143–58. **[G: U.S.]**

Banz, Rolf W. and Breen, William J. Sample-Dependent Results Using Accounting and Market Data: Some Evidence. *J. Finance*, September 1986, *41*(4), pp. 779–93. **[G: U.S.]**

Barnes, P. Financial Statement Analysis. **In** *Firth, M. and Keane, S. M., eds.*, 1986, pp. 171–81.

Baumol, William J. Optimal Depreciation Policy: Pricing the Products of Durable Assets. **In** *Baumol, W. J.*, 1986, pp. 111–29.

Baxter, W. T. Accounting Values: Sale Price versus Replacement Cost. **In** *Parker, R. H.; Harcourt, G. C. and Whittington, G., eds.*, 1986, *1967*, pp. 242–49.

Beaver, William H. and Demski, Joel S. The Nature of Income Measurement. **In** *Parker, R. H.; Harcourt, G. C. and Whittington, G., eds.*, 1986, *1979*, pp. 167–78.

Bell, Philip W. and Johnson, L. Todd. Current Value Accounting and the Simple Production Case: Edbejo and Other Companies in the Taxi Business. **In** *Parker, R. H.; Harcourt, G. C. and Whittington, G., eds.*, 1986, *1979*, pp. 278–313.

Blanchard, Garth A.; Chow, Chee W. and Noreen, Eric W. Information Asymmetry, Incentive Schemes, and Information Biasing: The Case of Hospital Budgeting under Rate Regulation. *Accounting Rev.*, January 1986, *61*(1), pp. 1–15. **[G: U.S.]**

Boritz, Jefim Efrim. The Effect of Research Method on Audit Planning and Review Judgments. *J. Acc. Res.*, Autumn 1986, *24*(2), pp. 335–48.

Borthick, A. Faye and Clark, Ronald L. The Role of Productive Thinking in Affecting Student Learning with Microcomputers in Accounting Education. *Accounting Rev.*, January 1986, *61*(1), pp. 143–57.

Bowen, Robert M.; Burgstahler, David and Daley, Lane A. Evidence on the Relationships between Earnings and Various Measures of Cash Flow. *Accounting Rev.*, October 1986, *61*(4), pp. 713–25.

Brooks, LeRoy D. and Buckmaster, Dale. The Impact of Inflation on the Monetary Stocks of the Firm. *J. Econ. Soc. Meas.*, April 1986, *14*(1), pp. 51–63. **[G: U.S.]**

Brown, Lawrence D. Evidence on the Incremental Information Content of Additional Firm Disclosures Made Concurrently with Earnings: Discussion. *J. Acc. Res.*, Supp. 1986, *24*, pp. 33–36. **[G: U.S.]**

Brownell, Peter and Hirst, Mark. Reliance on Accounting Information, Budgetary Participation, and Task Uncertainty: Tests of a Three-Way Interaction. *J. Acc. Res.*, Autumn 1986, *24*(2), pp. 241–49. **[G: U.S.]**

Brownell, Peter and McInnes, Morris. Budgetary Participation, Motivation, and Managerial Performance. *Accounting Rev.*, October 1986, *61*(4), pp. 587–600. **[G: U.S.]**

Bullock, John. The Audit Role in the Context of Financial Deregulation. **In** *Dale, R., ed.*, 1986, pp. 36–47. **[G: U.K.]**

Burgstahler, David and Jiambalvo, James. Sample Error Characteristics and Projection of Error to Audit Populations. *Accounting Rev.*, April 1986, *61*(2), pp. 233–48.

Butler, Stephen A. Anchoring in the Judgmental Evaluation of Audit Samples. *Accounting Rev.*, January 1986, *61*(1), pp. 101–11.

Cargile, Barney R. and Bublitz, Bruce. Factors Contributing to Published Research by Accounting Faculties. *Accounting Rev.*, January 1986, *61*(1), pp. 158–78. **[G: U.S.]**

Castanias, Richard P., II and Griffin, Paul A. The Effects of Foreign-Currency Translation Accounting on Security Analysts' Forecasts. *Managerial Dec. Econ.*, March 1986, *7*(1), pp. 3–10. **[G: U.S.]**

Caster, Paul and Simon, Daniel T. The Association between Selected Variables and Inventory Methods. *Quart. Rev. Econ. Bus.*, Summer 1986, *26*(2), pp. 84–93. **[G: U.S.]**

Chambers, R. J. Second Thoughts on Continuously Contemporary Accounting. **In** *Parker, R. H.; Harcourt, G. C. and Whittington, G., eds.*, 1986, *1970*, pp. 344–66.

Chan, K. Hung and Dodin, Bajis. A Decision Support System for Audit-Staff Scheduling with Precedence Constraints and Due Dates. *Accounting Rev.*, October 1986, *61*(4), pp. 726–34.

Chen, K. C. and D'Arcy, Stephen P. Market Sensitivity to Interest Rate Assumptions in Corporate Pension Plans. *J. Risk Ins.*, June 1986, *53*(2), pp. 209–25. **[G: U.S.]**

Chenhall, Robert H. Authoritarianism and Participative Budgeting: A Dyadic Analysis. *Accounting Rev.*, April 1986, *61*(2), pp. 263–72. **[G: U.S.]**

Chenhall, Robert H. and Morris, Deigan. The Impact of Structure, Environment, and Interdependence on the Perceived Usefulness of Management Accounting Systems. *Accounting Rev.*, January 1986, *61*(1), pp. 16–35.

Chua, Wai Fong. Radical Developments in Accounting Thought. *Accounting Rev.*, October 1986, *61*(4), pp. 601–32.

Comiskey, Eugene E. and Mulford, Charles W. Investment Decisions and the Equity Accounting Standard. *Accounting Rev.*, July 1986, *61*(3), pp. 519–25. **[G: U.S.]**

Connolly, Robert A. Assessing the Importance of Measurement Error in Capital Investment Models. *Managerial Dec. Econ.*, September 1986, *7*(3), pp. 177–85.

Danos, Paul and Eichenseher, John W. Long-term Trends toward Seller Concentration in the U.S. Audit Market. *Accounting Rev.*, October 1986, *61*(4), pp. 633–50. **[G: U.S.]**

DeAngelo, Linda Elizabeth. Accounting Numbers as Market Valuation Substitutes: A Study of Management Buyouts of Public Stockholders. *Accounting Rev.*, July 1986, *61*(3), pp. 400–420. **[G: U.S.]**

Dhaliwal, Dan S. Measurement of Financial Leverage in the Presence of Unfunded Pension Obligations. *Accounting Rev.*, October 1986, *61*(4), pp. 651–61.

Dopuch, Nicholas; Holthausen, Robert W. and Leftwich, Richard W. Abnormal Stock Returns Associated with Media Disclosures of 'Subject to' Qualified Audit Opinions. *J. Acc. Econ.*, June 1986, *8*(2), pp. 93–117. **[G: U.S.]**

Drexl, Andreas. Erhebungskosten versus Schätzgenauigkeit bei der Stichprobeninventur—Ein integrierender Ansatz. (With English summary.) *Z. Betriebswirtshaft*, June 1986, *56*(6), pp. 509–24.

Dworin, Lowell and Grimlund, Richard A. Dollar-Unit Sampling: A Comparison of the Quasi-Bayesian and Moment Bounds. *Accounting Rev.*, January 1986, *61*(1), pp. 36–57.

Dye, Ronald A. Proprietary and Nonproprietary Disclosures. *J. Bus.*, Part 1, April 1986, *59*(2), pp. 331–66.

Edwards, Edgar O. The State of Current Value Accounting. **In** *Parker, R. H.; Harcourt, G. C. and Whittington, G., eds.*, 1986, *1975*, pp. 264–77.

El-Gazzar, Samir; Lilien, Steve and Pastena, Victor. Accounting for Leases by Lessees. *J. Acc. Econ.*, October 1986, *8*(3), pp. 217–37. **[G: U.S.]**

Ellerman, David P. Property Appropriation and Economic Theory. **In** *Mirowski, P., ed.*, 1986, pp. 41–92.

Erikson, Walter E. Credible Accounting and Disclosure. **In** *Federal Home Loan Bank of San Francisco,* 1986, pp. 119–27. **[G: U.S.]**

Evans, Eric S. FMC Corporation: Inflation-Adjusted Performance Evaluation. **In** *Holzer, H. P. and Schoenfeld, H.-M. W., eds.*, 1986, pp. 73–86. **[G: U.S.]**

Farmer, Roger E. A. and Winter, Ralph A. The Role of Options in the Resolution of Agency Problems: A Comment [Theory of the Firm: Managerial Behaviour, Agency Costs and Ownership Structure]. *J. Finance,* December 1986, *41*(5), pp. 1157–70.

Filios, Vassilios P. The Conceptual Framework of a Human Resource Accounting System. *Rivista Int. Sci. Econ. Com.*, March 1986, *33*(3), pp. 281–92.

Fisher, Irving. The Economics of Accountancy. **In** *Parker, R. H.; Harcourt, G. C. and Whittington, G., eds.*, 1986, *1930*, pp. 66–81.

Flesher, Dale L. and Flesher, Tonya K. Ivar Kreuger's Contribution to U.S. Financial Reporting. *Accounting Rev.*, July 1986, *61*(3), pp. 421–34. **[G: U.S.]**

Fletcher, John C. Management Control and the Internal Auditor: The Borg-Warner Case. **In** *Holzer, H. P. and Schoenfeld, H.-M. W., eds.*, 1986, pp. 87–100.

Förschle, Gerhart and Kropp, Manfred. Die Bewertungsstetigkeit im Bilanzrichtlinien-Gesetz. (With English summary.) *Z. Betriebswirtshaft*, September 1986, *56*(9), pp. 873–93. **[G: W. Germany]**

Francis, Jere R. and Stokes, Donald J. Audit Prices, Product Differentiation, and Scale Economies: Further Evidence from the Australian Market. *J. Acc. Res.*, Autumn 1986, *24*(2), pp. 383–93. **[G: Australia]**

Frederick, David M. and Libby, Robert. Expertise and Auditors' Judgments of Conjunctive Events. *J. Acc. Res.*, Autumn 1986, *24*(2), pp. 270–90.

Freeman, Robert N. The Information Contained in the Components of Earnings: Discussion. *J. Acc. Res.*, Supp. 1986, *24*, pp. 65–68. **[G: U.S.]**

Frost, Peter A. and Tamura, Hirokuni. Accuracy of Auxiliary Information Interval Estimation in Statistical Auditing. *J. Acc. Res.*, Spring 1986, *24*(1), pp. 57–75.

Ged, Alain. Les nouvelles voies de recherche en comptabilité managériale. (The Most Promising Areas of Research in Managerial Accounting. With English summary.) *Écon. Soc.*, June 1986, *20*(6), pp. 147–80.

Gynther, Reg S. Why Use General Purchasing Power? **In** *Parker, R. H.; Harcourt, G. C. and Whittington, G., eds.*, 1986, *1974*, pp. 314–43.

Haglund, Eric. Revisorns roll. (The Role of the Accountant. With English summary.) *Ekon. Samfundets Tidskr.*, 1986, *39*(4), pp. 217–28.

Hahtola, Kauko. Onko toiminta-analyyttinen tutkimusote tärmännyt luonnontieteellisen filosofian muuriin? (Has the Action-Oriented Approach Reached the Barrier of Natural-Scientific Philosophy? With English summary.) *Liiketaloudellinen Aikak.*, 1986, *35*(4), pp. 376–83. **[G: Finland]**

Haka, Susan; Friedman, Lauren and Jones, Virginia. Functional Fixation and Interference Theory: A Theoretical and Empirical Investigation. *Accounting Rev.*, July 1986, *61*(3), pp. 455–74.

Hall, G. and Stark, A. W. Bankruptcy Risk and the Effects of Conservative Policy for 1979–81. *Int. J. Ind. Organ.*, September 1986, *4*(3), pp. 317–32. **[G: U.K.]**

Hassell, John M. and Jennings, Robert H. Relative Forecast Accuracy and the Timing of Earnings Forecast Announcements. *Accounting Rev.*, January 1986, *61*(1), pp. 58–75. **[G: U.S.]**

Haugen, Robert A. and Senbet, Lemma W. The Role of Options in the Resolution of Agency Problems: A Reply. *J. Finance,* December 1986, *41*(5), pp. 1171–73.

Heck, J. Louis and Bremser, Wayne G. Six Decades of *The Accounting Review:* A Summary of Author and Institutional Contributors. *Accounting Rev.*, October 1986, *61*(4), pp. 735–44.

Hilke, John C. Early Mandatory Disclosure Regulations. *Int. Rev. Law Econ.*, December 1986, *6*(2), pp. 229–39. **[G: U.S.]**

Holzer, H. Peter. Past Research on Performance Evaluation of International Subsidiaries. **In** *Holzer, H. P. and Schoenfeld, H.-M. W., eds.*, 1986, pp. 1–12.

Hoskin, Robert E.; Hughes, John S. and Ricks, William E. Evidence on the Incremental Information Content of Additional Firm Disclosures Made Concurrently with Earnings. *J. Acc. Res.*, Supp. 1986, *24,* pp. 1–32. **[G: U.S.]**

Hughes, Patricia J. Signalling by Direct Disclosure under Asymmetric Information. *J. Acc. Econ.*, June 1986, *8*(2), pp. 119–42.

Huss, H. Fenwick and Trader, Ramona L. A Note on Optimal Sample Sizes in Compliance Tests Using a Formal Bayesian Decision-Theoretic Approach for Finite and Infinite Populations. *J. Acc. Res.*, Autumn 1986, *24*(2), pp. 394–99.

Hutchinson, P. J. The Effect of the E.E.C. Fourth Directive on Corporate Financial Disclosure by European Industry. **In** *Hall, G., ed.*, 1986, pp. 44–58. **[G: EEC]**

Ijiri, Yuji. A Framework for Triple-Entry Book-keeping. *Accounting Rev.*, October 1986, *61*(4), pp. 745–59.

Jacobs, Fred A.; Hartgraves, Al L. and Beard, Larry H. Publication Productivity of Doctoral Alumni: A Time-adjusted Model. *Accounting Rev.*, January 1986, *61*(1), pp. 179–87. **[G: U.S.]**

Jennings, Ross. The Association of Operating Cash Flow and Accruals with Security Returns: Discussion. *J. Acc. Res.*, Supp. 1986, *24*, pp. 134–37. **[G: U.S.]**

Kang, K. Won and Park, Soong H. Managerial Accounting and Analysis in Multinational Enterprises: GoldStar Electronics. **In** *Holzer, H. P. and Schoenfeld, H.-M. W., eds.*, 1986, pp. 51–71. **[G: S. Korea]**

Kay, John A. and Mayer, Colin. On the Application of Accounting Rates of Returns. *Econ. J.*, March 1986, *96*(381), pp. 199–207.

Kennedy, Charles. Inflation Accounting: Retrospect and Prospect. **In** *Parker, R. H.; Harcourt, G. C. and Whittington, G., eds.*, 1986, *1978*, pp. 179–99. **[G: U.K.]**

King, Raymond D. and O'Keefe, Terrence B. Lobbying Activities and Insider Trading. *Accounting Rev.*, January 1986, *61*(1), pp. 76–90. **[G: U.S.]**

Kinney, William R., Jr. Audit Technology and Preferences for Auditing Standards. *J. Acc. Econ.*, March 1986, *8*(1), pp. 73–89. **[G: U.S.]**

Kinney, William R., Jr. Empirical Accounting Research Design for Ph.D. Students. *Accounting Rev.*, April 1986, *61*(2), pp. 338–50.

Kirkman, P. Working Capital Management. **In** *Firth, M. and Keane, S. M., eds.*, 1986, pp. 142–57. **[G: U.K.]**

Laitinen, Erkki K. Suomalaisten ja ulkomaisten vuosikertomusten välittämä yrityskuva. (Corporate Image as Reflected in the Annual Reports of Finnish and Foreign Firms. With English summary.) *Liiketaloudellinen Aikak.*, 1986, *35*(4), pp. 357–75. **[G: Finland]**

Landsman, Wayne. An Empirical Investigation of Pension Fund Property Rights. *Accounting Rev.*, October 1986, *61*(4), pp. 662–91. **[G: U.S.]**

Lanfermann, Josef. Performance Evaluation of International Subsidiaries in the Case of Acquisition/Disposal and Annual Audits from the Point of View of a German Wirtschaftsprüfer. **In** *Holzer, H. P. and Schoenfeld, H.-M. W., eds.*, 1986, pp. 189–215.

Lere, John C. Product Pricing Based on Accounting Costs [Theory of the Firm Facing Uncertain Demand]. *Accounting Rev.*, April 1986, *61*(2), pp. 318–24.

Liberty, Susan E. and Zimmerman, Jerold L. Labor Union Contract Negotiations and Accounting Choices. *Accounting Rev.*, October 1986, *61*(4), pp. 692–712. **[G: U.S.]**

Licata, Michael P.; Strawser, Robert H. and Welker, Robert B. A Note on Participation in Budgeting and Locus of Control. *Accounting Rev.*, January 1986, *61*(1), pp. 112–17.

Lipe, Robert C. The Information Contained in the Components of Earnings. *J. Acc. Res.*, Supp. 1986, *24*, pp. 37–64. **[G: U.S.]**

Lys, Thomas. Capital Analysis of Reserve Recognition Accounting: Discussion. *J. Acc. Res.*, Supp. 1986, *24*, pp. 109–11. **[G: U.S.]**

Macharzina, Klaus. European Financial Reporting: Standards and Efficiency Problems. **In** *Macharzina, K. and Staehle, W. H., eds.*, 1986, pp. 335–50. **[G: W. Europe]**

MacRae, C. Duncan. User Control Knowledge in a Tax Consulting System. **In** *Pau, L. F., ed.*, 1986, pp. 194–203.

Magliolo, Joseph. Capital Market Analysis of Reserve Recognition Accounting. *J. Acc. Res.*, Supp. 1986, *24*, pp. 69–108. **[G: U.S.]**

Mansury, R. The Measurement of Business Income: Part I: The Concepts of the Measurement in Theory. *Bull. Int. Fiscal Doc.*, February 1986, *40*(2), pp. 55–60.

Margheim, Loren L. Further Evidence on External Auditors' Reliance on Internal Auditors. *J. Acc. Res.*, Spring 1986, *24*(1), pp. 194–205. **[G: U.S.]**

Miller, Elwood L. Monsanto Company—Managing Change. **In** *Holzer, H. P. and Schoenfeld, H.-M. W., eds.*, 1986, pp. 31–50. **[G: U.S.]**

Miranti, Paul J., Jr. Associationalism, Statism, and Professional Regulation: Public Accountants and the Reform of the Financial Markets, 1896–1940. *Bus. Hist. Rev.*, Autumn 1986, *60*(3), pp. 438–68. **[G: U.S.]**

Miranti, Paul J., Jr. From Conflict to Concensus: The American Institute of Accountants and the Professionalization of Public Accountancy, 1886–1940. **In** *Atack, J., ed.*, 1986, pp. 93–100. **[G: U.S.]**

Morris, R. Some Implications of the Theory of Business Finance for External Financial Reporting. **In** *Firth, M. and Keane, S. M., eds.*, 1986, pp. 223–41.

Murdoch, Brock. The Information Content of FAS 33 Returns on Equity. *Accounting Rev.*, April 1986, *61*(2), pp. 273–87. **[G: U.S.]**

Murray, Dennis and Frazier, Katherine Beal. A Within-Subjects Tests of Expectancy Theory in a Public Accounting Environment. *J. Acc. Res.*, Autumn 1986, *24*(2), pp. 400–404. **[G: U.S.]**

Neuhauser, Lenz. Financial Reporting Systems of Multinational Companies—An External Auditor's Viewpoint. **In** *Holzer, H. P. and Schoenfeld, H.-M. W., eds.*, 1986, pp. 175–88.

O'Brien, Patricia C. The Relative Information Content of Accruals and Cash Flows: Combined Evidence at the Earnings Announcement and Annual Report Release Date: Discussion. *J. Acc. Res.*, Supp. 1986, *24*, pp. 201–03. **[G: U.S.]**

Olivéro, Bernard. Réflexion sur un système d'information comptable. (Comments on an Accounting Information System. With English summary.) *Écon. Soc.*, June 1986, *20*(6), pp. 204–22.

Palmrose, Zoe-Vonna. Audit Fees and Auditor Size: Further Evidence. *J. Acc. Res.*, Spring 1986, *24*(1), pp. 97–110. **[G: U.S.]**

Palmrose, Zoe-Vonna. The Effect of Nonaudit Services on the Pricing of Audit Services: Further Evidence. *J. Acc. Res.*, Autumn 1986, *24*(2), pp. 405–11. **[G: U.S.]**

Peles, Yoram C. A Note on Yield Variance and Mix Variance. *Accounting Rev.*, April 1986, *61*(2), pp. 325–29.

Pihlanto, Pekka. Laskentatoimen tutkimuksen uusia painotuksia. (New Accentuations in Accounting Research. With English summary.) *Liiketaloudellinen Aikak.*, 1986, *35*(1), pp. 48–57.

Pincus, Morton. The Incremental Information Content of Financial Statement Disclosures: The Case of LIFO Inventory Liquidations: Discussion. *J. Acc. Res.*, Supp. 1986, *24*, pp. 161–64. **[G: U.S.]**

Pollard, Ian. Corporate Reconstructions. **In** *Bruce, R., et al., eds.*, 1986, pp. 413–27. **[G: Australia]**

Postner, Harry H. Microbusiness Accounting and Macroeconomic Accounting: The Limits to Consistency. *Rev. Income Wealth*, September 1986, *32*(3), pp. 217–44.

Pownall, Grace. An Empirical Analysis of the Regulation of the Defense Contracting Industry: The Cost Accounting Standards Board. *J. Acc. Res.*, Autumn 1986, *24*(2), pp. 291–315. **[G: U.S.]**

Queissner, Eberhard. Praxisorientiertes Herstellkosten-Controlling mit Hilfe einer integrierten Kostenrechnung. (With English summary.) *Z. Betriebswirtshaft*, Apr.-May 1986, *56*(4/5), pp. 452–64.

Rahman, M. Zubaidur and Finnerty, Joseph E. International Accounting Standards and Transnational Corporations. *Rivista Int. Sci. Econ. Com.*, June-July 1986, *33*(6–7), pp. 697–714.

Rayburn, Judy. The Association of Operating Cash Flow and Accruals with Security Returns. *J. Acc. Res.*, Supp. 1986, *24*, pp. 112–33. **[G: U.S.]**

Ricks, William E. Firm Size Effects and the Association between Excess Returns and LIFO Tax Savings. *J. Acc. Res.*, Spring 1986, *24*(1), pp. 206–16. **[G: U.S.]**

Robbins, Walter A. and Austin, Kenneth R. Disclosure Quality in Governmental Financial Reports: An Assessment of the Appropriateness of a Compound Measure. *J. Acc. Res.*, Autumn 1986, *24*(2), pp. 412–21. **[G: U.S.]**

Roberts, Donald M. Stratified Sampling Using a Stochastic Model. *J. Acc. Res.*, Spring 1986, *24*(1), pp. 111–26.

Robinson, Terence. Depreciation Reserve Assessment. **In** *[Dorsey, J. N. and Wiggins, B. T.]*, 1986, pp. 189–206. **[G: U.S.]**

Rohrbach, Kermit John. Monetary Unit Acceptance Sampling. *J. Acc. Res.*, Spring 1986, *24*(1), pp. 127–50.

Rousseau, Patrick. Conversion des documents comptables et taux de change: proposition d'une nouvelle approch. (Translating Financial Statements and Exchange Rate: Proposals for a New Approach. With English summary.) *Écon. Soc.*, December 1986, *20*(12), pp. 83–103.

Rubino, R. J. Accounting Techniques Utilized for the Evaluation of International Subsidiaries: The IBM Case. **In** *Holzer, H. P. and Schoenfeld, H.-M. W., eds.*, 1986, pp. 13–30. **[G: U.S.]**

Salmi, Timo. Laskentatoimen ja rahoituksen kvantitatiivinen tutkimusprosessi ja kytkeytyminen lähioppialoihin. (Quantitative Research Process in Accounting and Financial Management, and Their Interaction with Related Disciplines. With English summary.) *Liiketaloudellinen Aikak.*, 1986, *35*(1), pp. 71–87.

Schnitkey, Gary D. and Sonka, Steven T. Systems Design Procedures for Farm Accounting. *Southern J. Agr. Econ.*, December 1986, *18*(2), pp. 207–13. **[G: U.S.]**

Schoenfeld, Hanns-Martin W. Performance Evaluation in Multinational Companies: Two European Examples. **In** *Holzer, H. P. and Schoenfeld, H.-M. W., eds.*, 1986, pp. 101–62. **[G: W. Germany; Netherlands]**

Schoenfeld, Hanns-Martin W. The Present State of Performance Evaluation in Multinational Companies. **In** *Holzer, H. P. and Schoenfeld, H.-M. W., eds.*, 1986, pp. 217–52.

Scott, M. FG. Some Economic Principles of Accounting: A Constructive Critique of the Sandilands Report. **In** *Parker, R. H.; Harcourt, G. C. and Whittington, G., eds.*, 1986, pp. 200–241.

Shriver, Keith A. Further Evidence on the Marginal Gains in Accuracy of Alternative Levels of Specificity of the Producer Price Indexes. *J. Acc. Res.*, Spring 1986, *24*(1), pp. 151–65. **[G: U.S.]**

Smieliauskas, Wally. A Note on a Comparison of Bayesian with Non-Bayesian Dollar-Unit Sampling Bounds for Overstatement Errors of Accounting Populations [Modified Multinomial Bounds for Larger Numbers of Errors in Audits]. *Accounting Rev.*, January 1986, *61*(1), pp. 118–28.

Smieliauskas, Wally. A Simulation Analysis of the Power Characteristics of Some Popular Estimators under Different Risk and Materiality Levels. *J. Acc. Res.*, Spring 1986, *24*(1), pp. 217–30.

Solomons, David. Economic and Accounting Concepts of Income. **In** *Parker, R. H.; Harcourt, G. C. and Whittington, G., eds.*, 1986, *1961*, pp. 153–66.

Stober, Thomas L. The Incremental Information Content of Financial Statement Disclosures: The Case of LIFO Inventory Liquidations. *J. Acc. Res.*, Supp. 1986, *24*, pp. 138–60. **[G: U.S.]**

Tamura, Hirokuni and Frost, Peter A. Tightening CAV (DUS) Bounds by Using a Parametric Model. *J. Acc. Res.*, Autumn 1986, *24*(2), pp. 364–71.

Thomas, Lynn R. and Swanson, Edward P. Additional Considerations When Using the FASB Data Bank of Changing Price Information. *Ac-*

counting Rev., April 1986, *61*(2), pp. 330–36. [G: U.S.]

Thomson, William and Francis, Peter N. Performance Auditing in the Midst of Litigation: A Case Study and Lessons Learned from the Arizona Experience. *Public Budg. Finance*, Summer 1986, *6*(2), pp. 104–14. [G: U.S.]

Titman, Sheridan and Trueman, Brett. Information Quality and the Valuation of New Issues. *J. Acc. Econ.*, June 1986, *8*(2), pp. 159–72.

Trueman, Brett. Why Do Managers Voluntarily Release Earnings Forecasts? *J. Acc. Econ.*, March 1986, *8*(1), pp. 53–71.

Tse, Senyo. Intra-Year Trends in the Degree of Association between Accounting Numbers and Security Prices. *Accounting Rev.*, July 1986, *61*(3), pp. 475–97. [G: U.S.]

Ture, Norman B. and Bonilla, Carlos E. ACRS-ITC, CCRS, and NCRS Cost Recovery in an Inflationary Economy. **In** *Landau, R. and Jorgenson, D. W., eds.*, 1986, pp. 171–89. [G: U.S.]

Vermaelen, Theo. Encouraging Information Disclosure. *Tijdschrift Econ. Manage.*, 1986, *31*(4), pp. 435–49. [G: Belgium]

Verrecchia, Robert E. Managerial Discretion in the Choice among Financial Reporting Alternatives. *J. Acc. Econ.*, October 1986, *8*(3), pp. 175–95.

Wagner, Franz W. Zum Informationsgehalt einer inflationsbereinigten Rechnungslegung. (With English summary.) *Z. Betriebswirtschaft*, March 1986, *56*(3), pp. 219–43.

Waymire, Gregory. Additional Evidence on the Accuracy of Analyst Forecasts before and after Voluntary Management Earnings Forecasts. *Accounting Rev.*, January 1986, *61*(1), pp. 129–42. [G: U.S.]

Weber, Ron. Data Models Research in Accounting: An Evaluation of Wholesale Distribution Software. *Accounting Rev.*, July 1986, *61*(3), pp. 498–518. [G: U.S.]

Wheeler, James E. and Outslay, Edmund. The Phantom Federal Income Taxes of General Dynamics Corporation. *Accounting Rev.*, October 1986, *61*(4), pp. 760–74. [G: U.S.]

Wilson, G. Peter. The Relative Information Content of Accruals and Cash Flows: Combined Evidence at the Earnings Announcement and Annual Report Release Date. *J. Acc. Res.*, Supp. 1986, *24*, pp. 165–200. [G: U.S.]

Wright, Charlotte J. and Groff, James E. Uses of Indexes and Data Bases for Information Release Analysis. *Accounting Rev.*, January 1986, *61*(1), pp. 91–100. [G: U.S.]

Yli-Olli, Paavo and Virtanen, Ilkka. Classification Pattern of Financial Ratios: A Comparative Analysis between U.S. and Finnish Firms on the Aggregate Level. *Liiketaloudellinen Aikak.*, 1986, *35*(2), pp. 112–32. [G: U.S.; Finland]

Young, Richard A. A Note on "Economically Optimal Performance Evaluation and Control Systems": The Optimality of Two-Tailed Investigations. *J. Acc. Res.*, Spring 1986, *24*(1), pp. 231–40.

Zimmer, Ian. Accounting for Interest by Real Estate Developers. *J. Acc. Econ.*, March 1986, *8*(1), pp. 37–51. [G: Australia]

600 Industrial Organization; Technological Change; Industry Studies

610 Industrial Organization and Public Policy

6100 General

Salgó, István. Economic Mechanism and Foreign Trade Organization in Hungary. *Acta Oecon.*, 1986, *36*(3–4), pp. 271–87. [G: Hungary]

611 Market Structure and Corporate Strategy

6110 Market Structure and Corporate Strategy

Adams, Jean W. and Heimforth, Keith. The Effect of Conglomerate Mergers on Changes in Industry Concentration. *Antitrust Bull.*, Spring 1986, *31*(1), pp. 133–53. [G: U.S.]

Adams, Walter and Brock, James W. Corporate Power and Economic Sabotage. *J. Econ. Issues*, December 1986, *20*(4), pp. 919–40. [G: U.S.]

Adams, Walter and Brock, James W. The Automobile Industry. **In** *Adams, W., ed.*, 1986, pp. 126–71. [G: U.S.]

Adams, Walter and Mueller, Hans. The Steel Industry. **In** *Adams, W., ed.*, 1986, pp. 74–125. [G: U.S.; OECD]

Adelman, M. A. Scarcity and World Oil Prices. *Rev. Econ. Statist.*, August 1986, *68*(3), pp. 387–97. [G: U.S.; Saudi Arabia]

Aftab, Khalid and Rahim, Eric. The Emergence of a Small-Scale Engineering Sector: The Case of Tubewell Production in the Pakistan Punjab. *J. Devel. Stud.*, October 1986, *23*(1), pp. 60–76. [G: Pakistan]

Akerlof, George A. The Market for "Lemons": Quality Uncertainty and the Market Mechanism. **In** *Barney, J. B. and Ouchi, W. G., eds.*, 1986, *1970*, pp. 27–39. [G: India]

Alchian, Armen A. and Demsetz, Harold. Production, Information Costs, and Economic Organization. **In** *Putterman, L., ed.*, 1986, *1972*, pp. 111–34.

Alessio, Frank J. Cost Support for Market Pricing: Challenges to Local-Exchange Companies. **In** *[Dorsey, J. N. and Wiggins, B. T.]*, 1986, pp. 119–22. [G: U.S.]

Alexander, Donald L. Diversification and Market Performance. *Rev. Ind. Organ.*, 1986, *3*(1), pp. 44–64. [G: U.S.]

Alexander, Jeffrey A.; Morrisey, Michael A. and Shortell, Stephen M. Physician Participation in the Administration and Governance of System and Freestanding Hospitals: A Comparison by Type of Ownership. **In** *Gray, B. H., ed.*, 1986, pp. 402–21. [G: U.S.]

Alexander, Robert J. Is the United States Substituting a Speculative Economy for a Productive

One? *J. Econ. Issues,* June 1986, *20*(2), pp. 365–74. **[G: U.S.]**

Allen, D. E.; Crook, J. N. and Reekie, W. Duncan. Technical Change, Economies of Scope and Contestable Markets: Lessons from a British R&D Consortium. *S. Afr. J. Econ.,* June 1986, *54*(2), pp. 181–93. **[G: U.K.]**

Amihud, Yakov; Dodd, Peter and Weinstein, Mark. Conglomerate Mergers, Managerial Motives and Stockholder Wealth. *J. Banking Finance,* October 1986, *10*(3), pp. 401–10.

Amoako-Adu, Ben and Yagil, Joseph. Stock Price Behavior between the Base, Announcement, and Consummation Dates of the Merger. *J. Econ. Bus.,* May 1986, *38*(2), pp. 105–11. **[G: Canada]**

Anderson, Evan E. Image Differentiation and Locational Proximity among Retail Firms. *Managerial Dec. Econ.,* March 1986, *7*(1), pp. 63–68.

Anderson, S. P. Equilibrium Existence in the Circle Model of Product Differentiation. **In** *Norman, G., ed.,* 1986, pp. 19–29.

Ando, Faith H. An Analysis of the Formation and Failure Rates of Minority-Owned Firms. *Rev. Black Polit. Econ.,* Fall 1986, *15*(2), pp. 51–71. **[G: U.S.]**

Angyal, Ádám. The Large Enterprise Syndrome. *Eastern Europ. Econ.,* Fall 1986, *25*(1), pp. 61–83. **[G: Hungary]**

Anthony, Robert N. Accounting Rates of Return: Note [On the Misuse of Accounting Rates of Return to Infer Monopoly Profits]. *Amer. Econ. Rev.,* March 1986, *76*(1), pp. 244–46.

Aoki, Masahiko. Horizontal vs. Vertical Information Structure of the Firm. *Amer. Econ. Rev.,* December 1986, *76*(5), pp. 971–83.

Apró, Éva. Collective Responsibility or Collective Scapegoat? *Eastern Europ. Econ.,* Fall 1986, *25*(1), pp. 39–60. **[G: Hungary]**

Archibald, G. C.; Eaton, B. C. and Lipsey, Richard G. Address Models of Value Theory. **In** *Stiglitz, J. E. and Mathewson, G. F., eds.,* 1986, pp. 3–47.

Armour, Henry Ogden and Teece, David J. Organizational Structure and Economic Performance: A Test of the Multidivisional Hypothesis. **In** *Barney, J. B. and Ouchi, W. G., eds.,* 1986, *1978,* pp. 187–204.

Armstrong, Donald E. The Sugar Case as a Reason for "Strengthening" the Combines Act: An Economic Perspective. **In** *Block, W., ed.,* 1986, pp. 71–93. **[G: Canada]**

Arvan, Lanny. Sunk Capacity Costs, Long-run Fixed Costs, and Entry Deterrence under Complete and Incomplete Information. *Rand J. Econ.,* Spring 1986, *17*(1), pp. 105–21.

Atack, Jeremy. Firm Size and Industrial Structure in the United States during the Nineteenth Century. *J. Econ. Hist.,* June 1986, *46*(2), pp. 463–75. **[G: U.S.]**

Atkinson, Scott E. and Kerkvliet, Joe. Measuring the Multilateral Allocation of Rents: Wyoming Low-Sulfur Coal. *Rand J. Econ.,* Autumn 1986, *17*(3), pp. 416–30. **[G: U.S.]**

Audretsch, David B. The Celler Kefauver Act and the Deterrent Effect. *Rev. Ind. Organ.,* 1986, *2*(4), pp. 322–38. **[G: U.S.]**

Audretsch, David B. and Woolf, Arthur G. The Industry Life Cycle and the Concentration Profits Relationship. *Amer. Econ.,* Fall 1986, *30*(2), pp. 46–51. **[G: U.S.]**

Backhaus, Klaus. Industrial Marketing—State of the Art in Germany. **In** *Backhaus, K. and Wilson, D. T., eds.,* 1986, pp. 3–14. **[G: W. Germany]**

Baden Fuller, C. W. F. Rising Concentration: The UK Grocery Trade 1970–1980. **In** *[Yamey, B.],* 1986, pp. 63–82. **[G: U.K.]**

Bailey, Elizabeth E. Price and Productivity Change Following Deregulation: The U.S. Experience. *Econ. J.,* March 1986, *96*(381), pp. 1–17. **[G: U.S.]**

Bakos, Zsigmond. Remarks Concerning the "Thoughts" of András Hegedüs Concerning "Large Enterprises and Socialism." *Eastern Europ. Econ.,* Fall 1986, *25*(1), pp. 18–25. **[G: Hungary]**

Baldwin, John R. and Gorecki, Paul K. The Relationship between Plant Scale and Product Diversity in Canadian Manufacturing Industries. *J. Ind. Econ.,* June 1986, *34*(4), pp. 373–88. **[G: Canada]**

Baldwin, John R.; Gorecki, Paul K. and McVey, John S. International Trade, Secondary Output and Concentration in Canadian Manufacturing Industries, 1979. *Appl. Econ.,* May 1986, *18*(5), pp. 529–43. **[G: Canada]**

Ballantine, John W.; Cleveland, Frederick W. and Koeller, C. Timothy. Profit Differences: A Management Approach. *J. Post Keynesian Econ.,* Winter 1985-86, *8*(2), pp. 277–97. **[G: U.S.]**

Barney, Jay B. and Ouchi, William G. Learning from Organizational Economics. **In** *Barney, J. B. and Ouchi, W. G., eds.,* 1986, pp. 423–45.

Barone, S. S., et al. Deregulation in the Canadian Airline Industry: Is There Room for a Large Regional Airline? *Logist. Transp. Rev.,* December 1986, *22*(4), pp. 421–48. **[G: Canada]**

Bartley, Jon W. and Boardman, Calvin M. Replacement-Cost–Adjusted Valuation Ratio as a Discriminator among Takeover Target and Nontarget Firms. *J. Econ. Bus.,* February 1986, *38*(1), pp. 41–55. **[G: U.S.]**

Baumol, William J. Contestable Markets: An Uprising in the Theory of Industry Structure. **In** *Baumol, W. J.,* 1986, *1982,* pp. 40–54.

Baumol, William J. Quasi-permanence of Price Reductions: A Policy for Prevention of Predatory Pricing. **In** *Baumol, W. J.,* 1986, pp. 165–90. **[G: U.S.]**

Baumol, William J.; Panzar, J. C. and Willig, Robert D. On the Theory of Perfectly-Contestable Markets. **In** *Stiglitz, J. E. and Mathewson, G. F., eds.,* 1986, pp. 339–65.

Baumol, William J. and Willig, Robert D. Contestability: Developments since the Book. *Oxford Econ. Pap.,* Suppl. Nov. 1986, *38,* pp. 9–36. **[G: U.S.]**

Baumol, William J. and Willig, Robert D. Contestability: Developments since the Book. **In** *Morris, D. J., et al., eds.*, 1986, pp. 9–36.

Beales, J. Howard, III. Comments [The Effects of the Advertising Substantiation Program on Advertising Agencies] [An Economic Analysis of the FTC's Ad Substantiation Program]. **In** *Ippolito, P. M. and Scheffman, D. T., eds.*, 1986, pp. 213–16. **[G: U.S.]**

Bebchuk, Lucian Arye. The Case for Facilitating Competing Tender Offers: A Last (?) Reply [The Proper Role of a Target's Management in Responding to a Tender Offer] [Auctions and Sunk Costs in Tender Offers]. *J. Law, Econ., Organ.*, Fall 1986, *2*(2), pp. 253–71.

Beck, Paul J. Internal Control Technologies within Industrial Organizations. *Managerial Dec. Econ.*, June 1986, *7*(2), pp. 81–89.

Beck, Roger L. Structure and Performance with Profit Measures Based on Stock Market Prices. *Southern Econ. J.*, October 1986, *53*(2), pp. 432–47. **[G: Canada]**

Beckenstein, Alan R. and Gabel, H. Landis. Predation Rules: An Economic and Behavioral Analysis. *Antitrust Bull.*, Spring 1986, *31*(1), pp. 29–49. **[G: U.S.]**

Beesley, Michael E. Commitment, Sunk Costs, and Entry to the Airline Industry: Reflections on Experience. *J. Transp. Econ. Policy*, May 1986, *20*(2), pp. 173–90. **[G: U.K.]**

Behrens, Peter. Industrial Policy and the Nature of the Firm: Comment. *J. Inst. Theoretical Econ.*, March 1986, *142*(1), pp. 109–13.

Berg, Hartmut. Thesen des Bundeskartellamtes zur "Nachfragemacht" im Lebensmittelhandel: Eine kritische Analyse. (Theses of the Federal Cartel Office Concerning "Buying Power" Positions in German Food Retailing: A Critical Assessment. With English summary.) **In** *Eucken, W. and Böhm, F., eds.*, 1986, pp. 183–200. **[G: W. Germany]**

Berg, Sanford V. and Romano, Richard E. Predatory Intent under Uncertainty. *Rev. Ind. Organ.*, 1986, *3*(1), pp. 1–9.

Berg, Sigbjørn Atle. Excess Capacity and the Degree of Collusion: The Norwegian Experience, 1967–82. *Int. J. Ind. Organ.*, March 1986, *4*(1), pp. 99–107. **[G: Norway]**

Bhattacharya, Sudipto; Chatterjee, Kalyan and Samuelson, Larry. Sequential Research and the Adoption of Innovations. *Oxford Econ. Pap.*, Suppl. Nov. 1986, *38*, pp. 219–43.

Blanchard, Olivier J. Market Structure and Macroeconomic Fluctuations: Comments. *Brookings Pap. Econ. Act.*, 1986, (2), pp. 323–28.

Blanchflower, David. Wages and Concentration in British Manufacturing. *Appl. Econ.*, September 1986, *18*(9), pp. 1025–38. **[G: U.K.]**

Blomström, Magnus. Foreign Investment and Productive Efficiency: The Case of Mexico. *J. Ind. Econ.*, September 1986, *35*(1), pp. 97–110. **[G: Mexico]**

Blomström, Magnus. Multinationals and Market Structure in Mexico. *World Devel.*, April 1986, *14*(4), pp. 523–30. **[G: Mexico]**

Böcker, Franz. Handelskonzentration: Ein partielles Phänomen?—oder: Irreführende Handelsstatistiken. (With English summary.) *Z. Betriebswirtshaft*, July 1986, *56*(7), pp. 654–60. **[G: W. Germany]**

Boeri, Tito. Monopolistic Competition, Differentiated Products and Peripheral Development. *Giorn. Econ.*, Mar.-Apr. 1986, *45*(3–4), pp. 201–23.

Bolton, Craig J. and Meiners, Roger E. The Politicization of the Electric Utility Industry. **In** *Moorhouse, J. C., ed.*, 1986, pp. 249–77. **[G: U.S.]**

Bonanno, Giacomo. Advertising, Perceived Quality and Strategic Entry Deterrence and Accommodation. *Metroecon.*, October 1986, *38*(3), pp. 257–80.

Bonanno, Giacomo. Vertical Differentiation with Cournot Competition. *Econ. Notes*, 1986, (2), pp. 68–91.

Bond, Eric W. The Effect of Used Markets with Endogenous Replacement of Durable Goods. *Southern Econ. J.*, October 1986, *53*(2), pp. 422–31.

Bonus, Holger. The Cooperative Association as a Business Enterprise: A Study in the Economics of Transactions. *J. Inst. Theoretical Econ.*, June 1986, *142*(2), pp. 310–39.

Borooah, V. K. and van der Ploeg, Frederick. Oligopoly Power in British Industry. *Appl. Econ.*, June 1986, *18*(6), pp. 583–98. **[G: U.K.]**

Bower, Lindsay. Complementary Inputs and Market Power. *Antitrust Bull.*, Spring 1986, *31*(1), pp. 51–90. **[G: U.S.]**

Boyd, John H. and Graham, Stanley L. Risk, Regulation, and Bank Holding Company Expansion into Nonbanking. *Fed. Res. Bank Minn. Rev.*, Spring 1986, *10*(2), pp. 2–17. **[G: U.S.]**

Bradley, Michael and Rosenzweig, Michael. Defensive Stock Repurchases and the Appraisal Remedy. *Yale Law J.*, December 1986, *96*(2), pp. 322–38.

Braga, Helson C. and Guimarães, Edson P. Estrutura industrial e exportação de manufaturados no Brasil: 1978. (With English summary.) *Pesquisa Planejamento Econ.*, April 1986, *16*(1), pp. 167–88. **[G: Brazil]**

Brander, James A. and Lewis, Tracy R. Oligopoly and Financial Structure: The Limited Liability Effect. *Amer. Econ. Rev.*, December 1986, *76*(5), pp. 956–70.

Brauchlin, Emil A. Role and Structure of Swiss Multinationals. **In** *Macharzina, K. and Staehle, W. H., eds.*, 1986, pp. 67–77. **[G: Switzerland]**

Brennan, Timothy J. and Kimmel, Sheldon. Joint Production and Monopoly Extension through Tying. *Southern Econ. J.*, October 1986, *53*(2), pp. 490–501. **[G: U.S.]**

Bresnahan, Timothy F. and Salop, Steven C. Quantifying the Competitive Effects of Production Joint Ventures. *Int. J. Ind. Organ.*, June 1986, *4*(2), pp. 155–75. **[G: U.S.]**

Brickman, Ronald. National Policies for Developing High Technology Industries: International

Comparisons: France. **In** *Rushing, F. W. and Brown, C. G., eds.*, 1986, pp. 71–87. **[G: France; OECD]**

Brittan, Samuel. Privatisation: A Policy in Search of a Rationale: A Comment. *Econ. J.*, March 1986, *96*(381), pp. 33–38. **[G: U.K.]**

Broadman, Harry G. Elements of Market Power in the Natural Gas Pipeline Industry. *Energy J.*, January 1986, *7*(1), pp. 119–38. **[G: U.S.]**

Brock, Gerald W. The Computer Industry. **In** *Adams, W., ed.*, 1986, pp. 239–60. **[G: U.S.]**

Brockhoff, Klaus. The Incentive Limits of Firms: A Comparative Institutional Assessment of Bureaucracy: Comment. **In** *Balassa, B. and Giersch, H., eds.*, 1986, pp. 231–34.

Bronsteen, Peter. Market Share and Market Power in the Domestic Lemon Industry. **In** *Zerbe, R. O., Jr., ed.*, 1986, pp. 13–28. **[G: U.S.]**

Brown, Kathryn J. and Klosterman, Richard E. Hospital Acquisitions and Their Effects: Florida, 1979–1982. **In** *Gray, B. H., ed.*, 1986, pp. 303–21. **[G: U.S.]**

Brown, Martin and Philips, Peter. Competition, Racism, and Hiring Practices among California Manufacturers, 1860–1882. *Ind. Lab. Relat. Rev.*, October 1986, *40*(1), pp. 61–74. **[G: U.S.]**

Brusco, Sebastiano. Small Firms and Industrial Districts: The Experience of Italy. *Econ. Int.*, May-Aug.-Nov. 1986, *39*(2–3–4), pp. 85–97. **[G: Italy]**

Bucovetsky, Sam and Chilton, John. Concurrent Renting and Selling in a Durable-Goods Monopoly under Threat of Entry. *Rand J. Econ.*, Summer 1986, *17*(2), pp. 261–75.

Bulmash, Samuel and Mehrez, Abraham. Mergers and Synergism—Some Chance-Constraint Perspectives. *Managerial Dec. Econ.*, March 1986, *7*(1), pp. 57–62.

Bumpass, Donald L. and Nichol, Patricia J. The 1984 Justice Department Guidelines toward Horizontal Mergers. *Rev. Ind. Organ.*, 1986, *3*(1), pp. 65–77. **[G: U.S.]**

Bunting, David and Young, Shik C. Recovery of Robinson–Patman Damages: Confusion and Resolution. *Antitrust Bull.*, Fall 1986, *31*(3), pp. 797–825. **[G: U.S.]**

Burington, Bart E. Consumer Coal in Guangzhou: A Case Study of Small-scale Enterprise Organization in China. *Comp. Econ. Stud.*, Winter 1986, *28*(4), pp. 37–59. **[G: China]**

Burns, Malcolm R. Predatory Pricing and Acquisition Cost of Competitors. *J. Polit. Econ.*, April 1986, *94*(2), pp. 266–96. **[G: U.S.]**

Buson, Roberto. La dimensione aziendale nella teoria dell'impresa. (Size in the Theory of the Firm. With English summary.) *Rivista Int. Sci. Econ. Com.*, December 1986, *33*(12), pp. 1219–31. **[G: Italy]**

Calvet, A. Louis and Lefoll, Jean. Industry and Firm-Specific Factors in Canadian Corporate Acquisitions. *Finance*, December 1986, *7*(2), pp. 203–30. **[G: Canada]**

Calzolari, Michele and Somaini, Eugenio. Ciclicitá del mark-up in un modello di oligopolio. Costi e prezzi nel settore manifatturiero italiano (1970–1982). (Mark-up Cycles in an Oligopoly Model. Costs and Prices in the Italian Manufacturing Industry [1970–1982]. With English summary.) *Polit. Econ.*, April 1986, *2*(1), pp. 81–120. **[G: Italy]**

Capitelli, René and Müller, Heinz H. Ein Beispiel zum Problem der Innovationsförderung. (Stimulating Innovation Activities: An Illustration. With English summary.) *Schweiz. Z. Volkswirtsch. Statist.*, September 1986, *122*(3), pp. 535–53.

Caplin, Andrew S. and Nalebuff, Barry J. Multidimensional Product Differentiation and Price Competition. *Oxford Econ. Pap.*, Suppl. Nov. 1986, *38*, pp. 129–45.

Carleton, Willard T. and Lakonishok, Josef. The Size Anomaly: Does Industry Group Matter? *J. Portfol. Manage.*, Spring 1986, *12*(3), pp. 36–40. **[G: U.S.]**

Carlos, Ann M. and Hoffman, Elizabeth. The North American Fur Trade: Bargaining to a Joint Profit Maximum under Incomplete Information, 1804–1821. *J. Econ. Hist.*, December 1986, *46*(4), pp. 967–86. **[G: Canada]**

Carlton, Dennis W. The Rigidity of Prices. *Amer. Econ. Rev.*, September 1986, *76*(4), pp. 637–58. **[G: U.S.]**

Carstensen, Erik. Den fremtidige arbejdsdeling på penge- og kapitalmarkedet. (The Future Structure of Financial Markets in Denmark. With English summary.) *Nationaløkon. Tidsskr.*, 1986, *124*(1), pp. 62–76. **[G: Denmark]**

Casey, Cornelius J. and Selling, Thomas I. The Effect of Task Predictability and Prior Probability Disclosure on Judgment Quality and Confidence. *Accounting Rev.*, April 1986, *61*(2), pp. 302–17.

Cassing, James H. and Hillman, Arye L. Shifting Comparative Advantage and Senescent Industry Collapse. *Amer. Econ. Rev.*, June 1986, *76*(3), pp. 516–23.

Casson, Mark. Foreign Divestment and International Rationalisation: The Sale of Chrysler (UK) to Peugeot. **In** *Coyne, J. and Wright, M., eds.*, 1986, pp. 102–39. **[G: U.K.]**

Casson, Mark. The Role of Vertical Integration in the Shipping Industry. *J. Transp. Econ. Policy*, January 1986, *20*(1), pp. 7–29. **[G: U.K.]**

Casson, Mark. Vertical Integration and Intra-firm Trade. **In** *Casson, M., et al.*, 1986, pp. 103–37.

Caves, Richard E. Exporting Behavior and Market Structure: Evidence from the United States. **In** *de Jong, H. W. and Shepherd, W. G., eds.*, *Bk. 1*, 1986, pp. 189–210. **[G: U.S.]**

Cecchetti, Stephen G. The Frequency of Price Adjustment: A Study of the Newsstand Prices of Magazines. *J. Econometrics*, April 1986, *31*(3), pp. 255–74. **[G: U.S.]**

Champsaur, Paul and Rochet, Jean-Charles. Concurrence par les prix et variété des produits. (Price Competition and Product Variety. With English summary.) *Ann. Écon. Statist.*,

Jan./Mar. 1986, (1), pp. 153–73.

Chandler, Alfred D., Jr. Technological and Organizational Underpinnings of Modern Industrial Multinational Enterprise: The Dynamics of Competitive Advantage. **In** *Teichova, A.; Lévy-Leboyer, M. and Nussbaum, H., eds.*, 1986, pp. 30–54. **[G: OECD]**

Chappell, Henry W., Jr.; Pietrowski, Jane T. and Wilder, Ronald P. R and D, Firm Size, and Concentration: Evidence from the FTC Line of Business Survey. *Quart. J. Bus. Econ.*, Spring 1986, *25*(2), pp. 32–50. **[G: U.S.]**

Chard, John S. Economic Effects of Exclusive Purchasing Arrangements in the Distribution of Goods. **In** *Pellegrini, L. and Reddy, S. K., eds.*, 1986, pp. 39–57.

Chen, K. C.; Cheng, David C. and Hite, Gailen L. Systematic Risk and Market Power: An Application of Tobin's *q*. *Quart. Rev. Econ. Bus.*, Autumn 1986, *26*(3), pp. 58–72. **[G: U.S.]**

Chetty, V. K. and Heckman, James J. A Dynamic Model of Aggregate Output Supply, Factor Demand and Entry and Exit for a Competitive Industry with Heterogeneous Plants. *J. Econometrics*, Oct./Nov. 1986, *33*(1/2), pp. 237–62. **[G: U.S.]**

Chou, Tein-Chen. Concentration, Profitability and Trade in a Simultaneous Equation Analysis: The Case of Taiwan. *J. Ind. Econ.*, June 1986, *34*(4), pp. 429–43. **[G: Taiwan]**

Clark, Jeffrey A. Market Structure, Risk, and Profitability: The Quiet Life Hypothesis Revisited. *Quart. Rev. Econ. Bus.*, Spring 1986, *26*(1), pp. 45–56. **[G: U.S.]**

Clark, Robert C. Tender Offers and Corporate Governance. **In** *Knowlton, W. and Zeckhauser, R., eds.*, 1986, pp. 251–80. **[G: U.S.]**

Coase, Ronald H. The Nature of the Firm. **In** *Putterman, L., ed.*, 1986, *1937*, pp. 72–85.

Coate, Malcolm B. An Analysis of Three Approaches to Market Definition. **In** *Zerbe, R. O., Jr., ed.*, 1986, pp. 29–43.

Coate, Malcolm B. Relative Market Share and Profitability. *J. Behav. Econ.*, Spring/Summer 1986, *15*(1/2), pp. 41–53.

Coate, Malcolm B. and Uri, Noel D. A Simultaneous Equations Model of Profitability, Concentration and Marketing Expense. *J. Behav. Econ.*, Fall 1986, *15*, pp. 1–15. **[G: U.S.]**

Coleman, James S. Processes of Concentration and Dispersal of Power in Social Systems. **In** *Coleman, J. S.*, 1986, *1974*, pp. 267–80.

Coleman, James S. and Babinec, Anthony. The Corporate Structure of the Economy and Its Effects on Income. **In** *Coleman, J. S.*, 1986, *1978*, pp. 281–301. **[G: U.S.]**

Comanor, William S. The Political Economy of the Pharmaceutical Industry. *J. Econ. Lit.*, September 1986, *24*(3), pp. 1178–1217. **[G: U.S.]**

Cossutta, Dario and Grillo, Michele. Excess Capacity, Sunk Costs and Collusion: A Non-cooperative Bargaining Game: Some Considerations on the European Car Industry. *Int. J. Ind. Organ.*, September 1986, *4*(3), pp. 251–70. **[G: W. Europe]**

Cotterill, Ronald W. Market Power in the Retail Food Industry: Evidence from Vermont. *Rev. Econ. Statist.*, August 1986, *68*(3), pp. 379–86. **[G: U.S.]**

Cowley, Peter R. Business Margins and Buyer/Seller Power. *Rev. Econ. Statist.*, May 1986, *68*(2), pp. 333–37. **[G: U.S.; Canada]**

Cowling, Keith and Mueller, Dennis C. The Social Costs of Monopoly Power. **In** *Mueller, D. C.*, 1986, *1978*, pp. 223–47. **[G: U.S.; U.K.]**

Coyne, John. Divestment by Management Buy-Out: Variant and Variety. **In** *Coyne, J. and Wright, M., eds.*, 1986, pp. 140–65. **[G: U.K.]**

Coyne, John and Wright, Mike. An Introduction to Divestment: The Conceptual Issues. **In** *Coyne, J. and Wright, M., eds.*, 1986, pp. 1–26.

Cramer, Curtis A. The Structural Implications of a Minimum Bill Provision in the Transportation of Natural Gas in the United States. *Int. J. Transport Econ.*, February 1986, *13*(1), pp. 77–86. **[G: U.S.]**

Crew, Michael A. and Crocker, Keith J. Vertically Integrated Governance Structures and Optimal Institutional Arrangements for Cogeneration. *J. Inst. Theoretical Econ.*, June 1986, *142*(2), pp. 340–59. **[G: U.S.]**

Crew, Michael A. and Rowley, Charles K. Deregulation as an Instrument in Industrial Policy. *J. Inst. Theoretical Econ.*, March 1986, *142*(1), pp. 52–70.

Dahmén, Erik. Företagarverksamheten i den ekonomiska teorien. (Entrepreneurial Activity in Economic Theory. With English summary.) *Ekon. Samfundets Tidskr.*, 1986, *39*(2), pp. 69–75.

Dahremöller, Axel. Konzentration im Einzelhandel: Eine Fehlinterpretation? (With English summary.) *Z. Betriebswirtshaft*, July 1986, *56*(7), pp. 661–74. **[G: W. Germany]**

Danielsen, Albert L. and Kamerschen, David R. A Methodological Study of Market Power and Market Shares in Intrastate Inter-LATA Telecommunications. **In** *[Dorsey, J. N. and Wiggins, B. T.]*, 1986, pp. 135–80. **[G: U.S.]**

Danos, Paul and Eichenseher, John W. Long-term Trends toward Seller Concentration in the U.S. Audit Market. *Accounting Rev.*, October 1986, *61*(4), pp. 633–50. **[G: U.S.]**

Davidson, Carl and Deneckere, Raymond J. Long-run Competition in Capacity, Short-run Competition in Price, and the Cournot Model. *Rand J. Econ.*, Autumn 1986, *17*(3), pp. 404–15.

Davies, John E. Competition, Contestability and the Liner Shipping Industry. *J. Transp. Econ. Policy*, September 1986, *20*(3), pp. 299–312. **[G: Canada]**

Davis, Gary. Strategic Trading: Rationalisation in U.S. Brewing. **In** *Coyne, J. and Wright, M., eds.*, 1986, pp. 73–101. **[G: U.S.]**

Davis, Lance E. and Huttenback, Robert A. Imperialism and Social Class (Apologies to Marx and Schumpeter): Imperial Investors in the

Age of High Imperialism. **In** *Wagener, H.-J. and Drukker, J. W., eds.*, 1986, pp. 156–85. **[G: U.K.]**

Demsetz, Harold. Corporate Control, Insider Trading, and Rates of Return. *Amer. Econ. Rev.*, May 1986, *76*(2), pp. 313–16. **[G: U.S.]**

Demsetz, Harold. Industry Structure, Market Rivalry, and Public Policy. **In** *Barney, J. B. and Ouchi, W. G., eds.*, 1986, *1973*, pp. 414–22. **[G: U.S.]**

Dennis, Debra K. and McConnell, John J. Corporate Mergers and Security Returns. *J. Finan. Econ.*, June 1986, *16*(2), pp. 143–87. **[G: U.S.]**

DeSerpa, Allan C. A Note on Second Degree Price Discrimination and Its Implications. *Rev. Ind. Organ.*, 1986, *2*(4), pp. 368–75.

Desreumaux, Alain. Formation des structures d'entreprise: revue des travaux et quelques hypothèses. (Determinants of Organizational Structures: A Review of Literature and Some Proposals. With English summary.) *Écon. Soc.*, June 1986, *20*(6), pp. 3–41.

Dickson, John P. Locational Interdependency: The Impact of Change on Retail Images. **In** *Pellegrini, L. and Reddy, S. K., eds.*, 1986, pp. 171–81. **[G: U.S.]**

Dickson, Vaughan A. Efficiencies, Market Power and Horizontal Merger. *Rev. Ind. Organ.*, 1986, *3*(1), pp. 10–24.

Dickson, Vaughan A. Goals of Oligopolistic Firms: Comment. *Southern Econ. J.*, April 1986, *52*(4), pp. 1151–57. **[G: U.S.]**

de Dios, Emmanuel S. Protection, Concentration, and the Direction of Foreign Investments. *Philippine Rev. Econ. Bus.*, Mar./June 1986, *23*(1/2), pp. 57–82. **[G: Philippines]**

Dixit, Avinash K. and Shapiro, Carl. Entry Dynamics with Mixed Strategies. **In** *[Dean, J.]*, 1986, pp. 63–79.

Dixon, Huw. Strategic Investment with Consistent Conjectures. **In** *Morris, D. J., et al., eds.*, 1986, pp. 111–28.

Dixon, Huw. Strategic Investment with Consistent Conjectures. *Oxford Econ. Pap.*, Suppl. Nov. 1986, *38*, pp. 111–28.

Dixon, Robert J. and Gunther, Alan. Margins, Concentration and Oligopolistic Interdependence. *Econ. Rec.*, June 1986, *62*(177), pp. 199–207. **[G: Australia]**

Dockner, Engelbert and Feichtinger, Gustav. Dynamic Advertising and Pricing in an Oligopoly: A Nash Equilibrium Approach. **In** *Başar, T., ed.*, 1986, pp. 238–51.

Domberger, Simon; Meadowcroft, Shirley A. and Thompson, David J. Competitive Tendering and Efficiency: The Case of Refuse Collection. *Fisc. Stud.*, November 1986, *7*(4), pp. 69–87. **[G: U.K.]**

Dominique, C.-René. A Practical Way of Assessing Firms' X-Efficiency and Ability to Compete in Mature Good Industries: The Case of Textiles and Apparel. *J. Econ. Devel.*, December 1986, *11*(2), pp. 25–40. **[G: Selected Countries]**

Domowitz, Ian; Hubbard, R. Glenn and Petersen, Bruce C. Business Cycles and the Relationship between Concentration and Price–Cost Margins. *Rand J. Econ.*, Spring 1986, *17*(1), pp. 1–17. **[G: U.S.]**

Domowitz, Ian; Hubbard, R. Glenn and Petersen, Bruce C. The Intertemporal Stability of the Concentration–Margins Relationship. *J. Ind. Econ.*, September 1986, *35*(1), pp. 13–34. **[G: U.S.]**

Donsimoni, Marie-Paule; Economides, Nicholas S. and Polemarchakis, Herakles M. Stable Cartels. *Int. Econ. Rev.*, June 1986, *27*(2), pp. 317–27.

Dorn, James A. Industrial Policy and the Nature of the Firm: Comment. *J. Inst. Theoretical Econ.*, March 1986, *142*(1), pp. 101–08.

Douglas, Susan P. Selling in Japan: Consumer Behavior and Distribution as Barriers to Imports: Comment. **In** *Pugel, T. A., ed.*, 1986, pp. 107–13. **[G: U.S.; Japan; W. Germany]**

Dow, Gregory K. Stability Analysis for Profit-Responsive Selection Mechanisms. *Math. Soc. Sci.*, October 1986, *12*(2), pp. 169–83.

Dowrick, Steve. von Stackelberg and Cournot Duopoly: Choosing Roles. *Rand J. Econ.*, Summer 1986, *17*(2), pp. 251–60.

Driver, Ciaran. The Scrapping Behaviour of Concentrated and Non-concentrated Industries in the UK. *Appl. Econ.*, March 1986, *18*(3), pp. 249–63. **[G: U.K.]**

Dunn, L. F. Work Disutility and Compensating Differentials: Estimation of Factors in the Link between Wages and Firm Size. *Rev. Econ. Statist.*, February 1986, *68*(1), pp. 67–73. **[G: U.S.]**

Eaton, Jonathan and Grossman, Gene M. The Provision of Information as Marketing Strategy. *Oxford Econ. Pap.*, Suppl. Nov. 1986, *38*, pp. 166–83.

Eaton, Jonathan and Grossman, Gene M. The Provision of Information as Marketing Strategy. **In** *Morris, D. J., et al., eds.*, 1986, pp. 166–83.

Eckbo, B. Espen. Mergers and the Market for Corporate Control: The Canadian Evidence. *Can. J. Econ.*, May 1986, *19*(2), pp. 236–60. **[G: Canada]**

Edwards, Franklin R. Concentration in Banking: Problem or Solution? **In** *Kaufman, G. G. and Kormendi, R. C., eds.*, 1986, pp. 145–68. **[G: U.S.]**

Eliashberg, Jehoshua and Jeuland, Abel P. The Impact of Competitive Entry in a Developing Market upon Dynamic Pricing Strategies. *Marketing Sci.*, Winter 1986, *5*(1), pp. 20–36.

Eliasson, Gunnar. International Competition, Productivity Change and the Organization of Production. **In** *de Jong, H. W. and Shepherd, W. G., eds., Bk. 1*, 1986, pp. 127–58. **[G: OECD]**

Eliasson, Gunnar. Schumpeterian Competition in Alternative Technological Regimes: Comment. **In** *Day, R. H. and Eliasson, G., eds.*, 1986, pp. 233–38.

Elzinga, Kenneth G. The Beer Industry. **In** *Ad-*

ams, W., ed., 1986, pp. 203–38. [G: U.S.]

Encaoua, David and Geroski, Paul A. Price Dynamics and Competition in Five OECD Countries. *OECD Econ. Stud.*, Spring 1986, (6), pp. 47–74. **[G: Canada; Japan; U.K.; U.S.; Sweden]**

Encaoua, David; Geroski, Paul A. and Jacquemin, Alexis. Strategic Competition and the Persistence of Dominant Firms: A Survey. **In** *Stiglitz, J. E. and Mathewson, G. F., eds.*, 1986, pp. 55–86.

Encaoua, David; Jacquemin, Alexis and Moreaux, Michel. Global Market Power and Diversification. *Econ. J.*, June 1986, *96*(382), pp. 525–33.

Ermann, Dan and Gabel, Jon. Investor-Owned Multihospital Systems: A Synthesis of Research Findings. **In** *Gray, B. H., ed.*, 1986, pp. 474–91. **[G: U.S.]**

Espitia, Manuel; Salas, Vicente and Vagüe, M. Jesús. Medidas de resultados empresariales: relevancia para los estudios sobre el poder de monopolio. (With English summary.) *Invest. Ecón.*, September 1986, *10*(3), pp. 427–48.

Esposito, Frances Ferguson. Industry Risk and Market Structure. *Rev. Ind. Organ.*, 1986, *2*(4), pp. 306–20. **[G: U.S.]**

Esposito, Frances Ferguson and Esposito, Louis. Excess Capacity and Market Structure in U.S. Manufacturing: New Evidence. *Quart. J. Bus. Econ.*, Summer 1986, *25*(3), pp. 3–14. **[G: U.S.]**

Fábri, Ervin. Change and Unchangeability in Stockpiling Processes in Hungary. *Acta Oecon.*, 1986, *37*(1–2), pp. 73–85. **[G: Hungary]**

Falus-Szikra, Katalin. Wage and Income Disparities between the First and Second Economies in Hungary. *Acta Oecon.*, 1986, *36*(1–2), pp. 91–103. **[G: Hungary]**

Farber, Stephen C. and Martin, Robert E. Market Structure and Pollution Control under Imperfect Surveillance. *J. Ind. Econ.*, December 1986, *35*(2), pp. 147–60. **[G: U.S.]**

Färe, Rolf. Addition and Efficiency. *Quart. J. Econ.*, November 1986, *101*(4), pp. 861–65.

Farrell, Joseph. Moral Hazard as an Entry Barrier. *Rand J. Econ.*, Autumn 1986, *17*(3), pp. 440–49.

Farrell, Joseph and Saloner, Garth. Installed Base and Compatibility: Innovation, Product Preannouncements, and Predation. *Amer. Econ. Rev.*, December 1986, *76*(5), pp. 940–55.

Favereau, Olivier. Compétitivité et emploi: trois niveaux d'analyse, trois paradoxes. (Competitivity and Employment: Three Levels of Analysis, Three Paradoxes. With English summary.) *Écon. Soc.*, January 1986, *20*(1), pp. 69–90.

Faxén, Karl-Olof. Quasi-monopoly Profits, Barriers to Entry and the Welfare State: Their Impact on Labor Markets in Industrialized Countries: Comment. **In** *Day, R. H. and Eliasson, G., eds.*, 1986, pp. 435–41. **[G: OECD]**

Fehl, Ulrich. Wettbewerbliche Dimensionen des Oligopolmarktes. (Competitive Dimensions of the Oligopoly Market. With English summary.) **In** *Eucken, W. and Böhm, F., eds.*, 1986, pp. 141–53.

Feinberg, Robert M. The Effects of European Competition Policy on Pricing and Profit Margins. *Kyklos*, 1986, *39*(2), pp. 267–87. **[G: EEC; W. Germany]**

Feinberg, Robert M. The Interaction of Foreign Exchange and Market Power Effects on German Domestic Prices. *J. Ind. Econ.*, September 1986, *35*(1), pp. 61–70. **[G: W. Germany]**

Feinberg, Robert M. Trademarks, Market Power, and Information. *Rev. Ind. Organ.*, 1986, *2*(4), pp. 376–85.

Feldman, Marshall M. A. Firm Size and Local Employment Change: Three Issues. *Reg. Stud.*, February 1986, *20*(1), pp. 73–77. **[G: U.S.]**

Fernández, Zulima. La estructura organizativa: un análisis contingente. (With English summary.) *Invest. Ecón.*, September 1986, *10*(3), pp. 467–82.

Finan, William F. and Amundsen, Chris B. Modeling U.S.–Japan Competition in Semiconductors. *J. Policy Modeling*, Fall 1986, *8*(3), pp. 305–26. **[G: U.S.; Japan]**

Finsinger, Jörg; Kraft, Kornelius and Pauly, Mark V. Some Observations on Greater Competition in the West German Health-insurance System from a U.S. Perspective. *Managerial Dec. Econ.*, September 1986, *7*(3), pp. 151–61. **[G: W. Germany; U.S.]**

FitzRoy, Felix R. and Mueller, Dennis C. Cooperation and Conflict in Contractual Organizations. **In** *Mueller, D. C.*, 1986, *1984*, pp. 52–77.

Fletcher, Daniel O. A Survey of Textbooks for Industrial Organization and Public Policy. *J. Econ. Educ.*, Spring 1986, *17*(2), pp. 141–51.

Fooladi, Iraj; Roberts, Gordon S. and Viscione, Jerry A. Captive Finance Subsidiaries: Overview and Synthesis. *Financial Rev.*, May 1986, *21*(2), pp. 259–75. **[G: U.S.]**

Franke, Günter. Zur Festlegung von Abstimmungsregeln im Insolvenzverfahren. (With English summary.) *Z. Betriebswirtshaft*, July 1986, *56*(7), pp. 614–30. **[G: U.S.; W. Germany]**

Franks, Julian R. and Harris, Robert S. The Role of the Mergers and Monopolies Commission in Merger Policy: Costs and Alternatives. *Oxford Rev. Econ. Policy*, Winter 1986, *2*(4), pp. 58–78. **[G: U.K.]**

Frasco, Gregg. Vertical Integration and Contractual Alternatives with a Perfectly Competitive Output Market: A Generalization. *Southern Econ. J.*, October 1986, *53*(2), pp. 509–14.

Fratoe, Frank A. A Sociological Analysis of Minority Business. *Rev. Black Polit. Econ.*, Fall 1986, *15*(2), pp. 5–29. **[G: U.S.]**

French, Michael. Structural Change and Competition in the United States Tire Industry, 1920–1937. *Bus. Hist. Rev.*, Spring 1986, *60*(1), pp. 28–54. **[G: U.S.]**

Frischtak, Claudio R. National Policies for Developing High Technology Industries: International Comparisons: Brazil. **In** *Rushing, F. W. and Brown, C. G., eds.*, 1986, pp. 31–69. **[G: Brazil]**

Fudenberg, Drew and Tirole, Jean. A "Signal-Jamming" Theory of Predation. *Rand J. Econ.*, Autumn 1986, *17*(3), pp. 366–76.

Fudenberg, Drew and Tirole, Jean. A Theory of Exit in Duopoly. *Econometrica*, July 1986, *54*(4), pp. 943–60.

Gabszewicz, Jean Jaskold, et al. Segmenting the Market: The Monopolist's Optimal Product Mix. *J. Econ. Theory*, August 1986, *39*(2), pp. 273–89.

Gaitanides, Michael. Strategic Planning and Structuring of Organization. **In** *Macharzina, K. and Staehle, W. H., eds.*, 1986, pp. 261–74.

Galbraith, Craig S. and Kay, Neil M. Towards a Theory of Multinational Enterprise. *J. Econ. Behav. Organ.*, March 1986, *7*(1), pp. 3–19.

Gallagher, C. C. and Stewart, H. Jobs and the Business Life-Cycle in the UK. *Appl. Econ.*, August 1986, *18*(8), pp. 875–900. **[G: U.K.]**

Garten, Helen A. Banking On the Market: Relying On Depositors to Control Bank Risks. *Yale J. Regul.*, Fall 1986, *4*(1), pp. 129–72. **[G: U.S.]**

Gee, J. M. A. and Jarvis, R. J. Costs and Social Welfare in the Theory of the Spatial Firm and Industry. **In** *Norman, G., ed.*, 1986, pp. 85–102.

Ghemawat, Pankaj and Caves, Richard E. Capital Commitment and Profitability: An Empirical Investigation. **In** *Morris, D. J., et al., eds.*, 1986, pp. 94–110.

Ghemawat, Pankaj and Caves, Richard E. Capital Commitment and Profitability: An Empirical Investigation. *Oxford Econ. Pap.*, Suppl. Nov. 1986, *38*, pp. 94–110. **[G: N. America]**

Ghertman, Michel. New Multinationals in Europe. **In** *Macharzina, K. and Staehle, W. H., eds.*, 1986, pp. 38–50. **[G: W. Europe]**

Ghosh, Avijit and McLafferty, Sara. Shopping Behavior and Optimal Store Locations in Multipurpose Trip Environments. **In** *Pellegrini, L. and Reddy, S. K., eds.*, 1986, pp. 157–70.

Giammarino, Ronald M. and Heinkel, Robert L. A Model of Dynamic Takeover Behavior. *J. Finance*, June 1986, *41*(2), pp. 465–80.

Gilbert, Richard J. Pre-emptive Competition. **In** *Stiglitz, J. E. and Mathewson, G. F., eds.*, 1986, pp. 90–123.

Giquel, Christine. Les accords dits "OEM" et les formes de coopération industrielle. (With English summary.) *Revue Écon. Polit.*, Nov.-Dec. 1986, *96*(6), pp. 666–87. **[G: OECD]**

Gisser, Micha. Price Leadership and Welfare Losses in U.S. Manufacturing. *Amer. Econ. Rev.*, September 1986, *76*(4), pp. 756–67. **[G: U.S.]**

Gisser, Micha. Welfare Implications of Oligopoly in U.S. Food Manufacturing: Reply. *Amer. J. Agr. Econ.*, February 1986, *68*(1), pp. 168–69. **[G: U.S.]**

Giuffra, Robert J., Jr. Investment Bankers' Fairness Opinions in Corporate Control Transactions. *Yale Law J.*, November 1986, *96*(1), pp. 119–41. **[G: U.S.]**

Glick, Mark and Ehrbar, Hans. An Econometric Model of Industrial Profit Rate Adjustment in the U.S. *Econ. Forum*, Winter 1986-1987, *16*(1), pp. 29–43. **[G: U.S.]**

Globerman, Steven and Schwindt, Richard. The Organization of Vertically Related Transactions in the Canadian Forest Products Industries. *J. Econ. Behav. Organ.*, June 1986, *7*(2), pp. 199–212. **[G: Canada]**

Gold, Bela. Technological Change and Vertical Integration. *Managerial Dec. Econ.*, September 1986, *7*(3), pp. 169–76.

Gold, Bela. Transformation Tendencies in the World Steel Industry and Adaptive Strategies. **In** *Goldberg, W. H., ed.*, 1986, pp. 461–91.

Goldberg, Robert C.; Hakkio, Craig S. and Moses, Leon N. Competition and Collusion, Side by Side: The Corrugated Container Antitrust Litigation. **In** *Grieson, R. E., ed.*, 1986, pp. 105–25. **[G: U.S.]**

Goldberg, Walter H. Ailing Steel: The Transoceanic Quarrel: Conclusions. **In** *Goldberg, W. H., ed.*, 1986, pp. 495–510.

Goldberg, Walter H. The Steel Industry of the United States of America. **In** *Goldberg, W. H., ed.*, 1986, pp. 165–89. **[G: U.S.]**

Goldschmidt, Douglas. The Entry of New Satellite Carriers in International Telecommunications: Some Interests of Developing Nations. **In** *Demac, D. A., ed.*, 1986, pp. 88–104.

Goldstein, Jonathan P. Markup Variability and Flexibility: Theory and Empirical Evidence. *J. Bus.*, Part 1, October 1986, *59*(4), pp. 599–621.

Gomes, Lawrence J. The Competitive and Anticompetitive Theories of Advertising: An Empirical Analysis. *Appl. Econ.*, June 1986, *18*(6), pp. 599–613. **[G: U.K.]**

Gorbunov, E. and Bulatova, I. Raising the Effectiveness of a "Small-Scale Economy." *Prob. Econ.*, October 1986, *29*(6), pp. 77–87.

Gordon, Jeffrey N. and Kornhauser, Lewis A. Takeover Defense Tactics: A Comment on Two Models. *Yale Law J.*, December 1986, *96*(2), pp. 295–321. **[G: U.S.]**

Gorecki, Paul K. The Importance of Being First: The Case of Prescription Drugs in Canada. *Int. J. Ind. Organ.*, December 1986, *4*(4), pp. 371–95. **[G: Canada]**

Gorre, Lucien. Nationalization of Insurance in France. **In** *Wasow, B. and Hill, R. D., eds.*, 1986, pp. 179–210. **[G: France]**

Grabowski, Henry G. and Mueller, Dennis C. Managerial and Stockholder Welfare Models of Firm Expenditures. **In** *Mueller, D. C.*, 1986, *1972*, pp. 81–107.

Granstrand, Ove. On Measuring and Modelling Innovative New Entry in Swedish Industry. **In** *Day, R. H. and Eliasson, G., eds.*, 1986, pp. 295–310. **[G: Sweden]**

Green, Chris. Mainstreams in Industrial Organization: Challenges and Tasks. **In** *de Jong, H.*

W. and Shepherd, W. G., eds., Bk. 1, 1986, pp. 113–20.

Green, Jerry R. Vertical Integration and Assurance of Markets. **In** *Stiglitz, J. E. and Mathewson, G. F., eds.*, 1986, pp. 177–207.

Greenaway, David and Tharakan, P. K. Mathew. Imperfect Competition, Adjustment Policy, and Commercial Policy. **In** *Greenaway, D. and Tharakan, P. K. M., eds.*, 1986, pp. 7–33.

Greenhut, Melvin L. On Demand Curves and Spatial Pricing. **In** *Norman, G., ed.*, 1986, pp. 65–76.

Greer, Douglas F. Acquiring in Order to Avoid Acquisition. *Antitrust Bull.*, Spring 1986, *31*(1), pp. 155–86. **[G: U.S.]**

Gribbin, J. Denys and Utton, Michael. The Treatment of Dominant Firms in the UK Competition Legislation. **In** *de Jong, H. W. and Shepherd, W. G., eds., Bk. 2*, 1986, pp. 243–72. **[G: U.K.]**

Grossman, Sanford J. and Hart, Oliver D. The Costs and Benefits of Ownership: A Theory of Vertical and Lateral Integration. *J. Polit. Econ.*, August 1986, *94*(4), pp. 691–719.

Günter, Bernd. Risk Management in Industrial Marketing Project-Cooperations—Some Comments on Joint Risk Handling. **In** *Backhaus, K. and Wilson, D. T., eds.*, 1986, pp. 274–93.

Haining, Robert. Intraurban Retail Price Competition: Corporate and Neighbourhood Aspects of Spatial Price Variation. **In** *Norman, G., ed.*, 1986, pp. 144–64. **[G: U.K.]**

Hall, G. and Stark, A. W. Bankruptcy Risk and the Effects of Conservative Policy for 1979–81. *Int. J. Ind. Organ.*, September 1986, *4*(3), pp. 317–32. **[G: U.K.]**

Hall, Lana and Sweeney, Jan. Profitability of Mergers in Food Manufacturing. *Appl. Econ.*, July 1986, *18*(7), pp. 709–27. **[G: U.S.]**

Hall, Robert E. Market Structure and Macroeconomic Fluctuations. *Brookings Pap. Econ. Act.*, 1986, (2), pp. 285–322. **[G: U.S.]**

Haller, Hans. Market Power, Objectives of the Firm, and Objectives of Shareholders. *J. Inst. Theoretical Econ.*, December 1986, *142*(4), pp. 716–26.

Hamilton, James L. and Lee, Soo Bock. The Paradox of Vertical Integration. *Southern Econ. J.*, July 1986, *53*(1), pp. 110–26.

Hamilton, James L. and Lee, Soo Bock. Vertical Merger, Market Foreclosure, and Economic Welfare. *Southern Econ. J.*, April 1986, *52*(4), pp. 948–61.

Hansen, Robert G. A Model of Intra-brand Competition and Related Pricing Policies for Manufacturers. *Info. Econ. Policy*, June 1986, *2*(2), pp. 119–35.

Harrigan, Kathryn Rudie. Strategic Flexibility. **In** *[Dean, J.]*, 1986, pp. 81–111. **[G: U.S.]**

Harris, Frederick H. deB. Market Structure and Price–Cost Performance under Endogenous Profit Risk. *J. Ind. Econ.*, September 1986, *35*(1), pp. 35–59. **[G: U.S.]**

Harris, Robert G. and Sullivan, Lawrence A. Horizontal Merger Policy: Promoting Competition and American Competitiveness. *Antitrust Bull.*, Winter 1986, *31*(4), pp. 871–933. **[G: U.S.]**

Hart, Peter E. and Pearce, Robert D. Growth Patterns of the World's Largest Firms, 1962–1982. *Weltwirtsch. Arch.*, 1986, *122*(1), pp. 65–79. **[G: Global]**

Hausman, Gerald L. The Merger Game Starts with Deception. *Challenge*, Sept./Oct. 1986, *29*(4), pp. 44–48. **[G: U.S.]**

Hawdon, David. The Economics of the Natural Gas Market and Its Competitiveness. **In** *Stevens, P., ed.*, 1986, pp. 14–33. **[G: Selected Countries]**

Hawes, Catherine and Phillips, Charles D. The Changing Structure of the Nursing Home Industry and the Impact of Ownership on Quality, Cost, and Access. **In** *Gray, B. H., ed.*, 1986, pp. 492–541. **[G: U.S.]**

Hax, Herbert. Japan's Industrial Policy for New Technologies: Comment. *J. Inst. Theoretical Econ.*, March 1986, *142*(1), pp. 181–83. **[G: Japan]**

Hazledine, Tim and Cahill, Sean. Welfare Implications of Oligopoly in U.S. Food Manufacturing: Comment. *Amer. J. Agr. Econ.*, February 1986, *68*(1), pp. 165–67. **[G: U.S.]**

Hederman, William F., Jr. A Comparative Analysis of Two Difficult Market Transitions: Telecommunications and Natural Gas. **In** *[Dorsey, J. N. and Wiggins, B. T.]*, 1986, pp. 207–14. **[G: U.S.]**

Hegedüs, András. Large Enterprises and Socialism (Thoughts While Reading Erzsébet Szalai's Book). *Eastern Europ. Econ.*, Fall 1986, *25*(1), pp. 3–17. **[G: Hungary]**

Hegedüs, András. Questions Waiting for Answers (In the Aftermath of a Debate). *Eastern Europ. Econ.*, Fall 1986, *25*(1), pp. 113–27. **[G: Hungary]**

Heggestad, Arnold A. and Shepherd, William G. The "Banking" Industry. **In** *Adams, W., ed.*, 1986, pp. 290–324. **[G: U.S.]**

Hendricks, Ann M. On the Currents in Mainstream Industrial Organization. **In** *de Jong, H. W. and Shepherd, W. G., eds., Bk. 1*, 1986, pp. 121–24.

Hennart, Jean-François. What Is Internalization? *Weltwirtsch. Arch.*, 1986, *122*(4), pp. 791–804.

Heywood, John S. Labor Quality and the Concentration–Earnings Hypothesis. *Rev. Econ. Statist.*, May 1986, *68*(2), pp. 342–46. **[G: U.S.]**

Hill, C. W. L. and Pickering, J. F. Conglomerate Mergers, Internal Organization and Competition Policy. *Int. Rev. Law Econ.*, June 1986, *6*(1), pp. 59–75. **[G: U.K.]**

Hill, Raymond D. Brazil: The Insurance Market Consolidation of the 1970s. **In** *Wasow, B. and Hill, R. D., eds.*, 1986, pp. 211–27. **[G: Brazil]**

Hillman, Arye L. and Katz, Eliakim. Domestic Uncertainty and Foreign Dumping. *Can. J. Econ.*, August 1986, *19*(3), pp. 403–16.

Hirschey, Mark. Mergers, Buyouts and Fakeouts. *Amer. Econ. Rev.*, May 1986, *76*(2), pp. 317–22.

Hobbs, Benjamin F. Mill Pricing versus Spatial

Price Discrimination under Bertrand and Cournot Spatial Competition. *J. Ind. Econ.*, December 1986, *35*(2), pp. 173–91.

Hoch, Róbert. The Maxi and the Mini (Thoughts on the Large Enterprise Debate). *Eastern Europ. Econ.*, Fall 1986, *25*(1), pp. 84–105. **[G: Hungary]**

Hodson, Randy and England, Paula. Industrial Structure and Sex Differences in Earnings. *Ind. Relat.*, Winter 1986, *25*(1), pp. 16–32. **[G: U.S.]**

Hofmann, Hans-Joachim. Mindestroptimale Betriebsgrössen und die Ursachen suboptimaler Kapazitäten. Eine empirische Untersuchung mit Hilfe der "Survivor-Technik." (Minimum Efficient Plant Size and the Determinants of Suboptimal Capacity: An Empirical Analysis Applying the "Survivor-Technique.". With English summary.) *Jahr. Nationalökon. Statist.*, March 1986, *201*(2), pp. 131–51. **[G: W. Germany]**

Hölker, Franz-J. Entmonopolisierung der energieversorgung? (Monopolies in the German Energy Sector. With English summary.) *Ann. Pub. Co-op. Econ.*, Oct.-Dec. 1986, *57*(4), pp. 513–21. **[G: W. Germany]**

Holmes, John. The Organization and Locational Structure of Production Subcontracting. **In** *Scott, A. J. and Storper, M., eds.*, 1986, pp. 80–106.

Holt, Charles A.; Langan, Loren W. and Villamil, Anne P. Market Power in Oral Double Auctions. *Econ. Inquiry*, January 1986, *24*(1), pp. 107–23.

Hood, Neil. Role and Structure of British Multinationals. **In** *Macharzina, K. and Staehle, W. H., eds.*, 1986, pp. 79–91. **[G: U.K.]**

Horn, Ernst-Jürgen; Klodt, Henning and Saunders, Christopher. Advanced Machine Tools: Production, Diffusion and Trade. **In** *Sharp, M., ed.*, 1986, pp. 46–86. **[G: OECD]**

Hörnell, Erik. Role and Structure of Swedish Multinationals. **In** *Macharzina, K. and Staehle, W. H., eds.*, 1986, pp. 93–103. **[G: Sweden]**

Horvat, Branko. Workers' Management and the Market. **In** *Stiglitz, J. E. and Mathewson, G. F., eds.*, 1986, pp. 297–309. **[G: Yugoslavia]**

Horwitch, Mel and Sakakibara, Kiyonori. The Changing Strategy–Technology Relationship in Technology-Based Industries: A Comparison of the United States and Japan. **In** *Rosenbloom, R. S., ed.*, 1986, pp. 83–135. **[G: U.S.; Japan]**

Hotta, Kazuyoshi. Historische Entwicklungslinien der Wettbewerbsdynamik im japanischen Markt. (With English summary.) *Z. Betriebswirtshaft*, June 1986, *56*(6), pp. 500–508. **[G: Japan]**

Howells, J. Industry-Academic Links in Research and Innovation: A National and Regional Development Perspective. *Reg. Stud.*, October 1986, *20*(5), pp. 472–76. **[G: U.K.]**

Hoy, Elizabeth W. and Gray, Bradford H. Trends in the Growth of the Major Investor-Owned Hospital Companies. **In** *Gray, B. H., ed.*, 1986, pp. 250–59. **[G: U.S.]**

Hubbard, R. Glenn. Market Structure and Macroeconomic Fluctuations: Comments. *Brookings Pap. Econ. Act.*, 1986, (2), pp. 328–36.

Hubbard, R. Glenn and Weiner, Robert J. Petroleum Regulation and Public Policy. **In** *Weiss, L. W. and Klass, M. W., eds.*, 1986, pp. 105–36. **[G: U.S.]**

Hung, Chao-Shun. The Effects of Entry on Spatial Pricing and Their Implications in Industrial Economics. *Atlantic Econ. J.*, September 1986, *14*(3), pp. 18–23.

Hviid, Morten. Udtømmelige ressourcer og karteller. (Theoretical Models of a Dominant Cartel in a Market for an Exhaustible Resource. With English summary.) *Nationaløkon. Tidsskr.*, 1986, *124*(3), pp. 396–415.

Ireland, N. and Stoneman, Paul L. Technological Diffusion, Expectations and Welfare. *Oxford Econ. Pap.*, July 1986, *38*(2), pp. 283–304.

Irving, Malcolm. Mergers, Acquisitions and Takeovers. **In** *Bruce, R., et al., eds.*, 1986, pp. 109–43. **[G: Australia]**

Irwin, Manley R. The Telecommunications Industry. **In** *Adams, W., ed.*, 1986, pp. 261–89. **[G: U.S.]**

Jackson, Marvin R. Industrial Output in Romania and Its Historical Regions, 1880 to 1930, Part II, 1913 to 1930. *J. Europ. Econ. Hist.*, Fall 1986, *15*(2), pp. 231–57. **[G: Romania]**

Jappelli, Tullio. The Estimation of the Degree of Oligopoly of the Italian Banking Sector. *Stud. Econ.*, 1986, *41*(30), pp. 91–105. **[G: Italy]**

Jensen, Michael C. Agency Costs of Free Cash Flow, Corporate Finance, and Takeovers. *Amer. Econ. Rev.*, May 1986, *76*(2), pp. 323–29. **[G: U.S.]**

Johansson, Börje and Larsson, Jan. Characteristics of the Firm and the Speed of Technology Adoption. *Ricerche Econ.*, Oct.-Dec. 1986, *40*(4), pp. 675–95.

John, Teresa A. Mergers and Investment Incentives. *J. Finan. Quant. Anal.*, December 1986, *21*(4), pp. 393–413.

de Jong, Henk W. European Industrial Organization: Entrepreneurial Economics in an Organizational Setting. **In** *de Jong, H. W. and Shepherd, W. G., eds., Bk. 1*, 1986, pp. 69–112. **[G: EEC]**

Jorde, Thomas M. Restoring Predictability to Merger Guideline Analysis. *Contemp. Policy Issues*, July 1986, *4*(3), pp. 1–21. **[G: U.S.]**

Jørgensen, Steffen. Optimal Dynamic Pricing in an Oligopolistic Market: A Survey. **In** *Başar, T., ed.*, 1986, pp. 179–237.

Joy, Stewart. Contestable Market Analysis in the Australian Domestic Airline Industry. *J. Transp. Econ. Policy*, May 1986, *20*(2), pp. 245–54. **[G: Australia]**

Judd, Kenneth L. and Petersen, Bruce C. Dynamic Limit Pricing and Internal Finance. *J. Econ. Theory*, August 1986, *39*(2), pp. 368–99.

Kahneman, Daniel; Knetsch, Jack L. and Thaler,

Richard H. Fairness as a Constraint on Profit Seeking: Entitlements in the Market. *Amer. Econ. Rev.*, September 1986, *76*(4), pp. 728–41.

Kalecki, Michal. The Vertically Integrated Firm as an Element in the New Economic Model. **In** *Kalecki, M.*, 1986, *1957*, pp. 38–40.

Kamann, Dirk-Jan F. Industrial Organisation, Innovation and Employment. **In** *Nijkamp, P., ed. (II)*, 1986, pp. 131–54.

Kaminsky, Graciela Laura. Uncertainty, Expectations of Devaluation, and the Real Exchange Rate. *J. Devel. Econ.*, November 1986, *24*(1), pp. 29–57. **[G: Argentina]**

Kass, David I. Antitakeover Measures—Obstructions to the Market for Corporate Control? Comment [Motivations for Hostile Tender Offers and the Market for Political Exchange]. *Contemp. Policy Issues*, July 1986, *4*(3), pp. 46–49.

Katz, Michael L. and Shapiro, Carl. How to License Intangible Property. *Quart. J. Econ.*, August 1986, *101*(3), pp. 567–89.

Katz, Michael L. and Shapiro, Carl. Product Compatibility Choice in a Market with Technological Progress. *Oxford Econ. Pap.*, Suppl. Nov. 1986, *38*, pp. 146–65.

Katz, Michael L. and Shapiro, Carl. Product Compatibility Choice in a Market with Technological Progress. **In** *Morris, D. J., et al., eds.*, 1986, pp. 146–65.

Kay, John A. and Mayer, Colin. On the Application of Accounting Rates of Returns. *Econ. J.*, March 1986, *96*(381), pp. 199–207.

Kay, John A. and Thompson, David J. Privatisation: A Policy in Search of a Rationale. *Econ. J.*, March 1986, *96*(381), pp. 18–32. **[G: U.K.]**

Kelly, J. Patrick and Geurts, Michael D. Increasing the Efficiency of Forecasting Seasonal Demand for Individual Products. **In** *Pellegrini, L. and Reddy, S. K., eds.*, 1986, pp. 183–95. **[G: U.S.]**

Kessides, Ioannis N. Advertising, Sunk Costs, and Barriers to Entry. *Rev. Econ. Statist.*, February 1986, *68*(1), pp. 84–95. **[G: U.S.]**

Keyes, Lucile. The Vertical Restraints Guidelines of the Department of Justice. *Rev. Ind. Organ.*, 1986, *2*(4), pp. 356–66. **[G: U.S.]**

Khemani, R. S. and Shapiro, Daniel M. The Determinants of New Plant Entry in Canada. *Appl. Econ.*, November 1986, *18*(11), pp. 1243–57. **[G: Canada]**

Kihlstrom, Richard E. The Informational Role of Mergers in the Context of a Complete Securities Market. **In** *[Dean, J.]*, 1986, pp. 171–85.

Kirchgässner, Gebhard. Innovations, Market Structure and Market Dynamics: Comment. *J. Inst. Theoretical Econ.*, March 1986, *142*(1), pp. 204–09. **[G: W. Germany]**

Kirchner, Christian. Deregulation as an Instrument in Industrial Policy: Comment. *J. Inst. Theoretical Econ.*, March 1986, *142*(1), pp. 75–78.

Kirman, William I. and Masson, Robert T. Capacity Signals and Entry Deterrence. *Int. J. Ind. Organ.*, March 1986, *4*(1), pp. 25–42.

Klein, Benjamin; Crawford, Robert G. and Alchian, Armen A. Vertical Integration, Appropriable Rents, and the Competitive Contracting Process. **In** *Barney, J. B. and Ouchi, W. G., eds.*, 1986, *1978*, pp. 39–71. **[G: U.S.]**

Knoeber, Charles R. Golden Parachutes, Shark Repellents, and Hostile Tender Offers. *Amer. Econ. Rev.*, March 1986, *76*(1), pp. 155–67. **[G: U.S.]**

Koch, James V. The Intercollegiate Athletics Industry. **In** *Adams, W., ed.*, 1986, pp. 325–46. **[G: U.S.]**

König, Heinz and Zimmermann, Klaus F. Innovations, Market Structure and Market Dynamics. *J. Inst. Theoretical Econ.*, March 1986, *142*(1), pp. 184–99. **[G: W. Germany]**

Koutsoyiannis, A. Goals of Oligopolistic Firms: Reply. *Southern Econ. J.*, April 1986, *52*(4), pp. 1158–61. **[G: U.S.]**

Krattenmaker, Thomas G. and Salop, Steven C. Competition and Cooperation in the Market for Exclusionary Rights. *Amer. Econ. Rev.*, May 1986, *76*(2), pp. 109–13.

Krause, David S. Ownership Control and Stock Market Performance. *J. Behav. Econ.*, Spring/Summer 1986, *15*(1/2), pp. 113–21. **[G: U.S.]**

Kroll, Mark and Johnson, Herb. A Note on Managerial Behavior and the Theory of the Firm. *J. Behav. Econ.*, Spring/Summer 1986, *15*(1/2), pp. 123–34.

Kulagin, G. A. Product Mix, Price, Profit. *Prob. Econ.*, September 1986, *29*(5), pp. 3–20. **[G: U.S.S.R.]**

Kwoka, John E., Jr. and Ravenscraft, David J. Cooperation *vs.* Rivalry: Price–Cost Margins by Line of Business. *Economica*, August 1986, *53*(211), pp. 351–63. **[G: U.S.]**

Kwoka, John E., Jr. and Warren-Boulton, Frederick R. Efficiencies, Failing Firms, and Alternatives to Merger: A Policy Synthesis. *Antitrust Bull.*, Summer 1986, *31*(2), pp. 431–50. **[G: U.S.]**

Langlois, Richard N. Rationality, Institutions, and Explanation. **In** *Langlois, R. N., ed.*, 1986, pp. 225–55.

Laulajainen, Risto and Gadde, Lars-Erik. Locational Avoidance: A Case Study of Three Swedish Retail Chains. *Reg. Stud.*, April 1986, *20*(2), pp. 131–40. **[G: Sweden]**

Law, Peter J. The Effect of Regulation on Wages and Intermediate Product Prices under Bilateral Monopoly. *Bull. Econ. Res.*, September 1986, *38*(3), pp. 221–36.

Lazear, Edward P. Retail Pricing and Clearance Sales. *Amer. Econ. Rev.*, March 1986, *76*(1), pp. 14–32.

Lecraw, Donald J. Industry Structure and Competition Policy. **In** *Block, W., ed.*, 1986, pp. 171–85. **[G: Canada]**

Lee, Jaymin. Market Performance in an Open Developing Economy: Technical and Allocative Efficiency of Korean Industries. *J. Ind. Econ.*, September 1986, *35*(1), pp. 81–96. **[G: S. Korea]**

Leffler, Keith B. and Sauer, Raymond, Jr. The Effects of the Advertising Substantiation Program on Advertising Agencies. **In** *Ippolito, P. M. and Scheffman, D. T., eds.*, 1986, pp. 177–95. **[G: U.S.]**

Leibenstein, Harvey. Intra-firm Effort Decisions and Sanctions: Hierarchy versus Peers. **In** *Gilad, B. and Kaish, S., eds., Vol. A*, 1986, pp. 213–31.

Leijonhufvud, Axel. Capitalism and the Factory System. **In** *Langlois, R. N., ed.*, 1986, pp. 203–23.

Levy, David T. and Haber, Lawrence J. An Advantage of the Multiproduct Firm: The Transferability of Firm-Specific Capital. *J. Econ. Behav. Organ.*, September 1986, *7*(3), pp. 291–302.

Lewis, Tracy R. Reputation and Contractual Performance in Long-term Projects. *Rand J. Econ.*, Summer 1986, *17*(2), pp. 141–57.

Libecap, Gary D. Deregulation as an Instrument in Industrial Policy: Comment. *J. Inst. Theoretical Econ.*, March 1986, *142*(1), pp. 71–74.

Lilien, Gary L. New Product Success in Business/Industrial Markets: Progress, Problems, and Research Program. **In** *Backhaus, K. and Wilson, D. T., eds.*, 1986, pp. 339–48.

Linda, Remo. Competition Policies and Measures of Dominant Power. **In** *de Jong, H. W. and Shepherd, W. G., eds., Bk. 2*, 1986, pp. 287–307. **[G: U.S.]**

Lindenberg, Siegwart. Individual Economic Ignorance versus Social Production Functions and Precarious Enlightenment: Comment on Tullock's View of Rent Seeking in Dictatorships. *J. Inst. Theoretical Econ.*, March 1986, *142*(1), pp. 20–26.

Littlechild, S. C. Three Types of Market Process. **In** *Langlois, R. N., ed.*, 1986, pp. 27–39.

Lloyd, Tom. The Importance of Giant Companies. *Lloyds Bank Rev.*, April 1986, (160), pp. 52–54. **[G: U.S.; U.K.]**

Lloyd, William P.; Jahera, John S. and Goldstein, Steven J. The Relation between Returns, Ownership Structure, and Market Value. *J. Finan. Res.*, Summer 1986, *9*(2), pp. 171–77. **[G: U.S.]**

Lo, Andrew W. Logit versus Discriminant Analysis: A Specification Test and Application to Corporate Bankruptcies. *J. Econometrics*, March 1986, *31*(2), pp. 151–78. **[G: U.S.]**

Loasby, Brian J. Organisation, Competition, and the Growth of Knowledge. **In** *Langlois, R. N., ed.*, 1986, pp. 41–57.

Lunn, John. An Empirical Analysis of Process and Product Patenting: A Simultaneous Equation Framework. *J. Ind. Econ.*, March 1986, *34*(3), pp. 319–30. **[G: U.S.]**

Lunn, John and Martin, Stephen. Market Structure, Firm Structure, and Research Development. *Quart. Rev. Econ. Bus.*, Spring 1986, *26*(1), pp. 31–44. **[G: U.S.]**

MacDonald, James M. Entry and Exit on the Competitive Fringe. *Southern Econ. J.*, January 1986, *52*(3), pp. 640–52. **[G: U.S.]**

Macey, Jonathan R. Takeover Defense Tactics and Legal Scholarship: Market Forces versus the Policymaker's Dilemma. *Yale Law J.*, December 1986, *96*(2), pp. 342–52.

Macharzina, Klaus. The European Microelectronics Industry and New Technologies. **In** *Macharzina, K. and Staehle, W. H., eds.*, 1986, pp. 241–56. **[G: W. Europe]**

Maggi, Rico and Haeni, Peter K. Spatial Concentration, Location and Competitiveness: The Case of Switzerland. *Reg. Stud.*, April 1986, *20*(2), pp. 141–49. **[G: Switzerland]**

Malatesta, Paul H. and Thompson, Rex. Stock Price Reactions to Partially Anticipated Events: Evidence on the Economic Impact of Corporate Acquisition Attempts. **In** *Chen, A. H., ed.*, 1986, pp. 119–48. **[G: U.S.]**

Malecki, Edward J. Technological Imperatives and Modern Corporate Strategy. **In** *Scott, A. J. and Storper, M., eds.*, 1986, pp. 67–79.

Malécot, Jean-François. Sait-on vraiment prévoir les défaillances d'entreprises? (Predicting Business Failure: Is It Really Possible? With English summary.) *Écon. Soc.*, December 1986, *20*(12), pp. 55–82. **[G: France]**

Mankiw, N. Gregory and Whinston, Michael D. Free Entry and Social Inefficiency. *Rand J. Econ.*, Spring 1986, *17*(1), pp. 48–58.

Manne, Henry G. Industrial Organization and Rent Seeking in Dictatorships: Comment. *J. Inst. Theoretical Econ.*, March 1986, *142*(1), pp. 16–19.

Mantakas, George. Duopolistic Conduct under Demand Uncertainty with Irreversible Capital Commitments. *Greek Econ. Rev.*, June 1986, *8*(1), pp. 21–40.

Marcus, Matityahu; Palmon, Dan and Yaari, Uzi. Growth and the Decision to Incorporate: A Financial Theory of the U.S. Tax System. **In** *Chen, A. H., ed.*, 1986, pp. 29–50. **[G: U.S.]**

Marin, Dalia. Exchange Rate and Industrial Profits: Austria's Revaluation Policy in the 1970s. *Appl. Econ.*, June 1986, *18*(6), pp. 675–89. **[G: Austria]**

Mariotti, Sergio and Ricotta, Enrico. Diversification, Agreements between Firms and Innovative Behaviour. *Ricerche Econ.*, Oct.-Dec. 1986, *40*(4), pp. 644–74. **[G: U.S.; Europe]**

Marris, Robin and Mueller, Dennis C. The Corporation, Competition, and the Invisible Hand. **In** *Mueller, D. C.*, 1986, *1980*, pp. 261–97.

Martin, Stephen. Causes and Effects of Vertical Integration. *Appl. Econ.*, July 1986, *18*(7), pp. 737–55. **[G: U.S.]**

Marvel, Howard P. and McCafferty, Stephen. The Political Economy of Resale Price Maintenance. *J. Polit. Econ.*, October 1986, *94*(5), pp. 1074–95. **[G: U.S.]**

Mason, Charles F. Predation by Noisy Advertising. *Rev. Ind. Organ.*, 1986, *3*(1), pp. 78–93.

Masson, Robert T. and Shaanan, Joseph. Excess Capacity and Limit Pricing: An Empirical Test. *Economica*, August 1986, *53*(211), pp. 365–78. **[G: U.S.]**

Masten, Scott E. Institutional Choice and the Organization of Production: The Make-or-Buy

Decision. *J. Inst. Theoretical Econ.*, September 1986, *142*(3), pp. 493–509.

Masten, Scott E. The Economic Institutions of Capitalism: A Review Article. *J. Inst. Theoretical Econ.*, June 1986, *142*(2), pp. 445–51.

Mathewson, G. Frank and Winter, Ralph A. The Economics of Vertical Restraints in Distribution. **In** *Stiglitz, J. E. and Mathewson, G. F., eds.*, 1986, pp. 211–36.

McChesney, Fred S. Assumptions, Empirical Evidence and Social Science Method. *Yale Law J.*, December 1986, *96*(2), pp. 339–41.

McFarland, Henry. Ramsey Pricing of Inputs with Downstream Monopoly Power and Regulation: Implications for Railroad Rate Setting. *J. Transp. Econ. Policy*, January 1986, *20*(1), pp. 81–90. **[G: U.S.]**

McKenzie, Richard B. Eminent Domain: A New Industrial Policy Tool. *J. Inst. Theoretical Econ.*, March 1986, *142*(1), pp. 27–38. **[G: U.S.]**

Measday, Walter S. and Martin, Stephen. The Petroleum Industry. **In** *Adams, W., ed.*, 1986, pp. 38–73. **[G: U.S.; OPEC]**

Mefford, Robert N. Introducing Management into the Production Function. *Rev. Econ. Statist.*, February 1986, *68*(1), pp. 96–104. **[G: U.S.]**

de Melo, Jaime and Urata, Shujiro. The Influence of Increased Foreign Competition on Industrial Concentration and Profitability. *Int. J. Ind. Organ.*, September 1986, *4*(3), pp. 287–304. **[G: Chile]**

Meyerson, Per-Martin. Quasi-monopoly Profits, Barriers to Entry and the Welfare State: Their Impact on Labor Markets in Industrialized Countries: Comment. **In** *Day, R. H. and Eliasson, G., eds.*, 1986, pp. 442–46. **[G: OECD]**

Milánovics, Szvetozár. The (Large) Enterprises and Socialism (Thoughts about András Hegedüs's Thoughts). *Eastern Europ. Econ.*, Fall 1986, *25*(1), pp. 26–38. **[G: Hungary]**

Miller, Debra Lynn. National Policies for Developing High Technology Industries: International Comparisons: Mexico. **In** *Rushing, F. W. and Brown, C. G., eds.*, 1986, pp. 173–99. **[G: Mexico]**

Miller, Edward M. Determinants of the Size of the Small Business Sector: They Are Labor Productivity, Wage Rates and Capital Intensity. *Amer. J. Econ. Soc.*, October 1986, *45*(4), pp. 390–402. **[G: U.S.]**

Milner, Chris. Optimal Intervention and Intra-industry Trade: The Case of Horizontally Differentiated Goods and Monopolistically Competitive Industries. **In** *Greenaway, D. and Tharakan, P. K. M., eds.*, 1986, pp. 47–67.

Mirman, Leonard J.; Tauman, Yair and Zang, Israel. Ramsey Prices, Average Cost Prices and Price Sustainability. *Int. J. Ind. Organ.*, June 1986, *4*(2), pp. 123–40.

Mitchell, William E. and Sorensen, Robert L. Pricing, Price Dispersion, and Information: The Discount Brokerage Industry. *J. Econ. Bus.*, December 1986, *38*(4), pp. 273–82. **[G: U.S.]**

Mittelsten Scheid, Jörg. The Family Business Remnant: Elixir of the Market Economy? **In** *Pohl, H. and Rudolph, B., eds.*, 1986, pp. 1–26.

Mixon, J. Wilson, Jr. and Uri, Noel D. On the Optimal Pricing Policy of a Dominant Firm. *De Economist*, 1986, *134*(2), pp. 225–27.

Montgomery, David B. Conjoint Calibration of the Customer/Competitor Interface in Industrial Markets. **In** *Backhaus, K. and Wilson, D. T., eds.*, 1986, pp. 297–319.

Morris, Derek J., et al. Strategic Behaviour and Industrial Competition: An Introduction. **In** *Morris, D. J., et al., eds.*, 1986, pp. 1–8.

Morris, Derek J., et al. Strategic Behaviour and Industrial Competition: An Introduction. *Oxford Econ. Pap.*, Suppl. Nov. 1986, *38*, pp. 1–8.

Mueller, Dennis C. A Theory of Conglomerate Mergers. **In** *Mueller, D. C.*, 1986, *1969*, pp. 155–70.

Mueller, Dennis C. Persistent Performance among Large Corporations. **In** *[Dean, J.]*, 1986, pp. 31–61. **[G: U.S.]**

Mueller, Dennis C. Power and Profit in Hierarchical Organizations. **In** *Mueller, D. C.*, 1986, *1980*, pp. 37–51.

Mueller, Dennis C. The Effects of Conglomerate Mergers: A Survey of the Empirical Evidence. **In** *Mueller, D. C.*, 1986, *1977*, pp. 187–219. **[G: U.S.]**

Mueller, Dennis C. The Persistence of Profits above the Norm. **In** *Mueller, D. C.*, 1986, *1977*, pp. 248–60. **[G: U.S.]**

Mueller, Willard F. Conglomerates: A "Nonindustry." **In** *Adams, W., ed.*, 1986, pp. 347–94. **[G: U.S.]**

Mulherin, J. Harold. Complexity in Long-term Contracts: An Analysis of Natural Gas Contractual Provisions. *J. Law, Econ., Organ.*, Spring 1986, *2*(1), pp. 105–17. **[G: U.S.]**

Mulherin, J. Harold. Specialized Assets, Governmental Regulation, and Organizational Structure in the Natural Gas Industry. *J. Inst. Theoretical Econ.*, September 1986, *142*(3), pp. 528–41. **[G: U.S.]**

Mulligan, James G. Technical Change and Scale Economies Given Stochastic Demand and Production. *Int. J. Ind. Organ.*, June 1986, *4*(2), pp. 189–201.

Nakao, Takeo. Industrial Organization in an International Framework. **In** *de Jong, H. W. and Shepherd, W. G., eds., Bk. 1*, 1986, pp. 159–87. **[G: OECD]**

Natke, Paul A. Market Imperfections and Import Pricing Behavior by Multinational Enterprises. *J. Econ. Devel.*, July 1986, *11*(1), pp. 105–18. **[G: Brazil]**

Negandhi, Anant R. Role and Structure of German Multinationals: A Comparative Profile. **In** *Macharzina, K. and Staehle, W. H., eds.*, 1986, pp. 51–66. **[G: W. Germany]**

Nelson, Richard R. Evolutionary Modelling of Economic Change. **In** *Stiglitz, J. E. and Mathewson, G. F., eds.*, 1986, pp. 450–71. **[G: U.S.]**

Nelson, Richard R. The Tension between Process Stories and Equilibrium Models: Analyzing the Productivity-Growth Slowdown of the 1970s. **In** *Langlois, R. N., ed.*, 1986, pp. 135–51.

Neumann, Manfred. Improved Competitiveness of Steel-Producing Firms by Means of Diversification. **In** *Goldberg, W. H., ed.*, 1986, pp. 439–43. **[G: W. Germany]**

Neven, D. 'Address' Models of Differentiation. **In** *Norman, G., ed.*, 1986, pp. 5–18.

Nguyen, Godefroy Dang. Telecommunications: A Challenge to the Old Order. **In** *Sharp, M., ed.*, 1986, pp. 87–133. **[G: OECD]**

Norman, George. Market Strategy with Variable Entry Threats. **In** *Norman, G., ed.*, 1986, pp. 103–24.

North, Douglass C. The New Institutional Economics. *J. Inst. Theoretical Econ.*, March 1986, *142* (1), pp. 230–37.

Nuti, Domenico Mario. Merger Conditions and the Measurement of Disequilibrium in Labour-Managed Economies. *Ann. Pub. Co-op. Econ.*, Jan.-March 1986, *57* (1), pp. 47–53.

O'Brien, D. P. Divestiture: The Case of AT&T. **In** *Coyne, J. and Wright, M., eds.*, 1986, pp. 166–201. **[G: U.S.]**

O'Driscoll, Gerald P., Jr. Competition as a Process: A Law and Economics Perspective. **In** *Langlois, R. N., ed.*, 1986, pp. 153–69. **[G: U.S.]**

Odagiri, Hiroyuki and Yamawaki, Hideki. A Study of Company Profit-Rate Time Series: Japan and the United States. *Int. J. Ind. Organ.*, March 1986, *4* (1), pp. 1–23. **[G: Japan; U.S.]**

Odle, Curt J. and Gorman, Raymond F. Collusion among Many Agents. *J. Econ. Bus.*, February 1986, *38* (1), pp. 57–64.

Ordover, Janusz A. and Willig, Robert D. Perspectives on Mergers and World Competition. **In** *Grieson, R. E., ed.*, 1986, pp. 201–18.

Oster, Clinton V., Jr. and Pickrell, Don H. Marketing Alliances and Competitive Strategy in the Airline Industry. *Logist. Transp. Rev.*, December 1986, *22* (4), pp. 371–87. **[G: U.S.]**

Owen, Bruce M. The Evolution of Clayton Section 7 Enforcement and the Beginnings of U.S. Industrial Policy. *Antitrust Bull.*, Summer 1986, *31* (2), pp. 409–29. **[G: U.S.]**

Owen, Bruce M. and Greenhalgh, Peter R. Competitive Considerations in Cable Television Franchising. *Contemp. Policy Issues*, April 1986, *4* (2), pp. 69–79. **[G: U.S.]**

Paba, Sergio. 'Brand-naming' as an Entry Strategy in the White Goods Industry. *Cambridge J. Econ.*, December 1986, *10* (4), pp. 305–18. **[G: W. Europe]**

Pagoulatos, Emilio and Sorensen, Robert L. What Determines the Elasticity of Industry Demand? *Int. J. Ind. Organ.*, September 1986, *4* (3), pp. 237–50. **[G: U.S.]**

Palepu, Krishna G. Predicting Takeover Targets: A Methodological and Empirical Analysis. *J. Acc. Econ.*, March 1986, *8* (1), pp. 3–35. **[G: U.S.]**

de Palma, André; Labbé, M. and Thisse, Jacques-François. On the Existence of Price Equilibria under Mill and Uniform Delivered Price Policies. **In** *Norman, G., ed.*, 1986, pp. 30–42.

Papanek, Gábor. Hungarian Enterprises Surviving Critical Financial Situations (A Retrospective Analysis). *Acta Oecon.*, 1986, *37* (3–4), pp. 305–23. **[G: Hungary]**

Pastena, Victor and Ruland, William. The Merger/Bankruptcy Alternative. *Accounting Rev.*, April 1986, *61* (2), pp. 288–301. **[G: U.S.]**

Patel, I. G. Free Enterprise in the Nehru Era. **In** *Patel, I. G.*, 1986, *1984*, pp. 165–81. **[G: India]**

Pattison, Robert V. Response to Financial Incentives among Investor-Owned and Not-for-Profit Hospitals: An Analysis Based on California Data, 1978–1982. **In** *Gray, B. H., ed.*, 1986, pp. 290–302. **[G: U.S.]**

Paulsson, Gunnar. Licensing Industrial Technology to Developing Countries: The Operations of Swedish Firms in India. *Aussenwirtschaft*, December 1986, *41* (4), pp. 533–49. **[G: India]**

Peck, Francis W. and Townsend, Alan R. Corporate Interaction in Oligopolistic Markets: The Role of Case Studies of Rationalisation. **In** *Danson, M., ed.*, 1986, pp. 49–63. **[G: U.K.]**

Peck, S. C. Econometric Aspects of Firm Growth Behaviour. **In** *[Yamey, B.]*, 1986, pp. 133–58.

Pellegrini, Luca. Sale or Return Agreements versus Outright Sales. **In** *Pellegrini, L. and Reddy, S. K., eds.*, 1986, pp. 59–72.

Pelton, Joseph N. INTELSAT: Responding to New Challenges. **In** *Demac, D. A., ed.*, 1986, pp. 58–74.

Perloff, Jeffrey M. and Salop, Steven C. Firm-Specific Information, Product Differentiation, and Industry Equilibrium. *Oxford Econ. Pap.*, Suppl. Nov. 1986, *38*, pp. 184–202.

Perloff, Jeffrey M. and Salop, Steven C. Firm-Specific Information, Product Differentiation, and Industry Equilibrium. **In** *Morris, D. J., et al., eds.*, 1986, pp. 184–202.

Pernia, Ernesto M. and Pernia, Joseph M. An Economic and Social Impact Analysis of Small Industry Promotion: A Philippine Experience. *World Devel.*, May 1986, *14* (5), pp. 637–51. **[G: Philippines]**

Perrakis, Stylianos and Warskett, George. Uncertainty, Economies of Scale, and Barrier to Entry. **In** *Morris, D. J., et al., eds.*, 1986, pp. 58–74.

Perrakis, Stylianos and Warskett, George. Uncertainty, Economies of Scale, and Barrier to Entry. *Oxford Econ. Pap.*, Suppl. Nov. 1986, *38*, pp. 58–74.

Perry, Martin K. and Groff, Robert H. Trademark Licensing in a Monopolistically Competitive Industry. *Rand J. Econ.*, Summer 1986, *17* (2), pp. 189–200.

Pethig, Rüdiger. Eminent Domain: A New Industrial Policy Tool: Comment. *J. Inst. Theoretical Econ.*, March 1986, *142* (1), pp. 44–51. **[G: W. Germany]**

Pindyck, Robert S. Capital Adjustment Costs,

Monopoly Power, and the Regulated Firm. **In** *Grieson, R. E., ed.*, 1986, pp. 219–30.

Pitelis, Christos N. Corporate Control, Social Choice and Capital Accumulation: An Asymmetrical Choice Approach. *Rev. Radical Polit. Econ.*, Fall 1986, *18*(3), pp. 85–100.

Pitelis, Christos N. and Sugden, Roger. The Separation of Ownership and Control in the Theory of the Firm: A Reappraisal. *Int. J. Ind. Organ.*, March 1986, *4*(1), pp. 69–86.

Polo, Michele. Recenti sviluppi nell'analisi della differenziazione del prodotto. (Recent Developments in the Analysis of Product Differentiation. With English summary.) *Giorn. Econ.*, Mar.-Apr. 1986, *45*(3–4), pp. 171–200.

Porter, Michael E. The Contributions of Industrial Organization to Strategic Management. **In** *Barney, J. B. and Ouchi, W. G., eds.*, 1986, *1981*, pp. 381–96.

Porter, Philip K.; Scully, Gerald W. and Slottje, Daniel J. Industrial Policy and the Nature of the Firm. *J. Inst. Theoretical Econ.*, March 1986, *142*(1), pp. 79–100. **[G: W. Europe]**

Porter, Robert H. The Impact of Government Policy on the U.S. Cigarette Industry. **In** *Ippolito, P. M. and Scheffman, D. T., eds.*, 1986, pp. 447–81. **[G: U.S.]**

Poulsen, Annette B. and Jarrell, Gregg A. Motivations for Hostile Tender Offers and the Market for Political Exchange. *Contemp. Policy Issues*, July 1986, *4*(3), pp. 30–45. **[G: U.S.]**

Pozdena, Randall J. Structure and Performance: Some Evidence from California Banking. *Fed. Res. Bank San Francisco Econ. Rev.*, Winter 1986, (1), pp. 5–17. **[G: U.S.]**

Pratten, Cliff. The Importance of Giant Companies. *Lloyds Bank Rev.*, January 1986, (159), pp. 33–48. **[G: U.S.; U.K.]**

Price, C. M. Regional Price Discrimination in the United Kingdom Gas Industry. **In** *Norman, G., ed.*, 1986, pp. 165–85. **[G: U.K.]**

Primeaux, Walter J., Jr. Competition between Electric Utilities. **In** *Moorhouse, J. C., ed.*, 1986, pp. 395–423. **[G: U.S.]**

Putterman, Louis G. The Economic Nature of the Firm: Overview. **In** *Putterman, L., ed.*, 1986, pp. 1–29.

Quiggin, John; Gargett, D. and Barrett, G. Exits from the Australian Dairy Industry: Causes and Predictions. *J. Agr. Econ.*, May 1986, *37*(2), pp. 233–42. **[G: Australia]**

Quirk, James P. and Terasawa, Katsuaki. Sample Selection and Cost Underestimation Bias in Pioneer Projects. *Land Econ.*, May 1986, *62*(2), pp. 192–200. **[G: U.S.]**

Quirmbach, Herman C. The Diffusion of New Technology and the Market for an Innovation. *Rand J. Econ.*, Spring 1986, *17*(1), pp. 33–47.

Quirmbach, Herman C. The Path of Price Changes in Vertical Integration. *J. Polit. Econ.*, October 1986, *94*(5), pp. 1110–19.

Quirmbach, Herman C. Vertical Integration: Scale Distortions, Partial Integration, and the Direction of Price Change. *Quart. J. Econ.*, February 1986, *101*(1), pp. 131–47.

Radner, Roy. The Internal Economy of Large Firms. *Econ. J.*, Supplement 1986, *96*, pp. 1–22.

Rangan, V. Kasturi. Relationship Management of Distributors: A Proposed Framework. **In** *Pellegrini, L. and Reddy, S. K., eds.*, 1986, pp. 103–17.

Rao, T. V. S. Ramomahan. Welfare Economics of Organizational Decisions and Its Implications for Industrial Economics. *Indian Econ. J.*, Oct.-Dec. 1986, *34*(2), pp. 87–105.

Read, Robert A. The Banana Industry: Oligopoly and Barriers to Entry. **In** *Casson, M., et al.*, 1986, pp. 317–42. **[G: Selected Countries]**

Read, Robert A. The Synthetic Fibre Industry: Innovation Integration and Market Structure. **In** *Casson, M., et al.*, 1986, pp. 197–223. **[G: Global]**

Reekie, W. Duncan. The Economics of Business and the Business of Economics. *S. Afr. J. Econ.*, December 1986, *54*(4), pp. 362–80. **[G: S. Africa]**

Reve, Torger and Stern, Louis W. The Relationship between Interorganizational Form, Transaction Climate, and Economic Performance in Vertical Interfirm Dyads. **In** *Pellegrini, L. and Reddy, S. K., eds.*, 1986, pp. 75–102. **[G: Norway]**

Révész, Gábor. On the Expansion and Functioning of the Direct Market Sector of the Hungarian Economy. *Acta Oecon.*, 1986, *36*(1–2), pp. 105–21. **[G: Hungary]**

Rey, Patrick and Tirole, Jean. Contraintes verticales: l'approche principal–agent. (Vertical Restraints: The Principal–Agent Approach. With English summary.) *Ann. Écon. Statist.*, Jan./Mar. 1986, (1), pp. 175–201.

Rey, Patrick and Tirole, Jean. The Logic of Vertical Restraints. *Amer. Econ. Rev.*, December 1986, *76*(5), pp. 921–39.

Rey, Patrick and Tirole, Jean. Vertical Restraints from a Principal–Agent Viewpoint. **In** *Pellegrini, L. and Reddy, S. K., eds.*, 1986, pp. 1–30.

Reynolds, Robert J. and Snapp, Bruce R. The Competitive Effects of Partial Equity Interests and Joint Ventures. *Int. J. Ind. Organ.*, June 1986, *4*(2), pp. 141–53.

Reynolds, Stanley S. Strategic Capital Investment in the American Aluminum Industry. *J. Ind. Econ.*, March 1986, *34*(3), pp. 225–45. **[G: U.S.]**

Rispoli, Maurizio. L'innovazione nella strategia delle piccole imprese. (Innovation in the Strategy of Small Firms. With English summary.) *Ricerche Econ.*, Apr.-Sept. 1986, *40*(2–3), pp. 489–509.

Roberts, John. A Signaling Model of Predatory Pricing. **In** *Morris, D. J., et al., eds.*, 1986, pp. 75–93.

Roberts, John. A Signaling Model of Predatory Pricing. *Oxford Econ. Pap.*, Suppl. Nov. 1986, *38*, pp. 75–93.

Rogowsky, Robert A. The Economic Effectiveness of Section 7 Relief. *Antitrust Bull.*, Spring 1986, *31*(1), pp. 187–233. **[G: U.S.]**

Roll, Richard. The Hubris Hypothesis of Corporate Takeovers. *J. Bus.*, Part 1, April 1986, *59*(2), pp. 197–216. **[G: U.S.]**

Roman, Z. Competition and Industrial Organisation in the Centrally Planned Economies. **In** *Stiglitz, J. E. and Mathewson, G. F., eds.*, 1986, pp. 315–35. **[G: CMEA]**

Roseveare, R. W. Public Enterprise: Studies in Organisational Structure: British Steel Corporation. **In** *Ramanadham, V. V., ed.*, 1986, pp. 21–50. **[G: U.K.]**

Ross, David R. Learning to Dominate. *J. Ind. Econ.*, June 1986, *34*(4), pp. 337–53.

Ross, Howard N. and Krausz, Joshua. Buyers' and Sellers' Prices and Administered Behavior. *Rev. Econ. Statist.*, August 1986, *68*(3), pp. 369–78. **[G: U.S.]**

Rotemberg, Julio J. and Saloner, Garth. A Supergame-Theoretic Model of Price Wars during Booms. *Amer. Econ. Rev.*, June 1986, *76*(3), pp. 390–407. **[G: U.S.]**

Rothschild, R. Raising Rivals' Costs: Regulation as a Competitive Strategy in Intra-industry Trade. **In** *Greenaway, D. and Tharakan, P. K. M., eds.*, 1986, pp. 34–46.

Rothschild, R. The Stability of Cartels in Spatial Markets. **In** *Norman, G., ed.*, 1986, pp. 43–51.

Rowley, J. William. Merger and Pre-merger Notification. **In** *Block, W., ed.*, 1986, pp. 21–40. **[G: Canada]**

Rugman, Alan M. European Multinationals: An International Comparison of Size and Performance. **In** *Macharzina, K. and Staehle, W. H., eds.*, 1986, pp. 15–22. **[G: OECD]**

Rugman, Alan M. New Theories of the Multinational Enterprise: An Assessment of Internationalization Theory. *Bull. Econ. Res.*, May 1986, *38*(2), pp. 101–18.

Russell, Allen M.; Rickard, John A. and Howroyd, T. D. The Effects of Delays on the Stability and Rate of Convergence to Equilibrium of Oligopolies. *Econ. Rec.*, June 1986, *62*(177), pp. 194–98.

Salop, Steven C. Measuring Ease of Entry. *Antitrust Bull.*, Summer 1986, *31*(2), pp. 551–70. **[G: U.S.]**

Salop, Steven C. Practices that (Credibly) Facilitate Oligopoly Co-ordination. **In** *Stiglitz, J. E. and Mathewson, G. F., eds.*, 1986, pp. 265–90.

Samuelson, William F. and Rosenthal, Leonard. Price Movements as Indicators of Tender Offer Success. *J. Finance*, June 1986, *41*(2), pp. 481–99. **[G: U.S.]**

Scheffman, David T. The Impact of Government Policy on the U.S. Cigarette Industry: Comments. **In** *Ippolito, P. M. and Scheffman, D. T., eds.*, 1986, pp. 483–84. **[G: U.S.]**

Scherer, F. M. Mergers, Sell-offs, and Managerial Behavior. **In** *[Dean, J.]*, 1986, pp. 143–70. **[G: U.S.]**

Scherer, F. M. On the Current State of Knowledge in Industrial Organization. **In** *de Jong, H. W. and Shepherd, W. G., eds., Bk. 1*, 1986, pp. 5–22.

Scherer, F. M. The Breakfast Cereal Industry. **In** *Adams, W., ed.*, 1986, pp. 172–202. **[G: U.S.]**

Schlesinger, Harris and Venezian, Emilio C. Insurance Markets with Loss-Prevention Activity: Profits, Market Structure, and Consumer Welfare. *Rand J. Econ.*, Summer 1986, *17*(2), pp. 227–38.

Schmalensee, Richard. Advertising and Market Structure. **In** *Stiglitz, J. E. and Mathewson, G. F., eds.*, 1986, pp. 373–96.

Schneider, Dieter. Ausweichhandlungen vor Regulierungen auf Finanzmärkten als Prüfstein wettbewerbspolitischer Konzepte. (Evasions of Regulations in Financial Markets as a Test of Concepts of Competition Policy. With English summary.) **In** *Eucken, W. and Böhm, F., eds.*, 1986, pp. 155–81.

Schoenberger, Erica. Competition, Competitive Strategy, and Industrial Change: The Case of Electronic Components. *Econ. Geogr.*, October 1986, *62*(4), pp. 321–33. **[G: Global]**

Schröter, Harm. A Typical Factor of German International Market Strategy: Agreements between the U.S. and German Electrotechnical Industries Up to 1939. **In** *Teichova, A.; Lévy-Leboyer, M. and Nussbaum, H., eds.*, 1986, pp. 160–70. **[G: U.S.; Germany]**

Schuster, Leo. Concentration and Competition in Banking. *J. Bank Res.*, Spring 1986, *17*(1), pp. 51–53. **[G: N. America; Japan; U.K.; W. Germany; France]**

Schwalbach, Joachim. Markteintrittsverhalten industrieller Unternehmen. (With English summary.) *Z. Betriebswirtschaft*, August 1986, *56*(8), pp. 713–27. **[G: W. Germany]**

Schwartz, Alan. Bebchuk on Minimum Offer Periods. *J. Law, Econ., Organ.*, Fall 1986, *2*(2), pp. 271–77.

Schwartz, Alan. Search Theory and the Tender Offer Auction. *J. Law, Econ., Organ.*, Fall 1986, *2*(2), pp. 229–53.

Schwartz, Marius. The Nature and Scope of Contestability Theory. *Oxford Econ. Pap.*, Suppl. Nov. 1986, *38*, pp. 37–57.

Schwartz, Marius. The Nature and Scope of Contestability Theory. **In** *Morris, D. J., et al., eds.*, 1986, pp. 37–57.

Schwartz, Marius and Thompson, Earl A. Divisionalization and Entry Deterrence. *Quart. J. Econ.*, May 1986, *101*(2), pp. 307–21.

Schwarz, Samuel. Self-destruction of a Government-Created Oligopoly: A Case Study of the New York City Bingo Market. *Amer. Econ.*, Fall 1986, *30*(2), pp. 33–36. **[G: U.S.]**

Schweitzer, Arthur. Detrimental Competition. *J. Econ. Issues*, September 1986, *20*(3), pp. 681–707.

Scott, Allen J. Industrial Organization and Location: Division of Labor, the Firm, and Spatial Process. *Econ. Geogr.*, July 1986, *62*(3), pp. 215–31.

Scott, John T. and Pascoe, George. Beyond Firm and Industry Effects on Profitability in Imperfect Markets. *Rev. Econ. Statist.*, May 1986, *68*(2), pp. 284–92. **[G: U.S.]**

Segura, Edilberto L. Fertilizer Pricing Principles.

In *Segura, E. L.; Shetty, Y. T. and Nishimizu, M., eds.*, 1986, pp. 22–47.

Selten, Reinhard. Elementary Theory of Slack-Ridden Imperfect Competition. **In** *Stiglitz, J. E. and Mathewson, G. F., eds.*, 1986, pp. 126–44.

Shaffer, Sherrill. A Reverse Structural Test for the Degree of Monopoly Power. *Atlantic Econ. J.*, March 1986, *14*(1), pp. 124.

Shaffer, Sherrill. Does Competition Imply Frequent Rank Turnover? *Scand. J. Econ.*, 1986, *88*(3), pp. 511–27.

Shapiro, Nina. Innovation, New Industries and New Firms. *Eastern Econ. J.*, Jan.-Mar. 1986, *12*(1), pp. 27–43.

Shaw, Richard W. and Simpson, Paul. The Persistence of Monopoly: An Investigation of the Effectiveness of the United Kingdom Monopolies Commission. *J. Ind. Econ.*, June 1986, *34*(4), pp. 355–72. **[G: U.K.]**

Shepherd, William G. Assessing "Predatory" Actions by Market Shares and Selectivity. *Antitrust Bull.*, Spring 1986, *31*(1), pp. 1–28. **[G: U.S.]**

Shepherd, William G. Illogic and Unreality: The Odd Case of Ultra-free Entry and Inert Markets. **In** *Grieson, R. E., ed.*, 1986, pp. 231–52. **[G: U.S.]**

Shepherd, William G. On the Core Concepts of Industrial Economics. **In** *de Jong, H. W. and Shepherd, W. G., eds., Bk. 1*, 1986, pp. 23–67. **[G: U.S.]**

Shepherd, William G. Tobin's *q* and the Structure–Performance Relationship: Comment. *Amer. Econ. Rev.*, December 1986, *76*(5), pp. 1205–10. **[G: U.S.]**

Shleifer, Andrei and Vishny, Robert W. Large Shareholders and Corporate Control. *J. Polit. Econ.*, Part 1, June 1986, *94*(3), pp. 461–88.

Shmanske, Stephen. News as a Public Good: Cooperative Ownership, Price Commitments, and the Success of the Associated Press. *Bus. Hist. Rev.*, Spring 1986, *60*(1), pp. 55–80. **[G: U.S.]**

Siebert, Horst. Steel Crisis: Consequences of the European Steel Policy after World War II: Closing Costs in Ailing Industries: Comment. *J. Inst. Theoretical Econ.*, March 1986, *142*(1), pp. 156–62. **[G: W. Europe]**

Simon, Denis Fred and Schive, Chi. National Policies for Developing High Technology Industries: International Comparisons: Taiwan. **In** *Rushing, F. W. and Brown, C. G., eds.*, 1986, pp. 201–26.

Simon, Julian L.; Primeaux, Walter J., Jr. and Rice, Edward. The Price Effects of Monopolistic Ownership in Newspapers. *Antitrust Bull.*, Spring 1986, *31*(1), pp. 113–31. **[G: U.S.]**

Simpson, Paul and Waterson, Michael. Cartel Problems: The Incentive to Lie about Costs. *Bull. Econ. Res.*, September 1986, *38*(3), pp. 209–19.

Simpson, Wayne. Unions, Industrial Concentration and Wages: A Re-examination. *Appl. Econ.*, March 1986, *18*(3), pp. 305–17. **[G: Canada]**

Sinha, Dipendra. The Theory of Contestable Markets and U.S. Airline Deregulation: A Survey. *Logist. Transp. Rev.*, December 1986, *22*(4), pp. 405–19. **[G: U.S.]**

Slade, Margaret E. Conjectures, Firm Characteristics, and Market Structure: An Empirical Assessment. *Int. J. Ind. Organ.*, December 1986, *4*(4), pp. 347–69. **[G: Canada]**

Slade, Margaret E. Exogeneity Tests of Market Boundaries Applied to Petroleum Products. *J. Ind. Econ.*, March 1986, *34*(3), pp. 291–303. **[G: U.S.]**

Slade, Margaret E. Measures of Market Power in Extractive Industries: The Legacy of *United States v. General Dynamics*. *Antitrust Bull.*, Spring 1986, *31*(1), pp. 91–111. **[G: U.S.]**

Slade, Margaret E. Static Profitability as a Measure of Deviations from the Competitive Norm. *Managerial Dec. Econ.*, June 1986, *7*(2), pp. 113–18.

Sleuwaegen, Leo E. On the Nature and Significance of Collusive Price Leadership. *Int. J. Ind. Organ.*, June 1986, *4*(2), pp. 177–88.

Sleuwaegen, Leo E. and Dehandschutter, Wim V. The Critical Choice between the Concentration Ratio and the *H*-Index in Assessing Industry Performance. *J. Ind. Econ.*, December 1986, *35*(2), pp. 193–208. **[G: U.S.]**

Smirlock, Michael and Brown, David. Collusion, Efficiency and Pricing Behavior: Evidence from the Banking Industry. *Econ. Inquiry*, January 1986, *24*(1), pp. 85–96. **[G: U.S.]**

Smirlock, Michael; Gilligan, Thomas and Marshall, William. Tobin's *q* and the Structure–Performance Relationship: Reply. *Amer. Econ. Rev.*, December 1986, *76*(5), pp. 1211–13. **[G: U.S.]**

Spence, Michael. Cost Reduction, Competition and Industry Performance. **In** *Stiglitz, J. E. and Mathewson, G. F., eds.*, 1986, pp. 475–515.

Spiller, Pablo T. Comments [The Effects of the Advertising Substantiation Program on Advertising Agencies] [An Economic Analysis of the FTC's Ad Substantiation Program]. **In** *Ippolito, P. M. and Scheffman, D. T., eds.*, 1986, pp. 217–20. **[G: U.S.]**

Spiller, Pablo T. and Huang, Cliff J. On the Extent of the Market: Wholesale Gasoline in the Northeastern United States. *J. Ind. Econ.*, December 1986, *35*(2), pp. 131–45. **[G: U.S.]**

Spinanger, Dean. Quasi-monopoly Profits, Barriers to Entry and the Welfare State: Their Impact on Labor Markets in Industrialized Countries. **In** *Day, R. H. and Eliasson, G., eds.*, 1986, pp. 411–34. **[G: OECD]**

Spinanger, Dean. Quasi-monopoly Profits, Barriers to Entry and the Welfare State: Their Impact on Labor Markets in Industrialized Countries: Reply. **In** *Day, R. H. and Eliasson, G., eds.*, 1986, pp. 447–48. **[G: OECD]**

Springer, Robert F. and Frech, H. E., III. Deterring Fraud: The Role of Resale Price Maintenance. *J. Bus.*, July 1986, *59*(3), pp. 433–49.

Spulber, Daniel F. Second-Best Pricing and Cooperation. *Rand J. Econ.*, Summer 1986, *17*(2), pp. 239–50.

Steindel, Charles. Tax Reform and the Merger and Acquisition Market: The Repeal of *General Utilities*. *Fed. Res. Bank New York Quart. Rev.*, Autumn 1986, *11*(3), pp. 31–35. **[G: U.S.]**

Stigler, George J. A Theory of Oligopoly. **In** *Stigler, G. J.*, 1986, *1964*, pp. 153–78.

Stigler, George J. Free Riders and Collective Action: An Appendix to Theories of Economic Regulation. **In** *Stigler, G. J.*, 1986, *1974*, pp. 67–75. **[G: U.S.]**

Stigler, George J. The Division of Labor Is Limited by the Extent of the Market. **In** *Stigler, G. J.*, 1986, *1951*, pp. 13–24.

Stigler, George J. The Dominant Firm and the Inverted Umbrella. **In** *Stigler, G. J.*, 1986, *1965*, pp. 179–83. **[G: U.S.]**

Stigler, George J. The Economies of Scale. **In** *Stigler, G. J.*, 1986, *1958*, pp. 25–45. **[G: U.S.]**

Stiglitz, Joseph E. New Developments in the Analysis of Market Structure: Introduction. **In** *Stiglitz, J. E. and Mathewson, G. F., eds.*, 1986, pp. vii–xxiv.

Stiglitz, Joseph E. Theory of Competition, Incentives and Risk. **In** *Stiglitz, J. E. and Mathewson, G. F., eds.*, 1986, pp. 399–446.

Stokey, Nancy L. The Dynamics of Industrywide Learning. **In** *[Arrow, K. J.], Vol. 2*, 1986, pp. 81–104.

Stollery, Kenneth R. Monopsony Processing in an Open-Access Fishery. *Marine Resource Econ.*, 1986, *3*(4), pp. 331–51. **[G: Global]**

Stopford, John M. International Competitiveness of European Industry. **In** *Macharzina, K. and Staehle, W. H., eds.*, 1986, pp. 5–14. **[G: W. Europe]**

Suominen, Seppo I. Dynamisk modell för vertikal integration. (A Dynamic Model of Vertical Integration. With English summary.) *Ekon. Samfundets Tidskr.*, 1986, *39*(4), pp. 239–46.

Suslow, Valerie Y. Estimating Monopoly Behavior with Competitive Recycling: An Application to Alcoa. *Rand J. Econ.*, Autumn 1986, *17*(3), pp. 389–403. **[G: U.S.]**

Sutton, John. Vertical Product Differentiation: Some Basic Themes. *Amer. Econ. Rev.*, May 1986, *76*(2), pp. 393–98.

Swidler, Steve. A Reexamination of Liquor Price and Consumption Differences between Public and Private Ownership States: Comment [Public versus Private Liquor Retailing: An Investigation into the Behavior of the State Governments]. *Southern Econ. J.*, July 1986, *53*(1), pp. 259–64. **[G: U.S.]**

Swidler, Steve. Consumption and Price Effects of State-run Liquor Monopolies. *Managerial Dec. Econ.*, March 1986, *7*(1), pp. 49–55. **[G: U.S.]**

Szalai, Erzsébet. The Structural Reasons for Antireform Attitudes (Comments on András Hegedüs's Article and the Subsequent Debate). *Eastern Europ. Econ.*, Fall 1986, *25*(1), pp. 106–12. **[G: Hungary]**

Tanigawa, Yasuhiko. On Mutual Share Holding by Corporations. *Econ. Stud. Quart.*, December 1986, *37*(4), pp. 319–35. **[G: Japan]**

Teece, David J. Assessing the Competition Faced by Oil Pipelines. *Contemp. Policy Issues*, October 1986, *4*(4), pp. 65–78. **[G: U.S.]**

Teece, David J. Firm Boundaries, Technological Innovation, and Strategic Management. **In** *[Dean, J.]*, 1986, pp. 187–99.

Teece, David J. Profiting from Technological Innovation: Implications for Integration, Collaboration, Licensing and Public Policy. *Ricerche Econ.*, Oct.-Dec. 1986, *40*(4), pp. 607–43. **[G: U.S.]**

Teece, David J. Transactions Cost Economics and the Multinational Enterprise: An Assessment. *J. Econ. Behav. Organ.*, March 1986, *7*(1), pp. 21–45. **[G: U.K.; U.S.]**

Thomas, Lacy Glenn. The Economics of Strategic Planning: A Survey of the Issues. **In** *[Dean, J.]*, 1986, pp. 1–27. **[G: U.S.]**

Thomas, R. E. Parent-to-Parent Divestment. **In** *Coyne, J. and Wright, M., eds.*, 1986, pp. 27–44. **[G: U.K.]**

Thompson, R. S. Entry and Market Characteristics: A Logit Study of Newspaper Launching in the Republic of Ireland. *J. Econ. Stud.*, 1986, *13*(2), pp. 14–22. **[G: Ireland]**

Tilton, John E. and Mueller, Dennis C. Research and Development Costs as a Barrier to Entry. **In** *Mueller, D. C.*, 1986, *1969*, pp. 108–18.

Tirole, Jean. Hierarchies and Bureaucracies: On the Role of Collusion in Organizations. *J. Law, Econ., Organ.*, Fall 1986, *2*(2), pp. 181–214.

Tirole, Jean. Procurement and Renegotiation. *J. Polit. Econ.*, April 1986, *94*(2), pp. 235–59.

Trapani, John M., III. Eminent Domain: A New Industrial Policy Tool: Comment. *J. Inst. Theoretical Econ.*, March 1986, *142*(1), pp. 39–43. **[G: U.S.]**

Tucker, Paul W. The Natural Gas Market: The Cyclical Process. **In** *Stevens, P., ed.*, 1986, pp. 5–13.

Tullock, Gordon. Industrial Organization and Rent Seeking in Dictatorships. *J. Inst. Theoretical Econ.*, March 1986, *142*(1), pp. 4–15.

Tye, William B. Stand-Alone Costs as an Indicator of Market Dominance and Rate Reasonableness under the Staggers Rail Act. *Int. J. Transport Econ.*, February 1986, *13*(1), pp. 21–40. **[G: U.S.]**

von Ungern-Sternberg, Thomas. Schumpeterian Competition in Alternative Technological Regimes: Comment. **In** *Day, R. H. and Eliasson, G., eds.*, 1986, pp. 239–41.

Uppal, J. S. Public Financial Institutions and Economic Concentration in India. *J. Devel. Econ.*, Jan.-Feb. 1986, *20*(1), pp. 135–44. **[G: India]**

Van Den Bulcke, Daniel. Role and Structure of Belgian Multinationals. **In** *Macharzina, K. and Staehle, W. H., eds.*, 1986, pp. 105–27. **[G: Belgium]**

Van Hulle, C. Corporate Restructuring. *Tijdschrift Econ. Manage.*, 1986, *31*(4), pp. 417–33. **[G: Belgium]**

Varaiya, Nikhil P. An Empirical Investigation of

the Bidding Firms' Gains from Corporate Takeovers. **In** *Chen, A. H., ed.*, 1986, pp. 149–78. **[G: U.S.]**

Várhegyi, Éva. Sources of the Growth of Enterprises in Hungary (An Empirical Investigation of Investment and Enterprise Growth). *Acta Oecon.*, 1986, *37*(3–4), pp. 267–84. **[G: Hungary]**

Vickers, John S. The Evolution of Market Structure When There Is a Sequence of Innovations. *J. Ind. Econ.*, September 1986, *35*(1), pp. 1–12.

Von Hohenbalken, Balder and West, Douglas S. Empirical Tests for Predatory Reputation. *Can. J. Econ.*, February 1986, *19*(1), pp. 160–78. **[G: Canada]**

Voos, Paula B. and Mishel, Lawrence R. The Union Impact on Profits in the Supermarket Industry. *Rev. Econ. Statist.*, August 1986, *68*(3), pp. 513–17. **[G: U.S.]**

Voszka, Éva. Company Liquidation without a Legal Successor. *Acta Oecon.*, 1986, *37*(1–2), pp. 59–71. **[G: Hungary]**

Vyas, Niren M. and Woodside, Arch G. Micro Analysis of Supplier Choice Strategies: Industrial Packaging Materials. **In** *Backhaus, K. and Wilson, D. T., eds.*, 1986, pp. 41–68.

Wada, Mitsuo. Selling in Japan: Consumer Behavior and Distribution as Barriers to Imports. **In** *Pugel, T. A., ed.*, 1986, pp. 91–105. **[G: U.S.; Japan; W. Germany]**

Wadhwani, Sushil B. Inflation, Bankruptcy, Default Premia and the Stock Market. *Econ. J.*, March 1986, *96*(381), pp. 120–38. **[G: U.K.]**

Wagner, Joachim. Zur Technologieintensität der Produktion in der Bundesrepublik Deutschland. (On the Technological Intensity of Production in the Federal Republic of Germany. With English summary.) *Ifo-Studien*, 1986, *32*(4), pp. 297–307. **[G: W. Germany]**

Warr, Peter G. and Jayasuriya, S. K. Welfare Effects of Mechanization: Monopoly and Indivisibility. *Pakistan Devel. Rev.*, Spring 1986, *25*(1), pp. 85–90.

Waterson, Michael. The Economics of Vertical Restraints on Retailers. **In** *Norman, G., ed.*, 1986, pp. 125–43.

Watt, J. Michael, et al. The Effects of Ownership and Multihospital System Membership on Hospital Functional Strategies and Economic Performance. **In** *Gray, B. H., ed.*, 1986, pp. 260–89. **[G: U.S.]**

Webb, L. Roy and de Jong, Piet. Competitive Bidding and the Price Mechanism. **In** *[Yamey, B.]*, 1986, pp. 109–29.

Weber, Lawrence R. Cross-Subsidization in a Competitive Environment. **In** *[Dorsey, J. N. and Wiggins, B. T.]*, 1986, pp. 67–71. **[G: U.S.]**

Weiss, Nitzan and Lee, Phil. Sustainability of the Multiproduct Monopoly and Ramsey-Optimal Pricing. *J. Inst. Theoretical Econ.*, September 1986, *142*(3), pp. 473–92.

von Weizsäcker, Carl Christian. Free Entry into Telecommunications. **In** *Snow, M. S.*, 1986, pp. 20–41.

Wernerfelt, Birger. Product Line Rivalry: Note. *Amer. Econ. Rev.*, September 1986, *76*(4), pp. 842–44.

Westfield, Fred M. Vertical Industry Structure: An Analytical Scheme. **In** *Grieson, R. E., ed.*, 1986, pp. 253–66.

Wheelwright, Ted. The World Food Industry. **In** *Wheelwright, T., ed.*, 1986, pp. 143–82. **[G: Global]**

Whitehall, Peter. Profit Variation in the Barbados Manufacturing Sector. *Soc. Econ. Stud.*, December 1986, *35*(4), pp. 67–91. **[G: Barbados]**

Wiggins, Steven N. Innovation, Market Structure and Market Dynamics: Comment. *J. Inst. Theoretical Econ.*, March 1986, *142*(1), pp. 200–203. **[G: W. Germany]**

Williamson, Oliver E. Hierarchical Control and Optimum Firm Size. **In** *Williamson, O. E.*, 1986, *1967*, pp. 32–53.

Williamson, Oliver E. Managerial Discretion and Business Behaviour. **In** *Williamson, O. E.*, 1986, *1963*, pp. 6–31.

Williamson, Oliver E. The Economics of Antitrust: Transaction Cost Considerations. **In** *Williamson, O. E.*, 1986, pp. 197–249.

Williamson, Oliver E. The Economics of Governance: Framework and Implications. **In** *Langlois, R. N., ed.*, 1986, pp. 171–202.

Williamson, Oliver E. The Incentive Limits of Firms: A Comparative Institutional Assessment of Bureaucracy. **In** *Balassa, B. and Giersch, H., eds.*, 1986, pp. 204–30.

Williamson, Oliver E. The Modern Corporation: Origins, Evolution, Attributes. **In** *Williamson, O. E.*, 1986, *1981*, pp. 131–73.

Williamson, Oliver E. The Multidivisional Structure. **In** *Barney, J. B. and Ouchi, W. G., eds.*, 1986, *1975*, pp. 163–87.

Williamson, Oliver E. The Vertical Integration of Production: Market Failure Considerations. **In** *Williamson, O. E.*, 1986, *1971*, pp. 85–100.

Williamson, Oliver E. Transaction-Cost Economics: The Governance of Contractual Relations. **In** *Barney, J. B. and Ouchi, W. G., eds.*, 1986, *1979*, pp. 98–129.

Williamson, Oliver E. Transforming Merger Policy: The Pound of New Perspectives. *Amer. Econ. Rev.*, May 1986, *76*(2), pp. 114–19. **[G: U.S.]**

Williamson, Oliver E. Vertical Integration and Related Variations on a Transaction-Cost Economics Theme. **In** *Stiglitz, J. E. and Mathewson, G. F., eds.*, 1986, pp. 149–74.

Williamson, Oliver E. and Bhargava, Narottam. Assessing and Classifying the Internal Structure and Control Apparatus of the Modern Corporation. **In** *Williamson, O. E.*, 1986, *1972*, pp. 54–80.

Williamson, Peter J. Multinational Enterprise Behaviour and Domestic Industry Adjustment under Import Threat. *Rev. Econ. Statist.*, August 1986, *68*(3), pp. 359–68. **[G: Australia]**

Willmore, Larry N. The Comparative Performance of Foreign and Domestic Firms in Brazil. *World Devel.*, April 1986, *14*(4), pp. 489–502. **[G: Brazil]**

Wilson, David T. Industrial Marketing—State of the Art in the USA. **In** *Backhaus, K. and Wilson, D. T., eds.*, 1986, pp. 15–21. **[G: U.S.]**

Wilson, David T. New Product Success in Business/Industrial Markets: A Buyer–Seller Perspective. **In** *Backhaus, K. and Wilson, D. T., eds.*, 1986, pp. 349–67.

Winter, Sidney G. Schumpeterian Competition in Alternative Technological Regimes: Reply. **In** *Day, R. H. and Eliasson, G., eds.*, 1986, pp. 242–45.

Winter, Sidney G. Schumpeterian Competition in Alternative Technological Regimes. **In** *Day, R. H. and Eliasson, G., eds.*, 1986, *1984*, pp. 199–232.

Winter, Sidney G. The Research Program of the Behavioral Theory of the Firm: Orthodox Critique and Evolutionary Perspective. **In** *Gilad, B. and Kaish, S., eds., Vol. A*, 1986, pp. 151–88.

Wintrobe, Ronald and Breton, Albert. Organizational Structure and Productivity. *Amer. Econ. Rev.*, June 1986, *76*(3), pp. 530–38.

Wolinsky, Asher. The Nature of Competition and the Scope of Firms. *J. Ind. Econ.*, March 1986, *34*(3), pp. 247–59.

Woolf, Arthur G. Market Structure and Minority Presence: Black-Owned Firms in Manufacturing. *Rev. Black Polit. Econ.*, Spring 1986, *14*(4), pp. 79–89. **[G: U.S.]**

Wright, Mike. Demergers: The Case of Bowater. **In** *Coyne, J. and Wright, M., eds.*, 1986, pp. 45–72. **[G: U.K.]**

Wright, Mike and Thompson, Steve. Vertical Disintegration and the Life-cycle of Firms and Industries. *Managerial Dec. Econ.*, June 1986, *7*(2), pp. 141–44. **[G: U.K.]**

Yamawaki, Hideki. Exports, Foreign Market Structure, and Profitability in Japanese and U.S. Manufacturing. *Rev. Econ. Statist.*, November 1986, *68*(4), pp. 618–27. **[G: Japan; U.S.]**

Yates, JoAnne. The Telegraph's Effect on Nineteenth Century Markets and Firms. **In** *Atack, J., ed.*, 1986, pp. 149–63. **[G: U.S.]**

You, Victor, et al. Mergers and Bidders' Wealth: Managerial and Strategic Factors. **In** *[Dean, J.]*, 1986, pp. 201–20. **[G: U.S.]**

Young, Dennis R. Entrepreneurship and the Behavior of Nonprofit Organizations: Elements of a Theory. **In** *Rose-Ackerman, S., ed.*, 1986, *1981*, pp. 161–84.

Zardkoohi, Asghar. Competition in the Production of Electricity. **In** *Moorhouse, J. C., ed.*, 1986, pp. 63–95. **[G: U.S.]**

Zardkoohi, Asghar and Sheer, Alain. A Reexamination of Liquor Price and Consumption Differences between Public and Private Ownership States: Reply [Public versus Private Liquor Retailing: An Investigation into the Behavior of the State Governments]. *Southern Econ. J.*, July 1986, *53*(1), pp. 265–68. **[G: U.S.]**

612 Public Policy Toward Monopoly and Competition

6120 Public Policy Toward Monopoly and Competition

Adams, Walter. Public Policy in a Free Enterprise Economy. **In** *Adams, W., ed.*, 1986, pp. 395–427. **[G: U.S.]**

Adams, Walter and Brock, James W. Corporate Power and Economic Sabotage. *J. Econ. Issues*, December 1986, *20*(4), pp. 919–40. **[G: U.S.]**

Ahiakpor, James C. W. Regulation and the Consumer Interest. **In** *Block, W., ed.*, 1986, pp. 141–54. **[G: Canada]**

Anderson, Richard K. and Enomoto, Carl E. Product Quality and Price Regulation: A General Equilibrium Analysis. *Economica*, February 1986, *53*(209), pp. 87–95.

Armstrong, Donald E. The Sugar Case as a Reason for "Strengthening" the Combines Act: An Economic Perspective. **In** *Block, W., ed.*, 1986, pp. 71–93. **[G: Canada]**

Aura, Matti. Är konkurrenslagstiftning effektiv? (Is Antitrust Legislation Efficient? With English summary.) *Ekon. Samfundets Tidskr.*, 1986, *39*(1), pp. 17–19. **[G: Finland]**

Baker, Donald I. and Blumenthal, William. Ideological Cycles and Unstable Antitrust Rules. *Antitrust Bull.*, Summer 1986, *31*(2), pp. 327–39. **[G: U.S.]**

Balmer, Thomas A. One Step Forward, Two Steps Back: Economic Analysis and Political Considerations in Antitrust Law Revision. *Antitrust Bull.*, Winter 1986, *31*(4), pp. 981–1001. **[G: U.S.]**

Baughcum, Alan. Deregulation, Divestiture, and Competition in U.S. Telecommunications: Lessons for Other Countries. **In** *Snow, M. S.*, 1986, pp. 69–105. **[G: U.S.]**

Baumol, William J. Quasi-permanence of Price Reductions: A Policy for Prevention of Predatory Pricing. **In** *Baumol, W. J.*, 1986, pp. 165–90. **[G: U.S.]**

Beck, Roger L. Comment: Does Competitive Dissipation Require a Short Patent Life? [The Scope and Duration of the Patent Right and the Nature of Research Rivalry]. **In** *Palmer, J., ed.*, 1986, pp. 121–29.

Beckenstein, Alan R. and Gabel, H. Landis. Predation Rules: An Economic and Behavioral Analysis. *Antitrust Bull.*, Spring 1986, *31*(1), pp. 29–49. **[G: U.S.]**

Beckenstein, Alan R. and Gabel, H. Landis. The Economics of Antitrust Compliance. *Southern Econ. J.*, January 1986, *52*(3), pp. 673–92. **[G: U.S.]**

Benson, Bruce L. and Greenhut, Melvin L. Special Interests, Bureaucrats, and Antitrust: An Explanation of the Antitrust Paradox. **In** *Grieson, R. E., ed.*, 1986, pp. 53–90. **[G: U.S.]**

Berg, Hartmut. Thesen des Bundeskartellamtes zur "Nachfragemacht" im Lebensmittelhandel: Eine kritische Analyse. (Theses of the Federal Cartel Office Concerning "Buying Power" Positions in German Food Retailing: A Critical Assessment. With English summary.) **In** *Eucken, W. and Böhm, F., eds.*, 1986, pp. 183–200. **[G: W. Germany]**

Berg, Sanford V. and Romano, Richard E. Predatory Intent under Uncertainty. *Rev. Ind. Organ.*, 1986, *3*(1), pp. 1–9.

Besen, Stanley M. Private Copying, Reproduction Costs, and the Supply of Intellectual Property. *Info. Econ. Policy,* 1986, *2*(1), pp. 5–22.

Bisang, Roberto, et al. Insulina y economía política: el difícil arte de la política pública. (With English summary.) *Desarrollo Econ.*, Oct.-Dec. 1986, *26*(103), pp. 369–88. **[G: Argentina]**

Block, Michael K. and Feinstein, Jonathan S. The Spillover Effect of Antitrust Enforcement. *Rev. Econ. Statist.*, February 1986, *68*(1), pp. 122–31. **[G: U.S.]**

Block, Walter. Reaction: The New Combines Investigation Act: Introduction. **In** *Block, W., ed.*, 1986, pp. xiii–xxix. **[G: Canada]**

Bower, Lindsay. Complementary Inputs and Market Power. *Antitrust Bull.*, Spring 1986, *31*(1), pp. 51–90. **[G: U.S.]**

Brenner, Gabrielle A. and Brenner, Reuven. Innovations and the Competition Act. **In** *Block, W., ed.*, 1986, pp. 117–38. **[G: Canada]**

Brittan, Samuel. Privatisation: A Policy in Search of a Rationale: A Comment. *Econ. J.*, March 1986, *96*(381), pp. 33–38. **[G: U.K.]**

Brock, Gerald W. The Regulatory Change in Telecommunications: The Dissolution of AT&T. **In** *Weiss, L. W. and Klass, M. W., eds.*, 1986, pp. 210–33. **[G: U.S.]**

Bronsteen, Peter. Market Share and Market Power in the Domestic Lemon Industry. **In** *Zerbe, R. O., Jr., ed.*, 1986, pp. 13–28. **[G: U.S.]**

Bumpass, Donald L. and Nichol, Patricia J. The 1984 Justice Department Guidelines toward Horizontal Mergers. *Rev. Ind. Organ.*, 1986, *3*(1), pp. 65–77. **[G: U.S.]**

Bunting, David and Young, Shik C. Recovery of Robinson–Patman Damages: Confusion and Resolution. *Antitrust Bull.*, Fall 1986, *31*(3), pp. 797–825. **[G: U.S.]**

Cairns, J.; Jennett, N. and Sloane, Peter J. The Economics of Professional Team Sports: A Survey of Theory and Evidence. *J. Econ. Stud.*, 1986, *13*(1), pp. 1–80.

Calvani, Terry and Tritell, Randolph W. Invocation of United States Import Relief Laws as an Antitrust Violation. *Antitrust Bull.*, Summer 1986, *31*(2), pp. 527–50. **[G: U.S.]**

Caves, Richard E. Vertical Restraints in Manufacturer–Distributor Relations: Incidence and Economic Effects. **In** *Grieson, R. E., ed.*, 1986, pp. 29–51. **[G: U.S.]**

Chard, John S. Economic Effects of Exclusive Purchasing Arrangements in the Distribution of Goods. **In** *Pellegrini, L. and Reddy, S. K., eds.*, 1986, pp. 39–57.

Cheung, Steven N. S. Property Rights and Invention. **In** *Palmer, J., ed.*, 1986, pp. 5–18. **[G: U.S.]**

Clark, Nolan Ezra. The Future of Antitrust Enforcement. *Antitrust Bull.*, Summer 1986, *31*(2), pp. 401–08. **[G: U.S.]**

Coate, Malcolm B. An Analysis of Three Approaches to Market Definition. **In** *Zerbe, R. O., Jr., ed.*, 1986, pp. 29–43.

Cochran, Neilsen. Divestiture: A Public Service Commissioner's Perspective. **In** *[Dorsey, J. N. and Wiggins, B. T.]*, 1986, pp. 13–15. **[G: U.S.]**

Comanor, William S. and Kirkwood, John B. Resale Price Maintenance and Antitrust Policy. **In** *Pellegrini, L. and Reddy, S. K., eds.*, 1986, *1985*, pp. 31–38.

Cramer, Curtis A. The Structural Implications of a Minimum Bill Provision in the Transportation of Natural Gas in the United States. *Int. J. Transport Econ.*, February 1986, *13*(1), pp. 77–86. **[G: U.S.]**

Cronin, F. J. and Wusterbarth, A. R. Economic Harm Ignored: Betamax Revisited. *Contemp. Policy Issues*, April 1986, *4*(2), pp. 54–68. **[G: U.S.]**

Crum, Michael R. and Allen, Benjamin J. U.S. Transportation Merger Policy: Evolution, Current Status, and Antitrust Considerations. *Int. J. Transport Econ.*, February 1986, *13*(1), pp. 41–75. **[G: U.S.]**

Dansby, Robert E. Comment: Liability and Compensation in the Sale of Quasi-public Goods [Audio Home Recording: Canadian Copyright Implications]. **In** *Palmer, J., ed.*, 1986, pp. 175–79. **[G: Canada]**

Delaunay, Jean-Claude. Questions posées à la théorie dite de la "régulation monopoliste." (Some Questions on the So-Called "Monopoly Regulation" Theory. With English summary.) *Écon. Soc.*, May 1986, *20*(5), pp. 209–31.

Demsetz, Harold. Industry Structure, Market Rivalry, and Public Policy. **In** *Barney, J. B. and Ouchi, W. G., eds.*, 1986, *1973*, pp. 414–22. **[G: U.S.]**

Dewey, Donald. Antitrust and Its Alternatives: A Compleat Guide to the Welfare Tradeoffs. **In** *Grieson, R. E., ed.*, 1986, pp. 1–27.

Douglas, George W. and Mullenix, James W. Cities and States as Agents in Restraint of Trade. *Antitrust Bull.*, Summer 1986, *31*(2), pp. 505–25. **[G: U.S.]**

Dulude, Louise Séguin. Patents, Licensing, and Antitrust: Comments. **In** *Palmer, J., ed.*, 1986, pp. 87–89. **[G: U.S.]**

Easterbrook, Frank H. Workable Antitrust Policy. *Mich. Law Rev.*, August 1986, *84*(8), pp. 1696–1713. **[G: U.S.]**

Enholm, Gregory B. and Malko, J. Robert. Cost-of-Equity Decisions by State Regulators of Ameritech's Subsidiaries. **In** *[Dorsey, J. N. and Wiggins, B. T.]*, 1986, pp. 17–27. **[G: U.S.]**

Erkkila, John. Copyright Law, Photocopying, and

Price Discrimination: Comment. In *Palmer, J., ed.*, 1986, pp. 201–03.

Feinberg, Robert M. The Effects of European Competition Policy on Pricing and Profit Margins. *Kyklos*, 1986, *39*(2), pp. 267–87. [G: EEC; W. Germany]

Feinberg, Robert M. Trademarks, Market Power, and Information. *Rev. Ind. Organ.*, 1986, *2*(4), pp. 376–85.

First, Harry. Japan's Antitrust Policy: Impact on Import Competition. In *Pugel, T. A., ed.*, 1986, pp. 63–76. [G: U.S.; Japan]

Flavell, C. J. Michael. The Monopoly Provision: Abuse of Dominant Position. In *Block, W., ed.*, 1986, pp. 43–58. [G: Canada]

Fox, Eleanor M. Antitrust in Its Second Century: The Phoenix Rises from Its Ashes. *Antitrust Bull.*, Summer 1986, *31*(2), pp. 383–99. [G: U.S.]

Fox, Eleanor M. Consumer Beware Chicago. *Mich. Law Rev.*, August 1986, *84*(8), pp. 1714–20. [G: U.S.]

Fox, Eleanor M. Lessons of Economics for Antitrust; Problems of Antitrust for Economists. In *de Jong, H. W. and Shepherd, W. G., eds., Bk. 2*, 1986, pp. 309–13. [G: U.S.]

Franks, Julian R. and Harris, Robert S. The Role of the Mergers and Monopolies Commission in Merger Policy: Costs and Alternatives. *Oxford Rev. Econ. Policy*, Winter 1986, *2*(4), pp. 58–78. [G: U.K.]

Frasco, Gregg. Vertical Integration and Contractual Alternatives with a Perfectly Competitive Output Market: A Generalization. *Southern Econ. J.*, October 1986, *53*(2), pp. 509–14.

Gellhorn, Ernest. Climbing the Antitrust Staircase. *Antitrust Bull.*, Summer 1986, *31*(2), pp. 341–57. [G: U.S.]

Ginsburg, Douglas H. The Reagan Administration's Legislative Initiative in Antitrust. *Antitrust Bull.*, Winter 1986, *31*(4), pp. 851–69. [G: U.S.]

Gist, Peter and Meadowcroft, Shirley A. Regulating for Competition: The Newly Liberalised Market for Private Branch Exchanges. *Fisc. Stud.*, August 1986, *7*(3), pp. 41–66. [G: U.K.]

Globerman, Steven. The Merger Provisions of Bill C-91: An Evaluation. In *Block, W., ed.*, 1986, pp. 103–14. [G: Canada]

Goldberg, Robert C.; Hakkio, Craig S. and Moses, Leon N. Competition and Collusion, Side by Side: The Corrugated Container Antitrust Litigation. In *Grieson, R. E., ed.*, 1986, pp. 105–25. [G: U.S.]

Gorecki, Paul K. Monopoly, Entry and Predatory Pricing: The Hoffman–La Roche Case. In *[Yamey, B.]*, 1986, pp. 159–77. [G: Canada]

Grabowski, Henry G. and Vernon, John. Longer Patents for Lower Imitation Barriers: The 1984 Drug Act. *Amer. Econ. Rev.*, May 1986, *76*(2), pp. 195–98. [G: U.S.]

Gramlich, Fred. Scrip Damages in Antitrust Case. *Antitrust Bull.*, Spring 1986, *31*(1), pp. 261–85. [G: U.S.]

de Grandpré, L. Philippe. Legal Powers. In *Block, W., ed.*, 1986, pp. 61–69. [G: Canada]

Granstrand, Ove. Innovator Protection and the Rate of Technical Progress: Comment. In *Day, R. H. and Eliasson, G., eds.*, 1986, pp. 293–94.

Gribbin, J. Denys and Utton, Michael. The Treatment of Dominant Firms in the UK Competition Legislation. In *de Jong, H. W. and Shepherd, W. G., eds., Bk. 2*, 1986, pp. 243–72. [G: U.K.]

Grieson, Ronald E. and Singh, Nirvikar. Resale Price Maintenance: A Simple Analysis. In *Grieson, R. E., ed.*, 1986, pp. 127–33.

Grossack, Irvin M. OPEC and the Antitrust Laws. *J. Econ. Issues*, September 1986, *20*(3), pp. 725–41.

Grossman, Gene M. and Shapiro, Carl. Research Joint Ventures: An Antitrust Analysis. *J. Law, Econ., Organ.*, Fall 1986, *2*(2), pp. 315–37. [G: U.S.]

Hall, Bronwyn H.; Griliches, Zvi and Hausman, Jerry A. Patents and R and D: Is There a Lag? *Int. Econ. Rev.*, June 1986, *27*(2), pp. 265–83. [G: U.S.]

Hall, Christopher D. Patents, Licensing, and Antitrust. In *Palmer, J., ed.*, 1986, pp. 59–86. [G: U.S.]

Harris, Robert G. and Sullivan, Lawrence A. Horizontal Merger Policy: Promoting Competition and American Competitiveness. *Antitrust Bull.*, Winter 1986, *31*(4), pp. 871–933. [G: U.S.]

Hay, Fenton. Canada's Role in International Negotiations Concerning Intellectual Property Laws. In *Palmer, J., ed.*, 1986, pp. 239–63. [G: Canada]

Hayes, Beth and Siegel, Daniel. Rate of Return Regulation with Price Flexibility. *J. Bus.*, Part 1, October 1986, *59*(4), pp. 537–53.

Hazlett, Thomas W. Competition vs. Franchise Monopoly in Cable Television. *Contemp. Policy Issues*, April 1986, *4*(2), pp. 80–97. [G: U.S.]

Hazlett, Thomas W. Regulation and the Communications Revolution: Introduction. *Contemp. Policy Issues*, April 1986, *4*(2), pp. 52–53. [G: U.S.]

Hill, C. W. L. and Pickering, J. F. Conglomerate Mergers, Internal Organization and Competition Policy. *Int. Rev. Law Econ.*, June 1986, *6*(1), pp. 59–75. [G: U.K.]

Hobbs, Caswell O. Antitrust in the Next Decade—A Role for the Federal Trade Commission? *Antitrust Bull.*, Summer 1986, *31*(2), pp. 451–80. [G: U.S.]

Hollander, Abraham. Collective Administration of Copyright: An Economic Analysis: Comments. In *Palmer, J., ed.*, 1986, pp. 153–55.

Hollander, Stanley C. and Sheffet, Mary Jane. The Robinson–Patman Act: Boon or Bane for Retailers? *Antitrust Bull.*, Fall 1986, *31*(3), pp. 759–95. [G: U.S.]

Hovenkamp, Herbert. Rhetoric and Skepticism in Antitrust Argument. *Mich. Law Rev.*, August 1986, *84*(8), pp. 1721–29. [G: U.S.]

Hutter, Michael. Transaction Cost and Communication: A Theory of Institutional Change, Applied to the Case of Patent Law. **In** *von der Schulenburg, J.-M. G. and Skogh, G., eds.*, 1986, pp. 113–29.

Irving, Colin. The "Errors" in Atlantic Sugar et al. V.R. **In** *Block, W., ed.*, 1986, pp. 95–100. **[G: Canada]**

Irwin, Manley R. The Telecommunications Industry. **In** *Adams, W., ed.*, 1986, pp. 261–89. **[G: U.S.]**

Iyori, Hiroshi. Antitrust and Industrial Policy in Japan: Competition and Cooperation. **In** *Saxonhouse, G. R. and Yamamura, K., eds.*, 1986, pp. 56–82. **[G: Japan]**

Jorde, Thomas M. Restoring Predictability to Merger Guideline Analysis. *Contemp. Policy Issues*, July 1986, *4*(3), pp. 1–21. **[G: U.S.]**

Joyce, Jon M. and McGuckin, Robert H. Assignment of Rights to Sue under *Illinois Brick:* An Empirical Assessment. *Antitrust Bull.*, Spring 1986, *31*(1), pp. 235–59. **[G: U.S.]**

Kamien, Morton I. and Tauman, Yair. Fees versus Royalties and the Private Value of a Patent. *Quart. J. Econ.*, August 1986, *101*(3), pp. 471–91.

Kareken, John H. Federal Bank Regulatory Policy: A Description and Some Observations. *J. Bus.*, January 1986, *59*(1), pp. 3–48. **[G: U.S.]**

Katz, Michael L. and Shapiro, Carl. How to License Intangible Property. *Quart. J. Econ.*, August 1986, *101*(3), pp. 567–89.

Katzenbach, Erhard. The Treatment of Dominance in German Antitrust Policy. **In** *de Jong, H. W. and Shepherd, W. G., eds., Bk. 2*, 1986, pp. 273–85. **[G: W. Germany]**

Kaufer, Erich. The Incentives to Innovate under Alternative Property Rights Assignments with Special Reference to the Patent System. *J. Inst. Theoretical Econ.*, March 1986, *142*(1), pp. 210–26.

Kay, John A. and Thompson, David J. Privatisation: A Policy in Search of a Rationale. *Econ. J.*, March 1986, *96*(381), pp. 18–32. **[G: U.K.]**

Keon, Jim. Audio Home Recording: Canadian Copyright Implications. **In** *Palmer, J., ed.*, 1986, pp. 157–73. **[G: Canada]**

Keyes, Lucile. The Vertical Restraints Guidelines of the Department of Justice. *Rev. Ind. Organ.*, 1986, *2*(4), pp. 356–66. **[G: U.S.]**

Kintner, Earl W. and Bauer, Joseph P. The Robinson–Patman Act: A Look Backwards, a View Forward. *Antitrust Bull.*, Fall 1986, *31*(3), pp. 571–609. **[G: U.S.]**

Kitch, Edmund W. Patents: Monopolies or Property Rights? **In** *Palmer, J., ed.*, 1986, pp. 31–49.

Klein, Christopher C. Strategic Sham Litigation: Economic Incentives in the Context of the Case Law. *Int. Rev. Law Econ.*, December 1986, *6*(2), pp. 241–53. **[G: U.S.]**

Krattenmaker, Thomas G. and Salop, Steven C. Anticompetitive Exclusion: Raising Rivals' Costs to Achieve Power over Price. *Yale Law J.*, December 1986, *96*(2), pp. 209–93. **[G: U.S.]**

Kudrle, Robert T. Antitrust and the Performance of the U.S. Economy. **In** *Redburn, F. S.; Buss, T. F. and Ledebur, L. C., eds.*, 1986, pp. 64–82. **[G: U.S.]**

Kwoka, John E., Jr. and Warren-Boulton, Frederick R. Efficiencies, Failing Firms, and Alternatives to Merger: A Policy Synthesis. *Antitrust Bull.*, Summer 1986, *31*(2), pp. 431–50. **[G: U.S.]**

Langenfeld, James. The Impact of Antitrust Guidelines on Business. *Contemp. Policy Issues*, July 1986, *4*(3), pp. 22–29. **[G: U.S.]**

Langenfeld, James and Scheffman, David T. Evolution or Revolution—What Is the Future of Antitrust? *Antitrust Bull.*, Summer 1986, *31*(2), pp. 287–300. **[G: U.S.]**

Lecraw, Donald J. Industry Structure and Competition Policy. **In** *Block, W., ed.*, 1986, pp. 171–85. **[G: Canada]**

Levin, Richard C. A New Look at the Patent System. *Amer. Econ. Rev.*, May 1986, *76*(2), pp. 199–202. **[G: U.S.]**

Liebowitz, S. J. Copyright Law, Photocopying, and Price Discrimination. **In** *Palmer, J., ed.*, 1986, pp. 181–200.

Liebowitz, S. J. International Policies and Intellectual Property: Comments. **In** *Palmer, J., ed.*, 1986, pp. 285–87.

Linda, Remo. Competition Policies and Measures of Dominant Power. **In** *de Jong, H. W. and Shepherd, W. G., eds., Bk. 2*, 1986, pp. 287–307. **[G: U.S.]**

Lipsky, Abbott B., Jr. Antitrust without Apology. *Antitrust Bull.*, Summer 1986, *31*(2), pp. 481–504. **[G: U.S.]**

Littlechild, S. C. The Incentives to Innovate under Alternative Property Rights Assignments with Special Reference to the Patent System: Comment. *J. Inst. Theoretical Econ.*, March 1986, *142*(1), pp. 227–29.

Lunn, John. An Empirical Analysis of Process and Product Patenting: A Simultaneous Equation Framework. *J. Ind. Econ.*, March 1986, *34*(3), pp. 319–30. **[G: U.S.]**

Macdonald, William A. Overview of Competition Law Changes, 1986-Style. **In** *Block, W., ed.*, 1986, pp. 3–19. **[G: Canada; U.S.]**

Marfels, Christian. Economic Criteria for the Application of Antitrust—Overview and Assessment of the Fifth Report of the Monopolies Commission of the Federal Republic of Germany. *Antitrust Bull.*, Winter 1986, *31*(4), pp. 1067–87. **[G: W. Germany]**

Margolis, Stephen E. Copyright and Computer Software: Comments. **In** *Palmer, J., ed.*, 1986, pp. 227–31. **[G: U.S.; Canada]**

Marvel, Howard P. and McCafferty, Stephen. The Political Economy of Resale Price Maintenance. *J. Polit. Econ.*, October 1986, *94*(5), pp. 1074–95. **[G: U.S.]**

Mathewson, G. Frank and Winter, Ralph A. The Economics of Vertical Restraints in Distribution. **In** *Stiglitz, J. E. and Mathewson, G. F., eds.*, 1986, pp. 211–36.

Mayer, Thomas. Regulating Banks: Comment. *J. Bus.*, January 1986, *59*(1), pp. 87–96. **[G: U.S.]**

McChesney, Fred S. Law's Honour Lost: The Plight of Antitrust. *Antitrust Bull.*, Summer 1986, *31*(2), pp. 359–82. **[G: U.S.]**

McFetridge, D. G. and Rafiquzzaman, M. The Scope and Duration of the Patent Right and the Nature of Research Rivalry. **In** *Palmer, J., ed.*, 1986, pp. 91–120.

McKee, Michael J. You Can't Always Get What You Want: Lessons from the Paris Convention Revision Exercise. **In** *Palmer, J., ed.*, 1986, pp. 265–72.

Meyer, David L. A Standard for Tailoring Noerr–Pennington Immunity More Closely to the First Amendment Mandate. *Yale Law J.*, March 1986, *95*(4), pp. 832–56. **[G: U.S.]**

Millstein, Ira M.; Birrell, George A. and Kessler, Jeffrey L. S. 1300-H.R. 4831—An Overdue Antitrust Reform. *Antitrust Bull.*, Winter 1986, *31*(4), pp. 955–80. **[G: U.S.]**

Mueller, Dennis C. United States' Antitrust: At the Crossroads. **In** *de Jong, H. W. and Shepherd, W. G., eds., Bk. 2*, 1986, pp. 215–41. **[G: U.S.]**

Noll, Roger G. State Regulatory Responses to Competition and Divestiture in the Telecommunications Industry. **In** *Grieson, R. E., ed.*, 1986, pp. 165–200. **[G: U.S.]**

Nussbaum, Helga. International Cartels and Multinational Enterprises. **In** *Teichova, A.; Lévy-Leboyer, M. and Nussbaum, H., eds.*, 1986, pp. 131–44. **[G: Global]**

O'Brien, D. P. Divestiture: The Case of AT&T. **In** *Coyne, J. and Wright, M., eds.*, 1986, pp. 166–201. **[G: U.S.]**

Ospina, Sylvia. Piracy of Satellite-Transmitted Copyright Material in the Americas: Bane or Boon? **In** *Demac, D. A., ed.*, 1986, pp. 166–98.

Owen, Bruce M. The Evolution of Clayton Section 7 Enforcement and the Beginnings of U.S. Industrial Policy. *Antitrust Bull.*, Summer 1986, *31*(2), pp. 409–29. **[G: U.S.]**

Owen, Bruce M. and Greenhalgh, Peter R. Competitive Considerations in Cable Television Franchising. *Contemp. Policy Issues*, April 1986, *4*(2), pp. 69–79. **[G: U.S.]**

Pakes, Ariel S. Patents as Options: Some Estimates of the Value of Holding European Patent Stocks. *Econometrica*, July 1986, *54*(4), pp. 755–84. **[G: France; U.K.; W. Germany]**

Palmer, John P. Copyright and Computer Software. **In** *Palmer, J., ed.*, 1986, pp. 205–25. **[G: Canada; U.S.]**

Paredes M., Ricardo. "Una revisión crítica a la literatura de colusión." (With English summary.) *Cuadernos Econ.*, August 1986, *23*(69), pp. 173–99.

Perry, Martin K. and Groff, Robert H. Trademark Licensing in a Monopolistically Competitive Industry. *Rand J. Econ.*, Summer 1986, *17*(2), pp. 189–200.

Peyton, David. A New View of Copyright. *J. Policy Anal. Manage.*, Fall 1986, *6*(1), pp. 92–98. **[G: U.S.]**

Pindyck, Robert S. Capital Adjustment Costs, Monopoly Power, and the Regulated Firm. **In** *Grieson, R. E., ed.*, 1986, pp. 219–30.

Ponsoldt, James F. The Unreasonableness of Coerced Cooperation: A Comment upon the *NCAA* Decision's Rejection of the Chicago School. *Antitrust Bull.*, Winter 1986, *31*(4), pp. 1003–44. **[G: U.S.]**

Priest, George L. What Economists Can Tell Lawyers about Intellectual Property: Comment [Property Rights and Invention]. **In** *Palmer, J., ed.*, 1986, pp. 19–24. **[G: U.S.]**

Ránki, Gy. and Tomaszewski, Jerzy. The Role of the State in Industry, Banking and Trade. **In** *Kaser, M. C. and Radice, E. A., eds.*, 1986, pp. 3–48. **[G: E. Europe]**

Reagan, Patricia B. Resale Price Maintenance: A Re-examination of the Outlets Hypothesis. **In** *Zerbe, R. O., Jr., ed.*, 1986, pp. 1–12.

Rey, Patrick and Tirole, Jean. Vertical Restraints from a Principal–Agent Viewpoint. **In** *Pellegrini, L. and Reddy, S. K., eds.*, 1986, pp. 1–30.

Roberts, John. A Signaling Model of Predatory Pricing. *Oxford Econ. Pap.*, Suppl. Nov. 1986, *38*, pp. 75–93.

Robinson, Kenneth. Maximizing the Public Benefits of the AT&T Breakup. *J. Policy Anal. Manage.*, Spring 1986, *5*(3), pp. 572–83. **[G: U.S.]**

Rogowsky, Robert A. The Economic Effectiveness of Section 7 Relief. *Antitrust Bull.*, Spring 1986, *31*(1), pp. 187–233. **[G: U.S.]**

Rolshoven, Hubertus. Antitrust Policy and the Rationalization of the U.S. Steel Industry. *J. Inst. Theoretical Econ.*, March 1986, *142*(1), pp. 134–37. **[G: U.S.]**

Rose-Ackerman, Susan. Unfair Competition and Corporate Income Taxation. **In** *Rose-Ackerman, S., ed.*, 1986, *1982*, pp. 394–414.

Ross, Thomas W. The Costs of Regulating Price Differences. *J. Bus.*, January 1986, *59*(1), pp. 143–56.

Roth, Timothy P. Antitrust Policy and the Rationalization of the U.S. Steel Industry. *J. Inst. Theoretical Econ.*, March 1986, *142*(1), pp. 114–30. **[G: U.S.]**

Rowley, J. William. Merger and Pre-merger Notification. **In** *Block, W., ed.*, 1986, pp. 21–40. **[G: Canada]**

Salop, Steven C. Measuring Ease of Entry. *Antitrust Bull.*, Summer 1986, *31*(2), pp. 551–70. **[G: U.S.]**

Schankerman, Mark and Pakes, Ariel S. Estimates of the Value of Patent Rights in European Countries during the Post-1950 Period. *Econ. J.*, December 1986, *96*(384), pp. 1052–76. **[G: U.K.; France; W. Germany]**

Scherer, F. M. Patents: Monopolies or Property Rights? Comment. **In** *Palmer, J., ed.*, 1986, pp. 51–58.

Schwartz, Marius. Errata [The Perverse Effects of the Robinson–Patman Act]. *Antitrust Bull.*, Winter 1986, *31*(4), pp. 1089. **[G: U.S.]**

Schwartz, Marius. The Nature and Scope of Contestability Theory. *Oxford Econ. Pap.*, Suppl. Nov. 1986, *38*, pp. 37–57.

Schwartz, Marius. The Perverse Effects of the Robinson–Patman Act. *Antitrust Bull.*, Fall 1986, *31* (3), pp. 733–57. **[G: U.S.]**

Scott, John T. and Pascoe, George. Beyond Firm and Industry Effects on Profitability in Imperfect Markets. *Rev. Econ. Statist.*, May 1986, *68* (2), pp. 284–92. **[G: U.S.]**

Shaw, Richard W. and Simpson, Paul. The Persistence of Monopoly: An Investigation of the Effectiveness of the United Kingdom Monopolies Commission. *J. Ind. Econ.*, June 1986, *34* (4), pp. 355–72. **[G: U.K.]**

Shepherd, William G. Assessing "Predatory" Actions by Market Shares and Selectivity. *Antitrust Bull.*, Spring 1986, *31* (1), pp. 1–28. **[G: U.S.]**

Shniderman, Harry L. The Robinson–Patman Act and the Supreme Court, 1978–85. *Antitrust Bull.*, Fall 1986, *31* (3), pp. 665–708. **[G: U.S.]**

Shughart, William F., II; Tollison, Robert D. and Goff, Brian L. Bureaucratic Structure and Congressional Control. *Southern Econ. J.*, April 1986, *52* (4), pp. 962–72. **[G: U.S.]**

Silcox, Clark R. and MacIntyre, A. Everette. The Robinson–Patman Act and Competitive Fairness: Balancing the Economic and Social Dimensions of Antitrust. *Antitrust Bull.*, Fall 1986, *31* (3), pp. 611–64. **[G: U.S.]**

Sims, Joe and Lande, Robert H. The End of Antitrust—Or a New Beginning? *Antitrust Bull.*, Summer 1986, *31* (2), pp. 301–22. **[G: U.S.]**

Slade, Margaret E. Exogeneity Tests of Market Boundaries Applied to Petroleum Products. *J. Ind. Econ.*, March 1986, *34* (3), pp. 291–303. **[G: U.S.]**

Slade, Margaret E. Measures of Market Power in Extractive Industries: The Legacy of *United States v. General Dynamics. Antitrust Bull.*, Spring 1986, *31* (1), pp. 91–111. **[G: U.S.]**

Smith, Douglas A. Collective Administration of Copyright: An Economic Analysis. **In** *Palmer, J., ed.*, 1986, pp. 137–51.

Smith, W. James and Vaughan, Michael B. Economic Welfare, Price and Profit: The Deterrent Effect of Alternative Antitrust Regimes. *Econ. Inquiry*, October 1986, *24* (4), pp. 615–29.

Spiller, Pablo T. Treble Damages and Optimal Suing Time. **In** *Zerbe, R. O., Jr., ed.*, 1986, pp. 45–56.

Stigler, George J. The Economic Effects of the Antitrust Laws. **In** *Stigler, G. J.*, 1986, *1966*, pp. 184–223. **[G: U.S.]**

Teece, David J. Profiting from Technological Innovation: Implications for Integration, Collaboration, Licensing and Public Policy. *Ricerche Econ.*, Oct.-Dec. 1986, *40* (4), pp. 607–43. **[G: U.S.]**

Temin, Peter. Is History Stranger Than Theory? The Origin of Telephone Separations. **In** *Parker, W. N., ed.*, 1986, pp. 50–59.

Thompson, Donald N. The "Abuse of Dominant Position" Provision. **In** *Block, W., ed.*, 1986, pp. 157–69. **[G: Canada]**

Timmins, Paul V. Divestiture as a Remedy in Private Actions Brought under Section 16 of the Clayton Act. *Mich. Law Rev.*, June 1986, *84* (7), pp. 1579–97. **[G: U.S.]**

Tollison, Robert D. Antitrust Policy and the Rationalization of the U.S. Steel Industry: Comment. *J. Inst. Theoretical Econ.*, March 1986, *142* (1), pp. 131–33. **[G: U.S.]**

Tye, William B. Stand-Alone Costs as an Indicator of Market Dominance and Rate Reasonableness under the Staggers Rail Act. *Int. J. Transport Econ.*, February 1986, *13* (1), pp. 21–40. **[G: U.S.]**

von Ungern-Sternberg, Thomas. Innovator Protection and the Rate of Technical Progress. **In** *Day, R. H. and Eliasson, G., eds.*, 1986, *1984*, pp. 277–91.

Walters, Stephen J. K. Reciprocity Reexamined: The Consolidated Foods Case. *J. Law Econ.*, October 1986, *29* (2), pp. 423–38. **[G: U.S.]**

Wassermann, Ursula. Patents and the Biotechnological Industry. *J. World Trade Law*, Nov.:Dec. 1986, *20* (6), pp. 705–13. **[G: Global]**

Weiss, Nitzan and Lee, Phil. Sustainability of the Multiproduct Monopoly and Ramsey-Optimal Pricing. *J. Inst. Theoretical Econ.*, September 1986, *142* (3), pp. 473–92.

Werden, Gregory J. and Simon, Marilyn J. An Economic Assessment of the Administration's Detrebling Proposal. *Antitrust Bull.*, Winter 1986, *31* (4), pp. 935–54. **[G: U.S.]**

West, Edwin G. Canada's Competition Act in the Light of U.S. Experience: A Cautionary Tale. **In** *Block, W., ed.*, 1986, pp. 187–201. **[G: Canada; U.S.]**

Whalley, John. International Aspects of Copyright Legislation in Canada: Economic Analysis of Policy Options. **In** *Palmer, J., ed.*, 1986, pp. 273–83. **[G: Canada]**

White, Ward H. Divestiture and the Local-Exchange Carrier. **In** *[Dorsey, J. N. and Wiggins, B. T.]*, 1986, pp. 89–95. **[G: U.S.]**

Whiting, Richard A. R–P: May It Rest in Peace. *Antitrust Bull.*, Fall 1986, *31* (3), pp. 709–32. **[G: U.S.]**

Williams, Michael A. An Economic Application of Bootstrap Statistical Methods: *Addyston Pipe* Revisited. *Amer. Econ.*, Fall 1986, *30* (2), pp. 52–58. **[G: U.S.]**

Williamson, Oliver E. On the Political Economy of Antitrust: Grounds for Cautious Optimism. **In** *Williamson, O. E.*, 1986, pp. 250–57. **[G: U.S.]**

Williamson, Oliver E. The Economics of Antitrust: Transaction Cost Considerations. **In** *Williamson, O. E.*, 1986, pp. 197–249.

Williamson, Oliver E. Transforming Merger Policy: The Pound of New Perspectives. *Amer. Econ. Rev.*, May 1986, *76* (2), pp. 114–19. **[G: U.S.]**

Yamamura, Kozo. Joint Research and Antitrust: Japanese vs. American Strategies. **In** *Patrick, H., ed.*, 1986, pp. 171–209. **[G: U.S.; Japan]**

Yamamura, Kozo and Vandenberg, Jan. Japan's Rapid-Growth Policy on Trial: The Television Case. **In** *Saxonhouse, G. R. and Yamamura, K., eds.*, 1986, pp. 238–83. **[G: U.S.; Japan]**

Yamey, Basil. The New Anti-trust Economics. **In** *[Seldon, A.]*, 1986, pp. 67–78. **[G: U.S.]**

Yandle, Bruce. Federal Trade Commission Output and Costs: Cycling through the Zone of Political Wrath. *Soc. Sci. Quart.*, September 1986, *67*(3), pp. 517–33. **[G: U.S.]**

Yandle, Bruce. The Evolution of Regulatory Activities in the 1970s and 1980s. **In** *Cagan, P., ed.*, 1986, pp. 105–45. **[G: U.S.]**

Yonce, Henry G. Regulating the Telecommunication "Bear" Markets. **In** *[Dorsey, J. N. and Wiggins, B. T.]*, 1986, pp. 3–6. **[G: U.S.]**

Young, Michael K. Japan's Antitrust Policy: Impact on Import Competition: Comment. **In** *Pugel, T. A., ed.*, 1986, pp. 77–90. **[G: U.S.; Japan]**

613 Regulation of Public Utilities

6130 Regulation of Public Utilities

Agnew, Carson E. and Gould, Richard G. Frequency Coordination and Spectrum Economics. **In** *Zerbe, R. O., Jr., ed.*, 1986, pp. 167–84.

Alessio, Frank J. Cost Support for Market Pricing: Challenges to Local-Exchange Companies. **In** *[Dorsey, J. N. and Wiggins, B. T.]*, 1986, pp. 119–22. **[G: U.S.]**

Andersson, Roland. Electricity Tariffs in Sweden—A Reply. *Energy Econ.*, January 1986, *8*(1), pp. 54–56. **[G: Sweden]**

Atkinson, Scott E. and Halvorsen, Robert. The Relative Efficiency of Public and Private Firms in a Regulated Environment: The Case of U.S. Electric Utilities. *J. Public Econ.*, April 1986, *29*(3), pp. 281–94. **[G: U.S.]**

Bailey, Elizabeth E. Price and Productivity Change Following Deregulation: The U.S. Experience. *Econ. J.*, March 1986, *96*(381), pp. 1–17. **[G: U.S.]**

Bailey, Richard. Gas Privatization and the Energy Strategy. *Nat. Westminster Bank Quart. Rev.*, August 1986, pp. 2–12. **[G: U.K.]**

Baughcum, Alan. Deregulation, Divestiture, and Competition in U.S. Telecommunications: Lessons for Other Countries. **In** *Snow, M. S.*, 1986, pp. 69–105. **[G: U.S.]**

Baysinger, Barry D. and Zardkoohi, Asghar. Technology, Residual Claimants, and Corporate Control. *J. Law, Econ., Organ.*, Fall 1986, *2*(2), pp. 339–49. **[G: U.S.]**

Bergougnoux, Jean; Careme, François and Mosconi, Jean-Jacques. Tarification et financement: quelques approches dans le cas d'Électricité de France. (Pricing and Financing Policies: The Electricité de France Approach. With English summary.) *Écon. Soc.*, July 1986, *20*(7), pp. 175–201. **[G: France]**

Bhagat, Sanjai and Frost, Peter A. Issuing Costs to Existing Shareholders in Competitive and Negotiated Underwritten Public Utility Equity Offerings. *J. Finan. Econ.*, Jan./Feb. 1986, *15*(1/2), pp. 233–59. **[G: U.S.]**

Billinghurst, Roy A. Repeal the Knowledge Tax. **In** *[Dorsey, J. N. and Wiggins, B. T.]*, 1986, pp. 59–65. **[G: U.S.]**

Bolton, Craig J. and Meiners, Roger E. The Politicization of the Electric Utility Industry. **In** *Moorhouse, J. C., ed.*, 1986, pp. 249–77. **[G: U.S.]**

Braeutigam, Ronald R. and Hubbard, R. Glenn. Natural Gas: The Regulatory Transition. **In** *Weiss, L. W. and Klass, M. W., eds.*, 1986, pp. 137–68. **[G: U.S.]**

Broadman, Harry G. Natural Gas Deregulation: The Need for Further Reform. *J. Policy Anal. Manage.*, Spring 1986, *5*(3), pp. 496–516. **[G: U.S.]**

Broadman, Harry G. and Toman, Michael A. Non-Price Provisions in Long-term Natural Gas Contracts. *Land Econ.*, May 1986, *62*(2), pp. 111–18. **[G: U.S.]**

Brock, Gerald W. The Regulatory Change in Telecommunications: The Dissolution of AT&T. **In** *Weiss, L. W. and Klass, M. W., eds.*, 1986, pp. 210–33. **[G: U.S.]**

Burns, Robert T. Separations of Costs and the Need for Reform. **In** *[Dorsey, J. N. and Wiggins, B. T.]*, 1986, pp. 99–104. **[G: U.S.]**

Byrnes, Patricia; Grosskopf, Shawna and Hayes, Kathy J. Efficiency and Ownership: Further Evidence. *Rev. Econ. Statist.*, May 1986, *68*(2), pp. 337–41. **[G: U.S.]**

Chao, Hung-po, et al. Multilevel Demand Subscription Pricing for Electric Power. *Energy Econ.*, October 1986, *8*(4), pp. 199–217.

Chappell, Henry W., Jr. and Wilder, Ronald P. Multiproduct Monopoly, Regulation, and Firm Costs: Comment. *Southern Econ. J.*, April 1986, *52*(4), pp. 1168–74. **[G: U.S.]**

Chen, Andrew H. and Merville, Larry J. An Analysis of Divestiture Effects Resulting from Deregulation. *J. Finance*, December 1986, *41*(5), pp. 997–1010. **[G: U.S.]**

Danielsen, Albert L. and Kamerschen, David R. A Methodological Study of Market Power and Market Shares in Intrastate Inter-LATA Telecommunications. **In** *[Dorsey, J. N. and Wiggins, B. T.]*, 1986, pp. 135–80. **[G: U.S.]**

Demsetz, Harold. Electric Power: Deregulation and the Public Interest: Foreword. **In** *Moorhouse, J. C., ed.*, 1986, pp. xv–xviii.

Eickhof, Norbert. Versorgungswirtschaft und Wettbewerbsordnung. (Public Utilities and the Competitive System. With English summary.) **In** *Eucken, W. and Böhm, F., eds.*, 1986, pp. 201–18. **[G: W. Germany]**

Ekelund, Robert B., Jr. and Saba, Richard P. Establishing Property Rights in Utility Franchises. **In** *Moorhouse, J. C., ed.*, 1986, pp. 425–45.

Etzioni, Amitai. Does Regulation Reduce Electricity Rates? A Research Note. *Policy Sci.*, December 1986, *19*(4), pp. 349–57. **[G: U.S.]**

Färe, Rolf and Logan, James. Regulation, Scale and Productivity: A Comment. *Int. Econ. Rev.*,

October 1986, *27*(3), pp. 777–81.

Ferguson, James D. Access Charges and the OCCs. **In** *[Dorsey, J. N. and Wiggins, B. T.]*, 1986, pp. 73–77. **[G: U.S.]**

Ferris, Stephen P.; Johnson, Dana J. and Shome, Dilip K. Regulatory Environment and Market Response to Public Utility Rate Decisions. *J. Finan. Res.*, Winter 1986, *9*(4), pp. 313–18. **[G: U.S.]**

Forbes, Ronald. Determinants of the Cost of Capital for the New York Power Authority. **In** *Saltzman, S. and Schuler, R. E., eds.*, 1986, pp. 288–307. **[G: U.S.]**

Fox, William F. and Hofler, Richard A. Using Homothetic Composed Error Frontiers to Measure Water Utility Efficiency. *Southern Econ. J.*, October 1986, *53*(2), pp. 461–77. **[G: U.S.]**

Freeman, S. David. Electric Utility Conservation Programs: Progress and Problems: Comments. **In** *Sawhill, J. C. and Cotton, R., eds.*, 1986, pp. 160–62. **[G: U.S.]**

Fuhr, Joseph P., Jr. Maintaining Universal Telephone Service under Deregulation. *J. Policy Anal. Manage.*, Spring 1986, *5*(3), pp. 583–90. **[G: U.S.]**

Gerstner, Eitan. Peak Load Pricing in Competitive Markets. *Econ. Inquiry*, April 1986, *24*(2), pp. 349–61.

Globerman, Steven and Stanbury, W. T. Changing the Telephone Pricing Structure: Allocative, Distributional and Political Considerations. *Can. Public Policy*, March 1986, *12*(1), pp. 214–26. **[G: Canada]**

Gordon, Richard L. Perspectives on Reforming Electric Utility Regulation. **In** *Moorhouse, J. C., ed.*, 1986, pp. 447–75. **[G: U.S.]**

Grennes, Thomas J. Electric Utility Regulation in an Open Economy. **In** *Moorhouse, J. C., ed.*, 1986, pp. 219–47. **[G: U.S.]**

Hajiran, Homayoun; Kamerschen, David R. and Legler, John B. The Economic and Political Determinants of the Requested–Granted Rate of Return in Public Utility Rate Cases. **In** *[Dorsey, J. N. and Wiggins, B. T.]*, 1986, pp. 29–56. **[G: U.S.]**

Hammond, Claire Holton. An Overview of Electric Utility Regulation. **In** *Moorhouse, J. C., ed.*, 1986, pp. 31–61.

Hammond, Elizabeth M.; Helm, Dieter R. and Thompson, David J. Competition in Electricity Supply: Has the Energy Act Failed? *Fisc. Stud.*, February 1986, *7*(1), pp. 11–33. **[G: U.K.]**

Hartley, Peter and Trengove, Chris D. Who Benefits from Public Utilities? *Econ. Rec.*, June 1986, *62*(177), pp. 163–79.

Hartman, Raymond S. and Doane, Michael J. The Estimation of the Effects of Utility-sponsored Conservation Programmes. *Appl. Econ.*, January 1986, *18*(1), pp. 1–25. **[G: U.S.]**

Hausman, William J.; Kemme, David M. and Neufeld, John L. The Relative Economic Efficiency of Private versus Municipal Waterworks in the 1890s. **In** *Atack, J., ed.*, 1986, pp. 13–27. **[G: U.S.]**

Hederman, William F., Jr. A Comparative Analysis of Two Difficult Market Transitions: Telecommunications and Natural Gas. **In** *[Dorsey, J. N. and Wiggins, B. T.]*, 1986, pp. 207–14. **[G: U.S.]**

Hemphill, Robert F. and Myers, Edward A. Electric Utility Conservation Programs: Progress and Problems. **In** *Sawhill, J. C. and Cotton, R., eds.*, 1986, pp. 137–59. **[G: U.S.]**

Henderson, J. Stephen. Price Discrimination Limits in Relation to the Death Spiral. *Energy J.*, July 1986, *7*(3), pp. 33–50.

Henderson, J. Stephen. The Effect of Regulation on Nonuniform Electricity Price Schedules in the United States. *J. Public Econ.*, April 1986, *29*(3), pp. 317–32. **[G: U.S.]**

Hill, R. Carter; Danielsen, Albert L. and Kamerschen, David R. Assessing the Feasibility of Modeling the Economic Impacts Associated with Changing Carrier Access and Customer Line Charges: A Generic Study of the Southern Region. **In** *[Dorsey, J. N. and Wiggins, B. T.]*, 1986, pp. 215–41. **[G: U.S.]**

Hjalmarsson, Lennart and Veiderpass, Ann. Electricity Tariffs in Sweden—A Comment. *Energy Econ.*, January 1986, *8*(1), pp. 51–53. **[G: Sweden]**

Hobbs, Benjamin F. and Schuler, Richard E. Deregulating the Distribution of Electricity: Price and Welfare Consequences of Spatial Oligopoly with Uniform Delivered Prices. *J. Reg. Sci.*, May 1986, *26*(2), pp. 235–65. **[G: U.S.]**

Hoskins, Colin and McFadyen, Stuart. The Canadian Broadcast Program Development Fund: An Evaluation and Some Recommendations. *Can. Public Policy*, March 1986, *12*(1), pp. 227–35. **[G: Canada]**

Huband, Frank L. A Survey of Alternative Electric Utility Supply and Use Technologies. **In** *Saltzman, S. and Schuler, R. E., eds.*, 1986, pp. 167–75. **[G: U.S.]**

Huber, Jack. Post-divestiture Telecommunications Pricing: Doing Business in the Competitive, Divested World. **In** *[Dorsey, J. N. and Wiggins, B. T.]*, 1986, pp. 123–28. **[G: U.S.]**

Hyman, Leonard S.; Kelley, Doris A. and Toole, Richard C. Financial Constraints on Electric Utilities in New York State: Technology, Institutional Structure, and Investors' Attitudes. **In** *Saltzman, S. and Schuler, R. E., eds.*, 1986, pp. 275–80. **[G: U.S.]**

Ito, Youichi. Telecommunications and Industrial Policies in Japan: Recent Developments. **In** *Snow, M. S.*, 1986, pp. 201–30. **[G: Japan]**

Jarrell, Gregg A. The Demand for Electric Utility Regulation. **In** *Moorhouse, J. C., ed.*, 1986, pp. 291–305. **[G: U.S.]**

Jonscher, Charles. Telecommunications Liberalization in the United Kingdom. **In** *Snow, M. S.*, 1986, pp. 153–72. **[G: U.K.]**

Joskow, Paul L. and Schmalensee, Richard. Incentive Regulation for Electric Utilities. *Yale J. Regul.*, Fall 1986, *4*(1), pp. 1–49. **[G: U.S.]**

Kafoglis, Milton Z. Tax Policy and Public Utility

Regulation. In *Moorhouse, J. C., ed.*, 1986, pp. 97–133. [G: U.S.]

Kahn, Alfred E. A Critique of Proposed Changes. In *Saltzman, S. and Schuler, R. E., eds.*, 1986, pp. 340–47. [G: U.S.]

Kaiser, Gordon E. Developments in Canadian Telecommunications Regulation. In *Snow, M. S.*, 1986, pp. 173–200. [G: Canada]

Kantor, Brian S. Electricity Pricing in Hong Kong: A Comment. *Hong Kong Econ. Pap.*, 1986, (17), pp. 91–107. [G: Hong Kong]

Karlson, Stephen H. Multiple-Output Production and Pricing in Electric Utilities. *Southern Econ. J.*, July 1986, *53*(1), pp. 73–86.

Keshava, G. P. A Review of the Theory of Electricity Pricing. *Indian Econ. J.*, Oct.-Dec. 1986, *34*(2), pp. 71–86.

Kokkelenberg, Edward C. and Choi, Jeong Poy. Factor Demands, Adjustment Costs and Regulation. *Appl. Econ.*, June 1986, *18*(6), pp. 631–43. [G: U.S.]

Kron, Philip C. The Electric Utility Financial Crisis from a Banker's Perspective. In *Saltzman, S. and Schuler, R. E., eds.*, 1986, pp. 281–87. [G: U.S.]

Kryzanowski, Lawrence and Jalilvand, Abolhassan. Statistical Tests of the Accuracy of Alternative Forecasts: Some Results for U.S. Utility Betas. *Financial Rev.*, May 1986, *21*(2), pp. 319–35. [G: U.S.]

Kunreuther, Howard and Bendixen, Lisa. Benefits Assessment for Regulatory Problems. In *Bentkover, J. D.; Covello, V. T. and Jeryl, M., eds.*, 1986, pp. 35–50. [G: U.S.]

Laffont, Jean-Jacques and Tirole, Jean. Using Cost Observation to Regulate Firms. *J. Polit. Econ.*, Part 1, June 1986, *94*(3), pp. 614–41.

Lamberton, Don M. Australian Regulatory Policy. In *Snow, M. S.*, 1986, pp. 231–52. [G: Australia]

Leggette, James A. Separation and Telecommunications Pricing Issues. In *[Dorsey, J. N. and Wiggins, B. T.]*, 1986, pp. 105–18. [G: U.S.]

Makhija, Anil K. and Thompson, Howard E. The Ratepayer and Stockholder under Alternative Regulatory Policies. *Land Econ.*, May 1986, *62*(2), pp. 119–33. [G: U.S.]

Mansell, Robin E. The Telecommunication Bypass Threat: Real or Imagined? *J. Econ. Issues*, March 1986, *20*(1), pp. 145–64.

Marx, Jane. Regulation of Electric Utilities and Affiliated Coal Companies—Determining Reasonable Expenses: Comment. *Natural Res. J.*, Fall 1986, *26*(4), pp. 851–69. [G: U.S.]

Matthews, Derek. Laissez-faire and the London Gas Industry in the Nineteenth Century: Another Look. *Econ. Hist. Rev., 2nd Ser.*, May 1986, *39*(2), pp. 244–63. [G: U.K.]

Mayo, John W. Multiproduct Monopoly, Regulation, and Firm Costs: Reply. *Southern Econ. J.*, April 1986, *52*(4), pp. 1175–78.

McCormick, Robert E. Inflation, Regulation, and Financial Adequacy. In *Moorhouse, J. C., ed.*, 1986, pp. 135–61. [G: U.S.]

McGuire, Robert A. and Ohsfeldt, Robert L. Public versus Private Water Delivery: A Critical Analysis of a Hedonic Cost Approach. *Public Finance Quart.*, July 1986, *14*(3), pp. 339–50.

Moorhouse, John C. The Uncertain Future of the Electric Power Industry. In *Moorhouse, J. C., ed.*, 1986, pp. 1–23. [G: U.S.]

Mountain, Dean C. and Hsiao, Cheng. Peak and Off-Peak Industrial Demand for Electricity: The Hopkinson Rate in Ontario, Canada. *Energy J.*, January 1986, *7*(1), pp. 149–68. [G: Canada]

Mulherin, J. Harold. Specialized Assets, Governmental Regulation, and Organizational Structure in the Natural Gas Industry. *J. Inst. Theoretical Econ.*, September 1986, *142*(3), pp. 528–41. [G: U.S.]

Muris, Timothy J. Regulatory Policymaking at the Federal Trade Commission: The Extent of Congressional Control. *J. Polit. Econ.*, August 1986, *94*(4), pp. 884–89. [G: U.S.]

Naughton, Michael C. The Efficiency and Equity Consequences of Two-Part Tariffs in Electricity Pricing. *Rev. Econ. Statist.*, August 1986, *68*(3), pp. 406–14. [G: U.S.]

Navarro, Peter. The Performance of Utility Commissions. In *Moorhouse, J. C., ed.*, 1986, pp. 337–58. [G: U.S.]

Neumann, Karl-Heinz. Economic Policy toward Telecommunications, Information, and the Media in West Germany. In *Snow, M. S.*, 1986, pp. 131–52. [G: W. Germany]

Noam, Eli M. Telecommunications Policy on Both Sides of the Atlantic: Divergence and Outlook. In *Snow, M. S.*, 1986, pp. 255–74.

Noll, Roger G. State Regulatory Responses to Competition and Divestiture in the Telecommunications Industry. In *Grieson, R. E., ed.*, 1986, pp. 165–200. [G: U.S.]

Noll, Roger G. The Political and Institutional Context of Communications Policy. In *Snow, M. S.*, 1986, pp. 42–65. [G: OECD]

Pashigian, B. Peter. Reply [The Effect of Environmental Regulation on Optimal Plant Size and Factor Shares]. *J. Law Econ.*, April 1986, *29*(1), pp. 201–09. [G: U.S.]

Pasour, E. C., Jr. Information, Incentives, and Regulation. In *Moorhouse, J. C., ed.*, 1986, pp. 359–79.

Percival, Robert V. Conservation and Renewable Energy Sources as Supply Alternatives for New York's Electric Utilities. In *Saltzman, S. and Schuler, R. E., eds.*, 1986, pp. 126–50. [G: U.S.]

Perkins, Clinton, Jr. Pricing for Today's Environment. In *[Dorsey, J. N. and Wiggins, B. T.]*, 1986, pp. 129–32. [G: U.S.]

Price, Alan K. Access Charges: A Local-Exchange Carrier's Perspective. In *[Dorsey, J. N. and Wiggins, B. T.]*, 1986, pp. 79–82. [G: U.S.]

Primeaux, Walter J., Jr. and Mann, Patrick C. Regulator Selection Methods and Electricity Prices. *Land Econ.*, February 1986, *62*(1), pp. 1–13. [G: U.S.]

Rees, Ray. Indivisibilities, Pricing and Investment: The Case of the Second Best. *J. Econ.*

(*Z. Nationalökon.)*, Supplementum 5, 1986, pp. 195–210.

Ringleb, Al H. Environmental Regulation of Electric Utilities. **In** *Moorhouse, J. C., ed.*, 1986, pp. 183–218. **[G: U.S.]**

Roberts, Mark J. Economies of Density and Size in the Production and Delivery of Electric Power. *Land Econ.*, November 1986, *62*(4), pp. 378–87. **[G: U.S.]**

Saltzman, Sidney and Schuler, Richard E. Electricity's Future: Sharpening the Debates. **In** *Saltzman, S. and Schuler, R. E., eds.*, 1986, pp. 348–62. **[G: U.S.]**

Schmidt, Ronald H. and Gunther, Jeffery W. Distributional Implications of Reducing Interstate Energy Price Differences. *Fed. Res. Bank Dallas Econ. Rev.*, November 1986, pp. 1–15. **[G: U.S.]**

Schuler, Richard E. The Institutional and Regulatory Structure for Providing Electric Service: A Conceptual Basis for Change. **In** *Saltzman, S. and Schuler, R. E., eds.*, 1986, pp. 311–29. **[G: U.S.]**

Scullion, Patrick J. Electric Utility Conservation Programs: Progress and Problems: Comments. **In** *Sawhill, J. C. and Cotton, R., eds.*, 1986, pp. 159–60. **[G: U.S.]**

Skinner, Frank. Communications in the New Era. **In** *[Dorsey, J. N. and Wiggins, B. T.]*, 1986, pp. 83–88. **[G: U.S.]**

Snow, Marcellus S. Communications Policy in Seven Developed Countries: Introduction, Background, and Conclusions. **In** *Snow, M. S.*, 1986, pp. 3–19. **[G: OECD]**

Snow, Marcellus S. Regulating Telecommunications, Information, and the Media: An Agenda for Future Comparative Research. **In** *Snow, M. S.*, 1986, pp. 275–94.

Srinagesh, Padmanabhan. Nonlinear Prices and the Regulated Firm. *Quart. J. Econ.*, February 1986, *101*(1), pp. 51–68.

Stalon, Charles G. Analysis and Synthesis in Quasi-judicial Multimember Regulatory Agencies. **In** *Saltzman, S. and Schuler, R. E., eds.*, 1986, pp. 330–39. **[G: U.S.]**

Stigler, George J. What Can Regulators Regulate? The Case of Electricity. **In** *Stigler, G. J.*, 1986, *1962*, pp. 224–42. **[G: U.S.]**

Taylor, Thomas N. and Schwarz, Peter M. A Residential Demand Charge: Evidence from the Duke Power Time-of-Day Pricing Experiment. *Energy J.*, April 1986, *7*(2), pp. 135–51. **[G: U.S.]**

Teeples, Ronald; Feigenbaum, Susan and Glyver, David. Public versus Private Water Delivery: Cost Comparisons. *Public Finance Quart.*, July 1986, *14*(3), pp. 351–66.

Trebing, Harry M. Apologetics of Deregulation in Energy and Telecommunications: An Institutionalist Assessment. *J. Econ. Issues*, September 1986, *20*(3), pp. 613–32.

Veall, Michael R. Time-of-Use Rates and Peak Period Electricity Consumption: An Empirical Note. *Energy Econ.*, October 1986, *8*(4), pp. 257–62. **[G: U.S.]**

Vietor, Richard H. K. Perspectives on the Bell System: Strategy, Structure, Technology, and Unionism. *Bus. Hist. Rev.*, Winter 1986, *60*(4), pp. 633–40. **[G: U.S.]**

Voge, Jean-Paul. A Survey of French Regulatory Policy. **In** *Snow, M. S.*, 1986, pp. 106–30. **[G: France]**

Volkonskii, V. A.; Kuzovkin, A. I. and Pomanskii, A. B. On Determining Time-of-Day Tariffs for Energy and Services. *Matekon*, Fall 1986, *23*(1), pp. 3–24. **[G: U.S.S.R.]**

Weingast, Barry R. and Moran, Mark J. Congress and Regulatory Agency Choice: Reply [Bureaucratic Discretion or Congressional Control? Regulatory Policymaking by the Federal Trade Commission]. *J. Polit. Econ.*, August 1986, *94*(4), pp. 890–94. **[G: U.S.]**

von Weizsäcker, Carl Christian. Free Entry into Telecommunications. **In** *Snow, M. S.*, 1986, pp. 20–41.

Wenders, John T. Economic Efficiency and Income Distribution in the Electric Utility Industry. *Southern Econ. J.*, April 1986, *52*(4), pp. 1056–67. **[G: U.S.]**

Wenders, John T. Efficiency, Subsidy, and Cross-Subsidy in Electric Utility Pricing. **In** *Moorhouse, J. C., ed.*, 1986, pp. 307–36. **[G: U.S.]**

White, Ward H. Divestiture and the Local-Exchange Carrier. **In** *[Dorsey, J. N. and Wiggins, B. T.]*, 1986, pp. 89–95. **[G: U.S.]**

Williams, Stephen F. It's Worse than You Thought: Further Flaws in Price Controls as a Device for Transferring Scarcity Rents. *J. Policy Anal. Manage.*, Fall 1986, *6*(1), pp. 106–09. **[G: U.S.]**

Williamson, Oliver E. Franchise Bidding for Natural Monopolies—In General and with Respect to CATV. **In** *Williamson, O. E.*, 1986, *1976*, pp. 258–97.

Winward, John. Nationalised Industry Consumer Councils. **In** *Moores, B., ed.*, 1986, pp. 217–28. **[G: U.K.]**

Woo, Chi-Keung; Hanser, Philip and Toyama, Nate. Estimating Hourly Electric Load with Generalized Least Square Procedures. *Energy J.*, April 1986, *7*(2), pp. 153–70.

Woo, Chi-Keung and Toyama, Nate. Service Reliability and the Optimal Interruptible Rate Option in Residential Electricity Pricing. *Energy J.*, July 1986, *7*(3), pp. 123–36.

Zardkoohi, Asghar. Competition in the Production of Electricity. **In** *Moorhouse, J. C., ed.*, 1986, pp. 63–95. **[G: U.S.]**

614 Public Enterprises

6140 Public Enterprises

Abromeit, Heidrun. Privatisation in Great Britain. *Ann. Pub. Co-op. Econ.*, Apr.-June 1986, *57*(2), pp. 153–79. **[G: U.K.]**

Ahiakpor, James C. W. The Capital Intensity of Foreign, Private Local and State Owned Firms in a Less Developed Country: Ghana. *J. Devel. Econ.*, Jan.-Feb. 1986, *20*(1), pp. 145–62. **[G: Ghana]**

Akhtar, Haq Nawaz. Manpower Development in Public Enterprises. **In** *U.N., Dept. of Technical Co-operation for Development,* 1986, pp. 149–61. **[G: Pakistan]**

Atkinson, Scott E. and Halvorsen, Robert. The Relative Efficiency of Public and Private Firms in a Regulated Environment: The Case of U.S. Electric Utilities. *J. Public Econ.*, April 1986, *29*(3), pp. 281–94. **[G: U.S.]**

Austin, James E. and Ickis, John C. Management, Managers, and Revolution. *World Devel.*, July 1986, *14*(7), pp. 775–90. **[G: Nicaragua]**

Bance, Philippe and Monnier, Lionel. The Privatization of Public Enterprises in France. *Ann. Pub. Co-op. Econ.*, Apr.-June 1986, *57*(2), pp. 181–203. **[G: France]**

Baqai, Moin. The Question of Subsidies in the Pricing Policy of Public Enterprises. **In** *U.N., Dept. of Technical Co-operation for Development,* 1986, pp. 107–15. **[G: Pakistan]**

Baxter, J. R. Public Enterprise: Studies in Organisational Structure: The Post Office. **In** *Ramanadham, V. V., ed.*, 1986, pp. 51–63. **[G: U.K.]**

Beg, H. U. Project Cost Overruns, Nature and Impact of Delays in Project Implementation. **In** *U.N., Dept. of Technical Co-operation for Development,* 1986, pp. 100–106. **[G: Pakistan]**

Behrens, Peter. Industrial Policy and the Nature of the Firm: Comment. *J. Inst. Theoretical Econ.*, March 1986, *142*(1), pp. 109–13.

Bennett, James T. and DiLorenzo, Thomas J. Credit Allocation and Capital Formation: The Political Economy of Indirect Taxation. **In** *Lee, D. R., ed.*, 1986, pp. 275–96. **[G: U.S.]**

Boardman, Anthony; Freedman, Ruth and Eckel, Catherine C. The Price of Government Ownership: A Study of the Domtar Takeover. *J. Public Econ.*, December 1986, *31*(3), pp. 269–85. **[G: Canada]**

Bokhari, Riyaz H. Public Enterprise: Studies in Organisational Structure: National Fertilizer Corporation of Pakistan Limited. **In** *Ramanadham, V. V., ed.*, 1986, pp. 181–210. **[G: Pakistan]**

Bös, Dieter. A Theory of the Privatization of Public Enterprises. *J. Econ. (Z. Nationalökon.),* Supplementum 5, 1986, pp. 17–40.

Braun, Armand. Role of the Public Sector in the Promotion of Science and Technology. **In** *U.N., Dept. of Technical Co-operation for Development,* 1986, pp. 182–245. **[G: OECD; France]**

Brean, Donald J. S. and Bird, Richard M. Fiscal Risk of State-Owned Enterprise. **In** *Herber, B. P., ed.*, 1986, pp. 333–42. **[G: LDCs; MDCs]**

Brede, Helmut and Hoppe, Ulrich. Outline of the Present Status of the Privatization Debate in the Federal German Republic. *Ann. Pub. Co-op. Econ.*, Apr.-June 1986, *57*(2), pp. 205–29. **[G: W. Germany]**

Briones, Leonor M. The Role of Government-Owned or Controlled Corporation in Development. *Philippine Econ. J.*, 1986, *25*(1–2), pp. 51–89. **[G: Philippines]**

Brittan, Samuel. Privatisation: A Policy in Search of a Rationale: A Comment. *Econ. J.*, March 1986, *96*(381), pp. 33–38. **[G: U.K.]**

Brox, James A. and Maclean, Wendy A. The Financial Behaviour of Canadian Private Corporations and Government Enterprise: A Flow of Funds Analysis. *Bull. Econ. Res.*, January 1986, *38*(1), pp. 49–66. **[G: Canada]**

Bruce, Alistair. State-to-Private Sector Divestment: The Case of Sealink. **In** *Coyne, J. and Wright, M., eds.*, 1986, pp. 202–44. **[G: U.K.]**

Burki, Shahid Javed. Role of Public Enterprises in the Economies of Developing Countries. **In** *U.N., Dept. of Technical Co-operation for Development,* 1986, pp. 37–50. **[G: Pakistan]**

Campbell, John L. The State, Capital Formation, and Industrial Planning: Financing Nuclear Energy in the United States and France. *Soc. Sci. Quart.*, December 1986, *67*(4), pp. 707–21. **[G: U.S.; France]**

Cavendish, Elizabeth A. Public Provision of the Performing Arts: A Case Study of the Federal Theatre Project in Connecticut. **In** *DiMaggio, P. J., ed.*, 1986, pp. 140–58. **[G: U.S.]**

Chang, C. Y. Bureaucracy and Modernization: A Case Study of the Special Economic Zones in China. **In** *Jao, Y. C. and Leung, C. K., eds.*, 1986, pp. 105–23. **[G: China]**

Cohen, Stephen S.; Halimi, Serge and Zysman, John. Institutions, Politics, and Industrial Policy in France. **In** *Barfield, C. E. and Schambra, W. A., eds.*, 1986, pp. 106–27. **[G: France]**

Crampes, Claude. Des instruments pour le controle des entreprises publiques. (Some Instruments to Regulate a Public Enterprise. With English summary.) *Revue Écon.*, September 1986, *37*(5), pp. 757–82.

Csikós-Nagy, Béla and Gadó, Ottó. Public Enterprises and Off-Budget Debt. **In** *Herber, B. P., ed.*, 1986, pp. 321–31. **[G: Hungary]**

Diokno, Benjamin E. Perspectives on the Performance Evaluation of State-Operated Enterprises. *Philippine Econ. J.*, 1986, *25*(1–2), pp. 98–110. **[G: Philippines]**

Domberger, Simon and Piggott, John. Privatization Policies and Public Enterprise: A Survey. *Econ. Rec.*, June 1986, *62*(177), pp. 145–62. **[G: U.S.; W. Germany; Canada; Australia]**

Dorn, James A. Industrial Policy and the Nature of the Firm: Comment. *J. Inst. Theoretical Econ.*, March 1986, *142*(1), pp. 101–08.

Eckel, Catherine C. and Vermaelen, Theo. Internal Regulation: The Effects of Government Ownership on the Value of the Firm. *J. Law Econ.*, October 1986, *29*(2), pp. 381–403. **[G: Canada]**

Ennara, Ragaa El-Hady. Fertilizer Pricing in Egypt. **In** *Segura, E. L.; Shetty, Y. T. and Nishimizu, M., eds.*, 1986, pp. 91–94. **[G: Egypt]**

Escarmelle, Jean-François and Hujoel, Luc. Privatization and Deregulation. Its Implementation in Belgium. *Ann. Pub. Co-op. Econ.*, Apr.-June 1986, *57*(2), pp. 253–73. **[G: Belgium]**

Flowerdew, A. D. J. Problems of Public Enterprises in the Transport Sector of Developing Countries. **In** *U.N., Dept. of Technical Co-operation for Development*, 1986, pp. 162–81. **[G: LDCs]**

Freibaum, Jerry. Commercial Space Policy: Theory and Practice. **In** *Demac, D. A., ed.*, 1986, pp. 156–65. **[G: U.S.]**

Gambaccini, Louis J. Public Enterprise: Studies in Organisational Structure: The Port Authority of New York and New Jersey. **In** *Ramanadham, V. V., ed.*, 1986, pp. 131–63. **[G: U.S.]**

Gorre, Lucien. Nationalization of Insurance in France. **In** *Wasow, B. and Hill, R. D., eds.*, 1986, pp. 179–210. **[G: France]**

Handoussa, Heba; Nishimizu, Mieko and Page, John M., Jr. Productivity Change in Egyptian Public Sector Industries after "The Opening," 1973–1979. *J. Devel. Econ.*, Jan.-Feb. 1986, *20*(1), pp. 53–73. **[G: Egypt]**

Hart, Jeffrey A. British Industrial Policy. **In** *Barfield, C. E. and Schambra, W. A., eds.*, 1986, pp. 128–60. **[G: U.K.]**

Hartley, Peter and Trengove, Chris D. Who Benefits from Public Utilities? *Econ. Rec.*, June 1986, *62*(177), pp. 163–79.

Haubrich, Joseph G. Does the Potency of Monetary Policy Vary with Capacity Utilization? A Comment. *Carnegie-Rochester Conf. Ser. Public Policy*, Spring 1986, *24*, pp. 333–37.

Hausman, William J.; Kemme, David M. and Neufeld, John L. The Relative Economic Efficiency of Private versus Municipal Waterworks in the 1890s. **In** *Atack, J., ed.*, 1986, pp. 13–27. **[G: U.S.]**

Hensher, David A. Privatisation: An Interpretative Essay. *Australian Econ. Pap.*, December 1986, *25*(47), pp. 147–74. **[G: Global]**

Herzog, Philippe. Public Enterprises Should Promote Social Efficiency. **In** *Adams, W. J. and Stoffaës, C., eds.*, 1986, pp. 127–32. **[G: France]**

Hirsch, Mario. The Doldrums of Europe's TV Landscape: Coronet as Catalyst. **In** *Demac, D. A., ed.*, 1986, pp. 114–29.

Hussain, Irtiza. Role of Financial Institutions in the Financing of Public Enterprises. **In** *U.N., Dept. of Technical Co-operation for Development*, 1986, pp. 65–83. **[G: Pakistan]**

James, Jeffrey. Bureaucratic, Engineering and Economic Men: Decision-Making for Technology in Tanzania's State-Owned Enterprises. **In** *[Streeten, P.]*, 1986, pp. 217–39. **[G: Tanzania]**

Jones, Leroy. Towards Performance Evaluation: Methodology for Public Enterprises, with Particular Reference to Pakistan. **In** *U.N., Dept. of Technical Co-operation for Development*, 1986, pp. 116–38. **[G: Pakistan]**

Jones, Patricio. Mining Development and the Origin of Capital. *CEPAL Rev.*, December 1986, (30), pp. 163–72. **[G: Latin America]**

Kamal, Salih, et al. Young Workers and Urban Services in Penang. **In** *Yeung, Y. M. and McGee, T. G., eds.*, 1986, pp. 119–63. **[G: Malaysia]**

Karataş, Cevat. Public Economic Enterprises in Turkey: Reform Proposals, Pricing and Investment Policies. *METU*, 1986, *13*(1/2), pp. 135–69. **[G: Turkey]**

Kay, John A. and Thompson, David J. Privatisation: A Policy in Search of a Rationale. *Econ. J.*, March 1986, *96*(381), pp. 18–32. **[G: U.K.]**

Kazi, A. G. N. Economic Performance of Public Enterprises. **In** *U.N., Dept. of Technical Cooperation for Development*, 1986, pp. 26–36. **[G: Pakistan]**

Kirkpatrick, Colin. The World Bank's Views on State Owned Enterprises in Less Developed Countries: A Critical Comment. *Rivista Int. Sci. Econ. Com.*, June-July 1986, *33*(6–7), pp. 685–96. **[G: LDCs]**

Kňakal, Jan. The Role of the Public Sector and Transnational Corporations in the Mining Development of Latin America. *CEPAL Rev.*, December 1986, (30), pp. 143–62.

Knowlton, Winthrop and Zeckhauser, Richard. American Society: Public and Private Responsibilities: Overview. **In** *Knowlton, W. and Zeckhauser, R., eds.*, 1986, pp. 3–14. **[G: U.S.]**

Koneczny, Walter. Problems Relating to the Increasing Debt of Off-Budget Public Corporations. *Ann. Pub. Co-op. Econ.*, September 1986, *57*(3), pp. 359–72. **[G: Austria]**

Kornai, János. The Soft Budget Constraint. *Kyklos*, 1986, *39*(1), pp. 3–30. **[G: Hungary; Yugoslavia; China; U.S.]**

Laitinen, Erkki K. Financial Ratio Model of a Public Enterprise. *Liiketaloudellinen Aikak.*, 1986, *35*(4), pp. 313–32. **[G: Finland]**

Langohr, Herwig M. and Viallet, Claude J. Compensation and Wealth Transfers in the French Nationalizations: 1981–1982. *J. Finan. Econ.*, December 1986, *17*(2), pp. 273–312. **[G: France]**

Lawarree, Jacques. Une comparaison empirique des performances des secteurs privé et public: le cas des collectes d'immondices en Belgique. (With English summary.) *Cah. Écon. Bruxelles*, First Trimester 1986, (109), pp. 3–31. **[G: Belgium]**

Lizzo, Emilio. The Privatization of State Holdings in Italy up to 1984. *Ann. Pub. Co-op. Econ.*, September 1986, *57*(3), pp. 315–43. **[G: Italy]**

Mallon, Richard. Public Enterprise Pricing Policies. **In** *U.N., Dept. of Technical Co-operation for Development*, 1986, pp. 84–99.

Manasan, Rosario G. and Buenaventura, Corazon R. A Macroeconomic Overview of Public Enterprise in the Philippines, 1975–84. *Philippine Econ. J.*, 1986, *25*(1–2), pp. 24–50. **[G: Philippines]**

Maramba, Felix K., Jr. Privatization: Imperative for Sustained Economic Development. *Philippine Econ. J.*, 1986, *25*(1–2), pp. 17–23. **[G: Philippines]**

Marsan, Veniero Ajmone. Public Enterprise: Studies in Organisational Structure: Instituto per la Ricostruzione Industriale. **In** *Ramanadham, V. V., ed.*, 1986, pp. 83–113. **[G: Italy]**

Milne, R. S. Ethnic Aspects of Privatization in Malaysia. **In** *Nevitte, N. and Kennedy, C. H., eds.*, 1986, pp. 119–34. **[G: Malaysia]**

Moore, Chris and Booth, Simon. From Comprehensive Regeneration to Privatization: The Search for Effective Area Strategies. **In** *Lever, W. and Moore, C., eds.*, 1986, pp. 76–91. **[G: U.K.]**

Mufti, Abdul Majid. Experience of Public Enterprises in Pakistan, with Particular Reference to Manufacturing Industries. **In** *U.N., Dept. of Technical Co-operation for Development*, 1986, pp. 51–56. **[G: Pakistan]**

Mulley, Corinne and Wright, Mike. Buy-Outs and the Privatisation of National Bus. *Fisc. Stud.*, August 1986, *7*(3), pp. 1–24. **[G: U.K.]**

Navajas, Fernando H. Bonos, incentivos gerenciales, eficiencia y control en la empresa pública. (Bonds, Managerial Incentives, Efficiency and Control in the Public Enterprise. With English summary.) *Económica (La Plata)*, Jan.-June 1986, *32*(1), pp. 81–118.

Nawab, Syed Ali. Organizational Arrangements for Systematic Monitoring of Performance of Public Enterprises. **In** *U.N., Dept. of Technical Co-operation for Development*, 1986, pp. 139–48. **[G: Pakistan]**

Neumann, Karl-Heinz. Economic Policy toward Telecommunications, Information, and the Media in West Germany. **In** *Snow, M. S.*, 1986, pp. 131–52. **[G: W. Germany]**

Nove, Alec. The Poverty of Micro-economics: An Essay on the Relationship of Theory and Policy. **In** *Nove, A.*, 1986, *1982*, pp. 39–47.

Petretto, Alessandro. L'approccio econometrico per la misurazione dei risultati delle imprese pubbliche locali. (Performance of Local Public Enterprises: An Econometric Measurement. With English summary.) *Polit. Econ.*, August 1986, *2*(2), pp. 203–24.

Pieper, Ernst. Public Enterprise: Studies in Organisational Structure: Salzgitter AG. **In** *Ramanadham, V. V., ed.*, 1986, pp. 114–30. **[G: W. Germany]**

Platzer, Renate. The Privatisation Debate in Austria. *Ann. Pub. Co-op. Econ.*, Apr.-June 1986, *57*(2), pp. 275–91. **[G: Austria]**

Porter, Philip K.; Scully, Gerald W. and Slottje, Daniel J. Industrial Policy and the Nature of the Firm. *J. Inst. Theoretical Econ.*, March 1986, *142*(1), pp. 79–100. **[G: W. Europe]**

Price, C. M. Regional Price Discrimination in the United Kingdom Gas Industry. **In** *Norman, G., ed.*, 1986, pp. 165–85. **[G: U.K.]**

Qureshi, D. M. Financing of Investments of Public Enterprises in Developing Countries. **In** *U.N., Dept. of Technical Co-operation for Development*, 1986, pp. 57–64. **[G: Pakistan]**

Ramanadham, V. V. Public Enterprise: Studies in Organisational Structure: Concluding Review. **In** *Ramanadham, V. V., ed.*, 1986, pp. 261–81.

Ramanadham, V. V. The Organisational Structure of a Public Enterprise: An Analysis. **In** *Ramanadham, V. V., ed.*, 1986, pp. 1–20.

Roca, Sergio G. State Enterprises in Cuba under the New System of Planning and Management (SDPE). **In** *Mesa-Lago, C., ed.*, 1986, pp. 153–79. **[G: Cuba]**

Roseveare, R. W. Public Enterprise: Studies in Organisational Structure: British Steel Corporation. **In** *Ramanadham, V. V., ed.*, 1986, pp. 21–50. **[G: U.K.]**

de los Santos-Guina, Carolina T. Approaches to Performance Evaluation of Public Enterprises. *Philippine Econ. J.*, 1986, *25*(1–2), pp. 90–97. **[G: Philippines]**

Saulniers, Alfred H. Entrepreneurs in Public Enterprises. **In** *Greenfield, S. M. and Strickon, A., eds.*, 1986, pp. 158–65.

Schimberni, Mario. State-Owned and Private Enterprises in Italy. **In** *Barfield, C. E. and Schambra, W. A., eds.*, 1986, pp. 206–09. **[G: Italy]**

Schultz, Knud H. and Mattos, Jorge A. S. Fertilizer Pricing in Brazil. **In** *Segura, E. L.; Shetty, Y. T. and Nishimizu, M., eds.*, 1986, pp. 185–95. **[G: Brazil]**

Scott, Frank A., Jr. Assessing USA Postal Ratemaking: An Application of Ramsey Prices. *J. Ind. Econ.*, March 1986, *34*(3), pp. 279–90. **[G: U.S.]**

Shackleton, J. R. Privatising the Third World. *Banca Naz. Lavoro Quart. Rev.*, December 1986, (159), pp. 429–39. **[G: LDCs]**

Sikorsky, Douglas. Public Enterprise (PE): How Is It Different from the Private Sector: A Review of the Literature. *Ann. Pub. Co-op. Econ.*, Oct.-Dec. 1986, *57*(4), pp. 477–511. **[G: U.S.; U.K.]**

Stefani, Giorgio. Privatizing Public Enterprises in Italy: The Case of State Holdings. *Ann. Pub. Co-op. Econ.*, Apr.-June 1986, *57*(2), pp. 231–51.

Stoffaës, Christian. French Industrial Policy: Postscript. **In** *Adams, W. J. and Stoffaës, C., eds.*, 1986, pp. 198–210. **[G: France]**

Supple, Barry. Ideology or Pragmatism? The Nationalization of Coal, 1916–46. **In** *[Coleman, D. C.]*, 1986, pp. 228–50. **[G: U.K.]**

Swidler, Steve. A Reexamination of Liquor Price and Consumption Differences between Public and Private Ownership States: Comment [Public versus Private Liquor Retailing: An Investigation into the Behavior of the State Governments]. *Southern Econ. J.*, July 1986, *53*(1), pp. 259–64. **[G: U.S.]**

Swidler, Steve. Consumption and Price Effects of State-run Liquor Monopolies. *Managerial Dec. Econ.*, March 1986, *7*(1), pp. 49–55. **[G: U.S.]**

Thiemeyer, Theo. Privatization: On the Many Senses in Which This Word Is Used in an International Discussion on Economic Theory. *Ann. Pub. Co-op. Econ.*, Apr.-June 1986, *57*(2), pp. 141–52.

614 Public Enterprises

Trimble, William F. The Naval Aircraft Factory, the American Aviation Industry, and Government Competition, 1919–1928. *Bus. Hist. Rev.*, Summer 1986, *60*(2), pp. 175–98. **[G: U.S.]**

Trivedi, Prajapati. Explaining Public versus Private Partitioning of the Economy. *Indian Econ. J.*, Oct.-Dec. 1986, *34*(2), pp. 112–24.

Tulkens, Henry. La performance productive d'un service public. Définitions, méthodes de mesure et application à la Régie des Postes en Belgique. (The Productive Performance of a Public Service. With English summary.) *L'Actual. Econ.*, June 1986, *62*(2), pp. 306–35. **[G: Belgium]**

Tulkens, Henry. The Performance Approach in Public Enterprise Economics: An Introduction and an Example. *Ann. Pub. Co-op. Econ.*, Oct.-Dec. 1986, *57*(4), pp. 429–43. **[G: Belgium]**

Viloria, Enrique. Public Enterprise: Studies in Organisational Structure: Corporación Venezolana de Guayana. **In** *Ramanadham, V. V., ed.*, 1986, pp. 164–80. **[G: Venezuela]**

Virole, Jean L. Public Enterprise: Studies in Organisational Structure: Electricité de France. **In** *Ramanadham, V. V., ed.*, 1986, pp. 64–82. **[G: France]**

Voge, Jean-Paul. A Survey of French Regulatory Policy. **In** *Snow, M. S.*, 1986, pp. 106–30. **[G: France]**

Voszka, Éva. Company Liquidation without a Legal Successor. *Acta Oecon.*, 1986, *37*(1–2), pp. 59–71. **[G: Hungary]**

Wadehra, B. L. Public Enterprise: Studies in Organisational Structure: Coal India Limited. **In** *Ramanadham, V. V., ed.*, 1986, pp. 211–33. **[G: India]**

Walzer, Michael. Toward a Theory of Social Assignments. **In** *Knowlton, W. and Zeckhauser, R., eds.*, 1986, pp. 79–96. **[G: U.S.]**

Ware, Roger. A Model of Public Enterprise with Entry. *Can. J. Econ.*, November 1986, *19*(4), pp. 642–55.

Ware, Roger and Winter, Ralph A. Public Pricing under Imperfect Competition. *Int. J. Ind. Organ.*, March 1986, *4*(1), pp. 87–97.

Wasow, Bernard. Effects of Nationalization on the Insurance Industry in India. **In** *Wasow, B. and Hill, R. D., eds.*, 1986, pp. 228–40. **[G: India]**

Werneck, Rogério L. F. A questão do controle da necessidade de financiamento das empresas estatais e o orç amento de dispêndios globais da SEST. (With English summary.) *Pesquisa Planejamento Econ.*, August 1986, *16*(2), pp. 381–411. **[G: Brazil]**

Winward, John. Nationalised Industry Consumer Councils. **In** *Moores, B., ed.*, 1986, pp. 217–28. **[G: U.K.]**

Wohlmuth, Karl. Practices and Policies of Host Countries towards Third World Multinationals: A Competitive Edge against Old Multinationals? **In** *Khan, K. M., ed.*, 1986, pp. 211–39. **[G: LDCs]**

Yoder, Sunny G. Economic Theories of For-Profit and Not-for-Profit Organizations. **In** *Gray, B. H., ed.*, 1986, pp. 19–25.

Zardkoohi, Asghar and Sheer, Alain. A Reexamination of Liquor Price and Consumption Differences between Public and Private Ownership States: Reply [Public versus Private Liquor Retailing: An Investigation into the Behavior of the State Governments]. *Southern Econ. J.*, July 1986, *53*(1), pp. 265–68. **[G: U.S.]**

Zeckhauser, Richard. The Muddled Responsibilities of Public and Private America. **In** *Knowlton, W. and Zeckhauser, R., eds.*, 1986, pp. 45–77. **[G: U.S.]**

615 Economics of Transportation

6150 Economics of Transportation

Allen, Benjamin J. and Voorhees, Roy Dale. The Logistics of Rail-Barge Transportation Involving Non-Integrated Firms: A Purchasing Case Study. *Logist. Transp. Rev.*, March 1986, *22*(1), pp. 69–82. **[G: U.S.]**

Allen, W. Bruce. Ramsey Pricing in the Transportation Industries. *Int. J. Transport Econ.*, October 1986, *13*(3), pp. 293–330. **[G: U.S.]**

Asch, Peter. Automobile Safety: Is Government Regulation Really Our Savior? *Yale J. Regul.*, Spring 1986, *3*(2), pp. 383–89. **[G: U.S.]**

Baber, Colin. Canals and the Economic Development of South Wales. **In** *Baber, C. and Williams, L. J., eds.*, 1986, pp. 24–42. **[G: U.K.]**

Bailey, Elizabeth E. Price and Productivity Change Following Deregulation: The U.S. Experience. *Econ. J.*, March 1986, *96*(381), pp. 1–17. **[G: U.S.]**

Barone, S. S., et al. Deregulation in the Canadian Airline Industry: Is There Room for a Large Regional Airline? *Logist. Transp. Rev.*, December 1986, *22*(4), pp. 421–48. **[G: Canada]**

Batten, David F. and Boyce, David E. Spatial Interaction, Transportation, and Interregional Commodity Flow Models. **In** *Nijkamp, P., ed. (I)*, 1986, pp. 357–406.

Bauchet, Pierre. Un service singulier: le transport maritime français. (With English summary.) *Revue Écon. Polit.*, Sept.-Oct. 1986, *96*(5), pp. 503–12. **[G: France]**

Bayliss, Brian T. The Structure of the Road Haulage Industry in the United Kingdom, and Optimum Scale. *J. Transp. Econ. Policy*, May 1986, *20*(2), pp. 153–72. **[G: U.K.]**

Beesley, Michael E. Commitment, Sunk Costs, and Entry to the Airline Industry: Reflections on Experience. *J. Transp. Econ. Policy*, May 1986, *20*(2), pp. 173–90. **[G: U.K.]**

Beilock, Richard P.; Garrod, Peter V. and Miklius, Walter. Freight Charge Variations in Truck Transport Markets: Price Discrimination or Competitive Pricing? *Amer. J. Agr. Econ.*, May 1986, *68*(2), pp. 226–36. **[G: U.S.]**

Beilock, Richard P. and Kilmer, Richard L. The Determinants of Full–Empty Truck Movements. *Amer. J. Agr. Econ.*, February 1986, *68*(1), pp. 67–76. **[G: U.S.]**

Bell, Philip W. and Johnson, L. Todd. Current Value Accounting and the Simple Production Case: Edbejo and Other Companies in the Taxi Business. **In** *Parker, R. H.; Harcourt, G. C. and Whittington, G., eds.*, 1986, *1979*, pp. 278–313.

Berg, George L., Jr. Rural Roads and Bridges—Link to Agriculture. **In** *Chicoine, D. L. and Walzer, N., eds.*, 1986, pp. 167–83. **[G: U.S.]**

Bivens, W. E., III. Rural Highway Finance: State and Local Innovation. **In** *Chicoine, D. L. and Walzer, N., eds.*, 1986, pp. 199–217. **[G: U.S.]**

Blair, Roger D.; Kaserman, David L. and McClave, James T. Motor Carrier Deregulation: The Florida Experiment. *Rev. Econ. Statist.*, February 1986, *68*(1), pp. 159–64. **[G: U.S.]**

Blumestock, James W. and Thomchick, Evelyn A. Deregulation and Airline Labor Relations. *Logist. Transp. Rev.*, December 1986, *22*(4), pp. 389–403. **[G: U.S.]**

Bly, P. H. and Oldfield, R. H. Competition between Minibuses and Regular Bus Services. *J. Transp. Econ. Policy*, January 1986, *20*(1), pp. 47–68. **[G: U.K.]**

Bolyard, Joan E. International Travel and Passenger Fares, 1981–85. *Surv. Curr. Bus.*, May 1986, *66*(5), pp. 42–46. **[G: U.S.]**

Bonus, Holger. Obstacles to Changing the Incentive System: The Case of the Federal Republic of Germany. **In** *Balassa, B. and Giersch, H., eds.*, 1986, pp. 378–91. **[G: W. Germany]**

Boucher, Michel. L'inspiration américaine de la déréglementation en transport routier. (With English summary.) *Can. Public Policy*, March 1986, *12*(1), pp. 189–201. **[G: U.S.]**

Boyer, Kenneth D. What Do We Understand about the Economics of Regulation: The Effects of U.S. Transport Deregulation. **In** *de Jong, H. W. and Shepherd, W. G., eds., Bk. 2*, 1986, pp. 317–45. **[G: U.S.]**

Boyer, Marcel and Dionne, Georges. Le tarification de l'assurance automobile et les incitations à la sécurité routière: Une étude empirique. (The Tariffication of Car Insurances and the Incentives for Road Safety: An Empirical Investigation. With English summary.) *Schweiz. Z. Volkswirtsch. Statist.*, September 1986, *122*(3), pp. 293–321. **[G: Canada]**

Brown, Edwin L. "...to Make a Man Feel Good": John Henry Mealing, Railroad Caller. *Labor Hist.*, Spring 1986, *27*(2), pp. 257–64. **[G: U.S.]**

Bruce, Alistair. State-to-Private Sector Divestment: The Case of Sealink. **In** *Coyne, J. and Wright, M., eds.*, 1986, pp. 202–44. **[G: U.K.]**

Buchanan, B. J. The Evolution of the English Turnpike Trusts: Lessons from a Case Study. *Econ. Hist. Rev., 2nd Ser.*, May 1986, *39*(2), pp. 223–43. **[G: U.K.]**

Burfoot, Tim. Quality Control in Thomas Cook. **In** *Moores, B., ed.*, 1986, pp. 166–78. **[G: U.K.]**

Card, David. Efficient Contracts with Costly Adjustment: Short-run Employment Determination for Airline Mechanics. *Amer. Econ. Rev.*, December 1986, *76*(5), pp. 1045–71. **[G: U.S.]**

Card, David. The Impact of Deregulation on the Employment and Wages of Airline Mechanics. *Ind. Lab. Relat. Rev.*, July 1986, *39*(4), pp. 527–38. **[G: U.S.]**

Cassing, James H. A Wicksellian Model of International Freights and Prices. *Int. J. Transport Econ.*, February 1986, *13*(1), pp. 7–19.

Casson, Mark. The Role of Vertical Integration in the Shipping Industry. *J. Transp. Econ. Policy*, January 1986, *20*(1), pp. 7–29. **[G: U.K.]**

Casson, Mark; Barry, David and Horner, Dennis. The Shipping Industry. **In** *Casson, M., et al.*, 1986, pp. 343–71.

de Castro, Newton. Produçao, distribuiçao e consumo: determinantes da demanda derivada por transporte e energia. (With English summary.) *Pesquisa Planejamento Econ.*, December 1986, *16*(3), pp. 713–44. **[G: Brazil]**

Chalk, Andrew. Market Forces and Aircraft Safety: The Case of the DC-10. *Econ. Inquiry*, January 1986, *24*(1), pp. 43–60. **[G: U.S.]**

Chicoine, David L. and Walzer, Norman. Financing Local Infrastructure in Nonmetropolitan Areas: Introduction. **In** *Chicoine, D. L. and Walzer, N., eds.*, 1986, pp. 1–15. **[G: U.S.]**

Chicoine, David L. and Walzer, Norman. Financing Rural Roads in the Midwest. **In** *Chicoine, D. L. and Walzer, N., eds.*, 1986, pp. 33–51. **[G: U.S.]**

Colegate, Raymond. Airline De-regulation in the United States Eight Years On: Review Article. *World Econ.*, December 1986, *9*(4), pp. 441–44. **[G: U.S.]**

Cook, Charles D. From Bull Path to Boulevard. **In** *Chicoine, D. L. and Walzer, N., eds.*, 1986, pp. 77–92. **[G: U.S.]**

Courant, Paul N. Welfare Effects of Marginal-Cost Taxation of Motor Freight Transportation: A Study of Infrastructure Pricing: Comment. **In** *Rosen, H. S., ed.*, 1986, pp. 128–34. **[G: U.S.]**

Craig, Robin. Trade and Shipping in South Wales—The Radcliffe Company, 1882–1921. **In** *Baber, C. and Williams, L. J., eds.*, 1986, pp. 171–91. **[G: U.K.]**

Crum, Michael R. and Allen, Benjamin J. U.S. Transportation Merger Policy: Evolution, Current Status, and Antitrust Considerations. *Int. J. Transport Econ.*, February 1986, *13*(1), pp. 41–75. **[G: U.S.]**

Cupingood, Leonard A. and Wei, William W. S. Seasonal Adjustment of Time Series Using One-Sided Filters. *J. Bus. Econ. Statist.*, October 1986, *4*(4), pp. 473–84. **[G: U.S.]**

Curtin, William J. Airline Labor Relations under Deregulation. **In** *Dennis, B. D., ed.*, 1986, pp. 158–64. **[G: U.S.]**

D'Souza, Amita. A Model of Infrastructural Interlinkages for India. *Indian Econ. Rev.*, July-Dec. 1986, *21*(2), pp. 115–48. **[G: India]**

Dahl, Carol A. Gasoline Demand Survey. *Energy J.*, January 1986, 7(1), pp. 67–82. **[G: U.S.]**

Davies, John E. Competition, Contestability and the Liner Shipping Industry. *J. Transp. Econ. Policy*, September 1986, *20*(3), pp. 299–312. **[G: Canada]**

Davies, John E. Peak Load Pricing in Liner Shipping. A Reply. *Int. J. Transport Econ.*, June 1986, *13*(2), pp. 235–36.

Diederich, Helmut. Entwicklung und Stand der Verkehrsbetriebslehre. (With English summary.) *Z. Betriebswirtshaft*, January 1986, *56*(1), pp. 51–88.

Evans, Carolyn. Airline Performance as Rated by Frequent Passengers. **In** *Moores, B., ed.*, 1986, pp. 67–76. **[G: Selected Countries]**

Falvey, Rodney E. and Rogers, Alan J. Fuel Prices, Sales Taxes and Passenger Car Market Shares in New Zealand, 1963–1978. *Econ. Rec.*, March 1986, *62*(176), pp. 52–59. **[G: New Zealand]**

Falvey, Rodney E., et al. Fuel Economy Standards and Automobile Prices. *J. Transp. Econ. Policy*, January 1986, *20*(1), pp. 31–45. **[G: U.S.]**

Fishlow, Albert. Growth and Productivity Change in the Canadian Railway Sector, 1871–1926: Comment. **In** *Engerman, S. L. and Gallman, R. E., eds.*, 1986, pp. 812–16. **[G: Canada]**

Florescu, Gabriela. Aspects of Modelling Transportation through the Dynamic Transportation Problem. *Econ. Computat. Cybern. Stud. Res.*, 1986, *21*(4), pp. 55–57.

Flowerdew, A. D. J. Problems of Public Enterprises in the Transport Sector of Developing Countries. **In** *U.N., Dept. of Technical Co-operation for Development*, 1986, pp. 162–81. **[G: LDCs]**

Fong, Peter K. W. An Evaluative Analysis of the Electronic Road Pricing System in Hong Kong. *Hong Kong Econ. Pap.*, 1986, (17), pp. 75–90. **[G: Hong Kong]**

Forsyth, Peter J. Economic Problems of International Transport for the South Pacific Island Economies. **In** *Cole, R. V. and Parry, T. G., eds.*, 1986, pp. 176–207. **[G: S. Pacific]**

Forsyth, Peter J.; Hill, Rob D. and Trengove, Chris D. Measuring Airline Efficiency. *Fisc. Stud.*, February 1986, *7*(1), pp. 61–81. **[G: Global]**

Fowkes, Tony. The UK Department of Transport Value of Time Project. *Int. J. Transport Econ.*, June 1986, *13*(2), pp. 197–207. **[G: U.K.]**

Frankel, E. G. Economic and Commercial Implications of the U.S. Shipping Act of 1984. *Logist. Transp. Rev.*, June 1986, *22*(2), pp. 99–114. **[G: U.S.]**

Frankena, Mark W. and Pautler, Paul A. Taxicab Regulation: An Economic Analysis. **In** *Zerbe, R. O., Jr., ed.*, 1986, pp. 129–65. **[G: U.S.]**

Freeman, Michael. Atlas of Industrializing Britain 1780–1914: Transport. **In** *Langton, J. and Morris, R. J., eds.*, 1986, pp. 80–93. **[G: U.K.]**

Frey, N. Gail; Krolick, Reuben H. and Tontz, Jay L. The Impact of Motor Carrier Deregulation: California Intrastate Agricultural Products. *Logist. Transp. Rev.*, September 1986, *22*(3), pp. 259–76. **[G: U.S.]**

Frost, L. E. A Reinterpretation of Victoria's Railway Construction Boom of the 1880s. *Australian Econ. Hist. Rev.*, March 1986, *26*(1), pp. 40–55. **[G: Australia]**

Fuchs, Victor R. and Leveson, Irving. Motor Accident Mortality and Compulsory Inspection of Vehicles. **In** *Fuchs, V. R.*, 1986, *1967*, pp. 169–80. **[G: U.S.]**

Fukan, Vladimír. Tasks of Progressive Conveyance Systems in the Transportation System of the State. *Czech. Econ. Digest.*, January 1986, (1), pp. 22–32. **[G: Czechoslovakia]**

Gambaccini, Louis J. Public Enterprise: Studies in Organisational Structure: The Port Authority of New York and New Jersey. **In** *Ramanadham, V. V., ed.*, 1986, pp. 131–63. **[G: U.S.]**

Gander, James P. Highway Speed and Uncertainty of Enforcement: The Traveling Salesman (or Trucker) Case. *Logist. Transp. Rev.*, March 1986, *22*(1), pp. 43–55. **[G: U.S.]**

Gardiner, J. Paul. Design Trajectories for Airplanes and Automobiles during the Past Fifty Years. **In** *Freeman, C., ed.*, 1986, pp. 121–42. **[G: OECD]**

Gardiner, J. Paul. Robust and Lean Designs with State-of-the-Art Automotive and Aircraft Examples. **In** *Freeman, C., ed.*, 1986, pp. 143–68. **[G: U.S.; W. Europe; Canada]**

Gathon, Henry-Jean. La mesure des gains de productivite globale dans les chemins de fer. Une comparaison internationale. (The Measurement of Global Productivity Gains in Railroads: An International Comparisons. With English summary.) *Ann. Pub. Co-op. Econ.*, Oct.-Dec. 1986, *57*(4), pp. 459–76. **[G: W. Europe; Japan]**

Giblin, Daniel. Customer Care in British Rail. **In** *Moores, B., ed.*, 1986, pp. 57–66. **[G: U.K.]**

Gil, Avishai. Some Labour Implications of Technological Change in Rail and Air Transport. *Int. Lab. Rev.*, Jan.-Feb. 1986, *125*(1), pp. 1–17. **[G: France; U.K.; Netherlands; W. Germany]**

Golbe, Devra L. Safety and Profits in the Airline Industry. *J. Ind. Econ.*, March 1986, *34*(3), pp. 305–18. **[G: U.S.]**

Goss, R. O. Peak Load Pricing in Liner Shipping. A Comment. *Int. J. Transport Econ.*, June 1986, *13*(2), pp. 221–34.

Graham, John D. and Lee, Younghee. Behavioral Response to Safety Regulation: The Case of Motorcycle Helmet-Wearing Legislation. *Policy Sci.*, October 1986, *19*(3), pp. 253–73. **[G: U.S.]**

Green, Alan G. Growth and Productivity Change in the Canadian Railway Sector, 1871–1926. **In** *Engerman, S. L. and Gallman, R. E., eds.*, 1986, pp. 779–812. **[G: Canada]**

Green, Trellis G. Specification Considerations for the Price Variable in Travel Cost Demand Models: Comment. *Land Econ.*, November 1986, *62*(4), pp. 416–18.

Greene, David L. The Market Share of Diesel

Cars in the USA, 1979–83. *Energy Econ.*, January 1986, *8*(1), pp. 13–21. **[G: U.S.]**

Grimm, Curtis M. Excess Branch Line Capacity in the U.S. Railroad Industry: A Simulation Model Approach. *Logist. Transp. Rev.*, September 1986, *22*(3), pp. 223–40. **[G: U.S.]**

Grimm, Curtis M. and Smith, Ken G. The Impact of Rail Regulatory Reform on Rates, Service Quality, and Management Performance: A Shipper Perspective. *Logist. Transp. Rev.*, March 1986, *22*(1), pp. 57–68. **[G: U.S.]**

Guria, Jagadish C. Traffic Flow Control for Backward Bending Cost Curves. *Int. J. Transport Econ.*, October 1986, *13*(3), pp. 331–50.

Hamill, Brian and Davies, Roger. Quality in British Airways. **In** *Moores, B., ed.*, 1986, pp. 77–87. **[G: U.K.]**

Hamlett, Cathy A.; Pautsch, Gregory R. and Baumel, C. Phillip. County Traffic Patterns and Prospects for Change. **In** *Chicoine, D. L. and Walzer, N., eds.*, 1986, pp. 93–108. **[G: U.S.]**

Haralambides, Hercules E. Estimation of Laid-Up Tonnage in Competitive Shipping Markets. *Logist. Transp. Rev.*, June 1986, *22*(2), pp. 184–92. **[G: Greece]**

Haralambides, Hercules E. Investment in Shipping and the Balance of Payments Short-run Equilibrium Freight Rate. *Int. J. Transport Econ.*, October 1986, *13*(3), pp. 351–57.

Harvey, A. C. and Durbin, J. The Effects of Seat Belt Legislation on British Road Casualties: A Case Study in Structural Time Series Modelling. *J. Roy. Statist. Soc.*, 1986, *149*(3), pp. 187–210. **[G: U.S.]**

Hauser, Robert J. Competitive Forces in the U.S. Inland Grain Transport Industry: A Regional Perspective. *Logist. Transp. Rev.*, June 1986, *22*(2), pp. 158–83. **[G: U.S.]**

Hayashi, Yoshitsugu; Isobe, Tomohiko and Tomita, Yasuo. Modelling the Long-term Effects of Transport and Land Use Policies on Industrial Locational Behaviour: A Discrete Choice Model System. *Reg. Sci. Urban Econ.*, February 1986, *16*(1), pp. 123–43. **[G: Japan]**

Hendricks, Wallace. Collective Bargaining in Regulated Industries. **In** *Lipsky, D. B. and Lewin, D., eds.*, 1986, pp. 21–42. **[G: U.S.]**

Henriet, Dominique and Rochet, Jean-Charles. La logique des systèmes bonus-malus en assurance automobile: une approche théorique. (The Logic of the System of Bonuses and Penalties in Automobile Insurance: A Theoretical Approach. With English summary.) *Ann. Écon. Statist.*, Jan./Mar. 1986, (1), pp. 133–52. **[G: France]**

Hill, Daniel Henry. Dynamics of Household Driving Demand. *Rev. Econ. Statist.*, February 1986, *68*(1), pp. 132–41. **[G: U.S.]**

Ho, Lok-Sang. On Electronic Road Pricing and Traffic Management in Hong Kong. *Hong Kong Econ. Pap.*, 1986, (17), pp. 64–74. **[G: Hong Kong]**

Hochmuth, Milton S. The European Aerospace Industry. **In** *Macharzina, K. and Staehle, W. H., eds.*, 1986, pp. 205–25. **[G: U.S.; U.K.; France; W. Germany]**

Hughes, David E. The Prahu and Unrecorded Inter-island Trade. *Bull. Indonesian Econ. Stud.*, August 1986, *22*(2), pp. 103–13. **[G: Indonesia]**

Jacobs, David and Fuller, Michael. The Social Construction of Drunken Driving: Modeling the Organizational Processing of DWI Defendants. *Soc. Sci. Quart.*, December 1986, *67*(4), pp. 785–802. **[G: U.S.]**

Jaffer, Susan M. and Thompson, David J. Deregulating Express Coaches: A Reassessment. *Fisc. Stud.*, November 1986, *7*(4), pp. 45–68. **[G: U.K.]**

Jansson, J. O. and Shneerson, D. The Effect of Capacity Costs and Demand Elasticities on the Structure of Liner Freight Rates. *Logist. Transp. Rev.*, March 1986, *22*(1), pp. 3–25. **[G: Global]**

Jara-Díaz, Sergio R. On the Relation between Users' Benefits and the Economic Effects of Transportation Activities. *J. Reg. Sci.*, May 1986, *26*(2), pp. 379–91.

Jordan, William A. Results of U.S. Airline Deregulation: Evidence from the Regulated Canadian Airlines. *Logist. Transp. Rev.*, December 1986, *22*(4), pp. 297–337. **[G: Canada; U.S.]**

Joy, Stewart. Contestable Market Analysis in the Australian Domestic Airline Industry. *J. Transp. Econ. Policy*, May 1986, *20*(2), pp. 245–54. **[G: Australia]**

Kahn, James A. Gasoline Prices and the Used Automobile Market: A Rational Expectations Asset Price Approach. *Quart. J. Econ.*, May 1986, *101*(2), pp. 323–39. **[G: U.S.]**

Kaplan, Daniel P. The Changing Airline Industry. **In** *Weiss, L. W. and Klass, M. W., eds.*, 1986, pp. 40–77. **[G: U.S.]**

Katz, Harry C. Management Approaches to Collective Bargaining: The Dynamics of Change in the U.S.: Discussion. **In** *Dennis, B. D., ed.*, 1986, pp. 179–80. **[G: U.S.]**

Keasey, K. and Mulley, Corinne. Deregulation and Privatisation of Local Buses in the United Kingdom. *Int. J. Transport Econ.*, June 1986, *13*(2), pp. 153–75. **[G: U.K.]**

Keeler, Theodore E. Public Policy and Productivity in the Trucking Industry: Some Evidence on the Effects of Highway Investments, Deregulation, and the 55 MPH Speed Limit. *Amer. Econ. Rev.*, May 1986, *76*(2), pp. 153–58. **[G: U.S.]**

Kenwood, A. G. Fixed Capital Formation in the Ports of the South Wales Coalfield, 1850–1913. **In** *Baber, C. and Williams, L. J., eds.*, 1986, pp. 117–27. **[G: U.K.]**

Kim, Moshe and Sachish, Arie. The Structure of Production, Technical Change and Productivity in a Port. *J. Ind. Econ.*, December 1986, *35*(2), pp. 209–23.

Kirby, Michael G. Airline Economics of "Scale" and Australian Domestic Air Transport Policy. *J. Transp. Econ. Policy*, September 1986, *20*(3), pp. 339–52. **[G: Australia]**

Kolsen, H. M. Transport Policy in Australia: The

Role of the Inter-state Commission. *J. Transp. Econ. Policy,* May 1986, *20*(2), pp. 275–82. **[G: Australia]**

Koo, Won W. and Uhm, Ihn H. A Spatial Equilibrium Analysis of U.S. Wheat Exports under Alternative Transport Costs and Trade Restrictions. *Logist. Transp. Rev.,* March 1986, *22*(1), pp. 27–41. **[G: OECD]**

Koshal, Rajindar K.; Koshal, Manjulika and Nandola, Kahandas. Effects of High Energy Prices on Traffic: Some Indian Experience. *Int. J. Transport Econ.,* October 1986, *13*(3), pp. 359–68. **[G: India]**

Kraft, Dennis J. H.; Oum, Tae H. and Tretheway, Michael W. Airline Seat Management. *Logist. Transp. Rev.,* June 1986, *22*(2), pp. 115–30.

Larsen, Melvin B. Rural Transportation: A Look at the Future. **In** *Chicoine, D. L. and Walzer, N., eds.,* 1986, pp. 219–33. **[G: U.S.]**

Leontief, Wassily. The Growth of Maritime Traffic and the Future of World Ports. **In** *Leontief, W.,* 1986, *1979,* pp. 379–91. **[G: Global]**

Lewchuk, W. The Motor Vehicle Industry. **In** *Elbaum, B. and Lazonick, W., eds.,* 1986, pp. 135–61. **[G: U.K.; U.S.]**

Lewis, Barbara and Owtram, Mike. Customer Satisfaction with Package Holidays. **In** *Moores, B., ed.,* 1986, pp. 201–13.

Livingstone, Ian. International Transport Costs and Industrial Development in the Least Developed African Countries. *Industry Devel.,* 1986, (19), pp. 1–54. **[G: Africa]**

Lorenz, Edward and Wilkinson, Frank. The Shipbuilding Industry 1880–1965. **In** *Elbaum, B. and Lazonick, W., eds.,* 1986, pp. 109–34. **[G: U.K.; OECD]**

Luhr, David R. Economics of Pavement Strategies for Rural Roads. **In** *Chicoine, D. L. and Walzer, N., eds.,* 1986, pp. 109–25.

Mackie, Peter J. and Simon, David. Do Road Projects Benefit Industry? A Case Study of the Humber Bridge. *J. Transp. Econ. Policy,* September 1986, *20*(3), pp. 377–84. **[G: U.K.]**

Maillet, Pierre. Obstacles to Changing the Incentive System: The Case of the Federal Republic of Germany: Comment. **In** *Balassa, B. and Giersch, H., eds.,* 1986, pp. 392–95. **[G: W. Germany]**

Marston, Geoffrey. The UN Convention on Registration of Ships. *J. World Trade Law,* Sept.-Oct. 1986, *20*(5), pp. 575–80. **[G: Global]**

Mason, Charles F. Cherries, Lemons, and the FTC, Revisited [The Market for 'Lemons'] [Cherries, Lemons, and the FTC: Minimum Quality Standards in the Retail Used Automobile Industry]. *Econ. Inquiry,* April 1986, *24*(2), pp. 363–65. **[G: U.S.]**

McCarthy, Patrick S. Shared Fleet Arrangements: Implications for Vehicle Demand Using a Simultaneous Equations Approach. *Int. J. Transport Econ.,* February 1986, *13*(1), pp. 87–103. **[G: U.S.]**

McFarland, Henry. Ramsey Pricing of Inputs with Downstream Monopoly Power and Regulation: Implications for Railroad Rate Setting. *J. Transp. Econ. Policy,* January 1986, *20*(1), pp. 81–90. **[G: U.S.]**

Menashe, Eliahu and Guttman, Joel M. Uncertainty, Continuous Modal Split, and the Value of Travel Time in Israel. *J. Transp. Econ. Policy,* September 1986, *20*(3), pp. 369–75. **[G: Israel]**

Menda, Jean-Luc. La spécialisation internationale de la France dans les échanges de services. (With English summary.) *Revue Écon. Polit.,* Sept.-Oct. 1986, *96*(5), pp. 527–40. **[G: France]**

Meyer, David L. A Standard for Tailoring Noerr–Pennington Immunity More Closely to the First Amendment Mandate. *Yale Law J.,* March 1986, *95*(4), pp. 832–56. **[G: U.S.]**

Moore, Thomas Gale. Rail and Trucking Deregulation. **In** *Weiss, L. W. and Klass, M. W., eds.,* 1986, pp. 14–39. **[G: U.S.]**

Moore, Thomas Gale. U.S. Airline Deregulation: Its Effects on Passengers, Capital, and Labor. *J. Law Econ.,* April 1986, *29*(1), pp. 1–28. **[G: U.S.]**

Mulley, Corinne and Wright, Mike. Buy-Outs and the Privatisation of National Bus. *Fisc. Stud.,* August 1986, *7*(3), pp. 1–24. **[G: U.K.]**

Naniopoulos, A. and Papaioannou, P. Evaluation of Bridging the Rion–Antirrion Crossing in Greece with Special Emphasis on the Application of the Concept of Community Interest. *Int. J. Transport Econ.,* October 1986, *13*(3), pp. 369–93. **[G: Greece]**

O'Neil, Brian F. Information—A Viable Substitute for Inventory. *Logist. Transp. Rev.,* March 1986, *22*(1), pp. 83–89.

Ohta, Makoto and Griliches, Zvi. Automobile Prices and Quality: Did the Gasoline Price Increases Change Consumer Tastes in the U.S.? *J. Bus. Econ. Statist.,* April 1986, *4*(2), pp. 187–98. **[G: U.S.]**

Olson, Dennis O. A Benefit–Cost Analysis of Improving Alaska's Dalton Highway. *Logist. Transp. Rev.,* June 1986, *22*(2), pp. 141–57. **[G: U.S.]**

Oreshin, V. Problems of Method in Planning the Production Infrastructure. *Prob. Econ.,* July 1986, *29*(3), pp. 81–93. **[G: U.S.S.R.]**

Oster, Clinton V., Jr. and Pickrell, Don H. Marketing Alliances and Competitive Strategy in the Airline Industry. *Logist. Transp. Rev.,* December 1986, *22*(4), pp. 371–87. **[G: U.S.]**

Otsuka, Keijiro; Kikuchi, Masao and Hayami, Yujiro. Community and Market in Contract Choice: The Jeepney in the Philippines. *Econ. Develop. Cult. Change,* January 1986, *34*(2), pp. 279–98. **[G: Philippines]**

Oum, Tae H.; Gillen, David W. and Noble, S. E. Demands for Fareclasses and Pricing in Airline Markets. *Logist. Transp. Rev.,* September 1986, *22*(3), pp. 195–222. **[G: U.S.]**

Parbhakar, K. J. Fuel Consumption for Road Transport in Quebec. *Energy Econ.,* July 1986, *8*(3), pp. 165–70. **[G: Canada]**

Peck, Merton J. Deregulation in the American

Economy. *Kobe Univ. Econ.*, 1986, (32), pp. 1–17. **[G: U.S.]**

Pelkmans, Jacques. Deregulation of European Air Transport. **In** *de Jong, H. W. and Shepherd, W. G., eds., Bk. 2,* 1986, pp. 347–85. **[G: EEC; U.S.]**

Perelman, Sergio. Frontiers d'efficacite et performance technique des chemins de fer. (Efficiency and Technical Performance Frontiers in Railroads. With English summary.) *Ann. Pub. Co-op. Econ.*, Oct.-Dec. 1986, *57*(4), pp. 445–58. **[G: W. Europe; Japan]**

Peterson, George E. Urban Road Reinvestment: The Effects of External Aid. *Amer. Econ. Rev.*, May 1986, *76*(2), pp. 159–64. **[G: U.S.]**

Phillips, Laurence T. The Railroad Industry: The Road to Recovery. *Bus. Econ.*, April 1986, *21*(2), pp. 52–56. **[G: U.S.]**

Pogue, Thomas F. Minnesota Highway User Taxes: Issues and Alternatives. **In** *Minnesota Tax Study Commission,* 1986, pp. 189–205. **[G: U.S.]**

Pratt, Michael D. and Hoffer, George E. The Efficacy of State Mandated Minimum Quality Certification: The Case of Used Vehicles. *Econ. Inquiry*, April 1986, *24*(2), pp. 313–18. **[G: U.S.]**

Pustay, Michael W. Pre-Reform Entry into the Interstate Motor Carrier Industry: An Appraisal. *J. Transp. Econ. Policy*, January 1986, *20*(1), pp. 69–80. **[G: U.S.]**

Rainer, Norbert. The Set of Trade and Transport Margin Matrices in the Austrian IO-System. **In** *Franz, A. and Rainer, N., eds.*, 1986, pp. 47–67. **[G: Austria]**

Rhodes, George F., Jr. and Westbrook, M. Daniel. Econometric Analysis of Costing System Components in Rail Rate Regulation. *J. Bus. Econ. Statist.*, July 1986, *4*(3), pp. 289–303. **[G: U.S.]**

Richardson, David H. The St. Lawrence Seaway and Power Project: An *Ex Post* Evaluation. *Public Finance*, 1986, *41*(1), pp. 8–41. **[G: U.S.; Canada]**

Sargious, Michel and Tam, Timmy. Potential Energy Savings in the Movement of Finished Products in Canada. *Logist. Transp. Rev.*, September 1986, *22*(3), pp. 277–88. **[G: Canada]**

Schmitt, Robert P. State and Federal Management Assistance. **In** *Chicoine, D. L. and Walzer, N., eds.*, 1986, pp. 127–41. **[G: U.S.]**

Scholer, Charles. Cost-Saving Techniques. **In** *Chicoine, D. L. and Walzer, N., eds.*, 1986, pp. 185–97. **[G: U.S.]**

Senauer, Benjamin; Kinsey, Jean and Roe, Terry. Imperfect Mileage Information and Changing Utility: A Model and Survey Results. *J. Cons. Aff.*, Winter 1986, *20*(2), pp. 155–72. **[G: U.S.]**

Sharp, Clifford; Button, Kenneth J. and Deadman, Derek. The Economics of Tolled Road Crossings. *J. Transp. Econ. Policy*, May 1986, *20*(2), pp. 255–74. **[G: U.S.; U.K.]**

Sickles, Robin C.; Good, David H. and Johnson, Richard L. Allocative Distortions and the Regulatory Transition of the U.S. Airline Industry. *J. Econometrics*, Oct./Nov. 1986, *33*(1/2), pp. 143–63. **[G: U.S.]**

Singell, Larry D. and Lillydahl, Jane H. An Empirical Analysis of the Commute to Work Patterns of Males and Females in Two-Earner Households. *Urban Stud.*, April 1986, *23*(2), pp. 119–29. **[G: U.S.]**

Sinha, Dipendra. The Theory of Contestable Markets and U.S. Airline Deregulation: A Survey. *Logist. Transp. Rev.*, December 1986, *22*(4), pp. 405–19. **[G: U.S.]**

Slater, Paul B. International Migration and Air Travel: Global Smoothing and Estimation. **In** *Slater, P. B.*, 1986, pp. 107–24. **[G: Selected Countries]**

Small, Kenneth A. and Winston, Clifford. Efficient Pricing and Investment Solutions to Highway Infrastructure Needs. *Amer. Econ. Rev.*, May 1986, *76*(2), pp. 165–69. **[G: U.S.]**

Small, Kenneth A. and Winston, Clifford. Welfare Effects of Marginal-Cost Taxation of Motor Freight Transportation: A Study of Infrastructure Pricing. **In** *Rosen, H. S., ed.*, 1986, pp. 113–28. **[G: U.S.]**

Srinivasan, R. Supply and Demand Model for Short-haul Air Services in India. *J. Quant. Econ.*, January 1986, *2*(1), pp. 93–110. **[G: India]**

Stanbury, W. T. and Tretheway, Michael W. Airline Deregulation: A Bibliography. *Logist. Transp. Rev.*, December 1986, *22*(4), pp. 449–89. **[G: U.S.; Canada]**

Starkie, David N. M. and Thompson, David J. Stansted: A Viable Investment? *Fisc. Stud.*, August 1986, *7*(3), pp. 76–82. **[G: U.K.]**

Studnicki-Gizbert, Konrad W. The Changing Nature of Transport Policy and Planning. *Int. J. Transport Econ.*, October 1986, *13*(3), pp. 263–91. **[G: LDCs]**

Takacs, Wendy E. and Tanzer, Ellen P. Structural Change in the Demand for Automobiles by Size Class. *Quart. Rev. Econ. Bus.*, Autumn 1986, *26*(3), pp. 48–57. **[G: U.S.]**

Talley, Wayne K. A Short-run Cost Analysis of Ocean Containerships. *Logist. Transp. Rev.*, June 1986, *22*(2), pp. 131–39. **[G: U.S.]**

Talley, Wayne K.; Agarwal, Vinod B. and Breakfield, James W. Economies of Density of Ocean Tanker Ships. *J. Transp. Econ. Policy*, January 1986, *20*(1), pp. 91–99.

Tarpgaard, Peter T. U.S. Shipping Subsidies and Ocean Shipping of Petroleum: Policy Choices. *Contemp. Policy Issues*, October 1986, *4*(4), pp. 79–92. **[G: U.S.]**

Taylor, Tom. Capital Formation by Railways in South Wales, 1836–1914. **In** *Baber, C. and Williams, L. J., eds.*, 1986, pp. 97–116. **[G: U.K.]**

TenEyck, Thomas E. and Lebo, Dennis E. Pennsylvania's Agricultural Access Study. **In** *Chicoine, D. L. and Walzer, N., eds.*, 1986, pp. 159–66. **[G: U.S.]**

Tolofari, Sonny R.; Button, Kenneth J. and Pitfield, David E. Shipping Costs and the Controversy over Open Registry. *J. Ind. Econ.*, June

1986, *34*(4), pp. 409–27.

Tretheway, Michael W. Airline Deregulation: Introduction. *Logist. Transp. Rev.*, December 1986, *22*(4), pp. 293–96. **[G: U.S.]**

Tullock, Gordon. The Case of Dutch Inland Shipping: Comment. *Int. Rev. Law Econ.*, June 1986, *6*(1), pp. 139–40. **[G: Netherlands]**

Tye, William B. Stand-Alone Costs as an Indicator of Market Dominance and Rate Reasonableness under the Staggers Rail Act. *Int. J. Transport Econ.*, February 1986, *13*(1), pp. 21–40. **[G: U.S.]**

Vellenga, David B. and Vellenga, Daniel R. Essential Airline Service since Deregulation: Selected States in the Northwestern and Southwestern U.S. *Logist. Transp. Rev.*, December 1986, *22*(4), pp. 339–70. **[G: U.S.]**

Verbeke, A. and Winkelmans, W. The Illusion of Belgian Sea Port Policy Evaluation of Structural Effectiveness and Development of a Policy Alternative. *Int. J. Transport Econ.*, June 1986, *13*(2), pp. 209–20. **[G: Belgium]**

Ville, Simon. Total Factor Productivity in the English Shipping Industry: The North-east Coal Trade, 1700–1850. *Econ. Hist. Rev., 2nd Ser.*, August 1986, *39*(3), pp. 355–70. **[G: U.K.]**

Viscencio-Brambilla, Hector and Fuller, Stephen. Effects of Port User Fees on Export Grain Flow Patterns. *Southern J. Agr. Econ.*, December 1986, *18*(2), pp. 25–37. **[G: U.S.]**

Voss, Paul R. Demographics and Rural Roads. **In** *Chicoine, D. L. and Walzer, N., eds.*, 1986, pp. 53–76. **[G: U.S.]**

Ward, Frank A. Specification Considerations for the Price Variable in Travel Cost Demand Models: Reply. *Land Econ.*, November 1986, *62*(4), pp. 419–21.

Williamson, Kenneth C.; Bloomberg, David J. and Peterson, Roger A. Commuter Air Carriers and Federal Equipment Loan Guarantees. *Logist. Transp. Rev.*, September 1986, *22*(3), pp. 241–58. **[G: U.S.]**

Wittman, Donald. The Price of Negligence under Differing Liability Rules. *J. Law Econ.*, April 1986, *29*(1), pp. 151–63. **[G: U.S.]**

Zador, Paul and Lund, Adrian. Re-Analyses of the Effects of No-Fault Auto Insurance on Fatal Crashes. *J. Risk Ins.*, June 1986, *53*(2), pp. 226–41.

616 Industrial Policy

6160 Industrial Policy

Adams, Walter and Martin, Stephen. Public Support of Innovative Activity: Lessons from U.S. Industrial Policy. **In** *de Jong, H. W. and Shepherd, W. G., eds., Bk. 2*, 1986, pp. 413–39. **[G: U.S.]**

Adams, William James. French Industrial Policy: Introduction. **In** *Adams, W. J. and Stoffaës, C., eds.*, 1986, pp. 3–9. **[G: U.S.; France]**

Adler, Emanuel. Ideological "Guerrillas" and the Quest for Technological Autonomy: Brazil's Domestic Computer Industry. *Int. Organ.*, Summer 1986, *40*(3), pp. 673–705. **[G: Brazil]**

Ahlbrandt, Roger S., Jr. State-Sponsored Partnership: Building a Hi-tech Center for Western Pennsylvania. **In** *Gondolf, E. W.; Marcus, I. M. and Dougherty, J. P., eds.*, 1986, pp. 172–82. **[G: U.S.]**

Amsden, Alice H. and Kim, Linsu. A Technological Perspective on the General Machinery Industry in the Republic of Korea. **In** *Fransman, M., ed.*, 1986, pp. 93–123. **[G: S. Korea]**

Androuais, Anne. Spatialisation du système productif japonais. (Spacialisation of the Japanese Productive System. With English summary.) *Écon. Soc.*, May 1986, *20*(5), pp. 125–53. **[G: Japan; ASEAN]**

Ariki, Soichiro. Post-War Industrial Policy in Japan. *Rivista Int. Sci. Econ. Com.*, May 1986, *33*(5), pp. 425–45. **[G: Japan]**

Armstrong, H. The Assignment of Regional Industrial Policy Powers. *Reg. Stud.*, June 1986, *20*(3), pp. 258–61. **[G: U.K.]**

Aron, Paul H. Industrial Policy in Japan: Implications for Technological Catch-up and Leadership: Comment. **In** *Pugel, T. A., ed.*, 1986, pp. 233–35. **[G: U.S.; Japan]**

Aujac, Henri. An Introduction to French Industrial Policy. **In** *Adams, W. J. and Stoffaës, C., eds.*, 1986, pp. 13–35. **[G: France]**

Bade, Franz-Josef. The De-industrialisation of the Federal Republic of Germany and Its Spatial Implications. **In** *Nijkamp, P., ed. (II)*, 1986, pp. 196–220. **[G: W. Germany; OECD]**

Baden, John; Blood, Tom and Stroup, Richard L. America's Version of the Melanesian Cargo Cults: The New Industrial Policy. **In** *Lee, D. R., ed.*, 1986, pp. 437–58. **[G: U.S.]**

Baer, Werner. Brazil: Diversifying Exports. **In** *Preeg, E. H. and Bendahmane, D. B., eds.*, 1986, pp. 101–07. **[G: Brazil]**

Balassa, Bela. Selective versus General Economic Policy in Postwar France. **In** *Adams, W. J. and Stoffaës, C., eds.*, 1986, pp. 97–102. **[G: France]**

Barnett, Richard R. A Perspective on De-industrialization. *Nat. Westminster Bank Quart. Rev.*, August 1986, pp. 13–20. **[G: U.K.]**

Bartlett, Bruce. Supply-Side Economics, Industrial Policy, and Rational Ignorance: Comment. **In** *Barfield, C. E. and Schambra, W. A., eds.*, 1986, pp. 272–74.

Behrens, Peter. Industrial Policy and the Nature of the Firm: Comment. *J. Inst. Theoretical Econ.*, March 1986, *142*(1), pp. 109–13.

Bennett, John. Korea: Maintaining Steady Growth. **In** *Preeg, E. H. and Bendahmane, D. B., eds.*, 1986, pp. 95–99. **[G: S. Korea]**

Benson, Bruce L. and Johnson, Ronald N. Capital Formation and Interstate Tax Competition. **In** *Lee, D. R., ed.*, 1986, pp. 407–36. **[G: U.S.]**

Best, Michael H. Strategic Planning, the New Competition and Industrial Policy. **In** *Nolan, P. and Paine, S., eds.*, 1986, pp. 182–97. **[G: U.K.]**

Bilger, François. Frankreich vor der ordnungspolitischen Wende? Die wirtschaftspolitischen Wahlprogramme der französischen Parteien. (France at the Economic Turning Point?

Economic Policy in the Election Platforms of the French Political Parties. With English summary.) **In** *Eucken, W. and Böhm, F., eds.*, 1986, pp. 3–43. **[G: France]**

Black, Andrew P. Industrial Policy in W. Germany. Policy in Search of a Goal? **In** *Hall, G., ed.*, 1986, pp. 84–127. **[G: W. Germany]**

Black, Michael and Worthington, Richard. The Center for Industrial Innovation at RPI: Critical Reflections on New York's Economic Recovery. **In** *Schoolman, M. and Magid, A., eds.*, 1986, pp. 257–80. **[G: U.S.]**

Blackhurst, Richard. GATT Surveillance of Industrial Policies. *Aussenwirtschaft*, September 1986, *41*(2/3), pp. 361–78. **[G: OECD]**

Blackhurst, Richard. GATT Surveillance of Industrial Policies. **In** *Hauser, H., ed. (II)*, 1986, pp. 199–216. **[G: OECD]**

Blumenthal, Sidney. Supply-Side Economics, Industrial Policy, and Rational Ignorance: Comment. **In** *Barfield, C. E. and Schambra, W. A., eds.*, 1986, pp. 270–72.

Bochkareva, V. K.; Bredikhin, N. P. and Kabanova, T. A. Optimizing the Development and Location of a Group of Interdependent Industries (A Case Study of the Chemical and Petrochemical Industries). *Matekon*, Winter 1986-87, *23*(2), pp. 57–73. **[G: U.S.S.R.]**

Boisot, Max. Industrial Policy and Industrial Culture: The Case of European Petrochemical. **In** *Macharzina, K. and Staehle, W. H., eds.*, 1986, pp. 163–84. **[G: W. Europe]**

Borrus, Michael and Zysman, John. National Policies for Developing High Technology Industries: International Comparisons: Japan. **In** *Rushing, F. W. and Brown, C. G., eds.*, 1986, pp. 111–42. **[G: Japan]**

Botos, Balázs. Changes in the Structure of Hungarian Industrial Foreign Trade: Review Article. *Acta Oecon.*, 1986, *37*(1–2), pp. 129–42. **[G: Hungary]**

Bradford, Calvin and Temali, Mihailo. City Venture Corporation: Initiatives in U.S. Cities. **In** *Bergman, E. M., ed.*, 1986, *1983*, pp. 185–204. **[G: U.S.]**

Braendgaard, Asger. Danish Industrial Policy: Liberalism Revised or Revisited. **In** *Hall, G., ed.*, 1986, pp. 165–82. **[G: Denmark]**

Brander, James A. Rationales for Strategic Trade and Industrial Policy. **In** *Krugman, P. R., ed.*, 1986, pp. 23–46.

Branson, William H. and Klevorick, Alvin K. Strategic Behavior and Trade Policy. **In** *Krugman, P. R., ed.*, 1986, pp. 241–55. **[G: U.S.]**

Brickman, Ronald. National Policies for Developing High Technology Industries: International Comparisons: France. **In** *Rushing, F. W. and Brown, C. G., eds.*, 1986, pp. 71–87. **[G: France; OECD]**

Brinkman, Richard L. The Genesis of a New Industrial Policy: Equity and Efficiency. *J. Econ. Issues*, June 1986, *20*(2), pp. 335–44. **[G: U.S.]**

Brittan, Samuel. Privatisation: A Policy in Search of a Rationale: A Comment. *Econ. J.*, March 1986, *96*(381), pp. 33–38. **[G: U.K.]**

Brown, Carole Ganz and Rushing, Francis W. National Policies for Developing High Technology Industries: International Comparisons: Introduction: Past Successes, Present Directions, and Future Issues. **In** *Rushing, F. W. and Brown, C. G., eds.*, 1986, pp. 1–8.

Budd, Alan P. Do We Need a National Investment Bank? *Nat. Westminster Bank Quart. Rev.*, August 1986, pp. 36–48. **[G: U.K.]**

Bulow, Jeremy I. and Summers, Lawrence H. A Theory of Dual Labor Markets with Application to Industrial Policy, Discrimination, and Keynesian Unemployment. *J. Lab. Econ.*, Part 1, July 1986, *4*(3), pp. 376–414.

Butler, Stuart. Free-Market Entrepreneurship: Political Realism within American Democracy. **In** *Gondolf, E. W.; Marcus, I. M. and Dougherty, J. P., eds.*, 1986, pp. 182–90. **[G: U.S.]**

Butt Philip, Alan. Europe's Industrial Policies: An Overview. **In** *Hall, G., ed.*, 1986, pp. 1–20. **[G: EEC]**

Carliner, Geoffrey. Industrial Policies for Emerging Industries. **In** *Krugman, P. R., ed.*, 1986, pp. 147–68. **[G: U.S.; France; Japan]**

Chai, C. H. The Economic System of a Special Economic Zone under Socialism. **In** *Jao, Y. C. and Leung, C. K., eds.*, 1986, pp. 141–59. **[G: China]**

Chan, Thomas; Chen, E. K. Y. and Chin, Steve. China's Special Economic Zones: Ideology, Policy and Practice. **In** *Jao, Y. C. and Leung, C. K., eds.*, 1986, pp. 87–104. **[G: China]**

Chang, C. Y. Bureaucracy and Modernization: A Case Study of the Special Economic Zones in China. **In** *Jao, Y. C. and Leung, C. K., eds.*, 1986, pp. 105–23. **[G: China]**

Chu, D. K. Y. The Special Economic Zones and the Problem of Territorial Containment. **In** *Jao, Y. C. and Leung, C. K., eds.*, 1986, pp. 21–38. **[G: China]**

Chung, Joseph S. National Policies for Developing High Technology Industries: International Comparisons: Korea. **In** *Rushing, F. W. and Brown, C. G., eds.*, 1986, pp. 143–72. **[G: S. Korea]**

Clausen, A. W. Promoting the Private Sector in Developing Countries: A Multilateral Approach: Address to the Institute of Directors: London, England: February 26, 1985. **In** *Clausen, A. W.*, 1986, pp. 361–80.

Cline, William R. U.S. Trade and Industrial Policy: The Experience of Textiles, Steel, and Automobiles. **In** *Krugman, P. R., ed.*, 1986, pp. 211–39. **[G: U.S.]**

Cohen, Stephen S.; Halimi, Serge and Zysman, John. Institutions, Politics, and Industrial Policy in France. **In** *Barfield, C. E. and Schambra, W. A., eds.*, 1986, pp. 106–27. **[G: France]**

Cohen, Stephen S. and Zysman, John. Can America Compete? *Challenge*, May/June 1986, *29*(2), pp. 56–64. **[G: U.S.]**

de Combret, François. What Can the United States Learn from the French Experience? **In**

Adams, W. J. and Stoffaës, C., eds., 1986, pp. 161–65. **[G: U.S.; France]**

Cox, Andrew. The State, Finance and Industry Relationship in Comparative Perspective. **In** *Cox, A., ed.*, 1986, pp. 1–59. **[G: OECD]**

Coyne, John and Wright, Mike. The Small Firm, Government Policy and Industrial Change. **In** *Hall, G., ed.*, 1986, pp. 284–306. **[G: U.K.]**

Crandall, Robert W. Investment and Productivity Growth in the Steel Industry: Some Implications for Industrial Policy. **In** *Goldberg, W. H., ed.*, 1986, pp. 191–204. **[G: U.S.]**

Crew, Michael A. and Rowley, Charles K. Deregulation as an Instrument in Industrial Policy. *J. Inst. Theoretical Econ.*, March 1986, *142*(1), pp. 52–70.

Curzon Price, Victoria. Industrial and Trade Policy in a Period of Rapid Structural Change. **In** *Hauser, H., ed. (II)*, 1986, pp. 39–61. **[G: EEC]**

Curzon Price, Victoria. Industrial and Trade Policy in a Period of Rapid Structural Change. *Aussenwirtschaft*, September 1986, *41*(2/3), pp. 201–23. **[G: EEC]**

Danson, Mike. The Longer Term Impact of Policies of Regeneration at the Local Level. **In** *Danson, M., ed.*, 1986, pp. 169–74. **[G: U.K.]**

Darity, William A., Jr. The Managerial Class and Industrial Policy. *Ind. Relat.*, Spring 1986, *25*(2), pp. 212–27. **[G: U.S.]**

Del Monte, Alfredo. The Impact of Italian Industrial Policy, 1960–1980. **In** *Hall, G., ed.*, 1986, pp. 128–64. **[G: Italy]**

Dewar, David; Todes, Alison and Watson, Vanessa. Industrial Decentralization Policy in South Africa: Rhetoric and Practice. *Urban Stud.*, October 1986, *23*(5), pp. 363–76. **[G: S. Africa]**

de Dios, Emmanuel S. Protection, Concentration, and the Direction of Foreign Investments. *Philippine Rev. Econ. Bus.*, Mar./June 1986, *23*(1/2), pp. 57–82. **[G: Philippines]**

Dominique, C.-René and Oral, Muhittin. Exporting to Northern Markets: The Making of an Industrial Competitiveness Index. *Industry Devel.*, 1986, (18), pp. 1–17. **[G: Global]**

Dorn, James A. Industrial Policy and the Nature of the Firm: Comment. *J. Inst. Theoretical Econ.*, March 1986, *142*(1), pp. 101–08.

Dumez, Hervé. De la politique industrielle: existe-t-elle, "et quelle serait sa vraie nature?" (Industrial Policy: Does It Exist and Which Is Its Real Nature? With English summary.) *Écon. Soc.*, December 1986, *20*(12), pp. 187–98.

Dyson, Kenneth. The State, Banks and Industry: The West German Case. **In** *Cox, A., ed.*, 1986, pp. 118–41. **[G: W. Germany]**

Eads, George C. and Nelson, Richard R. Japanese High Technology Policy: What Lessons for the United States? **In** *Patrick, H., ed.*, 1986, pp. 243–69. **[G: U.S.; Japan]**

Eaton, Jonathan and Grossman, Gene M. Optimal Trade and Industrial Policy under Oligopoly. *Quart. J. Econ.*, May 1986, *101*(2), pp. 383–406.

Eccleston, Bernard. The State, Finance and Industry in Japan. **In** *Cox, A., ed.*, 1986, pp. 60–79. **[G: Japan]**

Eizenstat, Stuart E. Political Institutions and Industrial Policy: Comment. **In** *Barfield, C. E. and Schambra, W. A., eds.*, 1986, pp. 333–36. **[G: U.S.]**

Etzioni, Amitai. The Reindustrialization of the United States of America. **In** *Redburn, F. S.; Buss, T. F. and Ledebur, L. C., eds.*, 1986, pp. 6–27. **[G: U.S.]**

Eussner, Ansgar. Agro-Industrial Co-operation between the European Community and the ACP Countries. *J. Common Market Stud.*, September 1986, *25*(1), pp. 51–73. **[G: EEC; Cameroon; Rwanda]**

Evans, Peter B. State, Capital, and the Transformation of Dependence: The Brazilian Computer Case. *World Devel.*, July 1986, *14*(7), pp. 791–808. **[G: Brazil]**

Fallows, James. Cultural and Historical Perspectives on Industrial Policy: Comment. **In** *Barfield, C. E. and Schambra, W. A., eds.*, 1986, pp. 87–90. **[G: U.S.]**

Fong, Glenn R. The Potential for Industrial Policy: Lessons from the Very High Speed Integrated Circuit Program. *J. Policy Anal. Manage.*, Winter 1986, *5*(2), pp. 264–91. **[G: U.S.]**

Franke, Günter. Zur Festlegung von Abstimmungsregeln im Insolvenzverfahren. (With English summary.) *Z. Betriebswirtschaft*, July 1986, *56*(7), pp. 614–30. **[G: U.S.; W. Germany]**

Fransman, Martin. International Competitiveness, Technical Change and the State: The Machine Tool Industry in Taiwan and Japan. *World Devel.*, December 1986, *14*(12), pp. 1375–96. **[G: Taiwan; Japan]**

Fransman, Martin. International Competitiveness, International Diffusion of Technology and the State: A Case Study from Taiwan and Japan. **In** *Fransman, M., ed.*, 1986, pp. 153–214. **[G: Taiwan; Japan]**

Fuchs, Peter. Past, Present, and Future Perfect? Casing Japan's Competitive Strategy. **In** *Finn, R. B., ed.*, 1986, pp. 17–37. **[G: Japan]**

Fujimori, Hideo. Industrial Policy and Technology Transfer: A Case Study of Automobile Industry in the Philippines. *Devel. Econ.*, December 1986, *24*(4), pp. 349–67. **[G: Philippines]**

Furlong, Paul. State, Finance and Industry in Italy. **In** *Cox, A., ed.*, 1986, pp. 142–71. **[G: Italy]**

Gold, Bela. Some International Differences in Approaches to Industrial Policy. *Contemp. Policy Issues*, January 1986, *4*(1), pp. 12–22. **[G: U.S.; Japan; W. Europe]**

Goldstein, Walter. The Changing Impact of International Trade on the Economy of New York State. **In** *Schoolman, M. and Magid, A., eds.*, 1986, pp. 167–203. **[G: U.S.]**

Goux, Christian. Parliament Should Play a Larger Role in Industrial Policy. **In** *Adams, W. J. and*

Stoffaës, C., eds., 1986, pp. 156–60. **[G: France]**

Grasso, Patrick G. Distributive Policies and the Politics of Economic Development. **In** *Redburn, F. S.; Buss, T. F. and Ledebur, L. C., eds.*, 1986, pp. 83–98. **[G: U.S.]**

Gray, H. Peter. Japan's Challenge to Technological Competition and Its Limitations: Comment. **In** *Pugel, T. A., ed.*, 1986, pp. 255–61. **[G: Japan; U.S.]**

Green, Diana. The State, Finance and Industry in France. **In** *Cox, A., ed.*, 1986, pp. 80–117. **[G: France]**

Guillaume, Henri. Implications of the New Indicative Planning. **In** *Adams, W. J. and Stoffaës, C., eds.*, 1986, pp. 119–26. **[G: France]**

Gupta, Amar. National Policies for Developing High Technology Industries: International Comparisons: India. **In** *Rushing, F. W. and Brown, C. G., eds.*, 1986, pp. 89–110. **[G: India]**

Hahne, Ulf and Mundkowski-Bek, Monika. Freie Unternehmenszonen—Patentrezept für strukturschwache Regionen? (Free Enterprise Zones—A Panacea for Structurally Handicapped Regions? With English summary.) *Konjunkturpolitik*, 1986, *32*(1/2), pp. 27–51. **[G: W. Germany]**

Haley, John O. Administrative Guidance versus Formal Regulation: Resolving the Paradox of Industrial Policy. **In** *Saxonhouse, G. R. and Yamamura, K., eds.*, 1986, pp. 107–28. **[G: Japan]**

Hall, Peter A. The State and Economic Decline. **In** *Elbaum, B. and Lazonick, W., eds.*, 1986, pp. 266–302. **[G: U.K.]**

Handoussa, Heba; Nishimizu, Mieko and Page, John M., Jr. Productivity Change in Egyptian Public Sector Industries after "The Opening," 1973–1979. *J. Devel. Econ.*, Jan.-Feb. 1986, *20*(1), pp. 53–73. **[G: Egypt]**

Harper, Edwin L. Political Institutions and Industrial Policy: Comment. **In** *Barfield, C. E. and Schambra, W. A., eds.*, 1986, pp. 336–40. **[G: U.S.]**

Harrison, Bennett. Deindustrialization: The Case against Capital Flight. **In** *Gondolf, E. W.; Marcus, I. M. and Dougherty, J. P., eds.*, 1986, pp. 96–108. **[G: U.S.]**

Harrison, Michael. France: A State-Managed Industrial Power. **In** *Preeg, E. H. and Bendahmane, D. B., eds.*, 1986, pp. 85–93. **[G: France]**

Harrison, Richard T. The Standard Capital Grants Scheme in Northern Ireland: A Review and Assessment. *Reg. Stud.*, April 1986, *20*(2), pp. 175–82. **[G: Ireland]**

Hart, Gary. Industrial Policy and the Major U.S. Parties. **In** *Barfield, C. E. and Schambra, W. A., eds.*, 1986, pp. 222–27. **[G: U.S.]**

Hart, Jeffrey A. British Industrial Policy. **In** *Barfield, C. E. and Schambra, W. A., eds.*, 1986, pp. 128–60. **[G: U.K.]**

Hart, Jeffrey A. West German Industrial Policy. **In** *Barfield, C. E. and Schambra, W. A., eds.*, 1986, pp. 161–86. **[G: W. Germany]**

Hauser, Heinz. International Trade Policy: Discussion to Session III. *Aussenwirtschaft*, September 1986, *41*(2/3), pp. 395–401. **[G: OECD]**

Hawkins, A. M. Can Africa Industrialize? **In** *Berg, R. J. and Whitaker, J. S., eds.*, 1986, pp. 279–307. **[G: Africa]**

Hawley, Ellis W. "Industrial Policy" in the 1920s and 1930s. **In** *Barfield, C. E. and Schambra, W. A., eds.*, 1986, pp. 63–86. **[G: U.S.]**

Heclo, Hugh. Industrial Policy and the Executive Capacities of Government. **In** *Barfield, C. E. and Schambra, W. A., eds.*, 1986, pp. 292–317. **[G: U.S.]**

Heikkila, Eric and Hutton, Thomas A. Toward an Evaluative Framework for Land Use Policy in Industrial Districts of the Urban Core: A Qualitative Analysis of the Exclusionary Zoning Approach. *Urban Stud.*, February 1986, *23*(1), pp. 47–60. **[G: Canada]**

Hendriks, Ad J. Local Entrepreneurial Initiatives and Central Government. **In** *Nijkamp, P., ed. (II)*, 1986, pp. 280–88. **[G: Netherlands]**

Herbst, Karl. The Regulatory Framework for Foreign Investment in the Special Economic Zones. **In** *Jao, Y. C. and Leung, C. K., eds.*, 1986, pp. 124–37. **[G: China]**

Herzog, Philippe. Public Enterprises Should Promote Social Efficiency. **In** *Adams, W. J. and Stoffaës, C., eds.*, 1986, pp. 127–32. **[G: France]**

Hudson, Ray and Sadler, David. Contesting Works Closures in Western Europe's Old Industrial Regions: Defending Place or Betraying Class? **In** *Scott, A. J. and Storper, M., eds.*, 1986, pp. 172–93. **[G: W. Europe]**

Hutchison, Terence W. Industrial Policy: A Note on the History of Ideas. *J. Inst. Theoretical Econ.*, March 1986, *142*(1), pp. 238–40.

Imai, Ken-ichi. Japan's Industrial Policy for High Technology Industry. **In** *Patrick, H., ed.*, 1986, pp. 137–69. **[G: Japan]**

Iyori, Hiroshi. Antitrust and Industrial Policy in Japan: Competition and Cooperation. **In** *Saxonhouse, G. R. and Yamamura, K., eds.*, 1986, pp. 56–82. **[G: Japan]**

Jao, Y. C. Banking and Currency in the Special Economic Zones: Problems and Prospects. **In** *Jao, Y. C. and Leung, C. K., eds.*, 1986, pp. 160–83. **[G: China]**

Johnson, Chalmers. The Institutional Foundations of Japanese Industrial Policy. **In** *Barfield, C. E. and Schambra, W. A., eds.*, 1986, pp. 187–205. **[G: Japan]**

Jones, A. and Kinner, D. R. Deindustrialisation: The Case of Humberside. **In** *Danson, M., ed.*, 1986, pp. 103–19. **[G: U.K.]**

Jordan, James V.; Sassone, Peter G. and Walkling, Ralph A. A New Test of State Industrial Development Policy. **In** *Redburn, F. S.; Buss, T. F. and Ledebur, L. C., eds.*, 1986, pp. 114–39. **[G: U.S.]**

Kalas, John W. Reindustrialization in New York: The Role of the State University. **In** *Schoolman, M. and Magid, A., eds.*, 1986, pp. 281–312. **[G: U.S.]**

Kasoff, Mark J. and Soskin, Mark D. Economic Development Prospects for New York's St. Lawrence River Basin. **In** *Schoolman, M. and Magid, A., eds.*, 1986, pp. 131–46. **[G: U.S.]**

Kay, John A. and Thompson, David J. Privatisation: A Policy in Search of a Rationale. *Econ. J.*, March 1986, *96*(381), pp. 18–32. **[G: U.K.]**

Kingston, William. Industrial Policy and Innovation in Europe. **In** *de Jong, H. W. and Shepherd, W. G., eds., Bk. 2*, 1986, pp. 441–61. **[G: W. Europe]**

Kirchner, Christian. Deregulation as an Instrument in Industrial Policy: Comment. *J. Inst. Theoretical Econ.*, March 1986, *142*(1), pp. 75–78.

Kitschelt, Herbert. Four Theories of Public Policy Making and Fast Breeder Reactor Development. *Int. Organ.*, Winter 1986, *40*(1), pp. 65–104. **[G: France; W. Germany; U.S.]**

Koshiro, Kazutoshi. Japan's Industrial Policy for New Technologies. *J. Inst. Theoretical Econ.*, March 1986, *142*(1), pp. 163–77. **[G: Japan]**

Kutscher, Ronald E. and Personick, Valerie A. Deindustrialization and the Shift to Services. *Mon. Lab. Rev.*, June 1986, *109*(6), pp. 3–13. **[G: U.S.]**

Kwok, R. Y. W. Structure and Policies in Industrial Planning in the Shenzhen Special Economic Zone. **In** *Jao, Y. C. and Leung, C. K., eds.*, 1986, pp. 39–64. **[G: China]**

Lafuente Felez, Alberto and Salas Fumás, Vicente. Incentivos y participación pública en al promoción de empresas. (With English summary.) *Invest. Ecón.*, May 1986, *10*(2), pp. 379–403. **[G: Spain]**

Lagrange, François. Industrial Policy Should Be Conducted at the Supranational Level. **In** *Adams, W. J. and Stoffaës, C., eds.*, 1986, pp. 133–42. **[G: France]**

Landesmann, Michael A. UK Policy and the International Economy: An Internationalist Perspective. **In** *Nolan, P. and Paine, S., eds.*, 1986, pp. 115–34. **[G: U.K.]**

Ledebur, Larry C. and Hamilton, William W. Cost-Effective Development Finance. **In** *Walzer, N. and Chicoine, D. L., eds.*, 1986, pp. 103–21. **[G: U.S.]**

Ledebur, Larry C. and Hamilton, William W. The Failure of Tax Concessions as Economic Development Incentives. **In** *Gold, S. D., ed.*, 1986, pp. 101–17. **[G: U.S.]**

Lehman, James and Willett, Thomas D. National Security and Industrial Policy: The Need for a Public Choice Perspective. *Contemp. Policy Issues*, January 1986, *4*(1), pp. 36–47. **[G: U.S.]**

Leung, C. K. Spatial Redeployment and the Special Economic Zones in China: An Overview. **In** *Jao, Y. C. and Leung, C. K., eds.*, 1986, pp. 1–18. **[G: China]**

Lever, William. Old Policies in a New Role. **In** *Lever, W. and Moore, C., eds.*, 1986, pp. 44–61. **[G: U.K.]**

Lever, William and Moore, Chris. Future Directions for Urban Policy. **In** *Lever, W. and Moore, C., eds.*, 1986, pp. 142–61. **[G: U.K.]**

Lévy, Raymond. Industrial Policy and the Steel Industry. **In** *Adams, W. J. and Stoffaës, C., eds.*, 1986, pp. 63–73. **[G: France]**

Libecap, Gary D. Deregulation as an Instrument in Industrial Policy: Comment. *J. Inst. Theoretical Econ.*, March 1986, *142*(1), pp. 71–74.

Liedholm, Carl and Mead, Donald C. Small-scale Industry. **In** *Berg, R. J. and Whitaker, J. S., eds.*, 1986, pp. 308–30. **[G: Sub-Saharan Africa]**

Lilley, William, III. Political Institutions and Industrial Policy: Comment. **In** *Barfield, C. E. and Schambra, W. A., eds.*, 1986, pp. 340–41. **[G: U.S.]**

Lincoln, Edward J. Japan: Over-Rating the Government's Influence. **In** *Preeg, E. H. and Bendahmane, D. B., eds.*, 1986, pp. 75–83. **[G: Japan]**

Lisle-Williams, Michael. The State, Finance and Industry in Britain. **In** *Cox, A., ed.*, 1986, pp. 231–81. **[G: U.K.]**

Macharzina, Klaus. The European Microelectronics Industry and New Technologies. **In** *Macharzina, K. and Staehle, W. H., eds.*, 1986, pp. 241–56. **[G: W. Europe]**

MacLaury, Bruce K. French Industrial Policy: Concluding Comments. **In** *Adams, W. J. and Stoffaës, C., eds.*, 1986, pp. 196–97. **[G: France]**

Magid, Alvin. Industrial Democracy and Reindustrialization: Cross-Cultural Perspectives. **In** *Schoolman, M. and Magid, A., eds.*, 1986, pp. 377–96. **[G: U.S.; Sweden; Spain; Yugoslavia]**

Malvy, Martin. Modernization: The Industrial Policy of Laurent Fabius. **In** *Adams, W. J. and Stoffaës, C., eds.*, 1986, pp. 115–18. **[G: France]**

Martin, Fernand. Repercussions of Industrial Redeployment upon the International Role of the Region of Montreal. **In** *Danson, M., ed.*, 1986, pp. 147–57. **[G: Canada]**

Mason, Colin M. and Harrison, Richard T. The Regional Impact of Public Policy towards Small Firms in the United Kingdom. **In** *Keeble, D. and Wever, E., eds.*, 1986, pp. 224–55. **[G: U.K.]**

Matz, Deborah and Ledebur, Larry C. The State Role in Economic Development. **In** *Walzer, N. and Chicoine, D. L., eds.*, 1986, pp. 85–102. **[G: U.S.]**

McCraw, Thomas K. Mercantilism and the Market: Antecedents of American Industrial Policy. **In** *Barfield, C. E. and Schambra, W. A., eds.*, 1986, pp. 33–62. **[G: U.S.]**

McCulloch, Rachel. Japan's Invisible Barriers to Trade: Comment. **In** *Pugel, T. A., ed.*, 1986, pp. 55–62. **[G: Japan; U.S.]**

McKenzie, Richard B. Capital Taxation and Industrial Policy. **In** *Lee, D. R., ed.*, 1986, pp. 459–75.

McKenzie, Richard B. Eminent Domain: A New Industrial Policy Tool. *J. Inst. Theoretical Econ.*, March 1986, *142*(1), pp. 27–38. **[G: U.S.]**

McLennan, Kenneth. The Case for a Non-targeted Approach to Industrial Strategy. **In** *Redburn, F. S.; Buss, T. F. and Ledebur, L. C., eds.*, 1986, pp. 45–63. **[G: U.S.; OECD]**

Mentré, Paul. The French Economy Should Be Deregulated. **In** *Adams, W. J. and Stoffaës, C., eds.*, 1986, pp. 143–55. **[G: OECD; France]**

Monteiro, Jorge Vianna, et al. A política industrial no Brasil no início da dé cada de 80: um estudo de indentificação. (With English summary.) *Pesquisa Planejamento Econ.*, August 1986, *16*(2), pp. 425–66. **[G: Brazil]**

Moore, Chris and Booth, Simon. From Comprehensive Regeneration to Privatization: The Search for Effective Area Strategies. **In** *Lever, W. and Moore, C., eds.*, 1986, pp. 76–91. **[G: U.K.]**

Moore, Chris and Booth, Simon. The Post-industrial Synthesis: Policies for Enterprise in Clydeside. **In** *Lever, W. and Moore, C., eds.*, 1986, pp. 62–75. **[G: U.K.]**

Moore, Chris and Booth, Simon. The Pragmatic Approach: Local Political Models of Regeneration. **In** *Lever, W. and Moore, C., eds.*, 1986, pp. 92–106. **[G: U.K.]**

Moore, Chris and Booth, Simon. Unlocking Enterprise: The Search for Synergy. **In** *Lever, W. and Moore, C., eds.*, 1986, pp. 107–19. **[G: U.K.]**

Morgan, Eleanor. Stimulating Investment—Government Incentives and the Financial Leasing Industry. **In** *Hall, G., ed.*, 1986, pp. 261–83. **[G: W. Europe; U.K.]**

Moriarty, Barry M. Regional Industrial Change, Industrial Restructuring, and U.S. Industrial Policy. *Rev. Reg. Stud.*, Fall 1986, *16*(3), pp. 1–10. **[G: U.S.]**

Murakami, Yasusuke. Technology in Transition: Two Perspectives on Industrial Policy. **In** *Patrick, H., ed.*, 1986, pp. 211–41.

Nau, Henry R. National Policies for High Technology Development and Trade: An International and Comparative Assessment. **In** *Rushing, F. W. and Brown, C. G., eds.*, 1986, pp. 9–29. **[G: India; Brazil; Mexico; S. Korea; Argentina]**

Nielsen, Erik Brinch. Indusatrieksportens muligheder—nichevirksomhed. (The Possibilities of Industrial Exports as Seen by a Niche Firm. With English summary.) *Nationaløkon. Tidsskr.*, 1986, *124*(2), pp. 156–65. **[G: Denmark]**

Norton, Roger D. Industrial Policy and American Renewal. *J. Econ. Lit.*, March 1986, *24*(1), pp. 1–40. **[G: U.S.]**

O'Suilleabhain, Michael. Industrial Policy in the Republic of Ireland: Review and Outlook. **In** *Hall, G., ed.*, 1986, pp. 183–208. **[G: Ireland]**

Odagiri, Hiroyuki. Industrial Policy in Theory and Reality. **In** *de Jong, H. W. and Shepherd, W. G., eds., Bk. 2*, 1986, pp. 387–412. **[G: Japan]**

Ohtsuka, Seiichiro. Japan's Invisible Barriers to Trade: Comment. **In** *Pugel, T. A., ed.*, 1986, [illegible]-54. **[G: U.S.; Japan]**

Okimoto, Daniel I. Regime Characteristics of Japanese Industrial Policy. **In** *Patrick, H., ed.*, 1986, pp. 35–95. **[G: Japan]**

Olson, Mancur. Supply-Side Economics, Industrial Policy, and Rational Ignorance. **In** *Barfield, C. E. and Schambra, W. A., eds.*, 1986, pp. 245–69.

Orlov, A. and Rubval'ter, D. Reforming Consumer Goods Production. *Prob. Econ.*, December 1986, *29*(8), pp. 54–72. **[G: U.S.S.R.]**

Owen, Bruce M. The Evolution of Clayton Section 7 Enforcement and the Beginnings of U.S. Industrial Policy. *Antitrust Bull.*, Summer 1986, *31*(2), pp. 409–29. **[G: U.S.]**

Pack, Howard and Westphal, Larry E. Industrial Strategy and Technological Change: Theory versus Reality. *J. Devel. Econ.*, June 1986, *22*(1), pp. 87–128. **[G: S. Korea]**

Pastor, Robert. Industrial Policy in International Perspective: Comment. **In** *Barfield, C. E. and Schambra, W. A., eds.*, 1986, pp. 210–12.

Patrick, Hugh. Japan's High Technology Industries: Introduction. **In** *Patrick, H., ed.*, 1986, pp. ix–xxi. **[G: Japan]**

Patrick, Hugh. Japanese High Technology Industrial Policy in Comparative Context. **In** *Patrick, H., ed.*, 1986, pp. 3–33. **[G: Japan]**

Patterson, James T. Cultural and Historical Perspectives on Industrial Policy: Comment. **In** *Barfield, C. E. and Schambra, W. A., eds.*, 1986, pp. 93–94. **[G: U.S.]**

Pepper, Thomas. Industrial Policy in Japan: Implications for Technological Catch-up and Leadership: Comment. **In** *Pugel, T. A., ed.*, 1986, pp. 229–32. **[G: U.S.; Japan]**

Pernia, Ernesto M. and Pernia, Joseph M. An Economic and Social Impact Analysis of Small Industry Promotion: A Philippine Experience. *World Devel.*, May 1986, *14*(5), pp. 637–51. **[G: Philippines]**

Perrin-Pelletier, François. Industrial Policy and the Automobile Industry. **In** *Adams, W. J. and Stoffaës, C., eds.*, 1986, pp. 74–81. **[G: France]**

Pethig, Rüdiger. Eminent Domain: A New Industrial Policy Tool: Comment. *J. Inst. Theoretical Econ.*, March 1986, *142*(1), pp. 44–51. **[G: W. Germany]**

Petitbó, Amadeu. Notas sobre desindustrializacion y crisis en la economia española. (Note on the De-industrialization and the Crisis in the Spanish Economy. With English summary.) *Écon. Soc.*, May 1986, *20*(5), pp. 69–99. **[G: Spain]**

Pettigrew, P. and Dann, S. Streamlining Regional Industrial Aid? *Reg. Stud.*, April 1986, *20*(2), pp. 182–84. **[G: Ireland]**

Phillips, David R. Special Economic Zones in China's Modernization: Changing Policies and Changing Fortunes. *Nat. Westminster Bank Quart. Rev.*, February 1986, pp. 37–49. **[G: China]**

Porter, Philip K.; Scully, Gerald W. and Slottje, Daniel J. Industrial Policy and the Nature of the Firm. *J. Inst. Theoretical Econ.*, March

1986, *142*(1), pp. 79–100. **[G: W. Europe]**

Porter, Roger B. Industrial Policy and the Role of Government in the Economy. **In** *Adams, W. J. and Stoffaës, C., eds.*, 1986, pp. 166–74. **[G: U.S.]**

Preeg, Ernest H. Implications for U.S. Trade and Aid Policy. **In** *Preeg, E. H. and Bendahmane, D. B., eds.*, 1986, pp. 109–14. **[G: U.S.]**

Premus, Robert. Attracting High-Tech Industry and Jobs: An Assessment of State Practices. **In** *Walzer, N. and Chicoine, D. L., eds.*, 1986, pp. 55–71. **[G: U.S.]**

Premus, Robert. High Technology and State Economic Development Strategies. **In** *Redburn, F. S.; Buss, T. F. and Ledebur, L. C., eds.*, 1986, pp. 99–113. **[G: U.S.]**

Pugel, Thomas A. Industrial Policy in Japan: Implications for Technological Catch-up and Leadership. **In** *Pugel, T. A., ed.*, 1986, pp. 209–27. **[G: U.S.; Japan]**

Rapp, William V. Japan's Invisible Barriers to Trade. **In** *Pugel, T. A., ed.*, 1986, pp. 21–45. **[G: Japan; U.S.]**

Rasmussen, David W. and Ledebur, Larry C. The Role of State Economic Development Programs in National Industry Policy. **In** *Redburn, F. S.; Buss, T. F. and Ledebur, L. C., eds.*, 1986, pp. 140–57. **[G: U.S.]**

Riegle, Donald. American Industrial Policy: Building on the Chrysler Experience. **In** *Adams, W. J. and Stoffaës, C., eds.*, 1986, pp. 175–80. **[G: U.S.]**

Rosen, George. Industrial Technologies and Industrial Policies in India: Or When Small Is *Not* Beautiful. **In** *Björkman, J. W., ed.*, 1986, pp. 60–68. **[G: India]**

Rothwell, Roy. Reindustrialisation, Innovation and Public Policy. **In** *Hall, P., ed.*, 1986, *1984*, pp. 65–83. **[G: OECD]**

Russell, Robert W. Congress and the Proposed Industrial Policy Structures. **In** *Barfield, C. E. and Schambra, W. A., eds.*, 1986, pp. 318–32. **[G: U.S.]**

Samuels, Richard J. Miti and the Market: The Japanese Oil Industry in Transition. *Rivista Int. Sci. Econ. Com.*, May 1986, *33*(5), pp. 447–64. **[G: Japan]**

Sato, Ryuzo. Japan's Challenge to Technological Competition and Its Limitations. **In** *Pugel, T. A., ed.*, 1986, pp. 237–54. **[G: Japan; U.S.]**

Saxonhouse, Gary R. Industrial Policy and Factor Markets: Biotechnology in Japan and the United States. **In** *Patrick, H., ed.*, 1986, pp. 97–135. **[G: U.S.; Japan]**

Schimberni, Mario. State-Owned and Private Enterprises in Italy. **In** *Barfield, C. E. and Schambra, W. A., eds.*, 1986, pp. 206–09. **[G: Italy]**

Schneider, William. Supply-Side Economics, Industrial Policy, and Rational Ignorance: Comment. **In** *Barfield, C. E. and Schambra, W. A., eds.*, 1986, pp. 274–79.

Schoolman, Morton. Solving the Dilemma of Statesmanship: Reindustrialization through an Evolving Democratic Plan. **In** *Schoolman, M. and Magid, A., eds.*, 1986, pp. 3–49. **[G: U.S.]**

Schultze, Charles L. Industrial Policy: A Dissent. **In** *Reynolds, L. G.; Masters, S. H. and Moser, C. H., eds.*, 1986, *1983*, pp. 164–75. **[G: U.S.]**

Shelp, Ronald Kent and Shelp, June Peno. Services as an Industrial Policy Issue. **In** *Redburn, F. S.; Buss, T. F. and Ledebur, L. C., eds.*, 1986, pp. 28–44. **[G: U.S.]**

Simai, Mihály. The Socio-economic Issues of Growth-Oriented Strategic Adjustment Programs. *Acta Oecon.*, 1986, *37*(3–4), pp. 155–67.

Sit, Victor F. S. Industries in Shenzhen: An Attempt at Open-Door Industrialization. **In** *Jao, Y. C. and Leung, C. K., eds.*, 1986, pp. 226–46. **[G: China]**

Solo, Robert A. Melman and Reich on Industrial Policy: Review Article. *Econ. Develop. Cult. Change*, January 1986, *34*(2), pp. 373–84. **[G: U.S.]**

Southwick, Lawrence, Jr. Local Economic Development and the State. **In** *Schoolman, M. and Magid, A., eds.*, 1986, pp. 147–64. **[G: U.S.]**

Stein, Herbert. Cultural and Historical Perspectives on Industrial Policy: Comment. **In** *Barfield, C. E. and Schambra, W. A., eds.*, 1986, pp. 90–92. **[G: U.S.]**

Steiner, Michael. Restructuring the Regions: The Austrian Experience. **In** *Danson, M., ed.*, 1986, pp. 137–46. **[G: Austria]**

Stern, Paula and Wechsler, Andrew. Escape Clause Relief and Recessions: An Economic and Legal Look at Section 201. **In** *Saxonhouse, G. R. and Yamamura, K., eds.*, 1986, pp. 195–217. **[G: U.S.]**

Stoffaës, Christian. French Industrial Policy: Postscript. **In** *Adams, W. J. and Stoffaës, C., eds.*, 1986, pp. 198–210. **[G: France]**

Stoffaës, Christian. Industrial Policy in the High-Technology Industries. **In** *Adams, W. J. and Stoffaës, C., eds.*, 1986, pp. 36–62. **[G: OECD]**

Tashiro, Yasuhisa. America's Industrial Policy Debate. **In** *Finn, R. B., ed.*, 1986, pp. 1–15. **[G: U.S.]**

Teitel, Simón and Thoumi, Francisco E. From Import Substitution to Exports: The Manufacturing Exports Experience of Argentina and Brazil. *Econ. Develop. Cult. Change*, April 1986, *34*(3), pp. 455–90. **[G: Brazil; Argentina]**

di Tella, Guido. La estrategia del desarrollo indirecto veinte años después. (With English summary.) *Desarrollo Econ.*, Apr.-June 1986, *26*(101), pp. 51–70. **[G: Argentina]**

Tomlinson, R. and Addleson, Mark. Trends in Industrial Decentralization: An Examination of Bell's Hypothesis. *S. Afr. J. Econ.*, December 1986, *54*(4), pp. 381–94. **[G: S. Africa]**

Tower, Edward. Industrial Policy in Less Developed Countries. *Contemp. Policy Issues*, January 1986, *4*(1), pp. 23–35. **[G: LDCs]**

Trapani, John M., III. Eminent Domain: A New Industrial Policy Tool: Comment. *J. Inst. Theo-*

retical Econ., March 1986, *142*(1), pp. 39–43. **[G: U.S.]**

Trivedi, Prajapati. Explaining Public versus Private Partitioning of the Economy. *Indian Econ. J.*, Oct.-Dec. 1986, *34*(2), pp. 112–24.

Uppal, J. S. Public Financial Institutions and Economic Concentration in India. *J. Devel. Econ.*, Jan.-Feb. 1986, *20*(1), pp. 135–44. **[G: India]**

Utton, Michael. Developments in British Industrial and Competition Policies. **In** *Hall, G., ed.*, 1986, pp. 59–83. **[G: U.K.]**

Vaughan, Roger J. and Pollard, Robert. Small Business and Economic Development. **In** *Walzer, N. and Chicoine, D. L., eds.*, 1986, pp. 122–38. **[G: U.S.]**

Weinstein, Michael M. Industrial Planning and Economic Policy-Making: Lessons from the 1930s. **In** *[Tarshis, L.]*, 1986, pp. 135–57. **[G: U.S.]**

Wellings, Paul and Black, Anthony. Industrial Decentralization under Apartheid: The Relocation of Industry to the South African Periphery. *World Devel.*, January 1986, *14*(1), pp. 1–38. **[G: S. Africa]**

Wells, Donald A. The Effects of Saudi Industrialization on Employment. *J. Energy Devel.*, Spring 1986, *11*(2), pp. 273–84. **[G: Saudi Arabia]**

Wernerfelt, Karsten. Industriens muligheder for at løse balanceproblemerne. (Suggestions for a Growth-Oriented Industrial Policy. With English summary.) *Nationaløkon. Tidsskr.*, 1986, *124*(2), pp. 147–55. **[G: Denmark]**

Wiarda, Howard J. Industrial Policy in International Perspective: Comment. **In** *Barfield, C. E. and Schambra, W. A., eds.*, 1986, pp. 212–13.

Wiewel, Wim and Mier, Robert. Enterprise Activities of Not-for-Profit Organizations: Surviving the New Federalism? **In** *Bergman, E. M., ed.*, 1986, pp. 205–25.

Wildavsky, Aaron. Industrial Policies in American Political Cultures. **In** *Barfield, C. E. and Schambra, W. A., eds.*, 1986, pp. 15–32. **[G: U.S.]**

Willett, Thomas D. The Economics and Politics of Industrial Policy: Some Lessons from the U.S. and Abroad. *Contemp. Policy Issues*, January 1986, *4*(1), pp. 10–11. **[G: U.S.]**

Williamson, Oliver E. Japan's Industrial Policy for New Technologies: Comment. *J. Inst. Theoretical Econ.*, March 1986, *142*(1), pp. 178–80. **[G: Japan]**

Wolf, Martin. Industrial and Trade Policy: Discussion to Session I. *Aussenwirtschaft*, September 1986, *41*(2/3), pp. 259–69.

Yago, Glenn, et al. Industrial Devolution in New York State. **In** *Schoolman, M. and Magid, A., eds.*, 1986, pp. 75–89. **[G: U.S.]**

Yamamura, Kozo. Caveat Emptor: The Industrial Policy of Japan. **In** *Krugman, P. R., ed.*, 1986, pp. 169–209. **[G: Japan]**

Yamamura, Kozo. Joint Research and Antitrust: Japanese vs. American Strategies. **In** *Patrick, H., ed.*, 1986, pp. 171–209. **[G: U.S.; Japan]**

Yamamura, Kozo and Vandenberg, Jan. Japan's Rapid-Growth Policy on Trial: The Television Case. **In** *Saxonhouse, G. R. and Yamamura, K., eds.*, 1986, pp. 238–83. **[G: U.S.; Japan]**

Yamauchi, Ichizo. Long-range Strategic Planning in Japanese R&D. **In** *Freeman, C., ed.*, 1986, pp. 169–85. **[G: Japan]**

Yusof, A. K. M. Public Enterprise: Studies in Organisational Structure: Urban Development Authority. **In** *Ramanadham, V. V., ed.*, 1986, pp. 234–49. **[G: Malaysia]**

Zehender, Wolfgang. Industrialisierung und regionale Kooperation in Schwarzafrika. (Industrialization and Regional Cooperation in Sub-Saharan Africa. With English summary.) *Konjunkturpolitik*, 1986, *32*(4), pp. 218–35. **[G: Africa]**

619 Economics of Regulation

6190 Economics of Regulation

Abromeit, Heidrun. Privatisation in Great Britain. *Ann. Pub. Co-op. Econ.*, Apr.-June 1986, *57*(2), pp. 153–79. **[G: U.K.]**

Adams, Walter and Brock, James W. Corporate Power and Economic Sabotage. *J. Econ. Issues*, December 1986, *20*(4), pp. 919–40. **[G: U.S.]**

Anderson, Eric E. Taxes vs. Quotas for Regulating Fisheries under Uncertainty: A Hybrid Discrete-Time Continuous-Time Model. *Marine Resource Econ.*, 1986, *3*(3), pp. 183–207.

Anderson, Richard K. and Enomoto, Carl E. Product Quality and Price Regulation: A General Equilibrium Analysis. *Economica*, February 1986, *53*(209), pp. 87–95.

Anderson, Ronald W. Regulation of Futures Trading in the United States and the United Kingdom. *Oxford Rev. Econ. Policy*, Winter 1986, *2*(4), pp. 41–57. **[G: U.S.; U.K.]**

Asch, Peter. Automobile Safety: Is Government Regulation Really Our Savior? *Yale J. Regul.*, Spring 1986, *3*(2), pp. 383–89. **[G: U.S.]**

Ashworth, John; Papps, Ivy and Storey, David J. Assessing the Effectiveness and Economic Efficiency of an E.E.C. Pollution Control Directive: The Control of Discharges of Mercury to the Aquatic Environment. **In** *von der Schulenburg, J.-M. G. and Skogh, G., eds.*, 1986, pp. 207–25. **[G: EEC]**

Axelrod, Howard. Predicting the Next Regulatory Crisis: An Issues Management Approach. **In** *Saltzman, S. and Schuler, R. E., eds.*, 1986, pp. 267–72.

Babbitt, Bruce and Rose, Jonathan. Building a Better Mousetrap: Health Care Reform and the Arizona Program. *Yale J. Regul.*, Spring 1986, *3*(2), pp. 243–82. **[G: U.S.]**

Bailey, Elizabeth E. Price and Productivity Change Following Deregulation: The U.S. Experience. *Econ. J.*, March 1986, *96*(381), pp. 1–17. **[G: U.S.]**

Barth, James R.; Cordes, Joseph J. and Yezer, Anthony M. J. Benefits and Costs of Legal Restrictions on Personal Loan Markets. *J. Law Econ.*, October 1986, *29*(2), pp. 357–80. **[G: U.S.]**

Baumann, Michael G. and Kalt, Joseph P. Intertemporal Consumer Surplus in Lagged-Adjustment Demand Models: An Application to Natural Gas Pricing. *Energy Econ.*, January 1986, *8*(1), pp. 2–12. **[G: U.S.]**

Baumol, William J. Minimum and Maximum Pricing Principles for Residual Regulation. **In** *Baumol, W. J.*, 1986, *1983*, pp. 151–64.

Baumol, William J. and Willig, Robert D. Contestability: Developments since the Book. *Oxford Econ. Pap.*, Suppl. Nov. 1986, *38*, pp. 9–36. **[G: U.S.]**

Bayley, Molly G. Technology Meets Regulation. **In** *Saunders, A. and White, L. J., eds.*, 1986, pp. 63–71. **[G: U.S.]**

Beales, J. Howard, III. Comments [The Effects of the Advertising Substantiation Program on Advertising Agencies] [An Economic Analysis of the FTC's Ad Substantiation Program]. **In** *Ippolito, P. M. and Scheffman, D. T., eds.*, 1986, pp. 213–16. **[G: U.S.]**

Becker, Gilbert. The Public Interest Hypothesis Revisited: A New Test of Peltzman's Theory of Regulation. *Public Choice*, 1986, *49*(3), pp. 223–34.

Benson, Bruce L. and Faminow, Merle D. Regulatory Transfers in Canadian/American Agriculture: The Case of Supply Management. *Cato J.*, Spring/Summer 1986, *6*(1), pp. 271–94. **[G: Canada]**

Benson, Bruce L. and Faminow, Merle D. The Incentives to Organize and Demand Regulation: Two Ends against the Middle. *Econ. Inquiry*, July 1986, *24*(3), pp. 473–84.

Bertsch, Gary K. Technology Transfers and Technology Controls: A Synthesis of the Western–Soviet Relationship. **In** *Amann, R. and Cooper, J., eds.*, 1986, pp. 115–34. **[G: U.S.S.R.; OECD]**

Bisang, Roberto, et al. Insulina y economía política: el difícil arte de la política pública. (With English summary.) *Desarrollo Econ.*, Oct.-Dec. 1986, *26*(103), pp. 369–88. **[G: Argentina]**

Blankart, Charles B. and Finsinger, Jörg. Regulation-Induced Price Instability in Swiss Motor Car Liability Insurance. **In** *Finsinger, J. and Pauly, M. V., eds.*, 1986, pp. 200–211. **[G: Switzerland]**

Blankart, Charles B. and Schneider, Friedrich. Insurance Regulation in Switzerland: An Outline with Special Reference to Life and Motor Car Liability Insurance. **In** *Finsinger, J. and Pauly, M. V., eds.*, 1986, pp. 189–99. **[G: Switzerland]**

Blumestock, James W. and Thomchick, Evelyn A. Deregulation and Airline Labor Relations. *Logist. Transp. Rev.*, December 1986, *22*(4), pp. 389–403. **[G: U.S.]**

Boyd, John H. and Graham, Stanley L. Risk, Regulation, and Bank Holding Company Expansion into Nonbanking. *Fed. Res. Bank Minn. Rev.*, Spring 1986, *10*(2), pp. 2–17. **[G: U.S.]**

Bradley, Michael D. and Jansen, Dennis W. Deposit Market Deregulation and Interest Rates. *Southern Econ. J.*, October 1986, *53*(2), pp. 478–89.

Brede, Helmut and Hoppe, Ulrich. Outline of the Present Status of the Privatization Debate in the Federal German Republic. *Ann. Pub. Co-op. Econ.*, Apr.-June 1986, *57*(2), pp. 205–29. **[G: W. Germany]**

Broadman, Harry G. Natural Gas Deregulation: The Need for Further Reform. *J. Policy Anal. Manage.*, Spring 1986, *5*(3), pp. 496–516. **[G: U.S.]**

Butters, Gerard R. The Impact of Product Recalls on the Wealth of Sellers: Comments. **In** *Ippolito, P. M. and Scheffman, D. T., eds.*, 1986, pp. 411–13. **[G: U.S.]**

Campbell, A. Hartwell. The Changing World of Regulation. **In** *[Dorsey, J. N. and Wiggins, B. T.]*, 1986, pp. 7–11. **[G: U.S.]**

Carter, Richard. Déréglementation: Faut-il dédommager les groupes qui sont pénalisés? (With English summary.) *Can. Public Policy*, June 1986, *12*(2), pp. 294–306.

Chen, Andrew H. and Merville, Larry J. An Analysis of Divestiture Effects Resulting from Deregulation. *J. Finance*, December 1986, *41*(5), pp. 997–1010. **[G: U.S.]**

Cherkes, Martin; Friedman, Joseph and Spivak, Avia. The Disinterest in Deregulation: Comment. *Amer. Econ. Rev.*, June 1986, *76*(3), pp. 559–63.

Christol, Carl Q. The Search for a Stable Regulatory Framework. **In** *Demac, D. A., ed.*, 1986, pp. 3–18.

Colegate, Raymond. Airline De-regulation in the United States Eight Years On: Review Article. *World Econ.*, December 1986, *9*(4), pp. 441–44. **[G: U.S.]**

Comanor, William S. The Political Economy of the Pharmaceutical Industry. *J. Econ. Lit.*, September 1986, *24*(3), pp. 1178–1217. **[G: U.S.]**

Cox, Charles C. and Kohn, Bruce A. Regulatory Implications of Computerized Communications in Securities Markets. **In** *Saunders, A. and White, L. J., eds.*, 1986, pp. 7–18. **[G: U.S.]**

Cox, Louis Anthony, Jr. Theory of Regulatory Benefits Assessment: Econometric and Expressed Preference Approaches. **In** *Bentkover, J. D.; Covello, V. T. and Jeryl, M., eds.*, 1986, pp. 85–159. **[G: U.S.]**

Crandall, Robert W. Economic Rents as a Barrier to Deregulation. *Cato J.*, Spring/Summer 1986, *6*(1), pp. 173–94. **[G: U.S.]**

Crew, Michael A. and Rowley, Charles K. Deregulation as an Instrument in Industrial Policy. *J. Inst. Theoretical Econ.*, March 1986, *142*(1), pp. 52–70.

Cummings, Ronald G.; Cox, Louis Anthony, Jr. and Freeman, A. Myrick, III. General Methods for Benefits Assessment. **In** *Bentkover, J. D.; Covello, V. T. and Jeryl, M., eds.*, 1986, pp. 161–91.

Curzon Price, Victoria. Industrial and Trade Policy in a Period of Rapid Structural Change.

Aussenwirtschaft, September 1986, *41*(2/3), pp. 201–23. **[G: EEC]**

Cyrnak, Anthony W. Chain Banks and Competition: The Effectiveness of Federal Reserve Policy in 1977. *Fed. Res. Bank San Francisco Econ. Rev.*, Spring 1986, (2), pp. 5–15. **[G: U.S.]**

Delaunay, Jean-Claude. Questions posées à la théorie dite de la "régulation monopoliste." (Some Questions on the So-Called "Monopoly Regulation" Theory. With English summary.) *Écon. Soc.*, May 1986, *20*(5), pp. 209–31.

DeMuth, Christopher C. The Case against Credit Card Interest Rate Regulation. *Yale J. Regul.*, Spring 1986, *3*(2), pp. 201–42. **[G: U.S.]**

Diamond, Douglas W. and Dybvig, Philip H. Banking Theory, Deposit Insurance, and Bank Regulation. *J. Bus.*, January 1986, *59*(1), pp. 55–68. **[G: U.S.]**

Doherty, Neil A. and Garven, James R. Price Regulation in Property-Liability Insurance: A Contingent-Claims Approach. *J. Finance*, December 1986, *41*(5), pp. 1031–50.

Domberger, Simon and Piggott, John. Privatization Policies and Public Enterprise: A Survey. *Econ. Rec.*, June 1986, *62*(177), pp. 145–62. **[G: U.S.; W. Germany; Canada; Australia]**

Edwards, Franklin R. Technology and New Regulatory Challenges in Futures Markets. **In** *Saunders, A. and White, L. J., eds.*, 1986, pp. 171–79. **[G: U.S.]**

Eisen, Roland. Wettbewerb und Regulierung in der Versicherung Die Rolle asymmetrischer Information. (Competition and Regulation in Insurance: The Role of Asymmetrical Information. With English summary.) *Schweiz. Z. Volkswirtsch. Statist.*, September 1986, *122*(3), pp. 339–58.

Escarmelle, Jean-François and Hujoel, Luc. Privatization and Deregulation. Its Implementation in Belgium. *Ann. Pub. Co-op. Econ.*, Apr.-June 1986, *57*(2), pp. 253–73. **[G: Belgium]**

Etzioni, Amitai. Does Regulation Reduce Electricity Rates? A Research Note. *Policy Sci.*, December 1986, *19*(4), pp. 349–57. **[G: U.S.]**

Evans, David S. The Differential Effect of Regulation across Plant Size: Comment [The Effect of Environmental Regulation on Optimal Plant Size and Factor Shares]. *J. Law Econ.*, April 1986, *29*(1), pp. 187–200. **[G: U.S.]**

Ferris, Stephen P.; Johnson, Dana J. and Shome, Dilip K. Regulatory Environment and Market Response to Public Utility Rate Decisions. *J. Finan. Res.*, Winter 1986, *9*(4), pp. 313–18. **[G: U.S.]**

Finsinger, Jörg. A State Controlled Market: The German Case. **In** *Finsinger, J. and Pauly, M. V., eds.*, 1986, pp. 111–60. **[G: W. Germany]**

Finsinger, Jörg and Pauly, Mark V. The Economics of Insurance Regulation: A Cross-National Study: Introduction. **In** *Finsinger, J. and Pauly, M. V., eds.*, 1986, pp. 1–23. **[G: OECD]**

Finsinger, Jörg and Waldmann, Reinhold. The French Automobile and Life Insurance Markets. **In** *Finsinger, J. and Pauly, M. V., eds.*, 1986, pp. 215–29. **[G: France]**

Fiorina, Morris P. Legislator Uncertainty, Legislative Control, and the Delegation of Legislative Power. *J. Law, Econ., Organ.*, Spring 1986, *2*(1), pp. 33–51. **[G: U.S.]**

Fischhoff, Baruch and Cox, Louis Anthony, Jr. Conceptual Framework for Regulatory Benefits Assessment. **In** *Bentkover, J. D.; Covello, V. T. and Jeryl, M., eds.*, 1986, pp. 51–84.

Foreman-Peck, James and Manning, Dorothy. Liberalisation as an Industrial Policy: The Case of Telecommunications Manufacturing. *Nat. Westminster Bank Quart. Rev.*, November 1986, pp. 20–33. **[G: U.S.; U.K.]**

Fournier, Gary M. The Determinants of Economic Rents in Television Broadcasting. *Antitrust Bull.*, Winter 1986, *31*(4), pp. 1045–66. **[G: U.S.]**

Frey, Bruno S. and Ramser, Hans J. Where Are the Limits of Regulation? *J. Inst. Theoretical Econ.*, September 1986, *142*(3), pp. 571–80.

Geehan, Randall. Economies of Scale in Insurance: Implications for Regulation. **In** *Wasow, B. and Hill, R. D., eds.*, 1986, pp. 137–59. **[G: Canada; U.S.; Australia]**

Giersch, Herbert. Weltwirtschaftliches Wachstum durch Liberalisierung. (Global Economic Growth by Liberalization. With English summary.) *Kyklos*, 1986, *39*(4), pp. 518–36. **[G: W. Europe]**

Ginsburg, Douglas H. The Reagan Administration's Legislative Initiative in Antitrust. *Antitrust Bull.*, Winter 1986, *31*(4), pp. 851–69. **[G: U.S.]**

Gist, Peter and Meadowcroft, Shirley A. Regulating for Competition: The Newly Liberalised Market for Private Branch Exchanges. *Fisc. Stud.*, August 1986, *7*(3), pp. 41–66. **[G: U.K.]**

Giuffra, Robert J., Jr. Investment Bankers' Fairness Opinions in Corporate Control Transactions. *Yale Law J.*, November 1986, *96*(1), pp. 119–41. **[G: U.S.]**

Goodman, Laurie S. The Interface between Technology and Regulation in Banking. **In** *Saunders, A. and White, L. J., eds.*, 1986, pp. 181–86.

Grabowski, Henry G. and Vernon, John. Longer Patents for Lower Imitation Barriers: The 1984 Drug Act. *Amer. Econ. Rev.*, May 1986, *76*(2), pp. 195–98. **[G: U.S.]**

Graham, John D. and Lee, Younghee. Behavioral Response to Safety Regulation: The Case of Motorcycle Helmet-Wearing Legislation. *Policy Sci.*, October 1986, *19*(3), pp. 253–73. **[G: U.S.]**

Haas-Wilson, Deborah. The Effect of Commercial Practice Restrictions: The Case of Optometry. *J. Law Econ.*, April 1986, *29*(1), pp. 165–86. **[G: U.S.]**

Haddock, David D. and Macey, Jonathan R. Controlling Insider Trading in Europe and America: The Economics of the Politics. **In** *von* der Schulenburg, J.-M. G. and Skogh, G., eds., 1986, pp. 149–67. **[G: W. Europe; U.S.]**

Haley, John O. Administrative Guidance versus Formal Regulation: Resolving the Paradox of Industrial Policy. **In** *Saxonhouse, G. R. and Yamamura, K., eds.*, 1986, pp. 107–28. **[G: Japan]**

Harper, Ian R. Why Financial Deregulation? *Australian Econ. Rev.*, 1st Quarter 1986, (73), pp. 37–49. **[G: Australia]**

Hartley, Keith; Lavers, R. J. and Maynard, A. K. Regulation and Development Times in the U.K. Pharmaceutical Industry. *Scot. J. Polit. Econ.*, November 1986, *33*(4), pp. 355–69. **[G: U.K.]**

Hayes, Beth and Siegel, Daniel. Rate of Return Regulation with Price Flexibility. *J. Bus.*, Part 1, October 1986, *59*(4), pp. 537–53.

Hazlett, Thomas W. Competition vs. Franchise Monopoly in Cable Television. *Contemp. Policy Issues*, April 1986, *4*(2), pp. 80–97. **[G: U.S.]**

Hazlett, Thomas W. Regulation and the Communications Revolution: Introduction. *Contemp. Policy Issues*, April 1986, *4*(2), pp. 52–53. **[G: U.S.]**

Henderson, J. Stephen. Price Discrimination Limits in Relation to the Death Spiral. *Energy J.*, July 1986, *7*(3), pp. 33–50.

Henderson, J. Stephen. The Effect of Regulation on Nonuniform Electricity Price Schedules in the United States. *J. Public Econ.*, April 1986, *29*(3), pp. 317–32. **[G: U.S.]**

Hendricks, Wallace. Collective Bargaining in Regulated Industries. **In** *Lipsky, D. B. and Lewin, D., eds.*, 1986, pp. 21–42. **[G: U.S.]**

Higgins, Richard S. and McChesney, Fred S. An Economic Analysis of the FTC's Ad Substantiation Program. **In** *Ippolito, P. M. and Scheffman, D. T., eds.*, 1986, pp. 197–211. **[G: U.S.]**

Higgins, Richard S. and McChesney, Fred S. Truth and Consequences: The Federal Trade Commission's Ad Substantiation Program. *Int. Rev. Law Econ.*, December 1986, *6*(2), pp. 151–68. **[G: U.S.]**

Higgins, Richard S. and Rubin, Paul H. Counterfeit Goods. *J. Law Econ.*, October 1986, *29*(2), pp. 211–30.

Hilke, John C. Early Mandatory Disclosure Regulations. *Int. Rev. Law Econ.*, December 1986, *6*(2), pp. 229–39. **[G: U.S.]**

Hirsch, Mario. The Doldrums of Europe's TV Landscape: Coronet as Catalyst. **In** *Demac, D. A., ed.*, 1986, pp. 114–29.

Hobbs, Benjamin F. and Schuler, Richard E. Deregulating the Distribution of Electricity: Price and Welfare Consequences of Spatial Oligopoly with Uniform Delivered Prices. *J. Reg. Sci.*, May 1986, *26*(2), pp. 235–65. **[G: U.S.]**

Holcombe, Randall G. and Holcombe, Lora P. The Market for Regulation. *J. Inst. Theoretical Econ.*, December 1986, *142*(4), pp. 684–96.

Hubbard, R. Glenn and Weiner, Robert J. Petroleum Regulation and Public Policy. **In** *Weiss, L. W. and Klass, M. W., eds.*, 1986, pp. 105–36. **[G: U.S.]**

Hubbard, R. Glenn and Weiner, Robert J. Regulation and Long-term Contracting in U.S. Natural Gas Markets. *J. Ind. Econ.*, September 1986, *35*(1), pp. 71–79. **[G: U.S.]**

Illy, Hans F. Regulation and Evasion: Street-Vendors in Manila. *Policy Sci.*, July 1986, *19*(1), pp. 61–81. **[G: Philippines]**

Ito, Youichi. Telecommunications and Industrial Policies in Japan: Recent Developments. **In** *Snow, M. S.*, 1986, pp. 201–30. **[G: Japan]**

Jaffer, Susan M. and Kay, John A. The Regulation of Shop Opening Hours in the United Kingdom. **In** *von der Schulenburg, J.-M. G. and Skogh, G., eds.*, 1986, pp. 169–83. **[G: U.K.]**

Jarrell, Gregg A. and Peltzman, Sam. The Impact of Product Recalls on the Wealth of Sellers. **In** *Ippolito, P. M. and Scheffman, D. T., eds.*, 1986, pp. 377–409. **[G: U.S.]**

Jehle, Geoffrey A. Regulation and the Public Interest in Banking. *J. Banking Finance*, December 1986, *10*(4), pp. 549–73. **[G: U.S.]**

Jordan, William A. Results of U.S. Airline Deregulation: Evidence from the Regulated Canadian Airlines. *Logist. Transp. Rev.*, December 1986, *22*(4), pp. 297–337. **[G: Canada; U.S.]**

Kalt, Joseph P. and Leone, Robert A. Regional Effects of Energy Price Decontrol: The Roles of Interregional Trade, Stockholding, and Microeconomic Incidence. *Rand J. Econ.*, Summer 1986, *17*(2), pp. 201–13. **[G: U.S.]**

Kane, Edward J. Technology and the Regulation of Financial Markets. **In** *Saunders, A. and White, L. J., eds.*, 1986, pp. 187–93.

Kareken, John H. Federal Bank Regulatory Policy: A Description and Some Observations. *J. Bus.*, January 1986, *59*(1), pp. 3–48. **[G: U.S.]**

Kaserman, David L. and Mayo, John W. The Ghosts of Deregulated Telecommunications: An Essay by Exorcists. *J. Policy Anal. Manage.*, Fall 1986, *6*(1), pp. 84–92. **[G: U.S.]**

Kaufman, George G. Federal Bank Regulatory Policy: Comment. *J. Bus.*, January 1986, *59*(1), pp. 69–77. **[G: U.S.]**

Keeley, Michael C. and Furlong, Frederick T. Bank Regulation and the Public Interest. *Fed. Res. Bank San Francisco Econ. Rev.*, Spring 1986, (2), pp. 55–71.

Kemp, Kathleen A. Lawyers, Politics, and Economic Regulation. *Soc. Sci. Quart.*, June 1986, *67*(2), pp. 267–82. **[G: U.S.]**

Kirchner, Christian. Deregulation as an Instrument in Industrial Policy: Comment. *J. Inst. Theoretical Econ.*, March 1986, *142*(1), pp. 75–78.

Kokkelenberg, Edward C. and Choi, Jeong Poy. Factor Demands, Adjustment Costs and Regulation. *Appl. Econ.*, June 1986, *18*(6), pp. 631–43. **[G: U.S.]**

Krattenmaker, Thomas G. and Salop, Steven C. Anticompetitive Exclusion: Raising Rivals' Costs to Achieve Power over Price. *Yale Law J.*, December 1986, *96*(2), pp. 209–93. **[G: U.S.]**

Kunreuther, Howard and Bendixen, Lisa. Benefits Assessment for Regulatory Problems. **In** *Bentkover, J. D.; Covello, V. T. and Jeryl, M., eds.*, 1986, pp. 35–50. **[G: U.S.]**

Laffont, Jean-Jacques and Tirole, Jean. Using Cost Observation to Regulate Firms. *J. Polit. Econ.*, Part 1, June 1986, *94*(3), pp. 614–41.

Lamberton, Don M. Australian Regulatory Policy. **In** *Snow, M. S.*, 1986, pp. 231–52. **[G: Australia]**

Law, Peter J. The Effect of Regulation on Wages and Intermediate Product Prices under Bilateral Monopoly. *Bull. Econ. Res.*, September 1986, *38*(3), pp. 221–36.

Lemon, J. Rodney. Regulatory Reform of Interstate Natural Gas Pipelines. *Contemp. Policy Issues*, October 1986, *4*(4), pp. 93–103. **[G: U.S.]**

Levin, Harvey J. Latecomer Cost Handicap: Importance in a Changing Regulatory Landscape. **In** *Demac, D. A., ed.*, 1986, pp. 251–79. **[G: U.S.]**

Libecap, Gary D. Deregulation as an Instrument in Industrial Policy: Comment. *J. Inst. Theoretical Econ.*, March 1986, *142*(1), pp. 71–74.

Litan, Robert E. and Nordhaus, William D. Regulatory Reform and OSHA Policy: Comments. *J. Policy Anal. Manage.*, Spring 1986, *5*(3), pp. 467–81. **[G: U.S.]**

Lizzo, Emilio. The Privatization of State Holdings in Italy up to 1984. *Ann. Pub. Co-op. Econ.*, September 1986, *57*(3), pp. 315–43. **[G: Italy]**

Macauley, Molly K. Out of Space? Regulation and Technical Change in Communications Satellites. *Amer. Econ. Rev.*, May 1986, *76*(2), pp. 280–84. **[G: U.S.]**

Maddox, Brenda. The Theology of Satellite Television: Dogmas That Are Holding Up the Progress of Satellite Television. **In** *Demac, D. A., ed.*, 1986, pp. 107–13. **[G: U.S.; W. Europe]**

Makhija, Anil K. and Thompson, Howard E. The Ratepayer and Stockholder under Alternative Regulatory Policies. *Land Econ.*, May 1986, *62*(2), pp. 119–33. **[G: U.S.]**

Mann, Michael D. International Legal Assistance in Securities Law Enforcement—Status and Perspectives. *Wirtsch. Recht*, 1986, *38*(2), pp. 157–92. **[G: U.S.]**

Maramba, Felix K., Jr. Privatization: Imperative for Sustained Economic Development. *Philippine Econ. J.*, 1986, *25*(1–2), pp. 17–23. **[G: Philippines]**

Mathewson, G. Frank and Winter, Ralph A. The Economics of Life Insurance Regulation: Valuation Constraints. **In** *Finsinger, J. and Pauly, M. V., eds.*, 1986, pp. 257–90. **[G: Canada]**

Mayer, Thomas. Regulating Banks: Comment. *J. Bus.*, January 1986, *59*(1), pp. 87–96. **[G: U.S.]**

McCormick, Robert E.; Shughart, William F., II and Tollison, Robert D. The Disinterest in Deregulation: Reply. *Amer. Econ. Rev.*, June 1986, *76*(3), pp. 564–65.

McCulloch, J. Huston. Bank Regulation and Deposit Insurance. *J. Bus.*, January 1986, *59*(1), pp. 79–85. **[G: U.S.]**

McFarland, Henry. Ramsey Pricing of Inputs with Downstream Monopoly Power and Regulation: Implications for Railroad Rate Setting. *J. Transp. Econ. Policy*, January 1986, *20*(1), pp. 81–90. **[G: U.S.]**

McGonagle, John J., Jr. The Uncertainty Principle and Regulation. **In** *Gilad, B. and Kaish, S., eds., Vol. B*, 1986, pp. 123–32. **[G: U.S.]**

McKenzie, Richard B. Eminent Domain: A New Industrial Policy Tool. *J. Inst. Theoretical Econ.*, March 1986, *142*(1), pp. 27–38. **[G: U.S.]**

Mendeloff, John. Regulatory Reform and OSHA Policy. *J. Policy Anal. Manage.*, Spring 1986, *5*(3), pp. 440–68. **[G: U.S.]**

Meyer, Peter B. The Corporate Person and Social Control: Responding to Deregulation. *Rev. Radical Polit. Econ.*, Fall 1986, *18*(3), pp. 65–84. **[G: U.S.]**

Minnerop, Henry F. and Stoll, Hans R. Technological Change in the Back Office: Implications for Structure and Regulation of the Securities Industry. **In** *Saunders, A. and White, L. J., eds.*, 1986, pp. 31–51. **[G: U.S.]**

Moylan, James J. and Ukman, Laren. Dispute Resolution Systems in the Commodity Futures Industry. *J. Futures Markets*, Winter 1986, *6*(4), pp. 659–70. **[G: U.S.]**

Mussa, Michael. Safety and Soundness as an Objective of Regulation of Depository Institutions: Comment. *J. Bus.*, January 1986, *59*(1), pp. 97–117. **[G: U.S.]**

Noam, Eli M. Telecommunications Policy on Both Sides of the Atlantic: Divergence and Outlook. **In** *Snow, M. S.*, 1986, pp. 255–74.

Noether, Monica. The Effect of Government Policy Changes on the Supply of Physicians: Expansion of a Competitive Fringe. *J. Law Econ.*, October 1986, *29*(2), pp. 231–62. **[G: U.S.]**

O'Driscoll, Gerald P., Jr. Deregulation and Monetary Reform. *Fed. Res. Bank Dallas Econ. Rev.*, July 1986, pp. 19–31. **[G: U.S.]**

Okediji, Olubunmi. Government Participation in the Nigerian Insurance Market: Regulatory or Competitive? *J. World Trade Law*, Sept.:Oct. 1986, *20*(5), pp. 540–53. **[G: Nigeria]**

Outreville, J.-François. The French Insurance Market. **In** *Finsinger, J. and Pauly, M. V., eds.*, 1986, pp. 230–53. **[G: France]**

Owen, Bruce M. and Gottlieb, Paul D. The Rise and Fall and Rise of Cable Television Regulation. **In** *Weiss, L. W. and Klass, M. W., eds.*, 1986, pp. 78–104. **[G: U.S.]**

Pauly, Mark V.; Kunreuther, Howard and Kleindorfer, Paul R. Regulation and Quality Competition in the U.S. Insurance Industry. **In** *Finsinger, J. and Pauly, M. V., eds.*, 1986, pp. 65–107. **[G: U.S.]**

Peck, Merton J. Deregulation in the American Economy. *Kobe Univ. Econ.*, 1986, (32), pp. 1–17. **[G: U.S.]**

Pethig, Rüdiger. Eminent Domain: A New Industrial Policy Tool: Comment. *J. Inst. Theoretical*

Econ., March 1986, *142*(1), pp. 44–51. **[G: W. Germany]**

Petzel, Todd E. Self-regulation and Futures Markets: Benefits from Technology Gains. **In** *Saunders, A. and White, L. J., eds.*, 1986, pp. 73–77. **[G: U.S.]**

Peyton, David. A New View of Copyright. *J. Policy Anal. Manage.*, Fall 1986, *6*(1), pp. 92–98. **[G: U.S.]**

Piga, Francesco. The CONSOB and the Transparency of Markets. *Rev. Econ. Cond. Italy*, May-Aug. 1986, (2), pp. 317–41. **[G: Italy]**

Pindyck, Robert S. Capital Adjustment Costs, Monopoly Power, and the Regulated Firm. **In** *Grieson, R. E., ed.*, 1986, pp. 219–30.

Platzer, Renate. The Privatisation Debate in Austria. *Ann. Pub. Co-op. Econ.*, Apr.-June 1986, *57*(2), pp. 275–91. **[G: Austria]**

Porter, Robert H. The Impact of Government Policy on the U.S. Cigarette Industry. **In** *Ippolito, P. M. and Scheffman, D. T., eds.*, 1986, pp. 447–81. **[G: U.S.]**

Pratt, Joseph A. Business and Public Policy: The Uses and Limits of Strategic–Structural Analysis. **In** *Atack, J., ed.*, 1986, pp. 103–18.

Price, Barry and Simowitz, Roslyn. In Defense of Government Regulation. *J. Econ. Issues*, March 1986, *20*(1), pp. 165–77.

Price, Robert S. Government Policy and International Natural Gas Trade. *J. Energy Devel.*, Spring 1986, *11*(2), pp. 189–211. **[G: OECD]**

Pyle, David H. Capital Regulation and Deposit Insurance. *J. Banking Finance*, June 1986, *10*(2), pp. 189–201.

Quinn, Robert and Yandle, Bruce. Expenditures on Air Pollution Control under Federal Regulation. *Rev. Reg. Stud.*, Fall 1986, *16*(3), pp. 11–16. **[G: U.S.]**

Redwood, John. How to Protect the Investor. *Lloyds Bank Rev.*, April 1986, (160), pp. 21–35. **[G: U.K.]**

Regan, Donald H. The Supreme Court and State Protectionism: Making Sense of the Dormant Commerce Clause. *Mich. Law Rev.*, May 1986, *84*(6), pp. 1091–1287. **[G: U.S.]**

Ricketts, Martin and Peacock, Alan. Bargaining and the Regulatory System. *Int. Rev. Law Econ.*, June 1986, *6*(1), pp. 3–16.

Rohatyn, Felix G. Needed: Restraints on the Takeover Mania. *Challenge*, May/June 1986, *29*(2), pp. 30–34. **[G: U.S.]**

Rolnick, Arthur J. and Weber, Warren E. Inherent Instability in Banking: The Free Banking Experience. *Cato J.*, Winter 1986, *5*(3), pp. 877–90. **[G: U.S.]**

Rolshoven, Hubertus. Antitrust Policy and the Rationalization of the U.S. Steel Industry. *J. Inst. Theoretical Econ.*, March 1986, *142*(1), pp. 134–37. **[G: U.S.]**

Rosengren, Eric S. Is There a Need for Regulation in the Government Securities Market? *New Eng. Econ. Rev.*, Sept./Oct. 1986, pp. 29–40. **[G: U.S.]**

Ross, Thomas W. Store Wars: The Chain Tax Movement. *J. Law Econ.*, April 1986, *29*(1), pp. 125–37. **[G: U.S.]**

Ross, Thomas W. The Costs of Regulating Price Differences. *J. Bus.*, January 1986, *59*(1), pp. 143–56.

Roth, Timothy P. Antitrust Policy and the Rationalization of the U.S. Steel Industry. *J. Inst. Theoretical Econ.*, March 1986, *142*(1), pp. 114–30. **[G: U.S.]**

Rothschild, R. Raising Rivals' Costs: Regulation as a Competitive Strategy in Intra-industry Trade. **In** *Greenaway, D. and Tharakan, P. K. M., eds.*, 1986, pp. 34–46.

Rutz, Roger D. Futures Markets: Comment. **In** *Saunders, A. and White, L. J., eds.*, 1986, pp. 85–90. **[G: U.S.]**

Sappington, David E. M. Commitment to Regulatory Bureaucracy. *Info. Econ. Policy*, December 1986, *2*(4), pp. 243–58.

Sappington, David E. M. Designing Incentives for Efficient Production in Large-scale Enterprises: The Case of Fertilizer Manufacturers. **In** *Segura, E. L.; Shetty, Y. T. and Nishimizu, M., eds.*, 1986, pp. 69–89. **[G: Egypt; India]**

Scheffman, David T. The Impact of Government Policy on the U.S. Cigarette Industry: Comments. **In** *Ippolito, P. M. and Scheffman, D. T., eds.*, 1986, pp. 483–84. **[G: U.S.]**

Schneider, Dieter. Ausweichhandlungen vor Regulierungen auf Finanzmärkten als Prüfstein wettbewerbspolitischer Konzepte. (Evasions of Regulations in Financial Markets as a Test of Concepts of Competition Policy. With English summary.) **In** *Eucken, W. and Böhm, F., eds.*, 1986, pp. 155–81.

Schramm, Carl J. Revisiting the Competition/Regulation Debate in Health Care Cost Containment. *Inquiry*, Fall 1986, *23*(3), pp. 236–42. **[G: U.S.]**

Schuck, Peter H. and Litan, Robert E. Regulatory Reform in the Third World: The Case of Peru. *Yale J. Regul.*, Fall 1986, *4*(1), pp. 51–78. **[G: Peru]**

von der Schulenburg, J.-Matthias Graf. Regulatory Measures to Enforce Quality Production of Self-employed Professionals—A Theoretical Study of a Dynamic Market Process. **In** *von der Schulenburg, J.-M. G. and Skogh, G., eds.*, 1986, pp. 133–47.

Schwartz, Marius. The Nature and Scope of Contestability Theory. *Oxford Econ. Pap.*, Suppl. Nov. 1986, *38*, pp. 37–57.

Schwartz, Robert A. Securities Markets: Comment. **In** *Saunders, A. and White, L. J., eds.*, 1986, pp. 57–59. **[G: U.S.]**

Scribner, Richard O. The Technological Revolution in Securities Trading: Can Regulation Keep Up? **In** *Saunders, A. and White, L. J., eds.*, 1986, pp. 19–29. **[G: U.S.]**

Skogh, Göran. The Regulation of the Swedish Insurance Industry. **In** *Finsinger, J. and Pauly, M. V., eds.*, 1986, pp. 163–86. **[G: Sweden]**

Snow, Marcellus S. Communications Policy in Seven Developed Countries: Introduction, Background, and Conclusions. **In** *Snow, M. S.*, 1986, pp. 3–19. **[G: OECD]**

Snow, Marcellus S. Regulating Telecommunications, Information, and the Media: An Agenda for Future Comparative Research. **In** *Snow, M. S.*, 1986, pp. 275–94.

Spencer, Lee B., Jr. Securities Markets: Comment. **In** *Saunders, A. and White, L. J., eds.*, 1986, pp. 53–55. **[G: U.S.]**

Spiller, Pablo T. Comments [The Effects of the Advertising Substantiation Program on Advertising Agencies] [An Economic Analysis of the FTC's Ad Substantiation Program]. **In** *Ippolito, P. M. and Scheffman, D. T., eds.*, 1986, pp. 217–20. **[G: U.S.]**

Stalon, Charles G. The Diminishing Role of Regulation in the Natural Gas Industry. *Energy J.*, April 1986, *7*(2), pp. 1–12. **[G: U.S.]**

Stanbury, W. T. and Tretheway, Michael W. Airline Deregulation: A Bibliography. *Logist. Transp. Rev.*, December 1986, *22*(4), pp. 449–89. **[G: U.S.; Canada]**

Starr, Kenneth W. Judicial Review in the Post-*Chevron* Era. *Yale J. Regul.*, Spring 1986, *3*(2), pp. 283–312. **[G: U.S.]**

Stefani, Giorgio. Privatizing Public Enterprises in Italy: The Case of State Holdings. *Ann. Pub. Co-op. Econ.*, Apr.-June 1986, *57*(2), pp. 231–51.

Stigler, George J. Free Riders and Collective Action: An Appendix to Theories of Economic Regulation. **In** *Stigler, G. J.*, 1986, *1974*, pp. 67–75. **[G: U.S.]**

Stigler, George J. The Regularities of Regulation. **In** *Dale, R., ed.*, 1986, pp. 1–12. **[G: U.S.]**

Stigler, George J. The Theory of Economic Regulation. **In** *Stigler, G. J.*, 1986, *1971*, pp. 243–64.

Stigler, George J. What Can Regulators Regulate? The Case of Electricity. **In** *Stigler, G. J.*, 1986, *1962*, pp. 224–42. **[G: U.S.]**

Strauss, Robert P. Business Taxes. **In** *Gold, S. D., ed.*, 1986, pp. 231–58. **[G: U.S.]**

Sunstein, Cass R. Deregulation and the Courts. *J. Policy Anal. Manage.*, Spring 1986, *5*(3), pp. 517–34. **[G: U.S.]**

Swidler, Steve. A Reexamination of Liquor Price and Consumption Differences between Public and Private Ownership States: Comment [Public versus Private Liquor Retailing: An Investigation into the Behavior of the State Governments]. *Southern Econ. J.*, July 1986, *53*(1), pp. 259–64. **[G: U.S.]**

Takigawa, Yoshio. Deregulation of Interest Rate and Bank Rate Policy. *Kobe Univ. Econ.*, 1986, (32), pp. 121–37.

Tapp, Julian. Regulation of the UK Insurance Industry. **In** *Finsinger, J. and Pauly, M. V., eds.*, 1986, pp. 27–61. **[G: U.K.]**

Tauzovich, B., et al. An Expert Advisory System for Government Regulations: Knowledge Acquisition Methodology. **In** *Pau, L. F., ed.*, 1986, pp. 205–12.

Telson, Michael L. Policy Issues in Oil and Gas Transportation Regulation. *Contemp. Policy Issues*, October 1986, *4*(4), pp. 60–64. **[G: U.S.]**

Terasawa, Yoshio. Opening Japanese Financial Markets: What Has Changed, What Will Change? Comment. **In** *Pugel, T. A., ed.*, 1986, pp. 137–39. **[G: Japan]**

Thiemeyer, Theo. Privatization: On the Many Senses in Which This Word Is Used in an International Discussion on Economic Theory. *Ann. Pub. Co-op. Econ.*, Apr.-June 1986, *57*(2), pp. 141–52.

Tollison, Robert D. Antitrust Policy and the Rationalization of the U.S. Steel Industry: Comment. *J. Inst. Theoretical Econ.*, March 1986, *142*(1), pp. 131–33. **[G: U.S.]**

Trapani, John M., III. Eminent Domain: A New Industrial Policy Tool: Comment. *J. Inst. Theoretical Econ.*, March 1986, *142*(1), pp. 39–43. **[G: U.S.]**

Trebing, Harry M. Apologetics of Deregulation in Energy and Telecommunications: An Institutionalist Assessment. *J. Econ. Issues*, September 1986, *20*(3), pp. 613–32.

Tretheway, Michael W. Airline Deregulation: Introduction. *Logist. Transp. Rev.*, December 1986, *22*(4), pp. 293–96. **[G: U.S.]**

Van den Bergh, Roger. Belgian Public Policy towards the Retailing Trade. **In** *von der Schulenburg, J.-M. G. and Skogh, G., eds.*, 1986, pp. 185–205. **[G: Belgium]**

Vanthienen, L. and Vermaelen, Theo. The Effect of Royal Decree 15 on Security Prices and Financing Decisions. *Tijdschrift Econ. Manage.*, 1986, *31*(4), pp. 541–82. **[G: Netherlands]**

Varela, Oscar and Olson, Richard E. A General Equilibrium Analysis of Financial Regulation. *J. Public Econ.*, August 1986, *30*(3), pp. 329–40.

de Villiers, J. U. and Scott, D. R. Research and Development Expenditure in Regulated and Unregulated Markets. *Managerial Dec. Econ.*, September 1986, *7*(3), pp. 197–201. **[G: S. Africa]**

Viscusi, W. Kip. Regulatory Reform and OSHA Policy: The Status of OSHA Reform: A Comment on Mendeloff's Proposals. *J. Policy Anal. Manage.*, Spring 1986, *5*(3), pp. 469–75. **[G: U.S.]**

Vitaliano, Donald F. Measuring the Efficiency Cost of Rent Control. *Amer. Real Estate Urban Econ. Assoc. J.*, Spring 1986, *14*(1), pp. 61–71. **[G: U.S.]**

Voge, Jean-Paul. A Survey of French Regulatory Policy. **In** *Snow, M. S.*, 1986, pp. 106–30. **[G: France]**

Wahlroos, Bror. Näringslivets liberalisering. Fri konkurrens kontra reglering. (Liberalization of the Industrial Sector. With English summary.) *Ekon. Samfundets Tidskr.*, 1986, *39*(1), pp. 7–15. **[G: Finland]**

Wald, Patricia M. The Realpolitik of Judicial Review in a Deregulation Era. *J. Policy Anal. Manage.*, Spring 1986, *5*(3), pp. 535–46. **[G: U.S.]**

Walters, Stephen J. K. Reciprocity Reexamined: The Consolidated Foods Case. *J. Law Econ.*, October 1986, *29*(2), pp. 423–38. **[G: U.S.]**

Ware, Roger and Winter, Ralph A. Public Pricing under Imperfect Competition. *Int. J. Ind. Organ.*, March 1986, *4*(1), pp. 87–97.

Weiss, Leonard W. The Regulatory Reform Movement. **In** *Weiss, L. W. and Klass, M. W., eds.*, 1986, pp. 1–13. **[G: U.S.]**

Wells, Donald R. and Scruggs, L. S. Historical Insights into the Deregulation of Money and Banking. *Cato J.*, Winter 1986, *5*(3), pp. 899–910. **[G: U.S.]**

White, Frederick L. and Stein, William. Legal and Regulatory Developments. *J. Futures Markets*, Fall 1986, *6*(3), pp. 503–04. **[G: U.S.]**

White, Lawrence H. Regulatory Sources of Instability in Banking [Inherent Instability in Banking: The Free Banking Experience]. *Cato J.*, Winter 1986, *5*(3), pp. 891–97. **[G: U.S.]**

White, Lawrence J. The Partial Deregulation of Banks and Other Depository Institutions. **In** *Weiss, L. W. and Klass, M. W., eds.*, 1986, pp. 169–209. **[G: U.S.]**

Williamson, Oliver E. Managerial Discretion and Business Behaviour. **In** *Williamson, O. E.*, 1986, *1963*, pp. 6–31.

Yandle, Bruce. Federal Trade Commission Output and Costs: Cycling through the Zone of Political Wrath. *Soc. Sci. Quart.*, September 1986, *67*(3), pp. 517–33. **[G: U.S.]**

Yandle, Bruce. The Evolution of Regulatory Activities in the 1970s and 1980s. **In** *Cagan, P., ed.*, 1986, pp. 105–45. **[G: U.S.]**

Yandle, Bruce and Young, Elizabeth. Regulating the Function, Not the Industry. *Public Choice*, 1986, *51*(1), pp. 59–70.

Zardkoohi, Asghar and Sheer, Alain. A Reexamination of Liquor Price and Consumption Differences between Public and Private Ownership States: Reply [Public versus Private Liquor Retailing: An Investigation into the Behavior of the State Governments]. *Southern Econ. J.*, July 1986, *53*(1), pp. 265–68. **[G: U.S.]**

620 Economics of Technological Change

621 Technological Change; Innovation; Research and Development

6210 General

Aganbegian, A. G. The General Course of Economic Policy. *Prob. Econ.*, October 1986, *29*(6), pp. 3–35.

Amann, Ronald. Technical Progress and Soviet Economic Development: Setting the Scene. **In** *Amann, R. and Cooper, J., eds.*, 1986, pp. 5–30. **[G: U.S.S.R.]**

Baark, Erik and Jamison, Andrew. The Technology and Culture Problematique. **In** *Baark, E. and Jamison, A., eds.*, 1986, pp. 1–34.

Bechtel, Stephen D., Jr. Technology and Its Role in Modern Society. **In** *Landau, R. and Rosenberg, N., eds.*, 1986, pp. 115–18.

Beck, Roger L. Comment: Does Competitive Dissipation Require a Short Patent Life? [The Scope and Duration of the Patent Right and the Nature of Research Rivalry]. **In** *Palmer, J., ed.*, 1986, pp. 121–29.

Bhalla, Ajit S. and James, Dilmus D. Technological Blending: Frontier Technology in Traditional Economic Sectors. *J. Econ. Issues*, June 1986, *20*(2), pp. 453–62.

Bhargava, S. N. India: Fiscal Incentives for the Development of Scientific Research and Locally Developed Technology. *Bull. Int. Fiscal Doc.*, Apr./May 1986, *40*(4/5), pp. 161–63. **[G: India]**

Bianchi, Lorenzo and Rispoli, Maurizio. Innovation Diffusion: Foreword. *Ricerche Econ.*, Oct.-Dec. 1986, *40*(4), pp. 579–84.

Blomström, Magnus. Foreign Investment and Productive Efficiency: The Case of Mexico. *J. Ind. Econ.*, September 1986, *35*(1), pp. 97–110. **[G: Mexico]**

Claeys, George. Ecology and Technology in Early Nineteenth Century American Utopianism: A Note on John Adolphus Etzler. *Sci. Soc.*, Summer 1986, *50*(2), pp. 219–25.

Comanor, William S. The Political Economy of the Pharmaceutical Industry. *J. Econ. Lit.*, September 1986, *24*(3), pp. 1178–1217. **[G: U.S.]**

Dahmén, Erik. Rights and Relations in Modern Economic Theory: Comment. **In** *Day, R. H. and Eliasson, G., eds.*, 1986, pp. 342–43.

Eads, George C. and Nelson, Richard R. Japanese High Technology Policy: What Lessons for the United States? **In** *Patrick, H., ed.*, 1986, pp. 243–69. **[G: U.S.; Japan]**

Eliasson, Gunnar. Micro Heterogeneity of Firms and the Stability of Industrial Growth: Reply. **In** *Day, R. H. and Eliasson, G., eds.*, 1986, pp. 112–14. **[G: Sweden]**

Eliasson, Gunnar. Micro Heterogeneity of Firms and the Stability of Industrial Growth. **In** *Day, R. H. and Eliasson, G., eds.*, 1986, *1984*, pp. 79–104. **[G: Sweden]**

Eliasson, Gunnar. Rights and Relations in Modern Economic Theory: Comment. **In** *Day, R. H. and Eliasson, G., eds.*, 1986, pp. 346–50.

Elzinga, Aant and Jamison, Andrew. The Other Side of the Coin: The Cultural Critique of Technology in India and Japan. **In** *Baark, E. and Jamison, A., eds.*, 1986, pp. 205–53. **[G: India; Japan]**

Florescu, M. Role of Cybernetics in Science and Technology Evolution. *Econ. Computat. Cybern. Stud. Res.*, 1986, *21*(1), pp. 7–13. **[G: Romania]**

Gangopadhyay, Shubhashis. Choice of Techniques, Employment and Poverty. *J. Quant. Econ.*, July 1986, *2*(2), pp. 199–212.

Gonçalves, Reinaldo. Technological Spill-Overs and Manpower Training: A Comparative Analysis of Multinational and National Enterprises in Brazilian Manufacturing. *J. Econ. Devel.*, July 1986, *11*(1), pp. 119–32. **[G: Brazil]**

Gray, H. Peter. Japan's Challenge to Technological Competition and Its Limitations: Comment. **In** *Pugel, T. A., ed.*, 1986, pp. 255–61. **[G: Japan; U.S.]**

Gray, H. Peter. North–South Technology Transfer: Two Neglected Problems. *J. Econ. Devel.*, July 1986, *11*(1), pp. 27–45. [G: LDCs]

Hall, P. H. The Theory and Practice of Innovation Policy: An Overview. **In** *Hall, P., ed.*, 1986, *1984*, pp. 1–34.

Hamilton, David. Technology and Institutions Are Neither. *J. Econ. Issues*, June 1986, *20*(2), pp. 525–32.

Haug, Peter. U.S. High Technology Multinationals and Silicon Glen. *Reg. Stud.*, April 1986, *20*(2), pp. 103–16. [G: U.S.; U.K.]

Hax, Herbert. Japan's Industrial Policy for New Technologies: Comment. *J. Inst. Theoretical Econ.*, March 1986, *142*(1), pp. 181–83. [G: Japan]

Heierli, U. Division of Labour and Appropriate Technology—From Adam Smith to E. F. Schumacher. **In** *Bassand, M., et al., eds.*, 1986, pp. 9–37.

Imai, Ken-ichi. Japan's Industrial Policy for High Technology Industry. **In** *Patrick, H., ed.*, 1986, pp. 137–69. [G: Japan]

Janiszewski, Hubert A. New Rules Concerning Technology Transfer in Poland. *J. World Trade Law*, Sept.:Oct. 1986, *20*(5), pp. 571–74. [G: Poland]

Katz, Michael L. and Shapiro, Carl. How to License Intangible Property. *Quart. J. Econ.*, August 1986, *101*(3), pp. 567–89.

Kaufer, Erich. The Incentives to Innovate under Alternative Property Rights Assignments with Special Reference to the Patent System. *J. Inst. Theoretical Econ.*, March 1986, *142*(1), pp. 210–26.

Kjærby, Finn. The Development of Agricultural Mechanisation in Tanzania. **In** *Boesen, J., et al., eds.*, 1986, pp. 173–90. [G: Tanzania]

Kline, Stephen J. and Rosenberg, Nathan. An Overview of Innovation. **In** *Landau, R. and Rosenberg, N., eds.*, 1986, pp. 275–305.

Koshiro, Kazutoshi. Japan's Industrial Policy for New Technologies. *J. Inst. Theoretical Econ.*, March 1986, *142*(1), pp. 163–77. [G: Japan]

Kuwahara, Yasuo. Technology Promotion in Japan. **In** *Hax, H.; Kraus, W. and Tsuchiya, K., eds.*, 1986, pp. 49–70. [G: U.S.; U.K.; Japan; W. Germany]

Lall, Sanjaya. Technological Development and Export Performance in LDCs: Leading Engineering and Chemical Firms in India. *Weltwirtsch. Arch.*, 1986, *122*(1), pp. 80–92. [G: India]

Lamberton, Don M.; Macdonald, Stuart and Mandeville, Thomas D. Information and Technological Change—A Research Program in Retrospect. **In** *Hall, P., ed.*, 1986, *1984*, pp. 231–43. [G: U.K.]

Landau, Ralph and Rosenberg, Nathan. The Positive Sum Strategy: Harnessing Technology for Economic Growth: Introduction. **In** *Landau, R. and Rosenberg, N., eds.*, 1986, pp. v–x.

Landes, David S. European Expansion: The History of Innovation and Performance. **In** *Gondolf, E. W.; Marcus, I. M. and Dougherty, J. P., eds.*, 1986, pp. 25–41.

Ledić, Michèle and Silberston, Aubrey. The Technological Balance of Payments in Perspective. **In** *Hall, P., ed.*, 1986, *1984*, pp. 104–34. [G: OECD]

Lee, Han Yu and Hayden, F. Gregory. DeGregori's *A Theory of Technology:* A Review Article. *J. Econ. Issues*, September 1986, *20*(3), pp. 799–804.

Levin, Henry M. and Rumberger, Russell. The Low-Skill Future of High Tech. **In** *Reynolds, L. G.; Masters, S. H. and Moser, C. H., eds.*, 1986, *1983*, pp. 190–96. [G: U.S.]

Littlechild, S. C. The Incentives to Innovate under Alternative Property Rights Assignments with Special Reference to the Patent System: Comment. *J. Inst. Theoretical Econ.*, March 1986, *142*(1), pp. 227–29.

Lyon, David. Marxist Misgivings about the Information Society: Help or Hinderance in Facing the Future? **In** *Jain, A. and Matejko, A., eds.*, 1986, pp. 245–58.

Maggs, Peter B. Legal Regulation of the Dissemination of Scientific and Technical Information in the USSR. **In** *Ioffe, O. S. and Janis, M. W., eds.*, 1986, pp. 103–26. [G: U.S.S.R.]

McFetridge, D. G. and Rafiquzzaman, M. The Scope and Duration of the Patent Right and the Nature of Research Rivalry. **In** *Palmer, J., ed.*, 1986, pp. 91–120.

McLoughlin, Peter F. M. A Theory of Technology—Continuity and Change in Human Development: A Review Article. *J. Econ. Issues*, September 1986, *20*(3), pp. 785–98.

Metcalfe, J. S. and Gibbons, Michael. Technological Variety and the Process of Competition. *Écon. Appl.*, 1986, *39*(3), pp. 493–520.

Meyerson, Per-Martin. Industrial Finance System in Europe, U.S. and Japan: Comment. **In** *Day, R. H. and Eliasson, G., eds.*, 1986, pp. 401–03. [G: Europe; U.S.; Japan]

Michie, Barry H. Problematics of Technology and Social Change. **In** *Björkman, J. W., ed.*, 1986, pp. 69–83. [G: S. Asia]

Mishan, Ezra J. Religion, Capitalism and Technology. **In** *Mishan, E. J.*, 1986, *1983*, pp. 194–224.

Mueller, Willard F. and Culbertson, John D. Inter-industry Technology Flows in the U.S. Food-processing Industries. *Managerial Dec. Econ.*, September 1986, *7*(3), pp. 163–68. [G: U.S.]

Mujahid-Mukhtar, Eshya and Mukhtar, Hanid. The Overall Rate of Return to Agricultural Research and Extension Investments in Pakistan: A Comment. *Pakistan J. Appl. Econ.*, Winter 1986, *5*(2), pp. 207–15. [G: Pakistan]

Nelson, Richard R. Evolutionary Modelling of Economic Change. **In** *Stiglitz, J. E. and Mathewson, G. F., eds.*, 1986, pp. 450–71. [G: U.S.]

Ozawa, Terutomo. Japanese Policy toward Foreign Multinationals: Implications for Trade and Competitiveness. **In** *Pugel, T. A., ed.*, 1986, pp. 141–62. [G: Japan]

Pack, Howard. The Technological Impact of World Bank Operations. **In** *Feinberg, R. E.,* *et al.*, 1986, pp. 161–75.

Pakes, Ariel S. Patents as Options: Some Estimates of the Value of Holding European Patent Stocks. *Econometrica*, July 1986, *54*(4), pp. 755–84. **[G: France; U.K.; W. Germany]**

Parker, William N. Industrial Finance System in Europe, U.S. and Japan: Comment. **In** *Day, R. H. and Eliasson, G., eds.*, 1986, pp. 397–400. **[G: Europe; U.S.; Japan]**

Patrick, Hugh. Japanese High Technology Industrial Policy in Comparative Context. **In** *Patrick, H., ed.*, 1986, pp. 3–33. **[G: Japan]**

Russo, John. Technological Displacement: Strategies of the Global Auto Industry. **In** *Gondolf, E. W.; Marcus, I. M. and Dougherty, J. P., eds.*, 1986, pp. 122–32. **[G: U.S.]**

Rybczynski, Tad M. Industrial Finance System in Europe, U.S. and Japan: Reply. **In** *Day, R. H. and Eliasson, G., eds.*, 1986, pp. 408–09. **[G: Europe; U.S.; Japan]**

Rybczynski, Tad M. Industrial Finance System in Europe, U.S. and Japan. **In** *Day, R. H. and Eliasson, G., eds.*, 1986, *1984*, pp. 385–96. **[G: Europe; U.S.; Japan]**

Sato, Ryuzo. Japan's Challenge to Technological Competition and Its Limitations. **In** *Pugel, T. A., ed.*, 1986, pp. 237–54. **[G: Japan; U.S.]**

Schoenberger, Erica. Competition, Competitive Strategy, and Industrial Change: The Case of Electronic Components. *Econ. Geogr.*, October 1986, *62*(4), pp. 321–33. **[G: Global]**

Sörbom, Per. The Reception of Western Technology in China and Japan. **In** *Baark, E. and Jamison, A., eds.*, 1986, pp. 35–56. **[G: China; Japan]**

Spence, Michael. Cost Reduction, Competition and Industry Performance. **In** *Stiglitz, J. E. and Mathewson, G. F., eds.*, 1986, pp. 475–515.

Spinanger, Dean. Industrial Finance System in Europe, U.S. and Japan: Comment. **In** *Day, R. H. and Eliasson, G., eds.*, 1986, pp. 404–07. **[G: Europe; U.S.; Japan]**

Stiglitz, Joseph E. Theory of Competition, Incentives and Risk. **In** *Stiglitz, J. E. and Mathewson, G. F., eds.*, 1986, pp. 399–446.

Stranahan, H. A. and Shonkwiler, J. Scott. Evaluating the Returns to Postharvest Research in the Florida Citrus-Processing Subsector. *Amer. J. Agr. Econ.*, February 1986, *68*(1), pp. 88–94. **[G: U.S.]**

von Weizsäcker, Carl Christian. Rights and Relations in Modern Economic Theory. **In** *Day, R. H. and Eliasson, G., eds.*, 1986, *1984*, pp. 317–41.

Williamson, Oliver E. Japan's Industrial Policy for New Technologies: Comment. *J. Inst. Theoretical Econ.*, March 1986, *142*(1), pp. 178–80. **[G: Japan]**

Winter, Sidney G. Micro Heterogeneity of Firms and the Stability of Industrial Growth: Comment. **In** *Day, R. H. and Eliasson, G., eds.*, 1986, pp. 105–11. **[G: Sweden]**

Wohlmuth, Karl. Practices and Policies of Host Countries towards Third World Multinationals: A Competitive Edge against Old Multinationals? **In** *Khan, K. M., ed.*, 1986, pp. 211–39. **[G: LDCs]**

Wrigley, Julia. Technical Education and Industry in the Nineteenth Century. **In** *Elbaum, B. and Lazonick, W., eds.*, 1986, pp. 162–88. **[G: U.K.]**

Ysander, Bengt-Christer. Rights and Relations in Modern Economic Theory: Comment. **In** *Day, R. H. and Eliasson, G., eds.*, 1986, pp. 344–45.

Zinam, Oleg. Impact of Ideology and Organizational Structures on Technology and Quality of Life. *Rivista Int. Sci. Econ. Com.*, January 1986, *33*(1), pp. 41–58. **[G: Global]**

6211 Technological Change and Innovation

Ács, János. The Development of the Steel Industry from the Viewpoint of Innovation Theory. **In** *Goldberg, W. H., ed.*, 1986, pp. 283–306. **[G: Global]**

Adamowicz, Wiktor. Production Technology in Canadian Agriculture. *Can. J. Agr. Econ.*, March 1986, *34*(1), pp. 87–104. **[G: Canada]**

Adler, Emanuel. Ideological "Guerrillas" and the Quest for Technological Autonomy: Brazil's Domestic Computer Industry. *Int. Organ.*, Summer 1986, *40*(3), pp. 673–705. **[G: Brazil]**

Ahiakpor, James C. W. The Capital Intensity of Foreign, Private Local and State Owned Firms in a Less Developed Country: Ghana. *J. Devel. Econ.*, Jan.-Feb. 1986, *20*(1), pp. 145–62. **[G: Ghana]**

Ahlbrandt, Roger S., Jr. State-Sponsored Partnership: Building a Hi-tech Center for Western Pennsylvania. **In** *Gondolf, E. W.; Marcus, I. M. and Dougherty, J. P., eds.*, 1986, pp. 172–82. **[G: U.S.]**

Ahmad, Aqueil and Wilke, Arthur S. Technology Transfer in the New International Economic Order: Options, Obstacles, and Dilemmas. **In** *McIntyre, J. R. and Papp, D. S., eds.*, 1986, pp. 77–94.

Ahmad, Syed. Sraffa Numeraire and Reswitching: A Note. *J. Macroecon.*, Summer 1986, *8*(3), pp. 381–85.

Akinola, Amos A. Dynamic Innovator–Imitator (IN–IM) Diffusion Model. *Can. J. Agr. Econ.*, March 1986, *34*(1), pp. 113–24. **[G: Nigeria]**

Allen, D. E.; Crook, J. N. and Reekie, W. Duncan. Technical Change, Economies of Scope and Contestable Markets: Lessons from a British R&D Consortium. *S. Afr. J. Econ.*, June 1986, *54*(2), pp. 181–93. **[G: U.K.]**

Amendola, Mario and Gaffard, J. L. Technology as an Environment: A Suggested Interpretation. *Écon. Appl.*, 1986, *39*(3), pp. 473–92.

Amsden, Alice H. and Kim, Linsu. A Technological Perspective on the General Machinery Industry in the Republic of Korea. **In** *Fransman, M., ed.*, 1986, pp. 93–123. **[G: S. Korea]**

Anderson, Ronald W. and Harris, Christopher J. A Model of Innovation with Application to New Financial Products. **In** *Morris, D. J., et* *al., eds.*, 1986, pp. 203–18.

Anderson, Ronald W. and Harris, Christopher J. A Model of Innovation with Application to New Financial Products. *Oxford Econ. Pap.*, Suppl. Nov. 1986, *38*, pp. 203–18.

Antle, John M. Aggregation, Expectations, and the Explanation of Technological Change. *J. Econometrics*, Oct./Nov. 1986, *33*(1/2), pp. 213–36. **[G: U.S.]**

Antonelli, Cristiano. The International Diffusion of Process Innovations and the Neotechnology Theory of International Trade. *Econ. Notes*, 1986, (1), pp. 60–83. **[G: Global]**

Aoki, Masahiko. The Macroeconomic Background for High-Tech Industrialization in Japan. **In** *Landau, R. and Rosenberg, N., eds.*, 1986, pp. 569–81. **[G: Japan]**

Arena, Richard and Froeschle, Claude. Formes de progrès technique, séquences d'équilibres temporaires et stabilité économique. (Forms of Technical Progress, Sequences of Temporary Equilibrium and Economic Stability. With English summary.) *Écon. Appl.*, 1986, *39*(3), pp. 415–47.

Arnold, Erik and Senker, Peter. Computer-Aided Design: Europe's Role and American Technology. **In** *Sharp, M., ed.*, 1986, pp. 10–45. **[G: W. Europe; U.S.]**

Arnold, Walter. Japan's Technology Transfer to Advanced Industrial Countries. **In** *McIntyre, J. R. and Papp, D. S., eds.*, 1986, pp. 161–86. **[G: Japan]**

Audretsch, David B. The Celler Kefauver Act and the Deterrent Effect. *Rev. Ind. Organ.*, 1986, 2(4), pp. 322–38. **[G: U.S.]**

Baark, Erik. Information Infrastructures in India and China. **In** *Baark, E. and Jamison, A., eds.*, 1986, pp. 86–141. **[G: India; China]**

Bairam, Erkin I. Returns to Scale, Technical Progress and Output Growth in Branches of Industry: The Case of Eastern Europe and the USSR, 1961–75. *Keio Econ. Stud.*, 1986, 23(1), pp. 63–78. **[G: CMEA]**

Barkai, Haim. Ricardo's Volte-Face on Machinery. *J. Polit. Econ.*, Part 1, June 1986, *94*(3), pp. 595–613.

Barras, Richard. A Comparison of Embodied Technical Change in Services and Manufacturing Industry. *Appl. Econ.*, September 1986, *18*(9), pp. 941–58. **[G: U.K.]**

Baumol, William J. On the Possibility of Continuing Expansion of Finite Resources. *Kyklos*, 1986, *39*(2), pp. 167–79.

Baumol, William J. Technological Change and the New Urban Equilibrium. **In** *Baumol, W. J.*, 1986, *1981*, pp. 191–205. **[G: U.S.]**

Bayley, Molly G. Technology Meets Regulation. **In** *Saunders, A. and White, L. J., eds.*, 1986, pp. 63–71. **[G: U.S.]**

Bender, Horst O. High Technology Marketing. **In** *Backhaus, K. and Wilson, D. T., eds.*, 1986, pp. 191–223.

Berger, Allen N. The Role of Interstate Banking in the Diffusion of Electronic Payments Technology: Rejoinder. **In** *Lawrence, C. and Shay, R. P., eds.*, 1986, pp. 105. **[G: U.S.]**

Berger, Allen N. and Humphrey, David B. The Role of Interstate Banking in the Diffusion of Electronic Payments Technology. **In** *Lawrence, C. and Shay, R. P., eds.*, 1986, pp. 13–52. **[G: U.S.]**

Berlan, Jean-Pierre. From the United States to a World System: Technological Change, International Trade, Agricultural Policy in the Twentieth Century. **In** *Maunder, A. and Renborg, U., eds.*, 1986, pp. 343–52. **[G: U.S.]**

Berman, Marc L. Technology and the Clearing Function. **In** *Saunders, A. and White, L. J., eds.*, 1986, pp. 167–69. **[G: U.S.]**

Bertsch, Gary K. Technology Transfers and Technology Controls: A Synthesis of the Western–Soviet Relationship. **In** *Amann, R. and Cooper, J., eds.*, 1986, pp. 115–34. **[G: U.S.S.R.; OECD]**

Bhalla, Ajit S. and James, Jeffrey. New Technology Revolution: Myth or Reality for Developing Countries? **In** *Hall, P., ed.*, 1986, *1984*, pp. 135–71. **[G: LDCs]**

Binswanger, Hans P. and Pingali, Prabhu. Agricultural Intensification and Technical Change in Sub-Saharan Africa. **In** *Maunder, A. and Renborg, U., eds.*, 1986, pp. 381–86. **[G: Sub-Saharan Africa]**

Birolo, Adriano. Crescita e mutamento strutturale: un'analisi preliminare. (Growth and Structural Change: A Preliminary Analysis. With English summary.) *Ricerche Econ.*, Apr.-Sept. 1986, *40*(2–3), pp. 286–302.

Birowo, Achmad T. Human Capital, Technology and Institutions: Discussion. **In** *Maunder, A. and Renborg, U., eds.*, 1986, pp. 386–87.

Blackburn, Clark Waring, Jr. The Tug Hill Approach: Circuit Riders and Technology. **In** *Chicoine, D. L. and Walzer, N., eds.*, 1986, pp. 143–57. **[G: U.S.]**

Bohn, Roger E. and Jaikumar, Ramchandran. The Development of Intelligent Systems for Industrial Use: An Empirical Investigation. **In** *Rosenbloom, R. S., ed.*, 1986, pp. 213–62.

Bonin, John P. and Fukuda, Wataru. The Multifactor Illyrian Firm Revisited. *J. Compar. Econ.*, June 1986, *10*(2), pp. 171–80.

Bouman, Huub and Verhoef, Bram. High-technology and Employment: Some Information on the Netherlands. **In** *Nijkamp, P., ed. (II)*, 1986, pp. 289–98. **[G: Netherlands]**

Boyer, Robert and Coriat, Benjamin. Technical Flexibility and Macro Stabilisation. *Ricerche Econ.*, Oct.-Dec. 1986, *40*(4), pp. 771–835. **[G: U.S.]**

Braginskii, O. B. Economic Evaluation of New Directions in Scientific and Technical Development. *Matekon*, Fall 1986, *23*(1), pp. 82–96.

Brandt, Gerhard. Technological Change, Labour Market, and Trade Union Policy. **In** *Jacobi, O., et al., eds. (I)*, 1986, pp. 50–70. **[G: U.S.; U.K.; Italy; W. Germany]**

Braverman, Avishay and Stiglitz, Joseph E. Landlords, Tenants and Technological Innovations. *J. Devel. Econ.*, October 1986, *23*(2), pp. 313–32.

Bresnahan, Timothy F. Measuring the Spillovers

from Technical Advance: Mainframe Computers in Financial Services. *Amer. Econ. Rev.*, September 1986, *76*(4), pp. 742–55. **[G: U.S.]**

Brotchie, John F. Industrial Interdependence via Information Technology and Transport Interaction—Employment Impacts. **In** *Nijkamp, P., ed. (II)*, 1986, pp. 115–30.

Brown, Carole Ganz and Rushing, Francis W. National Policies for Developing High Technology Industries: International Comparisons: Introduction: Past Successes, Present Directions, and Future Issues. **In** *Rushing, F. W. and Brown, C. G., eds.*, 1986, pp. 1–8.

Brown, Martin and Philips, Peter. Craft Labor and Mechanization in Nineteenth-Century American Canning. *J. Econ. Hist.*, September 1986, *46*(3), pp. 743–56. **[G: U.S.]**

Businaro, Ugo L. Applying the Biological Evolution Metaphor to Technological Innovation. **In** *Freeman, C., ed.*, 1986, pp. 104–20.

Butera, Federico and Della Rocca, Giuseppe. Technological Innovation, Organisation of Work, and Unions. **In** *Jacobi, O., et al., eds. (I)*, 1986, pp. 15–34. **[G: Italy]**

Cain, Louis P. and Paterson, Donald G. Biased Technical Change, Scale, and Factor Substitution in American Industry, 1850–1919. *J. Econ. Hist.*, March 1986, *46*(1), pp. 153–64. **[G: U.S.]**

Cairncross, Alec. Innovation, Imitation and Growth. **In** *Cairncross, A.*, 1986, pp. 108–23.

Cairncross, Alec. The Role of Technology and Natural Resources in the Development Process. **In** *Cairncross, A.*, 1986, *1979*, pp. 124–35. **[G: Japan]**

Cantalupi, Marco. Sull'estendibilità dell'approccio neo-austriaco a trattare il progresso tecnico: il caso dei modelli verticalmente integrati. (On the Extensibility of the Neo-Austrian Approach to Technical Progress: The Case of Vertically Integrated Models. With English summary.) *Giorn. Econ.*, Mar.-Apr. 1986, *45*(3–4), pp. 149–70.

Capitelli, René and Müller, Heinz H. Ein Beispiel zum Problem der Innovationsförderung. (Stimulating Innovation Activities: An Illustration. With English summary.) *Schweiz. Z. Volkswirtsch. Statist.*, September 1986, *122*(3), pp. 535–53.

Carlsson, Bo. The Development and Use of Machine Tools in Historical Perspective. **In** *Day, R. H. and Eliasson, G., eds.*, 1986, *1984*, pp. 247–70. **[G: U.K.]**

Cekota, Jaromir. Technological Change in the USSR (1959–72), Poland (1962–77), and Czechoslovakia (1962–77): An Application of the Contemporary Production Model to National Input–Output Data. **In** *Altmann, F.-L., ed.*, 1986, pp. 58–81. **[G: U.S.S.R.; Poland; Czechoslovakia]**

Chambers, Robert G. and Lee, Hyunok. Constrained Output Maximization and U.S. Agriculture. *Appl. Econ.*, April 1986, *18*(4), pp. 347–57. **[G: U.S.]**

Chiplin, B. Information Technology and Personal Financial Services. **In** *Carter, R. L.; Chiplin, B. and Lewis, M. K., eds.*, 1986, pp. 75–105. **[G: U.K.]**

Christol, Carl Q. The Search for a Stable Regulatory Framework. **In** *Demac, D. A., ed.*, 1986, pp. 3–18.

Cohen, S. I. Product Prices and Technological Choice: The Case of the International Cocoa Processing Industry. *J. Devel. Stud.*, April 1986, *22*(3), pp. 573–82.

Cohen, Stephen S. and Zysman, John. Can America Compete? *Challenge*, May/June 1986, *29*(2), pp. 56–64. **[G: U.S.]**

Cojocaru, G. and Ticovschi, Vl. Considerations about the Cybernetic Approach of the Transfer of Technology Process. *Econ. Computat. Cybern. Stud. Res.*, 1986, *21*(1), pp. 69–80.

Cole, Sam. The Global Impact of Information Technology. *World Devel.*, Oct./Nov. 1986, *14*(10/11), pp. 1277–92. **[G: Global]**

Coleman, D. C. and MacLeod, Christine. Attitudes to New Techniques: British Businessmen, 1800–1950. *Econ. Hist. Rev., 2nd Ser.*, November 1986, *39*(4), pp. 588–611. **[G: U.K.]**

Cooley, Mike and Murphy, Shaun. Jobs and Human-Centred Production. **In** *Nolan, P. and Paine, S., eds.*, 1986, pp. 284–90. **[G: U.K.]**

Coombs, Rod and Kleinknecht, Alfred. New Evidence on the Shift toward Process Innovation during the Long-Wave Upswing. **In** *Freeman, C., ed.*, 1986, pp. 78–103. **[G: OECD]**

Corona, Leonel. Long Waves and the International Diffusion of the Automated Labour Process: The Role of the Semi-industrialized Countries. **In** *Freeman, C., ed.*, 1986, pp. 194–213. **[G: LDCs]**

Cusumano, Michael A. Diversity and Innovation in Japanese Technology Management. **In** *Rosenbloom, R. S., ed.*, 1986, pp. 137–67. **[G: U.S.; Japan]**

Dahlman, Carl J. and Westphal, Larry E. The Acquisition of Technological Mastery in Industry. **In** *Adelman, I. and Taylor, J. E., eds.*, 1986, pp. 263–95. **[G: S. Korea]**

Dasgupta, Partha. The Theory of Technological Competition. **In** *Stiglitz, J. E. and Mathewson, G. F., eds.*, 1986, pp. 519–47.

Daunton, M. J. Labour and Technology in South Wales, 1870–1914. **In** *Baber, C. and Williams, L. J., eds.*, 1986, pp. 140–52. **[G: U.K.]**

David, Paul A. Technology Diffusion, Public Policy, and Industrial Competitiveness. **In** *Landau, R. and Rosenberg, N., eds.*, 1986, pp. 373–91.

David, Paul A. and Olsen, Trond E. Equilibrium Dynamics of Diffusion When Incremental Technological Innovations Are Foreseen. *Ricerche Econ.*, Oct.-Dec. 1986, *40*(4), pp. 738–70.

Day, Richard H. and Hanson, Kenneth A. Adaptive Economising, Technological Change and the Demand for Labour in Disequilibrium. **In** *Nijkamp, P., ed. (II)*, 1986, pp. 301–20.

De Gregori, Thomas R. Technology and Negative Entropy: Continuity or Catastrophe? *J. Econ.*

Issues, June 1986, *20*(2), pp. 463–69.
Demac, Donna A. Tracing New Orbits: Cooperation and Competition in Global Satellite Development: Introduction. **In** *Demac, D. A., ed.*, 1986, pp. xi–xviii.
Derakhshani, Shidan. Negotiating Transfer of Technology Agreements. *Finance Develop.*, December 1986, *23*(4), pp. 42–44.
Deriabin, A. Price and Scientific–Technical Progress. *Prob. Econ.*, July 1986, *29*(3), pp. 3–20. **[G: U.S.S.R.]**
Deutsch, Steven. International Experiences with Technological Change. *Mon. Lab. Rev.*, March 1986, *109*(3), pp. 36–40. **[G: OECD]**
Dizard, Wilson. The Role of International Satellite Networks. **In** *Demac, D. A., ed.*, 1986, pp. 222–50.
Dollar, David. Technological Innovations, Capital Mobility, and the Product Cycle in North–South Trade. *Amer. Econ. Rev.*, March 1986, *76*(1), pp. 177–90.
Dosi, Giovanni. Technology and Conditions of Macroeconomic Development. **In** *Freeman, C., ed.*, 1986, pp. 60–77.
Downing, John D. H. Cooperation and Competition in Satellite Communication: The Soviet Union. **In** *Demac, D. A., ed.*, 1986, pp. 283–304. **[G: CMEA; U.S.S.R.; France; India]**
Dudley, William C. Controlling Risk on Large-Dollar Wire Transfer Systems. **In** *Saunders, A. and White, L. J., eds.*, 1986, pp. 121–35. **[G: U.S.]**
Dutt, Amitava Krishna. Growth, Distribution and Technological Change. *Metroecon.*, June 1986, *38*(2), pp. 113–34.
Ebel, Karl-H. The Impact of Industrial Robots on the World of Work. *Int. Lab. Rev.*, Jan.-Feb. 1986, *125*(1), pp. 39–51. **[G: W. Europe; U.S.]**
Edwards, Franklin R. Technology and New Regulatory Challenges in Futures Markets. **In** *Saunders, A. and White, L. J., eds.*, 1986, pp. 171–79. **[G: U.S.]**
Edwards, Franklin R. Technology and Regulation: Commentary. **In** *Lawrence, C. and Shay, R. P., eds.*, 1986, pp. 144–48. **[G: U.S.]**
Elliott, John E. Modeling Technological and Institutional Change in Karl Marx's Theory of Capitalism. *J. Econ. Issues*, June 1986, *20*(2), pp. 403–12.
Enos, J. L. Public Policy in an Economy with Different Types of Agents. **In** *Hall, P., ed.*, 1986, *1984*, pp. 172–200.
Evans, William MacDonald. Canada's Space Policy. **In** *Demac, D. A., ed.*, 1986, pp. 130–40. **[G: Canada]**
Fairchild, Loretta and Sosin, Kim. Evaluating Differences in Technological Activity between Transnational and Domestic Firms in Latin America. *J. Devel. Stud.*, July 1986, *22*(4), pp. 697–708. **[G: Latin America]**
Farrell, Joseph and Saloner, Garth. Installed Base and Compatibility: Innovation, Product Preannouncements, and Predation. *Amer. Econ. Rev.*, December 1986, *76*(5), pp. 940–55.
Faulhaber, Gerald and Noam, Eli M. Services in Transition: The Impact of Information Technology on the Service Sector: Introduction. **In** *Faulhaber, G.; Noam, E. and Tasley, R., eds.*, 1986, pp. xiii–xix.
Fels, Gerhard. The Impact of New Technologies and the Development of Service Industries in the Federal Republic of Germany. **In** *Hax, H.; Kraus, W. and Tsuchiya, K., eds.*, 1986, pp. 115–24. **[G: W. Germany]**
Figlewski, Stephen. Futures Markets: Comment. **In** *Saunders, A. and White, L. J., eds.*, 1986, pp. 91–94. **[G: U.S.]**
Fischer, Manfred M. and Nijkamp, Peter. Technological Change and Regional Employment Research. **In** *Nijkamp, P., ed. (II)*, 1986, pp. 454–62.
Fishel, Walter L. and Kenney, Martin. Challenge to Studies of Biotechnology Impacts in the Social Sciences. **In** *Maunder, A. and Renborg, U., eds.*, 1986, pp. 353–60.
Flagel, Owen and Harmon, Bruce. Digital Thinking and Technological Progress. *J. Econ. Issues*, June 1986, *20*(2), pp. 551–60.
Flannery, Mark J. Technology and Banking: Commentary. **In** *Lawrence, C. and Shay, R. P., eds.*, 1986, pp. 93–97. **[G: U.S.]**
Flinn, J. C. and Ali, Mubarik. Technical Efficiency in Basmati Rice Production. *Pakistan J. Appl. Econ.*, Summer 1986, *5*(1), pp. 63–79. **[G: Pakistan]**
Foell, Wesley K. and Siddayao, Corazon Morales. Microcomputers and Energy Policy Analysis: Growth Prospects in Developing Countries. *World Devel.*, Oct./Nov. 1986, *14*(10/11), pp. 1311–27. **[G: Indonesia; Philippines]**
Foray, Dominique and Le Bas, Christian. Diffusion de l'innovation dans l'industrie et fonction de recherche technique: dichotomie ou intégration. (Innovation Diffusion in Industry and Technical Research Function: Dichotomy or Integration. With English summary.) *Écon. Appl.*, 1986, *39*(3), pp. 615–50.
Fox, Renée C. Medicine, Science, and Technology. **In** *Aiken, L. H. and Mechanic, D., eds.*, 1986, pp. 13–30.
Fransman, Martin. International Competitiveness, Technical Change and the State: The Machine Tool Industry in Taiwan and Japan. *World Devel.*, December 1986, *14*(12), pp. 1375–96. **[G: Taiwan; Japan]**
Fransman, Martin. International Competitiveness, International Diffusion of Technology and the State: A Case Study from Taiwan and Japan. **In** *Fransman, M., ed.*, 1986, pp. 153–214. **[G: Taiwan; Japan]**
Fransman, Martin. Machinery in Economic Development. **In** *Fransman, M., ed.*, 1986, pp. 1–53.
Freeman, Christopher. Design, Innovation and Long Cycles in Economic Development: Introduction. **In** *Freeman, C., ed.*, 1986, pp. 1–4.
Freeman, Christopher and Soete, Luc L. G. Innovation Diffusion and Employment Policies.

Ricerche Econ., Oct.-Dec. 1986, *40*(4), pp. 836–54. **[G: U.S.; U.K.; Japan; France; W. Germany]**

Freibaum, Jerry. Commercial Space Policy: Theory and Practice. **In** *Demac, D. A., ed.*, 1986, pp. 156–65. **[G: U.S.]**

Friedman, Benjamin M. Financing American Investment in New Technology. **In** *Landau, R. and Jorgenson, D. W., eds.*, 1986, pp. 205–19. **[G: U.S.]**

Fujimori, Hideo. Industrial Policy and Technology Transfer: A Case Study of Automobile Industry in the Philippines. *Devel. Econ.*, December 1986, *24*(4), pp. 349–67. **[G: Philippines]**

Fujimoto, Takao and Krause, Ulrich. Ergodic Price Setting with Technical Progress. **In** *Semmler, W., ed.*, 1986, pp. 115–24.

von Furstenberg, George M. High-Tech Industries and Economic Growth. *Bus. Econ.*, July 1986, *21*(3), pp. 43–45. **[G: U.S.]**

Ganiatsos, Tom. Transfer of Technology: Theory and Policy. **In** *[Patel, S.]*, 1986, pp. 229–51.

Gardiner, J. Paul. Design Trajectories for Airplanes and Automobiles during the Past Fifty Years. **In** *Freeman, C., ed.*, 1986, pp. 121–42. **[G: OECD]**

Gardiner, J. Paul. Robust and Lean Designs with State-of-the-Art Automotive and Aircraft Examples. **In** *Freeman, C., ed.*, 1986, pp. 143–68. **[G: U.S.; W. Europe; Canada]**

Gellman, Aaron. U.S. National Policies for High Technology Industries: Some Lessons Learned. **In** *Rushing, F. W. and Brown, C. G., eds.*, 1986, pp. 227–35. **[G: U.S.]**

Georgescu, D. M. Cybernetization and Robotization of the Operating Processes in the Wood and Building Materials Industry. *Econ. Computat. Cybern. Stud. Res.*, 1986, *21*(1), pp. 55–68. **[G: Romania]**

Giaoutzi, Maria. Technological Change and Employment Patterns: The Greek Case. **In** *Nijkamp, P., ed. (II)*, 1986, pp. 244–61. **[G: Greece]**

Gil, Avishai. Some Labour Implications of Technological Change in Rail and Air Transport. *Int. Lab. Rev.*, Jan.-Feb. 1986, *125*(1), pp. 1–17. **[G: France; U.K.; Netherlands; W. Germany]**

Ginzberg, Eli. Services: Certainties and Uncertainties. **In** *Faulhaber, G.; Noam, E. and Tasley, R., eds.*, 1986, pp. 1–5.

Gleave, David. The Impact of Innovations on Service Employment. **In** *Nijkamp, P., ed. (II)*, 1986, pp. 177–95. **[G: U.K.; U.S.]**

Goddard, John B. and Thwaites, Alfred T. New Technology and Regional Development Policy. **In** *Nijkamp, P., ed. (II)*, 1986, pp. 91–114. **[G: U.K.]**

Gold, Bela. Technological Change and Vertical Integration. *Managerial Dec. Econ.*, September 1986, *7*(3), pp. 169–76.

Goldschmidt, Douglas. The Entry of New Satellite Carriers in International Telecommunications: Some Interests of Developing Nations. **In** *Demac, D. A., ed.*, 1986, pp. 88–104.

Gomulka, Stanislaw. Do New Factories Embody Best Practice Technology?—New Evidence. **In** *Gomulka, S.*, 1986, *1976*, pp. 219–23. **[G: Poland]**

Gomulka, Stanislaw. Growth and the Import of Technology: Poland 1971–80. **In** *Gomulka, S.*, 1986, *1978*, pp. 195–218. **[G: E. Europe]**

Gomulka, Stanislaw. Slowdown in Soviet Industrial Growth: 1947–75 Reconsidered: Afterword. **In** *Gomulka, S.*, 1986, pp. 150–53. **[G: U.S.S.R.]**

Gomulka, Stanislaw. Slowdown in Soviet Industrial Growth: 1947–75 Reconsidered. **In** *Gomulka, S.*, 1986, *1977*, pp. 138–49. **[G: U.S.S.R.]**

González-Vega, Claudio. Human Capital, Technology and Institutions: Discussion. **In** *Maunder, A. and Renborg, U., eds.*, 1986, pp. 360–63. **[G: U.S.]**

Goodman, Laurie S. The Interface between Technology and Regulation in Banking. **In** *Saunders, A. and White, L. J., eds.*, 1986, pp. 181–86.

Goodman, S. E. and McHenry, W. K. Computing in the USSR: Recent Progress and Policies. *Soviet Econ.*, Oct.-Dec. 1986, *2*(4), pp. 327–54. **[G: U.S.S.R.]**

Grabowski, Richard; Sivan, David and Tracy, Ronald L. Technical Change in Taiwanese Agriculture. *Indian Econ. Rev.*, Jan.-June 1986, *21*(1), pp. 41–49. **[G: Taiwan]**

Grabowski, Richard; Tracy, Ronald L. and Sanchez, Onesimo. The Development of Technology in Taiwanese Agriculture. *J. Econ. Devel.*, December 1986, *11*(2), pp. 161–76. **[G: Taiwan]**

Granstrand, Ove. Innovator Protection and the Rate of Technical Progress: Comment. **In** *Day, R. H. and Eliasson, G., eds.*, 1986, pp. 293–94.

Guagnano, Greg, et al. Innovation Perception and Adoption of Solar Heating Technology. *J. Cons. Aff.*, Summer 1986, *20*(1), pp. 48–64. **[G: U.S.]**

Hagen, Everett E. More on the Employment Effects of Innovation: A Correction. *J. Devel. Econ.*, November 1986, *24*(1), pp. 201.

Hammann, Peter and Mittag, Heiko. The Marketing of Industrial Technology through Licensing. **In** *Backhaus, K. and Wilson, D. T., eds.*, 1986, pp. 224–42. **[G: W. Germany]**

Harlow, Ruth E. The EPA and Biotechnology Regulation: Coping with Scientific Uncertainty. *Yale Law J.*, January 1986, *95*(3), pp. 553–76. **[G: U.S.]**

Harris, Candee S. Establishing High-Technology Enterprises in Metropolitan Areas. **In** *Bergman, E. M., ed.*, 1986, pp. 165–84. **[G: U.S.]**

Harris, John R. Michael Alcock and the Transfer of Birmingham Technology to France before the Revolution. *J. Europ. Econ. Hist.*, Spring 1986, *15*(1), pp. 7–57. **[G: France]**

Harsh, S. B.; Kuhlmann, F. and Burg, F. Farm Level Information Systems as an Aid to Decision-makers. **In** *Maunder, A. and Renborg, U.*, *eds.*, 1986, pp. 727–33.

Hartley, Keith. Defence, Industry and Technology: Problems and Possibilities for European Collaboration. **In** *Hall, G., ed.*, 1986, pp. 245–60. **[G: EEC]**

Hattori, Tamio. Technology Transfer and Management Systems. *Devel. Econ.*, December 1986, *24*(4), pp. 314–25. **[G: Japan]**

Hazell, Peter and Anderson, Jock R. Public Policy toward Technical Change in Agriculture. **In** *Hall, P., ed.*, 1986, *1984*, pp. 201–30. **[G: Global]**

Helfgott, Roy B. America's Third Industrial Revolution. *Challenge*, Nov./Dec. 1986, *29*(5), pp. 41–46. **[G: U.S.]**

Hendriks, Ad J. Local Entrepreneurial Initiatives and Central Government. **In** *Nijkamp, P., ed. (II)*, 1986, pp. 280–88. **[G: Netherlands]**

Hepworth, Mark. The Geography of Technological Change in the Information Economy. *Reg. Stud.*, October 1986, *20*(5), pp. 407–24. **[G: Canada]**

Hesse, Dieter M. and Tarkka, Helena. The Demand for Capital, Labor and Energy in European Manufacturing Industry before and after the Oil Price Shocks. *Scand. J. Econ.*, 1986, *88*(3), pp. 529–46. **[G: W. Europe]**

Hill, Malcolm R. and McKay, Richard. Soviet Product Quality, State Standards and Technical Progress. **In** *Amann, R. and Cooper, J., eds.*, 1986, pp. 94–114. **[G: U.S.S.R.]**

Hoogteijling, Els; Gunning, Jan Willem and Nijkamp, Peter. Spatial Dimensions of Innovation and Employment: Some Dutch Results. **In** *Nijkamp, P., ed. (II)*, 1986, pp. 221–43. **[G: Netherlands]**

Horvitz, Paul M. Technological Innovation: Implications for Regulation of Financial Institutions. **In** *Lawrence, C. and Shay, R. P., eds.*, 1986, pp. 111–23. **[G: U.S.]**

Huband, Frank L. A Survey of Alternative Electric Utility Supply and Use Technologies. **In** *Saltzman, S. and Schuler, R. E., eds.*, 1986, pp. 167–75. **[G: U.S.]**

Hudson, Heather E. Access to Information Resources: The Development Context of the Space WARC. **In** *Demac, D. A., ed.*, 1986, pp. 209–21.

Hughes, Kirsty S. Exports and Innovation: A Simultaneous Model. *Europ. Econ. Rev.*, April 1986, *30*(2), pp. 383–99. **[G: U.K.]**

Hunt, Lester Charles. Energy and Capital: Substitutes or Complements? A Note on the Importance of Testing for Non-neutral Technical Progress. *Appl. Econ.*, July 1986, *18*(7), pp. 729–35. **[G: U.K.]**

Hunter, William C. and Timme, Stephen G. Technical Change, Organizational Form, and the Structure of Bank Production. *J. Money, Credit, Banking*, May 1986, *18*(2), pp. 152–66. **[G: U.S.]**

Iglesias, Enrique. Some Considerations on the Transfer of Technology: A Latin American Perspective. **In** *[Patel, S.]*, 1986, pp. 219–25. **[G: Latin America]**

Ikegami, Rywsuke. Changing Chinese Thinking about Technology Transfer. *Devel. Econ.*, December 1986, *24*(4), pp. 391–404. **[G: China]**

Ikemoto, Yukio. Technical Progress and Level of Technology in Asian Countries, 1970–80: A Translog Index Approach. *Devel. Econ.*, December 1986, *24*(4), pp. 368–90. **[G: Selected Asian]**

Ireland, N. and Stoneman, Paul L. Technological Diffusion, Expectations and Welfare. *Oxford Econ. Pap.*, July 1986, *38*(2), pp. 283–304.

Itq, Shqji. Modifying Imported Technology by Local Engineers: Hypotheses and Case Study of India. *Devel. Econ.*, December 1986, *24*(4), pp. 334–48. **[G: India]**

Itq, Shqji. Technology Transfer from Japan to Asian Developing Countries: Introduction. *Devel. Econ.*, December 1986, *24*(4), pp. 309–13. **[G: Japan]**

Jacobi, Otto; Kastendiek, Hans and Jessop, Bob. Between Erosion and Transformation: Industrial Relations Systems under the Impact of Technological Change. **In** *Jacobi, O., et al., eds. (I)*, 1986, pp. 1–12. **[G: W. Germany; U.K.; Italy]**

Jaikumar, Ramchandran and Bohn, Roger E. The Development of Intelligent Systems for Industrial Use: A Conceptual Framework. **In** *Rosenbloom, R. S., ed.*, 1986, pp. 169–211.

James, Jeffrey. Bureaucratic, Engineering and Economic Men: Decision-Making for Technology in Tanzania's State-Owned Enterprises. **In** *[Streeten, P.]*, 1986, pp. 217–39. **[G: Tanzania]**

Jayasuriya, S. K. and Shand, Richard T. Technical Change and Labor Absorption in Asian Agriculture: Some Emerging Trends. *World Devel.*, March 1986, *14*(3), pp. 415–28. **[G: LDCs; Asia]**

Johansson, Börje and Karlsson, Charlie. Industrial Applications of Information Technology: Speed of Introduction and Labour Force Competence. **In** *Nijkamp, P., ed. (II)*, 1986, pp. 401–28. **[G: Sweden]**

Johansson, Börje and Larsson, Jan. Characteristics of the Firm and the Speed of Technology Adoption. *Ricerche Econ.*, Oct.-Dec. 1986, *40*(4), pp. 675–95.

Jonscher, Charles. Information Technology and the United States Economy: Modeling and Measurement. **In** *Faulhaber, G.; Noam, E. and Tasley, R., eds.*, 1986, pp. 119–31. **[G: U.S.]**

Judy, Richard W. Computing in the USSR: A Comment. *Soviet Econ.*, Oct.-Dec. 1986 cat ds45, 2(4), pp. 355–67. **[G: U.S.S.R.]**

Kalas, John W. Reindustrialization in New York: The Role of the State University. **In** *Schoolman, M. and Magid, A., eds.*, 1986, pp. 281–312. **[G: U.S.]**

Kalirajan, K. Measuring Technical Efficiencies from Interdependent Multiple Outputs Frontiers. *J. Quant. Econ.*, July 1986, *2*(2), pp. 263–74. **[G: Philippines]**

Kalmbach, Peter and Kurz, Heinz D. Economic Dynamics and Innovation: Ricardo, Marx and Schumpeter on Technological Change and Unemployment. In *Wagener, H.-J. and Drukker, J. W., eds.*, 1986, pp. 71–92.

Kane, Edward J. Technology and the Regulation of Financial Markets. In *Saunders, A. and White, L. J., eds.*, 1986, pp. 187–93.

Kantorovich, L. V. Scientific–Technical Progress: Economic Problems. *Prob. Econ.*, February 1986, *28*(10), pp. 3–25. **[G: U.S.S.R.]**

Kareken, John H. Technology and Regulation: Commentary. In *Lawrence, C. and Shay, R. P., eds.*, 1986, pp. 149–55. **[G: U.S.]**

Karlson, Stephen H. Adoption of Competing Inventions by United States Steel Producers. *Rev. Econ. Statist.*, August 1986, *68*(3), pp. 415–22. **[G: U.S.]**

Katsoulacos, Y. Technical Change and Structural Unemployment. *Scot. J. Polit. Econ.*, August 1986, *33*(3), pp. 275–83.

Katz, Michael L. and Shapiro, Carl. Product Compatibility Choice in a Market with Technological Progress. In *Morris, D. J., et al., eds.*, 1986, pp. 146–65.

Katz, Michael L. and Shapiro, Carl. Product Compatibility Choice in a Market with Technological Progress. *Oxford Econ. Pap.*, Suppl. Nov. 1986, *38*, pp. 146–65.

Katz, Michael L. and Shapiro, Carl. Technology Adoption in the Presence of Network Externalities. *J. Polit. Econ.*, August 1986, *94*(4), pp. 822–41.

Katz, Milton. The Role of the Legal System in Technological Innovation and Economic Growth. In *Landau, R. and Rosenberg, N., eds.*, 1986, pp. 169–89. **[G: U.S.]**

Kawagoe, Toshihiko; Otsuka, Keijiro and Hayami, Yujiro. Induced Bias of Technical Change in Agriculture: The United States and Japan, 1880–1980. *J. Polit. Econ.*, Part 1, June 1986, *94*(3), pp. 523–44. **[G: U.S.; Japan]**

Kim, Moshe and Sachish, Arie. The Structure of Production, Technical Change and Productivity in a Port. *J. Ind. Econ.*, December 1986, *35*(2), pp. 209–23.

Kirchgässner, Gebhard. Innovations, Market Structure and Market Dynamics: Comment. *J. Inst. Theoretical Econ.*, March 1986, *142*(1), pp. 204–09. **[G: W. Germany]**

Klvačová, Eva. Scientific–Technological Progress and the System of Management of the National Economy. *Czech. Econ. Digest.*, June/July 1986, (4), pp. 71–89. **[G: Czechoslovakia]**

Komin, A. Technological Progress and Prices. *Prob. Econ.*, October 1986, *29*(6), pp. 36–49.

Komoda, Fumio. Japanese Studies on Technology Transfer to Developing Countries: A Survey. *Devel. Econ.*, December 1986, *24*(4), pp. 405–20. **[G: Japan]**

König, Heinz and Zimmermann, Klaus F. Innovations, Market Structure and Market Dynamics. *J. Inst. Theoretical Econ.*, March 1986, *142*(1), pp. 184–99. **[G: W. Germany]**

Kontorovich, Vladimir. Soviet Growth Slowdown: Econometric vs. Direct Evidence. *Amer. Econ. Rev.*, May 1986, *76*(2), pp. 181–85. **[G: U.S.S.R.]**

Koshiro, Kazutoshi. The Impact of New Technologies and the Development of Service Industries in Japan. In *Hax, H.; Kraus, W. and Tsuchiya, K., eds.*, 1986, pp. 84–114. **[G: Japan; U.S.; U.K.; W. Germany]**

Kranzberg, Melvin. The Technical Elements in International Technology Transfer: Historical Perspectives. In *McIntyre, J. R. and Papp, D. S., eds.*, 1986, pp. 31–45. **[G: U.S.; Japan; U.S.S.R.]**

Krasovskii, V. Current Priorities in the Investment Complex. *Prob. Econ.*, February 1986, *28*(10), pp. 26–42. **[G: U.S.S.R.]**

Krasovskii, V. and Fridman, L. Accumulation and Technical Progress in the USSR Economy. *Prob. Econ.*, March 1986, *28*(11), pp. 3–18. **[G: U.S.S.R.]**

Krommenacker, Raymond J. The Impact of Information Technology on Trade Interdependence. *J. World Trade Law*, July:Aug. 1986, *20*(4), pp. 381–400. **[G: Global]**

Kumar, Nagesh. Foreign Direct Investments and Technology Transfers among Developing Countries. In *Panchamukhi, V. R., et al.*, 1986, pp. 139–65. **[G: LDCs]**

Kunreuther, Howard. The Impact of Technology on the Insurance Industry: Discussion. In *Faulhaber, G.; Noam, E. and Tasley, R., eds.*, 1986, pp. 44–48. **[G: U.S.]**

Lacaze, Dominique. Théorie des prix et sélection de techniques ou de projets. (Price Theory and Selection of Techniques or Projects. With English summary.) *Revue Écon.*, July 1986, *37*(4), pp. 677–95.

Lakshmanan, T. R. and Chatterjee, Lata. Technical Change and Metropolitan Adjustments: Some Policy and Analytical Implications. *Reg. Sci. Urban Econ.*, February 1986, *16*(1), pp. 7–30.

Lakshmanan, T. R. and Chatterjee, Lata. Technical Change, Employment and Metropolitan Adjustment. In *Nijkamp, P., ed. (II)*, 1986, pp. 21–45.

Lambrecht, Philippe. Agriculture in a Turbulent World Economy: Theoretical Developments: Discussion. In *Maunder, A. and Renborg, U., eds.*, 1986, pp. 741–43.

Landau, Ralph. Technology, Economics, and Public Policy. In *Landau, R. and Jorgenson, D. W., eds.*, 1986, pp. 1–74. **[G: OECD]**

Landau, Ralph and Rosenberg, Nathan. The Positive Sum Strategy: Harnessing Technology for Economic Growth: Editors' Overview. In *Landau, R. and Rosenberg, N., eds.*, 1986, pp. 1–16.

Landesmann, Michael A. Conceptions of Technology and the Production Process. In *Baranzini, M. and Scazzieri, R., eds.*, 1986, pp. 281–310.

Langr, František. From His Address at the 28th International Engineering Fair in Brno, September 1986. *Czech. Econ. Digest.*, December 1986, (8), pp. 26–35. **[G: Czechoslovakia]**

Lau, Lawrence J. and Ma, Barry K. Choice of Technique in a Putty-Clay Model of Production. *Eastern Econ. J.*, July-Sept. 1986, *12*(3), pp. 321–26.

Lawrence, Colin and Shay, Robert P. Money and Technology. **In** *Lawrence, C. and Shay, R. P., eds.*, 1986, pp. 1–10. **[G: U.S.]**

Lawrence, Colin and Shay, Robert P. Technology and Financial Intermediation in Multiproduct Banking Firms: An Econometric Study of U.S. Banks, 1979–1982. **In** *Lawrence, C. and Shay, R. P., eds.*, 1986, pp. 53–92. **[G: U.S.]**

Lawrence, Colin and Shay, Robert P. Technology and Financial Intermediation in Multiproduct Banking Firms: An Econometric Study of U.S. Banks, 1979–1982: Rejoinder. **In** *Lawrence, C. and Shay, R. P., eds.*, 1986, pp. 106–07. **[G: U.S.]**

Layton, Roy A. Will Satellites and Optical Fiber Collide or Coexist? **In** *Demac, D. A., ed.*, 1986, pp. 19–29.

Lefebvre, Louis A., et al. L'impact de la technologie informatique sur la main-d'oeuvre dans les organisations. (The Impact of Information Technology on Human Resources in Organizations. With English summary.) *L'Actual. Econ.*, December 1986, *62*(4), pp. 557–78. **[G: Canada]**

Leijonhufvud, Axel. Capitalism and the Factory System. **In** *Langlois, R. N., ed.*, 1986, pp. 203–23.

Leontief, Wassily. Technological Change, Prices, Wages, and Rates of Return on Capital in the U.S. Economy. **In** *Leontief, W.*, 1986, *1985*, pp. 392–417. **[G: U.S.]**

Leontief, Wassily. Technology Change, Employment, the Rate of Return on Capital and Wages. **In** *Burton, D. F., et al., eds.*, 1986, pp. 47–53. **[G: U.S.]**

Leontief, Wassily. The Distribution of Work and Income. **In** *Leontief, W.*, 1986, *1982*, pp. 363–78. **[G: U.S.; Austria]**

Levin, Harvey J. Latecomer Cost Handicap: Importance in a Changing Regulatory Landscape. **In** *Demac, D. A., ed.*, 1986, pp. 251–79. **[G: U.S.]**

Lévy-Garboua, Louis. Innovations et diffusion des produits de consommation. (Innovations and the Diffusion of Consumer Goods. With English summary.) *Écon. Appl.*, 1986, *39*(3), pp. 521–82.

Levy, Robert A. and Jondrow, James M. The Adjustment of Employment to Technical Change in the Steel and Auto Industries. *J. Bus.*, July 1986, *59*(3), pp. 475–91. **[G: U.S.]**

Lewit, Eugene M. The Diffusion of Surgical Technology: Who's on First? *J. Health Econ.*, March 1986, *5*(1), pp. 99–102.

Linneman, Peter. Information Technology, Demographics, and the Retail Response: Discussion. **In** *Faulhaber, G.; Noam, E. and Tasley, R., eds.*, 1986, pp. 175–77. **[G: U.S.; OECD]**

Linneman, Peter. Technology and Financial Services: Regulatory Problems in a Deregulated Environment: Discussion. **In** *Faulhaber, G.; Noam, E. and Tasley, R., eds.*, 1986, pp. 73–75. **[G: U.S.]**

Lombardini, Siro. L'innovazione. (Innovation. With English summary.) *Rivista Int. Sci. Econ. Com.*, April 1986, *33*(4), pp. 319–32.

Macauley, Molly K. Out of Space? Regulation and Technical Change in Communications Satellites. *Amer. Econ. Rev.*, May 1986, *76*(2), pp. 280–84. **[G: U.S.]**

MacLeod, Christine. The 1690s Patents Boom: Invention or Stock-Jobbing? *Econ. Hist. Rev., 2nd Ser.*, November 1986, *39*(4), pp. 549–71. **[G: U.K.]**

Malecki, Edward J. High-Technology Sectors and Local Economic Development. **In** *Bergman, E. M., ed.*, 1986, *1983*, pp. 129–42. **[G: U.S.]**

Malecki, Edward J. Technological Imperatives and Modern Corporate Strategy. **In** *Scott, A. J. and Storper, M., eds.*, 1986, pp. 67–79.

Malecki, Edward J. and Varaiya, Pravin. Innovation and Changes in Regional Structure. **In** *Nijkamp, P., ed. (I)*, 1986, pp. 629–45.

Martin, W. J. Human Capital, Technology and Institutions: Discussion. **In** *Maunder, A. and Renborg, U., eds.*, 1986, pp. 363–65.

Marton, Katherin. Technology Transfer to Developing Countries via Multinationals. *World Econ.*, December 1986, *9*(4), pp. 409–26. **[G: OECD; LDCs]**

Marver, James D. Trends in Financing Innovation. **In** *Landau, R. and Rosenberg, N., eds.*, 1986, pp. 473–78.

Maslova, I.; Dadashev, A. and Moskovich, V. The Impact of Technological Progress on the Release and Redistribution of Workers. *Prob. Econ.*, July 1986, *29*(3), pp. 69–80. **[G: U.S.S.R.]**

Matějka, Karel. Czechoslovakia in Scientific–Technological Integration with the CMEA Countries. *Czech. Econ. Digest.*, Sept./Oct. 1986, (6), pp. 20–35. **[G: CMEA; Czechoslovakia]**

Mathé, Jean-Charles and Gontier, Jean-Louis. Gestion de la dimension technologique de l'entreprise. (Management of Technological Dimensions of the Firm. With English summary.) *Écon. Soc.*, December 1986, *20*(12), pp. 3–36.

Matthews, Ron. Technological Dynamism in India and Japan: The Case of Machine-Tool Manufacture. **In** *Baark, E. and Jamison, A., eds.*, 1986, pp. 142–204. **[G: India; Japan]**

McClintock, David W. Agricultural Technology Transfer in the Evolving North–South Dialogue. **In** *McIntyre, J. R. and Papp, D. S., eds.*, 1986, pp. 117–35. **[G: LDCs]**

McIntosh, James. Economic Growth and Technical Change in Britain 1950–1978. *Europ. Econ. Rev.*, February 1986, *30*(1), pp. 117–28. **[G: U.K.]**

McIntyre, John R. The Political Economy of International Technology Transfer: Introduction: Critical Perspectives on International Technology Transfer. **In** *McIntyre, J. R. and Papp, D. S., eds.*, 1986, pp. 3–24.

Meeks, Philip J. West–West Technology Transfer: The Dilemmas of Cooperation and Conflict. **In** *McIntyre, J. R. and Papp, D. S., eds.*, 1986, pp. 141–59. **[G: MDCs]**

Metcalfe, J. S. Technological Innovation and the

Competitive Process. **In** *Hall, P., ed.*, 1986, *1984*, pp. 35–64.

Mettler, Ruben F. Innovation, Job Creation, and Competitiveness. **In** *Landau, R. and Rosenberg, N., eds.*, 1986, pp. 517–25. **[G: U.S.]**

Meunier, François and Volle, M. The Effects of the New Communications Media on Employment. *Info. Econ. Policy*, September 1986, *2*(3), pp. 195–209. **[G: France]**

Minami, Ryoshin and Makino, Fumio. Choice of Technology: A Case Study of the Japanese Cotton Weaving Industry 1902–1938. *Hitotsubashi J. Econ.*, December 1986, *27*(2), pp. 111–32. **[G: Japan]**

Mine, Manabu. The Social Impact of Micro-electronics in Japan. *Int. Lab. Rev.*, July-Aug. 1986, *125*(4), pp. 473–97. **[G: Japan]**

Montgomery, William H. A Canadian Perspective on the 1985 ITU Space Conference. **In** *Demac, D. A., ed.*, 1986, pp. 201–08. **[G: Canada]**

Moss, Mitchell. Information Technology, Demographics, and the Retail Response: Discussion. **In** *Faulhaber, G.; Noam, E. and Tasley, R., eds.*, 1986, pp. 178–82. **[G: U.S.; OECD]**

Mountain, Dean C. Economies of Scale versus Technological Change: An Aggregate Production Function for Switzerland. *Rev. Econ. Statist.*, November 1986, *68*(4), pp. 707–11. **[G: Switzerland]**

Mulligan, James G. Technical Change and Scale Economies Given Stochastic Demand and Production. *Int. J. Ind. Organ.*, June 1986, *4*(2), pp. 189–201.

Murakami, Yasusuke. Technology in Transition: Two Perspectives on Industrial Policy. **In** *Patrick, H., ed.*, 1986, pp. 211–41.

Murota, Takeshi. History and Present of the Helical Waterwheel: Its Unique Position in the Modern Technology of Japan: Part I/Investigations for the Period of 1920–1942. *Hitotsubashi J. Econ.*, June 1986, *27*(1), pp. 11–33. **[G: Japan]**

Nardinelli, Clark. Technology and Unemployment: The Case of the Handloom Weavers. *Southern Econ. J.*, July 1986, *53*(1), pp. 87–94. **[G: U.K.]**

Nau, Henry R. International Technology Transfer: Security and Economic Considerations under the Reagan Administration. **In** *McIntyre, J. R. and Papp, D. S., eds.*, 1986, pp. 61–71. **[G: U.S.]**

Nau, Henry R. National Policies for High Technology Development and Trade: An International and Comparative Assessment. **In** *Rushing, F. W. and Brown, C. G., eds.*, 1986, pp. 9–29. **[G: India; Brazil; Mexico; S. Korea; Argentina]**

Nelson, Gerald C. Labor Intensity, Employment Growth and Technical Change: An Example from Starch Processing in Indonesia. *J. Devel. Econ.*, November 1986, *24*(1), pp. 111–17. **[G: Indonesia]**

Nelson, Michael. Technology Transfer in the Mining Sector: Options for the Latin American Mining Organization (OLAMI). *CEPAL Rev.*, December 1986, (30), pp. 137–42. **[G: Latin America]**

Nelson, Randy A. Capital Vintage, Time Trends, and Technical Change in the Electric Power Industry. *Southern Econ. J.*, October 1986, *53*(2), pp. 315–32. **[G: U.S.]**

Nijkamp, Peter. The Triangle of Industrial Dynamics, Labour Markets and Spatial Systems. **In** *Nijkamp, P., ed. (II)*, 1986, pp. 1–17.

Nijkamp, Peter and Poot, Jacques. Technological Change and Labour Migration in a General Spatial Interaction System. **In** *Nijkamp, P., ed. (II)*, 1986, pp. 358–70.

Nilsson, Björn. Microcomputers in the Statistical Environment of Developed and Developing Countries. *Statist. J.*, October 1986, *4*(2), pp. 127–43.

Norgaard, Richard B. and Leu, Gwo Jiun. Petroleum Accessibility and Drilling Technology: An Analysis of U.S. Development Costs from 1959 to 1978. *Land Econ.*, February 1986, *62*(1), pp. 14–25. **[G: U.S.]**

Norman, David A. Impact of Entrepreneurship and Innovation on the Distribution of Personal Computers. **In** *Landau, R. and Rosenberg, N., eds.*, 1986, pp. 437–39. **[G: U.S.]**

Norton, Seth W. and Norton, Will, Jr. Economies of Scale and the New Technology of Daily Newspapers: A Survivor Analysis. *Quart. Rev. Econ. Bus.*, Summer 1986, *26*(2), pp. 66–83. **[G: U.S.]**

Obzina, Jaromír. Stress on Effectiveness. *Czech. Econ. Digest.*, January 1986, (1), pp. 3–12. **[G: Czechoslovakia]**

Ogunleye, Ajibade. Self-reliant Development of Iron and Steel Technology in Africa. **In** *Onwuka, R. I. and Aluko, O., eds.*, 1986, pp. 35–41. **[G: Africa]**

Omichi, Masao. Nuclear Power in the United States and Japan. **In** *Finn, R. B., ed.*, 1986, pp. 51–75. **[G: U.S.; Japan]**

Ono, Akira. Technical Progress in Silk Industry in Prewar Japan—The Types of Borrowed Technology. *Hitotsubashi J. Econ.*, June 1986, *27*(1), pp. 1–10. **[G: Japan]**

Osterman, Paul. The Impact of Computers on the Employment of Clerks and Managers. *Ind. Lab. Relat. Rev.*, January 1986, *39*(2), pp. 175–86. **[G: U.S.]**

Pack, Howard and Westphal, Larry E. Industrial Strategy and Technological Change: Theory versus Reality. *J. Devel. Econ.*, June 1986, *22*(1), pp. 87–128. **[G: S. Korea]**

Panas, Epaminondas E. Biased Technological Progress and Theories of Induced Innovation: The Case of Greek Manufacturing, 1958–1975. *Greek Econ. Rev.*, June 1986, *8*(1), pp. 95–119. **[G: Greece]**

Parker, William N. The Development and Use of Machine Tools in Historical Perspective: Comment. **In** *Day, R. H. and Eliasson, G., eds.*, 1986, pp. 271–76. **[G: U.K.]**

Paulsson, Gunnar. Licensing Industrial Technology to Developing Countries: The Operations of Swedish Firms in India. *Aussenwirtschaft*,

December 1986, *41*(4), pp. 533–49. **[G: India]**

Pauly, Mark V. Information Technology and the U.S. Health Care Industry: A New Direction: Discussion. **In** *Faulhaber, G.; Noam, E. and Tasley, R., eds.*, 1986, pp. 21–25. **[G: U.S.]**

Pelton, Joseph N. INTELSAT: Responding to New Challenges. **In** *Demac, D. A., ed.*, 1986, pp. 58–74.

Perez, Carlota. Structural Change and Assimilation of New Technologies in the Economic and Social System. **In** *Freeman, C., ed.*, 1986, pp. 27–47.

Perrin, James M. High Technology and Uncompensated Hospital Care. **In** *Sloan, F. A.; Blumstein, J. F. and Perrin, J. M., eds.*, 1986, pp. 54–71. **[G: U.S.]**

Perry, William J. Cultivating Technological Innovation. **In** *Landau, R. and Rosenberg, N., eds.*, 1986, pp. 443–51. **[G: U.S.]**

Peterson, Willis and Kislev, Yoav. The Cotton Harvester in Retrospect: Labor Displacement or Replacement? *J. Econ. Hist.*, March 1986, *46*(1), pp. 199–216. **[G: U.S.]**

Pettit, Joseph M. Technological Education. **In** *Landau, R. and Rosenberg, N., eds.*, 1986, pp. 255–62. **[G: U.S.; Japan]**

Petzel, Todd E. Self-regulation and Futures Markets: Benefits from Technology Gains. **In** *Saunders, A. and White, L. J., eds.*, 1986, pp. 73–77. **[G: U.S.]**

Phillips, Almarin and Berlin, Mitchell. Technology and Financial Services: Regulatory Problems in a Deregulated Environment. **In** *Faulhaber, G.; Noam, E. and Tasley, R., eds.*, 1986, pp. 49–72. **[G: U.S.]**

Poznanski, Kazimierz. Patterns of Technology Imports: Interregional Comparison. *World Devel.*, June 1986, *14*(6), pp. 743–56. **[G: E. Europe; Latin America]**

Premus, Robert. Attracting High-Tech Industry and Jobs: An Assessment of State Practices. **In** *Walzer, N. and Chicoine, D. L., eds.*, 1986, pp. 55–71. **[G: U.S.]**

Premus, Robert. High Technology and State Economic Development Strategies. **In** *Redburn, F. S.; Buss, T. F. and Ledebur, L. C., eds.*, 1986, pp. 99–113. **[G: U.S.]**

Quadrio-Curzio, Alberto. Technological Scarcity: An Essay on Production and Structural Change. **In** *Baranzini, M. and Scazzieri, R., eds.*, 1986, pp. 311–38.

Quinn, James Brian. Technology Adoption: The Services Industries. **In** *Landau, R. and Rosenberg, N., eds.*, 1986, pp. 357–71. **[G: U.S.; U.K.; Japan; W. Germany; France]**

Quirmbach, Herman C. The Diffusion of New Technology and the Market for an Innovation. *Rand J. Econ.*, Spring 1986, *17*(1), pp. 33–47.

Rahman, K. M. Technology, Productivity and Employment in Rural Industries. **In** *Islam, R. and Muqtada, M., eds.*, 1986, pp. 197–207. **[G: Bangladesh]**

Rajan, Amin and Cooke, Geoffrey. The Impact of Information Technology on Employment in the Financial Services Industry. *Nat. Westminster Bank Quart. Rev.*, August 1986, pp. 21–35. **[G: U.K.]**

Reed, John S. and Moreno, Glen R. The Role of Large Banks in Financing Innovation. **In** *Landau, R. and Rosenberg, N., eds.*, 1986, pp. 443–65. **[G: U.S.]**

Reeder, Charles B. The Effect of Recent Macroeconomic Policies on Innovation and Productivity. **In** *Landau, R. and Rosenberg, N., eds.*, 1986, pp. 89–91. **[G: U.S.]**

Rispoli, Maurizio. L'innovazione nella strategia delle piccole imprese. (Innovation in the Strategy of Small Firms. With English summary.) *Ricerche Econ.*, Apr.-Sept. 1986, *40*(2–3), pp. 489–509.

Rohrer, Wayne C. Developing Third World Farming: Conflict between Modern Imperatives and Traditional Ways. *Econ. Develop. Cult. Change*, January 1986, *34*(2), pp. 299–314. **[G: Philippines; LDCs]**

Roman, Daniel D. Science Policy, Technology Transfer, Economic Impacts, and Sociological Implications in the West–West Context. **In** *McIntyre, J. R. and Papp, D. S., eds.*, 1986, pp. 187–202.

Root, William A. U.S. Policy on East–West Technology Trade: Past, Present, and Future. **In** *McIntyre, J. R. and Papp, D. S., eds.*, 1986, pp. 207–20. **[G: U.S.]**

Rosegger, Gerhard. Adjustment through Piecemeal Innovation—The U.S. Experience. **In** *Goldberg, W. H., ed.*, 1986, pp. 307–37. **[G: U.S.]**

Rosenberg, Nathan. The Impact of Technological Innovation: A Historical View. **In** *Landau, R. and Rosenberg, N., eds.*, 1986, pp. 17–32.

Rosenberg, Nathan and Frischtak, Claudio R. Technological Innovation and Long Waves. **In** *Freeman, C., ed.*, 1986, pp. 5–26.

Rothwell, Roy. Reindustrialisation, Innovation and Public Policy. **In** *Hall, P., ed.*, 1986, *1984*, pp. 65–83. **[G: OECD]**

Rouwendal, Jan. On the Production and Diffusion of Technological Change. **In** *Nijkamp, P., ed. (II)*, 1986, pp. 371–81.

Rozenova, L. The Role of Price in the Management of Technical Progress. *Prob. Econ.*, March 1986, *28*(11), pp. 39–56. **[G: U.S.S.R.]**

Rutz, Roger D. Futures Markets: Comment. **In** *Saunders, A. and White, L. J., eds.*, 1986, pp. 85–90. **[G: U.S.]**

Sapir, André. Trade in Investment-Related Technological Studies. *World Devel.*, May 1986, *14*(5), pp. 605–22. **[G: India]**

Sazzu, Antonio. Nuove prospettive per lo studio del progresso tecnologico. (New Developments in the Study of Technical Progress. With English summary.) *Econ. Polít.*, April 1986, *3*(1), pp. 129–58.

Scarbrough, Harry. The Politics of Technological Change at British Leyland. **In** *Jacobi, O., et al., eds. (I)*, 1986, pp. 95–115. **[G: U.K.]**

Schaffer, Ken. A Television Window on the Soviet Union. **In** *Demac, D. A., ed.*, 1986, pp. 305–11.

Schankerman, Mark and Pakes, Ariel S. Estimates of the Value of Patent Rights in European Countries during the Post-1950 Period. *Econ. J.*, December 1986, *96*(384), pp. 1052–76. **[G: U.K.; France; W. Germany]**

Scheffler, Richard M. Information Technology and the U.S. Health Care Industry: A New Direction. **In** *Faulhaber, G.; Noam, E. and Tasley, R., eds.*, 1986, pp. 7–20. **[G: U.S.]**

Schiefer, Gerhard. Agriculture in a Turbulent World Economy: Theoretical Developments: Discussion. **In** *Maunder, A. and Renborg, U., eds.*, 1986, pp. 743–45.

Schünemann, Thomas M. and Bruns, Thomas. Modellierung und Prognose der Diffusion von Industrierobotern in der Bundesrepublik Deutschland. (With English summary.) *Z. Betriebswirtshaft*, October 1986, *56*(10), pp. 953–88. **[G: W. Germany]**

Scribner, Richard O. The Technological Revolution in Securities Trading: Can Regulation Keep Up? **In** *Saunders, A. and White, L. J., eds.*, 1986, pp. 19–29. **[G: U.S.]**

Segal, Aaron. From Technology Transfer to Science and Technology Institutionalization. **In** *McIntyre, J. R. and Papp, D. S., eds.*, 1986, pp. 95–115. **[G: Selected Countries]**

Shaiken, Harley. Decentralized Production: A Technological Revolution with Political Issues. **In** *Gondolf, E. W.; Marcus, I. M. and Dougherty, J. P., eds.*, 1986, pp. 58–65.

Shaiken, Harley; Herzenberg, Stephen and Kuhn, Sarah. The Work Process under More Flexible Production. *Ind. Relat.*, Spring 1986, *25*(2), pp. 167–83. **[G: U.S.]**

Shapiro, Nina. Innovation, New Industries and New Firms. *Eastern Econ. J.*, Jan.-Mar. 1986, *12*(1), pp. 27–43.

Sharp, Margaret. Technology Gap or Management Gap? **In** *Sharp, M., ed.*, 1986, pp. 263–97. **[G: W. Europe]**

Shay, Robert P. Technology and Financial Services: Regulatory Problems in a Deregulated Environment: Discussion. **In** *Faulhaber, G.; Noam, E. and Tasley, R., eds.*, 1986, pp. 76–79. **[G: U.S.]**

Shelp, June Peno. Insurance Industry Technology. **In** *Wasow, B. and Hill, R. D., eds.*, 1986, pp. 57–66.

Shleifer, Andrei. Implementation Cycles. *J. Polit. Econ.*, December 1986, *94*(6), pp. 1163–90.

Sidhu, D. S. and Singh, A. J. Technological Change in Indian Agriculture. **In** *Dantwala, M. L., et al.*, 1986, pp. 140–61. **[G: India]**

Siggel, Eckhard. Technology Transfers to Developing Countries through Consulting Engineers: A Model and Empirical Observations from Canada. *Devel. Econ.*, September 1986, *24*(3), pp. 229–50. **[G: Canada; LDCs]**

Sigurdson, Jon. The High Technology Challenge and Policies in Japan and Sweden. **In** *Baark, E. and Jamison, A., eds.*, 1986, pp. 57–85. **[G: Japan; Sweden]**

Sikdar, Soumyen. Technological Change and the Labour-Managed Firm. *J. Quant. Econ.*, January 1986, *2*(1), pp. 111–18.

Simon, Denis Fred. The Technology Issue in Sino–U.S. Relations. **In** *McIntyre, J. R. and Papp, D. S., eds.*, 1986, pp. 241–55. **[G: U.S.; China]**

Simon, Julian L. Some Theory of Population Growth's Effect on Technical Change in an Industrial Context. *Australian Econ. Hist. Rev.*, September 1986, *26*(2), pp. 148–58.

Sinclair, P. J. N. Faster Technical Progress Need Not Imply Lower Optimal Savings. *Greek Econ. Rev.*, June 1986, *8*(1), pp. 60–65.

Slade, Margaret E. Total-Factor-Productivity Measurement When Equilibrium Is Temporary: A Monte Carlo Assessment. *J. Econometrics*, Oct./Nov. 1986, *33*(1/2), pp. 75–95.

Sláma, Jiří. Verbreitung von Innovationen im internationalen Vergleich Dargestellt am Beispiel der Oxygenstahlerzeugung. **In** *Altmann, F.-L., ed.*, 1986, pp. 101–29. **[G: OECD; CMEA]**

Sloan, Frank A., et al. Diffusion of Surgical Technology: An Exploratory Study. *J. Health Econ.*, March 1986, *5*(1), pp. 31–61. **[G: U.S.]**

Smidt, Seymour. Productivity, Technological Change, and Futures Trading. **In** *Saunders, A. and White, L. J., eds.*, 1986, pp. 79–84. **[G: U.S.]**

Smirlock, Michael. Technology and Banking: Commentary. **In** *Lawrence, C. and Shay, R. P., eds.*, 1986, pp. 98–104. **[G: U.S.]**

Smith, Gordon B. The Impact of Western Technology Transfer on the Soviet Union. **In** *McIntyre, J. R. and Papp, D. S., eds.*, 1986, pp. 221–39. **[G: U.S.S.R.]**

Snow, Marcellus S. Competition by Private Carriers in International Commercial Satellite Traffic: Conceptual and Historical Background. **In** *Demac, D. A., ed.*, 1986, pp. 33–57.

Sobell, Vladimir. Technology Flows within COMECON and Channels of Communication. **In** *Amann, R. and Cooper, J., eds.*, 1986, pp. 135–52. **[G: CMEA]**

Soete, Luc L. G. Long Cycles and the International Diffusion of Technology. **In** *Freeman, C., ed.*, 1986, pp. 214–30.

Solomou, Solomos. Innovation Clusters and Kondratieff Long Waves in Economic Growth. *Cambridge J. Econ.*, June 1986, *10*(2), pp. 101–12. **[G: U.S.]**

Sonis, Michael. Unified Theory of Innovation Diffusion, Dynamic Choice of Alternatives, Ecological Dynamics and Urban/Regional Growth and Decline. *Ricerche Econ.*, Oct.-Dec. 1986, *40*(4), pp. 696–723.

Sonka, Steven T. Computer-Aided Farm Management Systems: Will the Promise Be Fulfilled? **In** *Maunder, A. and Renborg, U., eds.*, 1986, pp. 717–26.

Souder, H. Ray and Damachi, Nicholas. Introduction of Computers to Management in Developing Countries. **In** *Damachi, U. G. and Seibel, H. D., eds.*, 1986, pp. 333–55.

Sternlieb, George and Hughes, James W. Information Technology, Demographics, and the Retail Response. **In** *Faulhaber, G.; Noam, E.*

and Tasley, R., eds., 1986, pp. 139–74. **[G: U.S.; OECD]**

Stoneman, Paul L. Technological Diffusion: The Viewpoint of Economic Theory. *Ricerche Econ.*, Oct.-Dec. 1986, *40*(4), pp. 585–606.

Stoneman, Paul L. and David, Paul A. Adoption Subsidies vs Information Provision as Instruments of Technology Policy. *Econ. J.*, Supplement 1986, *96*, pp. 142–50.

Storper, Michael. Technology and New Regional Growth Complexes: The Economics of Discontinuous Spatial Development. **In** *Nijkamp, P., ed. (II)*, 1986, pp. 46–75.

Sugai, Yoshihiko and Teixeira Filho, A. R. Impact on Farmers' Decision-Making by Farm Management and Computer Sciences in the Turbulent Economy. **In** *Maunder, A. and Renborg, U., eds.*, 1986, pp. 734–41. **[G: Brazil]**

Teece, David J. Firm Boundaries, Technological Innovation, and Strategic Management. **In** *[Dean, J.]*, 1986, pp. 187–99.

Teece, David J. Profiting from Technological Innovation: Implications for Integration, Collaboration, Licensing and Public Policy. *Ricerche Econ.*, Oct.-Dec. 1986, *40*(4), pp. 607–43. **[G: U.S.]**

Templé, Philippe. Le processus d'innovation dans les entreprises. (Innovation Process and Firms. With English summary.) *Écon. Appl.*, 1986, *39*(3), pp. 583–614. **[G: France]**

Thompson, Edward. Performers and Technological Change 25 Years after the Rome Convention. *Int. Lab. Rev.*, Sept.-Oct. 1986, *125*(5), pp. 575–90. **[G: OECD]**

Thorpe, Kenneth E. Information Technology and the U.S. Health Care Industry: A New Direction: Discussion. **In** *Faulhaber, G.; Noam, E. and Tasley, R., eds.*, 1986, pp. 26–30. **[G: U.S.]**

von Ungern-Sternberg, Thomas. Innovator Protection and the Rate of Technical Progress. **In** *Day, R. H. and Eliasson, G., eds.*, 1986, *1984*, pp. 277–91.

Unnevehr, Laurian J. Changing Comparative Advantage in Philippine Rice Production: 1966 to 1982. *Food Res. Inst. Stud.*, 1986, *20*(1), pp. 43–69. **[G: Philippines]**

Vernon, Raymond. The Curious Character of the International Technology Market: An Economic Perspective. **In** *McIntyre, J. R. and Papp, D. S., eds.*, 1986, pp. 47–51. **[G: U.S.]**

Vilenskii, M. V. Intensification of the Economy and the Acceleration of Technical Progress. *Prob. Econ.*, June 1986, *29*(2), pp. 24–42. **[G: U.S.S.R.]**

Vizas, Christopher J., II. The Reality of Change, Satellite Technology, Economics, and Institutional Resistance. **In** *Demac, D. A., ed.*, 1986, pp. 75–87.

Walker, David J. and Young, Douglas L. The Effect of Technical Progress on Erosion Damage and Economic Incentives for Soil Conservation. *Land Econ.*, February 1986, *62*(1), pp. 83–93. **[G: U.S.]**

Wallace, Neil. The Impact of New Payment Technologies: A Macro View. **In** *Lawrence, C. and Shay, R. P., eds.*, 1986, pp. 201–06. **[G: U.S.]**

Washio, Hiroaki. The Provision of Manuals and Japanese Private Technology Transfer. *Devel. Econ.*, December 1986, *24*(4), pp. 326–33. **[G: Japan]**

Watanabe, Susumu. Labour-Saving versus Work-Amplifying Effects of Micro-electronics. *Int. Lab. Rev.*, May-June 1986, *125*(3), pp. 243–59. **[G: W. Europe; U.S.; Japan; Brazil]**

Webber, Douglas, et al. Information Technology and Economic Recovery in Western Europe: The Role of the British, French and West German Governments. *Policy Sci.*, October 1986, *19*(3), pp. 319–46. **[G: U.K.; Japan; W. Germany; U.S.; France]**

Wells, John V. A Behavioral Analysis of Technological Change in the Computer Industry, 1930–1950. *J. Econ. Issues*, June 1986, *20*(2), pp. 533–39. **[G: U.S.]**

Wiggins, Steven N. Innovation, Market Structure and Market Dynamics: Comment. *J. Inst. Theoretical Econ.*, March 1986, *142*(1), pp. 200–203. **[G: W. Germany]**

Wildemann, Horst. Einführungsstrategien für neue Produktionstechnologien—dargestellt an CAD/CAM-Systemen und Flexiblen Fertigungssystemen. (With English summary.) *Z. Betriebswirtschaft*, Apr.-May 1986, *56*(4/5), pp. 337–69. **[G: W. Germany]**

Williams, Bruce. Technical Change and Employment. **In** *Hall, P., ed.*, 1986, *1984*, pp. 84–103. **[G: U.K.]**

Williams, J. T. Germplasm Resources. **In** *Swaminathan, M. S. and Sinha, S. K., eds.*, 1986, pp. 117–28.

Wilner, Gabriel M. An International Legal Framework for the Transfer of Technology. **In** *McIntyre, J. R. and Papp, D. S., eds.*, 1986, pp. 53–60.

Wong, Christine P. W. Intermediate Technology for Development: Small-scale Chemical Fertilizer Plants in China. *World Devel.*, Oct./Nov. 1986, *14*(10/11), pp. 1329–46. **[G: China]**

Yao, Dennis A. Information Technology and the United States Economy: Modeling and Measurement: Discussion. **In** *Faulhaber, G.; Noam, E. and Tasley, R., eds.*, 1986, pp. 132–37. **[G: U.S.]**

Young, David N. The Impact of Technology on the Insurance Industry. **In** *Faulhaber, G.; Noam, E. and Tasley, R., eds.*, 1986, pp. 31–43. **[G: U.S.]**

6212 Research and Development

Adams, Walter and Martin, Stephen. Public Support of Innovative Activity: Lessons from U.S. Industrial Policy. **In** *de Jong, H. W. and Shepherd, W. G., eds., Bk. 2*, 1986, pp. 413–39. **[G: U.S.]**

Allen, D. E.; Crook, J. N. and Reekie, W. Duncan. Technical Change, Economies of Scope and Contestable Markets: Lessons from a British R&D Consortium. *S. Afr. J. Econ.*, June 1986, *54*(2), pp. 181–93. **[G: U.K.]**

Andersson, Åke. Creativity, Complexity, and Economic Development. On the Role of Structural Instabilities in R&D-Analysis. *Ricerche Econ.*, Oct.-Dec. 1986, *40*(4), pp. 724–37.

Aron, Paul H. Industrial Policy in Japan: Implications for Technological Catch-up and Leadership: Comment. **In** *Pugel, T. A., ed.*, 1986, pp. 233–35. **[G: U.S.; Japan]**

Bernstein, Jeffrey I. The Effect of Direct and Indirect Tax Incentives on Canadian Industrial R&D Expenditures. *Can. Public Policy*, September 1986, *12*(3), pp. 438–48. **[G: Canada]**

Bhattacharya, Sudipto; Chatterjee, Kalyan and Samuelson, Larry. Sequential Research and the Adoption of Innovations. **In** *Morris, D. J., et al., eds.*, 1986, pp. 219–43.

Bhattacharya, Sudipto; Chatterjee, Kalyan and Samuelson, Larry. Sequential Research and the Adoption of Innovations. *Oxford Econ. Pap.*, Suppl. Nov. 1986, *38*, pp. 219–43.

Binswanger, Hans P. Evaluating Research System Performance and Targeting Research in Land-abundant Areas of Sub-Saharan Africa. *World Devel.*, April 1986, *14*(4), pp. 469–75. **[G: Sub-Saharan Africa]**

Boskin, Michael J. Budgets, Deficits, Technology and Economic Growth. **In** *Landau, R. and Jorgenson, D. W., eds.*, 1986, pp. 191–204. **[G: U.S.]**

Bozeman, Barry; Link, Albert N. and Zardkoohi, Asghar. An Economic Analysis of R&D Joint Ventures. *Managerial Dec. Econ.*, December 1986, *7*(4), pp. 263–66.

Braun, Armand. Role of the Public Sector in the Promotion of Science and Technology. **In** *U.N., Dept. of Technical Co-operation for Development*, 1986, pp. 182–245. **[G: OECD; France]**

Broadus, J. M. Asian Pacific Marine Minerals and Industry Structure. *Marine Resource Econ.*, 1986, *3*(1), pp. 63–88. **[G: Asia]**

Brockhoff, Klaus. Die Produktivität der Forschung und Entwicklung eines Industrieunternehmens. (With English summary.) *Z. Betriebswirtshaft*, June 1986, *56*(6), pp. 525–37. **[G: W. Germany]**

Brooks, Harvey. National Science Policy and Technological Innovation. **In** *Landau, R. and Rosenberg, N., eds.*, 1986, pp. 119–67. **[G: U.S.; U.K.; Japan; France; W. Germany]**

Brunner, E. and Schubert, U. Capital Mobility, Labour Demand and R&D Investment in Austria in a Multiregional Context: A First Attempt at Econometric Modelling. **In** *Nijkamp, P., ed. (II)*, 1986, pp. 429–53. **[G: Austria]**

Camagni, Roberto. The Economics of Industrial Revitalisation in Declining Metropolitan Areas. *Econ. Int.*, May-Aug.-Nov. 1986, *39*(2–3–4), pp. 316–34. **[G: Italy]**

Chappell, Henry W., Jr.; Pietrowski, Jane T. and Wilder, Ronald P. R and D, Firm Size, and Concentration: Evidence from the FTC Line of Business Survey. *Quart. J. Bus. Econ.*, Spring 1986, *25*(2), pp. 32–50. **[G: U.S.]**

Cheung, Steven N. S. Property Rights and Invention. **In** *Palmer, J., ed.*, 1986, pp. 5–18. **[G: U.S.]**

Chokki, Toshiaki. A History of the Machine Tool Industry in Japan. **In** *Fransman, M., ed.*, 1986, pp. 124–52. **[G: Japan]**

Chudnovsky, Daniel. The Entry into the Design and Production of Complex Capital Goods: The Experiences of Brazil, India and South Korea. **In** *Fransman, M., ed.*, 1986, pp. 54–92. **[G: S. Korea; Brazil; India]**

Cohen, Linda R. and Noll, Roger G. Government R&D Programs for Commercializing Space. *Amer. Econ. Rev.*, May 1986, *76*(2), pp. 269–73. **[G: U.S.]**

Connolly, Robert A.; Hirsch, Barry T. and Hirschey, Mark. Union Rent Seeking, Intangible Capital, and Market Value of the Firm. *Rev. Econ. Statist.*, November 1986, *68*(4), pp. 567–77. **[G: U.S.]**

Coover, H. W. Programmed Innovation—Strategy for Success. **In** *Landau, R. and Rosenberg, N., eds.*, 1986, pp. 399–416. **[G: U.S.]**

Crampes, Claude. Les inconvénients d'un dépôt de brevet pour une entreprise innovatrice. (The Disadvantage of Patenting. With English summary.) *L'Actual. Econ.*, December 1986, *62*(4), pp. 521–34.

Delbono, Flavio. Proprietà dell'equilibrio di Nash in modelli di competizione tecnologica. (Properties of Nash Equilibrium in R&D Models. With English summary.) *Rivista Int. Sci. Econ. Com.*, December 1986, *33*(12), pp. 1167–83.

Doi, Teruo. The Role of Intellectual Property Law in Bilateral Licensing Transactions between Japan and the United States. **In** *Saxonhouse, G. R. and Yamamura, K., eds.*, 1986, pp. 157–92. **[G: Japan; U.S.]**

Domsch, Michel and Gerpott, Torsten J. Aufstiegsklima von industriellen F & E-Einheiten und individuelle Arbeitsleistung und -zufriedenheit. (With English summary.) *Z. Betriebswirtshaft*, November 1986, *56*(11), pp. 1095–1116. **[G: W. Germany]**

Edelman, Gerald M. Profits and Prophecy: A Partial View of American Science Near the Millennium. **In** *Knowlton, W. and Zeckhauser, R., eds.*, 1986, pp. 223–48. **[G: U.S.]**

Eliasson, Gunnar. Schumpeterian Competition in Alternative Technological Regimes: Comment. **In** *Day, R. H. and Eliasson, G., eds.*, 1986, pp. 233–38.

Fels, Gerhard. Incentives for Entrepreneurship and Supporting Institutions: Comment. **In** *Balassa, B. and Giersch, H., eds.*, 1986, pp. 188–91.

Friedlaender, Ann F. Macroeconomics and Microeconomics of Innovation: The Role of the Technological Environment. **In** *Landau, R. and Rosenberg, N., eds.*, 1986, pp. 327–32.

Gomulka, Stanislaw. The Incompatibility of Socialism and Rapid Innovation. **In** *Gomulka, S.*, 1986, *1984*, pp. 42–61. **[G: U.S.S.R.; E. Europe]**

Gomulka, Stanislaw and Ostojić, Slobodan. Innovation Activity in the Yugoslav Economy. **In**

Gomulka, S., 1986, pp. 62–72. **[G: Yugoslavia]**

Gort, Michael and Wall, Richard A. The Evolution of Technologies and Investment in Innovation. *Econ. J.*, September 1986, *96*(383), pp. 741–57. **[G: U.S.]**

Grabowski, Henry G. and Vernon, John. Longer Patents for Lower Imitation Barriers: The 1984 Drug Act. *Amer. Econ. Rev.*, May 1986, *76*(2), pp. 195–98. **[G: U.S.]**

Granstrand, Ove. Innovator Protection and the Rate of Technical Progress: Comment. **In** *Day, R. H. and Eliasson, G., eds.*, 1986, pp. 293–94.

Granstrand, Ove. On Measuring and Modelling Innovative New Entry in Swedish Industry. **In** *Day, R. H. and Eliasson, G., eds.*, 1986, pp. 295–310. **[G: Sweden]**

Gremmen, Hans J. and Vollebergh, Ad H. J. An Input Approach to European Comparative Advantage in Advanced Products: A Study with Special Emphasis on the Netherlands. *Weltwirtsch. Arch.*, 1986, *122*(2), pp. 270–80. **[G: Netherlands; Global]**

Griliches, Zvi. Productivity, *R&D*, and the Basic Research at the Firm Level in the 1970's. *Amer. Econ. Rev.*, March 1986, *76*(1), pp. 141–54. **[G: U.S.]**

Grossman, Gene M. and Shapiro, Carl. Research Joint Ventures: An Antitrust Analysis. *J. Law, Econ., Organ.*, Fall 1986, *2*(2), pp. 315–37. **[G: U.S.]**

Hall, Bronwyn H.; Griliches, Zvi and Hausman, Jerry A. Patents and R and D: Is There a Lag? *Int. Econ. Rev.*, June 1986, *27*(2), pp. 265–83. **[G: U.S.]**

Hansen, Jørgen. Investeringsbehov og balanceproblemer. (Industrial Investments and Economic Imbalance in the Danish Economy. With English summary.) *Nationaløkon. Tidsskr.*, 1986, *124*(2), pp. 139–46. **[G: Denmark]**

Henning, Steven A. and Eddleman, B. R. Intra- and Inter-state Transferability of Soybean Variety Research. *Southern J. Agr. Econ.*, December 1986, *18*(2), pp. 7–13. **[G: U.S.]**

Holmer, Edwin C. The Chemical Industry: Challenges, Risks, and Rewards. **In** *Landau, R. and Rosenberg, N., eds.*, 1986, pp. 417–22. **[G: U.S.]**

Horton, Douglas. Assessing the Impact of International Agricultural Research and Development Programs. *World Devel.*, April 1986, *14*(4), pp. 453–68. **[G: LDCs]**

Horwitch, Mel and Sakakibara, Kiyonori. The Changing Strategy–Technology Relationship in Technology-Based Industries: A Comparison of the United States and Japan. **In** *Rosenbloom, R. S., ed.*, 1986, pp. 83–135. **[G: U.S.; Japan]**

Jaffe, Adam B. Technological Opportunity and Spillovers of *R&D:* Evidence from Firms' Patents, Profits, and Market Value. *Amer. Econ. Rev.*, December 1986, *76*(5), pp. 984–1001. **[G: U.S.]**

Joglekar, Prafulla and Paterson, Morton L. A Closer Look at the Returns and Risks of Pharmaceutical R&D. *J. Health Econ.*, June 1986, *5*(2), pp. 153–77. **[G: U.S.]**

Judd, M. Ann; Boyce, James K. and Evenson, Robert E. Investing in Agricultural Supply: The Determinants of Agricultural Research and Extension Investment. *Econ. Develop. Cult. Change,* October 1986, *35*(1), pp. 77–113. **[G: Global]**

Kaldor, Mary; Sharp, Margaret and Walker, William. Industrial Competitiveness and Britain's Defence. *Lloyds Bank Rev.*, October 1986, (162), pp. 31–49. **[G: U.K.]**

Kennedy, Donald. Basic Research in the Universities: How Much Utility? **In** *Landau, R. and Rosenberg, N., eds.*, 1986, pp. 263–74. **[G: U.S.]**

Khan, Mahmood Hasan and Akbari, Ather Hussain. Impact of Agricultural Research and Extension on Crop Productivity in Pakistan: A Production Function Approach. *World Devel.*, June 1986, *14*(6), pp. 757–62. **[G: Pakistan]**

Kingston, William. Industrial Policy and Innovation in Europe. **In** *de Jong, H. W. and Shepherd, W. G., eds., Bk. 2,* 1986, pp. 441–61. **[G: W. Europe]**

Kitch, Edmund W. Patents: Monopolies or Property Rights? **In** *Palmer, J., ed.*, 1986, pp. 31–49.

Klett, Daniel. The U.S. Tariff Act: Section 337: Off-Shore Assembly and the "Domestic Industry." *J. World Trade Law,* May:June 1986, *20*(3), pp. 294–312. **[G: U.S.]**

Klette, Tor and de Meza, David. Is the Market Biased against Risky R&D? *Rand J. Econ.*, Spring 1986, *17*(1), pp. 133–39.

Layton, Christopher. The High-tech Triangle. **In** *Morgan, R. and Bray, C., eds.*, 1986, pp. 184–204. **[G: U.K.; W. Germany; France]**

Ledyard, John O. Incentive Compatible Space Station Pricing. *Amer. Econ. Rev.*, May 1986, *76*(2), pp. 274–79. **[G: U.S.]**

Levitsky, Serge L. Copyrights and Trademarks in Soviet Economy: A Study in Contrasts. **In** *Ioffe, O. S. and Janis, M. W., eds.*, 1986, pp. 127–68. **[G: U.S.S.R.]**

Lichtenberg, Frank R. The Duration and Intensity of Investment in Independent Research and Development Projects. *J. Econ. Soc. Meas.*, October 1986, *14*(3), pp. 207–18. **[G: U.S.]**

Link, Albert N. and Neufeld, John L. Innovation versus Imitation: Investigating Alternative R&D Strategies. *Appl. Econ.*, December 1986, *18*(12), pp. 1359–63. **[G: U.S.]**

Lunn, John. An Empirical Analysis of Process and Product Patenting: A Simultaneous Equation Framework. *J. Ind. Econ.*, March 1986, *34*(3), pp. 319–30. **[G: U.S.]**

Lunn, John and Martin, Stephen. Market Structure, Firm Structure, and Research Development. *Quart. Rev. Econ. Bus.*, Spring 1986, *26*(1), pp. 31–44. **[G: U.S.]**

Malpas, Robert. Harnessing Technology for Growth. **In** *Landau, R. and Rosenberg, N., eds.*, 1986, pp. 105–13. **[G: OECD]**

Mansfield, Edwin. Microeconomics of Technological Innovation. **In** *Landau, R. and Rosenberg, N., eds.*, 1986, pp. 307–25. **[G: U.S.]**

Mansfield, Edwin. The R&D Tax Credit and Other Technology Policy Issues. *Amer. Econ. Rev.*, May 1986, *76*(2), pp. 190–94. **[G: U.S.; Canada; Sweden]**

Mariotti, Sergio and Ricotta, Enrico. Diversification, Agreements between Firms and Innovative Behaviour. *Ricerche Econ.*, Oct.-Dec. 1986, *40*(4), pp. 644–74. **[G: U.S.; Europe]**

Marsh, Robert M. and Mannari, Hiroshi. Entrepreneurship in Medium- and Large-scale Japanese Firms. **In** *Greenfield, S. M. and Strickon, A., eds.*, 1986, pp. 19–44.

Martinez, Stephen and Norton, George W. Evaluating Privately Funded Public Research: An Example with Poultry and Eggs. *Southern J. Agr. Econ.*, July 1986, *18*(1), pp. 129–40. **[G: U.S.]**

Maxwell, Simon. Farming Systems Research: Hitting a Moving Target. *World Devel.*, January 1986, *14*(1), pp. 65–77. **[G: LDCs]**

de Meza, David. Immiserising Invention: The Private and Social Returns to R&D under Oligopoly. *Int. J. Ind. Organ.*, December 1986, *4*(4), pp. 409–17.

Mohnen, Pierre A.; Nadiri, M. Ishaq and Prucha, Ingmar R. R&D, Production Structure and Rates of Return in the U.S., Japanese and German Manufacturing Sectors: A Non-separable Dynamic Factor Demand Model. *Europ. Econ. Rev.*, August 1986, *30*(4), pp. 749–71. **[G: U.S.; Japan; W. Germany]**

Mowery, David C. Industry Research, 1900–1950. **In** *Elbaum, B. and Lazonick, W., eds.*, 1986, pp. 189–222. **[G: U.K.]**

Nelson, Richard R. Incentives for Entrepreneurship and Supporting Institutions. **In** *Balassa, B. and Giersch, H., eds.*, 1986, pp. 173–87.

Nelson, Richard R. Institutions Supporting Technical Advance in Industry. *Amer. Econ. Rev.*, May 1986, *76*(2), pp. 186–89. **[G: U.S.]**

Nelson, Richard R. The Tension between Process Stories and Equilibrium Models: Analyzing the Productivity-Growth Slowdown of the 1970s. **In** *Langlois, R. N., ed.*, 1986, pp. 135–51.

Odagiri, Hiroyuki. Industrial Policy in Theory and Reality. **In** *de Jong, H. W. and Shepherd, W. G., eds., Bk. 2*, 1986, pp. 387–412. **[G: Japan]**

Okimoto, Daniel I. Regime Characteristics of Japanese Industrial Policy. **In** *Patrick, H., ed.*, 1986, pp. 35–95. **[G: Japan]**

Okimoto, Daniel I. The Japanese Challenge in High Technology. **In** *Landau, R. and Rosenberg, N., eds.*, 1986, pp. 541–67. **[G: Japan]**

Pake, G. E. From Research to Innovation at Xerox: A Manager's Principles and Some Examples. **In** *Rosenbloom, R. S., ed.*, 1986, pp. 1–32. **[G: U.S.]**

Pavitt, Keith L. R. Determinants of Innovative Activity. **In** *Landau, R. and Rosenberg, N., eds.*, 1986, pp. 393–97.

Pepper, Thomas. Industrial Policy in Japan: Implications for Technological Catch-up and Leadership: Comment. **In** *Pugel, T. A., ed.*, 1986, pp. 229–32. **[G: U.S.; Japan]**

Peters, Michael and Winter, Ralph A. Research and Development with Publicly Observable Outcomes. *J. Econ. Theory*, December 1986, *40*(2), pp. 349–63.

Priest, George L. What Economists Can Tell Lawyers about Intellectual Property: Comment [Property Rights and Invention]. **In** *Palmer, J., ed.*, 1986, pp. 19–24. **[G: U.S.]**

Pruitt, Bettye H. and Smith, George David. The Corporate Management of Innovation: Alcoa Research, Aircraft Alloys, and the Problem of Stress-Corrosion Cracking. **In** *Rosenbloom, R. S., ed.*, 1986, pp. 33–81. **[G: U.S.]**

Pugel, Thomas A. Industrial Policy in Japan: Implications for Technological Catch-up and Leadership. **In** *Pugel, T. A., ed.*, 1986, pp. 209–27. **[G: U.S.; Japan]**

Raipuria, Kalyan M. A Distributed Information and Research System (DIRS) for the Third World. **In** *Panchamukhi, V. R., et al.*, 1986, pp. 273–93.

Raipuria, Kalyan M. Third World in the 'Third Wave': Imperative of South–South Cooperation in Science and Technology. **In** *Panchamukhi, V. R., et al.*, 1986, pp. 166–214. **[G: Global]**

Rasmussen, Poul Nyrup. Hvad har vi Lært? (The Problem of Imbalance and Solutions Based on Concensus in the Society. With English summary.) *Nationaløkon. Tidsskr.*, 1986, *124*(2), pp. 223–33. **[G: Denmark]**

Reichert, Joachim. Die Wirkungen einer allgemeinen Lizenzpflicht auf den technologischen und technischen Fortschritt. (Effects of a General Licencing Duty on Technological and Technical Progress. With English summary.) *Jahr. Nationalökon. Statist.*, November 1986, *201*(6), pp. 605–17.

Rob, Rafael. The Design of Procurement Contracts. *Amer. Econ. Rev.*, June 1986, *76*(3), pp. 378–89.

Robinson, Austin. Incentives for Entrepreneurship and Supporting Institutions: Comment. **In** *Balassa, B. and Giersch, H., eds.*, 1986, pp. 192–96.

Rothwell, Roy. The Role of Small Firms in the Emergence of New Technologies. **In** *Freeman, C., ed.*, 1986, pp. 231–48. **[G: U.K.; U.S.]**

Rugman, Alan M. and Douglas, Sheila. The Strategic Management of Multinationals and World Product Mandating. *Can. Public Policy*, June 1986, *12*(2), pp. 320–28. **[G: Canada]**

Ruttan, Vernon W. Technical Change and Innovation in Agriculture. **In** *Landau, R. and Rosenberg, N., eds.*, 1986, pp. 333–56. **[G: U.S.; Japan]**

Saxonhouse, Gary R. Industrial Policy and Factor Markets: Biotechnology in Japan and the United States. **In** *Patrick, H., ed.*, 1986, pp. 97–135. **[G: U.S.; Japan]**

Schankerman, Mark and Nadiri, M. Ishaq. A Test of Static Equilibrium Models and Rates of Return to Quasi-fixed Factors, with an Application to the Bell System. *J. Econometrics*,

Oct./Nov. 1986, *33*(1/2), pp. 97–118.

Scherer, F. M. Patents: Monopolies or Property Rights? Comment. **In** *Palmer, J., ed.*, 1986, pp. 51–58.

Scholz, Lothar. Technology Promotion in the Federal Republic of Germany. **In** *Hax, H.; Kraus, W. and Tsuchiya, K., eds.*, 1986, pp. 71–83. **[G: W. Germany]**

Sharp, Margaret. Biotechnology: Watching and Waiting. **In** *Sharp, M., ed.*, 1986, pp. 161–212. **[G: OECD]**

Simon, Denis Fred and Schive, Chi. National Policies for Developing High Technology Industries: International Comparisons: Taiwan. **In** *Rushing, F. W. and Brown, C. G., eds.*, 1986, pp. 201–26.

Skorov, George. Science, Society and Endogenous Development. **In** *[Patel, S.]*, 1986, pp. 253–65.

Stoffaës, Christian. Industrial Policy in the High-Technology Industries. **In** *Adams, W. J. and Stoffaës, C., eds.*, 1986, pp. 36–62. **[G: OECD]**

Stöhr, Walter B. Towards a Framework for Evaluating the Effects of Technology Complexes and Science Parks. *Econ. Int.*, May-Aug.-Nov. 1986, *39*(2–3–4), pp. 299–311. **[G: U.S.]**

Sunley, Emil M. Federal Tax Policy and the Budget. **In** *Landau, R. and Jorgenson, D. W., eds.*, 1986, pp. 85–96. **[G: U.S.]**

Sveikauskas, Leo. The Contribution of R and D to Productivity Growth. *Mon. Lab. Rev.*, March 1986, *109*(3), pp. 16–20. **[G: U.S.]**

Swanson, Robert A. Entrepreneurship and Innovation: Biotechnology. **In** *Landau, R. and Rosenberg, N., eds.*, 1986, pp. 429–35. **[G: U.S.]**

Tilton, John E. and Mueller, Dennis C. Research and Development Costs as a Barrier to Entry. **In** *Mueller, D. C.*, 1986, *1969*, pp. 108–18.

Ulrich, Alvin; Furtan, Hartley and Schmitz, Andrew. Public and Private Returns from Joint Venture Research: An Example from Agriculture. *Quart. J. Econ.*, February 1986, *101*(1), pp. 103–29. **[G: Canada]**

von Ungern-Sternberg, Thomas. Innovator Protection and the Rate of Technical Progress. **In** *Day, R. H. and Eliasson, G., eds.*, 1986, *1984*, pp. 277–91.

von Ungern-Sternberg, Thomas. Schumpeterian Competition in Alternative Technological Regimes: Comment. **In** *Day, R. H. and Eliasson, G., eds.*, 1986, pp. 239–41.

Van Cayseele, Patrick. Spillovers and the Cost of Multiproject R&D. *Managerial Dec. Econ.*, June 1986, *7*(2), pp. 133–39.

Vickers, John S. The Evolution of Market Structure When There Is a Sequence of Innovations. *J. Ind. Econ.*, September 1986, *35*(1), pp. 1–12.

de Villiers, J. U. and Scott, D. R. Research and Development Expenditure in Regulated and Unregulated Markets. *Managerial Dec. Econ.*, September 1986, *7*(3), pp. 197–201. **[G: S. Africa]**

Wagner, Joachim. Zur Technologieintensität der Produktion in der Bundesrepublik Deutschland. (On the Technological Intensity of Production in the Federal Republic of Germany. With English summary.) *Ifo-Studien*, 1986, *32*(4), pp. 297–307. **[G: W. Germany]**

Weingarten, Fred W. and Wilk, Charles. Research and Development Policy in the United States: Implications for Satellite Communications. **In** *Demac, D. A., ed.*, 1986, pp. 141–55. **[G: U.S.]**

Winter, Sidney G. Schumpeterian Competition in Alternative Technological Regimes. **In** *Day, R. H. and Eliasson, G., eds.*, 1986, *1984*, pp. 199–232.

Winter, Sidney G. Schumpeterian Competition in Alternative Technological Regimes: Reply. **In** *Day, R. H. and Eliasson, G., eds.*, 1986, pp. 242–45.

Wise, W. S. The Calculation of Rates of Return on Agricultural Research from Production Functions. *J. Agr. Econ.*, May 1986, *37*(2), pp. 151–61. **[G: EEC]**

Wittwer, S. H. Research and Technology Needs for the Twenty-first Century. **In** *Swaminathan, M. S. and Sinha, S. K., eds.*, 1986, pp. 85–116.

Yamamura, Kozo. Joint Research and Antitrust: Japanese vs. American Strategies. **In** *Patrick, H., ed.*, 1986, pp. 171–209. **[G: U.S.; Japan]**

Yamauchi, Ichizo. Long-range Strategic Planning in Japanese R&D. **In** *Freeman, C., ed.*, 1986, pp. 169–85. **[G: Japan]**

Yu, Ben T. Comparative Productivity of Inventors in Emerging Research Organizations: Some Evidence from the U.S. Petroleum Industry. *Hong Kong Econ. Pap.*, 1986, (17), pp. 11–33. **[G: U.S.]**

Zschau, Ed. Government Policies for Innovation and Growth. **In** *Landau, R. and Rosenberg, N., eds.*, 1986, pp. 535–39. **[G: U.S.]**

630 Industry Studies

6300 General

Abalkin, L. Intensification and Economic Growth. *Prob. Econ.*, June 1986, *29*(2), pp. 64–78. **[G: U.S.S.R.]**

Ahluwalia, Isher Judge. Industrial Growth in India: Performance and Prospects. *J. Devel. Econ.*, September 1986, *23*(1), pp. 1–18. **[G: India]**

Amann, Ronald. Technical Progress and Soviet Economic Development: Setting the Scene. **In** *Amann, R. and Cooper, J., eds.*, 1986, pp. 5–30. **[G: U.S.S.R.]**

Baba, Masao. Changes in Industrial Structure and Investment Planning. *Ifo-Studien*, 1986, *32*(1–3), pp. 123–30. **[G: Japan]**

Bade, Franz-Josef. The De-industrialisation of the Federal Republic of Germany and Its Spatial Implications. **In** *Nijkamp, P., ed. (II)*, 1986, pp. 196–220. **[G: W. Germany; OECD]**

Bade, Franz-Josef. The Economic Importance of Small and Medium-sized Firms in the Federal Republic of Germany. **In** *Keeble, D. and*

Wever, E., eds., 1986, pp. 256–74. **[G: W. Germany]**

Black, Andrew P. Industrial Policy in W. Germany. Policy in Search of a Goal? **In** *Hall, G., ed.*, 1986, pp. 84–127. **[G: W. Germany]**

Blanchard, Olivier J. Market Structure and Macroeconomic Fluctuations: Comments. *Brookings Pap. Econ. Act.*, 1986, (2), pp. 323–28.

Blanchflower, David. Wages and Concentration in British Manufacturing. *Appl. Econ.*, September 1986, *18*(9), pp. 1025–38. **[G: U.K.]**

Blitzer, Charles R. and Eckaus, Richard S. Energy–Economy Interactions in Mexico: A Multiperiod General Equilibrium Model. *J. Devel. Econ.*, May 1986, *21*(2), pp. 259–81. **[G: Mexico]**

Boddy, Martin and Lovering, John. High Technology Industry in the Bristol Sub-Region: The Aerospace/Defence Nexus. *Reg. Stud.*, June 1986, *20*(3), pp. 217–31. **[G: U.K.]**

Boyer, Robert and Ralle, Pierre. L'insertion internationale conditionne-t-elle les formes nationales d'emploi? Convergences ou différenciations des pays européens. (Are Jobs Dependent on International Openness? Similarities and Differences between European Countries. With English summary.) *Écon. Soc.*, January 1986, *20*(1), pp. 145–68. **[G: EEC]**

Brewer, H. L. and Moomaw, Ronald L. Regional Economic Instability and Industrial Diversification in the U.S.: Comment. *Land Econ.*, November 1986, *62*(4), pp. 412–15. **[G: U.S.]**

Browne, Lynn E. Taking in Each Other's Laundry—The Service Economy. *New Eng. Econ. Rev.*, July/Aug. 1986, pp. 20–31. **[G: U.S.]**

Bukhval'd, E. and Pogrebinskaia, V. V. I. Lenin on the Dynamics of Reproduction and the Rates of the USSR's Economic Development. *Prob. Econ.*, April 1986, *28*(12), pp. 59–77. **[G: U.S.S.R.]**

Casson, Mark. Multinationals and World Trade: Introduction and Summary. **In** *Casson, M., et al.*, 1986, pp. 1–59. **[G: U.S.]**

Costrell, Robert M.; Duguay, Gerald E. and Treyz, George I. Labour Substitution and Complementarity among Age–Sex Groups. *Appl. Econ.*, July 1986, *18*(7), pp. 777–91. **[G: U.S.]**

Crémieux, Michel and Mezière, Dominique. Le financement des investissements d'utilisation rationnelle de l'énergie dans l'industrie (1975–1985). (Investments Financing for Rational Use of Energy in Industry [1975–1985]. With English summary.) *Écon. Soc.*, July 1986, *20*(7), pp. 159–74. **[G: France]**

Deardorff, Alan V. and Stern, Robert M. The Structure and Sample Results of the Michigan Computational Model of World Production and Trade. **In** *Srinivasan, T. N. and Whalley, J., eds.*, 1986, pp. 151–88. **[G: LDCs; MDCs]**

Dixon, Peter B. Prospects for Australian Industries and Occupations, 1985 to 1990. *Australian Econ. Rev.*, 1st Quarter 1986, (73), pp. 3–28. **[G: Australia]**

Dokopoulou, Evangelia. Small Manufacturing Firms and Regional Development in Greece: Patterns and Changes. **In** *Keeble, D. and Wever, E., eds.*, 1986, pp. 299–317. **[G: Greece]**

Dominique, C.-René and Oral, Muhittin. Exporting to Northern Markets: The Making of an Industrial Competitiveness Index. *Industry Devel.*, 1986, (18), pp. 1–17. **[G: Global]**

Donckels, Rik and Bert, Christiane. New Firms in the Local Economy: The Case of Belgium. **In** *Keeble, D. and Wever, E., eds.*, 1986, pp. 124–40. **[G: Belgium]**

Donckels, Rik and Degadt, Jan. Women in Small Business: The Belgian Experience. **In** *Donckels, R. and Meijer, J. N., eds.*, 1986, pp. 45–64. **[G: Belgium]**

Donckels, Rik and Meijer, Jane N. Women in Small Business: Focus on Europe: Introduction. **In** *Donckels, R. and Meijer, J. N., eds.*, 1986, pp. 1–9.

Driver, Ciaran. Spare Capacity and the Scope for Industrial Expansion. *Fisc. Stud.*, August 1986, *7*(3), pp. 67–75. **[G: U.K.]**

Drucker, Peter F. The Changed World Economy. *Foreign Aff.*, Spring 1986, *64*(4), pp. 768–91.

Erić, Milan, et al. Identification of Cycles in Yugoslav Industry during the Period 1953–1982. *Eastern Europ. Econ.*, Winter 1986-87, *25*(2), pp. 100–123. **[G: Yugoslavia]**

Evans, David S. The Differential Effect of Regulation across Plant Size: Comment [The Effect of Environmental Regulation on Optimal Plant Size and Factor Shares]. *J. Law Econ.*, April 1986, *29*(1), pp. 187–200. **[G: U.S.]**

Freeman, Richard B. In Search of Union Wage Concessions in Standard Data Sets. *Ind. Relat.*, Spring 1986, *25*(2), pp. 131–45. **[G: U.S.]**

Gertler, Meric S. Regional Dynamics of Manufacturing and Non-manufacturing Investment in Canada. *Reg. Stud.*, October 1986, *20*(6), pp. 523–34. **[G: Canada]**

Goldstein, Walter. The Changing Impact of International Trade on the Economy of New York State. **In** *Schoolman, M. and Magid, A., eds.*, 1986, pp. 167–203. **[G: U.S.]**

Guillen, Arturo. Mexico: crisis, industria y restructuracion del sistema productivo. (Mexico: Crisis, Industry and Restructuring of the Productive System. With English summary.) *Écon. Soc.*, May 1986, *20*(5), pp. 155–69. **[G: Mexico]**

Hall, Robert E. Market Structure and Macroeconomic Fluctuations. *Brookings Pap. Econ. Act.*, 1986, (2), pp. 285–322. **[G: U.S.]**

Hamilton, Clive. A Technique for Calculating Capital Coefficients in Newly Industrializing Countries, with Application to the Republic of Korea. *Devel. Econ.*, March 1986, *24*(1), pp. 56–70. **[G: S. Korea]**

Harris, Richard G. Market Structure and Trade Liberalization: A General Equilibrium Assessment. **In** *Srinivasan, T. N. and Whalley, J., eds.*, 1986, pp. 231–50. **[G: Canada]**

Hazilla, Michael and Kopp, Raymond J. Systematic Effects of Capital Service Price Definition on Perceptions of Input Substitution. *J. Bus.*

Econ. Statist., April 1986, 4(2), pp. 209–24. [G: U.S.]

Heikkila, Eric and Hutton, Thomas A. Toward an Evaluative Framework for Land Use Policy in Industrial Districts of the Urban Core: A Qualitative Analysis of the Exclusionary Zoning Approach. *Urban Stud.*, February 1986, *23*(1), pp. 47–60. **[G: Canada]**

Helliwell, John F., et al. The Supply Side in the OECD's Macroeconomic Model. *OECD Econ. Stud.*, Spring 1986, (6), pp. 75–131. **[G: OECD]**

Hendriks, Ad J. Local Entrepreneurial Initiatives and Central Government. **In** *Nijkamp, P., ed. (II)*, 1986, pp. 280–88. **[G: Netherlands]**

Herman, Arthur S. Productivity Continued to Increase in Many Industries during 1984. *Mon. Lab. Rev.*, March 1986, *109*(3), pp. 11–15. **[G: U.S.]**

Hersztajn-Moldau, Juan and Pelin, Eli Roberto. O custo dos recursos domésticos das exportações brasileiras em 1980. (With English summary.) *Pesquisa Planejamento Econ.*, April 1986, *16*(1), pp. 189–222. **[G: Brazil]**

Hubbard, R. Glenn. Market Structure and Macroeconomic Fluctuations: Comments. *Brookings Pap. Econ. Act.*, 1986, (2), pp. 328–36.

Hughes, Warren R. A Risk Appraisal of New Zealand's Export Industries Using Asset Pricing Models. *New Zealand Econ. Pap.*, 1986, *20*, pp. 61–75. **[G: New Zealand]**

Hunt, Lester Charles. Energy and Capital: Substitutes or Complements? A Note on the Importance of Testing for Non-neutral Technical Progress. *Appl. Econ.*, July 1986, *18*(7), pp. 729–35. **[G: U.K.]**

Illés, Iván. Structural Changes in the Hungarian Economy (1979–1985). *Acta Oecon.*, 1986, *36*(1–2), pp. 21–33. **[G: Hungary]**

Jackson, Marvin R. Industrial Output in Romania and Its Historical Regions, 1880 to 1930, Part II, 1913 to 1930. *J. Europ. Econ. Hist.*, Fall 1986, *15*(2), pp. 231–57. **[G: Romania]**

Jackson, Marvin R. Industrial Output in Romania and Its Historical Regions, 1880 to 1930: Part I—1880 to 1915. *J. Europ. Econ. Hist.*, Spring 1986, *15*(1), pp. 59–111. **[G: Romania]**

Jansson, Sune. Swedish Labour-Owned Industrial Firms: Some Empirical Observations. *Ann. Pub. Co-op. Econ.*, Jan.-March 1986, *57*(1), pp. 103–16. **[G: Sweden]**

Karbstein, Werner; Ludwig, Udo and Siehndel, Karl-Heinz. On the Data Basis for the Compilation of Inter-industry Balances of Gross Output: Some Experiences of the GDR. **In** *Franz, A. and Rainer, N., eds.*, 1986, pp. 471–84. **[G: E. Germany]**

Kletskii, V. I. What Should Be Included in the Economic Mechanism of the Twelfth Five-Year Plan? *Prob. Econ.*, January 1986, *28*(9), pp. 73–88. **[G: U.S.S.R.]**

Kohn, Martin J. and Leggett, Robert E. A Look at Soviet Capital Retirement Statistics: Unraveling Some Mysteries? *Comp. Econ. Stud.*, Summer 1986, *28*(2), pp. 21–35. **[G: U.S.S.R.]**

Kutscher, Ronald E. and Personick, Valerie A. Deindustrialization and the Shift to Services. *Mon. Lab. Rev.*, June 1986, *109*(6), pp. 3–13. **[G: U.S.]**

de Leeuw, Frank. An Indirect Technique for Measuring the Underground Economy: A Note on Revised Data. *Surv. Curr. Bus.*, September 1986, *66*(9), pp. 21–22. **[G: U.S.]**

Linneman, Peter and Wachter, Michael L. Rising Union Premiums and the Declining Boundaries among Noncompeting Groups. *Amer. Econ. Rev.*, May 1986, *76*(2), pp. 103–08. **[G: U.S.]**

Lizzo, Emilio. The Privatization of State Holdings in Italy up to 1984. *Ann. Pub. Co-op. Econ.*, September 1986, *57*(3), pp. 315–43. **[G: Italy]**

Lo, T. W. C. Foreign Investment in the Special Economic Zones: A Management Perspective. **In** *Jao, Y. C. and Leung, C. K., eds.*, 1986, pp. 184–200. **[G: China]**

Loviscek, Anthony L. and Yang, Chin-Wei. Determining the Strength of Industrial Grouping Methods. *Rev. Reg. Stud.*, Spring 1986, *16*(2), pp. 31–40. **[G: U.S.]**

Maij-Weggen, Hanja R. H. Actions of the European Parliament in Favour of Women in Small Business. **In** *Donckels, R. and Meijer, J. N., eds.*, 1986, pp. 10–15. **[G: W. Europe]**

Maki, Dennis R. The Effect of the Cost of Strikes on the Volume of Strike Activity. *Ind. Lab. Relat. Rev.*, July 1986, *39*(4), pp. 552–63. **[G: Canada]**

Marsden, David and Ryan, Paul. Where Do Young Workers Work? Youth Employment by Industry in Various European Economies. *Brit. J. Ind. Relat.*, March 1986, *24*(1), pp. 83–102. **[G: W. Europe]**

Marsden, James R. and Pingry, David E. Engineering Production Functions and the Testing of Quantitative Economic Hypotheses. *Economica*, November 1986, *53*(212), pp. 533–34.

McClain, David. Direct Investment in the United States: The European Experience. **In** *Gray, H. P., ed.*, 1986, pp. 309–43. **[G: Europe; U.S.]**

Meijer, Jane N.; Braaksma, Ro M. and van Uxem, Frits W. Contributing Wife: Partner in Business. **In** *Donckels, R. and Meijer, J. N., eds.*, 1986, pp. 65–77. **[G: Netherlands]**

Messerlin, Patrick A. and Becuwe, Stephane. Intra-industry Trade in the Long Run: The French Case, 1850–1913. **In** *Greenaway, D. and Tharakan, P. K. M., eds.*, 1986, pp. 191–215. **[G: France]**

Miernyk, William H. Long-range Forecasting with a Regional Input–Output Model. **In** *Sohn, I., ed.*, 1986, *1968*, pp. 81–92. **[G: U.S.]**

Miettinen, Asko. Contributing Spouses and the Dynamics of Entrepreneurial Families. **In** *Donckels, R. and Meijer, J. N., eds.*, 1986, pp. 78–86.

Naples, Michele I. The Unraveling of the Union–Capital Truce and the U.S. Industrial Productivity Crisis. *Rev. Radical Polit. Econ.*,

Spring/Summer 1986, *18*(1/2), pp. 110–31. **[G: U.S.]**

O'Brien, Patrick K. Do We Have a Typology for the Study of European Industrialization in the XIXth Century? *J. Europ. Econ. Hist.*, Fall 1986, *15*(2), pp. 291–333. **[G: Europe]**

O'Riordan, William K. An Alternative Measure of Employment Intensity. *Econ. Soc. Rev.*, October 1986, *18*(1), pp. 27–41. **[G: EEC]**

Pashigian, B. Peter. Reply [The Effect of Environmental Regulation on Optimal Plant Size and Factor Shares]. *J. Law Econ.*, April 1986, *29*(1), pp. 201–09. **[G: U.S.]**

Pernia, Ernesto M. and Pernia, Joseph M. An Economic and Social Impact Analysis of Small Industry Promotion: A Philippine Experience. *World Devel.*, May 1986, *14*(5), pp. 637–51. **[G: Philippines]**

Petitbó, Amadeu. Notas sobre desindustrialización y crisis en la economia española. (Note on the De-industrialization and the Crisis in the Spanish Economy. With English summary.) *Écon. Soc.*, May 1986, *20*(5), pp. 69–99. **[G: Spain]**

Ray, George F. The British Economy in the Long Term: The Changing Structure of the UK Economy. *Nat. Inst. Econ. Rev.*, November 1986, (118), pp. 82–88. **[G: U.K.]**

Riedel, James. Factor Proportions, Linkages, and the Open Developing Economy. **In** *Sohn, I., ed.*, 1986, *1975*, pp. 340–53. **[G: Taiwan]**

Rogovskii, E. A. and Rutkovskaia, E. A. A Method of Analyzing the Economic Return to Capital Investment. *Matekon*, Summer 1986, *22*(4), pp. 33–53. **[G: U.S.S.R.]**

Rothschild, Emma. A Divergence Hypothesis. *J. Devel. Econ.*, October 1986, *23*(2), pp. 205–26. **[G: U.S.]**

Rugman, Alan M. and McIlveen, John. Canadian Foreign Direct Investment in the United States. **In** *Gray, H. P., ed.*, 1986, pp. 289–307. **[G: Canada; U.S.]**

Sandesara, J. C. Industrial Production and Employment in the Seventh Plan—Two Quick Comments. *Indian Econ. J.*, Apr.-June 1986, *33*(4), pp. 92–97. **[G: India]**

Sandesara, J. C. and Bishnoi, T. R. Factor Income Shares in Medium and Large Public Limited Companies in India—1950–51 to 1978–79—A Statistical Analysis. *Indian Econ. J.*, Oct.-Dec. 1986, *34*(2), pp. 28–48. **[G: India]**

Seskin, Eugene P. and Sullivan, David F. Plant and Equipment Expenditures, the Four Quarters of 1986. *Surv. Curr. Bus.*, June 1986, *66*(6), pp. 17–20. **[G: U.S.]**

Shepherd, William G. Illogic and Unreality: The Odd Case of Ultra-free Entry and Inert Markets. **In** *Grieson, R. E., ed.*, 1986, pp. 231–52. **[G: U.S.]**

Simpson, David and Tsukui, Jinkichi. The Fundamental Structure of Input–Output Tables: An International Comparison. **In** *Sohn, I., ed.*, 1986, pp. 372–91. **[G: U.S.; Japan]**

Singh, Ajit. Crisis and Recovery in the Mexican Economy: The Role of the Capital Goods Sector. **In** *Fransman, M., ed.*, 1986, pp. 246–68. **[G: Mexico]**

Slater, Paul B. The Determination of Groups of Functionally Integrated Industries in the United States Using a 1967 Interindustry Flow Table. **In** *Slater, P. B.*, 1986, *1977*, pp. 13–17. **[G: U.S.]**

Smith, V. Kerry. Another View of the State of Engineering Production Functions. *Economica*, November 1986, *53*(212), pp. 529–32.

Smuts, Michael. The Growth of Black Business in South Africa. **In** *Smollan, R., ed.*, 1986, pp. 23–30. **[G: S. Africa]**

Solo, Robert A. Melman and Reich on Industrial Policy: Review Article. *Econ. Develop. Cult. Change*, January 1986, *34*(2), pp. 373–84. **[G: U.S.]**

Tecson, Gwendolyn R. Nontraditional Markets for Philippine Exports. *Philippine Rev. Econ. Bus.*, Sept.-Dec. 1986, *23*(3–4), pp. 191–242. **[G: Philippines]**

Tomlinson, R. and Addleson, Mark. Trends in Industrial Decentralization: An Examination of Bell's Hypothesis. *S. Afr. J. Econ.*, December 1986, *54*(4), pp. 381–94. **[G: S. Africa]**

Tybout, James. A Firm-Level Chronicle of Financial Crises in the Southern Cone. *J. Devel. Econ.*, December 1986, *24*(2), pp. 371–400. **[G: Chile; Argentina; Uruguay]**

Tyers, Rodney and Phillips, Prue. ASEAN in Pacific Basin Trade: Export Composition and Performance. **In** *Nemetz, P. N., ed.*, 1986, pp. 74–116. **[G: Pacific Basin; ASEAN]**

Vilenskii, M. V. Intensification of the Economy and the Acceleration of Technical Progress. *Prob. Econ.*, June 1986, *29*(2), pp. 24–42. **[G: U.S.S.R.]**

Vlachou, A. S. and Samouilidis, E. J. Interfuel Substitution: Results from Several Sectors of the Greek Economy. *Energy Econ.*, January 1986, *8*(1), pp. 39–45. **[G: Greece]**

Wallis, John Joseph and North, Douglass C. Measuring the Transaction Sector in the American Economy, 1870–1970. **In** *Engerman, S. L. and Gallman, R. E., eds.*, 1986, pp. 95–148. **[G: U.S.]**

Wellings, Paul and Black, Anthony. Industrial Decentralization under Apartheid: The Relocation of Industry to the South African Periphery. *World Devel.*, January 1986, *14*(1), pp. 1–38. **[G: S. Africa]**

Wever, Egbert. New Firm Formation in the Netherlands. **In** *Keeble, D. and Wever, E., eds.*, 1986, pp. 54–74. **[G: Netherlands]**

Wheeler, J. W. Japanese Foreign Direct Investment in the United States. **In** *Gray, H. P., ed.*, 1986, pp. 345–75. **[G: U.S.; Japan]**

Wibe, Sören. Observable and Non-observable Data: A Reply [Engineering Production Functions—A Survey]. *Economica*, November 1986, *53*(212), pp. 535–36.

Yan, Chiou-Shuang and Ames, Edward. Economic Interrelatedness. **In** *Sohn, I., ed.*, 1986, *1965*, pp. 392–405. **[G: U.S.]**

Zhuravlev, S. N. Structural Shifts in the Economy: Techniques for Evaluating Their Impact on Efficiency and Growth. *Matekon,* Winter 1986-87, *23*(2), pp. 3–31. **[G: U.S.S.R.]**

631 Industry Studies: Manufacturing

6310 General

Abd-El-Rahman, K. S. Réexamen de la définition et de la mesure des échanges croisés de produits similaires entre les nations. (Definition and Measurements of Two-way Trade in Similar Products: A Re-examination. With English summary.) *Revue Écon.,* January 1986, *37*(1), pp. 89–115. **[G: EEC]**

Abel, Andrew B. and Blanchard, Olivier J. The Present Value of Profits and Cyclical Movements in Investment. *Econometrica,* March 1986, *54*(2), pp. 249–73. **[G: U.S.]**

Abramovitz, Moses. Inventory Fluctuations in the United States since 1929: Comment. **In** *Gordon, R. J., ed.,* 1986, pp. 214–23. **[G: U.S.]**

Ady, Robert M. Criteria Used for Facility Location Selection. **In** *Walzer, N. and Chicoine, D. L., eds.,* 1986, pp. 72–84. **[G: U.S.]**

Ahiakpor, James C. W. The Capital Intensity of Foreign, Private Local and State Owned Firms in a Less Developed Country: Ghana. *J. Devel. Econ.,* Jan.-Feb. 1986, *20*(1), pp. 145–62. **[G: Ghana]**

Ahiakpor, James C. W. The Profits of Foreign Firms in a Less Developed Country: Ghana. *J. Devel. Econ.,* July-Aug. 1986, *22*(2), pp. 321–35. **[G: Ghana]**

Akrasanee, Narongchai and Ajanant, Juanjai. Manufacturing Industry Protection in Thailand: Issues and Empirical Studies. **In** *Findlay, C. and Garnaut, R., eds.,* 1986, pp. 77–98. **[G: Thailand]**

Alford, B. W. E. Lost Opportunities: British Business and Businessmen during the First World War. **In** *[Coleman, D. C.],* 1986, pp. 205–27. **[G: U.K.]**

Amsden, Alice H. The Direction of Trade—Past and Present—And the 'Learning Effects' of Exports to Different Directions. *J. Devel. Econ.,* October 1986, *23*(2), pp. 249–74. **[G: Japan; LDCs]**

Anderson, Kym and Garnaut, Ross. The Political Economy of Manufacturing Protection in Australia. **In** *Findlay, C. and Garnaut, R., eds.,* 1986, pp. 159–83. **[G: Australia]**

Andrikopoulos, Andreas A. and Brox, James A. Demand Systems for Energy Consumption by the Manufacturing Sector. *J. Econ. Bus.,* May 1986, *38*(2), pp. 141–53. **[G: Canada]**

Ariff, Mohamed and Hill, Hal. A Factor-Intensity Analysis of Structural Change in ASEAN Manufacturing. *Industry Devel.,* 1986, (19), pp. 77–101. **[G: ASEAN]**

Atack, Jeremy. Firm Size and Industrial Structure in the United States during the Nineteenth Century. *J. Econ. Hist.,* June 1986, *46*(2), pp. 463–75. **[G: U.S.]**

Auerbach, Alan J. Major Changes in Cyclical Behavior: Comment. **In** *Gordon, R. J., ed.,* 1986, pp. 573–75. **[G: U.S.; U.K.; France; W. Germany]**

Aujac, Henri. An Introduction to French Industrial Policy. **In** *Adams, W. J. and Stoffaës, C., eds.,* 1986, pp. 13–35. **[G: France]**

Aydalot, Philippe. The Location of New Firm Creation: The French Case. **In** *Keeble, D. and Wever, E., eds.,* 1986, pp. 105–23. **[G: France]**

Baily, Martin Neil. Productivity Growth and Materials Use in U.S. Manufacturing [Productivity and the Services of Capital and Labor]. *Quart. J. Econ.,* February 1986, *101*(1), pp. 185–95. **[G: U.S.]**

Baily, Martin Neil. The Cyclical Behavior of Industrial Labor Markets: A Comparison of the Prewar and Postwar Eras: Comment. **In** *Gordon, R. J., ed.,* 1986, pp. 621–66. **[G: U.S.]**

Bairam, Erkin I. Returns to Scale, Technical Progress and Output Growth in Branches of Industry: The Case of Eastern Europe and the USSR, 1961–75. *Keio Econ. Stud.,* 1986, *23*(1), pp. 63–78. **[G: CMEA]**

Balassa, Bela. Intra-industry Specialization: A Cross-Country Analysis. *Europ. Econ. Rev.,* February 1986, *30*(1), pp. 27–42. **[G: LDCs; MDCs]**

Balassa, Bela. The Determinants of Intra-industry Specialization in United States Trade. *Oxford Econ. Pap.,* July 1986, *38*(2), pp. 220–33. **[G: U.S.]**

Balassa, Bela. The Employment Effects of Trade in Manufactured Products between Developed and Developing Countries. *J. Policy Modeling,* Fall 1986, *8*(3), pp. 371–90.

Baldwin, John R. and Gorecki, Paul K. The Relationship between Plant Scale and Product Diversity in Canadian Manufacturing Industries. *J. Ind. Econ.,* June 1986, *34*(4), pp. 373–88. **[G: Canada]**

Baldwin, John R.; Gorecki, Paul K. and McVey, John S. International Trade, Secondary Output and Concentration in Canadian Manufacturing Industries, 1979. *Appl. Econ.,* May 1986, *18*(5), pp. 529–43. **[G: Canada]**

Barbera, Anthony J. and McConnell, Virginia D. Effects of Pollution Control on Industry Productivity: A Factor Demand Approach. *J. Ind. Econ.,* December 1986, *35*(2), pp. 161–72. **[G: U.S.]**

Barnett, Richard R. A Perspective on De-industrialization. *Nat. Westminster Bank Quart. Rev.,* August 1986, pp. 13–20. **[G: U.K.]**

Barras, Richard. A Comparison of Embodied Technical Change in Services and Manufacturing Industry. *Appl. Econ.,* September 1986, *18*(9), pp. 941–58. **[G: U.K.]**

Baruh, Joseph. Factor Proportions in Israel's Manufacturing Trade: 1965–1982. *J. Devel. Econ.,* November 1986, *24*(1), pp. 131–39. **[G: Israel]**

Beck, Roger L. Structure and Performance with Profit Measures Based on Stock Market Prices. *Southern Econ. J.,* October 1986, *53*(2), pp. 432–47. **[G: Canada]**

Beesley, Michael E. and Hamilton, R. T. Births and Deaths of Manufacturing Firms in the

Scottish Regions. *Reg. Stud.*, August 1986, *20*(4), pp. 281–88. [G: U.K.]

Bergés Lobera, Angel; Maravall, Fernando and Pérez Simarro, Ramón. Eficiencia técnica en las grandes empresas industriales de España y Europa. (With English summary.) *Invest. Ecón.*, September 1986, *10*(3), pp. 449–66. [G: EEC]

Bernanke, Ben S. Employment, Hours, and Earnings in the Depression: An Analysis of Eight Manufacturing Industries. *Amer. Econ. Rev.*, March 1986, *76*(1), pp. 82–109. [G: U.S.]

Bernanke, Ben S. and Powell, James L. The Cyclical Behavior of Industrial Labor Markets: A Comparison of the Prewar and Postwar Eras. **In** *Gordon, R. J., ed.*, 1986, pp. 583–621. [G: U.S.]

Berndt, Ernst R. and Hesse, Dieter M. Measuring and Assessing Capacity Utilization in the Manufacturing Sectors of Nine OECD Countries. *Europ. Econ. Rev.*, October 1986, *30*(5), pp. 961–89. [G: OECD]

Berndt, Ernst R. and Wood, David O. Energy Price Shocks and Productivity Growth in U.S. and UK Manufacturing. *Oxford Rev. Econ. Policy*, Autumn 1986, *2*(3), pp. 1–31. [G: U.K.; U.S.]

Berthelemy, Jean-Claude; Devezeaux de Lavergne, Jean-Guy and Ladoux, Norbert. Une analyse de la dynamique des comportements de substitution de facteurs dans cinq branches de l'économie française. (An Analysis of the Dynamics of Inputs Substitution in Five Sectors of French Economy. With English summary.) *Ann. Écon. Statist.*, Oct./Dec. 1986, (4), pp. 3–22. [G: France]

Bhalla, Ajit S. and James, Jeffrey. New Technology Revolution: Myth or Reality for Developing Countries? **In** *Hall, P., ed.*, 1986, *1984*, pp. 135–71. [G: LDCs]

Blackley, Paul R. Urban–Rural Variations in the Structure of Manufacturing Production. *Urban Stud.*, December 1986, *23*(6), pp. 471–83. [G: U.S.]

Blinder, Alan S. Can the Production Smoothing Model of Inventory Behavior Be Saved? *Quart. J. Econ.*, August 1986, *101*(3), pp. 431–53. [G: U.S.]

Blinder, Alan S. More on the Speed of Adjustment in Inventory Models. *J. Money, Credit, Banking*, August 1986, *18*(3), pp. 355–65.

Blinder, Alan S. and Holtz-Eakin, Douglas. Inventory Fluctuations in the United States since 1929. **In** *Gordon, R. J., ed.*, 1986, pp. 183–214. [G: U.S.]

Blinder, Alan S. and Holtz-Eakin, Douglas. Inventory Fluctuations in the United States since 1929: Reply. **In** *Gordon, R. J., ed.*, 1986, pp. 231–33. [G: U.S.]

Bluestone, Barry; Harrison, Bennett and Clayton-Matthews, Alan. Structure vs. Cycle in U.S. Manufacturing Job Growth. *Ind. Relat.*, Spring 1986, *25*(2), pp. 101–17. [G: U.S.]

Bongaerts, Jan C. and Heinrichs, Dirk. Deutsche Umweltschutzgesetze und Umweltschutzinvestitionen des produzierenden Gewerbes. (German Environmental Protection Legislation and Environmental Investment by West German Manufacturing Industries. With English summary.) *Konjunkturpolitik*, 1986, *32*(3), pp. 151–63. [G: W. Germany]

Borooah, V. K. and van der Ploeg, Frederick. Oligopoly Power in British Industry. *Appl. Econ.*, June 1986, *18*(6), pp. 583–98. [G: U.K.]

Botos, Balázs. Changes in the Structure of Hungarian Industrial Foreign Trade: Review Article. *Acta Oecon.*, 1986, *37*(1–2), pp. 129–42. [G: Hungary]

Boyer, Robert. Industrial Policy in Macroeconomic Perspective. **In** *Adams, W. J. and Stoffaës, C., eds.*, 1986, pp. 88–96. [G: France]

Boyer, Robert and Coriat, Benjamin. Technical Flexibility and Macro Stabilisation. *Ricerche Econ.*, Oct.-Dec. 1986, *40*(4), pp. 771–835. [G: U.S.]

Braga, Helson C. and Guimarães, Edson P. Estrutura industrial e exportação de manufaturados no Brasil: 1978. (With English summary.) *Pesquisa Planejamento Econ.*, April 1986, *16*(1), pp. 167–88. [G: Brazil]

Brown, Martin and Philips, Peter. Competition, Racism, and Hiring Practices among California Manufacturers, 1860–1882. *Ind. Lab. Relat. Rev.*, October 1986, *40*(1), pp. 61–74. [G: U.S.]

Browne, Lynn E. High Technology Industry in the World Marketplace. *New Eng. Econ. Rev.*, May/June 1986, pp. 21–25. [G: U.S.]

Bruno, Michael. Raw Materials, Profits, and the Productivity Slowdown: A Complementary Note [Productivity and the Services of Capital and Labor]. *Quart. J. Econ.*, February 1986, *101*(1), pp. 197–200. [G: U.S.]

Brusco, Sebastiano. Small Firms and Industrial Districts: The Experience of Italy. **In** *Keeble, D. and Wever, E., eds.*, 1986, pp. 184–202. [G: Italy]

Byrne, Dennis M. and King, Randall H. Wildcat Strikes in U.S. Manufacturing, 1960–1977. *J. Lab. Res.*, Fall 1986, *7*(4), pp. 387–401. [G: U.S.]

Cain, Louis P. and Paterson, Donald G. Biased Technical Change, Scale, and Factor Substitution in American Industry, 1850–1919. *J. Econ. Hist.*, March 1986, *46*(1), pp. 153–64. [G: U.S.]

Calzolari, Michele and Somaini, Eugenio. Ciclicitá del mark-up in un modello di oligopolio. Costi e prezzi nel settore manifatturiero italiano (1970–1982). (Mark-up Cycles in an Oligopoly Model. Costs and Prices in the Italian Manufacturing Industry [1970–1982]. With English summary.) *Polit. Econ.*, April 1986, *2*(1), pp. 81–120. [G: Italy]

Camagni, Roberto. The Economics of Industrial Revitalisation in Declining Metropolitan Areas. *Econ. Int.*, May-Aug.-Nov. 1986, *39*(2–3–4), pp. 316–34. [G: Italy]

Camba, Roberto, et al. L'evoluzione della struttura produttiva e imprenditoriale in una regione di antica industrializzazione: il caso del piemonte. (The Development of the Industrial System in an Old Industrialized Region: The Case of Piemonte. With English summary.) *Ricerche Econ.*, Jan.-Mar. 1986, *40*(1), pp. 130–59. **[G: Italy]**

Carlsson, Bo. The Development and Use of Machine Tools in Historical Perspective. **In** *Day, R. H. and Eliasson, G., eds.*, 1986, *1984*, pp. 247–70. **[G: U.K.]**

Carlton, Dennis W. The Rigidity of Prices. *Amer. Econ. Rev.*, September 1986, *76*(4), pp. 637–58. **[G: U.S.]**

Chandler, Alfred D., Jr. Technological and Organizational Underpinnings of Modern Industrial Multinational Enterprise: The Dynamics of Competitive Advantage. **In** *Teichova, A.; Lévy-Leboyer, M. and Nussbaum, H., eds.*, 1986, pp. 30–54. **[G: OECD]**

Chavas, Jean-Paul and Segerson, Kathleen. Singularity and Auotregressive Disturbances in Linear Logit Models. *J. Bus. Econ. Statist.*, April 1986, *4*(2), pp. 161–69. **[G: U.S.]**

Chen, K. C.; Cheng, David C. and Hite, Gailen L. Systematic Risk and Market Power: An Application of Tobin's *q*. *Quart. Rev. Econ. Bus.*, Autumn 1986, *26*(3), pp. 58–72. **[G: U.S.]**

Chetty, V. K. and Heckman, James J. A Dynamic Model of Aggregate Output Supply, Factor Demand and Entry and Exit for a Competitive Industry with Heterogeneous Plants. *J. Econometrics*, Oct./Nov. 1986, *33*(1/2), pp. 237–62. **[G: U.S.]**

Cholette, Pierre A. and Lamy, Robert. Multivariate ARIMA Forecasting of Irregular Time Series. *Int. J. Forecasting*, 1986, *2*(2), pp. 201–16. **[G: Canada]**

Chung, Joseph S. National Policies for Developing High Technology Industries: International Comparisons: Korea. **In** *Rushing, F. W. and Brown, C. G., eds.*, 1986, pp. 143–72. **[G: S. Korea]**

Clair, Robert T. The Labor-intensive Nature of Manufacturing High-Technology Capital Goods. *Fed. Res. Bank Dallas Econ. Rev.*, March 1986, pp. 11–19. **[G: U.S.]**

Cooper, Julian. The Civilian Production of the Soviet Defence Industry. **In** *Amann, R. and Cooper, J., eds.*, 1986, pp. 31–50. **[G: U.S.S.R.]**

Corona, Leonel. Long Waves and the International Diffusion of the Automated Labour Process: The Role of the Semi-industrialized Countries. **In** *Freeman, C., ed.*, 1986, pp. 194–213. **[G: LDCs]**

Coyne, John and Wright, Mike. The Small Firm, Government Policy and Industrial Change. **In** *Hall, G., ed.*, 1986, pp. 284–306. **[G: U.K.]**

Crandall, Robert W. The Transformation of U.S. Manufacturing. *Ind. Relat.*, Spring 1986, *25*(2), pp. 118–30. **[G: U.S.]**

Cuthbertson, Keith. The Behaviour of U.K. Export Prices of Manufactured Goods 1970–1983. *J. Appl. Econometrics*, July 1986, *1*(3), pp. 255–75. **[G: U.K.]**

Daly, Michael J. and Rao, P. Someshwar. Free Trade, Scale Economies and Productivity Growth in Canadian Manufacturing. *Manchester Sch. Econ. Soc. Stud.*, December 1986, *54*(4), pp. 391–402. **[G: Canada]**

Davis, Lance E. Measuring the Transaction Sector in the American Economy, 1870–1970: Comment. **In** *Engerman, S. L. and Gallman, R. E., eds.*, 1986, pp. 149–59. **[G: U.S.]**

De Long, James Bradford and Summers, Lawrence H. Improvements in Macroeconomic Stability: The Role of Wages and Prices: Comment. **In** *Gordon, R. J., ed.*, 1986, pp. 669–72. **[G: U.S.]**

Dean, Edwin; Boissevain, Harry and Thomas, James. Productivity and Labor Costs Trends in Manufacturing, 12 Countries. *Mon. Lab. Rev.*, March 1986, *109*(3), pp. 3–10. **[G: U.S.; Selected OECD]**

Dearden, Stephen. EEC Membership and the United Kingdom's Trade in Manufactured Goods. *Nat. Westminster Bank Quart. Rev.*, February 1986, pp. 15–25. **[G: U.K.; EEC]**

Del Monte, Alfredo and Giannola, Adriano. Relevance and Nature of Small and Medium-sized Firms in Southern Italy. **In** *Keeble, D. and Wever, E., eds.*, 1986, pp. 275–98. **[G: Italy]**

Dickson, Vaughan A. Goals of Oligopolistic Firms: Comment. *Southern Econ. J.*, April 1986, *52*(4), pp. 1151–57. **[G: U.S.]**

Dixon, Robert J. and Gunther, Alan. Margins, Concentration and Oligopolistic Interdependence. *Econ. Rec.*, June 1986, *62*(177), pp. 199–207. **[G: Australia]**

Domowitz, Ian; Hubbard, R. Glenn and Petersen, Bruce C. Business Cycles and the Relationship between Concentration and Price–Cost Margins. *Rand J. Econ.*, Spring 1986, *17*(1), pp. 1–17. **[G: U.S.]**

Domowitz, Ian; Hubbard, R. Glenn and Petersen, Bruce C. The Intertemporal Stability of the Concentration–Margins Relationship. *J. Ind. Econ.*, September 1986, *35*(1), pp. 13–34. **[G: U.S.]**

Dormont, Brigitte. Les ajustements de l'emploi dans la crise en France et en R.F.A. Une étude sur des données d'entreprises industrielles françaises et allemandes sur la période 1967–1979. (With English summary.) *Revue Écon. Polit.*, May-June 1986, *96*(3), pp. 256–80. **[G: France; W. Germany]**

Driver, Ciaran. The Scrapping Behaviour of Concentrated and Non-concentrated Industries in the UK. *Appl. Econ.*, March 1986, *18*(3), pp. 249–63. **[G: U.K.]**

Driver, Ciaran. Transformation of the CBI Capacity Utilization Series: Theory and Evidence. *Oxford Bull. Econ. Statist.*, November 1986, *48*(4), pp. 339–52. **[G: U.K.]**

Dumez, Hervé. De la politique industrielle: existe-t-elle, "et quelle serait sa vraie nature?" (Industrial Policy: Does It Exist and Which Is Its Real Nature? With English summary.) *Écon. Soc.*, December 1986, *20*(12), pp. 187–98.

Dunford, M. Integration and Unequal Development: The Case of Southern Italy, 1951–73.

In *Scott, A. J. and Storper, M., eds.*, 1986, pp. 225–45. **[G: Italy]**

Ebel, Karl-H. The Impact of Industrial Robots on the World of Work. *Int. Lab. Rev.*, Jan.-Feb. 1986, *125*(1), pp. 39–51. **[G: W. Europe; U.S.]**

Eichner, Alfred S. Post Keynesian View of Average Direct Cost: A Comment. *J. Post Keynesian Econ.*, Spring 1986, *8*(3), pp. 425–26.

Ershov, E. B. and Sadykov, I. S. A Study of Substitution Possibilities between Inputs and Their Relationship over Time in Soviet Industry. *Matekon*, Winter 1986-87, *23*(2), pp. 32–56. **[G: U.S.S.R.]**

Esposito, Frances Ferguson and Esposito, Louis. Excess Capacity and Market Structure in U.S. Manufacturing: New Evidence. *Quart. J. Bus. Econ.*, Summer 1986, *25*(3), pp. 3–14. **[G: U.S.]**

Ewers, Hans-Jürgen. Spatial Dimensions of Technological Developments and Employment Effects. In *Nijkamp, P., ed. (II)*, 1986, pp. 157–76. **[G: W. Germany]**

Fabricant, Solomon. Major Changes in Cyclical Behavior: Comment. In *Gordon, R. J., ed.*, 1986, pp. 575–78. **[G: U.S.; U.K.; W. Germany; France]**

Fal'tsman, F. Increasing the Return on Industry's Fixed Capital. *Prob. Econ.*, January 1986, *28*(9), pp. 18–36. **[G: U.S.S.R.]**

Farber, Stephen C. and Martin, Robert E. Market Structure and Pollution Control under Imperfect Surveillance. *J. Ind. Econ.*, December 1986, *35*(2), pp. 147–60. **[G: U.S.]**

Feinberg, Robert M. The Effects of European Competition Policy on Pricing and Profit Margins. *Kyklos*, 1986, *39*(2), pp. 267–87. **[G: EEC; W. Germany]**

Fieleke, Norman S. New England Manufacturing and International Trade. *New Eng. Econ. Rev.*, Sept./Oct. 1986, pp. 22–28. **[G: U.S.]**

Findlay, Christopher C. and Garnaut, Ross. The Political Economy of Manufacturing Protection: Experiences of ASEAN and Australia: Conclusions and Suggestions for Policy Action. In *Findlay, C. and Garnaut, R., eds.*, 1986, pp. 264–80. **[G: ASEAN; Australia]**

Fomby, Thomas B. A Comparison of Forecasting Accuracies of Alternative Regional Production Index Methodologies. *J. Bus. Econ. Statist.*, April 1986, *4*(2), pp. 177–86. **[G: U.S.]**

Frantzen, Dirk J. The Cyclical Behaviour of Manufacturing Prices in a Small Open Economy. *J. Ind. Econ.*, June 1986, *34*(4), pp. 389–408. **[G: Belgium]**

Freeman, Christopher and Soete, Luc L. G. Innovation Diffusion and Employment Policies. *Ricerche Econ.*, Oct.-Dec. 1986, *40*(4), pp. 836–54. **[G: U.S.; U.K.; Japan; France; W. Germany]**

Fullerton, Don and Lyon, Andrew B. Does the Tax System Favor Investment in High-Tech or Smoke-Stack Industries? *Econ. Inquiry*, July 1986, *24*(3), pp. 403–16. **[G: U.S.]**

Funke, Michael. Influences on the Profitability of the Manufacturing Sector in the UK—An Empirical Study. *Oxford Bull. Econ. Statist.*, May 1986, *48*(2), pp. 165–87. **[G: U.K.]**

von Furstenberg, George M. High-Tech Industries and Economic Growth. *Bus. Econ.*, July 1986, *21*(3), pp. 43–45. **[G: U.S.]**

Gallagher, C. C. and Stewart, H. Jobs and the Business Life-Cycle in the UK. *Appl. Econ.*, August 1986, *18*(8), pp. 875–900. **[G: U.K.]**

Garber, Steven and Klepper, Steven. Relative Price Changes in Recession: A Microeconometric Analysis of U.S. Manufacturing. *Int. Econ. Rev.*, February 1986, *27*(1), pp. 187–208. **[G: U.S.]**

Gershenberg, Irving. Labor, Capital, and Management Slack in Multinational and Local Firms in Kenyan Manufacturing. *Econ. Develop. Cult. Change*, October 1986, *35*(1), pp. 163–78. **[G: Kenya]**

Giannaros, Demetrios S. Determinants of Sectoral Investment in a Developing Capital Market Economy. *J. Econ. Devel.*, July 1986, *11*(1), pp. 133–56. **[G: Greece]**

Gilmer, Robert W. and Pulsipher, Allan G. Cyclical and Structural Change in Southern Manufacturing: Recent Evidence from the Tennessee Valley: Note. *Growth Change*, October 1986, *17*(4), pp. 61–69. **[G: U.S.]**

Giquel, Christine. Les accords dits "OEM" et les formes de coopération industrielle. (With English summary.) *Revue Écon. Polit.*, Nov.-Dec. 1986, *96*(6), pp. 666–87. **[G: OECD]**

Gisser, Micha. Price Leadership and Welfare Losses in U.S. Manufacturing. *Amer. Econ. Rev.*, September 1986, *76*(4), pp. 756–67. **[G: U.S.]**

Glasmeier, Amy K. High-Tech Industries and the Regional Division of Labor. *Ind. Relat.*, Spring 1986, *25*(2), pp. 197–211. **[G: U.S.]**

Glick, Mark and Ehrbar, Hans. An Econometric Model of Industrial Profit Rate Adjustment in the U.S. *Econ. Forum*, Winter 1986-1987, *16*(1), pp. 29–43. **[G: U.S.]**

Goldar, Bishwanath. Import Substitution, Industrial Concentration and Productivity Growth in Indian Manufacturing. *Oxford Bull. Econ. Statist.*, May 1986, *48*(2), pp. 143–64. **[G: India]**

Goldin, Claudia. Monitoring Costs and Occupational Segregation by Sex: A Historical Analysis. *J. Lab. Econ.*, January 1986, *4*(1), pp. 1–27. **[G: U.S.]**

Goldstein, Jonathan P. Markup Variability and Flexibility: Theory and Empirical Evidence. *J. Bus.*, Part 1, October 1986, *59*(4), pp. 599–621.

Gomulka, Stanislaw. Soviet Growth Slowdown: Duality, Maturity, and Innovation. *Amer. Econ. Rev.*, May 1986, *76*(2), pp. 170–74. **[G: U.S.S.R.]**

Goode, Frank M. The Efficacy of More Refined Demand Variables in Industrial Location Models: Note. *Growth Change*, January 1986, *17*(1), pp. 66–75. **[G: U.S.]**

Gould, Brian W. and Kulshreshtha, Surendra N. An Interindustry Analysis of Structural Change and Energy Use Linkages in the Saskatchewan

Economy. *Energy Econ.*, July 1986, *8*(3), pp. 186–96. [G: Canada]

Grabowski, Henry G. and Mueller, Dennis C. Managerial and Stockholder Welfare Models of Firm Expenditures. **In** *Mueller, D. C.*, 1986, *1972*, pp. 81–107.

Granberg, Alexander. Structural Changes and Intensification in Siberian Industry. *Prob. Econ.*, July 1986, *29*(3), pp. 39–60. [G: U.S.S.R.]

Grant, James H. and Nichols, Len M. On the Existence of a Market for Second Hand Physical Capital: An Empirical Test of the Keynesian and Neoclassical Assumptions. *J. Macroecon.*, Spring 1986, *8*(2), pp. 131–57. [G: U.S.]

Griliches, Zvi. Productivity, *R&D*, and the Basic Research at the Firm Level in the 1970's. *Amer. Econ. Rev.*, March 1986, *76*(1), pp. 141–54. [G: U.S.]

Griliches, Zvi and Hausman, Jerry A. Errors in Variables in Panel Data. *J. Econometrics*, February 1986, *31*(1), pp. 93–118. [G: U.S.]

Grubb, David B. Raw Materials, Profits, and the Productivity Slowdown: Some Doubts. *Quart. J. Econ.*, February 1986, *101*(1), pp. 175–84. [G: U.S.; W. Europe; Japan]

Hall, Stephen G.; Henry, S. G. B. and Wren-Lewis, Simon. Manufacturing Stocks and Forward-Looking Expectations in the UK. *Economica*, November 1986, *53*(212), pp. 447–65. [G: U.K.]

Hall, V. B. Major OECD Country Industrial Sector Interfuel Substitution Estimates, 1960–79. *Energy Econ.*, April 1986, *8*(2), pp. 74–89. [G: OECD]

Hamilton, R. T. The Extent and Nature of Diversification in New Zealand Manufacturing Industries. *New Zealand Econ. Pap.*, 1986, *20*, pp. 77–91. [G: New Zealand]

Handoussa, Heba; Nishimizu, Mieko and Page, John M., Jr. Productivity Change in Egyptian Public Sector Industries after "The Opening," 1973–1979. *J. Devel. Econ.*, Jan.-Feb. 1986, *20*(1), pp. 53–73. [G: Egypt]

Hannay, N. Bruce. Technology and Trade: A Study of U.S. Competitiveness in Seven Industries. **In** *Landau, R. and Rosenberg, N., eds.*, 1986, pp. 479–99. [G: U.S.]

Hanseman, Dennis J. A Quarterly Econometric Model of Factor Demands in Regional Manufacturing. *J. Reg. Sci.*, February 1986, *26*(1), pp. 161–77. [G: U.S.]

Hansen, Jørgen. Investeringsbehov og balanceproblemer. (Industrial Investments and Economic Imbalance in the Danish Economy. With English summary.) *Nationaløkon. Tidsskr.*, 1986, *124*(2), pp. 139–46. [G: Denmark]

Harris, Candee S. Establishing High-Technology Enterprises in Metropolitan Areas. **In** *Bergman, E. M., ed.*, 1986, pp. 165–84. [G: U.S.]

Harrison, Glenn W. and Rutström, E. E. The Effect of Manufacturing Sector Protection on ASEAN and Australia: A General Equilibrium Analysis. **In** *Findlay, C. and Garnaut, R., eds.*, 1986, pp. 184–213. [G: ASEAN; Australia]

Hart, Peter E. and Pearce, Robert D. Growth Patterns of the World's Largest Firms, 1962–1982. *Weltwirtsch. Arch.*, 1986, *122*(1), pp. 65–79. [G: Global]

Hayashi, Yoshitsugu; Isobe, Tomohiko and Tomita, Yasuo. Modelling the Long-term Effects of Transport and Land Use Policies on Industrial Locational Behaviour: A Discrete Choice Model System. *Reg. Sci. Urban Econ.*, February 1986, *16*(1), pp. 123–43. [G: Japan]

Hazilla, Michael and Kopp, Raymond J. Testing for Separable Functional Structure Using Temporary Equilibrium Models. *J. Econometrics*, Oct./Nov. 1986, *33*(1/2), pp. 119–41. [G: U.S.]

Henderson, J. Vernon. Efficiency of Resource Usage and City Size. *J. Urban Econ.*, January 1986, *19*(1), pp. 47–70. [G: Brazil; U.S.]

Hepworth, Mark. The Geography of Technological Change in the Information Economy. *Reg. Stud.*, October 1986, *20*(5), pp. 407–24. [G: Canada]

Hesse, Dieter M. and Tarkka, Helena. The Demand for Capital, Labor and Energy in European Manufacturing Industry before and after the Oil Price Shocks. *Scand. J. Econ.*, 1986, *88*(3), pp. 529–46. [G: W. Europe]

Hill, Hal. On the Transferability of United States Factor Intensity Classifications to LDC Manufacturing: Indonesia and Singapore Compared. *Singapore Econ. Rev.*, October 1986, *31*(2), pp. 67–78. [G: Indonesia; Singapore]

Hofmann, Hans-Joachim. Mindestroptimale Betriebsgrössen und die Ursachen suboptimaler Kapazitäten. Eine empirische Untersuchung mit Hilfe der "Survivor-Technik." (Minimum Efficient Plant Size and the Determinants of Suboptimal Capacity: An Empirical Analysis Applying the "Survivor-Technique.". With English summary.) *Jahr. Nationalökon. Statist.*, March 1986, *201*(2), pp. 131–51. [G: W. Germany]

Holmes, John. The Organization and Locational Structure of Production Subcontracting. **In** *Scott, A. J. and Storper, M., eds.*, 1986, pp. 80–106.

Holz, Arnold. Die Ausrüstungsinvestitionen der schweizerischen Industrie. Desaggregierte Hochrechnungen 1969–1985. (Equipment Investment of Swiss Industry. Disaggregated Estimations 1969 to 1985. With English summary.) *Schweiz. Z. Volkswirtsch. Statist.*, December 1986, *122*(4), pp. 677–96. [G: Switzerland]

Hotta, Kazuyoshi. Historische Entwicklungslinien der Wettbewerbsdynamik im japanischen Markt. (With English summary.) *Z. Betriebswirtschaft*, June 1986, *56*(6), pp. 500–508. [G: Japan]

Hua, Mingshu. The Inflationary Effect on the Structure of Trade. *Weltwirtsch. Arch.*, 1986, *122*(2), pp. 254–69. [G: U.S.]

Illeris, Sven. New Firm Creation in Denmark: The Importance of the Cultural Background. **In** *Keeble, D. and Wever, E., eds.*, 1986, pp. 141–50. [G: Denmark]

Ilmakunnas, Pekka. Stochastic Constraints on

Cost Function Parameters: Mixed and Hierarchical Approaches. *Empirical Econ.*, 1986, *11*(2), pp. 69–80.

Imai, Ken-ichi. Japan's Industrial Policy for High Technology Industry. **In** *Patrick, H., ed.*, 1986, pp. 137–69. **[G: Japan]**

Iqbal, Mahmood. Substitution of Labour, Capital and Energy in the Manufacturing Sector of Pakistan. *Empirical Econ.*, 1986, *11*(2), pp. 81–95. **[G: Pakistan]**

James, David E.; Musgrove, A. R. deL. and Stocks, K. J. Integration of an Economic Input–Output Model and a Linear Programming Technological Model for Energy Systems Analysis. *Energy Econ.*, April 1986, *8*(2), pp. 99–112. **[G: Australia]**

Jones, Ian S. Apprentice Training Costs in British Manufacturing Establishments: Some New Evidence. *Brit. J. Ind. Relat.*, November 1986, *24*(3), pp. 333–62. **[G: U.K.]**

Junge, G. and Zarinnejadan, Milad. A Rate-of-Return Model of Investment Behavior for Switzerland. *Empirical Econ.*, 1986, *11*(3), pp. 153–67. **[G: Switzerland]**

Kadekodi, Gopal K. Derived Demand Elasticities in a Multi-sectoral Production Framework. *J. Quant. Econ.*, January 1986, *2*(1), pp. 33–41. **[G: India]**

Kaldor, Mary; Sharp, Margaret and Walker, William. Industrial Competitiveness and Britain's Defence. *Lloyds Bank Rev.*, October 1986, (162), pp. 31–49. **[G: U.K.]**

Kaufman, Roger T. and Jacoby, Richard A. The Stock Market and the Productivity Slowdown: International Evidence. *Rev. Econ. Statist.*, February 1986, *68*(1), pp. 18–23. **[G: Selected OECD]**

Kavoussi, Rostam M. Trade Policy and Industrialization in an Oil-Exporting Country: The Case of Iran. *J. Devel. Areas*, July 1986, *20*(4), pp. 453–71. **[G: Iran]**

Kawasaki, Seiichi and Zimmermann, Klaus F. Testing the Rationality of Price Expectations for Manufacturing Firms. *Appl. Econ.*, December 1986, *18*(12), pp. 1335–47. **[G: W. Germany]**

Kawashima, Yoko and Tachibanaki, Toshiaki. The Effect of Discrimination and of Industry Segmentation on Japanese Wage Differentials in Relation to Education. *Int. J. Ind. Organ.*, March 1986, *4*(1), pp. 43–68. **[G: Japan]**

Kelkar, Vijay L. A View from the South: Growth of World Trade in Manufactures. **In** *[Patel, S.]*, 1986, pp. 105–21. **[G: MDCs; LDCs]**

Khan, Mahmud Jameel and Chowdhury, Nuimuddin. Trade, Industrialisation and Employment. **In** *Islam, R. and Muqtada, M., eds.*, 1986, pp. 89–117. **[G: Bangladesh]**

Khemani, R. S. and Shapiro, Daniel M. The Determinants of New Plant Entry in Canada. *Appl. Econ.*, November 1986, *18*(11), pp. 1243–57. **[G: Canada]**

Kim, W. Chan and Tschoegl, Adrian E. The Regional Balance of Industrialization: An Empirical Investigation of the Asian Pacific Area. *J. Devel. Areas*, January 1986, *20*(2), pp. 173–83. **[G: Asia; LDCs]**

King, Stephen R. Improvements in Macroeconomic Stability: The Role of Wages and Prices: Comment. **In** *Gordon, R. J., ed.*, 1986, pp. 665–69. **[G: U.S.]**

Koch, Paul D. and Ragan, James F., Jr. Investigating the Causal Relationship between Quits and Wages: An Exercise in Comparative Dynamics. *Econ. Inquiry*, January 1986, *24*(1), pp. 61–83. **[G: U.S.]**

Kokkelenberg, Edward C. and Bischoff, Charles W. Expectations and Factor Demand. *Rev. Econ. Statist.*, August 1986, *68*(3), pp. 423–31. **[G: U.S.]**

Kontorovich, Vladimir. Soviet Growth Slowdown: Econometric vs. Direct Evidence. *Amer. Econ. Rev.*, May 1986, *76*(2), pp. 181–85. **[G: U.S.S.R.]**

Koutsoyiannis, A. Goals of Oligopolistic Firms: Reply. *Southern Econ. J.*, April 1986, *52*(4), pp. 1158–61. **[G: U.S.]**

Kuehn, John A. and Braschler, Curtis. Technology and Foreign Trade Impacts on U.S. Manufacturing Employment 1975–80. *Growth Change*, October 1986, *17*(4), pp. 46–60. **[G: U.S.]**

Kuyvenhoven, Arie and Poot, Huib. The Structure of Indonesian Manufacturing Industry: An Input–Output Approach. *Bull. Indonesian Econ. Stud.*, August 1986, *22*(2), pp. 54–79. **[G: Indonesia]**

Kwoka, John E., Jr. and Ravenscraft, David J. Cooperation *vs.* Rivalry: Price–Cost Margins by Line of Business. *Economica*, August 1986, *53*(211), pp. 351–63. **[G: U.S.]**

Kwon, Jene K. Capital Utilization, Economies of Scale and Technical Change in the Growth of Total Factor Productivity: An Explanation of South Korean Manufacturing Growth. *J. Devel. Econ.*, November 1986, *24*(1), pp. 75–89. **[G: S. Korea]**

Landau, Ralph and Hatsopoulos, George N. Capital Formation in the United States and Japan. **In** *Landau, R. and Rosenberg, N., eds.*, 1986, pp. 583–606. **[G: U.S.; Japan]**

Landefeld, J. Steven and Seskin, Eugene P. A Comparison of Anticipatory Surveys and Econometric Models in Forecasting U.S. Business Investment. *J. Econ. Soc. Meas.*, April 1986, *14*(1), pp. 77–85. **[G: U.S.]**

Laumas, Prem S. and Williams, Martin. The Demand for Heterogeneous Capital and Labour Inputs in a Developing Economy. *Pakistan Devel. Rev.*, Summer 1986, *25*(2), pp. 127–40. **[G: India]**

Lazear, Edward P. The Cyclical Behavior of Industrial Labor Markets: A Comparison of the Prewar and Postwar Eras: Comment. **In** *Gordon, R. J., ed.*, 1986, pp. 626–32. **[G: U.S.]**

Lee, Fred S. Post Keynesian View of Average Direct Costs: A Critical Evaluation of the Theory and the Empirical Evidence. *J. Post Keynesian Econ.*, Spring 1986, *8*(3), pp. 400–424. **[G: U.S.]**

Lee, Jaymin. Determinants of Offshore Production in Developing Countries. *J. Devel. Econ.*, Jan.-Feb. 1986, *20*(1), pp. 1–13. **[G: LDCs]**

Lee, Jaymin. Market Performance in an Open Developing Economy: Technical and Allocative Efficiency of Korean Industries. *J. Ind. Econ.*, September 1986, *35*(1), pp. 81–96. **[G: S. Korea]**

Lee, Kiong-Hock. The Structure and Causes of Malaysian Manufacturing Sector Protection. **In** *Findlay, C. and Garnaut, R., eds.*, 1986, pp. 99–134. **[G: Malaysia]**

Leite, Sergio Pereira and Vaez-Zadeh, Reza. Credit Allocation and Investment Decisions: The Case of the Manufacturing Sector in Korea. *World Devel.*, January 1986, *14*(1), pp. 115–26. **[G: S. Korea]**

Leontief, Wassily. Air Pollution and the Economic Structure: Empirical Results of Input–Output Computations. **In** *Leontief, W.*, 1986, *1972*, pp. 273–93. **[G: U.S.]**

Leontief, Wassily. Domestic Production and Foreign Trade: The American Capital Position Reexamined. **In** *Leontief, W.*, 1986, *1953*, pp. 65–93. **[G: U.S.]**

Leontief, Wassily. Factor Proportions and the Structure of American Trade: Further Theoretical and Empirical Analysis. **In** *Leontief, W.*, 1986, *1956*, pp. 94–128. **[G: U.S.]**

Leontief, Wassily. Wages, Profits, Prices, and Taxes. **In** *Leontief, W.*, 1986, *1947*, pp. 55–64. **[G: U.S.]**

Leontief, Wassily and Hoffenberg, Marvin. The Economic Effects of Disarmament. **In** *Leontief, W.*, 1986, *1961*, pp. 188–203. **[G: U.S.]**

Lévy-Garboua, Louis. Innovations et diffusion des produits de consommation. (Innovations and the Diffusion of Consumer Goods. With English summary.) *Écon. Appl.*, 1986, *39*(3), pp. 521–82.

Liedholm, Carl and Mead, Donald C. Small-scale Industry. **In** *Berg, R. J. and Whitaker, J. S., eds.*, 1986, pp. 308–30. **[G: Sub-Saharan Africa]**

Little, Jane Sneddon. Intra-firm Trade and U.S. Protectionism: Thoughts Based on a Small Survey. *New Eng. Econ. Rev.*, Jan./Feb. 1986, pp. 42–51. **[G: U.S.]**

Lloyd, Tom. The Importance of Giant Companies. *Lloyds Bank Rev.*, April 1986, (160), pp. 52–54. **[G: U.S.; U.K.]**

Luger, Michael I. Depreciation Profiles and Depreciation Policy in a Spatial Context. *J. Reg. Sci.*, February 1986, *26*(1), pp. 141–59. **[G: U.S.]**

Lundberg, Lars and Hansson, Pär. Intra-industry Trade and Its Consequences for Adjustment. **In** *Greenaway, D. and Tharakan, P. K. M., eds.*, 1986, pp. 129–47. **[G: Sweden]**

MacCharles, Donald C. Canadian International Intra-industry Trade. **In** *Greenaway, D. and Tharakan, P. K. M., eds.*, 1986, pp. 148–73. **[G: Canada]**

Madhur, Srinivasa and Roy, Prannoy. Price Setting in Indian Industry. *J. Devel. Econ.*, March 1986, *20*(2), pp. 205–24. **[G: India]**

Mann, Catherine L. Prices, Profit Margins, and Exchange Rates. *Fed. Res. Bull.*, June 1986, *72*(6), pp. 366–79. **[G: U.S.]**

Marin, Dalia. Exchange Rate and Industrial Profits: Austria's Revaluation Policy in the 1970s. *Appl. Econ.*, June 1986, *18*(6), pp. 675–89. **[G: Austria]**

Mariotti, Sergio and Ricotta, Enrico. Diversification, Agreements between Firms and Innovative Behaviour. *Ricerche Econ.*, Oct.-Dec. 1986, *40*(4), pp. 644–74. **[G: U.S.; Europe]**

Martin, Fernand. Repercussions of Industrial Redeployment upon the International Role of the Region of Montreal. **In** *Danson, M., ed.*, 1986, pp. 147–57. **[G: Canada]**

Martin, Ronald L. Industrial Restructuring, Labour Shake-Out and the Geography of Recession. **In** *Danson, M., ed.*, 1986, pp. 1–22. **[G: U.K.]**

Martin, Stephen. Causes and Effects of Vertical Integration. *Appl. Econ.*, July 1986, *18*(7), pp. 737–55. **[G: U.S.]**

Masson, Robert T. and Shaanan, Joseph. Excess Capacity and Limit Pricing: An Empirical Test. *Economica*, August 1986, *53*(211), pp. 365–78. **[G: U.S.]**

McCallum, Bennett T. Inventory Fluctuations in the United States since 1929: Comment. **In** *Gordon, R. J., ed.*, 1986, pp. 223–31. **[G: U.S.]**

McCombie, John S. L. On Some Interpretations of the Relationship between Productivity and Output Growth. *Appl. Econ.*, November 1986, *18*(11), pp. 1215–25. **[G: OECD]**

McQuaid, Ronald William. Production Functions and the Disaggregation of Labor Inputs in Manufacturing Plants. *J. Reg. Sci.*, August 1986, *26*(3), pp. 595–603. **[G: U.S.]**

Mefford, Robert N. Introducing Management into the Production Function. *Rev. Econ. Statist.*, February 1986, *68*(1), pp. 96–104. **[G: U.S.]**

de Melo, Jaime and Urata, Shujiro. The Influence of Increased Foreign Competition on Industrial Concentration and Profitability. *Int. J. Ind. Organ.*, September 1986, *4*(3), pp. 287–304. **[G: Chile]**

Messerlin, Patrick A. Export-Credit Mercantilism à la Française. *World Econ.*, December 1986, *9*(4), pp. 385–408. **[G: France]**

Michel, Allen and Shaked, Israel. Industry Influence on Pension Funding. *J. Portfol. Manage.*, Spring 1986, *12*(3), pp. 71–77. **[G: U.S.]**

Miller, Edward M. Cross-sectional and Time-Series Biases in Factor Demand Studies: Explaining Energy–Capital Complementarity. *Southern Econ. J.*, January 1986, *52*(3), pp. 745–62. **[G: U.S.]**

Miller, Edward M. Determinants of the Size of the Small Business Sector: They Are Labor Productivity, Wage Rates and Capital Intensity. *Amer. J. Econ. Soc.*, October 1986, *45*(4), pp. 390–402. **[G: U.S.]**

Milone, Luciano Marcello. The Law of One Price: Further Empirical Evidence Concerning Italy and the United Kingdom. *Appl. Econ.*, June 1986, *18*(6), pp. 645–61. **[G: Italy; U.K.]**

Moghimzadeh, Mahmood and Kymn, Kern O. Cost Shares, Own, and Cross-Price Elasticities in U.S. Manufacturing with Disaggregated Energy Inputs. *Energy J.*, October 1986, *7*(4), pp. 65–80. **[G: U.S.]**

Mohnen, Pierre A.; Nadiri, M. Ishaq and Prucha, Ingmar R. R&D, Production Structure and Rates of Return in the U.S., Japanese and German Manufacturing Sectors: A Non-separable Dynamic Factor Demand Model. *Europ. Econ. Rev.*, August 1986, *30*(4), pp. 749–71. **[G: U.S.; Japan; W. Germany]**

Moomaw, Ronald L. Have Changes in Localization Economies Been Responsible for Declining Productivity Advantages in Large Cities? *J. Reg. Sci.*, February 1986, *26*(1), pp. 19–32. **[G: U.S.]**

Morrison, Catherine J. Productivity Measurement with Non-static Expectations and Varying Capacity Utilization: An Integrated Approach. *J. Econometrics*, Oct./Nov. 1986, *33*(1/2), pp. 51–74. **[G: U.S.]**

Morrison, Catherine J. Structural Models of Dynamic Factor Demands with Nonstatic Expectations: An Empirical Assessment of Alternative Expectations Specifications. *Int. Econ. Rev.*, June 1986, *27*(2), pp. 365–86. **[G: U.S.]**

Muellbauer, John. The Assessment: Productivity and Competitiveness in British Manufacturing. *Oxford Rev. Econ. Policy*, Autumn 1986, *2*(3), pp. i–xxv. **[G: U.K.]**

Mueller, Dennis C. Persistent Performance among Large Corporations. **In** *[Dean, J.]*, 1986, pp. 31–61. **[G: U.S.]**

Murty, M. N. Interfuel Substitution and Derived Demands for Inputs in the Manufacturing Sector of India. *J. Quant. Econ.*, January 1986, *2*(1), pp. 119–35. **[G: India]**

Neef, Arthur. International Trends in Productivity and Unit Labor Costs in Manufacturing. *Mon. Lab. Rev.*, December 1986, *109*(12), pp. 12–17. **[G: OECD]**

Nicholas, Stephen. The Hierarchical Division of Labour and the Growth of British Manufacturing Multinationals: 1870–1939. **In** *Teichova, A.; Lévy-Leboyer, M. and Nussbaum, H., eds.*, 1986, pp. 241–56. **[G: U.K.]**

Norton, Roger D. Industrial Policy and American Renewal. *J. Econ. Lit.*, March 1986, *24*(1), pp. 1–40. **[G: U.S.]**

Nove, Alec. The Soviet Industrial Enterprise. **In** *Nove, A.*, 1986, *1981*, pp. 169–79. **[G: U.S.S.R.]**

O'Farrell, Patrick N. The Nature of New Firms in Ireland: Empirical Evidence and Policy Implications. **In** *Keeble, D. and Wever, E., eds.*, 1986, pp. 151–83. **[G: Ireland]**

Ochoa, Eduardo M. Is Reswitching Empirically Relevant? U.S. Wage-Profit-Rate Frontiers, 1947–1972. *Econ. Forum*, Winter 1986-1987, *16*(1), pp. 45–67. **[G: U.S.]**

Odagiri, Hiroyuki and Yamawaki, Hideki. A Study of Company Profit-Rate Time Series: Japan and the United States. *Int. J. Ind. Organ.*, March 1986, *4*(1), pp. 1–23. **[G: Japan; U.S.]**

Öller, Lars-Erik. A Note on Exponentially Smoothed Seasonal Differences. *J. Bus. Econ. Statist.*, October 1986, *4*(4), pp. 485–89. **[G: U.S.]**

Orlov, Ia. The Role of Industry and Trade in Satisfying the Population's Demand. *Prob. Econ.*, April 1986, *28*(12), pp. 42–58. **[G: U.S.S.R.]**

Panas, Epaminondas E. Biased Technological Progress and Theories of Induced Innovation: The Case of Greek Manufacturing, 1958–1975. *Greek Econ. Rev.*, June 1986, *8*(1), pp. 95–119. **[G: Greece]**

Panchamukhi, V. R. Lima Target and the Interdependencies. **In** *Panchamukhi, V. R., et al.*, 1986, pp. 112–36. **[G: LDCs; MDCs]**

Pangestu, Mari and Boediono. The Structure and Causes of Manufacturing Sector Protection in Indonesia. **In** *Findlay, C. and Garnaut, R., eds.*, 1986, pp. 1–47. **[G: Indonesia]**

Parker, William N. The Development and Use of Machine Tools in Historical Perspective: Comment. **In** *Day, R. H. and Eliasson, G., eds.*, 1986, pp. 271–76. **[G: U.K.]**

Peck, Merton J. and Beggs, John J. Energy Conservation in American Industry. **In** *Sawhill, J. C. and Cotton, R., eds.*, 1986, pp. 59–91. **[G: U.S.]**

Perrons, Diane. Unequal Integration in Global Fordism: The Case of Ireland. **In** *Scott, A. J. and Storper, M., eds.*, 1986, pp. 246–64. **[G: Ireland]**

Perryman, M. Ray. Institutional Evolution in an Economy Characterized by Basic Industry Decline and Technological Expansion. *J. Econ. Issues*, June 1986, *20*(2), pp. 481–88. **[G: U.S.]**

Phipps, A. J. An Examination of Inter-industry Differences in the Relationship between Output and Employment in Australia. *Australian Bull. Lab.*, December 1986, *13*(1), pp. 35–50. **[G: Australia]**

Popović, Milenko. Uzroci retardacije jugoslovenske industrije. (Causes of Retardation of Yugoslav Industry. With English summary.) *Econ. Anal. Workers' Manage.*, 1986, *20*(3), pp. 257–74. **[G: Yugoslavia]**

Pratten, Cliff. The Importance of Giant Companies. *Lloyds Bank Rev.*, January 1986, (159), pp. 33–48. **[G: U.S.; U.K.]**

Prosperetti, Luigi and Borellini, Rosella. Produttività, orari di fatto e domanda di lavoro nell'industria manifatturiera italiana: un'analisi Cross-Section. (Productivity, Working Hours and Labour Demand in Manufacturing in Italy: A Cross Section Analysis. With English summary.) *Polit. Econ.*, August 1986, *2*(2), pp. 225–42. **[G: Italy]**

Prywes, Menahem. A Nested CES Approach to Capital–Energy Substitution. *Energy Econ.*, January 1986, *8*(1), pp. 22–28. **[G: U.S.]**

Rahmeyer, Fritz. Der Zusammenhang zwischen Lohn-, Produktivitäts- und Preisstruktur im verarbeitenden Gewerbe. (The Interrelation between the Relative Growth of Wages, Productivity and Prices in the Manufacturing Sector. With English summary.) *Z. Wirtschaft.*

Sozialwissen., 1986, *106*(5), pp. 467–93. **[G: W. Germany]**

Rao, B. Bhaskara. A Note on Employment, Labor Supply, and Real Wages in Market Disequilibrium. *J. Macroecon.*, Spring 1986, *8*(2), pp. 233–42. **[G: U.S.]**

Ray, George F. Services for Manufacturing. *Nat. Inst. Econ. Rev.*, August 1986, (117), pp. 30–32. **[G: U.K.]**

Reati, Angelo. The Rate of Profit and the Organic Composition of Capital in West German Industry from 1960 to 1981. *Rev. Radical Polit. Econ.*, Spring/Summer 1986, *18*(1/2), pp. 56–86. **[G: W. Germany]**

Rutgaizer, V. and Zhuravlev, S. N. Resources of the Personal Services Sphere. *Prob. Econ.*, November 1986, *29*(7), pp. 20–39. **[G: U.S.S.R.]**

Samuelson, Paul A. The Future of American Industry in a Changing Economy. **In** *Samuelson, P. A.*, 1986, *1984*, pp. 520–24. **[G: U.S.]**

Samuelson, Paul A. To Protect Manufacturing? **In** *Samuelson, P. A.*, 1986, *1981*, pp. 510–17.

Sarantis, Nicholas C. A Note on Employment, Labor Supply, and Real Wages in Market Disequilibrium: A Reply. *J. Macroecon.*, Spring 1986, *8*(2), pp. 243–45. **[G: U.S.]**

Sazanami, Yoko. Some Policy Implications of Intra-industry Trade for Japan. **In** *Greenaway, D. and Tharakan, P. K. M., eds.*, 1986, pp. 174–90. **[G: Selected Countries; Japan]**

Scherer, Alf. Intersectoral Efficiency between Agriculture and Industry in Six C.M.E.A. Countries: Introducing a Simple Equilibrium Model. *Econ. Planning*, 1986, *20*(1), pp. 1–27. **[G: CMEA]**

Seitz, H. Firms Responses to Changes in Demand: Some Insight from Survey-Data. *Empirical Econ.*, 1986, *11*(2), pp. 111–23. **[G: W. Germany]**

Shaiken, Harley. Decentralized Production: A Technological Revolution with Political Issues. **In** *Gondolf, E. W.; Marcus, I. M. and Dougherty, J. P., eds.*, 1986, pp. 58–65.

Shapiro, Matthew D. Capital Utilization and Capital Accumulation: Theory and Evidence. *J. Appl. Econometrics*, July 1986, *1*(3), pp. 211–34. **[G: U.S.]**

Shapiro, Matthew D. The Dynamic Demand for Capital and Labor. *Quart. J. Econ.*, August 1986, *101*(3), pp. 513–42. **[G: U.S.]**

Sharp, Margaret. Technology Gap or Management Gap? **In** *Sharp, M., ed.*, 1986, pp. 263–97. **[G: W. Europe]**

Shiells, Clinton R.; Stern, Robert M. and Deardorff, Alan V. Estimates of the Elasticities of Substitution between Imports and Home Goods for the United States. *Weltwirtsch. Arch.*, 1986, *122*(3), pp. 497–519. **[G: U.S.]**

Sit, Victor F. S. Industries in Shenzhen: An Attempt at Open-Door Industrialization. **In** *Jao, Y. C. and Leung, C. K., eds.*, 1986, pp. 226–46. **[G: China]**

Skarstein, Rune. Growth and Crisis in the Manufacturing Sector. **In** *Boesen, J., et al., eds.*, 1986, pp. 79–104. **[G: Tanzania]**

Smyth, David J. The Cyclical Response of Employment to Output Changes: United States Manufacturing Industries, 1948 to 1983. *Appl. Econ.*, May 1986, *18*(5), pp. 495–500. **[G: U.S.]**

Sokoloff, Kenneth L. Productivity Growth in Manufacturing during Early Industrialization: Evidence from the American Northeast, 1820–1860. **In** *Engerman, S. L. and Gallman, R. E., eds.*, 1986, pp. 679–729. **[G: U.S.]**

Spatz, Donald L. Issues in Asbestos Disease Compensation. **In** *Chelius, J., ed.*, 1986, pp. 287–311. **[G: U.S.]**

Stern, Paula and Wechsler, Andrew. Escape Clause Relief and Recessions: An Economic and Legal Look at Section 201. **In** *Saxonhouse, G. R. and Yamamura, K., eds.*, 1986, pp. 195–217. **[G: U.S.]**

Sugiura, Yoshio. Diffusion of Rotary Clubs in Japan, 1920–1940: A Case of Non-profit-Motivated Innovation Diffusion under a Decentralized Decision Making Structure. *Econ. Geogr.*, April 1986, *62*(2), pp. 125–43. **[G: Japan]**

Tan, Norma A. The Structure and Causes of Manufacturing Sector Protection in the Philippines. **In** *Findlay, C. and Garnaut, R., eds.*, 1986, pp. 48–76. **[G: Philippines]**

Tatom, John A. Domestic vs. International Explanations of Recent U.S. Manufacturing Developments. *Fed. Res. Bank St. Louis Rev.*, April 1986, *68*(4), pp. 5–18. **[G: U.S.]**

Tatom, John A. Why Has Manufacturing Employment Declined? *Fed. Res. Bank St. Louis Rev.*, December 1986, *68*(10), pp. 15–25. **[G: U.S.]**

Tay, Boon Nga. The Structure and Causes of Manufacturing Sector Protection in Singapore. **In** *Findlay, C. and Garnaut, R., eds.*, 1986, pp. 135–58. **[G: Singapore]**

Taylor, John B. Improvements in Macroeconomic Stability: The Role of Wages and Prices. **In** *Gordon, R. J., ed.*, 1986, pp. 639–65. **[G: U.S.]**

Taylor, John B. Improvements in Macroeconomic Stability: The Role of Wages and Prices: Reply. **In** *Gordon, R. J., ed.*, 1986, pp. 672–75. **[G: U.S.]**

Teitel, Simón and Thoumi, Francisco E. Da substituição de importações às exportações: as experiências argentina e brasileira no campo das exportações de manufaturados. (With English summary.) *Pesquisa Planejamento Econ.*, April 1986, *16*(1), pp. 129–66. **[G: Argentina; Brazil]**

Teubal, Morris; Halevi, Nadav and Tsiddon, D. Learning and the Rise of Israel's Exports of Sophisticated Products. *World Devel.*, December 1986, *14*(12), pp. 1397–1410. **[G: Israel]**

Thomas, Lacy Glenn. The Economics of Strategic Planning: A Survey of the Issues. **In** *[Dean, J.]*, 1986, pp. 1–27. **[G: U.S.]**

Tsao, Yuan. Translog Price Estimations of Singapore's Manufacturing Industries. *Devel. Econ.*, September 1986, *24*(3), pp. 251–71. **[G: Singapore]**

Voos, Paula B. and Mishel, Lawrence R. The Union Impact on Profits: Evidence from Industry Price–Cost Margin Data. *J. Lab. Econ.*, January 1986, *4*(1), pp. 105–33. **[G: U.S.]**

Voráček, Josef. Cooperation in the Engineering Industry. *Czech. Econ. Digest.*, June 1986, (5), pp. 28–32. **[G: CMEA]**

Wabe, J. Stuart. The Regional Impact of De-industrialization in the European Community. *Reg. Stud.*, February 1986, *20*(1), pp. 27–36. **[G: EEC]**

Warr, Peter G. Australian Protection and the ASEAN Countries. **In** *Findlay, C. and Garnaut, R., eds.*, 1986, pp. 248–63. **[G: ASEAN; Australia]**

Webber, M. J. and Rigby, D. L. The Rate of Profit in Canadian Manufacturing, 1950–1981. *Rev. Radical Polit. Econ.*, Spring/Summer 1986, *18*(1/2), pp. 33–55. **[G: Canada]**

Weissenberger, Edgar; Müller-Brockhausen, Gerd and Welsch, Heinz. A Factor Demand Model with Quasi-fixed Factors and Rational Expectations. *J. Econ. (Z. Nationalökon.)*, 1986, *46*(2), pp. 123–42. **[G: U.S.]**

Wells, John. Economic Recovery and Industrial Expansion in the U.K. **In** *Nolan, P. and Paine, S., eds.*, 1986, pp. 135–44. **[G: U.K.]**

West, Kenneth D. A Variance Bounds Test of the Linear Quadratic Inventory Model. *J. Polit. Econ.*, April 1986, *94*(2), pp. 374–401. **[G: U.S.]**

Wheat, Leonard F. The Determinants of 1963–77 Regional Manufacturing Growth: Why the South and West Grow. *J. Reg. Sci.*, November 1986, *26*(4), pp. 635–59. **[G: U.S.]**

Wheatcroft, S. G.; Davies, R. W. and Cooper, Julian. Soviet Industrialization Reconsidered: Some Preliminary Conclusions about Economic Development between 1926 and 1941. *Econ. Hist. Rev., 2nd Ser.*, May 1986, *39*(2), pp. 264–94. **[G: U.S.S.R.]**

Whitehall, Peter. Profit Variation in the Barbados Manufacturing Sector. *Soc. Econ. Stud.*, December 1986, *35*(4), pp. 67–91. **[G: Barbados]**

Williamson, Jeffrey G. Productivity Growth in Manufacturing during Early Industrialization: Evidence from the American Northeast, 1820–1860: Comment. **In** *Engerman, S. L. and Gallman, R. E., eds.*, 1986, pp. 729–33. **[G: U.S.]**

Williamson, Peter J. Multinational Enterprise Behaviour and Domestic Industry Adjustment under Import Threat. *Rev. Econ. Statist.*, August 1986, *68*(3), pp. 359–68. **[G: Australia]**

Willmore, Larry N. The Comparative Performance of Foreign and Domestic Firms in Brazil. *World Devel.*, April 1986, *14*(4), pp. 489–502. **[G: Brazil]**

Winiecki, Jan. The Overgrown Industrial Sector in Soviet-Type Economies: Explanations, Evidence, Consequences. *Comp. Econ. Stud.*, Winter 1986, *28*(4), pp. 13–36. **[G: Cent. Planned Econ.]**

Wong, Christine P. W. The Economics of Shortage and Problems of Reform in Chinese Industry. *J. Compar. Econ.*, December 1986, *10*(4), pp. 363–87. **[G: China]**

Woolf, Arthur G. Market Structure and Minority Presence: Black-Owned Firms in Manufacturing. *Rev. Black Polit. Econ.*, Spring 1986, *14*(4), pp. 79–89. **[G: U.S.]**

Wren-Lewis, Simon. An Econometric Model of U.K. Manufacturing Employment Using Survey Data on Expected Output. *J. Appl. Econometrics*, October 1986, *1*(4), pp. 297–316. **[G: U.K.]**

Yago, Glenn, et al. Industrial Devolution in New York State. **In** *Schoolman, M. and Magid, A., eds.*, 1986, pp. 75–89. **[G: U.S.]**

Yamawaki, Hideki. Exports, Foreign Market Structure, and Profitability in Japanese and U.S. Manufacturing. *Rev. Econ. Statist.*, November 1986, *68*(4), pp. 618–27. **[G: Japan; U.S.]**

Yankson, P. W. K. Small-Scale Industries in the Implementation of a Growth Centre Strategy of Regional Development: A Case-Study in Ghana. *Industry Devel.*, 1986, (17), pp. 65–89. **[G: Ghana]**

Zanetto, Gabriele. Sviluppo regionale e continuità culturale: il caso della beauce (Canada). (Regional Development and Cultural Continuity: The Case of the Beauce [Canada]. With English summary.) *Ricerche Econ.*, Apr.-Sept. 1986, *40*(2–3), pp. 537–55. **[G: Canada]**

Zarnowitz, Victor and Moore, Geoffrey H. Major Changes in Cyclical Behavior. **In** *Gordon, R. J., ed.*, 1986, pp. 519–72. **[G: U.S.; W. Germany; U.K.; France]**

Zimmermann, Klaus F. On Rationality of Business Expectations: A Micro Analysis of Qualitative Responses. *Empirical Econ.*, 1986, *11*(1), pp. 23–40. **[G: W. Germany]**

6312 Metals (iron, steel, and other)

Ács, János. The Development of the Steel Industry from the Viewpoint of Innovation Theory. **In** *Goldberg, W. H., ed.*, 1986, pp. 283–306. **[G: Global]**

Adams, Walter and Mueller, Hans. The Steel Industry. **In** *Adams, W., ed.*, 1986, pp. 74–125. **[G: U.S.; OECD]**

Atkinson, Michael. The Supply of Raw Materials to the South Wales Iron Industry, 1800–60. **In** *Baber, C. and Williams, L. J., eds.*, 1986, pp. 43–52. **[G: U.K.]**

Atsumi, Naoki. Voluntary Restraint Agreements: The Case of Automobiles and Steel. **In** *Finn, R. B., ed.*, 1986, pp. 39–49. **[G: U.S.; Japan]**

Benyon, Frank S. The EC–U.S. Steel Trade Crisis: Comment. **In** *Tsoukalis, L., ed.*, 1986, pp. 45–49. **[G: EEC; U.S.]**

Boylston, Benjamin C. Employee Involvement and Cultural Change at Bethlehem Steel. **In** *Rosow, J. M., ed.*, 1986, pp. 89–109. **[G: U.S.]**

Brand, Horst and Huffstutler, Clyde. Trends of Labor Productivity in Metal Stamping Industries. *Mon. Lab. Rev.*, May 1986, *109*(5), pp. 13–20. **[G: U.S.]**

Camens, Sam. Labor–Management Participation

Teams in the Basic Steel Industry. **In** *Rosow, J. M., ed.*, 1986, pp. 110–18. **[G: U.S.]**

Carruth, Alan A.; Oswald, Andrew J. and Findlay, Lewis. A Test of a Model of Trade Union Behaviour: The Coal and Steel Industries in Britain. *Oxford Bull. Econ. Statist.*, February 1986, *48*(1), pp. 1–18. **[G: U.K.]**

Cima, Lawrence R. The Excess Supply–Pure Demand Approach to International Commodity Trade: The Case of Japanese Steel Exports to the United States. *Econ. Inquiry*, October 1986, *24*(4), pp. 645–56. **[G: U.S.; Japan]**

Cline, William R. U.S. Trade and Industrial Policy: The Experience of Textiles, Steel, and Automobiles. **In** *Krugman, P. R., ed.*, 1986, pp. 211–39. **[G: U.S.]**

Cockerill, Anthony and Cole, Sara. Restructuring British Steel. **In** *Goldberg, W. H., ed.*, 1986, pp. 149–63. **[G: U.K.; France; W. Germany]**

Crandall, Robert W. Investment and Productivity Growth in the Steel Industry: Some Implications for Industrial Policy. **In** *Goldberg, W. H., ed.*, 1986, pp. 191–204. **[G: U.S.]**

Crandall, Robert W. The EC–U.S. Steel Trade Crisis. **In** *Tsoukalis, L., ed.*, 1986, pp. 17–35. **[G: U.S.; EEC]**

Dal Co, Mario. Recenti sviluppi della contrattazione collettiva negli Stati Uniti. (Concession Bargaining in the United States: Auto and Steel Industries. With English summary.) *Econ. Lavoro*, July-Sept. 1986, *20*(3), pp. 97–111. **[G: U.S.]**

Daunton, M. J. Labour and Technology in South Wales, 1870–1914. **In** *Baber, C. and Williams, L. J., eds.*, 1986, pp. 140–52. **[G: U.K.]**

Elbaum, Bernard. The Steel Industry before World War I. **In** *Elbaum, B. and Lazonick, W., eds.*, 1986, pp. 51–81. **[G: U.K.; U.S.]**

FitzRoy, Felix R. and Kraft, Kornelius. Profitability and Profit-Sharing. *J. Ind. Econ.*, December 1986, *35*(2), pp. 113–30. **[G: W. Germany]**

Foroutan, Faezeh. Determinants of European Community Imports of Steel Mill Products. *Appl. Econ.*, August 1986, *18*(8), pp. 863–73. **[G: EEC]**

Gerken, Egbert; Gross, Martin and Lächler, Ulrich. The Causes and Consequences of Steel Subsidization in Germany. *Europ. Econ. Rev.*, August 1986, *30*(4), pp. 773–804. **[G: W. Germany]**

Gold, Bela. Technological Change and Vertical Integration. *Managerial Dec. Econ.*, September 1986, *7*(3), pp. 169–76.

Gold, Bela. Transformation Tendencies in the World Steel Industry and Adaptive Strategies. **In** *Goldberg, W. H., ed.*, 1986, pp. 461–91.

Goldberg, Walter H. Ailing Steel: The Transoceanic Quarrel: Great Britain. **In** *Goldberg, W. H., ed.*, 1986, pp. 145–48. **[G: U.K.]**

Goldberg, Walter H. Ailing Steel: The Transoceanic Quarrel: The Federal Republic of Germany. **In** *Goldberg, W. H., ed.*, 1986, pp. 125–39. **[G: W. Germany]**

Goldberg, Walter H. Ailing Steel: The Transoceanic Quarrel: Conclusions. **In** *Goldberg, W. H., ed.*, 1986, pp. 495–510.

Goldberg, Walter H. Ailing Steel: The Transoceanic Quarrel: France. **In** *Goldberg, W. H., ed.*, 1986, pp. 141–43. **[G: France]**

Goldberg, Walter H. Ailing Steel: The Transoceanic Quarrel: The Problems. **In** *Goldberg, W. H., ed.*, 1986, pp. 3–35. **[G: Global]**

Goldberg, Walter H. Japan's Steel Industry. **In** *Goldberg, W. H., ed.*, 1986, pp. 247–60. **[G: Japan]**

Goldberg, Walter H. The European Steel Industry. **In** *Goldberg, W. H., ed.*, 1986, pp. 111–23. **[G: EEC]**

Goldberg, Walter H. The Steel Industry of the United States of America. **In** *Goldberg, W. H., ed.*, 1986, pp. 165–89. **[G: U.S.]**

Grossman, Gene M. Imports as a Cause of Injury: The Case of the U.S. Steel Industry. *J. Int. Econ.*, May 1986, *20*(3/4), pp. 201–23. **[G: U.S.]**

Guerci, Carlo Maria and Treichler, Sergio. Crisis, Adjustment and Outlook of the Steel Industry. **In** *Goldberg, W. H., ed.*, 1986, pp. 53–93. **[G: Selected Countries]**

Hirschhorn, Joel S. Restructuring of the United States Steel Industry Requires New Policies. **In** *Goldberg, W. H., ed.*, 1986, pp. 205–46. **[G: U.S.]**

Hogan, William T. The EC–U.S. Steel Trade Crisis: Comment. **In** *Tsoukalis, L., ed.*, 1986, pp. 42–44. **[G: U.S.; EEC]**

Hood, Neil and Young, Stephen. Foreign Direct Investment in the U.S. Automobile Industry. **In** *Gray, H. P., ed.*, 1986, pp. 163–90. **[G: U.S.]**

d'Iribarne, Philippe. Régulation sociale vie des entreprises et performances économiques. (Social Regulation, the Activity of Firms and Economic Performances. With English summary.) *Revue Écon.*, May 1986, *37*(3), pp. 429–54. **[G: France; Netherlands; U.S.; Cameroon]**

Karlson, Stephen H. Adoption of Competing Inventions by United States Steel Producers. *Rev. Econ. Statist.*, August 1986, *68*(3), pp. 415–22. **[G: U.S.]**

Kogut, Bruce. Steel and the European Communities. **In** *Macharzina, K. and Staehle, W. H., eds.*, 1986, pp. 185–203. **[G: EEC]**

Kohama, Hirohisa and Kajiwara, Hirokazu. Structural Change in Steel Trade and International Industrial Adjustments. *Devel. Econ.*, June 1986, *24*(2), pp. 109–30. **[G: Global]**

Kunzmann, Klaus R. Structural Problems of an Old Industrial Area: The Case of the Ruhr District. **In** *Goldberg, W. H., ed.*, 1986, pp. 409–33. **[G: W. Germany]**

Kymn, Kern O. and Palomba, Catherine A. The Strike Experience Model: Adaptive Expectations Applied to Strikes. *J. Behav. Econ.*, Spring/Summer 1986, *15*(1/2), pp. 135–48. **[G: U.S.]**

Lévy, Raymond. Industrial Policy and the Steel Industry. **In** *Adams, W. J. and Stoffaës, C., eds.*, 1986, pp. 63–73. **[G: France]**

Levy, Robert A. and Jondrow, James M. The Adjustment of Employment to Technical

Change in the Steel and Auto Industries. *J. Bus.*, July 1986, *59*(3), pp. 475–91. **[G: U.S.]**

Mangum, Garth L. and Kim, Sae Young. Survival of the U.S. Steel Industry in a Changing World Economy. *Econ. Forum,* Winter 1986-1987, *16*(1), pp. 81–103. **[G: U.S.]**

Mangum, Garth L.; Mangum, Stephen L. and Kim, Sae Young. The High Cost of Peace in Steel. *Challenge,* July/Aug. 1986, *29*(3), pp. 47–50. **[G: U.S.]**

Margolin, Stanley V. U.S. Environmental Laws and Their Impact on American Steel. **In** *Goldberg, W. H., ed.*, 1986, pp. 351–60. **[G: U.S.]**

Markusen, Ann Roell. Neither Ore, nor Coal, nor Markets: A Policy-Oriented View of Steel Sites in the USA. *Reg. Stud.*, October 1986, *20*(5), pp. 449–61. **[G: U.S.]**

Markusen, Ann Roell. The New International Division of Labor: The Changing Relationship of Brazilian and American Steel. **In** *Gondolf, E. W.; Marcus, I. M. and Dougherty, J. P., eds.*, 1986, pp. 67–78. **[G: U.S.; Brazil]**

Mendel, Julius S. The Effect of Exchange Rate Depreciation on the Metal and Engineering Industry. *Econ. Rec.*, Supplement 1986, pp. 89–93. **[G: Australia]**

Méndez, José A. The Short-run Trade and Employment Effects of Steel Import Restraints. *J. World Trade Law,* Sept.:Oct. 1986, *20*(5), pp. 554–66. **[G: U.S.]**

Messerlin, Patrick A. The EC–U.S. Steel Trade Crisis: Comment. **In** *Tsoukalis, L., ed.*, 1986, pp. 36–41. **[G: U.S.; EEC]**

Mueller, Hans. Whither the World Steel Industry? *World Econ.*, December 1986, *9*(4), pp. 444–48.

Mulloney, Peter. Unfair Trade and Foreign Subsidies: Steel "Chaos" in the United States. **In** *Gondolf, E. W.; Marcus, I. M. and Dougherty, J. P., eds.*, 1986, pp. 78–85. **[G: U.S.]**

Mürdter, Heinz. The Compilation of an Input–Output Table with Disaggregated Steel-Sectors—Framework and First Experience. **In** *Franz, A. and Rainer, N., eds.*, 1986, pp. 325–31. **[G: W. Germany]**

Neumann, Manfred. Improved Competitiveness of Steel-Producing Firms by Means of Diversification. **In** *Goldberg, W. H., ed.*, 1986, pp. 439–43. **[G: W. Germany]**

Ogunleye, Ajibade. Self-reliant Development of Iron and Steel Technology in Africa. **In** *Onwuka, R. I. and Aluko, O., eds.*, 1986, pp. 35–41. **[G: Africa]**

Persigehl, Elmer S. and Olsen, John G. Productivity in the Metal Doors, Sash, and Trim Industry. *Mon. Lab. Rev.*, March 1986, *109*(3), pp. 27–31. **[G: U.S.]**

Prais, S. J. Some International Comparisons of the Age of the Machine-Stock. *J. Ind. Econ.*, March 1986, *34*(3), pp. 261–77. **[G: France; Japan; U.K.; U.S.; W. Germany]**

Pruitt, Bettye H. and Smith, George David. The Corporate Management of Innovation: Alcoa Research, Aircraft Alloys, and the Problem of Stress-Corrosion Cracking. **In** *Rosenbloom, R. S., ed.*, 1986, pp. 33–81. **[G: U.S.]**

Rassekh, Farhad. Employment Effects of the Steel Trigger Price Mechanism on the Steel and Motor Vehicle Industries. *Atlantic Econ. J.*, March 1986, *14*(1), pp. 39–49. **[G: U.S.]**

Read, Robert A. The Copper Industry. **In** *Casson, M., et al.*, 1986, pp. 275–315. **[G: Global]**

Reynolds, Joy K. Steelworkers Press Organizing and Coordinated Bargaining. *Mon. Lab. Rev.*, November 1986, *109*(11), pp. 48–49.

Reynolds, Stanley S. Strategic Capital Investment in the American Aluminum Industry. *J. Ind. Econ.*, March 1986, *34*(3), pp. 225–45. **[G: U.S.]**

Riden, Philip. Atlas of Industrializing Britain 1780–1914: Iron and Steel. **In** *Langton, J. and Morris, R. J., eds.*, 1986, pp. 127–31. **[G: U.K.]**

Rolshoven, Hubertus. Antitrust Policy and the Rationalization of the U.S. Steel Industry. *J. Inst. Theoretical Econ.*, March 1986, *142*(1), pp. 134–37. **[G: U.S.]**

Rosegger, Gerhard. Adjustment through Piecemeal Innovation—The U.S. Experience. **In** *Goldberg, W. H., ed.*, 1986, pp. 307–37. **[G: U.S.]**

Roseveare, R. W. Public Enterprise: Studies in Organisational Structure: British Steel Corporation. **In** *Ramanadham, V. V., ed.*, 1986, pp. 21–50. **[G: U.K.]**

Roth, Timothy P. Antitrust Policy and the Rationalization of the U.S. Steel Industry. *J. Inst. Theoretical Econ.*, March 1986, *142*(1), pp. 114–30. **[G: U.S.]**

Schneider, Hans K. Steel Crisis: Consequences of the European Steel Policy after World War II. *J. Inst. Theoretical Econ.*, March 1986, *142*(1), pp. 138–51. **[G: W. Europe]**

Schröter, Lutz. "Steelworks Now!" The Conflicting Character of Modernisation: A Case Study of Hoesch in Dortmund. **In** *Goldberg, W. H., ed.*, 1986, pp. 361–408. **[G: W. Germany]**

Scott, Kenneth E. European Steel Policy after World War II: Comment. *J. Inst. Theoretical Econ.*, March 1986, *142*(1), pp. 152–55. **[G: W. Europe]**

Siebert, Horst. Steel Crisis: Consequences of the European Steel Policy after World War II: Closing Costs in Ailing Industries: Comment. *J. Inst. Theoretical Econ.*, March 1986, *142*(1), pp. 156–62. **[G: W. Europe]**

Sláma, Jiří. Verbreitung von Innovationen im internationalen Vergleich Dargestellt am Beispiel der Oxygenstahlerzeugung. **In** *Altmann, F.-L., ed.*, 1986, pp. 101–29. **[G: OECD; CMEA]**

Takano, Hiroshi and Horie, Shigeyashi. Responsibilities of the Steel Industry of Industrialised Countries: The Case of Japan. **In** *Goldberg, W. H., ed.*, 1986, pp. 445–59. **[G: Japan]**

Taniura, Taeko. Economic Development Effects of an Integrated Iron and Steel Works: A Case Study of Minas Gerais Steel in Brazil. *Devel. Econ.*, June 1986, *24*(2), pp. 169–93. **[G: Brazil]**

Teräsvirta, Timo. Model Selection Using Business Survey Data: Forecasting the Output of the Finnish Metal and Engineering Industries. *Int. J. Forecasting,* 1986, *2*(2), pp. 191–200. **[G: Finland]**

Tolliday, Steven. Steel and Rationalization Policies, 1918–1950. **In** *Elbaum, B. and Lazonick, W., eds.,* 1986, pp. 82–108. **[G: U.K.]**

Tollison, Robert D. Antitrust Policy and the Rationalization of the U.S. Steel Industry: Comment. *J. Inst. Theoretical Econ.,* March 1986, *142*(1), pp. 131–33. **[G: U.S.]**

Tsurumi, Hiroki; Wago, Hajime and Ilmakunnas, Pekka. Gradual Switching Multivariate Regression Models with Stochastic Cross-Equational Constraints and an Application to the *KLEM* Translog Production Model. *J. Econometrics,* April 1986, *31*(3), pp. 235–53. **[G: Japan]**

Wienert, Helmut. On the Development of Steel Consumption in Highly Industrialised Countries: The Case of the United States of America. **In** *Goldberg, W. H., ed.,* 1986, pp. 95–105. **[G: U.S.]**

6313 Machinery (tools, electrical equipment, computers, communication equipment, and appliances)

Adler, Emanuel. Ideological "Guerrillas" and the Quest for Technological Autonomy: Brazil's Domestic Computer Industry. *Int. Organ.,* Summer 1986, *40*(3), pp. 673–705. **[G: Brazil]**

Aftab, Khalid and Rahim, Eric. The Emergence of a Small-Scale Engineering Sector: The Case of Tubewell Production in the Pakistan Punjab. *J. Devel. Stud.,* October 1986, *23*(1), pp. 60–76. **[G: Pakistan]**

Alic, John A. and Harris, Martha Caldwell. Employment Lessons from the Electronics Industry. *Mon. Lab. Rev.,* February 1986, *109*(2), pp. 27–36. **[G: U.S.]**

Almon, Clopper. Investment in Input–Output Models and the Treatment of Secondary Products. **In** *Sohn, I., ed.,* 1986, *1970,* pp. 285–94. **[G: U.S.]**

Amsden, Alice H. and Kim, Linsu. A Technological Perspective on the General Machinery Industry in the Republic of Korea. **In** *Fransman, M., ed.,* 1986, pp. 93–123. **[G: S. Korea]**

Arnold, Erik and Senker, Peter. Computer-Aided Design: Europe's Role and American Technology. **In** *Sharp, M., ed.,* 1986, pp. 10–45. **[G: W. Europe; U.S.]**

Borrus, Michael and Zysman, John. National Policies for Developing High Technology Industries: International Comparisons: Japan. **In** *Rushing, F. W. and Brown, C. G., eds.,* 1986, pp. 111–42. **[G: Japan]**

Bouman, Huub and Verhoef, Bram. High-technology and Employment: Some Information on the Netherlands. **In** *Nijkamp, P., ed. (II),* 1986, pp. 289–98. **[G: Netherlands]**

Boyle, Fosten A. An Evolving Process of Participation: Honeywell and Teamsters Local 1145. **In** *Rosow, J. M., ed.,* 1986, pp. 146–68. **[G: U.S.]**

Brickman, Ronald. National Policies for Developing High Technology Industries: International Comparisons: France. **In** *Rushing, F. W. and Brown, C. G., eds.,* 1986, pp. 71–87. **[G: France; OECD]**

Brock, Gerald W. The Computer Industry. **In** *Adams, W., ed.,* 1986, pp. 239–60. **[G: U.S.]**

Broder, Albert. The Multinationalisation of the French Electrical Industry 1880–1914: Dependence and Its Causes. **In** *Hertner, P. and Jones, G., eds.,* 1986, pp. 169–91. **[G: France]**

Cain, Louis P. How Public Works Saved Private Enterprise: The Thomas & Betts Company in the Great Depression. **In** *Atack, J., ed.,* 1986, pp. 29–40. **[G: U.S.]**

Cartwright, David W. Improved Deflation of Purchases of Computers. *Surv. Curr. Bus.,* March 1986, *66*(3), pp. 7–10. **[G: U.S.]**

Cave, Martin. Computers in Soviet Management, 1963–1984. **In** *Altmann, F.-L., ed.,* 1986, pp. 133–50. **[G: U.S.S.R.]**

Chen, Tain-Jy and Tang, De-Piao. The Production Characteristics of Multinational Firms and the Effects of Tax Incentives: The Case of Taiwan's Electronics Industry. *J. Devel. Econ.,* November 1986, *24*(1), pp. 119–29. **[G: Taiwan]**

Chokki, Toshiaki. A History of the Machine Tool Industry in Japan. **In** *Fransman, M., ed.,* 1986, pp. 124–52. **[G: Japan]**

Chudnovsky, Daniel. The Entry into the Design and Production of Complex Capital Goods: The Experiences of Brazil, India and South Korea. **In** *Fransman, M., ed.,* 1986, pp. 54–92. **[G: S. Korea; Brazil; India]**

Cole, Rosanne, et al. Quality-adjusted Price Indexes for Computer Processors and Selected Peripheral Equipment. *Surv. Curr. Bus.,* January 1986, *66*(1), pp. 41–50. **[G: U.S.]**

Cole, Sam. The Global Impact of Information Technology. *World Devel.,* Oct./Nov. 1986, *14*(10/11), pp. 1277–92. **[G: Global]**

De Bondt, R., et al. The Computer Industry in Belgium. *Tijdschrift Econ. Manage.,* 1986, *31*(2), pp. 227–56. **[G: Belgium]**

Eads, George C. and Nelson, Richard R. Japanese High Technology Policy: What Lessons for the United States? **In** *Patrick, H., ed.,* 1986, pp. 243–69. **[G: U.S.; Japan]**

Engelbrecht, Hans-Jürgen. The Japanese Information Economy: Its Quantification and Analysis in a Macroeconomic Framework (with Comparisons to the U.S.). *Info. Econ. Policy,* December 1986, *2*(4), pp. 277–306. **[G: Japan; U.S.]**

Erber, Fabio Stefano. The Capital Goods Industry and the Dynamics of Economic Development in LDCs: The Case of Brazil. **In** *Fransman, M., ed.,* 1986, pp. 215–45. **[G: Brazil]**

Evans, Peter B. State, Capital, and the Transformation of Dependence: The Brazilian Computer Case. *World Devel.,* July 1986, *14*(7), pp. 791–808. **[G: Brazil]**

Finan, William F. and Amundsen, Chris B. Modeling U.S.–Japan Competition in Semiconductors. *J. Policy Modeling,* Fall 1986, *8*(3), pp. 305–26. **[G: U.S.; Japan]**

Fong, Glenn R. The Potential for Industrial Policy: Lessons from the Very High Speed Integrated Circuit Program. *J. Policy Anal. Manage.*, Winter 1986, *5*(2), pp. 264–91. **[G: U.S.]**

Foreman-Peck, James and Manning, Dorothy. Liberalisation as an Industrial Policy: The Case of Telecommunications Manufacturing. *Nat. Westminster Bank Quart. Rev.*, November 1986, pp. 20–33. **[G: U.S.; U.K.]**

Fransman, Martin. International Competitiveness, International Diffusion of Technology and the State: A Case Study from Taiwan and Japan. **In** *Fransman, M., ed.*, 1986, pp. 153–214. **[G: Taiwan; Japan]**

Fransman, Martin. International Competitiveness, Technical Change and the State: The Machine Tool Industry in Taiwan and Japan. *World Devel.*, December 1986, *14*(12), pp. 1375–96. **[G: Taiwan; Japan]**

Frischtak, Claudio R. National Policies for Developing High Technology Industries: International Comparisons: Brazil. **In** *Rushing, F. W. and Brown, C. G., eds.*, 1986, pp. 31–69. **[G: Brazil]**

Gellman, Aaron. U.S. National Policies for High Technology Industries: Some Lessons Learned. **In** *Rushing, F. W. and Brown, C. G., eds.*, 1986, pp. 227–35. **[G: U.S.]**

Gemünden, Hans Georg. "Promoters"—Key Persons for the Development and Marketing of Innovative Industrial Products. **In** *Backhaus, K. and Wilson, D. T., eds.*, 1986, pp. 134–66. **[G: W. Germany]**

Gupta, Amar. National Policies for Developing High Technology Industries: International Comparisons: India. **In** *Rushing, F. W. and Brown, C. G., eds.*, 1986, pp. 89–110. **[G: India]**

Harsh, S. B.; Kuhlmann, F. and Burg, F. Farm Level Information Systems as an Aid to Decision-makers. **In** *Maunder, A. and Renborg, U., eds.*, 1986, pp. 727–33.

Hertner, Peter. Financial Strategies and Adaptation to Foreign Markets: The German Electrotechnical Industry and Its Multinational Activities: 1890s to 1939. **In** *Teichova, A.; Lévy-Leboyer, M. and Nussbaum, H., eds.*, 1986, pp. 145–59. **[G: Germany]**

Hill, Malcolm R. and McKay, Richard. Soviet Product Quality, State Standards and Technical Progress. **In** *Amann, R. and Cooper, J., eds.*, 1986, pp. 94–114. **[G: U.S.S.R.]**

Horn, Ernst-Jürgen; Klodt, Henning and Saunders, Christopher. Advanced Machine Tools: Production, Diffusion and Trade. **In** *Sharp, M., ed.*, 1986, pp. 46–86. **[G: OECD]**

Horwitch, Mel and Sakakibara, Kiyonori. The Changing Strategy–Technology Relationship in Technology-Based Industries: A Comparison of the United States and Japan. **In** *Rosenbloom, R. S., ed.*, 1986, pp. 83–135. **[G: U.S.; Japan]**

Howland, Marie. Cyclical Startups and Closures in Key Industries of America's Cities and Suburbs. **In** *Bergman, E. M., ed.*, 1986, pp. 111–28. **[G: U.S.]**

Hume, John R. and Oglethorpe, Miles. Atlas of Industrializing Britain 1780–1914: Engineering. **In** *Langton, J. and Morris, R. J., eds.*, 1986, pp. 136–39. **[G: U.K.]**

Kang, K. Won and Park, Soong H. Managerial Accounting and Analysis in Multinational Enterprises: GoldStar Electronics. **In** *Holzer, H. P. and Schoenfeld, H.-M. W., eds.*, 1986, pp. 51–71. **[G: S. Korea]**

Keeble, David and Kelly, Timothy. New Firms and High-Technology Industry in the United Kingdom: The Case of Computer Electronics. **In** *Keeble, D. and Wever, E., eds.*, 1986, pp. 75–104. **[G: U.K.]**

Kelly, Deirdre. St. Lucia's Female Electronics Factory Workers: Key Components in an Export-oriented Industrialization Strategy. *World Devel.*, July 1986, *14*(7), pp. 823–38. **[G: St. Lucia]**

Kubát, Milan. At the Turn of Five-Year Plans. *Czech. Econ. Digest.*, January 1986, (1), pp. 13–21. **[G: Czechoslovakia]**

Lalor, Sean Eamon. Overview of the Micro-electronics Industry in Selected Developing Countries. *Industry Devel.*, 1986, (16), pp. 23–58. **[G: LDCs]**

Lambrecht, Philippe. Agriculture in a Turbulent World Economy: Theoretical Developments: Discussion. **In** *Maunder, A. and Renborg, U., eds.*, 1986, pp. 741–43.

Leahey, Philip J. Skilled Labor and the Rise of the Modern Corporation: The Case of the Electrical Industry. *Labor Hist.*, Winter 1985-86, *27*(1), pp. 31–53. **[G: U.S.]**

Łebkowski, Maciej and Monkiewicz, Jan. Information Industries in the CMEA Countries: A Foreign Trade Dimension. *Konjunkturpolitik*, 1986, *32*(5), pp. 308–24. **[G: CMEA]**

Levačić, Rosalind. Government Policies towards the Consumer Electronics Industry and Their Effects: A Comparison of Britain and France. **In** *Hall, G., ed.*, 1986, pp. 227–44. **[G: U.K.; France]**

Lewis, Jacqueline A. and Armstrong, Kathleen M. Skill Shortages and Recruitment Problems in West Midlands Engineering Industry. *Nat. Westminster Bank Quart. Rev.*, November 1986, pp. 45–57. **[G: U.K.]**

Macharzina, Klaus. The European Microelectronics Industry and New Technologies. **In** *Macharzina, K. and Staehle, W. H., eds.*, 1986, pp. 241–56. **[G: W. Europe]**

Matthews, Ron. Technological Dynamism in India and Japan: The Case of Machine-Tool Manufacture. **In** *Baark, E. and Jamison, A., eds.*, 1986, pp. 142–204. **[G: India; Japan]**

Megheşan, V.; Costake, D. and Marsanu, M. Prospects of the Development in the Calculation Technique Industry in Relation to the Demands of the Improvement of Planning and of Economic and Social System Management. *Econ. Computat. Cybern. Stud. Res.*, 1986, *21*(1), pp. 39–46. **[G: Romania]**

Mendel, Julius S. The Effect of Exchange Rate Depreciation on the Metal and Engineering Industry. *Econ. Rec.*, Supplement 1986, pp. 89–93. **[G: Australia]**

Miller, Debra Lynn. National Policies for Developing High Technology Industries: International Comparisons: Mexico. **In** *Rushing, F. W. and Brown, C. G., eds.*, 1986, pp. 173–99. **[G: Mexico]**

Moore, Gordon E. Entrepreneurship and Innovation: The Electronics Industry. **In** *Landau, R. and Rosenberg, N., eds.*, 1986, pp. 423–27. **[G: U.S.]**

Moses, Frederick, A. and Pugel, Thomas A. Foreign Direct Investment in the United States: The Electronics Industries. **In** *Gray, H. P., ed.*, 1986, pp. 111–61. **[G: U.S.]**

Norman, David A. Impact of Entrepreneurship and Innovation on the Distribution of Personal Computers. **In** *Landau, R. and Rosenberg, N., eds.*, 1986, pp. 437–39. **[G: U.S.]**

Palterovich, D. M. Machine Motors and Economic Motors. *Prob. Econ.*, April 1986, *28*(12), pp. 3–22. **[G: U.S.S.R.]**

Roach, Stephen S. Macrorealities of the Information Economy. **In** *Landau, R. and Rosenberg, N., eds.*, 1986, pp. 93–103. **[G: U.S.]**

Rothwell, Roy. The Role of Small Firms in the Emergence of New Technologies. **In** *Freeman, C., ed.*, 1986, pp. 231–48. **[G: U.K.; U.S.]**

Saxonhouse, Gary R. The National Security Clause of the Trade Expansion Act of 1962: Import Competition and the Machine Tool Industry. **In** *Saxonhouse, G. R. and Yamamura, K., eds.*, 1986, pp. 218–37. **[G: U.S.]**

Sayer, Andrew. Industrial Location on a World Scale: The Case of the Semiconductor Industry. **In** *Scott, A. J. and Storper, M., eds.*, 1986, pp. 107–23. **[G: Selected Countries]**

Schiefer, Gerhard. Agriculture in a Turbulent World Economy: Theoretical Developments: Discussion. **In** *Maunder, A. and Renborg, U., eds.*, 1986, pp. 743–45.

Schoenberger, Erica. Competition, Competitive Strategy, and Industrial Change: The Case of Electronic Components. *Econ. Geogr.*, October 1986, *62*(4), pp. 321–33. **[G: Global]**

Schröter, Harm. A Typical Factor of German International Market Strategy: Agreements between the U.S. and German Electrotechnical Industries Up to 1939. **In** *Teichova, A.; Lévy-Leboyer, M. and Nussbaum, H., eds.*, 1986, pp. 160–70. **[G: U.S.; Germany]**

Simon, Denis Fred and Schive, Chi. National Policies for Developing High Technology Industries: International Comparisons: Taiwan. **In** *Rushing, F. W. and Brown, C. G., eds.*, 1986, pp. 201–26.

Snell, Paul. Soviet Microprocessors and Microcomputers. **In** *Amann, R. and Cooper, J., eds.*, 1986, pp. 51–74. **[G: U.S.S.R.]**

Sobell, Vladimir. Technology Flows within COMECON and Channels of Communication. **In** *Amann, R. and Cooper, J., eds.*, 1986, pp. 135–52. **[G: CMEA]**

Sonka, Steven T. Computer-Aided Farm Management Systems: Will the Promise Be Fulfilled? **In** *Maunder, A. and Renborg, U., eds.*, 1986, pp. 717–26.

Stoffaës, Christian. Industrial Policy in the High-Technology Industries. **In** *Adams, W. J. and Stoffaës, C., eds.*, 1986, pp. 36–62. **[G: OECD]**

Sugai, Yoshihiko and Teixeira Filho, A. R. Impact on Farmers' Decision-Making by Farm Management and Computer Sciences in the Turbulent Economy. **In** *Maunder, A. and Renborg, U., eds.*, 1986, pp. 734–41. **[G: Brazil]**

Teräsvirta, Timo. Model Selection Using Business Survey Data: Forecasting the Output of the Finnish Metal and Engineering Industries. *Int. J. Forecasting*, 1986, *2*(2), pp. 191–200. **[G: Finland]**

Triplett, Jack E. The Economic Interpretation of Hedonic Methods. *Surv. Curr. Bus.*, January 1986, *66*(1), pp. 36–40. **[G: U.S.]**

Webber, Douglas, et al. Information Technology and Economic Recovery in Western Europe: The Role of the British, French and West German Governments. *Policy Sci.*, October 1986, *19*(3), pp. 319–46. **[G: U.K.; Japan; W. Germany; U.S.; France]**

Wells, John V. A Behavioral Analysis of Technological Change in the Computer Industry, 1930–1950. *J. Econ. Issues*, June 1986, *20*(2), pp. 533–39. **[G: U.S.]**

Wolf, Bernard M. The Bearing Industry: Rationalization in Europe. **In** *Casson, M., et al.*, 1986, pp. 175–95. **[G: OECD]**

Yamamura, Kozo. Joint Research and Antitrust: Japanese vs. American Strategies. **In** *Patrick, H., ed.*, 1986, pp. 171–209. **[G: U.S.; Japan]**

Yamamura, Kozo and Vandenberg, Jan. Japan's Rapid-Growth Policy on Trial: The Television Case. **In** *Saxonhouse, G. R. and Yamamura, K., eds.*, 1986, pp. 238–83. **[G: U.S.; Japan]**

6314 Transportation Equipment

Adams, Walter and Brock, James W. Corporate Power and Economic Sabotage. *J. Econ. Issues*, December 1986, *20*(4), pp. 919–40. **[G: U.S.]**

Adams, Walter and Brock, James W. The Automobile Industry. **In** *Adams, W., ed.*, 1986, pp. 126–71. **[G: U.S.]**

Atsumi, Naoki. Voluntary Restraint Agreements: The Case of Automobiles and Steel. **In** *Finn, R. B., ed.*, 1986, pp. 39–49. **[G: U.S.; Japan]**

Blanchard, Olivier J. and Melino, Angelo. The Cyclical Behavior of Prices and Quantities: The Case of the Automobile Market. *J. Monet. Econ.*, May 1986, *17*(3), pp. 379–407.

Blankart, Charles B. and Finsinger, Jörg. Regulation-Induced Price Instability in Swiss Motor Car Liability Insurance. **In** *Finsinger, J. and Pauly, M. V., eds.*, 1986, pp. 200–211. **[G: Switzerland]**

Borrus, Michael; Tyson, Laura D'Andrea and Zysman, John. Creating Advantage: How Government Policies Shape International Trade in the Semiconductor Industry. **In** *Krugman,*

P. R., ed., 1986, pp. 91–113. **[G: U.S.; Japan]**

Branson, William H. and Klevorick, Alvin K. Strategic Behavior and Trade Policy. **In** *Krugman, P. R., ed.*, 1986, pp. 241–55. **[G: U.S.]**

Bresnahan, Timothy F. and Salop, Steven C. Quantifying the Competitive Effects of Production Joint Ventures. *Int. J. Ind. Organ.*, June 1986, *4*(2), pp. 155–75. **[G: U.S.]**

Brumlop, Eva and Juergens, Ulrich. Rationalisation and Industrial Relations: A Case Study of Volkswagen. **In** *Jacobi, O., et al., eds. (I)*, 1986, pp. 73–94. **[G: W. Germany]**

Butters, Gerard R. The Impact of Product Recalls on the Wealth of Sellers: Comments. **In** *Ippolito, P. M. and Scheffman, D. T., eds.*, 1986, pp. 411–13. **[G: U.S.]**

Casson, Mark. Foreign Divestment and International Rationalisation: The Sale of Chrysler (UK) to Peugeot. **In** *Coyne, J. and Wright, M., eds.*, 1986, pp. 102–39. **[G: U.K.]**

Church, Roy. The Effects of American Multinationals on the British Motor Industry: 1911–83. **In** *Teichova, A.; Lévy-Leboyer, M. and Nussbaum, H., eds.*, 1986, pp. 116–30. **[G: U.K.]**

Clark, Gordon L. The Crisis of the Midwest Auto Industry. **In** *Scott, A. J. and Storper, M., eds.*, 1986, pp. 127–48. **[G: U.S.]**

Cline, William R. U.S. Trade and Industrial Policy: The Experience of Textiles, Steel, and Automobiles. **In** *Krugman, P. R., ed.*, 1986, pp. 211–39. **[G: U.S.]**

Cossutta, Dario and Grillo, Michele. Excess Capacity, Sunk Costs and Collusion: A Non-cooperative Bargaining Game: Some Considerations on the European Car Industry. *Int. J. Ind. Organ.*, September 1986, *4*(3), pp. 251–70. **[G: W. Europe]**

Cremeans, John E. and Mohr, Michael F. Industry Perspective: The Motor Vehicle Industry—Will the Recovery Last? *Bus. Econ.*, October 1986, *21*(4), pp. 37–42. **[G: Global]**

Cusumano, Michael A. Diversity and Innovation in Japanese Technology Management. **In** *Rosenbloom, R. S., ed.*, 1986, pp. 137–67. **[G: U.S.; Japan]**

Dal Co, Mario. Recenti sviluppi della contrattazione collettiva negli Stati Uniti. (Concession Bargaining in the United States: Auto and Steel Industries. With English summary.) *Econ. Lavoro*, July-Sept. 1986, *20*(3), pp. 97–111. **[G: U.S.]**

Einstein, Marcus E. and Franklin, James C. Computer Manufacturing Enters a New Era of Growth. *Mon. Lab. Rev.*, September 1986, *109*(9), pp. 9–16. **[G: U.S.]**

Ephlin, Donald F. United Auto Workers: Pioneers in Labor–Management Partnership. **In** *Rosow, J. M., ed.*, 1986, pp. 133–45. **[G: U.S.]**

Falvey, Rodney E. and Rogers, Alan J. Fuel Prices, Sales Taxes and Passenger Car Market Shares in New Zealand, 1963–1978. *Econ. Rec.*, March 1986, *62*(176), pp. 52–59. **[G: New Zealand]**

Falvey, Rodney E., et al. Fuel Economy Standards and Automobile Prices. *J. Transp. Econ. Policy*, January 1986, *20*(1), pp. 31–45. **[G: U.S.]**

Foreman-Peck, James. The Motor Industry. **In** *Casson, M., et al.*, 1986, pp. 141–73. **[G: Selected Countries]**

Fraser, Douglas A. A Labor Director Looks at the Board. **In** *Rosow, J. M., ed.*, 1986, pp. 56–72. **[G: U.S.]**

Fridenson, Patrick. The Growth of Multinational Activities in the French Motor Industry, 1890–1979. **In** *Hertner, P. and Jones, G., eds.*, 1986, pp. 157–68. **[G: France]**

Fujimori, Hideo. Industrial Policy and Technology Transfer: A Case Study of Automobile Industry in the Philippines. *Devel. Econ.*, December 1986, *24*(4), pp. 349–67. **[G: Philippines]**

Gardiner, J. Paul. Design Trajectories for Airplanes and Automobiles during the Past Fifty Years. **In** *Freeman, C., ed.*, 1986, pp. 121–42. **[G: OECD]**

Gardiner, J. Paul. Robust and Lean Designs with State-of-the-Art Automotive and Aircraft Examples. **In** *Freeman, C., ed.*, 1986, pp. 143–68. **[G: U.S.; W. Europe; Canada]**

Greene, David L. The Market Share of Diesel Cars in the USA, 1979–83. *Energy Econ.*, January 1986, *8*(1), pp. 13–21. **[G: U.S.]**

Hochmuth, Milton S. The European Aerospace Industry. **In** *Macharzina, K. and Staehle, W. H., eds.*, 1986, pp. 205–25. **[G: U.S.; U.K.; France; W. Germany]**

Howland, Marie. Cyclical Startups and Closures in Key Industries of America's Cities and Suburbs. **In** *Bergman, E. M., ed.*, 1986, pp. 111–28. **[G: U.S.]**

Jarrell, Gregg A. and Peltzman, Sam. The Impact of Product Recalls on the Wealth of Sellers. **In** *Ippolito, P. M. and Scheffman, D. T., eds.*, 1986, pp. 377–409. **[G: U.S.]**

Kahn, James A. Gasoline Prices and the Used Automobile Market: A Rational Expectations Asset Price Approach. *Quart. J. Econ.*, May 1986, *101*(2), pp. 323–39. **[G: U.S.]**

Levačić, Rosalind. Import Penetration and Barriers to Trade: The Case of the UK Television Set Market. *Appl. Econ.*, June 1986, *18*(6), pp. 615–30. **[G: U.K.]**

Levy, Robert A. and Jondrow, James M. The Adjustment of Employment to Technical Change in the Steel and Auto Industries. *J. Bus.*, July 1986, *59*(3), pp. 475–91. **[G: U.S.]**

Lewchuk, W. The Motor Vehicle Industry. **In** *Elbaum, B. and Lazonick, W., eds.*, 1986, pp. 135–61. **[G: U.K.; U.S.]**

Lorenz, Edward and Wilkinson, Frank. The Shipbuilding Industry 1880–1965. **In** *Elbaum, B. and Lazonick, W., eds.*, 1986, pp. 109–34. **[G: U.K.; OECD]**

Mayer, Robert N. and Zick, Cathleen D. Mandating Behavioral or Technological Change: The Case of Auto Safety. *J. Cons. Aff.*, Summer 1986, *20*(1), pp. 1–18. **[G: U.S.]**

McKinney, Joseph A. and Rowley, Keith A. The

Economic Impact of the Japanese Automobile Export Restraint. *Atlantic Econ. J.*, July 1986, *14*(2), pp. 9–15. **[G: Japan; U.S.]**

Moran, Larry R. Motor Vehicles, Model Year 1986. *Surv. Curr. Bus.*, November 1986, *66*(11), pp. 19–22. **[G: U.S.]**

Ohta, Makoto and Griliches, Zvi. Automobile Prices and Quality: Did the Gasoline Price Increases Change Consumer Tastes in the U.S.? *J. Bus. Econ. Statist.*, April 1986, *4*(2), pp. 187–98. **[G: U.S.]**

Perrin-Pelletier, François. Industrial Policy and the Automobile Industry. **In** *Adams, W. J. and Stoffaës, C., eds.*, 1986, pp. 74–81. **[G: France]**

Pruitt, Stephen W.; Reilly, Robert J. and Hoffer, George E. Security Market Anticipation of Consumer Preference Shifts: The Case of Automotive Recalls. *Quart. J. Bus. Econ.*, Autumn 1986, *25*(4), pp. 14–28. **[G: U.S.]**

Rassekh, Farhad. Employment Effects of the Steel Trigger Price Mechanism on the Steel and Motor Vehicle Industries. *Atlantic Econ. J.*, March 1986, *14*(1), pp. 39–49. **[G: U.S.]**

Reynolds, Morgan O. Unions and Jobs: The U.S. Auto Industry. *J. Lab. Res.*, Spring 1986, *7*(2), pp. 103–26. **[G: U.S.]**

Riegle, Donald. American Industrial Policy: Building on the Chrysler Experience. **In** *Adams, W. J. and Stoffaës, C., eds.*, 1986, pp. 175–80. **[G: U.S.]**

Rollier, Matteo. Changes of Industrial Relations at Fiat. **In** *Jacobi, O., et al., eds. (I)*, 1986, pp. 116–33. **[G: Italy]**

Russo, John. Technological Displacement: Strategies of the Global Auto Industry. **In** *Gondolf, E. W.; Marcus, I. M. and Dougherty, J. P., eds.*, 1986, pp. 122–32. **[G: U.S.]**

Scarbrough, Harry. The Politics of Technological Change at British Leyland. **In** *Jacobi, O., et al., eds. (I)*, 1986, pp. 95–115. **[G: U.K.]**

Senauer, Benjamin; Kinsey, Jean and Roe, Terry. Imperfect Mileage Information and Changing Utility: A Model and Survey Results. *J. Cons. Aff.*, Winter 1986, *20*(2), pp. 155–72. **[G: U.S.]**

Slaven, Anthony. Atlas of Industrializing Britain 1780–1914: Shipbuilding. **In** *Langton, J. and Morris, R. J., eds.*, 1986, pp. 132–35. **[G: U.K.]**

Stoney, P. J. M. The Employment Impact of the Merseyside Motor-Vehicle Assembly Industry. **In** *Danson, M., ed.*, 1986, pp. 65–81. **[G: U.K.]**

Stråth, Bo. Redundancy and Solidarity: Tripartite Politics and the Contraction of the West European Shipbuilding Industry. *Cambridge J. Econ.*, June 1986, *10*(2), pp. 147–63. **[G: W. Europe]**

Takacs, Wendy E. and Tanzer, Ellen P. Structural Change in the Demand for Automobiles by Size Class. *Quart. Rev. Econ. Bus.*, Autumn 1986, *26*(3), pp. 48–57. **[G: U.S.]**

Tesař, Vladimír. The Role and Problems of an Enterprise Director in the Czechoslovak Automobile Industry. *Int. Lab. Rev.*, July-Aug. 1986, *125*(4), pp. 435–45. **[G: Czechoslovakia]**

Trimble, William F. The Naval Aircraft Factory, the American Aviation Industry, and Government Competition, 1919–1928. *Bus. Hist. Rev.*, Summer 1986, *60*(2), pp. 175–98. **[G: U.S.]**

Tsurumi, Yoshi. Japanese and European Multinationals in America: A Case of Flexible Corporate Systems. **In** *Macharzina, K. and Staehle, W. H., eds.*, 1986, pp. 23–37. **[G: U.S.]**

Warren, Alfred S. Quality of Work Life at General Motors. **In** *Rosow, J. M., ed.*, 1986, pp. 119–32. **[G: U.S.]**

Watanabe, Susumu. Labour-Saving versus Work-Amplifying Effects of Micro-electronics. *Int. Lab. Rev.*, May-June 1986, *125*(3), pp. 243–59. **[G: W. Europe; U.S.; Japan; Brazil]**

Witt, Stephen F. and Johnson, S. Raymond. An Econometric Model of New-Car Demand in the UK. *Managerial Dec. Econ.*, March 1986, *7*(1), pp. 19–23. **[G: U.K.]**

Yamauchi, Ichizo. Long-range Strategic Planning in Japanese R&D. **In** *Freeman, C., ed.*, 1986, pp. 169–85. **[G: Japan]**

Young, Stephen. European Car Industry. **In** *Macharzina, K. and Staehle, W. H., eds.*, 1986, pp. 147–62. **[G: W. Europe]**

6315 Chemicals, Drugs, Plastics, Ceramics, Glass, Cement, and Rubber

Akridge, Jay T. and Hertel, Thomas W. Multiproduct Cost Relationships for Retail Fertilizer Plants. *Amer. J. Agr. Econ.*, November 1986, *68*(4), pp. 928–38. **[G: U.S.]**

Al-Gharabally, Tewfik. The Petrochemical Industries of the Arab Countries. **In** *El Mallakh, R., ed.*, 1986, pp. 79–89. **[G: Arab Countries]**

Al-Mady, Mohamed H. Economic Factors in the Manufacture of Petrochemicals in Saudi Arabia. **In** *El Mallakh, R., ed.*, 1986, pp. 71–78. **[G: U.S.; Saudi Arabia]**

Balbino, L. R. and Monteiro Marques, M. Fertilizer Pricing Policy in Portugal. **In** *Segura, E. L.; Shetty, Y. T. and Nishimizu, M., eds.*, 1986, pp. 102–08. **[G: Portugal]**

Bawa, H. S. The Pricing of Fertilizers in India. **In** *Segura, E. L.; Shetty, Y. T. and Nishimizu, M., eds.*, 1986, pp. 156–63. **[G: India]**

Berlin, Hans and Jönsson, Bengt. International Dissemination of New Drugs: A Comparative Study of Six Countries. *Managerial Dec. Econ.*, December 1986, *7*(4), pp. 235–42. **[G: W. Europe; U.S.]**

Bisang, Roberto, et al. Insulina y economía política: el difícil arte de la política pública. (With English summary.) *Desarrollo Econ.*, Oct.-Dec. 1986, *26*(103), pp. 369–88. **[G: Argentina]**

Bochkareva, V. K.; Bredikhin, N. P. and Kabanova, T. A. Optimizing the Development and Location of a Group of Interdependent Industries (A Case Study of the Chemical and Petrochemical Industries). *Matekon*, Winter 1986-87, *23*(2), pp. 57–73. **[G: U.S.S.R.]**

Boisot, Max. Industrial Policy and Industrial Culture: The Case of European Petrochemical. **In** *Macharzina, K. and Staehle, W. H., eds.*, 1986, pp. 163–84. **[G: W. Europe]**

Bokhari, Riyaz H. Public Enterprise: Studies in Organisational Structure: National Fertilizer Corporation of Pakistan Limited. **In** *Ramanadham, V. V., ed.*, 1986, pp. 181–210. **[G: Pakistan]**

Brada, Josef C. and Méndez, José A. Foreign Direct Investment in the U.S. Pharmaceutical Industry. **In** *Gray, H. P., ed.*, 1986, pp. 223–60. **[G: U.S.]**

Butters, Gerard R. The Impact of Product Recalls on the Wealth of Sellers: Comments. **In** *Ippolito, P. M. and Scheffman, D. T., eds.*, 1986, pp. 411–13. **[G: U.S.]**

Caselles-Moncho, Antonio. An Empirical Comparison of Cross-Impact Models for Forecasting Sales. *Int. J. Forecasting*, 1986, *2*(3), pp. 295–303. **[G: Spain]**

Castro Forero, Yesid. Fertilizer Pricing in Colombia. **In** *Segura, E. L.; Shetty, Y. T. and Nishimizu, M., eds.*, 1986, pp. 196–200. **[G: Colombia]**

Comanor, William S. The Political Economy of the Pharmaceutical Industry. *J. Econ. Lit.*, September 1986, *24*(3), pp. 1178–1217. **[G: U.S.]**

Conroy, Michael D. The Petrochemical Industry: Restructuring Challenges. **In** *El Mallakh, R., ed.*, 1986, pp. 62–69. **[G: U.S.]**

Coover, H. W. Programmed Innovation—Strategy for Success. **In** *Landau, R. and Rosenberg, N., eds.*, 1986, pp. 399–416. **[G: U.S.]**

Das, Sarojini and Das, Kumar. Cement Industry in India—A Spatio-Economic Analysis. *Indian Econ. J.*, Oct.-Dec. 1986, *34*(2), pp. 18–27. **[G: India]**

Desai, Gunvant M. Growth in Indian Fertilizer Consumption: Price and Non-price Policies. **In** *Segura, E. L.; Shetty, Y. T. and Nishimizu, M., eds.*, 1986, pp. 109–36. **[G: India]**

Dunn, L. F. Work Disutility and Compensating Differentials: Estimation of Factors in the Link between Wages and Firm Size. *Rev. Econ. Statist.*, February 1986, *68*(1), pp. 67–73. **[G: U.S.]**

Ennara, Ragaa El-Hady. Fertilizer Pricing in Egypt. **In** *Segura, E. L.; Shetty, Y. T. and Nishimizu, M., eds.*, 1986, pp. 91–94. **[G: Egypt]**

Etuk, O. E. U. Fertilizer Pricing in Nigeria. **In** *Segura, E. L.; Shetty, Y. T. and Nishimizu, M., eds.*, 1986, pp. 95–101. **[G: Nigeria]**

Evans, Peter B. Generalized Linkages in Industrial Development: A Reexamination of Basic Petrochemicals in Brazil. **In** *[Hirshman, A. O.]*, 1986, pp. 7–26. **[G: Brazil]**

Francois, John. Case Studies of Black Advancement: SA Cyanamid. **In** *Smollan, R., ed.*, 1986, pp. 205–10. **[G: S. Africa]**

French, Michael. Structural Change and Competition in the United States Tire Industry, 1920–1937. *Bus. Hist. Rev.*, Spring 1986, *60*(1), pp. 28–54. **[G: U.S.]**

Gorecki, Paul K. Monopoly, Entry and Predatory Pricing: The Hoffman–La Roche Case. **In** *[Yamey, B.]*, 1986, pp. 159–77. **[G: Canada]**

Gorecki, Paul K. The Importance of Being First: The Case of Prescription Drugs in Canada. *Int. J. Ind. Organ.*, December 1986, *4*(4), pp. 371–95. **[G: Canada]**

Grabowski, Henry G. and Vernon, John. Longer Patents for Lower Imitation Barriers: The 1984 Drug Act. *Amer. Econ. Rev.*, May 1986, *76*(2), pp. 195–98. **[G: U.S.]**

Hartley, Keith; Lavers, R. J. and Maynard, A. K. Regulation and Development Times in the U.K. Pharmaceutical Industry. *Scot. J. Polit. Econ.*, November 1986, *33*(4), pp. 355–69. **[G: U.K.]**

Hauser, John. Theory and Application of Defensive Strategy. **In** *[Dean, J.]*, 1986, pp. 114–39. **[G: U.S.]**

Holmer, Edwin C. The Chemical Industry: Challenges, Risks, and Rewards. **In** *Landau, R. and Rosenberg, N., eds.*, 1986, pp. 417–22. **[G: U.S.]**

Hutter, Michael. Transaction Cost and Communication: A Theory of Institutional Change, Applied to the Case of Patent Law. **In** *von der Schulenburg, J.-M. G. and Skogh, G., eds.*, 1986, pp. 113–29.

Jarrell, Gregg A. and Peltzman, Sam. The Impact of Product Recalls on the Wealth of Sellers. **In** *Ippolito, P. M. and Scheffman, D. T., eds.*, 1986, pp. 377–409. **[G: U.S.]**

Jerala, Tomislav. Fertilizer Pricing in Yugoslavia. **In** *Segura, E. L.; Shetty, Y. T. and Nishimizu, M., eds.*, 1986, pp. 204–18. **[G: Yugoslavia]**

Jeszeck, Charles. Structural Change in CB: The U.S. Tire Industry. *Ind. Relat.*, Fall 1986, *25*(3), pp. 229–47. **[G: U.S.]**

Joglekar, Prafulla and Paterson, Morton L. A Closer Look at the Returns and Risks of Pharmaceutical R&D. *J. Health Econ.*, June 1986, *5*(2), pp. 153–77. **[G: U.S.]**

Karlinger, Janos. Fertilizer Pricing in Hungary. **In** *Segura, E. L.; Shetty, Y. T. and Nishimizu, M., eds.*, 1986, pp. 201–03. **[G: Hungary]**

Kirim, Arman S. Transnational Corporations and Local Capital: Comparative Conduct and Performance in the Turkish Pharmaceutical Industry. *World Devel.*, April 1986, *14*(4), pp. 503–21. **[G: Turkey]**

Lall, Sanjaya. Technological Development and Export Performance in LDCs: Leading Engineering and Chemical Firms in India. *Weltwirtsch. Arch.*, 1986, *122*(1), pp. 80–92. **[G: India]**

Miller, Elwood L. Monsanto Company—Managing Change. **In** *Holzer, H. P. and Schoenfeld, H.-M. W., eds.*, 1986, pp. 31–50. **[G: U.S.]**

Moran, Patrick J. U.S.A.: Recent Developments Relating to the Taxation of International Technology Transfers in the Pharmaceutical Industry. *Bull. Int. Fiscal Doc.*, Apr./May 1986, *40*(4/5), pp. 210–14. **[G: U.S.]**

Mukherjee, S. K. Chemical Technology for Producing Fertilizer Nitrogen in the Year 2000.

In *Swaminathan, M. S. and Sinha, S. K., eds.*, 1986, pp. 227–37.

Narayan, Pratap. Fertilizer Pricing in India. **In** *Segura, E. L.; Shetty, Y. T. and Nishimizu, M., eds.*, 1986, pp. 137–55. **[G: India]**

Niaz, M. Shafi. The Fertilizer Pricing System in Pakistan. **In** *Segura, E. L.; Shetty, Y. T. and Nishimizu, M., eds.*, 1986, pp. 164–84. **[G: Pakistan]**

Niron, Suna. Fertilizer Pricing in Turkey. **In** *Segura, E. L.; Shetty, Y. T. and Nishimizu, M., eds.*, 1986, pp. 219–35. **[G: Turkey]**

Oner, Erhan. Ex-factory Pricing in Turkey. **In** *Segura, E. L.; Shetty, Y. T. and Nishimizu, M., eds.*, 1986, pp. 236–46. **[G: Turkey]**

Plumpe, Gottfried. Industry, Technical Progress and State: The Synthesis of Rubber in Germany 1906–1944/45. **In** *Pohl, H. and Rudolph, B., eds.*, 1986, pp. 97–124. **[G: Germany]**

Ponnamperuma, F. N. Role of Phosphorus in Global Food Production. **In** *Swaminathan, M. S. and Sinha, S. K., eds.*, 1986, pp. 239–65. **[G: Selected Countries]**

Prasad, R. Fertilizer Nitrogen: Requirements and Management. **In** *Swaminathan, M. S. and Sinha, S. K., eds.*, 1986, pp. 199–226. **[G: Global]**

Ramos, Manuel M. The Venezuelan Petrochemical Industry: Present and Plans. **In** *El Mallakh, R., ed.*, 1986, pp. 55–61. **[G: Venezuela]**

Sappington, David E. M. Designing Incentives for Efficient Production in Large-scale Enterprises: The Case of Fertilizer Manufacturers. **In** *Segura, E. L.; Shetty, Y. T. and Nishimizu, M., eds.*, 1986, pp. 69–89. **[G: Egypt; India]**

Schultz, Knud H. and Mattos, Jorge A. S. Fertilizer Pricing in Brazil. **In** *Segura, E. L.; Shetty, Y. T. and Nishimizu, M., eds.*, 1986, pp. 185–95. **[G: Brazil]**

Schut, Frederick T. and van Bergeijk, Peter A. G. International Price Discrimination: The Pharmaceutical Industry. *World Devel.*, September 1986, *14*(9), pp. 1141–50.

Segura, Edilberto L. Fertilizer Pricing Principles. **In** *Segura, E. L.; Shetty, Y. T. and Nishimizu, M., eds.*, 1986, pp. 22–47.

Segura, Edilberto L.; Shetty, Y. T. and Nishimizu, Mieko. International Seminar on Fertilizer Pricing Policies: Summary of Proceedings. **In** *Segura, E. L.; Shetty, Y. T. and Nishimizu, M., eds.*, 1986, pp. 1–20. **[G: LDCs]**

Sekhon, G. S. Needs and Resources of Potassium. **In** *Swaminathan, M. S. and Sinha, S. K., eds.*, 1986, pp. 267–82. **[G: Global]**

Srinivasan, T. N. Fertilizer Pricing in Developing Countries: A Market-Based Approach. **In** *Segura, E. L.; Shetty, Y. T. and Nishimizu, M., eds.*, 1986, pp. 48–68. **[G: LDCs]**

Veall, Michael R. Time-of-Use Rates and Peak Period Electricity Consumption: An Empirical Note. *Energy Econ.*, October 1986, *8*(4), pp. 257–62. **[G: U.S.]**

Warren, Kenneth. Atlas of Industrializing Britain 1780–1914: Chemicals. **In** *Langton, J. and Morris, R. J., eds.*, 1986, pp. 114–18. **[G: U.K.]**

Wheelwright, Ted. The World Drug Industry. **In** *Wheelwright, T., ed.*, 1986, pp. 89–125. **[G: LDCs]**

Wheelwright, Ted. The World Pesticide Industry. **In** *Wheelwright, T., ed.*, 1986, pp. 127–42. **[G: LDCs]**

Williams, Mansfield. Petrochemicals and Chemicals. **In** *Gray, H. P., ed.*, 1986, pp. 191–221. **[G: U.S.; OECD]**

Wong, Christine P. W. Intermediate Technology for Development: Small-scale Chemical Fertilizer Plants in China. *World Devel.*, Oct./Nov. 1986, *14*(10/11), pp. 1329–46. **[G: China]**

6316 Textiles, Leather, and Clothing

Anderson, Gary M. and Tollison, Robert D. Luddism as Cartel Enforcement. *J. Inst. Theoretical Econ.*, December 1986, *142*(4), pp. 727–38. **[G: U.K.]**

Aw, Bee Yan and Roberts, Mark J. Measuring Quality Change in Quota-Constrained Import Markets: The Case of U.S. Footwear. *J. Int. Econ.*, August 1986, *21*(1/2), pp. 45–60. **[G: U.S.]**

Blaug, Mark. The Productivity of Capital in the Lancashire Cotton Industry during the Nineteenth Century. **In** *Blaug, M.*, 1986, *1961*, pp. 51–87. **[G: U.K.]**

Chao, Kang. The Chinese–American Cotton-Textile Trade, 1830–1930. **In** *May, E. R. and Fairbank, J. K., eds.*, 1986, pp. 103–27. **[G: China; Japan; U.S.; U.K.]**

Cline, William R. U.S. Trade and Industrial Policy: The Experience of Textiles, Steel, and Automobiles. **In** *Krugman, P. R., ed.*, 1986, pp. 211–39. **[G: U.S.]**

Dominique, C.-René. A Practical Way of Assessing Firms' X-Efficiency and Ability to Compete in Mature Good Industries: The Case of Textiles and Apparel. *J. Econ. Devel.*, December 1986, *11*(2), pp. 25–40. **[G: Selected Countries]**

Gewen, Barry. Imports and Apparel: From Riches to Rags. **In** *Schoolman, M. and Magid, A., eds.*, 1986, pp. 53–73. **[G: U.S.]**

Greenaway, David. Estimating the Welfare Effects of Voluntary Export Restraints and Tariffs: An Application to Nonleather Footwear in the UK. *Appl. Econ.*, October 1986, *18*(10), pp. 1065–83. **[G: U.K.]**

Hall, Jacquelyn Dowd; Korstad, Robert and Leloudis, James. Cotton Mill People: Work, Community, and Protest in the Textile South, 1880–1940. *Amer. Hist. Rev.*, April 1986, *91*(2), pp. 245–86. **[G: U.S.]**

Hamilton, Carl. ASEAN Systems for Allocation of Export Licences under VERs. **In** *Findlay, C. and Garnaut, R., eds.*, 1986, pp. 235–47. **[G: ASEAN]**

Huberman, Michael. Invisible Handshakes in Lancashire: Cotton Spinning in the First Half of the Nineteenth Century. *J. Econ. Hist.*, December 1986, *46*(4), pp. 987–98. **[G: U.K.]**

Hughes, John S.; Magat, Wesley A. and Ricks,

William E. The Economic Consequences of the OSHA Cotton Dust Standards: An Analysis of Stock Price Behavior. *J. Law Econ.*, April 1986, *29*(1), pp. 29–59. **[G: U.S.]**

Jefferis, Keith and Thomas, Alan. Conditions for Financial Viability in Workers' Co-operatives: The Case of UK Clothing and Printing Co-ops. *Ann. Pub. Co-op. Econ.*, Jan.-March 1986, *57*(1), pp. 79–102. **[G: U.K.]**

Kibria, M. G. and Tisdell, Clem A. Life-Time Patterns of Capacity Utilization by Manufacturing Firms in an LDC: A Study of Jute Spinning in Bangladesh. *Indian Econ. Rev.*, Jan.-June 1986, *21*(1), pp. 1–19. **[G: Bangladesh]**

Kriedte, Peter. Demographic and Economic Rhythms: The Rise of the Silk Industry in Krefeld in the Eighteenth Century. *J. Europ. Econ. Hist.*, Fall 1986, *15*(2), pp. 259–89. **[G: Germany]**

Langdon, Steven. Industrial Dependence and Export Manufacturing in Kenya. **In** *Ravenhill, J., ed.*, 1986, pp. 181–212. **[G: Kenya]**

Laxton, Paul. Atlas of Industrializing Britain 1780–1914: Textiles. **In** *Langton, J. and Morris, R. J., eds.*, 1986, pp. 106–13. **[G: U.K.]**

Lazonick, William. The Cotton Industry. **In** *Elbaum, B. and Lazonick, W., eds.*, 1986, pp. 18–50. **[G: U.K.]**

Li, Lillian M. The Silk Export Trade and Economic Modernization in China and Japan. **In** *May, E. R. and Fairbank, J. K., eds.*, 1986, pp. 77–99. **[G: China; Japan]**

Mariotti, Sergio and Cainarca, Gian Carlo. The Evolution of Transaction Governance in the Textile–Clothing Industry. *J. Econ. Behav. Organ.*, December 1986, *7*(4), pp. 351–74. **[G: Italy]**

McLewin, Philip J. The Cockroaches of Paterson: A Study of Labor Conflict and Technological Change. *Rev. Radical Polit. Econ.*, Fall 1986, *18*(3), pp. 23–43. **[G: U.S.]**

Minami, Ryoshin and Makino, Fumio. Choice of Technology: A Case Study of the Japanese Cotton Weaving Industry 1902–1938. *Hitotsubashi J. Econ.*, December 1986, *27*(2), pp. 111–32. **[G: Japan]**

Mounfield, P. R. Atlas of Industrializing Britain 1780–1914: Leather Footwear. **In** *Langton, J. and Morris, R. J., eds.*, 1986, pp. 124–26. **[G: U.K.]**

Ono, Akira. Technical Progress in Silk Industry in Prewar Japan—The Types of Borrowed Technology. *Hitotsubashi J. Econ.*, June 1986, *27*(1), pp. 1–10. **[G: Japan]**

Pamuk, Şevket. The Decline and Resistance of Ottoman Cotton Textiles, 1820–1913. *Exploration Econ. Hist.*, April 1986, *23*(2), pp. 205–25. **[G: Turkey]**

Phillips, William H. The Labor Market of Southern Textile Mill Villages: Some Micro Evidence. *Exploration Econ. Hist.*, April 1986, *23*(2), pp. 103–23. **[G: U.S.]**

Read, Robert A. The Synthetic Fibre Industry: Innovation Integration and Market Structure. **In** *Casson, M., et al.*, 1986, pp. 197–223. **[G: Global]**

Reynolds, Bruce L. The East Asian "Textile Cluster" Trade, 1868–1973: A Comparative-Advantage Interpretation. **In** *May, E. R. and Fairbank, J. K., eds.*, 1986, pp. 129–50. **[G: U.S.; U.K.; China; India; Japan]**

Sampson, Gary P. Market Disturbances and the Multifibre Arrangement. **In** *Snape, R. H., ed.*, 1986, pp. 61–87.

Singleton, John. Lancashire's Last Stand: Declining Employment in the British Cotton Industry, 1950–70. *Econ. Hist. Rev., 2nd Ser.*, February 1986, *39*(1), pp. 92–107. **[G: U.K.]**

Thomson, Graeme. Market Disturbances and the Multifibre Arrangement: Comment. **In** *Snape, R. H., ed.*, 1986, pp. 88–92.

de la Torre, José. Corporate Adjustment Strategies in the European Clothing Industry. **In** *Macharzina, K. and Staehle, W. H., eds.*, 1986, pp. 227–39. **[G: W. Europe]**

Truman, Dorothy. The Museum of American Textile History: Archival Sources for Business History. *Bus. Hist. Rev.*, Winter 1986, *60*(4), pp. 641–50. **[G: U.S.]**

Yamauchi, Ichizo. Long-range Strategic Planning in Japanese R&D. **In** *Freeman, C., ed.*, 1986, pp. 169–85. **[G: Japan]**

6317 Forest Products, Lumber, Paper, and Printing and Publishing

Brown, James N. and Ashenfelter, Orley. Testing the Efficiency of Employment Contracts. *J. Polit. Econ.*, Part 2, June 1986, *94*(3), pp. S40–S87. **[G: U.S.]**

Defourny, Jacques. Une analyse financière comparée des coopératives de travailleurs et des entreprises capitalistes en France. (A Comparative Financial Analysis of Workers' Cooperatives and Capitalist Firms in France. With English summary.) *Ann. Pub. Co-op. Econ.*, Jan.-March 1986, *57*(1), pp. 55–78. **[G: France]**

Eike, Ann M. An Investigation of the Market for Paperback Romance Novels. *J. Cult. Econ.*, June 1986, *10*(1), pp. 25–36. **[G: U.S.]**

Georgescu, D. M. Cybernetization and Robotization of the Operating Processes in the Wood and Building Materials Industry. *Econ. Computat. Cybern. Stud. Res.*, 1986, *21*(1), pp. 55–68. **[G: Romania]**

Globerman, Steven and Schwindt, Richard. The Organization of Vertically Related Transactions in the Canadian Forest Products Industries. *J. Econ. Behav. Organ.*, June 1986, *7*(2), pp. 199–212. **[G: Canada]**

Jefferis, Keith and Thomas, Alan. Conditions for Financial Viability in Workers' Co-operatives: The Case of UK Clothing and Printing Co-ops. *Ann. Pub. Co-op. Econ.*, Jan.-March 1986, *57*(1), pp. 79–102. **[G: U.K.]**

Kaltenberg, Michael C. and Buongiorno, Joseph. Growth and Decline of the Paper Industry: An Econometric Analysis of U.S. Regions. *Appl. Econ.*, April 1986, *18*(4), pp. 379–97. **[G: U.S.]**

Lin, Winston T. Analysis of Lumber and Pulpwood Production in a Partial Adjustment

Model with Dynamic and Variable Speeds of Adjustment. *J. Bus. Econ. Statist.*, July 1986, *4*(3), pp. 305–16. **[G: U.S.]**

MaCurdy, Thomas E. and Pencavel, John H. Testing between Competing Models of Wage and Employment Determination in Unionized Markets. *J. Polit. Econ.*, Part 2, June 1986, *94*(3), pp. S3–S39. **[G: U.S.]**

Mickwitz, Gösta. Skogsindustrins aftonrodnad—eller omvandling? (The Forest Industry—Sunset or Restructure? With English summary.) *Ekon. Samfundets Tidskr.*, 1986, *39*(2), pp. 65–68.

Nautiyal, J. C. and Singh, B. K. Long-term Productivity and Factor Demand in the Canadian Pulp and Paper Industry. *Can. J. Agr. Econ.*, March 1986, *34*(1), pp. 21–44. **[G: Canada]**

Norton, Seth W. and Norton, Will, Jr. Economies of Scale and the New Technology of Daily Newspapers: A Survivor Analysis. *Quart. Rev. Econ. Bus.*, Summer 1986, *26*(2), pp. 66–83. **[G: U.S.]**

Pretzer, William S. "The British, Duff Green, the Rats and the Devil": Custom, Capitalism, and Conflict in the Washington Printing Trade, 1834–36. *Labor Hist.*, Winter 1985-86, *27*(1), pp. 5–30. **[G: U.S.]**

Simon, Julian L.; Primeaux, Walter J., Jr. and Rice, Edward. The Price Effects of Monopolistic Ownership in Newspapers. *Antitrust Bull.*, Spring 1986, *31*(1), pp. 113–31. **[G: U.S.]**

Singh, B. K. and Nautiyal, J. C. Adjustment Dynamics of Paper and Paperboard Consumption in Canada. *Can. J. Agr. Econ.*, March 1986, *34*(1), pp. 45–65. **[G: Canada]**

Thompson, R. S. Entry and Market Characteristics: A Logit Study of Newspaper Launching in the Republic of Ireland. *J. Econ. Stud.*, 1986, *13*(2), pp. 14–22. **[G: Ireland]**

6318 Food Processing, Tobacco, and Beverages

Allain, Annelies. The 'Hamburgerisation' of the World. **In** *Wheelwright, T., ed.*, 1986, pp. 183–90.

Armstrong, Donald E. The Sugar Case as a Reason for "Strengthening" the Combines Act: An Economic Perspective. **In** *Block, W., ed.*, 1986, pp. 71–93. **[G: Canada]**

Bivin, David G. Inventories and Interest Rates: A Critique of the Buffer Stock Model. *Amer. Econ. Rev.*, March 1986, *76*(1), pp. 168–76. **[G: U.S.]**

Brown, Martin and Philips, Peter. The Decline of the Piece-Rate System in California Canning: Technological Innovation, Labor Management, and Union Pressure, 1890–1947. *Bus. Hist. Rev.*, Winter 1986, *60*(4), pp. 564–601. **[G: U.S.]**

Brown, Martin and Philips, Peter. The Historical Origin of Job Ladders in the U.S. Canning Industry and Their Effects on the Gender Division of Labour. *Cambridge J. Econ.*, June 1986, *10*(2), pp. 129–45. **[G: U.S.]**

Burns, Malcolm R. Predatory Pricing and Acquisition Cost of Competitors. *J. Polit. Econ.*, April 1986, *94*(2), pp. 266–96. **[G: U.S.]**

Chalmin, Ph. The Strategy of a Multinational in the World Sugar Economy: The Case of Tate and Lyle: 1870–1980. **In** *Teichova, A.; Lévy-Leboyer, M. and Nussbaum, H., eds.*, 1986, pp. 103–15. **[G: Selected Countries]**

Chapman, Simon. The World Tobacco Industry. **In** *Wheelwright, T., ed.*, 1986, pp. 191–227. **[G: LDCs]**

Cochran, Sherman. Commercial Penetration and Economic Imperialism in China: An American Cigarette Company's Entrance into the Market. **In** *May, E. R. and Fairbank, J. K., eds.*, 1986, pp. 151–203. **[G: China]**

Cohen, S. I. Product Prices and Technological Choice: The Case of the International Cocoa Processing Industry. *J. Devel. Stud.*, April 1986, *22*(3), pp. 573–82.

Davis, Gary. Strategic Trading: Rationalisation in U.S. Brewing. **In** *Coyne, J. and Wright, M., eds.*, 1986, pp. 73–101. **[G: U.S.]**

Dias, Guilherme Leite da Silva. Markets and Trade: Discussion. **In** *Maunder, A. and Renborg, U., eds.*, 1986, pp. 577–78.

Dufour, Jean-Claude; Ghersi, Gérard and Saint-Louis, Robert. New Types of Multinational Firms in the Agribusiness Sector: Implications of Their Emergence in the Least Industrialised World. **In** *Maunder, A. and Renborg, U., eds.*, 1986, pp. 566–77.

Elzinga, Kenneth G. The Beer Industry. **In** *Adams, W., ed.*, 1986, pp. 203–38. **[G: U.S.]**

Eussner, Ansgar. Agro-Industrial Co-operation between the European Community and the ACP Countries. *J. Common Market Stud.*, September 1986, *25*(1), pp. 51–73. **[G: EEC; Cameroon; Rwanda]**

Gardella, Robert P. The Boom Years of the Fukien Tea Trade, 1842–1888. **In** *May, E. R. and Fairbank, J. K., eds.*, 1986, pp. 33–75. **[G: U.S.; U.K.; China; Australia]**

Georgianna, Daniel L. and Hogan, William V. Production Costs in Atlantic Fresh Fish Processing. *Marine Resource Econ.*, 1986, *2*(3), pp. 275–92. **[G: U.S.]**

Gisser, Micha. Welfare Implications of Oligopoly in U.S. Food Manufacturing: Reply. *Amer. J. Agr. Econ.*, February 1986, *68*(1), pp. 168–69. **[G: U.S.]**

Godley, Michael R. Bacchus in the East: The Chinese Grape Wine Industry, 1892–1938. *Bus. Hist. Rev.*, Autumn 1986, *60*(3), pp. 383–409. **[G: China]**

Gottfried, Robert R. The Potential Impact of High-Test Molasses from Energy Cane on the Rum Industry of Puerto Rico. *World Devel.*, Oct./Nov. 1986, *14*(10/11), pp. 1347–56. **[G: Puerto Rico]**

Hall, Lana and Sweeney, Jan. Profitability of Mergers in Food Manufacturing. *Appl. Econ.*, July 1986, *18*(7), pp. 709–27. **[G: U.S.]**

Hammer, Tove H. The History of the Rath Buy-out: A Role Expectations Analysis. **In** *Dennis, B. D., ed.*, 1986, pp. 205–13. **[G: U.S.]**

Hao, Yen-p'ing. Chinese Teas to America—A

Synopsis. **In** *May, E. R. and Fairbank, J. K., eds.*, 1986, pp. 11–31. **[G: U.S.; China]**

Hawkins, M. H. and Higginson, N. Marketing Research in the Canadian Food Retail and Processing Industry, 1950–1986. *Can. J. Agr. Econ.*, November 1986, *34*(3), pp. 287–311. **[G: Canada]**

Hazledine, Tim and Cahill, Sean. Welfare Implications of Oligopoly in U.S. Food Manufacturing: Comment. *Amer. J. Agr. Econ.*, February 1986, *68*(1), pp. 165–67. **[G: U.S.]**

Hillberg, Ann Marie. Limiting EC Grain Substitute Imports: A Simulation Model of the West German Manufactured Feed Economy. *Europ. Rev. Agr. Econ.*, 1986, *13*(1), pp. 43–56. **[G: W. Germany]**

Irving, Colin. The "Errors" in Atlantic Sugar et al. V.R. **In** *Block, W., ed.*, 1986, pp. 95–100. **[G: Canada]**

Johar, R. S. and Singh, Tarlok. Determinants of Investment in Liquor Industry in Punjab. *Margin*, October 1986, *19*(1), pp. 59–65. **[G: India]**

Johnson, Douglas A. Confronting Corporate Power: Strategies and Phases of the Nestlé Boycott. **In** *Wheelwright, T., ed.*, 1986, pp. 305–30.

Lee, Jonq-Ying and Brown, Mark G. Economic Effectiveness of Brand Advertising Programmes for U.S. Orange Juice in the European Market: An Error Component Analysis. *J. Agr. Econ.*, September 1986, *37*(3), pp. 385–94. **[G: U.S.]**

MacDonald, James M. Entry and Exit on the Competitive Fringe. *Southern Econ. J.*, January 1986, *52*(3), pp. 640–52. **[G: U.S.]**

Mellor, C. J. and Hessner, Catherine. Structural Change in the Yellow Fats Market. *Appl. Econ.*, June 1986, *18*(6), pp. 663–73. **[G: U.K.]**

Mueller, Willard F. and Culbertson, John D. Inter-industry Technology Flows in the U.S. Food-processing Industries. *Managerial Dec. Econ.*, September 1986, *7*(3), pp. 163–68. **[G: U.S.]**

Nelson, Gerald C. Labor Intensity, Employment Growth and Technical Change: An Example from Starch Processing in Indonesia. *J. Devel. Econ.*, November 1986, *24*(1), pp. 111–17. **[G: Indonesia]**

Opp, Karl-Dieter. The Evolution of a Prisoner's Dilemma in the Market. **In** *[Rapoport, A.]*, 1986, pp. 149–67. **[G: W. Germany]**

Pagoulatos, Emilio and Sorensen, Robert L. What Determines the Elasticity of Industry Demand? *Int. J. Ind. Organ.*, September 1986, *4*(3), pp. 237–50. **[G: U.S.]**

Porter, Robert H. The Impact of Government Policy on the U.S. Cigarette Industry. **In** *Ippolito, P. M. and Scheffman, D. T., eds.*, 1986, pp. 447–81. **[G: U.S.]**

Scheffman, David T. The Impact of Government Policy on the U.S. Cigarette Industry: Comments. **In** *Ippolito, P. M. and Scheffman, D. T., eds.*, 1986, pp. 483–84. **[G: U.S.]**

Schelling, Thomas C. Whose Business Is Good Behavior? **In** *Knowlton, W. and Zeckhauser, R., eds.*, 1986, pp. 153–80. **[G: U.S.]**

Scherer, F. M. The Breakfast Cereal Industry. **In** *Adams, W., ed.*, 1986, pp. 172–202. **[G: U.S.]**

Schmitz, Peter M. Markets and Trade: Discussion. **In** *Maunder, A. and Renborg, U., eds.*, 1986, pp. 578–80.

Termorshuizen, J. G.; Meulenberg, M. T. G. and Wierenga, B. Consumer Behaviour in Respect of Milk in the Netherlands. *Europ. Rev. Agr. Econ.*, 1986, *13*(1), pp. 1–22. **[G: Netherlands]**

Ulrich, Alvin; Furtan, Hartley and Schmitz, Andrew. Public and Private Returns from Joint Venture Research: An Example from Agriculture. *Quart. J. Econ.*, February 1986, *101*(1), pp. 103–29. **[G: Canada]**

Uri, Noel D. The Demand for Beverages and Interbeverage Substitution in the United States. *Bull. Econ. Res.*, January 1986, *38*(1), pp. 77–85. **[G: U.S.]**

Vaez-Zadeh, Reza and Leite, Sergio Pereira. Effectiveness of Selective Credit Controls: An Empirical Test Applied to India. *J. Devel. Stud.*, April 1986, *22*(3), pp. 558–72. **[G: India]**

Weir, R. B. Atlas of Industrializing Britain 1780–1914: Brewing and Distilling. **In** *Langton, J. and Morris, R. J., eds.*, 1986, pp. 119–23. **[G: U.K.]**

Wheelwright, Ted. The World Food Industry. **In** *Wheelwright, T., ed.*, 1986, pp. 143–82. **[G: Global]**

6319 Other Industries

Rimmington, Anthony. Soviet Biotechnology: The Case of Single Cell Protein. **In** *Amann, R. and Cooper, J., eds.*, 1986, pp. 75–93. **[G: U.S.S.R.]**

Saxonhouse, Gary R. Industrial Policy and Factor Markets: Biotechnology in Japan and the United States. **In** *Patrick, H., ed.*, 1986, pp. 97–135. **[G: U.S.; Japan]**

Sharp, Margaret. Biotechnology: Watching and Waiting. **In** *Sharp, M., ed.*, 1986, pp. 161–212. **[G: OECD]**

Swanson, Robert A. Entrepreneurship and Innovation: Biotechnology. **In** *Landau, R. and Rosenberg, N., eds.*, 1986, pp. 429–35. **[G: U.S.]**

632 Industry Studies: Extractive Industries

6320 General

Fraser, R. W. On the Relationship between Exploration and Extraction. *Australian Econ. Pap.*, June 1986, *25*(46), pp. 135–43.

Lucas, Robert E. B. Emigration, Employment, and Accumulation: The Miners of Southern Africa. **In** *Stark, O., ed.*, 1986, pp. 107–38. **[G: S. Africa]**

Martin, Stephen. Causes and Effects of Vertical Integration. *Appl. Econ.*, July 1986, *18*(7), pp. 737–55. **[G: U.S.]**

McDowell, John M. Foreign Direct Investment in U.S. Natural Resource Industries. **In** *Gray, H. P., ed.*, 1986, pp. 261–86. **[G: U.S.]**

6322 Mining (metal, coal, and other nonmetallic minerals)

Amigues, Jean-Pierre and Moreaux, Michel. Gravières et vins de Bordeaux. (Gravel Pits and Bordeaux Wines. With English summary.) *Ann. Écon. Statist.*, Jan./Mar. 1986, (1), pp. 75–105.

Anderson, David L. Marketing Arrangements for Western Canadian Coking Coal. *Can. Public Policy*, September 1986, *12*(3), pp. 473–83. **[G: Canada; Japan]**

Atkinson, Scott E. and Kerkvliet, Joe. Measuring the Multilateral Allocation of Rents: Wyoming Low-Sulfur Coal. *Rand J. Econ.*, Autumn 1986, *17*(3), pp. 416–30. **[G: U.S.]**

Banks, Ferdinand E. Short-term Price Formation in the U.S. Uranium Market: A Comment. *Energy J.*, July 1986, *7*(3), pp. 159–60. **[G: U.S.]**

Bodde, David L.; Quasebarth, Mollie V. and Thomasian, John B. The Economics of Strategic Choice: U.S. Uranium Enrichment in the World Market. *Energy J.*, October 1986, *7*(4), pp. 95–107. **[G: U.S.]**

Boyns, Trevor. Growth in the Coal Industry: The Cases of Powell Duffryn and the Ocean Coal Company, 1864–1913. **In** *Baber, C. and Williams, L. J., eds.*, 1986, pp. 153–70. **[G: U.K.]**

Broadus, J. M. Asian Pacific Marine Minerals and Industry Structure. *Marine Resource Econ.*, 1986, *3*(1), pp. 63–88. **[G: Asia]**

Burington, Bart E. Consumer Coal in Guangzhou: A Case Study of Small-scale Enterprise Organization in China. *Comp. Econ. Stud.*, Winter 1986, *28*(4), pp. 37–59. **[G: China]**

Cairns, Robert D. More on Depletion in the Nickel Industry. *J. Environ. Econ. Manage.*, March 1986, *13*(1), pp. 93–98. **[G: U.S.]**

Cairns, Robert D. and Lasserre, Pierre. Sectoral Supply of Minerals of Varying Quality. *Scand. J. Econ.*, 1986, *88*(4), pp. 605–26.

Carruth, Alan A.; Oswald, Andrew J. and Findlay, Lewis. A Test of a Model of Trade Union Behaviour: The Coal and Steel Industries in Britain. *Oxford Bull. Econ. Statist.*, February 1986, *48*(1), pp. 1–18. **[G: U.K.]**

Chen, Chia-Yon. The Optimal Adjustment to Mineral-supply Disruptions: The Case of Aluminum in Taiwan. *J. Policy Modeling*, Summer 1986, *8*(2), pp. 199–221. **[G: Taiwan]**

Clark, Allen L. and Clark, Jennifer Cook. Marine Metallic Mineral Resources of the Pacific Basin. *Marine Resource Econ.*, 1986, *3*(1), pp. 45–62. **[G: Pacific Basin]**

D'Souza, Amita. A Model of Infrastructural Interlinkages for India. *Indian Econ. Rev.*, July-Dec. 1986, *21*(2), pp. 115–48. **[G: India]**

Dubs, Marne A. Minerals of the Deep Sea: Myth and Reality. **In** *Pontecorvo, G., ed.*, 1986, pp. 85–121. **[G: France; Japan; U.S.S.R.; U.S.; India]**

Fishback, Price V. Did Coal Miners "Owe Their Souls to the Company Store"? Theory and Evidence from the Early 1900s. *J. Econ. Hist.*, December 1986, *46*(4), pp. 1011–29. **[G: U.S.]**

Goss, Barry A. The Forward Pricing Function of the London Metal Exchange. **In** *Goss, B. A., ed.*, 1986, pp. 157–73. **[G: U.K.]**

Gowaskie, Joe. John Mitchell and the Anthracite Mine Workers: Leadership Conservatism and Rank-and-File Militancy. *Labor Hist.*, Winter 1985-86, *27*(1), pp. 54–83. **[G: U.S.]**

Halvorsen, Robert and Smith, Tim R. Substitution Possibilities for Unpriced Natural Resources: Restricted Cost Functions for the Canadian Metal Mining Industry. *Rev. Econ. Statist.*, August 1986, *68*(3), pp. 398–405. **[G: Canada]**

Halvorson, Harold. The British Columbia Coal Industry. **In** *Nemetz, P. N., ed.*, 1986, pp. 293–306. **[G: Canada; Pacific Basin]**

Hennart, Jean-François. The Tin Industry. **In** *Casson, M., et al.*, 1986, pp. 225–73. **[G: Selected Countries]**

Holmes, Graeme. The First World War and Government Coal Control. **In** *Baber, C. and Williams, L. J., eds.*, 1986, pp. 206–21. **[G: U.K.]**

Hyde, Charles K. Undercover and Underground: Labor Spies and Mine Management in the Early Twentieth Century. *Bus. Hist. Rev.*, Spring 1986, *60*(1), pp. 1–27. **[G: U.S.]**

Johnson, Charles J.; Clark, Allen L. and Otto, James M. Pacific Ocean Minerals: The Next Twenty Years. **In** *Nemetz, P. N., ed.*, 1986, pp. 199–222. **[G: Pacific Basin]**

Jones, Patricio. Mining Development and the Origin of Capital. *CEPAL Rev.*, December 1986, (30), pp. 163–72. **[G: Latin America]**

Kenwood, A. G. Fixed Capital Formation in the Ports of the South Wales Coalfield, 1850–1913. **In** *Baber, C. and Williams, L. J., eds.*, 1986, pp. 117–27. **[G: U.K.]**

Kñakal, Jan. The Role of the Public Sector and Transnational Corporations in the Mining Development of Latin America. *CEPAL Rev.*, December 1986, (30), pp. 143–62.

Kolstad, Charles D. and Wolak, Frank A. Conjectural Variation and the Indeterminacy of Duopolistic Equilibria. *Can. J. Econ.*, November 1986, *19*(4), pp. 656–77. **[G: U.S.]**

Nelson, Michael. Technology Transfer in the Mining Sector: Options for the Latin American Mining Organization (OLAMI). *CEPAL Rev.*, December 1986, (30), pp. 137–42. **[G: Latin America]**

O'Faircheallaigh, Ciaran. Mineral Taxation, Mineral Revenues and Mine Investment in Zambia, 1964–83. *Amer. J. Econ. Soc.*, January 1986, *45*(1), pp. 53–67. **[G: Zambia]**

Penny, N. J. H. Migrant Labour and the South African Gold Mining Industry: A Study of Remittances. *S. Afr. J. Econ.*, September 1986, *54*(3), pp. 290–306. **[G: S. Africa]**

Poitras, G. Futures Hedging Policies for the South African Gold Mining Industry. *S. Afr.*

J. Econ., December 1986, *54*(4), pp. 395–405. **[G: S. Africa]**

Queripel, John; Richardson, Neville and Moerdyk, Alwyn. Case Studies of Black Advancement: Rand Mines. **In** *Smollan, R., ed.*, 1986, pp. 218–28. **[G: S. Africa]**

Read, Robert A. The Copper Industry. **In** *Casson, M., et al.*, 1986, pp. 275–315. **[G: Global]**

Rittenberg, Libby and Manuel, Ernest H., Jr. A Case Study of Decline in Labor Productivity: Underground Coal Mining Industry, 1960–1976. *Quart. J. Bus. Econ.*, Winter 1986, *25*(1), pp. 38–55. **[G: U.S.]**

Sanz Guerrero, Rolando. New Objectives for the Development of Mining Resources. *CEPAL Rev.*, December 1986, (30), pp. 173–200. **[G: Latin America]**

Schmitz, Christopher. The Rise of Big Business in the World Copper Industry 1870–1930. *Econ. Hist. Rev., 2nd Ser.*, August 1986, *39*(3), pp. 392–410. **[G: OECD]**

Seibel, Hans Dieter. Achievement Orientation: A Case Study in Multinational Firms in Africa. **In** *Damachi, U. G. and Seibel, H. D., eds.*, 1986, pp. 215–31. **[G: Liberia]**

Siddiqi, Toufiq A. Factors Affecting Steam Coal Trade in Asia and the Pacific. **In** *Nemetz, P. N., ed.*, 1986, pp. 275–92. **[G: Asia; Pacific Basin]**

Sloman, M. Setting up the NCB Enterprise Initiative. *Reg. Stud.*, April 1986, *20*(2), pp. 184–87. **[G: U.K.]**

Solomon, Barry D. and Pyrdol, John J. Delineating Coal Market Regions. *Econ. Geogr.*, April 1986, *62*(2), pp. 109–24. **[G: U.S.]**

Suissa, A. Le nouveau marché international du charbon. (The New International Market for Coal. With English summary.) *Écon. Soc.*, July 1986, *20*(7), pp. 77–93.

Supple, Barry. Ideology or Pragmatism? The Nationalization of Coal, 1916–46. **In** *[Coleman, D. C.]*, 1986, pp. 228–50. **[G: U.K.]**

Symons, M. V. Coal-Mining in the Llanelli Area—Years of Growth, 1800–64. **In** *Baber, C. and Williams, L. J., eds.*, 1986, pp. 53–64. **[G: U.K.]**

Wadehra, B. L. Public Enterprise: Studies in Organisational Structure: Coal India Limited. **In** *Ramanadham, V. V., ed.*, 1986, pp. 211–33. **[G: India]**

Weitz, Eric D. Class Formation and Labor Protest in the Mining Communities of Southern Illinois and the Ruhr, 1890–1925. *Labor Hist.*, Winter 1985-86, *27*(1), pp. 85–105. **[G: U.S.; Germany]**

Weston, C. Rae and McDonnell, Ross. An Analysis of Gold Futures Prices in Large and Small Markets. **In** *Goss, B. A., ed.*, 1986, pp. 175–89. **[G: U.S.; Australia; Canada]**

6323 Oil, Gas, and Other Fuels

Abushihada, Adnan. Arab Gas and the International Market. **In** *Stevens, P., ed.*, 1986, pp. 107–44. **[G: OPEC]**

Adelman, M. A. Lessons from the 1986 Oil Price Collapse: Comments. *Brookings Pap. Econ. Act.*, 1986, (2), pp. 272–76. **[G: OPEC]**

Adelman, M. A. Scarcity and World Oil Prices. *Rev. Econ. Statist.*, August 1986, *68*(3), pp. 387–97. **[G: U.S.; Saudi Arabia]**

Adelman, M. A. The Competitive Floor to World Oil Prices. *Energy J.*, October 1986, *7*(4), pp. 9–31. **[G: U.S.; U.K.; OPEC]**

Ager-Hanssen, Henrik. The Future of Norwegian Gas. **In** *Stevens, P., ed.*, 1986, pp. 34–47. **[G: Norway]**

Ahmadian, Majid. Oil Pricing Policies and Macroeconomy for an Oil-Based Economy. *Energy Econ.*, October 1986, *8*(4), pp. 251–56.

Al-Gharabally, Tewfik. The Petrochemical Industries of the Arab Countries. **In** *El Mallakh, R., ed.*, 1986, pp. 79–89. **[G: Arab Countries]**

Al-Mady, Mohamed H. Economic Factors in the Manufacture of Petrochemicals in Saudi Arabia. **In** *El Mallakh, R., ed.*, 1986, pp. 71–78. **[G: U.S.; Saudi Arabia]**

Al-Sahlawi, Mohammed A. Saudi and Gulf Cooperation Council Oil Supply: An Econometric Analysis. *J. Energy Devel.*, Spring 1986, *11*(2), pp. 263–72. **[G: Saudi Arabia; Kuwait; United Arab Emirates; Qatar]**

Amuzegar, Jahangir. The Oil Price Turmoil. *Finance Develop.*, June 1986, *23*(2), pp. 14–15. **[G: Global]**

Anders, Gary C. Oil, Economic Dependence, and Alaska's Development. *J. Energy Devel.*, Spring 1986, *11*(2), pp. 243–61. **[G: U.S.]**

de Araújo, João Lizardo and Ghirardi, André. Substituiçao de derivados do petróleo no Brasil: questoes urgentes. (With English summary.) *Pesquisa Planejamento Econ.*, December 1986, *16*(3), pp. 745–71. **[G: Brazil]**

Barrett, Scott A. The Economics of Oil Supply Dynamics: Theory and Practice. *Energy Econ.*, October 1986, *8*(4), pp. 237–50. **[G: Canada]**

Beltramo, Mark A.; Manne, Alan S. and Weyant, John P. A North American Gas Trade Model (GTM). *Energy J.*, July 1986, *7*(3), pp. 15–32. **[G: U.S.; Canada; Mexico]**

Bochkareva, V. K.; Bredikhin, N. P. and Kabanova, T. A. Optimizing the Development and Location of a Group of Interdependent Industries (A Case Study of the Chemical and Petrochemical Industries). *Matekon*, Winter 1986-87, *23*(2), pp. 57–73. **[G: U.S.S.R.]**

Bourcier, Philippe and Shirazi, Mohsen. Natural Gas: An Important but Underexploited Resource. *Finance Develop.*, June 1986, *23*(2), pp. 8–11.

Braeutigam, Ronald R. and Hubbard, R. Glenn. Natural Gas: The Regulatory Transition. **In** *Weiss, L. W. and Klass, M. W., eds.*, 1986, pp. 137–68. **[G: U.S.]**

Brierley, C. W. UK Gas Prospects. **In** *Stevens, P., ed.*, 1986, pp. 48–70. **[G: U.K.]**

Broadman, Harry G. Elements of Market Power in the Natural Gas Pipeline Industry. *Energy J.*, January 1986, *7*(1), pp. 119–38. **[G: U.S.]**

Brown, Stephen P. A. and Phillips, Keith R. Exchange Rates and World Oil Prices. *Fed. Res.*

Bank Dallas Econ. Rev., March 1986, pp. 1–10. [G: U.S.; Global]

Cadieux, François. Western Technology and Early Russian Pipelines, 1877–1917. *J. Europ. Econ. Hist.*, Fall 1986, *15*(2), pp. 335–44. [G: U.S.S.R.]

Carrié, Jean. World Surplus of Crude-Oil Primary Refining Capacity. **In** *El Mallakh, R., ed.*, 1986, pp. 19–27. [G: Global]

de Castro, Newton. Produção, distribuição e consumo: determinantes da demanda derivada por transporte e energia. (With English summary.) *Pesquisa Planejamento Econ.*, December 1986, *16*(3), pp. 713–44. [G: Brazil]

Chen, Yikun. China's Petroleum Refining and Petrochemical Industry in Progress. **In** *El Mallakh, R., ed.*, 1986, pp. 101–15. [G: China]

Cheng, Chu-yuan. The United States Petroleum Trade with China, 1876–1949. **In** *May, E. R. and Fairbank, J. K., eds.*, 1986, pp. 205–33. [G: U.S.; China]

Conroy, Michael D. The Petrochemical Industry: Restructuring Challenges. **In** *El Mallakh, R., ed.*, 1986, pp. 62–69. [G: U.S.]

Cook, P. Lesley. The Offshore Supplies Industry: Fast, Continuous and Incremental Change. **In** *Sharp, M., ed.*, 1986, pp. 213–62. [G: U.K.; France; Norway; Netherlands]

Czerniejewicz, Wilfried. Natural Gas in the Federal Republic of Germany: Facts and Prospects. *J. Energy Devel.*, Spring 1986, *11*(2), pp. 301–09. [G: W. Germany]

Dahl, Carol A. Gasoline Demand Survey. *Energy J.*, January 1986, *7*(1), pp. 67–82. [G: U.S.]

David, Frédéric. Le commerce international de produits pétroliers. (International Trade of Petroleum Products. With English summary.) *Écon. Soc.*, July 1986, *20*(7), pp. 95–113.

Dewes, John W. The Changing Petroleum Products Market: An Industry View. **In** *El Mallakh, R., ed.*, 1986, pp. 9–18. [G: Pacific Basin]

Dreyer, P. Importations gaziéres et commerce extérieur. (Gas Imports and Foreign Trade. With English summary.) *Écon. Soc.*, July 1986, *20*(7), pp. 63–76. [G: France]

Drollas, Leonidas P. The Search for Oil in the USA: An Econometric Approach. *Energy Econ.*, July 1986, *8*(3), pp. 155–64. [G: U.S.]

El Atta, Laila Hamed Abou. Egypt: A Profile of the Refining and Petrochemical Industry. **In** *El Mallakh, R., ed.*, 1986, pp. 91–100. [G: Egypt]

Eubanks, Larry S. and Mueller, Michael J. An Economic Analysis of Oklahoma's Oil and Gas Forced Pooling Law. *Natural Res. J.*, Summer 1986, *26*(3), pp. 469–91. [G: U.S.]

Evans, Peter B. Generalized Linkages in Industrial Development: A Reexamination of Basic Petrochemicals in Brazil. **In** *[Hirshman, A. O.]*, 1986, pp. 7–26. [G: Brazil]

Farmer, Richard D. Problems and Lessons in Estimating Supply Curves for Refined Petroleum Products. *J. Energy Devel.*, Autumn 1986, *12*(1), pp. 27–42. [G: U.S.]

Fieleke, Norman S. The Decline of the Oil Cartel. *New Eng. Econ. Rev.*, July/Aug. 1986, pp. 32–41. [G: OECD; OPEC]

Gately, Dermot. Lessons from the 1986 Oil Price Collapse. *Brookings Pap. Econ. Act.*, 1986, (2), pp. 237–71. [G: OPEC]

Griffin, James M. Lessons from the 1986 Oil Price Collapse: Comments. *Brookings Pap. Econ. Act.*, 1986, (2), pp. 276–82. [G: OPEC]

Griffin, James M. and Jones, Clifton T. Falling Oil Prices: Where Is the Floor? *Energy J.*, October 1986, *7*(4), pp. 37–50. [G: U.S.]

Haglund, David G. Protectionism and National Security: The Case of Canadian Uranium Exports to the United States. *Can. Public Policy*, September 1986, *12*(3), pp. 459–72. [G: U.S.; Canada]

Hall, Jane V. Financial Fragility and Restructuring of the U.S. Petroleum Industry. *Econ. Forum*, Winter 1986-1987, *16*(1), pp. 69–80. [G: U.S.]

Hall, Stephen G.; Henry, S. G. B. and Herbert, Rhys. Oil Prices and the Economy. *Nat. Inst. Econ. Rev.*, May 1986, (116), pp. 38–44. [G: U.K.]

Harris, A. H., et al. Who Gains from Structural Change? The Distribution of the Benefits of Oil in Aberdeen. *Urban Stud.*, August 1986, *23*(4), pp. 271–83. [G: U.K.]

Hawdon, David. The Economics of the Natural Gas Market and Its Competitiveness. **In** *Stevens, P., ed.*, 1986, pp. 14–33. [G: Selected Countries]

Helliwell, John F., et al. The Western Accord and Lower World Oil Prices. *Can. Public Policy*, June 1986, *12*(2), pp. 341–55. [G: Canada]

Herbert, John H. Data Analysis, Specification, and Estimation of an Aggregate Relationship for Sales of Natural Gas per Customer. *J. Econ. Soc. Meas.*, October 1986, *14*(3), pp. 165–74.

Hoffman, Elizabeth and Marsden, James R. Testing Informational Assumptions in Common Value Bidding Models. *Scand. J. Econ.*, 1986, *88*(4), pp. 627–41. [G: U.S.]

Hubbard, R. Glenn. Supply Shocks and Price Adjustment in the World Oil Market. *Quart. J. Econ.*, February 1986, *101*(1), pp. 85–102. [G: Global]

Hubbard, R. Glenn and Weiner, Robert J. Petroleum Regulation and Public Policy. **In** *Weiss, L. W. and Klass, M. W., eds.*, 1986, pp. 105–36. [G: U.S.]

Hubbard, R. Glenn and Weiner, Robert J. Regulation and Long-term Contracting in U.S. Natural Gas Markets. *J. Ind. Econ.*, September 1986, *35*(1), pp. 71–79. [G: U.S.]

Ionescu, V., et al. Model for Establishing the Competitiveness of the "SPOT" Lots in Crude Oil Imports. *Econ. Computat. Cybern. Stud. Res.*, 1986, *21*(3), pp. 23–25.

Jorgenson, Dale W. The Oil Price Decline and Economic Growth in Japan and the United States. *Keio Econ. Stud.*, 1986, *23*(1), pp. 1–19. [G: Japan; U.S.]

Kantor, Brian S. and Barr, G. D. I. The Impact of a Change in the Price of Petrol on the South

African Rate of Inflation. *J. Stud. Econ. Econometrics,* November 1986, (26), pp. 35–57. [G: S. Africa]

Kaser, Michael. Soviet Gas Supplies. **In** *Stevens, P., ed.,* 1986, pp. 71–88. [G: U.S.S.R.]

Khoja, Bakr A. Refining History and Priorities in Saudi Arabia. **In** *El Mallakh, R., ed.,* 1986, pp. 117–22. [G: Saudi Arabia]

Kobrin, Paul R. The Cost of OCS Bid Rejection. *Energy J.,* January 1986, *7*(1), pp. 83–97. [G: U.S.]

Kohli, Ulrich and Morey, Edward R. The U.S. Demand for Foreign Crude Oil: A Translog Approach. *J. Energy Devel.,* Autumn 1986, *12*(1), pp. 115–33. [G: U.S.]

Lee, Maw Lin. Nonbudgetary Constraints in Consumer Demand for Gasoline. *Appl. Econ.,* January 1986, *18*(1), pp. 101–12. [G: U.S.]

Lemon, J. Rodney. Regulatory Reform of Interstate Natural Gas Pipelines. *Contemp. Policy Issues,* October 1986, *4*(4), pp. 93–103. [G: U.S.]

Lodwick, Seeley G. The International Trading Environment in Petrochemicals. **In** *El Mallakh, R., ed.,* 1986, pp. 47–54. [G: U.S.]

Lomax, David F. The Investment Implications of China's Offshore Oil Development. *Nat. Westminster Bank Quart. Rev.,* February 1986, pp. 50–69. [G: China]

Lorentsen, Lorents and Roland, Kjell. The World Oil Market (WOM) Model: An Assessment of the Crude Oil Market through 2000. *Energy J.,* January 1986, *7*(1), pp. 23–34. [G: Global]

Lukman, Nasrun and McGlinchey, James M. The Indonesian Petroleum Industry: Current Problems and Future Prospects. *Bull. Indonesian Econ. Stud.,* December 1986, *22*(3), pp. 70–92. [G: Indonesia]

Lumsden, George Quincey, Jr. International Oil Trade through the Strait of of Hormuz. *J. Energy Devel.,* Autumn 1986, *12*(1), pp. 43–48. [G: Global]

Lynk, Edward L. On the Economics of the Oil Refining Industry in the United Kingdom. *Appl. Econ.,* January 1986, *18*(1), pp. 113–26. [G: U.K.]

Lynk, Edward L. and Webb, Michael G. An Unintended Consequence of the Taxation System for U.K. North Sea Oil. *Scot. J. Polit. Econ.,* February 1986, *33*(1), pp. 58–73. [G: U.K.]

Manne, Alan S. and Schrattenholzer, Leo. International Energy Workshop: Oil Price Projections. *Energy J.,* July 1986, *7*(3), pp. 109–14. [G: OECD]

Marshalla, Robert A. and Nesbitt, Dale M. Future World Oil Prices and Production Levels: An Economic Analysis. *Energy J.,* January 1986, *7*(1), pp. 1–22. [G: Global]

Mead, Walter J. The OPEC Cartel Thesis Reexamined: Price Constraints from Oil Substitutes. *J. Energy Devel.,* Spring 1986, *11*(2), pp. 213–42. [G: OPEC]

Mead, Walter J.; Moesidjord, Asbjorn and Sorensen, Philip E. Competition in Outer Shelf Oil and Gas Lease Auctions: A Statistical Analysis of Winning Bids. *Natural Res. J.,* Winter 1986, *26*(1), pp. 95–111. [G: U.S.]

Measday, Walter S. and Martin, Stephen. The Petroleum Industry. **In** *Adams, W., ed.,* 1986, pp. 38–73. [G: U.S.; OPEC]

Morse, Edward L. After the Fall: The Politics of Oil. *Foreign Aff.,* Spring 1986, *64*(4), pp. 792–811.

Mueller, Michael J. and Eubanks, Larry S. Institutional Effects on an In Situ Natural Resource Market: Forced Pooling in a Petroleum Reserves Market. *Southern Econ. J.,* October 1986, *53*(2), pp. 374–92. [G: U.S.]

Mulherin, J. Harold. Complexity in Long-term Contracts: An Analysis of Natural Gas Contractual Provisions. *J. Law, Econ., Organ.,* Spring 1986, *2*(1), pp. 105–17. [G: U.S.]

Mulherin, J. Harold. Specialized Assets, Governmental Regulation, and Organizational Structure in the Natural Gas Industry. *J. Inst. Theoretical Econ.,* September 1986, *142*(3), pp. 528–41. [G: U.S.]

Murphy, Frederic H.; Toman, Michael A. and Weiss, Howard J. An Integrated Analysis of U.S. Oil Security Policies. *Energy J.,* July 1986, *7*(3), pp. 67–82. [G: U.S.]

Norgaard, Richard B. and Leu, Gwo Jiun. Petroleum Accessibility and Drilling Technology: An Analysis of U.S. Development Costs from 1959 to 1978. *Land Econ.,* February 1986, *62*(1), pp. 14–25. [G: U.S.]

Odell, Peter R. Institutional Constraints on the Development of the Western European Natural Gas Market. **In** *Stevens, P., ed.,* 1986, pp. 89–106. [G: W. Europe]

Omorogbe, Yinka. Contractual Forms in the Oil Industry: The Nigerian Experience with Production-Sharing Contracts. *J. World Trade Law,* May:June 1986, *20*(3), pp. 342–49. [G: Nigeria]

Parbhakar, K. J. Fuel Consumption for Road Transport in Quebec. *Energy Econ.,* July 1986, *8*(3), pp. 165–70. [G: Canada]

Price, C. M. Regional Price Discrimination in the United Kingdom Gas Industry. **In** *Norman, G., ed.,* 1986, pp. 165–85. [G: U.K.]

Price, Robert S. Government Policy and International Natural Gas Trade. *J. Energy Devel.,* Spring 1986, *11*(2), pp. 189–211. [G: OECD]

Ramos, Manuel M. The Venezuelan Petrochemical Industry: Present and Plans. **In** *El Mallakh, R., ed.,* 1986, pp. 55–61. [G: Venezuela]

Roberts, John. The Effect of the Oil Price Collapse on the Gulf Cooperation Council Economies. *J. Energy Devel.,* Autumn 1986, *12*(1), pp. 103–14. [G: Middle East]

Rowse, John. Allocation of Canadian Natural Gas to Domestic and Export Markets. *Can. J. Econ.,* August 1986, *19*(3), pp. 417–42. [G: Canada]

Sagers, Matthew J. and Tretyakova, Albina. Constraints in Gas for Oil Substitution in the USSR: The Oil Refining Industry and Gas Storage. *Soviet Econ.,* Jan.-Mar. 1986, *2*(1), pp. 72–94. [G: U.S.S.R.]

Salehi-Isfahani, Djavad. Oil Supply and Economic Development Strategy: A Dynamic Planning Approach. *J. Devel. Econ.*, April 1986, *21*(1), pp. 1–23. **[G: Algeria]**

Salvatore, Dominick. Oil Import Costs and Domestic Inflation in Industrial Countries. *Weltwirtsch. Arch.*, 1986, *122*(2), pp. 281–91. **[G: OECD; LDCs]**

Samuels, Richard J. Miti and the Market: The Japanese Oil Industry in Transition. *Rivista Int. Sci. Econ. Com.*, May 1986, *33*(5), pp. 447–64. **[G: Japan]**

Sathaye, Jayant and Meyers, Stephen. Changes in Oil Demand in Oil-importing Developing Countries: The Case of the Philippines. *Energy J.*, April 1986, *7*(2), pp. 171–79. **[G: Philippines]**

Scanlan, Tony. The Competitive Floor to World Oil Prices: A Comment. *Energy J.*, October 1986, *7*(4), pp. 34–35. **[G: U.S.; U.K.; OPEC]**

Shipman, Ross L. Energy on the U.S.–Mexico Border. *Natural Res. J.*, Fall 1986, *26*(4), pp. 711–16. **[G: U.S.; Mexico]**

Siddayao, Corazon Morales. Petroleum Resources in the Pacific Rim: The Roles Played by Governments in Their Development and Trade. **In** *Nemetz, P. N., ed.*, 1986, pp. 234–74. **[G: Pacific Basin]**

Slade, Margaret E. Exogeneity Tests of Market Boundaries Applied to Petroleum Products. *J. Ind. Econ.*, March 1986, *34*(3), pp. 291–303. **[G: U.S.]**

Solomon, Barry D. The Socioeconomic Impacts of a Regional Synthetic Fuels Industry: An Integrated Econometric Analysis. **In** *Batey, P. W. and Madden, M., eds.*, 1986, pp. 167–86. **[G: U.S.]**

Stalon, Charles G. The Diminishing Role of Regulation in the Natural Gas Industry. *Energy J.*, April 1986, *7*(2), pp. 1–12. **[G: U.S.]**

Stocks, K. J. and Musgrove, A. R. deL. The Value of Australia's Natural Gas Resource—A Linear Programming Analysis. *Energy J.*, April 1986, *7*(2), pp. 91–106. **[G: Australia]**

Strøm, Trygve. Project Financing in the North Sea. *Écon. Soc.*, July 1986, *20*(7), pp. 145–57.

Székely, Alberto. The International Law of Submarine Transboundary Hydrocarbon Resources: Legal Limits to Behavior and Experience for the Gulf of Mexico. *Natural Res. J.*, Fall 1986, *26*(4), pp. 733–68. **[G: U.S.; Mexico]**

Székely, Alberto. Transboundary Oil and Gas: Selected Bibliography. *Natural Res. J.*, Fall 1986, *26*(4), pp. 833–50.

Tahmassebi, Hossein. World Energy Outlook through 2000. *J. Energy Devel.*, Autumn 1986, *12*(1), pp. 1–26. **[G: Global]**

Teece, David J. Assessing the Competition Faced by Oil Pipelines. *Contemp. Policy Issues*, October 1986, *4*(4), pp. 65–78. **[G: U.S.]**

Telson, Michael L. Policy Issues in Oil and Gas Transportation Regulation. *Contemp. Policy Issues*, October 1986, *4*(4), pp. 60–64. **[G: U.S.]**

Tiplitz, Charles. Optimal Seasonal Distillate Inventory. *Energy J.*, July 1986, *7*(3), pp. 83–97. **[G: U.S.]**

Toichi, Tsutomu and Ogawa, Yoshiki. Recent Problems in Japan's Oil Industry. **In** *El Mallakh, R., ed.*, 1986, pp. 129–44. **[G: Japan]**

Tucker, Paul W. The Natural Gas Market: The Cyclical Process. **In** *Stevens, P., ed.*, 1986, pp. 5–13.

Utton, Albert E. and McHugh, Paul D. On an Institutional Arrangement for Developing Oil and Gas in the Gulf of Mexico. *Natural Res. J.*, Fall 1986, *26*(4), pp. 717–32. **[G: U.S.; Mexico]**

Ver Hulst, N. and Laporte, J. M. Le rôle des banques dans les grands projets énergétiques. (The Role of Banks in Big Energetic Projects. With English summary.) *Écon. Soc.*, July 1986, *20*(7), pp. 129–43.

Vergara, Walter; Cordoba, Armando and Somoza, Marcial. Natural Gas as Transport Fuel: Notes on the Case of Colombia. *J. Energy Devel.*, Autumn 1986, *12*(1), pp. 67–83. **[G: Colombia]**

Wilkinson, Jack W. The Competitive Floor to World Oil Prices: A Comment. *Energy J.*, October 1986, *7*(4), pp. 32–33. **[G: U.S.; U.K.; OPEC]**

Williams, Mansfield. Petrochemicals and Chemicals. **In** *Gray, H. P., ed.*, 1986, pp. 191–221. **[G: U.S.; OECD]**

Woods, Thomas J. The Outlook for Gas Supply: Surviving the Short Term. *J. Energy Devel.*, Autumn 1986, *12*(1), pp. 49–66. **[G: U.S.]**

Yu, Ben T. Comparative Productivity of Inventors in Emerging Research Organizations: Some Evidence from the U.S. Petroleum Industry. *Hong Kong Econ. Pap.*, 1986, (17), pp. 11–33. **[G: U.S.]**

Zakariya, Hasan S. Financing Petroleum Development in the Third World: The Role of the Public International Sector. *J. World Trade Law*, July:Aug. 1986, *20*(4), pp. 417–40. **[G: LDCs]**

633 Industry Studies: Distributive Trades

6330 General

Anderson, James C. and Narus, James A. Toward a Better Understanding of Distribution Channel Working Relationships. **In** *Backhaus, K. and Wilson, D. T., eds.*, 1986, pp. 320–36.

Bamossy, Gary J. and Scammon, Debra L. Counterfeiting—A Worldwide Problem: What Is the Role of Channel Members? **In** *Pellegrini, L. and Reddy, S. K., eds.*, 1986, pp. 141–54. **[G: U.S.]**

Bohm, Robert A.; Herzog, Henry W., Jr. and Schlottmann, Alan M. Trade and Service Sector Development in the Rural South: The Case of the Tennessee–Tombigbee Corridor. *Rev. Reg. Stud.*, Spring 1986, *16*(2), pp. 41–49. **[G: U.S.]**

633 Industry Studies: Distributive Trades

Chard, John S. Economic Effects of Exclusive Purchasing Arrangements in the Distribution of Goods. **In** *Pellegrini, L. and Reddy, S. K., eds.*, 1986, pp. 39–57.

Cristini, Guido. Channel Alternatives in the Press Industry: A Comparative Analysis. **In** *Pellegrini, L. and Reddy, S. K., eds.*, 1986, pp. 119–39. **[G: W. Germany; U.K.; France; Italy]**

Darbinian, M. The Population's Demand and Ways of Satisfying It. *Prob. Econ.*, March 1986, *28*(11), pp. 76–91. **[G: U.S.S.R.]**

Douglas, Susan P. Selling in Japan: Consumer Behavior and Distribution as Barriers to Imports: Comment. **In** *Pugel, T. A., ed.*, 1986, pp. 107–13. **[G: U.S.; Japan; W. Germany]**

Grieson, Ronald E. and Singh, Nirvikar. Resale Price Maintenance: A Simple Analysis. **In** *Grieson, R. E., ed.*, 1986, pp. 127–33.

Mornande, Felipe G. Domestic Prices of Importable Goods in Chile and the Law of One Price: 1975–1982. *J. Devel. Econ.*, April 1986, *21*(1), pp. 131–47. **[G: Chile]**

Rangan, V. Kasturi. Relationship Management of Distributors: A Proposed Framework. **In** *Pellegrini, L. and Reddy, S. K., eds.*, 1986, pp. 103–17.

Reve, Torger and Stern, Louis W. The Relationship between Interorganizational Form, Transaction Climate, and Economic Performance in Vertical Interfirm Dyads. **In** *Pellegrini, L. and Reddy, S. K., eds.*, 1986, pp. 75–102. **[G: Norway]**

Wada, Mitsuo. Selling in Japan: Consumer Behavior and Distribution as Barriers to Imports. **In** *Pugel, T. A., ed.*, 1986, pp. 91–105. **[G: U.S.; Japan; W. Germany]**

6332 Wholesale Trade

Feldbæk, Ole. The Danish Trading Companies of the Seventeenth and Eighteenth Centuries. *Scand. Econ. Hist. Rev.*, 1986, *34*(3), pp. 204–18. **[G: Denmark]**

Spiller, Pablo T. and Huang, Cliff J. On the Extent of the Market: Wholesale Gasoline in the Northeastern United States. *J. Ind. Econ.*, December 1986, *35*(2), pp. 131–45. **[G: U.S.]**

6333 Retail Trade

Anderson, Evan E. Image Differentiation and Locational Proximity among Retail Firms. *Managerial Dec. Econ.*, March 1986, *7*(1), pp. 63–68.

Anderson, James E. and Gollop, Frank M. The Effect of Warranty Provisions on Used Car Prices. **In** *Ippolito, P. M. and Scheffman, D. T., eds.*, 1986, pp. 67–102. **[G: U.S.]**

Baden Fuller, C. W. F. Rising Concentration: The UK Grocery Trade 1970–1980. **In** *[Yamey, B.]*, 1986, pp. 63–82. **[G: U.K.]**

Berg, Hartmut. Thesen des Bundeskartellamtes zur "Nachfragemacht" im Lebensmittelhandel: Eine kritische Analyse. (Theses of the Federal Cartel Office Concerning "Buying Power" Positions in German Food Retailing: A Critical Assessment. With English summary.) **In** *Eucken, W. and Böhm, F., eds.*, 1986, pp. 183–200. **[G: W. Germany]**

Böcker, Franz. Handelskonzentration: Ein partielles Phänomen?—oder: Irreführende Handelsstatistiken. (With English summary.) *Z. Betriebswirtshaft*, July 1986, *56*(7), pp. 654–60. **[G: W. Germany]**

Cotterill, Ronald W. Market Power in the Retail Food Industry: Evidence from Vermont. *Rev. Econ. Statist.*, August 1986, *68*(3), pp. 379–86. **[G: U.S.]**

Dahremöller, Axel. Konzentration im Einzelhandel: Eine Fehlinterpretation? (With English summary.) *Z. Betriebswirtshaft*, July 1986, *56*(7), pp. 661–74. **[G: W. Germany]**

Dickson, John P. Locational Interdependency: The Impact of Change on Retail Images. **In** *Pellegrini, L. and Reddy, S. K., eds.*, 1986, pp. 171–81. **[G: U.S.]**

Fox, William F. Tax Structure and the Location of Economic Activity along State Borders. *Nat. Tax J.*, December 1986, *39*(4), pp. 387–401. **[G: U.S.]**

Geurts, Michael D. and Kelly, J. Patrick. Forecasting Retail Sales Using Alternative Models. *Int. J. Forecasting*, 1986, *2*(3), pp. 261–72. **[G: U.S.]**

Ghosh, Avijit and McLafferty, Sara. Shopping Behavior and Optimal Store Locations in Multipurpose Trip Environments. **In** *Pellegrini, L. and Reddy, S. K., eds.*, 1986, pp. 157–70.

Graziani, Augusto. Le commerce comme secteur productif et comme secteur improductif. (Retail Trade as a Productive Sector and as an Unproductive Sector. With English summary.) *Écon. Soc.*, Aug.-Sept. 1986, *20*(8–9), pp. 159–70.

Haining, Robert. Intraurban Retail Price Competition: Corporate and Neighbourhood Aspects of Spatial Price Variation. **In** *Norman, G., ed.*, 1986, pp. 144–64. **[G: U.K.]**

Haugen, Steven E. The Employment Expansion in Retail Trade, 1973–85. *Mon. Lab. Rev.*, August 1986, *109*(8), pp. 9–16. **[G: U.S.]**

Hawkins, M. H. and Higginson, N. Marketing Research in the Canadian Food Retail and Processing Industry, 1950–1986. *Can. J. Agr. Econ.*, November 1986, *34*(3), pp. 287–311. **[G: Canada]**

Hollander, Stanley C. and Sheffet, Mary Jane. The Robinson–Patman Act: Boon or Bane for Retailers? *Antitrust Bull.*, Fall 1986, *31*(3), pp. 759–95. **[G: U.S.]**

Holstius, Karin. Choice of Retailer in Non-equilibrium Competition. *Liiketaloudellinen Aikak.*, 1986, *35*(3), pp. 175–83. **[G: Finland]**

Jaffer, Susan M. and Kay, John A. The Regulation of Shop Opening Hours in the United Kingdom. **In** *von der Schulenburg, J.-M. G. and Skogh, G., eds.*, 1986, pp. 169–83. **[G: U.K.]**

Kelly, J. Patrick and Geurts, Michael D. Increasing the Efficiency of Forecasting Seasonal Demand for Individual Products. **In** *Pellegrini,*

L. and Reddy, S. K., eds.*, 1986, pp. 183–95. **[G: U.S.]**

Langenfeld, James. The Effect of Warranty Provisions on Used Car Prices: Comments. **In** *Ippolito, P. M. and Scheffman, D. T., eds.*, 1986, pp. 105–07. **[G: U.S.]**

Laulajainen, Risto and Gadde, Lars-Erik. Locational Avoidance: A Case Study of Three Swedish Retail Chains. *Reg. Stud.*, April 1986, *20*(2), pp. 131–40. **[G: Sweden]**

Linneman, Peter. Information Technology, Demographics, and the Retail Response: Discussion. **In** *Faulhaber, G.; Noam, E. and Tasley, R., eds.*, 1986, pp. 175–77. **[G: U.S.; OECD]**

Marvel, Howard P. and McCafferty, Stephen. The Political Economy of Resale Price Maintenance. *J. Polit. Econ.*, October 1986, *94*(5), pp. 1074–95. **[G: U.S.]**

Mikesell, John L. Retail Sales and Use Taxation in Minnesota. **In** *Minnesota Tax Study Commission*, 1986, pp. 155–87. **[G: U.S.]**

Moss, Mitchell. Information Technology, Demographics, and the Retail Response: Discussion. **In** *Faulhaber, G.; Noam, E. and Tasley, R., eds.*, 1986, pp. 178–82. **[G: U.S.; OECD]**

Pellegrini, Luca. Sale or Return Agreements versus Outright Sales. **In** *Pellegrini, L. and Reddy, S. K., eds.*, 1986, pp. 59–72.

Ross, Thomas W. Store Wars: The Chain Tax Movement. *J. Law Econ.*, April 1986, *29*(1), pp. 125–37. **[G: U.S.]**

Shaw, Gareth. Atlas of Industrializing Britain 1780–1914: Retail Patterns. **In** *Langton, J. and Morris, R. J., eds.*, 1986, pp. 180–84. **[G: U.K.]**

Silcox, Clark R. and MacIntyre, A. Everette. The Robinson–Patman Act and Competitive Fairness: Balancing the Economic and Social Dimensions of Antitrust. *Antitrust Bull.*, Fall 1986, *31*(3), pp. 611–64. **[G: U.S.]**

Slade, Margaret E. Conjectures, Firm Characteristics, and Market Structure: An Empirical Assessment. *Int. J. Ind. Organ.*, December 1986, *4*(4), pp. 347–69. **[G: Canada]**

Sternlieb, George and Hughes, James W. Information Technology, Demographics, and the Retail Response. **In** *Faulhaber, G.; Noam, E. and Tasley, R., eds.*, 1986, pp. 139–74. **[G: U.S.; OECD]**

Swidler, Steve. A Reexamination of Liquor Price and Consumption Differences between Public and Private Ownership States: Comment [Public versus Private Liquor Retailing: An Investigation into the Behavior of the State Governments]. *Southern Econ. J.*, July 1986, *53*(1), pp. 259–64. **[G: U.S.]**

Swidler, Steve. Consumption and Price Effects of State-run Liquor Monopolies. *Managerial Dec. Econ.*, March 1986, *7*(1), pp. 49–55. **[G: U.S.]**

Thomas, Owen. Ensuring Quality of Service for Sainsbury's Customers. **In** *Moores, B., ed.*, 1986, pp. 156–65. **[G: U.K.]**

Thurik, A. R. and Kleijweg, A. J. M. Procyclical Retail Labour Productivity. *Bull. Econ. Res.*, May 1986, *38*(2), pp. 169–75. **[G: Netherlands]**

Thury, Gerhard. The Consequences of Trading Day Variation and Calendar Effects for ARIMA Model Building and Seasonal Adjustment. *Empirica*, 1986, *13*(1), pp. 3–25. **[G: Austria]**

Van den Bergh, Roger. Belgian Public Policy towards the Retailing Trade. **In** *von der Schulenburg, J.-M. G. and Skogh, G., eds.*, 1986, pp. 185–205. **[G: Belgium]**

Von Hohenbalken, Balder and West, Douglas S. Empirical Tests for Predatory Reputation. *Can. J. Econ.*, February 1986, *19*(1), pp. 160–78. **[G: Canada]**

Voos, Paula B. and Mishel, Lawrence R. The Union Impact on Profits in the Supermarket Industry. *Rev. Econ. Statist.*, August 1986, *68*(3), pp. 513–17. **[G: U.S.]**

Waterson, Michael. The Economics of Vertical Restraints on Retailers. **In** *Norman, G., ed.*, 1986, pp. 125–43.

Zardkoohi, Asghar and Sheer, Alain. A Reexamination of Liquor Price and Consumption Differences between Public and Private Ownership States: Reply [Public versus Private Liquor Retailing: An Investigation into the Behavior of the State Governments]. *Southern Econ. J.*, July 1986, *53*(1), pp. 265–68. **[G: U.S.]**

634 Industry Studies: Construction

6340 Construction

Allen, Steven G. Union Work Rules and Efficiency in the Building Trades. *J. Lab. Econ.*, April 1986, *4*(2), pp. 212–42. **[G: U.S.]**

Allen, Steven G. Unionization and Productivity in Office Building and School Construction. *Ind. Lab. Relat. Rev.*, January 1986, *39*(2), pp. 187–201. **[G: U.S.]**

Aydalot, Philippe. The Location of New Firm Creation: The French Case. **In** *Keeble, D. and Wever, E., eds.*, 1986, pp. 105–23. **[G: France]**

Bajic, Vladimir. Factor Costs and Factor Use: Substitution among Urban Land and Capital Inputs in the Production of Single-Family Housing. *Appl. Econ.*, March 1986, *18*(3), pp. 291–303. **[G: Canada]**

Carliner, Michael S. The Impact of Tax Reform on Housing Demand and Residential Construction Activity. **In** *Follain, J. R., ed.*, 1986, pp. 113–33. **[G: U.S.]**

Falk, Barry. Unanticipated Money-Supply Growth and Single-Family Housing Starts in the U.S.: 1964–1983. *Housing Finance Rev.*, Summer 1986, *5*(1), pp. 15–23. **[G: U.S.]**

Gabriel, Stuart A. and Maoz, Ilan. Cyclical Fluctuations in the Israeli Housing Markets. *J. Urban Econ.*, May 1986, *19*(3), pp. 249–63. **[G: Israel]**

Goodman, John L., Jr. Reducing the Error in Monthly Housing Starts Estimates. *Amer. Real Estate Urban Econ. Assoc. J.*, Winter 1986, *14*(4), pp. 557–66. **[G: U.S.]**

634 Industry Studies: Construction

Lin, Winston T. Modeling and Forecasting U.S. Public Construction. *Int. J. Forecasting,* 1986, *2*(3), pp. 319–31. **[G: U.S.]**

Nourse, Hugh O. Rental Price Adjustment and Investment in the Office Market. *Amer. Real Estate Urban Econ. Assoc. J.,* Spring 1986, *14*(1), pp. 163–64. **[G: U.S.]**

Oshima, Harry T. The Construction Boom of the 1970s: The End of High Growth in the NICs and ASEAN? *Devel. Econ.,* September 1986, *24*(3), pp. 207–28. **[G: LDCs; Asia]**

Quirk, James P. and Terasawa, Katsuaki. Sample Selection and Cost Underestimation Bias in Pioneer Projects. *Land Econ.,* May 1986, *62*(2), pp. 192–200. **[G: U.S.]**

Rose, Joseph B. Legislative Support for Multi-employer Bargaining: The Canadian Experience. *Ind. Lab. Relat. Rev.,* October 1986, *40*(1), pp. 3–18. **[G: Canada]**

635 Industry Studies: Services and Related Industries

6350 General

Bailly, A. S. The Service Sector as a Stimulus to Endogenous Development: The Case of Switzerland. **In** *Bassand, M., et al., eds.,* 1986, pp. 112–22. **[G: Switzerland]**

Barras, Richard. A Comparison of Embodied Technical Change in Services and Manufacturing Industry. *Appl. Econ.,* September 1986, *18*(9), pp. 941–58. **[G: U.K.]**

Baumol, William J. Information Technology and the Service Sector: A Feedback Process? **In** *Faulhaber, G.; Noam, E. and Tasley, R., eds.,* 1986, pp. 183–93. **[G: U.S.]**

Baumol, William J. Services in Transition: The Impact of Information Technology on the Service Sector: Conclusion. **In** *Faulhaber, G.; Noam, E. and Tasley, R., eds.,* 1986, pp. 195–99. **[G: U.S.]**

Bernard, Jean-Thomas; Lessard, François and Thivierge, Simon. La demande d'énergie du secteur commercial quéeécois. (The Energy Demand of the Commercial Sector in Quebec. With English summary.) *L'Actual. Econ.,* March 1986, *62*(1), pp. 5–22. **[G: Canada]**

Bohm, Robert A.; Herzog, Henry W., Jr. and Schlottmann, Alan M. Trade and Service Sector Development in the Rural South: The Case of the Tennessee–Tombigbee Corridor. *Rev. Reg. Stud.,* Spring 1986, *16*(2), pp. 41–49. **[G: U.S.]**

Cazes, Bernard. La polarité biens-services dans une perspective longue. (With English summary.) *Revue Écon. Polit.,* Sept.-Oct. 1986, *96*(5), pp. 456–62.

Cocheba, Donald J.; Gilmer, Robert W. and Mack, Richard S. Causes and Consequences of Slow Growth in the Tennessee Valley's Service Sector. *Growth Change,* January 1986, *17*(1), pp. 51–65. **[G: U.S.]**

Dale, Barrie. Experience with Quality Circles and Quality Costs. **In** *Moores, B., ed.,* 1986, pp. 36–49. **[G: U.K.]**

Epstein, Richard A. Medical Malpractice, Imperfect Information, and the Contractual Foundation for Medical Services. *Law Contemp. Probl.,* Spring 1986, *49*(2), pp. 201–12. **[G: U.S.]**

Fels, Gerhard. The Impact of New Technologies and the Development of Service Industries in the Federal Republic of Germany. **In** *Hax, H.; Kraus, W. and Tsuchiya, K., eds.,* 1986, pp. 115–24. **[G: W. Germany]**

Gallagher, C. C. and Stewart, H. Jobs and the Business Life-Cycle in the UK. *Appl. Econ.,* August 1986, *18*(8), pp. 875–900. **[G: U.K.]**

Gardes, François. La consommation de services en France. (With English summary.) *Revue Écon. Polit.,* Sept.-Oct. 1986, *96*(5), pp. 463–75. **[G: France]**

Howe, Wayne J. The Business Services Industry Sets Pace in Employment Growth. *Mon. Lab. Rev.,* April 1986, *109*(4), pp. 29–36. **[G: U.S.]**

Keil, Stanley R. and Mack, Richard S. Identifying Export Potential in the Service Sector. *Growth Change,* April 1986, *17*(2), pp. 1–10. **[G: U.S.]**

Koshiro, Kazutoshi. The Impact of New Technologies and the Development of Service Industries in Japan. **In** *Hax, H.; Kraus, W. and Tsuchiya, K., eds.,* 1986, pp. 84–114. **[G: Japan; U.S.; U.K.; W. Germany]**

Lane, Chris. Putting People First—A Company-Wide Approach to Good Service. **In** *Moores, B., ed.,* 1986, pp. 50–53.

Lee, Clive. Atlas of Industrializing Britain 1780–1914: Services. **In** *Langton, J. and Morris, R. J., eds.,* 1986, pp. 140–43. **[G: U.K.]**

Menda, Jean-Luc. La spécialisation internationale de la France dans les échanges de services. (With English summary.) *Revue Écon. Polit.,* Sept.-Oct. 1986, *96*(5), pp. 527–40. **[G: France]**

Moores, Brian. Are They Being Served? Quality Consciousness in Service Industries: Introduction. **In** *Moores, B., ed.,* 1986, pp. 1–10.

Noyelle, Thierry J. Advanced Services in the System of Cities. **In** *Bergman, E. M., ed.,* 1986, *1983,* pp. 143–64. **[G: U.S.]**

Nusbaumer, Jacques. Les négociations internationales sur les services ou la quadrature du cercle. (With English summary.) *Revue Écon. Polit.,* Sept.-Oct. 1986, *96*(5), pp. 541–50.

Preel, Bernard. La gestion de l'emploi des services: pourquoi faut-il passer à l'analyse d'entreprise? (With English summary.) *Revue Écon. Polit.,* Sept.-Oct. 1986, *96*(5), pp. 490–502. **[G: OECD]**

Prieto, Francisco Javier. Services: A Disquieting Link between Latin America and the World Economy. *CEPAL Rev.,* December 1986, (30), pp. 17–36.

Quinn, James Brian. Technology Adoption: The Services Industries. **In** *Landau, R. and Rosenberg, N., eds.,* 1986, pp. 357–71. **[G: U.S.; U.K.; Japan; W. Germany; France]**

Rappoport, Peter. Inflation in the Service Sector. *Fed. Res. Bank New York Quart. Rev.,* Winter

1986-87, *11*(4), pp. 35–45. [G: U.S.]

Ray, George F. Productivity in Services. *Nat. Inst. Econ. Rev.*, February 1986, (115), pp. 44–47. [G: U.K.]

Ray, George F. Services for Manufacturing. *Nat. Inst. Econ. Rev.*, August 1986, (117), pp. 30–32. [G: U.K.]

Renard, François. La place des échanges de services dans la balance des paiements française. (With English summary.) *Revue Écon. Polit.*, Sept.-Oct. 1986, *96*(5), pp. 513–26. [G: France]

Sapir, André. Trade in Investment-Related Technological Studies. *World Devel.*, May 1986, *14*(5), pp. 605–22. [G: India]

Shelp, Ronald Kent. Services in the Economies of the Developing Countries. **In** *Wasow, B. and Hill, R. D., eds.*, 1986, pp. 3–28. [G: LDCs]

Shelp, Ronald Kent and Shelp, June Peno. Services as an Industrial Policy Issue. **In** *Redburn, F. S.; Buss, T. F. and Ledebur, L. C., eds.*, 1986, pp. 28–44. [G: U.S.]

Townroe, Peter M. Technological Change in the Service Sector: Urban and Regional Implications. **In** *Nijkamp, P., ed. (II)*, 1986, pp. 76–90. [G: U.K.]

6352 Electrical, Gas, Communication, and Information Services

Agnew, Carson E. and Gould, Richard G. Frequency Coordination and Spectrum Economics. **In** *Zerbe, R. O., Jr., ed.*, 1986, pp. 167–84.

Alessio, Frank J. Cost Support for Market Pricing: Challenges to Local-Exchange Companies. **In** *[Dorsey, J. N. and Wiggins, B. T.]*, 1986, pp. 119–22. [G: U.S.]

Andersson, Roland and Taylor, Lewis. The Social Cost of Unsupplied Electricity: A Critical Review. *Energy Econ.*, July 1986, *8*(3), pp. 139–46. [G: Sweden; U.K.; Chile; Canada]

Atkinson, Scott E. and Halvorsen, Robert. The Relative Efficiency of Public and Private Firms in a Regulated Environment: The Case of U.S. Electric Utilities. *J. Public Econ.*, April 1986, *29*(3), pp. 281–94. [G: U.S.]

Axelrod, Howard. Predicting the Next Regulatory Crisis: An Issues Management Approach. **In** *Saltzman, S. and Schuler, R. E., eds.*, 1986, pp. 267–72.

Baark, Erik. Information Infrastructures in India and China. **In** *Baark, E. and Jamison, A., eds.*, 1986, pp. 86–141. [G: India; China]

Bailey, Richard. Gas Privatization and the Energy Strategy. *Nat. Westminster Bank Quart. Rev.*, August 1986, pp. 2–12. [G: U.K.]

Barnett, Steve. A New York State Consumer Energy Mindset. **In** *Saltzman, S. and Schuler, R. E., eds.*, 1986, pp. 260–66. [G: U.S.]

Barrett, W. Brian; Heuson, Andrea J. and Kolb, Robert W. The Effect of Three Mile Island on Utility Bond Risk Premia: A Note. *J. Finance,* March 1986, *41*(1), pp. 255–61. [G: U.S.]

Baughcum, Alan. Deregulation, Divestiture, and Competition in U.S. Telecommunications: Lessons for Other Countries. **In** *Snow, M. S.*, 1986, pp. 69–105. [G: U.S.]

Baxter, J. R. Public Enterprise: Studies in Organisational Structure: The Post Office. **In** *Ramanadham, V. V., ed.*, 1986, pp. 51–63. [G: U.K.]

Billinghurst, Roy A. Repeal the Knowledge Tax. **In** *[Dorsey, J. N. and Wiggins, B. T.]*, 1986, pp. 59–65. [G: U.S.]

Bodde, David L.; Quasebarth, Mollie V. and Thomasian, John B. The Economics of Strategic Choice: U.S. Uranium Enrichment in the World Market. *Energy J.*, October 1986, *7*(4), pp. 95–107. [G: U.S.]

Bohi, Douglas R. and Darmstadter, Joel. The World Oil Market and New York Electricity. **In** *Saltzman, S. and Schuler, R. E., eds.*, 1986, pp. 97–110. [G: U.S.]

Bolton, Craig J. and Meiners, Roger E. The Politicization of the Electric Utility Industry. **In** *Moorhouse, J. C., ed.*, 1986, pp. 249–77. [G: U.S.]

Braeutigam, Ronald R. and Hubbard, R. Glenn. Natural Gas: The Regulatory Transition. **In** *Weiss, L. W. and Klass, M. W., eds.*, 1986, pp. 137–68. [G: U.S.]

Brock, Gerald W. The Regulatory Change in Telecommunications: The Dissolution of AT&T. **In** *Weiss, L. W. and Klass, M. W., eds.*, 1986, pp. 210–33. [G: U.S.]

Brotchie, John F. Industrial Interdependence via Information Technology and Transport Interaction—Employment Impacts. **In** *Nijkamp, P., ed. (II)*, 1986, pp. 115–30.

Burns, Robert T. Separations of Costs and the Need for Reform. **In** *[Dorsey, J. N. and Wiggins, B. T.]*, 1986, pp. 99–104. [G: U.S.]

Callan, Scott J. Decomposition of Total Factor Productivity Growth, Additional Evidence: The Case of the U.S. Electric Utility Industry, 1951–1978. *Quart. J. Bus. Econ.*, Summer 1986, *25*(3), pp. 55–71. [G: U.S.]

Cameron, Trudy Ann and White, K. J. The Demand for Computer Services: A Disaggregate Decision Model. *Managerial Dec. Econ.*, March 1986, *7*(1), pp. 37–41.

Campbell, John L. The State, Capital Formation, and Industrial Planning: Financing Nuclear Energy in the United States and France. *Soc. Sci. Quart.*, December 1986, *67*(4), pp. 707–21. [G: U.S.; France]

Cave, Martin. Computers in Soviet Management, 1963–1984. **In** *Altmann, F.-L., ed.*, 1986, pp. 133–50. [G: U.S.S.R.]

Chappell, Henry W., Jr. and Wilder, Ronald P. Multiproduct Monopoly, Regulation, and Firm Costs: Comment. *Southern Econ. J.*, April 1986, *52*(4), pp. 1168–74. [G: U.S.]

Cheah, Chee-Wah. Telecommunications in the South Pacific: The Economic Issues. **In** *Cole, R. V. and Parry, T. G., eds.*, 1986, pp. 208–25. [G: S. Pacific]

Christol, Carl Q. The Search for a Stable Regulatory Framework. **In** *Demac, D. A., ed.*, 1986, pp. 3–18.

Coates, Daniel E. and Mulligan, James G. The Efficiency of Electric Power Pools: Evidence from Firing Unit Data. *Appl. Econ.*, December 1986, *18*(12), pp. 1323–34. **[G: U.S.]**

Cochran, Neilsen. Divestiture: A Public Service Commissioner's Perspective. **In** *[Dorsey, J. N. and Wiggins, B. T.]*, 1986, pp. 13–15. **[G: U.S.]**

Cohen, Linda R. and Noll, Roger G. Government R&D Programs for Commercializing Space. *Amer. Econ. Rev.*, May 1986, *76*(2), pp. 269–73. **[G: U.S.]**

Conrad, Klaus and Henseler-Unger, Iris. The Economic Impact of Coal-fired versus Nuclear Power Plants: An Application of a General Equilibrium Model. *Energy J.*, October 1986, *7*(4), pp. 51–63. **[G: W. Germany]**

Cramer, Curtis A. The Structural Implications of a Minimum Bill Provision in the Transportation of Natural Gas in the United States. *Int. J. Transport Econ.*, February 1986, *13*(1), pp. 77–86. **[G: U.S.]**

Crane, Alan T. Nuclear Safety and Environmental Issues. **In** *Saltzman, S. and Schuler, R. E., eds.*, 1986, pp. 213–23. **[G: U.S.]**

Crew, Michael A. and Crocker, Keith J. Vertically Integrated Governance Structures and Optimal Institutional Arrangements for Cogeneration. *J. Inst. Theoretical Econ.*, June 1986, *142*(2), pp. 340–59. **[G: U.S.]**

Cristini, Guido. Channel Alternatives in the Press Industry: A Comparative Analysis. **In** *Pellegrini, L. and Reddy, S. K., eds.*, 1986, pp. 119–39. **[G: W. Germany; U.K.; France; Italy]**

Cronin, F. J. and Wusterbarth, A. R. Economic Harm Ignored: Betamax Revisited. *Contemp. Policy Issues*, April 1986, *4*(2), pp. 54–68. **[G: U.S.]**

D'Souza, Amita. A Model of Infrastructural Interlinkages for India. *Indian Econ. Rev.*, July-Dec. 1986, *21*(2), pp. 115–48. **[G: India]**

Danielsen, Albert L. and Kamerschen, David R. A Methodological Study of Market Power and Market Shares in Intrastate Inter-LATA Telecommunications. **In** *[Dorsey, J. N. and Wiggins, B. T.]*, 1986, pp. 135–80. **[G: U.S.]**

Davis, William E. New York's Electricity Supply: Present Capacity and Future Needs. **In** *Saltzman, S. and Schuler, R. E., eds.*, 1986, pp. 113–18. **[G: U.S.]**

Defris, Lorraine V.; Layton, Allan P. and Zehnwirth, Ben. The Impact of Economic Cycles on the Demand for International Telecommunications in Australia. *Info. Econ. Policy*, June 1986, *2*(2), pp. 105–17. **[G: Australia]**

DeLuca, Donald R. Survey Research on Energy-Related Issues. **In** *Saltzman, S. and Schuler, R. E., eds.*, 1986, pp. 227–59. **[G: U.S.]**

Demac, Donna A. Tracing New Orbits: Cooperation and Competition in Global Satellite Development: Introduction. **In** *Demac, D. A., ed.*, 1986, pp. xi–xviii.

Dizard, Wilson. The Role of International Satellite Networks. **In** *Demac, D. A., ed.*, 1986, pp. 222–50.

Downing, John D. H. Cooperation and Competition in Satellite Communication: The Soviet Union. **In** *Demac, D. A., ed.*, 1986, pp. 283–304. **[G: CMEA; U.S.S.R.; France; India]**

Dubin, Jeffrey A.; Miedema, Allen K. and Chandran, Ram V. Price Effects of Energy-Efficient Technologies: A Study of Residential Demand for Heating and Cooling. *Rand J. Econ.*, Autumn 1986, *17*(3), pp. 310–25.

Ekelund, Robert B., Jr. and Saba, Richard P. Establishing Property Rights in Utility Franchises. **In** *Moorhouse, J. C., ed.*, 1986, pp. 425–45.

Engelbrecht, Hans-Jürgen. From Newly Industrialising to Newly Informatising Country: The Primary Information Sector of the Republic of Korea 1975–1980. *Info. Econ. Policy*, September 1986, *2*(3), pp. 169–94. **[G: S. Korea]**

Engelbrecht, Hans-Jürgen. The Japanese Information Economy: Its Quantification and Analysis in a Macroeconomic Framework (with Comparisons to the U.S.). *Info. Econ. Policy*, December 1986, *2*(4), pp. 277–306. **[G: Japan; U.S.]**

Engle, Robert F., et al. Semiparametric Estimates of the Relation between Weather and Electricity Sales. *J. Amer. Statist. Assoc.*, June 1986, *81*(394), pp. 310–20. **[G: U.S.]**

Enholm, Gregory B. and Malko, J. Robert. Cost-of-Equity Decisions by State Regulators of Ameritech's Subsidiaries. **In** *[Dorsey, J. N. and Wiggins, B. T.]*, 1986, pp. 17–27. **[G: U.S.]**

Evans, David S. and Heckman, James J. A Test for Subadditivity of the Cost Function with an Application to the Bell System: Erratum. *Amer. Econ. Rev.*, September 1986, *76*(4), pp. 856–58.

Evans, William MacDonald. Canada's Space Policy. **In** *Demac, D. A., ed.*, 1986, pp. 130–40. **[G: Canada]**

Faulhaber, Gerald and Noam, Eli M. Services in Transition: The Impact of Information Technology on the Service Sector: Introduction. **In** *Faulhaber, G.; Noam, E. and Tasley, R., eds.*, 1986, pp. xiii–xix.

Feketekuty, Geza and Hauser, Kathryn. The Impact of Information Technology on Trade in Services. **In** *Faulhaber, G.; Noam, E. and Tasley, R., eds.*, 1986, pp. 81–97. **[G: U.S.]**

Ferguson, James D. Access Charges and the OCCs. **In** *[Dorsey, J. N. and Wiggins, B. T.]*, 1986, pp. 73–77. **[G: U.S.]**

Fisher, Ronald and Martin, Lawrence. Taxes and Telecommunications in an Era of Change. **In** *Minnesota Tax Study Commission*, 1986, pp. 223–49. **[G: U.S.]**

Forbes, Ronald. Determinants of the Cost of Capital for the New York Power Authority. **In** *Saltzman, S. and Schuler, R. E., eds.*, 1986, pp. 288–307. **[G: U.S.]**

Fortenberry, Robert E. Interexchange Issues. **In** *[Dorsey, J. N. and Wiggins, B. T.]*, 1986, pp. 181–87. **[G: U.S.]**

Fournier, Gary M. The Determinants of Economic Rents in Television Broadcasting. *Antitrust Bull.*, Winter 1986, *31*(4), pp. 1045–66. **[G: U.S.]**

Freeman, S. David. Electric Utility Conservation Programs: Progress and Problems: Comments. **In** *Sawhill, J. C. and Cotton, R., eds.*, 1986, pp. 160–62. **[G: U.S.]**

Freibaum, Jerry. Commercial Space Policy: Theory and Practice. **In** *Demac, D. A., ed.*, 1986, pp. 156–65. **[G: U.S.]**

Garbacz, Christopher. Seasonal and Regional Residential Electricity Demand. *Energy J.*, April 1986, *7*(2), pp. 121–34. **[G: U.S.]**

Gilmer, Robert W. and Mack, Richard S. Long-run Adjustment to Alternative Levels of Reliability in Electric Supply. *Energy J.*, October 1986, *7*(4), pp. 89–94.

Ginzberg, Eli. Services: Certainties and Uncertainties. **In** *Faulhaber, G.; Noam, E. and Tasley, R., eds.*, 1986, pp. 1–5.

Gist, Peter and Meadowcroft, Shirley A. Regulating for Competition: The Newly Liberalised Market for Private Branch Exchanges. *Fisc. Stud.*, August 1986, *7*(3), pp. 41–66. **[G: U.K.]**

Globerman, Steven and Stanbury, W. T. Changing the Telephone Pricing Structure: Allocative, Distributional and Political Considerations. *Can. Public Policy*, March 1986, *12*(1), pp. 214–26. **[G: Canada]**

Goldschmidt, Douglas. The Entry of New Satellite Carriers in International Telecommunications: Some Interests of Developing Nations. **In** *Demac, D. A., ed.*, 1986, pp. 88–104.

Goodman, S. E. and McHenry, W. K. Computing in the USSR: Recent Progress and Policies. *Soviet Econ.*, Oct.-Dec. 1986, *2*(4), pp. 327–54. **[G: U.S.S.R.]**

Grennes, Thomas J. Electric Utility Regulation in an Open Economy. **In** *Moorhouse, J. C., ed.*, 1986, pp. 219–47. **[G: U.S.]**

Guinn, Charles R. New York Electricity and Energy Forecasts. **In** *Saltzman, S. and Schuler, R. E., eds.*, 1986, pp. 52–66. **[G: U.S.]**

Hazlett, Thomas W. Competition vs. Franchise Monopoly in Cable Television. *Contemp. Policy Issues*, April 1986, *4*(2), pp. 80–97. **[G: U.S.]**

Hazlett, Thomas W. Regulation and the Communications Revolution: Introduction. *Contemp. Policy Issues*, April 1986, *4*(2), pp. 52–53. **[G: U.S.]**

Hederman, William F., Jr. A Comparative Analysis of Two Difficult Market Transitions: Telecommunications and Natural Gas. **In** *[Dorsey, J. N. and Wiggins, B. T.]*, 1986, pp. 207–14. **[G: U.S.]**

Hemphill, Robert F. and Myers, Edward A. Electric Utility Conservation Programs: Progress and Problems. **In** *Sawhill, J. C. and Cotton, R., eds.*, 1986, pp. 137–59. **[G: U.S.]**

Hewett, Ed. A., et al. Panel on the Economic and Political Consequences of Chernobyl' *Soviet Econ.*, Apr.-June 1986, *2*(2), pp. 97–130. **[G: U.S.S.R.]**

Hicks, Donald A. The Impact of Information Technology on Trade in Services: Discussion. **In** *Faulhaber, G.; Noam, E. and Tasley, R., eds.*, 1986, pp. 98–105. **[G: U.S.]**

Hill, R. Carter; Danielsen, Albert L. and Kamerschen, David R. Assessing the Feasibility of Modeling the Economic Impacts Associated with Changing Carrier Access and Customer Line Charges: A Generic Study of the Southern Region. **In** *[Dorsey, J. N. and Wiggins, B. T.]*, 1986, pp. 215–41. **[G: U.S.]**

Hiney, Robert A. Importing Canadian Electricity. **In** *Saltzman, S. and Schuler, R. E., eds.*, 1986, pp. 123–25. **[G: U.S.; Canada]**

Hirsch, Mario. The Doldrums of Europe's TV Landscape: Coronet as Catalyst. **In** *Demac, D. A., ed.*, 1986, pp. 114–29.

Hoskins, Colin and McFadyen, Stuart. The Canadian Broadcast Program Development Fund: An Evaluation and Some Recommendations. *Can. Public Policy*, March 1986, *12*(1), pp. 227–35. **[G: Canada]**

Hovey, Harry H., Jr. Air Pollution Impacts of Fossil Fuel-Fired Electrical Generation. **In** *Saltzman, S. and Schuler, R. E., eds.*, 1986, pp. 187–202. **[G: U.S.]**

Huband, Frank L. A Survey of Alternative Electric Utility Supply and Use Technologies. **In** *Saltzman, S. and Schuler, R. E., eds.*, 1986, pp. 167–75. **[G: U.S.]**

Huber, Jack. Post-divestiture Telecommunications Pricing: Doing Business in the Competitive, Divested World. **In** *[Dorsey, J. N. and Wiggins, B. T.]*, 1986, pp. 123–28. **[G: U.S.]**

Hudson, Heather E. Access to Information Resources: The Development Context of the Space WARC. **In** *Demac, D. A., ed.*, 1986, pp. 209–21.

Hyman, Leonard S.; Kelley, Doris A. and Toole, Richard C. Financial Constraints on Electric Utilities in New York State: Technology, Institutional Structure, and Investors' Attitudes. **In** *Saltzman, S. and Schuler, R. E., eds.*, 1986, pp. 275–80. **[G: U.S.]**

Irwin, Manley R. The Telecommunications Industry. **In** *Adams, W., ed.*, 1986, pp. 261–89. **[G: U.S.]**

Ito, Youichi. Telecommunications and Industrial Policies in Japan: Recent Developments. **In** *Snow, M. S.*, 1986, pp. 201–30. **[G: Japan]**

Jencks, Christopher. Should the News Be Sold for Profit? **In** *DiMaggio, P. J., ed.*, 1986, pp. 279–83.

Johansson, Börje and Karlsson, Charlie. Industrial Applications of Information Technology: Speed of Introduction and Labour Force Competence. **In** *Nijkamp, P., ed. (II)*, 1986, pp. 401–28. **[G: Sweden]**

Johnson, Nicholas and Adams, John. Electricity Demand Growth in New York State: The Uncertain Factor in the Electricity Planning Process. **In** *Saltzman, S. and Schuler, R. E., eds.*, 1986, pp. 67–76. **[G: U.S.]**

Jones, Ian S. The Application of Risk Analysis to the Appraisal of Optional Investment in the Electricity Supply Industry. *Appl. Econ.*, May 1986, *18*(5), pp. 509–28. **[G: U.K.]**

Jonscher, Charles. Information Technology and the United States Economy: Modeling and Measurement. In *Faulhaber, G.; Noam, E. and Tasley, R., eds.*, 1986, pp. 119–31. **[G: U.S.]**

Jonscher, Charles. Telecommunications Liberalization in the United Kingdom. In *Snow, M. S.*, 1986, pp. 153–72. **[G: U.K.]**

Judy, Richard W. Computing in the USSR: A Comment. *Soviet Econ.*, Oct.-Dec. 1986 cat ds45, *2*(4), pp. 355–67. **[G: U.S.S.R.]**

Kafoglis, Milton Z. Tax Policy and Public Utility Regulation. In *Moorhouse, J. C., ed.*, 1986, pp. 97–133. **[G: U.S.]**

Kahn, Alfred E. A Critique of Proposed Changes. In *Saltzman, S. and Schuler, R. E., eds.*, 1986, pp. 340–47. **[G: U.S.]**

Kaiser, Gordon E. Developments in Canadian Telecommunications Regulation. In *Snow, M. S.*, 1986, pp. 173–200. **[G: Canada]**

Kantor, Brian S. Electricity Pricing in Hong Kong: A Comment. *Hong Kong Econ. Pap.*, 1986, (17), pp. 91–107. **[G: Hong Kong]**

Karlson, Stephen H. Multiple-Output Production and Pricing in Electric Utilities. *Southern Econ. J.*, July 1986, *53*(1), pp. 73–86.

Karunaratne, Neil Dias. An Input–Output Approach to the Measurement of the Information Economy. *Econ. Planning*, 1986, *20*(2), pp. 87–103. **[G: Australia]**

Kaserman, David L. and Mayo, John W. The Ghosts of Deregulated Telecommunications: An Essay by Exorcists. *J. Policy Anal. Manage.*, Fall 1986, *6*(1), pp. 84–92. **[G: U.S.]**

Klein, Lawrence R. The Energy Crisis Ten Years Later. In *Saltzman, S. and Schuler, R. E., eds.*, 1986, pp. 18–31. **[G: U.S.]**

Kokkelenberg, Edward C. and Choi, Jeong Poy. Factor Demands, Adjustment Costs and Regulation. *Appl. Econ.*, June 1986, *18*(6), pp. 631–43. **[G: U.S.]**

Kraft, Philip and Dubnoff, Steven. Job Content, Fragmentation, and Control in Computer Software Work. *Ind. Relat.*, Spring 1986, *25*(2), pp. 184–96. **[G: U.S.]**

Kron, Philip C. The Electric Utility Financial Crisis from a Banker's Perspective. In *Saltzman, S. and Schuler, R. E., eds.*, 1986, pp. 281–87. **[G: U.S.]**

Kunisawa, Kiyonori and Horibe, Yasuichi. Forecasting International Telecommunications Traffic by the Data Translation Method. *Int. J. Forecasting*, 1986, *2*(4), pp. 427–34.

Kunreuther, Howard. The Impact of Technology on the Insurance Industry: Discussion. In *Faulhaber, G.; Noam, E. and Tasley, R., eds.*, 1986, pp. 44–48. **[G: U.S.]**

Lamberton, Don M. Australian Regulatory Policy. In *Snow, M. S.*, 1986, pp. 231–52. **[G: Australia]**

Layton, Allan P.; Defris, Lorraine V. and Zehnwirth, Ben. An International Comparison of Economic Leading Indicators of Telecommunications Traffic. *Int. J. Forecasting*, 1986, *2*(4), pp. 413–25. **[G: Australia; U.S.]**

Layton, Roy A. Will Satellites and Optical Fiber Collide or Coexist? In *Demac, D. A., ed.*, 1986, pp. 19–29.

Łebkowski, Maciej and Monkiewicz, Jan. Information Industries in the CMEA Countries: A Foreign Trade Dimension. *Konjunkturpolitik*, 1986, *32*(5), pp. 308–24. **[G: CMEA]**

Ledyard, John O. Incentive Compatible Space Station Pricing. *Amer. Econ. Rev.*, May 1986, *76*(2), pp. 274–79. **[G: U.S.]**

Leggette, James A. Separation and Telecommunications Pricing Issues. In *[Dorsey, J. N. and Wiggins, B. T.]*, 1986, pp. 105–18. **[G: U.S.]**

Lemon, J. Rodney. Regulatory Reform of Interstate Natural Gas Pipelines. *Contemp. Policy Issues*, October 1986, *4*(4), pp. 93–103. **[G: U.S.]**

Levačić, Rosalind. Government Policies towards the Consumer Electronics Industry and Their Effects: A Comparison of Britain and France. In *Hall, G., ed.*, 1986, pp. 227–44. **[G: U.K.; France]**

Levin, Harvey J. Latecomer Cost Handicap: Importance in a Changing Regulatory Landscape. In *Demac, D. A., ed.*, 1986, pp. 251–79. **[G: U.S.]**

Levin, Nissan; Tishler, Asher and Zahavi, Jacob. Evaluating Energy Options for Israel: A Case Study. *Energy J.*, January 1986, *7*(1), pp. 51–65. **[G: Israel]**

Lewin, Peter and Parsons, Steve G. Long-term versus Short-term Costs of Electricity Supply Interruptions: A Cautionary Note. *Energy J.*, April 1986, *7*(2), pp. 181–86.

Lewis, Pamela M. The Economic Impact of the Operation and Closure of a Nuclear Power Station. *Reg. Stud.*, October 1986, *20*(5), pp. 425–32. **[G: U.K.]**

Linneman, Peter. Information Technology, Demographics, and the Retail Response: Discussion. In *Faulhaber, G.; Noam, E. and Tasley, R., eds.*, 1986, pp. 175–77. **[G: U.S.; OECD]**

Macauley, Molly K. Out of Space? Regulation and Technical Change in Communications Satellites. *Amer. Econ. Rev.*, May 1986, *76*(2), pp. 280–84. **[G: U.S.]**

Maddox, Brenda. The Theology of Satellite Television: Dogmas That Are Holding Up the Progress of Satellite Television. In *Demac, D. A., ed.*, 1986, pp. 107–13. **[G: U.S.; W. Europe]**

Maggs, Peter B. Legal Regulation of the Dissemination of Scientific and Technical Information in the USSR. In *Ioffe, O. S. and Janis, M. W., eds.*, 1986, pp. 103–26. **[G: U.S.S.R.]**

Mansell, Robin E. The Telecommunication Bypass Threat: Real or Imagined? *J. Econ. Issues*, March 1986, *20*(1), pp. 145–64.

Marx, Jane. Regulation of Electric Utilities and Affiliated Coal Companies—Determining Reasonable Expenses: Comment. *Natural Res. J.*, Fall 1986, *26*(4), pp. 851–69. **[G: U.S.]**

Mayo, John W. Multiproduct Monopoly, Regulation, and Firm Costs: Reply. *Southern Econ. J.*, April 1986, *52*(4), pp. 1175–78.

McCormick, Robert E. Inflation, Regulation, and

Financial Adequacy. In *Moorhouse, J. C., ed.*, 1986, pp. 135–61. [G: U.S.]

Mead, Walter J. The OPEC Cartel Thesis Reexamined: Price Constraints from Oil Substitutes. *J. Energy Devel.*, Spring 1986, *11*(2), pp. 213–42. [G: OPEC]

Menneer, Peter. Broadcasting Research—Necessity or Nicety? In *Moores, B., ed.*, 1986, pp. 255–65. [G: U.K.]

Meunier, François and Volle, M. The Effects of the New Communications Media on Employment. *Info. Econ. Policy*, September 1986, *2*(3), pp. 195–209. [G: France]

Montgomery, William H. A Canadian Perspective on the 1985 ITU Space Conference. In *Demac, D. A., ed.*, 1986, pp. 201–08. [G: Canada]

Moorhouse, John C. The Uncertain Future of the Electric Power Industry. In *Moorhouse, J. C., ed.*, 1986, pp. 1–23. [G: U.S.]

Morgan, R. H. The Development of the Electricity Supply Industry in South Wales to 1939. In *Baber, C. and Williams, L. J., eds.*, 1986, pp. 222–36. [G: U.K.]

Moss, Mitchell. Information Technology, Demographics, and the Retail Response: Discussion. In *Faulhaber, G.; Noam, E. and Tasley, R., eds.*, 1986, pp. 178–82. [G: U.S.; OECD]

Mount, Timothy D. and Deehan, William J. Determinants of the Demand for Electricity in New York: Economic Conditions, Nuclear Power Costs, and Primary Fuel Prices. In *Saltzman, S. and Schuler, R. E., eds.*, 1986, pp. 77–96. [G: U.S.]

Mountain, Dean C. and Hsiao, Cheng. Peak and Off-Peak Industrial Demand for Electricity: The Hopkinson Rate in Ontario, Canada. *Energy J.*, January 1986, *7*(1), pp. 149–68. [G: Canada]

Nelson, Randy A. Capital Vintage, Time Trends, and Technical Change in the Electric Power Industry. *Southern Econ. J.*, October 1986, *53*(2), pp. 315–32. [G: U.S.]

Neumann, Karl-Heinz. Economic Policy toward Telecommunications, Information, and the Media in West Germany. In *Snow, M. S.*, 1986, pp. 131–52. [G: W. Germany]

Nguyen, Godefroy Dang. Telecommunications: A Challenge to the Old Order. In *Sharp, M., ed.*, 1986, pp. 87–133. [G: OECD]

Nguyen, Godefroy Dang and Arnold Erik. Videotex: Much Ado about Nothing? In *Sharp, M., ed.*, 1986, pp. 134–60. [G: U.K.; France; W. Germany; Canada]

Noam, Eli M. Telecommunications Policy on Both Sides of the Atlantic: Divergence and Outlook. In *Snow, M. S.*, 1986, pp. 255–74.

Noll, Roger G. State Regulatory Responses to Competition and Divestiture in the Telecommunications Industry. In *Grieson, R. E., ed.*, 1986, pp. 165–200. [G: U.S.]

Noll, Roger G. The Political and Institutional Context of Communications Policy. In *Snow, M. S.*, 1986, pp. 42–65. [G: OECD]

Omichi, Masao. Nuclear Power in the United States and Japan. In *Finn, R. B., ed.*, 1986, pp. 51–75. [G: U.S.; Japan]

Oreshin, V. Problems of Method in Planning the Production Infrastructure. *Prob. Econ.*, July 1986, *29*(3), pp. 81–93. [G: U.S.S.R.]

Ospina, Sylvia. Piracy of Satellite-Transmitted Copyright Material in the Americas: Bane or Boon? In *Demac, D. A., ed.*, 1986, pp. 166–98.

Owen, Bruce M. and Gottlieb, Paul D. The Rise and Fall and Rise of Cable Television Regulation. In *Weiss, L. W. and Klass, M. W., eds.*, 1986, pp. 78–104. [G: U.S.]

Owen, Bruce M. and Greenhalgh, Peter R. Competitive Considerations in Cable Television Franchising. *Contemp. Policy Issues*, April 1986, *4*(2), pp. 69–79. [G: U.S.]

Pauly, Mark V. Information Technology and the U.S. Health Care Industry: A New Direction: Discussion. In *Faulhaber, G.; Noam, E. and Tasley, R., eds.*, 1986, pp. 21–25. [G: U.S.]

Peavy, John W., III and Scott, Jonathan A. The AT&T Divestiture: Effect of Rating Changes on Bond Returns. *J. Econ. Bus.*, August 1986, *38*(3), pp. 255–71. [G: U.S.]

Pelton, Joseph N. INTELSAT: Responding to New Challenges. In *Demac, D. A., ed.*, 1986, pp. 58–74.

Percival, Robert V. Conservation and Renewable Energy Sources as Supply Alternatives for New York's Electric Utilities. In *Saltzman, S. and Schuler, R. E., eds.*, 1986, pp. 126–50. [G: U.S.]

Perkins, Clinton, Jr. Pricing for Today's Environment. In *[Dorsey, J. N. and Wiggins, B. T.]*, 1986, pp. 129–32. [G: U.S.]

Pogorel, Gérard. The Impact of Information Technology on Trade in Services: Discussion. In *Faulhaber, G.; Noam, E. and Tasley, R., eds.*, 1986, pp. 106–09. [G: U.S.]

Powell, Walter W. Should University Presses Compete with Commercial Scholarly Publishers? In *DiMaggio, P. J., ed.*, 1986, pp. 270–78. [G: U.S.]

Powell, Walter W. and Friedkin, Rebecca Jo. Politics and Programs: Organizational Factors in Public Television Decision Making. In *DiMaggio, P. J., ed.*, 1986, pp. 245–69. [G: U.S.]

Price, Alan K. Access Charges: A Local-Exchange Carrier's Perspective. In *[Dorsey, J. N. and Wiggins, B. T.]*, 1986, pp. 79–82. [G: U.S.]

Price, D. H. R. and Sharp, J. A. A Comparison of the Performance of Different Univariate Forecasting Methods in a Model of Capacity Acquisition in UK Electricity Supply. *Int. J. Forecasting*, 1986, *2*(3), pp. 333–48. [G: U.K.]

Primeaux, Walter J., Jr. Competition between Electric Utilities. In *Moorhouse, J. C., ed.*, 1986, pp. 395–423. [G: U.S.]

Raipuria, Kalyan M. A Distributed Information and Research System (DIRS) for the Third World. In *Panchamukhi, V. R., et al.*, 1986, pp. 273–93.

Richardson, David H. The St. Lawrence Seaway and Power Project: An *Ex Post* Evaluation.

Public Finance, 1986, *41*(1), pp. 8–41. [G: U.S.; Canada]

Ringleb, Al H. Environmental Regulation of Electric Utilities. **In** *Moorhouse, J. C., ed.*, 1986, pp. 183–218. [G: U.S.]

Roach, Stephen S. Macrorealities of the Information Economy. **In** *Landau, R. and Rosenberg, N., eds.*, 1986, pp. 93–103. [G: U.S.]

Roberts, Mark J. Economies of Density and Size in the Production and Delivery of Electric Power. *Land Econ.*, November 1986, *62*(4), pp. 378–87. [G: U.S.]

Robinson, Terence. Depreciation Reserve Assessment. **In** *[Dorsey, J. N. and Wiggins, B. T.]*, 1986, pp. 189–206. [G: U.S.]

Saltzman, Sidney and Schuler, Richard E. Electricity's Future: Sharpening the Debates. **In** *Saltzman, S. and Schuler, R. E., eds.*, 1986, pp. 348–62. [G: U.S.]

Schaffer, Ken. A Television Window on the Soviet Union. **In** *Demac, D. A., ed.*, 1986, pp. 305–11.

Schankerman, Mark and Nadiri, M. Ishaq. A Test of Static Equilibrium Models and Rates of Return to Quasi-fixed Factors, with an Application to the Bell System. *J. Econometrics*, Oct./Nov. 1986, *33*(1/2), pp. 97–118.

Scheffler, Richard M. Information Technology and the U.S. Health Care Industry: A New Direction. **In** *Faulhaber, G.; Noam, E. and Tasley, R., eds.*, 1986, pp. 7–20. [G: U.S.]

Schlesinger, James R. The Long-run Security of the Energy Supply. **In** *Saltzman, S. and Schuler, R. E., eds.*, 1986, pp. 32–39. [G: U.S.]

Schmalensee, Richard and Joskow, Paul L. Estimated Parameters as Independent Variables: An Application to the Costs of Electric Generating Units. *J. Econometrics*, April 1986, *31*(3), pp. 275–305. [G: U.S.]

Schuler, Richard E. Electricity in New York State: The First One Hundred Years as Prelude to the Future. **In** *Saltzman, S. and Schuler, R. E., eds.*, 1986, pp. 7–17. [G: U.S.]

Schuler, Richard E. The Institutional and Regulatory Structure for Providing Electric Service: A Conceptual Basis for Change. **In** *Saltzman, S. and Schuler, R. E., eds.*, 1986, pp. 311–29. [G: U.S.]

Scullion, Patrick J. Electric Utility Conservation Programs: Progress and Problems: Comments. **In** *Sawhill, J. C. and Cotton, R., eds.*, 1986, pp. 159–60. [G: U.S.]

Shaiken, Harley. Decentralized Production: A Technological Revolution with Political Issues. **In** *Gondolf, E. W.; Marcus, I. M. and Dougherty, J. P., eds.*, 1986, pp. 58–65.

Shelp, Ronald Kent. The Impact of Information Technology on Trade in Services: Discussion. **In** *Faulhaber, G.; Noam, E. and Tasley, R., eds.*, 1986, pp. 110–17. [G: U.S.]

Shmanske, Stephen. News as a Public Good: Cooperative Ownership, Price Commitments, and the Success of the Associated Press. *Bus. Hist. Rev.*, Spring 1986, *60*(1), pp. 55–80. [G: U.S.]

Sioshansi, Fereidoon P. Energy, Electricity, and the U.S. Economy: Emerging Trends. *Energy J.*, April 1986, *7*(2), pp. 81–90. [G: U.S.]

Skinner, Frank. Communications in the New Era. **In** *[Dorsey, J. N. and Wiggins, B. T.]*, 1986, pp. 83–88. [G: U.S.]

Snow, Marcellus S. Communications Policy in Seven Developed Countries: Introduction, Background, and Conclusions. **In** *Snow, M. S.*, 1986, pp. 3–19. [G: OECD]

Snow, Marcellus S. Competition by Private Carriers in International Commercial Satellite Traffic: Conceptual and Historical Background. **In** *Demac, D. A., ed.*, 1986, pp. 33–57.

Snow, Marcellus S. Regulating Telecommunications, Information, and the Media: An Agenda for Future Comparative Research. **In** *Snow, M. S.*, 1986, pp. 275–94.

Stafford, Robert T. Energy and the Environment: The View from Washington. **In** *Saltzman, S. and Schuler, R. E., eds.*, 1986, pp. 179–86. [G: U.S.]

Stalon, Charles G. Analysis and Synthesis in Quasi-judicial Multimember Regulatory Agencies. **In** *Saltzman, S. and Schuler, R. E., eds.*, 1986, pp. 330–39. [G: U.S.]

Stasiuk, William N. Some Public Health Concerns Associated with Electrical Energy Generation. **In** *Saltzman, S. and Schuler, R. E., eds.*, 1986, pp. 203–12. [G: U.S.]

Sternlieb, George and Hughes, James W. Information Technology, Demographics, and the Retail Response. **In** *Faulhaber, G.; Noam, E. and Tasley, R., eds.*, 1986, pp. 139–74. [G: U.S.; OECD]

Stone, Merlin. Keeping Customers by Keeping Them Happy—An Example from the Computer Industry. **In** *Moores, B., ed.*, 1986, pp. 266–77. [G: U.K.]

Stromback, C. Thorsten. Modelling Electricity Demand in Western Australia. *Australian Econ. Pap.*, June 1986, *25*(46), pp. 106–17. [G: W. Australia]

Sturgess, Brian. Media Policy in Europe—Cable Television. **In** *Hall, G., ed.*, 1986, pp. 209–26. [G: W. Europe; U.K.]

Stuzin, Lester M. Existing Electric Generating Capacity in New York State. **In** *Saltzman, S. and Schuler, R. E., eds.*, 1986, pp. 119–22. [G: U.S.]

Sueyoshi, Toshiyuki and Anselmo, Peter C. The Evans and Heckman Subadditivity Test: Comment. *Amer. Econ. Rev.*, September 1986, *76*(4), pp. 854–55.

Sutherland, Ronald J. A Portfolio Analysis Model of the Demand for Nuclear Power Plants. *Energy Econ.*, October 1986, *8*(4), pp. 218–26. [G: U.S.]

Taylor, Thomas N. and Schwarz, Peter M. A Residential Demand Charge: Evidence from the Duke Power Time-of-Day Pricing Experiment. *Energy J.*, April 1986, *7*(2), pp. 135–51. [G: U.S.]

Teece, David J. Assessing the Competition Faced by Oil Pipelines. *Contemp. Policy Issues*, October 1986, *4*(4), pp. 65–78. [G: U.S.]

Telson, Michael L. Policy Issues in Oil and Gas

Transportation Regulation. *Contemp. Policy Issues,* October 1986, *4*(4), pp. 60–64. **[G: U.S.]**

Terza, Joseph V. Determinants of Household Electricity Demand: A Two-Stage Probit Approach. *Southern Econ. J.,* April 1986, *52*(4), pp. 1131–39. **[G: U.S.]**

Thornton, Judith. Soviet Electric Power after Chernobyl': Economic Consequences and Options. *Soviet Econ.,* Apr.-June 1986, *2*(2), pp. 131–79. **[G: U.S.S.R.]**

Thorpe, Kenneth E. Information Technology and the U.S. Health Care Industry: A New Direction: Discussion. **In** *Faulhaber, G.; Noam, E. and Tasley, R., eds.,* 1986, pp. 26–30. **[G: U.S.]**

Tourinho, Octávio A. F. A expansão de longa prazo do sistema elétrico brasileiro: uma análise com o modelo PSE. (With English summary.) *Pesquisa Planejamento Econ.,* April 1986, *16*(1), pp. 87–127. **[G: Brazil]**

Trebing, Harry M. Apologetics of Deregulation in Energy and Telecommunications: An Institutionalist Assessment. *J. Econ. Issues,* September 1986, *20*(3), pp. 613–32.

Tudge, David T. Financial Initiatives to Enhance Competitiveness in an International Non-profit Cooperative: The Case of the New INTELSAT. *Ann. Pub. Co-op. Econ.,* Oct.-Dec. 1986, *57*(4), pp. 523–30. **[G: Global]**

von Tunzelmann, Nick. Atlas of Industrializing Britain 1780–1914: Coal and Steam Power. **In** *Langton, J. and Morris, R. J., eds.,* 1986, pp. 72–79. **[G: U.K.]**

Veall, Michael R. On Estimating the Effects of Peak Demand Pricing. *J. Appl. Econometrics,* January 1986, *1*(1), pp. 81–93. **[G: Canada]**

Veall, Michael R. Time-of-Use Rates and Peak Period Electricity Consumption: An Empirical Note. *Energy Econ.,* October 1986, *8*(4), pp. 257–62. **[G: U.S.]**

Vietor, Richard H. K. Perspectives on the Bell System: Strategy, Structure, Technology, and Unionism. *Bus. Hist. Rev.,* Winter 1986, *60*(4), pp. 633–40. **[G: U.S.]**

Virole, Jean L. Public Enterprise: Studies in Organisational Structure: Electricité de France. **In** *Ramanadham, V. V., ed.,* 1986, pp. 64–82. **[G: France]**

Vizas, Christopher J., II. The Reality of Change, Satellite Technology, Economics, and Institutional Resistance. **In** *Demac, D. A., ed.,* 1986, pp. 75–87.

Voge, Jean-Paul. A Survey of French Regulatory Policy. **In** *Snow, M. S.,* 1986, pp. 106–30. **[G: France]**

Wasserfallen, Walter; Gassmann, Jean-Marie and Gfeller, Andreas. Die Nachfrage nach Telefongesprächen—Erklärung und Prognose Eine empirische Untersuchung für die Schweiz. (The Demand for Telephone Services: Explanation and Forecast—An Empirical Investigation for Switzerland. With English summary.) *Schweiz. Z. Volkswirtsch. Statist.,* June 1986, *122*(2), pp. 187–97. **[G: Switzerland]**

Weber, Lawrence R. Cross-Subsidization in a Competitive Environment. **In** *[Dorsey, J. N. and Wiggins, B. T.],* 1986, pp. 67–71. **[G: U.S.]**

Weinberg, Alvin M. An Energy Traditionalist Talks to the Energy Nontraditionalists about Electricity and Nuclear Energy. **In** *Saltzman, S. and Schuler, R. E., eds.,* 1986, pp. 151–65. **[G: U.S.]**

Weingarten, Fred W. and Wilk, Charles. Research and Development Policy in the United States: Implications for Satellite Communications. **In** *Demac, D. A., ed.,* 1986, pp. 141–55. **[G: U.S.]**

von Weizsäcker, Carl Christian. Free Entry into Telecommunications. **In** *Snow, M. S.,* 1986, pp. 20–41.

Wenders, John T. Economic Efficiency and Income Distribution in the Electric Utility Industry. *Southern Econ. J.,* April 1986, *52*(4), pp. 1056–67. **[G: U.S.]**

Wenders, John T. Efficiency, Subsidy, and Cross-Subsidy in Electric Utility Pricing. **In** *Moorhouse, J. C., ed.,* 1986, pp. 307–36. **[G: U.S.]**

White, Ward H. Divestiture and the Local-Exchange Carrier. **In** *[Dorsey, J. N. and Wiggins, B. T.],* 1986, pp. 89–95. **[G: U.S.]**

Willett, Keith D. Environmental Management Costs Using a Best Available Control Technology BACT in the Electrical Generating Industry. *Managerial Dec. Econ.,* March 1986, *7*(1), pp. 29–36. **[G: U.S.]**

Williams, Raymond and Watts, Glenn. The Process of Working Together: CWA's/AT&T's Approach to QWL. **In** *Rosow, J. M., ed.,* 1986, pp. 75–88. **[G: U.S.]**

Williamson, Oliver E. Franchise Bidding for Natural Monopolies—In General and with Respect to CATV. **In** *Williamson, O. E.,* 1986, *1976,* pp. 258–97.

Yao, Dennis A. Information Technology and the United States Economy: Modeling and Measurement: Discussion. **In** *Faulhaber, G.; Noam, E. and Tasley, R., eds.,* 1986, pp. 132–37. **[G: U.S.]**

Yonce, Henry G. Regulating the Telecommunication "Bear" Markets. **In** *[Dorsey, J. N. and Wiggins, B. T.],* 1986, pp. 3–6. **[G: U.S.]**

Yorke, David. The Quality of Library Services. **In** *Moores, B., ed.,* 1986, pp. 278–87. **[G: U.K.]**

Young, David N. The Impact of Technology on the Insurance Industry. **In** *Faulhaber, G.; Noam, E. and Tasley, R., eds.,* 1986, pp. 31–43. **[G: U.S.]**

Zardkoohi, Asghar. Competition in the Production of Electricity. **In** *Moorhouse, J. C., ed.,* 1986, pp. 63–95. **[G: U.S.]**

6353 Personal Services

Brand, Horst and Ahmed, Ziaul Z. Beauty and Barber Shops: The Trend of Labor Productivity. *Mon. Lab. Rev.,* March 1986, *109*(3), pp. 21–26. **[G: U.S.]**

635 Industry Studies: Services and Related Industries

Brown, Ralph J. Implicit Inflation and Interest Rates in Discounting Personal Injury Economic Losses—Comment. *J. Risk Ins.*, September 1986, *53*(3), pp. 492–95. **[G: U.S.]**

Hammond, Christopher J. Estimating the Statistical Cost Curve: An Application of the Stochastic Frontier Technique. *Appl. Econ.*, September 1986, *18*(9), pp. 971–84. **[G: U.K.]**

Jones, David D. Rejoinder to Brown's Comment and a Reaction to Schilling's "Estimating the Present Value...." [Inflation Rates Implicit in Discounting Personal Injury Economic Losses]. *J. Risk Ins.*, September 1986, *53*(3), pp. 489–500. **[G: U.S.]**

Schilling, Don. Implicit Inflation and Interest Rates in Discounting Personal Injury Economic Losses—Rejoinder. *J. Risk Ins.*, September 1986, *53*(3), pp. 496–97. **[G: U.S.]**

Thurik, A. R. and van der Hoeven, W. H. M. Labor Productivity in the Hotel and Catering Sector. *Atlantic Econ. J.*, December 1986, *14*(4), pp. 105. **[G: U.S.]**

6354 Business and Legal Services

Beales, J. Howard, III. Comments [The Effects of the Advertising Substantiation Program on Advertising Agencies] [An Economic Analysis of the FTC's Ad Substantiation Program]. **In** *Ippolito, P. M. and Scheffman, D. T., eds.*, 1986, pp. 213–16. **[G: U.S.]**

Cox, Steven R.; Schroeter, John R. and Smith, Scott L. Attorney Advertising and the Quality of Routine Legal Services. *Rev. Ind. Organ.*, 1986, *2*(4), pp. 340–54. **[G: U.S.]**

Higgins, Richard S. and McChesney, Fred S. An Economic Analysis of the FTC's Ad Substantiation Program. **In** *Ippolito, P. M. and Scheffman, D. T., eds.*, 1986, pp. 197–211. **[G: U.S.]**

Leffler, Keith B. and Sauer, Raymond, Jr. The Effects of the Advertising Substantiation Program on Advertising Agencies. **In** *Ippolito, P. M. and Scheffman, D. T., eds.*, 1986, pp. 177–95. **[G: U.S.]**

Minnerop, Henry F. and Stoll, Hans R. Technological Change in the Back Office: Implications for Structure and Regulation of the Securities Industry. **In** *Saunders, A. and White, L. J., eds.*, 1986, pp. 31–51. **[G: U.S.]**

Siggel, Eckhard. Technology Transfers to Developing Countries through Consulting Engineers: A Model and Empirical Observations from Canada. *Devel. Econ.*, September 1986, *24*(3), pp. 229–50. **[G: Canada; LDCs]**

Spiller, Pablo T. Comments [The Effects of the Advertising Substantiation Program on Advertising Agencies] [An Economic Analysis of the FTC's Ad Substantiation Program]. **In** *Ippolito, P. M. and Scheffman, D. T., eds.*, 1986, pp. 217–20. **[G: U.S.]**

6355 Repair Services

Eastwood, David B. and Garner, Sammie G. Home Repairs: A Household Production Perspective. *J. Behav. Econ.*, Spring/Summer 1986, *15*(1/2), pp. 25–39. **[G: U.S.]**

Murphy, Patrick E. and Ross, Steven C. Local Consumer Information Systems for Services: A Test. *J. Cons. Aff.*, Winter 1986, *20*(2), pp. 249–66. **[G: U.S.]**

6356 Insurance

Abel, Andrew B. The Effect of Annuity Insurance and Savings and Inequality: Comment. *J. Lab. Econ.*, Part 2, July 1986, *4*(3), pp. S208–15.

Alter, George and Riley, James C. How to Bet on Lives: A Guide to Life Contingent Contracts in Early Modern Europe. **In** *Uselding, P., ed.*, 1986, pp. 1–53. **[G: Europe]**

Anderson, Dan R. and Weinrobe, Maurice. Insurance Issues Related to Mortgage Default Risks Associated with Natural Disasters. *J. Risk Ins.*, September 1986, *53*(3), pp. 501–13. **[G: U.S.]**

Bar-Niv, Ran and Bickelhaupt, David L. Research in International Risk and Insurance: Summary, Synthesis, and Prospects. *J. Risk Ins.*, March 1986, *53*(1), pp. 119–34.

Bardsley, Peter. A Note on the Viability of Rainfall Insurance—Reply [The Economics of Insuring Crops against Drought]. *Australian J. Agr. Econ.*, April 1986, *30*(1), pp. 70–75. **[G: Australia]**

Bassoco, Luz María; Cartas, Celso and Norton, Roger D. Sectoral Analysis of the Benefits of Subsidized Insurance in Mexico. **In** *Hazell, P.; Pomareda, C. and Valdés, A., eds.*, 1986, pp. 126–42. **[G: Mexico]**

Benjamini, Yael and Benjamini, Yoav. The Choice among Medical Insurance Plans. *Amer. Econ. Rev.*, March 1986, *76*(1), pp. 221–27. **[G: U.S.]**

Binswanger, Hans P. Risk Aversion, Collateral Requirements, and the Markets for Credit and Insurance in Rural Areas. **In** *Hazell, P.; Pomareda, C. and Valdés, A., eds.*, 1986, pp. 67–86.

Black, Jeanne T. The Employed Uninsured and the Role of Public Policy: Comment. *Inquiry*, Summer 1986, *23*(2), pp. 209–12. **[G: U.S.]**

Blankart, Charles B. and Finsinger, Jörg. Regulation-Induced Price Instability in Swiss Motor Car Liability Insurance. **In** *Finsinger, J. and Pauly, M. V., eds.*, 1986, pp. 200–211. **[G: Switzerland]**

Blankart, Charles B. and Schneider, Friedrich. Insurance Regulation in Switzerland: An Outline with Special Reference to Life and Motor Car Liability Insurance. **In** *Finsinger, J. and Pauly, M. V., eds.*, 1986, pp. 189–99. **[G: Switzerland]**

Blazenko, George. The Economics of Reinsurance. *J. Risk Ins.*, June 1986, *53*(2), pp. 258–77.

Boussard, Jean-Marc. Agriculture in a Turbulent World Economy: Theoretical Developments: Discussion. **In** *Maunder, A. and Renborg, U., eds.*, 1986, pp. 663–65.

Bovbjerg, Randall R. Insuring the Uninsured

through Private Action: Ideas and Initiatives. *Inquiry*, Winter 1986, *23*(4), pp. 403–18.

Bovbjerg, Randall R. and Koller, Christopher F. State Health Insurance Pools: Current Performance, Future Prospects. *Inquiry*, Summer 1986, *23*(2), pp. 111–21. **[G: U.S.]**

Boyer, Marcel and Dionne, Georges. Le tarification de l'assurance automobile et les incitations à la sécurité routière: Une étude empirique. (The Tariffication of Car Insurances and the Incentives for Road Safety: An Empirical Investigation. With English summary.) *Schweiz. Z. Volkswirtsch. Statist.*, September 1986, *122*(3), pp. 293–321. **[G: Canada]**

Briys, Eric. Insurance and Consumption: The Continuous Time Case. *J. Risk Ins.*, December 1986, *53*(4), pp. 718–23.

Brockett, Patrick L.; Cox, Samuel H., Jr. and Witt, Robert C. Insurance versus Self-Insurance: A Risk Management Perspective. *J. Risk Ins.*, June 1986, *53*(2), pp. 242–57.

Broverman, Samuel. The Rate of Return on Life Insurance and Annuities. *J. Risk Ins.*, September 1986, *53*(3), pp. 419–34.

Calcoen, F.; Eeckhoudt, L. and Outreville, J.-François. Indemnisation du chômage et revenus de remplacement: Une approche par la théorie de l'assurance. (Unemployment Insurance and Damage Insurance: An Approach through the Theory of Insurance. With English summary.) *Schweiz. Z. Volkswirtsch. Statist.*, September 1986, *122*(3), pp. 323–37.

Carlson, Severin and Lord, Blair. Unisex Retirement Benefits and the Market for Annuity "Lemons." *J. Risk Ins.*, September 1986, *53*(3), pp. 409–18.

Carpenter, Michael D., et al. Methodologies of Valuing Lost Earnings: A Review, a Criticism, and a Recommendation. *J. Risk Ins.*, March 1986, *53*(1), pp. 104–18. **[G: U.S.]**

Chassagne, Yvette. Insurance and Development. **In** *U.N., Dept. of International Econ. and Social Affairs*, 1986, pp. 61–64. **[G: LDCs]**

Chesney, Marc and Loubergé, Henri. Risk Aversion and the Composition of Wealth in the Demand for Full Insurance Coverage. *Schweiz. Z. Volkswirtsch. Statist.*, September 1986, *122*(3), pp. 359–70.

Crocker, Keith J. and Snow, Arthur. The Efficiency Effects of Categorical Discrimination in the Insurance Industry. *J. Polit. Econ.*, April 1986, *94*(2), pp. 321–44.

Cross, Mark L.; Davidson, Wallace N., III and Thornton, John H. The Impact of Captive Insurer Formation on the Parent Firm's Value. *J. Risk Ins.*, September 1986, *53*(3), pp. 471–83. **[G: U.S.]**

Curry, Timothy and Warshawsky, Mark. Life Insurance Companies in a Changing Environment. *Fed. Res. Bull.*, July 1986, *72*(7), pp. 449–60. **[G: U.S.]**

D'Arcy, Stephen P. Legislative Reform of the Medical Malpractice Tort System in Illinois. *J. Risk Ins.*, September 1986, *53*(3), pp. 538–50. **[G: U.S.]**

Dahlby, Bev and West, Douglas S. Price Dispersion in an Automobile Insurance Market. *J. Polit. Econ.*, April 1986, *94*(2), pp. 418–38. **[G: Canada]**

Dickinson, Gerard M. The Impact of International Insurance and Reinsurance on the Balance of Payments. **In** *Wasow, B. and Hill, R. D., eds.*, 1986, pp. 69–86.

Doherty, Neil A. and Garven, James R. Price Regulation in Property-Liability Insurance: A Contingent-Claims Approach. *J. Finance*, December 1986, *41*(5), pp. 1031–50.

Eisen, Roland. Wettbewerb und Regulierung in der Versicherung Die Rolle asymmetrischer Information. (Competition and Regulation in Insurance: The Role of Asymmetrical Information. With English summary.) *Schweiz. Z. Volkswirtsch. Statist.*, September 1986, *122*(3), pp. 339–58.

Ellis, Randall P. Rational Behavior in the Presence of Coverage Ceilings and Deductibles. *Rand J. Econ.*, Summer 1986, *17*(2), pp. 158–75. **[G: U.S.]**

Etheredge, Lynn. Ethics and the New Insurance Market. *Inquiry*, Fall 1986, *23*(3), pp. 308–15. **[G: U.S.]**

Finsinger, Jörg. A State Controlled Market: The German Case. **In** *Finsinger, J. and Pauly, M. V., eds.*, 1986, pp. 111–60. **[G: W. Germany]**

Finsinger, Jörg; Kraft, Kornelius and Pauly, Mark V. Some Observations on Greater Competition in the West German Health-insurance System from a U.S. Perspective. *Managerial Dec. Econ.*, September 1986, *7*(3), pp. 151–61. **[G: W. Germany; U.S.]**

Finsinger, Jörg and Pauly, Mark V. The Economics of Insurance Regulation: A Cross-National Study: Introduction. **In** *Finsinger, J. and Pauly, M. V., eds.*, 1986, pp. 1–23. **[G: OECD]**

Finsinger, Jörg and Waldmann, Reinhold. The French Automobile and Life Insurance Markets. **In** *Finsinger, J. and Pauly, M. V., eds.*, 1986, pp. 215–29. **[G: France]**

Fox, William F. Insurance Taxation in Minnesota. **In** *Minnesota Tax Study Commission*, 1986, pp. 251–78. **[G: U.S.]**

Freifelder, Leonard R. Estimation of Classification Factor Relativities: A Modelling Approach. *J. Risk Ins.*, March 1986, *53*(1), pp. 135–43. **[G: U.S.]**

Fuchs, Victor R. Paying the Piper, Calling the Tune. **In** *Fuchs, V. R.*, 1986, *1986*, pp. 332–56. **[G: U.S.]**

Funatsu, Hideki. Export Credit Insurance. *J. Risk Ins.*, December 1986, *53*(4), pp. 679–92.

Gardner, Bruce L. and Kramer, Randall A. Experience with Crop Insurance Programs in the United States. **In** *Hazell, P.; Pomareda, C. and Valdés, A., eds.*, 1986, pp. 195–222. **[G: U.S.]**

Geehan, Randall. Economies of Scale in Insurance: Implications for Regulation. **In** *Wasow, B. and Hill, R. D., eds.*, 1986, pp. 137–59. **[G: Canada; U.S.; Australia]**

Giaccotto, Carmelo. Stochastic Modelling of Interest Rates: Actuarial vs. Equilibrium Approach. *J. Risk Ins.*, September 1986, *53*(3), pp. 435–53. [G: U.S.]

Glaser, William A. Payment Systems and Their Effects. **In** *Aiken, L. H. and Mechanic, D., eds.*, 1986, pp. 481–99. [G: U.S.]

Glennon, Dennis and Lane, Julia. Imputing a Housewife's Earnings in a Wrongful Death and Injury Case. *J. Risk Ins.*, December 1986, *53*(4), pp. 734–43. [G: U.S.]

Globerman, Steven. Firm Size and Dynamic Efficiency in the Life Insurance Industry. *J. Risk Ins.*, June 1986, *53*(2), pp. 278–93. [G: U.S.; Canada]

Goodman, Laurie S. and Santomero, Anthony M. Variable-Rate Deposit Insurance: A Re-examination. *J. Banking Finance*, June 1986, *10*(2), pp. 203–18.

Gorre, Lucien. Nationalization of Insurance in France. **In** *Wasow, B. and Hill, R. D., eds.*, 1986, pp. 179–210. [G: France]

Grubel, Herbert G. Government Deposit Insurance, Moral Hazard and the International Debt Crisis. **In** *Giersch, H., ed.*, 1986, pp. 172–86. [G: U.S.]

Gudger, William M. and Avalos, Luis. Planning for the Efficient Operation of Crop Credit Insurance Schemes. **In** *Hazell, P.; Pomareda, C. and Valdés, A., eds.*, 1986, pp. 263–80.

Hamwi, Iskandar S. and Nissan, Edward. On the Use of Distributional Methods in Ratemaking—Reply [Determination of Net Rate in Property and Liability Insurance: An Alternative Approach]. *J. Risk Ins.*, June 1986, *53*(2), pp. 334. [G: U.S.]

Harrington, Scott E. and Nelson, Jack M. A Regression-Based Methodology for Solvency Surveillance in the Property-Liability Insurance Industry. *J. Risk Ins.*, December 1986, *53*(4), pp. 583–605. [G: U.S.]

Hazell, Peter; Bassoco, Luz María and Arcia, Gustavo. A Model for Evaluating Farmers' Demand for Insurance: Applications in Mexico and Panama. **In** *Hazell, P.; Pomareda, C. and Valdés, A., eds.*, 1986, pp. 35–66. [G: Mexico; Panama]

Hazell, Peter; Pomareda, Carlos and Valdés, Alberto. Crop Insurance for Agricultural Development: Issues and Experience: Epilogue. **In** *Hazell, P.; Pomareda, C. and Valdés, A., eds.*, 1986, pp. 293–97.

Hazell, Peter; Pomareda, Carlos and Valdés, Alberto. Crop Insurance for Agricultural Development: Issues and Experience: Introduction. **In** *Hazell, P.; Pomareda, C. and Valdés, A., eds.*, 1986, pp. 1–13.

Henriet, Dominique and Rochet, Jean-Charles. La logique des systèmes bonus-malus en assurance automobile: une approche théorique. (The Logic of the System of Bonuses and Penalties in Automobile Insurance: A Theoretical Approach. With English summary.) *Ann. Écon. Statist.*, Jan./Mar. 1986, (1), pp. 133–52. [G: France]

Hill, Raymond D. Brazil: The Insurance Market Consolidation of the 1970s. **In** *Wasow, B. and Hill, R. D., eds.*, 1986, pp. 211–27. [G: Brazil]

Hill, Raymond D. Insurance and Financial Intermediation. **In** *Wasow, B. and Hill, R. D., eds.*, 1986, pp. 120–34. [G: U.S.]

Horvitz, Sigmund A. Implications of Projecting Future Losses of Earning Capacity with Deterministic Models [Problems in the Use of Historical Data in Estimating Economic Loss in Wrongful Death and Injury Cases]. *J. Risk Ins.*, September 1986, *53*(3), pp. 530–37. [G: U.S.]

Hutter, Josef. Ein Modell zur kalkulatorischen Bewältigung von Änderungsrisiken im Schadenbereich eines Versicherungsunternehmens. (A Model with Consideration of Permanent Changes of the Global Risk Situation. With English summary.) *Schweiz. Z. Volkswirtsch. Statist.*, September 1986, *122*(3), pp. 261–91.

Johnston, Felton McC. Political Risk Insurance. **In** *Raddock, D. M., et al.*, 1986, pp. 186–96.

Kane, Edward J. Appearance and Reality in Deposit Insurance: The Case for Reform. *J. Banking Finance*, June 1986, *10*(2), pp. 175–88. [G: U.S.]

Kane, Edward J. Confronting Incentive Problems in U.S. Deposit Insurance: The Range of Alternative Solutions. **In** *Kaufman, G. G. and Kormendi, R. C., eds.*, 1986, pp. 97–120. [G: U.S.]

Karni, Edi and Zilcha, Itzhak. Risk Aversion in the Theory of Life Insurance: The Fisherian Model. *J. Risk Ins.*, December 1986, *53*(4), pp. 606–20.

Katz, Samuel I. Government Deposit Insurance, Moral Hazard and the International Debt Crisis: Comment. **In** *Giersch, H., ed.*, 1986, pp. 187–91. [G: U.S.]

Kotlikoff, Laurence J.; Shoven, John B. and Spivak, Avia. The Effect of Annuity Insurance and Savings and Inequality. *J. Lab. Econ.*, Part 2, July 1986, *4*(3), pp. S183–207.

Krogh, Harold C. and Levin, Murray S. Recent Trends: State Insurance Guaranty Funds and Insurance Company Insurance Assessment Operations. *J. Risk Ins.*, June 1986, *53*(2), pp. 335–55. [G: U.S.]

Kunreuther, Howard. The Impact of Technology on the Insurance Industry: Discussion. **In** *Faulhaber, G.; Noam, E. and Tasley, R., eds.*, 1986, pp. 44–48. [G: U.S.]

Lloyd, Alan G. and Mauldon, Roger G. Agricultural Instability and Alternative Government Policies: The Australian Experience. **In** *Hazell, P.; Pomareda, C. and Valdés, A., eds.*, 1986, pp. 156–77. [G: Australia]

Lopes, Mauro de Rezende and Dias, Guilherme Leite da Silva. The Brazilian Experience with Crop Insurance Programs. **In** *Hazell, P.; Pomareda, C. and Valdés, A., eds.*, 1986, pp. 240–62. [G: Brazil]

Mathewson, G. Frank and Winter, Ralph A. The Economics of Life Insurance Regulation: Valuation Constraints. **In** *Finsinger, J. and Pauly, M. V., eds.*, 1986, pp. 257–90. [G: Canada]

Mayers, David and Smith, Clifford W., Jr. Ownership Structure and Control: The Mutualization of Stock Life Insurance Companies. *J. Finan. Econ.*, May 1986, *16*(1), pp. 73–98. **[G: U.S.]**

McGee, Robert T. The Cycle in Property/Casualty Insurance. *Fed. Res. Bank New York Quart. Rev.*, Autumn 1986, *11*(3), pp. 22–30. **[G: U.S.]**

McGonagle, John J., Jr. The Uncertainty Principle and Regulation. **In** *Gilad, B. and Kaish, S., eds., Vol. B,* 1986, pp. 123–32. **[G: U.S.]**

McGuire, Thomas G. Financing Psychotherapy. *J. Risk Ins.*, September 1986, *53*(3), pp. 484–91. **[G: U.S.]**

Meador, Joseph W.; Madden, Gerald P. and Johnston, David J. On the Probability of Acquisition of Non-life Insurers. *J. Risk Ins.*, December 1986, *53*(4), pp. 621–43. **[G: U.S.]**

Nabholz, Max E. The Position of the International Reinsurer in Developing Countries. **In** *Wasow, B. and Hill, R. D., eds.*, 1986, pp. 29–56. **[G: MDCs; LDCs]**

Newhouse, Joseph P. Social Experiments in Health. **In** *Aiken, L. H. and Mechanic, D., eds.*, 1986, pp. 229–47. **[G: U.S.]**

Niewuwoudt, W. L. and Bullock, J. Bruce. The Demand for Crop Insurance. **In** *Maunder, A. and Renborg, U., eds.*, 1986, pp. 655–61. **[G: U.S.]**

Nye, David J. and Kolb, Robert W. Inflation, Interest Rates and Property-Liability Insurer Risk. *J. Risk Ins.*, March 1986, *53*(1), pp. 144–54.

Okediji, Olubunmi. Government Participation in the Nigerian Insurance Market: Regulatory or Competitive? *J. World Trade Law*, Sept.:Oct. 1986, *20*(5), pp. 540–53. **[G: Nigeria]**

Outreville, J.-François. The French Insurance Market. **In** *Finsinger, J. and Pauly, M. V., eds.*, 1986, pp. 230–53. **[G: France]**

Outreville, J.-François and Helie, Carole. More Evidence on the Systematic Underwriting Risk in Automobile Insurance. *J. Risk Ins.*, December 1986, *53*(4), pp. 755–66. **[G: Canada]**

Panjer, Harry H. Direct Calculation of Ruin Probabilities. *J. Risk Ins.*, September 1986, *53*(3), pp. 521–29.

Pauly, Mark V. Taxation, Health Insurance, and Market Failure in the Medical Economy. *J. Econ. Lit.*, June 1986, *24*(2), pp. 629–75. **[G: U.S.]**

Pauly, Mark V.; Kunreuther, Howard and Kleindorfer, Paul R. Regulation and Quality Competition in the U.S. Insurance Industry. **In** *Finsinger, J. and Pauly, M. V., eds.*, 1986, pp. 65–107. **[G: U.S.]**

Pomareda, Carlos. An Evaluation of the Impact of Credit Insurance on Bank Performance in Panama. **In** *Hazell, P.; Pomareda, C. and Valdés, A., eds.*, 1986, pp. 101–14. **[G: Panama]**

Pomareda, Carlos. The Financial Viability of Agricultural Insurance. **In** *Hazell, P.; Pomareda, C. and Valdés, A., eds.*, 1986, pp. 281–91. **[G: Selected Countries]**

Posner, James R. Trends in Medical Malpractice Insurance, 1970–1985. *Law Contemp. Probl.*, Spring 1986, *49*(2), pp. 37–56. **[G: U.S.]**

Pyle, David H. Capital Regulation and Deposit Insurance. *J. Banking Finance,* June 1986, *10*(2), pp. 189–201.

Quiggin, John. A Note on the Viability of Rainfall Insurance [The Economics of Insuring Crops against Drought]. *Australian J. Agr. Econ.*, April 1986, *30*(1), pp. 63–69. **[G: Australia]**

Radcliffe, Julian G. Y. Coverage of Political Risk by the Private Insurance Industry. **In** *Hauser, H., ed. (I),* 1986, pp. 135–39.

Ramsay, Colin M. An Optimum and Equitable Net Risk Premium Payment Plan. *J. Risk Ins.*, June 1986, *53*(2), pp. 294–300.

Robinson, Glen O. The Medical Malpractice Crisis of the 1970's: A Retrospective. *Law Contemp. Probl.*, Spring 1986, *49*(2), pp. 5–35. **[G: U.S.]**

Schlesinger, Harris and Venezian, Emilio C. Insurance Markets with Loss-Prevention Activity: Profits, Market Structure, and Consumer Welfare. *Rand J. Econ.*, Summer 1986, *17*(2), pp. 227–38.

Schmit, Joan T. A New View of the Requisites of Insurability. *J. Risk Ins.*, June 1986, *53*(2), pp. 320–29. **[G: U.S.]**

Shelp, June Peno. Insurance Industry Technology. **In** *Wasow, B. and Hill, R. D., eds.*, 1986, pp. 57–66.

Shihata, Ibrahim F. I. The Role of ICSID and the Projected Multilateral Investment Guarantee Agency (MIGA). **In** *Hauser, H., ed. (I),* 1986, pp. 105–22.

Siamwalla, Ammar. Approaches to Price Insurance for Farmers. **In** *Hazell, P.; Pomareda, C. and Valdés, A., eds.*, 1986, pp. 178–92.

Siamwalla, Ammar and Valdés, Alberto. Should Crop Insurance Be Subsidized? **In** *Hazell, P.; Pomareda, C. and Valdés, A., eds.*, 1986, pp. 117–25.

Simmons, LeRoy F. and Cross, Mark L. The Underwriting Cycle and the Risk Manager. *J. Risk Ins.*, March 1986, *53*(1), pp. 155–63. **[G: U.S.]**

Sinha, Tapen. The Effects of Survival Probabilities, Transactions Cost and the Attitude towards Risk on the Demand for Annuities. *J. Risk Ins.*, June 1986, *53*(2), pp. 301–07.

Skees, Jerry R. and Reed, Michael R. Rate Making for Farm-Level Crop Insurance: Implications for Adverse Selection. *Amer. J. Agr. Econ.*, August 1986, *68*(3), pp. 653–59.

Skogh, Göran. The Regulation of the Swedish Insurance Industry. **In** *Finsinger, J. and Pauly, M. V., eds.*, 1986, pp. 163–86. **[G: Sweden]**

Smith, Barry D. Analyzing the Tax Deductibility of Premiums Paid to Captive Insurers. *J. Risk Ins.*, March 1986, *53*(1), pp. 85–103. **[G: U.S.]**

Smith, Clifford W., Jr. On the Convergence of Insurance and Finance Research. *J. Risk Ins.*, December 1986, *53*(4), pp. 693–717.

Smith, Dean G. and Rose, Lawrence C. The Effects of Insurance Policy Limits on Product

Choice. *J. Risk Ins.*, September 1986, *53*(3), pp. 514–20. **[G: U.S.]**

Soejima, Aritoshi. Postwar Development of the Insurance Industry in Japan and Its Future Role in World Economy. **In** *Wasow, B. and Hill, R. D., eds.*, 1986, pp. 250–63. **[G: Japan]**

Spahr, Ronald W. and Escolas, Edmond L. Mortgage Guaranty Insurance: A Unique Style of Insurance. *J. Risk Ins.*, June 1986, *53*(2), pp. 308–19. **[G: U.S.]**

Stano, Miron. A Further Analysis of the "Variations in Practice Style" Phenomenon. *Inquiry*, Summer 1986, *23*(2), pp. 176–82. **[G: U.S.]**

Szegö, Giorgio. Bank Asset Management and Financial Insurance. *J. Banking Finance*, June 1986, *10*(2), pp. 295–307.

Szpiro, George G. Über das Risikoverhalten in der Schweiz. (About the Behavior under Risk in Switzerland. With English summary.) *Schweiz. Z. Volkswirtsch. Statist.*, September 1986, *122*(3), pp. 463–70. **[G: Switzerland]**

Szpiro, George G. Measuring Risk Aversion: An Alternative Approach. *Rev. Econ. Statist.*, February 1986, *68*(1), pp. 156–59. **[G: U.S.]**

Tapp, Julian. Regulation of the UK Insurance Industry. **In** *Finsinger, J. and Pauly, M. V., eds.*, 1986, pp. 27–61. **[G: U.K.]**

Trebilcock, Clive. The City, Entrepreneurship and Insurance: Two Pioneers in Invisible Exports—The Phoenix Fire Office and the Royal of Liverpool, 1800–90. **In** *[Coleman, D. C.]*, 1986, pp. 137–72. **[G: Selected Countries]**

Tsujii, Hiroshi. An Economic Analysis of Rice Insurance in Japan. **In** *Hazell, P.; Pomareda, C. and Valdés, A., eds.*, 1986, pp. 143–55. **[G: Japan]**

Venezian, Emilio C. Risk Management and Financial Regret. *J. Risk Ins.*, September 1986, *53*(3), pp. 395–408.

Venezian, Emilio C. Use of Risk Loads and Distributional Fitting in Ratemaking—Comment [Determination of Net Rate in Property and Liability Insurance: An Alternative Approach]. *J. Risk Ins.*, June 1986, *53*(2), pp. 330–33. **[G: U.S.]**

Viscusi, W. Kip. The Valuation of Risks to Life and Health: Guidelines for Policy Analysis. **In** *Bentkover, J. D.; Covello, V. T. and Jeryl, M., eds.*, 1986, pp. 8510. **[G: U.S.]**

Von Pischke, J. D. Can Crop Credit Insurance Address Risks in Agricultural Lending? **In** *Hazell, P.; Pomareda, C. and Valdés, A., eds.*, 1986, pp. 87–100.

Wasow, Bernard. Determinants of Insurance Penetration: A Cross-Country Analysis. **In** *Wasow, B. and Hill, R. D., eds.*, 1986, pp. 160–76. **[G: Selected Countries]**

Wasow, Bernard. Effects of Nationalization on the Insurance Industry in India. **In** *Wasow, B. and Hill, R. D., eds.*, 1986, pp. 228–40. **[G: India]**

Wasow, Bernard. Insurance and the Balance of Payments. **In** *Wasow, B. and Hill, R. D., eds.*, 1986, pp. 87–103. **[G: S. Korea; Portugal; India; Brazil; Taiwan]**

Wasow, Bernard. Insurance in Korea. **In** *Wasow, B. and Hill, R. D., eds.*, 1986, pp. 241–49. **[G: S. Korea]**

Weiss, Mary A. Analysis of Productivity at the Firm Level: An Application to Life Insurers. *J. Risk Ins.*, March 1986, *53*(1), pp. 49–84. **[G: U.S.]**

Welland, Deborah A. Workers' Compensation Liability Changes and the Distribution of Injury Claims. *J. Risk Ins.*, December 1986, *53*(4), pp. 662–78. **[G: U.S.]**

Wheaton, William C. The Impact of State Taxation on Life Insurance Company Growth. *Nat. Tax J.*, March 1986, *39*(1), pp. 85–95. **[G: U.S.]**

Wilensky, Gail R. Underwriting the Uninsured: Targeting Providers or Individuals. **In** *Sloan, F. A.; Blumstein, J. F. and Perrin, J. M., eds.*, 1986, pp. 148–66. **[G: U.S.]**

Williams, C. Arthur, Jr. Higher Interest Rates, Longer Lifetimes, and the Demand for Life Annuities. *J. Risk Ins.*, March 1986, *53*(1), pp. 164–71.

Williams, C. Arthur, Jr. 1985 Annual Report of the Editor of the *Journal of Risk and Insurance*. *J. Risk Ins.*, March 1986, *53*(1), pp. 23–27. **[G: U.S.]**

de Wit, G. W. The Politics of Rate Discrimination: An International Perspective. *J. Risk Ins.*, December 1986, *53*(4), pp. 644–61. **[G: Netherlands; U.S.]**

Witt, Robert C. The Evolution of Risk Management and Insurance: Change and Challenge. *J. Risk Ins.*, March 1986, *53*(1), pp. 9–22. **[G: U.S.]**

Wurmstich, Jörg-Dietrich. Coverage of Political Risk by National Insurance Agencies: The German Investment Guarantee Scheme. **In** *Hauser, H., ed. (1)*, 1986, pp. 123–33. **[G: W. Germany]**

Yamauchi, Toyoji. Evolution of the Crop Insurance Program in Japan. **In** *Hazell, P.; Pomareda, C. and Valdés, A., eds.*, 1986, pp. 223–39. **[G: Japan]**

Young, David N. The Impact of Technology on the Insurance Industry. **In** *Faulhaber, G.; Noam, E. and Tasley, R., eds.*, 1986, pp. 31–43. **[G: U.S.]**

Zador, Paul and Lund, Adrian. Re-Analyses of the Effects of No-Fault Auto Insurance on Fatal Crashes. *J. Risk Ins.*, June 1986, *53*(2), pp. 226–41.

Zweifel, Peter. Die Kosten-Versicherungs-Spirale im schweizerischen Gesundheitswesen. (The Cost–Insurance Spiral in the Swiss Health Care Sector. With English summary.) *Schweiz. Z. Volkswirtsch. Statist.*, September 1986, *122*(3), pp. 555–83. **[G: Switzerland]**

6357 Real Estate

Beaton, William and Sirmans, C. F. Do Syndications Pay More for Real Estate? *Amer. Real Estate Urban Econ. Assoc. J.*, Summer 1986, *14*(2), pp. 206–15. **[G: U.S.]**

Blackley, Dixie M.; Follain, James R. and Lee,

Haeduck. Evaluation of Hedonic Price Indexes for Thirty-four Large SMSAs. *Amer. Real Estate Urban Econ. Assoc. J.*, Summer 1986, *14*(2), pp. 179–205. [G: U.S.]

Cannaday, Roger E. and Colwell, Peter F. Real Estate Valuation Models: Lender and Equity Investor Criteria. *Amer. Real Estate Urban Econ. Assoc. J.*, Summer 1986, *14*(2), pp. 316–37.

Cannaday, Roger E. and Sunderman, Mark A. Estimation of Depreciation for Single-Family Appraisals. *Amer. Real Estate Urban Econ. Assoc. J.*, Summer 1986, *14*(2), pp. 255–73. [G: U.S.]

Chiang, Raymond; Lai, Tsong-Yue and Ling, David C. Retail Leasehold Interests: A Contingent Claim Analysis. *Amer. Real Estate Urban Econ. Assoc. J.*, Summer 1986, *14*(2), pp. 216–29.

Clauretie, Terrence M. and Harju, Melvin W. The Expanding Concept of Just Compensation and the Role of the Appraiser. *Amer. Real Estate Urban Econ. Assoc. J.*, Summer 1986, *14*(2), pp. 338–60. [G: U.S.]

Colwell, Peter F. and Marshall, David W. Market Share in the Real Estate Brokerage Industry. *Amer. Real Estate Urban Econ. Assoc. J.*, Winter 1986, *14*(4), pp. 583–99. [G: U.S.]

Crandall, Robert W. The Market for Housing Quality: Comments. **In** *Ippolito, P. M. and Scheffman, D. T., eds.*, 1986, pp. 103–04. [G: U.S.]

Erickson, Rodney A. and Syms, Paul M. The Effects of Enterprise Zones on Local Property Markets. *Reg. Stud.*, February 1986, *20*(1), pp. 1–14. [G: U.K.]

Evans, Alan W. and Beed, Clive. Transport Costs and Urban Property Values in the 1970s. *Urban Stud.*, April 1986, *23*(2), pp. 105–17. [G: Australia]

Farber, Stephen C. Market Segmentation and the Effects on Group Homes for the Handicapped on Residential Property Values. *Urban Stud.*, December 1986, *23*(6), pp. 519–25. [G: U.S.]

Fisher, Jeffrey D. and Lentz, George H. Tax Reform and the Value of Real Estate Income Property. *Amer. Real Estate Urban Econ. Assoc. J.*, Summer 1986, *14*(2), pp. 287–315. [G: U.S.]

Frew, James R. and Jud, G. Donald. The Value of a Real Estate Franchise. *Amer. Real Estate Urban Econ. Assoc. J.*, Summer 1986, *14*(2), pp. 374–83. [G: U.S.]

Froland, Charles; Gorlow, Robert and Sampson, Richard. The Market Risk of Real Estate. *J. Portfol. Manage.*, Spring 1986, *12*(3), pp. 12–19. [G: U.S.]

Halphen, Christine. U.S.A.: Effect of the 1985–1986 U.S. Tax Reform Bill on Foreign Investments in U.S. Real Estate. *Bull. Int. Fiscal Doc.*, March 1986, *40*(3), pp. 115–24. [G: U.S.]

Hartzell, David; Hekman, John and Miles, Mike. Diversification Categories in Investment Real Estate. *Amer. Real Estate Urban Econ. Assoc. J.*, Summer 1986, *14*(2), pp. 230–54. [G: U.S.]

Isakson, Hans R. The Nearest Neighbors Appraisal Technique: An Alternative to the Adjustment Grid Methods. *Amer. Real Estate Urban Econ. Assoc. J.*, Summer 1986, *14*(2), pp. 274–86. [G: U.S.]

Johnson, Linda L. and Loucks, Christine. The Effect of State Licensing Regulations on the Real Estate Brokerage Industry. *Amer. Real Estate Urban Econ. Assoc. J.*, Winter 1986, *14*(4), pp. 567–82. [G: U.S.]

Jud, G. Donald and Frew, James R. Real Estate Brokers, Housing Prices, and the Demand for Housing. *Urban Stud.*, February 1986, *23*(1), pp. 21–31. [G: U.S.]

Kane, Edward J. Wealth-Based Engels Curves for Financial and Real Estate Assets. **In** *Chen, A. H., ed.*, 1986, pp. 233–45. [G: U.S.]

Kowalski, Joseph G. and Colwell, Peter F. Market versus Assessed Value of Industrial Land. *Amer. Real Estate Urban Econ. Assoc. J.*, Summer 1986, *14*(2), pp. 361–73. [G: U.S.]

Lusht, Kenneth M. Real Estate Valuation and Appraisal. *Amer. Real Estate Urban Econ. Assoc. J.*, Summer 1986, *14*(2), pp. 175–78. [G: U.S.]

Mills, Edwin S. and Rosen, Harvey S. Tax Reform and Commercial Real Estate. **In** *Follain, J. R., ed.*, 1986, pp. 151–61. [G: U.S.]

Nourse, Hugh O. Rental Price Adjustment and Investment in the Office Market. *Amer. Real Estate Urban Econ. Assoc. J.*, Spring 1986, *14*(1), pp. 163–64. [G: U.S.]

Rosen, Kenneth T. and Smith, Lawrence B. The Resale Housing Market. *Amer. Real Estate Urban Econ. Assoc. J.*, Winter 1986, *14*(4), pp. 510–24. [G: U.S.]

Sack, Paul. Winners and Losers in Commercial Real Estate from the President's Proposals. **In** *Follain, J. R., ed.*, 1986, pp. 137–49. [G: U.S.]

Titman, Sheridan and Warga, Arthur D. Risk and the Performance of Real Estate Investment Trusts: A Multiple Index Approach. *Amer. Real Estate Urban Econ. Assoc. J.*, Fall 1986, *14*(3), pp. 414–31. [G: U.S.]

Vorst, Ton. The Relation between the Rent and Selling Price of a Building under Optimal Maintenance with Uncertainty. *J. Econ. Dynam. Control*, June 1986, *10*(1/2), pp. 315–20.

Webb, James R. and Rubens, Jack H. Portfolio Considerations in the Valuation of Real Estate. *Amer. Real Estate Urban Econ. Assoc. J.*, Fall 1986, *14*(3), pp. 465–95. [G: U.S.]

Weicher, John C. The Market for Housing Quality. **In** *Ippolito, P. M. and Scheffman, D. T., eds.*, 1986, pp. 39–65. [G: U.S.]

Wu, Chunchi and Colwell, Peter F. Equilibrium of Housing and Real Estate Brokerage Markets under Uncertainty. *Amer. Real Estate Urban Econ. Assoc. J.*, Spring 1986, *14*(1), pp. 1–23.

Zimmer, Ian. Accounting for Interest by Real Estate Developers. *J. Acc. Econ.*, March 1986, *8*(1), pp. 37–51. [G: Australia]

Zorn, Thomas S. and Larsen, James E. The Incentive Effects of Flat-Fee and Percentage Commissions for Real Estate Brokers. *Amer. Real Estate Urban Econ. Assoc. J.*, Spring 1986, *14*(1), pp. 24–47.

6358 Entertainment, Recreation, Tourism

Anderson, Terry L. and Johnson, Ronald N. The Problem of Instream Flows. *Econ. Inquiry*, October 1986, *24*(4), pp. 535–54.

Asch, Peter; Malkiel, Burton G. and Quandt, Richard E. Market Efficiency in Racetrack Betting: Further Evidence and a Correction. *J. Bus.*, January 1986, *59*(1), pp. 157–60. **[G: U.S.]**

Baumol, William J. Unnatural Value: Or Art Investment as Floating Crap Game. *Amer. Econ. Rev.*, May 1986, *76*(2), pp. 10–14. **[G: U.S.]**

Bolyard, Joan E. International Travel and Passenger Fares, 1981–85. *Surv. Curr. Bus.*, May 1986, *66*(5), pp. 42–46. **[G: U.S.]**

Cairns, J.; Jennett, N. and Sloane, Peter J. The Economics of Professional Team Sports: A Survey of Theory and Evidence. *J. Econ. Stud.*, 1986, *13*(1), pp. 1–80.

Cameron, S. The Supply and Demand for Cinema Tickets: Some U.K. Evidence. *J. Cult. Econ.*, June 1986, *10*(1), pp. 38–62. **[G: U.K.]**

Cavendish, Elizabeth A. Public Provision of the Performing Arts: A Case Study of the Federal Theatre Project in Connecticut. **In** *DiMaggio, P. J., ed.*, 1986, pp. 140–58. **[G: U.S.]**

Curry, Steve. The Economic Impact of the Tourist Industry in the United Republic of Tanzania: An Input–Output Analysis. *Industry Devel.*, 1986, (19), pp. 55–75. **[G: Tanzania]**

DiMaggio, Paul J. Can Culture Survive the Marketplace? **In** *DiMaggio, P. J., ed.*, 1986, pp. 65–92. **[G: U.S.]**

DiMaggio, Paul J. Cultural Entrepreneurship in Nineteenth-Century Boston. **In** *DiMaggio, P. J., ed.*, 1986, pp. 41–61. **[G: U.S.]**

DiMaggio, Paul J. Nonprofit Enterprise in the Arts: Introduction. **In** *DiMaggio, P. J., ed.*, 1986, pp. 3–13. **[G: U.S.]**

DiMaggio, Paul J. Support for the Arts from Independent Foundations. **In** *DiMaggio, P. J., ed.*, 1986, pp. 113–39. **[G: U.S.]**

Drahozal, Christopher R. The Impact of Free Agency on the Distribution of Playing Talent in Major League Baseball. *J. Econ. Bus.*, May 1986, *38*(2), pp. 113–21. **[G: U.S.]**

Dwyer, Larry. Tourism in the South Pacific. **In** *Cole, R. V. and Parry, T. G., eds.*, 1986, pp. 226–50. **[G: S. Pacific]**

Freedman, Marc R. The Elusive Promise of Management Cooperation in the Performing Arts. **In** *DiMaggio, P. J., ed.*, 1986, pp. 199–213. **[G: U.S.]**

Frey, Bruno S. The Salzburg Festival: An Economic Point of View. *J. Cult. Econ.*, December 1986, *10*(2), pp. 27–44. **[G: W. Germany]**

Gapinski, James H. The Lively Arts as Substitutes for the Lively Arts. *Amer. Econ. Rev.*, May 1986, *76*(2), pp. 20–25. **[G: U.S.; U.K.]**

Globerman, Steven. Potential Implications of Canadian–U.S. Trade Negotiations for Canadian Cultural Support Policies. **In** *C. D. Howe Institute*, 1986, pp. 123–34. **[G: Canada; U.S.]**

Grigalunas, Thomas A., et al. Estimating the Cost of Oil Spills: Lessons from the *Amoco Cadiz* Incident. *Marine Resource Econ.*, 1986, *2*(3), pp. 239–62. **[G: France]**

Hall, Christopher D. Market Enforced Information Asymmetry: A Study of Claiming Races. *Econ. Inquiry*, April 1986, *24*(2), pp. 271–91. **[G: U.S.]**

Hansmann, Henry B. Nonprofit Enterprise in the Performing Arts. **In** *DiMaggio, P. J., ed.*, 1986, pp. 17–40.

Johnson, Erwin H. The Impressario as Entrepreneur. **In** *Greenfield, S. M. and Strickon, A., eds.*, 1986, pp. 138–57.

Kaempfer, William H. and Pacey, Patricia L. Televising College Football: The Complementarity of Attendance and Viewing. *Soc. Sci. Quart.*, March 1986, *67*(1), pp. 176–85. **[G: U.S.]**

Knowlton, Winthrop. Members of the Audience: Public and Private Responsibilities to the Arts. **In** *Knowlton, W. and Zeckhauser, R., eds.*, 1986, pp. 137–51. **[G: U.S.]**

Koch, James V. The Intercollegiate Athletics Industry. **In** *Adams, W., ed.*, 1986, pp. 325–46. **[G: U.S.]**

König, Heinz. Work Incentives, Wage Differentials and the Supply of Human Resources: Comment. **In** *Balassa, B. and Giersch, H., eds.*, 1986, pp. 165–68. **[G: U.S.]**

McCormick, Robert E. and Tollison, Robert D. Crime and Income Distribution in a Basketball Economy. *Int. Rev. Law Econ.*, June 1986, *6*(1), pp. 115–24. **[G: U.S.]**

Medoff, Marshall H. Baseball Attendance and Fan Discrimination. *J. Behav. Econ.*, Spring/Summer 1986, *15*(1/2), pp. 149–55. **[G: U.S.]**

Montias, J. Michael. Public Support for the Performing Arts in Europe and the United States. **In** *DiMaggio, P. J., ed.*, 1986, pp. 287–319. **[G: OECD]**

Morrison, William G. and West, Edwin G. Child Exposure to the Performing Arts: The Implications for Adult Demand. *J. Cult. Econ.*, June 1986, *10*(1), pp. 17–24. **[G: U.S.]**

Morrison, William G. and West, Edwin G. Subsidies for the Performing Arts: Evidence on Voter Preference. *J. Behav. Econ.*, Fall 1986, *15*, pp. 57–72. **[G: Canada]**

Netzer, Dick. Dance in New York: Market and Subsidy Changes. *Amer. Econ. Rev.*, May 1986, *76*(2), pp. 15–19. **[G: U.S.]**

Owen, Bruce M. and Gottlieb, Paul D. The Rise and Fall and Rise of Cable Television Regulation. **In** *Weiss, L. W. and Klass, M. W., eds.*, 1986, pp. 78–104. **[G: U.S.]**

Peterson, Richard A. From Impresario to Arts Administrator: Formal Accountability in Nonprofit Cultural Organizations. **In** *DiMaggio, P. J., ed.*, 1986, pp. 161–83. **[G: U.S.]**

Rosensweig, Jeffrey A. Exchange Rates and Competition for Tourists. *New Eng. Econ. Rev.*,

July/Aug. 1986, pp. 57–67. [G: U.S.]

Round, Jeremy. The Good Food Guide. **In** *Moores, B., ed.*, 1986, pp. 193–200.

Schuster, J. Mark Davidson. Tax Incentives as Arts Policy in Western Europe. **In** *DiMaggio, P. J., ed.*, 1986, pp. 320–60. [G: W. Europe]

Scitovsky, Tibor. Subsidies for the Arts: The Economic Argument. **In** *Scitovsky, T.*, 1986, *1983*, pp. 149–59.

Scitovsky, Tibor. What's Wrong with the Arts Is What's Wrong with Society. **In** *Scitovsky, T.*, 1986, *1972*, pp. 37–46. [G: U.S.]

Shaw, Douglas V. Making Leisure Pay: Street Railway Owned Amusement Parks in the United States, 1900–1925. *J. Cult. Econ.*, December 1986, *10*(2), pp. 67–79. [G: U.S.]

Smith, Sharon P. and Smith, V. Kerry. Successful Movies: A Preliminary Empirical Analysis. *Appl. Econ.*, May 1986, *18*(5), pp. 501–07. [G: U.S.]

Spiggle, Susan. Measuring Social Values: A Content Analysis of Sunday Comics and Underground Comix. *J. Cons. Res.*, June 1986, *13*(1), pp. 100–113. [G: U.S.]

Spinanger, Dean. Work Incentives, Wage Differentials and the Supply of Human Resources. **In** *Balassa, B. and Giersch, H., eds.*, 1986, pp. 140–58. [G: U.S.]

Thompson, Nancy L. Financially Troubled Museums and the Law. **In** *DiMaggio, P. J., ed.*, 1986, pp. 214–42. [G: U.S.]

Touzin, Mia. The Sheraton Guest Experience. **In** *Moores, B., ed.*, 1986, pp. 181–92.

Useem, Michael and Kutner, Stephen I. Corporate Contributions to Culture and the Arts: The Organization of Giving and the Influence of the Chief Executive Officer and of Other Firms on Company Contributions in Massachusetts. **In** *DiMaggio, P. J., ed.*, 1986, pp. 93–112. [G: U.S.]

Walker, Bruce. The Demand for Professional League Football and the Success of Football League Teams: Some City Size Effects. *Urban Stud.*, June 1986, *23*(3), pp. 209–19. [G: U.K.]

Weinberg, Charles B. Arts Plan: Implementation, Evolution, and Usage. *Marketing Sci.*, Spring 1986, *5*(2), pp. 143–58. [G: U.S.]

White, Michael D. Self-interest Redistribution and the National Football League Players Association. *Econ. Inquiry*, October 1986, *24*(4), pp. 669–80. [G: U.S.]

Zolberg, Vera L. Tensions of Mission in American Art Museums. **In** *DiMaggio, P. J., ed.*, 1986, pp. 184–98. [G: U.S.]

636 Nonprofit Industries: Theory and Studies

6360 Nonprofit Industries: Theory and Studies

Abrams, Burton A. and Schmitz, Mark D. The Crowding-out Effect of Governmental Transfers on Private Charitable Contributions. **In** *Rose-Ackerman, S., ed.*, 1986, *1978*, pp. 303–12. [G: U.S.]

Andersen, Ronald M.; Banks, Martha J. and Aplington, Margaret. Success in Reaching the Communities and People Targeted for MHSP. **In** *Fleming, G. V. and Andersen, R. M., eds.*, 1986, pp. 45–67. [G: U.S.]

Andersen, Ronald M. and Fleming, Gretchen V. Expenditures for Medical Care. **In** *Fleming, G. V. and Andersen, R. M., eds.*, 1986, pp. 94–118. [G: U.S.]

Bell, Ralph. Utilization of Medical Care Services. **In** *Fleming, G. V. and Andersen, R. M., eds.*, 1986, pp. 80–93. [G: U.S.]

Bell, Ralph and Banks, Martha J. The MHSP Evaluation Data and Methods. **In** *Fleming, G. V. and Andersen, R. M., eds.*, 1986, pp. 27–44. [G: U.S.]

Ben-Ner, Avner. Nonprofit Organizations: Why Do They Exist in Market Economies? **In** *Rose-Ackerman, S., ed.*, 1986, pp. 94–113.

Blau, Judith R.; Newman, Laurie and Schwartz, Joseph E. Internal Economies of Scale in Performing Arts Organizations. *J. Cult. Econ.*, June 1986, *10*(1), pp. 63–76. [G: U.S.]

Clotfelter, Charles T. The Effect of Tax Simplification on Educational and Charitable Organizations. **In** *Federal Reserve Bank of Boston*, 1986, pp. 187–215. [G: U.S.]

Clotfelter, Charles T. and Salamon, Lester M. The Impact of the 1981 Tax Act on Individual Charitable Giving. **In** *Rose-Ackerman, S., ed.*, 1986, *1982*, pp. 207–23. [G: U.S.]

DiMaggio, Paul J. Can Culture Survive the Marketplace? **In** *DiMaggio, P. J., ed.*, 1986, pp. 65–92. [G: U.S.]

DiMaggio, Paul J. Cultural Entrepreneurship in Nineteenth-Century Boston. **In** *DiMaggio, P. J., ed.*, 1986, pp. 41–61. [G: U.S.]

DiMaggio, Paul J. Nonprofit Enterprise in the Arts: Introduction. **In** *DiMaggio, P. J., ed.*, 1986, pp. 3–13. [G: U.S.]

DiMaggio, Paul J. Support for the Arts from Independent Foundations. **In** *DiMaggio, P. J., ed.*, 1986, pp. 113–39. [G: U.S.]

Easley, David and O'Hara, Maureen. Optimal Nonprofit Firms. **In** *Rose-Ackerman, S., ed.*, 1986, pp. 85–93.

Elkan, Walter. Collecting for Galleries and Museums. *Nat. Westminster Bank Quart. Rev.*, February 1986, pp. 26–36. [G: U.K.]

Ernst, Richard L. and Zaidi, Mahmood A. On the Economics of Nonprofit Sellers: Output Policies in Community Hospitals. *Rev. Ind. Organ.*, 1986, *3*(1), pp. 25–43.

Fleming, Gretchen V. Appropriateness of Care. **In** *Fleming, G. V. and Andersen, R. M., eds.*, 1986, pp. 160–77. [G: U.S.]

Fleming, Gretchen V. Selection Effects in the MHSP Program. **In** *Fleming, G. V. and Andersen, R. M., eds.*, 1986, pp. 68–79. [G: U.S.]

Fleming, Gretchen V. and Andersen, Ronald M. Can Access Be Improved While Controlling Costs? Conclusion. **In** *Fleming, G. V. and Andersen, R. M., eds.*, 1986, pp. 195–208. [G: U.S.]

Foster, Richard W. Waiver Effects and Further Controls for Selection Bias. **In** *Fleming, G. V.*

and Andersen, R. M., eds., 1986, pp. 119–59. [G: U.S.]

Freedman, Marc R. The Elusive Promise of Management Cooperation in the Performing Arts. **In** *DiMaggio, P. J., ed.*, 1986, pp. 199–213. [G: U.S.]

Frey, Bruno S. The Salzburg Festival: An Economic Point of View. *J. Cult. Econ.*, December 1986, *10*(2), pp. 27–44. [G: W. Germany]

German, Rachel M. Health Care in the City: Setting the Stage for the Municipal Health Services Program. **In** *Fleming, G. V. and Andersen, R. M., eds.*, 1986, pp. 13–26. [G: U.S.]

Glenday, Graham; Gupta, Anil K. and Pawlak, Henry. Tax Incentives for Personal Charitable Contributions. *Rev. Econ. Statist.*, November 1986, *68*(4), pp. 688–93. [G: Canada]

Grant, James H. and Lindauer, David L. The Economics of Charity Life-Cycle Patterns of Alumnae Contributions. *Eastern Econ. J.*, Apr.-June 1986, *12*(2), pp. 129–41.

Grossman, Philip J. and Chan, Yoke-Fong. The Impact of CPF Savings on Charitable Contributions in Singapore: A Note. *Singapore Econ. Rev.*, October 1986, *31*(2), pp. 79–84. [G: Singapore]

Hansmann, Henry B. Nonprofit Enterprise in the Performing Arts. **In** *DiMaggio, P. J., ed.*, 1986, pp. 17–40.

Hansmann, Henry B. The Rationale for Exempting Nonprofit Organizations from Corporate Income Taxation. **In** *Rose-Ackerman, S., ed.*, 1986, *1981*, pp. 367–93. [G: U.S.]

Hansmann, Henry B. The Role of Nonprofit Enterprise. **In** *Rose-Ackerman, S., ed.*, 1986, *1980*, pp. 57–84. [G: U.S.]

Havenga, Richard. The Role of Non-profit Organisations in Education and Training. **In** *Smollan, R., ed.*, 1986, pp. 145–52. [G: S. Africa]

Hochman, Harold M. The Charitable Deduction: Comments. **In** *Rose-Ackerman, S., ed.*, 1986, pp. 297–99.

Hochman, Harold M. and Rodgers, James D. The Optimal Tax Treatment of Charitable Contributions. **In** *Rose-Ackerman, S., ed.*, 1986, *1977*, pp. 224–45. [G: U.S.]

Horowitz, Harold. The Federal and State Partnership in the Support of Culture in the U.S.A. *J. Cult. Econ.*, December 1986, *10*(2), pp. 1–26. [G: U.S.]

James, Estelle. Contract Failure and Information Asymmetry: Comments. **In** *Rose-Ackerman, S., ed.*, 1986, pp. 154–58.

James, Estelle. How Nonprofits Grow: A Model. **In** *Rose-Ackerman, S., ed.*, 1986, *1983*, pp. 185–95. [G: U.S.]

James, Estelle. The Private Nonprofit Provision of Education: A Theoretical Model and Application to Japan. *J. Compar. Econ.*, September 1986, *10*(3), pp. 255–76. [G: Japan]

Kieffer, Jarold A. The Older Volunteer Resource. **In** *Inst. Med. and Nat'l Res. Counc., Comm. on an Aging Society*, 1986, pp. 51–72. [G: U.S.]

Knowlton, Winthrop. Members of the Audience: Public and Private Responsibilities to the Arts. **In** *Knowlton, W. and Zeckhauser, R., eds.*, 1986, pp. 137–51. [G: U.S.]

Krashinsky, Michael. Transaction Costs and a Theory of the Nonprofit Organization. **In** *Rose-Ackerman, S., ed.*, 1986, pp. 114–32.

Lange, Mark; Luksetich, William and Jacobs, Philip. Managerial Objectives of Symphony Orchestras. *Managerial Dec. Econ.*, December 1986, *7*(4), pp. 273–78. [G: U.S.]

Legorreta, Judith Manfredo and Young, Dennis R. Why Organizations Turn Nonprofit: Lessons from Case Studies. **In** *Rose-Ackerman, S., ed.*, 1986, pp. 196–204. [G: U.S.]

Lindsey, Lawrence B. The Effect of the President's Tax Reform Proposal on Charitable Giving. *Nat. Tax J.*, March 1986, *39*(1), pp. 1–12. [G: U.S.]

Maule, Christopher J. Trade and Culture in Canada. *J. World Trade Law*, Nov.:Dec. 1986, *20*(6), pp. 615–23. [G: Canada]

McTighe, Michael J. "True Philanthropy" and the Limits of the Female Sphere: Poor Relief and Labor Organizations in Ante-Bellum Cleveland. *Labor Hist.*, Spring 1986, *27*(2), pp. 227–56. [G: U.S.]

Montias, J. Michael. Public Support for the Performing Arts in Europe and the United States. **In** *DiMaggio, P. J., ed.*, 1986, pp. 287–319. [G: OECD]

Morgan, James N. Unpaid Productive Activity over the Life Course. **In** *Inst. Med. and Nat'l Res. Counc., Comm. on an Aging Society*, 1986, pp. 73–109. [G: U.S.]

Morrison, William G. and West, Edwin G. Child Exposure to the Performing Arts: The Implications for Adult Demand. *J. Cult. Econ.*, June 1986, *10*(1), pp. 17–24. [G: U.S.]

Muurinen, Jaana-Marja. Modelling Non-profit Firms in Medicine. **In** *Culyer, A. J. and Jönsson, B., eds.*, 1986, pp. 86–98.

Netzer, Dick. Dance in New York: Market and Subsidy Changes. *Amer. Econ. Rev.*, May 1986, *76*(2), pp. 15–19. [G: U.S.]

Oster, Sharon. Contract Failure and Information Asymmetry: Comments. **In** *Rose-Ackerman, S., ed.*, 1986, pp. 152–54.

Paqué, Karl-Heinz. The Efficiency of Tax Incentives to Private Charitable Giving—Some Econometric Evidence for the Federal Republic of Germany. *Weltwirtsch. Arch.*, 1986, *122*(4), pp. 690–712. [G: W. Germany]

Peterson, Richard A. From Impresario to Arts Administrator: Formal Accountability in Nonprofit Cultural Organizations. **In** *DiMaggio, P. J., ed.*, 1986, pp. 161–83. [G: U.S.]

Posnett, John and Sandler, Todd. Joint Supply and the Finance of Charitable Activity. *Public Finance Quart.*, April 1986, *14*(2), pp. 209–22. [G: U.K.]

Powell, Walter W. Should University Presses Compete with Commercial Scholarly Publishers? **In** *DiMaggio, P. J., ed.*, 1986, pp. 270–78. [G: U.S.]

Powell, Walter W. and Friedkin, Rebecca Jo. Politics and Programs: Organizational Factors in Public Television Decision Making. **In** *DiMaggio, P. J., ed.*, 1986, pp. 245–69. **[G: U.S.]**

Reiner, Thomas and Wilson, Mark. Nonprofits in a Löschian Landscape. **In** *[Lösch, A.]*, 1986, pp. 243–55. **[G: U.S.]**

Ridler, Neil B. Cultural Identity and Public Policy: An Economic Analysis. *J. Cult. Econ.*, December 1986, *10*(2), pp. 45–56. **[G: Canada]**

Romero, Carol Jusenius. The Economics of Volunteerism: A Review. **In** *Inst. Med. and Nat'l Res. Counc., Comm. on an Aging Society*, 1986, pp. 23–50. **[G: U.S.]**

Rose-Ackerman, Susan. Charitable Giving and "Excessive" Fundraising. **In** *Rose-Ackerman, S., ed.*, 1986, *1982*, pp. 333–46.

Rose-Ackerman, Susan. Do Government Grants to Charity Reduce Private Donations? **In** *Rose-Ackerman, S., ed.*, 1986, *1981*, pp. 313–29.

Rose-Ackerman, Susan. The Economics of Nonprofit Institutions: Introduction. **In** *Rose-Ackerman, S., ed.*, 1986, pp. 3–17.

Rose-Ackerman, Susan. Unfair Competition and Corporate Income Taxation. **In** *Rose-Ackerman, S., ed.*, 1986, *1982*, pp. 394–414.

Schuster, J. Mark Davidson. Tax Incentives as Arts Policy in Western Europe. **In** *DiMaggio, P. J., ed.*, 1986, pp. 320–60. **[G: W. Europe]**

Schwarz, Samuel. Long-term Adjustments in Performing Arts Expenditures. *J. Cult. Econ.*, December 1986, *10*(2), pp. 57–66. **[G: U.S.]**

Schwarz, Samuel. Self-destruction of a Government-Created Oligopoly: A Case Study of the New York City Bingo Market. *Amer. Econ.*, Fall 1986, *30*(2), pp. 33–36. **[G: U.S.]**

Scitovsky, Tibor. Subsidies for the Arts: The Economic Argument. **In** *Scitovsky, T.*, 1986, *1983*, pp. 149–59.

Simon, John G. Charity and Dynasty under the Federal Tax System. **In** *Rose-Ackerman, S., ed.*, 1986, *1978*, pp. 246–64. **[G: U.S.]**

Smolensky, Eugene. Municipal Financing of the U.S. Fine Arts Museum: A Historical Rationale. *J. Econ. Hist.*, September 1986, *46*(3), pp. 757–68. **[G: U.S.]**

Steinberg, Richard. Should Donors Care about Fundraising? **In** *Rose-Ackerman, S., ed.*, 1986, pp. 347–64.

Steuerle, C. Eugene. The Effect of Tax Simplification on Educational and Charitable Organizations: Discussion. **In** *Federal Reserve Bank of Boston*, 1986, pp. 216–21. **[G: U.S.]**

Strnad, Jeff. The Charitable Contribution Deduction: A Politico-Economic Analysis. **In** *Rose-Ackerman, S., ed.*, 1986, pp. 265–96.

Thompson, Nancy L. Financially Troubled Museums and the Law. **In** *DiMaggio, P. J., ed.*, 1986, pp. 214–42. **[G: U.S.]**

Tullock, Gordon. Information without Profit. **In** *Tullock, G.*, 1986, *1966*, pp. 73–88.

Useem, Michael and Kutner, Stephen I. Corporate Contributions to Culture and the Arts: The Organization of Giving and the Influence of the Chief Executive Officer and of Other Firms on Company Contributions in Massachusetts. **In** *DiMaggio, P. J., ed.*, 1986, pp. 93–112. **[G: U.S.]**

Weisbrod, Burton A. Toward a Theory of the Voluntary Nonprofit Sector in a Three-Sector Economy. **In** *Rose-Ackerman, S., ed.*, 1986, *1977*, pp. 21–44.

Weisbrod, Burton A. and Dominguez, Nestor D. Demand for Collective Goods in Private Nonprofit Markets: Can Fundraising Expenditures Help Overcome Free-Rider Behavior? *J. Public Econ.*, June 1986, *30*(1), pp. 83–96. **[G: U.S.]**

Weisbrod, Burton A. and Schlesinger, Mark. Public, Private, Nonprofit Ownership and the Response to Asymmetric Information: The Case of Nursing Homes. **In** *Rose-Ackerman, S., ed.*, 1986, pp. 133–51. **[G: U.S.]**

Weiss, Jeffrey H. Donations: Can They Reduce a Donor's Welfare? **In** *Rose-Ackerman, S., ed.*, 1986, pp. 45–54.

Wiewel, Wim and Mier, Robert. Enterprise Activities of Not-for-Profit Organizations: Surviving the New Federalism? **In** *Bergman, E. M., ed.*, 1986, pp. 205–25.

Wolch, Jennifer R. and Geiger, Robert K. Urban Restructuring and the Not-for-Profit Sector. *Econ. Geogr.*, January 1986, *62*(1), pp. 3–18. **[G: U.S.]**

Yang, James T. Y. Collaboration between Nonprofit Universities and Commercial Enterprises: The Rationale for Exempting Nonprofit Universities from Federal Income Taxation. *Yale Law J.*, July 1986, *95*(8), pp. 1857–81. **[G: U.S.]**

Yoder, Sunny G. Economic Theories of For-Profit and Not-for-Profit Organizations. **In** *Gray, B. H., ed.*, 1986, pp. 19–25.

Young, Dennis R. Entrepreneurship and the Behavior of Nonprofit Organizations: Elements of a Theory. **In** *Rose-Ackerman, S., ed.*, 1986, *1981*, pp. 161–84.

Zolberg, Vera L. Tensions of Mission in American Art Museums. **In** *DiMaggio, P. J., ed.*, 1986, pp. 184–98. **[G: U.S.]**

640 Economic Capacity

641 Economic Capacity

6410 Economic Capacity

Bakalis, Steve and Hazari, Bharat R. A Note on Underutilization of Capital and Unemployment in a Harris–Todaro Framework. *Devel. Econ.*, September 1986, *24*(3), pp. 288–98. **[G: LDCs]**

Berg, Sigbjørn Atle. Excess Capacity and the Degree of Collusion: The Norwegian Experience, 1967–82. *Int. J. Ind. Organ.*, March 1986, *4*(1), pp. 99–107. **[G: Norway]**

Berndt, Ernst R. and Fuss, Melvyn A. Productivity Measurement with Adjustments for Variations in Capacity Utilization and Other Forms of Temporary Equilibrium. *J. Econometrics*, Oct./Nov. 1986, *33*(1/2), pp. 7–29. **[G: U.S.]**

Berndt, Ernst R. and Hesse, Dieter M. Measuring and Assessing Capacity Utilization in the Manufacturing Sectors of Nine OECD Countries. *Europ. Econ. Rev.*, October 1986, *30*(5), pp. 961–89. **[G: OECD]**

Betancourt, Roger R. A Generalization of Modern Production Theory. *Appl. Econ.*, August 1986, *18*(8), pp. 915–28.

Byrnes, Patricia; Grosskopf, Shawna and Hayes, Kathy J. Efficiency and Ownership: Further Evidence. *Rev. Econ. Statist.*, May 1986, *68*(2), pp. 337–41. **[G: U.S.]**

Carvalhais, Z. and Davis, M. H. A. Optimal Timing of Capacity Expansion. *J. Econ. Dynam. Control*, June 1986, *10*(1/2), pp. 89–91.

Cossutta, Dario and Grillo, Michele. Excess Capacity, Sunk Costs and Collusion: A Non-cooperative Bargaining Game: Some Considerations on the European Car Industry. *Int. J. Ind. Organ.*, September 1986, *4*(3), pp. 251–70. **[G: W. Europe]**

Driver, Ciaran. Spare Capacity and the Scope for Industrial Expansion. *Fisc. Stud.*, August 1986, *7*(3), pp. 67–75. **[G: U.K.]**

Driver, Ciaran. Transformation of the CBI Capacity Utilization Series: Theory and Evidence. *Oxford Bull. Econ. Statist.*, November 1986, *48*(4), pp. 339–52. **[G: U.K.]**

Evans, Paul. Does the Potency of Monetary Policy Vary with Capacity Utilization? *Carnegie-Rochester Conf. Ser. Public Policy*, Spring 1986, *24*, pp. 303–31. **[G: U.S.]**

Fal'tsman, F. Increasing the Return on Industry's Fixed Capital. *Prob. Econ.*, January 1986, *28*(9), pp. 18–36. **[G: U.S.S.R.]**

Helliwell, John F. and Chung, Alan. Aggregate Output with Variable Rates of Utilization of Employed Factors. *J. Econometrics*, Oct./Nov. 1986, *33*(1/2), pp. 285–310. **[G: Canada]**

Hulten, Charles R. Productivity Change, Capacity Utilization, and the Sources of Efficiency Growth. *J. Econometrics*, Oct./Nov. 1986, *33*(1/2), pp. 31–50.

Kibria, M. G. and Tisdell, Clem A. Life-Time Patterns of Capacity Utilization by Manufacturing Firms in an LDC: A Study of Jute Spinning in Bangladesh. *Indian Econ. Rev.*, Jan.-June 1986, *21*(1), pp. 1–19. **[G: Bangladesh]**

Kornai, János. The Reproduction of Shortage. **In** *Kornai, J.*, 1986, *1979*, pp. 6–32.

Masson, Robert T. and Shaanan, Joseph. Excess Capacity and Limit Pricing: An Empirical Test. *Economica*, August 1986, *53*(211), pp. 365–78. **[G: U.S.]**

Medikov, V. Ia. The Customary and the Unapparent in Capacity Utilization. *Prob. Econ.*, February 1986, *28*(10), pp. 79–90. **[G: U.S.S.R.]**

Morrison, Catherine J. Productivity Measurement with Non-static Expectations and Varying Capacity Utilization: An Integrated Approach. *J. Econometrics*, Oct./Nov. 1986, *33*(1/2), pp. 51–74. **[G: U.S.]**

Shapiro, Matthew D. Capital Utilization and Capital Accumulation: Theory and Evidence. *J. Appl. Econometrics*, July 1986, *1*(3), pp. 211–34. **[G: U.S.]**

700 Agriculture; Natural Resources

710 Agriculture

7100 General

von Ah, Joseph. Pressure on Natural Resources: Discussion. **In** *Maunder, A. and Renborg, U., eds.*, 1986, pp. 293–95.

Aricanli, Tosun. Agrarian Relations in Turkey: A Historical Sketch. **In** *Richards, A., ed.*, 1986, pp. 23–67. **[G: Turkey]**

Aspengren, Evald. Java and the World: A Study in the Relationship between the Rice Agriculture of Java and the World Economy in the 1930s. **In** *Nørlund, I.; Cederroth, S. and Gerdin, I., eds.*, 1986, pp. 230–63. **[G: Indonesia]**

Beilock, Richard P.; Polopolus, Leo C. and Correal, Mario. Ranking of Agricultural Economics Department by Citations. *Amer. J. Agr. Econ.*, August 1986, *68*(3), pp. 595–604. **[G: U.S.]**

Bertrand, Jean-Pierre. Pressure on Natural Resources: Discussion. **In** *Maunder, A. and Renborg, U., eds.*, 1986, pp. 295–96.

Bhaduri, Amit. Forced Commerce and Agrarian Growth. *World Devel.*, Special Issue, Feb. 1986, *14*(2), pp. 267–72.

Binswanger, Hans P. Agricultural Mechanization: A Comparative Historical Perspective. *World Bank Res. Observer*, January 1986, *1*(1), pp. 27–56. **[G: Selected Countries]**

Birowo, Achmad T. and Prabowo, Dibyo. The Pressure on Natural Resources in Indonesian Agricultural Development. **In** *Maunder, A. and Renborg, U., eds.*, 1986, pp. 284–93.

Blomqvist, Ake G. The Economics of Price Scissors: Comment. *Amer. Econ. Rev.*, December 1986, *76*(5), pp. 1188–91.

Bossier, Jacques. Human Capital, Technology and Institutions: Discussion. **In** *Maunder, A. and Renborg, U., eds.*, 1986, pp. 434–36.

Bratton, Michael. Farmer Organizations and Food Production in Zimbabwe. *World Devel.*, March 1986, *14*(3), pp. 367–84. **[G: Zimbabwe]**

Bromley, Daniel W. Natural Resources and Agricultural Development in the Tropics: Is Conflict Inevitable? **In** *Maunder, A. and Renborg, U., eds.*, 1986, pp. 319–27.

Camargo Barros, Geraldo. Growing Interdependencies and Uncertainties: Discussion. **In** *Maunder, A. and Renborg, U., eds.*, 1986, pp. 122–23.

Carter, Michael R. The Economics of Price Scissors: Comment. *Amer. Econ. Rev.*, December 1986, *76*(5), pp. 1192–94.

Cederroth, Sven and Gerdin, Ingela. Cultivating Poverty: The Case of the Green Revolution in Lombok. **In** *Nørlund, I.; Cederroth, S. and Gerdin, I., eds.*, 1986, pp. 124–50. **[G: Indonesia]**

Chataigner, Jean and Leon, Yves. Self-reliance or Dependence of Agricultural Economics Research in Developing Countries. **In** *Maunder, A. and Renborg, U., eds.*, 1986, pp. 417–23.

Dantwala, M. L. Strategy of Agricultural Development since Independence. **In** *Dantwala, M. L., et al.*, 1986, pp. 1–15. **[G: India]**

De Visscher, Guy. Growing Interdependencies and Uncertainties: Discussion. **In** *Maunder, A. and Renborg, U., eds.*, 1986, pp. 123–25.

Deere, Carmen Diana. Agrarian Reform, Peasant and Rural Production, and the Organization of Production in the Transition to Socialism. **In** *Fagen, R. R.; Deere, C. D. and Coraggio, J. L., eds.*, 1986, pp. 97–142. **[G: Selected LDCs]**

Dutt, Amitava Krishna. Stock Equilibrium in Flexprice Markets in Macromodels for Less Developed Economies: The Case of Food Speculation. *J. Devel. Econ.*, April 1986, *21* (1), pp. 89–109. **[G: LDCs]**

Eastwood, David B.; Brooker, John R. and Terry, Danny E. Household Nutrient Demand: Use of Characteristics Theory and a Common Attribute Model. *Southern J. Agr. Econ.*, December 1986, *18* (2), pp. 235–46. **[G: U.S.]**

Farrell, Kenneth R. and Capalbo, Susan M. Natural Resource and Environmental Dimensions of Agricultural Development. **In** *Maunder, A. and Renborg, U., eds.*, 1986, pp. 273–83. **[G: U.S.]**

FitzSimmons, Margaret. The New Industrial Agriculture: The Regional Integration of Specialty Crop Production. *Econ. Geogr.*, October 1986, *62* (4), pp. 334–53. **[G: U.S.]**

Fox, Karl A. Agricultural Economists as World Leaders in Applied Econometrics, 1917–33. *Amer. J. Agr. Econ.*, May 1986, *68* (2), pp. 381–86.

Furtan, W. H. Educational Institutions and Scholarship in the Twenty-First Century. *Can. J. Agr. Econ.*, June 1986, *33*, pp. 111–17. **[G: Canada]**

Grabowski, Richard and Sivan, David. The Supply of Labor in Agriculture and Food Prices: The Cases of Japan and Egypt. *World Devel.*, March 1986, *14* (3), pp. 441–47. **[G: Japan; Egypt]**

Grabowski, Richard; Tracy, Ronald L. and Sanchez, Onesimo. The Development of Technology in Taiwanese Agriculture. *J. Econ. Devel.*, December 1986, *11* (2), pp. 161–76. **[G: Taiwan]**

Gunter, Lewell F. Wage Determination for Regular Hired Farm Workers: An Empirical Analysis for Georgia. *Southern J. Agr. Econ.*, December 1986, *18* (2), pp. 197–206. **[G: U.S.]**

Henning, Steven A. and Eddleman, B. R. Intra- and Inter-state Transferability of Soybean Variety Research. *Southern J. Agr. Econ.*, December 1986, *18* (2), pp. 7–13. **[G: U.S.]**

Johnson, D. Gale. Agricultural Economics, Contributions: Discussion [Views on Agricultural Economics' Role in Economic Thought]. *Amer. J. Agr. Econ.*, May 1986, *68* (2), pp. 395–96. **[G: U.S.]**

Johnson, Glenn L. Scope of Agricultural Economics. **In** *Maunder, A. and Renborg, U., eds.*, 1986, pp. 21–34.

Johnson, Stan R. Future Challenges for Modeling in Agricultural Economics. *Amer. J. Agr. Econ.*, May 1986, *68* (2), pp. 387–94.

Johnston, Bruce F. Governmental Strategies for Agricultural Development. **In** *Berg, R. J. and Whitaker, J. S., eds.*, 1986, pp. 155–83. **[G: Africa]**

Kjaergaard, Thorkild. Origins of Economic Growth in European Societies since the XVIth Century: The Case of Agriculture. *J. Europ. Econ. Hist.*, Winter 1986, *15* (3), pp. 591–98. **[G: Europe]**

Kueh, Y. Y. Weather Cycles and Agricultural Instability in China. *J. Agr. Econ.*, January 1986, *37* (1), pp. 101–04. **[G: China]**

Lacombe, Philippe. Structure of Agriculture: Implications for Research and Policy. **In** *Maunder, A. and Renborg, U., eds.*, 1986, pp. 781–90.

Leonard, David K. Putting the Farmer in Control: Building Agricultural Institutions. **In** *Berg, R. J. and Whitaker, J. S., eds.*, 1986, pp. 184–214. **[G: Africa]**

Lundahl, Mats. U-ländernas jordbruk: dualism eller bristande jämlikhet? (Agriculture in Developing Countries: Dualism or Lacking Equality? With English summary.) *Ekon. Samfundets Tidskr.*, 1986, *39* (4), pp. 180–200. **[G: LDCs]**

Matthews, Alan. Structure of Agriculture and People in Rural Societies: Discussion. **In** *Maunder, A. and Renborg, U., eds.*, 1986, pp. 500–504.

Maxwell, Simon. The Social Scientist in Farming Systems Research. *J. Agr. Econ.*, January 1986, *37* (1), pp. 25–35.

McCalla, Alex F. and Josling, Timothy E. Agriculture in an Interdependent and Uncertain World: Implications for Markets and Prices. **In** *Maunder, A. and Renborg, U., eds.*, 1986, pp. 114–22.

McClintock, David W. Agricultural Technology Transfer in the Evolving North–South Dialogue. **In** *McIntyre, J. R. and Papp, D. S., eds.*, 1986, pp. 117–35. **[G: LDCs]**

Mellor, John W. Agriculture on the Road to Industrialization. **In** *Lewis, J. P. and Kallab, V., eds.*, 1986, pp. 67–89.

Michie, Barry H. Problematics of Technology and Social Change. **In** *Björkman, J. W., ed.*, 1986, pp. 69–83. **[G: S. Asia]**

Mwangi, Wilfred. Human Capital, Technology and Institutions: Discussion. **In** *Maunder, A. and Renborg, U., eds.*, 1986, pp. 436–38.

Nerlove, Marc. Agricultural Economics, Contributions: Discussion [Agricultural Economists as World Leaders in Applied Econometrics, 1917–33] [Future Challenges for Modeling in Agricultural Economics]. *Amer. J. Agr. Econ.*, May 1986, *68* (2), pp. 397–98.

Newby, Howard. The Changing Structure of Agriculture and the Future of Rural Society. **In** *Maunder, A. and Renborg, U., eds.*, 1986, pp. 493–500.

Niu, Ruofeng and Calkins, Peter H. Towards an Agricultural Economy for China in a New Age: Progress, Problems, Response, and Prospects. *Amer. J. Agr. Econ.*, May 1986, *68*(2), pp. 445–50. **[G: China]**

Nørlund, Irene. Rice Production in Colonial Vietnam, 1900–1930: Production, Consumption, Market Relations and Social Differentiation. **In** *Nørlund, I.; Cederroth, S. and Gerdin, I., eds.*, 1986, pp. 203–29. **[G: China]**

O'Brien, Patrick K. and Toniolo, Gianni. Sull'arretratezza dell'agricoltura italiana rispetto a quella del regno unito attorno al 1910. (On the Backwardness of Italian Agriculture Relative to the United Kingdom C.A. 1910. With English summary.) *Ricerche Econ.*, Apr.-Sept. 1986, *40*(2–3), pp. 266–85. **[G: U.K.; Italy]**

Odie-Ali, Stella. Women in Agriculture: The Case of Guyana. *Soc. Econ. Stud.*, June 1986, *35*(2), pp. 241–89. **[G: Guyana]**

Osburn, Donald. Human Capital, Technology and Institutions: Discussion. **In** *Maunder, A. and Renborg, U., eds.*, 1986, pp. 488–89.

Oshima, Harry T. The Transition from an Agricultural to an Industrial Economy in East Asia. *Econ. Develop. Cult. Change*, July 1986, *34*(4), pp. 783–809. **[G: Japan; Taiwan; S. Korea]**

Outhwaite, R. B. Progress and Backwardness in English Agriculture, 1500–1650. *Econ. Hist. Rev., 2nd Ser.*, February 1986, *39*(1), pp. 1–18. **[G: U.K.]**

Petit, Michel. The Status and the State of Agricultural Economics. **In** *Maunder, A. and Renborg, U., eds.*, 1986, pp. 793–803.

Pope, Rulon D. and Hallam, Arne. A Confusion of Agricultural Economists? A Professional Interest Survey and Essay. *Amer. J. Agr. Econ.*, August 1986, *68*(3), pp. 572–94. **[G: U.S.]**

Quizón, Jaime and Binswanger, Hans P. Modeling the Impact of Agricultural Growth and Government Policy on Income Distribution in India. *World Bank Econ. Rev.*, September 1986, *1*(1), pp. 103–48. **[G: India]**

Rao, J. Mohan. Agriculture in Recent Development Theory. *J. Devel. Econ.*, June 1986, *22*(1), pp. 41–86.

Rao, V. K. R. V. Balance between Agriculture and Industry in Economic Development. *Indian Econ. J.*, Oct.-Dec. 1986, *34*(2), pp. 1–8. **[G: Global]**

Rasmussen, Torben. The Green Revolution in the Southern Highlands. **In** *Boesen, J., et al., eds.*, 1986, pp. 191–205. **[G: Tanzania]**

Redclift, Michael. Sustainability and the Market: Survival Strategies on the Bolivian Frontier. *J. Devel. Stud.*, October 1986, *23*(1), pp. 93–105. **[G: Bolivia]**

Richards, Alan. Food, States, and Peasants: Introduction. **In** *Richards, A., ed.*, 1986, pp. 1–21.

Roberts, Michael K., et al. The Policy Consequences of the Green Revolution: The Latin American Case. **In** *Browne, W. P. and Hadwiger, D. F., eds.*, 1986, pp. 137–52. **[G: Latin America]**

Rohrer, Wayne C. Developing Third World Farming: Conflict between Modern Imperatives and Traditional Ways. *Econ. Develop. Cult. Change*, January 1986, *34*(2), pp. 299–314. **[G: Philippines; LDCs]**

Sah, Raaj Kumar and Stiglitz, Joseph E. The Economics of Price Scissors: Reply. *Amer. Econ. Rev.*, December 1986, *76*(5), pp. 1195–99.

Sajhau, Jean-Paul. Employment, Wages and Living Conditions in a Changing Industry—Plantations. *Int. Lab. Rev.*, Jan.-Feb. 1986, *125*(1), pp. 71–85. **[G: LDCs]**

Smith, Sheldon. Entrepreneurial Agriculture and the Involution of Agricultural Dynamics in the Americas. **In** *Greenfield, S. M. and Strickon, A., eds.*, 1986, pp. 96–123. **[G: Central America]**

Spencer, Dunstan S. C. Agricultural Research: Lessons of the Past, Strategies for the Future. **In** *Berg, R. J. and Whitaker, J. S., eds.*, 1986, pp. 215–41. **[G: Sub-Saharan Africa]**

Srivastava, U. K. Pressure on Natural Resources: Discussion. **In** *Maunder, A. and Renborg, U., eds.*, 1986, pp. 337–38.

Sumner, David. Human Capital, Technology and Institutions: Discussion. **In** *Maunder, A. and Renborg, U., eds.*, 1986, pp. 486–88.

Throsby, C. D. Agriculture in the Economy: The Evolution of Economists' Perceptions over Three Centuries. *Rev. Marketing Agr. Econ.*, December 1986, *54*(3), pp. 5–48.

Tyrchniewicz, Edward W. The Food Chain, Markets, and Prices: Implications for Research and Policy. **In** *Maunder, A. and Renborg, U., eds.*, 1986, pp. 776–80.

Watts, Michael. Geographers among the Peasants: Power, Politics, and Practice. *Econ. Geogr.*, October 1986, *62*(4), pp. 373–86. **[G: Africa]**

Zevin, L. Z., et al. Cooperation of CMEA Member-Countries and Developing Countries in the Resolution of the Food Problem. *Soviet E. Europ. Foreign Trade*, Fall-Winter 1986-87, *22*(3), pp. 1–209. **[G: CMEA; LDCs]**

711 Agricultural Supply and Demand Analysis

7110 Agricultural Supply and Demand Analysis

Abdou, Dyaa K.; Gardner, B. Delworth and Green, Richard D. To Violate or Not Violate the Law: An Example from Egyptian Agriculture. *Amer. J. Agr. Econ.*, February 1986, *68*(1), pp. 120–26. **[G: Egypt]**

Abdullah, Abu. Distributional Aspects of Fertilizer Pricing Policy. *Bangladesh Devel. Stud.*, March 1986, *14*(1), pp. 93–100. **[G: Bangladesh]**

Achoth, Lalith, et al. Output Growth Stability of Natural Rubber in India. *Margin*, January 1986, *18*(2), pp. 51–61. **[G: India]**

Adamowicz, Wiktor. Production Technology in Canadian Agriculture. *Can. J. Agr. Econ.*, March 1986, *34*(1), pp. 87–104. **[G: Canada]**

Adams, Richard M. Agriculture, Forestry, and Related Benefits of Air Pollution Control: A Review and Some Observations. *Amer. J. Agr. Econ.*, May 1986, *68*(2), pp. 464–72. **[G: U.S.]**

Adams, Richard M.; Callaway, J. M. and McCarl, Bruce A. Pollution, Agriculture and Social Welfare: The Case of Acid Deposition. *Can. J. Agr. Econ.*, March 1986, *34*(1), pp. 3–19. **[G: U.S.]**

Adams, Richard M.; Hamilton, Scott A. and McCarl, Bruce A. The Benefits of Pollution Control: The Case of Ozone and U.S. Agriculture. *Amer. J. Agr. Econ.*, November 1986, *68*(4), pp. 886–93. **[G: U.S.]**

Adelaja, Adesoji and Hoque, Anwarul. A Multiproduct Analysis of Energy Demand in Agricultural Subsectors. *Southern J. Agr. Econ.*, December 1986, *18*(2), pp. 51–63. **[G: U.S.]**

Alauddin, Mohammad and Tisdell, Clem A. Decomposition Methods, Agricultural Productivity Growth and Technological Change: A Critique Supported by Bangladeshi Data. *Oxford Bull. Econ. Statist.*, November 1986, *48*(4), pp. 353–72. **[G: Bangladesh]**

Alderman, Harold. Food Subsidies and State Policies in Egypt. **In** *Richards, A., ed.*, 1986, pp. 183–200. **[G: Egypt]**

Alston, Julian M. The Effects of the CAP on International Trade in Poultry Meat. *Europ. Rev. Agr. Econ.*, 1986, *13*(2), pp. 217–31. **[G: EEC]**

von Alvensleben, Reimar; Behr, Hans-Christoph and Jahn, Hans-Harald. Fruits and Vegetables in the European Community. **In** *Bale, M. D., ed.*, 1986, pp. 5–93. **[G: EEC]**

An, Xi-Ji. Pricing System Reform for Agricultural Products and Price Policy Adjustment in China (1979–1984). **In** *Maunder, A. and Renborg, U., eds.*, 1986, pp. 449–60. **[G: China]**

Antle, John M. Aggregation, Expectations, and the Explanation of Technological Change. *J. Econometrics*, Oct./Nov. 1986, *33*(1/2), pp. 213–36. **[G: U.S.]**

Antonovitz, Frances and Roe, Terry. A Theoretical and Empirical Approach to the Value of Information in Risky Markets. *Rev. Econ. Statist.*, February 1986, *68*(1), pp. 105–14. **[G: U.S.]**

Arregui, Jorge H. A Quarterly Model for the EEC Beef Sector. *J. Agr. Econ.*, May 1986, *37*(2), pp. 221–32. **[G: EEC]**

Audibert, Martine. Agricultural Non-wage Production and Health Status: A Case Study in a Tropical Environment. *J. Devel. Econ.*, December 1986, *24*(2), pp. 275–91. **[G: Cameroon]**

Ballenger, Nicole S. and Norton, Roger D. Optimization of Policy Goals in the Context of a Sector Model. *Agr. Econ. Res.*, Spring 1986, *38*(2), pp. 28–36. **[G: Mexico]**

Basu, Dipak R. Sen's Analysis of Famine: A Critique. *J. Devel. Stud.*, April 1986, *22*(3), pp. 598–603. **[G: Bengal]**

Batten, Dallas S. and Belongia, Michael T. Monetary Policy, Real Exchange Rates, and U.S. Agricultural Exports. *Amer. J. Agr. Econ.*, May 1986, *68*(2), pp. 422–27. **[G: U.S.]**

Bautista, Romeo M. Domestic Price Distortions and Agricultural Income in Developing Countries. *J. Devel. Econ.*, September 1986, *23*(1), pp. 19–39. **[G: Philippines]**

Belongia, Michael T. Estimating Exchange Rate Effects on Exports: A Cautionary Note. *Fed. Res. Bank St. Louis Rev.*, January 1986, *68*(1), pp. 5–16. **[G: U.S.]**

Berlan, Jean-Pierre. From the United States to a World System: Technological Change, International Trade, Agricultural Policy in the Twentieth Century. **In** *Maunder, A. and Renborg, U., eds.*, 1986, pp. 343–52. **[G: U.S.]**

Bessler, David A. and Kling, John L. Forecasting Vector Autoregressions with Bayesian Priors. *Amer. J. Agr. Econ.*, February 1986, *68*(1), pp. 144–51. **[G: U.S.]**

Bhide, Shashanka and Siddiqui, K. A. Foodgrain Output and Rainfall. *Margin*, July 1986, *18*(4), pp. 29–40. **[G: India]**

Binswanger, Hans P. Evaluating Research System Performance and Targeting Research in Land-abundant Areas of Sub-Saharan Africa. *World Devel.*, April 1986, *14*(4), pp. 469–75. **[G: Sub-Saharan Africa]**

Binswanger, Hans P. and Pingali, Prabhu. Agricultural Intensification and Technical Change in Sub-Saharan Africa. **In** *Maunder, A. and Renborg, U., eds.*, 1986, pp. 381–86. **[G: Sub-Saharan Africa]**

Birowo, Achmad T. Human Capital, Technology and Institutions: Discussion. **In** *Maunder, A. and Renborg, U., eds.*, 1986, pp. 386–87.

Bobst, Barry W. Implications for Food Demand of Changes in Competitive State within Marketing Channels. **In** *Capps, O., Jr. and Senauer, B., eds.*, 1986, pp. 269–80. **[G: U.S.]**

Boussard, Jean-Marc, et al. Productivité et inflation: le cas de l'agriculture française 1960–1982. With English summary.) *Revue Écon. Polit.*, Jan.-Feb. 1986, *96*(1), pp. 13–24. **[G: France]**

Boyce, James K. Kinked Exponential Models for Growth Rate Estimation. *Oxford Bull. Econ. Statist.*, November 1986, *48*(4), pp. 385–91. **[G: India; Bangladesh]**

Boyd, Milton S. and Brorsen, B. Wade. Dynamic Price Relationships for U.S. and EC Corn Gluten Feed and Related Markets. *Europ. Rev. Agr. Econ.*, 1986, *13*(2), pp. 199–215. **[G: U.S.; EEC]**

Brada, Josef C. The Variability of Crop Production in Private and Socialized Agriculture: Evidence from Eastern Europe. *J. Polit. Econ.*, Part 1, June 1986, *94*(3), pp. 545–63. **[G: Bulgaria; Czechoslovakia; Hungary; Poland; Romania]**

Bratton, Michael. Farmer Organizations and Food Production in Zimbabwe. *World Devel.*, March 1986, *14*(3), pp. 367–84. **[G: Zimbabwe]**

Braverman, Avishay and Hammer, Jeffrey S. Multimarket Analysis of Agricultural Pricing Policies in Senegal. **In** *Singh, I.; Squire, L. and Strauss, J., eds.*, 1986, pp. 233–54. **[G: Senegal]**

Breimyer, Harold F. Human Capital, Technology and Institutions: Discussion. **In** *Maunder, A.*

and Renborg, U., eds., 1986, pp. 460–62. [G: China]

Brown, Colin G. and Drynan, Ross G. On Some Aspects of Organizational Efficiency in the Queensland Cattle Slaughtering Industry. *Rev. Marketing Agr. Econ.*, August 1986, *54*(2), pp. 11–29. [G: Australia]

Brown, Mark G. The Demand for Fruit Juices: Market Participation and Quantity Demanded. *Western J. Agr. Econ.*, December 1986, *11*(2), pp. 179–83. [G: U.S.]

Brown, Mark G. and Lee, Jong-Ying. Orange and Grapefruit Juice Demand Forecasts. **In** *Capps, O., Jr. and Senauer, B., eds.*, 1986, pp. 215–32. [G: U.S.]

Brun, André. Agriculture in a Turbulent World Economy: Theoretical Developments: Discussion. **In** *Maunder, A. and Renborg, U., eds.*, 1986, pp. 712–14.

Buchholz, H. E. Agriculture in a Turbulent World Economy: Theoretical Developments: Discussion. **In** *Maunder, A. and Renborg, U., eds.*, 1986, pp. 604–06.

Bullock, J. Bruce and Womack, Abner. Changes in Domestic Demand for Food: Impacts on Southern Agriculture: Discussion. *Southern J. Agr. Econ.*, July 1986, *18*(1), pp. 37–39. [G: U.S.]

Buse, Rueben C. Is the Structure of the Demand for Food Changing? Implications for Projections. **In** *Capps, O., Jr. and Senauer, B., eds.*, 1986, pp. 105–29. [G: U.S.]

Capalbo, Susan M. and Denny, Michael G. S. Testing Long-run Productivity Models for the Canadian and U.S. Agricultural Sectors. *Amer. J. Agr. Econ.*, August 1986, *68*(3), pp. 615–25. [G: U.S.; Canada]

Capps, Oral, Jr. Changes in Domestic Demand for Food: Impacts on Southern Agriculture. *Southern J. Agr. Econ.*, July 1986, *18*(1), pp. 25–36. [G: U.S.]

Capps, Oral, Jr. and Cheng, Hsiang-Tai. The Missing Income Problem in Analyses of Engel Functions. *Western J. Agr. Econ.*, July 1986, *11*(1), pp. 31–39. [G: U.S.]

Capps, Oral, Jr. and Pearson, Joanne M. Analysis of Convenience and Nonconvenience Food Expenditures by U.S. Households with Projections to the Year 2000. **In** *Capps, O., Jr. and Senauer, B., eds.*, 1986, pp. 233–50. [G: U.S.]

del Castillo, Gustavo and Barajas de Vega, Rosario. U.S.–Mexican Agricultural Relations: The Upper Limits of Linkage Formation. **In** *Browne, W. P. and Hadwiger, D. F., eds.*, 1986, pp. 153–68. [G: U.S.; Mexico]

Castro Forero, Yesid. Fertilizer Pricing in Colombia. **In** *Segura, E. L.; Shetty, Y. T. and Nishimizu, M., eds.*, 1986, pp. 196–200. [G: Colombia]

Chadha, G. K. The Off-Farm Economic Structure of Agriculturally Growing Regions: A Study of Indian Punjab. **In** *Shand, R. T., ed., Vol. 2*, 1986, pp. 147–75. [G: India]

Chambers, Robert G. and Just, Richard E. A Critique of Exchange Rate Treatment in Agricultural Trade Models: Reply. *Amer. J. Agr. Econ.*, November 1986, *68*(4), pp. 994–97.

Chambers, Robert G. and Lee, Hyunok. Constrained Output Maximization and U.S. Agriculture. *Appl. Econ.*, April 1986, *18*(4), pp. 347–57. [G: U.S.]

Choksi, Armeane. Commodity Export Prices and the Real Exchange Rate in Developing Countries: Coffee in Colombia: Comment. **In** *Edwards, S. and Ahamed, L., eds.*, 1986, pp. 260–63. [G: Colombia]

Christiansen, Sofus. Wet Rice Cultivation: Some Reason Why. **In** *Nørlund, I.; Cederroth, S. and Gerdin, I., eds.*, 1986, pp. 15–27.

Chu, Ke-young and Morrison, Thomas K. World Non-Oil Primary Commodity Markets: A Medium-term Framework of Analysis. *Int. Monet. Fund Staff Pap.*, March 1986, *33*(1), pp. 139–84.

Coleman, J. R. A Policy Analysis of Exchange Rate Fluctuations on the Rural Sector: The Experience of the Canadian Red Meat Industry. *J. Agr. Econ.*, May 1986, *37*(2), pp. 253–66. [G: Canada]

Cowen, Michael. Change in State Power, International Conditions and Peasant Producers: The Case of Kenya. *J. Devel. Stud.*, January 1986, *22*(2), pp. 355–84. [G: Kenya]

Cox, Thomas L. and Wohlgenant, Michael K. Prices and Quality Effects in Cross-sectional Demand Analysis. *Amer. J. Agr. Econ.*, November 1986, *68*(4), pp. 908–19. [G: U.S.]

De Benedictis, Michele. Balancing Overproduction and Malnutrition: Discussion. **In** *Maunder, A. and Renborg, U., eds.*, 1986, pp. 265–68. [G: LDCs]

Delgado, Christopher L. A Variance Components Approach to Food Grain Market Integration in Northern Nigeria. *Amer. J. Agr. Econ.*, November 1986, *68*(4), pp. 970–79. [G: Nigeria]

Dommen, Arthur J. Increasing Food Production in Sub-Saharan Africa: Comment. *Amer. J. Agr. Econ.*, November 1986, *68*(4), pp. 998–99.

Dubgaard, Alex. Disaggregation of the Farm Sector in the Danish Input–Output Table. **In** *Franz, A. and Rainer, N., eds.*, 1986, pp. 427–45. [G: Denmark]

Dzhikiia, I. Ia. An Integrated Econometric Model for Forecasting Agricultural Production. *Matekon*, Spring 1986, 22(3), pp. 67–90. [G: U.S.S.R.]

Edwards, Clark. The Role of Natural Resources in Regional Agricultural Growth. **In** *Maunder, A. and Renborg, U., eds.*, 1986, pp. 692–702.

Edwards, Sebastian. Commodity Export Prices and the Real Exchange Rate in Developing Countries: Coffee in Colombia. **In** *Edwards, S. and Ahamed, L., eds.*, 1986, pp. 235–60. [G: Colombia]

Eicher, Carl K. Facing Up to Africa's Food Crisis. **In** *Ravenhill, J., ed.*, 1986, pp. 149–80. [G: Africa]

Eicher, Carl K. Strategic Issues in Combating Hunger and Poverty in Africa. **In** *Berg, R. J.*

and Whitaker, J. S., eds., 1986, pp. 242–75. **[G: Sub-Saharan Africa]**

Eicher, Carl K. and Staatz, John M. Food Security Policy in Sub-Saharan Africa. **In** *Maunder, A. and Renborg, U., eds.*, 1986, pp. 215–29. **[G: Sub-Saharan Africa]**

Ercolani, Paolo. Decline in the Share of the Agricultural Product: Measurements and Explanations. *Banca Naz. Lavoro Quart. Rev.*, March 1986, (156), pp. 103–28. **[G: Global]**

Evans, Scott F. and Lewis, Philip E. T. Demand, Supply and Adjustment of Farm Labour in Australia. *Australian Econ. Pap.*, December 1986, *25*(47), pp. 236–46. **[G: Australia]**

Ewing, Arthur F. Agriculture, Trade and Growth: Review Article. *J. World Trade Law*, Nov.:Dec. 1986, *20*(6), pp. 665–89. **[G: Global]**

Falgon, Claude. The Effect of Enlargement of the EC on Tunisian Fruits and Vegetables. **In** *Bale, M. D., ed.*, 1986, pp. 95–130. **[G: EEC; Tunisia]**

Faminow, Merle D. and Gum, Russell L. Feeder Cattle Price Differentials in Arizona Auction Markets. *Western J. Agr. Econ.*, December 1986, *11*(2), pp. 156–63. **[G: U.S.]**

Fischer, Günther, et al. The World Economy: Resilient for the Rich, Stubborn for the Starving. **In** *Maunder, A. and Renborg, U., eds.*, 1986, pp. 259–65. **[G: LDCs]**

Fishel, Walter L. and Kenney, Martin. Challenge to Studies of Biotechnology Impacts in the Social Sciences. **In** *Maunder, A. and Renborg, U., eds.*, 1986, pp. 353–60.

Fisher, Brian S. Agriculture in a Turbulent World Economy: Theoretical Developments: Discussion. **In** *Maunder, A. and Renborg, U., eds.*, 1986, pp. 606–09.

Fox, H. S. A. The Alleged Transformation from Two-field to Three-field Systems in Medieval England. *Econ. Hist. Rev., 2nd Ser.*, November 1986, *39*(4), pp. 526–48. **[G: U.K.]**

French, Ben C. and King, Gordon A. Demand and Price-Markup Functions for Canned Cling Peaches and Fruit Cocktail. *Western J. Agr. Econ.*, July 1986, *11*(1), pp. 8–18. **[G: U.S.]**

Garcia, Philip, et al. Measuring the Benefits of Environmental Change Using a Duality Approach: The Case of Ozone and Illinois Cash Grain Farms. *J. Environ. Econ. Manage.*, March 1986, *13*(1), pp. 69–80. **[G: U.S.]**

Garraty, John A. Agriculture in the Great Depression and in the 1970s. **In** *Berend, I. T. and Borchardt, K., eds.*, 1986, pp. 516–44. **[G: Global]**

Gersovitz, Mark. Agro-industrial Processing and Agricultural Pricing under Uncertainty. *Rev. Econ. Stud.*, January 1986, *53*(1), pp. 153–69. **[G: Senegal]**

Glover, David J. Agrarian Reform and Agro-Industry in Honduras. *Can. J. Devel. Stud.*, 1986, *7*(1), pp. 21–35. **[G: Honduras]**

Glushkov, N. Improving Pricing in the Agro–Industrial Complex (AIC). *Prob. Econ.*, August 1986, *29*(4), pp. 52–70. **[G: U.S.S.R.]**

González-Vega, Claudio. Human Capital, Technology and Institutions: Discussion. **In** *Maunder, A. and Renborg, U., eds.*, 1986, pp. 360–63. **[G: U.S.]**

Grabowski, Richard and Sanchez, Onesimo. Returns to Scale in Agriculture: An Empirical Investigation of Japanese Experience. *Europ. Rev. Agr. Econ.*, 1986, *13*(2), pp. 189–98. **[G: Japan]**

Grabowski, Richard; Sivan, David and Tracy, Ronald L. Technical Change in Taiwanese Agriculture. *Indian Econ. Rev.*, Jan.-June 1986, *21*(1), pp. 41–49. **[G: Taiwan]**

Grabowski, Richard; Tracy, Ronald L. and Sanchez, Onesimo. The Development of Technology in Taiwanese Agriculture. *J. Econ. Devel.*, December 1986, *11*(2), pp. 161–76. **[G: Taiwan]**

Greeley, Martin. Food, Technology and Employment: The Farm-Level Post-Harvest System in Developing Countries. *J. Agr. Econ.*, September 1986, *37*(3), pp. 333–47. **[G: LDCs]**

Grennes, Thomas J. and Lapp, John S. Neutrality of Inflation in the Agricultural Sector. *J. Int. Money Finance*, June 1986, *5*(2), pp. 231–43. **[G: U.S.]**

Griffin, Keith. Communal Land Tenure Systems and Their Role in Rural Development. **In** *[Streeten, P.]*, 1986, pp. 165–91. **[G: Selected Countries]**

Grigsby, S. Elaine and Arnade, Carlos Anthony. The Effect of Exchange Rate Distortions on Grain Export Markets, the Case of Argentina. *Amer. J. Agr. Econ.*, May 1986, *68*(2), pp. 434–40. **[G: Argentina]**

Guseman, Patricia K. and Sapp, Stephen G. Population Scale, Composition, and Income Effects on Per Capita and Aggregate Beef Consumption: A Temporal and Spatial Assessment. **In** *Capps, O., Jr. and Senauer, B., eds.*, 1986, pp. 185–213. **[G: U.S.]**

Gustafson, Cole R. Measuring the Productivity of Capital in United States Agriculture. *Southern J. Agr. Econ.*, December 1986, *18*(2), pp. 187–95. **[G: U.S.]**

Haley, Stephen L. and Abbott, Philip C. Estimation of Agricultural Production Functions on a World-Wide Basis. *Can. J. Agr. Econ.*, November 1986, *34*(3), pp. 433–54.

Hart, Gillian. Interlocking Transactions: Obstacles, Precursors or Instruments of Agrarian Capitalism. *J. Devel. Econ.*, September 1986, *23*(1), pp. 177–203.

Haughton, Jonathan. Farm Price Responsiveness and the Choice of Functional Form: An Application to Rice Cultivation West Malaysia. *J. Devel. Econ.*, December 1986, *24*(2), pp. 203–23. **[G: Malaysia]**

Havlicek, Joseph, Jr. Food Demand Analysis: Implications for Future Consumption: Discussion. **In** *Capps, O., Jr. and Senauer, B., eds.*, 1986, pp. 87–90. **[G: U.S.]**

Hayami, Yujiro. Poverty and Beyond: The Forces Shaping the Future in Asia. **In** *Maunder, A. and Renborg, U., eds.*, 1986, pp. 37–48. **[G: LDCs; MDCs]**

Hedlin, R. A. An Additional Perspective. *Can.*

J. Agr. Econ., June 1986, *33*, pp. 30–40. **[G: Canada]**

Hertel, Thomas W. and McKinzie, Lance. Pseudo Data as a Teaching Tool: Application to the Translog, Multiproduct Profit Function. *Western J. Agr. Econ.*, July 1986, *11*(1), pp. 19–30.

Horton, Douglas. Assessing the Impact of International Agricultural Research and Development Programs. *World Devel.*, April 1986, *14*(4), pp. 453–68. **[G: LDCs]**

Hossain, Mahabub and Quasem, Md. Abul. Growth of Fertilizer Consumption in Two Villages of Bangladesh 1977–84. *Bangladesh Devel. Stud.*, March 1986, *14*(1), pp. 59–74. **[G: Bangladesh]**

Houck, James P.. Views on Agricultural Economics' Role in Economic Thought. *Amer. J. Agr. Econ.*, May 1986, *68*(2), pp. 375–80. **[G: U.S.]**

Howell, David. Farming in South-east Wales c.1840–80. **In** *Baber, C. and Williams, L. J., eds.*, 1986, pp. 82–96. **[G: U.K.]**

Huang, Chung L. and Raunikar, Robert. Food Expenditure Patterns: Evidence from U.S. Household Data. **In** *Capps, O., Jr. and Senauer, B., eds.*, 1986, pp. 49–65. **[G: U.S.]**

Huang, Chung L.; Raunikar, Robert and Tyan, Holly L. Heteroscedasticity in Broiler Meat Expenditure Pattern Estimation. *Western J. Agr. Econ.*, December 1986, *11*(2), pp. 195–203. **[G: U.S.]**

Huang, Kuo S. and Haidacher, Richard C. Projecting Aggregate Food Expenditures to the Year 2000. **In** *Capps, O., Jr. and Senauer, B., eds.*, 1986, pp. 67–85. **[G: U.S.]**

Iakimets, Vladimir. Adjustment of Regional Agriculture to Expected Climatic Changes. **In** *Maunder, A. and Renborg, U., eds.*, 1986, pp. 160–67. **[G: U.S.S.R.]**

Islam, Nurul. World Food Security: National and International Measures for Stabilisation of Supplies. **In** *[Streeten, P.]*, 1986, pp. 192–216. **[G: Global]**

Jain, T. B. Allied Enterprises: I—Poultry. **In** *Dantwala, M. L., et al.*, 1986, pp. 199–208. **[G: India]**

Jakhade, V. M. and Sundaram, T. R. Role of Agriculture in the Indian National Economy. **In** *Dantwala, M. L., et al.*, 1986, pp. 16–58. **[G: India]**

Jayasuriya, S. K. and Shand, Richard T. Technical Change and Labor Absorption in Asian Agriculture: Some Emerging Trends. *World Devel.*, March 1986, *14*(3), pp. 415–28. **[G: LDCs; Asia]**

Jayasuriya, S. K.; Te, A. and Herdt, R. W. Mechanisation and Cropping Intensification: Economics of Machinery Use in Low-Wage Economies. *J. Devel. Stud.*, January 1986, *22*(2), pp. 327–35. **[G: LDCs]**

Johnson, Sam H., III. Agricultural Intensification in Thailand: Complementary Role of Infrastructure and Agricultural Policy. **In** *Easter, W. K., ed.*, 1986, pp. 111–27. **[G: Thailand]**

Johnson, Stan R., et al. Market Demand Functions. **In** *Capps, O., Jr. and Senauer, B., eds.*, 1986, pp. 1–33. **[G: Canada; U.S.]**

Ka, Chih-Ming and Selden, Mark. Original Accumulation, Equity and Late Industrialization: The Cases of Socialist China and Capitalist Taiwan. *World Devel.*, Oct./Nov. 1986, *14*(10/11), pp. 1293–1310. **[G: Taiwan; China]**

Kalirajan, K. and Shand, Richard T. Estimating Location-Specific and Firm-Specific Technical Efficiency: An Analysis of Malaysian Agriculture. *J. Econ. Devel.*, December 1986, *11*(2), pp. 147–60. **[G: Malaysia]**

Kashlon, A. S. Agricultural Price Policy and Terms of Trade. **In** *Dantwala, M. L., et al.*, 1986, pp. 358–72. **[G: India]**

Kasnakoglu, Haluk. Agricultural Price Support Policies in Turkey: An Empirical Investigation. **In** *Richards, A., ed.*, 1986, pp. 131–57. **[G: Turkey]**

Kawagoe, Toshihiko; Otsuka, Keijiro and Hayami, Yujiro. Induced Bias of Technical Change in Agriculture: The United States and Japan, 1880–1980. *J. Polit. Econ.*, Part 1, June 1986, *94*(3), pp. 523–44. **[G: U.S.; Japan]**

Kennedy, John O. S. Rules for Optimal Fertilizer Carryover: An Alternative Explanation. *Rev. Marketing Agr. Econ.*, August 1986, *54*(2), pp. 3–10. **[G: Australia]**

Khan, Mahmood Hasan and Akbari, Ather Hussain. Impact of Agricultural Research and Extension on Crop Productivity in Pakistan: A Production Function Approach. *World Devel.*, June 1986, *14*(6), pp. 757–62. **[G: Pakistan]**

Kinnucan, Henry and Sullivan, Gregory. Monopsonistic Food Processing and Farm Prices: The Case of the West Alabama Catfish Industry. *Southern J. Agr. Econ.*, December 1986, *18*(2), pp. 15–24. **[G: U.S.]**

Kirkpatrick, Colin and Diakosavvas, Dimitris. Food Insecurity and the Foreign Exchange Constraint in Sub-Saharan Africa. **In** *Maunder, A. and Renborg, U., eds.*, 1986, pp. 230–39. **[G: Sub-Saharan Africa]**

Kirschke, Dieter. Budget Costs of the EC's Agricultural Price Policy under Uncertainty. *Europ. Rev. Agr. Econ.*, 1986, *13*(1), pp. 57–74. **[G: EEC]**

Kjærby, Finn. The Development of Agricultural Mechanisation in Tanzania. **In** *Boesen, J., et al., eds.*, 1986, pp. 173–90. **[G: Tanzania]**

Klatzmann, Joseph. Balancing Overproduction and Malnutrition: Discussion. **In** *Maunder, A. and Renborg, U., eds.*, 1986, pp. 208–09.

Klemyshev, P. Scientific–Technical Progress and the Intensification of Agriculture. *Prob. Econ.*, May 1986, *29*(1), pp. 63–81. **[G: U.S.S.R.]**

Knudsen, Odin K. and Scandizzo, Pasquale L. The Demand for Calories in Developing Countries: Reply. *Amer. J. Agr. Econ.*, February 1986, *68*(1), pp. 180–81. **[G: LDCs]**

Kokoski, Mary F. An Empirical Analysis of Intertemporal and Demographic Variations in Consumer Preferences. *Amer. J. Agr. Econ.*, November 1986, *68*(4), pp. 894–907. **[G: U.S.]**

Kolstad, Charles D. and Burris, Anthony E. Imperfectly Competitive Equilibria in International Commodity Markets. *Amer. J. Agr. Econ.*, February 1986, *68*(1), pp. 27–36. **[G: Global]**

Koo, Won W. and Uhm, Ihn H. A Spatial Equilibrium Analysis of U.S. Wheat Exports under Alternative Transport Costs and Trade Restrictions. *Logist. Transp. Rev.*, March 1986, *22*(1), pp. 27–41. **[G: OECD]**

Kurian, N. J. Economics of Rice Production in India—An Interregional and Intertemporal Analysis. *J. Quant. Econ.*, January 1986, *2*(1), pp. 51–76. **[G: India]**

Kutil, Jaroslav. Topical Aspects of the Use of the Production Potential of Agriculture. *Czech. Econ. Digest.*, June/July 1986, (4), pp. 90–113. **[G: Czechoslovakia]**

Laxminarayan, H. Programmes for Agricultural Development in the Seventh Five-Year Plan. *Indian Econ. J.*, Apr.-June 1986, *33*(4), pp. 21–36. **[G: India]**

LeBlanc, Michael and Hrubovcak, James. Dynamic Input Demand: An Application to Agriculture. *Appl. Econ.*, July 1986, *18*(7), pp. 807–18. **[G: U.S.]**

Lee, Jonq-Ying; Brown, Mark G. and Schwartz, Brooke. The Demand for National Brand and Private Label Frozen Concentrated Orange Juice: A Switching Regressional Analysis. *Western J. Agr. Econ.*, July 1986, *11*(1), pp. 1–17. **[G: U.S.]**

Lee, Tenpao and Baumel, C. Phillip. Testing Asset Fixity for U.S. Agriculture: Comment. *Amer. J. Agr. Econ.*, May 1986, *68*(2), pp. 353–54. **[G: U.S.]**

Lemeshev, M. The Food Program and Protecting the Environment. *Prob. Econ.*, September 1986, *29*(5), pp. 57–75. **[G: U.S.S.R.]**

Lindström, Jan. Grain for Livestock and Livestock for Grain: Are the Agro-Pastoral Iramba Marginalising Themselves? **In** *Boesen, J., et al., eds.*, 1986, pp. 225–37. **[G: Tanzania]**

Lopez, Rigoberto A. The Use of Composite Price Expectations in Supply Response Models. *Can. J. Agr. Econ.*, November 1986, *34*(3), pp. 354–74. **[G: U.S.]**

Lucas, Robert E. B. Emigration, Employment, and Accumulation: The Miners of Southern Africa. **In** *Stark, O., ed.*, 1986, pp. 107–38. **[G: S. Africa]**

Malish, Anton F. Soviet Agricultural Policy in the 1980s. **In** *Browne, W. P. and Hadwiger, D. F., eds.*, 1986, pp. 77–90. **[G: U.S.S.R.]**

Manzanal, Mabel. El deterioro regional: una manifestación en la producción tabacalera correntina 1976–1981. (With English summary.) *Desarrollo Econ.*, Oct.-Dec. 1986, *26*(103), pp. 455–76. **[G: Argentina]**

Martin, Michael V. and McDonald, John A. Food Grain Policy in the Republic of Korea: The Economic Costs of Self-sufficiency. *Econ. Develop. Cult. Change*, January 1986, *34*(2), pp. 315–31. **[G: S. Korea]**

Martin, W. J. Human Capital, Technology and Institutions: Discussion. **In** *Maunder, A. and Renborg, U., eds.*, 1986, pp. 363–65.

McInnis, R. M. Output and Productivity in Canadian Agriculture, 1870–71 to 1926–27. **In** *Engerman, S. L. and Gallman, R. E., eds.*, 1986, pp. 737–70. **[G: Canada]**

McPherson, Malcolm. Why Do Researchers Continue to Ignore Risk in Tests of Farmer Efficiency? A Comment on Shapiro's Rejection of the Efficient But Poor Hypothesis [Efficiency Differentials in Peasant Agriculture and Their Implications for Development Policies]. *J. Devel. Stud.*, April 1986, *22*(3), pp. 604–07. **[G: Tanzania]**

Meester, Gerrit. Agriculture in a Turbulent World Economy: Theoretical Developments: Discussion. **In** *Maunder, A. and Renborg, U., eds.*, 1986, pp. 633–35.

Mellor, John W. and Paulino, Leonardo. Food Production Needs in a Consumption Perspective. **In** *Swaminathan, M. S. and Sinha, S. K., eds.*, 1986, pp. 1–24. **[G: Global]**

Miller, M. H. Soil Degradation in Eastern Canada: Its Extent and Impact. *Can. J. Agr. Econ.*, June 1986, *33*, pp. 7–18. **[G: Canada]**

Moseley, Anne E.; Spreen, Thomas H. and Pheasant, Jim W. A Mixed-Integer Programming Analysis of the Structure of a Florida-Based Cattle Feeding Industry. *Southern J. Agr. Econ.*, December 1986, *18*(2), pp. 125–37. **[G: U.S.]**

Msambichaka, L. A. Balancing Overproduction and Malnutrition: Discussion. **In** *Maunder, A. and Renborg, U., eds.*, 1986, pp. 239–42. **[G: Sub-Saharan Africa]**

Mujahid-Mukhtar, Eshya and Mukhtar, Hanid. The Overall Rate of Return to Agricultural Research and Extension Investments in Pakistan: A Comment. *Pakistan J. Appl. Econ.*, Winter 1986, *5*(2), pp. 207–15. **[G: Pakistan]**

Mujumdar, N. A. and Menon, K. A. Saving and Capital Formation in the Agricultural Sector: A Review. **In** *Dantwala, M. L., et al.* 1986, pp. 234–69. **[G: India]**

Mundlak, Yair. Agricultural Growth and the Price of Food. **In** *Maunder, A. and Renborg, U., eds.*, 1986, pp. 611–23. **[G: U.S.]**

Muqtada, M. Determinants and Possibilities of Employment Expansion in the Crop Sector. **In** *Islam, R. and Muqtada, M., eds.*, 1986, pp. 61–88. **[G: Bangladesh]**

Murshid, K. A. S. Instability in Foodgrain Production in Bangladesh: Nature, Levels, Trends. *Bangladesh Devel. Stud.*, June 1986, *14*(2), pp. 33–73. **[G: Bangladesh]**

Myers, Lester H. Food Demand Analysis: Implications for Future Consumption: Comments. **In** *Capps, O., Jr. and Senauer, B., eds.*, 1986, pp. 177–84. **[G: U.S.]**

Nagarajan, S. Disease Problems and Their Management. **In** *Swaminathan, M. S. and Sinha, S. K., eds.*, 1986, pp. 387–416. **[G: LDCs]**

Naik, Gopal and Dixon, Bruce L. A Monte Carlo Comparison of Alternative Estimators of Autocorrelated Simultaneous Systems Using A U.S. Pork Sector Model as the True Structure. *Western J. Agr. Econ.*, December 1986, *11*(2), pp. 134–45. **[G: U.S.]**

Nolan, Peter and Paine, Suzanne. Towards an

Appraisal of the Impact of Rural Reform in China, 1978–85. *Cambridge J. Econ.*, March 1986, *10*(1), pp. 83–99. **[G: China]**

Nove, Alec. Soviet Agriculture in the 1980s. **In** *Nove, A.*, 1986, *1982*, pp. 150–68. **[G: U.S.S.R.]**

Nyankori, James C. O. A Systematic Analysis of Household Food Consumption Behavior with Specific Emphasis on Predicting Aggregate Food Expenditures. **In** *Capps, O., Jr. and Senauer, B., eds.*, 1986, pp. 251–68. **[G: U.S.]**

O'Connell, Arturo A. La fiebre aftosa, el embargo sanitario norteamericano contra las importaciones de carne y el triángulo Argentina–Gran Bretaña–Estados Unidos en el Periodo entre las dos guerras mundiales. (With English summary.) *Desarrollo Econ.*, Apr.-June 1986, *26*(101), pp. 21–50. **[G: Argentina]**

O'Connell, John. A Hedonic Price Model of the Paris Carcase Lamb Market. *Europ. Rev. Agr. Econ.*, 1986, *13*(4), pp. 439–50. **[G: France]**

Odgaard, Rie. Tea—Does It Do the Peasant Women in Rungwe Any Good? **In** *Boesen, J., et al., eds.*, 1986, pp. 207–24. **[G: Tanzania]**

Oliveira, Joao do Carmo. Trade Policy, Market 'Distortions,' and Agriculture in the Process of Economic Development: Brazil, 1950–1974. *J. Devel. Econ.*, November 1986, *24*(1), pp. 91–109. **[G: Brazil]**

Orazem, Peter F. and Miranowski, John. An Indirect Test for the Specification of Expectation Regimes. *Rev. Econ. Statist.*, November 1986, *68*(4), pp. 603–09. **[G: U.S.]**

Orden, David. A Critique of Exchange Rate Treatment in Agricultural Trade Models: Comment. *Amer. J. Agr. Econ.*, November 1986, *68*(4), pp. 990–93.

Orden, David. Agriculture, Trade, and Macroeconomics: The U.S. Case. *J. Policy Modeling*, Spring 1986, *8*(1), pp. 27–51. **[G: U.S.]**

Orden, David. Money and Agriculture: The Dynamics of Money–Financial Market–Agricultural Trade Linkages. *Agr. Econ. Res.*, Summer 1986, *38*(3), pp. 14–28. **[G: U.S.]**

Orden, David. Public Policy, the Exchange Rate, and Agricultural Exports: Discussion [Monetary Policy, Real Exchange Rates, and U.S. Agricultural Exports] [The Consequences of a Floating Exchange Rate for the U.S. Wheat Market] [The Effect of Exchange Rate Distortions on Grain Export Markets, the Case of Argentina]. *Amer. J. Agr. Econ.*, May 1986, *68*(2), pp. 443–44.

Owen, Roger. Large Landowners, Agricultural Progress and the State in Egypt, 1800–1970: An Overview with Many Questions. **In** *Richards, A., ed.*, 1986, pp. 69–95. **[G: Egypt]**

Paarlberg, Philip L. and Abbott, Philip C. Oligopolistic Behavior by Public Agencies in International Trade: The World Wheat Market. *Amer. J. Agr. Econ.*, August 1986, *68*(3), pp. 528–43. **[G: OECD]**

Paarlberg, Philip L. and Webb, Alan J. Public Policy and the Reemergence of International Economic Influences on U.S. Agriculture. *Agr. Econ. Res.*, Winter 1986, *38*(1), pp. 45–56. **[G: U.S.]**

Pagoulatos, Emilio. Public Policy, the Exchange Rate, and Agricultural Exports: Discussion [Monetary Policy, Real Exchange Rates, and U.S. Agricultural Exports] [The Consequences of a Floating Exchange Rate for the U.S. Wheat Market] [The Effect of Exchange Rate Distortions on Grain Export Markets, the Case of Argentina]. *Amer. J. Agr. Econ.*, May 1986, *68*(2), pp. 441–42. **[G: U.S.; Argentina]**

Pal, S. P. and Singh, J. P. Food Security and Food Stocks in India. *Margin*, October 1986, *19*(1), pp. 30–41.

Palm, F. C. and Vogelvang, E. A Short-run Econometric Analysis of the International Coffee Market. *Europ. Rev. Agr. Econ.*, 1986, *13*(4), pp. 451–76. **[G: Global]**

Panayotou, Theodore. Investment, Growth and Employment in Thailand: From Agriculture to Rural Industry. **In** *Nemetz, P. N., ed.*, 1986, pp. 117–58. **[G: Thailand]**

Panchamukhi, V. R. Trade in Agricultural Commodities—A Profile of Two Decades: 1960–80. **In** *Dantwala, M. L., et al.*, 1986, pp. 432–59. **[G: India]**

Pathak, M. D. and Dhaliwal, G. S. Insect Control. **In** *Swaminathan, M. S. and Sinha, S. K., eds.*, 1986, pp. 357–86. **[G: Selected Countries]**

Penna, Julio A. Sources of Growth of Argentine Agriculture and Prospects for the 1990s. **In** *Maunder, A. and Renborg, U., eds.*, 1986, pp. 475–86. **[G: Argentina]**

Peters, G. H. Human Capital, Technology and Institutions: Discussion. **In** *Maunder, A. and Renborg, U., eds.*, 1986, pp. 462–63.

Pierce, John T. and Furuseth, Owen J. Constraints to Expanded Food Production: A North American Perspective. *Natural Res. J.*, Winter 1986, *26*(1), pp. 15–39. **[G: U.S.]**

Pitt, Mark M. and Rosenzweig, Mark R. Agricultural Prices, Food Consumption, and the Health and Productivity of Indonesian Farmers. **In** *Singh, I.; Squire, L. and Strauss, J., eds.*, 1986, pp. 153–82. **[G: Indonesia]**

Podkaminer, Leon. The Demand for Calories in Developing Countries: Comment. *Amer. J. Agr. Econ.*, February 1986, *68*(1), pp. 177–79. **[G: LDCs]**

Polopolus, Leo C. The Competitive Position of Southern Commodities in International Markets: A Synopsis. *Southern J. Agr. Econ.*, July 1986, *18*(1), pp. 75–78. **[G: U.S.]**

Ponnamperuma, F. N. Role of Phosphorus in Global Food Production. **In** *Swaminathan, M. S. and Sinha, S. K., eds.*, 1986, pp. 239–65. **[G: Selected Countries]**

Prasad, R. Fertilizer Nitrogen: Requirements and Management. **In** *Swaminathan, M. S. and Sinha, S. K., eds.*, 1986, pp. 199–226. **[G: Global]**

Price, David W. The Effects of Household Size and Composition on the Demand for Food. **In** *Capps, O., Jr. and Senauer, B., eds.*, 1986, pp. 131–48. **[G: U.S.]**

Price, Dorothy Z. Role of Integrated Decision Theory in Considering Future Food Consumption Patterns of the Elderly. **In** *Capps, O., Jr. and Senauer, B., eds.*, 1986, pp. 149–62. **[G: U.S.]**

Quiggin, John; Gargett, D. and Barrett, G. Exits from the Australian Dairy Industry: Causes and Predictions. *J. Agr. Econ.*, May 1986, *37*(2), pp. 233–42. **[G: Australia]**

Quizón, Jaime and Binswanger, Hans P. Modeling the Impact of Agricultural Growth and Government Policy on Income Distribution in India. *World Bank Econ. Rev.*, September 1986, *1*(1), pp. 103–48. **[G: India]**

Radice, E. A. Agriculture and Food. **In** *Kaser, M. C. and Radice, E. A., eds.*, 1986, pp. 366–97. **[G: E. Europe; Germany]**

Raikes, Phil. Eating the Carrot and Wielding the Stick: The Agricultural Sector in Tanzania. **In** *Boesen, J., et al., eds.*, 1986, pp. 105–41. **[G: Tanzania]**

Rajapatirana, Sarath. Commodity Export Prices and the Real Exchange Rate in Developing Countries: Coffee in Colombia: Comment. **In** *Edwards, S. and Ahamed, L., eds.*, 1986, pp. 263–66. **[G: Colombia]**

Rao, V. M. and Deshpande, R. S. Agricultural Production—Pace and Pattern of Growth. **In** *Dantwala, M. L., et al.*, 1986, pp. 89–106. **[G: India]**

Raunikar, Robert and Huang, Chung L. Implications of Factors Affecting Food Consumption. **In** *Capps, O., Jr. and Senauer, B., eds.*, 1986, pp. 91–103. **[G: U.S.]**

Rausser, Gordon C.; Chalfant, James A. and Stamoulis, Kostas G. Instability in Agricultural Markets: The U.S. Experience. **In** *Maunder, A. and Renborg, U., eds.*, 1986, pp. 595–604. **[G: U.S.]**

Rayner, A. J.; Whittaker, J. M. and Ingersent, K. A. Productivity Growth in Agriculture (Revisited): A Measurement Framework and Some Empirical Results. *J. Agr. Econ.*, May 1986, *37*(2), pp. 127–50. **[G: U.K.]**

Read, Robert A. The Banana Industry: Oligopoly and Barriers to Entry. **In** *Casson, M., et al.*, 1986, pp. 317–42. **[G: Selected Countries]**

Remenyi, J. V. Issues in Smallholder Tropical Dairying. *Bull. Indonesian Econ. Stud.*, April 1986, *22*(1), pp. 57–87. **[G: Indonesia]**

Riethmuller, Paul and Roe, Terry. Government Intervention in Commodity Markets: The Case of Japanese Rice and Wheat Policy. *J. Policy Modeling*, Fall 1986, *8*(3), pp. 327–49. **[G: Japan]**

Rivera Vilas, Luis Miguel. Un análisis empírico sobre la elaboración de expectativas de precios. (With English summary.) *Invest. Ecón.*, January 1986, *10*(1), pp. 201–10. **[G: Spain]**

Roberts, Roland K. Plant Nutrient Demand Functions for Tennessee with Prices of Jointly Applied Nutrients. *Southern J. Agr. Econ.*, December 1986, *18*(2), pp. 107–12. **[G: U.S.]**

Ruttan, Vernon W. Technical Change and Innovation in Agriculture. **In** *Landau, R. and Rosenberg, N., eds.*, 1986, pp. 333–56. **[G: U.S.; Japan]**

Sahota, Gian Singh. Fertilizer in Economic Development Revisited. *Indian J. Quant. Econ.*, 1986, *2*(2), pp. 15–81. **[G: Global]**

Salam, Abdul. Farm Labour Use and Its Determinants: Results from a Farm Survey in Pakistan. *Pakistan Econ. Soc. Rev.*, Summer 1986, *24*(1), pp. 1–21. **[G: Pakistan]**

Salathe, Larry and Langley, Suchada. An Empirical Analysis of Alternative Export Subsidy Programs for U.S. Wheat. *Agr. Econ. Res.*, Winter 1986, *38*(1), pp. 1–18. **[G: U.S.]**

Sanni, T. A. Vector Autoregression on Nigerian Money and Agricultural Aggregates. *Can. J. Agr. Econ.*, March 1986, *34*(1), pp. 67–85. **[G: Nigeria]**

Sarma, P. B. S. Water Resources and Their Role in Food Production. **In** *Swaminathan, M. S. and Sinha, S. K., eds.*, 1986, pp. 171–98. **[G: Global]**

Sarris, Alexander H. Uncertainty in Market Analysis. **In** *Maunder, A. and Renborg, U., eds.*, 1986, pp. 585–94.

Sarup, Shanti and Pandey, R. K. Inter-District Growth Analysis of Groundnut in Gujarat. *Margin*, January 1986, *18*(2), pp. 77–84. **[G: India]**

Sawant, S. D. Balancing Overproduction and Malnutrition: Discussion. **In** *Maunder, A. and Renborg, U., eds.*, 1986, pp. 243–45. **[G: Sub-Saharan Africa]**

Sawant, S. D. and Achuthan, C. V. Agriculture in Seventh Five Year Plan. *Indian Econ. J.*, Apr.-June 1986, *33*(4), pp. 37–52. **[G: India]**

Scherer, Alf. Intersectoral Efficiency between Agriculture and Industry in Six C.M.E.A. Countries: Introducing a Simple Equilibrium Model. *Econ. Planning*, 1986, *20*(1), pp. 1–27. **[G: CMEA]**

Schiff, Maurice. The Competitive Firm under Uncertainty: An Application to Canadian Wheat Production. *Can. J. Agr. Econ.*, July 1986, *34*(2), pp. 235–42. **[G: Canada]**

Schmitz, Andrew. Marketing Institutions in International Commodity Markets. *Southern J. Agr. Econ.*, July 1986, *18*(1), pp. 41–48. **[G: U.S.]**

Schrimper, Ronald A. Effects of Increasing Elderly Population on Future Food Demand and Consumption. **In** *Capps, O., Jr. and Senauer, B., eds.*, 1986, pp. 163–76. **[G: U.S.]**

Schwartz, Nancy E. The Consequences of a Floating Exchange Rate for the U.S. Wheat Market. *Amer. J. Agr. Econ.*, May 1986, *68*(2), pp. 428–33. **[G: U.S.]**

Segura, Edilberto L.; Shetty, Y. T. and Nishimizu, Mieko. International Seminar on Fertilizer Pricing Policies: Summary of Proceedings. **In** *Segura, E. L.; Shetty, Y. T. and Nishimizu, M., eds.*, 1986, pp. 1–20. **[G: LDCs]**

Sekhon, G. S. Needs and Resources of Potassium. **In** *Swaminathan, M. S. and Sinha, S. K., eds.*, 1986, pp. 267–82. **[G: Global]**

Sen, Amartya K. Food, Economics and Entitlements. *Lloyds Bank Rev.*, April 1986, (160), pp. 1–20.

Sen, Amartya K. Food, Economics and Entitlements. **In** *Maunder, A. and Renborg, U., eds.*, 1986, pp. 3–20.

Senauer, Benjamin; Sahn, David and Alderman, Harold. The Effect of the Value of Time on Food Consumption Patterns in Developing Countries: Evidence from Sri Lanka. *Amer. J. Agr. Econ.*, November 1986, *68*(4), pp. 920–27. **[G: Sri Lanka]**

Shah, C. H. Animal Husbandry. **In** *Dantwala, M. L., et al.*, 1986, pp. 162–98. **[G: India]**

Shepard, Lawrence. Cartelization of the California–Arizona Orange Industry, 1934–1981. *J. Law Econ.*, April 1986, *29*(1), pp. 83–123. **[G: U.S.]**

Shoemaker, Robbin and Somwaru, Agapi. Total Factor Productivity and Sources of Growth in the Dairy Sector. *Agr. Econ. Res.*, Fall 1986, *38*(4), pp. 1–13. **[G: U.S.]**

Shonkwiler, J. Scott and Spreen, Thomas H. Statistical Significance and Stability of the Hog Cycle. *Southern J. Agr. Econ.*, December 1986, *18*(2), pp. 227–33. **[G: U.S.]**

Shumway, C. Richard. Supply Relationships in the South—What Have We Learned? *Southern J. Agr. Econ.*, July 1986, *18*(1), pp. 11–19. **[G: U.S.]**

Sidhu, D. S. and Singh, A. J. Technological Change in Indian Agriculture. **In** *Dantwala, M. L., et al.*, 1986, pp. 140–61. **[G: India]**

Silver, Mick. The Economic Implications of Rising Food Prices: Friedman and the Price of Steaks. *J. Agr. Econ.*, September 1986, *37*(3), pp. 377–83. **[G: U.K.]**

Sinha, S. K. Energy Balance in Agriculture: The Developing World. **In** *Swaminathan, M. S. and Sinha, S. K., eds.*, 1986, pp. 57–83. **[G: LDCs]**

Sivakumar, M. V. K. and Virmani, S. M. Climate and Production in the Semi-arid and the Humid Tropics. **In** *Swaminathan, M. S. and Sinha, S. K., eds.*, 1986, pp. 129–69. **[G: LDCs]**

Sivanappan, R. K. and Rajagopalan, V. Irrigation Development Needs in India. **In** *Easter, W. K., ed.*, 1986, pp. 57–71. **[G: India]**

Slesser, M. Energy Balance in Agriculture: The Developed World. **In** *Swaminathan, M. S. and Sinha, S. K., eds.*, 1986, pp. 47–56. **[G: MDCs]**

Smil, Vaclav. Food Production and Quality of Diet in China. *Population Devel. Rev.*, March 1986, *12*(1), pp. 25–45. **[G: China]**

Somel, Kutlu. Agricultural Support Policies in Turkey, 1950–1980: An Overview. **In** *Richards, A., ed.*, 1986, pp. 97–130. **[G: Turkey]**

Spinks, Murray and Lehmer, Carola. An Economic Evaluation of Additional Measurement in Wool Processing. *Australian J. Agr. Econ.*, August/December 1986, *30*(2–3), pp. 162–72.

Srinivasan, T. N. Undernutrition: Extent and Distribution of Its Incidence. **In** *Maunder, A. and Renborg, U., eds.*, 1986, pp. 199–207. **[G: LDCs]**

St. Żegar, Józef. Peasant Farms in Economic and Social Crisis: The Case of Poland in the 1980s. **In** *Maunder, A. and Renborg, U., eds.*, 1986, pp. 139–45. **[G: Poland]**

Stacey, Robert C. Agricultural Investment and the Management of the Royal Demesne Manors, 1236–1240. *J. Econ. Hist.*, December 1986, *46*(4), pp. 919–34.

Stranahan, H. A. and Shonkwiler, J. Scott. Evaluating the Returns to Postharvest Research in the Florida Citrus-Processing Subsector. *Amer. J. Agr. Econ.*, February 1986, *68*(1), pp. 88–94. **[G: U.S.]**

Strauss, John. Does Better Nutrition Raise Farm Productivity? *J. Polit. Econ.*, April 1986, *94*(2), pp. 297–320. **[G: Sierra Leone]**

Stucki, Erwin. Agriculture in a Turbulent World Economy: Theoretical Developments: Discussion. **In** *Maunder, A. and Renborg, U., eds.*, 1986, pp. 714–16.

Subbarao, K. Farm Prices: A Survey of the Debate. **In** *Dantwala, M. L., et al.*, 1986, pp. 373–84. **[G: India]**

Suits, Daniel B. The Structure of American Industry: Agriculture. **In** *Adams, W., ed.*, 1986, pp. 1–37. **[G: U.S.]**

Sukhatme, P. V. Quantitative Dimensions of the Nutrition Problem. **In** *Swaminathan, M. S. and Sinha, S. K., eds.*, 1986, pp. 25–45. **[G: LDCs]**

Sumner, Daniel A. The Competitive Position of Southern Commodities: Some Trends and Underlying Forces. *Southern J. Agr. Econ.*, July 1986, *18*(1), pp. 49–59. **[G: U.S.]**

Sumner, David. Human Capital, Technology and Institutions: Discussion. **In** *Maunder, A. and Renborg, U., eds.*, 1986, pp. 486–88.

Swaminathan, M. S. Building National and Global Nutrition Security Systems. **In** *Swaminathan, M. S. and Sinha, S. K., eds.*, 1986, pp. 417–49. **[G: LDCs; MDCs]**

Thompson, C. Stassen. Supply Relationships in the South—What Have We Learned? Discussion. *Southern J. Agr. Econ.*, July 1986, *18*(1), pp. 21–23. **[G: U.S.]**

Thurman, Walter N. Endogeneity Testing in a Supply and Demand Framework. *Rev. Econ. Statist.*, November 1986, *68*(4), pp. 638–46. **[G: U.S.]**

Tims, Wouter. Balancing Overproduction and Malnutrition: Discussion. **In** *Maunder, A. and Renborg, U., eds.*, 1986, pp. 209–10.

Tomic, Dušan. Growing Interdependencies and Uncertainties: Discussion. **In** *Maunder, A. and Renborg, U., eds.*, 1986, pp. 145–48. **[G: Canada; Poland]**

Trant, Michael. Farm Producers, Past and Present. *Can. J. Agr. Econ.*, June 1986, *33*, pp. 122–44. **[G: Canada]**

Turner, Michael. Corn Crises in Britain in the Age of Malthus. **In** *Turner, M., ed.*, 1986, pp. 112–28. **[G: U.K.]**

Tweeten, Luther. Impact of Domestic Policy on Comparative Advantage of Agriculture in the South. *Southern J. Agr. Econ.*, July 1986, *18*(1), pp. 67–74. **[G: U.S.]**

Unnevehr, Laurian J. Changing Comparative Advantage in Philippine Rice Production: 1966 to 1982. *Food Res. Inst. Stud.*, 1986, *20*(1), pp. 43–69. **[G: Philippines]**

Unnevehr, Laurian J. Consumer Demand for Rice Grain Quality and Returns to Research for Quality Improvement in Southeast Asia. *Amer. J. Agr. Econ.*, August 1986, *68*(3), pp. 634–41. **[G: Philippines; Indonesia; Thailand]**

Vasavada, Utpal and Chambers, Robert G. Investment in U.S. Agriculture. *Amer. J. Agr. Econ.*, November 1986, *68*(4), pp. 950–60. **[G: U.S.]**

Vasavada, Utpal and Chambers, Robert G. Testing Asset Fixity for U.S. Agriculture: Reply. *Amer. J. Agr. Econ.*, May 1986, *68*(2), pp. 355–57. **[G: U.S.]**

Vere, D. T. and Muir, A. M. Pasture Improvement Adoption in South-eastern New South Wales. *Rev. Marketing Agr. Econ.*, April 1986, *54*(1), pp. 19–32. **[G: Australia]**

van Vuuren, Willem. Soil Erosion: The Case for Market Intervention. *Can. J. Agr. Econ.*, June 1986, *33*, pp. 41–62. **[G: Canada]**

Vyas, Vijay S. Balancing Overproduction and Malnutrition: Discussion. **In** *Maunder, A. and Renborg, U., eds.*, 1986, pp. 210–12.

Vyas, Vijay S. Balancing Overproduction and Malnutrition—Implications for Policy and Research. **In** *Maunder, A. and Renborg, U., eds.*, 1986, pp. 749–53.

Wells, Gary J.; Miller, Stephen E. and Thompson, C. Stassen. Farm Level Demand for Pecans Reconsidered. *Southern J. Agr. Econ.*, July 1986, *18*(1), pp. 157–60. **[G: U.S.]**

Wennergren, E. Boyd and Whitaker, Morris D. Foodgrain Sufficiency in Bangladesh: A Reappraisal and Policy Implications. *J. Devel. Areas*, October 1986, *21*(1), pp. 1–13. **[G: Bangladesh]**

van der Willigen, Tessa A. Cash Crop Production and the Balance of Trade in a Less Developed Economy: A Model of Temporary Equilibrium with Rationing. *Oxford Econ. Pap.*, November 1986, *38*(3), pp. 424–42.

Winter, George and Gunjal, Kisan. Computerized Delphi: An Application to Quota Value Determination in the Quebec Dairy Industry. *Can. J. Agr. Econ.*, November 1986, *34*(3), pp. 417–31. **[G: Canada]**

Wittwer, S. H. Research and Technology Needs for the Twenty-first Century. **In** *Swaminathan, M. S. and Sinha, S. K., eds.*, 1986, pp. 85–116.

Wohlgenant, Michael K. Global Behavior of Demand Elasticities for Food: Implications for Demand Projections. **In** *Capps, O., Jr. and Senauer, B., eds.*, 1986, pp. 35–48.

Wright, Gavin. Output and Productivity in Canadian Agriculture, 1870–71 to 1926–27: Comment. **In** *Engerman, S. L. and Gallman, R. E., eds.*, 1986, pp. 771–76. **[G: Canada]**

712 Agricultural Situation and Outlook

7120 Agricultural Situation and Outlook

Anderson, Kym. Economic Growth, Structural Change and the Political Economy of Protection. **In** *Anderson, K. and Hayami, Y.*, 1986, pp. 7–16. **[G: E. Asia]**

Anderson, Kym and Hayami, Yujiro. Lessons and Implications. **In** *Anderson, K. and Hayami, Y.*, 1986, pp. 111–19. **[G: E. Asia]**

Anderson, Kym and Hayami, Yujiro. The Political Economy of Agricultural Protection: East Asia in International Perspective: Introduction. **In** *Anderson, K. and Hayami, Y.*, 1986, pp. 1–6. **[G: Europe; Asia]**

Antlöv, Hans. Tradition and Transition Harvest and Social Change in Rural Java. **In** *Nørlund, I.; Cederroth, S. and Gerdin, I., eds.*, 1986, pp. 151–70. **[G: Indonesia]**

Balaam, David N. Self-sufficiency in Japanese Agriculture: Telescoping and Reconciling the Food Security–Efficiency Dilemma. **In** *Browne, W. P. and Hadwiger, D. F., eds.*, 1986, pp. 91–108. **[G: Japan]**

Barichello, Richard R. and Warley, T. K. Agriculture and Negotiation of a Free-Trade Area: Issues in Policy Harmonization. **In** *C. D. Howe Institute*, 1986, pp. 135–64. **[G: Canada; U.S.]**

Bauer, Siegfried. Agriculture in a Turbulent World Economy: A Survey of the 19th International Conference of Agricultural Economists, Malaga, Spain, 26 August–4 September, 1985. *Europ. Rev. Agr. Econ.*, 1986, *13*(2), pp. 249–61.

Belongia, Michael T. The Farm Sector in the 1980s: Sudden Collapse or Steady Downturn? *Fed. Res. Bank St. Louis Rev.*, November 1986, *68*(9), pp. 17–25. **[G: U.S.]**

Chhibber, Ajay and Wilton, John. Macroeconomic Policies and Agricultural Performance in Developing Countries. *Finance Develop.*, September 1986, *23*(3), pp. 6–9. **[G: LDCs]**

Dantwala, M. L. Strategy of Agricultural Development since Independence. **In** *Dantwala, M. L., et al.*, 1986, pp. 1–15. **[G: India]**

Dommen, Arthur J. Increasing Food Production in Sub-Saharan Africa: Comment. *Amer. J. Agr. Econ.*, November 1986, *68*(4), pp. 998–99.

Fearnside, Philip M. Agricultural Plans for Brazil's Grande Carajás Program: Lost Opportunity for Sustainable Local Development? *World Devel.*, March 1986, *14*(3), pp. 385–409. **[G: Brazil]**

Hazell, Peter; Pomareda, Carlos and Valdés, Alberto. Crop Insurance for Agricultural Development: Issues and Experience: Introduction. **In** *Hazell, P.; Pomareda, C. and Valdés, A., eds.*, 1986, pp. 1–13.

Ikerd, John E. U.S. Agriculture at a Crossroads: Implications for Agricultural Economics. *Southern J. Agr. Econ.*, July 1986, *18*(1), pp. 1–9. **[G: U.S.]**

Islam, Nurul. World Food Security: National and International Measures for Stabilisation of Supplies. **In** *[Streeten, P.]*, 1986, pp. 192–216. **[G: Global]**

Khachaturov, Tigran S. The Intensification of Land Use. *Prob. Econ.*, February 1986, *28*(10), pp. 43–59. **[G: U.S.S.R.]**

Kjeldsen-Kragh, S. Den internationale fødevaresituation. (The World Food Problem. With English summary.) *Nationaløkon. Tidsskr.*, 1986, *124*(1), pp. 107–22. **[G: Global]**

Klatzmann, Joseph. Balancing Overproduction and Malnutrition: Discussion. **In** *Maunder, A. and Renborg, U., eds.*, 1986, pp. 208–09.

Klemyshev, P. Scientific–Technical Progress and the Intensification of Agriculture. *Prob. Econ.*, May 1986, *29*(1), pp. 63–81. **[G: U.S.S.R.]**

Lardy, Nicholas R. Prospects and Some Policy Problems of Agricultural Development in China. *Amer. J. Agr. Econ.*, May 1986, *68*(2), pp. 451–57. **[G: China]**

Mellor, John W. Dealing with the Uncertainty of Growing Food Imbalances: International Structures and National Policies. **In** *Maunder, A. and Renborg, U., eds.*, 1986, pp. 191–98.

Morales, Edmundo. Coca and Cocaine Economy and Social Change in the Andes of Peru. *Econ. Develop. Cult. Change*, October 1986, *35*(1), pp. 143–61. **[G: Peru]**

Mukherjee, S. K. Chemical Technology for Producing Fertilizer Nitrogen in the Year 2000. **In** *Swaminathan, M. S. and Sinha, S. K., eds.*, 1986, pp. 227–37.

Nolan, Peter and Paine, Suzanne. Towards an Appraisal of the Impact of Rural Reform in China, 1978–85. *Cambridge J. Econ.*, March 1986, *10*(1), pp. 83–99. **[G: China]**

O'Relley, Z. Edward. The Changing Status of Collectivized and Private Agriculture under Central Planning: To Increase Output, State Socialist Hungary Combines Private with State Enterprises. *Amer. J. Econ. Soc.*, January 1986, *45*(1), pp. 9–16. **[G: Hungary]**

Otsuka, Keijiro and Hayami, Yujiro. Revealed Preference in Japan's Rice Policy. **In** *Anderson, K. and Hayami, Y.*, 1986, pp. 63–79. **[G: Japan]**

Overton, Mark. Atlas of Industrializing Britain 1780–1914: Agriculture. **In** *Langton, J. and Morris, R. J., eds.*, 1986, pp. 34–53. **[G: U.K.]**

Owens, Raymond E. The Agricultural Outlook for 1986...Continued Financial Weakness Seen. *Fed. Res. Bank Richmond Econ. Rev.*, Jan./Feb. 1986, *72*(1), pp. 29–34. **[G: U.S.]**

Pal, S. P. and Singh, J. P. Food Security and Food Stocks in India. *Margin*, October 1986, *19*(1), pp. 30–41.

Penna, Julio A. Sources of Growth of Argentine Agriculture and Prospects for the 1990s. **In** *Maunder, A. and Renborg, U., eds.*, 1986, pp. 475–86. **[G: Argentina]**

Picard, Louis A. Self-sufficiency, Delinkage, and Food Production: Limits on Agricultural Development in Africa. **In** *Browne, W. P. and Hadwiger, D. F., eds.*, 1986, pp. 121–36. **[G: Africa]**

Quasem, Md. Abul. The Impact of Privatisation on Entrepreneurial Development in Bangladesh Agriculture. *Bangladesh Devel. Stud.*, June 1986, *14*(2), pp. 1–19. **[G: Bangladesh]**

Redclift, Michael. Sustainability and the Market: Survival Strategies on the Bolivian Frontier. *J. Devel. Stud.*, October 1986, *23*(1), pp. 93–105. **[G: Bolivia]**

Robinson, Warren C. and Yamazaki, Fumiko. Agriculture, Population, and Economic Planning in Ethiopia, 1953–1980. *J. Devel. Areas*, April 1986, *20*(3), pp. 327–38. **[G: Ethiopia]**

Sen, Amartya K. Food, Economics and Entitlements. **In** *Maunder, A. and Renborg, U., eds.*, 1986, pp. 3–20.

Senauer, Benjamin and Young, Nathan. The Impact of Food Stamps on Food Expenditures: Rejection of the Traditional Model. *Amer. J. Agr. Econ.*, February 1986, *68*(1), pp. 37–43. **[G: U.S.]**

Sicular, Terry. Prospects and Some Policy Problems of Agricultural Development in China: Discussion [Towards an Agricultural Economy for China in a New Age: Progress, Problems, Response, and Prospects] [Prospects and Some Policy Problems of Agricultural Development in China]. *Amer. J. Agr. Econ.*, May 1986, *68*(2), pp. 458–60. **[G: China]**

Smith, Pamela. "Not Enough Hours, Our Accountant Tells Me": Trends in Children's, Women's and Men's Involvement in Canadian Agriculture. *Can. J. Agr. Econ.*, June 1986, *33*, pp. 161–95. **[G: Canada]**

Sumner, David. Human Capital, Technology and Institutions: Discussion. **In** *Maunder, A. and Renborg, U., eds.*, 1986, pp. 486–88.

Timmer, C. Peter. Prospects and Some Policy Problems of Agricultural Development in China: Discussion [Towards an Agricultural Economy for China in a New Age: Progress, Problems, Response, and Prospects] [Prospects and Some Policy Problems of Agricultural Development in China]. *Amer. J. Agr. Econ.*, May 1986, *68*(2), pp. 461–63. **[G: China]**

Tims, Wouter. Balancing Overproduction and Malnutrition: Discussion. **In** *Maunder, A. and Renborg, U., eds.*, 1986, pp. 209–10.

Trant, Michael. Farm Producers, Past and Present. *Can. J. Agr. Econ.*, June 1986, *33*, pp. 122–44. **[G: Canada]**

Vyas, Vijay S. Balancing Overproduction and Malnutrition: Discussion. **In** *Maunder, A. and Renborg, U., eds.*, 1986, pp. 210–12.

Wagstaff, Howard. The Employment Problem, Agricultural Change, and Policy Objectives in Industrially Advanced Countries. *J. Agr. Econ.*, May 1986, *37*(2), pp. 163–72. **[G: OECD]**

Weinbaum, Marvin G. Food Security and Agricultural Development Policies in the Middle East. **In** *Browne, W. P. and Hadwiger, D. F., eds.*, 1986, pp. 109–20. **[G: Middle East]**

Wennergren, E. Boyd and Whitaker, Morris D. Foodgrain Sufficiency in Bangladesh: A Reappraisal and Policy Implications. *J. Devel. Areas*, October 1986, *21*(1), pp. 1–13. **[G: Bangladesh]**

Williams, J. T. Germplasm Resources. **In** *Swaminathan, M. S. and Sinha, S. K., eds.*, 1986, pp. 117–28.

Wittwer, S. H. Research and Technology Needs

for the Twenty-first Century. In *Swaminathan, M. S. and Sinha, S. K., eds.*, 1986, pp. 85–116.

Zahid, Shahid N. and Hyder, Syed Sajjad. Pakistan's Agricultural Terms of Trade: 1973–74 to 1983–84. *Pakistan J. Appl. Econ.*, Winter 1986, *5*(2), pp. 91–141. **[G: Pakistan]**

713 Agricultural Policy, Domestic and International

7130 Agricultural Policy, Domestic and International

Abdou, Dyaa K.; Gardner, B. Delworth and Green, Richard D. To Violate or Not Violate the Law: An Example from Egyptian Agriculture. *Amer. J. Agr. Econ.*, February 1986, *68*(1), pp. 120–26. **[G: Egypt]**

Abdullah, Abu. Distributional Aspects of Fertilizer Pricing Policy. *Bangladesh Devel. Stud.*, March 1986, *14*(1), pp. 93–100. **[G: Bangladesh]**

Adams, Dale W. and Vogel, Robert C. Rural Financial Markets in Low-income Countries: Recent Controversies and Lessons. *World Devel.*, April 1986, *14*(4), pp. 477–87. **[G: LDCs]**

Adams, Richard H., Jr. Taxation, Control, and Agrarian Transition in Rural Egypt: A Local-Level View. In *Richards, A., ed.*, 1986, pp. 159–82. **[G: Egypt]**

Al-Zand, Osama A.; Coffin, G. and Dufour, Jean-Claude. Channel Conflict in the Agri-Food System. *Can. J. Agr. Econ.*, Proceedings 1986, *34*, pp. 22–31. **[G: Canada]**

Alderman, Harold. Food Subsidies and State Policies in Egypt. In *Richards, A., ed.*, 1986, pp. 183–200. **[G: Egypt]**

Alston, Julian M. A Note on Victoria's Hen Quota Transfer System. *Rev. Marketing Agr. Econ.*, April 1986, *54*(1), pp. 45–49. **[G: Australia]**

Alston, Julian M. Consequences of Deregulation in Victorian Egg Industry: A Reply. *Rev. Marketing Agr. Econ.*, December 1986, *54*(3), pp. 51–52. **[G: Australia]**

Alston, Julian M. Consequences of Deregulation in the Victorian Egg Industry. *Rev. Marketing Agr. Econ.*, April 1986, *54*(1), pp. 33–43. **[G: Australia]**

Alston, Julian M. The Effects of the CAP on International Trade in Poultry Meat. *Europ. Rev. Agr. Econ.*, 1986, *13*(2), pp. 217–31. **[G: EEC]**

von Alvensleben, Reimar; Behr, Hans-Christoph and Jahn, Hans-Harald. Fruits and Vegetables in the European Community. In *Bale, M. D., ed.*, 1986, pp. 5–93. **[G: EEC]**

An, Xi-Ji. Pricing System Reform for Agricultural Products and Price Policy Adjustment in China (1979–1984). In *Maunder, A. and Renborg, U., eds.*, 1986, pp. 449–60. **[G: China]**

Anderson, Kym. Economic Growth, Structural Change and the Political Economy of Protection. In *Anderson, K. and Hayami, Y.*, 1986, pp. 7–16. **[G: E. Asia]**

Anderson, Kym. The Peculiar Rationality of Beef Import Quotas in Japan and Korea. In *Anderson, K. and Hayami, Y.*, 1986, pp. 80–90. **[G: Japan; S. Korea]**

Anderson, Kym and Hayami, Yujiro. Lessons and Implications. In *Anderson, K. and Hayami, Y.*, 1986, pp. 111–19. **[G: E. Asia]**

Anderson, Kym and Hayami, Yujiro. The Political Economy of Agricultural Protection: East Asia in International Perspective: Introduction. In *Anderson, K. and Hayami, Y.*, 1986, pp. 1–6. **[G: Europe; Asia]**

Anderson, Kym; Hayami, Yujiro and Honma, Masayoshi. The Growth of Agricultural Protection. In *Anderson, K. and Hayami, Y.*, 1986, pp. 17–30. **[G: Japan]**

Anderson, Kym and Tyers, Rodney. Agricultural Policies of Industrial Countries and Their Effects on Traditional Food Exporters. *Econ. Rec.*, December 1986, *62*(179), pp. 385–99. **[G: Global]**

Anderson, Kym and Tyers, Rodney. International Effects of Agricultural Policies. In *Snape, R. H., ed.*, 1986, pp. 93–114. **[G: OECD]**

Anderson, Kym, et al. Details of Agricultural Protection Estimates, 1955–82. In *Anderson, K. and Hayami, Y.*, 1986, pp. 123–45. **[G: Europe; E. Asia; U.S.]**

Andrews, Margaret S. and Rausser, Gordon C. Some Political Economy Aspects of Macroeconomic Linkages with Agriculture. *Amer. J. Agr. Econ.*, May 1986, *68*(2), pp. 413–17. **[G: U.S.]**

Antle, John M. and Aitah, Ali S. Egypt's Multiproduct Agricultural Technology and Agricultural Policy. *J. Devel. Stud.*, July 1986, *22*(4), pp. 709–23. **[G: Egypt]**

Ashmead, Ralph. The Long-term Credit Agency Perspective. *Can. J. Agr. Econ.*, June 1986, *33*, pp. S26–36. **[G: Canada; U.S.]**

Bailey, R. C. Resolving Federal–Provincial Conflicts in Agri-Food Policy. *Can. J. Agr. Econ.*, Proceedings 1986, *34*, pp. 37–41. **[G: Canada]**

Balaam, David N. Self-sufficiency in Japanese Agriculture: Telescoping and Reconciling the Food Security–Efficiency Dilemma. In *Browne, W. P. and Hadwiger, D. F., eds.*, 1986, pp. 91–108. **[G: Japan]**

Balbino, L. R. and Monteiro Marques, M. Fertilizer Pricing Policy in Portugal. In *Segura, E. L.; Shetty, Y. T. and Nishimizu, M., eds.*, 1986, pp. 102–08. **[G: Portugal]**

Bale, Malcolm D. Horticultural Trade of the Expanded European Community: Implications for Mediterranean Countries: Overview. In *Bale, M. D., ed.*, 1986, pp. 1–3. **[G: EEC]**

Ballenger, Nicole S. and Norton, Roger D. Optimization of Policy Goals in the Context of a Sector Model. *Agr. Econ. Res.*, Spring 1986, *38*(2), pp. 28–36. **[G: Mexico]**

Barichello, Richard R. and Warley, T. K. Agriculture and Negotiation of a Free-Trade Area: Issues in Policy Harmonization. In *C. D. Howe Institute*, 1986, pp. 135–64. **[G: Canada; U.S.]**

Bassoco, Luz María; Cartas, Celso and Norton,

Roger D. Sectoral Analysis of the Benefits of Subsidized Insurance in Mexico. **In** *Hazell, P.; Pomareda, C. and Valdés, A., eds.*, 1986, pp. 126–42. **[G: Mexico]**

Basu, Dipak R. Sen's Analysis of Famine: A Critique. *J. Devel. Stud.*, April 1986, *22*(3), pp. 598–603. **[G: Bengal]**

Batie, Sandra S. and Sappington, Alyson G. Cross-compliance as a Soil Conservation Strategy: A Case Study. *Amer. J. Agr. Econ.*, November 1986, *68*(4), pp. 880–85. **[G: U.S.]**

Bautista, Romeo M. Domestic Price Distortions and Agricultural Income in Developing Countries. *J. Devel. Econ.*, September 1986, *23*(1), pp. 19–39. **[G: Philippines]**

Benson, Bruce L. and Faminow, Merle D. Regulatory Transfers in Canadian/American Agriculture: The Case of Supply Management. *Cato J.*, Spring/Summer 1986, *6*(1), pp. 271–94. **[G: Canada]**

Binswanger, Hans P. Risk Aversion, Collateral Requirements, and the Markets for Credit and Insurance in Rural Areas. **In** *Hazell, P.; Pomareda, C. and Valdés, A., eds.*, 1986, pp. 67–86.

Birowo, Achmad T. Human Capital, Technology and Institutions: Discussion. **In** *Maunder, A. and Renborg, U., eds.*, 1986, pp. 386–87.

Blais, Pierre. Notes for an Address on Agricultural Policy. *Can. J. Agr. Econ.*, Proceedings 1986, *34*, pp. 66–70. **[G: Canada]**

Bolin, Olof. Human Capital, Technology and Institutions: Discussion. **In** *Maunder, A. and Renborg, U., eds.*, 1986, pp. 414–15.

Bond, Gary E. The Farmers' View of New South Wales Rural Planning Policy. *Rev. Marketing Agr. Econ.*, December 1986, *54*(3), pp. 66–70. **[G: Australia]**

Booth, Anne. Agricultural Taxation: A Survey of Issues and Evidence. **In** *Shome, P., ed.*, 1986, pp. 117–40. **[G: S. Asia; S. E. Asia]**

Boss, Adrian. The Justification for Rural Planning. *Rev. Marketing Agr. Econ.*, December 1986, *54*(3), pp. 53–57. **[G: Australia]**

Boussard, Jean-Marc. Changing Environment and Structural Heterogeneity in Agriculture. **In** *Maunder, A. and Renborg, U., eds.*, 1986, pp. 531–41.

Boyle, G. E. An Exploratory Assessment of the Returns to Agricultural Research in Ireland 1963–1983. *Irish J. Agr. Econ. Rural Soc.*, 1986, *11*, pp. 57–71. **[G: Ireland]**

Braverman, Avishay and Guasch, J. Luis. Rural Credit Markets and Institutions in Developing Countries: Lessons for Policy Analysis from Practice and Modern Theory. *World Devel.*, Oct./Nov. 1986, *14*(10/11), pp. 1253–67. **[G: LDCs]**

Braverman, Avishay and Hammer, Jeffrey S. Multimarket Analysis of Agricultural Pricing Policies in Senegal. **In** *Singh, I.; Squire, L. and Strauss, J., eds.*, 1986, pp. 233–54. **[G: Senegal]**

Breimyer, Harold F. Human Capital, Technology and Institutions: Discussion. **In** *Maunder, A. and Renborg, U., eds.*, 1986, pp. 460–62. **[G: China]**

Brinkman, George L. Farming under Uncertainty in the 1980s: Some Lessons from Canada. **In** *Maunder, A. and Renborg, U., eds.*, 1986, pp. 127–38. **[G: Canada]**

Brinkman, George L. The Search for Common Ground in Agricultural Policy: How Far Have We Come? *Can. J. Agr. Econ.*, Proceedings 1986, *34*, pp. 71–76. **[G: Canada]**

Bronshtein, M. Toward a Conception of the Economic Mechanism of the AIC [Agro-Industrial Complex]. *Prob. Econ.*, December 1986, *29*(8), pp. 73–87. **[G: U.S.S.R.]**

Browne, William P. Issues of World Food and Trade: Perspectives and Projections. **In** *Browne, W. P. and Hadwiger, D. F., eds.*, 1986, pp. 1–13.

Bruce, C. J. and Kerr, William A. A Proposed Arbitration Mechanism to Ensure Free Trade in Livestock Products. *Can. J. Agr. Econ.*, November 1986, *34*(3), pp. 347–60. **[G: Canada; U.S.]**

Butler, Nicholas. The Common Agricultural Policy and World Food Trade. **In** *Browne, W. P. and Hadwiger, D. F., eds.*, 1986, pp. 45–57. **[G: EEC]**

Byerlee, Derek and Sain, Gustavo. Food Pricing Policy in Developing Countries: Bias against Agriculture or for Urban Consumers? *Amer. J. Agr. Econ.*, November 1986, *68*(4), pp. 961–69. **[G: LDCs]**

Camargo Barros, Geraldo. Growing Interdependencies and Uncertainties: Discussion. **In** *Maunder, A. and Renborg, U., eds.*, 1986, pp. 122–23.

Carter, C. A.; Loyns, R. M. A. and Ahmadi-Esfahani, Z. F. Varietal Licensing Standards and Canadian Wheat Exports. *Can. J. Agr. Econ.*, November 1986, *34*(3), pp. 361–77. **[G: Canada]**

Carter, Harold O. Agricultural Policy at the Crossroads—Again. *Contemp. Policy Issues*, January 1986, *4*(1), pp. 48.

del Castillo, Gustavo and Barajas de Vega, Rosario. U.S.–Mexican Agricultural Relations: The Upper Limits of Linkage Formation. **In** *Browne, W. P. and Hadwiger, D. F., eds.*, 1986, pp. 153–68. **[G: U.S.; Mexico]**

Castro Forero, Yesid. Fertilizer Pricing in Colombia. **In** *Segura, E. L.; Shetty, Y. T. and Nishimizu, M., eds.*, 1986, pp. 196–200. **[G: Colombia]**

Čerňa, Peter. Change in the System of Plan-Based Management of Agriculture. *Czech. Econ. Digest.*, June/July 1986, (4), pp. 31–38. **[G: Czechoslovakia]**

Chambers, Robert G. Domestic and International Agricultural Policy Interfaces. *Southern J. Agr. Econ.*, July 1986, *18*(1), pp. 61–66.

Charlton, Mark W. The Management of Canada's Bilateral Food Aid: An Organizational Perspective. *Can. J. Devel. Stud.*, 1986, *7*(1), pp. 7–19. **[G: Canada; LDCs]**

Chatterji, Monojit and Junankar, P. N. Agricultural Taxation in Less Developed Countries:

Effects of a Tax on Inefficiency. *J. Quant. Econ.*, July 1986, *2*(2), pp. 275–90.

Chicoine, David L. Farm Taxes. **In** *Gold, S. D., ed.*, 1986, pp. 307–31. **[G: U.S.]**

Considine, Jennifer I., et al. The Impact of a New Grading System on the Beef Cattle Industry: The Case of Canada. *Western J. Agr. Econ.*, December 1986, *11*(2), pp. 184–94. **[G: Canada]**

Cowen, Michael. Change in State Power, International Conditions and Peasant Producers: The Case of Kenya. *J. Devel. Stud.*, January 1986, *22*(2), pp. 355–84. **[G: Kenya]**

Dantwala, M. L. and Barmeda, J. N. Rural Development: Approaches and Issues. **In** *Dantwala, M. L., et al.*, 1986, pp. 460–78. **[G: India]**

De Benedictis, Michele. Balancing Overproduction and Malnutrition: Discussion. **In** *Maunder, A. and Renborg, U., eds.*, 1986, pp. 265–68. **[G: LDCs]**

De Visscher, Guy. Growing Interdependencies and Uncertainties: Discussion. **In** *Maunder, A. and Renborg, U., eds.*, 1986, pp. 123–25.

Desai, Gunvant M. Growth in Indian Fertilizer Consumption: Price and Non-price Policies. **In** *Segura, E. L.; Shetty, Y. T. and Nishimizu, M., eds.*, 1986, pp. 109–36. **[G: India]**

Dias, Guilherme Leite da Silva. Markets and Trade: Discussion. **In** *Maunder, A. and Renborg, U., eds.*, 1986, pp. 577–78.

Duffy, Patricia A.; Richardson, James W. and Smith, Edward G. Effects of Alternative Farm Programs and Levels of Price Variability on Texas Cotton Farms. *Southern J. Agr. Econ.*, December 1986, *18*(2), pp. 97–106. **[G: U.S.]**

Dumais, Mario. Agri-Food Policy in Canada: Aims, Stakes and Conflicts of Interest as Viewed by Quebec Farmers. *Can. J. Agr. Econ.*, Proceedings 1986, *34*, pp. 11–16. **[G: Canada]**

Eicher, Carl K. Facing Up to Africa's Food Crisis. **In** *Ravenhill, J., ed.*, 1986, pp. 149–80. **[G: Africa]**

Eicher, Carl K. Strategic Issues in Combating Hunger and Poverty in Africa. **In** *Berg, R. J. and Whitaker, J. S., eds.*, 1986, pp. 242–75. **[G: Sub-Saharan Africa]**

Eicher, Carl K. and Staatz, John M. Food Security Policy in Sub-Saharan Africa. **In** *Maunder, A. and Renborg, U., eds.*, 1986, pp. 215–29. **[G: Sub-Saharan Africa]**

Ennara, Ragaa El-Hady. Fertilizer Pricing in Egypt. **In** *Segura, E. L.; Shetty, Y. T. and Nishimizu, M., eds.*, 1986, pp. 91–94. **[G: Egypt]**

Etuk, O. E. U. Fertilizer Pricing in Nigeria. **In** *Segura, E. L.; Shetty, Y. T. and Nishimizu, M., eds.*, 1986, pp. 95–101. **[G: Nigeria]**

Evans, David B. The Credit Market and Rural Development: A Model of a Land Resettlement Scheme. *J. Devel. Econ.*, December 1986, *24*(2), pp. 317–29.

Falgon, Claude. The Effect of Enlargement of the EC on Tunisian Fruits and Vegetables. **In** *Bale, M. D., ed.*, 1986, pp. 95–130. **[G: EEC; Tunisia]**

Fane, George. International Effects of Agricultural Policies: Comment. **In** *Snape, R. H., ed.*, 1986, pp. 115–18. **[G: OECD]**

Fearnside, Philip M. Agricultural Plans for Brazil's Grande Carajás Program: Lost Opportunity for Sustainable Local Development? *World Devel.*, March 1986, *14*(3), pp. 385–409. **[G: Brazil]**

Feder, Gershon and Slade, Roger H. A Comparative Analysis of Some Aspects of the Training and Visit System of Agricultural Extension in India. *J. Devel. Stud.*, January 1986, *22*(2), pp. 406–28. **[G: India]**

Feder, Gershon and Slade, Roger H. The Impact of Agricultural Extension: The Training and Visit System in India. *World Bank Res. Observer*, July 1986, *1*(2), pp. 139–61. **[G: India]**

Fischer, Günther, et al. The World Economy: Resilient for the Rich, Stubborn for the Starving. **In** *Maunder, A. and Renborg, U., eds.*, 1986, pp. 259–65. **[G: LDCs]**

Frankel, Jeffrey A. Overshooting Agricultural Commodity Markets and Public Policy: Discussion [Macroeconomic Linkages, Taxes, and Subsidies in the U.S. Agricultural Sector] [Some Political Economy Aspects of Macroeconomic Linkages with Agriculture]. *Amer. J. Agr. Econ.*, May 1986, *68*(2), pp. 418–19. **[G: U.S.]**

García Alvarez-Coque, José María. La política de precios agrarios y el bienestar. (With English summary.) *Invest. Ecón.*, May 1986, *10*(2), pp. 227–50. **[G: Spain]**

Gardner, Bruce L. Farm Commodity Programs as Income Transfers. *Cato J.*, Spring/Summer 1986, *6*(1), pp. 251–61.

Gardner, Bruce L. Farm Policy and the Farm Problem. **In** *Cagan, P., ed.*, 1986, pp. 223–46. **[G: U.S.]**

Gardner, Bruce L. and Kramer, Randall A. Experience with Crop Insurance Programs in the United States. **In** *Hazell, P.; Pomareda, C. and Valdés, A., eds.*, 1986, pp. 195–222. **[G: U.S.]**

George, Aurelia and Saxon, Eric. The Politics of Agricultural Protection in Japan. **In** *Anderson, K. and Hayami, Y.*, 1986, pp. 91–110. **[G: Japan]**

Gibson, Richard E. Selection and Evaluation of Small Scale Rural Infrastructure Projects. *Bull. Indonesian Econ. Stud.*, April 1986, *22*(1), pp. 113–22. **[G: Indonesia]**

Gilbert, Christopher L. Commodity Price Stabilization: The Massell Model and Multiplicative Disturbances. *Quart. J. Econ.*, August 1986, *101*(3), pp. 635–40.

Glover, David J. Agrarian Reform and Agro-Industry in Honduras. *Can. J. Devel. Stud.*, 1986, *7*(1), pp. 21–35. **[G: Honduras]**

Gold, Hyam and Thakur, Ramesh. Australia and New Zealand: The Role of Agriculture in a Closer Economic Relationship. **In** *Browne,*

W. P. and Hadwiger, D. F., eds., 1986, pp. 63–75. **[G: Australia; New Zealand]**

Gold, Steven D. Minnesota's Farm Sector and the Taxation of Agriculture. **In** *Minnesota Tax Study Commission*, 1986, pp. 411–60. **[G: U.S.]**

Gould, Brian W. and Gunjal, Kisan. Production and Support Services. *Can. J. Agr. Econ.*, Proceedings 1986, *34*, pp. 58–60. **[G: Canada]**

Grabowski, Richard; Sivan, David and Tracy, Ronald L. Technical Change in Taiwanese Agriculture. *Indian Econ. Rev.*, Jan.-June 1986, *21*(1), pp. 41–49. **[G: Taiwan]**

Grammond, Gaston. The Search for a Common Base for Food Policies in Canada. *Can. J. Agr. Econ.*, Proceedings 1986, *34*, pp. 61–65. **[G: Canada]**

Grant, Walter V. Federal–Provincial Conflicts in Agri-Food Policy. *Can. J. Agr. Econ.*, Proceedings 1986, *34*, pp. 32–36. **[G: Canada]**

Groenewald, J. A. Structure of Agriculture and People in Rural Societies: Discussion. **In** *Maunder, A. and Renborg, U., eds.*, 1986, pp. 551–53. **[G: U.S.]**

Groenewegen, John R. A Perspective on Canadian Wheat Board Exports, Price Pooling, and West Coast Capacity Constraints. *Can. J. Agr. Econ.*, November 1986, *34*(3), pp. 331–46. **[G: Canada]**

Grube, Arthur H. Participation in Farm Commodity Programs: A Stochastic Dominance Analysis: Comment. *Amer. J. Agr. Econ.*, February 1986, *68*(1), pp. 185–88. **[G: U.S.]**

Gudger, William M. and Avalos, Luis. Planning for the Efficient Operation of Crop Credit Insurance Schemes. **In** *Hazell, P.; Pomareda, C. and Valdés, A., eds.*, 1986, pp. 263–80.

Gupta, Anand P. Taxation and Subsidies. **In** *Dantwala, M. L., et al.*, 1986, pp. 385–99. **[G: India]**

Hadwiger, Don F. Public Policy and Interdependence. **In** *Browne, W. P. and Hadwiger, D. F., eds.*, 1986, pp. 203–09.

Hall, Anthony L. Agricultural Plans for Brazil's Grande Carajás Program: Lost Opportunity for Sustainable Local Development? More of the Same in Brazilian Amazonia: A Comment. *World Devel.*, March 1986, *14*(3), pp. 411–14. **[G: Brazil]**

Hallam, David. The Eggs Authority: A Critical Appraisal. *J. Agr. Econ.*, May 1986, *37*(2), pp. 185–91. **[G: U.K.]**

Hamilton, Carl. Agricultural Protection in Sweden 1970–1980. *Europ. Rev. Agr. Econ.*, 1986, *13*(1), pp. 75–87. **[G: Sweden]**

Hayami, Yujiro. Poverty and Beyond: The Forces Shaping the Future in Asia. **In** *Maunder, A. and Renborg, U., eds.*, 1986, pp. 37–48. **[G: LDCs; MDCs]**

Hayami, Yujiro. The Roots of Agricultural Protectionism. **In** *Anderson, K. and Hayami, Y.*, 1986, pp. 31–38. **[G: E. Asia]**

Hayden, F. Gregory. Rejoinder to David Vail's Comments on National Agricultural Policy [A Geobased National Agricultural Policy for Rural Community Enhancement, Environmental Vitality, and Income Stabilization]. *J. Econ. Issues*, March 1986, *20*(1), pp. 191–201. **[G: U.S.]**

Hazell, Peter and Anderson, Jock R. Public Policy toward Technical Change in Agriculture. **In** *Hall, P., ed.*, 1986, *1984*, pp. 201–30. **[G: Global]**

Hazell, Peter; Bassoco, Luz María and Arcia, Gustavo. A Model for Evaluating Farmers' Demand for Insurance: Applications in Mexico and Panama. **In** *Hazell, P.; Pomareda, C. and Valdés, A., eds.*, 1986, pp. 35–66. **[G: Mexico; Panama]**

Hazell, Peter; Pomareda, Carlos and Valdés, Alberto. Crop Insurance for Agricultural Development: Issues and Experience: Epilogue. **In** *Hazell, P.; Pomareda, C. and Valdés, A., eds.*, 1986, pp. 293–97.

Hazell, Peter; Pomareda, Carlos and Valdés, Alberto. Crop Insurance for Agricultural Development: Issues and Experience: Introduction. **In** *Hazell, P.; Pomareda, C. and Valdés, A., eds.*, 1986, pp. 1–13.

Hedlund, Stefan and Lundahl, Mats. Emergency Considerations in Swedish Agriculture: A Retrospective Look. *Europ. Rev. Agr. Econ.*, 1986, *13*(1), pp. 89–105. **[G: Sweden]**

Heimlich, Ralph E. Agricultural Programs and Cropland Conversion, 1975–1981. *Land Econ.*, May 1986, *62*(2), pp. 174–81. **[G: U.S.]**

Herrmann, Roland. Free Riders and the Redistributive Effects of International Commodity Agreements: The Case of Coffee. *J. Policy Modeling*, Winter 1986, *8*(4), pp. 597–621. **[G: Global]**

Hillberg, Ann Marie. Limiting EC Grain Substitute Imports: A Simulation Model of the West German Manufactured Feed Economy. *Europ. Rev. Agr. Econ.*, 1986, *13*(1), pp. 43–56. **[G: W. Germany]**

Hillman, Jimmye S. and Faminow, Merle D. Inconsistencies in U.S. Trade and Agricultural Policies vis-a-vis Its Major Trading Partners. *Keio Econ. Stud.*, 1986, *23*(2), pp. 1–18. **[G: U.S.]**

Hoag, Dana L. and Young, Douglas L. Commodity and Conservation Policy Impacts on Risk and Returns. *Western J. Agr. Econ.*, December 1986, *11*(2), pp. 211–20. **[G: U.S.]**

Honma, Masayoshi and Hayami, Yujiro. Structure of Agricultural Protection in Industrial Countries. *J. Int. Econ.*, February 1986, *20*(1/2), pp. 115–29. **[G: U.S.; EEC; Japan]**

Honma, Masayoshi and Hayami, Yujiro. The Determinants of Agricultural Protection Levels: An Econometric Analysis: Explanatory Variables Used in the Regression Analysis. **In** *Anderson, K. and Hayami, Y.*, 1986, pp. 146–51. **[G: U.S.; Europe; E. Asia]**

Honma, Masayoshi and Hayami, Yujiro. The Determinants of Agricultural Protection Levels: An Econometric Analysis. **In** *Anderson, K. and Hayami, Y.*, 1986, pp. 39–49. **[G: Europe; U.S.; E. Asia]**

Horton, Douglas. Assessing the Impact of International Agricultural Research and Development Programs. *World Devel.*, April 1986, *14*(4), pp. 453–68. **[G: LDCs]**

Hughes Hallett, A. J. Commodity Market Stabilisation and "North–South" Income Transfers: An Empirical Investigation. *J. Devel. Econ.*, December 1986, *24*(2), pp. 293–316.

Idachaba, Francis S. The Evolution of National Agricultural Research Systems in Sub-Saharan Africa. **In** *Maunder, A. and Renborg, U., eds.*, 1986, pp. 368–80. **[G: Sub-Saharan Africa]**

Ikerd, John E. U.S. Agriculture at a Crossroads: Implications for Agricultural Economics. *Southern J. Agr. Econ.*, July 1986, *18*(1), pp. 1–9. **[G: U.S.]**

Ikpi, A. E. Growing Interdependencies and Uncertainties: Discussion. **In** *Maunder, A. and Renborg, U., eds.*, 1986, pp. 90–93. **[G: LDCs]**

Islam, Nurul. World Food Security: National and International Measures for Stabilisation of Supplies. **In** *[Streeten, P.]*, 1986, pp. 192–216. **[G: Global]**

Jain, T. B. Allied Enterprises: I—Poultry. **In** *Dantwala, M. L., et al.*, 1986, pp. 199–208. **[G: India]**

de Janvry, Alain. Integration of Agriculture in the National and World Economy: Implications for Agricultural Policies in Developing Countries. **In** *Maunder, A. and Renborg, U., eds.*, 1986, pp. 73–82. **[G: LDCs]**

Johnson, D. Gale. Agricultural Policies and World Trade: The U.S. and the European Community at Bay: Comment. **In** *Tsoukalis, L., ed.*, 1986, pp. 77–80. **[G: U.S.; EEC]**

Johnson, Sam H., III. Agricultural Intensification in Thailand: Complementary Role of Infrastructure and Agricultural Policy. **In** *Easter, W. K., ed.*, 1986, pp. 111–27. **[G: Thailand]**

Josling, Timothy E. Agricultural Policies and World Trade: The U.S. and the European Community at Bay. **In** *Tsoukalis, L., ed.*, 1986, pp. 50–70. **[G: U.S.; EEC]**

Judd, M. Ann; Boyce, James K. and Evenson, Robert E. Investing in Agricultural Supply: The Determinants of Agricultural Research and Extension Investment. *Econ. Develop. Cult. Change*, October 1986, *35*(1), pp. 77–113. **[G: Global]**

Ka, Chih-Ming and Selden, Mark. Original Accumulation, Equity and Late Industrialization: The Cases of Socialist China and Capitalist Taiwan. *World Devel.*, Oct./Nov. 1986, *14*(10/11), pp. 1293–1310. **[G: Taiwan; China]**

Kashlon, A. S. Agricultural Price Policy and Terms of Trade. **In** *Dantwala, M. L., et al.*, 1986, pp. 358–72. **[G: India]**

Kasnakoglu, Haluk. Agricultural Price Support Policies in Turkey: An Empirical Investigation. **In** *Richards, A., ed.*, 1986, pp. 131–57. **[G: Turkey]**

Kehoe, Timothy J. and Serra-Puche, Jaime. A General Equilibrium Analysis of Price Controls and Subsidies on Food in Mexico. *J. Devel. Econ.*, April 1986, *21*(1), pp. 65–87. **[G: Mexico]**

Keyzer, Michiel A. Short-run Impact of Trade Liberalization Measures on the Economy of Bangladesh: Exercises in Comparative Statics for the Year 1977. **In** *Srinivasan, T. N. and Whalley, J., eds.*, 1986, pp. 251–82. **[G: Bangladesh]**

Kirschke, Dieter. Budget Costs of the EC's Agricultural Price Policy under Uncertainty. *Europ. Rev. Agr. Econ.*, 1986, *13*(1), pp. 57–74. **[G: EEC]**

Koester, Ulrich. Regional Co-operation in the Food Sector among Developing Countries to Improve Food Security. **In** *Maunder, A. and Renborg, U., eds.*, 1986, pp. 100–113. **[G: Africa]**

Kornai, János and Dániel, Zsuzsa. The Chinese Economic Reform—as Seen by Hungarian Economists (Marginal Notes to Our Travel Diary). *Acta Oecon.*, 1986, *36*(3–4), pp. 289–305. **[G: China]**

Kramer, Randall A. and Pope, Rulon D. Participation in Farm Commodity Programs: A Stochastic Dominance Analysis: Reply. *Amer. J. Agr. Econ.*, February 1986, *68*(1), pp. 189–90. **[G: U.S.]**

Kutil, Jaroslav. Topical Aspects of the Use of the Production Potential of Agriculture. *Czech. Econ. Digest.*, June/July 1986, (4), pp. 90–113. **[G: Czechoslovakia]**

Lamo de Espinosa, Jaime. International Markets and Price Policy: The Instability of Agriculture. **In** *Maunder, A. and Renborg, U., eds.*, 1986, pp. 557–65.

Lardy, Nicholas R. Prospects and Some Policy Problems of Agricultural Development in China. *Amer. J. Agr. Econ.*, May 1986, *68*(2), pp. 451–57. **[G: China]**

Laxminarayan, H. Programmes for Agricultural Development in the Seventh Five-Year Plan. *Indian Econ. J.*, Apr.-June 1986, *33*(4), pp. 21–36. **[G: India]**

Learn, Elmer W. Agricultural Price and Income Policy: A Need for Change. *Contemp. Policy Issues*, January 1986, *4*(1), pp. 49–61. **[G: U.S.]**

Leathers, Howard D. and Chavas, Jean-Paul. Farm Debt, Default, and Foreclosure: An Economic Rationale for Policy Action. *Amer. J. Agr. Econ.*, November 1986, *68*(4), pp. 828–37.

LeBlanc, Michael and Hrubovcak, James. The Effects of Tax Policy on Aggregate Agricultural Investment. *Amer. J. Agr. Econ.*, November 1986, *68*(4), pp. 767–77. **[G: U.S.]**

Lerohl, M. L. Policy Formation and the Agri-Food System in Western Canada. *Can. J. Agr. Econ.*, Proceedings 1986, *34*, pp. 17–21. **[G: Canada]**

Lichtenberg, Erik and Zilberman, David. The Welfare Economics of Price Supports in U.S. Agriculture. *Amer. Econ. Rev.*, December 1986, *76*(5), pp. 1135–41. **[G: U.S.]**

Lloyd, Alan G. and Mauldon, Roger G. Agricultural Instability and Alternative Government Policies: The Australian Experience. **In** *Hazell, P.; Pomareda, C. and Valdés, A., eds.*, 1986, pp. 156–77. **[G: Australia]**

Lopes, Mauro de Rezende and Dias, Guilherme Leite da Silva. The Brazilian Experience with Crop Insurance Programs. **In** *Hazell, P.; Pomareda, C. and Valdés, A., eds.*, 1986, pp. 240–62. **[G: Brazil]**

Loseby, Margaret. The Contribution of the Common Agricultural Policy to Convergence within the EEC. *Econ. Notes*, 1986, (1), pp. 84–97. **[G: EEC]**

Lourenço, Joachim Silva. Origens, evolução e futuro da Política Agrícola Comum. (With English summary.) *Economia (Portugal)*, January 1986, *10*(1), pp. 67–89. **[G: EEC]**

Luyten, Paul. Agricultural Policies and World Trade: The U.S. and the European Community at Bay: Comment. **In** *Tsoukalis, L., ed.*, 1986, pp. 81–82. **[G: U.S.; EEC]**

Malish, Anton F. Soviet Agricultural Policy in the 1980s. **In** *Browne, W. P. and Hadwiger, D. F., eds.*, 1986, pp. 77–90. **[G: U.S.S.R.]**

Marcus, Alan J. and Modest, David M. The Valuation of a Random Number of Put Options: An Application to Agricultural Price Supports. *J. Finan. Quant. Anal.*, March 1986, *21*(1), pp. 73–86. **[G: U.S.]**

Martin, Michael V. and McDonald, John A. Food Grain Policy in the Republic of Korea: The Economic Costs of Self-sufficiency. *Econ. Develop. Cult. Change*, January 1986, *34*(2), pp. 315–31. **[G: S. Korea]**

Martinez, Stephen and Norton, George W. Evaluating Privately Funded Public Research: An Example with Poultry and Eggs. *Southern J. Agr. Econ.*, July 1986, *18*(1), pp. 129–40. **[G: U.S.]**

Matthews, Alan H. Agricultural Credit and Public Policy. *Irish J. Agr. Econ. Rural Soc.*, 1986, *11*, pp. 93–97. **[G: Ireland]**

Mayer, Leo V. Farm Exports and the Farm Economy: Economic and Political Interdependence. **In** *Browne, W. P. and Hadwiger, D. F., eds.*, 1986, pp. 17–27. **[G: U.S.]**

McCabe, Bernie. Economics of Quota Allocation within Supply Management Analysis of the Present Procedures for Quota Allocation. *Can. J. Agr. Econ.*, June 1986, *33*, pp. 196–204. **[G: Canada]**

McKinzie, Lance; Paarlberg, Philip L. and Huerta, Ivan P. Estimating a Complete Matrix of Demand Elasticities for Feed Components Using Pseudo Data: A Case Study of Dutch Compound Livestock Feeds. *Europ. Rev. Agr. Econ.*, 1986, *13*(1), pp. 23–42. **[G: Netherlands]**

McSweeny, William T. and Kramer, Randall A. The Integration of Farm Programs for Achieving Soil Conservation and Nonpoint Pollution Control Objectives. *Land Econ.*, May 1986, *62*(2), pp. 159–73.

Meester, Gerrit. Agriculture in a Turbulent World Economy: Theoretical Developments: Discussion. **In** *Maunder, A. and Renborg, U., eds.*, 1986, pp. 633–35.

Mellor, John W. Agriculture on the Road to Industrialization. **In** *Lewis, J. P. and Kallab, V., eds.*, 1986, pp. 67–89.

Meredith, David. State Controlled Marketing and Economic "Development": The Case of West African Produce during the Second World War. *Econ. Hist. Rev., 2nd Ser.*, February 1986, *39*(1), pp. 77–91. **[G: W. Africa]**

Mishra, S. N. Protection versus Underpricing of Agriculture in the Developing Countries: A Case Study of India. *Devel. Econ.*, June 1986, *24*(2), pp. 131–48. **[G: India]**

Monke, Eric, et al. Portugal on the Brink of Europe: The CAP and Portuguese Agriculture. *J. Agr. Econ.*, September 1986, *37*(3), pp. 317–31. **[G: Portugal]**

Msambichaka, L. A. Balancing Overproduction and Malnutrition: Discussion. **In** *Maunder, A. and Renborg, U., eds.*, 1986, pp. 239–42. **[G: Sub-Saharan Africa]**

Musgrave, Warren F. Should Agricultural Land Be Protected from Sub-division?—Economic Considerations. *Rev. Marketing Agr. Econ.*, December 1986, *54*(3), pp. 70–74. **[G: Australia]**

Mustapha, Nik Hashim. Pressure on the Malaysian Fisheries Arising from Current Modernisation Programmes and Management Conditions. **In** *Maunder, A. and Renborg, U., eds.*, 1986, pp. 328–37. **[G: Malaysia]**

Naqvi, Syed Nawab Haider and Cornelisse, Peter A. Public Policy and Wheat Market in Pakistan. *Pakistan Devel. Rev.*, Summer 1986, *25*(2), pp. 99–126. **[G: Pakistan]**

Narváez-Bueno, J. Human Capital, Technology and Institutions: Discussion. **In** *Maunder, A. and Renborg, U., eds.*, 1986, pp. 413–14. **[G: LDCs]**

Nolan, Peter and Paine, Suzanne. Towards an Appraisal of the Impact of Rural Reform in China, 1978–85. *Cambridge J. Econ.*, March 1986, *10*(1), pp. 83–99. **[G: China]**

Norton, Desmond. Smuggling under the Common Agricultural Policy: Northern Ireland and the Republic of Ireland. *J. Common Market Stud.*, June 1986, *24*(4), pp. 297–312. **[G: Ireland; EEC]**

O'Relley, Z. Edward. The Changing Status of Collectivized and Private Agriculture under Central Planning: To Increase Output, State Socialist Hungary Combines Private with State Enterprises. *Amer. J. Econ. Soc.*, January 1986, *45*(1), pp. 9–16. **[G: Hungary]**

Obstfeld, Maurice. Overshooting Agricultural Commodity Markets and Public Policy: Discussion [Macroeconomic Linkages, Taxes, and Subsidies in the U.S. Agricultural Sector] [Some Political Economy Aspects of Macroeconomic Linkages with Agriculture]. *Amer. J. Agr. Econ.*, May 1986, *68*(2), pp. 420–21. **[G: U.S.]**

Oliveira, Joao do Carmo. Trade Policy, Market 'Distortions,' and Agriculture in the Process of Economic Development: Brazil, 1950–1974. *J. Devel. Econ.*, November 1986, *24*(1), pp. 91–109. **[G: Brazil]**

Olson, Mancur. The Exploitation and Subsidization of Agriculture in Developing and Developed Countries. **In** *Maunder, A. and Renborg,*

U., eds., 1986, pp. 49–59.

Oner, Erhan. Ex-factory Pricing in Turkey. **In** *Segura, E. L.; Shetty, Y. T. and Nishimizu, M., eds.*, 1986, pp. 236–46. **[G: Turkey]**

Orgaz, Luis and Pérez Blanco, José M. La rentabilidad social de la inversión pública en regadio. (With English summary.) *Invest. Ecón.*, September 1986, *10*(3), pp. 545–77. **[G: Spain]**

Otsuka, Keijiro and Hayami, Yujiro. Revealed Preference in Japan's Rice Policy. **In** *Anderson, K. and Hayami, Y.*, 1986, pp. 63–79. **[G: Japan]**

Paarlberg, Philip L. and Abbott, Philip C. Oligopolistic Behavior by Public Agencies in International Trade: The World Wheat Market. *Amer. J. Agr. Econ.*, August 1986, *68*(3), pp. 528–43. **[G: OECD]**

Paarlberg, Philip L. and Webb, Alan J. Public Policy and the Reemergence of International Economic Influences on U.S. Agriculture. *Agr. Econ. Res.*, Winter 1986, *38*(1), pp. 45–56. **[G: U.S.]**

Pal, S. P. and Singh, J. P. Food Security and Food Stocks in India. *Margin*, October 1986, *19*(1), pp. 30–41.

Panayotou, Theodore. Investment, Growth and Employment in Thailand: From Agriculture to Rural Industry. **In** *Nemetz, P. N., ed.*, 1986, pp. 117–58. **[G: Thailand]**

Panchamukhi, V. R. Trade in Agricultural Commodities—A Profile of Two Decades: 1960–80. **In** *Dantwala, M. L., et al.*, 1986, pp. 432–59. **[G: India]**

Parmenter, B. R. What Does Manufacturing Protection Cost Farmers? A Review of Some Recent Australian Contributions. *Australian J. Agr. Econ.*, August/December 1986, *30*(2–3), pp. 118–27. **[G: Australia]**

Parsons, Kenneth H. The Relevance of the Ideas of John R. Commons for the Formulation of Agricultural Development Policies: Remarks upon Receipt of the Veblen–Commons Award. *J. Econ. Issues*, June 1986, *20*(2), pp. 281–95. **[G: U.S.]**

Pasour, E. C., Jr. Rent Seeking and Farm Commodity Programs: Is Education the Solution? [Farm Commodity Programs as Income Transfers]. *Cato J.*, Spring/Summer 1986, *6*(1), pp. 263–70.

Patel, I. G. On a Policy Framework for Indian Agriculture. **In** *Patel, I. G.*, 1986, *1980*, pp. 61–82. **[G: India]**

Pavaskar, Madhoo. Public Intervention in Agricultural Marketing. **In** *Dantwala, M. L., et al.*, 1986, pp. 329–57. **[G: India]**

Penna, Julio A. Sources of Growth of Argentine Agriculture and Prospects for the 1990s. **In** *Maunder, A. and Renborg, U., eds.*, 1986, pp. 475–86. **[G: Argentina]**

Peters, G. H. Human Capital, Technology and Institutions: Discussion. **In** *Maunder, A. and Renborg, U., eds.*, 1986, pp. 462–63.

Petit, Michel. Agricultural Policies and World Trade: The U.S. and the European Community at Bay: Comment. **In** *Tsoukalis, L., ed.*, 1986, pp. 71–76. **[G: U.S.; EEC]**

Picard, Louis A. Self-sufficiency, Delinkage, and Food Production: Limits on Agricultural Development in Africa. **In** *Browne, W. P. and Hadwiger, D. F., eds.*, 1986, pp. 121–36. **[G: Africa]**

Podkaminer, Leon. Persistent Disequilibrium in Poland's Consumer Markets: Some Hypothetical Explanations. *Comp. Econ. Stud.*, Fall 1986, *28*(3), pp. 1–16. **[G: Poland]**

Polopolus, Leo C. The Competitive Position of Southern Commodities in International Markets: A Synopsis. *Southern J. Agr. Econ.*, July 1986, *18*(1), pp. 75–78. **[G: U.S.]**

Pomareda, Carlos. An Evaluation of the Impact of Credit Insurance on Bank Performance in Panama. **In** *Hazell, P.; Pomareda, C. and Valdés, A., eds.*, 1986, pp. 101–14. **[G: Panama]**

Pomareda, Carlos. The Financial Viability of Agricultural Insurance. **In** *Hazell, P.; Pomareda, C. and Valdés, A., eds.*, 1986, pp. 281–91. **[G: Selected Countries]**

Quizón, Jaime and Binswanger, Hans P. Modeling the Impact of Agricultural Growth and Government Policy on Income Distribution in India. *World Bank Econ. Rev.*, September 1986, *1*(1), pp. 103–48. **[G: India]**

Raikes, Phil. Eating the Carrot and Wielding the Stick: The Agricultural Sector in Tanzania. **In** *Boesen, J., et al., eds.*, 1986, pp. 105–41. **[G: Tanzania]**

Rausser, Gordon C., et al. Macroeconomic Linkages, Taxes, and Subsidies in the U.S. Agricultural Sector. *Amer. J. Agr. Econ.*, May 1986, *68*(2), pp. 399–412. **[G: U.S.]**

Ray, Anandarup. Trade and Pricing Policies in World Agriculture. *Finance Develop.*, September 1986, *23*(3), pp. 2–5. **[G: Global]**

Riethmuller, Paul and Roe, Terry. Government Intervention in Commodity Markets: The Case of Japanese Rice and Wheat Policy. *J. Policy Modeling*, Fall 1986, *8*(3), pp. 327–49. **[G: Japan]**

Roemer, Michael. Simple Analytics of Segmented Markets: What Case for Liberalization? *World Devel.*, March 1986, *14*(3), pp. 429–39.

Rosaasen, Ken and Maley, Doug. Forward Planning: An Alternative Marketing Mechanism. *Can. J. Agr. Econ.*, June 1986, *33*, pp. 205–20. **[G: Canada]**

Salathe, Larry and Langley, Suchada. An Empirical Analysis of Alternative Export Subsidy Programs for U.S. Wheat. *Agr. Econ. Res.*, Winter 1986, *38*(1), pp. 1–18. **[G: U.S.]**

Sanderson, Fred H. The Common Agricultural Policy and World Food Trade: CAP Update. **In** *Browne, W. P. and Hadwiger, D. F., eds.*, 1986, pp. 58–61. **[G: EEC]**

Sawant, S. D. Balancing Overproduction and Malnutrition: Discussion. **In** *Maunder, A. and Renborg, U., eds.*, 1986, pp. 243–45. **[G: Sub-Saharan Africa]**

Schiff, Maurice. Growing Interdependencies and Uncertainties: Discussion. **In** *Maunder, A. and*

Renborg, U., eds., 1986, pp. 94–98.

Schmitt, Günther. "Renationalisierung" der gemeinsamen Agrarpolitik—Ein Ausweg aus der Krise? (With English summary.) *Z. Wirtschaft. Sozialwissen.*, 1986, *106*(3), pp. 253–73. **[G: EEC]**

Schmitt, Günther. The Role of Institutions in Formulation of Agricultural Policy: Their Repercussions on the Challenges of an Agriculture in a Turbulent World Economy. **In** *Maunder, A. and Renborg, U., eds.*, 1986, pp. 390–403.

Schmitz, Andrew. Marketing Institutions in International Commodity Markets. *Southern J. Agr. Econ.*, July 1986, *18*(1), pp. 41–48. **[G: U.S.]**

Schmitz, Andrew and Chambers, Robert G. Welfare and Trade Effects of Deficiency Payments. *J. Agr. Econ.*, January 1986, *37*(1), pp. 37–43. **[G: U.S.]**

Schmitz, Andrew; Sigurdson, Dale and Doering, Otto. Domestic Farm Policy and the Gains from Trade. *Amer. J. Agr. Econ.*, November 1986, *68*(4), pp. 820–27. **[G: U.S.]**

Schmitz, Peter M. Markets and Trade: Discussion. **In** *Maunder, A. and Renborg, U., eds.*, 1986, pp. 578–80.

Schuh, G. Edward. Maximizing U.S. Benefits from Agricultural Interdependence. **In** *Browne, W. P. and Hadwiger, D. F., eds.*, 1986, pp. 29–41. **[G: U.S.]**

Schuh, G. Edward. The International Capital Market as a Source of Instability in International Commodity Markets. **In** *Maunder, A. and Renborg, U., eds.*, 1986, pp. 83–90.

Seddon, David. Politics and the Price of Bread in Tunisia. **In** *Richards, A., ed.*, 1986, pp. 201–23. **[G: Tunisia]**

Sen, Amartya K. Food, Economics and Entitlements. **In** *Maunder, A. and Renborg, U., eds.*, 1986, pp. 3–20.

Shepard, Lawrence. Cartelization of the California–Arizona Orange Industry, 1934–1981. *J. Law Econ.*, April 1986, *29*(1), pp. 83–123. **[G: U.S.]**

Short, Cameron. Reducing the Cost of the Dairy Program. *Can. J. Agr. Econ.*, November 1986, *34*(3), pp. 379–97. **[G: Canada]**

Siamwalla, Ammar. Approaches to Price Insurance for Farmers. **In** *Hazell, P.; Pomareda, C. and Valdés, A., eds.*, 1986, pp. 178–92.

Siamwalla, Ammar and Valdés, Alberto. Should Crop Insurance Be Subsidized? **In** *Hazell, P.; Pomareda, C. and Valdés, A., eds.*, 1986, pp. 117–25.

Sicular, Terry. Agricultural Planning in China: The Case of Lee Willow Team No. 4. *Food Res. Inst. Stud.*, 1986, *20*(1), pp. 1–24. **[G: China]**

Sicular, Terry. Prospects and Some Policy Problems of Agricultural Development in China: Discussion [Towards an Agricultural Economy for China in a New Age: Progress, Problems, Response, and Prospects] [Prospects and Some Policy Problems of Agricultural Development in China]. *Amer. J. Agr. Econ.*, May 1986, *68*(2), pp. 458–60. **[G: China]**

Sicular, Terry. Using a Farm-Household Model to Analyze Labor Allocation on a Chinese Collective Farm. **In** *Singh, I.; Squire, L. and Strauss, J., eds.*, 1986, pp. 277–305. **[G: China]**

Simons, Scott. Land Fragmentation in Developing Countries: The Optimal Choice and Policy Implications. **In** *Maunder, A. and Renborg, U., eds.*, 1986, pp. 703–12.

Skees, Jerry R. and Reed, Michael R. Rate Making for Farm-Level Crop Insurance: Implications for Adverse Selection. *Amer. J. Agr. Econ.*, August 1986, *68*(3), pp. 653–59.

Soares, Fernando B. Structure of Agriculture and People in Rural Societies: Discussion. **In** *Maunder, A. and Renborg, U., eds.*, 1986, pp. 550–51. **[G: U.S.]**

Somel, Kutlu. Agricultural Support Policies in Turkey, 1950–1980: An Overview. **In** *Richards, A., ed.*, 1986, pp. 97–130. **[G: Turkey]**

Srivastava, U. K. Pressure on Natural Resources: Discussion. **In** *Maunder, A. and Renborg, U., eds.*, 1986, pp. 337–38.

Stacey, Robert C. Agricultural Investment and the Management of the Royal Demesne Manors, 1236–1240. *J. Econ. Hist.*, December 1986, *46*(4), pp. 919–34.

Strickland, Ken W. Policy Issues, Conflicts and Objectives at the Grassroots Levels. *Can. J. Agr. Econ.*, Proceedings 1986, *34*, pp. 1–10. **[G: Canada]**

Subbarao, K. Farm Prices: A Survey of the Debate. **In** *Dantwala, M. L., et al.*, 1986, pp. 373–84. **[G: India]**

Sumner, David. Human Capital, Technology and Institutions: Discussion. **In** *Maunder, A. and Renborg, U., eds.*, 1986, pp. 486–88.

Talbot, Ross B. The Role of World Food Organizations. **In** *Browne, W. P. and Hadwiger, D. F., eds.*, 1986, pp. 171–84. **[G: Selected Countries]**

Tatom, John A. How Federal Farm Spending Distorts Measures of Economic Activity. *Fed. Res. Bank St. Louis Rev.*, June/July 1986, *68*(6), pp. 16–22. **[G: U.S.]**

Taylor, Timothy G. and Shonkwiler, J. Scott. Alternative Stochastic Specifications of the Frontier Production Function in the Analysis of Agricultural Credit Programs and Technical Efficiency. *J. Devel. Econ.*, April 1986, *21*(1), pp. 149–60. **[G: Brazil]**

Thiele, Graham. The State and Rural Development in Tanzania: The Village Administration as a Political Field. *J. Devel. Stud.*, April 1986, *22*(3), pp. 540–57. **[G: Tanzania]**

Thies, Clifford F. A Note on the Role of Knowledge in Direct Voting on Milk Price Decontrol. *Public Choice*, 1986, *49*(2), pp. 191–94. **[G: U.S.]**

Thompson, Robert L. Recent Developments in United States Agricultural and Food Policy. *J. Agr. Econ.*, September 1986, *37*(3), pp. 311–16. **[G: U.S.]**

Timmer, C. Peter. Prospects and Some Policy Problems of Agricultural Development in China: Discussion [Towards an Agricultural Economy for China in a New Age: Progress,

Problems, Response, and Prospects] [Prospects and Some Policy Problems of Agricultural Development in China]. *Amer. J. Agr. Econ.*, May 1986, *68*(2), pp. 461–63. **[G: China]**

Tomic, Dušan. Growing Interdependencies and Uncertainties: Discussion. **In** *Maunder, A. and Renborg, U., eds.*, 1986, pp. 145–48. **[G: Canada; Poland]**

Treml, Vladimir G. Soviet Foreign Trade in Foodstuffs. *Soviet Econ.*, Jan.-Mar. 1986, *2*(1), pp. 19–50. **[G: U.S.S.R.]**

Trewin, Ray and Bhati, U. N. Consequences of Deregulation in Victorian Egg Industry: A Comment. *Rev. Marketing Agr. Econ.*, December 1986, *54*(3), pp. 49–51. **[G: Australia]**

Tsujii, Hiroshi. An Economic Analysis of Rice Insurance in Japan. **In** *Hazell, P.; Pomareda, C. and Valdés, A., eds.*, 1986, pp. 143–55. **[G: Japan]**

Tweeten, Luther. Impact of Domestic Policy on Comparative Advantage of Agriculture in the South. *Southern J. Agr. Econ.*, July 1986, *18*(1), pp. 67–74. **[G: U.S.]**

Tyers, Rodney. Details of the Simulation Model of World Grain and Meat Markets. **In** *Anderson, K. and Hayami, Y.*, 1986, pp. 152–61. **[G: EEC; Asia; U.S.]**

Tyers, Rodney and Anderson, Kym. The Price, Trade and Welfare Effects of Agricultural Protection. **In** *Anderson, K. and Hayami, Y.*, 1986, pp. 50–62. **[G: U.S.; Europe; E. Asia]**

Valdés, Alberto. Exchange Rates and Trade Policy: Help or Hindrance to Agricultural Growth? **In** *Maunder, A. and Renborg, U., eds.*, 1986, pp. 624–33. **[G: Peru; LDCs]**

Vamplew, Wray. Malthus and the Corn Laws. **In** *Turner, M., ed.*, 1986, pp. 129–39. **[G: U.K.]**

de Veer, Jan. National Agricultural Policies, Surplus Problems and International Instability. **In** *Maunder, A. and Renborg, U., eds.*, 1986, pp. 247–58.

Venkatesan, V. Rural Development Administration. **In** *Dantwala, M. L., et al.*, 1986, pp. 479–510. **[G: India]**

Von Pischke, J. D. Can Crop Credit Insurance Address Risks in Agricultural Lending? **In** *Hazell, P.; Pomareda, C. and Valdés, A., eds.*, 1986, pp. 87–100.

Wakefield, Joseph C. Federal Farm Programs for 1986–90. *Surv. Curr. Bus.*, April 1986, *66*(4), pp. 31–35. **[G: U.S.]**

Walker, Thomas S. and Jodha, N. S. How Small Farm Households Adapt to Risk. **In** *Hazell, P.; Pomareda, C. and Valdés, A., eds.*, 1986, pp. 17–34. **[G: India; Tanzania; El Salvador]**

Weinbaum, Marvin G. Food Security and Agricultural Development Policies in the Middle East. **In** *Browne, W. P. and Hadwiger, D. F., eds.*, 1986, pp. 109–20. **[G: Middle East]**

Wennergren, E. Boyd and Whitaker, Morris D. Foodgrain Sufficiency in Bangladesh: A Reappraisal and Policy Implications. *J. Devel. Areas*, October 1986, *21*(1), pp. 1–13. **[G: Bangladesh]**

von Witzke, Harald. Endogenous Supranational Policy Decisions: The Common Agricultural Policy of the European Community. *Public Choice*, 1986, *48*(2), pp. 157–74. **[G: EEC]**

Yamauchi, Toyoji. Evolution of the Crop Insurance Program in Japan. **In** *Hazell, P.; Pomareda, C. and Valdés, A., eds.*, 1986, pp. 223–39. **[G: Japan]**

Yan, Rui-Zhen. Economic Reform in Rural China. **In** *Maunder, A. and Renborg, U., eds.*, 1986, pp. 440–48. **[G: China]**

Zevin, L. Z., et al. Cooperation of CMEA Member-Countries and Developing Countries in the Resolution of the Food Problem. *Soviet E. Europ. Foreign Trade*, Fall-Winter 1986-87, *22*(3), pp. 1–209. **[G: CMEA; LDCs]**

Zietz, Joachim. Trade Liberalization in Cereals: Blessing or Curse to Developing Countries? *J. Econ. Devel.*, December 1986, *11*(2), pp. 103–22. **[G: LDCs]**

Zietz, Joachim and Valdés, Alberto. The Potential Benefits to LDCs of Trade Liberalization in Beef and Sugar by Industrialized Countries. *Weltwirtsch. Arch.*, 1986, *122*(1), pp. 93–112. **[G: Global]**

714 Agricultural Finance

7140 Agricultural Finance

Adams, Dale W. and Vogel, Robert C. Rural Financial Markets in Low-income Countries: Recent Controversies and Lessons. *World Devel.*, April 1986, *14*(4), pp. 477–87. **[G: LDCs]**

Ahmad, Ismail; Duft, Ken D. and Mittelhammer, Ron C. Analyzing Equity Capital Programs of Banks for Cooperatives. *Amer. J. Agr. Econ.*, November 1986, *68*(4), pp. 849–56. **[G: U.S.]**

Amougou, Thomas Balla and Ottou, Jean. The Phenomenon of Thrift and Loan Societies. **In** *U.N., Dept. of International Econ. and Social Affairs*, 1986, pp. 95–100. **[G: Cameroon]**

Arthur, Louise M. and Van Kooten, G. C. An Empirical Investigation of 1983 Farm Mortgagors in Western Canada. *Can. J. Agr. Econ.*, July 1986, *34*(2), pp. 195–207. **[G: Canada]**

Ashmead, Ralph. The Long-term Credit Agency Perspective. *Can. J. Agr. Econ.*, June 1986, *33*, pp. S26–36. **[G: Canada; U.S.]**

Ashmead, Ralph. The Myth and Reality of the Farm Finance Crisis. *Can. J. Agr. Econ.*, June 1986, *33*, pp. 63–75. **[G: Canada]**

Aukes, Robert G. Economic Structure and Capital Requirements for Agriculture: Comment [Land Prices and Farm-Based Returns]. *Can. J. Agr. Econ.*, July 1986, *34*(2), pp. 263–67. **[G: Canada]**

Aukes, Robert G. Economic/Accounting Confusion Underlying the Current Farm Financial Crisis. *Can. J. Agr. Econ.*, June 1986, *33*, pp. S43–68.

Bardsley, Peter. A Note on the Viability of Rainfall Insurance—Reply [The Economics of Insuring Crops against Drought]. *Australian J. Agr. Econ.*, April 1986, *30*(1), pp. 70–75. **[G: Australia]**

Barry, Peter J. and Robison, Lindon J. Economic versus Accounting Rates of Return for Farm Land. *Land Econ.*, November 1986, *62*(4), pp. 388–401. **[G: U.S.]**

Belongia, Michael T. The Farm Sector in the 1980s: Sudden Collapse or Steady Downturn? *Fed. Res. Bank St. Louis Rev.*, November 1986, *68*(9), pp. 17–25. **[G: U.S.]**

Binswanger, Hans P. Risk Aversion, Collateral Requirements, and the Markets for Credit and Insurance in Rural Areas. **In** *Hazell, P.; Pomareda, C. and Valdés, A., eds.*, 1986, pp. 67–86.

Binswanger, Hans P. and Rosenzweig, Mark R. Behavioural and Material Determinants of Production Relations in Agriculture. *J. Devel. Stud.*, April 1986, *22*(3), pp. 503–39.

Boehlje, Michael D. and Lowenberg-DeBoer, John. Integration of Production and Financial Theory in Analysing Farm Firm Behaviour. **In** *Maunder, A. and Renborg, U., eds.*, 1986, pp. 668–79.

Boussard, Jean-Marc. Agriculture in a Turbulent World Economy: Theoretical Developments: Discussion. **In** *Maunder, A. and Renborg, U., eds.*, 1986, pp. 663–65.

Boussard, Jean-Marc, et al. Productivité et inflation: le cas de l'agriculture française 1960–1982. With English summary.) *Revue Écon. Polit.*, Jan.-Feb. 1986, *96*(1), pp. 13–24. **[G: France]**

Braverman, Avishay and Guasch, J. Luis. Rural Credit Markets and Institutions in Developing Countries: Lessons for Policy Analysis from Practice and Modern Theory. *World Devel.*, Oct./Nov. 1986, *14*(10/11), pp. 1253–67. **[G: LDCs]**

Breimyer, Harold F. The Asset Devaluation Problem. *Southern J. Agr. Econ.*, July 1986, *18*(1), pp. 79–82.

Bryant, W. Keith. A Portfolio Analysis of Poor Rural Wage—Working Families' Assets and Debts. *Amer. J. Agr. Econ.*, May 1986, *68*(2), pp. 237–45. **[G: U.S.]**

Calomiris, Charles W.; Hubbard, R. Glenn and Stock, James H. The Farm Debt Crisis and Public Policy. *Brookings Pap. Econ. Act.*, 1986, (2), pp. 441–79. **[G: U.S.]**

Caves, Richard E. and Petersen, Bruce C. Cooperatives' Tax "Advantages": Growth, Retained Earnings, and Equity Rotation. *Amer. J. Agr. Econ.*, May 1986, *68*(2), pp. 207–13. **[G: U.S.]**

Clark, J. H. The Financial Crisis of Farming: The Educators' Perspective. *Can. J. Agr. Econ.*, June 1986, *33*, pp. S16–25. **[G: Canada]**

Collins, Robert A. and Barry, Peter J. Risk Analysis with Single-Index Portfolio Models: An Application to Farm Planning. *Amer. J. Agr. Econ.*, February 1986, *68*(1), pp. 152–61. **[G: U.S.]**

Cuevas, Carlos E. and Graham, Douglas H. Rationing Agricultural Credit in Developing Countries: The Role and Determinants of Transaction Costs for Borrowers. **In** *Maunder, A. and Renborg, U., eds.*, 1986, pp. 680–86. **[G: Bangladesh; Peru; Ecuador; Honduros; Panama]**

Drabenstott, Mark. Agriculture in a Turbulent World Economy: Theoretical Developments: Discussion. **In** *Maunder, A. and Renborg, U., eds.*, 1986, pp. 686–88.

Egger, Philippe. Banking for the Rural Poor: Lessons from Some Innovative Savings and Credit Schemes. *Int. Lab. Rev.*, July-Aug. 1986, *125*(4), pp. 447–62. **[G: Bangladesh; India; Nepal; Zimbabwe]**

Ehrensaft, Philip and Bollman, Ray D. Large Farms: The Leading Edge of Structural Change. *Can. J. Agr. Econ.*, June 1986, *33*, pp. 145–60. **[G: Canada]**

Eswaran, Mukesh and Kotwal, Ashok. Access to Capital and Agrarian Production Organisation. *Econ. J.*, June 1986, *96*(382), pp. 482–98.

Evans, David B. The Credit Market and Rural Development: A Model of a Land Resettlement Scheme. *J. Devel. Econ.*, December 1986, *24*(2), pp. 317–29.

Friedman, Benjamin M. The Farm Debt Crisis and Public Policy: Comments. *Brookings Pap. Econ. Act.*, 1986, (2), pp. 480–84. **[G: U.S.]**

Gadgil, Madhukar. Agriculture in a Turbulent World Economy: Theoretical Developments: Discussion. **In** *Maunder, A. and Renborg, U., eds.*, 1986, pp. 688–90.

Gardner, Bruce L. and Kramer, Randall A. Experience with Crop Insurance Programs in the United States. **In** *Hazell, P.; Pomareda, C. and Valdés, A., eds.*, 1986, pp. 195–222. **[G: U.S.]**

Glover, Glenn H. Agribusiness in the Agricultural Financial Crisis. *Southern J. Agr. Econ.*, July 1986, *18*(1), pp. 103–08. **[G: U.S.]**

Gudger, William M. and Avalos, Luis. Planning for the Efficient Operation of Crop Credit Insurance Schemes. **In** *Hazell, P.; Pomareda, C. and Valdés, A., eds.*, 1986, pp. 263–80.

Harwell, R. Lynn and Rosson, C. Parr, III. Financial Crisis in Agriculture, a Southern Perspective: Discussion. *Southern J. Agr. Econ.*, July 1986, *18*(1), pp. 109–12. **[G: U.S.]**

Hayden, F. Gregory. Family Farmland Reserve: A State Government Program for Restructuring Farm Debt. *J. Econ. Issues*, March 1986, *20*(1), pp. 179–90.

Hill, G. P. and Seagraves, J. A. Agricultural Finance and Inflation: An Examination of Alternative Methods with Reference to British Experience. *J. Agr. Econ.*, May 1986, *37*(2), pp. 173–83. **[G: U.K.]**

Iqbal, Farrukh. The Demand and Supply of Funds among Agricultural Households in India. **In** *Singh, I.; Squire, L. and Strauss, J., eds.*, 1986, pp. 183–205. **[G: India]**

Kim, Sung-Hoon. Rural Savings Mobilization: The Asian Experience. **In** *U.N., Dept. of International Econ. and Social Affairs*, 1986, pp. 50–60. **[G: Asia]**

Leathers, Howard D. and Chavas, Jean-Paul.

Farm Debt, Default, and Foreclosure: An Economic Rationale for Policy Action. *Amer. J. Agr. Econ.*, November 1986, *68*(4), pp. 828–37.

Lloyd, Alan G. and Mauldon, Roger G. Agricultural Instability and Alternative Government Policies: The Australian Experience. **In** *Hazell, P.; Pomareda, C. and Valdés, A., eds.*, 1986, pp. 156–77. **[G: Australia]**

Lopes, Mauro de Rezende and Dias, Guilherme Leite da Silva. The Brazilian Experience with Crop Insurance Programs. **In** *Hazell, P.; Pomareda, C. and Valdés, A., eds.*, 1986, pp. 240–62. **[G: Brazil]**

Loree, J. Wilson. Farm Financial Situation from an Extension Educator's Point of View. *Can. J. Agr. Econ.*, June 1986, *33*, pp. S37–42.

Love, Ross O. The Role of Extension in Dealing with Farm Families in Financial Crisis. *Southern J. Agr. Econ.*, July 1986, *18*(1), pp. 83–92. **[G: U.S.]**

Lowenberg-DeBoer, John and Boehlje, Michael D. The Impact of Farmland Price Changes on Farm Size and Financial Structure. *Amer. J. Agr. Econ.*, November 1986, *68*(4), pp. 838–48. **[G: U.S.]**

Martin, Preston. Statement to the Senate Committee on Banking, Housing, and Urban Affairs, March 11, 1986. *Fed. Res. Bull.*, May 1986, *72*(5), pp. 313–15. **[G: U.S.]**

Martin, Preston. Statement to the U.S. House Subcommittee on Financial Institutions Supervision, Regulation and Insurance of the Committee on Banking, Finance and Urban Affairs, April 9, 1986. *Fed. Res. Bull.*, June 1986, *72*(6), pp. 382–89. **[G: U.S.]**

Matthews, Alan H. Agricultural Credit and Public Policy. *Irish J. Agr. Econ. Rural Soc.*, 1986, *11*, pp. 93–97. **[G: Ireland]**

McRorie, H. D. Crisis in Farm Finance—Banker's Perspective. *Can. J. Agr. Econ.*, June 1986, *33*, pp. S5–15. **[G: Canada]**

Melichar, Emanuel. Agricultural Banks under Stress. *Fed. Res. Bull.*, July 1986, *72*(7), pp. 437–48. **[G: U.S.]**

Niewuwoudt, W. L. and Bullock, J. Bruce. The Demand for Crop Insurance. **In** *Maunder, A. and Renborg, U., eds.*, 1986, pp. 655–61. **[G: U.S.]**

Owens, Raymond E. The Agricultural Outlook for 1986...Continued Financial Weakness Seen. *Fed. Res. Bank Richmond Econ. Rev.*, Jan./Feb. 1986, *72*(1), pp. 29–34. **[G: U.S.]**

Pederson, Glenn D. and Bertelsen, Diane. Financial Risk Management Alternatives in a Whole-Farm Setting. *Western J. Agr. Econ.*, July 1986, *11*(1), pp. 67–75. **[G: U.S.]**

Pomareda, Carlos. An Evaluation of the Impact of Credit Insurance on Bank Performance in Panama. **In** *Hazell, P.; Pomareda, C. and Valdés, A., eds.*, 1986, pp. 101–14. **[G: Panama]**

Quiggin, John. A Note on the Viability of Rainfall Insurance [The Economics of Insuring Crops against Drought]. *Australian J. Agr. Econ.*, April 1986, *30*(1), pp. 63–69. **[G: Australia]**

Ruttan, Vernon W. Assistance to Expand Agricultural Production. *World Devel.*, January 1986, *14*(1), pp. 39–63. **[G: LDCs]**

Sakellis, M. G. An Empirical Analysis of Savings Behaviour of the Greek Agricultural Households. *Europ. Rev. Agr. Econ.*, 1986, *13*(2), pp. 169–88. **[G: Greece]**

Severn, Alan K. Taxation of Federal Land Banks: Competitive Effects. *Quart. J. Bus. Econ.*, Autumn 1986, *25*(4), pp. 41–55. **[G: U.S.]**

Shepard, Lawrence. The Farm Debt Crisis: Temporary or Chronic? *Contemp. Policy Issues*, January 1986, *4*(1), pp. 62–71. **[G: U.S.]**

Shivamaggi, H. B. Credit for Agricultural and Rural Development. **In** *Dantwala, M. L., et al.*, 1986, pp. 270–307. **[G: India]**

Taylor, Timothy G.; Drummond, H. Evan and Gomes, Aloisio T. Agricultural Credit Programs and Production Efficiency: An Analysis of Traditional Farming in Southeastern Minas Gerais, Brazil. *Amer. J. Agr. Econ.*, February 1986, *68*(1), pp. 110–19. **[G: Brazil]**

Taylor, Timothy G. and Shonkwiler, J. Scott. Alternative Stochastic Specifications of the Frontier Production Function in the Analysis of Agricultural Credit Programs and Technical Efficiency. *J. Devel. Econ.*, April 1986, *21*(1), pp. 149–60. **[G: Brazil]**

Taylor, William. Statement to the U.S. House Subcommittee on Conservation, Credit, and Rural Development of the Committee on Agriculture, April 9, 1986. *Fed. Res. Bull.*, June 1986, *72*(6), pp. 389–93. **[G: U.S.]**

U.N. Food and Agricultural Organization. Savings Mobilization for Agricultural and Rural Development in Africa. **In** *U.N., Dept. of International Econ. and Social Affairs*, 1986, pp. 87–94. **[G: Africa]**

Unnevehr, Laurian J. and Zain, Djumilah. Marketing Efficiency, Informal Credit, and the Role of Government Loan Programs: Cassava Trade in Indonesia. *J. Devel. Areas*, April 1986, *20*(3), pp. 369–78. **[G: Indonesia]**

Von Pischke, J. D. Can Crop Credit Insurance Address Risks in Agricultural Lending? **In** *Hazell, P.; Pomareda, C. and Valdés, A., eds.*, 1986, pp. 87–100.

Wilson, Gene and Sullivan, Gene D. Agricultural Banks in the Southeast and Nation: A Study in Contrasts. *Southern J. Agr. Econ.*, July 1986, *18*(1), pp. 93–101. **[G: U.S.]**

715 Agricultural Markets and Marketing; Cooperatives

7150 Agricultural Markets and Marketing; Cooperatives

Abbott, John C. Alternative Forms of Marketing Enterprise for the Developing Countries. **In** *Maunder, A. and Renborg, U., eds.*, 1986, pp. 404–13. **[G: LDCs]**

Ahmad, Ismail; Duft, Ken D. and Mittelhammer, Ron C. Analyzing Equity Capital Programs of Banks for Cooperatives. *Amer. J. Agr. Econ.*, November 1986, *68*(4), pp. 849–56. **[G: U.S.]**

715 Agricultural Markets and Marketing; Cooperatives

Al-Zand, Osama A. The Food Marketing Cost Index—An Alternative Estimate of Food Price Changes. *Can. J. Agr. Econ.*, July 1986, *34*(2), pp. 227–33. **[G: Canada]**

Alexander, Jennifer. Information and Price Setting in a Rural Javanese Market. *Bull. Indonesian Econ. Stud.*, April 1986, *22*(1), pp. 88–112. **[G: Indonesia]**

Alexander, Vickie J.; Musser, Wesley N. and Mason, George. Futures Markets and Firm Decisions under Price, Production, and Financial Uncertainty. *Southern J. Agr. Econ.*, December 1986, *18*(2), pp. 39–49. **[G: U.S.]**

Alston, Julian M. A Note on Victoria's Hen Quota Transfer System. *Rev. Marketing Agr. Econ.*, April 1986, *54*(1), pp. 45–49. **[G: Australia]**

Alston, Julian M. Consequences of Deregulation in the Victorian Egg Industry. *Rev. Marketing Agr. Econ.*, April 1986, *54*(1), pp. 33–43. **[G: Australia]**

Alston, Julian M.; Nguyen, S. T. and Tunstall, A. W. Assessing Accuracy of Livestock Market Reporters: Some Evidence on Pigs in Victoria. *Rev. Marketing Agr. Econ.*, April 1986, *54*(1), pp. 7–17. **[G: Australia]**

Anaman, Kwabena A. and Boggess, William G. A Stochastic Dominance Analysis of Alternative Marketing Strategies for Mixed Crop Farms in North Florida. *Southern J. Agr. Econ.*, December 1986, *18*(2), pp. 257–66. **[G: U.S.]**

Beilock, Richard P. and Kilmer, Richard L. The Determinants of Full–Empty Truck Movements. *Amer. J. Agr. Econ.*, February 1986, *68*(1), pp. 67–76. **[G: U.S.]**

Blanchard, Ian. The Continental European Cattle Trade, 1400–1600. *Econ. Hist. Rev., 2nd Ser.*, August 1986, *39*(3), pp. 427–60. **[G: Europe]**

Bond, Gary E. and Thompson, Stanley R. Optimal Commodity Hedging within the Capital Asset Pricing Model. *J. Futures Markets,* Fall 1986, *6*(3), pp. 421–31. **[G: Australia]**

Boyd, Milton S. and Brorsen, B. Wade. Dynamic Price Relationships for U.S. and EC Corn Gluten Feed and Related Markets. *Europ. Rev. Agr. Econ.*, 1986, *13*(2), pp. 199–215. **[G: U.S.; EEC]**

Branson, Robert E., et al. Marketing Implications from the National Consumer Beef Study. *Western J. Agr. Econ.*, July 1986, *11*(1), pp. 82–91. **[G: U.S.]**

Bronsteen, Peter. Market Share and Market Power in the Domestic Lemon Industry. **In** *Zerbe, R. O., Jr., ed.*, 1986, pp. 13–28. **[G: U.S.]**

Brown, James G. Improving Agroindusteries in Developing Countries. *Finance Develop.*, June 1986, *23*(2), pp. 42–44. **[G: LDCs]**

Brown, Stewart L. A Reformulation of the Portfolio Model of Hedging: Reply. *Amer. J. Agr. Econ.*, November 1986, *68*(4), pp. 1010–12. **[G: U.S.]**

Camargo Barros, Geraldo. Growing Interdependencies and Uncertainties: Discussion. **In** *Maunder, A. and Renborg, U., eds.*, 1986, pp. 122–23.

Caves, Richard E. and Petersen, Bruce C. Cooperatives' Tax "Advantages": Growth, Retained Earnings, and Equity Rotation. *Amer. J. Agr. Econ.*, May 1986, *68*(2), pp. 207–13. **[G: U.S.]**

De Visscher, Guy. Growing Interdependencies and Uncertainties: Discussion. **In** *Maunder, A. and Renborg, U., eds.*, 1986, pp. 123–25.

Dias, Guilherme Leite da Silva. Markets and Trade: Discussion. **In** *Maunder, A. and Renborg, U., eds.*, 1986, pp. 577–78.

Dutt, Amitava Krishna. Stock Equilibrium in Flexprice Markets in Macromodels for Less Developed Economies: The Case of Food Speculation. *J. Devel. Econ.*, April 1986, *21*(1), pp. 89–109. **[G: LDCs]**

Echchihab, Slimane. L'évaluation des contrats à terme sur le sucre à la Bourse de commerce de Paris. (The Pricing of Sugar Futures Contracts on the Paris Commodity Exchange. With English summary.) *Finance*, June 1986, *7*(1), pp. 41–56. **[G: France]**

Elam, Emmett W.; Miller, Stephen E. and Holder, Shelby H. Simple and Multiple Cross-Hedging of Rice Bran. *Southern J. Agr. Econ.*, July 1986, *18*(1), pp. 123–28. **[G: U.S.]**

Falgon, Claude. The Effect of Enlargement of the EC on Tunisian Fruits and Vegetables. **In** *Bale, M. D., ed.*, 1986, pp. 95–130. **[G: EEC; Tunisia]**

Faminow, Merle D. and Gum, Russell L. Feeder Cattle Price Differentials in Arizona Auction Markets. *Western J. Agr. Econ.*, December 1986, *11*(2), pp. 156–63. **[G: U.S.]**

Fletcher, Stanley M. and Terza, Joseph V. Analyzing Farmers' Selection of Available Marketing Alternatives Using the Multivariate Probit Model. *Can. J. Agr. Econ.*, July 1986, *34*(2), pp. 243–52. **[G: U.S.]**

Frankel, Jeffrey A. Expectations and Commodity Price Dynamics: The Overshooting Model. *Amer. J. Agr. Econ.*, May 1986, *68*(2), pp. 344–48.

Frankel, Jeffrey A. Overshooting Agricultural Commodity Markets and Public Policy: Discussion [Macroeconomic Linkages, Taxes, and Subsidies in the U.S. Agricultural Sector] [Some Political Economy Aspects of Macroeconomic Linkages with Agriculture]. *Amer. J. Agr. Econ.*, May 1986, *68*(2), pp. 418–19. **[G: U.S.]**

Freebairn, John W. The Exchange Rate and the Trade Account: Comment. *Econ. Rec.*, Supplement 1986, pp. 108–10. **[G: Australia]**

Fryar, Edward O., Jr. Residual Supplier Model of Coarse Grains Trade: Comment. *Amer. J. Agr. Econ.*, November 1986, *68*(4), pp. 1028–29. **[G: Selected Countries]**

Garcia, Philip; Leuthold, Raymond M. and Zapata, Hector. Lead-Lag Relationships between Trading Volume and Price Variability: New Evidence. *J. Futures Markets,* Spring 1986, *6*(1), pp. 1–10. **[G: U.S.]**

Gay, Gerald D.; Hunter, William C. and Kolb, Robert W. A Comparative Analysis of Futures Contract Margins. *J. Futures Markets,* Summer 1986, *6*(2), pp. 307–24. **[G: U.S.]**

Gillis, Kevin. A Note on the Definition of Basis. *Can. J. Agr. Econ.*, July 1986, *34*(2), pp. 253–56.

Gisser, Micha. Welfare Implications of Oligopoly in U.S. Food Manufacturing: Reply. *Amer. J. Agr. Econ.*, February 1986, *68*(1), pp. 168–69. **[G: U.S.]**

Glover, David J. Agrarian Reform and Agro-Industry in Honduras. *Can. J. Devel. Stud.*, 1986, *7*(1), pp. 21–35. **[G: Honduras]**

Glover, David J. Multinational Corporations and Third World Agriculture. **In** *Moran, T. H., ed.*, 1986, pp. 113–29. **[G: LDCs]**

Glover, Glenn H. Agribusiness in the Agricultural Financial Crisis. *Southern J. Agr. Econ.*, July 1986, *18*(1), pp. 103–08. **[G: U.S.]**

Glushkov, N. Improving Pricing in the Agro–Industrial Complex (AIC). *Prob. Econ.*, August 1986, *29*(4), pp. 52–70. **[G: U.S.S.R.]**

Gottfried, Robert R. The Potential Impact of High-Test Molasses from Energy Cane on the Rum Industry of Puerto Rico. *World Devel.*, Oct./Nov. 1986, *14*(10/11), pp. 1347–56. **[G: Puerto Rico]**

Grennes, Thomas J. and Lapp, John S. Neutrality of Inflation in the Agricultural Sector. *J. Int. Money Finance*, June 1986, *5*(2), pp. 231–43. **[G: U.S.]**

Groenewegen, John R. A Perspective on Canadian Wheat Board Exports, Price Pooling, and West Coast Capacity Constraints. *Can. J. Agr. Econ.*, November 1986, *34*(3), pp. 331–46. **[G: Canada]**

Hammer, Jeffrey S. 'Subsistence First': Farm Allocation Decisions in Senegal. *J. Devel. Econ.*, October 1986, *23*(2), pp. 355–69. **[G: Senegal]**

Hanf, C.-Hennig and Kühl, Rainer. Possibilities and Limits of Individual Marketing on Family Farm Firms. *Europ. Rev. Agr. Econ.*, 1986, *13*(2), pp. 149–67. **[G: W. Germany]**

Harwell, R. Lynn and Rosson, C. Parr, III. Financial Crisis in Agriculture, a Southern Perspective: Discussion. *Southern J. Agr. Econ.*, July 1986, *18*(1), pp. 109–12. **[G: U.S.]**

Hauser, Robert J. and Eales, James S. On Marketing Strategies with Options: A Technique to Measure Risk and Return. *J. Futures Markets*, Summer 1986, *6*(2), pp. 273–88. **[G: U.S.]**

Hawkins, M. H. and Higginson, N. Marketing Research in the Canadian Food Retail and Processing Industry, 1950–1986. *Can. J. Agr. Econ.*, November 1986, *34*(3), pp. 287–311. **[G: Canada]**

Hazledine, Tim and Cahill, Sean. Welfare Implications of Oligopoly in U.S. Food Manufacturing: Comment. *Amer. J. Agr. Econ.*, February 1986, *68*(1), pp. 165–67. **[G: U.S.]**

Hessner, Catherine and Mellor, C. J. An Empirical Analysis of the Relationship between Advertising and Sales: A Case Study of the Liquid Milk Market. *J. Agr. Econ.*, May 1986, *37*(2), pp. 193–206. **[G: U.K.]**

Heytens, Paul J. Testing Market Integration. *Food Res. Inst. Stud.*, 1986, *20*(1), pp. 25–41. **[G: Nigeria]**

Jones, Bruce L. A Model of Cooperative Finance: Comment. *Amer. J. Agr. Econ.*, February 1986, *68*(1), pp. 170–72.

Kahl, Kandice H. A Reformulation of the Portfolio Model of Hedging: Comment. *Amer. J. Agr. Econ.*, November 1986, *68*(4), pp. 1007–09. **[G: U.S.]**

Kahl, Kandice H. and Tomek, William G. Forward-Pricing Models for Futures Markets: Some Statistical and Interpretive Issues. *Food Res. Inst. Stud.*, 1986, *20*(1), pp. 71–85. **[G: U.S.]**

Khan, Arshad M. Conformity with Large Speculators: A Test of Efficiency in the Grain Futures Market. *Atlantic Econ. J.*, September 1986, *14*(3), pp. 51–55.

Kinnucan, Henry and Forker, Olan D. Seasonality in the Consumer Response to Milk Advertising with Implications for Milk Promotion Policy. *Amer. J. Agr. Econ.*, August 1986, *68*(3), pp. 562–71. **[G: U.S.]**

Koester, Ulrich. Regional Co-operation in the Food Sector among Developing Countries to Improve Food Security. **In** *Maunder, A. and Renborg, U., eds.*, 1986, pp. 100–113. **[G: Africa]**

Lamo de Espinosa, Jaime. International Markets and Price Policy: The Instability of Agriculture. **In** *Maunder, A. and Renborg, U., eds.*, 1986, pp. 557–65.

Lee, Jonq-Ying and Brown, Mark G. Economic Effectiveness of Brand Advertising Programmes for U.S. Orange Juice in the European Market: An Error Component Analysis. *J. Agr. Econ.*, September 1986, *37*(3), pp. 385–94. **[G: U.S.]**

Martin, W. and Shaw, I. The Effect of Exchange Rate Changes on the Value of Australia's Major Agricultural Exports. *Econ. Rec.*, Supplement 1986, pp. 101–07. **[G: Australia]**

McCabe, Bernie. Economics of Quota Allocation within Supply Management Analysis of the Present Procedures for Quota Allocation. *Can. J. Agr. Econ.*, June 1986, *33*, pp. 196–204. **[G: Canada]**

Meredith, David. State Controlled Marketing and Economic "Development": The Case of West African Produce during the Second World War. *Econ. Hist. Rev., 2nd Ser.*, February 1986, *39*(1), pp. 77–91. **[G: W. Africa]**

Miller, Stephen E. Forward Cash Contracting of Cotton. *J. Futures Markets*, Summer 1986, *6*(2), pp. 249–59. **[G: U.S.]**

Miller, Stephen E. Forward Contracting versus Hedging under Price and Yield Uncertainty. *Southern J. Agr. Econ.*, December 1986, *18*(2), pp. 139–46. **[G: U.S.]**

Milonas, Nikolaos T. A Note on Agricultural Options and the Variance of Futures Prices. *J. Futures Markets*, Winter 1986, *6*(4), pp. 671–76. **[G: U.S.]**

Milonas, Nikolaos T. Liquidity and Price Variability in Futures Markets. *Financial Rev.*, May 1986, *21*(2), pp. 211–37. **[G: U.S.]**

Milonas, Nikolaos T. Price Variability and the Maturity Effect in Futures Markets. *J. Futures Markets,* Fall 1986, *6*(3), pp. 443–60. **[G: U.S.]**

Moseley, Anne E.; Spreen, Thomas H. and Pheasant, Jim W. A Mixed-Integer Programming Analysis of the Structure of a Florida-Based Cattle Feeding Industry. *Southern J. Agr. Econ.,* December 1986, *18*(2), pp. 125–37. **[G: U.S.]**

Naqvi, Syed Nawab Haider and Cornelisse, Peter A. Public Policy and Wheat Market in Pakistan. *Pakistan Devel. Rev.,* Summer 1986, *25*(2), pp. 99–126. **[G: Pakistan]**

Narváez-Bueno, J. Human Capital, Technology and Institutions: Discussion. **In** *Maunder, A. and Renborg, U., eds.,* 1986, pp. 413–14. **[G: LDCs]**

O'Connell, John. A Hedonic Price Model of the Paris Carcase Lamb Market. *Europ. Rev. Agr. Econ.,* 1986, *13*(4), pp. 439–50. **[G: France]**

Obstfeld, Maurice. Overshooting Agricultural Commodity Markets and Public Policy: Discussion [Macroeconomic Linkages, Taxes, and Subsidies in the U.S. Agricultural Sector] [Some Political Economy Aspects of Macroeconomic Linkages with Agriculture]. *Amer. J. Agr. Econ.,* May 1986, *68*(2), pp. 420–21. **[G: U.S.]**

Oellermann, Charles M. and Farris, Paul L. Trader Concentration Effects in Live Cattle Futures. *J. Futures Markets,* Winter 1986, *6*(4), pp. 565–74. **[G: U.S.]**

Pangeti, Evelyn. Agribusiness in Colonial Zimbabwe: The Case of the Lowveld. **In** *Teichova, A.; Lévy-Leboyer, M. and Nussbaum, H., eds.,* 1986, pp. 326–38. **[G: Zimbabwe]**

Pashigian, B. Peter. The Political Economy of Futures Market Regulation. *J. Bus.,* Part 2, April 1986, *59*(2), pp. S55–84. **[G: U.S.]**

Paul, Allen B. Liquidation Bias in Futures Price Spreads. *Amer. J. Agr. Econ.,* May 1986, *68*(2), pp. 313–21. **[G: U.S.]**

Pavaskar, Madhoo. Public Intervention in Agricultural Marketing. **In** *Dantwala, M. L., et al.,* 1986, pp. 329–57. **[G: India]**

Polopolus, Leo C. The Competitive Position of Southern Commodities in International Markets: A Synopsis. *Southern J. Agr. Econ.,* July 1986, *18*(1), pp. 75–78. **[G: U.S.]**

Purcell, Wayne D. and Hudson, Michael A. The Certificate System for Delivery in Live Cattle: Conceptual Issues and Measures of Performance. *J. Futures Markets,* Fall 1986, *6*(3), pp. 461–75. **[G: U.S.]**

Quilkey, J. J. Promotion of Primary Products—A View from the Cloister. *Australian J. Agr. Econ.,* April 1986, *30*(1), pp. 38–52.

Rajaraman, Indira. Testing the Rationality of Futures Prices for Selected LDC Agricultural Exports. *J. Futures Markets,* Winter 1986, *6*(4), pp. 523–40. **[G: U.S.; LDCs]**

Ravallion, Martin. Testing Market Integration. *Amer. J. Agr. Econ.,* February 1986, *68*(1), pp. 102–09. **[G: Bangladesh]**

Remenyi, J. V. Issues in Smallholder Tropical Dairying. *Bull. Indonesian Econ. Stud.,* April 1986, *22*(1), pp. 57–87. **[G: Indonesia]**

Richardson, Bob. Some Current Issues in the Marketing of Agricultural Products. *Australian J. Agr. Econ.,* August/December 1986, *30*(2–3), pp. 89–102. **[G: Australia]**

Roemer, Michael. Simple Analytics of Segmented Markets: What Case for Liberalization? *World Devel.,* March 1986, *14*(3), pp. 429–39.

Rosaasen, Ken and Maley, Doug. Forward Planning: An Alternative Marketing Mechanism. *Can. J. Agr. Econ.,* June 1986, *33*, pp. 205–20. **[G: Canada]**

Schmitz, Andrew. Marketing Institutions in International Commodity Markets. *Southern J. Agr. Econ.,* July 1986, *18*(1), pp. 41–48. **[G: U.S.]**

Schmitz, Peter M. Markets and Trade: Discussion. **In** *Maunder, A. and Renborg, U., eds.,* 1986, pp. 578–80.

Sexton, Richard J. The Formation of Cooperatives: A Game-Theoretic Approach with Implications for Cooperative Finance, Decision Making, and Stability. *Amer. J. Agr. Econ.,* May 1986, *68*(2), pp. 214–25.

Sheldon, I. M. The Early Development of the London Meat Futures Exchange: Some Interview Results. *J. Agr. Econ.,* January 1986, *37*(1), pp. 97–99.

Shepard, Lawrence. Cartelization of the California–Arizona Orange Industry, 1934–1981. *J. Law Econ.,* April 1986, *29*(1), pp. 83–123. **[G: U.S.]**

Shonkwiler, J. Scott. Are Livestock Futures Prices Rational Forecasts? *Western J. Agr. Econ.,* December 1986, *11*(2), pp. 123–28. **[G: U.S.]**

Smith, Edward G.; Knutson, Ronald D. and Richardson, James W. Input and Marketing Economies: Impact on Structural Change in Cotton Farming on the Texas High Plains. *Amer. J. Agr. Econ.,* August 1986, *68*(3), pp. 716–20. **[G: U.S.]**

Subbarao, K. Agricultural Marketing. **In** *Dantwala, M. L., et al.,* 1986, pp. 308–28. **[G: India]**

Tecson, Gwendolyn R. Export Markets for Philippine Diversified Agriculture and Labor-Intensive Industries. *Philippine Rev. Econ. Bus.,* Mar./June 1986, *23*(1/2), pp. 1–56. **[G: Philippines]**

Thompson, Sarahelen. Returns to Storage in Coffee and Cocoa Futures Markets. *J. Futures Markets,* Winter 1986, *6*(4), pp. 541–64. **[G: U.S.; U.K.; LDCs]**

Torok, Stephen J. and Huffman, Wallace E. U.S.–Mexican Trade in Winter Vegetables and Illegal Immigration. *Amer. J. Agr. Econ.,* May 1986, *68*(2), pp. 246–60. **[G: U.S.; Mexico]**

Tyers, Rodney. Details of the Simulation Model of World Grain and Meat Markets. **In** *Anderson, K. and Hayami, Y.,* 1986, pp. 152–61. **[G: EEC; Asia; U.S.]**

Unnevehr, Laurian J. and Zain, Djumilah. Marketing Efficiency, Informal Credit, and the Role of Government Loan Programs: Cassava Trade in Indonesia. *J. Devel. Areas,* April

1986, *20*(3), pp. 369–78. **[G: Indonesia]**

VanSickle, John J. and Ladd, George W. A Model of Cooperative Finance: Reply. *Amer. J. Agr. Econ.*, February 1986, *68*(1), pp. 173–76.

Viscencio-Brambilla, Hector and Fuller, Stephen. Effects of Port User Fees on Export Grain Flow Patterns. *Southern J. Agr. Econ.*, December 1986, *18*(2), pp. 25–37. **[G: U.S.]**

Williams, R. E. Perspectives on Milk Marketing. *J. Agr. Econ.*, September 1986, *37*(3), pp. 295–309. **[G: U.K.]**

Wilson, John. The Political Economy of Contract Farming. *Rev. Radical Polit. Econ.*, Winter 1986, *18*(4), pp. 47–70. **[G: U.S.]**

7151 Corporate Agriculture

Brown, Colin G. and Drynan, Ross G. On Some Aspects of Organizational Efficiency in the Queensland Cattle Slaughtering Industry. *Rev. Marketing Agr. Econ.*, August 1986, *54*(2), pp. 11–29. **[G: Australia]**

Dias, Guilherme Leite da Silva. Markets and Trade: Discussion. **In** *Maunder, A. and Renborg, U., eds.*, 1986, pp. 577–78.

Dufour, Jean-Claude; Ghersi, Gérard and Saint-Louis, Robert. New Types of Multinational Firms in the Agribusiness Sector: Implications of Their Emergence in the Least Industrialised World. **In** *Maunder, A. and Renborg, U., eds.*, 1986, pp. 566–77.

Jain, T. B. Allied Enterprises: I—Poultry. **In** *Dantwala, M. L., et al.*, 1986, pp. 199–208. **[G: India]**

Mbilinyi, Marjorie. Agribusiness and Casual Labor in Tanzania. *African Econ. Hist.*, 1986, (15), pp. 107–41. **[G: Tanzania]**

Schmitz, Peter M. Markets and Trade: Discussion. **In** *Maunder, A. and Renborg, U., eds.*, 1986, pp. 578–80.

Shoemaker, Robbin and Somwaru, Agapi. Total Factor Productivity and Sources of Growth in the Dairy Sector. *Agr. Econ. Res.*, Fall 1986, *38*(4), pp. 1–13. **[G: U.S.]**

Stranahan, H. A. and Shonkwiler, J. Scott. Evaluating the Returns to Postharvest Research in the Florida Citrus-Processing Subsector. *Amer. J. Agr. Econ.*, February 1986, *68*(1), pp. 88–94. **[G: U.S.]**

716 Farm Management

7160 Farm Management

Adamowicz, Wiktor. Production Technology in Canadian Agriculture. *Can. J. Agr. Econ.*, March 1986, *34*(1), pp. 87–104. **[G: Canada]**

Adams, John. Peasant Rationality: Individuals, Groups, Cultures. *World Devel.*, Special Issue, Feb. 1986, *14*(2), pp. 273–82.

Ahuja, Kanta. Agricultural Labour and Rural Employment. **In** *Dantwala, M. L., et al.*, 1986, pp. 400–431. **[G: India]**

Akinola, Amos A. An Application of Bass's Model in the Analysis of Diffusion of Cocoa-Spraying Chemicals among Nigerian Cocoa Farmers. *J. Agr. Econ.*, September 1986, *37*(3), pp. 395–404. **[G: Nigeria]**

Akinola, Amos A. Dynamic Innovator–Imitator (IN–IM) Diffusion Model. *Can. J. Agr. Econ.*, March 1986, *34*(1), pp. 113–24. **[G: Nigeria]**

Alexander, Vickie J.; Musser, Wesley N. and Mason, George. Futures Markets and Firm Decisions under Price, Production, and Financial Uncertainty. *Southern J. Agr. Econ.*, December 1986, *18*(2), pp. 39–49. **[G: U.S.]**

Anderson, James L. and Wilen, James E. Implications of Private Salmon Aquaculture on Prices, Production, and Management of Salmon Resources. *Amer. J. Agr. Econ.*, November 1986, *68*(4), pp. 866–79. **[G: U.S.]**

Anderson, Jock R.; Dillon, John L. and Hardaker, J. Brian. Farmers and Risk. **In** *Maunder, A. and Renborg, U., eds.*, 1986, pp. 638–48.

Antle, John M. and Aitah, Ali S. Egypt's Multiproduct Agricultural Technology and Agricultural Policy. *J. Devel. Stud.*, July 1986, *22*(4), pp. 709–23. **[G: Egypt]**

Antle, John M. and Hatchett, Stephen A. Dynamic Input Decisions in Econometric Product Models. *Amer. J. Agr. Econ.*, November 1986, *68*(4), pp. 939–49. **[G: U.S.]**

Atwood, Joseph, et al. Performance of Risk-Income Models Outside the Original Data Set. *Southern J. Agr. Econ.*, December 1986, *18*(2), pp. 113–23. **[G: U.S.]**

Barry, Peter J. and Robison, Lindon J. Economic versus Accounting Rates of Return for Farm Land. *Land Econ.*, November 1986, *62*(4), pp. 388–401. **[G: U.S.]**

Belongia, Michael T. The Farm Sector in the 1980s: Sudden Collapse or Steady Downturn? *Fed. Res. Bank St. Louis Rev.*, November 1986, *68*(9), pp. 17–25. **[G: U.S.]**

Bhaduri, Amit. Forced Commerce and Agrarian Growth. *World Devel.*, Special Issue, Feb. 1986, *14*(2), pp. 267–72.

Binswanger, Hans P. and Pingali, Prabhu. Agricultural Intensification and Technical Change in Sub-Saharan Africa. **In** *Maunder, A. and Renborg, U., eds.*, 1986, pp. 381–86. **[G: Sub-Saharan Africa]**

Binswanger, Hans P. and Rosenzweig, Mark R. Behavioural and Material Determinants of Production Relations in Agriculture. *J. Devel. Stud.*, April 1986, *22*(3), pp. 503–39.

Birowo, Achmad T. Human Capital, Technology and Institutions: Discussion. **In** *Maunder, A. and Renborg, U., eds.*, 1986, pp. 386–87.

Bode, Frederick A. and Ginter, Donald E. Regional Patterns of Intercounty Farm Investment in Antebellum Georgia. **In** *Uselding, P., ed.*, 1986, pp. 241–69. **[G: U.S.]**

Boehlje, Michael D. and Lowenberg-DeBoer, John. Integration of Production and Financial Theory in Analysing Farm Firm Behaviour. **In** *Maunder, A. and Renborg, U., eds.*, 1986, pp. 668–79.

Boussard, Jean-Marc. Agriculture in a Turbulent World Economy: Theoretical Developments: Discussion. **In** *Maunder, A. and Renborg, U.,* *eds.*, 1986, pp. 663–65.

Boussard, Jean-Marc. Changing Environment and Structural Heterogeneity in Agriculture. **In** *Maunder, A. and Renborg, U., eds.*, 1986, pp. 531–41.

Boyle, G. E. An Exploratory Assessment of the Returns to Agricultural Research in Ireland 1963–1983. *Irish J. Agr. Econ. Rural Soc.*, 1986, *11*, pp. 57–71. **[G: Ireland]**

Braden, John B. and Eales, James S. The Adoption of Reduced Tillage: The Role of Human Capital and Other Variables: Comment. *Amer. J. Agr. Econ.*, February 1986, *68*(1), pp. 182–83. **[G: U.S.]**

Braverman, Avishay and Stiglitz, Joseph E. Cost-Sharing Arrangements under Sharecropping: Moral Hazard, Incentive Flexibility, and Risk. *Amer. J. Agr. Econ.*, August 1986, *68*(3), pp. 642–52.

Braverman, Avishay and Stiglitz, Joseph E. Landlords, Tenants and Technological Innovations. *J. Devel. Econ.*, October 1986, *23*(2), pp. 313–32.

Bravo-Ureta, Boris E. Technical Efficiency Measures for Dairy Farms Based on a Probabilistic Frontier Function Model. *Can. J. Agr. Econ.*, November 1986, *34*(3), pp. 399–415. **[G: Canada]**

Breimyer, Harold F. The Asset Devaluation Problem. *Southern J. Agr. Econ.*, July 1986, *18*(1), pp. 79–82.

Brewer, A. C. and Mead, R. Continuous Second Order Models of Spatial Variation with Application to the Efficiency of Field Crop Experiments. *J. Roy. Statist. Soc.*, 1986, *149*(4), pp. 314–36.

Brinkman, George L. Farming under Uncertainty in the 1980s: Some Lessons from Canada. **In** *Maunder, A. and Renborg, U., eds.*, 1986, pp. 127–38. **[G: Canada]**

Brown, Colin G. and Drynan, Ross G. On Some Aspects of Organizational Efficiency in the Queensland Cattle Slaughtering Industry. *Rev. Marketing Agr. Econ.*, August 1986, *54*(2), pp. 11–29. **[G: Australia]**

Brown, Colin G. and Drynan, Ross G. Plant Location Analysis Using Discrete Stochastic Programming. *Australian J. Agr. Econ.*, April 1986, *30*(1), pp. 1–22. **[G: Australia]**

Buccola, Steven T. Testing for Nonnormality in Farm Net Returns. *Amer. J. Agr. Econ.*, May 1986, *68*(2), pp. 334–43. **[G: U.S.]**

Buccola, Steven T. and McCarl, Bruce A. Small-Sample Evaluation of Mean-Variance Production Function Estimators. *Amer. J. Agr. Econ.*, August 1986, *68*(3), pp. 732–38.

Burt, Oscar R. Farm-Level Economics of Soil Conservation in the Palouse Area of the Northwest: Reply. *Amer. J. Agr. Econ.*, May 1986, *68*(2), pp. 367–69. **[G: U.S.]**

Byerlee, Derek and Hesse de Polanco, Edith. Farmers' Stepwise Adoption of Technological Packages: Evidence from the Mexican Altiplano. *Amer. J. Agr. Econ.*, August 1986, *68*(3), pp. 519–27. **[G: Mexico]**

Calomiris, Charles W.; Hubbard, R. Glenn and Stock, James H. The Farm Debt Crisis and Public Policy. *Brookings Pap. Econ. Act.*, 1986, (2), pp. 441–79. **[G: U.S.]**

Caswell, Margriet F. and Zilberman, David. The Effects of Well Depth and Land Quality on the Choice of Irrigation Technology. *Amer. J. Agr. Econ.*, November 1986, *68*(4), pp. 798–811. **[G: U.S.]**

Chambers, Robert G. and Lee, Hyunok. Constrained Output Maximization and U.S. Agriculture. *Appl. Econ.*, April 1986, *18*(4), pp. 347–57. **[G: U.S.]**

Chand, Ramesh and Kaul, J. L. A Note on the Use of the Cobb–Douglas Profit Function. *Amer. J. Agr. Econ.*, February 1986, *68*(1), pp. 162–64.

Chavas, Jean-Paul and Klemme, Richard M. Aggregate Milk Supply Response and Investment Behavior on U.S. Dairy Farms. *Amer. J. Agr. Econ.*, February 1986, *68*(1), pp. 55–66. **[G: U.S.]**

Chicoine, David L. Farm Taxes. **In** *Gold, S. D., ed.*, 1986, pp. 307–31. **[G: U.S.]**

Coles, Charles. Use of a Lotus 1-2-3 Spreadsheet Program in Farm Management Extension. *Can. J. Agr. Econ.*, June 1986, *33*, pp. 100–106.

Collender, Robert Neil and Chalfant, James A. An Alternative Approach to Decisions under Uncertainty Using the Empirical Moment-Generating Function. *Amer. J. Agr. Econ.*, August 1986, *68*(3), pp. 727–31.

Collins, Robert A. and Barry, Peter J. Risk Analysis with Single-Index Portfolio Models: An Application to Farm Planning. *Amer. J. Agr. Econ.*, February 1986, *68*(1), pp. 152–61. **[G: U.S.]**

Condominas, Georges. Ritual Technology in Mnong Gar Swidden Agriculture. **In** *Nørlund, I.; Cederroth, S. and Gerdin, I., eds.*, 1986, pp. 28–46. **[G: Vietnam]**

Corner, Lorraine. The Prospects for Off-Farm Employment as an Anti-poverty Strategy among Malaysian Paddy Farm Households: Macro and Micro Views. **In** *Shand, R. T., ed., Vol. 2*, 1986, pp. 45–67. **[G: Malaysia]**

Dawson, P. J. Family Labour Supply: Some Empirical Results from Agriculture: A Reply. *Appl. Econ.*, August 1986, *18*(8), pp. 835–36. **[G: U.K.]**

Dinar, Ariel; Knapp, Keith C. and Rhoades, James D. Production Function for Cotton with Dated Irrigation Quantities and Qualities. *Water Resources Res.*, October 1986, *22*(11), pp. 1519–25. **[G: U.S.]**

Drabenstott, Mark. Agriculture in a Turbulent World Economy: Theoretical Developments: Discussion. **In** *Maunder, A. and Renborg, U., eds.*, 1986, pp. 686–88.

Driver, H. C. and Onwona, S. O. Profiles in Management and Performance for Assessment of Information Needs. *Can. J. Agr. Econ.*, July 1986, *34*(2), pp. 155–76. **[G: Canada]**

Duffy, Patricia A.; Richardson, James W. and Smith, Edward G. Effects of Alternative Farm Programs and Levels of Price Variability on

Texas Cotton Farms. *Southern J. Agr. Econ.*, December 1986, *18*(2), pp. 97–106. [G: U.S.]

Ehrensaft, Philip and Bollman, Ray D. Large Farms: The Leading Edge of Structural Change. *Can. J. Agr. Econ.*, June 1986, *33*, pp. 145–60. [G: Canada]

El-Nazer, Talaat and McCarl, Bruce A. The Choice of Crop Rotation: A Modeling Approach and Case Study. *Amer. J. Agr. Econ.*, February 1986, *68*(1), pp. 127–36. [G: U.S.]

Elahi, Mahboob and Khan, Mahmud Jameel. Rural Labour Market with Special Reference to Hired Labour in Pakistan's Punjab. **In** *Hirashima, S. and Muqtada, M., eds.*, 1986, pp. 75–118. [G: Pakistan]

England, R. A. Reducing the Nitrogen Input on Arable Farms. *J. Agr. Econ.*, January 1986, *37*(1), pp. 13–24. [G: U.K.]

Eswaran, Mukesh and Kotwal, Ashok. Access to Capital and Agrarian Production Organisation. *Econ. J.*, June 1986, *96*(382), pp. 482–98.

Flinn, J. C. and Ali, Mubarik. Technical Efficiency in Basmati Rice Production. *Pakistan J. Appl. Econ.*, Summer 1986, *5*(1), pp. 63–79. [G: Pakistan]

Ford, Barry L.; Nealon, Jack and Tortora, Robert D. Area Frame Estimators in Agricultural Surveys: Sampling versus Nonsampling Errors. *Agr. Econ. Res.*, Spring 1986, *38*(2), pp. 1–10. [G: U.S.]

Fraser, R. W. Supply Responses, Risk Aversion and Covariances in Agriculture. *Australian J. Agr. Econ.*, August/December 1986, *30*(2–3), pp. 153–56.

Fraser, R. W. Unreliable Markets and Perishable Products. *J. Agr. Econ.*, January 1986, *37*(1), pp. 89–95.

Frawley, J. and Reidy, K. An Approach to Identify Different Categories of Farmer: An Illustration of the Use of Discriminant Analysis. *Irish J. Agr. Econ. Rural Soc.*, 1986, *11*, pp. 35–47. [G: Ireland]

Friedman, Benjamin M. The Farm Debt Crisis and Public Policy: Comments. *Brookings Pap. Econ. Act.*, 1986, (2), pp. 480–84. [G: U.S.]

Fu, T. T.; Fletcher, Stanley M. and Epperson, J. E. Acreage Planting Decision Analysis of South Carolina Tomatoes: Nerlovian versus Just Risk Model. *Southern J. Agr. Econ.*, December 1986, *18*(2), pp. 65–71. [G: U.S.]

Gadgil, Madhukar. Agriculture in a Turbulent World Economy: Theoretical Developments: Discussion. **In** *Maunder, A. and Renborg, U., eds.*, 1986, pp. 688–90.

Gangopadhyay, Shubhashis and Sengupta, Kunal. Interlinkages in Rural Markets. *Oxford Econ. Pap.*, March 1986, *38*(1), pp. 112–21.

Gardner, Bruce L. Farm Policy and the Farm Problem. **In** *Cagan, P., ed.*, 1986, pp. 223–46. [G: U.S.]

Gersovitz, Mark. Agro-industrial Processing and Agricultural Pricing under Uncertainty. *Rev. Econ. Stud.*, January 1986, *53*(1), pp. 153–69. [G: Senegal]

Gillmor, Desmond A. Behavioural Studies in Agriculture: Goals, Values and Enterprise Choice. *Irish J. Agr. Econ. Rural Soc.*, 1986, *11*, pp. 19–33. [G: Ireland]

Grabowski, Richard and Belbase, K. An Analysis of Optimal Scale and Factor Intensity in Nepalese Agriculture: An Application of a Ray–Homothetic Production Function. *Appl. Econ.*, October 1986, *18*(10), pp. 1051–63. [G: Nepal]

Greeley, Martin. Food, Technology and Employment: The Farm-Level Post-Harvest System in Developing Countries. *J. Agr. Econ.*, September 1986, *37*(3), pp. 333–47. [G: LDCs]

Groenewald, J. A. Structure of Agriculture and People in Rural Societies: Discussion. **In** *Maunder, A. and Renborg, U., eds.*, 1986, pp. 551–53. [G: U.S.]

Hammer, Jeffrey S. 'Subsistence First': Farm Allocation Decisions in Senegal. *J. Devel. Econ.*, October 1986, *23*(2), pp. 355–69. [G: Senegal]

Hanf, C.-Hennig and Kühl, Rainer. Possibilities and Limits of Individual Marketing on Family Farm Firms. *Europ. Rev. Agr. Econ.*, 1986, *13*(2), pp. 149–67. [G: W. Germany]

Harsh, S. B.; Kuhlmann, F. and Burg, F. Farm Level Information Systems as an Aid to Decision-makers. **In** *Maunder, A. and Renborg, U., eds.*, 1986, pp. 727–33.

Haughton, Jonathan. Farm Price Responsiveness and the Choice of Functional Form: An Application to Rice Cultivation West Malaysia. *J. Devel. Econ.*, December 1986, *24*(2), pp. 203–23. [G: Malaysia]

Hazell, Peter; Bassoco, Luz María and Arcia, Gustavo. A Model for Evaluating Farmers' Demand for Insurance: Applications in Mexico and Panama. **In** *Hazell, P.; Pomareda, C. and Valdés, A., eds.*, 1986, pp. 35–66. [G: Mexico; Panama]

Herath, H. M. G. An Exploratory Study of Off-Farm Employment and Incomes in Sri Lanka. **In** *Shand, R. T., ed., Vol. 2*, 1986, pp. 209–33. [G: Sri Lanka]

Higgins, James. Input Demand and Output Supply on Irish Farms—A Micro-economic Approach. *Europ. Rev. Agr. Econ.*, 1986, *13*(4), pp. 477–93. [G: Ireland]

Higgins, James. Investment Behaviour on Irish Farms—A Cross-Sectional Analysis. *Irish J. Agr. Econ. Rural Soc.*, 1986, *11*, pp. 49–56. [G: Ireland]

Hildreth, Clifford and Knowles, Glen J. Farmers' Utility Functions. **In** *[de Finetti, B.]*, 1986, pp. 291–317. [G: U.S.]

Hildreth, R. J. Agriculture in a Turbulent World Economy: Theoretical Developments: Discussion. **In** *Maunder, A. and Renborg, U., eds.*, 1986, pp. 661–63.

Hillberg, Ann Marie. Limiting EC Grain Substitute Imports: A Simulation Model of the West German Manufactured Feed Economy. *Europ. Rev. Agr. Econ.*, 1986, *13*(1), pp. 43–56. [G: W. Germany]

Ho, Samuel P. S. Off-Farm Employment and Farm Households in Taiwan. **In** *Shand, R. T.*, *ed., Vol. 1*, 1986, pp. 95–133. **[G: Taiwan]**

Hoag, Dana L. and Young, Douglas L. Commodity and Conservation Policy Impacts on Risk and Returns. *Western J. Agr. Econ.*, December 1986, *11*(2), pp. 211–20. **[G: U.S.]**

Howell, David. Farming in South-east Wales c.1840–80. **In** *Baber, C. and Williams, L. J., eds.*, 1986, pp. 82–96. **[G: U.K.]**

Hrubovcak, James. Measuring Implicit Rental Rates for Farm Capital. *Agr. Econ. Res.*, Winter 1986, *38*(1), pp. 19–33. **[G: U.S.]**

Huang, Cliff J.; Tang, Anthony M. and Bagi, Faquir S. Two View of Efficiency in Indian Agriculture. *Can. J. Agr. Econ.*, July 1986, *34*(2), pp. 209–26. **[G: India]**

Huffman, Wallace E. Changes in Human Capital, Technology, and Institutions: Implications for Policy and Research. **In** *Maunder, A. and Renborg, U., eds.*, 1986, pp. 769–75.

Hunek, Tadeusz. Farmers and Rural Societies in Uncertain Food Production Systems. **In** *Maunder, A. and Renborg, U., eds.*, 1986, pp. 505–12.

Iqbal, Farrukh. The Demand and Supply of Funds among Agricultural Households in India. **In** *Singh, I.; Squire, L. and Strauss, J., eds.*, 1986, pp. 183–205. **[G: India]**

Jayasuriya, S. K.; Te, A. and Herdt, R. W. Mechanisation and Cropping Intensification: Economics of Machinery Use in Low-Wage Economies. *J. Devel. Stud.*, January 1986, *22*(2), pp. 327–35. **[G: LDCs]**

Johnson, Donald A. and Boehlje, Michael D. Managing Risk by Coordinating Investment, Marketing, and Production Strategies: Reply. *Western J. Agr. Econ.*, December 1986, *11*(2), pp. 235–36.

Johnson, James and Baum, Kenneth. Whole Farm Survey Data for Economic Indicators and Performance Measures. *Agr. Econ. Res.*, Summer 1986, *38*(3), pp. 1–13. **[G: U.S.]**

Kada, Ryohei. Off-Farm Employment and the Rural–Urban Interface in Japanese Economic Development. **In** *Shand, R. T., ed., Vol. 1*, 1986, pp. 75–93. **[G: Japan]**

Kalirajan, K. Measuring Technical Efficiencies from Interdependent Multiple Outputs Frontiers. *J. Quant. Econ.*, July 1986, *2*(2), pp. 263–74. **[G: Philippines]**

Kalirajan, K. and Shand, Richard T. Estimating Location-Specific and Firm-Specific Technical Efficiency: An Analysis of Malaysian Agriculture. *J. Econ. Devel.*, December 1986, *11*(2), pp. 147–60. **[G: Malaysia]**

Karp, Larry; Sadeh, Arye and Griffin, Wade L. Cycles in Agricultural Production: The Case of Aquaculture. *Amer. J. Agr. Econ.*, August 1986, *68*(3), pp. 553–61.

Kasim, Sukor and Najimudin, Mustafa. Evolution of Sources of Income in the Muda Irrigation Scheme, Malaysia, 1972/73 to 1981/82. **In** *Shand, R. T., ed., Vol. 2*, 1986, pp. 21–43. **[G: Malaysia]**

Kennedy, John O. S. Rules for Optimal Fertilizer Carryover: An Alternative Explanation. *Rev. Marketing Agr. Econ.*, August 1986, *54*(2), pp. 3–10. **[G: Australia]**

Kerr, John and Kalirajan, K. Measuring Production Risk Using a Modified RCRM Model. **In** *Maunder, A. and Renborg, U., eds.*, 1986, pp. 649–54. **[G: India]**

Khuda, B. Off-Farm Employment in Traditional and Developed Villages of Bangladesh. **In** *Shand, R. T., ed., Vol. 2*, 1986, pp. 193–207. **[G: Bangladesh]**

Kiker, Clyde and Lieblich, Mark. Financial Analysis of On-Farm Grain Drying. *Southern J. Agr. Econ.*, December 1986, *18*(2), pp. 73–83. **[G: U.S.]**

Kinnucan, Henry; Cacho, Oscar and Hanson, Gregory D. Effects of Selected Tax Policies on Management and Growth of a Catfish Enterprise. *Southern J. Agr. Econ.*, December 1986, *18*(2), pp. 215–25.

Kirkland, Jack J. and Mittelhammer, Ron C. A Nonlinear Programming Analysis of Production Response to Multiple Component Milk Pricing. *Amer. J. Agr. Econ.*, February 1986, *68*(1), pp. 44–54. **[G: U.S.]**

Kirschke, Dieter. Budget Costs of the EC's Agricultural Price Policy under Uncertainty. *Europ. Rev. Agr. Econ.*, 1986, *13*(1), pp. 57–74. **[G: EEC]**

Kjærby, Finn. The Development of Agricultural Mechanisation in Tanzania. **In** *Boesen, J., et al., eds.*, 1986, pp. 173–90. **[G: Tanzania]**

Kurian, N. J. Economics of Rice Production in India—An Interregional and Intertemporal Analysis. *J. Quant. Econ.*, January 1986, *2*(1), pp. 51–76. **[G: India]**

LaFrance, Jeffrey T. and Watts, Myles J. The Value of Protein in Feed Barley for Beef, Diary, and Swine Feeding. *Western J. Agr. Econ.*, July 1986, *11*(1), pp. 76–81. **[G: U.S.]**

Lambrecht, Philippe. Agriculture in a Turbulent World Economy: Theoretical Developments: Discussion. **In** *Maunder, A. and Renborg, U., eds.*, 1986, pp. 741–43.

Leathers, Howard D. and Chavas, Jean-Paul. Farm Debt, Default, and Foreclosure: An Economic Rationale for Policy Action. *Amer. J. Agr. Econ.*, November 1986, *68*(4), pp. 828–37.

Lee, Hyunok and Chambers, Robert G. Expenditure Constraints and Profit Maximization in U.S. Agriculture. *Amer. J. Agr. Econ.*, November 1986, *68*(4), pp. 857–65. **[G: U.S.]**

Lehmann, David. Sharecropping and the Capitalist Transition in Agriculture: Some Evidence from the Highlands of Ecuador. *J. Devel. Econ.*, October 1986, *23*(2), pp. 333–54. **[G: Ecuador]**

Leibenstein, Harvey. The Theory of Underemployment in Densely Populated Backward Areas. **In** *Akerlof, G. A. and Yellen, J. L., eds.*, 1986, *1963*, pp. 22–40.

Lianos, Theodore P. and Parliarou, Despina. Farm Size Structure in Greek Agriculture. *Europ. Rev. Agr. Econ.*, 1986, *13*(2), pp. 233–48. **[G: Greece]**

Liapis, Peter S. and Moffitt, L. Joe. Economic

Analysis of Cotton Integrated Pest Management Strategies: Reply. *Southern J. Agr. Econ.*, July 1986, *18*(1), pp. 173–74.

Lichtenberg, Erik and Zilberman, David. The Econometrics of Damage Control: Why Specification Matters. *Amer. J. Agr. Econ.*, May 1986, *68*(2), pp. 261–73.

Lopez, Ramon E. Structural Models of the Farm Household That Allow for Interdependent Utility and Profit-Maximization Decisions. **In** *Singh, I.; Squire, L. and Strauss, J., eds.*, 1986, pp. 306–25. **[G: Canada]**

Love, Ross O. The Role of Extension in Dealing with Farm Families in Financial Crisis. *Southern J. Agr. Econ.*, July 1986, *18*(1), pp. 83–92. **[G: U.S.]**

Lowenberg-DeBoer, John and Boehlje, Michael D. The Impact of Farmland Price Changes on Farm Size and Financial Structure. *Amer. J. Agr. Econ.*, November 1986, *68*(4), pp. 838–48. **[G: U.S.]**

Malfliet, Katlijn. The Economic Function and Purpose of Personal Property and Its Legal Implementation. **In** *Ioffe, O. S. and Janis, M. W., eds.*, 1986, pp. 79–101. **[G: U.S.S.R.]**

Martin, Philip L. Western Farm Labor Issues. *Contemp. Policy Issues*, January 1986, *4*(1), pp. 72–86. **[G: U.S.]**

Maxwell, Simon. Farming Systems Research: Hitting a Moving Target. *World Devel.*, January 1986, *14*(1), pp. 65–77. **[G: LDCs]**

McCamley, Francis and Kliebenstein, James B. Two Simple Stochastic Efficiency Tests for MOTAD Solutions. *Can. J. Agr. Econ.*, July 1986, *34*(2), pp. 177–94.

McCarl, Bruce A. and Apland, Jeffrey. Validation of Linear Programming Models. *Southern J. Agr. Econ.*, December 1986, *18*(2), pp. 155–64.

McClelland, John W.; Wetzstein, Michael E. and Musser, Wesley N. Returns to Scale and Size in Agricultural Economics. *Western J. Agr. Econ.*, December 1986, *11*(2), pp. 129–33.

McGrann, James M., et al. Microcomputer Budget Management System. *Southern J. Agr. Econ.*, July 1986, *18*(1), pp. 151–56.

McKinzie, Lance; Paarlberg, Philip L. and Huerta, Ivan P. Estimating a Complete Matrix of Demand Elasticities for Feed Components Using Pseudo Data: A Case Study of Dutch Compound Livestock Feeds. *Europ. Rev. Agr. Econ.*, 1986, *13*(1), pp. 23–42. **[G: Netherlands]**

McPherson, Malcolm. Why Do Researchers Continue to Ignore Risk in Tests of Farmer Efficiency? A Comment on Shapiro's Rejection of the Efficient But Poor Hypothesis [Efficiency Differentials in Peasant Agriculture and Their Implications for Development Policies]. *J. Devel. Stud.*, April 1986, *22*(3), pp. 604–07. **[G: Tanzania]**

Miller, Bill R.; Arraes, Ronaldo A. and Pesti, Gene M. Formulation of Broiler Finishing Rations by Quadratic Programming. *Southern J. Agr. Econ.*, July 1986, *18*(1), pp. 141–50. **[G: U.S.]**

Miller, Stephen E. Forward Contracting versus Hedging under Price and Yield Uncertainty. *Southern J. Agr. Econ.*, December 1986, *18*(2), pp. 139–46. **[G: U.S.]**

Moffitt, L. Joe. Risk-Efficient Thresholds for Pest Control Decisions. *J. Agr. Econ.*, January 1986, *37*(1), pp. 69–75.

Moffitt, L. Joe, et al. Economic Impact of Public Pest Information: Soybean Insect Forecasts in Illinois. *Amer. J. Agr. Econ.*, May 1986, *68*(2), pp. 274–79. **[G: U.S.]**

Mui, H. W.; Bradford, G. L. and Ali, M. M. Modeling the Demand for Durable Inputs: Distributed Lags and Causality. *Southern J. Agr. Econ.*, December 1986, *18*(2), pp. 273–79. **[G: U.S.]**

Musser, Wesley N.; McCarl, Bruce A. and Smith, G. Scott. An Investigation of the Relationship between Constraint Omission and Risk Aversion in Firm Risk Programming Models. *Southern J. Agr. Econ.*, December 1986, *18*(2), pp. 147–54. **[G: U.S.]**

Musser, Wesley N.; Tew, Bernard V. and White, Fred C. Choice of Depreciation Methods for Farm Firms. *Amer. J. Agr. Econ.*, November 1986, *68*(4), pp. 980–89. **[G: U.S.]**

Musser, Wesley N., et al. Beliefs of Farmers and Adoption of Integrated Pest Management. *Agr. Econ. Res.*, Winter 1986, *38*(1), pp. 34–44. **[G: U.S.]**

Nabi, Ijaz. Contracts, Resource Use and Productivity in Sharecropping. *J. Devel. Stud.*, January 1986, *22*(2), pp. 429–42. **[G: Pakistan]**

Niewuwoudt, W. L. and Bullock, J. Bruce. The Demand for Crop Insurance. **In** *Maunder, A. and Renborg, U., eds.*, 1986, pp. 655–61. **[G: U.S.]**

Nutt, Perry J.; Reed, Michael R. and Skees, Jerry R. Farm Level Corn Acreage Response Estimation. *Southern J. Agr. Econ.*, December 1986, *18*(2), pp. 1–5. **[G: U.S.]**

Odgaard, Rie. Tea—Does It Do the Peasant Women in Rungwe Any Good? **In** *Boesen, J., et al., eds.*, 1986, pp. 207–24. **[G: Tanzania]**

Oshima, Harry T. Off-Farm Employment and Incomes in Postwar East Asian Growth. **In** *Shand, R. T., ed., Vol. 1*, 1986, pp. 25–74. **[G: Japan; Taiwan; S. Korea]**

Paranavitana, C. Family Labour Supply: Some Empirical Results from Agriculture: Comment. *Appl. Econ.*, August 1986, *18*(8), pp. 829–34. **[G: U.K.]**

Park, Fun Koo. Off-Farm Employment in Korea: Current Status and Future Prospects. **In** *Shand, R. T., ed., Vol. 1*, 1986, pp. 135–52. **[G: S. Korea]**

Pederson, Glenn D. and Bertelsen, Diane. Financial Risk Management Alternatives in a Whole-Farm Setting. *Western J. Agr. Econ.*, July 1986, *11*(1), pp. 67–75. **[G: U.S.]**

Perry, Gregory M. Managing Risk by Coordinating Investment, Marketing, and Production Strategies: Comment. *Western J. Agr. Econ.*,

December 1986, *11*(2), pp. 232–34.

Perry, Gregory M., et al. Analyzing Tenure Arrangements and Crop Rotations Using Farm Simulation and Probit Analysis. *Southern J. Agr. Econ.*, December 1986, *18*(2), pp. 165–74. **[G: U.S.]**

Pescaru, V. Demands of the Cybernetization of Informational and Decisional Systems in Agriculture. *Econ. Computat. Cybern. Stud. Res.*, 1986, *21*(3), pp. 5–11. **[G: Romania]**

Phillips, Joseph M. and Marble, Robert P. Farmer Education and Efficiency: A Frontier Production Function Approach. *Econ. Educ. Rev.*, 1986, *5*(3), pp. 257–64. **[G: Guatemala]**

van Poollen, H. Walter and Leung, PingSun. Analyzing the Effect of Changing Feed–Beef Price Relationships on Beef Production Management Strategies in Hawaii: A Dynamic Programming Approach. *Western J. Agr. Econ.*, July 1986, *11*(1), pp. 106–14. **[G: U.S.]**

Quibria, M. G. and Rashid, Salim. Sharecropping in Dual Agrarian Economies: A Synthesis. *Oxford Econ. Pap.*, March 1986, *38*(1), pp. 94–111.

Rahm, Michael R. and Huffman, Wallace E. The Adoption of Reduced Tillage: The Role of Human Capital and Other Variables: Reply. *Amer. J. Agr. Econ.*, February 1986, *68*(1), pp. 184. **[G: U.S.]**

Ramaratnam, S. Sri, et al. Risk Attitudes and Farm/Producer Attributes: A Case Study of Texas Coastal Bend Grain Sorghum Producers. *Southern J. Agr. Econ.*, December 1986, *18*(2), pp. 85–95. **[G: U.S.]**

Rivera Vilas, Luis Miguel. El criterio de Baumol: una aplicación a la planificación comercial de variedades. (With English summary.) *Invest. Ecón.*, May 1986, *10*(2), pp. 309–25. **[G: Spain]**

Robinson, G. N. A Synthetic Model of Agricultural Supply. *J. Agr. Econ.*, January 1986, *37*(1), pp. 45–58.

Roe, Terry and Graham-Tomasi, Theodore. Yield Risk in a Dynamic Model of the Agricultural Household. **In** *Singh, I.; Squire, L. and Strauss, J., eds.*, 1986, pp. 255–76. **[G: Dominican Republic]**

Ross, Randolph W. Innovation in Spreadsheet Analysis and Farm Management. *Can. J. Agr. Econ.*, June 1986, *33*, pp. 80–85.

Salam, Abdul. Farm Labour Use and Its Determinants: Results from a Farm Survey in Pakistan. *Pakistan Econ. Soc. Rev.*, Summer 1986, *24*(1), pp. 1–21. **[G: Pakistan]**

Sandrey, Ron A. and Zwart, A. C. Dynamics of Herd Build-up in a New Industry: Commercial Red Deer Production in New Zealand. *Western J. Agr. Econ.*, July 1986, *11*(1), pp. 92–99. **[G: New Zealand]**

Satish, S. Relative Economic Efficiencies in Indian Agriculture: A Case Study of Cotton in Karnataka. *Indian J. Quant. Econ.*, 1986, *2*(1), pp. 45–55. **[G: India]**

Schiefer, Gerhard. Agriculture in a Turbulent World Economy: Theoretical Developments: Discussion. **In** *Maunder, A. and Renborg, U., eds.*, 1986, pp. 743–45.

Schiff, Maurice. The Competitive Firm under Uncertainty: An Application to Canadian Wheat Production. *Can. J. Agr. Econ.*, July 1986, *34*(2), pp. 235–42. **[G: Canada]**

Schnitkey, Gary D. and Sonka, Steven T. Systems Design Procedures for Farm Accounting. *Southern J. Agr. Econ.*, December 1986, *18*(2), pp. 207–13. **[G: U.S.]**

Scott, R. Douglas, III; Cochran, Mark J. and Nicholson, W. F., Jr. Economic Analysis of Cotton Integrated Pest Management Strategies: A Comment. *Southern J. Agr. Econ.*, July 1986, *18*(1), pp. 169–71.

Seckler, David W. Institutionalism and Agricultural Development in India. *J. Econ. Issues*, December 1986, *20*(4), pp. 1011–27. **[G: India]**

Sevilla Guzman, E. Structure of Agriculture and People in Rural Societies: Discussion. **In** *Maunder, A. and Renborg, U., eds.*, 1986, pp. 527–29.

Shahabuddin, Quazi and Mestelman, Stuart. Uncertainty and Disaster-Avoidance Behaviour in Peasant Farming: Evidence from Bangladesh. *J. Devel. Stud.*, July 1986, 22(4), pp. 740–52. **[G: Bangladesh]**

Siamwalla, Ammar. Approaches to Price Insurance for Farmers. **In** *Hazell, P.; Pomareda, C. and Valdés, A., eds.*, 1986, pp. 178–92.

Sicular, Terry. Agricultural Planning in China: The Case of Lee Willow Team No. 4. *Food Res. Inst. Stud.*, 1986, *20*(1), pp. 1–24. **[G: China]**

Sicular, Terry. Using a Farm-Household Model to Analyze Labor Allocation on a Chinese Collective Farm. **In** *Singh, I.; Squire, L. and Strauss, J., eds.*, 1986, pp. 277–305. **[G: China]**

Simons, Scott. Land Fragmentation in Developing Countries: The Optimal Choice and Policy Implications. **In** *Maunder, A. and Renborg, U., eds.*, 1986, pp. 703–12.

Singh, Inderjit and Janakiram, Subramanian. Agricultural Household Modeling in a Multicrop Environment: Case Studies in Korea and Nigeria. **In** *Singh, I.; Squire, L. and Strauss, J., eds.*, 1986, pp. 95–115. **[G: S. Korea; Nigeria]**

Singh, Inderjit; Squire, Lyn and Strauss, John. Agricultural Household Models: Methodological Issues. **In** *Singh, I.; Squire, L. and Strauss, J., eds.*, 1986, pp. 48–70.

Singh, Inderjit; Squire, Lyn and Strauss, John. Agricultural Household Models: Introduction. **In** *Singh, I.; Squire, L. and Strauss, J., eds.*, 1986, pp. 3–14.

Singh, Inderjit; Squire, Lyn and Strauss, John. Agricultural Household Models: The Basic Model: Theory, Empirical Results, and Policy Conclusions. **In** *Singh, I.; Squire, L. and Strauss, J., eds.*, 1986, pp. 17–47. **[G: Selected Countries]**

Skees, Jerry R. and Reed, Michael R. Rate Making for Farm-Level Crop Insurance: Implications for Adverse Selection. *Amer. J. Agr. Econ.*, August 1986, *68*(3), pp. 653–59.

Smith, Edward G.; Knutson, Ronald D. and Richardson, James W. Input and Marketing Economies: Impact on Structural Change in Cotton Farming on the Texas High Plains. *Amer. J. Agr. Econ.*, August 1986, *68*(3), pp. 716–20. **[G: U.S.]**

Smith, Hilary H. The Choice of Part-time Farming in Texas. *Fed. Res. Bank Dallas Econ. Rev.*, September 1986, pp. 10–19. **[G: U.S.]**

Smith, Joyotee. Moral Hazard, Costly Supervision, and Agricultural Mechanization. *J. Devel. Areas*, October 1986, *21*(1), pp. 75–85. **[G: Philippines]**

Smith, Victor E. and Strauss, John. Simulating the Rural Economy in a Subsistence Environment: Sierra Leone. **In** *Singh, I.; Squire, L. and Strauss, J., eds.*, 1986, pp. 206–32. **[G: Sierra Leone]**

Soares, Fernando B. Structure of Agriculture and People in Rural Societies: Discussion. **In** *Maunder, A. and Renborg, U., eds.*, 1986, pp. 550–51. **[G: U.S.]**

Sonka, Steven T. Computer-Aided Farm Management Systems: Will the Promise Be Fulfilled? **In** *Maunder, A. and Renborg, U., eds.*, 1986, pp. 717–26.

St. Żegar, Józef. Peasant Farms in Economic and Social Crisis: The Case of Poland in the 1980s. **In** *Maunder, A. and Renborg, U., eds.*, 1986, pp. 139–45. **[G: Poland]**

Stefanou, Spiro E.; Mangel, Marc and Wilen, James E. Information in Agricultural Pest Control. *J. Agr. Econ.*, January 1986, *37*(1), pp. 77–88.

Strauss, John. Does Better Nutrition Raise Farm Productivity? *J. Polit. Econ.*, April 1986, *94*(2), pp. 297–320. **[G: Sierra Leone]**

Strauss, John. Estimating the Determinants of Food Consumption and Caloric Availability in Rural Sierra Leone. **In** *Singh, I.; Squire, L. and Strauss, J., eds.*, 1986, pp. 116–52. **[G: Sierra Leone]**

Strauss, John. The Theory and Comparative Statics of Agricultural Household Models: A General Approach. **In** *Singh, I.; Squire, L. and Strauss, J., eds.*, 1986, pp. 71–91.

Sugai, Yoshihiko and Teixeira Filho, A. R. Impact on Farmers' Decision-Making by Farm Management and Computer Sciences in the Turbulent Economy. **In** *Maunder, A. and Renborg, U., eds.*, 1986, pp. 734–41. **[G: Brazil]**

Swanson, Earl R. Structure of Agriculture and People in Rural Societies: Discussion. **In** *Maunder, A. and Renborg, U., eds.*, 1986, pp. 526–27.

Talpaz, Hovav; Penson, John B., Jr. and Harpaz, Avraham. Activity Selection under Conditions of Risk and Instability: Consideration of Frequency. *J. Agr. Econ.*, January 1986, *37*(1), pp. 59–67.

Taylor, C. Robert. Risk Aversion versus Expected Profit Maximization with a Progressive Income Tax. *Amer. J. Agr. Econ.*, February 1986, *68*(1), pp. 137–43. **[G: U.S.]**

Taylor, Daniel B., et al. Farm-Level Economics of Soil Conservation in the Palouse Area of the Northwest: Comment. *Amer. J. Agr. Econ.*, May 1986, *68*(2), pp. 364–66. **[G: U.S.]**

Taylor, Timothy G.; Drummond, H. Evan and Gomes, Aloisio T. Agricultural Credit Programs and Production Efficiency: An Analysis of Traditional Farming in Southeastern Minas Gerais, Brazil. *Amer. J. Agr. Econ.*, February 1986, *68*(1), pp. 110–19. **[G: Brazil]**

Taylor, Timothy G. and Shonkwiler, J. Scott. Alternative Stochastic Specifications of the Frontier Production Function in the Analysis of Agricultural Credit Programs and Technical Efficiency. *J. Devel. Econ.*, April 1986, *21*(1), pp. 149–60. **[G: Brazil]**

Tisdell, Clem A. Levels of Pest Control and Uncertainty of Benefits. *Australian J. Agr. Econ.*, August/December 1986, *30*(2–3), pp. 157–61.

Tisdell, Clem A. and De Silva, N. T. M. H. Supply-Maximising and Variation-Minimising Replacement Cycles of Perennial Crops and Similar Assets: Theory Illustrated by Coconut Cultivation. *J. Agr. Econ.*, May 1986, *37*(2), pp. 243–51.

Tomic, Dušan. Growing Interdependencies and Uncertainties: Discussion. **In** *Maunder, A. and Renborg, U., eds.*, 1986, pp. 145–48. **[G: Canada; Poland]**

Trapp, James N. A Methodology for Estimating Integrated Forecasting/Decision Model Parameters Using Linear Programming. *Southern J. Agr. Econ.*, December 1986, *18*(2), pp. 247–55. **[G: U.S.]**

Trapp, James N. Investment and Disinvestment Principles with Nonconstant Prices and Varying Firm Size Applied to Beef-Breeding Herds. *Amer. J. Agr. Econ.*, August 1986, *68*(3), pp. 691–703.

Tulchin, Joseph S. The Relationship between Labour and Capital in Rural Argentina, 1880–1914. **In** *di Tella, G. and Platt, D. C. M., eds.*, 1986, pp. 15–38. **[G: Argentina]**

Turner, Michael. English Open Fields and Enclosures: Retardation or Productivity Improvements. *J. Econ. Hist.*, September 1986, *46*(3), pp. 669–92. **[G: U.K.]**

Turvey, C. G. and Driver, H. C. Economic Analysis and Properties of the Risk Aversion Coefficient in Constrained Mathematical Optimization. *Can. J. Agr. Econ.*, March 1986, *34*(1), pp. 125–37.

Tweeten, Luther. Agricultural Structure in a Service Economy. **In** *Maunder, A. and Renborg, U., eds.*, 1986, pp. 542–50. **[G: U.S.]**

Van Kooten, G. C.; Schoney, Richard A. and Hayward, Keith A. An Alternative Approach to the Evaluation of Goal Hierarchies among Farmers. *Western J. Agr. Econ.*, July 1986, *11*(1), pp. 40–49. **[G: Canada]**

Vasavada, Utpal and Chambers, Robert G. Investment in U.S. Agriculture. *Amer. J. Agr. Econ.*, November 1986, *68*(4), pp. 950–60. **[G: U.S.]**

Vuorela, Ulla. No Sugar—No Tea! A Women's

Cooperative in Crisis: Some Experiences from Manyoni Town in Singida Region. **In** *Boesen, J., et al., eds.*, 1986, pp. 253–68. **[G: Tanzania]**

Walker, Thomas S. and Jodha, N. S. How Small Farm Households Adapt to Risk. **In** *Hazell, P.; Pomareda, C. and Valdés, A., eds.*, 1986, pp. 17–34. **[G: India; Tanzania; El Salvador]**

Whitby, Martin and Hanley, Nick. Problems of Agricultural Externalities: A Conceptual Model with Implications for Research. *J. Agr. Econ.*, January 1986, *37*(1), pp. 1–11.

Wilson, John. The Political Economy of Contract Farming. *Rev. Radical Polit. Econ.*, Winter 1986, *18*(4), pp. 47–70. **[G: U.S.]**

Winter, George and Gunjal, Kisan. Computerized Delphi: An Application to Quota Value Determination in the Quebec Dairy Industry. *Can. J. Agr. Econ.*, November 1986, *34*(3), pp. 417–31. **[G: Canada]**

Wise, W. S. The Calculation of Rates of Return on Agricultural Research from Production Functions. *J. Agr. Econ.*, May 1986, *37*(2), pp. 151–61. **[G: EEC]**

Zacharias, Thomas P. and Grube, Arthur H. Integrated Pest Management Strategies for Approximately Optimal Control of Corn Rootworm and Soybean Cyst Nematode. *Amer. J. Agr. Econ.*, August 1986, *68*(3), pp. 704–15. **[G: U.S.]**

Zimet, David J. and Spreen, Thomas H. A Target MOTAD Analysis of a Crop and Livestock Farm in Jefferson County, Florida. *Southern J. Agr. Econ.*, December 1986, *18*(2), pp. 175–85. **[G: U.S.]**

Zulauf, Carl R. Changes in Selected Characteristics of U.S. Farms during the 1970s and Early 1980s: An Investigation Based on Current and Constant Dollar Sales Categories. *Southern J. Agr. Econ.*, July 1986, *18*(1), pp. 113–22. **[G: U.S.]**

717 Land Reform and Land Use

7170 General

Barry, Peter J. and Robison, Lindon J. Economic versus Accounting Rates of Return for Farm Land. *Land Econ.*, November 1986, *62*(4), pp. 388–401. **[G: U.S.]**

van Dijk, G.; Smit, L. and Veerman, C. P. Land Prices and Technological Development. *Europ. Rev. Agr. Econ.*, 1986, *13*(4), pp. 495–515. **[G: Netherlands]**

Ruttan, Vernon W. Assistance to Expand Agricultural Production. *World Devel.*, January 1986, *14*(1), pp. 39–63. **[G: LDCs]**

7171 Land Ownership and Tenure; Land Reform

Abdullah, Abu. Distributional Aspects of Fertilizer Pricing Policy. *Bangladesh Devel. Stud.*, March 1986, *14*(1), pp. 93–100. **[G: Bangladesh]**

Adams, Richard H., Jr. Taxation, Control, and Agrarian Transition in Rural Egypt: A Local-Level View. **In** *Richards, A., ed.*, 1986, pp. 159–82. **[G: Egypt]**

Alston, Lee J. Race Etiquette in the South: The Role of Tenancy. **In** *Uselding, P., ed.*, 1986, pp. 199–211. **[G: U.S.]**

Bandiyono, Suko and Conroy, John D. Employment and Income from Non-agricultural Sources in Rural East Java: Some Preliminary Findings. **In** *Shand, R. T., ed., Vol. 1*, 1986, pp. 327–67. **[G: Indonesia]**

Berck, Peter and Levy, Amnon. The Costs of Equal Land Distribution: The Case of the Israeli Moshavim. *Amer. J. Agr. Econ.*, August 1986, *68*(3), pp. 605–14. **[G: Israel]**

Binswanger, Hans P. and Rosenzweig, Mark R. Behavioural and Material Determinants of Production Relations in Agriculture. *J. Devel. Stud.*, April 1986, *22*(3), pp. 503–39.

Braverman, Avishay and Stiglitz, Joseph E. Cost-Sharing Arrangements under Sharecropping: Moral Hazard, Incentive Flexibility, and Risk. *Amer. J. Agr. Econ.*, August 1986, *68*(3), pp. 642–52.

Braverman, Avishay and Stiglitz, Joseph E. Landlords, Tenants and Technological Innovations. *J. Devel. Econ.*, October 1986, *23*(2), pp. 313–32.

Brown, Keith C. and Brown, Deborah J. Heterogenous Expectations and Farmland Prices: Reply. *Amer. J. Agr. Econ.*, November 1986, *68*(4), pp. 1003–06. **[G: U.S.]**

Brus, Włodzimierz. Postwar Reconstruction and Socio-economic Transformation. **In** *Kaser, M. C. and Radice, E. A., eds.*, 1986, pp. 564–641. **[G: E. Europe]**

Cain, Mead. Landholding and Fertility: A Rejoinder [On the Relationship between Landholding and Fertility]. *Population Stud.*, July 1986, *40*(2), pp. 313–17. **[G: LDCs]**

Cain, Mead. Risk and Fertility: A Reply to Robinson. *Population Stud.*, July 1986, *40*(2), pp. 299–304. **[G: Bangladesh]**

del Castillo, Gustavo and Barajas de Vega, Rosario. U.S.–Mexican Agricultural Relations: The Upper Limits of Linkage Formation. **In** *Browne, W. P. and Hadwiger, D. F., eds.*, 1986, pp. 153–68. **[G: U.S.; Mexico]**

Chaudhry, M. Ghaffar. Landlessness and Rural Poverty in Underdeveloped Countries: Comments. *Pakistan Devel. Rev.*, Autumn 1986, *25*(3), pp. 395–97. **[G: LDCs]**

Commander, Simon and Peek, Peter. Oil Exports, Agrarian Change and the Rural Labor Process: The Ecuadorian Sierra in the 1970s. *World Devel.*, January 1986, *14*(1), pp. 79–96. **[G: Ecuador]**

Conway, A. G. Land Leasing—Findings of a Study in the West Region of the Republic of Ireland. *Irish J. Agr. Econ. Rural Soc.*, 1986, *11*, pp. 1–18. **[G: Ireland]**

Dantwala, M. L. Agrarian Structure and Agrarian Relations in India. **In** *Dantwala, M. L., et al.*, 1986, pp. 59–88. **[G: India]**

Datta, Samar K.; O'Hara, Donald J. and Nugent, Jeffrey B. Choice of Agricultural Tenancy in the Presence of Transaction Costs. *Land Econ.*,

May 1986, 62(2), pp. 145–58. **[G: India]**

Gifford, Adam, Jr. and Kenney, Roy W. Contracting and Sharecropping: An Empirical Test. *Atlantic Econ. J.*, July 1986, 14(2), pp. 81. **[G: U.S.]**

Griffin, Keith. Communal Land Tenure Systems and Their Role in Rural Development. **In** *[Streeten, P.]*, 1986, pp. 165–91. **[G: Selected Countries]**

Hirashima, S. and Muqtada, M. Issues on Employment, Poverty and Hired Labour in South and Southeast Asia: An Introduction. **In** *Hirashima, S. and Muqtada, M., eds.*, 1986, pp. 1–19. **[G: S. Asia; S. E. Asia]**

Hoffman, Philip T. Taxes and Agrarian Life in Early Modern France: Land Sales, 1550–1730. *J. Econ. Hist.*, March 1986, 46(1), pp. 37–55. **[G: France]**

Hossain, Mahabub. A Note on the Trend of Landlessness in Bangladesh. *Bangladesh Devel. Stud.*, June 1986, 14(2), pp. 93–100. **[G: Bangladesh]**

Ka, Chih-Ming and Selden, Mark. Original Accumulation, Equity and Late Industrialization: The Cases of Socialist China and Capitalist Taiwan. *World Devel.*, Oct./Nov. 1986, 14(10/11), pp. 1293–1310. **[G: Taiwan; China]**

Khan, Mahmood Hasan. Landlessness and Rural Poverty in Underdeveloped Countries. *Pakistan Devel. Rev.*, Autumn 1986, 25(3), pp. 271–94. **[G: LDCs]**

Lehmann, David. Sharecropping and the Capitalist Transition in Agriculture: Some Evidence from the Highlands of Ecuador. *J. Devel. Econ.*, October 1986, 23(2), pp. 333–54. **[G: Ecuador]**

Lin, Kuo-Ching and Pasour, E. C., Jr. Heterogenous Expectations and Farmland Prices: Comment. *Amer. J. Agr. Econ.*, November 1986, 68(4), pp. 1000–1002. **[G: U.S.]**

Livingstone, Ian. The Common Property Problem and Pastoralist Economic Behaviour. *J. Devel. Stud.*, October 1986, 23(1), pp. 5–19.

Manzanal, Mabel. El deterioro regional: una manifestación en la producción tabacalera correntina 1976–1981. (With English summary.) *Desarrollo Econ.*, Oct.-Dec. 1986, 26(103), pp. 455–76. **[G: Argentina]**

Nabi, Ijaz. Contracts, Resource Use and Productivity in Sharecropping. *J. Devel. Stud.*, January 1986, 22(2), pp. 429–42. **[G: Pakistan]**

Oakley, Stewart P. Reconstructing Scandinavian Farms 1660–1860: Sources in Denmark, Iceland, Norway and Sweden. *Scand. Econ. Hist. Rev.*, 1986, 34(3), pp. 181–203. **[G: Denmark; Iceland; Norway; Sweden]**

Otsuka, Keijiro. Economics of Share Contract: A Survey in the Light of Theory of Agency–Principal Relationships. (In Japanese. With English summary.) *Econ. Stud. Quart.*, December 1986, 37(4), pp. 351–72.

Owen, Roger. Large Landowners, Agricultural Progress and the State in Egypt, 1800–1970: An Overview with Many Questions. **In** *Richards, A., ed.*, 1986, pp. 69–95. **[G: Egypt]**

Perry, Gregory M., et al. Analyzing Tenure Arrangements and Crop Rotations Using Farm Simulation and Probit Analysis. *Southern J. Agr. Econ.*, December 1986, 18(2), pp. 165–74. **[G: U.S.]**

Quibria, M. G. and Rashid, Salim. Sharecropping in Dual Agrarian Economies: A Synthesis. *Oxford Econ. Pap.*, March 1986, 38(1), pp. 94–111.

Quiggin, John. Common Property, Private Property and Regulation: The Case of Dryland Salinity. *Australian J. Agr. Econ.*, August/December 1986, 30(2–3), pp. 103–17. **[G: Australia]**

Qureshi, Sarfraz Khan. Landlessness and Rural Poverty in Underdeveloped Countries: Comments. *Pakistan Devel. Rev.*, Autumn 1986, 25(3), pp. 398–402. **[G: LDCs]**

Robinson, Warren C. High Fertility as Risk-Insurance. *Population Stud.*, July 1986, 40(2), pp. 289–98. **[G: Bangladesh]**

Stokes, C. Shannon; Schutjer, Wayne A. and Bulatao, Rodolfo A. Is the Relationship between Landholding and Fertility Spurious? A Response. *Population Stud.*, July 1986, 40(2), pp. 305–11. **[G: LDCs]**

Vilas, Carlos M. Sobre la estrategia económica de la Revolución Sandinista. (With English summary.) *Desarrollo Econ.*, Apr.-June 1986, 26(101), pp. 121–42. **[G: Nicaragua]**

Ward, J. T. Compensation for Maori Land Rights. A Case Study of the Otago Tenths. *New Zealand Econ. Pap.*, 1986, 20, pp. 3–16. **[G: New Zealand]**

Wennergren, E. Boyd. Land Redistribution as a Development Strategy in Bangladesh. *Land Econ.*, February 1986, 62(1), pp. 74–82. **[G: Bangladesh]**

Wiradi, Gunawan. Landlessness, Tenancy and Off-Farm Employment in Rural Java: A Study of Twelve Villages. **In** *Shand, R. T., ed., Vol. 1*, 1986, pp. 309–26. **[G: Indonesia]**

Zulauf, Carl R. Changes in Selected Characteristics of U.S. Farms during the 1970s and Early 1980s: An Investigation Based on Current and Constant Dollar Sales Categories. *Southern J. Agr. Econ.*, July 1986, 18(1), pp. 113–22. **[G: U.S.]**

7172 Land Development; Land Use; Irrigation Policy

Abrol, I. P. Salt-Affected Soils: Problems and Prospects in Developing Countries. **In** *Swaminathan, M. S. and Sinha, S. K., eds.*, 1986, pp. 283–305. **[G: Global]**

Alston, Julian M. An Analysis of Growth of U.S. Farmland Prices, 1963–82. *Amer. J. Agr. Econ.*, February 1986, 68(1), pp. 1–9. **[G: U.S.]**

Amigues, Jean-Pierre and Moreaux, Michel. Gravières et vins de Bordeaux. (Gravel Pits and Bordeaux Wines. With English summary.) *Ann. Écon. Statist.*, Jan./Mar. 1986, (1), pp. 75–105.

Andersen, Søren Munk. The Need of Central Water Management in Irrigation Systems. **In** *Nørlund, I.; Cederroth, S. and Gerdin, I., eds.*, 1986, pp. 307–21.

Andrus, Chip. The Economics of Erosion Control in a Subtropical Watershed: Comment. *Land Econ.*, August 1986, *62*(3), pp. 329–30. **[G: Dominican Republic]**

Anthonio, Q. B. O. and Akinyosoye, V. O. The Changing Structure of Nigeria's Agriculture and Prospects for the River Basin Development Reorganisation Programme. **In** *Maunder, A. and Renborg, U., eds.*, 1986, pp. 151–59. **[G: Nigeria]**

Apinantara, Adul and Sriswasdilek, Jerachone. An Evaluation of River Pump and Tank Irrigation Systems in Northeast Thailand. **In** *Easter, W. K., ed.*, 1986, pp. 147–75. **[G: Thailand]**

Basu, Kaushik. The Market for Land: An Analysis of Interim Transactions. *J. Devel. Econ.*, Jan.-Feb. 1986, *20*(1), pp. 163–77. **[G: LDCs]**

Beasley, Steven D.; Workman, William G. and Williams, Nancy A. Estimating Amenity Values of Urban Fringe Farmland: A Contingent Valuation Approach: Note. *Growth Change*, October 1986, *17*(4), pp. 70–78. **[G: U.S.]**

Bond, Gary E. The Farmers' View of New South Wales Rural Planning Policy. *Rev. Marketing Agr. Econ.*, December 1986, *54*(3), pp. 66–70. **[G: Australia]**

Bosch, Darrell J.; Eidman, Vernon R. and Gill, Eric E. Compensating Irrigators for Restricting Water Use: An Expected Utility Analysis. *Western J. Agr. Econ.*, December 1986, *11*(2), pp. 146–55. **[G: U.S.]**

Bossier, Jacques. Human Capital, Technology and Institutions: Discussion. **In** *Maunder, A. and Renborg, U., eds.*, 1986, pp. 434–36.

Bowen, Richard L. and Young, Robert A. Allocative Impacts of Alternative Methods of Charging for Irrigation Water in Egypt. **In** *Easter, W. K., ed.*, 1986, pp. 211–23. **[G: Egypt]**

Breimyer, Harold F. The Asset Devaluation Problem. *Southern J. Agr. Econ.*, July 1986, *18*(1), pp. 79–82.

Brun, André. Agriculture in a Turbulent World Economy: Theoretical Developments: Discussion. **In** *Maunder, A. and Renborg, U., eds.*, 1986, pp. 712–14.

Bryde, John A. The Decline in Paddy Cultivation in a Dry Zone Village of Sri Lanka. **In** *Nørlund, I.; Cederroth, S. and Gerdin, I., eds.*, 1986, pp. 81–116. **[G: Sri Lanka]**

Burt, Oscar R. Econometric Modeling of the Capitalization Formula for Farmland Prices. *Amer. J. Agr. Econ.*, February 1986, *68*(1), pp. 10–26. **[G: U.S.]**

Burt, Oscar R. Farm-Level Economics of Soil Conservation in the Palouse Area of the Northwest: Reply. *Amer. J. Agr. Econ.*, May 1986, *68*(2), pp. 367–69. **[G: U.S.]**

Butcher, Walter R. and Wandschneider, Philip R. Competition between Irrigation and Hydropower in the Pacific Northwest. **In** *Frederick, K. D., ed.*, 1986, pp. 25–66. **[G: U.S.]**

Caswell, Margriet F. and Zilberman, David. The Effects of Well Depth and Land Quality on the Choice of Irrigation Technology. *Amer. J. Agr. Econ.*, November 1986, *68*(4), pp. 798–811. **[G: U.S.]**

Christiansson, Carl. Soil Erosion and Conservation in the Drylands. **In** *Boesen, J., et al., eds.*, 1986, pp. 143–57. **[G: Tanzania]**

Clark, Richard T. and Raitt, Daryll D. Cross Compliance for Erosion Control: Anticipating Efficiency and Distributive Impacts: Comment. *Amer. J. Agr. Econ.*, November 1986, *68*(4), pp. 1013–15. **[G: U.S.]**

Coward, E. Walter, Jr. Direct or Indirect Alternatives for Irrigation Investment and the Creation of Property. **In** *Easter, W. K., ed.*, 1986, pp. 225–44. **[G: Philippines; Indonesia]**

Csáki, Csaba. Land Utilisation and Agricultural Development: The Case of Hungary. **In** *Maunder, A. and Renborg, U., eds.*, 1986, pp. 299–306. **[G: Hungary]**

Danielson, Leon E. and Leitch, Jay A. Private vs Public Economics of Prairie Wetland Allocation. *J. Environ. Econ. Manage.*, March 1986, *13*(1), pp. 81–92. **[G: U.S.]**

Dinar, Ariel and Knapp, Keith C. A Dynamic Analysis of Optimal Water Use under Saline Conditions. *Western J. Agr. Econ.*, July 1986, *11*(1), pp. 58–66. **[G: U.S.]**

Dinar, Ariel; Knapp, Keith C. and Rhoades, James D. Production Function for Cotton with Dated Irrigation Quantities and Qualities. *Water Resources Res.*, October 1986, *22*(11), pp. 1519–25. **[G: U.S.]**

Dinar, Ariel and Yaron, Dan. Treatment Optimization of Municipal Wastewater and Reuse for Regional Irrigation. *Water Resources Res.*, March 1986, *22*(3), pp. 331–38. **[G: Israel]**

Dinehart, Stephen J. Cross-Compliance for Erosion Control: Anticipating Efficiency and Distributive Impacts: Comment. *Amer. J. Agr. Econ.*, May 1986, *68*(2), pp. 349–50. **[G: U.S.]**

Easter, K. William. Irrigation Investment, Technology, and Management Strategies for Development: Introduction and Conceptual Model. **In** *Easter, W. K., ed.*, 1986, pp. 1–11.

Easter, K. William. Irrigation Policies for Future Growth in Agriculture. **In** *Easter, W. K., ed.*, 1986, pp. 245–55.

Easter, K. William and Welsch, Delane E. Implementing Irrigation Projects: Operational and Institutional Problems. **In** *Easter, W. K., ed.*, 1986, pp. 33–56.

Easter, K. William and Welsch, Delane E. Priorities for Irrigation Planning and Investment. **In** *Easter, W. K., ed.*, 1986, pp. 13–32.

Ervin, David E.; Heffernan, William D. and Green, Gary P. Cross Compliance for Erosion Control: Anticipating Efficiency and Distributive Impacts: Reply. *Amer. J. Agr. Econ.*, November 1986, *68*(4), pp. 1016–17. **[G: U.S.]**

Ervin, David E.; Heffernan, William D. and Green, Gary P. Cross-Compliance for Erosion Control: Anticipating Efficiency and Distributive Impacts: Reply. *Amer. J. Agr. Econ.*, May 1986, *68*(2), pp. 351–52.

Evans, Alan W. The Supply of Land: A Pedagogic Comment. *Urban Stud.*, December 1986, *23*(6), pp. 527–30.

Foster, William E., et al. Distributional Welfare Implications of an Irrigation Water Subsidy. *Amer. J. Agr. Econ.*, November 1986, *68*(4), pp. 778–86. **[G: U.S.]**

Hamilton, Joel R. and Gardner, Richard L. Value Added and Secondary Benefits in Regional Projection Evaluation: Irrigation Development in the Snake River Basin. *Ann. Reg. Sci.*, March 1986, *20*(1), pp. 1–11. **[G: U.S.]**

Hammer, Jeffrey S. 'Subsistence First': Farm Allocation Decisions in Senegal. *J. Devel. Econ.*, October 1986, *23*(2), pp. 355–69. **[G: Senegal]**

Harris, Thomas R. and Mapp, Harry P. Stochastic Dominance Comparison of Water-Conserving Irrigation Strategies. *Amer. J. Agr. Econ.*, May 1986, *68*(2), pp. 298–305. **[G: U.S.]**

Harwell, R. Lynn and Rosson, C. Parr, III. Financial Crisis in Agriculture, a Southern Perspective: Discussion. *Southern J. Agr. Econ.*, July 1986, *18*(1), pp. 109–12. **[G: U.S.]**

Hawkins, C. A. The Conservation of Agricultural Land and the Realities of Farm Economics: A Case Study in the Fragmentation of Good Agricultural Land. *Rev. Marketing Agr. Econ.*, December 1986, *54*(3), pp. 57–65. **[G: Australia]**

Hayden, F. Gregory. Rejoinder to David Vail's Comments on National Agricultural Policy [A Geobased National Agricultural Policy for Rural Community Enhancement, Environmental Vitality, and Income Stabilization]. *J. Econ. Issues*, March 1986, *20*(1), pp. 191–201. **[G: U.S.]**

Heimlich, Ralph E. Agricultural Programs and Cropland Conversion, 1975–1981. *Land Econ.*, May 1986, *62*(2), pp. 174–81. **[G: U.S.]**

Hesselberg, Jan. Lack of Maintenance of Irrigation Facilities Experiences from Southern Sri Lanka. **In** *Nørlund, I.; Cederroth, S. and Gerdin, I., eds.*, 1986, pp. 72–80. **[G: Sri Lanka]**

Houston, Jack E., Jr. and Whittlesey, Norman K. Modeling Agricultural Water Markets for Hydropower Production in the Pacific Northwest. *Western J. Agr. Econ.*, December 1986, *11*(2), pp. 221–31. **[G: U.S.]**

Huffaker, Ray G. and Gardner, B. Delworth. The Distribution of Economic Rents Arising from Subsidized Water When Land Is Leased. *Amer. J. Agr. Econ.*, May 1986, *68*(2), pp. 306–12. **[G: U.S.]**

Johnson, Sam H., III. Agricultural Intensification in Thailand: Complementary Role of Infrastructure and Agricultural Policy. **In** *Easter, W. K., ed.*, 1986, pp. 111–27. **[G: Thailand]**

Kamuanga, Mulumba. Irrigation Investment in Africa: Major Issues in the Design and Implementation of Large Schemes. **In** *Maunder, A. and Renborg, U., eds.*, 1986, pp. 424–34. **[G: Africa]**

Kanbur, S. M. Ravi. Risk Aversion and Risk in Irrigation: A Theoretical Analysis. *J. Quant. Econ.*, January 1986, *2*(1), pp. 43–49.

Kasim, Sukor and Najimudin, Mustafa. Evolution of Sources of Income in the Muda Irrigation Scheme, Malaysia, 1972/73 to 1981/82. **In** *Shand, R. T., ed., Vol. 2*, 1986, pp. 21–43. **[G: Malaysia]**

Khachaturov, Tigran S. The Intensification of Land Use. *Prob. Econ.*, February 1986, *28*(10), pp. 43–59. **[G: U.S.S.R.]**

Khan, Qaiser M. Poverty and Household Responses in Rural Bangladesh. **In** *Abegaz, B., ed.*, 1986, pp. 55–71. **[G: Bangladesh]**

Kiker, Clyde and Lynne, Gary. An Economic Model of Soil Conservation: Comment. *Amer. J. Agr. Econ.*, August 1986, *68*(3), pp. 739–42.

Kramer, Randall A. An International Overview of Soil Conservation Policy. **In** *Maunder, A. and Renborg, U., eds.*, 1986, pp. 307–13. **[G: Global]**

Lundqvist, Jan. Irrigation Development and Central Control: Some Features of Sri Lankan Development. **In** *Nørlund, I.; Cederroth, S. and Gerdin, I., eds.*, 1986, pp. 52–71. **[G: Sri Lanka]**

McConnell, Kenneth E. An Economic Model of Soil Conservation: Reply. *Amer. J. Agr. Econ.*, August 1986, *68*(3), pp. 743–44.

McSweeny, William T. and Kramer, Randall A. Soil Conservation with Uncertain Revenues and Input Supplies: Reply. *Amer. J. Agr. Econ.*, May 1986, *68*(2), pp. 361–63.

McSweeny, William T. and Kramer, Randall A. The Integration of Farm Programs for Achieving Soil Conservation and Nonpoint Pollution Control Objectives. *Land Econ.*, May 1986, *62*(2), pp. 159–73.

Mingay, G. E. The Course of Rents in the Age of Malthus. **In** *Turner, M., ed.*, 1986, pp. 85–95. **[G: U.K.]**

Musgrave, Warren F. Should Agricultural Land Be Protected from Sub-division?—Economic Considerations. *Rev. Marketing Agr. Econ.*, December 1986, *54*(3), pp. 70–74. **[G: Australia]**

Mwangi, Wilfred. Human Capital, Technology and Institutions: Discussion. **In** *Maunder, A. and Renborg, U., eds.*, 1986, pp. 436–38.

Nagnju, Dimyati. The Asian Development Bank Approach to Research Design for Irrigation Projects. **In** *Easter, W. K., ed.*, 1986, pp. 177–91. **[G: Thailand]**

Nazarenko, Victor. Land Resources and Distribution of Agricultural Production in the USSR. **In** *Maunder, A. and Renborg, U., eds.*, 1986, pp. 170–77. **[G: U.S.S.R.]**

Nutt, Perry J.; Reed, Michael R. and Skees, Jerry R. Farm Level Corn Acreage Response Estimation. *Southern J. Agr. Econ.*, December 1986, *18*(2), pp. 1–5. **[G: U.S.]**

Oberai, A. S. Land Settlement Policies and Population Redistribution in Developing Countries: Performance, Problems and Prospects. *Int. Lab. Rev.*, Mar.-Apr. 1986, *125*(2), pp. 141–61. **[G: LDCs]**

Odgaard, Rie. Tea—Does It Do the Peasant

Women in Rungwe Any Good? **In** *Boesen, J., et al., eds.*, 1986, pp. 207–24. **[G: Tanzania]**

von Oppen, M.; Rao, Subba K. V. and Engelhardt, T. Alternatives for Improving Small-scale Irrigation Systems in Alfisol Watersheds in India. **In** *Easter, W. K., ed.*, 1986, pp. 73–89. **[G: India]**

Orazem, Peter F. and Miranowski, John. An Indirect Test for the Specification of Expectation Regimes. *Rev. Econ. Statist.*, November 1986, *68*(4), pp. 603–09. **[G: U.S.]**

Orgaz, Luis and Pérez Blanco, José M. La rentabilidad social de la inversión pública en regadio. (With English summary.) *Invest. Ecón.*, September 1986, *10*(3), pp. 545–77. **[G: Spain]**

Palanisami, K. and Easter, K. William. Management, Production, and Rehabilitation in South Indian Irrigation Tanks. **In** *Easter, W. K., ed.*, 1986, pp. 91–109. **[G: India]**

Pardew, Jolie B.; Shane, Ronald L. and Yanagida, John F. Structural Hedonic Prices of Land Parcels in Transition from Agriculture in a Western Community. *Western J. Agr. Econ.*, July 1986, *11*(1), pp. 50–57. **[G: U.S.]**

Perry, James A. and Dixon, Robert K. An Interdisciplinary Approach to Community Resource Management: Preliminary Field Test in Thailand. *J. Devel. Areas*, October 1986, *21*(1), pp. 31–47. **[G: Thailand]**

Peterson, Willis. Land Quality and Prices. *Amer. J. Agr. Econ.*, November 1986, *68*(4), pp. 812–19. **[G: U.S.]**

Pfeifer, Karen. The Development of Commercial Agriculture in Algeria, 1830–1970. **In** *Uselding, P., ed.*, 1986, pp. 271–308. **[G: Algeria]**

Pohoryles, Samuel. Agricultural Emancipation in a Semi-Arid Ecosystem. *Konjunkturpolitik*, 1986, *32*(3), pp. 164–78. **[G: Israel]**

Redclift, Michael. Sustainability and the Market: Survival Strategies on the Bolivian Frontier. *J. Devel. Stud.*, October 1986, *23*(1), pp. 93–105. **[G: Bolivia]**

Renfro, Raymond Z. H. and Sparling, Edward W. Private Tubewell and Canal Water Trade on Pakistan Punjab Watercourses. **In** *Easter, W. K., ed.*, 1986, pp. 193–210. **[G: Pakistan]**

Romero, Carlos. Pressure on Natural Resources: Discussion. **In** *Maunder, A. and Renborg, U., eds.*, 1986, pp. 313–15.

Sarma, P. B. S. Water Resources and Their Role in Food Production. **In** *Swaminathan, M. S. and Sinha, S. K., eds.*, 1986, pp. 171–98. **[G: Global]**

Sawant, S. D. Irrigation and Water Use. **In** *Dantwala, M. L., et al.*, 1986, pp. 107–39. **[G: India]**

Seckler, David W. Institutionalism and Agricultural Development in India. *J. Econ. Issues*, December 1986, *20*(4), pp. 1011–27. **[G: India]**

Sengupta, Jati K. and Khalili, Monsour. Efficiency in Water Allocation under Stochastic Demand. *Appl. Econ.*, January 1986, *18*(1), pp. 37–48. **[G: U.S.]**

Sewastynowicz, James. "Two-Step" Migration and Upward Mobility on the Frontier: The Safety Valve Effect in Pejibaye, Costa Rica. *Econ. Develop. Cult. Change*, July 1986, *34*(4), pp. 731–53. **[G: Costa Rica]**

Shonkwiler, J. Scott and Reynolds, J. E. A Note on the Use of Hedonic Price Models in the Analysis of Land Prices at the Urban Fringe. *Land Econ.*, February 1986, *62*(1), pp. 58–63.

Shortle, James S. and Stefanou, Spiro E. Soil Conservation with Uncertain Revenues and Input Supplies: Comment. *Amer. J. Agr. Econ.*, May 1986, *68*(2), pp. 358–60.

Simons, Scott. Land Fragmentation in Developing Countries: The Optimal Choice and Policy Implications. **In** *Maunder, A. and Renborg, U., eds.*, 1986, pp. 703–12.

Sivanappan, R. K. and Rajagopalan, V. Irrigation Development Needs in India. **In** *Easter, W. K., ed.*, 1986, pp. 57–71. **[G: India]**

Solow, Robert M. Resources and Economic Growth. **In** *Szenberg, M., ed.*, 1986, *1978*, pp. 57–68.

Southgate, Douglas. The Economics of Erosion Control in a Subtropical Watershed: Reply. *Land Econ.*, August 1986, *62*(3), pp. 331–32. **[G: Dominican Republic]**

Spooner, B. The Significance of Desertification. **In** *Swaminathan, M. S. and Sinha, S. K., eds.*, 1986, pp. 337–56.

Stucki, Erwin. Agriculture in a Turbulent World Economy: Theoretical Developments: Discussion. **In** *Maunder, A. and Renborg, U., eds.*, 1986, pp. 714–16.

Swedborg, Erik. Growing Interdependencies and Uncertainties: Discussion. **In** *Maunder, A. and Renborg, U., eds.*, 1986, pp. 184–87. **[G: U.S.S.R.]**

Szabolcs, I. Salt-Affected Soils: Problems and Prospects in Developed Countries. **In** *Swaminathan, M. S. and Sinha, S. K., eds.*, 1986, pp. 307–36. **[G: Selected MDCs]**

Talbot, Lee M. Demographic Factors in Resource Depletion and Environmental Degradation in East African Rangeland. *Population Devel. Rev.*, September 1986, *12*(3), pp. 441–51. **[G: Kenya]**

Taylor, Daniel B., et al. Farm-Level Economics of Soil Conservation in the Palouse Area of the Northwest: Comment. *Amer. J. Agr. Econ.*, May 1986, *68*(2), pp. 364–66. **[G: U.S.]**

Taylor, Donald C. Reduced Pressure Irrigation Investment Economics. *Water Resources Res.*, February 1986, *22*(2), pp. 121–28. **[G: U.S.]**

Therkildsen, Ole. State, Donors and Villagers in Rural Water Management. **In** *Boesen, J., et al., eds.*, 1986, pp. 293–307. **[G: Tanzania]**

Thoroe, Carsten. Pressure on Natural Resources: Discussion. **In** *Maunder, A. and Renborg, U., eds.*, 1986, pp. 315–17.

Trant, Michael. Farm Producers, Past and Present. *Can. J. Agr. Econ.*, June 1986, *33*, pp. 122–44. **[G: Canada]**

Tubpun, Yuavares. The Economics of Small Tank Irrigation in Northeast Thailand. **In** *Easter, W. K., ed.*, 1986, pp. 129–46. **[G: Thailand]**

Tweeten, Luther. A Note on Explaining Farmland Price Changes in the Seventies and Eighties: Research Review. *Agr. Econ. Res.*, Fall 1986, *38*(4), pp. 25–30. [G: U.S.]

Vere, D. T. and Muir, A. M. Pasture Improvement Adoption in South-eastern New South Wales. *Rev. Marketing Agr. Econ.*, April 1986, *54*(1), pp. 19–32. [G: Australia]

Young, Robert A.; Daubert, John T. and Morel-Seytoux, Hubert J. Evaluating Institutional Alternatives for Managing an Interrelated Stream-Aquifer System. *Amer. J. Agr. Econ.*, November 1986, *68*(4), pp. 787–97. [G: U.S.]

718 Rural Economics

7180 Rural Economics

Abdullah, Abu. Distributional Aspects of Fertilizer Pricing Policy. *Bangladesh Devel. Stud.*, March 1986, *14*(1), pp. 93–100. [G: Bangladesh]

Acharya, Meena. Changing Division of Labor and Participation. **In** *Björkman, J. W., ed.*, 1986, pp. 128–40. [G: India; S. Asia]

Adams, John. Peasant Rationality: Individuals, Groups, Cultures. *World Devel.*, Special Issue, Feb. 1986, *14*(2), pp. 273–82.

Adams, Richard H., Jr. Bureaucrats, Peasants and the Dominant Coalition: An Egyptian Case Study. *J. Devel. Stud.*, January 1986, *22*(2), pp. 336–54. [G: Egypt]

Adams, Richard H., Jr. Corrigenda [Bureaucrats, Peasants and the Dominant Coalition: An Egyptian Case Study]. *J. Devel. Stud.*, October 1986, *23*(1), pp. 4. [G: Egypt]

Adams, Richard H., Jr. Taxation, Control, and Agrarian Transition in Rural Egypt: A Local-Level View. **In** *Richards, A., ed.*, 1986, pp. 159–82. [G: Egypt]

Ahn, Byong Man and Boyer, William W. Political Efficacy and Trust in Rural South Korea. *J. Devel. Areas*, July 1986, *20*(4), pp. 439–52. [G: S. Korea]

Alexander, Jennifer. Information and Price Setting in a Rural Javanese Market. *Bull. Indonesian Econ. Stud.*, April 1986, *22*(1), pp. 88–112. [G: Indonesia]

Amougou, Thomas Balla and Ottou, Jean. The Phenomenon of Thrift and Loan Societies. **In** *U.N., Dept. of International Econ. and Social Affairs*, 1986, pp. 95–100. [G: Cameroon]

Antlöv, Hans. Tradition and Transition Harvest and Social Change in Rural Java. **In** *Nørlund, I.; Cederroth, S. and Gerdin, I., eds.*, 1986, pp. 151–70. [G: Indonesia]

Århem, Kaj. Pastoralism under Pressure: The Ngorongoro Maasai. **In** *Boesen, J., et al., eds.*, 1986, pp. 239–51. [G: Tanzania]

Bairagi, Radheshyam. Food Crisis, Nutrition, and Female Children in Rural Bangladesh. *Population Devel. Rev.*, June 1986, *12*(2), pp. 307–15. [G: Bangladesh]

Bandiyono, Suko and Conroy, John D. Employment and Income from Non-agricultural Sources in Rural East Java: Some Preliminary Findings. **In** *Shand, R. T., ed., Vol. 1*, 1986, pp. 327–67. [G: Indonesia]

Bautista, Germelino M. The Structure of Employment Opportunities in Three Philippine Villages. **In** *Hirashima, S. and Muqtada, M., eds.*, 1986, pp. 119–50. [G: Philippines]

Bauwens, A. L. G. M. and Douw, L. Rural Development: A Minor Problem in the Netherlands? *Europ. Rev. Agr. Econ.*, 1986, *13*(3), pp. 343–66. [G: Netherlands]

Berg, George L., Jr. Rural Roads and Bridges—Link to Agriculture. **In** *Chicoine, D. L. and Walzer, N., eds.*, 1986, pp. 167–83. [G: U.S.]

Bivens, W. E., III. Rural Highway Finance: State and Local Innovation. **In** *Chicoine, D. L. and Walzer, N., eds.*, 1986, pp. 199–217. [G: U.S.]

Boss, Adrian. The Justification for Rural Planning. *Rev. Marketing Agr. Econ.*, December 1986, *54*(3), pp. 53–57. [G: Australia]

Boyer, George R. The Poor Law, Migration, and Economic Growth. *J. Econ. Hist.*, June 1986, *46*(2), pp. 419–30. [G: U.K.]

Brand, C. Rural Animation and Self-reliant Development: Experiences in the Isère Region of France. **In** *Bassand, M., et al., eds.*, 1986, pp. 161–74. [G: France]

Brun, André. France: Rural Development in a Dynamic Context. *Europ. Rev. Agr. Econ.*, 1986, *13*(3), pp. 309–26. [G: France]

Bryant, W. Keith. A Portfolio Analysis of Poor Rural Wage—Working Families' Assets and Debts. *Amer. J. Agr. Econ.*, May 1986, *68*(2), pp. 237–45. [G: U.S.]

Bryde, John A. The Decline in Paddy Cultivation in a Dry Zone Village of Sri Lanka. **In** *Nørlund, I.; Cederroth, S. and Gerdin, I., eds.*, 1986, pp. 81–116. [G: Sri Lanka]

Cain, Mead. Risk and Fertility: A Reply to Robinson. *Population Stud.*, July 1986, *40*(2), pp. 299–304. [G: Bangladesh]

Caldwell, John C.; Reddy, P. H. and Caldwell, Pat. Periodic High Risk as a Cause of Fertility Decline in a Changing Rural Environment: Survival Strategies in the 1980–1983 South Indian Drought. *Econ. Develop. Cult. Change*, July 1986, *34*(4), pp. 677–701. [G: India]

Cantarero, Rodrigo F. and Colburn, Forrest D. The Structural Basis of Rural Employment in Postrevolutionary Nicaragua. *J. Devel. Areas*, October 1986, *21*(1), pp. 49–61. [G: Nicaragua]

Castillo, L.; Gascon, F. and Jayasuriya, S. K. Off-Farm Employment of Farm Households in Laguna, Philippines. **In** *Shand, R. T., ed., Vol. 2*, 1986, pp. 133–46. [G: Philippines]

Ceña, Felisa and Fernandez-Cavada, Jose Luis. Spain: Rural Development under Rapid Depopulation. *Europ. Rev. Agr. Econ.*, 1986, *13*(3), pp. 415–32. [G: Spain]

Chadha, G. K. The Off-Farm Economic Structure of Agriculturally Growing Regions: A Study of Indian Punjab. **In** *Shand, R. T., ed., Vol. 2*, 1986, pp. 147–75. [G: India]

Chalamwong, Yongyuth. Rural Labour Supply in Thailand: A Recent Experience. **In** *Shand, R. T., ed., Vol. 1,* 1986, pp. 257–71. **[G: Thailand]**

Charsombut, Pradit. The Potential for Increases in Income and Employment in Thai Rural Household Manufacturing Enterprises. **In** *Shand, R. T., ed., Vol. 1,* 1986, pp. 231–55. **[G: Thailand]**

Chaudhry, M. Ghaffar. Landlessness and Rural Poverty in Underdeveloped Countries: Comments. *Pakistan Devel. Rev.*, Autumn 1986, *25*(3), pp. 395–97. **[G: LDCs]**

Chicoine, David L. and Walzer, Norman. Financing Local Infrastructure in Nonmetropolitan Areas: Introduction. **In** *Chicoine, D. L. and Walzer, N., eds.*, 1986, pp. 1–15. **[G: U.S.]**

Chicoine, David L. and Walzer, Norman. Financing Rural Roads in the Midwest. **In** *Chicoine, D. L. and Walzer, N., eds.*, 1986, pp. 33–51. **[G: U.S.]**

Chowdhury, Nuimuddin. Improved and New Products in Rural Industries: Implications for the Expansion of Demand and Employment. **In** *Islam, R. and Muqtada, M., eds.*, 1986, pp. 169–95. **[G: Bangladesh]**

Chulasai, Luechai; Bhekasut, Suwarat and Shusuwan, Thongchai. Family Labour, Hired Labour and Employment Linkages in Rural Thailand. **In** *Hirashima, S. and Muqtada, M., eds.*, 1986, pp. 151–75. **[G: Thailand]**

Clay, Edward J. Rural Public Works and Food-for-Work: A Survey. *World Devel.*, Oct./Nov. 1986, *14*(10/11), pp. 1237–52. **[G: LDCs]**

Cloke, Paul and Edwards, Gareth. Rurality in England and Wales 1981: A Replication of the 1971 Index. *Reg. Stud.*, August 1986, *20*(4), pp. 289–306. **[G: U.K.]**

Commander, Simon and Peek, Peter. Oil Exports, Agrarian Change and the Rural Labor Process: The Ecuadorian Sierra in the 1970s. *World Devel.*, January 1986, *14*(1), pp. 79–96. **[G: Ecuador]**

Condominas, Georges. Ritual Technology in Mnong Gar Swidden Agriculture. **In** *Nørlund, I.; Cederroth, S. and Gerdin, I., eds.*, 1986, pp. 28–46. **[G: Vietnam]**

Conway, A. G. and O'Hara, P. Education of Farm Children. *Econ. Soc. Rev.*, July 1986, *17*(4), pp. 253–76. **[G: Ireland]**

Cook, Charles D. From Bull Path to Boulevard. **In** *Chicoine, D. L. and Walzer, N., eds.*, 1986, pp. 77–92. **[G: U.S.]**

Cook, Scott. The 'Managerial' vs. the 'Labor' Function, Capital Accumulation, and the Dynamics of Simple Commodity Production in Rural Oaxaca, Mexico. **In** *Greenfield, S. M. and Strickon, A., eds.*, 1986, pp. 54–95. **[G: Mexico]**

Cook, Scott and Binford, Leigh. Petty Commodity Production, Capital Accumulation, and Peasant Differentiation: Lenin vs. Chayanov in Rural Mexico. *Rev. Radical Polit. Econ.*, Winter 1986, *18*(4), pp. 1–31. **[G: Mexico]**

Corner, Lorraine. The Prospects for Off-Farm Employment as an Anti-poverty Strategy among Malaysian Paddy Farm Households: Macro and Micro Views. **In** *Shand, R. T., ed., Vol. 2,* 1986, pp. 45–67. **[G: Malaysia]**

Dantwala, M. L. and Barmeda, J. N. Rural Development: Approaches and Issues. **In** *Dantwala, M. L., et al.*, 1986, pp. 460–78. **[G: India]**

De Benedictis, Michele. Italy: Fragmentation of Policies and Research Effort. *Europ. Rev. Agr. Econ.*, 1986, *13*(3), pp. 327–41. **[G: Italy]**

Deb, Nibaran Chandra. Consumption Pattern in Rural Bangladesh. *Bangladesh Devel. Stud.*, March 1986, *14*(1), pp. 1–28. **[G: Bangladesh]**

Deere, Carmen Diana. Agrarian Reform, Peasant and Rural Production, and the Organization of Production in the Transition to Socialism. **In** *Fagen, R. R.; Deere, C. D. and Coraggio, J. L., eds.*, 1986, pp. 97–142. **[G: Selected LDCs]**

Egger, Philippe. Banking for the Rural Poor: Lessons from Some Innovative Savings and Credit Schemes. *Int. Lab. Rev.*, July-Aug. 1986, *125*(4), pp. 447–62. **[G: Bangladesh; India; Nepal; Zimbabwe]**

Elahi, Mahboob and Khan, Mahmud Jameel. Rural Labour Market with Special Reference to Hired Labour in Pakistan's Punjab. **In** *Hirashima, S. and Muqtada, M., eds.*, 1986, pp. 75–118. **[G: Pakistan]**

Epstein, T. Scarlett. Cracks in the Wall: Changing Gender Roles in Rural South Asia. **In** *Björkman, J. W., ed.*, 1986, pp. 17–32. **[G: S. Asia]**

Eswaran, Mukesh and Kotwal, Ashok. Access to Capital and Agrarian Production Organisation. *Econ. J.*, June 1986, *96*(382), pp. 482–98.

Evans, David B. The Credit Market and Rural Development: A Model of a Land Resettlement Scheme. *J. Devel. Econ.*, December 1986, *24*(2), pp. 317–29.

Evans, Scott F. and Lewis, Philip E. T. Demand, Supply and Adjustment of Farm Labour in Australia. *Australian Econ. Pap.*, December 1986, *25*(47), pp. 236–46. **[G: Australia]**

Fabella, Raul V. Rural Non-Farm Employment in the Philippines: Composition, Growth and Seasonality. **In** *Shand, R. T., ed., Vol. 2,* 1986, pp. 69–97. **[G: Philippines]**

Gangopadhyay, Shubhashis and Sengupta, Kunal. Interlinkages in Rural Markets. *Oxford Econ. Pap.*, March 1986, *38*(1), pp. 112–21.

Ghosh, Dipak. Monetary Dualism in Developing Economies. *Écon. Soc.*, February 1986, *20*(2), pp. 19–30. **[G: LDCs]**

Giessübel, Rainer and Spitzer, Hartwig. Fed. Rep. of Germany: Rural Development under Federal Government. *Europ. Rev. Agr. Econ.*, 1986, *13*(3), pp. 283–307. **[G: W. Germany]**

Gravers, Mikael. On the Systematic Character of the Thai State: The Properties of Precapitalist Class Relations and the Effects of Capitalist Penetration. **In** *Nørlund, I.; Cederroth, S. and Gerdin, I., eds.*, 1986, pp. 280–306. **[G: Thailand]**

Greeley, Martin. Rural Energy Technology Assessment: A Sri Lankan Case Study. *World Devel.*, December 1986, *14*(12), pp. 1411–21. **[G: Sri Lanka]**

Green, Gary P. Capital Flows in Rural Areas: An Analysis of the Impact of Banking Centralization on Lending Policies. *Soc. Sci. Quart.*, June 1986, *67*(2), pp. 365–78. **[G: U.S.]**

Greer, Joel and Thorbecke, Erik. A Methodology for Measuring Food Poverty Applied to Kenya. *J. Devel. Econ.*, November 1986, *24*(1), pp. 59–74. **[G: Kenya]**

Greer, Joel and Thorbecke, Erik. Food Poverty Profile Applied to Kenyan Smallholders. *Econ. Develop. Cult. Change*, October 1986, *35*(1), pp. 115–41. **[G: Kenya]**

Guttman, Joel M. and Haruvi, Nava. Cooperation and Part-Time Farming in the Israeli Moshav. *Amer. J. Agr. Econ.*, February 1986, *68*(1), pp. 77–87. **[G: Israel]**

Haggis, Jane, et al. By the Teeth: A Critical Examination of James Scott's *The Moral Economy of the Peasant. World Devel.*, December 1986, *14*(12), pp. 1435–55. **[G: India]**

Hamlett, Cathy A.; Pautsch, Gregory R. and Baumel, C. Phillip. County Traffic Patterns and Prospects for Change. **In** *Chicoine, D. L. and Walzer, N., eds.*, 1986, pp. 93–108. **[G: U.S.]**

Harris, G. T. and Vitols, M. Unemployment in Australian Rural Towns. *Australian Bull. Lab.*, December 1986, *13*(1), pp. 51–60. **[G: Australia]**

Hart, Gillian. Exclusionary Labour Arrangements: Interpreting Evidence on Employment Trends in Rural Java. *J. Devel. Stud.*, July 1986, *22*(4), pp. 681–96. **[G: Java]**

Hart, Gillian. Interlocking Transactions: Obstacles, Precursors or Instruments of Agrarian Capitalism. *J. Devel. Econ.*, September 1986, *23*(1), pp. 177–203.

Havnevik, Kjell J. A Resource Overlooked—Crafts and Small-scale Industries. **In** *Boesen, J., et al., eds.*, 1986, pp. 269–91. **[G: Tanzania]**

Hayden, F. Gregory. Rejoinder to David Vail's Comments on National Agricultural Policy [A Geobased National Agricultural Policy for Rural Community Enhancement, Environmental Vitality, and Income Stabilization]. *J. Econ. Issues*, March 1986, *20*(1), pp. 191–201. **[G: U.S.]**

Herath, H. M. G. An Exploratory Study of Off-Farm Employment and Incomes in Sri Lanka. **In** *Shand, R. T., ed., Vol. 2*, 1986, pp. 209–33. **[G: Sri Lanka]**

Higgins, James. The Distribution of Income on Irish Farms. *Irish J. Agr. Econ. Rural Soc.*, 1986, *11*, pp. 73–91. **[G: Ireland]**

Hirashima, S. and Muqtada, M. Issues on Employment, Poverty and Hired Labour in South and Southeast Asia: An Introduction. **In** *Hirashima, S. and Muqtada, M., eds.*, 1986, pp. 1–19. **[G: S. Asia; S. E. Asia]**

Hodge, Ian D. The Scope and Context of Rural Development. *Europ. Rev. Agr. Econ.*, 1986, *13*(3), pp. 271–82. **[G: EEC]**

Hodge, Ian D. and Whitby, Martin. The U.K.: Rural Development, Issues and Analysis. *Europ. Rev. Agr. Econ.*, 1986, *13*(3), pp. 391–413. **[G: U.K.]**

Hossain, Mahabub. Employment Generation through Cottage Industries: Potentials and Constraints. **In** *Islam, R. and Muqtada, M., eds.*, 1986, pp. 119–50. **[G: Bangladesh]**

Islam, Rizwanul. Non-farm Employment in Rural Asia: Issues and Evidence. **In** *Shand, R. T., ed., Vol. 1*, 1986, pp. 153–73. **[G: Bangladesh; Sri Lanka; Pakistan; Thailand; India]**

Islam, Rizwanul. Rural Unemployment and Underemployment: A Review. **In** *Islam, R. and Muqtada, M., eds.*, 1986, pp. 11–20. **[G: Bangladesh]**

Iyengar, N. S. and Suryanarayana, M. H. On Growth and Equity in Indian Planning during 1962–62 to 1973–74. *Indian Econ. J.*, Apr.-June 1986, *33*(4), pp. 53–83. **[G: India]**

Jones, Barclay Gibbs. Urban Support for Rural Development in Kenya. *Econ. Geogr.*, July 1986, *62*(3), pp. 201–14. **[G: Kenya]**

Kasim, Sukor and Najimudin, Mustafa. Evolution of Sources of Income in the Muda Irrigation Scheme, Malaysia, 1972/73 to 1981/82. **In** *Shand, R. T., ed., Vol. 2*, 1986, pp. 21–43. **[G: Malaysia]**

Kasryno, Faisal. Impact of Off-Farm Employment on Agricultural Labour Absorption and Wages in Indonesia. **In** *Shand, R. T., ed., Vol. 1*, 1986, pp. 273–307. **[G: Indonesia]**

Kemp, Sharon F. How Women's Work Is Perceived: Hunger or Humiliation. **In** *Björkman, J. W., ed.*, 1986, pp. 84–99. **[G: India]**

Khan, Mahmood Hasan. Landlessness and Rural Poverty in Underdeveloped Countries. *Pakistan Devel. Rev.*, Autumn 1986, *25*(3), pp. 271–94. **[G: LDCs]**

Khan, Qaiser M. Poverty and Household Responses in Rural Bangladesh. **In** *Abegaz, B., ed.*, 1986, pp. 55–71. **[G: Bangladesh]**

Khuda, B. Off-Farm Employment in Traditional and Developed Villages of Bangladesh. **In** *Shand, R. T., ed., Vol. 2*, 1986, pp. 193–207. **[G: Bangladesh]**

Kikuchi, Masao. Growing Impact of Off-Farm Employment on a Rural Economy: Changes in Labour Utilization and Income Earning Structure in a Philippine Rice Village. **In** *Shand, R. T., ed., Vol. 2*, 1986, pp. 99–131. **[G: Philippines]**

Kim, Sung-Hoon. Rural Savings Mobilization: The Asian Experience. **In** *U.N., Dept. of International Econ. and Social Affairs*, 1986, pp. 50–60. **[G: Asia]**

Kubo, Yuji. Urban Concentration and Rural Growth: A Two-Sector Analysis. *J. Reg. Sci.*, August 1986, *26*(3), pp. 379–93.

Larsen, Melvin B. Rural Transportation: A Look at the Future. **In** *Chicoine, D. L. and Walzer, N., eds.*, 1986, pp. 219–33. **[G: U.S.]**

Lehmann, David. Sharecropping and the Capitalist Transition in Agriculture: Some Evidence from the Highlands of Ecuador. *J. Devel. Econ.*, October 1986, *23*(2), pp. 333–54. **[G: Ecuador]**

Leite, Pedro Sisnando. Forces That Will Shape Future Rural Development: The Case of Northeastern Brazil. **In** *Maunder, A. and Renborg, U., eds.*, 1986, pp. 60–69. **[G: Brazil]**

Lele, Uma. Women and Structural Transformation. *Econ. Develop. Cult. Change,* January 1986, *34*(2), pp. 195–221. **[G: LDCs]**

Livingstone, Ian. The Common Property Problem and Pastoralist Economic Behaviour. *J. Devel. Stud.*, October 1986, *23*(1), pp. 5–19.

London, Bruce and Anderson, Kristine L. Rural–Urban Hierarchy and National Development: The Role of Elites in the Distribution of Scarce Resources to the Thai Hinterland. *Soc. Sci. Quart.*, September 1986, *67*(3), pp. 545–60. **[G: Thailand]**

Luhr, David R. Economics of Pavement Strategies for Rural Roads. **In** *Chicoine, D. L. and Walzer, N., eds.*, 1986, pp. 109–25.

Matthews, Alan. Ireland: Rural Development in Agrarian Society. *Europ. Rev. Agr. Econ.*, 1986, *13*(3), pp. 367–89. **[G: Ireland]**

Mazumdar, Dipak and Sawit, M. Husein. Trends in Rural Wages, West Java, 1977–83. *Bull. Indonesian Econ. Stud.*, December 1986, *22*(3), pp. 93–105. **[G: Indonesia]**

McIntosh, James; Satchell, Stephen E. and Nasim, Anjum. Differential Mortality in Rural Bangladesh. *J. Appl. Econometrics,* October 1986, *1*(4), pp. 345–53. **[G: Bangladesh]**

Mohtadi, Hamid. Rural Stratification, Rural to Urban Migration, and Urban Inequality: Evidence from Iran. *World Devel.*, June 1986, *14*(6), pp. 713–25. **[G: Iran]**

Moock, Peter R. and Leslie, Joanne. Childhood Malnutrition and Schooling in the Terai Region of Nepal. *J. Devel. Econ.*, Jan.-Feb. 1986, *20*(1), pp. 33–52. **[G: Nepal]**

Morales, Edmundo. Coca and Cocaine Economy and Social Change in the Andes of Peru. *Econ. Develop. Cult. Change,* October 1986, *35*(1), pp. 143–61. **[G: Peru]**

Muqtada, M. Poverty and Inequality: Trends and Causes. **In** *Islam, R. and Muqtada, M., eds.*, 1986, pp. 41–60. **[G: Bangladesh]**

Muqtada, M. and Alam, M. Mustafa. Hired Labour and Rural Labour Market in Bangladesh. **In** *Hirashima, S. and Muqtada, M., eds.*, 1986, pp. 21–73. **[G: Bangladesh]**

Nair, Kusum. Impact of New Technologies in Agriculture in South Asia. **In** *Björkman, J. W., ed.*, 1986, pp. 53–59. **[G: S. Asia]**

Newby, Howard. Locality and Rurality: The Restructuring of Rural Social Relations. *Reg. Stud.*, June 1986, *20*(3), pp. 209–15. **[G: U.K.]**

Nishimura, Hiroyuki. The Rural–Urban Balance in Rural Development. **In** *Maunder, A. and Renborg, U., eds.*, 1986, pp. 513–25. **[G: LDCs; MDCs]**

Nolan, Peter and Paine, Suzanne. Towards an Appraisal of the Impact of Rural Reform in China, 1978–85. *Cambridge J. Econ.*, March 1986, *10*(1), pp. 83–99. **[G: China]**

Oakley, Stewart P. Reconstructing Scandinavian Farms 1660–1860: Sources in Denmark, Iceland, Norway and Sweden. *Scand. Econ. Hist. Rev.*, 1986, *34*(3), pp. 181–203. **[G: Denmark; Iceland; Norway; Sweden]**

Oberai, A. S. Land Settlement Policies and Population Redistribution in Developing Countries: Performance, Problems and Prospects. *Int. Lab. Rev.*, Mar.-Apr. 1986, *125*(2), pp. 141–61. **[G: LDCs]**

Odie-Ali, Stella. Women in Agriculture: The Case of Guyana. *Soc. Econ. Stud.*, June 1986, *35*(2), pp. 241–89. **[G: Guyana]**

Olson, Mancur. The Exploitation and Subsidization of Agriculture in Developing and Developed Countries. **In** *Maunder, A. and Renborg, U., eds.*, 1986, pp. 49–59.

Onchan, Tongroj and Chalamwong, Yongyuth. Rural Off-Farm Income and Employment in Thailand: Current Evidence, Future Trends and Implications. **In** *Shand, R. T., ed., Vol. 1*, 1986, pp. 199–230. **[G: Thailand]**

Oshima, Harry T. Off-Farm Employment and Incomes in Postwar East Asian Growth. **In** *Shand, R. T., ed., Vol. 1*, 1986, pp. 25–74. **[G: Japan; Taiwan; S. Korea]**

Oshima, Harry T. The Transition from an Agricultural to an Industrial Economy in East Asia. *Econ. Develop. Cult. Change,* July 1986, *34*(4), pp. 783–809. **[G: Japan; Taiwan; S. Korea]**

Osmani, S. R. and Deb, Nibaran Chandra. Demand for Products of Rural Industries. **In** *Islam, R. and Muqtada, M., eds.*, 1986, pp. 151–67. **[G: Bangladesh]**

Otsuka, Keijiro; Kikuchi, Masao and Hayami, Yujiro. Community and Market in Contract Choice: The Jeepney in the Philippines. *Econ. Develop. Cult. Change,* January 1986, *34*(2), pp. 279–98. **[G: Philippines]**

Pal, Padmaja; Chakravarty, S. R. and Bhattacharya, N. Poverty in Rural India: A Decomposition Analysis. *Indian Econ. Rev.*, July-Dec. 1986, *21*(2), pp. 149–84. **[G: India]**

Panayotou, Theodore. Investment, Growth and Employment in Thailand: From Agriculture to Rural Industry. **In** *Nemetz, P. N., ed.*, 1986, pp. 117–58. **[G: Thailand]**

Panda, Manoj Kumar. Fixing Income and Price Targets for the Poor in India. *J. Devel. Econ.*, March 1986, *20*(2), pp. 287–97. **[G: India]**

Panpiemras, Kosit and Phongpaichit, Pasuk. Policy Guidelines for Human Resource Development and Employment Generation in Thailand. **In** *Shand, R. T., ed., Vol. 1*, 1986, pp. 175–98. **[G: Thailand]**

Penny, N. J. H. Migrant Labour and the South African Gold Mining Industry: A Study of Remittances. *S. Afr. J. Econ.*, September 1986, *54*(3), pp. 290–306. **[G: S. Africa]**

Perry, James A. and Dixon, Robert K. An Interdisciplinary Approach to Community Resource Management: Preliminary Field Test in Thailand. *J. Devel. Areas,* October 1986, *21*(1), pp. 31–47. **[G: Thailand]**

Quibria, M. G. and Rashid, Salim. Sharecropping in Dual Agrarian Economies: A Synthesis. *Oxford Econ. Pap.*, March 1986, *38*(1), pp. 94–111.

Qureshi, Sarfraz Khan. Landlessness and Rural Poverty in Underdeveloped Countries: Comments. *Pakistan Devel. Rev.*, Autumn 1986, *25*(3), pp. 398–402. **[G: LDCs]**

Radwan, Samir. Rural Labor Markets in Egypt. **In** *Richards, A., ed.*, 1986, pp. 265–82. **[G: Egypt]**

Rahman, Atiq. Poverty Alleviation and the Most Disadvantaged Groups in Bangladesh Agriculture. *Bangladesh Devel. Stud.*, March 1986, *14*(1), pp. 29–58. **[G: Bangladesh]**

Rahman, K. M. Technology, Productivity and Employment in Rural Industries. **In** *Islam, R. and Muqtada, M., eds.*, 1986, pp. 197–207. **[G: Bangladesh]**

Rahman, Rushidan Islam. Time Budget Studies and the Measurement of Time Spent on Child Care by Rural Women in Bangladesh: A Note on Methodology. *Bangladesh Devel. Stud.*, March 1986, *14*(1), pp. 107–16. **[G: Bangladesh]**

Rajaraman, Indira. Offered Wage and Recipient Attribute: Wage Functions for Rural Labour in India. *J. Devel. Econ.*, November 1986, *24*(1), pp. 179–95. **[G: India]**

Rao, J. Mohan. Agriculture in Recent Development Theory. *J. Devel. Econ.*, June 1986, *22*(1), pp. 41–86.

Rao, M. S. A. Migration, Agricultural Development, and Deprivation: A Case Study of a Tribal Situation in India. **In** *Glazier, I. A. and De Rosa, L., eds.*, 1986, pp. 58–75. **[G: India]**

Rayappa, P. Hanumantha. Some Dimensions of Off-Farm Employment in Rural Karnataka, India. **In** *Shand, R. T., ed., Vol. 2*, 1986, pp. 177–92. **[G: India]**

Redclift, Michael. Sustainability and the Market: Survival Strategies on the Bolivian Frontier. *J. Devel. Stud.*, October 1986, *23*(1), pp. 93–105. **[G: Bolivia]**

Reid, J. Norman and Sullivan, Patrick J. The Rural Infrastructure Problem: A National Perspective. **In** *Chicoine, D. L. and Walzer, N., eds.*, 1986, pp. 17–32. **[G: U.S.]**

Rietveld, Piet. Non-agricultural Activities and Income Distribution in Rural Java. *Bull. Indonesian Econ. Stud.*, December 1986, *22*(3), pp. 106–17. **[G: Indonesia]**

Roberts, Brian. Atlas of Industrializing Britain 1780–1914: Rural Settlements. **In** *Langton, J. and Morris, R. J., eds.*, 1986, pp. 54–59. **[G: U.K.]**

Robinson, Warren C. High Fertility as Risk-Insurance. *Population Stud.*, July 1986, *40*(2), pp. 289–98. **[G: Bangladesh]**

Rohrer, Wayne C. Developing Third World Farming: Conflict between Modern Imperatives and Traditional Ways. *Econ. Develop. Cult. Change*, January 1986, *34*(2), pp. 299–314. **[G: Philippines; LDCs]**

Salvatore, Ricardo D. Control del trabajo y discriminación: el sistema de contratistas en Mendoza, Argentina, 1880–1920. (With English summary.) *Desarrollo Econ.*, July-Sept. 1986, *26*(102), pp. 229–53. **[G: Argentina]**

Schildkrout, Enid. Children as Entrepreneurs: Case Studies from Kano, Nigeria. **In** *Greenfield, S. M. and Strickon, A., eds.*, 1986, pp. 195–223. **[G: Nigeria]**

Scholer, Charles. Cost-Saving Techniques. **In** *Chicoine, D. L. and Walzer, N., eds.*, 1986, pp. 185–97. **[G: U.S.]**

Sevilla Guzman, E. Structure of Agriculture and People in Rural Societies: Discussion. **In** *Maunder, A. and Renborg, U., eds.*, 1986, pp. 527–29.

Sewastynowicz, James. "Two-Step" Migration and Upward Mobility on the Frontier: The Safety Valve Effect in Pejibaye, Costa Rica. *Econ. Develop. Cult. Change*, July 1986, *34*(4), pp. 731–53. **[G: Costa Rica]**

Shahabuddin, Quazi; Mestelman, Stuart and Feeny, David. Peasant Behaviour towards Risk and Socio-Economic and Structural Characteristics of Farm Households in Bangladesh. *Oxford Econ. Pap.*, March 1986, *38*(1), pp. 122–30. **[G: Bangladesh]**

Shand, Richard T. Off-Farm Employment in the Development of Rural Asia: Issues. **In** *Shand, R. T., ed., Vol. 1*, 1986, pp. 1–24. **[G: Asia]**

Shand, Richard T. and Chew, T. A. Off-Farm Employment in the Kemubu Project in Kelantan, Malaysia. **In** *Shand, R. T., ed., Vol. 2*, 1986, pp. 1–20. **[G: Malaysia]**

Shand, Richard T. and Teck-Ann, Chew. The Off-Farm Labour Supply of Padi Farmers in Kelantan, Malaysia. *Singapore Econ. Rev.*, October 1986, *31*(2), pp. 23–33. **[G: Malaysia]**

Shivamaggi, H. B. Credit for Agricultural and Rural Development. **In** *Dantwala, M. L., et al.*, 1986, pp. 270–307. **[G: India]**

Singh, Inderjit; Squire, Lyn and Strauss, John. A Survey of Agricultural Household Models: Recent Findings and Policy Implications. *World Bank Econ. Rev.*, September 1986, *1*(1), pp. 149–79. **[G: Selected Countries]**

Smale, Melinda; Saupe, William E. and Salant, Priscilla. Farm Family Characteristics and the Viability of Farm Households in Wisconsin, Mississippi, and Tennessee. *Agr. Econ. Res.*, Spring 1986, *38*(2), pp. 11–27. **[G: U.S.]**

Smith, Hilary H. The Choice of Part-time Farming in Texas. *Fed. Res. Bank Dallas Econ. Rev.*, September 1986, pp. 10–19. **[G: U.S.]**

Smith, Pamela. "Not Enough Hours, Our Accountant Tells Me": Trends in Children's, Women's and Men's Involvement in Canadian Agriculture. *Can. J. Agr. Econ.*, June 1986, *33*, pp. 161–95. **[G: Canada]**

Stiglitz, Joseph E. The New Development Economics. *World Devel.*, Special Issue, Feb. 1986, *14*(2), pp. 257–65.

Swanson, Earl R. Structure of Agriculture and People in Rural Societies: Discussion. **In** *Maunder, A. and Renborg, U., eds.*, 1986, pp. 526–27.

TenEyck, Thomas E. and Lebo, Dennis E. Pennsylvania's Agricultural Access Study. **In** *Chicoine, D. L. and Walzer, N., eds.*, 1986, pp. 159–66. **[G: U.S.]**

Thakur, D. S. Estimation of Poverty in India—An Empirical Investigation. *Margin,* October 1986, *19*(1), pp. 66–80. **[G: India]**

Therkildsen, Ole. State, Donors and Villagers in Rural Water Management. **In** *Boesen, J., et al., eds.*, 1986, pp. 293–307. **[G: Tanzania]**

Thiele, Graham. The State and Rural Development in Tanzania: The Village Administration as a Political Field. *J. Devel. Stud.*, April 1986, *22*(3), pp. 540–57. **[G: Tanzania]**

Timmer, C. Peter. *Redesigning Rural Development* from a Food Policy Perspective: Review Article. *Econ. Develop. Cult. Change,* July 1986, *34*(4), pp. 855–60.

Tulchin, Joseph S. The Relationship between Labour and Capital in Rural Argentina, 1880–1914. **In** *di Tella, G. and Platt, D. C. M., eds.*, 1986, pp. 15–38. **[G: Argentina]**

Ulack, Richard. Ties to Origin, Remittances, and Mobility: Evidence from Rural and Urban Areas in the Philippines. *J. Devel. Areas,* April 1986, *20*(3), pp. 339–55. **[G: Philippines]**

Uner, Sunday. Migration and Labor Transformation in Rural Turkey. **In** *Richards, A., ed.*, 1986, pp. 225–64. **[G: Turkey]**

Uppal, J. S. Income Distribution and Poverty in Indonesia. *J. Econ. Devel.*, December 1986, *11*(2), pp. 177–96. **[G: Indonesia]**

Venkatesan, V. Rural Development Administration. **In** *Dantwala, M. L., et al.*, 1986, pp. 479–510. **[G: India]**

Voss, Paul R. Demographics and Rural Roads. **In** *Chicoine, D. L. and Walzer, N., eds.*, 1986, pp. 53–76. **[G: U.S.]**

Vuorela, Ulla. No Sugar—No Tea! A Women's Cooperative in Crisis: Some Experiences from Manyoni Town in Singida Region. **In** *Boesen, J., et al., eds.*, 1986, pp. 253–68. **[G: Tanzania]**

Whitby, Martin. Rural Development in Europe: Some Surveys of Literature: An Editorial Post-script. *Europ. Rev. Agr. Econ.*, 1986, *13*(3), pp. 433–38. **[G: EEC]**

Wiradi, Gunawan. Landlessness, Tenancy and Off-Farm Employment in Rural Java: A Study of Twelve Villages. **In** *Shand, R. T., ed., Vol. 1*, 1986, pp. 309–26. **[G: Indonesia]**

Wrigley, E. A. Men on the Land and Men in the Countryside: Employment in Agriculture in Early-Nineteenth-Century England. **In** *[Laslett, P.]*, 1986, pp. 295–336. **[G: U.K.]**

Yotopoulos, Pan A. and Mergos, George J. Family Labor Allocation in the Agricultural Household. *Food Res. Inst. Stud.*, 1986, *20*(1), pp. 87–104. **[G: Philippines]**

Zulauf, Carl R. Changes in Selected Characteristics of U.S. Farms during the 1970s and Early 1980s: An Investigation Based on Current and Constant Dollar Sales Categories. *Southern J. Agr. Econ.*, July 1986, *18*(1), pp. 113–22. **[G: U.S.]**

720 Natural Resources

7200 General

Georgescu-Roegen, Nicholas. Man and Production. **In** *Baranzini, M. and Scazzieri, R., eds.*, 1986, pp. 247–80.

Krutilla, John V. Reflections on Man's Relation to Nature. **In** *[Crutchfield, J. A.]*, 1986, pp. 1–24.

Wooster, Warren S. Immiscible Investigators: Oceanographers, Meteorologists, and Fishery Scientists. **In** *[Crutchfield, J. A.]*, 1986, pp. 374–86.

721 Natural Resources

7210 General

Achoth, Lalith, et al. Output Growth Stability of Natural Rubber in India. *Margin,* January 1986, *18*(2), pp. 51–61. **[G: India]**

Adams, Richard M. Agriculture, Forestry, and Related Benefits of Air Pollution Control: A Review and Some Observations. *Amer. J. Agr. Econ.*, May 1986, *68*(2), pp. 464–72. **[G: U.S.]**

Agthe, Donald E., et al. A Simultaneous Equation Demand Model for Block Rates. *Water Resources Res.*, January 1986, *22*(1), pp. 1–4. **[G: U.S.]**

Ahmadian, Majid. Oil Pricing Policies and Macroeconomy for an Oil-Based Economy. *Energy Econ.*, October 1986, *8*(4), pp. 251–56.

Al-Qunaibet, Mohammad H. and Johnston, Richard S. Reply [Municipal Demand for Water in Kuwait: Methodological Issues and Empirical Results]. *Water Resources Res.*, May 1986, *22*(5), pp. 835–36. **[G: Kuwait]**

Amigues, Jean-Pierre and Moreaux, Michel. Gravières et vins de Bordeaux. (Gravel Pits and Bordeaux Wines. With English summary.) *Ann. Écon. Statist.*, Jan./Mar. 1986, (1), pp. 75–105.

Anders, Gary C. Oil, Economic Dependence, and Alaska's Development. *J. Energy Devel.*, Spring 1986, *11*(2), pp. 243–61. **[G: U.S.]**

Anderson, Dennis. Declining Tree Stocks in African Countries. *World Devel.*, July 1986, *14*(7), pp. 853–63. **[G: Africa]**

Anderson, Eric E. Taxes vs. Quotas for Regulating Fisheries under Uncertainty: A Hybrid Discrete-Time Continuous-Time Model. *Marine Resource Econ.*, 1986, *3*(3), pp. 183–207.

Anderson, F. J. Valuing a Depletable Resource Endowment in an Open Economy. *Can. J. Econ.*, November 1986, *19*(4), pp. 730–44.

Anderson, Lee G. Economically Optimal Total Allowable Catches in the Absence of Stock–Recruitment Relationships. **In** *[Crutchfield, J. A.]*, 1986, pp. 309–30.

Anderson, Lee G. and Lee, Dwight R. Optimal Governing Instrument, Operation Level, and Enforcement in Natural Resource Regulation: The Case of the Fishery. *Amer. J. Agr. Econ.*, August 1986, *68*(3), pp. 678–90.

Anderson, Terry L. and Johnson, Ronald N. The Problem of Instream Flows. *Econ. Inquiry,* October 1986, *24*(4), pp. 535–54.

Asheim, Geir B. Hartwick's Rule in Open Economies. *Can. J. Econ.,* August 1986, *19*(3), pp. 395–402.

Bailey, Conner; Cycon, Dean E. and Morris, Michael. Fisheries Development in the Third World: The Role of International Agencies. *World Devel.,* Oct./Nov. 1986, *14*(10/11), pp. 1269–75. **[G: LDCs]**

Barrett, Scott A. The Economics of Oil Supply Dynamics: Theory and Practice. *Energy Econ.,* October 1986, *8*(4), pp. 237–50. **[G: Canada]**

Baskerville, Gordon L. Forest and Wildlife Management. **In** *Economic Council of Canada,* 1986, pp. 33–46. **[G: Canada]**

Baumol, William J. On the Possibility of Continuing Expansion of Finite Resources. *Kyklos,* 1986, *39*(2), pp. 167–79.

Bell, Frederick W. Competition from Fish Farming in Influencing Rent Dissipation: The Crawfish Fishery. *Amer. J. Agr. Econ.,* February 1986, *68*(1), pp. 95–101. **[G: U.S.]**

Bell, Frederick W. Mitigating the Tragedy of the Commons. *Southern Econ. J.,* January 1986, *52*(3), pp. 653–64. **[G: U.S.]**

Ben-Zvi, M. and Bachmat, Y. Location of an Interface Observation Well: A Bayesian Approach. *Water Resources Res.,* October 1986, *22*(11), pp. 1503–08.

Bird, Peter J. W. N. Econometric Estimation of World Salmon Demand. *Marine Resource Econ.,* 1986, *3*(2), pp. 169–82. **[G: OECD]**

Bolle, Friedel. On the Oligopolistic Extraction of Non-renewable Common-Pool Resources. *Economica,* November 1986, *53*(212), pp. 519–27.

Bosch, Darrell J.; Eidman, Vernon R. and Gill, Eric E. Compensating Irrigators for Restricting Water Use: An Expected Utility Analysis. *Western J. Agr. Econ.,* December 1986, *11*(2), pp. 146–55. **[G: U.S.]**

Boskin, Michael J., et al. New Estimates of the Value of Federal Mineral Rights and Land: Erratum. *Amer. Econ. Rev.,* September 1986, *76*(4), pp. 859. **[G: U.S.]**

Boyd, Roy and Daniels, Barbara J. Errata [Capital Gains Treatment of Timber Income: Incidence and Welfare Implications]. *Land Econ.,* February 1986, *62*(1), pp. ii. **[G: U.S.]**

Bradley, Michael D. and Carpenter, Michael C. Subsiding Land and Falling Ground-Water Tables: Public Policy, Private Liability, and Legal Remedy. *Econ. Geogr.,* July 1986, *62*(3), pp. 241–53. **[G: U.S.]**

Brander, J. R. G. and Cook, B. A. The Market as a Commons: A Further Comment [The Market as an Open Access Commons: A Neglected Aspect of Excess Capacity]. *De Economist,* 1986, *134*(2), pp. 214–24.

Branson, William H. Natural Resources and the Macroeconomy: A Theoretical Framework: Discussion: An International Macroeconomic Perspective. **In** *Neary, J. P. and van Wijnbergen, S., eds.,* 1986, pp. 50–52.

Broadman, Harry G. Natural Gas Deregulation: The Need for Further Reform. *J. Policy Anal. Manage.,* Spring 1986, *5*(3), pp. 496–516. **[G: U.S.]**

Broadus, J. M. Asian Pacific Marine Minerals and Industry Structure. *Marine Resource Econ.,* 1986, *3*(1), pp. 63–88. **[G: Asia]**

Brookshire, David S.; Eubanks, Larry S. and Sorg, Cindy F. Existence Values and Normative Economics: Implications for Valuing Water Resources. *Water Resources Res.,* October 1986, *22*(11), pp. 1509–18.

Brown, Gardner, Jr. When Do Bells and Whistles Make Finer Music? Static versus Dynamic Models in Fishery Management. **In** *[Crutchfield, J. A.],* 1986, pp. 331–50.

Brun, André. Agriculture in a Turbulent World Economy: Theoretical Developments: Discussion. **In** *Maunder, A. and Renborg, U., eds.,* 1986, pp. 712–14.

Bryant, Richard R. U.S. Residential Demand for Wood. *Energy J.,* July 1986, *7*(3), pp. 137–47. **[G: U.S.]**

Buchholz, Wolfgang. Kie Elastizitä t des Grenznutzens als Determinante optimaler Allokation. (The Elasticity of Marginal Utility as a Determinant of Optimal Allocation. With English summary.) *Jahr. Nationalökon. Statist.,* January 1986, *201*(1), pp. 66–80.

Buresh, James C. State and Federal Land Use Regulation: An Application to Groundwater and Nonpoint Source Pollution Control. *Yale Law J.,* June 1986, *95*(7), pp. 1433–58. **[G: U.S.]**

Burness, H. S. and Cummings, Ronald G. Thermodynamic and Economic Concepts as Related to Resource-Use Policies: Reply. *Land Econ.,* August 1986, *62*(3), pp. 323–24.

Butcher, Walter R. and Wandschneider, Philip R. Competition between Irrigation and Hydropower in the Pacific Northwest. **In** *Frederick, K. D., ed.,* 1986, pp. 25–66. **[G: U.S.]**

Cairncross, Alec. The Role of Technology and Natural Resources in the Development Process. **In** *Cairncross, A.,* 1986, *1979,* pp. 124–35. **[G: Japan]**

Cairns, Robert D. A Model of Exhaustible Resource Exploitation with Ricardian Rent. *J. Environ. Econ. Manage.,* December 1986, *13*(4), pp. 313–24.

Cairns, Robert D. Intergenerational Equity and Heterogeneous Resources. *Scand. J. Econ.,* 1986, *88*(2), pp. 401–16.

Cairns, Robert D. More on Depletion in the Nickel Industry. *J. Environ. Econ. Manage.,* March 1986, *13*(1), pp. 93–98. **[G: U.S.]**

Cairns, Robert D. and Lasserre, Pierre. Sectoral Supply of Minerals of Varying Quality. *Scand. J. Econ.,* 1986, *88*(4), pp. 605–26.

Camara, Antonio S.; Viegas, M. Graca and Amaro, Ana. Interfacing System Dynamics and Multiobjective Programming for Regional Water Resources Planning. *Ann. Reg. Sci.,* November 1986, *20*(3), pp. 104–13. **[G: Portugal]**

Capalbo, Susan M. Temporary Equilibrium Production Models for a Common-Property Renewable-Resource Sector. *J. Econometrics*, Oct./Nov. 1986, *33*(1/2), pp. 263–84.

Carroll, John E. Water Resources Management as an Issue in Environmental Diplomacy. *Natural Res. J.*, Spring 1986, *26*(2), pp. 207–20. **[G: U.S.; Canada]**

Chambers, Robert G. and Strand, Ivar E., Jr. Estimating Parameters of a Renewable Resource Model without Population Data. *Marine Resource Econ.*, 1986, *2*(3), pp. 263–74. **[G: U.S.]**

Charles, Anthony T. Coastal State Fishery Development: Foreign Fleets and Optimal Investment Dynamics. *J. Devel. Econ.*, December 1986, *24*(2), pp. 331–58.

Charney, Jonathan I. The Unfinished Business of the Law of the Sea Conference. **In** *Pontecorvo, G., ed.*, 1986, pp. 238–64.

Chesnokov, B. Use Value of Natural Resources and Commodity–Monetary Relations. *Prob. Econ.*, December 1986, *29*(8), pp. 88–101. **[G: U.S.S.R.]**

Chicoine, David L.; Deller, Steven C. and Ramamurthy, Ganapathi. Water Demand Estimation under Block Rate Pricing: A Simultaneous Equation Approach. *Water Resources Res.*, June 1986, *22*(6), pp. 859–63. **[G: U.S.]**

Christiansson, Carl. Soil Erosion and Conservation in the Drylands. **In** *Boesen, J., et al., eds.*, 1986, pp. 143–57. **[G: Tanzania]**

Christy, Francis T., Jr. Special Characteristics and Problems of Small-scale Fisheries Management in Developing Countries. **In** *[Crutchfield, J. A.]*, 1986, pp. 118–51.

Chu, D. K. Y. Government Policies, Economic Development, and Possible Environmental Effects as the Land–Water Interfaces of Guangdong Province, China. *Marine Resource Econ.*, 1986, *3*(1), pp. 29–44. **[G: China]**

Cicin-Sain, Biliana, et al. Conflictual Interdependence: United States–Mexican Relations on Fishery Resources. *Natural Res. J.*, Fall 1986, *26*(4), pp. 769–92. **[G: U.S.; Mexico]**

Clark, Allen L. and Clark, Jennifer Cook. Marine Metallic Mineral Resources of the Pacific Basin. *Marine Resource Econ.*, 1986, *3*(1), pp. 45–62. **[G: Pacific Basin]**

Clark, Colin W. and Kirkwood, Geoffrey P. On Uncertain Renewable Resource Stocks: Optimal Harvest Policies and the Value of Stock Surveys. *J. Environ. Econ. Manage.*, September 1986, *13*(3), pp. 235–44.

Clawson, Marion. Application of Economics to the Problems of Natural Resource Use, Development, and Policy. **In** *[Crutchfield, J. A.]*, 1986, pp. 25–41.

Clemhout, S. and Wan, Henry Y., Jr. Common-Property Exploitations under Risks of Resource Extinctions. **In** *Başar, T., ed.*, 1986, pp. 267–88.

Clingan, Thomas A., Jr. The United States and the Law of the Sea Conference. **In** *Pontecorvo, G., ed.*, 1986, pp. 219–37. **[G: U.S.]**

Cocklin, C.; Lonergan, S. C. and Smit, B. The Economics of Forest Energy Plantations: An Empirical Enquiry. *Econ. Geogr.*, October 1986, *62*(4), pp. 354–72. **[G: Canada]**

Comolli, Paul M. Exhaustible Resources and International Trade. *Eastern Econ. J.*, July-Sept. 1986, *12*(3), pp. 291–96.

Conrad, Jon M. Resource Development and Environmental Risk. **In** *[Crutchfield, J. A.]*, 1986, pp. 296–308.

Conrad, Jon M. and Adu-Asamoah, Richard. Single and Multispecies Systems: The Case of Tuna in the Eastern Tropical Atlantic. *J. Environ. Econ. Manage.*, March 1986, *13*(1), pp. 50–68. **[G: Global]**

Copes, Parzival. A Critical Review of the Individual Quota as a Device in Fisheries Management. *Land Econ.*, August 1986, *62*(3), pp. 278–91. **[G: EEC; U.S.; Canada]**

Cornes, Richard; Mason, Charles F. and Sandler, Todd. The Commons and the Optimal Number of Firms. *Quart. J. Econ.*, August 1986, *101*(3), pp. 641–46.

Crabbé, Philippe. Gray and Hotelling: A Reply [The Contribution of L. C. Gray to the Economic Theory of Exhaustible Natural Resources and Its Roots in the History of Economic Thought]. *J. Environ. Econ. Manage.*, September 1986, *13*(3), pp. 295–300.

Crutchfield, Stephen R. U.S. Demand for Selected Groundfish Products, 1967–80: Comment. *Amer. J. Agr. Econ.*, November 1986, *68*(4), pp. 1018–20. **[G: U.S.]**

Cummings, Ronald G. and Pearse, Spencer R. The Intertemporal Problem: Comment. **In** *Bromley, D. W., ed.*, 1986, pp. 21–28.

Curran, Peter Anthony. Italian Legislation on Deep Sea Mining. *J. World Trade Law*, Nov.:Dec. 1986, *20*(6), pp. 713–16. **[G: Italy]**

Cycon, Dean E. Managing Fisheries in Developing Nations: A Plea for Appropriate Development. *Natural Res. J.*, Winter 1986, *26*(1), pp. 1–14. **[G: LDCs]**

Dagenais, Camille. Dams and the Environment. **In** *Economic Council of Canada*, 1986, pp. 63–67.

Daly, Herman E. Thermodynamic and Economic Concepts as Related to Resource-Use Policies: Comment. *Land Econ.*, August 1986, *62*(3), pp. 319–22.

Danielson, Leon E. and Leitch, Jay A. Private vs Public Economics of Prairie Wetland Allocation. *J. Environ. Econ. Manage.*, March 1986, *13*(1), pp. 81–92. **[G: U.S.]**

Dasgupta, Partha. Natural Resources and the Macroeconomy: A Theoretical Framework: Discussion: A Natural Resources Perspective. **In** *Neary, J. P. and van Wijnbergen, S., eds.*, 1986, pp. 53.

Deller, Steven C.; Chicoine, David L. and Ramamurthy, Ganapathi. Instrumental Variables Approach to Rural Water Service Demand. *Southern Econ. J.*, October 1986, *53*(2), pp. 333–46. **[G: U.S.]**

van Dijk, G.; Smit, L. and Veerman, C. P. Land Prices and Technological Development. *Eu-*

rop. Rev. Agr. Econ., 1986, *13*(4), pp. 495–515. **[G: Netherlands]**

Dinar, Ariel and Knapp, Keith C. A Dynamic Analysis of Optimal Water Use under Saline Conditions. *Western J. Agr. Econ.*, July 1986, *11*(1), pp. 58–66. **[G: U.S.]**

Djalal, Hasjim. A Southeast Asian Perspective. **In** *Pontecorvo, G., ed.*, 1986, pp. 199–216. **[G: S. E. Asia]**

Dubs, Marne A. Minerals of the Deep Sea: Myth and Reality. **In** *Pontecorvo, G., ed.*, 1986, pp. 85–121. **[G: France; Japan; U.S.S.R.; U.S.; India]**

Dworsky, Leonard B. The Great Lakes: 1955–1985. *Natural Res. J.*, Spring 1986, *26*(2), pp. 291–336. **[G: U.S.; Canada]**

Eales, James S. and Wilen, James E. An Examination of Fishing Location Choice in the Pink Shrimp Fishery. *Marine Resource Econ.*, 1986, *2*(4), pp. 331–51. **[G: U.S.]**

Edwards, Clark. The Role of Natural Resources in Regional Agricultural Growth. **In** *Maunder, A. and Renborg, U., eds.*, 1986, pp. 692–702.

Elton, G. R. Piscatorial Politics in the Early Parliaments of Elizabeth I. **In** *[Coleman, D. C.]*, 1986, pp. 1–20. **[G: U.K.]**

Emerson, Craig. Fiscal Arrangements for Mineral Development. **In** *Shome, P., ed.*, 1986, pp. 141–59. **[G: Indonesia; Philippines; Papua New Guinea; Australia]**

Eubanks, Larry S. and Mueller, Michael J. An Economic Analysis of Oklahoma's Oil and Gas Forced Pooling Law. *Natural Res. J.*, Summer 1986, *26*(3), pp. 469–91. **[G: U.S.]**

Flemming, John S. Booming Sectors and Structural Change in Australia and Britain: A Comparison: Comment. **In** *Neary, J. P. and van Wijnbergen, S., eds.*, 1986, pp. 284–87. **[G: U.K.; Australia]**

Forsyth, Peter J. Booming Sectors and Structural Change in Australia and Britain: A Comparison. **In** *Neary, J. P. and van Wijnbergen, S., eds.*, 1986, pp. 251–84. **[G: Australia; U.K.]**

Foster, William E., et al. Distributional Welfare Implications of an Irrigation Water Subsidy. *Amer. J. Agr. Econ.*, November 1986, *68*(4), pp. 778–86. **[G: U.S.]**

Fox, William F. and Hofler, Richard A. Using Homothetic Composed Error Frontiers to Measure Water Utility Efficiency. *Southern Econ. J.*, October 1986, *53*(2), pp. 461–77. **[G: U.S.]**

Fraser, R. W. On the Relationship between Exploration and Extraction. *Australian Econ. Pap.*, June 1986, *25*(46), pp. 135–43.

Frederick, Kenneth D. Scarce Water and Institutional Change: Overview. **In** *Frederick, K. D., ed.*, 1986, pp. 1–24. **[G: U.S.]**

Freeman, David A. A Model for Water Pricing. *J. Bus. Econ. Statist.*, January 1986, *4*(1), pp. 131–33.

French, David. Confronting an Unsolvable Problem: Deforestation in Malawi. *World Devel.*, April 1986, *14*(4), pp. 531–40. **[G: Malawi]**

Friedman, Julia Mason. Taxation of Timberland. **In** *Minnesota Tax Study Commission*, 1986, pp. 399–410. **[G: U.S.]**

Gaudet, Gérard and Lasserre, Pierre. Capital Income Taxation, Depletion Allowances, and Nonrenewable Resource Extraction. *J. Public Econ.*, March 1986, *29*(2), pp. 241–53.

Georgianna, Daniel L. and Hogan, William V. Production Costs in Atlantic Fresh Fish Processing. *Marine Resource Econ.*, 1986, *2*(3), pp. 275–92. **[G: U.S.]**

Gilbert, Alison and Hafkamp, Wim. Natural Resource Accounting in a Multi-objective Context. *Ann. Reg. Sci.*, November 1986, *20*(3), pp. 10–37. **[G: EEC]**

Gilland, Bernard. On Resources and Economic Development. *Population Devel. Rev.*, June 1986, *12*(2), pp. 295–305. **[G: Global]**

Gligo, Nicolo. The Preparation of Natural and Cultural Heritage Inventories and Accounts. *CEPAL Rev.*, April 1986, (28), pp. 171–86.

Gofman, K. G. and Gusev, A. A. On Some Controversial Questions in the Methodology for Optimizing Natural Resource Use. *Matekon*, Spring 1986, *22*(3), pp. 24–34.

Graham-Tomasi, Theodore; Runge, Carlisle Ford and Hyde, William F. Foresight and Expectations in Models of Natural Resource Markets. *Land Econ.*, August 1986, *62*(3), pp. 234–49.

Gray, H. Peter. "Natural Resource Pricing," Allocative Efficiency and Protection. *Weltwirtsch. Arch.*, 1986, *122*(2), pp. 365–70.

Guariso, G.; Rinaldi, S. and Soncini-Sessa, R. The Management of Lake Como: A Multiobjective Analysis. *Water Resources Res.*, February 1986, *22*(2), pp. 109–20. **[G: Italy]**

Gulland, J. A. Predictability of Living Marine Resources. **In** *Mason, J.; Mathias, P. and Westcott, J. H., eds.*, 1986, pp. 127–41. **[G: Japan; U.S.; U.K.; S. Africa]**

Gupta, Tirath. Allied Enterprises: III—Forestry in India: Problems and Potentials for Development. **In** *Dantwala, M. L., et al.*, 1986, pp. 223–33. **[G: India]**

Hafkamp, Wim and Nijkamp, Peter. Integrated Economic–Environmental–Energy Policy and Conflict Analysis. *J. Policy Modeling*, Winter 1986, *8*(4), pp. 551–76. **[G: Netherlands]**

Hagan, Philip and Henry, Gary. Potential Effects of Differing Management Programs on the Southern Bluefin Tuna Fishery. *Marine Resource Econ.*, 1986, *3*(4), pp. 353–89. **[G: Japan; Australia; New Zealand]**

Halvorsen, Robert and Smith, Tim R. Substitution Possibilities for Unpriced Natural Resources: Restricted Cost Functions for the Canadian Metal Mining Industry. *Rev. Econ. Statist.*, August 1986, *68*(3), pp. 398–405. **[G: Canada]**

Hämäläinen, Raimo P.; Ruusunen, Jukka and Kaitala, Veijo. Myopic Stackelberg Equilibria and Social Coordination in a Share Contract Fishery. *Marine Resource Econ.*, 1986, *3*(3), pp. 209–35.

Hamilton, Andrew L. Fresh Water Issues: Comments. In *Economic Council of Canada*, 1986, pp. 24–27. [G: Canada]

Handl, Günther. National Uses of Transboundary Air Resources: The International Entitlement Issue Reconsidered. *Natural Res. J.*, Summer 1986, *26*(3), pp. 405–67. [G: OECD]

Hannesson, Rögnvaldur. The Effect of the Discount Rate on the Optimal Exploitation of Renewable Resources. *Marine Resource Econ.*, 1986, *3*(4), pp. 319–29.

Hansen, Robert G. Sealed-Bid versus Open Auctions: The Evidence. *Econ. Inquiry*, January 1986, *24*(1), pp. 125–42. [G: U.S.]

Hartje, Volkmar J. Zur Erhaltung genetischer Ressourcen. Eine ökonomische Analyse von Institutionen und Instrumenten. (With English summary.) *Z. Wirtschaft. Sozialwissen.*, 1986, *106*(3), pp. 229–52. [G: W. Germany]

Hartwick, John M.; Kemp, Murray C. and Long, Ngo Van. Set-Up Costs and Theory of Exhaustible Resources. *J. Environ. Econ. Manage.*, September 1986, *13*(3), pp. 212–24.

Heal, Geoffrey. The Intertemporal Problem. In *Bromley, D. W., ed.*, 1986, pp. 1–20.

Heinonen, Pertti and Herve, Sirpa. Improvement of Water Statistics with Particular Reference to Water Quality. *Statist. J.*, October 1986, *4*(2), pp. 183–93. [G: Finland]

Hite, James C. Interbasin Water Transfers in Riparian Doctrine States: The Case of Interregional Compensation. *Growth Change*, October 1986, *17*(4), pp. 10–24. [G: U.S.]

Houston, Jack E., Jr. and Whittlesey, Norman K. Modeling Agricultural Water Markets for Hydropower Production in the Pacific Northwest. *Western J. Agr. Econ.*, December 1986, *11*(2), pp. 221–31. [G: U.S.]

Howe, Charles W. Project Benefits and Costs from National and Regional Viewpoints: Methodological Issues and Case Study of the Colorado-Big Thompson Project. *Natural Res. J.*, Winter 1986, *26*(1), pp. 77–94. [G: U.S.]

Howe, Charles W.; Schurmeier, Dennis R. and Shaw, William Douglas, Jr. Innovative Approaches to Water Allocation: The Potential for Water Markets. *Water Resources Res.*, April 1986, *22*(4), pp. 439–45. [G: U.S.]

Howe, Charles W.; Schurmeier, Dennis R. and Shaw, William Douglas, Jr. Innovations in Water Management: Lessons from the Colorado–Big Thompson Project and Northern Colorado Water Conservancy District. In *Frederick, K. D., ed.*, 1986, pp. 171–200. [G: U.S.]

Hrezo, Margaret S.; Bridgeman, Phyllis G. and Walker, William R. Integrating Drought Planning into Water Resources Management. *Natural Res. J.*, Winter 1986, *26*(1), pp. 141–67. [G: U.S.]

Hubbard, R. Glenn. Supply Shocks and Price Adjustment in the World Oil Market. *Quart. J. Econ.*, February 1986, *101*(1), pp. 85–102. [G: Global]

Huffaker, Ray G. and Gardner, B. Delworth. The "Hammer" Clause of the Reclamation Reform Act of 1982. *Natural Res. J.*, Winter 1986, *26*(1), pp. 41–67. [G: U.S.]

Huffaker, Ray G. and Gardner, B. Delworth. The Distribution of Economic Rents Arising from Subsidized Water When Land Is Leased. *Amer. J. Agr. Econ.*, May 1986, *68*(2), pp. 306–12. [G: U.S.]

Huppert, Daniel D. and Squires, Dale. Potential Economic Benefits and Optimum Fleet Size in the Pacific Coast Trawl Fleet. *Marine Resource Econ.*, 1986, *3*(4), pp. 297–318. [G: U.S.]

Hviid, Morten. Udtømmelige ressourcer og karteller. (Theoretical Models of a Dominant Cartel in a Market for an Exhaustible Resource. With English summary.) *Nationaløkon. Tidsskr.*, 1986, *124*(3), pp. 396–415.

Izac, A.-M. N. Resource Policies, Property Rights and Conflicts of Interest. *Australian J. Agr. Econ.*, April 1986, *30*(1), pp. 23–37.

James, David E. A Hypothetical Case Study: The Lake Burley Fishery Project. In *Dixon, J. A. and Hufschmidt, M. M., eds.*, 1986, pp. 11–38. [G: U.S.]

Jayal, N. D. Research Priorities for Planning Water Resource Development. *Can. J. Devel. Stud.*, 1986, *7*(1), pp. 37–46. [G: LDCs]

Johnson, Charles J.; Clark, Allen L. and Otto, James M. Pacific Ocean Minerals: The Next Twenty Years. In *Nemetz, P. N., ed.*, 1986, pp. 199–222. [G: Pacific Basin]

Jones, Ronald W. Natural Resources and the Macroeconomy: A Theoretical Framework: Discussion: A Trade Theoretic Perspective. In *Neary, J. P. and van Wijnbergen, S., eds.*, 1986, pp. 46–50.

Jonsson, Sigfus. International Saltfish Markets and the Icelandic Economy ca. 1900–1940. *Scand. Econ. Hist. Rev.*, 1986, *34*(1), pp. 20–40. [G: Iceland]

Kabir, M. and Ridler, Neil B. The Market for Atlantic Salmon. *Atlantic Econ. J.*, March 1986, *14*(1), pp. 125. [G: Canada]

Kaitala, Veijo. Game Theory Models of Fisheries Management—A Survey. In *Başar, T., ed.*, 1986, pp. 252–66.

Karp, Larry; Sadeh, Arye and Griffin, Wade L. Cycles in Agricultural Production: The Case of Aquaculture. *Amer. J. Agr. Econ.*, August 1986, *68*(3), pp. 553–61.

Kennedy, John O. S. and Watkins, James W. Time-Dependent Quotas for the Southern Bluefish Tuna Fishery. *Marine Resource Econ.*, 1986, *2*(4), pp. 293–313. [G: Australia; Japan]

Kher, Lov Kumar and Sorooshian, Soroosh. Identification of Water Demand Models from Noisy Data. *Water Resources Res.*, March 1986, *22*(3), pp. 322–30. [G: U.S.]

Kirn, Jackie Krolopp and Marts, Marion E. The Skagit–High Ross Controversy: Negotiation and Settlement. *Natural Res. J.*, Spring 1986, *26*(2), pp. 261–89. [G: U.S.; Canada]

Knedlik, Will R. Introduction to U.S.–Mexico Transboundary Resource Issues. *Natural Res. J.*, Fall 1986, *26*(4), pp. 661–68. [G: U.S.; Mexico]

Kolm, Serge-Christophe. L'allocation des ressources naturalles et le libéralisme. (The Allocation of Natural Resources and the Theory of Liberalism. With English summary.) *Revue Écon.*, March 1986, *37*(2), pp. 207–41.

Kovenock, Dan. Property and Income Taxation in an Economy with an Austrian Sector. *Land Econ.*, May 1986, *62*(2), pp. 201–09.

Kromm, David E. and White, Stephen E. Public Preferences for Recommendations Made by the High Plains–Ogallala Aquifer Study. *Soc. Sci. Quart.*, December 1986, *67*(4), pp. 841–54. [G: U.S.]

Krzysztofowicz, Roman. Expected Utility, Benefit, and Loss Criteria for Seasonal Water Supply Planning. *Water Resources Res.*, March 1986, *22*(3), pp. 303–12. [G: U.S.]

Krzysztofowicz, Roman. Optimal Water Supply Planning Based on Seasonal Runoff Forecasts. *Water Resources Res.*, March 1986, *22*(3), pp. 313–21. [G: U.S.]

Kukushkin, G. Planning the Rational Utilization of Natural Resources. *Prob. Econ.*, January 1986, *28*(9), pp. 50–61. [G: U.S.S.R.]

Kula, Erhun. The Developing Framework for the Economic Evaluation of Forestry in the United Kingdom. *J. Agr. Econ.*, September 1986, *37*(3), pp. 365–76. [G: U.K.]

Langton, John. Atlas of Industrializing Britain 1780–1914: The Physical Environment. **In** *Langton, J. and Morris, R. J., eds.*, 1986, pp. 2–9. [G: U.K.]

Lawson, Rowena. Strategies for Fisheries Development. **In** *[Crutchfield, J. A.]*, 1986, pp. 152–84. [G: Selected Countries]

Laxton, Paul. Atlas of Industrializing Britain 1780–1914: Wind and Water Power. **In** *Langton, J. and Morris, R. J., eds.*, 1986, pp. 69–71. [G: U.K.]

Lee, Seung-Dong. On the Theory of an Exhaustible Resource Extractive Multinational Firm. *Can. J. Econ.*, November 1986, *19*(4), pp. 716–29.

LeMarquand, David G. Preconditions to Cooperation in Canada–United States Boundary Water. *Natural Res. J.*, Spring 1986, *26*(2), pp. 221–42. [G: U.S.; Canada]

Lewis, Tracy R.; Linsey, Robin and Ware, Roger. Long-term Bilateral Monopoly: The Case of an Exhaustible Resource. *Rand J. Econ.*, Spring 1986, *17*(1), pp. 89–104.

van Lierop, Wal F. J. and Braat, Leon. Multiobjective Modelling of Economic–Ecological Interactions and Conflicts. *Ann. Reg. Sci.*, November 1986, *20*(3), pp. 114–29.

Lin, Biing-Hwan; Johnston, Richard S. and Rettig, R. Bruce. U.S. Demand for Selected Groundfish Products, 1967–80: Comment. *Amer. J. Agr. Econ.*, November 1986, *68*(4), pp. 1021–24. [G: U.S.]

Livingston, Marie Leigh and Miller, Thomas A. A Framework for Analyzing the Impact of Western Instream Water Rights on Choice Domains: Transferability, Externalities, and Consumptive Use. *Land Econ.*, August 1986, *62*(3), pp. 269–77. [G: U.S.]

Loomis, John B.; Sorg, Cindy F. and Donnelly, Dennis M. Evaluating Regional Demand Models for Estimating Recreation Use and Economic Benefits: A Case Study. *Water Resources Res.*, April 1986, *22*(4), pp. 431–38. [G: U.S.]

Loury, Glenn C. A Theory of 'Oil'igopoly: Cournot Equilibrium in Exhaustible Resource Markets with Fixed Supplies. *Int. Econ. Rev.*, June 1986, *27*(2), pp. 285–301.

Lower, Ann K. Engineering, Vested Interests, and Threshold Choice: Pipelines, Coal, and the Railroads. *J. Econ. Issues,* June 1986, *20*(2), pp. 471–80. [G: U.S.]

Maidment, David R. and Miaou, Shaw-Pin. Daily Water Use in Nine Cities. *Water Resources Res.*, June 1986, *22*(6), pp. 845–51. [G: U.S.]

Main, Robert S. Impacts, Costs, and Techniques for Mitigation of Contaminated Groundwater: A Review: Comment. *Water Resources Res.*, March 1986, *22*(3), pp. 429–30. [G: U.S.]

Mäler, Karl-Göran. On the Intergenerational Allocation of Natural Resources: Comment. *Scand. J. Econ.*, 1986, *88*(1), pp. 151–52.

Manz, Peter. Forestry Economics in the Steady State: The Contribution of J. H. von Thünen. *Hist. Polit. Econ.*, Summer 1986, *18*(2), pp. 281–90.

Martin, William E. and Thomas, John F. Policy Relevance in Studies of Urban Residential Water Demand. *Water Resources Res.*, December 1986, *22*(13), pp. 1735–41. [G: Kuwait; Australia; U.S.]

Martin, William E.; Thomas, John F. and Macpherson, Duncan K. Municipal Demand for Water in Kuwait: Methodological Issues and Empirical Results: Comment. *Water Resources Res.*, May 1986, *22*(5), pp. 832–34. [G: Kuwait]

Mason, Charles F. Exploration, Information, and Regulation in an Exhaustible Mineral Industry. *J. Environ. Econ. Manage.*, June 1986, *13*(2), pp. 153–66.

Matulich, Scott C. and Hanson, Jeffrey E. Modeling Supply Response in Bioeconomic Research: An Example from Wildlife Enhancement. *Land Econ.*, August 1986, *62*(3), pp. 292–305. [G: U.S.]

Mawdsley, Andrés Aguilar. Law of the Sea: The Latin American View. **In** *Pontecorvo, G., ed.*, 1986, pp. 158–98. [G: Latin America]

McDowell, John M. Foreign Direct Investment in U.S. Natural Resource Industries. **In** *Gray, H. P., ed.*, 1986, pp. 261–86. [G: U.S.]

McGuire, Robert A. and Ohsfeldt, Robert L. Public versus Private Water Delivery: A Critical Analysis of a Hedonic Cost Approach. *Public Finance Quart.*, July 1986, *14*(3), pp. 339–50.

Mead, Walter J.; Moesidjord, Asbjorn and Sorensen, Philip E. Competition in Outer Shelf Oil and Gas Lease Auctions: A Statistical Analysis of Winning Bids. *Natural Res. J.*, Winter 1986, *26*(1), pp. 95–111. [G: U.S.]

Mickwitz, Gösta. Skogsindustrin bör kräva luftvård. (The Forest Industry Should Demand

Air Pollution Control. With English summary.) *Ekon. Samfundets Tidskr.*, 1986, *39*(4), pp. 179–80. **[G: Finland]**

Mickwitz, Gösta. Skogsindustrins aftonrodnad—eller omvandling? (The Forest Industry—Sunset or Restructure? With English summary.) *Ekon. Samfundets Tidskr.*, 1986, *39*(2), pp. 65–68.

Milliman, Scott R. Optimal Fishery Management in the Presence of Illegal Activity. *J. Environ. Econ. Manage.*, December 1986, *13*(4), pp. 363–81.

Mitra, Tapan and Wan, Henry Y., Jr. On the Faustmann Solution to the Forest Management Problem. *J. Econ. Theory,* December 1986, *40*(2), pp. 229–49.

Monette, Marcel. L'Économique des pêcheries: une revue de la littérature. (The Literature on Fishery Economies: A Survey. With English summary.) *L'Actual. Econ.*, June 1986, *62*(2), pp. 289–305.

Morey, Edward R. A Generalized Harvest Function for Fishing: Allocating Effort among Common Property Cod Stocks (A Generalized Harvest Function). *J. Environ. Econ. Manage.*, March 1986, *13*(1), pp. 30–49. **[G: Europe]**

Moy, Wai-See; Cohon, Jared L. and ReVelle, Charles S. A Programming Model for Analysis of the Reliability, Resilience, and Vulnerability of a Water Supply Resevoir. *Water Resources Res.*, April 1986, *22*(4), pp. 489–98.

Mueller, Michael J. and Eubanks, Larry S. Institutional Effects on an In Situ Natural Resource Market: Forced Pooling in a Petroleum Reserves Market. *Southern Econ. J.*, October 1986, *53*(2), pp. 374–92. **[G: U.S.]**

Mulherin, J. Harold. Specialized Assets, Governmental Regulation, and Organizational Structure in the Natural Gas Industry. *J. Inst. Theoretical Econ.*, September 1986, *142*(3), pp. 528–41. **[G: U.S.]**

Munro, Gordon R. The Management of Shared Fishery Resources under Extended Jurisdiction. *Marine Resource Econ.*, 1986, *3*(4), pp. 271–96. **[G: Global]**

Muraoka, Dennis D. and Watson, Richard B. Improving the Efficiency of Federal Timber Sale Procedures: An Update. *Natural Res. J.*, Winter 1986, *26*(1), pp. 69–76. **[G: U.S.]**

Mustapha, Nik Hashim. Pressure on the Malaysian Fisheries Arising from Current Modernisation Programmes and Management Conditions. **In** *Maunder, A. and Renborg, U., eds.*, 1986, pp. 328–37. **[G: Malaysia]**

Neary, J. Peter and van Wijnbergen, Sweder J. G. Natural Resources and the Macroeconomy: Introduction. **In** *Neary, J. P. and van Wijnbergen, S., eds.*, 1986, pp. 1–11.

Neary, J. Peter and van Wijnbergen, Sweder J. G. Natural Resources and the Macroeconomy: A Theoretical Framework. **In** *Neary, J. P. and van Wijnbergen, S., eds.*, 1986, pp. 13–45.

Nilsson, Per. Wood—The Other Energy Crisis. **In** *Boesen, J., et al., eds.*, 1986, pp. 159–72. **[G: Tanzania]**

Njenga, Frank X. Historical Background of the Evolution of the Exclusive Economic Zone and the Contribution of Africa. **In** *Pontecorvo, G., ed.*, 1986, pp. 125–57. **[G: Africa]**

Nordhaus, William D. Resources, Technology, and Development: Will the Table Be Bare When Poor Countries Get There? *Indian Econ. Rev.*, July-Dec. 1986, *21*(2), pp. 81–94.

Norgaard, Richard B. Thermodynamic and Economic Concepts as Related to Resource-Use Policies: Synthesis. *Land Econ.*, August 1986, *62*(3), pp. 325–28.

O'Faircheallaigh, Ciaran. Mineral Taxation in Less Developed Countries: Papua New Guinea's Balanced System. *Amer. J. Econ. Soc.*, July 1986, *45*(3), pp. 291–95.

Ovsienko, Iu. V. and Sobolev, I. I. On Valuing Forests in a Way Which Takes Account of Their Ecological Significance. *Matekon,* Summer 1986, *22*(4), pp. 54–74.

Paté-Cornell, M. Elisabeth and Tagaras, George. Risk Costs for New Dams: Economic Analysis and Effects of Monitoring. *Water Resources Res.*, January 1986, *22*(1), pp. 5–14. **[G: U.S.]**

Pearse, Peter H. Fresh Water Issues. **In** *Economic Council of Canada*, 1986, pp. 15–24. **[G: Canada]**

Perrings, Charles. Conservation of Mass and Instability in a Dynamic Economy-Environment System. *J. Environ. Econ. Manage.*, September 1986, *13*(3), pp. 199–211.

Perry, James A. and Dixon, Robert K. An Interdisciplinary Approach to Community Resource Management: Preliminary Field Test in Thailand. *J. Devel. Areas*, October 1986, *21*(1), pp. 31–47. **[G: Thailand]**

Pierce, John T. and Furuseth, Owen J. Constraints to Expanded Food Production: A North American Perspective. *Natural Res. J.*, Winter 1986, *26*(1), pp. 15–39. **[G: U.S.]**

van der Ploeg, Frederick. Inefficiency of Oligopolistic Resource Markets with ISO-Elastic Demand, Zero Extraction Costs and Stochastic Renewal. *J. Econ. Dynam. Control,* June 1986, *10*(1/2), pp. 309–14.

Plummer, Mark L. Supply Uncertainty, Option Price, and Option Value: An Extension. *Land Econ.*, August 1986, *62*(3), pp. 313–18.

Pontecorvo, Giulio. Division of the Spoils: Hydrocarbons and Living Resources. **In** *Pontecorvo, G., ed.*, 1986, pp. 15–28. **[G: U.S.; Canada; Greenland]**

Pontecorvo, Giulio. Opportunity, Abundance, Scarcity: An Overview. **In** *Pontecorvo, G., ed.*, 1986, pp. 3–14.

Pontecorvo, Giulio. Supply, Demand, and Common Property: The Historical Dynamics of the Fisheries of Georges Bank—Some Preliminary Observations. **In** *[Crutchfield, J. A.]*, 1986, pp. 97–117. **[G: U.S.]**

Postel, Sandra L. Needed: A New Water Policy. *Challenge*, Jan./Feb. 1986, *28*(6), pp. 43–49. **[G: U.S.]**

Quirk, James P. The Intertemporal Problem: Comment. **In** *Bromley, D. W., ed.*, 1986, pp. 29–36.

Raiatskas, R. L.; Chiakanavichius, L. P. and Radushis, V. Iu. On the Methodology for Estimating the Economic Cost of Environmental Pollution. *Matekon,* Spring 1986, *22*(3), pp. 3–23.

Raut, K. C. Allied Enterprises: II—Fisheries. **In** *Dantwala, M. L., et al.*, 1986, pp. 209–22. **[G: India]**

Ray, George F. The British Economy in the Long Term: Natural Resources. *Nat. Inst. Econ. Rev.*, November 1986, (118), pp. 53–58. **[G: Global]**

Richardson, Edward J. and Gates, John M. Economic Benefits of American Lobster Fishery Management Regulations. *Marine Resource Econ.*, 1986, *2*(4), pp. 353–82. **[G: U.S.]**

Rosenman, Robert E. The Optimal Tax for Maximum Economic Yield: Fishery Regulation under Rational Expectations. *J. Environ. Econ. Manage.*, December 1986, *13*(4), pp. 348–62.

Ross, David A. Ocean Science: Its Place in the New Order of the Oceans. **In** *Pontecorvo, G., ed.*, 1986, pp. 65–84.

Runge, Carlisle Ford. Common Property and Collective Action in Economic Development. *World Devel.*, May 1986, *14*(5), pp. 623–35. **[G: LDCs]**

Sadler, Barry. The Management of Canada–U.S. Boundary Waters: Retrospect and Prospect. *Natural Res. J.*, Spring 1986, *26*(2), pp. 359–76. **[G: Canada; U.S.]**

Samples, Karl C.; Dixon, John A. and Gowen, Marcia M. Information Disclosure and Endangered Species Valuation. *Land Econ.*, August 1986, *62*(3), pp. 306–12. **[G: U.S.]**

Samuelson, Larry. The Multinational Firm and Exhaustible Resources. *Economica*, May 1986, *53*(210), pp. 191–207.

Samuelson, Paul A. Land and the Rate of Interest. **In** *Samuelson, P. A.*, 1986, *1979*, pp. 664–82.

Samuelson, Paul A. Stochastic Land Valuation: Total Return as Martingale Implying Price Changes—A Negatively Correlated Walk. **In** *Samuelson, P. A.*, 1986, pp. 527–36.

Sandiford, Frances. An Analysis of Multiobjective Decision-Making for the Scottish Inshore Fishery. *J. Agr. Econ.*, May 1986, *37*(2), pp. 207–19. **[G: U.K.]**

Sarma, P. B. S. Water Resources and Their Role in Food Production. **In** *Swaminathan, M. S. and Sinha, S. K., eds.*, 1986, pp. 171–98. **[G: Global]**

Sasseville, Jean-Louis. Fresh Water Issues: Comments. **In** *Economic Council of Canada*, 1986, pp. 27–31.

Schachter, Oscar. Concepts and Realities in the New Law of the Sea. **In** *Pontecorvo, G., ed.*, 1986, pp. 29–59.

Schramm, Gunter. Practical Approaches for Estimating Resource Depletion Costs. **In** *[Crutchfield, J. A.]*, 1986, pp. 272–95.

Schrank, William E.; Roy, Noel and Tsoa, Eugene. Employment Prospects in a Commercially Viable Newfoundland Fishery: An Application of 'An Econometric Model of the Newfoundland Groundfishery.' *Marine Resource Econ.*, 1986, *3*(3), pp. 237–63. **[G: Canada]**

Scitovsky, Tibor. Can Changing Consumer Tastes Save Resources? **In** *Scitovsky, T.*, 1986, *1979*, pp. 117–27. **[G: U.S.; Europe]**

Scott, Anthony. Catch Quotas and Shares in the Fishstock as Property Rights. **In** *[Crutchfield, J. A.]*, 1986, pp. 61–96.

Sengupta, Jati K. and Khalili, Monsour. Efficiency in Water Allocation under Stochastic Demand. *Appl. Econ.*, January 1986, *18*(1), pp. 37–48. **[G: U.S.]**

Sewell, W. R. Derrick. Large-scale Water Transfers in North America: Solution or Disaster? **In** *[Crutchfield, J. A.]*, 1986, pp. 214–48. **[G: U.S.; Canada]**

Sewell, W. R. Derrick and Utton, Albert E. "Getting to Yes" in United States–Canadian Water Disputes. *Natural Res. J.*, Spring 1986, *26*(2), pp. 201–05. **[G: U.S.; Canada]**

Shabman, Leonard and Cox, William E. Costs of Water Management Institutions: The Case of Southeastern Virginia. **In** *Frederick, K. D., ed.*, 1986, pp. 134–70. **[G: U.S.]**

Sinclair, P. J. N. Faster Technical Progress Need Not Imply Lower Optimal Savings. *Greek Econ. Rev.*, June 1986, *8*(1), pp. 60–65.

Slade, Margaret E. Taxation of Non-renewable Resources at Various Stages of Production. *Can. J. Econ.*, May 1986, *19*(2), pp. 281–97.

Smith, Gerald Alonzo. Gray and Hotelling: A Comment [The Contribution of L. C. Gray to the Economic Theory of Exhaustible Natural Resources and Its Roots in the History of Economic Thought]. *J. Environ. Econ. Manage.*, September 1986, *13*(3), pp. 292–94.

Smith, J. Barry. Stochastic Steady-State Replenishable Resource Management Policies. *Marine Resource Econ.*, 1986, *3*(2), pp. 155–68.

Snipp, C. Matthew. American Indians and Natural Resource Development: Indigenous Peoples' Land, Now Sought after, Has Produced New Indian–White Problems. *Amer. J. Econ. Soc.*, October 1986, *45*(4), pp. 457–74. **[G: U.S.]**

Solow, Robert M. On the Intergenerational Allocation of Natural Resources. *Scand. J. Econ.*, 1986, *88*(1), pp. 141–49.

Solow, Robert M. Resources and Economic Growth. **In** *Szenberg, M., ed.*, 1986, *1978*, pp. 57–68.

Srivastava, U. K. Pressure on Natural Resources: Discussion. **In** *Maunder, A. and Renborg, U., eds.*, 1986, pp. 337–38.

Stepleton, Bonnie M. Texas Groundwater Legislation: Conservation of Groundwater or Drought by Process: Note. *Natural Res. J.*, Fall 1986, *26*(4), pp. 871–81. **[G: U.S.]**

Stoffer, David S. Estimation and Identification of Space-Time ARMAX Models in the Presence of Missing Data. *J. Amer. Statist. Assoc.*, September 1986, *81*(395), pp. 762–62. **[G: U.S.; France; Ivory Coast; Senegal; Morocco]**

Stokes, Robert L. Improving the Relevance of Fisheries Economics through Political Analysis: Some Suggested Approaches. **In** *[Crutch-*

field, J. A.], 1986, pp. 42–58.

Stollery, Kenneth R. Monopsony Processing in an Open-Access Fishery. *Marine Resource Econ.*, 1986, *3*(4), pp. 331–51. **[G: Global]**

Stollery, Kenneth R. A Short-run Model of Capital Stuffing in the Pacific Halibut Fishery. *Marine Resource Econ.*, 1986, *3*(2), pp. 137–53. **[G: Canada]**

Stucki, Erwin. Agriculture in a Turbulent World Economy: Theoretical Developments: Discussion. **In** *Maunder, A. and Renborg, U., eds.*, 1986, pp. 714–16.

Stynes, Daniel J.; Peterson, George L. and Rosenthal, Donald H. Log Transformation Bias in Estimating Travel Cost Models. *Land Econ.*, February 1986, *62*(1), pp. 94–103. **[G: U.S.]**

Sutinen, Jon G. and Hennessey, Timothy M. Enforcement: The Neglected Element in Fishery Management. **In** *[Crutchfield, J. A.]*, 1986, pp. 185–213. **[G: U.S.]**

Svensson, Lars E. O. On the Intergenerational Allocation of Natural Resources: Comment. *Scand. J. Econ.*, 1986, *88*(1), pp. 153–55.

Swainson, Neil A. The Columbia River Treaty—Where Do We Go from Here? *Natural Res. J.*, Spring 1986, *26*(2), pp. 243–59. **[G: U.S.; Canada]**

Swaminathan, M. S. Building National and Global Nutrition Security Systems. **In** *Swaminathan, M. S. and Sinha, S. K., eds.*, 1986, pp. 417–49. **[G: LDCs; MDCs]**

Székely, Alberto. The International Law of Submarine Transboundary Hydrocarbon Resources: Legal Limits to Behavior and Experience for the Gulf of Mexico. *Natural Res. J.*, Fall 1986, *26*(4), pp. 733–68. **[G: U.S.; Mexico]**

Székely, Alberto. Transboundary Oil and Gas: Selected Bibliography. *Natural Res. J.*, Fall 1986, *26*(4), pp. 833–50.

Székely, Alberto. Transboundary Resources: A View from Mexico. *Natural Res. J.*, Fall 1986, *26*(4), pp. 669–94. **[G: Mexico; U.S.]**

Tarlock, A. Dan. A Word of Caution about Water Conservation: Editorial. *Natural Res. J.*, Fall 1986, *26*(4), pp. 659–60. **[G: U.S.]**

Tate, D. M. Structural Change Implications for Industrial Water Use. *Water Resources Res.*, October 1986, *22*(11), pp. 1526–30. **[G: Canada]**

Taylor, Donald C. Reduced Pressure Irrigation Investment Economics. *Water Resources Res.*, February 1986, *22*(2), pp. 121–28. **[G: U.S.]**

Teeples, Ronald; Feigenbaum, Susan and Glyer, David. Public versus Private Water Delivery: Cost Comparisons. *Public Finance Quart.*, July 1986, *14*(3), pp. 351–66.

Therkildsen, Ole. State, Donors and Villagers in Rural Water Management. **In** *Boesen, J., et al., eds.*, 1986, pp. 293–307. **[G: Tanzania]**

Thompson, Russell G. and Singleton, F. D., Jr. Wastewater Treatment Costs and Outlays in Organic Petrochemicals: Standards versus Taxes with Methodology Suggestions for Marginal Cost Pricing and Analysis. *Water Resources Res.*, April 1986, *22*(4), pp. 467–74. **[G: U.S.]**

Timberlake, Lloyd. Guarding Africa's Renewable Resources. **In** *Berg, R. J. and Whitaker, J. S., eds.*, 1986, pp. 111–28. **[G: Africa]**

Tisdell, Clem A. Conflicts about Living Marine Resources in Southeast Asian and Australian Waters: Turtles and Dugong as Cases. *Marine Resource Econ.*, 1986, *3*(1), pp. 89–109. **[G: Asia; Australia]**

Tisdell, Clem A. and De Silva, N. T. M. H. Supply-Maximising and Variation-Minimising Replacement Cycles of Perennial Crops and Similar Assets: Theory Illustrated by Coconut Cultivation. *J. Agr. Econ.*, May 1986, *37*(2), pp. 243–51.

Toman, Michael A. "Depletion Effects" and Nonrenewable Resource Supply: A Diagrammatic Supply. *Land Econ.*, November 1986, *62*(4), pp. 341–52.

Toman, Michael A. Existence and Transversality Conditions for a General 'Unbounded-Horizon' Model of the Mining Firm. *J. Econ. Dynam. Control*, September 1986, *10*(3), pp. 395–414.

Townsend, Ralph E. A Critique of Models of the American Lobster Fishery. *J. Environ. Econ. Manage.*, September 1986, *13*(3), pp. 277–91. **[G: U.S.]**

Tsoa, Eugene; Shrank, William E. and Roy, Noel. U.S. Demand for Selected Groundfish Products, 1967–80: Reply. *Amer. J. Agr. Econ.*, November 1986, *68*(4), pp. 1025–27. **[G: U.S.]**

Tullock, Gordon. Transitional Gains and Transfers. *Cato J.*, Spring/Summer 1986, *6*(1), pp. 143–54.

Utton, Albert E. and McHugh, Paul D. On an Institutional Arrangement for Developing Oil and Gas in the Gulf of Mexico. *Natural Res. J.*, Fall 1986, *26*(4), pp. 717–32. **[G: U.S.; Mexico]**

Valencia, Mark J. and Marsh, James Barney. Southeast Asia: Marine Resources, Extended Maritime Jurisdiction, and Development. *Marine Resource Econ.*, 1986, *3*(1), pp. 3–27. **[G: S.E. Asia]**

Vaux, H. J., Jr. Water Scarcity and Gains from Trade in Kern County, California. **In** *Frederick, K. D., ed.*, 1986, pp. 67–101. **[G: U.S.]**

Vislie, Jon. Joint Production and Market Structure: The Case of Oil and Natural Gas. *J. Econ. (Z. Nationalökon.)*, 1986, *46*(2), pp. 163–73.

Wahl, Richard W. and Davis, Robert K. Satisfying Southern California's Thirst for Water: Efficient Alternatives. **In** *Frederick, K. D., ed.*, 1986, pp. 102–33. **[G: U.S.]**

Wallace, Stein W. and Brekke, Karl. Optimal Fleet Size When National Quotas Can Be Traded. *Marine Resource Econ.*, 1986, *2*(4), pp. 315–29. **[G: Norway]**

Wanakule, Nisai; Mays, Larry W. and Lasdon, Leon S. Optimal Management of Large-Scale Aquifers: Methodology and Applications. *Water Resources Res.*, April 1986, *22*(4), pp. 447–65. **[G: U.S.]**

Wandschneider, Philip R. Neoclassical and Institutionalist Explanations of Changes in Northwest Water Institutions. *J. Econ. Issues*, March 1986, *20*(1), pp. 87–107.

Wang, Der Hsiung; Goodreau, Louis J. and Mueller, Joseph J. Economics of Atlantic Sea Scallop Management. *Marine Resource Econ.*, 1986, *3*(2), pp. 111–35. **[G: U.S.]**

Ward, Frank A. and Loomis, John B. The Travel Cost Demand Model as an Environmental Policy Assessment Tool: A Review of Literature. *Western J. Agr. Econ.*, December 1986, *11*(2), pp. 164–78.

Wilen, James E. and Brown, Gardner, Jr. Optimal Recovery Paths for Perturbations of Trophic Level Bioeconomic Systems. *J. Environ. Econ. Manage.*, September 1986, *13*(3), pp. 225–34.

Williams, Martin and Suh, Byung. The Demand for Urban Water by Customer Class. *Appl. Econ.*, December 1986, *18*(12), pp. 1275–89. **[G: U.S.]**

Young, Robert A.; Daubert, John T. and Morel-Seytoux, Hubert J. Evaluating Institutional Alternatives for Managing an Interrelated Stream-Aquifer System. *Amer. J. Agr. Econ.*, November 1986, *68*(4), pp. 787–97. **[G: U.S.]**

Young, Trevor and Allen, P. Geoffrey. Methods for Valuing Countryside Amenity: An Overview. *J. Agr. Econ.*, September 1986, *37*(3), pp. 349–64.

7211 Recreational Aspects of Natural Resources

Anderson, Glen D. and Bishop, Richard C. The Valuation Problem. **In** *Bromley, D. W., ed.*, 1986, pp. 89–137.

Brower, Sidney. Planners in the Neighborhood: A Cautionary Tale. **In** *Taylor, R. B., ed.*, 1986, pp. 181–214. **[G: U.S.]**

Caulkins, Peter P.; Bishop, Richard C. and Bouwes, Nicolaas, Sr. The Travel Cost Model for Lake Recreation: A Comparison of Two Methods for Incorporating Site Quality and Substitution Effects. *Amer. J. Agr. Econ.*, May 1986, *68*(2), pp. 291–97. **[G: U.S.]**

Duffell, J. Roger. The Car Excursion to Informal Outdoor Recreation Sites: Comparative Studies in the West Midlands Region in 1966 to 1978. *Reg. Stud.*, October 1986, *20*(6), pp. 505–21. **[G: U.K.]**

Freeman, A. Myrick, III. The Valuation Problem: Comment. **In** *Bromley, D. W., ed.*, 1986, pp. 139–49.

Green, Trellis G. Specification Considerations for the Price Variable in Travel Cost Demand Models: Comment. *Land Econ.*, November 1986, *62*(4), pp. 416–18.

Kealy, Mary Jo and Bishop, Richard C. Theoretical and Empirical Specifications Issues in Travel Cost Demand Studies. *Amer. J. Agr. Econ.*, August 1986, *68*(3), pp. 660–67. **[G: U.S.]**

McConnell, Kenneth E. The Valuation Problem: Comment. **In** *Bromley, D. W., ed.*, 1986, pp. 151–61.

Sandrey, Ron A. Non-Market Valuation in New Zealand: An Empirical Analysis of Vehicle Bias. *New Zealand Econ. Pap.*, 1986, *20*, pp. 53–60. **[G: New Zealand]**

Smith, V. Kerry; Desvousges, William H. and Fisher, Ann. A Comparison of Direct and Indirect Methods for Estimating Environmental Benefits. *Amer. J. Agr. Econ.*, May 1986, *68*(2), pp. 280–90. **[G: U.S.]**

Ward, Frank A. Specification Considerations for the Price Variable in Travel Cost Demand Models: Reply. *Land Econ.*, November 1986, *62*(4), pp. 419–21.

722 Conservation and Pollution

7220 Conservation and Pollution

Abrol, I. P. Salt-Affected Soils: Problems and Prospects in Developing Countries. **In** *Swaminathan, M. S. and Sinha, S. K., eds.*, 1986, pp. 283–305. **[G: Global]**

Adams, Richard M. Agriculture, Forestry, and Related Benefits of Air Pollution Control: A Review and Some Observations. *Amer. J. Agr. Econ.*, May 1986, *68*(2), pp. 464–72. **[G: U.S.]**

Adams, Richard M.; Callaway, J. M. and McCarl, Bruce A. Pollution, Agriculture and Social Welfare: The Case of Acid Deposition. *Can. J. Agr. Econ.*, March 1986, *34*(1), pp. 3–19. **[G: U.S.]**

Adams, Richard M.; Hamilton, Scott A. and McCarl, Bruce A. The Benefits of Pollution Control: The Case of Ozone and U.S. Agriculture. *Amer. J. Agr. Econ.*, November 1986, *68*(4), pp. 886–93. **[G: U.S.]**

von Ah, Joseph. Pressure on Natural Resources: Discussion. **In** *Maunder, A. and Renborg, U., eds.*, 1986, pp. 293–95.

Alper, Donald K. and Monahan, Robert L. Regional Transboundary Negotiations Leading to the Skagit River Treaty: Analysis and Future Application. *Can. Public Policy*, March 1986, *12*(1), pp. 163–74. **[G: Canada; U.S.]**

Alschuler, John H., Jr. Local Energy Conservation Programs: Comments. **In** *Sawhill, J. C. and Cotton, R., eds.*, 1986, pp. 200–201. **[G: U.S.]**

Anderson, Dennis. Declining Tree Stocks in African Countries. *World Devel.*, July 1986, *14*(7), pp. 853–63. **[G: Africa]**

Anderson, Glen D. and Bishop, Richard C. The Valuation Problem. **In** *Bromley, D. W., ed.*, 1986, pp. 89–137.

Anderson, Lee G. Economically Optimal Total Allowable Catches in the Absence of Stock–Recruitment Relationships. **In** *[Crutchfield, J. A.]*, 1986, pp. 309–30.

Anderson, Lee G. and Lee, Dwight R. Optimal Governing Instrument, Operation Level, and Enforcement in Natural Resource Regulation: The Case of the Fishery. *Amer. J. Agr. Econ.*, August 1986, *68*(3), pp. 678–90.

Anderson, Terry L. and Johnson, Ronald N. The Problem of Instream Flows. *Econ. Inquiry*,

October 1986, *24*(4), pp. 535–54.

Andrus, Chip. The Economics of Erosion Control in a Subtropical Watershed: Comment. *Land Econ.*, August 1986, *62*(3), pp. 329–30. **[G: Dominican Republic]**

Århem, Kaj. Pastoralism under Pressure: The Ngorongoro Maasai. **In** *Boesen, J., et al., eds.*, 1986, pp. 239–51. **[G: Tanzania]**

Arrow, Kenneth J. Valuing Environmental Goods: An Assessment of the Contingent Valuation Method: The Review Panel's Assessment: Comments. **In** *Cummings, R. G.; Brookshire, D. S. and Schulze, W. D., eds.*, 1986, pp. 180–85.

Ashworth, John; Papps, Ivy and Storey, David J. Assessing the Effectiveness and Economic Efficiency of an E.E.C. Pollution Control Directive: The Control of Discharges of Mercury to the Aquatic Environment. **In** *von der Schulenburg, J.-M. G. and Skogh, G., eds.*, 1986, pp. 207–25. **[G: EEC]**

Assaf, George B.; Kroetch, Brent G. and Mathur, Subodh C. Nonmarket Valuations of Accidental Oil Spills: A Survey of Economic and Legal Principles. *Marine Resource Econ.*, 1986, *2*(3), pp. 211–37. **[G: U.S.]**

Barbera, Anthony J. and McConnell, Virginia D. Effects of Pollution Control on Industry Productivity: A Factor Demand Approach. *J. Ind. Econ.*, December 1986, *35*(2), pp. 161–72. **[G: U.S.]**

Baskerville, Gordon L. Forest and Wildlife Management. **In** *Economic Council of Canada*, 1986, pp. 33–46. **[G: Canada]**

Batie, Sandra S. and Sappington, Alyson G. Cross-compliance as a Soil Conservation Strategy: A Case Study. *Amer. J. Agr. Econ.*, November 1986, *68*(4), pp. 880–85. **[G: U.S.]**

Beavis, Brian and Dobbs, Ian M. The Dynamics of Optimal Environmental Regulation. *J. Econ. Dynam. Control*, September 1986, *10*(3), pp. 415–23.

Bentkover, Judith D. The Role of Benefits Assessment in Public Policy Development. **In** *Bentkover, J. D.; Covello, V. T. and Jeryl, M., eds.*, 1986, pp. 1–12. **[G: U.S.]**

Bertrand, Jean-Pierre. Pressure on Natural Resources: Discussion. **In** *Maunder, A. and Renborg, U., eds.*, 1986, pp. 295–96.

Birowo, Achmad T. and Prabowo, Dibyo. The Pressure on Natural Resources in Indonesian Agricultural Development. **In** *Maunder, A. and Renborg, U., eds.*, 1986, pp. 284–93.

Bishop, Richard C. and Heberlein, Thomas A. Does Contingent Valuation Work? **In** *Cummings, R. G.; Brookshire, D. S. and Schulze, W. D., eds.*, 1986, pp. 123–47.

Bongaerts, Jan C. and Heinrichs, Dirk. Deutsche Umweltschutzgesetze und Umweltschutzinvestitionen des produzierenden Gewerbes. (German Environmental Protection Legislation and Environmental Investment by West German Manufacturing Industries. With English summary.) *Konjunkturpolitik*, 1986, *32*(3), pp. 151–63. **[G: W. Germany]**

Bonus, Holger. Obstacles to Changing the Incentive System: The Case of the Federal Republic of Germany. **In** *Balassa, B. and Giersch, H., eds.*, 1986, pp. 378–91. **[G: W. Germany]**

Bradley, Michael D. and Carpenter, Michael C. Subsiding Land and Falling Ground-Water Tables: Public Policy, Private Liability, and Legal Remedy. *Econ. Geogr.*, July 1986, *62*(3), pp. 241–53. **[G: U.S.]**

Briassoulis, Helen. Integrated Economic-Environmental-Policy Modeling at the Regional and Multiregional Level: Methodological Characteristics and Issues. *Growth Change*, July 1986, *17*(3), pp. 22–34. **[G: Netherlands; U.S.; Canada]**

Bromley, Daniel W. Natural Resources and Agricultural Development in the Tropics: Is Conflict Inevitable? **In** *Maunder, A. and Renborg, U., eds.*, 1986, pp. 319–27.

Bruce, James P. Addressing Environmental Issues in the Future: Comments. **In** *Economic Council of Canada*, 1986, pp. 98–99.

Bryson, John. State Government Conservation Programs: Comments. **In** *Sawhill, J. C. and Cotton, R., eds.*, 1986, pp. 234–35. **[G: U.S.]**

Buresh, James C. State and Federal Land Use Regulation: An Application to Groundwater and Nonpoint Source Pollution Control. *Yale Law J.*, June 1986, *95*(7), pp. 1433–58. **[G: U.S.]**

Burrows, Paul. Nonconvexity Induced by External Costs on Production: Theoretical Curio or Policy Dilemma? *J. Environ. Econ. Manage.*, June 1986, *13*(2), pp. 101–28.

Butler, Richard V. and Maher, Michael D. The Control of Externalities: Abatement vs. Damage Prevention. *Southern Econ. J.*, April 1986, *52*(4), pp. 1088–1102.

Caldwell, John C.; Reddy, P. H. and Caldwell, Pat. Periodic High Risk as a Cause of Fertility Decline in a Changing Rural Environment: Survival Strategies in the 1980–1983 South Indian Drought. *Econ. Develop. Cult. Change*, July 1986, *34*(4), pp. 677–701. **[G: India]**

Carter, Anne P. Energy, Environment, and Economic Growth. **In** *Sohn, I., ed.*, 1986, *1974*, pp. 417–31. **[G: U.S.]**

Chant, Donald A. Management and Disposal of Toxic Wastes. **In** *Economic Council of Canada*, 1986, pp. 47–56. **[G: Canada]**

Charney, Jonathan I. The Unfinished Business of the Law of the Sea Conference. **In** *Pontecorvo, G., ed.*, 1986, pp. 238–64.

Christiansson, Carl. Soil Erosion and Conservation in the Drylands. **In** *Boesen, J., et al., eds.*, 1986, pp. 143–57. **[G: Tanzania]**

Chu, D. K. Y. Government Policies, Economic Development, and Possible Environmental Effects as the Land–Water Interfaces of Guangdong Province, China. *Marine Resource Econ.*, 1986, *3*(1), pp. 29–44. **[G: China]**

Claeys, George. Ecology and Technology in Early Nineteenth Century American Utopianism: A Note on John Adolphus Etzler. *Sci. Soc.*, Summer 1986, *50*(2), pp. 219–25.

Clark, Richard T. and Raitt, Daryll D. Cross

Compliance for Erosion Control: Anticipating Efficiency and Distributive Impacts: Comment. *Amer. J. Agr. Econ.*, November 1986, *68*(4), pp. 1013–15. **[G: U.S.]**

Clausen, A. W. Sustainable Development: The Global Imperative: Fairfield Osborn Memorial Lecture in Environmental Science: Washington, D.C.: November 12, 1981. **In** *Clausen, A. W.*, 1986, pp. 21–35.

Cohen, Mark A. The Costs and Benefits of Oil Spill Prevention and Enforcement. *J. Environ. Econ. Manage.*, June 1986, *13*(2), pp. 167–88. **[G: U.S.]**

Conrad, Jon M. Resource Development and Environmental Risk. **In** *[Crutchfield, J. A.]*, 1986, pp. 296–308.

Crandall, Robert W. Economic Rents as a Barrier to Deregulation. *Cato J.*, Spring/Summer 1986, *6*(1), pp. 173–94. **[G: U.S.]**

Crane, Alan T. Nuclear Safety and Environmental Issues. **In** *Saltzman, S. and Schuler, R. E., eds.*, 1986, pp. 213–23. **[G: U.S.]**

Dagenais, Camille. Dams and the Environment. **In** *Economic Council of Canada*, 1986, pp. 63–67.

Daly, George and Mayor, Thomas. Equity, Efficiency and Environmental Quality. *Public Choice*, 1986, *51*(2), pp. 141–59. **[G: U.S.]**

Dinar, Ariel and Yaron, Dan. Treatment Optimization of Municipal Wastewater and Reuse for Regional Irrigation. *Water Resources Res.*, March 1986, *22*(3), pp. 331–38. **[G: Israel]**

Dinehart, Stephen J. Cross-Compliance for Erosion Control: Anticipating Efficiency and Distributive Impacts: Comment. *Amer. J. Agr. Econ.*, May 1986, *68*(2), pp. 349–50. **[G: U.S.]**

Dixon, John A. The Role of Economics in Valuing Environmental Effects of Development Projects. **In** *Dixon, J. A. and Hufschmidt, M. M., eds.*, 1986, pp. 3–10.

Dixon, John A. and Meister, Anton D. Time Horizons, Discounting, and Computational Aids. **In** *Dixon, J. A. and Hufschmidt, M. M., eds.*, 1986, pp. 39–55.

Dorfman, Robert. Benefit–Cost Analysis of Environmental Protection Programs in Less Developed Countries. **In** *Adelman, I. and Taylor, J. E., eds.*, 1986, pp. 103–23. **[G: LDCs]**

Downing, Paul B. and White, Lawrence J. Innovation in Pollution Control. *J. Environ. Econ. Manage.*, March 1986, *13*(1), pp. 18–29.

Duncan, Angus. Local Energy Conservation Programs: Comments. **In** *Sawhill, J. C. and Cotton, R., eds.*, 1986, pp. 201–03. **[G: U.S.]**

Endres, Alfred. Charges, Permits and Pollutant Interactions. *Eastern Econ. J.*, July-Sept. 1986, *12*(3), pp. 327–36.

England, Richard W. Production, Distribution, and Environmental Quality: Mr. Sraffa Reinterpreted as an Ecologist. *Kyklos*, 1986, *39*(2), pp. 230–44.

Ervin, David E.; Heffernan, William D. and Green, Gary P. Cross Compliance for Erosion Control: Anticipating Efficiency and Distributive Impacts: Reply. *Amer. J. Agr. Econ.*, November 1986, *68*(4), pp. 1016–17. **[G: U.S.]**

Ervin, David E.; Heffernan, William D. and Green, Gary P. Cross-Compliance for Erosion Control: Anticipating Efficiency and Distributive Impacts: Reply. *Amer. J. Agr. Econ.*, May 1986, *68*(2), pp. 351–52.

Evans, David S. The Differential Effect of Regulation across Plant Size: Comment [The Effect of Environmental Regulation on Optimal Plant Size and Factor Shares]. *J. Law Econ.*, April 1986, *29*(1), pp. 187–200. **[G: U.S.]**

Farber, Kit D. and Rutledge, Gary L. Pollution Abatement and Control Expenditures. *Surv. Curr. Bus.*, July 1986, *66*(7), pp. 94–105. **[G: U.S.]**

Farber, Stephen C. and Martin, Robert E. Market Structure and Pollution Control under Imperfect Surveillance. *J. Ind. Econ.*, December 1986, *35*(2), pp. 147–60. **[G: U.S.]**

Farrell, Kenneth R. and Capalbo, Susan M. Natural Resource and Environmental Dimensions of Agricultural Development. **In** *Maunder, A. and Renborg, U., eds.*, 1986, pp. 273–83. **[G: U.S.]**

Feinstein, Jerald L. An Expert System Used to Prevent the Disclosure of Sensitive Information at the United States Environmental Protection Agency. **In** *Pau, L. F., ed.*, 1986, pp. 213–20. **[G: U.S.]**

Fenge, Terry and Smith, L. Graham. Reforming the Federal Environmental Assessment and Review Process. *Can. Public Policy*, December 1986, *12*(4), pp. 596–605. **[G: Canada]**

Florio, James J. Congress as Reluctant Regulator: Hazardous Waste Policy in the 1980's. *Yale J. Regul.*, Spring 1986, *3*(2), pp. 351–82. **[G: U.S.]**

Fox, Irving K. Management and Disposal of Toxic Wastes: Comments. **In** *Economic Council of Canada*, 1986, pp. 56–59. **[G: Canada]**

Frederick, Kenneth D. Scarce Water and Institutional Change: Overview. **In** *Frederick, K. D., ed.*, 1986, pp. 1–24. **[G: U.S.]**

Freeman, A. Myrick, III. Estimating the Benefits of Environmental Regulations. **In** *Bentkover, J. D.; Covello, V. T. and Jeryl, M., eds.*, 1986, pp. 211–29.

Freeman, A. Myrick, III. On Assessing the State of the Arts of the Contingent Valuation Method of Valuing Environmental Changes. **In** *Cummings, R. G.; Brookshire, D. S. and Schulze, W. D., eds.*, 1986, pp. 148–61.

Freeman, A. Myrick, III. The Valuation Problem: Comment. **In** *Bromley, D. W., ed.*, 1986, pp. 139–49.

Freeman, A. Myrick, III. Uncertainty and Option Value in Environmental Policy. **In** *[Crutchfield, J. A.]*, 1986, pp. 251–71.

French, David. Confronting an Unsolvable Problem: Deforestation in Malawi. *World Devel.*, April 1986, *14*(4), pp. 531–40. **[G: Malawi]**

Galster, George C. Nuclear Power Plants and Residential Property Values: A Comment on Short-run vs. Long-run Considerations. *J. Reg. Sci.*, November 1986, *26*(4), pp. 803–05. **[G: U.S.]**

Gamble, Hays B. and Downing, Roger H. Nuclear Power Plants and Residential Property Values: A Comment on Short-run vs. Long-run Considerations: A Reply. *J. Reg. Sci.*, November 1986, *26*(4), pp. 807–08. **[G: U.S.]**

Garcia, Philip, et al. Measuring the Benefits of Environmental Change Using a Duality Approach: The Case of Ozone and Illinois Cash Grain Farms. *J. Environ. Econ. Manage.*, March 1986, *13*(1), pp. 69–80. **[G: U.S.]**

Gerking, Shelby and Stanley, Linda R. An Economic Analysis of Air Pollution and Health: The Case of St. Louis. *Rev. Econ. Statist.*, February 1986, *68*(1), pp. 115–21. **[G: U.S.]**

Gibbons, John H.; Gwin, Holly L. and Pool, Richard B. Energy Conservation in the Federal Government. **In** *Sawhill, J. C. and Cotton, R., eds.*, 1986, pp. 237–57. **[G: U.S.]**

Gordon, Roberta G. Legal Incentives for Reduction, Reuse, and Recycling: A New Approach to Hazardous Waste Management. *Yale Law J.*, March 1986, *95*(4), pp. 810–31. **[G: U.S.]**

Grenier, Pierre. Management and Disposal of Toxic Wastes: Comments. **In** *Economic Council of Canada*, 1986, pp. 59–61. **[G: Canada]**

Griffin, Karen. State Government Conservation Programs. **In** *Sawhill, J. C. and Cotton, R., eds.*, 1986, pp. 205–32. **[G: U.S.]**

Griffith, James J. and Knoeber, Charles R. Why Do Corporations Contribute to the Nature Conservancy? *Public Choice*, 1986, *49*(1), pp. 69–77. **[G: U.S.]**

Grigalunas, Thomas A., et al. Estimating the Cost of Oil Spills: Lessons from the *Amoco Cadiz* Incident. *Marine Resource Econ.*, 1986, *2*(3), pp. 239–62. **[G: France]**

Hahn, Robert W. Trade-offs in Designing Markets with Multiple Objectives. *J. Environ. Econ. Manage.*, March 1986, *13*(1), pp. 1–12.

Hamilton, Andrew L. Fresh Water Issues: Comments. **In** *Economic Council of Canada*, 1986, pp. 24–27. **[G: Canada]**

Handl, Günther. National Uses of Transboundary Air Resources: The International Entitlement Issue Reconsidered. *Natural Res. J.*, Summer 1986, *26*(3), pp. 405–67. **[G: OECD]**

Hare, F. Kenneth. Air Quality and the Energy–Environment Interface. **In** *Economic Council of Canada*, 1986, pp. 69–75. **[G: Canada]**

Harlow, Ruth E. The EPA and Biotechnology Regulation: Coping with Scientific Uncertainty. *Yale Law J.*, January 1986, *95*(3), pp. 553–76. **[G: U.S.]**

Harris, Thomas R. and Mapp, Harry P. Stochastic Dominance Comparison of Water-Conserving Irrigation Strategies. *Amer. J. Agr. Econ.*, May 1986, *68*(2), pp. 298–305. **[G: U.S.]**

Hayden, F. Gregory. Rejoinder to David Vail's Comments on National Agricultural Policy [A Geobased National Agricultural Policy for Rural Community Enhancement, Environmental Vitality, and Income Stabilization]. *J. Econ. Issues*, March 1986, *20*(1), pp. 191–201. **[G: U.S.]**

Hedges, Roman and Reeb, Donald J. Acid Rain: Public Policy in the Face of Uncertainty. **In** *Schoolman, M. and Magid, A., eds.*, 1986, pp. 357–74. **[G: U.S.]**

Hedlin, R. A. An Additional Perspective. *Can. J. Agr. Econ.*, June 1986, *33*, pp. 30–40. **[G: Canada]**

Heimlich, Ralph E. Agricultural Programs and Cropland Conversion, 1975–1981. *Land Econ.*, May 1986, *62*(2), pp. 174–81. **[G: U.S.]**

Hettelingh, Jean-Paul and Hordijk, Leen. Environmental Conflicts: The Case of Acid Rain in Europe. *Ann. Reg. Sci.*, November 1986, *20*(3), pp. 38–52. **[G: Europe]**

Hewett, Ed. A., et al. Panel on the Economic and Political Consequences of Chernobyl' *Soviet Econ.*, Apr.-June 1986, *2*(2), pp. 97–130. **[G: U.S.S.R.]**

Hirst, Eric. State Government Conservation Programs: Comments. **In** *Sawhill, J. C. and Cotton, R., eds.*, 1986, pp. 232–34. **[G: U.S.]**

Hoag, Dana L. and Young, Douglas L. Commodity and Conservation Policy Impacts on Risk and Returns. *Western J. Agr. Econ.*, December 1986, *11*(2), pp. 211–20. **[G: U.S.]**

Hovey, Harry H., Jr. Air Pollution Impacts of Fossil Fuel-Fired Electrical Generation. **In** *Saltzman, S. and Schuler, R. E., eds.*, 1986, pp. 187–202. **[G: U.S.]**

Howe, Charles W.; Schurmeier, Dennis R. and Shaw, William Douglas, Jr. Innovations in Water Management: Lessons from the Colorado–Big Thompson Project and Northern Colorado Water Conservancy District. **In** *Frederick, K. D., ed.*, 1986, pp. 171–200. **[G: U.S.]**

Isaacs, Colin E. Managing the Legacy: Proceedings of a Colloquium on the Environment, December 1985: International Perspectives: Comments. **In** *Economic Council of Canada*, 1986, pp. 9–11.

Janssen, Ron and Hafkamp, Wim. A Decision Support System for Conflict Analysis on Environmental Effects of Energy Conversion. *Ann. Reg. Sci.*, November 1986, *20*(3), pp. 67–85.

Kahneman, Daniel. Valuing Environmental Goods: An Assessment of the Contingent Valuation Method: The Review Panel's Assessment: Comments. **In** *Cummings, R. G.; Brookshire, D. S. and Schulze, W. D., eds.*, 1986, pp. 185–94.

Kehne, Jeffrey. Encouraging Safety through Insurance-Based Incentives: Financial Responsibility for Hazardous Wastes. *Yale Law J.*, December 1986, *96*(2), pp. 403–27. **[G: U.S.]**

Kiker, Clyde and Lynne, Gary. An Economic Model of Soil Conservation: Comment. *Amer. J. Agr. Econ.*, August 1986, *68*(3), pp. 739–42.

Kim, Sung-Hoon and Dixon, John A. Economic Valuation of Environmental Quality Aspects of Upland Agricultural Projects in Korea. **In** *Dixon, J. A. and Hufschmidt, M. M., eds.*, 1986, pp. 63–82. **[G: S. Korea]**

Kneese, Allen V. Environmental Preservation and Economic Growth. **In** *Economic Council of Canada*, 1986, pp. 79–87. **[G: U.S.]**

Kohn, Robert E. A Note on the Dolbear Theorem. *Public Finance*, 1986, *41*(2), pp. 285–88.

Kohn, Robert E. Aggregating Goods and Pollutants. *J. Environ. Econ. Manage.*, September 1986, *13*(3), pp. 245–54.

Kohn, Robert E. The Rate of Emission and the Optimal Scale of the Polluting Firm. *Can. J. Econ.*, August 1986, *19*(3), pp. 574–81.

Kolosov, A. Environmental Protection and the Intensification of the Economy. *Prob. Econ.*, November 1986, *29*(7), pp. 40–54.

Kolstad, Charles D. Empirical Properties of Economic Incentives and Command-and-Control Regulations for Air Pollution Control. *Land Econ.*, August 1986, *62*(3), pp. 250–68. **[G: U.S.]**

Kramer, Randall A. An International Overview of Soil Conservation Policy. **In** *Maunder, A. and Renborg, U., eds.*, 1986, pp. 307–13. **[G: Global]**

Krupnick, Alan J. Costs of Alternative Policies for the Control of Nitrogen Dioxide in Baltimore. *J. Environ. Econ. Manage.*, June 1986, *13*(2), pp. 189–97. **[G: U.S.]**

Kukushkin, G. Planning the Rational Utilization of Natural Resources. *Prob. Econ.*, January 1986, *28*(9), pp. 50–61. **[G: U.S.S.R.]**

Kunreuther, Howard and Kleindorfer, Paul R. A Sealed-Bid Auction Mechanism for Siting Noxious Facilities. *Amer. Econ. Rev.*, May 1986, *76*(2), pp. 295–99.

Lakshmanan, T. R. and Bolton, Roger. Regional Energy and Environmental Analysis. **In** *Nijkamp, P., ed. (I)*, 1986, pp. 581–628. **[G: U.S.; OECD]**

Lam, K. C. Environmental Protection in the Shenzhen Special Economic Zone: Achievements, Problems and Implications. **In** *Jao, Y. C. and Leung, C. K., eds.*, 1986, pp. 65–83. **[G: China]**

Lang, Winfried. Environmental Protection: The Challenge for International Law. *J. World Trade Law*, Sept.:Oct. 1986, *20*(5), pp. 489–96.

Larkin, Andrew. Environmental Impact and Institutional Adjustment: Application of Foster's Principles to Solid Waste Disposal. *J. Econ. Issues*, March 1986, *20*(1), pp. 43–61.

Lave, Lester B. The Cost of Abating Sulfur, Nitrogen, and Ozone Air Pollutants. *Amer. J. Agr. Econ.*, May 1986, *68*(2), pp. 473–78. **[G: U.S.]**

Lawarree, Jacques. Une comparaison empirique des performances des secteurs privé et public: le cas des collectes d'immondices en Belgique. (With English summary.) *Cah. Écon. Bruxelles*, First Trimester 1986, (109), pp. 3–31. **[G: Belgium]**

Layton, Christopher. Conserving the Planet or Rushing to Disaster? *J. World Trade Law*, Nov.:Dec. 1986, *20*(6), pp. 701–05. **[G: Global]**

Lee, Dwight R. and Misiolek, Walter S. Substituting Pollution Taxation for General Taxation: Some Implications for Efficiency in Pollutions Taxation. *J. Environ. Econ. Manage.*, December 1986, *13*(4), pp. 338–47.

Lee, Henry. Local Energy Conservation Programs. **In** *Sawhill, J. C. and Cotton, R., eds.*, 1986, pp. 163–200. **[G: U.S.]**

Lee, James and Goodland, Robert. Economic Development and the Environment. *Finance Develop.*, December 1986, *23*(4), pp. 36–39. **[G: LDCs]**

Leipert, Christian. Social Costs of Economic Growth. *J. Econ. Issues*, March 1986, *20*(1), pp. 109–31. **[G: W. Germany]**

Lemeshev, M. The Food Program and Protecting the Environment. *Prob. Econ.*, September 1986, *29*(5), pp. 57–75. **[G: U.S.S.R.]**

Leontief, Wassily. Air Pollution and the Economic Structure: Empirical Results of Input–Output Computations. **In** *Leontief, W.*, 1986, *1972*, pp. 273–93. **[G: U.S.]**

Leontief, Wassily. Environmental Repercussions and the Economic Structure: An Input–Output Approach. **In** *Leontief, W.*, 1986, *1970*, pp. 241–60.

Leontief, Wassily. National Income, Economic Structure, and Environmental Externalities. **In** *Leontief, W.*, 1986, *1973*, pp. 261–72.

van Lierop, Wal F. J. and Braat, Leon. Multiobjective Modelling of Economic–Ecological Interactions and Conflicts. *Ann. Reg. Sci.*, November 1986, *20*(3), pp. 114–29.

Lieu, T. S. Impacts of Air Pollution Control Costs: An Input–Output Approach. *Ann. Reg. Sci.*, July 1986, *20*(2), pp. 55–65. **[G: U.S.]**

Linder, Stephen H. Better Regulatory Compliance through Environmental Auditing: A Reform Whose Time Has Passed. *J. Policy Anal. Manage.*, Spring 1986, *5*(3), pp. 590–94. **[G: U.S.]**

Loaiciga, Hugo A. and Mariñno, Miguel A. Risk Analysis for Reservoir Operation. *Water Resources Res.*, April 1986, *22*(4), pp. 483–88. **[G: U.S.]**

Lyon, Randolph M. Equilibrium Properties of Auctions and Alternative Procedures for Allocating Transferable Permits. *J. Environ. Econ. Manage.*, June 1986, *13*(2), pp. 129–52.

MacNeill, James W. Managing the Legacy: Proceedings of a Colloquium on the Environment, December 1985: International Perspectives. **In** *Economic Council of Canada*, 1986, pp. 3–9.

Magnan de Bornier, Jean. The Coase Theorem and the Empty Core: A Reexamination. *Int. Rev. Law Econ.*, December 1986, *6*(2), pp. 265–71.

Maillet, Pierre. Obstacles to Changing the Incentive System: The Case of the Federal Republic of Germany: Comment. **In** *Balassa, B. and Giersch, H., eds.*, 1986, pp. 392–95. **[G: W. Germany]**

Main, Robert S. Impacts, Costs, and Techniques for Mitigation of Contaminated Groundwater: A Review: Comment. *Water Resources Res.*, March 1986, *22*(3), pp. 429–30. **[G: U.S.]**

Mar, Brian W. Complexity, Interdisciplinary Research, and Multiobjective Risk: Hopes or Pitfalls for Environmental Management? **In** *[Crutchfield, J. A.]*, 1986, pp. 353–73.

Margolin, Stanley V. U.S. Environmental Laws and Their Impact on American Steel. **In** *Gold-*

berg, W. H., ed., 1986, pp. 351–60. **[G: U.S.]**

Marsan, André A. Managing the Legacy: Proceedings of a Colloquium on the Environment, December 1985: International Perspectives: Comments. **In** *Economic Council of Canada*, 1986, pp. 11–13.

McConnell, Kenneth E. An Economic Model of Soil Conservation: Reply. *Amer. J. Agr. Econ.*, August 1986, *68*(3), pp. 743–44.

McConnell, Kenneth E. The Valuation Problem: Comment. **In** *Bromley, D. W., ed.*, 1986, pp. 151–61.

McConnell, Virginia D. Automobile Use and Locational Interdependencies. *J. Reg. Sci.*, August 1986, *26*(3), pp. 475–98.

McConnell, Virginia D.; Cumberland, John H. and Gordon, Patrice. Forecasting Municipal Waste Treatment Effluent and Costs: An Application to the Chesapeake Bay. *Rev. Reg. Stud.*, Spring 1986, *16*(2), pp. 11–22. **[G: U.S.]**

McSweeny, William T. and Kramer, Randall A. Soil Conservation with Uncertain Revenues and Input Supplies: Reply. *Amer. J. Agr. Econ.*, May 1986, *68*(2), pp. 361–63.

McSweeny, William T. and Kramer, Randall A. The Integration of Farm Programs for Achieving Soil Conservation and Nonpoint Pollution Control Objectives. *Land Econ.*, May 1986, *62*(2), pp. 159–73.

Mendelsohn, Robert. Economic Evaluation of Air Pollution Damage and Control: Discussion [Agriculture, Forestry, and Related Benefits of Air Pollution Control: A Review and Some Observations] [The Cost of Abating Sulfur, Nitrogen, and Ozone Air Pollutants]. *Amer. J. Agr. Econ.*, May 1986, *68*(2), pp. 482–84. **[G: U.S.]**

Mendelsohn, Robert. Regulating Heterogeneous Emissions. *J. Environ. Econ. Manage.*, December 1986, *13*(4), pp. 301–12.

Mestelman, Stuart. General Equilibrium Modelling of Industries with Production Externalities. *Can. J. Econ.*, August 1986, *19*(3), pp. 522–25.

Mickwitz, Gösta. Skogsindustrin bör kräva luftvård. (The Forest Industry Should Demand Air Pollution Control. With English summary.) *Ekon. Samfundets Tidskr.*, 1986, *39*(4), pp. 179–80. **[G: Finland]**

Miller, M. H. Soil Degradation in Eastern Canada: Its Extent and Impact. *Can. J. Agr. Econ.*, June 1986, *33*, pp. 7–18. **[G: Canada]**

Mitchell, Robert Cameron and Carson, Richard T. Property Rights, Protest, and the Siting of Hazardous Waste Facilities. *Amer. Econ. Rev.*, May 1986, *76*(2), pp. 285–90. **[G: U.S.]**

Mitchell, Robert Cameron and Carson, Richard T. Some Comments on the State of the Arts Assessment of the Contigent Valuation Method Draft Report: Appendix. **In** *Cummings, R. G.; Brookshire, D. S. and Schulze, W. D., eds.*, 1986, pp. 237–45.

Moffitt, L. Joe, et al. Economic Impact of Public Pest Information: Soybean Insect Forecasts in Illinois. *Amer. J. Agr. Econ.*, May 1986, *68*(2), pp. 274–79. **[G: U.S.]**

von Moltke, Konrad. Air Quality and the Energy–Environment Interface: Comments. **In** *Economic Council of Canada*, 1986, pp. 75–78. **[G: W. Europe]**

Muraro, Gilberto. The Economics of Unidirectional Transfrontier Pollution Revisited. *Ricerche Econ.*, Apr.-Sept. 1986, *40*(2–3), pp. 510–24.

Nachtnebel, H. P.; Hanisch, P. and Duckstein, L. Multicriterion Analysis of Small Hydropower Plants under Fuzzy Objectives. *Ann. Reg. Sci.*, November 1986, *20*(3), pp. 86–103. **[G: Austria]**

Nagarajan, S. Disease Problems and Their Management. **In** *Swaminathan, M. S. and Sinha, S. K., eds.*, 1986, pp. 387–416. **[G: LDCs]**

Nalven, Joseph. Transboundary Environmental Problem Solving: Social Process, Cultural Perception. *Natural Res. J.*, Fall 1986, *26*(4), pp. 793–818. **[G: U.S.; Mexico]**

Nemetz, Peter N. Federal Environmental Regulation in Canada. *Natural Res. J.*, Summer 1986, *26*(3), pp. 551–608. **[G: Canada]**

Nijkamp, Peter and Rietveld, Piet. Conflicting Objectives in Environmental Management, an Introduction. *Ann. Reg. Sci.*, November 1986, *20*(3), pp. 1–9.

Norgaard, Richard B. Environmental Evaluation Techniques and Optimization in an Uncertain World. *Land Econ.*, May 1986, *62*(2), pp. 210–13.

O'Hare, Michael. Environmental Management. **In** *Knowlton, W. and Zeckhauser, R., eds.*, 1986, pp. 99–135. **[G: U.S.]**

Owens, Emiel W. Social Control of Pesticides—Some Health Effects. *Int. J. Soc. Econ.*, 1986, *13*(1/2), pp. 93–97. **[G: U.S.]**

Pashigian, B. Peter. Reply [The Effect of Environmental Regulation on Optimal Plant Size and Factor Shares]. *J. Law Econ.*, April 1986, *29*(1), pp. 201–09. **[G: U.S.]**

Pathak, M. D. and Dhaliwal, G. S. Insect Control. **In** *Swaminathan, M. S. and Sinha, S. K., eds.*, 1986, pp. 357–86. **[G: Selected Countries]**

Pearse, Peter H. Fresh Water Issues. **In** *Economic Council of Canada*, 1986, pp. 15–24. **[G: Canada]**

Percival, Robert V. Conservation and Renewable Energy Sources as Supply Alternatives for New York's Electric Utilities. **In** *Saltzman, S. and Schuler, R. E., eds.*, 1986, pp. 126–50. **[G: U.S.]**

Pillet, Gonzague. From External Effects to Energy Externality: New Proposals in Environmental Economics. *Hitotsubashi J. Econ.*, June 1986, *27*(1), pp. 77–97.

Pontecorvo, Giulio. Division of the Spoils: Hydrocarbons and Living Resources. **In** *Pontecorvo, G., ed.*, 1986, pp. 15–28. **[G: U.S.; Canada; Greenland]**

Portney, Paul R. and Mullahy, John. Urban Air Quality and Acute Respiratory Illness. *J. Urban Econ.*, July 1986, *20*(1), pp. 21–38. **[G: U.S.]**

Postel, Sandra L. Needed: A New Water Policy. *Challenge,* Jan./Feb. 1986, *28*(6), pp. 43–49. **[G: U.S.]**

Quiggin, John. Common Property, Private Property and Regulation: The Case of Dryland Salinity. *Australian J. Agr. Econ.,* August/December 1986, *30*(2–3), pp. 103–17. **[G: Australia]**

Quinn, Robert and Yandle, Bruce. Expenditures on Air Pollution Control under Federal Regulation. *Rev. Reg. Stud.,* Fall 1986, *16*(3), pp. 11–16. **[G: U.S.]**

Radice, E. A. Energy and Materials. **In** *Kaser, M. C. and Radice, E. A., eds.,* 1986, pp. 398–415. **[G: E. Europe; Germany]**

Raiatskas, R. L.; Chiakanavichius, L. P. and Radushis, V. Iu. On the Methodology for Estimating the Economic Cost of Environmental Pollution. *Matekon,* Spring 1986, *22*(3), pp. 3–23.

Randall, Alan. The Possibility of Satisfactory Benefit Estimation with Contingent Markets. **In** *Cummings, R. G.; Brookshire, D. S. and Schulze, W. D., eds.,* 1986, pp. 114–22.

Ranson, Thomas Baldwin. Swaney on Economics, Ecology, and Entropy. *J. Econ. Issues,* September 1986, *20*(3), pp. 837–39.

Raucher, Robert L. The Benefits and Costs of Policies Related to Groundwater Contamination. *Land Econ.,* February 1986, *62*(1), pp. 33–45. **[G: U.S.]**

Regens, James L. and Rycroft, Robert W. Options for Financing Acid Rain Controls. *Natural Res. J.,* Summer 1986, *26*(3), pp. 519–49. **[G: U.S.]**

Rennie, D. A. Soil Degradation, a Western Perspective. *Can. J. Agr. Econ.,* June 1986, *33,* pp. 19–29. **[G: Canada]**

Ribaudo, Marc O. Consideration of Offsite Impacts in Targeting Soil Conservation Programs. *Land Econ.,* November 1986, *62*(4), pp. 402–11. **[G: U.S.]**

Ringleb, Al H. Environmental Regulation of Electric Utilities. **In** *Moorhouse, J. C., ed.,* 1986, pp. 183–218. **[G: U.S.]**

Romero, Carlos. Pressure on Natural Resources: Discussion. **In** *Maunder, A. and Renborg, U., eds.,* 1986, pp. 313–15.

Rosen, Sherwin. Valuing Environmental Goods: An Assessment of the Contingent Valuation Method: The Review Panel's Assessment: Comments. **In** *Cummings, R. G.; Brookshire, D. S. and Schulze, W. D., eds.,* 1986, pp. 194–97.

Rosenfeld, Arthur H. Energy Conservation in the Federal Government: Comments. **In** *Sawhill, J. C. and Cotton, R., eds.,* 1986, pp. 260–62. **[G: U.S.]**

Russell, Clifford S. A Note on the Efficiency Ranking of Two Second-best Policy Instruments for Pollution Control. *J. Environ. Econ. Manage.,* March 1986, *13*(1), pp. 13–17.

Russell, Clifford S. and Kneese, Allen V. Revisiting the Scientific, Technical, and Economic Basis for Coastal Zone Management. **In** *[Crutchfield, J. A.],* 1986, pp. 387–402.

Rutledge, Gary L. and Stergioulas, Nikolaos A. Plant and Equipment Expenditures by Business for Pollution Abatement, 1985 and 1986. *Surv. Curr. Bus.,* December 1986, *66*(12), pp. 20–22. **[G: U.S.]**

Samples, Karl C.; Dixon, John A. and Gowen, Marcia M. Information Disclosure and Endangered Species Valuation. *Land Econ.,* August 1986, *62*(3), pp. 306–12. **[G: U.S.]**

Sapru, R. K. Relevance of International Economic Issues to the Human Environment. *Indian Econ. J.,* Jan.-Mar. 1986, *33*(3), pp. 81–84.

Sasseville, Jean-Louis. Fresh Water Issues: Comments. **In** *Economic Council of Canada,* 1986, pp. 27–31.

Schramm, Gunter. Practical Approaches for Estimating Resource Depletion Costs. **In** *[Crutchfield, J. A.],* 1986, pp. 272–95.

Scott, Anthony. The Canadian–American Problem of Acid Rain. *Natural Res. J.,* Spring 1986, *26*(2), pp. 337–58. **[G: U.S.; Canada]**

Segerson, Kathleen. Economic Evaluation of Air Pollution Damage and Control: Discussion [Agriculture, Forestry, and Related Benefits of Air Pollution Control: A Review and Some Observations] [The Cost of Abating Sulfur, Nitrogen, and Ozone Air Pollutants]. *Amer. J. Agr. Econ.,* May 1986, *68*(2), pp. 479–81. **[G: U.S.]**

Seidman, Laurence S. Why an Incentive Anti-inflation Plan Should Be Implemented. **In** *Colander, D. C., ed.,* 1986, pp. 201–07. **[G: U.S.]**

Sewell, W. R. Derrick. Addressing Environmental Issues in the Future: Comments. **In** *Economic Council of Canada,* 1986, pp. 99–101.

Shabman, Leonard and Cox, William E. Costs of Water Management Institutions: The Case of Southeastern Virginia. **In** *Frederick, K. D., ed.,* 1986, pp. 134–70. **[G: U.S.]**

Shortle, James S. and Dunn, James W. The Relative Efficiency of Agricultural Source Water Pollution Control Policies. *Amer. J. Agr. Econ.,* August 1986, *68*(3), pp. 668–77.

Shortle, James S. and Stefanou, Spiro E. Soil Conservation with Uncertain Revenues and Input Supplies: Comment. *Amer. J. Agr. Econ.,* May 1986, *68*(2), pp. 358–60.

Shortle, James S. and Willett, Keith D. The Incidence of Water Pollution Control Costs: Partial vs. General Equilibrium Computations. *Growth Change,* April 1986, *17*(2), pp. 32–43. **[G: U.S.]**

Sieber, René and Wetterwald, Paul. Environmental Protection and Direct Foreign Investment with Specific Factors of Production: The Case of the Small Open Economy. *Schweiz. Z. Volkswirtsch. Statist.,* December 1986, *122*(4), pp. 611–25.

Sláma, Jiří. An International Comparison of Sulphur Dioxide Emissions. *J. Compar. Econ.,* September 1986, *10*(3), pp. 277–92. **[G: Europe]**

Smith, V. Kerry. To Keep or Toss the Contingent Valuation Method. **In** *Cummings, R. G.; Brookshire, D. S. and Schulze, W. D., eds.,* 1986, pp. 162–79.

Smith, V. Kerry and Desvousges, William H. Asymmetries in the Valuation of Risk and the Siting of Hazardous Waste Disposal Facilities. *Amer. Econ. Rev.*, May 1986, *76*(2), pp. 291–94. **[G: U.S.]**

Smith, V. Kerry and Desvousges, William H. The Value of Avoiding a *Lulu:* Hazardous Waste Disposal Sites. *Rev. Econ. Statist.*, May 1986, *68*(2), pp. 293–99. **[G: U.S.]**

Smith, V. Kerry; Desvousges, William H. and Fisher, Ann. A Comparison of Direct and Indirect Methods for Estimating Environmental Benefits. *Amer. J. Agr. Econ.*, May 1986, *68*(2), pp. 280–90. **[G: U.S.]**

Smith, Vernon L. Valuing Environmental Goods: An Assessment of the Contingent Valuation Method: The Review Panel's Assessment: Comments. **In** *Cummings, R. G.; Brookshire, D. S. and Schulze, W. D., eds.*, 1986, pp. 197–204.

Southgate, Douglas. The Economics of Erosion Control in a Subtropical Watershed: Reply. *Land Econ.*, August 1986, *62*(3), pp. 331–32. **[G: Dominican Republic]**

Speth, James Gustave. Addressing Environmental Issues in the Future. **In** *Economic Council of Canada,* 1986, pp. 91–98.

Spooner, B. The Significance of Desertification. **In** *Swaminathan, M. S. and Sinha, S. K., eds.*, 1986, pp. 337–56.

Srivastava, U. K. Pressure on Natural Resources: Discussion. **In** *Maunder, A. and Renborg, U., eds.*, 1986, pp. 337–38.

Stafford, Robert T. Energy and the Environment: The View from Washington. **In** *Saltzman, S. and Schuler, R. E., eds.*, 1986, pp. 179–86. **[G: U.S.]**

Starr, Kenneth W. Judicial Review in the Post-*Chevron* Era. *Yale J. Regul.*, Spring 1986, *3*(2), pp. 283–312. **[G: U.S.]**

Stasiuk, William N. Some Public Health Concerns Associated with Electrical Energy Generation. **In** *Saltzman, S. and Schuler, R. E., eds.*, 1986, pp. 203–12. **[G: U.S.]**

Sullivan, Arthur M. Liability Rules for Toxics Cleanup. *J. Urban Econ.*, September 1986, *20*(2), pp. 191–204. **[G: U.S.]**

Sutinen, Jon G. and Hennessey, Timothy M. Enforcement: The Neglected Element in Fishery Management. **In** *[Crutchfield, J. A.]*, 1986, pp. 185–213. **[G: U.S.]**

Swaigen, John Z. Environmental Preservation and Economic Growth: Comments. **In** *Economic Council of Canada,* 1986, pp. 87–88.

Swaney, James A. Entropy and the Institutional Dichotomy: A Reply [Economics, Ecology, and Entropy]. *J. Econ. Issues*, September 1986, *20*(3), pp. 841–43.

Szabolcs, I. Salt-Affected Soils: Problems and Prospects in Developed Countries. **In** *Swaminathan, M. S. and Sinha, S. K., eds.*, 1986, pp. 307–36. **[G: Selected MDCs]**

Talbot, Lee M. Demographic Factors in Resource Depletion and Environmental Degradation in East African Rangeland. *Population Devel. Rev.*, September 1986, *12*(3), pp. 441–51. **[G: Kenya]**

Taylor, D.; Diprose, G. and Duffy, M. EC Environmental Policy and the Control of Water Pollution: The Implementation of Directive 76/464 in Perspective. *J. Common Market Stud.*, March 1986, *24*(3), pp. 225–46. **[G: EEC]**

Thompson, Grant P. Energy Conservation in the Federal Government: Comments. **In** *Sawhill, J. C. and Cotton, R., eds.*, 1986, pp. 257–60. **[G: U.S.]**

Thompson, Russell G. and Singleton, F. D., Jr. Wastewater Treatment Costs and Outlays in Organic Petrochemicals: Standards versus Taxes with Methodology Suggestions for Marginal Cost Pricing and Analysis. *Water Resources Res.*, April 1986, *22*(4), pp. 467–74. **[G: U.S.]**

Thornton, Judith. Soviet Electric Power after Chernobyl': Economic Consequences and Options. *Soviet Econ.*, Apr.-June 1986, *2*(2), pp. 131–79. **[G: U.S.S.R.]**

Thoroe, Carsten. Pressure on Natural Resources: Discussion. **In** *Maunder, A. and Renborg, U., eds.*, 1986, pp. 315–17.

Tietenberg, Thomas H. Uncommon Sense: The Program to Reform Pollution Control Policy. **In** *Weiss, L. W. and Klass, M. W., eds.*, 1986, pp. 269–303. **[G: U.S.]**

Timberlake, Lloyd. Guarding Africa's Renewable Resources. **In** *Berg, R. J. and Whitaker, J. S., eds.*, 1986, pp. 111–28. **[G: Africa]**

Tisdell, Clem A. Conflicts about Living Marine Resources in Southeast Asian and Australian Waters: Turtles and Dugong as Cases. *Marine Resource Econ.*, 1986, *3*(1), pp. 89–109. **[G: Asia; Australia]**

Tisdell, Clem A. Cost–Benefit Analysis, the Environment and Informational Constraints in LDCs. *J. Econ. Devel.*, December 1986, *11*(2), pp. 63–81. **[G: LDCs]**

Vaux, H. J., Jr. Water Scarcity and Gains from Trade in Kern County, California. **In** *Frederick, K. D., ed.*, 1986, pp. 67–101. **[G: U.S.]**

van Vuuren, Willem. Soil Erosion: The Case for Market Intervention. *Can. J. Agr. Econ.*, June 1986, *33*, pp. 41–62. **[G: Canada]**

Wahl, Richard W. and Davis, Robert K. Satisfying Southern California's Thirst for Water: Efficient Alternatives. **In** *Frederick, K. D., ed.*, 1986, pp. 102–33. **[G: U.S.]**

Walker, David J. and Young, Douglas L. The Effect of Technical Progress on Erosion Damage and Economic Incentives for Soil Conservation. *Land Econ.*, February 1986, *62*(1), pp. 83–93. **[G: U.S.]**

Weinschenk, Günther. Pressure on Natural Resources—Implications for Research and Policy. **In** *Maunder, A. and Renborg, U., eds.*, 1986, pp. 754–68.

Wheelwright, Ted. The World Pesticide Industry. **In** *Wheelwright, T., ed.*, 1986, pp. 127–42. **[G: LDCs]**

Whitby, Martin and Hanley, Nick. Problems of Agricultural Externalities: A Conceptual Model with Implications for Research. *J. Agr. Econ.*,

January 1986, *37*(1), pp. 1–11.

Willett, Keith D. Environmental Management Costs Using a Best Available Control Technology BACT in the Electrical Generating Industry. *Managerial Dec. Econ.*, March 1986, *7*(1), pp. 29–36. **[G: U.S.]**

Wilman, Elizabeth A. Environmental Preservation and Economic Growth: Comments. **In** *Economic Council of Canada*, 1986, pp. 88–90.

Wollen, Deborah. Reformation of the Burden of Proof. *Natural Res. J.*, Spring 1986, *26*(2), pp. 377–89. **[G: U.S.]**

Young, Trevor and Allen, P. Geoffrey. Methods for Valuing Countryside Amenity: An Overview. *J. Agr. Econ.*, September 1986, *37*(3), pp. 349–64.

Zaikov, G. Political and Economic Problems of Accounting for Ecological Factors in Social Production. *Prob. Econ.*, January 1986, *28*(9), pp. 3–17. **[G: U.S.S.R.]**

Zimmermann, Klaus F. Beschäftigungspolitik mit der Umwelt? Eine angebotsorientierte Kritik und umweltpolitische Perspektive. (With English summary.) *Z. Wirtschaft. Sozialwissen.*, 1986, *106*(1), pp. 41–61. **[G: W. Germany]**

723 Energy

7230 Energy

Abushihada, Adnan. Arab Gas and the International Market. **In** *Stevens, P., ed.*, 1986, pp. 107–44. **[G: OPEC]**

Adelaja, Adesoji and Hoque, Anwarul. A Multiproduct Analysis of Energy Demand in Agricultural Subsectors. *Southern J. Agr. Econ.*, December 1986, *18*(2), pp. 51–63. **[G: U.S.]**

Adelman, M. A. Lessons from the 1986 Oil Price Collapse: Comments. *Brookings Pap. Econ. Act.*, 1986, (2), pp. 272–76. **[G: OPEC]**

Adelman, M. A. Scarcity and World Oil Prices. *Rev. Econ. Statist.*, August 1986, *68*(3), pp. 387–97. **[G: U.S.; Saudi Arabia]**

Adelman, M. A. The Competitive Floor to World Oil Prices. *Energy J.*, October 1986, *7*(4), pp. 9–31. **[G: U.S.; U.K.; OPEC]**

Ager-Hanssen, Henrik. The Future of Norwegian Gas. **In** *Stevens, P., ed.*, 1986, pp. 34–47. **[G: Norway]**

Ahm, Byong-hun, et al. Integrated National Energy Planning: A Case Study of the Republic of Korea. *Energy J.*, April 1986, *7*(2), pp. 13–35. **[G: S. Korea]**

Al-Gharabally, Tewfik. The Petrochemical Industries of the Arab Countries. **In** *El Mallakh, R., ed.*, 1986, pp. 79–89. **[G: Arab Countries]**

Al-Mady, Mohamed H. Economic Factors in the Manufacture of Petrochemicals in Saudi Arabia. **In** *El Mallakh, R., ed.*, 1986, pp. 71–78. **[G: U.S.; Saudi Arabia]**

Alschuler, John H., Jr. Local Energy Conservation Programs: Comments. **In** *Sawhill, J. C. and Cotton, R., eds.*, 1986, pp. 200–201. **[G: U.S.]**

Amuzegar, Jahangir. The Oil Price Turmoil. *Finance Develop.*, June 1986, *23*(2), pp. 14–15. **[G: Global]**

Andersson, Roland and Taylor, Lewis. The Social Cost of Unsupplied Electricity: A Critical Review. *Energy Econ.*, July 1986, *8*(3), pp. 139–46. **[G: Sweden; U.K.; Chile; Canada]**

Andrikopoulos, Andreas A. and Brox, James A. Demand Systems for Energy Consumption by the Manufacturing Sector. *J. Econ. Bus.*, May 1986, *38*(2), pp. 141–53. **[G: Canada]**

de Araújo, João Lizardo and Ghirardi, André. Substituiçao de derivados do petróleo no Brasil: questoes urgentes. (With English summary.) *Pesquisa Planejamento Econ.*, December 1986, *16*(3), pp. 745–71. **[G: Brazil]**

Arushanian, I. I.; Belen'kii, V. Z. and Biriukova, E. S. A Closed Dynamic Model of Stationary Growth for Variant Analysis of the Interrelations between the Energy System and the Economy of the USSR. *Matekon*, Spring 1986, *22*(3), pp. 35–66. **[G: U.S.S.R.]**

Aslaksen, Iulie and Bjerkholt, Olav. Certainty Equivalence Methods in the Macroeconomic Management of Petroleum Resources. **In** *Neary, J. P. and van Wijnbergen, S., eds.*, 1986, pp. 170–95. **[G: Norway]**

Axelrod, Regina S. and Wilson, Hugh A. Citizen Participation and Nuclear Power: The Shoreham Experience. *J. Energy Devel.*, Spring 1986, *11*(2), pp. 311–31. **[G: U.S.]**

Bailey, Richard. Gas Privatization and the Energy Strategy. *Nat. Westminster Bank Quart. Rev.*, August 1986, pp. 2–12. **[G: U.K.]**

Barkai, Haim. The Energy Sector in the 1960s and 1970s. **In** *Ben-Porath, Y., ed.*, 1986, pp. 264–75. **[G: Israel]**

Bator, Francis. Patterns of Energy Use: Comments. **In** *Sawhill, J. C. and Cotton, R., eds.*, 1986, pp. 56–58. **[G: U.S.]**

Baumann, Michael G. and Kalt, Joseph P. Intertemporal Consumer Surplus in Lagged-Adjustment Demand Models: An Application to Natural Gas Pricing. *Energy Econ.*, January 1986, *8*(1), pp. 2–12. **[G: U.S.]**

Baxter, Lester W., et al. An Efficiency Analysis of Household Energy Use. *Energy Econ.*, April 1986, *8*(2), pp. 62–73. **[G: U.S.]**

Beenstock, Michael and Dalziel, Alan. The Demand for Energy in the UK: A General Equilibrium Analysis. *Energy Econ.*, April 1986, *8*(2), pp. 90–98. **[G: U.K.]**

Beltramo, Mark A.; Manne, Alan S. and Weyant, John P. A North American Gas Trade Model (GTM). *Energy J.*, July 1986, *7*(3), pp. 15–32. **[G: U.S.; Canada; Mexico]**

Bernard, Jean-Thomas; Lessard, François and Thivierge, Simon. La demande d'énergie du secteur commercial quéeécois. (The Energy Demand of the Commercial Sector in Quebec. With English summary.) *L'Actual. Econ.*, March 1986, *62*(1), pp. 5–22. **[G: Canada]**

Berndt, Ernst R. and Watkins, G. C. Modeling Energy Demand: The Choice between Input and Output Energy Measures. *Energy J.*, April 1986, *7*(2), pp. 69–79.

Berndt, Ernst R. and Wood, David O. Energy Price Shocks and Productivity Growth in U.S. and UK Manufacturing. *Oxford Rev. Econ. Policy,* Autumn 1986, *2* (3), pp. 1–31. **[G: U.K.; U.S.]**

Bitsakis, J. Aspects of Energy–Economy Interactions in South Africa. *S. Afr. J. Econ.,* June 1986, *54* (2), pp. 172–80. **[G: S. Africa]**

Blitzer, Charles R. Energy–Economy Interactions in Developing Countries. *Energy J.,* January 1986, *7* (1), pp. 35–50. **[G: LDCs]**

Blitzer, Charles R. and Eckaus, Richard S. Energy–Economy Interactions in Mexico: A Multiperiod General Equilibrium Model. *J. Devel. Econ.,* May 1986, *21* (2), pp. 259–81. **[G: Mexico]**

Blitzer, Charles R. and Eckaus, Richard S. Modeling Energy–Economy Interactions in Small Developing Countries: A Case Study of Sri Lanka. *J. Policy Modeling,* Winter 1986, *8* (4), pp. 471–501. **[G: Sri Lanka]**

Blum, Edward H. Financial Barriers to Investment in Conservation: Comments. **In** *Sawhill, J. C. and Cotton, R., eds.,* 1986, pp. 132–33. **[G: U.S.]**

Bodde, David L.; Quasebarth, Mollie V. and Thomasian, John B. The Economics of Strategic Choice: U.S. Uranium Enrichment in the World Market. *Energy J.,* October 1986, *7* (4), pp. 95–107. **[G: U.S.]**

Bohi, Douglas R. and Darmstadter, Joel. The World Oil Market and New York Electricity. **In** *Saltzman, S. and Schuler, R. E., eds.,* 1986, pp. 97–110. **[G: U.S.]**

Bohi, Douglas R. and Toman, Michael A. Oil Supply Disruptions and the Role of the International Energy Agency. *Energy J.,* April 1986, *7* (2), pp. 37–50. **[G: Global]**

Bourcier, Philippe and Shirazi, Mohsen. Natural Gas: An Important but Underexploited Resource. *Finance Develop.,* June 1986, *23* (2), pp. 8–11.

Bowman, Ann O'M. and Franke, James L. Explaining Adoption of Conservation Programs by Local Governments. *Rev. Reg. Stud.,* Fall 1986, *16* (3), pp. 17–24. **[G: U.S.]**

Braeutigam, Ronald R. and Hubbard, R. Glenn. Natural Gas: The Regulatory Transition. **In** *Weiss, L. W. and Klass, M. W., eds.,* 1986, pp. 137–68. **[G: U.S.]**

Brierley, C. W. UK Gas Prospects. **In** *Stevens, P., ed.,* 1986, pp. 48–70. **[G: U.K.]**

Broadman, Harry G. and Toman, Michael A. Non-Price Provisions in Long-term Natural Gas Contracts. *Land Econ.,* May 1986, *62* (2), pp. 111–18. **[G: U.S.]**

Brown, Jonathan C. Foreign Oil Companies, Oil Workers, and the Mexican Revolutionary State in the 1920s. **In** *Teichova, A.; Lévy-Leboyer, M. and Nussbaum, H., eds.,* 1986, pp. 257–69. **[G: Mexico]**

Bryant, Richard R. Regional Energy Source Substitution: Wood Fuels in Missouri. *Growth Change,* July 1986, *17* (3), pp. 71–84. **[G: U.S.]**

Bryant, Richard R. U.S. Residential Demand for Wood. *Energy J.,* July 1986, *7* (3), pp. 137–47. **[G: U.S.]**

Bryson, John. State Government Conservation Programs: Comments. **In** *Sawhill, J. C. and Cotton, R., eds.,* 1986, pp. 234–35. **[G: U.S.]**

Burness, H. S. and Cummings, Ronald G. Thermodynamic and Economic Concepts as Related to Resource-Use Policies: Reply. *Land Econ.,* August 1986, *62* (3), pp. 323–24.

Butcher, Walter R. and Wandschneider, Philip R. Competition between Irrigation and Hydropower in the Pacific Northwest. **In** *Frederick, K. D., ed.,* 1986, pp. 25–66. **[G: U.S.]**

Campbell, John L. The State, Capital Formation, and Industrial Planning: Financing Nuclear Energy in the United States and France. *Soc. Sci. Quart.,* December 1986, *67* (4), pp. 707–21. **[G: U.S.; France]**

Carrié, Jean. World Surplus of Crude-Oil Primary Refining Capacity. **In** *El Mallakh, R., ed.,* 1986, pp. 19–27. **[G: Global]**

Carter, Anne P. Energy, Environment, and Economic Growth. **In** *Sohn, I., ed.,* 1986, *1974,* pp. 417–31. **[G: U.S.]**

de Castro, Newton. Produção, distribuição e consumo: determinantes da demanda derivada por transporte e energia. (With English summary.) *Pesquisa Planejamento Econ.,* December 1986, *16* (3), pp. 713–44. **[G: Brazil]**

Chappell, Henry W., Jr. and Wilder, Ronald P. Multiproduct Monopoly, Regulation, and Firm Costs: Comment. *Southern Econ. J.,* April 1986, *52* (4), pp. 1168–74. **[G: U.S.]**

Chen, Yikun. China's Petroleum Refining and Petrochemical Industry in Progress. **In** *El Mallakh, R., ed.,* 1986, pp. 101–15. **[G: China]**

Chen, Zhao-Ying. Decision Support System for Management of Oil Pipeline. **In** *Pau, L. F., ed.,* 1986, pp. 103–06.

Cheng, Chu-yuan. The United States Petroleum Trade with China, 1876–1949. **In** *May, E. R. and Fairbank, J. K., eds.,* 1986, pp. 205–33. **[G: U.S.; China]**

Coates, Daniel E. and Mulligan, James G. The Efficiency of Electric Power Pools: Evidence from Firing Unit Data. *Appl. Econ.,* December 1986, *18* (12), pp. 1323–34. **[G: U.S.]**

Cocklin, C.; Lonergan, S. C. and Smit, B. The Economics of Forest Energy Plantations: An Empirical Enquiry. *Econ. Geogr.,* October 1986, *62* (4), pp. 354–72. **[G: Canada]**

Conrad, Klaus and Henseler-Unger, Iris. Applied General Equilibrium Modeling for Long-term Energy Policy in Germany. *J. Policy Modeling,* Winter 1986, *8* (4), pp. 531–49. **[G: W. Germany]**

Conrad, Klaus and Henseler-Unger, Iris. The Economic Impact of Coal-fired versus Nuclear Power Plants: An Application of a General Equilibrium Model. *Energy J.,* October 1986, *7* (4), pp. 51–63. **[G: W. Germany]**

Conroy, Michael D. The Petrochemical Industry: Restructuring Challenges. **In** *El Mallakh, R., ed.,* 1986, pp. 62–69. **[G: U.S.]**

Cook, P. Lesley. The Offshore Supplies Industry:

Fast, Continuous and Incremental Change. **In** *Sharp, M., ed.*, 1986, pp. 213–62. **[G: U.K.; France; Norway; Netherlands]**

Cooper, Richard N. Global Economic Policy in a World of Energy Shortage. **In** *Cooper, R. N.*, 1986, *1982*, pp. 53–69.

Coronel, Gustavo. Venezuela: Oil, Democracy, and the Quest for Sound Political Leadership. **In** *Raddock, D. M., et al.*, 1986, pp. 94–109. **[G: Venezuela]**

Costanza, Robert. Embodied Energy and Economic Valuation. **In** *Sohn, I., ed.*, 1986, *1980*, pp. 432–44. **[G: U.S.]**

Crane, Alan T. Nuclear Safety and Environmental Issues. **In** *Saltzman, S. and Schuler, R. E., eds.*, 1986, pp. 213–23. **[G: U.S.]**

Crémieux, Michel and Mezière, Dominique. Le financement des investissements d'utilisation rationnelle de l'énergie dans l'industrie (1975–1985). (Investments Financing for Rational Use of Energy in Industry [1975–1985]. With English summary.) *Écon. Soc.*, July 1986, *20*(7), pp. 159–74. **[G: France]**

Czerniejewicz, Wilfried. Natural Gas in the Federal Republic of Germany: Facts and Prospects. *J. Energy Devel.*, Spring 1986, *11*(2), pp. 301–09. **[G: W. Germany]**

Daly, Herman E. Thermodynamic and Economic Concepts as Related to Resource-Use Policies: Comment. *Land Econ.*, August 1986, *62*(3), pp. 319–22.

Darvish, Tikva and Eckstein, Shlomo. Evaluation of an Energy Project under Uncertainty: The Case of the Mediterranean–Dead Sea Project. *J. Policy Modeling*, Fall 1986, *8*(3), pp. 391–413. **[G: Israel]**

Davis, William E. New York's Electricity Supply: Present Capacity and Future Needs. **In** *Saltzman, S. and Schuler, R. E., eds.*, 1986, pp. 113–18. **[G: U.S.]**

DeLuca, Donald R. Survey Research on Energy-Related Issues. **In** *Saltzman, S. and Schuler, R. E., eds.*, 1986, pp. 227–59. **[G: U.S.]**

Der Hovanessian, Aida. Economic Forces Affecting the Middle East. **In** *Roukis, G. S. and Montana, P. J., eds.*, 1986, pp. 47–70. **[G: OPEC]**

Desai, Dinesh. Energy–GDP Relationship and Capital Intensity in LDCs. *Energy Econ.*, April 1986, *8*(2), pp. 113–17. **[G: LDCs]**

Dewes, John W. The Changing Petroleum Products Market: An Industry View. **In** *El Mallakh, R., ed.*, 1986, pp. 9–18. **[G: Pacific Basin]**

Dick, Hermann, et al. Effect of Oil Price Increases on Developing Countries—A Reply. *Energy Econ.*, January 1986, *8*(1), pp. 48–50. **[G: Ivory Coast; Kenya; S. Korea; Turkey]**

Donnelly, W. A. Response [The Australian Demand for Petrol]. *Int. J. Transport Econ.*, February 1986, *13*(1), pp. 109. **[G: Australia]**

Douthitt, Robin A. The Demand for Residential Space and Water Heating Fuel by Energy Conserving Households. *J. Cons. Aff.*, Winter 1986, *20*(2), pp. 231–48. **[G: U.S.]**

Dubin, Jeffrey A. A Nested Logit Model of Space and Water Heat System Choice. *Marketing Sci.*, Spring 1986, *5*(2), pp. 112–24. **[G: U.S.]**

Dubin, Jeffrey A. Will Mandatory Conservation Promote Energy Efficiency in the Selection of Household Appliance Stocks? *Energy J.*, January 1986, *7*(1), pp. 99–118. **[G: U.S.]**

Dubin, Jeffrey A.; Miedema, Allen K. and Chandran, Ram V. Price Effects of Energy-Efficient Technologies: A Study of Residential Demand for Heating and Cooling. *Rand J. Econ.*, Autumn 1986, *17*(3), pp. 310–25.

Duncan, Angus. Local Energy Conservation Programs: Comments. **In** *Sawhill, J. C. and Cotton, R., eds.*, 1986, pp. 201–03. **[G: U.S.]**

Ebinger, Charles K. The Brazilian Energy Sector. **In** *Hartland-Thunberg, P. and Ebinger, C. K., eds.*, 1986, pp. 131–53. **[G: Brazil]**

Edwards, Sebastian. Adjustment to Windfall Gains: A Comparative Analysis of Oil-Exporting Countries: Comment. **In** *Neary, J. P. and van Wijnbergen, S., eds.*, 1986, pp. 93–95. **[G: OPEC]**

Ehrenberger, Vlastimil. Economization—A Priority. *Czech. Econ. Digest.*, June/July 1986, (4), pp. 12–18. **[G: Czechoslovakia]**

Einhorn, Michael A. The Effects of Energy Prices upon Appliance Efficiencies and Building Insulation. *Energy J.*, July 1986, *7*(3), pp. 115–22.

El Atta, Laila Hamed Abou. Egypt: A Profile of the Refining and Petrochemical Industry. **In** *El Mallakh, R., ed.*, 1986, pp. 91–100. **[G: Egypt]**

El Mallakh, Ragaei. The Middle East, Pacific Basin, and the United States: Refining and Petrochemicals: Introduction. **In** *El Mallakh, R., ed.*, 1986, pp. 1–7.

Engle, Robert F., et al. Semiparametric Estimates of the Relation between Weather and Electricity Sales. *J. Amer. Statist. Assoc.*, June 1986, *81*(394), pp. 310–20. **[G: U.S.]**

Fieleke, Norman S. The Decline of the Oil Cartel. *New Eng. Econ. Rev.*, July/Aug. 1986, pp. 32–41. **[G: OECD; OPEC]**

Fishlow, Albert. Latin American Adjustment to the Oil Shocks of 1973 and 1979. **In** *Hartlyn, J. and Morley, S. A., eds.*, 1986, pp. 54–84. **[G: Selected LDCs]**

Flaig, Gebhard. Ein Modell der Elektrizitätsnachfrage privater Haushalte mit indirekt beobachteten Variablen. (A Model of the Household Demand for Electricity with Indirectly Observed Variables. With English summary.) *Ifo-Studien*, 1986, *32*(4), pp. 275–96. **[G: W. Germany]**

Flemming, John S. Booming Sectors and Structural Change in Australia and Britain: A Comparison: Comment. **In** *Neary, J. P. and van Wijnbergen, S., eds.*, 1986, pp. 284–87. **[G: U.K.; Australia]**

Foell, Wesley K. and Siddayao, Corazon Morales. Microcomputers and Energy Policy Analysis: Growth Prospects in Developing Countries. *World Devel.*, Oct./Nov. 1986, *14*(10/11), pp. 1311–27. **[G: Indonesia; Philippines]**

Forsyth, Peter J. Booming Sectors and Structural

Change in Australia and Britain: A Comparison. In *Neary, J. P. and van Wijnbergen, S., eds.*, 1986, pp. 251–84. **[G: Australia; U.K.]**

Freeman, S. David. Electric Utility Conservation Programs: Progress and Problems: Comments. In *Sawhill, J. C. and Cotton, R., eds.*, 1986, pp. 160–62. **[G: U.S.]**

Frijns, Jean M. G. The Dutch Disease in the Netherlands: Comment. In *Neary, J. P. and van Wijnbergen, S., eds.*, 1986, pp. 136–41. **[G: Netherlands]**

Fry, Gene R. Heinze. The Economics of Home Solar Water Heating and the Role of Solar Tax Credits. *Land Econ.*, May 1986, *62*(2), pp. 134–44. **[G: U.S.]**

Gately, Dermot. Lessons from the 1986 Oil Price Collapse. *Brookings Pap. Econ. Act.*, 1986, (2), pp. 237–71. **[G: OPEC]**

Gelb, Alan. Adjustment to Windfall Gains: A Comparative Analysis of Oil-Exporting Countries. In *Neary, J. P. and van Wijnbergen, S., eds.*, 1986, pp. 54–93. **[G: OPEC]**

Gelb, Alan. The Oil Syndrome: Adjustment to Windfall Gains in Oil-Exporting Countries. In *Lal, D. and Wolf, M., eds.*, 1986, pp. 115–30. **[G: Selected Countries]**

George, David L. and Southwell, Priscilla L. Opinion on the Diablo Canyon Nuclear Power Plant: The Effects of Situation and Socialization. *Soc. Sci. Quart.*, December 1986, *67*(4), pp. 722–35. **[G: U.S.]**

Gibbons, John H.; Gwin, Holly L. and Pool, Richard B. Energy Conservation in the Federal Government. In *Sawhill, J. C. and Cotton, R., eds.*, 1986, pp. 237–57. **[G: U.S.]**

Gilbert, Richard J. and Mork, Knut Anton. Efficient Pricing during Oil Supply Disruptions. *Energy J.*, April 1986, *7*(2), pp. 51–68.

Gilland, Bernard. On Resources and Economic Development. *Population Devel. Rev.*, June 1986, *12*(2), pp. 295–305. **[G: Global]**

Gilmer, Robert W. and Mack, Richard S. Long-run Adjustment to Alternative Levels of Reliability in Electric Supply. *Energy J.*, October 1986, *7*(4), pp. 89–94.

Gisser, Micha and Goodwin, Thomas H. Crude Oil and the Macroeconomy: Tests of Some Popular Notions: A Note. *J. Money, Credit, Banking*, February 1986, *18*(1), pp. 95–103. **[G: U.S.]**

Gould, Brian W. The Impact of Structural Change within an Economy on Resource Use: An Input–Output Analysis. *Appl. Econ.*, May 1986, *18*(5), pp. 457–77. **[G: Canada]**

Gould, Brian W. and Kulshreshtha, Surendra N. An Interindustry Analysis of Structural Change and Energy Use Linkages in the Saskatchewan Economy. *Energy Econ.*, July 1986, *8*(3), pp. 186–96. **[G: Canada]**

Greeley, Martin. Rural Energy Technology Assessment: A Sri Lankan Case Study. *World Devel.*, December 1986, *14*(12), pp. 1411–21. **[G: Sri Lanka]**

Green, Rodney D., et al. The Demand for Heating Fuels: A Disaggregated Modeling Approach. *Atlantic Econ. J.*, December 1986, *14*(4), pp. 1–14. **[G: U.S.]**

Griffin, James M. Lessons from the 1986 Oil Price Collapse: Comments. *Brookings Pap. Econ. Act.*, 1986, (2), pp. 276–82. **[G: OPEC]**

Griffin, James M. and Jones, Clifton T. Falling Oil Prices: Where Is the Floor? *Energy J.*, October 1986, *7*(4), pp. 37–50. **[G: U.S.]**

Griffin, Karen. State Government Conservation Programs. In *Sawhill, J. C. and Cotton, R., eds.*, 1986, pp. 205–32. **[G: U.S.]**

Guagnano, Greg, et al. Innovation Perception and Adoption of Solar Heating Technology. *J. Cons. Aff.*, Summer 1986, *20*(1), pp. 48–64. **[G: U.S.]**

Guinn, Charles R. New York Electricity and Energy Forecasts. In *Saltzman, S. and Schuler, R. E., eds.*, 1986, pp. 52–66. **[G: U.S.]**

Hafkamp, Wim and Nijkamp, Peter. Integrated Economic–Environmental–Energy Policy and Conflict Analysis. *J. Policy Modeling*, Winter 1986, *8*(4), pp. 551–76. **[G: Netherlands]**

Hall, Stephen G.; Henry, S. G. B. and Herbert, Rhys. Oil Prices and the Economy. *Nat. Inst. Econ. Rev.*, May 1986, (116), pp. 38–44. **[G: U.K.]**

Hall, V. B. Major OECD Country Industrial Sector Interfuel Substitution Estimates, 1960–79. *Energy Econ.*, April 1986, *8*(2), pp. 74–89. **[G: OECD]**

Halvorson, Harold. The British Columbia Coal Industry. In *Nemetz, P. N., ed.*, 1986, pp. 293–306. **[G: Canada; Pacific Basin]**

Hanna, David R. Petroleum Product Trade East of Suez. In *El Mallakh, R., ed.*, 1986, pp. 37–45. **[G: Middle East]**

Hartland-Thunberg, Penelope. Causes and Consequences of the World Debt Crisis. In *Hartland-Thunberg, P. and Ebinger, C. K., eds.*, 1986, pp. 1–22.

Hartman, Raymond S. and Doane, Michael J. Household Discount Rates Revisited. *Energy J.*, January 1986, *7*(1), pp. 139–48. **[G: U.S.]**

Hartman, Raymond S. and Doane, Michael J. The Estimation of the Effects of Utility-sponsored Conservation Programmes. *Appl. Econ.*, January 1986, *18*(1), pp. 1–25. **[G: U.S.]**

Hawdon, David. The Economics of the Natural Gas Market and Its Competitiveness. In *Stevens, P., ed.*, 1986, pp. 14–33. **[G: Selected Countries]**

Helliwell, John F., et al. The Western Accord and Lower World Oil Prices. *Can. Public Policy*, June 1986, *12*(2), pp. 341–55. **[G: Canada]**

Hemphill, Robert F. and Myers, Edward A. Electric Utility Conservation Programs: Progress and Problems. In *Sawhill, J. C. and Cotton, R., eds.*, 1986, pp. 137–59. **[G: U.S.]**

Herbert, John H. Data Analysis, Specification, and Estimation of an Aggregate Relationship for Sales of Natural Gas per Customer. *J. Econ. Soc. Meas.*, October 1986, *14*(3), pp. 165–74.

Hesse, Dieter M. and Tarkka, Helena. The Demand for Capital, Labor and Energy in European Manufacturing Industry before and after the Oil Price Shocks. *Scand. J. Econ.*, 1986, *88*(3), pp. 529–46. **[G: W. Europe]**

Hewett, Ed. A., et al. Panel on the Economic and Political Consequences of Chernobyl' *Soviet Econ.*, Apr.-June 1986, *2*(2), pp. 97–130. **[G: U.S.S.R.]**

Hill, John K. Energy's Contribution to the Growth of Employment in Texas, 1972–1982. *Fed. Res. Bank Dallas Econ. Rev.*, May 1986, pp. 11–18. **[G: U.S.]**

Hirst, Eric. State Government Conservation Programs: Comments. **In** *Sawhill, J. C. and Cotton, R., eds.*, 1986, pp. 232–34. **[G: U.S.]**

Hogan, William W. Patterns of Energy Use. **In** *Sawhill, J. C. and Cotton, R., eds.*, 1986, pp. 19–53. **[G: U.S.]**

Hölker, Franz-J. Entmonopolisierung der energieversorgung? (Monopolies in the German Energy Sector. With English summary.) *Ann. Pub. Co-op. Econ.*, Oct.-Dec. 1986, *57*(4), pp. 513–21. **[G: W. Germany]**

Hopkins, J. Wallace. Energy Security: The Most Important Element of Energy Security. **In** *Preeg, E. H. and Bendahmane, D. B., eds.*, 1986, pp. 17–20.

Horwich, George. Energy Security: Relying on Unfettered Decentralized Market Decisions. **In** *Preeg, E. H. and Bendahmane, D. B., eds.*, 1986, pp. 20–25. **[G: U.S.]**

Houston, Jack E., Jr. and Whittlesey, Norman K. Modeling Agricultural Water Markets for Hydropower Production in the Pacific Northwest. *Western J. Agr. Econ.*, December 1986, *11*(2), pp. 221–31. **[G: U.S.]**

Hovey, Harry H., Jr. Air Pollution Impacts of Fossil Fuel-Fired Electrical Generation. **In** *Saltzman, S. and Schuler, R. E., eds.*, 1986, pp. 187–202. **[G: U.S.]**

Huband, Frank L. A Survey of Alternative Electric Utility Supply and Use Technologies. **In** *Saltzman, S. and Schuler, R. E., eds.*, 1986, pp. 167–75. **[G: U.S.]**

Hubbard, R. Glenn and Weiner, Robert J. Oil Supply Shocks and International Policy Coordination. *Europ. Econ. Rev.*, February 1986, *30*(1), pp. 91–106.

Hubbard, R. Glenn and Weiner, Robert J. Petroleum Regulation and Public Policy. **In** *Weiss, L. W. and Klass, M. W., eds.*, 1986, pp. 105–36. **[G: U.S.]**

Hughes, Gordon A. A New Method for Estimating the Effects of Fuel Taxes: An Application to Thailand. *World Bank Econ. Rev.*, September 1986, *1*(1), pp. 65–101. **[G: Thailand]**

Hunt, Lester Charles. Energy and Capital: Substitutes or Complements? A Note on the Importance of Testing for Non-neutral Technical Progress. *Appl. Econ.*, July 1986, *18*(7), pp. 729–35. **[G: U.K.]**

Hwang, Jiunn T. Multiplicative Errors-in-Variables Models with Applications to Recent Data Released by the U.S. Department of Energy. *J. Amer. Statist. Assoc.*, September 1986, *81*(395), pp. 680–88. **[G: U.S.]**

Ikenberry, G. John. The Irony of State Strength: Comparative Responses to the Oil Shocks in the 1970s. *Int. Organ.*, Winter 1986, *40*(1), pp. 105–37. **[G: U.S.; W. Germany; Japan; France]**

Iqbal, Mahmood. Substitution of Labour, Capital and Energy in the Manufacturing Sector of Pakistan. *Empirical Econ.*, 1986, *11*(2), pp. 81–95. **[G: Pakistan]**

Itteilag, Richard L. and Swanson, Christina A. Residential Gas Cooling: A Life-Cycle Approach. *Energy J.*, October 1986, *7*(4), pp. 81–88. **[G: U.S.]**

James, David E.; Musgrove, A. R. deL. and Stocks, K. J. Integration of an Economic Input–Output Model and a Linear Programming Technological Model for Energy Systems Analysis. *Energy Econ.*, April 1986, *8*(2), pp. 99–112. **[G: Australia]**

Janssen, Ron and Hafkamp, Wim. A Decision Support System for Conflict Analysis on Environmental Effects of Energy Conversion. *Ann. Reg. Sci.*, November 1986, *20*(3), pp. 67–85.

Jenkins, Barbara. Reexamining the "Obsolescing Bargain": A Study of Canada's National Energy Program. *Int. Organ.*, Winter 1986, *40*(1), pp. 139–65. **[G: Canada]**

Johnson, L. W. A Note on Australian Petrol Demand. *Int. J. Transport Econ.*, February 1986, *13*(1), pp. 105–08. **[G: Australia]**

Johnson, Nicholas and Adams, John. Electricity Demand Growth in New York State: The Uncertain Factor in the Electricity Planning Process. **In** *Saltzman, S. and Schuler, R. E., eds.*, 1986, pp. 67–76. **[G: U.S.]**

Jorgenson, Dale W. The Great Transition: Energy and Economic Change. *Energy J.*, July 1986, *7*(3), pp. 1–13. **[G: OECD]**

Kalt, Joseph P. and Leone, Robert A. Regional Effects of Energy Price Decontrol: The Roles of Interregional Trade, Stockholding, and Microeconomic Incidence. *Rand J. Econ.*, Summer 1986, *17*(2), pp. 201–13. **[G: U.S.]**

Kaser, Michael. Soviet Gas Supplies. **In** *Stevens, P., ed.*, 1986, pp. 71–88. **[G: U.S.S.R.]**

Khoja, Bakr A. Refining History and Priorities in Saudi Arabia. **In** *El Mallakh, R., ed.*, 1986, pp. 117–22. **[G: Saudi Arabia]**

Kitschelt, Herbert. Four Theories of Public Policy Making and Fast Breeder Reactor Development. *Int. Organ.*, Winter 1986, *40*(1), pp. 65–104. **[G: France; W. Germany; U.S.]**

Klein, Lawrence R. The Energy Crisis Ten Years Later. **In** *Saltzman, S. and Schuler, R. E., eds.*, 1986, pp. 18–31. **[G: U.S.]**

Kok, M. and van Oostvoorn, F. On the Use of Interactive Multi-objective Linear Programming Methods for Long Term Energy Planning. *Ann. Reg. Sci.*, November 1986, *20*(3), pp. 53–66. **[G: Netherlands]**

Koshal, Rajindar K.; Koshal, Manjulika and Nandola, Kahandas. Effects of High Energy Prices on Traffic: Some Indian Experience. *Int. J. Transport Econ.*, October 1986, *13*(3), pp. 359–68. **[G: India]**

Kremers, Jeroen J. M. The Dutch Disease in the Netherlands. **In** *Neary, J. P. and van*

Wijnbergen, S., eds., 1986, pp. 96–136. [G: Netherlands]

Kushman, John E. and Anderson, Joan Gray. A Model of Individual Household Temperature Demand and Energy-Related Welfare Changes Using Satiety. *Energy Econ.*, July 1986, *8*(3), pp. 147–54. [G: U.S.]

Lakshmanan, T. R. and Bolton, Roger. Regional Energy and Environmental Analysis. **In** *Nijkamp, P., ed. (I)*, 1986, pp. 581–628. [G: U.S.; OECD]

Lantzke, Ulf. Energy Supply in the European Community. **In** *Hax, H.; Kraus, W. and Tsuchiya, K., eds.*, 1986, pp. 42–48. [G: EEC]

Laquatra, Joseph. Housing Market Capitalization of Thermal Integrity. *Energy Econ.*, July 1986, *8*(3), pp. 134–38. [G: U.S.]

Lee, Henry. Local Energy Conservation Programs. **In** *Sawhill, J. C. and Cotton, R., eds.*, 1986, pp. 163–200. [G: U.S.]

Lenjosek, Gordon and Whalley, John. A Small Open Economy Model Applied to an Evaluation of Canadian Energy Policies Using 1980 Data. *J. Policy Modeling*, Spring 1986, *8*(1), pp. 89–110. [G: Canada]

Levin, Nissan; Tishler, Asher and Zahavi, Jacob. Evaluating Energy Options for Israel: A Case Study. *Energy J.*, January 1986, *7*(1), pp. 51–65. [G: Israel]

Lipton, Michael. Recession, Rent and Debt: Quasi-Ricardian and Quasi-Keynesian Components of Non-recovery. **In** *[Streeten, P.]*, 1986, pp. 58–86.

Loaiciga, Hugo A. and Mariñno, Miguel A. Risk Analysis for Reservoir Operation. *Water Resources Res.*, April 1986, *22*(4), pp. 483–88. [G: U.S.]

Lodwick, Seeley G. The International Trading Environment in Petrochemicals. **In** *El Mallakh, R., ed.*, 1986, pp. 47–54. [G: U.S.]

Lomax, David F. The Investment Implications of China's Offshore Oil Development. *Nat. Westminster Bank Quart. Rev.*, February 1986, pp. 50–69. [G: China]

Loungani, Prakash. Oil Price Shocks and the Dispersion Hypothesis. *Rev. Econ. Statist.*, August 1986, *68*(3), pp. 536–39. [G: U.S.]

Lower, Ann K. Engineering, Vested Interests, and Threshold Choice: Pipelines, Coal, and the Railroads. *J. Econ. Issues*, June 1986, *20*(2), pp. 471–80. [G: U.S.]

Lu, Yingzhong. Energy Prospects and Policies in the PRC. *Energy J.*, July 1986, *7*(3), pp. 99–108. [G: China]

Lukman, Nasrun and McGlinchey, James M. The Indonesian Petroleum Industry: Current Problems and Future Prospects. *Bull. Indonesian Econ. Stud.*, December 1986, *22*(3), pp. 70–92. [G: Indonesia]

Lynk, Edward L. and Webb, Michael G. An Unintended Consequence of the Taxation System for U.K. North Sea Oil. *Scot. J. Polit. Econ.*, February 1986, *33*(1), pp. 58–73. [G: U.K.]

Magat, Wesley A.; Payne, John W. and Brucato, Peter F., Jr. How Important Is Information Format? An Experimental Study of Home Energy Audit Programs. *J. Policy Anal. Manage.*, Fall 1986, *6*(1), pp. 20–34. [G: U.S.]

Malin, Clement B. The World Oil Market: Preparing for Future Surprises. **In** *Preeg, E. H. and Bendahmane, D. B., eds.*, 1986, pp. 9–12.

Manne, Alan S. and Schrattenholzer, Leo. International Energy Workshop: Oil Price Projections. *Energy J.*, July 1986, *7*(3), pp. 109–14. [G: OECD]

Marquez, Jaime. Oil-Price Effects in Theory and Practice. *J. Devel. Econ.*, November 1986, *24*(1), pp. 1–27. [G: Global]

Marquez, Jaime. The International Transmission of Oil-Price Effects and OPEC's Pricing Policy. *J. Econ. Bus.*, August 1986, *38*(3), pp. 237–53.

Marshalla, Robert A. and Nesbitt, Dale M. Future World Oil Prices and Production Levels: An Economic Analysis. *Energy J.*, January 1986, *7*(1), pp. 1–22. [G: Global]

Martin, Ricardo and van Wijnbergen, Sweder J. G. Shadow Prices and the Intertemporal Aspects of Remittances and Oil Revenues in Egypt. **In** *Neary, J. P. and van Wijnbergen, S., eds.*, 1986, pp. 142–68. [G: Egypt]

Mayo, John W. Multiproduct Monopoly, Regulation, and Firm Costs: Reply. *Southern Econ. J.*, April 1986, *52*(4), pp. 1175–78.

McCarl, H. N.; Preda, G. and Carlea, F. Substituting Energy Technologies. *Econ. Computat. Cybern. Stud. Res.*, 1986, *21*(2), pp. 19–25. [G: OECD]

Mead, Walter J. The OPEC Cartel Thesis Reexamined: Price Constraints from Oil Substitutes. *J. Energy Devel.*, Spring 1986, *11*(2), pp. 213–42. [G: OPEC]

Measday, Walter S. and Martin, Stephen. The Petroleum Industry. **In** *Adams, W., ed.*, 1986, pp. 38–73. [G: U.S.; OPEC]

Miller, Edward M. Cross-sectional and Time-Series Biases in Factor Demand Studies: Explaining Energy–Capital Complementarity. *Southern Econ. J.*, January 1986, *52*(3), pp. 745–62. [G: U.S.]

Moghimzadeh, Mahmood and Kymn, Kern O. Cost Shares, Own, and Cross-Price Elasticities in U.S. Manufacturing with Disaggregated Energy Inputs. *Energy J.*, October 1986, *7*(4), pp. 65–80. [G: U.S.]

Moorhouse, John C. The Uncertain Future of the Electric Power Industry. **In** *Moorhouse, J. C., ed.*, 1986, pp. 1–23. [G: U.S.]

Morgan, R. H. The Development of the Electricity Supply Industry in South Wales to 1939. **In** *Baber, C. and Williams, L. J., eds.*, 1986, pp. 222–36. [G: U.K.]

Mount, Timothy D. and Deehan, William J. Determinants of the Demand for Electricity in New York: Economic Conditions, Nuclear Power Costs, and Primary Fuel Prices. **In** *Saltzman, S. and Schuler, R. E., eds.*, 1986, pp. 77–96. [G: U.S.]

Mountain, Dean C. Impact of Higher Energy Prices on Wage Rates, Return to Capital, Energy Intensity and Productivity: A Regional Profit Specification. *Energy Econ.*, July 1986, *8*(3), pp. 171–76. **[G: Canada]**

Moy, Wai-See; Cohon, Jared L. and ReVelle, Charles S. A Programming Model for Analysis of the Reliability, Resilience, and Vulnerability of a Water Supply Resevoir. *Water Resources Res.*, April 1986, *22*(4), pp. 489–98.

Munk, A. O. An Alternative View of the Oil Price Future. **In** *El Mallakh, R., ed.*, 1986, pp. 177–80.

Murphy, Frederic H.; Toman, Michael A. and Weiss, Howard J. An Integrated Analysis of U.S. Oil Security Policies. *Energy J.*, July 1986, *7*(3), pp. 67–82. **[G: U.S.]**

Nachtnebel, H. P.; Hanisch, P. and Duckstein, L. Multicriterion Analysis of Small Hydropower Plants under Fuzzy Objectives. *Ann. Reg. Sci.*, November 1986, *20*(3), pp. 86–103. **[G: Austria]**

Neary, J. Peter and van Wijnbergen, Sweder J. G. Natural Resources and the Macroeconomy: Introduction. **In** *Neary, J. P. and van Wijnbergen, S., eds.*, 1986, pp. 1–11.

Newbery, David M. G. Certainty Equivalence Methods in the Macroeconomic Management of Petroleum Resources: Comment. **In** *Neary, J. P. and van Wijnbergen, S., eds.*, 1986, pp. 195–200. **[G: Norway]**

Niculescu, I. and Boconcios, Rodica. Mathematical Model for Optimizing the Functioning of the National Energy System. *Econ. Computat. Cybern. Stud. Res.*, 1986, *21*(2), pp. 27–32.

Nilsson, Per. Wood—The Other Energy Crisis. **In** *Boesen, J., et al., eds.*, 1986, pp. 159–72. **[G: Tanzania]**

Nordhaus, William D. Resources, Technology, and Development: Will the Table Be Bare When Poor Countries Get There? *Indian Econ. Rev.*, July-Dec. 1986, *21*(2), pp. 81–94.

Norgaard, Richard B. Thermodynamic and Economic Concepts as Related to Resource-Use Policies: Synthesis. *Land Econ.*, August 1986, *62*(3), pp. 325–28.

Norgaard, Richard B. and Leu, Gwo Jiun. Petroleum Accessibility and Drilling Technology: An Analysis of U.S. Development Costs from 1959 to 1978. *Land Econ.*, February 1986, *62*(1), pp. 14–25. **[G: U.S.]**

Numminen, Kalevi. Finlands energiekonomi nu och i framtiden. (Finnish Energy Economy Now and in the Future. With English summary.) *Ekon. Samfundets Tidskr.*, 1986, *39*(3), pp. 149–61. **[G: Finland]**

Odell, Peter R. Institutional Constraints on the Development of the Western European Natural Gas Market. **In** *Stevens, P., ed.*, 1986, pp. 89–106. **[G: W. Europe]**

Omichi, Masao. Nuclear Power in the United States and Japan. **In** *Finn, R. B., ed.*, 1986, pp. 51–75. **[G: U.S.; Japan]**

Ott, Mack and Tatom, John A. Are Energy Prices Cyclical? *Energy Econ.*, October 1986, *8*(4), pp. 227–36. **[G: U.S.]**

Peck, Merton J. and Beggs, John J. Energy Conservation in American Industry. **In** *Sawhill, J. C. and Cotton, R., eds.*, 1986, pp. 59–91. **[G: U.S.]**

Percival, Robert V. Conservation and Renewable Energy Sources as Supply Alternatives for New York's Electric Utilities. **In** *Saltzman, S. and Schuler, R. E., eds.*, 1986, pp. 126–50. **[G: U.S.]**

Pesaran, M. Hashem. A Macro Model of an Oil Exporter: Nigeria: Comment. **In** *Neary, J. P. and van Wijnbergen, S., eds.*, 1986, pp. 225–28. **[G: Nigeria]**

Pešout, Jaroslav. Statistics on the Production and Use of New, Renewable and Secondary Forms of Energy in Czechoslovakia. *Statist. J.*, May 1986, *4*(1), pp. 59–70. **[G: Czechoslovakia]**

Polzin, Paul E. The Specification of Price in Studies of Consumer Demand under Block Price Scheduling: Reply. *Land Econ.*, August 1986, *62*(3), pp. 335. **[G: U.S.]**

Pop, M. G. M., et al. Entropy and Development: A Regional Approach to Energy Problems. *Econ. Computat. Cybern. Stud. Res.*, 1986, *21*(2), pp. 11–18.

Preda, G. Glossary of Terms in the Field of Energy Conservation Economy. *Econ. Computat. Cybern. Stud. Res.*, 1986, *21*(2), pp. 33–90. **[G: Global]**

Price, Robert S. Government Policy and International Natural Gas Trade. *J. Energy Devel.*, Spring 1986, *11*(2), pp. 189–211. **[G: OECD]**

Prior, M. J. Fuel Markets in Urban Bangladesh. *World Devel.*, July 1986, *14*(7), pp. 865–72. **[G: Bangladesh]**

Prywes, Menahem. A Nested CES Approach to Capital–Energy Substitution. *Energy Econ.*, January 1986, *8*(1), pp. 22–28. **[G: U.S.]**

Pugliaresi, Lucian. The Iran–Iraq War: A Way Out. **In** *Preeg, E. H. and Bendahmane, D. B., eds.*, 1986, pp. 32–34. **[G: U.S.; Middle East]**

Puiu, Al. and Preda, G. Energy Conservation Technologies—Economic and Social Aspects. *Econ. Computat. Cybern. Stud. Res.*, 1986, *21*(4), pp. 5–12. **[G: Romania]**

Purvis, Douglas D. Indonesia's Other Dutch Disease: Economic Effects of the Petroleum Boom: Comment. **In** *Neary, J. P. and van Wijnbergen, S., eds.*, 1986, pp. 321–23. **[G: Indonesia]**

Quandt, William B. Two Kinds of Threats to U.S. Energy Supplies. **In** *Preeg, E. H. and Bendahmane, D. B., eds.*, 1986, pp. 27–32. **[G: U.S.; Middle East]**

Quick, Perry D. Financial Barriers to Investment in Conservation: Comments. **In** *Sawhill, J. C. and Cotton, R., eds.*, 1986, pp. 133–35. **[G: U.S.]**

Quigley, John M. "Blind Spots" in Perspective: Comment. *J. Policy Anal. Manage.*, Winter 1986, *5*(2), pp. 228–33. **[G: U.S.]**

Radice, E. A. Energy and Materials. **In** *Kaser, M. C. and Radice, E. A., eds.*, 1986, pp. 398–415. **[G: E. Europe; Germany]**

Raffiee, Kambiz. The Specification of Price in Studies of Consumer Demand under Block Price Scheduling: Comment. *Land Econ.*, August 1986, *62*(3), pp. 333–34. **[G: U.S.]**

Ramain, Patrice. The Energy Demand Elasticity in Relation to Gross Domestic Product: A Relevant Indicator? *Energy Econ.*, January 1986, *8*(1), pp. 29–38. **[G: OECD]**

Ramos, Manuel M. The Venezuelan Petrochemical Industry: Present and Plans. **In** *El Mallakh, R., ed.*, 1986, pp. 55–61. **[G: Venezuela]**

Ramstetter, Eric D. Interaction between Japanese Policy Priorities: Energy and Trade in the 1980s. *J. Energy Devel.*, Spring 1986, *11*(2), pp. 285–300. **[G: Japan]**

Reilly, Barry. A Note on Demand Elasticities for Energy Imports. *Econ. Soc. Rev.*, January 1986, *17*(2), pp. 147–58. **[G: Ireland]**

Richardson, James A. Severance Tax Reform. **In** *Gold, S. D., ed.*, 1986, pp. 277–90. **[G: U.S.]**

Roberts, Mark J. Economies of Density and Size in the Production and Delivery of Electric Power. *Land Econ.*, November 1986, *62*(4), pp. 378–87. **[G: U.S.]**

Robison, H. David and Silver, Stephen J. The Impact of Changing Oil Prices on Interfuel Substitution: Ethanol's Prospects in the United States to 1995. *J. Policy Modeling*, Summer 1986, *8*(2), pp. 241–53. **[G: U.S.]**

Romînu, I., et al. Economic Efficiency of Investment in Energy Conservation. *Econ. Computat. Cybern. Stud. Res.*, 1986, *21*(2), pp. 5–10.

Rosenfeld, Arthur H. Energy Conservation in the Federal Government: Comments. **In** *Sawhill, J. C. and Cotton, R., eds.*, 1986, pp. 260–62. **[G: U.S.]**

Rowse, John. Allocation of Canadian Natural Gas to Domestic and Export Markets. *Can. J. Econ.*, August 1986, *19*(3), pp. 417–42. **[G: Canada]**

Rushdi, Ali Ahmed. Interfuel Substitution in the Residential Sector of South Australia. *Energy Econ.*, July 1986, *8*(3), pp. 177–85. **[G: Australia]**

Sagers, Matthew J. and Tretyakova, Albina. Constraints in Gas for Oil Substitution in the USSR: The Oil Refining Industry and Gas Storage. *Soviet Econ.*, Jan.-Mar. 1986, *2*(1), pp. 72–94. **[G: U.S.S.R.]**

Salvatore, Dominick. Oil Import Costs and Domestic Inflation in Industrial Countries. *Weltwirtsch. Arch.*, 1986, *122*(2), pp. 281–91. **[G: OECD; LDCs]**

Sametz, Arnold W. Financial Barriers to Investment in Conservation. **In** *Sawhill, J. C. and Cotton, R., eds.*, 1986, pp. 95–132. **[G: U.S.]**

Saqqaf, Abdulaziz. Energy Production and Consumption in the Yemen Arab Republic. **In** *El Mallakh, R., ed.*, 1986, pp. 145–61. **[G: Yemen]**

Saul, Eduard. We Know Our Responsibility. *Czech. Econ. Digest.*, March 1986, (2), pp. 13–23. **[G: CMEA]**

Sav, G. Thomas. On Subsidies for Energy-Saving Durables. *Amer. Econ.*, Spring 1986, *30*(1), pp. 56–59.

Sav, G. Thomas. The Failure of Solar Tax Incentives: A Dynamic Analysis. *Energy J.*, July 1986, *7*(3), pp. 51–66. **[G: U.S.]**

Sawhill, John C. and Cotton, Richard. Energy Conservation: Successes and Failures: Introduction. **In** *Sawhill, J. C. and Cotton, R., eds.*, 1986, pp. 1–17.

Scanlan, Tony. The Competitive Floor to World Oil Prices: A Comment. *Energy J.*, October 1986, *7*(4), pp. 34–35. **[G: U.S.; U.K.; OPEC]**

Schlesinger, James R. The Long-run Security of the Energy Supply. **In** *Saltzman, S. and Schuler, R. E., eds.*, 1986, pp. 32–39. **[G: U.S.]**

Schmidt, Ronald H. and Gunther, Jeffery W. Distributional Implications of Reducing Interstate Energy Price Differences. *Fed. Res. Bank Dallas Econ. Rev.*, November 1986, pp. 1–15. **[G: U.S.]**

Schotta, Charles. Middle East Economic Cooperation: Energy Product Trade. **In** *El Mallakh, R., ed.*, 1986, pp. 29–36. **[G: Middle East]**

Schuler, Richard E. Electricity in New York State: The First One Hundred Years as Prelude to the Future. **In** *Saltzman, S. and Schuler, R. E., eds.*, 1986, pp. 7–17. **[G: U.S.]**

Schurr, Sam H. Patterns of Energy Use: Comments. **In** *Sawhill, J. C. and Cotton, R., eds.*, 1986, pp. 53–56. **[G: U.S.]**

Scullion, Patrick J. Electric Utility Conservation Programs: Progress and Problems: Comments. **In** *Sawhill, J. C. and Cotton, R., eds.*, 1986, pp. 159–60. **[G: U.S.]**

Sengupta, Mritunjoy. The Choice between Coal and Nuclear Power in India: A Cost–Benefit Approach. *J. Energy Devel.*, Autumn 1986, *12*(1), pp. 85–102. **[G: India]**

Shabad, Theodore. Selected Recent Books on Soviet Energy. *Soviet Econ.*, Apr.-June 1986, *2*(2), pp. 186–91. **[G: U.S.S.R.]**

Shipman, Ross L. Energy on the U.S.–Mexico Border. *Natural Res. J.*, Fall 1986, *26*(4), pp. 711–16. **[G: U.S.; Mexico]**

Shukla, P. R. and Moulik, T. K. Impact of Biomass Availability on Selection of Optimal Energy Systems and Cost of Energy. *Energy J.*, April 1986, *7*(2), pp. 107–20. **[G: India]**

Siddayao, Corazon Morales. Petroleum Resources in the Pacific Rim: The Roles Played by Governments in Their Development and Trade. **In** *Nemetz, P. N., ed.*, 1986, pp. 234–74. **[G: Pacific Basin]**

Siddiqi, Toufiq A. Factors Affecting Steam Coal Trade in Asia and the Pacific. **In** *Nemetz, P. N., ed.*, 1986, pp. 275–92. **[G: Asia; Pacific Basin]**

Sinha, S. K. Energy Balance in Agriculture: The Developing World. **In** *Swaminathan, M. S. and Sinha, S. K., eds.*, 1986, pp. 57–83. **[G: LDCs]**

Sioshansi, Fereidoon P. Energy, Electricity, and the U.S. Economy: Emerging Trends. *Energy J.*, April 1986, *7*(2), pp. 81–90. **[G: U.S.]**

Sláma, Jiří. An International Comparison of Sulphur Dioxide Emissions. *J. Compar. Econ.*,

September 1986, *10*(3), pp. 277–92. **[G: Europe]**

Slater, Paul B. Petroleum Trade in 1970: An Exploratory Analysis. **In** *Slater, P. B.*, 1986, *1975*, pp. 7–12. **[G: Global]**

Slesser, M. Energy Balance in Agriculture: The Developed World. **In** *Swaminathan, M. S. and Sinha, S. K., eds.*, 1986, pp. 47–56. **[G: MDCs]**

Small, Kenneth A. Effects of the 1979 Gasoline Shortages on Philadelphia Housing Prices. *J. Urban Econ.*, May 1986, *19*(3), pp. 371–81. **[G: U.S.]**

Smil, Vaclav. China and Japan in the New Energy Era. **In** *Nemetz, P. N., ed.*, 1986, pp. 223–33. **[G: China; Japan]**

Smith, Alasdair. Shadow Prices and the Intertemporal Aspects of Remittances and Oil Revenues in Egypt: Comment. **In** *Neary, J. P. and van Wijnbergen, S., eds.*, 1986, pp. 168–69. **[G: Egypt]**

Solomon, Barry D. The Socioeconomic Impacts of a Regional Synthetic Fuels Industry: An Integrated Econometric Analysis. **In** *Batey, P. W. and Madden, M., eds.*, 1986, pp. 167–86. **[G: U.S.]**

Stafford, Robert T. Energy and the Environment: The View from Washington. **In** *Saltzman, S. and Schuler, R. E., eds.*, 1986, pp. 179–86. **[G: U.S.]**

Stalon, Charles G. The Diminishing Role of Regulation in the Natural Gas Industry. *Energy J.*, April 1986, *7*(2), pp. 1–12. **[G: U.S.]**

Stasiuk, William N. Some Public Health Concerns Associated with Electrical Energy Generation. **In** *Saltzman, S. and Schuler, R. E., eds.*, 1986, pp. 203–12. **[G: U.S.]**

Stern, Paul C. Blind Spots in Policy Analysis: What Economics Doesn't Say about Energy Use. *J. Policy Anal. Manage.*, Winter 1986, *5*(2), pp. 200–227. **[G: U.S.]**

Stocks, K. J. and Musgrove, A. R. deL. The Value of Australia's Natural Gas Resource—A Linear Programming Analysis. *Energy J.*, April 1986, *7*(2), pp. 91–106. **[G: Australia]**

Strøm, Trygve. Project Financing in the North Sea. *Écon. Soc.*, July 1986, *20*(7), pp. 145–57.

Stromback, C. Thorsten. Modelling Electricity Demand in Western Australia. *Australian Econ. Pap.*, June 1986, *25*(46), pp. 106–17. **[G: W. Australia]**

Struckmeyer, Charles S. The Impact of Energy Price Shocks on Capital Formation and Economic Growth in a Putty–Clay Technology. *Southern Econ. J.*, July 1986, *53*(1), pp. 127–40.

Supple, Barry. Ideology or Pragmatism? The Nationalization of Coal, 1916–46. **In** *[Coleman, D. C.]*, 1986, pp. 228–50. **[G: U.K.]**

Sutherland, Ronald J. A Portfolio Analysis Model of the Demand for Nuclear Power Plants. *Energy Econ.*, October 1986, *8*(4), pp. 218–26. **[G: U.S.]**

Swanson, David A. Missing Survey Data in End-Use Energy Models: An Overlooked Problem. *Energy J.*, July 1986, *7*(3), pp. 149–57. **[G: U.S.]**

Swartz, Stephen and Welsch, Roy E. Applications of Bounded-Influence and Diagnostic Methods in Energy Modeling. **In** *Belsley, D. A. and Kuh, E., eds.*, 1986, pp. 154–90. **[G: U.S.]**

Tahmassebi, Hossein. Future Energy Trends in a Changing Market Environment. **In** *El Mallakh, R., ed.*, 1986, pp. 163–75. **[G: Global]**

Tahmassebi, Hossein. World Energy Outlook through 2000. *J. Energy Devel.*, Autumn 1986, *12*(1), pp. 1–26. **[G: Global]**

Takayama, T. and Labys, Walter C. Spatial Equilibrium Analysis. **In** *Nijkamp, P., ed. (I)*, 1986, pp. 171–99.

Tarpgaard, Peter T. U.S. Shipping Subsidies and Ocean Shipping of Petroleum: Policy Choices. *Contemp. Policy Issues*, October 1986, *4*(4), pp. 79–92. **[G: U.S.]**

Taylor, Lance; Yurukoglu, Kadir T. and Chaudhry, Shahid A. A Macro Model of an Oil Exporter: Nigeria. **In** *Neary, J. P. and van Wijnbergen, S., eds.*, 1986, pp. 201–24. **[G: Nigeria]**

Taylor, Thomas N. and Schwarz, Peter M. A Residential Demand Charge: Evidence from the Duke Power Time-of-Day Pricing Experiment. *Energy J.*, April 1986, *7*(2), pp. 135–51. **[G: U.S.]**

Terza, Joseph V. Determinants of Household Electricity Demand: A Two-Stage Probit Approach. *Southern Econ. J.*, April 1986, *52*(4), pp. 1131–39. **[G: U.S.]**

Thomas, Brinley. Was There an Energy Crisis in Great Britain in the 17th Century? *Exploration Econ. Hist.*, April 1986, *23*(2), pp. 124–52. **[G: U.K.]**

Thompson, Grant P. Energy Conservation in the Federal Government: Comments. **In** *Sawhill, J. C. and Cotton, R., eds.*, 1986, pp. 257–60. **[G: U.S.]**

Thornton, Judith. Soviet Electric Power after Chernobyl': Economic Consequences and Options. *Soviet Econ.*, Apr.-June 1986, *2*(2), pp. 131–79. **[G: U.S.S.R.]**

Toichi, Tsutomu and Ogawa, Yoshiki. Recent Problems in Japan's Oil Industry. **In** *El Mallakh, R., ed.*, 1986, pp. 129–44. **[G: Japan]**

Tourinho, Octávio A. F. A expansão de longa prazo do sistema elétrico brasileiro: uma análise com o modelo PSE. (With English summary.) *Pesquisa Planejamento Econ.*, April 1986, *16*(1), pp. 87–127. **[G: Brazil]**

Trehan, Bharat. Oil Prices, Exchange Rates and the U.S. Economy: An Empirical Investigation. *Fed. Res. Bank San Francisco Econ. Rev.*, Fall 1986, (4), pp. 25–43. **[G: U.S.]**

Tsuchiya, Kiyoshi. Middle Eastern Oil and the Japanese Economy. **In** *Hax, H.; Kraus, W. and Tsuchiya, K., eds.*, 1986, pp. 29–41. **[G: Japan]**

Tucker, Paul W. The Natural Gas Market: The Cyclical Process. **In** *Stevens, P., ed.*, 1986, pp. 5–13.

Udokang, Okon. The Energy Question and Africa's Role in a NIEO. **In** *Onwuka, R. I. and*

Aluko, O., eds., 1986, pp. 165–86. **[G: Africa]**

Urano, Hiroshi. Security of Oil Supplies: Japan's Options. **In** *Finn, R. B., ed.*, 1986, pp. 149–71. **[G: Middle East; Japan; Selected Countries]**

Ver Hulst, N. and Laporte, J. M. Le rôle des banques dans les grands projets énergétiques. (The Role of Banks in Big Energetic Projects. With English summary.) *Econ. Soc.*, July 1986, *20*(7), pp. 129–43.

Virén, Matti. Estimating the Output Effects of Energy Price and Real Interest Rate Shocks: A Cross-Country Study. *Schweiz. Z. Volkswirtsch. Statist.*, December 1986, *122*(4), pp. 627–39. **[G: OECD]**

Vlachou, A. S. and Samouilidis, E. J. Interfuel Substitution: Results from Several Sectors of the Greek Economy. *Energy Econ.*, January 1986, *8*(1), pp. 39–45. **[G: Greece]**

Volkonskii, V. A.; Kuzovkin, A. I. and Pomanskii, A. B. On Determining Time-of-Day Tariffs for Energy and Services. *Matekon*, Fall 1986, *23*(1), pp. 3–24. **[G: U.S.S.R.]**

Wadehra, B. L. Public Enterprise: Studies in Organisational Structure: Coal India Limited. **In** *Ramanadham, V. V., ed.*, 1986, pp. 211–33. **[G: India]**

Warr, Peter G. Indonesia's Other Dutch Disease: Economic Effects of the Petroleum Boom. **In** *Neary, J. P. and van Wijnbergen, S., eds.*, 1986, pp. 288–320.

Weinberg, Alvin M. An Energy Traditionalist Talks to the Energy Nontraditionalists about Electricity and Nuclear Energy. **In** *Saltzman, S. and Schuler, R. E., eds.*, 1986, pp. 151–65. **[G: U.S.]**

Wendt, E. Allan. Oil Products: Prospects for an Open Trading Regime. **In** *El Mallakh, R., ed.*, 1986, pp. 123–27.

Westoby, Richard. Effect of Oil Price Increases on Developing Countries—A Comment. *Energy Econ.*, January 1986, *8*(1), pp. 46–47. **[G: Ivory Coast; Kenya; S. Korea; Turkey]**

Weyant, John P. The World Oil Market: Lessons of the Past. **In** *Preeg, E. H. and Bendahmane, D. B., eds.*, 1986, pp. 13–15.

Wilkinson, Jack W. The Competitive Floor to World Oil Prices: A Comment. *Energy J.*, October 1986, *7*(4), pp. 32–33. **[G: U.S.; U.K.; OPEC]**

Williams, Stephen F. It's Worse than You Thought: Further Flaws in Price Controls as a Device for Transferring Scarcity Rents. *J. Policy Anal. Manage.*, Fall 1986, *6*(1), pp. 106–09. **[G: U.S.]**

Wionczek, Miguel S. Energy and International Security in the 1980s: Realities or Misperceptions? **In** *[Patel, S.]*, 1986, pp. 75–84.

Woo, Chi-Keung; Hanser, Philip and Toyama, Nate. Estimating Hourly Electric Load with Generalized Least Square Procedures. *Energy J.*, April 1986, *7*(2), pp. 153–70.

Woo, Chi-Keung and Toyama, Nate. Service Reliability and the Optimal Interruptible Rate Option in Residential Electricity Pricing. *Energy J.*, July 1986, *7*(3), pp. 123–36.

Yergin, Daniel. The World Oil Market: How We Have Changed since 1973. **In** *Preeg, E. H. and Bendahmane, D. B., eds.*, 1986, pp. 5–9.

Zakariya, Hasan S. Financing Petroleum Development in the Third World: The Role of the Public International Sector. *J. World Trade Law*, July:Aug. 1986, *20*(4), pp. 417–40. **[G: LDCs]**

730 Economic Geography

731 Economic Geography

7310 Economic Geography

Altman, Morris. Resource Endowments and Location Theory in Economic History: A Case Study of Quebec and Ontario at the Turn of the Twentieth Century. *J. Econ. Hist.*, December 1986, *46*(4), pp. 999–1009. **[G: Canada]**

Bonin, Serge. A Cartographic Approach to the Problem of Internal Migration in Sardinia in the Eighteenth Century: Part 2. **In** *Glazier, I. A. and De Rosa, L., eds.*, 1986, pp. 371–78. **[G: Italy]**

Bradley, Michael D. and Carpenter, Michael C. Subsiding Land and Falling Ground-Water Tables: Public Policy, Private Liability, and Legal Remedy. *Econ. Geogr.*, July 1986, *62*(3), pp. 241–53. **[G: U.S.]**

Dahmann, Donald C. Geographical Mobility Research with Panel Data. *Growth Change*, July 1986, *17*(3), pp. 35–48. **[G: U.S.]**

Day, John. A Cartographic Approach to the Problem of Internal Migration in Sardinia in the Eighteenth Century: Part 1. **In** *Glazier, I. A. and De Rosa, L., eds.*, 1986, pp. 365–70. **[G: Italy]**

FitzSimmons, Margaret. The New Industrial Agriculture: The Regional Integration of Specialty Crop Production. *Econ. Geogr.*, October 1986, *62*(4), pp. 334–53. **[G: U.S.]**

Gould, Peter. August Lösch as a Child of His Time. **In** *[Lösch, A.]*, 1986, pp. 7–19.

Hannon, Bruce; Costanza, Robert and Herendeen, Robert A. Measures of Energy Cost and Value in Ecosystems. *J. Environ. Econ. Manage.*, December 1986, *13*(4), pp. 391–401.

Hiltner, John; Smith, Bruce W. and Sullivan, James A. The Utilization of Social and Recreational Services by the Elderly: A Case Study of Northwestern Ohio. *Econ. Geogr.*, July 1986, *62*(3), pp. 232–40. **[G: U.S.]**

Hwang, Hong and Mai, Chao-cheng. Welfare-Maximizing Location versus Profit-Maximizing Locations. *Ann. Reg. Sci.*, March 1986, *20*(1), pp. 54–64.

Kohsaka, Hiroyuki. The Location Process of Central Place System within a Circular City. *Econ. Geogr.*, July 1986, *62*(3), pp. 254–66.

Komorowski, Stanislaw M. Lösch Revisited. **In** *[Lösch, A.]*, 1986, pp. 21–34.

Laulajainen, Risto and Gadde, Lars-Erik. Locational Avoidance: A Case Study of Three Swedish Retail Chains. *Reg. Stud.*, April 1986, *20*(2), pp. 131–40. **[G: Sweden]**

Mehretu, Assefa. Towards a Framework for Spatial Resolution of Structural Polarity in African Development. *Econ. Geogr.*, January 1986, *62*(1), pp. 30–51. **[G: Africa]**

Osborne, Martin J. and Pitchik, Carolyn. The Nature of Equilibrium in a Location Model. *Int. Econ. Rev.*, February 1986, *27*(1), pp. 223–37.

Pinder, D. A. Small Firms, Regional Development and the European Investment Bank. *J. Common Market Stud.*, March 1986, *24*(3), pp. 171–86. **[G: EEC]**

Ponsard, Claude. August Lösch: A Famous, but Ignored Economist. **In** *[Lösch, A.]*, 1986, pp. 35–45.

Puu, Tönu and Weidlich, Wolfgang. The Stability of Hexagonal Tessellations. **In** *[Lösch, A.]*, 1986, pp. 133–58.

Robson, Brian. Research Issues in the Changing Urban and Regional System. *Reg. Stud.*, June 1986, *20*(3), pp. 203–07. **[G: U.K.]**

Schoenberger, Erica. Competition, Competitive Strategy, and Industrial Change: The Case of Electronic Components. *Econ. Geogr.*, October 1986, *62*(4), pp. 321–33. **[G: Global]**

Scott, Allen J. Industrial Organization and Location: Division of Labor, the Firm, and Spatial Process. *Econ. Geogr.*, July 1986, *62*(3), pp. 215–31.

Scott, Allen J. and Storper, Michael. Industrial Change and Territorial Organization: A Summing Up. **In** *Scott, A. J. and Storper, M., eds.*, 1986, pp. 301–11.

Solomon, Barry D. and Pyrdol, John J. Delineating Coal Market Regions. *Econ. Geogr.*, April 1986, *62*(2), pp. 109–24. **[G: U.S.]**

Timmermans, Harry. Locational Choice Behaviour of Entrepreneurs: An Experimental Analysis. *Urban Stud.*, June 1986, *23*(3), pp. 231–40.

Upton, Graham J. G. Distance and Directional Analyses of Settlement Patterns. *Econ. Geogr.*, April 1986, *62*(2), pp. 167–79. **[G: Argentina]**

Watts, Michael. Geographers among the Peasants: Power, Politics, and Practice. *Econ. Geogr.*, October 1986, *62*(4), pp. 373–86. **[G: Africa]**

Wheeler, James O. Similarities in the Corporate Structure of American Cities. *Growth Change*, July 1986, *17*(3), pp. 13–21. **[G: U.S.]**

800 Manpower; Labor; Population

8000 General

Stafford, Frank. Forestalling the Demise of Empirical Economics: The Role of Microdata in Labor Economics Research. **In** *Ashenfelter, O. and Layard, R., eds., Vol. 1*, 1986, pp. 387–423.

Swanson, Dorothy. Annual Bibliography on American Labor History, 1985: Periodicals, Dissertations, and Research in Progress. *Labor Hist.*, Fall 1986, *27*(4), pp. 529–41. **[G: U.S.]**

Venkateswarlu, Tadiboyina. Labor Economics: Survey of Course Outlines in Universities in Canada and the United States of America. *Amer. Econ.*, Spring 1986, *30*(1), pp. 78–85. **[G: Canada; U.S.]**

810 Manpower Training and Development; Labor Force and Supply

811 Manpower Training and Development

8110 Manpower Training and Development

Bassi, Laurie J. and Ashenfelter, Orley. The Effect of Direct Job Creation and Training Programs on Low-Skilled Workers. **In** *Danziger, S. H. and Weinberg, D. H., eds.*, 1986, pp. 133–51. **[G: U.S.]**

Bendick, Marc, Jr. Government's Role in the Job Transitions of U.S. Dislocated Workers. **In** *Redburn, F. S.; Buss, T. F. and Ledebur, L. C., eds.*, 1986, pp. 158–75. **[G: U.S.]**

Bezdek, Roger H. Long-Range U.S. Manpower Forecasts in Retrospect: How Accurate Were We? *Econ. Planning*, 1986, *20*(1), pp. 52–67. **[G: U.S.]**

Bisesi, Michael. Public Policy and Human Venture Capital: Forging a More Productive Business–Education Link. *J. Policy Anal. Manage.*, Summer 1986, *5*(4), pp. 820–24. **[G: U.S.]**

Bishop, John H. and Montgomery, Mark. Evidence on Firm Participation in Employment Subsidy Programs. *Ind. Relat.*, Winter 1986, *25*(1), pp. 56–64. **[G: U.S.]**

Bottazzi, Gianfranco and Moscati, Roberto. I contratti di formazione lavoro nel mezzogiorno: riflessioni sui risultati di una ricerca. (Implementation of the "Employment and Training Contracts" in Southern Italy. With English summary.) *Econ. Lavoro*, Oct.-Dec. 1986, *20*(4), pp. 87–104. **[G: Italy]**

Burtless, Gary and Orr, Larry L. Are Classical Experiments Needed for Manpower Policy? *J. Human Res.*, Fall 1986, *21*(4), pp. 606–39. **[G: U.S.]**

Casey, Bernard. The Dual Apprenticeship System and the Recruitment and Retention of Young Persons in West Germany. *Brit. J. Ind. Relat.*, March 1986, *24*(1), pp. 63–81. **[G: W. Germany]**

Castley, Robert and Alfthan, Torkel. Training for Industrial Development: How Governments Can Help. *Int. Lab. Rev.*, Sept.-Oct. 1986, *125*(5), pp. 545–60. **[G: LDCs]**

Chan, Lean Heng. Young Workers Education Project: Development of a Participatory Urban Services Centre in Penang, Malaysia. **In** *Yeung, Y. M. and McGee, T. G., eds.*, 1986, pp. 165–90. **[G: Malaysia]**

Daly, Anne. Education and Productivity: A Comparison of Great Britain and the United States. *Brit. J. Ind. Relat.*, July 1986, *24*(2), pp. 251–66. **[G: U.K.; U.S.]**

Davis, Norman. Training for Change. **In** *Hart, P. E., ed.*, 1986, pp. 82–98. **[G: U.K.]**

Dickinson, Katherine P.; Johnson, Terry R. and West, Richard W. An Analysis of the Impact of CETA Programs on Participants' Earnings. *J. Human Res.*, Winter 1986, *21*(1), pp. 64–91. **[G: U.S.]**

Etheredge, Dennis. The Role of the Private Sector in Education and Training. **In** *Smollan, R., ed.*, 1986, pp. 138–44. **[G: S. Africa]**

Ford, G. W. Learning from Japan: The Concept of Skill Formation. *Australian Bull. Lab.*, March 1986, *12*(2), pp. 119–27. **[G: Australia; Japan]**

Fraser, Douglas A. A Challenge to the United States: Job Creation and Employment Security. **In** *Burton, D. F., et al., eds.*, 1986, pp. 11–26. **[G: U.S.]**

Germe, J. F. Employment Policies and the Entry of Young People into the Labour Market in France. *Brit. J. Ind. Relat.*, March 1986, *24*(1), pp. 29–42. **[G: France]**

Glazer, Nathan. Education and Training Programs and Poverty. **In** *Danziger, S. H. and Weinberg, D. H., eds.*, 1986, pp. 152–73. **[G: U.S.]**

Gonçalves, Reinaldo. Technological Spill-Overs and Manpower Training: A Comparative Analysis of Multinational and National Enterprises in Brazilian Manufacturing. *J. Econ. Devel.*, July 1986, *11*(1), pp. 119–32. **[G: Brazil]**

Hansen, Gary B. U.S. Employment and Training Policy: A Twenty-five Year Review, 1960–1985. *Econ. Lavoro*, July-Sept. 1986, *20*(3), pp. 141–47. **[G: U.S.]**

Hartshorne, Ken. The Role of the State in Education and Training. **In** *Smollan, R., ed.*, 1986, pp. 117–37. **[G: S. Africa]**

Jain, S. K. The Need for an Operational Thrust to Human Resources Development. *Int. Lab. Rev.*, Nov.-Dec. 1986, *125*(6), pp. 627–40.

Jencks, Christopher. Education and Training Programs and Poverty: Comment. **In** *Danziger, S. H. and Weinberg, D. H., eds.*, 1986, pp. 173–79. **[G: U.S.]**

Kalas, John W. Reindustrialization in New York: The Role of the State University. **In** *Schoolman, M. and Magid, A., eds.*, 1986, pp. 281–312. **[G: U.S.]**

King, Kenneth. Manpower, Technology, and Employment in Africa: Internal and External Policy Agendas. **In** *Berg, R. J. and Whitaker, J. S., eds.*, 1986, pp. 422–50. **[G: Africa]**

Kostin, L. A. The Development of Vocational Guidance in the USSR. *Int. Lab. Rev.*, Nov.-Dec. 1986, *125*(6), pp. 715–29. **[G: U.S.S.R.]**

Kriulin, G. A. Disability Prevention and Vocational Rehabilitation of the Disabled in the Byelorussian SSR. *Int. Lab. Rev.*, Mar.-Apr. 1986, *125*(2), pp. 209–25. **[G: U.S.S.R.]**

LaLonde, Robert J. Evaluating the Econometric Evaluations of Training Programs with Experimental Data. *Amer. Econ. Rev.*, September 1986, *76*(4), pp. 604–20. **[G: U.S.]**

Lambooy, Jan G. and van der Vegt, Chris. Segmentation Theories and Manpower Policy in Dutch Cities. **In** *Nijkamp, P., ed. (II)*, 1986, pp. 262–79. **[G: Netherlands]**

Manevich, E. L. The Economic Mechanism and the Use of Labor Resources. *Prob. Econ.*, September 1986, *29*(5), pp. 41–56. **[G: U.S.S.R.]**

Mangum, Stephen L. and Ball, David. Skill Transfer and Military Occupational Training. **In** *Hills, S. M., ed.*, 1986, pp. 133–47. **[G: U.S.]**

Marnie, Sheila. Transition from School to Work: Satisfying Pupils' Aspirations and the Needs of the Economy. **In** *Lane, D., ed.*, 1986, pp. 209–22. **[G: U.S.S.R.]**

Matulovich, Michael. Organisational Programmes of Black Advancement: Training Needs and Techniques. **In** *Smollan, R., ed.*, 1986, pp. 189–202. **[G: S. Africa]**

McArthur, Andrew and McGregor, Alan. Policies for the Disadvantaged in the Labour Market. **In** *Lever, W. and Moore, C., eds.*, 1986, pp. 120–41. **[G: U.K.]**

Moerdyk, Alwyn. Planning and Implementing a Black Advancement Programme. **In** *Smollan, R., ed.*, 1986, pp. 155–77. **[G: S. Africa]**

Picker, Harvey. Adult Education and Jobs. **In** *Burton, D. F., et al., eds.*, 1986, pp. 199–203. **[G: U.S.]**

Prais, S. J. Training for Change: Comment. **In** *Hart, P. E., ed.*, 1986, pp. 98–102. **[G: U.K.]**

Prais, S. J. and Steedman, Hilary. Vocational Training in France and Britain: The Building Trades. *Nat. Inst. Econ. Rev.*, May 1986, (116), pp. 45–55. **[G: U.K.; France]**

Psacharopoulos, George and Arriagada, Ana María. The Educational Composition of the Labour Force: An International Comparison. *Int. Lab. Rev.*, Sept.-Oct. 1986, *125*(5), pp. 561–74. **[G: Global]**

Ridder, G. An Event History Approach to the Evaluation of Training, Recruitment and Employment Programmes. *J. Appl. Econometrics*, April 1986, *1*(2), pp. 109–26. **[G: Netherlands]**

Ripley, Randall B. and Franklin, Grace A. The Private Sector, Public Employment and Training Programs, and Economic Revitalization. **In** *Redburn, F. S.; Buss, T. F. and Ledebur, L. C., eds.*, 1986, pp. 176–99. **[G: U.S.]**

Roukis, George S. and Montana, Patrick J. Development and Human Resources Management in the Arab Oil Rich Gulf States. **In** *Roukis, G. S. and Montana, P. J., eds.*, 1986, pp. 169–96. **[G: Middle East]**

Schober-Brinkmann, Karen. The Crisis of Youth Employment and Training in West Germany: Public Intervention and the Response of Employers and Trade Unions. *Econ. Lavoro*, Oct.-Dec. 1986, *20*(4), pp. 117–27. **[G: W. Germany]**

Seeborg, Irmtraud Streker; Seeborg, Michael C. and Zegeye, Abera. Training and Labor Market Outcomes of Disadvantaged Blacks. *Ind.*

Relat., Winter 1986, *25*(1), pp. 33–44. **[G: U.S.]**

Shaw, Paul F. Saudi Arabian Manpower Requirements. **In** *Roukis, G. S. and Montana, P. J., eds.*, 1986, pp. 95–112. **[G: Saudi Arabia]**

Spellman, Ruth. Education and Training Initiatives in the United Kingdom and Macro-economic Policies. **In** *Burton, D. F., et al., eds.*, 1986, pp. 205–25. **[G: U.K.]**

Thornton, Craig and Maynard, Rebecca. The Economics of Transitional Employment and Supported Employment. **In** *Berkowitz, M. and Hill, M. A., eds.*, 1986, pp. 142–70. **[G: U.S.]**

Vaganov, Boris. Fifty Years since the Creation of the All-Union Foreign Trade Academy of the Ministry of Foreign Trade of the USSR. *Soviet E. Europ. Foreign Trade*, Summer 1986, *22*(2), pp. 28–38. **[G: U.S.S.R.]**

Van Horn, Carl E.; Beauregard, Robert A. and Ford, David S. Local Economic Development and Job Targeting. **In** *Bergman, E. M., ed.*, 1986, pp. 226–47. **[G: U.S.]**

812 Occupation

8120 Occupation

Acar, Feride. Working Women in a Changing Society: The Case of Jordanian Academics. *METU*, 1986, *13*(3–4), pp. 307–24. **[G: Jordan]**

Adams, John and Paul, Linda. The Informal Sector in India: Work, Gender, and Technology. **In** *Björkman, J. W., ed.*, 1986, pp. 33–52. **[G: India]**

Al-Tuhaih, Salem M. The Vicious Cycle of Manpower in Kuwait. **In** *Roukis, G. S. and Montana, P. J., eds.*, 1986, pp. 123–38.

Albelda, Randy P. Occupational Segregation by Race and Gender, 1958–1981. *Ind. Lab. Relat. Rev.*, April 1986, *39*(3), pp. 404–11. **[G: U.S.]**

Altonji, Joseph G. Efficiency Wage Theories: A Partial Evaluation: Comment. **In** *Fischer, S., ed.*, 1986, pp. 276–85. **[G: U.S.]**

Anderstig, Christer and Hårsman, Björn. On Occupation Structure and Location Pattern in the Stockholm Region. *Reg. Sci. Urban Econ.*, February 1986, *16*(1), pp. 97–122. **[G: Sweden]**

Appelbaum, Eileen and Granrose, Cherlyn Skromme. Hospital Employment under Revised Medicare Payment Schedules. *Mon. Lab. Rev.*, August 1986, *109*(8), pp. 37–45. **[G: U.S.]**

Atkinson, Scott E. and Tschirhart, John. Flexible Modelling of Time to Failure in Risky Careers. *Rev. Econ. Statist.*, November 1986, *68*(4), pp. 558–66. **[G: U.S.]**

Bandiyono, Suko and Conroy, John D. Employment and Income from Non-agricultural Sources in Rural East Java: Some Preliminary Findings. **In** *Shand, R. T., ed., Vol. 1*, 1986, pp. 327–67. **[G: Indonesia]**

Becker, William E. and Williams, Arlington W. Assessing Personnel Practices in Higher Education: A Case Study in the Hiring of Female. *Econ. Educ. Rev.*, 1986, *5*(3), pp. 265–72.

Bianchi, Suzanne M. and Rytina, Nancy. The Decline in Occupational Sex Segregation during the 1970s: Census and CPS Comparisons. *Demography*, February 1986, *23*(1), pp. 79–86. **[G: U.S.]**

Blomqvist, Ake G. International Migration of Educated Manpower and Social Rates of Return to Education in LDCs. *Int. Econ. Rev.*, February 1986, *27*(1), pp. 165–74. **[G: LDCs]**

Bradbury, Katharine L. and Browne, Lynn E. Black Men in the Labor Market. *New Eng. Econ. Rev.*, Mar./Apr. 1986, pp. 32–42. **[G: U.S.]**

Carter, Susan B. Occupational Segregation, Teachers' Wages, and American Economic Growth. *J. Econ. Hist.*, June 1986, *46*(2), pp. 373–83. **[G: U.S.]**

Chang, Cyril F. and Tuckman, Howard P. Price-Induced Substitution of Faculty in Academe: Does Mission Make a Difference? *Econ. Educ. Rev.*, 1986, *5*(2), pp. 197–204. **[G: U.S.]**

Chiswick, Barry R. Family Effects in Simple Models of Education, Occupational Status and Earnings: Findings from the Wisconsin and Kalamazoo Studies: Comment. *J. Lab. Econ.*, Part 2, July 1986, *4*(3), pp. 116–20. **[G: U.S.]**

Chulasai, Luechai; Bhekasut, Suwarat and Shusuwan, Thongchai. Family Labour, Hired Labour and Employment Linkages in Rural Thailand. **In** *Hirashima, S. and Muqtada, M., eds.*, 1986, pp. 151–75. **[G: Thailand]**

Conway, Hugh and Anderson, Ewan. Kuwait's Labor Force: An Historical Perspective, Industrial Development, and Measures to Stabilize the Expatriate Labor Force. **In** *Roukis, G. S. and Montana, P. J., eds.*, 1986, pp. 139–56. **[G: Kuwait]**

Cooper, Kathleen M. NABE's Role: Fostering the Professional Growth of Business Economists. *Bus. Econ.*, April 1986, *21*(2), pp. 25–27. **[G: U.S.]**

Cotler, Julio. The Political Radicalization of Working-Class Youth in Peru. *CEPAL Rev.*, August 1986, (29), pp. 107–18. **[G: Peru]**

Craver, Earlene. The Emigration of the Austrian Economists. *Hist. Polit. Econ.*, Spring 1986, *18*(1), pp. 1–32. **[G: Austria]**

Creedy, John and Whitfield, K. Earnings and Job Mobility: Professional Chemists in Britain. *J. Econ. Stud.*, 1986, *13*(2), pp. 23–37. **[G: U.K.]**

Cromwell, Jerry and Mitchell, Janet B. Physician-Induced Demand for Surgery. *J. Health Econ.*, December 1986, *5*(4), pp. 293–313. **[G: U.S.]**

Culler, Steven D. and Ohsfeldt, Robert L. The Determinants of the Provision of Charity Medical Care by Physicians. *J. Human Res.*, Winter 1986, *21*(1), pp. 138–56. **[G: U.S.]**

Datcher-Loury, Linda and Loury, Glenn C. The Effects of Attitudes and Aspirations on the Labor Supply of Young Men. **In** *Freeman,*

R. B. and Holzer, H. J., eds., 1986, pp. 377–99. **[G: U.S.]**

Deery, Stephen, et al. The Labour Market Experience of Redundant Workers: A Study of a Plant Closure. *Australian Bull. Lab.*, June 1986, *12*(3), pp. 173–94. **[G: Australia]**

Dixon, Peter B. Prospects for Australian Industries and Occupations, 1985 to 1990. *Australian Econ. Rev.*, 1st Quarter 1986, (73), pp. 3–28. **[G: Australia]**

Dussault, Ginette. Valeurs sociales, ségrégation professionnelle et discrimination. (Social Values, Occupational Segregation and Discrimination. With English summary.) *Écon. Soc.*, April 1986, *20*(4), pp. 141–64. **[G: France]**

Elahi, Mahboob and Khan, Mahmud Jameel. Rural Labour Market with Special Reference to Hired Labour in Pakistan's Punjab. **In** *Hirashima, S. and Muqtada, M., eds.*, 1986, pp. 75–118. **[G: Pakistan]**

Elliott, Robert F. and Murphy, Phillip D. The Determinants of the Coverage of PBR Systems in Britain. *J. Econ. Stud.*, 1986, *13*(3), pp. 38–50. **[G: U.K.]**

Engerman, Stanley L. Population and Labor in the British Caribbean in the Early Nineteenth Century: Comment. **In** *Engerman, S. L. and Gallman, R. E., eds.*, 1986, pp. 625–29. **[G: Caribbean]**

Fagan, Thomas W. Comparative Costs of Alternative Forces in the U.S. Army. **In** *Gilroy, C. L., ed.*, 1986, pp. 347–60. **[G: U.S.]**

Farley, Pamela J. Theories of the Price and Quantity of Physician Services: A Synthesis and Critique. *J. Health Econ.*, December 1986, *5*(4), pp. 315–33. **[G: U.S.]**

Filer, Randall K. The "Starving Artist"—Myth or Reality? Earnings of Artists in the United States. *J. Polit. Econ.*, February 1986, *94*(1), pp. 56–75. **[G: U.S.]**

Filer, Randall K. The Role of Personality and Tastes in Determining Occupational Structure. *Ind. Lab. Relat. Rev.*, April 1986, *39*(3), pp. 412–24. **[G: U.S.]**

Friedlander, Dov and Moshe, Eliahu Ben. Occupations, Migration, Sex Ratios, and Nuptiality in Nineteenth Century English Communities: A Model of Relationships. *Demography*, February 1986, *23*(1), pp. 1–12. **[G: U.K.]**

Friedman, Gerald. Population and Labor in the British Caribbean in the Early Nineteenth Century: Comment. **In** *Engerman, S. L. and Gallman, R. E., eds.*, 1986, pp. 629–37. **[G: Caribbean]**

Gil, Avishai. Some Labour Implications of Technological Change in Rail and Air Transport. *Int. Lab. Rev.*, Jan.-Feb. 1986, *125*(1), pp. 1–17. **[G: France; U.K.; Netherlands; W. Germany]**

Ginsburgh, Victor; Perelman, Sergio and Pestieau, Pierre. Les prestations des salariés en heures supplémentaires Résultats d'une enquête. (With English summary.) *Cah. Écon. Bruxelles*, 4th Trimester 1986, (112), pp. 109–25. **[G: Belgium]**

Glasmeier, Amy K. High-Tech Industries and the Regional Division of Labor. *Ind. Relat.*, Spring 1986, *25*(2), pp. 197–211. **[G: U.S.]**

Gloeckner, Eduard. Underemployment and Potential Unemployment of the Technical Intelligentsia: Distortions between Education and Occupation. **In** *Lane, D., ed.*, 1986, pp. 223–36. **[G: U.S.S.R.]**

Goldberg, Lawrence and Greenston, Peter. Economic Analysis of Army Enlistments: Policy Implications. **In** *Gilroy, C. L., ed.*, 1986, pp. 61–94. **[G: U.S.]**

Goldberg, Lawrence and Greenston, Peter. Economic Analysis of Army Enlistments: Policy Implications: Reply. **In** *Gilroy, C. L., ed.*, 1986, pp. 97–99. **[G: U.S.]**

Goldberg, Michael A. Hedging Your Great Grandchildren's Bets: The Case of Overseas Chinese Investment in Real Estate around the Cities of the Pacific Rim. **In** *Nemetz, P. N., ed.*, 1986, pp. 159–98. **[G: S. E. Asia; ASEAN; Hong Kong]**

Goldin, Claudia. Monitoring Costs and Occupational Segregation by Sex: A Historical Analysis. *J. Lab. Econ.*, January 1986, *4*(1), pp. 1–27. **[G: U.S.]**

Grimes, Paul W. Occupational Mobility and Racial Equity in the Labor Market. *J. Behav. Econ.*, Spring/Summer 1986, *15*(1/2), pp. 54–69. **[G: U.S.]**

Grissmer, David W. and Fernandez, Judith C. Meeting Occupational and Total Manpower Requirements at Least Cost: A Nonlinear Programing Approach. **In** *Gilroy, C. L., ed.*, 1986, pp. 361–83. **[G: U.S.]**

Harris, G. T. and Rashid, Zakariah bin Abdul. The Employment Performance of Developing Countries during the 1970s. *Devel. Econ.*, September 1986, *24*(3), pp. 272–87. **[G: LDCs]**

Hart, Peter E. and Trinder, C. Employment Protection, National Insurance, Income Tax and Youth Unemployment. **In** *Hart, P. E., ed.*, 1986, pp. 29–44. **[G: U.K.]**

Hauser, Robert M. and Sewell, William H. Family Effects in Simple Models of Education, Occupational Status and Earnings: Findings from the Wisconsin and Kalamazoo Studies. *J. Lab. Econ.*, Part 2, July 1986, *4*(3), pp. S83–115. **[G: U.S.]**

Higman, B. W. Population and Labor in the British Caribbean in the Early Nineteenth Century. **In** *Engerman, S. L. and Gallman, R. E., eds.*, 1986, pp. 605–25. **[G: Caribbean]**

Hoffman, Emily P. A Review of Two Studies of Elasticity in Academe. *Econ. Educ. Rev.*, 1986, *5*(2), pp. 219–24. **[G: U.S.]**

Hogan, Paul F. Army Reenlistment and Extension Decisions by Occupation: Comment. **In** *Gilroy, C. L., ed.*, 1986, pp. 257–60.

Horne, David K. and Weltin, Mary M. Motivation and Career Intentions. *J. Behav. Econ.*, Fall 1986, *15*, pp. 29–42. **[G: U.S.]**

Horowitz, Stanley A. Experience and Readiness. **In** *Gilroy, C. L., ed.*, 1986, pp. 321–27. **[G: U.S.]**

Hoskins, W. Lee. Professional Certification: An Idea in Search of a Problem. *Bus. Econ.*, April

1986, *21*(2), pp. 15–20. [G: U.S.]

Jackson, John L. Long-run Effects of Military Service during the Vietnam War. **In** *Hills, S. M., ed.*, 1986, pp. 113–32. [G: U.S.]

Jensen, Gail A. and Morrisey, Michael A. The Role of Physicians in Hospital Production. *Rev. Econ. Statist.*, August 1986, *68*(3), pp. 432–42. [G: U.S.]

Johnson, Michael P. Work, Culture, and the Slave Community: Slave Occupations in the Cotton Belt in 1860. *Labor Hist.*, Summer 1986, *27*(3), pp. 325–55. [G: U.S.]

Kahan, Arcadius. Jewish Life in the United States: Perspectives from Economics. **In** *Kahan, A.*, 1986, *1981*, pp. 128–48. [G: U.S.]

Kahl, Anne and Clark, Donald E. Employment in Health Services: Long-term Trends and Projections. *Mon. Lab. Rev.*, August 1986, *109*(8), pp. 17–36. [G: U.S.]

Katz, Lawrence F. Efficiency Wage Theories: A Partial Evaluation. **In** *Fischer, S., ed.*, 1986, pp. 235–76. [G: U.S.]

Kearl, J. R. and Pope, Clayne L. Choices, Rents, and Luck: Economic Mobility of Nineteenth-Century Utah Households. **In** *Engerman, S. L. and Gallman, R. E., eds.*, 1986, pp. 215–56. [G: U.S.]

Kikuchi, Masao. Growing Impact of Off-Farm Employment on a Rural Economy: Changes in Labour Utilization and Income Earning Structure in a Philippine Rice Village. **In** *Shand, R. T., ed., Vol. 2*, 1986, pp. 99–131. [G: Philippines]

Killingsworth, Mark R. and Heckman, James J. Female Labor Supply: A Survey. **In** *Ashenfelter, O. and Layard, R., eds., Vol. 1*, 1986, pp. 103–204. [G: U.S.; U.K.; Canada; Germany]

Köllö, János. The Impact of the Labour Market on the Employment Structure in Hungary. *Acta Oecon.*, 1986, *36*(3–4), pp. 197–208. [G: Hungary]

Kraft, Philip and Dubnoff, Steven. Job Content, Fragmentation, and Control in Computer Software Work. *Ind. Relat.*, Spring 1986, *25*(2), pp. 184–96. [G: U.S.]

Kriegler, Roy. The Employment Outlook for Data Processing Occupations. *Australian Bull. Lab.*, March 1986, *12*(2), pp. 91–101. [G: Australia]

Kulcsár, R. Results of the First Nationwide Prestige Survey in Hungary. *Acta Oecon.*, 1986, *36*(1–2), pp. 155–67. [G: Hungary]

Lakhani, Hyder and Gilroy, Curtis L. Army Reenlistment and Extension Decisions by Occupation. **In** *Gilroy, C. L., ed.*, 1986, pp. 225–56. [G: U.S.]

Langrehr, Virginia B. and Langrehr, Frederick W. Course Requirements, Job Responsibilities, and Compensation for Financial Counselors: The Not-for-Profit Industry View. *J. Cons. Aff.*, Summer 1986, *20*(1), pp. 131–41. [G: U.S.]

Latack, Janina C. and D'Amico, Ronald J. Career Mobility among Young Men: A Search for Patterns. **In** *Hills, S. M., ed.*, 1986, pp. 91–112. [G: U.S.]

Laurent, André. The Elimination of Sex Discrimination in Occupational Social Security Schemes in the EEC. *Int. Lab. Rev.*, Nov.-Dec. 1986, *125*(6), pp. 675–83. [G: EEC]

Lebergott, Stanley. Revised Estimates of the United States Workforce, 1800–1860: Comment. **In** *Engerman, S. L. and Gallman, R. E., eds.*, 1986, pp. 671–73. [G: U.S.]

Lefebvre, Louis A., et al. L'impact de la technologie informatique sur la main-d'oeuvre dans les organisations. (The Impact of Information Technology on Human Resources in Organizations. With English summary.) *L'Actual. Econ.*, December 1986, *62*(4), pp. 557–78. [G: Canada]

Leigh, J. Paul. Wage Differentials and Risk of Death: Comment. *Econ. Inquiry*, July 1986, *24*(3), pp. 505–08. [G: U.S.]

Leonard, Jonathan S. The Effectiveness of Equal Employment Law and Affirmative Action Regulation. **In** *Ehrenberg, R. G., ed., Pt. B*, 1986, pp. 319–50. [G: U.S.]

Levin, Henry M. and Rumberger, Russell. The Low-Skill Future of High Tech. **In** *Reynolds, L. G.; Masters, S. H. and Moser, C. H., eds.*, 1986, *1983*, pp. 190–96. [G: U.S.]

Lewis, Gregory B. and Emmert, Mark A. The Sexual Division of Labor in Federal Employment. *Soc. Sci. Quart.*, March 1986, *67*(1), pp. 143–55. [G: U.S.]

Lillard, Lee; Smith, James P. and Welch, Finis. What Do We Really Know about Wages? The Importance of Nonreporting and Census Imputation. *J. Polit. Econ.*, Part 1, June 1986, *94*(3), pp. 489–506. [G: U.S.]

Low, Stuart A. and McPheters, Lee R. Wage Differentials and Risk of Death: Reply. *Econ. Inquiry*, July 1986, *24*(3), pp. 509–11. [G: U.S.]

Mangum, Stephen L. and Ball, David. Skill Transfer and Military Occupational Training. **In** *Hills, S. M., ed.*, 1986, pp. 133–47. [G: U.S.]

Martínez, Javier and Valenzuela, Eduardo. Chilean Youth and Social Exclusion. *CEPAL Rev.*, August 1986, (29), pp. 93–105. [G: Chile]

Mason, Jerry and Poduska, Bud. Financial Planner or Financial Counselor: The Differences Are Significant. *J. Cons. Aff.*, Summer 1986, *20*(1), pp. 142–47.

Massiah, Joycelin. Establishing a Programme of Women and Development Studies in the University of the West Indies. *Soc. Econ. Stud.*, March 1986, *35*(1), pp. 151–97. [G: Jamaica]

Massiah, Joycelin. Work in the Lives of Caribbean Women. *Soc. Econ. Stud.*, June 1986, *35*(2), pp. 177–240. [G: Barbados; Antigua; St. Vincent]

McCormick, Barry. Evidence about the Comparative Earnings of Asian and West Indian Workers in Great Britain. *Scot. J. Polit. Econ.*, May 1986, *33*(2), pp. 97–110. [G: U.K.]

McNiel, Douglas W. and Swofford, James L. Competition in the Medical Profession—An

Application of the Theory of Regulation: Comment. *Southern Econ. J.*, January 1986, *52*(3), pp. 857–66. **[G: U.S.]**

Medoff, Marshall H. Baseball Attendance and Fan Discrimination. *J. Behav. Econ.*, Spring/Summer 1986, *15*(1/2), pp. 149–55. **[G: U.S.]**

Miller, Ann R. Internal Migration and the Changing Structure of Employment in the United States in 1900: Machine Readable Census Samples as a New Source for Historical Research. **In** *Glazier, I. A. and De Rosa, L., eds.*, 1986, pp. 336–55. **[G: U.S.]**

Morton, John D. BLS White-Collar Pay Survey Now Covers Small Firms. *Mon. Lab. Rev.*, October 1986, *109*(10), pp. 26–30. **[G: U.S.]**

Muqtada, M. and Alam, M. Mustafa. Hired Labour and Rural Labour Market in Bangladesh. **In** *Hirashima, S. and Muqtada, M., eds.*, 1986, pp. 21–73. **[G: Bangladesh]**

Nelson, K. Labor Demand, Labor Supply and the Suburbanization of Low-wage Office Work. **In** *Scott, A. J. and Storper, M., eds.*, 1986, pp. 149–71. **[G: U.S.]**

Noether, Monica. The Effect of Government Policy Changes on the Supply of Physicians: Expansion of a Competitive Fringe. *J. Law Econ.*, October 1986, *29*(2), pp. 231–62. **[G: U.S.]**

Noether, Monica. The Growing Supply of Physicians: Has the Market Become More Competitive? *J. Lab. Econ.*, October 1986, *4*(4), pp. 503–37. **[G: U.S.]**

Noyelle, Thierry J. Advanced Services in the System of Cities. **In** *Bergman, E. M., ed.*, 1986, *1983*, pp. 143–64. **[G: U.S.]**

Ojo, Folayan. Manpower Development in West Africa. **In** *Damachi, U. G. and Seibel, H. D., eds.*, 1986, pp. 33–68. **[G: W. Africa]**

Orazem, Peter F. and Mattila, J. Peter. Occupational Entry and Uncertainty: Males Leaving High School. *Rev. Econ. Statist.*, May 1986, *68*(2), pp. 265–73. **[G: U.S.]**

Parrish, John B. Are Women Taking Over the Professions? *Challenge*, Jan./Feb. 1986, *28*(6), pp. 54–58. **[G: U.S.]**

Paul, Chris W., II and Goodwin, Randall. Competition in the Medical Profession—An Application of the Theory of Regulation: Reply. *Southern Econ. J.*, January 1986, *52*(3), pp. 867–70. **[G: U.S.]**

Piore, Michael J. The Effects of Attitudes and Aspirations on the Labor Supply of Young Men: Comment. **In** *Freeman, R. B. and Holzer, H. J., eds.*, 1986, pp. 399–401. **[G: U.S.]**

Powell, Dorian. Caribbean Women and Their Response to Familial Experience. *Soc. Econ. Stud.*, June 1986, *35*(2), pp. 83–130. **[G: Barbados; St. Vincent; Antigua]**

Prekel, Truida. The Role of Black Women in the Economy. **In** *Smollan, R., ed.*, 1986, pp. 31–51. **[G: S. Africa]**

Quan, Nguyen T. Characteristics of Blue Collar and White Collar Jobs and Pecuniary Returns. *J. Behav. Econ.*, Spring/Summer 1986, *15*(1/2), pp. 157–74. **[G: U.S.]**

Raisian, John; Ward, Michael P. and Welch, Finis. Pay Equity and Comparable Worth. *Contemp. Policy Issues*, April 1986, *4*(2), pp. 4–20. **[G: U.S.]**

Rama, Germán W. Latin American Youth between Development and Crisis. *CEPAL Rev.*, August 1986, (29), pp. 17–39. **[G: Latin America]**

Rayappa, P. Hanumantha. Some Dimensions of Off-Farm Employment in Rural Karnataka, India. **In** *Shand, R. T., ed., Vol. 2*, 1986, pp. 177–92. **[G: India]**

Register, Charles A. Nurses' Earnings, Monopsony, Compensating Differentials, and Comparable Worth. *Atlantic Econ. J.*, September 1986, *14*(3), pp. 86. **[G: U.S.]**

Robinson, Olive. Employment Protection, National Insurance, Income Tax and Youth Unemployment: Comment. **In** *Hart, P. E., ed.*, 1986, pp. 45–49. **[G: U.K.]**

Rosenberg, Sam. Racial Differentials in Younger Male Occupational Mobility over the Business Cycle, 1966–1975. **In** *Dennis, B. D., ed.*, 1986, pp. 391–99. **[G: U.S.]**

Rostker, Bernard. Economic Analysis of Army Enlistments: Policy Implications: Comment. **In** *Gilroy, C. L., ed.*, 1986, pp. 95–96. **[G: U.S.]**

Schroeder, Sandra J. and Finlay, William. Internal Labor Markets, Professional Domination, and Gender: A Comparison of Laboratory Employees in Hospitals and Chemical/Oil Firms. *Soc. Sci. Quart.*, December 1986, *67*(4), pp. 827–40. **[G: U.S.]**

Shand, Richard T. and Chew, T. A. Off-Farm Employment in the Kemubu Project in Kelantan, Malaysia. **In** *Shand, R. T., ed., Vol. 2*, 1986, pp. 1–20. **[G: Malaysia]**

Shapiro, Carl. Investment, Moral Hazard, and Occupational Licensing. *Rev. Econ. Stud.*, October 1986, *53*(5), pp. 843–62.

Shughart, William F., II; Tollison, Robert D. and Goff, Brian L. Pigskins and Publications. *Atlantic Econ. J.*, July 1986, *14*(2), pp. 46–50. **[G: U.S.]**

Soltow, Lee. Choices, Rents, and Luck: Economic Mobility of Nineteenth-Century Utah Households: Comment. **In** *Engerman, S. L. and Gallman, R. E., eds.*, 1986, pp. 256–58. **[G: U.S.]**

Staten, Michael and Umbeck, John. A Study of Signaling Behavior in Occupational Disease Claims. *J. Law Econ.*, October 1986, *29*(2), pp. 263–86. **[G: U.S.]**

Swierenga, Robert P. Dutch International Migration and Occupational Change: A Structural Analysis of Multinational Linked Files. **In** *Glazier, I. A. and De Rosa, L., eds.*, 1986, pp. 95–124. **[G: Netherlands; U.S.]**

Thomas, D. A. War and the Economy: The South Wales Experience. **In** *Baber, C. and Williams, L. J., eds.*, 1986, pp. 251–77. **[G: U.K.]**

Thompson, Edward. Performers and Technological Change 25 Years after the Rome Convention. *Int. Lab. Rev.*, Sept.-Oct. 1986, *125*(5), pp. 575–90. **[G: OECD]**

Tuckman, Howard P. and Chang, Cyril F. Own-Price and Cross Elasticities of Demand for College Faculty. *Southern Econ. J.*, January 1986, *52*(3), pp. 735–44. **[G: U.S.]**

Wall, Richard A. Work, Welfare and the Family: An Illustration of the Adaptive Family Economy. **In** *[Laslett, P.]*, 1986, pp. 261–94. **[G: U.K.]**

Wasow, Bernard. Insurance and the Balance of Payments. **In** *Wasow, B. and Hill, R. D., eds.*, 1986, pp. 87–103. **[G: S. Korea; Portugal; India; Brazil; Taiwan]**

Webber, M. J. Regional Production and the Production of Regions: The Case of Steeltown. **In** *Scott, A. J. and Storper, M., eds.*, 1986, pp. 197–224. **[G: Canada]**

Weesie, Jeroen and Wippler, Reinhard. Cumulative Effects of Sequential Decisions in Organizations. **In** *[Rapoport, A.]*, 1986, pp. 257–79.

Weiss, Laurence. Efficiency Wage Theories: A Partial Evaluation: Comment. **In** *Fischer, S., ed.*, 1986, pp. 285–87. **[G: U.S.]**

Weiss, Thomas. Revised Estimates of the United States Workforce, 1800–1860: Reply. **In** *Engerman, S. L. and Gallman, R. E., eds.*, 1986, pp. 673–74. **[G: U.S.]**

Weiss, Thomas. Revised Estimates of the United States Workforce, 1800–1860. **In** *Engerman, S. L. and Gallman, R. E., eds.*, 1986, pp. 641–71. **[G: U.S.]**

Wilson, Paul R.; Chappell, Duncan and Lincoln, Robyn. Policing Physician Abuse in BC: An Analysis of Current Policies. *Can. Public Policy*, March 1986, *12*(1), pp. 236–44. **[G: Canada]**

Wilson, R. A. Is It Worth Becoming an Architect? *Appl. Econ.*, January 1986, *18*(1), pp. 59–69. **[G: U.S.]**

Woo, Jennie Hay. Graduate Degrees and Job Success: Managers in One U.S. Corporation. *Econ. Educ. Rev.*, 1986, *5*(3), pp. 227–37. **[G: U.S.]**

Zalokar, Nadja. Generational Differences in Female Occupational Attainment—Have the 1970's Changed Women's Opportunities? *Amer. Econ. Rev.*, May 1986, *76*(2), pp. 378–81. **[G: U.S.]**

813 Labor Force

8130 General

Al-Tuhaih, Salem M. The Vicious Cycle of Manpower in Kuwait. **In** *Roukis, G. S. and Montana, P. J., eds.*, 1986, pp. 123–38.

Altonji, Joseph G. and Paxson, Christina H. Job Characteristics and Hours of Work. **In** *Ehrenberg, R. G., ed., Pt. A*, 1986, pp. 1–55. **[G: U.S.]**

Arrufat, Jose Luis and Zabalza, Antonio. Female Labor Supply with Taxation, Random Preferences, and Optimization Errors. *Econometrica*, January 1986, *54*(1), pp. 47–63. **[G: U.K.]**

Ashenfelter, Orley and Card, David. Why Have Unemployment Rates in Canada and the United States Diverged? *Economica*, Supplement 1986, *53*(210(S)), pp. S171–95. **[G: U.S.; Canada]**

Bade, Franz-Josef. The De-industrialisation of the Federal Republic of Germany and Its Spatial Implications. **In** *Nijkamp, P., ed. (II)*, 1986, pp. 196–220. **[G: W. Germany; OECD]**

Ball, Nicole. Converting the Workforce: Defence Industry Conversion in the Industrialised Countries. *Int. Lab. Rev.*, July-Aug. 1986, *125*(4), pp. 401–22. **[G: OECD]**

Ben-Porath, Yoram. Diversity in Population and in the Labor Force. **In** *Ben-Porath, Y., ed.*, 1986, pp. 153–70. **[G: Israel]**

Bentzel, Ragnar. Incentives in the United Kingdom: Comment. **In** *Balassa, B. and Giersch, H., eds.*, 1986, pp. 296–300. **[G: U.K.]**

Blau, David M. and Robins, Philip K. Labor Supply Response to Welfare Programs: A Dynamic Analysis. *J. Lab. Econ.*, January 1986, *4*(1), pp. 82–104. **[G: U.S.]**

Bloch, Laurence, et al. Analyse macro-économique des taux d'activité et flexion conjonctrelle. (Macroeconomic Analysis of Activity Rates and Short Term Flexion Impact. With English summary.) *Écon. Appl.*, 1986, *39*(4), pp. 665–703.

Bloom, David E. and Freeman, Richard B. The Effects of Rapid Population Growth on Labor Supply and Employment in Developing Countries. *Population Devel. Rev.*, September 1986, *12*(3), pp. 381–414. **[G: LDCs]**

Blundell, Richard and Walker, Ian. A Life-Cycle Consistent Empirical Model of Family Labour Supply Using Cross-Section Data. *Rev. Econ. Stud.*, August 1986, *53*(4), pp. 539–58. **[G: U.K.]**

Blundell, Richard, et al. A Labour Supply Model for the Simulation of Tax and Benefit Reforms. **In** *Blundell, R. and Walker, I., eds.*, 1986, pp. 267–93. **[G: U.K.]**

Boss, Alfred. Social Insurance: Incentives and Disincentives to Save and to Work: Comment. **In** *Balassa, B. and Giersch, H., eds.*, 1986, pp. 81–85. **[G: OECD]**

Bouillaguet-Bernard, Patricia and Gauvin, Annie. Le travail des femmes dans la crise en France. (Women's Work throughout the Crisis in France. With English summary.) *Écon. Soc.*, April 1986, *20*(4), pp. 105–40. **[G: France]**

Bourguignon, François. Female Participation and Taxation in France. **In** *Blundell, R. and Walker, I., eds.*, 1986, pp. 243–66. **[G: France]**

Braslavsky, Cecilia. Youth in Argentina: Between the Legacy of the Past and the Construction of the Future. *CEPAL Rev.*, August 1986, (29), pp. 41–54. **[G: Argentina]**

Brown, C. V., et al. Payment Systems, Demand Constraints and Their Implications for Research into Labour Supply. **In** *Blundell, R. and Walker, I., eds.*, 1986, pp. 190–216. **[G: U.K.]**

Browne, Lynn E. Taking in Each Other's Laundry—The Service Economy. *New Eng. Econ. Rev.*, July/Aug. 1986, pp. 20–31. **[G: U.S.]**

Bruni, Michele and Franciosi, Franco B. Scenari alternativi di domanda e di offerta di lavoro.

(Alternative Scenarios of Labour Demand and Supply. With English summary.) *Econ. Lavoro*, July-Sept. 1986, *20*(3), pp. 113–36. **[G: U.S.; Italy]**

Bubnova, E. M. Demographic Waves and Labor Resources. *Prob. Econ.*, July 1986, 29(3), pp. 61–68. **[G: U.S.S.R.]**

Buss, Terry F. Assessing the Accuracy of BLS Local Unemployment Rates: A Case Study. *Ind. Lab. Relat. Rev.*, January 1986, *39*(2), pp. 241–50. **[G: U.S.]**

Cain, Glen G. Married Women in the Labor Force. **In** *Reynolds, L. G.; Masters, S. H. and Moser, C. H., eds.*, 1986, pp. 41–50. **[G: U.S.]**

Cantarero, Rodrigo F. and Colburn, Forrest D. The Structural Basis of Rural Employment in Postrevolutionary Nicaragua. *J. Devel. Areas*, October 1986, *21*(1), pp. 49–61. **[G: Nicaragua]**

Carcaterra, Rose. Facts and Projections at a Glance. **In** *Burton, D. F., et al., eds.*, 1986, pp. 265–84. **[G: U.S.]**

Carter, Susan B. The Female Labor Force and American Economic Growth, 1890–1980: Comment. **In** *Engerman, S. L. and Gallman, R. E., eds.*, 1986, pp. 594–99. **[G: U.S.]**

Chiswick, Barry R. Labor Supply and Investment in Child Quality: A Study of Jewish and Non-Jewish Women. *Rev. Econ. Statist.*, November 1986, *68*(4), pp. 700–703. **[G: U.S.]**

Chmura, Christine. The Industrial Mix of Employment in the Fifth District, 1950–1985. *Fed. Res. Bank Richmond Econ. Rev.*, May/June 1986, *72*(3), pp. 26–34. **[G: U.S.]**

Choate, Pat. Looking Forward—Jobs and Workers. **In** *Burton, D. F., et al., eds.*, 1986, pp. 85–102. **[G: U.S.]**

Conway, Hugh and Anderson, Ewan. Kuwait's Labor Force: An Historical Perspective, Industrial Development, and Measures to Stabilize the Expatriate Labor Force. **In** *Roukis, G. S. and Montana, P. J., eds.*, 1986, pp. 139–56. **[G: Kuwait]**

Cotler, Julio. The Political Radicalization of Working-Class Youth in Peru. *CEPAL Rev.*, August 1986, (29), pp. 107–18. **[G: Peru]**

Danziger, Sheldon H. and Gottschalk, Peter. Work, Poverty, and the Working Poor: A Multifaceted Problem. *Mon. Lab. Rev.*, September 1986, *109*(9), pp. 17–21. **[G: U.S.]**

Devaney, Barbara L. An Analysis of Variations in U.S. Fertility and Female Labor Force Participation Trends: A Reply. *Demography*, February 1986, *23*(1), pp. 141–42. **[G: U.S.]**

Devens, Richard M., Jr. Displaced Workers: One Year Later. *Mon. Lab. Rev.*, July 1986, *109*(7), pp. 40–43. **[G: U.S.]**

Devens, Richard M., Jr. Displaced Workers: One Year Later: Errata. *Mon. Lab. Rev.*, September 1986, *109*(9), pp. 41. **[G: U.S.]**

Dornbusch, Rudiger. Unemployment: Europe's Challenge of the '80s. *Challenge*, Sept./Oct. 1986, *29*(4), pp. 11–18. **[G: Europe; U.S.]**

Engerman, Stanley L. Population and Labor in the British Caribbean in the Early Nineteenth Century: Comment. **In** *Engerman, S. L. and Gallman, R. E., eds.*, 1986, pp. 625–29. **[G: Caribbean]**

Fabella, Raul V. Rural Non-Farm Employment in the Philippines: Composition, Growth and Seasonality. **In** *Shand, R. T., ed., Vol. 2*, 1986, pp. 69–97. **[G: Philippines]**

Fenn, P. T. and Vlachonikolis, I. G. Male Labour Force Participation Following Illness or Injury. *Economica*, August 1986, *53*(211), pp. 379–91. **[G: U.K.]**

Ferguson, Brian S. Labour Force Substitution and the Effects of an Aging Population. *Appl. Econ.*, August 1986, *18*(8), pp. 901–13. **[G: Canada]**

Flaim, Paul O. Work Schedules of Americans: An Overview of New Findings. *Mon. Lab. Rev.*, November 1986, *109*(11), pp. 3–6.

Friedman, Gerald. Population and Labor in the British Caribbean in the Early Nineteenth Century: Comment. **In** *Engerman, S. L. and Gallman, R. E., eds.*, 1986, pp. 629–37. **[G: Caribbean]**

Germe, J. F. Employment Policies and the Entry of Young People into the Labour Market in France. *Brit. J. Ind. Relat.*, March 1986, *24*(1), pp. 29–42. **[G: France]**

van Ginneken, Wouter. Full Employment in OECD Countries: Why Not? *Int. Lab. Rev.*, Jan.-Feb. 1986, *125*(1), pp. 19–37. **[G: OECD]**

Goldin, Claudia. The Female Labor Force and American Economic Growth, 1890–1980. **In** *Engerman, S. L. and Gallman, R. E., eds.*, 1986, pp. 557–94. **[G: U.S.]**

Greenwood, Michael J. and McDowell, John M. The Factor Market Consequences of U.S. Immigration. *J. Econ. Lit.*, December 1986, *24*(4), pp. 1738–72. **[G: U.S.]**

Hamermesh, Daniel S. Incentives for the Homogenization of Time Use. **In** *Balassa, B. and Giersch, H., eds.*, 1986, pp. 124–39.

Harris, G. T. and Rashid, Zakariah bin Abdul. The Employment Performance of Developing Countries during the 1970s. *Devel. Econ.*, September 1986, *24*(3), pp. 272–87. **[G: LDCs]**

Hayghe, Howard V. Military and Civilian Wives: Update on the Labor Force Gap. *Mon. Lab. Rev.*, December 1986, *109*(12), pp. 31–33. **[G: U.S.]**

Hayghe, Howard V. Rise in Mothers' Labor Force Activity Includes Those with Infants. *Mon. Lab. Rev.*, February 1986, *109*(2), pp. 43–45. **[G: U.S.]**

Higman, B. W. Population and Labor in the British Caribbean in the Early Nineteenth Century. **In** *Engerman, S. L. and Gallman, R. E., eds.*, 1986, pp. 605–25. **[G: Caribbean]**

Hogue, Carma R. and Flaim, Paul O. Measuring Gross Flows in the Labor Force: An Overview of a Special Conference. *J. Bus. Econ. Statist.*, January 1986, *4*(1), pp. 111–21. **[G: U.S.]**

Hong, Evelyn. Women, Consumers and Development. **In** *Wheelwright, T., ed.*, 1986, pp. 67–87. **[G: Asia]**

Ichniowski, Bernard E. and Preston, Anne E.

New Trends in Part-time Employment. **In** *Dennis, B. D., ed.*, 1986, pp. 60–67. **[G: U.S.]**

Isserman, Andrew, et al. Regional Labor Market Analysis. **In** *Nijkamp, P., ed. (I)*, 1986, pp. 543–80.

Jansen, Mary A. Emotional Disorders and the Labour Force: Prevalence, Costs, Prevention and Rehabilitation. *Int. Lab. Rev.*, Sept.-Oct. 1986, *125*(5), pp. 605–15. **[G: U.S.]**

Janssen, Martin. Social Insurance: Incentives and Disincentives to Save and to Work. **In** *Balassa, B. and Giersch, H., eds.*, 1986, pp. 67–80. **[G: OECD]**

Jatobá, Jorge. The Labour Market in a Recession-Hit Region: The North-East of Brazil. *Int. Lab. Rev.*, Mar.-Apr. 1986, *125*(2), pp. 227–41. **[G: Brazil]**

Johnson, William R. and Skinner, Jonathan. Labor Supply and Marital Separation. *Amer. Econ. Rev.*, June 1986, *76*(3), pp. 455–69. **[G: U.S.]**

Jones, David R. and Martin, Ronald L. Voluntary and Involuntary Turnover in the Labour Force. *Scot. J. Polit. Econ.*, May 1986, *33*(2), pp. 124–44. **[G: U.K.]**

Joshi, Heather. Participation in Paid Work: Evidence from the Women and Employment Survey. **In** *Blundell, R. and Walker, I., eds.*, 1986, pp. 217–42. **[G: U.K.]**

Kasryno, Faisal. Impact of Off-Farm Employment on Agricultural Labour Absorption and Wages in Indonesia. **In** *Shand, R. T., ed., Vol. 1*, 1986, pp. 273–307. **[G: Indonesia]**

Katzman, Rubén. Youth and Unemployment in Montevideo. *CEPAL Rev.*, August 1986, (29), pp. 119–31. **[G: Uruguay]**

König, Heinz. Incentives for the Homogenization of Time Use: Comment. **In** *Balassa, B. and Giersch, H., eds.*, 1986, pp. 162–65.

Krashevski, Richard S. What Is Full Employment? *Challenge*, Nov./Dec. 1986, *29*(5), pp. 33–40. **[G: U.S.]**

Krejči, Jeroslav. The Bohemian–Moravian War Economy. **In** *Kaser, M. C. and Radice, E. A., eds.*, 1986, pp. 452–92. **[G: Bohemia; Moravia]**

Kutscher, Ronald E. and Personick, Valerie A. Deindustrialization and the Shift to Services. *Mon. Lab. Rev.*, June 1986, *109*(6), pp. 3–13. **[G: U.S.]**

Lambrinos, James and Appel, David. Workers' Compensation and Employment: An Industry Analysis. **In** *Berkowitz, M. and Hill, M. A., eds.*, 1986, pp. 124–41. **[G: U.S.]**

Lebergott, Stanley. Revised Estimates of the United States Workforce, 1800–1860: Comment. **In** *Engerman, S. L. and Gallman, R. E., eds.*, 1986, pp. 671–73. **[G: U.S.]**

Leonard, Jonathan S. Labor Supply Incentives and Disincentives for Disabled Persons. **In** *Berkowitz, M. and Hill, M. A., eds.*, 1986, pp. 64–94. **[G: U.S.]**

Mahmud, Raisul A. International Migration and the Domestic Economy. **In** *Islam, R. and Muqtada, M., eds.*, 1986, pp. 247–78. **[G: Bangladesh]**

Manevich, E. L. The Economic Mechanism and the Use of Labor Resources. *Prob. Econ.*, September 1986, *29*(5), pp. 41–56. **[G: U.S.S.R.]**

Mark, Jerome A. Developments in Labor Statistics. *Bus. Econ.*, July 1986, *21*(3), pp. 16–20. **[G: U.S.]**

Marks, Denton and Vining, Aidan. Prison Labor Markets: The Supply Issue. *Policy Sci.*, July 1986, *19*(1), pp. 83–111. **[G: U.S.]**

Marnie, Sheila. Transition from School to Work: Satisfying Pupils' Aspirations and the Needs of the Economy. **In** *Lane, D., ed.*, 1986, pp. 209–22. **[G: U.S.S.R.]**

Martin, Fernand. Repercussions of Industrial Redeployment upon the International Role of the Region of Montreal. **In** *Danson, M., ed.*, 1986, pp. 147–57. **[G: Canada]**

Martínez, Javier and Valenzuela, Eduardo. Chilean Youth and Social Exclusion. *CEPAL Rev.*, August 1986, (29), pp. 93–105. **[G: Chile]**

McCallum, John. Unemployment in OECD Countries in the 1980s. *Econ. J.*, December 1986, *96*(384), pp. 942–60. **[G: OECD]**

McGregor, Alan and Mather, Frank. Developments in Glasgow's Labour Market. **In** *Lever, W. and Moore, C., eds.*, 1986, pp. 22–43. **[G: U.K.]**

McMahon, Patrick J. An International Comparison of Labor Force Participation, 1977–84. *Mon. Lab. Rev.*, May 1986, *109*(5), pp. 3–12. **[G: W. Germany; N. America; Japan; Australia; Sweden]**

McQuaid, Ronald William. Production Functions and the Disaggregation of Labor Inputs in Manufacturing Plants. *J. Reg. Sci.*, August 1986, *26*(3), pp. 595–603. **[G: U.S.]**

Mellor, Earl F. Shift Work and Flexitime: How Prevalent Are They? *Mon. Lab. Rev.*, November 1986, *109*(11), pp. 14–21. **[G: U.S.]**

Mikhailuk, V. Ways of Increasing the Social Effectiveness of Women's Labor. *Prob. Econ.*, January 1986, *28*(9), pp. 62–72. **[G: U.S.S.R.]**

Minford, Patrick. Incentives in the United Kingdom. **In** *Balassa, B. and Giersch, H., eds.*, 1986, pp. 279–95. **[G: U.K.]**

Molho, Ian. A Time Series Study of Household Participation Decisions through Boom and Slump. *Oxford Econ. Pap.*, March 1986, *38*(1), pp. 141–59. **[G: U.K.]**

Morishima, Motohiro. Job Satisfaction and Desire to Quit: Differences in the Determinants of Two Responses. **In** *Dennis, B. D., ed.*, 1986, pp. 80–91. **[G: Japan]**

Moser, James W. Labor Market Transitions: Cyclic, Trend, and Seasonal Effects for Prime-Age Men. *Ind. Lab. Relat. Rev.*, January 1986, *39*(2), pp. 251–63. **[G: U.S.]**

Norwood, Janet L. Jobs in the 1980's and Beyond. **In** *Burton, D. F., et al., eds.*, 1986, pp. 55–83. **[G: U.S.]**

O'Brien, A. Maureen and Hawley, Clifford B. The Labor Force Participation Behavior of

Married Women under Conditions of Constraints on Borrowing. *J. Human Res.*, Spring 1986, *21*(2), pp. 267–78. **[G: U.S.]**

Osterman, Paul. Technology and White-Collar Employment: A Research Strategy. **In** *Dennis, B. D., ed.*, 1986, pp. 52–59. **[G: U.S.]**

Pandit, Kavita. Sectoral Allocation of Labor Force with Development and the Effect of Trade Activity. *Econ. Geogr.*, April 1986, *62*(2), pp. 144–54.

Pencavel, John H. Labor Supply of Men: A Survey. **In** *Ashenfelter, O. and Layard, R., eds.*, *Vol. 1*, 1986, pp. 3–102. **[G: U.S.; U.K.; Canada; Germany]**

Phillips, Robyn S. and Vidal, Avis C. Restructuring and Growth Transitions of Metropolitan Economies: The Context for Economic Development Policy. **In** *Bergman, E. M., ed.*, 1986, *1983*, pp. 59–83. **[G: U.S.]**

Poterba, James M. and Summers, Lawrence H. Reporting Errors and Labor Market Dynamics. *Econometrica*, November 1986, *54*(6), pp. 1319–38. **[G: U.S.]**

Preel, Bernard. La gestion de l'emploi des services: pourquoi faut-il passer à l'analyse d'entreprise? (With English summary.) *Revue Écon. Polit.*, Sept.-Oct. 1986, *96*(5), pp. 490–502. **[G: OECD]**

Prescott, David; Swidinsky, Robert and Wilton, David A. Labour Supply Estimates for Low-Income Female Heads of Household Using Mincome Data. *Can. J. Econ.*, February 1986, *19*(1), pp. 134–41. **[G: Canada]**

Psacharopoulos, George and Arriagada, Ana María. The Educational Composition of the Labour Force: An International Comparison. *Int. Lab. Rev.*, Sept.-Oct. 1986, *125*(5), pp. 561–74. **[G: Global]**

Purnell, Susanna. The Labor Force in Oman. **In** *Roukis, G. S. and Montana, P. J., eds.*, 1986, pp. 113–22. **[G: Oman]**

Radice, E. A. Territorial Changes, Population Movements and Labour Supplies. **In** *Kaser, M. C. and Radice, E. A., eds.*, 1986, pp. 309–28. **[G: E. Europe]**

Rama, Germán W. Latin American Youth between Development and Crisis. *CEPAL Rev.*, August 1986, (29), pp. 17–39. **[G: Latin America]**

Ransom, Roger L. and Sutch, Richard. The Labor of Older Americans: Retirement of Men on and off the Job, 1870–1937. *J. Econ. Hist.*, March 1986, *46*(1), pp. 1–30. **[G: U.S.]**

Reicher Madeira, Felicia. Youth in Brazil: Old Assumptions and New Approaches. *CEPAL Rev.*, August 1986, (29), pp. 55–78. **[G: Brazil]**

Robins, Philip K. and West, Richard W. Sample Attrition and Labor Supply Response in Experimental Panel Data: A Study of Alternative Correction Procedures. *J. Bus. Econ. Statist.*, July 1986, *4*(3), pp. 329–38. **[G: U.S.]**

Roca, Maria L. Women Veterans Total 1 Million in First Half of 1986. *Mon. Lab. Rev.*, December 1986, *109*(12), pp. 30–31. **[G: U.S.]**

Romer, Christina D. Spurious Volatility in Historical Unemployment Data. *J. Polit. Econ.*, February 1986, *94*(1), pp. 1–37. **[G: U.S.]**

Ross, Russell T. Analysis of the 1980 Sydney Survey of Work Patterns of Married Women: Further Results. *Econ. Rec.*, September 1986, *62*(178), pp. 325–37. **[G: Australia]**

Rothschild, Kurt W. Incentives for the Homogenization of Time Use: Comment. **In** *Balassa, B. and Giersch, H., eds.*, 1986, pp. 159–61.

Schaich, Eberhard and Zimmermann, Peter. Zur Erfassung der Arbeitslosigkeit: Kritik derzeit praktizierter Verfahrensweisen und Erweiterungsvorschläge. (Measuring Unemployment in West Germany: Actual Procedures and Possible Improvements. With English summary.) *Jahr. Nationalökon. Statist.*, September 1986, *201*(5), pp. 498–517. **[G: W. Germany]**

Schultz, T. Paul. The Value and Allocation of Time in High-Income Countries: Implications for Fertility. *Population Devel. Rev.*, Supp. 1986, *12*, pp. 87–108. **[G: U.S.]**

Scott, Alison MacEwen. Women and Industrialisation: Examining the 'Female Marginalisation' Thesis. *J. Devel. Stud.*, July 1986, *22*(4), pp. 649–80. **[G: Peru; Brazil]**

Shank, Susan E. Employment Up, Unemployment Stable in the First Half of 1986. *Mon. Lab. Rev.*, August 1986, *109*(8), pp. 3–8. **[G: U.S.]**

Shank, Susan E. and Getz, Patricia M. Employment and Unemployment: Developments in 1985. *Mon. Lab. Rev.*, February 1986, *109*(2), pp. 3–12. **[G: U.S.]**

Shaw, Paul F. Saudi Arabian Manpower Requirements. **In** *Roukis, G. S. and Montana, P. J., eds.*, 1986, pp. 95–112. **[G: Saudi Arabia]**

Silvera, Rachel and Outin, Jean-Luc. Excédents de main-d'oeuvre et dispositifs de cessation anticipée d'activité. (Excess Labour and Early Retirement. With English summary.) *Écon. Soc.*, April 1986, *20*(4), pp. 305–43. **[G: France]**

Smith, David P. An Analysis of Variations in U.S. Fertility and Female Labor Force Participation Trends: Comment. *Demography*, February 1986, *23*(1), pp. 137–39. **[G: U.S.]**

Smith, Shirley J. The Growing Diversity of Work Schedules. *Mon. Lab. Rev.*, November 1986, *109*(11), pp. 7–13. **[G: U.S.]**

Sneessens, Henri R. and Drèze, Jacques H. What, If Anything, Have We Learned from the Rise of Unemployment in Belgium, 1974–1983. *Cah. Écon. Bruxelles*, 2nd/3rd Trimester 1986, (110/111), pp. 21–66. **[G: Belgium]**

Standing, Guy. Meshing Labour Flexibility with Security: An Answer to British Unemployment? *Int. Lab. Rev.*, Jan.-Feb. 1986, *125*(1), pp. 87–106. **[G: EEC]**

Stasny, Elizabeth A. Estimating Gross Flows Using Panel Data with Nonresponse: An Example from the Canadian Labour Force Survey. *J. Amer. Statist. Assoc.*, March 1986, *81*(393), pp. 42–47. **[G: Canada]**

Virgo, John. Youth Unemployment Issues: Western Europe and the United States. *Rivista Int. Sci. Econ. Com.*, June-July 1986, *33*(6–7), pp. 565–84. **[G: U.S.; W. Europe]**

Way, Philip K. White-Collar Labor Market Changes: Discussion. **In** *Dennis, B. D., ed.*, 1986, pp. 68–71. **[G: U.S.]**

Weiss, Thomas. Revised Estimates of the United States Workforce, 1800–1860: Reply. **In** *Engerman, S. L. and Gallman, R. E., eds.*, 1986, pp. 673–74. **[G: U.S.]**

Weiss, Thomas. Revised Estimates of the United States Workforce, 1800–1860. **In** *Engerman, S. L. and Gallman, R. E., eds.*, 1986, pp. 641–71. **[G: U.S.]**

Whitley, J. D. and Wilson, R. A. The Impact on Employment of a Reduction in the Length of the Working Week. *Cambridge J. Econ.*, March 1986, *10*(1), pp. 43–59. **[G: U.K.]**

Yamada, Tadashi and Yamada, Tetsuji. Fertility and Labor Force Participation of Married Women: Empirical Evidence from the 1980 Population Census of Japan. *Quart. Rev. Econ. Bus.*, Summer 1986, *26*(2), pp. 35–46. **[G: Japan]**

8131 Agriculture

Ahuja, Kanta. Agricultural Labour and Rural Employment. **In** *Dantwala, M. L., et al.*, 1986, pp. 400–431. **[G: India]**

Chaudhri, D. P. Human Capital, Structures of Production and the Basic Needs. **In** *Maunder, A. and Renborg, U., eds.*, 1986, pp. 466–74.

Commander, Simon and Peek, Peter. Oil Exports, Agrarian Change and the Rural Labor Process: The Ecuadorian Sierra in the 1970s. *World Devel.*, January 1986, *14*(1), pp. 79–96. **[G: Ecuador]**

Dantwala, M. L. Agrarian Structure and Agrarian Relations in India. **In** *Dantwala, M. L., et al.*, 1986, pp. 59–88. **[G: India]**

Dawson, P. J. Family Labour Supply: Some Empirical Results from Agriculture: A Reply. *Appl. Econ.*, August 1986, *18*(8), pp. 835–36. **[G: U.K.]**

Evans, Scott F. and Lewis, Philip E. T. Demand, Supply and Adjustment of Farm Labour in Australia. *Australian Econ. Pap.*, December 1986, *25*(47), pp. 236–46. **[G: Australia]**

Grabowski, Richard and Sivan, David. The Supply of Labor in Agriculture and Food Prices: The Cases of Japan and Egypt. *World Devel.*, March 1986, *14*(3), pp. 441–47. **[G: Japan; Egypt]**

Hossain, Mahabub. Employment Generation through Cottage Industries: Potentials and Constraints. **In** *Islam, R. and Muqtada, M., eds.*, 1986, pp. 119–50. **[G: Bangladesh]**

Islam, Rizwanul. Rural Unemployment and Underemployment: A Review. **In** *Islam, R. and Muqtada, M., eds.*, 1986, pp. 11–20. **[G: Bangladesh]**

Lele, Uma. Women and Structural Transformation. *Econ. Develop. Cult. Change*, January 1986, *34*(2), pp. 195–221. **[G: LDCs]**

Lukinov, I. The Effect of Scientific-Technological and Social Progress on Development in Agrarian Labour. **In** *Maunder, A. and Renborg, U., eds.*, 1986, pp. 178–84. **[G: U.S.S.R.]**

Martin, Philip L. Western Farm Labor Issues. *Contemp. Policy Issues*, January 1986, *4*(1), pp. 72–86. **[G: U.S.]**

McInnis, R. M. Output and Productivity in Canadian Agriculture, 1870–71 to 1926–27. **In** *Engerman, S. L. and Gallman, R. E., eds.*, 1986, pp. 737–70. **[G: Canada]**

Muqtada, M. Determinants and Possibilities of Employment Expansion in the Crop Sector. **In** *Islam, R. and Muqtada, M., eds.*, 1986, pp. 61–88. **[G: Bangladesh]**

Paranavitana, C. Family Labour Supply: Some Empirical Results from Agriculture: Comment. *Appl. Econ.*, August 1986, *18*(8), pp. 829–34. **[G: U.K.]**

Pitt, Mark M. and Rosenzweig, Mark R. Agricultural Prices, Food Consumption, and the Health and Productivity of Indonesian Farmers. **In** *Singh, I.; Squire, L. and Strauss, J., eds.*, 1986, pp. 153–82. **[G: Indonesia]**

Renshaw, Edward F. Trends in Manufacturing Employment and Reflections on Infrastructure Investment, Tax and Expenditure Policy in New York State. **In** *Schoolman, M. and Magid, A., eds.*, 1986, pp. 91–114. **[G: U.S.]**

Salam, Abdul. Farm Labour Use and Its Determinants: Results from a Farm Survey in Pakistan. *Pakistan Econ. Soc. Rev.*, Summer 1986, *24*(1), pp. 1–21. **[G: Pakistan]**

Shand, Richard T. and Teck-Ann, Chew. The Off-Farm Labour Supply of Padi Farmers in Kelantan, Malaysia. *Singapore Econ. Rev.*, October 1986, *31*(2), pp. 23–33. **[G: Malaysia]**

Sicular, Terry. Using a Farm-Household Model to Analyze Labor Allocation on a Chinese Collective Farm. **In** *Singh, I.; Squire, L. and Strauss, J., eds.*, 1986, pp. 277–305. **[G: China]**

Smith, Pamela. "Not Enough Hours, Our Accountant Tells Me": Trends in Children's, Women's and Men's Involvement in Canadian Agriculture. *Can. J. Agr. Econ.*, June 1986, *33*, pp. 161–95. **[G: Canada]**

Soskiev, A. Social and Economic Problems of Labor Power Reproduction in Agriculture. *Prob. Econ.*, May 1986, *29*(1), pp. 82–91. **[G: U.S.S.R.]**

Swedborg, Erik. Growing Interdependencies and Uncertainties: Discussion. **In** *Maunder, A. and Renborg, U., eds.*, 1986, pp. 184–87. **[G: U.S.S.R.]**

Wright, Gavin. Output and Productivity in Canadian Agriculture, 1870–71 to 1926–27: Comment. **In** *Engerman, S. L. and Gallman, R. E., eds.*, 1986, pp. 771–76. **[G: Canada]**

Wrigley, E. A. Men on the Land and Men in the Countryside: Employment in Agriculture in Early–Nineteenth-Century England. **In** *[Laslett, P.]*, 1986, pp. 295–336. **[G: U.K.]**

8132 Manufacturing

Barnett, Richard R. A Perspective on De-industrialization. *Nat. Westminster Bank Quart. Rev.*, August 1986, pp. 13–20. **[G: U.K.]**

Browne, Lynn E. High Technology Industry in

the World Marketplace. *New Eng. Econ. Rev.*, May/June 1986, pp. 21–25. [G: U.S.]

Dean, Edwin; Boissevain, Harry and Thomas, James. Productivity and Labor Costs Trends in Manufacturing, 12 Countries. *Mon. Lab. Rev.*, March 1986, *109*(3), pp. 3–10. [G: U.S.; Selected OECD]

Driver, Ciaran; Kilpatrick, Andrew and Naisbitt, Barry. The Employment Effects of UK Manufacturing Trade Expansion with the EEC and the Newly Industrialising Countries. *Europ. Econ. Rev.*, April 1986, *30*(2), pp. 427–38. [G: U.K.]

Dunford, M. Integration and Unequal Development: The Case of Southern Italy, 1951–73. **In** *Scott, A. J. and Storper, M., eds.*, 1986, pp. 225–45. [G: Italy]

Gregory, Mary; Lobban, Peter and Thomson, Andrew. Bargaining Structure, Pay Settlements and Perceived Pressures in Manufacturing 1979–84: Further Analysis from the CBI Databank. *Brit. J. Ind. Relat.*, July 1986, *24*(2), pp. 215–32. [G: U.K.]

Hills, Stephen M. and Shapiro, David. Inter-industry Mobility and Wage Changes in the 1970s: A Longitudinal Analysis of the Construction, Auto, and Steel Industries. **In** *Dennis, B. D., ed.*, 1986, pp. 400–408. [G: U.S.]

Kelly, Deirdre. St. Lucia's Female Electronics Factory Workers: Key Components in an Export-oriented Industrialization Strategy. *World Devel.*, July 1986, *14*(7), pp. 823–38. [G: St. Lucia]

Tatom, John A. Why Has Manufacturing Employment Declined? *Fed. Res. Bank St. Louis Rev.*, December 1986, *68*(10), pp. 15–25. [G: U.S.]

Webber, M. J. Regional Production and the Production of Regions: The Case of Steeltown. **In** *Scott, A. J. and Storper, M., eds.*, 1986, pp. 197–224. [G: Canada]

Williams, Donald R. Contributed Papers: Labor Economics and Labor Markets: Discussion. **In** *Dennis, B. D., ed.*, 1986, pp. 418–23.

Wren-Lewis, Simon. An Econometric Model of U.K. Manufacturing Employment Using Survey Data on Expected Output. *J. Appl. Econometrics*, October 1986, *1*(4), pp. 297–316. [G: U.K.]

8133 Service

Alpert, William T. and Ozawa, Martha N. Fringe Benefits of Workers in Nonmanufacturing Industries: They Vary by Employee Income, the Marginal Tax Rate, Union Status and Firm Size. *Amer. J. Econ. Soc.*, April 1986, *45*(2), pp. 173–88. [G: U.S.]

Gleave, David. The Impact of Innovations on Service Employment. **In** *Nijkamp, P., ed. (II)*, 1986, pp. 177–95. [G: U.K.; U.S.]

Haugen, Steven E. The Employment Expansion in Retail Trade, 1973–85. *Mon. Lab. Rev.*, August 1986, *109*(8), pp. 9–16. [G: U.S.]

Howe, Wayne J. The Business Services Industry Sets Pace in Employment Growth. *Mon. Lab. Rev.*, April 1986, *109*(4), pp. 29–36. [G: U.S.]

Nelson, K. Labor Demand, Labor Supply and the Suburbanization of Low-wage Office Work. **In** *Scott, A. J. and Storper, M., eds.*, 1986, pp. 149–71. [G: U.S.]

Shelp, Ronald Kent. Services in the Economies of the Developing Countries. **In** *Wasow, B. and Hill, R. D., eds.*, 1986, pp. 3–28. [G: LDCs]

8134 Professional

Acar, Feride. Working Women in a Changing Society: The Case of Jordanian Academics. *METU*, 1986, *13*(3–4), pp. 307–24. [G: Jordan]

Alexander, Jeffrey A.; Morrisey, Michael A. and Shortell, Stephen M. Physician Participation in the Administration and Governance of System and Freestanding Hospitals: A Comparison by Type of Ownership. **In** *Gray, B. H., ed.*, 1986, pp. 402–21. [G: U.S.]

Bosk, Charles L. Professional Responsibility and Medical Error. **In** *Aiken, L. H. and Mechanic, D., eds.*, 1986, pp. 460–77. [G: U.S.]

Breyer, Friedrich; Mühlenkamp, Holger and Adam, Hans. Determinants of the Utilization of Physician Services in the System of Statutory Health Insurance in Germany. **In** *von der Schulenburg, J.-M. G., ed.*, 1986, pp. 196–216. [G: W. Germany]

Chang, Cyril F. and Tuckman, Howard P. Price-Induced Substitution of Faculty in Academe: Does Mission Make a Difference? *Econ. Educ. Rev.*, 1986, *5*(2), pp. 197–204. [G: U.S.]

Chesterman, Esther. Implications of the New South Wales Doctors' Dispute: Discussion. **In** *Butler, J. R. G. and Doessel, D. P., eds.*, 1986, pp. 79–80. [G: Australia]

Filer, Randall K. The "Starving Artist"—Myth or Reality? Earnings of Artists in the United States. *J. Polit. Econ.*, February 1986, *94*(1), pp. 56–75. [G: U.S.]

Freidson, Eliot. The Medical Profession in Transition. **In** *Aiken, L. H. and Mechanic, D., eds.*, 1986, pp. 63–79. [G: U.S.]

Fuchs, Victor R. The Supply of Surgeons and the Demand for Operations. **In** *Fuchs, V. R.*, 1986, *1978*, pp. 126–47. [G: U.S.]

Fuchs, Victor R. and Kramer, Marcia J. Determinants of Expenditures for Physicians' Services. **In** *Fuchs, V. R.*, 1986, *1972*, pp. 67–107. [G: U.S.]

Garbarino, Joseph W. Faculty Collective Bargaining: A Status Report. **In** *Lipset, S. M., ed.*, 1986, pp. 265–84. [G: U.S.]

Glandon, Gerald L. and Morrisey, Michael A. Redefining the Hospital–Physician Relationship under Prospective Payment. *Inquiry*, Summer 1986, *23*(2), pp. 166–75. [G: U.S.]

Gloeckner, Eduard. Underemployment and Potential Unemployment of the Technical Intelligentsia: Distortions between Education and Occupation. **In** *Lane, D., ed.*, 1986, pp. 223–36. [G: U.S.S.R.]

Hoffman, Emily P. A Review of Two Studies of Elasticity in Academe. *Econ. Educ. Rev.*, 1986, *5*(2), pp. 219–24. **[G: U.S.]**

Kemp, Kathleen A. Lawyers, Politics, and Economic Regulation. *Soc. Sci. Quart.*, June 1986, *67*(2), pp. 267–82. **[G: U.S.]**

Morrisey, Michael A.; Alexander, Jeffrey A. and Shortell, Stephen M. Medical Staff Size, Hospital Privileges, and Compensation Arrangements: A Comparison of System Hospitals. **In** *Gray, B. H., ed.*, 1986, pp. 422–57. **[G: U.S.]**

Musacchio, Robert A., et al. Hospital Ownership and the Practice of Medicine: Evidence from the Physician's Perspective. **In** *Gray, B. H., ed.*, 1986, pp. 385–401. **[G: U.S.]**

Noether, Monica. The Effect of Government Policy Changes on the Supply of Physicians: Expansion of a Competitive Fringe. *J. Law Econ.*, October 1986, *29*(2), pp. 231–62. **[G: U.S.]**

Noether, Monica. The Growing Supply of Physicians: Has the Market Become More Competitive? *J. Lab. Econ.*, October 1986, *4*(4), pp. 503–37. **[G: U.S.]**

Parrish, John B. Are Women Taking Over the Professions? *Challenge*, Jan./Feb. 1986, *28*(6), pp. 54–58. **[G: U.S.]**

Pensabene, Tony S. Implications of the New South Wales Doctors' Dispute. **In** *Butler, J. R. G. and Doessel, D. P., eds.*, 1986, pp. 67–78. **[G: Australia]**

Prekel, Truida. The Role of Black Women in the Economy. **In** *Smollan, R., ed.*, 1986, pp. 31–51. **[G: S. Africa]**

Raipuria, Kalyan M. Third World in the 'Third Wave': Imperative of South–South Cooperation in Science and Technology. **In** *Panchamukhi, V. R., et al.*, 1986, pp. 166–214. **[G: Global]**

Rassuli, Ali and Roy, Raj. Sex Discrimination in the Audiology Profession: It Explains Two-thirds of the $9,500 Difference between Male and Female Earnings. *Amer. J. Econ. Soc.*, April 1986, *45*(2), pp. 189–200. **[G: U.S.]**

Reader, W. J. 'At the Head of All the New Professions': The Engineer in Victorian Society. **In** *[Coleman, D. C.]*, 1986, pp. 173–84. **[G: U.K.]**

von der Schulenburg, J.-Matthias Graf. Regulatory Measures to Enforce Quality Production of Self-employed Professionals—A Theoretical Study of a Dynamic Market Process. **In** *von der Schulenburg, J.-M. G. and Skogh, G., eds.*, 1986, pp. 133–47.

Tuckman, Howard P. and Chang, Cyril F. Own-Price and Cross Elasticities of Demand for College Faculty. *Southern Econ. J.*, January 1986, *52*(3), pp. 735–44. **[G: U.S.]**

Yang, Bong-min. Do Physicians Induce Patient Demand for Medical Care? An Empirical Analysis. *J. Econ. Devel.*, December 1986, *11*(2), pp. 83–102. **[G: U.S.]**

8135 Government Employees

Black, Matthew and Fraker, Thomas. First-Term Attrition of High School Graduates in the Military. **In** *Gilroy, C. L., ed.*, 1986, pp. 261–91. **[G: U.S.]**

Borjas, George J. The Earnings of State Government Employees in the United States. *J. Urban Econ.*, March 1986, *19*(2), pp. 156–73. **[G: U.S.]**

Borjas, George J. and Welch, Finis. The Postservice Earnings of Military Retirees. **In** *Gilroy, C. L., ed.*, 1986, pp. 295–313. **[G: U.S.]**

Borjas, George J. and Welch, Finis. The Postservice Earnings of Military Retirees: Evidence from the U.S. Air Force. **In** *Ehrenberg, R. G., ed., Pt. A*, 1986, pp. 57–83. **[G: U.S.]**

Britton, Andrew. Employment Policy in the Public Sector. **In** *Hart, P. E., ed.*, 1986, pp. 128–46. **[G: U.K.]**

Brown, Charles. Recruiting Goals, Enlistment Supply, and Enlistments in the U.S. Army: Comment. **In** *Gilroy, C. L., ed.*, 1986, pp. 124–26. **[G: U.S.]**

Callaghan, W. H. Employment Policy in the Public Sector: Comment. **In** *Hart, P. E., ed.*, 1986, pp. 147–51. **[G: U.K.]**

Dale, Charles. The Changing Structure of the U.S. Economy: Its Effects on Army Enlistments. **In** *Gilroy, C. L., ed.*, 1986, pp. 149–65. **[G: U.S.]**

Daula, Thomas V. and Baldwin, Robert H. Reenlistment Decision Models: Implications for Policy Making. **In** *Gilroy, C. L., ed.*, 1986, pp. 203–21. **[G: U.S.]**

Daula, Thomas V. and Smith, D. Alton. Recruiting Goals, Enlistment Supply, and Enlistments in the U.S. Army. **In** *Gilroy, C. L., ed.*, 1986, pp. 101–23. **[G: U.S.]**

Dertouzos, James N. Microeconomic Foundations of Recruiter Behavior: Implications for Aggregate Enlistment Models. **In** *Gilroy, C. L., ed.*, 1986, pp. 127–45. **[G: U.S.]**

Doering, Zahava D. Attrition and Retention in the Army Reserve and National Guard: An Empirical Analysis: Comment. **In** *Gilroy, C. L., ed.*, 1986, pp. 198–201. **[G: U.S.]**

Gilroy, Curtis L. Army Manpower Economics: Introduction. **In** *Gilroy, C. L., ed.*, 1986, pp. xi–xvii. **[G: U.S.]**

Goldberg, Lawrence and Greenston, Peter. Economic Analysis of Army Enlistments: Policy Implications. **In** *Gilroy, C. L., ed.*, 1986, pp. 61–94. **[G: U.S.]**

Goldberg, Lawrence and Greenston, Peter. Economic Analysis of Army Enlistments: Policy Implications: Reply. **In** *Gilroy, C. L., ed.*, 1986, pp. 97–99. **[G: U.S.]**

Goldberg, Matthew S. Microeconomic Foundations of Recruiter Behavior: Implications for Aggregate Enlistment Models: Comment. **In** *Gilroy, C. L., ed.*, 1986, pp. 146–47. **[G: U.S.]**

Greene, Kenneth V. and Moulton, George D. Municipal Employee Residency Requirement Statutes: An Economic Analysis. **In** *Zerbe, R. O., Jr., ed.*, 1986, pp. 185–204. **[G: U.S.]**

Grissmer, David W. and Fernandez, Judith C. Meeting Occupational and Total Manpower Requirements at Least Cost: A Nonlinear Programing Approach. **In** *Gilroy, C. L., ed.*, 1986, pp. 361–83. **[G: U.S.]**

Grissmer, David W. and Kirby, Sheila Nataraj. Attrition and Retention in the Army Reserve and National Guard: An Empirical Analysis. **In** *Gilroy, C. L., ed.*, 1986, pp. 169–97. **[G: U.S.]**

Hale, Robert. The Changing Structure of the U.S. Economy: Its Effects on Army Enlistments: Comment. **In** *Gilroy, C. L., ed.*, 1986, pp. 166–68. **[G: U.S.]**

Hirsch, Werner Z. and Rufolo, Anthony M. Residence Laws and Unionization in Municipal Labor Markets: The Case of Firefighters. *J. Lab. Res.*, Winter 1986, *7*(1), pp. 41–58. **[G: U.S.]**

Hogan, Paul F. Army Reenlistment and Extension Decisions by Occupation: Comment. **In** *Gilroy, C. L., ed.*, 1986, pp. 257–60.

Horowitz, Stanley A. Experience and Readiness. **In** *Gilroy, C. L., ed.*, 1986, pp. 321–27. **[G: U.S.]**

Hosek, James R. and Peterson, Christine E. Enlistment Decisions of Young Men. **In** *Gilroy, C. L., ed.*, 1986, pp. 1–56. **[G: U.S.]**

Kennedy, Charles H. Policies of Redistributional Preference in Pakistan. **In** *Nevitte, N. and Kennedy, C. H., eds.*, 1986, pp. 63–93. **[G: Pakistan]**

Lakhani, Hyder and Gilroy, Curtis L. Army Reenlistment and Extension Decisions by Occupation. **In** *Gilroy, C. L., ed.*, 1986, pp. 225–56. **[G: U.S.]**

Leila, Ali; Yassin, El Sayeed and Palmer, Monte. Job Satisfaction as an Indicator of Bureaucratic Performance in Egypt. *Can. J. Devel. Stud.*, 1986, *7*(1), pp. 105–16. **[G: Egypt]**

Lewin, David. Public Employee Unionism in the 1980s: An Analysis of Transformation. **In** *Lipset, S. M., ed.*, 1986, pp. 241–64. **[G: U.S.]**

Lewis, Gregory B. and Emmert, Mark A. The Sexual Division of Labor in Federal Employment. *Soc. Sci. Quart.*, March 1986, *67*(1), pp. 143–55. **[G: U.S.]**

Mehay, Stephen L. and Gonzalez, Rodolfo A. The Relative Effect of Unionization and Interjurisdictional Competition on Municipal Wages. *J. Lab. Res.*, Winter 1986, *7*(1), pp. 79–93. **[G: U.S.]**

Nelson, Gary R. Compensation and Force Structure: A Comment. **In** *Gilroy, C. L., ed.*, 1986, pp. 385–91. **[G: U.S.]**

Oberst, Robert. Policies of Ethnic Preference in Sri Lanka. **In** *Nevitte, N. and Kennedy, C. H., eds.*, 1986, pp. 135–54. **[G: Sri Lanka]**

Oechsler, Walter A. Public Administration and Civil Service in Europe—Approaches to Reform. **In** *Macharzina, K. and Staehle, W. H., eds.*, 1986, pp. 369–79. **[G: W. Europe]**

Oi, Walter Y. The Postservice Earnings of Military Retirees: Comment. **In** *Gilroy, C. L., ed.*, 1986, pp. 314–19. **[G: U.S.]**

Premdas, Ralph R. Politics of Preference in the Caribbean: The Case of Guyana. **In** *Nevitte, N. and Kennedy, C. H., eds.*, 1986, pp. 155–87. **[G: Guyana]**

Rostker, Bernard. Economic Analysis of Army Enlistments: Policy Implications: Comment. **In** *Gilroy, C. L., ed.*, 1986, pp. 95–96. **[G: U.S.]**

Singer, Neil M. Retirement Changes and Military Force Manning: A Sensitivity Analysis. **In** *Gilroy, C. L., ed.*, 1986, pp. 329–46. **[G: U.S.]**

Stromsdorfer, Ernst W. Enlistment Decisions of Young Men: Comment. **In** *Gilroy, C. L., ed.*, 1986, pp. 57–60. **[G: U.S.]**

Utgoff, Kathleen P. First-Term Attrition of High School Graduates in the Military: Comment. **In** *Gilroy, C. L., ed.*, 1986, pp. 292–93. **[G: U.S.]**

Warner, John T. Reenlistment Decision Models: Implications for Policy Making: Comment. **In** *Gilroy, C. L., ed.*, 1986, pp. 222–24. **[G: U.S.]**

Yandle, Bruce. The Evolution of Regulatory Activities in the 1970s and 1980s. **In** *Cagan, P., ed.*, 1986, pp. 105–45. **[G: U.S.]**

8136 Construction

Allen, Steven G. Unionization and Productivity in Office Building and School Construction. *Ind. Lab. Relat. Rev.*, January 1986, *39*(2), pp. 187–201. **[G: U.S.]**

Hills, Stephen M. and Shapiro, David. Inter-industry Mobility and Wage Changes in the 1970s: A Longitudinal Analysis of the Construction, Auto, and Steel Industries. **In** *Dennis, B. D., ed.*, 1986, pp. 400–408. **[G: U.S.]**

O'Connell, John F. The Effects of Davis–Bacon on Labor Cost and Union Wages. *J. Lab. Res.*, Summer 1986, *7*(3), pp. 239–53. **[G: U.S.]**

Williams, Donald R. Contributed Papers: Labor Economics and Labor Markets: Discussion. **In** *Dennis, B. D., ed.*, 1986, pp. 418–23.

Jackson, John L. Long-run Effects of Military Service during the Vietnam War. **In** *Hills, S. M., ed.*, 1986, pp. 113–32. **[G: U.S.]**

Mangum, Stephen L. and Ball, David. Skill Transfer and Military Occupational Training. **In** *Hills, S. M., ed.*, 1986, pp. 133–47. **[G: U.S.]**

820 Labor Markets; Public Policy

8200 General

Clarke, Paul. Teaching Economics to the 13–16 Age Range: Employment, Unemployment and Inflation. **In** *Whitehead, D. J., ed.*, 1986, pp. 102–09.

Epstein, Eugene. The Share Economy: An Idea Whose Time Came Long Ago. *Challenge*, Jan./Feb. 1986, *28*(6), pp. 62–64.

Kadish, Elisa. Discrimination in Employment: A Selective Bibliography. *Law Contemp. Probl.*, Autumn 1986, *49*(4), pp. 211–35. **[G: U.S.]**

821 Labor Economics

8210 Labor Economics: Theory and Empirical Studies Illustrating Theory

Abraham, Katharine G. and Katz, Lawrence F. Cyclical Unemployment: Sectoral Shifts or Aggregate Disturbances? *J. Polit. Econ.*, Part 1, June 1986, *94*(3), pp. 507–22.

Adams, Charles; Fenton, Paul R. and Larsen, Flemming. Differences in Employment Behavior among Industrial Countries. **In** *International Monetary Fund, Research Department*, 1986, pp. 1–50. **[G: OECD]**

Adnett, N. J. On the Job Search in a Recession. *Appl. Econ.*, March 1986, *18*(3), pp. 333–45. **[G: U.K.]**

Aizenman, Joshua. Stabilization Policies and the Information Content of Real Wages. *Economica*, May 1986, *53*(210), pp. 181–90.

Akerlof, George A. Labor Contracts as Partial Gift Exchange. **In** *Akerlof, G. A. and Yellen, J. L., eds.*, 1986, *1982*, pp. 66–92.

Akerlof, George A. and Yellen, Janet L. Efficiency Wage Models of the Labor Market. **In** *Akerlof, G. A. and Yellen, J. L., eds.*, 1986, pp. 1–21. **[G: U.S.]**

Albrecht, James W.; Axell, Bo and Lang, Harald. General Equilibrium Wage and Price Distributions. *Quart. J. Econ.*, November 1986, *101*(4), pp. 687–706.

Albrecht, James W. and Jovanovic, Boyan. The Efficiency of Search under Competition and Monopsony. *J. Polit. Econ.*, December 1986, *94*(6), pp. 1246–57.

Altonji, Joseph G. Econometric Approaches to the Specification of Life-Cycle Labour Supply and Commodity Demand Behaviour: Comment. *Econometric Rev.*, 1986, *5*(1), pp. 147–51.

Altonji, Joseph G. Efficiency Wage Theories: A Partial Evaluation: Comment. **In** *Fischer, S., ed.*, 1986, pp. 276–85. **[G: U.S.]**

Altonji, Joseph G. Intertemporal Substitution in Labor Supply: Evidence from Micro Data. *J. Polit. Econ.*, Part 2, June 1986, *94*(3), pp. S176–S215.

Altonji, Joseph G. and Paxson, Christina H. Job Characteristics and Hours of Work. **In** *Ehrenberg, R. G., ed., Pt. A*, 1986, pp. 1–55. **[G: U.S.]**

Alvi, Eskander. The Production Process in a Competitive Economy: Comment. *Amer. Econ. Rev.*, December 1986, *76*(5), pp. 1200–1202.

Andersen, Torben M. Fagforeninger, lønudvikling og arbejdsløshed. (Trade Unions and the Wage–Employment Nexus. With English summary.) *Nationaløkon. Tidsskr.*, 1986, *124*(3), pp. 241–58. **[G: Denmark]**

Andrews, Martyn and Nickell, Stephen J. A Disaggregated Disequilibrium Model of the Labour Market. *Oxford Econ. Pap.*, November 1986, *38*(3), pp. 386–402. **[G: U.K.]**

Apostolakis, Bobby E. Labor Subsidies in a Neoclassical Framework and an Empirical Extension. *Ricerche Econ.*, Jan.-Mar. 1986, *40*(1), pp. 31–49. **[G: Greece]**

Apostolakis, Bobby E. Taxes, Labor Subsidies, and Employment Equilibrium: A Synthesis. *Stud. Econ.*, 1986, *41*(30), pp. 71–89.

Arnaudo, A. A., et al. Tipología del Desempleo en la Argentina 1950–84. (Typology of Argentine Unemployment 1950–84. With English summary.) *Económica (La Plata)*, July-December 1986, *32*(2), pp. 143–63. **[G: Argentina]**

Arrufat, Jose Luis and Zabalza, Antonio. Female Labor Supply with Taxation, Random Preferences, and Optimization Errors. *Econometrica*, January 1986, *54*(1), pp. 47–63. **[G: U.K.]**

Artus, Patrick and Bismut, Claude. Exchange Rate and Wage–Price Dynamics: A Theoretical Analysis and an Econometric Investigation. *Europ. Econ. Rev.*, February 1986, *30*(1), pp. 57–90. **[G: U.S.; Japan; W. Germany; France; U.K.]**

Ashenfelter, Orley and Card, David. Why Have Unemployment Rates in Canada and the United States Diverged? **In** *Bean, C. R.; Layard, P. R. G. and Nickell, S. J., eds.*, 1986, pp. 171–95. **[G: U.S.; Canada]**

Assenmacher, Walter. Die Dynamik der Inflations- und Beschäftigungsentwicklung. Eine theoretische und ökonometrische Analyse. (The Dynamism of Inflationary and Employment Trends: A Theoretical and Econometric Analysis. With English summary.) *Kredit Kapital*, 1986, *19*(4), pp. 540–68.

Azariadis, Costas. Theories of Wage Rigidity: Comment. **In** *Butkiewicz, J. L.; Koford, K. J. and Miller, J. B., eds.*, 1986, pp. 216–19.

Bakalis, Steve and Hazari, Bharat R. A Note on Underutilization of Capital and Unemployment in a Harris–Todaro Framework. *Devel. Econ.*, September 1986, *24*(3), pp. 288–98. **[G: LDCs]**

Balducci, Renato. Sussidi, occupazione e crescita. (Unemployment Benefits, Employment and Growth. With English summary.) *Giorn. Econ.*, Nov.-Dec. 1986, *45*(11–12), pp. 617–38.

Ballot, Gérard and Piatechi, Cyrille. Turnover, productivité et hiérarchie dans le marché interne du travail. (Turnover, Productivity and Hierarchy in the Internal Market. With English summary.) *Revue Écon.*, March 1986, *37*(2), pp. 285–306.

Barbera, Anthony J. A Comparison of Alternative Wage Equations. *Quart. Rev. Econ. Bus.*, Spring 1986, *26*(1), pp. 74–87. **[G: U.S.]**

Barmby, Tim. Estimating Labour Supply Functions in a Linear Expenditure System Framework. *Bull. Econ. Res.*, May 1986, *38*(2), pp. 183–87. **[G: U.K.]**

Barro, Robert J. Payroll-Tax Financed Social Insurance with Variable Retirement: Comment. *Scand. J. Econ.*, 1986, *88*(1), pp. 55–58.

Barron, John M. and Loewenstein, Mark A. On Imperfect Evaluation and Earning Differentials. *Econ. Inquiry*, October 1986, *24*(4), pp. 595–614. **[G: U.S.]**

Barron, John M.; McAfee, R. Preston and Speaker, Paul J. Unemployment Insurance and the Entitlement Effect: A Tax Incidence Approach. *Int. Econ. Rev.*, February 1986, *27*(1), pp. 175–85.

Bartoli, Henri. La flexibilité du travial et les limites de la flexibilisation. (Labour Flexibility and the Limits of Flexibilization. With English summary.) *Rivista Int. Sci. Econ. Com.*, September 1986, *33*(9), pp. 833–58.

Battinelli, Andrea. Variable Working Hours in a Simple Model of Macroeconomic Equilibrium with Rationing. *Econ. Lavoro,* Jan.-Mar. 1986, *20*(1), pp. 3–22.

Baumol, William J. Marx and the Iron Law of Wages. **In** *Baumol, W. J.,* 1986, *1983,* pp. 259–64.

Baumol, William J. On the Stochastic Unemployment Distribution Model and the Long-run Phillips Curve. **In** *Baumol, W. J.,* 1986, *1978,* pp. 206–23.

Bean, Charles R.; Layard, Richard and Nickell, Stephen J. The Rise in Unemployment: A Multi-country Study. **In** *Bean, C. R.; Layard, P. R. G. and Nickell, S. J., eds.,* 1986, pp. 1–22. **[G: OECD]**

Beckerman, Wilfred and Jenkinson, Tim. How Rigid Are Wages Anyway? **In** *Beckerman, W., ed.,* 1986, pp. 21–42. **[G: U.S.; U.K.; Japan]**

Bentzel, Ragnar. Payroll-Tax Financed Social Insurance with Variable Retirement: Comment. *Scand. J. Econ.,* 1986, *88*(1), pp. 51–54.

Berkovitch, Elazar. Implicit Labor Contracts to Explain Turnover. *J. Lab. Econ.,* Part 1, July 1986, *4*(3), pp. 341–54.

Bernanke, Ben S. Employment, Hours, and Earnings in the Depression: An Analysis of Eight Manufacturing Industries. *Amer. Econ. Rev.,* March 1986, *76*(1), pp. 82–l09. **[G: U.S.]**

Berninghaus, Siegfried. Job Search with Belated Information and Wage Signalling. *J. Econ. Dynam. Control,* December 1986, *10*(4), pp. 495–508.

Berninghaus, Siegfried; Lippman, Steven A. and McCall, John J. An Equilibrium Model of Turnover with Belated Information. *Info. Econ. Policy,* September 1986, *2*(3), pp. 221–39.

Betson, David M. and Greenberg, David H. Labor Supply and Tax Rates: Comment. *Amer. Econ. Rev.,* June 1986, *76*(3), pp. 551–56.

Bewley, Truman F. The Share Economy in General Equilibrium. *J. Compar. Econ.,* December 1986, *10*(4), pp. 457–59.

Blair, Christine E. and Rodrigues, Anthony P. A Model of Wage Contract Bargaining with Imperfect Information and Strikes. *Eastern Econ. J.,* July-Sept. 1986, *12*(3), pp. 251–56.

Blanchard, Olivier J. The Wage Price Spiral. *Quart. J. Econ.,* August 1986, *101*(3), pp. 543–65.

Blanchard, Olivier J. and Summers, Lawrence H. Hysteresis and the European Unemployment Problem. **In** *Fischer, S., ed.,* 1986, pp. 15–78. **[G: U.S.; U.K.; W. Germany; France]**

Blau, David M. and Robins, Philip K. Job Search, Wage Offers, and Unemployment Insurance. *J. Public Econ.,* March 1986, *29*(2), pp. 173–97. **[G: U.S.]**

Blau, David M. and Robins, Philip K. Labor Supply Response to Welfare Programs: A Dynamic Analysis. *J. Lab. Econ.,* January 1986, *4*(1), pp. 82–104. **[G: U.S.]**

Blaug, Mark. Another Look at the Labour Reduction Problem in Marx. **In** *Blaug, M.,* 1986, *1982,* pp. 197–208.

Blomquist, N. Sören. Nonlinear Taxes and the Intertemporal Allocation of Hours of Work. **In** *Blundell, R. and Walker, I., eds.,* 1986, pp. 318–34.

Blomqvist, Ake G. Higher Education and the Markets for Educated Labour in LDCs: Theoretical Approaches and Implications. *Pakistan Devel. Rev.,* Autumn 1986, *25*(3), pp. 249–73. **[G: LDCs]**

Blundell, Richard. Econometric Approaches to the Specification of Life-Cycle Labour Supply and Commodity Demand Behaviour: Reply. *Econometric Rev.,* 1986, *5*(1), pp. 163–70.

Blundell, Richard. Econometric Approaches to the Specification of Life-Cycle Labour Supply and Commodity Demand Behaviour. *Econometric Rev.,* 1986, *5*(1), pp. 89–146.

Blundell, Richard and Meghir, Costas. Selection Criteria for a Microeconometric Model of Labour Supply. *J. Appl. Econometrics,* January 1986, *1*(1), pp. 55–80. **[G: U.K.]**

Blundell, Richard and Walker, Ian. A Life-Cycle Consistent Empirical Model of Family Labour Supply Using Cross-Section Data. *Rev. Econ. Stud.,* August 1986, *53*(4), pp. 539–58. **[G: U.K.]**

Blundell, Richard, et al. A Labour Supply Model for the Simulation of Tax and Benefit Reforms. **In** *Blundell, R. and Walker, I., eds.,* 1986, pp. 267–93. **[G: U.K.]**

Boddy, Raford and Alwan, Rami. Work Shifts and the Cyclical Behavior of Productivity and Real Wages. *J. Macroecon.,* Summer 1986, *8*(3), pp. 355–63.

Boddy, Raford; Frantz, Roger S. and Poe-Tierney, Barbara. The Marginal Productivity Theory: Production Line and Machine Level by Work-Shift and Time of Day. *J. Behav. Econ.,* Spring/Summer 1986, *15*(1/2), pp. 1–23. **[G: Mexico; U.S.]**

Bohanon, Cecil E. and Van Cott, T. Norman. Labor Supply and Tax Rates: Comment. *Amer. Econ. Rev.,* March 1986, *76*(1), pp. 277–79.

Bonin, John P. Implicit-Contract Theory in Illyria: Comment [The Economics of a Labor-Managed Enterprise in the Short Run: An "Implict Contracts" Approach]. *J. Compar. Econ.,* March 1986, *10*(1), pp. 79–85.

Borjas, George J. The Sensitivity of Labor Demand Functions to Choice of Dependent Variable. *Rev. Econ. Statist.,* February 1986, *68*(1), pp. 58–66. **[G: U.S.]**

Bosworth, Barry P. Financial Markets and Macroeconomic Fluctuations: Comment. **In** *Butkiewicz, J. L.; Koford, K. J. and Miller, J. B., eds.,* 1986, pp. 133–35.

Bourguignon, François. Female Participation and Taxation in France. **In** *Blundell, R. and Walker, I., eds.,* 1986, pp. 243–66. **[G: France]**

Bowles, Samuel. The Production Process in a Competitive Economy: Reply. *Amer. Econ. Rev.,* December 1986, *76*(5), pp. 1203–04.

Bowles, Samuel. The Production Process in a Competitive Economy: Walrasian, Neo-Hobbesian, and Marxian Models. **In** *Putterman, L., ed.*, 1986, *1985*, pp. 329–55.

Brotchie, John F. Industrial Interdependence via Information Technology and Transport Interaction—Employment Impacts. **In** *Nijkamp, P., ed. (II)*, 1986, pp. 115–30.

Brown, James N. and Ashenfelter, Orley. Testing the Efficiency of Employment Contracts. *J. Polit. Econ.*, Part 2, June 1986, *94*(3), pp. S40–S87. **[G: U.S.]**

Brown, William. A Symposium on the Role and Influence of Trade Unions in a Recession: Comments. *Brit. J. Ind. Relat.*, July 1986, *24*(2), pp. 208–09. **[G: U.K.]**

Browning, Martin. Econometric Approaches to the Specification of Life-Cycle Labour Supply and Commodity Demand Behaviour: Comment. *Econometric Rev.*, 1986, *5*(1), pp. 153–58.

Brunello, Giorgio. Enterprise Unionism in the McDonald–Solow Model: A Brief Note. *Econ. Stud. Quart.*, September 1986, *37*(3), pp. 259–64.

Brunetta, Renato and Venturini, Alessandra. La variabile temporale nella transizione tra società industriale e post-industriale. (Work Time Variables in the Transition to Post-Industrial Society. With English summary.) *Econ. Lavoro*, Jan.-Mar. 1986, *20*(1), pp. 23–44.

Brunner, Karl. Theories of Wage Rigidity: Comment. **In** *Butkiewicz, J. L.; Koford, K. J. and Miller, J. B., eds.*, 1986, pp. 209–15.

Bruno, Michael. Aggregate Supply and Demand Factors in OECD Unemployment: An Update. **In** *Bean, C. R.; Layard, P. R. G. and Nickell, S. J., eds.*, 1986, pp. 35–52. **[G: OECD]**

Buchanan, James M. Justice and Equal Treatment. **In** *Buchanan, J. M.*, 1986, *1983*, pp. 140–58.

Budd, Alan P. On Keynesian Unemployment and the Unemployment of Keynes. **In** *Burton, J., et al.*, 1986, pp. 139–52.

Bulow, Jeremy I. and Summers, Lawrence H. A Theory of Dual Labor Markets with Application to Industrial Policy, Discrimination, and Keynesian Unemployment. *J. Lab. Econ.*, Part 1, July 1986, *4*(3), pp. 376–414.

Burtless, Gary. Social Security, Unanticipated Benefit Increases, and the Timing of Retirement. *Rev. Econ. Stud.*, October 1986, *53*(5), pp. 781–805. **[G: U.S.]**

Calvo, Guillermo A. and Wellisz, Stanislaw. Hierarchy, Ability, and Income Distribution. **In** *Akerlof, G. A. and Yellen, J. L., eds.*, 1986, *1979*, pp. 115–34.

Cantor, Richard. A Macroeconomic Model with Auction Markets and Nominal Contracts. *Amer. Econ. Rev.*, March 1986, *76*(1), pp. 204–11.

Card, David. An Empirical Model of Wage Indexation Provisions in Union Contracts. *J. Polit. Econ.*, Part 2, June 1986, *94*(3), pp. S144–75. **[G: Canada]**

Carlberg, Michael. Makroökonomik der Kapitalmangel-Arbeitslosigkeit. (Macroeconomics of Unemployment Due to Lack of Capital. With English summary.) *Kredit Kapital*, 1986, *19*(3), pp. 313–24.

Carmichael, H. Lorne. Reputations for Safety: Market Performance and Policy Remedies. *J. Lab. Econ.*, October 1986, *4*(4), pp. 458–72.

Casey, Bernard. A Symposium on the Role and Influence of Trade Unions in a Recession: Comments. *Brit. J. Ind. Relat.*, July 1986, *24*(2), pp. 212–13. **[G: U.K.]**

Catinat, Michel; Cette, Gilbert and Taddéi, Dominique. Réduction-réorganisation du temps de travail. (Reduction and Reorganisation of Working Time: A Macroeconomic Model of Disequilibrium. With English summary.) *Écon. Appl.*, 1986, *39*(4), pp. 757–92.

Chalamwong, Yongyuth. Rural Labour Supply in Thailand: A Recent Experience. **In** *Shand, R. T., ed., Vol. 1*, 1986, pp. 257–71. **[G: Thailand]**

Challier, Marie-Christine. Travail atypique et théorie du risque. (Non-typical Labour and Theory of Risk. With English summary.) *Revue Écon.*, September 1986, *37*(5), pp. 805–31.

Chapman, P. G. Alternative Trade Union Objective Functions in the Theory of Wage Bargaining. *Manchester Sch. Econ. Soc. Stud.*, December 1986, *54*(4), pp. 367–79.

Chatterji, Monojit. Unions, Employment and the Inflation Tax. *Econ. J.*, June 1986, *96*(382), pp. 342–51.

Chiang, Shin-Hwan. Cost Savings, Wages and the Growth of the Firm. *Econ. J.*, September 1986, *96*(383), pp. 798–807.

Chillemi, Ottorino. Salari e produttività dei lavoratori qualificati. Rapporti di lavoro a lungo termine e aspettative. (Wage and Productivity Profiles with Specific Human Capital and Imperfect Information. With English summary.) *Econ. Polít.*, December 1986, *3*(3), pp. 339–53.

Chiswick, Carmel U. The Efficiency-Wage Hypothesis: Applying a General Model of the Interactions between Labor Quantity and Quality. *J. Devel. Econ.*, March 1986, *20*(2), pp. 311–23.

Clemenz, Gerhard. The Impact of Imperfect Monitoring on the Efficiency Wage Hypothesis. *Empirica*, 1986, *13*(2), pp. 203–19.

Colander, David C. Financial Markets and Macroeconomic Fluctuations: Comment. **In** *Butkiewicz, J. L.; Koford, K. J. and Miller, J. B., eds.*, 1986, pp. 145–49.

Cole, William E. and Sanders, Richard D. Internal Migration and Urban Employment: Reply. *Amer. Econ. Rev.*, June 1986, *76*(3), pp. 570–72. **[G: Mexico; India; Colombia; Nigeria]**

Coles, Jeffrey L. Nonconvexity in General Equilibrium Labor Markets. *J. Lab. Econ.*, Part 1, July 1986, *4*(3), pp. 415–37.

Collier, Paul and Knight, J. B. Wage Structure and Labour Turnover. *Oxford Econ. Pap.*, March 1986, *38*(1), pp. 77–93.

Colombino, Ugo. Orari di lavoro come strumento di selezione in un modello con informazione asimmetrica. (Hours of Work as a Selection Mechanism in a Model with Asymmetric Information. With English summary.) *Econ. Lavoro,* Jan.-Mar. 1986, *20*(1), pp. 77–86.

Connelly, Rachel. A Framework for Analyzing the Impact of Cohort Size on Education and Labor Earnings. *J. Human Res.,* Fall 1986, *21*(4), pp. 543–62.

Contini, B.; Galeotti, Marcello and Cugno, F. Inflation and the Irregular Economy: A Dynamic Analysis. *Metroecon.,* February 1986, *38*(1), pp. 67–84.

Cooper, Russell. Share Contracts and Macroeconomic Externalities. *J. Compar. Econ.,* December 1986, *10*(4), pp. 421–26.

Coyte, Peter C. The Supply of Individual Hours and Labor Force Participation under Uncertainty. *Econ. Inquiry,* January 1986, *24*(1), pp. 155–71.

Cross, Rod. Phelps, Hysteresis, and the Natural Rate of Unemployment. *Quart. J. Bus. Econ.,* Winter 1986, *25*(1), pp. 56–64.

Cugno, Franco and Ferrero, Mario. Partecipazione ai profitti e sussidi all'occupazione: un'analisi comparativa. (Profit Shares and Employment Subsidies, a Comparative Analysis. With English summary.) *Polit. Econ.,* December 1986, *2*(3), pp. 291–322.

Danziger, Leif. Relative-Price Seasonality, Wage Indexation and the Perfect Price Index. *Europ. Econ. Rev.,* December 1986, *30*(6), pp. 1145–67.

Dasgupta, Partha and Ray, Debraj. Inequality as a Determinant of Malnutrition and Unemployment: Theory. *Econ. J.,* December 1986, *96*(384), pp. 1011–34.

Davidson, Paul. Financial Markets and Macroeconomic Fluctuations: Comment. **In** *Butkiewicz, J. L.; Koford, K. J. and Miller, J. B., eds.,* 1986, pp. 135–43.

De Long, James Bradford and Summers, Lawrence H. Is Increased Price Flexibility Stabilizing? *Amer. Econ. Rev.,* December 1986, *76*(5), pp. 1031–44.

De Neubourg, Chris. Unidentified Floating Unemployment (UFU) and the Specification of the UV-Curve. *Rech. Écon. Louvain,* 1986, *52*(3–4), pp. 227–55. **[G: Netherlands]**

Deane, Phyllis. Microeconomic Incentives and Macroeconomic Decline: Comment. **In** *Balassa, B. and Giersch, H., eds.,* 1986, pp. 54–58.

Dehez, Pierre and Fitoussi, Jean-Paul. Wage Indexation and Macroeconomic Fluctuations. **In** *Beckerman, W., ed.,* 1986, pp. 201–17.

Del Vecchio, Vincenzo and Garonna, Paolo. L'aggiustamento alla recessione in condizioni di incertezza: riduzione di orario, Part-Time e disoccupazione. (Adjustment to the Recession under Uncertainty. With English summary.) *Econ. Lavoro,* Apr.-June 1986, *20*(2), pp. 31–49.

Dendrinos, Dimitrios S. On the Incongruous Spatial Employment Dynamics. **In** *Nijkamp, P., ed. (II),* 1986, pp. 321–39.

Diamond, Peter A. Intertemporal Aspects of Learning New Techniques: Implications for Efficiency and Distribution: Comment. *Scand. J. Econ.,* 1986, *88*(1), pp. 189–94.

Diamond, Peter A. and Mirrlees, James A. Payroll-Tax Financed Social Insurance with Variable Retirement. *Scand. J. Econ.,* 1986, *88*(1), pp. 25–50.

Doeringer, Peter B. Internal Labor Markets and Noncompeting Groups. *Amer. Econ. Rev.,* May 1986, *76*(2), pp. 48–52.

Dolado, Juan J. Costes variables de ajuste en funciones de empleo a corto plazo en la industria. (With English summary.) *Invest. Ecón.,* May 1986, *10*(2), pp. 219–226. **[G: OECD]**

Dolado, Juan J.; Malo de Molina, José Luis and Zabalza, Antonio. Spanish Industrial Unemployment: Some Explanatory Factors. **In** *Bean, C. R.; Layard, P. R. G. and Nickell, S. J., eds.,* 1986, pp. 313–33. **[G: Spain]**

Dooley, David and Catalano, Ralph. Do Economic Variables Generate Psychological Problems? Different Methods, Different Answers. **In** *MacFadyen, A. J. and MacFadyen, H. W., eds.,* 1986, pp. 503–46.

Dormont, Brigitte and Sevestre, Patrick. Modèles dynamiques de demande de travail: spécification et estimation sur données de panel. (Dynamic Labor Demand Models: Specification and Estimation Using Panel Data. With English summary.) *Revue Écon.,* May 1986, *37*(3), pp. 455–87. **[G: France]**

Dowell, Richard S. and McLaren, Keith R. An Intertemporal Analysis of the Interdependence between Risk Preference, Retirement, and Work Rate Decisions. *J. Polit. Econ.,* Part 1, June 1986, *94*(3), pp. 667–82.

Drago, Robert. Work Discipline and Lay-Offs: Is There a Trade-off between Wages and Job Security? *J. Lab. Res.,* Summer 1986, *7*(3), pp. 285–92.

Drazen, Allan. Optimal Minimum Wage Legislation. *Econ. J.,* September 1986, *96*(383), pp. 774–84.

Driehuis, Wim. Unemployment in the Netherlands, 1960–1983. *Economica,* Supplement 1986, *53*(210(S)), pp. S297–312. **[G: Netherlands]**

Driehuis, Wim. Unemployment in the Netherlands, 1960–1983. **In** *Bean, C. R.; Layard, P. R. G. and Nickell, S. J., eds.,* 1986, pp. 297–312. **[G: Netherlands]**

Dudley, Leonard. Implicit Labor Contracts and Public Choice: A General Equilibrium Approach. *J. Law Econ.,* April 1986, *29*(1), pp. 61–82. **[G: OECD; LDCs]**

Dunn, L. F. and Youngblood, Stuart A. Absenteeism as a Mechanism for Approaching an Optimal Labor Market Equilibrium: An Empirical Study. *Rev. Econ. Statist.,* November 1986, *68*(4), pp. 668–74. **[G: U.S.]**

Eberts, Randall W. and Stone, Joe A. On the Contract Curve: A Test of Alternative Models of Collective Bargaining. *J. Lab. Econ.,* January 1986, *4*(1), pp. 66–81. **[G: U.S.]**

Elliott, J. Walter and Sherony, Keith R. Employer Search Activities and Short-run Aggregate Labor Supply. *Southern Econ. J.*, January 1986, *52*(3), pp. 693–705. **[G: U.S.]**

Elliott, Robert F. and Murphy, Phillip D. The Theory of Net Advantages. *Scot. J. Polit. Econ.*, February 1986, *33*(1), pp. 46–57.

Ethier, Wilfred J. Illegal Immigration. *Amer. Econ. Rev.*, May 1986, *76*(2), pp. 258–62.

Ethier, Wilfred J. Illegal Immigration: The Host-Country Problem. *Amer. Econ. Rev.*, March 1986, *76*(1), pp. 56–71.

Extejt, Marian M. Contributed Papers: Organizational Behavior and Personnel: Discussion. **In** *Dennis, B. D., ed.*, 1986, pp. 108–11.

Fagan, G. and Murphy, A. Employers' Social Insurance Contributions and Employment. *Econ. Soc. Rev.*, October 1986, *18*(1), pp. 43–56. **[G: Ireland]**

Farmer, Karl. Gleichgewichtskonzept, Investitionsfunktion und Unterbeschäftigungsgleichgewicht. (Equilibrium Concepts, Investment Function and Unemployment Equilibrium. With English summary.) *Z. Wirtschaft. Sozialwissen.*, 1986, *106*(5), pp. 441–65.

Favereau, Olivier; Py, Jacques and Sollogoub, Michel. Les modèles français et allemand de marché interne du travail: essai de formalisation. (An Attempt to Formalise French and German Internal Labour Markets. With English summary.) *Écon. Appl.*, 1986, *39*(4), pp. 819–846. **[G: France; W. Germany]**

Fehr, Ernest. A Theory of Involuntary Equilibrium Unemployment. *J. Inst. Theoretical Econ.*, June 1986, *142*(2), pp. 405–30.

Fethke, Gary and Policano, Andrew. Will Wage Setters Ever Stagger Decisions? [Wage Contingencies, the Pattern of Negotiation and Aggregate Implications of Alternative Contract Structures]. *Quart. J. Econ.*, November 1986, *101*(4), pp. 867–77.

Filer, Randall K. The Effects of Nonpecuniary Compensation on Estimates of Labor Supply Functions. *Quart. Rev. Econ. Bus.*, Spring 1986, *26*(1), pp. 17–30.

Fischer, Edwin O. and Jammernegg, Werner. Empirical Investigation of a Catastrophe Theory Extension of the Phillips Curve. *Rev. Econ. Statist.*, February 1986, *68*(1), pp. 9–17. **[G: U.S.]**

Fischer, Stanley. Long-term Contracts, Rational Expectations, and the Optimal Money Supply Rule. **In** *Fischer, S.*, 1986, *1977*, pp. 365–81.

Fischer, Stanley. Wage Indexation and Macroeconomic Stability. **In** *Fischer, S.*, 1986, *1977*, pp. 159–91.

Flinn, Christopher J. Econometric Analysis of CPS-Type Unemployment Data. *J. Human Res.*, Fall 1986, *21*(4), pp. 456–84. **[G: Italy]**

Flug, Karnit and Galor, Oded. Minimum Wage in a General Equilibrium Model of International Trade and Human Capital. *Int. Econ. Rev.*, February 1986, *27*(1), pp. 149–64.

Foster, James E. and Wan, Henry Y., Jr. Involuntary Unemployment as a Principal–Agent Equilibrium. **In** *Akerlof, G. A. and Yellen, J. L., eds.*, 1986, *1984*, pp. 57–65.

Franz, Wolfgang and König, Heinz. The Nature and Causes of Unemployment in the Federal Republic of Germany since the 1970s: An Empirical Investigation. **In** *Bean, C. R.; Layard, P. R. G. and Nickell, S. J., eds.*, 1986, pp. 219–44. **[G: W. Germany]**

Fremdling, Rainer. Microeconomic Incentives and Macroeconomic Decline: Comment. **In** *Balassa, B. and Giersch, H., eds.*, 1986, pp. 59–62.

Frenkel, Roberto. Salários e inflação na América Latina: resultados de pesquisas recentes na Argentina, Brasil, Chile, Colômbia e Costa Rica. (With English summary.) *Pesquisa Planejamento Econ.*, April 1986, *16*(1), pp. 21–59. **[G: Argentina; Brazil; Chile; Colombia; Costa Rica]**

Gahvari, Firouz. Labor Supply and Tax Rates: Comment. *Amer. Econ. Rev.*, March 1986, *76*(1), pp. 280–83.

Garfinkel, Irwin and Masters, Stanley. Welfare and Work Incentives. **In** *Reynolds, L. G.; Masters, S. H. and Moser, C. H., eds.*, 1986, pp. 277–87. **[G: U.S.]**

Garner, C. Alan. Equity in Economic Relationships: Towards a Positive Theory. *J. Econ. Behav. Organ.*, September 1986, *7*(3), pp. 253–64.

Genosko, Joachim. Verkürzte Wochenarbeitszeit und Pensionierungszeitpunkt. (Weekly Work-Time Reductions and Age of Retirement. With English summary.) *Jahr. Nationalökon. Statist.*, March 1986, *201*(2), pp. 190–93.

Gifford, Adam, Jr. and Kenney, Roy W. The Production of Information through Labor Market Contests. *J. Law, Econ., Organ.*, Fall 1986, *2*(2), pp. 305–13.

Grady, Stephen W. and Hutchinson, Gillian. A Symposium on the Role and Influence of Trade Unions in a Recession: Comments. *Brit. J. Ind. Relat.*, July 1986, *24*(2), pp. 209–12. **[G: U.K.]**

Greenwald, Bruce C. Adverse Selection in the Labour Market. *Rev. Econ. Stud.*, July 1986, *53*(3), pp. 325–47.

Gregory, R. G. Wages Policy and Unemployment in Australia. **In** *Bean, C. R.; Layard, P. R. G. and Nickell, S. J., eds.*, 1986, pp. 53–74. **[G: Australia]**

Groenewegen, John and van Paridon, Kees. Theory and Practice of the Dutch Labor Market: The 1985 Conference of the Dutch Study Circle for Post Keynesian Economics. *J. Econ. Issues*, September 1986, *20*(3), pp. 825–33.

Gronau, Reuben. Home Production—A Survey. **In** *Ashenfelter, O. and Layard, R., eds., Vol. 1*, 1986, pp. 273–304. **[G: U.S.]**

Grubb, David B. Topics in the OECD Phillips Curve. *Econ. J.*, March 1986, *96*(381), pp. 55–79. **[G: OECD]**

Gui, Benedetto. "Insiders," "Outsiders" e partecipazione nella problematica occuzapionale. Alcuni rilievi critici alla proposta di Weitzman. ("Insiders," "Outsiders" and the Share Economy: A Comment. With English summary.) *Polit. Econ.*, December 1986, *2*(3), pp. 323–37.

Guiso, Luigi and Terlizzese, Daniele. Shock temporanei e aggiustamento dinamico: una interpretazione contrattuale della cassa integrazione guadagni. (Temporary Shocks and Dynamic Adjustment: A Contractual Interpretation of the Wage Supplementation Fund. With English summary.) *Giorn. Econ.*, Nov.-Dec. 1986, *45*(11–12), pp. 653–80. **[G: Italy]**

Gupta, M. R. Shadow Wage Rate in a Dynamic Harris–Todaro Model. *Oxford Econ. Pap.*, March 1986, *38*(1), pp. 131–40.

Gustman, Alan L. and Steinmeier, Thomas L. A Structural Retirement Model. *Econometrica*, May 1986, *54*(3), pp. 555–84. **[G: U.S.]**

Gwartney, James and Stroup, Richard L. Labor Supply and Tax Rates: Reply. *Amer. Econ. Rev.*, March 1986, *76*(1), pp. 284–85.

Gwartney, James and Stroup, Richard L. Labor Supply and Tax Rates: Reply. *Amer. Econ. Rev.*, June 1986, *76*(3), pp. 557–58.

Gylfason, Thorvaldur and Lindbeck, Assar. Endogenous Unions and Governments: A Game-Theoretic Approach. *Europ. Econ. Rev.*, February 1986, *30*(1), pp. 5–26.

Haag, Günter. A Stochastic Theory for Residential and Labour Mobility Including Travel Networks. **In** *Nijkamp, P., ed. (II)*, 1986, pp. 340–57.

Hafer, R. W. Inflation Uncertainty and a Test of the Friedman Hypothesis. *J. Macroecon.*, Summer 1986, *8*(3), pp. 365–72. **[G: U.S.]**

Hahn, Frank H. and Solow, Robert M. Is Wage Flexibility a Good Thing? **In** *Beckerman, W., ed.*, 1986, pp. 1–19.

Hall, Robert E. Hysteresis and the European Unemployment Problem: Comment. **In** *Fischer, S., ed.*, 1986, pp. 85–88. **[G: U.S.; U.K.; W. Germany; France]**

Hall, Stephen G., et al. Forecasting Employment: The Role of Forward-Looking Behaviour. *Int. J. Forecasting*, 1986, *2*(4), pp. 435–45. **[G: U.K.]**

Haltiwanger, John and Waldman, Michael. Insurance and Labor Market Contracting: An Analysis of the Capital Market Assumption. *J. Lab. Econ.*, Part 1, July 1986, *4*(3), pp. 355–75.

Ham, John C. On the Interpretation of Unemployment in Empirical Labour Supply Analysis. **In** *Blundell, R. and Walker, I., eds.*, 1986, pp. 121–42. **[G: U.K.]**

Ham, John C. Testing Whether Unemployment Represents Intertemporal Labour Supply Behaviour. *Rev. Econ. Stud.*, August 1986, *53*(4), pp. 559–78.

Hamada, Fumimasa. A Macroeconomic Model with the Rate of Unemployment as a Risk Probability under the Government Budget Restraint. *Keio Econ. Stud.*, 1986, *23*(1), pp. 49–62.

Hamada, Koichi and Kurosaka, Yoshio. Trends in Unemployment, Wages and Productivity: The Case of Japan. **In** *Bean, C. R.; Layard, P. R. G. and Nickell, S. J., eds.*, 1986, pp. 275–96. **[G: Japan]**

Hamermesh, Daniel S. Incentives for the Homogenization of Time Use. **In** *Balassa, B. and Giersch, H., eds.*, 1986, pp. 124–39.

Hamermesh, Daniel S. Inflation and Labour Market Adjustment. *Economica*, February 1986, *53*(209), pp. 63–73. **[G: U.S.]**

Hammermesh, Daniel S. The Demand for Labor in the Long Run. **In** *Ashenfelter, O. and Layard, R., eds., Vol. 1*, 1986, pp. 429–71.

Hartog, Joop. Allocation and the Earnings Function. *Empirical Econ.*, 1986, *11*(2), pp. 97–110. **[G: Netherlands]**

Harvey, A. C., et al. Stochastic Trends in Dynamic Regression Models: An Application to the Employment–Output Equations. *Econ. J.*, December 1986, *96*(384), pp. 975–85. **[G: U.K.]**

Hatton, T. J. Rational Expectations and Labour Market Equilibrium in Britain 1855–1913. *Oxford Econ. Pap.*, March 1986, *38*(1), pp. 160–73. **[G: U.K.]**

Heckman, James J. and MaCurdy, Thomas E. Labor Econometrics. **In** *Griliches, Z. and Intriligator, M. D., eds.*, 1986, pp. 1917–77.

Heckman, James J. and Singer, Burton. Econometric Analysis of Longitudinal Data. **In** *Griliches, Z. and Intriligator, M. D., eds.*, 1986, pp. 1689–1763.

Heneman, Robert L. Contributed Papers: Organizational Behavior and Personnel: Discussion. **In** *Dennis, B. D., ed.*, 1986, pp. 104–07.

Herce San Miguel, José Antonio. Presupuesto de Seguridad Social y oferta de factores en una economía de generaciones sucesivas. (With English summary.) *Invest. Ecón.*, January 1986, *10*(1), pp. 37–64.

Hersoug, Tor; Kjaer, Knut N. and Rødseth, Asbjorn. Wages, Taxes and the Utility-Maximizing Trade Union: A Confrontation with Norwegian Data. *Oxford Econ. Pap.*, November 1986, *38*(3), pp. 403–23. **[G: Norway]**

Hoel, Michael. Employment and Allocation Effects of Reducing the Length of the Workday. *Economica*, February 1986, *53*(209), pp. 75–85.

Hoel, Michael and Vale, Bent. Effects on Unemployment of Reduced Working Time in an Economy Where Firms Set Wages. *Europ. Econ. Rev.*, October 1986, *30*(5), pp. 1097–1104.

Hollander, Abraham and Lacroix, Robert. Unionism, Information Disclosure and Profit-sharing. *Southern Econ. J.*, January 1986, *52*(3), pp. 706–17.

Hollander, Samuel. Marx and Malthusianism: Reply. *Amer. Econ. Rev.*, June 1986, *76*(3), pp. 548–50.

Holmlund, Bertil. Centralized Wage Setting, Wage Drift and Stabilization Policies under Trade Unionism. *Oxford Econ. Pap.*, July 1986, *38*(2), pp. 243–58. **[G: Sweden]**

Horn, Henrik and Svensson, Lars E. O. Trade Unions and Optimal Labour Contracts. *Econ. J.*, June 1986, *96*(382), pp. 323–41.

Hosios, Arthur J. Layoffs, Recruitment, and Interfirm Mobility. *J. Lab. Econ.*, October 1986, *4*(4), pp. 473–502.

Howitt, Peter. Wage Flexibility and Employment. *Eastern Econ. J.*, July-Sept. 1986, *12*(3), pp. 237–42.

Huang, Wei-Chiao and Ray, Subhash C. Labor Supply, Voluntary Work, and Charitable Contributions in a Model of Utility Maximization. *Eastern Econ. J.*, July-Sept. 1986, *12*(3), pp. 257–63.

Hughes, Gerard. Employers' Social Insurance Contributions and Employment: Reply. *Econ. Soc. Rev.*, October 1986, *18*(1), pp. 57–68. [G: Ireland]

Hui, Weng T. and Trivedi, Pravin K. Duration Dependence, Targeted Employment Subsidies and Unemployment Benefits. *J. Public Econ.*, October 1986, *31*(1), pp. 105–29.

Hujer, Reinhard. Ökonometrische "Switch"-Modelle: Methodische Ansätze und empirische Analysen. (Econometric Switch-Models: Methodical and Empirical Analysis. With English summary.) *Jahr. Nationalökon. Statist.*, May 1986, *201*(3), pp. 229–56. [G: W. Germany]

Humphrey, Thomas M. Some Recent Developments in Phillips Curve Analysis. In *Humphreys, T. M.*, 1986, *1978*, pp. 119–27.

Humphrey, Thomas M. The Early History of the Phillips Curve. In *Humphreys, T. M.*, 1986, *1985*, pp. 91–98.

Humphrey, Thomas M. The Evolution and Policy Implications of Phillips Curve Analysis. In *Humphreys, T. M.*, 1986, *1985*, pp. 99–118.

Hutchens, Robert M. Delayed Payment Contracts and a Firm's Propensity to Hire Older Workers. *J. Lab. Econ.*, October 1986, *4*(4), pp. 439–57. [G: U.S.]

Isaac, Alan G. Reversing the Phillips' Curve: A Microfoundation. *J. Macroecon.*, Spring 1986, *8*(2), pp. 221–26.

Isserman, Andrew, et al. Regional Labor Market Analysis. In *Nijkamp, P., ed. (I)*, 1986, pp. 543–80.

Ito, Takatoshi. Implicit Contracts and Risk Aversion. In *[Arrow, K. J.], Vol. 2*, 1986, pp. 265–87.

Jackman, Richard and Layard, Richard. A Wage-Tax, Worker-Subsidy Policy for Reducing the 'Natural' Rate of Unemployment. In *Beckerman, W., ed.*, 1986, pp. 153–69.

Jackman, Richard; Layard, Richard and Pissarides, Christopher A. Policies for Reducing the Natural Rate of Unemployment. In *Butkiewicz, J. L.; Koford, K. J. and Miller, J. B., eds.*, 1986, pp. 111–33.

Jenkinson, Tim. Testing Neo-Classical Theories of Labour Demand: An Application of Cointegration Techniques. *Oxford Bull. Econ. Statist.*, August 1986, *48*(3), pp. 241–51. [G: U.K.]

Jespersen, Jesper. "Wage Fixing" and "Demand Management": The Cures for Stagflation—New Keynesianism. *Econ. Lavoro*, Apr.-June 1986, *20*(2), pp. 125–33. [G: OECD]

Jha, Raghbendra. Optimal Labour Supply and the Accumulation of Human and Financial Capital with Capital Market Imperfections. *Indian Econ. Rev.*, Jan.-June 1986, *21*(1), pp. 21–39.

Johnson, G. E. and Layard, Richard. The Natural Rate of Unemployment: Explanation and Policy. In *Ashenfelter, O. and Layard, R., eds., Vol. 2*, 1986, pp. 921–99. [G: OECD]

Jones, Stephen R. G. Unemployment Insurance and Involuntary Unemployment: The Case of Adverse Selection. *J. Public Econ.*, August 1986, *30*(3), pp. 317–28.

Jungenfelt, Karl G. Intertemporal Aspects of Learning New Techniques: Implications for Efficiency and Distribution. *Scand. J. Econ.*, 1986, *88*(1), pp. 157–87.

Kaiser, Carl P. Unemployment Insurance and the Theory of Labor Demand. *Eastern Econ. J.*, Apr.-June 1986, *12*(2), pp. 115–28.

Kalmbach, Peter and Kurz, Heinz D. Economic Dynamics and Innovation: Ricardo, Marx and Schumpeter on Technological Change and Unemployment. In *Wagener, H.-J. and Drukker, J. W., eds.*, 1986, pp. 71–92.

Kato, Takao. "Bumping," Layoffs, and Worksharing. *Econ. Inquiry*, October 1986, *24*(4), pp. 657–68.

Katsoulacos, Y. Technical Change and Structural Unemployment. *Scot. J. Polit. Econ.*, August 1986, *33*(3), pp. 275–83.

Katz, Eliakim. A Diagramatic Illustration of the Labour Cooperative, a Note. *Amer. Econ.*, Spring 1986, *30*(1), pp. 73–74.

Katz, Eliakim; Spiegel, Uriel and Ziderman, Adrian. The Remuneration Package and Pareto Inefficiency in the Labour Market. *Europ. Econ. Rev.*, December 1986, *30*(6), pp. 1197–1205.

Katz, Eliakim and Stark, Oded. On the Shadow Wage of Urban Jobs in Less-Developed Countries. *J. Urban Econ.*, September 1986, *20*(2), pp. 121–27. [G: LDCs]

Katz, Eliakim and Ziderman, Adrian. Incomplete Information, Non-wage Benefits and Desirable-Worker Self Selection. *Australian Econ. Pap.*, December 1986, *25*(47), pp. 252–56.

Katz, Eliakim and Ziderman, Adrian. Towards a Theory of Incremental Wage Scales. *Appl. Econ.*, October 1986, *18*(10), pp. 1047–50. [G: U.S.]

Katz, Lawrence F. Efficiency Wage Theories: A Partial Evaluation. In *Fischer, S., ed.*, 1986, pp. 235–76. [G: U.S.]

Keizer, P. Wage Formation in the Context of Collective Bargaining. *De Economist*, 1986, *134*(2), pp. 191–213.

Kennan, John. Hysteresis and the European Unemployment Problem: Comment. In *Fischer, S., ed.*, 1986, pp. 78–85. [G: OECD]

Kiefer, Nicholas M. Econometric Approaches to the Specification of Life-Cycle Labour Supply and Commodity Demand Behaviour: Comment. *Econometric Rev.*, 1986, *5*(1), pp. 159–62.

Killingsworth, Mark R. A Simple Structural Model of Heterogeneous Preferences and Compensating Wage Differentials. In *Blundell,*

R. and Walker, I., eds., 1986, pp. 303–17. **[G: U.S.]**

Killingsworth, Mark R. and Heckman, James J. Female Labor Supply: A Survey. **In** *Ashenfelter, O. and Layard, R., eds., Vol. 1*, 1986, pp. 103–204. **[G: U.S.; U.K.; Canada; Germany]**

Kimbrough, Kent P. Inflation, Employment, and Welfare in the Presence of Transactions Costs. *J. Money, Credit, Banking*, May 1986, *18*(2), pp. 127–40.

König, Heinz. Incentives for the Homogenization of Time Use: Comment. **In** *Balassa, B. and Giersch, H., eds.*, 1986, pp. 162–65.

Kooreman, Peter and Kapteyn, Arie. Estimation of Rationed and Unrationed Household Labour Supply Functions Using Flexible Functional Forms. *Econ. J.*, June 1986, *96*(382), pp. 398–412. **[G: Netherlands]**

Kuhn, Peter. Wages, Effort, and Incentive Compatibility in Life-Cycle Employment Contracts. *J. Lab. Econ.*, January 1986, *4*(1), pp. 28–49.

Kuran, Timur. Anticipated Inflation and Aggregate Employment: The Case of Costly Price Adjustment. *Econ. Inquiry*, April 1986, *24*(2), pp. 293–311.

Kurz, Mordecai. On Asymmetric Information, Unemployment, and Inflexible Wages. **In** *[Arrow, K. J.], Vol. 2*, 1986, pp. 219–49.

Lancaster, Tony. Some Remarks on Wage and Duration Econometrics. **In** *Blundell, R. and Walker, I., eds.*, 1986, pp. 15–22.

Latham, Roger W. and Naisbitt, Barry. A Note on Progression and Leisure. *Public Finance*, December 1986, *41*(3), pp. 440–46.

Lavoie, Marc. Chômage classique et chômage keynésien: un prétexte aux politiques d'austérité. (Classical Unemployment and Keynesian Unemployment: A Pretext for Policies of Austerity. With English summary.) *Écon. Appl.*, 1986, *39*(2), pp. 203–38.

Layard, Richard. Financial Markets and Macroeconomic Fluctuations: Reply. **In** *Butkiewicz, J. L.; Koford, K. J. and Miller, J. B., eds.*, 1986, pp. 149–52.

Layard, Richard. Theories of Wage Rigidity: Comment. **In** *Butkiewicz, J. L.; Koford, K. J. and Miller, J. B., eds.*, 1986, pp. 215–16.

Layard, Richard and Nickell, Stephen J. Unemployment in Britain. **In** *Bean, C. R.; Layard, P. R. G. and Nickell, S. J., eds.*, 1986, pp. 121–69. **[G: U.K.]**

Lazear, Edward P. Raids and Offer Matching. **In** *Ehrenberg, R. G., ed., Pt. A*, 1986, pp. 141–65. **[G: U.S.]**

Lazear, Edward P. Salaries and Piece Rates. *J. Bus.*, July 1986, *59*(3), pp. 405–31.

Lazear, Edward P. and Moore, Robert L. Incentives, Productivity, and Labor Contracts. **In** *Akerlof, G. A. and Yellen, J. L., eds.*, 1986, *1984*, pp. 135–56. **[G: U.S.]**

Leap, Terry L. and Grigsby, David W. A Conceptualization of Collective Bargaining Power. *Ind. Lab. Relat. Rev.*, January 1986, *39*(2), pp. 202–13.

Ledent, Jacques. Consistent Modelling of Employment, Population, Labour Force, and Unemployment in the Statistical Analysis of Regional Growth. **In** *Batey, P. W. and Madden, M., eds.*, 1986, pp. 25–36.

Lee, Ronald D. The Value and Allocation of Time in High-Income Countries: Implications for Fertility: Comment. *Population Devel. Rev.*, Supp. 1986, *12*, pp. 108–10.

Leibenstein, Harvey. The Theory of Underemployment in Densely Populated Backward Areas. **In** *Akerlof, G. A. and Yellen, J. L., eds.*, 1986, *1963*, pp. 22–40.

Leigh, J. Paul and Lust, John. Punctuality and Tardiness in Supplying Labor. *Atlantic Econ. J.*, July 1986, *14*(2), pp. 16–25. **[G: U.S.]**

Leontief, Wassily. Technology Change, Employment, the Rate of Return on Capital and Wages. **In** *Burton, D. F., et al., eds.*, 1986, pp. 47–53. **[G: U.S.]**

Levine, David P. A Note on Wage Determination and Capital Accumulation. *J. Post Keynesian Econ.*, Spring 1986, *8*(3), pp. 463–77.

Lewis, H. Gregg. Union Relative Wage Effects. **In** *Ashenfelter, O. and Layard, R., eds., Vol. 2*, 1986, pp. 1139–81. **[G: U.S.]**

Li, Elizabeth H. Compensating Differentials for Cyclical and Noncyclical Unemployment: The Interaction between Investors' and Employees' Risk Aversion. *J. Lab. Econ.*, April 1986, *4*(2), pp. 277–300. **[G: U.S.]**

Lindbeck, Assar and Snower, Dennis J. Wage Rigidity, Union Activity and Unemployment. **In** *Beckerman, W., ed.*, 1986, pp. 97–125.

Lindbeck, Assar and Snower, Dennis J. Wage Setting, Unemployment, and Insider–Outsider Relations. *Amer. Econ. Rev.*, May 1986, *76*(2), pp. 235–39.

Lockwood, Ben. Transferable Skills, Job Matching, and the Inefficiency of the 'Natural' Rate of Unemployment. *Econ. J.*, December 1986, *96*(384), pp. 961–74.

Lopez, Ramon E. Structural Models of the Farm Household That Allow for Interdependent Utility and Profit-Maximization Decisions. **In** *Singh, I.; Squire, L. and Strauss, J., eds.*, 1986, pp. 306–25. **[G: Canada]**

Lorenz, Wilhelm. Labor Supply, Household Production and Consumption: A Diagrammatic Presentation. *J. Inst. Theoretical Econ.*, December 1986, *142*(4), pp. 745–52.

Loungani, Prakash. Oil Price Shocks and the Dispersion Hypothesis. *Rev. Econ. Statist.*, August 1986, *68*(3), pp. 536–39. **[G: U.S.]**

Lubian, Diego. Interessi nel tasso "naturale": una interpretazione della elevata e persistente disoccupazione attuale. (Hysteresis in the "Natural" Rate of Employment: An Interpretation of the High and Persistent Present Unemployment. With English summary.) *Giorn. Econ.*, Jan.-Feb. 1986, *45*(1–2), pp. 55–72. **[G: U.S.; U.K.; Japan; Italy; W. Germany]**

Lubrano, Michel. Bayesian Analysis of Single Market Disequilibrium Models: An Application to Unemployment in the U.S. Labour

Market. In *Blundell, R. and Walker, I., eds.*, 1986, pp. 75–102. **[G: U.S.]**

Luger, Michael I. and Stahl, Dale O., II. Specification Errors in Models of Aggregate Labor Supply. *Rev. Econ. Statist.*, May 1986, *68*(2), pp. 274–83. **[G: U.S.]**

MaCurdy, Thomas E. and Pencavel, John H. Testing between Competing Models of Wage and Employment Determination in Unionized Markets. *J. Polit. Econ.*, Part 2, June 1986, *94*(3), pp. S3–S39. **[G: U.S.]**

Malcomson, James M. Work Incentives, Hierarchy, and Internal Labor Markets. In *Akerlof, G. A. and Yellen, J. L., eds.*, 1986, *1984*, pp. 157–78.

Malinvaud, Edmond. Jusqu'ou la rigueur salariale devrait-elle aller? Une exploration théorique de la question. (The Search for the Appropriate Real Wage. With English summary.) *Revue Écon.*, March 1986, *37*(2), pp. 181–205.

Malinvaud, Edmond. The Rise of Unemployment in France. In *Bean, C. R.; Layard, P. R. G. and Nickell, S. J., eds.*, 1986, pp. 197–217. **[G: France]**

Manning, Alan. The Profitability of Private Information in Unionised Capitalist Enterprises. *Econ. J.*, Supplement 1986, *96*, pp. 122–33.

Marini, Giancarlo. Employment Fluctuations and Demand Management. *Economica*, May 1986, *53*(210), pp. 209–18.

Martin, James E. and Peterson, Melanie M. Two-Tier Wage Structures and Attitude Differences. In *Dennis, B. D., ed.*, 1986, pp. 72–79. **[G: U.S.]**

Matsukawa, Shigeru. The Equilibrium Distribution of Wage Settlements and Economic Stability. *Int. Econ. Rev.*, June 1986, *27*(2), pp. 415–37.

Matusz, Steven J. Implicit Contracts, Unemployment and International Trade. *Econ. J.*, June 1986, *96*(382), pp. 307–22.

Mauleón, Iñaki. El déficit público y el mercado de trabajo en España: algunas conexiones e implicaciones. (With English summary.) *Invest. Ecón.*, September 1986, *10*(3), pp. 483–504. **[G: Spain]**

McCombie, John S. L. Why Cutting Real Wages Will Not Necessarily Reduce Unemployment—Keynes and the "Postulates of the Classical Economics." *J. Post Keynesian Econ.*, Winter 1985-86, *8*(2), pp. 233–48.

McDonald, Ian M. Can the Risk-Shifting Employment Model Explain Fluctuating Employment? *Econ. Inquiry*, January 1986, *24*(1), pp. 25–41.

McElwain, Adrienne M. and Swofford, James L. The Social Security Payroll Tax and the Life-Cycle Work Pattern. *J. Human Res.*, Spring 1986, *21*(2), pp. 279–87. **[G: U.S.]**

McKenna, Christopher J. Equilibrium Wage Offers and Turnovers in a Simple Search Market. *Econ. J.*, September 1986, *96*(383), pp. 785–97.

Megdal, Sharon Bernstein. Comparable Worth: Some Issues for Consideration. *Contemp. Policy Issues*, April 1986, *4*(2), pp. 40–51.

Mincer, Jacob. Wage Changes in Job Changes. In *Ehrenberg, R. G., ed., Pt. A*, 1986, pp. 171–97. **[G: U.S.]**

Mirlesse, D. and Royer, D. Dynamique du chômage et attractions du plein-emploi. (Unemployment Dynamics and Full-Employment Attractions. With English summary.) *Écon. Appl.*, 1986, *39*(2), pp. 369–99.

Mitchell, Daniel J. B. Explanations of Wage Inflexibility: Institutions and Incentives. In *Beckerman, W., ed.*, 1986, pp. 43–76. **[G: U.S.]**

Miyazaki, Hajime. Labor–Management Bargaining: Contract Curves and Slutsky Equations. *J. Polit. Econ.*, December 1986, *94*(6), pp. 1225–45.

Modigliani, Franco; Padoa Schioppa, F. and Rossi, N. Aggregate Unemployment in Italy, 1960–1983. In *Bean, C. R.; Layard, P. R. G. and Nickell, S. J., eds.*, 1986, pp. 245–73. **[G: Italy]**

Moffitt, Robert. Work Incentives in Transfer Programs (Revisited): A Study of the AFDC Program. In *Ehrenberg, R. G., ed., Pt. B*, 1986, pp. 389–439. **[G: U.S.]**

Molho, Ian. A Time Series Study of Household Participation Decisions through Boom and Slump. *Oxford Econ. Pap.*, March 1986, *38*(1), pp. 141–59. **[G: U.K.]**

Mookherjee, Dilip. Involuntary Unemployment and Worker Moral Hazard. *Rev. Econ. Stud.*, October 1986, *53*(5), pp. 739–54.

Morgan, Peter B. A Note on "Job Search: The Choice of Intensity." *J. Polit. Econ.*, April 1986, *94*(2), pp. 439–42.

Morley, Samuel A. Salários relativos, estrutura da força de trabalho e distribuição de renda a curto e longo prazo. (With English summary.) *Pesquisa Planejamento Econ.*, December 1986, *16*(3), pp. 599–619.

Mortensen, Dale T. Job Search and Labor Market Analysis. In *Ashenfelter, O. and Layard, R., eds., Vol. 2*, 1986, pp. 849–919.

Mukherji, Anjan and Sanyal, Amal. Price Flexibility and Unemployment: Microeconomics of Some Old-Fashioned Questions. *Keio Econ. Stud.*, 1986, *23*(2), pp. 19–35.

Mulder, C. B. and van der Ploeg, Frederick. Trade Unions, Investment and Employment in a Small Open Economy: A Dutch Perspective. *Rech. Écon. Louvain*, 1986, *52*(3–4), pp. 313–38. **[G: Netherlands; OECD]**

Murphy, Kevin J. Incentives, Learning, and Compensation: A Theoretical and Empirical Investigation of Managerial Labor Contracts. *Rand J. Econ.*, Spring 1986, *17*(1), pp. 59–76. **[G: U.S.]**

Myatt, Anthony E. On the Non-existence of a Natural Rate of Unemployment and Kaleckian Micro Underpinnings to the Phillips Curve. *J. Post Keynesian Econ.*, Spring 1986, *8*(3), pp. 447–62.

Nakagome, Masaki. The Spatial Labour Market and Spatial Competition. *Reg. Stud.*, August 1986, *20*(4), pp. 307–12.

Narendranathan, Wiji and Nickell, Stephen J. Estimating the Parameters of Interest in a Job

Search Model. **In** *Blundell, R. and Walker, I., eds.*, 1986, pp. 1–14.

Nickell, Stephen J. Dynamic Models of Labour Demand. **In** *Ashenfelter, O. and Layard, R., eds., Vol. 1,* 1986, pp. 473–522.

Nijkamp, Peter. The Triangle of Industrial Dynamics, Labour Markets and Spatial Systems. **In** *Nijkamp, P., ed. (II),* 1986, pp. 1–17.

Nijkamp, Peter and Poot, Jacques. Technological Change and Labour Migration in a General Spatial Interaction System. **In** *Nijkamp, P., ed. (II),* 1986, pp. 358–70.

Nordhaus, William D. Can the Share Economy Cure Our Macroeconomic Woes? Probably Not. *J. Compar. Econ.*, December 1986, *10*(4), pp. 448–53.

Nordhaus, William D. Introduction to the Share Economy. *J. Compar. Econ.*, December 1986, *10*(4), pp. 416–20. **[G: U.S.]**

O'Connell, John F. An Alternative Theory of Labor Union Growth. *Amer. Econ.*, Spring 1986, *30*(1), pp. 51–55.

Olson, Mancur. Microeconomic Incentives and Macroeconomic Decline. **In** *Balassa, B. and Giersch, H., eds.*, 1986, pp. 40–53.

Osberg, Lars, et al. Job Mobility, Wage Determination and Market Segmentation in the Presence of Sample Selection Bias. *Can. J. Econ.*, May 1986, *19*(2), pp. 319–46. **[G: Canada]**

Oswald, Andrew J. A Symposium on the Role and Influence of Trade Unions in a Recession: Comments. *Brit. J. Ind. Relat.*, July 1986, *24*(2), pp. 213–14. **[G: U.K.]**

Oswald, Andrew J. Is Wage Rigidity Caused by 'Lay-offs by Seniority'? **In** *Beckerman, W., ed.*, 1986, pp. 77–95. **[G: U.K.]**

Oswald, Andrew J. Unemployment Insurance and Labor Contracts under Asymmetric Information: Theory and Facts. *Amer. Econ. Rev.*, June 1986, *76*(3), pp. 365–77. **[G: U.S.]**

Oswald, Andrew J. Wage Determination and Recession: A Report on Recent Work. *Brit. J. Ind. Relat.*, July 1986, *24*(2), pp. 181–94.

Paauw, Douglas S. and Islam, Muhammad M. Leisure-Income Choice and the Development of a Dual Economy. *J. Econ. Devel.*, July 1986, *11*(1), pp. 7–25.

Parsons, Donald O. The Employment Relationship: Job Attachment, Work Effort, and the Nature of Contracts. **In** *Ashenfelter, O. and Layard, R., eds., Vol. 2,* 1986, pp. 789–848. **[G: U.S.]**

Pedersen, Peter J. and Westergård-Nielsen, Niels. A Longitudinal Study of Unemployment: History Dependence and Insurance Effects. **In** *Blundell, R. and Walker, I., eds.*, 1986, pp. 44–59. **[G: Denmark]**

Pencavel, John H. Labor Supply of Men: A Survey. **In** *Ashenfelter, O. and Layard, R., eds., Vol. 1,* 1986, pp. 3–102. **[G: U.S.; U.K.; Canada; Germany]**

Perrings, Charles. Income Redistribution and Labour Surplus in the Classical Theory of Labour Migration. *Manchester Sch. Econ. Soc. Stud.*, September 1986, *54*(3), pp. 283–97.

Perry, George L. Policy Lessons from the Postwar Period. **In** *Beckerman, W., ed.*, 1986, pp. 127–51. **[G: OECD]**

Peston, Maurice H. The Elementary Macroeconomic Consequences of Differing Public and Private Sector Wages. *Public Finance*, 1986, *41*(2), pp. 173–81.

Peterson, William. Keynesian Policies for Voluntary Unemployment. *Rech. Écon. Louvain*, 1986, *52*(3–4), pp. 399–411. **[G: U.K.]**

Pichelmann, Karl and Wagner, Michael. Labour Surplus as a Signal for Real-Wage Adjustment: Austria, 1968–1984. **In** *Bean, C. R.; Layard, P. R. G. and Nickell, S. J., eds.*, 1986, pp. 75–87. **[G: Austria]**

Pissarides, Christopher A. Theories of Wage Rigidity: Comment. **In** *Butkiewicz, J. L.; Koford, K. J. and Miller, J. B., eds.*, 1986, pp. 206–09.

Pissarides, Christopher A. Trade Unions and the Efficiency of the Natural Rate of Unemployment. *J. Lab. Econ.*, October 1986, *4*(4), pp. 582–95.

Plaut, Steven E. Implicit Contracts in the Absence of Enforcement: Note. *Amer. Econ. Rev.*, March 1986, *76*(1), pp. 257–58.

Poterba, James M. and Summers, Lawrence H. Reporting Errors and Labor Market Dynamics. *Econometrica*, November 1986, *54*(6), pp. 1319–38. **[G: U.S.]**

Potestio, Paola. Una nota sul modello di economia partecipativa di M. Weitzman. (A Note on Weitzman's Share Economy. With English summary.) *Polit. Econ.*, December 1986, *2*(3), pp. 339–60.

Pyatt, Graham. Inertia in Labor Markets. *Eastern Econ. J.*, July-Sept. 1986, *12*(3), pp. 243–50.

Qadir, Asghar. Higher Education and the Markets for Educated Labour in LDCs: Theoretical Approaches and Implications: Comments. *Pakistan Devel. Rev.*, Autumn 1986, *25*(3), pp. 277–78. **[G: LDCs]**

Quan, Nguyen T. Characteristics of Blue Collar and White Collar Jobs and Pecuniary Returns. *J. Behav. Econ.*, Spring/Summer 1986, *15*(1/2), pp. 157–74. **[G: U.S.]**

Quandt, Richard E. and Rosen, Harvey S. Some Further Results on Rosen and Quandt's Labor Market Model: Queries and Disagreements [Estimating a Disequilibrium Aggregate Labor Market Model]. *Europ. Econ. Rev.*, April 1986, *30*(2), pp. 457–59. **[G: U.S.]**

Quandt, Richard E. and Rosen, Harvey S. Unemployment, Disequilibrium and the Short Run Phillips Curve: An Econometric Approach. *J. Appl. Econometrics*, July 1986, *1*(3), pp. 235–53. **[G: U.S.]**

Raaum, Oddbjørn. Wage Formation in a Two-Sector Open Economy with Two Strong Unions. *Rech. Écon. Louvain*, 1986, *52*(3–4), pp. 283–311.

Ramirez, Miguel D. Marx and Malthusianism: Comment. *Amer. Econ. Rev.*, June 1986, *76*(3), pp. 543–47.

Rao, B. Bhaskara. A Note on Employment, Labor Supply, and Real Wages in Market Disequilibrium. *J. Macroecon.*, Spring 1986, *8*(2), pp. 233–42. **[G: U.S.]**

Reati, Angelo. The Deviation of Prices from Labour Values: An Extension to the Non-competitive Case. *Cambridge J. Econ.*, March 1986, *10*(1), pp. 35–42.

Rees, Albert. Information Networks in Labor Markets. **In** *Reynolds, L. G.; Masters, S. H. and Moser, C. H., eds.*, 1986, *1966*, pp. 60–65.

Rice, Patricia G. Juvenile Unemployment, Relative Wages and Social Security: The Econometric Evidence. **In** *Blundell, R. and Walker, I., eds.*, 1986, pp. 60–74. **[G: U.K.]**

Rivera-Batiz, Francisco L. Can Border Industries Be a Substitute for Immigration? *Amer. Econ. Rev.*, May 1986, *76*(2), pp. 263–68. **[G: U.S.; Mexico]**

Roemer, Michael. Simple Analytics of Segmented Markets: What Case for Liberalization? *World Devel.*, March 1986, *14*(3), pp. 429–39.

Rosen, Sherwin. The Theory of Equalizing Differences. **In** *Ashenfelter, O. and Layard, R., eds., Vol. 1*, 1986, pp. 641–92.

Rossana, Robert J. Wage and Hiring Dynamics with Storable Output. *J. Macroecon.*, Summer 1986, *8*(3), pp. 313–28.

Rothschild, Kurt W. Incentives for the Homogenization of Time Use: Comment. **In** *Balassa, B. and Giersch, H., eds.*, 1986, pp. 159–61.

Rouzaud, Catherine. Approches théoriques récentes du chômage imputable à l'absence d'ajustement du salaire. (Recent Wage Rigidity Explanations of Unemployment. With English summary.) *Écon. Appl.*, 1986, *39*(4), pp. 793–817.

Rudebusch, Glenn D. Testing for Labor Market Equilibrium with an Exact Excess Demand Disequilibrium Model. *Rev. Econ. Statist.*, August 1986, *68*(3), pp. 468–76. **[G: U.S.]**

Salop, Steven C. A Model of the Natural Rate of Unemployment. **In** *Akerlof, G. A. and Yellen, J. L., eds.*, 1986, *1979*, pp. 93–101.

Sarantis, Nicholas C. A Note on Employment, Labor Supply, and Real Wages in Market Disequilibrium: A Reply. *J. Macroecon.*, Spring 1986, *8*(2), pp. 243–45. **[G: U.S.]**

Schippers, Joop J. and Siegers, Jacques I. Women's Relative Wage Rate in the Netherlands, 1950–1983: A Test of Alternative Discrimination Theories. *De Economist*, 1986, *134*(2), pp. 165–80. **[G: Netherlands]**

Schultz, T. Paul. The Value and Allocation of Time in High-Income Countries: Implications for Fertility. *Population Devel. Rev.*, Supp. 1986, *12*, pp. 87–108. **[G: U.S.]**

Schultze, Charles L. The Cyclical Flexibility of Wages. *Amer. Econ. Rev.*, December 1986, *76*(5), pp. 1152–53. **[G: U.S.]**

Schwab, Stewart. Is Statistical Discrimination Efficient? *Amer. Econ. Rev.*, March 1986, *76*(1), pp. 228–34.

Segal, Martin. Post-Institutionalism in Labor Economics: The Forties and Fifties Revisited. *Ind. Lab. Relat. Rev.*, April 1986, *39*(3), pp. 388–403.

Seidman, Laurence S. Financial Markets and Macroeconomic Fluctuations: Comment. **In** *Butkiewicz, J. L.; Koford, K. J. and Miller, J. B., eds.*, 1986, pp. 143–44.

Sgro, Pasquale M. Factor Substitution and Discrimination in Labor Markets. *Southern Econ. J.*, April 1986, *52*(4), pp. 1103–14.

Shaffer, Sherrill. An Alternative Theory of Upward Sloping Age-Earnings Profiles. *Australian Econ. Pap.*, June 1986, *25*(46), pp. 118–21.

Shapiro, Carl. Investment, Moral Hazard, and Occupational Licensing. *Rev. Econ. Stud.*, October 1986, *53*(5), pp. 843–62.

Shapiro, Carl and Stiglitz, Joseph E. Equilibrium Unemployment as a Worker Discipline Device. **In** *Akerlof, G. A. and Yellen, J. L., eds.*, 1986, *1984*, pp. 45–56.

Smith, Richard J. and Blundell, Richard. An Exogeneity Test for a Simultaneous Equation Tobit Model with an Application to Labor Supply. *Econometrica*, May 1986, *54*(3), pp. 679–85. **[G: U.K.]**

Smith, Robert Stewart. The Economics of Job Displacement. **In** *Berkowitz, M. and Hill, M. A., eds.*, 1986, pp. 171–95.

Sneessens, Henri R. and Drèze, Jacques H. A Discussion of Belgian Unemployment, Combining Traditional Concepts and Disequilibrium Econometrics. **In** *Bean, C. R.; Layard, P. R. G. and Nickell, S. J., eds.*, 1986, pp. 89–119. **[G: Belgium]**

Snow, Arthur and Warren, Ronald S., Jr. Price Level Uncertainty, Saving, and Labor Supply. *Econ. Inquiry*, January 1986, *24*(1), pp. 97–106.

Solimano, Andrés. Salarios Reales y Empleo Bajo Distintos Regímenes Macroeconómicos. Una Aplicación para Chile y Brasil. (With English summary.) *Cuadernos Econ.*, December 1986, *23*(70), pp. 343–71. **[G: Chile; Brazil]**

Solow, Robert M. Another Possible Source of Wage Stickiness. **In** *Akerlof, G. A. and Yellen, J. L., eds.*, 1986, *1979*, pp. 41–44.

Solow, Robert M. Unemployment: Getting the Questions Right. **In** *Bean, C. R.; Layard, P. R. G. and Nickell, S. J., eds.*, 1986, pp. 23–34.

Solow, Robert M. Unemployment: Getting the Questions Right. *Economica*, Supplement 1986, *53*(210(S)), pp. S23–34.

Sparks, Roger. A Model of Involuntary Unemployment and Wage Rigidity: Worker Incentives and the Threat of Dismissal. *J. Lab. Econ.*, October 1986, *4*(4), pp. 560–81.

Steele, G. R. A Note on Labour Market Monopsony. *Indian Econ. J.*, Oct.-Dec. 1986, *34*(2), pp. 59–64.

Steindl, Alois, et al. On the Optimality of Cyclical Employment Policies: A Numerical Investigation. *J. Econ. Dynam. Control*, December 1986, *10*(4), pp. 457–66.

Stenius, Marianne and Virén, Matti. A Reply [Estimating a Disequilibrium Aggregate Labor Market Model] [Some Further Results on Rosen and Quandt's Labor Market Model]. *Eu-*

rop. Econ. Rev., April 1986, 30(2), pp. 461–62. **[G: U.S.]**

Stern, Jon. Repeat Unemployment Spells: The Effect of Unemployment Benefits on Unemployment Entry. **In** *Blundell, R. and Walker, I., eds.*, 1986, pp. 23–43. **[G: U.K.]**

Stern, Nicholas. On the Specification of Labour Supply Functions. **In** *Blundell, R. and Walker, I., eds.*, 1986, pp. 143–89.

Stewart, Mark B. A Symposium on the Role and Influence of Trade Unions in a Recession: Comments. *Brit. J. Ind. Relat.*, July 1986, *24*(2), pp. 205–08. **[G: U.K.]**

Stiglitz, Joseph E. Financial Markets and Macroeconomic Fluctuations: Comment. **In** *Butkiewicz, J. L.; Koford, K. J. and Miller, J. B., eds.*, 1986, pp. 144–45.

Stiglitz, Joseph E. Theories of Wage Rigidity. **In** *Butkiewicz, J. L.; Koford, K. J. and Miller, J. B., eds.*, 1986, pp. 153–206.

Stiglitz, Joseph E. Theories of Wage Rigidity: Reply. **In** *Butkiewicz, J. L.; Koford, K. J. and Miller, J. B., eds.*, 1986, pp. 219–21.

Sumner, Michael T. and Ward, Robert. Nonlinear Estimates of the UK Phillips Curve. *Econ. Notes*, 1986, (2), pp. 62–67. **[G: U.K.]**

Svejnar, Jan. Bargaining Power, Fear of Disagreement, and Wage Settlements: Theory and Evidence from U.S. Industry. *Econometrica*, September 1986, *54*(5), pp. 1055–78. **[G: U.S.]**

Svensson, Lars-Gunnar. National Income and Marginal Taxes. *Scand. J. Econ.*, 1986, *88*(4), pp. 565–81.

Tabellini, Guido. Rules, Discretion and the Provision of Employment Incentives. *Giorn. Econ.*, May-June 1986, *45*(5–6), pp. 243–50.

Tabuchi, Takatoshi. Urban Agglomeration, Capital Augmenting Technology, and Labor Market Equilibrium. *J. Urban Econ.*, September 1986, *20*(2), pp. 211–28. **[G: Japan]**

Taubman, Paul and Wachter, Michael L. Segmented Labor Markets. **In** *Ashenfelter, O. and Layard, R., eds., Vol. 2*, 1986, pp. 1183–1217.

Tedeschi, Piero. Wage, Effort, Monitoring Profiles and Agency Models. *Giorn. Econ.*, May-June 1986, *45*(5–6), pp. 251–62.

Tobin, James. Inflation and Unemployment in the Share Economy. *J. Compar. Econ.*, December 1986, *10*(4), pp. 460–63.

Todaro, Michael P. Internal Migration and Urban Employment: Comment. *Amer. Econ. Rev.*, June 1986, *76*(3), pp. 566–69. **[G: Mexico; India; Colombia; Nigeria]**

Topel, Robert. Job Mobility, Search, and Earnings Growth: A Reinterpretation of Human Capital Earnings Functions. **In** *Ehrenberg, R. G., ed., Pt. A*, 1986, pp. 199–233. **[G: U.S.]**

Tracy, Joseph S. Unions and the Share Economy. *J. Compar. Econ.*, December 1986, *10*(4), pp. 433–37.

Tunali, Insan. A General Structure for Models of Double-Selection and an Application to a Joint Migration/Earnings Process with Remigration. **In** *Ehrenberg, R. G., ed., Pt. B*, 1986, pp. 235–83. **[G: Turkey]**

Viscusi, W. Kip. Moral Hazard an Merit Rating over Time: An Analysis of Optimal Intertemporal Wage Structures. *Southern Econ. J.*, April 1986, *52*(4), pp. 1068–79.

Walz, Daniel T. and Spencer, Roger W. Expectations and the Phillips Curve: An Ex-Ante Approach. *Atlantic Econ. J.*, July 1986, *14*(2), pp. 26–30. **[G: U.S.]**

Weiss, Andrew M. Job Queues and Layoffs in Labor Markets with Flexible Wages. **In** *Akerlof, G. A. and Yellen, J. L., eds.*, 1986, *1980*, pp. 102–14. **[G: U.S.]**

Weiss, Laurence. Asymmetric Adjustment Costs and Sectoral Shifts. **In** *[Arrow, K. J.], Vol. 2*, 1986, pp. 251–64.

Weiss, Laurence. Efficiency Wage Theories: A Partial Evaluation: Comment. **In** *Fischer, S., ed.*, 1986, pp. 285–87. **[G: U.S.]**

Weitzman, Martin L. The Share Economy Symposium: A Reply. *J. Compar. Econ.*, December 1986, *10*(4), pp. 469–73.

Weitzman, Martin L. The Simple Macroeconomics of Profit-Sharing. **In** *Beckerman, W., ed.*, 1986, pp. 171–99.

Williamson, Oliver E. Transaction-Cost Economics: The Governance of Contractual Relations. **In** *Williamson, O. E.*, 1986, *1979*, pp. 101–30.

Williamson, Oliver E. What Is Transaction Cost Economics? **In** *Williamson, O. E.*, 1986, pp. 174–91.

Wilson, Thomas. Real Wages and Unemployment. *Banca Naz. Lavoro Quart. Rev.*, March 1986, (156), pp. 85–102. **[G: U.S.; U.K.]**

Wright, Randall. Job Search and Cyclical Unemployment. *J. Polit. Econ.*, February 1986, *94*(1), pp. 38–55.

Yaniv, Gideon. Absenteeism, Overtime, and the Compressed Workweek. *J. Behav. Econ.*, Spring/Summer 1986, *15*(1/2), pp. 211–19.

Yu, Eden S. H. and Ingene, Charles A. Resource Allocation in a General Equilibrium Model of Production under Uncertainty: The Case of Variable Supply of Labor. *J. Econ. Theory*, December 1986, *40*(2), pp. 329–37.

Zenezini, Maurizio. I salari e la curva di Phillips: alcune considerazioni sull'esperienza italiana e un commento ad un articolo di onofri e salituro. (Wages and Phillips Curve: A Comment. With English summary.) *Polit. Econ.*, December 1986, *2*(3), pp. 401–34. **[G: Italy]**

822 Public Policy; Role of Government

8220 General

Auld, Douglas. Human Resources and Social Support Policy in Canada. *Can. Public Policy*, Supp. February 1986, *12*, pp. 84–91. **[G: Canada]**

van den Berg, Ger P. Labor Law as a Restraint on the Soviet Economy. **In** *Ioffe, O. S. and Janis, M. W., eds.*, 1986, pp. 41–56. **[G: U.S.S.R.]**

Burbridge, Lynn C. Changes in Equal Employment Enforcement: What Enforcement Statistics Tell Us. *Rev. Black Polit. Econ.*, Summer 1986, *15*(1), pp. 71–80. **[G: U.S.]**

Bysiewicz, Shirley Raissi and Shelley, Louise I. Women in the Soviet Economy: Proclamations and Practice. **In** *Ioffe, O. S. and Janis, M. W., eds.*, 1986, pp. 57–77. **[G: U.S.S.R.]**

Carroll, Thomas M. Do Right-to-Work Laws Matter? Reply. *Southern Econ. J.*, October 1986, *53*(2), pp. 525–28. **[G: U.S.]**

Clark, Gordon L. Restructuring the U.S. Economy: The NLRB, the Saturn Project, and Economic Justice. *Econ. Geogr.*, October 1986, *62*(4), pp. 289–306. **[G: U.S.]**

Deakin, Simon. Labour Law and the Developing Employment Relationship in the UK. *Cambridge J. Econ.*, September 1986, *10*(3), pp. 225–46.

Endres, Anthony M. and Cook, Malcolm. Administering 'The Unemployed Difficulty': The N.S.W. Government Labour Bureau 1892–1912. *Australian Econ. Hist. Rev.*, March 1986, *26*(1), pp. 56–70. **[G: Australia]**

Horowitz, Donald L. The Deprivitization of Labor Relations Law. *Law Contemp. Probl.*, Autumn 1986, *49*(4), pp. 1–8. **[G: U.S.]**

Hughes, Helen. The Right to Work. *Australian Bull. Lab.*, September 1986, *12*(4), pp. 234–43. **[G: Australia]**

Lampert, Nick. Job Security and the Law in the USSR. **In** *Lane, D., ed.*, 1986, pp. 256–77. **[G: U.S.S.R.]**

Lewis, Gregory B. and Emmert, Mark A. The Sexual Division of Labor in Federal Employment. *Soc. Sci. Quart.*, March 1986, *67*(1), pp. 143–55. **[G: U.S.]**

Luskin, David. The Case for Subsidising Extra Jobs: A Comment. *Econ. J.*, March 1986, *96*(381), pp. 212–15. **[G: U.K.]**

Moore, William J.; Dunlevy, James A. and Newman, Robert J. Do Right to Work Laws Matter? Comment. *Southern Econ. J.*, October 1986, *53*(2), pp. 515–24. **[G: U.S.]**

Nelson, Richard R. State Labor Legislation Enacted in 1985. *Mon. Lab. Rev.*, January 1986, *109*(1), pp. 34–54. **[G: U.S.]**

Piore, Michael J. A Critique of Reagan's Labor Policy. *Challenge*, Mar./Apr. 1986, *29*(1), pp. 48–54. **[G: U.S.]**

Servais, J. M. Flexibility and Rigidity in International Labour Standards. *Int. Lab. Rev.*, Mar.-Apr. 1986, *125*(2), pp. 193–208.

8221 Wages and Hours

Abbott, Michael G. Labour Economics Research of the Macdonald Commission: A Review of Volumes 17 and 18. *Can. Public Policy*, December 1986, *12*(4), pp. 628–39. **[G: Canada]**

Bloom, David E. and Freeman, Richard B. The Effects of Rapid Population Growth on Labor Supply and Employment in Developing Countries. *Population Devel. Rev.*, September 1986, *12*(3), pp. 381–414. **[G: LDCs]**

Cameron, Trudy Ann. Some Reflections on Comparable Worth. *Contemp. Policy Issues*, April 1986, *4*(2), pp. 33–39. **[G: U.S.]**

Carrica, J. L. Just Wages: The Law and Morality. *Int. J. Soc. Econ.*, 1986, *13*(9), pp. 17–24.

Colombino, Ugo. Orari di lavoro come strumento di selezione in un modello con informazione asimmetrica. (Hours of Work as a Selection Mechanism in a Model with Asymmetric Information. With English summary.) *Econ. Lavoro*, Jan.-Mar. 1986, *20*(1), pp. 77–86.

Cox, James C. and Oaxaca, Ronald L. Minimum Wage Effects with Output Stabilization. *Econ. Inquiry*, July 1986, *24*(3), pp. 443–54. **[G: U.S.]**

DePoy, Marilyn; Huber, Vandra and Mangum, Stephen L. Comparable Worth Is in the Eye of the Beholder. *J. Policy Anal. Manage.*, Fall 1986, *6*(1), pp. 98–101. **[G: U.S.]**

Drazen, Allan. Optimal Minimum Wage Legislation. *Econ. J.*, September 1986, *96*(383), pp. 774–84.

Ehrenberg, Ronald G. Workers' Rights: Rethinking Protective Labor Legislation. **In** *Ehrenberg, R. G., ed., Pt. B*, 1986, pp. 285–317. **[G: U.S.]**

Faxén, Karl-Olof. Quasi-monopoly Profits, Barriers to Entry and the Welfare State: Their Impact on Labor Markets in Industrialized Countries: Comment. **In** *Day, R. H. and Eliasson, G., eds.*, 1986, pp. 435–41. **[G: OECD]**

Flug, Karnit and Galor, Oded. Minimum Wage in a General Equilibrium Model of International Trade and Human Capital. *Int. Econ. Rev.*, February 1986, *27*(1), pp. 149–64.

Gregory, R. G. Wages Policy and Unemployment in Australia. *Economica*, Supplement 1986, *53*(210(S)), pp. S53–74. **[G: Australia]**

Guiso, Luigi and Terlizzese, Daniele. Shock temporanei e aggiustamento dinamico: una interpretazione contrattuale della cassa integrazione guadagni. (Temporary Shocks and Dynamic Adjustment: A Contractual Interpretation of the Wage Supplementation Fund. With English summary.) *Giorn. Econ.*, Nov.-Dec. 1986, *45*(11–12), pp. 653–80. **[G: Italy]**

Hince, Kevin. Wage Fixing in a Period of Change: The New Zealand Case. *Int. Lab. Rev.*, July-Aug. 1986, *125*(4), pp. 463–72. **[G: New Zealand]**

Johnson, George and Solon, Gary. Estimates of the Direct Effects of Comparable Worth Policy. *Amer. Econ. Rev.*, December 1986, *76*(5), pp. 1117–25. **[G: U.S.]**

Laurent, André. The Elimination of Sex Discrimination in Occupational Social Security Schemes in the EEC. *Int. Lab. Rev.*, Nov.-Dec. 1986, *125*(6), pp. 675–83. **[G: EEC]**

Lerda, Juan Carlos. A política salarial do período 1979/85: alguns aspectos dinâmicos. (With English summary.) *Pesquisa Planejamento Econ.*, August 1986, *16*(2), pp. 467–92. **[G: Brazil]**

Megdal, Sharon Bernstein. Comparable Worth: Some Issues for Consideration. *Contemp. Policy Issues*, April 1986, *4*(2), pp. 40–51.

Meyerson, Per-Martin. Quasi-monopoly Profits,

Barriers to Entry and the Welfare State: Their Impact on Labor Markets in Industrialized Countries: Comment. **In** *Day, R. H. and Eliasson, G., eds.*, 1986, pp. 442–46. **[G: OECD]**

O'Connell, John F. The Effects of Davis–Bacon on Labor Cost and Union Wages. *J. Lab. Res.*, Summer 1986, *7*(3), pp. 239–53. **[G: U.S.]**

O'Neill, June. Issues Surrounding Comparable Worth: Introduction. *Contemp. Policy Issues*, April 1986, *4*(2), pp. 1–3. **[G: U.S.]**

Oi, Walter Y. Neglected Women and Other Implications of Comparable Worth. *Contemp. Policy Issues*, April 1986, *4*(2), pp. 21–32. **[G: U.S.; Japan]**

Paulsen, George E. Ghost of the NRA: Drafting National Wage and Hour Legislation in 1937. *Soc. Sci. Quart.*, June 1986, *67*(2), pp. 241–54. **[G: U.S.]**

Raisian, John; Ward, Michael P. and Welch, Finis. Pay Equity and Comparable Worth. *Contemp. Policy Issues*, April 1986, *4*(2), pp. 4–20. **[G: U.S.]**

Register, Charles A. and Williams, Donald R. Some Evidence on the Impact of State-Level Equal Rights Legislation. *Soc. Sci. Quart.*, December 1986, *67*(4), pp. 869–76. **[G: U.S.]**

Reid, Frank. Combatting Unemployment through Work Time Reductions. *Can. Public Policy*, June 1986, *12*(2), pp. 275–85. **[G: Canada]**

Santiago, Carlos E. Closing the Gap: The Employment and Unemployment Effects of Minimum Wage Policy in Puerto Rico. *J. Devel. Econ.*, October 1986, *23*(2), pp. 293–311. **[G: Puerto Rico]**

Spinanger, Dean. Quasi-monopoly Profits, Barriers to Entry and the Welfare State: Their Impact on Labor Markets in Industrialized Countries: Reply. **In** *Day, R. H. and Eliasson, G., eds.*, 1986, pp. 447–48. **[G: OECD]**

Spinanger, Dean. Quasi-monopoly Profits, Barriers to Entry and the Welfare State: Their Impact on Labor Markets in Industrialized Countries. **In** *Day, R. H. and Eliasson, G., eds.*, 1986, pp. 411–34. **[G: OECD]**

Spinanger, Dean. Work Incentives, Wage Differentials and the Supply of Human Resources. **In** *Balassa, B. and Giersch, H., eds.*, 1986, pp. 140–58. **[G: U.S.]**

Stigler, George J. The Economics of Minimum Wage Legislation. **In** *Stigler, G. J.*, 1986, *1946*, pp. 3–12. **[G: U.S.]**

8222 Workmen's Compensation and Vocational Rehabilitation

Barth, Peter S. On Efforts to Reform Workers' Compensation for Occupational Diseases. **In** *Chelius, J., ed.*, 1986, pp. 327–45. **[G: U.S.]**

Berkowitz, Monroe. The Administration of Workers' Compensation. **In** *Chelius, J., ed.*, 1986, pp. 237–49. **[G: U.S.]**

Berkowitz, Monroe and Hill, M. Anne. Disability and the Labor Market: An Overview. **In** *Berkowitz, M. and Hill, M. A., eds.*, 1986, pp. 1–28. **[G: U.S.]**

Boden, Leslie I. Problems in Occupational Disease Compensation. **In** *Chelius, J., ed.*, 1986, pp. 313–25. **[G: U.S.]**

Burkhauser, Richard V. Disability Policy in the United States, Sweden, and the Netherlands. **In** *Berkowitz, M. and Hill, M. A., eds.*, 1986, pp. 262–84. **[G: U.S.; Sweden; Netherlands]**

Burton, John F., Jr. and Krueger, Alan B. Interstate Variations in the Employers' Costs of Workers' Compensation, with Particular Reference to Connecticut, New Jersey, and New York. **In** *Chelius, J., ed.*, 1986, pp. 111–208. **[G: U.S.]**

Butler, Richard J. and Worrall, John D. The Costs of Workers' Compensation Insurance: Private versus Public. *J. Law Econ.*, October 1986, *29*(2), pp. 329–56. **[G: U.S.]**

Chelius, James R. The Status and Direction of Workers' Compensation: An Introduction to Current Issues. **In** *Chelius, J., ed.*, 1986, pp. 1–15. **[G: U.S.]**

Collignon, Frederick C. The Role of Reasonable Accommodation in Employing Disabled Persons in Private Industry. **In** *Berkowitz, M. and Hill, M. A., eds.*, 1986, pp. 196–241. **[G: U.S.]**

Halpern, Janice and Hausman, Jerry A. Choice under Uncertainty: Labour Supply and the Decision to Apply for Disability Insurance. **In** *Blundell, R. and Walker, I., eds.*, 1986, pp. 294–302. **[G: U.S.]**

Hunt, H. Allan. Two Rounds of Workers' Compensation Reform in Michigan. **In** *Chelius, J., ed.*, 1986, pp. 55–84. **[G: U.S.]**

Johnson, William G. The Rehabilitation Act and Discrimination against Handicapped Workers: Does the Cure Fit the Disease? **In** *Berkowitz, M. and Hill, M. A., eds.*, 1986, pp. 242–61. **[G: U.S.]**

Keefe, Steve. The Minnesota Experience with Workers' Compensation Reform. **In** *Chelius, J., ed.*, 1986, pp. 17–43. **[G: U.S.]**

Kriulin, G. A. Disability Prevention and Vocational Rehabilitation of the Disabled in the Byelorussian SSR. *Int. Lab. Rev.*, Mar.-Apr. 1986, *125*(2), pp. 209–25. **[G: U.S.S.R.]**

Lambrinos, James and Appel, David. Workers' Compensation and Employment: An Industry Analysis. **In** *Berkowitz, M. and Hill, M. A., eds.*, 1986, pp. 124–41. **[G: U.S.]**

Leonard, Jonathan S. Labor Supply Incentives and Disincentives for Disabled Persons. **In** *Berkowitz, M. and Hill, M. A., eds.*, 1986, pp. 64–94. **[G: U.S.]**

Lewis, John H. The Politics of Workers' Compensation Reform. **In** *Chelius, J., ed.*, 1986, pp. 85–103. **[G: U.S.]**

McIntosh, Barbara. Accident Compensation as a Factor Influencing Managerial Perceptions and Behavior in New Zealand. **In** *Chelius, J., ed.*, 1986, pp. 347–72. **[G: New Zealand]**

Murray, Michael L. An Alternative to Workers' Compensation—24 Hour Benefits. *J. Risk Ins.*, December 1986, *53*(4), pp. 744–54. **[G: U.S.]**

Price, Daniel N. Workers' Compensation: Coverage, Benefits, and Costs, 1983. *Soc. Sec. Bull.*, February 1986, *49*(2), pp. 5–11. **[G: U.S.]**

Richards, John and Carruth, Alan A. Short-Time Working and the Unemployment Benefit System in Great Britain. *Oxford Bull. Econ. Statist.*, February 1986, *48*(1), pp. 41–59. **[G: U.K.]**

Smith, Robert Stewart. The Economics of Job Displacement. **In** *Berkowitz, M. and Hill, M. A., eds.*, 1986, pp. 171–95.

Spatz, Donald L. Issues in Asbestos Disease Compensation. **In** *Chelius, J., ed.*, 1986, pp. 287–311. **[G: U.S.]**

Staten, Michael. Discussion of Papers on Recent State Reforms. **In** *Chelius, J., ed.*, 1986, pp. 105–09.

Staten, Michael and Umbeck, John. A Study of Signaling Behavior in Occupational Disease Claims. *J. Law Econ.*, October 1986, *29*(2), pp. 263–86. **[G: U.S.]**

Tebb, Alan. The 1982 Changes in California. **In** *Chelius, J., ed.*, 1986, pp. 45–54. **[G: U.S.]**

Thornton, Craig and Maynard, Rebecca. The Economics of Transitional Employment and Supported Employment. **In** *Berkowitz, M. and Hill, M. A., eds.*, 1986, pp. 142–70. **[G: U.S.]**

Tinsley, LaVerne C. Key Workers' Compensation Laws Enacted by States in 1985. *Mon. Lab. Rev.*, January 1986, *109*(1), pp. 61–66. **[G: U.S.]**

Viscusi, W. Kip. The Valuation of Risks to Life and Health: Guidelines for Policy Analysis. **In** *Bentkover, J. D.; Covello, V. T. and Jeryl, M., eds.*, 1986, pp. 8510. **[G: U.S.]**

Weaver, Carolyn L. Social Security Disability Policy in the 1980s and Beyond. **In** *Berkowitz, M. and Hill, M. A., eds.*, 1986, pp. 29–63. **[G: U.S.]**

Williams, C. Arthur, Jr. Workers' Compensation Insurance Rates: Their Determination and Regulation: A Regional Perspective. **In** *Chelius, J., ed.*, 1986, pp. 209–35. **[G: U.S.]**

Worrall, John D. Nominal Costs, Nominal Prices, and Nominal Profits. **In** *Chelius, J., ed.*, 1986, pp. 251–56. **[G: U.S.]**

Worrall, John D. and Butler, Richard J. Some Lessons from the Workers' Compensation Program. **In** *Berkowitz, M. and Hill, M. A., eds.*, 1986, pp. 95–123. **[G: U.S.]**

8223 Factory Act and Safety Legislation

Barth, Peter S. On Efforts to Reform Workers' Compensation for Occupational Diseases. **In** *Chelius, J., ed.*, 1986, pp. 327–45. **[G: U.S.]**

Boden, Leslie I. Problems in Occupational Disease Compensation. **In** *Chelius, J., ed.*, 1986, pp. 313–25. **[G: U.S.]**

Carmichael, H. Lorne. Reputations for Safety: Market Performance and Policy Remedies. *J. Lab. Econ.*, October 1986, *4*(4), pp. 458–72.

Chelius, James R. The Status and Direction of Workers' Compensation: An Introduction to Current Issues. **In** *Chelius, J., ed.*, 1986, pp. 1–15. **[G: U.S.]**

Cotter, Diane M. Work-related Deaths in 1984: BLS Survey Findings. *Mon. Lab. Rev.*, May 1986, *109*(5), pp. 42–46. **[G: U.S.]**

Cox, Louis Anthony, Jr. Theory of Regulatory Benefits Assessment: Econometric and Expressed Preference Approaches. **In** *Bentkover, J. D.; Covello, V. T. and Jeryl, M., eds.*, 1986, pp. 85–159. **[G: U.S.]**

Craigie, Rowen; Cumpston, Richard and Sams, Dennis. Accident Compensation Reform. *Australian Econ. Rev.*, 3rd Quarter 1986, (75), pp. 9–30. **[G: Australia]**

Curington, William P. Safety Regulation and Workplace Injuries. *Southern Econ. J.*, July 1986, *53*(1), pp. 51–72. **[G: U.S.]**

Dewees, Donald N. and Daniels, Ronald J. The Cost of Protecting Occupational Health: The Asbestos Case. *J. Human Res.*, Summer 1986, *21*(3), pp. 381–96. **[G: U.S.; Canada]**

Dickens, William T. Safety Regulation and "Irrational" Behavior. **In** *Gilad, B. and Kaish, S., eds., Vol. A*, 1986, pp. 325–48.

Elisburg, Donald. Federal Occupational Disease Legislation: A Current Review. **In** *Chelius, J., ed.*, 1986, pp. 257–85. **[G: U.S.]**

Fishback, Price V. Workplace Safety during the Progressive Era: Fatal Accidents in Bituminous Coal Mining, 1912–1923. *Exploration Econ. Hist.*, July 1986, *23*(3), pp. 269–98. **[G: U.S.]**

House, James S. and Cottington, Eric M. Health and the Workplace. **In** *Aiken, L. H. and Mechanic, D., eds.*, 1986, pp. 392–416. **[G: U.S.]**

Hughes, John S.; Magat, Wesley A. and Ricks, William E. The Economic Consequences of the OSHA Cotton Dust Standards: An Analysis of Stock Price Behavior. *J. Law Econ.*, April 1986, *29*(1), pp. 29–59. **[G: U.S.]**

Jahnke, Wilfried. Simulation verschiedener Strategien zur Verringerung der Arbeitslosigkeit. (Simulation of Alternative Policies to Reduce Unemployment. With English summary.) *Z. Wirtschaft. Sozialwissen.*, 1986, *106*(6), pp. 557–78. **[G: W. Germany]**

Leger, J. P. Safety and the Organisation of Work in South African Gold Mines: A Crisis of Control. *Int. Lab. Rev.*, Sept.-Oct. 1986, *125*(5), pp. 591–603. **[G: S. Africa]**

Linsenmayer, Tadd. ILO Adopts Asbestos Standard; Focuses on Employment Issues. *Mon. Lab. Rev.*, October 1986, *109*(10), pp. 31–32.

Litan, Robert E. and Nordhaus, William D. Regulatory Reform and OSHA Policy: Comments. *J. Policy Anal. Manage.*, Spring 1986, *5*(3), pp. 467–81. **[G: U.S.]**

McIntosh, Barbara. Accident Compensation as a Factor Influencing Managerial Perceptions and Behavior in New Zealand. **In** *Chelius, J., ed.*, 1986, pp. 347–72. **[G: New Zealand]**

Mendeloff, John. Regulatory Reform and OSHA Policy. *J. Policy Anal. Manage.*, Spring 1986, *5*(3), pp. 440–68. **[G: U.S.]**

Moye, William T. BLS and Alice Hamilton: Pioneers in Industrial Health. *Mon. Lab. Rev.*, June 1986, *109*(6), pp. 24–27. **[G: U.S.]**

822 Public Policy; Role of Government

Norman, N. R. Accident Compensation Reform: Comment. *Australian Econ. Rev.*, 3rd Quarter 1986, (75), pp. 31–32. [G: Australia]

Sass, Robert. The Need to Broaden the Legal Concept of Risk in Workplace Health and Safety. *Can. Public Policy*, June 1986, *12*(2), pp. 286–93. [G: Canada]

Schroeder, Elinor P. Legislative and Judicial Responses to the Inadequacy of Compensation for Occupational Disease. *Law Contemp. Probl.*, Autumn 1986, *49*(4), pp. 151–82. [G: U.S.]

Smith, Robert Stewart. Greasing the Squeaky Wheel: The Relative Productivity of OSHA Complaint Inspections. *Ind. Lab. Relat. Rev.*, October 1986, *40*(1), pp. 35–47. [G: U.S.]

Spatz, Donald L. Issues in Asbestos Disease Compensation. In *Chelius, J., ed.*, 1986, pp. 287–311. [G: U.S.]

Szasz, Andrew. The Reversal of Federal Policy toward Worker Safety and Health. *Sci. Soc.*, Spring 1986, *50*(1), pp. 25–51. [G: U.S.]

Viscusi, W. Kip. Reforming OSHA Regulation of Workplace Risks. In *Weiss, L. W. and Klass, M. W., eds.*, 1986, pp. 234–68. [G: U.S.]

Viscusi, W. Kip. Regulatory Reform and OSHA Policy: The Status of OSHA Reform: A Comment on Mendeloff's Proposals. *J. Policy Anal. Manage.*, Spring 1986, *5*(3), pp. 469–75. [G: U.S.]

Viscusi, W. Kip. The Structure and Enforcement of Job Safety Regulation. *Law Contemp. Probl.*, Autumn 1986, *49*(4), pp. 127–50. [G: U.S.]

Weiss, Peter; Maier, Gunther and Gerking, Shelby. The Economic Evaluation of Job Safety: A Methodological Survey and Some Estimates for Austria. *Empirica*, 1986, *13*(1), pp. 53–67. [G: Austria]

8224 Unemployment Insurance

Abbott, Michael G. Labour Economics Research of the Macdonald Commission: A Review of Volumes 17 and 18. *Can. Public Policy*, December 1986, *12*(4), pp. 628–39. [G: Canada]

Adams, James D. Equilibrium Taxation and Experience Rating in a Federal System of Unemployment Insurance. *J. Public Econ.*, February 1986, *29*(1), pp. 51–77.

Balducci, Renato. Sussidi, occupazione e crescita. (Unemployment Benefits, Employment and Growth. With English summary.) *Giorn. Econ.*, Nov.-Dec. 1986, *45*(11–12), pp. 617–38.

Barron, John M.; McAfee, R. Preston and Speaker, Paul J. Unemployment Insurance and the Entitlement Effect: A Tax Incidence Approach. *Int. Econ. Rev.*, February 1986, *27*(1), pp. 175–85.

Blau, David M. and Robins, Philip K. Job Search, Wage Offers, and Unemployment Insurance. *J. Public Econ.*, March 1986, *29*(2), pp. 173–97. [G: U.S.]

Brown, Eleanor P. Unemployment Insurance Taxes and Cyclical Layoff Incentives. *J. Lab. Econ.*, January 1986, *4*(1), pp. 50–65. [G: U.S.]

Calcoen, F.; Eeckhoudt, L. and Outreville, J.-François. Indemnisation du chômage et revenus de remplacement: Une approche par la théorie de l'assurance. (Unemployment Insurance and Damage Insurance: An Approach through the Theory of Insurance. With English summary.) *Schweiz. Z. Volkswirtsch. Statist.*, September 1986, *122*(3), pp. 323–37.

Englander, Fred and Director, Steven M. Benefits Levels, Enforcement Stringency, and the Level of Initial Claims for Unemployment Insurance. *Southern Econ. J.*, April 1986, *52*(4), pp. 1140–44. [G: U.S.]

Gregory, R. G. Wages Policy and Unemployment in Australia. In *Bean, C. R.; Layard, P. R. G. and Nickell, S. J., eds.*, 1986, pp. 53–74. [G: Australia]

Hedges, Janice Neipert. Work Sharing: New Experiences: Discussion. In *Dennis, B. D., ed.*, 1986, pp. 453–56. [G: U.S.]

Jones, Stephen R. G. Unemployment Insurance and Involuntary Unemployment: The Case of Adverse Selection. *J. Public Econ.*, August 1986, *30*(3), pp. 317–28.

Kaiser, Carl P. Unemployment Insurance and the Theory of Labor Demand. *Eastern Econ. J.*, Apr.-June 1986, *12*(2), pp. 115–28.

Kerachsky, Stuart, et al. An Evaluation of Short-Time Compensation Programs. In *Dennis, B. D., ed.*, 1986, pp. 424–32. [G: U.S.]

Kesselman, Jonathan R. The Royal Commission's Proposals for Income Security Reform. *Can. Public Policy*, Supp. February 1986, *12*, pp. 101–12. [G: Canada]

Kingston, Jerry L.; Burgess, Paul L. and St. Louis, Robert D. Unemployment Insurance Overpayments: Evidence and Implication. *Ind. Lab. Relat. Rev.*, April 1986, *39*(3), pp. 323–36. [G: U.S.]

Lardaro, Leonard. Unused Benefit Weeks as a Work Disincentive: Does the Entitlement Effect of UI Always Offset the Work Disincentive Effect? In *Dennis, B. D., ed.*, 1986, pp. 409–17. [G: U.S.]

Leigh, J. Paul. Unemployment Insurance and the Duration of Unemployment: The Case for Reciprocal Effects. *J. Post Keynesian Econ.*, Spring 1986, *8*(3), pp. 387–99. [G: U.S.]

Meltz, Noah M. Work-Sharing: New Experiences: Discussion. In *Dennis, B. D., ed.*, 1986, pp. 449–52. [G: U.S.]

Metcalf, David. Employment-Subsidies and Redundancies. In *Blundell, R. and Walker, I., eds.*, 1986, pp. 103–20. [G: U.K.]

Micklewright, John. Unemployment and Incentives to Work: Policy and Evidence in the 1980s. In *Hart, P. E., ed.*, 1986, pp. 104–20. [G: U.K.]

Miller, Nancy, et al. Social Security Programs in the United States. *Soc. Sec. Bull.*, January 1986, *49*(1), pp. 5–59. [G: U.S.]

Morand, Martin J. Work Sharing: New Experiences: Discussion. **In** *Dennis, B. D., ed.*, 1986, pp. 457–64. **[G: U.S.]**

Morris, Nick. Unemployment and Incentives to Work: Policy and Evidence in the 1980s: Comment. **In** *Hart, P. E., ed.*, 1986, pp. 121–26. **[G: U.K.]**

Oaxaca, Ronald L. and Taylor, Carol A. Simulating the Impacts of Economic Programs on Urban Areas: The Case of Unemployment Insurance Benefits. *J. Urban Econ.*, January 1986, *19*(1), pp. 23–46. **[G: U.S.]**

Oswald, Andrew J. Unemployment Insurance and Labor Contracts under Asymmetric Information: Theory and Facts. *Amer. Econ. Rev.*, June 1986, *76*(3), pp. 365–77. **[G: U.S.]**

Pedersen, Peter J. and Westergård-Nielsen, Niels. A Longitudinal Study of Unemployment: History Dependence and Insurance Effects. **In** *Blundell, R. and Walker, I., eds.*, 1986, pp. 44–59. **[G: Denmark]**

Pini, Paolo. Durata di ricerca di un posto di lavoro e sussidi di disoccupazione. (Duration of Unemployment and Unemployment Benefits. With English summary.) *Ricerche Econ.*, Jan.-Mar. 1986, *40*(1), pp. 50–81. **[G: U.S.; U.K.; Italy]**

Rice, Patricia G. Juvenile Unemployment, Relative Wages and Social Security: The Econometric Evidence. **In** *Blundell, R. and Walker, I., eds.*, 1986, pp. 60–74. **[G: U.K.]**

Runner, Diana. Changes in Unemployment Insurance Legislation during 1985. *Mon. Lab. Rev.*, January 1986, *109*(1), pp. 55–60. **[G: U.S.]**

Schiff, Frank W. Issues in Assessing Work-Sharing. **In** *Dennis, B. D., ed.*, 1986, pp. 433–40. **[G: U.S.]**

Scott, Cuthbert L., III. Effects of Differing Unemployment Insurance Taxable Wage Bases on System Capacity. *J. Risk Ins.*, September 1986, *53*(3), pp. 454–70. **[G: U.S.]**

Spenceley, G. F. R. Responses to Unemployment in Australia: The 1930s and Now. **In** *Berend, I. T. and Borchardt, K., eds.*, 1986, pp. 82–105. **[G: Australia]**

St. Louis, Robert D.; Burgess, Paul L. and Kingston, Jerry L. Reported vs. Actual Job Search by Unemployment Insurance Claimants. *J. Human Res.*, Winter 1986, *21*(1), pp. 92–117. **[G: U.S.]**

Stern, Jon. Repeat Unemployment Spells: The Effect of Unemployment Benefits on Unemployment Entry. **In** *Blundell, R. and Walker, I., eds.*, 1986, pp. 23–43. **[G: U.K.]**

Williams, Donald R. Contributed Papers: Labor Economics and Labor Markets: Discussion. **In** *Dennis, B. D., ed.*, 1986, pp. 418–23.

Wright, Randall. The Redistributive Roles of Unemployment Insurance and the Dynamics of Voting. *J. Public Econ.*, December 1986, *31*(3), pp. 377–99.

Yaniv, Gideon. Fraudulent Collection of Unemployment Benefits: A Theoretical Analysis with Reference to Income Tax Evasion. *J. Public Econ.*, August 1986, *30*(3), pp. 369–83.

Zalusky, John. Labor's Interest and Concerns with Short-Time Compensation. **In** *Dennis, B. D., ed.*, 1986, pp. 441–48. **[G: U.S.]**

8225 Government Employment Policies (including employment services)

Bellemare, Diane and Poulin-Simon, Lise. Le plein emploi: objectif et stratégie économique. (Full Employment: An Objective and an Economic Strategy. With English summary.) *Écon. Soc.*, April 1986, *20*(4), pp. 345–90. **[G: Canada]**

Bendick, Marc, Jr. Government's Role in the Job Transitions of U.S. Dislocated Workers. **In** *Redburn, F. S.; Buss, T. F. and Ledebur, L. C., eds.*, 1986, pp. 158–75. **[G: U.S.]**

Bishop, John H. and Montgomery, Mark. Evidence on Firm Participation in Employment Subsidy Programs. *Ind. Relat.*, Winter 1986, *25*(1), pp. 56–64. **[G: U.S.]**

Bottazzi, Gianfranco and Moscati, Roberto. I contratti di formazione lavoro nel mezzogiorno: riflessioni sui risultati di una ricerca. (Implementation of the "Employment and Training Contracts" in Southern Italy. With English summary.) *Econ. Lavoro*, Oct.-Dec. 1986, *20*(4), pp. 87–104. **[G: Italy]**

Burkhauser, Richard V. Disability Policy in the United States, Sweden, and the Netherlands. **In** *Berkowitz, M. and Hill, M. A., eds.*, 1986, pp. 262–84. **[G: U.S.; Sweden; Netherlands]**

Buvinić, Mayra. Projects for Women in Third World: Explaining Their Misbehavior. *World Devel.*, May 1986, *14*(5), pp. 653–64. **[G: LDCs]**

Calmfors, Lars and Horn, Henrik. Employment Policies and Centralized Wage-Setting. *Economica*, August 1986, *53*(211), pp. 281–302.

Canto, Victor A.; Kadlec, Charles W. and Laffer, Arthur B. The Productive Employment Program: A New Approach to Fighting Unemployment. **In** *Canto, V. A.; Kadlec, C. W. and Laffer, A. B., eds.*, 1986, pp. 160–88. **[G: U.S.]**

Cassels, John. Unemployment and Labour Market Policies: Introduction. **In** *Hart, P. E., ed.*, 1986, pp. 1–4.

Chambers, Julius L. and Goldstein, Barry. Title VII: The Continuing Challenge of Establishing Fair Employment Practices. *Law Contemp. Probl.*, Autumn 1986, *49*(4), pp. 9–23. **[G: U.S.]**

Clay, Edward J. Rural Public Works and Food-for-Work: A Survey. *World Devel.*, Oct./Nov. 1986, *14*(10/11), pp. 1237–52. **[G: LDCs]**

Cooley, Mike and Murphy, Shaun. Jobs and Human-Centred Production. **In** *Nolan, P. and Paine, S., eds.*, 1986, pp. 284–90. **[G: U.K.]**

De Wachter, Marcia and Somers, Yolanda. Job Creation Programs in an International Comparison. *Rech. Écon. Louvain*, 1986, *52*(3–4), pp. 413–37. **[G: EEC]**

Deshpande, L. K. The Seventh Plan and Some Aspects of Employment. *Indian Econ. J.*, Apr.-June 1986, *33*(4), pp. 98–105. **[G: India]**

Garonna, Paolo. Youth Unemployment, Labour

Market Deregulation and Union Stategies in Italy. *Brit. J. Ind. Relat.*, March 1986, *24*(1), pp. 43–61. **[G: Italy]**

Gateau, Gilles and Tremblay, Diane. TUC et travaux communautaires: les enjeux de l'insertion/exclusion des jeunes. (Community Jobs and TUC: Integration or Exclusion of Youth? With English summary.) *Écon. Soc.*, April 1986, *20*(4), pp. 261–304.

Hansen, Gary B. U.S. Employment and Training Policy: A Twenty-five Year Review, 1960–1985. *Econ. Lavoro*, July-Sept. 1986, *20*(3), pp. 141–47. **[G: U.S.]**

Hart, Peter E. and Trinder, C. Employment Protection, National Insurance, Income Tax and Youth Unemployment. **In** *Hart, P. E., ed.*, 1986, pp. 29–44. **[G: U.K.]**

Kasarda, John D. Transforming Cities and Employment Policy for Displaced Workers. **In** *Bergman, E. M., ed.*, 1986, *1983*, pp. 286–307. **[G: U.S.]**

Kesselman, Jonathan R. The Royal Commission's Proposals for Income Security Reform. *Can. Public Policy*, Supp. February 1986, *12*, pp. 101–12. **[G: Canada]**

King, Kenneth. Manpower, Technology, and Employment in Africa: Internal and External Policy Agendas. **In** *Berg, R. J. and Whitaker, J. S., eds.*, 1986, pp. 422–50. **[G: Africa]**

Layard, Richard; Metcalf, David and O'Brien, Richard. A New Deal for the Long-term Unemployed. **In** *Hart, P. E., ed.*, 1986, pp. 181–90. **[G: U.K.]**

Levin, Martin and Ferman, Barbara. The Political Hand: Policy Implementation and Youth Employment Programs. *J. Policy Anal. Manage.*, Winter 1986, *5*(2), pp. 311–25. **[G: U.S.]**

Lindley, Robert. Labour Demand: Microeconomic Aspects of State Intervention. **In** *Hart, P. E., ed.*, 1986, pp. 154–75. **[G: U.K.]**

Lobban, Peter. A New Deal for the Long-term Unemployed: Comment. **In** *Hart, P. E., ed.*, 1986, pp. 191–92. **[G: U.K.]**

McArthur, Andrew and McGregor, Alan. Policies for the Disadvantaged in the Labour Market. **In** *Lever, W. and Moore, C., eds.*, 1986, pp. 120–41. **[G: U.K.]**

Metcalf, David. Employment-Subsidies and Redundancies. **In** *Blundell, R. and Walker, I., eds.*, 1986, pp. 103–20. **[G: U.K.]**

Michon, François. Flexibilité et Partages. Les enjeux de la Solidarité. (Flexibilities and Work Sharing. A Search for Solidarity. With English summary.) *Écon. Soc.*, April 1986, *20*(4), pp. 77–104.

Odling-Smee, John. Labour Demand: Microeconomic Aspects of State Intervention: Comment. **In** *Hart, P. E., ed.*, 1986, pp. 176–79. **[G: U.K.]**

Panpiemras, Kosit and Phongpaichit, Pasuk. Policy Guidelines for Human Resource Development and Employment Generation in Thailand. **In** *Shand, R. T., ed., Vol. 1*, 1986, pp. 175–98. **[G: Thailand]**

Petit, Pascal. Full-employment Policies in Stagnation: France in the 1980s. *Cambridge J. Econ.*, December 1986, *10*(4), pp. 393–406. **[G: France]**

Reed, Merl E. Black Workers, Defense Industries, and Federal Agencies in Pennsylvania, 1941–1945. *Labor Hist.*, Summer 1986, *27*(3), pp. 356–84. **[G: U.S.]**

Ridder, G. An Event History Approach to the Evaluation of Training, Recruitment and Employment Programmes. *J. Appl. Econometrics*, April 1986, *1*(2), pp. 109–26. **[G: Netherlands]**

Ripley, Randall B. and Franklin, Grace A. The Private Sector, Public Employment and Training Programs, and Economic Revitalization. **In** *Redburn, F. S.; Buss, T. F. and Ledebur, L. C., eds.*, 1986, pp. 176–99. **[G: U.S.]**

Robertson, James. How the Cities Can Finance New Enterprise. *Lloyds Bank Rev.*, July 1986, (161), pp. 32–43.

Robinson, Olive. Employment Protection, National Insurance, Income Tax and Youth Unemployment: Comment. **In** *Hart, P. E., ed.*, 1986, pp. 45–49. **[G: U.K.]**

Smith, Robert Stewart. The Economics of Job Displacement. **In** *Berkowitz, M. and Hill, M. A., eds.*, 1986, pp. 171–95.

Steindl, Alois, et al. On the Optimality of Cyclical Employment Policies: A Numerical Investigation. *J. Econ. Dynam. Control*, December 1986, *10*(4), pp. 457–66.

Stiglitz, Joseph E. Financial Markets and Macroeconomic Fluctuations: Comment. **In** *Butkiewicz, J. L.; Koford, K. J. and Miller, J. B., eds.*, 1986, pp. 144–45.

Thornton, Craig and Maynard, Rebecca. The Economics of Transitional Employment and Supported Employment. **In** *Berkowitz, M. and Hill, M. A., eds.*, 1986, pp. 142–70. **[G: U.S.]**

Tobin, James. High Time to Restore the Employment Act of 1946. *Challenge*, May/June 1986, *29*(2), pp. 4–12. **[G: U.S.]**

8226 Employment in the Public Sector

Avila, Jorge C. Reducción del Empleo Público Redundante, Capital Humano y Ajuste en una Economía Abierta. (Reducing Government Overmanning, Human Capital and Open-Economy Adjustment. With English summary.) *Económica (La Plata)*, July-December 1986, *32*(2), pp. 165–205. **[G: Argentina]**

Britton, Andrew. Employment Policy in the Public Sector. **In** *Hart, P. E., ed.*, 1986, pp. 128–46. **[G: U.K.]**

Callaghan, W. H. Employment Policy in the Public Sector: Comment. **In** *Hart, P. E., ed.*, 1986, pp. 147–51. **[G: U.K.]**

Ehrenberg, Ronald G. and Schwarz, Joshua L. Public-Sector Labor Markets. **In** *Ashenfelter, O. and Layard, R., eds., Vol. 2*, 1986, pp. 1219–68. **[G: U.S.]**

Eisinger, Peter. Local Civil Service Employment and Black Socioeconomic Mobility. *Soc. Sci. Quart.*, March 1986, *67*(1), pp. 169–75. **[G: U.S.]**

Horne, David K. and Weltin, Mary M. Motivation and Career Intentions. *J. Behav. Econ.*, Fall 1986, *15*, pp. 29–42. **[G: U.S.]**

Kerns, Wilmer L. Federal Employees' Retirement System Act of 1986. *Soc. Sec. Bull.*, November 1986, *49*(11), pp. 5–10. **[G: U.S.]**

Lewis, Gregory B. Gender and Promotions: Promotion Chances of White Men and Women in Federal White-Collar Employment. *J. Human Res.*, Summer 1986, *21*(3), pp. 406–19. **[G: U.S.]**

Shome, Parthasarathi. The Impact of Social Security Institutions on Resource Allocation. **In** *Shome, P., ed.*, 1986, pp. 198–219. **[G: Malaysia; Singapore; Thailand; India; Sri Lanka]**

Vatter, Harold G. and Walker, John F. Real Public Sector Employment Growth, Wagner's Law, and Economic Growth in the United States. *Public Finance*, 1986, *41*(1), pp. 116–38. **[G: U.S.]**

823 Labor Mobility; National and International Migration

8230 Labor Mobility; National and International Migration

Ahmed, Salehuddin. Rural–Urban Migration: Policy Simulations in a Dual Economy Model of Bangladesh. *Devel. Econ.*, March 1986, *24*(1), pp. 26–43. **[G: Bangladesh]**

Alba, Richard D. and Trent, Katherine. Population Loss and Change in the North: An Examination of New York's Migration to the Sunbelt. *Soc. Sci. Quart.*, December 1986, *67*(4), pp. 690–706. **[G: U.S.]**

Antel, John J. Human Capital Investment Specialization and the Wage Effects of Voluntary Labor Mobility. *Rev. Econ. Statist.*, August 1986, *68*(3), pp. 477–83. **[G: U.S.]**

Arnold, R. The Dynamics and Quality of Trans-Tasman Migration, 1885–1910. *Australian Econ. Hist. Rev.*, March 1986, *26*(1), pp. 1–20. **[G: Australia]**

Arnott, Richard J. and Gersovitz, Mark. Social Welfare Underpinnings of Urban Bias and Unemployment. *Econ. J.*, June 1986, *96*(382), pp. 413–24.

Becker, Charles M.; Mills, Edwin S. and Williamson, Jeffrey G. Dynamics of Rural–Urban Migration in India: 1960–1981. *Indian J. Quant. Econ.*, 1986, *2*(1), pp. 1–43. **[G: India]**

Becker, Charles M.; Mills, Edwin S. and Williamson, Jeffrey G. Modeling Indian Migration and City Growth, 1960–2000. *Econ. Develop. Cult. Change*, October 1986, *35*(1), pp. 1–33. **[G: India]**

Ben-Porath, Yoram. The Entwined Growth of Population and Product, 1922–1982. **In** *Ben-Porath, Y., ed.*, 1986, pp. 27–41. **[G: Israel]**

Bhagwati, Jagdish N. Incentives and Disincentives: International Migration. **In** *Balassa, B. and Giersch, H., eds.*, 1986, pp. 89–111. **[G: U.S.; W. Germany]**

Blau, David M. Self-employment, Earnings, and Mobility in Peninsular Malaysia. *World Devel.*, July 1986, *14*(7), pp. 839–52. **[G: Malaysia]**

Blomqvist, Ake G. International Migration of Educated Manpower and Social Rates of Return to Education in LDCs. *Int. Econ. Rev.*, February 1986, *27*(1), pp. 165–74. **[G: LDCs]**

Borjas, George J. Immigrants and the U.S. Labor Market. **In** *Pozo, S., ed.*, 1986, pp. 7–20. **[G: U.S.]**

Borjas, George J. The Self-Employment Experience of Immigrants. *J. Human Res.*, Fall 1986, *21*(4), pp. 485–506. **[G: U.S.]**

Boyer, George R. The Poor Law, Migration, and Economic Growth. *J. Econ. Hist.*, June 1986, *46*(2), pp. 419–30. **[G: U.K.]**

Camagni, Roberto. Innovation and the Urban Life-cycle: Production, Location and Income Distribution Aspects. **In** *Nijkamp, P., ed. (II)*, 1986, pp. 382–400. **[G: Italy]**

Canto, Victor A. and Udwadia, Firdaus E. The Effect of Immigration Quotas on the Average Quality of Migrating Labor and Income Distribution. *Southern Econ. J.*, January 1986, *52*(3), pp. 785–93.

Carvajal, Manuel J. and Upadhiaya, Anita. Propensity to Migrate Differentials by Poverty Status: An Empirical Test for Costa Rica. *J. Econ. Devel.*, December 1986, *11*(2), pp. 123–46. **[G: Costa Rica]**

Charney, Alberta H. and Taylor, Carol A. Integrated State–Substate Econometric Modeling: Design and Utilization for Long-run Economic Analysis. **In** *Perryman, M. R. and Schmidt, J. R., eds.*, 1986, pp. 43–92. **[G: U.S.]**

Chiswick, Barry R. Human Capital and the Labor Market Adjustment of Immigrants: Testing Alternative Hypotheses. **In** *Stark, O., ed.*, 1986, pp. 1–26. **[G: U.S.]**

Chiswick, Barry R. Illegal Aliens: A Preliminary Report on an Employee–Employer Survey. *Amer. Econ. Rev.*, May 1986, *76*(2), pp. 253–57. **[G: U.S.]**

Chiswick, Barry R. Is the New Immigration Less Skilled Than the Old? *J. Lab. Econ.*, April 1986, *4*(2), pp. 168–92. **[G: U.S.]**

Choucri, Nazli. The Hidden Economy: A New View of Remittances in the Arab World. *World Devel.*, June 1986, *14*(6), pp. 697–712. **[G: Middle East]**

Clark, Don P. and Thompson, Henry. Immigration, International Capital Flows, and Long Run Income Distribution in Canada. *Atlantic Econ. J.*, December 1986, *14*(4), pp. 24–29. **[G: Canada]**

Cole, William E. and Sanders, Richard D. Internal Migration and Urban Employment: Reply. *Amer. Econ. Rev.*, June 1986, *76*(3), pp. 570–72. **[G: Mexico; India; Colombia; Nigeria]**

Conway, Hugh and Anderson, Ewan. Kuwait's Labor Force: An Historical Perspective, Industrial Development, and Measures to Stabilize the Expatriate Labor Force. **In** *Roukis, G. S. and Montana, P. J., eds.*, 1986, pp. 139–56. **[G: Kuwait]**

Cortese, Antonio. La presenza straniera in Italia

al 1981: considerazioni sulla qualità dei risultati del censimento demografico. (Immigrants' Presence in Italy: An Evaluation of the 1981 Census Data. With English summary.) *Econ. Lavoro,* Oct.-Dec. 1986, *20*(4), pp. 39–58. **[G: Italy]**

Craver, Earlene. The Emigration of the Austrian Economists. *Hist. Polit. Econ.,* Spring 1986, *18*(1), pp. 1–32. **[G: Austria]**

Cushing, Brian J. Accounting for Spatial Relationships in Models of Interstate Population Migration. *Ann. Reg. Sci.,* July 1986, *20*(2), pp. 66–73. **[G: U.S.]**

Dahrendorf, Ralf, et al. Labour Market Flexibility. Report by a High-Level Group of Experts to the Secretary-General. *Econ. Lavoro,* July-Sept. 1986, *20*(3), pp. 3–19. **[G: OECD]**

Dendrinos, Dimitrios S. On the Incongruous Spatial Employment Dynamics. **In** *Nijkamp, P., ed. (II),* 1986, pp. 321–39.

van Dijk, Jouke and Folmer, Hendrik. The Consequences of Interregional Labor Migration for the Regional Labor Market: Theory, Methodology and Dutch Experience. *Rev. Econ. Statist.,* February 1986, *68*(1), pp. 74–83. **[G: Netherlands]**

Djajić, Slobodan. International Migration, Remittances and Welfare in a Dependent Economy. *J. Devel. Econ.,* May 1986, *21*(2), pp. 229–34.

Egan, Mary Lou and Bendick, Marc, Jr. The Urban–Rural Dimension in National Economic Development. *J. Devel. Areas,* January 1986, *20*(2), pp. 203–21. **[G: LDCs]**

Eichengreen, Barry and Gemery, Henry A. The Earnings of Skilled and Unskilled Immigrants at the End of the Nineteenth Century. *J. Econ. Hist.,* June 1986, *46*(2), pp. 441–54. **[G: U.S.]**

Engerman, Stanley L. Slavery and Emancipation in Comparative Perspective: A Look at Some Recent Debates. *J. Econ. Hist.,* June 1986, *46*(2), pp. 317–39. **[G: U.S.; Caribbean]**

Esser, Hartmut. Ethnic Segmentation as the Unintended Result of Intentional Action. **In** *[Rapoport, A.],* 1986, pp. 281–96.

Ethier, Wilfred J. Illegal Immigration. *Amer. Econ. Rev.,* May 1986, *76*(2), pp. 258–62.

Ethier, Wilfred J. Illegal Immigration: The Host-Country Problem. *Amer. Econ. Rev.,* March 1986, *76*(1), pp. 56–71.

Ethier, Wilfred J. International Trade Theory and International Migration. **In** *Stark, O., ed.,* 1986, pp. 27–74.

Galor, Oded. Time Preference and International Labor Migration. *J. Econ. Theory,* February 1986, *38*(1), pp. 1–20.

Ghezzi, Stefano. Mercato duale e mobilità del lavoro: un'applicazione del modello Modigliani–Tarantelli. (Labour Mobility in a Dualistic Labour Market. The Modigliani–Tarantelli Model. With English summary.) *Econ. Lavoro,* July-Sept. 1986, *20*(3), pp. 21–37. **[G: Italy]**

Gordon, Ian. What Contribution Can Labour Migration Make to Reducing Unemployment? Comment. **In** *Hart, P. E., ed.,* 1986, pp. 75–79. **[G: U.K.]**

Goss, Ernst P. and Paul, Chris. Age and Work Experience in the Decision to Migrate. *J. Human Res.,* Summer 1986, *21*(3), pp. 397–405.

Graves, Philip E. and Sexton, Robert L. Development, Mobility and Slavery: Real Income and Spatial Equilibration in the Postbellum South. *Amer. Econ.,* Spring 1986, *30*(1), pp. 36–39. **[G: U.S.]**

Green, A. E., et al. What Contribution Can Labour Migration Make to Reducing Unemployment? **In** *Hart, P. E., ed.,* 1986, pp. 52–74. **[G: U.K.]**

Greenwood, Michael J.; Hunt, Gary L. and McDowell, John M. Migration and Employment Change: Empirical Evidence on the Spatial and Temporal Dimensions of the Linkage. *J. Reg. Sci.,* May 1986, *26*(2), pp. 223–34. **[G: U.S.]**

Greenwood, Michael J. and McDowell, John M. The Factor Market Consequences of U.S. Immigration. *J. Econ. Lit.,* December 1986, *24*(4), pp. 1738–72. **[G: U.S.]**

Grubb, Farley. Redemptioner Immigration to Pennsylvania: Evidence on Contract Choice and Profitability. *J. Econ. Hist.,* June 1986, *46*(2), pp. 407–18. **[G: U.S.]**

Haag, Günter. A Stochastic Theory for Residential and Labour Mobility Including Travel Networks. **In** *Nijkamp, P., ed. (II),* 1986, pp. 340–57.

Haag, Günter and Weidlich, Wolfgang. A Dynamic Migration Theory and Its Evaluation for Concrete Systems. *Reg. Sci. Urban Econ.,* February 1986, *16*(1), pp. 57–80. **[G: Canada]**

Hardjono, Joan. Transmigration: Looking to the Future. *Bull. Indonesian Econ. Stud.,* August 1986, *22*(2), pp. 28–53. **[G: Indonesia]**

Helgeson, Ann. Geographical Mobility—Its Implications for Employment. **In** *Lane, D., ed.,* 1986, pp. 145–75. **[G: U.S.S.R.]**

Herzog, Henry W., Jr.; Schlottmann, Alan M. and Johnson, Donald L. High-Technology Jobs and Worker Mobility. *J. Reg. Sci.,* August 1986, *26*(3), pp. 445–59. **[G: U.S.]**

Hills, Stephen M. Adjusting to the Structure of Jobs: Geographic Mobility. **In** *Hills, S. M., ed.,* 1986, pp. 63–78. **[G: U.S.]**

Inglis, Paul A. and Stromback, C. Thorsten. Migrants' Unemployment: The Determinants of Employment Success. *Econ. Rec.,* September 1986, *62*(178), pp. 310–24. **[G: Australia]**

James, Franklin J. and Blair, John P. Labor Mobility in National Policy and Local Economies. **In** *Bergman, E. M., ed.,* 1986, *1983,* pp. 271–85. **[G: U.S.]**

Jasso, Guillermina and Rosenzweig, Mark R. Family Reunification and the Immigration Multiplier: U.S. Immigration Law, Origin-Country Conditions, and the Reproduction of Immigrants. *Demography,* August 1986, *23*(3), pp. 291–311. **[G: U.S.]**

Jasso, Guillermina and Rosenzweig, Mark R. What's in a Name? Country-of-Origin Influences on the Earnings of Immigrants in the United States. **In** *Stark, O., ed.*, 1986, pp. 75–106. **[G: U.S.]**

Jones, Barclay Gibbs. Urban Support for Rural Development in Kenya. *Econ. Geogr.*, July 1986, *62*(3), pp. 201–14. **[G: Kenya]**

Jun, Il Soo and Chang, Hui S. Functional Forms and the Relevance of Contiguous Migration in the Study of Migration and Employment Growth. *Ann. Reg. Sci.*, July 1986, *20*(2), pp. 17–27. **[G: U.S.]**

Kahan, Arcadius. Jewish Life in the United States: Perspectives from Economics. **In** *Kahan, A.*, 1986, *1981*, pp. 128–48. **[G: U.S.]**

Kahan, Arcadius. The First Wave of Jewish Immigration from Eastern Europe to the United States. **In** *Kahan, A.*, 1986, pp. 118–27. **[G: U.S.]**

Katz, Eliakim and Stark, Oded. Labor Migration and Risk Aversion in Less Developed Countries. *J. Lab. Econ.*, January 1986, *4*(1), pp. 134–49.

Katz, Eliakim and Stark, Oded. On the Shadow Wage of Urban Jobs in Less-Developed Countries. *J. Urban Econ.*, September 1986, *20*(2), pp. 121–27. **[G: LDCs]**

Kennedy, John M.; De Jong, Gordon F. and Lichter, Daniel T. Updating Local Area Population Projections with Current Migration Estimates. *J. Econ. Soc. Meas.*, July 1986, *14*(2), pp. 107–20. **[G: U.S.]**

King, Allan G.; Lowell, B. Lindsay and Bean, Frank D. The Effects of Hispanic Immigrants on the Earnings of Native Hispanic Americans. *Soc. Sci. Quart.*, December 1986, *67*(4), pp. 673–89. **[G: U.S.]**

Kirwan, Frank and Harrigan, Frank. Swedish–Finnish Return Migration, Extent, Timing, and Information Flows. *Demography*, August 1986, *23*(3), pp. 313–27. **[G: U.S.; Finland; Sweden]**

Kirwan, Frank and Holden, Darryl. Emigrants' Remittances, Non-traded Goods and Economic Welfare in the Source Country. *J. Econ. Stud.*, 1986, *13*(2), pp. 52–58.

Klau, Friedrich and Mittelstädt, Axel. Labour Market Flexibility. *OECD Econ. Stud.*, Spring 1986, (6), pp. 7–45. **[G: OECD]**

Ledent, Jacques. A Model of Urbanization with Nonlinear Migration Flows. *Int. Reg. Sci. Rev.*, December 1986, *10*(3), pp. 221–42. **[G: U.S.]**

Ledent, Jacques. Forecasting Interregional Migration: An Economic–Demographic Approach. **In** *Isserman, A. M., ed.*, 1986, pp. 53–77. **[G: Canada; U.S.]**

Lichter, Daniel T.; Heaton, Tim B. and Fuguitt, Glenn V. Convergence in Black and White Population Redistribution in the United States. *Soc. Sci. Quart.*, March 1986, *67*(1), pp. 21–38. **[G: U.S.]**

Liu, Pak-Wai. Human Capital, Job Matching and Earnings Growth between Jobs: An Empirical Analysis. *Appl. Econ.*, October 1986, *18*(10), pp. 1135–47. **[G: Singapore]**

Lucas, Robert E. B. Emigration, Employment, and Accumulation: The Miners of Southern Africa. **In** *Stark, O., ed.*, 1986, pp. 107–38. **[G: S. Africa]**

Mahmud, Raisul A. International Migration and the Domestic Economy. **In** *Islam, R. and Muqtada, M., eds.*, 1986, pp. 247–78. **[G: Bangladesh]**

McCrohan, Kevin F. The Revenue Loss Due to Undocumented Alien Earnings: Estimates for 1980. *J. Econ. Soc. Meas.*, December 1986, *14*(4), pp. 311–24. **[G: U.S.]**

McDevitt, Thomas M., et al. Migration Plans of the Rural Populations of Third World Countries: A Probit Analysis of Micro-Level Data from Asia, Africa, and Latin America. *J. Devel. Areas*, July 1986, *20*(4), pp. 473–90. **[G: Colombia; Egypt; Thailand]**

Miller, Ann R. Internal Migration and the Changing Structure of Employment in the United States in 1900: Machine Readable Census Samples as a New Source for Historical Research. **In** *Glazier, I. A. and De Rosa, L., eds.*, 1986, pp. 336–55. **[G: U.S.]**

Miller, Paul W. Immigrant Unemployment in the First Year of Australian Labour Market Activity. *Econ. Rec.*, March 1986, *62*(176), pp. 82–87. **[G: Australia]**

Mohtadi, Hamid. Rural Stratification, Rural to Urban Migration, and Urban Inequality: Evidence from Iran. *World Devel.*, June 1986, *14*(6), pp. 713–25. **[G: Iran]**

Molho, Ian. Theories of Migration: A Review. *Scot. J. Polit. Econ.*, November 1986, *33*(4), pp. 396–419.

Morrill, Richard; Downing, Jeanne and Leon, William. Attribute Preferences and the Nonmetropolitan Migration Decision. *Ann. Reg. Sci.*, March 1986, *20*(1), pp. 33–53. **[G: U.S.]**

Morrison, Peter A. and DaVanzo, Julie. The Prism of Migration: Dissimilarities between Return and Onward Movers. *Soc. Sci. Quart.*, September 1986, *67*(3), pp. 504–16. **[G: U.S.]**

Neuman, Shoshana and Ziderman, Adrian. Testing the Dual Labor Market Hypothesis: Evidence from the Israel Labor Mobility Survey. *J. Human Res.*, Spring 1986, *21*(2), pp. 230–37. **[G: Israel]**

Nijkamp, Peter and Poot, Jacques. Technological Change and Labour Migration in a General Spatial Interaction System. **In** *Nijkamp, P., ed. (II)*, 1986, pp. 358–70.

Ó Gráda, Cormac. Across the Briny Ocean: Some Thoughts on Irish Emigration to America, 1800–1850. **In** *Glazier, I. A. and De Rosa, L., eds.*, 1986, pp. 79–94. **[G: U.S.; Ireland]**

Oberai, A. S. Land Settlement Policies and Population Redistribution in Developing Countries: Performance, Problems and Prospects. *Int. Lab. Rev.*, Mar.-Apr. 1986, *125*(2), pp. 141–61. **[G: LDCs]**

Osberg, Lars, et al. Job Mobility, Wage Determination and Market Segmentation in the Presence of Sample Selection Bias. *Can. J. Econ.*, May 1986, *19*(2), pp. 319–46. **[G: Canada]**

Panagariya, Arvind and Succar, Patricia. The Harris–Todaro Model and Economies of Scale. *Southern Econ. J.*, April 1986, *52*(4), pp. 984–98.

Parra Sandoval, Rodrigo. The Missing Future: Colombian Youth. *CEPAL Rev.*, August 1986, (29), pp. 79–92. **[G: Colombia]**

Penny, N. J. H. Migrant Labour and the South African Gold Mining Industry: A Study of Remittances. *S. Afr. J. Econ.*, September 1986, *54*(3), pp. 290–306. **[G: S. Africa]**

Perrings, Charles. Income Redistribution and Labour Surplus in the Classical Theory of Labour Migration. *Manchester Sch. Econ. Soc. Stud.*, September 1986, *54*(3), pp. 283–97.

Poot, Jacques. A System Approach to Modelling the Inter-urban Exchange of Workers in New Zealand. *Scot. J. Polit. Econ.*, August 1986, *33*(3), pp. 249–74. **[G: New Zealand]**

Puth, Robert C. Human Mobility as a Source of American Economic Growth. *Quart. Rev. Econ. Bus.*, Spring 1986, *26*(1), pp. 57–73. **[G: U.S.]**

Rivera-Batiz, Francisco L. Can Border Industries Be a Substitute for Immigration? *Amer. Econ. Rev.*, May 1986, *76*(2), pp. 263–68. **[G: U.S.; Mexico]**

Rivera-Batiz, Francisco L. International Migration, Remittances and Economic Welfare in the Source Country. *J. Econ. Stud.*, 1986, *13*(3), pp. 3–19.

Roukis, George S. and Montana, Patrick J. Development and Human Resources Management in the Arab Oil Rich Gulf States. **In** *Roukis, G. S. and Montana, P. J., eds.*, 1986, pp. 169–96. **[G: Middle East]**

Russell, Sharon Stanton. Remittances from International Migration: A Review in Perspective. *World Devel.*, June 1986, *14*(6), pp. 677–96. **[G: LDCs]**

Schatz, Klaus-Werner. Incentives and Disincentives: International Migration: Comment. **In** *Balassa, B. and Giersch, H., eds.*, 1986, pp. 112–17. **[G: U.S.; W. Germany]**

Schoenman, Julie A. and Sloan, Frank A. Why Have Surgeons Moved to the Country? *Quart. Rev. Econ. Bus.*, Autumn 1986, *26*(3), pp. 25–47. **[G: U.S.]**

Shaw, R. Paul. Fiscal versus Traditional Market Variables in Canadian Migration. *J. Polit. Econ.*, Part 1, June 1986, *94*(3), pp. 648–66. **[G: Canada]**

Shughart, William F., II; Tollison, Robert D. and Kimenyi, Mwangi S. The Political Economy of Immigration Restriction. *Yale J. Regul.*, Fall 1986, *4*(1), pp. 79–97. **[G: U.S.]**

Shukla, Vibhooti and Stark, Oded. Urban External Economies and Optimal Migration. **In** *Stark, O., ed.*, 1986, pp. 139–46.

Slesnick, Daniel T. Welfare Distributional Change and the Measurement of Social Mobility. *Rev. Econ. Statist.*, November 1986, *68*(4), pp. 586–93. **[G: U.S.]**

Smith, Nina and Smith, Valdemar. Mobilitet og uddannelse. (Mobility in the Danish Labour Market. With English summary.) *Nationaløkon. Tidsskr.*, 1986, *124*(3), pp. 340–52. **[G: Denmark]**

Speare, Alden, Jr. and Harris, John. Education, Earnings, and Migration in Indonesia. *Econ. Develop. Cult. Change*, January 1986, *34*(2), pp. 223–44. **[G: Indonesia]**

Staines, Brian. The Movement of Population from South Wales with Specific Reference to the Effects of the Industrial Transference Scheme, 1928–37. **In** *Baber, C. and Williams, L. J., eds.*, 1986, pp. 237–50. **[G: U.K.]**

Stark, Oded. Migration, Markets, Clusters and Cooperation. **In** *Stark, O., ed.*, 1986, pp. xi–xiv.

Stark, Oded; Taylor, J. Edward and Yitzhaki, Shlomo. Remittances and Inequality. *Econ. J.*, September 1986, *96*(383), pp. 722–40. **[G: Mexico]**

Stewart, Charles T., Jr. and Lee, Jin-Hsia. Urban Concentration and Sectoral Income Distribution. *J. Devel. Areas*, April 1986, *20*(3), pp. 357–68. **[G: LDCs]**

Stewart, James B. and Hyclak, Thomas J. The Effects of Immigrants, Women, and Teenagers on the Relative Earnings of Black Males. *Rev. Black Polit. Econ.*, Summer 1986, *15*(1), pp. 93–101. **[G: U.S.]**

Straubhaar, Thomas. The Determinants of Workers' Remittances: The Case of Turkey. *Weltwirtsch. Arch.*, 1986, *122*(4), pp. 728–40. **[G: Turkey]**

Swierenga, Robert P. Dutch International Migration and Occupational Change: A Structural Analysis of Multinational Linked Files. **In** *Glazier, I. A. and De Rosa, L., eds.*, 1986, pp. 95–124. **[G: Netherlands; U.S.]**

Tapvong, Churai. Duality in Factor Endowments, International Trade, and Factor Prices: An Analysis of Labour Migration. *Indian Econ. J.*, Jan.-Mar. 1986, *33*(3), pp. 46–52.

Taylor, J. Edward. Differential Migration, Networks, Information and Risk. **In** *Stark, O., ed.*, 1986, pp. 147–71.

Todaro, Michael P. Internal Migration and Urban Employment: Comment. *Amer. Econ. Rev.*, June 1986, *76*(3), pp. 566–69. **[G: Mexico; India; Colombia; Nigeria]**

Topel, Robert H. Local Labor Markets. *J. Polit. Econ.*, Part 2, June 1986, *94*(3), pp. S111–43. **[G: U.S.]**

Torok, Stephen J. and Huffman, Wallace E. U.S.–Mexican Trade in Winter Vegetables and Illegal Immigration. *Amer. J. Agr. Econ.*, May 1986, *68*(2), pp. 246–60. **[G: U.S.; Mexico]**

Tunali, Insan. A General Structure for Models of Double-Selection and an Application to a Joint Migration/Earnings Process with Remigration. **In** *Ehrenberg, R. G., ed., Pt. B*, 1986, pp. 235–83. **[G: Turkey]**

Ulack, Richard. Ties to Origin, Remittances, and Mobility: Evidence from Rural and Urban Areas in the Philippines. *J. Devel. Areas*, April 1986, *20*(3), pp. 339–55. **[G: Philippines]**

Uner, Sunday. Migration and Labor Transformation in Rural Turkey. **In** *Richards, A., ed.*, 1986, pp. 225–64. **[G: Turkey]**

Vasegh-Daneshvary, Nasser; Herzog, Henry W., Jr. and Schlottmann, Alan M. College Educated Immigrants in the American Labor Force: A Study of Locational Behavior. *Southern Econ. J.*, January 1986, *52*(3), pp. 818–31. **[G: U.S.]**

Vedder, Richard, et al. Demonstrating Their Freedom: The Post-emancipation Migration of Black Americans. **In** *Uselding, P., ed.*, 1986, pp. 213–39. **[G: U.S.]**

Vining, Daniel R., Jr. Population Redistribution towards Core Areas of Less Developed Countries, 1950–1980. *Int. Reg. Sci. Rev.*, April 1986, *10*(1), pp. 1–45. **[G: LDCs]**

Wahba, Mohamed A. and Al-Musfir, Muhammad S. Managing Human Resources in the United Arab Emirates: A Review of Trends and Problems. **In** *Roukis, G. S. and Montana, P. J., eds.*, 1986, pp. 157–68. **[G: United Arab Emirates]**

Watson, William G. An Estimate of the Welfare Gain from Fiscal Equalization. *Can. J. Econ.*, May 1986, *19*(2), pp. 298–308. **[G: Canada]**

Williamson, Jeffrey G. The Impact of the Irish on British Labor Markets during the Industrial Revolution. *J. Econ. Hist.*, September 1986, *46*(3), pp. 693–720. **[G: U.K.; Ireland]**

Wong, Kar-yiu. The Economic Analysis of International Migration: A Generalization. *Can. J. Econ.*, May 1986, *19*(2), pp. 357–62.

Zacchia, C. Possibilities and Constraints of Endogenous Industrial Development. **In** *Bassand, M., et al., eds.*, 1986, pp. 146–60. **[G: Europe]**

824 Labor Market Studies, Wages, Employment

8240 General

Abbott, Michael G. Labour Economics Research of the Macdonald Commission: A Review of Volumes 17 and 18. *Can. Public Policy*, December 1986, *12*(4), pp. 628–39. **[G: Canada]**

Al-Tuhaih, Salem M. The Vicious Cycle of Manpower in Kuwait. **In** *Roukis, G. S. and Montana, P. J., eds.*, 1986, pp. 123–38.

Andrews, Martyn and Nickell, Stephen J. A Disaggregated Disequilibrium Model of the Labour Market. *Oxford Econ. Pap.*, November 1986, *38*(3), pp. 386–402. **[G: U.K.]**

Baily, Martin Neil. The Cyclical Behavior of Industrial Labor Markets: A Comparison of the Prewar and Postwar Eras: Comment. **In** *Gordon, R. J., ed.*, 1986, pp. 621–66. **[G: U.S.]**

Bernanke, Ben S. Employment, Hours, and Earnings in the Depression: An Analysis of Eight Manufacturing Industries. *Amer. Econ. Rev.*, March 1986, *76*(1), pp. 82–109. **[G: U.S.]**

Bernanke, Ben S. and Powell, James L. The Cyclical Behavior of Industrial Labor Markets: A Comparison of the Prewar and Postwar Eras. **In** *Gordon, R. J., ed.*, 1986, pp. 583–621. **[G: U.S.]**

Blandy, Richard and Kain, Peter. The Australian Labour Market, September 1986. *Australian Bull. Lab.*, September 1986, *12*(4), pp. 199–220. **[G: Australia]**

Blandy, Richard and Sloan, Judith. The Australian Labour Market March 1986. *Australian Bull. Lab.*, March 1986, *12*(2), pp. 82–90. **[G: Australia]**

Boyer, George R. The Old Poor Law and the Agricultural Labor Market in Southern England: An Empirical Analysis. *J. Econ. Hist.*, March 1986, *46*(1), pp. 113–35. **[G: U.K.]**

Brandt, Gerhard. Technological Change, Labour Market, and Trade Union Policy. **In** *Jacobi, O., et al., eds. (I)*, 1986, pp. 50–70. **[G: U.S.; U.K.; Italy; W. Germany]**

Brown, Martin and Philips, Peter. The Historical Origin of Job Ladders in the U.S. Canning Industry and Their Effects on the Gender Division of Labour. *Cambridge J. Econ.*, June 1986, *10*(2), pp. 129–45. **[G: U.S.]**

Brunello, Giorgio. The Italian and the Japanese Labour Markets: A Time Series Representation. *Giorn. Econ.*, July-Aug. 1986, *45*(7–8), pp. 389–406. **[G: Italy; Japan]**

Burton, Daniel F., Jr. Policy Options and the Changing World of Work. **In** *Burton, D. F., et al., eds.*, 1986, pp. 229–63. **[G: U.S.]**

Chiswick, Barry R. Family Effects in Simple Models of Education, Occupational Status and Earnings: Findings from the Wisconsin and Kalamazoo Studies: Comment. *J. Lab. Econ.*, Part 2, July 1986, *4*(3), pp. 116–20. **[G: U.S.]**

Chulasai, Luechai; Bhekasut, Suwarat and Shusuwan, Thongchai. Family Labour, Hired Labour and Employment Linkages in Rural Thailand. **In** *Hirashima, S. and Muqtada, M., eds.*, 1986, pp. 151–75. **[G: Thailand]**

Conway, Hugh and Anderson, Ewan. Kuwait's Labor Force: An Historical Perspective, Industrial Development, and Measures to Stabilize the Expatriate Labor Force. **In** *Roukis, G. S. and Montana, P. J., eds.*, 1986, pp. 139–56. **[G: Kuwait]**

Costrell, Robert M.; Duguay, Gerald E. and Treyz, George I. Labour Substitution and Complementarity among Age–Sex Groups. *Appl. Econ.*, July 1986, *18*(7), pp. 777–91. **[G: U.S.]**

Dahrendorf, Ralf, et al. Labour Market Flexibility. Report by a High-Level Group of Experts to the Secretary-General. *Econ. Lavoro*, July-Sept. 1986, *20*(3), pp. 3–19. **[G: OECD]**

Fagan, G. and Murphy, A. Employers' Social Insurance Contributions and Employment. *Econ. Soc. Rev.*, October 1986, *18*(1), pp. 43–56. **[G: Ireland]**

Favereau, Olivier; Py, Jacques and Sollogoub, Michel. Les modèles français et allemand de marché interne du travail: essai de formalisation. (An Attempt to Formalise French and German Internal Labour Markets. With English summary.) *Écon. Appl.*, 1986, *39*(4), pp. 819–846. **[G: France; W. Germany]**

Faxén, Karl-Olof. Quasi-monopoly Profits, Barriers to Entry and the Welfare State: Their Impact on Labor Markets in Industrialized Countries: Comment. **In** *Day, R. H. and Eliasson, G., eds.*, 1986, pp. 435–41. **[G: OECD]**

Freeman, Richard B. Individual Mobility and Union Voice in the Labor Market. **In** *Putterman, L., ed.*, 1986, *1976*, pp. 156–64.

Ghezzi, Stefano. Mercato duale e mobilità del lavoro: un'applicazione del modello Modigliani–Tarantelli. (Labour Mobility in a Dualistic Labour Market. The Modigliani–Tarantelli Model. With English summary.) *Econ. Lavoro,* July-Sept. 1986, *20*(3), pp. 21–37. **[G: Italy]**

Glennon, Dennis, et al. Incorporating Labour Market Structure in Regional Econometric Models. *Appl. Econ.*, May 1986, *18*(5), pp. 545–55. **[G: U.S.]**

Groenewegen, John and van Paridon, Kees. Theory and Practice of the Dutch Labor Market: The 1985 Conference of the Dutch Study Circle for Post Keynesian Economics. *J. Econ. Issues,* September 1986, *20*(3), pp. 825–33.

Hall, Robert E. Hysteresis and the European Unemployment Problem: Comment. **In** *Fischer, S., ed.*, 1986, pp. 85–88. **[G: U.S.; U.K.; W. Germany; France]**

Hamermesh, Daniel S. Incentives for the Homogenization of Time Use. **In** *Balassa, B. and Giersch, H., eds.*, 1986, pp. 124–39.

Harris, A. H., et al. Who Gains from Structural Change? The Distribution of the Benefits of Oil in Aberdeen. *Urban Stud.*, August 1986, *23*(4), pp. 271–83. **[G: U.K.]**

Hauser, Robert M. and Sewell, William H. Family Effects in Simple Models of Education, Occupational Status and Earnings: Findings from the Wisconsin and Kalamazoo Studies. *J. Lab. Econ.*, Part 2, July 1986, *4*(3), pp. S83–115. **[G: U.S.]**

Hills, Stephen M. How Fluid Is the U.S. Labor Market? **In** *Hills, S. M., ed.*, 1986, pp. 149–59. **[G: U.S.]**

Hirashima, S. and Muqtada, M. Issues on Employment, Poverty and Hired Labour in South and Southeast Asia: An Introduction. **In** *Hirashima, S. and Muqtada, M., eds.*, 1986, pp. 1–19. **[G: S. Asia; S. E. Asia]**

Horvath, Francis W. Work at Home: New Findings from the Current Population Survey. *Mon. Lab. Rev.*, November 1986, *109*(11), pp. 31–35. **[G: U.S.]**

Huberman, Michael. Invisible Handshakes in Lancashire: Cotton Spinning in the First Half of the Nineteenth Century. *J. Econ. Hist.*, December 1986, *46*(4), pp. 987–98. **[G: U.K.]**

Hughes, Helen. The Right to Work. *Australian Bull. Lab.*, September 1986, *12*(4), pp. 234–43. **[G: Australia]**

Jacoby, Sanford M. and Mitchell, Daniel J. B. Alternative Sources of Labor Market Data. **In** *Dennis, B. D., ed.*, 1986, pp. 42–49. **[G: U.S.]**

Johnson, Omotunde E. G. Labor Markets, External Developments, and Unemployment in Developing Countries. **In** *International Monetary Fund, Research Department,* 1986, pp. 51–72. **[G: LDCs; MDCs]**

Jones, Stuart. The History of Black Involvement in the South African Economy. **In** *Smollan, R., ed.*, 1986, pp. 1–22. **[G: S. Africa]**

Kahnert, Friedrich. Re-examining Urban Poverty and Employment. *Finance Develop.*, March 1986, *23*(1), pp. 44–47. **[G: LDCs]**

Kennan, John. Hysteresis and the European Unemployment Problem: Comment. **In** *Fischer, S., ed.*, 1986, pp. 78–85. **[G: OECD]**

Kenyon, Peter. The Australian Labour Market, June 1986. *Australian Bull. Lab.*, June 1986, *12*(3), pp. 131–53. **[G: Australia]**

Khan, Shaheen. The Determinants of Urban Activity Rates. *Pakistan Econ. Soc. Rev.*, Summer 1986, *24*(1), pp. 23–44. **[G: Pakistan]**

Klau, Friedrich and Mittelstädt, Axel. Labour Market Flexibility. *OECD Econ. Stud.*, Spring 1986, (6), pp. 7–45. **[G: OECD]**

König, Heinz. Incentives for the Homogenization of Time Use: Comment. **In** *Balassa, B. and Giersch, H., eds.*, 1986, pp. 162–65.

Kooreman, Peter and Kapteyn, Arie. Estimation of Rationed and Unrationed Household Labour Supply Functions Using Flexible Functional Forms. *Econ. J.*, June 1986, *96*(382), pp. 398–412. **[G: Netherlands]**

Kosters, Marvin H. Free Markets Bring Change and Growth. *Challenge*, Mar./Apr. 1986, *29*(1), pp. 55–64. **[G: U.S.; U.K.; Italy; France; W. Germany]**

Kovács, G. J. Job-Creating Capacity of the Private Sector in Hungary between 1981–1985. *Acta Oecon.*, 1986, *37*(3–4), pp. 341–54. **[G: Hungary]**

Lazear, Edward P. The Cyclical Behavior of Industrial Labor Markets: A Comparison of the Prewar and Postwar Eras: Comment. **In** *Gordon, R. J., ed.*, 1986, pp. 626–32. **[G: U.S.]**

Leontief, Wassily. The Distribution of Work and Income. **In** *Leontief, W.*, 1986, *1982*, pp. 363–78. **[G: U.S.; Austria]**

Linneman, Peter and Wachter, Michael L. Rising Union Premiums and the Declining Boundaries among Noncompeting Groups. *Amer. Econ. Rev.*, May 1986, *76*(2), pp. 103–08. **[G: U.S.]**

Luskin, David. The Case for Subsidising Extra Jobs: A Comment. *Econ. J.*, March 1986, *96*(381), pp. 212–15. **[G: U.K.]**

Mark, Jerome A. Developments in Labor Statistics. *Bus. Econ.*, July 1986, *21*(3), pp. 16–20. **[G: U.S.]**

Marsden, David and Ryan, Paul. Where Do Young Workers Work? Youth Employment by Industry in Various European Economies. *Brit. J. Ind. Relat.*, March 1986, *24*(1), pp. 83–102. **[G: W. Europe]**

Martin, Philip L. Western Farm Labor Issues. *Contemp. Policy Issues*, January 1986, *4*(1), pp. 72–86. **[G: U.S.]**

Maslova, I.; Dadashev, A. and Moskovich, V. The Impact of Technological Progress on the Release and Redistribution of Workers. *Prob.*

Econ., July 1986, *29*(3), pp. 69–80. **[G: U.S.S.R.]**

Meyerson, Per-Martin. Quasi-monopoly Profits, Barriers to Entry and the Welfare State: Their Impact on Labor Markets in Industrialized Countries: Comment. **In** *Day, R. H. and Eliasson, G., eds.*, 1986, pp. 442–46. **[G: OECD]**

Michon, François. Flexibilité et Partages. Les enjeux de la Solidarité. (Flexibilities and Work Sharing. A Search for Solidarity. With English summary.) *Écon. Soc.*, April 1986, *20*(4), pp. 77–104.

Mitchell, Daniel J. B. Wages and Keynes: Lessons from the Past. *Eastern Econ. J.*, July-Sept. 1986, *12*(3), pp. 199–208. **[G: U.S.]**

Moulton, Brent R. An Analysis of Female Work Experience Data Derived from Social Security Records. *J. Econ. Soc. Meas.*, April 1986, *14*(1), pp. 65–75. **[G: U.S.]**

Muqtada, M. and Alam, M. Mustafa. Hired Labour and Rural Labour Market in Bangladesh. **In** *Hirashima, S. and Muqtada, M., eds.*, 1986, pp. 21–73. **[G: Bangladesh]**

Neuman, Shoshana and Ziderman, Adrian. Testing the Dual Labor Market Hypothesis: Evidence from the Israel Labor Mobility Survey. *J. Human Res.*, Spring 1986, *21*(2), pp. 230–37. **[G: Israel]**

Nijman, T. E. and Palm, F. C. The Construction and Use of Approximations for Missing Quarterly Observations: A Model-based Approach. *J. Bus. Econ. Statist.*, January 1986, *4*(1), pp. 47–58. **[G: Netherlands]**

Osberg, Lars, et al. Job Mobility, Wage Determination and Market Segmentation in the Presence of Sample Selection Bias. *Can. J. Econ.*, May 1986, *19*(2), pp. 319–46. **[G: Canada]**

Peterson, Willis and Kislev, Yoav. The Cotton Harvester in Retrospect: Labor Displacement or Replacement? *J. Econ. Hist.*, March 1986, *46*(1), pp. 199–216. **[G: U.S.]**

Phillips, William H. The Labor Market of Southern Textile Mill Villages: Some Micro Evidence. *Exploration Econ. Hist.*, April 1986, *23*(2), pp. 103–23. **[G: U.S.]**

Piore, Michael J. Perspectives on Labor Market Flexibility. *Ind. Relat.*, Spring 1986, *25*(2), pp. 146–66. **[G: U.S.; W. Europe]**

Rama, Germán W. Latin American Youth between Development and Crisis. *CEPAL Rev.*, August 1986, (29), pp. 17–39. **[G: Latin America]**

Richards, John and Carruth, Alan A. Short-Time Working and the Unemployment Benefit System in Great Britain. *Oxford Bull. Econ. Statist.*, February 1986, *48*(1), pp. 41–59. **[G: U.K.]**

Rothschild, Kurt W. Incentives for the Homogenization of Time Use: Comment. **In** *Balassa, B. and Giersch, H., eds.*, 1986, pp. 159–61.

Roukis, George S. and Montana, Patrick J. Development and Human Resources Management in the Arab Oil Rich Gulf States. **In** *Roukis, G. S. and Montana, P. J., eds.*, 1986, pp. 169–96. **[G: Middle East]**

Rudebusch, Glenn D. Testing for Labor Market Equilibrium with an Exact Excess Demand Disequilibrium Model. *Rev. Econ. Statist.*, August 1986, *68*(3), pp. 468–76. **[G: U.S.]**

Seeborg, Irmtraud Streker; Seeborg, Michael C. and Zegeye, Abera. Training and Labor Market Outcomes of Disadvantaged Blacks. *Ind. Relat.*, Winter 1986, *25*(1), pp. 33–44. **[G: U.S.]**

Spinanger, Dean. Quasi-monopoly Profits, Barriers to Entry and the Welfare State: Their Impact on Labor Markets in Industrialized Countries. **In** *Day, R. H. and Eliasson, G., eds.*, 1986, pp. 411–34. **[G: OECD]**

Spinanger, Dean. Quasi-monopoly Profits, Barriers to Entry and the Welfare State: Their Impact on Labor Markets in Industrialized Countries: Reply. **In** *Day, R. H. and Eliasson, G., eds.*, 1986, pp. 447–48. **[G: OECD]**

Svensson, Lennart. Class Struggle in a Welfare State in Crisis: From Radicalism to Neoliberalism in Sweden. **In** *Edwards, R.; Garonna, P. and Tödtling, F., eds.*, 1986, pp. 269–308. **[G: Sweden]**

Thiede, Reinhold; Pickard, Stephanie and Helberger, Christof. Arbeit und Einkommen in der alternativen Wirtschaft—Empirische Grundlagen für die aktuelle Diskussion. (Work and Incomes in the "Alternative Economy." With English summary.) *Jahr. Nationalökon. Statist.*, November 1986, *201*(6), pp. 618–41. **[G: W. Germany]**

Weinstein, Paul. Sources of Labor Statistics in an Era of Budget Cutbacks: What Are Alternative Sources for I.R. Data? Discussion. **In** *Dennis, B. D., ed.*, 1986, pp. 50–51. **[G: U.S.]**

Weiss, Andrew M. Job Queues and Layoffs in Labor Markets with Flexible Wages. **In** *Akerlof, G. A. and Yellen, J. L., eds.*, 1986, *1980*, pp. 102–14. **[G: U.S.]**

8241 Geographic Labor Market Studies

Abraham, Katharine G. Why Is the Unemployment Rate So Very High near Full Employment? Comments. *Brookings Pap. Econ. Act.*, 1986, (2), pp. 384–89. **[G: U.S.]**

Adams, J. C. and Kraithman, D. A. Unemployment in a Relatively Prosperous Region: The Hertfordshire Experience. **In** *Danson, M., ed.*, 1986, pp. 121–35. **[G: U.K.]**

Armington, Catherine. Trends in Midwest Business Employment. **In** *Walzer, N. and Chicoine, D. L., eds.*, 1986, pp. 15–33. **[G: U.S.]**

Benhayoun, Gilbert. L'emploi et le chômage des jeunes analyse urbaine. (With English summary.) *Revue Écon. Polit.*, May-June 1986, *96*(3), pp. 281–99. **[G: France]**

Charney, Alberta H. and Taylor, Carol A. Integrated State–Substate Econometric Modeling: Design and Utilization for Long-run Economic Analysis. **In** *Perryman, M. R. and Schmidt, J. R., eds.*, 1986, pp. 43–92. **[G: U.S.]**

Chmura, Christine. The Industrial Mix of Employment in the Fifth District, 1950–1985. *Fed. Res. Bank Richmond Econ. Rev.*, May/June

1986, *72*(3), pp. 26–34. **[G: U.S.]**

Dunford, M. Integration and Unequal Development: The Case of Southern Italy, 1951–73. **In** *Scott, A. J. and Storper, M., eds.*, 1986, pp. 225–45. **[G: Italy]**

Elahi, Mahboob and Khan, Mahmud Jameel. Rural Labour Market with Special Reference to Hired Labour in Pakistan's Punjab. **In** *Hirashima, S. and Muqtada, M., eds.*, 1986, pp. 75–118. **[G: Pakistan]**

Goddard, John B. and Thwaites, Alfred T. New Technology and Regional Development Policy. **In** *Nijkamp, P., ed. (II)*, 1986, pp. 91–114. **[G: U.K.]**

Gruben, William C. and Phillips, Keith R. Understanding the Texas Unemployment Rate. *Fed. Res. Bank Dallas Econ. Rev.*, November 1986, pp. 17–30. **[G: U.S.]**

Helgeson, Ann. Geographical Mobility—Its Implications for Employment. **In** *Lane, D., ed.*, 1986, pp. 145–75. **[G: U.S.S.R.]**

Hill, John K. Energy's Contribution to the Growth of Employment in Texas, 1972–1982. *Fed. Res. Bank Dallas Econ. Rev.*, May 1986, pp. 11–18. **[G: U.S.]**

Hills, Stephen M. Adjusting to the Structure of Jobs: Geographic Mobility. **In** *Hills, S. M., ed.*, 1986, pp. 63–78. **[G: U.S.]**

Hunt, E. H. Industrialization and Regional Inequality: Wages in Britain, 1760–1914. *J. Econ. Hist.*, December 1986, *46*(4), pp. 935–66. **[G: U.K.]**

Jatobá, Jorge. The Labour Market in a Recession-Hit Region: The North-East of Brazil. *Int. Lab. Rev.*, Mar.-Apr. 1986, *125*(2), pp. 227–41. **[G: Brazil]**

Jones, A. and Kinner, D. R. Deindustrialisation: The Case of Humberside. **In** *Danson, M., ed.*, 1986, pp. 103–19. **[G: U.K.]**

Klarich, Nina M. Private-Sector Economic Development Activities in the Chicago Metro Area. **In** *Walzer, N. and Chicoine, D. L., eds.*, 1986, pp. 214–25. **[G: U.S.]**

Ledent, Jacques. Consistent Modelling of Employment, Population, Labour Force, and Unemployment in the Statistical Analysis of Regional Growth. **In** *Batey, P. W. and Madden, M., eds.*, 1986, pp. 25–36.

Lewis, Jacqueline A. and Armstrong, Kathleen M. Skill Shortages and Recruitment Problems in West Midlands Engineering Industry. *Nat. Westminster Bank Quart. Rev.*, November 1986, pp. 45–57. **[G: U.K.]**

Little, Jane Sneddon. The Effects of Foreign Direct Investment on U.S. Employment during Recession and Structural Change. *New Eng. Econ. Rev.*, Nov./Dec. 1986, pp. 40–48. **[G: U.S.]**

Owen, D. W.; Coombes, M. G. and Gillespie, A. E. The Urban–Rural Shift and Employment Change in Britain, 1971–81. **In** *Danson, M., ed.*, 1986, pp. 23–47. **[G: U.K.]**

Peck, Francis W. and Townsend, Alan R. Corporate Interaction in Oligopolistic Markets: The Role of Case Studies of Rationalisation. **In** *Danson, M., ed.*, 1986, pp. 49–63. **[G: U.K.]**

Rones, Philip L. An Analysis of Regional Employment Growth, 1973–85. *Mon. Lab. Rev.*, July 1986, *109*(7), pp. 3–14. **[G: U.S.]**

Stoney, P. J. M. The Employment Impact of the Merseyside Motor-Vehicle Assembly Industry. **In** *Danson, M., ed.*, 1986, pp. 65–81. **[G: U.K.]**

Summers, Lawrence H. Why Is the Unemployment Rate So Very High near Full Employment? *Brookings Pap. Econ. Act.*, 1986, (2), pp. 339–83. **[G: U.S.]**

Topel, Robert H. Local Labor Markets. *J. Polit. Econ.*, Part 2, June 1986, *94*(3), pp. S111–43. **[G: U.S.]**

Wachter, Michael L. Why Is the Unemployment Rate So Very High near Full Employment? Comments. *Brookings Pap. Econ. Act.*, 1986, (2), pp. 389–94.

Wasylenko, Michael. The Effect of Business Climate on Employment Growth. **In** *Minnesota Tax Study Commission*, 1986, pp. 51–73. **[G: U.S.]**

Wasylenko, Michael. The Effect of Business Climate on Employment Growth: A Review of the Evidence. **In** *Walzer, N. and Chicoine, D. L., eds.*, 1986, pp. 34–54. **[G: U.S.]**

8242 Wage, Hours, and Fringe Benefit Studies

Abdelkarim, Abbas. Toward the Political Economy of Wage Determination: A Case Study of Sudanese Agricultural Labor Markets. **In** *Zarembka, P., ed.*, 1986, pp. 95–126. **[G: Sudan]**

Abedian, Iraj and Standish, B. Market Imperfections and Unemployment: A Model of the South African Labour Market 1900–1940. *S. Afr. J. Econ.*, December 1986, *54*(4), pp. 406–17. **[G: S. Africa]**

Albers, Sönke. Controlling Independent Manufacturer Representatives by Using Commission Rate Functions Depending on Achieved Sales Volume. **In** *Backhaus, K. and Wilson, D. T., eds.*, 1986, pp. 88–112.

Allen, Steven G. and Clark, Robert L. Unions, Pension Wealth, and Age-Compensation Profiles. *Ind. Lab. Relat. Rev.*, July 1986, *39*(4), pp. 502–18. **[G: U.S.]**

Allen, Steven G.; Clark, Robert L. and Sumner, Daniel A. Postretirement Adjustments of Pension Benefits. *J. Human Res.*, Winter 1986, *21*(1), pp. 118–37. **[G: U.S.]**

Alpert, William T. and Ozawa, Martha N. Fringe Benefits of Workers in Nonmanufacturing Industries: They Vary by Employee Income, the Marginal Tax Rate, Union Status and Firm Size. *Amer. J. Econ. Soc.*, April 1986, *45*(2), pp. 173–88. **[G: U.S.]**

Altonji, Joseph G. Efficiency Wage Theories: A Partial Evaluation: Comment. **In** *Fischer, S., ed.*, 1986, pp. 276–85. **[G: U.S.]**

Altonji, Joseph G. and Paxson, Christina H. Job Characteristics and Hours of Work. **In** *Ehrenberg, R. G., ed., Pt. A*, 1986, pp. 1–55. **[G: U.S.]**

Amir, Shmuel. Educational Structure and Wage

Differentials of the Labor Force in the 1970s. **In** *Ben-Porath, Y., ed.*, 1986, pp. 137–52. **[G: Israel]**

Antel, John J. Human Capital Investment Specialization and the Wage Effects of Voluntary Labor Mobility. *Rev. Econ. Statist.*, August 1986, *68*(3), pp. 477–83. **[G: U.S.]**

Arrufat, Jose Luis and Zabalza, Antonio. Female Labor Supply with Taxation, Random Preferences, and Optimization Errors. *Econometrica*, January 1986, *54*(1), pp. 47–63. **[G: U.K.]**

Atkinson, John. Working Time and Employment: A Negotiable Issue? Comment. **In** *Hart, P. E., ed.*, 1986, pp. 22–26. **[G: U.K.]**

Avery, Robert B.; Elliehausen, Gregory E. and Gustafson, Thomas A. Pensions and Social Security in Household Portfolios: Evidence from the *1983 Survey of Consumer Finances*. **In** *Adams, F. G. and Wachter, S. M., eds.*, 1986, pp. 127–60. **[G: U.S.]**

Bandiyono, Suko and Conroy, John D. Employment and Income from Non-agricultural Sources in Rural East Java: Some Preliminary Findings. **In** *Shand, R. T., ed., Vol. 1*, 1986, pp. 327–67. **[G: Indonesia]**

Bane, Mary Jo and Ellwood, David T. Slipping into and out of Poverty: The Dynamics of Spells. *J. Human Res.*, Winter 1986, *21*(1), pp. 1–23. **[G: U.S.]**

Barron, John M. and Loewenstein, Mark A. On Imperfect Evaluation and Earning Differentials. *Econ. Inquiry*, October 1986, *24*(4), pp. 595–614. **[G: U.S.]**

Beckerman, Wilfred and Jenkinson, Tim. How Rigid Are Wages Anyway? **In** *Beckerman, W., ed.*, 1986, pp. 21–42. **[G: U.S.; U.K.; Japan]**

Beenstock, Michael and Warburton, Peter. Wages and Unemployment in Interwar Britain. *Exploration Econ. Hist.*, April 1986, *23*(2), pp. 153–72. **[G: U.K.]**

Behrman, Jere R. and Taubman, Paul. Birth Order, Schooling, and Earnings. *J. Lab. Econ.*, Part 2, July 1986, *4*(3), pp. S121–45. **[G: U.S.]**

Bell, Linda A. Wage Rigidity in West Germany: A Comparison with the U.S. Experience. *Fed. Res. Bank New York Quart. Rev.*, Autumn 1986, *11*(3), pp. 11–21. **[G: W. Germany; U.S.]**

Ben-Porath, Yoram. Diversity in Population and in the Labor Force. **In** *Ben-Porath, Y., ed.*, 1986, pp. 153–70. **[G: Israel]**

Benjamin, Daniel K. Combinations of Workmen: Trade Unions in the American Economy. **In** *Lipset, S. M., ed.*, 1986, pp. 201–20. **[G: U.S.]**

Bentzel, Ragnar. Incentives in the United Kingdom: Comment. **In** *Balassa, B. and Giersch, H., eds.*, 1986, pp. 296–300. **[G: U.K.]**

Benyon, Frank S. The EC–U.S. Steel Trade Crisis: Comment. **In** *Tsoukalis, L., ed.*, 1986, pp. 45–49. **[G: EEC; U.S.]**

Blackaby, David H. An Analysis of the Male Racial Earnings Differential in the UK, Using the General Household Survey. *Appl. Econ.*, November 1986, *18*(11), pp. 1233–42. **[G: U.K.]**

Blakemore, Arthur E.; Hunt, Janet C. and Kiker, B. F. Collective Bargaining and Union Membership Effects on the Wages of Male Youths. *J. Lab. Econ.*, April 1986, *4*(2), pp. 193–211. **[G: U.S.]**

Blanchflower, David. Wages and Concentration in British Manufacturing. *Appl. Econ.*, September 1986, *18*(9), pp. 1025–38. **[G: U.K.]**

Blanchflower, David. What Effect Do Unions Have on Relative Wages in Great Britain? *Brit. J. Ind. Relat.*, July 1986, *24*(2), pp. 195–204. **[G: U.K.]**

Blau, David M. Self-employment, Earnings, and Mobility in Peninsular Malaysia. *World Devel.*, July 1986, *14*(7), pp. 839–52. **[G: Malaysia]**

Blinder, Alan S. His and Hers: Gender Differences in Work and Income, 1959–1979: Comment. *J. Lab. Econ.*, Part 2, July 1986, *4*(3), pp. S273–77.

Blinder, Alan S. Macroeconomic Implications of Profit Sharing: Comment. **In** *Fischer, S., ed.*, 1986, pp. 335–43. **[G: Japan]**

Borjas, George J. The Earnings of State Government Employees in the United States. *J. Urban Econ.*, March 1986, *19*(2), pp. 156–73. **[G: U.S.]**

Borjas, George J. and Welch, Finis. The Postservice Earnings of Military Retirees: Evidence from the U.S. Air Force. **In** *Ehrenberg, R. G., ed., Pt. A*, 1986, pp. 57–83. **[G: U.S.]**

Borjas, George J. and Welch, Finis. The Postservice Earnings of Military Retirees. **In** *Gilroy, C. L., ed.*, 1986, pp. 295–313. **[G: U.S.]**

Bosch, Gerhard. The Dispute over the Reduction of the Working Week in West Germany. *Cambridge J. Econ.*, September 1986, *10*(3), pp. 271–90. **[G: W. Germany]**

Bound, John; Griliches, Zvi and Hall, Bronwyn H. Wages, Schooling and IQ of Brothers and Sisters: Do the Family Factors Differ? *Int. Econ. Rev.*, February 1986, *27*(1), pp. 77–105. **[G: U.S.]**

Brown, C. V., et al. Payment Systems, Demand Constraints and Their Implications for Research into Labour Supply. **In** *Blundell, R. and Walker, I., eds.*, 1986, pp. 190–216. **[G: U.K.]**

Brown, Martin and Philips, Peter. The Decline of the Piece-Rate System in California Canning: Technological Innovation, Labor Management, and Union Pressure, 1890–1947. *Bus. Hist. Rev.*, Winter 1986, *60*(4), pp. 564–601. **[G: U.S.]**

Brown, Martin and Philips, Peter. The Decline of Piece Rates in California Canneries: 1890–1960. *Ind. Relat.*, Winter 1986, *25*(1), pp. 81–91. **[G: U.S.]**

Brown, William. A Symposium on the Role and Influence of Trade Unions in a Recession: Comments. *Brit. J. Ind. Relat.*, July 1986, *24*(2), pp. 208–09. **[G: U.K.]**

Browne, Lynn E. Taking in Each Other's Laundry—The Service Economy. *New Eng. Econ. Rev.*, July/Aug. 1986, pp. 20–31. **[G: U.S.]**

Capecchi, Vittorio. Organizzazione e politiche del

tempo: un primo confronto tra Giappone ed Europa. (Work Time Organization and Policies. A Comparison between Japan and Europe. With English summary.) *Econ. Lavoro*, Jan.-Mar. 1986, *20*(1), pp. 45–76. **[G: Japan; W. Europe]**

Card, David. Efficient Contracts with Costly Adjustment: Short-run Employment Determination for Airline Mechanics. *Amer. Econ. Rev.*, December 1986, *76*(5), pp. 1045–71. **[G: U.S.]**

Card, David. The Impact of Deregulation on the Employment and Wages of Airline Mechanics. *Ind. Lab. Relat. Rev.*, July 1986, *39*(4), pp. 527–38. **[G: U.S.]**

Carr, Darrell E. Overtime Work: An Expanded View. *Mon. Lab. Rev.*, November 1986, *109*(11), pp. 36–39. **[G: U.S.]**

Carruth, Alan A.; Oswald, Andrew J. and Findlay, Lewis. A Test of a Model of Trade Union Behaviour: The Coal and Steel Industries in Britain. *Oxford Bull. Econ. Statist.*, February 1986, *48*(1), pp. 1–18. **[G: U.K.]**

Carter, Susan B. Occupational Segregation, Teachers' Wages, and American Economic Growth. *J. Econ. Hist.*, June 1986, *46*(2), pp. 373–83. **[G: U.S.]**

Casey, Bernard. A Symposium on the Role and Influence of Trade Unions in a Recession: Comments. *Brit. J. Ind. Relat.*, July 1986, *24*(2), pp. 212–13. **[G: U.K.]**

Castillo, L.; Gascon, F. and Jayasuriya, S. K. Off-Farm Employment of Farm Households in Laguna, Philippines. **In** *Shand, R. T., ed., Vol. 2*, 1986, pp. 133–46. **[G: Philippines]**

Chadha, G. K. The Off-Farm Economic Structure of Agriculturally Growing Regions: A Study of Indian Punjab. **In** *Shand, R. T., ed., Vol. 2*, 1986, pp. 147–75. **[G: India]**

Charsombut, Pradit. The Potential for Increases in Income and Employment in Thai Rural Household Manufacturing Enterprises. **In** *Shand, R. T., ed., Vol. 1*, 1986, pp. 231–55. **[G: Thailand]**

Chiswick, Barry R. Illegal Aliens: A Preliminary Report on an Employee–Employer Survey. *Amer. Econ. Rev.*, May 1986, *76*(2), pp. 253–57. **[G: U.S.]**

Christovich, Leslie and Stallworth, Lamont E. The Equal Employment Opportunity Act and Its Administration: The Claimant's Perspective. **In** *Dennis, B. D., ed.*, 1986, pp. 472–77. **[G: U.S.]**

Clark, Robert L. and McDermed, Ann A. Earnings and Pension Compensation: The Effect of Eligibility. *Quart. J. Econ.*, May 1986, *101*(2), pp. 341–61. **[G: U.S.]**

Cling, Jean-Pierre and Meunier, François. La désinflation en France: Le point de vue de l'économètre. (The French Disinflation. With English summary.) *Revue Écon.*, November 1986, *37*(6), pp. 1093–1125. **[G: France]**

Cohen, Yinon and Tyree, Andrea. Escape from Poverty: Determinants of Intergenerational Mobility of Sons and Daughters of the Poor. *Soc. Sci. Quart.*, December 1986, *67*(4), pp. 803–13. **[G: U.S.]**

Cohn, Elchanan and Kiker, B. F. Socioeconomic Background, Schooling, Experience and Monetary Rewards in the United States. *Economica*, November 1986, *53*(212), pp. 497–503. **[G: U.S.]**

Cooper, Russell. Macroeconomic Implications of Profit Sharing: Comment. **In** *Fischer, S., ed.*, 1986, pp. 343–51. **[G: Japan]**

Corner, Lorraine. The Prospects for Off-Farm Employment as an Anti-poverty Strategy among Malaysian Paddy Farm Households: Macro and Micro Views. **In** *Shand, R. T., ed., Vol. 2*, 1986, pp. 45–67. **[G: Malaysia]**

Crandall, Robert W. The EC–U.S. Steel Trade Crisis. **In** *Tsoukalis, L., ed.*, 1986, pp. 17–35. **[G: U.S.; EEC]**

Creedy, John and Whitfield, K. Earnings and Job Mobility: Professional Chemists in Britain. *J. Econ. Stud.*, 1986, *13*(2), pp. 23–37. **[G: U.K.]**

Cunningham, James S. and Donovan, Elaine. Patterns of Union Membership and Relative Wages. *J. Lab. Res.*, Spring 1986, *7*(2), pp. 127–44. **[G: U.S.]**

Datcher-Loury, Linda. Racial Differences in the Stability of High Earnings among Young Men. *J. Lab. Econ.*, Part 1, July 1986, *4*(3), pp. 301–16. **[G: U.S.]**

Datcher-Loury, Linda and Loury, Glenn C. The Effects of Attitudes and Aspirations on the Labor Supply of Young Men. **In** *Freeman, R.B. and Holzer, H. J., eds.*, 1986, pp. 377–99. **[G: U.S.]**

De Long, James Bradford and Summers, Lawrence H. Improvements in Macroeconomic Stability: The Role of Wages and Prices: Comment. **In** *Gordon, R. J., ed.*, 1986, pp. 669–72. **[G: U.S.]**

De Luca, Paolo. Punto unico, politica dei redditi, struttura del salario. (Income Policies and Wage Indexing in Italy. With English summary.) *Econ. Lavoro*, Oct.-Dec. 1986, *20*(4), pp. 21–37. **[G: Italy]**

Defourny, Jacques. Une analyse financière comparée des coopératives de travailleurs et des entreprises capitalistes en France. (A Comparative Financial Analysis of Workers' Cooperatives and Capitalist Firms in France. With English summary.) *Ann. Pub. Co-op. Econ.*, Jan.-March 1986, *57*(1), pp. 55–78. **[G: France]**

Dex, Shirley. Earnings Differentials of Second Generation West Indian and White School Leavers in Britain. *Manchester Sch. Econ. Soc. Stud.*, June 1986, *54*(2), pp. 162–79. **[G: U.K.]**

Diamond, Arthur M., Jr. What Is a Citation Worth? *J. Human Res.*, Spring 1986, *21*(2), pp. 200–215. **[G: U.S.]**

Dickinson, Katherine P.; Johnson, Terry R. and West, Richard W. An Analysis of the Impact of CETA Programs on Participants' Earnings. *J. Human Res.*, Winter 1986, *21*(1), pp. 64–91. **[G: U.S.]**

Dolado, Juan J.; Malo de Molina, José Luis and

Zabalza, Antonio. Spanish Industrial Unemployment: Some Explanatory Factors. *Economica,* Supplement 1986, *53*(210(S)), pp. S313–34. **[G: Spain]**

Dolton, P. J. and Makepeace, G. H. Sample Selection and Male–Female Earnings Differentials in the Graduate Labour Market. *Oxford Econ. Pap.*, July 1986, *38*(2), pp. 317–41. **[G: U.S.]**

Dooley, Martin D. The Overeducated Canadian? Changes in the Relationship among Earnings, Education, and Age for Canadian Men: 1971–81. *Can. J. Econ.*, February 1986, *19*(1), pp. 142–59. **[G: Canada]**

Duda, Helga and Tödtling, Franz. Austrian Trade Unions in the Economic Crisis. **In** *Edwards, R.; Garonna, P. and Tödtling, F., eds.*, 1986, pp. 227–68. **[G: Austria]**

Dunn, L. F. Work Disutility and Compensating Differentials: Estimation of Factors in the Link between Wages and Firm Size. *Rev. Econ. Statist.*, February 1986, *68*(1), pp. 67–73. **[G: U.S.]**

Dunn, L. F. and Youngblood, Stuart A. Absenteeism as a Mechanism for Approaching an Optimal Labor Market Equilibrium: An Empirical Study. *Rev. Econ. Statist.*, November 1986, *68*(4), pp. 668–74. **[G: U.S.]**

Dutkowsky, Donald H. and Gianturco, David J. On the Inflation-Unit Labor Cost Relation. *J. Econ. Bus.*, May 1986, *38*(2), pp. 173–81. **[G: U.S.]**

Eccleston, Bernard. Malthus, Wages and the Labour Market in England, 1790–1830. **In** *Turner, M., ed.*, 1986, pp. 143–56.

Edwards, Richard and Swaim, Paul. Union–Nonunion Earnings Differentials and the Decline of Private-Sector Unionism. *Amer. Econ. Rev.*, May 1986, *76*(2), pp. 97–102. **[G: U.S.]**

Ehrenberg, Ronald G. Black Youth Nonemployment: Duration and Job Search: Comment. **In** *Freeman, R. B. and Holzer, H. J., eds.*, 1986, pp. 70–73. **[G: U.S.]**

Ehrenberg, Ronald G. Workers' Rights: Rethinking Protective Labor Legislation. **In** *Ehrenberg, R. G., ed., Pt. B*, 1986, pp. 285–317. **[G: U.S.]**

Ehrenberg, Ronald G. and Schwarz, Joshua L. Public-Sector Labor Markets. **In** *Ashenfelter, O. and Layard, R., eds., Vol. 2*, 1986, pp. 1219–68. **[G: U.S.]**

Eichengreen, Barry and Gemery, Henry A. The Earnings of Skilled and Unskilled Immigrants at the End of the Nineteenth Century. *J. Econ. Hist.*, June 1986, *46*(2), pp. 441–54. **[G: U.S.]**

Elahi, Mahboob and Khan, Mahmud Jameel. Rural Labour Market with Special Reference to Hired Labour in Pakistan's Punjab. **In** *Hirashima, S. and Muqtada, M., eds.*, 1986, pp. 75–118. **[G: Pakistan]**

Elliott, Robert F. and Murphy, Phillip D. The Determinants of the Coverage of PBR Systems in Britain. *J. Econ. Stud.*, 1986, *13*(3), pp. 38–50. **[G: U.K.]**

Elliott, Robert F. and Murphy, Phillip D. The Theory of Net Advantages. *Scot. J. Polit. Econ.*, February 1986, *33*(1), pp. 46–57.

Etter, Christian. Versicherungsaspekte des Arbeitsverhältnisses: Der Einfluss impliziter Arbeitsverträge auf Löhne und Beschäftigung. Eine empirische Untersuchung für die Schweiz. (The Insurance Character of the Employer–Employee Relationship: The Influence of Implicit Labour Contracts on Wage Formation and Employment. An Empirical Analysis for Switzerland. With English summary.) *Schweiz. Z. Volkswirtsch. Statist.*, September 1986, *122*(3), pp. 405–24. **[G: Switzerland]**

Extejt, Marian M. Contributed Papers: Organizational Behavior and Personnel: Discussion. **In** *Dennis, B. D., ed.*, 1986, pp. 108–11.

Fagan, Thomas W. Comparative Costs of Alternative Forces in the U.S. Army. **In** *Gilroy, C. L., ed.*, 1986, pp. 347–60. **[G: U.S.]**

Falus-Szikra, Katalin. Wage and Income Disparities between the First and Second Economies in Hungary. *Acta Oecon.*, 1986, *36*(1–2), pp. 91–103. **[G: Hungary]**

Faustini, Gino. A New Method of Indexing Wages. *Rev. Econ. Cond. Italy,* Jan.-Apr. 1986, (1), pp. 65–84. **[G: Italy]**

Fauvel, Yvon. L'Incidence des régimes publics de pensions sur la consommation: une extension du modèle de Feldstein et une évaluation empirique pour le Canada. (The Effect of Public Pension Plans on Consumption. With English summary.) *L'Actual. Econ.*, June 1986, *62*(2), pp. 210–35. **[G: Canada]**

Feldman, Marshall M. A. Firm Size and Local Employment Change: Three Issues. *Reg. Stud.*, February 1986, *20*(1), pp. 73–77. **[G: U.S.]**

Ferber, Marianne A. What Is the Worth of "Comparable Worth"? *J. Econ. Educ.*, Fall 1986, *17*(4), pp. 267–82. **[G: U.S.]**

Ferber, Marianne A.; Green, Carole A. and Spaeth, Joe L. Work Power and Earnings of Women and Men. *Amer. Econ. Rev.*, May 1986, *76*(2), pp. 53–56. **[G: U.S.]**

Feuille, Peter and Delaney, John Thomas. Collective Bargaining, Interest Arbitration, and Police Salaries. *Ind. Lab. Relat. Rev.*, January 1986, *39*(2), pp. 228–40. **[G: U.S.]**

Filer, Randall K. The "Starving Artist"—Myth or Reality? Earnings of Artists in the United States. *J. Polit. Econ.*, February 1986, *94*(1), pp. 56–75. **[G: U.S.]**

Flaim, Paul O. Work Schedules of Americans: An Overview of New Findings. *Mon. Lab. Rev.*, November 1986, *109*(11), pp. 3–6.

Flinn, Christopher J. Wages and Job Mobility of Young Workers. *J. Polit. Econ.*, Part 2, June 1986, *94*(3), pp. S88–S110. **[G: U.S.]**

Fournier, Gary M. and Rasmussen, David W. Salaries in Public Education: The Impact of Geographic Cost-of-Living Differentials. *Public Finance Quart.*, April 1986, *14*(2), pp. 179–98. **[G: U.S.]**

Franz, Wolfgang and König, Heinz. The Nature and Causes of Unemployment in the Federal Republic of Germany since the 1970s: An Empirical Investigation. *Economica,* Supplement 1986, *53*(210(S)), pp. S219–44. **[G: W. Germany]**

Freedman, Audrey and Goldstein, Kenneth. Labor Market Data from the Conference Board. **In** *Dennis, B. D., ed.,* 1986, pp. 34–41. **[G: U.S.]**

Freeman, Richard B. Effects of Unions on the Economy. **In** *Lipset, S. M., ed.,* 1986, pp. 177–200.

Freeman, Richard B. In Search of Union Wage Concessions in Standard Data Sets. *Ind. Relat.,* Spring 1986, *25*(2), pp. 131–45. **[G: U.S.]**

Freeman, Richard B. The Effect of the Union Wage Differential on Management Opposition and Union Organizing Success. *Amer. Econ. Rev.,* May 1986, *76*(2), pp. 92–96. **[G: U.S.]**

Frenkel, Roberto. Salarios e inflación en América Latina. Resultados de investigaciones recientes en la Argentina, Brasil, Colombia, Costa Rica y Chile. (With English summary.) *Desarrollo Econ.,* Jan.-Mar. 1986, *25*(100), pp. 587–622. **[G: Argentina; Brazil; Colombia; Costa Rica; Chile]**

Friedenberg, Howard L. and DePass, Rudolph E. Regional Nonfarm Wages and Salaries: Three Years of Expansion. *Surv. Curr. Bus.,* April 1986, *66*(4), pp. 37–38. **[G: U.S.]**

Fuchs, Victor R. His and Hers: Gender Differences in Work and Income, 1959–1979. *J. Lab. Econ.,* Part 2, July 1986, *4*(3), pp. S245–72. **[G: U.S.]**

Gannicott, Kenneth. Women, Wages, and Discrimination: Some Evidence from Taiwan. *Econ. Develop. Cult. Change,* July 1986, *34*(4), pp. 721–30. **[G: Taiwan]**

Garonna, Paolo and Pisani, Elena. Italian Unions in Transition: The Crisis of Political Unionism. **In** *Edwards, R.; Garonna, P. and Tödtling, F., eds.,* 1986, pp. 114–72. **[G: OECD; Italy]**

Geroski, Paul A. and Stewart, Mark B. Specification-induced Uncertainty in the Estimation of Trade Union Wage Differentials from Industry-level Data. *Economica,* February 1986, *53*(209), pp. 29–39. **[G: U.K.]**

Ginsburgh, Victor; Perelman, Sergio and Pestieau, Pierre. Les prestations des salariés en heures supplémentaires Résultats d'une enquête. (With English summary.) *Cah. Écon. Bruxelles,* 4th Trimester 1986, (112), pp. 109–25. **[G: Belgium]**

Glaude, Michel. Ancienneté, expérience et théorie dualiste du marché du travail: une étude sur données individuelles. (Tenure, Experience and Dual Labour Market Theory. With English summary.) *Écon. Appl.,* 1986, *39*(4), pp. 847–76. **[G: France]**

Grady, Stephen W. and Hutchinson, Gillian. A Symposium on the Role and Influence of Trade Unions in a Recession: Comments. *Brit. J. Ind. Relat.,* July 1986, *24*(2), pp. 209–12. **[G: U.K.]**

Gregory, Mary; Lobban, Peter and Thomson, Andrew. Bargaining Structure, Pay Settlements and Perceived Pressures in Manufacturing 1979–84: Further Analysis from the CBI Databank. *Brit. J. Ind. Relat.,* July 1986, *24*(2), pp. 215–32. **[G: U.K.]**

Gregory, R. G. Wages Policy and Unemployment in Australia. *Economica,* Supplement 1986, *53*(210(S)), pp. S53–74. **[G: Australia]**

Gregory, R. G. Wages Policy and Unemployment in Australia. **In** *Bean, C. R.; Layard, P. R. G. and Nickell, S. J., eds.,* 1986, pp. 53–74. **[G: Australia]**

Grenier, Gilles and Lacroix, Guy. Les revenus et la langue: le cas de la capitale nationale. (Earnings and Language: The Case of the National Capital. With English summary.) *L'Actual. Econ.,* September 1986, *62*(3), pp. 365–84. **[G: Canada]**

Griliches, Zvi. Birth Order, Schooling, and Earnings: Comment. *J. Lab. Econ.,* Part 2, July 1986, *4*(3), pp. S146–50. **[G: U.S.]**

Gunter, Lewell F. Wage Determination for Regular Hired Farm Workers: An Empirical Analysis for Georgia. *Southern J. Agr. Econ.,* December 1986, *18*(2), pp. 197–206. **[G: U.S.]**

Haberman, Steven. Improvements in State Pension Rights for Women. **In** *von der Schulenburg, J.-M. G., ed.,* 1986, pp. 130–65. **[G: U.K.]**

Hall, Stephen G. An Application of the Granger & Engle Two-Step Estimation Procedure to United Kingdom Aggregate Wage Data. *Oxford Bull. Econ. Statist.,* August 1986, *48*(3), pp. 229–39. **[G: U.K.]**

Ham, John C. Testing Whether Unemployment Represents Intertemporal Labour Supply Behaviour. *Rev. Econ. Stud.,* August 1986, *53*(4), pp. 559–78.

Hamada, Koichi and Kurosaka, Yoshio. Trends in Unemployment, Wages and Productivity: The Case of Japan. **In** *Bean, C. R.; Layard, P. R. G. and Nickell, S. J., eds.,* 1986, pp. 275–96. **[G: Japan]**

Hamada, Koichi and Kurosaka, Yoshio. Trends in Unemployment, Wages and Productivity: The Case of Japan. *Economica,* Supplement 1986, *53*(210(S)), pp. S275–96. **[G: Japan]**

Hamermesh, Daniel S. Inflation and Labour Market Adjustment. *Economica,* February 1986, *53*(209), pp. 63–73. **[G: U.S.]**

Harrison, Bennett; Tilly, Chris and Bluestone, Barry. Wage Inequality Takes a Great U-Turn. *Challenge,* Mar./Apr. 1986, *29*(1), pp. 26–32. **[G: U.S.]**

Hartog, Joop. Allocation and the Earnings Function. *Empirical Econ.,* 1986, *11*(2), pp. 97–110. **[G: Netherlands]**

Hartog, Joop. Earnings Functions: Beyond Human Capital. *Appl. Econ.,* December 1986, *18*(12), pp. 1291–1309. **[G: Netherlands]**

Hartog, Joop and Theeuwes, Jules. Participation and Hours of Work: Two Stages in the Life-Cycle of Married Women. *Europ. Econ. Rev.,* August 1986, *30*(4), pp. 833–57. **[G: Netherlands]**

Heckman, James J. and Hotz, V. Joseph. An Investigation of the Labor Market Earnings of Panamanian Males: Evaluating the Sources of

Inequality. *J. Human Res.*, Fall 1986, *21*(4), pp. 507–42. **[G: Panama]**

Hendricks, Wallace and Kahn, Lawrence M. Wage Indexation and Compensating Wage Differentials. *Rev. Econ. Statist.*, August 1986, *68*(3), pp. 484–92. **[G: U.S.]**

Heneman, Robert L. Contributed Papers: Organizational Behavior and Personnel: Discussion. **In** *Dennis, B. D., ed.*, 1986, pp. 104–07.

Henry, S. G. B. and Wren-Lewis, Simon. The Labour Market. *Nat. Inst. Econ. Rev.*, February 1986, (115), pp. 52–63. **[G: U.K.]**

Herath, H. M. G. An Exploratory Study of Off-Farm Employment and Incomes in Sri Lanka. **In** *Shand, R. T., ed., Vol. 2*, 1986, pp. 209–33. **[G: Sri Lanka]**

Hersoug, Tor; Kjaer, Knut N. and Rødseth, Asbjorn. Wages, Taxes and the Utility-Maximizing Trade Union: A Confrontation with Norwegian Data. *Oxford Econ. Pap.*, November 1986, *38*(3), pp. 403–23. **[G: Norway]**

Heywood, John S. Labor Quality and the Concentration–Earnings Hypothesis. *Rev. Econ. Statist.*, May 1986, *68*(2), pp. 342–46. **[G: U.S.]**

Hill, Herbert. Equal Employment Opportunity Act and Its Administration: An Appraisal of the Commission and the Act: Discussion. **In** *Dennis, B. D., ed.*, 1986, pp. 478–85. **[G: U.S.]**

Hills, Stephen M. and Shapiro, David. Inter-industry Mobility and Wage Changes in the 1970s: A Longitudinal Analysis of the Construction, Auto, and Steel Industries. **In** *Dennis, B. D., ed.*, 1986, pp. 400–408. **[G: U.S.]**

Hirsch, Werner Z. and Rufolo, Anthony M. Effects of State Income Taxes on Fringe Benefits Demand of Policeman and Firemen. *Nat. Tax J.*, June 1986, *39*(2), pp. 211–19. **[G: U.S.]**

Hirsch, Werner Z. and Rufolo, Anthony M. Residence Laws and Unionization in Municipal Labor Markets: The Case of Firefighters. *J. Lab. Res.*, Winter 1986, *7*(1), pp. 41–58. **[G: U.S.]**

Ho, Samuel P. S. Off-Farm Employment and Farm Households in Taiwan. **In** *Shand, R. T., ed., Vol. 1*, 1986, pp. 95–133. **[G: Taiwan]**

Hodson, Randy and England, Paula. Industrial Structure and Sex Differences in Earnings. *Ind. Relat.*, Winter 1986, *25*(1), pp. 16–32. **[G: U.S.]**

Hogan, William T. The EC–U.S. Steel Trade Crisis: Comment. **In** *Tsoukalis, L., ed.*, 1986, pp. 42–44. **[G: U.S.; EEC]**

Holden, Kenneth and Peel, David A. Expectations Formation, Public Forecasts and the Wage Equation. *Econ. Modelling*, April 1986, *3*(2), pp. 129–34. **[G: U.K.]**

Holden, Kenneth and Peel, David A. The Impact of Benefits on Unemployment in Britain in the Interwar Period: Some Further Empirical Evidence. *J. Macroecon.*, Spring 1986, *8*(2), pp. 227–32. **[G: U.K.]**

Holland, A. Steven. Wage Indexation and the Effect of Inflation Uncertainty on Employment: An Empirical Analysis. *Amer. Econ. Rev.*, March 1986, *76*(1), pp. 235–43. **[G: U.S.]**

Holzer, Harry J. Are Unemployed Black Youth Income Maximizers? *Southern Econ. J.*, January 1986, *52*(3), pp. 777–84. **[G: U.S.]**

Holzer, Harry J. Black Youth Nonemployment: Duration and Job Search. **In** *Freeman, R. B. and Holzer, H. J., eds.*, 1986, pp. 23–70. **[G: U.S.]**

Holzer, Harry J. Reservation Wages and Their Labor Market Effects for Black and White Male Youth. *J. Human Res.*, Spring 1986, *21*(2), pp. 157–77. **[G: U.S.]**

Horowitz, Stanley A. Experience and Readiness. **In** *Gilroy, C. L., ed.*, 1986, pp. 321–27. **[G: U.S.]**

Horvitz, Sigmund A. Implications of Projecting Future Losses of Earning Capacity with Deterministic Models [Problems in the Use of Historical Data in Estimating Economic Loss in Wrongful Death and Injury Cases]. *J. Risk Ins.*, September 1986, *53*(3), pp. 530–37. **[G: U.S.]**

Hoyman, Michele. Equal Employment Opportunity Act and Its Administration: An Appraisal of the Commission and the Act: Discussion. **In** *Dennis, B. D., ed.*, 1986, pp. 486–89.

Hughes, Gerard. Employers' Social Insurance Contributions and Employment: Reply. *Econ. Soc. Rev.*, October 1986, *18*(1), pp. 57–68. **[G: Ireland]**

Hunt, E. H. Atlas of Industrializing Britain 1780–1914: Wages. **In** *Langton, J. and Morris, R. J., eds.*, 1986, pp. 60–68. **[G: U.K.]**

Hunt, H. Allan. Two Rounds of Workers' Compensation Reform in Michigan. **In** *Chelius, J., ed.*, 1986, pp. 55–84. **[G: U.S.]**

Hunt, Janet C., et al. Wages, Union Membership, and Public Sector Bargaining Legislation: Simultaneous Equations with an Ordinal Qualitative Variable. *J. Lab. Res.*, Summer 1986, *7*(3), pp. 255–67. **[G: U.S.]**

Hutchens, Robert M. The Effects of the Omnibus Budget Reconciliation Act of 1981 on AFDC Recipients: A Review of Studies. **In** *Ehrenberg, R. G., ed., Pt. B*, 1986, pp. 351–87. **[G: U.S.]**

Ichniowski, Bernard E. and Preston, Anne E. New Trends in Part-time Employment. **In** *Dennis, B. D., ed.*, 1986, pp. 60–67. **[G: U.S.]**

Islam, Iyanatul and Kirkpatrick, Colin. Export-Led Development, Labour-Market Conditions and the Distribution of Income: The Case of Singapore. *Cambridge J. Econ.*, June 1986, *10*(2), pp. 113–27. **[G: Singapore]**

Islam, Rizwanul. Non-farm Employment in Rural Asia: Issues and Evidence. **In** *Shand, R. T., ed., Vol. 1*, 1986, pp. 153–73. **[G: Bangladesh; Sri Lanka; Pakistan; Thailand; India]**

Jacoby, Sanford M. and Mitchell, Daniel J. B. Management Attitudes toward Two-Tier Pay Plans. *J. Lab. Res.*, Summer 1986, *7*(3), pp. 221–37. **[G: U.S.]**

Jarousse, Jean-Pierre and Mingat, Alain. Un réexamen du modèle de gains de mincer. (A Re-appraisal of Mincer's Earnings Model. With English summary.) *Revue Écon.*, November

1986, *37*(6), pp. 999–1031. **[G: France]**

Jasso, Guillermina and Rosenzweig, Mark R. What's in a Name? Country-of-Origin Influences on the Earnings of Immigrants in the United States. **In** *Stark, O., ed.*, 1986, pp. 75–106. **[G: U.S.]**

Johnson, G. E. and Layard, Richard. The Natural Rate of Unemployment: Explanation and Policy. **In** *Ashenfelter, O. and Layard, R., eds., Vol. 2*, 1986, pp. 921–99. **[G: OECD]**

Johnson, William R. and Skinner, Jonathan. Labor Supply and Marital Separation. *Amer. Econ. Rev.*, June 1986, *76*(3), pp. 455–69. **[G: U.S.]**

Joshi, Heather. Participation in Paid Work: Evidence from the Women and Employment Survey. **In** *Blundell, R. and Walker, I., eds.*, 1986, pp. 217–42. **[G: U.K.]**

Kada, Ryohei. Off-Farm Employment and the Rural–Urban Interface in Japanese Economic Development. **In** *Shand, R. T., ed., Vol. 1*, 1986, pp. 75–93. **[G: Japan]**

Kasim, Sukor and Najimudin, Mustafa. Evolution of Sources of Income in the Muda Irrigation Scheme, Malaysia, 1972/73 to 1981/82. **In** *Shand, R. T., ed., Vol. 2*, 1986, pp. 21–43. **[G: Malaysia]**

Kasryno, Faisal. Impact of Off-Farm Employment on Agricultural Labour Absorption and Wages in Indonesia. **In** *Shand, R. T., ed., Vol. 1*, 1986, pp. 273–307. **[G: Indonesia]**

Katz, Eliakim and Ziderman, Adrian. Towards a Theory of Incremental Wage Scales. *Appl. Econ.*, October 1986, *18*(10), pp. 1047–50. **[G: U.S.]**

Katz, Lawrence F. Efficiency Wage Theories: A Partial Evaluation. **In** *Fischer, S., ed.*, 1986, pp. 235–76. **[G: U.S.]**

Kawashima, Yoko and Tachibanaki, Toshiaki. The Effect of Discrimination and of Industry Segmentation on Japanese Wage Differentials in Relation to Education. *Int. J. Ind. Organ.*, March 1986, *4*(1), pp. 43–68. **[G: Japan]**

Kikuchi, Masao. Growing Impact of Off-Farm Employment on a Rural Economy: Changes in Labour Utilization and Income Earning Structure in a Philippine Rice Village. **In** *Shand, R. T., ed., Vol. 2*, 1986, pp. 99–131. **[G: Philippines]**

Killingsworth, Mark R. A Simple Structural Model of Heterogeneous Preferences and Compensating Wage Differentials. **In** *Blundell, R. and Walker, I., eds.*, 1986, pp. 303–17. **[G: U.S.]**

King, Allan G.; Lowell, B. Lindsay and Bean, Frank D. The Effects of Hispanic Immigrants on the Earnings of Native Hispanic Americans. *Soc. Sci. Quart.*, December 1986, *67*(4), pp. 673–89. **[G: U.S.]**

King, Stephen R. Improvements in Macroeconomic Stability: The Role of Wages and Prices: Comment. **In** *Gordon, R. J., ed.*, 1986, pp. 665–69. **[G: U.S.]**

Kleiman, Ephraim. Indexation in the Labor Market. **In** *Ben-Porath, Y., ed.*, 1986, pp. 302–19. **[G: Israel]**

Klein, Bruce W. Missed Work and Lost Hours, May 1985. *Mon. Lab. Rev.*, November 1986, *109*(11), pp. 26–30. **[G: U.S.]**

Klodt, Henning. Lohnquote und Beschäftigung—Die Lohnlücke. (Labour Share and Employment—The Wage-Gap. With English summary.) *Jahr. Nationalökon. Statist.*, September 1986, *201*(5), pp. 480–97. **[G: W. Germany; OECD]**

Koch, Paul D. and Ragan, James F., Jr. Investigating the Causal Relationship between Quits and Wages: An Exercise in Comparative Dynamics. *Econ. Inquiry*, January 1986, *24*(1), pp. 61–83. **[G: U.S.]**

Kohlöffel, Klaus and Zietemann, Ulrich. Betriebswirtschaftliche Aspekte von arbeitszeitverkürzenden Massnahmen. (With English summary.) *Z. Betriebswirtschaft*, October 1986, *56*(10), pp. 1030–38.

Köllö, János. The Impact of the Labour Market on the Employment Structure in Hungary. *Acta Oecon.*, 1986, *36*(3–4), pp. 197–208. **[G: Hungary]**

König, Heinz. Work Incentives, Wage Differentials and the Supply of Human Resources: Comment. **In** *Balassa, B. and Giersch, H., eds.*, 1986, pp. 165–68. **[G: U.S.]**

Lal, Deepak. Stolper–Samuleson–Rybczynski in the Pacific: Real Wages and Real Exchange Rates in the Philippines, 1956–1978. *J. Devel. Econ.*, April 1986, *21*(1), pp. 181–204. **[G: Philippines]**

Lang, Kevin and Ruud, Paul A. Returns to Schooling, Implicit Discount Rates and Black–White Wage Differentials. *Rev. Econ. Statist.*, February 1986, *68*(1), pp. 41–47. **[G: U.S.]**

Lassibille, Gérard. L'influence des événements familiaux dans la formation des revenus. (The Effect of Family Events on Earnings. With English summary.) *Ann. Écon. Statist.*, Apr./June 1986, (2), pp. 101–16. **[G: France]**

Laurent, André. The Elimination of Sex Discrimination in Occupational Social Security Schemes in the EEC. *Int. Lab. Rev.*, Nov.-Dec. 1986, *125*(6), pp. 675–83. **[G: EEC]**

Layard, Richard and Nickell, Stephen J. Unemployment in Britain. *Economica*, Supplement 1986, *53*(210(S)), pp. S121–69. **[G: U.K.]**

Lazear, Edward P. Raids and Offer Matching. **In** *Ehrenberg, R. G., ed., Pt. A*, 1986, pp. 141–65. **[G: U.S.]**

Lazear, Edward P. Salaries and Piece Rates. *J. Bus.*, July 1986, *59*(3), pp. 405–31.

Lazear, Edward P. and Moore, Robert L. Incentives, Productivity, and Labor Contracts. **In** *Akerlof, G. A. and Yellen, J. L., eds.*, 1986, *1984*, pp. 135–56. **[G: U.S.]**

Leibig, Michael T. The Deprivitization of Employee Benefit and Labor Law: The Surprising Conservative Erosion of Trusts and of the Competitive Labor Model. *Law Contemp. Probl.*, Autumn 1986, *49*(4), pp. 183–209. **[G: U.S.]**

Leigh, J. Paul. Are Compensating Wages Paid for Time spent Commuting? *Appl. Econ.*, November 1986, *18*(11), pp. 1203–13. **[G: U.S.]**

Leontief, Wassily. Technological Change, Prices,

Wages, and Rates of Return on Capital in the U.S. Economy. In *Leontief, W.*, 1986, *1985*, pp. 392–417. **[G: U.S.]**

Lewis, H. Gregg. Union Relative Wage Effects. In *Ashenfelter, O. and Layard, R., eds., Vol. 2*, 1986, pp. 1139–81. **[G: U.S.]**

Lilien, David M. and Hall, Robert E. Cyclical Fluctuations in the Labor Market. In *Ashenfelter, O. and Layard, R., eds., Vol. 2*, 1986, pp. 1001–35. **[G: U.S.]**

Lillard, Lee; Smith, James P. and Welch, Finis. What Do We Really Know about Wages? The Importance of Nonreporting and Census Imputation. *J. Polit. Econ.*, Part 1, June 1986, *94*(3), pp. 489–506. **[G: U.S.]**

Lim, Chong Yah, et al. Report of the Central Provident Fund Study Group. *Singapore Econ. Rev.*, April 1986, *31*(1), pp. ii–107. **[G: Singapore]**

Liu, Pak-Wai. Human Capital, Job Matching and Earnings Growth between Jobs: An Empirical Analysis. *Appl. Econ.*, October 1986, *18*(10), pp. 1135–47. **[G: Singapore]**

Lubrano, Michel. Bayesian Analysis of Single Market Disequilibrium Models: An Application to Unemployment in the U.S. Labour Market. In *Blundell, R. and Walker, I., eds.*, 1986, pp. 75–102. **[G: U.S.]**

Luizer, James and Thornton, Robert. Concentration in the Labor Market for Public School Teachers. *Ind. Lab. Relat. Rev.*, July 1986, *39*(4), pp. 573–84. **[G: U.S.]**

Maani, Sholeh A. and Studenmund, A. H. The Critical Wage, Unemployment Duration, and Wage Expectations: The Case of Chile. *Ind. Lab. Relat. Rev.*, January 1986, *39*(2), pp. 264–76. **[G: Chile]**

Maier, Gunther and Weiss, Peter. The Importance of Regional Factors in the Determination of Earnings: The Case of Austria. *Int. Reg. Sci. Rev.*, December 1986, *10*(3), pp. 211–20. **[G: Austria]**

Maki, Dennis R. and Meredith, Lindsay N. The Effect of U.S. and Canadian Wage and Productivity Differentials and FDI Status on the Canadian Propensity to Import U.S. Sourced Products. *Weltwirtsch. Arch.*, 1986, *122*(1), pp. 164–72. **[G: U.S.; Canada]**

Marcus, Richard D. Earnings and the Decision to Return to School. *Econ. Educ. Rev.*, 1986, *5*(3), pp. 309–17. **[G: U.S.]**

Margo, Robert A. Race and Human Capital: Comment. *Amer. Econ. Rev.*, December 1986, *76*(5), pp. 1221–24. **[G: U.S.]**

Marsden, David and Richardson, Ray. Youth Pay and Employers' Recruitment Practices for Young Workers in Western Europe. *Brit. J. Ind. Relat.*, March 1986, *24*(1), pp. 25–27. **[G: W. Europe]**

Marshall, Ray. Reversing the Downtrend in Real Wages. *Challenge*, May/June 1986, *29*(2), pp. 48–55. **[G: U.S.]**

Martin, James E. and Peterson, Melanie M. Two-Tier Wage Structures and Attitude Differences. In *Dennis, B. D., ed.*, 1986, pp. 72–79. **[G: U.S.]**

Mazumdar, Dipak and Sawit, M. Husein. Trends in Rural Wages, West Java, 1977–83. *Bull. Indonesian Econ. Stud.*, December 1986, *22*(3), pp. 93–105. **[G: Indonesia]**

McCormick, Barry. Evidence about the Comparative Earnings of Asian and West Indian Workers in Great Britain. *Scot. J. Polit. Econ.*, May 1986, *33*(2), pp. 97–110. **[G: U.K.]**

McCrohan, Kevin F. The Revenue Loss Due to Undocumented Alien Earnings: Estimates for 1980. *J. Econ. Soc. Meas.*, December 1986, *14*(4), pp. 311–24. **[G: U.S.]**

McMahon, Patrick J. An International Comparison of Labor Force Participation, 1977–84. *Mon. Lab. Rev.*, May 1986, *109*(5), pp. 3–12. **[G: W. Germany; N. America; Japan; Australia; Sweden]**

McMahon, Patrick J. and Tschetter, John H. The Declining Middle Class: A Further Analysis. *Mon. Lab. Rev.*, September 1986, *109*(9), pp. 22–27. **[G: U.S.]**

Mehay, Stephen L. and Gonzalez, Rodolfo A. The Relative Effect of Unionization and Interjurisdictional Competition on Municipal Wages. *J. Lab. Res.*, Winter 1986, *7*(1), pp. 79–93. **[G: U.S.]**

Mellor, Earl F. Shift Work and Flexitime: How Prevalent Are They? *Mon. Lab. Rev.*, November 1986, *109*(11), pp. 14–21. **[G: U.S.]**

Mellor, Earl F. Weekly Earnings in 1985: A Look at More Than 200 Occupations. *Mon. Lab. Rev.*, September 1986, *109*(9), pp. 28–32. **[G: U.S.]**

Mellor, Earl F. and Haugen, Steven E. Hourly Paid Workers: Who They Are and What They Earn. *Mon. Lab. Rev.*, February 1986, *109*(2), pp. 20–26. **[G: U.S.]**

Messerlin, Patrick A. The EC–U.S. Steel Trade Crisis: Comment. In *Tsoukalis, L., ed.*, 1986, pp. 36–41. **[G: U.S.; EEC]**

Metcalf, David. Employment-Subsidies and Redundancies. In *Blundell, R. and Walker, I., eds.*, 1986, pp. 103–20. **[G: U.K.]**

Michl, Thomas R. The Productivity Slowdown and the Elasticity of Demand for Labor. *Rev. Econ. Statist.*, August 1986, *68*(3), pp. 532–36. **[G: U.S.]**

Mincer, Jacob. Wage Changes in Job Changes. In *Ehrenberg, R. G., ed., Pt. A*, 1986, pp. 171–97. **[G: U.S.]**

Minde, Kjell Bjørn and Ramstad, Jan. The Development of Real Wages in Norway about 1730–1910. *Scand. Econ. Hist. Rev.*, 1986, *34*(2), pp. 90–121. **[G: Norway]**

Minford, Patrick. Incentives in the United Kingdom. In *Balassa, B. and Giersch, H., eds.*, 1986, pp. 279–95. **[G: U.K.]**

Mitchell, Daniel J. B. Explanations of Wage Inflexibility: Institutions and Incentives. In *Beckerman, W., ed.*, 1986, pp. 43–76. **[G: U.S.]**

Mitchell, Daniel J. B. Union vs. Nonunion Wage Norm Shifts. *Amer. Econ. Rev.*, May 1986, *76*(2), pp. 249–52. **[G: U.S.]**

Mitchell, Jean M. and Butler, J. S. Arthritis and the Earnings of Men: An Analysis Incorporating Selection Bias. *J. Health Econ.*, March 1986, *5*(1), pp. 81–98. **[G: U.S.]**

Morgan, James N. Unpaid Productive Activity over the Life Course. **In** *Inst. Med. and Nat'l Res. Counc., Comm. on an Aging Society*, 1986, pp. 73–109. **[G: U.S.]**

Morrisey, Michael A.; Alexander, Jeffrey A. and Shortell, Stephen M. Medical Staff Size, Hospital Privileges, and Compensation Arrangements: A Comparison of System Hospitals. **In** *Gray, B. H., ed.*, 1986, pp. 422–57. **[G: U.S.]**

Moulton, Brent R. Human Capital Accumulation and Trends in the Male–Female Wage Gap in the United States, 1956–1983. *Eastern Econ. J.*, July-Sept. 1986, *12*(3), pp. 265–71. **[G: U.S.]**

Musgrove, Philip. Desigualdad en la distribución del ingreso en diez ciudades sudamericanas: descomposición e interpretación del coefficiente de gini. (With English summary.) *Cuadernos Econ.*, August 1986, *23*(69), pp. 201–27. **[G: Latin America]**

Nelson, Gary R. Compensation and Force Structure: A Comment. **In** *Gilroy, C. L., ed.*, 1986, pp. 385–91. **[G: U.S.]**

Nelson, K. Labor Demand, Labor Supply and the Suburbanization of Low-wage Office Work. **In** *Scott, A. J. and Storper, M., eds.*, 1986, pp. 149–71. **[G: U.S.]**

Neusser, Klaus. Time Series Representation of the Austrian Labor Market. *Weltwirtsch. Arch.*, 1986, *122*(2), pp. 292–312. **[G: Austria]**

Newman, Winn and Owens, Christine L. Wage Discrimination: A Family Issue. **In** *Hewlett, S. A.; Ilchman, A. S. and Sweeney, J. J., eds.*, 1986, pp. 161–68. **[G: U.S.]**

Noguchi, Yukio. Overcommitment in Pensions: The Japanese Experience. **In** *Rose, R. and Shiratori, R., eds.*, 1986, pp. 173–92. **[G: Japan]**

Nord, Stephen. An Analysis of the Effects of Higher Education on Wage Differentials between Blacks and Whites by Gender in the United States. *Appl. Econ.*, February 1986, *18*(2), pp. 173–89. **[G: U.S.]**

O'Connell, John F. The Effects of Davis–Bacon on Labor Cost and Union Wages. *J. Lab. Res.*, Summer 1986, *7*(3), pp. 239–53. **[G: U.S.]**

O'Neill, June. Issues Surrounding Comparable Worth: Introduction. *Contemp. Policy Issues*, April 1986, *4*(2), pp. 1–3. **[G: U.S.]**

O'Relley, Z. Edward. Economic Reform, the Search for Economic Efficiency, and the Expansion of the Second Economy in Hungary. **In** *Altmann, F.-L., ed.*, 1986, pp. 218–37. **[G: Hungary]**

Ohsfeldt, Robert L. and Culler, Steven D. Differences in Income between Male and Female Physicians. *J. Health Econ.*, December 1986, *5*(4), pp. 335–46. **[G: U.S.]**

Oi, Walter Y. Neglected Women and Other Implications of Comparable Worth. *Contemp. Policy Issues*, April 1986, *4*(2), pp. 21–32. **[G: U.S.; Japan]**

Oi, Walter Y. The Postservice Earnings of Military Retirees: Comment. **In** *Gilroy, C. L., ed.*, 1986, pp. 314–19. **[G: U.S.]**

Onchan, Tongroj and Chalamwong, Yongyuth. Rural Off-Farm Income and Employment in Thailand: Current Evidence, Future Trends and Implications. **In** *Shand, R. T., ed., Vol. 1*, 1986, pp. 199–230. **[G: Thailand]**

Oshima, Harry T. Off-Farm Employment and Incomes in Postwar East Asian Growth. **In** *Shand, R. T., ed., Vol. 1*, 1986, pp. 25–74. **[G: Japan; Taiwan; S. Korea]**

Oshima, Harry T.; de Borja, Elizabeth and Paz, Wilhelmina. Rising National Income per Worker and Falling Real Wages in the Philippines in the 1970s. *Philippine Rev. Econ. Bus.*, Sept.-Dec. 1986, *23*(3–4), pp. 151–90. **[G: Philippines]**

Osterman, Paul. The Impact of Computers on the Employment of Clerks and Managers. *Ind. Lab. Relat. Rev.*, January 1986, *39*(2), pp. 175–86. **[G: U.S.]**

Østrup, Finn. Problemstillinger ved indretning af et pensionssystem. (A Comparison between Differnt Old-Age Pension Schemes. With English summary.) *Nationaløkon. Tidsskr.*, 1986, *124*(3), pp. 294–303.

Oswald, Andrew J. A Symposium on the Role and Influence of Trade Unions in a Recession: Comments. *Brit. J. Ind. Relat.*, July 1986, *24*(2), pp. 213–14. **[G: U.K.]**

Oswald, Andrew J. Is Wage Rigidity Caused by 'Lay-offs by Seniority'? **In** *Beckerman, W., ed.*, 1986, pp. 77–95. **[G: U.K.]**

Oswald, Andrew J. Unemployment Insurance and Labor Contracts under Asymmetric Information: Theory and Facts. *Amer. Econ. Rev.*, June 1986, *76*(3), pp. 365–77. **[G: U.S.]**

Oswald, Andrew J. Wage Determination and Recession: A Report on Recent Work. *Brit. J. Ind. Relat.*, July 1986, *24*(2), pp. 181–94.

Park, Fun Koo. Off-Farm Employment in Korea: Current Status and Future Prospects. **In** *Shand, R. T., ed., Vol. 1*, 1986, pp. 135–52. **[G: S. Korea]**

Parmenter, B. R. Taxation of Non-cash Fringe Benefits. *Australian Econ. Rev.*, 4th Quarter 1986, (76), pp. 30–33. **[G: Australia]**

Parsons, Donald O. The Employment Relationship: Job Attachment, Work Effort, and the Nature of Contracts. **In** *Ashenfelter, O. and Layard, R., eds., Vol. 2*, 1986, pp. 789–848. **[G: U.S.]**

Patrizi, Vincenzo. Measures of Concealed Employment: Pitfalls and Insights. *Econ. Lavoro*, Apr.-June 1986, *20*(2), pp. 91–111. **[G: Italy]**

Peck, Merton J. Is Japan Really a Share Economy? *J. Compar. Econ.*, December 1986, *10*(4), pp. 427–32. **[G: Japan]**

Pérez-López, Jorge F. The Economics of Cuban Joint Ventures. **In** *Mesa-Lago, C., ed.*, 1986, pp. 181–207. **[G: Cuba]**

Perry, George L. Policy Lessons from the Postwar Period. **In** *Beckerman, W., ed.*, 1986, pp. 127–51. **[G: OECD]**

Perry, George L. Shifting Wage Norms and Their

Implications. *Amer. Econ. Rev.*, May 1986, *76*(2), pp. 245–48. **[G: U.S.]**

Petersen, Jørn Henrik. Pensionsfinansiering i vækstsammenhaeng. (Pension Finance Based on a Pay-as-You-Go System versus a System Based on Previous Savings and Capital Accumulation. With English summary.) *Nationaløkon. Tidsskr.*, 1986, *124*(3), pp. 304–15. **[G: Denmark]**

Pichelmann, Karl and Wagner, Michael. Labour Surplus as a Signal for Real-Wage Adjustment: Austria, 1968–1984. *Economica*, Supplement 1986, *53*(210(S)), pp. S75–87. **[G: Austria]**

Piore, Michael J. The Effects of Attitudes and Aspirations on the Labor Supply of Young Men: Comment. **In** *Freeman, R. B. and Holzer, H. J., eds.*, 1986, pp. 399–401. **[G: U.S.]**

Plowman, David; Siebert, Calvin D. and Zaidi, Mahmood A. Market and Spillover Forces in Wage Award Determination in Australia. *Appl. Econ.*, February 1986, *18*(2), pp. 191–203. **[G: Australia]**

Podgursky, Michael. Unions, Establishment Size, and Intra-industry Threat Effects. *Ind. Lab. Relat. Rev.*, January 1986, *39*(2), pp. 277–84. **[G: U.S.]**

Pope, Ralph A. Economies of Scale in Large State and Municipal Retirement Systems. *Public Budg. Finance*, Autumn 1986, *6*(3), pp. 70–80.

Prescott, David; Swidinsky, Robert and Wilton, David A. Labour Supply Estimates for Low-Income Female Heads of Household Using Mincome Data. *Can. J. Econ.*, February 1986, *19*(1), pp. 134–41. **[G: Canada]**

Price, Daniel N. Cash Benefits for Short-Term Sickness: Thirty-five Years of Data, 1948–83. *Soc. Sec. Bull.*, May 1986, *49*(5), pp. 5–19. **[G: U.S.]**

Price, Daniel N. Workers' Compensation: Coverage, Benefits, and Costs, 1983. *Soc. Sec. Bull.*, February 1986, *49*(2), pp. 5–11. **[G: U.S.]**

Quan, Nguyen T. Characteristics of Blue Collar and White Collar Jobs and Pecuniary Returns. *J. Behav. Econ.*, Spring/Summer 1986, *15* (1/2), pp. 157–74. **[G: U.S.]**

Rahmeyer, Fritz. Der Zusammenhang zwischen Lohn-, Produktivitäts- und Preisstruktur im verarbeitenden Gewerbe. (The Interrelation between the Relative Growth of Wages, Productivity and Prices in the Manufacturing Sector. With English summary.) *Z. Wirtschaft. Sozialwissen.*, 1986, *106*(5), pp. 467–93. **[G: W. Germany]**

Raisian, John; Ward, Michael P. and Welch, Finis. Pay Equity and Comparable Worth. *Contemp. Policy Issues*, April 1986, *4*(2), pp. 4–20. **[G: U.S.]**

Rajaraman, Indira. Offered Wage and Recipient Attribute: Wage Functions for Rural Labour in India. *J. Devel. Econ.*, November 1986, *24*(1), pp. 179–95. **[G: India]**

Rassuli, Ali and Roy, Raj. Sex Discrimination in the Audiology Profession: It Explains Two-thirds of the $9,500 Difference between Male and Female Earnings. *Amer. J. Econ. Soc.*, April 1986, *45*(2), pp. 189–200. **[G: U.S.]**

Rees, Hedley and Shah, Anup. An Empirical Analysis of Self-employment in the U.K. *J. Appl. Econometrics*, January 1986, *1*(1), pp. 95–108. **[G: U.K.]**

Register, Charles A. Racial Employment and Earnings Differentials: The Impact of the Reagan Administration. *Rev. Black Polit. Econ.*, Summer 1986, *15*(1), pp. 59–69. **[G: U.S.]**

Register, Charles A. and Williams, Donald R. Some Evidence on the Impact of State-Level Equal Rights Legislation. *Soc. Sci. Quart.*, December 1986, *67*(4), pp. 869–76. **[G: U.S.]**

Reicher Madeira, Felicia. Youth in Brazil: Old Assumptions and New Approaches. *CEPAL Rev.*, August 1986, (29), pp. 55–78. **[G: Brazil]**

Reichlin, Lucrezia. Un approccio istituzionale alla determinazione del salario: il caso Italiano. (An Institutional Approach to Wage Determination in Italy. With English summary.) *Polit. Econ.*, December 1986, *2*(3), pp. 361–99. **[G: Italy]**

Reynolds, Morgan O. Unions and Jobs: The U.S. Auto Industry. *J. Lab. Res.*, Spring 1986, *7*(2), pp. 103–26. **[G: U.S.]**

Rubery, Jill. Trade Unions in the 1980s: The Case of the United Kingdom. **In** *Edwards, R.; Garonna, P. and Tödtling, F., eds.*, 1986, pp. 61–113. **[G: U.K.]**

Rubin, Marc. Occupation and Earnings Inequality: Some Contrasts between Workers and Management in Soviet Industry. *Econ. Planning*, 1986, *20*(3), pp. 206–30. **[G: U.S.S.R.]**

Rzhanitsyna, L. Intensifying the Stimulation of the Effectiveness of Labor. *Prob. Econ.*, May 1986, *29*(1), pp. 50–62. **[G: U.S.S.R.]**

Saffer, Henry. Wages and Hazardous Working Conditions. *Appl. Econ.*, August 1986, *18*(8), pp. 819–27. **[G: U.S.]**

Sajhau, Jean-Paul. Employment, Wages and Living Conditions in a Changing Industry—Plantations. *Int. Lab. Rev.*, Jan.-Feb. 1986, *125*(1), pp. 71–85. **[G: LDCs]**

Salisbury, Dallas L. and Witte, Hazel A. Employee Benefits and Assistance to Working Parents. **In** *Hewlett, S. A.; Ilchman, A. S. and Sweeney, J. J., eds.*, 1986, pp. 125–37. **[G: U.S.]**

San, Gee. The Early Labor Force Experience of College Students and Their Post-college Success. *Econ. Educ. Rev.*, 1986, *5*(1), pp. 65–76. **[G: U.S.]**

Sandesara, J. C. and Bishnoi, T. R. Factor Income Shares in Medium and Large Public Limited Companies in India—1950–51 to 1978–79—A Statistical Analysis. *Indian Econ. J.*, Oct.-Dec. 1986, *34*(2), pp. 28–48. **[G: India]**

Saunders, George. Impact of Interest Arbitration on Canadian Federal Employees' Wages. *Ind. Relat.*, Fall 1986, *25*(3), pp. 320–27. **[G: Canada]**

Schippers, Joop J. and Siegers, Jacques I. Women's Relative Wage Rate in the Netherlands, 1950–1983: A Test of Alternative Discrimination Theories. *De Economist,* 1986, *134*(2), pp. 165–80. **[G: Netherlands]**

Schwartz, Saul. Earnings Capacity and the Trend in Inequality among Black Men. *J. Human Res.*, Winter 1986, *21*(1), pp. 44–63. **[G: U.S.]**

Schwartz, Saul. The Relative Earnings of Vietnam and Korean-Era Veterans. *Ind. Lab. Relat. Rev.*, July 1986, *39*(4), pp. 564–72. **[G: U.S.]**

Scofea, Laura. BLS Area Wage Surveys Will Cover More Areas. *Mon. Lab. Rev.*, June 1986, *109*(6), pp. 19–23. **[G: U.S.]**

Scoville, James G. The Traditional Industrial Sector in Developing Countries: An Update on Its Role and Functioning. *Amer. J. Econ. Soc.*, July 1986, *45*(3), pp. 313–28. **[G: LDCs]**

Shah, Anup. Education and Earnings Inequality across British Labour Markets. *Appl. Econ.*, February 1986, *18*(2), pp. 205–17. **[G: U.K.]**

Shand, Richard T. and Chew, T. A. Off-Farm Employment in the Kemubu Project in Kelantan, Malaysia. **In** *Shand, R. T., ed., Vol. 2*, 1986, pp. 1–20. **[G: Malaysia]**

Shank, Susan E. Preferred Hours of Work and Corresponding Earnings. *Mon. Lab. Rev.*, November 1986, *109*(11), pp. 40–44. **[G: U.S.]**

Shannon, Russell and Wallace, Myles S. Wages and Inflation: An Investigation into Causality. *J. Post Keynesian Econ.*, Winter 1985-86, *8*(2), pp. 182–91. **[G: U.S.]**

Shapiro, David and Hills, Stephen M. Adjusting to Recession: Labor Market Dynamics in the Construction, Automobile, and Steel Industries. **In** *Hills, S. M., ed.*, 1986, pp. 37–62. **[G: U.S.]**

Shaw, R. Paul. Unemployment and Low Family Incomes in Canada. *Can. Public Policy*, June 1986, *12*(2), pp. 368–86. **[G: Canada]**

Simpson, Wayne. Analysis of Part-Time Pay in Canada. *Can. J. Econ.*, November 1986, *19*(4), pp. 798–807. **[G: Canada]**

Simpson, Wayne. Unions, Industrial Concentration and Wages: A Re-examination. *Appl. Econ.*, March 1986, *18*(3), pp. 305–17. **[G: Canada]**

Singer, Neil M. Retirement Changes and Military Force Manning: A Sensitivity Analysis. **In** *Gilroy, C. L., ed.*, 1986, pp. 329–46. **[G: U.S.]**

Sloan, Frank A. and Adamache, Killard W. Taxation and the Growth of Nonwage Compensation. *Public Finance Quart.*, April 1986, *14*(2), pp. 115–37. **[G: U.S.]**

Sloane, Peter J. The Male/Female Earnings Differential in Britain and Europe: Are There Lessons for the United States? **In** *Hewlett, S. A.; Ilchman, A. S. and Sweeney, J. J., eds.*, 1986, pp. 139–60. **[G: U.K.; EEC]**

Smith, Arthur B., Jr. Equal Employment Opportunity Act and Its Administration: A Management Perspective. **In** *Dennis, B. D., ed.*, 1986, pp. 465–71. **[G: U.S.]**

Smith, James P. Race and Human Capital: Reply. *Amer. Econ. Rev.*, December 1986, *76*(5), pp. 1225–29. **[G: U.S.]**

Smith, Shirley J. The Growing Diversity of Work Schedules. *Mon. Lab. Rev.*, November 1986, *109*(11), pp. 7–13. **[G: U.S.]**

Sneessens, Henri R. and Drèze, Jacques H. A Discussion of Belgian Unemployment, Combining Traditional Concepts and Disequilibrium Econometrics. *Economica*, Supplement 1986, *53*(210(S)), pp. S89–119. **[G: Belgium]**

Sneessens, Henri R. and Drèze, Jacques H. What, If Anything, Have We Learned from the Rise of Unemployment in Belgium, 1974–1983. *Cah. Écon. Bruxelles*, 2nd/3rd Trimester 1986, (110/111), pp. 21–66. **[G: Belgium]**

Snyder, Donald C. Defined Benefit or Defined Contribution Plans: Which Way Are Private Pensions Headed? *Soc. Sec. Bull.*, September 1986, *49*(9), pp. 14. **[G: U.S.]**

Snyder, Donald C. Pension Status of Recently Retired Workers on Their Longest Job: Findings from the New Beneficiary Survey. *Soc. Sec. Bull.*, August 1986, *49*(8), pp. 5–21. **[G: U.S.]**

Snyder, Donald C. Spend It or Save It? *Soc. Sec. Bull.*, September 1986, *49*(9), pp. 15–16. **[G: U.S.]**

Sorensen, Elaine. Implementing Comparable Worth: A Survey of Recent Job Evaluation Studies. *Amer. Econ. Rev.*, May 1986, *76*(2), pp. 364–67. **[G: U.S.]**

Speare, Alden, Jr. and Harris, John. Education, Earnings, and Migration in Indonesia. *Econ. Develop. Cult. Change*, January 1986, *34*(2), pp. 223–44. **[G: Indonesia]**

Spinanger, Dean. Work Incentives, Wage Differentials and the Supply of Human Resources. **In** *Balassa, B. and Giersch, H., eds.*, 1986, pp. 140–58. **[G: U.S.]**

Stewart, James B. and Hyclak, Thomas J. The Effects of Immigrants, Women, and Teenagers on the Relative Earnings of Black Males. *Rev. Black Polit. Econ.*, Summer 1986, *15*(1), pp. 93–101. **[G: U.S.]**

Stewart, Mark B. A Symposium on the Role and Influence of Trade Unions in a Recession: Comments. *Brit. J. Ind. Relat.*, July 1986, *24*(2), pp. 205–08. **[G: U.K.]**

Studenmund, A. H. and Maani, Sholeh A. Erratum [The Critical Wage, Unemployment Duration, and Wage Expectations: The Case of Chile]. *Ind. Lab. Relat. Rev.*, October 1986, *40*(1), pp. 128. **[G: Chile]**

Tamburi, Giovanni and Mouton, Pierre. The Uncertain Frontier between Private and Public Pension Schemes. *Int. Lab. Rev.*, Mar.-Apr. 1986, *125*(2), pp. 127–40.

Taylor, John B. Improvements in Macroeconomic Stability: The Role of Wages and Prices: Reply. **In** *Gordon, R. J., ed.*, 1986, pp. 672–75. **[G: U.S.]**

Taylor, John B. Improvements in Macroeconomic Stability: The Role of Wages and Prices. **In** *Gordon, R. J., ed.*, 1986, pp. 639–65. **[G: U.S.]**

Tokman, Víctor E. Creación de empleo productivo: una tarea impostergable. (With English summary.) *Desarrollo Econ.*, Oct.-Dec. 1986, *26*(103), pp. 339–67. **[G: Latin America]**

Topel, Robert. Job Mobility, Search, and Earnings Growth: A Reinterpretation of Human Capital Earnings Functions. **In** *Ehrenberg, R. G., ed., Pt. A*, 1986, pp. 199–233. **[G: U.S.]**

Tremblay, Carol Horton. Regional Wage Differentials: Has the South Risen Again? A Comment. *Rev. Econ. Statist.*, February 1986, *68*(1), pp. 175–78. **[G: U.S.]**

Tremblay, Carol Horton. The Impact of School and College Expenditures on the Wages of Southern and Non-Southern Workers. *J. Lab. Res.*, Spring 1986, *7*(2), pp. 201–11. **[G: U.S.]**

Tunali, Insan. A General Structure for Models of Double-Selection and an Application to a Joint Migration/Earnings Process with Remigration. **In** *Ehrenberg, R. G., ed., Pt. B*, 1986, pp. 235–83. **[G: Turkey]**

Uthoff, Andras W. Changes in Earnings Inequality and Labour Market Segmentation: Metropolitan Santiago 1969–78. *J. Devel. Stud.*, January 1986, *22*(2), pp. 300–326. **[G: Chile]**

Vaillancourt, François and Henriques, Irene. The Returns to University Schooling in Canada. *Can. Public Policy*, September 1986, *12*(3), pp. 449–58. **[G: Canada]**

Verbon, Harrie A. A. and van Winden, Frans. Public Pensions and Political Decision-Making. **In** *von der Schulenburg, J.-M. G., ed.*, 1986, pp. 32–53. **[G: Netherlands]**

Vijverberg, Wim P. M. Consistent Estimates of the Wage Equation When Individuals Choose among Income-Earning Activities. *Southern Econ. J.*, April 1986, *52*(4), pp. 1028–42. **[G: Malaysia]**

Vroman, Wayne. Transfer Payments, Sample Selection, and Male Black–White Earnings Differences. *Amer. Econ. Rev.*, May 1986, *76*(2), pp. 351–54. **[G: U.S.]**

Wachter, Michael L. Union Wage Rigidity: The Default Settings of Labor Law. *Amer. Econ. Rev.*, May 1986, *76*(2), pp. 240–44.

Walsh, John M. Sources of Labor Market Data from BNA. **In** *Dennis, B. D., ed.*, 1986, pp. 26–33. **[G: U.S.]**

Weiss, Laurence. Efficiency Wage Theories: A Partial Evaluation: Comment. **In** *Fischer, S., ed.*, 1986, pp. 285–87. **[G: U.S.]**

Weiss, Peter; Maier, Gunther and Gerking, Shelby. The Economic Evaluation of Job Safety: A Methodological Survey and Some Estimates for Austria. *Empirica*, 1986, *13*(1), pp. 53–67. **[G: Austria]**

Weiss, Yoram. The Determination of Life Cycle Earnings: A Survey. **In** *Ashenfelter, O. and Layard, R., eds., Vol. 1*, 1986, pp. 603–40.

Weitzman, Martin L. Macroeconomic Implications of Profit Sharing. **In** *Fischer, S., ed.*, 1986, pp. 291–335. **[G: Japan]**

White, Michael. Working Time and Employment: A Negotiable Issue? **In** *Hart, P. E., ed.*, 1986, pp. 5–22. **[G: W. Europe]**

White, Michael D. Self-interest Redistribution and the National Football League Players Association. *Econ. Inquiry*, October 1986, *24*(4), pp. 669–80. **[G: U.S.]**

Williams, Donald R. Contributed Papers: Labor Economics and Labor Markets: Discussion. **In** *Dennis, B. D., ed.*, 1986, pp. 418–23.

Williams, Donald R. and Register, Charles A. Regional Variations in Earnings and the Gender Composition of Employment: Is "Women's Work" Undervalued? *J. Econ. Issues*, December 1986, *20*(4), pp. 1121–34. **[G: U.S.]**

Willis, Robert J. Wage Determinants: A Survey and Reinterpretation of Human Capital Earnings Functions. **In** *Ashenfelter, O. and Layard, R., eds., Vol. 1*, 1986, pp. 525–602. **[G: U.S.]**

Wiradi, Gunawan. Landlessness, Tenancy and Off-Farm Employment in Rural Java: A Study of Twelve Villages. **In** *Shand, R. T., ed., Vol. 1*, 1986, pp. 309–26. **[G: Indonesia]**

Withers, Glenn A.; Pitman, D. and Whittingham, B. Wage Adjustments and Labour Market Systems: A Cross-Country Analysis. *Econ. Rec.*, December 1986, *62*(179), pp. 415–26. **[G: Australia; U.K.; U.S.; Sweden]**

Wong, Yue-chim. Entrepreneurship, Marriage, and Earnings. *Rev. Econ. Statist.*, November 1986, *68*(4), pp. 693–99. **[G: Hong Kong]**

Woods, John. Working Women and Pensions. *Soc. Sec. Bull.*, May 1986, *49*(5), pp. 33–34. **[G: U.S.]**

Yaniv, Gideon. Absenteeism, Overtime, and the Compressed Workweek. *J. Behav. Econ.*, Spring/Summer 1986, *15*(1/2), pp. 211–19.

Young, Karen M. Creating the Idea of Ownership: Lessons from Employee Ownership Success Stories. **In** *Dennis, B. D., ed.*, 1986, pp. 214–20. **[G: U.S.]**

Zachmann, Roberto. Reduction of Working Time as a Means to Reduce Unemployment: A Micro-economic Perspective. *Int. Lab. Rev.*, Mar.-Apr. 1986, *125*(2), pp. 163–75.

8243 Employment Studies; Unemployment and Vacancies; Retirements and Quits

Abedian, Iraj and Standish, B. Market Imperfections and Unemployment: A Model of the South African Labour Market 1900–1940. *S. Afr. J. Econ.*, December 1986, *54*(4), pp. 406–17. **[G: S. Africa]**

Abraham, Katharine G. Structural/Frictional vs. Deficient Demand Unemployment: Reply. *Amer. Econ. Rev.*, March 1986, *76*(1), pp. 273–76. **[G: U.S.]**

Abraham, Katharine G. Why Is the Unemployment Rate So Very High near Full Employment? Comments. *Brookings Pap. Econ. Act.*, 1986, (2), pp. 384–89. **[G: U.S.]**

Abraham, Katharine G. and Katz, Lawrence F. Cyclical Unemployment: Sectoral Shifts or Aggregate Disturbances? *J. Polit. Econ.*, Part 1, June 1986, *94*(3), pp. 507–22.

Adams, Charles; Fenton, Paul R. and Larsen, Flemming. Differences in Employment Behavior among Industrial Countries. **In** *Interna-*

tional Monetary Fund, Research Department, 1986, pp. 1–50. **[G: OECD]**

Adnett, N. J. On the Job Search in a Recession. *Appl. Econ.*, March 1986, *18*(3), pp. 333–45. **[G: U.K.]**

Ahuja, Kanta. Agricultural Labour and Rural Employment. **In** *Dantwala, M. L., et al.*, 1986, pp. 400–431. **[G: India]**

Akerlof, George A. and Yellen, Janet L. Efficiency Wage Models of the Labor Market. **In** *Akerlof, G. A. and Yellen, J. L., eds.*, 1986, pp. 1–21. **[G: U.S.]**

Aldcroft, Derek H. Great Britain—The Constraints to Full Employment in the 1930s and 1980s. **In** *Berend, I. T. and Borchardt, K., eds.*, 1986, pp. 106–24. **[G: U.K.]**

Alic, John A. and Harris, Martha Caldwell. Employment Lessons from the Electronics Industry. *Mon. Lab. Rev.*, February 1986, *109*(2), pp. 27–36. **[G: U.S.]**

Allen, Stuart D.; Sulock, Joseph M. and Sabo, William A. The Political Business Cycle: How Significant? *Public Finance Quart.*, January 1986, *14*(1), pp. 107–12. **[G: U.S.]**

Amin, A. T. M. Nurul. Urban Informal Sector: Employment Potentials and Problems. **In** *Islam, R. and Muqtada, M., eds.*, 1986, pp. 209–46. **[G: Bangladesh]**

Amin, A. T. M. Nurul. Urban Unemployment and Underemployment. **In** *Islam, R. and Muqtada, M., eds.*, 1986, pp. 21–39. **[G: Bangladesh]**

Andersen, P. S. Keynesian and Classical Unemployment: Evidence from the Current Cycle. *Eastern Econ. J.*, July-Sept. 1986, *12*(3), pp. 223–36. **[G: OECD]**

Anderson, Kathryn H.; Burkhauser, Richard V. and Quinn, Joseph F. Do Retirement Dreams Come True? The Effect of Unanticipated Events on Retirement Plans. *Ind. Lab. Relat. Rev.*, July 1986, *39*(4), pp. 518–26. **[G: U.S.]**

Anderstig, Christer and Hårsman, Björn. On Occupation Structure and Location Pattern in the Stockholm Region. *Reg. Sci. Urban Econ.*, February 1986, *16*(1), pp. 97–122. **[G: Sweden]**

Appelbaum, Eileen and Granrose, Cherlyn Skromme. Hospital Employment under Revised Medicare Payment Schedules. *Mon. Lab. Rev.*, August 1986, *109*(8), pp. 37–45. **[G: U.S.]**

Arnaudo, A. A., et al. Tipología del Desempleo en la Argentina 1950–84. (Typology of Argentine Unemployment 1950–84. With English summary.) *Económica (La Plata)*, July-December 1986, *32*(2), pp. 143–63. **[G: Argentina]**

Ashenfelter, Orley and Card, David. Why Have Unemployment Rates in Canada and the United States Diverged? **In** *Bean, C. R.; Layard, P. R. G. and Nickell, S. J., eds.*, 1986, pp. 171–95. **[G: U.S.; Canada]**

Ashenfelter, Orley and Card, David. Why Have Unemployment Rates in Canada and the United States Diverged? *Economica*, Supplement 1986, *53*(210(S)), pp. S171–95. **[G: U.S.; Canada]**

Atkinson, John. Working Time and Employment: A Negotiable Issue? Comment. **In** *Hart, P. E., ed.*, 1986, pp. 22–26. **[G: U.K.]**

Atkinson, Scott E. and Tschirhart, John. Flexible Modelling of Time to Failure in Risky Careers. *Rev. Econ. Statist.*, November 1986, *68*(4), pp. 558–66. **[G: U.S.]**

Bade, Franz-Josef. The De-industrialisation of the Federal Republic of Germany and Its Spatial Implications. **In** *Nijkamp, P., ed. (II)*, 1986, pp. 196–220. **[G: W. Germany; OECD]**

Balassa, Bela. The Employment Effects of Trade in Manufactured Products between Developed and Developing Countries. *J. Policy Modeling*, Fall 1986, *8*(3), pp. 371–90.

Ball, Nicole. Converting the Workforce: Defence Industry Conversion in the Industrialised Countries. *Int. Lab. Rev.*, July-Aug. 1986, *125*(4), pp. 401–22. **[G: OECD]**

Ballen, John and Freeman, Richard B. Transitions between Employment and Nonemployment. **In** *Freeman, R. B. and Holzer, H. J., eds.*, 1986, pp. 75–112. **[G: U.S.]**

Bandiyono, Suko and Conroy, John D. Employment and Income from Non-agricultural Sources in Rural East Java: Some Preliminary Findings. **In** *Shand, R. T., ed., Vol. 1*, 1986, pp. 327–67. **[G: Indonesia]**

Barbera, Anthony J. A Comparison of Alternative Wage Equations. *Quart. Rev. Econ. Bus.*, Spring 1986, *26*(1), pp. 74–87. **[G: U.S.]**

Bates, Timothy. Characteristics of Minorities Who Are Entering Self-Employment. *Rev. Black Polit. Econ.*, Fall 1986, *15*(2), pp. 31–49. **[G: U.S.]**

Bautista, Germelino M. The Structure of Employment Opportunities in Three Philippine Villages. **In** *Hirashima, S. and Muqtada, M., eds.*, 1986, pp. 119–50. **[G: Philippines]**

Beach, C. M. and Kaliski, S. F. Structural Unemployment, Demographic Change or Industrial Structure? *Can. Public Policy*, June 1986, *12*(2), pp. 356–67. **[G: Canada]**

Bean, Charles R.; Layard, Richard and Nickell, Stephen J. The Rise in Unemployment: A Multi-country Study. *Economica*, Supplement 1986, *53*(210(S)), pp. S1–22. **[G: OECD]**

Bean, Charles R.; Layard, Richard and Nickell, Stephen J. The Rise in Unemployment: A Multi-country Study. **In** *Bean, C. R.; Layard, P. R. G. and Nickell, S. J., eds.*, 1986, pp. 1–22. **[G: OECD]**

Beenstock, Michael and Warburton, Peter. Wages and Unemployment in Interwar Britain. *Exploration Econ. Hist.*, April 1986, *23*(2), pp. 153–72. **[G: U.K.]**

Bendick, Marc, Jr. Government's Role in the Job Transitions of U.S. Dislocated Workers. **In** *Redburn, F. S.; Buss, T. F. and Ledebur, L. C., eds.*, 1986, pp. 158–75. **[G: U.S.]**

Benhayoun, Gilbert. L'emploi et le chômage des jeunes analyse urbaine. (With English summary.) *Revue Écon. Polit.*, May-June 1986, *96*(3), pp. 281–99. **[G: France]**

Bickford, Deborah J.; Clapp, John M. and Vehorn, Charles L. An Econometric Analysis of

Regional Employment Effects of Federal Economic Development Programs. *Growth Change*, January 1986, *17*(1), pp. 1–16. **[G: U.S.]**

Black, Matthew and Fraker, Thomas. First-Term Attrition of High School Graduates in the Military. **In** *Gilroy, C. L., ed.*, 1986, pp. 261–91. **[G: U.S.]**

Blanchard, Olivier J. and Summers, Lawrence H. Hysteresis and the European Unemployment Problem. **In** *Fischer, S., ed.*, 1986, pp. 15–78. **[G: U.S.; U.K.; W. Germany; France]**

Blanchard, Olivier J., et al. Employment and Growth in Europe: A Two-Handed Approach. **In** *Blanchard, O.; Dornbusch, R. and Layard, R., eds.*, 1986, pp. 95–124. **[G: W. Europe]**

Blank, Rebecca M. and Blinder, Alan S. Macroeconomics, Income Distribution, and Poverty. **In** *Danziger, S. H. and Weinberg, D. H., eds.*, 1986, pp. 180–208. **[G: U.S.]**

Blau, David M. Self-employment, Earnings, and Mobility in Peninsular Malaysia. *World Devel.*, July 1986, *14*(7), pp. 839–52. **[G: Malaysia]**

Blau, David M. and Robins, Philip K. Labor Supply Response to Welfare Programs: A Dynamic Analysis. *J. Lab. Econ.*, January 1986, *4*(1), pp. 82–104. **[G: U.S.]**

Bloch, Laurence, et al. Analyse macro-économique des taux d'activité et flexion conjonctrelle. (Macroeconomic Analysis of Activity Rates and Short Term Flexion Impact. With English summary.) *Écon. Appl.*, 1986, *39*(4), pp. 665–703.

Bluestone, Barry; Harrison, Bennett and Clayton-Matthews, Alan. Structure vs. Cycle in U.S. Manufacturing Job Growth. *Ind. Relat.*, Spring 1986, *25*(2), pp. 101–17. **[G: U.S.]**

Bodson, Paul and Stafford, Jean. L'adaptation au chômage prolongé. Un paradoxe social. (Adjustment to Long Duration Unemployment: A Social Paradox. With English summary.) *Écon. Soc.*, April 1986, *20*(4), pp. 187–219. **[G: Canada]**

Boldy, Duncan. Unemployment and Health in Australia: A Policy Perspective: Discussion. **In** *Butler, J. R. G. and Doessel, D. P., eds.*, 1986, pp. 35. **[G: Australia]**

Borjas, George J. The Demographic Determinants of the Demand for Black Labor. **In** *Freeman, R. B. and Holzer, H. J., eds.*, 1986, pp. 191–230. **[G: U.S.]**

Borjas, George J. The Self-Employment Experience of Immigrants. *J. Human Res.*, Fall 1986, *21*(4), pp. 485–506. **[G: U.S.]**

Borjas, George J. The Sensitivity of Labor Demand Functions to Choice of Dependent Variable. *Rev. Econ. Statist.*, February 1986, *68*(1), pp. 58–66. **[G: U.S.]**

Bouillaguet-Bernard, Patricia; Gandon, Marie-Pierre and Outin, Jean-Luc. Chômage de longue durée et pauvreté en France. (Long Duration Unemployment and Poverty in France. With English summary.) *Écon. Soc.*, April 1986, *20*(4), pp. 221–59. **[G: France]**

Bouman, Huub and Verhoef, Bram. High-technology and Employment: Some Information on the Netherlands. **In** *Nijkamp, P., ed. (II)*, 1986, pp. 289–98. **[G: Netherlands]**

Bound, John. NBER-Mathematica Survey of Inner-city Black Youth: An Analysis of the Undercount of Older Youths. **In** *Freeman, R. B. and Holzer, H. J., eds.*, 1986, pp. 443–59. **[G: U.S.]**

Boykin, Robert H. Statement to the U.S. House Subcommittee on Domestic Monetary Policy of the Committee on Banking, Finance and Urban Affairs, March 19, 1986. *Fed. Res. Bull.*, May 1986, *72*(5), pp. 316–18. **[G: U.S.]**

Bradbury, Katharine L. and Browne, Lynn E. Black Men in the Labor Market. *New Eng. Econ. Rev.*, Mar./Apr. 1986, pp. 32–42. **[G: U.S.]**

Bradford, Calvin and Temali, Mihailo. City Venture Corporation: Initiatives in U.S. Cities. **In** *Bergman, E. M., ed.*, 1986, *1983*, pp. 185–204. **[G: U.S.]**

Bradley, John. Unemployment and Fiscal Activism in a Small Open Economy. *Rech. Écon. Louvain*, 1986, *52*(3–4), pp. 339–72. **[G: Ireland]**

Branson, William H. The Limits of Monetary Coordination as Exchange Rate Policy. *Brookings Pap. Econ. Act.*, 1986, (1), pp. 175–94. **[G: U.S.]**

Britton, Andrew. Can Fiscal Expansion Cut Unemployment? *Nat. Inst. Econ. Rev.*, February 1986, (115), pp. 83–99. **[G: U.K.]**

Britton, Andrew. Employment Policy in the Public Sector. **In** *Hart, P. E., ed.*, 1986, pp. 128–46. **[G: U.K.]**

Britton, Andrew. The British Economy in the Long Term: Output Growth and Unemployment. *Nat. Inst. Econ. Rev.*, November 1986, (118), pp. 89–104. **[G: U.K.]**

Britton, Andrew. The Budget and Unemployment. *Fisc. Stud.*, May 1986, *7*(2), pp. 11–20. **[G: U.K.]**

Brooks, Clive and Volker, Paul. The Probability of Leaving Unemployment: The Influence of Duration, Destination and Demographics. *Econ. Rec.*, September 1986, *62*(178), pp. 296–309. **[G: Australia]**

Brown, Charles. Do Better Jobs Make Better Workers? Absenteeism from Work among Inner-city Black Youths: Comment. **In** *Freeman, R. B. and Holzer, H. J., eds.*, 1986, pp. 295–98. **[G: U.S.]**

Brown, Charles. Recruiting Goals, Enlistment Supply, and Enlistments in the U.S. Army: Comment. **In** *Gilroy, C. L., ed.*, 1986, pp. 124–26. **[G: U.S.]**

Brown, Martin and Philips, Peter. Competition, Racism, and Hiring Practices among California Manufacturers, 1860–1882. *Ind. Lab. Relat. Rev.*, October 1986, *40*(1), pp. 61–74. **[G: U.S.]**

Browne, Lynn E. Taking in Each Other's Laundry—The Service Economy. *New Eng. Econ. Rev.*, July/Aug. 1986, pp. 20–31. **[G: U.S.]**

Brunello, Giorgio. Unemployment and Employment Adjustment after the First Oil Shock in

Japan. *Rivista Int. Sci. Econ. Com.*, May 1986, *33*(5), pp. 465–91. **[G: Japan]**

Bruni, Michele and Franciosi, Franco B. Scenari alternativi di domanda e di offerta di lavoro. (Alternative Scenarios of Labour Demand and Supply. With English summary.) *Econ. Lavoro*, July-Sept. 1986, *20*(3), pp. 113–36. **[G: U.S.; Italy]**

Bruno, Michael. Aggregate Supply and Demand Factors in OECD Unemployment: An Update. **In** *Bean, C. R.; Layard, P. R. G. and Nickell, S. J., eds.*, 1986, pp. 35–52. **[G: OECD]**

Bruno, Michael. Aggregate Supply and Demand Factors in OECD Unemployment: An Update. *Economica*, Supplement 1986, *53*(210(S)), pp. S35–52. **[G: OECD]**

Bruno, Michael. Stagflation in the Industrial Countries: An Updated Overview. *Hitotsubashi J. Econ.*, Spec. Iss. Oct. 1986, *27*, pp. 57–74. **[G: OECD]**

Burge, James D. Worksharing: A "Win–Win" Concept. **In** *Burton, D. F., et al., eds.*, 1986, pp. 135–45. **[G: U.S.]**

Burtless, Gary. Social Security, Unanticipated Benefit Increases, and the Timing of Retirement. *Rev. Econ. Stud.*, October 1986, *53*(5), pp. 781–805. **[G: U.S.]**

Buss, Terry F. Assessing the Accuracy of BLS Local Unemployment Rates: A Case Study. *Ind. Lab. Relat. Rev.*, January 1986, *39*(2), pp. 241–50. **[G: U.S.]**

Buss, Terry F. Unemployment Rates and Their Implications for Human Resource Planning. *J. Econ. Soc. Meas.*, April 1986, *14*(1), pp. 1–18. **[G: U.S.]**

Butler, Richard J. and McDonald, James B. Trends in Unemployment Duration Data. *Rev. Econ. Statist.*, November 1986, *68*(4), pp. 545–57. **[G: U.S.]**

Caire, Guy. Contrainte extérieure et emploi: trois discours. (Foreign Constraint and Employment: Three Approaches. With English summary.) *Écon. Soc.*, January 1986, *20*(1), pp. 11–44. **[G: OECD]**

Callaghan, W. H. Employment Policy in the Public Sector: Comment. **In** *Hart, P. E., ed.*, 1986, pp. 147–51. **[G: U.K.]**

Canto, Victor A.; Kadlec, Charles W. and Laffer, Arthur B. The Productive Employment Program: A New Approach to Fighting Unemployment. **In** *Canto, V. A.; Kadlec, C. W. and Laffer, A. B., eds.*, 1986, pp. 160–88. **[G: U.S.]**

Carcaterra, Rose. Facts and Projections at a Glance. **In** *Burton, D. F., et al., eds.*, 1986, pp. 265–84. **[G: U.S.]**

Card, David. The Impact of Deregulation on the Employment and Wages of Airline Mechanics. *Ind. Lab. Relat. Rev.*, July 1986, *39*(4), pp. 527–38. **[G: U.S.]**

Carey, Max L. and Hazelbaker, Kim L. Employment Growth in the Temporary Help Industry. *Mon. Lab. Rev.*, April 1986, *109*(4), pp. 37–44. **[G: U.S.]**

Caroleo, Flora E. and Pinto, Antonio. Il mercato del lavoro nel mezzogiorno e le politiche del lavoro. (Labour Policy and Labour Market in the South of Italy. With English summary.) *Econ. Lavoro*, Apr.-June 1986, *20*(2), pp. 69–90. **[G: Italy]**

Casey, Bernard. The Dual Apprenticeship System and the Recruitment and Retention of Young Persons in West Germany. *Brit. J. Ind. Relat.*, March 1986, *24*(1), pp. 63–81. **[G: W. Germany]**

Castillo, L.; Gascon, F. and Jayasuriya, S. K. Off-Farm Employment of Farm Households in Laguna, Philippines. **In** *Shand, R. T., ed., Vol. 2*, 1986, pp. 133–46. **[G: Philippines]**

Chalamwong, Yongyuth. Rural Labour Supply in Thailand: A Recent Experience. **In** *Shand, R. T., ed., Vol. 1*, 1986, pp. 257–71. **[G: Thailand]**

Chamberlain, Gary. Transitions between Employment and Nonemployment: Comment. **In** *Freeman, R. B. and Holzer, H. J., eds.*, 1986, pp. 113–14. **[G: U.S.]**

Chapman, Bruce J. and Prior, Heather. Sex Differences in Labour Turnover in the Australian Public Service. *Econ. Rec.*, December 1986, *62*(179), pp. 497–505. **[G: Australia]**

Charsombut, Pradit. The Potential for Increases in Income and Employment in Thai Rural Household Manufacturing Enterprises. **In** *Shand, R. T., ed., Vol. 1*, 1986, pp. 231–55. **[G: Thailand]**

Choate, Pat. Looking Forward—Jobs and Workers. **In** *Burton, D. F., et al., eds.*, 1986, pp. 85–102. **[G: U.S.]**

Chowdhury, Nuimuddin. Improved and New Products in Rural Industries: Implications for the Expansion of Demand and Employment. **In** *Islam, R. and Muqtada, M., eds.*, 1986, pp. 169–95. **[G: Bangladesh]**

Christovich, Leslie and Stallworth, Lamont E. The Equal Employment Opportunity Act and Its Administration: The Claimant's Perspective. **In** *Dennis, B. D., ed.*, 1986, pp. 472–77. **[G: U.S.]**

Clark, Gordon L. The Crisis of the Midwest Auto Industry. **In** *Scott, A. J. and Storper, M., eds.*, 1986, pp. 127–48. **[G: U.S.]**

Collignon, Frederick C. The Role of Reasonable Accommodation in Employing Disabled Persons in Private Industry. **In** *Berkowitz, M. and Hill, M. A., eds.*, 1986, pp. 196–241. **[G: U.S.]**

Córdova, Efrén. From Full-time Wage Employment to Atypical Employment: A Major Shift in the Evolution of Labour Relations? *Int. Lab. Rev.*, Nov.-Dec. 1986, *125*(6), pp. 641–57.

Corner, Lorraine. The Prospects for Off-Farm Employment as an Anti-poverty Strategy among Malaysian Paddy Farm Households: Macro and Micro Views. **In** *Shand, R. T., ed., Vol. 2*, 1986, pp. 45–67. **[G: Malaysia]**

Crandall, Robert W. The Transformation of U.S. Manufacturing. *Ind. Relat.*, Spring 1986, *25*(2), pp. 118–30. **[G: U.S.]**

Culp, Jerome McCristal, Jr. and Dunson, Bruce H. Brothers of a Different Color: A Preliminary Look at Employer Treatment of White and

Black Youth. **In** *Freeman, R. B. and Holzer, H. J., eds.*, 1986, pp. 233–59. **[G: U.S.]**

D'Amico, Ronald J. and Golon, Jeff. The Displaced Worker: Consequences of Career Interruption among Young Men. **In** *Hills, S. M., ed.*, 1986, pp. 7–36. **[G: U.S.]**

Dale, Charles. The Changing Structure of the U.S. Economy: Its Effects on Army Enlistments. **In** *Gilroy, C. L., ed.*, 1986, pp. 149–65. **[G: U.S.]**

Damania, D. The Impact of Non-domestic Property Taxes on Employment: A Comment [The Effect of Business Rates on the Location of Employment] [The Determinants of Employment in Counties: Some Evidence on the Importance of Local Authority Fiscal Policy and Government Regional Policy in England and Wales]. *Urban Stud.*, October 1986, *23*(5), pp. 413–18. **[G: U.K.]**

Danziger, Sheldon H. and Gottschalk, Peter. Families with Children Have Fared Worst. *Challenge*, Mar./Apr. 1986, *29*(1), pp. 40–47. **[G: U.S.]**

Darity, William A., Jr. and Myers, Samuel L., Jr. Welfare and Work: Microeconomic vs. Macroeconomic Considerations [The Political Economy of Work-for-Welfare]. *Cato J.*, Spring/Summer 1986, *6*(1), pp. 245–50. **[G: U.S.]**

Datcher-Loury, Linda and Loury, Glenn C. The Effects of Attitudes and Aspirations on the Labor Supply of Young Men. **In** *Freeman, R. B. and Holzer, H. J., eds.*, 1986, pp. 377–99. **[G: U.S.]**

Daula, Thomas V. and Baldwin, Robert H. Reenlistment Decision Models: Implications for Policy Making. **In** *Gilroy, C. L., ed.*, 1986, pp. 203–21. **[G: U.S.]**

Daula, Thomas V. and Smith, D. Alton. Recruiting Goals, Enlistment Supply, and Enlistments in the U.S. Army. **In** *Gilroy, C. L., ed.*, 1986, pp. 101–23. **[G: U.S.]**

Davies, R. W. The Ending of Mass Unemployment in the USSR. **In** *Lane, D., ed.*, 1986, pp. 19–35. **[G: U.S.S.R.]**

Davies, R. W. and Wheatcroft, S. G. A Note on the Sources of Unemployment Statistics. **In** *Lane, D., ed.*, 1986, pp. 36–49. **[G: U.S.S.R.]**

Davis, John and Minford, Patrick. Germany and the European Disease. *Rech. Écon. Louvain*, 1986, *52*(3–4), pp. 373–98. **[G: W. Germany]**

Davis, Norman. Training for Change. **In** *Hart, P. E., ed.*, 1986, pp. 82–98. **[G: U.K.]**

De Neubourg, Chris. Unidentified Floating Unemployment (UFU) and the Specification of the UV-Curve. *Rech. Écon. Louvain*, 1986, *52*(3–4), pp. 227–55. **[G: Netherlands]**

De Wachter, Marcia and Somers, Yolanda. Job Creation Programs in an International Comparison. *Rech. Écon. Louvain*, 1986, *52*(3–4), pp. 413–37. **[G: EEC]**

Deery, Stephen, et al. The Labour Market Experience of Redundant Workers: A Study of a Plant Closure. *Australian Bull. Lab.*, June 1986, *12*(3), pp. 173–94. **[G: Australia]**

DeFreitas, Gregory. A Time-Series Analysis of Hispanic Unemployment. *J. Human Res.*, Winter 1986, *21*(1), pp. 24–43. **[G: U.S.]**

Del Monte, Alfredo and Giannola, Adriano. Relevance and Nature of Small and Medium-sized Firms in Southern Italy. **In** *Keeble, D. and Wever, E., eds.*, 1986, pp. 275–98. **[G: Italy]**

Dertouzos, James N. Microeconomic Foundations of Recruiter Behavior: Implications for Aggregate Enlistment Models. **In** *Gilroy, C. L., ed.*, 1986, pp. 127–45. **[G: U.S.]**

Deshpande, L. K. The Seventh Plan and Some Aspects of Employment. *Indian Econ. J.*, Apr.-June 1986, *33*(4), pp. 98–105. **[G: India]**

Devens, Richard M., Jr. Displaced Workers: One Year Later: Errata. *Mon. Lab. Rev.*, September 1986, *109*(9), pp. 41. **[G: U.S.]**

Devens, Richard M., Jr. Displaced Workers: One Year Later. *Mon. Lab. Rev.*, July 1986, *109*(7), pp. 40–43. **[G: U.S.]**

Doering, Zahava D. Attrition and Retention in the Army Reserve and National Guard: An Empirical Analysis: Comment. **In** *Gilroy, C. L., ed.*, 1986, pp. 198–201. **[G: U.S.]**

Dokopoulou, Evangelia. Small Manufacturing Firms and Regional Development in Greece: Patterns and Changes. **In** *Keeble, D. and Wever, E., eds.*, 1986, pp. 299–317. **[G: Greece]**

Dolado, Juan J. Costes variables de ajuste en funciones de empleo a corto plazo en la industria. (With English summary.) *Invest. Ecón.*, May 1986, *10*(2), pp. 219–226. **[G: OECD]**

Dolado, Juan J. and Malo de Molina, José Luis. An Expectational Model of Labour Demand in Spanish Industry: An Encompassing Approach. *Greek Econ. Rev.*, December 1986, *8*(2), pp. 218–44. **[G: Spain]**

Dolado, Juan J.; Malo de Molina, José Luis and Zabalza, Antonio. Spanish Industrial Unemployment: Some Explanatory Factors. *Economica*, Supplement 1986, *53*(210(S)), pp. S313–34. **[G: Spain]**

Dolado, Juan J.; Malo de Molina, José Luis and Zabalza, Antonio. Spanish Industrial Unemployment: Some Explanatory Factors. **In** *Bean, C. R.; Layard, P. R. G. and Nickell, S. J., eds.*, 1986, pp. 313–33. **[G: Spain]**

Dormont, Brigitte. Emploi et contrainte de débouchés: estimation d'un modèle de demande de travail à deux régimes sur données microéconomiques. (Demand Constraints and Employment: Estimation of a Two-Regime Labour Demand Function on Microeconomic Data. With English summary.) *Écon. Appl.*, 1986, *39*(4), pp. 705–37. **[G: France]**

Dormont, Brigitte. Les ajustements de l'emploi dans la crise en France et en R.F.A. Une étude sur des données d'entreprises industrielles françaises et allemandes sur la période 1967–1979. (With English summary.) *Revue Écon. Polit.*, May-June 1986, *96*(3), pp. 256–80. **[G: France; W. Germany]**

Dormont, Brigitte and Sevestre, Patrick. Modèles dynamiques de demande de travail: spécification et estimation sur données de panel. (Dynamic Labor Demand Models: Specification and Estimation Using Panel Data. With English summary.) *Revue Écon.*, May 1986, *37*(3), pp. 455–87. **[G: France]**

Dornbusch, Rudiger. Sound Currency and Full Employment. **In** *Dornbusch, R.*, 1986, *1985*, pp. 205–31. **[G: U.K.]**

Dornbusch, Rudiger. Unemployment: Europe's Challenge of the '80s. *Challenge*, Sept./Oct. 1986, *29*(4), pp. 11–18. **[G: Europe; U.S.]**

Drèze, Jacques H., et al. Per una minore disoccupazione in Europa: il ruolo della formazione di capitale. (For a Reduction of Unemployment in Europe: The Role of the Capital Formation. With English summary.) *Giorn. Econ.*, Sept.-Oct. 1986, *45*(9–10), pp. 479–514. **[G: EEC]**

Driehuis, Wim. Unemployment in the Netherlands, 1960–1983. **In** *Bean, C. R.; Layard, P. R. G. and Nickell, S. J., eds.*, 1986, pp. 297–312. **[G: Netherlands]**

Driehuis, Wim. Unemployment in the Netherlands, 1960–1983. *Economica*, Supplement 1986, *53*(210(S)), pp. S297–312. **[G: Netherlands]**

Driver, Ciaran; Kilpatrick, Andrew and Naisbitt, Barry. The Employment Effects of UK Manufacturing Trade Expansion with the EEC and the Newly Industrialising Countries. *Europ. Econ. Rev.*, April 1986, *30*(2), pp. 427–38. **[G: U.K.]**

Dutkowsky, Donald H. and Atesoglu, H. Sonmez. Unanticipated Money Growth and Unemployment: Post-Sample Forecasts. *Southern Econ. J.*, October 1986, *53*(2), pp. 413–21. **[G: U.S.]**

Eagan, Vince. Notes on Implicit Contracts and the Racial Unemployment Differential. *Rev. Black Polit. Econ.*, Summer 1986, *15*(1), pp. 81–91. **[G: U.S.]**

Edmondson, William and Schluter, Gerald. Demand Foundations of Food and Fiber Sector Employment in the South. *Growth Change*, October 1986, *17*(4), pp. 1–9. **[G: U.S.]**

Ehrenberg, Ronald G. Black Youth Nonemployment: Duration and Job Search: Comment. **In** *Freeman, R. B. and Holzer, H. J., eds.*, 1986, pp. 70–73. **[G: U.S.]**

Ellwood, David T. The Spatial Mismatch Hypothesis: Are There Teenage Jobs Missing in the Ghetto? **In** *Freeman, R. B. and Holzer, H. J., eds.*, 1986, pp. 147–85. **[G: U.S.]**

Englander, Fred and Director, Steven M. Benefits Levels, Enforcement Stringency, and the Level of Initial Claims for Unemployment Insurance. *Southern Econ. J.*, April 1986, *52*(4), pp. 1140–44. **[G: U.S.]**

Etter, Christian. Versicherungsaspekte des Arbeitsverhältnisses: Der Einfluss impliziter Arbeitsverträge auf Löhne und Beschäftigung. Eine empirische Untersuchung für die Schweiz. (The Insurance Character of the Employer–Employee Relationship: The Influence of Implicit Labour Contracts on Wage Formation and Employment. An Empirical Analysis for Switzerland. With English summary.) *Schweiz. Z. Volkswirtsch. Statist.*, September 1986, *122*(3), pp. 405–24. **[G: Switzerland]**

Ewers, Hans-Jürgen. Spatial Dimensions of Technological Developments and Employment Effects. **In** *Nijkamp, P., ed. (II)*, 1986, pp. 157–76. **[G: W. Germany]**

Extejt, Marian M. Contributed Papers: Organizational Behavior and Personnel: Discussion. **In** *Dennis, B. D., ed.*, 1986, pp. 108–11.

Fabella, Raul V. Rural Non-Farm Employment in the Philippines: Composition, Growth and Seasonality. **In** *Shand, R. T., ed., Vol. 2*, 1986, pp. 69–97. **[G: Philippines]**

Feldman, Marshall M. A. Firm Size and Local Employment Change: Three Issues. *Reg. Stud.*, February 1986, *20*(1), pp. 73–77. **[G: U.S.]**

Fels, Gerhard. The Impact of New Technologies and the Development of Service Industries in the Federal Republic of Germany. **In** *Hax, H.; Kraus, W. and Tsuchiya, K., eds.*, 1986, pp. 115–24. **[G: W. Germany]**

Ferguson, Ronald and Filer, Randall K. Do Better Jobs Make Better Workers? Absenteeism from Work among Inner-city Black Youths. **In** *Freeman, R. B. and Holzer, H. J., eds.*, 1986, pp. 261–95. **[G: U.S.]**

Feroldi, Mathieu and Sterdyniak, Henri. Maximiser l'emploi: la réponse de modèles macroéconomiques. (Maximizing the Employment: The Macroeconomics Models Response. With English summary.) *Écon. Soc.*, January 1986, *20*(1), pp. 235–63. **[G: France]**

Filer, Randall K. The Effects of Nonpecuniary Compensation on Estimates of Labor Supply Functions. *Quart. Rev. Econ. Bus.*, Spring 1986, *26*(1), pp. 17–30.

Fischer, Manfred M. and Nijkamp, Peter. Technological Change and Regional Employment Research. **In** *Nijkamp, P., ed. (II)*, 1986, pp. 454–62.

Flinn, Christopher J. Econometric Analysis of CPS-Type Unemployment Data. *J. Human Res.*, Fall 1986, *21*(4), pp. 456–84. **[G: Italy]**

Flinn, Christopher J. Wages and Job Mobility of Young Workers. *J. Polit. Econ.*, Part 2, June 1986, *94*(3), pp. S88–S110. **[G: U.S.]**

Flückiger, Yves; Schönenberger, Alain and Zarinnejadan, Milad. Measuring Different Types of Unemployment in Switzerland. *Schweiz. Z. Volkswirtsch. Statist.*, March 1986, *122*(1), pp. 17–35. **[G: Switzerland]**

Foot, David K. and Li, Jeanne C. Youth Employment in Canada: A Misplaced Priority? *Can. Public Policy*, September 1986, *12*(3), pp. 499–506. **[G: Canada]**

Franz, Wolfgang and König, Heinz. The Nature and Causes of Unemployment in the Federal Republic of Germany since the 1970s: An Empirical Investigation. **In** *Bean, C. R.; Layard, P. R. G. and Nickell, S. J., eds.*, 1986, pp. 219–44. **[G: W. Germany]**

Franz, Wolfgang and König, Heinz. The Nature and Causes of Unemployment in the Federal Republic of Germany since the 1970s: An Empirical Investigation. *Economica*, Supplement

1986, *53*(210(S)), pp. S219–44. **[G: W. Germany]**

Fraser, Douglas A. A Challenge to the United States: Job Creation and Employment Security. **In** *Burton, D. F., et al., eds.*, 1986, pp. 11–26. **[G: U.S.]**

Freeman, Christopher and Soete, Luc L. G. Innovation Diffusion and Employment Policies. *Ricerche Econ.*, Oct.-Dec. 1986, *40*(4), pp. 836–54. **[G: U.S.; U.K.; Japan; France; W. Germany]**

Freeman, Richard B. and Holzer, Harry J. The Black Youth Employment Crisis: Summary of Findings. **In** *Freeman, R. B. and Holzer, H. J., eds.*, 1986, pp. 3–20. **[G: U.S.]**

Freeman, Richard B. and Holzer, Harry J. Young Blacks and Jobs—What We Now Know. **In** *Reynolds, L. G.; Masters, S. H. and Moser, C. H., eds.*, 1986, *1985*, pp. 128–37. **[G: U.S.]**

Gallagher, C. C. and Stewart, H. Jobs and the Business Life-Cycle in the UK. *Appl. Econ.*, August 1986, *18*(8), pp. 875–900. **[G: U.K.]**

Garonna, Paolo. Youth Unemployment, Labour Market Deregulation and Union Stategies in Italy. *Brit. J. Ind. Relat.*, March 1986, *24*(1), pp. 43–61. **[G: Italy]**

Germe, J. F. Employment Policies and the Entry of Young People into the Labour Market in France. *Brit. J. Ind. Relat.*, March 1986, *24*(1), pp. 29–42. **[G: France]**

Gerson, J. Unemployment in South Africa: A Reply. *S. Afr. J. Econ.*, December 1986, *54*(4), pp. 418–29. **[G: S. Africa]**

Gerster, Hans J. Kritische Beurteilung der Arbeitsmarktinterpretationen auf der Grundlage saisonbereinigter Daten. (A Statistical Evaluation of the Labor Market—Interpretations Based on Seasonally Adjusted Data. With English summary.) *Jahr. Nationalökon. Statist.*, March 1986, *201*(2), pp. 152–74. **[G: W. Germany]**

Giaoutzi, Maria. Technological Change and Employment Patterns: The Greek Case. **In** *Nijkamp, P., ed. (II)*, 1986, pp. 244–61. **[G: Greece]**

Gil, Avishai. Some Labour Implications of Technological Change in Rail and Air Transport. *Int. Lab. Rev.*, Jan.-Feb. 1986, *125*(1), pp. 1–17. **[G: France; U.K.; Netherlands; W. Germany]**

van Ginneken, Wouter. Full Employment in OECD Countries: Why Not? *Int. Lab. Rev.*, Jan.-Feb. 1986, *125*(1), pp. 19–37. **[G: OECD]**

Glasmeier, Amy K. High-Tech Industries and the Regional Division of Labor. *Ind. Relat.*, Spring 1986, *25*(2), pp. 197–211. **[G: U.S.]**

Glazer, Nathan. Education and Training Programs and Poverty. **In** *Danziger, S. H. and Weinberg, D. H., eds.*, 1986, pp. 152–73. **[G: U.S.]**

Gleave, David. The Impact of Innovations on Service Employment. **In** *Nijkamp, P., ed. (II)*, 1986, pp. 177–95. **[G: U.K.; U.S.]**

Goldberg, Lawrence and Greenston, Peter. Economic Analysis of Army Enlistments: Policy Implications: Reply. **In** *Gilroy, C. L., ed.*, 1986, pp. 97–99. **[G: U.S.]**

Goldberg, Lawrence and Greenston, Peter. Economic Analysis of Army Enlistments: Policy Implications. **In** *Gilroy, C. L., ed.*, 1986, pp. 61–94. **[G: U.S.]**

Goldberg, Matthew S. Microeconomic Foundations of Recruiter Behavior: Implications for Aggregate Enlistment Models: Comment. **In** *Gilroy, C. L., ed.*, 1986, pp. 146–47. **[G: U.S.]**

Goldberg, Walter H. Ailing Steel: The Transoceanic Quarrel: The Federal Republic of Germany. **In** *Goldberg, W. H., ed.*, 1986, pp. 125–39. **[G: W. Germany]**

Goldstein, Harvey A. The Changing International Division of Labor and Regional Employment Cycles in the U.S. *Rev. Reg. Stud.*, Winter 1986, *16*(1), pp. 31–43. **[G: U.S.]**

Gordon, Ian. What Contribution Can Labour Migration Make to Reducing Unemployment? Comment. **In** *Hart, P. E., ed.*, 1986, pp. 75–79. **[G: U.K.]**

Gramlich, Edward M. Fighting Poverty: What Works and What Doesn't: The Main Themes. **In** *Danziger, S. H. and Weinberg, D. H., eds.*, 1986, pp. 341–47. **[G: U.S.]**

Green, A. E., et al. What Contribution Can Labour Migration Make to Reducing Unemployment? **In** *Hart, P. E., ed.*, 1986, pp. 52–74. **[G: U.K.]**

Greenwood, Michael J.; Hunt, Gary L. and McDowell, John M. Migration and Employment Change: Empirical Evidence on the Spatial and Temporal Dimensions of the Linkage. *J. Reg. Sci.*, May 1986, *26*(2), pp. 223–34. **[G: U.S.]**

Gregory, R. G. Wages Policy and Unemployment in Australia. *Economica*, Supplement 1986, *53*(210(S)), pp. S53–74. **[G: Australia]**

Gregory, R. G. Wages Policy and Unemployment in Australia. **In** *Bean, C. R.; Layard, P. R. G. and Nickell, S. J., eds.*, 1986, pp. 53–74. **[G: Australia]**

Grissmer, David W. and Kirby, Sheila Nataraj. Attrition and Retention in the Army Reserve and National Guard: An Empirical Analysis. **In** *Gilroy, C. L., ed.*, 1986, pp. 169–97. **[G: U.S.]**

Groenewald, J. A. Structure of Agriculture and People in Rural Societies: Discussion. **In** *Maunder, A. and Renborg, U., eds.*, 1986, pp. 551–53. **[G: U.S.]**

Gustman, Alan L. and Steinmeier, Thomas L. A Disaggregated, Structural Analysis of Retirement by Race, Difficulty of Work and Health. *Rev. Econ. Statist.*, August 1986, *68*(3), pp. 509–13. **[G: U.S.]**

Gustman, Alan L. and Steinmeier, Thomas L. A Structural Retirement Model. *Econometrica*, May 1986, *54*(3), pp. 555–84. **[G: U.S.]**

Haberman, Steven. Improvements in State Pension Rights for Women. **In** *von der Schulenburg, J.-M. G., ed.*, 1986, pp. 130–65. **[G: U.K.]**

Hale, Robert. The Changing Structure of the U.S. Economy: Its Effects on Army Enlistments: Comment. **In** *Gilroy, C. L., ed.*, 1986, pp. 166–68. **[G: U.S.]**

Hall, Stephen G., et al. Forecasting Employment: The Role of Forward-Looking Behaviour. *Int. J. Forecasting*, 1986, *2*(4), pp. 435–45. **[G: U.K.]**

Halpern, Janice and Hausman, Jerry A. Choice under Uncertainty: Labour Supply and the Decision to Apply for Disability Insurance. **In** *Blundell, R. and Walker, I., eds.*, 1986, pp. 294–302. **[G: U.S.]**

Ham, John C. On the Interpretation of Unemployment in Empirical Labour Supply Analysis. **In** *Blundell, R. and Walker, I., eds.*, 1986, pp. 121–42. **[G: U.K.]**

Hamada, Koichi and Kurosaka, Yoshio. Trends in Unemployment, Wages and Productivity: The Case of Japan. *Economica*, Supplement 1986, *53*(210(S)), pp. S275–96. **[G: Japan]**

Hamada, Koichi and Kurosaka, Yoshio. Trends in Unemployment, Wages and Productivity: The Case of Japan. **In** *Bean, C. R.; Layard, P. R. G. and Nickell, S. J., eds.*, 1986, pp. 275–96. **[G: Japan]**

Hamermesh, Daniel S. The Demographic Determinants of the Demand for Black Labor: Comment. **In** *Freeman, R. B. and Holzer, H. J., eds.*, 1986, pp. 230–32. **[G: U.S.]**

Hammond, Elizabeth M. and Morris, C. Nick. What Price Equality? The Cost of Changing the Age of Retirement. *Fisc. Stud.*, August 1986, *7*(3), pp. 25–40. **[G: U.K.]**

Hanson, Philip. The Serendipitous Soviet Achievement of Full Employment: Labour Shortage and Labour Hoarding in the Soviet Economy. **In** *Lane, D., ed.*, 1986, pp. 83–111. **[G: U.S.S.R.]**

Harris, G. T. and Rashid, Zakariah bin Abdul. The Employment Performance of Developing Countries during the 1970s. *Devel. Econ.*, September 1986, *24*(3), pp. 272–87. **[G: LDCs]**

Harris, G. T. and Vitols, M. Unemployment in Australian Rural Towns. *Australian Bull. Lab.*, December 1986, *13*(1), pp. 51–60. **[G: Australia]**

Harrison, Mark. Lessons of Soviet Planning for Full Employment. **In** *Lane, D., ed.*, 1986, pp. 69–82. **[G: U.S.S.R.]**

Hart, Gillian. Exclusionary Labour Arrangements: Interpreting Evidence on Employment Trends in Rural Java. *J. Devel. Stud.*, July 1986, *22*(4), pp. 681–96. **[G: Java]**

Hart, Peter E., et al. Measures to Reduce Youth Unemployment in Britain, France and West Germany. *Nat. Inst. Econ. Rev.*, August 1986, (117), pp. 43–51. **[G: U.K.; France; W. Germany]**

Hatton, T. J. Structural Aspects of Unemployment in Britain between the World Wars. **In** *Uselding, P., ed.*, 1986, pp. 54–92. **[G: U.K.]**

Haugen, Steven E. The Employment Expansion in Retail Trade, 1973–85. *Mon. Lab. Rev.*, August 1986, *109*(8), pp. 9–16. **[G: U.S.]**

Hedges, Janice Neipert. Work Sharing: New Experiences: Discussion. **In** *Dennis, B. D., ed.*, 1986, pp. 453–56. **[G: U.S.]**

Heneman, Robert L. Contributed Papers: Organizational Behavior and Personnel: Discussion. **In** *Dennis, B. D., ed.*, 1986, pp. 104–07.

Henry, S. G. B. and Wren-Lewis, Simon. The Labour Market. *Nat. Inst. Econ. Rev.*, February 1986, (115), pp. 52–63. **[G: U.K.]**

Herath, H. M. G. An Exploratory Study of Off-Farm Employment and Incomes in Sri Lanka. **In** *Shand, R. T., ed., Vol. 2*, 1986, pp. 209–33. **[G: Sri Lanka]**

Hibbs, Douglas A., Jr. Political Parties and Macroeconomic Policies and Outcomes in the United States. *Amer. Econ. Rev.*, May 1986, *76*(2), pp. 66–70. **[G: U.S.]**

Hill, Herbert. Equal Employment Opportunity Act and Its Administration: An Appraisal of the Commission and the Act: Discussion. **In** *Dennis, B. D., ed.*, 1986, pp. 478–85. **[G: U.S.]**

Hills, Stephen M. The Changing Labor Market: A Longitudinal Study of Young Men: Introduction. **In** *Hills, S. M., ed.*, 1986, pp. 1–6. **[G: U.S.]**

Hirsch, Werner Z. and Rufolo, Anthony M. Residence Laws and Unionization in Municipal Labor Markets: The Case of Firefighters. *J. Lab. Res.*, Winter 1986, *7*(1), pp. 41–58. **[G: U.S.]**

Ho, Samuel P. S. Off-Farm Employment and Farm Households in Taiwan. **In** *Shand, R. T., ed., Vol. 1*, 1986, pp. 95–133. **[G: Taiwan]**

Hoel, Michael and Vale, Bent. Effects on Unemployment of Reduced Working Time in an Economy Where Firms Set Wages. *Europ. Econ. Rev.*, October 1986, *30*(5), pp. 1097–1104.

van der Hoeven, W. H. M. and Hundepool, A. J. A Method for Seasonally Adjusted Time Series with Variation in the Seasonal Amplitude. *J. Bus. Econ. Statist.*, October 1986, *4*(4), pp. 455–71. **[G: Netherlands]**

Hogan, Paul F. Army Reenlistment and Extension Decisions by Occupation: Comment. **In** *Gilroy, C. L., ed.*, 1986, pp. 257–60.

Hogue, Carma R. and Flaim, Paul O. Measuring Gross Flows in the Labor Force: An Overview of a Special Conference. *J. Bus. Econ. Statist.*, January 1986, *4*(1), pp. 111–21. **[G: U.S.]**

Holden, Kenneth and Peel, David A. The Impact of Benefits on Unemployment in Britain in the Interwar Period: Some Further Empirical Evidence. *J. Macroecon.*, Spring 1986, *8*(2), pp. 227–32. **[G: U.K.]**

Holland, A. Steven. Wage Indexation and the Effect of Inflation Uncertainty on Employment: An Empirical Analysis. *Amer. Econ. Rev.*, March 1986, *76*(1), pp. 235–43. **[G: U.S.]**

Holzer, Harry J. Are Unemployed Black Youth Income Maximizers? *Southern Econ. J.*, January 1986, *52*(3), pp. 777–84. **[G: U.S.]**

Holzer, Harry J. Black Youth Nonemployment: Duration and Job Search. **In** *Freeman, R. B. and Holzer, H. J., eds.*, 1986, pp. 23–70. **[G: U.S.]**

Holzer, Harry J. Reservation Wages and Their

Labor Market Effects for Black and White Male Youth. *J. Human Res.*, Spring 1986, *21* (2), pp. 157–77. **[G: U.S.]**

Hoogteijling, Els; Gunning, Jan Willem and Nijkamp, Peter. Spatial Dimensions of Innovation and Employment: Some Dutch Results. **In** *Nijkamp, P., ed. (II)*, 1986, pp. 221–43. **[G: Netherlands]**

Horowitz, Stanley A. Experience and Readiness. **In** *Gilroy, C. L., ed.*, 1986, pp. 321–27. **[G: U.S.]**

Hosek, James R. and Peterson, Christine E. Enlistment Decisions of Young Men. **In** *Gilroy, C. L., ed.*, 1986, pp. 1–56. **[G: U.S.]**

Hossain, Mahabub. Employment Generation through Cottage Industries: Potentials and Constraints. **In** *Islam, R. and Muqtada, M., eds.*, 1986, pp. 119–50. **[G: Bangladesh]**

Howe, Wayne J. Temporary Help Workers: Who They Are, What Jobs They Hold. *Mon. Lab. Rev.*, November 1986, *109* (11), pp. 45–47. **[G: U.S.]**

Howe, Wayne J. The Business Services Industry Sets Pace in Employment Growth. *Mon. Lab. Rev.*, April 1986, *109* (4), pp. 29–36. **[G: U.S.]**

Hoyman, Michele. Equal Employment Opportunity Act and Its Administration: An Appraisal of the Commission and the Act: Discussion. **In** *Dennis, B. D., ed.*, 1986, pp. 486–89.

Hudson, Ray and Sadler, David. Contesting Works Closures in Western Europe's Old Industrial Regions: Defending Place or Betraying Class? **In** *Scott, A. J. and Storper, M., eds.*, 1986, pp. 172–93. **[G: W. Europe]**

Hughes, Peter R. and Hutchinson, Gillian. The Changing Picture of Male Unemployment in Great Britain 1972–1981. *Oxford Bull. Econ. Statist.*, November 1986, *48* (4), pp. 309–30. **[G: U.K.]**

Hutchens, Robert M. Delayed Payment Contracts and a Firm's Propensity to Hire Older Workers. *J. Lab. Econ.*, October 1986, *4* (4), pp. 439–57. **[G: U.S.]**

Iams, Howard M. Characteristics of the Longest Job for New Disabled Workers: Findings from the New Beneficiary Survey. *Soc. Sec. Bull.*, December 1986, *49* (12), pp. 13–18. **[G: U.S.]**

Ichniowski, Bernard E. and Preston, Anne E. New Trends in Part-time Employment. **In** *Dennis, B. D., ed.*, 1986, pp. 60–67. **[G: U.S.]**

Inglis, Paul A. and Stromback, C. Thorsten. Migrants' Unemployment: The Determinants of Employment Success. *Econ. Rec.*, September 1986, *62* (178), pp. 310–24. **[G: Australia]**

Islam, Rizwanul. Non-farm Employment in Rural Asia: Issues and Evidence. **In** *Shand, R. T., ed., Vol. 1*, 1986, pp. 153–73. **[G: Bangladesh; Sri Lanka; Pakistan; Thailand; India]**

Islam, Rizwanul. Rural Unemployment and Underemployment: A Review. **In** *Islam, R. and Muqtada, M., eds.*, 1986, pp. 11–20. **[G: Bangladesh]**

Islam, Rizwanul and Muqtada, M. Employment and Poverty Alleviation: An Overview. **In** *Islam, R. and Muqtada, M., eds.*, 1986, pp. 1–10. **[G: Bangladesh]**

Jackson, Peter and Montgomery, Edward. Layoffs, Discharges and Youth Unemployment. **In** *Freeman, R. B. and Holzer, H. J., eds.*, 1986, pp. 115–41. **[G: U.S.]**

Jadresić, Esteban. Evolución del empleo y desempleo en Chile, 1970–85. Series anuales y trimestrales. (Employment and Unemployment in Chile, 1970–85: Yearly and Quarterly Series. With English summary.) *Colección Estud. CIEPLAN*, December 1986, (20), pp. 147–93. **[G: Chile]**

Jahnke, Wilfried. Simulation verschiedener Strategien zur Verringerung der Arbeitslosigkeit. (Simulation of Alternative Policies to Reduce Unemployment. With English summary.) *Z. Wirtschaft. Sozialwissen.*, 1986, *106* (6), pp. 557–78. **[G: W. Germany]**

James-Bryan, Meryl. Youth in the English-speaking Caribbean: The High Cost of Dependent Development. *CEPAL Rev.*, August 1986, (29), pp. 133–52. **[G: Caribbean]**

James, Franklin J. and Blair, John P. Labor Mobility in National Policy and Local Economies. **In** *Bergman, E. M., ed.*, 1986, *1983*, pp. 271–85. **[G: U.S.]**

Jencks, Christopher. Education and Training Programs and Poverty: Comment. **In** *Danziger, S. H. and Weinberg, D. H., eds.*, 1986, pp. 173–79. **[G: U.S.]**

Johnson, G. E. and Layard, Richard. The Natural Rate of Unemployment: Explanation and Policy. **In** *Ashenfelter, O. and Layard, R., eds., Vol. 2*, 1986, pp. 921–99. **[G: OECD]**

Johnston, R. J. The State, the Region, and the Division of Labor. **In** *Scott, A. J. and Storper, M., eds.*, 1986, pp. 265–80.

Jones, David R. and MacKay, P. R. Labour Adjustment and the Limits to Voluntary Choice. **In** *Danson, M., ed.*, 1986, pp. 83–102. **[G: U.K.]**

Jones, David R. and Martin, Ronald L. Voluntary and Involuntary Turnover in the Labour Force. *Scot. J. Polit. Econ.*, May 1986, *33* (2), pp. 124–44. **[G: U.K.]**

Kada, Ryohei. Off-Farm Employment and the Rural–Urban Interface in Japanese Economic Development. **In** *Shand, R. T., ed., Vol. 1*, 1986, pp. 75–93. **[G: Japan]**

Kahl, Anne and Clark, Donald E. Employment in Health Services: Long-term Trends and Projections. *Mon. Lab. Rev.*, August 1986, *109* (8), pp. 17–36. **[G: U.S.]**

Kamal, Salih, et al. Young Workers and Urban Services in Penang. **In** *Yeung, Y. M. and McGee, T. G., eds.*, 1986, pp. 119–63. **[G: Malaysia]**

Kannappan, Subbiah. The Economic Significance of the Social Structure for Urban Labor Markets with Special Reference to India. **In** *Dennis, B. D., ed.*, 1986, pp. 324–35. **[G: India]**

Kasarda, John D. Transforming Cities and Employment Policy for Displaced Workers. **In**

Bergman, E. M., ed., 1986, *1983*, pp. 286–307. **[G: U.S.]**

Kasryno, Faisal. Impact of Off-Farm Employment on Agricultural Labour Absorption and Wages in Indonesia. **In** *Shand, R. T., ed., Vol. 1*, 1986, pp. 273–307. **[G: Indonesia]**

Katzman, Rubén. Youth and Unemployment in Montevideo. *CEPAL Rev.*, August 1986, (29), pp. 119–31. **[G: Uruguay]**

Keeble, David and Kelly, Timothy. New Firms and High-Technology Industry in the United Kingdom: The Case of Computer Electronics. **In** *Keeble, D. and Wever, E., eds.*, 1986, pp. 75–104. **[G: U.K.]**

Kerachsky, Stuart, et al. An Evaluation of Short-Time Compensation Programs. **In** *Dennis, B. D., ed.*, 1986, pp. 424–32. **[G: U.S.]**

Khan, Mahmud Jameel and Chowdhury, Nuimuddin. Trade, Industrialisation and Employment. **In** *Islam, R. and Muqtada, M., eds.*, 1986, pp. 89–117. **[G: Bangladesh]**

Khuda, B. Off-Farm Employment in Traditional and Developed Villages of Bangladesh. **In** *Shand, R. T., ed., Vol. 2*, 1986, pp. 193–207. **[G: Bangladesh]**

Kieffer, Jarold A. The Older Volunteer Resource. **In** *Inst. Med. and Nat'l Res. Counc., Comm. on an Aging Society*, 1986, pp. 51–72. **[G: U.S.]**

Kikuchi, Masao. Growing Impact of Off-Farm Employment on a Rural Economy: Changes in Labour Utilization and Income Earning Structure in a Philippine Rice Village. **In** *Shand, R. T., ed., Vol. 2*, 1986, pp. 99–131. **[G: Philippines]**

King, J. E. How Large Is the Structural Element in the Current Unemployment. *Australian Bull. Lab.*, March 1986, *12*(2), pp. 102–18. **[G: Australia]**

Klodt, Henning. Lohnquote und Beschäftigung—Die Lohnlücke. (Labour Share and Employment—The Wage-Gap. With English summary.) *Jahr. Nationalökon. Statist.*, September 1986, *201*(5), pp. 480–97. **[G: W. Germany; OECD]**

Knoester, Anthonie. Okun's Law Revisited. *Weltwirtsch. Arch.*, 1986, *122*(4), pp. 657–66. **[G: W. Germany; Netherlands; U.K.; U.S.]**

Koch, Paul D. and Ragan, James F., Jr. Investigating the Causal Relationship between Quits and Wages: An Exercise in Comparative Dynamics. *Econ. Inquiry*, January 1986, *24*(1), pp. 61–83. **[G: U.S.]**

Köllö, János. The Impact of the Labour Market on the Employment Structure in Hungary. *Acta Oecon.*, 1986, *36*(3–4), pp. 197–208. **[G: Hungary]**

Koshiro, Kazutoshi. The Impact of New Technologies and the Development of Service Industries in Japan. **In** *Hax, H.; Kraus, W. and Tsuchiya, K., eds.*, 1986, pp. 84–114. **[G: Japan; U.S.; U.K.; W. Germany]**

Kosters, Marvin H. Job Changes and Displaced Workers: An Examination of Employment Adjustment Experience. **In** *Cagan, P., ed.*, 1986, pp. 275–305. **[G: U.S.]**

Kraft, Kornelius. Exit and Voice in the Labor Market: An Empirical Study of Quits. *J. Inst. Theoretical Econ.*, December 1986, *142*(4), pp. 697–715. **[G: W. Germany]**

Krashevski, Richard S. What Is Full Employment? *Challenge*, Nov./Dec. 1986, *29*(5), pp. 33–40. **[G: U.S.]**

Kuehn, John A. and Braschler, Curtis. Technology and Foreign Trade Impacts on U.S. Manufacturing Employment 1975–80. *Growth Change*, October 1986, *17*(4), pp. 46–60. **[G: U.S.]**

Kutscher, Ronald E. and Personick, Valerie A. Deindustrialization and the Shift to Services. *Mon. Lab. Rev.*, June 1986, *109*(6), pp. 3–13. **[G: U.S.]**

Kuwahara, Yasuo. Technology Promotion in Japan. **In** *Hax, H.; Kraus, W. and Tsuchiya, K., eds.*, 1986, pp. 49–70. **[G: U.S.; U.K.; Japan; W. Germany]**

Lakhani, Hyder and Gilroy, Curtis L. Army Reenlistment and Extension Decisions by Occupation. **In** *Gilroy, C. L., ed.*, 1986, pp. 225–56. **[G: U.S.]**

Lambooy, Jan G. and van der Vegt, Chris. Segmentation Theories and Manpower Policy in Dutch Cities. **In** *Nijkamp, P., ed. (II)*, 1986, pp. 262–79. **[G: Netherlands]**

Lambrinos, James and Appel, David. Workers' Compensation and Employment: An Industry Analysis. **In** *Berkowitz, M. and Hill, M. A., eds.*, 1986, pp. 124–41. **[G: U.S.]**

Lampert, Nick. Job Security and the Law in the USSR. **In** *Lane, D., ed.*, 1986, pp. 256–77. **[G: U.S.S.R.]**

Lane, David. Marxist-Leninism: An Ideology for Full Employment in Socialist States? **In** *Lane, D., ed.*, 1986, pp. 1–16. **[G: U.S.S.R.]**

Lapp, John S. The Secular Behavior of Aggregate Retirement Flows. *Atlantic Econ. J.*, March 1986, *14*(1), pp. 30–38. **[G: U.S.]**

Laroque, Guy. Le chômage des années 1970 était-il classique? (The Unemployment of the 1970's: A Classical Unemployment Régime? With English summary.) *L'Actual. Econ.*, September 1986, *62*(3), pp. 349–64. **[G: France]**

Layard, Richard; Metcalf, David and O'Brien, Richard. A New Deal for the Long-term Unemployed. **In** *Hart, P. E., ed.*, 1986, pp. 181–90. **[G: U.K.]**

Layard, Richard and Nickell, Stephen J. Unemployment in Britain. *Economica*, Supplement 1986, *53*(210(S)), pp. S121–69. **[G: U.K.]**

Layard, Richard and Nickell, Stephen J. Unemployment in Britain. **In** *Bean, C. R.; Layard, P. R. G. and Nickell, S. J., eds.*, 1986, pp. 121–69. **[G: U.K.]**

Lazear, Edward P. Raids and Offer Matching. **In** *Ehrenberg, R. G., ed., Pt. A*, 1986, pp. 141–65. **[G: U.S.]**

Lazear, Edward P. Retirement from the Labor Force. **In** *Ashenfelter, O. and Layard, R., eds., Vol. 1*, 1986, pp. 305–55. **[G: U.S.]**

Lebergott, Stanley. Discussion [New Estimates of Prewar Gross National Product and Unemployment] [The Reliability of Historical Macroeconomic Data for Comparing Cyclical Stability]. *J. Econ. Hist.*, June 1986, *46*(2), pp. 367–71. **[G: U.S.]**

Lee, Kiong-Hock. Affective, Cognitive and Vocational Skills: The Employers' Perspective. *Econ. Educ. Rev.*, 1986, *5*(4), pp. 395–401. **[G: Malaysia]**

Lehmann, Rainer H. and Verhine, Robert E. Educação e obtenção de empregos industriais no Brasil: para um modelo causal aprimorado. (With English summary.) *Pesquisa Planejamento Econ.*, December 1986, *16*(3), pp. 621–46. **[G: Brazil]**

Leibenstein, Harvey. The Theory of Underemployment in Densely Populated Backward Areas. **In** *Akerlof, G. A. and Yellen, J. L., eds.*, 1986, *1963*, pp. 22–40.

Leigh, J. Paul. Unemployment Insurance and the Duration of Unemployment: The Case for Reciprocal Effects. *J. Post Keynesian Econ.*, Spring 1986, *8*(3), pp. 387–99. **[G: U.S.]**

Leigh, J. Paul and Lust, John. Punctuality and Tardiness in Supplying Labor. *Atlantic Econ. J.*, July 1986, *14*(2), pp. 16–25. **[G: U.S.]**

Leijon, Anna-Greta. Labor–Management Relations and the Jobs Problem: The Swedish Experience. **In** *Burton, D. F., et al., eds.*, 1986, pp. 175–86. **[G: Sweden]**

Leonard, Jonathan S. The Effectiveness of Equal Employment Law and Affirmative Action Regulation. **In** *Ehrenberg, R. G., ed., Pt. B*, 1986, pp. 319–50. **[G: U.S.]**

Leonard, Jonathan S. The Spatial Mismatch Hypothesis: Are There Teenage Jobs Missing in the Ghetto? Comment. **In** *Freeman, R. B. and Holzer, H. J., eds.*, 1986, pp. 185–90. **[G: U.S.]**

Leonard, Jonathan S. Unions, Turnover, and Employment Variation. **In** *Lipsky, D. B. and Lewin, D., eds.*, 1986, pp. 119–51. **[G: U.S.]**

Leopold, J. W. and Beaumont, P. B. Trade Unions, Consultation and Redundancies. **In** *Danson, M., ed.*, 1986, pp. 159–67. **[G: U.K.]**

Lesage, James P. and Magura, Michael. Econometric Modeling of Interregional Labour Market Linkages. *J. Reg. Sci.*, August 1986, *26*(3), pp. 367–77. **[G: U.S.]**

Lever, William. Old Policies in a New Role. **In** *Lever, W. and Moore, C., eds.*, 1986, pp. 44–61. **[G: U.K.]**

Lever, William and Mather, Frank. The Changing Structure of Business and Employment in the Conurbation. **In** *Lever, W. and Moore, C., eds.*, 1986, pp. 1–21. **[G: U.K.]**

Levy, Robert A. and Jondrow, James M. The Adjustment of Employment to Technical Change in the Steel and Auto Industries. *J. Bus.*, July 1986, *59*(3), pp. 475–91. **[G: U.S.]**

Lewin, David. Public Employee Unionism in the 1980s: An Analysis of Transformation. **In** *Lipset, S. M., ed.*, 1986, pp. 241–64. **[G: U.S.]**

Lilien, David M. and Hall, Robert E. Cyclical Fluctuations in the Labor Market. **In** *Ashenfelter, O. and Layard, R., eds., Vol. 2*, 1986, pp. 1001–35. **[G: U.S.]**

Lindley, Robert. Labour Demand: Microeconomic Aspects of State Intervention. **In** *Hart, P. E., ed.*, 1986, pp. 154–75. **[G: U.K.]**

Lloyd, John. Pressures and Policies in the European Labor Market. **In** *Burton, D. F., et al., eds.*, 1986, pp. 159–73. **[G: OECD]**

Lobban, Peter. A New Deal for the Long-term Unemployed: Comment. **In** *Hart, P. E., ed.*, 1986, pp. 191–92. **[G: U.K.]**

Loungani, Prakash. Oil Price Shocks and the Dispersion Hypothesis. *Rev. Econ. Statist.*, August 1986, *68*(3), pp. 536–39. **[G: U.S.]**

Lovell, Michael C. A Quick Fix for the Unemployment Estimate. *Brookings Pap. Econ. Act.*, 1986, (2), pp. 520–32. **[G: U.S.]**

Lubian, Diego. Interessi nel tasso "naturale": una interpretazione della elevata e persistente disoccupazione attuale. (Hysteresis in the "Natural" Rate of Employment: An Interpretation of the High and Persistent Present Unemployment. With English summary.) *Giorn. Econ.*, Jan.-Feb. 1986, *45*(1–2), pp. 55–72. **[G: U.S.; U.K.; Japan; Italy; W. Germany]**

Lubrano, Michel. Bayesian Analysis of Single Market Disequilibrium Models: An Application to Unemployment in the U.S. Labour Market. **In** *Blundell, R. and Walker, I., eds.*, 1986, pp. 75–102. **[G: U.S.]**

Lucas, Robert E. B. Emigration, Employment, and Accumulation: The Miners of Southern Africa. **In** *Stark, O., ed.*, 1986, pp. 107–38. **[G: S. Africa]**

Lynch, Lisa M. Household Costs of Unemployment. **In** *Hills, S. M., ed.*, 1986, pp. 79–89. **[G: U.S.]**

Maani, Sholeh A. and Studenmund, A. H. The Critical Wage, Unemployment Duration, and Wage Expectations: The Case of Chile. *Ind. Lab. Relat. Rev.*, January 1986, *39*(2), pp. 264–76. **[G: Chile]**

Malinvaud, Edmond. The Rise of Unemployment in France. **In** *Bean, C. R.; Layard, P. R. G. and Nickell, S. J., eds.*, 1986, pp. 197–217. **[G: France]**

Malinvaud, Edmond. The Rise of Unemployment in France. *Economica*, Supplement 1986, *53*(210(S)), pp. S197–217. **[G: France]**

Malle, Silvana. Heterogeneity of the Soviet Labour Market as a Limit to a More Efficient Utilisation of Manpower. **In** *Lane, D., ed.*, 1986, pp. 122–42. **[G: U.S.S.R.]**

Marsden, David and Richardson, Ray. Youth Pay and Employers' Recruitment Practices for Young Workers in Western Europe. *Brit. J. Ind. Relat.*, March 1986, *24*(1), pp. 25–27. **[G: W. Europe]**

Marshall, Ray. Employment and Industrial Relations. **In** *Burton, D. F., et al., eds.*, 1986, pp. 27–43. **[G: OECD]**

Martin, Ronald L. In What Sense a 'Jobs Boom'? Employment Recovery, Government Policy and the Regions. *Reg. Stud.*, October 1986, *20*(5), pp. 463–72. **[G: U.K.]**

Martin, Ronald L. Industrial Restructuring, Labour Shake-Out and the Geography of Recession. **In** *Danson, M., ed.*, 1986, pp. 1–22. **[G: U.K.]**

Martínez, Javier and Valenzuela, Eduardo. Chilean Youth and Social Exclusion. *CEPAL Rev.*, August 1986, (29), pp. 93–105. **[G: Chile]**

Massiah, Joycelin. Work in the Lives of Caribbean Women. *Soc. Econ. Stud.*, June 1986, *35*(2), pp. 177–240. **[G: Barbados; Antigua; St. Vincent]**

Maxwell, Nan L. The Effect of Human Capital and Labor Market Segments on Retirement Income: A Policy Analysis. *Soc. Sci. Quart.*, March 1986, *67*(1), pp. 53–68. **[G: U.S.]**

Maxwell, Nan L. and D'Amico, Ronald J. Employment and Wage Effects of Involuntary Job Separation: Male–Female Differences. *Amer. Econ. Rev.*, May 1986, *76*(2), pp. 373–77. **[G: U.S.]**

McCallum, John. Unemployment in OECD Countries in the 1980s. *Econ. J.*, December 1986, *96*(384), pp. 942–60. **[G: OECD]**

McCormick, Barry. Employment Opportunities, Earnings, and the Journey to Work of Minority Workers in Great Britain. *Econ. J.*, June 1986, *96*(382), pp. 375–97. **[G: U.K.]**

McMahon, Patrick J. and Tschetter, John H. The Declining Middle Class: A Further Analysis. *Mon. Lab. Rev.*, September 1986, *109*(9), pp. 22–27. **[G: U.S.]**

Medoff, James L. Layoffs, Discharges and Youth Unemployment: Comment. **In** *Freeman, R. B. and Holzer, H. J., eds.*, 1986, pp. 142–43. **[G: U.S.]**

Meitzen, Mark E. Differences in Male and Female Job-quitting Behavior. *J. Lab. Econ.*, April 1986, *4*(2), pp. 151–67. **[G: U.S.]**

Meltz, Noah M. Work-Sharing: New Experiences: Discussion. **In** *Dennis, B. D., ed.*, 1986, pp. 449–52. **[G: U.S.]**

Metcalf, David. Employment-Subsidies and Redundancies. **In** *Blundell, R. and Walker, I., eds.*, 1986, pp. 103–20. **[G: U.K.]**

Mettler, Ruben F. Innovation, Job Creation, and Competitiveness. **In** *Landau, R. and Rosenberg, N., eds.*, 1986, pp. 517–25. **[G: U.S.]**

Meunier, François and Volle, M. The Effects of the New Communications Media on Employment. *Info. Econ. Policy*, September 1986, *2*(3), pp. 195–209. **[G: France]**

Micklewright, John. Unemployment and Incentives to Work: Policy and Evidence in the 1980s. **In** *Hart, P. E., ed.*, 1986, pp. 104–20. **[G: U.K.]**

Miller, Paul W. Immigrant Unemployment in the First Year of Australian Labour Market Activity. *Econ. Rec.*, March 1986, *62*(176), pp. 82–87. **[G: Australia]**

Miller, Paul W. Unemployment Patterns in the Youth Labour Market. *Australian Econ. Pap.*, December 1986, *25*(47), pp. 222–35. **[G: Australia]**

Mincer, Jacob. Wage Changes in Job Changes. **In** *Ehrenberg, R. G., ed., Pt. A*, 1986, pp. 171–97. **[G: U.S.]**

Modigliani, Franco; Padoa Schioppa, F. and Rossi, N. Aggregate Unemployment in Italy, 1960–1983. *Economica*, Supplement 1986, *53*(210(S)), pp. S245–73. **[G: Italy]**

Modigliani, Franco; Padoa Schioppa, F. and Rossi, N. Aggregate Unemployment in Italy, 1960–1983. **In** *Bean, C. R.; Layard, P. R. G. and Nickell, S. J., eds.*, 1986, pp. 245–73. **[G: Italy]**

Morand, Martin J. Work Sharing: New Experiences: Discussion. **In** *Dennis, B. D., ed.*, 1986, pp. 457–64. **[G: U.S.]**

Morgan, James N. Unpaid Productive Activity over the Life Course. **In** *Inst. Med. and Nat'l Res. Counc., Comm. on an Aging Society*, 1986, pp. 73–109. **[G: U.S.]**

Morishima, Motohiro. Job Satisfaction and Desire to Quit: Differences in the Determinants of Two Responses. **In** *Dennis, B. D., ed.*, 1986, pp. 80–91. **[G: Japan]**

Morlicchio, Enrica. Effetti sociali della disoccupazione nelle ricerche sociologiche inglesi degli anni trenta. (British Sociological Research in the Thirties on the Social Effects of Unemployment. With English summary.) *Econ. Lavoro*, July-Sept. 1986, *20*(3), pp. 81–95. **[G: U.K.]**

Morris, Nick. Unemployment and Incentives to Work: Policy and Evidence in the 1980s: Comment. **In** *Hart, P. E., ed.*, 1986, pp. 121–26. **[G: U.K.]**

Morton, John D. BLS White-Collar Pay Survey Now Covers Small Firms. *Mon. Lab. Rev.*, October 1986, *109*(10), pp. 26–30. **[G: U.S.]**

Moser, James W. Demographic and Time Patterns in Layoffs and Quits. *J. Human Res.*, Spring 1986, *21*(2), pp. 178–99. **[G: U.S.]**

Moser, James W. Labor Market Transitions: Cyclic, Trend, and Seasonal Effects for Prime-Age Men. *Ind. Lab. Relat. Rev.*, January 1986, *39*(2), pp. 251–63. **[G: U.S.]**

Muqtada, M. Determinants and Possibilities of Employment Expansion in the Crop Sector. **In** *Islam, R. and Muqtada, M., eds.*, 1986, pp. 61–88. **[G: Bangladesh]**

Myers, George C.; Manton, Kenneth G. and Bacellar, Helena. Sociodemographic Aspects of Future Unpaid Productive Roles. **In** *Inst. Med. and Nat'l Res. Counc., Comm. on an Aging Society*, 1986, pp. 110–47. **[G: U.S.]**

Naisbitt, Barry. Employment Functions and the Slowdown in UK Productivity Growth. *Bull. Econ. Res.*, January 1986, *38*(1), pp. 67–75. **[G: U.K.]**

Nardinelli, Clark. Technology and Unemployment: The Case of the Handloom Weavers. *Southern Econ. J.*, July 1986, *53*(1), pp. 87–94. **[G: U.K.]**

Nardone, Thomas J. Part-time Workers: Who Are They? *Mon. Lab. Rev.*, February 1986, *109*(2), pp. 13–19. **[G: U.S.]**

Nash, June. Deunionization: Economic Dislocation in an American Community. **In** *Gondolf, E. W.; Marcus, I. M. and Dougherty, J. P., eds.*, 1986, pp. 132–41. **[G: U.S.]**

Nelson, Gerald C. Labor Intensity, Employment Growth and Technical Change: An Example from Starch Processing in Indonesia. *J. Devel.*

Econ., November 1986, *24*(1), pp. 111–17. **[G: Indonesia]**

Nickell, Stephen J. Dynamic Models of Labour Demand. **In** *Ashenfelter, O. and Layard, R., eds., Vol. 1*, 1986, pp. 473–522.

Nishikawa, Shunsaku and Shimada, Haruo. Recent Changes in Unemployment in the Japanese Labor Market. **In** *Hax, H.; Kraus, W. and Tsuchiya, K., eds.*, 1986, pp. 125–44. **[G: Japan; OECD]**

Nolan, Brian. Unemployment and the Size Distribution of Income. *Economica*, November 1986, *53*(212), pp. 421–45. **[G: U.K.]**

Norwood, Janet L. Jobs in the 1980's and Beyond. **In** *Burton, D. F., et al., eds.*, 1986, pp. 55–83. **[G: U.S.]**

Noyelle, Thierry J. Advanced Services in the System of Cities. **In** *Bergman, E. M., ed.*, 1986, *1983*, pp. 143–64. **[G: U.S.]**

O'Farrell, Patrick N. The Nature of New Firms in Ireland: Empirical Evidence and Policy Implications. **In** *Keeble, D. and Wever, E., eds.*, 1986, pp. 151–83. **[G: Ireland]**

O'Riordan, William K. An Alternative Measure of Employment Intensity. *Econ. Soc. Rev.*, October 1986, *18*(1), pp. 27–41. **[G: EEC]**

Odling-Smee, John. Labour Demand: Microeconomic Aspects of State Intervention: Comment. **In** *Hart, P. E., ed.*, 1986, pp. 176–79. **[G: U.K.]**

Onchan, Tongroj and Chalamwong, Yongyuth. Rural Off-Farm Income and Employment in Thailand: Current Evidence, Future Trends and Implications. **In** *Shand, R. T., ed., Vol. 1*, 1986, pp. 199–230. **[G: Thailand]**

van Opstal, Rocus and Theeuwes, Jules. Duration of Unemployment in the Dutch Youth Labour Market. *De Economist*, 1986, *134*(3), pp. 351–67. **[G: Netherlands]**

Osberg, Lars; Apostle, Richard and Clairmont, Don. The Incidence and Duration of Individual Unemployment: Supply Side or Demand Side? *Cambridge J. Econ.*, March 1986, *10*(1), pp. 13–33. **[G: Canada]**

Osborne, R. D. and Cormack, R. J. Unemployment and Religion in Northern Ireland. *Econ. Soc. Rev.*, April 1986, *17*(3), pp. 215–25. **[G: Ireland]**

Osterman, Paul. Brothers of a Different Color: A Preliminary Look at Employer Treatment of White and Black Youth: Comment. **In** *Freeman, R. B. and Holzer, H. J., eds.*, 1986, pp. 259–60. **[G: U.S.]**

Ostry, Sylvia. The International Anatomy of Unemployment. **In** *Burton, D. F., et al., eds.*, 1986, pp. 149–57. **[G: OECD]**

Oswald, Andrew J. Is Wage Rigidity Caused by 'Lay-offs by Seniority'? **In** *Beckerman, W., ed.*, 1986, pp. 77–95. **[G: U.K.]**

Palazzi, Paolo and Piacentini, Paolo. Direct and Indirect Labor and Demand for Workers and Working Hours. *Rivista Int. Sci. Econ. Com.*, December 1986, *33*(12), pp. 1207–18. **[G: U.S.]**

Panpiemras, Kosit and Phongpaichit, Pasuk. Policy Guidelines for Human Resource Development and Employment Generation in Thailand. **In** *Shand, R. T., ed., Vol. 1*, 1986, pp. 175–98. **[G: Thailand]**

Park, Fun Koo. Off-Farm Employment in Korea: Current Status and Future Prospects. **In** *Shand, R. T., ed., Vol. 1*, 1986, pp. 135–52. **[G: S. Korea]**

Parra Sandoval, Rodrigo. The Missing Future: Colombian Youth. *CEPAL Rev.*, August 1986, (29), pp. 79–92. **[G: Colombia]**

Parry, Robert T. Statement to the U.S. House Subcommittee on Domestic Monetary Policy of the Committee on Banking, Finance and Urban Affairs, March 19, 1986. *Fed. Res. Bull.*, May 1986, *72*(5), pp. 318–21. **[G: U.S.]**

Parsons, Donald O. The Employment Relationship: Job Attachment, Work Effort, and the Nature of Contracts. **In** *Ashenfelter, O. and Layard, R., eds., Vol. 2*, 1986, pp. 789–848. **[G: U.S.]**

Patrizi, Vincenzo. Measures of Concealed Employment: Pitfalls and Insights. *Econ. Lavoro*, Apr.-June 1986, *20*(2), pp. 91–111. **[G: Italy]**

Pedersen, Peter J. and Westergård-Nielsen, Niels. A Longitudinal Study of Unemployment: History Dependence and Insurance Effects. **In** *Blundell, R. and Walker, I., eds.*, 1986, pp. 44–59. **[G: Denmark]**

Perrons, Diane. Unequal Integration in Global Fordism: The Case of Ireland. **In** *Scott, A. J. and Storper, M., eds.*, 1986, pp. 246–64. **[G: Ireland]**

Perry, George L. Policy Lessons from the Postwar Period. **In** *Beckerman, W., ed.*, 1986, pp. 127–51. **[G: OECD]**

Petit, Pascal. Full-employment Policies in Stagnation: France in the 1980s. *Cambridge J. Econ.*, December 1986, *10*(4), pp. 393–406. **[G: France]**

Phillips, Robyn S. and Vidal, Avis C. Restructuring and Growth Transitions of Metropolitan Economies: The Context for Economic Development Policy. **In** *Bergman, E. M., ed.*, 1986, *1983*, pp. 59–83. **[G: U.S.]**

Phipps, A. J. An Examination of Inter-industry Differences in the Relationship between Output and Employment in Australia. *Australian Bull. Lab.*, December 1986, *13*(1), pp. 35–50. **[G: Australia]**

Pichelmann, Karl and Wagner, Michael. Labour Surplus as a Signal for Real-Wage Adjustment: Austria, 1968–1984. *Economica*, Supplement 1986, *53*(210(S)), pp. S75–87. **[G: Austria]**

Pichelmann, Karl and Wagner, Michael. Labour Surplus as a Signal for Real-Wage Adjustment: Austria, 1968–1984. **In** *Bean, C. R.; Layard, P. R. G. and Nickell, S. J., eds.*, 1986, pp. 75–87. **[G: Austria]**

Pini, Paolo. Durata di ricerca di un posto di lavoro e sussidi di disoccupazione. (Duration of Unemployment and Unemployment Benefits. With English summary.) *Ricerche Econ.*, Jan.-Mar. 1986, *40*(1), pp. 50–81. **[G: U.S.; U.K.; Italy]**

Piore, Michael J. The Effects of Attitudes and Aspirations on the Labor Supply of Young Men:

Comment. **In** *Freeman, R. B. and Holzer, H. J., eds.*, 1986, pp. 399–401. **[G: U.S.]**

Pirog-Good, Maureen A. Modeling Employment and Crime Relationships. *Soc. Sci. Quart.*, December 1986, *67*(4), pp. 767–84. **[G: U.S.]**

Portes, Alejandro; Blitzer, Silvia and Curtis, John. The Urban Informal Sector in Uruguay: Its Internal Structure, Characteristics, and Effects. *World Devel.*, June 1986, *14*(6), pp. 727–41. **[G: Uruguay]**

Poterba, James M. and Summers, Lawrence H. Reporting Errors and Labor Market Dynamics. *Econometrica*, November 1986, *54*(6), pp. 1319–38. **[G: U.S.]**

Pozo, Susan and Woodbury, Stephen A. Pensions, Social Security, and Asset Accumulation. *Eastern Econ. J.*, July-Sept. 1986, *12*(3), pp. 273–81. **[G: U.S.]**

Prais, S. J. Training for Change: Comment. **In** *Hart, P. E., ed.*, 1986, pp. 98–102. **[G: U.K.]**

Prescott, David; Swidinsky, Robert and Wilton, David A. Labour Supply Estimates for Low-Income Female Heads of Household Using Mincome Data. *Can. J. Econ.*, February 1986, *19*(1), pp. 134–41. **[G: Canada]**

Quandt, Richard E. and Rosen, Harvey S. Some Further Results on Rosen and Quandt's Labor Market Model: Queries and Disagreements [Estimating a Disequilibrium Aggregate Labor Market Model]. *Europ. Econ. Rev.*, April 1986, *30*(2), pp. 457–59. **[G: U.S.]**

Quinn, D. J. Accessibility and Job Search: A Study of Unemployed School Leavers. *Reg. Stud.*, April 1986, *20*(2), pp. 163–73. **[G: U.K.]**

Radwan, Samir. Rural Labor Markets in Egypt. **In** *Richards, A., ed.*, 1986, pp. 265–82. **[G: Egypt]**

Rahman, K. M. Technology, Productivity and Employment in Rural Industries. **In** *Islam, R. and Muqtada, M., eds.*, 1986, pp. 197–207. **[G: Bangladesh]**

Rajan, Amin and Cooke, Geoffrey. The Impact of Information Technology on Employment in the Financial Services Industry. *Nat. Westminster Bank Quart. Rev.*, August 1986, pp. 21–35. **[G: U.K.]**

Rassekh, Farhad. Employment Effects of the Steel Trigger Price Mechanism on the Steel and Motor Vehicle Industries. *Atlantic Econ. J.*, March 1986, *14*(1), pp. 39–49. **[G: U.S.]**

Rayappa, P. Hanumantha. Some Dimensions of Off-Farm Employment in Rural Karnataka, India. **In** *Shand, R. T., ed., Vol. 2*, 1986, pp. 177–92. **[G: India]**

Rebitzer, James B. Establishment Size and Job Tenure. *Ind. Relat.*, Fall 1986, *25*(3), pp. 292–302. **[G: U.S.]**

Rees, Albert. An Essay on Youth Joblessness. *J. Econ. Lit.*, June 1986, *24*(2), pp. 613–28. **[G: U.S.]**

Reicher Madeira, Felicia. Youth in Brazil: Old Assumptions and New Approaches. *CEPAL Rev.*, August 1986, (29), pp. 55–78. **[G: Brazil]**

Reid, Frank. Combatting Unemployment through Work Time Reductions. *Can. Public Policy*, June 1986, *12*(2), pp. 275–85. **[G: Canada]**

Renshaw, Edward F. Trends in Manufacturing Employment and Reflections on Infrastructure Investment, Tax and Expenditure Policy in New York State. **In** *Schoolman, M. and Magid, A., eds.*, 1986, pp. 91–114. **[G: U.S.]**

Rice, Patricia G. Juvenile Unemployment, Relative Wages and Social Security: The Econometric Evidence. **In** *Blundell, R. and Walker, I., eds.*, 1986, pp. 60–74. **[G: U.K.]**

Rice, Patricia G. Juvenile Unemployment, Relative Wages and Social Security in Great Britain. *Econ. J.*, June 1986, *96*(382), pp. 352–74. **[G: U.K.]**

Richards, Craig E. Race and Demographic Trends: The Employment of Minority Teachers in California Public Schools. *Econ. Educ. Rev.*, 1986, *5*(1), pp. 57–64. **[G: U.S.]**

Richards, Peter J. Preserving Jobs under Economic Stabilisation Programmes: Can There Be an Employment Target? *Int. Lab. Rev.*, July-Aug. 1986, *125*(4), pp. 423–34. **[G: LDCs]**

Richardson, Bronwyn. Unemployment and Health in Australia: A Policy Perspective. **In** *Butler, J. R. G. and Doessel, D. P., eds.*, 1986, pp. 1–34. **[G: Australia]**

Riechel, Klaus-Walter. Labor Market Disequilibrium and the Scope for Work-Sharing: A Case Study of the Netherlands. *Int. Monet. Fund Staff Pap.*, September 1986, *33*(3), pp. 509–40. **[G: Netherlands]**

Rimler, Judit. Economic Obsolescence and Employment (A Comparative Analysis of the Hungarian and Dutch Economies). *Acta Oecon.*, 1986, *36*(1–2), pp. 123–40. **[G: Hungary; Netherlands]**

Roberts, Markley. A Labor Agenda for Jobs. **In** *Burton, D. F., et al., eds.*, 1986, pp. 119–33. **[G: U.S.]**

Robertson, Matthew. Long-term Unemployment in the Canadian Labor Market: A Longitudinal Perspective. *Amer. J. Econ. Soc.*, July 1986, *45*(3), pp. 277–89. **[G: Canada]**

Rocherieux, François. La dynamique macro-économique de l'internationalisation et des caractéristiques de l'emploi. (The Macroeconomic Dynamics of Internationalization and Employment Characteristics. With English summary.) *Écon. Soc.*, January 1986, *20*(1), pp. 169–209. **[G: France]**

Romer, Christina D. New Estimates of Prewar Gross National Product and Unemployment. *J. Econ. Hist.*, June 1986, *46*(2), pp. 341–52. **[G: U.S.]**

Romer, Christina D. Spurious Volatility in Historical Unemployment Data. *J. Polit. Econ.*, February 1986, *94*(1), pp. 1–37. **[G: U.S.]**

Rosen, Ellen. Women: Disproportionate Losers in Jobs and Status. **In** *Gondolf, E. W.; Marcus, I. M. and Dougherty, J. P., eds.*, 1986, pp. 143–51. **[G: U.S.]**

Rostker, Bernard. Economic Analysis of Army Enlistments: Policy Implications: Comment. **In**

Gilroy, C. L., ed., 1986, pp. 95–96. **[G: U.S.]**

Royer, Jacques. The Long-term Employment Impact of Disarmament Policies: Some Findings from an Econometric Model. *Int. Lab. Rev.*, May-June 1986, *125*(3), pp. 279–303. **[G: Global]**

Rubery, Jill. Trade Unions in the 1980s: The Case of the United Kingdom. **In** *Edwards, R.; Garonna, P. and Tödtling, F., eds.*, 1986, pp. 61–113. **[G: U.K.]**

Russo, John. Technological Displacement: Strategies of the Global Auto Industry. **In** *Gondolf, E. W.; Marcus, I. M. and Dougherty, J. P., eds.*, 1986, pp. 122–32. **[G: U.S.]**

Sajhau, Jean-Paul. Employment, Wages and Living Conditions in a Changing Industry—Plantations. *Int. Lab. Rev.*, Jan.-Feb. 1986, *125*(1), pp. 71–85. **[G: LDCs]**

Salinas, Patricia Wilson. Urban Growth, Subemployment, and Mobility. **In** *Bergman, E. M., ed.*, 1986, pp. 248–70. **[G: U.S.]**

San, Gee. The Early Labor Force Experience of College Students and Their Post-college Success. *Econ. Educ. Rev.*, 1986, *5*(1), pp. 65–76. **[G: U.S.]**

Sandesara, J. C. Industrial Production and Employment in the Seventh Plan—Two Quick Comments. *Indian Econ. J.*, Apr.-June 1986, *33*(4), pp. 92–97. **[G: India]**

Santiago, Carlos E. Closing the Gap: The Employment and Unemployment Effects of Minimum Wage Policy in Puerto Rico. *J. Devel. Econ.*, October 1986, *23*(2), pp. 293–311. **[G: Puerto Rico]**

Santoni, Gary J. The Employment Act of 1946: Some History Notes. *Fed. Res. Bank St. Louis Rev.*, November 1986, *68*(9), pp. 5–16. **[G: U.S.]**

Schaich, Eberhard and Zimmermann, Peter. Zur Erfassung der Arbeitslosigkeit: Kritik derzeit praktizierter Verfahrensweisen und Erweiterungsvorschläge. (Measuring Unemployment in West Germany: Actual Procedures and Possible Improvements. With English summary.) *Jahr. Nationalökon. Statist.*, September 1986, *201*(5), pp. 498–517. **[G: W. Germany]**

Schiff, Frank W. Issues in Assessing Work-Sharing. **In** *Dennis, B. D., ed.*, 1986, pp. 433–40. **[G: U.S.]**

Schober-Brinkmann, Karen. The Crisis of Youth Employment and Training in West Germany: Public Intervention and the Response of Employers and Trade Unions. *Econ. Lavoro*, Oct.-Dec. 1986, *20*(4), pp. 117–27. **[G: W. Germany]**

Schrank, William E.; Roy, Noel and Tsoa, Eugene. Employment Prospects in a Commercially Viable Newfoundland Fishery: An Application of 'An Econometric Model of the Newfoundland Groundfishery.' *Marine Resource Econ.*, 1986, *3*(3), pp. 237–63. **[G: Canada]**

Schröter, Lutz. "Steelworks Now!" The Conflicting Character of Modernisation: A Case Study of Hoesch in Dortmund. **In** *Goldberg, W. H., ed.*, 1986, pp. 361–408. **[G: W. Germany]**

Schwartz, Arthur R.; Cohen, Malcolm S. and Grimes, Donald R. Structural/Frictional vs. Deficient Demand Unemployment: Comment. *Amer. Econ. Rev.*, March 1986, *76*(1), pp. 268–72. **[G: U.S.]**

Schweke, William and Jones, David R. European Job Creation in the Wake of Plant Closing and Layoffs. *Mon. Lab. Rev.*, October 1986, *109*(10), pp. 18–22. **[G: W. Europe]**

Scitovsky, Tibor. Excess Demand for Job Importance and Its Implications. **In** *Scitovsky, T.*, 1986, *1981*, pp. 136–48. **[G: U.S.]**

Scoville, James G. Economic Analysis of Labor Market Premiums for Traditional Skills in LDCs. **In** *Dennis, B. D., ed.*, 1986, pp. 346–52. **[G: LDCs]**

Sellier, François and Silvestre, Jean-Jacques. Unions' Policies in the Economic Crisis in France. **In** *Edwards, R.; Garonna, P. and Tödtling, F., eds.*, 1986, pp. 173–226. **[G: France]**

Shack-Marquez, Janice. Effects of Repeated Interviewing on Estimation of Labor Force Status. *J. Econ. Soc. Meas.*, December 1986, *14*(4), pp. 379–98. **[G: U.S.]**

Shand, Richard T. Off-Farm Employment in the Development of Rural Asia: Issues. **In** *Shand, R. T., ed., Vol. 1*, 1986, pp. 1–24. **[G: Asia]**

Shand, Richard T. and Chew, T. A. Off-Farm Employment in the Kemubu Project in Kelantan, Malaysia. **In** *Shand, R. T., ed., Vol. 2*, 1986, pp. 1–20. **[G: Malaysia]**

Shank, Susan E. Employment Up, Unemployment Stable in the First Half of 1986. *Mon. Lab. Rev.*, August 1986, *109*(8), pp. 3–8. **[G: U.S.]**

Shank, Susan E. and Getz, Patricia M. Employment and Unemployment: Developments in 1985. *Mon. Lab. Rev.*, February 1986, *109*(2), pp. 3–12. **[G: U.S.]**

Shapiro, David and Hills, Stephen M. Adjusting to Recession: Labor Market Dynamics in the Construction, Automobile, and Steel Industries. **In** *Hills, S. M., ed.*, 1986, pp. 37–62. **[G: U.S.]**

Shaw, R. Paul. Unemployment and Low Family Incomes in Canada. *Can. Public Policy*, June 1986, *12*(2), pp. 368–86. **[G: Canada]**

Shelp, Ronald Kent. Services in the Economies of the Developing Countries. **In** *Wasow, B. and Hill, R. D., eds.*, 1986, pp. 3–28. **[G: LDCs]**

Shome, Parthasarathi. Effects of Tax Incentives on Investment and Employment: Appendix: The Broad Goals of Tax Incentives. **In** *Shome, P., ed.*, 1986, pp. 43–47. **[G: Thailand; Malaysia; Philippines]**

Sickles, Robin C. and Taubman, Paul. An Analysis of the Health and Retirement Status of the Elderly. *Econometrica*, November 1986, *54*(6), pp. 1339–56. **[G: U.S.]**

Silvera, Rachel and Outin, Jean-Luc. Excédents de main-d'oeuvre et dispositifs de cessation anticipée d'activité. (Excess Labour and Early Retirement. With English summary.) *Écon.*

Soc., April 1986, *20*(4), pp. 305–43. **[G: France]**

Singer, Neil M. Retirement Changes and Military Force Manning: A Sensitivity Analysis. **In** *Gilroy, C. L., ed.*, 1986, pp. 329–46. **[G: U.S.]**

Singleton, John. Lancashire's Last Stand: Declining Employment in the British Cotton Industry, 1950–70. *Econ. Hist. Rev., 2nd Ser.*, February 1986, *39*(1), pp. 92–107. **[G: U.K.]**

Sjogren, Jane. Retirement Age Women and Men: Income Sources and Work. *Eastern Econ. J.*, July-Sept. 1986, *12*(3), pp. 283–90. **[G: U.S.]**

Smith, Arthur B., Jr. Equal Employment Opportunity Act and Its Administration: A Management Perspective. **In** *Dennis, B. D., ed.*, 1986, pp. 465–71. **[G: U.S.]**

Smith, Shirley J. Work Experience Profile, 1984: The Effects of Recovery Continue. *Mon. Lab. Rev.*, February 1986, *109*(2), pp. 37–43. **[G: U.S.]**

Smyth, David J. The Cyclical Response of Employment to Output Changes: United States Manufacturing Industries, 1948 to 1983. *Appl. Econ.*, May 1986, *18*(5), pp. 495–500. **[G: U.S.]**

Sneessens, Henri R. and Drèze, Jacques H. A Discussion of Belgian Unemployment, Combining Traditional Concepts and Disequilibrium Econometrics. *Economica*, Supplement 1986, *53*(210(S)), pp. S89–119. **[G: Belgium]**

Sneessens, Henri R. and Drèze, Jacques H. A Discussion of Belgian Unemployment, Combining Traditional Concepts and Disequilibrium Econometrics. **In** *Bean, C. R.; Layard, P. R. G. and Nickell, S. J., eds.*, 1986, pp. 89–119. **[G: Belgium]**

Sneessens, Henri R. and Drèze, Jacques H. What, If Anything, Have We Learned from the Rise of Unemployment in Belgium, 1974–1983. *Cah. Écon. Bruxelles*, 2nd/3rd Trimester 1986, (110/111), pp. 21–66. **[G: Belgium]**

Soares, Fernando B. Structure of Agriculture and People in Rural Societies: Discussion. **In** *Maunder, A. and Renborg, U., eds.*, 1986, pp. 550–51. **[G: U.S.]**

Solon, Gary. Effects of Rotation Group Bias on Estimation of Unemployment. *J. Bus. Econ. Statist.*, January 1986, *4*(1), pp. 105–09. **[G: U.S.]**

Solow, Robert M. The Unemployment of Nations. *Bus. Econ.*, January 1986, *21*(1), pp. 5–12. **[G: U.S.; EEC]**

Spenceley, G. F. R. Responses to Unemployment in Australia: The 1930s and Now. **In** *Berend, I. T. and Borchardt, K., eds.*, 1986, pp. 82–105. **[G: Australia]**

St. Louis, Robert D.; Burgess, Paul L. and Kingston, Jerry L. Reported vs. Actual Job Search by Unemployment Insurance Claimants. *J. Human Res.*, Winter 1986, *21*(1), pp. 92–117. **[G: U.S.]**

Standing, Guy. Labour Flexibility and Older Worker Marginalisation: The Need for a New Strategy. *Int. Lab. Rev.*, May-June 1986, *125*(3), pp. 329–48. **[G: EEC]**

Standing, Guy. Meshing Labour Flexibility with Security: An Answer to British Unemployment? *Int. Lab. Rev.*, Jan.-Feb. 1986, *125*(1), pp. 87–106. **[G: EEC]**

Stenius, Marianne and Virén, Matti. A Reply [Estimating a Disequilibrium Aggregate Labor Market Model] [Some Further Results on Rosen and Quandt's Labor Market Model]. *Europ. Econ. Rev.*, April 1986, *30*(2), pp. 461–62. **[G: U.S.]**

Stern, Jon. Repeat Unemployment Spells: The Effect of Unemployment Benefits on Unemployment Entry. **In** *Blundell, R. and Walker, I., eds.*, 1986, pp. 23–43. **[G: U.K.]**

Stinson, John F., Jr. Moonlighting by Women Jumped to Record Highs. *Mon. Lab. Rev.*, November 1986, *109*(11), pp. 22–25. **[G: U.S.]**

Stobernack, Michael. Umfang und Struktur der stillen Reserve auf dem Arbeitsmarkt. Eine Schätzung auf der Grundlage des Sozio-ökonomischen Panels. (Size and Structure of Hidden Unemployment in the Federal Republic of Germany. With English summary.) *Konjunkturpolitik*, 1986, *32*(4), pp. 195–217. **[G: W. Germany; U.S.]**

Storey, David J. and Amin, Ash. Employment Creation at a Local Level in the U.K. *Econ. Lavoro*, July-Sept. 1986, *20*(3), pp. 63–80. **[G: U.K.]**

Stromsdorfer, Ernst W. Enlistment Decisions of Young Men: Comment. **In** *Gilroy, C. L., ed.*, 1986, pp. 57–60. **[G: U.S.]**

Studenmund, A. H. and Maani, Sholeh A. Erratum [The Critical Wage, Unemployment Duration, and Wage Expectations: The Case of Chile]. *Ind. Lab. Relat. Rev.*, October 1986, *40*(1), pp. 128. **[G: Chile]**

Summers, Lawrence H. Why Is the Unemployment Rate So Very High near Full Employment? *Brookings Pap. Econ. Act.*, 1986, (2), pp. 339–83. **[G: U.S.]**

Taira, Koji. Diverse Entrepreneurial Traditions and Implications for Internal and External Labor Markets. **In** *Dennis, B. D., ed.*, 1986, pp. 336–45. **[G: Japan]**

Tatom, John A. Why Has Manufacturing Employment Declined? *Fed. Res. Bank St. Louis Rev.*, December 1986, *68*(10), pp. 15–25. **[G: U.S.]**

Taylor, Jim. The Use of Unemployment and Vacancy Data in Analysing Unemployment. *Rech. Écon. Louvain*, 1986, *52*(3–4), pp. 257–82. **[G: U.K.]**

Theeuwes, Jules. Unemployment and Labour Market Transition Probabilities. *Rech. Écon. Louvain*, 1986, *52*(3–4), pp. 209–26. **[G: Netherlands]**

Thomas, D. A. War and the Economy: The South Wales Experience. **In** *Baber, C. and Williams, L. J., eds.*, 1986, pp. 251–77. **[G: U.K.]**

Till, Thomas E. The Share of Southeastern Black Counties in the Southern Rural Renaissance: Were They Bypassed by Factory Job Gains, 1959–77? *Growth Change*, April 1986, *17*(2), pp. 44–55. **[G: U.S.]**

Tokman, Víctor E. Adjustment and Employment

in Latin America: The Current Challenges. *Int. Lab. Rev.*, Sept.-Oct. 1986, *125*(5), pp. 533–43. **[G: Latin America]**

Tokman, Víctor E. Creación de empleo productivo: una tarea impostergable. (With English summary.) *Desarrollo Econ.*, Oct.-Dec. 1986, *26*(103), pp. 339–67. **[G: Latin America]**

Topel, Robert. Job Mobility, Search, and Earnings Growth: A Reinterpretation of Human Capital Earnings Functions. **In** *Ehrenberg, R. G., ed., Pt. A,* 1986, pp. 199–233. **[G: U.S.]**

Townroe, Peter M. Technological Change in the Service Sector: Urban and Regional Implications. **In** *Nijkamp, P., ed. (II),* 1986, pp. 76–90. **[G: U.K.]**

Townsend, Alan R. Spatial Aspects of the Growth of Part-Time Employment in Britain. *Reg. Stud.*, August 1986, *20*(4), pp. 313–30. **[G: U.K.]**

Tweeten, Luther. Agricultural Structure in a Service Economy. **In** *Maunder, A. and Renborg, U., eds.*, 1986, pp. 542–50. **[G: U.S.]**

Utgoff, Kathleen P. First-Term Attrition of High School Graduates in the Military: Comment. **In** *Gilroy, C. L., ed.*, 1986, pp. 292–93. **[G: U.S.]**

Van Horn, Carl E.; Beauregard, Robert A. and Ford, David S. Local Economic Development and Job Targeting. **In** *Bergman, E. M., ed.*, 1986, pp. 226–47. **[G: U.S.]**

Virgo, John. Youth Unemployment Issues: Western Europe and the United States. *Rivista Int. Sci. Econ. Com.*, June-July 1986, *33*(6–7), pp. 565–84. **[G: U.S.; W. Europe]**

Wachter, Michael L. Why Is the Unemployment Rate So Very High near Full Employment? Comments. *Brookings Pap. Econ. Act.*, 1986, (2), pp. 389–94.

Wagstaff, Howard. The Employment Problem, Agricultural Change, and Policy Objectives in Industrially Advanced Countries. *J. Agr. Econ.*, May 1986, *37*(2), pp. 163–72. **[G: OECD]**

Warner, John T. Reenlistment Decision Models: Implications for Policy Making: Comment. **In** *Gilroy, C. L., ed.*, 1986, pp. 222–24. **[G: U.S.]**

Way, Philip K. White-Collar Labor Market Changes: Discussion. **In** *Dennis, B. D., ed.*, 1986, pp. 68–71. **[G: U.S.]**

Webber, M. J. Regional Production and the Production of Regions: The Case of Steeltown. **In** *Scott, A. J. and Storper, M., eds.*, 1986, pp. 197–224. **[G: Canada]**

Weir, David R. The Reliability of Historical Macroeconomic Data for Comparing Cyclical Stability. *J. Econ. Hist.*, June 1986, *46*(2), pp. 353–65. **[G: U.S.]**

Wells, Donald A. The Effects of Saudi Industrialization on Employment. *J. Energy Devel.*, Spring 1986, *11*(2), pp. 273–84. **[G: Saudi Arabia]**

White, Michael. Working Time and Employment: A Negotiable Issue? **In** *Hart, P. E., ed.*, 1986, pp. 5–22. **[G: W. Europe]**

Whitley, J. D. and Wilson, R. A. The Impact on Employment of a Reduction in the Length of the Working Week. *Cambridge J. Econ.*, March 1986, *10*(1), pp. 43–59. **[G: U.K.]**

Wicker, Elmus R. Terminating Hyperinflation in the Dismembered Habsburg Monarchy. *Amer. Econ. Rev.*, June 1986, *76*(3), pp. 350–64. **[G: Poland; Austria; Hungary]**

Williams, Bruce. Technical Change and Employment. **In** *Hall, P., ed.*, 1986, *1984*, pp. 84–103. **[G: U.K.]**

Winpisinger, William. Surplus Labor: An Appeal for an International Trade Program. **In** *Gondolf, E. W.; Marcus, I. M. and Dougherty, J. P., eds.*, 1986, pp. 111–21. **[G: U.S.]**

Wiradi, Gunawan. Landlessness, Tenancy and Off-Farm Employment in Rural Java: A Study of Twelve Villages. **In** *Shand, R. T., ed., Vol. 1,* 1986, pp. 309–26. **[G: Indonesia]**

Wonnacott, R. J. On the Employment Effects of Free Trade with the United States. *Can. Public Policy*, March 1986, *12*(1), pp. 258–63. **[G: Canada; U.S.]**

Wood, P. A. The Anatomy of Job Loss and Job Creation: Some Speculations on the Role of the 'Producer Service' Sector. *Reg. Stud.*, February 1986, *20*(1), pp. 37–46. **[G: U.K.]**

Wood, Stephen. Recruitment Systems and the Recession. *Brit. J. Ind. Relat.*, March 1986, *24*(1), pp. 103–20. **[G: U.K.; W. Germany]**

Wren-Lewis, Simon. An Econometric Model of U.K. Manufacturing Employment Using Survey Data on Expected Output. *J. Appl. Econometrics,* October 1986, *1*(4), pp. 297–316. **[G: U.K.]**

Yago, Glenn, et al. Industrial Devolution in New York State. **In** *Schoolman, M. and Magid, A., eds.*, 1986, pp. 75–89. **[G: U.S.]**

Zachmann, Roberto. Reduction of Working Time as a Means to Reduce Unemployment: A Micro-economic Perspective. *Int. Lab. Rev.*, Mar.-Apr. 1986, *125*(2), pp. 163–75.

Zalokar, Nadja. Generational Differences in Female Occupational Attainment—Have the 1970's Changed Women's Opportunities? *Amer. Econ. Rev.*, May 1986, *76*(2), pp. 378–81. **[G: U.S.]**

Zalusky, John. Labor's Interest and Concerns with Short-Time Compensation. **In** *Dennis, B. D., ed.*, 1986, pp. 441–48. **[G: U.S.]**

Zoll, Rainer and Neumann, Enno. Workers' Reactions to Crisis. **In** *Jacobi, O., et al., eds. (I),* 1986, pp. 261–75. **[G: W. Germany]**

825 Productivity Studies: Labor, Capital, and Total Factor

8250 Productivity Studies: Labor, Capital, and Total Factor

Abalkin, L. The Interaction of the Productive Forces and Production Relations. *Prob. Econ.*, April 1986, *28*(12), pp. 23–41. **[G: U.S.S.R.]**

Ahluwalia, Isher Judge. Industrial Growth in India: Performance and Prospects. *J. Devel. Econ.*, September 1986, *23*(1), pp. 1–18. **[G: India]**

825 Productivity Studies: Labor, Capital, and Total Factor

Akerlof, George A. and Yellen, Janet L. Efficiency Wage Models of the Labor Market. **In** *Akerlof, G. A. and Yellen, J. L., eds.*, 1986, pp. 1–21. **[G: U.S.]**

Allen, Steven G. The Effect of Unionism on Productivity in Privately and Publicly Owned Hospitals and Nursing Homes. *J. Lab. Res.*, Winter 1986, *7*(1), pp. 59–68. **[G: U.S.]**

Allen, Steven G. Unionization and Productivity in Office Building and School Construction. *Ind. Lab. Relat. Rev.*, January 1986, *39*(2), pp. 187–201. **[G: U.S.]**

Amann, Ronald. Technical Progress and Soviet Economic Development: Setting the Scene. **In** *Amann, R. and Cooper, J., eds.*, 1986, pp. 5–30. **[G: U.S.S.R.]**

Baily, Martin Neil. Productivity Growth and Materials Use in U.S. Manufacturing [Productivity and the Services of Capital and Labor]. *Quart. J. Econ.*, February 1986, *101*(1), pp. 185–95. **[G: U.S.]**

Baily, Martin Neil. The Cyclical Behavior of Industrial Labor Markets: A Comparison of the Prewar and Postwar Eras: Comment. **In** *Gordon, R. J., ed.*, 1986, pp. 621–66. **[G: U.S.]**

Bairam, Erkin I. Returns to Scale, Technical Progress and Output Growth in Branches of Industry: The Case of Eastern Europe and the USSR, 1961–75. *Keio Econ. Stud.*, 1986, *23*(1), pp. 63–78. **[G: CMEA]**

Barbera, Anthony J. and McConnell, Virginia D. Effects of Pollution Control on Industry Productivity: A Factor Demand Approach. *J. Ind. Econ.*, December 1986, *35*(2), pp. 161–72. **[G: U.S.]**

Barsky, A. D. and Belagurova, E. A. Toward an Analysis of the Principles Governing the Formation of Material Incentive Funds. *Matekon*, Spring 1986, *22*(3), pp. 91–110. **[G: U.S.S.R.]**

Batstone, Eric. Labour and Productivity. *Oxford Rev. Econ. Policy*, Autumn 1986, *2*(3), pp. 32–43. **[G: U.K.]**

Baumol, William J. Information Technology and the Service Sector: A Feedback Process? **In** *Faulhaber, G.; Noam, E. and Tasley, R., eds.*, 1986, pp. 183–93. **[G: U.S.]**

Baumol, William J. Services in Transition: The Impact of Information Technology on the Service Sector: Conclusion. **In** *Faulhaber, G.; Noam, E. and Tasley, R., eds.*, 1986, pp. 195–99. **[G: U.S.]**

Belongia, Michael T. The Farm Sector in the 1980s: Sudden Collapse or Steady Downturn? *Fed. Res. Bank St. Louis Rev.*, November 1986, *68*(9), pp. 17–25. **[G: U.S.]**

Bernanke, Ben S. and Powell, James L. The Cyclical Behavior of Industrial Labor Markets: A Comparison of the Prewar and Postwar Eras. **In** *Gordon, R. J., ed.*, 1986, pp. 583–621. **[G: U.S.]**

Berndt, Ernst R. and Fuss, Melvyn A. Productivity Measurement with Adjustments for Variations in Capacity Utilization and Other Forms of Temporary Equilibrium. *J. Econometrics*, Oct./Nov. 1986, *33*(1/2), pp. 7–29. **[G: U.S.]**

Berndt, Ernst R. and Wood, David O. Energy Price Shocks and Productivity Growth in U.S. and UK Manufacturing. *Oxford Rev. Econ. Policy*, Autumn 1986, *2*(3), pp. 1–31. **[G: U.K.; U.S.]**

Blanchard, Olivier J. and Summers, Lawrence H. Hysteresis and the European Unemployment Problem. **In** *Fischer, S., ed.*, 1986, pp. 15–78. **[G: U.S.; U.K.; W. Germany; France]**

Blattenberger, G. and Lad, F. A Subjective Bayesian Characterization of Evidence on New Views of Worker Productivity. *Metroecon.*, June 1986, *38*(2), pp. 135–56. **[G: U.S.]**

Blaug, Mark. The Productivity of Capital in the Lancashire Cotton Industry during the Nineteenth Century. **In** *Blaug, M.*, 1986, *1961*, pp. 51–87. **[G: U.K.]**

Boddy, Raford and Alwan, Rami. Work Shifts and the Cyclical Behavior of Productivity and Real Wages. *J. Macroecon.*, Summer 1986, *8*(3), pp. 355–63.

Boddy, Raford; Frantz, Roger S. and Poe-Tierney, Barbara. The Marginal Productivity Theory: Production Line and Machine Level by Work-Shift and Time of Day. *J. Behav. Econ.*, Spring/Summer 1986, *15*(1/2), pp. 1–23. **[G: Mexico; U.S.]**

Brand, Horst and Ahmed, Ziaul Z. Beauty and Barber Shops: The Trend of Labor Productivity. *Mon. Lab. Rev.*, March 1986, *109*(3), pp. 21–26. **[G: U.S.]**

Brand, Horst and Huffstutler, Clyde. Trends of Labor Productivity in Metal Stamping Industries. *Mon. Lab. Rev.*, May 1986, *109*(5), pp. 13–20. **[G: U.S.]**

Brockhoff, Klaus. Die Produktivität der Forschung und Entwicklung eines Industrieunternehmens. (With English summary.) *Z. Betriebswirtshaft*, June 1986, *56*(6), pp. 525–37. **[G: W. Germany]**

Brown, Martin and Philips, Peter. Craft Labor and Mechanization in Nineteenth-Century American Canning. *J. Econ. Hist.*, September 1986, *46*(3), pp. 743–56. **[G: U.S.]**

Bruno, Michael. Raw Materials, Profits, and the Productivity Slowdown: A Complementary Note [Productivity and the Services of Capital and Labor]. *Quart. J. Econ.*, February 1986, *101*(1), pp. 197–200. **[G: U.S.]**

Bukhval'd, E. and Pogrebinskaia, V. V. I. Lenin on the Dynamics of Reproduction and the Rates of the USSR's Economic Development. *Prob. Econ.*, April 1986, *28*(12), pp. 59–77. **[G: U.S.S.R.]**

Callan, Scott J. Decomposition of Total Factor Productivity Growth, Additional Evidence: The Case of the U.S. Electric Utility Industry, 1951–1978. *Quart. J. Bus. Econ.*, Summer 1986, *25*(3), pp. 55–71. **[G: U.S.]**

Capalbo, Susan M. and Denny, Michael G. S. Testing Long-run Productivity Models for the Canadian and U.S. Agricultural Sectors. *Amer. J. Agr. Econ.*, August 1986, *68*(3), pp. 615–25. **[G: U.S.; Canada]**

Cockerill, Anthony and Cole, Sara. Restructuring

British Steel. **In** *Goldberg, W. H., ed.*, 1986, pp. 149–63. **[G: U.K.; France; W. Germany]**

Cole, Sam. The Global Impact of Information Technology. *World Devel.*, Oct./Nov. 1986, *14*(10/11), pp. 1277–92. **[G: Global]**

Contino, Ronald. Productivity Gains through Labor–Management Cooperation at the N.Y.C. Department of Sanitation Bureau of Motor Equipment. **In** *Rosow, J. M., ed.*, 1986, pp. 169–86. **[G: U.S.]**

Dale, Barrie. Experience with Quality Circles and Quality Costs. **In** *Moores, B., ed.*, 1986, pp. 36–49. **[G: U.K.]**

Daly, Anne. Education and Productivity: A Comparison of Great Britain and the United States. *Brit. J. Ind. Relat.*, July 1986, *24*(2), pp. 251–66. **[G: U.K.; U.S.]**

Daly, Michael J. and Rao, P. Someshwar. Free Trade, Scale Economies and Productivity Growth in Canadian Manufacturing. *Manchester Sch. Econ. Soc. Stud.*, December 1986, *54*(4), pp. 391–402. **[G: Canada]**

Dean, Edwin; Boissevain, Harry and Thomas, James. Productivity and Labor Costs Trends in Manufacturing, 12 Countries. *Mon. Lab. Rev.*, March 1986, *109*(3), pp. 3–10. **[G: U.S.; Selected OECD]**

Defourny, Jacques. Une analyse financière comparée des coopératives de travailleurs et des entreprises capitalistes en France. (A Comparative Financial Analysis of Workers' Cooperatives and Capitalist Firms in France. With English summary.) *Ann. Pub. Co-op. Econ.*, Jan.-March 1986, *57*(1), pp. 55–78. **[G: France]**

Dutkowsky, Donald H. and Gianturco, David J. On the Inflation-Unit Labor Cost Relation. *J. Econ. Bus.*, May 1986, *38*(2), pp. 173–81. **[G: U.S.]**

Edwards, Richard and Podgursky, Michael. The Unraveling Accord: American Unions in Crisis. **In** *Edwards, R.; Garonna, P. and Tödtling, F., eds.*, 1986, pp. 14–60. **[G: U.S.]**

Ehrenberg, Ronald G. and Schwarz, Joshua L. Public-Sector Labor Markets. **In** *Ashenfelter, O. and Layard, R., eds., Vol. 2*, 1986, pp. 1219–68. **[G: U.S.]**

Ekpo-Ufot, Abel. Personnel Functions, Practices and Productivity in Nigeria. **In** *Damachi, U. G. and Seibel, H. D., eds.*, 1986, pp. 292–314. **[G: Nigeria]**

Filer, Randall K. People and Productivity: Effort Supply as Viewed by Economists and Psychologists. **In** *Gilad, B. and Kaish, S., eds., Vol. A*, 1986, pp. 261–87.

Fishlow, Albert. Growth and Productivity Change in the Canadian Railway Sector, 1871–1926: Comment. **In** *Engerman, S. L. and Gallman, R. E., eds.*, 1986, pp. 812–16. **[G: Canada]**

Frantz, Roger S. X-Efficiency in Behavioral Economics. **In** *Gilad, B. and Kaish, S., eds., Vol. A*, 1986, pp. 307–23.

Freeman, Richard B. and Medoff, James L. The Two Faces of Unionism. **In** *Reynolds, L. G.; Masters, S. H. and Moser, C. H., eds.*, 1986, *1979*, pp. 374–90. **[G: U.S.]**

Fulco, Lawrence J. U.S. Productivity Growth Since 1982: The Post-recession Experience. *Mon. Lab. Rev.*, December 1986, *109*(12), pp. 18–22. **[G: U.S.]**

Gathon, Henry-Jean. La mesure des gains de productivite globale dans les chemins de fer. Une comparaison internationale. (The Measurement of Global Productivity Gains in Railroads: An International Comparisons. With English summary.) *Ann. Pub. Co-op. Econ.*, Oct.-Dec. 1986, *57*(4), pp. 459–76. **[G: W. Europe; Japan]**

Gloeckner, Eduard. Underemployment and Potential Unemployment of the Technical Intelligentsia: Distortions between Education and Occupation. **In** *Lane, D., ed.*, 1986, pp. 223–36. **[G: U.S.S.R.]**

Goldar, Bishwanath. Import Substitution, Industrial Concentration and Productivity Growth in Indian Manufacturing. *Oxford Bull. Econ. Statist.*, May 1986, *48*(2), pp. 143–64. **[G: India]**

Gomulka, Stanislaw. Growth and the Import of Technology: Poland 1971–80. **In** *Gomulka, S.*, 1986, *1978*, pp. 195–218. **[G: E. Europe]**

Green, Alan G. Growth and Productivity Change in the Canadian Railway Sector, 1871–1926. **In** *Engerman, S. L. and Gallman, R. E., eds.*, 1986, pp. 779–812. **[G: Canada]**

Griliches, Zvi. Productivity, *R&D*, and the Basic Research at the Firm Level in the 1970's. *Amer. Econ. Rev.*, March 1986, *76*(1), pp. 141–54. **[G: U.S.]**

Grossbard-Shechtman, Amyra. Marriage and Productivity: An Interdisciplinary Analysis. **In** *Gilad, B. and Kaish, S., eds., Vol. A*, 1986, pp. 289–302.

Grubb, David B. Raw Materials, Profits, and the Productivity Slowdown: Some Doubts. *Quart. J. Econ.*, February 1986, *101*(1), pp. 175–84. **[G: U.S.; W. Europe; Japan]**

Hall, Robert E. Hysteresis and the European Unemployment Problem: Comment. **In** *Fischer, S., ed.*, 1986, pp. 85–88. **[G: U.S.; U.K.; W. Germany; France]**

Hamada, Koichi and Kurosaka, Yoshio. Trends in Unemployment, Wages and Productivity: The Case of Japan. *Economica*, Supplement 1986, *53*(210(S)), pp. S275–96. **[G: Japan]**

Handoussa, Heba; Nishimizu, Mieko and Page, John M., Jr. Productivity Change in Egyptian Public Sector Industries after "The Opening," 1973–1979. *J. Devel. Econ.*, Jan.-Feb. 1986, *20*(1), pp. 53–73. **[G: Egypt]**

Hanson, Philip. The Serendipitous Soviet Achievement of Full Employment: Labour Shortage and Labour Hoarding in the Soviet Economy. **In** *Lane, D., ed.*, 1986, pp. 83–111. **[G: U.S.S.R.]**

Herman, Arthur S. Productivity Continued to Increase in Many Industries during 1984. *Mon. Lab. Rev.*, March 1986, *109*(3), pp. 11–15. **[G: U.S.]**

Hulten, Charles R. Productivity Change, Capacity Utilization, and the Sources of Efficiency Growth. *J. Econometrics*, Oct./Nov. 1986, *33*(1/2), pp. 31–50.

Ichniowski, Casey. The Effects of Grievance Activity on Productivity. *Ind. Lab. Relat. Rev.*, October 1986, *40*(1), pp. 75–89. **[G: U.S.]**

Ikemoto, Yukio. Technical Progress and Level of Technology in Asian Countries, 1970–80: A Translog Index Approach. *Devel. Econ.*, December 1986, *24*(4), pp. 368–90. **[G: Selected Asian]**

Jackson, John L. Long-run Effects of Military Service during the Vietnam War. **In** *Hills, S. M., ed.*, 1986, pp. 113–32. **[G: U.S.]**

Jonscher, Charles. Information Technology and the United States Economy: Modeling and Measurement. **In** *Faulhaber, G.; Noam, E. and Tasley, R., eds.*, 1986, pp. 119–31. **[G: U.S.]**

Jorgenson, Dale W. Microeconomics and Productivity. **In** *Landau, R. and Rosenberg, N., eds.*, 1986, pp. 57–76. **[G: U.S.]**

Kalecki, Michal. Observations on Labour Productivity. **In** *Kalecki, M.*, 1986, *1960*, pp. 54–59.

Kamaev, V. Intensification and the Quality of Economic Growth. *Prob. Econ.*, March 1986, *28*(11), pp. 19–38. **[G: U.S.S.R.]**

Kaufman, Roger T. and Jacoby, Richard A. The Stock Market and the Productivity Slowdown: International Evidence. *Rev. Econ. Statist.*, February 1986, *68*(1), pp. 18–23. **[G: Selected OECD]**

Kennan, John. Hysteresis and the European Unemployment Problem: Comment. **In** *Fischer, S., ed.*, 1986, pp. 78–85. **[G: OECD]**

Kim, Moshe and Sachish, Arie. The Structure of Production, Technical Change and Productivity in a Port. *J. Ind. Econ.*, December 1986, *35*(2), pp. 209–23.

Klein, Burton H. Dynamic Competition and Productivity Advances. **In** *Landau, R. and Rosenberg, N., eds.*, 1986, pp. 77–88. **[G: U.S.]**

Kremp, E. and Le Dem, J. Competitiveness and Employment in the Large Industrialized Countries. **In** *Artus, P. and Guvenen, O., eds.*, 1986, pp. 159–80. **[G: U.S.; France; W. Germany; Japan]**

Kwon, Jene K. Capital Utilization, Economies of Scale and Technical Change in the Growth of Total Factor Productivity: An Explanation of South Korean Manufacturing Growth. *J. Devel. Econ.*, November 1986, *24*(1), pp. 75–89. **[G: S. Korea]**

Laumas, Prem S. and Williams, Martin. The Demand for Heterogeneous Capital and Labour Inputs in a Developing Economy. *Pakistan Devel. Rev.*, Summer 1986, *25*(2), pp. 127–40. **[G: India]**

Lazear, Edward P. The Cyclical Behavior of Industrial Labor Markets: A Comparison of the Prewar and Postwar Eras: Comment. **In** *Gordon, R. J., ed.*, 1986, pp. 626–32. **[G: U.S.]**

Lazear, Edward P. and Moore, Robert L. Incentives, Productivity, and Labor Contracts. **In** *Akerlof, G. A. and Yellen, J. L., eds.*, 1986, *1984*, pp. 135–56. **[G: U.S.]**

Le Pen, Claude. La productivité des services publics non marchands: quelques réflexions méthodologiques. (With English summary.) *Revue Écon. Polit.*, Sept.-Oct. 1986, *96*(5), pp. 476–89. **[G: France]**

Lefebvre, Louis A., et al. L'impact de la technologie informatique sur la main-d'oeuvre dans les organisations. (The Impact of Information Technology on Human Resources in Organizations. With English summary.) *L'Actual. Econ.*, December 1986, *62*(4), pp. 557–78. **[G: Canada]**

Leibenstein, Harvey. Intra-firm Effort Decisions and Sanctions: Hierarchy versus Peers. **In** *Gilad, B. and Kaish, S., eds., Vol. A*, 1986, pp. 213–31.

Leibenstein, Harvey. The Theory of Underemployment in Densely Populated Backward Areas. **In** *Akerlof, G. A. and Yellen, J. L., eds.*, 1986, *1963*, pp. 22–40.

Loginov, V. and Novitskii, N. Factors and Trends in the Intensification of Socialist Reproduction. *Prob. Econ.*, June 1986, 29(2), pp. 3–23. **[G: U.S.S.R.]**

Lovell, Malcolm R., Jr. Obstacles to Competitiveness: A Challenge to Labor and Management. **In** *Burton, D. F., et al., eds.*, 1986, pp. 105–17. **[G: U.S.]**

Lukinov, I. The Effect of Scientific-Technological and Social Progress on Development in Agrarian Labour. **In** *Maunder, A. and Renborg, U., eds.*, 1986, pp. 178–84. **[G: U.S.S.R.]**

Mark, Jerome A. Problems Encountered in Measuring Single- and Multifactor Productivity. *Mon. Lab. Rev.*, December 1986, *109*(12), pp. 3–11. **[G: U.S.]**

Marshall, Ray. Reversing the Downtrend in Real Wages. *Challenge*, May/June 1986, *29*(2), pp. 48–55. **[G: U.S.]**

McCombie, John S. L. On Some Interpretations of the Relationship between Productivity and Output Growth. *Appl. Econ.*, November 1986, *18*(11), pp. 1215–25. **[G: OECD]**

McInnis, R. M. Output and Productivity in Canadian Agriculture, 1870–71 to 1926–27. **In** *Engerman, S. L. and Gallman, R. E., eds.*, 1986, pp. 737–70. **[G: Canada]**

McLennan, Kenneth. The Case for a Non-targeted Approach to Industrial Strategy. **In** *Redburn, F. S.; Buss, T. F. and Ledebur, L. C., eds.*, 1986, pp. 45–63. **[G: U.S.; OECD]**

Mefford, Robert N. The Effect of Unions on Productivity in a Multinational Manufacturing Firm. *Ind. Lab. Relat. Rev.*, October 1986, *40*(1), pp. 105–14. **[G: U.S.]**

Meunier, François and Volle, M. The Effects of the New Communications Media on Employment. *Info. Econ. Policy*, September 1986, *2*(3), pp. 195–209. **[G: France]**

Michl, Thomas R. The Productivity Slowdown and the Elasticity of Demand for Labor. *Rev. Econ. Statist.*, August 1986, *68*(3), pp. 532–36. **[G: U.S.]**

Miller, Edward M. Determinants of the Size of the Small Business Sector: They Are Labor Productivity, Wage Rates and Capital Intensity. *Amer. J. Econ. Soc.*, October 1986, *45*(4), pp. 390–402. **[G: U.S.]**

Moores, Brian. Are They Being Served? Quality Consciousness in Service Industries: Introduction. **In** *Moores, B., ed.*, 1986, pp. 1–10.

Morrison, Catherine J. Productivity Measurement with Non-static Expectations and Varying Capacity Utilization: An Integrated Approach. *J. Econometrics*, Oct./Nov. 1986, *33*(1/2), pp. 51–74. **[G: U.S.]**

Moseley, Fred. The Intensity of Labor and the Productivity Slowdown [Productivity Growth and Capitalist Stagnation]. *Sci. Soc.*, Summer 1986, *50*(2), pp. 210–18.

Mountain, Dean C. Impact of Higher Energy Prices on Wage Rates, Return to Capital, Energy Intensity and Productivity: A Regional Profit Specification. *Energy Econ.*, July 1986, *8*(3), pp. 171–76. **[G: Canada]**

Muellbauer, John. The Assessment: Productivity and Competitiveness in British Manufacturing. *Oxford Rev. Econ. Policy*, Autumn 1986, *2*(3), pp. i–xxv. **[G: U.K.]**

Naisbitt, Barry. Employment Functions and the Slowdown in UK Productivity Growth. *Bull. Econ. Res.*, January 1986, *38*(1), pp. 67–75. **[G: U.K.]**

Naples, Michele I. The Unraveling of the Union–Capital Truce and the U.S. Industrial Productivity Crisis. *Rev. Radical Polit. Econ.*, Spring/Summer 1986, *18*(1/2), pp. 110–31. **[G: U.S.]**

Neef, Arthur. International Trends in Productivity and Unit Labor Costs in Manufacturing. *Mon. Lab. Rev.*, December 1986, *109*(12), pp. 12–17. **[G: OECD]**

Nijkamp, Peter. The Triangle of Industrial Dynamics, Labour Markets and Spatial Systems. **In** *Nijkamp, P., ed. (II)*, 1986, pp. 1–17.

Nishimizu, Mieko and Page, John M., Jr. Productivity Change and Dynamic Comparative Advantage. *Rev. Econ. Statist.*, May 1986, *68*(2), pp. 241–47. **[G: Thailand]**

Ochoa, Eduardo M. An Input–Output Study of Labor Productivity in the U.S. Economy, 1947–72. *J. Post Keynesian Econ.*, Fall 1986, *9*(1), pp. 111–37. **[G: U.S.]**

Persigehl, Elmer S. and Olsen, John G. Productivity in the Metal Doors, Sash, and Trim Industry. *Mon. Lab. Rev.*, March 1986, *109*(3), pp. 27–31. **[G: U.S.]**

Piacentini, Paolo. Produttivitá e domanda di lavoro nell'industria manifatturiera italiana: un commento all'articolo di Presperetti e Borellini. (Productivity and Labour Demand in Italian Manufacturing. With English summary.) *Polit. Econ.*, December 1986, *2*(3), pp. 435–40. **[G: Italy]**

Pietsch, Anna-Jutta. Shortage of Labour and Motivation Problems of Soviet Workers. **In** *Lane, D., ed.*, 1986, pp. 176–90. **[G: U.S.S.R.]**

Pitt, Mark M. and Rosenzweig, Mark R. Agricultural Prices, Food Consumption, and the Health and Productivity of Indonesian Farmers. **In** *Singh, I.; Squire, L. and Strauss, J., eds.*, 1986, pp. 153–82. **[G: Indonesia]**

Preel, Bernard. La gestion de l'emploi des services: pourquoi faut-il passer à l'analyse d'entreprise? (With English summary.) *Revue Écon. Polit.*, Sept.-Oct. 1986, *96*(5), pp. 490–502. **[G: OECD]**

Prosperetti, Luigi and Borellini, Rosella. Produttività, orari di fatto e domanda di lavoro nell'industria manifatturiera italiana: un'analisi Cross-Section. (Productivity, Working Hours and Labour Demand in Manufacturing in Italy: A Cross Section Analysis. With English summary.) *Polit. Econ.*, August 1986, *2*(2), pp. 225–42. **[G: Italy]**

Quinn, James Brian. Technology Adoption: The Services Industries. **In** *Landau, R. and Rosenberg, N., eds.*, 1986, pp. 357–71. **[G: U.S.; U.K.; Japan; W. Germany; France]**

Rahman, K. M. Technology, Productivity and Employment in Rural Industries. **In** *Islam, R. and Muqtada, M., eds.*, 1986, pp. 197–207. **[G: Bangladesh]**

Rahmeyer, Fritz. Der Zusammenhang zwischen Lohn-, Produktivitäts- und Preisstruktur im verarbeitenden Gewerbe. (The Interrelation between the Relative Growth of Wages, Productivity and Prices in the Manufacturing Sector. With English summary.) *Z. Wirtschaft. Sozialwissen.*, 1986, *106*(5), pp. 467–93. **[G: W. Germany]**

Ray, George F. Productivity in Services. *Nat. Inst. Econ. Rev.*, February 1986, (115), pp. 44–47. **[G: U.K.]**

Rayner, A. J.; Whittaker, J. M. and Ingersent, K. A. Productivity Growth in Agriculture (Revisited): A Measurement Framework and Some Empirical Results. *J. Agr. Econ.*, May 1986, *37*(2), pp. 127–50. **[G: U.K.]**

Reynolds, Morgan O. Trade Unions in the Production Process Reconsidered. *J. Polit. Econ.*, April 1986, *94*(2), pp. 443–47.

Rittenberg, Libby and Manuel, Ernest H., Jr. A Case Study of Decline in Labor Productivity: Underground Coal Mining Industry, 1960–1976. *Quart. J. Bus. Econ.*, Winter 1986, *25*(1), pp. 38–55. **[G: U.S.]**

Roach, Stephen S. Macrorealities of the Information Economy. **In** *Landau, R. and Rosenberg, N., eds.*, 1986, pp. 93–103. **[G: U.S.]**

Rossi, Vanessa, et al. Exchange Rates, Productivity and International Competitiveness. *Oxford Rev. Econ. Policy*, Autumn 1986, *2*(3), pp. 56–73. **[G: U.K.; U.S.]**

Rothschild, Emma. A Divergence Hypothesis. *J. Devel. Econ.*, October 1986, *23*(2), pp. 205–26. **[G: U.S.]**

Rutland, Peter. Productivity Campaigns in Soviet Industry. **In** *Lane, D., ed.*, 1986, pp. 191–208. **[G: U.S.S.R.]**

Shoemaker, Robbin and Somwaru, Agapi. Total Factor Productivity and Sources of Growth in the Dairy Sector. *Agr. Econ. Res.*, Fall 1986, *38*(4), pp. 1–13. **[G: U.S.]**

Skarstein, Rune. Growth and Crisis in the Manufacturing Sector. **In** *Boesen, J., et al., eds.*, 1986, pp. 79–104. **[G: Tanzania]**

Slade, Margaret E. Total-Factor-Productivity

Measurement When Equilibrium Is Temporary: A Monte Carlo Assessment. *J. Econometrics*, Oct./Nov. 1986, *33*(1/2), pp. 75–95.

Sokoloff, Kenneth L. Productivity Growth in Manufacturing during Early Industrialization: Evidence from the American Northeast, 1820–1860. **In** *Engerman, S. L. and Gallman, R. E., eds.*, 1986, pp. 679–729. **[G: U.S.]**

Soskiev, A. Social and Economic Problems of Labor Power Reproduction in Agriculture. *Prob. Econ.*, May 1986, *29*(1), pp. 82–91. **[G: U.S.S.R.]**

Spechler, Martin C. Social Influences on Growth and Productivity in the West, 1965–1984. **In** *Gilad, B. and Kaish, S., eds., Vol. B*, 1986, pp. 163–200. **[G: OECD]**

Sveikauskas, Leo. The Contribution of R and D to Productivity Growth. *Mon. Lab. Rev.*, March 1986, *109*(3), pp. 16–20. **[G: U.S.]**

Swedborg, Erik. Growing Interdependencies and Uncertainties: Discussion. **In** *Maunder, A. and Renborg, U., eds.*, 1986, pp. 184–87. **[G: U.S.S.R.]**

Tabuchi, Takatoshi. Urban Agglomeration, Capital Augmenting Technology, and Labor Market Equilibrium. *J. Urban Econ.*, September 1986, *20*(2), pp. 211–28. **[G: Japan]**

Tatom, John A. Domestic vs. International Explanations of Recent U.S. Manufacturing Developments. *Fed. Res. Bank St. Louis Rev.*, April 1986, *68*(4), pp. 5–18. **[G: U.S.]**

Tatom, John A. Why Has Manufacturing Employment Declined? *Fed. Res. Bank St. Louis Rev.*, December 1986, *68*(10), pp. 15–25. **[G: U.S.]**

Thurik, A. R. and van der Hoeven, W. H. M. Labor Productivity in the Hotel and Catering Sector. *Atlantic Econ. J.*, December 1986, *14*(4), pp. 105. **[G: U.S.]**

Thurik, A. R. and Kleijweg, A. J. M. Procyclical Retail Labour Productivity. *Bull. Econ. Res.*, May 1986, *38*(2), pp. 169–75. **[G: Netherlands]**

Tokman, Víctor E. Creación de empleo productivo: una tarea impostergable. (With English summary.) *Desarrollo Econ.*, Oct.-Dec. 1986, *26*(103), pp. 339–67. **[G: Latin America]**

Tomer, John F. Productivity and Organizational Behavior: Where Human Capital Theory Fails. **In** *Gilad, B. and Kaish, S., eds., Vol. A*, 1986, pp. 233–55.

Tulkens, Henry. La performance productive d'un service public. Définitions, méthodes de mesure et application à la Régie des Postes en Belgique. (The Productive Performance of a Public Service. With English summary.) *L'Actual. Econ.*, June 1986, *62*(2), pp. 306–35. **[G: Belgium]**

Tyler, Peter and Rhodes, John. The Census of Production as an Indicator of Regional Differences in Productivity and Profitability in the United Kingdom. *Reg. Stud.*, August 1986, *20*(4), pp. 331–39. **[G: U.K.]**

Vasavada, Utpal and Chambers, Robert G. Investment in U.S. Agriculture. *Amer. J. Agr. Econ.*, November 1986, *68*(4), pp. 950–60. **[G: U.S.]**

Ville, Simon. Total Factor Productivity in the English Shipping Industry: The North-east Coal Trade, 1700–1850. *Econ. Hist. Rev., 2nd Ser.*, August 1986, *39*(3), pp. 355–7C. **[G: U.K.]**

Warke, Thomas W. International Variation in Labor Quality. *Rev. Econ. Statist.*, November 1986, *68*(4), pp. 704–06. **[G: Global]**

Wasow, Bernard. Insurance and the Balance of Payments. **In** *Wasow, B. and Hill, R. D., eds.*, 1986, pp. 87–103. **[G: S. Korea; Portugal; India; Brazil; Taiwan]**

Watanabe, Susumu. Labour-Saving versus Work-Amplifying Effects of Micro-electronics. *Int. Lab. Rev.*, May-June 1986, *125*(3), pp. 243–59. **[G: W. Europe; U.S.; Japan; Brazil]**

Watt, J. Michael, et al. The Effects of Ownership and Multihospital System Membership on Hospital Functional Strategies and Economic Performance. **In** *Gray, B. H., ed.*, 1986, pp. 260–89. **[G: U.S.]**

Weiss, Mary A. Analysis of Productivity at the Firm Level: An Application to Life Insurers. *J. Risk Ins.*, March 1986, *53*(1), pp. 49–84. **[G: U.S.]**

Williamson, Jeffrey G. Productivity Growth in Manufacturing during Early Industrialization: Evidence from the American Northeast, 1820–1860: Comment. **In** *Engerman, S. L. and Gallman, R. E., eds.*, 1986, pp. 729–33. **[G: U.S.]**

Wintrobe, Ronald and Breton, Albert. Organizational Structure and Productivity. *Amer. Econ. Rev.*, June 1986, *76*(3), pp. 530–38.

Wolff, Edward N. The Productivity Slowdown and the Fall in the U.S. Rate of Profit, 1947–76. *Rev. Radical Polit. Econ.*, Spring/Summer 1986, *18*(1/2), pp. 87–109. **[G: U.S.]**

Woo, Jennie Hay. Graduate Degrees and Job Success: Managers in One U.S. Corporation. *Econ. Educ. Rev.*, 1986, *5*(3), pp. 227–37. **[G: U.S.]**

Wren-Lewis, Simon. An Econometric Model of U.K. Manufacturing Employment Using Survey Data on Expected Output. *J. Appl. Econometrics*, October 1986, *1*(4), pp. 297–316. **[G: U.K.]**

Wright, Gavin. Output and Productivity in Canadian Agriculture, 1870–71 to 1926–27: Comment. **In** *Engerman, S. L. and Gallman, R. E., eds.*, 1986, pp. 771–76. **[G: Canada]**

Yao, Dennis A. Information Technology and the United States Economy: Modeling and Measurement: Discussion. **In** *Faulhaber, G.; Noam, E. and Tasley, R., eds.*, 1986, pp. 132–37. **[G: U.S.]**

Young, John A. Global Competition—The New Reality: Results of the President's Commission on Industrial Competitiveness. **In** *Landau, R. and Rosenberg, N., eds.*, 1986, pp. 501–09. **[G: U.S.]**

Zhuravlev, S. N. Structural Shifts in the Economy: Techniques for Evaluating Their Impact on Efficiency and Growth. *Matekon*, Winter 1986-87, *23*(2), pp. 3–31. **[G: U.S.S.R.]**

826 Labor Markets: Demographic Characteristics

8260 Labor Markets: Demographic Characteristics

Acar, Feride. Working Women in a Changing Society: The Case of Jordanian Academics. *METU*, 1986, *13*(3–4), pp. 307–24. **[G: Jordan]**

Acharya, Meena. Changing Division of Labor and Participation. **In** *Björkman, J. W., ed.*, 1986, pp. 128–40. **[G: India; S. Asia]**

Adams, John and Paul, Linda. The Informal Sector in India: Work, Gender, and Technology. **In** *Björkman, J. W., ed.*, 1986, pp. 33–52. **[G: India]**

Al-Tuhaih, Salem M. The Vicious Cycle of Manpower in Kuwait. **In** *Roukis, G. S. and Montana, P. J., eds.*, 1986, pp. 123–38.

Amanshauser, Wilfried; Grünwald, Doris and Pichelmann, Karl. The Youth Labour Market Problem in Austria Some: Basic Features. *Econ. Lavoro*, Oct.-Dec. 1986, *20*(4), pp. 129–35. **[G: Austria]**

Amin, A. T. M. Nurul. Urban Unemployment and Underemployment. **In** *Islam, R. and Muqtada, M., eds.*, 1986, pp. 21–39. **[G: Bangladesh]**

Amir, Shmuel. Educational Structure and Wage Differentials of the Labor Force in the 1970s. **In** *Ben-Porath, Y., ed.*, 1986, pp. 137–52. **[G: Israel]**

Anderson, Barbara A. and Silver, Brian D. Sex Differentials in Mortality in the Soviet Union: Regional Differences in Length of Working Life in Comparative Perspective. *Population Stud.*, July 1986, *40*(2), pp. 191–214. **[G: U.S.S.R.]**

Ballen, John and Freeman, Richard B. Transitions between Employment and Nonemployment. **In** *Freeman, R. B. and Holzer, H. J., eds.*, 1986, pp. 75–112. **[G: U.S.]**

Beach, C. M. and Kaliski, S. F. Structural Unemployment, Demographic Change or Industrial Structure? *Can. Public Policy*, June 1986, *12*(2), pp. 356–67. **[G: Canada]**

Ben-Porath, Yoram. Diversity in Population and in the Labor Force. **In** *Ben-Porath, Y., ed.*, 1986, pp. 153–70. **[G: Israel]**

Benhayoun, Gilbert. L'emploi et le chômage des jeunes analyse urbaine. (With English summary.) *Revue Écon. Polit.*, May-June 1986, *96*(3), pp. 281–99. **[G: France]**

Björkman, James Warner. Themes, Schemes, and Dreams: An Introduction to the Changing Division of Labor in South Asia. **In** *Björkman, J. W., ed.*, 1986, pp. 1–16. **[G: S. Asia]**

Black, Matthew and Fraker, Thomas. First-Term Attrition of High School Graduates in the Military. **In** *Gilroy, C. L., ed.*, 1986, pp. 261–91. **[G: U.S.]**

Blinder, Alan S. His and Hers: Gender Differences in Work and Income, 1959–1979: Comment. *J. Lab. Econ.*, Part 2, July 1986, *4*(3), pp. S273–77.

Bloch, Laurence, et al. Analyse macro-économique des taux d'activité et flexion conjonctrelle. (Macroeconomic Analysis of Activity Rates and Short Term Flexion Impact. With English summary.) *Écon. Appl.*, 1986, *39*(4), pp. 665–703.

Bloom, David E. and Freeman, Richard B. The Effects of Rapid Population Growth on Labor Supply and Employment in Developing Countries. *Population Devel. Rev.*, September 1986, *12*(3), pp. 381–414. **[G: LDCs]**

Borjas, George J. The Demographic Determinants of the Demand for Black Labor. **In** *Freeman, R. B. and Holzer, H. J., eds.*, 1986, pp. 191–230. **[G: U.S.]**

Borjas, George J. and Welch, Finis. The Postservice Earnings of Military Retirees. **In** *Gilroy, C. L., ed.*, 1986, pp. 295–313. **[G: U.S.]**

Bound, John. NBER-Mathematica Survey of Inner-city Black Youth: An Analysis of the Undercount of Older Youths. **In** *Freeman, R. B. and Holzer, H. J., eds.*, 1986, pp. 443–59. **[G: U.S.]**

Bourguignon, François. Female Participation and Taxation in France. **In** *Blundell, R. and Walker, I., eds.*, 1986, pp. 243–66. **[G: France]**

Braslavsky, Cecilia. Youth in Argentina: Between the Legacy of the Past and the Construction of the Future. *CEPAL Rev.*, August 1986, (29), pp. 41–54. **[G: Argentina]**

Brown, C. V., et al. Payment Systems, Demand Constraints and Their Implications for Research into Labour Supply. **In** *Blundell, R. and Walker, I., eds.*, 1986, pp. 190–216. **[G: U.K.]**

Brown, Charles. Do Better Jobs Make Better Workers? Absenteeism from Work among Inner-city Black Youths: Comment. **In** *Freeman, R. B. and Holzer, H. J., eds.*, 1986, pp. 295–98. **[G: U.S.]**

Bysiewicz, Shirley Raissi and Shelley, Louise I. Women in the Soviet Economy: Proclamations and Practice. **In** *Ioffe, O. S. and Janis, M. W., eds.*, 1986, pp. 57–77. **[G: U.S.S.R.]**

Cain, Glen G. Married Women in the Labor Force. **In** *Reynolds, L. G.; Masters, S. H. and Moser, C. H., eds.*, 1986, pp. 41–50. **[G: U.S.]**

Cain, Glen G. The Economic Analysis of Labor Market Discrimination: A Survey. **In** *Ashenfelter, O. and Layard, R., eds., Vol. 1*, 1986, pp. 693–785. **[G: U.S.]**

Carcaterra, Rose. Facts and Projections at a Glance. **In** *Burton, D. F., et al., eds.*, 1986, pp. 265–84. **[G: U.S.]**

Carter, Susan B. The Female Labor Force and American Economic Growth, 1890–1980: Comment. **In** *Engerman, S. L. and Gallman, R. E., eds.*, 1986, pp. 594–99. **[G: U.S.]**

Casey, Bernard. The Dual Apprenticeship System and the Recruitment and Retention of Young Persons in West Germany. *Brit. J. Ind. Relat.*, March 1986, *24*(1), pp. 63–81. **[G: W. Germany]**

Castillo, L.; Gascon, F. and Jayasuriya, S. K.

Off-Farm Employment of Farm Households in Laguna, Philippines. **In** *Shand, R. T., ed., Vol. 2*, 1986, pp. 133–46. **[G: Philippines]**

Chamberlain, Gary. Transitions between Employment and Nonemployment: Comment. **In** *Freeman, R. B. and Holzer, H. J., eds.*, 1986, pp. 113–14. **[G: U.S.]**

Chan, Lean Heng. Young Workers Education Project: Development of a Participatory Urban Services Centre in Penang, Malaysia. **In** *Yeung, Y. M. and McGee, T. G., eds.*, 1986, pp. 165–90. **[G: Malaysia]**

Chapman, Bruce J. and Prior, Heather. Sex Differences in Labour Turnover in the Australian Public Service. *Econ. Rec.*, December 1986, *62*(179), pp. 497–505. **[G: Australia]**

Costrell, Robert M.; Duguay, Gerald E. and Treyz, George I. Labour Substitution and Complementarity among Age–Sex Groups. *Appl. Econ.*, July 1986, *18*(7), pp. 777–91. **[G: U.S.]**

Cotler, Julio. The Political Radicalization of Working-Class Youth in Peru. *CEPAL Rev.*, August 1986, (29), pp. 107–18. **[G: Peru]**

Culp, Jerome McCristal, Jr. and Dunson, Bruce H. Brothers of a Different Color: A Preliminary Look at Employer Treatment of White and Black Youth. **In** *Freeman, R. B. and Holzer, H. J., eds.*, 1986, pp. 233–59. **[G: U.S.]**

D'Amico, Ronald J. and Golon, Jeff. The Displaced Worker: Consequences of Career Interruption among Young Men. **In** *Hills, S. M., ed.*, 1986, pp. 7–36. **[G: U.S.]**

Dagum, Camilo; Grenier, Gilles and Bédard, Mario. Répartition du revenu selon le sexe dans quatre agglomérations urbaines du Canada: Exemple d'application de données des déclarations de revenus des particuliers. (An Analysis of Income Distribution by Sex in Four Canadian Metropolitan Areas, Using Personal Income Tax Records. With English summary.) *L'Actual. Econ.*, March 1986, *62*(1), pp. 23–42. **[G: Canada]**

Dale, Charles. The Changing Structure of the U.S. Economy: Its Effects on Army Enlistments. **In** *Gilroy, C. L., ed.*, 1986, pp. 149–65. **[G: U.S.]**

Datcher-Loury, Linda and Loury, Glenn C. The Effects of Attitudes and Aspirations on the Labor Supply of Young Men. **In** *Freeman, R. B. and Holzer, H. J., eds.*, 1986, pp. 377–99. **[G: U.S.]**

Daula, Thomas V. and Baldwin, Robert H. Reenlistment Decision Models: Implications for Policy Making. **In** *Gilroy, C. L., ed.*, 1986, pp. 203–21. **[G: U.S.]**

Devaney, Barbara L. An Analysis of Variations in U.S. Fertility and Female Labor Force Participation Trends: A Reply. *Demography*, February 1986, *23*(1), pp. 141–42. **[G: U.S.]**

Devens, Richard M., Jr. Displaced Workers: One Year Later: Errata. *Mon. Lab. Rev.*, September 1986, *109*(9), pp. 41. **[G: U.S.]**

Devens, Richard M., Jr. Displaced Workers: One Year Later. *Mon. Lab. Rev.*, July 1986, *109*(7), pp. 40–43. **[G: U.S.]**

Doering, Zahava D. Attrition and Retention in the Army Reserve and National Guard: An Empirical Analysis: Comment. **In** *Gilroy, C. L., ed.*, 1986, pp. 198–201. **[G: U.S.]**

Dooley, Martin D. The Overeducated Canadian? Changes in the Relationship among Earnings, Education, and Age for Canadian Men: 1971–81. *Can. J. Econ.*, February 1986, *19*(1), pp. 142–59. **[G: Canada]**

Ehrenberg, Ronald G. Black Youth Nonemployment: Duration and Job Search: Comment. **In** *Freeman, R. B. and Holzer, H. J., eds.*, 1986, pp. 70–73. **[G: U.S.]**

Ellwood, David T. The Spatial Mismatch Hypothesis: Are There Teenage Jobs Missing in the Ghetto? **In** *Freeman, R. B. and Holzer, H. J., eds.*, 1986, pp. 147–85. **[G: U.S.]**

Ferguson, Brian S. Labour Force Substitution and the Effects of an Aging Population. *Appl. Econ.*, August 1986, *18*(8), pp. 901–13. **[G: Canada]**

Ferguson, Ronald and Filer, Randall K. Do Better Jobs Make Better Workers? Absenteeism from Work among Inner-city Black Youths. **In** *Freeman, R. B. and Holzer, H. J., eds.*, 1986, pp. 261–95. **[G: U.S.]**

Flinn, Christopher J. Wages and Job Mobility of Young Workers. *J. Polit. Econ.*, Part 2, June 1986, *94*(3), pp. S88–S110. **[G: U.S.]**

Foot, David K. and Li, Jeanne C. Youth Employment in Canada: A Misplaced Priority? *Can. Public Policy*, September 1986, *12*(3), pp. 499–506. **[G: Canada]**

Franz, Wolfgang and König, Heinz. The Nature and Causes of Unemployment in the Federal Republic of Germany since the 1970s: An Empirical Investigation. *Economica*, Supplement 1986, *53*(210(S)), pp. S219–44. **[G: W. Germany]**

Franz, Wolfgang and König, Heinz. The Nature and Causes of Unemployment in the Federal Republic of Germany since the 1970s: An Empirical Investigation. **In** *Bean, C. R.; Layard, P. R. G. and Nickell, S. J., eds.*, 1986, pp. 219–44. **[G: W. Germany]**

Freeman, Richard B. Who Escapes? The Relation of Churchgoing and Other Background Factors to the Socioeconomic Performance of Black Male Youths from Inner-city Tracts. **In** *Freeman, R. B. and Holzer, H. J., eds.*, 1986, pp. 353–76. **[G: U.S.]**

Freeman, Richard B. and Holzer, Harry J. The Black Youth Employment Crisis: Summary of Findings. **In** *Freeman, R. B. and Holzer, H. J., eds.*, 1986, pp. 3–20. **[G: U.S.]**

Freeman, Richard B. and Holzer, Harry J. Young Blacks and Jobs—What We Now Know. **In** *Reynolds, L. G.; Masters, S. H. and Moser, C. H., eds.*, 1986, *1985*, pp. 128–37. **[G: U.S.]**

Fuchs, Victor R. His and Hers: Gender Differences in Work and Income, 1959–1979. *J. Lab. Econ.*, Part 2, July 1986, *4*(3), pp. S245–72. **[G: U.S.]**

Gannicott, Kenneth. Women, Wages, and Discrimination: Some Evidence from Taiwan.

Econ. Develop. Cult. Change, July 1986, *34*(4), pp. 721–30. [G: Taiwan]

Garonna, Paolo. Youth Unemployment, Labour Market Deregulation and Union Stategies in Italy. *Brit. J. Ind. Relat.*, March 1986, *24*(1), pp. 43–61. [G: Italy]

Garonna, Paolo and Ryan, Paul. Youth Labour, Industrial Relations and Deregulation in Advanced Economies. *Econ. Lavoro*, Oct.-Dec. 1986, *20*(4), pp. 3–19. [G: U.S.; U.K.; Italy]

Gateau, Gilles and Tremblay, Diane. TUC et travaux communautaires: les enjeux de l'insertion/exclusion des jeunes. (Community Jobs and TUC: Integration or Exclusion of Youth? With English summary.) *Écon. Soc.*, April 1986, *20*(4), pp. 261–304.

Germe, J. F. Employment Policies and the Entry of Young People into the Labour Market in France. *Brit. J. Ind. Relat.*, March 1986, *24*(1), pp. 29–42. [G: France]

Glazer, Nathan. Education and Training Programs and Poverty. **In** *Danziger, S. H. and Weinberg, D. H., eds.*, 1986, pp. 152–73. [G: U.S.]

Goldin, Claudia. The Female Labor Force and American Economic Growth, 1890–1980. **In** *Engerman, S. L. and Gallman, R. E., eds.*, 1986, pp. 557–94. [G: U.S.]

Grissmer, David W. and Kirby, Sheila Nataraj. Attrition and Retention in the Army Reserve and National Guard: An Empirical Analysis. **In** *Gilroy, C. L., ed.*, 1986, pp. 169–97. [G: U.S.]

Gronau, Reuben. Home Production—A Survey. **In** *Ashenfelter, O. and Layard, R., eds., Vol. 1*, 1986, pp. 273–304. [G: U.S.]

Grossbard-Shechtman, Amyra. Marriage and Productivity: An Interdisciplinary Analysis. **In** *Gilad, B. and Kaish, S., eds., Vol. A*, 1986, pp. 289–302.

Guyer, Jane I. Women's Role in Development. **In** *Berg, R. J. and Whitaker, J. S., eds.*, 1986, pp. 393–421. [G: Africa]

Haberman, Steven. Improvements in State Pension Rights for Women. **In** *von der Schulenburg, J.-M. G., ed.*, 1986, pp. 130–65. [G: U.K.]

Hale, Robert. The Changing Structure of the U.S. Economy: Its Effects on Army Enlistments: Comment. **In** *Gilroy, C. L., ed.*, 1986, pp. 166–68. [G: U.S.]

Hamada, Koichi and Kurosaka, Yoshio. Trends in Unemployment, Wages and Productivity: The Case of Japan. **In** *Bean, C. R.; Layard, P. R. G. and Nickell, S. J., eds.*, 1986, pp. 275–96. [G: Japan]

Hamermesh, Daniel S. The Demographic Determinants of the Demand for Black Labor: Comment. **In** *Freeman, R. B. and Holzer, H. J., eds.*, 1986, pp. 230–32. [G: U.S.]

Hart, Peter E. and Trinder, C. Employment Protection, National Insurance, Income Tax and Youth Unemployment. **In** *Hart, P. E., ed.*, 1986, pp. 29–44. [G: U.K.]

Hart, Peter E., et al. Measures to Reduce Youth Unemployment in Britain, France and West Germany. *Nat. Inst. Econ. Rev.*, August 1986, (117), pp. 43–51. [G: U.K.; France; W. Germany]

Hartog, Joop and Theeuwes, Jules. Participation and Hours of Work: Two Stages in the Life-Cycle of Married Women. *Europ. Econ. Rev.*, August 1986, *30*(4), pp. 833–57. [G: Netherlands]

Hayghe, Howard V. Rise in Mothers' Labor Force Activity Includes Those with Infants. *Mon. Lab. Rev.*, February 1986, *109*(2), pp. 43–45. [G: U.S.]

Holzer, Harry J. Black Youth Nonemployment: Duration and Job Search. **In** *Freeman, R. B. and Holzer, H. J., eds.*, 1986, pp. 23–70. [G: U.S.]

Hosek, James R. and Peterson, Christine E. Enlistment Decisions of Young Men. **In** *Gilroy, C. L., ed.*, 1986, pp. 1–56. [G: U.S.]

Iams, Howard M. Employment of Retired-Worker Women. *Soc. Sec. Bull.*, March 1986, *49*(3), pp. 5–13. [G: U.S.]

Jackson, John L. Long-run Effects of Military Service during the Vietnam War. **In** *Hills, S. M., ed.*, 1986, pp. 113–32. [G: U.S.]

Jackson, Peter and Montgomery, Edward. Layoffs, Discharges and Youth Unemployment. **In** *Freeman, R. B. and Holzer, H. J., eds.*, 1986, pp. 115–41. [G: U.S.]

James-Bryan, Meryl. Youth in the English-speaking Caribbean: The High Cost of Dependent Development. *CEPAL Rev.*, August 1986, (29), pp. 133–52. [G: Caribbean]

Jencks, Christopher. Education and Training Programs and Poverty: Comment. **In** *Danziger, S. H. and Weinberg, D. H., eds.*, 1986, pp. 173–79. [G: U.S.]

Joshi, Heather. Gender Inequality in the Labour Market and the Domestic Division of Labour. **In** *Nolan, P. and Paine, S., eds.*, 1986, pp. 258–69. [G: U.K.]

Joshi, Heather. Participation in Paid Work: Evidence from the Women and Employment Survey. **In** *Blundell, R. and Walker, I., eds.*, 1986, pp. 217–42. [G: U.K.]

Kamal, Salih, et al. Young Workers and Urban Services in Penang. **In** *Yeung, Y. M. and McGee, T. G., eds.*, 1986, pp. 119–63. [G: Malaysia]

Kannappan, Subbiah. The Economic Significance of the Social Structure for Urban Labor Markets with Special Reference to India. **In** *Dennis, B. D., ed.*, 1986, pp. 324–35. [G: India]

Kasarda, John D. Transforming Cities and Employment Policy for Displaced Workers. **In** *Bergman, E. M., ed.*, 1986, *1983*, pp. 286–307. [G: U.S.]

Katzman, Rubén. Youth and Unemployment in Montevideo. *CEPAL Rev.*, August 1986, (29), pp. 119–31. [G: Uruguay]

Killingsworth, Mark R. and Heckman, James J. Female Labor Supply: A Survey. **In** *Ashenfelter, O. and Layard, R., eds., Vol. 1*, 1986, pp. 103–204. [G: U.S.; U.K.; Canada; Germany]

Kohlhase, Janet E. Labor Supply and Housing

Demand for One- and Two-Earner Households. *Rev. Econ. Statist.*, February 1986, *68*(1), pp. 48–57. **[G: U.S.]**

Lambooy, Jan G. and van der Vegt, Chris. Segmentation Theories and Manpower Policy in Dutch Cities. **In** *Nijkamp, P., ed. (II)*, 1986, pp. 262–79. **[G: Netherlands]**

Lapp, John S. The Secular Behavior of Aggregate Retirement Flows. *Atlantic Econ. J.*, March 1986, *14*(1), pp. 30–38. **[G: U.S.]**

Latack, Janina C. and D'Amico, Ronald J. Career Mobility among Young Men: A Search for Patterns. **In** *Hills, S. M., ed.*, 1986, pp. 91–112. **[G: U.S.]**

Lele, Uma. Women and Structural Transformation. *Econ. Develop. Cult. Change*, January 1986, *34*(2), pp. 195–221. **[G: LDCs]**

Leonard, Jonathan S. The Spatial Mismatch Hypothesis: Are There Teenage Jobs Missing in the Ghetto? Comment. **In** *Freeman, R. B. and Holzer, H. J., eds.*, 1986, pp. 185–90. **[G: U.S.]**

Lerman, Robert I. Do Welfare Programs Affect the Schooling and Work Patterns of Young Black Men? **In** *Freeman, R. B. and Holzer, H. J., eds.*, 1986, pp. 403–38. **[G: U.S.]**

Linneman, Peter. Information Technology, Demographics, and the Retail Response: Discussion. **In** *Faulhaber, G.; Noam, E. and Tasley, R., eds.*, 1986, pp. 175–77. **[G: U.S.; OECD]**

Lynch, Lisa M. Household Costs of Unemployment. **In** *Hills, S. M., ed.*, 1986, pp. 79–89. **[G: U.S.]**

Marnie, Sheila. Transition from School to Work: Satisfying Pupils' Aspirations and the Needs of the Economy. **In** *Lane, D., ed.*, 1986, pp. 209–22. **[G: U.S.S.R.]**

Marsden, David and Richardson, Ray. Youth Pay and Employers' Recruitment Practices for Young Workers in Western Europe. *Brit. J. Ind. Relat.*, March 1986, *24*(1), pp. 25–27. **[G: W. Europe]**

Marsden, David and Ryan, Paul. Where Do Young Workers Work? Youth Employment by Industry in Various European Economies. *Brit. J. Ind. Relat.*, March 1986, *24*(1), pp. 83–102. **[G: W. Europe]**

Martínez, Javier and Valenzuela, Eduardo. Chilean Youth and Social Exclusion. *CEPAL Rev.*, August 1986, (29), pp. 93–105. **[G: Chile]**

Maxwell, Nan L. and D'Amico, Ronald J. Employment and Wage Effects of Involuntary Job Separation: Male–Female Differences. *Amer. Econ. Rev.*, May 1986, *76*(2), pp. 373–77. **[G: U.S.]**

McGregor, Alan and Mather, Frank. Developments in Glasgow's Labour Market. **In** *Lever, W. and Moore, C., eds.*, 1986, pp. 22–43. **[G: U.K.]**

McMahon, Patrick J. An International Comparison of Labor Force Participation, 1977–84. *Mon. Lab. Rev.*, May 1986, *109*(5), pp. 3–12. **[G: W. Germany; N. America; Japan; Australia; Sweden]**

Medoff, James L. Layoffs, Discharges and Youth Unemployment: Comment. **In** *Freeman, R. B. and Holzer, H. J., eds.*, 1986, pp. 142–43. **[G: U.S.]**

Meitzen, Mark E. Differences in Male and Female Job-quitting Behavior. *J. Lab. Econ.*, April 1986, *4*(2), pp. 151–67. **[G: U.S.]**

Mellor, Earl F. and Haugen, Steven E. Hourly Paid Workers: Who They Are and What They Earn. *Mon. Lab. Rev.*, February 1986, *109*(2), pp. 20–26. **[G: U.S.]**

Montgomery, Mark R. and Trussell, James. Models of Marital Status and Childbearing. **In** *Ashenfelter, O. and Layard, R., eds., Vol. 1*, 1986, pp. 205–71. **[G: U.S.]**

Moss, Mitchell. Information Technology, Demographics, and the Retail Response: Discussion. **In** *Faulhaber, G.; Noam, E. and Tasley, R., eds.*, 1986, pp. 178–82. **[G: U.S.; OECD]**

Myers, Samuel L., Jr. Do Welfare Programs Affect the Schooling and Work Patterns of Young Black Men? Comment. **In** *Freeman, R. B. and Holzer, H. J., eds.*, 1986, pp. 438–41. **[G: U.S.]**

Nardone, Thomas J. Part-time Workers: Who Are They? *Mon. Lab. Rev.*, February 1986, *109*(2), pp. 13–19. **[G: U.S.]**

Nelson, K. Labor Demand, Labor Supply and the Suburbanization of Low-wage Office Work. **In** *Scott, A. J. and Storper, M., eds.*, 1986, pp. 149–71. **[G: U.S.]**

Nishikawa, Shunsaku and Shimada, Haruo. Recent Changes in Unemployment in the Japanese Labor Market. **In** *Hax, H.; Kraus, W. and Tsuchiya, K., eds.*, 1986, pp. 125–44. **[G: Japan; OECD]**

Norwood, Janet L. Jobs in the 1980's and Beyond. **In** *Burton, D. F., et al., eds.*, 1986, pp. 55–83. **[G: U.S.]**

O'Brien, A. Maureen and Hawley, Clifford B. The Labor Force Participation Behavior of Married Women under Conditions of Constraints on Borrowing. *J. Human Res.*, Spring 1986, *21*(2), pp. 267–78. **[G: U.S.]**

Oi, Walter Y. The Postservice Earnings of Military Retirees: Comment. **In** *Gilroy, C. L., ed.*, 1986, pp. 314–19. **[G: U.S.]**

Olsen, Randall J.; Smith, D. Alton and Farkas, George. Structural and Reduced-Form Models of Choice among Alternatives in Continuous Time: Youth Employment under a Guaranteed Jobs Program. *Econometrica*, March 1986, *54*(2), pp. 375–94. **[G: U.S.]**

van Opstal, Rocus and Theeuwes, Jules. Duration of Unemployment in the Dutch Youth Labour Market. *De Economist*, 1986, *134*(3), pp. 351–67. **[G: Netherlands]**

Osterman, Paul. Brothers of a Different Color: A Preliminary Look at Employer Treatment of White and Black Youth: Comment. **In** *Freeman, R. B. and Holzer, H. J., eds.*, 1986, pp. 259–60. **[G: U.S.]**

Parra Sandoval, Rodrigo. The Missing Future: Colombian Youth. *CEPAL Rev.*, August 1986, (29), pp. 79–92. **[G: Colombia]**

Pearson, Ruth. Multinational Companies and the Sexual Division of Labour: A Historical Perspective. **In** *Teichova, A.; Lévy-Leboyer, M.*

and Nussbaum, H., eds., 1986, pp. 339–50.

Pencavel, John H. Labor Supply of Men: A Survey. **In** *Ashenfelter, O. and Layard, R., eds., Vol. 1*, 1986, pp. 3–102. **[G: U.S.; U.K.; Canada; Germany]**

Pietsch, Anna-Jutta. Shortage of Labour and Motivation Problems of Soviet Workers. **In** *Lane, D., ed.*, 1986, pp. 176–90. **[G: U.S.S.R.]**

Piore, Michael J. The Effects of Attitudes and Aspirations on the Labor Supply of Young Men: Comment. **In** *Freeman, R. B. and Holzer, H. J., eds.*, 1986, pp. 399–401. **[G: U.S.]**

Portes, Alejandro; Blitzer, Silvia and Curtis, John. The Urban Informal Sector in Uruguay: Its Internal Structure, Characteristics, and Effects. *World Devel.*, June 1986, *14*(6), pp. 727–41. **[G: Uruguay]**

Pozo, Susan and Woodbury, Stephen A. Pensions, Social Security, and Asset Accumulation. *Eastern Econ. J.*, July-Sept. 1986, *12*(3), pp. 273–81. **[G: U.S.]**

Prekel, Truida. The Role of Black Women in the Economy. **In** *Smollan, R., ed.*, 1986, pp. 31–51. **[G: S. Africa]**

Rama, Germán W. Latin American Youth between Development and Crisis. *CEPAL Rev.*, August 1986, (29), pp. 17–39. **[G: Latin America]**

Rees, Albert. An Essay on Youth Joblessness. *J. Econ. Lit.*, June 1986, *24*(2), pp. 613–28. **[G: U.S.]**

Reicher Madeira, Felicia. Youth in Brazil: Old Assumptions and New Approaches. *CEPAL Rev.*, August 1986, (29), pp. 55–78. **[G: Brazil]**

Rice, Patricia G. Juvenile Unemployment, Relative Wages and Social Security: The Econometric Evidence. **In** *Blundell, R. and Walker, I., eds.*, 1986, pp. 60–74. **[G: U.K.]**

Rice, Patricia G. Juvenile Unemployment, Relative Wages and Social Security in Great Britain. *Econ. J.*, June 1986, *96*(382), pp. 352–74. **[G: U.K.]**

Robinson, Olive. Employment Protection, National Insurance, Income Tax and Youth Unemployment: Comment. **In** *Hart, P. E., ed.*, 1986, pp. 45–49. **[G: U.K.]**

Rosenberg, Sam. Racial Differentials in Younger Male Occupational Mobility over the Business Cycle, 1966–1975. **In** *Dennis, B. D., ed.*, 1986, pp. 391–99. **[G: U.S.]**

Schober-Brinkmann, Karen. The Crisis of Youth Employment and Training in West Germany: Public Intervention and the Response of Employers and Trade Unions. *Econ. Lavoro*, Oct.-Dec. 1986, *20*(4), pp. 117–27. **[G: W. Germany]**

Scitovsky, Tibor. The Economy's Impact on Family and Social Relations in America. **In** *Scitovsky, T.*, 1986, *1984*, pp. 160–82. **[G: U.S.]**

Scott, Alison MacEwen. Women and Industrialisation: Examining the 'Female Marginalisation' Thesis. *J. Devel. Stud.*, July 1986, *22*(4), pp. 649–80. **[G: Peru; Brazil]**

Shank, Susan E. Employment Up, Unemployment Stable in the First Half of 1986. *Mon. Lab. Rev.*, August 1986, *109*(8), pp. 3–8. **[G: U.S.]**

Shank, Susan E. and Getz, Patricia M. Employment and Unemployment: Developments in 1985. *Mon. Lab. Rev.*, February 1986, *109*(2), pp. 3–12. **[G: U.S.]**

Shaw, R. Paul. Unemployment and Low Family Incomes in Canada. *Can. Public Policy*, June 1986, *12*(2), pp. 368–86. **[G: Canada]**

Smith, David P. An Analysis of Variations in U.S. Fertility and Female Labor Force Participation Trends: Comment. *Demography*, February 1986, *23*(1), pp. 137–39. **[G: U.S.]**

Smith, Shirley J. Work Experience Profile, 1984: The Effects of Recovery Continue. *Mon. Lab. Rev.*, February 1986, *109*(2), pp. 37–43. **[G: U.S.]**

Spenceley, G. F. R. Responses to Unemployment in Australia: The 1930s and Now. **In** *Berend, I. T. and Borchardt, K., eds.*, 1986, pp. 82–105. **[G: Australia]**

Stanback, Howard. Blacks: Paying the Costs of Economic Change. **In** *Gondolf, E. W.; Marcus, I. M. and Dougherty, J. P., eds.*, 1986, pp. 152–60. **[G: U.S.]**

Standing, Guy. Labour Flexibility and Older Worker Marginalisation: The Need for a New Strategy. *Int. Lab. Rev.*, May-June 1986, *125*(3), pp. 329–48. **[G: EEC]**

Sternlieb, George and Hughes, James W. Information Technology, Demographics, and the Retail Response. **In** *Faulhaber, G.; Noam, E. and Tasley, R., eds.*, 1986, pp. 139–74. **[G: U.S.; OECD]**

Stromsdorfer, Ernst W. Enlistment Decisions of Young Men: Comment. **In** *Gilroy, C. L., ed.*, 1986, pp. 57–60. **[G: U.S.]**

Sweeney, John J. Collective Bargaining's Role in the Determination of Family Policy. **In** *Hewlett, S. A.; Ilchman, A. S. and Sweeney, J. J., eds.*, 1986, pp. 17–22. **[G: U.S.]**

Utgoff, Kathleen P. First-Term Attrition of High School Graduates in the Military: Comment. **In** *Gilroy, C. L., ed.*, 1986, pp. 292–93. **[G: U.S.]**

Warner, John T. Reenlistment Decision Models: Implications for Policy Making: Comment. **In** *Gilroy, C. L., ed.*, 1986, pp. 222–24. **[G: U.S.]**

Wilson, William Julius and Neckerman, Kathryn M. Poverty and Family Structure: The Widening Gap between Evidence and Public Policy Issues. **In** *Danziger, S. H. and Weinberg, D. H., eds.*, 1986, pp. 232–59. **[G: U.S.]**

830 Trade Unions; Collective Bargaining; Labor–Management Relations

8300 General

Cebula, Richard J. On the Impact of Right-to-Work Laws: A Reply. *Urban Stud.*, February 1986, *23*(1), pp. 69. **[G: U.S.]**

Garonna, Paolo and Pisani, Elena. Italian Unions in Transition: The Crisis of Political Unionism.

In *Edwards, R.; Garonna, P. and Tödtling, F., eds.*, 1986, pp. 114–72. **[G: OECD; Italy]**

Horowitz, Donald L. The Deprivitization of Labor Relations Law. *Law Contemp. Probl.*, Autumn 1986, *49*(4), pp. 1–8. **[G: U.S.]**

Howe, Carolyn. The Politics of Class Compromise in an International Context: Considerations for a New Strategy for Labor. *Rev. Radical Polit. Econ.*, Fall 1986, *18*(3), pp. 1–22. **[G: U.S.]**

Molitor, Bruno. Sozialpolitik in der Marktwirtschaft. (Social Policy in the Market Economy. With English summary.) **In** *Eucken, W. and Böhm, F., eds.*, 1986, pp. 59–71.

Ostrosky, Anthony L. The Impact of Right-to-Work Laws on the Cost of Living in the United States: A Comment. *Urban Stud.*, February 1986, *23*(1), pp. 67. **[G: U.S.]**

Oswald, Rudolph A. Joint Labor–Management Programs: A Labor Viewpoint. **In** *Rosow, J. M., ed.*, 1986, pp. 26–40. **[G: U.S.]**

Rubery, Jill. Trade Unions in the 1980s: The Case of the United Kingdom. **In** *Edwards, R.; Garonna, P. and Tödtling, F., eds.*, 1986, pp. 61–113. **[G: U.K.]**

831 Trade Unions

8310 Trade Unions

Abraham, Katharine G. Why Is the Unemployment Rate So Very High near Full Employment? Comments. *Brookings Pap. Econ. Act.*, 1986, (2), pp. 384–89. **[G: U.S.]**

Accornero, Aris. Social Change and Trade Union Movement in the 1970s. **In** *Jacobi, O., et al., eds. (I)*, 1986, pp. 219–37. **[G: Italy]**

Allen, Steven G. The Effect of Unionism on Productivity in Privately and Publicly Owned Hospitals and Nursing Homes. *J. Lab. Res.*, Winter 1986, *7*(1), pp. 59–68. **[G: U.S.]**

Allen, Steven G. Union Work Rules and Efficiency in the Building Trades. *J. Lab. Econ.*, April 1986, *4*(2), pp. 212–42. **[G: U.S.]**

Allen, Steven G. Unionization and Productivity in Office Building and School Construction. *Ind. Lab. Relat. Rev.*, January 1986, *39*(2), pp. 187–201. **[G: U.S.]**

Allen, Steven G. and Clark, Robert L. Unions, Pension Wealth, and Age-Compensation Profiles. *Ind. Lab. Relat. Rev.*, July 1986, *39*(4), pp. 502–18. **[G: U.S.]**

Andersen, Torben M. Fagforeninger, lønudvikling og arbejdsløshed. (Trade Unions and the Wage–Employment Nexus. With English summary.) *Nationaløkon. Tidsskr.*, 1986, *124*(3), pp. 241–58. **[G: Denmark]**

Bain, George. A Symposium on the Role and Influence of Trade Unions in a Recession: Introduction. *Brit. J. Ind. Relat.*, July 1986, *24*(2), pp. 157–59. **[G: U.K.]**

Barkin, Solomon. Selected Aspects of the CIO Experience. **In** *Dennis, B. D., ed.*, 1986, pp. 187–95. **[G: U.S.]**

Barnard, John. Rebirth of the United Automobile Workers: The General Motors Tool and Diemakers' Strike of 1939. *Labor Hist.*, Spring 1986, *27*(2), pp. 165–87. **[G: U.S.]**

Batstone, Eric. Bureaucracy, Oligarchy, and Incorporation in Shop Steward Organisations in the 1980s. **In** *Jacobi, O., et al., eds. (I)*, 1986, pp. 137–60. **[G: U.S.]**

Benjamin, Daniel K. Combinations of Workmen: Trade Unions in the American Economy. **In** *Lipset, S. M., ed.*, 1986, pp. 201–20. **[G: U.S.]**

Bennett, James T. and DiLorenzo, Thomas J. Tax-Funded Unionism: The Unemployment Connection. *J. Lab. Res.*, Fall 1986, *7*(4), pp. 363–85. **[G: U.S.]**

Benson, Herman. The Fight for Union Democracy. **In** *Lipset, S. M., ed.*, 1986, pp. 323–70. **[G: U.S.]**

Black, Dan A. and Parker, Darrell F. Unions, Seniority, and Public Choice. *J. Lab. Res.*, Fall 1986, *7*(4), pp. 337–48.

Blakemore, Arthur E.; Hunt, Janet C. and Kiker, B. F. Collective Bargaining and Union Membership Effects on the Wages of Male Youths. *J. Lab. Econ.*, April 1986, *4*(2), pp. 193–211. **[G: U.S.]**

Blanchflower, David. Wages and Concentration in British Manufacturing. *Appl. Econ.*, September 1986, *18*(9), pp. 1025–38. **[G: U.K.]**

Blanchflower, David. What Effect Do Unions Have on Relative Wages in Great Britain? *Brit. J. Ind. Relat.*, July 1986, *24*(2), pp. 195–204. **[G: U.K.]**

Blanchflower, David and Cubbin, John S. Strike Propensities at the British Workplace. *Oxford Bull. Econ. Statist.*, February 1986, *48*(1), pp. 19–39. **[G: U.K.]**

Block, Richard N. and Wolkinson, Benjamin W. Delay in the Union Election Campaign Revisited: A Theoretical and Empirical Analysis. **In** *Lipsky, D. B. and Lewin, D., eds.*, 1986, pp. 43–81. **[G: U.S.]**

Bloom, David E. Empirical Models of Arbitrator Behavior under Conventional Arbitration. *Rev. Econ. Statist.*, November 1986, *68*(4), pp. 578–85. **[G: U.S.]**

Bluestone, Irving. Changes in U.S. Labor–Management Relations. **In** *Dennis, B. D., ed.*, 1986, pp. 165–70.

Bognanno, Mario F. Contributed Papers: Unions and Collective Bargaining: Discussion. **In** *Dennis, B. D., ed.*, 1986, pp. 296–99. **[G: U.S.]**

Booth, Alison. Estimating the Probability of Trade Union Membership: A Study of Men and Women in Britain. *Economica*, February 1986, *53*(209), pp. 41–61. **[G: U.K.]**

Borland, Jeff. The Ross–Dunlop Debate Revisited. *J. Lab. Res.*, Summer 1986, *7*(3), pp. 293–307.

Bosch, Gerhard. The Dispute over the Reduction of the Working Week in West Germany. *Cambridge J. Econ.*, September 1986, *10*(3), pp. 271–90. **[G: W. Germany]**

Boyle, Fosten A. An Evolving Process of Participation: Honeywell and Teamsters Local 1145. **In** *Rosow, J. M., ed.*, 1986, pp. 146–68. **[G: U.S.]**

Boyle, Kevin. Rite of Passage: The 1939 General

Motors Tool and Die Strike. *Labor Hist.*, Spring 1986, *27*(2), pp. 188–203. **[G: U.S.]**

Brandt, Gerhard. Technological Change, Labour Market, and Trade Union Policy. **In** *Jacobi, O., et al., eds. (I)*, 1986, pp. 50–70. **[G: U.S.; U.K.; Italy; W. Germany]**

Brown, Martin and Philips, Peter. The Decline of the Piece-Rate System in California Canning: Technological Innovation, Labor Management, and Union Pressure, 1890–1947. *Bus. Hist. Rev.*, Winter 1986, *60*(4), pp. 564–601. **[G: U.S.]**

Brown, William. A Symposium on the Role and Influence of Trade Unions in a Recession: Comments. *Brit. J. Ind. Relat.*, July 1986, *24*(2), pp. 208–09. **[G: U.K.]**

Brown, William. The Changing Role of Trade Unions in the Management of Labour. *Brit. J. Ind. Relat.*, July 1986, *24*(2), pp. 161–68. **[G: U.K.]**

Brunello, Giorgio. Enterprise Unionism in the McDonald–Solow Model: A Brief Note. *Econ. Stud. Quart.*, September 1986, *37*(3), pp. 259–64.

Brush, Brian C. and Crane, Steven E. Wage Share, Market Power and Unionism: Rejoinder. *Manchester Sch. Econ. Soc. Stud.*, March 1986, *54*(1), pp. 190–12. **[G: U.S.]**

Butera, Federico and Della Rocca, Giuseppe. Technological Innovation, Organisation of Work, and Unions. **In** *Jacobi, O., et al., eds. (I)*, 1986, pp. 15–34. **[G: Italy]**

Byrne, Dennis M. and King, Randall H. Wildcat Strikes in U.S. Manufacturing, 1960–1977. *J. Lab. Res.*, Fall 1986, *7*(4), pp. 387–401. **[G: U.S.]**

Campbell, Duncan C. U.S. Firms and Black Labor in South Africa: Creating a Structure for Change. *J. Lab. Res.*, Winter 1986, *7*(1), pp. 1–18. **[G: S. Africa]**

Cappelli, Peter and Chalykoff, John. The Effects of Management Industrial Relations Strategy: Results of a Recent Survey. **In** *Dennis, B. D., ed.*, 1986, pp. 171–78. **[G: U.S.]**

Carrieri, Mimmo and Donolo, Carlo. The Political System as a Problem for the Trade Unions in Italy: 1975–1983. **In** *Jacobi, O., et al., eds. (II)*, 1986, pp. 191–209. **[G: Italy]**

Carroll, Thomas M. Do Right-to-Work Laws Matter? Reply. *Southern Econ. J.*, October 1986, *53*(2), pp. 525–28. **[G: U.S.]**

Carruth, Alan A.; Oswald, Andrew J. and Findlay, Lewis. A Test of a Model of Trade Union Behaviour: The Coal and Steel Industries in Britain. *Oxford Bull. Econ. Statist.*, February 1986, *48*(1), pp. 1–18. **[G: U.K.]**

Casey, Bernard. A Symposium on the Role and Influence of Trade Unions in a Recession: Comments. *Brit. J. Ind. Relat.*, July 1986, *24*(2), pp. 212–13. **[G: U.K.]**

Cebula, Richard J. Right-to-Work Laws and Geographic Differences in Living Costs: Reply. *Amer. J. Econ. Soc.*, April 1986, *45*(2), pp. 252–54. **[G: U.S.]**

Champlin, Frederic C. Contributed Papers: Unions and Collective Bargaining: Discussion. **In** *Dennis, B. D., ed.*, 1986, pp. 300–303. **[G: U.S.]**

Chapman, P. G. Alternative Trade Union Objective Functions in the Theory of Wage Bargaining. *Manchester Sch. Econ. Soc. Stud.*, December 1986, *54*(4), pp. 367–79.

Chatterji, Monojit. Unions, Employment and the Inflation Tax. *Econ. J.*, June 1986, *96*(382), pp. 342–51.

Cohen, Lizabeth and Chapman, Herrick. Recent Dissertations: In American and European Labor History. *Labor Hist.*, Fall 1986, *27*(4), pp. 545–48. **[G: W. Europe; U.S.]**

Connolly, Robert A.; Hirsch, Barry T. and Hirschey, Mark. Union Rent Seeking, Intangible Capital, and Market Value of the Firm. *Rev. Econ. Statist.*, November 1986, *68*(4), pp. 567–77. **[G: U.S.]**

Cousineau, Jean-Michel and Lacroix, Robert. Imperfect Information and Strikes: An Analysis of Canadian Experience, 1967–82. *Ind. Lab. Relat. Rev.*, April 1986, *39*(3), pp. 377–87. **[G: Canada]**

Crouch, Colin. Conservative Industrial Relations Policy: Towards Labour Exclusion? **In** *Jacobi, O., et al., eds. (II)*, 1986, pp. 131–53. **[G: U.K.]**

Cunningham, James S. and Donovan, Elaine. Patterns of Union Membership and Relative Wages. *J. Lab. Res.*, Spring 1986, *7*(2), pp. 127–44. **[G: U.S.]**

Curtin, William J. Airline Labor Relations under Deregulation. **In** *Dennis, B. D., ed.*, 1986, pp. 158–64. **[G: U.S.]**

Dal Co, Mario. Recenti sviluppi della contrattazione collettiva negli Stati Uniti. (Concession Bargaining in the United States: Auto and Steel Industries. With English summary.) *Econ. Lavoro*, July-Sept. 1986, *20*(3), pp. 97–111. **[G: U.S.]**

Dasso, James D. Employer Postcertification Polls to Determine Union Support. *Mich. Law Rev.*, August 1986, *84*(8), pp. 1770–90. **[G: U.S.]**

Date-Bah, Eugenia. Contemporary Industrial Relations Problems in Ghana 1972–1979. **In** *Damachi, U. G. and Seibel, H. D., eds.*, 1986, pp. 159–70. **[G: Ghana]**

Domowitz, Ian; Hubbard, R. Glenn and Petersen, Bruce C. The Intertemporal Stability of the Concentration–Margins Relationship. *J. Ind. Econ.*, September 1986, *35*(1), pp. 13–34. **[G: U.S.]**

Dompierre, Michael B. The Role of Unions in African Economic Development. *Devel. Econ.*, March 1986, *24*(1), pp. 71–85. **[G: Africa]**

Dow, Christopher. Trade Unions and Inflation. *Lloyds Bank Rev.*, January 1986, (159), pp. 1–21. **[G: U.K.]**

Dubofsky, Melvyn. Industrial Relations: Comparing the 1980s with the 1920s. **In** *Dennis, B. D., ed.*, 1986, pp. 227–36. **[G: U.S.]**

Duda, Helga and Tödtling, Franz. Austrian Trade Unions in the Economic Crisis. **In** *Edwards, R.; Garonna, P. and Tödtling, F., eds.*, 1986, pp. 227–68. **[G: Austria]**

Eberts, Randall W. and Stone, Joe A. Teacher

Unions and the Cost of Public Education. *Econ. Inquiry*, October 1986, *24*(4), pp. 631–43. **[G: U.S.]**

Edwards, Richard. The Decline of American Unionism in Comparative Perspective. *Econ. Rev. (Keizai Kenkyu)*, October 1986, *37*(4), pp. 289–98. **[G: U.S.]**

Edwards, Richard. Unions in Crisis and Beyond: Introduction. **In** *Edwards, R.; Garonna, P. and Tödtling, F., eds.*, 1986, pp. 1–13.

Edwards, Richard and Podgursky, Michael. The Unraveling Accord: American Unions in Crisis. **In** *Edwards, R.; Garonna, P. and Tödtling, F., eds.*, 1986, pp. 14–60. **[G: U.S.]**

Edwards, Richard and Swaim, Paul. Union–Nonunion Earnings Differentials and the Decline of Private-Sector Unionism. *Amer. Econ. Rev.*, May 1986, *76*(2), pp. 97–102. **[G: U.S.]**

Ehrenberg, Ronald G. and Schwarz, Joshua L. Public-Sector Labor Markets. **In** *Ashenfelter, O. and Layard, R., eds., Vol. 2*, 1986, pp. 1219–68. **[G: U.S.]**

Ephlin, Donald F. United Auto Workers: Pioneers in Labor–Management Partnership. **In** *Rosow, J. M., ed.*, 1986, pp. 133–45. **[G: U.S.]**

Extejt, Marian M. Contributed Papers: Organizational Behavior and Personnel: Discussion. **In** *Dennis, B. D., ed.*, 1986, pp. 108–11.

Farber, Henry S. The Analysis of Union Behavior. **In** *Ashenfelter, O. and Layard, R., eds., Vol. 2*, 1986, pp. 1039–89. **[G: U.S.]**

Fashoyin, Tayo. Management of Industrial Conflict in Africa: A Comparative Analysis of Kenya, Nigeria and Tanzania. **In** *Damachi, U. G. and Seibel, H. D., eds.*, 1986, pp. 171–211. **[G: Nigeria; Kenya; Tanzania]**

Fink, Gary M. Historical Analysis: Industrial Relations Eras: Discussion. **In** *Dennis, B. D., ed.*, 1986, pp. 246–49. **[G: U.S.]**

Fiorito, Jack. Union Voting and Politics. **In** *Dennis, B. D., ed.*, 1986, pp. 270–78. **[G: U.S.]**

Fiorito, Jack and Gallagher, Daniel G. Job Content, Job Status, and Unionism. **In** *Lipsky, D. B. and Lewin, D., eds.*, 1986, pp. 261–316.

Fiorito, Jack and Greer, Charles R. Gender Differences in Union Membership, Preferences, and Beliefs. *J. Lab. Res.*, Spring 1986, *7*(2), pp. 145–64. **[G: U.S.]**

Fischer, Stanley. Contracts, Credibility, and Disinflation. **In** *Fischer, S.*, 1986, *1985*, pp. 221–45. **[G: U.S.]**

Fjällström, Harry. A Trade Unionist's Reply. *Int. Lab. Rev.*, Jan.-Feb. 1986, *125*(1), pp. 119–22. **[G: Sweden]**

Fones-Wolf, Elizabeth. Industrial Recreation, the Second World War, and the Revival of Welfare Capitalism, 1934–1960. *Bus. Hist. Rev.*, Summer 1986, *60*(2), pp. 232–57. **[G: U.S.]**

Freeman, Richard B. Effects of Unions on the Economy. **In** *Lipset, S. M., ed.*, 1986, pp. 177–200.

Freeman, Richard B. In Search of Union Wage Concessions in Standard Data Sets. *Ind. Relat.*, Spring 1986, *25*(2), pp. 131–45. **[G: U.S.]**

Freeman, Richard B. Individual Mobility and Union Voice in the Labor Market. **In** *Putterman, L., ed.*, 1986, *1976*, pp. 156–64.

Freeman, Richard B. The Effect of the Union Wage Differential on Management Opposition and Union Organizing Success. *Amer. Econ. Rev.*, May 1986, *76*(2), pp. 92–96. **[G: U.S.]**

Freeman, Richard B. Unionism Comes to the Public Sector. *J. Econ. Lit.*, March 1986, *24*(1), pp. 41–86. **[G: U.S.]**

Freeman, Richard B. and Medoff, James L. The Two Faces of Unionism. **In** *Reynolds, L. G.; Masters, S. H. and Moser, C. H., eds.*, 1986, *1979*, pp. 374–90. **[G: U.S.]**

Galenson, Walter. The Historical Role of American Trade Unionism. **In** *Lipset, S. M., ed.*, 1986, pp. 39–73. **[G: U.S.]**

Garonna, Paolo. Youth Unemployment, Labour Market Deregulation and Union Stategies in Italy. *Brit. J. Ind. Relat.*, March 1986, *24*(1), pp. 43–61. **[G: Italy]**

Gärtner, Manfred and Heri, Erwin W. Causes and Consequences of Labor Militancy or The Common Factor in Industrial Conflict and Unionization Dynamics. *Rivista Int. Sci. Econ. Com.*, December 1986, *33*(12), pp. 1185–1205. **[G: W. Germany]**

Gaudio, Ricardo and Domeniconi, Hector. Las primeras elecciones sindicales en la transición democrática. (With English summary.) *Desarrollo Econ.*, Oct.-Dec. 1986, *26*(103), pp. 423–54. **[G: Argentina]**

Geroski, Paul A. and Stewart, Mark B. Specification-induced Uncertainty in the Estimation of Trade Union Wage Differentials from Industry-level Data. *Economica*, February 1986, *53*(209), pp. 29–39. **[G: U.K.]**

Goldschmidt, Steven M. and Stuart, Leland E. The Extent and Impact of Educational Policy Bargaining. *Ind. Lab. Relat. Rev.*, April 1986, *39*(3), pp. 350–60. **[G: U.S.]**

Gowaskie, Joe. John Mitchell and the Anthracite Mine Workers: Leadership Conservatism and Rank-and-File Militancy. *Labor Hist.*, Winter 1985-86, *27*(1), pp. 54–83. **[G: U.S.]**

Grady, Stephen W. and Hutchinson, Gillian. A Symposium on the Role and Influence of Trade Unions in a Recession: Comments. *Brit. J. Ind. Relat.*, July 1986, *24*(2), pp. 209–12. **[G: U.K.]**

Gramm, Cynthia L. The Determinants of Strike Incidence and Severity: A Micro-level Study. *Ind. Lab. Relat. Rev.*, April 1986, *39*(3), pp. 361–76. **[G: U.S.]**

Guzda, Henry P. Constitutional Convention Marks and Golden Anniversary of the UAW. *Mon. Lab. Rev.*, October 1986, *109*(10), pp. 23–25.

Halpern, Martin. Taft–Hartley and the Defeat of the Progressive Alternative in the United Auto Workers. *Labor Hist.*, Spring 1986, *27*(2), pp. 204–26. **[G: U.S.]**

Hammer, Tove H. and Stern, Robert N. A Yo-Yo Model of Cooperation: Union Participation in Management at the Rath Packing Company. *Ind. Lab. Relat. Rev.*, April 1986, *39*(3), pp. 337–49. **[G: U.S.]**

Hedges, Janice Neipert. Work Sharing: New Experiences: Discussion. **In** *Dennis, B. D., ed.*, 1986, pp. 453–56. **[G: U.S.]**

Hedlund, Jeffrey D. An Economic Case for Mandatory Bargaining over Partial Termination and Plant Relocation Decisions. *Yale Law J.*, April 1986, *95*(5), pp. 949–68. **[G: U.S.]**

Heine, Hartwig. Some Current Strategy Problems of the Italian Trade Unions. **In** *Jacobi, O., et al., eds. (I)*, 1986, pp. 176–95. **[G: Italy; W. Germany]**

Heneman, Robert L. Contributed Papers: Organizational Behavior and Personnel: Discussion. **In** *Dennis, B. D., ed.*, 1986, pp. 104–07.

Henley, Andrew. Wage Share, Market Power and Unionism: A Reply. *Manchester Sch. Econ. Soc. Stud.*, March 1986, *54*(1), pp. 104–08. **[G: U.S.]**

Hersoug, Tor; Kjaer, Knut N. and Rødseth, Asbjorn. Wages, Taxes and the Utility-Maximizing Trade Union: A Confrontation with Norwegian Data. *Oxford Econ. Pap.*, November 1986, *38*(3), pp. 403–23. **[G: Norway]**

Hobson, Charles J. and Dworkin, James B. West German Labor Unrest: Are Unions Losing Ground to Worker Councils? *Mon. Lab. Rev.*, February 1986, *109*(2), pp. 46–48. **[G: W. Germany]**

Hodson, Randy and England, Paula. Industrial Structure and Sex Differences in Earnings. *Ind. Relat.*, Winter 1986, *25*(1), pp. 16–32. **[G: U.S.]**

Hollander, Abraham and Lacroix, Robert. Unionism, Information Disclosure and Profit-sharing. *Southern Econ. J.*, January 1986, *52*(3), pp. 706–17.

Holmlund, Bertil. Centralized Wage Setting, Wage Drift and Stabilization Policies under Trade Unionism. *Oxford Econ. Pap.*, July 1986, *38*(2), pp. 243–58. **[G: Sweden]**

Horn, Henrik and Svensson, Lars E. O. Trade Unions and Optimal Labour Contracts. *Econ. J.*, June 1986, *96*(382), pp. 323–41.

Hunt, Janet C., et al. Wages, Union Membership, and Public Sector Bargaining Legislation: Simultaneous Equations with an Ordinal Qualitative Variable. *J. Lab. Res.*, Summer 1986, *7*(3), pp. 255–67. **[G: U.S.]**

Hurd, Richard W. and Kriesky, Jill K. "The Rise and Demise of PATCO" Reconstructed. *Ind. Lab. Relat. Rev.*, October 1986, *40*(1), pp. 115–22. **[G: U.S.]**

Hutt, William H. The 'Power' of Labour Unions. **In** *[Seldon, A.]*, 1986, pp. 41–63.

Huxley, Christopher; Kettler, David and Struthers, James. Is Canada's Experience "Especially Instructive"? **In** *Lipset, S. M., ed.*, 1986, pp. 113–32. **[G: Canada; U.S.]**

Hyman, Richard. British Industrial Relations: The Limits of Corporatism. **In** *Jacobi, O., et al., eds. (II)*, 1986, pp. 79–104. **[G: U.K.]**

Iwuji, Eleazar C. Peaceful Settlement of Trade Disputes. **In** *Damachi, U. G. and Seibel, H. D., eds.*, 1986, pp. 146–58. **[G: Nigeria]**

Jacobi, Otto. Economic Development and Trade Union Collective Bargaining Policy since the Middle of the 1970s. **In** *Jacobi, O., et al., eds. (II)*, 1986, pp. 213–35. **[G: W. Germany]**

Jacobi, Otto. Trade Unions, Industrial Relations and Structural Economic 'Ruptures.' **In** *Jacobi, O., et al., eds. (II)*, 1986, pp. 32–60.

Jacobi, Otto; Kastendiek, Hans and Jessop, Bob. Between Erosion and Transformation: Industrial Relations Systems under the Impact of Technological Change. **In** *Jacobi, O., et al., eds. (I)*, 1986, pp. 1–12. **[G: W. Germany; U.K.; Italy]**

Jacoby, Sanford M. Historical Analysis: Industrial Relations Eras: Discussion. **In** *Dennis, B. D., ed.*, 1986, pp. 243–45. **[G: U.S.]**

Jermier, John M., et al. Paying Dues: Police Unionism in a "Right-to-Work" Environment. *Ind. Relat.*, Fall 1986, *25*(3), pp. 265–75. **[G: U.S.]**

Jessop, Bob; Jacobi, Otto and Kastendiek, Hans. Corporatist and Liberal Responses to the Crisis of Postwar Capitalism. **In** *Jacobi, O., et al., eds. (II)*, 1986, pp. 1–13.

Jeszeck, Charles. Structural Change in CB: The U.S. Tire Industry. *Ind. Relat.*, Fall 1986, *25*(3), pp. 229–47. **[G: U.S.]**

Kahn, Shulamit. Trends in Union Membership in the Postwar Period: The Case of the ILGWU. **In** *Dennis, B. D., ed.*, 1986, pp. 279–86. **[G: U.S.]**

Kahn, Shulamit; Lang, Kevin and Kadev, Donna. National Union Leader Performance and Turnover in Building Trades. *Ind. Relat.*, Fall 1986, *25*(3), pp. 276–91. **[G: U.S.]**

Kassalow, Everett M. Trade Unionism: Once More into the Future. **In** *Dennis, B. D., ed.*, 1986, pp. 1–13. **[G: U.S.]**

Kastendiek, Hans; Kastendiek, Hella and Reister, Hugo. Institutional Strategies for Trade Union Participation: An Assessment of the Incorporation Thesis. **In** *Jacobi, O., et al., eds. (II)*, 1986, pp. 258–87. **[G: W. Germany]**

Katz, Harry C. Management Approaches to Collective Bargaining: The Dynamics of Change in the U.S.: Discussion. **In** *Dennis, B. D., ed.*, 1986, pp. 179–80. **[G: U.S.]**

Kirkland, Lane. "It Has All Been Said Before . . ." **In** *Lipset, S. M., ed.*, 1986, pp. 393–404. **[G: U.S.]**

Kleiman, Ephraim. Indexation in the Labor Market. **In** *Ben-Porath, Y., ed.*, 1986, pp. 302–19. **[G: Israel]**

Kochan, Thomas A.; McKersie, Robert B. and Chalykoff, John. The Effects of Corporate Strategy and Workplace Innovations on Union Representation. *Ind. Lab. Relat. Rev.*, July 1986, *39*(4), pp. 487–501. **[G: U.S.]**

Kraft, Kornelius. Exit and Voice in the Labor Market: An Empirical Study of Quits. *J. Inst. Theoretical Econ.*, December 1986, *142*(4), pp. 697–715. **[G: W. Germany]**

Krislov, Joseph. Unions in the Next Century: An Exploratory Essay. *J. Lab. Res.*, Spring 1986, *7*(2), pp. 165–73. **[G: Global]**

Kymn, Kern O. and Palomba, Catherine A. The Strike Experience Model: Adaptive Expectations Applied to Strikes. *J. Behav. Econ.*,

Spring/Summer 1986, *15*(1/2), pp. 135–48. **[G: U.S.]**

Laber, Pamela. The U.S. Labor Movement and Working Women: An Alliance for the Future. **In** *Hewlett, S. A.; Ilchman, A. S. and Sweeney, J. J., eds.*, 1986, pp. 179–85. **[G: U.S.]**

Labig, Chalmer E., Jr. and Helburn, I. B. Union and Management Policy Influences on Grievance Initiation. *J. Lab. Res.*, Summer 1986, *7*(3), pp. 269–84. **[G: U.S.]**

Lee, Dwight R. Union Myopia and the Taxation of Capital. **In** *Lee, D. R., ed.*, 1986, pp. 297–322. **[G: U.S.]**

Leibig, Michael T. The Deprivitization of Employee Benefit and Labor Law: The Surprising Conservative Erosion of Trusts and of the Competitive Labor Model. *Law Contemp. Probl.*, Autumn 1986, *49*(4), pp. 183–209. **[G: U.S.]**

Leigh, Duane E. Union Preferences, Job Satisfaction, and the Union-Voice Hypothesis. *Ind. Relat.*, Winter 1986, *25*(1), pp. 65–71. **[G: U.S.]**

Leonard, Jonathan S. Unions, Turnover, and Employment Variation. **In** *Lipsky, D. B. and Lewin, D., eds.*, 1986, pp. 119–51. **[G: U.S.]**

Leopold, J. W. and Beaumont, P. B. Trade Unions, Consultation and Redundancies. **In** *Danson, M., ed.*, 1986, pp. 159–67. **[G: U.K.]**

Lever, Jeffrey. The Trade Unions and Black Advancement. **In** *Smollan, R., ed.*, 1986, pp. 52–70. **[G: S. Africa]**

Lewin, David. Public Employee Unionism in the 1980s: An Analysis of Transformation. **In** *Lipset, S. M., ed.*, 1986, pp. 241–64. **[G: U.S.]**

Lewin, David and Lipsky, David B. Current Research on Industrial Relations Regulation, Bargaining Theory, Progressive Discipline, and Occupational Influences on Unionism. **In** *Lipsky, D. B. and Lewin, D., eds.*, 1986, pp. 1–19.

Lewis, H. Gregg. Union Relative Wage Effects. **In** *Ashenfelter, O. and Layard, R., eds., Vol. 2*, 1986, pp. 1139–81. **[G: U.S.]**

Linneman, Peter and Wachter, Michael L. Rising Union Premiums and the Declining Boundaries among Noncompeting Groups. *Amer. Econ. Rev.*, May 1986, *76*(2), pp. 103–08. **[G: U.S.]**

Lipset, Seymour Martin. Labor Unions in the Public Mind. **In** *Lipset, S. M., ed.*, 1986, pp. 287–321. **[G: U.S.]**

Lipset, Seymour Martin. North American Labor Movements: A Comparative Perspective. **In** *Lipset, S. M., ed.*, 1986, pp. 421–52. **[G: OECD]**

Livingston, Craig H. Capital Strategies for Labor. **In** *Dennis, B. D., ed.*, 1986, pp. 221–26. **[G: U.S.]**

MaCurdy, Thomas E. and Pencavel, John H. Testing between Competing Models of Wage and Employment Determination in Unionized Markets. *J. Polit. Econ.*, Part 2, June 1986, *94*(3), pp. S3–S39. **[G: U.S.]**

Marshall, Ray. America and Japan: Industrial Relations in a Time of Change. **In** *Lipset, S. M., ed.*, 1986, pp. 133–49. **[G: Japan; U.S.]**

Martin, James E. Predictors of Individual Propensity to Strike. *Ind. Lab. Relat. Rev.*, January 1986, *39*(2), pp. 214–27. **[G: U.S.]**

Martin, James E.; Magenau, John M. and Peterson, Mark F. Variables Related to Patterns of Union Stewards' Commitment. *J. Lab. Res.*, Fall 1986, *7*(4), pp. 323–36. **[G: U.S.]**

Martin, James E. and Peterson, Melanie M. Two-Tier Wage Structures and Attitude Differences. **In** *Dennis, B. D., ed.*, 1986, pp. 72–79. **[G: U.S.]**

Masters, Marick F. and Zardkoohi, Asghar. The Determinants of Labor PAC Allocations to Legislators. *Ind. Relat.*, Fall 1986, *25*(3), pp. 328–38. **[G: U.S.]**

McShane, Steven L. A Path Analysis of Participation in Union Administration [Union Government in the U.S.: Research Past and Future]. *Ind. Relat.*, Winter 1986, *25*(1), pp. 72–80. **[G: U.S.]**

McShane, Steven L. General Union Attitude: A Construct Validation. *J. Lab. Res.*, Fall 1986, *7*(4), pp. 403–17. **[G: Canada]**

McTighe, Michael J. "True Philanthropy" and the Limits of the Female Sphere: Poor Relief and Labor Organizations in Ante-Bellum Cleveland. *Labor Hist.*, Spring 1986, *27*(2), pp. 227–56. **[G: U.S.]**

Mefford, Robert N. The Effect of Unions on Productivity in a Multinational Manufacturing Firm. *Ind. Lab. Relat. Rev.*, October 1986, *40*(1), pp. 105–14. **[G: U.S.]**

Mehay, Stephen L. and Gonzalez, Rodolfo A. The Relative Effect of Unionization and Interjurisdictional Competition on Municipal Wages. *J. Lab. Res.*, Winter 1986, *7*(1), pp. 79–93. **[G: U.S.]**

Meltz, Noah M. Work-Sharing: New Experiences: Discussion. **In** *Dennis, B. D., ed.*, 1986, pp. 449–52. **[G: U.S.]**

Mishel, Lawrence R. The Structural Determinants of Union Bargaining Power. *Ind. Lab. Relat. Rev.*, October 1986, *40*(1), pp. 90–104. **[G: U.S.]**

Mitchell, Daniel J. B. Union vs. Nonunion Wage Norm Shifts. *Amer. Econ. Rev.*, May 1986, *76*(2), pp. 249–52. **[G: U.S.]**

Moore, William J.; Dunlevy, James A. and Newman, Robert J. Do Right to Work Laws Matter? Comment. *Southern Econ. J.*, October 1986, *53*(2), pp. 515–24. **[G: U.S.]**

Morand, Martin J. Work Sharing: New Experiences: Discussion. **In** *Dennis, B. D., ed.*, 1986, pp. 457–64. **[G: U.S.]**

Moses, John A. Standing on Marx's Shoulders—The Legacy of Marx in the West German Trade Union Movement. **In** *Dowdy, E., ed.*, 1986, pp. 24–47. **[G: W. Germany]**

Mulder, C. B. and van der Ploeg, Frederick. Trade Unions, Investment and Employment in a Small Open Economy: A Dutch Perspective. *Rech. Écon. Louvain*, 1986, *52*(3–4), pp. 313–38. **[G: Netherlands; OECD]**

Northrup, Herbert R. Reply [The Rise and Demise of PATCO]. *Ind. Lab. Relat. Rev.*, October 1986, *40*(1), pp. 122–27. **[G: U.S.]**

O'Connell, John F. An Alternative Theory of Labor Union Growth. *Amer. Econ.*, Spring 1986, *30*(1), pp. 51–55.

Oswald, Andrew J. A Symposium on the Role and Influence of Trade Unions in a Recession: Comments. *Brit. J. Ind. Relat.*, July 1986, *24*(2), pp. 213–14. **[G: U.K.]**

Oswald, Andrew J. Wage Determination and Recession: A Report on Recent Work. *Brit. J. Ind. Relat.*, July 1986, *24*(2), pp. 181–94.

Panitch, Leo. Trade Unions and the Capitalist State. **In** *Panitch, L.*, 1986, *1981*, pp. 187–214.

Papadimitriou, Zissis. Changing Skill Requirements and Trade Union Bargaining. **In** *Jacobi, O., et al., eds. (I)*, 1986, pp. 35–49.

Patton, David B.; Marrone, John J. and Hindman, Hugh D. Unions and Politics: 1984 and Beyond. **In** *Dennis, B. D., ed.*, 1986, pp. 490–94. **[G: U.S.]**

Pissarides, Christopher A. Trade Unions and the Efficiency of the Natural Rate of Unemployment. *J. Lab. Econ.*, October 1986, *4*(4), pp. 582–95.

Podgursky, Michael. Unions, Establishment Size, and Intra-industry Threat Effects. *Ind. Lab. Relat. Rev.*, January 1986, *39*(2), pp. 277–84. **[G: U.S.]**

Pretzer, William S. "The British, Duff Green, the Rats and the Devil": Custom, Capitalism, and Conflict in the Washington Printing Trade, 1834–36. *Labor Hist.*, Winter 1985-86, *27*(1), pp. 5–30. **[G: U.S.]**

Raaum, Oddbjørn. Wage Formation in a Two-Sector Open Economy with Two Strong Unions. *Rech. Écon. Louvain*, 1986, *52*(3–4), pp. 283–311.

Raskin, A. H. Labor: A Movement in Search of a Mission. **In** *Lipset, S. M., ed.*, 1986, pp. 3–38. **[G: U.S.]**

Regalia, Ida. Centralisation or Decentralisation? An Analysis of Organisational Changes in the Italian Trade Union Movement at a Time of Crisis. **In** *Jacobi, O., et al., eds. (I)*, 1986, pp. 196–218. **[G: Italy]**

Regini, Marino. Political Bargaining in Western Europe during the Economic Crisis of the 1980s. **In** *Jacobi, O., et al., eds. (II)*, 1986, pp. 61–76.

Reshef, Yonatan. Political Exchange in Israel: Histadrut–State Relations. *Ind. Relat.*, Fall 1986, *25*(3), pp. 303–19. **[G: Israel]**

Reynolds, Morgan O. The Case for Ending the Legal Privileges and Immunities of Trade Unions. **In** *Lipset, S. M., ed.*, 1986, pp. 221–38. **[G: U.S.]**

Reynolds, Morgan O. Trade Unions in the Production Process Reconsidered. *J. Polit. Econ.*, April 1986, *94*(2), pp. 443–47.

Reynolds, Morgan O. Unions and Jobs: The U.S. Auto Industry. *J. Lab. Res.*, Spring 1986, *7*(2), pp. 103–26. **[G: U.S.]**

Reynolds, Morgan O. and Edwards, Mary. Right-to-Work Laws and Geographic Differences in Living Costs: Comment. *Amer. J. Econ. Soc.*, April 1986, *45*(2), pp. 247–52. **[G: U.S.]**

Roberts, Markley. A Labor Agenda for Jobs. **In** *Burton, D. F., et al., eds.*, 1986, pp. 119–33. **[G: U.S.]**

Rogin, Lawrence. Historical Analysis: Industrial Relations Eras: Discussion. **In** *Dennis, B. D., ed.*, 1986, pp. 250–53. **[G: U.S.]**

Rosswurm, Steven and Gilpin, Toni. The FBI and the Farm Equipment Workers: FBI Surveillance Records as a Source for CIO Union History. *Labor Hist.*, Fall 1986, *27*(4), pp. 485–505. **[G: U.S.]**

Russo, John. Technological Displacement: Strategies of the Global Auto Industry. **In** *Gondolf, E. W.; Marcus, I. M. and Dougherty, J. P., eds.*, 1986, pp. 122–32. **[G: U.S.]**

Sampson, Anthony A. The Shift to Indirect Taxation in a Unionized Economy. *Bull. Econ. Res.*, January 1986, *38*(1), pp. 87–91.

Sampson, Anthony A. Voting in Unions with Seniority Rules. *Bull. Econ. Res.*, September 1986, *38*(3), pp. 271–76.

Sapsford, David. Some Further Evidence on the Role of Profits in Union Growth Equations. *Appl. Econ.*, January 1986, *18*(1), pp. 27–36. **[G: Ireland]**

Sellier, François and Silvestre, Jean-Jacques. Unions' Policies in the Economic Crisis in France. **In** *Edwards, R.; Garonna, P. and Tödtling, F., eds.*, 1986, pp. 173–226. **[G: France]**

Simpson, Wayne. Unions, Industrial Concentration and Wages: A Re-examination. *Appl. Econ.*, March 1986, *18*(3), pp. 305–17. **[G: Canada]**

Southall, Humphrey. Atlas of Industrializing Britain 1780–1914: Unionization. **In** *Langton, J. and Morris, R. J., eds.*, 1986, pp. 189–93. **[G: U.K.]**

Staehle, Wolfgang H. Industrial Relations and Europe's Multinationals. **In** *Macharzina, K. and Staehle, W. H., eds.*, 1986, pp. 129–42. **[G: W. Europe]**

Steele, Mairi; Miller, Kenneth and Gennard, John. The Trade Union Act, 1984: Political Fund Ballots. *Brit. J. Ind. Relat.*, November 1986, *24*(3), pp. 443–67. **[G: U.K.]**

Stepina, Lee P. and Fiorito, Jack. Toward a Comprehensive Theory of Union Growth and Decline. *Ind. Relat.*, Fall 1986, *25*(3), pp. 248–64. **[G: U.S.]**

Stewart, Mark B. A Symposium on the Role and Influence of Trade Unions in a Recession: Comments. *Brit. J. Ind. Relat.*, July 1986, *24*(2), pp. 205–08. **[G: U.K.]**

Summers, Lawrence H. Why Is the Unemployment Rate So Very High near Full Employment? *Brookings Pap. Econ. Act.*, 1986, (2), pp. 339–83. **[G: U.S.]**

Svejnar, Jan. Bargaining Power, Fear of Disagreement, and Wage Settlements: Theory and Evidence from U.S. Industry. *Econometrica*, September 1986, *54*(5), pp. 1055–78. **[G: U.S.]**

Svensson, Lennart. Class Struggle in a Welfare

State in Crisis: From Radicalism to Neoliberalism in Sweden. **In** *Edwards, R.; Garonna, P. and Tödtling, F., eds.*, 1986, pp. 269–308. **[G: Sweden]**

Terry, Michael. How Do We Know If Shop Stewards Are Getting Weaker? *Brit. J. Ind. Relat.*, July 1986, *24*(2), pp. 169–79. **[G: U.K.]**

Terry, Michael. Shop Stewards and Management: Collective Bargaining as Co-operation. **In** *Jacobi, O., et al., eds. (I)*, 1986, pp. 161–75.

Tinsley, Kevin. Teaching Economics to the 13–16 Age Range: Trade Unions. **In** *Whitehead, D. J., ed.*, 1986, pp. 95–99.

Touraine, Alain. Unionism as a Social Movement. **In** *Lipset, S. M., ed.*, 1986, pp. 151–73.

Tracy, Joseph S. An Investigation into the Determinants of U.S. Strike Activity. *Amer. Econ. Rev.*, June 1986, *76*(3), pp. 423–36. **[G: U.S.]**

Troy, Leo. The Rise and Fall of American Trade Unions: The Labor Movement from FDR to RR. **In** *Lipset, S. M., ed.*, 1986, pp. 75–109. **[G: OECD]**

Tyler, Gus. Labor at the Crossroads. **In** *Lipset, S. M., ed.*, 1986, pp. 373–92. **[G: U.S.]**

Voos, Paula B. and Mishel, Lawrence R. The Union Impact on Profits in the Supermarket Industry. *Rev. Econ. Statist.*, August 1986, *68*(3), pp. 513–17. **[G: U.S.]**

Voos, Paula B. and Mishel, Lawrence R. The Union Impact on Profits: Evidence from Industry Price–Cost Margin Data. *J. Lab. Econ.*, January 1986, *4*(1), pp. 105–33. **[G: U.S.]**

Wachter, Michael L. Union Wage Rigidity: The Default Settings of Labor Law. *Amer. Econ. Rev.*, May 1986, *76*(2), pp. 240–44.

Wachter, Michael L. Why Is the Unemployment Rate So Very High near Full Employment? Comments. *Brookings Pap. Econ. Act.*, 1986, (2), pp. 389–94.

Walker, J. Malcolm and Lawler, John J. Union Campaign Activities and Voter Preferences. *J. Lab. Res.*, Winter 1986, *7*(1), pp. 19–40. **[G: U.S.]**

Weitz, Eric D. Class Formation and Labor Protest in the Mining Communities of Southern Illinois and the Ruhr, 1890–1925. *Labor Hist.*, Winter 1985-86, *27*(1), pp. 85–105. **[G: U.S.; Germany]**

Weitzman, Martin L. The Simple Macroeconomics of Profit-Sharing. **In** *Beckerman, W., ed.*, 1986, pp. 171–99.

Wesman, Elizabeth C. Labor Unions and Title VII: A Case Study of Organizational Response to Environmental Change. **In** *Dennis, B. D., ed.*, 1986, pp. 92–103. **[G: U.S.]**

White, Michael D. Self-interest Redistribution and the National Football League Players Association. *Econ. Inquiry*, October 1986, *24*(4), pp. 669–80. **[G: U.S.]**

Wilhite, Allen and Theilmann, John. Unions, Corporations, and Political Campaign Contributions: The 1982 House Elections. *J. Lab. Res.*, Spring 1986, *7*(2), pp. 175–85. **[G: U.S.]**

Winckler, Georg and Amann, Erwin. Exchange Rate Policy in the Presence of a Strong Trade Union. *J. Econ. (Z. Nationalökon.)*, Supplementum 5, 1986, pp. 259–80.

Zalusky, John. Labor's Interest and Concerns with Short-Time Compensation. **In** *Dennis, B. D., ed.*, 1986, pp. 441–48. **[G: U.S.]**

832 Collective Bargaining

8320 General

Addison, John T. Job Security in the United States: Law, Collective Bargaining, Policy, and Practice. *Brit. J. Ind. Relat.*, November 1986, *24*(3), pp. 381–418. **[G: U.S.]**

Atkinson, John. Working Time and Employment: A Negotiable Issue? Comment. **In** *Hart, P. E., ed.*, 1986, pp. 22–26. **[G: U.K.]**

Benjamin, Daniel K. Combinations of Workmen: Trade Unions in the American Economy. **In** *Lipset, S. M., ed.*, 1986, pp. 201–20. **[G: U.S.]**

Bhagwati, Jagdish N. U.S. Immigration Policy: What Next? **In** *Pozo, S., ed.*, 1986, pp. 111–28. **[G: U.S.]**

Blair, Christine E. and Rodrigues, Anthony P. A Model of Wage Contract Bargaining with Imperfect Information and Strikes. *Eastern Econ. J.*, July-Sept. 1986, *12*(3), pp. 251–56.

Bloom, David E. Empirical Models of Arbitrator Behavior under Conventional Arbitration. *Rev. Econ. Statist.*, November 1986, *68*(4), pp. 578–85. **[G: U.S.]**

Bloom, David E. and Cavanagh, Christopher L. An Analysis of the Selection of Arbitrators. *Amer. Econ. Rev.*, June 1986, *76*(3), pp. 408–22. **[G: U.S.]**

Bognanno, Mario F. Contributed Papers: Unions and Collective Bargaining: Discussion. **In** *Dennis, B. D., ed.*, 1986, pp. 296–99. **[G: U.S.]**

Briggs, Vernon M., Jr. The Imperative of Immigration Reform. **In** *Pozo, S., ed.*, 1986, pp. 43–71. **[G: U.S.]**

Brown, William. The Changing Role of Trade Unions in the Management of Labour. *Brit. J. Ind. Relat.*, July 1986, *24*(2), pp. 161–68. **[G: U.K.]**

Cella, Gian Primo and Treu, Tiziano. Collective and Political Bargaining. **In** *Jacobi, O., et al., eds. (II)*, 1986, pp. 171–90. **[G: Italy]**

Champlin, Frederic C. Contributed Papers: Unions and Collective Bargaining: Discussion. **In** *Dennis, B. D., ed.*, 1986, pp. 300–303. **[G: U.S.]**

Champlin, Frederic C. and Bognanno, Mario F. A Model of Arbitration and the Incentive to Bargain. **In** *Lipsky, D. B. and Lewin, D., eds.*, 1986, pp. 153–90.

Chiswick, Barry R. The Illegal Alien Policy Dilemma. **In** *Pozo, S., ed.*, 1986, pp. 73–87. **[G: U.S.]**

Dal Co, Mario and Perulli, Paolo. The Trilateral Agreement of 1983: Social Pact or Political Truce? **In** *Jacobi, O., et al., eds. (II)*, 1986, pp. 157–70. **[G: Italy]**

Date-Bah, Eugenia. Contemporary Industrial Relations Problems in Ghana 1972–1979. **In** *Damachi, U. G. and Seibel, H. D., eds.*, 1986, pp. 159–70. **[G: Ghana]**

Dunlop, John T. A Decade of National Experience. **In** *Rosow, J. M., ed.*, 1986, pp. 12–25. **[G: U.S.]**

Farber, Henry S. The Analysis of Union Behavior. **In** *Ashenfelter, O. and Layard, R., eds., Vol. 2*, 1986, pp. 1039–89. **[G: U.S.]**

Farber, Henry S. and Bazerman, Max H. The General Basis of Arbitrator Behavior: An Empirical Analysis of Conventional and Final-Offer Arbitration. *Econometrica,* July 1986, *54*(4), pp. 819–44.

Farber, Henry S. and Bazerman, Max H. The General Basis of Arbitrator Behavior: An Empirical Analysis of Conventional and Final-Offer Arbitration. *Econometrica,* November 1986, *54*(6), pp. 1503–28.

Fiorito, Jack. Union Voting and Politics. **In** *Dennis, B. D., ed.*, 1986, pp. 270–78. **[G: U.S.]**

Freeman, Richard B. Effects of Unions on the Economy. **In** *Lipset, S. M., ed.*, 1986, pp. 177–200.

Friedman, Debra. The Principal–Agent Problem in Labor–Management Negotiations. **In** *Lawler, E. J., ed.*, 1986, pp. 89–106.

Garbarino, Joseph W. Faculty Collective Bargaining: A Status Report. **In** *Lipset, S. M., ed.*, 1986, pp. 265–84. **[G: U.S.]**

Hedlund, Jeffrey D. An Economic Case for Mandatory Bargaining over Partial Termination and Plant Relocation Decisions. *Yale Law J.*, April 1986, *95*(5), pp. 949–68. **[G: U.S.]**

Hendricks, Wallace. Collective Bargaining in Regulated Industries. **In** *Lipsky, D. B. and Lewin, D., eds.*, 1986, pp. 21–42. **[G: U.S.]**

Horwitz, Ralph. Collective Bargaining or Economic Pluralism. **In** *[Hutt, W. H.]*, 1986, pp. 105–24.

Hurd, Richard W. and Kriesky, Jill K. "The Rise and Demise of PATCO" Reconstructed. *Ind. Lab. Relat. Rev.*, October 1986, *40*(1), pp. 115–22. **[G: U.S.]**

Hutt, William H. The Principle of Social Justice. **In** *[Hutt, W. H.]*, 1986, pp. 53–86.

Jacobi, Otto. Trade Unions, Industrial Relations and Structural Economic 'Ruptures.' **In** *Jacobi, O., et al., eds. (II)*, 1986, pp. 32–60.

Keizer, P. Wage Formation in the Context of Collective Bargaining. *De Economist,* 1986, *134*(2), pp. 191–213.

Kennan, John. The Economics of Strikes. **In** *Ashenfelter, O. and Layard, R., eds., Vol. 2*, 1986, pp. 1091–1137. **[G: U.S.]**

Labig, Chalmer E., Jr. and Helburn, I. B. Union and Management Policy Influences on Grievance Initiation. *J. Lab. Res.*, Summer 1986, *7*(3), pp. 269–84. **[G: U.S.]**

Lawler, Edward J. and Bacharach, Samuel B. Power Dependence in Collective Bargaining. **In** *Lipsky, D. B. and Lewin, D., eds.*, 1986, pp. 191–212.

Leap, Terry L. and Grigsby, David W. A Conceptualization of Collective Bargaining Power. *Ind. Lab. Relat. Rev.*, January 1986, *39*(2), pp. 202–13.

Lewin, David and Lipsky, David B. Current Research on Industrial Relations Regulation, Bargaining Theory, Progressive Discipline, and Occupational Influences on Unionism. **In** *Lipsky, D. B. and Lewin, D., eds.*, 1986, pp. 1–19.

Lindbeck, Assar and Snower, Dennis J. Wage Rigidity, Union Activity and Unemployment. **In** *Beckerman, W., ed.*, 1986, pp. 97–125.

Matsukawa, Shigeru. The Equilibrium Distribution of Wage Settlements and Economic Stability. *Int. Econ. Rev.*, June 1986, *27*(2), pp. 415–37.

Mitchell, Daniel J. B. Explanations of Wage Inflexibility: Institutions and Incentives. **In** *Beckerman, W., ed.*, 1986, pp. 43–76. **[G: U.S.]**

Mueckenberger, Ulrich. Labour Law and Industrial Relations. **In** *Jacobi, O., et al., eds. (II)*, 1986, pp. 236–57. **[G: W. Germany]**

Mueller-Jentsch, Walther. Labour Conflicts and Class Struggles. **In** *Jacobi, O., et al., eds. (I)*, 1986, pp. 238–60. **[G: W. Germany]**

Oswald, Andrew J. Is Wage Rigidity Caused by 'Lay-offs by Seniority'? **In** *Beckerman, W., ed.*, 1986, pp. 77–95. **[G: U.K.]**

Panitch, Leo. Profits and Politics: Labour and the Crisis of British Capitalism. **In** *Panitch, L.*, 1986, *1977*, pp. 78–108. **[G: U.K.]**

Panitch, Leo. Socialists and the Labour Party: A Reappraisal. **In** *Panitch, L.*, 1986, *1979*, pp. 109–31. **[G: U.K.]**

Papadimitriou, Zissis. Changing Skill Requirements and Trade Union Bargaining. **In** *Jacobi, O., et al., eds. (I)*, 1986, pp. 35–49.

Piore, Michael J. Can International Migration Be Controlled? **In** *Pozo, S., ed.*, 1986, pp. 21–42. **[G: U.S.]**

Pozo, Susan. The Many Guises of Immigration Reform. **In** *Pozo, S., ed.*, 1986, pp. 1–6. **[G: U.S.]**

Terry, Michael. Shop Stewards and Management: Collective Bargaining as Co-operation. **In** *Jacobi, O., et al., eds. (I)*, 1986, pp. 161–75.

Tracy, Joseph S. Unions and the Share Economy. *J. Compar. Econ.*, December 1986, *10*(4), pp. 433–37.

Treble, John G. How New Is Final-Offer Arbitration? *Ind. Relat.*, Winter 1986, *25*(1), pp. 92–94.

White, Michael. Working Time and Employment: A Negotiable Issue? **In** *Hart, P. E., ed.*, 1986, pp. 5–22. **[G: W. Europe]**

8321 Collective Bargaining in the Private Sector

Albåge, Lars-Gunnar. Recents Trends in Collective Bargaining in Sweden. An Employer's View. *Int. Lab. Rev.*, Jan.-Feb. 1986, *125*(1), pp. 107–18. **[G: Sweden]**

Barnard, John. Rebirth of the United Automobile Workers: The General Motors Tool and Diemakers' Strike of 1939. *Labor Hist.*, Spring 1986, *27*(2), pp. 165–87. **[G: U.S.]**

Blakemore, Arthur E.; Hunt, Janet C. and Kiker,

B. F. Collective Bargaining and Union Membership Effects on the Wages of Male Youths. *J. Lab. Econ.*, April 1986, *4*(2), pp. 193–211. [G: U.S.]

Blanchflower, David and Cubbin, John S. Strike Propensities at the British Workplace. *Oxford Bull. Econ. Statist.*, February 1986, *48*(1), pp. 19–39. [G: U.K.]

Bluestone, Irving. Changes in U.S. Labor–Management Relations. **In** *Dennis, B. D., ed.*, 1986, pp. 165–70.

Bluestone, Irving. Joint Action and Collective Bargaining—and Vice Versa. **In** *Rosow, J. M., ed.*, 1986, pp. 41–55. [G: U.S.]

Borum, Joan and Conley, James. Wage Restraints Continue in 1985 Major Contracts. *Mon. Lab. Rev.*, April 1986, *109*(4), pp. 22–28. [G: U.S.]

Boyle, Kevin. Rite of Passage: The 1939 General Motors Tool and Die Strike. *Labor Hist.*, Spring 1986, *27*(2), pp. 188–203. [G: U.S.]

Brown, James N. and Ashenfelter, Orley. Testing the Efficiency of Employment Contracts. *J. Polit. Econ.*, Part 2, June 1986, *94*(3), pp. S40–S87. [G: U.S.]

Byrne, Dennis M. and King, Randall H. Wildcat Strikes in U.S. Manufacturing, 1960–1977. *J. Lab. Res.*, Fall 1986, *7*(4), pp. 387–401. [G: U.S.]

Cappelli, Peter and Chalykoff, John. The Effects of Management Industrial Relations Strategy: Results of a Recent Survey. **In** *Dennis, B. D., ed.*, 1986, pp. 171–78. [G: U.S.]

Card, David. An Empirical Model of Wage Indexation Provisions in Union Contracts. *J. Polit. Econ.*, Part 2, June 1986, *94*(3), pp. S144–75. [G: Canada]

Curtin, William J. Airline Labor Relations under Deregulation. **In** *Dennis, B. D., ed.*, 1986, pp. 158–64. [G: U.S.]

Dal Co, Mario. Recenti sviluppi della contrattazione collettiva negli Stati Uniti. (Concession Bargaining in the United States: Auto and Steel Industries. With English summary.) *Econ. Lavoro*, July-Sept. 1986, *20*(3), pp. 97–111. [G: U.S.]

Deitsch, Clarence R. and Dilts, David A. Factors Affecting Pre-arbitral Settlement of Rights Disputes: Predicting the Method of Rights Dispute Resolution. *J. Lab. Res.*, Winter 1986, *7*(1), pp. 69–78. [G: U.S.]

Dilts, David A. Strike Activity in the United States: An Analysis of the Stocks and Flows. *J. Lab. Res.*, Spring 1986, *7*(2), pp. 187–99. [G: U.S.]

Dompierre, Michael B. The Role of Unions in African Economic Development. *Devel. Econ.*, March 1986, *24*(1), pp. 71–85. [G: Africa]

Donahue, Steven M. Communications Workers Focus on Bargaining with AT&T. *Mon. Lab. Rev.*, July 1986, *109*(7), pp. 37–39. [G: U.S.]

Fashoyin, Tayo. Management of Industrial Conflict in Africa: A Comparative Analysis of Kenya, Nigeria and Tanzania. **In** *Damachi, U. G. and Seibel, H. D., eds.*, 1986, pp. 171–211. [G: Nigeria; Kenya; Tanzania]

Fjällström, Harry. A Trade Unionist's Reply. *Int. Lab. Rev.*, Jan.-Feb. 1986, *125*(1), pp. 119–22. [G: Sweden]

Fraser, Douglas A. A Labor Director Looks at the Board. **In** *Rosow, J. M., ed.*, 1986, pp. 56–72. [G: U.S.]

Freeman, Richard B. In Search of Union Wage Concessions in Standard Data Sets. *Ind. Relat.*, Spring 1986, *25*(2), pp. 131–45. [G: U.S.]

Geroski, Paul A. and Stewart, Mark B. Specification-induced Uncertainty in the Estimation of Trade Union Wage Differentials from Industry-level Data. *Economica*, February 1986, *53*(209), pp. 29–39. [G: U.K.]

Gregory, Mary; Lobban, Peter and Thomson, Andrew. Bargaining Structure, Pay Settlements and Perceived Pressures in Manufacturing 1979–84: Further Analysis from the CBI Databank. *Brit. J. Ind. Relat.*, July 1986, *24*(2), pp. 215–32. [G: U.K.]

Gunderson, Morley; Kervin, John and Reid, Frank. Logit Estimates of Strike Incidence from Canadian Contract Data. *J. Lab. Econ.*, April 1986, *4*(2), pp. 257–76. [G: Canada]

Hendricks, Wallace and Kahn, Lawrence M. Wage Indexation and Compensating Wage Differentials. *Rev. Econ. Statist.*, August 1986, *68*(3), pp. 484–92. [G: U.S.]

Hince, Kevin. Wage Fixing in a Period of Change: The New Zealand Case. *Int. Lab. Rev.*, July-Aug. 1986, *125*(4), pp. 463–72. [G: New Zealand]

Hobson, Charles J. and Dworkin, James B. West German Labor Unrest: Are Unions Losing Ground to Worker Councils? *Mon. Lab. Rev.*, February 1986, *109*(2), pp. 46–48. [G: W. Germany]

Ichniowski, Casey. The Effects of Grievance Activity on Productivity. *Ind. Lab. Relat. Rev.*, October 1986, *40*(1), pp. 75–89. [G: U.S.]

Iwuji, Eleazar C. Peaceful Settlement of Trade Disputes. **In** *Damachi, U. G. and Seibel, H. D., eds.*, 1986, pp. 146–58. [G: Nigeria]

Jacobi, Otto. Economic Development and Trade Union Collective Bargaining Policy since the Middle of the 1970s. **In** *Jacobi, O., et al., eds. (II)*, 1986, pp. 213–35. [G: W. Germany]

Jacoby, Sanford M. and Mitchell, Daniel J. B. Management Attitudes toward Two-Tier Pay Plans. *J. Lab. Res.*, Summer 1986, *7*(3), pp. 221–37. [G: U.S.]

Jeszeck, Charles. Structural Change in CB: The U.S. Tire Industry. *Ind. Relat.*, Fall 1986, *25*(3), pp. 229–47. [G: U.S.]

Katz, Harry C. Management Approaches to Collective Bargaining: The Dynamics of Change in the U.S.: Discussion. **In** *Dennis, B. D., ed.*, 1986, pp. 179–80. [G: U.S.]

Kaufman, Roger T. and Woglom, Geoffrey. The Degree of Indexation in Major U.S. Union Contracts. *Ind. Lab. Relat. Rev.*, April 1986, *39*(3), pp. 439–48. [G: U.S.]

Knight, Thomas R. Feedback and Grievance Resolution. *Ind. Lab. Relat. Rev.*, July 1986, *39*(4), pp. 585–98. **[G: U.S.]**

Kochan, Thomas A. and Katz, Harry C. Collective Bargaining, Work Organization, and Worker Participation: The Return of Plant-Level Bargaining. **In** *Reynolds, L. G.; Masters, S. H. and Moser, C. H., eds.*, 1986, *1983*, pp. 453–58.

Kymn, Kern O. and Palomba, Catherine A. The Strike Experience Model: Adaptive Expectations Applied to Strikes. *J. Behav. Econ.*, Spring/Summer 1986, *15*(1/2), pp. 135–48. **[G: U.S.]**

Leibenstein, Harvey. Intra-firm Effort Decisions and Sanctions: Hierarchy versus Peers. **In** *Gilad, B. and Kaish, S., eds., Vol. A*, 1986, pp. 213–31.

Leopold, J. W. and Beaumont, P. B. Trade Unions, Consultation and Redundancies. **In** *Danson, M., ed.*, 1986, pp. 159–67. **[G: U.K.]**

Liberty, Susan E. and Zimmerman, Jerold L. Labor Union Contract Negotiations and Accounting Choices. *Accounting Rev.*, October 1986, *61*(4), pp. 692–712. **[G: U.S.]**

Maki, Dennis R. The Effect of the Cost of Strikes on the Volume of Strike Activity. *Ind. Lab. Relat. Rev.*, July 1986, *39*(4), pp. 552–63. **[G: Canada]**

Mangum, Garth L.; Mangum, Stephen L. and Kim, Sae Young. The High Cost of Peace in Steel. *Challenge*, July/Aug. 1986, *29*(3), pp. 47–50. **[G: U.S.]**

Matkin, James. The Future of Industrial Relations in Canada. *Can. Public Policy*, Supp. February 1986, *12*, pp. 127–32. **[G: Canada]**

Mishel, Lawrence R. The Structural Determinants of Union Bargaining Power. *Ind. Lab. Relat. Rev.*, October 1986, *40*(1), pp. 90–104. **[G: U.S.]**

Mitchell, Daniel J. B. Union vs. Nonunion Wage Norm Shifts. *Amer. Econ. Rev.*, May 1986, *76*(2), pp. 249–52. **[G: U.S.]**

Owusu-Gyapong, Anthony. Alternative Estimating Techniques for Panel Data on Strike Activity. *Rev. Econ. Statist.*, August 1986, *68*(3), pp. 526–31. **[G: Canada]**

Palmer, Gill. Donavan, the Commission of Industrial Relations and Post-Liberal Rationalisation. *Brit. J. Ind. Relat.*, July 1986, *24*(2), pp. 267–96. **[G: U.K.]**

Reynolds, Joy K. Steelworkers Press Organizing and Coordinated Bargaining. *Mon. Lab. Rev.*, November 1986, *109*(11), pp. 48–49.

Rose, Joseph B. Legislative Support for Multi-employer Bargaining: The Canadian Experience. *Ind. Lab. Relat. Rev.*, October 1986, *40*(1), pp. 3–18. **[G: Canada]**

Rosow, Jerome M. Teamwork: Pros, Cons, and Prospects for the Future. **In** *Rosow, J. M., ed.*, 1986, pp. 3–11. **[G: U.S.]**

Ruben, George. Labor and Management Continue to Combat Mutual Problems in 1985. *Mon. Lab. Rev.*, January 1986, *109*(1), pp. 3–15. **[G: U.S.]**

Schlein, David J.; Brown, Phyllis I. and Sleemi, Fehmida. Collective Bargaining during 1986: Pressures to Curb Costs Remain. *Mon. Lab. Rev.*, January 1986, *109*(1), pp. 16–33. **[G: U.S.]**

Schwartz, Stephen. Holdings on the 1934 West Coast Maritime Strike in the San Francisco Headquarters Archive, Sailors' Union of the Pacific: A Descriptive Summary. *Labor Hist.*, Summer 1986, *27*(3), pp. 427–30. **[G: U.S.]**

Simpson, Wayne. Unions, Industrial Concentration and Wages: A Re-examination. *Appl. Econ.*, March 1986, *18*(3), pp. 305–17. **[G: Canada]**

Sockell, Donna. The Scope of Mandatory Bargaining: A Critique and a Proposal. *Ind. Lab. Relat. Rev.*, October 1986, *40*(1), pp. 19–34. **[G: U.S.]**

Sweeney, John J. Collective Bargaining's Role in the Determination of Family Policy. **In** *Hewlett, S. A.; Ilchman, A. S. and Sweeney, J. J., eds.*, 1986, pp. 17–22. **[G: U.S.]**

Tracy, Joseph S. An Investigation into the Determinants of U.S. Strike Activity. *Amer. Econ. Rev.*, June 1986, *76*(3), pp. 423–36. **[G: U.S.]**

Voos, Paula B. Cooperative Labor Relations and the Collective Bargaining Environment. **In** *Dennis, B. D., ed.*, 1986, pp. 287–95. **[G: U.S.]**

Walsh, John M. Sources of Labor Market Data from BNA. **In** *Dennis, B. D., ed.*, 1986, pp. 26–33. **[G: U.S.]**

Williams, Lynn. Collective Bargaining Prospects. **In** *Dennis, B. D., ed.*, 1986, pp. 14–25. **[G: U.S.]**

8322 Collective Bargaining in the Public Sector

Becker, Brian E. and Olson, Craig A. The Impact of Strikes on Shareholder Equity. *Ind. Lab. Relat. Rev.*, April 1986, *39*(3), pp. 425–38. **[G: U.S.]**

Cousineau, Jean-Michel and Lacroix, Robert. Imperfect Information and Strikes: An Analysis of Canadian Experience, 1967–82. *Ind. Lab. Relat. Rev.*, April 1986, *39*(3), pp. 377–87. **[G: Canada]**

Delaney, John Thomas. Impasses and Teacher Contract Outcomes. *Ind. Relat.*, Winter 1986, *25*(1), pp. 45–55. **[G: U.S.]**

Delaney, John Thomas; Feuille, Peter and Hendricks, Wallace. The Regulation of Bargaining Disputes: A Cost–Benefit Analysis of Interest Arbitration in the Public Sector. **In** *Lipsky, D. B. and Lewin, D., eds.*, 1986, pp. 83–118. **[G: U.S.]**

Eberts, Randall W. and Stone, Joe A. On the Contract Curve: A Test of Alternative Models of Collective Bargaining. *J. Lab. Econ.*, January 1986, *4*(1), pp. 66–81. **[G: U.S.]**

Feuille, Peter and Delaney, John Thomas. Collective Bargaining, Interest Arbitration, and Police Salaries. *Ind. Lab. Relat. Rev.*, January 1986, *39*(2), pp. 228–40. **[G: U.S.]**

Freeman, Richard B. Unionism Comes to the Public Sector. *J. Econ. Lit.*, March 1986, *24*(1), pp. 41–86. **[G: U.S.]**

Garnett, Tom. Scope of Bargaining in the Federal Sector: A Management View. **In** *Dennis, B. D., ed.*, 1986, pp. 378–83. **[G: U.S.]**

Goldschmidt, Steven M. and Stuart, Leland E. The Extent and Impact of Educational Policy Bargaining. *Ind. Lab. Relat. Rev.*, April 1986, *39*(3), pp. 350–60. **[G: U.S.]**

Gramm, Cynthia L. The Determinants of Strike Incidence and Severity: A Micro-level Study. *Ind. Lab. Relat. Rev.*, April 1986, *39*(3), pp. 361–76. **[G: U.S.]**

Herman, E. Edward and Leftwich, Howard M. Mediation and Fact-Finding under the 1983 Ohio Public Employee Collective Bargaining Act. **In** *Dennis, B. D., ed.*, 1986, pp. 316–23. **[G: U.S.]**

Horton, Raymond D. Fiscal Stress and Labor Power. **In** *Dennis, B. D., ed.*, 1986, pp. 304–15. **[G: U.S.]**

Hunt, Janet C., et al. Wages, Union Membership, and Public Sector Bargaining Legislation: Simultaneous Equations with an Ordinal Qualitative Variable. *J. Lab. Res.*, Summer 1986, *7*(3), pp. 255–67. **[G: U.S.]**

Karim, Ahmad and Stone, Thomas H. Mediation Outcomes and Sources of Impasse: An Empirical Investigation. *J. Lab. Res.*, Summer 1986, *7*(3), pp. 309–18. **[G: Bangladesh]**

Lampert, Nick. Job Security and the Law in the USSR. **In** *Lane, D., ed.*, 1986, pp. 256–77. **[G: U.S.S.R.]**

Lewin, David. Public Employee Unionism in the 1980s: An Analysis of Transformation. **In** *Lipset, S. M., ed.*, 1986, pp. 241–64. **[G: U.S.]**

Loewenberg, J. Joseph. What's $13 Billion among Friends? The 1984 Postal Arbitration. **In** *Dennis, B. D., ed.*, 1986, pp. 369–77. **[G: U.S.]**

Martin, James E. Predictors of Individual Propensity to Strike. *Ind. Lab. Relat. Rev.*, January 1986, *39*(2), pp. 214–27. **[G: U.S.]**

Matkin, James. The Future of Industrial Relations in Canada. *Can. Public Policy*, Supp. February 1986, *12*, pp. 127–32. **[G: Canada]**

Northrup, Herbert R. Reply [The Rise and Demise of PATCO]. *Ind. Lab. Relat. Rev.*, October 1986, *40*(1), pp. 122–27. **[G: U.S.]**

Olson, Craig A. Strikes, Strike Penalties, and Arbitration in Six States. *Ind. Lab. Relat. Rev.*, July 1986, *39*(4), pp. 539–51. **[G: U.S.]**

Ruben, George. Labor and Management Continue to Combat Mutual Problems in 1985. *Mon. Lab. Rev.*, January 1986, *109*(1), pp. 3–15. **[G: U.S.]**

Saunders, George. Impact of Interest Arbitration on Canadian Federal Employees' Wages. *Ind. Relat.*, Fall 1986, *25*(3), pp. 320–27. **[G: Canada]**

Schlein, David J.; Brown, Phyllis I. and Sleemi, Fehmida. Collective Bargaining during 1986: Pressures to Curb Costs Remain. *Mon. Lab. Rev.*, January 1986, *109*(1), pp. 16–33. **[G: U.S.]**

833 Labor–Management Relations

8330 General

Albåge, Lars-Gunnar. Recents Trends in Collective Bargaining in Sweden. An Employer's View. *Int. Lab. Rev.*, Jan.-Feb. 1986, *125*(1), pp. 107–18. **[G: Sweden]**

Banderet, M. E. Discipline at the Workplace: A Comparative Study of Law and Practice: 1. The Sources and Substance of Disciplinary Law. *Int. Lab. Rev.*, May-June 1986, *125*(3), pp. 261–78. **[G: OECD]**

Barrère-Maurisson, Marie-Agnès. Gestion de la main-d'œuvre et formes familiales: du paternalisme à la recherche de flexiblité. (Labour Force Management and Family Forms: From Paternalism to a Search for Flexibility. With English summary.) *Écon. Soc.*, April 1986, *20*(4), pp. 165–86.

Barsky, A. D. and Belagurova, E. A. Toward an Analysis of the Principles Governing the Formation of Material Incentive Funds. *Matekon*, Spring 1986, *22*(3), pp. 91–110. **[G: U.S.S.R.]**

Batstone, Eric. Bureaucracy, Oligarchy, and Incorporation in Shop Steward Organisations in the 1980s. **In** *Jacobi, O., et al., eds. (I)*, 1986, pp. 137–60. **[G: U.S.]**

Block, Richard N. and Wolkinson, Benjamin W. Delay in the Union Election Campaign Revisited: A Theoretical and Empirical Analysis. **In** *Lipsky, D. B. and Lewin, D., eds.*, 1986, pp. 43–81. **[G: U.S.]**

Bloom, David E. Empirical Models of Arbitrator Behavior under Conventional Arbitration. *Rev. Econ. Statist.*, November 1986, *68*(4), pp. 578–85. **[G: U.S.]**

Cable, John. Worker Participation and Productivity—An Econometric Analysis: Comment [Mitarbeiterbeteiligung bei deutschen Industrieaktiengesellschaften—Ein Kommentar]. *Z. Betriebswirtshaft*, Apr.-May 1986, *56*(4/5), pp. 435–43. **[G: W. Germany]**

Charlesworth, Andrew. Atlas of Industrializing Britain 1780–1914: Labour Protest 1780–1850. **In** *Langton, J. and Morris, R. J., eds.*, 1986, pp. 185–89. **[G: U.K.]**

Crouch, Colin. Conservative Industrial Relations Policy: Towards Labour Exclusion? **In** *Jacobi, O., et al., eds. (II)*, 1986, pp. 131–53. **[G: U.K.]**

Damachi, Ukandi G. Industrial Relations: A Development Dilemma. **In** *Damachi, U. G. and Seibel, H. D., eds.*, 1986, pp. 115–45. **[G: Africa]**

Date-Bah, Eugenia. Contemporary Industrial Relations Problems in Ghana 1972–1979. **In** *Damachi, U. G. and Seibel, H. D., eds.*, 1986, pp. 159–70. **[G: Ghana]**

Deakin, Simon. Labour Law and the Developing Employment Relationship in the UK. *Cambridge J. Econ.*, September 1986, *10*(3), pp. 225–46.

Deutsch, Steven. International Experiences with

Technological Change. *Mon. Lab. Rev.*, March 1986, *109*(3), pp. 36–40. **[G: OECD]**

Dunlop, John T. A Decade of National Experience. **In** *Rosow, J. M., ed.*, 1986, pp. 12–25. **[G: U.S.]**

Ebel, Karl-H. The Impact of Industrial Robots on the World of Work. *Int. Lab. Rev.*, Jan.-Feb. 1986, *125*(1), pp. 39–51. **[G: W. Europe; U.S.]**

Favereau, Olivier. Compétitivité et emploi: trois niveaux d'analyse, trois paradoxes. (Competitivity and Employment: Three Levels of Analysis, Three Paradoxes. With English summary.) *Écon. Soc.*, January 1986, *20*(1), pp. 69–90.

FitzRoy, Felix R. and Kraft, Kornelius. Participation and Productivity: Issues of Methodology and Stability [Mitarbeiterbeteiligung bei deutschen Industrieaktiengesellschaften—Ein Kommentar]. *Z. Betriebswirtshaft*, Apr.-May 1986, *56*(4/5), pp. 444–51. **[G: W. Germany]**

Garonna, Paolo and Ryan, Paul. Youth Labour, Industrial Relations and Deregulation in Advanced Economies. *Econ. Lavoro*, Oct.-Dec. 1986, *20*(4), pp. 3–19. **[G: U.S.; U.K.; Italy]**

Hewlett, Sylvia Ann. Family and Work: Bridging the Gap: Conclusions: A Policy Agenda for the United States. **In** *Hewlett, S. A.; Ilchman, A. S. and Sweeney, J. J., eds.*, 1986, pp. 187–91. **[G: U.S.]**

Holland, David C. Self-management in Poland since Martial Law. *Econ. Anal. Workers' Manage.*, 1986, *20*(3), pp. 275–306. **[G: Poland]**

Hollander, Abraham and Lacroix, Robert. Unionism, Information Disclosure and Profit-sharing. *Southern Econ. J.*, January 1986, *52*(3), pp. 706–17.

Hyman, Richard. British Industrial Relations: The Limits of Corporatism. **In** *Jacobi, O., et al., eds. (II)*, 1986, pp. 79–104. **[G: U.K.]**

Jacoby, Sanford M. Progressive Discipline in American Industry: Its Origins, Development, and Consequences. **In** *Lipsky, D. B. and Lewin, D., eds.*, 1986, pp. 213–60. **[G: U.K.; U.S.]**

Jones, Derek C. The Scope and Nature of Feasible Initiatives in Workplace Democratization and Participation. **In** *Nolan, P. and Paine, S., eds.*, 1986, pp. 270–83. **[G: U.K.]**

Kamerman, Sheila B. Maternity, Paternity, and Parenting Policies: How Does the United States Compare? **In** *Hewlett, S. A.; Ilchman, A. S. and Sweeney, J. J., eds.*, 1986, pp. 53–65. **[G: U.S.]**

Kerr, Clark. A New Industrial Relations? A Four- (or Perhaps Six-) Sector Approach to an Answer. **In** *Rosow, J. M., ed.*, 1986, pp. xi–xvi. **[G: U.S.]**

Knight, Thomas R. Feedback and Grievance Resolution. *Ind. Lab. Relat. Rev.*, July 1986, *39*(4), pp. 585–98. **[G: U.S.]**

Labig, Chalmer E., Jr. and Helburn, I. B. Union and Management Policy Influences on Grievance Initiation. *J. Lab. Res.*, Summer 1986, *7*(3), pp. 269–84. **[G: U.S.]**

Lagergren, Stina. The Influence of ILO Standards on Swedish Law and Practice. *Int. Lab. Rev.*, May-June 1986, *125*(3), pp. 305–28. **[G: Sweden]**

Landes, David S. What Do Bosses Really Do? *J. Econ. Hist.*, September 1986, *46*(3), pp. 585–623. **[G: U.K.]**

Lewin, David and Lipsky, David B. Current Research on Industrial Relations Regulation, Bargaining Theory, Progressive Discipline, and Occupational Influences on Unionism. **In** *Lipsky, D. B. and Lewin, D., eds.*, 1986, pp. 1–19.

Lovell, Malcolm R., Jr. Obstacles to Competitiveness: A Challenge to Labor and Management. **In** *Burton, D. F., et al., eds.*, 1986, pp. 105–17. **[G: U.S.]**

Luker, Stuart. Teaching Economics to the 16–19 Age Range: Industrial Relations. **In** *Whitehead, D. J., ed.*, 1986, pp. 187–93.

Magid, Alvin. Industrial Democracy and Reindustrialization: Cross-Cultural Perspectives. **In** *Schoolman, M. and Magid, A., eds.*, 1986, pp. 377–96. **[G: U.S.; Sweden; Spain; Yugoslavia]**

Marshall, Ray. America and Japan: Industrial Relations in a Time of Change. **In** *Lipset, S. M., ed.*, 1986, pp. 133–49. **[G: Japan; U.S.]**

Marshall, Ray. Employment and Industrial Relations. **In** *Burton, D. F., et al., eds.*, 1986, pp. 27–43. **[G: OECD]**

McIntosh, Barbara. Accident Compensation as a Factor Influencing Managerial Perceptions and Behavior in New Zealand. **In** *Chelius, J., ed.*, 1986, pp. 347–72. **[G: New Zealand]**

Osterman, Paul. Technology and White-Collar Employment: A Research Strategy. **In** *Dennis, B. D., ed.*, 1986, pp. 52–59. **[G: U.S.]**

Panitch, Leo. The Importance of Workers' Control for Revolutionary Change. **In** *Panitch, L.*, 1986, *1977*, pp. 215–24.

Piore, Michael J. Perspectives on Labor Market Flexibility. *Ind. Relat.*, Spring 1986, *25*(2), pp. 146–66. **[G: U.S.; W. Europe]**

Remer, Andreas. Personnel Management in Western Europe—Development, Situation and Concepts. **In** *Macharzina, K. and Staehle, W. H., eds.*, 1986, pp. 351–67. **[G: W. Europe]**

Roberts, Markley. A Labor Agenda for Jobs. **In** *Burton, D. F., et al., eds.*, 1986, pp. 119–33. **[G: U.S.]**

Rzhanitsyna, L. Intensifying the Stimulation of the Effectiveness of Labor. *Prob. Econ.*, May 1986, *29*(1), pp. 50–62. **[G: U.S.S.R.]**

Salisbury, Dallas L. and Witte, Hazel A. Employee Benefits and Assistance to Working Parents. **In** *Hewlett, S. A.; Ilchman, A. S. and Sweeney, J. J., eds.*, 1986, pp. 125–37. **[G: U.S.]**

Scitovsky, Tibor. Inequalities: Open and Hidden, Measured and Unmeasurable. **In** *Scitovsky, T.*, 1986, *1973*, pp. 26–34.

Shaw, Paul F. Saudi Arabian Manpower Requirements. **In** *Roukis, G. S. and Montana, P. J., eds.*, 1986, pp. 95–112. **[G: Saudi Arabia]**

Shimada, Haruo. Japan's Postwar Industrial

Growth and Labor–Management Relations. **In** *Reynolds, L. G.; Masters, S. H. and Moser, C. H., eds.*, 1986, *1982*, pp. 468–73. **[G: Japan]**

Strümpel, Burkhard and Yuchtman-Yaar, E. Collective Values and Involvement in the Economy. **In** *Gilad, B. and Kaish, S., eds., Vol. B*, 1986, pp. 215–32. **[G: W. Germany; Israel]**

Szul, Roman. Workers' Self-management in Poland. *Econ. Anal. Workers' Manage.*, 1986, *20*(2), pp. 169–93. **[G: Poland]**

Tarantelli, Ezio. Erratum [The Regulation of Inflation and Unemployment]. *Ind. Relat.*, Spring 1986, *25*(2), pp. 94. **[G: OECD]**

Tarantelli, Ezio. The Regulation of Inflation and Unemployment. *Ind. Relat.*, Winter 1986, *25*(1), pp. 1–15. **[G: OECD]**

Urry, John. Capitalist Production, Scientific Management and the Service Class. **In** *Scott, A. J. and Storper, M., eds.*, 1986, pp. 43–66. **[G: U.S.; U.K.]**

Wahba, Mohamed A. and Al-Musfir, Muhammad S. Managing Human Resources in the United Arab Emirates: A Review of Trends and Problems. **In** *Roukis, G. S. and Montana, P. J., eds.*, 1986, pp. 157–68. **[G: United Arab Emirates]**

Weesie, Jeroen and Wippler, Reinhard. Cumulative Effects of Sequential Decisions in Organizations. **In** *[Rapoport, A.]*, 1986, pp. 257–79.

8331 Labor–Management Relations in the Private Sector

Addison, John T. Job Security in the United States: Law, Collective Bargaining, Policy, and Practice. *Brit. J. Ind. Relat.*, November 1986, *24*(3), pp. 381–418. **[G: U.S.]**

Banderet, M. E. Discipline at the Workplace: A Comparative Study of Law and Practice: 2. Procedure. *Int. Lab. Rev.*, July-Aug. 1986, *125*(4), pp. 383–99.

Blinder, Alan S. Macroeconomic Implications of Profit Sharing: Comment. **In** *Fischer, S., ed.*, 1986, pp. 335–43. **[G: Japan]**

Bluestone, Irving. Changes in U.S. Labor–Management Relations. **In** *Dennis, B. D., ed.*, 1986, pp. 165–70.

Bluestone, Irving. Joint Action and Collective Bargaining—and Vice Versa. **In** *Rosow, J. M., ed.*, 1986, pp. 41–55. **[G: U.S.]**

Blumestock, James W. and Thomchick, Evelyn A. Deregulation and Airline Labor Relations. *Logist. Transp. Rev.*, December 1986, *22*(4), pp. 389–403. **[G: U.S.]**

Boyle, Fosten A. An Evolving Process of Participation: Honeywell and Teamsters Local 1145. **In** *Rosow, J. M., ed.*, 1986, pp. 146–68. **[G: U.S.]**

Boylston, Benjamin C. Employee Involvement and Cultural Change at Bethlehem Steel. **In** *Rosow, J. M., ed.*, 1986, pp. 89–109. **[G: U.S.]**

Brera, Paolo. Austro-Keynesism in a Monetarist Decade: Or, Will Austria's 'Social Partnership' Live through the 1980s? (With a Game Theory Postscript). *Rivista Int. Sci. Econ. Com.*, June-July 1986, *33*(6–7), pp. 667–84. **[G: Austria]**

Brown, Martin and Philips, Peter. The Decline of the Piece-Rate System in California Canning: Technological Innovation, Labor Management, and Union Pressure, 1890–1947. *Bus. Hist. Rev.*, Winter 1986, *60*(4), pp. 564–601. **[G: U.S.]**

Brumlop, Eva and Juergens, Ulrich. Rationalisation and Industrial Relations: A Case Study of Volkswagen. **In** *Jacobi, O., et al., eds. (I)*, 1986, pp. 73–94. **[G: W. Germany]**

Burge, James D. Worksharing: A "Win-Win" Concept. **In** *Burton, D. F., et al., eds.*, 1986, pp. 135–45. **[G: U.S.]**

Butera, Federico and Della Rocca, Giuseppe. Technological Innovation, Organisation of Work, and Unions. **In** *Jacobi, O., et al., eds. (I)*, 1986, pp. 15–34. **[G: Italy]**

Camens, Sam. Labor–Management Participation Teams in the Basic Steel Industry. **In** *Rosow, J. M., ed.*, 1986, pp. 110–18. **[G: U.S.]**

Campbell, Duncan C. U.S. Firms and Black Labor in South Africa: Creating a Structure for Change. *J. Lab. Res.*, Winter 1986, *7*(1), pp. 1–18. **[G: S. Africa]**

Cappelli, Peter and Chalykoff, John. The Effects of Management Industrial Relations Strategy: Results of a Recent Survey. **In** *Dennis, B. D., ed.*, 1986, pp. 171–78. **[G: U.S.]**

Clark, Gordon L. Restructuring the U.S. Economy: The NLRB, the Saturn Project, and Economic Justice. *Econ. Geogr.*, October 1986, *62*(4), pp. 289–306. **[G: U.S.]**

Clunies Ross, Anthony. Wages and Shares: Review Article. *J. Econ. Stud.*, 1986, *13*(2), pp. 65–70.

Cooper, Russell. Macroeconomic Implications of Profit Sharing: Comment. **In** *Fischer, S., ed.*, 1986, pp. 343–51. **[G: Japan]**

Córdova, Efrén. From Full-time Wage Employment to Atypical Employment: A Major Shift in the Evolution of Labour Relations? *Int. Lab. Rev.*, Nov.-Dec. 1986, *125*(6), pp. 641–57.

Coyne, John. Divestment by Management Buy-Out: Variant and Variety. **In** *Coyne, J. and Wright, M., eds.*, 1986, pp. 140–65. **[G: U.K.]**

Curtin, William J. Airline Labor Relations under Deregulation. **In** *Dennis, B. D., ed.*, 1986, pp. 158–64. **[G: U.S.]**

Dale, Barrie. Experience with Quality Circles and Quality Costs. **In** *Moores, B., ed.*, 1986, pp. 36–49. **[G: U.K.]**

Dalton, Amy H. and Marcis, John G. The Determinants of Job Satisfaction for Young Males and Females. *Atlantic Econ. J.*, September 1986, *14*(3), pp. 85. **[G: U.S.]**

Damachi, Ukandi G. Workers' Participation in Management. **In** *Damachi, U. G. and Seibel, H. D., eds.*, 1986, pp. 315–30. **[G: Nigeria]**

Damachi, Ukandi G. and Seibel, Hans Dieter. Workers' Participation in Technological and Organisational Development: The Human Resources for a Suggestion Programme in Nige-

rian Industry. **In** *Damachi, U. G. and Seibel, H. D., eds.*, 1986, pp. 69–85. **[G: Nigeria]**
Davis, Evan H. Profit Sharing and Employee Share Ownership. *Fisc. Stud.*, May 1986, *7*(2), pp. 54–62. **[G: U.K.]**
Defourny, Jacques. The Economic Performance of Self-Managed Firms: A Comparative Perspective. *Ann. Pub. Co-op. Econ.*, Jan.-March 1986, *57*(1), pp. 3–9.
Doeringer, Peter B.; Moss, Philip I. and Terkla, David G. Capitalism and Kinship: Do Institutions Matter in the Labor Market? *Ind. Lab. Relat. Rev.*, October 1986, *40*(1), pp. 48–60. **[G: U.S.]**
Drago, Robert. Participatory Management in Capitalist Firms: An Analysis of "Quality Circles." *Econ. Anal. Workers' Manage.*, 1986, *20*(3), pp. 233–49. **[G: U.S.]**
Drago, Robert. Quality Circles: Lessons from the United States. *Australian Bull. Lab.*, September 1986, *12*(4), pp. 244–51. **[G: U.S.]**
Ekpo-Ufot, Abel. Personnel Functions, Practices and Productivity in Nigeria. **In** *Damachi, U. G. and Seibel, H. D., eds.*, 1986, pp. 292–314. **[G: Nigeria]**
Ellerman, David P. Horizon Problems and Property Rights in Labor-Managed Firms. *J. Compar. Econ.*, March 1986, *10*(1), pp. 62–78.
Ephlin, Donald F. United Auto Workers: Pioneers in Labor–Management Partnership. **In** *Rosow, J. M., ed.*, 1986, pp. 133–45. **[G: U.S.]**
Extejt, Marian M. Contributed Papers: Organizational Behavior and Personnel: Discussion. **In** *Dennis, B. D., ed.*, 1986, pp. 108–11.
Farrell, Judy. Corporate Concern for Working Parents. **In** *Hewlett, S. A.; Ilchman, A. S. and Sweeney, J. J., eds.*, 1986, pp. 169–78.
Fashoyin, Tayo. Management of Industrial Conflict in Africa: A Comparative Analysis of Kenya, Nigeria and Tanzania. **In** *Damachi, U. G. and Seibel, H. D., eds.*, 1986, pp. 171–211. **[G: Nigeria; Kenya; Tanzania]**
Filer, Randall K. People and Productivity: Effort Supply as Viewed by Economists and Psychologists. **In** *Gilad, B. and Kaish, S., eds., Vol. A*, 1986, pp. 261–87.
FitzRoy, Felix R. and Kraft, Kornelius. Profitability and Profit-Sharing. *J. Ind. Econ.*, December 1986, *35*(2), pp. 113–30. **[G: W. Germany]**
Flisfisch, Angel. Reflexiones algo oblicuas sobre el tema de la concertación. (With English summary.) *Desarrollo Econ.*, Apr.-June 1986, *26*(101), pp. 3–20. **[G: Latin America]**
Fones-Wolf, Elizabeth. Industrial Recreation, the Second World War, and the Revival of Welfare Capitalism, 1934–1960. *Bus. Hist. Rev.*, Summer 1986, *60*(2), pp. 232–57. **[G: U.S.]**
Franko, Lawrence G. Expansion of Japanese Companies Abroad: The Management of Cross-Cultural Interface: Comment. **In** *Pugel, T. A., ed.*, 1986, pp. 201–05. **[G: U.S.; Japan]**
Fraser, Douglas A. A Labor Director Looks at the Board. **In** *Rosow, J. M., ed.*, 1986, pp. 56–72. **[G: U.S.]**
Freeman, Richard B. The Effect of the Union Wage Differential on Management Opposition and Union Organizing Success. *Amer. Econ. Rev.*, May 1986, *76*(2), pp. 92–96. **[G: U.S.]**
Gärtner, Manfred and Heri, Erwin W. Causes and Consequences of Labor Militancy or The Common Factor in Industrial Conflict and Unionization Dynamics. *Rivista Int. Sci. Econ. Com.*, December 1986, *33*(12), pp. 1185–1205. **[G: W. Germany]**
Gilardi, Jean-Claude. Le détermination des critères de choix utilsés par le travailleur. (The Determination of the Criteria Influencing Worker's Choice. With English summary.) *Écon. Soc.*, December 1986, *20*(12), pp. 155–86.
Gitlow, Abraham L. and Gitlow, Howard S. Labor–Management Relations: A Vital Piece of the Quality Puzzle. *Rivista Int. Sci. Econ. Com.*, June-July 1986, *33*(6–7), pp. 545–64.
Gospel, Howard F. Comparative Patterns of Labor–Management Relations: Great Britain, the U.S., and Japan. **In** *Atack, J., ed.*, 1986, pp. 119–31. **[G: U.S.; U.K.; Japan]**
Granrose, Cherlyn Skromme; Appelbaum, Eileen and Singh, Virendra. Saving Jobs through Worker Buyouts: Economic and Qualitative Outcomes for Workers in Worker-Owned, QWL, and Non-QWL Supermarkets. **In** *Dennis, B. D., ed.*, 1986, pp. 196–204. **[G: U.S.]**
Guest, David E. Workers' Participation and Personnel Policy in the United Kingdom: Some Case Studies. *Int. Lab. Rev.*, Nov.-Dec. 1986, *125*(6), pp. 685–702. **[G: U.K.]**
Guimaræs, Roberto P. Co-operativism and Popular Participation: New Considerations Regarding an Old Subject. *CEPAL Rev.*, April 1986, (28), pp. 187–201. **[G: Latin America]**
Gunn, Christopher. Workers' Self-management in the United States: Contemporary Cases and Comments. *Econ. Anal. Workers' Manage.*, 1986, *20*(4), pp. 337–56. **[G: U.S.]**
Gustavsen, Björn. Evolving Patterns of Enterprise Organisation: The Move toward Greater Flexibility. *Int. Lab. Rev.*, July-Aug. 1986, *125*(4), pp. 367–82.
Hammer, Tove H. The History of the Rath Buyout: A Role Expectations Analysis. **In** *Dennis, B. D., ed.*, 1986, pp. 205–13. **[G: U.S.]**
Hammer, Tove H. and Stern, Robert N. A Yo-Yo Model of Cooperation: Union Participation in Management at the Rath Packing Company. *Ind. Lab. Relat. Rev.*, April 1986, *39*(3), pp. 337–49. **[G: U.S.]**
Hashi, Iraj and Hussain, Athar. The Employee Investment Funds in Sweden. *Nat. Westminster Bank Quart. Rev.*, May 1986, pp. 17–27. **[G: Sweden]**
Hayashi, Kichiro. Expansion of Japanese Companies Abroad: The Management of Cross-Cultural Interface. **In** *Pugel, T. A., ed.*, 1986, pp. 175–99. **[G: Japan; U.S.]**
Helfgott, Roy B. America's Third Industrial Revolution. *Challenge*, Nov./Dec. 1986, *29*(5), pp. 41–46. **[G: U.S.]**
Heneman, Robert L. Contributed Papers: Orga-

nizational Behavior and Personnel: Discussion. In *Dennis, B. D., ed.*, 1986, pp. 104–07.

Himmelstrand, Ulf; Brulin, Göran and Swedberg, Richard. Control, Motivation, and Structure: The "New Managerial Philosophies" vs. Industrial Democracy. *Econ. Anal. Workers' Manage.*, 1986, *20*(1), pp. 1–21. **[G: Sweden]**

Hobson, Charles J. and Dworkin, James B. West German Labor Unrest: Are Unions Losing Ground to Worker Councils? *Mon. Lab. Rev.*, February 1986, *109*(2), pp. 46–48. **[G: W. Germany]**

Horvat, Branko. Industrial Partnership: Utopia or Necessity? *Econ. Anal. Workers' Manage.*, 1986, *20*(3), pp. 251–55.

Hyde, Charles K. Undercover and Underground: Labor Spies and Mine Management in the Early Twentieth Century. *Bus. Hist. Rev.*, Spring 1986, *60*(1), pp. 1–27. **[G: U.S.]**

Iwuji, Eleazar C. Peaceful Settlement of Trade Disputes. In *Damachi, U. G. and Seibel, H. D., eds.*, 1986, pp. 146–58. **[G: Nigeria]**

Jacoby, Sanford M. Employee Attitude Testing at Sears, Roebuck and Company, 1938–1960. *Bus. Hist. Rev.*, Winter 1986, *60*(4), pp. 602–32. **[G: U.S.]**

Jones, Ian S. Apprentice Training Costs in British Manufacturing Establishments: Some New Evidence. *Brit. J. Ind. Relat.*, November 1986, *24*(3), pp. 333–62. **[G: U.K.]**

Jossa, Bruno. Considerazioni su di un "tipo ideale" di cooperativi di produzione. (With English summary.) *Stud. Econ.*, 1986, *41*(28), pp. 3–22.

Kastendiek, Hans; Kastendiek, Hella and Reister, Hugo. Institutional Strategies for Trade Union Participation: An Assessment of the Incorporation Thesis. In *Jacobi, O., et al., eds. (II)*, 1986, pp. 258–87. **[G: W. Germany]**

Katz, Harry C. Management Approaches to Collective Bargaining: The Dynamics of Change in the U.S.: Discussion. In *Dennis, B. D., ed.*, 1986, pp. 179–80. **[G: U.S.]**

Kochan, Thomas A.; McKersie, Robert B. and Chalykoff, John. The Effects of Corporate Strategy and Workplace Innovations on Union Representation. *Ind. Lab. Relat. Rev.*, July 1986, *39*(4), pp. 487–501. **[G: U.S.]**

Kraft, Philip and Dubnoff, Steven. Job Content, Fragmentation, and Control in Computer Software Work. *Ind. Relat.*, Spring 1986, *25*(2), pp. 184–96. **[G: U.S.]**

Leahey, Philip J. Skilled Labor and the Rise of the Modern Corporation: The Case of the Electrical Industry. *Labor Hist.*, Winter 1985-86, *27*(1), pp. 31–53. **[G: U.S.]**

Lee, Dwight R. Union Myopia and the Taxation of Capital. In *Lee, D. R., ed.*, 1986, pp. 297–322. **[G: U.S.]**

Leibenstein, Harvey. Intra-firm Effort Decisions and Sanctions: Hierarchy versus Peers. In *Gilad, B. and Kaish, S., eds., Vol. A*, 1986, pp. 213–31.

Leibig, Michael T. The Deprivitization of Employee Benefit and Labor Law: The Surprising Conservative Erosion of Trusts and of the Competitive Labor Model. *Law Contemp. Probl.*, Autumn 1986, *49*(4), pp. 183–209. **[G: U.S.]**

Leijon, Anna-Greta. Labor–Management Relations and the Jobs Problem: The Swedish Experience. In *Burton, D. F., et al., eds.*, 1986, pp. 175–86. **[G: Sweden]**

Livingston, Craig H. Capital Strategies for Labor. In *Dennis, B. D., ed.*, 1986, pp. 221–26. **[G: U.S.]**

Maij-Weggen, Hanja R. H. Actions of the European Parliament in Favour of Women in Small Business. In *Donckels, R. and Meijer, J. N., eds.*, 1986, pp. 10–15. **[G: W. Europe]**

Maruo, Naomi. The Development of the Welfare Mix in Japan. In *Rose, R. and Shiratori, R., eds.*, 1986, pp. 64–79. **[G: Japan]**

McLewin, Philip J. The Cockroaches of Paterson: A Study of Labor Conflict and Technological Change. *Rev. Radical Polit. Econ.*, Fall 1986, *18*(3), pp. 23–43. **[G: U.S.]**

Mine, Manabu. The Social Impact of Micro-electronics in Japan. *Int. Lab. Rev.*, July-Aug. 1986, *125*(4), pp. 473–97. **[G: Japan]**

Morishima, Motohiro. Job Satisfaction and Desire to Quit: Differences in the Determinants of Two Responses. In *Dennis, B. D., ed.*, 1986, pp. 80–91. **[G: Japan]**

Naples, Michele I. The Unraveling of the Union–Capital Truce and the U.S. Industrial Productivity Crisis. *Rev. Radical Polit. Econ.*, Spring/Summer 1986, *18*(1/2), pp. 110–31. **[G: U.S.]**

Negandhi, Anant R. Role and Structure of German Multinationals: A Comparative Profile. In *Macharzina, K. and Staehle, W. H., eds.*, 1986, pp. 51–66. **[G: W. Germany]**

Palmer, Gill. Donavan, the Commission of Industrial Relations and Post-Liberal Rationalisation. *Brit. J. Ind. Relat.*, July 1986, *24*(2), pp. 267–96. **[G: U.K.]**

Purg, Danica. Workers' Participation in Management of Enterprises in the Netherlands—Achievements and Problems. *Econ. Anal. Workers' Manage.*, 1986, *20*(1), pp. 89–100. **[G: Netherlands]**

Reagan, Patricia B. and Stulz, René M. Risk-Bearing, Labor Contracts, and Capital Markets. In *Chen, A. H., ed.*, 1986, pp. 217–31.

Rebitzer, James B. Establishment Size and Job Tenure. *Ind. Relat.*, Fall 1986, *25*(3), pp. 292–302. **[G: U.S.]**

Reid, Frank. Combatting Unemployment through Work Time Reductions. *Can. Public Policy*, June 1986, *12*(2), pp. 275–85. **[G: Canada]**

Richardson, Ray and Nejad, Aaron. Employee Share Ownership Schemes in the UK—An Evaluation. *Brit. J. Ind. Relat.*, July 1986, *24*(2), pp. 233–50. **[G: U.K.]**

Rollier, Matteo. Changes of Industrial Relations at Fiat. In *Jacobi, O., et al., eds. (I)*, 1986, pp. 116–33. **[G: Italy]**

Roos, Poul. Workers' Participation and Personnel Policy in Denmark. *Int. Lab. Rev.*, Nov.-Dec. 1986, *125*(6), pp. 703–13. **[G: Denmark]**

Rosow, Jerome M. Teamwork: Pros, Cons, and

Prospects for the Future. **In** *Rosow, J. M., ed.*, 1986, pp. 3–11. **[G: U.S.]**

Saffer, Henry. Wages and Hazardous Working Conditions. *Appl. Econ.*, August 1986, *18*(8), pp. 819–27. **[G: U.S.]**

Sass, Robert. The Need to Broaden the Legal Concept of Risk in Workplace Health and Safety. *Can. Public Policy*, June 1986, *12*(2), pp. 286–93. **[G: Canada]**

Scarbrough, Harry. The Politics of Technological Change at British Leyland. **In** *Jacobi, O., et al., eds. (I)*, 1986, pp. 95–115. **[G: U.K.]**

Schroeder, Elinor P. Legislative and Judicial Responses to the Inadequacy of Compensation for Occupational Disease. *Law Contemp. Probl.*, Autumn 1986, *49*(4), pp. 151–82. **[G: U.S.]**

Schroeder, Sandra J. and Finlay, William. Internal Labor Markets, Professional Domination, and Gender: A Comparison of Laboratory Employees in Hospitals and Chemical/Oil Firms. *Soc. Sci. Quart.*, December 1986, *67*(4), pp. 827–40. **[G: U.S.]**

Seibel, Hans Dieter. Achievement Orientation: A Case Study in Multinational Firms in Africa. **In** *Damachi, U. G. and Seibel, H. D., eds.*, 1986, pp. 215–31. **[G: Liberia]**

Shaiken, Harley; Herzenberg, Stephen and Kuhn, Sarah. The Work Process under More Flexible Production. *Ind. Relat.*, Spring 1986, *25*(2), pp. 167–83. **[G: U.S.]**

Smith, Robert Stewart. Greasing the Squeaky Wheel: The Relative Productivity of OSHA Complaint Inspections. *Ind. Lab. Relat. Rev.*, October 1986, *40*(1), pp. 35–47. **[G: U.S.]**

Staehle, Wolfgang H. Industrial Relations and Europe's Multinationals. **In** *Macharzina, K. and Staehle, W. H., eds.*, 1986, pp. 129–42. **[G: W. Europe]**

Stråth, Bo. Redundancy and Solidarity: Tripartite Politics and the Contraction of the West European Shipbuilding Industry. *Cambridge J. Econ.*, June 1986, *10*(2), pp. 147–63. **[G: W. Europe]**

Tomer, John F. Productivity and Organizational Behavior: Where Human Capital Theory Fails. **In** *Gilad, B. and Kaish, S., eds., Vol. A*, 1986, pp. 233–55.

Trowbridge, Alexander B. A Management Look at Labor Relations. **In** *Lipset, S. M., ed.*, 1986, pp. 405–18. **[G: U.S.]**

Tsurumi, Yoshi. Japanese and European Multinationals in America: A Case of Flexible Corporate Systems. **In** *Macharzina, K. and Staehle, W. H., eds.*, 1986, pp. 23–37. **[G: U.S.]**

Vratusa, Anton. Problems of Labour Participation, with Particular Reference to the System of Self-management in Yugoslavia. **In** *U.N., Dept. of Technical Co-operation for Development*, 1986, pp. 246–60. **[G: Yugoslavia]**

Warren, Alfred S. Quality of Work Life at General Motors. **In** *Rosow, J. M., ed.*, 1986, pp. 119–32. **[G: U.S.]**

Watanabe, Takehiko and Mochizuki, Hiroshi. Perception Gap between the U.S. and Japan: Delegation and Sharing of Authority and Responsibility. **In** *Finn, R. B., ed.*, 1986, pp. 85–100. **[G: U.S.; Japan]**

Weitz, Eric D. Class Formation and Labor Protest in the Mining Communities of Southern Illinois and the Ruhr, 1890–1925. *Labor Hist.*, Winter 1985-86, *27*(1), pp. 85–105. **[G: U.S.; Germany]**

Weitzman, Martin L. Macroeconomic Implications of Profit Sharing. **In** *Fischer, S., ed.*, 1986, pp. 291–335. **[G: Japan]**

Whitt, J. Allen and Rothschild-Whitt, Joyce. Workers' Cooperatives: The Marxian and Non-Marxian Heritage. **In** *Jain, A. and Matejko, A., eds.*, 1986, pp. 228–44.

Williams, Raymond and Watts, Glenn. The Process of Working Together: CWA's/AT&T's Approach to QWL. **In** *Rosow, J. M., ed.*, 1986, pp. 75–88. **[G: U.S.]**

Young, Karen M. Creating the Idea of Ownership: Lessons from Employee Ownership Success Stories. **In** *Dennis, B. D., ed.*, 1986, pp. 214–20. **[G: U.S.]**

Young, Kelvin. The Management of Craft Work: A Case Study of an Oil Refinery. *Brit. J. Ind. Relat.*, November 1986, *24*(3), pp. 363–80. **[G: U.K.]**

Zafiris, Nicos. The Sharing of the Firm's Risks between Capital and Labour. *Ann. Pub. Co-op. Econ.*, Jan.-March 1986, *57*(1), pp. 35–46.

Zonderman, David A. From Mill Village to Industrial City: Letters from Vermont Factory Operatives. *Labor Hist.*, Spring 1986, *27*(2), pp. 265–85. **[G: U.S.]**

8332 Labor–Management Relations in the Public Sector

Burington, Bart E. Consumer Coal in Guangzhou: A Case Study of Small-scale Enterprise Organization in China. *Comp. Econ. Stud.*, Winter 1986, *28*(4), pp. 37–59. **[G: China]**

Chase, William. Workers' Control and Socialist Democracy. *Sci. Soc.*, Summer 1986, *50*(2), pp. 226–38. **[G: U.S.S.R.]**

Contino, Ronald. Productivity Gains through Labor–Management Cooperation at the N.Y.C. Department of Sanitation Bureau of Motor Equipment. **In** *Rosow, J. M., ed.*, 1986, pp. 169–86. **[G: U.S.]**

Héthy, Lajos. New Developments in Collective Forms of Work Organisation in Socialist Countries. *Int. Lab. Rev.*, Nov.-Dec. 1986, *125*(6), pp. 659–74. **[G: E. Europe]**

Kalecki, Michal. Observations on Labour Productivity. **In** *Kalecki, M.*, 1986, *1960*, pp. 54–59.

Kalecki, Michal. Workers' Councils and Central Planning. **In** *Kalecki, M.*, 1986, *1956*, pp. 25–37.

Kessler, Ian. Shop Stewards in Local Government Revisited. *Brit. J. Ind. Relat.*, November 1986, *24*(3), pp. 419–41. **[G: U.K.]**

Lampert, Nick. Job Security and the Law in the USSR. **In** *Lane, D., ed.*, 1986, pp. 256–77. **[G: U.S.S.R.]**

Leila, Ali; Yassin, El Sayeed and Palmer, Monte.

Job Satisfaction as an Indicator of Bureaucratic Performance in Egypt. *Can. J. Devel. Stud.*, 1986, *7*(1), pp. 105–16. **[G: Egypt]**

Loewenberg, J. Joseph. What's $13 Billion among Friends? The 1984 Postal Arbitration. **In** *Dennis, B. D., ed.*, 1986, pp. 369–77. **[G: U.S.]**

Luizer, James and Thornton, Robert. Concentration in the Labor Market for Public School Teachers. *Ind. Lab. Relat. Rev.*, July 1986, *39*(4), pp. 573–84. **[G: U.S.]**

Matejko, Alexander J. Marxists against a Polish Anarchosyndicalist: The Case of Jan Wolski. **In** *Jain, A. and Matejko, A., eds.*, 1986, pp. 178–227. **[G: Poland]**

Ramanadham, V. V. Public Enterprise: Studies in Organisational Structure: The Yugoslav Enterprise. **In** *Ramanadham, V. V., ed.*, 1986, pp. 250–60. **[G: Yugoslavia]**

Stephan, Paul B., III. Comrades' Courts and Labor Discipline since Brezhnev. **In** *Ioffe, O. S. and Janis, M. W., eds.*, 1986, pp. 213–32. **[G: U.S.S.R.]**

Teague, Elizabeth. The USSR Law on Work Collectives: Workers' Control or Workers Controlled? **In** *Lane, D., ed.*, 1986, pp. 239–55. **[G: U.S.S.R.]**

840 Demographic Economics

841 Demographic Economics

8410 Demographic Economics

Abegaz, Berhanu. Mass Poverty, Demography, and Development Strategy: A Selective Survey. **In** *Abegaz, B., ed.*, 1986, pp. 1–54. **[G: LDCs]**

Abel, Andrew B. The Effect of Annuity Insurance and Savings and Inequality: Comment. *J. Lab. Econ.*, Part 2, July 1986, *4*(3), pp. S208–15.

Abeysinghe, Tilak. Rising Needs and Falling Family Size: Implications from Marx on Demographic Transition. *Rev. Soc. Econ.*, December 1986, *44*(3), pp. 281–93.

Ahlburg, Dennis A. Forecasting Regional Births: An Economic–Demographic Approach. **In** *Isserman, A. M., ed.*, 1986, pp. 31–51. **[G: U.S.]**

Ahlburg, Dennis A. Population and Economic Development in the Island Nations of the South Pacific. **In** *Cole, R. V. and Parry, T. G., eds.*, 1986, pp. 21–70. **[G: S. Pacific]**

Ahmad, Nigar. Changes in Female Roles in Pakistan: Are the Volume and Pace Adequate? Comments. *Pakistan Devel. Rev.*, Autumn 1986, *25*(3), pp. 364–66. **[G: Pakistan]**

Akin, John S., et al. Breastfeeding Patterns and Determinants in the Near East: An Analysis for Four Countries. *Population Stud.*, July 1986, *40*(2), pp. 247–62. **[G: Jordan; Yemen; Tunisia; Egypt]**

Al-Osh, Mohamed. Birth Forecasting Based on Birth Order Probabilities, with Application to U.S. Data. *J. Amer. Statist. Assoc.*, September 1986, *81*(395), pp. 645–56. **[G: U.S.]**

Alba, Francisco and Potter, Joseph E. Population and Development in Mexico since 1940: An Interpretation. *Population Devel. Rev.*, March 1986, *12*(1), pp. 47–75. **[G: Mexico]**

Alba, Richard D. and Trent, Katherine. Population Loss and Change in the North: An Examination of New York's Migration to the Sunbelt. *Soc. Sci. Quart.*, December 1986, *67*(4), pp. 690–706. **[G: U.S.]**

Alonso, William. Intuition, Science, and the Application of Regional Models. **In** *Isserman, A. M., ed.*, 1986, pp. 261–69.

Anderson, Annelise. Social Security in Aging Societies: Comment. *Population Devel. Rev.*, Supp. 1986, *12*, pp. 313–17. **[G: U.S.]**

Anderson, Barbara A. and Silver, Brian D. Infant Mortality in the Soviet Union: Regional Differences and Measurement Issues. *Population Devel. Rev.*, December 1986, *12*(4), pp. 705–38. **[G: U.S.S.R.]**

Anderson, Barbara A. and Silver, Brian D. Sex Differentials in Mortality in the Soviet Union: Regional Differences in Length of Working Life in Comparative Perspective. *Population Stud.*, July 1986, *40*(2), pp. 191–214. **[G: U.S.S.R.]**

Andorka, Rudolf. The Decline of Fertility in Europe: Review Symposium. *Population Devel. Rev.*, June 1986, *12*(2), pp. 329–34. **[G: Europe]**

Arnold, Fred and Liu, Zhaoxiang. Sex Preference, Fertility, and Family Planning in China. *Population Devel. Rev.*, June 1986, *12*(2), pp. 221–46. **[G: China]**

Arnold, Roger A. Marriage, Divorce, and Property Rights: A Natural Rights Framework. **In** *Peden, J. R. and Glahe, F. R., eds.*, 1986, pp. 195–227.

Bairagi, Radheshyam. Food Crisis, Nutrition, and Female Children in Rural Bangladesh. *Population Devel. Rev.*, June 1986, *12*(2), pp. 307–15. **[G: Bangladesh]**

Bane, Mary Jo. Household Composition and Poverty. **In** *Danziger, S. H. and Weinberg, D. H., eds.*, 1986, pp. 209–31. **[G: U.S.]**

Barkai, Avraham. German-Jewish Migration in the Nineteenth Century, 1830–1910. **In** *Glazier, I. A. and De Rosa, L., eds.*, 1986, pp. 202–19. **[G: Germany]**

Barrère-Maurisson, Marie-Agnès. Gestion de la main-d'œuvre et formes familiales: du paternalisme à la recherche de flexiblité. (Labour Force Management and Family Forms: From Paternalism to a Search for Flexibility. With English summary.) *Écon. Soc.*, April 1986, *20*(4), pp. 165–86.

Bartel, Ann and Taubman, Paul. Some Economic and Demographic Consequences of Mental Illness. *J. Lab. Econ.*, April 1986, *4*(2), pp. 243–56. **[G: U.S.]**

Batina, Raymond G. The Optimal Linear Income Tax with Tax Credits Contingent on Fertility. *J. Public Econ.*, July 1986, *30*(2), pp. 219–35.

Beaumont, Paul, et al. The ECESIS Economic–Demographic Model of the United States. **In** *Isserman, A. M., ed.*, 1986, pp. 203–38. **[G: U.S.]**

Beauroy, Jacques. Family Patterns and Relations of Bishop's Lynn Will-Makers in the Fourteenth Century. **In** *[Laslett, P.]*, 1986, pp. 23–42. **[G: U.K.]**

Becker, Charles M.; Mills, Edwin S. and Williamson, Jeffrey G. Dynamics of Rural–Urban Migration in India: 1960–1981. *Indian J. Quant. Econ.*, 1986, *2*(1), pp. 1–43. **[G: India]**

Becker, Gary S. and Barro, Robert J. Altruism and the Economic Theory of Fertility. *Population Devel. Rev.*, Supp. 1986, *12*, pp. 69–76.

Becker, Gary S. and Tomes, Nigel. Human Capital and the Rise and Fall of Families. *J. Lab. Econ.*, Part 2, July 1986, *4*(3), pp. S1–39. **[G: U.S.; Switzerland; Norway; Sweden; U.K.]**

Becker, Stan; Chowdhury, Alauddin and Leridon, Henri. Seasonal Patterns of Reproduction in Matlab, Bangladesh. *Population Stud.*, November 1986, *40*(3), pp. 457–72. **[G: Bangladesh]**

Behrman, Jere R.; Pollak, Robert A. and Taubman, Paul. Do Parents Favor Boys? *Int. Econ. Rev.*, February 1986, *27*(1), pp. 33–54. **[G: U.S.]**

Behrman, Jere R. and Taubman, Paul. Birth Order, Schooling, and Earnings. *J. Lab. Econ.*, Part 2, July 1986, *4*(3), pp. S121–45. **[G: U.S.]**

Bell, David E. Population Policy: Choices for the United States. **In** *Menken, J., ed.*, 1986, pp. 207–28. **[G: U.S.]**

Beller, Andrea H. and Graham, John W. Child Support Awards: Differentials and Trends by Race and Marital Status. *Demography*, May 1986, *23*(2), pp. 231–45. **[G: U.S.]**

Beller, Andrea H. and Graham, John W. The Determinants of Child Support Income. *Soc. Sci. Quart.*, June 1986, *67*(2), pp. 353–64. **[G: U.S.]**

Ben-Porat, A. Formation of the Working Class in the U.S.A. and Palestine, 1881–1920: A Comparative Study. *Sci. Soc.*, Winter 1986-1987, *50*(4), pp. 440–63.

Ben-Porath, Yoram. The Entwined Growth of Population and Product, 1922–1982. **In** *Ben-Porath, Y., ed.*, 1986, pp. 27–41. **[G: Israel]**

Bernstam, Mikhail S. Competitive Human Markets, Interfamily Transfers, and Below-Replacement Fertility. *Population Devel. Rev.*, Supp. 1986, *12*, pp. 111–36. **[G: U.S.; U.S.S.R.]**

Bhagwati, Jagdish N. U.S. Immigration Policy: What Next? **In** *Pozo, S., ed.*, 1986, pp. 111–28. **[G: U.S.]**

Blau, David M. Fertility, Child Nutrition, and Child Mortality in Nicaragua: An Economic Analysis of Interrelationships. *J. Devel. Areas*, January 1986, *20*(2), pp. 185–201. **[G: Nicaragua]**

Blau, Francine D. Immigration and the U.S. Taxpayer. **In** *Pozo, S., ed.*, 1986, pp. 89–110. **[G: U.S.]**

Bloom, David E. and Freeman, Richard B. The Effects of Rapid Population Growth on Labor Supply and Employment in Developing Countries. *Population Devel. Rev.*, September 1986, *12*(3), pp. 381–414. **[G: LDCs]**

Bloom, David E. and Reddy, P. H. Age Patterns of Women at Marriage, Cohabitation, and First Birth in India. *Demography*, November 1986, *23*(4), pp. 509–23. **[G: India]**

Bonfield, Lloyd. Normative Rules and Property Transmission: Reflections on the Link between Marriage and Inheritance in Early Modern England. **In** *[Laslett, P.]*, 1986, pp. 155–76. **[G: U.K.]**

Bongaarts, John. The Transition in Reproductive Behavior in the Third World. **In** *Menken, J., ed.*, 1986, pp. 105–32. **[G: LDCs]**

Bonin, Serge. A Cartographic Approach to the Problem of Internal Migration in Sardinia in the Eighteenth Century: Part 2. **In** *Glazier, I. A. and De Rosa, L., eds.*, 1986, pp. 371–78. **[G: Italy]**

Borjas, George J. Immigrants and the U.S. Labor Market. **In** *Pozo, S., ed.*, 1986, pp. 7–20. **[G: U.S.]**

Boserup, Ester. Economic Growth with Below-Replacement Fertility: Comment. *Population Devel. Rev.*, Supp. 1986, *12*, pp. 238–43. **[G: U.S.]**

Boswell, Thomas D. The Characteristics of Internal Migration to and from New Providence Island (Greater Nassau), Bahamas 1960–1970. *Soc. Econ. Stud.*, March 1986, *35*(1), pp. 111–50. **[G: Bahamas]**

Boulier, Bryan L. and Mankiw, N. Gregory. An Econometric Investigation of Easterlin's 'Synthesis Framework': The Philippines and the United States. *Population Stud.*, November 1986, *40*(3), pp. 473–86. **[G: Philippines; U.S.]**

Bourgeois-Pichat, Jean. The Unprecedented Shortage of Births in Europe. *Population Devel. Rev.*, Supp. 1986, *12*, pp. 3–25. **[G: Europe]**

Boyle, Phelim P. and Gráda, Cormac Ó. Fertility Trends, Excess Mortality, and the Great Irish Famine. *Demography*, November 1986, *23*(4), pp. 543–62. **[G: Ireland]**

Brady, J. E. and Parker, A. J. The Socio-Demographic Spatial Structure of Dublin in 1981. *Econ. Soc. Rev.*, July 1986, *17*(4), pp. 229–52. **[G: Ireland]**

Braslavsky, Cecilia. Youth in Argentina: Between the Legacy of the Past and the Construction of the Future. *CEPAL Rev.*, August 1986, (29), pp. 41–54. **[G: Argentina]**

Briggs, John W. Fertility and Cultural Change among Families in Italy and America. *Amer. Hist. Rev.*, December 1986, *91*(5), pp. 1129–45. **[G: U.S.]**

Brodsky, Vivien. Widows in Late Elizabethan London: Remarriage, Economic Opportunity and Family Orientations. **In** *[Laslett, P.]*, 1986, pp. 122–54. **[G: U.K.]**

Brueckner, Jan K. A Switching Regression Analysis of Urban Population Densities. *J. Urban Econ.*, March 1986, *19*(2), pp. 174–89. **[G: U.S.]**

Bubnova, E. M. Demographic Waves and Labor Resources. *Prob. Econ.*, July 1986, *29*(3), pp. 61–68. **[G: U.S.S.R.]**

Bucht, Birgitta and El-Badry, M. A. Reflections on Recent Levels and Trends of Fertility and Mortality in Egypt. *Population Stud.*, March 1986, *40*(1), pp. 101–13. **[G: Egypt]**

Bumpass, Larry L.; Rindfuss, Ronald R. and Palmore, James A. Determinants of Korean Birth Intervals: The Confrontation of Theory and Data. *Population Stud.*, November 1986, *40*(3), pp. 403–23. **[G: S. Korea]**

Burkhauser, Richard V.; Holden, Karen C. and Myers, Daniel A. Marital Disruption and Poverty: The Role of Survey Procedures in Artificially Creating Poverty. *Demography*, November 1986, *23*(4), pp. 621–31. **[G: U.S.]**

Butler, David R. Teaching Economics to the 13–16 Age Range: Population. **In** *Whitehead, D. J., ed.*, 1986, pp. 92–95. **[G: U.K.]**

Cain, Mead. Landholding and Fertility: A Rejoinder [On the Relationship between Landholding and Fertility]. *Population Stud.*, July 1986, *40*(2), pp. 313–17. **[G: LDCs]**

Cain, Mead. Risk and Fertility: A Reply to Robinson. *Population Stud.*, July 1986, *40*(2), pp. 299–304. **[G: Bangladesh]**

Cain, Mead. The Consequences of Reproductive Failure: Dependence, Mobility, and Mortality among the Elderly of Rural South Asia. *Population Stud.*, November 1986, *40*(3), pp. 375–88. **[G: Bangladesh]**

Caldwell, John C. Routes to Low Mortality in Poor Countries. *Population Devel. Rev.*, June 1986, *12*(2), pp. 171–220. **[G: Costa Rica; Sri Lanka; Kerala]**

Caldwell, John C.; Reddy, P. H. and Caldwell, Pat. Periodic High Risk as a Cause of Fertility Decline in a Changing Rural Environment: Survival Strategies in the 1980–1983 South Indian Drought. *Econ. Develop. Cult. Change*, July 1986, *34*(4), pp. 677–701. **[G: India]**

Canto, Victor A. and Udwadia, Firdaus E. The Effect of Immigration Quotas on the Average Quality of Migrating Labor and Income Distribution. *Southern Econ. J.*, January 1986, *52*(3), pp. 785–93.

Carlson, Elwood. Using the Melbourne Family Survey in Migration Research: Reply [The Impact of International Migration upon the Timing of Marriage and Childbearing]. *Demography*, August 1986, *23*(3), pp. 469–71. **[G: Australia]**

Carter, Lawrence R. and Lee, Ronald D. Joint Forecasts of U.S. Marital Fertility, Nuptiality, Births, and Marriages Using Time Series Models. *J. Amer. Statist. Assoc.*, December 1986, *81*(396), pp. 902–11. **[G: U.S.]**

Carvajal, Manuel J. and Upadhiaya, Anita. Propensity to Migrate Differentials by Poverty Status: An Empirical Test for Costa Rica. *J. Econ. Devel.*, December 1986, *11*(2), pp. 123–46. **[G: Costa Rica]**

Casterline, John B.; Williams, Lindy and McDonald, Peter. The Age Difference between Spouses: Variations among Developing Countries. *Population Stud.*, November 1986, *40*(3), pp. 353–74. **[G: LDCs]**

Chapman, Steven H.; LaPlante, Mitchell P. and Wilensky, Gail R. Life Expectancy and Health Status of the Aged. *Soc. Sec. Bull.*, October 1986, *49*(10), pp. 24–48. **[G: U.S.]**

Chiswick, Barry R. Family Effects in Simple Models of Education, Occupational Status and Earnings: Findings from the Wisconsin and Kalamazoo Studies: Comment. *J. Lab. Econ.*, Part 2, July 1986, *4*(3), pp. 116–20. **[G: U.S.]**

Chiswick, Barry R. Immigration as a Counter to Below-Replacement Fertility in the United States: Comment. *Population Devel. Rev.*, Supp. 1986, *12*, pp. 269–70. **[G: U.S.]**

Chiswick, Barry R. Labor Supply and Investment in Child Quality: A Study of Jewish and Non-Jewish Women. *Rev. Econ. Statist.*, November 1986, *68*(4), pp. 700–703. **[G: U.S.]**

Chiswick, Carmel U. Economic Growth with Below-Replacement Fertility: Comment. *Population Devel. Rev.*, Supp. 1986, *12*, pp. 244–47.

Christainsen, Gregory B. and Williams, Walter E. Welfare, Family Cohesiveness, and Out-of-Wedlock Births. **In** *Peden, J. R. and Glahe, F. R., eds.*, 1986, pp. 381–424. **[G: U.S.]**

Cigno, Alessandro. Fertility and the Tax–Benefit System: A Reconsideration of the Theory of Family Taxation. *Econ. J.*, December 1986, *96*(384), pp. 1035–51.

Čizmić, Ivan. Emigration from Yugoslavia prior to World War II. **In** *Glazier, I. A. and De Rosa, L., eds.*, 1986, pp. 255–67. **[G: Yugoslavia]**

Clausen, A. W. Economic Growth and Economic and Social Development: Address to the National Leaders' Seminar on Population and Development: Nairobi, Kenya: July 11, 1984. **In** *Clausen, A. W.*, 1986, pp. 283–308.

Clausen, A. W. Economic Growth and Economic and Social Development: Address to the International Population Conference: Mexico City, Mexico: August 7, 1984. **In** *Clausen, A. W.*, 1986, pp. 309–18.

Coale, Ansley J. Demographic Effects of Below-Replacement Fertility and Their Social Implications. *Population Devel. Rev.*, Supp. 1986, *12*, pp. 203–16. **[G: U.S.]**

Coale, Ansley J. Population Trends and Economic Development. **In** *Menken, J., ed.*, 1986, pp. 96–104. **[G: LDCs]**

Coale, Ansley J. and Kisker, Ellen Eliason. Mortality Crossovers: Reality or Bad Data? *Population Stud.*, November 1986, *40*(3), pp. 389–401. **[G: Global]**

Cohen, Joel E. Population Forecasts and Confidence Intervals for Sweden: A Comparison of Model-based and Empirical Approaches. *Demography*, February 1986, *23*(1), pp. 105–26. **[G: Sweden]**

Compton, Paul A. and Power, John P. Estimates of the Religious Composition of Northern Ireland Local Government Districts in 1981 and Change in the Geographical Pattern of Religious Composition between 1971 and 1981.

Econ. Soc. Rev., January 1986, *17*(2), pp. 87–105. **[G: Ireland]**

Connelly, Rachel. A Framework for Analyzing the Impact of Cohort Size on Education and Labor Earnings. *J. Human Res.*, Fall 1986, *21*(4), pp. 543–62.

Connerly, Charles E. and Frank, James E. Predicting Support for Local Growth Controls. *Soc. Sci. Quart.*, September 1986, *67*(3), pp. 572–86. **[G: U.S.]**

Cook, Charles D. From Bull Path to Boulevard. **In** *Chicoine, D. L. and Walzer, N., eds.*, 1986, pp. 77–92. **[G: U.S.]**

Cortese, Antonio. La presenza straniera in Italia al 1981: considerazioni sulla qualità dei risultati del censimento demografico. (Immigrants' Presence in Italy: An Evaluation of the 1981 Census Data. With English summary.) *Econ. Lavoro*, Oct.-Dec. 1986, *20*(4), pp. 39–58. **[G: Italy]**

Cotler, Julio. The Political Radicalization of Working-Class Youth in Peru. *CEPAL Rev.*, August 1986, (29), pp. 107–18. **[G: Peru]**

Ćtrnáct, Pavel. What Will the Czechoslovak Population Be in the Year 2000? *Czech. Econ. Digest.*, Oct./Nov. 1986, (7), pp. 40–43. **[G: Czechoslovakia]**

Cushing, Brian J. Accounting for Spatial Relationships in Models of Interstate Population Migration. *Ann. Reg. Sci.*, July 1986, *20*(2), pp. 66–73. **[G: U.S.]**

Cutright, Phillips and Smith, Herbert L. Trends in Illegitimacy among Five English-Speaking Populations: 1940–1980. *Demography*, November 1986, *23*(4), pp. 563–78. **[G: U.K.; U.S.; Canada; Australia]**

Dahmann, Donald C. Geographical Mobility Research with Panel Data. *Growth Change*, July 1986, *17*(3), pp. 35–48. **[G: U.S.]**

Daly, Herman E. Population Growth and Economic Development: Policy Questions. *Population Devel. Rev.*, September 1986, *12*(3), pp. 582–85.

Danziger, Sheldon H. and Gottschalk, Peter. Families with Children Have Fared Worst. *Challenge*, Mar./Apr. 1986, *29*(1), pp. 40–47. **[G: U.S.]**

DaVanzo, Julie and Habicht, Jean-Pierre. Infant Mortality Decline in Malaysia, 1946–1975: The Roles of Changes in Variables and Changes in the Structure of Relationships. *Demography*, May 1986, *23*(2), pp. 143–60. **[G: Malaysia]**

David, Paul A. Altruism and the Economic Theory of Fertility: Comment. *Population Devel. Rev.*, Supp. 1986, *12*, pp. 77–86.

David, Paul A. and Sanderson, Warren C. Rudimentary Contraceptive Methods and the American Transition to Marital Fertility Control, 1855–1915. **In** *Engerman, S. L. and Gallman, R. E., eds.*, 1986, pp. 307–79. **[G: U.S.]**

Davis, Kingsley. Low Fertility in Evolutionary Perspective. *Population Devel. Rev.*, Supp. 1986, *12*, pp. 48–65. **[G: OECD]**

Day, John. A Cartographic Approach to the Problem of Internal Migration in Sardinia in the Eighteenth Century: Part 1. **In** *Glazier, I. A. and De Rosa, L., eds.*, 1986, pp. 365–70. **[G: Italy]**

Day, L. H. The Age of Women at Completion of Childbearing: Australian Differentials by Religion and Country of Birth. *Population Stud.*, July 1986, *40*(2), pp. 237–45. **[G: Australia]**

Deaton, Angus S. and Muellbauer, John. On Measuring Child Costs: With Applications to Poor Countries. *J. Polit. Econ.*, August 1986, *94*(4), pp. 720–44. **[G: Sri Lanka; Indonesia]**

Demeny, Paul. Population and the Invisible Hand. *Demography*, November 1986, *23*(4), pp. 473–87.

Demeny, Paul. Pronatalist Policies in Low-Fertility Countries: Patterns, Performance, and Prospects. *Population Devel. Rev.*, Supp. 1986, *12*, pp. 335–58. **[G: U.S.]**

Demeny, Paul. The World Demographic Situation. **In** *Menken, J., ed.*, 1986, pp. 27–66. **[G: Global]**

Devaney, Barbara L. An Analysis of Variations in U.S. Fertility and Female Labor Force Participation Trends: A Reply. *Demography*, February 1986, *23*(1), pp. 141–42. **[G: U.S.]**

Di Comité, Luigi. Aspects of Italian Emigration, 1881–1915. **In** *Glazier, I. A. and De Rosa, L., eds.*, 1986, pp. 148–59. **[G: Italy]**

Diamond, Ian D.; McDonald, John W. and Shah, Iqbal H. Proportional Hazards Models for Current Status Data: Application to the Study of Differentials in Age at Weaning in Pakistan. *Demography*, November 1986, *23*(4), pp. 607–20. **[G: Pakistan]**

van Dijk, Jouke and Oosterhaven, J. Regional Impacts of Migrants' Expenditures: An Input–Output/Vacancy-Chain Approach. **In** *Batey, P. W. and Madden, M., eds.*, 1986, pp. 122–47. **[G: Netherlands]**

Dinkel, Reiner. Declining Life Expectancy in a Highly Developed Nation: Paradox or Statistical Artifact? **In** *[Rapoport, A.]*, 1986, pp. 311–21. **[G: U.S.S.R.; W. Germany; Sweden]**

Dinkel, Reiner. Social Security and Intergenerational Equity. **In** *von der Schulenburg, J.-M. G., ed.*, 1986, pp. 77–107. **[G: W. Germany]**

Duleep, Harriet Orcutt. Incorporating Longitudinal Aspects into Mortality Research Using Social Security Administrative Record Data. *J. Econ. Soc. Meas.*, July 1986, *14*(2), pp. 121–33. **[G: U.S.]**

Dupâquier, Jacques. Geographic and Social Mobility in France in the Nineteenth and Twentieth Centuries. **In** *Glazier, I. A. and De Rosa, L., eds.*, 1986, pp. 356–64. **[G: France]**

Dutton, Diana B. Social Class, Health, and Illness. **In** *Aiken, L. H. and Mechanic, D., eds.*, 1986, pp. 31–62. **[G: U.S.]**

Dynarski, Mark. Household Formation and Suburbanization, 1970–1980. *J. Urban Econ.*, January 1986, *19*(1), pp. 71–87. **[G: U.S.]**

Earle, Peter. Age and Accumulation in the London Business Community, 1665–1720. **In** *[Coleman, D. C.]*, 1986, pp. 38–63. **[G: U.K.]**

Easterlin, Richard A. Economic Preconceptions and Demographic Research: A Comment [The Fertility Revolution: A Supply–Demand Analysis]. *Population Devel. Rev.*, September 1986, *12*(3), pp. 517–28. **[G: Sri Lanka; Colombia; China; India]**

Engelen, Th. L. M. and Hillebrand, J. H. A. Fertility and Nuptiality in the Netherlands, 1850–1960. *Population Stud.*, November 1986, *40*(3), pp. 487–503. **[G: Netherlands]**

Engerman, Stanley L. Population and Labor in the British Caribbean in the Early Nineteenth Century: Comment. **In** *Engerman, S. L. and Gallman, R. E., eds.*, 1986, pp. 625–29. **[G: Caribbean]**

Englová, Jana. The Effects of Migration on the Demarcation of Industrial Areas. **In** *Glazier, I. A. and De Rosa, L., eds.*, 1986, pp. 271–75. **[G: Austria]**

Entwisle, Barbara; Mason, William M. and Hermalin, Albert I. The Multilevel Dependence of Contraceptive Use on Socioeconomic Development and Family Planning Program Strength. *Demography*, May 1986, *23*(2), pp. 199–216. **[G: LDCs]**

Erickson, Charlotte. The Uses of Passenger Lists for the Study of British and Irish Emigration. **In** *Glazier, I. A. and De Rosa, L., eds.*, 1986, pp. 318–35. **[G: U.S.; U.K.; Ireland]**

Espenshade, Thomas J. Population Dynamics with Immigration and Low Fertility. *Population Devel. Rev.*, Supp. 1986, *12*, pp. 248–61. **[G: U.S.]**

Espenshade, Thomas J. and Calhoun, Charles A. The Dollar and Cents of Parenthood. *J. Policy Anal. Manage.*, Summer 1986, *5*(4), pp. 813–17. **[G: U.S.]**

Essemyr, Mats. Food, Fare and Nutrition. Some Reflections on the Historical Development of Food Consumption. *Scand. Econ. Hist. Rev.*, 1986, *34*(2), pp. 76–89. **[G: Sweden]**

Evans, M. D. R. American Fertility Pattern: A Comparison of White and Nonwhite Cohorts Born 1903–56. *Population Devel. Rev.*, June 1986, *12*(2), pp. 267–93. **[G: U.S.]**

Felderer, Bernhard. August Lösch on Population Waves. **In** *[Lösch, A.]*, 1986, pp. 47–53.

Firebaugh, Glenn. Is the Density–Fertility Relation a Statistical Artifact? A Reply [Population Density and Fertility in 22 Indian Villages]. *Demography*, May 1986, *23*(2), pp. 285–89. **[G: India]**

Fogel, Robert William. Nutrition and the Decline in Mortality since 1700: Some Preliminary Findings. **In** *Engerman, S. L. and Gallman, R. E., eds.*, 1986, pp. 439–527. **[G: U.S.]**

Folbre, Nancy. Cleaning House: New Perspectives on Households and Economic Development. *J. Devel. Econ.*, June 1986, *22*(1), pp. 5–40.

Folbre, Nancy. Hearts and Spades: Paradigms of Household Economics. *World Devel.*, Special Issue, Feb. 1986, *14*(2), pp. 245–55.

Forte, Francesco. Ten Paradoxes Facing African Countries. *Atlantic Econ. J.*, March 1986, *14*(1), pp. 1–7. **[G: LDCs; Africa]**

Franklin, Peter. Peasant Widows' "Liberation" and Remarriage before the Black Death. *Econ. Hist. Rev., 2nd Ser.*, May 1986, *39*(2), pp. 186–204. **[G: U.K.]**

Freedman, Ronald. On Underestimating the Rate of Social Change: A Cautionary Note [Policy Options after the Demographic Transition: The Case of Taiwan]. *Population Devel. Rev.*, September 1986, *12*(3), pp. 529–32. **[G: Taiwan]**

Freedman, Ronald. Policy Options after the Demographic Transition: The Case of Taiwan. *Population Devel. Rev.*, March 1986, *12*(1), pp. 77–100. **[G: Taiwan]**

Fricke, Thomas E.; Syed, Sabiha H. and Smith, Peter C. Rural Punjabi Social Organization and Marriage Timing Strategies in Pakistan. *Demography*, November 1986, *23*(4), pp. 489–508. **[G: Pakistan]**

Friedlander, Dov and Moshe, Eliahu Ben. Occupations, Migration, Sex Ratios, and Nuptiality in Nineteenth Century English Communities: A Model of Relationships. *Demography*, February 1986, *23*(1), pp. 1–12. **[G: U.K.]**

Friedman, Gerald. Population and Labor in the British Caribbean in the Early Nineteenth Century: Comment. **In** *Engerman, S. L. and Gallman, R. E., eds.*, 1986, pp. 629–37. **[G: Caribbean]**

Fuchs, Victor R. Low-Level Radiation and Infant Mortality. **In** *Fuchs, V. R.*, 1986, *1981*, pp. 200–213. **[G: U.S.]**

Fuchs, Victor R. Some Economic Aspects of Mortality in Developed Countries. **In** *Fuchs, V. R.*, 1986, *1974*, pp. 181–99. **[G: OECD]**

Furstenberg, Frank F., Jr. and Brooks-Gunn, Jeanne. Teenage Childbearing: Causes, Consequences, and Remedies. **In** *Aiken, L. H. and Mechanic, D., eds.*, 1986, pp. 307–34. **[G: U.S.]**

Gabriel, Stuart A. and Sabatello, Eitan F. Palestinian Migration from the West Bank and Gaza: Economic and Demographic Analyses. *Econ. Develop. Cult. Change*, January 1986, *34*(2), pp. 245–62. **[G: Israel]**

Gage, Timothy B.; Dyke, Bennett and MacCluer, Jean W. Estimating Mortality Level for Small Populations: An Evaluation of a Pair of Two-Census Methods. *Population Stud.*, July 1986, *40*(2), pp. 263–73.

Gallaway, Lowell and Vedder, Richard. Inflation, Migration, and Divorce in Contemporary America. **In** *Peden, J. R. and Glahe, F. R., eds.*, 1986, pp. 285–307. **[G: U.S.]**

Galloway, Patrick R. Long-term Fluctuations in Climate and Population in the Preindustrial Era. *Population Devel. Rev.*, March 1986, *12*(1), pp. 1–24. **[G: China; Europe]**

Gilks, Walter R. The Relationship between Birth History and Current Fertility in Developing Countries. *Population Stud.*, November 1986, *40*(3), pp. 437–55. **[G: LDCs]**

Gilland, Bernard. On Resources and Economic Development. *Population Devel. Rev.*, June 1986, *12*(2), pp. 295–305. **[G: Global]**

Goldberg, Michael A. Hedging Your Great Grandchildren's Bets: The Case of Overseas

Chinese Investment in Real Estate around the Cities of the Pacific Rim. **In** *Nemetz, P. N., ed.*, 1986, pp. 159–98. **[G: S. E. Asia; ASEAN; Hong Kong]**

Goldman, Noreen and Lord, Graham. A New Look at Entropy and the Life Table. *Demography,* May 1986, *23*(2), pp. 275–82.

Goldstone, J. A. The Demographic Revolution in England: A Re-examination. *Population Stud.*, March 1986, *40*(1), pp. 5–33. **[G: U.K.]**

Gramlich, Edward M. Fighting Poverty: What Works and What Doesn't: The Main Themes. **In** *Danziger, S. H. and Weinberg, D. H., eds.*, 1986, pp. 341–47. **[G: U.S.]**

Gray, Alan. Sectional Growth Balance Analysis for Non-stable Closed Populations. *Population Stud.*, November 1986, *40*(3), pp. 425–36. **[G: LDCs]**

Greenberg, Carol and Renfro, Charles. An Econometric–Demographic Model of New York State. **In** *Isserman, A. M., ed.*, 1986, pp. 105–25. **[G: U.S.]**

Greenhalgh, Susan. Shifts in China's Population Policy, 1984–86: Views from the Central, Provincial, and Local Levels. *Population Devel. Rev.*, September 1986, *12*(3), pp. 491–515. **[G: China]**

Greenwood, Michael J. and McDowell, John M. The Factor Market Consequences of U.S. Immigration. *J. Econ. Lit.*, December 1986, *24*(4), pp. 1738–72. **[G: U.S.]**

Griliches, Zvi. Birth Order, Schooling, and Earnings: Comment. *J. Lab. Econ.*, Part 2, July 1986, *4*(3), pp. S146–50. **[G: U.S.]**

Grossbard-Shechtman, Amyra. Economic Behavior, Marriage and Fertility: Two Lessons from Polygyny. *J. Econ. Behav. Organ.*, December 1986, *7*(4), pp. 415–24. **[G: Nigeria]**

Grossbard-Shechtman, Amyra and Neuman, Shoshana. Economic Behavior, Marriage and Religiosity. *J. Behav. Econ.*, Spring/Summer 1986, *15*(1/2), pp. 71–85. **[G: Israel]**

Guzda, Henry P. Ellis Island a Welcome Site? Only after Years of Reform. *Mon. Lab. Rev.*, July 1986, *109*(7), pp. 30–36. **[G: U.S.]**

Haag, Günter and Weidlich, Wolfgang. A Dynamic Migration Theory and Its Evaluation for Concrete Systems. *Reg. Sci. Urban Econ.*, February 1986, *16*(1), pp. 57–80. **[G: Canada]**

Haines, Michael R. New Results on the Decline in Household Fertility in the United States from 1750 to 1900: Comment. **In** *Engerman, S. L. and Gallman, R. E., eds.*, 1986, pp. 426–33. **[G: U.S.]**

Haines, Michael R. Rudimentary Contraceptive Methods and the American Transition to Marital Fertility Control, 1855–1915: Comment. **In** *Engerman, S. L. and Gallman, R. E., eds.*, 1986, pp. 379–83. **[G: U.S.]**

Hammer, Jeffrey S. Children and Savings in Less Developed Countries. *J. Devel. Econ.*, September 1986, *23*(1), pp. 107–18. **[G: LDCs]**

Hammer, Jeffrey S. Population Growth and Savings in LDCs: A Survey Article. *World Devel.*, May 1986, *14*(5), pp. 579–91. **[G: LDCs]**

Hardjono, Joan. Transmigration: Looking to the Future. *Bull. Indonesian Econ. Stud.*, August 1986, *22*(2), pp. 28–53. **[G: Indonesia]**

Hart, John Fraser. Population Trends in the Midwest. **In** *Walzer, N. and Chicoine, D. L., eds.*, 1986, pp. 1–14. **[G: U.S.]**

Hassan, Syed Fayyaz and Pasha, Hafiz A. Land Densities in Karachi. *Pakistan J. Appl. Econ.*, Winter 1986, *5*(2), pp. 143–62. **[G: Pakistan]**

Hatcher, John. Mortality in the Fifteenth Century: Some New Evidence. *Econ. Hist. Rev., 2nd Ser.*, February 1986, *39*(1), pp. 19–38. **[G: U.K.]**

Hauser, Robert M. and Sewell, William H. Family Effects in Simple Models of Education, Occupational Status and Earnings: Findings from the Wisconsin and Kalamazoo Studies. *J. Lab. Econ.*, Part 2, July 1986, *4*(3), pp. S83–115. **[G: U.S.]**

Hayes, Kathy J. Local Public Goods Demands and Demographic Effects. *Appl. Econ.*, October 1986, *18*(10), pp. 1039–45. **[G: U.S.]**

Heer, David M. Immigration as a Counter to Below-Replacement Fertility in the United States. *Population Devel. Rev.*, Supp. 1986, *12*, pp. 262–69. **[G: U.S.]**

Henderson, J. Vernon. Urbanization in a Developing Country: City Size and Population Composition. *J. Devel. Econ.*, July-Aug. 1986, *22*(2), pp. 269–93. **[G: Brazil]**

Herzog, Henry W., Jr. and Schlottmann, Alan M. State and Local Tax Deductibility and Metropolitan Migration. *Nat. Tax J.*, June 1986, *39*(2), pp. 189–200. **[G: U.S.]**

Herzog, Henry W., Jr. and Schlottmann, Alan M. The Metro Rating Game: What Can Be Learned from the Recent Migrants? *Growth Change,* January 1986, *17*(1), pp. 37–50. **[G: U.S.]**

Higman, B. W. Population and Labor in the British Caribbean in the Early Nineteenth Century. **In** *Engerman, S. L. and Gallman, R. E., eds.*, 1986, pp. 605–25. **[G: Caribbean]**

Hirschman, Charles. The Recent Rise in Malay Fertility: A New Trend or a Temporary Lull in a Fertility Transition? *Demography,* May 1986, *23*(2), pp. 161–84. **[G: Malaysia]**

van der Hoeven, W. H. M. and Hundepool, A. J. A Method for Seasonally Adjusted Time Series with Variation in the Seasonal Amplitude. *J. Bus. Econ. Statist.*, October 1986, *4*(4), pp. 455–71. **[G: Netherlands]**

Hollander, Samuel. Marx and Malthusianism: Reply. *Amer. Econ. Rev.*, June 1986, *76*(3), pp. 548–50.

Horton, Susan. Child Nutrition and Family Size in the Philippines. *J. Devel. Econ.*, September 1986, *23*(1), pp. 161–76. **[G: Philippines]**

Horvitz, Sigmund A. Implications of Projecting Future Losses of Earning Capacity with Deterministic Models [Problems in the Use of Historical Data in Estimating Economic Loss in Wrongful Death and Injury Cases]. *J. Risk Ins.*, September 1986, *53*(3), pp. 530–37. **[G: U.S.]**

Humphrey, Thomas M. The Dismal Science Revisited. **In** *Humphreys, T. M.*, 1986, *1973*, pp. 312–23.

Huzel, J. P. The Demographic Impact of the Old Poor Laws: More Reflections on Malthus. **In** *Turner, M., ed.*, 1986, pp. 40–59. **[G: U.K.]**

Imhof, Arthur E. Is Japan Following Europe towards a Society of Singles? Possible Impacts of the Rapid Increase in Life Expectancy on Japanese Social Structure—As Seen by a European Historical-Demographer. *Keio Econ. Stud.*, 1986, *23*(1), pp. 21–47. **[G: Japan]**

Isard, Walter and Smith, Christine. Economic–Demographic Linkages in an Interregional Model. **In** *Isserman, A. M., ed.*, 1986, pp. 159–75. **[G: Australia]**

Isiugo-Abanihe, Uche C. Child Fostering and High Fertility Interrelationships in West Africa. **In** *Abegaz, B., ed.*, 1986, pp. 73–100. **[G: W. Africa]**

Isserman, Andrew. Forecasting Birth and Migration Rates: The Theoretical Foundation. **In** *Isserman, A. M., ed.*, 1986, pp. 3–30. **[G: U.S.]**

James-Bryan, Meryl. Youth in the English-speaking Caribbean: The High Cost of Dependent Development. *CEPAL Rev.*, August 1986, (29), pp. 133–52. **[G: Caribbean]**

Jasso, Guillermina and Rosenzweig, Mark R. Family Reunification and the Immigration Multiplier: U.S. Immigration Law, Origin-Country Conditions, and the Reproduction of Immigrants. *Demography*, August 1986, *23*(3), pp. 291–311. **[G: U.S.]**

Jasso, Guillermina and Rosenzweig, Mark R. What's in a Name? Country-of-Origin Influences on the Earnings of Immigrants in the United States. **In** *Stark, O., ed.*, 1986, pp. 75–106. **[G: U.S.]**

Jensen, Eric. Population Density and Fertility: A Comment. *Demography*, May 1986, *23*(2), pp. 283–84. **[G: India]**

Johnson, William R. and Skinner, Jonathan. Labor Supply and Marital Separation. *Amer. Econ. Rev.*, June 1986, *76*(3), pp. 455–69. **[G: U.S.]**

Jones, Barclay Gibbs. Urban Support for Rural Development in Kenya. *Econ. Geogr.*, July 1986, *62*(3), pp. 201–14. **[G: Kenya]**

Jones, Huw, et al. Peripheral Counter-Urbanization: Findings from an Integration of Census and Survey Data in Northern Scotland. *Reg. Stud.*, February 1986, *20*(1), pp. 15–26. **[G: U.K.]**

Jud, G. Donald and Bennett, D. Gordon. Public Schools and the Pattern of Intraurban Residential Mobility. *Land Econ.*, November 1986, *62*(4), pp. 362–70. **[G: U.S.]**

Jun, Il Soo and Chang, Hui S. Functional Forms and the Relevance of Contiguous Migration in the Study of Migration and Employment Growth. *Ann. Reg. Sci.*, July 1986, *20*(2), pp. 17–27. **[G: U.S.]**

Kahan, Arcadius. A Day in the Ghetto. **In** *Kahan, A.*, 1986, pp. 170–84. **[G: Poland]**

Kahan, Arcadius. The First Wave of Jewish Immigration from Eastern Europe to the United States. **In** *Kahan, A.*, 1986, pp. 118–27. **[G: U.S.]**

Kahan, Arcadius. The Impact of Industrialization in Tsarist Russia on the Socioeconomic Conditions of the Jewish Population. **In** *Kahan, A.*, 1986, pp. 1–69. **[G: U.S.S.R.]**

Kahan, Arcadius. The Urbanization Process of the Jews in Nineteenth-Century Europe. **In** *Kahan, A.*, 1986, pp. 70–81. **[G: Europe]**

Kahimbaara, J. A. The Population Density Gradient and the Spatial Structure of a Third World City: Nairobi, A Case Study. *Urban Stud.*, August 1986, *23*(4), pp. 307–22. **[G: Kenya]**

Kamphoefner, Walter D. At the Crossroads of Economic Development: Background Factors Affecting Emigration from Nineteenth-Century Germany. **In** *Glazier, I. A. and De Rosa, L., eds.*, 1986, pp. 174–201. **[G: Germany]**

Kasun, Jacqueline R. The State and Adolescent Sexual Behavior. **In** *Peden, J. R. and Glahe, F. R., eds.*, 1986, pp. 329–64. **[G: U.S.]**

Katz, Eliakim and Stark, Oded. On Fertility, Migration and Remittances in LDCs. *World Devel.*, January 1986, *14*(1), pp. 133–35. **[G: LDCs]**

Katzman, Rubén. Youth and Unemployment in Montevideo. *CEPAL Rev.*, August 1986, (29), pp. 119–31. **[G: Uruguay]**

Kearl, J. R. and Pope, Clayne L. Unobservable Family and Individual Contributions to the Distributions of Income and Wealth. *J. Lab. Econ.*, Part 2, July 1986, *4*(3), pp. S48–79. **[G: U.S.]**

Kelley, Allen C. Population Growth and Economic Development: Policy Questions. *Population Devel. Rev.*, September 1986, *12*(3), pp. 563–68.

Kemp, Murray C. and Kondo, Hitoshi. Overlapping Generations, Competitive Efficiency and Optimal Population. *J. Public Econ.*, July 1986, *30*(2), pp. 237–47.

Kennedy, Charles H. Policies of Redistributional Preference in Pakistan. **In** *Nevitte, N. and Kennedy, C. H., eds.*, 1986, pp. 63–93. **[G: Pakistan]**

Kennedy, John M.; De Jong, Gordon F. and Lichter, Daniel T. Updating Local Area Population Projections with Current Migration Estimates. *J. Econ. Soc. Meas.*, July 1986, *14*(2), pp. 107–20. **[G: U.S.]**

Keyfitz, Nathan. The Family That Does Not Reproduce Itself. *Population Devel. Rev.*, Supp. 1986, *12*, pp. 139–54. **[G: OECD]**

Khan, M. R. Prospects and Problems of Integration of Family Planning with Health Services in Bangladesh. *Bangladesh Devel. Stud.*, June 1986, *14*(2), pp. 101–08. **[G: Bangladesh]**

Kiernan, Kathleen E. Teenage Marriage and Marital Breakdown: A Longitudinal Study. *Population Stud.*, March 1986, *40*(1), pp. 35–54. **[G: U.K.]**

Kirsch, Henry. University Youth as Social Protagonist in Latin America. *CEPAL Rev.*, August 1986, (29), pp. 191–202. **[G: Latin America]**

Kirwan, Frank and Harrigan, Frank. Swedish–Finnish Return Migration, Extent, Timing, and Information Flows. *Demography*, August 1986, *23*(3), pp. 313–27. **[G: U.S.; Finland; Sweden]**

Kleiner, Robert J., et al. International Migration and Internal Migration: A Comprehensive Theoretical Approach. **In** *Glazier, I. A. and De Rosa, L., eds.*, 1986, pp. 305–17.

Klinger, Andras and Kepecs, Joszef. Methodological Aspects of the 1984 Hungarian Microcensus. *Statist. J.*, May 1986, *4*(1), pp. 1–18. **[G: Hungary]**

Kondo, Hitoshi. On Pitfalls in the Construction of Family-based Models of Population Growth: A Note. *Europ. Econ. Rev.*, April 1986, *30*(2), pp. 439–47.

Kono, Shigemi. Perspective on Nuptiality and Fertility: Comment. *Population Devel. Rev.*, Supp. 1986, *12*, pp. 171–75. **[G: OECD]**

Kooreman, Peter and Kapteyn, Arie. Estimation of Rationed and Unrationed Household Labour Supply Functions Using Flexible Functional Forms. *Econ. J.*, June 1986, *96*(382), pp. 398–412. **[G: Netherlands]**

Koponen, Juhani. Population Growth in Historical Perspective: The Key Role of Changing Fertility. **In** *Boesen, J., et al., eds.*, 1986, pp. 31–57. **[G: Tanzania]**

Kotlikoff, Laurence J.; Shoven, John B. and Spivak, Avia. The Effect of Annuity Insurance and Savings and Inequality. *J. Lab. Econ.*, Part 2, July 1986, *4*(3), pp. S183–207.

Lam, David. The Dynamics of Population Growth, Differential Fertility, and Inequality. *Amer. Econ. Rev.*, December 1986, *76*(5), pp. 1103–16. **[G: Brazil]**

Land, Kenneth C. Methods for National Population Forecasts: A Review. *J. Amer. Statist. Assoc.*, December 1986, *81*(396), pp. 888–901. **[G: U.S.]**

Lang, M. New Urban and Rural Definitions for the U.S. Census of Population. *Reg. Stud.*, February 1986, *20*(1), pp. 77–83. **[G: U.S.]**

Lassibille, Gérard. L'influence des événements familiaux dans la formation des revenus. (The Effect of Family Events on Earnings. With English summary.) *Ann. Écon. Statist.*, Apr./June 1986, (2), pp. 101–16. **[G: France]**

Latham, A. J. H. Southeast Asia: A Preliminary Survey, 1800–1914. **In** *Glazier, I. A. and De Rosa, L., eds.*, 1986, pp. 11–29. **[G: S. E. Asia]**

Lavely, William R. Age Patterns of Chinese Marital Fertility, 1950–1981. *Demography*, August 1986, *23*(3), pp. 419–34. **[G: China]**

Lawton, Richard. Atlas of Industrializing Britain 1780–1914: Population. **In** *Langton, J. and Morris, R. J., eds.*, 1986, pp. 10–29. **[G: U.K.]**

Lazear, Edward P. and Michael, Robert T. Estimating the Personal Distribution of Income with Adjustment for Within-Family Variation. *J. Lab. Econ.*, Part 2, July 1986, *4*(3), pp. S216–39. **[G: U.S.]**

Le Bras, Hervé and Todd, Emmanuel. Mountains, Rivers and the Family: Comments on a Map from the 1975 French Census. **In** *[Laslett, P.]*, 1986, pp. 379–87. **[G: France]**

Le Grand, Julian and Rabin, Matthew. Trends in British Health Inequality, 1931–83. **In** *Culyer, A. J. and Jönsson, B., eds.*, 1986, pp. 112–27. **[G: U.K.]**

Ledent, Jacques. Forecasting Interregional Migration: An Economic–Demographic Approach. **In** *Isserman, A. M., ed.*, 1986, pp. 53–77. **[G: Canada; U.S.]**

Lee, Ronald D. The Value and Allocation of Time in High-Income Countries: Implications for Fertility: Comment. *Population Devel. Rev.*, Supp. 1986, *12*, pp. 108–10.

Leete, R. and Kwok, K. K. Demographic Changes in East Malaysia and Their Relationship with Those in the Peninsula 1960–80. *Population Stud.*, March 1986, *40*(1), pp. 83–100. **[G: Malaysia]**

Leibowitz, Arleen; Eisen, Marvin and Chow, Winston K. An Economic Model of Teenage Pregnancy Decision-making. *Demography*, February 1986, *23*(1), pp. 67–77. **[G: U.S.]**

Leontief, Wassily. Population Growth and Economic Development: Illustrative Projections. **In** *Leontief, W.*, 1986, *1979*, pp. 338–62. **[G: Global]**

Leppel, Karen. A Trinomial Logit Analysis of Household Composition. *Amer. Real Estate Urban Econ. Assoc. J.*, Winter 1986, *14*(4), pp. 537–56. **[G: U.S.]**

Levine, David. The Decline of Fertility in Europe: Review Symposium. *Population Devel. Rev.*, June 1986, *12*(2), pp. 335–40. **[G: Europe]**

Levy, Frank S. and Michel, Richard C. An Economic Bust for the Baby Boom. *Challenge*, Mar./Apr. 1986, *29*(1), pp. 33–39. **[G: U.S.]**

Levy, Victor. Seasonal Fertility Cycles in Rural Egypt: Behavioral and Biological Linkages. *Demography*, February 1986, *23*(1), pp. 13–30. **[G: Egypt]**

Lewbel, Arthur. Additive Separability and Equivalent Scales [Demographic Variables in Demand Analysis]. *Econometrica*, January 1986, *54*(1), pp. 219–22. **[G: U.K.]**

Lichter, Daniel T.; Heaton, Tim B. and Fuguitt, Glenn V. Convergence in Black and White Population Redistribution in the United States. *Soc. Sci. Quart.*, March 1986, *67*(1), pp. 21–38. **[G: U.S.]**

Lindert, Peter H. Nutrition and the Decline in Mortality since 1700: Some Preliminary Findings: Comment. **In** *Engerman, S. L. and Gallman, R. E., eds.*, 1986, pp. 527–37. **[G: U.S.]**

Linneman, Peter. Information Technology, Demographics, and the Retail Response: Discussion. **In** *Faulhaber, G.; Noam, E. and Tasley, R., eds.*, 1986, pp. 175–77. **[G: U.S.; OECD]**

Luptáčik, M. and Schmoranz, I. Economic Consequences of a Change in Demographic Patterns: An Integrated Approach. **In** *Batey, P. W. and Madden, M., eds.*, 1986, pp. 107–21. **[G: Austria]**

Mageean, Deirdre. Ulster Emigration to Philadelphia, 1847–1865: A Preliminary Analysis Using Passenger Lists. **In** *Glazier, I. A. and De Rosa, L., eds.*, 1986, pp. 276–86. **[G: Ireland; U.S.]**

Magnusson, Lars. Malthus in Scandinavia, 1799. **In** *Turner, M., ed.*, 1986, pp. 60–70. **[G: Sweden]**

Mammo, Abate and Morgan, S. Philip. Childlessness in Rural Ethiopia. *Population Devel. Rev.*, September 1986, *12*(3), pp. 533–46. **[G: Ethiopia]**

Martínez, Javier and Valenzuela, Eduardo. Chilean Youth and Social Exclusion. *CEPAL Rev.*, August 1986, (29), pp. 93–105. **[G: Chile]**

Martínez, Javier and Valenzuela, Eduardo. Working-class Youth and Anomy. *CEPAL Rev.*, August 1986, (29), pp. 171–81. **[G: Latin America]**

Martínez Moreno, Carlos. Thinking about Youth. *CEPAL Rev.*, August 1986, (29), pp. 153–70. **[G: Latin America]**

Marton, Adam. Synthetic Estimates for Small Areas: Problems and Results of a Simulation Experiment. *Statist. J.*, May 1986, *4*(1), pp. 71–80.

Masson, André. A Cohort Analysis of Wealth–Age Profiles Generated by a Simulation Model in France (1949–75). *Econ. J.*, March 1986, *96*(381), pp. 173–90. **[G: France]**

McCormick, Marie C. Implications of Recent Changes in Infant Mortality. **In** *Aiken, L. H. and Mechanic, D., eds.*, 1986, pp. 282–306. **[G: U.S.]**

McDevitt, Thomas M., et al. Migration Plans of the Rural Populations of Third World Countries: A Probit Analysis of Micro-Level Data from Asia, Africa, and Latin America. *J. Devel. Areas*, July 1986, *20*(4), pp. 473–90. **[G: Colombia; Egypt; Thailand]**

McIntosh, C. Alison. Recent Pronatalist Policies in Western Europe. *Population Devel. Rev.*, Supp. 1986, *12*, pp. 318–34. **[G: W. Europe]**

McIntosh, James; Satchell, Stephen E. and Nasim, Anjum. Differential Mortality in Rural Bangladesh. *J. Appl. Econometrics*, October 1986, *1*(4), pp. 345–53. **[G: Bangladesh]**

McNicoll, Geoffrey. Economic Growth with Below-Replacement Fertility. *Population Devel. Rev.*, Supp. 1986, *12*, pp. 217–38. **[G: U.S.]**

Medoff, Marshall H. An Evaluation of the Effectiveness of Suicide Prevention Center. *J. Behav. Econ.*, Fall 1986, *15*, pp. 43–55. **[G: U.S.]**

Mehta, Rajesh. Role of Inter-sectoral Approach for Health Services in Developing Economies. **In** *Panchamukhi, V. R., et al.*, 1986, pp. 245–69. **[G: India; Indonesia; Japan; Philippines; Thailand]**

Meiners, Nancy. New York State Economic and Demographic Forecasts to 2003. **In** *Saltzman, S. and Schuler, R. E., eds.*, 1986, pp. 45–51. **[G: U.S.]**

Menken, Jane. World Population and U.S. Policy: The Choices Ahead: Introduction and Overview. **In** *Menken, J., ed.*, 1986, pp. 6–26. **[G: U.S.]**

Mera, Koichi. Population Stabilization and National Spatial Policy of Public Investment: The Japanese Experience. *Int. Reg. Sci. Rev.*, April 1986, *10*(1), pp. 47–65. **[G: Japan]**

Mercer, A. J. Relative Trends in Mortality from Related Respiratory and Airborne Infectious Diseases. *Population Stud.*, March 1986, *40*(1), pp. 129–45. **[G: U.K.]**

Michael, Robert T. and Tuma, Nancy. [Erratum] Entry into Marriage and Parenthood by Young Men and Women. *Demography*, August 1986, *23*(3), pp. 289. **[G: U.S.]**

Miller, Warren B. Proception: An Import Fertility Behavior. *Demography*, November 1986, *23*(4), pp. 579–94.

Montgomery, Mark R.; Richards, Toni and Braun, Henry I. Child Health, Breast-Feeding, and Survival in Malaysia: A Random-Effects Logit Approach. *J. Amer. Statist. Assoc.*, June 1986, *81*(394), pp. 297–309. **[G: Malaysia]**

Montgomery, Mark R. and Trussell, James. Models of Marital Status and Childbearing. **In** *Ashenfelter, O. and Layard, R., eds., Vol. 1*, 1986, pp. 205–71. **[G: U.S.]**

Moore, Thomas Gale. Economic Growth with Below-Replacement Fertility: Comment. *Population Devel. Rev.*, Supp. 1986, *12*, pp. 243–44. **[G: U.S.]**

Moore, Thomas Gale. Social Security in Aging Societies: Comment. *Population Devel. Rev.*, Supp. 1986, *12*, pp. 295.

Moreh, Jacob. Women, Men, and Society. *Kyklos*, 1986, *39*(2), pp. 209–29.

Morrill, Richard; Downing, Jeanne and Leon, William. Attribute Preferences and the Nonmetropolitan Migration Decision. *Ann. Reg. Sci.*, March 1986, *20*(1), pp. 33–53. **[G: U.S.]**

Morrison, Peter A. and DaVanzo, Julie. The Prism of Migration: Dissimilarities between Return and Onward Movers. *Soc. Sci. Quart.*, September 1986, *67*(3), pp. 504–16. **[G: U.S.]**

Mosk, Carl and Johansson, S. Ryan. Income and Mortality: Evidence from Modern Japan. *Population Devel. Rev.*, September 1986, *12*(3), pp. 415–40. **[G: Japan]**

Moss, Mitchell. Information Technology, Demographics, and the Retail Response: Discussion. **In** *Faulhaber, G.; Noam, E. and Tasley, R., eds.*, 1986, pp. 178–82. **[G: U.S.; OECD]**

Myers, George C.; Manton, Kenneth G. and Bacellar, Helena. Sociodemographic Aspects of Future Unpaid Productive Roles. **In** *Inst. Med. and Nat'l Res. Counc., Comm. on an Aging Society*, 1986, pp. 110–47. **[G: U.S.]**

Nerlove, Marc; Razin, Assaf and Sadka, Efraim. Endogenous Population with Public Goods and Malthusian Fixed Resources: Efficiency or Market Failure. *Int. Econ. Rev.*, October 1986, *27*(3), pp. 601–09.

Nerlove, Marc; Razin, Assaf and Sadka, Efraim. Some Welfare Theoretic Implications of Endogenous Fertility. *Int. Econ. Rev.*, February 1986, *27*(1), pp. 3–31.

Nerlove, Marc; Razin, Assaf and Sadka, Efraim. Tamaño de población socialmente óptimo. (With English summary.) *Cuadernos Econ.*, April 1986, *23*(68), pp. 3–23.

Newman, Stephen C. A Generalization of Life Expectancy Which Incorporates the Age Distribution of the Population and Its Use in the Measurement of the Impact of Mortality Reduction. *Demography*, May 1986, *23*(2), pp. 261–74.

Ng, Yew-Kwang. On the Welfare Economics of Population Control. *Population Devel. Rev.*, June 1986, *12*(2), pp. 247–66.

Ó Gráda, Cormac. Across the Briny Ocean: Some Thoughts on Irish Emigration to America, 1800–1850. **In** *Glazier, I. A. and De Rosa, L., eds.*, 1986, pp. 79–94. **[G: U.S.; Ireland]**

Oberai, A. S. Land Settlement Policies and Population Redistribution in Developing Countries: Performance, Problems and Prospects. *Int. Lab. Rev.*, Mar.-Apr. 1986, *125*(2), pp. 141–61. **[G: LDCs]**

Oberly, James W. Westward Who? Estimates of Native White Interstate Migration after the War of 1812. *J. Econ. Hist.*, June 1986, *46*(2), pp. 431–40. **[G: U.S.]**

Ostergren, Robert C. Swedish Migration to North America in Transatlantic Perspective. **In** *Glazier, I. A. and De Rosa, L., eds.*, 1986, pp. 125–47. **[G: Sweden; U.S.]**

Ostfeld, Adrian M. Applications of Social Science to Clinical Medicine and Health Policy: Cardiovascular Disease. **In** *Aiken, L. H. and Mechanic, D., eds.*, 1986, pp. 129–56. **[G: U.S.]**

Outhwaite, R. B. Marriage as Business: Opinions on the Rise in Aristocratic Bridal Portions in Early Modern England. **In** *[Coleman, D. C.]*, 1986, pp. 21–37. **[G: U.K.]**

Palmer, John P. The Social Cost of Adoption Agencies. *Int. Rev. Law Econ.*, December 1986, *6*(2), pp. 189–203. **[G: U.S.]**

Pampel, Fred C., Jr. and Pillai, Vijayan K. Patterns and Determinants of Infant Mortality in Developed Nations, 1950–1975. *Demography*, November 1986, *23*(4), pp. 525–42. **[G: OECD]**

Parra Sandoval, Rodrigo. The Missing Future: Colombian Youth. *CEPAL Rev.*, August 1986, (29), pp. 79–92. **[G: Colombia]**

Peery, J. Craig. The Family: Federal Policy and Private Alternatives. **In** *Peden, J. R. and Glahe, F. R., eds.*, 1986, pp. 425–47. **[G: U.S.]**

Peters, H. Elizabeth. Marriage and Divorce: Informational Constraints and Private Contracting. *Amer. Econ. Rev.*, June 1986, *76*(3), pp. 437–54. **[G: U.S.]**

Pickering, Ruth M.; Murray, G. D. and Forbes, J. F. Pre-term Foetal Life Times in Scotland. *Population Stud.*, March 1986, *40*(1), pp. 115–27. **[G: U.K.]**

Plane, David A. and Rogerson, Peter A. Dynamic Flow Modeling with Interregional Dependency Effects: An Application to Structural Change in the U.S. Migration System. *Demography*, February 1986, *23*(1), pp. 91–104. **[G: U.S.]**

Plaut, Thomas. Economic–Demographic Interactions in the Growth of Texas. **In** *Isserman, A. M., ed.*, 1986, pp. 81–104. **[G: U.S.]**

Pollak, Robert A. A Reformulation of the Two-Sex Problem. *Demography*, May 1986, *23*(2), pp. 247–59.

Poos, L. R. Population Turnover in Medieval Essex: The Evidence of Some Early–Fourteenth-Century Tithing Lists. **In** *[Laslett, P.]*, 1986, pp. 1–22. **[G: U.K.]**

Potter, Joseph E. Population Growth and Economic Development: Policy Questions. *Population Devel. Rev.*, September 1986, *12*(3), pp. 578–81.

Powell, Dorian. Caribbean Women and Their Response to Familial Experience. *Soc. Econ. Stud.*, June 1986, *35*(2), pp. 83–130. **[G: Barbados; St. Vincent; Antigua]**

Powell, Richard A. Teaching Economics to the 16–19 Age Range: Population and Demography. **In** *Whitehead, D. J., ed.*, 1986, pp. 182–86. **[G: U.K.]**

Pradel de Lamaze, François. Malthusianism in South-west France in the Nineteenth and Twentieth Centuries. **In** *Turner, M., ed.*, 1986, pp. 71–81. **[G: France]**

Premdas, Ralph R. Politics of Preference in the Caribbean: The Case of Guyana. **In** *Nevitte, N. and Kennedy, C. H., eds.*, 1986, pp. 155–87. **[G: Guyana]**

Presser, Harriet B. Changing Values and Falling Birth Rates: Comment. *Population Devel. Rev.*, Supp. 1986, *12*, pp. 196–200. **[G: OECD]**

Preston, Samuel H. Are the Economic Consequences of Population Growth a Sound Basis for Population Policy? **In** *Menken, J., ed.*, 1986, pp. 67–95.

Preston, Samuel H. Changing Values and Falling Birth Rates. *Population Devel. Rev.*, Supp. 1986, *12*, pp. 176–95. **[G: OECD]**

Preston, Samuel H. The Decline of Fertility in Non-European Industrialized Countries. *Population Devel. Rev.*, Supp. 1986, *12*, pp. 26–47. **[G: Australia; Canada; Japan; New Zealand; U.S.]**

Preston, Samuel H. The Relation between Actual and Intrinsic Growth Rates. *Population Stud.*, November 1986, *40*(3), pp. 343–51.

Puskás, Julianna. Hungarian Migration Patterns, 1880–1930: From Macroanalysis to Microanalysis. **In** *Glazier, I. A. and De Rosa, L., eds.*, 1986, pp. 231–54. **[G: Hungary; U.S.]**

Quah, Euston. Persistent Problems in Measuring Household Production: Definition, Quantifying Joint Activities and Valuation Issues Are Solvable. *Amer. J. Econ. Soc.*, April 1986, *45*(2), pp. 235–45.

Radice, E. A. Territorial Changes, Population Movements and Labour Supplies. **In** *Kaser, M. C. and Radice, E. A., eds.*, 1986, pp. 309–28. **[G: E. Europe]**

Rahman, Rushidan Islam. Time Budget Studies

and the Measurement of Time Spent on Child Care by Rural Women in Bangladesh: A Note on Methodology. *Bangladesh Devel. Stud.*, March 1986, *14*(1), pp. 107–16. **[G: Bangladesh]**

Rama, Germán W. Latin American Youth between Development and Crisis. *CEPAL Rev.*, August 1986, (29), pp. 17–39. **[G: Latin America]**

Ramirez, Miguel D. Marx and Malthusianism: Comment. *Amer. Econ. Rev.*, June 1986, *76*(3), pp. 543–47.

Rao, M. S. A. Migration, Agricultural Development, and Deprivation: A Case Study of a Tribal Situation in India. **In** *Glazier, I. A. and De Rosa, L., eds.*, 1986, pp. 58–75. **[G: India]**

Ray, Ranjan. Demographic Variables and Equivalence Scales in a Flexible Demand System: The Case of AIDS. *Appl. Econ.*, March 1986, *18*(3), pp. 265–78. **[G: U.K.]**

Reicher Madeira, Felicia. Youth in Brazil: Old Assumptions and New Approaches. *CEPAL Rev.*, August 1986, (29), pp. 55–78. **[G: Brazil]**

Ricardo-Campbell, Rita. U.S. Social Security under Low Fertility. *Population Devel. Rev.*, Supp. 1986, *12*, pp. 296–312.

Riessman, Catherine Kohler and Nathanson, Constance A. The Management of Reproduction: Social Construction of Risk and Responsibility. **In** *Aiken, L. H. and Mechanic, D., eds.*, 1986, pp. 251–81. **[G: U.S.]**

Riley, James C. Insects and the European Mortality Decline. *Amer. Hist. Rev.*, October 1986, *91*(4), pp. 833–58. **[G: Europe]**

Robinson, Warren C. High Fertility as Risk-Insurance. *Population Stud.*, July 1986, *40*(2), pp. 289–98. **[G: Bangladesh]**

Rogers, Andrei and Williams, Pamela. Multistate Demoeconomic Modeling and Projection. **In** *Isserman, A. M., ed.*, 1986, pp. 177–202. **[G: Australia]**

van Roon, Ger. Cycles, Turning Phases and Societal Structures: Historical Perspective and Current Problems. **In** *Freeman, C., ed.*, 1986, pp. 48–59. **[G: U.K.; U.S.; W. Europe]**

Rosen, Sherwin. Unobservable Family and Individual Contributions to the Distributions of Income and Wealth: Comment. *J. Lab. Econ.*, Part 2, July 1986, *4*(3), pp. S80–82.

Rosenzweig, Mark R. Birth Spacing and Sibling Inequality: Asymmetric Information within the Family. *Int. Econ. Rev.*, February 1986, *27*(1), pp. 55–76. **[G: U.S.]**

Rosenzweig, Mark R. Program Interventions, Intrahousehold Distribution and the Welfare of Individuals: Modeling Household Behavior. *World Devel.*, Special Issue, Feb. 1986, *14*(2), pp. 233–43. **[G: India; Indonesia; Philippines]**

Rosenzweig, Mark R. and Wolpin, Kenneth I. Evaluating the Effects of Optimally Distributed Public Programs: Child Health and Family Planning Interventions. *Amer. Econ. Rev.*, June 1986, *76*(3), pp. 470–82. **[G: Philippines]**

Rubin, Rose M. and Riney, Bobye J. Second-Earner Net Income Model and Simulated Income Distributions for Dual-Earner Households. *Soc. Sci. Quart.*, June 1986, *67*(2), pp. 432–41. **[G: U.S.]**

Ruggiero, Kristin. Social and Psychological Factors in Migration from Italy to Argentina: From the Waldensian Valleys to San Gustavo. **In** *Glazier, I. A. and De Rosa, L., eds.*, 1986, pp. 160–73. **[G: Italy; Argentina]**

Ryder, Norman B. Observations on the History of Cohort Fertility in the United States. *Population Devel. Rev.*, December 1986, *12*(4), pp. 617–43. **[G: U.S.]**

Safa, Helen I. Economic Autonomy and Sexual Equality in Caribbean Society. *Soc. Econ. Stud.*, September 1986, *35*(3), pp. 1–21. **[G: Caribbean]**

Sai, Fred T. Population and Health: Africa's Most Basic Resource and Development Problem. **In** *Berg, R. J. and Whitaker, J. S., eds.*, 1986, pp. 129–52. **[G: Africa]**

Samuelson, Paul A. Complete Genetic Models for Altruism, Kin Selection and Like-Gene Selection. **In** *Samuelson, P. A.*, 1986, *1983*, pp. 710–22.

Samuelson, Paul A. Fisher's "Reproductive Value" as an Economic Specimen in Merton's Zoo. **In** *Samuelson, P. A.*, 1986, *1980*, pp. 752–68.

Samuelson, Paul A. Generalizing Fisher's "Reproductive Value": Overlapping and Nonoverlapping Generations with Competing Genotypes. **In** *Samuelson, P. A.*, 1986, *1978*, pp. 777–81.

Samuelson, Paul A. Generalizing Fisher's "Reproductive Value": Linear Differential and Difference Equations of "Dilute" Biological Systems. **In** *Samuelson, P. A.*, 1986, *1977*, pp. 769–72.

Samuelson, Paul A. Generalizing Fisher's "Reproductive Value": "Incipient" and "Penultimate" Reproductive-Value Functions When Environment Limits Growth; Linear Approximants for Nonlinear Mendelian Mating Models. **In** *Samuelson, P. A.*, 1986, *1978*, pp. 782–86.

Samuelson, Paul A. Generalizing Fisher's "Reproductive Value": Nonlinear, Homogeneous, Biparental Systems. **In** *Samuelson, P. A.*, 1986, *1978*, pp. 773–76.

Samuelson, Paul A. Modes of Thought in Economics and Biology. **In** *Samuelson, P. A.*, 1986, *1985*, pp. 723–29.

Sander, William. Farm Women, Work, and Fertility. *Quart. J. Econ.*, August 1986, *101*(3), pp. 653–57. **[G: U.S.]**

Sander, William. On the Economics of Marital Instability in the United Kingdom. *Scot. J. Polit. Econ.*, November 1986, *33*(4), pp. 370–81. **[G: U.K.]**

Santow, Gig. The Impact of International Migration upon the Timing of Marriage and Childbearing: A Comment. *Demography*, August 1986, *23*(3), pp. 467–68. **[G: Australia]**

Sathar, Zeba A. Changes in Female Roles in Pakistan: Are the Volume and Pace Adequate? Comments. *Pakistan Devel. Rev.*, Autumn 1986, *25*(3), pp. 367–69. **[G: Pakistan]**

Schofield, Roger. Did the Mothers Really Die? Three Centuries of Maternal Mortality in 'The World We Have Lost.' **In** *[Laslett, P.]*, 1986, pp. 231–60. **[G: Sweden; U.K.]**

Schultz, T. Paul. Richard A. Easterlin and Eileen M. Crimmins: The Fertility Revolution: A Supply–Demand Analysis. *Population Devel. Rev.*, March 1986, *12* (1), pp. 127–40. **[G: Sri Lanka; Colombia; China; India]**

Schultz, T. Paul. The Value and Allocation of Time in High-Income Countries: Implications for Fertility. *Population Devel. Rev.*, Supp. 1986, *12*, pp. 87–108. **[G: U.S.]**

Schultz, Theodore W. The Changing Economy and the Family. *J. Lab. Econ.*, Part 2, July 1986, *4* (3), pp. S278–87.

Scitovsky, Tibor. The Economy's Impact on Family and Social Relations in America. **In** *Scitovsky, T.*, 1986, *1984*, pp. 160–82. **[G: U.S.]**

Sewastynowicz, James. "Two-Step" Migration and Upward Mobility on the Frontier: The Safety Valve Effect in Pejibaye, Costa Rica. *Econ. Develop. Cult. Change*, July 1986, *34* (4), pp. 731–53. **[G: Costa Rica]**

Shah, Nasra M. Changes in Female Roles in Pakistan: Are the Volume and Pace Adequate? *Pakistan Devel. Rev.*, Autumn 1986, *25* (3), pp. 339–63. **[G: Pakistan]**

Shields, Michael P. and Tracy, Ronald L. Four Themes in Fertility Research. *Southern Econ. J.*, July 1986, *53* (1), pp. 201–16. **[G: U.S.]**

Simmons, George B. Family Planning Programs. **In** *Menken, J., ed.*, 1986, pp. 175–206. **[G: Global]**

Simon, Julian L. Population Growth and Economic Development: Policy Questions. *Population Devel. Rev.*, September 1986, *12* (3), pp. 569–77.

Simon, Julian L. Some Theory of Population Growth's Effect on Technical Change in an Industrial Context. *Australian Econ. Hist. Rev.*, September 1986, *26* (2), pp. 148–58.

Simon, Julian L. and Steinmann, Gunter. A Model of Supply, Demand and Technical Progress [Phelps's Technical Progress Model Generalized]. **In** *Simon, J. L.*, 1986, *1981*, pp. 102–14.

Simon, Julian L. and Steinmann, Gunter. The Effects of Population Size and Growth through Learning-by-Doing [The Economic Implications of Learning-by-Doing for Population Size and Growth]. **In** *Simon, J. L.*, 1986, *1984*, pp. 83–101.

Sirageldin, Ismail. The Potential for Economic–Demographic Development: Whither Theory? *Pakistan Devel. Rev.*, Spring 1986, *25* (1), pp. 1–42. **[G: LDCs]**

Skeldon, Ronald. On Migration Patterns in India during the 1970s. *Population Devel. Rev.*, December 1986, *12* (4), pp. 759–79. **[G: India]**

Slater, Paul B. Biplots of 1959–1961 United States Metropolitan Mortality. **In** *Slater, P. B.*, 1986, *1979*, pp. 43–50. **[G: U.S.]**

Slater, Paul B. Comparisons of Aggregation Procedures for Interaction Data: An Illustration Using a College Student International Flow Table. **In** *Slater, P. B.*, 1986, *1981*, pp. 29–36. **[G: Selected Countries]**

Slater, Paul B. International Migration and Air Travel: Global Smoothing and Estimation. **In** *Slater, P. B.*, 1986, pp. 107–24. **[G: Selected Countries]**

Slater, Paul B. Origin and Destination Entropies of U.S. 1965–70 Age–Sex-Specific Intercounty Migration Flows. **In** *Slater, P. B.*, 1986, *1984*, pp. 51–56. **[G: U.S.]**

Slater, Paul B. Point-to-Point Migration Functions and Gravity Model Renormalization: Approaches to Aggregation in Spatial Interaction Modeling. **In** *Slater, P. B.*, 1986, *1985*, pp. 57–76. **[G: U.S.]**

Slater, Paul B. World Population Distribution: Smoothed Representations. **In** *Slater, P. B.*, 1986, pp. 77–106. **[G: Global]**

Smil, Vaclav. Food Production and Quality of Diet in China. *Population Devel. Rev.*, March 1986, *12* (1), pp. 25–45. **[G: China]**

Smith, David P. An Analysis of Variations in U.S. Fertility and Female Labor Force Participation Trends: Comment. *Demography*, February 1986, *23* (1), pp. 137–39. **[G: U.S.]**

Smith, James D. Estimating the Personal Distribution of Income with Adjustment for Within-Family Variation: Comment. *J. Lab. Econ.*, Part 2, July 1986, *4* (3), pp. S239–44. **[G: U.S.]**

Smith, R. M. Marriage Processes in the English Past: Some Continuities. **In** *[Laslett, P.]*, 1986, pp. 43–99. **[G: U.K.]**

Smith, Stanley K. A Review and Evaluation of the Housing Unit Method of Population Estimation. *J. Amer. Statist. Assoc.*, June 1986, *81* (394), pp. 287–96. **[G: U.S.]**

Smith, Stanley K. Accounting for Migration in Cohort-Component Projections of State and Local Populations. *Demography*, February 1986, *23* (1), pp. 127–35. **[G: U.S.]**

Smith, Stanley K. Using Medicare Data for Short-run Projections of the Elderly Population. *J. Econ. Soc. Meas.*, April 1986, *14* (1), pp. 37–49. **[G: U.S.]**

Smith, Tony E. An Axiomatic Foundation for Poisson Frequency Analyses of Weakly Interacting Populations. *Reg. Sci. Urban Econ.*, May 1986, *16* (2), pp. 269–307.

Smith, Wayne R. and Pryor, Edward T. The Census of Canada: Current Situation and Future Developments. *Statist. J.*, May 1986, *4* (1), pp. 19–30. **[G: Canada]**

Sora, V.; Hristache, I. and Despa, M. Stable Population-Reference Model in the Analysis of the Structure by Age. *Econ. Computat. Cybern. Stud. Res.*, 1986, *21* (1), pp. 33–37. **[G: Romania]**

Soskiev, A. Social and Economic Problems of Labor Power Reproduction in Agriculture. *Prob. Econ.*, May 1986, *29* (1), pp. 82–91. **[G: U.S.S.R.]**

Spooner, Frank. Batavia, 1673–1790: A City of Colonial Growth and Migration. **In** *Glazier, I. A. and De Rosa, L., eds.*, 1986, pp. 30–57. **[G: Indonesia]**

Stampfer, Shaul. The Geographic Background of East European Jewish Migration to the United States before World War I. **In** *Glazier, I. A. and De Rosa, L., eds.*, 1986, pp. 220–30. **[G: E. Europe; U.S.]**

Stapleton, B. Malthus: The Origins of the Principle of Population? **In** *Turner, M., ed.*, 1986, pp. 19–39. **[G: U.K.]**

Steckel, Richard H. A Peculiar Population: The Nutrition, Health, and Mortality of American Slaves from Childhood to Maturity. *J. Econ. Hist.*, September 1986, *46*(3), pp. 721–41. **[G: U.S.]**

Steckel, Richard H. Birth Weights and Infant Mortality among American Slaves. *Exploration Econ. Hist.*, April 1986, *23*(2), pp. 173–98. **[G: U.S.]**

Steinmann, Gunter and Simon, Julian L. The Optimum Rate of Population Growth [On the Optimum Theoretical Rate of Population Growth]. **In** *Simon, J. L.*, 1986, *1985*, pp. 115–39.

Sternlieb, George and Hughes, James W. Information Technology, Demographics, and the Retail Response. **In** *Faulhaber, G.; Noam, E. and Tasley, R., eds.*, 1986, pp. 139–74. **[G: U.S.; OECD]**

Stokes, C. Shannon; Schutjer, Wayne A. and Bulatao, Rodolfo A. Is the Relationship between Landholding and Fertility Spurious? A Response. *Population Stud.*, July 1986, *40*(2), pp. 305–11. **[G: LDCs]**

Stone, Richard. Demographic Input–Output: An Extension of Social Accounting. **In** *Sohn, I., ed.*, 1986, *1970*, pp. 151–72. **[G: U.K.]**

Swan, George Steven. The Political Economy of American Family Policy, 1945–85. *Population Devel. Rev.*, December 1986, *12*(4), pp. 739–58. **[G: U.S.]**

Swidler, Steve. The Old-Age Security Motive for Having Children and the Effect of Social Security on Completed Family Size. *Quart. Rev. Econ. Bus.*, Summer 1986, *26*(2), pp. 14–34. **[G: U.S.]**

Szreter, S. R. S. The First Scientific Social Structure of Modern Britain, 1875–1883. **In** *[Laslett, P.]*, 1986, pp. 337–54. **[G: U.K.]**

Talbot, Lee M. Demographic Factors in Resource Depletion and Environmental Degradation in East African Rangeland. *Population Devel. Rev.*, September 1986, *12*(3), pp. 441–51. **[G: Kenya]**

Taylor, Carol A. The Effects of Refining Demographic–Economic Interactions in Regional Econometric Models. **In** *Isserman, A. M., ed.*, 1986, pp. 127–55. **[G: U.S.]**

Tedford, John R.; Capps, Oral, Jr. and Havlicek, Joseph, Jr. Adult Equivalent Scales Once More—A Developmental Approach. *Amer. J. Agr. Econ.*, May 1986, *68*(2), pp. 322–33. **[G: U.S.]**

Teitelbaum, Michael S. Intersections: Immigration and Demographic Change and Their Impact on the United States. **In** *Menken, J., ed.*, 1986, pp. 133–74. **[G: U.S.]**

Thomas, Brinley. The Industrial Revolution and the Welsh Language. **In** *Baber, C. and Williams, L. J., eds.*, 1986, pp. 6–21. **[G: U.K.]**

Thornton, Arland, et al. Intergenerational Relations and Reproductive Behavior in Taiwan. *Demography*, May 1986, *23*(2), pp. 185–97. **[G: Taiwan]**

Tilly, Charles. The Decline of Fertility in Europe: Review. *Population Devel. Rev.*, June 1986, *12*(2), pp. 323–28. **[G: Europe]**

Timmer, C. Peter. *Redesigning Rural Development* from a Food Policy Perspective: Review Article. *Econ. Develop. Cult. Change*, July 1986, *34*(4), pp. 855–60.

Treas, Judith and Logue, Barbara. Economic Development and the Older Population. *Population Devel. Rev.*, December 1986, *12*(4), pp. 645–73.

Tullock, Gordon. Population Paradoxes. **In** *Tullock, G.*, 1986, pp. 183–92.

Uner, Sunday. Migration and Labor Transformation in Rural Turkey. **In** *Richards, A., ed.*, 1986, pp. 225–64. **[G: Turkey]**

Vasegh-Daneshvary, Nasser; Herzog, Henry W., Jr. and Schlottmann, Alan M. College Educated Immigrants in the American Labor Force: A Study of Locational Behavior. *Southern Econ. J.*, January 1986, *52*(3), pp. 818–31. **[G: U.S.]**

Vaupel, J. W. How Change in Age-specific Mortality Affects Life Expectancy. *Population Stud.*, March 1986, *40*(1), pp. 147–57. **[G: Sweden; Selected Countries]**

Vecoli, Rudolph J. The Formation of Chicago's "Little Italies." **In** *Glazier, I. A. and De Rosa, L., eds.*, 1986, pp. 287–301. **[G: U.S.]**

Viazzo, Pier Paolo. Illegitimacy and the European Marriage Pattern: Comparative Evidence from the Alpine Area. **In** *[Laslett, P.]*, 1986, pp. 100–121. **[G: Switzerland]**

Vining, Daniel R., Jr. Population Redistribution towards Core Areas of Less Developed Countries, 1950–1980. *Int. Reg. Sci. Rev.*, April 1986, *10*(1), pp. 1–45. **[G: LDCs]**

Voss, Paul R. Demographics and Rural Roads. **In** *Chicoine, D. L. and Walzer, N., eds.*, 1986, pp. 53–76. **[G: U.S.]**

Wachter, Kenneth W. Ergodicity and Inverse Projection. *Population Stud.*, July 1986, *40*(2), pp. 275–87.

Wahl, Jenny Bourne. New Results on the Decline in Household Fertility in the United States from 1750 to 1900. **In** *Engerman, S. L. and Gallman, R. E., eds.*, 1986, pp. 391–425. **[G: U.S.]**

Warwick, Donald P. The Indonesian Family Planning Program: Government Influence and Client Choice. *Population Devel. Rev.*, September 1986, *12*(3), pp. 453–90. **[G: Indonesia]**

Wascher, William L.; Burch, Susan W. and Goodman, John L., Jr. Economic Implications of Changing Population Trends. *Fed. Res. Bull.*, December 1986, *72*(12), pp. 815–26.

Weaver, Carolyn L. Social Security in Aging Societies. *Population Devel. Rev.*, Supp. 1986, *12*, pp. 273–94. **[G: OECD]**

Westoff, Charles F. Perspective on Nuptiality and Fertility. *Population Devel. Rev.*, Supp. 1986, *12*, pp. 155–70. **[G: OECD]**

White, Averille. Profiles: Women in the Caribbean Project. *Soc. Econ. Stud.*, June 1986, *35*(2), pp. 59–81. **[G: Barbados; Antigua; St. Vincent]**

Williamson, Jeffrey G. Regional Economic–Demographic Modeling: Progress and Prospects. **In** *Isserman, A. M., ed.*, 1986, pp. 241–60. **[G: LDCs]**

Willis, Robert J. Human Capital and the Rise and Fall of Families: Comment. *J. Lab. Econ.*, Part 2, July 1986, *4*(3), pp. S40–47.

Wilson, Chris. The Proximate Determinants of Marital Fertility in England 1600–1799. **In** *[Laslett, P.]*, 1986, pp. 203–30. **[G: U.K.]**

Wilson, William Julius and Neckerman, Kathryn M. Poverty and Family Structure: The Widening Gap between Evidence and Public Policy Issues. **In** *Danziger, S. H. and Weinberg, D. H., eds.*, 1986, pp. 232–59. **[G: U.S.]**

Wolf, Arthur P. The Preeminent Role of Government Intervention in China's Family Revolution. *Population Devel. Rev.*, March 1986, *12*(1), pp. 101–16. **[G: China]**

Wolfe, Barbara L. and Behrman, Jere R. Child Quantity and Quality in a Developing Country: Family Background, Endogenous Tastes, and Biological Supply Factors. *Econ. Develop. Cult. Change*, July 1986, *34*(4), pp. 703–20. **[G: Nicaragua]**

Wong, Yue-chim. Entrepreneurship, Marriage, and Earnings. *Rev. Econ. Statist.*, November 1986, *68*(4), pp. 693–99. **[G: Hong Kong]**

Wood, Charles H. and McCracken, Stephen D. Underdevelopment, Urban Growth and Collective Social Action in Sao Paulo, Brazil. **In** *Abegaz, B., ed.*, 1986, pp. 101–40. **[G: Brazil]**

Wrigley, E. A. Malthus's Model of a Pre-industrial Economy. **In** *Turner, M., ed.*, 1986, pp. 3–18. **[G: U.K.]**

Yamada, Tadashi and Yamada, Tetsuji. Fertility and Labor Force Participation of Married Women: Empirical Evidence from the 1980 Population Census of Japan. *Quart. Rev. Econ. Bus.*, Summer 1986, *26*(2), pp. 35–46. **[G: Japan]**

Yellin, Joel and Samuelson, Paul A. Comparison of Linear and Nonlinear Models for Human Population Dynamics. **In** *Samuelson, P. A.*, 1986, *1977*, pp. 730–51.

Yotopoulos, Pan A. and Mergos, George J. Family Labor Allocation in the Agricultural Household. *Food Res. Inst. Stud.*, 1986, *20*(1), pp. 87–104. **[G: Philippines]**

Zeng, Yi. Changes in Family Structure in China: A Simulation Study. *Population Devel. Rev.*, December 1986, *12*(4), pp. 675–703. **[G: China]**

850 Human Capital; Value of Human Life

851 Human Capital; Value of Human Life

8510 Human Capital; Value of Human Life

Akhtar, Haq Nawaz. Manpower Development in Public Enterprises. **In** *U.N., Dept. of Technical Co-operation for Development*, 1986, pp. 149–61. **[G: Pakistan]**

Amir, Shmuel. Educational Structure and Wage Differentials of the Labor Force in the 1970s. **In** *Ben-Porath, Y., ed.*, 1986, pp. 137–52. **[G: Israel]**

Antel, John J. Human Capital Investment Specialization and the Wage Effects of Voluntary Labor Mobility. *Rev. Econ. Statist.*, August 1986, *68*(3), pp. 477–83. **[G: U.S.]**

Avila, Jorge C. Reducción del Empleo Público Redundante, Capital Humano y Ajuste en una Economía Abierta. (Reducing Government Overmanning, Human Capital and Open-Economy Adjustment. With English summary.) *Económica (La Plata)*, July-December 1986, *32*(2), pp. 165–205. **[G: Argentina]**

Becker, Gary S. and Tomes, Nigel. Human Capital and the Rise and Fall of Families. *J. Lab. Econ.*, Part 2, July 1986, *4*(3), pp. S1–39. **[G: U.S.; Switzerland; Norway; Sweden; U.K.]**

Behrman, Jere R.; Pollak, Robert A. and Taubman, Paul. Do Parents Favor Boys? *Int. Econ. Rev.*, February 1986, *27*(1), pp. 33–54. **[G: U.S.]**

Behrman, Jere R. and Taubman, Paul. Birth Order, Schooling, and Earnings. *J. Lab. Econ.*, Part 2, July 1986, *4*(3), pp. S121–45. **[G: U.S.]**

Beladi, Hamid; Brunner, Lawrence P. and Zuberi, Habib A. The Rates of Return on Investment in Education in Michigan. *Atlantic Econ. J.*, December 1986, *14*(4), pp. 50–64. **[G: U.S.]**

Bellante, Don and Saba, Richard P. Human Capital and Life-Cycle Effects on Risk Aversion. *J. Finan. Res.*, Spring 1986, *9*(1), pp. 41–51. **[G: U.S.]**

Bielby, William T. and Baron, James N. Sex Segregation within Occupations. *Amer. Econ. Rev.*, May 1986, *76*(2), pp. 43–47. **[G: U.S.]**

Birdsall, Nancy and Meesook, Oey Astra. Children's Education and the Intergenerational Transmission of Inequality: A Simulation. *Econ. Educ. Rev.*, 1986, *5*(3), pp. 239–56. **[G: Brazil]**

Björkman, James Warner. Health Policies and Human Capital: The Case of Pakistan. *Pakistan Devel. Rev.*, Autumn 1986, *25*(3), pp. 281–330. **[G: Pakistan]**

Blaug, Mark. The Economics of Education in English Classical Political Economy: A Re-examination. **In** *Blaug, M.*, 1986, *1975*, pp. 150–83.

Blomqvist, Ake G. Health Policies and Human Capital: The Case of Pakistan: Comments. *Pakistan Devel. Rev.*, Autumn 1986, *25*(3), pp. 331–34. **[G: Pakistan]**

Blomqvist, Ake G. Higher Education and the Markets for Educated Labour in LDCs: Theoretical Approaches and Implications. *Pakistan Devel. Rev.*, Autumn 1986, *25*(3), pp. 249–73. **[G: LDCs]**

Blomqvist, Ake G. International Migration of Educated Manpower and Social Rates of Return to Education in LDCs. *Int. Econ. Rev.*, February 1986, *27*(1), pp. 165–74. **[G: LDCs]**

Bouman, Huub and Verhoef, Bram. High-technology and Employment: Some Information on the Netherlands. **In** *Nijkamp, P., ed. (II)*, 1986, pp. 289–98. **[G: Netherlands]**

Bound, John; Griliches, Zvi and Hall, Bronwyn H. Wages, Schooling and IQ of Brothers and Sisters: Do the Family Factors Differ? *Int. Econ. Rev.*, February 1986, *27*(1), pp. 77–105. **[G: U.S.]**

Brown, Ralph J. Implicit Inflation and Interest Rates in Discounting Personal Injury Economic Losses—Comment. *J. Risk Ins.*, September 1986, *53*(3), pp. 492–95. **[G: U.S.]**

Carpenter, Michael D., et al. Methodologies of Valuing Lost Earnings: A Review, a Criticism, and a Recommendation. *J. Risk Ins.*, March 1986, *53*(1), pp. 104–18. **[G: U.S.]**

Chaudhri, D. P. Human Capital, Structures of Production and the Basic Needs. **In** *Maunder, A. and Renborg, U., eds.*, 1986, pp. 466–74.

Chillemi, Ottorino. Salari e produttività dei lavoratori qualificati. Rapporti di lavoro a lungo termine e aspettative. (Wage and Productivity Profiles with Specific Human Capital and Imperfect Information. With English summary.) *Econ. Polít.*, December 1986, *3*(3), pp. 339–53.

Chiswick, Barry R. Human Capital and the Labor Market Adjustment of Immigrants: Testing Alternative Hypotheses. **In** *Stark, O., ed.*, 1986, pp. 1–26. **[G: U.S.]**

Cohen, Jacob. Fritz Machlup's Swan Song. *Econ. Educ. Rev.*, 1986, *5*(3), pp. 319–23.

Cohn, Elchanan and Kiker, B. F. Socioeconomic Background, Schooling, Experience and Monetary Rewards in the United States. *Economica*, November 1986, *53*(212), pp. 497–503. **[G: U.S.]**

Connelly, Rachel. A Framework for Analyzing the Impact of Cohort Size on Education and Labor Earnings. *J. Human Res.*, Fall 1986, *21*(4), pp. 543–62.

Corman, Hope. The Demand for Education for Home Production. *Econ. Inquiry*, April 1986, *24*(2), pp. 213–30. **[G: U.S.]**

Damachi, Ukandi G. and Seibel, Hans Dieter. Workers' Participation in Technological and Organisational Development: The Human Resources for a Suggestion Programme in Nigerian Industry. **In** *Damachi, U. G. and Seibel, H. D., eds.*, 1986, pp. 69–85. **[G: Nigeria]**

Dardanoni, Valentino. A Note on a Simple Model of Health Investment [On the Concept of Health Capital and the Demand for Health]. *Bull. Econ. Res.*, January 1986, *38*(1), pp. 97–100.

Dooley, Martin D. The Overeducated Canadian? Changes in the Relationship among Earnings, Education, and Age for Canadian Men: 1971–81. *Can. J. Econ.*, February 1986, *19*(1), pp. 142–59. **[G: Canada]**

Eliasson, Gunnar. On the Stability of Economic Organizational Forms and the Importance of Human Capital: A Proposition about the Endogenous, Market Induced Disintegration of the Non-market Sector. **In** *Day, R. H. and Eliasson, G., eds.*, 1986, pp. 454–67.

Enaohwo, J. Okpako and Osakwe, H. O. An Analysis of the Private Rate of Return to Vocational Nursing Education in Nigeria. *Econ. Educ. Rev.*, 1986, *5*(1), pp. 77–81. **[G: Nigeria]**

Etheredge, Dennis. The Role of the Private Sector in Education and Training. **In** *Smollan, R., ed.*, 1986, pp. 138–44. **[G: S. Africa]**

Filer, John H. Human Capital. **In** *Burton, D. F., et al., eds.*, 1986, pp. 3–9. **[G: U.S.]**

Francois, John. Case Studies of Black Advancement: SA Cyanamid. **In** *Smollan, R., ed.*, 1986, pp. 205–10. **[G: S. Africa]**

Freeman, Richard B. Demand for Education. **In** *Ashenfelter, O. and Layard, R., eds., Vol. 1*, 1986, pp. 357–86. **[G: U.S.]**

Frey, Bruno S. and Buhofer, Heinz. A Market for Men, Or: There Is No Such Thing as a Free Lynch. *J. Inst. Theoretical Econ.*, December 1986, *142*(4), pp. 739–44. **[G: Europe]**

Gloeckner, Eduard. Underemployment and Potential Unemployment of the Technical Intelligentsia: Distortions between Education and Occupation. **In** *Lane, D., ed.*, 1986, pp. 223–36. **[G: U.S.S.R.]**

Goss, Ernst P. and Paul, Chris. Age and Work Experience in the Decision to Migrate. *J. Human Res.*, Summer 1986, *21*(3), pp. 397–405.

Gremmen, Hans J. and Vollebergh, Ad H. J. An Input Approach to European Comparative Advantage in Advanced Products: A Study with Special Emphasis on the Netherlands. *Weltwirtsch. Arch.*, 1986, *122*(2), pp. 270–80. **[G: Netherlands; Global]**

Griliches, Zvi. Birth Order, Schooling, and Earnings: Comment. *J. Lab. Econ.*, Part 2, July 1986, *4*(3), pp. S146–50. **[G: U.S.]**

Hartog, Joop. Allocation and the Earnings Function. *Empirical Econ.*, 1986, *11*(2), pp. 97–110. **[G: Netherlands]**

Hartog, Joop. Earnings Functions: Beyond Human Capital. *Appl. Econ.*, December 1986, *18*(12), pp. 1291–1309. **[G: Netherlands]**

Havenga, Richard. The Role of Non-profit Organisations in Education and Training. **In** *Smollan, R., ed.*, 1986, pp. 145–52. **[G: S. Africa]**

Huffman, Wallace E. Changes in Human Capital, Technology, and Institutions: Implications for Policy and Research. **In** *Maunder, A. and Renborg, U., eds.*, 1986, pp. 769–75.

Huijsman, R., et al. An Empirical Analysis of College Enrollment in the Netherlands. *De Econ-*

omist, 1986, *134*(2), pp. 181–90. **[G: Netherlands]**

Ioannides, Yannis M. Heritability of Ability, Intergenerational Transfers and the Distribution of Wealth. *Int. Econ. Rev.*, October 1986, *27*(3), pp. 611–23.

Jain, S. K. The Need for an Operational Thrust to Human Resources Development. *Int. Lab. Rev.*, Nov.-Dec. 1986, *125*(6), pp. 627–40.

Jarousse, Jean-Pierre and Mingat, Alain. Un réexamen du modèle de gains de mincer. (A Re-appraisal of Mincer's Earnings Model. With English summary.) *Revue Écon.*, November 1986, *37*(6), pp. 999–1031. **[G: France]**

Johansson, Börje and Karlsson, Charlie. Industrial Applications of Information Technology: Speed of Introduction and Labour Force Competence. **In** *Nijkamp, P., ed. (II)*, 1986, pp. 401–28. **[G: Sweden]**

Jones, David D. Rejoinder to Brown's Comment and a Reaction to Schilling's "Estimating the Present Value...." [Inflation Rates Implicit in Discounting Personal Injury Economic Losses]. *J. Risk Ins.*, September 1986, *53*(3), pp. 489–500. **[G: U.S.]**

Kawashima, Yoko and Tachibanaki, Toshiaki. The Effect of Discrimination and of Industry Segmentation on Japanese Wage Differentials in Relation to Education. *Int. J. Ind. Organ.*, March 1986, *4*(1), pp. 43–68. **[G: Japan]**

Kodde, David A. Uncertainty and the Demand for Education. *Rev. Econ. Statist.*, August 1986, *68*(3), pp. 460–67. **[G: Netherlands]**

Kraft, Kornelius. Wettbewerbssituation und Marktzutrittsbarrieren bei spezifischen Qualifikationen. (Competition and Barriers to Entry in the Case of Specific Qualifications. With English summary.) *Z. Wirtschaft. Sozialwissen.*, 1986, *106*(4), pp. 387–414. **[G: W. Germany]**

Kroch, Eugene and Sjoblom, Kriss. Education and the National Wealth of the United States. *Rev. Income Wealth,* March 1986, *32*(1), pp. 87–106. **[G: U.S.]**

Lang, Kevin and Kropp, David. Human Capital versus Sorting: The Effects of Compulsory Attendance Laws. *Quart. J. Econ.*, August 1986, *101*(3), pp. 609–24. **[G: U.S.]**

Lang, Kevin and Ruud, Paul A. Returns to Schooling, Implicit Discount Rates and Black–White Wage Differentials. *Rev. Econ. Statist.*, February 1986, *68*(1), pp. 41–47. **[G: U.S.]**

Lassibille, Gérard. L'influence des événements familiaux dans la formation des revenus. (The Effect of Family Events on Earnings. With English summary.) *Ann. Écon. Statist.*, Apr./June 1986, (2), pp. 101–16. **[G: France]**

Lazear, Edward P. and Moore, Robert L. Incentives, Productivity, and Labor Contracts. **In** *Akerlof, G. A. and Yellen, J. L., eds.*, 1986, *1984*, pp. 135–56. **[G: U.S.]**

Lehmann, Rainer H. and Verhine, Robert E. Educação e obtenção de empregos industriais no Brasil: para um modelo causal aprimorado. (With English summary.) *Pesquisa Planejamento Econ.*, December 1986, *16*(3), pp. 621–46. **[G: Brazil]**

Leigh, J. Paul. Wage Differentials and Risk of Death: Comment. *Econ. Inquiry*, July 1986, *24*(3), pp. 505–08. **[G: U.S.]**

Liu, Pak-Wai. Human Capital, Job Matching and Earnings Growth between Jobs: An Empirical Analysis. *Appl. Econ.*, October 1986, *18*(10), pp. 1135–47. **[G: Singapore]**

Low, Stuart A. and McPheters, Lee R. Wage Differentials and Risk of Death: Reply. *Econ. Inquiry*, July 1986, *24*(3), pp. 509–11. **[G: U.S.]**

Lubian, Diego. Interessi nel tasso "naturale": una interpretazione della elevata e persistente disoccupazione attuale. (Hysteresis in the "Natural" Rate of Employment: An Interpretation of the High and Persistent Present Unemployment. With English summary.) *Giorn. Econ.*, Jan.-Feb. 1986, *45*(1–2), pp. 55–72. **[G: U.S.; U.K.; Japan; Italy; W. Germany]**

Malle, Silvana. Heterogeneity of the Soviet Labour Market as a Limit to a More Efficient Utilisation of Manpower. **In** *Lane, D., ed.*, 1986, pp. 122–42. **[G: U.S.S.R.]**

Marcus, Richard D. Earnings and the Decision to Return to School. *Econ. Educ. Rev.*, 1986, *5*(3), pp. 309–17. **[G: U.S.]**

Margo, Robert A. Race and Human Capital: Comment. *Amer. Econ. Rev.*, December 1986, *76*(5), pp. 1221–24. **[G: U.S.]**

Margo, Robert A. Race, Educational Attainment, and the 1940 Census. *J. Econ. Hist.*, March 1986, *46*(1), pp. 189–98. **[G: U.S.]**

Maxwell, Nan L. The Effect of Human Capital and Labor Market Segments on Retirement Income: A Policy Analysis. *Soc. Sci. Quart.*, March 1986, *67*(1), pp. 53–68. **[G: U.S.]**

Maxwell, Nan L. and D'Amico, Ronald J. Employment and Wage Effects of Involuntary Job Separation: Male–Female Differences. *Amer. Econ. Rev.*, May 1986, *76*(2), pp. 373–77. **[G: U.S.]**

Moerdyk, Alwyn. Planning and Implementing a Black Advancement Programme. **In** *Smollan, R., ed.*, 1986, pp. 155–77. **[G: S. Africa]**

Moulton, Brent R. Human Capital Accumulation and Trends in the Male–Female Wage Gap in the United States, 1956–1983. *Eastern Econ. J.*, July-Sept. 1986, *12*(3), pp. 265–71. **[G: U.S.]**

Mubbashar, Malik H. Health Policies and Human Capital: The Case of Pakistan: Comments. *Pakistan Devel. Rev.*, Autumn 1986, *25*(3), pp. 335–37. **[G: Pakistan]**

Neuman, Shoshana. Religious Observance within a Human Capital Framework: Theory and Application. *Appl. Econ.*, November 1986, *18*(11), pp. 1193–1202. **[G: Israel]**

Noether, Monica. The Growing Supply of Physicians: Has the Market Become More Competitive? *J. Lab. Econ.*, October 1986, *4*(4), pp. 503–37. **[G: U.S.]**

Nord, Stephen. An Analysis of the Effects of Higher Education on Wage Differentials between Blacks and Whites by Gender in the United States. *Appl. Econ.*, February 1986, *18*(2), pp. 173–89. **[G: U.S.]**

Orazem, Peter F. and Mattila, J. Peter. Occupational Entry and Uncertainty: Males Leaving High School. *Rev. Econ. Statist.*, May 1986, *68*(2), pp. 265–73. **[G: U.S.]**

Osburn, Donald. Human Capital, Technology and Institutions: Discussion. **In** *Maunder, A. and Renborg, U., eds.*, 1986, pp. 488–89.

Pascoe, Anthony. Case Studies of Black Advancement: Barclays National Bank. **In** *Smollan, R., ed.*, 1986, pp. 211–17. **[G: S. Africa]**

Phillips, Joseph M. and Marble, Robert P. Farmer Education and Efficiency: A Frontier Production Function Approach. *Econ. Educ. Rev.*, 1986, *5*(3), pp. 257–64. **[G: Guatemala]**

Prais, S. J. and Steedman, Hilary. Vocational Training in France and Britain: The Building Trades. *Nat. Inst. Econ. Rev.*, May 1986, (116), pp. 45–55. **[G: U.K.; France]**

Psacharopoulos, George and Arriagada, Ana María. The Educational Composition of the Labour Force: An International Comparison. *Int. Lab. Rev.*, Sept.-Oct. 1986, *125*(5), pp. 561–74. **[G: Global]**

Qadir, Asghar. Higher Education and the Markets for Educated Labour in LDCs: Theoretical Approaches and Implications: Comments. *Pakistan Devel. Rev.*, Autumn 1986, *25*(3), pp. 277–78. **[G: LDCs]**

Queripel, John; Richardson, Neville and Moerdyk, Alwyn. Case Studies of Black Advancement: Rand Mines. **In** *Smollan, R., ed.*, 1986, pp. 218–28. **[G: S. Africa]**

Schilling, Don. Implicit Inflation and Interest Rates in Discounting Personal Injury Economic Losses—Rejoinder. *J. Risk Ins.*, September 1986, *53*(3), pp. 496–97. **[G: U.S.]**

Schwartz, Saul. Earnings Capacity and the Trend in Inequality among Black Men. *J. Human Res.*, Winter 1986, *21*(1), pp. 44–63. **[G: U.S.]**

Scitovsky, Tibor. Excess Demand for Job Importance and Its Implications. **In** *Scitovsky, T.*, 1986, *1981*, pp. 136–48. **[G: U.S.]**

Shah, Anup. Education and Earnings Inequality across British Labour Markets. *Appl. Econ.*, February 1986, *18*(2), pp. 205–17. **[G: U.K.]**

Shanker, Albert. Business and Schools: The Inevitable Partnership. **In** *Burton, D. F., et al., eds.*, 1986, pp. 189–98. **[G: U.S.]**

Shapiro, Carl. Investment, Moral Hazard, and Occupational Licensing. *Rev. Econ. Stud.*, October 1986, *53*(5), pp. 843–62.

Smith, James P. Race and Human Capital: Reply. *Amer. Econ. Rev.*, December 1986, *76*(5), pp. 1225–29. **[G: U.S.]**

Sumner, David. Human Capital, Technology and Institutions: Discussion. **In** *Maunder, A. and Renborg, U., eds.*, 1986, pp. 486–88.

Tomer, John F. Productivity and Organizational Behavior: Where Human Capital Theory Fails. **In** *Gilad, B. and Kaish, S., eds., Vol. A*, 1986, pp. 233–55.

Topel, Robert. Job Mobility, Search, and Earnings Growth: A Reinterpretation of Human Capital Earnings Functions. **In** *Ehrenberg, R. G., ed., Pt. A*, 1986, pp. 199–233. **[G: U.S.]**

Tremblay, Carol Horton. The Impact of School and College Expenditures on the Wages of Southern and Non-Southern Workers. *J. Lab. Res.*, Spring 1986, *7*(2), pp. 201–11. **[G: U.S.]**

Uthoff, Andras W. Changes in Earnings Inequality and Labour Market Segmentation: Metropolitan Santiago 1969–78. *J. Devel. Stud.*, January 1986, *22*(2), pp. 300–326. **[G: Chile]**

Vaillancourt, François and Henriques, Irene. The Returns to University Schooling in Canada. *Can. Public Policy*, September 1986, *12*(3), pp. 449–58. **[G: Canada]**

Vasegh-Daneshvary, Nasser; Herzog, Henry W., Jr. and Schlottmann, Alan M. College Educated Immigrants in the American Labor Force: A Study of Locational Behavior. *Southern Econ. J.*, January 1986, *52*(3), pp. 818–31. **[G: U.S.]**

Vijverberg, Wim P. M. Consistent Estimates of the Wage Equation When Individuals Choose among Income-Earning Activities. *Southern Econ. J.*, April 1986, *52*(4), pp. 1028–42. **[G: Malaysia]**

Wagstaff, Adam. The Demand for Health: A Simplified Grossman Model [On the Concept of Health Capital and the Demand for Health]. *Bull. Econ. Res.*, January 1986, *38*(1), pp. 93–95.

Weiss, Yoram. The Determination of Life Cycle Earnings: A Survey. **In** *Ashenfelter, O. and Layard, R., eds., Vol. 1*, 1986, pp. 603–40.

Willis, Robert J. Human Capital and the Rise and Fall of Families: Comment. *J. Lab. Econ.*, Part 2, July 1986, *4*(3), pp. S40–47.

Willis, Robert J. Wage Determinants: A Survey and Reinterpretation of Human Capital Earnings Functions. **In** *Ashenfelter, O. and Layard, R., eds., Vol. 1*, 1986, pp. 525–602. **[G: U.S.]**

Wilson, R. A. Is It Worth Becoming an Architect? *Appl. Econ.*, January 1986, *18*(1), pp. 59–69. **[G: U.S.]**

Wolfson, Murray; Orzech, Ze'ev B. and Hanna, Susan S. Karl Marx and the Depletion of Human Capital as Open-Access Resource. *Hist. Polit. Econ.*, Fall 1986, *18*(3), pp. 497–514.

Wong, Yue-chim. Entrepreneurship, Marriage, and Earnings. *Rev. Econ. Statist.*, November 1986, *68*(4), pp. 693–99. **[G: Hong Kong]**

Woo, Jennie Hay. Graduate Degrees and Job Success: Managers in One U.S. Corporation. *Econ. Educ. Rev.*, 1986, *5*(3), pp. 227–37. **[G: U.S.]**

Zalokar, Nadja. Generational Differences in Female Occupational Attainment—Have the 1970's Changed Women's Opportunities? *Amer. Econ. Rev.*, May 1986, *76*(2), pp. 378–81. **[G: U.S.]**

900 Welfare Programs; Consumer Economics; Urban and Regional Economics

910 Welfare; Health; Education

9100 General

Allardt, Erik. The Civic Conception of the Welfare State in Scandinavia. **In** *Rose, R. and Shiratori, R., eds.*, 1986, pp. 107–25. **[G: Scandinavia]**

Auld, Douglas. Human Resources and Social Support Policy in Canada. *Can. Public Policy,* Supp. February 1986, *12*, pp. 84–91. **[G: Canada]**

Bernstein, Irving. The Emergence of the American Welfare State: The New Deal and the New Frontier–Great Society. *Econ. Lavoro,* July-Sept. 1986, *20*(3), pp. 137–40. **[G: U.S.]**

Bryson, Phillip J. and Perry, Philip J. *Sozialpolitik:* East German Social Welfare Policies. *Comp. Econ. Stud.*, Summer 1986, *28*(2), pp. 1–20. **[G: E. Germany]**

Burkett, John P. PQLI as a Measure of Comparative Performance: Comment. *Comp. Econ. Stud.*, Summer 1986, *28*(2), pp. 59–68.

Dauderstädt, Michael. Internationale Konkurrenz und Wohlfahrtsstaat. Überlegungen am Beispiel Portugal. (International Competition and the Welfare State—The Case of Portugal. With English summary.) *Konjunkturpolitik,* 1986, *32*(6), pp. 349–80. **[G: Portugal]**

Dye, Ronald A. and Antle, Rick. Cost-Minimizing Welfare Programs. *J. Public Econ.*, July 1986, *30*(2), pp. 259–65.

Eisenstadt, Shmuel. The Israeli Welfare System—A Nation with a Difference. **In** *Rose, R. and Shiratori, R., eds.*, 1986, pp. 156–72. **[G: Israel]**

Frederiksen, John. Manøvremulighederne for velfærdsudgifterne. (The Room for Manoeuvre with Regard to Welfare Activities. With English summary.) *Nationaløkon. Tidsskr.*, 1986, *124*(3), pp. 284–93. **[G: Denmark]**

Gács, Endre. Hungary's Social Expenditures in International Comparison. *Acta Oecon.*, 1986, *36*(1–2), pp. 141–54. **[G: Hungary; OECD]**

Greenberg, David H. and Robins, Philip K. The Changing Role of Social Experiments in Policy Analysis. *J. Policy Anal. Manage.*, Winter 1986, *5*(2), pp. 340–62. **[G: U.S.]**

Heller, Peter S. and Hemming, Richard. Aging and Social Expenditure in Major Industrial Countries. *Finance Develop.*, December 1986, *23*(4), pp. 18–21. **[G: OECD]**

Katz, Israel. Changing Social Policy: Israel 1985–86: Preface. **In** *Kop, Y., ed.*, 1986, pp. ix–xv. **[G: Israel]**

Kelman, Steven. A Case for In-Kind Transfers. *Econ. Philos.*, April 1986, *2*(1), pp. 55–73.

Kop, Yaakov. Allocation for Services in 1985—Summary. **In** *Kop, Y., ed.*, 1986, pp. xvii–xxiii. **[G: Israel]**

Kop, Yaakov; Blankett, Joel and Sharon, Dalit. Government Expenditure on Social Services. **In** *Kop, Y., ed.*, 1986, pp. 1–107. **[G: Israel]**

Lindbeck, Assar. Limits to the Welfare State. *Challenge,* Jan./Feb. 1986, *28*(6), pp. 31–36.

Maddison, Angus. Marx and Bismarck: Capitalism and Government 1883–1983. **In** *Wagener, H.-J. and Drukker, J. W., eds.*, 1986, pp. 196–213. **[G: OECD]**

Maruo, Naomi. The Development of the Welfare Mix in Japan. **In** *Rose, R. and Shiratori, R., eds.*, 1986, pp. 64–79. **[G: Japan]**

Molitor, Bruno. Sozialpolitik in der Marktwirtschaft. (Social Policy in the Market Economy. With English summary.) **In** *Eucken, W. and Böhm, F., eds.*, 1986, pp. 59–71.

Mouly, Jean. Where Social Welfare and Economics Meet. *Int. Lab. Rev.*, May-June 1986, *125*(3), pp. 349–55.

Ofer, Gur. Public Spending on Civilian Services. **In** *Ben-Porath, Y., ed.*, 1986, pp. 192–208. **[G: Israel]**

Rose, Richard. Common Goals but Different Roles: The State's Contribution to the Welfare Mix. **In** *Rose, R. and Shiratori, R., eds.*, 1986, pp. 13–39. **[G: OECD]**

Rose, Richard. The Dynamics of the Welfare Mix in Britain. **In** *Rose, R. and Shiratori, R., eds.*, 1986, pp. 80–106. **[G: U.K.]**

Rose, Richard and Shiratori, Rei. Welfare in Society: Three Worlds or One? **In** *Rose, R. and Shiratori, R., eds.*, 1986, pp. 3–12. **[G: OECD]**

Schneider, Friedrich. The Influence of Political Institutions on Social Security Policies: A Public Choice View. **In** *von der Schulenburg, J.-M. G., ed.*, 1986, pp. 13–31. **[G: OECD]**

Shiratori, Rei. The Future of the Welfare State. **In** *Rose, R. and Shiratori, R., eds.*, 1986, pp. 193–206. **[G: OECD]**

Tavitian, M. Robert. Politiques sociales et interdépendance économique. Les dangers da la notion de contrainte extérieure. (The Impact of Economic Interdependence on Social Policies—Constraints or Opportunities. With English summary.) *Écon. Soc.*, January 1986, *20*(1), pp. 45–68. **[G: W. Europe]**

Wagner, Richard E. The Welfare State, Capital Formation, and Tax-Transfer Politics. **In** *Lee, D. R., ed.*, 1986, pp. 241–73. **[G: U.S.]**

911 General Welfare Programs

9110 General Welfare Programs

Anderson, Terry L. and Hill, Peter J. Constraining the Transfer Society: Constitutional and Moral Dimensions. *Cato J.*, Spring/Summer 1986, *6*(1), pp. 317–39.

Barkai, Haim. Income and Income Maintenance Policy. **In** *Kop, Y., ed.*, 1986, pp. 135–45. **[G: Israel]**

Baudelot, Olga. Child Care in France. **In** *Hewlett, S. A.; Ilchman, A. S. and Sweeney, J. J., eds.*, 1986, pp. 39–51. **[G: France]**

Beller, Andrea H. and Graham, John W. Child Support Awards: Differentials and Trends by

Race and Marital Status. *Demography*, May 1986, *23*(2), pp. 231–45. **[G: U.S.]**

Berger, Brigitte. On the Limits of the Welfare State: The Case of Foster Care. **In** *Peden, J. R. and Glahe, F. R., eds.*, 1986, pp. 365–79. **[G: U.S.]**

Blau, Francine D. Immigration and the U.S. Taxpayer. **In** *Pozo, S., ed.*, 1986, pp. 89–110. **[G: U.S.]**

Blumstein, James F. Providing Hospital Care to Indigent Patients: Hill–Burton as a Case Study and a Paradigm. **In** *Sloan, F. A.; Blumstein, J. F. and Perrin, J. M., eds.*, 1986, pp. 94–107. **[G: U.S.]**

Boyer, George R. The Old Poor Law and the Agricultural Labor Market in Southern England: An Empirical Analysis. *J. Econ. Hist.*, March 1986, *46*(1), pp. 113–35. **[G: U.K.]**

Browning, Edgar K. On the Welfare Cost of Transfers. **In** *Tullock, G.*, 1986, *1974*, pp. 102–06.

Browning, Edgar K. and Johnson, William R. The Cost of Reducing Economic Inequality. *Cato J.*, Spring/Summer 1986, *6*(1), pp. 85–109. **[G: U.S.]**

Burtless, Gary. Public Spending for the Poor: Trends, Prospects, and Economic Limits. **In** *Danziger, S. H. and Weinberg, D. H., eds.*, 1986, pp. 18–49. **[G: U.S.]**

Buvinić, Mayra. Projects for Women in Third World: Explaining Their Misbehavior. *World Devel.*, May 1986, *14*(5), pp. 653–64. **[G: LDCs]**

Christainsen, Gregory B. and Williams, Walter E. Welfare, Family Cohesiveness, and Out-of-Wedlock Births. **In** *Peden, J. R. and Glahe, F. R., eds.*, 1986, pp. 381–424. **[G: U.S.]**

Clarke, R. Community Development as an Element of a Strategy for Development from Below: Community Organisations in Scotland. **In** *Bassand, M., et al., eds.*, 1986, pp. 187–99. **[G: U.K.]**

Cox, J. P. Economic Growth and Income Support Policy in Australia. *Econ. Rec.*, September 1986, *62*(178), pp. 268–85. **[G: Australia]**

Craig, Steven G. and Inman, Robert P. Education, Welfare and the "New" Federalism: State Budgeting in a Federalist Public Economy. **In** *Rosen, H. S., ed.*, 1986, pp. 187–222. **[G: U.S.]**

Cuomo, Mario M. The Least of These. **In** *Hewlett, S. A.; Ilchman, A. S. and Sweeney, J. J., eds.*, 1986, pp. 23–29. **[G: U.S.]**

Danziger, Sheldon H.; Haveman, Robert H. and Plotnick, Robert D. Antipoverty Policy: Effects on the Poor and the Nonpoor. **In** *Danziger, S. H. and Weinberg, D. H., eds.*, 1986, pp. 50–77. **[G: U.S.]**

Danziger, Sheldon H. and Weinberg, Daniel H. Fighting Poverty: What Works and What Doesn't: Introduction. **In** *Danziger, S. H. and Weinberg, D. H., eds.*, 1986, pp. 1–17. **[G: U.S.]**

Darity, William A., Jr. and Myers, Samuel L., Jr. Welfare and Work: Microeconomic vs. Macroeconomic Considerations [The Political of Work-for-Welfare]. *Cato J.*, Spring/Summer 1986, *6*(1), pp. 245–50. **[G: U.S.]**

Davis, Carlton G., et al. Effects of Food Stamp Program Participation and Other Sociodemographic Characteristics on Food Expenditure Patterns of Elderly Minority Households. *Rev. Black Polit. Econ.*, Summer 1986, *15*(1), pp. 3–25. **[G: U.S.]**

Dellaportas, George. The Effectiveness of Public Assistance Payments (1970–80) in Reducing Poverty Reconsidered: The 'Safety Net' Was Still Very Leaky in 1980, But Less So, and More Working Poor May Have Been Aided. *Amer. J. Econ. Soc.*, January 1986, *45*(1), pp. 1–8. **[G: U.S.]**

Devaney, Barbara L. and Fraker, Thomas. Cashing Out Food Stamps: Impact on Food Expenditures and Diet Quality. *J. Policy Anal. Manage.*, Summer 1986, *5*(4), pp. 725–41. **[G: Puerto Rico]**

Digby, Anne. Malthus and Reform of the English Poor Law. **In** *Turner, M., ed.*, 1986, pp. 157–69. **[G: U.K.]**

Dorn, James A. The Transfer Society: Introduction. *Cato J.*, Spring/Summer 1986, *6*(1), pp. 1–17. **[G: U.S.]**

Duncan, Greg J. and Hoffman, Saul D. Welfare Dynamics and the Nature of Need. *Cato J.*, Spring/Summer 1986, *6*(1), pp. 31–54. **[G: U.S.]**

Edelman, Marian Wright. Federal Programs That Serve Children and Families. **In** *Hewlett, S. A.; Ilchman, A. S. and Sweeney, J. J., eds.*, 1986, pp. 105–16. **[G: U.S.]**

van't Eind, Gerrit Jan, et al. Evaluating the Distribution of Public Expenditure. *Rev. Income Wealth*, September 1986, *32*(3), pp. 299–312. **[G: Netherlands]**

Ellwood, David T. and Summers, Lawrence H. Poverty in America: Is Welfare the Answer or the Problem? **In** *Danziger, S. H. and Weinberg, D. H., eds.*, 1986, pp. 78–105. **[G: U.S.]**

Fishelson, Gideon. Allocation for Services and Equity. **In** *Kop, Y., ed.*, 1986, pp. 159–66. **[G: Israel]**

Fraker, Thomas; Devaney, Barbara L. and Cavin, Edward. An Evaluation of the Effect of Cashing Out Food Stamps on Food Expenditures. *Amer. Econ. Rev.*, May 1986, *76*(2), pp. 230–34. **[G: U.S.]**

Friedlander, Daniel, et al. Initial Findings from the Demonstration of State Work/Welfare Initiatives. *Amer. Econ. Rev.*, May 1986, *76*(2), pp. 224–29. **[G: U.S.]**

Friedman, Dana E. Painting the Child Care Landscape: A Palette of Inadequacy and Innovation. **In** *Hewlett, S. A.; Ilchman, A. S. and Sweeney, J. J., eds.*, 1986, pp. 67–89. **[G: U.S.]**

Gabriel, Stuart A. Housing Policy. **In** *Kop, Y., ed.*, 1986, pp. 227–59. **[G: Israel]**

Garfinkel, Irwin and Masters, Stanley. Welfare and Work Incentives. **In** *Reynolds, L. G.; Masters, S. H. and Moser, C. H., eds.*, 1986, pp. 277–87. **[G: U.S.]**

Ginzberg, Eli. Progress, So Very Slow. **In** *Hew-*

lett, S. A.; Ilchman, A. S. and Sweeney, J. J., eds., 1986, pp. 117–23. **[G: U.S.]**

Glazer, Nathan. Welfare and "Welfare" in America. **In** *Rose, R. and Shiratori, R., eds.*, 1986, pp. 40–63. **[G: U.S.]**

Gramlich, Edward M. Fighting Poverty: What Works and What Doesn't: The Main Themes. **In** *Danziger, S. H. and Weinberg, D. H., eds.*, 1986, pp. 341–47. **[G: U.S.]**

Grasso, Patrick G. Distributive Policies and the Politics of Economic Development. **In** *Redburn, F. S.; Buss, T. F. and Ledebur, L. C., eds.*, 1986, pp. 83–98. **[G: U.S.]**

Gwartney, James and Stroup, Richard L. Transfers, Equality, and the Limits of Public Policy. *Cato J.*, Spring/Summer 1986, *6*(1), pp. 111–37. **[G: U.S.]**

Hamilton, Charles V. and Hamilton, Dona C. Social Policies, Civil Rights, and Poverty. **In** *Danziger, S. H. and Weinberg, D. H., eds.*, 1986, pp. 287–311. **[G: U.S.]**

Hansmann, Henry B. The Role of Nonprofit Enterprise. **In** *Rose-Ackerman, S., ed.*, 1986, *1980*, pp. 57–84. **[G: U.S.]**

Haveman, Robert H. What Antipoverty Policies Cost the Nonpoor. *Challenge*, Jan./Feb. 1986, *28*(6), pp. 37–42. **[G: U.S.]**

Hewlett, Sylvia Ann. Family and Work: Bridging the Gap: Conclusions: A Policy Agenda for the United States. **In** *Hewlett, S. A.; Ilchman, A. S. and Sweeney, J. J., eds.*, 1986, pp. 187–91. **[G: U.S.]**

Holloway, Thomas M. and Reeb, Jane S. Sources of Change in Federal Transfer Payments to Persons: An Update. *Surv. Curr. Bus.*, June 1986, *66*(6), pp. 21–25. **[G: U.S.]**

Howenstine, E. Jay. Foreign Housing Voucher Systems: Evolution and Strategies. *Mon. Lab. Rev.*, May 1986, *109*(5), pp. 21–27. **[G: W. Europe; Canada]**

Hum, Derek P. J. UISP and the Macdonald Commission: Reform and Restraint. *Can. Public Policy*, Supp. February 1986, *12*, pp. 92–100. **[G: Canada]**

Hurl, Lorna F. Privatization of Social Services: Time to Move the Debate Along. *Can. Public Policy*, September 1986, *12*(3), pp. 507–12. **[G: Canada]**

Hurl, Lorna F. and Tucker, David J. Limitations of an Act of Faith: An Analysis of the Macdonald Commission's Stance on Social Services. *Can. Public Policy*, December 1986, *12*(4), pp. 606–21. **[G: Canada]**

Hutchens, Robert M. The Effects of the Omnibus Budget Reconciliation Act of 1981 on AFDC Recipients: A Review of Studies. **In** *Ehrenberg, R. G., ed., Pt. B*, 1986, pp. 351–87. **[G: U.S.]**

Ilchman, Alice S. Family and Work: Bridging the Gap: Introduction. **In** *Hewlett, S. A.; Ilchman, A. S. and Sweeney, J. J., eds.*, 1986, pp. 1–6. **[G: U.S.]**

James, Franklin J. and Blair, John P. Labor Mobility in National Policy and Local Economies. **In** *Bergman, E. M., ed.*, 1986, *1983*, pp. 271–85. **[G: U.S.]**

Johnson, Gary T. Rent Paying Ability and Racial Settlement Patterns: A Review and Analysis of Recent Housing Allowance Evidence. *Amer. J. Econ. Soc.*, January 1986, *45*(1), pp. 17–26. **[G: U.S.]**

Kahn, Arthur L. Characteristics of Supplemental Security Income Recipients, December 1984. *Soc. Sec. Bull.*, April 1986, *49*(4), pp. 5–11. **[G: U.S.]**

Kasun, Jacqueline R. The State and Adolescent Sexual Behavior. **In** *Peden, J. R. and Glahe, F. R., eds.*, 1986, pp. 329–64. **[G: U.S.]**

Kesselman, Jonathan R. The Royal Commission's Proposals for Income Security Reform. *Can. Public Policy*, Supp. February 1986, *12*, pp. 101–12. **[G: Canada]**

Knapp, Martin. The Relative Cost-Effectiveness of Public, Voluntary and Private Providers of Residential Child Care. **In** *Culyer, A. J. and Jönsson, B., eds.*, 1986, pp. 171–99. **[G: U.S.]**

Kodras, Janet E. The Spatial Perspective in Welfare Analysis [Transfers and Poverty: Cause and/or Effect?]. *Cato J.*, Spring/Summer 1986, *6*(1), pp. 77–83. **[G: U.S.]**

Kondratas, S. Anna. The Political Economy of Work-for-Welfare. *Cato J.*, Spring/Summer 1986, *6*(1), pp. 229–43. **[G: U.S.]**

Ladd, Helen F. Education, Welfare and the "New" Federalism: State Budgeting in a Federalist Public Economy: Comment. **In** *Rosen, H. S., ed.*, 1986, pp. 222–27. **[G: U.S.]**

Laffer, Arthur B. The Tightening Grip of the Poverty Trap. **In** *Canto, V. A.; Kadlec, C. W. and Laffer, A. B., eds.*, 1986, pp. 141–59. **[G: U.S.]**

Leijon, Anna-Greta. The Origins, Progress, and Future of Swedish Family Policy. **In** *Hewlett, S. A.; Ilchman, A. S. and Sweeney, J. J., eds.*, 1986, pp. 31–38. **[G: Sweden]**

Lerman, Robert I. Do Welfare Programs Affect the Schooling and Work Patterns of Young Black Men? **In** *Freeman, R. B. and Holzer, H. J., eds.*, 1986, pp. 403–38. **[G: U.S.]**

Levy, Frank S. and Michel, Richard C. Work for Welfare: How Much Good Will It Do? *Amer. Econ. Rev.*, May 1986, *76*(2), pp. 399–404. **[G: U.S.]**

Lilla, Mark. The Political Psychology of Economic Transfers [Transfers, Equality, and the Limits of Public Policy]. *Cato J.*, Spring/Summer 1986, *6*(1), pp. 139–42. **[G: U.S.]**

McCaleb, Thomas S. Ideology as the Ultimate Enforcement Mechanism [Constraining the Transfer Society: Constitutional and Moral Dimensions]. *Cato J.*, Spring/Summer 1986, *6*(1), pp. 341–45.

McCready, Douglas J. Privatized Social Service Systems: Are There Any Justifications? *Can. Public Policy*, March 1986, *12*(1), pp. 253–57. **[G: Canada]**

Mead, Lawrence M. Legal Rights and Welfare Change, 1960–1980: Comment. **In** *Danziger, S. H. and Weinberg, D. H., eds.*, 1986, pp. 283–86. **[G: U.S.]**

Miller, Nancy, et al. Social Security Programs in the United States. *Soc. Sec. Bull.*, January 1986, *49*(1), pp. 5–59. **[G: U.S.]**

Moffitt, Robert. The Lagged Effect of the 1981 Federal AFDC Legislation on Work Effort [Evaluating the Effects of Changes in AFDC: Methodological Issues and Challenges]. *J. Policy Anal. Manage.*, Spring 1986, *5*(3), pp. 596–97. **[G: U.S.]**

Moffitt, Robert. Work Incentives in the AFDC System: An Analysis of the 1981 Reforms. *Amer. Econ. Rev.*, May 1986, *76*(2), pp. 219–23. **[G: U.S.]**

Moffitt, Robert. Work Incentives in Transfer Programs (Revisited): A Study of the AFDC Program. **In** *Ehrenberg, R. G., ed., Pt. B*, 1986, pp. 389–439. **[G: U.S.]**

Morrow, Anne M. M. The Measurement of Inflation Experienced by the Poor, 1970–80. *Can. Public Policy*, March 1986, *12*(1), pp. 245–52. **[G: Canada]**

Moynihan, Daniel Patrick. Government and Family Policy. **In** *Hewlett, S. A.; Ilchman, A. S. and Sweeney, J. J., eds.*, 1986, pp. 7–15. **[G: U.S.]**

Murray, Charles. *Losing Ground* Two Years Later. *Cato J.*, Spring/Summer 1986, *6*(1), pp. 19–29.

Musgrave, Richard A. The Role of Social Insurance in an Overall Programme for Social Welfare. **In** *Musgrave, R. A., Vol. 2*, 1986, *1967*, pp. 67–81. **[G: U.S.]**

Musgrave, Richard A.; Heller, Peter S. and Peterson, George E. Cost-Effectiveness of Alternative Income Maintenance Schemes. **In** *Musgrave, R. A., Vol. 2*, 1986, *1970*, pp. 82–102. **[G: U.S.]**

Myers, Samuel L., Jr. Do Welfare Programs Affect the Schooling and Work Patterns of Young Black Men? Comment. **In** *Freeman, R. B. and Holzer, H. J., eds.*, 1986, pp. 438–41. **[G: U.S.]**

O'Neill, June. Transfers and Poverty: Cause and/or Effect? *Cato J.*, Spring/Summer 1986, *6*(1), pp. 55–76. **[G: U.S.]**

Peery, J. Craig. The Family: Federal Policy and Private Alternatives. **In** *Peden, J. R. and Glahe, F. R., eds.*, 1986, pp. 425–47. **[G: U.S.]**

Plotnick, Robert D. An Interest Group Model of Direct Income Redistribution. *Rev. Econ. Statist.*, November 1986, *68*(4), pp. 594–602. **[G: U.S.]**

Roberti, Paolo. Equità e politiche sociali. (Equity and Social Policy. With English summary.) *Econ. Lavoro*, Apr.-June 1986, *20*(2), pp. 51–68. **[G: U.S.]**

Robins, Philip K. Child Support, Welfare Dependency, and Poverty. *Amer. Econ. Rev.*, September 1986, *76*(4), pp. 768–88. **[G: U.S.]**

Robins, Philip K. and West, Richard W. Sample Attrition and Labor Supply Response in Experimental Panel Data: A Study of Alternative Correction Procedures. *J. Bus. Econ. Statist.*, July 1986, *4*(3), pp. 329–38. **[G: U.S.]**

Schuck, Peter H. Designing Hospital Care Subsidies for the Poor. **In** *Sloan, F. A.; Blumstein, J. F. and Perrin, J. M., eds.*, 1986, pp. 72–93. **[G: U.S.]**

Sen, Amartya K. Food, Economics and Entitlements. *Lloyds Bank Rev.*, April 1986, (160), pp. 1–20.

Senauer, Benjamin and Young, Nathan. The Impact of Food Stamps on Food Expenditures: Rejection of the Traditional Model. *Amer. J. Agr. Econ.*, February 1986, *68*(1), pp. 37–43. **[G: U.S.]**

Smeeding, Timothy M. Nonmoney Income and the Elderly: The Case of the 'Tweeners. *J. Policy Anal. Manage.*, Summer 1986, *5*(4), pp. 707–24. **[G: U.S.]**

Sosin, Michael R. Legal Rights and Welfare Change, 1960–1980. **In** *Danziger, S. H. and Weinberg, D. H., eds.*, 1986, pp. 260–83. **[G: U.S.]**

Spicker, Paul. The Case for Supplementary Benefit. *Fisc. Stud.*, November 1986, *7*(4), pp. 28–44. **[G: U.K.]**

Thomson, David. Welfare and the Historians. **In** *[Laslett, P.]*, 1986, pp. 355–78.

Tucker, Harvey J. and Herzik, Eric B. The Persisting Problem of Region in American State Policy Research. *Soc. Sci. Quart.*, March 1986, *67*(1), pp. 84–97. **[G: U.S.]**

Tullock, Gordon. Aid in Kind. **In** *Tullock, G.*, 1986, pp. 128–35.

Tullock, Gordon. Information without Profit. **In** *Tullock, G.*, 1986, *1966*, pp. 73–88.

Tullock, Gordon. Local Redistribution. **In** *Tullock, G.*, 1986, pp. 113–27.

Tullock, Gordon. More on the Welfare Cost of Transfers. **In** *Tullock, G.*, 1986, *1974*, pp. 107–10.

Tullock, Gordon. Reasons for Redistribution. **In** *Tullock, G.*, 1986, *1981*, pp. 15–41.

Tullock, Gordon. The Charity of the Uncharitable. **In** *Tullock, G.*, 1986, *1971*, pp. 57–69.

Tullock, Gordon. The Cost of Transfers. **In** *Tullock, G.*, 1986, *1971*, pp. 89–101.

Tullock, Gordon. The Economics of Wealth and Poverty: Introduction. **In** *Tullock, G.*, 1986, pp. 1–11.

Tullock, Gordon. Transitional Gains and Transfers. *Cato J.*, Spring/Summer 1986, *6*(1), pp. 143–54.

Upp, Melinda. Fast Facts and Figures about Social Security. *Soc. Sec. Bull.*, June 1986, *49*(6), pp. 5–19. **[G: U.S.]**

Weicher, John C. The Reagan Domestic Budget Cuts: Proposals, Outcomes, and Effects. **In** *Cagan, P., ed.*, 1986, pp. 7–44. **[G: U.S.]**

Wolf, Douglas and Greenberg, David H. The Dynamics of Welfare Fraud: An Econometric Duration Model in Discrete Time. *J. Human Res.*, Fall 1986, *21*(4), pp. 437–55. **[G: U.S.]**

Zapf, Wolfgang. Development, Structure, and Prospects of the German Social State. **In** *Rose, R. and Shiratori, R., eds.*, 1986, pp. 126–55. **[G: W. Germany]**

912 Economics of Education

9120 Economics of Education

Adelman, Irma. Education and Economic Development: A Comparative Perspective. **In** *Adel-*

man, I. and Taylor, J. E., eds., 1986, pp. 296–318. **[G: LDCs; China]**

Anderson, Gerard F. and Lave, Judith R. Financing Graduate Medical Education Using Multiple Regression to Set Payment Rates. *Inquiry*, Summer 1986, *23*(2), pp. 191–99. **[G: U.S.]**

Arcelus, F. J. and Levine, A. L. Merit Goods and Public Choice: The Case of Higher Education. *Public Finance*, December 1986, *41*(3), pp. 303–15.

Auten, Gerald E. and Rudney, Gabriel G. Tax Reform and Individual Giving to Higher Education. *Econ. Educ. Rev.*, 1986, *5*(2), pp. 167–78. **[G: U.S.]**

Baudelot, Olga. Child Care in France. **In** *Hewlett, S. A.; Ilchman, A. S. and Sweeney, J. J., eds.*, 1986, pp. 39–51. **[G: France]**

Baum, Donald N. A Simultaneous Equations Model of the Demand for and Production of Local Public Services: The Case of Education. *Public Finance Quart.*, April 1986, *14*(2), pp. 157–78. **[G: U.S.]**

Baum, Sandra R. and Schwartz, Saul. Equity, Envy, and Higher Education. *Soc. Sci. Quart.*, September 1986, *67*(3), pp. 491–503. **[G: U.S.]**

Becker, William E. and Williams, Arlington W. Assessing Personnel Practices in Higher Education: A Case Study in the Hiring of Female. *Econ. Educ. Rev.*, 1986, *5*(3), pp. 265–72.

Behrendt, Amy; Eisenach, Jeffrey and Johnson, William R. Selectivity Bias and the Determinants of SAT Scores. *Econ. Educ. Rev.*, 1986, *5*(4), pp. 363–71. **[G: U.S.]**

Beladi, Hamid; Brunner, Lawrence P. and Zuberi, Habib A. The Rates of Return on Investment in Education in Michigan. *Atlantic Econ. J.*, December 1986, *14*(4), pp. 50–64. **[G: U.S.]**

Berk, Marc L.; Horgan, Constance M. and Meyers, Samuel M. The Reporting of Stigmatizing Health Conditions: A Comparison of Proxy and Self-reporting. *J. Econ. Soc. Meas.*, October 1986, *14*(3), pp. 197–205. **[G: U.S.]**

Birdsall, Nancy and Meesook, Oey Astra. Children's Education and the Intergenerational Transmission of Inequality: A Simulation. *Econ. Educ. Rev.*, 1986, *5*(3), pp. 239–56. **[G: Brazil]**

Bisesi, Michael. Public Policy and Human Venture Capital: Forging a More Productive Business–Education Link. *J. Policy Anal. Manage.*, Summer 1986, *5*(4), pp. 820–24. **[G: U.S.]**

Blaug, Mark. The Economics of Education in English Classical Political Economy: A Re-examination. **In** *Blaug, M.*, 1986, *1975*, pp. 150–83.

Blomqvist, Ake G. Higher Education and the Markets for Educated Labour in LDCs: Theoretical Approaches and Implications. *Pakistan Devel. Rev.*, Autumn 1986, *25*(3), pp. 249–73. **[G: LDCs]**

Bound, John. NBER-Mathematica Survey of Inner-city Black Youth: An Analysis of the Undercount of Older Youths. **In** *Freeman, R. B. and Holzer, H. J., eds.*, 1986, pp. 443–59. **[G: U.S.]**

Bowman, Mary Jean; Millot, Benoît and Schiefelbein, Ernesto. An Adult Life Cycle Perspective on Public Subsidies to Higher Education in Three Countries. *Econ. Educ. Rev.*, 1986, *5*(2), pp. 135–45. **[G: Chile; France; Malaysia]**

Braslavsky, Cecilia. Youth in Argentina: Between the Legacy of the Past and the Construction of the Future. *CEPAL Rev.*, August 1986, (29), pp. 41–54. **[G: Argentina]**

Brazer, Harvey E. and McCarty, Therese A. Municipal Overburden: An Empirical Analysis. *Econ. Educ. Rev.*, 1986, *5*(4), pp. 353–61. **[G: U.S.]**

Carter, Susan B. Occupational Segregation, Teachers' Wages, and American Economic Growth. *J. Econ. Hist.*, June 1986, *46*(2), pp. 373–83. **[G: U.S.]**

Chan, Lean Heng. Young Workers Education Project: Development of a Participatory Urban Services Centre in Penang, Malaysia. **In** *Yeung, Y. M. and McGee, T. G., eds.*, 1986, pp. 165–90. **[G: Malaysia]**

Chang, Cyril F. and Tuckman, Howard P. Price-Induced Substitution of Faculty in Academe: Does Mission Make a Difference? *Econ. Educ. Rev.*, 1986, *5*(2), pp. 197–204. **[G: U.S.]**

Chressanthis, George A. The Impacts of Tuition Rate Changes on College Undergraduate Headcounts and Credit Hours over Time—A Case Study. *Econ. Educ. Rev.*, 1986, *5*(2), pp. 205–17. **[G: U.S.]**

Clotfelter, Charles T. The Effect of Tax Simplification on Educational and Charitable Organizations. **In** *Federal Reserve Bank of Boston*, 1986, pp. 187–215. **[G: U.S.]**

Cohen, Steven B. Data Collection Organization Effect in the National Medical Care Utilization and Expenditure Survey. *J. Econ. Soc. Meas.*, December 1986, *14*(4), pp. 367–78. **[G: U.S.]**

Cohn, Elchanan. Implementation of Federal Chapter 2 Block Grants to Education in South Carolina. **In** *Cohn, E., ed.*, 1986, *1985*, pp. 215–25. **[G: U.S.]**

Coleman, James S. Rawls, Nozick, and Educational Equality. **In** *Coleman, J. S.*, 1986, *1976*, pp. 365–74.

Coleman, Jules L. and Kraus, Jody. Rethinking the Theory of Legal Rights. *Yale Law J.*, June 1986, *95*(7), pp. 1335–71.

Collier, Paul and Mayer, Colin. An Investigation of University Selection Procedures. *Econ. J.*, Supplement 1986, *96*, pp. 163–70. **[G: U.K.]**

Conway, A. G. and O'Hara, P. Education of Farm Children. *Econ. Soc. Rev.*, July 1986, *17*(4), pp. 253–76. **[G: Ireland]**

Corman, Hope. The Demand for Education for Home Production. *Econ. Inquiry*, April 1986, *24*(2), pp. 213–30. **[G: U.S.]**

Cothran, Dan A. Some Sources of "Budgetary Uncontrollability": The Interaction of Automatic Funding and Program Flexibility. *Public Budg. Finance*, Summer 1986, *6*(2), pp. 45–62. **[G: U.S.]**

Coughlin, Cletus C. and Erekson, O. Homer. Determinants of State Aid and Voluntary Support of Higher Education. *Econ. Educ. Rev.*, 1986, *5*(2), pp. 179–90. **[G: U.S.]**

Court, David and Kinyanjui, Kabiru. African Education: Problems in a High-Growth Sector. **In** *Berg, R. J. and Whitaker, J. S., eds.*, 1986, pp. 361–92. **[G: Africa]**

Craig, Steven G. and Inman, Robert P. Education, Welfare and the "New" Federalism: State Budgeting in a Federalist Public Economy. **In** *Rosen, H. S., ed.*, 1986, pp. 187–222. **[G: U.S.]**

Craven, B. M.; Dick, B. and Wood, B. The Behaviour of a Resource Reducing Bureau. A Case Study of an English Polytechnic. *Appl. Econ.*, January 1986, *18*(1), pp. 87–99. **[G: U.K.]**

Dagenais, Denyse L. Analyse de la performance d'étudiants au baccalauréat en administration en fonction de leurs caractéristiques à l'entrée. (An Analysis of the Student's Performance in a B.A.A. Program. With English summary.) *L'Actual. Econ.*, June 1986, *62*(2), pp. 185–209. **[G: Canada]**

Daly, Anne. Education and Productivity: A Comparison of Great Britain and the United States. *Brit. J. Ind. Relat.*, July 1986, *24*(2), pp. 251–66. **[G: U.K.; U.S.]**

Dresch, Stephen P. The Educational Credit Trust: A Proposal for Reconstitution and Reform of the Student Loan System. *Econ. Educ. Rev.*, 1986, *5*(1), pp. 1–16. **[G: U.S.]**

Dye, Richard F. Aid Sources for Higher Education: Taxes and Other Determinants. *Econ. Educ. Rev.*, 1986, *5*(2), pp. 191–95.

Eberts, Randall W. and Stone, Joe A. Teacher Unions and the Cost of Public Education. *Econ. Inquiry*, October 1986, *24*(4), pp. 631–43. **[G: U.S.]**

Egbert, Robert L.; Kluender, Mary M. and Roach, James L. Rural Elementary School Districts in Nebraska: Their Application for ECIA Funds as Related to Demographic and Economic Issues. **In** *Cohn, E., ed.*, 1986, *1985*, pp. 189–95. **[G: U.S.]**

Ehrenberg, Ronald G. and Luzadis, Rebecca A. The Social Security Student Benefit Program and Family Decisions. *Econ. Educ. Rev.*, 1986, *5*(2), pp. 119–28. **[G: U.S.]**

van't Eind, Gerrit Jan, et al. Evaluating the Distribution of Public Expenditure. *Rev. Income Wealth*, September 1986, *32*(3), pp. 299–312. **[G: Netherlands]**

Elmore, Richard F. Implementation of Chapter 2 in Washington State. **In** *Cohn, E., ed.*, 1986, *1985*, pp. 245–52. **[G: U.S.]**

Eyler, Janet. Implementation of Chapter 2 in Tennessee. **In** *Cohn, E., ed.*, 1986, *1985*, pp. 227–35. **[G: U.S.]**

Fournier, Gary M. and Rasmussen, David W. Salaries in Public Education: The Impact of Geographic Cost-of-Living Differentials. *Public Finance Quart.*, April 1986, *14*(2), pp. 179–98. **[G: U.S.]**

Freeman, Richard B. Demand for Education. **In** *Ashenfelter, O. and Layard, R., eds., Vol. 1*, 1986, pp. 357–86. **[G: U.S.]**

Friedman, Dana E. Painting the Child Care Landscape: A Palette of Inadequacy and Innovation. **In** *Hewlett, S. A.; Ilchman, A. S. and Sweeney, J. J., eds.*, 1986, pp. 67–89. **[G: U.S.]**

Frykenberg, Robert Eric. Modern Education in South India, 1784–1854: Its Roots and Its Role as a Vehicle of Integration under Company Raj. *Amer. Hist. Rev.*, February 1986, *91*(1), pp. 37–65. **[G: India]**

Garbarino, Joseph W. Faculty Collective Bargaining: A Status Report. **In** *Lipset, S. M., ed.*, 1986, pp. 265–84. **[G: U.S.]**

Ginzberg, Eli. Progress, So Very Slow. **In** *Hewlett, S. A.; Ilchman, A. S. and Sweeney, J. J., eds.*, 1986, pp. 117–23. **[G: U.S.]**

Glazer, Nathan. Education and Training Programs and Poverty. **In** *Danziger, S. H. and Weinberg, D. H., eds.*, 1986, pp. 152–73. **[G: U.S.]**

Goldschmidt, Steven M. and Stuart, Leland E. The Extent and Impact of Educational Policy Bargaining. *Ind. Lab. Relat. Rev.*, April 1986, *39*(3), pp. 350–60. **[G: U.S.]**

Gramlich, Edward M. Evaluation of Education Projects: The Case of the Perry Preschool Program. *Econ. Educ. Rev.*, 1986, *5*(1), pp. 17–24. **[G: U.S.]**

Grant, James H. and Lindauer, David L. The Economics of Charity Life-Cycle Patterns of Alumnae Contributions. *Eastern Econ. J.*, Apr.-June 1986, *12*(2), pp. 129–41.

Hanushek, Eric A. The Economics of Schooling: Production and Efficiency in Public Schools. *J. Econ. Lit.*, September 1986, *24*(3), pp. 1141–77. **[G: U.S.]**

Harford, Jon D. and Marcus, Richard D. Tuition and U.S. Private College Characteristics: The Hedonic Approach. *Econ. Educ. Rev.*, 1986, *5*(4), pp. 415–30. **[G: U.S.]**

Hartshorne, Ken. The Role of the State in Education and Training. **In** *Smollan, R., ed.*, 1986, pp. 117–37. **[G: S. Africa]**

Haubert, Maxime. Adult Education and Grass-Roots Organisations in Latin America: The Contribution of the International Co-operative University. *Int. Lab. Rev.*, Mar.-Apr. 1986, *125*(2), pp. 177–92. **[G: Latin America]**

Hewlett, Sylvia Ann. Family and Work: Bridging the Gap: Conclusions: A Policy Agenda for the United States. **In** *Hewlett, S. A.; Ilchman, A. S. and Sweeney, J. J., eds.*, 1986, pp. 187–91. **[G: U.S.]**

Hoffman, Emily P. A Review of Two Studies of Elasticity in Academe. *Econ. Educ. Rev.*, 1986, *5*(2), pp. 219–24. **[G: U.S.]**

Hough, J. R. and Warburton, S. J. U.K. Research into School Costs and Resources. *Econ. Educ. Rev.*, 1986, *5*(4), pp. 383–94. **[G: U.K.]**

Huijsman, R., et al. An Empirical Analysis of College Enrollment in the Netherlands. *De Economist*, 1986, *134*(2), pp. 181–90. **[G: Netherlands]**

James, Estelle. The Private Nonprofit Provision of Education: A Theoretical Model and Application to Japan. *J. Compar. Econ.*, September

1986, *10*(3), pp. 255–76. **[G: Japan]**

Jamison, Dean T. Child Malnutrition and School Performance in China. *J. Devel. Econ.*, March 1986, *20*(2), pp. 299–309. **[G: China]**

Jencks, Christopher. Education and Training Programs and Poverty: Comment. **In** *Danziger, S. H. and Weinberg, D. H., eds.*, 1986, pp. 173–79. **[G: U.S.]**

Jimenez, Emmanuel. The Public Subsidization of Education and Health in Developing Countries: A Review of Equity and Efficiency. *World Bank Res. Observer,* January 1986, *1*(1), pp. 111–29. **[G: LDCs]**

Jimenez, Emmanuel. The Structure of Educational Costs: Multiproduct Cost Functions for Primary and Secondary Schools in Latin America. *Econ. Educ. Rev.*, 1986, *5*(1), pp. 25–39. **[G: Bolivia; Paraguay]**

Jones, L. R.; Thompson, Fred and Zumeta, William. Reform of Budget Control in Higher Education. *Econ. Educ. Rev.*, 1986, *5*(2), pp. 147–58. **[G: U.S.]**

Jones, L. R.; Thompson, Fred and Zumeta, William. Reform of Budget Control in Higher Education: Reply. *Econ. Educ. Rev.*, 1986, *5*(2), pp. 165–66. **[G: U.S.]**

Jud, G. Donald and Bennett, D. Gordon. Public Schools and the Pattern of Intraurban Residential Mobility. *Land Econ.*, November 1986, *62*(4), pp. 362–70. **[G: U.S.]**

Kagan, Jerome. The Ethics of a Public Preschool. **In** *Hewlett, S. A.; Ilchman, A. S. and Sweeney, J. J., eds.*, 1986, pp. 101–04. **[G: U.S.]**

Katzman, Martin T. Implementation of Chapter 2 of ECIA in Texas. **In** *Cohn, E., ed.*, 1986, *1985,* pp. 237–43. **[G: U.S.]**

Kearney, C. Philip. Michigan's Experiences with the Federal Education Block Grant. **In** *Cohn, E., ed.*, 1986, *1985*, pp. 181–88. **[G: U.S.]**

Kesselring, Randall G. and Strein, Charles T. A Test of the Williamson Hypothesis for Universities. *J. Behav. Econ.*, Spring/Summer 1986, *15*(1/2), pp. 103–12. **[G: U.S.]**

Khan, Shahrukh Rafi; Mahmood, Naushin and Hussain, Fazal. An Appraisal of School Level Enrollments and Facilities in Pakistan 1970/71–1982/83. *Pakistan Econ. Soc. Rev.*, Winter 1986, *24*(2), pp. 83–112. **[G: Pakistan]**

Khan, Shahrukh Rafi; Mahmood, Naushin and Siddiqui, Rehana. An Assessment of the Distribution of Public-Sector Educational Investment in Pakistan: 1970-71–1982-83. *Pakistan Devel. Rev.*, Summer 1986, *25*(2), pp. 175–92. **[G: Pakistan]**

Kodde, David A. Uncertainty and the Demand for Education. *Rev. Econ. Statist.*, August 1986, *68*(3), pp. 460–67. **[G: Netherlands]**

Kostin, L. A. The Development of Vocational Guidance in the USSR. *Int. Lab. Rev.*, Nov.-Dec. 1986, *125*(6), pp. 715–29. **[G: U.S.S.R.]**

Kourilsky, Marilyn. School Reform: The Role of the Economic Educator. *J. Econ. Educ.*, Summer 1986, *17*(3), pp. 213–17.

Kuriloff, Peter J. The Distributive and Educational Consequences of Chapter 2 Block Grants in Pennsylvania. **In** *Cohn, E., ed.*, 1986, *1985,* pp. 197–214. **[G: U.S.]**

Ladd, Helen F. Education, Welfare and the "New" Federalism: State Budgeting in a Federalist Public Economy: Comment. **In** *Rosen, H. S., ed.*, 1986, pp. 222–27. **[G: U.S.]**

Lang, Kevin and Kropp, David. Human Capital versus Sorting: The Effects of Compulsory Attendance Laws. *Quart. J. Econ.*, August 1986, *101*(3), pp. 609–24. **[G: U.S.]**

Lankford, R. Hamilton. Property Taxes, Tax-Cost Illusion and Desired Education Expenditures. *Public Choice,* 1986, *49*(1), pp. 79–97. **[G: U.S.]**

Lee, Kiong-Hock. Affective, Cognitive and Vocational Skills: The Employers' Perspective. *Econ. Educ. Rev.*, 1986, *5*(4), pp. 395–401. **[G: Malaysia]**

Lee, Ronald D. The Value and Allocation of Time in High-Income Countries: Implications for Fertility: Comment. *Population Devel. Rev.*, Supp. 1986, *12*, pp. 108–10.

Levin, Henry M. Are Block Grants the Answer to the Federal Role in Education? **In** *Cohn, E., ed.*, 1986, pp. 261–69. **[G: U.S.]**

Levin, Henry M. Are Longer School Sessions a Good Investment? *Contemp. Policy Issues,* July 1986, *4*(3), pp. 63–75. **[G: U.S.]**

Link, Charles R. and Mulligan, James G. The Merits of a Longer School Day. *Econ. Educ. Rev.*, 1986, *5*(4), pp. 373–81. **[G: U.S.]**

Liu, Ben-chieh; Mulvey, Thomas and Hsieh, Chang-Tzeh. Effects of Educational Expenditures on Regional Inequality in the Social Quality of Life. *Amer. J. Econ. Soc.*, April 1986, *45*(2), pp. 131–44. **[G: U.S.]**

Luizer, James and Thornton, Robert. Concentration in the Labor Market for Public School Teachers. *Ind. Lab. Relat. Rev.*, July 1986, *39*(4), pp. 573–84. **[G: U.S.]**

MacDowell, Michael A. The School-Reform Debate: Response. *J. Econ. Educ.*, Summer 1986, *17*(3), pp. 210–12.

Margo, Robert A. Educational Achievement in Segregated School Systems: The Effects of "Separate-but-Equal." *Amer. Econ. Rev.*, September 1986, *76*(4), pp. 794–801. **[G: U.S.]**

Marsden, W. E. Atlas of Industrializing Britain 1780–1914: Education. **In** *Langton, J. and Morris, R. J., eds.*, 1986, pp. 206–11. **[G: U.K.]**

McKenzie, Hermione. The Educational Experiences of Caribbean Women. *Soc. Econ. Stud.*, September 1986, *35*(3), pp. 65–105. **[G: St. Vincent; Antigua; Barbados]**

McKeown, Mary P. Issues in Higher Education Budgeting Policy [An Adult Life Cycle Perspective on Public Subsidies to Higher Education in Three Countries] [Reform of Budget Control in Higher Education]. *Econ. Educ. Rev.*, 1986, *5*(2), pp. 159–63. **[G: U.S.]**

Megdal, Sharon Bernstein. Estimating a Public School Expenditure Model under Binding Spending Limitations. *J. Urban Econ.*, May 1986, *19*(3), pp. 277–95. **[G: U.S.]**

Melck, Antony. On Subsidizing Education with

Block Grants. **In** *Cohn, E., ed.*, 1986, *1985*, pp. 253–59. **[G: U.S.]**

Miller, L. Scott. The School-Reform Debate. *J. Econ. Educ.*, Summer 1986, *17*(3), pp. 204–09.

Mingat, Alain and Tan, Jee-Peng. Expanding Education through User Charges: What Can Be Achieved in Malawi and Other LDCs? *Econ. Educ. Rev.*, 1986, *5*(3), pp. 273–86. **[G: LDCs; Malawi]**

Mitch, David F. The Impact of Subsidies to Elementary Schooling on Enrolment Rates in Nineteenth-century England. *Econ. Hist. Rev., 2nd Ser.*, August 1986, *39*(3), pp. 371–91. **[G: U.K.]**

Moisset, Jean. Éducation et développement: à la recherche d'un nouveau paradigme. (With English summary.) *Can. J. Devel. Stud.*, 1986, *7*(1), pp. 65–79. **[G: LDCs]**

Montmarquette, Claude and Houle, Rachel. An Empirical Note on Selectivity Bias in Educational Production Functions. *J. Econ. Educ.*, Spring 1986, *17*(2), pp. 99–105. **[G: Canada]**

Moock, Peter R. and Leslie, Joanne. Childhood Malnutrition and Schooling in the Terai Region of Nepal. *J. Devel. Econ.*, Jan.-Feb. 1986, *20*(1), pp. 33–52. **[G: Nepal]**

Moore, Peter G. Positioning Business Schools in the UK. *Lloyds Bank Rev.*, April 1986, (160), pp. 36–51. **[G: U.K.; U.S.]**

Moores, Brian. Are They Being Served? Quality Consciousness in Service Industries: Epilogue. **In** *Moores, B., ed.*, 1986, pp. 288–95.

Nelson, Michael A. Voter Perceptions of the Cost of Government: The Case of Local School Expenditures in Louisiana. *Public Finance Quart.*, January 1986, *14*(1), pp. 48–68. **[G: U.S.]**

Ofer, Gur. National Expenditure on Education and Health. **In** *Kop, Y., ed.*, 1986, pp. 111–34. **[G: Israel]**

Ojo, Folayan. Manpower Development in West Africa. **In** *Damachi, U. G. and Seibel, H. D., eds.*, 1986, pp. 33–68. **[G: W. Africa]**

Pettit, Joseph M. Technological Education. **In** *Landau, R. and Rosenberg, N., eds.*, 1986, pp. 255–62. **[G: U.S.; Japan]**

Plank, David N. State Action and the Distribution of School Enrollments in Brazil, 1970. *Econ. Educ. Rev.*, 1986, *5*(4), pp. 403–14. **[G: Brazil]**

Poulson, Barry W. Education and the Family during the Industrial Revolution. **In** *Peden, J. R. and Glahe, F. R., eds.*, 1986, pp. 135–58. **[G: U.S.]**

Prais, S. J. and Steedman, Hilary. Vocational Training in France and Britain: The Building Trades. *Nat. Inst. Econ. Rev.*, May 1986, (116), pp. 45–55. **[G: U.K.; France]**

Proctor, Allen J. Short-Term Borrowing by Local School Districts. *Fed. Res. Bank New York Quart. Rev.*, Summer 1986, *11*(2), pp. 30–41. **[G: U.S.]**

Psacharopoulos, George. Welfare Effects of Government Intervention in Education. *Contemp. Policy Issues*, July 1986, *4*(3), pp. 51–62. **[G: Africa]**

Qadir, Asghar. Higher Education and the Markets for Educated Labour in LDCs: Theoretical Approaches and Implications: Comments. *Pakistan Devel. Rev.*, Autumn 1986, *25*(3), pp. 277–78. **[G: LDCs]**

Ranson, Thomas Baldwin. Planning Education for Economic Progress: Distinguishing Occupational Demands from Technological Possibilities. *J. Econ. Issues*, December 1986, *20*(4), pp. 1053–65. **[G: U.S.]**

Ravitch, Diane. American Education: Public and Private Responsibilities. **In** *Knowlton, W. and Zeckhauser, R., eds.*, 1986, pp. 203–21. **[G: U.S.]**

Reisman, A., et. al. On the Voids in U.S. National Education Statistics. *J. Econ. Soc. Meas.*, December 1986, *14*(4), pp. 357–65. **[G: U.S.]**

Richards, Craig E. Race and Demographic Trends: The Employment of Minority Teachers in California Public Schools. *Econ. Educ. Rev.*, 1986, *5*(1), pp. 57–64. **[G: U.S.]**

Rodrique, André. La contribution de l'amélioration du bien-être au processus de croissance dans les pays en développement. (The Contribution of Welfare to Economic Growth. With English summary.) *L'Actual. Econ.*, March 1986, *62*(1), pp. 64–87. **[G: LDCs]**

Rose, James. Implementation of Federal ECIA Block Grants to Education in Colorado. **In** *Cohn, E., ed.*, 1986, *1985*, pp. 171–79. **[G: U.S.]**

Rothbard, Murray N. The Progressive Era and the Family. **In** *Peden, J. R. and Glahe, F. R., eds.*, 1986, pp. 109–34. **[G: U.S.]**

Ruel, R. F. and Taylor, P. J. The Economic Impacts of Institutions of Higher Education: A Survey of Studies. *Brit. Rev. Econ. Issues*, Autumn 1986, *8*(19), pp. 41–63. **[G: U.K.]**

San, Gee. The Early Labor Force Experience of College Students and Their Post-college Success. *Econ. Educ. Rev.*, 1986, *5*(1), pp. 65–76. **[G: U.S.]**

Sarkar, B. N. Enrolment and Primary Education Force in Rural India. *Margin*, April 1986, *18*(3), pp. 72–89. **[G: India]**

Sav, G. Thomas. The Politics of Race in Higher Education: Governing Boards and Constituents. *Public Choice*, 1986, *48*(2), pp. 147–55. **[G: U.S.]**

Schultz, T. Paul. The Value and Allocation of Time in High-Income Countries: Implications for Fertility. *Population Devel. Rev.*, Supp. 1986, *12*, pp. 87–108. **[G: U.S.]**

Schwartz, J. Brad. Wealth Neutrality in Higher Education: The Effects of Student Grants. *Econ. Educ. Rev.*, 1986, *5*(2), pp. 107–17. **[G: U.S.]**

Sengupta, Jati K. and Sfeir, Raymond E. Production Frontier Estimates of Scale in Public Schools in California. *Econ. Educ. Rev.*, 1986, *5*(3), pp. 297–307. **[G: U.S.]**

Shanker, Albert. Business and Schools: The Inevitable Partnership. **In** *Burton, D. F., et al., eds.*, 1986, pp. 189–98. **[G: U.S.]**

Shanker, Albert. Early Childhood Education and the Public Schools. **In** *Hewlett, S. A.; Ilchman, A. S. and Sweeney, J. J., eds.*, 1986, pp. 91–99. **[G: U.S.]**

Shughart, William F., II; Tollison, Robert D. and Goff, Brian L. Pigskins and Publications. *Atlantic Econ. J.*, July 1986, *14*(2), pp. 46–50. **[G: U.S.]**

Siegfried, John J. The Effects of Student Higher Education Grants. *Econ. Educ. Rev.*, 1986, *5*(2), pp. 129–33. **[G: U.S.]**

Solomon, Lewis C. Economic Perspectives on Educational Policy: Introduction. *Contemp. Policy Issues*, July 1986, *4*(3), pp. 50.

Spellman, Ruth. Education and Training Initiatives in the United Kingdom and Macro-economic Policies. **In** *Burton, D. F., et al., eds.*, 1986, pp. 205–25. **[G: U.K.]**

Steuerle, C. Eugene. The Effect of Tax Simplification on Educational and Charitable Organizations: Discussion. **In** *Federal Reserve Bank of Boston*, 1986, pp. 216–21. **[G: U.S.]**

Strauss, Robert P. and Sawyer, Elizabeth A. Some New Evidence on Teacher and Student Competencies. *Econ. Educ. Rev.*, 1986, *5*(1), pp. 41–48. **[G: U.S.]**

Thembela, Alex. Educational Obstacles to Black Advancement. **In** *Smollan, R., ed.*, 1986, pp. 73–80. **[G: S. Africa]**

Throsby, C. D. Cost Functions for Australian Universities. *Australian Econ. Pap.*, December 1986, *25*(47), pp. 175–92. **[G: Australia]**

Throsby, C. D. Economic Aspects of the Foreign Student Question. *Econ. Rec.*, December 1986, *62*(179), pp. 400–414. **[G: Australia]**

Toma, Eugenia Froedge. Rent Seeking, Federal Mandates, and the Quality of Public Education. *Atlantic Econ. J.*, July 1986, *14*(2), pp. 37–45. **[G: U.S.]**

Toma, Eugenia Froedge. State University Boards of Trustees: A Principal-Agent Perspective. *Public Choice*, 1986, *49*(2), pp. 155–63. **[G: U.S.]**

Tremblay, Carol Horton. The Impact of School and College Expenditures on the Wages of Southern and Non-Southern Workers. *J. Lab. Res.*, Spring 1986, *7*(2), pp. 201–11. **[G: U.S.]**

Tuckman, Howard P. and Chang, Cyril F. Own-Price and Cross Elasticities of Demand for College Faculty. *Southern Econ. J.*, January 1986, *52*(3), pp. 735–44. **[G: U.S.]**

Wainscott, Stephen H. and Woodard, J. David. School Finance and School Desegregation: Ten-Year Effects in Southern School Districts. *Soc. Sci. Quart.*, September 1986, *67*(3), pp. 587–95. **[G: U.S.]**

Wedeman, Sara Capen; Passman, Vicki Fay and Day, James Meredith. Education Block Grants: Introduction to the Debate. **In** *Cohn, E., ed.*, 1986, *1985*, pp. 163–70. **[G: U.S.]**

Weiler, William C. A Sequential Logit Model of the Access Effects of Higher Education Institutions. *Econ. Educ. Rev.*, 1986, *5*(1), pp. 49–55. **[G: U.S.]**

Wilkinson, Bruce W. Elementary and Secondary Education Policy in Canada: A Survey. *Can. Public Policy*, December 1986, *12*(4), pp. 535–72. **[G: Canada]**

Wrigley, Julia. Technical Education and Industry in the Nineteenth Century. **In** *Elbaum, B. and Lazonick, W., eds.*, 1986, pp. 162–88. **[G: U.K.]**

913 Economics of Health (including medical subsidy programs)

9130 Economics of Health (including medical subsidy programs)

Abernethy, Margaret A. A Contingency Approach to the Design and Use of Budgeting in a Public Teaching Hospital. **In** *Butler, J. R. G. and Doessel, D. P., eds.*, 1986, pp. 107–32. **[G: Australia]**

Adamache, Killard W. and Rossiter, Louis F. The Entry of HMOs into the Medicare Market: Implications for TEFRA's Mandate. *Inquiry*, Winter 1986, *23*(4), pp. 349–64. **[G: U.S.]**

Akin, John S., et al. The Demand for Primary Health Care Services in the Bicol Region of the Philippines. *Econ. Develop. Cult. Change*, July 1986, *34*(4), pp. 755–82. **[G: Philippines]**

Alexander, Jeffrey A.; Morrisey, Michael A. and Shortell, Stephen M. Physician Participation in the Administration and Governance of System and Freestanding Hospitals: A Comparison by Type of Ownership. **In** *Gray, B. H., ed.*, 1986, pp. 402–21. **[G: U.S.]**

Allen, Steven G. The Effect of Unionism on Productivity in Privately and Publicly Owned Hospitals and Nursing Homes. *J. Lab. Res.*, Winter 1986, *7*(1), pp. 59–68. **[G: U.S.]**

Altman, Drew E. Two Views of a Changing Health Care System. **In** *Aiken, L. H. and Mechanic, D., eds.*, 1986, pp. 100–112. **[G: U.S.]**

Andersen, Ronald M.; Banks, Martha J. and Aplington, Margaret. Success in Reaching the Communities and People Targeted for MHSP. **In** *Fleming, G. V. and Andersen, R. M., eds.*, 1986, pp. 45–67. **[G: U.S.]**

Andersen, Ronald M. and Fleming, Gretchen V. Expenditures for Medical Care. **In** *Fleming, G. V. and Andersen, R. M., eds.*, 1986, pp. 94–118. **[G: U.S.]**

Anderson, Gerard F. and Lave, Judith R. Financing Graduate Medical Education Using Multiple Regression to Set Payment Rates. *Inquiry*, Summer 1986, *23*(2), pp. 191–99. **[G: U.S.]**

Appelbaum, Eileen and Granrose, Cherlyn Skromme. Hospital Employment under Revised Medicare Payment Schedules. *Mon. Lab. Rev.*, August 1986, *109*(8), pp. 37–45. **[G: U.S.]**

Atiyah, P. S. Medical Malpractice and the Contract/Tort Boundary. *Law Contemp. Probl.*, Spring 1986, *49*(2), pp. 287–303. **[G: U.S.]**

Atri, Said and Lahiri, Kajal. Quality Change and the Demand for Hospital Care: An Econometric Reexamination. *Atlantic Econ. J.*, December 1986, *14*(4), pp. 15–23. **[G: U.S.]**

Audibert, Martine. Agricultural Non-wage Production and Health Status: A Case Study in a Tropical Environment. *J. Devel. Econ.*, December 1986, *24*(2), pp. 275–91. **[G: Cameroon]**

Babbitt, Bruce and Rose, Jonathan. Building a Better Mousetrap: Health Care Reform and the Arizona Program. *Yale J. Regul.*, Spring 1986, *3*(2), pp. 243–82. **[G: U.S.]**

Bairagi, Radheshyam. Food Crisis, Nutrition, and Female Children in Rural Bangladesh. *Population Devel. Rev.*, June 1986, *12*(2), pp. 307–15. **[G: Bangladesh]**

Banks, Martha J. The Sample Design and Its Effect on the Data. **In** *Fleming, G. V. and Andersen, R. M., eds.*, 1986, pp. 228–49. **[G: U.S.]**

Bartel, Ann and Taubman, Paul. Some Economic and Demographic Consequences of Mental Illness. *J. Lab. Econ.*, April 1986, *4*(2), pp. 243–56. **[G: U.S.]**

Bays, Carson W. The Determinants of Hospital Size: A Survivor Analysis. *Appl. Econ.*, April 1986, *18*(4), pp. 359–77. **[G: U.S.]**

Bell, Ralph. Utilization of Medical Care Services. **In** *Fleming, G. V. and Andersen, R. M., eds.*, 1986, pp. 80–93. **[G: U.S.]**

Bell, Ralph and Banks, Martha J. The MHSP Evaluation Data and Methods. **In** *Fleming, G. V. and Andersen, R. M., eds.*, 1986, pp. 27–44. **[G: U.S.]**

Benjamini, Yael and Benjamini, Yoav. The Choice among Medical Insurance Plans. *Amer. Econ. Rev.*, March 1986, *76*(1), pp. 221–27. **[G: U.S.]**

Bentkover, Judith D. The Role of Benefits Assessment in Public Policy Development. **In** *Bentkover, J. D.; Covello, V. T. and Jeryl, M., eds.*, 1986, pp. 1–12. **[G: U.S.]**

Berlin, Hans and Jönsson, Bengt. International Dissemination of New Drugs: A Comparative Study of Six Countries. *Managerial Dec. Econ.*, December 1986, *7*(4), pp. 235–42. **[G: W. Europe; U.S.]**

Björkman, James Warner. Health Policies and Human Capital: The Case of Pakistan. *Pakistan Devel. Rev.*, Autumn 1986, *25*(3), pp. 281–330. **[G: Pakistan]**

Black, Jeanne T. The Employed Uninsured and the Role of Public Policy: Comment. *Inquiry*, Summer 1986, *23*(2), pp. 209–12. **[G: U.S.]**

Blanchard, Garth A.; Chow, Chee W. and Noreen, Eric W. Information Asymmetry, Incentive Schemes, and Information Biasing: The Case of Hospital Budgeting under Rate Regulation. *Accounting Rev.*, January 1986, *61*(1), pp. 1–15. **[G: U.S.]**

Blau, David M. Fertility, Child Nutrition, and Child Mortality in Nicaragua: An Economic Analysis of Interrelationships. *J. Devel. Areas*, January 1986, *20*(2), pp. 185–201. **[G: Nicaragua]**

Blomqvist, Ake G. Health Policies and Human Capital: The Case of Pakistan: Comments. *Pakistan Devel. Rev.*, Autumn 1986, *25*(3), pp. 331–34. **[G: Pakistan]**

Blumenthal, David. The Social Responsibility of Physicians in a Changing Health Care System. *Inquiry*, Fall 1986, *23*(3), pp. 268–74. **[G: U.S.]**

Blumstein, James F. Providing Hospital Care to Indigent Patients: Hill–Burton as a Case Study and a Paradigm. **In** *Sloan, F. A.; Blumstein, J. F. and Perrin, J. M., eds.*, 1986, pp. 94–107. **[G: U.S.]**

Boldy, Duncan. Unemployment and Health in Australia: A Policy Perspective: Discussion. **In** *Butler, J. R. G. and Doessel, D. P., eds.*, 1986, pp. 35. **[G: Australia]**

Bombardier, Claire, et al. The Utilization of Surgical Operations. **In** *Fuchs, V. R.*, 1986, *1977*, pp. 108–25. **[G: U.S.]**

Bosanquet, Nick. Inconsistencies of the NHS: Buchanan Revisited. **In** *Culyer, A. J. and Jönsson, B., eds.*, 1986, pp. 101–11. **[G: U.K.]**

Bosk, Charles L. Professional Responsibility and Medical Error. **In** *Aiken, L. H. and Mechanic, D., eds.*, 1986, pp. 460–77. **[G: U.S.]**

Bovbjerg, Randall R. Insuring the Uninsured through Private Action: Ideas and Initiatives. *Inquiry*, Winter 1986, *23*(4), pp. 403–18.

Bovbjerg, Randall R. and Koller, Christopher F. State Health Insurance Pools: Current Performance, Future Prospects. *Inquiry*, Summer 1986, *23*(2), pp. 111–21. **[G: U.S.]**

Bowden, David; Williams, Glen and Stevens, Geoff. Medical Quality Assurance in Brighton Health Authority—Can American Translate into English? **In** *Moores, B., ed.*, 1986, pp. 104–14. **[G: U.K.]**

Breyer, Friedrich. Krankenhaus-Kostenstudien. (With English summary.) *Z. Betriebswirtshaft*, March 1986, *56*(3), pp. 260–86. **[G: U.S.]**

Breyer, Friedrich; Mühlenkamp, Holger and Adam, Hans. Determinants of the Utilization of Physician Services in the System of Statutory Health Insurance in Germany. **In** *von der Schulenburg, J.-M. G., ed.*, 1986, pp. 196–216. **[G: W. Germany]**

Brock, Dan W. and Buchanan, Allen. Ethical Issues in For-Profit Health Care. **In** *Gray, B. H., ed.*, 1986, pp. 224–49. **[G: U.S.]**

Brown, George W. Applications of Social Science to Clinical Medicine and Health Policy: Mental Illness. **In** *Aiken, L. H. and Mechanic, D., eds.*, 1986, pp. 175–203. **[G: U.S.; U.K.]**

Brown, Kathryn J. and Klosterman, Richard E. Hospital Acquisitions and Their Effects: Florida, 1979–1982. **In** *Gray, B. H., ed.*, 1986, pp. 303–21. **[G: U.S.]**

Brown, Ralph J. Implicit Inflation and Interest Rates in Discounting Personal Injury Economic Losses—Comment. *J. Risk Ins.*, September 1986, *53*(3), pp. 492–95. **[G: U.S.]**

Burrows, Colin. A Contingency Approach to the Design and Use of Budgeting in a Public Teaching Hospital: Discussion. **In** *Butler, J. R. G. and Doessel, D. P., eds.*, 1986, pp. 133–35. **[G: Australia]**

Buss, Emily. Getting Beyond Discrimination: A

Regulatory Solution to the Problem of Fetal Hazards in the Workplace. *Yale Law J.*, January 1986, *95*(3), pp. 577–98. **[G: U.S.]**

Butler, J. R. G. The Allocation of Hospital Costs to Type of Case: Discussion. **In** *Butler, J. R. G. and Doessel, D. P., eds.*, 1986, pp. 210–12. **[G: Australia]**

Cairns, John A. Demand for Abortion Services in the Private Sector and Excess Demand in the Public Sector. **In** *Culyer, A. J. and Jönsson, B., eds.*, 1986, pp. 152–67. **[G: U.K.]**

Carroll, Norman V.; Siridhara, Chanaporn and Fincham, Jack E. Perceived Risks and Pharmacists' Generic Substitution Behavior. *J. Cons. Aff.*, Summer 1986, *20*(1), pp. 36–47. **[G: U.S.]**

Catsambas, Thanos and Foster, Susan. Spending Money Sensibly: The Case of Essential Drugs. *Finance Develop.*, December 1986, *23*(4), pp. 29–32. **[G: LDCs]**

Chang, Cyril F. and Tuckman, Howard P. Econometric Analysis of the Hospital Size/Patient Load Relation. *Appl. Econ.*, July 1986, *18*(7), pp. 793–805. **[G: U.S.]**

Chant, David. The Allocation of Hospital Costs to Type of Case. **In** *Butler, J. R. G. and Doessel, D. P., eds.*, 1986, pp. 188–209. **[G: Australia]**

Chapman, Steven H.; LaPlante, Mitchell P. and Wilensky, Gail R. Life Expectancy and Health Status of the Aged. *Soc. Sec. Bull.*, October 1986, *49*(10), pp. 24–48. **[G: U.S.]**

Chernichovsky, Dov and Zmora, Irit. A Hedonic Prices Approach to Hospitalization Costs: The Case of Israel. *J. Health Econ.*, June 1986, *5*(2), pp. 179–91. **[G: Israel]**

Chesterman, Esther. Implications of the New South Wales Doctors' Dispute: Discussion. **In** *Butler, J. R. G. and Doessel, D. P., eds.*, 1986, pp. 79–80. **[G: Australia]**

Ching, Panfila. Public Provision and Demand for Health Services: A Case Study of Bicol. *Philippine Rev. Econ. Bus.*, Sept.-Dec. 1986, *23*(3–4), pp. 293–322. **[G: Philippines]**

Coelen, Craig G. Hospital Ownership and Comparative Hospital Costs. **In** *Gray, B. H., ed.*, 1986, pp. 322–53. **[G: U.S.]**

Cohen, Joel and Holahan, John. An Evaluation of Current Approaches to Nursing Home Capital Reimbursement. *Inquiry*, Spring 1986, *23*(1), pp. 23–39. **[G: U.S.]**

Cohodes, Donald R. America: The Home of the Free, the Land of the Uninsured. *Inquiry*, Fall 1986, *23*(3), pp. 227–35. **[G: U.S.]**

Coleman, James S.; Wu, Shi-Chang and Feld, Scott L. Constitutional Power in Experimental Health Service and Delivery Systems. **In** *Coleman, J. S.*, 1986, *1977*, pp. 226–46. **[G: U.S.]**

Cone, Kenneth R. and Dranove, David. Why Did States Enact Hospital Rate-Setting Laws? *J. Law Econ.*, October 1986, *29*(2), pp. 287–302. **[G: U.S.]**

Cromwell, Jerry; Hurdle, Sylvia and Wedig, Gerard. Impacts of Economic and Programmatic Changes on Medicaid Enrollments. *Rev. Econ. Statist.*, May 1986, *68*(2), pp. 232–40. **[G: U.S.]**

Cromwell, Jerry and Mitchell, Janet B. Physician-Induced Demand for Surgery. *J. Health Econ.*, December 1986, *5*(4), pp. 293–313. **[G: U.S.]**

Culler, Steven D. and Ehrenfried, David. On the Feasibility and Usefulness of Physician DRGs. *Inquiry*, Spring 1986, *23*(1), pp. 40–55. **[G: U.S.]**

Culler, Steven D. and Ohsfeldt, Robert L. The Determinants of the Provision of Charity Medical Care by Physicians. *J. Human Res.*, Winter 1986, *21*(1), pp. 138–56. **[G: U.S.]**

Cullis, John G. and Jones, Philip R. Rationing by Waiting Lists: An Implication. *Amer. Econ. Rev.*, March 1986, *76*(1), pp. 250–56. **[G: U.K.]**

Culyer, A. J. and Jönsson, Bengt. Public and Private Health Services: Complementarities and Conflicts: Introduction. **In** *Culyer, A. J. and Jönsson, B., eds.*, 1986, pp. 1–7.

Cunningham, Frances C. Hospital Output and the Use of Diagnosis Related Groups for Purposes of Economic and Financial Analysis: Discussion. **In** *Butler, J. R. G. and Doessel, D. P., eds.*, 1986, pp. 182–87. **[G: Australia]**

Curtis, Rick. The Role of State Governments in Assuring Access to Care. *Inquiry*, Fall 1986, *23*(3), pp. 277–85. **[G: U.S.]**

Custer, William S. Hospital Attributes and Physician Prices. *Southern Econ. J.*, April 1986, *52*(4), pp. 1010–27. **[G: U.S.]**

D'Arcy, Stephen P. Legislative Reform of the Medical Malpractice Tort System in Illinois. *J. Risk Ins.*, September 1986, *53*(3), pp. 538–50. **[G: U.S.]**

Danzon, Patricia M. The Frequency and Severity of Medical Malpractice Claims: New Evidence. *Law Contemp. Probl.*, Spring 1986, *49*(2), pp. 57–84. **[G: U.S.]**

Dardanoni, Valentino. A Note on a Simple Model of Health Investment [On the Concept of Health Capital and the Demand for Health]. *Bull. Econ. Res.*, January 1986, *38*(1), pp. 97–100.

Darling, Helen. The Role of the Federal Government in Assuring Access to Health Care. *Inquiry*, Fall 1986, *23*(3), pp. 286–95. **[G: U.S.]**

Dasgupta, Partha and Ray, Debraj. Inequality as a Determinant of Malnutrition and Unemployment: Theory. *Econ. J.*, December 1986, *96*(384), pp. 1011–34.

Davis, Karen. Research and Policy Formulation. **In** *Aiken, L. H. and Mechanic, D., eds.*, 1986, pp. 113–25. **[G: U.S.]**

Deeble, J. S. The Economics and Financing of Hospitals in Australia: Comment. *Australian Econ. Rev.*, 3rd Quarter 1986, (75), pp. 73–74. **[G: Australia]**

Dewees, Donald N. and Daniels, Ronald J. The Cost of Protecting Occupational Health: The Asbestos Case. *J. Human Res.*, Summer 1986, *21*(3), pp. 381–96. **[G: U.S.; Canada]**

Doessel, D. P. Medical Diagnosis as a Problem

in the Economics of Information. *Info. Econ. Policy*, 1986, *2*(1), pp. 49–68. **[G: Australia]**

Doessel, D. P. The Economics of Reducing Hypertension through Reduction of Sodium Intake: Discussion. **In** *Butler, J. R. G. and Doessel, D. P., eds.*, 1986, pp. 242–47. **[G: Australia]**

Dooley, David and Catalano, Ralph. Do Economic Variables Generate Psychological Problems? Different Methods, Different Answers. **In** *MacFadyen, A. J. and MacFadyen, H. W., eds.*, 1986, pp. 503–46.

Dranove, David; Satterthwaite, Mark and Sindelar, Jody. The Effect of Injecting Price Competition into the Hospital Market: The Case of Preferred Provider Organizations. *Inquiry*, Winter 1986, *23*(4), pp. 419–31.

Duleep, Harriet Orcutt. Measuring the Effect of Income on Adult Mortality Using Longitudinal Administrative Record Data. *J. Human Res.*, Spring 1986, *21*(2), pp. 238–51. **[G: U.S.]**

Dusansky, Richard, et al. On Increasing the Supply of Nurses: An Interstate Analysis. *Atlantic Econ. J.*, September 1986, *14*(3), pp. 34–44. **[G: U.S.]**

Dutton, Diana B. Social Class, Health, and Illness. **In** *Aiken, L. H. and Mechanic, D., eds.*, 1986, pp. 31–62. **[G: U.S.]**

van't Eind, Gerrit Jan, et al. Evaluating the Distribution of Public Expenditure. *Rev. Income Wealth*, September 1986, *32*(3), pp. 299–312. **[G: Netherlands]**

Ellis, Randall P. Rational Behavior in the Presence of Coverage Ceilings and Deductibles. *Rand J. Econ.*, Summer 1986, *17*(2), pp. 158–75. **[G: U.S.]**

Ellis, Randall P. and McGuire, Thomas G. Cost Sharing and Patterns of Mental Health Care Utilization. *J. Human Res.*, Summer 1986, *21*(3), pp. 359–79.

Ellis, Randall P. and McGuire, Thomas G. Provider Behavior under Prospective Reimbursement: Cost Sharing and Supply. *J. Health Econ.*, June 1986, *5*(2), pp. 129–51.

Epstein, Richard A. Medical Malpractice, Imperfect Information, and the Contractual Foundation for Medical Services. *Law Contemp. Probl.*, Spring 1986, *49*(2), pp. 201–12. **[G: U.S.]**

Erickson, Rodney A.; Gavin, Norma I. and Cordes, Sam M. Service Industries in Interregional Trade: The Economic Impacts of the Hospital Sector. *Growth Change*, January 1986, *17*(1), pp. 17–27. **[G: U.S.]**

Ermann, Dan and Gabel, Jon. Investor-Owned Multihospital Systems: A Synthesis of Research Findings. **In** *Gray, B. H., ed.*, 1986, pp. 474–91. **[G: U.S.]**

Ernst, Richard L. and Zaidi, Mahmood A. On the Economics of Nonprofit Sellers: Output Policies in Community Hospitals. *Rev. Ind. Organ.*, 1986, *3*(1), pp. 25–43.

Essemyr, Mats. Food, Fare and Nutrition. Some Reflections on the Historical Development of Food Consumption. *Scand. Econ. Hist. Rev.*, 1986, *34*(2), pp. 76–89. **[G: Sweden]**

Estes, Carroll L. and Lee, Philip R. Health Problems and Policy Issues of Old Age. **In** *Aiken, L. H. and Mechanic, D., eds.*, 1986, pp. 335–55. **[G: U.S.]**

Etheredge, Lynn. Ethics and the New Insurance Market. *Inquiry*, Fall 1986, *23*(3), pp. 308–15. **[G: U.S.]**

Fandel, Günter and Hegermann, Holger. Kapazitätssteuerung im Krankenhaus Ein Ansatz zur Verbesserung der Kapazitätsauslastung in der klinischen Diagnostik. (With English summary.) *Z. Betriebswirtshaft*, November 1986, *56*(11), pp. 1129–47. **[G: W. Germany]**

Farley, Pamela J. Theories of the Price and Quantity of Physician Services: A Synthesis and Critique. *J. Health Econ.*, December 1986, *5*(4), pp. 315–33. **[G: U.S.]**

Farnand, Lawrence J.; Jacobs, Philip and Dickson, W. Michael. An Evaluation of a Program to Regulate Rural Hospital Costs: The Finger Lakes Hospital Experimental Payment Program. *Inquiry*, Summer 1986, *23*(2), pp. 200–208. **[G: U.S.]**

Farrell, Phillip and Fuchs, Victor R. Schooling and Health: The Cigarette Connection. **In** *Fuchs, V. R.*, 1986, *1982*, pp. 243–54. **[G: U.S.]**

Feder, Judith and Hadley, Jack. Cutbacks, Recession, and Hospitals' Care for the Urban Poor. **In** *Peterson, G. E. and Lewis, C. W., eds.*, 1986, pp. 37–61. **[G: U.S.]**

Feick, Lawrence F.; Hermann, Robert O. and Warland, Rex H. Search for Nutrition Information: A Probit Analysis of the Use of Different Information Sources. *J. Cons. Aff.*, Winter 1986, *20*(2), pp. 173–92. **[G: U.S.]**

Feldman, Roger and Dowd, Bryan. Is There a Competitive Market for Hospital Services? *J. Health Econ.*, September 1986, *5*(3), pp. 277–92. **[G: U.S.]**

Fenn, P. T. and Vlachonikolis, I. G. Male Labour Force Participation Following Illness or Injury. *Economica*, August 1986, *53*(211), pp. 379–91. **[G: U.K.]**

Fine, Max W. and Sunshine, Jonathan H. Malpractice Reform through Consumer Choice and Consumer Education: Are New Concepts Marketable? *Law Contemp. Probl.*, Spring 1986, *49*(2), pp. 213–22. **[G: U.S.]**

Finsinger, Jörg; Kraft, Kornelius and Pauly, Mark V. Some Observations on Greater Competition in the West German Health-insurance System from a U.S. Perspective. *Managerial Dec. Econ.*, September 1986, *7*(3), pp. 151–61. **[G: W. Germany; U.S.]**

Fleming, Gretchen V. Appropriateness of Care. **In** *Fleming, G. V. and Andersen, R. M., eds.*, 1986, pp. 160–77. **[G: U.S.]**

Fleming, Gretchen V. Selection Effects in the MHSP Program. **In** *Fleming, G. V. and Andersen, R. M., eds.*, 1986, pp. 68–79. **[G: U.S.]**

Fleming, Gretchen V. and Andersen, Ronald M. Can Access Be Improved While Controlling Costs? Conclusion. **In** *Fleming, G. V. and Andersen, R. M., eds.*, 1986, pp. 195–208. **[G: U.S.]**

Fogel, Robert William. Nutrition and the Decline in Mortality since 1700: Some Preliminary Findings. **In** *Engerman, S. L. and Gallman, R. E., eds.*, 1986, pp. 439–527. **[G: U.S.]**

Folland, Sherman T. Health Care Need, Economics and Social Justice. *Int. J. Soc. Econ.*, 1986, *13*(1/2), pp. 98–116.

Foster, Richard W. Waiver Effects and Further Controls for Selection Bias. **In** *Fleming, G. V. and Andersen, R. M., eds.*, 1986, pp. 119–59. **[G: U.S.]**

Fox, Renée C. Medicine, Science, and Technology. **In** *Aiken, L. H. and Mechanic, D., eds.*, 1986, pp. 13–30.

Frank, Richard G. and Kamlet, Mark S. Quality, Quantity and Total Expenditures on Publicly Provided Goods: The Case of Public Mental Hospitals. *J. Public Econ.*, April 1986, *29*(3), pp. 295–316. **[G: U.S.]**

Frank, Richard G. and Lave, Judith R. The Effect of Benefit Design on the Length of Stay of Medicaid Psychiatric Patients. *J. Human Res.*, Summer 1986, *21*(3), pp. 321–37. **[G: U.S.]**

Fraser, Irene; Koontz, Theodore and Moran, William C. Medicare Reimbursement for Hospice Care: An Approach for Analyzing Cost Consequences. *Inquiry*, Summer 1986, *23*(2), pp. 141–53. **[G: U.S.]**

Freidson, Eliot. The Medical Profession in Transition. **In** *Aiken, L. H. and Mechanic, D., eds.*, 1986, pp. 63–79. **[G: U.S.]**

Frumkin, Robert N. Health Insurance Trends in Cost Control and Coverage. *Mon. Lab. Rev.*, September 1986, *109*(9), pp. 3–8. **[G: U.S.]**

Fuchs, Victor R. Economics, Health, and Postindustrial Society. **In** *Fuchs, V. R.*, 1986, *1979*, pp. 272–99.

Fuchs, Victor R. From Bismarck to Woodcock. **In** *Fuchs, V. R.*, 1986, *1976*, pp. 257–71. **[G: U.S.]**

Fuchs, Victor R. Health Care and the United States Economic System. **In** *Fuchs, V. R.*, 1986, *1972*, pp. 11–31. **[G: U.S.]**

Fuchs, Victor R. Low-Level Radiation and Infant Mortality. **In** *Fuchs, V. R.*, 1986, *1981*, pp. 200–213. **[G: U.S.]**

Fuchs, Victor R. Paying the Piper, Calling the Tune. **In** *Fuchs, V. R.*, 1986, *1986*, pp. 332–56. **[G: U.S.]**

Fuchs, Victor R. Physician-Induced Demand: A Parable: Editorial. *J. Health Econ.*, December 1986, *5*(4), pp. 367.

Fuchs, Victor R. Setting Priorities in Health Education and Promotion. **In** *Fuchs, V. R.*, 1986, *1983*, pp. 32–46. **[G: U.S.]**

Fuchs, Victor R. Some Economic Aspects of Mortality in Developed Countries. **In** *Fuchs, V. R.*, 1986, *1974*, pp. 181–99. **[G: OECD]**

Fuchs, Victor R. The Battle for Control of Health Care. **In** *Fuchs, V. R.*, 1986, *1982*, pp. 300–309.

Fuchs, Victor R. The Health Economy: Introduction. **In** *Fuchs, V. R.*, 1986, pp. 1–8.

Fuchs, Victor R. The Supply of Surgeons and the Demand for Operations. **In** *Fuchs, V. R.*, 1986, *1978*, pp. 126–47. **[G: U.S.]**

Fuchs, Victor R. Though Much Is Taken. **In** *Fuchs, V. R.*, 1986, *1984*, pp. 310–31. **[G: U.S.]**

Fuchs, Victor R. Time Preference and Health. **In** *Fuchs, V. R.*, 1986, *1982*, pp. 214–42. **[G: U.S.]**

Fuchs, Victor R. and Kramer, Marcia J. Determinants of Expenditures for Physicians' Services. **In** *Fuchs, V. R.*, 1986, *1972*, pp. 67–107. **[G: U.S.]**

Fuchs, Victor R. and Leveson, Irving. Motor Accident Mortality and Compulsory Inspection of Vehicles. **In** *Fuchs, V. R.*, 1986, *1967*, pp. 169–80. **[G: U.S.]**

Furstenberg, Frank F., Jr. and Brooks-Gunn, Jeanne. Teenage Childbearing: Causes, Consequences, and Remedies. **In** *Aiken, L. H. and Mechanic, D., eds.*, 1986, pp. 307–34. **[G: U.S.]**

Garber, Alan M.; Fuchs, Victor R. and Silverman, James F. Case Mix, Costs, and Outcomes. **In** *Fuchs, V. R.*, 1986, *1984*, pp. 148–65. **[G: U.S.]**

Gaumer, Gary. Medicare Patient Outcomes and Hospital Organizational Mission. **In** *Gray, B. H., ed.*, 1986, pp. 354–74. **[G: U.S.]**

Gerking, Shelby and Stanley, Linda R. An Economic Analysis of Air Pollution and Health: The Case of St. Louis. *Rev. Econ. Statist.*, February 1986, *68*(1), pp. 115–21. **[G: U.S.]**

German, Rachel M. Health Care in the City: Setting the Stage for the Municipal Health Services Program. **In** *Fleming, G. V. and Andersen, R. M., eds.*, 1986, pp. 13–26. **[G: U.S.]**

Glandon, Gerald L. and Morrisey, Michael A. Redefining the Hospital–Physician Relationship under Prospective Payment. *Inquiry*, Summer 1986, *23*(2), pp. 166–75. **[G: U.S.]**

Glaser, William A. Payment Systems and Their Effects. **In** *Aiken, L. H. and Mechanic, D., eds.*, 1986, pp. 481–99. **[G: U.S.]**

Goldstone, Len and Illsley, Veronica. Measuring the Quality of Nursing Care—The Monitor Experience. **In** *Moores, B., ed.*, 1986, pp. 125–37. **[G: U.K.]**

Goss, John. The Economics of Reducing Hypertension through Reduction of Sodium Intake. **In** *Butler, J. R. G. and Doessel, D. P., eds.*, 1986, pp. 213–41. **[G: Australia]**

Gottlieb, Symond R. V. Ensuring Access to Health Care: What Communities Can Do to Make a Difference through Private Sector Coalition. *Inquiry*, Fall 1986, *23*(3), pp. 322–29. **[G: U.S.]**

Grannemann, Thomas W.; Brown, Randall S. and Pauly, Mark V. Estimating Hospital Costs: A Multiple-Output Analysis. *J. Health Econ.*, June 1986, *5*(2), pp. 107–27. **[G: U.S.]**

Gravelle, Hugh S. E. Insurance and Corrective Taxes in the Health Care Market. *J. Econ. (Z. Nationalökon.)*, Supplementum 5, 1986, pp. 99–120.

Gray, Bradford H. and Osterweis, Marian. Ethical Issues in a Social Context. **In** *Aiken, L. H. and Mechanic, D., eds.*, 1986, pp. 543–64. **[G: U.S.]**

Gray, D.; MacAdam, D. and Boldy, Duncan. A Comparative Cost Analysis of Terminal Cancer Care. **In** *Butler, J. R. G. and Doessel, D. P., eds.*, 1986, pp. 136–52. **[G: Australia]**

Greer, Joel and Thorbecke, Erik. A Methodology for Measuring Food Poverty Applied to Kenya. *J. Devel. Econ.*, November 1986, *24*(1), pp. 59–74. **[G: Kenya]**

Grossman, Jerome H. Community Commitment, Competition, and the Future of Academic Medical Centers. *Inquiry*, Fall 1986, *23*(3), pp. 245–52. **[G: U.S.]**

Gustman, Alan L. and Steinmeier, Thomas L. A Disaggregated, Structural Analysis of Retirement by Race, Difficulty of Work and Health. *Rev. Econ. Statist.*, August 1986, *68*(3), pp. 509–13. **[G: U.S.]**

Haas-Wilson, Deborah. The Effect of Commercial Practice Restrictions: The Case of Optometry. *J. Law Econ.*, April 1986, *29*(1), pp. 165–86. **[G: U.S.]**

Hall, Jane; Hall, Nellie and Tweedie, Richard. A Longitudinal Study of Health Changes Following the Introduction of Medicare. **In** *Butler, J. R. G. and Doessel, D. P., eds.*, 1986, pp. 81–102. **[G: U.S.]**

Halleck, Seymour L. Responsibility and Excuse in Medicine and Law: A Utilitarian Perspective. *Law Contemp. Probl.*, Summer 1986, *49*(3), pp. 127–46.

Hardwick, Jill. Hospital Case Mix Standardisation: A Comparison of the Resource Need Index and Information Theory Measures. **In** *Butler, J. R. G. and Doessel, D. P., eds.*, 1986, pp. 36–63. **[G: Australia]**

Harlow, Ruth E. The EPA and Biotechnology Regulation: Coping with Scientific Uncertainty. *Yale Law J.*, January 1986, *95*(3), pp. 553–76. **[G: U.S.]**

Hart, Nicky. Inequalities in Health: The Individual versus the Environment. *J. Roy. Statist. Soc.*, 1986, *149*(3), pp. 228–46. **[G: U.K.]**

Havighurst, Clark C. Altering the Applicable Standard of Care. *Law Contemp. Probl.*, Spring 1986, *49*(2), pp. 265–75. **[G: U.S.]**

Hawes, Catherine and Phillips, Charles D. The Changing Structure of the Nursing Home Industry and the Impact of Ownership on Quality, Cost, and Access. **In** *Gray, B. H., ed.*, 1986, pp. 492–541. **[G: U.S.]**

Hayes, Maurice. Your Good Health: Access to Health and Health Care in Northern Ireland. *Reg. Stud.*, October 1986, *20*(6), pp. 493–504. **[G: Ireland]**

Heggenhougen, Harald Kristian. Health Services: Official and Unofficial. **In** *Boesen, J., et al., eds.*, 1986, pp. 309–17. **[G: Tanzania]**

Horrocks, Peter. The Approach of the NHS Health Advisory Service in England and Wales. **In** *Moores, B., ed.*, 1986, pp. 115–24. **[G: U.K.]**

Horton, Susan. Child Nutrition and Family Size in the Philippines. *J. Devel. Econ.*, September 1986, *23*(1), pp. 161–76. **[G: Philippines]**

House, James S. and Cottington, Eric M. Health and the Workplace. **In** *Aiken, L. H. and Mechanic, D., eds.*, 1986, pp. 392–416. **[G: U.S.]**

Hoy, Elizabeth W. and Gray, Bradford H. Trends in the Growth of the Major Investor-Owned Hospital Companies. **In** *Gray, B. H., ed.*, 1986, pp. 250–59. **[G: U.S.]**

Hughes, Edward F. X., et al. Surgical Work Loads in a Community Practice. **In** *Fuchs, V. R.*, 1986, pp. 49–66. **[G: U.S.]**

Iversen, Tor. An Interaction Model of Public and Private Health Services: Surgical Waiting Lists. **In** *Culyer, A. J. and Jönsson, B., eds.*, 1986, pp. 131–51.

Jacobs, Bruce and Weissert, William G. Helping Protect the Elderly and the Public against the Catastrophic Costs of Long-term Care. *J. Policy Anal. Manage.*, Winter 1986, *5*(2), pp. 378–83. **[G: U.S.]**

Jamison, Dean T. Child Malnutrition and School Performance in China. *J. Devel. Econ.*, March 1986, *20*(2), pp. 299–309. **[G: China]**

Jansen, Mary A. Emotional Disorders and the Labour Force: Prevalence, Costs, Prevention and Rehabilitation. *Int. Lab. Rev.*, Sept.-Oct. 1986, *125*(5), pp. 605–15. **[G: U.S.]**

Jensen, Gail A. and Morrisey, Michael A. Medical Staff Specialty Mix and Hospital Production. *J. Health Econ.*, September 1986, *5*(3), pp. 253–76. **[G: U.S.]**

Jensen, Gail A. and Morrisey, Michael A. The Role of Physicians in Hospital Production. *Rev. Econ. Statist.*, August 1986, *68*(3), pp. 432–42. **[G: U.S.]**

Jimenez, Emmanuel. The Public Subsidization of Education and Health in Developing Countries: A Review of Equity and Efficiency. *World Bank Res. Observer*, January 1986, *1*(1), pp. 111–29. **[G: LDCs]**

Johnsen, Dawn E. The Creation of Fetal Rights: Conflicts with Women's Constitutional Rights to Liberty, Privacy, and Equal Protection. *Yale Law J.*, January 1986, 95(3), pp. 599–625. **[G: U.S.]**

Judge, Ken. Value for Money in the British Residential Care Industry. **In** *Culyer, A. J. and Jönsson, B., eds.*, 1986, pp. 200–218. **[G: U.K.]**

Kahl, Anne and Clark, Donald E. Employment in Health Services: Long-term Trends and Projections. *Mon. Lab. Rev.*, August 1986, *109*(8), pp. 17–36. **[G: U.S.]**

Kern, Rosemary Gibson. The Unfinished Agenda for Medicaid Reform. **In** *Kern, R. G. and Windham, S. R.*, 1986, pp. 51–66. **[G: U.S.]**

Khan, M. R. Prospects and Problems of Integration of Family Planning with Health Services in Bangladesh. *Bangladesh Devel. Stud.*, June 1986, *14*(2), pp. 101–08. **[G: Bangladesh]**

Kimenyi, Mwangi S. and Shughart, William F., II. Economics of Suicide: Rational or Irrational Choice. *Atlantic Econ. J.*, March 1986, *14*(1), pp. 121. **[G: U.S.]**

Klatzmann, Joseph. Balancing Overproduction and Malnutrition: Discussion. **In** *Maunder, A. and Renborg, U., eds.*, 1986, pp. 208–09.

Klees, Barbara and Warfield, Carter. Actuarial

Status of the HI and SMI Trust Funds. *Soc. Sec. Bull.*, July 1986, *49*(7), pp. 10–18. [G: U.S.]

Kleindorfer, Paul R. and von der Schulenburg, J.-Matthias Graf. Intergenerational Equity and Fund Balances for Statutory Health Insurance. **In** *von der Schulenburg, J.-M. G., ed.*, 1986, pp. 108–29.

Knapp, Martin. The Relative Cost-Effectiveness of Public, Voluntary and Private Providers of Residential Child Care. **In** *Culyer, A. J. and Jönsson, B., eds.*, 1986, pp. 171–99. [G: U.S.]

de Kobbe, P. Measurement of Malnutrition in the Third World. *J. Agr. Econ.*, September 1986, *37*(3), pp. 405–19. [G: LDCs]

Kraft, Kornelius and von der Schulenburg, J.-Matthias Graf. Co-insurance and Supplier-Induced Demand in Medical Care: What Do We Have to Expect as the Physician's Response to Increased Out-of-Pocket Payments? *J. Inst. Theoretical Econ.*, June 1986, *142*(2), pp. 360–79. [G: Switzerland]

Krasker, William S. Two-Stage Bounded-Influence Estimators for Simultaneous-Equations Models. *J. Bus. Econ. Statist.*, October 1986, *4*(4), pp. 437–44. [G: U.S.]

Lagoe, Ronald J. A Community-Based Analysis of Regional Differences in Hospital Stays by Diagnosis Related Group. *Inquiry*, Summer 1986, *23*(2), pp. 183–90. [G: U.S.]

Lamberton, C. E.; Ellingson, W. D. and Spear, K. R. Factors Determining the Demand for Nursing Home Services. *Quart. Rev. Econ. Bus.*, Winter 1986 , *26*(4), pp. 74–90. [G: U.S.]

Le Grand, Julian and Rabin, Matthew. Trends in British Health Inequality, 1931–83. **In** *Culyer, A. J. and Jönsson, B., eds.*, 1986, pp. 112–27. [G: U.K.]

Lee, Eun Sul, et al. Complex Survey Data Analysis: Estimation of Standard Errors Using Pseudostrata. *J. Econ. Soc. Meas.*, July 1986, *14*(2), pp. 135–44. [G: U.S.]

Leu, Robert E. The Public–Private Mix and International Health Care Costs. **In** *Culyer, A. J. and Jönsson, B., eds.*, 1986, pp. 41–63. [G: OECD]

Levin, Henry M. A Benefit–Cost Analysis of Nutritional Programs for Anemia Reduction. *World Bank Res. Observer*, July 1986, *1*(2), pp. 219–45. [G: Indonesia; Kenya; Mexico]

Lewit, Eugene M. The Diffusion of Surgical Technology: Who's on First? *J. Health Econ.*, March 1986, *5*(1), pp. 99–102.

Light, Donald W. Surplus versus Cost Containment: The Changing Context for Health Providers. **In** *Aiken, L. H. and Mechanic, D., eds.*, 1986, pp. 519–42. [G: U.S.]

Lindert, Peter H. Nutrition and the Decline in Mortality since 1700: Some Preliminary Findings: Comment. **In** *Engerman, S. L. and Gallman, R. E., eds.*, 1986, pp. 527–37. [G: U.S.]

de Lissovoy, Greg, et al. Preferred Provider Organizations: Today's Models and Tomorrow's Prospects. *Inquiry*, Spring 1986, *23*(1), pp. 7–15. [G: U.S.]

Liu, Korbin, et al. The Feasibility of Using Case Mix and Prospective Payment for Medicare Skilled Nursing Facilities. *Inquiry*, Winter 1986, *23*(4), pp. 365–70.

Long, Stephen H.; Settle, Russell F. and Stuart, Bruce C. Reimbursement and Access to Physicians' Services under Medicaid. *J. Health Econ.*, September 1986, *5*(3), pp. 235–51. [G: U.S.]

Longo, Daniel R., et al. Compliance of Multihospital Systems with Standards of the Joint Commission on Accreditation of Hospitals. **In** *Gray, B. H., ed.*, 1986, pp. 375–84. [G: U.S.]

Luft, Harold S. Economic Incentives and Constraints in Clinical Practice. **In** *Aiken, L. H. and Mechanic, D., eds.*, 1986, pp. 500–518. [G: U.S.]

Luft, Harold S., et al. The Role of Specialized Clinical Services in Competition among Hospitals. *Inquiry*, Spring 1986, *23*(1), pp. 83–94. [G: U.S.]

Lyttle, Christopher. Methodology for Imputing Missing Values, MHSP. **In** *Fleming, G. V. and Andersen, R. M., eds.*, 1986, pp. 250–62. [G: U.S.]

Manning, Willard G., Jr. and Wells, Kenneth B. Preliminary Results of a Controlled Trial of the Effect of a Prepaid Group Practice on the Outpatient Use of Mental Health Services. *J. Human Res.*, Summer 1986, *21*(3), pp. 293–320. [G: U.S.]

Marmor, Theodore R.; Schlesinger, Mark and Smithey, Richard W. A New Look at Nonprofits: Health Care Policy in a Competitive Age. *Yale J. Regul.*, Spring 1986, *3*(2), pp. 313–49. [G: U.S.]

Marshall, James and Graham, Saxon. Applications of Social Science to Clinical Medicine and Health Policy: Cancer. **In** *Aiken, L. H. and Mechanic, D., eds.*, 1986, pp. 157–74. [G: U.S.]

McGuire, Thomas G. Financing Psychotherapy. *J. Risk Ins.*, September 1986, *53*(3), pp. 484–91. [G: U.S.]

McGuire, Thomas G. and Scheffler, Richard M. Research Issues in Reimbursement of Mental Health Services: Conference Overview. *J. Human Res.*, Summer 1986, *21*(3), pp. 289–92. [G: U.S.]

McIntosh, James; Satchell, Stephen E. and Nasim, Anjum. Differential Mortality in Rural Bangladesh. *J. Appl. Econometrics*, October 1986, *1*(4), pp. 345–53. [G: Bangladesh]

McKay, Niccie L. Industry Effects of Medical Device Regulation: The Case of Diagnostic Imaging Equipment. *J. Policy Anal. Manage.*, Fall 1986, *6*(1), pp. 35–44. [G: U.S.]

McNiel, Douglas W. and Swofford, James L. Competition in the Medical Profession—An Application of the Theory of Regulation: Comment. *Southern Econ. J.*, January 1986, *52*(3), pp. 857–66. [G: U.S.]

Measham, Anthony R. Health and Development: The Bank's Experience. *Finance Develop.*, December 1986, *23*(4), pp. 26–29. **[G: LDCs]**

Mechanic, David and Aiken, Linda H. Social Science, Medicine, and Health Policy. **In** *Aiken, L. H. and Mechanic, D., eds.*, 1986, pp. 1–9.

Medoff, Marshall H. An Evaluation of the Effectiveness of Suicide Prevention Center. *J. Behav. Econ.*, Fall 1986, *15*, pp. 43–55. **[G: U.S.]**

Mehta, Rajesh. Role of Inter-sectoral Approach for Health Services in Developing Economies. **In** *Panchamukhi, V. R., et al.*, 1986, pp. 245–69. **[G: India; Indonesia; Japan; Philippines; Thailand]**

Mercer, A. J. Relative Trends in Mortality from Related Respiratory and Airborne Infectious Diseases. *Population Stud.*, March 1986, *40*(1), pp. 129–45. **[G: U.K.]**

Merrill, Jeffrey C. and Somers, Stephen A. The Changing Health Care System: A Challenge for Foundations. *Inquiry*, Fall 1986, *23*(3), pp. 316–21. **[G: U.S.]**

Meyer, Jack A. Financing Uncompensated Care with All-Payer Rate Regulation. **In** *Sloan, F. A.; Blumstein, J. F. and Perrin, J. M., eds.*, 1986, pp. 167–84. **[G: U.S.]**

Meyer, Jack A. and Kern, Rosemary Gibson. The Changing Structure of the Health Care System. **In** *Cagan, P., ed.*, 1986, pp. 191–222. **[G: U.S.]**

Meyer, Jack A. and Lewin, Marion Ein. Poverty and Social Welfare: An Agenda for Change. *Inquiry*, Summer 1986, *23*(2), pp. 122–33.

Miller, Nancy, et al. Social Security Programs in the United States. *Soc. Sec. Bull.*, January 1986, *49*(1), pp. 5–59. **[G: U.S.]**

Mitchell, Jean M. and Butler, J. S. Arthritis and the Earnings of Men: An Analysis Incorporating Selection Bias. *J. Health Econ.*, March 1986, *5*(1), pp. 81–98. **[G: U.S.]**

Montgomery, Mark R.; Richards, Toni and Braun, Henry I. Child Health, Breast-Feeding, and Survival in Malaysia: A Random-Effects Logit Approach. *J. Amer. Statist. Assoc.*, June 1986, *81*(394), pp. 297–309. **[G: Malaysia]**

Moock, Peter R. and Leslie, Joanne. Childhood Malnutrition and Schooling in the Terai Region of Nepal. *J. Devel. Econ.*, Jan.-Feb. 1986, *20*(1), pp. 33–52. **[G: Nepal]**

Morrisey, Michael A.; Alexander, Jeffrey A. and Shortell, Stephen M. Medical Staff Size, Hospital Privileges, and Compensation Arrangements: A Comparison of System Hospitals. **In** *Gray, B. H., ed.*, 1986, pp. 422–57. **[G: U.S.]**

Mougeot, Michel. Régulation des dépenses de sante et décentralisation des décisions. (With English summary.) *Revue Écon. Polit.*, July-Aug. 1986, *96*(4), pp. 359–83. **[G: France]**

Moye, William T. BLS and Alice Hamilton: Pioneers in Industrial Health. *Mon. Lab. Rev.*, June 1986, *109*(6), pp. 24–27. **[G: U.S.]**

Mubbashar, Malik H. Health Policies and Human Capital: The Case of Pakistan: Comments. *Pakistan Devel. Rev.*, Autumn 1986, *25*(3), pp. 335–37. **[G: Pakistan]**

Musacchio, Robert A., et al. Hospital Ownership and the Practice of Medicine: Evidence from the Physician's Perspective. **In** *Gray, B. H., ed.*, 1986, pp. 385–401. **[G: U.S.]**

Muurinen, Jaana-Marja. Modelling Non-profit Firms in Medicine. **In** *Culyer, A. J. and Jönsson, B., eds.*, 1986, pp. 86–98.

Myers, Beverlee A. Public Subsidies for Hospital Care of the Poor: Medicaid and Other Myths of Equity. **In** *Sloan, F. A.; Blumstein, J. F. and Perrin, J. M., eds.*, 1986, pp. 126–47. **[G: U.S.]**

Nawaz, Shuja. Riverblindness Controlled. *Finance Develop.*, June 1986, *23*(2), pp. 32–34. **[G: W. Africa]**

Newhouse, Joseph P. Social Experiments in Health. **In** *Aiken, L. H. and Mechanic, D., eds.*, 1986, pp. 229–47. **[G: U.S.]**

Noether, Monica. The Effect of Government Policy Changes on the Supply of Physicians: Expansion of a Competitive Fringe. *J. Law Econ.*, October 1986, *29*(2), pp. 231–62. **[G: U.S.]**

Noether, Monica. The Growing Supply of Physicians: Has the Market Become More Competitive? *J. Lab. Econ.*, October 1986, *4*(4), pp. 503–37. **[G: U.S.]**

O'Connell, Jeffrey. Neo-No-Fault Remedies for Medical Injuries: Coordinated Statutory and Contractual Alternatives. *Law Contemp. Probl.*, Spring 1986, *49*(2), pp. 125–41.

O'Driscoll, Gerald P., Jr. Competition as a Process: A Law and Economics Perspective. **In** *Langlois, R. N., ed.*, 1986, pp. 153–69. **[G: U.S.]**

Ofer, Gur. National Expenditure on Education and Health. **In** *Kop, Y., ed.*, 1986, pp. 111–34. **[G: Israel]**

Ohsfeldt, Robert L. and Culler, Steven D. Differences in Income between Male and Female Physicians. *J. Health Econ.*, December 1986, *5*(4), pp. 335–46. **[G: U.S.]**

Ostfeld, Adrian M. Applications of Social Science to Clinical Medicine and Health Policy: Cardiovascular Disease. **In** *Aiken, L. H. and Mechanic, D., eds.*, 1986, pp. 129–56. **[G: U.S.]**

Owens, Emiel W. Social Control of Pesticides—Some Health Effects. *Int. J. Soc. Econ.*, 1986, *13*(1/2), pp. 93–97. **[G: U.S.]**

Palmer, George R. Hospital Output and the Use of Diagnosis Related Groups for Purposes of Economic and Financial Analysis. **In** *Butler, J. R. G. and Doessel, D. P., eds.*, 1986, pp. 159–81. **[G: Australia]**

Palmer, George R. The Economics and Financing of Hospitals in Australia. *Australian Econ. Rev.*, 3rd Quarter 1986, (75), pp. 60–72. **[G: Australia]**

Pattison, Robert V. Response to Financial Incentives among Investor-Owned and Not-for-Profit Hospitals: An Analysis Based on California Data, 1978–1982. **In** *Gray, B. H., ed.*, 1986, pp. 290–302. **[G: U.S.]**

Paul, Chris W., II and Goodwin, Randall. Competition in the Medical Profession—An Application of the Theory of Regulation: Reply.

Southern Econ. J., January 1986, *52*(3), pp. 867–70. **[G: U.S.]**

Pauly, Mark V. Information Technology and the U.S. Health Care Industry: A New Direction: Discussion. **In** *Faulhaber, G.; Noam, E. and Tasley, R., eds.*, 1986, pp. 21–25. **[G: U.S.]**

Pauly, Mark V. Taxation, Health Insurance, and Market Failure in the Medical Economy. *J. Econ. Lit.*, June 1986, *24*(2), pp. 629–75. **[G: U.S.]**

Pedersen, Kjeld Møller. Sygehusenes økonomiske situation. (The Development of the Danish Health Care Sector. With English summary.) *Nationaløkon. Tidsskr.*, 1986, *124*(3), pp. 316–39. **[G: Denmark]**

Pensabene, Tony S. Implications of the New South Wales Doctors' Dispute. **In** *Butler, J. R. G. and Doessel, D. P., eds.*, 1986, pp. 67–78. **[G: Australia]**

Perez-Chopra, Marisol and Grimes, Richard M. Inflation and Health Care Costs in Metropolitan Areas. *J. Econ. Soc. Meas.*, December 1986, *14*(4), pp. 341–55. **[G: U.S.]**

Perrin, James M. High Technology and Uncompensated Hospital Care. **In** *Sloan, F. A.; Blumstein, J. F. and Perrin, J. M., eds.*, 1986, pp. 54–71. **[G: U.S.]**

Petersen, Niels Christian. A Public Choice Analysis of Parallel Public–Private Provision of Health Care. **In** *Culyer, A. J. and Jönsson, B., eds.*, 1986, pp. 67–85.

Phelps, Charles E. Cross-Subsidies and Charge-Shifting in American Hospitals. **In** *Sloan, F. A.; Blumstein, J. F. and Perrin, J. M., eds.*, 1986, pp. 108–25. **[G: U.S.]**

Phelps, Charles E. Induced Demand—Can We Ever Know Its Extent? Editorial. *J. Health Econ.*, December 1986, *5*(4), pp. 355–65.

Pickering, Ruth M.; Murray, G. D. and Forbes, J. F. Pre-term Foetal Life Times in Scotland. *Population Stud.*, March 1986, *40*(1), pp. 115–27. **[G: U.K.]**

Portney, Paul R. and Mullahy, John. Urban Air Quality and Acute Respiratory Illness. *J. Urban Econ.*, July 1986, *20*(1), pp. 21–38. **[G: U.S.]**

Posner, James R. Trends in Medical Malpractice Insurance, 1970–1985. *Law Contemp. Probl.*, Spring 1986, *49*(2), pp. 37–56. **[G: U.S.]**

Poullier, Jean-Pierre. Levels and Trends in the Public–Private Mix of the Industrialized Countries' Health Systems. **In** *Culyer, A. J. and Jönsson, B., eds.*, 1986, pp. 11–40. **[G: OECD]**

Price, Daniel N. Workers' Compensation: Coverage, Benefits, and Costs, 1983. *Soc. Sec. Bull.*, February 1986, *49*(2), pp. 5–11. **[G: U.S.]**

Primeaux, Walter J., Jr. and Wilderman, Robert. Using Personality Traits as a Means of Reducing the Economic Costs of Alcoholism. *J. Behav. Econ.*, Fall 1986, *15*, pp. 73–78. **[G: U.S.]**

Register, Charles A. Nurses' Earnings, Monopsony, Compensating Differentials, and Comparable Worth. *Atlantic Econ. J.*, September 1986, *14*(3), pp. 86. **[G: U.S.]**

Reinhardt, Uwe E. The Nature of Equity Financing. **In** *Gray, B. H., ed.*, 1986, pp. 67–73. **[G: U.S.]**

Reinhardt, Uwe E. Uncompensated Hospital Care. **In** *Sloan, F. A.; Blumstein, J. F. and Perrin, J. M., eds.*, 1986, pp. 1–15. **[G: U.S.]**

Relman, Arnold S. and Reinhardt, Uwe E. An Exchange on For-Profit Health Care. **In** *Gray, B. H., ed.*, 1986, pp. 209–23. **[G: U.S.]**

Richards, Hamish. Investment in Public Health Provision in the Mining Valleys of South Wales, 1860–1914. **In** *Baber, C. and Williams, L. J., eds.*, 1986, pp. 128–39. **[G: U.K.]**

Richardson, Bronwyn. A Comparative Cost Analysis of Terminal Cancer Care: Discussion. **In** *Butler, J. R. G. and Doessel, D. P., eds.*, 1986, pp. 153–58. **[G: Australia]**

Richardson, Bronwyn. Unemployment and Health in Australia: A Policy Perspective. **In** *Butler, J. R. G. and Doessel, D. P., eds.*, 1986, pp. 1–34. **[G: Australia]**

Richardson, J. A Longitudinal Study of Health Changes Following the Introduction of Medicare: Discussion. **In** *Butler, J. R. G. and Doessel, D. P., eds.*, 1986, pp. 103–06. **[G: Australia]**

Riessman, Catherine Kohler and Nathanson, Constance A. The Management of Reproduction: Social Construction of Risk and Responsibility. **In** *Aiken, L. H. and Mechanic, D., eds.*, 1986, pp. 251–81. **[G: U.S.]**

Riley, James C. Insects and the European Mortality Decline. *Amer. Hist. Rev.*, October 1986, *91*(4), pp. 833–58. **[G: Europe]**

Robinson, Glen O. Rethinking the Allocation of Medical Malpractice Risks between Patients and Providers. *Law Contemp. Probl.*, Spring 1986, *49*(2), pp. 173–99. **[G: U.S.]**

Robinson, Glen O. The Medical Malpractice Crisis of the 1970's: A Retrospective. *Law Contemp. Probl.*, Spring 1986, *49*(2), pp. 5–35. **[G: U.S.]**

Rodrique, André. La contribution de l'amélioration du bien-être au processus de croissance dans les pays en développement. (The Contribution of Welfare to Economic Growth. With English summary.) *L'Actual. Econ.*, March 1986, *62*(1), pp. 64–87. **[G: LDCs]**

Rosenzweig, Mark R. and Wolpin, Kenneth I. Evaluating the Effects of Optimally Distributed Public Programs: Child Health and Family Planning Interventions. *Amer. Econ. Rev.*, June 1986, *76*(3), pp. 470–82. **[G: Philippines]**

Rosko, Michael D. and Broyles, Robert W. The Impact of the New Jersey All-Payer DRG System. *Inquiry*, Spring 1986, *23*(1), pp. 67–75. **[G: U.S.]**

Ross, Mary and Hayes, Carol. Consolidated Omnibus Budget Reconciliation Act of 1985. *Soc. Sec. Bull.*, August 1986, *49*(8), pp. 22–31. **[G: U.S.]**

Roth, Alvin E. On the Allocation of Residents to Rural Hospitals: A General Property of Two-Sided Matching Markets. *Econometrica*, March 1986, *54*(2), pp. 425–27.

Russo, J. Edward, et al. Nutrition Information in the Supermarket. *J. Cons. Res.*, June 1986, *13*(1), pp. 48–70. **[G: U.S.]**

Sai, Fred T. Population and Health: Africa's Most Basic Resource and Development Problem. **In** *Berg, R. J. and Whitaker, J. S., eds.*, 1986, pp. 129–52. **[G: Africa]**

Salkever, David S.; Steinwachs, Donald M. and Rupp, Agnes. Hospital Cost and Efficiency under per Service and per Case Payment in Maryland: A Tale of the Carrot and the Stick. *Inquiry*, Spring 1986, *23*(1), pp. 56–66. **[G: U.S.]**

Schaafsma, Joseph. Average Hospital Size and the Total Operating Expenditures for B_1 Beds Distributed over H_1 Hospitals. *Appl. Econ.*, March 1986, *18*(3), pp. 279–90. **[G: Canada]**

Schaub, Thomas. Bestimmungsfaktoren der Kosten eines Allgemeinspitals. (Determinants of General Hospital Costs. With English summary.) *Schweiz. Z. Volkswirtsch. Statist.*, December 1986, *122*(4), pp. 641–56. **[G: Switzerland]**

Scheffler, Richard M. Information Technology and the U.S. Health Care Industry: A New Direction. **In** *Faulhaber, G.; Noam, E. and Tasley, R., eds.*, 1986, pp. 7–20. **[G: U.S.]**

Scheffler, Richard M. and Watts, Carolyn A. Determinants of Inpatient Mental Health Use in a Heavily Insured Population. *J. Human Res.*, Summer 1986, *21*(3), pp. 338–58. **[G: U.S.]**

Schelling, Thomas C. Whose Business Is Good Behavior? **In** *Knowlton, W. and Zeckhauser, R., eds.*, 1986, pp. 153–80. **[G: U.S.]**

Schilling, Don. Implicit Inflation and Interest Rates in Discounting Personal Injury Economic Losses—Rejoinder. *J. Risk Ins.*, September 1986, *53*(3), pp. 496–97. **[G: U.S.]**

Schlesinger, Mark; Dorwart, Robert A. and Pulice, Richard T. Competitive Bidding and States' Purchase of Services: The Case of Mental Health Care in Massachusetts. *J. Policy Anal. Manage.*, Winter 1986, *5*(2), pp. 245–63. **[G: U.S.]**

Schoenman, Julie A. and Sloan, Frank A. Why Have Surgeons Moved to the Country? *Quart. Rev. Econ. Bus.*, Autumn 1986, *26*(3), pp. 25–47. **[G: U.S.]**

Schramm, Carl J. Revisiting the Competition/Regulation Debate in Health Care Cost Containment. *Inquiry*, Fall 1986, *23*(3), pp. 236–42. **[G: U.S.]**

Schuck, Peter H. Designing Hospital Care Subsidies for the Poor. **In** *Sloan, F. A.; Blumstein, J. F. and Perrin, J. M., eds.*, 1986, pp. 72–93. **[G: U.S.]**

Schut, Frederick T. and van Bergeijk, Peter A. G. International Price Discrimination: The Pharmaceutical Industry. *World Devel.*, September 1986, *14*(9), pp. 1141–50.

Seay, J. David, et al. Holding Fast to the Good: The Future of the Voluntary Hospital. *Inquiry*, Fall 1986, *23*(3), pp. 253–60. **[G: U.S.]**

Seldon, James R. Hospital Cost-Shifting under Fractional Reimbursement. *Atlantic Econ. J.*, March 1986, *14*(1), pp. 50–58.

Sen, Amartya K. Food, Economics and Entitlements. *Lloyds Bank Rev.*, April 1986, (160), pp. 1–20.

Sheingold, Steven and Buchberger, Thomas. Implications of Medicare's Prospective Payment System for the Provision of Uncompensated Hospital Care. *Inquiry*, Winter 1986, *23*(4), pp. 371–81. **[G: U.S.]**

Sherlock, Douglas B. Indigent Care in Rational Markets. *Inquiry*, Fall 1986, *23*(3), pp. 261–67. **[G: U.S.]**

Sherman, H. David. Interpreting Hospital Performance with Financial Statement Analysis. *Accounting Rev.*, July 1986, *61*(3), pp. 526–50. **[G: U.S.]**

Sickles, Robin C. and Taubman, Paul. An Analysis of the Health and Retirement Status of the Elderly. *Econometrica*, November 1986, *54*(6), pp. 1339–56. **[G: U.S.]**

Sintonen, Harri. Comparing the Productivity of Public and Private Dentistry. **In** *Culyer, A. J. and Jönsson, B., eds.*, 1986, pp. 219–34. **[G: Finland]**

Sloan, Frank A. Uncompensated Hospital Care: Rights and Responsibilities: Conclusion. **In** *Sloan, F. A.; Blumstein, J. F. and Perrin, J. M., eds.*, 1986, pp. 185–89. **[G: U.S.]**

Sloan, Frank A.; Valvona, Joseph and Mullner, Ross. Identifying the Issues: A Statistical Profile. **In** *Sloan, F. A.; Blumstein, J. F. and Perrin, J. M., eds.*, 1986, pp. 16–53. **[G: U.S.]**

Sloan, Frank A., et al. Diffusion of Surgical Technology: An Exploratory Study. *J. Health Econ.*, March 1986, *5*(1), pp. 31–61. **[G: U.S.]**

Smil, Vaclav. Food Production and Quality of Diet in China. *Population Devel. Rev.*, March 1986, *12*(1), pp. 25–45. **[G: China]**

Smith, Dean G. and Rose, Lawrence C. The Effects of Insurance Policy Limits on Product Choice. *J. Risk Ins.*, September 1986, *53*(3), pp. 514–20. **[G: U.S.]**

Smith, Stanley K. Using Medicare Data for Short-run Projections of the Elderly Population. *J. Econ. Soc. Meas.*, April 1986, *14*(1), pp. 37–49. **[G: U.S.]**

Smythe, Tony and Cook, Judith. Community Health Councils. **In** *Moores, B., ed.*, 1986, pp. 229–40. **[G: U.K.]**

Somers, Anne R. The Changing Demand for Health Services: A Historical Perspective and Some Thoughts for the Future. *Inquiry*, Winter 1986, *23*(4), pp. 395–402.

Spatz, Donald L. Issues in Asbestos Disease Compensation. **In** *Chelius, J., ed.*, 1986, pp. 287–311. **[G: U.S.]**

Srinivasan, T. N. Undernutrition: Extent and Distribution of Its Incidence. **In** *Maunder, A. and Renborg, U., eds.*, 1986, pp. 199–207. **[G: LDCs]**

Stano, Miron. A Further Analysis of the "Variations in Practice Style" Phenomenon. *Inquiry*, Summer 1986, *23*(2), pp. 176–82. **[G: U.S.]**

Starr, Paul. Health Care for the Poor: The Past Twenty Years. **In** *Danziger, S. H. and Wein-*

berg, D. H., eds., 1986, pp. 106–32. [G: U.S.]

Stasiuk, William N. Some Public Health Concerns Associated with Electrical Energy Generation. **In** *Saltzman, S. and Schuler, R. E., eds.*, 1986, pp. 203–12. [G: U.S.]

Steckel, Richard H. A Peculiar Population: The Nutrition, Health, and Mortality of American Slaves from Childhood to Maturity. *J. Econ. Hist.*, September 1986, *46*(3), pp. 721–41. [G: U.S.]

Steckel, Richard H. and Jensen, Richard A. New Evidence on the Causes of Slave and Crew Mortality in the Atlantic Slave Trade. *J. Econ. Hist.*, March 1986, *46*(1), pp. 57–77. [G: W. Africa; Caribbean]

Stevens, Rosemary. The Changing Hospital. **In** *Aiken, L. H. and Mechanic, D., eds.*, 1986, pp. 80–99. [G: U.S.]

Stoddart, Greg L., et al. Tobacco Taxes and Health Care Costs: Do Canadian Smokers Pay Their Way? *J. Health Econ.*, March 1986, *5*(1), pp. 63–80. [G: Canada]

Sukhatme, P. V. Quantitative Dimensions of the Nutrition Problem. **In** *Swaminathan, M. S. and Sinha, S. K., eds.*, 1986, pp. 25–45. [G: LDCs]

Sunga, Preetom S. and Swinamer, Janet L. Health Care Accounts—A Conceptual Framework and an Illustrative Example. *Rev. Income Wealth*, September 1986, *32*(3), pp. 277–98. [G: Canada]

Swartz, Katherine. Interpreting the Estimates from Four National Surveys of the Number of People without Health Insurance. *J. Econ. Soc. Meas.*, October 1986, *14*(3), pp. 233–42. [G: U.S.]

Szasz, Andrew. The Reversal of Federal Policy toward Worker Safety and Health. *Sci. Soc.*, Spring 1986, *50*(1), pp. 25–51. [G: U.S.]

Tatchell, Michael. Hospital Case Mix Standardisation: A Comparison of the Resource Need Index and Information Theory Measures: Discussion. **In** *Butler, J. R. G. and Doessel, D. P., eds.*, 1986, pp. 64–66. [G: Australia]

Taube, Carl A., et al. Validity of Medicaid Household Respondent Reporting of Ambulatory Visits for Mental Disorders. *J. Econ. Soc. Meas.*, October 1986, *14*(3), pp. 243–56. [G: U.S.]

Thompson, Andy. What the Patient Thinks. **In** *Moores, B., ed.*, 1986, pp. 91–103. [G: U.K.]

Thomson, William and Francis, Peter N. Performance Auditing in the Midst of Litigation: A Case Study and Lessons Learned from the Arizona Experience. *Public Budg. Finance,* Summer 1986, *6*(2), pp. 104–14. [G: U.S.]

Thorpe, Kenneth E. Information Technology and the U.S. Health Care Industry: A New Direction: Discussion. **In** *Faulhaber, G.; Noam, E. and Tasley, R., eds.*, 1986, pp. 26–30. [G: U.S.]

Tims, Wouter. Balancing Overproduction and Malnutrition: Discussion. **In** *Maunder, A. and Renborg, U., eds.*, 1986, pp. 209–10.

Torrance, George W. Measurement of Health State Utilities for Economic Appraisal: A Review. *J. Health Econ.*, March 1986, *5*(1), pp. 1–30.

Townsend, Jessica. Hospitals and Their Communities: A Report on Three Case Studies. **In** *Gray, B. H., ed.*, 1986, pp. 458–73. [G: U.S.]

Tresnowski, Bernard R. The Coming Crisis in Costs and Financing: Long-term Care. *Inquiry,* Winter 1986, *23*(4), pp. 345–46.

Tullock, Gordon. Giving Life [Avoiding Difficult Decisions]. **In** *Tullock, G.*, 1986, *1979*, pp. 158–69.

Tussing, A. Dale and Wojtowycz, Martha A. The Agency Role of the Physician in Ireland, Britain, and the USA. *Policy Sci.*, October 1986, *19*(3), pp. 275–96. [G: U.K.; U.S.; Ireland]

Vertrees, James and Manton, Kenneth G. The Complexity of Chronic Disease at Later Ages: Practical Implications for Prospective Payment and Data Collection. *Inquiry,* Summer 1986, *23*(2), pp. 154–65. [G: U.S.]

Vogel, Ronald J. and Christianson, Jon B. The Evaluation of Economic Development Projects Where Military Conflict Is Present: Investing in Health Care in El Salvador. *J. Policy Anal. Manage.*, Winter 1986, *5*(2), pp. 292–310. [G: El Salvador]

Vyas, Vijay S. Balancing Overproduction and Malnutrition: Discussion. **In** *Maunder, A. and Renborg, U., eds.*, 1986, pp. 210–12.

Wagstaff, Adam. The Demand for Health: A Simplified Grossman Model [On the Concept of Health Capital and the Demand for Health]. *Bull. Econ. Res.*, January 1986, *38*(1), pp. 93–95.

Wagstaff, Adam. The Demand for Health: Some New Empirical Evidence. *J. Health Econ.*, September 1986, *5*(3), pp. 195–233. [G: U.K.]

Ware, John E., Jr. The Assessment of Health Status. **In** *Aiken, L. H. and Mechanic, D., eds.*, 1986, pp. 204–28. [G: U.S.]

Waser, Otto and Zweifel, Peter. Innovation in Health Insurance: Bonus Systems in Western Germany. **In** *von der Schulenburg, J.-M. G., ed.*, 1986, pp. 169–95. [G: W. Germany]

Watt, J. Michael, et al. The Effects of Ownership and Multihospital System Membership on Hospital Functional Strategies and Economic Performance. **In** *Gray, B. H., ed.*, 1986, pp. 260–89. [G: U.S.]

Weigel, Van B. The Basic Needs Approach: Overcoming the Poverty of *Homo oeconomicus. World Devel.*, December 1986, *14*(12), pp. 1423–34.

Weisbrod, Burton A. and Schlesinger, Mark. Public, Private, Nonprofit Ownership and the Response to Asymmetric Information: The Case of Nursing Homes. **In** *Rose-Ackerman, S., ed.*, 1986, pp. 133–51. [G: U.S.]

Welch, W. P. The Elasticity of Demand for Health Maintenance Organizations. *J. Human Res.*, Spring 1986, *21*(2), pp. 252–66. [G: U.S.]

Welch, W. P. and Frank, Richard G. The Predictors of HMO Enrollee Populations: Results from a National Sample. *Inquiry,* Spring 1986, *23*(1), pp. 16–22. **[G: U.S.]**

Wheelwright, Ted. The World Drug Industry. **In** *Wheelwright, T., ed.*, 1986, pp. 89–125. **[G: LDCs]**

Wilensky, Gail R. Underwriting the Uninsured: Targeting Providers or Individuals. **In** *Sloan, F. A.; Blumstein, J. F. and Perrin, J. M., eds.*, 1986, pp. 148–66. **[G: U.S.]**

Wilson, Paul R.; Chappell, Duncan and Lincoln, Robyn. Policing Physician Abuse in BC: An Analysis of Current Policies. *Can. Public Policy,* March 1986, *12*(1), pp. 236–44. **[G: Canada]**

Windham, Susan R. The Massachusetts Medicaid Case Management Program. **In** *Kern, R. G. and Windham, S. R.*, 1986, pp. 3–17. **[G: U.S.]**

Windham, Susan R. and Griswold, Paula. The Commonwealth Health Care Corporation: A Medicaid Cost-Containment Experiment in Boston. **In** *Kern, R. G. and Windham, S. R.*, 1986, pp. 18–40. **[G: U.S.]**

Windham, Susan R. and Griswold, Paula. The Hospital Payment System in Massachusetts. **In** *Kern, R. G. and Windham, S. R.*, 1986, pp. 41–50. **[G: U.S.]**

Wright, Virginia Baxter. Will Quitting Smoking Help Medicare Solve Its Financial Problems? *Inquiry,* Spring 1986, *23*(1), pp. 76–82. **[G: U.S.]**

Wyszewianski, Leon. Financially Catastrophic and High-Cost Cases: Definitions, Distinctions, and Their Implications for Policy Formulation. *Inquiry,* Winter 1986, *23*(4), pp. 382–94. **[G: U.S.]**

Yang, Bong-min. Do Physicians Induce Patient Demand for Medical Care? An Empirical Analysis. *J. Econ. Devel.*, December 1986, *11*(2), pp. 83–102. **[G: U.S.]**

Yen, Gili and Benham, Lee. The Best of All Monopoly Profits Is a Quiet Life. *J. Health Econ.*, December 1986, *5*(4), pp. 347–53. **[G: U.S.]**

Yoder, Sunny G. Economic Theories of For-Profit and Not-for-Profit Organizations. **In** *Gray, B. H., ed.*, 1986, pp. 19–25.

York, Christopher C. Business and "the Common." *Inquiry,* Fall 1986, *23*(3), pp. 299–307. **[G: U.S.]**

Zuckerman, Stephen; Koller, Christopher F. and Bovbjerg, Randall R. Information on Malpractice: A Review of Empirical Research on Major Policy Issues. *Law Contemp. Probl.*, Spring 1986, *49*(2), pp. 85–111. **[G: U.S.]**

Zweifel, Peter. Die Kosten-Versicherungs-Spirale im schweizerischen Gesundheitswesen. (The Cost–Insurance Spiral in the Swiss Health Care Sector. With English summary.) *Schweiz. Z. Volkswirtsch. Statist.*, September 1986, *122*(3), pp. 555–83. **[G: Switzerland]**

914 Economics of Poverty

9140 Economics of Poverty

Abegaz, Berhanu. Mass Poverty, Demography, and Development Strategy: A Selective Survey. **In** *Abegaz, B., ed.*, 1986, pp. 1–54. **[G: LDCs]**

Adelman, Irma. A Poverty-Focused Approach to Development Policy. **In** *Lewis, J. P. and Kallab, V., eds.*, 1986, pp. 49–65. **[G: LDCs]**

Annis, Sheldon. The Shifting Grounds of Poverty Lending at the World Bank. **In** *Feinberg, R. E., et al.*, 1986, pp. 87–109.

Bane, Mary Jo. Household Composition and Poverty. **In** *Danziger, S. H. and Weinberg, D. H., eds.*, 1986, pp. 209–31. **[G: U.S.]**

Bane, Mary Jo and Ellwood, David T. Slipping into and out of Poverty: The Dynamics of Spells. *J. Human Res.*, Winter 1986, *21*(1), pp. 1–23. **[G: U.S.]**

Barrow, Christine. Finding the Support: A Study of Strategies for Survival. *Soc. Econ. Stud.*, June 1986, *35*(2), pp. 131–76. **[G: Barbados]**

Beckmann, David. The World Bank and Poverty in the 1980s. *Finance Develop.*, September 1986, *23*(3), pp. 26–29.

Blank, Rebecca M. and Blinder, Alan S. Macroeconomics, Income Distribution, and Poverty. **In** *Danziger, S. H. and Weinberg, D. H., eds.*, 1986, pp. 180–208. **[G: U.S.]**

Blaylock, James R. and Smallwood, David M. An Alternative Approach to Defining and Assessing Poverty Thresholds. *Western J. Agr. Econ.*, July 1986, *11*(1), pp. 100–105. **[G: U.S.]**

Bouillaguet-Bernard, Patricia; Gandon, Marie-Pierre and Outin, Jean-Luc. Chômage de longue durée et pauvreté en France. (Long Duration Unemployment and Poverty in France. With English summary.) *Écon. Soc.*, April 1986, *20*(4), pp. 221–59. **[G: France]**

Browning, Edgar K. and Johnson, William R. The Cost of Reducing Economic Inequality. *Cato J.*, Spring/Summer 1986, *6*(1), pp. 85–109. **[G: U.S.]**

Brunner, Ronald D. Case-wise Policy Information Systems: Redefining Poverty. *Policy Sci.*, September 1986, *19*(2), pp. 201–23. **[G: U.S.]**

Bryant, W. Keith. A Portfolio Analysis of Poor Rural Wage—Working Families' Assets and Debts. *Amer. J. Agr. Econ.*, May 1986, *68*(2), pp. 237–45. **[G: U.S.]**

Burkhauser, Richard V.; Holden, Karen C. and Myers, Daniel A. Marital Disruption and Poverty: The Role of Survey Procedures in Artificially Creating Poverty. *Demography,* November 1986, *23*(4), pp. 621–31. **[G: U.S.]**

Burtless, Gary. Public Spending for the Poor: Trends, Prospects, and Economic Limits. **In** *Danziger, S. H. and Weinberg, D. H., eds.*, 1986, pp. 18–49. **[G: U.S.]**

Carvajal, Manuel J. and Upadhiaya, Anita. Propensity to Migrate Differentials by Poverty Status: An Empirical Test for Costa Rica. *J. Econ. Devel.*, December 1986, *11*(2), pp. 123–46. **[G: Costa Rica]**

Chazan, Naomi. Ethnicity in Economic Crisis: Development Strategies and Patterns of Ethnicity in Africa. **In** *Thompson, D. L. and Ronen, D., eds.*, 1986, pp. 137–58. **[G: Africa]**

Clausen, A. W. Accelerating Growth and Reducing Poverty: A Multilateral Strategy for Development: Address to the Atlantik-Brücke and the Deutsche Gesellschaft für Auswärtige Politik: Bonn, Federal Republic of Germany: April 18, 1983. **In** *Clausen, A. W.*, 1986, pp. 157–75.

Clausen, A. W. Address to the Overseas Press Club of America Annual Awards Dinner: New York, New York: April 24, 1985. **In** *Clausen, A. W.*, 1986, pp. 381–90.

Clausen, A. W. Poverty in the Developing Countries, 1985: Address at the Martin Luther King, Jr., Center: Atlanta, Georgia: January 11, 1985. **In** *Clausen, A. W.*, 1986, pp. 347–60.

Cohen, Yinon and Tyree, Andrea. Escape from Poverty: Determinants of Intergenerational Mobility of Sons and Daughters of the Poor. *Soc. Sci. Quart.*, December 1986, *67*(4), pp. 803–13. **[G: U.S.]**

Cuomo, Mario M. The Least of These. **In** *Hewlett, S. A.; Ilchman, A. S. and Sweeney, J. J., eds.*, 1986, pp. 23–29. **[G: U.S.]**

Danziger, Sheldon H. and Gottschalk, Peter. Do Rising Tides Lift All Boats? The Impact of Secular and Cyclical Changes on Poverty. *Amer. Econ. Rev.*, May 1986, *76*(2), pp. 405–10. **[G: U.S.]**

Danziger, Sheldon H. and Gottschalk, Peter. Families with Children Have Fared Worst. *Challenge*, Mar./Apr. 1986, *29*(1), pp. 40–47. **[G: U.S.]**

Danziger, Sheldon H. and Gottschalk, Peter. Work, Poverty, and the Working Poor: A Multifaceted Problem. *Mon. Lab. Rev.*, September 1986, *109*(9), pp. 17–21. **[G: U.S.]**

Danziger, Sheldon H.; Haveman, Robert H. and Plotnick, Robert D. Antipoverty Policy: Effects on the Poor and the Nonpoor. **In** *Danziger, S. H. and Weinberg, D. H., eds.*, 1986, pp. 50–77. **[G: U.S.]**

Danziger, Sheldon H. and Weinberg, Daniel H. Fighting Poverty: What Works and What Doesn't: Introduction. **In** *Danziger, S. H. and Weinberg, D. H., eds.*, 1986, pp. 1–17. **[G: U.S.]**

Dellaportas, George. The Effectiveness of Public Assistance Payments (1970–80) in Reducing Poverty Reconsidered: The 'Safety Net' Was Still Very Leaky in 1980, But Less So, and More Working Poor May Have Been Aided. *Amer. J. Econ. Soc.*, January 1986, *45*(1), pp. 1–8. **[G: U.S.]**

Dilnot, Andrew W. and Stark, Graham K. The Poverty Trap, Tax Cuts, and the Reform of Social Security. *Fisc. Stud.*, February 1986, *7*(1), pp. 1–10. **[G: U.K.]**

Donaldson, David and Weymark, John A. Properties of Fixed-Population Poverty Indices. *Int. Econ. Rev.*, October 1986, *27*(3), pp. 667–88.

Dorn, James A. The Transfer Society: Introduction. *Cato J.*, Spring/Summer 1986, *6*(1), pp. 1–17. **[G: U.S.]**

Duncan, Greg J. and Hoffman, Saul D. Welfare Dynamics and the Nature of Need. *Cato J.*, Spring/Summer 1986, *6*(1), pp. 31–54. **[G: U.S.]**

Dutton, Diana B. Social Class, Health, and Illness. **In** *Aiken, L. H. and Mechanic, D., eds.*, 1986, pp. 31–62. **[G: U.S.]**

Edelman, Marian Wright. Federal Programs That Serve Children and Families. **In** *Hewlett, S. A.; Ilchman, A. S. and Sweeney, J. J., eds.*, 1986, pp. 105–16. **[G: U.S.]**

Ellwood, David T. and Summers, Lawrence H. Poverty in America: Is Welfare the Answer or the Problem? **In** *Danziger, S. H. and Weinberg, D. H., eds.*, 1986, pp. 78–105. **[G: U.S.]**

Glazer, Nathan. Welfare and "Welfare" in America. **In** *Rose, R. and Shiratori, R., eds.*, 1986, pp. 40–63. **[G: U.S.]**

Gramlich, Edward M. Fighting Poverty: What Works and What Doesn't: The Main Themes. **In** *Danziger, S. H. and Weinberg, D. H., eds.*, 1986, pp. 341–47. **[G: U.S.]**

Greer, Joel and Thorbecke, Erik. A Methodology for Measuring Food Poverty Applied to Kenya. *J. Devel. Econ.*, November 1986, *24*(1), pp. 59–74. **[G: Kenya]**

Greer, Joel and Thorbecke, Erik. Food Poverty Profile Applied to Kenyan Smallholders. *Econ. Develop. Cult. Change*, October 1986, *35*(1), pp. 115–41. **[G: Kenya]**

Gwartney, James and Stroup, Richard L. Transfers, Equality, and the Limits of Public Policy. *Cato J.*, Spring/Summer 1986, *6*(1), pp. 111–37. **[G: U.S.]**

Hamilton, Charles V. and Hamilton, Dona C. Social Policies, Civil Rights, and Poverty. **In** *Danziger, S. H. and Weinberg, D. H., eds.*, 1986, pp. 287–311. **[G: U.S.]**

Haveman, Robert H. What Antipoverty Policies Cost the Nonpoor. *Challenge*, Jan./Feb. 1986, *28*(6), pp. 37–42. **[G: U.S.]**

Hayami, Yujiro. Poverty and Beyond: The Forces Shaping the Future in Asia. **In** *Maunder, A. and Renborg, U., eds.*, 1986, pp. 37–48. **[G: LDCs; MDCs]**

Heclo, Hugh. The Political Foundations of Antipoverty Policy. **In** *Danziger, S. H. and Weinberg, D. H., eds.*, 1986, pp. 312–40. **[G: U.S.]**

Ilchman, Alice S. Family and Work: Bridging the Gap: Introduction. **In** *Hewlett, S. A.; Ilchman, A. S. and Sweeney, J. J., eds.*, 1986, pp. 1–6. **[G: U.S.]**

Islam, Iyanatul and Khan, Habibullah. Income Inequality, Poverty and Socioeconomic Development in Bangladesh: An Empirical Investigation. *Bangladesh Devel. Stud.*, June 1986, *14*(2), pp. 75–92. **[G: Bangladesh]**

Islam, Iyanatul and Khan, Habibullah. Spatial Patterns of Inequality and Poverty in Indonesia. *Bull. Indonesian Econ. Stud.*, August 1986, *22*(2), pp. 80–102. **[G: Indonesia]**

Islam, Rizwanul and Muqtada, M. Employment and Poverty Alleviation: An Overview. **In** *Islam, R. and Muqtada, M., eds.*, 1986, pp. 1–10. **[G: Bangladesh]**

Kahnert, Friedrich. Re-examining Urban Poverty and Employment. *Finance Develop.*, March 1986, *23*(1), pp. 44–47. **[G: LDCs]**

Kaufmann, Daniel and Lindauer, David L. A Model of Income Transfers for the Urban Poor. *J. Devel. Econ.*, July-Aug. 1986, *22*(2), pp. 337–50. **[G: El Salvador]**

Khan, Qaiser M. Poverty and Household Responses in Rural Bangladesh. **In** *Abegaz, B., ed.*, 1986, pp. 55–71. **[G: Bangladesh]**

Kodras, Janet E. The Spatial Perspective in Welfare Analysis [Transfers and Poverty: Cause and/or Effect?]. *Cato J.*, Spring/Summer 1986, *6*(1), pp. 77–83. **[G: U.S.]**

Laffer, Arthur B. The Tightening Grip of the Poverty Trap. **In** *Canto, V. A.; Kadlec, C. W. and Laffer, A. B., eds.*, 1986, pp. 141–59. **[G: U.S.]**

Levitt, Ian. Atlas of Industrializing Britain 1780–1914: Poor Law and Pauperism. **In** *Langton, J. and Morris, R. J., eds.*, 1986, pp. 160–63. **[G: U.K.]**

Levy, Frank S. and Michel, Richard C. Work for Welfare: How Much Good Will It Do? *Amer. Econ. Rev.*, May 1986, *76*(2), pp. 399–404. **[G: U.S.]**

Lilla, Mark. The Political Psychology of Economic Transfers [Transfers, Equality, and the Limits of Public Policy]. *Cato J.*, Spring/Summer 1986, *6*(1), pp. 139–42. **[G: U.S.]**

Loury, Glenn C. Public and Private Responsibilities in the Struggle against Poverty. **In** *Knowlton, W. and Zeckhauser, R., eds.*, 1986, pp. 181–202. **[G: U.S.]**

MacKinnon, Mary. Poor Law Policy, Unemployment, and Pauperism. *Exploration Econ. Hist.*, July 1986, *23*(3), pp. 299–336. **[G: U.K.]**

Meyer, Jack A. and Lewin, Marion Ein. Poverty and Social Welfare: An Agenda for Change. *Inquiry*, Summer 1986, *23*(2), pp. 122–33.

Mittar, Vishwa. Income Distribution and Poverty in the Urban Informal Sector. *Margin*, January 1986, *18*(2), pp. 29–41. **[G: India]**

Morris, Nick and Preston, Ian. Inequality, Poverty and the Redistribution of Income. *Bull. Econ. Res.*, November 1986, *38*(4), pp. 275–344. **[G: U.K.]**

Moynihan, Daniel Patrick. Government and Family Policy. **In** *Hewlett, S. A.; Ilchman, A. S. and Sweeney, J. J., eds.*, 1986, pp. 7–15. **[G: U.S.]**

Muqtada, M. Poverty and Inequality: Trends and Causes. **In** *Islam, R. and Muqtada, M., eds.*, 1986, pp. 41–60. **[G: Bangladesh]**

Murray, Charles. *Losing Ground* Two Years Later. *Cato J.*, Spring/Summer 1986, *6*(1), pp. 19–29.

O'Neill, June. Transfers and Poverty: Cause and/or Effect? *Cato J.*, Spring/Summer 1986, *6*(1), pp. 55–76. **[G: U.S.]**

Pal, Padmaja; Chakravarty, S. R. and Bhattacharya, N. Poverty in Rural India: A Decomposition Analysis. *Indian Econ. Rev.*, July-Dec. 1986, *21*(2), pp. 149–84. **[G: India]**

Panda, Manoj Kumar. Fixing Income and Price Targets for the Poor in India. *J. Devel. Econ.*, March 1986, *20*(2), pp. 287–97. **[G: India]**

Patel, I. G. The Poorest Billion. **In** *Patel, I. G.*, 1986, *1978*, pp. 156–64.

Rahman, Atiq. Poverty Alleviation and the Most Disadvantaged Groups in Bangladesh Agriculture. *Bangladesh Devel. Stud.*, March 1986, *14*(1), pp. 29–58. **[G: Bangladesh]**

Robins, Philip K. Child Support, Welfare Dependency, and Poverty. *Amer. Econ. Rev.*, September 1986, *76*(4), pp. 768–88. **[G: U.S.]**

Sen, Pranab Kumar. The Gini Coefficient and Poverty Indexes: Some Reconciliations. *J. Amer. Statist. Assoc.*, December 1986, *81*(396), pp. 1050–57.

Shapiro, Aharon. The Treatment of Poverty in the Talmud. *Int. J. Soc. Econ.*, 1986, *13*(6), pp. 54–59.

Sharif, Mohammed. The Concept and Measurement of Subsistence: A Survey of the Literature. *World Devel.*, May 1986, *14*(5), pp. 555–77.

Thakur, D. S. Estimation of Poverty in India—An Empirical Investigation. *Margin*, October 1986, *19*(1), pp. 66–80. **[G: India]**

Thanawala, Kishor. Some Aspects of Poverty in Less Developed Countries. *Indian J. Quant. Econ.*, 1986, *2*(1), pp. 83–92. **[G: China; India; Burma; Pakistan; Bangladesh]**

Thompson, Michael and Wildavsky, Aaron. A Poverty of Distinction: From Economic Homogeneity to Cultural Heterogeneity in the Classification of Poor People. *Policy Sci.*, September 1986, *19*(2), pp. 163–99. **[G: U.S.]**

Till, Thomas E. The Share of Southeastern Black Counties in the Southern Rural Renaissance: Were They Bypassed by Factory Job Gains, 1959–77? *Growth Change*, April 1986, *17*(2), pp. 44–55. **[G: U.S.]**

Uppal, J. S. Income Distribution and Poverty in Indonesia. *J. Econ. Devel.*, December 1986, *11*(2), pp. 177–96. **[G: Indonesia]**

Wagner, Richard E. Wealth Transfers in a Rent-Seeking Polity. *Cato J.*, Spring/Summer 1986, *6*(1), pp. 155–71.

Weinberg, Daniel H. A Poverty Research Agenda for the Next Decade. **In** *Danziger, S. H. and Weinberg, D. H., eds.*, 1986, pp. 348–57. **[G: U.S.]**

Wilson, William Julius and Neckerman, Kathryn M. Poverty and Family Structure: The Widening Gap between Evidence and Public Policy Issues. **In** *Danziger, S. H. and Weinberg, D. H., eds.*, 1986, pp. 232–59. **[G: U.S.]**

915 Social Security

9150 Social Security

Abel, Andrew B. Capital Accumulation and Uncertain Lifetimes with Adverse Selection. *Econometrica*, September 1986, *54*(5), pp. 1079–97.

Anderson, Annelise. Social Security in Aging Societies: Comment. *Population Devel. Rev.*, Supp. 1986, *12*, pp. 313–17. **[G: U.S.]**

Anderson, Kathryn H.; Burkhauser, Richard V. and Quinn, Joseph F. Do Retirement Dreams Come True? The Effect of Unanticipated

Events on Retirement Plans. *Ind. Lab. Relat. Rev.*, July 1986, *39*(4), pp. 518–26. **[G: U.S.]**

Avery, Robert B.; Elliehausen, Gregory E. and Gustafson, Thomas A. Pensions and Social Security in Household Portfolios: Evidence from the *1983 Survey of Consumer Finances*. **In** *Adams, F. G. and Wachter, S. M., eds.*, 1986, pp. 127–60. **[G: U.S.]**

Ball, Robert M. The Future of Social Security. **In** *Dennis, B. D., ed.*, 1986, pp. 128–35. **[G: U.S.]**

Ballantyne, Harry C. Actuarial Status of the OASI and DI Trust Funds. *Soc. Sec. Bull.*, July 1986, *49*(7), pp. 5–9. **[G: U.S.]**

Barro, Robert J. Payroll-Tax Financed Social Insurance with Variable Retirement: Comment. *Scand. J. Econ.*, 1986, *88*(1), pp. 55–58.

Barro, Robert J. and Sahasakul, Chaipat. Average Marginal Tax Rates from Social Security and the Individual Income Tax. *J. Bus.*, Part 1, October 1986, *59*(4), pp. 555–66. **[G: U.S.]**

Barten, A. P. and d'Alcantara, G. Simulating Economic Policy with the COMET Model. **In** *Artus, P. and Guvenen, O., eds.*, 1986, pp. 229–37. **[G: EEC]**

Bentzel, Ragnar. Payroll-Tax Financed Social Insurance with Variable Retirement: Comment. *Scand. J. Econ.*, 1986, *88*(1), pp. 51–54.

Boss, Alfred. Social Insurance: Incentives and Disincentives to Save and to Work: Comment. **In** *Balassa, B. and Giersch, H., eds.*, 1986, pp. 81–85. **[G: OECD]**

Briden, George and Zedella, John. Social Security and Household Savings: Comment. *Amer. Econ. Rev.*, March 1986, *76*(1), pp. 286–88.

Burkhauser, Richard V. Social Security in Panama: A Multiperiod Analysis of Income Distribution. *J. Devel. Econ.*, April 1986, *21*(1), pp. 53–64. **[G: Panama]**

Burtless, Gary. Social Security, Unanticipated Benefit Increases, and the Timing of Retirement. *Rev. Econ. Stud.*, October 1986, *53*(5), pp. 781–805. **[G: U.S.]**

Burtless, Gary and Moffitt, Robert. Social Security, Earnings Tests, and Age at Retirement. *Public Finance Quart.*, January 1986, *14*(1), pp. 3–27. **[G: U.S.]**

Chapman, Steven H.; LaPlante, Mitchell P. and Wilensky, Gail R. Life Expectancy and Health Status of the Aged. *Soc. Sec. Bull.*, October 1986, *49*(10), pp. 24–48. **[G: U.S.]**

Cohen, Wilbur J. Social Security after 50 Years. **In** *Dennis, B. D., ed.*, 1986, pp. 123–27. **[G: U.S.]**

Coughlin, Richard M. Understanding (and Misunderstanding) Social Security: Behavioral Insights into Public Policy. **In** *Gilad, B. and Kaish, S., eds., Vol. B*, 1986, pp. 133–58. **[G: U.S.]**

Cox, J. P. Economic Growth and Income Support Policy in Australia. *Econ. Rec.*, September 1986, *62*(178), pp. 268–85. **[G: Australia]**

Diamond, Peter A. and Mirrlees, James A. Payroll-Tax Financed Social Insurance with Variable Retirement. *Scand. J. Econ.*, 1986, *88*(1), pp. 25–50.

Dilnot, Andrew W. and Stark, Graham K. The Poverty Trap, Tax Cuts, and the Reform of Social Security. *Fisc. Stud.*, February 1986, *7*(1), pp. 1–10. **[G: U.K.]**

Dinkel, Reiner. Social Security and Intergenerational Equity. **In** *von der Schulenburg, J.-M. G., ed.*, 1986, pp. 77–107. **[G: W. Germany]**

Dixon, Daryl A. Suggested Refinements of the Treasury Costings of the Occupational Superannuation Tax Expenditures. *Australian Tax Forum*, 1986, *3*(2), pp. 223–32. **[G: Australia]**

Durán Heras, Almudena. Características de la población y equilibrio financiero del sistema de pensiones. (With English summary.) *Invest. Ecón.*, January 1986, *10*(1), pp. 97–126. **[G: Spain]**

Ehrenberg, Ronald G. and Luzadis, Rebecca A. The Social Security Student Benefit Program and Family Decisions. *Econ. Educ. Rev.*, 1986, *5*(2), pp. 119–28. **[G: U.S.]**

Enríquez de Salamanca Navarro, Rafael. Combinación óptima de los métodos financieros de un sistema de pensiones. (With English summary.) *Invest. Ecón.*, January 1986, *10*(1), pp. 127–40. **[G: Spain]**

Ferrara, Peter J. Intergenerational Transfers and Super IRA's. *Cato J.*, Spring/Summer 1986, *6*(1), pp. 195–220.

Fisher, Paul. Social Security after 50 Years: Looking Back and Looking Ahead: Discussion. **In** *Dennis, B. D., ed.*, 1986, pp. 154–57. **[G: U.S.]**

Flowers, Marilyn R. Social Security, Saving, and Our Legacy to the Future. **In** *Lee, D. R., ed.*, 1986, pp. 195–224. **[G: U.S.]**

Freebairn, John W. The Economics of Superannuation: Comment. *Australian Econ. Rev.*, 3rd Quarter 1986, (75), pp. 87–88. **[G: Australia]**

Gohmann, Stephen F. A Test of the Perceived Fairness of the Actuarial Adjustment to Social Security Benefits. *Nat. Tax J.*, June 1986, *39*(2), pp. 237–40. **[G: U.S.]**

Haberman, Steven. Improvements in State Pension Rights for Women. **In** *von der Schulenburg, J.-M. G., ed.*, 1986, pp. 130–65. **[G: U.K.]**

Halpern, Janice and Hausman, Jerry A. Choice under Uncertainty: A Model of Applications for the Social Security Disability Insurance Program. *J. Public Econ.*, November 1986, *31*(2), pp. 131–61. **[G: U.S.]**

Hammond, Elizabeth M. and Morris, C. Nick. What Price Equality? The Cost of Changing the Age of Retirement. *Fisc. Stud.*, August 1986, *7*(3), pp. 25–40. **[G: U.K.]**

Herce San Miguel, José Antonio. Presupuesto de Seguridad Social y oferta de factores en una economía de generaciones sucesivas. (With English summary.) *Invest. Ecón.*, January 1986, *10*(1), pp. 37–64.

Holler, Manfred J. Intergeneration Solutions to the Social Security Dilemma. **In** *von der*

Schulenburg, J.-M. G., ed., 1986, pp. 54–74.

Holloway, Thomas M. and Reeb, Jane S. Sources of Change in Federal Transfer Payments to Persons: An Update. *Surv. Curr. Bus.*, June 1986, *66*(6), pp. 21–25. **[G: U.S.]**

Hu, Sheng Cheng. Uncertain Life Span, Risk Aversion, and the Demand for Pension Annuities. *Southern Econ. J.*, April 1986, *52*(4), pp. 933–47.

Hubbard, R. Glenn. Pension Wealth and Individual Saving: Some New Evidence. *J. Money, Credit, Banking,* May 1986, *18*(2), pp. 167–78. **[G: U.S.]**

Hum, Derek P. J. UISP and the Macdonald Commission: Reform and Restraint. *Can. Public Policy,* Supp. February 1986, *12*, pp. 92–100. **[G: Canada]**

Hurl, Lorna F. and Tucker, David J. Limitations of an Act of Faith: An Analysis of the Macdonald Commission's Stance on Social Services. *Can. Public Policy,* December 1986, *12*(4), pp. 606–21. **[G: Canada]**

Iams, Howard M. Characteristics of the Longest Job for New Disabled Workers: Findings from the New Beneficiary Survey. *Soc. Sec. Bull.*, December 1986, *49*(12), pp. 13–18. **[G: U.S.]**

Iams, Howard M. Employment of Retired-Worker Women. *Soc. Sec. Bull.*, March 1986, *49*(3), pp. 5–13. **[G: U.S.]**

Irick, Christine. An Overview of OASDI Revenue, Expenditures, and Beneficiaries, 1974–85. *Soc. Sec. Bull.*, June 1986, *49*(6), pp. 21–28. **[G: U.S.]**

Janssen, Martin. Social Insurance: Incentives and Disincentives to Save and to Work. **In** *Balassa, B. and Giersch, H., eds.*, 1986, pp. 67–80. **[G: OECD]**

Kahn, Arthur L. Characteristics of Supplemental Security Income Recipients, December 1984. *Soc. Sec. Bull.*, April 1986, *49*(4), pp. 5–11. **[G: U.S.]**

Karni, Edi and Zilcha, Itzhak. Welfare and Comparative Statics Implications of Fair Social Security: A Steady-state Analysis. *J. Public Econ.*, August 1986, *30*(3), pp. 341–57.

Kerns, Wilmer L. Federal Employees' Retirement System Act of 1986. *Soc. Sec. Bull.*, November 1986, *49*(11), pp. 5–10. **[G: U.S.]**

Klees, Barbara and Warfield, Carter. Actuarial Status of the HI and SMI Trust Funds. *Soc. Sec. Bull.*, July 1986, *49*(7), pp. 10–18. **[G: U.S.]**

Koskela, Erkki and Virén, Matti. Social Security and Household Saving in an International Cross-section: Some Further Evidence. *Liiketaloudellinen Aikak.*, 1986, *35*(2), pp. 105–11. **[G: OECD]**

Koskela, Erkki and Virén, Matti. Social Security and Household Saving: Reply. *Amer. Econ. Rev.*, March 1986, *76*(1), pp. 289–90.

Lim, Chong Yah, et al. Report of the Central Provident Fund Study Group. *Singapore Econ. Rev.*, April 1986, *31*(1), pp. ii–l07. **[G: Singapore]**

Lindemans, A. and Willekens, F. The Possible Consequences of a Regional Financing System of Social Security. *Tijdschrift Econ. Manage.*, 1986, *31*(2), pp. 203–26.

Lingg, Barbara A. Beneficiaries Affected by the Annual Earnings Test in 1982. *Soc. Sec. Bull.*, May 1986, *49*(5), pp. 25–32. **[G: U.S.]**

López García, Miguel Angel. Pensiones de la Seguridad Social y bienestar. Un análisis de los períodos transitorios. (With English summary.) *Invest. Ecón.*, January 1986, *10*(1), pp. 65–95.

Marnata, Françoise and Sarrazin, Chantal. Les pays nordiques: protection sociale et contrainte extérieure. (Nordic Countries: Social Welfare and External Constraint. With English summary.) *Écon. Soc.*, January 1986, *20*(1), pp. 211–34. **[G: Denmark; Sweden; Norway; Finland]**

McElwain, Adrienne M. and Swofford, James L. The Social Security Payroll Tax and the Life-Cycle Work Pattern. *J. Human Res.*, Spring 1986, *21*(2), pp. 279–87. **[G: U.S.]**

McIntosh, C. Alison. Recent Pronatalist Policies in Western Europe. *Population Devel. Rev.*, Supp. 1986, *12*, pp. 318–34. **[G: W. Europe]**

Mesa-Lago, Carmelo. Social Security and Development in Latin America. *CEPAL Rev.*, April 1986, (28), pp. 135–50. **[G: Latin America]**

Miller, Nancy, et al. Social Security Programs in the United States. *Soc. Sec. Bull.*, January 1986, *49*(1), pp. 5–59. **[G: U.S.]**

Moore, Thomas Gale. Social Security in Aging Societies: Comment. *Population Devel. Rev.*, Supp. 1986, *12*, pp. 295.

Moulton, Brent R. An Analysis of Female Work Experience Data Derived from Social Security Records. *J. Econ. Soc. Meas.*, April 1986, *14*(1), pp. 65–75. **[G: U.S.]**

Musgrave, Richard A. A Reappraisal of Financing Social Security. **In** *Musgrave, R. A., Vol. 2*, 1986, *1981*, pp. 103–22. **[G: U.S.]**

Musgrave, Richard A. The Role of Social Insurance in an Overall Programme for Social Welfare. **In** *Musgrave, R. A., Vol. 2*, 1986, *1967*, pp. 67–81. **[G: U.S.]**

Noguchi, Yukio. Overcommitment in Pensions: The Japanese Experience. **In** *Rose, R. and Shiratori, R., eds.*, 1986, pp. 173–92. **[G: Japan]**

Okochi, Kazuo. Changes in Social Security and Value Orientation. **In** *Hax, H.; Kraus, W. and Tsuchiya, K., eds.*, 1986, pp. 163–72. **[G: Japan]**

Østrup, Finn. Problemstillinger ved indretning af et pensionssystem. (A Comparison between Differnt Old-Age Pension Schemes. With English summary.) *Nationaløkon. Tidsskr.*, 1986, *124*(3), pp. 294–303.

Petersen, Jørn Henrik. Pensionsfinansiering i vækstsammenhaeng. (Pension Finance Based on a Pay-as-You-Go System versus a System Based on Previous Savings and Capital Accumulation. With English summary.) *Nationaløkon. Tidsskr.*, 1986, *124*(3), pp. 304–15. **[G: Denmark]**

Petersen, Jørn Henrik. Three Precursors of Modern Theories of Old-Age Pensions: A Contribution to the History of Social-Policy Doctrines. *Hist. Polit. Econ.*, Fall 1986, *18*(3), pp. 405–17.

Podger, A. S. The Economics of Superannuation. *Australian Econ. Rev.*, 3rd Quarter 1986, (75), pp. 75–86. **[G: Australia]**

Pope, Ralph A. Economies of Scale in Large State and Municipal Retirement Systems. *Public Budg. Finance*, Autumn 1986, *6*(3), pp. 70–80.

Ricardo-Campbell, Rita. U.S. Social Security under Low Fertility. *Population Devel. Rev.*, Supp. 1986, *12*, pp. 296–312.

Ricketts, Jean Marie. Worldwide Trends and Developments in Social Security, 1983–85. *Soc. Sec. Bull.*, September 1986, *49*(9), pp. 5–11. **[G: Global]**

Robertson, A. Haeworth. Ferrara's Super IRA Proposal: A Critique [Intergenerational Transfers and Super IRA's]. *Cato J.*, Spring/Summer 1986, *6*(1), pp. 221–28.

Ross, Mary and Hayes, Carol. Consolidated Omnibus Budget Reconciliation Act of 1985. *Soc. Sec. Bull.*, August 1986, *49*(8), pp. 22–31. **[G: U.S.]**

Schneider, Friedrich. The Influence of Political Institutions on Social Security Policies: A Public Choice View. **In** *von der Schulenburg, J.-M. G., ed.*, 1986, pp. 13–31. **[G: OECD]**

von der Schulenburg, J.-Matthias Graf. Social Security at the Crossroads. **In** *von der Schulenburg, J.-M. G., ed.*, 1986, pp. 3–10.

Seidman, Bert. Social Security after 50 Years: Looking Back and Looking Ahead: Discussion. **In** *Dennis, B. D., ed.*, 1986, pp. 143–45. **[G: U.S.]**

Seidman, Laurence S. A Phase-down of Social Security: The Transition in a Life Cycle Growth Model. *Nat. Tax J.*, March 1986, *39*(1), pp. 97–107.

Shirai, Taishiro. Changes in Social Security and Value Orientation: Comments. **In** *Hax, H.; Kraus, W. and Tsuchiya, K., eds.*, 1986, pp. 172–76. **[G: Japan]**

Shome, Parthasarathi. The Impact of Social Security Institutions on Resource Allocation. **In** *Shome, P., ed.*, 1986, pp. 198–219. **[G: Malaysia; Singapore; Thailand; India; Sri Lanka]**

Siegfried, John J. The Effects of Student Higher Education Grants. *Econ. Educ. Rev.*, 1986, *5*(2), pp. 129–33. **[G: U.S.]**

Snyder, Donald C. Pension Status of Recently Retired Workers on Their Longest Job: Findings from the New Beneficiary Survey. *Soc. Sec. Bull.*, August 1986, *49*(8), pp. 5–21. **[G: U.S.]**

Stein, Bruno. Social Security after 50 Years: Looking Back and Looking Ahead: Discussion. **In** *Dennis, B. D., ed.*, 1986, pp. 151–53. **[G: U.S.]**

Swidler, Steve. The Old-Age Security Motive for Having Children and the Effect of Social Security on Completed Family Size. *Quart. Rev. Econ. Bus.*, Summer 1986, *26*(2), pp. 14–34. **[G: U.S.]**

Tamburi, Giovanni and Mouton, Pierre. The Uncertain Frontier between Private and Public Pension Schemes. *Int. Lab. Rev.*, Mar.-Apr. 1986, *125*(2), pp. 127–40.

Thomson, Lawrence H. The Social Security Reform Debate in the United States. *Invest. Ecón.*, January 1986, *10*(1), pp. 3–36. **[G: U.S.]**

Tullock, Gordon. Bismarckism. **In** *Lee, D. R., ed.*, 1986, pp. 225–40. **[G: U.S.]**

Upp, Melinda. Fast Facts and Figures about Social Security. *Soc. Sec. Bull.*, June 1986, *49*(6), pp. 5–19. **[G: U.S.]**

Vaughn, William M. Social Security after 50 Years: Looking Back and Looking Ahead: Discussion. **In** *Dennis, B. D., ed.*, 1986, pp. 146–50. **[G: U.S.]**

Veall, Michael R. Public Pensions as Optimal Social Contracts. *J. Public Econ.*, November 1986, *31*(2), pp. 237–51.

Verbon, Harrie A. A. Altruism, Political Power and Public Pensions. *Kyklos*, 1986, *39*(3), pp. 343–58.

Verbon, Harrie A. A. and van Winden, Frans. Public Pensions and Political Decision-Making. **In** *von der Schulenburg, J.-M. G., ed.*, 1986, pp. 32–53. **[G: Netherlands]**

Warlick, Jennifer L. and Burkhauser, Richard V. Who Gets What from Social Security? Analyzing the Redistributive Effects of Government Transfer Programs. *J. Econ. Educ.*, Summer 1986, *17*(3), pp. 187–94. **[G: U.S.]**

Wartonick, Daniel. Social Security Reform Proposals in the United Kingdom: The White Paper. *Soc. Sec. Bull.*, May 1986, *49*(5), pp. 21–24. **[G: U.K.]**

Weaver, Carolyn L. Social Security in Aging Societies. *Population Devel. Rev.*, Supp. 1986, *12*, pp. 273–94. **[G: OECD]**

Weaver, Carolyn L. Social Security Disability Policy in the 1980s and Beyond. **In** *Berkowitz, M. and Hill, M. A., eds.*, 1986, pp. 29–63. **[G: U.S.]**

Weaver, Carolyn L. Social Security's Outlook at 50: A Critical Assessment. **In** *Dennis, B. D., ed.*, 1986, pp. 136–42. **[G: U.S.]**

Ycas, Martynas A. Asset Holdings of the Newly Disabled: Findings from the New Beneficiary Survey. *Soc. Sec. Bull.*, December 1986, *49*(12), pp. 5–12. **[G: U.S.]**

Zapf, Wolfgang. Development, Structure, and Prospects of the German Social State. **In** *Rose, R. and Shiratori, R., eds.*, 1986, pp. 126–55. **[G: W. Germany]**

916 Economics of Law; Economics of Crime

9160 Economics of Law; Economics of Crime

Abdou, Dyaa K.; Gardner, B. Delworth and Green, Richard D. To Violate or Not Violate the Law: An Example from Egyptian Agriculture. *Amer. J. Agr. Econ.*, February 1986, *68*(1), pp. 120–26. **[G: Egypt]**

Aranson, Peter H. Economic Efficiency and the Common Law: A Critical Survey. **In** *von der Schulenburg, J.-M. G. and Skogh, G., eds.*, 1986, pp. 51–84.

Assaf, George B.; Kroetch, Brent G. and Mathur, Subodh C. Nonmarket Valuations of Accidental Oil Spills: A Survey of Economic and Legal Principles. *Marine Resource Econ.*, 1986, *2*(3), pp. 211–37. **[G: U.S.]**

Bamossy, Gary J. and Scammon, Debra L. Counterfeiting—A Worldwide Problem: What Is the Role of Channel Members? **In** *Pellegrini, L. and Reddy, S. K., eds.*, 1986, pp. 141–54. **[G: U.S.]**

Banderet, M. E. Discipline at the Workplace: A Comparative Study of Law and Practice: 1. The Sources and Substance of Disciplinary Law. *Int. Lab. Rev.*, May-June 1986, *125*(3), pp. 261–78. **[G: OECD]**

Banderet, M. E. Discipline at the Workplace: A Comparative Study of Law and Practice: 2. Procedure. *Int. Lab. Rev.*, July-Aug. 1986, *125*(4), pp. 383–99.

Beckenstein, Alan R. and Gabel, H. Landis. The Economics of Antitrust Compliance. *Southern Econ. J.*, January 1986, *52*(3), pp. 673–92. **[G: U.S.]**

Beller, Andrea H. and Graham, John W. The Determinants of Child Support Income. *Soc. Sci. Quart.*, June 1986, *67*(2), pp. 353–64. **[G: U.S.]**

Benson, Herman. The Fight for Union Democracy. **In** *Lipset, S. M., ed.*, 1986, pp. 323–70. **[G: U.S.]**

Bertsch, Gary K. The Extraterritoriality Issue in the Transatlantic Context: A Question of Law or Diplomacy? Comment. **In** *Tsoukalis, L., ed.*, 1986, pp. 152–57. **[G: U.S.; EEC]**

Boyes, William J. and Faith, Roger L. Some Effects of the Bankruptcy Reform Act of 1978. *J. Law Econ.*, April 1986, *29*(1), pp. 139–49. **[G: U.S.]**

Braithwaite, John. Consumers as Victims of Corporate Crime. **In** *Wheelwright, T., ed.*, 1986, pp. 331–42.

Breton, Albert and Wintrobe, Ronald. The Bureaucracy of Murder Revisited. *J. Polit. Econ.*, October 1986, *94*(5), pp. 905–26.

Brietzke, Paul H. Another Law and Economics. **In** *Zerbe, R. O., Jr., ed.*, 1986, pp. 57–109.

Brooks, Thornton H.; McGinn, M. Daniel and Cary, William P. H. Second Generation Problems Facing Employers in Employment Discrimination Cases: Continuing Violations, Pendent State Claims, and Double Attorneys' Fees. *Law Contemp. Probl.*, Autumn 1986, *49*(4), pp. 24–51. **[G: U.S.]**

Brown, Stephen J. and Klein, Roger W. Model Selection in the Federal Courts: An Application of the Posterior Odds Ratio Criterion. **In** *[de Finetti, B.]*, 1986, pp. 141–56. **[G: U.S.]**

Butler, Henry N. General Incorporation in Nineteenth Century England: Interaction of Common Law and Legislative Processes. *Int. Rev. Law Econ.*, December 1986, *6*(2), pp. 169–88. **[G: U.K.]**

Cagan, Phillip. Financial Regulation: Comment. *J. Bus.*, January 1986, *59*(1), pp. 49–54. **[G: U.S.]**

Cameron, S. An Empirical Study of Malicious False Fire Alarm Calls. *Int. Rev. Law Econ.*, June 1986, *6*(1), pp. 33–44. **[G: U.K.]**

Chambers, Julius L. and Goldstein, Barry. Title VII: The Continuing Challenge of Establishing Fair Employment Practices. *Law Contemp. Probl.*, Autumn 1986, *49*(4), pp. 9–23. **[G: U.S.]**

Charney, Jonathan I. The Unfinished Business of the Law of the Sea Conference. **In** *Pontecorvo, G., ed.*, 1986, pp. 238–64.

Cheung, Steven N. S. Property Rights and Invention. **In** *Palmer, J., ed.*, 1986, pp. 5–18. **[G: U.S.]**

Clauretie, Terrence M. and Harju, Melvin W. The Expanding Concept of Just Compensation and the Role of the Appraiser. *Amer. Real Estate Urban Econ. Assoc. J.*, Summer 1986, *14*(2), pp. 338–60. **[G: U.S.]**

Cooper, Graeme S. Income Tax Law and Contributive Justice: Some Thoughts on Defining and Expressing a Consistent Theory of Tax Justice and Its Limitations. *Australian Tax Forum*, 1986, *3*(3), pp. 297–332.

Crane, Steven E. and Nourzad, Farrokh. Federal Income Tax Evasion. **In** *Lindholm, R. W., ed.*, 1986, pp. 140–62. **[G: U.S.]**

Craswell, Richard and Calfee, John E. Deterrence and Uncertain Legal Standards. *J. Law, Econ., Organ.*, Fall 1986, *2*(2), pp. 279–303.

Culp, Jerome McCristal, Jr. Causation, Economists, and the Dinosaur: A Response to [Causal Judgment in Attributive and Explanatory Contexts]. *Law Contemp. Probl.*, Summer 1986, *49*(3), pp. 23–46.

Demaret, Paul. The Extraterritoriality Issue in the Transatlantic Context: A Question of Law or Diplomacy? **In** *Tsoukalis, L., ed.*, 1986, pp. 124–48. **[G: U.S.; EEC]**

Dickens, William T. Crime and Punishment Again: The Economic Approach with a Psychological Twist. *J. Public Econ.*, June 1986, *30*(1), pp. 97–107.

Doi, Teruo. The Role of Intellectual Property Law in Bilateral Licensing Transactions between Japan and the United States. **In** *Saxonhouse, G. R. and Yamamura, K., eds.*, 1986, pp. 157–92. **[G: Japan; U.S.]**

Dray, W. H. Causal Judgment in Attributive and Explanatory Contexts. *Law Contemp. Probl.*, Summer 1986, *49*(3), pp. 13–22.

Dulude, Louise Séguin. Patents, Licensing, and Antitrust: Comments. **In** *Palmer, J., ed.*, 1986, pp. 87–89. **[G: U.S.]**

Dye, Ronald A. An Economic Analysis of Bankruptcy Statutes. *Econ. Inquiry*, July 1986, *24*(3), pp. 417–28.

Erkkila, John. Copyright Law, Photocopying, and Price Discrimination: Comment. **In** *Palmer, J., ed.*, 1986, pp. 201–03.

Ethier, Wilfred J. Illegal Immigration: The Host-Country Problem. *Amer. Econ. Rev.*, March 1986, *76*(1), pp. 56–71.

Farran, Andrew. The Interplay of Law and Economics in International Trade Regulation. **In** *Snape, R. H., ed.*, 1986, pp. 193–217.

Feige, Edgar L. A Re-examination of the "Underground Economy" in the United States: A Comment. *Int. Monet. Fund Staff Pap.*, December 1986, *33*(4), pp. 768–81. **[G: Selected Countries]**

Fisher, Franklin M. Statisticians, Econometricians, and Adversary Proceedings. *J. Amer. Statist. Assoc.*, June 1986, *81*(394), pp. 277–86. **[G: U.S.]**

Forbes, Kevin F. Limited Liability and the Development of the Business Corporation. *J. Law, Econ., Organ.*, Spring 1986, *2*(1), pp. 163–77. **[G: U.S.]**

Gardiner, Frances K. Community Security: The Irish Problem. *Econ. Soc. Rev.*, October 1986, *18*(1), pp. 1–15.

Gentry, James Theodore. The Panopticon Revisited: The Problem of Monitoring Private Prisons. *Yale Law J.*, December 1986, *96*(2), pp. 353–75. **[G: U.S.]**

George, Peter and Sworden, Philip. The Courts and the Development of Trade in Upper Canada, 1830–1860. *Bus. Hist. Rev.*, Summer 1986, *60*(2), pp. 258–80. **[G: Canada]**

Geyikdagi, Yasar M. and Geyikdagi, Necla V. The Economics of Street Crime. *Rivista Int. Sci. Econ. Com.*, August 1986, *33*(8), pp. 813–18.

Graetz, Michael J.; Reinganum, Jennifer F. and Wilde, Louis L. The Tax Compliance Game: Toward an Interactive Theory of Law Enforcement. *J. Law, Econ., Organ.*, Spring 1986, *2*(1), pp. 1–32. **[G: U.S.]**

Gravelle, Hugh S. E. Default Risk and the Optimal Pricing of Court Enforcement Services. **In** *von der Schulenburg, J.-M. G. and Skogh, G., eds.*, 1986, pp. 85–112.

Greenberg, Stephanie W. and Rohe, William M. Informal Social Control and Crime Prevention in Modern Urban Neighborhoods. **In** *Taylor, R. B., ed.*, 1986, pp. 79–118.

Grossack, Irvin M. OPEC and the Antitrust Laws. *J. Econ. Issues*, September 1986, *20*(3), pp. 725–41.

Gyimah-Brempong, Kwabena. Empirical Models of Criminal Behavior: How Significant a Factor Is Race? *Rev. Black Polit. Econ.*, Summer 1986, *15*(1), pp. 27–43. **[G: U.S.]**

Hall, Christopher D. Patents, Licensing, and Antitrust. **In** *Palmer, J., ed.*, 1986, pp. 59–86. **[G: U.S.]**

Halleck, Seymour L. Responsibility and Excuse in Medicine and Law: A Utilitarian Perspective. *Law Contemp. Probl.*, Summer 1986, *49*(3), pp. 127–46.

Hamada, Koichi; Ishida, Hidetoh and Murakami, Masahiro. The Evolution and Economic Consequences of Product Liability Rules in Japan. **In** *Saxonhouse, G. R. and Yamamura, K., eds.*, 1986, pp. 83–106. **[G: Japan]**

Hay, Fenton. Canada's Role in International Negotiations Concerning Intellectual Property Laws. **In** *Palmer, J., ed.*, 1986, pp. 239–63. **[G: Canada]**

Hemenway, David; Wolf, Kate and Lang, Janet. An Arson Epidemic. *J. Behav. Econ.*, Fall 1986, *15*, pp. 17–28. **[G: U.S.]**

Higgins, Richard S. and Rubin, Paul H. Counterfeit Goods. *J. Law Econ.*, October 1986, *29*(2), pp. 211–30.

Hilf, Meinhard. International Trade Disputes and the Individual: Private Party Involvement in National and International Procedures Regarding Unfair Foreign Trade Practices. *Aussenwirtschaft*, September 1986, *41*(2/3), pp. 441–66. **[G: Global]**

Hollander, Abraham. Collective Administration of Copyright: An Economic Analysis: Comments. **In** *Palmer, J., ed.*, 1986, pp. 153–55.

Horton, Paul and Alexander, Lawrence. Freedom of Contract and the Family: A Skeptical Appraisal. **In** *Peden, J. R. and Glahe, F. R., eds.*, 1986, pp. 229–55. **[G: U.S.]**

Hourihan, Kevin. Community Policing in Cork: Awareness, Attitudes and Correlates. *Econ. Soc. Rev.*, October 1986, *18*(1), pp. 17–26. **[G: Ireland]**

Huber, Peter W. The Bhopalization of American Tort Law. **In** *Landau, R. and Rosenberg, N., eds.*, 1986, pp. 191–212. **[G: U.S.]**

Hutter, Michael. Transaction Cost and Communication: A Theory of Institutional Change, Applied to the Case of Patent Law. **In** *von der Schulenburg, J.-M. G. and Skogh, G., eds.*, 1986, pp. 113–29.

Ioffe, Olimpiad S. Soviet Law and the New Economic Experiment. **In** *Ioffe, O. S. and Janis, M. W., eds.*, 1986, pp. 3–28. **[G: U.S.S.R.]**

Jack, R. B. A Review of the Legal Problems. **In** *Dale, R., ed.*, 1986, pp. 48–63. **[G: U.K.]**

Jacobs, David and Fuller, Michael. The Social Construction of Drunken Driving: Modeling the Organizational Processing of DWI Defendants. *Soc. Sci. Quart.*, December 1986, *67*(4), pp. 785–802. **[G: U.S.]**

Jensen, Michael C.; Meckling, William H. and Holderness, Clifford G. Analysis of Alternative Standing Doctrines. *Int. Rev. Law Econ.*, December 1986, *6*(2), pp. 205–16. **[G: U.S.]**

Katz, Milton. The Role of the Legal System in Technological Innovation and Economic Growth. **In** *Landau, R. and Rosenberg, N., eds.*, 1986, pp. 169–89. **[G: U.S.]**

Kitch, Edmund W. Patents: Monopolies or Property Rights? **In** *Palmer, J., ed.*, 1986, pp. 31–49.

Kraakman, Reiner H. Gatekeepers: The Anatomy of a Third-Party Enforcement Strategy. *J. Law, Econ., Organ.*, Spring 1986, *2*(1), pp. 53–104.

Lagergren, Stina. The Influence of ILO Standards on Swedish Law and Practice. *Int. Lab. Rev.*, May-June 1986, *125*(3), pp. 305–28. **[G: Sweden]**

Laycock, Douglas. Continuing Violations, Disparate Impact in Compensation, and Other Title VII Issues. *Law Contemp. Probl.*, Autumn 1986, *49*(4), pp. 53–61. **[G: U.S.]**

Laycock, Douglas. Statistical Proof and Theories

of Discrimination. *Law Contemp. Probl.*, Autumn 1986, *49*(4), pp. 97–106. **[G: U.S.]**

Liebowitz, S. J. Copyright Law, Photocopying, and Price Discrimination. **In** *Palmer, J., ed.*, 1986, pp. 181–200.

Liebowitz, S. J. International Policies and Intellectual Property: Comments. **In** *Palmer, J., ed.*, 1986, pp. 285–87.

Lui, Francis T. A Dynamic Model of Corruption Deterrence. *J. Public Econ.*, November 1986, *31*(2), pp. 215–36.

Margolis, Stephen E. Copyright and Computer Software: Comments. **In** *Palmer, J., ed.*, 1986, pp. 227–31. **[G: U.S.; Canada]**

Marks, Denton and Vining, Aidan. Prison Labor Markets: The Supply Issue. *Policy Sci.*, July 1986, *19*(1), pp. 83–111. **[G: U.S.]**

McChesney, Fred S. Law's Honour Lost: The Plight of Antitrust. *Antitrust Bull.*, Summer 1986, *31*(2), pp. 359–82. **[G: U.S.]**

McCormick, Robert E. and Tollison, Robert D. Crime and Income Distribution in a Basketball Economy. *Int. Rev. Law Econ.*, June 1986, *6*(1), pp. 115–24. **[G: U.S.]**

McKee, Michael J. You Can't Always Get What You Want: Lessons from the Paris Convention Revision Exercise. **In** *Palmer, J., ed.*, 1986, pp. 265–72.

Mercuro, Nicholas. Contributions to Law and Economics: A Survey of Recent Books. *J. Econ. Educ.*, Fall 1986, *17*(4), pp. 295–306.

de Meza, David. The Efficiency of Liability Law. *Int. Rev. Law Econ.*, June 1986, *6*(1), pp. 107–13.

Milliman, Scott R. Optimal Fishery Management in the Presence of Illegal Activity. *J. Environ. Econ. Manage.*, December 1986, *13*(4), pp. 363–81.

Morales, Edmundo. Coca and Cocaine Economy and Social Change in the Andes of Peru. *Econ. Develop. Cult. Change,* October 1986, *35*(1), pp. 143–61. **[G: Peru]**

Moylan, James J. and Ukman, Laren. Dispute Resolution Systems in the Commodity Futures Industry. *J. Futures Markets,* Winter 1986, *6*(4), pp. 659–70. **[G: U.S.]**

Nadel, Mark S. Rings of Privacy: Unsolicited Telephone Calls and the Right of Privacy. *Yale J. Regul.*, Fall 1986, *4*(1), pp. 99–128.

Nas, Tevfik F.; Price, Albert C. and Weber, Charles T. A Policy-oriented Theory of Corruption. *Amer. Polit. Sci. Rev.*, March 1986, *80*(1), pp. 107–19.

Netter, Jeffry M.; Hersch, Philip L. and Manson, William D. An Economic Analysis of Adverse Possession Statutes. *Int. Rev. Law Econ.*, December 1986, *6*(2), pp. 217–28. **[G: U.S.]**

Norris, Barbara A. Multiple Regression Analysis in Title VII Cases: A Structural Approach to Attacks of "Missing Factors" and "Pre-act Discrimination." *Law Contemp. Probl.*, Autumn 1986, *49*(4), pp. 63–96. **[G: U.S.]**

Orland, Leonard. Perspectives on Soviet Economic Crime. **In** *Ioffe, O. S. and Janis, M. W., eds.*, 1986, pp. 169–211. **[G: U.S.S.R.]**

Pacheco, Fernando and Santos, Pedro. Corrupçao: Uma abordagem pela teoria do controle. (With English summary.) *Economia (Portugal)*, January 1986, *10*(1), pp. 47–66.

Palmer, John P. Copyright and Computer Software. **In** *Palmer, J., ed.*, 1986, pp. 205–25. **[G: Canada; U.S.]**

Parsons, Ross W. Income Taxation—An Institution in Decay? *Australian Tax Forum,* 1986, *3*(3), pp. 233–66.

Petersmann, Ernst-Ulrich. Trade Policy as a Constitutional Problem. On the "Domestic Policy Functions" of International Trade Rules. *Aussenwirtschaft*, September 1986, *41*(2/3), pp. 405–39. **[G: Global]**

Peterson, Richard E. and Seo, K. K. Crime Trends—East and West. *Int. J. Soc. Econ.*, 1986, *13*(1/2), pp. 68–76. **[G: U.S.; Japan; U.K.]**

Phegan, Colin. The Interplay of Law and Economics in International Trade Regulation: Comment. **In** *Snape, R. H., ed.*, 1986, pp. 218–21.

Pirog-Good, Maureen A. Modeling Employment and Crime Relationships. *Soc. Sci. Quart.*, December 1986, *67*(4), pp. 767–84. **[G: U.S.]**

Png, I. P. L. Optimal Subsidies and Damages in the Presence of Judicial Error. *Int. Rev. Law Econ.*, June 1986, *6*(1), pp. 101–05.

Priest, George L. What Economists Can Tell Lawyers about Intellectual Property: Comment [Property Rights and Invention]. **In** *Palmer, J., ed.*, 1986, pp. 19–24. **[G: U.S.]**

Rea, Samuel A., Jr. Damages for Buyer Breach. *Int. Rev. Law Econ.*, June 1986, *6*(1), pp. 77–86.

Rebelo, Sérgio. Optimização do controlo da evasao fiscal: O caso do imposto sobre o lucro das empresas. (With English summary.) *Economia (Portugal)*, October 1986, *10*(3), pp. 415–45.

Regan, Donald H. The Supreme Court and State Protectionism: Making Sense of the Dormant Commerce Clause. *Mich. Law Rev.*, May 1986, *84*(6), pp. 1091–1287. **[G: U.S.]**

Robertson, Michael. Legal Obstacles to Black Advancement. **In** *Smollan, R., ed.*, 1986, pp. 104–14. **[G: S. Africa]**

Roessler, Frieder. Competition and Trade Policies. The Constitutional Function of International Economic Law: Discussion to Session IV. *Aussenwirtschaft,* September 1986, *41*(2/3), pp. 467–74. **[G: Global]**

Roper, Brian A. Market Forces, Privatisation and Prisons: A Polar Case for Government Policy. *Int. J. Soc. Econ.*, 1986, *13*(1/2), pp. 77–92. **[G: U.K.]**

Rose-Ackerman, Susan. Efficiency, Equity and Inalienability. **In** *von der Schulenburg, J.-M. G. and Skogh, G., eds.*, 1986, pp. 11–37.

Rose-Ackerman, Susan. I'd Rather Be Liable than You: A Note on Property Rules and Liability Rules. *Int. Rev. Law Econ.*, December 1986, *6*(2), pp. 255–63.

Rosenthal, Douglas E. The Extraterritoriality Issue in the Transatlantic Context: A Question of Law or Diplomacy? Comment. **In** *Tsoukalis,*

L., ed., 1986, pp. 149–52. [G: U.S.; EEC]

Ross, H. Laurence and LaFree, Gary D. Deterrence in Criminology and Social Policy. **In** *Smelser, N. J. and Gerstein, D. R., eds.*, 1986, pp. 129–52.

Roth, Allan. Legal Environment. **In** *Gray, H. P., ed.*, 1986, pp. 43–69. **[G: U.S.]**

Rubin, Paul H. Costs and Benefits of a Duty to Rescue. *Int. Rev. Law Econ.*, December 1986, *6*(2), pp. 273–76.

Samuels, Warren J. and Mercuro, Nicholas. Wealth Maximization and Judicial Decision-Making: The Issues Further Clarified [Posnerian Law and Economics on the Bench]. *Int. Rev. Law Econ.*, June 1986, *6*(1), pp. 133–37. **[G: U.S.]**

Sandelin, Bo and Skogh, Göran. Property Crimes and the Police: An Empirical Analysis of Swedish Data. *Scand. J. Econ.*, 1986, *88*(3), pp. 547–61. **[G: Sweden]**

Scherer, F. M. Patents: Monopolies or Property Rights? Comment. **In** *Palmer, J., ed.*, 1986, pp. 51–58.

Schmalbeck, Richard. The Trouble with Statistical Evidence. *Law Contemp. Probl.*, Summer 1986, *49*(3), pp. 221–36.

Scholsem, Jean-Claude. The Extraterritoriality Issue in the Transatlantic Context: A Question of Law or Diplomacy? Comment. **In** *Tsoukalis, L., ed.*, 1986, pp. 158–62. **[G: U.S.; EEC]**

Seger, Martha R. Statement to the U.S. House Subcommittee on Financial Institutions Supervision, Regulation and Insurance of the Committee on Banking, Finance and Urban Affairs, May 14, 1986. *Fed. Res. Bull.*, July 1986, *72*(7), pp. 467–72. **[G: U.S.]**

Servais, J. M. Flexibility and Rigidity in International Labour Standards. *Int. Lab. Rev.*, Mar.-Apr. 1986, *125*(2), pp. 193–208.

Shavell, S. The Judgment Proof Problem. *Int. Rev. Law Econ.*, June 1986, *6*(1), pp. 45–58.

Smith, Douglas A. Collective Administration of Copyright: An Economic Analysis. **In** *Palmer, J., ed.*, 1986, pp. 137–51.

Spicer, Michael W. Civilization at a Discount: The Problem of Tax Evasion. *Nat. Tax J.*, March 1986, *39*(1), pp. 13–20. **[G: U.S.]**

Stell, Lance K. Close Encounters of the Lethal Kind: The Use of Deadly Force in Self-Defense. *Law Contemp. Probl.*, Winter 1986, *49*(1), pp. 113–24.

Stephen, Frank H. Decision Making under Uncertainty: In Defence of Shackle. *J. Econ. Stud.*, 1986, *13*(5), pp. 45–57.

Stigler, George J. The Economic Effects of the Antitrust Laws. **In** *Stigler, G. J.*, 1986, *1966*, pp. 184–223. **[G: U.S.]**

Swan, George Steven. The Political Economy of American Family Policy, 1945–85. *Population Devel. Rev.*, December 1986, *12*(4), pp. 739–58. **[G: U.S.]**

Tanzi, Vito. The Underground Economy in the United States: Reply to Comments. *Int. Monet. Fund Staff Pap.*, December 1986, *33*(4), pp. 799–811. **[G: Selected Countries; U.S.]**

Thomas, J. J. The Underground Economy in the United States: A Comment. *Int. Monet. Fund Staff Pap.*, December 1986, *33*(4), pp. 782–89. **[G: U.S.; Selected Countries]**

Thompson, James W. and Cataldo, James. Market Incentives for Criminal Behavior: Comment. **In** *Freeman, R. B. and Holzer, H. J., eds.*, 1986, pp. 347–51. **[G: U.S.]**

Tullock, Gordon. Giving Justice. **In** *Tullock, G.*, 1986, *1980*, pp. 145–57.

Tullock, Gordon. Negotiated Settlement. **In** *von der Schulenburg, J.-M. G. and Skogh, G., eds.*, 1986, pp. 39–50.

Usher, Dan. Police, Punishment, and Public Goods. *Public Finance*, 1986, *41*(1), pp. 96–115.

Viscusi, W. Kip. Market Incentives for Criminal Behavior. **In** *Freeman, R. B. and Holzer, H. J., eds.*, 1986, pp. 301–46. **[G: U.S.]**

Viscusi, W. Kip. The Risks and Rewards of Criminal Activity: A Comprehensive Test of Criminal Deterrence. *J. Lab. Econ.*, Part 1, July 1986, *4*(3), pp. 317–40. **[G: U.S.]**

Viscusi, W. Kip. The Structure and Enforcement of Job Safety Regulation. *Law Contemp. Probl.*, Autumn 1986, *49*(4), pp. 127–50. **[G: U.S.]**

Werden, Gregory J. and Simon, Marilyn J. An Economic Assessment of the Administration's Detrebling Proposal. *Antitrust Bull.*, Winter 1986, *31*(4), pp. 935–54. **[G: U.S.]**

Whalley, John. International Aspects of Copyright Legislation in Canada: Economic Analysis of Policy Options. **In** *Palmer, J., ed.*, 1986, pp. 273–83. **[G: Canada]**

Wiles, Peter. Political and Moral Aspects of the Two Economies. **In** *Höhmann, H.-H.; Nove, A. and Vogel, H., eds.*, 1986, pp. 198–213. **[G: U.S.S.R.]**

Wilner, Gabriel M. An International Legal Framework for the Transfer of Technology. **In** *McIntyre, J. R. and Papp, D. S., eds.*, 1986, pp. 53–60.

Witt, Ulrich. Evolution and Stability of Cooperation without Enforceable Contracts. *Kyklos*, 1986, *39*(2), pp. 245–66.

Witte, Ann D. The Underground Economy in the United States and Western Europe. **In** *Lindholm, R. W., ed.*, 1986, pp. 204–29. **[G: U.S.; W. Europe]**

Wittman, Donald. The Price of Negligence under Differing Liability Rules. *J. Law Econ.*, April 1986, *29*(1), pp. 151–63. **[G: U.S.]**

Yaniv, Gideon. Fraudulent Collection of Unemployment Benefits: A Theoretical Analysis with Reference to Income Tax Evasion. *J. Public Econ.*, August 1986, *30*(3), pp. 369–83.

Yarbrough, Marilyn V. Disparate Impact, Disparate Treatment, and the Displaced Homemaker. *Law Contemp. Probl.*, Autumn 1986, *49*(4), pp. 107–26. **[G: U.S.]**

Zilberfarb, Ben-Zion. Estimates of the Underground Economy in the United States, 1930–80: A Comment. *Int. Monet. Fund Staff Pap.*, December 1986, *33*(4), pp. 790–98. **[G: Selected Countries; U.S.]**

917 Economics of Minorities; Economics of Discrimination

9170 Economics of Minorities; Economics of Discrimination

Abbott, Michael G. Labour Economics Research of the Macdonald Commission: A Review of Volumes 17 and 18. *Can. Public Policy,* December 1986, *12*(4), pp. 628–39. **[G: Canada]**

Abedian, Iraj. Economic Obstacles to Black Advancement. **In** *Smollan, R., ed.,* 1986, pp. 81–97. **[G: S. Africa]**

Acharya, Meena. Changing Division of Labor and Participation. **In** *Björkman, J. W., ed.,* 1986, pp. 128–40. **[G: India; S. Asia]**

Adams, John and Paul, Linda. The Informal Sector in India: Work, Gender, and Technology. **In** *Björkman, J. W., ed.,* 1986, pp. 33–52. **[G: India]**

Agócs, Carol. Affirmative Action, Canadian Style: A Reconnaissance. *Can. Public Policy,* March 1986, *12*(1), pp. 148–62. **[G: Canada]**

Ahmad, Nigar. Changes in Female Roles in Pakistan: Are the Volume and Pace Adequate? Comments. *Pakistan Devel. Rev.,* Autumn 1986, *25*(3), pp. 364–66. **[G: Pakistan]**

Albelda, Randy P. Occupational Segregation by Race and Gender, 1958–1981. *Ind. Lab. Relat. Rev.,* April 1986, *39*(3), pp. 404–11. **[G: U.S.]**

Alston, Lee J. Race Etiquette in the South: The Role of Tenancy. **In** *Uselding, P., ed.,* 1986, pp. 199–211. **[G: U.S.]**

Amir, Shmuel. Educational Structure and Wage Differentials of the Labor Force in the 1970s. **In** *Ben-Porath, Y., ed.,* 1986, pp. 137–52. **[G: Israel]**

Anderson, Patricia. Conclusion: Women in the Caribbean. *Soc. Econ. Stud.,* June 1986, *35*(2), pp. 291–337. **[G: Caribbean]**

Ando, Faith H. An Analysis of the Formation and Failure Rates of Minority-Owned Firms. *Rev. Black Polit. Econ.,* Fall 1986, *15*(2), pp. 51–71. **[G: U.S.]**

Ashenfelter, Orley and Hannan, Timothy. Sex Discrimination and Product Market Competition: The Case of the Banking Industry. *Quart. J. Econ.,* February 1986, *101*(1), pp. 149–73. **[G: U.S.]**

Ballen, John and Freeman, Richard B. Transitions between Employment and Nonemployment. **In** *Freeman, R. B. and Holzer, H. J., eds.,* 1986, pp. 75–112. **[G: U.S.]**

Barrett, Nancy S. Obstacles to Economic Parity for Women. **In** *Reynolds, L. G.; Masters, S. H. and Moser, C. H., eds.,* 1986, *1982,* pp. 238–44. **[G: U.S.]**

Barrow, Christine. Finding the Support: A Study of Strategies for Survival. *Soc. Econ. Stud.,* June 1986, *35*(2), pp. 131–76. **[G: Barbados]**

Bates, Timothy. Characteristics of Minorities Who Are Entering Self-Employment. *Rev. Black Polit. Econ.,* Fall 1986, *15*(2), pp. 31–49. **[G: U.S.]**

Becker, William E. and Williams, Arlington W. Assessing Personnel Practices in Higher Education: A Case Study in the Hiring of Female. *Econ. Educ. Rev.,* 1986, *5*(3), pp. 265–72.

Ben-Porath, Yoram. Diversity in Population and in the Labor Force. **In** *Ben-Porath, Y., ed.,* 1986, pp. 153–70. **[G: Israel]**

Bianchi, Suzanne M. and Rytina, Nancy. The Decline in Occupational Sex Segregation during the 1970s: Census and CPS Comparisons. *Demography,* February 1986, *23*(1), pp. 79–86. **[G: U.S.]**

Bielby, William T. and Baron, James N. Sex Segregation within Occupations. *Amer. Econ. Rev.,* May 1986, *76*(2), pp. 43–47. **[G: U.S.]**

Björkman, James Warner. Themes, Schemes, and Dreams: An Introduction to the Changing Division of Labor in South Asia. **In** *Björkman, J. W., ed.,* 1986, pp. 1–16. **[G: S. Asia]**

Blackaby, David H. An Analysis of the Male Racial Earnings Differential in the UK, Using the General Household Survey. *Appl. Econ.,* November 1986, *18*(11), pp. 1233–42. **[G: U.K.]**

Borjas, George J. The Demographic Determinants of the Demand for Black Labor. **In** *Freeman, R. B. and Holzer, H. J., eds.,* 1986, pp. 191–230. **[G: U.S.]**

Bouillaguet-Bernard, Patricia and Gauvin, Annie. Le travail des femmes dans la crise en France. (Women's Work throughout the Crisis in France. With English summary.) *Écon. Soc.,* April 1986, *20*(4), pp. 105–40. **[G: France]**

Boulding, Kenneth E. Toward a Theory of Discrimination. **In** *Reynolds, L. G.; Masters, S. H. and Moser, C. H., eds.,* 1986, *1976,* pp. 199–204.

Bound, John. NBER-Mathematica Survey of Inner-city Black Youth: An Analysis of the Undercount of Older Youths. **In** *Freeman, R. B. and Holzer, H. J., eds.,* 1986, pp. 443–59. **[G: U.S.]**

Bound, John; Griliches, Zvi and Hall, Bronwyn H. Wages, Schooling and IQ of Brothers and Sisters: Do the Family Factors Differ? *Int. Econ. Rev.,* February 1986, *27*(1), pp. 77–105. **[G: U.S.]**

Bradbury, Katharine L. and Browne, Lynn E. Black Men in the Labor Market. *New Eng. Econ. Rev.,* Mar./Apr. 1986, pp. 32–42. **[G: U.S.]**

Brimmer, Andrew F. Trends, Prospects, and Strategies for Black Economic Progress. *Rev. Black Polit. Econ.,* Spring 1986, *14*(4), pp. 91–97. **[G: U.S.]**

Brooks, Thornton H.; McGinn, M. Daniel and Cary, William P. H. Second Generation Problems Facing Employers in Employment Discrimination Cases: Continuing Violations, Pendent State Claims, and Double Attorneys' Fees. *Law Contemp. Probl.,* Autumn 1986, *49*(4), pp. 24–51. **[G: U.S.]**

Brown, Charles. Do Better Jobs Make Better Workers? Absenteeism from Work among Inner-city Black Youths: Comment. **In** *Freeman,*

R. B. and Holzer, H. J., eds., 1986, pp. 295–98. **[G: U.S.]**

Brown, Edwin L. "...to Make a Man Feel Good": John Henry Mealing, Railroad Caller. *Labor Hist.*, Spring 1986, *27*(2), pp. 257–64. **[G: U.S.]**

Brown, Lorenzo. Why Should Black-Owned Businesses Hire Predominately Black Labor Forces? *Rev. Black Polit. Econ.*, Fall 1986, *15*(2), pp. 113–21. **[G: U.S.]**

Brown, Martin and Philips, Peter. Competition, Racism, and Hiring Practices among California Manufacturers, 1860–1882. *Ind. Lab. Relat. Rev.*, October 1986, *40*(1), pp. 61–74. **[G: U.S.]**

Brown, Martin and Philips, Peter. The Historical Origin of Job Ladders in the U.S. Canning Industry and Their Effects on the Gender Division of Labour. *Cambridge J. Econ.*, June 1986, *10*(2), pp. 129–45. **[G: U.S.]**

Buchanan, James M. Justice and Equal Treatment. **In** *Buchanan, J. M.*, 1986, *1983*, pp. 140–58.

Burbridge, Lynn C. Changes in Equal Employment Enforcement: What Enforcement Statistics Tell Us. *Rev. Black Polit. Econ.*, Summer 1986, *15*(1), pp. 71–80. **[G: U.S.]**

Buss, Emily. Getting Beyond Discrimination: A Regulatory Solution to the Problem of Fetal Hazards in the Workplace. *Yale Law J.*, January 1986, *95*(3), pp. 577–98. **[G: U.S.]**

Buvinić, Mayra. Projects for Women in Third World: Explaining Their Misbehavior. *World Devel.*, May 1986, *14*(5), pp. 653–64. **[G: LDCs]**

Bysiewicz, Shirley Raissi and Shelley, Louise I. Women in the Soviet Economy: Proclamations and Practice. **In** *Ioffe, O. S. and Janis, M. W., eds.*, 1986, pp. 57–77. **[G: U.S.S.R.]**

Cain, Glen G. The Economic Analysis of Labor Market Discrimination: A Survey. **In** *Ashenfelter, O. and Layard, R., eds., Vol. 1*, 1986, pp. 693–785. **[G: U.S.]**

Cameron, Trudy Ann. Some Reflections on Comparable Worth. *Contemp. Policy Issues*, April 1986, *4*(2), pp. 33–39. **[G: U.S.]**

Campbell, Duncan C. U.S. Firms and Black Labor in South Africa: Creating a Structure for Change. *J. Lab. Res.*, Winter 1986, *7*(1), pp. 1–18. **[G: S. Africa]**

Carson, Emmett D. The Black Underclass Concept: Self-Help vs. Government Intervention. *Amer. Econ. Rev.*, May 1986, *76*(2), pp. 347–50. **[G: U.S.]**

Carter, Susan B. Occupational Segregation, Teachers' Wages, and American Economic Growth. *J. Econ. Hist.*, June 1986, *46*(2), pp. 373–83. **[G: U.S.]**

Chamberlain, Gary. Transitions between Employment and Nonemployment: Comment. **In** *Freeman, R. B. and Holzer, H. J., eds.*, 1986, pp. 113–14. **[G: U.S.]**

Chambers, Julius L. and Goldstein, Barry. Title VII: The Continuing Challenge of Establishing Fair Employment Practices. *Law Contemp. Probl.*, Autumn 1986, *49*(4), pp. 9–23. **[G: U.S.]**

Chapman, Bruce J. and Prior, Heather. Sex Differences in Labour Turnover in the Australian Public Service. *Econ. Rec.*, December 1986, *62*(179), pp. 497–505. **[G: Australia]**

Charoux, Eric. The Identification of Black Management Potential. **In** *Smollan, R., ed.*, 1986, pp. 178–88. **[G: S. Africa]**

Chen, Gavin M. Minority Business Development: An International Comparison. *Rev. Black Polit. Econ.*, Fall 1986, *15*(2), pp. 93–111. **[G: W. Europe; U.S.; Canada]**

Chevillard, Nicole and Leconte, Sébastien. Slavery and Women. **In** *Coontz, S. and Henderson, P., eds.*, 1986, pp. 156–68. **[G: Africa]**

Chevillard, Nicole and Leconte, Sébastien. The Dawn of Lineage Societies: The Origin of Women's Oppression. **In** *Coontz, S. and Henderson, P., eds.*, 1986, pp. 76–107. **[G: Africa]**

Christovich, Leslie and Stallworth, Lamont E. The Equal Employment Opportunity Act and Its Administration: The Claimant's Perspective. **In** *Dennis, B. D., ed.*, 1986, pp. 472–77. **[G: U.S.]**

Cole, John A. and Reuben, Lucy J. Linkages between Minority Business Characteristics an Minority Banks' Locations. *Rev. Black Polit. Econ.*, Fall 1986, *15*(2), pp. 73–92. **[G: U.S.]**

Collignon, Frederick C. The Role of Reasonable Accommodation in Employing Disabled Persons in Private Industry. **In** *Berkowitz, M. and Hill, M. A., eds.*, 1986, pp. 196–241. **[G: U.S.]**

Coontz, Stephanie and Henderson, Peta. Property Forms, Political Power, and Female Labour in the Origins of Class and State Societies. **In** *Coontz, S. and Henderson, P., eds.*, 1986, pp. 108–55.

Culp, Jerome McCristal, Jr. Federal Courts and the Enforcement of Title VII. *Amer. Econ. Rev.*, May 1986, *76*(2), pp. 355–58. **[G: U.S.]**

Culp, Jerome McCristal, Jr. and Dunson, Bruce H. Brothers of a Different Color: A Preliminary Look at Employer Treatment of White and Black Youth. **In** *Freeman, R. B. and Holzer, H. J., eds.*, 1986, pp. 233–59. **[G: U.S.]**

Curtis, Fred. Class, Race, and Income Distribution: Analyzing "White South Africa." **In** *Zarembka, P., ed.*, 1986, pp. 33–67. **[G: S. Africa]**

Curtis, Fred. Understanding the Current Crisis in South Africa—Class, Race and Marxist Analysis: A Review Essay. *Rev. Radical Polit. Econ.*, Winter 1986, *18*(4), pp. 109–19. **[G: S. Africa]**

Datcher-Loury, Linda. Racial Differences in the Stability of High Earnings among Young Men. *J. Lab. Econ.*, Part 1, July 1986, *4*(3), pp. 301–16. **[G: U.S.]**

Datcher-Loury, Linda and Loury, Glenn C. The Effects of Attitudes and Aspirations on the Labor Supply of Young Men. **In** *Freeman,*

R. B. and Holzer, H. J., eds., 1986, pp. 377–99. **[G: U.S.]**

Davis, Carlton G., et al. Effects of Food Stamp Program Participation and Other Sociodemographic Characteristics on Food Expenditure Patterns of Elderly Minority Households. *Rev. Black Polit. Econ.*, Summer 1986, *15*(1), pp. 3–25. **[G: U.S.]**

DeFreitas, Gregory. A Time-Series Analysis of Hispanic Unemployment. *J. Human Res.*, Winter 1986, *21*(1), pp. 24–43. **[G: U.S.]**

Deshpande, Rohit; Hoyer, Wayne D. and Donthu, Naveen. The Intensity of Ethnic Affiliation: A Study of the Sociology of Hispanic Consumption. *J. Cons. Res.*, September 1986, *13*(2), pp. 214–20. **[G: U.S.]**

Dex, Shirley. Earnings Differentials of Second Generation West Indian and White School Leavers in Britain. *Manchester Sch. Econ. Soc. Stud.*, June 1986, *54*(2), pp. 162–79. **[G: U.K.]**

Donckels, Rik and Degadt, Jan. Women in Small Business: The Belgian Experience. **In** *Donckels, R. and Meijer, J. N., eds.*, 1986, pp. 45–64. **[G: Belgium]**

Donckels, Rik and Meijer, Jane N. Women in Small Business: Focus on Europe: Introduction. **In** *Donckels, R. and Meijer, J. N., eds.*, 1986, pp. 1–9.

Dussault, Ginette. Valeurs sociales, ségrégation professionnelle et discrimination. (Social Values, Occupational Segregation and Discrimination. With English summary.) *Écon. Soc.*, April 1986, *20*(4), pp. 141–64. **[G: France]**

Eagan, Vince. Notes on Implicit Contracts and the Racial Unemployment Differential. *Rev. Black Polit. Econ.*, Summer 1986, *15*(1), pp. 81–91. **[G: U.S.]**

Ehrenberg, Ronald G. Black Youth Nonemployment: Duration and Job Search: Comment. **In** *Freeman, R. B. and Holzer, H. J., eds.*, 1986, pp. 70–73. **[G: U.S.]**

Ehrenberg, Ronald G. Workers' Rights: Rethinking Protective Labor Legislation. **In** *Ehrenberg, R. G., ed., Pt. B*, 1986, pp. 285–317. **[G: U.S.]**

Eisinger, Peter. Local Civil Service Employment and Black Socioeconomic Mobility. *Soc. Sci. Quart.*, March 1986, *67*(1), pp. 169–75. **[G: U.S.]**

Ellwood, David T. The Spatial Mismatch Hypothesis: Are There Teenage Jobs Missing in the Ghetto? **In** *Freeman, R. B. and Holzer, H. J., eds.*, 1986, pp. 147–85. **[G: U.S.]**

Epstein, T. Scarlett. Cracks in the Wall: Changing Gender Roles in Rural South Asia. **In** *Björkman, J. W., ed.*, 1986, pp. 17–32. **[G: S. Asia]**

Esser, Hartmut. Ethnic Segmentation as the Unintended Result of Intentional Action. **In** *[Rapoport, A.]*, 1986, pp. 281–96.

Etheredge, Dennis. The Role of the Private Sector in Education and Training. **In** *Smollan, R., ed.*, 1986, pp. 138–44. **[G: S. Africa]**

Extejt, Marian M. Contributed Papers: Organizational Behavior and Personnel: Discussion. **In** *Dennis, B. D., ed.*, 1986, pp. 108–11.

Ferber, Marianne A. What Is the Worth of "Comparable Worth"? *J. Econ. Educ.*, Fall 1986, *17*(4), pp. 267–82. **[G: U.S.]**

Ferber, Marianne A.; Green, Carole A. and Spaeth, Joe L. Work Power and Earnings of Women and Men. *Amer. Econ. Rev.*, May 1986, *76*(2), pp. 53–56. **[G: U.S.]**

Ferguson, Ronald and Filer, Randall K. Do Better Jobs Make Better Workers? Absenteeism from Work among Inner-city Black Youths. **In** *Freeman, R. B. and Holzer, H. J., eds.*, 1986, pp. 261–95. **[G: U.S.]**

Fiorito, Jack and Greer, Charles R. Gender Differences in Union Membership, Preferences, and Beliefs. *J. Lab. Res.*, Spring 1986, *7*(2), pp. 145–64. **[G: U.S.]**

Folbre, Nancy. Hearts and Spades: Paradigms of Household Economics. *World Devel.*, Special Issue, Feb. 1986, *14*(2), pp. 245–55.

Foot, David K. and Li, Jeanne C. Youth Employment in Canada: A Misplaced Priority? *Can. Public Policy*, September 1986, *12*(3), pp. 499–506. **[G: Canada]**

Francois, John. Case Studies of Black Advancement: SA Cyanamid. **In** *Smollan, R., ed.*, 1986, pp. 205–10. **[G: S. Africa]**

Fratoe, Frank A. A Sociological Analysis of Minority Business. *Rev. Black Polit. Econ.*, Fall 1986, *15*(2), pp. 5–29. **[G: U.S.]**

Freeman, Richard B. Who Escapes? The Relation of Churchgoing and Other Background Factors to the Socioeconomic Performance of Black Male Youths from Inner-city Tracts. **In** *Freeman, R. B. and Holzer, H. J., eds.*, 1986, pp. 353–76. **[G: U.S.]**

Freeman, Richard B. and Holzer, Harry J. The Black Youth Employment Crisis: Summary of Findings. **In** *Freeman, R. B. and Holzer, H. J., eds.*, 1986, pp. 3–20. **[G: U.S.]**

Freeman, Richard B. and Holzer, Harry J. Young Blacks and Jobs—What We Now Know. **In** *Reynolds, L. G.; Masters, S. H. and Moser, C. H., eds.*, 1986, *1985*, pp. 128–37. **[G: U.S.]**

Gannicott, Kenneth. Women, Wages, and Discrimination: Some Evidence from Taiwan. *Econ. Develop. Cult. Change*, July 1986, *34*(4), pp. 721–30. **[G: Taiwan]**

Goffee, Robert and Scase, Richard. Women, Business Start-up and Economic Recession. **In** *Donckels, R. and Meijer, J. N., eds.*, 1986, pp. 21–32. **[G: U.K.]**

Goldin, Claudia. Monitoring Costs and Occupational Segregation by Sex: A Historical Analysis. *J. Lab. Econ.*, January 1986, *4*(1), pp. 1–27. **[G: U.S.]**

Grimes, Paul W. Occupational Mobility and Racial Equity in the Labor Market. *J. Behav. Econ.*, Spring/Summer 1986, *15*(1/2), pp. 54–69. **[G: U.S.]**

Grofman, Bernard; Migalski, Michael and Noviello, Nicholas. Effects of Multimember Districts on Black Representation in State Legislatures. *Rev. Black Polit. Econ.*, Spring 1986, *14*(4), pp. 64–78. **[G: U.S.]**

Guyer, Jane I. Women's Role in Development. **In** *Berg, R. J. and Whitaker, J. S., eds.*, 1986, pp. 393–421. **[G: Africa]**

Hajba, Sirpa. Male and Female Entrepreneurs: Similarities and Differences. **In** *Donckels, R. and Meijer, J. N., eds.*, 1986, pp. 16–20.

Hamermesh, Daniel S. The Demographic Determinants of the Demand for Black Labor: Comment. **In** *Freeman, R. B. and Holzer, H. J., eds.*, 1986, pp. 230–32. **[G: U.S.]**

Hamilton, Charles V. and Hamilton, Dona C. Social Policies, Civil Rights, and Poverty. **In** *Danziger, S. H. and Weinberg, D. H., eds.*, 1986, pp. 287–311. **[G: U.S.]**

Hartog, Joop and Theeuwes, Jules. Participation and Hours of Work: Two Stages in the Life-Cycle of Married Women. *Europ. Econ. Rev.*, August 1986, *30*(4), pp. 833–57. **[G: Netherlands]**

Hartshorne, Ken. The Role of the State in Education and Training. **In** *Smollan, R., ed.*, 1986, pp. 117–37. **[G: S. Africa]**

Havenga, Richard. The Role of Non-profit Organisations in Education and Training. **In** *Smollan, R., ed.*, 1986, pp. 145–52. **[G: S. Africa]**

Hayghe, Howard V. Military and Civilian Wives: Update on the Labor Force Gap. *Mon. Lab. Rev.*, December 1986, *109*(12), pp. 31–33. **[G: U.S.]**

Hayghe, Howard V. Rise in Mothers' Labor Force Activity Includes Those with Infants. *Mon. Lab. Rev.*, February 1986, *109*(2), pp. 43–45. **[G: U.S.]**

Heneman, Robert L. Contributed Papers: Organizational Behavior and Personnel: Discussion. **In** *Dennis, B. D., ed.*, 1986, pp. 104–07.

Hill, Herbert. Equal Employment Opportunity Act and Its Administration: An Appraisal of the Commission and the Act: Discussion. **In** *Dennis, B. D., ed.*, 1986, pp. 478–85. **[G: U.S.]**

Hinds, Dudley S. and Ordway, Nicholas. The Influence of Race on Rezoning Decisions: Equality of Treatment in Black and White Census Tracts, 1955–1980. *Rev. Black Polit. Econ.*, Spring 1986, *14*(4), pp. 51–63. **[G: U.S.]**

Hodson, Randy and England, Paula. Industrial Structure and Sex Differences in Earnings. *Ind. Relat.*, Winter 1986, *25*(1), pp. 16–32. **[G: U.S.]**

Holmquist, Carin and Sundin, Elisabeth. Female Entrepreneurs: A Newly Discovered Group. **In** *Donckels, R. and Meijer, J. N., eds.*, 1986, pp. 33–44. **[G: Sweden]**

Holzer, Harry J. Are Unemployed Black Youth Income Maximizers? *Southern Econ. J.*, January 1986, *52*(3), pp. 777–84. **[G: U.S.]**

Holzer, Harry J. Black Youth Nonemployment: Duration and Job Search. **In** *Freeman, R. B. and Holzer, H. J., eds.*, 1986, pp. 23–70. **[G: U.S.]**

Holzer, Harry J. Reservation Wages and Their Labor Market Effects for Black and White Male Youth. *J. Human Res.*, Spring 1986, *21*(2), pp. 157–77. **[G: U.S.]**

Hong, Evelyn. Women, Consumers and Development. **In** *Wheelwright, T., ed.*, 1986, pp. 67–87. **[G: Asia]**

Hoyman, Michele. Equal Employment Opportunity Act and Its Administration: An Appraisal of the Commission and the Act: Discussion. **In** *Dennis, B. D., ed.*, 1986, pp. 486–89.

Iams, Howard M. Employment of Retired-Worker Women. *Soc. Sec. Bull.*, March 1986, *49*(3), pp. 5–13. **[G: U.S.]**

Jackson, Peter and Montgomery, Edward. Layoffs, Discharges and Youth Unemployment. **In** *Freeman, R. B. and Holzer, H. J., eds.*, 1986, pp. 115–41. **[G: U.S.]**

Johnsen, Dawn E. The Creation of Fetal Rights: Conflicts with Women's Constitutional Rights to Liberty, Privacy, and Equal Protection. *Yale Law J.*, January 1986, *95*(3), pp. 599–625. **[G: U.S.]**

Johnson, Gary T. Rent Paying Ability and Racial Settlement Patterns: A Review and Analysis of Recent Housing Allowance Evidence. *Amer. J. Econ. Soc.*, January 1986, *45*(1), pp. 17–26. **[G: U.S.]**

Johnson, George and Solon, Gary. Estimates of the Direct Effects of Comparable Worth Policy. *Amer. Econ. Rev.*, December 1986, *76*(5), pp. 1117–25. **[G: U.S.]**

Johnson, William G. The Rehabilitation Act and Discrimination against Handicapped Workers: Does the Cure Fit the Disease? **In** *Berkowitz, M. and Hill, M. A., eds.*, 1986, pp. 242–61. **[G: U.S.]**

Jones, Stuart. The History of Black Involvement in the South African Economy. **In** *Smollan, R., ed.*, 1986, pp. 1–22. **[G: S. Africa]**

Joshi, Heather. Gender Inequality in the Labour Market and the Domestic Division of Labour. **In** *Nolan, P. and Paine, S., eds.*, 1986, pp. 258–69. **[G: U.K.]**

Kadish, Elisa. Discrimination in Employment: A Selective Bibliography. *Law Contemp. Probl.*, Autumn 1986, *49*(4), pp. 211–35. **[G: U.S.]**

Kaempfer, William H. and Lowenberg, Anton D. A Model of the Political Economy of International Investment Sanctions: The Case of South Africa. *Kyklos*, 1986, *39*(3), pp. 377–96. **[G: S. Africa]**

Kahan, Arcadius. Jewish Life in the United States: Perspectives from Economics. **In** *Kahan, A.*, 1986, *1981*, pp. 128–48. **[G: U.S.]**

Kahan, Arcadius. Notes on Jewish Entrepreneurship in Tsarist Russia. **In** *Kahan, A.*, 1986, *1983*, pp. 82–100. **[G: U.S.S.R.]**

Kahan, Arcadius. The First Wave of Jewish Immigration from Eastern Europe to the United States. **In** *Kahan, A.*, 1986, pp. 118–27. **[G: U.S.]**

Kahan, Arcadius. The Soviet Jews. **In** *Kahan, A.*, 1986, pp. 196–205. **[G: U.S.S.R.]**

Kahan, Arcadius. The Urbanization Process of the Jews in Nineteenth-Century Europe. **In** *Kahan, A.*, 1986, pp. 70–81. **[G: Europe]**

Kawashima, Yoko and Tachibanaki, Toshiaki. The Effect of Discrimination and of Industry Segmentation on Japanese Wage Differentials in Relation to Education. *Int. J. Ind. Organ.*,

March 1986, *4*(1), pp. 43–68. **[G: Japan]**

Kelly, Deirdre. St. Lucia's Female Electronics Factory Workers: Key Components in an Export-oriented Industrialization Strategy. *World Devel.*, July 1986, *14*(7), pp. 823–38. **[G: St. Lucia]**

Kemp, Sharon F. How Women's Work Is Perceived: Hunger or Humiliation. **In** *Björkman, J. W., ed.*, 1986, pp. 84–99. **[G: India]**

Kennedy, Charles H. Policies of Redistributional Preference in Pakistan. **In** *Nevitte, N. and Kennedy, C. H., eds.*, 1986, pp. 63–93. **[G: Pakistan]**

King, Allan G.; Lowell, B. Lindsay and Bean, Frank D. The Effects of Hispanic Immigrants on the Earnings of Native Hispanic Americans. *Soc. Sci. Quart.*, December 1986, *67*(4), pp. 673–89. **[G: U.S.]**

Knopff, Rainer. On Proving Discrimination: Statistical Methods and Unfolding Policy Logics. *Can. Public Policy*, December 1986, *12*(4), pp. 573–83. **[G: Canada]**

Laber, Pamela. The U.S. Labor Movement and Working Women: An Alliance for the Future. **In** *Hewlett, S. A.; Ilchman, A. S. and Sweeney, J. J., eds.*, 1986, pp. 179–85. **[G: U.S.]**

Lang, Kevin. A Language Theory of Discrimination. *Quart. J. Econ.*, May 1986, *101*(2), pp. 363–82. **[G: U.S.]**

Lang, Kevin and Ruud, Paul A. Returns to Schooling, Implicit Discount Rates and Black–White Wage Differentials. *Rev. Econ. Statist.*, February 1986, *68*(1), pp. 41–47. **[G: U.S.]**

Lateef, Shahida. Ethnicity in India: Implications for Women. **In** *Björkman, J. W., ed.*, 1986, pp. 100–111.

Laurent, André. The Elimination of Sex Discrimination in Occupational Social Security Schemes in the EEC. *Int. Lab. Rev.*, Nov.-Dec. 1986, *125*(6), pp. 675–83. **[G: EEC]**

Laycock, Douglas. Continuing Violations, Disparate Impact in Compensation, and Other Title VII Issues. *Law Contemp. Probl.*, Autumn 1986, *49*(4), pp. 53–61. **[G: U.S.]**

Laycock, Douglas. Statistical Proof and Theories of Discrimination. *Law Contemp. Probl.*, Autumn 1986, *49*(4), pp. 97–106. **[G: U.S.]**

Lele, Uma. Women and Structural Transformation. *Econ. Develop. Cult. Change*, January 1986, *34*(2), pp. 195–221. **[G: LDCs]**

Leonard, Jonathan S. The Effectiveness of Equal Employment Law and Affirmative Action Regulation. **In** *Ehrenberg, R. G., ed., Pt. B*, 1986, pp. 319–50. **[G: U.S.]**

Leonard, Jonathan S. The Spatial Mismatch Hypothesis: Are There Teenage Jobs Missing in the Ghetto? Comment. **In** *Freeman, R. B. and Holzer, H. J., eds.*, 1986, pp. 185–90. **[G: U.S.]**

Leonard, Jonathan S. What Was Affirmative Action? *Amer. Econ. Rev.*, May 1986, *76*(2), pp. 359–63. **[G: U.S.]**

Lerman, Robert I. Do Welfare Programs Affect the Schooling and Work Patterns of Young Black Men? **In** *Freeman, R. B. and Holzer, H. J., eds.*, 1986, pp. 403–38. **[G: U.S.]**

Lever, Jeffrey. The Trade Unions and Black Advancement. **In** *Smollan, R., ed.*, 1986, pp. 52–70. **[G: S. Africa]**

Lewis, Gregory B. Gender and Promotions: Promotion Chances of White Men and Women in Federal White-Collar Employment. *J. Human Res.*, Summer 1986, *21*(3), pp. 406–19. **[G: U.S.]**

Lewis, Gregory B. and Emmert, Mark A. The Sexual Division of Labor in Federal Employment. *Soc. Sci. Quart.*, March 1986, *67*(1), pp. 143–55. **[G: U.S.]**

Link, Charles R. and Mulligan, James G. The Merits of a Longer School Day. *Econ. Educ. Rev.*, 1986, *5*(4), pp. 373–81. **[G: U.S.]**

Maij-Weggen, Hanja R. H. Actions of the European Parliament in Favour of Women in Small Business. **In** *Donckels, R. and Meijer, J. N., eds.*, 1986, pp. 10–15. **[G: W. Europe]**

Manikyamba, P. The Participatory Predicament: Women in Indian Politics. **In** *Björkman, J. W., ed.*, 1986, pp. 112–27. **[G: India]**

Margo, Robert A. Educational Achievement in Segregated School Systems: The Effects of "Separate-but-Equal." *Amer. Econ. Rev.*, September 1986, *76*(4), pp. 794–801. **[G: U.S.]**

Margo, Robert A. Race and Human Capital: Comment. *Amer. Econ. Rev.*, December 1986, *76*(5), pp. 1221–24. **[G: U.S.]**

Margo, Robert A. Race, Educational Attainment, and the 1940 Census. *J. Econ. Hist.*, March 1986, *46*(1), pp. 189–98. **[G: U.S.]**

Massiah, Joycelin. Establishing a Programme of Women and Development Studies in the University of the West Indies. *Soc. Econ. Stud.*, March 1986, *35*(1), pp. 151–97. **[G: Jamaica]**

Massiah, Joycelin. Postscript: The Utility of WICP Research in Social Policy Formation. *Soc. Econ. Stud.*, September 1986, *35*(3), pp. 157–200.

Massiah, Joycelin. Women in the Caribbean Project: An Overview. *Soc. Econ. Stud.*, June 1986, *35*(2), pp. 1–29.

Massiah, Joycelin. Work in the Lives of Caribbean Women. *Soc. Econ. Stud.*, June 1986, *35*(2), pp. 177–240. **[G: Barbados; Antigua; St. Vincent]**

Matulovich, Michael. Organisational Programmes of Black Advancement: Training Needs and Techniques. **In** *Smollan, R., ed.*, 1986, pp. 189–202. **[G: S. Africa]**

McCormick, Barry. Employment Opportunities, Earnings, and the Journey to Work of Minority Workers in Great Britain. *Econ. J.*, June 1986, *96*(382), pp. 375–97. **[G: U.K.]**

McCormick, Barry. Evidence about the Comparative Earnings of Asian and West Indian Workers in Great Britain. *Scot. J. Polit. Econ.*, May 1986, *33*(2), pp. 97–110. **[G: U.K.]**

McDougall, Gerald S. and Bunce, Harold. Urban Services and the Suburbanization of Blacks. *Soc. Sci. Quart.*, September 1986, *67*(3), pp. 596–603. **[G: U.S.]**

McKenzie, Hermione. The Educational Experiences of Caribbean Women. *Soc. Econ. Stud.*,

September 1986, *35*(3), pp. 65–105. [G: St. Vincent; Antigua; Barbados]

McNally, M. Federal Initiatives for Economic Development of Reservations. *Reg. Stud.*, February 1986, *20*(1), pp. 83–89. [G: U.S.]

McTighe, Michael J. "True Philanthropy" and the Limits of the Female Sphere: Poor Relief and Labor Organizations in Ante-Bellum Cleveland. *Labor Hist.*, Spring 1986, *27*(2), pp. 227–56. [G: U.S.]

Means, Gordon P. Ethnic Preference Policies in Malaysia. **In** *Nevitte, N. and Kennedy, C. H., eds.*, 1986, pp. 95–118. [G: Malaysia]

Medoff, James L. Layoffs, Discharges and Youth Unemployment: Comment. **In** *Freeman, R. B. and Holzer, H. J., eds.*, 1986, pp. 142–43. [G: U.S.]

Medoff, Marshall H. Baseball Attendance and Fan Discrimination. *J. Behav. Econ.*, Spring/Summer 1986, *15*(1/2), pp. 149–55. [G: U.S.]

Megdal, Sharon Bernstein. Comparable Worth: Some Issues for Consideration. *Contemp. Policy Issues*, April 1986, *4*(2), pp. 40–51.

Meijer, Jane N.; Braaksma, Ro M. and van Uxem, Frits W. Contributing Wife: Partner in Business. **In** *Donckels, R. and Meijer, J. N., eds.*, 1986, pp. 65–77. [G: Netherlands]

Meitzen, Mark E. Differences in Male and Female Job-quitting Behavior. *J. Lab. Econ.*, April 1986, *4*(2), pp. 151–67. [G: U.S.]

Michael, Robert T. and Tuma, Nancy. [Erratum] Entry into Marriage and Parenthood by Young Men and Women. *Demography,* August 1986, *23*(3), pp. 289. [G: U.S.]

Michie, Barry H. Problematics of Technology and Social Change. **In** *Björkman, J. W., ed.*, 1986, pp. 69–83. [G: S. Asia]

Mikhailuk, V. Ways of Increasing the Social Effectiveness of Women's Labor. *Prob. Econ.*, January 1986, *28*(9), pp. 62–72. [G: U.S.S.R.]

Miller, Dennis D. Is It Height of Sex Discrimination? *Challenge,* Sept./Oct. 1986, *29*(4), pp. 59–61. [G: U.S.]

Miller, Paul W. Unemployment Patterns in the Youth Labour Market. *Australian Econ. Pap.*, December 1986, *25*(47), pp. 222–35. [G: Australia]

Milne, R. S. Ethnic Aspects of Privatization in Malaysia. **In** *Nevitte, N. and Kennedy, C. H., eds.*, 1986, pp. 119–34. [G: Malaysia]

Moerdyk, Alwyn. Planning and Implementing a Black Advancement Programme. **In** *Smollan, R., ed.*, 1986, pp. 155–77. [G: S. Africa]

Mohtadi, Hamid. Rural Stratification, Rural to Urban Migration, and Urban Inequality: Evidence from Iran. *World Devel.*, June 1986, *14*(6), pp. 713–25. [G: Iran]

Moulton, Brent R. Human Capital Accumulation and Trends in the Male–Female Wage Gap in the United States, 1956–1983. *Eastern Econ. J.*, July-Sept. 1986, *12*(3), pp. 265–71. [G: U.S.]

Myers, Samuel L., Jr. Do Welfare Programs Affect the Schooling and Work Patterns of Young Black Men? Comment. **In** *Freeman, R. B. and Holzer, H. J., eds.*, 1986, pp. 438–41. [G: U.S.]

Nevitte, Neil and Kennedy, Charles H. The Analysis of Policies of Ethnic Preference in Developing States. **In** *Nevitte, N. and Kennedy, C. H., eds.*, 1986, pp. 1–13.

Newman, Winn and Owens, Christine L. Wage Discrimination: A Family Issue. **In** *Hewlett, S. A.; Ilchman, A. S. and Sweeney, J. J., eds.*, 1986, pp. 161–68. [G: U.S.]

Nord, Stephen. An Analysis of the Effects of Higher Education on Wage Differentials between Blacks and Whites by Gender in the United States. *Appl. Econ.*, February 1986, *18*(2), pp. 173–89. [G: U.S.]

Norris, Barbara A. Multiple Regression Analysis in Title VII Cases: A Structural Approach to Attacks of "Missing Factors" and "Pre-act Discrimination." *Law Contemp. Probl.*, Autumn 1986, *49*(4), pp. 63–96. [G: U.S.]

O'Neill, June. Issues Surrounding Comparable Worth: Introduction. *Contemp. Policy Issues,* April 1986, *4*(2), pp. 1–3. [G: U.S.]

Oberst, Robert. Policies of Ethnic Preference in Sri Lanka. **In** *Nevitte, N. and Kennedy, C. H., eds.*, 1986, pp. 135–54. [G: Sri Lanka]

Odie-Ali, Stella. Women in Agriculture: The Case of Guyana. *Soc. Econ. Stud.*, June 1986, *35*(2), pp. 241–89. [G: Guyana]

Ohsfeldt, Robert L. and Culler, Steven D. Differences in Income between Male and Female Physicians. *J. Health Econ.*, December 1986, *5*(4), pp. 335–46. [G: U.S.]

Oi, Walter Y. Neglected Women and Other Implications of Comparable Worth. *Contemp. Policy Issues,* April 1986, *4*(2), pp. 21–32. [G: U.S.; Japan]

Osborne, R. D. and Cormack, R. J. Unemployment and Religion in Northern Ireland. *Econ. Soc. Rev.*, April 1986, *17*(3), pp. 215–25. [G: Ireland]

Osterman, Paul. Brothers of a Different Color: A Preliminary Look at Employer Treatment of White and Black Youth: Comment. **In** *Freeman, R. B. and Holzer, H. J., eds.*, 1986, pp. 259–60. [G: U.S.]

Parrish, John B. Are Women Taking Over the Professions? *Challenge,* Jan./Feb. 1986, *28*(6), pp. 54–58. [G: U.S.]

Pascoe, Anthony. Case Studies of Black Advancement: Barclays National Bank. **In** *Smollan, R., ed.*, 1986, pp. 211–17. [G: S. Africa]

Piore, Michael J. The Effects of Attitudes and Aspirations on the Labor Supply of Young Men: Comment. **In** *Freeman, R. B. and Holzer, H. J., eds.*, 1986, pp. 399–401. [G: U.S.]

Pirog-Good, Maureen A. Modeling Employment and Crime Relationships. *Soc. Sci. Quart.*, December 1986, *67*(4), pp. 767–84. [G: U.S.]

Prekel, Truida. The Role of Black Women in the Economy. **In** *Smollan, R., ed.*, 1986, pp. 31–51. [G: S. Africa]

Premdas, Ralph R. Politics of Preference in the Caribbean: The Case of Guyana. **In** *Nevitte, N. and Kennedy, C. H., eds.*, 1986, pp. 155–87. [G: Guyana]

Prescott, David; Swidinsky, Robert and Wilton, David A. Labour Supply Estimates for Low-Income Female Heads of Household Using Mincome Data. *Can. J. Econ.*, February 1986, *19*(1), pp. 134–41. **[G: Canada]**

Queripel, John; Richardson, Neville and Moerdyk, Alwyn. Case Studies of Black Advancement: Rand Mines. **In** *Smollan, R., ed.*, 1986, pp. 218–28. **[G: S. Africa]**

Raisian, John; Ward, Michael P. and Welch, Finis. Pay Equity and Comparable Worth. *Contemp. Policy Issues*, April 1986, *4*(2), pp. 4–20. **[G: U.S.]**

Rassuli, Ali and Roy, Raj. Sex Discrimination in the Audiology Profession: It Explains Two-thirds of the $9,500 Difference between Male and Female Earnings. *Amer. J. Econ. Soc.*, April 1986, *45*(2), pp. 189–200. **[G: U.S.]**

Reed, Merl E. Black Workers, Defense Industries, and Federal Agencies in Pennsylvania, 1941–1945. *Labor Hist.*, Summer 1986, *27*(3), pp. 356–84. **[G: U.S.]**

Rees, Albert. An Essay on Youth Joblessness. *J. Econ. Lit.*, June 1986, *24*(2), pp. 613–28. **[G: U.S.]**

Register, Charles A. Racial Employment and Earnings Differentials: The Impact of the Reagan Administration. *Rev. Black Polit. Econ.*, Summer 1986, *15*(1), pp. 59–69. **[G: U.S.]**

Register, Charles A. and Williams, Donald R. Some Evidence on the Impact of State-Level Equal Rights Legislation. *Soc. Sci. Quart.*, December 1986, *67*(4), pp. 869–76. **[G: U.S.]**

Reynolds, Morgan O. On *The Economics of the Colour Bar.* **In** *[Hutt, W. H.]*, 1986, pp. 125–52.

Richards, Craig E. Race and Demographic Trends: The Employment of Minority Teachers in California Public Schools. *Econ. Educ. Rev.*, 1986, *5*(1), pp. 57–64. **[G: U.S.]**

Roback, Jennifer. The Political Economy of Segregation: The Case of Segregated Streetcars. *J. Econ. Hist.*, December 1986, *46*(4), pp. 893–917. **[G: U.S.]**

Robertson, Michael. Legal Obstacles to Black Advancement. **In** *Smollan, R., ed.*, 1986, pp. 104–14. **[G: S. Africa]**

Roca, Maria L. Women Veterans Total 1 Million in First Half of 1986. *Mon. Lab. Rev.*, December 1986, *109*(12), pp. 30–31. **[G: U.S.]**

Rosen, Ellen. Women: Disproportionate Losers in Jobs and Status. **In** *Gondolf, E. W.; Marcus, I. M. and Dougherty, J. P., eds.*, 1986, pp. 143–51. **[G: U.S.]**

Rosenberg, Sam. Racial Differentials in Younger Male Occupational Mobility over the Business Cycle, 1966–1975. **In** *Dennis, B. D., ed.*, 1986, pp. 391–99. **[G: U.S.]**

Rothchild, Donald. State and Ethnicity in Africa: A Policy Perspective. **In** *Nevitte, N. and Kennedy, C. H., eds.*, 1986, pp. 15–61. **[G: Africa]**

Safa, Helen I. Economic Autonomy and Sexual Equality in Caribbean Society. *Soc. Econ. Stud.*, September 1986, *35*(3), pp. 1–21. **[G: Caribbean]**

Salvatore, Ricardo D. Control del trabajo y discriminación: el sistema de contratistas en Mendoza, Argentina, 1880–1920. (With English summary.) *Desarrollo Econ.*, July-Sept. 1986, *26*(102), pp. 229–53. **[G: Argentina]**

Sander, William. Farm Women, Work, and Fertility. *Quart. J. Econ.*, August 1986, *101*(3), pp. 653–57. **[G: U.S.]**

Sathar, Zeba A. Changes in Female Roles in Pakistan: Are the Volume and Pace Adequate? Comments. *Pakistan Devel. Rev.*, Autumn 1986, *25*(3), pp. 367–69. **[G: Pakistan]**

Sav, G. Thomas. The Politics of Race in Higher Education: Governing Boards and Constituents. *Public Choice*, 1986, *48*(2), pp. 147–55. **[G: U.S.]**

Schippers, Joop J. and Siegers, Jacques I. Women's Relative Wage Rate in the Netherlands, 1950–1983: A Test of Alternative Discrimination Theories. *De Economist*, 1986, *134*(2), pp. 165–80. **[G: Netherlands]**

Schlemmer, Lawrence. Organisational and Social Obstacles to Black Advancement. **In** *Smollan, R., ed.*, 1986, pp. 98–103. **[G: S. Africa]**

Schwab, Stewart. Is Statistical Discrimination Efficient? *Amer. Econ. Rev.*, March 1986, *76*(1), pp. 228–34.

Schwartz, Saul. Earnings Capacity and the Trend in Inequality among Black Men. *J. Human Res.*, Winter 1986, *21*(1), pp. 44–63. **[G: U.S.]**

Scott, Alison MacEwen. Women and Industrialisation: Examining the 'Female Marginalisation' Thesis. *J. Devel. Stud.*, July 1986, *22*(4), pp. 649–80. **[G: Peru; Brazil]**

Seeborg, Irmtraud Streker; Seeborg, Michael C. and Zegeye, Abera. Training and Labor Market Outcomes of Disadvantaged Blacks. *Ind. Relat.*, Winter 1986, *25*(1), pp. 33–44. **[G: U.S.]**

Semyonov, Moshe. The Socioeconomic Status of Noncitizen Arab Workers in the Israeli Labor Market: Costs and Benefits. *Soc. Sci. Quart.*, June 1986, *67*(2), pp. 411–18. **[G: Israel]**

Sgro, Pasquale M. Factor Substitution and Discrimination in Labor Markets. *Southern Econ. J.*, April 1986, *52*(4), pp. 1103–14.

Shah, Nasra M. Changes in Female Roles in Pakistan: Are the Volume and Pace Adequate? *Pakistan Devel. Rev.*, Autumn 1986, *25*(3), pp. 339–63. **[G: Pakistan]**

Sloane, Peter J. The Male/Female Earnings Differential in Britain and Europe: Are There Lessons for the United States? **In** *Hewlett, S. A.; Ilchman, A. S. and Sweeney, J. J., eds.*, 1986, pp. 139–60. **[G: U.K.; EEC]**

Smith, Arthur B., Jr. Equal Employment Opportunity Act and Its Administration: A Management Perspective. **In** *Dennis, B. D., ed.*, 1986, pp. 465–71. **[G: U.S.]**

Smith, James P. Race and Human Capital: Reply. *Amer. Econ. Rev.*, December 1986, *76*(5), pp. 1225–29. **[G: U.S.]**

Smuts, Michael. The Growth of Black Business in South Africa. **In** *Smollan, R., ed.*, 1986, pp. 23–30. **[G: S. Africa]**

Snipp, C. Matthew. American Indians and Natural Resource Development: Indigenous Peoples' Land, Now Sought after, Has Produced New Indian–White Problems. *Amer. J. Econ. Soc.*, October 1986, *45*(4), pp. 457–74. **[G: U.S.]**

Snipp, C. Matthew. The Changing Political and Economic Status of the American Indians: From Captive Nations to Internal Colonies. *Amer. J. Econ. Soc.*, April 1986, *45*(2), pp. 145–57. **[G: U.S.]**

Sorensen, Elaine. Implementing Comparable Worth: A Survey of Recent Job Evaluation Studies. *Amer. Econ. Rev.*, May 1986, *76*(2), pp. 364–67. **[G: U.S.]**

Squires, Gregory D. Inequality in Metropolitan Industrial Revenue Bond Programs. *Rev. Black Polit. Econ.*, Spring 1986, *14*(4), pp. 37–50. **[G: U.S.]**

Stanback, Howard. Blacks: Paying the Costs of Economic Change. **In** *Gondolf, E. W.; Marcus, I. M. and Dougherty, J. P., eds.*, 1986, pp. 152–60. **[G: U.S.]**

Stewart, James B. and Hyclak, Thomas J. The Effects of Immigrants, Women, and Teenagers on the Relative Earnings of Black Males. *Rev. Black Polit. Econ.*, Summer 1986, *15*(1), pp. 93–101. **[G: U.S.]**

Stinson, John F., Jr. Moonlighting by Women Jumped to Record Highs. *Mon. Lab. Rev.*, November 1986, *109*(11), pp. 22–25. **[G: U.S.]**

Struyk, Raymond J. and Turner, Margery A. Exploring the Effects of Racial Preferences on Urban Housing Markets. *J. Urban Econ.*, March 1986, *19*(2), pp. 131–47. **[G: U.S.]**

Sweeney, John J. Collective Bargaining's Role in the Determination of Family Policy. **In** *Hewlett, S. A.; Ilchman, A. S. and Sweeney, J. J., eds.*, 1986, pp. 17–22. **[G: U.S.]**

Theilmann, John and Wilhite, Allen. Differences in Campaign Funds: A Racial Explanation. *Rev. Black Polit. Econ.*, Summer 1986, *15*(1), pp. 45–58. **[G: U.S.]**

Thembela, Alex. Educational Obstacles to Black Advancement. **In** *Smollan, R., ed.*, 1986, pp. 73–80. **[G: S. Africa]**

Thompson, James W. and Cataldo, James. Market Incentives for Criminal Behavior: Comment. **In** *Freeman, R. B. and Holzer, H. J., eds.*, 1986, pp. 347–51. **[G: U.S.]**

Tridimas, G. Effective Demand and the Switch from Direct to Indirect Taxes in South Africa. *S. Afr. J. Econ.*, September 1986, *54*(3), pp. 263–72. **[G: S. Africa]**

Tullock, Gordon. Reasons for Redistribution. **In** *Tullock, G.*, 1986, *1981*, pp. 15–41.

Vedder, Richard, et al. Demonstrating Their Freedom: The Post-emancipation Migration of Black Americans. **In** *Uselding, P., ed.*, 1986, pp. 213–39. **[G: U.S.]**

Virgo, John. Youth Unemployment Issues: Western Europe and the United States. *Rivista Int. Sci. Econ. Com.*, June-July 1986, *33*(6–7), pp. 565–84. **[G: U.S.; W. Europe]**

Viscusi, W. Kip. Market Incentives for Criminal Behavior. **In** *Freeman, R. B. and Holzer, H. J., eds.*, 1986, pp. 301–46. **[G: U.S.]**

Vroman, Wayne. Transfer Payments, Sample Selection, and Male Black–White Earnings Differences. *Amer. Econ. Rev.*, May 1986, *76*(2), pp. 351–54. **[G: U.S.]**

Walker, Juliet E. K. Racism, Slavery, and Free Enterprise: Black Entrepreneurship in the United States before the Civil War. *Bus. Hist. Rev.*, Autumn 1986, *60*(3), pp. 343–82. **[G: U.S.]**

Ward, J. T. Compensation for Maori Land Rights. A Case Study of the Otago Tenths. *New Zealand Econ. Pap.*, 1986, *20*, pp. 3–16. **[G: New Zealand]**

Wellings, Paul and Black, Anthony. Industrial Decentralization under Apartheid: The Relocation of Industry to the South African Periphery. *World Devel.*, January 1986, *14*(1), pp. 1–38. **[G: S. Africa]**

Wesman, Elizabeth C. Labor Unions and Title VII: A Case Study of Organizational Response to Environmental Change. **In** *Dennis, B. D., ed.*, 1986, pp. 92–103. **[G: U.S.]**

Wharton, Clifton R., Jr. The Future of the Black Community: Human Capital, Family Aspirations, and Individual Motivation. *Rev. Black Polit. Econ.*, Spring 1986, *14*(4), pp. 9–16. **[G: U.S.]**

White, Averille. Profiles: Women in the Caribbean Project. *Soc. Econ. Stud.*, June 1986, *35*(2), pp. 59–81. **[G: Barbados; Antigua; St. Vincent]**

Wilhite, Allen and Theilmann, John. Women, Blacks, and PAC Discrimination. *Soc. Sci. Quart.*, June 1986, *67*(2), pp. 283–98. **[G: U.S.]**

Williams, Donald R. and Register, Charles A. Regional Variations in Earnings and the Gender Composition of Employment: Is "Women's Work" Undervalued? *J. Econ. Issues*, December 1986, *20*(4), pp. 1121–34. **[G: U.S.]**

Wilson, William Julius and Neckerman, Kathryn M. Poverty and Family Structure: The Widening Gap between Evidence and Public Policy Issues. **In** *Danziger, S. H. and Weinberg, D. H., eds.*, 1986, pp. 232–59. **[G: U.S.]**

de Wit, G. W. The Politics of Rate Discrimination: An International Perspective. *J. Risk Ins.*, December 1986, *53*(4), pp. 644–61. **[G: Netherlands; U.S.]**

Woods, John. Working Women and Pensions. *Soc. Sec. Bull.*, May 1986, *49*(5), pp. 33–34. **[G: U.S.]**

Woolf, Arthur G. Market Structure and Minority Presence: Black-Owned Firms in Manufacturing. *Rev. Black Polit. Econ.*, Spring 1986, *14*(4), pp. 79–89. **[G: U.S.]**

Yamada, Tadashi and Yamada, Tetsuji. Fertility and Labor Force Participation of Married Women: Empirical Evidence from the 1980 Population Census of Japan. *Quart. Rev. Econ.*

Bus., Summer 1986, *26*(2), pp. 35–46. [G: Japan]

Yarbrough, Marilyn V. Disparate Impact, Disparate Treatment, and the Displaced Homemaker. *Law Contemp. Probl.*, Autumn 1986, *49*(4), pp. 107–26. [G: U.S.]

Yinger, John. Measuring Racial Discrimination with Fair Housing Audits: Caught in the Act. *Amer. Econ. Rev.*, December 1986, *76*(5), pp. 881–93. [G: U.S.]

918 Economics of Aging

9180 Economics of Aging

Béland, Francois. Living Arrangement Preferences among the Quebec Elderly: Findings and Policy Implications. *Can. Public Policy*, March 1986, *12*(1), pp. 175–88. [G: Canada]

Burtless, Gary and Moffitt, Robert. Social Security, Earnings Tests, and Age at Retirement. *Public Finance Quart.*, January 1986, *14*(1), pp. 3–27. [G: U.S.]

Cain, Mead. The Consequences of Reproductive Failure: Dependence, Mobility, and Mortality among the Elderly of Rural South Asia. *Population Stud.*, November 1986, *40*(3), pp. 375–88. [G: Bangladesh]

Davis, Carlton G., et al. Effects of Food Stamp Program Participation and Other Sociodemographic Characteristics on Food Expenditure Patterns of Elderly Minority Households. *Rev. Black Polit. Econ.*, Summer 1986, *15*(1), pp. 3–25. [G: U.S.]

Estes, Carroll L. and Lee, Philip R. Health Problems and Policy Issues of Old Age. **In** *Aiken, L. H. and Mechanic, D., eds.*, 1986, pp. 335–55. [G: U.S.]

Fuchs, Victor R. Though Much Is Taken. **In** *Fuchs, V. R.*, 1986, *1984*, pp. 310–31. [G: U.S.]

Heller, Peter S. and Hemming, Richard. Aging and Social Expenditure in Major Industrial Countries. *Finance Develop.*, December 1986, *23*(4), pp. 18–21. [G: OECD]

Hiltner, John; Smith, Bruce W. and Sullivan, James A. The Utilization of Social and Recreational Services by the Elderly: A Case Study of Northwestern Ohio. *Econ. Geogr.*, July 1986, *62*(3), pp. 232–40. [G: U.S.]

Jacobs, Bruce and Weissert, William G. Helping Protect the Elderly and the Public against the Catastrophic Costs of Long-term Care. *J. Policy Anal. Manage.*, Winter 1986, *5*(2), pp. 378–83. [G: U.S.]

Kieffer, Jarold A. The Older Volunteer Resource. **In** *Inst. Med. and Nat'l Res. Counc., Comm. on an Aging Society*, 1986, pp. 51–72. [G: U.S.]

Lamberton, C. E.; Ellingson, W. D. and Spear, K. R. Factors Determining the Demand for Nursing Home Services. *Quart. Rev. Econ. Bus.*, Winter 1986 , *26*(4), pp. 74–90. [G: U.S.]

Leutz, Walter. Long-term Care for the Elderly: Public Dreams and Private Realities. *Inquiry*, Summer 1986, *23*(2), pp. 134–40.

Maxwell, Nan L. The Effect of Human Capital and Labor Market Segments on Retirement Income: A Policy Analysis. *Soc. Sci. Quart.*, March 1986, *67*(1), pp. 53–68. [G: U.S.]

Moore, Thomas Gale. Social Security in Aging Societies: Comment. *Population Devel. Rev.*, Supp. 1986, *12*, pp. 295.

Myers, George C.; Manton, Kenneth G. and Bacellar, Helena. Sociodemographic Aspects of Future Unpaid Productive Roles. **In** *Inst. Med. and Nat'l Res. Counc., Comm. on an Aging Society*, 1986, pp. 110–47. [G: U.S.]

Price, Dorothy Z. Role of Integrated Decision Theory in Considering Future Food Consumption Patterns of the Elderly. **In** *Capps, O., Jr. and Senauer, B., eds.*, 1986, pp. 149–62. [G: U.S.]

Ransom, Roger L. and Sutch, Richard. The Labor of Older Americans: Retirement of Men on and off the Job, 1870–1937. *J. Econ. Hist.*, March 1986, *46*(1), pp. 1–30. [G: U.S.]

Schrimper, Ronald A. Effects of Increasing Elderly Population on Future Food Demand and Consumption. **In** *Capps, O., Jr. and Senauer, B., eds.*, 1986, pp. 163–76. [G: U.S.]

Sjogren, Jane. Retirement Age Women and Men: Income Sources and Work. *Eastern Econ. J.*, July-Sept. 1986, *12*(3), pp. 283–90. [G: U.S.]

Smeeding, Timothy M. Nonmoney Income and the Elderly: The Case of the 'Tweeners. *J. Policy Anal. Manage.*, Summer 1986, *5*(4), pp. 707–24. [G: U.S.]

Standing, Guy. Labour Flexibility and Older Worker Marginalisation: The Need for a New Strategy. *Int. Lab. Rev.*, May-June 1986, *125*(3), pp. 329–48. [G: EEC]

Torrey, Barbara Boyle and Taeuber, Cynthia M. The Importance of Asset Income among the Elderly. *Rev. Income Wealth*, December 1986, *32*(4), pp. 443–49. [G: U.S.]

Treas, Judith and Logue, Barbara. Economic Development and the Older Population. *Population Devel. Rev.*, December 1986, *12*(4), pp. 645–73.

Tullock, Gordon. Bismarckism. **In** *Lee, D. R., ed.*, 1986, pp. 225–40. [G: U.S.]

Vertrees, James and Manton, Kenneth G. The Complexity of Chronic Disease at Later Ages: Practical Implications for Prospective Payment and Data Collection. *Inquiry*, Summer 1986, *23*(2), pp. 154–65. [G: U.S.]

Weaver, Carolyn L. Social Security in Aging Societies. *Population Devel. Rev.*, Supp. 1986, *12*, pp. 273–94. [G: OECD]

Weisbrod, Burton A. and Schlesinger, Mark. Public, Private, Nonprofit Ownership and the Response to Asymmetric Information: The Case of Nursing Homes. **In** *Rose-Ackerman, S., ed.*, 1986, pp. 133–51. [G: U.S.]

Yarbrough, Marilyn V. Disparate Impact, Disparate Treatment, and the Displaced Homemaker. *Law Contemp. Probl.*, Autumn 1986, *49*(4), pp. 107–26. [G: U.S.]

920 Consumer Economics

921 Consumer Economics; Levels and Standards of Living

9210 General

Abel, Andrew B. The Effect of Annuity Insurance and Savings and Inequality: Comment. *J. Lab. Econ.*, Part 2, July 1986, *4*(3), pp. S208–15.

Altonji, Joseph G. Econometric Approaches to the Specification of Life-Cycle Labour Supply and Commodity Demand Behaviour: Comment. *Econometric Rev.*, 1986, *5*(1), pp. 147–51.

Anderson, Paul F. On Method in Consumer Research: A Critical Relativist Perspective. *J. Cons. Res.*, September 1986, *13*(2), pp. 155–73.

Battalio, Raymond C.; Kagel, John H. and Phillips, Owen R. Optimal Prices and Animal Consumers in Congested Markets. *Econ. Inquiry*, April 1986, *24*(2), pp. 181–93.

Behrman, Jere R.; Pollak, Robert A. and Taubman, Paul. Do Parents Favor Boys? *Int. Econ. Rev.*, February 1986, *27*(1), pp. 33–54. **[G: U.S.]**

Bellante, Don and Saba, Richard P. Human Capital and Life-Cycle Effects on Risk Aversion. *J. Finan. Res.*, Spring 1986, *9*(1), pp. 41–51. **[G: U.S.]**

Blundell, Richard. Econometric Approaches to the Specification of Life-Cycle Labour Supply and Commodity Demand Behaviour: Reply. *Econometric Rev.*, 1986, *5*(1), pp. 163–70.

Blundell, Richard. Econometric Approaches to the Specification of Life-Cycle Labour Supply and Commodity Demand Behaviour. *Econometric Rev.*, 1986, *5*(1), pp. 89–146.

Browning, Martin. Econometric Approaches to the Specification of Life-Cycle Labour Supply and Commodity Demand Behaviour: Comment. *Econometric Rev.*, 1986, *5*(1), pp. 153–58.

Davis, Harry L.; Hoch, Stephen J. and Ragsdale, E. K. Easton. An Anchoring and Adjustment Model of Spousal Predictions. *J. Cons. Res.*, June 1986, *13*(1), pp. 25–37. **[G: U.S.]**

Deaton, Angus S. and Muellbauer, John. On Measuring Child Costs: With Applications to Poor Countries. *J. Polit. Econ.*, August 1986, *94*(4), pp. 720–44. **[G: Sri Lanka; Indonesia]**

Dunson, Bruce H. and Jackson, Peter. The Distributional Aspects of Inflation. *Quart. Rev. Econ. Bus.*, Winter 1986, *26*(4), pp. 62–73.

Eriksson, Erik Anders. Generalized Extreme Value Discrete Choice Demand Models: Existence and Uniqueness of Market Equilibria. *Reg. Sci. Urban Econ.*, November 1986, *16*(4), pp. 547–72.

Farrell, John P. On Polish Disequilibria: Comment [Estimates of the Disequilibria in Poland's Consumer Markets]. *Rev. Econ. Statist.*, May 1986, *68*(2), pp. 355–57. **[G: Poland]**

Feick, Lawrence F.; Hermann, Robert O. and Warland, Rex H. Search for Nutrition Information: A Probit Analysis of the Use of Different Information Sources. *J. Cons. Aff.*, Winter 1986, *20*(2), pp. 173–92. **[G: U.S.]**

Fox, Karl A. An Eco-behavioral Approach to Social Systems Accounting, Time-Allocation Matrices, and Measures of the Quality of Life. In *MacFadyen, A. J. and MacFadyen, H. W., eds.*, 1986, pp. 549–81. **[G: U.S.]**

Fry, Gene R. Heinze. The Economics of Home Solar Water Heating and the Role of Solar Tax Credits. *Land Econ.*, May 1986, *62*(2), pp. 134–44. **[G: U.S.]**

Hartman, Raymond S. and Doane, Michael J. Household Discount Rates Revisited. *Energy J.*, January 1986, *7*(1), pp. 139–48. **[G: U.S.]**

Hodkinson, Steve. Teaching Economics to the 13–16 Age Range: Economics Teaching and Consumer Education. In *Whitehead, D. J., ed.*, 1986, pp. 44–47.

Holstius, Karin. Choice of Retailer in Non-equilibrium Competition. *Liiketaloudellinen Aikak.*, 1986, *35*(3), pp. 175–83. **[G: Finland]**

Kiefer, Nicholas M. Econometric Approaches to the Specification of Life-Cycle Labour Supply and Commodity Demand Behaviour: Comment. *Econometric Rev.*, 1986, *5*(1), pp. 159–62.

de Kobbe, P. Measurement of Malnutrition in the Third World. *J. Agr. Econ.*, September 1986, *37*(3), pp. 405–19. **[G: LDCs]**

Kotlikoff, Laurence J.; Shoven, John B. and Spivak, Avia. The Effect of Annuity Insurance and Savings and Inequality. *J. Lab. Econ.*, Part 2, July 1986, *4*(3), pp. S183–207.

LaFrance, Jeffrey T. The Structure of Constant Elasticity Demand Models. *Amer. J. Agr. Econ.*, August 1986, *68*(3), pp. 543–52.

Lee, Lung-Fei and Pitt, Mark M. Microeconometric Demand Systems with Binding Nonnegativity Constraints: The Dual Approach. *Econometrica*, September 1986, *54*(5), pp. 1237–42.

Leigh, J. Paul. Accounting for Tastes: Correlates of Risk and Time Preferences. *J. Post Keynesian Econ.*, Fall 1986, *9*(1), pp. 17–31.

Levy, Shlomit. Psycho-economic Wellbeing: The Case of Israel. In *MacFadyen, A. J. and MacFadyen, H. W., eds.*, 1986, pp. 585–617. **[G: Israel]**

McCain, Roger A. Game Theory and Cultivation of Taste. *J. Cult. Econ.*, June 1986, *10*(1), pp. 1–16.

McCracken, Grant. Culture and Consumption: A Theoretical Account of the Structure and Movement of the Cultural Meaning of Consumer Goods. *J. Cons. Res.*, June 1986, *13*(1), pp. 71–84. **[G: U.S.]**

Mishan, Ezra J. GNP: Measurement or Mirage? In *Mishan, E. J.*, 1986, *1984*, pp. 108–23.

Moffitt, Robert. The Econometrics of Piecewise-Linear Budget Constraints: A Survey and Exposition of the Maximum Likelihood Method. *J. Bus. Econ. Statist.*, July 1986, *4*(3), pp. 317–28. **[G: U.K.; U.S.; Sweden]**

Morgan, James N. Research on Choices with Alternatives, Related Choices, Related Choosers, and Use of Economic Insights. **In** *Gilad, B. and Kaish, S., eds., Vol. A,* 1986, pp. 127–43.

Neuman, Shoshana. Religious Observance within a Human Capital Framework: Theory and Application. *Appl. Econ.,* November 1986, *18*(11), pp. 1193–1202. **[G: Israel]**

Okochi, Kazuo. Changes in Social Security and Value Orientation. **In** *Hax, H.; Kraus, W. and Tsuchiya, K., eds.,* 1986, pp. 163–72. **[G: Japan]**

Ortmeyer, David L. and Peek, Joe. An Ex Ante View of Household Portfolio Choice: The Role of Expected Capital Gains. *Rev. Econ. Statist.,* May 1986, *68*(2), pp. 207–16. **[G: U.S.]**

Podkaminer, Leon. On Polish Disequilbria: Reply [Estimates of the Disequilibria in Poland's Consumer Markets]. *Rev. Econ. Statist.,* May 1986, *68*(2), pp. 358. **[G: Poland]**

Podkaminer, Leon. Persistent Disequilibrium in Poland's Consumer Markets: Some Hypothetical Explanations. *Comp. Econ. Stud.,* Fall 1986, *28*(3), pp. 1–16. **[G: Poland]**

Quah, Euston. Persistent Problems in Measuring Household Production: Definition, Quantifying Joint Activities and Valuation Issues Are Solvable. *Amer. J. Econ. Soc.,* April 1986, *45*(2), pp. 235–45.

van Raaij, W. Fred. Developments in Consumer Behavior Research. **In** *Gilad, B. and Kaish, S., eds., Vol. A,* 1986, pp. 67–88.

Rosenzweig, Mark R. Program Interventions, Intrahousehold Distribution and the Welfare of Individuals: Modeling Household Behavior. *World Devel.,* Special Issue, Feb. 1986, *14*(2), pp. 233–43. **[G: India; Indonesia; Philippines]**

Rutgaizer, V. and Zhuravlev, S. N. Resources of the Personal Services Sphere. *Prob. Econ.,* November 1986, *29*(7), pp. 20–39. **[G: U.S.S.R.]**

Scitovsky, Tibor. Can Changing Consumer Tastes Save Resources? **In** *Scitovsky, T.,* 1986, *1979,* pp. 117–27. **[G: U.S.; Europe]**

Scitovsky, Tibor. Notes on the Producer Society. **In** *Scitovsky, T.,* 1986, *1972,* pp. 47–69.

Scitovsky, Tibor. The Desire for Excitement in Modern Society. **In** *Scitovsky, T.,* 1986, *1981,* pp. 128–35.

Sellar, Christine; Chavas, Jean-Paul and Stoll, John R. Specification of the Logit Model: The Case of Valuation of Nonmarket Goods. *J. Environ. Econ. Manage.,* December 1986, *13*(4), pp. 382–90. **[G: U.S.]**

Sen, Amartya K. Economic Distance and the Living Standard. **In** *[Patel, S.],* 1986, pp. 63–74. **[G: India; China; Mexico; Sri Lanka; Brazil]**

Shirai, Taishiro. Changes in Social Security and Value Orientation: Comments. **In** *Hax, H.; Kraus, W. and Tsuchiya, K., eds.,* 1986, pp. 172–76. **[G: Japan]**

Shiratori, Rei. The Future of the Welfare State. **In** *Rose, R. and Shiratori, R., eds.,* 1986, pp. 193–206. **[G: OECD]**

Sirgy, M. Joseph. A Quality-of-Life Derived from Maslow's Developmental Perspective: 'Quality' Is Related to Progressive Satisfaction of Hierarchy of Needs, Lower Order and Higher. *Amer. J. Econ. Soc.,* July 1986, *45*(3), pp. 329–42.

Slesnick, Daniel T. Welfare Distributional Change and the Measurement of Social Mobility. *Rev. Econ. Statist.,* November 1986, *68*(4), pp. 586–93. **[G: U.S.]**

Sproles, George B. The Concept of Quality and the Efficiency of Markets: Issues and Comments. *J. Cons. Res.,* June 1986, *13*(1), pp. 146–48. **[G: U.S.]**

Tedford, John R.; Capps, Oral, Jr. and Havlicek, Joseph, Jr. Adult Equivalent Scales Once More—A Developmental Approach. *Amer. J. Agr. Econ.,* May 1986, *68*(2), pp. 322–33. **[G: U.S.]**

Wall, Richard A. Work, Welfare and the Family: An Illustration of the Adaptive Family Economy. **In** *[Laslett, P.],* 1986, pp. 261–94. **[G: U.K.]**

Wärneryd, Karl-Erik. Advertising and Consumer Behavior. **In** *Gilad, B. and Kaish, S., eds., Vol. A,* 1986, pp. 89–126.

Wish, Naomi Bailin. Are We Really Measuring the Quality of Life? Well-being Has Subjective Dimensions as Well as Objective Ones. *Amer. J. Econ. Soc.,* January 1986, *45*(1), pp. 93–99.

Wish, Naomi Bailin. Some Issues about the "Quality" of Sunbelt/Frostbelt Life: Factor Analysis of the Better Data Demonstrates That This Dichotomy Is Hopelessly Biased. *Amer. J. Econ. Soc.,* July 1986, *45*(3), pp. 343–57. **[G: U.S.]**

Ycas, Martynas A. Asset Holdings of the Newly Disabled: Findings from the New Beneficiary Survey. *Soc. Sec. Bull.,* December 1986, *49*(12), pp. 5–12. **[G: U.S.]**

9211 Living Standards, Composition of Overall Expenditures, and Empirical Consumption and Savings Studies

Akhtar, Sajjad. Savings–Income Relationships in Urban Pakistan: Evidence from HIES 1979. *Pakistan J. Appl. Econ.,* Summer 1986, *5*(1), pp. 13–46. **[G: Pakistan]**

Allardt, Erik. The Civic Conception of the Welfare State in Scandinavia. **In** *Rose, R. and Shiratori, R., eds.,* 1986, pp. 107–25. **[G: Scandinavia]**

Ando, Albert. Why Is Japan's Saving Rate So Apparently High? Comment. **In** *Fischer, S., ed.,* 1986, pp. 211–20. **[G: Japan; U.S.]**

Arellano, José Pablo and Marfán, Manuel. Ahorro-inversión y relaciones financieras en la actual crisis económica chilena. (Savings, Investment, and Financial Relations in the Present Chilean Economic Crisis. With English summary.) *Colección Estud. CIEPLAN,* December 1986, (20), pp. 61–93. **[G: Chile]**

Avery, Robert B. and Elliehausen, Gregory E. Financial Characteristics of High-Income Families. *Fed. Res. Bull.,* March 1986, *72*(3), pp. 164–77. **[G: U.S.]**

Avery, Robert B.; Elliehausen, Gregory E. and Gustafson, Thomas A. Pensions and Social Security in Household Portfolios: Evidence from the *1983 Survey of Consumer Finances.* **In** *Adams, F. G. and Wachter, S. M., eds.*, 1986, pp. 127–60. **[G: U.S.]**

Avery, Robert B., et al. The Use of Cash and Transaction Accounts by American Families. *Fed. Res. Bull.*, February 1986, *72*(2), pp. 87–108. **[G: U.S.]**

Bane, Mary Jo and Ellwood, David T. Slipping into and out of Poverty: The Dynamics of Spells. *J. Human Res.*, Winter 1986, *21*(1), pp. 1–23. **[G: U.S.]**

Barrow, Christine. Finding the Support: A Study of Strategies for Survival. *Soc. Econ. Stud.*, June 1986, *35*(2), pp. 131–76. **[G: Barbados]**

Barth, James R.; Iden, George R. and Russek, Frank S. Government Debt, Government Spending, and Private Sector Behavior: Comment. *Amer. Econ. Rev.*, December 1986, *76*(5), pp. 1158–67. **[G: U.S.]**

Basemann, R. L., et al. Correction [On Deviations between Neoclassical and GFT-Based True Cost-of-Living Indexes Derived from the Same Demand Function System]. *J. Econometrics*, July 1986, *32*(2), pp. 293.

Bernheim, B. Douglas; Shleifer, Andrei and Summers, Lawrence H. The Strategic Bequest Motive. *J. Lab. Econ.*, Part 2, July 1986, *4*(3), pp. S151–82. **[G: U.S.]**

Bhalla, Surjit S. and Glewwe, Paul. Growth and Equity in Developing Countries: A Reinterpretation of the Sri Lankan Experience. *World Bank Econ. Rev.*, September 1986, *1*(1), pp. 35–63. **[G: Sri Lanka; LDCs]**

Bhatt, V. V. Resource Mobilization in Developing Countries: Financial Institutions and Policies. **In** *U.N., Dept. of Tech. Co-op. for Devel., Devel. Admin. Div.*, 1986, pp. 99–121. **[G: LDCs]**

Bivens, Gordon E. and Volker, Carol B. A Value-Added Approach to Household Production: The Special Case of Meal Preparation. *J. Cons. Res.*, September 1986, *13*(2), pp. 272–79. **[G: U.S.]**

Boje, Per. The Standard of Living in Scandinavia 1750–1914. *Scand. Econ. Hist. Rev.*, 1986, *34*(2), pp. 73–75. **[G: Scandinavia]**

Boje, Per. The Standard of Living in Denmark 1750–1914. *Scand. Econ. Hist. Rev.*, 1986, *34*(2), pp. 171–79. **[G: Denmark]**

Boskin, Michael J. Theoretical and Empirical Issues in the Measurement, Evaluation, and Interpretation of Postwar U.S. Saving. **In** *Adams, F. G. and Wachter, S. M., eds.*, 1986, pp. 11–43. **[G: U.S.]**

Boss, Alfred. Social Insurance: Incentives and Disincentives to Save and to Work: Comment. **In** *Balassa, B. and Giersch, H., eds.*, 1986, pp. 81–85. **[G: OECD]**

Bourne, Compton. The Propensities to Consume Labour and Property Incomes in the Commonwealth Caribbean. *J. Devel. Stud.*, April 1986, *22*(3), pp. 583–97. **[G: Jamaica; Guyana]**

Bowyer, Linda E.; Thompson, A. Frank and Srinivasan, Venkat. The Ohio Banking Crisis: A Lesson in Consumer Finance. *J. Cons. Aff.*, Winter 1986, *20*(2), pp. 290–99. **[G: U.S.]**

Breuss, Fritz and Wüger, Michael. Consumer Climate Data in Macroeconomic Consumption Functions. *Empirica*, 1986, *13*(1), pp. 27–51. **[G: Austria]**

Briden, George and Zedella, John. Social Security and Household Savings: Comment. *Amer. Econ. Rev.*, March 1986, *76*(1), pp. 286–88.

Bronsard, Camille and Salvas-Bronsard, Lise. Commodity and Asset Demands with and without Quantity Constraints in the Labour Market. *J. Appl. Econometrics*, April 1986, *1*(2), pp. 185–208. **[G: U.S.; Canada]**

Canlas, Dante B. Some Preliminary Evidence on the Short-Run Aggregate Demand Effects of Fiscal Policy. *Philippine Rev. Econ. Bus.*, Mar./June 1986, *23*(1/2), pp. 143–50. **[G: Philippines]**

Cannadine, David. Conspicuous Consumption by the Landed Classes, 1790–1830. **In** *Turner, M., ed.*, 1986, pp. 96–111. **[G: U.K.]**

Carter, R. L.; Chiplin, B. and Lewis, M. K. Personal Saving and Finance. **In** *Carter, R. L.; Chiplin, B. and Lewis, M. K., eds.*, 1986, pp. 1–26. **[G: U.K.]**

Carter, R. L. and Diacon, S. R. Personal Investment Markets. **In** *Carter, R. L.; Chiplin, B. and Lewis, M. K., eds.*, 1986, pp. 196–228. **[G: U.K.]**

Cebula, Richard J. An Exploratory Note on Interstate Living-Cost Differentials. *Rev. Reg. Stud.*, Spring 1986, *16*(2), pp. 58–59.

Chadeau, Ann and Roy, Caroline. Relating Households' Final Consumption to Household Activities: Substitutability or Complementarity between Market and Non-market Production. *Rev. Income Wealth*, December 1986, *32*(4), pp. 387–407. **[G: France]**

Chadha, G. K. The Off-Farm Economic Structure of Agriculturally Growing Regions: A Study of Indian Punjab. **In** *Shand, R. T., ed., Vol. 2*, 1986, pp. 147–75. **[G: India]**

Chandavarkar, Anand G. The Non-institutional Financial Sector in Developing Countries: Macro-economic Implications for Savings Policies. **In** *U.N., Dept. of International Econ. and Social Affairs*, 1986, pp. 81–86. **[G: LDCs]**

Cheema, Aftab Ahmad and Malik, Muhammad Hussain. Income-Specific Inflation Rates in Pakistan. *Pakistan Devel. Rev.*, Spring 1986, *25*(1), pp. 73–84. **[G: Pakistan]**

Darbinian, M. The Population's Demand and Ways of Satisfying It. *Prob. Econ.*, March 1986, *28*(11), pp. 76–91. **[G: U.S.S.R.]**

Deaton, Angus S. Demand Analysis. **In** *Griliches, Z. and Intriligator, M. D., eds.*, 1986, pp. 1767–1839.

Deaton, Angus S. The Role of Consumption in Economic Fluctuations: Comment. **In** *Gordon, R. J., ed.*, 1986, pp. 255–59. **[G: U.S.]**

van Dijk, Jouke and Oosterhaven, J. Regional Impacts of Migrants' Expenditures: An Input–Output/Vacancy-Chain Approach. **In** *Batey, P. W. and Madden, M., eds.*, 1986, pp. 122–47. **[G: Netherlands]**

Douglas, Susan P. Selling in Japan: Consumer Behavior and Distribution as Barriers to Imports: Comment. **In** *Pugel, T. A., ed.*, 1986, pp. 107–13. **[G: U.S.; Japan; W. Germany]**

Fauvel, Yvon. L'Incidence des régimes publics de pensions sur la consommation: une extension du modèle de Feldstein et une évaluation empirique pour le Canada. (The Effect of Public Pension Plans on Consumption. With English summary.) *L'Actual. Econ.*, June 1986, *62*(2), pp. 210–35. **[G: Canada]**

Fischer, Bernhard and Langhammer, Rolf J. Determinanten der Sparkapitalbildung in Entwicklungsländern. (Determinants of Savings Mobilization in Developing Countries. With English summary.) *Konjunkturpolitik*, 1986, *32*(5), pp. 282–307. **[G: LDCs]**

Flowers, Marilyn R. Social Security, Saving, and Our Legacy to the Future. **In** *Lee, D. R., ed.*, 1986, pp. 195–224. **[G: U.S.]**

Fornero, Elsa. Teoria del ciclo vitale del risparmio e assicurazioni di rendita vitalizia: Un'applicazione al caso italiano. (Life Cycle Theory of Savings and Lifetime Annuity Insurance: An Application to the Italian Case. With English summary.) *Giorn. Econ.*, July-Aug. 1986, *45*(7–8), pp. 341–61. **[G: Italy]**

Fournier, Gary M. and Rasmussen, David W. Real Economic Development in the South: The Implications of Regional Cost of Living Differences. *Rev. Reg. Stud.*, Winter 1986, *16*(1), pp. 6–13. **[G: U.S.]**

Foxley R., Juan. Determinantes económicos del ahorro nacional: Chile 1963–1983. (With English summary.) *Cuadernos Econ.*, April 1986, *23*(68), pp. 119–27. **[G: Chile]**

Frick, H. A Note on a Dynamic Adjustment Equation for a Poisson Distributed Lag Model. *Empirical Econ.*, 1986, *11*(1), pp. 65–67.

Gazioğlu, Şaziye. Government Deficits, Consumption and Inflation in Turkey. *METU*, 1986, *13*(1/2), pp. 117–34. **[G: Turkey]**

Glewwe, Paul. The Distribution of Income in Sri Lanka in 1969–70 and 1980–81: A Decomposition Analysis. *J. Devel. Econ.*, December 1986, *24*(2), pp. 255–74. **[G: Sri Lanka]**

Gordon, Roger H. and Slemrod, Joel. An Empirical Examination of Municipal Financial Policy. **In** *Rosen, H. S., ed.*, 1986, pp. 53–78. **[G: U.S.]**

Grebler, Leo. Household Saving in an Era of Financial Turmoil, 1975–1984. *J. Econ. Soc. Meas.*, July 1986, *14*(2), pp. 91–105. **[G: U.S.]**

Guay, Richard and Raynauld, Jacques. L'hypothèse du revenu permanent avec attentes rationnelles: une évaluation économétrique canadienne. (The Rational Expectations–Permanent Income Hypothesis: A Canadian Econometric Evaluation. With English summary.) *L'Actual. Econ.*, March 1986, *62*(1), pp. 43–63. **[G: Canada]**

Hadjimatheou, George. Unemployment and Consumption: A Review of Theory and Evidence. *Brit. Rev. Econ. Issues,* Spring 1986, *8*(18), pp. 51–73. **[G: U.S.]**

Hakim, Leonardo and Wallich, Christine. OECD Deficits, Debt, and Savings Structure and Trends, 1965–81: A Survey of the Evidence. **In** *Lal, D. and Wolf, M., eds.*, 1986, pp. 292–360. **[G: OECD]**

Hall, Jane; Hall, Nellie and Tweedie, Richard. A Longitudinal Study of Health Changes Following the Introduction of Medicare. **In** *Butler, J. R. G. and Doessel, D. P., eds.*, 1986, pp. 81–102. **[G: U.S.]**

Hall, Robert E. The Role of Consumption in Economic Fluctuations. **In** *Gordon, R. J., ed.*, 1986, pp. 237–55. **[G: U.S.]**

Hammer, Jeffrey S. Children and Savings in Less Developed Countries. *J. Devel. Econ.*, September 1986, *23*(1), pp. 107–18. **[G: LDCs]**

Hammer, Jeffrey S. Population Growth and Savings in LDCs: A Survey Article. *World Devel.*, May 1986, *14*(5), pp. 579–91. **[G: LDCs]**

Hanley, Susan B. Standard of Living in Nineteenth-Century Japan: Reply to Yasuba. *J. Econ. Hist.*, March 1986, *46*(1), pp. 225–26. **[G: Japan]**

Hartzenberg, G. M. Errata [The Individual Welfare Function of Income]. *J. Stud. Econ. Econometrics*, November 1986, (26), pp. 1. **[G: Belgium; Netherlands]**

Hartzenberg, G. M. The Individual Welfare Function of Income. *J. Stud. Econ. Econometrics*, August 1986, (25), pp. 51–78. **[G: Netherlands; Belgium]**

Hayashi, Fumio. Why Is Japan's Saving Rate So Apparently High? **In** *Fischer, S., ed.*, 1986, pp. 147–210. **[G: U.S.; Japan]**

Heien, Dale and Nuckton, Carole. A Note on the Savings Rate [National Savings in the U.S.]. *J. Econ. Soc. Meas.*, April 1986, *14*(1), pp. 87–89. **[G: U.S.]**

Heikkinen, Sakari. On Private Consumption and the Standard of Living in Finland, 1860–1912. *Scand. Econ. Hist. Rev.*, 1986, *34*(2), pp. 122–34. **[G: Finland]**

Holt, Charles A. and Sherman, Roger. Quality Uncertainty and Bundling. **In** *Ippolito, P. M. and Scheffman, D. T., eds.*, 1986, pp. 221–50.

Hong, Evelyn. Women, Consumers and Development. **In** *Wheelwright, T., ed.*, 1986, pp. 67–87. **[G: Asia]**

Horioka, Charles Yuji. Why Is Japan's Private Savings Rate So High? *Finance Develop.*, December 1986, *23*(4), pp. 22–25. **[G: Japan]**

Hu, Sheng Cheng. Uncertain Life Span, Risk Aversion, and the Demand for Pension Annuities. *Southern Econ. J.*, April 1986, *52*(4), pp. 933–47.

Hubbard, R. Glenn. Pension Wealth and Individual Saving: Some New Evidence. *J. Money, Credit, Banking*, May 1986, *18*(2), pp. 167–78. **[G: U.S.]**

Ilchman, Alice S. Family and Work: Bridging the Gap: Introduction. **In** *Hewlett, S. A.; Ilchman, A. S. and Sweeney, J. J., eds.*, 1986, pp. 1–6. **[G: U.S.]**

Islam, Iyanatul and Khan, Habibullah. Spatial Patterns of Inequality and Poverty in Indonesia. *Bull. Indonesian Econ. Stud.*, August 1986, *22*(2), pp. 80–102. **[G: Indonesia]**

Iyengar, N. S. and Suryanarayana, M. H. On Growth and Equity in Indian Planning during 1962–62 to 1973–74. *Indian Econ. J.*, Apr.-June 1986, *33*(4), pp. 53–83. **[G: India]**

Janssen, Martin. Social Insurance: Incentives and Disincentives to Save and to Work. **In** *Balassa, B. and Giersch, H., eds.*, 1986, pp. 67–80. **[G: OECD]**

Johnson, David. Consumption, Permanent Income, and Financial Wealth in Canada: Empirical Evidence on the Intertemporal Approach to the Current Account. *Can. J. Econ.*, May 1986, *19*(2), pp. 189–206. **[G: Canada]**

Joshi, Heather. Participation in Paid Work: Evidence from the Women and Employment Survey. **In** *Blundell, R. and Walker, I., eds.*, 1986, pp. 217–42. **[G: U.K.]**

Juster, F. Thomas. Macroeconomic Insights from a Behavioral Perspective. **In** *Gilad, B. and Kaish, S., eds., Vol. B*, 1986, pp. 51–81. **[G: U.S.]**

Kahan, Arcadius. Jewish Life in the United States: Perspectives from Economics. **In** *Kahan, A.*, 1986, *1981*, pp. 128–48. **[G: U.S.]**

Kahan, Arcadius. The Soviet Jews. **In** *Kahan, A.*, 1986, pp. 196–205. **[G: U.S.S.R.]**

Kaneer, Kirk. Distribution of Consumption Examined Using Aggregate Expenditure Shares. *Mon. Lab. Rev.*, April 1986, *109*(4), pp. 50–53. **[G: U.S.]**

Khan, Qaiser M. Poverty and Household Responses in Rural Bangladesh. **In** *Abegaz, B., ed.*, 1986, pp. 55–71. **[G: Bangladesh]**

Kihlstrom, Richard E. Advertising and Consumer Learning: Comments. **In** *Ippolito, P. M. and Scheffman, D. T., eds.*, 1986, pp. 171–76. **[G: U.S.]**

King, Mervyn A. Capital Market "Imperfections" and the Consumption Function. *Scand. J. Econ.*, 1986, *88*(1), pp. 59–80. **[G: U.K.]**

King, Robert G. The Role of Consumption in Economic Fluctuations: Comment. **In** *Gordon, R. J., ed.*, 1986, pp. 259–63. **[G: U.S.]**

Knudsen, Odin K. and Scandizzo, Pasquale L. The Demand for Calories in Developing Countries: Reply. *Amer. J. Agr. Econ.*, February 1986, *68*(1), pp. 180–81. **[G: LDCs]**

Kormendi, Roger C. and Meguire, Philip. Government Debt, Government Spending, and Private Sector Behavior: Reply. *Amer. Econ. Rev.*, December 1986, *76*(5), pp. 1180–87. **[G: U.S.]**

Koskela, Erkki and Virén, Matti. Social Security and Household Saving in an International Cross-section: Some Further Evidence. *Liiketaloudellinen Aikak.*, 1986, *35*(2), pp. 105–11. **[G: OECD]**

Koskela, Erkki and Virén, Matti. Social Security and Household Saving: Reply. *Amer. Econ. Rev.*, March 1986, *76*(1), pp. 289–90.

Koskela, Erkki and Virén, Matti. Testing the Direct Substitutability Hypotheses of Saving. *Appl. Econ.*, February 1986, *18*(2), pp. 143–55. **[G: OECD]**

Kotowitz, Y. and Mathewson, G. Frank. Advertising and Consumer Learning. **In** *Ippolito, P. M. and Scheffman, D. T., eds.*, 1986, pp. 109–34. **[G: U.S.]**

Lefebvre, Bruno and Mouillart, Michel. Logement et épargne des ménages: le modèle Fanie. (Housing Markets and Saving of Households: The Fanie Model. With English summary.) *Revue Écon.*, May 1986, *37*(3), pp. 521–70. **[G: France]**

Leijon, Anna-Greta. The Origins, Progress, and Future of Swedish Family Policy. **In** *Hewlett, S. A.; Ilchman, A. S. and Sweeney, J. J., eds.*, 1986, pp. 31–38. **[G: Sweden]**

Leinweber, Ladislav. Consumption of the Population in the 7th Five-Year Plan Period. *Czech. Econ. Digest.*, December 1986, (8), pp. 40–58. **[G: Czechoslovakia]**

Lelart, Michel. Informal Savings in Africa. **In** *Association of African Central Banks*, 1986, pp. 13–59. **[G: Africa]**

Lerman, Paul. The Effect of Marginal Tax Rates on the Advantage of Tax-Sheltered Savings Plans. *J. Cons. Aff.*, Summer 1986, *20*(1), pp. 106–17. **[G: U.S.]**

Lévy-Garboua, Louis. Innovations et diffusion des produits de consommation. (Innovations and the Diffusion of Consumer Goods. With English summary.) *Écon. Appl.*, 1986, *39*(3), pp. 521–82.

Lewbel, Arthur. Additive Separability and Equivalent Scales [Demographic Variables in Demand Analysis]. *Econometrica*, January 1986, *54*(1), pp. 219–22. **[G: U.K.]**

Lindbeck, Assar. Pure Profits as Forced Saving: Comment. *Scand. J. Econ.*, 1986, *88*(1), pp. 131–35. **[G: France]**

Lundberg, Erik. Pure Profits as Forced Saving: Comment. *Scand. J. Econ.*, 1986, *88*(1), pp. 137–40. **[G: France]**

Mackay, Robert J. Comments [Quality Uncertainty and Bundling] [Product Quality, Consumer Information and "Lemons" in Experimental Markets] [An Experimental Study of Warranty Coverage and Dispute Resolution in Competitive Markets]. **In** *Ippolito, P. M. and Scheffman, D. T., eds.*, 1986, pp. 373–74. **[G: U.S.]**

Makin, John H. Savings Rates in Japan and the United States: The Roles of Tax Policy and Other Factors. **In** *Adams, F. G. and Wachter, S. M., eds.*, 1986, pp. 91–126. **[G: OECD]**

Malinvaud, Edmond. Pure Profits as Forced Saving. *Scand. J. Econ.*, 1986, *88*(1), pp. 109–30. **[G: France]**

de Melo, Jaime and Tybout, James. The Effects of Financial Liberalization on Savings and Investment in Uruguay. *Econ. Develop. Cult. Change*, April 1986, *34*(3), pp. 561–87. **[G: Uruguay]**

Mieszkowski, Peter M. An Empirical Examination of Municipal Financial Policy: Comment. **In** *Rosen, H. S., ed.*, 1986, pp. 79–81. **[G: U.S.]**

Miller, Ross M. Comments [Quality Uncertainty and Bundling] [Product Quality, Consumer Information and "Lemons" in Experimental Markets] [An Experimental Study of Warranty

Coverage and Dispute Resolution in Competitive Markets]. **In** *Ippolito, P. M. and Scheffman, D. T., eds.*, 1986, pp. 375–76. **[G: U.S.]**

Modigliani, Franco. Life Cycle, Individual Thrift, and the Wealth of Nations. *Amer. Econ. Rev.*, June 1986, *76*(3), pp. 297–313. **[G: OECD]**

Modigliani, Franco; Jappelli, Tullio and Pagano, M. Errata corrige [The Impact of Fiscal Policy and Inflation on National Saving: The Italian Case]. *Banca Naz. Lavoro Quart. Rev.*, March 1986, (156), pp. 129. **[G: Italy]**

Montgomery, Edward. Where Did All the Saving Go? A Look at the Recent Decline in the Personal Saving Rate. *Econ. Inquiry*, October 1986, *24*(4), pp. 681–97. **[G: U.S.]**

Mujumdar, N. A. and Menon, K. A. Saving and Capital Formation in the Agricultural Sector: A Review. **In** *Dantwala, M. L., et al.*, 1986, pp. 234–69. **[G: India]**

Murphy, Neil B. and Rogers, Ronald C. Life Cycle and the Adoption of Consumer Financial Innovation: An Empirical Study of the Adoption Process. *J. Bank Res.*, Spring 1986, *17*(1), pp. 3–8. **[G: U.S.]**

Myhre, Jan Eivind. Research into Norwegian Living Conditions in the Period 1750–1914. *Scand. Econ. Hist. Rev.*, 1986, *34*(2), pp. 159–66. **[G: Norway]**

Nakhaeizadeh, Gholamreza. The Effects of Various Treatments of Truncation Remainders in the Estimation of the Consumption Function: A Bayesian Approach. *Bull. Econ. Res.*, May 1986, *38*(2), pp. 119–36. **[G: W. Germany]**

Newell, William H. Inheritance on the Maturing Frontier: Butler County, Ohio, 1803–1865. **In** *Engerman, S. L. and Gallman, R. E., eds.*, 1986, pp. 261–97. **[G: U.S.]**

Newell, William H. Inheritance on the Maturing Frontier: Butler County, Ohio, 1803–1865: Reply. **In** *Engerman, S. L. and Gallman, R. E., eds.*, 1986, pp. 300–301. **[G: U.S.]**

Nunnenkamp, Peter. Liberalisierung der Finanzmärkte und Ersparnisbildung in Indonesien. (Liberalization of the Financial Markets and Savings in Indonesia. With English summary.) *Kredit Kapital*, 1986, *19*(3), pp. 417–40. **[G: Indonesia]**

Olsson, Ulf. Recent Research in Sweden on the Standard of Living during the Eighteenth and Nineteenth Centuries. *Scand. Econ. Hist. Rev.*, 1986, *34*(2), pp. 153–58. **[G: Sweden]**

Orlov, Ia. The Role of Industry and Trade in Satisfying the Population's Demand. *Prob. Econ.*, April 1986, *28*(12), pp. 42–58. **[G: U.S.S.R.]**

Oshima, Harry T. Off-Farm Employment and Incomes in Postwar East Asian Growth. **In** *Shand, R. T., ed., Vol. 1*, 1986, pp. 25–74. **[G: Japan; Taiwan; S. Korea]**

Owen, P. Dorian. Wealth-Composition and Cross-Equation Effects in the U.K. Personal Sector's Expenditure and Portfolio Behaviour. *Manchester Sch. Econ. Soc. Stud.*, March 1986, *54*(1), pp. 65–98. **[G: U.K.]**

Owens, Emiel W. Demographic Trends and Saving Propensities "A Revisit with Life Cycle Theory." *Atlantic Econ. J.*, December 1986, *14*(4), pp. 106.

Patterson, K. D. The Stability of Some Annual Consumption Functions. *Oxford Econ. Pap.*, March 1986, *38*(1), pp. 1–30. **[G: U.K.]**

Paul, M. Thomas. Savings Behaviour in India (1951–52 to 1981–82). *Margin*, July 1986, *18*(4), pp. 41–68. **[G: India]**

Pearce, I. F. and Thomas, S. H. Personal Savings and Transactions Balance Changes. *Manchester Sch. Econ. Soc. Stud.*, December 1986, *54*(4), pp. 380–90. **[G: U.K.]**

Peart, Derek. Linking the Formal and Informal Sectors: Introduction of a Partner System in Jamaica. **In** *U.N., Dept. of International Econ. and Social Affairs*, 1986, pp. 113–14. **[G: Jamaica]**

Peek, Joe. Household Wealth Composition: The Impact of Capital Gains. *New Eng. Econ. Rev.*, Nov./Dec. 1986, pp. 26–39. **[G: U.S.]**

Persson, Torsten. Capital Market "Imperfections" and the Consumption Function: Comment. *Scand. J. Econ.*, 1986, *88*(1), pp. 81–83. **[G: U.K.]**

Petschnig, Mária. The Changing Role of Private Savings. *Acta Oecon.*, 1986, *37*(1–2), pp. 103–21. **[G: Hungary]**

Pitelis, Christos N. Corporate Control, Social Choice and Capital Accumulation: An Asymmetrical Choice Approach. *Rev. Radical Polit. Econ.*, Fall 1986, *18*(3), pp. 85–100.

Podkaminer, Leon. The Demand for Calories in Developing Countries: Comment. *Amer. J. Agr. Econ.*, February 1986, *68*(1), pp. 177–79. **[G: LDCs]**

Quah, Euston. Valuing and Measuring Contributions to Family Production: Some Results Using Contingent Evaluation. *Indian J. Quant. Econ.*, 1986, *2*(2), pp. 101–19. **[G: U.S.]**

Rashid, Muhammad and Gandhi, Devinder K. Tax and Savings Implications of the Canadian Registered Retirement Savings Plans. *Financial Rev.*, November 1986, *21*(4), pp. 463–71. **[G: Canada]**

Rasmussen, Poul Nyrup. Hvad har vi Lært? (The Problem of Imbalance and Solutions Based on Concensus in the Society. With English summary.) *Nationaløkon. Tidsskr.*, 1986, *124*(2), pp. 223–33. **[G: Denmark]**

Ray, Ranjan. Demographic Variables and Equivalence Scales in a Flexible Demand System: The Case of AIDS. *Appl. Econ.*, March 1986, *18*(3), pp. 265–78. **[G: U.K.]**

Richardson, J. A Longitudinal Study of Health Changes Following the Introduction of Medicare: Discussion. **In** *Butler, J. R. G. and Doessel, D. P., eds.*, 1986, pp. 103–06. **[G: Australia]**

Romer, Paul M. Why Is Japan's Saving Rate So Apparently High? Comment. **In** *Fischer, S., ed.*, 1986, pp. 220–33. **[G: Japan; U.S.]**

Rosenqvist, Gunnar. Paneldata, stokastiska diskreta valmodeller och märkesval. (Panel Data, Stochastic Discrete Choice Models and Brand Choice. With English summary.) *Ekon.*

Samfundets Tidskr., 1986, *39*(4), pp. 247–53. **[G: Finland]**

Ruggles, Richard and Ruggles, Nancy D. The Integration of Macro and Micro Data for the Household Sector. *Rev. Income Wealth,* September 1986, *32*(3), pp. 245–76. **[G: U.S.]**

Sakellis, M. G. An Empirical Analysis of Savings Behaviour of the Greek Agricultural Households. *Europ. Rev. Agr. Econ.*, 1986, *13*(2), pp. 169–88. **[G: Greece]**

Sandhu, H. S. and Khosla, M. Cross-country Comparison of Household Demand and Savings Patterns—An Application of Extended Linear Expenditure System. *Indian J. Quant. Econ.*, 1986, *2*(1), pp. 67–82. **[G: India; Greece; U.S.]**

Sarma, I. R. K. Does the Saving Behaviour of the Indian Household Sector Conform to the Planners' Expectation? *Margin,* July 1986, *18*(4), pp. 88–94. **[G: India]**

Sato, Kazuo. Economic Laws and the Household Economy in Japan: Lags in Policy Response to Economic Changes. **In** *Saxonhouse, G. R. and Yamamura, K., eds.*, 1986, pp. 3–55. **[G: Japan]**

Schaumann, Alexander. Opsparing og finansieringskanaler. (Private Saving, Pension-Schemes and Channels of Business Financing. With English summary.) *Nationaløkon. Tidsskr.*, 1986, *124*(2), pp. 189–95. **[G: Denmark]**

Scholl, John D. Consumer Expenditures with Respect to Transitory Income. *Atlantic Econ. J.*, March 1986, *14*(1), pp. 126. **[G: U.S.]**

Scitovsky, Tibor. The Economy's Impact on Family and Social Relations in America. **In** *Scitovsky, T.*, 1986, *1984*, pp. 160–82. **[G: U.S.]**

Scitovsky, Tibor. Why the U.S. Saving Rate Is Low—A Conflict between the National Accountant's and the Individual Saver's Perceptions. **In** *[Tarshis, L.]*, 1986, pp. 125–34. **[G: U.S.]**

Seibel, Hans Dieter and Marx, Michael. Mobilization of Personal Savings through Co-operative Societies or Indigenous Savings and Credit Associations: Case Studies from Nigeria. **In** *U.N., Dept. of International Econ. and Social Affairs,* 1986, pp. 107–12. **[G: Nigeria]**

Sharif, Mohammed. The Concept and Measurement of Subsistence: A Survey of the Literature. *World Devel.*, May 1986, *14*(5), pp. 555–77.

Silber, Jacques G. Variability in the Experienced Rates of Inflation and Price Index Linkage to Social Welfare. *Appl. Econ.*, January 1986, *18*(1), pp. 49–58. **[G: Israel]**

Skinner, C. J.; Holmes, D. J. and Smith, T. M. F. The Effect of Sample Design on Principal Component Analysis. *J. Amer. Statist. Assoc.*, September 1986, *81*(395), pp. 789–98. **[G: U.K.]**

Soikkanen, Hannu. Finnish Research on Changes in the Standard of Living. *Scand. Econ. Hist. Rev.*, 1986, *34*(2), pp. 167–70. **[G: Finland]**

Soltow, Lee. Inheritance on the Maturing Frontier: Butler County, Ohio, 1803–1865: Comment. **In** *Engerman, S. L. and Gallman, R. E., eds.*, 1986, pp. 297–300. **[G: U.S.]**

Starck, Christian C. Indexation and Household Saving Behavior: Some Empirical Evidence from Finnish Data. *Weltwirtsch. Arch.*, 1986, *122*(4), pp. 713–27. **[G: Finland]**

Starck, Christian C. Penningmarknadsindexering och hushållens sparande. (Financial Market Indexation and Household Savings Behaviour. With English summary.) *Ekon. Samfundets Tidskr.*, 1986, *39*(4), pp. 229–37. **[G: Finland]**

Stoker, Thomas M. Simple Tests of Distributional Effects on Macroeconomic Equations. *J. Polit. Econ.*, August 1986, *94*(4), pp. 763–95.

Stoker, Thomas M. The Distributional Welfare Effects of Rising Prices in the United States: The 1970's Experience. *Amer. Econ. Rev.*, June 1986, *76*(3), pp. 335–49. **[G: U.S.]**

Tachibanaki, Toshiaki and Shimono, Keiko. Saving and the Life-Cycle: A Cohort Analysis. *J. Public Econ.*, October 1986, *31*(1), pp. 1–24. **[G: Japan]**

Torrey, Barbara Boyle and Taeuber, Cynthia M. The Importance of Asset Income among the Elderly. *Rev. Income Wealth*, December 1986, *32*(4), pp. 443–49. **[G: U.S.]**

von Ungern-Sternberg, Thomas. Inflation and the Consumption Function. *Weltwirtsch. Arch.*, 1986, *122*(4), pp. 741–44. **[G: U.K.]**

V'iugin, O. V. Modeling and Forecasting Household Savings to Take Account of Supply and Demand. *Matekon*, Fall 1986, *23*(1), pp. 64–81. **[G: Hungary; E. Germany; U.S.S.R.; Czechoslovakia]**

Veall, Michael R. and Zimmermann, Klaus F. A Monthly Dynamic Consumer Expenditure System for Germany with Different Kinds of Households. *Rev. Econ. Statist.*, May 1986, *68*(2), pp. 256–64. **[G: W. Germany]**

Venieris, Yiannis P. and Gupta, Dipak K. Income Distribution and Sociopolitical Instability as Determinants of Savings: A Cross-sectional Model. *J. Polit. Econ.*, August 1986, *94*(4), pp. 873–83. **[G: Global]**

Venti, Steven F. and Wise, David A. Tax-Deferred Accounts, Constrained Choice and Estimation of Individual Saving. *Rev. Econ. Stud.*, August 1986, *53*(4), pp. 579–601. **[G: U.S.]**

Wada, Mitsuo. Selling in Japan: Consumer Behavior and Distribution as Barriers to Imports. **In** *Pugel, T. A., ed.*, 1986, pp. 91–105. **[G: U.S.; Japan; W. Germany]**

Weissenberger, Edgar. Consumption Innovations and Income Innovations: The Case of the United Kingdom and Germany. *Rev. Econ. Statist.*, February 1986, *68*(1), pp. 1–8. **[G: U.K.; W. Germany]**

Wood, Charles H. and McCracken, Stephen D. Underdevelopment, Urban Growth and Collective Social Action in Sao Paulo, Brazil. **In** *Abegaz, B., ed.*, 1986, pp. 101–40. **[G: Brazil]**

Wüger, Michael. The Influence of the Personal Income Distribution on Private Demand in Austria. *Empirica*, 1986, *13*(2), pp. 155–72. **[G: Austria]**

Yasuba, Yasukichi. Standard of Living in Japan before Industrialization: From What Level Did Japan Begin? A Comment. *J. Econ. Hist.*, March 1986, *46*(1), pp. 217–24. [G: Japan]

Zelko, Jaroslav. Living Standard and Life Style: Points of Intersection. *Czech. Econ. Digest.*, May 1986, (3), pp. 3–10. [G: Czechoslovakia]

9212 Expenditure Patterns and Consumption of Specific Items

Aczel, Amir D. and Fullam, Timothy J. Time Series Analysis of U.S. Consumption of Motor Gasoline. *Amer. Econ.*, Spring 1986, *30*(1), pp. 21–27. [G: U.S.]

Agthe, Donald E., et al. A Simultaneous Equation Demand Model for Block Rates. *Water Resources Res.*, January 1986, *22*(1), pp. 1–4. [G: U.S.]

Ahtola, Juha; Ekholm, Anders and Somervuori, Antti. Bayes Estimates for the Price and Income Elasticities of Alcoholic Beverages in Finland from 1955 to 1980. *J. Bus. Econ. Statist.*, April 1986, *4*(2), pp. 199–208. [G: Finland]

Aivazian, Varouj A., et al. An Empirical Portfolio Analysis of Financial Asset Substitutability: The Case of the U.S. Household Sector. *Quart. Rev. Econ. Bus.*, Summer 1986, *26*(2), pp. 47–65. [G: U.S.]

Al-Qunaibet, Mohammad H. and Johnston, Richard S. Reply [Municipal Demand for Water in Kuwait: Methodological Issues and Empirical Results]. *Water Resources Res.*, May 1986, *22*(5), pp. 835–36. [G: Kuwait]

Andersen, Ronald M. and Fleming, Gretchen V. Expenditures for Medical Care. **In** *Fleming, G. V. and Andersen, R. M., eds.*, 1986, pp. 94–118. [G: U.S.]

Andrikopoulos, Andreas A. and Brox, James A. The Demand for Deposits and Risk Sensitivity: The Case for Greece, 1955–1980. *Empirical Econ.*, 1986, *11*(4), pp. 197–206. [G: Greece]

Atri, Said and Lahiri, Kajal. Quality Change and the Demand for Hospital Care: An Econometric Reexamination. *Atlantic Econ. J.*, December 1986, *14*(4), pp. 15–23. [G: U.S.]

Baccouche, Rafiq and Laisney, François. Analyse microéconomique de la réforme de la TVA de juillet 1982 en France. (Microeconomic Analysis of the French VAT Reform of July 1982. With English summary.) *Ann. Écon. Statist.*, Apr./June 1986, (2), pp. 37–74. [G: France]

Baltagi, Badi H. and Levin, Dan. Estimating Dynamic Demand for Cigarettes Using Panel Data: The Effects of Bootlegging, Taxation and Advertising Reconsidered. *Rev. Econ. Statist.*, February 1986, *68*(1), pp. 148–55.

Barkai, Haim. The Energy Sector in the 1960s and 1970s. **In** *Ben-Porath, Y., ed.*, 1986, pp. 264–75. [G: Israel]

Baumann, Michael G. and Kalt, Joseph P. Intertemporal Consumer Surplus in Lagged-Adjustment Demand Models: An Application to Natural Gas Pricing. *Energy Econ.*, January 1986, *8*(1), pp. 2–12. [G: U.S.]

Baxter, Lester W., et al. An Efficiency Analysis of Household Energy Use. *Energy Econ.*, April 1986, *8*(2), pp. 62–73. [G: U.S.]

Bean, Charles R. The Estimation of "Surprise" Models and the "Surprise" Consumption Function. *Rev. Econ. Stud.*, August 1986, *53*(4), pp. 497–516. [G: U.S.]

Bird, Peter J. W. N. Econometric Estimation of World Salmon Demand. *Marine Resource Econ.*, 1986, *3*(2), pp. 169–82. [G: OECD]

Bobst, Barry W. Implications for Food Demand of Changes in Competitive State within Marketing Channels. **In** *Capps, O., Jr. and Senauer, B., eds.*, 1986, pp. 269–80. [G: U.S.]

Boehm, Thomas P. and Ihlanfeldt, Keith R. The Improvement Expenditures of Urban Homeowners: An Empirical Analysis. *Amer. Real Estate Urban Econ. Assoc. J.*, Spring 1986, *14*(1), pp. 48–60. [G: U.S.]

Borooah, V. K. and Sharpe, D. R. Aggregate Consumption and the Distribution of Income in the United Kingdom: An Econometric Analysis. *Econ. J.*, June 1986, *96*(382), pp. 449–66. [G: U.K.]

Branson, Robert E., et al. Marketing Implications from the National Consumer Beef Study. *Western J. Agr. Econ.*, July 1986, *11*(1), pp. 82–91. [G: U.S.]

Breuss, Fritz and Wüger, Michael. Consumer Climate Data in Macroeconomic Consumption Functions. *Empirica*, 1986, *13*(1), pp. 27–51. [G: Austria]

Brown, Mark G. and Lee, Jong-Ying. Orange and Grapefruit Juice Demand Forecasts. **In** *Capps, O., Jr. and Senauer, B., eds.*, 1986, pp. 215–32. [G: U.S.]

Bryant, W. Keith. Assets and Debts in a Consumer Portfolio. *J. Cons. Aff.*, Summer 1986, *20*(1), pp. 19–35. [G: U.S.]

Bullock, J. Bruce and Womack, Abner. Changes in Domestic Demand for Food: Impacts on Southern Agriculture: Discussion. *Southern J. Agr. Econ.*, July 1986, *18*(1), pp. 37–39. [G: U.S.]

Buse, Rueben C. Is the Structure of the Demand for Food Changing? Implications for Projections. **In** *Capps, O., Jr. and Senauer, B., eds.*, 1986, pp. 105–29. [G: U.S.]

Capps, Oral, Jr. Changes in Domestic Demand for Food: Impacts on Southern Agriculture. *Southern J. Agr. Econ.*, July 1986, *18*(1), pp. 25–36. [G: U.S.]

Capps, Oral, Jr. and Cheng, Hsiang-Tai. The Missing Income Problem in Analyses of Engel Functions. *Western J. Agr. Econ.*, July 1986, *11*(1), pp. 31–39. [G: U.S.]

Capps, Oral, Jr. and Pearson, Joanne M. Analysis of Convenience and Nonconvenience Food Expenditures by U.S. Households with Projections to the Year 2000. **In** *Capps, O., Jr. and Senauer, B., eds.*, 1986, pp. 233–50. [G: U.S.]

Carroll, Norman V.; Siridhara, Chanaporn and Fincham, Jack E. Perceived Risks and Pharmacists' Generic Substitution Behavior. *J.*

Cons. Aff., Summer 1986, *20*(1), pp. 36–47. **[G: U.S.]**

Caves, Richard E. Information Structures of Product Markets. *Econ. Inquiry*, April 1986, *24*(2), pp. 195–212. **[G: U.S.]**

Chandrakanth, M. G.; Gurumurthy and Satakopan, Usha. A Quantitative Analysis of the Pattern of Consumer Purchases. *Indian Econ. Rev.*, Jan.-June 1986, *21*(1), pp. 71–77. **[G: India]**

Chetty, V. K. and Haliburn, C. Estimation of Price and Income Elasticities of Demand for Food Grains in an Economy with Public Distribution Schemes. *Indian Econ. Rev.*, July-Dec. 1986, *21*(2), pp. 95–114. **[G: India]**

Chicoine, David L.; Deller, Steven C. and Ramamurthy, Ganapathi. Water Demand Estimation under Block Rate Pricing: A Simultaneous Equation Approach. *Water Resources Res.*, June 1986, *22*(6), pp. 859–63. **[G: U.S.]**

Chicoine, David L. and Ramamurthy, Ganapathi. Evidence on the Specification of Price in the Study of Domestic Water Demand. *Land Econ.*, February 1986, *62*(1), pp. 28–32. **[G: U.S.]**

Chowdhury, Nuimuddin. Improved and New Products in Rural Industries: Implications for the Expansion of Demand and Employment. **In** *Islam, R. and Muqtada, M., eds.*, 1986, pp. 169–95. **[G: Bangladesh]**

Collier, Irwin L., Jr. Effective Purchasing Power in a Quantity Constrained Economy: An Estimate for the German Democratic Republic. *Rev. Econ. Statist.*, February 1986, *68*(1), pp. 24–32. **[G: E. Germany]**

Cox, Thomas L. and Wohlgenant, Michael K. Prices and Quality Effects in Cross-sectional Demand Analysis. *Amer. J. Agr. Econ.*, November 1986, *68*(4), pp. 908–19. **[G: U.S.]**

Crutchfield, Stephen R. U.S. Demand for Selected Groundfish Products, 1967–80: Comment. *Amer. J. Agr. Econ.*, November 1986, *68*(4), pp. 1018–20. **[G: U.S.]**

Curry, David J. and Faulds, David J. Indexing Product Quality: Issues, Theory, and Results [The Concept of Quality and the Efficiency of Markets for Consumer Products]. *J. Cons. Res.*, June 1986, *13*(1), pp. 134–45. **[G: U.S.]**

Dahl, Carol A. Gasoline Demand Survey. *Energy J.*, January 1986, *7*(1), pp. 67–82. **[G: U.S.]**

Davis, Carlton G., et al. Effects of Food Stamp Program Participation and Other Sociodemographic Characteristics on Food Expenditure Patterns of Elderly Minority Households. *Rev. Black Polit. Econ.*, Summer 1986, *15*(1), pp. 3–25. **[G: U.S.]**

Deaton, Angus S. Demand Analysis. **In** *Griliches, Z. and Intriligator, M. D., eds.*, 1986, pp. 1767–1839.

Deb, Nibaran Chandra. Consumption Pattern in Rural Bangladesh. *Bangladesh Devel. Stud.*, March 1986, *14*(1), pp. 1–28. **[G: Bangladesh]**

Deller, Steven C.; Chicoine, David L. and Ramamurthy, Ganapathi. Instrumental Variables Approach to Rural Water Service Demand. *Southern Econ. J.*, October 1986, *53*(2), pp. 333–46. **[G: U.S.]**

Desai, Gunvant M. Growth in Indian Fertilizer Consumption: Price and Non-price Policies. **In** *Segura, E. L.; Shetty, Y. T. and Nishimizu, M., eds.*, 1986, pp. 109–36. **[G: India]**

Deshpande, Rohit; Hoyer, Wayne D. and Donthu, Naveen. The Intensity of Ethnic Affiliation: A Study of the Sociology of Hispanic Consumption. *J. Cons. Res.*, September 1986, *13*(2), pp. 214–20. **[G: U.S.]**

Devaney, Barbara L. and Fraker, Thomas. Cashing Out Food Stamps: Impact on Food Expenditures and Diet Quality. *J. Policy Anal. Manage.*, Summer 1986, *5*(4), pp. 725–41. **[G: Puerto Rico]**

Dick, Trevor J. O. Consumer Behavior in the Nineteenth Century and Ontario Workers, 1885–1889. *J. Econ. Hist.*, June 1986, *46*(2), pp. 477–88. **[G: Canada]**

Donnelly, W. A. Response [The Australian Demand for Petrol]. *Int. J. Transport Econ.*, February 1986, *13*(1), pp. 109. **[G: Australia]**

Douthitt, Robin A. The Demand for Residential Space and Water Heating Fuel by Energy Conserving Households. *J. Cons. Aff.*, Winter 1986, *20*(2), pp. 231–48. **[G: U.S.]**

Drobny, Andres and Speight, Alan. Consumption and Income: Some Simple Exercises with Panel Data. *Appl. Econ.*, July 1986, *18*(7), pp. 757–75. **[G: Austria]**

Dubin, Jeffrey A. A Nested Logit Model of Space and Water Heat System Choice. *Marketing Sci.*, Spring 1986, *5*(2), pp. 112–24. **[G: U.S.]**

Dubin, Jeffrey A. Will Mandatory Conservation Promote Energy Efficiency in the Selection of Household Appliance Stocks? *Energy J.*, January 1986, *7*(1), pp. 99–118. **[G: U.S.]**

Dubin, Jeffrey A.; Miedema, Allen K. and Chandran, Ram V. Price Effects of Energy-Efficient Technologies: A Study of Residential Demand for Heating and Cooling. *Rand J. Econ.*, Autumn 1986, *17*(3), pp. 310–25.

Dynarski, Mark. Residential Attachment and Housing Demand. *Urban Stud.*, February 1986, *23*(1), pp. 11–20. **[G: U.S.]**

Eastwood, David B.; Brooker, John R. and Terry, Danny E. Household Nutrient Demand: Use of Characteristics Theory and a Common Attribute Model. *Southern J. Agr. Econ.*, December 1986, *18*(2), pp. 235–46. **[G: U.S.]**

Eike, Ann M. An Investigation of the Market for Paperback Romance Novels. *J. Cult. Econ.*, June 1986, *10*(1), pp. 25–36. **[G: U.S.]**

Einhorn, Michael A. The Effects of Energy Prices upon Appliance Efficiencies and Building Insulation. *Energy J.*, July 1986, *7*(3), pp. 115–22.

Engle, Robert F., et al. Semiparametric Estimates of the Relation between Weather and Electricity Sales. *J. Amer. Statist. Assoc.*, June 1986, *81*(394), pp. 310–20. **[G: U.S.]**

Fayyad, Salam K. A Microeconomic System-Wide Approach to the Estimation of the Demand for Money. *Fed. Res. Bank St. Louis Rev.*, Aug./Sept. 1986, *68*(7), pp. 22–33. **[G: U.S.]**

Flaig, Gebhard. Ein Modell der Elektrizitätsnachfrage privater Haushalte mit indirekt beobachteten Variablen. (A Model of the Household Demand for Electricity with Indirectly Observed Variables. With English summary.) *Ifo-Studien*, 1986, *32*(4), pp. 275–96. **[G: W. Germany]**

French, Ben C. and King, Gordon A. Demand and Price-Markup Functions for Canned Cling Peaches and Fruit Cocktail. *Western J. Agr. Econ.*, July 1986, *11*(1), pp. 8–18. **[G: U.S.]**

Fuchs, Victor R. The Supply of Surgeons and the Demand for Operations. **In** *Fuchs, V. R.*, 1986, *1978*, pp. 126–47. **[G: U.S.]**

Fuchs, Victor R. and Kramer, Marcia J. Determinants of Expenditures for Physicians' Services. **In** *Fuchs, V. R.*, 1986, *1972*, pp. 67–107. **[G: U.S.]**

Garbacz, Christopher. Seasonal and Regional Residential Electricity Demand. *Energy J.*, April 1986, *7*(2), pp. 121–34. **[G: U.S.]**

García Alba, Pascual. Especificación de un sistema de demanda y su aplicación a México. (Specification of a Demand System and Application to Mexican Data. With English summary.) *Estud. Econ.*, July-Dec. 1986, *1*(2), pp. 305–35. **[G: Mexico]**

Gardes, François. La consommation de services en France. (With English summary.) *Revue Écon. Polit.*, Sept.-Oct. 1986, *96*(5), pp. 463–75. **[G: France]**

Gieseman, Raymond and Rogers, John. Consumer Expenditures: Results from the Diary and Interview Surveys. *Mon. Lab. Rev.*, June 1986, *109*(6), pp. 14–18. **[G: U.S.]**

Gilmer, Robert W. and Mack, Richard S. Long-run Adjustment to Alternative Levels of Reliability in Electric Supply. *Energy J.*, October 1986, *7*(4), pp. 89–94.

Green, Rodney D., et al. The Demand for Heating Fuels: A Disaggregated Modeling Approach. *Atlantic Econ. J.*, December 1986, *14*(4), pp. 1–14. **[G: U.S.]**

Green, Trellis G. Specification Considerations for the Price Variable in Travel Cost Demand Models: Comment. *Land Econ.*, November 1986, *62*(4), pp. 416–18.

Greene, David L. The Market Share of Diesel Cars in the USA, 1979–83. *Energy Econ.*, January 1986, *8*(1), pp. 13–21. **[G: U.S.]**

Grootaert, Christiaan. The Use of Multiple Diaries in a Household Expenditure Survey in Hong Kong. *J. Amer. Statist. Assoc.*, December 1986, *81*(396), pp. 938–44. **[G: Hong Kong]**

Guseman, Patricia K. and Sapp, Stephen G. Population Scale, Composition, and Income Effects on Per Capita and Aggregate Beef Consumption: A Temporal and Spatial Assessment. **In** *Capps, O., Jr. and Senauer, B., eds.*, 1986, pp. 185–213. **[G: U.S.]**

Harrison, Beth. Spending Patterns of Older Persons Revealed in Expenditure Survey. *Mon. Lab. Rev.*, October 1986, *109*(10), pp. 15–17. **[G: U.S.]**

Hartman, Raymond S. and Doane, Michael J. The Estimation of the Effects of Utility-sponsored Conservation Programmes. *Appl. Econ.*, January 1986, *18*(1), pp. 1–25. **[G: U.S.]**

Hassan, Zuhair A. and Johnson, Stan R. Consistency of Elasticities from Multiple Levels of Budgeting Process. *Can. J. Agr. Econ.*, July 1986, *34*(2), pp. 257–62. **[G: Canada]**

Hauser, John. Theory and Application of Defensive Strategy. **In** *[Dean, J.]*, 1986, pp. 114–39. **[G: U.S.]**

Hauser, John and Urban, Glen L. The Value Priority Hypotheses for Consumer Budget Plans. *J. Cons. Res.*, March 1986, *12*(4), pp. 446–62. **[G: U.S.]**

Hayes, Kathy J. Third-Order Translog Utility Functions. *J. Bus. Econ. Statist.*, July 1986, *4*(3), pp. 339–46. **[G: U.S.]**

Heikkinen, Sakari. On Private Consumption and the Standard of Living in Finland, 1860–1912. *Scand. Econ. Hist. Rev.*, 1986, *34*(2), pp. 122–34. **[G: Finland]**

Herbert, John H. Data Analysis, Specification, and Estimation of an Aggregate Relationship for Sales of Natural Gas per Customer. *J. Econ. Soc. Meas.*, October 1986, *14*(3), pp. 165–74.

Hill, Daniel Henry. Dynamics of Household Driving Demand. *Rev. Econ. Statist.*, February 1986, *68*(1), pp. 132–41. **[G: U.S.]**

Hjorth-Andersen, Chr. Hedoniske regressioner: Hvad koster en meter bil? (Hedonic Regressions. With English summary.) *Nationaløkon. Tidsskr.*, 1986, *124*(1), pp. 89–106. **[G: Denmark]**

Hjorth-Andersen, Chr. More on Multidimensional Quality: A Reply [The Concept of Quality and the Efficiency of Markets for Consumer Products]. *J. Cons. Res.*, June 1986, *13*(1), pp. 149–54. **[G: U.S.]**

Holder, Carlos. Consumption Expenditure on Durables in Barbados 1960–82. *Appl. Econ.*, November 1986, *18*(11), pp. 1227–32. **[G: Barbados]**

Huang, Chung L. and Raunikar, Robert. Food Expenditure Patterns: Evidence from U.S. Household Data. **In** *Capps, O., Jr. and Senauer, B., eds.*, 1986, pp. 49–65. **[G: U.S.]**

Huang, Chung L.; Raunikar, Robert and Tyan, Holly L. Heteroscedasticity in Broiler Meat Expenditure Pattern Estimation. *Western J. Agr. Econ.*, December 1986, *11*(2), pp. 195–203. **[G: U.S.]**

Hutton, R. Bruce, et al. Effects of Cost-Related Feedback on Consumer Knowledge and Consumption Behavior: A Field Experimental Approach. *J. Cons. Res.*, December 1986, *13*(3), pp. 327–36. **[G: U.S.; Canada]**

Jerala, Tomislav. Fertilizer Pricing in Yugoslavia. **In** *Segura, E. L.; Shetty, Y. T. and Nishimizu, M., eds.*, 1986, pp. 204–18. **[G: Yugoslavia]**

Johnson, L. W. A Note on Australian Petrol Demand. *Int. J. Transport Econ.*, February 1986, *13*(1), pp. 105–08. **[G: Australia]**

Kabir, M. and Ridler, Neil B. The Market for

Atlantic Salmon. *Atlantic Econ. J.*, March 1986, *14*(1), pp. 125. **[G: Canada]**

Kahn, E.; Sathaye, Jayant and Robbins, D. An Engineering–Economic Approach to Estimating the Price Elasticity of Residential Electricity Demand. *Energy Econ.*, April 1986, *8*(2), pp. 118–26. **[G: U.S.]**

Karapostolis, Vasilis. Socio-Occupational Groups and Consumer Behaviour in Greece. *Int. J. Soc. Econ.*, 1986, *13*(10), pp. 17–25. **[G: Greece]**

Katz, Michael L. and Shapiro, Carl. Consumer Shopping Behavior in the Retail Coffee Market. **In** *Ippolito, P. M. and Scheffman, D. T., eds.*, 1986, pp. 415–43. **[G: U.S.]**

Keen, Michael. Zero Expenditures and the Estimation of Engel Curves. *J. Appl. Econometrics*, July 1986, *1*(3), pp. 277–86. **[G: U.K.]**

Kessler, Denis; Perelman, Sergio and Pestieau, Pierre. Public Debt, Tax, and Consumption: A Test on O.E.C.D. Countries. *Public Finance*, 1986, *41*(1), pp. 63–70. **[G: OECD]**

Kim, H. Youn. Estimating Consumer Demand in Korea. *J. Devel. Econ.*, March 1986, *20*(2), pp. 325–38. **[G: S. Korea]**

Kinnucan, Henry and Forker, Olan D. Seasonality in the Consumer Response to Milk Advertising with Implications for Milk Promotion Policy. *Amer. J. Agr. Econ.*, August 1986, *68*(3), pp. 562–71. **[G: U.S.]**

Kokoski, Mary F. An Empirical Analysis of Intertemporal and Demographic Variations in Consumer Preferences. *Amer. J. Agr. Econ.*, November 1986, *68*(4), pp. 894–907. **[G: U.S.]**

Kushman, John E. and Anderson, Joan Gray. A Model of Individual Household Temperature Demand and Energy-Related Welfare Changes Using Satiety. *Energy Econ.*, July 1986, *8*(3), pp. 147–54. **[G: U.S.]**

Lancaster, Tony and Chesher, Andrew. Erratum [Residuals Tests and Plots with a Job Matching Illustration]. *Ann. Écon. Statist.*, Apr./June 1986, (2), pp. 171.

Lee, Jonq-Ying. Imputed Missing Incomes and Marginal Propensity to Consume Food. *Western J. Agr. Econ.*, December 1986, *11*(2), pp. 115–22. **[G: U.S.]**

Lee, Jonq-Ying and Brown, Mark G. Economic Effectiveness of Brand Advertising Programmes for U.S. Orange Juice in the European Market: An Error Component Analysis. *J. Agr. Econ.*, September 1986, *37*(3), pp. 385–94. **[G: U.S.]**

Lee, Jonq-Ying and Brown, Mark G. Food Expenditures at Home and Away from Home in the United States—A Switching Regression Analysis. *Rev. Econ. Statist.*, February 1986, *68*(1), pp. 142–47. **[G: U.S.]**

Lee, Jonq-Ying; Brown, Mark G. and Schwartz, Brooke. The Demand for National Brand and Private Label Frozen Concentrated Orange Juice: A Switching Regressional Analysis. *Western J. Agr. Econ.*, July 1986, *11*(1), pp. 1–17. **[G: U.S.]**

Lee, Maw Lin. Nonbudgetary Constraints in Consumer Demand for Gasoline. *Appl. Econ.*, January 1986, *18*(1), pp. 101–12. **[G: U.S.]**

Levedahl, J. William. Profit Maximizing Pricing of Cents Off Coupons: Promotion or Price Discrimination? *Quart. J. Bus. Econ.*, Autumn 1986, *25*(4), pp. 56–70. **[G: U.S.]**

Lin, Biing-Hwan; Johnston, Richard S. and Rettig, R. Bruce. U.S. Demand for Selected Groundfish Products, 1967–80: Comment. *Amer. J. Agr. Econ.*, November 1986, *68*(4), pp. 1021–24. **[G: U.S.]**

Magat, Wesley A.; Payne, John W. and Brucato, Peter F., Jr. How Important Is Information Format? An Experimental Study of Home Energy Audit Programs. *J. Policy Anal. Manage.*, Fall 1986, *6*(1), pp. 20–34. **[G: U.S.]**

Magnusson, Lars. Drinking and the Verlag System 1820–1850: The Significance of Taverns and Drink in Eskilstuna before Industrialisation. *Scand. Econ. Hist. Rev.*, 1986, *34*(1), pp. 1–19. **[G: Sweden]**

Malish, Anton F. Soviet Agricultural Policy in the 1980s. **In** *Browne, W. P. and Hadwiger, D. F., eds.*, 1986, pp. 77–90. **[G: U.S.S.R.]**

Martin, Michael V. and McDonald, John A. Food Grain Policy in the Republic of Korea: The Economic Costs of Self-sufficiency. *Econ. Develop. Cult. Change*, January 1986, *34*(2), pp. 315–31. **[G: S. Korea]**

Martin, William E. and Thomas, John F. Policy Relevance in Studies of Urban Residential Water Demand. *Water Resources Res.*, December 1986, *22*(13), pp. 1735–41. **[G: Kuwait; Australia; U.S.]**

Martin, William E.; Thomas, John F. and Macpherson, Duncan K. Municipal Demand for Water in Kuwait: Methodological Issues and Empirical Results: Comment. *Water Resources Res.*, May 1986, *22*(5), pp. 832–34. **[G: Kuwait]**

McCarthy, Patrick S. Shared Fleet Arrangements: Implications for Vehicle Demand Using a Simultaneous Equations Approach. *Int. J. Transport Econ.*, February 1986, *13*(1), pp. 87–103. **[G: U.S.]**

Mellor, C. J. and Hessner, Catherine. Structural Change in the Yellow Fats Market. *Appl. Econ.*, June 1986, *18*(6), pp. 663–73. **[G: U.K.]**

Miron, Jeffrey A. Seasonal Fluctuations and the Life Cycle–Permanent Income Model of Consumption. *J. Polit. Econ.*, December 1986, *94*(6), pp. 1258–79. **[G: U.S.]**

Moran, Larry R. Motor Vehicles, Model Year 1986. *Surv. Curr. Bus.*, November 1986, *66*(11), pp. 19–22. **[G: U.S.]**

Mullahy, John. Specification and Testing of Some Modified Count Data Models. *J. Econometrics*, December 1986, *33*(3), pp. 341–65. **[G: U.S.]**

Myers, Lester H. Food Demand Analysis: Implications for Future Consumption: Comments. **In** *Capps, O., Jr. and Senauer, B., eds.*, 1986, pp. 177–84. **[G: U.S.]**

Neldner, Manfred. Preisniveauschwankungen und privater Konsum: Zur empirischen Bedeutung des Pigou-Effekts in der Bundesrepublik

Deutschland. (Price Level Changes and Private Consumption: The Empirical Relevance of the Pigou-Effect in West Germany. With English summary.) *Weltwirtsch. Arch.*, 1986, *122*(3), pp. 534–51. **[G: W. Germany]**

Niron, Suna. Fertilizer Pricing in Turkey. **In** *Segura, E. L.; Shetty, Y. T. and Nishimizu, M., eds.*, 1986, pp. 219–35. **[G: Turkey]**

Nyankori, James C. O. A Systematic Analysis of Household Food Consumption Behavior with Specific Emphasis on Predicting Aggregate Food Expenditures. **In** *Capps, O., Jr. and Senauer, B., eds.*, 1986, pp. 251–68. **[G: U.S.]**

Ohta, Makoto and Griliches, Zvi. Automobile Prices and Quality: Did the Gasoline Price Increases Change Consumer Tastes in the U.S.? *J. Bus. Econ. Statist.*, April 1986, *4*(2), pp. 187–98. **[G: U.S.]**

Osmani, S. R. and Deb, Nibaran Chandra. Demand for Products of Rural Industries. **In** *Islam, R. and Muqtada, M., eds.*, 1986, pp. 151–67. **[G: Bangladesh]**

Parbhakar, K. J. Fuel Consumption for Road Transport in Quebec. *Energy Econ.*, July 1986, *8*(3), pp. 165–70. **[G: Canada]**

Pashardes, Panos. Myopic and Forward Looking Behavior in a Dynamic Demand System. *Int. Econ. Rev.*, June 1986, *27*(2), pp. 387–97. **[G: U.K.]**

Pitt, Mark M. and Rosenzweig, Mark R. Agricultural Prices, Food Consumption, and the Health and Productivity of Indonesian Farmers. **In** *Singh, I.; Squire, L. and Strauss, J., eds.*, 1986, pp. 153–82. **[G: Indonesia]**

Polzin, Paul E. The Specification of Price in Studies of Consumer Demand under Block Price Scheduling: Reply. *Land Econ.*, August 1986, *62*(3), pp. 335. **[G: U.S.]**

Price, David W. The Effects of Household Size and Composition on the Demand for Food. **In** *Capps, O., Jr. and Senauer, B., eds.*, 1986, pp. 131–48. **[G: U.S.]**

Price, Dorothy Z. Role of Integrated Decision Theory in Considering Future Food Consumption Patterns of the Elderly. **In** *Capps, O., Jr. and Senauer, B., eds.*, 1986, pp. 149–62. **[G: U.S.]**

Prior, M. J. Fuel Markets in Urban Bangladesh. *World Devel.*, July 1986, *14*(7), pp. 865–72. **[G: Bangladesh]**

Raffiee, Kambiz. The Specification of Price in Studies of Consumer Demand under Block Price Scheduling: Comment. *Land Econ.*, August 1986, *62*(3), pp. 333–34. **[G: U.S.]**

Raunikar, Robert and Huang, Chung L. Implications of Factors Affecting Food Consumption. **In** *Capps, O., Jr. and Senauer, B., eds.*, 1986, pp. 91–103. **[G: U.S.]**

Ray, Ranjan. Flexibility in Dynamic Demand Modelling and Its Implications for Testing Restrictions. *Manchester Sch. Econ. Soc. Stud.*, March 1986, *54*(1), pp. 1–21. **[G: U.K.]**

Ray, Ranjan. On Setting Indirect Taxes in India Using the Ramsey Approach: Evidence from Household Budget Data. *J. Quant. Econ.*, July 1986, *2*(2), pp. 249–62. **[G: India]**

Ray, Ranjan. Redistribution through Commodity Taxes: The Nonlinear Engel Curve Case. *Public Finance*, 1986, *41*(2), pp. 277–84. **[G: India]**

Rushdi, Ali Ahmed. Interfuel Substitution in the Residential Sector of South Australia. *Energy Econ.*, July 1986, *8*(3), pp. 177–85. **[G: Australia]**

Russo, J. Edward, et al. Nutrition Information in the Supermarket. *J. Cons. Res.*, June 1986, *13*(1), pp. 48–70. **[G: U.S.]**

Safyurtlu, A. N.; Johnson, Stan R. and Hassan, Zuhair A. Recent Evidence on Market Demand Systems for Food in Canada. *Can. J. Agr. Econ.*, November 1986, *34*(3), pp. 475–93. **[G: Canada]**

Sandrey, Ron A. Non-Market Valuation in New Zealand: An Empirical Analysis of Vehicle Bias. *New Zealand Econ. Pap.*, 1986, *20*, pp. 53–60. **[G: New Zealand]**

Sappington, David E. M. Consumer Shopping Behavior in the Retail Coffee Market: Comments. **In** *Ippolito, P. M. and Scheffman, D. T., eds.*, 1986, pp. 445–46. **[G: U.S.]**

Saqqaf, Abdulaziz. Energy Production and Consumption in the Yemen Arab Republic. **In** *El Mallakh, R., ed.*, 1986, pp. 145–61. **[G: Yemen]**

Schmidt, Ronald H. and Gunther, Jeffery W. Distributional Implications of Reducing Interstate Energy Price Differences. *Fed. Res. Bank Dallas Econ. Rev.*, November 1986, pp. 1–15. **[G: U.S.]**

Schrimper, Ronald A. Effects of Increasing Elderly Population on Future Food Demand and Consumption. **In** *Capps, O., Jr. and Senauer, B., eds.*, 1986, pp. 163–76. **[G: U.S.]**

Scitovsky, Tibor. What's Wrong with the Arts Is What's Wrong with Society. **In** *Scitovsky, T.*, 1986, *1972*, pp. 37–46. **[G: U.S.]**

Senauer, Benjamin; Kinsey, Jean and Roe, Terry. Imperfect Mileage Information and Changing Utility: A Model and Survey Results. *J. Cons. Aff.*, Winter 1986, *20*(2), pp. 155–72. **[G: U.S.]**

Senauer, Benjamin; Sahn, David and Alderman, Harold. The Effect of the Value of Time on Food Consumption Patterns in Developing Countries: Evidence from Sri Lanka. *Amer. J. Agr. Econ.*, November 1986, *68*(4), pp. 920–27. **[G: Sri Lanka]**

Senauer, Benjamin and Young, Nathan. The Impact of Food Stamps on Food Expenditures: Rejection of the Traditional Model. *Amer. J. Agr. Econ.*, February 1986, *68*(1), pp. 37–43. **[G: U.S.]**

Singh, B. K. and Nautiyal, J. C. Adjustment Dynamics of Paper and Paperboard Consumption in Canada. *Can. J. Agr. Econ.*, March 1986, *34*(1), pp. 45–65. **[G: Canada]**

Singh, Inderjit and Janakiram, Subramanian. Agricultural Household Modeling in a Multicrop Environment: Case Studies in Korea and Nigeria. **In** *Singh, I.; Squire, L. and Strauss, J., eds.*, 1986, pp. 95–115. **[G: S. Korea; Nigeria]**

Singh, Satya Prakash and Singh, Raghbir. Consumption of Milk Products and Income. *Margin*, October 1986, *19*(1), pp. 50–58. **[G: India]**

Smil, Vaclav. Food Production and Quality of Diet in China. *Population Devel. Rev.*, March 1986, *12*(1), pp. 25–45. **[G: China]**

Smith, Victor E. and Strauss, John. Simulating the Rural Economy in a Subsistence Environment: Sierra Leone. **In** *Singh, I.; Squire, L. and Strauss, J., eds.*, 1986, pp. 206–32. **[G: Sierra Leone]**

Somers, Anne R. The Changing Demand for Health Services: A Historical Perspective and Some Thoughts for the Future. *Inquiry*, Winter 1986, *23*(4), pp. 395–402.

Spriggs, John and Van Kooten, G. C. Estimating Systems of Nonlinear Equations in a Single Equation Framework. *Can. J. Agr. Econ.*, March 1986, *34*(1), pp. 105–11. **[G: Canada]**

Strauss, John. Estimating the Determinants of Food Consumption and Caloric Availability in Rural Sierra Leone. **In** *Singh, I.; Squire, L. and Strauss, J., eds.*, 1986, pp. 116–52. **[G: Sierra Leone]**

Stromback, C. Thorsten. Modelling Electricity Demand in Western Australia. *Australian Econ. Pap.*, June 1986, *25*(46), pp. 106–17. **[G: W. Australia]**

Takacs, Wendy E. and Tanzer, Ellen P. Structural Change in the Demand for Automobiles by Size Class. *Quart. Rev. Econ. Bus.*, Autumn 1986, *26*(3), pp. 48–57. **[G: U.S.]**

Tansel, Aysit. An Engel Curve Analysis of Household Expenditure in Turkey 1978–79. *METU*, 1986, *13*(3–4), pp. 239–57. **[G: Turkey]**

Termorshuizen, J. G.; Meulenberg, M. T. G. and Wierenga, B. Consumer Behaviour in Respect of Milk in the Netherlands. *Europ. Rev. Agr. Econ.*, 1986, *13*(1), pp. 1–22. **[G: Netherlands]**

Terza, Joseph V. Determinants of Household Electricity Demand: A Two-Stage Probit Approach. *Southern Econ. J.*, April 1986, *52*(4), pp. 1131–39. **[G: U.S.]**

Tirelli, Daniele. A Comparative Study of the Allocative Choices of Consumption, Saving and Leisure in Six European Countries. *Econ. Lavoro*, Oct.-Dec. 1986, *20*(4), pp. 59–86. **[G: Selected European]**

Tirelli, Daniele. An Empirical Analysis of Italian Households' Expenditure on Leisure and Consumption. *Econ. Notes*, 1986, (2), pp. 17–42. **[G: Italy]**

Tsay, Ruey S. Time Series Model Specification in the Presence of Outliers. *J. Amer. Statist. Assoc.*, March 1986, *81*(393), pp. 132–41. **[G: U.K.]**

Tsoa, Eugene; Shrank, William E. and Roy, Noel. U.S. Demand for Selected Groundfish Products, 1967–80: Reply. *Amer. J. Agr. Econ.*, November 1986, *68*(4), pp. 1025–27. **[G: U.S.]**

Unnevehr, Laurian J. Consumer Demand for Rice Grain Quality and Returns to Research for Quality Improvement in Southeast Asia. *Amer. J. Agr. Econ.*, August 1986, *68*(3), pp. 634–41. **[G: Philippines; Indonesia; Thailand]**

Uri, Noel D. The Demand for Beverages and Interbeverage Substitution in the United States. *Bull. Econ. Res.*, January 1986, *38*(1), pp. 77–85. **[G: U.S.]**

Uys, P. W. Demand for Meat in South Africa: A Non-additive Dynamic Linear Expenditure Model. *S. Afr. J. Econ.*, June 1986, *54*(2), pp. 207–19. **[G: S. Africa]**

Walton, Whitney. "To Triumph before Feminine Taste": Bourgeois Women's Consumption and Hand Methods of Production in Mid-Nineteenth-Century Paris. *Bus. Hist. Rev.*, Winter 1986, *60*(4), pp. 541–63. **[G: France]**

Ward, Frank A. Specification Considerations for the Price Variable in Travel Cost Demand Models: Reply. *Land Econ.*, November 1986, *62*(4), pp. 419–21.

Wasserfallen, Walter; Gassmann, Jean-Marie and Gfeller, Andreas. Die Nachfrage nach Telefongesprächen—Erklärung und Prognose Eine empirische Untersuchung für die Schweiz. (The Demand for Telephone Services: Explanation and Forecast—An Empirical Investigation for Switzerland. With English summary.) *Schweiz. Z. Volkswirtsch. Statist.*, June 1986, *122*(2), pp. 187–97. **[G: Switzerland]**

Weissenberger, Edgar. An Intertemporal System of Dynamic Consumer Demand Functions. *Europ. Econ. Rev.*, August 1986, *30*(4), pp. 859–91. **[G: U.K.]**

Wennergren, E. Boyd and Whitaker, Morris D. Foodgrain Sufficiency in Bangladesh: A Reappraisal and Policy Implications. *J. Devel. Areas*, October 1986, *21*(1), pp. 1–13. **[G: Bangladesh]**

Williams, Martin and Suh, Byung. The Demand for Urban Water by Customer Class. *Appl. Econ.*, December 1986, *18*(12), pp. 1275–89. **[G: U.S.]**

Witt, Stephen F. and Johnson, S. Raymond. An Econometric Model of New-Car Demand in the UK. *Managerial Dec. Econ.*, March 1986, *7*(1), pp. 19–23. **[G: U.K.]**

de Witte, M. A. C. and Cramer, J. S. Functional Form of Engel Curve for Foodstuffs. *Europ. Econ. Rev.*, August 1986, *30*(4), pp. 909–13. **[G: Netherlands]**

9213 Consumer Protection

Abraham, Martin and Asher, Allan. Dangerous Products: Consumer Interpol. **In** *Wheelwright, T., ed.*, 1986, pp. 261–75.

Anderson, James E. and Gollop, Frank M. The Effect of Warranty Provisions on Used Car Prices. **In** *Ippolito, P. M. and Scheffman, D. T., eds.*, 1986, pp. 67–102. **[G: U.S.]**

Asch, Peter. Automobile Safety: Is Government Regulation Really Our Savior? *Yale J. Regul.*, Spring 1986, *3*(2), pp. 383–89. **[G: U.S.]**

Asher, Allan. The Future of the Consumer Movement. **In** *Wheelwright, T., ed.*, 1986, pp. 359–74.

Atiyah, P. S. Medical Malpractice and the Contract/Tort Boundary. *Law Contemp. Probl.*, Spring 1986, *49*(2), pp. 287–303. **[G: U.S.]**

Barnett, Steve. A New York State Consumer Energy Mindset. **In** *Saltzman, S. and Schuler, R. E., eds.*, 1986, pp. 260–66. **[G: U.S.]**

Bosk, Charles L. Professional Responsibility and Medical Error. **In** *Aiken, L. H. and Mechanic, D., eds.*, 1986, pp. 460–77. **[G: U.S.]**

Braithwaite, John. Consumers as Victims of Corporate Crime. **In** *Wheelwright, T., ed.*, 1986, pp. 331–42.

Bray, Ann Marie and Smith, Dolores S. The Consumer Advisory Council in Its First Decade: An Overview. *Fed. Res. Bull.*, November 1986, *72*(11), pp. 757–65. **[G: U.S.]**

Butters, Gerard R. The Impact of Product Recalls on the Wealth of Sellers: Comments. **In** *Ippolito, P. M. and Scheffman, D. T., eds.*, 1986, pp. 411–13. **[G: U.S.]**

Chapman, Simon. The World Tobacco Industry. **In** *Wheelwright, T., ed.*, 1986, pp. 191–227. **[G: LDCs]**

Cox, Louis Anthony, Jr. Theory of Regulatory Benefits Assessment: Econometric and Expressed Preference Approaches. **In** *Bentkover, J. D.; Covello, V. T. and Jeryl, M., eds.*, 1986, pp. 85–159. **[G: U.S.]**

Crandall, Robert W. The Market for Housing Quality: Comments. **In** *Ippolito, P. M. and Scheffman, D. T., eds.*, 1986, pp. 103–04. **[G: U.S.]**

Crocker, Keith J. A Reexamination of the "Lemons" Market When Warranties Are Not Prepurchase Quality Signals. *Info. Econ. Policy*, June 1986, *2*(2), pp. 147–62.

DeMuth, Christopher C. The Case against Credit Card Interest Rate Regulation. *Yale J. Regul.*, Spring 1986, *3*(2), pp. 201–42. **[G: U.S.]**

Dickens, William T. Safety Regulation and "Irrational" Behavior. **In** *Gilad, B. and Kaish, S., eds., Vol. A*, 1986, pp. 325–48.

Epstein, Richard A. Medical Malpractice, Imperfect Information, and the Contractual Foundation for Medical Services. *Law Contemp. Probl.*, Spring 1986, *49*(2), pp. 201–12. **[G: U.S.]**

Farrell, Joseph. Voluntary Disclosure: Robustness of the Unraveling Result, and Comments on Its Importance. **In** *Grieson, R. E., ed.*, 1986, pp. 91–103. **[G: U.S.]**

Fine, Max W. and Sunshine, Jonathan H. Malpractice Reform through Consumer Choice and Consumer Education: Are New Concepts Marketable? *Law Contemp. Probl.*, Spring 1986, *49*(2), pp. 213–22. **[G: U.S.]**

Fuchs, Victor R. and Leveson, Irving. Motor Accident Mortality and Compulsory Inspection of Vehicles. **In** *Fuchs, V. R.*, 1986, *1967*, pp. 169–80. **[G: U.S.]**

Gander, James P. Highway Speed and Uncertainty of Enforcement: The Traveling Salesman (or Trucker) Case. *Logist. Transp. Rev.*, March 1986, *22*(1), pp. 43–55. **[G: U.S.]**

Golbe, Devra L. Safety and Profits in the Airline Industry. *J. Ind. Econ.*, March 1986, *34*(3), pp. 305–18. **[G: U.S.]**

Grabowski, Henry G. and Vernon, John. Longer Patents for Lower Imitation Barriers: The 1984 Drug Act. *Amer. Econ. Rev.*, May 1986, *76*(2), pp. 195–98. **[G: U.S.]**

Graham, John D. and Lee, Younghee. Behavioral Response to Safety Regulation: The Case of Motorcycle Helmet-Wearing Legislation. *Policy Sci.*, October 1986, *19*(3), pp. 253–73. **[G: U.S.]**

Hamada, Koichi; Ishida, Hidetoh and Murakami, Masahiro. The Evolution and Economic Consequences of Product Liability Rules in Japan. **In** *Saxonhouse, G. R. and Yamamura, K., eds.*, 1986, pp. 83–106. **[G: Japan]**

Harvey, A. C. and Durbin, J. The Effects of Seat Belt Legislation on British Road Casualties: A Case Study in Structural Time Series Modelling. *J. Roy. Statist. Soc.*, 1986, *149*(3), pp. 187–210. **[G: U.S.]**

Havighurst, Clark C. Altering the Applicable Standard of Care. *Law Contemp. Probl.*, Spring 1986, *49*(2), pp. 265–75. **[G: U.S.]**

Higgins, Richard S. and Rubin, Paul H. Counterfeit Goods. *J. Law Econ.*, October 1986, *29*(2), pp. 211–30.

Huber, Peter W. The Bhopalization of American Tort Law. **In** *Landau, R. and Rosenberg, N., eds.*, 1986, pp. 191–212. **[G: U.S.]**

Ippolito, Pauline M. Consumer Protection Economics: A Selective Survey. **In** *Ippolito, P. M. and Scheffman, D. T., eds.*, 1986, pp. 1–33. **[G: U.S.]**

Jarrell, Gregg A. and Peltzman, Sam. The Impact of Product Recalls on the Wealth of Sellers. **In** *Ippolito, P. M. and Scheffman, D. T., eds.*, 1986, pp. 377–409. **[G: U.S.]**

Johnson, Douglas A. Confronting Corporate Power: Strategies and Phases of the Nestlé Boycott. **In** *Wheelwright, T., ed.*, 1986, pp. 305–30.

Katz, Milton. The Role of the Legal System in Technological Innovation and Economic Growth. **In** *Landau, R. and Rosenberg, N., eds.*, 1986, pp. 169–89. **[G: U.S.]**

Kroll, Robert J. and Stampfl, Ronald W. Orientations toward Consumerism: A Test of a Two-Dimensional Theory. *J. Cons. Aff.*, Winter 1986, *20*(2), pp. 214–30. **[G: U.S.]**

Kunreuther, Howard and Bendixen, Lisa. Benefits Assessment for Regulatory Problems. **In** *Bentkover, J. D.; Covello, V. T. and Jeryl, M., eds.*, 1986, pp. 35–50. **[G: U.S.]**

Langenfeld, James. The Effect of Warranty Provisions on Used Car Prices: Comments. **In** *Ippolito, P. M. and Scheffman, D. T., eds.*, 1986, pp. 105–07. **[G: U.S.]**

Lynch, Michael, et al. Product Quality, Consumer Information and "Lemons" in Experimental Markets. **In** *Ippolito, P. M. and Scheffman, D. T., eds.*, 1986, pp. 251–306.

Mackay, Robert J. Comments [Quality Uncertainty and Bundling] [Product Quality, Consumer Information and "Lemons" in Experimental Markets] [An Experimental Study of

Warranty Coverage and Dispute Resolution in Competitive Markets]. **In** *Ippolito, P. M. and Scheffman, D. T., eds.*, 1986, pp. 373–74. **[G: U.S.]**

Mason, Charles F. Cherries, Lemons, and the FTC, Revisited [The Market for 'Lemons'] [Cherries, Lemons, and the FTC: Minimum Quality Standards in the Retail Used Automobile Industry]. *Econ. Inquiry*, April 1986, *24*(2), pp. 363–65. **[G: U.S.]**

Mayer, Robert N. and Zick, Cathleen D. Mandating Behavioral or Technological Change: The Case of Auto Safety. *J. Cons. Aff.*, Summer 1986, *20*(1), pp. 1–18. **[G: U.S.]**

McKay, Niccie L. Industry Effects of Medical Device Regulation: The Case of Diagnostic Imaging Equipment. *J. Policy Anal. Manage.*, Fall 1986, *6*(1), pp. 35–44. **[G: U.S.]**

Merciai, Patrizio. Consumer Protection and the United Nations. *J. World Trade Law*, Mar.:Apr. 1986, *20*(2), pp. 206–31. **[G: Global]**

Miller, Ross M. Comments [Quality Uncertainty and Bundling] [Product Quality, Consumer Information and "Lemons" in Experimental Markets] [An Experimental Study of Warranty Coverage and Dispute Resolution in Competitive Markets]. **In** *Ippolito, P. M. and Scheffman, D. T., eds.*, 1986, pp. 375–76. **[G: U.S.]**

O'Connell, Jeffrey. Neo-No-Fault Remedies for Medical Injuries: Coordinated Statutory and Contractual Alternatives. *Law Contemp. Probl.*, Spring 1986, *49*(2), pp. 125–41.

Palfrey, Thomas R. and Romer, Thomas. An Experimental Study of Warranty Coverage and Dispute Resolution in Competitive Markets. **In** *Ippolito, P. M. and Scheffman, D. T., eds.*, 1986, pp. 307–72. **[G: U.S.]**

Peterson, Esther. The United Nations and Consumer Guidelines. **In** *Wheelwright, T., ed.*, 1986, pp. 343–51.

Peterson, Richard L. Creditors' Use of Collection Remedies. *J. Finan. Res.*, Spring 1986, *9*(1), pp. 71–86. **[G: U.S.]**

Posner, James R. Trends in Medical Malpractice Insurance, 1970–1985. *Law Contemp. Probl.*, Spring 1986, *49*(2), pp. 37–56. **[G: U.S.]**

Pratt, Michael D. and Hoffer, George E. The Efficacy of State Mandated Minimum Quality Certification: The Case of Used Vehicles. *Econ. Inquiry*, April 1986, *24*(2), pp. 313–18. **[G: U.S.]**

Robinson, Glen O. Rethinking the Allocation of Medical Malpractice Risks between Patients and Providers. *Law Contemp. Probl.*, Spring 1986, *49*(2), pp. 173–99. **[G: U.S.]**

Robinson, Glen O. The Medical Malpractice Crisis of the 1970's: A Retrospective. *Law Contemp. Probl.*, Spring 1986, *49*(2), pp. 5–35. **[G: U.S.]**

Schelling, Thomas C. Whose Business Is Good Behavior? **In** *Knowlton, W. and Zeckhauser, R., eds.*, 1986, pp. 153–80. **[G: U.S.]**

Seger, Martha R. Statement to the U.S. House Subcommittee on Consumer Affairs and Coinage of the Committee on Banking, Finance and Urban Affairs, August 12, 1986. *Fed. Res. Bull.*, October 1986, *72*(10), pp. 697–700. **[G: U.S.]**

Viscusi, W. Kip; Magat, Wesley A. and Huber, Joel C. Informational Regulation of Consumer Health Risks: An Empirical Evaluation of Hazard Warnings. *Rand J. Econ.*, Autumn 1986, *17*(3), pp. 351–65. **[G: U.S.]**

Warren, Michael. Consumers' Association: *Which?* Why and How. **In** *Moores, B., ed.*, 1986, pp. 241–52. **[G: U.K.]**

Weicher, John C. The Market for Housing Quality. **In** *Ippolito, P. M. and Scheffman, D. T., eds.*, 1986, pp. 39–65. **[G: U.S.]**

Winward, John. Nationalised Industry Consumer Councils. **In** *Moores, B., ed.*, 1986, pp. 217–28. **[G: U.K.]**

Wood, John T. D. Consumer Affairs in Transition. **In** *Wheelwright, T., ed.*, 1986, pp. 353–58.

Zuckerman, Stephen; Koller, Christopher F. and Bovbjerg, Randall R. Information on Malpractice: A Review of Empirical Research on Major Policy Issues. *Law Contemp. Probl.*, Spring 1986, *49*(2), pp. 85–111. **[G: U.S.]**

930 Urban Economics

9300 General

Barnes, Sandra T. Political Entrepreneurs in a West African City. **In** *Greenfield, S. M. and Strickon, A., eds.*, 1986, pp. 224–61. **[G: Nigeria]**

Goose, N. R. In Search of the Urban Variable: Towns and the English Economy, 1500–1650. *Econ. Hist. Rev., 2nd Ser.*, May 1986, *39*(2), pp. 165–85. **[G: U.K.]**

Hardoy, Jorge E. and Satterthwaite, David. A Survey of Empirical Material on the Factors Affecting the Development of Small and Intermediate Urban Centres. **In** *Hardoy, J. E. and Satterthwaite, D., eds.*, 1986, pp. 279–334. **[G: LDCs]**

Hardoy, Jorge E. and Satterthwaite, David. Small and Intermediate Urban Centres: Their Role in National and Regional Development in the Third World: Some Tentative Conclusions. **In** *Hardoy, J. E. and Satterthwaite, D., eds.*, 1986, pp. 398–411.

Kahan, Arcadius. A Day in the Ghetto. **In** *Kahan, A.*, 1986, pp. 170–84. **[G: Poland]**

Wood, Charles H. and McCracken, Stephen D. Underdevelopment, Urban Growth and Collective Social Action in Sao Paulo, Brazil. **In** *Abegaz, B., ed.*, 1986, pp. 101–40. **[G: Brazil]**

Yusof, A. K. M. Public Enterprise: Studies in Organisational Structure: Urban Development Authority. **In** *Ramanadham, V. V., ed.*, 1986, pp. 234–49. **[G: Malaysia]**

931 Urban Economics and Public Policy

9310 Urban Economics and Public Policy

Ahlbrandt, Roger S., Jr. Using Research to Build Stronger Neighborhoods: A Study of Pittsburgh's Neighborhoods. **In** *Taylor, R. B., ed.*, 1986, pp. 285–309. **[G: U.S.]**

Amin, A. T. M. Nurul. Urban Informal Sector: Employment Potentials and Problems. **In** *Islam, R. and Muqtada, M., eds.*, 1986, pp. 209–46. **[G: Bangladesh]**

Amin, A. T. M. Nurul. Urban Unemployment and Underemployment. **In** *Islam, R. and Muqtada, M., eds.*, 1986, pp. 21–39. **[G: Bangladesh]**

Andersen, Ronald M.; Banks, Martha J. and Aplington, Margaret. Success in Reaching the Communities and People Targeted for MHSP. **In** *Fleming, G. V. and Andersen, R. M., eds.*, 1986, pp. 45–67. **[G: U.S.]**

Andersen, Ronald M. and Fleming, Gretchen V. Expenditures for Medical Care. **In** *Fleming, G. V. and Andersen, R. M., eds.*, 1986, pp. 94–118. **[G: U.S.]**

Anderson, John E. Property Taxes and the Timing of Urban Land Development. *Reg. Sci. Urban Econ.*, November 1986, *16*(4), pp. 483–92.

Anderstig, Christer and Hårsman, Björn. On Occupation Structure and Location Pattern in the Stockholm Region. *Reg. Sci. Urban Econ.*, February 1986, *16*(1), pp. 97–122. **[G: Sweden]**

Andrews, Howard F. The Effects of Neighbourhood Social Mix on Adolescents' Social Networks and Recreational Activities. *Urban Stud.*, December 1986, *23*(6), pp. 501–17. **[G: Canada]**

Arnott, Richard J. and Gersovitz, Mark. Social Welfare Underpinnings of Urban Bias and Unemployment. *Econ. J.*, June 1986, *96*(382), pp. 413–24.

Arnott, Richard J.; Pines, David and Sadka, Efraim. The Effects of an Equiproportional Transport Improvement in a Fully-Closed Monocentric City. *Reg. Sci. Urban Econ.*, August 1986, *16*(3), pp. 387–406.

Bairoch, Paul and Goertz, Gary. Factors of Urbanisation in the Nineteenth Century Developed Countries: A Descriptive and Econometric Analysis. *Urban Stud.*, August 1986, *23*(4), pp. 285–305. **[G: MDCs]**

Banham, John M. M. Paying for Local Government. *Lloyds Bank Rev.*, July 1986, (161), pp. 1–18. **[G: U.K.]**

Bartik, Timothy J. Neighborhood Revitalization's Effects on Tenants and the Benefit–Cost Analysis of Government Neighborhood Programs. *J. Urban Econ.*, March 1986, *19*(2), pp. 234–48. **[G: U.S.]**

Baumol, William J. Technological Change and the New Urban Equilibrium. **In** *Baumol, W. J.*, 1986, *1981*, pp. 191–205. **[G: U.S.]**

Beasley, Steven D.; Workman, William G. and Williams, Nancy A. Estimating Amenity Values of Urban Fringe Farmland: A Contingent Valuation Approach: Note. *Growth Change*, October 1986, *17*(4), pp. 70–78. **[G: U.S.]**

Becker, Charles M.; Mills, Edwin S. and Williamson, Jeffrey G. Dynamics of Rural–Urban Migration in India: 1960–1981. *Indian J. Quant. Econ.*, 1986, *2*(1), pp. 1–43. **[G: India]**

Becker, Charles M.; Mills, Edwin S. and Williamson, Jeffrey G. Modeling Indian Migration and City Growth, 1960–2000. *Econ. Develop. Cult. Change*, October 1986, *35*(1), pp. 1–33. **[G: India]**

Bell, Michael E. and Bowman, John H. Property Tax Differences among Minnesota Cities: The Effect of Property Tax Relief Programs. **In** *Minnesota Tax Study Commission*, 1986, pp. 349–59. **[G: U.S.]**

Bell, Ralph. Utilization of Medical Care Services. **In** *Fleming, G. V. and Andersen, R. M., eds.*, 1986, pp. 80–93. **[G: U.S.]**

Bell, Ralph and Banks, Martha J. The MHSP Evaluation Data and Methods. **In** *Fleming, G. V. and Andersen, R. M., eds.*, 1986, pp. 27–44. **[G: U.S.]**

Ben-Akiva, Moshe and de Palma, André. Analysis of a Dynamic Residential Location Choice Model with Transaction Costs. *J. Reg. Sci.*, May 1986, *26*(2), pp. 321–41.

Bendick, Marc, Jr. and Rasmussen, David W. Enterprise Zones and Inner-city Economic Revitalization. **In** *Peterson, G. E. and Lewis, C. W., eds.*, 1986, pp. 97–129. **[G: U.S.]**

Bergman, Edward M. Policy Realities and Development Potentials in Local Economies. **In** *Bergman, E. M., ed.*, 1986, pp. 1–14. **[G: U.S.]**

Bergman, Edward M. and Goldstein, Harvey A. Dynamics, Structural Change, and Economic Development Paths. **In** *Bergman, E. M., ed.*, 1986, *1983*, pp. 84–110. **[G: U.S.]**

Berliant, Marcus C. A Utility Representation for a Preference Relation on a σ-Algebra. *Econometrica*, March 1986, *54*(2), pp. 359–62.

Bjorklund, E. M. The Danwei: Socio-Spatial Characteristics of Work Units in China's Urban Society. *Econ. Geogr.*, January 1986, *62*(1), pp. 19–29. **[G: China]**

Blackley, Paul R. Urban–Rural Variations in the Structure of Manufacturing Production. *Urban Stud.*, December 1986, *23*(6), pp. 471–83. **[G: U.S.]**

Blackley, Paul R. and Greytak, David. Comparative Advantage and Industrial Location: An Intrametropolitan Evaluation. *Urban Stud.*, June 1986, *23*(3), pp. 221–30. **[G: U.S.]**

Boehm, Thomas P. and Ihlanfeldt, Keith R. Residential Mobility and Neighborhood Quality. *J. Reg. Sci.*, May 1986, *26*(2), pp. 411–24. **[G: U.S.]**

Bound, John. NBER-Mathematica Survey of Inner-city Black Youth: An Analysis of the Undercount of Older Youths. **In** *Freeman, R. B. and Holzer, H. J., eds.*, 1986, pp. 443–59. **[G: U.S.]**

Bradford, Calvin and Temali, Mihailo. City Venture Corporation: Initiatives in U.S. Cities. **In** *Bergman, E. M., ed.*, 1986, *1983*, pp. 185–204. **[G: U.S.]**

Brady, J. E. and Parker, A. J. The Socio-Demographic Spatial Structure of Dublin in 1981.

Econ. Soc. Rev., July 1986, *17*(4), pp. 229–52. **[G: Ireland]**

Bramley, Glen. Defining Equal Standards in Local Public Services. *Urban Stud.*, October 1986, *23*(5), pp. 391–412. **[G: U.K.]**

Brewer, H. L. and Moomaw, Ronald L. Regional Economic Instability and Industrial Diversification in the U.S.: Comment. *Land Econ.*, November 1986, *62*(4), pp. 412–15. **[G: U.S.]**

Bridbury, A. R. Dr. Rigby's Comment: A Reply [English Provincial Towns in the Later Middle Ages]. *Econ. Hist. Rev., 2nd Ser.*, August 1986, *39*(3), pp. 417–22. **[G: U.K.]**

Brouwer, Floor and Nijkamp, Peter. Mixed Qualitative Calculus as a Tool in Policy Modeling: A Dynamic Simulation Model of Urban Decline. *J. Policy Modeling*, Spring 1986, *8*(1), pp. 69–88.

Brower, Sidney. Planners in the Neighborhood: A Cautionary Tale. **In** *Taylor, R. B., ed.*, 1986, pp. 181–214. **[G: U.S.]**

Brown, Barbara. Modal Choice, Location Demand, and Income. *J. Urban Econ.*, September 1986, *20*(2), pp. 128–39.

Brown, Charles. Do Better Jobs Make Better Workers? Absenteeism from Work among Inner-city Black Youths: Comment. **In** *Freeman, R. B. and Holzer, H. J., eds.*, 1986, pp. 295–98. **[G: U.S.]**

Brueckner, Jan K. A Switching Regression Analysis of Urban Population Densities. *J. Urban Econ.*, March 1986, *19*(2), pp. 174–89. **[G: U.S.]**

Burkhead, Jesse, et al. Metropolitan and Fiscal Policy: The Record of 40 Years. *Urban Stud.*, February 1986, *23*(1), pp. 1–8. **[G: U.S.]**

Cain, Louis P. From Mud to Metropolis: Chicago before the Fire. **In** *Uselding, P., ed.*, 1986, pp. 93–129. **[G: U.S.]**

Camagni, Roberto. The Economics of Industrial Revitalisation in Declining Metropolitan Areas. *Econ. Int.*, May-Aug.-Nov. 1986, *39*(2–3–4), pp. 316–34. **[G: Italy]**

Camagni, Roberto. Innovation and the Urban Life-cycle: Production, Location and Income Distribution Aspects. **In** *Nijkamp, P., ed. (II)*, 1986, pp. 382–400. **[G: Italy]**

Camagni, Roberto; Diappi, Lidia and Leonardi, Giorgio. Urban Growth and Decline in a Hierarchical System: A Supply-oriented Dynamic Approach. *Reg. Sci. Urban Econ.*, February 1986, *16*(1), pp. 145–60.

Chan, Lean Heng. Young Workers Education Project: Development of a Participatory Urban Services Centre in Penang, Malaysia. **In** *Yeung, Y. M. and McGee, T. G., eds.*, 1986, pp. 165–90. **[G: Malaysia]**

Chavis, David M. and Wandersman, Abraham. Roles for Research and the Researcher in Neighborhood Development. **In** *Taylor, R. B., ed.*, 1986, pp. 215–49.

Cheshire, Paul; Carbonaro, Gianni and Hay, Dennis. Problems of Urban Decline and Growth in EEC Countries: Or Measuring Degrees of Elephantness. *Urban Stud.*, April 1986, *23*(2), pp. 131–49. **[G: EEC]**

Clapp, John M. Interdependent Behavior with Relocation Costs: The Comparative Statics of Spatial History. *J. Reg. Sci.*, February 1986, *26*(1), pp. 33–46.

Clarke, Susan E. Urban America, Inc.: Corporatist Convergence of Power in American Cities? **In** *Bergman, E. M., ed.*, 1986, pp. 37–58. **[G: U.S.]**

Connerly, Charles E. and Frank, James E. Predicting Support for Local Growth Controls. *Soc. Sci. Quart.*, September 1986, *67*(3), pp. 572–86. **[G: U.S.]**

Cooke, Philip. The Changing Urban and Regional System in the United Kingdom. *Reg. Stud.*, June 1986, *20*(3), pp. 243–51. **[G: U.K.]**

Cooley, Mike and Murphy, Shaun. Jobs and Human-Centred Production. **In** *Nolan, P. and Paine, S., eds.*, 1986, pp. 284–90. **[G: U.K.]**

Dendrinos, Dimitrios S. and Sonis, Michael. Variational Principles and Conservation Conditions in Volterra's Ecology and in Urban Relative Dynamics. *J. Reg. Sci.*, May 1986, *26*(2), pp. 359–77.

Dewar, David; Todes, Alison and Watson, Vanessa. Industrial Decentralization Policy in South Africa: Rhetoric and Practice. *Urban Stud.*, October 1986, *23*(5), pp. 363–76. **[G: S. Africa]**

Douglas, George W. and Mullenix, James W. Cities and States as Agents in Restraint of Trade. *Antitrust Bull.*, Summer 1986, *31*(2), pp. 505–25. **[G: U.S.]**

Dowall, David. Metropolitan and Fiscal Policy: The Record of 40 Years: Discussion: The Future of Policy. *Urban Stud.*, February 1986, *23*(1), pp. 8–9. **[G: U.S.]**

Duffy, Neal E. The Determination of an Appropriate Urban Production Function: A Statistical Approach. *Rev. Reg. Stud.*, Fall 1986, *16*(3), pp. 42–49. **[G: U.S.]**

Dynarski, Mark. Household Formation and Suburbanization, 1970–1980. *J. Urban Econ.*, January 1986, *19*(1), pp. 71–87. **[G: U.S.]**

Egan, Mary Lou and Bendick, Marc, Jr. The Urban–Rural Dimension in National Economic Development. *J. Devel. Areas*, January 1986, *20*(2), pp. 203–21. **[G: LDCs]**

Ellwood, David T. The Spatial Mismatch Hypothesis: Are There Teenage Jobs Missing in the Ghetto? **In** *Freeman, R. B. and Holzer, H. J., eds.*, 1986, pp. 147–85. **[G: U.S.]**

Erickson, Rodney A. and Syms, Paul M. The Effects of Enterprise Zones on Local Property Markets. *Reg. Stud.*, February 1986, *20*(1), pp. 1–14. **[G: U.K.]**

Evans, Alan W. Comparisons of Agglomeration: Or What Chinitz Really Said [Contrasts in Agglomeration: New York and Pittsburgh Reconsidered]. *Urban Stud.*, October 1986, *23*(5), pp. 387–89. **[G: U.S.]**

Evans, Alan W. The Supply of Land: A Pedagogic Comment. *Urban Stud.*, December 1986, *23*(6), pp. 527–30.

Evans, Diana Yiannakis. Sunbelt versus Frostbelt: The Evolution of Regional Conflict over Federal Aid to Cities in the House of Representatives. *Soc. Sci. Quart.*, March 1986, *67*(1), pp. 108–17. **[G: U.S.]**

Evans, Tony. Teaching Economics to the 13–16 Age Range: Producing a Local Economy Resources Pack. **In** *Whitehead, D. J., ed.*, 1986, pp. 34–38. **[G: U.K.]**

Feder, Judith and Hadley, Jack. Cutbacks, Recession, and Hospitals' Care for the Urban Poor. **In** *Peterson, G. E. and Lewis, C. W., eds.*, 1986, pp. 37–61. **[G: U.S.]**

Ferguson, Ronald and Filer, Randall K. Do Better Jobs Make Better Workers? Absenteeism from Work among Inner-city Black Youths. **In** *Freeman, R. B. and Holzer, H. J., eds.*, 1986, pp. 261–95. **[G: U.S.]**

Fleming, Gretchen V. Appropriateness of Care. **In** *Fleming, G. V. and Andersen, R. M., eds.*, 1986, pp. 160–77. **[G: U.S.]**

Fleming, Gretchen V. Selection Effects in the MHSP Program. **In** *Fleming, G. V. and Andersen, R. M., eds.*, 1986, pp. 68–79. **[G: U.S.]**

Fleming, Gretchen V. and Andersen, Ronald M. Can Access Be Improved While Controlling Costs? Conclusion. **In** *Fleming, G. V. and Andersen, R. M., eds.*, 1986, pp. 195–208. **[G: U.S.]**

Foster, Richard W. Waiver Effects and Further Controls for Selection Bias. **In** *Fleming, G. V. and Andersen, R. M., eds.*, 1986, pp. 119–59. **[G: U.S.]**

Freeman, Richard B. Who Escapes? The Relation of Churchgoing and Other Background Factors to the Socioeconomic Performance of Black Male Youths from Inner-city Tracts. **In** *Freeman, R. B. and Holzer, H. J., eds.*, 1986, pp. 353–76. **[G: U.S.]**

Fried, Marc. The Neighborhood in Metropolitan Life: Its Psychosocial Significance. **In** *Taylor, R. B., ed.*, 1986, pp. 331–63. **[G: U.S.]**

Fujita, Masahisa. Optimal Location of Public Facilities: Area Dominance Approach. *Reg. Sci. Urban Econ.*, May 1986, *16*(2), pp. 241–68.

Galloway, Thomas D. and Landis, John D. How Cities Expand: Does State Law Make a Difference? *Growth Change*, October 1986, *17*(4), pp. 25–45. **[G: U.S.]**

German, Rachel M. Health Care in the City: Setting the Stage for the Municipal Health Services Program. **In** *Fleming, G. V. and Andersen, R. M., eds.*, 1986, pp. 13–26. **[G: U.S.]**

Getis, Arthur. The Economic Health of Municipalities within a Metropolitan Region: The Case of Chicago. *Econ. Geogr.*, January 1986, *62*(1), pp. 52–73. **[G: U.S.]**

Glickman, Norman J. and Wilson, Robert H. National Contexts for Urban Economic Policy. **In** *Bergman, E. M., ed.*, 1986, pp. 15–36. **[G: OECD]**

Goldberg, Kalman and Scott, Robert C. Intrametropolitan Fiscal Relations: Special Taxing Districts. *J. Urban Econ.*, November 1986, *20*(3), pp. 341–55. **[G: U.S.]**

Gori, Enrico; Pastacaldi, Andrea and Vitali, Letizia. Models of Spatial Choice: The Case of Banking Services in Urban Areas. *Econ. Notes*, 1986, (2), pp. 129–39.

Greenberg, Stephanie W. and Rohe, William M. Informal Social Control and Crime Prevention in Modern Urban Neighborhoods. **In** *Taylor, R. B., ed.*, 1986, pp. 79–118.

Greene, Kenneth V. and Moulton, George D. Municipal Employee Residency Requirement Statutes: An Economic Analysis. **In** *Zerbe, R. O., Jr., ed.*, 1986, pp. 185–204. **[G: U.S.]**

Greiner, John M. and Peterson, George E. Do Budget Reductions Stimulate Public Sector Productivity? Evidence from Proposition 2½ in Massachusetts. **In** *Peterson, G. E. and Lewis, C. W., eds.*, 1986, pp. 63–95. **[G: U.S.]**

Grimaud, André. Équilibre spatial et effets de voisinage. Une généralisation de l'analyse au cas bidimensionnel. (Spatial Equilibrium and Neighbourhood Effects: A Generalization of the Analysis of the Bidimensional Case. With English summary.) *Revue Écon.*, January 1986, *37*(1), pp. 67–88.

Hadwin, J. F. From Dissonance to Harmony on the Late Medieval Town? *Econ. Hist. Rev., 2nd Ser.*, August 1986, *39*(3), pp. 423–26. **[G: U.K.]**

Hall, John Stuart. Retrenchment in Phoenix, Arizona. **In** *Peterson, G. E. and Lewis, C. W., eds.*, 1986, pp. 185–207. **[G: U.S.]**

Hamnett, Chris. The Changing Socio-economic Structure of London and the South East, 1961–1981. *Reg. Stud.*, October 1986, *20*(5), pp. 391–405. **[G: U.K.]**

Hardoy, Jorge E. and Satterthwaite, David. Government Policies and Small and Intermediate Urban Centres. **In** *Hardoy, J. E. and Satterthwaite, D., eds.*, 1986, pp. 335–97. **[G: LDCs]**

Hardoy, Jorge E. and Satterthwaite, David. Why Small and Intermediate Urban Centres? **In** *Hardoy, J. E. and Satterthwaite, D., eds.*, 1986, pp. 1–17.

Harris, Candee S. Establishing High-Technology Enterprises in Metropolitan Areas. **In** *Bergman, E. M., ed.*, 1986, pp. 165–84. **[G: U.S.]**

Heikkila, Eric and Hutton, Thomas A. Toward an Evaluative Framework for Land Use Policy in Industrial Districts of the Urban Core: A Qualitative Analysis of the Exclusionary Zoning Approach. *Urban Stud.*, February 1986, *23*(1), pp. 47–60. **[G: Canada]**

Henderson, J. Vernon. Efficiency of Resource Usage and City Size. *J. Urban Econ.*, January 1986, *19*(1), pp. 47–70. **[G: Brazil; U.S.]**

Henderson, J. Vernon. Urbanization in a Developing Country: City Size and Population Composition. *J. Devel. Econ.*, July-Aug. 1986, *22*(2), pp. 269–93. **[G: Brazil]**

Hirsch, Werner Z. Interindustry Relations of a Metropolitan Area. **In** *Sohn, I., ed.*, 1986, *1959*, pp. 354–71. **[G: U.S.]**

Hofmann, Michael. The Informal Sector in an Intermediate City: A Case in Egypt. *Econ. Develop. Cult. Change*, January 1986, *34*(2), pp. 263–77. **[G: Egypt]**

Hoggart, Keith. Property Tax Resources and Political Party Control in England 1974–1984. *Urban Stud.*, February 1986, *23*(1), pp. 33–46. [G: U.K.]

Howland, Marie. Cyclical Startups and Closures in Key Industries of America's Cities and Suburbs. **In** *Bergman, E. M., ed.*, 1986, pp. 111–28. [G: U.S.]

Hyclak, Thomas J. Productivity and City Size: Some Historical Evidence. *Eastern Econ. J.*, Jan.-Mar. 1986, *12*(1), pp. 45–51. [G: U.S.]

Illy, Hans F. Regulation and Evasion: Street-Vendors in Manila. *Policy Sci.*, July 1986, *19*(1), pp. 61–81. [G: Philippines]

James, Franklin J. and Blair, John P. Labor Mobility in National Policy and Local Economies. **In** *Bergman, E. M., ed.*, 1986, *1983*, pp. 271–85. [G: U.S.]

Johansson, Börje. Spatial Dynamics and Metropolitan Change: Introduction. *Reg. Sci. Urban Econ.*, February 1986, *16*(1), pp. 1–6.

Jones, Huw, et al. Peripheral Counter-Urbanization: Findings from an Integration of Census and Survey Data in Northern Scotland. *Reg. Stud.*, February 1986, *20*(1), pp. 15–26. [G: U.K.]

de Jong, Mark and Lambooy, Jan G. Urban Dynamics and the New Firm: The Position of Amsterdam in the Northern Rimcity. **In** *Keeble, D. and Wever, E., eds.*, 1986, pp. 203–23. [G: Netherlands]

Jud, G. Donald and Bennett, D. Gordon. Public Schools and the Pattern of Intraurban Residential Mobility. *Land Econ.*, November 1986, *62*(4), pp. 362–70. [G: U.S.]

Judd, Dennis R. and Ready, Randy L. Entrepreneurial Cities and the New Politics of Economic Development. **In** *Peterson, G. E. and Lewis, C. W., eds.*, 1986, pp. 209–47. [G: U.S.]

Kahimbaara, J. A. The Population Density Gradient and the Spatial Structure of a Third World City: Nairobi, A Case Study. *Urban Stud.*, August 1986, *23*(4), pp. 307–22. [G: Kenya]

Kahnert, Friedrich. Re-examining Urban Poverty and Employment. *Finance Develop.*, March 1986, *23*(1), pp. 44–47. [G: LDCs]

Kamal, Salih, et al. Young Workers and Urban Services in Penang. **In** *Yeung, Y. M. and McGee, T. G., eds.*, 1986, pp. 119–63. [G: Malaysia]

Karamoy, Amir and Dias, Gillian. Delivery of Urban Services in Kampungs in Jakarta and Ujung Pandang. **In** *Yeung, Y. M. and McGee, T. G., eds.*, 1986, pp. 191–210. [G: Indonesia]

Kasarda, John D. Transforming Cities and Employment Policy for Displaced Workers. **In** *Bergman, E. M., ed.*, 1986, *1983*, pp. 286–307. [G: U.S.]

Katz, Eliakim and Stark, Oded. On the Shadow Wage of Urban Jobs in Less-Developed Countries. *J. Urban Econ.*, September 1986, *20*(2), pp. 121–27. [G: LDCs]

Kaufmann, Daniel and Lindauer, David L. A Model of Income Transfers for the Urban Poor. *J. Devel. Econ.*, July-Aug. 1986, *22*(2), pp. 337–50. [G: El Salvador]

Keil, Stanley R. and Mack, Richard S. Identifying Export Potential in the Service Sector. *Growth Change*, April 1986, *17*(2), pp. 1–10. [G: U.S.]

Kellerman, Aharon and Krakover, Shaul. Multisectoral Urban Growth in Space and Time: An Empirical Approach. *Reg. Stud.*, April 1986, *20*(2), pp. 117–29. [G: U.S.]

Kemp, Kathleen A. Race, Ethnicity, Class and Urban Spatial Conflict: Chicago as a Crucial Test Case. *Urban Stud.*, June 1986, *23*(3), pp. 197–208. [G: U.S.]

Khan, Shaheen. The Determinants of Urban Activity Rates. *Pakistan Econ. Soc. Rev.*, Summer 1986, *24*(1), pp. 23–44. [G: Pakistan]

Kim, Tschangho John. Modeling the Density Variations of Urban Land Uses with Transportation Network Congestion. *J. Urban Econ.*, May 1986, *19*(3), pp. 264–76.

Klarich, Nina M. Private-Sector Economic Development Activities in the Chicago Metro Area. **In** *Walzer, N. and Chicoine, D. L., eds.*, 1986, pp. 214–25. [G: U.S.]

Kohsaka, Hiroyuki. The Location Process of Central Place System within a Circular City. *Econ. Geogr.*, July 1986, *62*(3), pp. 254–66.

Koppel, Bruce. Janus in Metropolis: An Essay on the Political Economy of Urban Resources. *Devel. Econ.*, March 1986, *24*(1), pp. 3–25.

Kuan, Hsin-chi; Lau, Siu-kai and Ho, Kam-fai. Organizing Participatory Urban Services: The Mutual-Aid Committees in Hong Kong. **In** *Yeung, Y. M. and McGee, T. G., eds.*, 1986, pp. 239–54. [G: Hong Kong]

Kubo, Yuji. Urban Concentration and Rural Growth: A Two-Sector Analysis. *J. Reg. Sci.*, August 1986, *26*(3), pp. 379–93.

Kurre, James A. Additional Evidence on the Incubator Hypothesis: Detroit, 1970–75. *Urban Stud.*, October 1986, *23*(5), pp. 429–34. [G: U.S.]

Kutay, Aydan. Optimum Office Location and the Comparative Statics of Information Economies. *Reg. Stud.*, October 1986, *20*(6), pp. 551–63.

Lakshmanan, T. R. and Chatterjee, Lata. Technical Change and Metropolitan Adjustments: Some Policy and Analytical Implications. *Reg. Sci. Urban Econ.*, February 1986, *16*(1), pp. 7–30.

Lakshmanan, T. R. and Chatterjee, Lata. Technical Change, Employment and Metropolitan Adjustment. **In** *Nijkamp, P., ed. (II)*, 1986, pp. 21–45.

Lambooy, Jan G. and van der Vegt, Chris. Segmentation Theories and Manpower Policy in Dutch Cities. **In** *Nijkamp, P., ed. (II)*, 1986, pp. 262–79. [G: Netherlands]

Lapointe, Alain and Desrosiers, Jacques. Modeling Residential Choice. *J. Reg. Sci.*, August 1986, *26*(3), pp. 348–66. [G: Canada]

Lau, Siu-kai; Kuan, Hsin-chi and Ho, Kam-fai. Leaders, Officials, and Citizens in Urban Service Delivery: A Comparative Study of Four Localities in Hong Kong. **In** *Yeung, Y. M. and*

McGee, T. G., eds., 1986, pp. 211–37. **[G: Hong Kong]**

Lawarree, Jacques. Une comparaison empirique des performances des secteurs privé et public: le cas des collectes d'immondices en Belgique. (With English summary.) *Cah. Écon. Bruxelles*, First Trimester 1986, (109), pp. 3–31. **[G: Belgium]**

Ledent, Jacques. A Model of Urbanization with Nonlinear Migration Flows. *Int. Reg. Sci. Rev.*, December 1986, *10*(3), pp. 221–42. **[G: U.S.]**

Leigh, J. Paul. Are Compensating Wages Paid for Time spent Commuting? *Appl. Econ.*, November 1986, *18*(11), pp. 1203–13. **[G: U.S.]**

Leonard, Jonathan S. The Spatial Mismatch Hypothesis: Are There Teenage Jobs Missing in the Ghetto? Comment. **In** *Freeman, R. B. and Holzer, H. J., eds.*, 1986, pp. 185–90. **[G: U.S.]**

Leonardi, Giorgio and Casti, J. Agglomerative Tendencies in the Distribution of Populations. *Reg. Sci. Urban Econ.*, February 1986, *16*(1), pp. 43–56.

Lever, William and Mather, Frank. The Changing Structure of Business and Employment in the Conurbation. **In** *Lever, W. and Moore, C., eds.*, 1986, pp. 1–21. **[G: U.K.]**

Lever, William and Moore, Chris. Future Directions for Urban Policy. **In** *Lever, W. and Moore, C., eds.*, 1986, pp. 142–61. **[G: U.K.]**

Liebschutz, Sarah F. and Taddiken, Alan J. The Effects of Reagan Administration Budget Cuts on Human Services in Rochester, New York. **In** *Peterson, G. E. and Lewis, C. W., eds.*, 1986, pp. 131–54. **[G: U.S.]**

Lines, Jon J.; Parker, Ellen L. and Perry, David C. Building the Twentieth-Century Public Works Machine: Robert Moses and the Public Authority. **In** *Schoolman, M. and Magid, A., eds.*, 1986, pp. 231–55. **[G: U.S.]**

London, Bruce and Anderson, Kristine L. Rural–Urban Hierarchy and National Development: The Role of Elites in the Distribution of Scarce Resources to the Thai Hinterland. *Soc. Sci. Quart.*, September 1986, *67*(3), pp. 545–60. **[G: Thailand]**

Lyttle, Christopher. Methodology for Imputing Missing Values, MHSP. **In** *Fleming, G. V. and Andersen, R. M., eds.*, 1986, pp. 250–62. **[G: U.S.]**

Malecki, Edward J. High-Technology Sectors and Local Economic Development. **In** *Bergman, E. M., ed.*, 1986, *1983*, pp. 129–42. **[G: U.S.]**

McArthur, Andrew and McGregor, Alan. Policies for the Disadvantaged in the Labour Market. **In** *Lever, W. and Moore, C., eds.*, 1986, pp. 120–41. **[G: U.K.]**

McConnell, Virginia D. Automobile Use and Locational Interdependencies. *J. Reg. Sci.*, August 1986, *26*(3), pp. 475–98.

McDougall, Gerald S. and Bunce, Harold. Urban Services and the Suburbanization of Blacks. *Soc. Sci. Quart.*, September 1986, *67*(3), pp. 596–603. **[G: U.S.]**

McGee, T. G. and Yeung, Y. M. Participatory Urban Services in Asia. **In** *Yeung, Y. M. and McGee, T. G., eds.*, 1986, pp. 9–27. **[G: Asia]**

McHone, W. Warren. Supply-Side Considerations in the Location of Industry in Suburban Communities: Empirical Evidence from the Philadelphia SMSA. *Land Econ.*, February 1986, *62*(1), pp. 64–73. **[G: U.S.]**

McPherson, Marlys and Silloway, Glenn. The Role of the Small Commercial Center in the Urban Neighborhood. **In** *Taylor, R. B., ed.*, 1986, pp. 144–76. **[G: U.S.]**

Megdal, Sharon Bernstein. Property Taxes and Firm Location: Evidence from Proposition 13: Comment. **In** *Rosen, H. S., ed.*, 1986, pp. 108–12. **[G: U.S.]**

Mindick, Burton. Neighborhood Mobilization: A Study of the Implementation of an Experimental Intervention. **In** *Taylor, R. B., ed.*, 1986, pp. 250–79. **[G: U.S.]**

Mirucki, Jean. Planned Economic Development and Loglinearity in the Rank-Size Distribution of Urban Systems: The Soviet Experience. *Urban Stud.*, April 1986, *23*(2), pp. 151–56. **[G: U.S.S.R.]**

Mittar, Vishwa. Income Distribution and Poverty in the Urban Informal Sector. *Margin*, January 1986, *18*(2), pp. 29–41. **[G: India]**

Mohtadi, Hamid. Rural Stratification, Rural to Urban Migration, and Urban Inequality: Evidence from Iran. *World Devel.*, June 1986, *14*(6), pp. 713–25. **[G: Iran]**

Montanari, Armando. Planning and Urban Growth in Southern Europe. *J. Europ. Econ. Hist.*, Spring 1986, *15*(1), pp. 183–95. **[G: Greece; Italy; Portugal; Spain; Turkey]**

Moomaw, Ronald L. Have Changes in Localization Economies Been Responsible for Declining Productivity Advantages in Large Cities? *J. Reg. Sci.*, February 1986, *26*(1), pp. 19–32. **[G: U.S.]**

Moor, G. and Parnell, R. Private Sector Involvement in Local Authority Service Delivery. *Reg. Stud.*, June 1986, *20*(3), pp. 253–57. **[G: U.K.]**

Moore, Chris and Booth, Simon. From Comprehensive Regeneration to Privatization: The Search for Effective Area Strategies. **In** *Lever, W. and Moore, C., eds.*, 1986, pp. 76–91. **[G: U.K.]**

Moore, Chris and Booth, Simon. The Post-industrial Synthesis: Policies for Enterprise in Clydeside. **In** *Lever, W. and Moore, C., eds.*, 1986, pp. 62–75. **[G: U.K.]**

Moore, Chris and Booth, Simon. The Pragmatic Approach: Local Political Models of Regeneration. **In** *Lever, W. and Moore, C., eds.*, 1986, pp. 92–106. **[G: U.K.]**

Moore, Chris and Booth, Simon. Unlocking Enterprise: The Search for Synergy. **In** *Lever, W. and Moore, C., eds.*, 1986, pp. 107–19. **[G: U.K.]**

Moore, Eric G. and Clark, W. A. V. Stable Structure and Local Variation: A Comparison of Household Flows in Four Metropolitan Areas. *Urban Stud.*, June 1986, *23*(3), pp. 185–96. **[G: U.S.]**

Morris, R. J. Atlas of Industrializing Britain 1780–1914: Urbanization. **In** *Langton, J. and Morris, R. J., eds.*, 1986, pp. 164–79. **[G: U.K.]**

Morrow-Jones, Hazel A. Neighbourhood Change and the Federal Housing Administration: Some Theoretical and Empirical Issues. *Urban Stud.*, October 1986, *23*(5), pp. 419–28. **[G: U.S.]**

Mutlu, Servet. City-Forming Propensities in a Central Place Hierarchy: Application of Beckmann–McPherson Model to the Turkish Urban System. *Ann. Reg. Sci.*, July 1986, *20*(2), pp. 28–43. **[G: Turkey]**

Noyelle, Thierry J. Advanced Services in the System of Cities. **In** *Bergman, E. M., ed.*, 1986, *1983*, pp. 143–64. **[G: U.S.]**

Oaxaca, Ronald L. and Taylor, Carol A. Simulating the Impacts of Economic Programs on Urban Areas: The Case of Unemployment Insurance Benefits. *J. Urban Econ.*, January 1986, *19*(1), pp. 23–46. **[G: U.S.]**

Ozo, A. O. Residential Location and Intra-urban Mobility in a Developing Country: Some Empirical Observations from Benin City, Nigeria. *Urban Stud.*, December 1986, *23*(6), pp. 457–70. **[G: Nigeria]**

Park, Soo-Young; Kim, Yong-Woong and Yang, Ok-Hyee. The *Saemaul* Self-help Activity System. **In** *Yeung, Y. M. and McGee, T. G., eds.*, 1986, pp. 59–71. **[G: S. Korea]**

Park, Soo-Young; Kim, Yong-Woong and Yang, Ok-Hyee. Urban Services and the Poor: The Case of Korea. **In** *Yeung, Y. M. and McGee, T. G., eds.*, 1986, pp. 29–57. **[G: S. Korea]**

Penny, P. E. An Opposing View on Site Rating [The Site Value Tax: An Evaluation]. *S. Afr. J. Econ.*, December 1986, *54*(4), pp. 430–31. **[G: S. Africa]**

Peterson, George E. Urban Policy and the Cyclical Behavior of Cities. **In** *Peterson, G. E. and Lewis, C. W., eds.*, 1986, pp. 11–35. **[G: U.S.]**

Phillips, Robyn S. and Vidal, Avis C. Restructuring and Growth Transitions of Metropolitan Economies: The Context for Economic Development Policy. **In** *Bergman, E. M., ed.*, 1986, *1983*, pp. 59–83. **[G: U.S.]**

Pines, David and Sadka, Efraim. Comparative Statics Analysis of a Fully Closed City. *J. Urban Econ.*, July 1986, *20*(1), pp. 1–20.

Platt, D. C. M. Domestic Finance in the Growth of Buenos Aires, 1880–1914. **In** *di Tella, G. and Platt, D. C. M., eds.*, 1986, pp. 1–14. **[G: Argentina]**

Portes, Alejandro; Blitzer, Silvia and Curtis, John. The Urban Informal Sector in Uruguay: Its Internal Structure, Characteristics, and Effects. *World Devel.*, June 1986, *14*(6), pp. 727–41. **[G: Uruguay]**

Quigley, John M. The Evaluation of Complex Urban Policies: Simulating the Willingness to Pay for the Benefits of Subsidy Programs. *Reg. Sci. Urban Econ.*, February 1986, *16*(1), pp. 31–42.

Quinn, D. J. Accessibility and Job Search: A Study of Unemployed School Leavers. *Reg. Stud.*, April 1986, *20*(2), pp. 163–73. **[G: U.K.]**

ten Raa, Thijs. The Initial Value Problem for the Trading Cycle in Euclidian Space. *Reg. Sci. Urban Econ.*, November 1986, *16*(4), pp. 527–46.

Raimondo, Henry J. and Stuart, Robert C. Variations in Soviet City Finance. *Growth Change*, April 1986, *17*(2), pp. 56–67. **[G: U.S.S.R.]**

Ramos, Exaltacion and Roman, Ma. A. A. Community Participation Model. **In** *Yeung, Y. M. and McGee, T. G., eds.*, 1986, pp. 97–117. **[G: Philippines]**

Ramos, Exaltacion and Roman, Ma. A. A. Participatory Urban Services in the Philippines. **In** *Yeung, Y. M. and McGee, T. G., eds.*, 1986, pp. 73–96. **[G: Philippines]**

Rich, Richard C. Neighborhood-Based Participation in the Planning Process: Promise and Reality. **In** *Taylor, R. B., ed.*, 1986, pp. 41–73. **[G: U.S.]**

Rigby, S. H. Late Medieval Urban Prosperity: The Evidence of the Lay Subsidies [English Provincial Towns in the Later Middle Ages] [The Medieval Lay Subsidies and Economic History]. *Econ. Hist. Rev., 2nd Ser.*, August 1986, *39*(3), pp. 411–16. **[G: U.K.]**

Robertson, James. How the Cities Can Finance New Enterprise. *Lloyds Bank Rev.*, July 1986, (161), pp. 32–43.

Robson, Brian. Research Issues in the Changing Urban and Regional System. *Reg. Stud.*, June 1986, *20*(3), pp. 203–07. **[G: U.K.]**

Rodriguez-Bachiller, Agustin. Discontiguous Urban Growth and the New Urban Economics: A Review. *Urban Stud.*, April 1986, *23*(2), pp. 79–104.

Rohe, William M. and Gates, Lauren B. Neighborhood Planning in America: Accomplishments and Limitations. **In** *Taylor, R. B., ed.*, 1986, pp. 5–40. **[G: U.S.]**

Salinas, Patricia Wilson. Urban Growth, Subemployment, and Mobility. **In** *Bergman, E. M., ed.*, 1986, pp. 248–70. **[G: U.S.]**

Schweizer, Urs. Suburbanisierung als Folge fiskalischer Inäquivalenz. (Suburbanisation Caused by Fiscal Inequivalence. With English summary.) *Schweiz. Z. Volkswirtsch. Statist.*, March 1986, *122*(1), pp. 1–15.

Scotchmer, Suzanne. The Short-run and Long-run Benefits of Environmental Improvement. *J. Public Econ.*, June 1986, *30*(1), pp. 61–81.

Scoville, James G. The Traditional Industrial Sector in Developing Countries: An Update on Its Role and Functioning. *Amer. J. Econ. Soc.*, July 1986, *45*(3), pp. 313–28. **[G: LDCs]**

Shannon, W. Wayne, et al. The Public Sector in Stamford, Connecticut: Responses to a Changing Federal Role. **In** *Peterson, G. E. and Lewis, C. W., eds.*, 1986, pp. 155–83. **[G: U.S.]**

Shefer, Daniel. Utility Changes in Housing and Neighborhood Services for Households Moving into and out of Distressed Neighborhoods. *J. Urban Econ.*, January 1986, *19*(1), pp. 107–24. **[G: Israel]**

Shonkwiler, J. Scott and Reynolds, J. E. A Note on the Use of Hedonic Price Models in the Analysis of Land Prices at the Urban Fringe. *Land Econ.*, February 1986, *62*(1), pp. 58–63.

Shukla, Vibhooti and Stark, Oded. Urban External Economies and Optimal Migration. **In** *Stark, O., ed.*, 1986, pp. 139–46.

Sinn, Hans-Werner. Vacant Land and the Role of Government Intervention. *Reg. Sci. Urban Econ.*, August 1986, *16*(3), pp. 353–85.

Smith, V. Kerry and Desvousges, William H. The Value of Avoiding a *Lulu:* Hazardous Waste Disposal Sites. *Rev. Econ. Statist.*, May 1986, *68*(2), pp. 293–99. **[G: U.S.]**

Solomon, D. The Site Value Tax: A Reply [The Site Value Tax: An Evaluation]. *S. Afr. J. Econ.*, December 1986, *54*(4), pp. 432–36. **[G: S. Africa]**

Sonstelie, Jon C. and Portney, Paul R. Profit Maximizing Communities and the Theory of Local Public Expenditure: Reply. *J. Urban Econ.*, September 1986, *20*(2), pp. 250–55.

Southwick, Lawrence, Jr. Local Economic Development and the State. **In** *Schoolman, M. and Magid, A., eds.*, 1986, pp. 147–64. **[G: U.S.]**

Steen, Robert C. Nonubiquitous Transportation and Urban Population Density Gradients. *J. Urban Econ.*, July 1986, *20*(1), pp. 97–106. **[G: U.S.]**

Stewart, Charles T., Jr. and Lee, Jin-Hsia. Urban Concentration and Sectoral Income Distribution. *J. Devel. Areas*, April 1986, *20*(3), pp. 357–68. **[G: LDCs]**

Strauss, Robert P. and Harkins, Peter B. The Net Fiscal Impact of Selected Federal Block Grant Programs. *J. Reg. Sci.*, February 1986, *26*(1), pp. 63–85. **[G: U.S.]**

Stull, William J. The Urban Economics of Adam Smith. *J. Urban Econ.*, November 1986, *20*(3), pp. 291–311.

Sullivan, Arthur M. A General Equilibrium Model with Agglomerative Economies and Decentralized Employment. *J. Urban Econ.*, July 1986, *20*(1), pp. 55–74.

Swanstrom, Todd. Strategic Planning in a White Collar City: The Case of Albany. **In** *Schoolman, M. and Magid, A., eds.*, 1986, pp. 117–29. **[G: U.S.]**

Tabuchi, Takatoshi. Urban Agglomeration Economies in a Linear City. *Reg. Sci. Urban Econ.*, August 1986, *16*(3), pp. 421–36.

Tabuchi, Takatoshi. Urban Agglomeration, Capital Augmenting Technology, and Labor Market Equilibrium. *J. Urban Econ.*, September 1986, *20*(2), pp. 211–28. **[G: Japan]**

Taylor, Carol A. Spatial Utility Equilibrium and City Size Distribution in a Central Place System. *J. Urban Econ.*, January 1986, *19*(1), pp. 1–22. **[G: U.S.]**

Taylor, Ralph B. Urban Neighborhoods: Research and Policy: Epilogue. **In** *Taylor, R. B., ed.*, 1986, pp. 364–72. **[G: U.S.]**

Thompson, James W. and Cataldo, James. Market Incentives for Criminal Behavior: Comment. **In** *Freeman, R. B. and Holzer, H. J., eds.*, 1986, pp. 347–51. **[G: U.S.]**

Timmermans, Harry. Locational Choice Behaviour of Entrepreneurs: An Experimental Analysis. *Urban Stud.*, June 1986, *23*(3), pp. 231–40.

Tran, Dang T. Locational Factors in the Declining Industrial Competitive Advantage of the New York Urban Region. *J. Reg. Sci.*, February 1986, *26*(1), pp. 121–39. **[G: U.S.]**

Urry, John. Locality Research: The Case of Lancaster. *Reg. Stud.*, June 1986, *20*(3), pp. 233–42. **[G: U.K.]**

Van Horn, Carl E.; Beauregard, Robert A. and Ford, David S. Local Economic Development and Job Targeting. **In** *Bergman, E. M., ed.*, 1986, pp. 226–47. **[G: U.S.]**

Vavouras, Ioannis S. Local Government Investment Planning: A Proposed Approach Applied to Greece. *Comp. Econ. Stud.*, Winter 1986, *28*(4), pp. 1–11. **[G: Greece]**

Vecoli, Rudolph J. The Formation of Chicago's "Little Italies." **In** *Glazier, I. A. and De Rosa, L., eds.*, 1986, pp. 287–301. **[G: U.S.]**

Viscusi, W. Kip. Market Incentives for Criminal Behavior. **In** *Freeman, R. B. and Holzer, H. J., eds.*, 1986, pp. 301–46. **[G: U.S.]**

Walker, Bruce. The Demand for Professional League Football and the Success of Football League Teams: Some City Size Effects. *Urban Stud.*, June 1986, *23*(3), pp. 209–19. **[G: U.K.]**

Warren, Donald I. The Helping Roles of Neighbors: Some Empirical Patterns. **In** *Taylor, R. B., ed.*, 1986, pp. 310–30. **[G: U.S.]**

Wheeler, James O. Similarities in the Corporate Structure of American Cities. *Growth Change*, July 1986, *17*(3), pp. 13–21. **[G: U.S.]**

White, Michelle J. Property Taxes and Firm Location: Evidence from Proposition 13. **In** *Rosen, H. S., ed.*, 1986, pp. 83–107. **[G: U.S.]**

White, Michelle J. Sex Differences in Urban Commuting Patterns. *Amer. Econ. Rev.*, May 1986, *76*(2), pp. 368–72. **[G: U.S.]**

Wiewel, Wim and Mier, Robert. Enterprise Activities of Not-for-Profit Organizations: Surviving the New Federalism? **In** *Bergman, E. M., ed.*, 1986, pp. 205–25.

Wildasin, David E. Spatial Variation of the Marginal Utility of Income and Unequal Treatment of Equals. *J. Urban Econ.*, January 1986, *19*(1), pp. 125–29.

Wish, Naomi Bailin. Are We Really Measuring the Quality of Life? Well-being Has Subjective Dimensions as Well as Objective Ones. *Amer. J. Econ. Soc.*, January 1986, *45*(1), pp. 93–99.

Wolch, Jennifer R. and Geiger, Robert K. Urban Restructuring and the Not-for-Profit Sector. *Econ. Geogr.*, January 1986, *62*(1), pp. 3–18. **[G: U.S.]**

Worrall, Leslie. The Analysis and Management of Urban Change: The Role of Local Information Systems. *J. Econ. Soc. Meas.*, December 1986, *14*(4), pp. 257–70. **[G: U.K.]**

Yeung, Y. M. and McGee, T. G. Community Participation in Delivering Urban Services in Asia: Conclusions. **In** *Yeung, Y. M. and McGee, T. G., eds.*, 1986, pp. 255–62. **[G: Asia]**

Yinger, John. On Fiscal Disparities across Cities. *J. Urban Econ.*, May 1986, *19*(3), pp. 316–37.

Zhang, Zeyu. A Mirror for Urban Economic Reforms. *Chinese Econ. Stud.*, Winter 1985-86, *19*(2), pp. 86–92. **[G: China]**

Zoványi, Gábor. Structural Chan ge in a System of Urban Places: The 20th-Century Evolution of Hungary's Urban Settlement Network. *Reg. Stud.*, February 1986, *20*(1), pp. 47–71. **[G: Hungary]**

932 Housing Economics

9320 Housing Economics (including nonurban housing)

Anas, Alex and Cho, Joong Rae. Existence and Uniqueness of Price Equilibria: Theory and Application to Discrete Choice Models. *Reg. Sci. Urban Econ.*, May 1986, *16*(2), pp. 211–39.

Anas, Alex and Eum, Sung Jick. Disequilibrium Models of Single Family Housing Prices and Transactions: The Case of Chicago, 1972–1976. *J. Urban Econ.*, July 1986, *20*(1), pp. 75–96. **[G: U.S.]**

Arnott, Richard J.; Davidson, Russell and Pines, David. Spatial Aspects of Housing Quality, Density, and Maintenance. *J. Urban Econ.*, March 1986, *19*(2), pp. 190–217.

Bajic, Vladimir. Factor Costs and Factor Use: Substitution among Urban Land and Capital Inputs in the Production of Single-Family Housing. *Appl. Econ.*, March 1986, *18*(3), pp. 291–303. **[G: Canada]**

Barney, L. Dwayne and White, Harry. The Optimal Mortgage Payment Path under Price Uncertainty. *Amer. Real Estate Urban Econ. Assoc. J.*, Fall 1986, *14*(3), pp. 406–13.

Barrow, Michael and Robinson, Ray. Housing and Tax Capitalisation. *Urban Stud.*, February 1986, *23*(1), pp. 61–66. **[G: U.K.]**

Bartik, Timothy J. Neighborhood Revitalization's Effects on Tenants and the Benefit–Cost Analysis of Government Neighborhood Programs. *J. Urban Econ.*, March 1986, *19*(2), pp. 234–48. **[G: U.S.]**

Ben-Akiva, Moshe and de Palma, André. Analysis of a Dynamic Residential Location Choice Model with Transaction Costs. *J. Reg. Sci.*, May 1986, *26*(2), pp. 321–41.

Bentham, Graham. Socio-Tenurial Polarization in the United Kingdom, 1953–83: The Income Evidence. *Urban Stud.*, April 1986, *23*(2), pp. 157–62. **[G: U.K.]**

Bhattacharya, Anand K. The Joint Effect of Housing Start and Inflation Announcements on GNMA Futures Prices. *J. Futures Markets*, Winter 1986, *6*(4), pp. 645–57. **[G: U.S.]**

Blackley, Dixie M.; Follain, James R. and Lee, Haeduck. Evaluation of Hedonic Price Indexes for Thirty-four Large SMSAs. *Amer. Real Estate Urban Econ. Assoc. J.*, Summer 1986, *14*(2), pp. 179–205. **[G: U.S.]**

Boehm, Thomas P. and Ihlanfeldt, Keith R. Residential Mobility and Neighborhood Quality. *J. Reg. Sci.*, May 1986, *26*(2), pp. 411–24. **[G: U.S.]**

Boehm, Thomas P. and Ihlanfeldt, Keith R. The Improvement Expenditures of Urban Homeowners: An Empirical Analysis. *Amer. Real Estate Urban Econ. Assoc. J.*, Spring 1986, *14*(1), pp. 48–60. **[G: U.S.]**

Börsch-Supan, Axel. Household Formation, Housing Prices, and Public Policy Impacts. *J. Public Econ.*, July 1986, *30*(2), pp. 145–64. **[G: U.S.]**

Börsch-Supan, Axel. On the West German Tenants' Protection Legislation. *J. Inst. Theoretical Econ.*, June 1986, *142*(2), pp. 380–404. **[G: W. Germany]**

Bosch, Jean-Claude; Morris, James R. and Wyatt, Steve B. The Investment in Housing as a Forward Market Transaction: Implications for Tenure Choice and Portfolio Selection. *Amer. Real Estate Urban Econ. Assoc. J.*, Fall 1986, *14*(3), pp. 385–405.

Braid, Ralph M. The Comparative Statics of a Filtering Model of Housing with Two Income Groups. *Reg. Sci. Urban Econ.*, August 1986, *16*(3), pp. 437–48.

Brown, Barbara. Modal Choice, Location Demand, and Income. *J. Urban Econ.*, September 1986, *20*(2), pp. 128–39.

Brueckner, Jan K. Reply [Creative Financing and House Prices: A Theoretical Inquiry into the Capitalization Issue]. *Amer. Real Estate Urban Econ. Assoc. J.*, Spring 1986, *14*(1), pp. 158–62.

Brueckner, Jan K. The Downpayment Constraint and Housing Tenure Choice: A Simplified Exposition. *Reg. Sci. Urban Econ.*, November 1986, *16*(4), pp. 519–25.

Cameron, Trudy Ann. Permanent and Transitory Income in Model of Housing Demand. *J. Urban Econ.*, September 1986, *20*(2), pp. 205–10.

Caniglia, Alan S. A Common Fallacy about In-Kind Subsidies: A Housing Program Application. *Eastern Econ. J.*, Apr.-June 1986, *12*(2), pp. 149–57.

Cannaday, Roger E. and Sunderman, Mark A. Estimation of Depreciation for Single-Family Appraisals. *Amer. Real Estate Urban Econ. Assoc. J.*, Summer 1986, *14*(2), pp. 255–73. **[G: U.S.]**

Carliner, Michael S. The Impact of Tax Reform on Housing Demand and Residential Construction Activity. **In** *Follain, J. R., ed.*, 1986, pp. 113–33. **[G: U.S.]**

Case, Karl E. The Market for Single-Family Homes in the Boston Area. *New Eng. Econ. Rev.*, May/June 1986, pp. 38–48. **[G: U.S.]**

Cebula, Richard J. The Urban Family Budget: Reply [The Urban Family Housing Budget in SMSAs]. *Soc. Sci. Quart.*, March 1986, *67*(1), pp. 213. **[G: U.S.]**

Chressanthis, George A. The Impact of Zoning

Changes on Housing Prices: A Time Series Analysis. *Growth Change*, July 1986, *17*(3), pp. 49–70.

van Clark, W. A. V. and Lierop, Wal F. J. Residential Mobility and Household Location Modelling. **In** *Nijkamp, P., ed. (I)*, 1986, pp. 97–132.

Clauretie, Terrence M.; Sirmans, C. F. and Merkle, Paul E. The Effect of Bond Issues on Housing Markets. *Housing Finance Rev.*, Winter 1986, *5*(3), pp. 207–17. **[G: U.S.]**

Crandall, Robert W. The Market for Housing Quality: Comments. **In** *Ippolito, P. M. and Scheffman, D. T., eds.*, 1986, pp. 103–04. **[G: U.S.]**

Dale-Johnson, David and Findlay, M. Chapman, III. Creative Financing and Housing Prices: On a Theoretical Inquiry into the Capitalization Issue: Comment. *Amer. Real Estate Urban Econ. Assoc. J.*, Spring 1986, *14*(1), pp. 153–57.

De Borger, Bruno. Estimating the Benefits of Public-Housing Programs: A Characteristics Approach. *J. Reg. Sci.*, November 1986, *26*(4), pp. 761–73. **[G: Belgium]**

De Borger, Bruno. Household Attributes and the Demand for Housing Characteristics. *Tijdschrift Econ. Manage.*, 1986, *31*(2), pp. 181–202. **[G: Belgium]**

De Borger, Bruno. In-kind Redistribution and Demand-Oriented Housing Subsidies: Some Micro-simulation Results. *Public Finance Quart.*, July 1986, *14*(3), pp. 235–61.

Dynarski, Mark. Residential Attachment and Housing Demand. *Urban Stud.*, February 1986, *23*(1), pp. 11–20. **[G: U.S.]**

Eastwood, David B. and Garner, Sammie G. Home Repairs: A Household Production Perspective. *J. Behav. Econ.*, Spring/Summer 1986, *15*(1/2), pp. 25–39. **[G: U.S.]**

Emmi, Philip C. On the Stability of Housing Sector Interaction: Evidence from 42 Metropolitan Areas. *J. Reg. Sci.*, November 1986, *26*(4), pp. 745–60. **[G: U.S.]**

Englund, Peter. Transaction Costs, Capital-Gains Taxes, and Housing Demand. *J. Urban Econ.*, November 1986, *20*(3), pp. 274–90.

Evans, Alan W. and Beed, Clive. Transport Costs and Urban Property Values in the 1970s. *Urban Stud.*, April 1986, *23*(2), pp. 105–17. **[G: Australia]**

Falk, Barry. The Impact of Federally Sponsored Credit Agencies' Policy Instruments on Housing and Credit Markets. *Housing Finance Rev.*, Fall 1986, *5*(2), pp. 99–118. **[G: U.S.]**

Falk, Barry. Unanticipated Money-Supply Growth and Single-Family Housing Starts in the U.S.: 1964–1983. *Housing Finance Rev.*, Summer 1986, *5*(1), pp. 15–23. **[G: U.S.]**

Farber, Stephen C. Market Segmentation and the Effects on Group Homes for the Handicapped on Residential Property Values. *Urban Stud.*, December 1986, *23*(6), pp. 519–25. **[G: U.S.]**

Fender, John. Local Taxation and Housing Finance: A Proposal for Reform. *Lloyds Bank Rev.*, October 1986, (162), pp. 17–30. **[G: U.K.]**

Fisch, Oscar. A Neoclassical Model of Housing Quality Growth: An Interpretation. *J. Reg. Sci.*, February 1986, *26*(1), pp. 103–20.

Follain, James R. The Impact of the President's Proposals and H.R. 3838 on the Housing Market. **In** *Follain, J. R., ed.*, 1986, pp. 61–85. **[G: U.S.]**

Follain, James R. What Are the Issues and What Is at Stake? **In** *Follain, J. R., ed.*, 1986, pp. 3–8. **[G: U.S.]**

Follain, James R. and Brueckner, Jan K. Federal Income Taxation and Real Estate: Tax Distortions and Their Impacts. **In** *Follain, J. R., ed.*, 1986, pp. 9–25. **[G: U.S.]**

Fortura, Peter and Kushner, Joseph. Canadian Inter-city House Price Differentials. *Amer. Real Estate Urban Econ. Assoc. J.*, Winter 1986, *14*(4), pp. 525–36. **[G: Canada]**

Fox, Alan, et al. The Effects of Tax Reform on Metropolitan Housing. **In** *Follain, J. R., ed.*, 1986, pp. 165–85. **[G: U.S.]**

Gabriel, Stuart A. Housing Policy. **In** *Kop, Y., ed.*, 1986, pp. 227–59. **[G: Israel]**

Gabriel, Stuart A. and Maoz, Ilan. Cyclical Fluctuations in the Israeli Housing Markets. *J. Urban Econ.*, May 1986, *19*(3), pp. 249–63. **[G: Israel]**

Gahvari, Firouz. Demand and Supply of Housing in the U.S.: 1929–1978. *Econ. Inquiry*, April 1986, *24*(2), pp. 333–47. **[G: U.S.]**

Galster, George C. Nuclear Power Plants and Residential Property Values: A Comment on Short-run vs. Long-run Considerations. *J. Reg. Sci.*, November 1986, *26*(4), pp. 803–05. **[G: U.S.]**

Gamble, Hays B. and Downing, Roger H. Nuclear Power Plants and Residential Property Values: A Comment on Short-run vs. Long-run Considerations: A Reply. *J. Reg. Sci.*, November 1986, *26*(4), pp. 807–08. **[G: U.S.]**

Gerber, Robert I. Efficiency of Markets for Heterogeneous, Indivisible Housing. *Reg. Sci. Urban Econ.*, August 1986, *16*(3), pp. 407–19.

Gerber, Robert I. The Comparative Static Response of Rental Housing to a Price Change: Inflation and Government Policy. *J. Reg. Sci.*, November 1986, *26*(4), pp. 731–43.

Goodman, Allen C. Neighborhood Impacts on Housing Prices. **In** *Taylor, R. B., ed.*, 1986, pp. 123–43. **[G: U.S.]**

Goodman, Allen C. and Kawai, Masahiro. Functional Form, Sample Selection, and Housing Demand. *J. Urban Econ.*, September 1986, *20*(2), pp. 155–67. **[G: U.S.]**

Goodman, John L., Jr. Reducing the Error in Monthly Housing Starts Estimates. *Amer. Real Estate Urban Econ. Assoc. J.*, Winter 1986, *14*(4), pp. 557–66. **[G: U.S.]**

Goodwin, Thomas H. Inflation, Risk, Taxes, and the Demand for Owner-Occupied Housing. *Rev. Econ. Statist.*, May 1986, *68*(2), pp. 197–206. **[G: U.S.]**

Goodwin, Thomas H. The Impact of Credit Rationing on Housing Investment: A Multi-Market Disequilibrium Approach. *Int. Econ. Rev.*, June 1986, *27*(2), pp. 445–64. **[G: U.S.]**

Guenther, Robert. Tax Reform and Its Role in the Emerging Dual Market for Housing. **In** *Follain, J. R., ed.*, 1986, pp. 233–36. **[G: U.S.]**

Guttentag, Jack M. Home Equity Conversion in 1986: Some Perspectives on a New Approach. *Housing Finance Rev.*, Summer 1986, *5*(1), pp. 61–64.

Hassan, Syed Fayyaz and Pasha, Hafiz A. Land Densities in Karachi. *Pakistan J. Appl. Econ.*, Winter 1986, *5*(2), pp. 143–62. **[G: Pakistan]**

Haurin, Donald R. and Hendershott, Patric H. Affordability and the Value of Creative Finance: An Application to Seller Financed Transactions. *Housing Finance Rev.*, Winter 1986, *5*(3), pp. 189–206. **[G: U.S.]**

Hemenway, David; Wolf, Kate and Lang, Janet. An Arson Epidemic. *J. Behav. Econ.*, Fall 1986, *15*, pp. 17–28. **[G: U.S.]**

Hendershott, Patric H. and Ling, David C. Likely Impacts of the Administration's Tax Proposals and H.R. 3838. **In** *Follain, J. R., ed.*, 1986, pp. 87–112. **[G: U.S.]**

Henderson, J. Vernon and Ioannides, Yannis M. Tenure Choice and the Demand for Housing. *Economica*, May 1986, *53*(210), pp. 231–46. **[G: U.S.]**

Herzog, Henry W., Jr. and Schlottmann, Alan M. The Metro Rating Game: What Can Be Learned from the Recent Migrants? *Growth Change*, January 1986, *17*(1), pp. 37–50. **[G: U.S.]**

Hinds, Dudley S. and Ordway, Nicholas. The Influence of Race on Rezoning Decisions: Equality of Treatment in Black and White Census Tracts, 1955–1980. *Rev. Black Polit. Econ.*, Spring 1986, *14*(4), pp. 51–63. **[G: U.S.]**

Hobson, Paul A. R. The Incidence of Heterogeneous Residential Property Taxes. *J. Public Econ.*, April 1986, *29*(3), pp. 363–73.

Honda, Nakaji and Mimaki, Tadashi. Multiobjective Decision Method Using Heuristic Rules. **In** *Pau, L. F., ed.*, 1986, pp. 157–65.

Horowitz, Joel L. Bidding Models of Housing Markets. *J. Urban Econ.*, September 1986, *20*(2), pp. 168–90. **[G: U.S.]**

Howenstine, E. Jay. Foreign Housing Voucher Systems: Evolution and Strategies. *Mon. Lab. Rev.*, May 1986, *109*(5), pp. 21–27. **[G: W. Europe; Canada]**

Howland, Marie. Cyclical Startups and Closures in Key Industries of America's Cities and Suburbs. **In** *Bergman, E. M., ed.*, 1986, pp. 111–28. **[G: U.S.]**

Ihlanfeldt, Keith R. and Jackson, John D. Systematic Assessment Error and Intrajurisdiction Property Tax Capitalization: Reply. *Southern Econ. J.*, January 1986, *52*(3), pp. 836–42. **[G: U.S.]**

Ihlanfeldt, Keith R. and Martinez-Vazquez, Jorge. Alternative Value Estimates of Owner-Occupied Housing: Evidence on Sample Selection Bias and Systematic Errors. *J. Urban Econ.*, November 1986, *20*(3), pp. 356–69. **[G: U.S.]**

Irvine, Ian. Inflation, Taxation, Capital Markets and the Demand for Housing in Ireland. *Econ. Soc. Rev.*, July 1986, *17*(4), pp. 277–92. **[G: Ireland]**

Isakson, Hans R. The Nearest Neighbors Appraisal Technique: An Alternative to the Adjustment Grid Methods. *Amer. Real Estate Urban Econ. Assoc. J.*, Summer 1986, *14*(2), pp. 274–86. **[G: U.S.]**

Itteilag, Richard L. and Swanson, Christina A. Residential Gas Cooling: A Life-Cycle Approach. *Energy J.*, October 1986, *7*(4), pp. 81–88. **[G: U.S.]**

Jackson, John D.; Jones, Charlotte A. and Balsmeir, Philip W. An Empirical Analysis of Tenant Selection under Federal Rent Supplement Programs: A First Step. *Amer. Real Estate Urban Econ. Assoc. J.*, Spring 1986, *14*(1), pp. 72–90. **[G: U.S.]**

Johansen, Hans Chr. and Boje, Per. Working Class Housing in Odense 1750–1914. *Scand. Econ. Hist. Rev.*, 1986, *34*(2), pp. 135–52. **[G: Denmark]**

Johnson, Gary T. Rent Paying Ability and Racial Settlement Patterns: A Review and Analysis of Recent Housing Allowance Evidence. *Amer. J. Econ. Soc.*, January 1986, *45*(1), pp. 17–26. **[G: U.S.]**

Jud, G. Donald and Bennett, D. Gordon. Public Schools and the Pattern of Intraurban Residential Mobility. *Land Econ.*, November 1986, *62*(4), pp. 362–70. **[G: U.S.]**

Jud, G. Donald and Frew, James R. Real Estate Brokers, Housing Prices, and the Demand for Housing. *Urban Stud.*, February 1986, *23*(1), pp. 21–31. **[G: U.S.]**

Kaneko, Mamoru and Yamamoto, Yoshitsugu. The Existence and Computation of Competitive Equilibria in Markets with an Indivisible Commodity. *J. Econ. Theory*, February 1986, *38*(1), pp. 118–36.

Kanemoto, Yoshitsugu and Nakamura, Ryohei. A New Approach to the Estimation of Structural Equations in Hedonic Models. *J. Urban Econ.*, March 1986, *19*(2), pp. 218–33. **[G: Japan]**

Kohlhase, Janet E. Labor Supply and Housing Demand for One- and Two-Earner Households. *Rev. Econ. Statist.*, February 1986, *68*(1), pp. 48–57. **[G: U.S.]**

Laquatra, Joseph. Housing Market Capitalization of Thermal Integrity. *Energy Econ.*, July 1986, *8*(3), pp. 134–38. **[G: U.S.]**

Lea, Michael J. and Zorn, Peter M. Adjustable-Rate Mortgages, Economic Fluctuations, and Lender Portfolio Change. *Amer. Real Estate Urban Econ. Assoc. J.*, Fall 1986, *14*(3), pp. 432–47. **[G: U.S.]**

Lee, Dwight R. Government Policy and the Distortions in Family Housing. **In** *Peden, J. R. and Glahe, F. R., eds.*, 1986, pp. 309–27. **[G: U.S.]**

Lefebvre, Bruno and Mouillart, Michel. Logement et épargne des ménages: le modèle Fanie. (Housing Markets and Saving of Households: The Fanie Model. With English summary.) *Revue Écon.*, May 1986, *37*(3), pp. 521–70. **[G: France]**

Leppel, Karen. A Trinomial Logit Analysis of Household Composition. *Amer. Real Estate Urban Econ. Assoc. J.*, Winter 1986, *14*(4), pp. 537–56. **[G: U.S.]**

Lerman, Donald L. and Lerman, Robert I. Imputed Incomes from Owner-Occupied Housing and Income Inequality. *Urban Stud.*, August 1986, *23*(4), pp. 323–31. **[G: U.S.]**

Lim, Chong Yah, et al. Report of the Central Provident Fund Study Group. *Singapore Econ. Rev.*, April 1986, *31*(1), pp. ii–l07. **[G: Singapore]**

Linneman, Peter. A New Look at the Homeownership Decision. *Housing Finance Rev.*, Winter 1986, *5*(3), pp. 159–87. **[G: U.S.]**

Linneman, Peter. An Empirical Test of the Efficiency of the Housing Market. *J. Urban Econ.*, September 1986, *20*(2), pp. 140–54. **[G: U.S.]**

Luger, Michael I. The Rent Control Paradox: Explanations and Prescriptions. *Rev. Reg. Stud.*, Fall 1986, *16*(3), pp. 25–41. **[G: U.S.]**

Malatesta, Paul H. and Hess, Alan C. Discount Mortgage Financing and Housing Prices. *Housing Finance Rev.*, Summer 1986, *5*(1), pp. 25–41. **[G: U.S.]**

Mark, Jonathan H. and Goldberg, Michael A. A Study of the Impacts of Zoning on Housing Values over Time. *J. Urban Econ.*, November 1986, *20*(3), pp. 257–73. **[G: Canada]**

Marks, Denton. The Effect of Rent Control on the Price of Rental Housing: Reply. *Land Econ.*, February 1986, *62*(1), pp. 106–09. **[G: U.S.]**

Mayo, Stephen K. Sources of Inefficiency in Subsidized Housing Programs: A Comparison of U.S. and German Experience. *J. Urban Econ.*, September 1986, *20*(2), pp. 229–49. **[G: U.S.; W. Germany]**

Mayo, Stephen K.; Malpezzi, Stephen and Gross, David J. Shelter Strategies for the Urban Poor in Developing Countries. *World Bank Res. Observer*, July 1986, *1*(2), pp. 183–203. **[G: LDCs]**

McCulloch, J. Huston. Risk Characteristics and Underwriting Standards for Price Level Adjusted Mortgages versus Other Mortgage Instruments. *Housing Finance Rev.*, Fall 1986, *5*(2), pp. 65–97. **[G: U.S.]**

McKenna, William F. Tax Reform Must Consider the Realities of Housing. **In** *Follain, J. R., ed.*, 1986, pp. 213–17. **[G: U.S.]**

McLure, Charles E., Jr. The Tax Treatment of Owner-Occupied Housing: The Achilles' Heel of Tax Reform? **In** *Follain, J. R., ed.*, 1986, pp. 219–32. **[G: U.S.]**

Megbolugbe, Isaac F. Econometric Analysis of Housing Trait Prices in a Third World City. *J. Reg. Sci.*, August 1986, *26*(3), pp. 533–47. **[G: Nigeria]**

Miyazaki, Shigetaka; Judge, George and Yancey, Thomas. Estimation of Location Parameters under Nonnormal Errors and Quadratic Loss. *J. Bus. Econ. Statist.*, April 1986, *4*(2), pp. 263–68. **[G: U.S.]**

Moore, Eric G. and Clark, W. A. V. Stable Structure and Local Variation: A Comparison of Household Flows in Four Metropolitan Areas. *Urban Stud.*, June 1986, *23*(3), pp. 185–96. **[G: U.S.]**

Morrow-Jones, Hazel A. Neighbourhood Change and the Federal Housing Administration: Some Theoretical and Empirical Issues. *Urban Stud.*, October 1986, *23*(5), pp. 419–28. **[G: U.S.]**

Moulton, Brent R. Random Group Effects and the Precision of Regression Estimates. *J. Econometrics*, August 1986, *32*(3), pp. 385–97. **[G: U.S.]**

Muth, Richard F. The Supply of Mortgage Lending. *J. Urban Econ.*, January 1986, *19*(1), pp. 88–106. **[G: U.S.]**

Ostrosky, Anthony L. A Further Note on the Urban Family Budget [The Urban Family Housing Budget in SMSAs]. *Soc. Sci. Quart.*, March 1986, *67*(1), pp. 212–13. **[G: U.S.]**

Ozo, A. O. Residential Location and Intra-urban Mobility in a Developing Country: Some Empirical Observations from Benin City, Nigeria. *Urban Stud.*, December 1986, *23*(6), pp. 457–70. **[G: Nigeria]**

Parsons, George Russell. An Almost Ideal Demand System for Housing Attributes. *Southern Econ. J.*, October 1986, *53*(2), pp. 347–63. **[G: U.S.]**

Pasha, Hafiz A. Seasonal Housing Markets: The Pilgrimage to Mecca. *Int. Reg. Sci. Rev.*, December 1986, *10*(3), pp. 193–210. **[G: Saudi Arabia]**

Pickles, Andrew and Davies, Richard B. Household Factors and Discrimination in Housing Consumption: Further Developments in the Analysis of Tenure Choice within Housing Careers. *Reg. Sci. Urban Econ.*, November 1986, *16*(4), pp. 493–517. **[G: U.S.]**

Plaut, Steven E. Mortgage Design in Imperfect Capital Markets. *J. Urban Econ.*, July 1986, *20*(1), pp. 107–19.

Pugh, Cedric. Housing Theory and Policy. *Int. J. Soc. Econ.*, 1986, *13*(4/5), pp. 1–104. **[G: Singapore; Norway; China]**

Reichert, Alan K. and Moore, James S. Using Latent Root Regression to Identify Nonpredictive Collinearity in Statistical Appraisal Models. *Amer. Real Estate Urban Econ. Assoc. J.*, Spring 1986, *14*(1), pp. 136–52. **[G: U.S.]**

Rodriguez-Bachiller, Agustin. Discontiguous Urban Growth and the New Urban Economics: A Review. *Urban Stud.*, April 1986, *23*(2), pp. 79–104.

Rosen, Kenneth T. and Smith, Lawrence B. The Resale Housing Market. *Amer. Real Estate Urban Econ. Assoc. J.*, Winter 1986, *14*(4), pp. 510–24. **[G: U.S.]**

Rosenthal, Leslie. Regional House Price Interactions in the UK, 1975–81: A Cross-Spectral Analysis. *Appl. Econ.*, September 1986, *18*(9), pp. 1011–23. **[G: U.K.]**

Rushdi, Ali Ahmed. Interfuel Substitution in the Residential Sector of South Australia. *Energy Econ.*, July 1986, *8*(3), pp. 177–85. **[G: Australia]**

Santerre, Rexford E. The Effect of Rent Control on the Price of Rental Housing: Comment. *Land Econ.*, February 1986, *62*(1), pp. 104–05. **[G: U.S.]**

Schwartz, Seymour I.; Zorn, Peter M. and Hansen, David E. Research Design Issues and Pitfalls in Growth Control Studies. *Land Econ.*, August 1986, *62*(3), pp. 223–33. **[G: U.S.]**

Scotchmer, Suzanne. The Short-run and Long-run Benefits of Environmental Improvement. *J. Public Econ.*, June 1986, *30*(1), pp. 61–81.

Seiders, David F. Should Tax Laws Be Used to Stimulate Investment in Housing? **In** *Follain, J. R., ed.*, 1986, pp. 207–12. **[G: U.S.]**

Shefer, Daniel. Utility Changes in Housing and Neighborhood Services for Households Moving into and out of Distressed Neighborhoods. *J. Urban Econ.*, January 1986, *19*(1), pp. 107–24. **[G: Israel]**

Shlay, Anne B. Taking Apart the American Dream: The Influence of Income and Family Composition on Residential Evaluations. *Urban Stud.*, August 1986, *23*(4), pp. 253–70. **[G: U.S.]**

Silver, Steven. A Logit Model of Values, Attitudes and Home Ownership. *J. Behav. Econ.*, Spring/Summer 1986, *15*(1/2), pp. 175–90.

Singell, Larry D. and Lillydahl, Jane H. An Empirical Analysis of the Commute to Work Patterns of Males and Females in Two-Earner Households. *Urban Stud.*, April 1986, *23*(2), pp. 119–29. **[G: U.S.]**

Slater, J. R. Income, Location and Housing in Greater London. *Urban Stud.*, August 1986, *23*(4), pp. 333–41. **[G: U.K.]**

Slater, Paul B. Disaggregated Spatial–Temporal Anayses of Residential Sales Prices. **In** *Slater, P. B.*, 1986, *1974*, pp. 1–6. **[G: U.S.]**

Small, Kenneth A. Effects of the 1979 Gasoline Shortages on Philadelphia Housing Prices. *J. Urban Econ.*, May 1986, *19*(3), pp. 371–81. **[G: U.S.]**

Stinson, Thomas F. and Vanderwall, Kathleen M. The Impact of Existing Property Tax Relief Programs on Taxes Paid on Owner-Occupied Housing in Minnesota. **In** *Minnesota Tax Study Commission*, 1986, pp. 361–74. **[G: U.S.]**

Stover, Mark Edward. The Price Elasticity of the Supply of Single-Family Detached Urban Housing. *J. Urban Econ.*, November 1986, *20*(3), pp. 331–40. **[G: U.S.]**

Strassmann, W. Paul. Types of Neighbourhood and Home-Based Enterprises: Evidence from Lima, Peru. *Urban Stud.*, December 1986, *23*(6), pp. 485–500. **[G: Peru]**

Struyk, Raymond J. and Turner, Margery A. Exploring the Effects of Racial Preferences on Urban Housing Markets. *J. Urban Econ.*, March 1986, *19*(2), pp. 131–47. **[G: U.S.]**

Vitaliano, Donald F. Measuring the Efficiency Cost of Rent Control. *Amer. Real Estate Urban Econ. Assoc. J.*, Spring 1986, *14*(1), pp. 61–71. **[G: U.S.]**

Vorst, Ton. The Relation between the Rent and Selling Price of a Building under Optimal Maintenance with Uncertainty. *J. Econ. Dynam. Control*, June 1986, *10*(1/2), pp. 315–20.

Weicher, John C. Simple Measures of Inadequate Housing. *J. Econ. Soc. Meas.*, October 1986, *14*(3), pp. 175–95. **[G: U.S.]**

Weicher, John C. The Market for Housing Quality. **In** *Ippolito, P. M. and Scheffman, D. T., eds.*, 1986, pp. 39–65. **[G: U.S.]**

White, Michelle J. Property Taxes and Urban Housing Abandonment. *J. Urban Econ.*, November 1986, *20*(3), pp. 312–30. **[G: U.S.]**

Wu, Chunchi and Colwell, Peter F. Equilibrium of Housing and Real Estate Brokerage Markets under Uncertainty. *Amer. Real Estate Urban Econ. Assoc. J.*, Spring 1986, *14*(1), pp. 1–23.

Yinger, John. Measuring Racial Discrimination with Fair Housing Audits: Caught in the Act. *Amer. Econ. Rev.*, December 1986, *76*(5), pp. 881–93. **[G: U.S.]**

Zorn, Peter M.; Hansen, David E. and Schwartz, Seymour I. Mitigating the Price Effects of Growth Control: A Case Study of Davis, California. *Land Econ.*, February 1986, *62*(1), pp. 46–57. **[G: U.S.]**

Zorn, Thomas S. and Larsen, James E. The Incentive Effects of Flat-Fee and Percentage Commissions for Real Estate Brokers. *Amer. Real Estate Urban Econ. Assoc. J.*, Spring 1986, *14*(1), pp. 24–47.

933 Urban Transportation Economics

9330 Urban Transportation Economics

Armstrong-Wright, Alan. Urban Transport in LDCs. *Finance Develop.*, September 1986, *23*(3), pp. 45–48. **[G: LDCs]**

Arnott, Richard J.; Pines, David and Sadka, Efraim. The Effects of an Equiproportional Transport Improvement in a Fully-Closed Monocentric City. *Reg. Sci. Urban Econ.*, August 1986, *16*(3), pp. 387–406.

Bly, P. H. and Oldfield, R. H. Competition between Minibuses and Regular Bus Services. *J. Transp. Econ. Policy*, January 1986, *20*(1), pp. 47–68. **[G: U.K.]**

Dick, H. W. and Rimmer, P. J. Urban Public Transport in Southeast Asia: A Case Study of Technological Imperialism? *Int. J. Transport Econ.*, June 1986, *13*(2), pp. 177–96. **[G: S.E. Asia]**

Dodgson, J. S. Benefits of Changes in Urban Public Transport Subsidies in the Major Australian Cities. *Econ. Rec.*, June 1986, *62*(177), pp. 224–35. **[G: Australia]**

Evans, Alan W. and Beed, Clive. Transport Costs and Urban Property Values in the 1970s. *Urban Stud.*, April 1986, *23*(2), pp. 105–17. **[G: Australia]**

Foster, Christopher and Golay, Jeanne. Some Curious Old Practices and Their Relevance to Equilibrium in Bus Competition. *J. Transp.*

Econ. Policy, May 1986, *20*(2), pp. 191–216. **[G: U.K.]**

Frankena, Mark W. and Pautler, Paul A. Taxicab Regulation: An Economic Analysis. **In** *Zerbe, R. O., Jr., ed.*, 1986, pp. 129–65. **[G: U.S.]**

Galvez, Tristan E. Competition on an Urban Bus Route: A Comment. *J. Transp. Econ. Policy*, January 1986, *20*(1), pp. 101–06. **[G: U.K.]**

Glaister, Stephen. A Rejoinder [Competition on an Urban Bus Route]. *J. Transp. Econ. Policy*, January 1986, *20*(1), pp. 107–08. **[G: U.K.]**

Glaister, Stephen. Bus Deregulation, Competition and Vehicle Size. *J. Transp. Econ. Policy*, May 1986, *20*(2), pp. 217–44. **[G: U.K.]**

Hau, Timothy D. Distributional Cost–Benefit Analysis in Discrete Choice. *J. Transp. Econ. Policy*, September 1986, *20*(3), pp. 313–38. **[G: U.S.]**

Hensher, David A. Sequential and Full Information Maximum Likelihood Estimation of a Nested Logit Model. *Rev. Econ. Statist.*, November 1986, *68*(4), pp. 657–67. **[G: Australia]**

Kim, Tschangho John. Modeling the Density Variations of Urban Land Uses with Transportation Network Congestion. *J. Urban Econ.*, May 1986, *19*(3), pp. 264–76.

McConnell, Virginia D. Automobile Use and Locational Interdependencies. *J. Reg. Sci.*, August 1986, *26*(3), pp. 475–98.

McCormick, Barry. Employment Opportunities, Earnings, and the Journey to Work of Minority Workers in Great Britain. *Econ. J.*, June 1986, *96*(382), pp. 375–97. **[G: U.K.]**

Peterson, George E. Urban Road Reinvestment: The Effects of External Aid. *Amer. Econ. Rev.*, May 1986, *76*(2), pp. 159–64. **[G: U.S.]**

Putman, S. H. Complexity in Urban Systems Modelling: The Effects of Transit on Urban Form. **In** *Batey, P. W. and Madden, M., eds.*, 1986, pp. 54–73. **[G: U.S.]**

Singell, Larry D. and Lillydahl, Jane H. An Empirical Analysis of the Commute to Work Patterns of Males and Females in Two-Earner Households. *Urban Stud.*, April 1986, *23*(2), pp. 119–29. **[G: U.S.]**

Steen, Robert C. Nonubiquitous Transportation and Urban Population Density Gradients. *J. Urban Econ.*, July 1986, *20*(1), pp. 97–106. **[G: U.S.]**

Talley, Wayne K. and Anderson, Eric E. An Urban Transit Firm Providing Transit, Paratransit and Contracted-out Services: A Cost Analysis. *J. Transp. Econ. Policy*, September 1986, *20*(3), pp. 353–68. **[G: U.S.]**

Viton, Philip A. The Question of Efficiency in Urban Bus Transportation. *J. Reg. Sci.*, August 1986, *26*(3), pp. 499–513.

Webster, F. V. Transport in Towns: Some of the Options. *J. Transp. Econ. Policy*, May 1986, *20*(2), pp. 129–52. **[G: U.K.]**

White, Michelle J. Sex Differences in Urban Commuting Patterns. *Amer. Econ. Rev.*, May 1986, *76*(2), pp. 368–72. **[G: U.S.]**

940 Regional Economics

941 Regional Economics

9410 General

Ashby, Lowell D. The Region: Place or Process? *Rev. Reg. Stud.*, Winter 1986, *16*(1), pp. 1–5.

Batey, P. W. J. and Madden, M. Integrated Analysis of Regional Systems: Introduction. **In** *Batey, P. W. and Madden, M., eds.*, 1986, pp. 1–7.

Brugger, E. A. and Stuckey, B. Self-reliant Development in Europe: Introduction. **In** *Bassand, M., et al., eds.*, 1986, pp. 1–5.

Brun, André. France: Rural Development in a Dynamic Context. *Europ. Rev. Agr. Econ.*, 1986, *13*(3), pp. 309–26. **[G: France]**

Bryden, J. Political and Cultural Aspects of Self-reliant Development. **In** *Bassand, M., et al., eds.*, 1986, pp. 125–29.

Danson, Mike. The Longer Term Impact of Policies of Regeneration at the Local Level. **In** *Danson, M., ed.*, 1986, pp. 169–74. **[G: U.K.]**

Friedmann, J. Regional Development in Industrialised Countries: Endogenous or Self-reliant? **In** *Bassand, M., et al., eds.*, 1986, pp. 203–16.

Hardoy, Jorge E. and Satterthwaite, David. A Survey of Empirical Material on the Factors Affecting the Development of Small and Intermediate Urban Centres. **In** *Hardoy, J. E. and Satterthwaite, D., eds.*, 1986, pp. 279–334. **[G: LDCs]**

Hardoy, Jorge E. and Satterthwaite, David. Government Policies and Small and Intermediate Urban Centres. **In** *Hardoy, J. E. and Satterthwaite, D., eds.*, 1986, pp. 335–97. **[G: LDCs]**

Hardoy, Jorge E. and Satterthwaite, David. Small and Intermediate Urban Centres: Their Role in National and Regional Development in the Third World: Some Tentative Conclusions. **In** *Hardoy, J. E. and Satterthwaite, D., eds.*, 1986, pp. 398–411.

Hardoy, Jorge E. and Satterthwaite, David. Why Small and Intermediate Urban Centres? **In** *Hardoy, J. E. and Satterthwaite, D., eds.*, 1986, pp. 1–17.

Isard, Walter. Frontiers in Regional Science: Comments by the Guest Editor. *Reg. Sci. Urban Econ.*, May 1986, *16*(2), pp. 161–64.

Keeble, David and Wever, Egbert. New Firms and Regional Development in Europe: Introduction. **In** *Keeble, D. and Wever, E., eds.*, 1986, pp. 1–34.

Matthews, Alan. Ireland: Rural Development in Agrarian Society. *Europ. Rev. Agr. Econ.*, 1986, *13*(3), pp. 367–89. **[G: Ireland]**

Mawson, John and Miller, David. The Alternative Regional Strategy: A New Regional Policy for Labour. **In** *Nolan, P. and Paine, S., eds.*, 1986, pp. 234–52. **[G: U.K.]**

McNally, M. Federal Initiatives for Economic Development of Reservations. *Reg. Stud.*, February 1986, *20*(1), pp. 83–89. **[G: U.S.]**

Moore, Chris and Booth, Simon. From Comprehensive Regeneration to Privatization: The Search for Effective Area Strategies. **In** *Lever, W. and Moore, C., eds.*, 1986, pp. 76–91. **[G: U.K.]**

Moore, Chris and Booth, Simon. The Post-industrial Synthesis: Policies for Enterprise in Clydeside. **In** *Lever, W. and Moore, C., eds.*, 1986, pp. 62–75. **[G: U.K.]**

Nijkamp, Peter. The Triangle of Industrial Dynamics, Labour Markets and Spatial Systems. **In** *Nijkamp, P., ed. (II),* 1986, pp. 1–17.

Nijkamp, Peter and Mills, Edwin S. Advances in Regional Economics. **In** *Nijkamp, P., ed. (I),* 1986, pp. 1–17.

Ó Huallacháin, Breandán. The Role of Foreign Direct Investment in the Development of Regional Industrial Systems: Current Knowledge and Suggestions for a Future American Research Agenda. *Reg. Stud.*, April 1986, *20*(2), pp. 151–62. **[G: U.S.]**

Quévit, Michel. Institutional and Financial Prerequisites for Endogenous Development Strategies. **In** *Bassand, M., et al., eds.*, 1986, pp. 103–11.

Sen, Ashish. Maximum Likelihood Estimation of Gravity Model Parameters. *J. Reg. Sci.*, August 1986, *26*(3), pp. 461–74.

Sexton, Robert L. Regional Choice and Economic History. *Econ. Forum,* Winter 1986-1987, *16*(1), pp. 159–66. **[G: U.S.]**

Stark, Oded; Taylor, J. Edward and Yitzhaki, Shlomo. Remittances and Inequality. *Econ. J.*, September 1986, *96*(383), pp. 722–40. **[G: Mexico]**

Steiner, Michael. Restructuring the Regions: The Austrian Experience. **In** *Danson, M., ed.*, 1986, pp. 137–46. **[G: Austria]**

Stöhr, Walter B. Changing External Conditions and a Paradigm Shift in Regional Development Strategies? **In** *Bassand, M., et al., eds.*, 1986, pp. 59–73.

Walzer, Norman and Chicoine, David L. Financing Economic Development in the 1980s: Issues and Trends: Introduction. **In** *Walzer, N. and Chicoine, D. L., eds.*, 1986, pp. xv–xxvii.

9411 Theory of Regional Economics

Allen, Ralph C.; Rabianski, Joseph S. and Stone, Jack H. A Managerial Model of the Effect of Product Market Structure on Firm Location. *J. Reg. Sci.*, May 1986, *26*(2), pp. 393–409.

Anderson, S. P. Equilibrium Existence in the Circle Model of Product Differentiation. **In** *Norman, G., ed.*, 1986, pp. 19–29.

Andersson, Åke and Kuenne, Robert E. Regional Economic Dynamics. **In** *Nijkamp, P., ed. (I),* 1986, pp. 201–53.

Anselin, Luc. Some Further Notes on Spatial Models and Regional Science [Non-nested Tests on the Weight Structure in Spatial Autoregressive Models: Some Monte-Carlo Results]. *J. Reg. Sci.*, November 1986, *26*(4), pp. 799–802.

Bagchi, Arunabha. Some Economic Applications of Dynamic Stackelberg Games. **In** *Başar, T., ed.*, 1986, pp. 88–102.

Bassand, M. The Socio-cultural Dimension of Self-reliant Development. **In** *Bassand, M., et al., eds.*, 1986, pp. 130–45. **[G: Switzerland]**

Batten, David F. Technical Progress and the Implicit Dynamics of Löschian Spatial Demand. **In** *[Lösch, A.],* 1986, pp. 177–202.

Beckmann, Martin J. Competitive Mill and Uniform Pricing. **In** *Norman, G., ed.*, 1986, pp. 52–64.

Beckmann, Martin J. and Thisse, Jacques-François. The Location of Production Activities. **In** *Nijkamp, P., ed. (I),* 1986, pp. 21–95.

Blackley, Paul R. and Greytak, David. Comparative Advantage and Industrial Location: An Intrametropolitan Evaluation. *Urban Stud.*, June 1986, *23*(3), pp. 221–30. **[G: U.S.]**

Boeri, Tito. Monopolistic Competition, Differentiated Products and Peripheral Development. *Giorn. Econ.*, Mar.-Apr. 1986, *45*(3–4), pp. 201–23.

Bossert, Walter and Buhl, Hans Ulrich. On Sufficient Conditions for Interior Location in the Triangle Space: A Comment [On a Foundation of the Economic Theory of Location—Transport Distance vs. Technological Substitution]. *J. Reg. Sci.*, November 1986, *26*(4), pp. 809–14.

Braid, Ralph M. Stackelberg Price Leadership in Spatial Competition. *Int. J. Ind. Organ.*, December 1986, *4*(4), pp. 439–49.

Brugger, E. A. Endogenous Development: A Concept between Utopia and Reality. **In** *Bassand, M., et al., eds.*, 1986, pp. 38–58. **[G: Switzerland]**

Caplin, Andrew S. and Nalebuff, Barry J. Multidimensional Product Differentiation and Price Competition. **In** *Morris, D. J., et al., eds.*, 1986, pp. 129–45.

Capozza, D. R. and Van Order, Robert. Spatial Competition with Cross-Hauling. **In** *Norman, G., ed.*, 1986, pp. 77–84.

Clapp, John M. Interdependent Behavior with Relocation Costs: The Comparative Statics of Spatial History. *J. Reg. Sci.*, February 1986, *26*(1), pp. 33–46.

Costa, Paolo. Regional Science *Ante Litteram:* Some Early Italian Contributions to Regional Economics. *Ricerche Econ.*, Apr.-Sept. 1986, *40*(2–3), pp. 525–36. **[G: Italy]**

Dafermos, Stella. Isomorphic Multiclass Spatial Price and Multimodal Traffic Network Equilibrium Models. *Reg. Sci. Urban Econ.*, May 1986, *16*(2), pp. 197–209.

Dow, Sheila C. The Capital Account and Regional Balance of Payments Problems. *Urban Stud.*, June 1986, *23*(3), pp. 173–84.

Drezner, Z.; Thisse, Jacques-François and Wesolowsky, George O. The Minimax-Min Location Problem. *J. Reg. Sci.*, February 1986, *26*(1), pp. 87–101.

Economides, Nicholas S. Nash Equilibrium in Duopoly with Products Defined by Two Characteristics. *Rand J. Econ.*, Autumn 1986, *17*(3), pp. 431–39.

Ekelund, Robert B., Jr. and Shieh, Yeung-Nan. Dupuit, Spatial Economics and Optimal Resource Allocation: A French Tradition. *Economica,* November 1986, *53*(212), pp. 483–96.

Eswaran, Mukesh and Ware, Roger. On the Shape of Market Areas in Löschian Spatial Models. *J. Reg. Sci.*, May 1986, *26*(2), pp. 307–19.

Ewers, Hans-Jürgen. Spatial Dimensions of Technological Developments and Employment Effects. **In** *Nijkamp, P., ed. (II),* 1986, pp. 157–76. **[G: W. Germany]**

Fischer, Manfred M. and Nijkamp, Peter. Technological Change and Regional Employment Research. **In** *Nijkamp, P., ed. (II),* 1986, pp. 454–62.

Fujita, Masahisa. Optimal Location of Public Facilities: Area Dominance Approach. *Reg. Sci. Urban Econ.*, May 1986, *16*(2), pp. 241–68.

Fujita, Masahisa and Thisse, Jacques-François. Spatial Competition with a Land Market: Hotelling and Von Thunen Unified. *Rev. Econ. Stud.*, October 1986, *53*(5), pp. 819–41.

Funck, Rolf H. August Lösch and the Concept of Region. **In** *[Lösch, A.]*, 1986, pp. 55–66.

Gabszewicz, Jean Jaskold and Garella, Paolo. 'Subjective' Price Search and Price Competition. *Int. J. Ind. Organ.*, September 1986, *4*(3), pp. 305–16.

Gee, J. M. A. and Jarvis, R. J. Costs and Social Welfare in the Theory of the Spatial Firm and Industry. **In** *Norman, G., ed.*, 1986, pp. 85–102.

Gori, Enrico; Pastacaldi, Andrea and Vitali, Letizia. Models of Spatial Choice: The Case of Banking Services in Urban Areas. *Econ. Notes,* 1986, (2), pp. 129–39.

Gould, Peter. August Lösch as a Child of His Time. **In** *[Lösch, A.]*, 1986, pp. 7–19.

Greenberg, Joseph and Weber, Shlomo. Strong Tiebout Equilibrium under Restricted Preferences Domain. *J. Econ. Theory,* February 1986, *38*(1), pp. 101–17.

Greenhut, Melvin L. On Demand Curves and Spatial Pricing. **In** *Norman, G., ed.*, 1986, pp. 65–76.

Greenhut, Melvin L.; Mai, Chao-cheng and Norman, George. Impacts on Optimum Location of Different Pricing Strategies, Market Structures and Customer Distributions over Space. *Reg. Sci. Urban Econ.*, August 1986, *16*(3), pp. 329–51.

Greenhut, Melvin L. and Norman, George. Spatial Pricing with a General Cost Function; the Effects of Taxes on Imports. *Int. Econ. Rev.*, October 1986, *27*(3), pp. 761–76.

Griffith, Daniel A. Central Place Structures Using Constant Elasticity of Substitution Demand Cones: The Infinite Plane. *Econ. Geogr.*, January 1986, *62*(1), pp. 74–84.

Haag, Günter. A Stochastic Theory for Residential and Labour Mobility Including Travel Networks. **In** *Nijkamp, P., ed. (II),* 1986, pp. 340–57.

Haining, Robert. Intraurban Retail Price Competition: Corporate and Neighbourhood Aspects of Spatial Price Variation. **In** *Norman, G., ed.*, 1986, pp. 144–64. **[G: U.K.]**

Haining, Robert. Spatial Models and Regional Science: A Comment on Anselin's Paper and Research Directions [Non-nested Tests on the Weight Structure in Spatial Autoregressive Models: Some Monte-Carlo Results]. *J. Reg. Sci.*, November 1986, *26*(4), pp. 793–98.

Henderson, J. Vernon. The Timing of Regional Development. *J. Devel. Econ.*, October 1986, *23*(2), pp. 275–92.

Hobbs, Benjamin F. Mill Pricing versus Spatial Price Discrimination under Bertrand and Cournot Spatial Competition. *J. Ind. Econ.*, December 1986, *35*(2), pp. 173–91.

Hung, Chao-Shun. The Effects of Entry on Spatial Pricing and Their Implications in Industrial Economics. *Atlantic Econ. J.*, September 1986, *14*(3), pp. 18–23.

Hwang, Hong and Mai, Chao-cheng. Welfare-Maximizing Location versus Profit-Maximizing Locations. *Ann. Reg. Sci.*, March 1986, *20*(1), pp. 54–64.

Isard, Walter. Reflections on the Relevance of Integrated Multiregion Models: Lessons from Physics. *Reg. Sci. Urban Econ.*, May 1986, *16*(2), pp. 165–80.

Isserman, Andrew, et al. Regional Labor Market Analysis. **In** *Nijkamp, P., ed. (I),* 1986, pp. 543–80.

Johansson, Börje and Karlsson, Charlie. Industrial Applications of Information Technology: Speed of Introduction and Labour Force Competence. **In** *Nijkamp, P., ed. (II),* 1986, pp. 401–28. **[G: Sweden]**

Johansson, Börje and Leonardi, Giorgio. Public Facility Location: A Multiregional and Multiauthority Decision Context. **In** *Nijkamp, P., ed. (I),* 1986, pp. 133–70.

Jordan, James V.; Sassone, Peter G. and Walkling, Ralph A. A New Test of State Industrial Development Policy. **In** *Redburn, F. S.; Buss, T. F. and Ledebur, L. C., eds.*, 1986, pp. 114–39. **[G: U.S.]**

Kamann, Dirk-Jan F. Industrial Organisation, Innovation and Employment. **In** *Nijkamp, P., ed. (II),* 1986, pp. 131–54.

Klaassen, Leo H. The Influence of Non-economic Factors on the Intensity of Spatial Interaction: The Influence of Language Differences. **In** *[Lösch, A.]*, 1986, pp. 229–42. **[G: Belgium]**

Knudson, Daniel C. and Fotheringham, A. Stewart. Matrix Comparison, Goodness-of-Fit, and Spatial Interaction Modeling. *Int. Reg. Sci. Rev.*, August 1986, *10*(2), pp. 127–47.

Kohsaka, Hiroyuki. An Analysis of Two-Center Competition. *J. Reg. Sci.*, February 1986, *26*(1), pp. 179–88.

Komorowski, Stanislaw M. Lösch Revisited. **In** *[Lösch, A.]*, 1986, pp. 21–34.

Kuklinski, Antoni. August Lösch—The Prominent Classic of Regional Studies. **In** *[Lösch, A.]*, 1986, pp. 275–83.

Kutay, Aydan. Optimum Office Location and the

Comparative Statics of Information Economies. *Reg. Stud.*, October 1986, *20*(6), pp. 551–63.

Lakshmanan, T. R. and Bolton, Roger. Regional Energy and Environmental Analysis. **In** *Nijkamp, P., ed. (I)*, 1986, pp. 581–628. **[G: U.S.; OECD]**

Lederer, Phillip J. and Hurter, Arthur P., Jr. Competition of Firms: Discriminatory Pricing and Location. *Econometrica*, May 1986, *54*(3), pp. 623–40.

Löfgren, Karl Gustaf. The Spatial Monopsony: A Theoretical Analysis. *J. Reg. Sci.*, November 1986, *26*(4), pp. 707–30.

Malecki, Edward J. Technological Imperatives and Modern Corporate Strategy. **In** *Scott, A. J. and Storper, M., eds.*, 1986, pp. 67–79.

Malecki, Edward J. and Varaiya, Pravin. Innovation and Changes in Regional Structure. **In** *Nijkamp, P., ed. (I)*, 1986, pp. 629–45.

McGuire, Martin C. Private Production, Collective Consumption, and Regional Population Structure: The Interactions between Public and Private Good Provision as Determinants of Community Composition. *J. Reg. Sci.*, November 1986, *26*(4), pp. 677–705.

Moore, Giora. Spatial Monopolistic Competition versus Spatial Monopoly: A Comment. *J. Econ. Theory*, February 1986, *38*(1), pp. 185.

Nagurney, Anna. An Algorithm for the Single Commodity Spatial Price Equilibrium Problem. *Reg. Sci. Urban Econ.*, November 1986, *16*(4), pp. 573–88.

Nakagome, Masaki. A Note on the Stability Property of Spatial Competition. *J. Reg. Sci.*, August 1986, *26*(3), pp. 605–11.

Nakagome, Masaki. The Spatial Labour Market and Spatial Competition. *Reg. Stud.*, August 1986, *20*(4), pp. 307–12.

Neven, D. 'Address' Models of Differentiation. **In** *Norman, G., ed.*, 1986, pp. 5–18.

Nijkamp, Peter and Rietveld, Piet. Multiple Objective Decision Analysis in Regional Economics. **In** *Nijkamp, P., ed. (I)*, 1986, pp. 493–541.

Norman, George. Market Strategy with Variable Entry Threats. **In** *Norman, G., ed.*, 1986, pp. 103–24.

Norman, George. Spatial Pricing and Differentiated Markets: Introduction. **In** *Norman, G., ed.*, 1986, pp. 1–4.

Orishimo, Isao. Reception of the Löschian Theory in Japan, and Consideration of Its Implications for Japanese Regional Planning Policy. **In** *[Lösch, A.]*, 1986, pp. 91–100. **[G: Japan]**

Osborne, Martin J. and Pitchik, Carolyn. The Nature of Equilibrium in a Location Model. *Int. Econ. Rev.*, February 1986, 27(1), pp. 223–37.

de Palma, André; Labbé, M. and Thisse, Jacques-François. On the Existence of Price Equilibria under Mill and Uniform Delivered Price Policies. **In** *Norman, G., ed.*, 1986, pp. 30–42.

Parr, John B. Economic Flows in Lösch's Modified Urban System. **In** *[Lösch, A.]*, 1986, pp. 103–22.

Perryman, M. Ray and Perryman, Nancy S. The Regional Business Cycle: A Theoretical Exposition with Time Series, Cross Sectional, and Predictive Applications. **In** *Perryman, M. R. and Schmidt, J. R., eds.*, 1986, pp. 125–58. **[G: U.S.]**

Pines, David and Sadka, Efraim. Comparative Statics Analysis of a Fully Closed City. *J. Urban Econ.*, July 1986, *20*(1), pp. 1–20.

Ponsard, Claude. August Lösch: A Famous, but Ignored Economist. **In** *[Lösch, A.]*, 1986, pp. 35–45.

Puu, Tönu. Multiplier-Accelerator Models Revisited. *Reg. Sci. Urban Econ.*, February 1986, *16*(1), pp. 81–95.

Puu, Tönu and Weidlich, Wolfgang. The Stability of Hexagonal Tessellations. **In** *[Lösch, A.]*, 1986, pp. 133–58.

ten Raa, Thijs. The Initial Value Problem for the Trading Cycle in Euclidian Space. *Reg. Sci. Urban Econ.*, November 1986, *16*(4), pp. 527–46.

Reiner, Thomas and Wilson, Mark. Nonprofits in a Löschian Landscape. **In** *[Lösch, A.]*, 1986, pp. 243–55. **[G: U.S.]**

ReVelle, Charles S. The Maximum Capture or "Sphere of Influence" Location Problem: Hotelling Revisited on a Network. *J. Reg. Sci.*, May 1986, *26*(2), pp. 343–58.

Richardson, Harry W. and Townroe, Peter M. Regional Policies in Developing Countries. **In** *Nijkamp, P., ed. (I)*, 1986, pp. 647–78.

Rothschild, R. The Stability of Cartels in Spatial Markets. **In** *Norman, G., ed.*, 1986, pp. 43–51.

Salant, David J. Equilibrium in a Spatial Model of Imperfect Competition with Sequential Choice of Locations and Quantities. *Can. J. Econ.*, November 1986, *19*(4), pp. 685–715.

Scott, Allen J. Industrial Organization and Location: Division of Labor, the Firm, and Spatial Process. *Econ. Geogr.*, July 1986, *62*(3), pp. 215–31.

Shieh, Yeung-Nan. Industrial Location and the Divorce of Management and Ownership: Comment. *Ann. Reg. Sci.*, March 1986, *20*(1), pp. 81–84.

Smith, Christine. An Empirically Implementable Integrated Multiregional Model for Australia. *Reg. Sci. Urban Econ.*, May 1986, *16*(2), pp. 181–95. **[G: Australia]**

Sonis, Michael. A Contribution to the Central Place Theory: Super-imposed Hierarchies, Structural Stability, Structural Changes and Catastrophes in Central Place Hierarchical Dynamics. **In** *[Lösch, A.]*, 1986, pp. 159–76. **[G: W. Germany]**

Sonis, Michael. Unified Theory of Innovation Diffusion, Dynamic Choice of Alternatives, Ecological Dynamics and Urban/Regional Growth and Decline. *Ricerche Econ.*, Oct.-Dec. 1986, *40*(4), pp. 696–723.

Stiens, G. The Strategy of Endogenous Development in the Light of German History. **In** *Bassand, M., et al., eds.*, 1986, pp. 77–89. **[G: W. Germany]**

Storper, Michael. Technology and New Regional Growth Complexes: The Economics of Discontinuous Spatial Development. **In** *Nijkamp, P., ed. (II),* 1986, pp. 46–75.

Takayama, T. and Labys, Walter C. Spatial Equilibrium Analysis. **In** *Nijkamp, P., ed. (I),* 1986, pp. 171–99.

Taylor, Carol A. Spatial Utility Equilibrium and City Size Distribution in a Central Place System. *J. Urban Econ.,* January 1986, *19*(1), pp. 1–22. **[G: U.S.]**

Thill, Jean-Claude. A Note on Multipurpose and Multistop Shopping, Sales, and Market Areas of Firms. *J. Reg. Sci.,* November 1986, *26*(4), pp. 775–84.

Thore, Sten. Spatial Disequilibrium. *J. Reg. Sci.,* November 1986, *26*(4), pp. 661–75.

Waterson, Michael. The Economics of Vertical Restraints on Retailers. **In** *Norman, G., ed.,* 1986, pp. 125–43.

Wilson, John D. A Theory of Interregional Tax Competition. *J. Urban Econ.,* May 1986, *19*(3), pp. 296–315.

Ziegler, Joseph A. Location, Theory of Production, and Variable Transportation Rates. *J. Reg. Sci.,* November 1986, *26*(4), pp. 785–91.

9412 Regional Economic Studies

Adams, J. C. and Kraithman, D. A. Unemployment in a Relatively Prosperous Region: The Hertfordshire Experience. **In** *Danson, M., ed.,* 1986, pp. 121–35. **[G: U.K.]**

Ady, Robert M. Criteria Used for Facility Location Selection. **In** *Walzer, N. and Chicoine, D. L., eds.,* 1986, pp. 72–84. **[G: U.S.]**

Ahlbrandt, Roger S., Jr. State-Sponsored Partnership: Building a Hi-tech Center for Western Pennsylvania. **In** *Gondolf, E. W.; Marcus, I. M. and Dougherty, J. P., eds.,* 1986, pp. 172–82. **[G: U.S.]**

Aitken, P. and Sparks, L. The Scottish Development Agency: A Case for Co-ordination? *Reg. Stud.,* October 1986, *20*(5), pp. 476–80. **[G: U.K.]**

Altman, Morris. Resource Endowments and Location Theory in Economic History: A Case Study of Quebec and Ontario at the Turn of the Twentieth Century. *J. Econ. Hist.,* December 1986, *46*(4), pp. 999–1009. **[G: Canada]**

Amirahmadi, Hooshang. Regional Planning in Iran: A Survey of Problems and Policies. *J. Devel. Areas,* July 1986, *20*(4), pp. 501–29. **[G: Iran]**

Amos, Orley M., Jr. Substate and SMSA Personal Income Inequality and Regional Development. *Rev. Reg. Stud.,* Spring 1986, *16*(2), pp. 23–30. **[G: U.S.]**

Anders, Gary C. Oil, Economic Dependence, and Alaska's Development. *J. Energy Devel.,* Spring 1986, *11*(2), pp. 243–61. **[G: U.S.]**

Aradeon, David; Aina, Tade Akin and Umo, Joe. South-west Nigeria. **In** *Hardoy, J. E. and Satterthwaite, D., eds.,* 1986, pp. 228–78. **[G: Nigeria]**

Armington, Catherine. Trends in Midwest Business Employment. **In** *Walzer, N. and Chicoine, D. L., eds.,* 1986, pp. 15–33. **[G: U.S.]**

Armstrong, H. The Assignment of Regional Industrial Policy Powers. *Reg. Stud.,* June 1986, *20*(3), pp. 258–61. **[G: U.K.]**

Atkinson, Michael. The Supply of Raw Materials to the South Wales Iron Industry, 1800–60. **In** *Baber, C. and Williams, L. J., eds.,* 1986, pp. 43–52. **[G: U.K.]**

Attaran, Mohsen. Industrial Diversity and Economic Performance in U.S. Areas. *Ann. Reg. Sci.,* July 1986, *20*(2), pp. 44–54. **[G: U.S.]**

Aydalot, Philippe. The Location of New Firm Creation: The French Case. **In** *Keeble, D. and Wever, E., eds.,* 1986, pp. 105–23. **[G: France]**

Baber, Colin. Canals and the Economic Development of South Wales. **In** *Baber, C. and Williams, L. J., eds.,* 1986, pp. 24–42. **[G: U.K.]**

Bade, Franz-Josef. The De-industrialisation of the Federal Republic of Germany and Its Spatial Implications. **In** *Nijkamp, P., ed. (II),* 1986, pp. 196–220. **[G: W. Germany; OECD]**

Bailly, A. S. The Service Sector as a Stimulus to Endogenous Development: The Case of Switzerland. **In** *Bassand, M., et al., eds.,* 1986, pp. 112–22. **[G: Switzerland]**

Bauwens, A. L. G. M. and Douw, L. Rural Development: A Minor Problem in the Netherlands? *Europ. Rev. Agr. Econ.,* 1986, *13*(3), pp. 343–66. **[G: Netherlands]**

Beesley, Michael E. and Hamilton, R. T. Births and Deaths of Manufacturing Firms in the Scottish Regions. *Reg. Stud.,* August 1986, *20*(4), pp. 281–88. **[G: U.K.]**

Benvenuti, S. Casini and Cavalieri, A. Applications of a Biregional Input–Output Model in Regional Policy Analysis. **In** *Batey, P. W. and Madden, M., eds.,* 1986, pp. 201–15. **[G: Italy]**

Bhooshan, B. S. Bangalore, Mandya and Mysore Districts, Karnataka State, South India. **In** *Hardoy, J. E. and Satterthwaite, D., eds.,* 1986, pp. 131–84. **[G: India]**

Bickford, Deborah J.; Clapp, John M. and Vehorn, Charles L. An Econometric Analysis of Regional Employment Effects of Federal Economic Development Programs. *Growth Change,* January 1986, *17*(1), pp. 1–16. **[G: U.S.]**

Blum, Ulrich C. H. The Impact of Location and Centrality on Regional Income: The German Experience, 1976 to 1980. **In** *[Lösch, A.],* 1986, pp. 219–28. **[G: W. Germany]**

Blum, Ulrich C. H. and Kowalski, Jan S. On the Efficiency of Regional Production in Poland, 1976–1982. *Ann. Reg. Sci.,* March 1986, *20*(1), pp. 12–32. **[G: Poland]**

Boddy, Martin and Lovering, John. High Technology Industry in the Bristol Sub-Region: The Aerospace/Defence Nexus. *Reg. Stud.,* June 1986, *20*(3), pp. 217–31. **[G: U.K.]**

Bohm, Robert A.; Herzog, Henry W., Jr. and Schlottmann, Alan M. Trade and Service Sector Development in the Rural South: The Case of the Tennessee–Tombigbee Corridor. *Rev. Reg. Stud.*, Spring 1986, *16*(2), pp. 41–49. **[G: U.S.]**

Booth, Douglas E. Long Waves and Uneven Regional Growth. *Southern Econ. J.*, October 1986, *53*(2), pp. 448–60. **[G: U.S.]**

Bowman, Ann O'M. and Franke, James L. Explaining Adoption of Conservation Programs by Local Governments. *Rev. Reg. Stud.*, Fall 1986, *16*(3), pp. 17–24. **[G: U.S.]**

Boykin, Robert H. Statement to the U.S. House Subcommittee on Domestic Monetary Policy of the Committee on Banking, Finance and Urban Affairs, March 19, 1986. *Fed. Res. Bull.*, May 1986, *72*(5), pp. 316–18. **[G: U.S.]**

Brand, C. Rural Animation and Self-reliant Development: Experiences in the Isère Region of France. **In** *Bassand, M., et al., eds.*, 1986, pp. 161–74. **[G: France]**

Brewer, H. L. and Moomaw, Ronald L. Regional Economic Instability and Industrial Diversification in the U.S.: Comment. *Land Econ.*, November 1986, *62*(4), pp. 412–15. **[G: U.S.]**

Brown, Colin G. and Drynan, Ross G. Plant Location Analysis Using Discrete Stochastic Programming. *Australian J. Agr. Econ.*, April 1986, *30*(1), pp. 1–22. **[G: Australia]**

Brusco, Sebastiano. Small Firms and Industrial Districts: The Experience of Italy. *Econ. Int.*, May-Aug.-Nov. 1986, *39*(2–3–4), pp. 85–97. **[G: Italy]**

Bryant, Richard R. Regional Energy Source Substitution: Wood Fuels in Missouri. *Growth Change*, July 1986, *17*(3), pp. 71–84. **[G: U.S.]**

Buss, Terry F. Unemployment Rates and Their Implications for Human Resource Planning. *J. Econ. Soc. Meas.*, April 1986, *14*(1), pp. 1–18. **[G: U.S.]**

Camagni, Roberto. The Economics of Industrial Revitalisation in Declining Metropolitan Areas. *Econ. Int.*, May-Aug.-Nov. 1986, *39*(2–3–4), pp. 316–34. **[G: Italy]**

Camara, Antonio S.; Viegas, M. Graca and Amaro, Ana. Interfacing System Dynamics and Multiobjective Programming for Regional Water Resources Planning. *Ann. Reg. Sci.*, November 1986, *20*(3), pp. 104–13. **[G: Portugal]**

Camba, Roberto, et al. L'evoluzione della struttura produttiva e imprenditoriale in una regione di antica industrializzazione: il caso del piemonte. (The Development of the Industrial System in an Old Industrialized Region: The Case of Piemonte. With English summary.) *Ricerche Econ.*, Jan.-Mar. 1986, *40*(1), pp. 130–59. **[G: Italy]**

Cameron, Gordon. Regional Policy for the Areas of Economic Decline: The Case of Wallonia (Belgium): Comments. *Econ. Int.*, May-Aug.-Nov. 1986, *39*(2–3–4), pp. 362–66. **[G: U.K.]**

Cebula, Richard J. On the Impact of Right-to-Work Laws: A Reply. *Urban Stud.*, February 1986, *23*(1), pp. 69. **[G: U.S.]**

Chichkanov, V. Problems and Prospects of the Development of Productive Forces in the Far East. *Prob. Econ.*, November 1986, *29*(7), pp. 74–91.

Chinitz, Benjamin. The Regional Transformation of the American Economy. *Urban Stud.*, October 1986, *23*(5), pp. 377–85. **[G: U.S.]**

Chinitz, Benjamin. The Regional Transformation of the American Economy. *Amer. Econ. Rev.*, May 1986, *76*(2), pp. 300–303. **[G: U.S.]**

Chu, D. K. Y. The Special Economic Zones and the Problem of Territorial Containment. **In** *Jao, Y. C. and Leung, C. K., eds.*, 1986, pp. 21–38. **[G: China]**

Clark, G. Regional Planning in Developing Countries: A Consultant's Perspective. *Reg. Stud.*, October 1986, *20*(6), pp. 584–90. **[G: LDCs]**

Clark, Gordon L. The Crisis of the Midwest Auto Industry. **In** *Scott, A. J. and Storper, M., eds.*, 1986, pp. 127–48. **[G: U.S.]**

Clarke, R. Community Development as an Element of a Strategy for Development from Below: Community Organisations in Scotland. **In** *Bassand, M., et al., eds.*, 1986, pp. 187–99. **[G: U.K.]**

Cocheba, Donald J.; Gilmer, Robert W. and Mack, Richard S. Causes and Consequences of Slow Growth in the Tennessee Valley's Service Sector. *Growth Change*, January 1986, *17*(1), pp. 51–65. **[G: U.S.]**

Connaughton, John E. and Madsen, Ronald A. Recession and Recovery: A State and Regional Analysis. *Rev. Reg. Stud.*, Spring 1986, *16*(2), pp. 1–10. **[G: U.S.]**

Conyers, Diana. In Search of the Practical Academic: Lessons from the Study of Regional Administration. *Reg. Stud.*, October 1986, *20*(6), pp. 579–84.

Cooke, Philip. The Changing Urban and Regional System in the United Kingdom. *Reg. Stud.*, June 1986, *20*(3), pp. 243–51. **[G: U.K.]**

Crandall, Robert W. The Transformation of U.S. Manufacturing. *Ind. Relat.*, Spring 1986, *25*(2), pp. 118–30. **[G: U.S.]**

Cushing, Brian J. Accounting for Spatial Relationships in Models of Interstate Population Migration. *Ann. Reg. Sci.*, July 1986, *20*(2), pp. 66–73. **[G: U.S.]**

Damania, D. The Impact of Non-domestic Property Taxes on Employment: A Comment [The Effect of Business Rates on the Location of Employment] [The Determinants of Employment in Counties: Some Evidence on the Importance of Local Authority Fiscal Policy and Government Regional Policy in England and Wales]. *Urban Stud.*, October 1986, *23*(5), pp. 413–18. **[G: U.K.]**

Das, Sarojini and Das, Kumar. Cement Industry in India—A Spatio-Economic Analysis. *Indian Econ. J.*, Oct.-Dec. 1986, *34*(2), pp. 18–27. **[G: India]**

Daunton, M. J. Labour and Technology in South Wales, 1870–1914. **In** *Baber, C. and Williams, L. J., eds.*, 1986, pp. 140–52. **[G: U.K.]**

De Benedictis, Michele. Italy: Fragmentation of Policies and Research Effort. *Europ. Rev. Agr. Econ.*, 1986, *13*(3), pp. 327–41. **[G: Italy]**

Del Monte, Alfredo. The Impact of Italian Industrial Policy, 1960–1980. **In** *Hall, G., ed.*, 1986, pp. 128–64. **[G: Italy]**

Del Monte, Alfredo and Giannola, Adriano. Relevance and Nature of Small and Medium-sized Firms in Southern Italy. **In** *Keeble, D. and Wever, E., eds.*, 1986, pp. 275–98. **[G: Italy]**

Dewar, David; Todes, Alison and Watson, Vanessa. Industrial Decentralization Policy in South Africa: Rhetoric and Practice. *Urban Stud.*, October 1986, *23*(5), pp. 363–76. **[G: S. Africa]**

Dholakia, Ravindra H. Removing the Residual in Standardization Procedure. *Rev. Reg. Stud.*, Winter 1986, *16*(1), pp. 44–46.

van Dijk, Jouke and Folmer, Hendrik. The Consequences of Interregional Labor Migration for the Regional Labor Market: Theory, Methodology and Dutch Experience. *Rev. Econ. Statist.*, February 1986, *68*(1), pp. 74–83. **[G: Netherlands]**

van Dijk, Jouke and Oosterhaven, J. Regional Impacts of Migrants' Expenditures: An Input–Output/Vacancy-Chain Approach. **In** *Batey, P. W. and Madden, M., eds.*, 1986, pp. 122–47. **[G: Netherlands]**

Dokopoulou, Evangelia. Small Manufacturing Firms and Regional Development in Greece: Patterns and Changes. **In** *Keeble, D. and Wever, E., eds.*, 1986, pp. 299–317. **[G: Greece]**

Donckels, Rik and Bert, Christiane. New Firms in the Local Economy: The Case of Belgium. **In** *Keeble, D. and Wever, E., eds.*, 1986, pp. 124–40. **[G: Belgium]**

Duffell, J. Roger. The Car Excursion to Informal Outdoor Recreation Sites: Comparative Studies in the West Midlands Region in 1966 to 1978. *Reg. Stud.*, October 1986, *20*(6), pp. 505–21. **[G: U.K.]**

Dunford, M. Integration and Unequal Development: The Case of Southern Italy, 1951–73. **In** *Scott, A. J. and Storper, M., eds.*, 1986, pp. 225–45. **[G: Italy]**

Dunham, Constance R. Regional Banking Competition. *New Eng. Econ. Rev.*, July/Aug. 1986, pp. 3–19. **[G: U.S.]**

Edmondson, William and Schluter, Gerald. Demand Foundations of Food and Fiber Sector Employment in the South. *Growth Change*, October 1986, *17*(4), pp. 1–9. **[G: U.S.]**

El Agraa, Omer M. A., et al. The Gezira Region, the Sudan. **In** *Hardoy, J. E. and Satterthwaite, D., eds.*, 1986, pp. 80–130. **[G: Sudan]**

Engelbourg, Saul and Schachter, Gustav. Two "Souths": The United States and Italy since the 1860's. *J. Europ. Econ. Hist.*, Winter 1986, *15*(3), pp. 563–89. **[G: U.S.; Italy]**

Erickson, Rodney A.; Gavin, Norma I. and Cordes, Sam M. Service Industries in Interregional Trade: The Economic Impacts of the Hospital Sector. *Growth Change*, January 1986, *17*(1), pp. 17–27. **[G: U.S.]**

Eskelinen, Heikki. The Challenge of Deindustrialisation: Changing Patterns in the Regional Division of Labour in Finland. *Econ. Int.*, May-Aug.-Nov. 1986, *39*(2–3–4), pp. 282–91. **[G: Finland]**

Fearnside, Philip M. Agricultural Plans for Brazil's Grande Carajás Program: Lost Opportunity for Sustainable Local Development? *World Devel.*, March 1986, *14*(3), pp. 385–409. **[G: Brazil]**

Feenberg, Daniel R. and Rosen, Harvey S. The Deductibility of State and Local Taxes: Impact Effects by State and Income Class. *Growth Change*, April 1986, *17*(2), pp. 11–31. **[G: U.S.]**

Feldman, Marshall M. A. Firm Size and Local Employment Change: Three Issues. *Reg. Stud.*, February 1986, *20*(1), pp. 73–77. **[G: U.S.]**

Fieleke, Norman S. New England Manufacturing and International Trade. *New Eng. Econ. Rev.*, Sept./Oct. 1986, pp. 22–28. **[G: U.S.]**

Findeis, Jill L. and Whittlesey, Norman K. Trade-Offs in Resource Use: Implications for State Economic Development. *Rev. Reg. Stud.*, Spring 1986, *16*(2), pp. 50–57. **[G: U.S.]**

Fournier, Gary M. and Rasmussen, David W. Real Economic Development in the South: The Implications of Regional Cost of Living Differences. *Rev. Reg. Stud.*, Winter 1986, *16*(1), pp. 6–13. **[G: U.S.]**

Fox, William F. Tax Structure and the Location of Economic Activity along State Borders. *Nat. Tax J.*, December 1986, *39*(4), pp. 387–401. **[G: U.S.]**

Geisslhofer, A. Endogenous Regional Development and Regional Animation in Peripheral Areas. **In** *Bassand, M., et al., eds.*, 1986, pp. 175–86. **[G: Austria]**

Gertler, Meric S. Regional Dynamics of Manufacturing and Non-manufacturing Investment in Canada. *Reg. Stud.*, October 1986, *20*(6), pp. 523–34. **[G: Canada]**

Getis, Arthur. The Economic Health of Municipalities within a Metropolitan Region: The Case of Chicago. *Econ. Geogr.*, January 1986, *62*(1), pp. 52–73. **[G: U.S.]**

Giaoutzi, Maria. Technological Change and Employment Patterns: The Greek Case. **In** *Nijkamp, P., ed. (II)*, 1986, pp. 244–61. **[G: Greece]**

Giessübel, Rainer and Spitzer, Hartwig. Fed. Rep. of Germany: Rural Development under Federal Government. *Europ. Rev. Agr. Econ.*, 1986, *13*(3), pp. 283–307. **[G: W. Germany]**

Gilmer, Robert W. and Pulsipher, Allan G. Cyclical and Structural Change in Southern Manufacturing: Recent Evidence from the Tennessee Valley: Note. *Growth Change*, October 1986, *17*(4), pp. 61–69. **[G: U.S.]**

Glasmeier, Amy K. High-Tech Industries and the Regional Division of Labor. *Ind. Relat.*, Spring 1986, *25*(2), pp. 197–211. **[G: U.S.]**

Goddard, John B. and Thwaites, Alfred T. New Technology and Regional Development Policy. **In** *Nijkamp, P., ed. (II)*, 1986, pp. 91–114. **[G: U.K.]**

Goldstein, Harvey A. The Changing International

Division of Labor and Regional Employment Cycles in the U.S. *Rev. Reg. Stud.*, Winter 1986, *16*(1), pp. 31–43. **[G: U.S.]**

Good, David F. Uneven Development in the Nineteenth Century: A Comparison of the Habsburg Empire and the United States. *J. Econ. Hist.*, March 1986, *46*(1), pp. 137–51. **[G: Europe; U.S.]**

Goode, Frank M. The Efficacy of More Refined Demand Variables in Industrial Location Models: Note. *Growth Change*, January 1986, *17*(1), pp. 66–75. **[G: U.S.]**

Gordon, Ian. What Contribution Can Labour Migration Make to Reducing Unemployment? Comment. **In** *Hart, P. E., ed.*, 1986, pp. 75–79. **[G: U.K.]**

Granberg, Alexander. Structural Changes and Intensification in Siberian Industry. *Prob. Econ.*, July 1986, *29*(3), pp. 39–60. **[G: U.S.S.R.]**

Green, A. E., et al. What Contribution Can Labour Migration Make to Reducing Unemployment? **In** *Hart, P. E., ed.*, 1986, pp. 52–74. **[G: U.K.]**

Greenwood, Michael J.; Hunt, Gary L. and McDowell, John M. Migration and Employment Change: Empirical Evidence on the Spatial and Temporal Dimensions of the Linkage. *J. Reg. Sci.*, May 1986, *26*(2), pp. 223–34. **[G: U.S.]**

Gruben, William C. and Phillips, Keith R. Understanding the Texas Unemployment Rate. *Fed. Res. Bank Dallas Econ. Rev.*, November 1986, pp. 17–30. **[G: U.S.]**

Gulácsi, Gábor and Juhász, Pál. Development of Settlements, Decentralization and Communal Management in Hungary. *Acta Oecon.*, 1986, *37*(1–2), pp. 31–46. **[G: Hungary]**

Hahne, Ulf. Changes in the International Division of Labour and Prospects for Endogenous Development. **In** *Bassand, M., et al., eds.*, 1986, pp. 90–102. **[G: W. Germany]**

Hahne, Ulf and Mundkowski-Bek, Monika. Freie Unternehmenszonen—Patentrezept für strukturschwache Regionen? (Free Enterprise Zones—A Panacea for Structurally Handicapped Regions? With English summary.) *Konjunkturpolitik*, 1986, *32*(1/2), pp. 27–51. **[G: W. Germany]**

Hall, Anthony L. Agricultural Plans for Brazil's Grande Carajás Program: Lost Opportunity for Sustainable Local Development? More of the Same in Brazilian Amazonia: A Comment. *World Devel.*, March 1986, *14*(3), pp. 411–14. **[G: Brazil]**

Hardjono, Joan. Transmigration: Looking to the Future. *Bull. Indonesian Econ. Stud.*, August 1986, *22*(2), pp. 28–53. **[G: Indonesia]**

Harrington, James W., Jr.; Burns, Karen and Cheung, Man. Market-Oriented Foreign Investment and Regional Development: Canadian Companies in Western New York. *Econ. Geogr.*, April 1986, *62*(2), pp. 155–66. **[G: U.S.]**

Harris, A. H., et al. Who Gains from Structural Change? The Distribution of the Benefits of Oil in Aberdeen. *Urban Stud.*, August 1986, *23*(4), pp. 271–83. **[G: U.K.]**

Harrison, Richard T. The Standard Capital Grants Scheme in Northern Ireland: A Review and Assessment. *Reg. Stud.*, April 1986, *20*(2), pp. 175–82. **[G: Ireland]**

Harrison, Richard T. and Mason, Colin M. The Regional Impact of the Small Firms Loan Guarantee Scheme in the United Kingdom. *Reg. Stud.*, October 1986, *20*(6), pp. 535–49. **[G: U.K.]**

Hart, John Fraser. Population Trends in the Midwest. **In** *Walzer, N. and Chicoine, D. L., eds.*, 1986, pp. 1–14. **[G: U.S.]**

Haug, Peter. U.S. High Technology Multinationals and Silicon Glen. *Reg. Stud.*, April 1986, *20*(2), pp. 103–16. **[G: U.S.; U.K.]**

Hayashi, Yoshitsugu; Isobe, Tomohiko and Tomita, Yasuo. Modelling the Long-term Effects of Transport and Land Use Policies on Industrial Locational Behaviour: A Discrete Choice Model System. *Reg. Sci. Urban Econ.*, February 1986, *16*(1), pp. 123–43. **[G: Japan]**

Hayes, Maurice. Your Good Health: Access to Health and Health Care in Northern Ireland. *Reg. Stud.*, October 1986, *20*(6), pp. 493–504. **[G: Ireland]**

Heim, Carol E. Interwar Responses to Regional Decline. **In** *Elbaum, B. and Lazonick, W., eds.*, 1986, pp. 240–65. **[G: U.K.]**

Henderson, J. Vernon. Efficiency of Resource Usage and City Size. *J. Urban Econ.*, January 1986, *19*(1), pp. 47–70. **[G: Brazil; U.S.]**

Hepworth, Mark. The Geography of Technological Change in the Information Economy. *Reg. Stud.*, October 1986, *20*(5), pp. 407–24. **[G: Canada]**

Herzog, Henry W., Jr.; Schlottmann, Alan M. and Johnson, Donald L. High-Technology Jobs and Worker Mobility. *J. Reg. Sci.*, August 1986, *26*(3), pp. 445–59. **[G: U.S.]**

Hill, John K. Energy's Contribution to the Growth of Employment in Texas, 1972–1982. *Fed. Res. Bank Dallas Econ. Rev.*, May 1986, pp. 11–18. **[G: U.S.]**

Hite, James C. Interbasin Water Transfers in Riparian Doctrine States: The Case of Interregional Compensation. *Growth Change*, October 1986, *17*(4), pp. 10–24. **[G: U.S.]**

Hodge, Ian D. and Whitby, Martin. The U.K.: Rural Development, Issues and Analysis. *Europ. Rev. Agr. Econ.*, 1986, *13*(3), pp. 391–413. **[G: U.K.]**

Hoehn, Thomas and Reichle, Marc. Einkommensdisparitä ten im Zentren-Peripherie-Kontext in der Schweiz. (Income Inequalities in Switzerland: A Centre-Periphery Approach. With English summary.) *Schweiz. Z. Volkswirtsch. Statist.*, June 1986, *122*(2), pp. 143–61. **[G: Switzerland]**

Hofmann, Michael. The Informal Sector in an Intermediate City: A Case in Egypt. *Econ. Develop. Cult. Change*, January 1986, *34*(2), pp. 263–77. **[G: Egypt]**

Hoogteijling, Els; Gunning, Jan Willem and Nijkamp, Peter. Spatial Dimensions of Innovation and Employment: Some Dutch Results. In *Nijkamp, P., ed. (II)*, 1986, pp. 221–43. **[G: Netherlands]**

Hotopp, Susan. Business Location 1860 and 1870: Evidence from the Manufacturing Censuses. In *Atack, J., ed.*, 1986, pp. 85–91. **[G: U.S.]**

Howells, J. Industry-Academic Links in Research and Innovation: A National and Regional Development Perspective. *Reg. Stud.*, October 1986, *20*(5), pp. 472–76. **[G: U.K.]**

Hudson, Ray and Sadler, David. Contesting Works Closures in Western Europe's Old Industrial Regions: Defending Place or Betraying Class? In *Scott, A. J. and Storper, M., eds.*, 1986, pp. 172–93. **[G: W. Europe]**

Hunt, E. H. Industrialization and Regional Inequality: Wages in Britain, 1760–1914. *J. Econ. Hist.*, December 1986, *46*(4), pp. 935–66. **[G: U.K.]**

Hutchinson, William K. Regional Exports of the United States to Foreign Countries: A Structural Analysis, 1870–1910. In *Uselding, P., ed.*, 1986, pp. 131–54. **[G: U.S.]**

Illeris, Sven. New Firm Creation in Denmark: The Importance of the Cultural Background. In *Keeble, D. and Wever, E., eds.*, 1986, pp. 141–50. **[G: Denmark]**

Islam, Iyanatul and Khan, Habibullah. Spatial Patterns of Inequality and Poverty in Indonesia. *Bull. Indonesian Econ. Stud.*, August 1986, *22*(2), pp. 80–102. **[G: Indonesia]**

Jatobá, Jorge. The Labour Market in a Recession-Hit Region: The North-East of Brazil. *Int. Lab. Rev.*, Mar.-Apr. 1986, *125*(2), pp. 227–41. **[G: Brazil]**

Jones, A. and Kinner, D. R. Deindustrialisation: The Case of Humberside. In *Danson, M., ed.*, 1986, pp. 103–19. **[G: U.K.]**

Jones, David R. and Martin, Ronald L. Voluntary and Involuntary Turnover in the Labour Force. *Scot. J. Polit. Econ.*, May 1986, *33*(2), pp. 124–44. **[G: U.K.]**

Jones, Huw, et al. Peripheral Counter-Urbanization: Findings from an Integration of Census and Survey Data in Northern Scotland. *Reg. Stud.*, February 1986, *20*(1), pp. 15–26. **[G: U.K.]**

Jones, J. An Examination of the Thinking behind Government Regional Policy in the UK since 1945. *Reg. Stud.*, June 1986, *20*(3), pp. 261–66. **[G: U.K.]**

Jordan, James V.; Sassone, Peter G. and Walkling, Ralph A. A New Test of State Industrial Development Policy. In *Redburn, F. S.; Buss, T. F. and Ledebur, L. C., eds.*, 1986, pp. 114–39. **[G: U.S.]**

Kalt, Joseph P. and Leone, Robert A. Regional Effects of Energy Price Decontrol: The Roles of Interregional Trade, Stockholding, and Microeconomic Incidence. *Rand J. Econ.*, Summer 1986, *17*(2), pp. 201–13. **[G: U.S.]**

Kaltenberg, Michael C. and Buongiorno, Joseph. Growth and Decline of the Paper Industry: An Econometric Analysis of U.S. Regions. *Appl. Econ.*, April 1986, *18*(4), pp. 379–97. **[G: U.S.]**

Koo, Won W. and Uhm, Ihn H. A Spatial Equilibrium Analysis of U.S. Wheat Exports under Alternative Transport Costs and Trade Restrictions. *Logist. Transp. Rev.*, March 1986, *22*(1), pp. 27–41. **[G: OECD]**

Korte, Werner B. Small and Medium-sized Establishments in Western Europe. In *Keeble, D. and Wever, E., eds.*, 1986, pp. 35–53. **[G: EEC]**

Kregel, J. A. Disarmonie e linee di riequilibrio nello sviluppo economico delle zone montane: Comments. *Econ. Int.*, May-Aug.-Nov. 1986, *39*(2–3–4), pp. 406–10. **[G: Italy]**

Kuehn, John A. and Braschler, Curtis. Technology and Foreign Trade Impacts on U.S. Manufacturing Employment 1975–80. *Growth Change*, October 1986, *17*(4), pp. 46–60. **[G: U.S.]**

Kunzmann, Klaus R. Structural Problems of an Old Industrial Area: The Case of the Ruhr District. In *Goldberg, W. H., ed.*, 1986, pp. 409–33. **[G: W. Germany]**

Kwok, R. Y. W. Structure and Policies in Industrial Planning in the Shenzhen Special Economic Zone. In *Jao, Y. C. and Leung, C. K., eds.*, 1986, pp. 39–64. **[G: China]**

Lagoe, Ronald J. A Community-Based Analysis of Regional Differences in Hospital Stays by Diagnosis Related Group. *Inquiry*, Summer 1986, *23*(2), pp. 183–90. **[G: U.S.]**

Laulajainen, Risto and Gadde, Lars-Erik. Locational Avoidance: A Case Study of Three Swedish Retail Chains. *Reg. Stud.*, April 1986, *20*(2), pp. 131–40. **[G: Sweden]**

Lee, Clive. Atlas of Industrializing Britain 1780–1914: Regional Structure and Change. In *Langton, J. and Morris, R. J., eds.*, 1986, pp. 30–33. **[G: U.K.]**

Leete, R. and Kwok, K. K. Demographic Changes in East Malaysia and Their Relationship with Those in the Peninsula 1960–80. *Population Stud.*, March 1986, *40*(1), pp. 83–100. **[G: Malaysia]**

Leite, Pedro Sisnando. Forces That Will Shape Future Rural Development: The Case of Northeastern Brazil. In *Maunder, A. and Renborg, U., eds.*, 1986, pp. 60–69. **[G: Brazil]**

Leontief, Wassily. The Economic Impact—Industrial and Regional—of an Arms Cut. In *Leontief, W.*, 1986, *1965*, pp. 204–40. **[G: U.S.]**

Leung, C. K. Spatial Redeployment and the Special Economic Zones in China: An Overview. In *Jao, Y. C. and Leung, C. K., eds.*, 1986, pp. 1–18. **[G: China]**

Leven, Charles L. Analysis and Policy Implications of Regional Decline. *Amer. Econ. Rev.*, May 1986, *76*(2), pp. 308–12. **[G: U.S.]**

Lever, William. Old Policies in a New Role. In *Lever, W. and Moore, C., eds.*, 1986, pp. 44–61. **[G: U.K.]**

Lever, William and Mather, Frank. The Changing Structure of Business and Employment in the Conurbation. In *Lever, W. and Moore, C., eds.*, 1986, pp. 1–21. **[G: U.K.]**

Lever, William and Moore, Chris. Future Directions for Urban Policy. In *Lever, W. and*

Moore, C., eds., 1986, pp. 142–61. **[G: U.K.]**

Lewis, Pamela M. The Economic Impact of the Operation and Closure of a Nuclear Power Station. *Reg. Stud.*, October 1986, *20*(5), pp. 425–32. **[G: U.K.]**

Little, Jane Sneddon. Recent Trends in Foreign Direct Investment in the United States: An Overview. **In** *Gray, H. P., ed.*, 1986, pp. 9–41. **[G: U.S.]**

Liu, Ben-chieh; Mulvey, Thomas and Hsieh, Chang-Tzeh. Effects of Educational Expenditures on Regional Inequality in the Social Quality of Life. *Amer. J. Econ. Soc.*, April 1986, *45*(2), pp. 131–44. **[G: U.S.]**

Loviscek, Anthony L. and Yang, Chin-Wei. Determining the Strength of Industrial Grouping Methods. *Rev. Reg. Stud.*, Spring 1986, *16*(2), pp. 31–40. **[G: U.S.]**

Lowery, David; Brunn, Stanley D. and Webster, Gerald. From Stable Disparity to Dynamic Equity: The Spatial Distribution of Federal Expenditures, 1971–1983. *Soc. Sci. Quart.*, March 1986, *67*(1), pp. 98–107. **[G: U.S.]**

Luger, Michael I. Depreciation Profiles and Depreciation Policy in a Spatial Context. *J. Reg. Sci.*, February 1986, *26*(1), pp. 141–59. **[G: U.S.]**

MacGregor, Bryan D., et al. The Development of High Technology Industry in Newbury District. *Reg. Stud.*, October 1986, *20*(5), pp. 433–47. **[G: U.K.]**

Maggi, Rico and Haeni, Peter K. Spatial Concentration, Location and Competitiveness: The Case of Switzerland. *Reg. Stud.*, April 1986, *20*(2), pp. 141–49. **[G: Switzerland]**

Maier, Gunther and Weiss, Peter. The Importance of Regional Factors in the Determination of Earnings: The Case of Austria. *Int. Reg. Sci. Rev.*, December 1986, *10*(3), pp. 211–20. **[G: Austria]**

Malecki, Edward J. High-Technology Sectors and Local Economic Development. **In** *Bergman, E. M., ed.*, 1986, *1983*, pp. 129–42. **[G: U.S.]**

Manzanal, Mabel. El deterioro regional: una manifestación en la producción tabacalera correntina 1976–1981. (With English summary.) *Desarrollo Econ.*, Oct.-Dec. 1986, *26*(103), pp. 455–76. **[G: Argentina]**

Manzanal, Mabel and Vapnarsky, Cesar A. The Development of the Upper Valley of the Rio Negro and Its Periphery within the Comahue Region, Argentina. **In** *Hardoy, J. E. and Satterthwaite, D., eds.*, 1986, pp. 18–79. **[G: Argentina]**

Markusen, Ann Roell. Neither Ore, nor Coal, nor Markets: A Policy-Oriented View of Steel Sites in the USA. *Reg. Stud.*, October 1986, *20*(5), pp. 449–61. **[G: U.S.]**

Martellato, Dino and Scandola, Massimo. Grado di apertura e attivazione in un modello interregionale per l'italia. (Tracing the Pattern of Location and Trade with an Interregional Model for Italy. With English summary.) *Ricerche Econ.*, Apr.-Sept. 1986, *40*(2–3), pp. 328–59. **[G: Italy]**

Martin, Fernand. Repercussions of Industrial Redeployment upon the International Role of the Region of Montreal. **In** *Danson, M., ed.*, 1986, pp. 147–57. **[G: Canada]**

Martin, Ronald L. In What Sense a 'Jobs Boom'? Employment Recovery, Government Policy and the Regions. *Reg. Stud.*, October 1986, *20*(5), pp. 463–72. **[G: U.K.]**

Martin, Ronald L. Industrial Restructuring, Labour Shake-Out and the Geography of Recession. **In** *Danson, M., ed.*, 1986, pp. 1–22. **[G: U.K.]**

Mason, Colin M. and Harrison, Richard T. The Regional Impact of Public Policy towards Small Firms in the United Kingdom. **In** *Keeble, D. and Wever, E., eds.*, 1986, pp. 224–55. **[G: U.K.]**

Matz, Deborah and Ledebur, Larry C. The State Role in Economic Development. **In** *Walzer, N. and Chicoine, D. L., eds.*, 1986, pp. 85–102. **[G: U.S.]**

McHone, W. Warren. Supply-Side Considerations in the Location of Industry in Suburban Communities: Empirical Evidence from the Philadelphia SMSA. *Land Econ.*, February 1986, *62*(1), pp. 64–73. **[G: U.S.]**

McNeill, D. Regional Planners—Without Power or Purpose? *Reg. Stud.*, October 1986, *20*(6), pp. 575–79. **[G: LDCs]**

Mehretu, Assefa. Towards a Framework for Spatial Resolution of Structural Polarity in African Development. *Econ. Geogr.*, January 1986, *62*(1), pp. 30–51. **[G: Africa]**

Mera, Koichi. Population Stabilization and National Spatial Policy of Public Investment: The Japanese Experience. *Int. Reg. Sci. Rev.*, April 1986, *10*(1), pp. 47–65. **[G: Japan]**

Miller, H. Max; Brown, E. Evan and Centner, Terence J. Southern Appalachian Handicraft Industry: Implications for Regional Economic Development. *Rev. Reg. Stud.*, Fall 1986, *16*(3), pp. 50–58. **[G: U.S.]**

Misra, H. N. Rae Bareli, Sultanpur and Pratapgarh Districts, Uttar Pradesh State, North India. **In** *Hardoy, J. E. and Satterthwaite, D., eds.*, 1986, pp. 185–227. **[G: India]**

Moore, Chris and Booth, Simon. Unlocking Enterprise: The Search for Synergy. **In** *Lever, W. and Moore, C., eds.*, 1986, pp. 107–19. **[G: U.K.]**

Moriarty, Barry M. Regional Industrial Change, Industrial Restructuring, and U.S. Industrial Policy. *Rev. Reg. Stud.*, Fall 1986, *16*(3), pp. 1–10. **[G: U.S.]**

Morse, George W. and Farmer, Michael C. Location and Investment Effects of a Tax Abatement Program. *Nat. Tax J.*, June 1986, *39*(2), pp. 229–36. **[G: U.S.]**

Mutti, John H. and Morgan, William E. Interstate Tax Exportation within the United States: An Appraisal of the Literature. *Int. Reg. Sci. Rev.*, August 1986, *10*(2), pp. 89–112. **[G: U.S.]**

Newby, Howard. Locality and Rurality: The Restructuring of Rural Social Relations. *Reg. Stud.*, June 1986, *20*(3), pp. 209–15. **[G: U.K.]**

Nijkamp, Peter. Infrastructure and Regional Development: A Multidimensional Policy Analysis. *Empirical Econ.*, 1986, *11*(1), pp. 1–21. **[G: Netherlands]**

Norton, Roger D. Industrial Policy and American Renewal. *J. Econ. Lit.*, March 1986, *24*(1), pp. 1–40. **[G: U.S.]**

O'Farrell, Patrick N. Entrepreneurship and Regional Development: Some Conceptual Issues. *Reg. Stud.*, October 1986, *20*(6), pp. 565–74. **[G: U.K.]**

Ostrosky, Anthony L. The Impact of Right-to-Work Laws on the Cost of Living in the United States: A Comment. *Urban Stud.*, February 1986, *23*(1), pp. 67. **[G: U.S.]**

Owen, D. W.; Coombes, M. G. and Gillespie, A. E. The Urban–Rural Shift and Employment Change in Britain, 1971–81. **In** *Danson, M., ed.*, 1986, pp. 23–47. **[G: U.K.]**

Parry, Robert T. Statement to the U.S. House Subcommittee on Domestic Monetary Policy of the Committee on Banking, Finance and Urban Affairs, March 19, 1986. *Fed. Res. Bull.*, May 1986, *72*(5), pp. 318–21. **[G: U.S.]**

Peck, Francis W. and Townsend, Alan R. Corporate Interaction in Oligopolistic Markets: The Role of Case Studies of Rationalisation. **In** *Danson, M., ed.*, 1986, pp. 49–63. **[G: U.K.]**

Perryman, M. Ray. Institutional Evolution in an Economy Characterized by Basic Industry Decline and Technological Expansion. *J. Econ. Issues*, June 1986, *20*(2), pp. 481–88. **[G: U.S.]**

Pettigrew, P. and Dann, S. Streamlining Regional Industrial Aid? *Reg. Stud.*, April 1986, *20*(2), pp. 182–84. **[G: Ireland]**

Pillai, P. P. Macro-Economic Behaviour of Kerala Economy: A Preliminary Exercise. *Margin*, January 1986, *18*(2), pp. 85–94. **[G: India]**

Premus, Robert. Attracting High-Tech Industry and Jobs: An Assessment of State Practices. **In** *Walzer, N. and Chicoine, D. L., eds.*, 1986, pp. 55–71. **[G: U.S.]**

Premus, Robert. High Technology and State Economic Development Strategies. **In** *Redburn, F. S.; Buss, T. F. and Ledebur, L. C., eds.*, 1986, pp. 99–113. **[G: U.S.]**

Price, C. M. Regional Price Discrimination in the United Kingdom Gas Industry. **In** *Norman, G., ed.*, 1986, pp. 165–85. **[G: U.K.]**

Quévit, Michel. Regional Policy for the Areas of Economic Decline: The Case of Wallonia (Belgium). *Econ. Int.*, May-Aug.-Nov. 1986, *39*(2–3–4), pp. 341–61. **[G: Belgium]**

Rabeau, Yves. Le statu quo est-il préférable à la régionalisation de la politique de stabilisation? (With English summary.) *Can. Public Policy*, June 1986, *12*(2), pp. 329–40. **[G: Canada]**

Rao, K. P. C. Structural Changes, Sectoral Performance and Inter-Sectoral Linkages in Andhra Pradesh Economy. *Margin*, January 1986, *18*(2), pp. 62–76. **[G: India]**

Ravallion, Martin. Testing Market Integration. *Amer. J. Agr. Econ.*, February 1986, *68*(1), pp. 102–09. **[G: Bangladesh]**

Riefler, Roger F. Comparative Cyclic Behavior of an Agricultural Economy: Nebraska in the 70s and 80s. *Rev. Reg. Stud.*, Winter 1986, *16*(1), pp. 24–30. **[G: U.S.]**

Roberts, R. O. Banks and the Economic Development of South Wales before 1914. **In** *Baber, C. and Williams, L. J., eds.*, 1986, pp. 65–80. **[G: U.K.]**

Robson, Brian. Research Issues in the Changing Urban and Regional System. *Reg. Stud.*, June 1986, *20*(3), pp. 203–07. **[G: U.K.]**

Rones, Philip L. An Analysis of Regional Employment Growth, 1973–85. *Mon. Lab. Rev.*, July 1986, *109*(7), pp. 3–14. **[G: U.S.]**

Round, J. I. Social Accounting for Regional Economic Systems. **In** *Batey, P. W. and Madden, M., eds.*, 1986, pp. 90–106. **[G: Malaysia]**

Schmidt, Ronald H. and Gunther, Jeffery W. Distributional Implications of Reducing Interstate Energy Price Differences. *Fed. Res. Bank Dallas Econ. Rev.*, November 1986, pp. 1–15. **[G: U.S.]**

Schramm, Gunter. Regional Cooperation and Economic Development. *Ann. Reg. Sci.*, July 1986, *20*(2), pp. 1–16. **[G: Africa]**

Schröter, Lutz. "Steelworks Now!" The Conflicting Character of Modernisation: A Case Study of Hoesch in Dortmund. **In** *Goldberg, W. H., ed.*, 1986, pp. 361–408. **[G: W. Germany]**

Smith, Stanley K. Accounting for Migration in Cohort-Component Projections of State and Local Populations. *Demography*, February 1986, *23*(1), pp. 127–35. **[G: U.S.]**

Solomon, Barry D. and Pyrdol, John J. Delineating Coal Market Regions. *Econ. Geogr.*, April 1986, *62*(2), pp. 109–24. **[G: U.S.]**

Staines, Brian. The Movement of Population from South Wales with Specific Reference to the Effects of the Industrial Transference Scheme, 1928–37. **In** *Baber, C. and Williams, L. J., eds.*, 1986, pp. 237–50. **[G: U.K.]**

Stöhr, Walter B. Towards a Framework for Evaluating the Effects of Technology Complexes and Science Parks. *Econ. Int.*, May-Aug.-Nov. 1986, *39*(2–3–4), pp. 299–311. **[G: U.S.]**

Stoney, P. J. M. The Employment Impact of the Merseyside Motor-Vehicle Assembly Industry. **In** *Danson, M., ed.*, 1986, pp. 65–81. **[G: U.K.]**

Storey, David J. and Amin, Ash. Employment Creation at a Local Level in the U.K. *Econ. Lavoro*, July-Sept. 1986, *20*(3), pp. 63–80. **[G: U.K.]**

Symons, M. V. Coal-Mining in the Llanelli Area—Years of Growth, 1800–64. **In** *Baber, C. and Williams, L. J., eds.*, 1986, pp. 53–64. **[G: U.K.]**

Taylor, Jim. L'efficacite economique des aides au developpement regional: le cas Francais: Comments. *Econ. Int.*, May-Aug.-Nov. 1986, *39*(2–3–4), pp. 278–81. **[G: France]**

Taylor, Tom. Capital Formation by Railways in South Wales, 1836–1914. **In** *Baber, C. and*

Williams, L. J., eds., 1986, pp. 97–116. **[G: U.K.]**

Thomas, Brinley. The Industrial Revolution and the Welsh Language. **In** *Baber, C. and Williams, L. J., eds.*, 1986, pp. 6–21. **[G: U.K.]**

Thomas, D. A. War and the Economy: The South Wales Experience. **In** *Baber, C. and Williams, L. J., eds.*, 1986, pp. 251–77. **[G: U.K.]**

Till, Thomas E. The Share of Southeastern Black Counties in the Southern Rural Renaissance: Were They Bypassed by Factory Job Gains, 1959–77? *Growth Change*, April 1986, *17*(2), pp. 44–55. **[G: U.S.]**

Timmermans, Harry. Locational Choice Behaviour of Entrepreneurs: An Experimental Analysis. *Urban Stud.*, June 1986, *23*(3), pp. 231–40.

Topel, Robert H. Local Labor Markets. *J. Polit. Econ.*, Part 2, June 1986, *94*(3), pp. S111–43. **[G: U.S.]**

Townroe, Peter M. Technological Change in the Service Sector: Urban and Regional Implications. **In** *Nijkamp, P., ed. (II)*, 1986, pp. 76–90. **[G: U.K.]**

Townsend, Alan R. Spatial Aspects of the Growth of Part-Time Employment in Britain. *Reg. Stud.*, August 1986, *20*(4), pp. 313–30. **[G: U.K.]**

Tran, Dang T. Locational Factors in the Declining Industrial Competitive Advantage of the New York Urban Region. *J. Reg. Sci.*, February 1986, *26*(1), pp. 121–39. **[G: U.S.]**

Tremblay, Carol Horton. Regional Wage Differentials: Has the South Risen Again? A Comment. *Rev. Econ. Statist.*, February 1986, *68*(1), pp. 175–78. **[G: U.S.]**

Tucker, Harvey J. and Herzik, Eric B. The Persisting Problem of Region in American State Policy Research. *Soc. Sci. Quart.*, March 1986, *67*(1), pp. 84–97. **[G: U.S.]**

Tyler, Peter and Rhodes, John. The Census of Production as an Indicator of Regional Differences in Productivity and Profitability in the United Kingdom. *Reg. Stud.*, August 1986, *20*(4), pp. 331–39. **[G: U.K.]**

Uno, Kimiko. Regional Translog Production Functions with Capital and Labor Inputs Differentiated by Educational Attainment: The Case of Japanese Industry, 1968–77. *Reg. Sci. Urban Econ.*, August 1986, *16*(3), pp. 449–62. **[G: Japan]**

Upton, Graham J. G. Distance and Directional Analyses of Settlement Patterns. *Econ. Geogr.*, April 1986, *62*(2), pp. 167–79. **[G: Argentina]**

Vereş, I.; Pepelea, P. and Chirică, C. Cybernetization and Monitorizing a District-Fundamental Factors of the Territory Best Social–Economic Development. *Econ. Computat. Cybern. Stud. Res.*, 1986, *21*(1), pp. 47–53. **[G: Romania]**

Vining, Daniel R., Jr. Population Redistribution towards Core Areas of Less Developed Countries, 1950–1980. *Int. Reg. Sci. Rev.*, April 1986, *10*(1), pp. 1–45. **[G: LDCs]**

Wabe, J. Stuart. The Regional Impact of Deindustrialization in the European Community. *Reg. Stud.*, February 1986, *20*(1), pp. 27–36. **[G: EEC]**

Wagener, Hans-Jürgen. The Political Economy of Soviet Nationalities and Regions. **In** *Höhmann, H.-H.; Nove, A. and Vogel, H., eds.*, 1986, pp. 146–71. **[G: U.S.S.R.]**

Wang, Jici and Bradbury, John H. The Changing Industrial Geography of the Chinese Special Economic Zones. *Econ. Geogr.*, October 1986, *62*(4), pp. 307–20. **[G: China]**

Wasylenko, Michael. The Effect of Business Climate on Employment Growth. **In** *Minnesota Tax Study Commission*, 1986, pp. 51–73. **[G: U.S.]**

Wasylenko, Michael. The Effect of Business Climate on Employment Growth: A Review of the Evidence. **In** *Walzer, N. and Chicoine, D. L., eds.*, 1986, pp. 34–54. **[G: U.S.]**

Wellings, Paul and Black, Anthony. Industrial Decentralization under Apartheid: The Relocation of Industry to the South African Periphery. *World Devel.*, January 1986, *14*(1), pp. 1–38. **[G: S. Africa]**

Wever, Egbert. New Firm Formation in the Netherlands. **In** *Keeble, D. and Wever, E., eds.*, 1986, pp. 54–74. **[G: Netherlands]**

Wheat, Leonard F. State Industrial Growth: Comment [Business Climate, Taxes and Expenditures, and State Industrial Growth in the United States]. *Southern Econ. J.*, April 1986, *52*(4), pp. 1179–84. **[G: U.S.]**

Wheat, Leonard F. The Determinants of 1963–77 Regional Manufacturing Growth: Why the South and West Grow. *J. Reg. Sci.*, November 1986, *26*(4), pp. 635–59. **[G: U.S.]**

Williams, L. John. The Climacteric of the 1890s . **In** *Baber, C. and Williams, L. J., eds.*, 1986, pp. 192–203. **[G: U.K.]**

Wrigley, Neil and Brouwer, Floor. Qualitative Statistical Models for Regional Economic Analysis. **In** *Nijkamp, P., ed. (I)*, 1986, pp. 443–90. **[G: U.K.; Ireland; Netherlands]**

Yankson, P. W. K. Small-Scale Industries in the Implementation of a Growth Centre Strategy of Regional Development: A Case-Study in Ghana. *Industry Devel.*, 1986, (17), pp. 65–89. **[G: Ghana]**

Young, Ruth C. Industrial Location and Regional Change: The United States and New York State. *Reg. Stud.*, August 1986, *20*(4), pp. 341–69. **[G: U.S.]**

Zacchia, C. Possibilities and Constraints of Endogenous Industrial Development. **In** *Bassand, M., et al., eds.*, 1986, pp. 146–60. **[G: Europe]**

Zanetto, Gabriele. Sviluppo regionale e continuità culturale: il caso della beauce (Canada). (Regional Development and Cultural Continuity: The Case of the Beauce [Canada]. With English summary.) *Ricerche Econ.*, Apr.-Sept. 1986, *40*(2–3), pp. 537–55. **[G: Canada]**

Zech, Charles E. Sub-national Foreign Export Development and Its Impact on Productivity. *Growth Change*, July 1986, *17*(3), pp. 1–12. **[G: U.S.]**

9413 Regional Economic Models and Forecasts

Ahlburg, Dennis A. Forecasting Regional Births: An Economic–Demographic Approach. **In** *Isserman, A. M., ed.*, 1986, pp. 31–51. **[G: U.S.]**

Alonso, William. Intuition, Science, and the Application of Regional Models. **In** *Isserman, A. M., ed.*, 1986, pp. 261–69.

Andersson, Åke and Kuenne, Robert E. Regional Economic Dynamics. **In** *Nijkamp, P., ed. (I)*, 1986, pp. 201–53.

Barnard, Jerald R. and Kennedy, James E. A Method for Analyzing the Changing Impact of the Business Cycle on Regional Economies. **In** *Perryman, M. R. and Schmidt, J. R., eds.*, 1986, pp. 159–78. **[G: U.S.]**

Batten, David F. and Boyce, David E. Spatial Interaction, Transportation, and Interregional Commodity Flow Models. **In** *Nijkamp, P., ed. (I)*, 1986, pp. 357–406.

Beckmann, Martin J. From Lösch to Continuous Flow Models. **In** *[Lösch, A.]*, 1986, pp. 123–31.

Bennett, Robert J. and Hordijk, Leen. Regional Econometric and Dynamic Models. **In** *Nijkamp, P., ed. (I)*, 1986, pp. 407–41.

Benvenuti, S. Casini and Cavalieri, A. Applications of a Biregional Input–Output Model in Regional Policy Analysis. **In** *Batey, P. W. and Madden, M., eds.*, 1986, pp. 201–15. **[G: Italy]**

Bickford, Deborah J.; Clapp, John M. and Vehorn, Charles L. An Econometric Analysis of Regional Employment Effects of Federal Economic Development Programs. *Growth Change*, January 1986, *17*(1), pp. 1–16. **[G: U.S.]**

Blackley, Paul R. and Greytak, David. Comparative Advantage and Industrial Location: An Intrametropolitan Evaluation. *Urban Stud.*, June 1986, *23*(3), pp. 221–30. **[G: U.S.]**

Blommestein, Hans and Nijkamp, Peter. Testing the Spatial Scale and the Dynamic Structure in Regional Models (A Contribution to Spatial Econometric Specification Analysis.) *J. Reg. Sci.*, February 1986, *26*(1), pp. 1–17. **[G: Netherlands]**

Briassoulis, Helen. Integrated Economic-Environmental-Policy Modeling at the Regional and Multiregional Level: Methodological Characteristics and Issues. *Growth Change*, July 1986, *17*(3), pp. 22–34. **[G: Netherlands; U.S.; Canada]**

Brooking, Carl G. Regional Econometric Models: The Forecasting Record. **In** *Perryman, M. R. and Schmidt, J. R., eds.*, 1986, pp. 229–39. **[G: U.S.]**

Brunner, E. and Schubert, U. Capital Mobility, Labour Demand and R&D Investment in Austria in a Multiregional Context: A First Attempt at Econometric Modelling. **In** *Nijkamp, P., ed. (II)*, 1986, pp. 429–53. **[G: Austria]**

Camagni, Roberto. Innovation and the Urban Life-cycle: Production, Location and Income Distribution Aspects. **In** *Nijkamp, P., ed. (II)*, 1986, pp. 382–400. **[G: Italy]**

Cañada Vicinay, Juan. Influencias interregionales: un procedimiento de análisis y medida. (With English summary.) *Invest. Ecón.*, May 1986, *10*(2), pp. 279–308.

Charney, Alberta H. and Taylor, Carol A. Integrated State–Substate Econometric Modeling: Design and Utilization for Long-run Economic Analysis. **In** *Perryman, M. R. and Schmidt, J. R., eds.*, 1986, pp. 43–92. **[G: U.S.]**

Chatterji, Manas. August Lösch and Spatial Regularities in the Developing Countries. **In** *[Lösch, A.]*, 1986, pp. 203–17. **[G: India]**

Clapp, John M., et al. Regional Policy Handles in Econometric Models: Evidence from U.S. Development Outlays. *Reg. Sci. Urban Econ.*, November 1986, *16*(4), pp. 589–604. **[G: U.S.]**

van Clark, W. A. V. and Lierop, Wal F. J. Residential Mobility and Household Location Modelling. **In** *Nijkamp, P., ed. (I)*, 1986, pp. 97–132.

van Dijk, Jouke and Oosterhaven, J. Regional Impacts of Migrants' Expenditures: An Input–Output/Vacancy-Chain Approach. **In** *Batey, P. W. and Madden, M., eds.*, 1986, pp. 122–47. **[G: Netherlands]**

Fomby, Thomas B. A Comparison of Forecasting Accuracies of Alternative Regional Production Index Methodologies. *J. Bus. Econ. Statist.*, April 1986, *4*(2), pp. 177–86. **[G: U.S.]**

Glennon, Dennis, et al. Incorporating Labour Market Structure in Regional Econometric Models. *Appl. Econ.*, May 1986, *18*(5), pp. 545–55. **[G: U.S.]**

Gould, Brian W. The Impact of Structural Change within an Economy on Resource Use: An Input–Output Analysis. *Appl. Econ.*, May 1986, *18*(5), pp. 457–77. **[G: Canada]**

Gould, Brian W. The Impacts of Prairie Branch Line Rehabilitation: An Application of Interregional Input–Output Analysis. *Can. J. Agr. Econ.*, November 1986, *34*(3), pp. 313–30. **[G: Canada]**

Hafkamp, Wim and Nijkamp, Peter. Integrated Economic–Environmental–Energy Policy and Conflict Analysis. *J. Policy Modeling*, Winter 1986, *8*(4), pp. 551–76. **[G: Netherlands]**

Hanseman, Dennis J. A Quarterly Econometric Model of Factor Demands in Regional Manufacturing. *J. Reg. Sci.*, February 1986, *26*(1), pp. 161–77. **[G: U.S.]**

Hewings, Geoffrey J. D. Problems of Integration in the Modelling of Regional Systems. **In** *Batey, P. W. and Madden, M., eds.*, 1986, pp. 37–53.

Hewings, Geoffrey J. D. and Jensen, Rodney C. Regional Interregional and Multiregional Input–Output Analysis. **In** *Nijkamp, P., ed. (I)*, 1986, pp. 295–355.

Hirsch, Werner Z. Interindustry Relations of a Metropolitan Area. **In** *Sohn, I., ed.*, 1986, *1959*, pp. 354–71. **[G: U.S.]**

Isard, Walter and Smith, Christine. Economic–Demographic Linkages in an Interregional

Model. In *Isserman, A. M., ed.*, 1986, pp. 159–75. **[G: Australia]**

Johnson, Nicholas and Adams, John. Electricity Demand Growth in New York State: The Uncertain Factor in the Electricity Planning Process. In *Saltzman, S. and Schuler, R. E., eds.*, 1986, pp. 67–76. **[G: U.S.]**

Johnson, Thomas G. A Dynamic Input–Output Model for Small Regions. *Rev. Reg. Stud.*, Winter 1986, *16*(1), pp. 14–23.

Kinal, Terrence and Ratner, Jonathan. A VAR Forecasting Model of a Regional Economy: Its Construction and Comparative Accuracy. *Int. Reg. Sci. Rev.*, August 1986, *10*(2), pp. 113–26. **[G: U.S.]**

Kort, John R.; Cartwright, Joseph V. and Beemiller, Richard M. Linking Regional Economic Models for Policy Analysis. In *Perryman, M. R. and Schmidt, J. R., eds.*, 1986, pp. 93–124. **[G: U.S.]**

Kushnirsky, F. I. Regional Growth in the Soviet Economy: A Model and Analysis. *J. Reg. Sci.*, February 1986, *26*(1), pp. 47–62. **[G: U.S.S.R.]**

Ledent, Jacques. Consistent Modelling of Employment, Population, Labour Force, and Unemployment in the Statistical Analysis of Regional Growth. In *Batey, P. W. and Madden, M., eds.*, 1986, pp. 25–36.

Ledent, Jacques. Forecasting Interregional Migration: An Economic–Demographic Approach. In *Isserman, A. M., ed.*, 1986, pp. 53–77. **[G: Canada; U.S.]**

Leistritz, F. L.; Chase, R. A. and Murdock, S. H. Socioeconomic Impact Models: A Review of Analytical Methods and Policy Implications. In *Batey, P. W. and Madden, M., eds.*, 1986, pp. 148–66.

Leontief, Wassily and Strout, Alan. Multiregional Input–Output Analysis. In *Leontief, W.*, 1986, *1963*, pp. 129–61. **[G: U.S.]**

Lesage, James P. and Magura, Michael. Econometric Modeling of Interregional Labour Market Linkages. *J. Reg. Sci.*, August 1986, *26*(3), pp. 367–77. **[G: U.S.]**

Lieu, T. S. Impacts of Air Pollution Control Costs: An Input–Output Approach. *Ann. Reg. Sci.*, July 1986, *20*(2), pp. 55–65. **[G: U.S.]**

Luptáčik, M. and Schmoranz, I. Economic Consequences of a Change in Demographic Patterns: An Integrated Approach. In *Batey, P. W. and Madden, M., eds.*, 1986, pp. 107–21. **[G: Austria]**

Martellato, Dino and Scandola, Massimo. Grado di apertura e attivazione in un modello interregionale per l'italia. (Tracing the Pattern of Location and Trade with an Interregional Model for Italy. With English summary.) *Ricerche Econ.*, Apr.-Sept. 1986, *40*(2–3), pp. 328–59. **[G: Italy]**

Mathis, Stephen A. and Posatko, Robert C. Local Government Expenditures and Private Sector Output: Theory and Evidence on Crowding Out at the Regional Level. *Quart. Rev. Econ. Bus.*, Autumn 1986, *26*(3), pp. 105–15. **[G: U.S.]**

McQuaid, Ronald William. Production Functions and the Disaggregation of Labor Inputs in Manufacturing Plants. *J. Reg. Sci.*, August 1986, *26*(3), pp. 595–603. **[G: U.S.]**

Miernyk, William H. Long-range Forecasting with a Regional Input–Output Model. In *Sohn, I., ed.*, 1986, *1968*, pp. 81–92. **[G: U.S.]**

Miller, Ronald E. Upper Bounds on the Sizes of Interregional Feedbacks in Multiregional Input–Output Models. *J. Reg. Sci.*, May 1986, *26*(2), pp. 285–306.

Mountain, Dean C. Impact of Higher Energy Prices on Wage Rates, Return to Capital, Energy Intensity and Productivity: A Regional Profit Specification. *Energy Econ.*, July 1986, *8*(3), pp. 171–76. **[G: Canada]**

Münzenmaier, Werner. Some Notes on the Appropriate Definition of Sectors in Regional Input–Output Tables, Especially for the Federal Republic of Germany. In *Franz, A. and Rainer, N., eds.*, 1986, pp. 23–46. **[G: W. Germany]**

Nijkamp, Peter and Poot, Jacques. Technological Change and Labour Migration in a General Spatial Interaction System. In *Nijkamp, P., ed. (II)*, 1986, pp. 358–70.

Nijkamp, Peter and Rietveld, Piet. Multiple Objective Decision Analysis in Regional Economics. In *Nijkamp, P., ed. (I)*, 1986, pp. 493–541.

Nijkamp, Peter; Rietveld, Piet and Snickars, Folke. Regional and Multiregional Economic Models: A Survey. In *Nijkamp, P., ed. (I)*, 1986, pp. 257–94.

Pagoulatos, A.; Mattas, K. and Debertin, D. L. A Comparison of Some Alternatives to Input–Output Multipliers. *Land Econ.*, November 1986, *62*(4), pp. 371–77. **[G: U.S.]**

Pedreño Muñoz, Andrés. Deducción de las tablas input–output: consideraciones críticas a través de la contrastación "survey–nonsurvey." (With English summary.) *Invest. Ecón.*, September 1986, *10*(3), pp. 579–99. **[G: Spain]**

Perryman, M. Ray and Perryman, Nancy S. The Regional Business Cycle: A Theoretical Exposition with Time Series, Cross Sectional, and Predictive Applications. In *Perryman, M. R. and Schmidt, J. R., eds.*, 1986, pp. 125–58. **[G: U.S.]**

Plane, David A. and Rogerson, Peter A. Dynamic Flow Modeling with Interregional Dependency Effects: An Application to Structural Change in the U.S. Migration System. *Demography*, February 1986, *23*(1), pp. 91–104. **[G: U.S.]**

Plaut, Thomas. State and Local Fiscal Analysis with an Econometric Model of Texas. In *Batey, P. W. and Madden, M., eds.*, 1986, pp. 187–200. **[G: U.S.]**

Polenske, Karen R. The Implementation of a Multiregional Input–Output Model for the United States. In *Sohn, I., ed.*, 1986, *1972*, pp. 93–107. **[G: U.S.]**

Puu, Tönu and Weidlich, Wolfgang. The Stability of Hexagonal Tessellations. In *[Lösch, A.]*, 1986, pp. 133–58.

Ralston, Scott N.; Hastings, Steven E. and Brucker, Sharon M. Improving Regional I-O Models: Evidence against Uniform Regional Purchase Coefficients across Rows. *Ann. Reg. Sci.*, March 1986, *20*(1), pp. 65–80. **[G: U.S.]**

Rogers, Andrei and Williams, Pamela. Multistate Demoeconomic Modeling and Projection. **In** *Isserman, A. M., ed.*, 1986, pp. 177–202. **[G: Australia]**

Round, J. I. Social Accounting for Regional Economic Systems. **In** *Batey, P. W. and Madden, M., eds.*, 1986, pp. 90–106. **[G: Malaysia]**

Rouwendal, Jan. On the Production and Diffusion of Technological Change. **In** *Nijkamp, P., ed. (II)*, 1986, pp. 371–81.

Schmidt, James R. A General Framework for Interpolation, Distribution, and Extrapolation of a Time Series by Related Series. **In** *Perryman, M. R. and Schmidt, J. R., eds.*, 1986, pp. 181–94. **[G: U.S.]**

Slater, Paul B. Comparisons of Aggregation Procedures for Interaction Data: An Illustration Using a College Student International Flow Table. **In** *Slater, P. B.*, 1986, *1981*, pp. 29–36. **[G: Selected Countries]**

Slater, Paul B. Point-to-Point Migration Functions and Gravity Model Renormalization: Approaches to Aggregation in Spatial Interaction Modeling. **In** *Slater, P. B.*, 1986, *1985*, pp. 57–76. **[G: U.S.]**

Smith, Christine. An Empirically Implementable Integrated Multiregional Model for Australia. *Reg. Sci. Urban Econ.*, May 1986, *16*(2), pp. 181–95. **[G: Australia]**

Solomon, Barry D. The Socioeconomic Impacts of a Regional Synthetic Fuels Industry: An Integrated Econometric Analysis. **In** *Batey, P. W. and Madden, M., eds.*, 1986, pp. 167–86. **[G: U.S.]**

Stevens, Benjamin H. and Treyz, George I. A Multiregional Model Forecast for the United States through 1995. *Amer. Econ. Rev.*, May 1986, *76*(2), pp. 304–07. **[G: U.S.]**

Stone, J. R. N. and Weale, Martin. Two Populations and Their Economies. **In** *Batey, P. W. and Madden, M., eds.*, 1986, pp. 74–89.

Swartz, Stephen and Welsch, Roy E. Applications of Bounded-Influence and Diagnostic Methods in Energy Modeling. **In** *Belsley, D. A. and Kuh, E., eds.*, 1986, pp. 154–90. **[G: U.S.]**

Takayama, T. and Labys, Walter C. Spatial Equilibrium Analysis. **In** *Nijkamp, P., ed. (I)*, 1986, pp. 171–99.

Taylor, Carol A. The Effects of Refining Demographic–Economic Interactions in Regional Econometric Models. **In** *Isserman, A. M., ed.*, 1986, pp. 127–55. **[G: U.S.]**

Weber, Richard E. Regional Econometric Modeling and the New Jersey State Model. **In** *Perryman, M. R. and Schmidt, J. R., eds.*, 1986, pp. 13–39. **[G: U.S.]**

Wegener, M. Integrated Forecasting Models of Urban and Regional Systems. **In** *Batey, P. W. and Madden, M., eds.*, 1986, pp. 9–24.

Williamson, Jeffrey G. Regional Economic–Demographic Modeling: Progress and Prospects. **In** *Isserman, A. M., ed.*, 1986, pp. 241–60. **[G: LDCs]**

Wrigley, Neil and Brouwer, Floor. Qualitative Statistical Models for Regional Economic Analysis. **In** *Nijkamp, P., ed. (I)*, 1986, pp. 443–90. **[G: U.K.; Ireland; Netherlands]**

Zech, Charles E. Sub-national Foreign Export Development and Its Impact on Productivity. *Growth Change*, July 1986, *17*(3), pp. 1–12. **[G: U.S.]**

Topical Guide
To Classification Schedule

TOPICAL GUIDE TO CLASSIFICATION SCHEDULE

This index refers to the subject index *group, category,* or *subcategory* in which the listed topic may be found. The subject index classifications include, in most cases, related topics as well. The term *category* generally indicates that the topic may be found in all of the *subcategories* of the 3-digit code; the term *group,* indicates that the topics may be found in all of the *subcategories* in the 2-digit code. The classification schedule (p. xxxv) serves to refer the user to cross references.

ABSENTEEISM: 8240
ACCELERATOR: 0233
ACCOUNTING: firm, 5410; national income, 2210, 2212; social, 2250
ADMINISTERED PRICES: theory, 0226; empirical studies, 6110; industry, 6354
ADMINISTRATION: 513 category; business, 5131; and planning, programming, and budgeting: national, 5132, 3226, state and local, 3241; public, 5132
ADVERTISING: industry, 6354; and marketing, 5310
AFFLUENT SOCIETY: 0510, 0110
AGENT THEORY, 0228
AGING: economics of, 9180
AGGREGATION: 2118; in input-output analysis, 2220; from micro to macro, 0220, 0230
AGREEMENTS: collective, 832 category; commodity, 4220, 7130; international trade, 4220
AGRIBUSINESS: *see* CORPORATE AGRICULTURE
AGRICULTURAL: commodity exchanges, 3132, 7150; cooperatives, 7150; credit, 7140; research and innovation, 621 category; employment, 8131; marketing, 7150; outlook, 7120; productivity, 7110, 7160; situation, 7120; supply and demand analysis, 7110; surpluses, 7130
AGRICULTURE: 710 group; government programs and policy, 7130; and development, 7100, 1120
AIR TRANSPORTATION: 6150
AIRPORT: 6150, 9410
AIRCRAFT MANUFACTURING: 6314
ALLOCATION: welfare aspects, 0242; and general equilibrium, 0210
ALUMINUM INDUSTRY: 6312
ANCIENT ECONOMIC HISTORY: 043 category
ANCIENT ECONOMIC THOUGHT: 0311; individuals, 0322
ANTITRUST POLICY: 6120
APPLIANCE INDUSTRY: 6313
APPRENTICESHIP: 8110
ARBITRATION: labor, 832 category
ASSISTANCE: foreign, 4430
ATOMIC ENERGY: conservation and pollution, 7220; industries, 6352, 7230
AUCTION MARKETS: theory, 0227
AUSTRIAN SCHOOL: 0315; individuals, 0322
AUTOMATION: employment: empirical studies, 8243, theory, 8210
AUTOMOBILE MANUFACTURING: 6314

BALANCE OF PAYMENTS: 431 category; accounting, 4310; empirical studies, 4313; theory, 4312
BANK FOR INTERNATIONAL SETTLEMENTS: 4320
BANKS: central, 3116; commercial, 3120; investment, 3140; other, 3140; portfolios, 3120; savings and loan, 3140; savings, 3140; supervision and regulation of, 3120, 3140, 3116
BARGAINING: collective, 832 category; theory, 0262
BAYESIAN ANALYSIS: 2115
BENEFIT–COST ANALYSIS: theory 0242; applied, see individual fields
BEQUESTS: empirical, 9211; theoretical, 0243
BEVERAGE INDUSTRIES: 6318
BIBLIOGRAPHY: 0110; see also the GENERAL heading under each subject
BIOGRAPHY: businessmen, 040 group; history of thought, 0322
BOND MARKET: 3132
BOOK PUBLISHING: 6352
BOYCOTTS, LABOR: 833 category; 832 category
BRAIN DRAIN: 8230, 8410
BRAND PREFERENCE: 5310; and consumers, 9212
BREAK-EVEN ANALYSIS: 5120
BRETTON WOODS AGREEMENT: 4320
BUDGETS: consumers, 9211; governments: theory, 3212, national studies, 3226, state and local studies, 3241
BUILDING: construction industry, 6340; materials industry, 6317

Building societies: 3152 and 3140
Bureaucracy, theory of, 0252
Business: credit, 3153; finance, 5210
Business cycle: and growth, 1312; empirical studies, 1313; policy, 1331; theory of, 1312; unemployment, 1312, 8210
Business services: 6354

Capacity of industry: 6410
Capital: expenditure by firm, 5220; gains tax, 3230; human, 8510; international movements of: short term, 431 category; long term, 441 category; and personal savings, 9211
Capital asset pricing: 3131
Capital budgeting: 5200
Capital markets: 313 category; efficiency of, 3131; studies and regulation, 3132; theory, 3131
Capital-output ratios: and growth, 111 category; empirical, 2212
Capital theory: distributive shares: aggregate, 0235, factor, 0224; firm, 0223; and growth, 111 category; and technological progress, 6211
Capitalist system: 0510
Cartels: 6110; international, 4220
Catholic economics: 0321; individuals, 0322
Cattle industry: 7110
Cement industry: 6315
Census: population, 8410; regional, 2280
Central banks: 3116
Centrally planned economies: country studies, 124 category; planning, 113 category; systems, 0520; theory, 027 category
Ceramics industry: 6315
Cereals: supply and demand, 7110; marketing, 7150; processing, 6318, 7151
Check-off system: 832 category
Chemical industry: 6315
Child labor legislation: 8221
Choice: consumer, 0222; social, 025 category
Christian socialism: 0317; individuals, 0322
Civil service employment: 8135, legislation, 8226
Classical school: 0314; individuals, 0322
Closed shop: 8310; 832 category
Clothing industry: 6316
Clubs, theory of: 0252
Coal mining: 6322, 7230
Codetermination: 0510
Collective bargaining: 832 category
Collective decision: studies, 0252; theory, 0251
Collective farm: 7130; socialist, 0520; Kibbutz, 0510
Collusion, government policy toward: 6120
COMECON: 4230, 4233
Commercial banks: 3120
Commercial policy: *see* International Trade Controls
Committees: theory of, 0252
Commodity agreements: 4220, agricultural, 7130
Commodity markets, 3132
Communication equipment industry: 6313
Communication industries: 6352; regulation of, 6130
Communist school: 0317; individuals, 0322
Communist system: 0520
Community relations of the firm: 5140
Company unions: 8310
Comparative cost theory: 4112
Comparative economic history: 0412
Comparative economic systems: 0530
Competition: 0225; government policy toward, 6120; imperfect, 0226; and innovation, 0225, 0226; non-price, 0226; spatial, 9411
Computational techniques: 2134; and computer programs, 2140
Computer industry: hardware, 6313; software, 6352
Computer programs: 2140
Concentration of industry: 6110; government policy toward, 6120
Conservation: 7220
Construction industry: 6340; labor force, 8136
Consumer demand: theory, 0222
Consumer: economics, 921 category; expenditure on specific items, 9212; motivation, 9210; overall expenditure, 9211; protection, 9213; savings, 9211
Consumer finance: 3151
Consumer price index: 2270; method, 2118
Consumer's surplus: 0222, 0240
Consumption: empirical studies, 9211; function, 0232
Control theory: applications, 1331 and 2120; technical use, 2132
Convertibility of currencies: 4320
Cooperatives: 0510; agricultural marketing, 7150; housing, 9320
Copper: manufacturing, 6312; mining, 6322
Corporate agriculture: 7151
Cost: 0223
Cost of living: index, 2270; index construction methods, 2118; studies, 9211
Cotton: crop, 7110; manufacturing, 6316; marketing, 7150
Countervailing power: 0510, 0110
Country studies: centrally planned economies, 124 category; comparative, 1230; developed, 122 category; developing, 121 category
Credit: business, 3153; consumer, 3151; farm, 7140; housing, 3152

CREDITOR NATION: 4430
CRIME, ECONOMICS OF: 9160
CRUDE OIL INDUSTRY: 6323, 7230
CUSTOMS UNIONS: 423 category
CYCLE: *see* BUSINESS CYCLE

DAIRY PRODUCTS: 7110; marketing, 7150; processing, 7151
DAMS: 7210
DEBT: consumer, 3151; international, 4430; public: national, 3228, state and local, 3243
DEBTOR NATION: 4430
DECISION THEORY: 5110
DEFENSE CONTRACTS: 1140
DEFENSE ECONOMICS: 1140
DEFLATION: *see* INFLATION
DEINDUSTRIALIZATION: 6160
DEMAND: aggregate consumption, 0232; aggregate investment, 0233; factor, 0223; individual and household, 0222
DEMOGRAPHY: 8410; and cycles, 8410, 1313; and development, 1120; and growth, 111 category
DEPOSIT INSURANCE: 3120, 3140
DEPRECIATION: accounting, 5410; and taxation, 3230
DEPRESSED AREAS: 941 category; and poverty: rural, 7180, urban, 9310
DEVALUATION: 4314
DEVELOPING COUNTRIES: *see* COUNTRY STUDIES
DEVELOPMENT: agricultural, 7100, 1120; aid, 4430; and growth, 1120; in particular countries, 120 group; and research, 6212; and trade, 4114
DIFFERENTIATION OF PRODUCT: and advertising, 5310; theory, 0226
DIFFUSION: economic geography, 7310; spatial, 941 category; technological, 6211
DIRECT CONTROLS: 1332
DISARMAMENT: 1140
DISABILITY: fringe benefits, 8242; insurance, 6356, 9130; workmen's compensation, 8222
DISCRIMINATION: age, race, and sex, 9170; in education, 9120; in employment, 9170; in housing, 9320; price: empirical studies, 6110, theory, 0226; spatial, 9411
DISCRIMINANT ANALYSIS: 2114
DISEQUILIBRIUM THEORY: 021 category
DISGUISED UNEMPLOYMENT: 8210; and development, 8131, 1120
DISMISSAL COMPENSATION: 8242
DISSONANCE ANALYSIS: 5310
DISTRIBUTED LAGS: 2113
DISTRIBUTION: aggregate theory, 0235; empirical studies of income, 2213; empirical studies of wealth, 2240; factor theory, 0224
DIVIDENDS: 5210

DRAFT: 1140
DRAWING RIGHTS: 4320
DRUG INDUSTRY: 6315
DUOPOLY: 0226
DUMPING: 4220

ECONOMETRIC METHODS: 211 category; construction, analysis, and use of models, 2120
ECONOMETRIC MODELS: 132 category
ECONOMIC: current conditions and outlook, 120 group, 1330; imperialism, 4420
ECONOMIC DATA: 220 group
ECONOMIC FLUCTUATIONS: *see* BUSINESS CYCLES
ECONOMIC HISTORY: 040 group; development of the discipline, 0411
ECONOMIC PLANNING: 113 category
ECONOMIC SYSTEMS: 050 group
ECONOMIC THEORY: 020 group
ECONOMIC THOUGHT: history of, 030 group
ECONOMICS: relation to other disciplines, 0113; social values, 0114, 050 group; teaching, 0111
ECONOMIES OF SCALE: 0223; determinants of market structure, 6110
ECONOMIST: role of, 0112
EDUCATION: economics of, 9120; investment in, 8510; manpower training, 8110
ELASTICITY: of demand, 0222; of supply, 0223
ELECTRICAL EQUIPMENT INDUSTRY: 6313
ELECTRIC ENERGY: conservation, 7220; pollution, 7220; resource, 7230; utilities: industry studies, 6352, regulation of, 6130
EMPIRICAL METHOD: 0360, 0115
EMPLOYEE PARTICIPATION IN MANAGEMENT: in market economies, 0510; in socialist economies, 0520
EMPLOYMENT: data and levels, 8240, 8243; geographic, 8241; by industry, 813 category; services (private), 6354 (public policy), 8225; studies (general), 8243, studies (public sector), 8226; subsidies, 8240
EMPLOYMENT POLICY: 8225
ENERGY: conservation, 7220; industries, 632 group, 6352; sources, 7230
ENTERTAINMENT INDUSTRY: 6358
ENTREPRENEURSHIP: and development, 1120; in firms, 5140; in market economies, 0510; and profit, 0224
ENVIRONMENT: 7220
EQUILIBRIUM: general, 0210; in macroeconomics, 0230; partial, 0225, 0226
ESTATE TAX: 3230
EUROCURRENCIES: 4320
EUROPEAN ECONOMIC COMMUNITY: 4233
EUROPEAN FREE TRADE ASSOCIATION: 4233
EXCESS PROFITS TAX: 3230

Exchange rates: *see* Foreign exchange
Excise tax: 3230
Executives: 5130
Expenditure, government: national, 3221; state and local, 3241; theory, 3212; and welfare, 0243
Expenditure, personal: 921 category
Experimental economic methods: 215 category
Exports: policies, 4220; restrictions, 4220; role in development, 4114; trade patterns, 4210
Externalities: theory, 0244; for applications *see* individual fields
Extractive industries: 632 category

Factor analysis: 2114
Factor proportions: 0223; and growth, 111 category
Factors of production and distributive shares: *see* Distribution
Fair trade: 6120
Family allowances: 9110
Family, economics of: *see* Household, economics of
Farm: finance, 7140; management, 7160
Farm machinery industry: 6313
Farm mechanization: 7160
Farmers' cooperatives: 7150
Federal Reserve Board and System: 3116
Federal-state financial relations: 3250
Feed processing industry: 7151
Fertility: 8410
Fertilizer: industry, 6315; use, 7160
Feudalism: 0430
Fiber crops: 7110; manufacturing, 6316; marketing, 7150
Financial accounts: 2230
Financial intermediaries: 3140
Financial intermediation: 3130
Financial statistics: 2230
Firm: financial structure, 5210; goals and objectives, 5140; investment, 5220; administrative organization, 5130; organization theory, 5110; regulation, 613 category; theory of, 0223
Fiscal policy: 3216; and fiscal theory, 3210
Fiscal theory: 3212
Fisheries: 7210
Flood control: 7220
Flow of funds accounts: 2230
Fluctuations: *see* Business cycles
Food: consumption, 9212; and nutrition standards, 9130; and population, 8410; processing industry, 6318, 7151
Food-stamp plan: 9110, 9140
Forecasting: 132 category; for a country, 1322; methods and theory, 1324, 2120; for a region, 9413; for a specific sector, 1323
Foreign assistance: 4430
Foreign debt: 4430
Foreign exchange: control, 4220; markets, 4314; rates, 4314
Foreign investment: studies, 4412; theory, 4411
Foreign trade: *see* International trade
Forest products industries: 6317
Forests: 7210; conservation, 7220
Foundations: non-profit organizations, 6360
Fringe benefits: 8242
Fruits: 7110; marketing of, 7150
Full-cost pricing: 0226, 5140
Furniture industry: 6317
Futures markets: 3132
Futurists: 2260

Game theory: 0262; game theoretic decision theory, 5110; and general equilibrium, 0210; in oligopoly, 0226; in social choice, 0251
Gas: conservation, 7220; pollution, 7220; resources, 7230; utilities: industry studies, 6352, regulation of, 6130
General Agreement on Tariffs and Trade (GATT): 4220, 7130
General Economics: 010 group
General equilibrium theory: 0210
Gift tax: 3230
Glass manufacturing: 6315
Goals and objectives of firms: 5140
Gold mining: 6322
Gold standard: 4320
Government bonds: market, 3132; national, 3228; state and local, 3243
Government employees: 8135
Government expenditures: *see* Expenditures, government
Grants-in-aid: 3250
Grievance procedures: 832 category; 833 category
Group of twenty: 4320
Growth: 111 category and 2260; country studies: LDCs, 121 category, MDCs, 122 category; centrally planned economies, 124 category; of firm, 0223; indicators, 2260; LDCs, 1120; MDCs, 2260; and technological change, 6211; theoretical models: one and two sector, 1112, monetary, 1114, multisector, 1113; socialist, 027 category or 1132

Harbors: *see* Ports
Health, economics of: 9130
Health insurance: 9130, 6356; by the firm, 8242; medicaid, 9130; medicare, 9130

HIGHWAYS: 6150
HISTORICAL SCHOOL: 0318; individuals, 0322
HISTORICISM: 0360
HISTORY: *see* ECONOMIC HISTORY
HISTORY OF ECONOMIC THOUGHT: 030 group
HOLDING COMPANIES: 6110; public utility, 6130
HOURS OF LABOR: regulation, 8221; studies, 824 category
HOUSEHOLD, ECONOMICS OF: and consumer economics, 921 category; and employment and leisure, 8210; household formation, 8410; consumption theory, 0222
HOUSING: 9320; mortgage credit, 3152; statistics, 2240, 2250
HUMAN CAPITAL: 8510

IMPERFECT COMPETITION: 0226
IMPERIALISM: 4420; and capitalism, 0510
IMPORT-SUBSTITUTION: empirical studies, 4220; theory, 4114
IMPORTS: restrictions, 4220; trade patterns, 4210
INCENTIVES: in socialist systems, 0520, 0271; wage, 8242
INCOME: and employment theory, 0230; national accounting, 2212; personal distribution, 2213
INCOME TAX: national, 3230; state and local, 3242; theory, 3212
INCOMES POLICY: 1332
INDEX NUMBERS THEORY: 2118
INDEXATION: 1342
INDICATORS: of business conditions, 1330; of productivity, 2260
INDIFFERENCE ANALYSIS: 0222
INDUSTRIAL: capacity, 6410; location, 9411
INDUSTRIAL AND MARKET STRUCTURES: 6110
INDUSTRIAL POLICY: 6160
INDUSTRIAL RELATIONS: 833 category; legislation, 822 category, 833 category
INDUSTRIALIZATION: and development, 1120; historical studies, 040 group
INDUSTRY STUDIES: 630 group
INEQUALITY: age, race, and sex, 9170; income distribution, 2213; regional, 9412; welfare aspects: studies, 9110, 9140; theory, 0243
INFLATION AND DEFLATION: 134 category; theory, 1342; and wages, 1342, 8210
INFORMATION: and imperfect competition, 0226; and labor market theory, 8210; and marketing, 5310; statistical theory, 2114; theory, 0261
INFORMATION SERVICES: industry, 6352
INHERITANCE: redistributive aspects, theory 0243; savings and asset studies, 9211; tax, 3230
INNOVATION: 6211
INPUT–OUTPUT: mathematical structure, 0210; models and empirical studies, 2220; regional, 9413
INSTITUTIONALISM: 0360
INSTITUTIONALIST SCHOOL: 0318; individuals, 0322
INSURANCE: industry, 6356; social security, 9150
INTEGRATION, INTERNATIONAL ECONOMIC: policies and studies, 4233; theory, 4232
INTEREST: and capital, 0224, 0235; empirical studies and policy, 3116; monetary theories, 3112
INTERGOVERNMENTAL FINANCIAL RELATIONS: 3250
INTERNAL ORGANIZATION OF FIRM: 5130
INTERNAL TRANSFER PRICING: 5120
INTERNATIONAL: adjustment mechanisms, 431 category; capital movements: long term, 441 category, short term and speculative, 4312, 4313; economics, 400 group; lending, private, 4330; lending, public, 4430; liquidity, 4320; movement of factors theory, 4112 specialization, 4112; trade controls, 4220; trade patterns, 4210; trade theory, 4112
INTERNATIONAL BANK FOR RECONSTRUCTION AND DEVELOPMENT: 4430
INTERNATIONAL MONETARY ARRANGEMENTS: 4320
INTERNATIONAL MONETARY FUND (IMF): 4320
INTERNATIONAL TRADE ORGANIZATION (ITO): 4220
INTERTEMPORAL CHOICE: macroeconomics of, 0239; microeconomics of, 0229
INVENTORY: and business cycles, 131 category; policies of the firm, 5120; theory, 0223, 0233, 5220
INVESTMENT: by individual firm and/or industry, 5220; component of national income, 2212; function, 0233; and rate of return, 5220; relation to savings, 0233; in socialist system, 027 category; theory, 0223, 0233
INVESTMENT BANK: 3140

JOB SEARCH: theory, 8210

KEYNESIAN ECONOMICS: 023 category

LABOR: demand studies, 8243; demand theory, 8210; in economic development, 1120, 8210; supply of, *see* LABOR FORCE; theory of, 8210, 0223
LABOR DISPUTES: 832 category
LABOR ECONOMICS: 800 group
LABOR FORCE: 8130; agricultural, 8131; construction, 8136; government, 8135; manufacturing, 8132; professional, 8134; recruiting and training, 8110; services, 8133
LABOR LEGISLATION: 822 category
LABOR MARKET: demographic characteristics, 8260; studies, 824 category; theory, 8210
LABOR PRODUCTIVITY: 8250
LABOR-MANAGEMENT RELATIONS: 833 category

LABOR TURNOVER: 8243
LABOR UNIONS: *see* TRADE UNIONS
LAND: development and use, 7172; ownership and tenure, 7171; reform, 7171; taxes, 3242
LAUSANNE SCHOOL: 0316; individuals, 0322
LAW AND CRIME, ECONOMICS OF: 9160
LEASE–PURCHASE DECISIONS: 5210
LEATHER MANUFACTURING: 6316
LEISURE: and living standards, 9210; theory of, 8210; and utility, 0222
LENDING: international (public), 4430; (private) 4330
LESS DEVELOPED COUNTRIES: *see* COUNTRY STUDIES
LICENSING: 6120
LIFE-CYCLE THEORY: 0232
LINEAR AND NONLINEAR PROGRAMMING: 2135
LIQUIDITY PREFERENCE: 3112
LIVESTOCK: 7110; marketing of, 7150
LIVING STANDARDS: studies, 9211; rural, 7180
LOANABLE FUNDS THEORY OF INTEREST: 3112
LOCATION ECONOMICS: 9411, 7310
LUMBER INDUSTRY: 6317

MACHINE TOOLS MANUFACTURING: 6313
MACHINERY MANUFACTURING: 6313
MANAGEMENT: of farm, 7160; of firm, 5120; of personnel, 5130
MANAGERIAL ECONOMICS: 5120
MANPOWER TRAINING: 8110
MANUFACTURING INDUSTRIES: 631 category
MARGINAL: cost, 0223; efficiency of capital, 0224; productivity, 0224
MARGINALISM: 0315, 0360
MARKET: equilibrium, 0225; 0226; research, 5310; structure, 6110
MARKETING: 5310
MARKOV CHAIN: 2114
MARSHALLIAN SCHOOL: 0315; individuals, 0322
MARXIST SCHOOL: 0317; for individuals belonging to this group, 0322
MASS TRANSIT: 6150; urban, 9330
MATHEMATICAL PROGRAMMING: 2135
MATHEMATICAL METHODS AND MODELS: 213 category, 0115
MEDICAL CARE: *see* HEALTH, ECONOMICS OF
MEDICAL SUBSIDY PROGRAMS: 9130
MEDIEVAL: economic thought, 0311; individuals, 0322; economic history, 043 category
MERCANTILISTS: 0313; for individuals belonging to this group, 0322
MERCHANT MARINE: 6150
MERGERS: 6110; government policy toward, 6120
METAL MANUFACTURING: 6312
METHODS: 0115; experimental economic methods, 215 category
METHODOLOGY OF ECONOMICS: 0360
METROPOLITAN PLANNING STUDIES: *see* REGIONAL PLANNING
METROPOLITANIZATION: 9310
MICRODATA: 2290
MIGRATION: of labor, 8230; of population, 8410
MILITARY PROCUREMENT: 1140
MINERALS: 7210; energy producing minerals, 7230
MINING INDUSTRIES: 632 category, 7210; energy producing mining, 7320
MINORITIES: 9170
MOBILITY: *see* MIGRATION
MONETARY: growth theory, 1114; policy, 3116; theories of cycles, 3112, 1310; theory, 3112
MONEY: demand for, 3112; markets, 3130, 3132; supply of, 3112
MONOPOLISTIC COMPETITION: 0226
MONOPOLY: 0226; control of, 6120
MONOPSONY: 0226
MONTE CARLO METHOD: 2112
MORBIDITY RATES: 8410
MORTALITY RATES: 8410
MORTGAGE MARKET: 3152, 9320
MOTIVATION: consumer, 0222; and marketing, 5310; profit maximization, 0223, 5140
MOTION PICTURE INDUSTRY: 6358
MULTINATIONAL CORPORATION: 4420
MULTIPLIER: 0232; balanced budget, 3212; foreign trade, 4112; investment, 0233
MULTICOLLINEARITY: 2113
MULTIVARIATE ANALYSIS: 2114

NATALITY RATES: 8410
NATIONAL INCOME: accounting, 2212; distribution of, 2213; international comparisons of, 1230; theory and procedures, 2210
NATIONAL WEALTH: 2240
NATIONALIZATION OF INDUSTRY: domestic, 6140; foreign, 4420
NATURAL GAS: conservation, 7230; industry, 6323, 7230; resources, 7230; utilities, 6130, 7230
NATURAL RESOURCES: 7210; conservation, 7220; and population, 8410; recreational aspects, 7211; energy producing resources, 7230
NEGATIVE INCOME TAX: studies, 3230, 9140, 9110; theory, 3212
NEOCLASSICAL SCHOOL: 0315; individuals, 0322
NEW INTERNATIONAL ECONOMIC ORDER: 400 group
NEWSPAPER PUBLISHING: 6317
NON-MARXIST SOCIALISM: 0317, 0321
NON-PROFIT ORGANIZATIONS: 6360
NUTRITION: 9130

OCCUPATION: classification, 8120; safety, 8223; wage differentials, 8120, 8210, 8242

OLD AGE: assistance, 9110; and health, 9130; and poverty, 9140; retirement incidence, 8243; social security, 9150
OLDER WORKERS: 9180; discrimination, 9170; as part of labor force, 8260; retirement and pensions, 8242; social security, 9150
OLIGOPOLY: 0226
OLIGOPSONY: 0226
OPEN ECONOMY MACROECONOMICS: 430 group
OPEN MARKET OPERATIONS: 3116
OPERATIONS RESEARCH: 5110, 5120
OPTIMIZATION TECHNIQUES: 2132
ORGANIZATION: theory, 5110
OVERPRODUCTION THEORY OF CYCLES: 1312
OVERTIME PAY: 8242

PARITY PRICES AND INCOMES, AGRICULTURE: 7130
PARKING, URBAN: 9330
PAPER INDUSTRY: 6317
PATENTS: 6120; technology aspects, 6210
PEAK LOAD PRICING: 6131
PENSIONS, PRIVATE: 8242; investment of, 3140
PERIODICALS, ECONOMIC: 0110
PERMANENT INCOME HYPOTHESIS: studies, 9211; theory, 0232
PERSONAL SERVICES INDUSTRY: 6353
PERSONNEL MANAGEMENT: 5130
PHILANTHROPY: and welfare, 0243
PHILLIPS CURVE: 8210; and inflation, 1342
PHYSIOCRATS: 0312; individuals, 0322
PLANNING: 1130; policy, 1136; regional, 9412; regional models, 9413; theory, 1132; urban, 9310
PLASTICS MANUFACTURING: 6315
POLITICAL ARITHMETICIANS: 0312; for individuals belonging to this group, 0322
POLLUTION: 7220; energy industries, 7230
POPULATION: 8410; and development, 1120; and growth, 111 category; limits to growth, 2260; and pollution, 7220
PORTFOLIO SELECTION: 3131
PORTS: regional, 9410; shipping aspect, 6150; urban, 9310
POSITIVE ECONOMICS: 0360
POST OFFICE: 6140
POULTRY: 7110; marketing of, 7150
POVERTY: 9140; rural, 7180; urban, 9140
PRE-CLASSICAL SCHOOLS: 0312; individuals, 0322
PRICE AND INCOMES POLICY: 1332
PRICE CONTROL: 1332
PRICE LEVELS AND INDEXES: 2270; hedonic, 0222; method, 2118
PRINTING INDUSTRY: 6317
PRODUCERS' COOPERATIVES: agricultural, 7150; market economies, 0510; socialist economies, 0520, 6110
PRODUCTION: agricultural, 7110; factors of, 0223; function and income distribution, 0224, 0235; functions: aggregate, 0234, firm and industry, 0223; theory: aggregate (supply), 0234, firm, 0223
PRODUCTION INDEX: 2260; method of, 2118
PRODUCTIVITY: agricultural, 7110; and growth, 2260; labor, capital, and total factor, 8250; measurement of, 2260
PROFESSIONAL LICENSING: 6120 and 8134
PROFIT-SHARING: 0510
PROFITS: and distribution of income, 0235, 2213; and factor share, 0224; maximization, 5140; 0223; tax on: empirical studies, 3230, theory, 3212
PROGRAMMING MODELS: mathematical, 2135
PROPERTY RIGHTS: 0510; and welfare aspects, 0244
PROPERTY TAX: studies, 3242; theory, 3212
PROTECTION: commercial policy, 4220; consumer, 9213; and development, 4114; non-tariff barriers, 4220; theory, 4113
PUBLIC ENTERPRISE: 6140; administration of, 5131
PUBLIC EXPENDITURE: *see* EXPENDITURES
PUBLIC FINANCE: 320 group
PUBLIC GOODS: 0240, 3212
PUBLIC HOUSING: 9320
PUBLIC INVESTMENT: theory, 3212; and welfare aspects, 024 category
PUBLIC REVENUE: *see* REVENUE
PUBLIC SECTOR: 0240, 3212; centralization, 3200; growth, 3200
PUBLIC UTILITIES: 6130; energy related, 7230
PUBLIC WORKS: expenditure: national, 3221, state and local, 3241; and stabilization policy, 1331, 3212
PUBLISHING INDUSTRY: 6317

QUALITY OF LIFE: environmental, 7220; individual, 9211; and social indicators, 2250; in the workplace, 833 category
QUANTITATIVE MODELS: *see* ECONOMETRIC MODELS, INPUT–OUTPUT MODELS, AND PROGRAMMING MODELS
QUANTITY THEORY OF MONEY: 3112
QUEUING THEORY: 2114
QUIT RATES: 8243
QUOTAS: *see* COMMERCIAL POLICY

RACIAL GROUPS: and discrimination, 9170; in the labor force, 8260; in population, 8410
RADIO: broadcasting industry, 6352; equipment manufacturing, 6313
RAILROAD INDUSTRY: 6150

Railways, urban: 9330
Rate base: public utilities, 6130; railroads, 6150
Rate of return: on capital, 5220; on human capital, 8510; on international capital, 4412; of public utilities, 6130; of railroads, 6150; on securities, 3132
Rational expectations: 0230, 3112; and inflation, 1342
Real estate services: 6357
Reclamation, land: 7172
Recreation: 9210; and natural resources, 7211
Redevelopment: housing, 9330; urban, 9310
Redistribution: and taxes, 3212; and welfare, 0243
Rediscount policy: 3116; and effect on commercial banks, 3120
Regional economics: general, 9410; models, 9413; planning, 9412; studies, 9412; theory, 9411
Regional trade associations: 4233
Regional monetary arrangements: 4320
Regulation: economics of, 6190; effects on industry, 6190; and public utilities, 6130
Relative income hypothesis: 0232
Rent: consumers' expenditure for, 9212; control, 1332; theory, 0224
Rent seeking: theory of, 0252
Repair services: 6355
Research and development: 6212; and innovation, 6210; and taxes, 3230; and technological change, 6210
Reserve requirements: 3116, 3120
Restrictive agreements: 6120
Retail price index: 2270
Retail trade: 6333
Retirement decision: 8243
Retirement pensions: *see* Pensions
Retraining: 8110
Revaluation of currency: 4314
Revealed preference: 0222
Rubber manufacturing: 6315
Rural economics: 7180

Safety of workers: 8223
Sales tax: incidence, 3212; national, 3230; state and local, 3242
Sampling methods and errors: 2117
Savings: corporate, 5210; empirical studies, 9211; function, 0232; personal, 9211; relation to investment, 0233, 5220; share of national income, 2212
Savings and loan associations: 3140
Security markets: 3132
Selective controls, monetary: 3116; and stabilization, 1331; theory, 3112
Service industries: 635 category
Shifting of taxes, theory: 3212
Shipbuilding: 6314
Shipping: 6150
Shopping centers: 6333, 9410
Sick benefits: 8242
Silver mining: 6322
Silver standards: 4320
Single time series analysis: 2116
Slave labor: *see* Country and historical studies
Social choice: 025 category
Social experiments: design of, 2119; experimental economic methods, 215 category
Social indicators: 2250
Social security: 9150
Social welfare: 0240; function, 0240, 0251
Socialist school: 0317; individuals, 0322
Socialist economics: country studies, 124 category; planning, 113 category; systems, 0520; theory, 027 category
Soil improvement: 7172
Space program: 3221, 6212
Spatial competition: 9410
Spectral analysis: *see* Time series
Stability conditions in dynamic systems: 2133
Stabilization: theory and policies, 1331; agricultural, 7130; fiscal, 3210; and inflation, 1340; monetary, 3110
Stagflation: 1331, 1342
Standard of living: 9211; and social indicators, 2250
State and local finance: borrowing, 3243; expenditures and budgets, 3241; general, 3240; taxation, 3242
State trading in international markets: 4220
Statistical: data, 220 category and individual subject areas; methods, 211 category
Sterling area: 4320
Stock markets: 3132
Strikes: collective bargaining, 832 category; and trade unions, 8310
Structural unemployment: 8210
Subsidies: 3230, 3242; agricultural, 7130; export, 4220; and fiscal theory, 3212; food stamps, 9110; and housing, 9320
Substitution of factors of production: 0223
Supply: aggregate, 0234; factor, 0223; firm and industry, 0223; money, 3112
Surplus: agricultural products, 7130
Survey methods: 2117
Swedish school: 0321; for individuals belonging to this group, 0322

Tariff: policy, 4220; studies, 4220; theory, 4113
Taxes: and income distribution, 2213, 3212; na-

tional, 3230; state and local, 3242; theory, 3212; and welfare, 0243
TEACHING OF ECONOMICS: 0112
TECHNICAL ASSISTANCE, INTERNATIONAL: *see* ASSISTANCE, FOREIGN
TECHNOLOGICAL CHANGE: 6211; and competition, 0225, 0226; and development, 1120; effect on employment: theory, 8210, empirical studies, 8243; and growth, 111 category; and market structure, 6110
TELEVISION: equipment manufacturing, 6314; transmission industry, 6352
TENURE: land, 7171
TERMS OF TRADE: 4210
TEXTILE MANUFACTURING: 6316
TIME: and household economics, 0222; and human capital, 8510; and work choice, 8210
TIME SERIES: 2116
TIN MANUFACTURING: 6312
TOBACCO, MANUFACTURING: 6318
TOURISM: industry, 6358; effect on balance of payments, 4313
TRADE AGREEMENTS: agricultural, 7130; international, 4220
TRADE BARRIERS: *see* PROTECTION
TRADE UNIONS: 8310; and collective bargaining, 832 category
TRANSFER PAYMENTS: and fiscal policy, 3212; intergovernmental, 3250; national government, 3230; redistributive effects: studies, 2213; theory, 0243; state and local government, 3242
TRANSFER PRICING: 5210; multinational, 4420, 5210
TRANSFER PROBLEM, INTERNATIONAL: capital, 4411; labor, 8230; technology, 6210, 4420
TRANSPORTATION: 6150; and congestion, 7220, 0244; urban, 9320
TRANSPORTATION EQUIPMENT MANUFACTURING: 6314
TRUSTS, INDUSTRIAL: 6110; government policy toward, 6120
TURNOVER TAX: effect on international trade, 4220; studies, 3230; theory, 3212

UNCERTAINTY: theory, 0261
UNDERCONSUMPTION THEORY: 1312
UNDEREMPLOYMENT: 0230
UNDERGROUND ECONOMY: and GNP, 2212; and crime, 9160
UNEMPLOYMENT: 8243; insurance, 8224
UNION-MANAGEMENT RELATIONS: *see* INDUSTRIAL RELATIONS
UNIONS: *see* TRADE UNIONS
URBAN: general, 9310; transportation, 9330
UTILITY THEORY: 0222

VALUATION: of the firm, 5220; and portfolio theory, 3131
VACANCIES: *see* UNEMPLOYMENT
VALUE OF HUMAN LIFE: and human capital, 8510; and life insurance, 6356; and medical costs, 9130
VEGETABLES: 7110; marketing of, 7150
VELOCITY OF MONEY: 3112
VETERANS: benefits, 3230, 9110; reconversion to civilian life, 1140
VITAL STATISTICS: 8410
VOCATIONAL EDUCATION: 8110
VOLUNTEER ARMY: 1140
VOTING: 0252

WAGES: controls, 1332; differentials, 8210; factor payments, 0224; fringe benefits, 8242; guaranteed annual, 8242; levels, 8242; as part of macro models, 0230; regulation, 8221; and stabilization policy, 1331; theory, 8210
WAR ECONOMICS: 1140
WATER: irrigation, 7172; resources, 7210; transportation, 6150; utilities, 6130
WEALTH: national and individual distribution, 2240; saving and asset studies, 9211; theories of wealth distribution, 0243
WELFARE ECONOMICS: theory of, 024 category; and international trade theory, 4113
WELFARE PROGRAMS: 9110
WHOLESALE PRICE INDEX: 2270
WHOLESALE TRADE: 6332
WOMEN: as demographic component in labor force, 8260; discrimination, 9170; labor force participation, 8130; as a minority, 9170; *see* also HOUSEHOLD, ECONOMICS OF
WOOL: manufacturing, 6316
WORK-LEISURE CHOICE: 8210
WORKMEN'S COMPENSATION: 8222
WORLD GROWTH MODELS: 2260

YOUTH LABOR: as demographic component, 8260